1944

BRITANNICA

BOOK OF

THE YEAR

A Record of the March of Events of 1943

1944
BRITANNICA
BOOK OF
THE YEAR

• Prepared Under the Editorial Direction of
Walter Yust, Editor of
Encyclopædia Britannica

PUBLISHED BY

ENCYCLOPÆDIA BRITANNICA, INC.

CHICAGO · LONDON · TORONTO

The editor of the BRITANNICA BOOK OF THE YEAR acknowledges with gratitude the privilege of using 144 pictures from *Life*. Acknowledgments of the copyright ownership of all illustrations may be found on the following three pages.

THE EDITOR

TABLE OF CONTENTS

LIST OF ILLUSTRATIONS

(Acknowledgment of Copyright is to be found in the Parentheses. Asterisks denote Illustrations from *Life*)

INTRODUCTION

A CONSIDERABLE *part of the work which made this seventh Book of the Year possible was done by John V. Dodge, assistant to the editor, before he was called to the service of his country in January 1944. The book was completed by those of us who could not be useful on the firing line, on the broad seas, on the bomb-shattered hills, muddy trails and dripping jungles of strange lands. The book will be distributed throughout those parts of the world where people are free to read whatever they wish and free to think as they please.*

It will stand as a testimonial to the great sacrifice and courage of those men and women who have, for the time being, been drawn into the insane conflict forced upon the world by small men who do not dare to allow people to read whatever they wish or to be free to think as they please.

The cruel circumstance growing out of enemy decadence, out of the cunning of political and diplomatic expedience, everywhere, in the year 1943, is reflected in this volume. The brave and good works of the John V. Dodges of this world are, however, the memorably significant record of the book, and it is this record which gives promise that the honesty and liberality of those rare men and women who helped create and perpetuate America's very special kind of democracy might again be recovered, for today, for tomorrow, not only for America but for anywhere, where happy families might hope to survive the arrogant domination of state and statesmen.

*   *   *   *

The Book of the Year was made not only by its authoritative contributors, but by the checkers, the proofreaders, the young women of the working files; by Miss Wilma Morgan, who assembled the hundreds of illustrations; by Mrs. Ruth L. Breed, who made the necessary contacts with the Book of the Year's 500 contributors; and by Mrs. Mae H. MacKay, who, with her assistant, Mrs. Harriet Milburn, directed the work of more than 30 staff assistants to speed the articles to the rolling presses.

WALTER YUST

EDITORS AND CONTRIBUTORS

WALTER YUST, EDITOR OF ENCYCLOPÆDIA BRITANNICA AND OF THE BRITANNICA BOOK OF THE YEAR

JOHN V. DODGE, *Assistant Editor of the Book of the Year*

LIBRARIAN CONSULTANTS

ANNE FRASER LEIDENDEKER, *Department Librarian, Science and Industry Department, Public Library, Los Angeles, Calif.*

CHARLES F. MCCOMBS, *Superintendent, Main Reading Room, New York Public Library.*

WINIFRED VER NOOY, *Reference Librarian, University of Chicago.*

(Initials and names of contributors to the Britannica Book of the Year with the principal articles written by them. The arrangement is alphabetical by initials.)

A.Al.	**ARTHUR ASPINALL.** Lecturer in Modern History, University of Reading, Reading, Eng.	**Great Britain and Northern Ireland, United Kingdom of** (*in part*)
A.B.Ho.	**A. B. HOLTON.** Superintendent, Technical Service Department, The Sherwin-Williams Co., Cleveland, Ohio.	**Paints and Varnishes**
A.Bm.	**ADELE BLOOM.** Acting Executive Secretary, The American Association for Social Security, Inc.	**Social Security** (*in part*)
A.B.Mo.	**ALBERT BURTON MOORE, M.S., M.A., Ph.D.** Professor of History and Dean of the Graduate School, University of Alabama, University, Ala. Author of *History of Alabama*; etc.	**Alabama** (*in part*)
A.C.Ch.	**ARTHUR C. CHRISTIE, M.D., M.S.** Professor of Clinical Radiology, Georgetown University Medical School, Washington, D.C.	**X-Ray**
A.C.I.	**A. C. IVY, M.D.** Nathan Smith Davis Professor in Physiology and Professor of Pharmacology, Northwestern University Medical School, Chicago, Ill.	**Physiology**
A.Da.	**ALLISON DANZIG.** Member of Sports Staff, *The New York Times*, New York, N.Y. Author of *The Racquet Game*; etc.	**Football** (*in part*)
A.D.An.	**ARTHUR D. ANDERSON.** Editor, *Boot and Shoe Recorder*, Boston, Mass. Author of *Shoe and Leather Lexicon*.	**Shoe Industry**
A.E.Du.	**ARTHUR E. DuBOIS.** Chief, Heraldic Section, Office of the Quartermaster General, War Department, Washington, D.C.	**Decorations, Military and Naval**
A.E.Gi.	**AUGUSTUS E. GIEGENGACK.** Public Printer of the United States.	**Printing Office, U.S. Government**
A.E.Sh.	**AUSTIN E. SMITH, M.D., C.M., M.Sc.** Secretary, Council on Pharmacy and Chemistry, American Medical Association.	**Chemotherapy**
A.G.Bl.	**A. G. BLACK.** Governor, Farm Credit Administration, U.S. Department of Agriculture, Kansas City, Mo.	**Farm Credit Administration**
A.G.Bn.	**ANSCO G. BRUINIER, JR.** Technical Advertising Manager, Dyestuffs Division, Organic Chemicals Department, E. I. du Pont de Nemours & Company, Inc., Wilmington, Del.	**Dyestuffs**
A.G.R.	**ALEXANDER G. RUTHVEN, Ph.D., Sc.D., LL.D.** President, University of Michigan, Ann Arbor, Mich.	**Michigan, University of**
A.G.S.	**ANTONE G. SINGSEN, M.S.** Manager, Department of Public Information, Connecticut Plan for Hospital Care.	**Insurance** (*in part*)
A.H.F.	**ABNER H. FERGUSON.** Commissioner, Federal Housing Administration, National Housing Agency, Washington, D.C.	**National Housing Agency** (*in part*)
A.J.Hp.	**ANGUS JOHN HARROP, M.A., Litt.D., Ph.D.** Representative in England of the University of New Zealand. Editor of *The New Zealand News*, London, Eng.	**New Zealand, Dominion of**
A.J.Li.	**ALFRED J. LIEBMANN, Ph.D.** President, Schenley Research Institute, Lawrenceburg, Ind.	**Liquors, Alcoholic** (*in part*)
A.J.Lo.	**ALFRED J. LOTKA.** Assistant Statistician, Metropolitan Life Insurance Company, New York, N.Y.	**Birth Statistics, etc.**
A.J.M.	**A. J. MUSTE, M.A.** Executive Secretary, Fellowship of Reconciliation. Co-editor, *Fellowship*. Associate Editor, *The Presbyterian Tribune*.	**Pacifism**
A.K.B.	**A. K. BRYCESON.** "Hotspur" of *The Daily Telegraph and Morning Post*, London, Eng.	**Horse Racing** (*in part*)
A.L.Bs.	**ANDREW L. BOUWHUIS, S.J.** Librarian, Canisius College, Buffalo, N.Y. President, Catholic Library Association.	**Catholic Library Association**
A.LeR.L.	**ALAIN LEROY LOCKE, Ph.D.** Professor of Philosophy, Howard University, Washington, D.C. Author of *Race Contacts and Interracial Relations; The New Negro; The Negro in America; The Negro and His Music; Negro Art: Past and Present.*	**Negroes (American)**
A.M.Bv.	**ALEXANDER M. BAYKOV, D.Jur., Ph.D.** Honorary Research Fellow, Birmingham University. Former Lecturer in Russian Economics, Czech University, Prague, Czechoslovakia.	**Moscow**
A.M.Ds.	**AUDREY M. DAVIES, J.D.** Librarian, Institute of Public Administration, New York, N.Y.	**Municipal Government** (*in part*)
A.Mu.	**ARTHUR MURRAY.** President, National Institute of Social Dancing. Author of *How to Become a Good Dancer; Modern Dancing; Dance Book*; etc.	**Dance** (*in part*)
A.My.	**AUGUST MAFFRY, Ph.D.** Chief, International Economics and Statistics Unit, Bureau of Foreign and Domestic Commerce, Department of Commerce, Washington, D.C.	**International Trade** (*in part*)
A.N.Ws.	**A. N. WILLIAMS.** President, The Western Union Telegraph Company, New York, N.Y.	**Telegraphy**
A.O.	**ALTON OCHSNER, M.D.** Chief, Section on Surgery, Ochsner Clinic, New Orleans, La. William Henderson. Professor of Surgery, School of Medicine, Tulane University of Louisiana, New Orleans, La.	**Surgery**
A.P.U.	**ABBOTT PAYSON USHER, Ph.D.** Professor of Economics, Harvard University, Cambridge, Mass. Corresponding Secretary, American Academy of Arts and Sciences.	**American Academy of Arts and Sciences**

Code	Contributor	Topic
Ar.B.	**ARTHUR BEACHAM.** Assistant Lecturer, Department of Economics, Queen's University, Belfast, Ire.	Ireland, Northern (*in part*)
A.R.N.	**ALBERT RAY NEWSOME, Ph.D.** Professor and Head of the Department of History, University of North Carolina, Chapel Hill, N.C.	North Carolina
A.T.B.	**ALLEN T. BURNS.** Member of the board of directors, Community Chests and Councils, Inc.	Community Chest
A.T.M.	**A. T. MITCHELSON.** Senior Irrigation Engineer, Division of Irrigation, Soil Conservation Service, U.S. Department of Agriculture, Berkeley, Calif.	Irrigation
A.Ws.	**AUBREY WILLIAMS.** Administrator, National Youth Administration, Washington, D.C., 1938-43.	National Youth Administration
A.Y.A.	**ABDULLAH YUSUF ALI, M.A., LL.M., C.B.E.** Former Revenue Minister, Hyderabad State. Author of *The Message of Islam*; *Cultural History of British India*; etc.	Islam
B.B.	**BAKER BROWNELL, A.M.** Professor of Philosophy and of Contemporary Thought, Northwestern University, Evanston, Ill.	Philosophy
B.B.W.	**BENJAMIN B. WALLACE, Ph.D.** Adviser to U.S. Tariff Commission on international trade policies.	Tariffs
B.C.B.	**BEN C. BROSHEER.** Associate Editor, *American Machinist*, New York, N.Y.	Machinery and Machine Tools
B.C.S.	**BARRY C. SMITH.** General Director, The Commonwealth Fund.	Commonwealth Fund, The
B.Cu.	**BRYSSON CUNNINGHAM, D.Sc.** Editor of *The Dock and Harbour Authority*.	Canals and Inland Waterways (*in part*), etc.
B.De.	**BYRON DEFENBACH.** Author of *Idaho: the Place and Its People* and other northwest history.	Idaho
B.Gm.	**BESSIE GRAHAM.** Director, Temple University Library School, Philadelphia, Pa., 1925-40. Author of *The Bookman's Manual* and *Famous Literary Prizes and Their Winners*.	Literary Prizes
B.H.P.	**BEN H. PARKER, Sc.D.** Associate Professor of Geology, Colorado School of Mines, Golden, Colo.	Geology (*in part*)
B.O.M.	**BYRON O. McCOY.** Hydraulic Engineer, Chas. T. Main, Inc., Boston, Mass. Associate Member, American Society of Civil Engineers.	Dams
B.Pr.	**BYRON PRICE.** Director, Office of Censorship, Washington, D.C.	Censorship
Br.S.	**BRUCE SMITH, M.A.** Acting Director, Institute of Public Administration, New York, N.Y.	Crime (*in part*), etc.
B.Sk.	**BEN SHUPACK.** Secretary, The Soaring Society of America.	Gliding
B.Ta.	**BOOTH TARKINGTON, Litt.D.** Honorary Chairman of the National Membership Committee of The Seeing Eye. Pulitzer prize winner for literature.	Seeing Eye, The
B.We.	**BENJAMIN WERNE, S.J.D.** Lecturer in Government Regulation and Law, New York University, New York, N.Y.	Supreme Court of the United States
B.Wp.	**BLANTON WINSHIP.** Major General, U.S.A. Coordinator, Inter-American Defense Board, Washington, D.C.	Inter-American Defense Board
B.W.T.	**BENJAMIN W. THORON.** Director, Division of Territories and Island Possessions, U.S. Department of the Interior, Washington, D.C.	Hawaii
B.Y.	**BARNEY YANOFSKY.** Editor of *Foreign Service* and Director of Public Relations, Veterans of Foreign Wars of the United States, Kansas City, Mo.	Veterans of Foreign Wars
B.Z.R.	**B. Z. RAPPAPORT, M.D.** Assistant Professor of Medicine and Acting Head of Allergy Clinic, University of Illinois College of Medicine, Chicago, Ill.	Allergy
C.A.Bn.	**CHARLES A. BRESKIN.** Editor and Managing Director, *Modern Plastics*, New York, N.Y.	Plastics Industry
C.A.Sr.	**CHARLES A. SEGNER.** Associate Administrator, National Physicians Committee for the Extension of Medical Service, Inc.	Taxation, etc.
C.A.T.	**C. A. THAYER.** Former President and Director, American Spice Trade Association, New York, N.Y.	Spices
C.B.C.	**CHRISTOPHER B. COLEMAN, Ph.D.** Director, Indiana State Historical Bureau, Indianapolis, Ind.	Indiana
C.B.F.M.	**C. B. F. MACAULEY.** Fairchild Engine and Airplane Corporation. Technical Member, Institute of Aeronautical Sciences. Author of *The Helicopters Are Coming*.	Aviation, Civil
C.B.H.	**CHARLES B. HENDERSON, LL.M.** Chairman of the Board, Reconstruction Finance Corporation, Washington, D.C.	Reconstruction Finance Corporation
C.B.S.	**CARL B. SWISHER, Ph.D.** Thomas P. Stran Professor of Political Science, Johns Hopkins University, Baltimore, Md. Author of *Roger B. Taney*; *Stephen J. Field, Craftsman of the Law*.	Baltimore; Maryland
C.Bs.	**CHESTER BOWLES.** Administrator, Office of Price Administration, Washington, D.C.	Price Administration, Office of; Rationing
C.Bu.	**CARLYLE BURROWS.** Assistant Art Editor and Critic, *The New York Herald Tribune*, New York, N.Y.	Sculpture
C.Cs.	**CHARLOTTE CAPERS.** Acting Director, Mississippi Department of Archives and History, Jackson, Miss.	Mississippi
C.Cy.	**CHARLES CLAY.** National Secretary, Canadian Authors' Association, Ottawa, Ont. Author of *Swampy Cree Legends*; *Young Voyageur*; etc.	Canadian Literature
C.D.Hu.	**CHARLES D. HURD, Ph.D., Sc.D.** Professor of Chemistry, Northwestern University, Evanston, Ill.	Chemistry
C.D.Sp.	**CHARLES D. SPENCER.** News Editor, *The National Underwriter*. Business Manager, *The Accident & Health Review*.	Insurance (*in part*)
C.E.A.	**CHARLES E. ALLRED, M.S.A., Ph.D.** Head, Department of Agricultural Economics and Rural Sociology, University of Tennessee, Knoxville, Tenn.	Tennessee
C.E.B.	**C. EDWARD BEHRE.** Assistant to the Chief, Forest Service, U.S. Department of Agriculture, Washington, D.C.	Forests (*in part*)
C.E.G.	**CECIL EDWARD GOLDING, LL.D.** Joint Secretary, Examiners' Committee, Chartered Insurance Institute.	Insurance (*in part*)
C.E.R.S.	**CHARLES ELY ROSE SHERRINGTON, M.A.** Secretary, British Railways Research Service. Former Lecturer in Transport, London School of Economics, London University, London, Eng.	Railroads (*in part*)
C.F.Lo.	**C. FRANCES LOOMIS.** Director, Program Department, Camp Fire Girls, Inc.	Camp Fire Girls
C.F.McC.	**CHARLES FLOWERS McCOMBS.** Chief Bibliographer, New York Public Library, New York, N.Y.	Libraries (*in part*)
C.Fo.	**CHARLES FOX, M.A.** Former Director of Training, University of Cambridge, Cambridge, Eng. Author of *Educational Psychology*; *The Mind and Its Body*; etc.	Cambridge University
C.G.A.	**C. G. ABBOT.** Secretary, Smithsonian Institution, Washington, D.C.	Smithsonian Institution
C.H.Bd.	**C. H. BINFORD, M.D.** Surgeon, U.S. Public Health Service. Pathologist, U.S. Marine Hospital, New Orleans, La.	Leprosy
C.I.B.	**CHESTER I. BARNARD.** President, United Service Organizations, Inc. President, New Jersey Bell Telephone Company.	United Service Organizations
C.J.Br.	**CHARLES J. BRAND.** Executive Secretary and Treasurer, The National Fertilizer Association, Washington, D.C.	Fertilizers
C.L.B.	**CLEMENT LINCOLN BOUVÉ.** Register of Copyrights, Washington, D.C.	Copyright
C.L.G.	**CHESTER L. GUTHRIE.** Lieutenant (jg), U.S.N.R. Head, Administrative History Section, Bureau of Medicine and Surgery, Navy Department, Washington, D.C.	Mexico; Puerto Rico; Virgin Islands
C.L.Ps.	**CHARLES L. PARSONS.** Secretary, American Chemical Society.	American Chemical Society
C.M.An.	**CARLETON M. ALLEN.** Lecturer on Wool and Woollen Textiles, Boston University, Boston, Mass.	Wool
C.M.Br.	**C. M. BREDER, JR., Sc.D.** Acting Director, New York Aquarium, 1938-40; Director, 1941-43. Research Associate, American Museum of Natural History, New York, N.Y.	Aquariums

C.M.Cl.	**CONSTANCE MARGARET CORNELL.** Writer and Lecturer on international affairs.	**Mediterranean, British Possessions in the** (*in part*), etc.
C.M.G.	**CHARLES M. GRIFFITH, M.D.** Medical Director, Veterans' Administration, Washington, D.C.	**Rehabilitation and Occupational Therapy for Wounded Soldiers**
C.Mh.	**CONSTANCE MURDOCH.** Secretary, Spelman Fund of New York.	**Spelman Fund of New York**
C.M.Pn.	**CARL M. PETERSON, M.D.** Secretary, Council on Industrial Health, American Medical Association.	**Industrial Health**
C.M.R.	**C. M. RITTENHOUSE.** National Director, Girl Scouts.	**Girl Scouts**
C.P.Co.	**CONWAY P. COE.** U.S. Commissioner of Patents, Washington, D.C.	**Patents**
C.P.S.	**CLIFFORD P. SMITH.** Editor, Bureau of History and Records, The First Church of Christ, Scientist, Boston, Mass.	**Christian Science**
C.S.Kr.	**CHESTER S. KEEFER, M.D.** Director, Robert Dawson Evans Memorial Hospital; Physician-in-chief, Massachusetts Memorial Hospitals, Boston, Mass. Wade Professor of Medicine, Boston University, Boston, Mass. Consulting Physician, U.S. Public Health Service, U.S. Marine Hospital, Brighton, Mass.	**Penicillin**
C.Sn.	**CARMEL SNOW.** Editor of *Harper's Bazaar*, New York, N.Y.	**Fashion and Dress**
C.V.N.	**CATHERINE V. NIMITZ.** Music Librarian, Public Library, Washington, D.C. Secretary-Treasurer, Music Library Association.	**Music Library Association**
C.W.Gl.	**CHARLES W. GILMORE.** Curator of Vertebrate Palaeontology, United States National Museum, Smithsonian Institution, Washington, D.C.	**Palaeontology**
C.W.Ra.	**CHARLES W. RAMSDELL, Jr.** Author of various historical works.	**Texas**
C.W.S.	**CARL W. STOCKS.** Editor, *Bus Transportation*, New York, N.Y.	**Motor Transportation** (*in part*)
C.Z.	**CARL ZEISBERG.** Former President, United States Table Tennis Association.	**Table Tennis**
D.A.Dy.	**DENNIS A. DOOLEY.** State Librarian of Massachusetts. President, National Association of State Libraries.	**National Association of State Libraries**
D.An.	**DEAN ACHESON, M.A.** Assistant Secretary of State, Washington, D.C.	**International Trade** (*in part*)
D.B.B.	**DORIS B. BERNSTEIN.** Division of Research and Statistics, Board of Governors of the Federal Reserve System, Washington, D.C.	**Exchange Control and Exchange Rates, etc.**
D.Bru.	**DAVID BRUNT, M.A., Sc.D.** Professor of Meteorology, Imperial College of Science and Technology, London, Eng.	**Meteorology** (*in part*)
D.B.S.	**DAVID BARNARD STEINMAN, Ph.D.** Authority on the design and construction of long-span bridges.	**Bridges**
D.C.H.J.	**D. C. HENRIK JONES.** Librarian and Information Officer, The Library Association, London, Eng.	**Libraries** (*in part*)
D.C.Sn.	**DOROTHY CONSTANCE STRATTON, M.A., Ph.D.** Lieutenant Commander, Women's Reserve, United States Coast Guard Reserve. Director, SPARS.	**Coast Guard, U.S.** (*in part*)
D. de S.P.	**DAVID de SOLA POOL, D.Ph.** Rabbi, Spanish and Portuguese Synagogue Shearith Israel, New York, N.Y.	**Jewish Religious Life**
D.D.L.	**DON D. LESCOHIER, Ph.D.** Professor of Economics, University of Wisconsin, Madison, Wis.	**Employment; Wages and Hours** (*in part*), etc.
D.D.W.	**DAVID DUNCAN WALLACE, A.M., Ph.D., Litt.D., LL.D.** Professor of History and Economics, Wofford College, Spartanburg, S.C.	**South Carolina**
D.F.Tr.	**DOROTHEA F. TURNER, M.S.** Instructor in Medicine, Department of Medicine, The University of Chicago, Chicago, Ill. Chairman, Diet Therapy Section, American Dietetic Association.	**Dietetics**
D.G.Wo.	**DOUGLAS G. WOOLF.** First Vice-President, Textile Research Institute, Inc.	**Cotton** (*in part*) **Textile Industry**
D.Ka.	**DANIEL KATZ, Ph.D.** Chairman, Department of Psychology, Brooklyn College, Brooklyn, N.Y.	**Psychology**
D.Ko.	**DAVID KARNO.** Cable Editor, *The Chicago Daily News*, Chicago, Ill.	**World War II**
D.L.Br.	**DWIGHT L. BOLINGER.** Chairman of the New Words Committee of the American Dialect Society which prepared the article. Professor Bolinger is Assistant Professor of Spanish, University of Southern California, Los Angeles, Calif.	**Words and Meanings, New**
D.Rd.	**DONALD WINSLOW ROWLAND, Ph.D.** Professor of Hispanic American and United States History, University of Southern California, Los Angeles, Calif.	**Central America Nicaragua, etc.**
D.R.G.	**DAVID ROBERT GENT.** Rugby Football Critic *The Sunday Times*, London, Eng.	**Football** (*in part*)
D.Rn.	**DOROTHY R. ROSENMAN (Mrs. Samuel I. Rosenman).** Chairman, National Committee on Housing.	**Building and Construction Industry** (*in part*) **Housing** (*in part*)
D.S.Mr.	**DILLON SEYMOUR MYER, M.A.** Director, War Relocation Authority, Washington, D.C.	**War Relocation Authority**
D.S.Mu.	**DAVID SAVILLE MUZZEY, Ph.D.** Emeritus Professor of History, Columbia University, New York, N.Y.	**United States** (*in part*)
D.St.	**DANIEL STARCH, M.A., Ph.D.** Consultant in Business Research. Former Lecturer and Professor at Harvard University and the University of Wisconsin.	**Advertising**
D.T.H.	**DALLAS T. HERNDON.** Executive Secretary, Arkansas History Commission, Little Rock, Ark.	**Arkansas**
D.V.	**DOUGLAS VEALE, M.A., C.B.E.** Registrar of Oxford University, Oxford, Eng.	**Oxford University**
D.W.B.	**D. W. BELL.** Under Secretary of the Treasury, Washington, D.C.	**War Debts**
D.W.G.	**DON W. GUDAKUNST, M.D., Dr.P.H.** Medical Director, National Foundation for Infantile Paralysis, Inc., New York, N.Y.	**Infantile Paralysis**
E.A.P.	**EDGAR ALLISON PEERS, M.A.** Professor of Spanish, University of Liverpool, Liverpool, Eng. Author of *A History of the Romantic Movement in Spain*; etc.	**Portugal** (*in part*), etc.
E.A.Wr.	**ERIC ANDERSON WALKER.** Vere Harmsworth Professor of Imperial and Naval History, Cambridge University, Cambridge, Eng. Former King George V Professor of History, Cape Town, South Africa.	**South Africa, The Union of** (*in part*)
E.Bd.	**EDWIN BORCHARD, Ph.D., LL.D.** Professor of International Law, Yale University, New Haven, Conn.	**International Law**
E.B.Du.	**EDWARD B. DUNFORD, LL.D.** Attorney, Legal Department, The Anti-Saloon League of America	**Anti-Saloon League**
E.B.L.	**EDGAR B. LANDIS.** Trust Officer, Chemical Bank & Trust Company, New York, N.Y. Former member of the Faculty of Columbia University Extension, American Institute of Banking.	**Banking** (*in part*)
E.B.Ph.	**EARLE B. PHELPS.** Professor of Sanitary Science, College of Physicians and Surgeons, Columbia University, New York, N.Y.	**Public Health Engineering**
E.C.Ar.	**E. C. AUCHTER.** Agricultural Research Administrator, U.S. Department of Agriculture, Washington, D.C.	**Agricultural Research Administration**
E.C.D.M.	**E. CHARLES D. MARRIAGE.** Librarian, Nevada State Library, Carson City, Nev.	**Nevada**
E.C.Gr.	**E. C. GRIFFITH, M.A., Ph.D.** Associate Professor of Economics, University of Georgia, Athens, Ga.	**Georgia**
E.Ck.	**EVANS CLARK.** Executive Director, The Twentieth Century Fund.	**Postwar Planning, etc.**
E.Cul.	**ELY CULBERTSON.** Editor, *The Bridge World*. President, World Federation, Inc. Author of *Total Peace*.	**Contract Bridge**
E.D.H.	**EVETT D. HESTER.** Economic Adviser, Office of the United States High Commissioner to the Philippine Islands, Office of the Secretary of the Interior, Washington, D.C.	**Philippines, Commonwealth of the**
E.E.B.	**EDWARD E. BENNETT, Ph.D.** Professor of History and Political Science, Montana State University, Missoula, Mont.	**Montana**

Fr.Ro.	**FREDERICK ROTHE.** Chairman, Committee on Handball, New York Athletic Club, New York, N.Y.	**Hand-ball**
F.R.Y.	**F. R. YERBURY.** Managing Director, The Building Centre, London, Eng.	**Housing** (*in part*)
F.Sm.	**FRED SMITH.** Assistant to the Secretary of the Treasury, Washington, D.C.	**War Bonds**
F.T.Hi.	**FRANK T. HINES.** Brigadier General, U.S.A. Administrator of Veterans' Affairs, Washington, D.C.	**Veterans' Administration**
F.W.Ga.	**FREDERIC WILLIAM GANZERT, M.A., Ph.D.** Associate Professor of History and Political Science, University of Utah, Salt Lake City, Utah.	**Utah**
F.W.Rr.	**F. W. REICHELDERFER, D.Sc.** Chief, Weather Bureau, United States Department of Commerce, Washington, D.C.	**Meteorology** (*in part*)
G.A.Bs.	**GEORGE A. BARNES.** Assistant to the Director, Office of War Information, Washington, D.C.	**War Information, Office of**
G.A.Ro.	**GAR A. ROUSH, M.S.** Editor, *Mineral Industry*, New York, N.Y.	**Copper; Nickel; etc.**
G.A.Si.	**GORDON A. SISCO, M.A., D.D.** Secretary, The United Church of Canada.	**United Church of Canada**
G.B.En.	**GEORGE B. EUSTERMAN, M.D.** Head of Section in Medicine, Mayo Clinic, Rochester, Minn. Professor of Medicine, Mayo Foundation, University of Minnesota Graduate School, Minneapolis, Minn.	**Alimentary System, Disorders of**
G.D.H.C.	**GEORGE DOUGLAS HOWARD COLE, M.A.** Director of the Nuffield College Social Reconstruction Survey. Reader in Economics, Oxford University, Oxford, Eng. Chairman of the Fabian Society.	**Labour Party; Wages and Hours** (*in part*), **etc.**
G.E.Ho.	**G. E. HOFMEISTER.** Vice-President, Continental Casualty Company, Chicago, Ill.	**Insurance** (*in part*)
G.Gr.	**GILBERT GROSVENOR, M.A., Litt.D., LL.D.** President and Editor, National Geographic Society, Washington, D.C.	**National Geographic Society**
G.J.B.F.	**GEORGE J. B. FISHER.** Colonel, U.S.A. Assistant Commandant, Chemical Warfare School, Edgewood Arsenal, Md.	**Warfare, Incendiary**
G.J.N.	**GEORGE JEAN NATHAN.** Critic. Author of *The Critic and the Drama; Encyclopaedia of the Theatre; Materia Critica*; etc.	**Theatre** (*in part*)
G.J.R.	**G. J. RENIER, Ph.D.** Reader in Dutch History and Institutions, University of London, London, Eng.	**Wilhelmina**
G.L.W.	**GEORGE L. WARREN.** Executive Secretary, President's Advisory Committee on Political Refugees, New York, N.Y.	**Refugees**
G.M.C.	**GEORGE MORRISON COATES, M.D.** Professor of Otorhinology, Graduate School of Medicine, University of Pennsylvania, Philadelphia, Pa. Editor in Chief, *Archives of Otolaryngology*.	**Ear, Nose and Throat, Diseases of**
G.M.Hy.	**GRANT M. HYDE, M.A.** Director, School of Journalism, University of Wisconsin, Madison, Wis.	**Newspapers and Magazines** (*in part*)
G.M.J.	**G. McSTAY JACKSON.** President, G. McStay Jackson, Inc., Chicago, Ill.	**Interior Decoration**
G.N.C.	**GEORGE NORMAN CLARK.** Regius Professor of Modern History, University of Cambridge, Cambridge, Eng. Doctor Honoris Causa, University of Utrecht, Utrecht, Netherlands.	**Netherlands** (*in part*), **etc.**
G.P.	**G. PARR, M.A.** Editor, *Electronic Engineering*. Hon. Secretary, The Television Society.	**Television** (*in part*)
G.Pl.	**GANSON PURCELL.** Chairman, Securities and Exchange Commission, Philadelphia, Pa.	**Securities and Exchange Commission**
G.R.G.	**G. R. GEARY, K.C.** Barrister and Solicitor, Toronto, Ont.	**Toronto**
G.S.Br.	**G. STEWART BROWN.** Vice-Chairman in charge of Public Relations, American Red Cross.	**Red Cross** (*in part*)
G.S.F.	**GARLAND S. FERGUSON.** Chairman, Federal Trade Commission, Washington, D.C.	**Federal Trade Commission**
G.St.	**GLEB STRUVE.** Reader in Russian Literature, School of Slavonic and East European Studies, University of London, London, Eng. Author of *Soviet Russian Literature*.	**Russian Literature**
G.W.Do.	**GEORGE W. DOUGLAS, A.M., Litt.D.** Former Chief Editorial writer of *The Philadelphia Evening Public Ledger*, Philadelphia, Pa. Author of *The Book of Days; The Many-Sided Roosevelt*; etc.	**New York Pennsylvania, etc.**
H.A.H.	**HOWARD ARCHIBALD HUBBARD, Ph.D.** Professor of History, University of Arizona, Tucson, Ariz.	**Arizona**
H.A.Ms.	**H. A. MILLIS, A.M., Ph.D.** Chairman, National Labor Relations Board, Washington, D.C.	**National Labor Relations Board**
H.Bec.	**HOWARD BECKER, A.M., Ph.D.** Professor of Sociology, University of Wisconsin, Madison, Wis. Book Review Editor, *American Sociological Review*. Co-author of *Systematic Sociology; Social Thought from Lore to Science*; etc.	**Sociology**
H.Bu.	**HERMAN N. BUNDESEN, M.D.** President, Board of Health, Chicago, Ill.	**Epidemics and Public Health Control**
H.B.V.W.	**H. B. VAN WESEP.** Office of Publications, The Rockefeller Foundation, New York, N.Y.	**Rockefeller Foundation**
H.C.D.	**HAROLD COLLETT DENT.** Editor of *The Times Educational Supplement*, London, Eng.	**Education** (*in part*)
H.D.G.	**H. DON GUSSOW.** Editor, *Confectionery-Ice Cream World*, New York, N.Y.	**Candy**
H.E.Ba.	**HARRY E. BARNARD, Ph.D., D.Sc.** Former Research Director, National Farm Chemurgic Council.	**Flour and Flour Milling**
He.Br.	**HENRY BRUÈRE.** President, Bowery Savings Bank, New York, N.Y.	**Banking** (*in part*)
H.E.Dl.	**HERBERT EDWARD DOUGALL, Ph.D.** Professor of Finance, Northwestern University, Evanston, Ill.	**Railroads** (*in part*)
H.Eh.	**HERBERT EMMERICH.** Commissioner, Federal Public Housing Authority, National Housing Agency, Washington, D.C.	**National Housing Agency** (*in part*)
H.F.D.	**HALLIE FLANAGAN DAVIS, A.M., L.H.D.** Dean and Professor of Theatre, Smith College, Northampton, Mass.	**Smith College**
H.F.Ms.	**H. FREEMAN MATTHEWS, A.M.** Chief, Division of European Affairs, Department of State, Washington, D.C.	**European Advisory Commission**
H.Fx.	**HOWARD FOX, M.D.** Emeritus Professor of Dermatology and Syphilology, College of Medicine, New York University, New York, N.Y.	**Dermatology**
H.G.Mo.	**HAROLD G. MOULTON, Ph.D., LL.D.** President, Brookings Institution, Washington, D.C.	**Brookings Institution**
H.G.Rn.	**H. G. RAWLINSON, M.A., C.I.E.** Former Principal, Deccan College, Poona, India.	**Ceylon** (*in part*) **India** (*in part*)
H.G.S.	**H. GERRISH SMITH.** President, Shipbuilding Council of America, New York, N.Y.	**Shipbuilding** (*in part*)
H.H.A.	**HENRY H. ARNOLD.** General, U.S.A. Commanding General, Army Air Forces, Washington, D.C.	**Air Forces of the World** (*in part*)
H.Ha.	**HARRY HANSEN.** Literary Editor, *New York World-Telegram*. Author of *Midwest Portraits; The Adventures of the Fourteen Points; Your Life Lies Before You; The Chicago*. Editor, *O. Henry Prize Stories*, 1936–1940.	**American Literature Pulitzer Prizes**
H.H.Be.	**HUGH H. BENNETT, LL.D., D.Sc.** Chief, Soil Conservation Service, U.S. Department of Agriculture, Washington, D.C.	**Soil Erosion and Soil Conservation**
H.H.L.	**HERBERT H. LEHMAN.** Director General, United Nations Relief and Rehabilitation Administration, Washington, D.C.	**United Nations Relief and Rehabilitation Administration**
H.Hy.	**HUGH HARLEY.** Secretary, Brewing Industry Foundation, New York, N.Y.	**Brewing and Beer**
H.I'A.F.	**HUGH I'ANSON FAUSSET.** English critic, biographer and novelist. Author of *Walt Whitman; Between the Tides; A Modern Prelude; William Cowper*; etc.	**English Literature**
H.J.A.	**H. J. ANSLINGER.** Commissioner of Narcotics, United States Treasury Department, Washington, D.C.	**Drugs and Drug Traffic** (*in part*)
H.J.De.	**HERMAN J. DEUTSCH, Ph.D.** Professor of History, State College of Washington, Pullman, Wash.	**Washington**
H.Js.	**HARLEAN JAMES.** Executive Secretary, American Planning and Civic Association, Washington, D.C.	**Washington, D.C., etc.**
H.J.Z.	**HENRY J. ZETTELMAN, M.S., M.D.** Former Coach of Fencing; Faculty Advisor, Northwestern University, Evanston, Ill.	**Fencing**

H.Ko.	**HANS KOHN, D. Jur.** Sydenham Clark Parsons Professor of History, Smith College, Northampton, Mass. Author of *The Idea of Nationalism, a Study of Its Origins and Background; Force or Reason; Revolutions and Dictatorships;* etc.	**Communism Czechoslovakia, etc.**
H.L.	**SIR HARRY LINDSAY, K.C.I.E., C.B.E.,** Director, Imperial Institute, South Kensington, London, Eng. Trade Commissioner for Burma.	**Burma**
H.L.B.	**HOWARD LANDIS BEVIS, S.J.D.** President, Ohio State University, Columbus, Ohio.	**Ohio State University**
H.L.G.	**HAROLD L. GEORGE.** Major General, U.S.A. Commanding General, Air Transport Command, Army Air Forces, Washington, D.C.	**Air Transport Command**
H.L.St.	**HERBERT L. STONE.** Editor, *Yachting,* New York, N.Y. Author of *America's Cup Races,* etc.	**Motor-Boat Racing Yachting**
H.M.Ft.	**HERBERT M. FAUST.** Director, Salvage Division, War Production Board, Washington, D.C.	**Salvage Drives, U.S.**
H.Ne.	**HELEN NEWMAN.** Associate Librarian, Supreme Court of the U.S., Washington, D.C. Executive Secretary and Treasurer, American Association of Law Libraries.	**American Association of Law Libraries**
H.N.MacC.	**HENRY N. MacCRACKEN, M.A., Ph.D., LL.D., L.H.D.** President, Vassar College, Poughkeepsie, N.Y.	**Vassar College**
Ho.J.B.	**HORACE J. BRIDGES, D.Litt.** Leader, The Chicago Ethical Society, Chicago, Ill.	**Ethical Culture Movement**
H.P.D.	**HARLAN PAUL DOUGLASS, A.M., D.D.** Editor, *Christendom.* Author of *A Decade of Objective Progress in Church Unity,* etc.	**Christian Unity Religion**
H.P.R.	**HOMER PRICE RAINEY, Ph.D., LL.D.** President, University of Texas, Austin, Tex.	**Texas, University of**
H.R.B.	**HORACE ROBERT BYERS, S.M., Sc.D.** Professor of Meteorology, The University of Chicago, Chicago, Ill. Executive Secretary, Institute of Meteorology, The University of Chicago, Chicago, Ill. Author of *Synoptic and Aeronautical Meteorology* and numerous scientific articles.	**Drought**
H.R.Bd.	**H. R. BLANFORD, O.B.E.** Former Chief Conservator of Forests, Burma. Editor-Secretary, Empire Forestry Association, London, Eng.	**Forests** (*in part*)
H.R.P.	**HELENA R. POUCH (Mrs. William H. Pouch).** President General, National Society Daughters of the American Revolution, Washington, D.C.	**Daughters of the American Revolution, National Society of**
H.R.V.	**HENRY R. VIETS, M.D.** Lecturer on Neurology, Harvard Medical School. Neurologist, Massachusetts General Hospital. Librarian, Boston Medical Library, Boston, Mass.	**Psychiatry**
H.Sn.	**HARRY SIMONS.** Editor and Publisher, *The Clothing Trade Journal,* New York, N.Y.	**Clothing Industry**
H.T.	**HENRY TETLOW.** Henry Tetlow Company, Washington, D.C.	**Soap, Perfumery and Cosmetics**
H.Ta.	**HAZEL TAYLOR.** Director, Women's Interest, AAF and WASP Public Relations; Air WAC Liaison, AAF Group, Bureau of Public Relations, War Department, Washington, D.C.	**Women's Airforce Service Pilots**
H.T.Ch.	**HUNG-TI CHU, Ph.D.** Research Associate, Chinese News Service.	**Chiang Kai-shek; China**
H.W.At.	**HEINZ WOLFGANG ARNDT.** Assistant Lecturer in Economics, Manchester University. Former Research Assistant, Royal Institute of International Affairs, London, Eng.	**Citrine, Sir Walter McLennan; Morrison, Herbert Stanley**
H.W.Ba.	**H. W. BASHORE.** Commissioner, Bureau of Reclamation, U.S. Department of the Interior, Washington, D.C.	**Aqueducts**
H.W.Ch.	**HARRY WOODBURN CHASE, Ph.D., LL.D., Litt.D.** Chancellor, New York University, New York, N.Y.	**New York University**
H.W.Do.	**HAROLD W. DODDS, Litt.D., LL.D.** President, Princeton University, Princeton, N.J.	**Princeton University**
H.W.L.	**HARRY W. LAIDLER.** Executive Director, League for Industrial Democracy.	**Socialism** (*in part*)
H.Z.	**HOWARD ZAHNISER.** Book Editor, *Nature Magazine,* Washington, D.C.	**Wild Life Conservation**
I.A.Rs.	**IVOR ARMSTRONG RICHARDS, M.A., Litt.D.** University Lecturer and Director, Commission on English Language Studies, Harvard University, Cambridge, Mass. Author of *Basic English and Its Uses;* etc.	**Basic English**
I.Bn.	**INNIS BROWN.** Former Managing Editor, *The American Golfer,* New York, N.Y. Co-author of *A Guide to Good Golf* and *Swinging into Golf.*	**Golf**
I.Bo.	**ISAIAH BOWMAN, Ph.D., LL.D.** President, Johns Hopkins University, Baltimore, Md.	**Johns Hopkins University**
I.Br.	**IVOR BROWN.** Editor of the *Observer,* London, Eng. Professor of Drama to the Royal Society of Literature.	**Theatre** (*in part*)
I.B.W.S.	**IDA B. WISE SMITH.** President, National Woman's Christian Temperance Union.	**Woman's Christian Temperance Union, National**
I.Gg.	**ISAAC GREGG.** Director, Press Relations, Office of the Postmaster General, Washington, D.C.	**Post Office** (*in part*)
I.L.Bl.	**IRENE L. BLUNT.** Secretary, The National Federation of Textiles, Inc., New York, N.Y.	**Linen and Flax, etc.**
I.L.K.	**ISAAC LEON KANDEL, M.A., Ph.D., Litt.D.** Professor of Education, Teachers College, Columbia University, New York, N.Y. Editor, *Educational Yearbook.*	**Education** (*in part*)
I.St.	**IRVIN STEWART, Ph.D.** Executive Secretary, Office of Scientific Research and Development; Executive Secretary, National Defense Research Committee. Executive Secretary, Committee on Medical Research, Washington, D.C.	**Scientific Research and Development, Office of**
J.A.G.	**J. A. GARY.** Editor, *Furniture Age,* Chicago, Ill.	**Furniture Industry**
J.A.Ma.	**J. ARTHUR MATHEWSON, K.C.** Of Mathewson, Wilson and Smith, Barristers, Montreal, Que.	**Montreal**
J.A.Mi.	**JOHN ANDERSON MILLER.** Member of Editorial Staff, American Society of Mechanical Engineers.	**Electric Transportation**
J.A.My.	**J. A. MYERS, M.D.** Professor of Medicine and Preventive Medicine and Public Health, University of Minnesota Medical School, Minneapolis, Minn.	**Tuberculosis**
J.A.S.R.	**J. A. S. RITSON.** Professor of Mining, Royal School of Mines, South Kensington. Member of Council of the Institutions of Mining and Metallurgy and Mining Engineers, London, Eng.	**Coal** (*in part*)
J.B.Bl.	**JOHN B. BLANDFORD, JR.** Administrator, National Housing Agency, Washington, D.C.	**National Housing Agency** (*in part*)
J.B.E.	**JOSEPH B. EASTMAN, LL.D.** Director, Office of Defense Transportation, Office for Emergency Management, Washington, D.C.	**Defense Transportation, Office of**
J.B.Mn.	**JOHN B. MARTIN.** Acting Director, Office of Civilian Defense, Washington, D.C.	**Civilian Defense** (*in part*)
J.Br.	**JAMES BREWSTER.** State Librarian, Connecticut State Library, Hartford, Conn.	**Connecticut**
J.C.He.	**JOSEPH CLARENCE HEMMEON, A.M., Ph.D.** William Dow Professor of Political Economy and Chairman, Department of Economics and Political Science, McGill University, Montreal, Que.	**Ontario Quebec, etc.**
J.C.Mn.	**JAMES C. MALIN, Ph.D.** Professor of History, University of Kansas, Lawrence, Kan.	**Kansas**
J.C.Ms.	**J. CLYDE MARQUIS, M.S.A., D.Ag.** American Representative and Vice-President, International Institute of Agriculture, Rome, Italy, 1935-41. Former Director of Economic Information, U.S. Department of Agriculture, Washington, D.C.	**Agriculture** (*in part*) **Cheese; Corn Hops; Hogs, etc.**
J.E.Ds.	**JOSEPH E. DAVIES.** Chairman, President's War Relief Control Board, Washington, D.C.	**War Relief, U.S.**
J.E.H.	**J. EDGAR HOOVER, LL.M.** Director, Federal Bureau of Investigation, U.S. Department of Justice, Washington, D.C.	**Federal Bureau of Investigation**
J.E.Mo.	**JOY ELMER MORGAN, D.Sc. in Ed.** Editor of the *Journal of the National Education Association,* Washington, D.C.	**National Education Association**
J.E.Ms.	**J. E. MASTERS.** Grand Secretary, Benevolent and Protective Order of Elks.	**Elks, Benevolent and Protective Order of**

J.F.B.	**JAMES F. BYRNES.** Former Justice, U.S. Supreme Court. Director of War Mobilization, Washington, D.C.	**Emergency Management, Office for**
J.F.D.	**JOHN FOSTER DULLES, LL.D.** Chairman, Commission on a Just and Durable Peace.	**Christian Mission on World Order**
J.Fe.	**JAMES FORGIE.** Internationally known authority on tunnels.	**Tunnels**
J.F.H.	**JOHNSON F. HAMMOND, M.D.** Lieutenant Colonel, U.S.A. Editor, *Bulletin of the U.S. Army Medical Department*, Washington, D.C.	**Medicine** (*in part*)
J.F.Ws.	**JOHN F. WILLIAMS.** Major General, U.S.A. Chief, National Guard Bureau, War Department, Washington, D.C.	**National Guard**
J.G.Bo.	**JOHN G. BOWMAN, A.M., LL.D., Litt.D.** Chancellor of the University of Pittsburgh, Pittsburgh, Pa.	**Pittsburgh**
J.H.A.	**J. HADEN ALLDREDGE.** Chairman, Interstate Commerce Commission, Washington, D.C.	**Interstate Commerce Commission**
J.H.Bn.	**J. HOWARD BROWN, Ph.D.** Associate Professor of Bacteriology, School of Medicine, The Johns Hopkins University, Baltimore, Md.	**Bacteriology**
J.H.Fa.	**JOHN H. FAHEY.** Commissioner, Federal Home Loan Bank Administration, National Housing Agency, Washington, D.C.	**National Housing Agency** (*in part*)
J.H.Fy.	**JOHN HARVEY FURBAY, A.M., Ph.D.** Professor of Education and Chairman, Department of Education, Mills College, Mills College, Calif. Adviser on Liberia, Office of War Information, Washington, D.C. Former President, College of West Africa.	**Liberia**
J.H.Hg.	**J. H. HILLDRING.** Major General, U.S.A. Director, Civil Affairs Division, War Department, Washington, D.C.	**Allied Military Government**
J.H.L.	**JOHN HOWLAND LATHROP, Ph.D., D.D.** Minister of the First Unitarian Congregational Society in Brooklyn, N.Y.	**Unitarian Church**
J.I.C.	**JOHN I. COOPER, M.A., Ph.D.** Assistant Professor of History, McGill University, Montreal, Que.	**Alberta Canada** (*in part*), **etc.**
J.J.Dn.	**J. J. DONOVAN.** Acting Director, Civil Service Assembly of the United States and Canada.	**Civil Service, U.S.**
J.J.Sw.	**JAMES JOHNSON SWEENEY.** Lecturer, Fine Arts Institute, New York University, New York, N.Y. Author of *Alexander Calder; Plastic Redirections in Twentieth Century Painting; John Miro*; etc.	**Painting**
J.LaF.	**JOHN LaFARGE, S.J.** Executive Editor, *America*, National Catholic Weekly, New York, N.Y.	**Pius XII Roman Catholic Church, etc.**
J.L.F.	**J. L. FRAZIER.** Editor, *The Inland Printer*, Chicago, Ill.	**Printing**
J.L.Fy.	**JAMES LAWRENCE FLY.** Chairman, Federal Communications Commission; Chairman, Board of War Communications, Washington, D.C.	**Federal Communications Commission War Communications, Board of**
J.L.He.	**JOHN L. HERVEY.** Author of *Racing in America; American Race Horses; The Old Gray Mare of Long Island*; etc.	**Horse Racing** (*in part*)
J.L.J.	**J. L. JOHNSTON.** Librarian, Provincial Library, Winnipeg, Man.	**Manitoba**
J.L.K.	**J. L. KEITH, M.A., O.B.E.** Colonial Service 1919-37. African Research Survey 1937-39.	**British East Africa** (*in part*) **Rhodesia** (*in part*), **etc.**
J.L.N.	**JOHN LLOYD NEWCOMB, Hon.D.Sc., LL.D.** President, University of Virginia, Charlottesville, Va.	**Virginia, University of**
J.M.Ca.	**J. M. CALLAHAN, A.M., Ph.D.** Research Professor of History, West Virginia University, Morgantown, W.Va.	**West Virginia**
J.McAt.	**JOHN McALMONT.** Civil Servant, London, Eng.	**Social Security** (*in part*)
J.M.L.	**JAMES MILLER LEAKE, Ph.D.** Professor of History and Political Science, University of Florida, Gainesville, Fla.	**Florida**
J.P.D.	**JAMES P. DAWSON.** Writer on baseball and boxing, *The New York Times*, New York, N.Y.	**Boxing**
J.P.J.	**JOHN PRICE JONES.** President and Treasurer, The John Price Jones Corporation, New York, N.Y. Author of *The Yearbook of Philanthropy*.	**Donations and Bequests**
J.R.Cl.	**J. REUBEN CLARK, JR.** First Counselor, Church of Jesus Christ of Latter-Day Saints, Salt Lake City, Utah.	**Mormons**
J.R.Hr.	**J. R. HELLER, JR.** Medical Director; Chief, Venereal Disease Division, U.S. Public Health Service, Washington, D.C.	**Venereal Diseases**
J.R.J.	**JAMES R. JOY, Litt.D., LL.D.** Librarian and Historian, The Methodist Historical Society in the City of New York.	**Methodist Church**
J.R.Tu.	**JOHN R. TUNIS.** Writer on tennis.	**Tennis**
J.S.Br.	**JOHN STEWART BRYAN, M.A., Litt.D., LL.D.** President and Publisher, *Richmond Times Dispatch* and *Richmond News Leader*, Richmond, Va.	**Virginia**
J.S.G.	**JAMES STEELE GOW, Ed.M.** Director, The Maurice and Laura Falk Foundation, Pittsburgh, Pa.	**Falk Foundation, The Maurice and Laura**
J.S.L.	**JOHN S. LUNDY, M.D.** Professor of Anaesthesia, University of Minnesota Graduate School, Minneapolis, Minn. Head, Section on Anaesthesia, Mayo Clinic, Rochester, Minn.	**Anaesthesia**
J.S.M.	**JOHN S. McCAIN.** Vice Admiral, U.S.N. Deputy Chief of Naval Operations (Air), Navy Department, Washington, D.C.	**Air Forces of the World** (*in part*)
J.Sn.	**JOHN SNURE, JR.** Current Information Officer, Selective Service System, Washington, D.C.	**Selective Service, U.S.**
J.Sto.	**JAMES STOKLEY.** Author of *Science Remakes Our World*.	**Radio Detection**
J.T.Ar.	**JOHN TAYLOR ARMS, S.M., M.A., Litt.D.** President, Society of American Etchers. First Vice-President, National Academy of Design.	**Etching**
J.T.W.	**JOHN T. WINTERICH.** Colonel, Signal Corps, War Department, Washington, D.C. Author of *A Primer of Book Collecting*; etc.	**Book-collecting**
J.V.L.H.	**JOHN V. L. HOGAN.** President, Interstate Broadcasting Co., Inc. (WQXR). President, Faximile, Inc. Author of *The Outline of Radio*.	**Radio** (*in part*) **Television** (*in part*)
J.W.Bl.	**JAMES WASHINGTON BELL, Ph.D.** Professor of Banking, Northwestern University, Evanston, Ill. Secretary-Treasurer and Editor of *Proceedings*, American Economic Association.	**American Economic Association**
J.W.Mt.	**JAMES W. MOFFITT.** Secretary, Oklahoma Historical Society, Oklahoma City, Okla.	**Oklahoma**
J.W.Sc.	**JAMES WALTER SCHADE.** Manager of Government Laboratories, University of Akron, Akron, Ohio.	**Rubber**
J.W.T.Y.	**JOHN WILLIAM THEODORE YOUNGS, M.A., Ph.D.** Assistant Professor of Mathematics, Purdue University, Lafayette, Ind.	**Mathematics**
K.B.S.	**KATHLEEN B. STEBBINS.** Secretary and Advertising Manager, Special Libraries Association.	**Special Libraries Association**
K.E.M.	**KATHARINE ELIZABETH McBRIDE, Ph.D., LL.D., L.H.D.** President, Bryn Mawr College, Bryn Mawr, Pa.	**Bryn Mawr College**
K.F.L.	**KATHARINE F. LENROOT.** Chief, Children's Bureau, U.S. Department of Labor, Washington, D.C.	**Child Welfare**
K.S.L.	**KENNETH SCOTT LATOURETTE, D.D., Ph.D.** Professor of Missions and Oriental History, Yale University, New Haven, Conn.	**Missions, Foreign**
K.Sm.	**KAZIMIERZ SMOGORZEWSKI.** Polish Journalist in Paris, Berlin, etc. Founder and Editor, *Free Europe*. Author of *Poland's Access to the Sea*; etc.	**Poland** (*in part*)
K.T.C.	**KARL T. COMPTON, M.S., Ph.D., D.Sc., LL.D.** President, Massachusetts Institute of Technology, Cambridge, Mass.	**Massachusetts Institute of Technology**
L.A.L.	**LEROY A. LINCOLN.** President, Metropolitan Life Insurance Company, New York, N.Y.	**Insurance** (*in part*)

L.A.M.	**LOUIS A. MERILLAT, M.D.V., V.S.** Editor, *Journal of the American Veterinary Medical Association* and *American Journal of Veterinary Research*. Author of *Veterinary Military History of the United States*, etc.	**Veterinary Medicine**
L.A.McA.	**LEWIS A. McARTHUR, M.A.** President and Director, Oregon Historical Society, Portland, Ore. Member and Secretary, Oregon Geographic Board.	**Oregon**
L.A.We.	**LUTHER ALLAN WEIGLE, Ph.D., D.D., Litt.D., S.T.D., LL.D., J.U.D.** Dean of the Divinity School, Yale University, New Haven, Conn. President, Federal Council of Churches.	**Church Membership** **Sunday Schools**
L.Be.	**LEWIS BEESON, M.A., Ph.D.** Acting Superintendent, Minnesota Historical Society, St. Paul, Minn.	**Minnesota**
L.C.S.	**LOUIS CARTER SMITH, LL.M.** Secretary-Treasurer, National Archery Association of the United States, Boston, Mass.	**Archery**
L. de B.H.	**L. de BREDA HANDLEY.** Honorary Coach, Women's Swimming Association of New York. Author of *Swimming for Women*; etc.	**Swimming**
L.D.Sh.	**LESLIE D. SHAFFER.** Secretary, American Friends Fellowship Council.	**Friends, Religious** **Society of**
L.D.U.	**LENT D. UPSON, Ph.D.** Director, Detroit Bureau of Governmental Research, Inc.	**Detroit**
L.Du	**LEONARD DUDENEY.** Parliamentary Gallery and Lobby correspondent 1918-43.	**Conservative Party,** **Great Britain** **George VI, etc.**
L.D.V.	**LEON DE VALINGER, JR., A.M.** State Archivist, Dover, Del.	**Delaware**
L.Ef.	**LOUIS EFFRAT.** Member of sports staff, *The New York Times*, New York, N.Y.	**Billiards**
L.E.L.	**LEWIS E. LAWES, Hon. D.Sc.** Former Warden, Sing Sing Prison, Ossining, N.Y. Chief Business Consultant, Government Division, War Production Board, New York, N.Y.	**Prisons**
L.E.T.	**LEON E. TRUESDELL, Ph.D., Sc.D.** Chief, Population Division, United States Bureau of the Census, Washington, D.C. Author of *Farm Population of the U.S.* and *The Canadian Born in the United States*.	**Census, 1940**
L.Gn.	**LESTER GIBSON,** Director of News Bureau, American Bankers Association.	**American Bankers** **Association**
L.Gu.	**LUTHER GULICK, Ph.D., Litt.D.** Director, Institute of Public Administration, New York, N.Y.	**Municipal Government** *(in part)*
L.G.V.V.	**LEWIS GEORGE VANDER VELDE, Ph.D.** Professor of History and Director of the Michigan Historical Collections, University of Michigan, Ann Arbor, Mich.	**Michigan**
L.H.L.	**LEWIS HARPER LEECH, M.A.** Editorial writer, *The Chicago Daily News*, Chicago, Ill.	**Chicago; Illinois**
L.J.Br.	**LYMAN J. BRIGGS, Ph.D., LL.D., Sc.D., Eng.D.** Director, National Bureau of Standards, U.S. Department of Commerce, Washington, D.C.	**Standards, National** **Bureau of**
L.K.F.	**LAWRENCE K. FOX.** Secretary, South Dakota State Historical Society, Pierre, S.D.	**South Dakota**
L.M.A.	**LILLIAN M. AINSWORTH.** Secretary, State Department of Public Welfare, Montpelier, Vt.	**Vermont**
L.M.F.	**LEONARD M. FANNING, M.A.** Author of *The Rise of American Oil*.	**Petroleum**
L.Mh.	**LUCILE MARSH.** Editor, *Dance Magazine*, New York, N.Y.	**Dance** *(in part)*
L.Mo.	**LUIS MONGUIÓ.** Instructor in Romance Languages, Mills College, Oakland, Calif.	**Spanish-American** **Literature**
L.M.S.M.	**LEROY M. S. MINER, D.M.D., M.D.** Dean of Harvard University Dental School, Boston, Mass.	**Dentistry**
L.O.	**LELAND OLDS.** Chairman, Federal Power Commission, Washington, D.C.	**Federal Power** **Commission**
L.O.C.	**LEO OTIS COLBERT, Sc.D.** Rear Admiral U.S.C. & G.S. Director, U.S. Coast and Geodetic Survey, Department of Commerce, Washington, D.C.	**Coast and Geodetic** **Survey, U. S.**
L.O.P.	**LOUELLA O. PARSONS.** Motion Picture Editor, International News Service. Author of *The Gay Illiterate*.	**Motion Pictures** *(in part)*
L.Sl.	**LEVERETT SALTONSTALL, LL.D.** Overseer of Harvard University. Governor of Massachusetts.	**Massachusetts**
L.S.Ro.	**L. S. ROWE, Ph.D., LL.D.** Director General, Pan American Union, Washington, D.C.	**Pan American Union**
L.T.S.	**LEONARD THOMAS SCOTT.** Colonial Administrative Service.	**Aden** *(in part)*
L.W.Ba.	**LORNE W. BARCLAY.** National Director of Publications, Boy Scouts of America.	**Boy Scouts**
L.W.L.	**LANE W. LANCASTER, Ph.D.** Professor of Political Science, University of Nebraska, Lincoln, Neb.	**Nebraska**
L.W.M.	**LON W. MORREY, D.D.S.** Director, Bureau of Public Relations, American Dental Association, Chicago, Ill.	**American Dental** **Association**
L.Wo.	**LEO WOLMAN, D.Ph.** Professor of Economics, Columbia University, New York, N.Y.	**Labour Unions** *(in part)*
M.Ab.	**MILTON ABELSON, M.C.S.** Economic Analyst, Bureau of Foreign and Domestic Commerce, Department of Commerce, Washington, D.C.	**Foreign Investments** **in the United States**
M.A.Hs.	**MINNETTA A. HASTINGS (Mrs. William A. Hastings).** President, National Congress of Parents and Teachers.	**Parents and Teachers,** **National Congress of**
M.C.Ml.	**MATTHEW C. MITCHELL, Ph.D.** Associate Professor of Political Science, Brown University, Providence, R. I.	**Rhode Island**
M.C.P.	**MARION CAROLINE PFUND, Ph.D.** Professor of Home Economics, New York State College of Home Economics and School of Nutrition, Cornell University, Ithaca, N.Y.	**Food Research** **Home Economics**
M.Dn.	**MITCHELL DAWSON, D.J.** Lawyer, writer. Former Editor, *Chicago Bar Record*, Chicago, Ill.	**American Bar Association** **Law**
M.Do.	**MAURICE DOBB, M.A., Ph.D.** Lecturer in Economics, Cambridge University, Cambridge, Eng. Visiting Lecturer in Soviet Economic History, School of Slavonic and East European Studies, University of London, London, Eng. Author of *Russian Economic Development Since the Revolution*; etc.	**Union of Soviet** **Socialist Republics** *(in part)*
M.E.H.	**MARTIN E. HANKE, Ph.D.** Associate Professor of Biochemistry, The University of Chicago, Chicago, Ill.	**Biochemistry**
M.F.C.	**MICHELE F. CANTARELLA.** Associate Professor of Italian Language and Literature, Smith College, Northampton, Mass. Now on leave.	**Italian Literature**
M.Fd.	**MAXWELL FINLAND, M.D.** Associate Physician, Thorndike Memorial Laboratory; Physician in Chief, Fourth Medical Service, Boston City Hospital. Assistant Professor of Medicine, Harvard Medical School, Boston, Mass.	**Pneumonia**
M.Fe.	**MAURICE FANSHAWE.** Chief Intelligence Officer, Central Office, League of Nations Union of Great Britain.	**League of Nations** **Mandates**
M.Fi.	**MORRIS FISHBEIN, M.D.** Editor, *The Journal of the American Medical Association* and *Hygeia*, Chicago, Ill. Editor of medical articles, *Britannica Book of the Year*.	**Medicine, etc.**
M.G.G.	**MARTIN G. GLAESER, Ph.D.** Professor of Economics, University of Wisconsin, Madison, Wis.	**Public Utilities**
M.Gt.	**MILTON GILBERT, M.A., Ph.D.** Acting Chief, Division of Research and Statistics, Bureau of Foreign and Domestic Commerce, Department of Commerce, Washington, D.C.	**Budget, National** **National Debt, etc.**
M.Ha.	**MANNEL HAHN.** Promotional Manager, *The Rotarian* and *Revista Rotaria*. Author of *U.S. Post Office, 1851-60*; *U.S. Postal Markings, 1847-51*; *So You're Collecting Stamps*; etc.	**Philately**
M.H.E.	**MARIE H. ERWIN.** Historian, Wyoming State Historical Department, Cheyenne, Wyo.	**Wyoming**
M.H.McA.	**MILDRED H. McAFEE, LL.D., L.H.D.** Captain, U.S.N.R. Director, Women's Reserve, U.S.N.R. President, Wellesley College, Wellesley, Mass.	**Wellesley College** **Women's Reserve of** **the Navy**
M.H.T.	**MILTON HALSEY THOMAS, A.M.** Curator of Columbiana, Columbia University, New York, N.Y.	**Columbia University**

M.J.Hs.	**MELVILLE J. HERSKOVITS, A.M., Ph.D.** Professor of Anthropology, Northwestern University, Evanston, Ill.	**Anthropology**
M.Jo.	**MELVIN JONES.** Secretary-General, International Association of Lions Clubs, Chicago, Ill.	**Lions Clubs**
M.Js.	**MARVIN JONES.** War Food Administrator, Washington, D.C.	**War Food Administration**
M.Lb.	**MAX LOEB.** Chief of Field Division, Illinois Liquor Control Commission.	**Liquors, Alcoholic** (*in part*)
M.L.W.	**M. L. WILSON.** Director of Extension Work, U.S. Department of Agriculture, Washington, D.C.	**Four-H Clubs**
M.O.P.	**MILDRED OTHMER PETERSON.** Special Writer, American Library Association.	**American Library Association**
M.Pr.	**MARTIN POPPER.** Executive Secretary, National Lawyers Guild.	**National Lawyers Guild**
M.P.W.	**MILTON P. WOODARD.** Sports Writer, *The Chicago Sun*, Chicago, Ill.	**Basketball; Track and Field Sports, etc.**
M.Sr.	**MARGARET SANGER.** Honorary Chairman, Planned Parenthood Federation, Inc.	**Birth Control**
M.S.Ss.	**MARY S. SIMS.** Executive, National Interpretation and Support Committee, National Board, Young Womens Christian Associations of the United States of America.	**Young Womens Christian Association**
M.T.	**MICHAEL TIERNEY, M.A.** Professor of Greek, University College, Dublin, Eire. Member of Council of State, Eire. Vice-Chairman, Seanad Eireann, 1938-43.	**Eire** (*in part*)
M.T.M.	**MALCOLM T. MacEACHERN, M.D.** Associate Director, American College of Surgeons.	**American College of Surgeons**
N.A.R.	**NELSON A. ROCKEFELLER.** Coordinator of Inter-American Affairs, Washington, D.C.	**Inter-American Affairs, Office of the Coordinator of**
N.B.D.	**NEWTON B. DRURY.** Director, National Park Service, U.S. Department of the Interior, Washington, D.C.	**National Parks and Monuments**
N.C.B.	**NELSON C. BROWN, M.F.** Professor in charge of Forest Utilization, New York State College of Forestry, Syracuse University, Syracuse, N.Y.	**Lumber** (*in part*)
N.E.C.	**NORMAN E. CRUMP.** City Editor, *London Sunday Times*, London, Eng.	**Bank of England**
N.E.W.	**N. E. WAYSON, M.D.** Medical Officer in Charge, Plague Investigations, U.S. Public Health Service, San Francisco, Calif.	**Plague, Bubonic and Pneumonic**
N.F.	**NORMAN FRENCH.** Editor, *The Timber Trades Journal and Sawmill Advertiser*.	**Lumber** (*in part*)
N.H.H.	**N. H. HECK, D.Sc.** Assistant to the Director, U.S. Coast and Geodetic Survey, Department of Commerce, Washington, D.C.	**Seismology**
N.Ke.	**NORMAN KEEP.** Head of the Senior Day School and Evening Building Department, London County Council School of Building, Brixton, London, Eng.	**Building and Construction Industry** (*in part*)
N.L.P.	**NEWTON LACY PIERCE, M.S., Ph.D.** Assistant Professor of Astronomy, Princeton University, Princeton, N.J.	**Astronomy**
N.S.	**NOEL SARGENT.** Secretary, National Association of Manufacturers.	**National Association of Manufacturers**
N.T.	**NORMAN THOMAS, Litt.D.** Socialist presidential candidate, 1940.	**Socialism** (*in part*)
N.T.R.	**NELLIE TAYLOE ROSS.** Director of the United States Mint.	**Coinage**
O.E.P.	**OWEN E. PENCE, A.M.** Director, Bureau of Records, Studies and Trends, National Council of the Young Men's Christian Associations of the United States, New York, N.Y.	**Young Men's Christian Association**
O.G.L.	**ORIN GRANT LIBBY, Ph.D.** Professor of American History, University of North Dakota, Grand Forks, N.D.	**North Dakota**
O.J.W.	**OSCAR J. WILE.** Senior Partner, Oscar J. Wile & Company, New York, N.Y. Author of *Wine Without Frills; What, When and How to Serve*.	**Wines**
O.M.T.	**OWEN MEREDITH TWEEDY, O.B.E.** Former Assistant Oriental Secretary, the British Embassy, Cairo, Egypt. Director, Middle East Bureau of the Ministry of Information, Cairo, Egypt, 1941-43.	**Anglo-Egyptian Sudan** (*in part*) **Egypt** (*in part*)
O.P.P.	**O. P. PEARSON.** Chief Statistician, Automotive Council for War Production, Detroit, Mich.	**Automobile Industry in the War**
P.B.F.	**PHILIP B. FLEMING.** Major General, U.S.A. Administrator, Federal Works Agency, Washington, D.C.	**Federal Works Agency**
P.Bn.	**PRESTON BENSON.** Journalist for the *Star*, London, Eng. Author of *Unknown Country*.	**Crime** (*in part*) **London**
P.Bt.	**PAUL BROCKETT.** Executive Secretary, National Academy of Sciences, Washington, D.C.	**National Academy of Sciences**
P.By.	**PAUL BELLAMY.** Editor, *Cleveland Plain Dealer*, Cleveland, Ohio.	**Cleveland; Ohio**
P.Dg.	**PAUL DEARING.** Assistant Director of Public Relations, National Catholic Community Service.	**Catholic Community Service, National**
P.D.W.	**PAUL D. WHITE, M.D.** Lecturer on Medicine, Harvard University Medical School; Physician, Massachusetts General Hospital, Boston, Mass.	**Heart and Heart Diseases**
P.E.	**PAUL EDWARDS.** Editor, *Trailer Topics Magazine*.	**Trailer Coaches**
P.E.R.	**PHILIP E. RYAN, M.A.** Director, Civilian Relief, Insular and Foreign Operations, American Red Cross.	**Prisoners of War Red Cross** (*in part*)
P.F.T.	**PAUL F. TANNER.** Director, Youth Department, National Catholic Welfare Conference, Washington, D.C.	**Catholic Organizations for Youth**
P.G.H.	**PAUL G. HOFFMAN.** Chairman, Committee for Economic Development. President, The Studebaker Corporation, South Bend, Ind.	**Committee for Economic Development**
P.Ly.	**PHILIP LOVEJOY.** General Secretary, Rotary International.	**Rotary International**
P.My.	**PHILIP MURRAY.** President, Congress of Industrial Organizations.	**Congress of Industrial Organizations**
P.N.R.	**PAUL NORTH RICE.** Chief, Reference Department, The New York Public Library, New York, N.Y. Executive Secretary, The Association of Research Libraries.	**Association of Research Libraries**
P.T.	**PAUL TITUS, M.D.** Secretary-Treasurer, American Board of Obstetrics and Gynecology.	**Gynaecology and Obstetrics**
P.V.M.	**PAUL V. McNUTT, LL.D.** Chairman, War Manpower Commission; Federal Security Administrator, Washington, D.C.	**Federal Security Agency**
R.A.G.	**R. A. GIBSON.** Deputy Commissioner, Northwest Territories.	**Northwest Territories**
R.A.Ga.	**RUTH A. GALLAHER, Ph.D.** Associate Editor of the State Historical Society of Iowa. Author of *Legal and Political Status of Women in Iowa*, etc.	**Iowa**
R.B.B.	**RALPH B. BRYAN.** Editor, *Hide and Leather and Shoes*, Chicago, Ill.	**Leather**
R.B.E.	**R. B. ELEAZER, A.M.** Former Educational Director, Commission on Interracial Co-operation, Inc., Atlanta, Ga.	**Lynchings**
R.B.Kr.	**R. B. KOEBER.** Manager, Research Department, San Francisco Chamber of Commerce, San Francisco, Calif.	**San Francisco**
R.C.R-G.	**RAYMOND CHARLES ROBERTSON-GLASGOW.** Cricket Correspondent of the *Sunday Observer*.	**Cricket**
R.D.Hu.	**ROCKWELL D. HUNT, A.M., Ph.D., LL.D., Litt.D.** Dean of the Graduate School and Professor of Economics, University of Southern California, Los Angeles, Calif.	**Southern California, University of**
R.E.E.H.	**REUBEN E. E. HARKNESS, Ph.D.** President, American Baptist Historical Society.	**Baptist Church**
R.E.Rh.	**ROBERT E. RALEIGH.** Acting Director, The Traffic Institute, Northwestern University, Evanston, Ill.	**Accidents** (*in part*)
R.F.K.	**ROBERT F. KELLEY.** Sports Writer, *The New York Times*, New York, N.Y. Assistant Secretary, United States Polo Association.	**Polo**

R.Fs.	**ROBERT FOSS.** Publicity Director and Editor, News Bureau, University of Wisconsin, Madison, Wis.	**Wisconsin, University of**
R.G.Ha.	**ROSWELL GRAY HAM, Ph.D., LL.D.** President, Mount Holyoke College, South Hadley, Mass.	**Mount Holyoke College**
R.G.Hu.	**RAY G. HULBURT, D.O.** Editor, American Osteopathic Association.	**Osteopathy**
R.G.M.	**R. G. MACDONALD.** Secretary-Treasurer, Technical Association of the Pulp and Paper Industry, New York, N.Y.	**Paper and Pulp Industry**
R.G.S.	**ROBERT G. SPROUL, LL.D.** President, University of California, Berkeley, Calif.	**California, University of**
R.Har.	**RICHARD HARTSHORNE, Ph.D.** Professor of Geography, University of Wisconsin, Madison, Wis.	**Geography**
R.H.F.	**REGINALD H. FIEDLER.** Chief, Marine Industries Section, Foreign Economic Administration, Washington, D.C.	**Fisheries**
R.Hs.	**RALPH HAYES.** Executive Director, New York Community Trust. Director; member of Executive Committee, National War Fund.	**Community Trusts**
R.H.Sd.	**ROLLIN H. SANFORD.** Head Crew Coach, Cornell University, Ithaca, N.Y.	**Rowing**
R.Is.	**RAPHAEL ISAACS, M.A., M.D.** Director, Research Laboratory of Haematology and Attending Physician in Haematology, Michael Reese Hospital, Chicago, Ill.	**Anaemia**
R.J.B.	**ROBERT J. BRAIDWOOD, A.M., Ph.D.** Archaeologist, The Oriental Institute and the Department of Anthropology, The University of Chicago, Chicago, Ill.	**Archaeology** (*in part*)
R.L.Fo.	**R. L. FORNEY.** General Secretary, National Safety Council, Chicago, Ill.	**Accidents** (*in part*)
R.L.Fy.	**ROSS LEE FINNEY.** American Composer. Editor, Smith College Music Archives. 1938 Pulitzer Scholarship, Guggenheim Fellowship. Professor of Music, Smith College, Northampton, Mass. and Mt. Holyoke College, South Hadley, Mass.	**Music** (*in part*)
R.L.Ss.	**ROBERT L. SAMMONS.** Economic Analyst, Bureau of Foreign and Domestic Commerce, Department of Commerce, Washington, D.C.	**U. S. Investments Abroad**
R.L.W.	**RAY LYMAN WILBUR, A.M., M.D., LL.D., Sc.D.** Chancellor, Stanford University, Stanford University, Calif.	**Stanford University**
R.M.Le.	**ROBERT M. LESTER.** Secretary, Carnegie Corporation of New York.	**Carnegie Trusts**
R.Nt.	**ROLF NUGENT.** Director, Department of Consumer Credit Studies, Russell Sage Foundation, New York, N.Y.	**Consumer Credit**
Ro.Sto.	**ROBERT STOKES.** Secretary, Press and Publications Board, Church Assembly, London, Eng. Editor of the Official Year Book of the Church of England.	**Church of England**
R.P.Br.	**RALPH P. BIEBER, Ph.D.** Professor of History, Washington University, St. Louis, Mo.	**Missouri**
R.Ra.	**ROBERT RAE.** Professor of Agriculture, University of Reading, Reading, Eng.	**Agriculture** (*in part*)
R.R.P.	**RAYE R. PLATT.** Research Associate, American Geographical Society.	**American Geographical Society**
R.R.W.	**RUSSELL R. WAESCHE.** Vice Admiral, U.S.N. Commandant, U.S. Coast Guard.	**Coast Guard, U.S.** (*in part*)
R.S.S.	**ROBERT SIDNEY SMITH, A.M., Ph.D.** Assistant Professor of Economics, Duke University, Durham, N.C. Author of *The Spanish Guild Merchant*; etc.	**Spanish Literature**
R.S.T.	**ROBERT S. THOMAS, M.A.** Military Historian, Army War College, Washington, D.C.	**Camouflage Munitions of War**
R.T.B.	**ROBERT T. BEALL.** Principal Economist, Rural Electrification Administration, U.S. Department of Agriculture, St. Louis, Mo.	**Rural Electrification**
R.Tu.	**RAY TUCKER.** Writer of syndicated column, "The National Whirligig."	**Democratic Party Republican Party Roosevelt, Franklin Delano, etc.**
S.An.	**SIRI ANDREWS.** Assistant Professor, School of Librarianship, University of Washington, Seattle, Wash.	**Children's Books**
S.A.W.	**SARA A. WHITEHURST (Mrs. John L. Whitehurst).** President, General Federation of Women's Clubs.	**Women's Clubs, General Federation of**
S.B.F.	**SIDNEY B. FAY, Ph.D., Litt.D., L.H.D.** Professor of History, Harvard University and Radcliffe College, Cambridge, Mass.	**Germany, etc.**
S.B.Wi.	**S. B. WILLIAMS.** Editor, *Electrical World*, New York, N.Y.	**Electrical Industries**
S.C.G.	**SARAH CHOKLA GROSS.** Secretary, Theatre Library Association.	**Theatre Library Association**
S.C.Ha.	**SIDNEY CHANDLER HAYWARD, M.A.** Secretary of Dartmouth College, Hanover, N.H.	**Dartmouth College**
S.D.McC.	**S. D. McCOMB.** Manager, Marine Office of America, New York, N.Y.	**Insurance** (*in part*)
S.J.Bu.	**SOLON JUSTUS BUCK, Ph.D.** Archivist of the United States. Author of *The Granger Movement*; etc.	**Archives, National**
S.J.Hy.	**S. J. HAWLEY, M.D.** Director, Department of Roentgenology and Radiotherapy, George F. Geisinger Memorial Hospital, Danville, Pa. Consulting Radiologist, Danville State Hospital, Danville, Pa.	**Radiology**
S.J.McK.	**S. JUSTUS McKINLEY, Ph.D.** Professor of Social Sciences, Emerson College, Boston, Mass.	**Boston**
S.Lea.	**STEPHEN LEACOCK, Ph.D., Litt.D., LL.D., D.C.L.** Professor Emeritus, McGill University, Montreal, Que.	**Canada** (*in part*), **etc.**
S.McC.C.	**SAMUEL McCREA CAVERT, D.D.** General Secretary, The Federal Council of the Churches of Christ in America.	**Federal Council of the Churches of Christ in America**
S.McC.L.	**SAMUEL McCUNE LINDSAY, Ph.D., LL.D.** Professor Emeritus of Social Legislation, Columbia University, New York, N.Y.	**International Labour Organization**
S.M.Ha.	**SHELBY M. HARRISON, LL.D.** General Director, Russell Sage Foundation, New York, N.Y.	**Russell Sage Foundation**
S.P.J.	**S. PAUL JOHNSTON.** Washington Manager, Curtiss-Wright Corporation. Former Co-ordinator of Research, National Advisory Committee for Aeronautics. Former Editor, *Aviation*.	**Air Forces of the World** (*in part*)
S.R.C.	**SIDNEY R. CAMPION.** Barrister-at-Law and Journalist. Press Officer to the British General Post Office. Former Chief of the Allied Newspapers Parliamentary Press Gallery Staff.	**Newspapers and Magazines** (*in part*) **Post Office** (*in part*)
S.R.S.	**SAMUEL RAY SCHOLES, Ph.D.** Professor of Glass Technology, New York State College of Ceramics, Alfred University, Alfred, N.Y.	**Glass**
S.S.H.	**S. S. HUEBNER, Ph.D., Sc.D.** President, American College of Life Underwriters. Professor of Insurance and Commerce, Wharton School of Finance and Commerce, University of Pennsylvania, Philadelphia, Pa. Chairman, Board of the American Institute for Property and Liability Underwriters, Inc.	**Stocks and Bonds**
S.So.	**SAMUEL SOSKIN, M.D., M.A., Ph.D.** Director of Metabolic and Endocrine Research and Medical Director, Michael Reese Hospital; Professorial Lecturer in Physiology, School of Medicine, Division of Biological Sciences, The University of Chicago, Chicago, Ill.	**Endocrinology**
S.Sp.	**SIGMUND SPAETH, Ph.D.** President, National Association for American Composers and Conductors, New York, N.Y. Author of *The Art of Enjoying Music; A Guide to Great Orchestral Music*; etc.	**Music** (*in part*)
S.Tf.	**SOL TAISHOFF.** Editor and General Manager, *Broadcasting*. Vice-President, Telecommunications Reports, Washington, D.C.	**Radio** (*in part*)
T.H.MacD.	**THOMAS H. MacDONALD.** Commissioner, Public Roads Administration, Federal Works Agency, Washington, D.C.	**Roads and Highways**
T.H.O.	**THOMAS H. OSGOOD, M.A., M.S., Ph.D.** Head, Department of Physics, Michigan State College of Agriculture and Applied Science, East Lansing, Mich. Co-author of *An Outline of Atomic Physics*.	**Physics**
T.J.D.	**THOMAS J. DEEGAN.** Publicist, New York, N.Y.	**Cycling; Lacrosse**
T.Pk.	**THOMAS PARK, Ph.D.** Associate Professor of Zoology and Associate Dean of The Division of the Biological Sciences, The University of Chicago, Chicago, Ill. Zoological Editor of *Ecology*.	**Zoology** (*in part*)

1943

JANUARY
S	M	T	W	T	F	S
.	.	.	.	.	1	2
3	4	5	6	7	8	9
10	11	12	13	14	15	16
17	18	19	20	21	22	23
24	25	26	27	28	29	30
31						

FEBRUARY
S	M	T	W	T	F	S
.	1	2	3	4	5	6
7	8	9	10	11	12	13
14	15	16	17	18	19	20
21	22	23	24	25	26	27
28						

MARCH
S	M	T	W	T	F	S
.	1	2	3	4	5	6
7	8	9	10	11	12	13
14	15	16	17	18	19	20
21	22	23	24	25	26	27
28	29	30	31			

APRIL
S	M	T	W	T	F	S
.	.	.	.	1	2	3
4	5	6	7	8	9	10
11	12	13	14	15	16	17
18	19	20	21	22	23	24
25	26	27	28	29	30	

MAY
S	M	T	W	T	F	S
.	.	.	.	.	.	1
2	3	4	5	6	7	8
9	10	11	12	13	14	15
16	17	18	19	20	21	22
23	24	25	26	27	28	29
30	31					

JUNE
S	M	T	W	T	F	S
.	.	1	2	3	4	5
6	7	8	9	10	11	12
13	14	15	16	17	18	19
20	21	22	23	24	25	26
27	28	29	30			

JULY
S	M	T	W	T	F	S
.	.	.	.	1	2	3
4	5	6	7	8	9	10
11	12	13	14	15	16	17
18	19	20	21	22	23	24
25	26	27	28	29	30	31

AUGUST
S	M	T	W	T	F	S
1	2	3	4	5	6	7
8	9	10	11	12	13	14
15	16	17	18	19	20	21
22	23	24	25	26	27	28
29	30	31				

SEPTEMBER
S	M	T	W	T	F	S
.	.	.	1	2	3	4
5	6	7	8	9	10	11
12	13	14	15	16	17	18
19	20	21	22	23	24	25
26	27	28	29	30		

OCTOBER
S	M	T	W	T	F	S
.	.	.	.	.	1	2
3	4	5	6	7	8	9
10	11	12	13	14	15	16
17	18	19	20	21	22	23
24	25	26	27	28	29	30
31						

NOVEMBER
S	M	T	W	T	F	S
.	1	2	3	4	5	6
7	8	9	10	11	12	13
14	15	16	17	18	19	20
21	22	23	24	25	26	27
28	29	30				

DECEMBER
S	M	T	W	T	F	S
.	.	.	1	2	3	4
5	6	7	8	9	10	11
12	13	14	15	16	17	18
19	20	21	22	23	24	25
26	27	28	29	30	31	

1944

JANUARY
S	M	T	W	T	F	S
.	.	.	.	.	.	1
2	3	4	5	6	7	8
9	10	11	12	13	14	15
16	17	18	19	20	21	22
23	24	25	26	27	28	29
30	31					

FEBRUARY
S	M	T	W	T	F	S
.	.	1	2	3	4	5
6	7	8	9	10	11	12
13	14	15	16	17	18	19
20	21	22	23	24	25	26
27	28	29				

MARCH
S	M	T	W	T	F	S
.	.	.	1	2	3	4
5	6	7	8	9	10	11
12	13	14	15	16	17	18
19	20	21	22	23	24	25
26	27	28	29	30	31	

APRIL
S	M	T	W	T	F	S
.	.	.	.	.	.	1
2	3	4	5	6	7	8
9	10	11	12	13	14	15
16	17	18	19	20	21	22
23	24	25	26	27	28	29
30						

MAY
S	M	T	W	T	F	S
.	1	2	3	4	5	6
7	8	9	10	11	12	13
14	15	16	17	18	19	20
21	22	23	24	25	26	27
28	29	30	31			

JUNE
S	M	T	W	T	F	S
.	.	.	.	1	2	3
4	5	6	7	8	9	10
11	12	13	14	15	16	17
18	19	20	21	22	23	24
25	26	27	28	29	30	

JULY
S	M	T	W	T	F	S
.	.	.	.	.	.	1
2	3	4	5	6	7	8
9	10	11	12	13	14	15
16	17	18	19	20	21	22
23	24	25	26	27	28	29
30	31					

AUGUST
S	M	T	W	T	F	S
.	.	1	2	3	4	5
6	7	8	9	10	11	12
13	14	15	16	17	18	19
20	21	22	23	24	25	26
27	28	29	30	31		

SEPTEMBER
S	M	T	W	T	F	S
.	.	.	.	.	1	2
3	4	5	6	7	8	9
10	11	12	13	14	15	16
17	18	19	20	21	22	23
24	25	26	27	28	29	30

OCTOBER
S	M	T	W	T	F	S
1	2	3	4	5	6	7
8	9	10	11	12	13	14
15	16	17	18	19	20	21
22	23	24	25	26	27	28
29	30	31				

NOVEMBER
S	M	T	W	T	F	S
.	.	.	1	2	3	4
5	6	7	8	9	10	11
12	13	14	15	16	17	18
19	20	21	22	23	24	25
26	27	28	29	30		

DECEMBER
S	M	T	W	T	F	S
.	.	.	.	.	1	2
3	4	5	6	7	8	9
10	11	12	13	14	15	16
17	18	19	20	21	22	23
24	25	26	27	28	29	30
31						

1945

JANUARY
S	M	T	W	T	F	S
.	1	2	3	4	5	6
7	8	9	10	11	12	13
14	15	16	17	18	19	20
21	22	23	24	25	26	27
28	29	30	31			

FEBRUARY
S	M	T	W	T	F	S
.	.	.	.	1	2	3
4	5	6	7	8	9	10
11	12	13	14	15	16	17
18	19	20	21	22	23	24
25	26	27	28			

MARCH
S	M	T	W	T	F	S
.	.	.	.	1	2	3
4	5	6	7	8	9	10
11	12	13	14	15	16	17
18	19	20	21	22	23	24
25	26	27	28	29	30	31

APRIL
S	M	T	W	T	F	S
1	2	3	4	5	6	7
8	9	10	11	12	13	14
15	16	17	18	19	20	21
22	23	24	25	26	27	28
29	30					

MAY
S	M	T	W	T	F	S
.	.	1	2	3	4	5
6	7	8	9	10	11	12
13	14	15	16	17	18	19
20	21	22	23	24	25	26
27	28	29	30	31		

JUNE
S	M	T	W	T	F	S
.	.	.	.	.	1	2
3	4	5	6	7	8	9
10	11	12	13	14	15	16
17	18	19	20	21	22	23
24	25	26	27	28	29	30

JULY
S	M	T	W	T	F	S
1	2	3	4	5	6	7
8	9	10	11	12	13	14
15	16	17	18	19	20	21
22	23	24	25	26	27	28
29	30	31				

AUGUST
S	M	T	W	T	F	S
.	.	.	1	2	3	4
5	6	7	8	9	10	11
12	13	14	15	16	17	18
19	20	21	22	23	24	25
26	27	28	29	30	31	

SEPTEMBER
S	M	T	W	T	F	S
.	.	.	.	.	.	1
2	3	4	5	6	7	8
9	10	11	12	13	14	15
16	17	18	19	20	21	22
23	24	25	26	27	28	29
30						

OCTOBER
S	M	T	W	T	F	S
.	1	2	3	4	5	6
7	8	9	10	11	12	13
14	15	16	17	18	19	20
21	22	23	24	25	26	27
28	29	30	31			

NOVEMBER
S	M	T	W	T	F	S
.	.	.	.	1	2	3
4	5	6	7	8	9	10
11	12	13	14	15	16	17
18	19	20	21	22	23	24
25	26	27	28	29	30	

DECEMBER
S	M	T	W	T	F	S
.	.	.	.	.	.	1
2	3	4	5	6	7	8
9	10	11	12	13	14	15
16	17	18	19	20	21	22
23	24	25	26	27	28	29
30	31					

THE year 1944 of the Christian Era corresponds to the year of Creation 5704–5705 of the Jewish calendar; to the year 1363–64 of the Mohammedan hegira; to the 168th of the United States; and to the 176th year of the *Encyclopædia Britannica.*

JANUARY, 1944

1 New Year's day.
6 Epiphany, or Twelfth Night.
8 Jackson day.
10 Second session of 78th U.S. congress convenes.
13 Festival of St. Veronica.
20 Eve of St. Agnes.
25 Total eclipse of the sun, invisible at Washington, D.C.
26 Foundation day, Australia.
27 Feast of St. Chrysostom.

FEBRUARY

2 Candlemas. Purification of the Virgin.
2 Ground-Hog day.
6 Septuagesima Sunday.
8 Boy Scout day, U.S.A.
12 Birth of Abraham Lincoln, 1809.
14 St. Valentine's day.
20 Quinquagesima Sunday.
22 Shrove Tuesday. Mardi Gras.
22 Washington's birthday, 1732.
23 Ash Wednesday.
24 Feast of St. Matthias.

MARCH

1 St. David's day, patron saint of Wales.
2 Texas Independence day.
11 400th anniversary, birth of Torquato Tasso, Italian poet.
12 Girl Scout day, U.S.A.
15 Ides of March.
17 St. Patrick's day, patron saint of Ireland.
18 Centenary, birth of Nicolas Andreievich Rimsky-Korsakov, Russian composer.
20 Equinox (5:49 P.M. Greenwich civil time); beginning of spring.
25 Annunciation. Quarter day.
30 Seward day, Alaska.

APRIL

1 All Fools' day.
2 Palm Sunday.
6 Army day.
6 Maundy Thursday.
7 Good Friday.
8 Jewish Passover; 1st day.
9 Easter Sunday.
14 Pan-American day.
16 Centenary, birth of Anatole France, French author.
23 St. George's day.
25 St. Mark's day.
26 Confederate Memorial day (also May 10, June 3).

MAY

1 May day. International labour festival.
5 Cinco de Mayo, Mexican holiday.
14 Rogation Sunday.
14 Mother's day, U.S.A.
18 Ascension day.
24 Empire day. 125th anniversary, birth of Queen Victoria.
24 Centenary, first public demonstration of the telegraph.
27 St. Bede's day.
28 Shebuoth (Jewish Pentecost).
28 Pentecost (Whitsunday).
30 Memorial or Decoration day, U.S.A.
31 125th anniversary, birth of Walt Whitman, U.S. poet.
31 Union day, South Africa.

JUNE

4 Trinity Sunday.
8 Corpus Christi.
9 Trooping the colour in honour of King George VI's birthday. His majesty was actually born on Dec. 14.
11 Feast of St. Barnabas.
14 Flag day, U.S.A.
18 Father's day, U.S.A.
21 Solstice (1:03 P.M. Greenwich civil time); beginning of summer.
22 Fourth anniversary, signing of Franco-German armistice.
24 St. John's day.

28 25th anniversary, signing of the Treaty of Versailles and foundation of the League of Nations.
30 St. Paul's day.

JULY

1 Dominion day, Canada.
4 Independence day, U.S.A.
7 Seventh anniversary, beginning of Chinese-Japanese war.
14 Bastille day.
15 St. Swithin's day.
20 Annular eclipse of the sun, invisible at Washington, D.C.
22 Feast of St. Mary Magdalene.
26 St. Anne's day.

AUGUST

1 200th anniversary, birth of Jean Baptiste de Lamarck, French scientist.
1 Swiss Independence day.
6 Feast of the Transfiguration.
10 Feast of St. Lawrence.
15 Assumption.
16 175th anniversary, birth of Napoleon Bonaparte.
24 Feast of St. Bartholomew.

SEPTEMBER

1 Fifth anniversary, beginning of World War II.
3 Fifth anniversary, entrance of Great Britain into World War II.
4 Labor day, U.S.A. and Canada.
16 Mexican Independence day.
17 Constitution day, U.S.A.
18 Rosh Hashanah (Jewish New Year), beginning year 5705.
23 Equinox (4:02 A.M. Greenwich civil time); beginning of fall.
25 Dominion day, New Zealand.
27 Yom Kippur (Jewish Day of Atonement).
29 Michaelmas. Quarter day.
30 Feast of St. Jerome.

OCTOBER

2 Succoth (Jewish Feast of Tabernacles), 1st day.
4 Feast of St. Francis of Assisi.
12 Columbus day.
14 300th anniversary, birth of William Penn, founder of Pennsylvania.
15 Centenary, birth of Friedrich Wilhelm Nietzsche, German philosopher.
21 Trafalgar day.
25 St. Crispin and St. Crispinian.
27 Navy day, U.S.A.
31 Hallowe'en.

NOVEMBER

1 All Saints' day. All Hallows.
3 150th anniversary, birth of William Cullen Bryant, U.S. poet.
5 Guy Fawkes' day.
7 General election day, U.S.A.
9 Lord Mayor's show, London.
10 U.S. Marine Corps day.
11 Armistice day.
16 Feast of St. Edmund.
17 75th anniversary, opening of the Suez canal.
21 250th Anniversary, birth of François Marie Arouet de Voltaire, French philosopher.
22 St. Cecilia's day.
30 St. Andrew's day, patron saint of Scotland.
30 Thanksgiving day, U.S.A.

DECEMBER

3 First Sunday in Advent.
5 U.S.S.R. Constitution day.
6 Feast of St. Nicholas.
7 Third anniversary, Japanese attack on Pearl Harbor.
8 Immaculate Conception.
8 U.S. declaration of war on Japan; 3rd anniversary.
14 Admission of Alabama to the Union; 125th anniversary.
16 Mohammedan year 1364 begins.
17 Aviation day, U.S.A.
21 Forefathers' day.
21 Solstice (11:15 P.M. Greenwich civil time); beginning of winter.
25 Christmas.
26 Boxing day. English bank holiday.
28 Childermas. Holy Innocents' day.

CALENDAR OF EVENTS, 1943

For elections and disasters of 1943, see under those headings in the text. For obituaries of prominent persons who died during 1943, see under the entry Obituaries.

JANUARY

1 Twenty-two axis divisions were trapped in Stalingrad area where Russians forged great steel ring about Volga city; Russian recapture of Velikie Lukie on northern front and Elista on Caucasus front announced.

German people were told by Hitler in his annual New Year's message that winter of 1943 would be hard, but no harder than winter of 1942.

Heavy U.S. air raid on Japanese-held Wake island Dec. 23-24, 1942, disclosed by Adm. Nimitz.

"Supreme necessity" of planning for peace was emphasized by Pres. Roosevelt on first anniversary of United Nations pact.

Gen. Zhukov's replacement of Marshal Timoshenko as Russian commander on the southern front was revealed in Russian press.

2 Allied air forces destroyed 28 axis planes and damaged 34 others in aerial battles over Tunisia.

United States White Book issued by state dep't said that prior to Pearl Harbor Japan proposed meeting of Pres. Roosevelt and Premier Konoye on warship in Pacific, but that plan failed because both governments could not reach preliminary understanding.

Ten per cent cut in value of fuel oil coupons for 17 eastern states was ordered by Price Administrator Henderson.

3 Caucasus town of Mozdok was retaken by Russian armies, soviet communiqué announced.

Docks at St. Nazaire, nazi U-boat base, were hammered by U.S. daylight raiders, escorted by 300 Allied fighter planes.

Allied forces crushed all Japanese resistance in Buna Mission sector and moved toward Sanananda area, United Nations communiqué said.

4 U.S. air and land forces opened offensive on Guadalcanal, U.S. navy announced.

5 Russian armies captured Tsimlyansk in Don river

loop in big drive toward Rostov, Moscow announced.

Casualties of U.S. armed forces since outbreak of war totalled 61,126, OWI announced.

7 Pres. Roosevelt, in speech before joint session of 78th congress, predicted substantial Allied victories in 1943 and outlined postwar "freedom from want and fear" plan.

OPA ban on pleasure driving by holders of A, B and C gasoline ration cards in 17 eastern states went into effect.

8 Allied fliers smashed Japanese convoy attempting to land troops at Lae in New Guinea in 2-day battle and downed 39 enemy planes.

9 Gen. MacArthur awarded D.S.C. to Lt. Gen. Robert L. Eichelberger, who was revealed as commander of U.S. troops in Papua.

Maj. Gen. Carl A. Spaatz of U.S. army air force assumed command of newly-created Allied air force in North Africa, Gen. Eisenhower announced.

11 Pres. Roosevelt asked congress for wartime budget of $108,903,047,923 for fiscal year of 1944.

Loss of aircraft carrier "Hornet" in battle of Santa Cruz Islands, Oct. 26, 1942, disclosed by U.S. navy.

Georgievsk, Pyatigorsk and Mineralne Vodi, in Caucasus, were retaken by Red army.

Edward J. Flynn was nominated as U.S. minister to Australia by Pres. Roosevelt; Wiley Blount Rutledge, Jr., associate justice of U.S. court of appeals, was named to U.S. supreme court; Prentiss M. Brown, former Michigan senator, was named OPA administrator.

12 U.S. air squadrons destroyed 36 axis planes in heavy raid over Tripoli.

13 Charles E. Bedeaux, industrialist who developed factory "speed-up" system, was arrested in French North Africa on charge of trading with enemy, Washington dispatches reported.

14 Pres. Roosevelt and Prime Minister Churchill met in Casablanca to confer on war strategy.

15 U.S. air forces shot down 30 Japanese planes and damaged three enemy destroyers

in Solomons area.

16 Russians opened new offensive on Voronezh front, Moscow communiqué announced.

R.A.F. bombers dumped large cargoes of 2-ton block busters on Berlin in first raid on reich capital since Nov. 1941.

Iraq declared war on Germany, Italy and Japan.

17 Millerovo, rail junction north of Donets river, was recaptured by Russian forces.

British 8th army resumed offensive in Libya, advancing 40 mi. beyond original German positions in Wadi Zemzem area.

18 German siege around Leningrad was eased as Russians smashed through 9 mi. of fortifications to recapture Schlusselburg fortress, a soviet communiqué announced.

Postmaster Gen'l Frank C. Walker was unanimously elected chairman of Democratic national committee, succeeding Edward J. Flynn.

U.S. supreme court upheld lower bench verdict finding American Medical association guilty of violating anti-trust law; A.M.A. was charged with conspiracy to block activities of co-operative health group.

19 Fourteen axis vessels trying to run supplies to Tripoli were sunk and three others damaged by Allied ships in 3-day battle, admiralty announced.

Claims that Germany was building 20 to 30 submarines monthly, or at rate twice as fast as Allies could sink them—were made in dispatch from London.

Marcel Peyrouton was named governor general of Algeria by Gen. Giraud.

Third daughter was born to Crown Princess Juliana in Ottawa, first member of any European royal family born in North America.

20 Chile severed relations with Germany, Italy and Japan.

British 8th army, closing in on Tripoli, captured near-by Homs and Tarhuna.

41 children and 6 teachers were killed in London schoolhouse by bomb during German air raid.

Majority of striking anthra-

cite miners, heeding Pres. Roosevelt's warning to resume jobs or face government action, voted to return to pits, ending 22-day strike.

21 Maj. Gen. Alexander M. Patch of U.S. army succeeded Maj. Gen. Alexander A. Vandegrift of marine corps on Guadalcanal.

22 Germans lost Salsk to Russian column advancing swiftly toward Rostov.

Fall of Sanananda was announced by Allied command in Australia.

23 Tripoli fell to British 8th army as Gen. Rommel beat hurried retreat toward Tunisia for a last stand.

Russian forces smashed through German lines in Caucasus to recapture Armavir.

24 Allied war strategy for 1943 called for "unconditional surrender" of axis, Roosevelt declared at end of 10-day parley with Churchill at Casablanca.

25 U.S. troops occupied Kairouan pass in Tunisia.

27 U.S. daylight raiders blasted naval bases of Wilhelmshaven and Emden in first aerial attack on Germany proper.

German troops in Marseilles killed at least 300 men and women who resisted nazi order to evacuate their homes in city's old port, European dispatches asserted.

28 White House statement disclosed that Pres. Roosevelt visited Liberia after leaving Casablanca; Pres. Roosevelt and Pres. Vargas conferred aboard U.S. destroyer at Natal, Brazil.

U.S. casualties in Tunisia totalled 1,258 dead, wounded and missing, Sec'y Stimson disclosed.

Mobilization of reich's entire civilian population for war effort was ordered by Hitler.

29 Gen. Giraud rejected political union with de Gaullists, declaring co-operation would extend only to military and economic spheres.

Ernst Kaltenbrunner was appointed head of German gestapo, succeeding late Reinhard Heydrich, Berne dispatch said.

30 R.A.F. planes staged two daylight raids on Berlin,

JANUARY—*Continued*

disrupting nazi plans to celebrate 10th anniversary of Hitler's accession to power; Hamburg was battered by 4-ton bombs.

Dr. Goebbels, reading proclamation by Hitler, warned Germans they faced "bolshevik" enslavement unless they fought to bitter end.

Russian armies recaptured Tikhoretsk and Maikop, a special soviet communiqué announced.

Adm. Karl Doenitz, U-boat commander, succeeded Grand Adm. Erich Raeder as commander-in-chief of German navy.

Cruiser "Chicago" was sunk by Japanese in Solomons area.

31 **Complete destruction of German army** of 330,000 in Stalingrad trap and capture of Reich Marshal Friedrich von Paulus and 16 other generals was announced in special Russian communiqué.

Ground fighting flared in Tunisia when U.S. tank and infantry forces struck at German positions at Faid pass and at Maknassy farther south.

Mussolini ousted Marshal Ugo Cavallero from post as chief of Italian general staff, replacing him with Gen. Vittorio Ambrosio.

FEBRUARY

1 **OWI denied Tokyo claim** that 2 U.S. battleships and 3 cruisers were sunk in Solomons.

Pres. Roosevelt withdrew nomination of Edward J. Flynn as minister to Australia at latter's request.

2 **Churchill and Turkish President** Ismet Inönü conferred at Adana, and agreed on measures to help Turkey strengthen her defenses, British foreign office announced.

Liquidation of last pocket of nazi resistance in Stalingrad area announced by Russians.

3 **Three days of mourning** for German soldiers killed at Stalingrad was decreed by nazi propaganda ministry.

Order banning hard liquor in U.S. army camps and military establishments was issued by war dep't.

4 **Closing of approximately 100,000 German restaurants,** amusement centres and department stores to release all possible labour for national emergency was ordered by economics ministry.

Unconditional release of 27 former communist deputies held in North African prisons was ordered by Gen. Giraud in move to correct political abuses.

5 **Mussolini ousted 12** of his most important aides, including Count Ciano, and himself assumed "entire burden" for conduct of military and political affairs.

Lt. Gen. Frank M. Andrews assumed command of U.S. forces in European theatre of war.

"War committee" was set up by Gen. Giraud to replace imperial council as ruling body in French North Africa.

6 **Creation of North African theatre of operations** under supreme command of Lt. Gen. Dwight D. Eisenhower of U.S. army was announced by Allied headquarters; Maj. Gen. Lewis H. Brereton was made commander of U.S. forces in middle east.

7 **Shoe rationing** at initial rate of approximately 3 pairs yearly per person decreed by OPA.

Appointment of Count Ciano as Italian ambassador to Vatican was announced by Rome radio.

8 **Strongly fortified nazi base of Kursk** was captured by Russians.

OPA announced ban of recapping tires would be lifted March 1.

9 **Minimum 48-hour work week** in war industries was decreed by Pres. Roosevelt; extension of 48-hr. week to 32 areas with labour shortages was announced by WMC chief Paul V. McNutt.

Belgorod was captured by Red army column pressing toward Kharkov.

U. S. troops won complete

control of Guadalcanal as Japanese abandoned island, Sec'y Knox declared.

10 **Mohandas K. Gandhi** started 21-day fast in protest against his confinement in Aga Khan's palace in Poona.

11 **Prime Minister Churchill** pledged Allies would make nazis "burn and bleed" on fronts other than Russia, in statement before commons.

Japanese were decisively defeated in 12-day battle near Wau, New Guinea, and fled toward Salamaua, according to Allied communiqué.

Thurman Arnold was named by Pres. Roosevelt to become associate justice of circuit court of District of Columbia.

12 **Russian armies** reoccupied Krasnodar.

Soviet weekly bulletin published in Washington hinted that U.S.S.R.'s postwar territorial claims would include the 3 Baltic states and Bessarabia.

U.S. marine corps announced establishment of new women's reserve with Mrs. Ruth Cheney Streeter as director.

13 **French battleship "Richelieu,"** accompanied by three other French warships, reached New York city and other Atlantic ports for repair and refitting, it was learned.

14 **Rostov and Voroshilovgrad** fell to Russian armies.

Americans in the Faid-Sened area of Tunisian front retreated under heavy German tank blows.

15 **Risto Ryti** was re-elected president of Finland on first ballot.

Maj. Gen. Ira C. Eaker was appointed commander of 8th U.S. army air force, succeeding Maj. Gen. Carl A. Spaatz, who had been assigned to North African theatre of war.

16 **Soviet troops captured Kharkov,** anchor of German line on southern Russian front.

U.S. forces in central Tunisia were routed by Marshal Rommel's panzer divisions which staged swift 22-mi. advance to outskirts of Sbeitla.

WPB chief Nelson ousted Ferdinand Eberstadt as WPB vice-chairman and appointed Charles E. Wilson as executive vice-chairman.

Archbishop Spellman of New York conferred with Gen. Francisco Franco in Madrid.

18 **Rommel's panzers,** led by new giant Mark VI tanks, hurled U.S. and French troops back to Algerian border and occupied towns of Feriana, Kasserine and Sbeitla.

Japanese forces opened offensives in seven different areas in China, Chungking announced.

Mme. Chiang Kai-shek challenged "prevailing opinion" that defeat of Hitler was first concern of United Nations and called for decisive blows against Japan in speeches before both houses of U.S. congress.

Sales of canned meat and fish were frozen by OPA.

19 **At joint conference with Mme. Chiang Kai-shek,** Pres. Roosevelt pledged that U.S. would rush more arms to China "as fast as Lord will let us."

U.S. had shipped more than 2,900,000 tons of material to soviet union since beginning of Russian aid program, Edward R. Stettinius, Jr., lend-lease administrator, disclosed.

20 **Both Krasnograd and Pavlograd** fell to Russian columns sweeping westward in Ukraine.

German mechanized units in Tunisia pierced Anglo-American defenses and occupied strategic Kasserine pass.

21 **Loss of 2,710-ton "Argonaut,"** largest U.S. submarine, and its crew of 102, was announced by navy dep't.

Point rationing of canned foods starting March 1 was announced by OPA.

The pictures on this page are, left to right:

FEBRUARY—Continued

Marshal Timoshenko opened new Russian offensive on Lake Ilmen sector south of Leningrad.

Prime Minister Sikorski of Polish government-in-exile charged Russian agents were waging active political warfare in Poland in effort to wean people away from "democracy."

22 **850 men of U.S. armed forces** were lost when U-boats sank two merchant vessels in North Atlantic early in February, navy dep't disclosed.

23 **Stalin said that Red army alone** was bearing whole weight of war in absence of second front and added that Germans had suffered 9,000,000 casualties, including 4,000,000 dead.

Capture of Sumy in Ukraine capped Russian advance of 82 mi. in seven days.

Anglo-U.S. forces halted German drive on Thala in Tunisia, after 24-hr. battle.

24 **Adolf Hitler** warned he would force workers from occupied lands to help nazi war effort and that he would not spare foreign lives in struggle.

25 **U.S. forces occupied Kasserine Gap** in central Tunisia after Rommel's forces withdrew to shorten their communications.

26 **Disclosure that U.S.** was exporting large supplies of oil, cotton and food to Spain was made by Carlton J. H. Hayes, U.S. ambassador to Madrid; U.S. state dep't asserted oil for Spain came from Caribbean and not from U.S. and was hauled in Spanish tankers.

Sumner Welles declared in Toronto speech that U.S. would not wait for end of war, but would press United Nations to open immediately preliminary talks on postwar peace aims.

The pictures on this page are, left to right:

27 **Charges that nearly 3,-400,000 persons** had been killed or had died in prison in nine nazi-occupied countries were made in statement by Inter-Allied Information committee of United Nations.

28 **German armies counter-attacking in Donets basin** recaptured Losovaya and Kramatorsk, nazi high command announced.

MARCH

1 **R.A.F. rained 900 tons of bombs** over Berlin in concentrated 30-minute attack, leaving fires that could be seen 180 miles distant; 19 British bombers were lost in raid.

U.S. army forces pierced axis lines at outlet of Kasserine pass and recaptured Tunisian town of Sbeitla.

Russian forces captured Demyansk and 301 other localities in Lake Ilmen sector, Moscow communiqué said.

U.S. supreme court reversed conviction of George Sylvester Viereck, German propagandist, and criticized prosecution for remarks prejudicial to fair trial.

President Risto Ryti of Finland said his country longed for peace, but urged Finns to continue fighting alongside Germany.

Appointment of Maj. Gen. Harry C. Ingles as deputy commander of U.S. army forces in Europe was announced in London.

Juan José de Amezaga assumed office as president of Uruguay.

3 **Red army took Rzhev** after prolonged and violent battle.

Mohandas K. Gandhi ended his 21-day hunger strike.

Sec'y Knox asked for navy of 2,250,000 men by 1944, estimating that navy casualties would approximate 10% of total personnel.

4 **Allied bombers** destroyed entire Japanese convoy of 22 ships, including 10 warships and 12 transports, in battle of Bismarck sea, beginning March 2; 82 Japanese planes were downed and 15,000 troops aboard transports were virtually annihilated.

Red army regained control of Velikie Luki rail link to Moscow and routed two German garrisons below Lake Ilmen area.

5 **Edwin J. Linkomies** became premier of Finland at head of coalition cabinet.

British Colonial Secretary Oliver Stanley, answering U.S. critics, said Britain would not agree to any scheme for international postwar rule of her colonies.

6 **Russians captured Gzhatsk** in drive to iron out deep bulge protecting Smolensk.

Stalin was given rank of marshal of soviet union, Moscow radio announced.

7 **War Manpower Commission** abolished 4-H draft classification, thus making possible military draft of men between 38 and 45.

8 **Vice-President Wallace** warned that world could be plunged into third great war unless democracies and U.S.S.R. came to "satisfactory understanding."

Complaints that soviet government was concealing from Russian people importance of lend-lease aid shipped to Russia were voiced by Adm. Standley, U.S. ambassador at Moscow.

Ruml pay-as-you-go income tax plan was rejected by house ways and means committee by 15–9 vote.

Ismet Inönü was unanimously re-elected president of Turkey by national assembly.

9 **Surprise drive by nazi army** of 375,000 in Kharkov area compelled Russians to retreat 80 mi. to protect over-extended communications, Russians said.

10 **Pres. Roosevelt asked congress** to consider two reports of National Resources Planning board suggesting "cradle to grave" social security and broader government participation in business.

Inadequate planning by government agencies, conflicting authority and government reluctance to adopt unpopular policies were listed as three basic weaknesses in U.S. war program by Truman investigating committee.

11 **Pres. Roosevelt signed bill extending Lend-Lease act** for another year after measure won congressional approval.

Edward R. Stettinius, Jr., lend-lease chief, disclosed that U.S. had sent to its allies from March 1941, to March 1942, 30 out of every 100 bombers produced, 38 of every 100 fighter planes, 28 of every 100 light tanks and 33 of every 100 medium tanks.

French guerrilla patriots slew 532 German soldiers in France in 10-week period.

12 **Arrival of Anthony Eden,** British foreign secretary, in Washington for parleys on war and postwar problems was announced by White House.

OPA announced point rationing of meats, cheese, edible fats and oil, butter and canned fish beginning March 29.

House rebuffed Pres. Roosevelt by approving measure to revoke president's order limiting salaries to $25,000 net yearly.

Red army occupied Vyazma in drive toward Smolensk.

13 **Japanese lost 64 ships** in Solomons campaign while U.S. lost only 32 vessels, navy dep't asserted.

14 **Recapture of Kharkov** by reich armies on southern Russian front was announced by German high command.

15 **Gen. Giraud** announced readiness to meet Gen. de Gaulle for conference on measures to unite rival pro-Allied French movements.

16 **U.S., British and Canadian high-ranking naval officers** in Washington reached complete agreement in conference on anti-submarine campaign.

Martial law was reported proclaimed throughout Savoie region, where French guerrillas battled Vichy police and axis troops.

OPA chief Prentiss M. Brown warned widespread inflation would result if WLB met demands of coal miners for wage increases.

   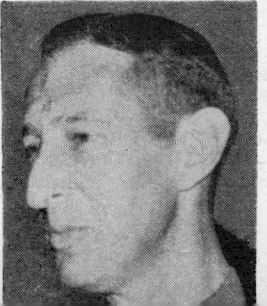 

MARCH—*Continued*

17 Restoration of laws of French republic to North Africa were decreed by Gen. Giraud.

Japan's shipping losses between Dec. 7, 1941, and March 1, 1943, were estimated by Sec'y Knox at 1,857,000 gross tons out of original tonnage of 6,369,000.

Gafsa fell to U.S. infantrymen in 30-mi. advance toward El Guettar in Tunisian hills.

Sveinn Bjoernsson was re-elected regent by Iceland parliament.

Nazi broadcasts said British 8th army in Tunisia had launched offensive against Mareth line.

Gen. Franco voiced fears, in speech to cortes, that "Red Revolution" would engulf Europe if U.S.S.R. defeated reich.

18 El Guettar was captured by U.S. tank forces advancing in central Tunisia.

19 Eight members of Capone gang were indicted in New York city on charges of fleecing moving picture union and employers of $2,500,000; Frank Nitti, alleged leader of movie racket, was found shot to death in Chicago suburb five hours after indictment.

Plans to ease restrictions on consumers' goods and permit manufacture of refrigerators, electric irons, etc., were announced by WPB chief Donald Nelson.

Promotion of Lt. Gen. Henry H. Arnold, commander of U.S. army air forces, to rank of full general was approved by senate.

20 De Gaulle and Giraud French factions clashed over control of French Guiana, with both sides claiming authority over South American colony.

Chinese forces recaptured Hwajung, city in eastern Hunan province, and slowed Japanese offensive south of Yangtze river.

Shortages of meat, butter and vegetables in large metropolitan centres were revealed in nation-wide survey as result of pre-ration buying.

Polish gov't-in-exile reported that nazis killed 35,000 Jews in "liquidation" of ghettoes of five Polish towns.

21 Prime Minister Churchill proposed postwar councils of nations for Europe and Asia, under which small nations would be grouped in federations; he advocated 4-year social reform

plan, but cautioned countrymen not to sidetrack winning of war to discussion of postwar plans.

Adolf Hitler asserted Germans had lost only 542,000 dead since war started, declared "Red peril" was world's greatest menace and said eastern front had been stabilized.

Russians admitted German recapture of Belgorod, 50 mi. north of Kharkov.

OPA suddenly halted sales of butter, edible fats and oils.

22 WLB rejected, by 8-to-4 vote, A.F. of L.'s petition to scrap "Little Steel" formula for wage increases.

23 British 8th army punctured Rommel's Mareth line at coast and outflanked it from south, as U.S. forces occupied Maknassy in drive to cut axis rear communications.

Complete occupation by Allied troops of Mambare river area in New Guinea was announced by Allied headquarters; U.S. Flying Fortresses blasted Rabaul, New Britain.

Danes overwhelmingly rejected national socialism in parliamentary elections, giving 1,898,360 votes to democratic parties and only 67,977 votes to two pro-German parties.

24 OPA announced point values for rationed foods, disclosing that total weekly average ration of meat, butter and hard cheese per individual would be 2 lb.

25 Swiss reports said Allied air offensive over axis-held Europe had cut German plane production 30% and steel and coal output 50%.

R.A.F. raiders bombed Campo Leone and Cisterna, two suburbs of Rome.

Chester C. Davis was named food administrator by Pres. Roosevelt.

Gov. John C. Vivian ordered immediate halt in Colorado military draft of men engaged in farming, stock raising and dairying.

26 British Foreign Sec'y Anthony Eden promised Chinese that Allies would give them more military assistance, in speech before Maryland general assembly.

Soviet Russia extended its fisheries agreement with Japan for another year.

27 U.S. troops punched 20-mi. hole in axis lines in central Tunisia and captured

position of Fondouk.

Berlin was blasted by 900 tons of bombs by R.A.F. planes.

Undersec'y of State Sumner Welles denied Gen. Giraud's abrogation of Crémieux decrees discriminated against Jewish population of North Africa.

28 British 8th army breached Mareth line at three points, forcing hasty axis retreat toward Gabes.

Plan for postwar world currency union to increase freedom of international trade was prepared by John Maynard Keynes, British economist.

29 Jurisdiction over all labour disputes, whether in war or non-war industries, was claimed by WLB.

30 Tunisian port of Gabes fell to British 8th army.

31 Madrid reports said German occupation authorities asked for additional 100,000 Frenchmen to rush construction of "Mediterranean wall" of fortifications.

APRIL

2 Visit of Gen. Mark Wayne Clark to Gen. Luis M. Orgaz Yoldi, high commissioner for Spanish Morocco, was revealed in U.S. army communiqué.

3 Germany lost 850,000 dead and 343,525 prisoners in Russian winter offensive, while Red army recaptured 185,328 sq.mi. of territory, soviet communiqué said.

Men in 38-to-45 age group should leave non-deferrable occupations by May 1 or face possibility of induction, Gen. Hershey warned.

4 Railroad bridge spanning Oder river at Frankfurt was blown up as new wave of sabotage swept through occupied areas, Stockholm reports said.

Allies stepped up aerial blows against Hitler's "Festung Europa" as Flying Fortresses pounded Naples while R.A.F. force hammered Kiel and Antwerp.

Both U.S. and British air forces were denounced by Marshal Pétain as authors of "unjustifiable" bombing raids on France.

Allied bombers sank or damaged 12 Japanese warships and merchant craft after three big raids in four days on enemy shipping concentrated at Kavieng, New Ireland.

5 Wilhelmstrasse announced that Daladier,

Blum, Gamelin and Reynaud had been removed to German prisons in move to balk Anglo-U.S. "plot" to kidnap these French leaders and set up exiled government outside France.

Gen. de Gaulle postponed scheduled trip to North Africa "for military reasons" at request of Gen. Eisenhower.

6 U.S. proposals for establishment of United Nations fund for postwar currency stabilization were made public by Sec'y Morgenthau.

7 Elements of U.S. 2nd army corps and British 8th army formed junction at Djebel Chemsi after cracking axis lines in southern Tunisia.

Four Allied ships, including destroyer, were sunk by Japanese air armada of 98 planes off Guadalcanal; U.S. squadrons shot down 34 enemy planes.

Naval fund of $24,551,070,000 for 1944 was requested of congress by Pres. Roosevelt.

Pres. Enrique Peñaranda declared Bolivia at war against axis and decreed general mobilization.

Lord Keynes' proposal for postwar banking and currency plan to expand world trade was published in British White Paper.

8 WMC chief McNutt was authorized to issue regulations preventing job transfers for higher pay unless change would aid war effort.

Common Wealth party, with platform of nationalization of British resources, won first seat in house of commons.

9 Plans to establish immediate price ceilings and controls on wheat, cotton, fresh fish, fresh fruits and other commodities were announced by OPA.

John L. Lewis protested that Pres. Roosevelt's order freezing wages was unfair to coal miners.

10 Hitler and Mussolini concluded four-day conference.

11 Public debt extension bill, containing repeal of Pres. Roosevelt's order limiting salaries to $25,000 yearly net after taxes, became law.

Desert junction of Kairouan was taken by Anglo-U.S. armoured units of British 1st army.

12 British 8th army advanced 48 mi. in single day and captured Sousse, Tunisian port.

British budget calling for £5,756,114,000 was introduced to commons by Sir Kingsley

APRIL—*Continued*

Wood, chancellor of exchequer.

New draft order issued by Paul V. McNutt, WMC chairman, said all able-bodied men between 18 and 38, excepting 3,200,000 deferred for essential war work, would be inducted into armed forces by end of 1943.

General freight rate increases granted in 1942 to railroads were revoked by ICC.

14 **Gen. MacArthur** warned that powerful Japanese naval forces were within "striking distance" of Australia; Gen. Thomas Blamey said that Japanese had massed 200,000 men in island arc above Australia.

15 **OWI report said food for U.S. civilians** in summer of 1943 would be 6% lower than in 1942.

16 **Senate voted** to deprive Pres. Roosevelt of right to devalue currency.

Cautious program under which Martinique and Guadeloupe would join Allies but would not "rebel" against "French government" was made public by French Commissioner Adm. Georges Robert.

Spain's readiness to mediate in interests of "just" peace were voiced by Count Francisco Gomez de Jordana.

Polish government-in-exile asked inquiry into German report that Russians had "massacred" 10,000 Polish officers near Smolensk.

17 **Regulations designed to freeze 27,000,000 U.S. workers** to their jobs were issued by WMC chief Paul V. McNutt.

Carlo Scorza was made secretary general of Italian fascist party, succeeding Aldo Vidussoni.

18 **Regent Nicholas Horthy** renewed pledges to Adolf Hitler that Hungary would help fight off Allied invasion, Berlin radio said.

Reports that Russians had slain 10,000 Polish prisoners near Smolensk, were denounced by soviet radio as "hideous gestapo frameup."

19 **Lend-lease equipment** totalling 126,184 tons had been shipped to North Africa in first four months after Allied landings, lend-lease chief Edward R. Stettinius, Jr., announced.

20 **Pres. Roosevelt and Pres. Avila Camacho** met in Monterrey, Mexico.

Aircraft carrier "Hornet" was revealed by U.S. war dep't as "Shangri-La" from which U.S. planes took off to bomb Tokyo in April 1942; "Hornet" was subsequently sunk.

Gen. Draja Mikhailovitch denied dealing with axis leaders.

21 **Japanese execution** of several of eight captured U.S. airmen who participated in Tokyo raid announced by Pres. Roosevelt.

Nazis were warned by British that use of poison gas on Russian front would bring immediate British reprisals.

Capture of Enfidaville on Tunisian coast by British 8th army was announced in Allied communiqué.

22 **Japan hinted more reprisals** if U.S. planes again bombed Tokyo, declaring that all U.S. fliers captured on such expeditions would be given "one-way ticket to hell."

Twenty giant six-engined German transport planes carrying troops and gasoline to Tunisia were shot down by Allied warplanes.

23 **U.S. reduced size of legation in Helsinki** as relations with Finland worsened.

Prime Minister Churchill denounced Japanese execution of U.S. fliers, asserting that Britain would help U.S. in bombing Japan.

Navy department revealed U. S. forces had occupied and established base on Ellice Islands in Southwest Pacific.

24 **General offensive** was launched by Allied forces on all Tunisian fronts.

26 **Moscow, angered at Polish intimation** that Russians "massacred" 10,000 Polish prisoners, broke off relations with Polish government-in-exile in London.

Categorical denial of nazi claim that U.S. aircraft carrier "Ranger" had been sunk by nazi U-boat was issued by U.S. navy department.

27 **Chairman Donald Nelson** of WPB denied that his allotment of critical war materials to synthetic rubber plants delayed production in aviation gasoline.

Sec'y Knox admitted that Allies had lost 1,000,000 tons of shipping in 1942, but said reports that losses totalled 1,000,000 tons monthly were incorrect.

Proposal that U.S. spend $7,695,000,000 on public works after war to cushion shock of expected economic recession was contained in Part II of National Resources Planning board report.

29 **Creation of joint U.S.-Mexico economic committee** to help remedy dislocation in Mexico's wartime economy was announced by state department.

30 **John L. Lewis** ignored Pres. Roosevelt's back-to-work order and soft coal miners went on strike.

OPA Administrator Prentiss M. Brown announced program to halt inflation by rolling back prices that got "out of hand" and by extending price control to "every important commodity."

U.S. state department severed political ties with pro-Vichy regime on Martinique and Guadeloupe.

New British-Canadian plan for convoy protection in North Atlantic designed to cover merchantmen with air "umbrella" over entire route was announced in Ottawa.

MAY

1 **Premier Stalin lauded Allied air attacks** on axis centres in Italy and Germany, declaring these raids presaged opening of second front.

Istanbul dispatches said King Boris left Sofia on May day after anti-German demonstrations swept Bulgarian capital.

Sir Basil Brooke was named prime minister of Northern Ireland.

Gen. Kenji Doihara was named commander of Japan's eastern defense area and concurrently supreme war councillor, Tokyo radio announced.

Pres. Roosevelt authorized Fuel Administrator Ickes to seize all coal mines because striking miners "perilled" national interest; all anthracite mines in eastern Pennsylvania were made idle by walkout of 80,000 miners.

2 **John L. Lewis called 15-day truce** in coal strike 30 min. before Pres. Roosevelt went on nation-wide broadcast to denounce miners' walkout as blow at war effort.

3 **Mateur fell** to U.S. Tunisian forces which consolidated positions only 19 mi. from Bizerte.

Pulitzer prizes went to Thornton Wilder, drama; and Upton Sinclair, novel.

4 **Russell Islands,** northwest of Guadalcanal, were occupied by U.S. forces in February, U.S. navy department announced.

5 **Premier Stalin expressed desire** to see strong and independent Poland established after war.

Fuel Administrator Ickes was given power to seize all coal stocks to protect war plants and civilian users in case of emergency.

6 **Japanese submarine campaign** was dismissed as inconsequential by Adm. Halsey, who branded as "flat lie" foe's claims of destroying 50,000 tons of Allied shipping.

Lt. Gen. Jacob L. Devers was named commander of U.S. forces in European theatre, succeeding Lt. Gen. Frank M. Andrews, killed in plane crash.

Allied warplanes staged 2,500 sorties in single day over axis lines in Tunisia.

7 **Tunis and Bizerte** fell to British and U.S. forces 181 days after Allied landings in North Africa.

Gen. Charles Mast was appointed by Gen. Giraud as resident general of Tunisia.

Maj. Gen. Idwal H. Edwards was appointed acting chief of staff to U.S. forces in European war theatre.

Sole purpose of Swedish foreign policy was to keep out of war, contended Swedish foreign minister Christian E. Guenther in defense of his neutrality program.

Occupation of Aleutian island of Amchitka by U.S. forces in January was announced by U.S. navy department, which also declared that Adak, another Aleutian isle, had been occupied earlier.

Plans to use subsidies to bring about 10% cut in retail prices of meat, coffee and butter were announced by Price Administrator Prentiss Brown.

8 **Allied communiqué revealed** that Maj. Gen. Omar N. Bradley commanded U.S. 2nd corps during entire operation that led to capture of Bizerte.

9 **400 U.S. planes raided Sicilian port of Palermo,** hitting auto works, war industries and arsenal.

6

CALENDAR OF EVENTS • 1943

MAY—*Continued*

Spanish dictator Franco appealed to Allies and axis to make peace, declaring that war had reached deadlock and that neither side could win.

Withdrawal of British and Indian forces from Buthidaung, a Burma outpost, was announced in British communiqué.

10 Axis defeat in Tunisia was ignored but hardships of German soldiers on eastern front and misery caused by Allied bombings were stressed by Adolf Hitler in message to people.

11 Prime Minister Churchill arrived in Washington for conferences with Pres. Roosevelt on plans for second front.

Marsala was left in flames after concentrated air blow by 300 U.S. planes; Catania and Pantelleria were bombed anew by Allied air forces.

German high command disclosed that Gen. Erwin Rommel, head of famed Afrika Korps, had been on leave in reich for past two months because of ill health.

U.S. forces landed on Japanese-held island of Attu in Aleutians.

Disclosure that U.S. plane production exceeded that of all other nations combined was made by Pres. Roosevelt.

12 All axis resistance in Tunisia ended, thus closing chapter of war in Africa; Col. Gen. von Arnim and other axis military leaders surrendered to Allies; U.S. 2nd corps and French allies took 37,998 prisoners in Bizerte zone.

Swedish dispatches said rioting occurred in Berlin among relatives of German troops who were captured or killed in Tunisia.

At least four and possibly 10 U-boats were sunk by Allied escort ships and planes after 8-day running battle in Atlantic with pack of 25 axis submarines that attacked convoy, admiralty announced.

WLB's power to make wage adjustments to correct "gross inequities" was restored by Director James F. Byrnes of Economic Stabilization board.

13 Allied headquarters revealed that Gen. MacArthur and Adm. Halsey had met and decided on close co-operation on future military moves in Southwest Pacific battle zones.

Two-year extension of administration's program for reciprocal trade pacts was approved in house of representatives by 342-to-65 vote.

Shipping losses in North African campaign amounted to only 2.16% of total traffic, Allied headquarters in Africa announced.

14 Allied communiqué said that all remaining axis troops in North Africa were now prisoners.

New blows to aid U.S.S.R. and China were promised by Prime Minister Churchill in broadcast from Washington.

299 persons perished when Japanese submarine torpedoed Australian hospital ship "Centaur."

15 Sidi Lamine was appointed bey of Tunis, succeeding Sidi Mohammed al Mounsaf, who was ousted by Gen. Giraud for compromising his position during axis occupation, French communiqué announced.

16 Ruhr valley was flooded after R.A.F. bombings breached Eder, Sorpe and Moehne dams.

18 Pres. Roosevelt opened United Nations food conference in Hot Springs, Va., with appeal to waive food tariffs.

Axis casualties in Africa since June 1940 numbered 1820,000 men against 220,000 for Great Britain, Maj. Clement Attlee told commons.

British admiralty revealed that "highly expendable" escort aircraft carriers were providing Atlantic convoys with air cover.

19 Prime Minister Churchill told U.S. congress Britain would help raze Japanese cities, but asserted destruction of Germany must come first.

United Mine Workers of America applied for reaffiliation with A.F. of L.

20 Joseph E. Davies presented Premier Stalin with personal letter from Pres. Roosevelt.

21 Berlin was bombed for third night in row by British Mosquito bombers.

22 Dissolution of Comintern (Communist International) was decided upon by praesidium of Comintern's own executive committee in Moscow.

All except three of U.S. warships sunk and damaged at Pearl Harbor had been refloated and repaired and were back in service, U.S. announced.

40% slash in gas rations for buses, trucks and taxis in eastern seaboard states was ordered by ODT to meet new gas shortage.

700 ships built in U.S. yards in first 20 weeks of 1943 nearly equalled production figure for entire year of 1942, Adm. Emory S. Land asserted.

Wildcat strike staged in protest against NLRB wage decision halted work at Akron's three major rubber plants.

Trebling of British bomber production in 12 months was announced by Oliver Lyttelton, minister of production.

23 Destruction of 305 axis planes in four days by Allied air forces operating in central Mediterranean area was announced by U.S. press agency.

R.A.F. dropped 2,000 tons of bombs on Dortmund, bringing to 100,000 tons the weight of explosives loosed over Germany by R.A.F. bomber command since war began.

Italian isle of Pantelleria was raked with block busters and other heavy explosives in four Allied raids in 48 hours.

25 Italian people were advised to quit war by Prime Minister Churchill in joint press conference with Pres. Roosevelt.

26 Adm. William A. Glassford was named U.S. minister to French West Africa.

27 British and U.S. military leaders reached "complete agreement" on future operations in all war theatres, Pres. Roosevelt announced.

U.S. casualties in North African campaign were 2,184 dead, 9,437 wounded and 6,937 missing or prisoners, war department said.

Majority of 52,000 wildcat strikers in Akron rubber plants heeded Pres. Roosevelt's ultimatum to end walkout and returned to jobs.

International Association of Machinists, comprising membership of 565,000, decided to leave A.F. of L., charging that latter "protected" unions which violated I.A.M. jurisdiction.

28 Russian force of 150,000 men drove wedge into German defenses in small Kuban salient held by nazis, Berlin radio announced.

James F. Byrnes was made director of Office of War Mobilization, new agency created by Pres. Roosevelt to assume overall direction of war effort on home front.

30 Japanese imperial headquarters admitted entire Japanese garrison on Attu had been wiped out by U.S. attacking forces.

31 British foreign office spokesman said French warships interned in Alexandria had joined Allies.

Routing of 75,000 Japanese troops with heavy losses on front southwest of Ichang was announced in Chungking communiqué.

JUNE

1 Gen. de Gaulle's insistence on removal of ex-Vichy officials from office in French Africa forced resignation of Marcel Peyrouton as governor general of Algeria.

Gen. Ezio Rossi was removed as chief of staff of Italian army by Premier Mussolini.

The pictures on this page are, left to right:

DEVERS............May 6
BRADLEY............May 8
HALSEY............May 13
DAVIES............May 20
GIRAUD............June 3

JUNE—Continued

Soft coal miners resumed strike in 25 states as result of deadlock between U.M.W. negotiators and Appalachian operators.

2 Senate approved house bill to extend reciprocal trade agreements for two years.

Pope Pius XII urged belligerent nations to obey laws of war and refrain from aerial reprisals.

3 Pres. Roosevelt ordered striking miners to return to work by June 7.

Resolutions for creating "new world order" based on freedom from want were approved by delegates at final session of United Nations Food conference.

French Committee of National Liberation was created as instrument to govern French empire with Generals de Gaulle and Giraud serving as co-presidents.

4 Argentine army officers staged swift coup d'état, overthrew Castillo regime and seized government.

530,000 striking coal miners were ordered to return to work on June 7 by John L. Lewis, U.M.W. chief.

Smith-Connally bill, providing drastic curbs on strikes in government operated plants, was passed by house of representatives by 231–141 vote.

5 Gen. Arturo Rawson was proclaimed president of Argentina.

Gen. Noguès resigned post as resident general of French Morocco.

7 Gen. Pedro Pablo Ramírez became president of Argentina after Gen. Arturo Rawson stepped down in his favour.

The pictures on this page are, left to right:

8 Los Angeles declared out of bounds by army and navy authorities as result of rioting between "zoot-suiters" and servicemen.

9 Axis forces on Pantelleria rejected Allied terms for unconditional surrender.

Director James F. Byrnes of OWM announced that he would take hand in shaping future federal tax policy; Byrnes also disclosed that Bernard M. Baruch had been appointed to his personal staff.

10 Pay-as-you-go tax measure, passed by both houses of congress, was signed by Pres. Roosevelt, and was scheduled to become operative July 1.

Premier John Curtin of Australia confidently declared Allied defensive strategy in Pacific had ended and that period for offensive operations against Japanese had arrived.

11 Bomb-ruined island of Pantelleria surrendered to Allied forces; axis forces of more than 10,000 were taken prisoners by Allied occupation units.

12 Italian island of Lampedusa, near fallen Pantelleria, surrendered to Allies after synchronized air and sea bombardment.

250,000 Yugoslav guerrillas were awaiting signal for invasion, Gen. Draja Mikhailovitch broadcast from his secret headquarters.

13 Garrison of 140 Italian sailors and soldiers on tiny isle of Linosa in Mediterranean surrendered without fight.

Revolution as an instrument of labour policy was condemned by Pope Pius XII, who also protested against "calumnious assertions" that Vatican had wanted war.

14 Ruling compelling school children to salute flag was reversed by supreme court, which declared decision violated spirit and letter of Bill of Rights.

Senate voted MacKellar bill, intended to "investigate" qualifications of 30,000 federal jobholders.

15 Buckingham palace officials revealed that King George VI was visiting British forces in North Africa.

16 77 Japanese planes were shot down by U.S. pilots in great aerial battle over Guadalcanal, while surface ships and shore batteries destroyed 17 more; U.S. losses were only six planes.

OPA Administrator Prentiss M. Brown asserted it would be impossible to roll back farm prices without federal subsidies.

17 Standard Oil Co. of Calif. agreed to drop contract for oil drilling on naval Elk Hills tract, Sec'y Knox said, after deal had been declared "illegal and invalid" by official of justice department.

18 Japanese lost 40,000 men killed or wounded in 40-day battle for control of upper Yangtze river, Chinese army spokesman asserted.

Appointment of Field Marshal Sir Archibald Wavell as viceroy of India was announced by British government.

Argentine presidential elections were suspended by Gen. Ramírez, who also banned use of word "provisional" in referring to his rule.

Demands of coal miners for wage boost based on portal-to-portal travel time was rejected by WLB.

21 Coal miners started third wartime strike after operators and U.M.W. officials reached deadlock on contract parleys.

25 Negroes and nine whites were killed and hundreds were injured in race riots in Detroit.

Proposal that midwest farmers kill pigs to divert grain for N.Y. state's livestock and fowl was made by Gov. Dewey at annual governors' conference.

22 Coal strike was called off by John L. Lewis, who extended truce until Oct. 31.

23 Pres. Roosevelt said he would ask congress to lift age ceiling for non-combatant military service to 65 in measure designed to quell strikes in government-owned or operated plants.

Economic Stabilization Director Fred M. Vinson rejected general wage increase of eight cents hourly for 1,100,000 non-operating railway employees.

24 German aerodrome at Sedes near Salonika in Greece was raided by Liberator bombers of U.S. 9th army air force.

Ray Atherton was named U.S. minister to Canada and to Luxembourg government-in-exile, established on Canadian soil.

25 Both houses of congress overrode Pres. Roosevelt's veto of Smith-Connally anti-strike bill.

20,000,000 bushels of corn in midwest elevators were requisitioned by War Food Administration in move to ease processing shortage.

28 Hundreds of R.A.F. planes carried nonstop aerial offensive over occupied Europe into 10th day, blasting Cologne and Hamburg with 2,000 tons of bombs; 25 R.A.F. bombers were lost.

Chester C. Davis resigned as war food administrator and stated program to halt inflation would not work; Judge Marvin Jones succeeded Davis.

Appointment of Carl Elbridge Newton as head of federal agency to operate seized coal mines was announced by Fuel Administrator Ickes.

29 Vice-President Wallace charged Sec'y of Commerce Jesse Jones with employing "obstructionist" tactics against the Board of Economic Warfare while Jones accused vice-president of "malice" and "misstatements."

Army appropriations bill of $71,507,678,873 for 1943–44 fiscal year was passed by senate.

30 U.S. army, navy and air forces launched offensive to drive Japanese out of New Guinea and northern group of Solomon Islands, and captured Trobriand and Woodlark islands in early stages of drive.

Axis powers were warned by Prime Minister Churchill that Allied attacks against European mainland were imminent "before leaves of autumn fall."

JUNE—Continued

Treasury report for 1942-43 fiscal year disclosed U.S. government expenditures of approximately $76,000,000,000.

U.S. troops occupied Rendova Island after wiping out Japanese garrison there.

JULY

1 Death sentence of Max Stephan, who aided escaped nazi flier, was commuted to life imprisonment by Pres. Roosevelt.

New Irish Dail Eireann reelected Eamon de Valera premier of Eire government.

3 Australian jungle forces joined U.S. troops at Nassau bay on New Guinea coast in drive on Salamaua, Allied communiqué said.

Flames visible for 150 miles shot up from Cologne after 45-minute R.A.F. bombing attack; Hamburg was also attacked by British bombers.

4 Fully loaded glider was towed 3,500 mi. across Atlantic in 28 hours, R.A.F. authorities announced.

Small British force landed on Crete, destroyed installations and returned to home base.

Charges that Representative Edward E. Cox (Dem., Ga.) was conspiring with "radio monopoly" and Wall street interests to wreck FCC were made by Lawrence Fly, FCC chairman.

5 Germans ended 101-day lull on Russian front by opening offensive in Orel-Kursk-Belgorod sectors.

Slashes in OPA fiscal appropriations and OWI domestic funds were approved by senate.

Japanese cession of six states of Malaya and Burma to Thailand as reward for that kingdom's "collaboration" was announced by Tokyo radio.

U.S. shock troops landed near Bairoko and Zanana (New Georgia island) in drive on Munda air strip.

6 At least nine Japanese warships—and possibly two others—were sunk in battle of Kula Gulf, July 5–6, as against announced loss of one U.S. cruiser, Allied communiqué said.

7 Gen. Henri Giraud reached Washington and conferred with Pres. Roosevelt.

Russians admitted German penetration near Belgorod, but contended nazis failed to achieve major breakthrough.

8 Senate abandoned fight against administration's price rollback subsidies as congress recessed until Sept. 14.

9 Pres. Roosevelt, parrying question of recognition of French committee, said that as 95% of French were under German rule, there was no France.

Losses of Allied merchantmen to U-boats in June were lowest of war, joint Anglo-U.S. statement said.

10 U.S., British and Canadian troops invaded Sicily, consolidated beachheads on southern shores and drove forward along 100-mi. front under cover of air-sea bombardments.

Gen. Eisenhower urged French not to commit rash actions but to wait for their day of liberation.

Truman committee report charged that Curtiss-Wright subsidiary caused government to accept allegedly defective engines.

11 Three Italian airfields and city of Pachino were captured by Allied troops in Sicily; Syracuse and nine other Sicilian towns were also captured, Allied communiqué announced.

German armies fell back before sharp Russian counter-thrusts in Kursk-Orel sector.

12 Japan lost four more warships in another engagement with U.S. naval units in Kula Gulf area.

13 Gen. Montgomery's British 8th army captured Augusta on Sicily's east coast while Gen. Patton's American 7th army joined British and Canadian forces at Ragusa.

Gen. Giraud disclosed that French troops were fighting alongside Allied forces in Sicily.

Adm. Georges Robert resigned as high commissioner for Martinique and Henri-Etienne Hoppenot was named as his successor, U.S. state department announced.

14 Stanislaw Mikolajczyk was named premier of Polish government-in-exile, replacing late Gen. Sikorski.

15 Pres. Roosevelt abolished Board of Economic Warfare, curbed foreign operations of RFC, and created new agency called Office of Economic Warfare; he rebuked both Vice-President Wallace and Jesse H. Jones for public airing of their inter-agency quarrels.

Recapture of 110 towns and villages in substantial advances on Orel front was announced in soviet communiqué.

U.S. and Australian troops recaptured Mubo area in New Guinea, Allied communiqué announced.

U.S. commercial airlines, in statement of policy, said they favoured free competition and international freedom of air transit in peaceful flight.

16 Italy was warned to overthrow fascism or suffer tragic ruin of war in joint statement by Pres. Roosevelt and Prime Minister Churchill.

Navy disclosed that planes based on "baby flat-top" (escort carrier) had sunk at least two submarines and probably eight others in Atlantic battle with 11 U-boats.

17 Seven Japanese vessels were sunk and 49 planes were shot down by 200 Allied planes attacking Buin-Faisi area of Bougainville island during battle on July 16–17.

Anglo-U.S. military occupation rule was set up in Sicily with Gen. Sir Harold R. L. G. Alexander as military governor.

Agrigento fell to vanguards of Gen. Patton's U.S. 7th army driving along south coast of Sicily, Allied communiqué said.

More than 500 Allied bombers converged upon Naples, wrecking arsenals, torpedo plant and damaging railways, aerodromes and oil refineries.

19 Rome was raided for first time by 500 U.S. daylight bombers that hammered at railway yards, airfields and other military targets.

Germans abandoned 130 villages and populated places to advancing Red army forces driving on big nazi base of Orel.

Hitler and Mussolini conferred in northern Italy on axis military plans.

Japanese naval and air base at Paramoshiri, in Kurile Islands, was bombed by U.S. army Liberators.

"Big Inch," world's longest oil pipe line, extending from Longview, Tex., to Phoenixville, Pa., was dedicated.

20 Japanese cruiser and two destroyers were sunk by U.S. planes in dawn battle in Vella Gulf, northwest of New Georgia.

U.S. and Canadian troops captured Enna, important communications hub in central Sicily.

21 Gen. de Gaulle said Fighting French movement was "nonpolitical revolt" against German rule and would be discontinued after war.

22 Allied bombers attacked Surabaya in Netherlands East Indies during 2,400-mile round-trip flight.

U.S. 7th army smashed inland through Sicily and captured Palermo.

C.I.O. Pres. Philip Murray and A.F. of L. Pres. William Green warned Pres. Roosevelt that their unions would drop support of his price-wage stabilization program unless steps were taken to roll back retail food prices.

23 Pres. Roosevelt said Rome was bombed to save U.S. and British lives and not in spirit of retaliation for damage done to English landmarks.

24 U.S. forces captured port of Marsala and rounded up 50,000 prisoners in western portion of Sicily, Allied communiqué announced.

German naval base at Trondheim, Norway, was raided by unescorted bombers of U.S. 8th air force.

Vatican radio denied axis reports that Pope Pius XII had protested to Pres. Roosevelt over bombing of Rome.

25 Benito Mussolini resigned as dictator of Italy; King Victor Emmanuel III named Marshal Pietro Badoglio as successor to the fallen duce.

Vice-President Wallace called upon U.S. to take initiative in planning war-proof postwar world and assailed "small but powerful groups which put money and power first and people last."

26 Berne dispatches said crowds paraded in large Italian cities clamouring for peace; Marshal Badoglio was reported to have proclaimed martial law throughout Italy.

27 Italy was given choice by Prime Minister Churchill of breaking alliance with Germany or of being "seared and scarred and blackened" by Allied war machine.

OWI was rebuked by Pres. Roosevelt for referring, in short-wave broadcast to Europe, to King Victor Emmanuel III as "moronic little king" and to Marshal Badoglio as "high-ranking fascist."

Ivan M. Maisky, soviet ambassador to Britain, was named by Premier Stalin vice-commissar for foreign affairs.

JULY—*Continued*

28 **Striking workers in northern Italy** demanded that Badoglio government sign peace with Allies; Rome radio announced abolition of fascism in Italy.

Pres. Roosevelt hailed fall of Mussolini as "first crack in axis" and reiterated demand for unconditional surrender of all three axis partners.

Pope Pius XII was quoted in Vatican broadcast as having denounced one-man rule of government.

29 **Nicosia on axis defense line** at Mt. Etna, Sicily, was stormed and captured by U.S. infantry.

Italians were offered honourable peace by Gen. Eisenhower if they would rid their country of Germans.

R.A.F. squadrons unloosed 2,300 tons of bombs on Hamburg in 8th Allied air attack on German port in six days.

30 **Peace demonstrators in Milan** stormed Cellari jail and released 200 political prisoners, Swiss dispatches said.

Pres. Roosevelt warned neutral countries not to give asylum to fleeing axis "war criminals."

31 **Allies warned Italians** that they would resume offensive in earnest, asserting that their failure to make peace aided Germany.

French Committee of National Liberation appointed Gen. de Gaulle chairman of national defense committee and Gen. Giraud commander-in-chief of all French forces.

Pres. Roosevelt asked "truly stiff program" of additional taxes, savings, or both" in asserting that estimate of $100,-000,000,000 for 1943–1944 fiscal year still stood.

AUGUST

1 **Force of 175 U.S. Liberator bombers** flying at low altitude devastated oil refineries in Ploesti region of Rumania with 300 tons of explosives.

Fear of heavy Allied air raids led nazis to order immediate evacuation from Berlin of civilians non-essential to war effort, Swedish dispatches said.

Fedor Guseff was named to succeed Ivan Maisky as Russian ambassador to Great Britain.

New York city authorities took quick action to quell incipient riots in Harlem area.

2 **Date for induction of fathers** into U.S. military service was set for Oct. 1 by Chairman Paul V. McNutt of WMC.

U.S. army test pilot in England was credited with travelling at 780 m.p.h. in vertical 5-mi. dive.

3 **Outbreak of strikes in Milan,** Genoa and Turin and anti-war demonstrations in northern Italy were reported in Berne dispatches.

5 **Sicilian port of Catania** fell to British 8th army.

Red army captured both Orel and Belgorod in drive that shattered axis defenses in south central Russia.

Sweden cancelled transit of German troops and war materials through her territory to Finland and Norway.

U.S. soldiers and marines captured Munda on New Georgia island.

6 **Troina, key axis stronghold in Sicily,** was occupied by U.S. 7th army after heavy fighting.

7 **U.S. naval forces sank three of four Japanese warships** that attempted to carry supplies to beleaguered garrison at Vila on Kolombangara island, in battle on night of Aug. 6–7.

8 **Occupation of Adrano,** Bronte, Biancavilla and Belpasso by British 8th army in Sicily was announced in Allied communiqué.

Former French liner "Normandie" was refloated at 49° list in New York pier.

U.S. troops, landing behind axis lines on north Sicilian coast, enabled main body of U.S. 7th army to capture Sant' Agata di Militello and San Fratello.

9 **Gen. MacArthur** declared that decisive Allied victories destroyed Japan's offensive power in Southwest Pacific.

10 **Prime Minister Churchill arrived in Quebec** for conferences with Allied high command.

Bozidar Pouritch succeeded Milos Trifunovitch as prime minister of Yugoslav government-in-exile.

12 **Evacuation of German troops from Sicily** to Italian mainland was underway.

U.S. bombers attacked Kurile Islands in North Pacific.

Chuguyev, 22 mi. from Kharkov, fell to Russian troops, a Moscow communiqué said.

13 **Lt. Gen. Patton's 7th U. S. army** captured Randazzo in Sicily.

U.S. bombers crippled Littorio and San Lorenzo railway yards of Rome with 500-ton bombload.

14 **Badoglio government** announced decision to declare Rome open city, according to Vatican City broadcast, but United Nations were silent on this unilateral action.

Key Japanese base of Salamaua in New Guinea was virtually ruined by 177-ton bombing attack by Allied warplanes, Allied communiqué said.

15 **Red army force of 60,000** overran German defense bastion of Karachaev.

U.S. forces by-passed Kolombangara island to occupy Vella Lavella island in central Solomons.

U.S. and Canadian forces occupied Kiska and found that all Japanese forces had fled island before Allied landings.

16 **Working week of U.S. coal miners** was raised from 42 to 48 hours in move to increase lagging coal production.

17 **All Sicily fell to Allied armies** 38 days after invasion began; U.S. troops occupied Stromboli and Lipari, two islands of Aeolian group in Tyrrhenian sea north of Sicily.

Dispatches from Italo-Swiss frontier said German military had assumed administration of martial law in northern Italy.

307 German fighter planes and 59 Flying Fortresses were shot down in aerial battle between U.S. and German air forces during U.S. air raids on Regensburg and Schweinfurt.

120 Japanese aircraft were destroyed, 50 more were damaged and 1,500 enemy airmen and ground crewmen were killed in surprise Allied air raid on New Guinea base of Wewak, Aug. 16–17.

Pres. Roosevelt arrived in Quebec for conferences with Prime Minister Churchill on Allied war plans.

18 **NWLB was empowered by Pres. Roosevelt** to take special sanctions against both workers and employers defying board's orders.

Coastal targets at Gioia Tauro and Palmi on southern por-

tion of Italian mainland were shelled by U.S. warships.

19 **Brig. Gen. Howard C. Davidson** was named commander of 10th U.S. air force in India, succeeding Maj. Gen. Clayton L. Bissell.

21 **Japanese retreat from outer defenses of Salamaua** to inner lines protecting base's aerodrome was disclosed in Allied communiqué.

Andrei A. Gromyko was named soviet ambassador to U.S., replacing Maxim Litvinov.

23 **Kharkov was recaptured** in Russian drive to free entire Donets basin.

Fires visible for more than 200 mi. raged in Berlin after estimated 700 R.A.F. planes rocked German capital with 1,800 tons of bombs.

24 **Pres. Roosevelt and Prime Minister Churchill,** concluding their Quebec conference, expressed hope that it would be possible to hold Anglo-U.S.-Soviet parleys.

Heinrich Himmler was named German interior minister, thus receiving virtual dictatorial powers to curb unrest in reich.

Lt. Gen. Hugh A. Drum was named chairman of Inter-American Defense board, to run concurrently with post as commander of Eastern Defense Command and 1st army.

25 **Adolf Hitler** and reichswehr generals were warned by Pres. Roosevelt that "surrender would pay them better now than later."

Establishment of separate Allied Southeast Asia Command and appointment of Lord Louis Mountbatten as its commander was announced.

26 **U.S., Britain and Canada** recognized French Committee of National Liberation as administrative authority for French overseas territory, but not as government of France or French empire.

Lord Louis Mountbatten arrived in Washington for conferences with U.S. military and naval chieftains.

27 **Rumours that U.S.S.R. and Germany were envisaging separate peace** were branded as fifth column propaganda by Brendan Bracken, British information minister.

28 **Allied headquarters** announced that all Japanese resistance on New Georgia island had ended.

AUGUST—*Continued*

Stockholm reports said Danish cabinet had refused to accept German demands that would place all Denmark under nazi control.

Arrest of Albert Lebrun, former French president, by gestapo agents was reported in French frontier dispatches.

29 Danes revolted against German measures placing country under martial law and scuttled major part of their fleet to foil nazi seizure.

Escape from Rome of Count Ciano, his wife and three children was reported by German broadcast.

30 Soviet armies recaptured Taganrog, southern anchor of German line in U.S.S.R.

Resignation of Premier Eric Scavenius' cabinet and internment of Danish royal family at Amalienborg under German military guard reported in Swedish dispatches.

Sec'y Hull branded statements by Drew Pearson, columnist, that secretary of state was anti-Russian as "monstrous and diabolical falsehoods."

Argentina's bid for lend-lease arms was flatly rejected by Sec'y Hull who sharply criticized Ramírez government's foreign policy on hemispheric defense.

31 Yelnya and Dorogobuzh fell to Russians opening direct drive on Smolensk, main German defense bastion on central Russian front.

Pres. Roosevelt reiterated statement by Sec'y Hull that charges by Drew Pearson, columnist, that Hull was anti-soviet were false.

Swedish vessels gave protection to 11 Danish warships fleeing to Swedish harbours.

Prime Minister Churchill invited soviet union to join with Britain and U.S. in "necessary and urgent" conference of foreign ministers.

Gen. Eisenhower was named for promotion to permanent rank of full general.

SEPTEMBER

1 Marcus island was raided by U.S. naval task force and carrier-based planes.

Pope Pius, in broadcast on fourth anniversary of World War II, called for "worthy peace" and generous treatment of defeated nations.

2 Annihilation of 40,100 German troops in Taganrog sector was claimed in Russian communiqué; Russian armies captured Sumy and cut Bryansk-Kiev railway.

Unescorted U.S. Flying Fortresses bombed Brenner pass in 1,500-mi. round-trip flight.

3 Italy was invaded by British and Canadian troops who established bridgehead in Calabria and advanced toward Palmi.

10th U.S. air force bombers raided Car Nicobar island, 200 mi. northwest of Sumatra, in 2,000-mi. round-trip flight across Indian ocean.

Sec'y Knox asserted that 2,500,000 tons of Japanese shipping had been sunk since Pearl Harbor.

4 Capture of Reggio di Calabria and Villa San Giovanni by British 8th army announced in Allied communiqué.

William M. Jeffers resigned as U.S. rubber director.

5 Japanese evacuation of important seaplane base at Rekata bay on Santa Isabel island in Solomons was announced by Allied spokesman.

6 Surprise Allied amphibious landings isolated Japanese forces in Salamaua-Lae area, Allied communiqué announced.

U.S. and Britain should continue co-operation for postwar organization and peace, Prime Minister Churchill declared in speech at Harvard university.

7 Statement urging U.S. participation in postwar co-operative organization was unanimously approved by Republican postwar advisory council meeting at Mackinac Island, Michigan.

8 Italy surrendered unconditionally to United Na-tions; Gen. Eisenhower revealed that he had concluded secret armistice with Badoglio government on Sept. 3; Italy's capitulation was branded a "cowardly betrayal" by Berlin newspapers.

Stalino fell to Russians as Red army cleared out nazi forces in Donets basin.

Arctic island of Spitsbergen was bombarded by German warships.

9 Allied 5th army troops landed and established bridgeheads in Salerno region south of Naples.

Approximately 1,800 Allied planes flew 4,000 sorties over English Channel in successful raids on 14 important targets in northern France.

U.S. refusal to give Argentina lend-lease arms resulted in resignation of Foreign Minister Segundo Storni from Ramírez cabinet.

Badoglio informed Hitler that Italy had been forced to ask for armistice to avoid total ruin, Rome broadcast disclosed.

German bomber sank 35,000-ton Italian battleship "Roma" as it was steaming toward Allied port.

10 Rome was shelled and occupied by German troops; elimination of Italy as belligerent was unimportant from military standpoint, Hitler asserted.

Allied 5th army beat off five powerful German counter-attacks on Salerno bridgehead.

James M. Landis was named by Pres. Roosevelt as head of all U.S. economic operations in middle east with status of minister.

11 Italian General Vittorio Ruggiero surrendered to German forces which occupied Lombardy.

Major part of Italy's fleet, including four battleships, nine cruisers and 11 destroyers, surrendered to Allies at Malta, London reports said.

Italian people were urged to strike hard against German soldiers on Italian soil in joint statement by Prime Minister Churchill and Pres. Roosevelt.

Capture of port of Salerno by Allied 5th army was announced in Allied communiqué.

Vice-President Wallace asserted that "democracy first" program should be basis for world peace and attacked international cartels as "creators of secret super-governments."

King Victor Emmanuel and Premier Badoglio appealed to Italians not to resist Allied forces but to defend homeland against "German aggression."

12 Steady stream of Allied reinforcements poured into Salerno to aid 5th army locked in battle with German forces.

Occupation of Brindisi by British troops was announced in Allied communiqué.

Eight more Italian destroyers and 14 submarines surrendered to Allies at Malta, British naval authorities said.

Mussolini was freed by nazi parachute troops who overwhelmed Italian jailers and took him to German-held territory.

Australian and U.S. forces captured Salamaua, important Japanese base in New Guinea.

Sec'y Hull declared international postwar co-operation should be based on willingness of member nations to use force, if necessary, to keep the peace.

13 Kuomintang's central executive committee named Generalissimo Chiang Kai-shek as president of Chungking government.

14 German tank, artillery and troop attacks hurled back Allied 5th army on Salerno bridgehead; Allied air forces staged 2,000 sorties over German positions there.

16 Split was captured by partisan armies, Yugoslav communiqué said.

SEPTEMBER—*Continued*

Novorossisk was recaptured by Russian armies in Kuban drive.

Japanese-held base of Lae fell to Australian troops pushing westward across northern coastline of New Guinea.

17 Pres. Roosevelt told congress that he and Churchill were agreed on time and places for launching of new blows against axis in Europe and Asia.

Assaults by Allied air and land forces compelled German troops to retreat from Salerno area as Allied 5th and British 8th armies established contact.

Bryansk was recaptured by Russians.

Yugoslav partisan units attacked Adriatic port of Fiume, according to Yugoslav communiqué.

Creation of labour pool to ease manpower shortage was suggested in report by Bernard M. Baruch to War Mobilization chief Byrnes.

18 Allied 5th army widened Salerno bridgehead and captured Roccadaspide.

Pavlograd was occupied by Red army divisions speeding toward Dnieper river, Russian communiqué said.

A speaker believed to be Benito Mussolini, heard over German radio, denounced King Victor Emmanuel and "fascist traitors" and urged Italians to take up arms again by side of Germany and Japan.

Battipaglia and Altavilla fell to Allied 5th army forging ahead in Salerno area.

19 German garrisons were driven out of Sardinia by two Italian divisions, Allies disclosed.

The pictures on this page are, left to right:

Yugoslav communiqué reported Germans launched big land drive to oust partisans from Fiume and Split.

Expansion of U.S. fleet into mightiest navy in history, possessing 14,072 surface vessels totalling almost 5,000,000 tons and having 18,000 naval planes, was announced in naval production report.

20 Gen. Marshall and Adm. King warned in talk before joint session of congressional military affairs committees, that delaying father draft would entail risk of prolonging war.

Willkie announced willingness to "accept" presidential nomination in 1944 campaign from "liberal" Republican party.

Landing of French forces on Corsica was announced by Gen. Giraud in special communiqué.

Allied occupation of most of Sorrento peninsula dominating Bay of Naples was announced in Allied communiqué.

21 Prime Minister Churchill told commons that Allies would invade Europe from west in due time and join U.S.S.R. in ridding world of German tyranny; he said Italy had "irretrievably" lost her empire.

House of representatives voted 360 to 29 to approve Fulbright resolution calling for U.S. participation in international machinery to preserve postwar peace.

Allied landings on the Aegean islands of Cos, Samos and Leros was announced in British middle east communiqué.

22 Allied forces made new landings above Finschhafen in new drive against Japanese-held New Guinea base.

Complete annihilation of Japanese garrison on Arundel island was announced in Allied communiqué.

Japan announced plans for evacuating unnecessary government offices, factories and civilians from Tokyo as air-raid emergency measure.

British midget submarines sneaked into Norway fjord and crippled German battleship "Tirpitz" with torpedo attacks.

23 Establishment of nazi-sponsored Italian government with Mussolini as premier and Gen. Graziani as defense minister was announced in German broadcast.

24 Churchill reshuffled cabinet, naming Sir John Anderson chancellor of exchequer and Lord Beaverbrook lord privy seal.

German troops, pinned against east coastal strip of Corsica by attacking French units, sped up evacuation from island.

25 Russian armies recaptured Smolensk and Roslavl and battled way into suburbs of Kiev.

Pres. Roosevelt announced resignation of Sumner Welles as undersecretary of state and appointed Edward R. Stettinius, Jr., as his successor; president also disclosed creation of Office of Foreign Economic Administration with Leo T. Crowley as director of new agency.

26 Berlin radio admitted that Russian forces had crossed Dnieper river at some points.

Thunderbolt fighter squadrons flew record round trip of 600 mi. in escorting Flying Fortresses that smashed Emden with 1,000 tons of bombs in daylight raid.

27 Foggia and its network of Italian air bases fell to British 8th army after 24-mi. advance.

Seven Japanese ships were sunk and 60 planes were destroyed in surprise Allied air raid on Wewak.

28 Reappearance in North Atlantic of U-boats fitted with heavy anti-aircraft guns was confirmed by R.C.A.F. headquarters in Ottawa.

Nazi seizure of Corfu and recapture of Split from Yugoslav partisans were announced in German communiqué.

29 Stockholm dispatches reported Germans were starting evacuation of Baltic states.

30 Representative Edward E. Cox (Dem., Ga.) resigned as chairman of committee investigating FCC.

OCTOBER

1 Allied 5th army occupied Naples.

German U-boat pack, using deadlier type of torpedo, was reported to have sunk 10 Allied vessels bound for Canada in September battle.

U. S. bomber armada staged 1,800-mi. round-trip flight from North African bases to raid Wiener-Neustadt and Munich area.

Ruhr steel centre of Hagen was target of 1,000-ton bomb salvo unloosed by giant R.A.F. night raiders.

Adm. William H. Standley resigned as U.S. ambassador to Moscow and W. Averell Harriman was appointed his successor.

2 New Guinea base of Finschhafen fell to Australia's veteran 9th division.

Sinking in Nov. 1942 of 18,700-ton British liner "Ceramic" with more than 500 passengers aboard was disclosed by Cape Town naval authorities.

3 German communiqué admitted nazi armies had evacuated Kuban city of Taman.

4 Bastia was occupied by French troops in Corsican campaign.

Frankfurt-on-Main was raided twice in 24 hours, with U.S. Flying Fortresses hammering the city by day while R.A.F. bombers unloaded 500 tons of explosives over the city by night.

5 Aegean island of Cos was recaptured from British by German landing parties after two-day battle.

All German troops were cleared from Corsica.

500 persons died when Allied submarine sank Japanese steamer off coast of Korea, Japanese radio said.

61 Japanese planes were destroyed during U.S. sea and air attack on Wake island.

6 Right of Associated Press to limit membership was upheld in federal district court decision but news agency was directed to modify its membership by-laws.

OCTOBER—*Continued*

7 **Russian armies crossed Dnieper river** and established three bridgeheads on west bank, Moscow announced.

At least 100 persons were killed and scores of others injured by explosion of German time bomb in Naples post office.

8 **Fall of Capua** to Allied 5th army was announced in United Nations communiqué.

U.S. bombers raiding Bremen and nearby Vegesack shot down 130 nazi fighter planes while American combat aircraft destroyed 12 more; total U.S. losses in air battle were 30 bombers and three fighters.

Premier Tojo took over personal control of munitions and commerce ministries in Japanese cabinet.

9 **U.S. bombers based in Britain** staged 1,800-mi. round-trip flight to raid Gdynia, Danzig and East Prussian targets.

Clearing of all German troops from Caucasus was announced by Premier Stalin.

Eight airfields in Greece, Crete and Rhodes were raided by U.S. bombers based in North Africa.

Strategic base of Vila on Kolombangara island was occupied by U.S. forces.

10 **102 German planes were shot down** by U.S. bombers and fighters during bombing expedition over Muenster and Coesfeld.

11 **New York Yankees** defeated St. Louis Cardinals, four games to one, to win baseball's world series.

Congress was asked by Pres. Roosevelt to repeal Chinese exclusion laws.

12 **Portugal agreed to allow Britain** use of Azores as anti-submarine bases to protect United Nations convoys in Atlantic.

Yugoslavs in London reported that partisan armies had occupied suburbs of Zagreb and were within 23 mi. of Belgrade.

U.S. air forces attacked Japanese base of Rabaul, destroying or damaging 177 planes and sinking or damaging 123 ships and harbour craft.

13 **Badoglio government** declared war on Germany, at 3 P.M. Greenwich time.

14 **U.S. 8th air force** lost 60 Flying Fortresses and 593

men in raid on Schweinfurt, but shot down 104 nazi planes.

Dnieper bend stronghold of Zaporozhe was captured by Russian forces battling way south toward Crimea and Black sea.

Allied 5th army threw several bridgeheads across Volturno after sharp fighting.

Selective service bureau warned that all draft evaders would be put into 1-A classification after Nov. 1.

German government filed formal protest with Portugal against grant to Britain of naval and air bases in Azores.

Berlin broadcast asserted that Gen. Rommel had been put in charge of operations against Yugoslav partisans.

15 **Gen. Arnold asserted** that heavy damage to targets in U.S. raid on Schweinfurt Oct. 14 was worth loss of 60 Flying Fortresses.

U.S. war department announced that Gen. Albert Coady Wedemeyer would serve as deputy chief of staff to Adm. Lord Louis Mountbatten in southeast Asia.

Argentine government lifted ban on Jewish newspapers after Pres. Roosevelt said act was "obviously anti-semitic."

Wendell Willkie made bid for G.O.P. presidential nomination with demand that Pres. Roosevelt and entire administration be voted out of office in 1944.

16 **Allied armies** surged over Volturno-Calore line and captured six key towns on Italian front.

Pres. Ramírez summarily dismissed all Argentine public officials who had signed anti-axis manifesto calling for "effective democracy."

Chicago's first passenger subway was dedicated in elaborate ceremony.

17 **OWI disclosed** U.S. army air force destroyed 7,312 enemy planes against loss of 1,867 from start of war to Sept. 1, 1943.

Anti-axis sources in Greece reported outbreak of civil war among three leading Greek guerrilla organizations.

18 **104 Japanese planes** were shot down by Allied pilots during series of aerial battles extending from New Guinea to Solomons, United Nations communiqué announced.

U-boats preying on U.S. coastwise shipping had sunk only three vessels in preceding 15 months, Vice-Adm. Adolphus Andrews disclosed.

Sec'y Hull and Foreign Minister Eden arrived in Moscow for tripartite talks with Russian Foreign Commissar Molotov.

Count Carlo Sforza arrived in Italy for conversations with leaders of Badoglio government.

Swedish dispatches said that Count Bent Holstein, rich pronazi Dane, had agreed to form new Danish government.

German-held rail hub of Skoplje in Yugoslavia was raided by Allied bombers based in Africa.

R.A.F. bombers poured 1,500 tons of high explosives over Hanover in fourth heavy attack on that city in 30 days.

19 **Control of both banks of Volturno river** from Tyrrhenian sea to Capua was secured by Allied 5th army.

Canada signed agreement to ship lend-lease material to soviet union, it was disclosed by U.S. state department.

Tarawa, principal air base on Japanese-held Gilbert islands, was bombed by U.S. navy planes.

20 **Vice-President Wallace** called on congress to legislate against railway transport "monopolies" and to eliminate regional-rate discrimination.

21 **Adm. Sir John H. D. Cunningham** was named commander-in-chief of Allied fleet in Mediterranean, succeeding his cousin Sir Andrew Browne Cunningham.

French Committee of National Liberation restored Crémieux decree, thus returning citizenship to disfranchised Algerian-born Jews.

Prentiss M. Brown resigned as head of Office of Price Administration.

22 **Brig. Gen. R. E. Laycock** succeeded Lord Louis Mountbatten as chief of British combined operations.

221 tons of Allied bombs were dropped on Japanese troop concentrations in Sattelberg, New Guinea.

23 **Red army troops recaptured Melitopol** after 11 days of savage street fighting.

Heads of five railway operating brotherhoods unanimously ordered strike vote on grounds

that wage increase offered members was inadequate.

24 **Gen. Harold R. L. G. Alexander** said difficult terrain slowed Allied advance in Italy.

25 **Dnepropetrovsk was recaptured** by Russian army in bold attack that smashed German lines for 25 mi. along Dnieper river.

Allied 5th army occupied Sparanise and drew up to foot of southern slopes of Mt. Massico.

Nearly 300 U.S. planes attacked Rabaul, ripping airfield and destroying 123 enemy planes, Allied headquarters announced.

26 **Gen. Jean-Marie-Joseph Bergeret,** former Darlan aide, was jailed by French Committee of National Liberation on charges of treason.

Japanese diet was told by Emperor Hirohito that Japan's situation was "truly grave."

Director Leo T. Crowley merged four government bureaus into his Office of Foreign Economic Administration.

27 **Allied forces landed on Mono and Stirling islands** in first phase of Solomons campaign to drive Japanese from Bougainville.

17 supporters of Gen. Mikhailovitch were executed by partisans on charges of aiding enemy, partisan broadcast announced.

28 **U.S. paratroopers** spearheaded Allied invasion of Choiseul island in Solomons.

29 **Genoa's rail yards and factories** were bombed by U.S. Flying Fortresses based in Mediterranean airfields.

31 **Count Sforza** gave limited endorsement to Badoglio rule, but hinted that he desired abdication of King Victor Emmanuel III.

Japanese-held Bougainville island was invaded by U.S. marines who swarmed ashore at Empress Augusta bay on island's west shore.

NOVEMBER

1 **Moscow parleys** concluded by U.S. Sec'y of State Hull, British Foreign Sec'y Eden and Foreign Commissar Molotov, who agreed (1) to carry on Anglo-U.S.-Russian collaboration after war and (2) to compel axis enemies to surrender unconditionally. Conferees also established machinery for closer military co-operation, created European Advisory commission and Italian Advisory council,

NOVEMBER—*Continued*

guaranteed restoration of Austrian independence and established principle that German war criminals would be tried in countries where crimes were committed.

Russian armies cut off last land escape route of German armies in Crimea by capturing Perekop, Moscow communiqué announced.

Congress was warned to retain food subsidies by Pres. Roosevelt, who said he would veto any bill which sought to prohibit use of them.

Sec'y Ickes was authorized by Pres. Roosevelt to seize coal mines after walkout of 530,000 coal miners who staged fourth big strike of 1943.

2 **Republican party** marked up impressive gains in elections throughout scattered districts of U.S.

Estimated 50,000 tons of Japanese shipping were sunk outright, 44,000 more tons were damaged and 67 Japanese planes were shot down during Allied air attack on Rabaul.

One Japanese cruiser and four destroyers were sunk in naval battle between U.S. and Japanese naval units off Bougainville.

3 **Striking coal miners** were ordered to return to work by John L. Lewis after Sec'y Ickes gave tentative approval to $1.50 daily wage boost.

U-boat base of Wilhelmshaven was showered with 1,000 tons of bombs during raid by 400 U.S. bombers.

Towering smoke columns rose from Duesseldorf, which was struck by more than 2,000 tons of bombs during R.A.F. raid.

Clause of Moscow agreement recognizing need for establishing world peace organization was embodied in postwar resolution sponsored by senate foreign relations committee.

4 **Isernia,** important German defense key in central Italy, was captured by Gen. Montgomery's British 8th army.

Russians said German casualties in four months of battle that started July 5 totalled 2,700,000 men, including 900,000 dead and 98,000 prisoners.

5 **U.S. senate** went on record by 85–5 vote as favouring postwar collaboration to secure and maintain world peace and establish new world peace organization.

Estimated 500 U.S. bombers flew through deadly curtain of

anti-aircraft to raze Gelsenkirchen.

Pay increase for coal miners arranged by Sec'y Ickes and United Mine Workers was approved 11 to 1 by WLB.

6 **Bernard M. Baruch** was named to head new unit within OWM for dealing with war and postwar adjustment problems.

Russian armies recaptured Kiev, which they had lost to German invaders in Sept. 1941.

U.S. housewives were warned by OPA chief Chester Bowles that food prices would be substantially increased if congress refused to sanction further subsidies.

8 **Nazi party leaders** were assured by Adolf Hitler in speech on 20th anniversary of Munich putsch that he would never capitulate and that he would exact retribution from England for Allied bombings of reich cities.

9 **Delegates of 44 nations** convening in Washington signed agreement establishing United Nations Relief and Rehabilitation administration.

Prime Minister Churchill warned that campaigns scheduled for 1944 to destroy German armies would entail "greatest sacrifices" of war for Anglo-U.S. armies.

Gen. Giraud resigned from French Committee of National Liberation, but retained command of French armies in field; Gen. de Gaulle was left with full powers in reshuffle of French committee.

10 **Gov. Bricker of Ohio** announced he would enter Ohio presidential preference primaries.

Strategic bridge and railroad yards of Bolzano, Italy, were attacked by U.S. bombers of northwest Africa air force.

11 **German industrial centre** of Muenster was raided by U.S. bombers.

Outbreak of rioting led French officials to arrest Lebanon leaders who had proclaimed independence of French-mandated Arab state.

One Japanese cruiser and two destroyers were bombed and sunk at Rabaul by Allied fliers.

Herbert H. Lehman was unanimously elected director general of UNRRA.

Nassau jury acquitted Alfred de Marigny of charge of slay-

ing his father-in-law, Sir Harry Oakes.

13 **Rail junction of Zhitomir** was captured by Russian units driving west of Kiev.

Marshal Badoglio organized "technical" government to carry on administrative affairs, but vowed to take no part in policy-making; the next day he said he would resign as premier when Rome was liberated, but pledged loyalty to King Victor Emmanuel.

14 **Railway yards at Sofia** were attacked by U.S. bombers based in Italy.

15 **Buckingham palace** announced appointment of duke of Gloucester to succeed Lord Gowrie as governor-general of Australia.

16 **Strong formations of U.S. bombers,** flying unescorted on 1,300-mi. round-trip flight, raided strategic targets in Norway.

17 **Dodecanese island of Leros** was recaptured by Germans, British admitted.

Land-based U.S. planes raided Japanese-held Marshall and Gilbert Islands, Nov. 16 and 17.

18 **Sec'y Hull** said Moscow parleys would lay foundations for world peace in address before joint session of senate and house of representatives.

Nearly 1,000 four-motored R.A.F. bombers dropped record load of 2,500 tons of explosives on Berlin and Ludwigshafen.

Ninety tons of explosives were dropped on Japanese-held island of Nauru by U.S. carrier-based planes.

19 **Zhitomir was recaptured** by German armies as Russians retreated in their first major reverse in four months of battle on eastern front.

German chemical plants at Leverkusen were heavily bombed by R.A.F. squadrons.

20 **U.S. marines invaded Gilbert Islands,** landing on Tarawa and Makin atolls.

21 **French Committee of National Liberation** ordered release of arrested Lebanese leaders and promised action to give mandated area independence.

22 **Landing of U.S. marines on Abemama,** third atoll in Gilbert group, was announced in U.S. naval communiqué.

23 **Gilbert Islands** were occupied by U.S. marines after bitter and sanguinary 76-hour battle.

24 **Toulon and Sofia** were raided by bombers of 15th U.S. air force.

U.S. escort carrier "Liscome Bay" was sunk by Japanese submarine in Makin battle.

25 **U.S. naval forces** sank four Japanese destroyers in dawn battle northwest of Bougainville.

26 **German stronghold of Gomel** was captured by Russian troops.

Satelberg mission, last Japanese stronghold on Huon peninsula of New Guinea, was seized by Australian troops.

Estimated 500 U.S. bombers accompanied by equal number of escort planes delivered shattering attack on German port of Bremen.

Charges that U.S. was spending $6,000,000,000 on wasteful and unnecessary projects in South America were made in 176-page report to senate by Sen. Hugh A. Butler.

Gen. Eisenhower revealed that he had denounced Gen. Patton for striking shell-shocked U.S. soldier, but upheld retention of Patton in his command on grounds that latter was valuable and loyal.

Pres. Roosevelt, Prime Minister Churchill and Generalissimo Chiang Kai-shek completed five day parley in Cairo and drafted specific program designed to (1) strip Japan of all her possessions gained since 1914, (2) restore to China all of her territory seized by Japan, (3) grant independence to Korea, (4) expel Japan from all territory acquired by "violence and greed," and (5) compel Japan to surrender unconditionally.

27 **Devastated Berlin** was raided for fifth night in row by R.A.F. formations which unloosed 1,000 tons on German capital.

WMC was charged by OWI Director Elmer Davis with creating "public confusion" by withholding and concealing news.

Declaration of state of belligerency between Colombia and Germany was approved by Colombian senate.

28 **German defenses across Sangro river** in Italy were pierced by British 8th army's drive.

29 **Thirteen U.S. bombers** and 16 fighters failed to re-

CALENDAR OF EVENTS·1943

14

NOVEMBER—Continued

turn from third big November raid on German port of Bremen.

Japanese supply base of Bonga on northeastern New Guinea coast was occupied by Australian forces.

30 King Victor Emmanuel was shorn of his titles as king of Albania and emperor of Ethiopia by Badoglio government.

Lt. Gen. Alexander A. Vandegrift was named to succeed Lt. Gen. Thomas Holcomb as commandant of U.S. marine corps, as of Jan. 1, 1944.

DECEMBER

1 Pres. Roosevelt, Premier Stalin and Prime Minister Churchill completed four-day conference in Teheran and reached complete agreement on measures to destroy German military power and to set up enduring postwar peace organization.

Industrial centre of Solingen in Germany was bombed for second day in row by U.S. four-engined planes.

Moscow admitted retreating Russian armies had evacuated Korosten.

Swedish exchange liner "Gripsholm" arrived in New York with 1,439 Americans and Canadians released from Japanese internment camps.

Total U.S. casualties incurred in Gilbert Islands invasion were 3,772; 1,026 marines were killed and 2,557 wounded in Tarawa battle.

2 Britain was urged by Prime Minister Jan Christiaan Smuts of South Africa to bolster her position in Europe lest she become a weak and unequal partner with U.S. and U.S.S.R.

More than 500 R.A.F. bombers broke through strong enemy fighter plane and anti-aircraft defenses to rain 1,680 short tons of explosives on Berlin, leaving fires visible 200 mi. away.

Seventeen Allied ships were sunk and 1,000 casualties were suffered in surprise German air attack on Allied merchantmen in Italian port of Bari.

3 WPB announced 8,789 planes, including more than 1,000 four-engined bombers, were produced by U.S. aircraft factories in Nov. 1943.

Allied 5th army bent back German lines over Mount Camino range after 72 hours of fierce battle in drive toward Rome.

4 R.A.F. bomber formations tricked Germans by feinting attack on Berlin, then swooping on Leipzig to batter that city with 1,680-short-ton salvo of explosives.

Yugoslav partisans announced they had set up provisional regime in opposition to Yugoslav government-in-exile sitting in Cairo.

U.S. shipyards delivered 25,284,287 tons of merchant shipping between Jan. 1 and Dec. 1, 1943, exceeding 24,000,000-ton goal set for year, Adm. Vickery announced.

Bolivia's declaration of war against axis nations, approved by Bolivian congress on Nov. 26, was formally disclosed.

Two Japanese cruisers, four other ships and 72 planes were destroyed by U.S. task force in raid on Marshall Islands.

Japanese-held Nauru Island was severely bombed and shelled by U.S. carrier planes and warships.

6 Turkey edged closer to camp of United Nations as President Inönü conferred with Pres. Roosevelt and Prime Minister Churchill for three days in Cairo.

7 OWM Director Byrnes warned that failure to retain food subsidies would lead to widespread inflation and result in hardships to people with fixed incomes.

8 Wareo junction fell to Australian troops driving westward along New Guinea coast.

9 Chinese forces recaptured Changteh in vigorous counterattack and pressed drive to expel Japanese from "rice bowl" area.

Znamenka, German-held rail centre southwest of Kremenchug, was captured by Russians.

Senate overruled Director of Economic Stabilization Vinson and approved by 74-to-4 vote pay increase of 8 cents per hour for nonoperating railroad employees.

Joint Allied statement asserted that more U-boats than Allied merchantmen were sunk in Nov. 1943.

Sec'y Hull announced that U.S. would aid Gen. Josep Brozovitch (Tito) and his Yugoslav partisan forces as well as Gen. Mikhailovitch.

10 Sofia was heavily bombed by Allied warplanes.

House foreign affairs committee was told by Breckinridge Long, U.S. assistant secretary of state, in secret session, that 580,000 victims of Hitler persecution had been admitted to U.S. in 10 years.

Pres. Roosevelt signed bill placing pre-Pearl Harbor fathers at bottom of draft list, overruling WMC Chairman Paul McNutt, who objected that measure would sabotage U.S. manpower program.

11 Hungary, Rumania and Bulgaria were solemnly warned by Sec'y Hull to quit war or suffer consequences.

138 nazi fighter planes were shot down trying to intercept U.S. bombers, escorted by combat planes, that staged paralyzing aerial attack on German U-boat base of Emden.

12 German counteroffensive in Kiev area was halted by Russian troops.

Russo-Czech treaty of friendship and mutual assistance was signed in Moscow by Foreign Commissar Molotov and Czech Ambassador Zdenek Fierlinger as Pres. Eduard Beneš witnessed ceremony.

Sec'y Stimson and Sec'y Knox stressed U.S. army-navy regulations did not ban officers from accepting "draft" nomination for president.

13 Swiss dispatches described nazi secret weapon as 12-ton rocket shell with range of 160 mi. to be fired from French coast over England.

14 Axis airfields in Greece and merchant ships in Piraeus harbour were attacked by 300 U.S. planes.

Load of 356 tons of explosives was dropped by more than 100 U.S. bombers on small Japanese-held port of Arawe.

Fall of Cherkassy to soviet troops was announced in Moscow communiqué.

15 Five railroad operating brotherhoods announced they would go on strike Dec. 30 because their demands for 30% pay increases were not met.

U.S. forces landed at Arawe on New Britain Island in new Pacific offensive designed to neutralize Japanese air base of Rabaul.

16 British government announced that Prime Minister Churchill was ill of pneumonia somewhere in middle east.

Safe return of Pres. Roosevelt to U.S. after conferences in middle east was announced by White House.

Berlin was aglow with many fires after R.A.F. bombers showered battered German capital with 1,680 short tons of explosives.

18 Three German soldiers and one Russian were sentenced to hang after they were found guilty by a Kharkov military tribunal of participating in mass slayings of Russian prisoners and civilians.

San Pietro in Fine fell to Allied 5th army in Italy after 72 hours of bitter battle.

19 Large formations of U.S. bombers attached to U.S. 15th air force accomplished "heavy and accurate" bombings of military objectives in Augsburg, Germany and Innsbruck, Austria.

20 New drive against German base of Vitebsk was opened by Russian armies, Moscow announced.

The pictures on this page are, left to right:

BOWLES .... Nov. 6
BRICKER .... Nov. 10
MARIGNY .... Nov. 11
LEHMAN .... Nov. 11
INÖNÜ .... Dec. 6

DECEMBER—*Continued*

Bombers of U.S. 8th air force struck Bremen with 1,200 tons of bombs.

Bolivian government of Pres. Peñaranda was overthrown in military coup and replaced by five-man junta.

Moscow radio announced that "The Internationale" would be replaced by new soviet anthem.

More than 2,250 tons of bombs were cascaded over Frankfurt by estimated 800–900 R.A.F. four-motored planes in one of heaviest raids of 1943, on German chemical and arms centre; R.A.F. bombers also battered Mannheim-Ludwigshafen industrial targets.

21 U.S. army headquarters in Central Pacific disclosed that Gen. Marshall had toured Pacific battle areas and had conferred with Gen. MacArthur.

Japanese air strip at Arawe was captured by troops of U.S. 6th army in New Britain, Allied communiqué announced.

Pierre-Étienne Flandin, Marcel Peyrouton, Pierre Boisson and two other Frenchmen suspected of Vichyite tendencies were arrested on treason charges by French Committee of National Liberation.

22 Thirty-eight German planes and 21 U.S. bombers were shot down during U.S. bombing raids over northwest Germany.

Yugoslav partisan government forbade King Peter to return to homeland during war and deprived his government of all rights.

Seven men accused of conspiring to extort $1,000,000 from motion picture industry were found guilty by New York federal court jury.

Mgr. Bernard W. Griffin was appointed archbishop of Westminster.

German foreign office hinted that reprisals would be taken against U.S. and British prisoners of war in Germany because Russians executed three German soldiers accused of wanton slayings.

23 Pres. Roosevelt suggested dropping "New Deal" label for his administration in favour of "Win the War" slogan.

U.S. war department revealed that 346 of 581 bomber crewmen whose planes were shot down over Germany during Schweinfurt raid were alive and prisoners of war.

Yugoslav partisan government was labelled as "work of impostors" by Yugoslav regime representing King Peter.

Premier Raid Soli told Lebanese chamber of deputies that France had agreed to give up her mandated controls over Syria and Lebanon on Jan. 1, 1944.

24 Gen. Eisenhower was named to command Allied armies slated to invade western Europe; Lt. Gen. Spaatz was appointed overall commander of U.S. strategic bombing air force operating against reich; Gen. Montgomery was appointed to lead British troops under Eisenhower; Gen. Sir Henry Maitland Wilson was picked to succeed Eisenhower as Allied commander in Mediterranean theatre of operations; and Gen. Alexander was named commander of all Allied forces in Italy.

Pres. Roosevelt declared in Christmas eve broadcast that "Big Four"—U.S., Britain, U.S.S.R. and China—were agreed to use force "for as long as may be necessary," to maintain postwar peace.

Pope Pius XII urged world leaders to shun hatred and vengeance and pleaded for just peace maintained by employment of force if necessary.

"Rocket coast" of France was smashed by estimated 3,000 Allied warplanes in attacks on "special military installations."

Tempelhof area of Berlin was systematically bombed by R.A.F. squadrons which unloosed 1,120 tons of bombs on reich capital.

Gorodok, fortified town protecting German-held Vitebsk 17 mi. away, fell to advancing Russian troops.

Two railway brotherhoods numbering 230,000 members agreed to arbitration by Pres. Roosevelt and called off scheduled strike.

Thirty Japanese planes were shot down by Allied pilots, in air battle over Rabaul, Allied headquarters announced.

25 German supply route linking Vitebsk and Polotsk was cut by Russian armies.

Deadlock between plant operators and C.I.O. steelworkers on latter's demands for pay boosts led to walkout of 70,000 steelworkers in four states.

26 26,000-ton German battleship "Scharnhorst" was sunk off North Cape, Norway, after running battle with British warships.

27 15,000 Germans were killed as Russia's 1st Ukrainian army rolled back nazi forces 25 mi. on a front 50 mi. wide, Moscow communiqué announced.

Pres. Roosevelt ordered Sec'y Stimson to seize all U.S. railroads and put them under army rule in move to thwart strike threat.

Fair Employment Practice committee called on Pres. Roosevelt to compel 16 southeast railroads and seven unions to cease discrimination in employment of Negroes.

Allied headquarters announced that U.S. marines had landed at two points around Cape Gloucester, New Britain Island.

Prediction that Allies would win European war in 1944 was made by Gen. Eisenhower.

Appointment of Air Chief Marshal Sir Arthur Tedder as deputy supreme commander of Allied invasion army under Gen. Eisenhower was announced by British government, which also revealed that Gen. Sir Bernard Paget had been named commander-in-chief in middle east under Gen. Sir Henry Maitland Wilson.

28 Majority of 170,000 striking steelworkers returned to jobs after WLB approved Pres. Roosevelt's suggestions that retroactive pay be guaranteed.

Maj. Gen. Doolittle was named to command U.S. 8th air force in England; Lt. Gen. Devers was appointed commander of all U.S. forces in Mediterranean; Lt. Gen. Eaker was named to command all Allied air forces in Mediterranean and Gen. Nathan F. Twining was named commander of U.S. 15th air force in Mediterranean.

29 Korosten, Ukraine rail hub, was recaptured by Gen. Nikolai Vatutin's 1st Ukrainian army.

Berlin reeled under weight of 2,240 tons of explosives dropped by great swarm of R.A.F. heavy bombers.

Canadians occupied Ortona in Italy after nine days of house-to-house fighting.

Adm. Sir Bertram Ramsay and Air Chief Marshal Trafford L. Leigh-Mallory were named naval and air chiefs respectively under Gen. Eisenhower.

Scheduled walkout of U.S. railway workers averted as last of three brotherhoods cancelled strike orders.

30 Russian armies in Ukraine routed 22 German divisions and swarmed through broken nazi lines on 186-mi. front.

More than 1,300 U.S. bombers and fighters smashed targets in southwest Germany.

Cape Gloucester aerodrome on New Britain Island fell to U.S. marines who captured both of Japanese-held landing strips after 48 hours of battle.

31 Zhitomir was recaptured by Russian armies in powerful drive toward Polish frontier.

Adolf Hitler warned that there would be "no victors or losers, but merely survivors and annihilated" in World War II.

All political parties in Argentina were ordered dissolved by government decree.

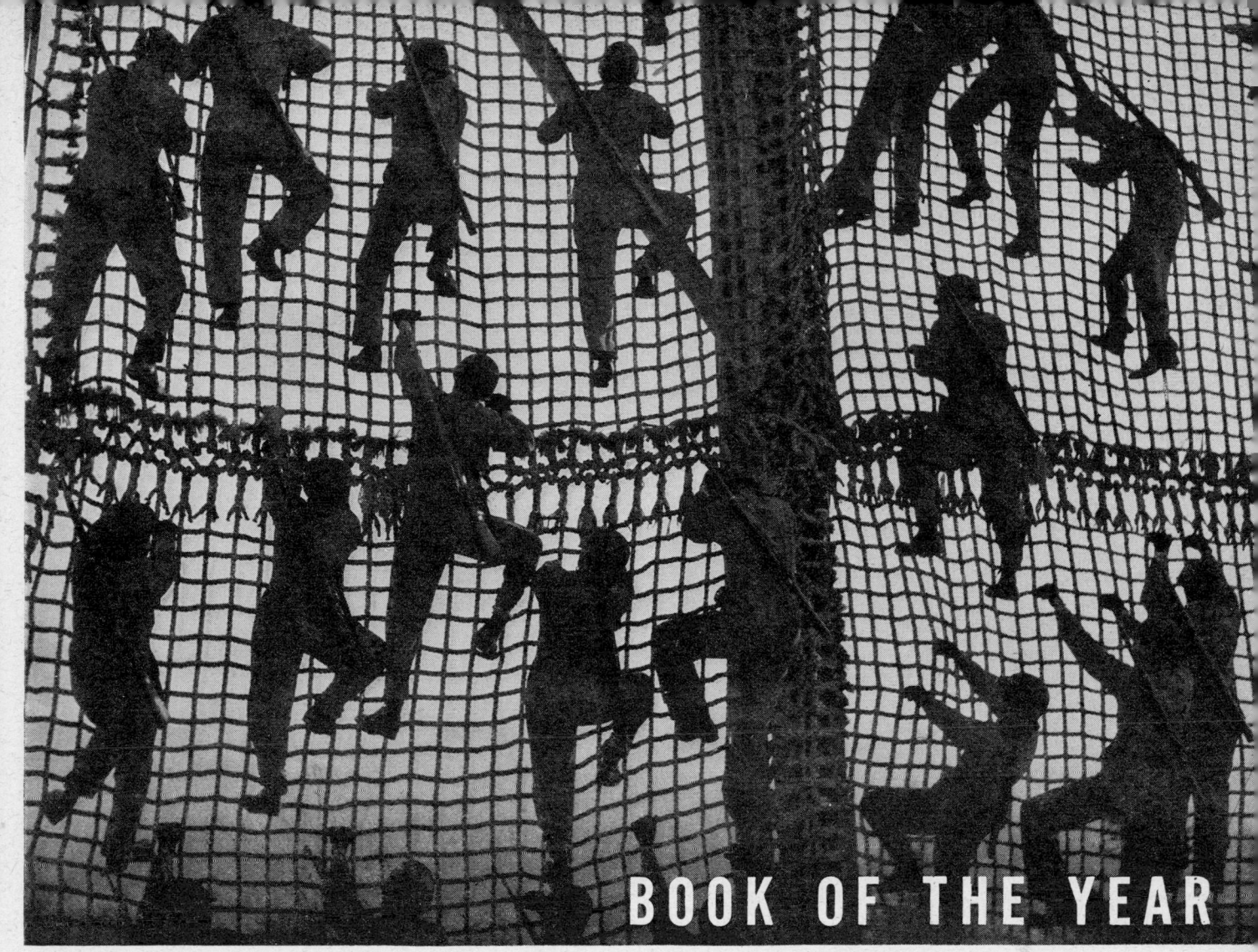

BOOK OF THE YEAR

Abd-el-Aziz-IV (1878–1943), sultan of Morocco, was born Feb. 24 in Marrakesh, Morocco. After his father's death in 1894, he became nominal head of the government with real power vested in his chamberlain, Si Ahmed-ben-Musa. After the latter's death in 1900, the young sultan ruled until 1908, when recurrent local revolts forced him to abdicate. He died in Tetuan, Spanish Morocco, June 9. (See *Encyclopædia Britannica*.)

Aberhart, William (1878–1943), Canadian politician, was born Dec. 30 on a farm near Kippen, Ont. After studying at Hamilton Normal school and Queen's university, he settled in Calgary, where he organized a Bible class that later expanded into the Calgary Prophetic institute. He became widely known for his religious broadcasts made in behalf of the institute. In 1935, he took over the premiership of Alberta as head of the Social Credit party, which promised monthly dividends of $25 for every man and woman; in the elections that year his party won 56 of the 63 seats in the Alberta legislature. Aberhart's program was based on the theories of social credit propounded in London by Major C. H. Douglas. Later, provincial and dominion courts and the privy council ruled his legislation unconstitutional, and in 1938 he set up a modified form of social credit. Aberhart was re-elected in 1940. He died in Vancouver, B.C., May 23, 1943.

Abrasives. Such data as were received in 1943 are abstracted as in the accompanying table.

Corundum.—It is possible that a moderate domestic supply might be developed following investigations of deposits in the United States, mostly in the southern Atlantic coast states.

Diamonds.—Demand continued high, but no information was made public on supplies. (*See* under DIAMONDS.)

Emery.—The area around Peekskill, N.Y. turned out the largest emery output since 1918.

Flint.—Sales of grinding pebbles increased from 13,561 tons in 1941 to 15,487 tons in 1942, while tube-mill liners dropped from 3,411 tons to 2,576 tons.

United States Production of Abrasives
(In short tons, or as indicated)

	1939	1940	1941	1942
Aluminous Abrasives				
Corundum*	2,029	2,989	4,021‡	?
Emery	765	1,046	4,876	5,277
Carbon Abrasives				
Industrial diamonds, carats*	3,590,111	3,809,856	2,911,117‡	?
Silica Abrasives				
Quartz	34,959	31,865	41,685	65,878
Sand (abrasive)	668,027	856,309	1,001,814	?
Sand and sandstone (ground)	310,512	342,218	487,665	527,886
Tripoli	33,474	30,212	29,301	17,536
Silica Stone Abrasives				
Grindstones	7,917	8,790	13,573	19,175
Millstones (value)	$11,084	$6,558	$15,579	$10,391
Pulpstones	2,517	4,533	1,963	1,918
Sharpening stones	620	?	?	?
Silicate Abrasives				
Garnet	4,056	4,716	5,501	4,357
Pumice	89,159	82,407	117,310	126,522
Artificial Abrasives				
Silicon carbide†	24,206	33,042	44,962	61,681
Aluminum oxide†	50,468	98,531	147,759	183,633
Metallic abrasives† . . .	42,015	50,016	86,309	125,264

*Imports; no domestic production. †Includes Canada also. ‡Jan.–Sept. only.

Garnet.—Sales declined in 1942, but were still well above the 1939 level.

Grindstones, Pulpstones and Millstones.—Sales of grindstones were increased 41% in quantity in 1942, but declined 3% in value, while pulpstones decreased in quantity but increased slightly in value. The value of millstones sold declined by one-third.

Pumice.—Sales of pumice made a new record high, with an increase of 11% over 1941.

Sharpening Stones.—Sales increased in 1942, but no data were published.   (G. A. Ro.)

Abyssinia: *see* ETHIOPIA.
Academic Freedom: *see* EDUCATION.
Academy of Arts and Letters, American: *see* AMERICAN ACADEMY OF ARTS AND LETTERS.
Academy of Arts and Sciences, American: *see* AMERICAN ACADEMY OF ARTS AND SCIENCES.
Academy of Political and Social Science, American: *see* AMERICAN ACADEMY OF POLITICAL AND SOCIAL SCIENCE.
Accident Insurance: *see* INSURANCE.

Accidents. Accidents throughout the United States during 1943 dropped 1.5% from 1942. Estimates for the year indicated 94,500 accidental deaths and about 9,000,000 disabling injuries.

The greatest reduction was in motor vehicle accidents, where deaths dropped 18%. (See *Traffic Accidents and Accident Prevention,* below.) Fatal accidents in industry decreased 3%. Home fatalities, on the contrary, showed a rise of 5% and there was a 3% advance in public accident deaths not involving motor vehicles.

The National Safety council estimated that 1943 accident losses, as measured in actual time off and in permanent disabilities and deaths, were the equivalent of 380,000,000 man-days of production.

Accident reductions from 1942, although not large, reflected a considerable measure of success in safety, because there were many circumstances tending toward increased accident totals. Only in the field of traffic did the exposure to accidents decrease. Here a reduction in motor vehicle mileage of 21% approximately equalled the drop in motor vehicle accidents.

The decline in industrial accidents was achieved in the face of increasing industrial employment, including large groups of inexperienced workers operating in unfamiliar trades.

The accident toll would undoubtedly have been much higher in 1943 except for the greatly increased attention given to safety by organizations and individuals throughout the United States. This interest was reflected in many ways: the inauguration or improvement of safety programs in war industries; the adoption of safety as an activity by numerous industrial, civic and service associations; greatly expanded use of safety educational material by newspapers, magazines and the radio.

Industry realized more clearly in 1943 that accident prevention was a "round-the-clock" problem, and that a worker hurt in an off-the-job accident was just as surely an industrial casualty as if he had been hurt at his machine. Consequently, industrial leaders undertook to educate employees in traffic and home accident prevention, through educational literature and other means.

The outstanding safety event of 1943 was the National Safety congress held in Chicago in October. This gathering included some 10,000 delegates, who came from every state in the union and represented every phase of the safety movement. There were 175 sessions held during the three-day convention, and more than 500 safety experts participated.

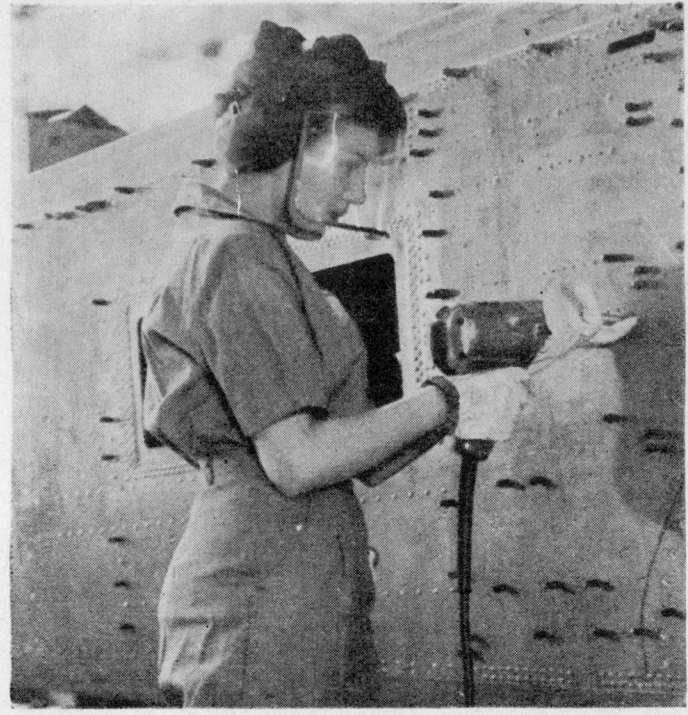

PLASTIC SHIELD to protect the faces of U.S. aircraft workers

Many units of the armed services developed and carried out extensive programs of safety among their personnel. Responsibility for such programs was commonly placed in the hands of men drawn from industry and from public agencies, with a background of many years' experience in industrial and traffic safety. (*See* also DEATH STATISTICS; DISASTERS; INDUSTRIAL HEALTH.)   (R. L. Fo.)

Traffic Accidents and Accident Prevention.—The year 1943 was marked by an increasing emphasis on the training of drivers —for purposes of accident prevention and in order to help fill the army's needs—and on making preparations in the fields of highway engineering and traffic law enforcement for the postwar period when the yearly traffic toll was expected to approach, if not exceed, the alarming all-time high mark of 40,000 reached in 1941. The total of 23,300 deaths in 1943 was 18% less than in 1942, and 42% less than in 1941, when the nation's traffic death toll reached an all-time high. In addition to the fatalities, 1943 traffic accidents resulted in 800,000 nonfatal injuries, 60,000 of which left some permanent impairment.

A valuable impetus to the driver education movement was given during 1943 when the U.S. army made a request that pre-induction driver education courses be set up in the high schools of the country. With the lowering of the induction age to 18 years and the corresponding increase in the flow into the army of young men with no civilian job experience useful from a military point of view, the problem of army training was considerably accentuated.

The war department and the U.S. office of education prepared teaching materials in the field of driver education as adapted to army needs, and these materials were distributed to a large number of high schools.

Four training institutes for state driver education leaders were held during the summer of 1943. The driver education program was carried on actively in 22 states, and more than 7,000 high schools signified their intention of including pre-induction driver education in their curricula.

Three staff members of the New York University Center for Safety Education and one staff member each from the National

Conservation bureau, the National Safety council and the American Automobile association devoted considerable time to instruction in connection with the driver training work.

Consultant services on the establishment of driver education courses were provided by war department representatives and by pre-induction training officers stationed in the service commands.

There was an intensification of traffic during 1943 in war production centres and in the vicinity of military posts, and as a result both military and civilian authorities devoted a great deal of attention to the matter of preventing traffic accidents as one phase of the over-all program to conserve essential manpower and vitally needed equipment and materials. Plans for maintaining close liaison in solving the critical traffic problems in areas where much of the highway travel was of emergency character were developed at meetings held in all of the service commands under the joint sponsorship of the army and the Highway Traffic Advisory committee to the war department. Discussions emphasized the need for closer co-ordination of the traffic control efforts of military and state officials.

In four cities—Norfolk, Va., Seattle, Wash., Charleston, S.C., and Baltimore, Md.—which were among those designated by the army transportation corps as being in greatest need of traffic control assistance, the Safety division of the International Association of Chiefs of Police made extensive traffic control surveys which were followed by detailed recommendations dealing with the traffic problem and the procedure for facilitating traffic flow and preventing accidents.

The need for more men for the fighting fronts put an increasingly heavier drain on police manpower during 1943, and in the field of traffic control and accident prevention this had serious effects. Trained men were badly needed to take the place of those who had gone into the armed services. The training of traffic enforcement personnel was continued as a means of meeting an immediate situation and of planning for the postwar period.

The Northwestern University Traffic institute, leading training agency for traffic police, conducted two four-month courses in traffic police administration as the major feature of its training program, and in addition held two short courses (of two weeks each) on the Northwestern campus and assisted in traffic training work in a number of police departments and at several colleges throughout the country.

Eleven organizations co-operated in sponsoring the sixth National Institute for Wartime Traffic Training from June 21 to July 2, 1943, at Ohio State university in Columbus. The eleven organizations were: the National Conservation bureau, the American Automobile association, the International Association of Chiefs of Police, the Automotive Safety foundation, the National Safety council, the American Association of Motor Vehicle Administrators, Northwestern University Traffic institute, the Yale University Bureau for Street Traffic Research, the American Association of State Highway Officials, the Institute of Traffic Engineers and Ohio State university.

Progress was made during 1943 in the construction of express highways designed to speed traffic movement and to help prevent accidents. The Defense Highway act of 1941, through which funds had been made available for a number of important highway projects either completed or under construction, also set the stage for the building of more than 1,000 mi. of expressways in and around metropolitan areas in the immediate postwar period.

During 1943 the Willow Run bomber plant near Detroit, the war department's Pentagon building near Washington, D.C., and an ordnance plant near Denver obtained expressway connections under this act. The Ramona freeway in Los Angeles and a

Deaths from Accidents in the U.S., 1943 and 1942

	1943	1942	Change
All accidents	94,500	95,889	—1.5%
Motor vehicle*	23,300	28,309	—18.0%
Public, civilian (except motor vehicle) .	15,500	15,000	+3.0%
Home, civilian	33,000	31,500	+5.0%
Occupational, civilian	18,000	18,500	—3.0%
Military personnel	9,500	6,600	+44.0%

*The motor vehicle death totals include some deaths also included in occupational, home and military personnel. This duplication amounted to about 4,800 deaths in 1943 and 4,000 in 1942.
The 1942 all-accident and motor vehicle totals are U.S. census bureau figures. All others are National Safety council estimates.

Pittsburgh downtown expressway belt also progressed substantially toward completion in 1943.

Five state legislatures adopted limited-access highway legislation in 1943 permitting construction of expressways. This brought the total number of states with such enactments to 17.

The year saw the expansion of programs for staggered working hours and group riding which helped to conserve essential highway transportation for the war effort. With more people per car riding to and from war plants, the need for preventing traffic accidents to save the lives of and to avoid injuries to war workers became more urgent than ever before.   (R. E. RH.)

Acheson, Dean Gooderham

(1893–   ), U.S. government official, was born in April in Middletown, Conn. He graduated from Yale university, 1915, and received a law degree from Harvard three years later. He served as a naval ensign in World War I, and later became private secretary to Louis D. Brandeis, associate justice of the U.S. supreme court. In 1921, he entered the private practice of law, which he followed until May 19, 1933, when he was appointed undersecretary of the treasury. This appointment terminated with his resignation later that year, when he returned to his law practice. He continued his work as attorney until Feb. 1, 1941, when he received an appointment as assistant secretary of state. With the formation of the United Nations Relief and Rehabilitation administration in 1943, Acheson was chosen as the U.S. member of the UNRRA council. He delivered the opening address before the assemblage of international delegates which met at Atlantic City in Nov. 1943.

Aden.

Aden is a British colony, seaport and territory in southwest Arabia, situated in 12° 47′ N. and 45° 10′ E., including Perim island in the strait of Bab-el-Mandeb between Africa and Arabia; area 80 sq.mi.; pop. (est. 1939) 48,338. Aden protectorate, including Socotra in the Indian ocean, 112,000 sq.mi.; pop. (est.) 600,000. Governor (1943): Sir J. Hathorn Hall. Language: English and Arabic; religion: predominantly Mohammedan.

History.—With the end of axis resistance in Africa and the subsequent surrender of Italy in 1943 the war receded from Aden, although conditions created by the war still continued to engage the active attention of the government. In the early part of 1943 the almost complete failure of the spring rains in the protectorate was the cause of grave concern, and it soon became apparent that a serious shortage of foodstuffs would result. Prompt action by the Aden government, assisted by the middle east supply centre and financed by the British government, resulted in the early amelioration of conditions.

The development of the Audali plateau, at a height of approximately 7,000 ft., as a market garden for the town of Aden during the summer months received great impetus during 1943 and provided additional supplies of fresh vegetables and potatoes during the hot season.

From the beginning of the war until the end of Nov. 1943 the people of Aden made monetary contributions to the prosecution of the war and to war charities amounting to approximately £73,000, a particularly generous response in view of the small population. In addition, up to June 1943 the government of Aden had lent to his majesty's government, free of interest, the sum of £105,000. (L. T. S.)

Finance.—Revenue (1941–42) Rs.46,71,758; expenditure (1941–42) Rs.39,53,932; currency, legal tender rupee: (Rs.1) = 1s. 6d., or approximately 30 cents U.S. in 1943. Rs.100,000 = 1 lakh, written Rs.1,00,000; Rs.10,000,000 = 1 crore = 100 lakhs, written Rs.1,00,00,000.

Trade and Communication.—External trade 1939 (merchandise and treasure on private account): imports, by sea Rs.5,78,-56,697; by land Rs.22,76,258; exports, by sea Rs.3,37,72,025; by land Rs.22,11,555; (treasure) imports Rs.37,00,871; exports Rs.20,22,690. Communications: shipping (1939) 2,004 merchant vessels (1,300 British) entered, total tonnage 8,005,763 net tons; motor vehicles registered (Sept. 30, 1939) 733 cars and taxis, 207 commercial vehicles.

Production.—In 1938–39, tobacco (approx. value of crop) Rs.500,000; salt 282,994 tons; (export) 248,784 tons; coffee (export) 5,401.27 short tons.

Adjusted Compensation: *see* VETERANS' ADMINISTRATION.
Adult Education: *see* EDUCATION.

Advertising.

United States. — During 1943, the United States' second year of World War II, the rapid expansion of war demands on manpower and production had a telling effect on business and hence upon advertising. Greatest single factor, perhaps, was the shortage of paper and printing materials. By the end of 1943 a War Production board edict had cut paper supply to publishing and printing industries to 75% of normal consumption. Newspaper publishers experimented with lightweight stock to stretch quotas.

In spite of shortages, volume of advertising increased greatly. Although profits were higher, they were largely absorbed by excess profit taxes. Both institutional and industrial advertising increased tremendously. In the United States, advertising expenditures were $2,100,000,000 as compared with $1,820,000,000 in 1942, an increase of 15%. Newspaper linage increased 12.5%. Dollar volume of magazine advertising increased 30%; radio increased 32.3%; farm paper advertising increased 39.9%; outdoor decreased 5.6%; direct mail increased 8.3%.[1]

It was estimated by the war advertising council that more than $300,000,000 in space had been contributed for the promotion of war themes. Nearly 100 separate home-front information campaigns on food, manpower conservation, finance, United States army, housing, Red Cross and bond drives were conducted in co-operation with the Office of War Information and 17 other major government departments.

A survey conducted by the American Marketing association showed that 86% of management and advertising executives believed business had a responsibility in disseminating information to the home front, expressing a strong preference for voluntary contributions of advertising space and time, rather than appropriation of government funds for this purpose.

To conserve natural resources, the War Production board ordered in September a national brown-out which replaced the general black-out regulation in coastal cities. This permitted advertisers to operate outdoor and indoor displays and show windows between dusk and 10 P.M., with the exception of places of public service while they were open for business.

Copy and Layout.—Most significant change in copy was a distinct improvement in the tone of war advertising and in the quality of appeal. Much of the copy became more realistic and informative. Advertising became aware of public and government sentiment against commercializing patriotism in print and boasts of contributions toward winning the war and took steps to eliminate such criticisms. Postwar themes were used extensively. Toward the end of 1943, the war was mentioned less frequently.

Magazines.—In spite of rationing of paper, magazines as a whole carried the largest advertising volume in their history—105 magazines grossed $227,000,000 as compared with $174,582,-984 in 1942 and $196,687,538 in 1929. An additional $50,000,000 worth was refused because of paper shortage. (*See* NEWSPAPERS AND MAGAZINES.)

Ten publishers, including *Newsweek, Life* and the *New Yorker,* put out and distributed free of charge miniature editions for servicemen overseas. They carried substantially the same editorial matter but no advertising.

Newspapers.—Efforts to tighten classified sections, editorial columns and the like had been exhausted by the end of 1943 and the next move was toward curtailment of local retail and national advertising. Some papers adopted a 1,000-line ceiling and limited the number of insertions. Optional insertion dates, limited space and other restrictions on national advertising had been imposed, and by the end of 1943 strict rationing plans were being formulated.

Stringent limitations on classified were universal. Agate type, limited display, limitation on number of lines, dropping of out-of-town help-wanted advertisements and so on helped to save paper. Further cuts were made through compact writing and editing of editorials, shorter stories, fewer features and slashing of comics, women's pages and financial news. Saturday editions were streamlined to six or eight pages; Sunday gravure sections were changed to tabloid size by many papers. Comparatively few newspapers froze circulations; some discontinued circulation promotion. More papers raised both per-copy and subscription rates. Newspapers supported government war projects by selling advertising for war loans and other campaigns and by increased use of informative institutional advertising.

Radio.—*See* RADIO.

Retail.—The use of institutional advertisements increased greatly among an overwhelming number of retail advertisers. Promotional copy using comparative prices and emphasizing big sales and special events was eliminated by practically all stores, resulting in the reduction of buying of scarce articles.

Of all retail advertising, 85.9% was in newspapers; 4.2% in radio; direct mail 4.5%; and other 4.7%.

Direct Mail.—This medium held up fairly well but changed somewhat in its nature. Printed promotion geared itself largely to the war effort and users of direct mail tied in their appeals with the various major wartime projects.

The Graphic Arts Victory committee issued a guide book which was helpful in supplying information to users of printed promotion in tying up their printing with the war effort. The Graphic Arts Victory committee was also instrumental in assisting all types of organizations in successfully using the convention-by-mail method, resulting in hundreds of conventions being cancelled which contributed greatly in relieving transportation problems. The committee also pointed out many ways to make paper really "stretch." Catalogues, directories and shopping newspapers were assigned paper quotas limiting them to 85% of 1941 usage.

Display.—Display advertisers keenly felt the effects of restrictions. A War Production board order in October banned the use of new fibreboard containers for shipping displays. The industry protested, charging the order unjustly discriminated against the

---

[1] January-September. No later figures available.

entire graphic arts industry, particularly the advertising display branch, and claimed it would practically eliminate this advertising medium. Little hope for immediate relief was in sight at the end of 1943.

Transportation.—This medium showed the largest percentage of gain over previous years of any major media. Volume was up more than 20% over 1942, grossing approximately $10,000,000. Sixteen per cent of this was local and 40% national advertising. Many cities were completely "sold out" with practically all space reserved for months ahead. Rate increases were prevalent. Most national advertising continued to be on branded goods, chiefly foods and drugs.

The industry's War Campaigns pool contributed approximately 100,000 free spaces per month to the government for war messages. Carded vehicles increased slightly, numbering 85,000. Riders exceeded 22,000,000,000 as against 18,000,000,000 in 1942.

Outdoor.—Traffic Audit bureau tabulations were resumed in 1943. Reports for the May 15–June 30 period based on 105 cities showed that, compared with 1939–41 audits, 65 cities increased in effective circulation, 36 decreased, while 4 remained the same.

Consumer.—Copy for the woman consumer reached down-to-earth realism in the face of shortages. Food advertisements gave as much information about nutrition as food editorials, as well as many friendly helps on making scarce foods go farther, maintaining the health of the family and getting variety out of short stocks on grocers' shelves. Other copy taught consumers how to get more wear out of many everyday commodities.

A survey of buying habits disclosed that 58.8% of housewives visited more stores to obtain food products and 55.7% went to more stores for meat. Changes in buying habits extended to practically all purchases. Despite shortages, housewives kept their homes well supplied by means of substitution and shopping around.

Branded products, however, were menaced by two factors: (1) unavailability of branded goods and the offering of substitutes, and (2) compulsory grade labelling in fixing price ceilings. These factors were partly offset by advertising of brand names and by adjustments in grade labelling in relation to quality.

Research.—Due to an increased demand for factual data, government agencies effectively used private research organizations. For 11 months of 1943, 41 special reports were compiled as

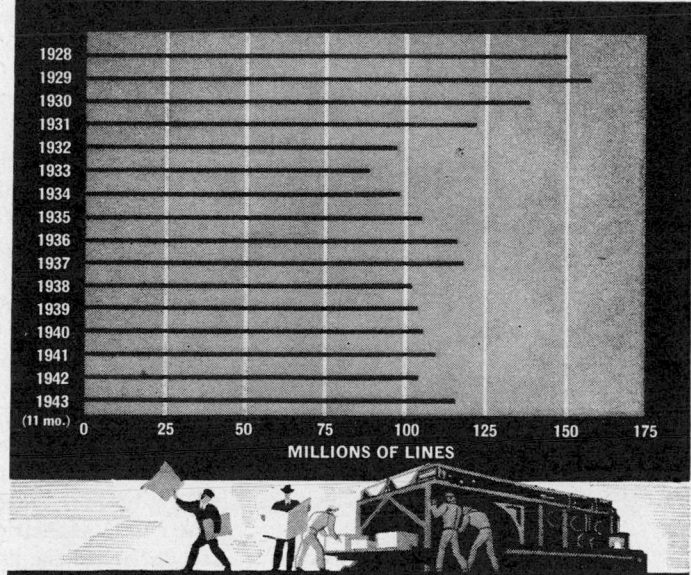

NEWSPAPER ADVERTISING (total linage in 52 cities of the United States): average per month. Compiled by Media Records, Inc.

against 23 in 1942, in response to specific requests from various agencies. Data on 57 commodities were compiled relating to consumer sales, rationing, allocation of vital war materials, price freezes and price ceilings.

A study made by the Association of National Advertisers revealed that the public wanted modest, informational advertisements with a description of postwar products, data on war-winning projects and information on how to co-operate with them. This study also showed that people were aware of the job business was doing in the war effort and that they wanted companies to continue advertising because names should be kept in the public eye. Forty-seven per cent believed advertised products were superior to nonadvertised ones. Interest in what manufacturers were doing to help in the war was definitely on the downgrade, however.

Another study made among farmers showed that three-quarters of those questioned thought (1) business advertising helped them, (2) private management ran business better than government could, (3) government-owned plants should be sold to manufacturers after the war and not run in competition with business. Both studies reported that a very high percentage of persons felt that business' war effort was good.

Great Britain.—With government advertising still leading in total spending, British advertising during the first nine months of 1943 amounted to approximately $40,882,000 as compared with $39,672,000 for the same period in 1942, a gain of 3%. Most conspicuous change in advertising of private commodities was the decline of cigarette advertising. Other goods on which advertising decreased were biscuits and baked products, soaps, furniture, whiskey and other products rationed or short in supply. Volume of advertising actually increased, however, on some short-supply articles, such as shoes, hosiery, chocolate, tea, textiles, motor cars and tires.

Despite drastic paper restrictions, British magazines increased in circulation. Lighter weight paper, readjustment in format and typography, suspension of some publications to support others for the duration and a slight boost in paper quotas helped to supply the increased demand.

In doing a wartime job, advertising in Great Britain ceased to be aggressively competitive and became educational and helpful.

The British war office produced a series of grim posters aimed at reducing serious accidents caused by improper handling of ammunition taken from defective but unspent grenades and similar objects picked up from practice ranges. Subjects of the posters were the result of a careful study of the situation by the public relations department.

Canada.—In addition to restrictions already imposed on newspapers and periodicals, limitations of as much as 50%, aimed to curb over-all use of printed matter, were levied by a Canadian Wartime Price and Trade board order. Business reply postcards and envelopes, blotters, jumbo size or multi-sheet calendars, and new catalogues or price lists illustrating goods or services were banned. Display of printed poster or card advertising was limited as to size of poster and place of display. Exceptions, however, were on printed matter for religious, charitable and similar groups when it contained no advertising.

South America.—*Argentina.*—Advertising volume in Argentina remained practically the same as for 1942. Stringent governmental supervision over pharmaceutical advertising in all media was introduced and advertisements for medicinal products had to be approved in complete form before publication.

Paper shortage was acute but toward the end of 1943, through improvements in shipping and local newsprint manufacture, the situation had eased somewhat. The bulk of Argentine advertising was devoted to local industry. Orders for strict control of broadcasting were issued in June, which included limitation of length of commercials, use of pure Spanish only, approval of scripts of programs by the Department of Radiocommunicaciones, licensing of speakers and artists, barring of audiences from studios and many other extreme measures. (*See* also NEWSPAPERS AND MAGAZINES; RADIO.)   (D. ST.)

Aero-otitis and Aerosinusitis: *see* EAR, NOSE AND THROAT, DISEASES OF.

Afghanistan.

A Moslem kingdom lying between India and Iran; area 250,000 sq.mi.; pop. (est. 1940) 10,000,000; chief towns: Kabul (cap., 80,000), Kandahar (60,000), Herat (50,000), Mazar-i-Sharif (30,000). Ruler: Mohammed Zahir Shah; languages: Persian, Pushtu, and some Turki in the north; religion: Mohammedan.

History.—There was little change in internal affairs during the year. On Nov. 26, 1942, the 9-year-old crown prince, Mohammed Akbar Khan, died. Foreign policy continued along the same lines of neutrality and friendship with Afghanistan's neighbours, and at the beginning of 1943 the Saadabad Pact with Turkey, Iran, and Iraq was automatically renewed for a further five years, as none of its signatories had denounced it six months before expiration.

A new departure was taken by the appointment on June 1 of the first Afghan minister to the U.S.A., Abdul Hosayn Aziz, who had formerly represented his country in Moscow. On Oct. 24 it was learned that negotiations for a treaty of alliance between China and Afghanistan had been completed in Ankara.

(C. M. CL.)

Education.—Confined chiefly to Kabul. Elementary schools exist throughout the country, but secondary schools exist only in Kabul and provincial capitals. Both are free. There were, in 1940, 130 primary schools and 1 normal school for teachers in Kabul. In addition there were 4 secondary schools and 13 military schools. Technical, art, commercial and medical schools exist for higher education. The Kabul university was established in 1932; only a medical faculty existed in 1940.

Finance.—Revenue and expenditure about 150,000,000 (Afghan) rupees; currency: Rs. 3.95 (Afghan) = Rs. 1 (Indian) = 30.12 cents U.S. (July 1943).

Trade and Communication.—(1939–40) Exports to India: Afghan merchandise Rs. 3,97,06,681; treasure Rs. 16,655; non-Afghan merchandise Rs. 2,008. Imports: Indian produce Rs. 72,79,399; other produce (imported through India and in transit) Rs. 1,96,25,197. Persian lambskin is one of the most important exports. Other exports are carpets, fruit, wool and cotton. Roads: trade routes, Kabul to Peshawar (India) 210 mi.; and Kandahar to Chaman, 70 mi.; there are about 2,265 mi. of unmetalled roads connecting the chief towns.

At the beginning of 1941 there were five wireless stations in the country.

Agriculture.—Wheat, rice, millet, maize, sheep, Persian lambskin, wool (1938) 6,800 metric tons.

BIBLIOGRAPHY.—Sir Percy Sykes, *A History of Afghanistan*, 2 vols. (1940).

A. F. of L.: *see* AMERICAN FEDERATION OF LABOR.
Africa, British East: *see* BRITISH EAST AFRICA.
Africa, British South: *see* BRITISH SOUTH AFRICAN PROTECTORATES.
Africa, British West: *see* BRITISH WEST AFRICA.
Africa, French Equatorial: *see* FRENCH COLONIAL EMPIRE.
Africa, French North: *see* FRENCH COLONIAL EMPIRE.
Africa, French West: *see* FRENCH COLONIAL EMPIRE.

Africa, Italian East: *see* ITALIAN COLONIAL EMPIRE.
Africa, Portuguese East and West: *see* PORTUGUESE COLONIAL EMPIRE.
Africa, Spanish West: *see* SPANISH COLONIAL EMPIRE.
Africa, Union of South: *see* SOUTH AFRICA, THE UNION OF.
Agricultural and Industrial Chemistry, Bureau of: *see* AGRICULTURAL RESEARCH ADMINISTRATION.

Agricultural Research Administration.

Among other steps in a major reorganization of the U.S. department of agriculture in Dec. 1941, seven bureaus of agricultural science were brought together into a unified group under an administrator of agricultural research, who was charged with the general supervision and direction of their scientific work. Together, these bureaus, each of which retained its identity, constituted the Agricultural Research administration. The step was a significant one in scientific organization, making possible closer co-ordination of a wide range of research and more effective pooling of resources of knowledge, personnel and material for simultaneous attack on major problems. Hastened by World War II, which made quick action on urgent problems imperative, the move was in line with a growing trend toward greater co-ordination and less sharply defined departmentalization in research.

The agencies in the Agricultural Research administration and their principal functions as of 1943 were as follows:

Bureau of Agricultural and Industrial Chemistry.—In addition to several general research divisions, it operated the four regional research laboratories: eastern, at Philadelphia, Pa.; northern, at Peoria, Ill.; southern, at New Orleans, La.; western, at Albany, Calif. These laboratories were concerned largely with developing new and wider industrial uses for agricultural products and by-products.
Bureau of Animal Industry.—Conducted research on the diseases and parasites and the breeding, feeding and management of domestic animals, including poultry, as well as on livestock products; conducted disease eradication work; administered certain quarantine and regulatory measures.
Bureau of Dairy Industry.—Conducted research on the breeding, feeding and management of dairy cattle and the manufacture and utilization of dairy products and by-products.
Bureau of Entomology and Plant Quarantine.—Conducted research on injurious insects and on honeybees; administered certain quarantine and regulatory laws and conducted control and eradication campaigns relating to insect pests and plant diseases.
Bureau of Human Nutrition and Home Economics.—Conducted research on nutrition, the nutritive values of foods, food preparation and preservation, textiles, clothing, household equipment and family economics.
Bureau of Plant Industry, Soils, and Agricultural Engineering.—Conducted research on the breeding, management, diseases, and introduction and adaptation of crop and other economic plants; the surveying, classifying and mapping of soils; the development and use of fertilizers; the development and use of farm machinery, buildings and equipment.
Office of Experiment Stations.—Administered federal grants to state and territorial agricultural experiment stations, co-ordinated their work with that of the department of agriculture, and operated the federal experiment station at Mayaguez, Puerto Rico.

The Agricultural Research administration also had charge of the Beltsville research centre, Beltsville, Md. (near Washington, D.C.), where extensive research facilities—laboratories, greenhouses, farm buildings, fields, orchards and woodland—were located. Nine regional research laboratories in various parts of the country, called Bankhead-Jones laboratories from the legislation which created them, were being administered by the bureaus or directly by the administrator in 1943. In addition, field stations operated by the bureaus were widely distributed over the United States, and much work was carried on co-operatively at state experiment stations. The purpose of this decentralization was to have the experimental work adequately represent the wide range of environments in the United States as well as to adapt it to regional and local needs.

Work of the Agricultural Research administration in 1943 was concerned almost entirely with war problems related to agriculture and to the needs of the armed forces and the civilian population. By mobilizing research facilities, personnel and the knowledge accumulated from previous research, practical solutions for many of these problems were worked out with unusual rapidity. Among the scores of developments resulting directly from this research were revolutionary new methods of destroying injurious insects, particularly disease-carrying lice and malarial mosquitoes; new, highly effective insect repellants; safe and satisfactory ways of dehydrating vegetables and meats for overseas shipment in large quantities; great increases in the production of oil, fibre and drug crops formerly for the most part imported and therefore relatively unfamiliar to United States farmers; the safeguarding of wartime diets from the health standpoint by sound scientific findings; wartime changes in livestock rations based on research; new methods of combatting livestock diseases and parasites; new or improved machinery for handling various crops; new processes for making industrial products such as alcohol, rubber substitutes, plastics and cork substitute from farm products and by-products; and methods for making the production of the new drug, penicillin (*q.v.*), commercially possible. (E. C. Ar.)

Agriculture.

Crop Production.—The gross production of crops in the United States in 1943 was estimated by the U.S. department of agriculture as 6% less than the record-breaking crops of 1942 but nearly 5% more than any previous year. In comparison with the average of the five years 1937–41, production of the 53 principal crops was up 9%. The favourable returns of 1942 and 1943 were due to several factors: (1) better than average growing seasons; (2) improved farm practices; (3) changes in the Farm Adjustment program; (4) higher prices of farm products; and (5) willingness of farmers and their families to work long hours to aid the war effort. The chief handicaps were shortage of labour, farm machinery and other supplies, and changing government policies and regulations.

Comparing the production of the war years with the ten-year pre-drought period of 1923–32 the production of 53 principal crops was: 1939—102.8%; 1940—107.4%; 1941—109.9%; 1942—124.1% and 1943—116.8%. It will be seen that the record production of 1942 was almost one-fourth greater than in the 1923–32 period. The increase in the production of vegetables for market was 144.4% in 1942 and 138.5% in 1943; in vegetables for canning and drying 225.1% in 1942 and 199.8% in 1943. These increases were the result of expansion of acreage as well as more favourable seasons which assured high yields. Had the United States experienced the bad weather of the years 1933–36 the results would have been disastrous. Compared to the pre-drought period of 1923–32 as 100 the production of 53 crops in 1933 was 88.9%; 1934—71.7%; 1935—95.2% and 1936—79.5%.

The expansion of crop production in acreage continued after 1939, but the total for 52 crops harvested, 347,498,000 ac., was less in 1943 than the average of the five years 1929–33, the high year being 1932, when 361,794,000 ac. were cultivated. Early in the 1943 season there were great difficulties in some areas from floods and to a less extent from drought. About 13,500,000 ac. of crops were lost in 1943, nearly 2,000,000 ac. more than in 1942.

Crop yields were mostly lower in 1943 than in 1942 but higher than in any of the years 1937–41. Compared with the pre-drought average, 1923–32, the yields of all crops, except vegetables, was 124% compared to 130% in 1942 and a range of 114 to 122 in the previous five years. Potatoes gave a record yield of 140 bu. per acre.

The crop season of 1943, as previously noted, was marked by several losses from floods and drought in widely scattered areas. In May heavy rains from Oklahoma to Michigan delayed planting, and June brought floods in the lower Missouri valley. July and August were mostly hot and dry, with severe droughts in Arkansas and in a belt extending from New Jersey southward

LUNCHEON FOR WHEAT HARVESTERS near East Grand Forks, Minn., in the summer of 1943

into Virginia. The dry summer favoured farm work and enabled farmers with a scarcity of labour to complete their harvesting and to do an unusual amount of fall plowing. The lack of good rains reduced the feed in pastures and ranges and accentuated the feed shortage.

Fruit production in 1943 was the smallest since 1938, about 12% below 1942. The yield of fruit was about 11% below 1942. Exceptionally small crops of apples, pears, peaches, cherries and strawberries were harvested. Early spring freezes and bad weather during pollination periods were the principal causes for the small crops. Grapes, however, produced the largest crop on record and the output of all citrus fruits was high. Truck crops of all kinds showed about 10% less total than in 1942, which was offset to some extent by the great increase in victory gardens. The production of feed crops, hay and grain was not large in proportion to the large numbers of livestock on farms. The feed shortage in the eastern states was particularly severe in late summer, partly because of the drought in the Atlantic coast states from Virginia northward. While the total hay crop was the second largest ever produced, the supply per unit of livestock was less than in previous years.

Table I.—Index Numbers of the Volume of Agricultural Production through Two War Periods*

(1935-39=100)

	1915	1920	1925	1930	1935	1940	1941	1942	1943
Crops									
Food grains	147	126	95	109	81	110	131	139	108
Feed grains and hay	126	149	128	83	91	114	126	141	127
Truck crops	35	51	74	91	92	110	116	127	115
Fruits and nuts	73	76	74	89	95	110	113	115	106
Vegetables	85	91	79	90	104	101	100	106	125
Sugar crops	73	98	73	85	89	104	97	110	86
Total crops	95	102	99	96	89	107	109	123	113
Livestock									
Meat animals	92	99	107	100	90	118	118	133	151
Poultry and eggs	78	78	93	106	92	109	116	131	153
Dairy products	70	72	85	94	98	105	110	114	112
Total livestock	81	85	96	99	93	112	115	126	138
Grand total	86	92	97	98	91	110	113	125	128

*From estimates by the bureau of agricultural economics, U.S. department of agriculture

The expansion of agricultural production compared to other years is indicated by the index numbers of the volume of agricultural production shown in Table I. This shows the decline in the production of food grains as compared to all crops and livestock and the very striking increase in the vegetable crops. These changes indicate a fundamental change of diet in the United States, namely, the consumption of more fresh vegetables in salads and sandwiches and a shift away from surplus-grain production.

Livestock Products.—The total production of livestock and livestock products made a new high record in 1943, although the total milk production dropped slightly below 1942. The total numbers of all livestock increased through the year, partly as the result of several years of good feed production on pastures and ranges. The increases in hogs and cattle more than offset the decreases in sheep, horses and mules. The large supplies of feed grains in 1942 led farmers to expand herds except where the shortage of labour was a retarding force, as on the sheep ranges and on many dairy farms. The hog expansion was beyond all expectations, with the spring and fall pig crops amounting to 127,000,000 head compared to the ten-year average of 73,148,000 head. This large increase, combined with full feeding to heavy weights because of the very favourable corn-hog ratio, led to record runs of hogs at the stockyards and slaughter houses in the late fall of 1943. The rationing points on pork were reduced in an effort to move the excess pork into consumption and thus relieve storage facilities. This flood of pork and the general feed shortage led the War Food administration to reduce the goals for 1944 to a total of 105,000,000 pigs. The ceiling price on corn was stated to be the chief factor in leading hog growers to feed their pigs to maximum weights, since at the ceiling prices for live hogs of $13.75 per 100 lb. at Chicago it was more profitable for them to feed their corn than to sell it. One result was that the processing plants using corn for industrial purposes were unable to get supplies until the government intervened and moved some of its stocks. There was also a large demand for corn in the eastern states that could not be filled from the usual midwest sources.

Milk production declined in 1943 from the record production of

119,240,000,000 lb. in 1942 to about 118,000,000,000 lb. A lower average yield per cow was believed to be due to the shortage of feed in the eastern dairy areas and drought in others. The percentage of the dairy cows being milked declined during 1943, reflecting the labour shortage on dairy farms. In the fall the government moved to check the decline in milk production by proposing subsidy payments and larger supplies of feed. Butter production was about 1% more in 1943 than in 1942 but was below the 1935-39 average and insufficient to meet the full needs for all civilian, military and lend-lease requirements. Cheese production declined for the same reasons, and some cheese factories shifted to butter-making where cream supplies could be obtained. The rationing of both butter and cheese became more severe during the later months of 1943. The production of evaporated, condensed and dry-skimmed milk continued higher than in 1942, although the shortage of fluid milk was also reflected in these products.

In calling for a goal of 122,000,000,000 lb. of milk for 1944, the War Food administration recognized the necessity of increasing the output per cow about 30 lb. of milk over 1943 levels and 60 lb. over the five-year average. In order to attain this increase, higher prices to producers, better supplies of feed and more fertilizer for pastures and hay crop were proposed.

The total numbers of chickens on farms and chickens raised reached a new high record in 1943, about 15% above 1942 and 28% above the ten-year average. Egg production likewise made a new high record of about 5,000,000,000 doz. or 12% more than 1942 and 45% above the average. The goal for 1944 was set at 5,000,000,000 doz., but the feed shortage was such that a culling of flocks had begun before the end of 1943. Farmers were advised to reduce the number of broilers to be fed to save feed for laying flocks.

The grand total of meat production of all kinds in 1943 was about 13% above 1942 and nearly 50% above the average of 1935-39. Military and lend-lease requirements amounted to about 25% of the total, leaving less than a normal supply for civilians. Thus a continuation of the rationing system was necessary. The total available for civilians, however, was about 128 lb. per capita in 1943—only 5.9 lb. less than was consumed

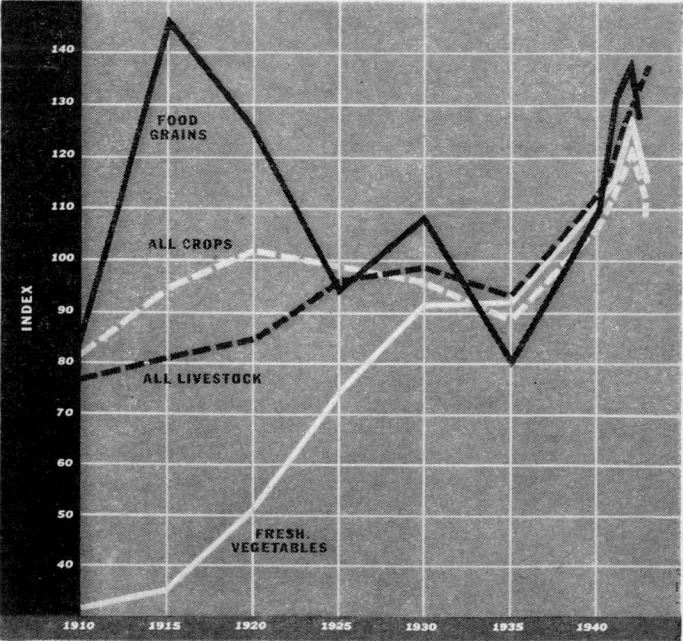

INDEX NUMBERS of U.S. production of food grains, all crops, all livestock and fresh vegetables through World Wars I and II. Food grains declined, while vegetables increased greatly. All crops and livestock made great advances after 1940

FLOODWATERS OF THE WABASH RIVER pouring across a farm late in May 1943. Planting in many parts of the midwest was delayed three weeks and early crops were ruined by the floods

in 1942. This compared with an average consumption of 126 lb. per capita in the period 1935–39.

Total food production for 1943 was estimated by the U.S. department of agriculture to be 5% above 1942 and 32% above 1935–39. The record output of livestock products more than offset the decline in crop production. It was also estimated that civilian food consumption per capita in 1943 was 5% above the average for 1935–39. The 1943 civilian food supply, while short in meats and dairy products, was richer in essential nutrients than in 1935–39 with a few exceptions.

Table II.—*Production Figures of Selected U.S. Crops, 1933–43*
(ooos omitted)

Year	Corn bu.	Oats bu.	Wheat bu.	Cotton bales	Tame Hay tons	Rice bu.	Tobacco lb.	Potatoes bu.
1933	2,399,632	733,166	551,683	13,049	66,530	37,651	1,371,131	342,306
1934	1,461,123	542,306	526,393	9,636	55,270	39,047	1,081,629	406,105
1935	2,303,747	1,194,902	626,344	10,638	78,138	38,784	1,297,155	386,380
1936	1,507,089	785,506	626,766	12,399	63,536	49,002	1,154,131	331,918
1937	2,644,995	1,146,258	873,993	18,946	73,785	53,364	1,553,405	393,289
1938	2,542,238	1,053,839	930,801	11,943	80,299	52,303	1,378,534	371,617
1939	2,619,137	937,215	754,971	11,817	75,726	52,306	1,848,654	364,016
1940	2,449,200	1,235,628	816,698	12,566	86,312	52,754	1,451,966	397,722
1941	2,672,541	1,176,107	945,937	10,744	82,358	54,028	1,261,364	357,783
1942	3,175,154	1,358,730	981,327	12,824	92,245	66,363	1,412,437	371,150
1943*	3,055,605	1,148,692	835,816	11,478	85,872	69,019	1,394,290	469,545

* Preliminary.

Stocks and Reserves.—The ever-normal granary idea and the widespread belief that the United States was a country of perennial surpluses led the public to question the necessity of rationing. While the U.S. produced surpluses for export before World War II and even in greater amounts in the decade before World War I, these surpluses were seldom accumulated for more than a half year, since the storage and marketing facilities required constant in-and-out movement. A large world wheat crop in the western hemisphere caused a large carry-over of wheat to accumulate in 1941 and 1942, a total about equal to a year's domestic U.S. consumption. Up to the spring of 1943 the policy of the government was to limit production to domestic requirements. Then suddenly the need for wheat for food became evident, and acreage and marketing restrictions were removed for both the 1943 spring seeding and for the fall seeding for harvest in 1944. In July the government decided to raise the goal 26% above that

for the 1943 acreage. In addition to the unexpected demand for wheat for feed, more than 125,000,000 bu. were used for making alcohol. The U.S. export market was practically closed, taking only about 35,000,000 bu. Canada, with a surplus of nearly 700,000,000 bu., was able to supply Great Britain's needs without difficulty.

The carry-over stocks of other grains—corn, barley, etc.—amounted as usual to only a small part of the year's production and were simply carried from harvest to time of use, with the usual reserves for seed and ordinary needs. The reservoir of food was on the farms and in the marketing channels—grain elevators, storehouses, cold storage plants and other distribution agencies. Aside from the grains and flour and feeds for livestock, the food reserves of large U.S. cities were very small, sufficient for only one to three weeks at most. Stocks of meats, fats, eggs and dairy products were equivalent to two or three weeks' consumption. In 1943 the storehouses were overcrowded because of reserves purchased and held by the government for the use of the military forces and lend-lease obligations. Some representatives of occupied countries purchased supplies to be used for relief and found it necessary to move them because of the cost of storage, spoilage and the need of the storage facilities for current use. Therefore the production in 1943 represented the food supply in general terms. In the case of perishables such as eggs, milk and its products and vegetables this was particularly true. The development of preserved, frozen and dehydrated products gave some promise of being able to carry over the surpluses in useful form, but these processes had yet to be fully developed in order that such preserved products might compete with the fresh product. (*See* also UNITED STATES.)

Lend-Lease Food Requirements.—Purchases, shipments, resale and transfers were so numerous and involved in 1943 that the quarterly reports on lend-lease to congress gave only some general measures of value and estimated percentages of the U.S. supply. As a general estimate lend-lease shipments were reported by the government to have amounted to about 6% of the U.S. domestic supply in 1942 and were expected not to exceed 10% in 1943, with the same amount allocated up to June 30, 1944. Values alone were not a full indication because of the many highly concentrated forms being shipped, such as the dehydrated foods, to save shipping space. The grand total value of exports shipped to June 30, 1943 was reported as $9,-882,000,000, of which foods and other agricultural products amounted to $2,085,000,000 in value. This was the largest single item, exceeded only by ammunition and aircraft and parts, which totalled $2,716,000,000. During the first year of the operation of lend-lease, foodstuffs constituted 30% of the total, while during the second year these goods had declined to 18% of the total because of the great increase in shipments of munitions. The

Table III.—Farmers' Average Prices, Certain U.S. Crops, on Selected Dates
(in cents per unit)

	Wheat per bu.	Corn per bu.	Oats per bu.	Barley per bu.	Rye per bu.	Buck-wheat per bu.	Pota-toes per bu.	Eggs per doz.	Cot-ton per lb.
Oct. average, 1909–13 . . .	88.1	64.8	38.4	60.5	72.0	71.1	65.0	23.8	12.10
Oct. 15, 1936 .	106.8	97.9	43.1	84.2	80.4	78.3	97.9	27.6	12.23
Oct. 15, 1937 .	88.7	58.9	28.8	52.0	63.8	62.4	48.5	25.2	8.10
Oct. 15, 1938 .	52.2	41.9	22.1	36.1	32.9	54.5	51.0	27.1	8.53
Oct. 15, 1939 .	70.3	47.6	30.3	42.2	45.1	62.7	66.4	22.9	8.73
Oct. 15, 1940 .	68.2	59.4	28.3	38.2	40.5	54.4	52.0	23.7	9.35
Oct. 15, 1941 .	91.0	64.9	38.9	49.1	51.3	64.3	67.2	31.8	16.55
Oct. 15, 1942 .	103.5	77.5	43.2	57.6	52.9	77.0	102.5	37.4	18.87
Sept. 15, 1943 .	130.0	109.0	69.6	96.5	94.9	111.0	134.0	41.6	20.20

food was sent principally to the United Kingdom and the soviet union, which together had received 93% of all goods shipments through June 1943. At times the need for food was so critical in the soviet union that foods were given preference over munitions for shipping space. From the outbreak of war the United Kingdom had by the end of 1943 increased its production from 40% to 70% of its requirements. Of the other 30%, the United States supplied about one-third, or 10% of the British consumption. Since supplies were being maintained at the very minimum of necessity, this part was a vital factor in assuring the continuation of British life.

The soviet union had lost about 40% of its most fertile crop land by 1943. Shipments to the soviet union were designed to aid the armies but did little to improve the inadequate diet of civilians. Food was shipped to North and West Africa to carry the civilian population over until the 1943 harvest, the Germans having removed most of the remainder of the 1942 crops. Seeds for planting formed a large part of the shipments early in 1943 and by the middle of the year other shipments had begun to decline.

While the total amount of food shipped under lend-lease was only 10% of the U.S. supply in 1943, the part of all foods was not in this proportion. Of some products as high as 30% of the U.S. supply was shipped, canned fish for example, while of butter only seven-tenths of 1% of the supply was exported.

In June the War Food administration tentatively allocated the available food to be produced from July 1, 1943 to June 30, 1944 as follows: for civilians 75%; for the armed forces 13%; for lend-lease 10%; and for U.S. territories and special needs 2%. This meant a slightly smaller civilian supply than in 1942 but more than in 1935–39.

Farm Income.—The gross farm income was estimated by the U.S. department of agriculture to be $22,700,000,000 in 1943—the largest on record and more than $4,000,000,000 above the $18,628,000,000 income of 1942. This high return was the result of the record volume of production which sold at the high prices. The gross income figures presented a more favourable situation than the facts justified because of the rapid advances in production costs. Production expenses in 1943 were estimated at $10,200,000,000, leaving $12,475,000,000 as the net income of farm operators. The gross farm income included cash income from sales, government payments, the value of products retained for human consumption on the farm and a rental value for the farm home. A part of the income of people on farms was obtained from nonfarm sources and in years prior to 1943 this had

amounted to 30% of the net income of persons on farms. No annual estimates were made, but special studies indicated that the total may have been more than $3,250,000,000 in 1942 and even greater in 1943. There was also a considerable income of nonfarm people from agriculture, estimated to have been about $1,700,000,000 in 1942. When comparing farm and nonfarm incomes these items must be considered. The total net income from agriculture per person on farms in 1943 was estimated to be about $430, compared to $368 in 1942 and $232 in 1941. Similar estimates of the income of persons not on farms placed their average income at about $1,428 for 1943 compared to $1,022 in 1942. The income of persons in agriculture in terms of percentage of the national income was estimated to be more than 12% in 1943 compared to 9.5% in 1942. The total farm population included only 21.7% of the total population in 1942 and a somewhat smaller part in 1943 since many persons had left the farms. The total number of people on farms was smaller in 1943 than in 1910. The high total was reached in 1916, when farm population was put at 32,530,000 persons. The decline was almost constant to 29,000,000 in 1943.

Government payments were a relatively small factor in the total farm income. In 1942 they amounted to $697,000,000. The previous high total was in 1939, when $807,000,000 was paid. The expenses that increased most during the war years were wages for labour and other current operating expenses. Interest on mortgages was down because the total mortgage debt of farmers was much below the high level of 1921 to 1929 inclusive. Expenditures for buildings and machinery were checked by the difficulties of getting materials and machines. Taxes were lower in 1942 than in 1941, as inventories had not been increased.

Table IV.—U.S. Farm Income, 1943 and 1942

	Jan.–Oct. 1943*	Jan.–Oct. 1942
All crops	$6,144,000,000	$4,856,000,000
Food grains	813,000,000	730,000,000
Feed grains and hay	812,000,000	613,000,000
Cotton and cotton-seed	987,000,000	887,000,000
Oil-bearing crops	512,000,000	297,000,000
Tobacco	395,000,000	367,000,000
Vegetables	1,398,000,000	988,000,000
Fruits and nuts	890,000,000	664,000,000
All livestock	9,174,000,000	7,247,000,000
Meat animals	4,806,000,000	3,893,000,000
Dairy products	2,311,000,000	1,925,000,000
Poultry and eggs	1,866,000,000	1,238,000,000
Government payments	582,000,000	564,000,000
Total	15,318,000,000	12,103,000,000

*Preliminary.

Prices of Farm Products.—Farmers received prices that averaged about 20% higher in 1943 than in 1942. The index of all farm products as estimated by the U.S. department of agriculture rose from 157 for the year 1942 to 192 in Dec. 1943. In 1939 the index was 92, having declined from 121 in 1937 and a previous high point of 156 in 1925. Farm prices did not reach their high peak in 1929 preceding the depression but stood at 146 for that year. The usual war influence was seen when World War II began and the index rose to 98 in 1940; to 122 in 1941; and to 157 in 1942. This general average index for the prices of all groups of farm products does not indicate the variations between different products which were as follows: truck crops, 264; chickens and eggs, 212; meat animals, 203; fruits, 197; dairy products, 187; cotton, 171 and grains, 162. All efforts to stabilize farm prices were not effective, and these prices followed the same general course as in World War I, but did not reach the high levels they did in 1919, when the index was 228, dropping the next year to 157. Different products reached high levels in 1919, grains for example being 233 as compared to 162 in 1943 and cotton 247 compared to 171. This generally lower price level was the basic cause of the efforts to increase prices to farmers, to secure greater production. The question became involved in the controversy over the method of payment, whether by subsidies or by higher ceilings.

The farmer's true price position—the relation between the price he receives for his product and the prices he pays for the labour and materials that he buys—was indicated by the index of the ratio of prices received to prices paid which is the basis of "parity." This index for 1943 stood at 116 compared to 104 in 1942, 92 in 1941 and 78 in 1940. Not since 1920 had this index reached 100 until the United States entered World War II in 1941. The prices farmers had to pay for commodities they had to buy for living and production, and interest and taxes were slightly below the level of prices of farm products, except for labour which stood at 280 compared to farm prices at 192. At the same time the cost of living index was 124 and the income of industrial workers 316. The cost of food rose faster than nonfood items in the cost of living index, which the government sought to control by price rollbacks.

Agriculture and World War II.

The output of U.S. crops and livestock in 1942 and 1943 demonstrated that the requirements of civilians, military and lend-lease aid to the Allies were met. Any extra food for relief had to come from a reserve built up through careful rationing, or a change in the diet habits of the American people, unless a renewed campaign for higher production was to be undertaken as a national policy. An analysis of the factors needed for greater food production reduced them to land, labour and machinery.

The land available for expanded production was not of the best fertility in 1943, and the costs of production would be higher than on the better lands being used in 1943, but a somewhat higher food price level would not be entirely out of line with wages and incomes and would probably lead to more economic use of food. The machinery needed could be produced quickly if the facilities being used in 1943 for ships and certain types of munitions were diverted to this use. Intensive fabrication of repair parts and the widespread development of repair stations were used enough to indicate that they would be effective in stretching machinery for the duration. Farm machines are seldom wholly worn out; they are simply discarded for newer types when the replacements become expensive.

The crux of the problem in 1943 was labour. Agriculture lacked several million trained men to bring it to a state of higher

FOUR-H BOY AND GIRL helping harvest corn during the agricultural labour shortage of 1943

Estimates varied greatly as to the number of men who had left the farms. The U.S. department of agriculture estimates showed that the number of farm workers on farms in Jan. 1943 was 8,171,000 and in July, 11,750,000. The difference between these numbers was the number who were hired for summer work. They came principally from small towns and villages where they had other employment that they could leave for the summer period. Out of these millions could be recruited possibly a part of the replacements needed until World War II ended and some of the millions who left the farms returned.

Crop Insurance.

The government experiment in crop insurance got a severe setback in 1943. Congress withdrew support for the work from the appropriation act of June 1943–44, and by the end of the year had not restored anything to continue the work in 1944 after July 1. Only sufficient funds were provided to complete the contracts for 1943.

The reasons given for the action were that the use of the law was too limited and the expenses too large to justify its continuance. Losses greatly exceeded the premiums. About 500,000 farmers were assisted in the four years 1939 to 1942 when they had crop failures, while many others had protection though they did not suffer losses. Out of 1,633 counties in which wheat was insured in 1942, 245 counties paid no losses and 308 paid losses less than one-fourth of their premiums. In 961 counties or more than half of them, losses paid were less than the premiums.

The basic law providing for the work still stood and a new and revised plan was proposed. Insurance authorities stated that the work had not been tested over sufficient time to provide an adequate basis for determining premiums and the best method of operation. The original idea was for the government to provide for administration while the premiums were to cover the risks. Participation was voluntary, which made it necessary to enlist the interest of the farmers in large numbers, and since the plan was untried this was found very difficult to do quickly.

The principal problems met with were: how to secure larger participation; how to determine risks with the limited data on many farms; how to spread the risk to cover bad years and the changes in operators. Acreage abandonment offered another problem on which there was insufficient data to determine a safe rate of premium. A three-year contract was adopted in 1943 to spread the risk. The system was tried only on wheat to any considerable extent. In 1943 there were 487,000 wheat contracts or about one-third of the wheat growers who were eligible. For cotton, only about 10% of the producers were listed and losses the first year were about 166% of the premiums. Proposals were made to use insurance in connection with war-emergency crops as a safeguard for those who were expanding acreage. It was estimated that

Table V.—U.S. Production and Yield per Acre for 1943 and 1942 Crops

Crop	1943 yield* per acre	1943 production*	1942 yield per acre	1942 production
Field crops				
Corn, bu.	32.4	3,055,605,000	35.5	3,175,154,000
Wheat, bu.	16.8	835,816,000	19.8	981,327,000
Oats, bu.	30.3	1,148,692,000	35.9	1,358,730,000
Barley, bu.	21.9	330,212,000	25.4	426,150,000
Rye, bu.	11.6	33,314,000	14.9	57,341,000
Flaxseed, bu.	8.8	51,486,000	9.2	40,660,000
Rice, bu.	45.5	69,019,000	44.9	66,363,000
Hay, all tame, tons.	1.42	85,872,000	1.53	92,245,000
Beans, dry edible, bags	8.96	22,770,000	9.95	19,608,000
Soybeans, bu.	18.0	..	19.5	..
Peanuts, lb.	660.7	2,769,000,000	644.4	2,206,935,000
Potatoes, bu.	139.6	469,545,000	136.9	371,150,000
Sweet potatoes, bu.	80.9	74,704,000	92.4	65,380,000
Tobacco, lb.	948	1,394,290,000	1,024	1,412,437,000
Sugar-beets, short tons	12.6	7,524,000	12.3	11,681,000
Cotton, bales	254.2†	11,478,000	272.5†	12,824,000
Fruit crops				
Apples, bu.	..	90,057,000	..	128,597,000
Peaches, bu.	..	42,000,000	..	66,380,000
Pears, bu.	..	23,753,000	..	30,717,000
Grapes, tons.	..	2,796,950	..	2,402,150

*Estimated.   †Pounds.

efficiency. The combined loss of the young men to the military forces and to war industries was the greatest weakening factor.

the cost to the government would be about $100,000,000 for the seven important crops, potatoes, flax, hemp, peanuts, dry beans and peas and soybeans.   (J. C. Ms.)

Great Britain.—While the government's agricultural policy remained the same, namely, the maximum production of bread corn, potatoes and sugar beet with the maintenance of milk production, county war agricultural committees were instructed to pay more attention to the efficiency of livestock production. These committees were given the additional powers necessary and appointments of livestock and milk production officers were made. The problem facing these officers was to raise to as high a standard and as quickly as possible the general level of efficiency of production. In the direction of milk production a number of important steps were taken. First, milk recording was taken over by the Milk Marketing board, and a national milk records scheme was introduced at the beginning of 1943. The enrolment under the scheme up to October was encouraging and indicated that more and more farmers were realizing that a system of milk recording in their own herds was the first essential in a sound breeding policy and economic production. Secondly, a classification of all dairy herds was being undertaken and farms were to be placed in grades. Concentration of effort would be directed toward helping and where necessary stimulating those who were most in need of such help with a consequent raising of the level of their cattle and their own efficiency as producers. The third important measure was that county committees prepared a register of bull breeding herds, the purpose of which was to make arrangements whereby a wide dispersion, among the ordinary dairy farmers, of good bull calves from the best herds could be brought about.

Every effort was being made to prevent any further decrease in the numbers of pigs and poultry so that the existing nucleus of breeding stock could be retained. Steps were also taken to stimulate sheep production especially in the mountainous areas.

From a figure of some 50,000 tractors in 1939 there were in 1943 about 125,000 in use on British farms. With this there had also been a large increase in the number of tractor-drawn implements and other machinery such as excavators. Part of this increase in tractors and machinery was in the hands of individual farmers, but county agricultural committees owned some 8% of the tractors and carried out tillage and other operations for farmers on a contract basis. All tractors and machinery, owned privately or otherwise, had to be used to the maximum, and committees had power of direction in regard to all machinery. Voluntary machinery pools were formed by farmers in many areas, as a form of mutual help, and were operating with marked success.

Weather conditions were variable throughout Britain in 1943; the drier areas suffered from insufficient rain throughout the growing period but other areas had a plentiful supply. The hay crop was good and in many areas got in under excellent conditions. Harvest conditions were early and good in the south but difficult in other parts, but on the whole the weight of threshed grain was again expected to be high.

The structure for the control of prices remained and only minor changes in individual products were made. In milk production an increased bonus was given for milk from tuberculin-tested herds.

British Empire.—Curtailment of world markets, shipping difficulties and restricted manpower supplies continued to be the primary problems of dominion farming during 1943. In Canada the shift to livestock and dairy farming continued and greatly benefited farmers, especially in Ontario and Quebec, while the problem of the wheat surplus in the prairie provinces was partly eased by export to the deficit areas of eastern Canada and to the United States. In New Zealand exports continued to be restricted to those covered by the war agreement with Britain, but the increas-

ingly difficult manpower situation was the most serious impediment to farm production both for the export and for the domestic market. In Australia, wheat production continued to outstrip demand and the urgent problem was to direct farm production into new channels to meet the situation created by the loss of the export market and by the new task of provisioning the large body of United States troops on Australian soil. South Africa continued to be without an export market for its deciduous and citrus fruit, and it was difficult also to export all the wool clip sold under agreement with the British government. The loss of the overseas trade was, however, to some extent made up by the increase in domestic demands which resulted from the changed situation in the North African sphere of hostilities.   (R. Ra.)

Other Countries.—The world-wide situation with respect to food production in World War II was almost the reverse of that of World War I. In the first war the central European countries were in a vulnerable position and the Allies controlled most of the food-exporting areas of Europe as well as all of those in the rest of the world. At the close of 1943, after four years of war, the enemy countries still held almost all of Europe and a vast area in the east, and surrounded China. For two years Germany had controlled the breadbasket of Russia, the Ukraine and the Danube basin. For a time the enemy blocked the seaway through the Mediterranean to the east, forcing all ships to take the long route around Africa or risk sinking. Japan controlled one-third of the world's supplies of oils and fats and most of the rubber.

Only the western hemisphere was free to the United Nations, together with Australia, New Zealand and South Africa. While these countries were normally surplus producing, their output was not equal to the extra requirements without expansion to the maximum. The soviet union, normally more than self-sufficient, became in the second year of World War II critically short of food because of the German invasion. While the blockade of Europe was tightly held, there was no prospect of weakening Germany by food shortage until late in 1943, when the Russians threatened the Danube basin and advanced in the Ukraine.

Food products from the United States fed about 10% of the British people, but more important was the fact that the United States was able to supply certain vital necessities, which though not used in great quantity were very essential to keep up the diet of the people.

The Russians' need for food was unexpected at the beginning of the war. While the exports of the soviet union had never risen to the levels of the old Russia, it was believed that it had ample supplies to support both its armies and civilians. But the fact that millions of Russians had lived close to the margin of subsistence, mainly on grains and potatoes, made them particularly vulnerable when the area for these crops was suddenly reduced by the loss of large areas to the Germans. This loss amounted to nearly 40% of the best grain land, 80% of the sugar beet area, 60% of the hogs and 40% of the cattle producing country. The losses in animals in the areas invaded were very severe. Only by depriving the civilians of supplies did the soviet armies keep supplied with enough food to carry on. Most of the people lived and worked on rations 20% to 40% below U.S. normal requirements. The removal of a large number of industrial workers to the east beyond the Urals and the development of new lands there helped greatly to meet the situation. Lend-lease shipments were used chiefly by the armies and war workers rather than by civilians. Food shipments increased in 1943 as the supplies of munitions became more nearly equal to the requirements of the armies.

In China the people of each region are chiefly dependent on the food produced in that region. Free China lost a large part of its best land. Many refugees crowded into Free China, but most of the millions remained where they had lived and gleaned a subsistence from the earth. The poor distribution system was taxed to the limit to supply the armies and war industries. Another difficulty was inflation, which made it almost impossible for many to buy sufficient food.

In India the famine in Bengal and Calcutta was the result of poor crops, lack of transportation, inflation of prices and the steady growth of population compared with food production. While the loss of the rice imports from Burma was serious it was not the principal factor. The fear of Japanese invasion led producers to hoard their limited supplies, and the refugees in towns and cities were unable to buy food at the high prices. There had been a part of the population on the margin of starvation at all times, and despite imports of food by the government there was constant malnutrition. (*See* also FAMINES.)

The food shortages in the invaded countries were not well known in 1943, but enough information came from all of these countries to indicate that the mass of the people were living very near to the lowest margin of existence. This meant in general terms that about one year's supplies would be needed to re-establish a normal food supply. Such a large amount could not be provided at once by the surplus producing countries but had to come from restored production within the areas plus such surpluses as could be shipped in from the distant parts of the world.

The axis countries, Germany and Italy, and most of the invaded countries in Europe had their agriculture at a high state of development in 1939 when the war started. Germany was close to 90% self-sufficient, Italy 80%, with its colonies, and the other European countries were in better status than for a generation previous. Every effort was made by the Germans to keep up farm production, and there were excellent crops in 1942 and 1943. Continental Europe as a whole produced about 90% as much food in 1941–42 as before the war, and the people were getting about four-fifths of prewar diets according to estimates by the U.S. department of agriculture. While livestock numbers were reduced from 10% to 25% in those areas dependent upon imported feedstuffs, there was not the wholesale slaughter that some early reports indicated.

The rationing systems in the several countries were set up to favour the armies and the essential workers over others whose health was less essential to the war effort. Many of the poorer classes were reduced to mere subsistence, and there were many deaths from malnutrition. The deaths in Greece and Poland were the result of the removal of food as an instrument of war, rather than of a shortage in production. The farmer-peasants in all of the invaded countries remained on their farms to a large extent. While they lost their stored stocks and some of their animals to the invaders they were able to keep up a good degree of production in the areas distant from the main highways where the armies travelled. Even in the Ukraine the farm tractors were removed eastward in advance of the German armies; livestock was shipped and seed stocks thereby protected. As quickly as the areas were rescued by the advancing Russian armies the farmers resumed operations. While more farmers were disturbed in World War II than ever before in modern times, on the whole the rural population remained as it was before the invasion. Able-bodied men were forced to follow the armies, but 70% to 90% of the farm work on eastern European farms is done by women and children in wartime.

The detailed estimates of postwar relief needs by 1943 had been constantly revised downward from the first calculations made in 1941 and 1942 before the organization of the United Nations Relief and Rehabilitation conference at Atlantic City in Nov. 1943. These revisions were made necessary by the fact that available supplies were not in view and also because crop production in Europe continued at a fairly high level in 1942 and

1943. The need was expected to depend, to a considerable extent, on the time of year when hostilities ceased and it became possible to send food supplies into the various invaded countries.

United States agricultural policy had not been changed in 1943 to take the relief need into consideration except as represented by lend-lease requirements, but the subject was being closely studied. As early as 1941 some private organizations had begun to agitate for a special campaign of production of foods to be stored and held for relief purposes, but the difficulty of meeting these current needs prevented action in this direction. Some groups were planning animal breeding in anticipation of the needs of Europe after the war and a beginning was made in some localities. (*See* also AGRICULTURAL RESEARCH ADMINISTRATION; CENSUS, 1940; CHEMURGY; DROUGHT; FERTILIZERS; HORTICULTURE; IRRIGATION; LAW; LIVESTOCK; MARKET GARDENING; PRICES; RATIONING; SOIL EROSION AND SOIL CONSERVATION; TRUCK FARMING; WAR FOOD ADMINISTRATION, etc.; also under principal crops.) (J. C. Ms.)

Agriculture, U.S. Department of: *see* GOVERNMENT DEPARTMENTS AND BUREAUS.

Air Conditioning.
In the United States, where most air conditioning equipment is produced, the wartime controls were further strengthened in 1943 to insure that air conditioning would only be manufactured with a minimum of critical materials and installed in applications that would directly help the war. This result was achieved by requiring individual and detailed application for priority assistance and permission to purchase through the War Production board.

Comfort air conditioning sales and installations were non-existent except for a relatively small number of individual room coolers manufactured in 1941, which were released from "frozen" inventory after the armed services had purchased all they required.

Refrigeration machinery in a number of large air conditioning systems in department stores and government buildings was removed, reconditioned by the manufacturers and installed in war plants, for industrial refrigeration and air conditioning applications.

The refrigerant Freon-12 which is almost exclusively used in all air conditioning systems, except for the largest systems utilizing centrifugal compressors, became critical in supply in 1943 due to its use in a new insecticide, aerosol, developed for the use of the armed services. This required some systems to shut down although many systems were converted to use the refrigerant methyl chloride.

Nonmilitary applications of air conditioning continued in new black-out plants; in precision manufacturing, assembling and testing; in the storage of vital materials, tools, dies and instruments; in research and development laboratories, especially of the "stratosphere" type; and in the processing of foodstuffs.

Military applications increased as a result of the severe requirements in the hot climates of Africa and the South Pacific. Some of the principal applications were bombsight storage, repair and calibration; in special buildings for celestial navigation training; in Link-Trainer buildings; for the storage of wool and fur flying suits; in parachute drying and storage; in airport control towers; aeroplane engine test buildings; photographic development rooms and mobile units; and radar rooms; powder magazines; ready-rooms for aviators and other special applications aboard ships; also, in armament instrument inspection and adjustment; in armament fire control buildings; plotting rooms; operating rooms and convalescent rooms in military hospitals, hospital ships and hospital cars; portable food refrigeration units.

Stabilization to wartime conditions permitted some manufacturers to start postwar plans for air conditioning. (*See* also PUBLIC HEALTH ENGINEERING.)   (F. H. F.)

Aircraft Carriers: *see* AIR FORCES OF THE WORLD; NAVIES OF THE WORLD.

Air Forces of the World.

U.S. Army.—The U.S. army air forces became, in 1943, the greatest air arm in the world. Nearly all its objectives for the year were realized or surpassed. The 15th air force was added to the 14 already established and committed to battle in the Mediterranean theatre. By December, A.A.F. personnel numbered in excess of 2,300,000, an approximate increase of 1,000,000 over the preceding year.

Several significant changes, tending to make the A.A.F. a more cohesive unit, took place during 1943. In March, a complete streamlining of the headquarters organization, on a functional basis, was effected. The coequal status of air power with land power was established in July. This recognized the principle of the concentration of aircraft as a striking unit, under the theatre commander, as opposed to its dissipation in small operations. It facilitated the further development of the strategic and tactical concepts of air warfare. In October, authority was procured to integrate into the A.A.F. all military personnel attached to it from other arms and services of the army.

Combat operations during the year increased greatly in size, scope and effectiveness. Losses were never out of proportion to the damage done to enemy objectives, nor were they sufficient in any single case to turn our bombers back from their objective. The German air force was forced to abandon its offensive tactics and to concentrate on defense against our bombardment. The industrial potential of axis-occupied Europe was reduced by effective precision daylight bombing missions against aircraft plants, oil refineries, bearing plants, rubber factories and numerous other war industries. The bombardment of Pantelleria became a milestone in aerial warfare when that island surrendered to Allied airmen on June 12. The ever-growing importance of air power in tactical operations was evidenced by the co-operation given to ground forces in the establishment of the Salerno beachhead and the drive up the Italian mainland. American airborne and parachute operations met with signal success in the invasion of Italy and the investment of Lae, New Guinea, in September.

Several new aeroplane types were put into production during 1943. Many modifications to increase range and effectiveness were made on those in use to meet changing combat conditions. By such modifications, the army air forces everywhere maintained qualitative superiority over enemy aircraft. American pilots in various theatres destroyed from 2 to 9 enemy aircraft for every one lost in combat during the past year.

The strategic bombardment of the enemy by the U.S. army air forces proved the validity of two basic operational principles: It is feasible to conduct precision daylight bombing operations against selected military or industrial targets despite the antiaircraft artillery and fighter defenses of the enemy. Presently developed aerial bombs can destroy or render unserviceable any enemy industrial installations essential for the conduct of war. None of the innovations and new tactics attempted by the enemy during the year could disprove these two principles. (H. H. A.)

U.S. Navy.—In Jan. 1943, the grave news was released identifying the aircraft carrier which had been sunk in the battle of Santa Cruz on Oct. 26, 1942, as the U.S.S. "Hornet." Its loss, however, was offset by the gratifying achievements of the navy's carrier-borne planes in the invasion of Africa on Nov. 8, 1942. More significant even than its performance was the very presence

of naval aviation in the Mediterranean. It cogently demonstrated the expanded scope of the navy's air force since Pearl Harbor.

During 1943, naval aircraft and pilots were found wherever U.S. task forces were operating, whether off Alaska, patrolling our own coasts or striking at Wake, Marcus, Rabaul and the Gilbert Islands.

By Feb. 13, all organized enemy resistance in Guadalcanal had collapsed and on that same day the Corsair (F4U) made its official debut in the Southwest Pacific. This plane has since proved superior to the Jap Zero in every way. The equally fast and deadly Hellcat (F6F) was introduced to the Japanese in the Marcus Island raid of Sept. 1, 1943.

These two formidable fighters greatly accelerated U.S. aerial attacking power in the Pacific and were inflicting tremendous losses on the Japanese, the ratio of their plane losses to U.S. averaging about five to one. In an exceptionally well co-ordinated attack by army, navy, marine corps and New Zealand fliers over Guadalcanal on June 17, 1943, a total of 94 planes were destroyed at a loss of only six for the Allies. In the 37-day Munda campaign—June 30 to Aug. 7—358 Japanese planes were destroyed to the loss of 93 U.S. planes. Navy and marine corps planes composed about two-thirds of the air power employed. U.S. planes dropped tons of bombs on Wake and aided the fleet and marine landing force in capturing Tarawa.

Perhaps most sensational was the achievement of U.S. carrier-based units in two November raids on Rabaul. On Nov. 5, six heavy enemy cruisers were knocked out, and two light cruisers and two destroyers were torpedoed or bombed. Six days later U.S. airmen came back, sinking a Jap light cruiser and two destroyers and damaging 11 other destroyers.

More and better planes, aircraft carriers and advance bases made naval aviation daily more menacing to the enemy. On March 16, 1943, Admiral Ernest J. King, commander in chief of the fleet, became chairman of a conference of American, British and Canadian officers held in Washington to formulate means of combating German submarines. One method adopted was the use of small aircraft carriers to patrol convoy lanes too remote for land-based planes to guard. Naval aviators of one of the baby flat-tops attacked 14 submarines and sank at least three, although it is probable that nine subs were sunk by that carrier. Planes from another baby flat-top played a vital role in the taking of Attu from the Japs in May 1943.

In July, Rear Admiral John Sidney McCain, chief of the bureau of aeronautics, was promoted to vice-admiral and appointed Deputy Chief of Naval Operations (Air). Rear Admiral DeWitt C. Ramsey was named chief of the bureau of aeronautics. The change was designed to better correlate and co-ordinate all operational phases of naval aviation, leaving with the bureau of aeronautics the job of continuing to design, procure and maintain the finest planes and aircraft equipment for the specialized work naval aviation has to perform.

At the outbreak of World War I, naval aviation had 54 planes, 31 pilots and 163 enlisted men. When Pearl Harbor was attacked 5,420 officer aviators and 806 enlisted pilots comprised the navy's air arm. At the end of 1943, naval aviation had grown to 30,000 pilots and 27,500 planes.   (J. S. M.)

The World.[1]—The aeroplane of 1942 looked and acted much the same as had its predecessors of 1940 and 1941. At the end of 1943, a similar statement can be made. Improvement of design detail had been continuous. The fighters and bombers of both sides were better military machines at the end of the year than they were at the beginning of the year. But nothing radical

---

[1] All assertions or opinions contained in this section of this article are the private ones of the writer, and are not to be construed as official or reflecting the views of any organization or government service.

enough to guarantee air superiority by the United Nations or the axis put in an appearance during the year 1943.

There were hints here and there that by another year the situation might be changed. Research projects that were initiated in the first year or two of World War II were beginning to bear fruit.

Germany went to war in 1939 only after she was satisfied that her aircraft production and her aviation reserves were adequate for the job to be done. The program, big as it was, contemplated a war of relatively short duration. Research never stopped, but new developments were put on shelves until needed. After it became evident that the war would not be over in 1941, a period of intensive research was inaugurated. This was made coincident with a great retooling program designed to permit the modernization of the luftwaffe by 1943, doubtless impeded seriously by the bombings of German production centres in the summer and fall of 1943. It seemed probable, however, that from plants hidden deep in Germany, would come a new series of planes of radical design, the offspring of wartime research. The spring and summer of 1944 should reveal the secret weapons on which Hitler might be counting for a last desperate effort.

But meanwhile, anti-axis air people had not been idle. When war came, British research activity lagged behind the German. Active air forces were inadequate to meet the attack. Following the destructive raids of 1940–41, and the terrific losses at Dunkirk, production was paramount, development had to wait. Once factories were decentralized and reconstructed, and after lend-lease began to furnish some relief to the hard-pressed British industry, engineering and technical talent again became available for research and development. The results would doubtless show up in service aircraft in 1944, to meet whatever new threats German science might have developed.

As the year closed, came the first public hints of the nature of some of the expected surprises. It had long been known that all first-rate aeronautical powers were experimenting with rocket or jet types of propulsion. The veil of secrecy, heretofore drawn tightly about all such projects, was lifted a little in 1943.

Rocket-driven missiles are not entirely new. There are records of early use against besieged cities. The modern counterpart is the anti-tank "bazooka." In 1943, rocket bombs were fired from aeroplanes. The Russians used them effectively against ground forces from the Stormoviks, and latterly the German fighters, on the defensive against U.S. and British heavy bombers, were so equipped. These were true rockets, containing a propellent in the tail which was ignited to develop a high velocity jet of burning gases to drive them. When the charge was exhausted, the projectile fell to earth.

This type of rocket engine had only limited application to full-size aircraft, so far. Short-time, high intensity jets might be used to give extra thrust at take-off to help get heavily loaded aeroplanes into the air. There was some indication that the Germans used this method to launch bombers. It was also possible to utilize the power of such jets to give momentary extra performance in flight. For example, a fighter pilot in a tight spot might touch off a rocket thrust augmentor to get away from, or to overtake, an enemy plane. The extra push is short lived, however, as the amount of fuel that can usually be carried for such purposes is quickly exhausted.

The so-called "sustained jet" type of propulsion was the novelty announced in the press at the end of the year. It replaced entirely the conventional engine and propeller combination. This type of aeroplane was built around an open-ended tube. Air is sucked in at the forward opening, compressed in a blower of some sort, heated by engine exhaust gas or by open gasoline burners, and blown out the stern opening. The reaction to the hot air blast provided the thrust to drive the plane forward.

The first public disclosure of this type came in 1941 when the Italian-built Caproni-Campiani CC-22 flew from Milan to Rome. Its performance was not impressive, but it proved to be a prototype for later development.

How far the British and the Germans had actually gone was in 1943 a closely guarded secret. It was known that machines were extensively test-flown both in England and in America. The Bell Aircraft company of Buffalo announced its collaboration with the General Electric company on the application of the British Whittle engine. There was reason to suspect that German jet-driven planes had been observed in flight, but whether any had fallen into Allied hands was unknown. There was intensive activity on both sides, and the chances were that before 1944 ended some extraordinary speeds at high altitudes would be possible.

The general trend toward increasing the fire power of all fighters continued during the year. More and more 20-mm. cannon were carried by British Hurricanes and Spitfires. Rumours of 40-mm. were heard. Some sources indicated that German experimental installations of 70-mm. cannon had been identified. In view of the announced arming of a U.S. Mitchell bomber with a 75-mm. cannon, such enemy installations did not appear improbable.

The practice of arming fighter aircraft with sizable bombs also continued in development. The application was somewhat limited, but most 1943 fighters carried a belly bomb rack, sometimes two wing racks. For ferry work, or for long range bomber escort missions, auxiliary fuel tanks (dropped when empty) could be carried in the bomb racks.

Apart from the above, little else in the realm of radical technical development turned up. Tactics changed, and operations of all kinds were intensified, but these were matters of degree rather than of novelty.

It was impossible to estimate with any accuracy production rates and numerical strength of opposing air forces. The interpretation of losses, reported from several sources, and the evaluation of the effects of material shortages and of bombing on production were equally difficult.

By the end of 1942, it was generally conceded that Allied aircraft production had surpassed the axis effort. If that was true, then 1943 certainly widened the gap with a phenomenal U.S. and British aircraft output matched against Hitler's shrinking and bomb-shattered industry. It appeared probable that the bulk of 1943 German production was of fighter types. Since the initiative in the air was lost in 1942, fewer bombers came from the factories of the reich. The need was for interceptors to beat off British and American bomber attacks.

What was probably a reasonably accurate estimate of aviation losses came from a British source. The total score for the European theatre of operations (excluding the Russian front) for the war up to mid-Dec. 1943, is as follows:

	Axis	Allied
Aircraft destroyed in combat or by AA gunfire	18,785	12,706
Personnel*	31,328	52,092

*Note that Allied losses of men are higher than for the axis. This is on account of the increased use of big bombers where crews average 8 to 12 men each.

Trends in current enemy aircraft design are established from examples that fall into Allied hands, and from aerial photographs taken in combat and on reconnaissance. Up to the close of 1943, there had been no marked indication of deterioration either in design or in matériel in captured equipment, German or Japanese. Fuels and lubricants were still first class. Metals and other materials of construction were generally as good as those of the

FLYING FORTRESSES returning from a mass U.S. raid on Stuttgart, Germany, Sept. 6, 1943. One of the engines of the plane from which the photograph was taken is dead

Allied nations. There was a hint of experimental wood construction in Germany, as a possible indication of shortage of light metals.

The following notes on various models in use by the several air forces are not complete. They are intended to give a brief survey of the newer types that came into combat use during the year 1943. Older types are listed and newest improvements noted.

THE AXIS POWERS

Germany.—The war communiqués of 1943 carried only names of German aircraft familiar in the reports of 1941 and 1942. Over Regensburg, Marienburg and Schweinfurt, the fighter swarms were Messerschmitt Me-109's and Me-110's, and Focke-Wulf FW-190's. Constant improvement of all these types was in evidence—higher speed (they all do about 400 m.p.h. at altitude), more fire power (cannon and rockets), and heavier armour. The Me's continued to use liquid cooled, direct injection inverted Vee engines (in 1943, rated at 1,350 h.p.); the FW's, twin-row radials, air cooled (about 1,750 h.p. at 18,000 ft.). Simplicity of design and rugged construction marked all recent models.

One trend for future fighters showed up in the Me-210. This was a compact monoplane with small central fuselage, powered with two nacelle-mounted DB-601 engines of 1,270 h.p. each. Pilot and gunner sit in a streamlined "greenhouse" high on the nose. Both engines and both cockpits were heavily armoured. Two 7.9 machine guns and two 20-mm. cannon were fitted in the nose. There was provision for a medium-sized bomb (500 lb., estimated), also in the nose. Most interesting armament feature was the mounting of two guns (approximately 50 cal.) in small remote-controlled "barbettes" on either side of the fuselage, for side and rear protection. All up, the Me-210 weighed over 21,000 lb. Its speed at 18,000 ft. was about 370 m.p.h. Rumours indicated that certain structural troubles cut production of this model short, but that a revised and improved design, the Me-410, of substantially the same type replaced it. The probabilities were that the 410 would carry guns of high calibre, 37 mm. or even larger.

Another high altitude fighter-bomber of somewhat similar pattern was described, the Junkers Ju-86P. It was said to have supercharged cockpits. Power plants were the Junkers Jumo diesel, with exhaust driven superchargers. It was well armed and armoured, and could carry a 2,200-lb. bomb.

The old Ju-87 (Stuka) dive bomber was modernized, and was in service in 1943. Its Jumo 211 engine was stepped up to 1,300 h.p. At a gross weight of 14,300 lb. it could manage 4,000 lb. of bombs for short ranges. Reports indicated that it was fitted experimentally with a 37-mm. cannon.

In early 1943, a large bomber appeared at extremely high altitudes over England. This was later identified as the Heinkel He-177. It was reported to be capable of carrying some 2,000 incendiary bombs, or a single 7,700-lb. "block buster." The crew consisted of seven or eight. Defensive armament was provided by 11 machine guns. Notable feature was the mounting of four 1,000-h.p. engines, each pair coupled to a single large propeller.

Only other large bombers in use at the close of 1943 by the luftwaffe appeared to be the Junkers Ju-90 and the Focke-Wulf FW-200 Kurier. Both were 4-engine machines of prewar vintage, modernized. They were used mainly for long-range bombing of convoys at sea.

The famous Junkers Ju-88, and Dornier Do-217 types were in service in improved models. The FW-189 twin-engine fighter that appeared early in 1942 was reported as widely used on observation missions on the Russian front.

One new ground attack type was identified, the Henschel Hs-129. It was probably under-powered, with its two 450-h.p. Argus air-cooled Vee engines. It carried a battery of machine guns and a 15-mm. or 30-mm. cannon under the fuselage. The under-part of the plane was well armoured for protection against ground fire.

Most novel development of the year was the appearance of extremely large powered glider transports. The usage of towed gliders was apparently abandoned in favour of the powered types. The older Gotha 242 twin-tail boom cargo sailplane used in Crete and in North Africa, came out with two small 14-cylinder radial engines (800 h.p. each) fitted in wing nacelles. A tricycle type undercarriage replaced the former belly skids. The rear portion of the body opened up as a door to permit loading. Loaded to its limit, the machine might require assistance for take-off, but once in the air, would be flyable on its own power.

The largest machines of the power glider type ever built were the Me-323's, powered version of the Me-321 glider, which were used to carry troops across the Mediterranean and were shot down in large numbers by U.S. and British fighters. These large and unwieldy machines had a span of 181 ft. and were 93 ft. long. A ten-wheeled landing gear was built directly into the bottom of the fuselage. The latter was of very large cross section, about 10 ft. wide and 13 ft. deep. A three-ton truck, a light tank, or up to 120 men could be loaded. Large doors in the nose and tail gave access to the interior. The two pilots sit in an armoured cockpit high on the nose. Power was furnished by six Gnôme-Rhône 14-cylinder engines of 965 h.p. each, strung out along the leading edge of the wing. Chances are that, when loaded to its maximum (about 40,000 lb.) some assistance for take-off, either by towing or by rockets, was necessary. Construction was of steel tube, wood and fabric.

The Blohm and Voss 222 6-engine flying boat appeared occasionally in 1943. It was used as a long range reconnaissance plane or as a troop transport. For the first mission, it was said to have a range of nearly 4,500 mi. As a transport, it could carry 80 men and their equipment, disposed on two decks. For protection, it carried three power-driven gun turrets along the top of the hull. In appearance, it resembled the big Short Sunderland of the British coastal command.

What use the Germans made of the captured French aircraft industry was not entirely clear. The factories which had not been dismantled and transported into Germany were probably employed on supplying parts for German production. One or two large planes, designed and started prewar, were reported to have been completed and flown. In this group was the Farman 2234, a 55,000-lb. civil transport with four Hispano-Suiza 12-cylinder X-type engines. Generally speaking, however, the French aircraft industry appeared to have lost its identity.

Italy.—Before capitulation, Italy contributed very little to the axis air effort in 1943. Italy's main manufacturing plants had been bombed to the point of minimum enthusiasm for production. Early in the year, a pair of reasonably good single-seater fighters appeared, the Reggione Re-2001 and the Macchi C-202. The former was a small machine (36-ft. span) powered with a DB-601 German engine. It carried two 50-cal. guns in the nose

and two 30's in the wings. Top speed was about 350 m.p.h. The Macchi C-202 showed strong German influence throughout. The resemblance to an Me-109 was strong. With a DB-601 engine, it was good for about 330 m.p.h.

Savoia-Marchetti turned out a big 3-engine (Alfa Romeo 128, 950 h.p.) troop transport that was used in North Africa. It was of the usual Italian mixed steel-wood-fabric construction. It grossed 38,000 lb. and had a speed of 230 m.p.h.

One big 4-engine bomber appeared, the Piaggio P-108. It was powered with four P7RC35 engines of 1,350 h.p. each. Top speed was about 290 m.p.h. Most interesting feature was cabin supercharging for high altitude use.

Two or three twin-engine seaplanes of conventional design were seen in the Mediterranean as torpedo carriers. The Fiat RS-14 grossed 16,000 lb., was powered with two 870-h.p. engines. The Cant 1018 was probably the most modern of the lot. It was used mainly for reconnaissance or as a medium bomber. The Savoia-Marchetti SM-84 carried two full-size naval torpedoes. It was powered with three Alfa Romeo engines.

Japan.—The fighter pilots of the Japanese army and naval air services proved tough opponents. They fly with a blind acceptance of orders which makes them dangerous. In groups under skilled command, they do well. If flight commanders are shot down, and flights disintegrate, individual pilots, left on their own, show lack of initiative and inability to cope with circumstances beyond their original orders. Naval pilots seem better trained, more resourceful than their army counterparts. Most of the action in the South Pacific was fought by naval air units with land-based army groups in support.

The work of the Jap torpedo and low-level bombers was excellent. Their high altitude bombing was far less accurate than that by U.S. fliers. Reconnaissance and patrol effectivity over long ranges at sea was high.

NEWEST AND DEADLIEST of the U.S. navy's fighters in 1943, the Grumman "Hellcat" made its battle debut Sept. 1, in the raid on Marcus Island. The "Hellcat," successor to the navy's famous "Wildcat," was designed from specifications made by combat fliers

HEAVY BOMBERS of the U.S. 8th air forces streaming through the upper air, trailing vapour plumes on their way to bomb Bremen Nov. 26, 1943

The Japanese aircraft industry showed unexpected strength in its ability to turn out machines with constant improvements at high rates of production. No accurate figures were ever tabulated on the extent of the Japanese aircraft industry, or of its output. Putting together information from German, Italian and American sources, by 1941 there were at least 17 major aircraft manufacturing plants in Japan proper. It was estimated that the capacity of these factories was between 500 to 1,000 units a month.

During the four or five years prior to the outbreak of the war, Japan acquired a large number of licences to manufacture European aircraft and accessories, including Italian Fiat bombers, German Heinkel and Junkers bombers, and the German Messerschmitt Me-109 and Me-110 fighters. Reports indicated that the latest German fighter designs, including the FW-190 and the Me-210 were released to the Japanese. It was known that Japanese concerns took licences to build the Swiss Oerlikon and the French Hispano aircraft cannons. But there was no indication of exact duplication of any of these machines. Resemblances existed, but all appeared to have been skilfully modified to meet the requirements of Japanese tactics and production.

In the early stages of the war, Japanese pilots were given little in the way of personal protection. To improve aeroplane performance, extras, such as armour plate, bullet-proof fuel tanks, etc., were omitted. The fanatic fatalism of the pilots favoured such a philosophy of design. During 1943, however, the practical lessons of war resulted in the appearance of armour and protected fuel tanks on newer aircraft. Even body armour was found on shot-down pilots.

The Japanese had a system of designating their aircraft models which tied them directly to the year of manufacture. The two digits which follow the name of any Japanese aeroplane indicate the year in which it was made, not in terms of the Christian calendar, but referred to their own. Thus OO indicates the year 2600 of the Japanese empire, which corresponds to 1940. This is the origin of the designation "Zero" for the Mitsubishi fighter that was reported so frequently in the press.

When the U.S. navy came into daily contact with the Japanese in the Pacific, the 10- to 16-letter words attached to the various aircraft proved too hard to remember, and laid a heavy burden on U.S. communications systems. Accordingly, all Jap planes were described by simple four- or five-letter words—male and female proper names. Thus, "Hamp," "Rufe" and "Zeke" were fighters; "Kate," "Betty" and "Nell," torpedo bombers; "Emily" and "Mavis," flying boats, etc.

"Nate," "Oscar" and "Zeke" were the oldest in the fighter category. The first two saw service in China before Pearl Harbor. They were largely replaced by later types. "Zeke" was best known as the original "Zero." Carrier-based, it was often seen in the Pacific. Land-based, it operated in the Aleutians. One was captured intact and was extensively studied by U.S. pilots and technicians. It was a small, highly manoeuvrable monoplane of simple but excellent design. Its single engine was a 14-cylinder air-cooled radial. It carried two 7.7-mm. machine guns in the fuselage, and two 20-mm. cannon in the wings. "Rufe" was a modification of "Zeke." The retractable landing gear was replaced by a single float for operation from cruiser catapults.

"Hamp" was an improved "Zero" used widely in the South Pacific from both carriers and land bases. It lacked armour or bullet-proof tanks, but was a dangerous opponent because of its high manoeuvrability and considerable fire power. It was small (36 ft. 6 in. span). With an improved 14-cylinder air-cooled radial engine, it did over 350 m.p.h. at 17,000 ft.

"Kate," "Betty" and "Nell" were torpedo carriers. "Kate" and "Nell" did the damage at Pearl Harbor, and "Nell" sank the "Prince of Wales" and "Repulse." "Kate" was single-engined, carrier-based. It resembled closely the U.S. Douglas TBD. "Nell" was big (82-ft. span) and had two engines. It was supposed to have been developed out of the German Junkers Ju-88, but bore little family resemblance. Top speed was about 230 m.p.h.

"Betty" was a late type, shore-based. It was of the same general size, outline and armament as "Nell." It differed in that a certain amount of armour was installed for crew protection. Also, bullet-proof tanks were fitted. Its main mission appeared to be for high-level bombardment.

"Val I" and "Val II" were in the dive-bomber class. They were single-engine monoplanes with fixed, faired landing gear.

"Sally" and "Lily" were land-based army bombers, both twin-engine, resembling the Martin Maryland. They had deep-bellied bomb bays, and were well protected with mobile guns in turrets fore and aft and below. They were active mainly in Burma and China.

"Dave," "Pete" and "Dinah" were all reconnaissance types. The first was a single-engine twin-float navy seaplane fitted with a few small bombs and with light protective armament. It was fairly slow, 216 m.p.h. at 7,500 ft. "Dave" was obsolete at the close of 1943, having been replaced by "Pete," a single-float, single-engine biplane for catapult use from warships. It was a good performer, with fast climb and an absolute ceiling of over 33,000 ft. "Dinah" was an army model, with two 14-cylinder radial engines. It did about 300 m.p.h. at 17,000 ft. It was used for ground attack against troops.

The transport "Topsy" looked much like a U.S. Douglas DC-2. It was reported as a paratroop carrier in the South Pacific. It had a span of 74 ft. Speed was about 260 m.p.h. at 10,000 ft. Its range with normal load was about 1,200 mi.

Biggest Jap aircraft were "Mavis" and "Emily," both 4-engine flying boats. Their normal mission was for long-range patrol. Without bombs or torpedoes, the range of "Mavis" was said to be over 5,000 mi. "Emily" appeared to be quite similar to the U.S. navy's Consolidated Coronado (PB₂Y).

On the other end of the scale were two tiny seaplanes, "Slim" and "Glen," both supposed to be designed for basing on submarines. It might have been one of these machines that dropped incendiary bombs into U.S. territory near Seattle, early in the war.

There was some indication that the Japanese did some glider building. After 1937, the Fukuda Mayeda Light Aircraft works at Asaki were building training gliders of common German types. No usage of gliders in actual service was reported up to the end of 1943.

U.S. FLYING FORTRESSES returning to their North African base after bombing German planes and fuel dumps at Tunis airport, burning in the distance

THE ALLIES

The military aircraft of the United Nations on the fighting fronts were in the same process of slow evolution that characterized axis aviation during 1943. A few new names appeared in British lists, and the Russian picture, although dim in detail, showed a somewhat clearer outline than it did in 1942.

Great Britain.—British aircraft manufacturing staged an almost complete recovery in 1943. Bombed-out plants were running again, often in new and widely scattered locations. What bombing attacks occurred in 1943 were so light that they were not at all disruptive to industry. A high degree of production liaison was maintained with the U.S. Technical and production missions were exchanged to the mutual benefit of both sides. The extent of the recovery could be judged by the ability of the R.A.F. to stage continuous raids of the magnitude of those that wrecked Berlin. Obviously, there was no shortage of planes, personnel or matériel by the end of 1943.

Assistance to Great Britain via lend-lease channels continued on a large scale. Deliveries of practically all current U.S. types were made throughout 1943. The roster of American aircraft in service with the R.A.F., the R.C.A.F. and the R.A.A.F. in various theatres includes:

Fighters:—Bell Airacobra, Curtiss Tomahawk, Curtiss Kittyhawk, Curtiss Warhawk, Grumman Martlet, Lockheed Lightning, North American Mustang, Republic Thunderbolt.
Bombers:—Boeing Fortress, Consolidated Liberator, Douglas Boston, Martin Maryland, Martin Baltimore, Martin Marauder, North American Mitchell.
Dive Bombers:—Brewster Bermuda, Vought-Sikorsky Chesapeake, Vultee Vengeance and Curtiss Helldiver.
Reconnaissance:—Lockheed Hudson, Lockheed Ventura.
Co-operation:—Fairchild Argus, Vultee Vigilant.
Trainers:—North American Harvard, Vought-Sikorsky Kingfisher.
Patrol:—Consolidated Catalina (flying boat).

No new names figured in lists of big British bombers. Little mentioned in 1943 dispatches were the Hampdens, the Whitleys and the Wellingtons that bore the brunt of 1940–41 bombing attacks. These machines were largely replaced by the bigger 4-engine Halifax, Stirling and Lancaster types. These were the machines that carried the "block-busters" to Berlin in night raids. They were big planes (of 99-ft., 99-ft. and 102-ft. wing spans, respectively). Halifax and Lancaster were powered with four Rolls-Royce Merlin XX liquid-cooled engines each. Stirling was fitted with air-cooled Bristol Hercules engines. An alternate Lancaster (II) appeared in 1943 with Hercules engines instead of the Merlins, probably due to the greater availability of the Bristol engines.

In the light, fast bomber category, the Mosquito proved to be the world's best. It was small (54-ft. span). It was powered with two Rolls-Royce Merlin XXI engines of 1,280 h.p. each. Its speed was said to be in the 400-m.p.h. range. It was built of wood, and was in quantity production in Canada as well as in England. It could carry four 500-lb. bombs. As an alternate, fighter armament was four 20-mm. cannon and four .303-in. machine guns. Mosquitos performed brilliant actions over Norway, and made many destructive daylight raids on Berlin.

In the single-seat fighter class, Spitfire and Hurricane reigned supreme up to the close of 1943. Both showed continuous improvement in performance and in fire-power. The Westland Whirlwind (twin-engine fighter) which first appeared in 1942 continued in limited production. Its forte was defensive fighting at night. It carried four 20-mm. cannon in the nose. A new single-engine fighter came into service in quantity in 1943, the Hawker Typhoon. It was designed for high-altitude work as a defense against the FW-190. Its 2,400-h.p. Napier Sabre engine was the most powerful single unit in use in England. Speed was over 400 m.p.h. Armament was either four 20-mm. cannon or 12 machine guns.

The Bristol Beaufighter, evolved from the earlier Blenheim

light bomber, figured in 1943 actions both in the European theatre and in the middle east. It fought very successfully against the Italians in the later phases of the Mediterranean campaigns. It was a twin-engine (Bristol Hercules III) two-place machine. It could do over 330 m.p.h. at 14,000 ft. Range was quite good, with reasonable bomb and armament loads. The Bristol Beaufort, also evolved from the Blenheim, figured in many cross-Channel attacks against the axis-held French coast.

For naval use, the older Fairey Fulmar, an adaptation of the prewar Fairey Battle, was in service up to the end of 1943. The old biplane Swordfish continued to appear on carrier decks, although the newer Albacore seemed to be replacing it. A modification of the Spitfire, the Seafire, was put into wide carrier use as a deck fighter. Its characteristics appeared to be much the same as its land-based prototype.

In the big flying-boat field, nothing newer than the Short Sunderland put in an appearance. Its normal gross weight was over 45,000 lb. Span was 113 ft. It was powered with four Bristol Pegasus XXII engines. Speed was 210 m.p.h. at 6,250 ft.

That the British industry was making postwar plans to enter the big commercial transport field was indicated by announcement late in 1943 of the Avro York, a 50-passenger modification of the Lancaster bomber. It was indicated that the commercial version might be produced in Canada.

Russia.—For many years, Russian aviation had been an enigma. A vast activity was suspected, but few people from other countries saw much of it first hand. In 1943, because of somewhat closer co-operation with Americans and British, some facts emerged, but the picture was far from complete up to the close of the year.

It was announced that nearly 7,000 U.S. aeroplanes were delivered to the Russian air force under lend-lease. Curtiss Warhawks, Bell Airacobras, Martin Marauders, Douglas A-20's and North American Mustangs were included. A German source guessed that soviet factories were turning out over 20,000 planes a year. Even if this figure is discounted, the Russian air force was probably of formidable proportions at the end of 1943. That it took the command of the air away from the luftwaffe in the campaigns of 1943 was certain.

Based on reports from a number of scattered sources, it appeared that the Russians had standardized their own production on a relatively small number of basic types. In the single-engine single-seat fighter class, the YAK series (odd numbers) was built around a liquid-cooled Vee engine, the LAGG series was powered with an air-cooled radial type. The YAK fighters resembled the British Spitfire or the U.S. P-40, with long tapered noses and pilot's cockpit well aft. The YAK-1 appeared early in the war with Germany. Improvements were constant. The YAK-9 was the last reported model in 1943.

The LAGG series resembled the U.S. P-47 (Thunderbolt), although it appeared to be somewhat smaller in power and dimension. The LAGG-3 was similar in design but was said to be built of wood.

Little was known of the armament of either YAK or LAGG. It was a fair guess, however, that they carry both cannon and machine guns comparable to any in use by fighters of the same class elsewhere.

For ground attack and army co-operation, two types predominated—the famous Stormovik (IL-2) and the PE-2. Stormovik was a clean-cut single-engine single-seater of 49-ft. span. The engine was an M-38 12-cylinder inverted-Vee, water-cooled, at 1,300 h.p. It could do 280 m.p.h. at 13,000 ft. It was characterized by fairly thick tapered wings with two large bulges below to house the undercarriage. It normally carried two 32-mm. cannon and four machine guns in the wings. Alternately, it could be fitted with bombs or rockets. It was heavily armoured against ground fire.

The PE-2 was a twin-engine type resembling the Messerschmitt-110 and -210. It was used either as a fast reconnaissance or a dive bomber. For the latter purpose it was fitted with "venetian blind" diving brakes. Engines were liquid-cooled, M-105 Hispano-Suiza, 12-cylinder Vee type of 1.100 h.p. each. Span was 60 ft. It carried a crew of two or three. Top speed was around 300 m.p.h. The PE-2B was similar to PE-2, but was fitted out as a fighter with a heavy battery of cannons and machine guns in the nose.

In the medium bomber field, the Russian DB3F compared with the U.S. B-25 Mitchells. It was similar to the machine (ZKB-26) that flew non-stop from Moscow to Miscou Island (New Brunswick) in April 1939. It was a midwing monoplane with two liquid-cooled M-88 engines of 1,100 h.p. each. Armament consisted of 7.6-mm. or 12.7-mm. machine guns. A considerable bomb load (two tons for relatively short ranges) was carried. These were the first soviet aircraft used to bomb Berlin.

The big 4-engine DB-7's designed by Tupelov were reported to have engaged in several raids against Berlin, Danzig and the Balkan cities early in 1943. They were said to have up to 8,000 lb. as bomb-load for long ranges. The type was characterized by very large inboard nacelles. Each housed a landing gear unit, and the radiators for both outboard engines. A machine-gun position was located in the tail of each of the larger nacelles. A crew of nine was carried. This machine compared in size with the U.S. Consolidated Liberator. (*See* also AIRPORTS AND FLYING FIELDS; AIR TRANSPORT COMMAND; AVIATION, CIVIL; BUSINESS REVIEW; MUNITIONS OF WAR; WORLD WAR II.) (S. P. J.)

Air Mail: *see* POST OFFICE.

Airports and Flying Fields.

The U.S. tradition is to build for peaceful commerce instead of for war, but to so build public facilities, particularly those federally created or aided, that they can be converted quickly and easily to military use when the national safety is imperilled.

Airport construction in 1943 was primarily aimed at satisfying the needs of the armed forces; however, the understanding reached between the federal and city governments was to enable the latter, at the same time, to develop plans which would make it possible to adapt military airport facilities to the needs of postwar commercial aviation.

Many military airports are not suitable for large communities, primarily because they are so far from these communities. Yet, in instances where postwar airport development is possible, plans were being made to enable municipalities to continue airport construction in a manner suitable for efficient and economical operation of civilian air transportation. It was not to be expected, however, that the air forces would leave a large number of newly equipped airports for commercial use after World War II. Here are some of the reasons why:

1. Many military airports are too distant from cities to be suitable for scheduled air line use.
2. Many military airports are designed primarily for mass formation flights; therefore, in their present state, these are unsuitable for economical civilian use.
3. The very nature of commercial airports requires a higher factor of safety and they must of necessity be designed accordingly.
4. Point three will determine, therefore, the location of building areas which in the case of army airports are widely dispersed for the purpose of protection, etc.

Existing air line companies however, were expected, at the close of World War II, to increase their facilities to several times the prewar standing. Numerous feeder line services would be fran-chised; the much-talked-about air freight services would quickly add considerably to airport traffic as adequate cargo planes came to hand. New land-based transoceanic services would be inaugurated; many progressive industrial concerns would conduct business by air with their own multi-engined aircraft. All these various services must be adequately accommodated at major air terminals.

The ultimate facilities should simulate, to a greater degree, those used for railroad passenger terminals as well as transoceanic passenger accommodations, and also, to some extent, provide freight service facilities until such time as increased business makes the building of separate air freight terminals necessary.

Redesign of Transport Airports for Increased Efficiency.— The air liners of the U.S. make several hundred thousand landings and take-offs each year. The length of runways, position of taxiways, approaches and other factors of design cause excessive wear and tear on flying equipment that adds materially to the maintenance and overhaul costs.

A majority of the transport airports in 1943 had an average runway length of 3,800 ft. and a width of 150 f†. In designing the taxiways, little consideration was given generally to their position with respect to the runway length or the manoeuvring of large aircraft upon the ground. As a result, when a transport plane landed, it invariably rolled past the turnoff point on the landing runway or had to be sharply braked to slow the plane in time for the turnoff.

When a landing aircraft overrolls a taxiway, the pilot must then come to a stop and by using alternate applications of power on his two engines and severe braking, turn the plane through 180°. The 150-ft.-wide runway necessitates a sharp turn with the consequent torque action on the rubber of the inboard wheel.

The average taxiway or runway intersection has rather short radii of turns and the taxiways are rarely over 100 ft. in width. These conditions cause a pilot to bring his ship almost to a stop before he can negotiate the turn off the runway and a series of irregular applications of single engine power to negotiate the relatively narrow taxiway. The lack of identification and guide lights for taxiways and runway intersections causes overroll and excessive braking as well as excessive use of the engines while landing and taxiing to the ramps during the hours of darkness. These same factors affect the operation of taxiing from a ramp to the runway ends for take-offs.

The additional engine wear and extra gasoline needed for excessive use of engines in ground manoeuvres and the higher degree of wear on brake linings and tires caused by short stops and sharp turns in several hundred thousand landings and take-offs cost the air lines and other operators no small amount each year. The poor location of turnoffs and taxiways seriously hampers the use of each port because of the added length of time it takes a plane to clear the runway for the next landing or take-off.

It would certainly be worth while to investigate each field from the standpoint of efficiency for ground manoeuvres and to press the proper agencies for design corrections to the taxiways, runway widths, lengths and airport lighting.

The growth of private flying and of air transport activities would certainly force the municipalities served by the air lines to provide numerous small airports for private craft and force the building of airports specifically designed for and exclusively used by the air lines.

There were in addition two important problems facing the air transport industry that must also be solved in the immediate future. The immediate need to relieve "stacking" and congestion at large terminals and to provide instrument landing systems at a majority of the fields served by scheduled air transport were too pressing to permit them to continue unsolved.

Federal Aid to Airport Development.—The Airports service of the Civil Aeronautics administration is charged with fostering airport development throughout the United States, its territories and possessions.

This service plans and co-ordinates all civil airport development and correlates these plans with those of the army, navy and other federal agencies. It recommends the allocation and supervises the expenditure of funds appropriated for airport development, and determines the necessity for all other federal expenditures for civil airport development. It supervises and directs the CAA airport program engaged in the construction of public airports essential for the prosecution of the war. It prepares and distributes to federal agencies, states, cities and other civic bodies typical airport plans, designs, specifications and bulletins pertaining to the planning and construction of airports. It reviews civil airport project applications, plans and specifications involving the expenditure of federal money, and processes certificates of necessity for such development in accordance with Section 303 of the Civil Aeronautics act. It collects and maintains current information on all civil airports in the United States. It conducts studies on airport zoning and advises on legal, financial and engineering matters concerning civil airports.

In 1931 the CAA reported to congress that the 2,300 airports in the U.S. should be increased to 3,500 in the succeeding six years, with particular emphasis on the larger type fields. In 1940 it revised this need, on the basis of world conditions, to urge a total of 4,000 fields, stressing particularly the need for major airports in the interest of national defense and proposing a $600,-000,000 program in the succeeding three to six years. It requested $80,000,000 for the immediate launching of a program which would be limited solely to landing facilities, omitting buildings and other refinements. Congress thereupon made its first direct appropriation ($40,000,000) to the CAA for airport improvements, limiting them to sites rated as preferentially important by the armed forces. All airports built since were certified as essential to the war effort by the secretaries of war, navy and commerce.

These construction projects were being carried out in any of three ways: (1) by commercial contract, with engineering and supervision by the corps of engineers, U.S. army; (2) by commercial contract, with engineering and supervision by the bureau of yards and docks, U.S. navy; (3) by commercial contract with engineering and supervision by the CAA airways engineering division.

When the CAA received its first airport appropriation, in 1941, there were in all the United States only 76 "major" airports, *i.e.*, fields having paved runways of 3,500 ft. or longer, the types needed by heavy, fast military aircraft. These had been increased at the close of 1943 to more than 850 such fields, in addition to a secret number of purely military air bases.

Snow as an Airport Problem.—Snow can effectively block an airport from income operations while costs go on as usual. Sometimes rolling will make a snow-covered field temporarily usable, but the packed snow has to thaw some time and then it may give with the load. The best solution, when equipment permits, is to melt it or to move it away. Scraping it into piles or windrows makes additional hazards on the field, but when this is absolutely necessary such piles should be adequately marked with flags and lights. These and all other lights on an airport must be kept uncovered and in a constant state of efficiency—which in itself is a considerable job in a snowstorm.

The airport manager, pilot and ground crewmen must always regard snow and freezing weather with suspicion. Loose stones or hard instruments should be removed from runways before a freeze or they may become keen tire cutters when points protrude from a frozen surface. Severe tire damage may also be caused by frozen ruts. Wheel chocks and tools are easily misplaced in bad weather and can become quickly hidden by a covering of snow. Such blind hazards have caused serious accidents when hit by taxiing aircraft. In freezing weather it is the airport operator's responsibility to make frequent checks on the condition of the runways, and to close the airport as soon as it becomes dangerous for use. The retarding effect of soft snow on take-offs may result in normally adequate runways proving too short. Wet snow or splashed slush may freeze in the wheels or undercarriage and cause disaster. Ice and slush create skidding hazards.

No aircraft should be allowed to leave the ground in freezing weather until it is certain that there is no snow or coating of frost, or water which may freeze upon the wings, since the flying characteristics of an aircraft may be materially altered thereby.

Airport Maintenance.—Perhaps this phase of airport management is more important than maintenance of field surfaces, structures and equipment. Practice has shown that there is but one completely satisfactory method of keeping the maintenance program of an airport up to par. The method is based on periodical inspection procedure.

Each superintendent or foreman should be provided with comprehensive report forms covering periodical inspection of all facilities and equipment under his direct charge. The airport budget should always include adequate sums for maintenance and replacement. Neglect of this item will invariably be costly because of the progressive deterioration which neglect brings. Runway surfaces and marking should be watched closely and repaired or painted regularly. Buildings and equipment should be kept in new condition at all times. Lighting, traffic control and similar facilities must be kept in good order for maximum safety of operations. Servicing equipment and personnel must be kept at maximum efficiency.

Airport Fires.—Changes in the construction material and size of aeroplanes, and in the size of hangars, have gradually changed the whole problem of fighting fires at airports. All-metal aeroplanes of huge size can have minor fires within their cabins that will not endanger aeroplanes in the same hangar, but if these fires are not quickly controlled by firemen using special portable equipment, the large gasoline loads of such planes will cause fires of an entirely different character. Open fires in hangars are best combated by sprinkler systems of the "deluge" type, which pour down thousands of gallons of water a minute. Still different types of equipment are required for paint shop and gas storage fires.

At Washington National airport, automatic fire fighting is part of the hangar design. The hangar is protected from fire by a "deluge" system which is a sort of big brother to the average sprinkler system. Every 10 feet, large nozzles are installed, and every 40 feet is a pneumatically-controlled switch which opens with a sudden rise of temperature of three degrees in the space of 20 seconds. This provision is to take care of explosions, fires and similar situations. The hangar is divided into areas, and the nozzles in each area are turned on independently. When all nozzles are going, a total of 5,000 gal. of water a minute flood the hangar. (*See* also Air Forces of the World; Aviation, Civil.)

(E. M. E.)

Air Transport Command.

The air transport command is part of the United States army air forces. It was established May 29, 1941, to ferry aircraft for the British from the United States to Canada. It was known then as the ferrying command. On July 1, 1942, the ferrying command was reorganized and renamed the air transport command.

Above, left: OFFICERS entering a giant Skymaster (C-54) cargo plane of the Air Transport Command at a West African base

Above, right: U.S. AIR TRANSPORT COMMAND PLANES after taking off from the airfield at Natal, Brazil, in the summer of 1943 for Africa and points east

Below, left: C-46 "COMMANDO" of the U.S. Air Transport Command being loaded with cargo destined for a war zone in 1943. An army lift truck speeds the loading

Below, right: QUARTERS of the Air Transport Command at a servicing outpost in Equatorial Africa

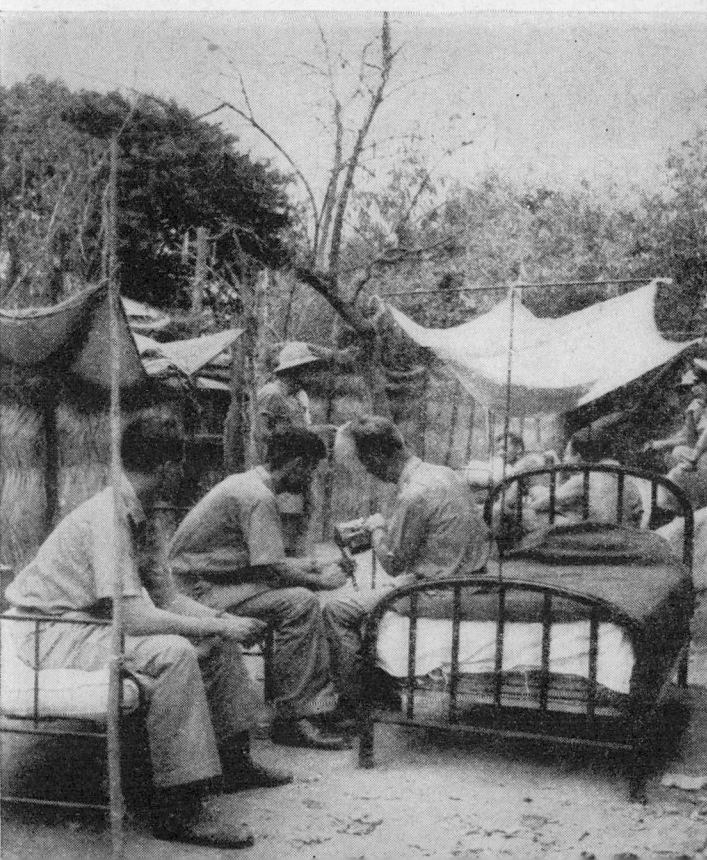

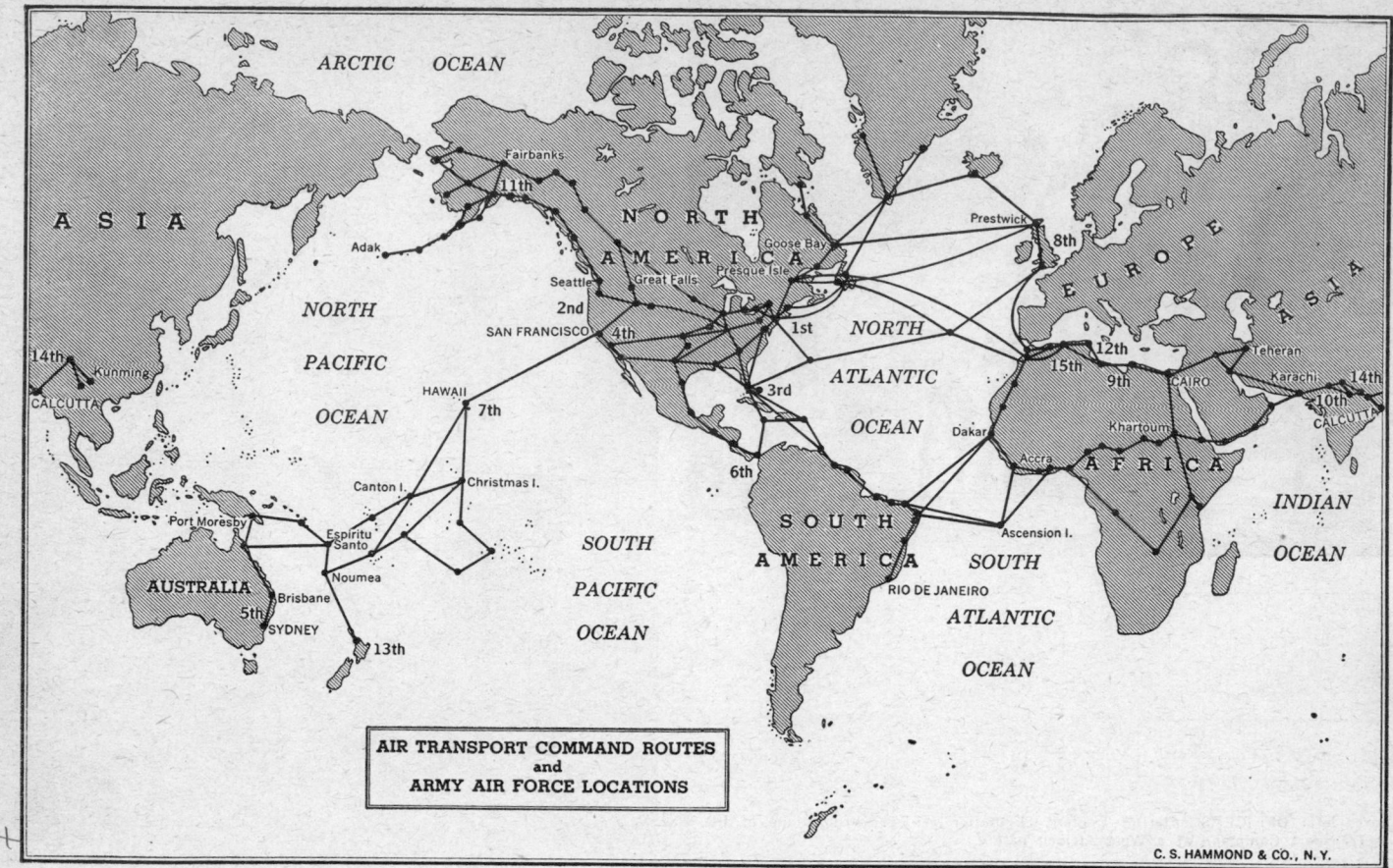

AIR TRANSPORT COMMAND ROUTES
and
ARMY AIR FORCE LOCATIONS

C. S. HAMMOND & CO., N. Y.

In a military letter under date of April 10, 1943, Gen. Henry H. Arnold, commanding general of the army air forces, set forth the mission of the ATC in these terms:

1. The ferrying of all aircraft within the United States and to destinations outside the United States, pursuant to existing directives.

2. The transportation by air of personnel, matériel, mail, strategic materials and other cargoes for all war department agencies (except those served by troop carrier command units) and for any government agency of the United States or governments of the United Nations, subject to established priorities.

3. The control, maintenance and operation of establishments and facilities on air routes outside the United States which are or which may be made the responsibility of the commanding general, army air forces, or which are assigned to the air transport command, and airports of embarkation for routes over which the air transport command operates.

4. The utilization to the fullest extent possible, both within and without the United States, of the service, facilities and personnel of the civil air carriers.

5. The performance of duties presently performed by the air transport command which were heretofore transferred to it from the military director of civil aviation.

6. The provision of assistance for movements overseas of combat units in accordance with existing directives.

7. The administration of priorities for air travel and the movement of cargoes on aircraft operated by or under contract for the air transport command and on civil air carriers (except as presently administered by the naval air transport service) in accordance with policies and procedures established by proper authority.

Operations of the ATC expanded so greatly in 1943 that miles flown in a single day equalled more than 30 trips around the globe at the equator. Mileage of the command's routes totalled 112,000.

When the command was founded, it consisted of two officers and a clerk. By late 1943, ATC personnel approached six figures.

The late Maj. Gen. Robert Olds, then a colonel, was the first commanding officer. In April, 1942, he was succeeded by Col. Harold L. George, who was made a brigadier general shortly thereafter and was promoted to major general in Aug. 1942.

During 1943, 35 pilots were awarded Distinguished Flying Crosses after each logged more than 1,000 hr. on command flights.

Among them, they amassed the equivalent in flying time of four solid years over oceans, mountains, jungles.

The command consists of headquarters in Washington, the ferrying division with headquarters in Cincinnati, the domestic transportation division, with headquarters in New York, and nine foreign wings. These wings are the Caribbean, South Atlantic, Central African, North African, European, North Atlantic, Alaskan, Pacific and India-China.   (H. L. G.)

A.L.A.: *see* AMERICAN LIBRARY ASSOCIATION.

Alabama. Alabama is one of the "deep south" states of the United States, admitted to the union 1819. Area, 51,609 sq.mi.; pop. (1940) 2,832,961. Capital, Montgomery (78,-084). Cities with larger population were Birmingham (267,583) and Mobile (78,720). Of the state's population in 1940, 855,941 were urban, or 30.2%. There were, in 1940, 1,847,850 whites; 983,290 Negroes; 574 of other races; 2,821,004 native-born; 11,-957 foreign-born; 47.2% of the total population was rural.

History.—Chauncey Sparks, Democrat, was elected governor Nov. 3, 1942, to succeed Frank M. Dixon. Eight of the nine congressional representatives, all Democrats, were re-elected. The new representative, from the ninth district, defeated Luther Patrick, the incumbent, in the Democratic primaries run-off election in June. Aside from Gov. Sparks, the principal state officers elected in Nov. 1942 were: Handy C. Ellis, lieutenant governor; Warren C. Lusk, treasurer; John Brandon, auditor; Howell Turner, secretary of state; Joe N. Poole, commissioner of agriculture; and Elbert B. Norton, superintendent of education.

Education.—State appropriations in 1943 amounted to $18,-770,631. Total revenues from all sources in 1942–43 were $34,-400,044. Illiteracy among whites between 10 and 20 years (1942) was 0.95%, Negroes 5.02%. There are seven state-supported institutions of higher education for whites and three for Negroes.

Charities and Correction.—The state supports many philanthropic and penal institutions: institutions for the deaf and blind of both races; hospitals for the insane of both races; a school for feeble-minded children; training schools for wayward white boys and girls; a reformatory school for Negro boys, etc.

Banking and Finance.—On Dec. 31, 1942, there were 66 national banks in the state, the same as in the preceding year, and 150 state banks and trust companies, a decrease of one from the 1941 figure. These 216 banks, together with their 21 branches (of which 19 belonged to the national banks), had a capital account of $54,444,000, deposits of $691,828,000 and total resources of $747,396,000. Total net receipts of the state from all sources in the fiscal year ending Sept. 30, 1942, were $102,870,-268.66 and total net disbursements were $91,439,096.16.

Agriculture.—The yield of corn, cotton, potatoes, peanuts and tobacco increased considerably in 1943; that of oats and hay declined.

Table I.—*Leading Agricultural Products of Alabama, 1943 and 1942*

Crop	1943 (est.)	1942
Corn, bu.	45,080,000	43,960,000
Oats, bu.	4,182,000	4,800,000
Cotton, bales	950,000	925,000
Potatoes, bu.	5,170,000	3,922,000
Peanuts, lb.	510,675,000	335,400,000
Tame and wild hay, tons	817,000	829,000
Tobacco, lb.	265,000	215,000

Manufacturing.—In 1939, by the federal biennial census of manufactures, there were 2,052 manufacturing establishments hiring 126,215 workers and producing goods valued at $574,670,-690. The leading manufactures were cotton textiles (valued at about $92,000,000; spindles in operation, 1,835,909), iron and steel and electricity. Corporation and municipal production of electricity amounted to about 900,000 h.p., and the TVA plants were capable of producing slightly more. There were more than 6,000 mi. of rural electric lines. Other important industries: lumber, blast furnace products, cast iron pipes and fittings, coke oven products, cotton seed oil and meal, paper, aluminum, cement, chemicals, fertilizers, meat packing and shipbuilding. War demands caused expansion of old industries and the rise of new industries, such as powder, aluminum and chemical manufacturing in 1941 and 1942.

Mineral Production.—The total value of Alabama's mineral

Table II.—*Principal Mineral Products of Alabama, 1939 and 1938*

Mineral	Value, 1939	Value, 1938
Pig iron	$43,902,681	$29,190,091
Coal	27,708,000	26,769,000
Coke	10,917,559	9,888,292
Iron ore	9,971,024	7,341,620
Cement	6,690,765	6,114,246
Stone	2,516,584	1,809,379
Clay products	2,306,712	1,487,067

production in 1939 was $54,124,382; in 1938 it was $46,296,293.
(A. B. Mo.; X.)

Alaska. Alaska is one of the two incorporated territories of the United States. Area, 586,400 sq.mi., approximately one-fifth the area of the 48 states. The territory lies between the meridians 130° W. and 173° E. longitude and between the parallels of 51° and 72° N. latitude. The civilian population of the territory (72,524 in the 1940 census as against 59,278 in 1938) was estimated to have increased in 1943 to approximately 90,000.

History.—In 1943 the U.S. army drove the Japanese invaders

BLEAK MOUNTAINS through which U.S. forces filed to attack Japanese positions on Attu Island after their landing on the tiny Aleutian outpost May 11, 1943

MIDGET SUBMARINES blown up by the Japanese before they evacuated Kiska in Aug. 1943

from Alaskan soil. On May 11, American forces landed on the Aleutian island of Attu, held by the Japanese since June of 1942. Desperate fighting continued throughout the mountainous island until the morning of May 29, when final large scale Japanese resistance was crushed. Few prisoners were taken, practically all of the 2,300 Japanese having been killed during the heavy fighting or having died in mass suicides undertaken when the Japanese cause became hopeless. In August a strong U.S. and Canadian force landed on Kiska, which had been the most strongly defended of the Aleutian islands held by the Japanese, to discover the invaders had abandoned the island. (*See* also WORLD WAR II.)

The Alaska highway, first overland transportation route between Alaska and continental United States, was dedicated in Nov. 1942, and during 1943 carried a heavy volume of military traffic. Also during 1943 there was intensive development of the Fort Norman oil fields in northwestern Canada, and under the direction of the U.S. army a pipe line was constructed from the oil fields to Whitehorse, where a refinery was being built. Construction of feeder pipe lines to transport refined petroleum products from Whitehorse along the route of the Alaska highway was rushed. In 1943 an additional connecting link of the Alaska highway was provided when under military supervision a road was built from a point on the highway west of Whitehorse to Haines, a seaport in southeastern Alaska. (*See* ROADS AND HIGHWAYS.)

The changed military status resulting from Allied victories in the Aleutians was reflected in the autumn of 1943 when the Alaska Defense Command of the army was abolished and there was set up instead the Alaskan department, operating as an independent unit instead of under the Western Defense Command.

Education.—School enrolment increased slightly in 1943 as compared with 1942, the figures being 5,349 in 1943 and 5,092 in 1942.

Fisheries and Mineral Production.—A very favourable season in the Bristol bay red salmon district was chiefly responsible for the increase in the pack of canned salmon in 1943, the total number of cases for the year being 5,450,000 as compared with 5,075,000 in 1942. Taking of fur seals in the Pribilof islands, suspended in 1942 because of the Japanese occupation of some of the nearby Aleutian islands, was resumed in 1943. Under government supervision, 117,164 seal skins were taken during the 1943 season, constituting an all-time record.

Production of gold, the mining of which had formerly ranked second in commercial importance to fisheries, continued to decline in 1943 under wartime restrictions.   (E. L. B.)

Alaska Highway: *see* ROADS AND HIGHWAYS.

Albania, a kingdom in the western part of the Balkan peninsula, occupied in 1939 by Italy. Area 10,631 sq.mi.; pop. (census 1930) 1,003,068; (estimate 1939) 1,063,000. Capital, Tirana. Chief cities: Tirana (30,806); Scutari (29,209); Koritsa (22,787); Elbasan (13,796); Valona (9,100). Religion: Mohammedans (688,280); Orthodox Christians (210,313); Roman Catholics (104,184). Prime minister (1943): Ekrem Libohova.

History.—World War II and the Italian capitulation in 1943 threw Albania into a turmoil, especially because the Allies had pledged repeatedly the restoration of a free Albania. Prime Minister Churchill reiterated this pledge in the house of commons on Nov. 4, 1943, promising an Albania "free from her Axis yoke and restored to her independence." He disclosed at the same time that British officers were co-operating with Albanian guerrillas. The Albanian guerrillas were fighting in three groups, of which the group in the centre near Tirana, under the command of Myslim Peza, was the most formidable. In the north the guerrillas operated under Col. Muharrem Bajraktari, ex-commander in the British-trained gendarmery, while the guerrillas in the south were commanded by Col. Bilal Nivica. The Albanian premier, Ekrem Libohova, formerly foreign minister under King Zog, had not been able to popularize the Italian connection. Unrest in the country was generally widespread and increased after Mussolini's downfall.

There existed no Albanian government in exile and Albania was not recognized officially as one of the United Nations. The former king of Albania, Ahmed Beg Zogu, who became King Zog I of Albania in Sept. 1928, left the country at the time of the Italian occupation in 1939 and in 1943 continued to live in England.

Education.—Though primary education is nominally compulsory, illiteracy was still very high in 1943, especially among women. In 1939 there existed 663 state elementary schools with 38,988 male and 17,948 female pupils and 19 secondary schools with 4,810 male and 1,425 female students. There were no institutions of higher education.

Trade and Finance.—The value of the foreign trade for 1938 amounted to $9,644,000. Imports amounted to $6,719,000, of which 37.2% came from Italy and 6% from the United States. The total exports amounted to $2,925,000, of which 68.4% went to Italy and 4.5% to the United States. The major import articles were cotton and cotton goods, corn, benzine and woollen goods; the main exports were wool, hides and furs, cheese, cattle, eggs and bitumen. Of the mineral wealth of the country aluminum and petroleum were of importance. In 1939, 229,278 tons of crude petroleum were produced. With the economic life of the country still on a very primitive level there exists practically no modern industry. Albania has no railroads but a good highway system, improved by the Italians for strategic reasons. The Albanian currency in 1943 was pegged to the Italian currency, an Albanian franc equalling 6.25 lire (32.89 cents U.S., June 1941). The external debt of Albania amounted to $15,000,000 in 1938. (*See* also ITALIAN COLONIAL EMPIRE.) (H. Ko.)

Alberta.
The most westerly of the three prairie provinces of Canada (*q.v.*). Area, 255,285 sq.mi.; pop. (1941) 796,169, of which the greater part was rural. The largest city is Edmonton (92,404), the provincial capital. Local administration is in the hands of a provincial parliament. Alberta returns to Ottawa 17 members for the house of commons and 6 senators.

History.—On May 23, 1943, William Aberhart, the provincial premier, died. As he was both the founder and leader of the party in power, the Social Credit, his death was of great political moment. E. C. Manning, formerly minister of trade and industry, was sworn in as premier on May 31. In December, the government carried an important by-election in Red Deer, thus indicating its vigour under the new leadership.

Agriculture.—The wheat yield was estimated in 1943 to be somewhat over 82,000,000 bu.; oats, 10,000,000 bu.; barley, 4,600,000 bu.; flaxseed, 2,300,000 bu. Wartime demands powerfully stimulated cattle raising and dairy farming. In 1943, Alberta led Canada in hog production, while dairy products were expected to reach the record value of $33,000,000.

Mineral Production.—In the first nine months of 1943, 6,443,276 tons of coal were mined, or 3% above the output of the corresponding period last year. The output of petroleum in the first nine months of 1943 was 7,308,669 bbl. Experiments in deep drilling were undertaken in order to expand this output. In 1940, over 26,000,000 cu.ft. of natural gas was produced. (J. I. C.)

Alcohol, Industrial.
The military and civil requirements for industrial alcohol in the U.S. increased in 1943. It became evident that all facilities were needed for its manufacture, including those formerly used for alcoholic liquors. From a total requirement of about 175,000,000 gal. in 1941, the need was raised to 356,000,000 for 1942, to about 400,000,000 gal. for 1943 and to 632,000,000 gal. for 1944. At the beginning of 1943 the production capacity was about 490,000,000 gal. and by the end of the year it had increased to nearly 593,000,000 gal. This situation indicated that all production facilities would have to be used during 1944 and also that a large reduction in the stocks of alcohol would be made. These stocks were reported to be 138,000,000 gal. in July 1943 and had been reduced to 80,000,000 gal. by the end of the year. It was estimated by the War Production board that about 40,000,000 gal. more would be taken from these stocks in 1944, bringing them down to the minimum for working reserves. The needs for 1944 were expected to be 50% more than called for in the original program. This made it doubtful that any spirits could be produced for drinking in the year.

The increasing demand came from the synthetic rubber uses, which increased rapidly during 1943. The needs for other war uses had first call on supplies but did not amount to so large a total.

The sources of alcohol were expanded at a rapid rate during 1943 by the increased use of wheat. In 1941–42 only about 2,000,000 bu. were used, in 1942–43 the amount had increased to 54,000,000 bu. and for 1943–44 it was estimated to be 110,000,000 bu. Since the stocks of wheat were so large, the use of wheat was limited only by the facilities. By taking over the liquormaking plants this raw material could be used to a larger extent. The department of agriculture reported that new methods of distilling were being developed which promised to make it possible on a commercial scale to get more alcohol from less malt and also to be able to separate the protein for livestock feed before the alcohol was removed, thus saving it for replacement of corn, which is needed for feed. The protein had heretofore been obtained only from the distiller's slops.

Another prospect for increasing production was in the larger use of molasses from the Caribbean if the imports of this raw material could be increased. The War Production board also proposed that Great Britain resume the making of alcohol from molasses from the Caribbean to replace some of the alcohol heretofore provided under lend-lease arrangements. Many new plants were expected to come into larger production during the year 1944, thereby, with more strict allocations, meeting the vital needs for all purposes. (J. C. Ms.)

Alcoholic Intoxication: *see* INTOXICATION, ALCOHOLIC.
Alcoholic Liquor: *see* BREWING AND BEER; LIQUORS, ALCOHOLIC; WINES.
"Alcoholics Anonymous": *see* INTOXICATION, ALCOHOLIC.
Aleutian Islands: *see* ALASKA; WORLD WAR II.

Alexander, Sir Harold Rupert Leofric George
(1891–   ), British army officer, is the 3rd son of the 4th earl of Caledon. He was educated at Harrow and Sandhurst. He received his commission in the Irish Guards in 1911. At the end of World War I he was commanding a battalion with the rank of lieutenant-colonel. In 1919 he commanded a landwehr of the Lettish army during the confused fighting in the Baltic provinces. In 1934 he was given command of a brigade in India, and in the following year he saw service in the Loe-Agra and Mohmand operations. In 1938 he became major-general and was given the 1st division. In Sept. 1939 he took the 1st division to France with the B.E.F. Later as lieutenant-general he was promoted to command the 1st corps. At Dunkirk it fell to him to organize the final defense and evacuation, and he was among the last men to leave the beach. After Dunkirk he was made

general officer commanding in chief, southern command, serving in this capacity till he went to Burma in Feb. 1942 as general officer commanding at a critical period in the campaign. In Aug. 1942 General Alexander was sent to the middle east as commander in chief, in time to break the full-scale attack launched by the enemy at the end of August against the El Alamein position. Under his command the 8th army won its decisive victory of Oct. 23–Nov. 4 and pursued the defeated German and Italian forces under Marshal Rommel to Tobruk, Bengasi, Tripoli and the border of Tunisia. In Feb. 1943 General Alexander was appointed deputy commander in chief to General Eisenhower of the Allied armies in North Africa. All British, American and French troops in Tunisia were formed into the 18th army group and were placed under his orders. After the capture of Tunis and the axis surrender, General Alexander, as commander of the 15th British, Canadian and American group, directed the invasion of Italy in July and the invasion of the mainland of Italy in Sept. 1943.

Alfalfa. The 1943 crop of alfalfa hay in the United States fell 11% below the record crop of 1942. The 1943 crop was 32,465,000 tons compared to 36,478,000 tons in 1942 and 26,709,000 tons average for the period 1932–41 as estimated by the U.S. department of agriculture. The acreage harvested in 1943 was 95% of that of 1942 and considerably above the average. The 1943 crop was somewhat spotted and the quality of the early crop damaged by rains though the late crop was of high quality. The highest yields were in California, mostly on irrigated land, at 4.40 tons per acre, followed by Oregon 2.50 tons, Arizona 2.70, New Mexico 2.70 and Texas 2.50. None of the central or plains states exceeded 2.30 tons per acre.

U.S. Production of Alfalfa Hay in Leading States, 1943 and 1942 and the 10-Yr. Average
(in thousands of tons)

States	1943	1942	10-yr. average	States	1943	1942	10-yr. average
California . .	3,819	3,440	3,228	Nebraska . .	1,343	1,593	1,272
Minnesota . .	3,036	3,170	1,889	Colorado . .	1,327	1,369	1,197
Iowa . . .	2,329	3,018	1,696	Montana . .	1,159	1,253	965
Wisconsin . .	2,132	2,859	1,860	Illinois . . .	963	1,481	921
Michigan . .	1,902	2,268	1,701	New York . .	897	1,035	618
Idaho . . .	1,853	1,852	1,887	Ohio . . .	829	1,107	800
Kansas . . .	1,408	1,628	946	Indiana . .	814	1,038	618

No other state produced more than 1,000,000 tons in 1942.

The production of alfalfa seed, estimated at 1,114,900 bu., was 15% larger than 1942 but 3% below the 10-year average. A larger acreage was harvested for seed in 1943 than in 1942. (*See* also Hay.) (J. C. Ms.)

Algeria: *see* French Colonial Empire.

Aliens. Listed below are ten countries in rank order of registered aliens in the U.S. as of Dec. 31, 1940:

Italy, including Sicily and Sardinia	695,472
Canada	447,898
Poland	442,547
Mexico	416,690
Russia, including Russia in Asia	366,827
Germany	314,870
Great Britain, including England, Scotland, and Wales	291,557
Austria	191,600
Eire	158,154
Hungary	116,701
Total	3,442,316

Further studies indicated that more than 80% of the registered aliens were living in the following ten states: New York, 1,234,-995; California, 531,882; Pennsylvania, 365,229; Massachusetts, 360,416; Illinois, 320,053; Michigan, 296,834; New Jersey, 276,-026; Texas, 209,450; Ohio, 200,322; Connecticut, 157,120.

Of the nearly 5,000,000 aliens who registered under the Alien

Registration act of 1940, approximately half were eligible for U.S. citizenship. The registration and unsettled world conditions tended to increase their desire to achieve United States citizenship. In the fiscal year 1943, 115,664 declarations of intention were filed as compared with 221,796 in 1942, and 224,123 in 1941. Petitions for naturalization numbered 375,700, which is the highest number filed during any fiscal year since June 30, 1906, when the federal government took over supervision of this activity.

Certificates of naturalization were issued to 318,933 persons, also a record number, during the fiscal year of 1943. The nations to which these new citizens formerly owed allegiance were: British empire, 93,827; Poland, 42,077; Italy, 36,118; soviet Russia, 25,444; Germany, 17,774; Czechoslovakia, 12,979; Sweden, 9,448; Yugoslavia, 8,471; Greece, 6,938; Hungary, 4,792; and all other countries, 59,640.

The Second War Powers act, approved March 27, 1942, made available an expeditious naturalization procedure to noncitizens serving in the armed forces of the United States. The statute provided a judicial naturalization process for those members of the armed forces who are residing within the jurisdiction of a naturalization court and an administrative naturalization process for those serving abroad with the armed forces. During the fiscal year ended June 30, 1943, 36,049 members of the military and naval forces residing in the United States, Alaska, Hawaii, Puerto Rico and the Virgin Islands of the United States were admitted to citizenship on the basis of petitions filed with naturalization courts. Of this total, 35,416 were granted citizenship while residing in continental United States or Alaska, 586 while on duty in Hawaii and 47 during service in Puerto Rico or the Virgin Islands of the United States.

In addition, a total of 1,425 persons serving abroad with the armed forces of the United States were admitted to citizenship under the administrative naturalization procedure authorized by the Second War Powers act of March 27, 1942. Naturalization was granted in such cases by designated representatives of the immigration and naturalization service.

Alien Enemies.—Under the Nationality act of 1940 alien enemies include natives, citizens, denizens and subjects of the countries against whom the United States declared war. In 1943 these countries were Japan, Germany, Italy, Hungary, Rumania and Bulgaria. By authority of presidential proclamations of Dec. 7 and 8, 1941, and Jan. 14, 1942, a series of regulations was promulgated by the department of justice affecting the conduct of citizens or subjects of Japan, Germany and Italy 14 years of age or older. On Oct. 12, 1942, aliens of Italian nationality, except those already interned or under parole, were excepted from the regulations for alien enemies by order of the attorney general.

Dangerous alien enemies who were ordered interned by the attorney general were kept in internment camps which are operated by the immigration and naturalization service. At the end of the 1943 fiscal year, 9,220 alien enemies were in the custody of the service of whom 5,988 were from the continental United States or Puerto Rico, 2,349 from Latin America, and 883 from Alaska, Hawaii and other Pacific islands. Sixteen detention stations were in operation at the end of the year. One of the internment camps, at Crystal City, Texas, was used solely for the internment of families of enemy nationalities, and at the end of the fiscal year 1943, 1,282 individuals were interned there, consisting of 367 men, 358 women and 557 children.

During 1943, 5,323 enemy aliens were apprehended under presidential warrants of arrest. Of this number, 2,311 were paroled upon formal orders of the attorney general, including 979 Japanese, 895 Germans, 434 Italians and 3 of miscellaneous nationality; and 266 Japanese, 294 Germans, 170 Italians and 12 of miscellaneous nationality were unconditionally released. Those

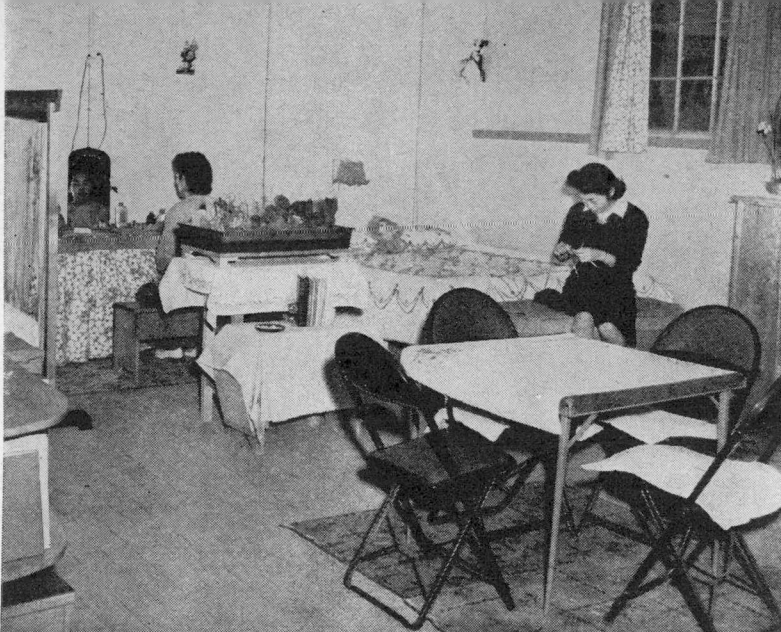

APARTMENT for Japanese in a U.S. relocation centre at Granada, Colorado

DEMOCRACY IN PRACTICE at a Japanese relocation centre in 1943. A Japanese evacuee leads a discussion of the centre's problems at a meeting attended also by the centre's U.S. advisers

EDITING the mimeographed newspaper of the Japanese relocation authority at Granada, Colorado

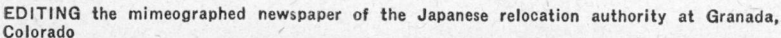

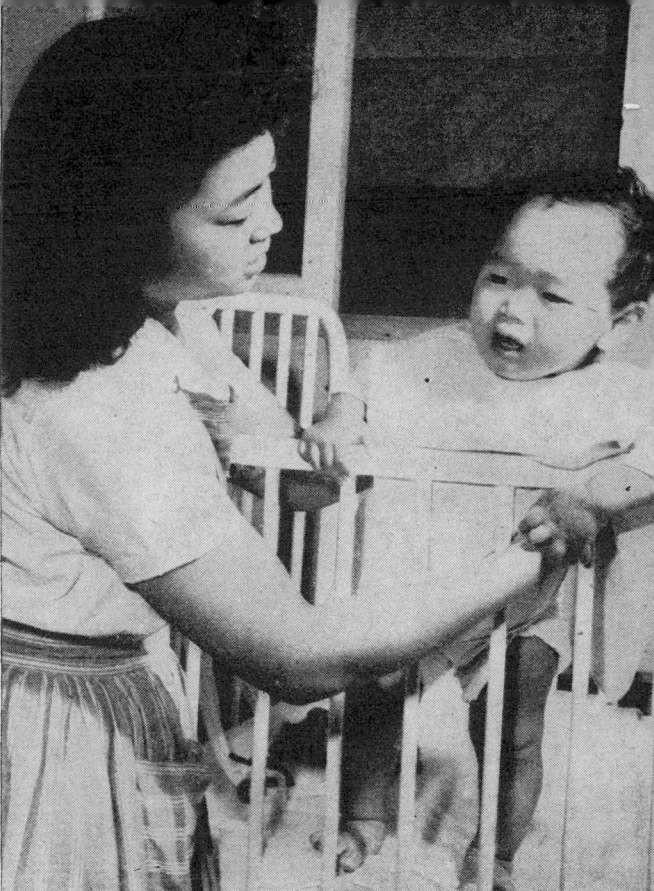

JAPANESE-AMERICAN NURSES' AIDE STUDENT at the Poston, Ariz., relocation centre hospital in 1943, attending a young patient

JAPANESE TRUCK FARMERS weeding onions in the spring of 1943 at a relocation centre in California

paroled were required to make regular reports to civilian supervisors and to district parole officers of the immigration and naturalization service who conducted periodic investigations in each such case. Aliens of enemy nationality might be naturalized under prescribed safeguards. The case of each enemy alien applicant for naturalization was thoroughly investigated by the immigration and naturalization service, and favourable recommendations were made to the courts only with respect to those petitioners for naturalization whose loyalty was established without question.

New Legislation.—During 1943 the following laws affecting aliens were passed by congress:

By far the most important measure approved by congress affecting aliens was the repeal in Dec. 1943, of the Chinese Exclusion laws. This legislation originated in 1882 and was retained on the statute books for 61 years, during which time it was subjected to many amendments and revisions. The congressional action at this time was designed to place the Chinese people on a parity with other nations for immigration purposes. The new legislation also removed the previously established prohibitions against naturalization of persons of the Chinese race as American citizens, and established an immigration quota permitting admission of a limited number of Chinese into the United States.

The act of July 13, 1943, authorized deportation under certain conditions to the country where the alien's recognized government in exile was located, or to a country proximate to the one of which the alien was a citizen or subject, or, with the consent of the country of which the alien was a citizen or subject, to any other country.

The act of April 29, 1943, permitted the entry of native-born agricultural workers from any western hemisphere country under certain exemptions and conditions.   (E. G. H.)

Japanese Relocation.—When the United States entered the war in Dec. 1941, there were more than 100,000 persons of Japanese ancestry living in the far western states. Approximately two-thirds of them, born in the United States, were American citizens. The aliens, *Issei,* are an older group who came to the United States as labourers and farm workers. Their average age is around 60. The citizens, *Nisei,* are largely a young group, most of them educated or being educated in American schools. Their average age is around 22.

The problems created by the determination in March 1942, to remove from the defense zones of the Pacific coast all persons of Japanese ancestry, continued into 1943. The policy of permanent relocation in civilian activities outside of the coastal defense zones was continued by the War Relocation authority which established offices in many of the larger midwestern cities in an endeavour to assist the evacuees in finding employment.

By the end of 1943, approximately 20,000 Japanese had been released from the relocation centres on indefinite leave to accept employment. This represented the placement of the great majority of eligible *Nisei* and the War Relocation authority was faced with the far more difficult problem of re-establishing the loyal aliens still retained in the camps.

The National Student Relocation council reported that 870 Japanese-American students had been accepted by 362 colleges and universities which had been approved by the army and navy. Minor objections to the admission of *Nisei* students to some eastern and midwestern colleges were reported.

Disturbances within certain of the camps, especially Poston in Arizona and Manzanar in California, which occurred late in 1942, led the War Relocation authority to the conviction that disorders were being instigated by a minority of disloyal elements who were taking advantage of the inevitable social disorganization of relo-

cation. In the original evacuation, stress had been placed upon retaining family units intact. In some of these families, there were younger persons who, while citizens of the United States, had been educated in Japan, and in others, older aliens who had never completely abandoned their loyalty to Japan. As their potentialities for mischief became more clearly evident, the War Relocation authority issued an order in July 1943, to segregate evacuees of doubtful loyalty to Tulelake centre in California.

An investigation of the disorders was undertaken by the Committee on Un-American Activities (Dies committee) of the house of representatives. Representatives John Costello (Dem.) of California, Carl E. Mundt (Rep.) of South Dakota and Herman Eberharter (Dem.) of Pennsylvania constituted the sub-committee which held hearings in the western states. The Dies subcommittee presented a report to congress listing several major complaints about the camps:

1. That Japanese of doubtful loyalty were being released.
2. That there were thousands in camps who had requested repatriation to Japan.
3. That loyal and disloyal Japanese were intermingling without segregation.
4. That the Japanese were being supplied food through the quartermaster corps of the army in greater variety and quantity than that available to the average American consumer.
5. That the discipline in the various relocation centres was very lax.

The committee failed to deny or affirm most of these charges, contenting itself with three recommendations:

1. That the disloyal be segregated from the loyal Japanese (already undertaken by the War Relocation authority).
2. That a special board be set up to investigate the loyalty of evacuees seeking release from the centres.
3. That the War Relocation authority inaugurate a thoroughgoing program of Americanization in the centres.

The third member of the sub-committee rendered a minority report taking to task the majority for not having clearly refuted most of the charges which brought about the investigation. Congressman Eberharter stated that the testimony before the committee showed conclusively:

1. That the Japanese being released from the camps were adequately investigated by the War Relocation authority and there was no evidence of laxness.
2. That a very limited number of Japanese had shown any desire for repatriation.
3. That segregation was taking place on the initiative of the War Relocation authority.
4. That all rationing restrictions were being applied to the camps without discrimination. Food costs averaged about 40 cents per person a day and the centres refrained from purchasing commodities where there were local shortages.
5. That evidence produced before the sub-committee indicated that there was much less crime of any kind in the relocation centres than in the average American community of the same size.

The Utah legislature in Feb. 1943 passed an alien property restriction bill denying the right of real property ownership to aliens ineligible to citizenship. This was vetoed by the governor and followed by a later bill of less stringent nature. Arkansas passed a similar anti-evacuee land ownership act which was later held unconstitutional by the attorney general of the state. In March the Arizona legislature passed a bill requiring three consecutive days of advertising by any business man doing business with Japanese. This law was held unconstitutional in the state superior court in July. In April the Iowa state legislature passed a resolution requesting the withdrawal of War Relocation authority students from Iowa colleges.

In the latter part of Jan. 1943, the army again accepted enlistments of *Nisei,* which resulted in 1,100 volunteers from the United States and 2,600 from Hawaii. It was estimated that the total number of Japanese-Americans in the armed forces of the U.S. exceeded 8,000. These *Nisei* were trained in separate camps in two sections of the United States. The first *Nisei* battalion which went into action on the Italian front received praise from its Caucasian officers. During July the Women's Army corps was open for enlistment of *Nisei* girls.

In March the Western Defense Command eliminated much of Arizona from military area No. 1. This was followed by an announcement from the War Relocation authority that evacuees from this area would be permitted to return to their homes; the return took place without disorder.

At the time army enlistment was open to *Nisei*, a declaration of loyalty to the United States was required of all Japanese of draft age (total 20,679). Of these, about 24% declined to affirm their loyalty to the United States. These statements, however, did not constitute affirmation of loyalty to Japan. It was this group which had been transferred to the Tulelake centre. The ratio of so-called disloyal answers varied greatly as between the different camps, with Manzanar showing a refusal to affirm loyalty of almost 50% as against a percentage of 2.2 for Granada, Colorado. It should be remembered that the residents of Manzanar were about two months earlier fired on by the United States army, in order to terminate disorder, and two residents killed.

Several court cases grew out of relocation. The Korematsu, Hirabayashi and Yasui cases challenging the legality of the curfew and evacuation orders were heard by the 9th circuit court of appeals in San Francisco which refused to render a decision and referred the cases directly to the United States supreme court. The supreme court held that the defendants were guilty of violating curfew regulations, but refused to render a decision on evacuation, indicating that the court was probably divided on the latter point.

The suit of the Native Sons of the Golden West to have the names of all American-born Japanese withdrawn from voting lists was disposed of by an adverse decision of the 9th circuit court of appeals, followed by a refusal by the United States supreme court to review the case, on the ground that the right of American-born Japanese to citizenship had been previously determined. A number of civil cases were in the courts dealing with Japanese who were evacuated in the midst of contractual obligations which thereafter remained unperformed.

In July War Mobilization Director James F. Byrnes issued a statement to congress, in response to a resolution of inquiry, stating that the restrictions on persons of Japanese ancestry would be continued as long as military necessity demanded, and denying that evacuees were being given preferential treatment, or that disloyal Japanese were being released.

The year 1943 closed with considerable agitation against Japanese-Americans on the west coast. (*See* also CENSUS, 1940; WAR RELOCATION AUTHORITY.) (W. W. B.)

Alimentary System, Disorders of. The Stomach and Duodenum.

—The well-known preponderance of duodenal ulcer over gastric ulcer and the major importance of nonsurgical methods of treating ulcer were attested by F. H. Lahey's report. Of 7,000 patients with peptic ulcer submitted to treatment in the hospital, 6,550 had duodenal ulcer. Only 6.59% of these and 18.1% of the 450 patients with gastric ulcer were submitted to operation.

W. L. Palmer contended that alkalosis induced by soluble alkali, which is characterized by an increase in sodium, total base, pH, and in the bicarbonate content of the blood, does not develop if the function of the kidney is normal and if the amount of water supplied daily is sufficiently great to eliminate the alkali as rapidly as it is absorbed. The alkalosis observed during the administration of calcium carbonate is identical with that seen in patients with obstruction of the lower end of the stomach and can be prevented by administration of sufficient amounts of sodium chloride despite the continued use of the alkali. Chemically this alkalosis is characterized by a decrease in the concentration of chlorides, sodium and total alkali in the blood and by elevation of the pH and of the bicarbonate content of the blood.

As the result of an analysis made of 2,111 cases of grossly bleeding gastric and duodenal ulcer, including 75 personally observed cases, in all of which the patients were treated by the prompt and frequent feeding program, E. A. Rasberry, Jr. and T. G. Miller reported a gross mortality rate of 1.9%. These observers concluded that, in the absence of coincident perforation, such procedure is superior to any other form of conservative treatment or to surgical intervention.

Conservatism characterized the current literature on gastritis in 1943, not only with respect to incidence and clinical significance but also to its potentiality as a precursor to other diseases, especially carcinoma. In the gastroscopic examinations of 50 patients with uncomplicated duodenal ulcer, H. J. Tumen and M. M. Lieberthal found that 33 had an associated chronic gastritis. They concluded that gastritis did not regularly influence the clinical course of duodenal ulcer. Moreover, it was impossible to postulate the presence or absence of associated gastritis on the basis of the nature of the symptoms or the character of the response to treatment.

Absence of free hydrochloric acid in the gastric secretion is not an infrequent occurrence. The role that such acid plays in normal function consists chiefly of activation of pepsin, swelling of protein, stimulation of motor and secretory functions, and solution of iron. It also has a bactericidal effect. Previous investigators showed that the usual doses of dilute hydrochloric acid are ineffective in appreciably modifying the gastric acidity in achlorhydric states. A. E. Koehler and E. Windsor made exhaustive observations on the effect of the addition of acid to a representative ground meal at body temperature in vitro. It was determined that the usual amount of acid used in replacement therapy had but little effect on the pH of the meal, that the swelling of proteins as a step in solution and digestion is not appreciably influenced by even the maximal therapeutic doses of acid, and that the pH is not sufficiently lowered to have any bactericidal effect. It also was found that anacidity or hyperacidity had no effect on destruction of thiamin.

The Biliary Tract.—A modified technique for the determination of serum bilirubin which is more accurate than standard methods and provides for separate measurements of the fractions which give direct and indirect van den Bergh reactions was devised by B. Sepulveda and A. E. Osterberg. The various factors underlying a recurrence or persistence of symptoms after removal of the gall bladder were reviewed by H. K. Gray and W. S. Sharpe. The significance of calculi and inflammatory or obstructive lesions of the cystic duct was exemplified in their study of 44 cases in which the lesion was found at operation.

The diagnostic significance of the amount of urobilinogen excreted in urine and faeces is generally recognized. The investigations of Frederick Steigmann and Josephine Dyniewicz confirmed the superiority of Watson's method with respect to urinary urobilinogen. They also concluded that the value of the determination of the amount of faecal urobilinogen in random specimens by this method was equal to that of determinations on stools collected for four days.

Intestine.—Numerous articles stressed the effect of tropical diseases and their sequelae on the intestinal tract. Dysentery, and acute abdominal diseases such as acute appendicitis, acute cholecystitis, acute pancreatitis, even intestinal obstruction, may be simulated during the acute stages of malignant tertian malaria. Bacillary dysentery may persist in a chronic form and closely resemble chronic ulcerative colitis. Diarrhoea may be the result of amoebiasis or helminthic infestation. The clinical features of intestinal bilharziasis as observed in Southern Rhodesia were instructively described by M. Gelfand.

BIBLIOGRAPHY.—F. H. Lahey and S. F. Marshall, "The Surgical Management of Some of the More Complicated Problems of Peptic Ulcer," *Surg., Gynec. & Obst.*, 76:641–648 (June 1943); W. L. Palmer, "Alkalosis in Antacid Therapy," (editorial), *Gastroenterology*, 1:892–893 (Sept. 1943); E. A. Rasberry, Jr. and T. G. Miller, "The Prompt-feeding Program for Bleeding Gastric and Duodenal Ulcer," *Gastroenterology*, 1:911–921 (Oct. 1943); H. J. Tumen and M. M. Lieberthal, "The Significance of the Gastroscopic Findings in Patients with Duodenal Ulcer," *Gastroenterology*, 1:555–564 (June 1943); A. E. Koehler and E. Windsor, "Effectiveness of Replacement Therapy in Achlorhydria," *Ann. Int. Med.*, 18:182–192 (Feb. 1943); B. Sepulveda and A. E. Osterberg, "Serum Bilirubin; Its Clinical Importance and a Recommended Procedure for the Determination of Indirect and Direct Values," *Proc. Staff Meet., Mayo Clin.*, 18:252–258 (July 28, 1943); H. K. Gray and W. S. Sharpe, "Biliary Dyskinesia; Role Played by a Remnant of the Cystic Duct," *Arch. Surg.*, 46:564–571 (Apr. 1943); Frederick Steigmann and Josephine M. Dyniewicz, "Studies of Urobilinogen: I. The Daily Urobilinogen Excretion in Urine and Feces in Health and Disease: An Evaluation of Watson's and Sparkman's Methods," *Gastroenterology*, 1:743–764 (Aug. 1943); M. Gelfand, "Clinical Features of Intestinal Bilharziasis (S. mansoni)," *Clin. Proc.*, 1:247–252 (Aug. 1942).   (G. B. EN.)

Allen, Terry de la Mesa

(1888–   ), U.S. army officer, was born April 1 at Ft. Douglas, Utah. After several years' study at the U.S. Military academy, he enrolled at the Catholic University of America, where he received the A.B. degree in 1912. He was commissioned a second lieutenant of cavalry the same year. In World War I he served with the A.E.F., taking part in the St. Mihiel and Meuse-Argonne offensives, and after the armistice he remained overseas in the army of occupation. During the period between wars he undertook advanced study at the Cavalry school, the Command and General Staff school, the Infantry school and the Army War college. By the time the United States entered World War II he had reached the rank of brigadier general. In 1942 he was made a major general and given command of the 1st infantry division, which took part in the campaigns of Tunisia and Sicily. For his achievements in North Africa Allen received the distinguished service medal and the *Croix de guerre*.

In the fall of 1943 he was recalled to the United States to command the 104th division.

Allergy.

The following new allergic causes for nasal symptoms were discovered: Vegetable gums (Gelfand), used in cosmetics; Spanish moss (Dean), often the upholstery of inexpensive furniture. Blumstein reported two cases of hay fever with nasal symptoms in May and June due to the ailanthus (tree of heaven) pollen. Hoersh emphasized the possibility of sensitization of infants by food odours in his report of nine cases of infantile eczema due to vapours or odours of cooked or uncooked food. Respiratory allergy due to such causes had been previously reported in 1942 by Urbach. Another unusual cause of eczema was reported by Keil who found that a resinous material used in finishing cotton fabrics caused skin sensitization.

For severe, intractable asthma Barach advised the following combination of previously described methods for the purpose of inducing bronchial relaxation: helium and oxygen for one to six hours daily, aminophyllin rectally, dilaudid in small doses, potassium iodide by mouth, and the inhalation of epinephrine (1:100). Only 17% of the cases thus treated failed to respond, 57% were rapidly relieved and 25% were classified merely as "helped."

The use of histamine associated with a modified horse serum was given added importance by the report of Cohen and Friedman, who found that the sera of patients treated with the histamine-horse serum conjugate contained specific antibodies capable of neutralizing histamine.

BIBLIOGRAPHY.—A. J. Hoersh, "Allergy to Food Odors. Its Relation to the Management of Infantile Eczema," *J. Allergy*, 14:335–39 (1943); A. L. Barach, "Repeated Bronchial Relaxation in the Treatment of Intractable Asthma," *ibid.*, 14:296–309 (1943); M. B. Cohen and H. J. Freedman, "Antibodies to Histamine Induced in Human Beings by Histamine Conjugates," *ibid.*, 14:195–202 (1943).   (B. Z. R.)

Allied Military Government.

International law requires military forces to establish some form of organized control in the war-torn areas they occupy. In addition to humanitarian considerations, effective and immediate establishment of some form of government is an aid to the prosecution of the war effort. Pursuant to these considerations, the United Kingdom and the United States moved jointly to provide the necessary personnel and equipment for this purpose. Military control of civil affairs, planned well in advance of actual tactical operations, was a development of World War II. Heretofore, the organization of occupied areas was an improvised arrangement devoid of preparation for the problems to be faced.

Intensive training programs for both U.S. and British military personnel were carried out and plans were formulated for active service in anticipation of tactical developments. The burden of civil administration of enemy occupied territory, prior to the invasion of Sicily and the Italian mainland, fell largely to the British. With the invasion of Italian territory, truly Anglo-American military government became a joint enterprise.

Responsibilities, assignments and personnel were divided among the officers of the United States and the British empire without discrimination.

Allied military government officers were included in the first assault forces in Sicily and Italy and so effective was their work that they won highest praise from tactical commanders in the field. Effective and immediate control over areas occupied by Allied military government, first referred to as AMGOT, later as AMG, relieved tactical commanders of the necessity of detaching combat personnel for this purpose and assured them of a stabilized condition in the rear echelons.

Upon the invasion of Sicily and Italy, AMG officers introduced emergency measures to effect immediate relief of the civilian population and establish order in the rear of the fighting zones. This process was repeated as the battle lines entered new areas.

The returning of civilian populations to their cities, towns and homes was a primary consideration. In some areas only a few score inhabitants of large cities were to be found when Allied forces entered. The population had fled to the mountains and taken refuge there. Many of the cities and towns had suffered extensive war damage and AMG officers set out to restore as quickly as possible essential utilities, such as waterworks, sewerage systems and power plants. The debris of the cities was moved as rapidly as possible and improvised housing facilities for the homeless established.

Foodstuffs were made available to the civilian public through channels of trade and strict rationing was enforced. Only when need was actually apparent was direct relief granted.

Public health measures were inaugurated to prevent epidemics, curtail contagious diseases and to protect Allied military personnel as well as the local citizens. In several areas it was necessary to bury the dead, both military and civilian, left in the wake of the fighting forces. Civilian hospital facilities were restored as rapidly as possible and the co-operation of civilian medical and health agencies was invited and secured. The injured were hospitalized or treated. Special rations, including milk, were secured for children and nursing and pregnant mothers. Malarial control agencies, never wholly effective under the fascist regime, were implemented and co-ordinated.

Transportation facilities were restored as expeditiously as possible, roads and railroads repaired, bridges rebuilt, and war-damaged harbours cleaned out. In this work, native civilians were enrolled at reasonable wages. Prisoners of war were also used to the extent permitted under international law. Communication facilities and the postal system were opened for limited service.

Policing of occupied areas was promptly inaugurated. Local

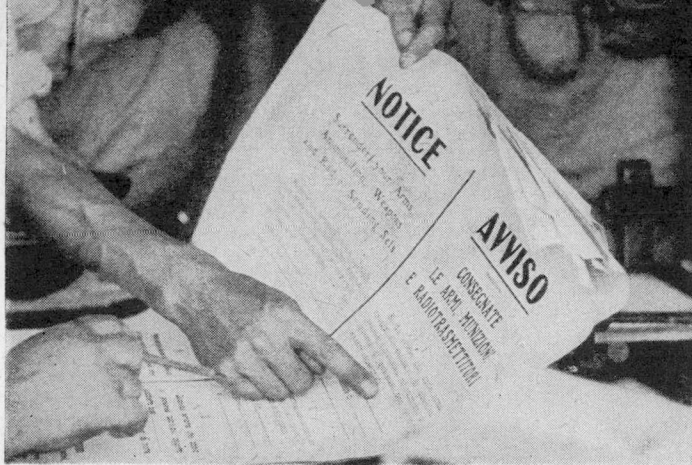

ALLIED PROCLAMATION warning Sicilians to surrender their weapons and radio transmitters

SICILIAN POLICEMAN helping an Allied soldier post a proclamation of the Allied Military Government of occupied nations in 1943

AMERICAN MILITARY GOVERNOR of Noto, Sicily, discussing local problems with a group of Italian civilians after U.S. occupation of the town in July 1943

STANDARD CLOTHES manufactured in the United States in 1943 for children of Allied-occupied countries

PROCLAMATIONS by the U.S. military governor posted on the streets of Palermo after the Sicilian city's fall July 22, 1943

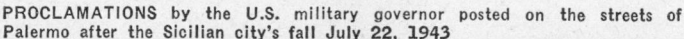

police establishments were reorganized and utilized whenever possible. Looting and other disorders were quickly eliminated. Military courts were set up for local offenses requiring immediate action. Proclamations and instructions were issued to the civil population informing them of their responsibilities and privileges. Legal administration extended to such fields as juvenile delinquency, and the supervision or reconstruction of penal and corrective institutions. Civil courts were re-established whenever practical after the elimination of fascist elements. Steps were taken to reform and reorganize bar associations under pre-fascist regulations.

All financial institutions were originally closed by AMG. In some instances local supplies of stamps and currency had been burned by the retreating enemy, while securities and other valuables had been removed. AMG introduced fresh and adequate supplies of stamps and currency, exchange rates were posted and as soon as feasible banks were reopened. In a number of re-opened banks, deposits had increased materially. Financial officers of the AMG also took over the supervision of postal savings, insurance companies and similar institutions. All civil incomes, taxes and disbursements were placed in the hands of the AMG.

Initial political activities of the AMG consisted, to a large extent, of releasing the political prisoners of the fascists and rescinding fascist decrees, racial and religious laws and edicts. Political activity of the populations of the occupied areas was allowed after the early stages of the operations, in such degrees as was consistent with maintenance of public order. With the exception of the removal of known or suspected fascists, the administration of civil agencies was left largely undisturbed.

The AMG took every possible precaution to preserve cultural and art treasures left behind by the retreating enemy. Educational institutions were reorganized and reopened as rapidly as possible. Committees of responsible non-fascist educators were appointed to serve with AMG in eliminating propaganda text books and in reorganizing school curricula. Plans were made for the reopening of universities as rapidly as adequate buildings could be found and non-fascist faculties recruited.

(J. H. HG.)

Allocations and Allotments: see PRIORITIES AND ALLOCATIONS.

Alloys: see MAGNESIUM; METALLURGY; MOLYBDENUM; MONAZITE; NICKEL; TITANIUM; VANADIUM.

Aluminum.
Statistics from all of the producing countries being lacking, there is nothing that can be added to the production table presented in previous years.

All of the belligerents in World War II, which designation includes all of the important producers of aluminum, enlarged

World Production of Aluminum
(Metric tons)

	1937	1938	1939	1940	1941
Canada.	42,500	66,000	75,000	95,000	200,000
France	34,500	45,300	50,000	50,000	60,000
Germany	127,500	161,100	200,000	240,000	270,000
Great Britain .	19,400	23,300	25,000	32,000	35,000
Italy	22,000	25,800	32,400	36,000	40,000
Japan	10,500	17,000	23,000	32,000	40,000
Norway	23,000	29,000	31,100	20,000	35,000
Switzerland . .	24,000	27,000	28,000	29,000	28,000
U.S.S.R. . . .	37,700	43,800	50,000	55,000	50,000
United States .	133,000	130,400	148,700	187,600	280,000
Others	7,200	10,400	7,400	7,500	6,000
Total	482,300	581,600	672,400	785,000	1,045,000

their production capacity, but so far as was known in 1943, the United States made the largest additions. The only information that was made public regarding current production was an official announcement in August 1943, that the output in July was 150,-892,000 lb. (73,292,000 lb. in government owned plants and 77,600,000 lb. in privately owned plants) and that the total output for January-July was 515,899,725 lb. The fact that the July output was more than double the monthly average for January-July indicated that extensive increases in output were made during the first half of the year. Also, it was reported that some plant capacity was not in operation because of labour shortage. This would indicate that the current production capacity of the United States was in 1943 at least three times that of 1941, when output was 280,000 metric tons, and was in excess of the world output of 1940. Assuming the July rate of output to continue during the remainder of the year, the 1943 total would be just about double the 1941 output.

Canadian capacity was similarly increased, and was unofficially reported to be about 450,000 tons a year. United States government purchases in Canada since 1941 exceeded 600,000 metric tons, about one-third of which had been delivered up to May 1943.

As a result of these developments the aluminum supply was improved to such an extent that the War Production board lifted the restrictions on some uses; furthermore, development work on many marginal bauxite deposits was stopped, and construction work on several new fabrication plants suspended. Not only had metal production caught up with demand, but scrap became so plentiful that its disposition was a major problem. (See also BUSINESS REVIEW; METALLURGY.)

(G. A. Ro.)

Ambassadors and Envoys.
The following is a list of ambassadors and envoys to and from the United States and to and from Great Britain Jan. 1, 1944.

To and From the United States

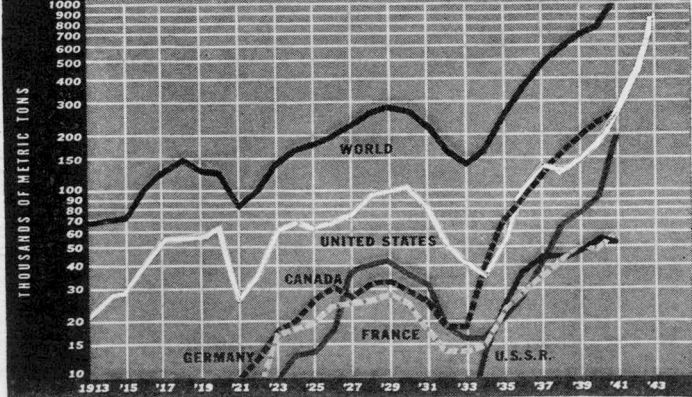

ALUMINUM PRODUCTION OF THE WORLD and the chief producing countries, as compiled by *The Mineral Industry*

To the United States	Country	From the United States
Aziz, Abdol H.	Afghanistan .	Engert, Cornelius Van H.
*Espil, Felipe A. (absent)	Argentina .	.*Armour, Norman
Dixon, Sir Owen	Australia . .	Johnson, Nelson T.
*Straten-Ponthoz, Count Robert van der	Belgium . . .	*Biddle, Anthony J. D., Jr.[3]
*Guachalla, Dr. Luis F.[1]	Bolivia . . .	*Boal, Pierre de L.[4]
*Martins, Carlos	Brazil	.*Caffery, Jefferson
*McCarthy, Leighton	Canada	.*Atherton, Ray
*Michels, Rodolfo	Chile	*Bowers, Claude G.
*Wei Tao-ming, Dr.	China	*Gauss, Clarence E.
*Turbay, Gabriel	Colombia . . .	.*Lane, Arthur Bliss
*Escalante, Carlos M.	Costa Rica . .	*Des Portes, Fay A.
*Concheso, Dr. Aurelio F. . . .	Cuba	.*Braden, Spruille
*Hurban, Vladimír	Czechoslovakia	*Biddle, Anthony J. D., Jr.[3]
Kauffmann, Henrik de.	Denmark . . .	. . . .

To the United States	Country	From the United States
*Copello, Anselmo	Dominican Rep.	*Warren, Avra M.
*Alfaro, Capt. Colón E.	Ecuador	*Scotten, Robert M.
Hassan Bey, Mahmoud	Egypt	Kirk, Alexander C.
Brennan, Robert	Eire (Ireland)	Gray, David
*Castro, Dr. Hector D.	El Salvador	*Thurston, Walter
Kaiv, Johannes[2]	Estonia	
Ephrem, Blatta	Ethiopia	Caldwell, John K.
Procopé, Hjalmar J.	Finland	Schoenfeld, H. F. Arthur
*Halifax, Viscount	Great Britain	*Winant, John G.
*Diamantopoulos, Cimon P.	Greece	*MacVeagh, Lincoln[5]
*Recinos, Dr. Adrian	Guatemala	*Long, Boaz
*Liautaud, André	Haiti	*White, John C.
*Caceres, Dr Julian R.	Honduras	*Erwin, John D.
Thors, Thor	Iceland	Morris, Leland B.
Shayesteh, Mohammed	Iran	Dreyfus, L. G., Jr.
Jawdat, Ali	Iraq	Henderson, Loy W.
Bilmanis, Dr. Alfred	Latvia	
	Liberia	Walton, Lester A.
Žadeikis, Povilas	Lithuania	
Le Gallais, Hugues	Luxembourg	Biddle, Anthony J. D. Jr.[3]
*Castillo Nájera, Dr. Francisco	Mexico	*Messersmith, George S.
*Loudon, Dr. A.	Netherlands	*Biddle, Anthony J. D., Jr.[3]
Nash, Walter (absent)	New Zealand	Burdett, William C.[6]
*Sevilla Sacasa, Guillermo	Nicaragua	*Stewart, James B.
*Munthe de Morgenstierne, Wilhelm	Norway	*Biddle, Anthony J. D., Jr.[3]
*Jiménez, E. A.	Panama	*Vacant
*Velázquez, Dr. Celso R.	Paraguay	*Frost, Wesley
*Freyre y Santander, Manuel de	Peru	*Vacant
*Ciechanowski, Jan	Poland	*Biddle, Anthony J. D., Jr.[3]
Bianchi, João A. de	Portugal	Norweb, R. Henry[7]
*Cárdenas, Juan F. de	Spain	*Hayes, Carlton J. H.
Boström, W.	Sweden	Johnson, Herschel V.
Bruggmann, Charles	Switzerland	Harrison, Leland
Seni Pramoj, Rajawongse	Thailand	
*Ertegün, Mehmet M.	Turkey	*Steinhardt, Laurence A.
Close, Ralph W. (absent)	Union of South Africa	Vacant
*Gromyko, Andrei A.	U.S.S.R.	*Harriman, W. Averell
*Blanco, Dr. Juan C.	Uruguay	*Dawson, William
*Escalante, Dr. Diógenes	Venezuela	*Corrigan, Frank P.
*Fotitch, Constantin	Yugoslavia	*MacVeagh, Lincoln[5]

*=ambassadors; unstarred, envoys.
[1]Resigned Jan. 1944.
[2]Acting consul general in New York City.
[3]Resigned Jan. 22, 1944. Chargés d'Affaires carried on his work as ambassador to the governments of Belgium, Czechoslovakia, the Netherlands, Norway and Poland and as minister to the government of Luxembourg, all established in England.
[4]Recalled Jan. 1944.
[5]Accredited to the governments of Greece and Yugoslavia established in Egypt.
[6]Died Jan. 13, 1944.
[7]With the personal rank of ambassador.

The following special diplomatic appointments were made during 1943:

	Name	Title
French Committee of National Liberation	Wilson, Edwin C.[1]	U.S. representative
Advisory Council to the Allied Control Commission for Italy	Murphy, Robt.[1]	U.S. member
United Nations European Advisory Commission	Winant, John G.	U.S. representative
Middle East and Middle East Supply Centre	Landis, James M.[2]	American Director of Economic Operations in the Middle East and Principal American Civilian Representative at the Middle East Supply Centre
French West Africa	Glassford, William A., Vice Admiral[2]	Personal representative of the president

[1]With the personal rank of ambassador.
[2]With the personal rank of minister.

To and From Great Britain

To Great Britain	Country	From Great Britain
Sardar Ahmed Ali Khan	Afghanistan	Squire, G. F.
*Cárcano, Dr. Miguel Angel	Argentina	*Kelly, Sir D. V.

To Great Britain	Country	From Great Britain
*de Marchienne, Baron de Cartier	Belgian Govt. (in London)	*Oliphant, Sir Lancelot
Patiño, Antenor	Bolivia	Rees, Thomas I.
*de Aragão, J. J. Moniz	Brazil	*Charles, Sir Noel N. H.
*Bianchi, Manuel	Chile	*Orde, Sir Charles W.
*Koo, Dr. V. K. Wellington	China	*Seymour, Sir H.
Jaramillo Arango, Dr. Jaime	Colombia	Snow, T. M.
(Vacant)	Costa Rica	§Patron, F. J.
de Blanck, Guillermo	Cuba	Ogilvie-Forbes, Sir G. A. D.
*Lobkowicz, Maximilian	Czechoslovak Provis. Govt. (in London)	[1]Nicholls, P. B. B.
[2]Reventlow, Count Eduard	Denmark	
Pérez-Alfonseca, Dr. Ricardo	Dominican Republic	Andrews, C. F. W.
Freile Larrea, Carlos	Ecuador	Hallett, L. C. Hughes
*Hassan Nashat Pasha	Egypt	*Killearn, Lord
Gabre, Belata Ayela	Ethiopia	Howe, R. G.
[3]Viénot, Pierre	French C'ttee of National Liberation (in Algiers)	[3]Cooper, Alfred Duff
*Aghnides, Thanassis	Greek Govt. (in Cairo)	*Leeper, R. W. A.
§Arévalo, Dr. Ismael Gónzalez (Guatemala and Nicaragua)	Guatemala, Honduras, Nicaragua and Salvador	Leche, J. H. (ad int.)
	Haiti	Tuson, A. A. L.
	Honduras	§Kemball, C. G.
Benediktsson, Pétur	Iceland	Shepherd, E. H. G.
Seyed Hassan Taqizadeh	Iran	Bullard, Sir R. W.
Sayid Daud al Haidari	Iraq	*Cornwallis, Sir Kinahan
‡de Lynden, Baron Robert Aernout	Liberia	§Trant, J. P.
§Clasen, André (ad int.)	Luxembourg Govt. (in London)	Oliphant, Sir Lancelot
Diaz, Dr. Alfonso de Rosenzweig	Mexico	Bateman, C. Harold
Gen. Shingha Shumshere Jung Bahadur Rana	Nepal	Betham, Lt. Col. G. L.
*van Verduynen, Jonkheer E. Michiels	Netherlands Govt. (in London)	*Bland, Sir G. N. M.
Herdocia, Dr. Constantino (absent: see Guatemala)	Nicaragua	§Leake, J. R. M.
*Colban, E. A.	Norwegian Govt. (in London)	*Collier, L.
§Parras, Dr. Demetrio (ad int.)	Panama	Irving, S. G.
(Vacant)	Paraguay	Brickell, D. F. H.
Benavides, Alfredo	Peru	Forbes, V. C. W.
*Raczyński, Count Edward	Polish Govt. (in London)	*O'Malley, Sir O. St. C.
*The Duke of Palmella	Portugal	*Campbell, Sir Ronald
(Vacant)	Salvador	§Joint, E. J.
Sheikh Hafiz Wahba	Saudi Arabia	Jordan, S. R.
*The Duke of Alba	Spain	*Hoare, Sir Samuel
Prytz, Björn Gustaf	Sweden	Mallet, V. A. L.
Thurnheer, Walter	Switzerland	Norton, C. J.
	Syria and the Lebanon	Spears, Maj. Gen. Sir E. L.
*Orbay, Huseyin Rauf	Turkey	*Knatchbull-Hugessen, Sir H. M.
*Gousev, Feodor Tarasovitch	U.S.S.R.	*Clark Kerr, Sir Archibald
*Winant, John G.	United States	*Halifax, Viscount
Castellanos, Dr. Daniel	Uruguay	Vereker, G. G. M.
	Vatican	Osborne, Sir F. d'A. G.
Pocaterra, José Rafael	Venezuela	Gainer, D. St. C.
*Jevtić, Bogoljub	Yugoslav Govt. (in Cairo)	*Stevenson, R. C. Skrine

*=Ambassador; unstarred=Envoy-Extraordinary; ‡=Minister Resident; §=Chargé d'Affaires.
[1]British representative.
[2]Recognized by H.M. government as continuing to be responsible for the protection of such Danish interests as are not under enemy control.
[3]Delegate (with personal rank of ambassador).
Persons no longer in the foregoing list but still accepted by H.M. government as personally possessing diplomatic privileges:

Torma, August	Estonia
Zarine, Charles	Latvia
Balutis, Bronius	Lithuania

Amblygonite: see LITHIUM MINERALS.

American Academy of Arts and Letters.

The American Academy of Arts and Letters was founded in 1904 by the National Institute of Arts and Letters, in order to make the institute more efficient in carrying out the purposes for which it was organized, namely the protection and furtherance of literature and the fine arts and to give greater definiteness to its work. The membership of the academy is limited to 50, chosen only from the members of the institute.

On May 12, 1943, the academy and institute held a second joint public ceremonial at which new members of the institute were inducted, ten $1,000 "arts and letters" grants were given and medals awarded. An exhibition of the works by newly elected members, recipients of the "arts and letters" grants, and sculpture by Carl Milles, recipient of the "award of merit medal," was opened in the art gallery and museum. This continued through June 23. On October 22 the annual meeting of the academy took place, at which the election of five new members was announced and officers were elected for the ensuing year.

The officers of the academy for 1943–44 were: Walter Damrosch, president; James Truslow Adams, chancellor and treasurer; Van Wyck Brooks, secretary. The other six directors were William Adams Delano, Charles Dana Gibson, Sinclair Lewis, Paul Manship, Deems Taylor and Chauncey B. Tinker.   (F. Gn.)

American Academy of Arts and Sciences.

The academy is limited to 800 fellows and 130 foreign honorary members, divided among four classes: mathematical and physical sciences, natural and physiological sciences, the social arts, the humanities. The officers for 1943 were: president, Harlow Shapley; corresponding secretary, Abbott P. Usher; recording secretary, Hudson Hoagland; treasurer, Horace S. Ford. The following papers were presented at the monthly meetings: George Sarton, "Leonardo, Man of Science"; Otto Benesch, "Leonardo da Vinci and the Beginning of Scientific Drawing"; Charles W. Eliot, "City Planning"; Ross A. McFarland, "Human Problems in Aviation"; Henry M. Wriston, "The Problem of the Liberal Arts College"; Paul C. Mangelsdorf, "Economic Plants as Weapons of War"; Manley O. Hudson, "International Organization after the War"; Francisco Castillo Najera, "Mexican-American Cultural Relations"; Kirtley F. Mather, "Earthquakes, Volcanoes, and Mountain Systems of Mexico"; George Sarton, "Nicholas Copernicus"; Fred L. Whipple, "The Solar System"; Bart J. Bok, "The Milky Way and the Metagalaxies." The following paper was read by title: Frederic T. Lewis, "The Advent of the Microscope in America, with notes on its Earlier History." Grants in aid of research were made from the Rumford fund, the C. M. Warren fund and from the Permanent Science fund.
    (A. P. U.)

American Academy of Political and Social Science.

On April 9 and 10, 1943, there was held the 47th annual meeting of the academy with the general subject "The United Nations and the Future." Other meetings of 1943 included a session on February 13th on "The Future of Western Europe" addressed by Paul van Zeeland, formerly Prime Minister of Belgium, M. P. L. Steenberghe, chairman of the economic, financial and shipping mission of the kingdom of The Netherlands, and others; a gathering on Oct. 6 on "American Business After the War" with addresses by James B. Carey, secretary of the C.I.O., Stuart Chase, and Paul G. Hoffman, president of the Studebaker corporations and chairman of the committee for economic development; and a meeting on Nov. 22 on "The East and the West" addressed by Joseph C. Grew, former United States ambassador to Japan, Pearl S. Buck, and Dr. Y. C. James Yen.

During 1943 the six bimonthly issues of The Annals had the following titles: "Nutrition and Food Supply: The War and After" (January); "Southeastern Asia and the Philippines" (March); "Our Servicemen and Economic Security" (May); "The United Nations and the Future" (July); "The American Family in World War II" (September); "Transportation: War and Postwar" (November). The academy also publishes a pamphlet series; during 1943 there appeared No. 13 entitled "The Core of a Continent" which consists of five addresses by Henryk Strasburger, minister of finance of Poland.

Student memberships, offered for the fourth year in 1943, totalled 268. Under this arrangement students enrolled in educational institutions receive all of the privileges of regular membership at a cost of only $3.00 per year instead of the usual $5.00.

The same arrangement was made for members of the armed services of the United States and 226 persons had taken advantage of this offer.

The officers for 1943 were: Ernest Minor Patterson, president; J. P. Lichtenberger, secretary; Charles J. Rhoads, treasurer; Thomas S. Hopkins, assistant treasurer; Herbert Hoover, Carl Kelsey and C. A. Dykstra, vice-presidents. Headquarters are at 3457 Walnut St., Philadelphia 4, Pa.   (E. M. P.)

American Association for the Advancement of Science.

The officers of the American Association for the Advancement of Science for 1943 were: Dr. Isaiah Bowman, president of the Johns Hopkins university, president; Forest Ray Moulton, permanent secretary; Otis W. Caldwell, general secretary; William E. Wrather, treasurer; Sam Woodley, assistant secretary; retiring president, Arthur H. Compton.

The vice-presidents were: F. D. Murnaghan, for the section on mathematics; J. W. Beams, for the section on physics; Arthur J. Hill, for the section on chemistry; Otto Struve, for the section on astronomy; John K. Wright, for the section on geology and geography; Carl R. Moore, for the section on zoological sciences; William J. Robbins, for the section on botanical sciences; Robert Lowie, for the section on anthropology; Herbert Woodrow, for the section on psychology; F. Stuart Chapin, for the section on social and economic sciences; Henry E. Sigerist, for the section on historical and philological sciences; Thorndike Saville, for the section on engineering; P. D. Lamson, for the section on medical sciences; R. E. Buchanan, for the section on agriculture; and Harold F. Clark, for the section on education.

The membership increased to 24,800 by the admission of 2,688 new members.

The annual meeting scheduled to be held in New York beginning Dec. 27 was cancelled because of lack of railway transportation facilities and no summer meeting was held. The Theobald Smith Award for a distinguished contribution to medical science by a person under 35 years of age was awarded to Dr. Sidney C. Madden, of the University of Rochester school of medicine and dentistry and Strong Memorial hospital, for his work on plasma proteins.

The publications of the association include 18 technical quarto volumes, the ones on Human Malaria and Relapsing Fever being widely used by the medical corps of the United States army and navy in the tropics. Its nontechnical science series includes Multiple Human Births—Twins and Supertwins, Strange Malady—the Story of Allergy, Alcohol Explored and Man's Food: its Rhyme or Reason. Its serial publications are the A.A.A.S. Bulletin and The Scientific Monthly. Each member of the association receives with his membership subscriptions to the A.A.A.S. Bulletin and to either The Scientific Monthly or the weekly journal Science.   (F. R. Mo.)

American Association of Law Libraries.

The American Association of Law Libraries during 1943 continued monthly publication of the *Index to Legal Periodicals* and completed the sixth 3-year bound cumulation covering the period August 1940 to July 1943. The *Law Library Journal* also published by the Association was curtailed from six to five issues. In 1944 it will appear quarterly.

Founded in 1906, the American Association of Law Libraries was incorporated in 1935 under the laws of the District of Columbia "as a nonprofit organization to promote librarianship, to develop and increase the usefulness of law libraries, to cultivate the science of law librarianship, and to foster a spirit of co-operation among the members of the profession." The Association in 1943 had a membership of over 500 bar association, county, court, government, law school and state law librarians in the United States and Canada.

The officers for the year 1943-44 were: president, Alfred Morrison, law librarian, University of Cincinnati; president-elect, William S. Johnston, librarian, Chicago Law institute; executive secretary and treasurer, Miss Helen Newman, associate librarian, supreme court of the United States; and members of the executive committee, Mrs. Bernita J. Long, law librarian, University of Illinois (retiring president); Miss Jean Ashman, law librarian, Indiana university; Arthur C. Pulling, law librarian, Harvard Law school; and William R. Roalfe, law librarian, Duke university (on leave), Office of Price Administration, Washington, D.C.   (H. NE.)

American Bankers Association.

During the association's year 1942-43, the major portion of its activities was given over to assisting the nation's war effort. The association, serving as the liaison agent between 14,000 banks and the various agencies and departments of the government in Washington, assisted the banks in providing the following war services: U.S. treasury financing, in which the banks sold 85% of all war bonds bought by the public and in addition bought many billions more for their own account; ration coupon banking, in which the banks handled the accounting and clearing procedure involved in the use of ration coupons by the public; freezing the funds of enemy aliens; serving as tax collection agencies for the bureau of internal revenue; financing war production factories by means of some $7,000,000,000 of war loans and commitments; financing farmers in increasing their production to meet the goals of the Food-for-Victory program; establishing banking facilities for service men in army camps and naval stations, and providing trust services for men in the armed forces.

At the association's war service meeting held in New York city, Sept. 13-15, 1943, the following officers were elected for the ensuing association year: president, A. L. M. Wiggins, president, Bank of Hartsville, Hartsville, S.C.; vice-president, W. Randolph Burgess, vice-chairman, National City Bank of New York, New York city; treasurer, Wilmer J. Waller, president, Hamilton National bank, Washington, D.C.; president, national bank division, F. Raymond Peterson, president, First National Bank of Paterson, Paterson, N.J.; president, state bank division, Wood Netherland, vice-president, Mercantile-Commerce Bank and Trust company, Saint Louis, Mo.; president, savings division, Fred F. Lawrence, treasurer, Maine Savings bank, Portland, Me.; president, trust division, Henry A. Theis, vice-president, Guaranty Trust company, New York city; president, state secretaries section, Lauder W. Hodges, executive manager, California Bankers association, San Francisco, Calif.

The association's secretary, Richard W. Hill, and its executive manager, Dr. Harold Stonier, both of New York city, would continue in office through the year 1943-44.   (L. GN.)

American Bar Association.

As part of its war program the association jointly sponsored, with the war and navy departments, free legal assistance offices for soldiers, sailors and their dependents; prepared and distributed 33,000 copies of a manual of law of civilian defense; and stimulated the volunteer service of lawyers in the administration of the selective service system. Problems dominating the discussions at the 1943 meeting in Chicago were: (1) legal procedures and structure of an international organization to maintain peace, and (2) the control and prevention of administrative absolutism by governmental bureaus. Officers elected for 1943: Joseph Welles Henderson, president; Guy Richards Crump, chairman of the house of delegates; Harry S. Knight, secretary; John H. Voorhees, treasurer; Joseph D. Stecher, assistant secretary.

Awards.—The annual medal was awarded to John J. Parker, senior judge of the United States circuit court of appeals for the 4th circuit, for distinguished service to American jurisprudence. The Ross prize of $3,000 went to Lester Bernhardt Orfield, professor of law, University of Nebraska, for an essay on "What Should Be the Function of the States in our System of Government?" Awards of merit were given to the State Bar Association of California, the District of Columbia Bar association, the Bar Association of the County of Bergen, New Jersey, and honorable mention to the Missouri State Bar association.   (M. DN.)

American Bible Society.

The 127th annual meeting of the American Bible society was held in May 1943. John T. Manson was president; Gilbert Darlington, treasurer. General secretaries were Rev. Dr. Eric M. North, Rev. Dr. Frederick W. Cropp (on leave), Frank H. Mann, M.A., and Rome A. Betts, M.A., Rev. Dr. Francis C. Stifler was editorial and recording secretary.

The society distributes about 5,000,000 volumes of Scripture annually in the United States and an equal number in other lands. In co-operation with the British and Foreign Bible society, the Scottish Bible society and other missionary organizations, the Scriptures were translated into 1,058 languages up to the end of 1942 and about 21,000,000 volumes were distributed in 1942 throughout the world.   (F. C. ST.)

American Chemical Society.

The society operates under a national charter from the 75th congress. In 1943 the presidency passed from Dr. Harry N. Holmes of Oberlin college to Dr. Per K. Frolich of the Standard Oil Development Co., with Dr. Thomas Midgley of the Ethyl Corp. as president-elect. National meetings in Detroit and Pittsburgh showed attendances of 3,719 and 3,537 with 327 and 365 papers, respectively. The 102 local sections were more active than ever. The awards of the society: Kenneth Sanborn Pitzer, American Chemical society award in pure chemistry (sponsored by Alpha Chi Sigma fraternity); Herbert E. Carter, Eli Lilly and Co. award; Earle O. Whittier, Borden award; no award, A.C.S. Women's award (Garvan medal); Charles Glenn King, Pittsburgh award; John Frank Schairer, Hillebrand award; Carl S. Marvel, Nichols medal; Raymond R. Ridgway, Schoellkopf medal; Conrad Arnold Elvehjem, Willard Gibbs medal. Membership passed 36,000.   (C. L. PS.)

American College of Surgeons.

The college was founded in 1913 by 500 surgeons of the United States and Canada, under the leadership of Dr. Franklin H. Martin, to elevate the standards of surgery and to stimulate high professional and ethical ideals. The fellowship for 1944 numbered approximately 14,000; 605 were received into fellowship in 1943. Chairman, board of regents, Dr.

Irvin Abell, Louisville, Kentucky; president in 1941 until the succeeding presidential meeting (the 1942 and 1943 clinical congresses and inaugural ceremonies were cancelled because of the war), Dr. W. Edward Gallie, Toronto, Ontario; president-elect, Dr. Irvin Abell, Louisville, Kentucky; treasurer, Dr. Dallas B. Phemister, Chicago, Illinois; secretary, Dr. Frederick A. Besley, Waukegan, Illinois; associate director and chairman, administrative board, Dr. Malcolm T. MacEachern, Chicago, Illinois; associate director, Dr. Bowman C. Crowell, Chicago, Illinois; assistant director, Dr. E. W. Williamson, Chicago, Illinois. The organization originated hospital standardization, 1918, formulating minimum standards for approval and starting periodic surveys; 3,253 hospitals in United States, Canada, and other countries were on the 1943 approved list; 392 cancer clinics in hospitals and 1,101 medical services in industry were approved in 1943. Hospitals approved for graduate training in surgery and surgical specialties in 1943 numbered 222. An approved list of medical motion picture films is issued yearly. The college maintains a medical library and literary research department. Committees on cancer, archives of cancer, fractures and other traumas, and the Hall of the Art and Science of Surgery function through a department of clinical research. War sessions were held in 1943 in 20 cities throughout the United States, with a combined attendance of nearly 14,000 physicians, medical students, and hospital executives. A similar series of War sessions was planned for March and April 1944, in 22 cities in the United States and Canada.

(M. T. M.)

American Dental Association.

The American Dental association, founded in 1859 at Niagara Falls, N.Y. is the second national dental association to be formed in the United States, the first being the American Society of Dental Surgeons, established in 1840 and disbanded in 1856. The Civil War split the American Dental association's membership, and in 1869 the Southern Dental association was organized. In 1897 the two organizations merged to form the National Dental association, which in 1922 adopted the original title, The American Dental association.

The American Dental association is composed of 58 state and territorial societies which in turn are formed of approximately 440 component societies organized in cities, counties and districts. The 58,000 members, through their state and local societies, annually elect their delegates, about 280, who in turn elect the association's president, three vice-presidents, secretary, treasurer and 13 trustees.

The association endeavours to cultivate and promote the art and science of dentistry, to direct and encourage dental research, to improve dental education, to disseminate knowledge of dentistry, and to enlighten and direct public opinion in relation to oral hygiene and the care of the oral cavity.

In 1942 the association voted to discontinue its annual conventions for the duration of the war, therefore, the 1943 meeting held in Cincinnati, Ohio, Oct. 11–13, was devoted exclusively to association business affairs.

The officers elected for the year 1944 were: president, Captain C. Raymond Wells; president-elect, Dr. Walter H. Scherer; first vice-president, Dr. Holly C. Jarvis; second vice-president, Dr. H. B. Higgins; third vice-president, Dr. F. A. Pierson; secretary, Dr. Harry B. Pinney; treasurer, Dr. Roscoe H. Volland.

(L. W. M.)

American Economic Association.

This nation-wide professional organization of economists was founded in 1885 to encourage economic research and stimulate thought and discussion of economic problems. It was composed in 1943 of 3,786 members and 1,275 library, corporate and other subscribers. Publications consisted of a quarterly journal, the *American Economic Review*, the *Papers and Proceedings* of the annual meetings, occasional monographs on special subjects, a *Directory* of its members and an information booklet.

The 56th annual meeting scheduled to be held in Washington, D.C., Jan. 20–23, 1944, was not to be considered a national meeting, though held jointly with the American Political Science association and the American Society for Public Administration, since only members in that vicinity and outside participants were expected to attend.

Officers for the year 1944: president, Joseph Stancliffe Davis, Stanford university; vice-presidents, Edward Hastings Chamberlin, Harvard university; Charles Oscar Hardy, Federal Reserve bank, Kansas City, Mo.; elected members of the executive committee, William L. Crum, Harvard university; Leonard L. Watkins, University of Michigan; Corwin D. Edwards, Washington, D.C.; Carl S. Shoup, Columbia university; Frank Whitson Fetter, Haverford college; Theodore W. Schultz, University of Chicago; secretary-treasurer and editor of *Proceedings*, James Washington Bell, Northwestern university; managing editor of the *American Economic Review*, Paul T. Homan, Cornell university.

(J. W. Bl.)

American Federation of Labor.

The American Federation of Labor reached the highest numerical point in its history in 1943 with a paid-up membership of 6,564,141 on Aug. 31. During 1943 the activities of the federation were directed principally toward extension of organization and in furthering the war effort of the country. The success of the organizing work was reflected in the gain in membership, and the report of the federation for the year which ended Aug. 31, 1943, focused attention on the dual purpose of the federation to maintain and extend uninterrupted war production and to plan for the postwar period, which would directly concern the welfare of the wage earners who would be faced with the necessity for a return to peacetime levels of production.

In planning for the postwar period the federation also continued its contacts in the international labour field wherever possible so that the workers of all nations might be protected in the peace negotiations.

In the administration of the war effort federation representatives served on various government boards and agencies charted with policy making and administration, such as the Combined War Labor board, National War Labor board, Manpower board, War Production board, Price Control and Rationing boards, the President's Committee on Fair Employment Practices, etc.

One of the principal responsibilities of the national federation was in the legislative field, not only to secure the enactment of desirable measures but also to guard against legislation which would react against the best interests of the wage earners. Special energy was directed to secure the repeal of anti-labour measures enacted and to prevent a spread of anti-strike and other labour-restricting legislation in both the national and state legislatures. (*See* also Congress of Industrial Organizations; Labour Unions; Strikes and Lock-outs; United States.)

(W. G.)

American Geographical Society.

During 1943 a large part of the work of the research and cartographic staffs of the American Geographical society was devoted to special projects of various agencies of the federal government in connection with the prosecution of the war and preparations for postwar planning.

At the request of instructors in the special training courses for members of the armed forces, the society issued two volumes of reprints of articles originally published in the *Geographical Review* under the titles of "Readings in the Geography of France, Germany, Flanders and the Netherlands" and "Readings in the Geography of the Mediterranean Area" and also republished a volume by its director, Dr. John Kirtland Wright, entitled "The Geographical Basis of European History," originally published in 1928 by Henry Holt and company.

At the suggestion of the commission on cartography of the Pan American Institute of Geography and History, the society sponsored and issued invitations to a consultation on geodetic surveying, aeronautical charts and topographic maps held in Washington and New York Sept. 29 to Oct. 14 and attended by representatives of the official mapping agencies of the governments of the South American republics, Mexico and Canada.

The society awarded two of its gold medals in 1943—the Cullum Geographical medal to Arthur R. Hinks, for 30 years secretary of the Royal Geographical society of London, and the Charles P. Daly medal to Sir Halford J. Mackinder, noted British political geographer. Dr. Christovam Leite de Castro, secretary-general of the National Council of Geography of Brazil, and Señor Manuel Medina, chief of the office of geography of the Mexican government, were elected honorary corresponding members.

The society's annual book publication was *Mirror for Americans: Likeness of the Eastern Seaboard, 1810,* by Professor Ralph H. Brown of the University of Minnesota—a portrait of the eastern seaboard of the United States a century and a quarter ago based on an exhaustive study of contemporary materials and written in the style of the period as from the hand of an imaginary contemporary geographer. In addition there was published a study of the geography, strategic position, resources, trade, etc. of Japan at the outbreak of the war by Professor Guy-Harold Smith of Ohio State university and Dr. Dorothy Good of the society's staff under the title *Japan: A Geographical View.*

In the *Geographical Review,* the society's quarterly journal, special attention was given to articles, book reviews, and notes on areas and topics of interest in connection with the war. Publication was continued of *Current Geographical Publications*—a classified list of books, articles, maps and photographs of geographical interest selected monthly for inclusion in the society's research catalogue and photograph index. (R. R. P.)

American Indians: *see* INDIANS, AMERICAN.

American Iron and Steel Institute.
Most of the activities of the American Iron and Steel institute during 1943 continued to relate directly or indirectly to the steel industry's contributions to the U.S. war effort. Through its committees formed of executives, operating men and technicians of companies in the steel industry, it served as a ready and efficient liaison between war agencies and steel producers. Another long-established institute activity, the collection and compilation of iron and steel statistics, likewise proved valuable to war agencies.

Among the most significant activities during 1943 were the accomplishments of certain committees in connection with the further development of alloy steels for war uses, and the preparation and publication of a manual of packaging and loading standards for overseas shipment of steel products. Publication of the packaging manual culminated three years of intensive research into the problem of delivering steel mill products overseas in first-class condition under even the most severe conditions of wartime transportation. (W. S. To.)

American Law Institute.
Since its organization in Feb. 1923, the chief work of the American Law Institute has been a *Restatement of the Law,* best described as an orderly statement of the common law. While the sections into which the restatement is divided are written in statutory form, they are not presented to legislatures for adoption. The object of the restatement is to clarify and simplify the common law, but not to prevent its continued development by judicial decision. Prior to 1942, 16 volumes of the restatement were published, including the law of contracts, conflict of laws, agency, trusts, restitution, torts and security, besides large portions of the law of property.

During 1943 work on the fourth and fifth volumes of the restatement of the law of property went forward, as also did work on the sales division of the Code of Commercial Law, and on an international bill (declaration) of rights to further education on postwar problems and for possible use in the postwar settlement.

Aside from the official members—those holding the leading judicial, bar and law school faculty positions—there were in 1943, 825 life members, membership being a distinct professional honour. The governing body is a council of 33. The members meet each year in Washington, D.C. All legal and other official publications of the institute must be first approved by the council and by a meeting of members. The president in 1943 was George Wharton Pepper; William Draper Lewis was director and chief of the editorial staff. The executive office was in 1943 at 3400 Chestnut st., Philadelphia, Pa. (W. D. L.)

American Legion.
An organization of American veterans of both World Wars I and II. It was originally chartered as a World War I veterans' organization by congress in 1919. It became a two-war organization Oct. 29, 1942, when President Roosevelt signed Public Act 767, making honourably discharged veterans of World War II eligible for membership.

The accomplishments of the American Legion in 1943 included: (1) launching of a vigorous fight on behalf of disabled veterans of World War II, particularly battle casualties, to eliminate the delays ranging from 3 to 11 months in the settlements of their rightful claims for government compensation following their discharges from hospitals; (2) giving leadership by national convention action to public opinion that American postwar foreign policy must be one of participation in the establishment and maintenance of an association of free and sovereign nations, implemented by whatever force may be necessary to maintain world peace and prevent a recurrence of war; (3) creation of an American Legion postwar planning commission; (4) authorization and setting up of the machinery for raising an Americanism endowment fund of $10,000,000 or more by public subscription, to aid in the preservation of the American way of life; (5) setting up a comprehensive program of services to the members of the armed forces and their families, financed by an appropriation of $250,000.

Other 1943 achievements were: (1) designation of the major legislative program for 1944 to be universal service in time of war, adoption of a permanent policy of universal military training, postwar planning, and adequate protection of disabled veterans of World Wars I and II and their dependents; (2) taking a firm stand that all governmental functions concerning or affecting war veterans of the United States be unified and placed under the exclusive control of the Veterans' administration, and that all legislation relating to war veterans should be considered by single committees in the house of representatives and the senate; (3) launching by official government request of a nationwide "America Alert" program to impress upon all citizens that the end of

WARREN H. ATHERTON, elected president of the American Legion Sept. 23, 1943

the war is not in sight, that the signal for the relaxation of the war effort on the home front must come from the battlefronts, and that the necessity of protection through civilian defense is continuous until the end of the war; (4) maintenance despite war conditions of youth-training programs such as junior baseball, Boys' States, national high school oratorical contest, and others, to build character for future good citizenship; (5) launching of a program of visual parent education in the wartime care of children to combat the spread of juvenile delinquency; (6) selling hundreds of millions of war bonds and stamps through Legion drives; (7) distribution to members of the armed forces abroad of more than a million decks of playing cards collected by the Legion's fun and honour society, the Forty and Eight; (8) furnishing approximately 18,000 sets of new records, 48 records to the set, to members of the armed forces abroad for their entertainment, as the result of shellac made available through hundreds of thousands of old phonograph records collected over the nation; (9) drafting an orderly program of demobilization with recommendations for muster out pay, vocational training, and placing of honourably discharged veterans into jobs without unnecessary delays; (10) continuation of its normal child welfare, rehabilitation, Americanism and community service activities.

All membership records of the American Legion again were broken during 1943. On Dec. 31, 1943, a new all-time high enrolment of 1,172,971 members was reached. At the same time the number of posts rose to a new high of 11,941. The American Legion auxiliary showed a membership of 534,630 in 9,375 units. The Sons of The American Legion closed the year with an enrolment of 37,267 in 3,488 squadrons. The Forty and Eight membership rolled to a new high of 48,971 in 717 voitures. The Eight and Forty also broke all former records with a membership of 8,300 in 300 salons.

At the annual national convention in Omaha, Neb., Warren H. Atherton, Stockton, Cal., attorney, was elected national commander.   (W. H. An.)

American Library Association.
Established in 1876, the A.L.A. is the official organization in the United States and Canada of librarians and others interested in the educational, social and cultural responsibilities of libraries. It is affiliated with more than 50 other library associations in the United States and other countries and works closely with many organizations concerned with education, recreation, research and public service. Its activities were carried on in 1943 by a headquarters staff of 76 persons and by more than 80 committees and boards of over 600 volunteer workers, all interested in various aspects or types of library service. Its program includes information and advisory services, personnel service, field work, annual and midwinter conferences, and the non-profit publication of numerous professional books and pamphlets. It publishes also the following periodicals: *A.L.A. Bulletin, Booklist, College and Research Libraries, Hospital Book Guide, Subscription Books Bulletin* and *Journal of Documentary Reproduction,* the latter discontinued for the duration of World War II. Althea H. Warren, Public library, Los Angeles, Calif., was president, 1943–44. The headquarters are located at 520 North Michigan avenue, Chicago, Illinois, with a newly established International Relations office in the Library of Congress annex, Washington, D.C., made possible through a Rockefeller foundation grant.

The association's income in 1942–43 (excluding cash balance of $88,000 on Sept. 1, 1942) was $639,500. Income from membership dues, conference, sale of publications, advertising, subscriptions, etc. was about $170,000; $391,000 came from outside sources in the form of grants for special purposes, and $78,500 was endowment income. The association's endowment was approximately $2,111,900.

Because of the war, the usual conferences were not held in 1943, but a National Institute on war and postwar problems and issues was conducted in Chicago, Jan. 30–31, 1943, followed during the year by 18 regional and numerous local institutes throughout the country. The annual Newbery medal was presented to Elizabeth Janet Gray for her children's story, *Adam of the Road,* and the annual Caldecott medal to Virginia Lee Burton for her picture book, *The Little House.* The annual trustee citations of merit were presented to Mrs. George H. Tomlinson, trustee of the Evanston (Ill.) Public library and Ora L. Wildermuth, trustee of the Gary (Ind.) Public library.

A "Conference in Print" was planned for early 1944, with librarians and others offering suggestions and conducting discussions in the *A.L.A. Bulletin* on the theme "Preparing for Postwar Library Service."

Among the studies and projects under A.L.A. supervision for 1943–44 were: a survey of resources of the principal libraries in the Kansas City area, preparatory to the establishment of a new library; a survey of the U.S. Army Medical library under a grant from the Rockefeller foundation; the preparation of an extensive guide to comparative literature and understanding in co-operation with the American Association of Colleges and the National Council of Teachers of English; a study of war activities of college and research libraries to augment 1942's similar survey of public libraries; the publication of a report "Government Publishing in Wartime," following a complete study of the subject, which was submitted to the office of war information as a program for action; reviewing of the problems of priorities, manpower and related subjects in co-operation with the Library Service Division of the Office of Education; and the publication of three volumes on *Classification and Pay Plans for Libraries in Institutions of Higher Education* following the study in 1942 on pay plans for public libraries.

A.L.A. also sponsored or assisted with the following war and postwar activities: the Victory Book campaign through which some 17,000,000 books were collected in two years; the publication of book lists, studies, plans and surveys on war related subjects, including *Post-War Standards for Public Libraries,* to serve as the basis for postwar library planning in this field as would similar plans in process for school, college and university libraries; and the *Library War Guide,* issued monthly by OWI and describing ways in which libraries could further the government war program.

With recommendations from A.L.A., OWI established United States reference libraries in London, England; Sydney and Melbourne, Australia; Wellington, New Zealand; Johannesburg, Union of South Africa; and Bombay, India. These libraries were designed to serve writers, the press, radio, U.S. missions, local government agencies, educational, scientific and cultural institutions and organizations.

Among the A.L.A.'s international activities are the direction of the American libraries in Mexico City, Managua, and Montevideo; the administration of a grant of $150,000 for the purchase of books by U.S. authors to be sent to Latin American libraries; the collection of some $160,000 worth of scholarly American periodicals to assist in replenishing libraries in foreign countries following the war; plans, surveys and studies regarding international postwar co-operation among libraries; the sponsorship of British Book Week, Oct. 24 to 30, 1943, as a reciprocal gesture to British libraries, which had purchased $100,000 worth of U.S. books to interpret the United States to the British people; the maintenance of close co-operation between the Library Association of Great Britain and other foreign libraries; and the assistance given to various libraries of Latin America, particularly the National library of Peru, which was destroyed by fire on May 10, 1943.   (M. O. P.)

American Literature.
The new books of 1943 in the U.S. revealed the strong development of several tendencies that either had been marked or foreshadowed in the preceding year. Of immediate interest to the reader was the great increase of books dealing with the war and written both by correspondents and men in the armed services. They showed that the time between the planning, writing and publication of a book had been materially reduced, that the authors were free to write anything that did not injure military plans and that World War II was being reported more fully than any war in history. The illustrations were copious and took full advantage of the strides in photography. Next in importance came discussion of American policy and books in this category, especially Wendell Willkie's *One World* and Walter Lippmann's *U. S. Foreign Policy,* attained larger circulation than any one war book. Allied with this was the growth of sympathetic interpretation of Russian affairs, in which Mr. Willkie's book was an influence. Then came the rise in the number of technical manuals and popular discussions of mechanical subjects, especially those devoted to constructing and flying aeroplanes. Finally the acceleration of a new religious and spiritual interest was marked. At the end of the year it appeared that the flood of new technical works had passed its peak and that they would suffice, except for necessary revisions, for the needs of students and industry. The Russian trend, however, pointed to an increase in books on this subject and the events of the war and discussions of postwar plans were bound to keep the number of books on these subjects unusually high, though publishers, hard-pressed for white paper, were inclined to adopt a more selective attitude toward the end of the year.

The War.—Never before has news of fighting been brought so fully and so quickly to the civilians back home. War correspondents led in this with *Battle for the Solomons* by Ira Wolfert; *Guadalcanal Diary* by Richard Tregaskis; *Retreat with Stilwell* by Jack Belden; *Southwest Passage* by John Lardner; *Grim Reapers* by Stanley Johnston; *Singapore Is Silent* by George Weller. The experiences of soldiers in Africa were reported sympathetically by Ernie Pyle in *Here Is Your War,* while Ralph Ingersoll described the observations of a captain of engineers in *The Battle Is the Pay-Off.* How Americans defended their posts was the subject of *Last Man Off Wake Island* by W. L. J. Bayler and Cecil Carnes, and Col. Robert L. Scott, Jr., wrote the best book of aviation experiences in *God Is My Co-Pilot.* The rescue of the party led by Capt. Eddie Rickenbacker was fully described in two books, including Rickenbacker's own *Seven Came Through.* Lieut. Juanita Redmond wrote *I Served on Bataan* and Carlos P. Romulo, Manila newspaper owner and Pulitzer prize winner for reporting, told his dramatic story in *I Saw the Fall of the Philippines.* Other books gave personal experiences with the Japanese, including *Tokyo Record* by Otto D. Tolischus; *Exchange Ship* by Max Hill; *My War with Japan* by Carroll Alcott; *Hong Kong Story* by Gwen Dew and *Shanghai Lawyer* by N. F. Allman. An account of the preparations for bombing Tokyo and the flight from the "Hornet" was the subject of Capt. Ted W. Lawson's *Thirty Seconds Over Tokyo.* Walter Simmons recorded the personal story of *Joe Foss, Flying Marine.* The Aleutian campaign was represented in *Bridge to Victory* by Howard Handleman, while Robert Carse described the merchant marine in *Lifeline.* A man of peace, Archbishop Francis J. Spellman of New York, journeyed through the lines and told the story of his trip to Africa, Rome, Spain, etc., in *Action This Day.* And when Lieut. John Mason Brown, U.S.N.R., published *To All Hands,* the public could read the talks broadcast on board ship during the Sicilian adventure.

In many instances books of observation and experience also promoted points of view and practically every correspondent who expressed himself on the subject favoured international co-operation after the war. Among the best eye-witness accounts of Russia in wartime was *Moscow Dateline* by Henry C. Cassidy. Russia was an important subject in Wendell Willkie's *One World* and Eve Curie's *Journey Among Warriors,* while personal experiences formed the basis of *Round Trip to Russia* by Walter Graebner, *Twelve Months That Changed the World* by Larry Lesueur and *Dynamite Cargo: Convoy to Russia* by Fred Herman. Maurice Hindus added another sympathetic book about the Russian people in *Mother Russia.* Analytical books also had their place: Albert Rhys Williams published *The Russians: the Land, the People and Why They Fight;* William Henry Chamberlain, author of a conservative study of soviet Russia wrote *The Russian Enigma;* David J. Dallin, one-time member of the revolutionary government added *Russia and Postwar Europe* to his earlier study of soviet foreign policy. Repercussions of communist policies in the United States were discussed in *America, Russia and the Communist Party in the Postwar World* by John L. Childs, George S. Counts and other critics of communism. *Ancient Russia* by George Vernadsky was the first volume in a series of histories; a translation was also published of Paul Miliukov's *Outline of Russian Culture.* Collections of contemporary and classical Russian literature were edited by Mark Van Doren, Ivar Spector, John Cournos and Bernard Guilbert Guerney, and new editions of works by Tolstoy and Dostoievski were published in the United States.

An argument for international co-operation was presented by John T. Whitaker in *We Cannot Escape History.* Thomas J. Hamilton criticized American policies toward Spain in *Appeasement's Child: the Franco Regime in Spain.* With American correspondents withdrawn from Germany, the eye-witness accounts of life there decreased, but books reflected information received from underground sources in the occupied countries, of which one of the most remarkable was Etta Shiber's account of how she helped rescue nearly 200 British soldiers from the nazis in *Paris Underground*. Other authors were busy discussing nazi methods and postwar attitudes toward Germany. Frank Munk exposed totalitarian economic methods in *The Legacy of Nazism*. Heinz Pol explained the German threat to postwar peace in *The Hidden Enemy*. Helmut Kuhn, another refugee teaching in the United States, wrote *Freedom Forgotten and Remembered*. A searching study of propaganda was made in *The Goebbels Experiment* by Derrick Sington and Arthur Weidenfeld. Bernadotte E. Schmitt asked pointedly: *What Shall We Do With Germany?* Adolf Sturmthal showed the menace of totalitarian methods in *The Tragedy of European Labor, 1918-1939*. The nazi treatment of a peaceful people was described in *Juggernaut Over Holland* by its foreign minister, Eelco N. van Kleffens. In addition to these and many similar studies one publisher sponsored *Hitler's Speeches*, a complete translation, edited by Norman Baynes with a foreword by Lord Astor.

Louis Adamic precipitated a bitter controversy among Yugoslavs by supporting Tito and his partisans in *My Native Land*. Betty Wason gave an excellent account of Greece in *Miracle in Hellas*, while Agnes Smedley in *Battle Hymn of China*, gave a remarkable first-hand account of the endurance and suffering of the Chinese soldier.

An earnest attitude toward American problems, foreign and domestic, distinguished both writers and readers. That publishers were not always aware of the eagerness of the public was proved by the delay attending the publication of *Under Cover: My Four Years in the Nazi Underworld of America* by John Roy Carlson (pseud.). A number of publishers refused to print the book because they thought the subject-matter had been fully reported in the newspapers, yet when issued the book sold half a million copies in a few months and continued selling in large editions well into 1944. But only a few readers heard about *Alien Enemies and Alien Friends in the United States*, by Ernst W. Puttkammer. Henry A. Wallace, vice-president, elaborated his theory of postwar plans in *The Century of the Common Man* and two separate publications were made of *The World of the Four Freedoms* by Sumner Welles, one with an introduction by Nicholas Murray Butler. One of the most persistent publicists for a postwar plan was the card expert, Ely Culbertson, who presented his ideas in *Total Peace*. Carl Sandburg's running comment on American affairs appeared as *Home Front Memo*. Among many books attention was given *The Postwar Plans of the United Nations* by Lewis L. Lorwin; *The Peace We Fight For* by Hiram Motherwell; *Make This the Last War* by Michael Straight; *Preview of History* by Raymond Gram Swing; *The Road to Peace and Freedom* by Irving Brant and *Building for Peace at Home and Abroad* by Maxwell S. Stewart. American political and social ideas and ideals found a brilliant exposition in a Socratic dialogue by Charles A. Beard called *The Republic: Conversations on Fundamentals*. Gustavus Myers, who pioneered years ago with his *History of the Great American Fortunes*, did not live to see the publication of his *History of Bigotry in the United States*.

Contemporary America was closely examined in numbers of books. *The Tennessee Valley Authority* by C. Herman Pritchett, *Radio Networks and the Federal Government* by Thomas Porter Robinson, *The Economic Control of the Motion Picture Industry* by Mae D. Huettig and *The Impact of Federal Taxes* by Roswell Magill discussed four important subjects of the day. A ripple of interest followed publication of an argument for primitive treatment of the soil in *Plowman's Folly* by Edward H. Faulkner. William R. Van Dersel issued *The American Land, Its History*

and Its Uses. Industrialists eager for a return to uncontrolled competition found something to worry about in *Business as a System of Power* by Robert A. Brady, with a foreword by Robert S. Lynd, a consideration of the totalitarian menace hidden in big business enterprises. How the newspapers served the nation in wartime was described by many writers in *Journalism in Wartime*, edited by Frank Luther Mott. *American Society in Wartime* was similarly edited by William F. Ogburn.

With so much concentration on modern problems history seemed to mark time and few books attained prominence, although publishing records show that 465 new titles of historical works were registered for copyright. Many, however, were in the textbook field. Biography is the major element in *Lee's Lieutenants: A Study in Command* by Douglas Southall Freeman, but the personalities and events are so intertwined that it was also the best work of the year in American history. Mr. Freeman completed the second volume: *Cedar Mountain to Chancellorsville*. Carl Van Doren's *Mutiny in January* described a Revolutionary episode from documents made available for the first time. Bernard de Voto described many dramatic episodes in *The Year of Decision: 1846*. History, biography and autobiography were happily combined by Vincent Sheean in *Between the Thunder and the Sun*. *Lincoln and the Patronage* by Harry J. Carman and Reinhard H. Luthin explored a political phase of Lincoln's career, and *Swedish Immigrants in Lincoln's Time* by Nels Hokanson showed where Lincoln obtained some of his support. *The Third Term Tradition; Its Rise and Fall* by Charles W. Stein closed a long debate. American mercantile history was represented by *A History of Macy's of New York, 1858-1919* by Ralph Merle Hower and aviation by *The First Century of Flight in America* by Jeremiah Milbank, Jr.

Biography and Autobiography.—Books in this category seemed to attain a higher level of writing than fiction. Books with a special meaning for intellectuals included *Connecticut Yankee* by Wilbur Lucius Cross, Yale educator and three times governor, who traced the changing educational and social life of New England. There were also *A Threshold in the Sun* by Lloyd Morris, filled with literary memories and modern points of view; *The World of Yesterday*, a brilliant analysis of the cultural twilight of Austria, completed just before despair drove the author, Stefan Zweig, out of this world. John Erskine's *The Complete Life* might be termed cultural guidance based on personal experiences. Albert J. Nock, a writer with strong classical convictions, called his unenthusiastic commentary on contemporary affairs *The Memoirs of a Superfluous Man*, while Harold L. Ickes, secretary of the interior, wryly called his memoirs of political controversy *The Autobiography of a Curmudgeon*. Ferris Greenslet, a Boston publisher, wrote more cheerfully about books, authors and fishing in *Under the Bridge*, while Albert Spalding, violinist, recalled the brilliant musical life of Europe in prewar days in *Rise to Follow*. The appearance of Sir Thomas Beecham as conductor of opera and orchestras lent interest to his own story, *A Mingled Chime*. Education and affairs were described by Henry Johnson in *The Other Side of Main Street; a History Teacher from Sauk Center* and Stephen Duggan's *A Professor at Large*. Social history was recorded in *Exploring the Dangerous Trades* by Alice Hamilton. Industry had its say in Tom Girdler's *Boot Straps*, in which he stoutly defended his policy of opposition to certain labour unions before the war. From far-off Asia a graduate of Johns Hopkins, Gordon S. Seagrave, now lieut. colonel of the United States medical corps, described his work under primitive conditions in *Burma Surgeon*, adding a chapter on his experiences in the Stilwell campaign. A Chicago man, Max Thorek, described his career in *A Surgeon's World*. One of the few autobiographical books with a touch of

THE BATTLE OF GUADALCANAL WON, U.S. marines lined the island's beaches in Feb. 1943 to board barges carrying them to troopships. A detailed story of the battle was the subject of Richard Tregaskis' *Guadalcanal Diary*, an outstanding U.S. war book of 1943

wit was H. L. Mencken's *Heathen Days*. An exciting life in many fields was revealed by C. Kay-Scott in *Life Is Too Short;* Lee Simonson described his career of designing for the theatre in *Part of a Lifetime;* Edward R. Hewitt, son of Abram S. Hewitt and himself an inventor of prominence, recalled New York experiences in *Those Were the Days*, while Roy Chapman Andrews recalled the happy experiences of a naturalist in *Under a Lucky Star*.

In biography half a dozen books dealt with phases of the life and writings of Thomas Jefferson, prompted by the 200th anniversary of his birth, which fell on April 13, 1943. None, however, was a work of lasting value. Saul K. Padover, who had published a biography of Jefferson in 1942, issued *The Complete Jefferson*, but despite its usefulness for reference purposes it was not complete. *The Philosophy of Jefferson*, by Adrienne Koch, won the Woodbridge prize in philosophy at Columbia university. Work of varying quality included *Jefferson: the Road to Glory* by Marie Kimball; *Thomas Jefferson* by Hendrik Van Loon, with his characteristic drawings; *Jefferson Himself* edited by Bernard Mayo, and *Thomas Jefferson, Then and Now*, a "national symposium" edited by James Waterman Wise. Princeton university and the New York *Times* announced that they would sponsor a project to publish the writings and letters of Jefferson in many volumes, with the co-operation of a committee of historians and representatives of learned societies.

Original work in biography was done by Rackham Holt in *George Washington Carver*, a sensitive study of the Tuskegee scientist. *Walt Whitman, an American* by Henry Seidel Canby, was a rational interpretation of the man and his poems and in effect also a study in criticism; the author contended that theories of an abnormal sex life remained unproved. In *Pioneer to the Past* Charles Breasted described the career of his father, James Henry Breasted, the archaeologist. Henry Knox Sherrill, bishop of Massachusetts, wrote sympathetically of his predecessor in *William Lawrence: Later Years of a Happy Life*. A Confederate statesman received another biography in *Judah P. Benjamin* by Robert Douthat Meade. A man who contributed to American culture was remembered in *Charles T. Griffes: The Life of an American Composer* by Edward M. Maisel; Mortimer Smith wrote *The Life of Ole Bull*, and E. E. Reynolds published *Baden-Powell*. Isaac Don Levine wrote an authorized biography in *Mitchell:*

Pioneer of Air Power, and Helen Jones Campbell practically vindicated the accused in *The Case for Mrs. Suratt*. Of minor interest were *Henry Ford* by William A. Simonds; *Mark Twain, Man of Legend* by Delancey Ferguson and *Young Lady Randolph* by Rene Kraus. Both biography and history were served in *The Wright Brothers* by Fred C. Kelly, in which he argued the case of priority in aeroplane invention for the Wrights. A man of the early republic was recalled in *Benjamin Tallmadge* by Charles Swain Hall. Raymond B. Nixon described a famous orator in *Henry W. Grady, Spokesman of the New South,* and Arthur Upham Pope praised a contemporary diplomat in *Maxim Litvinoff*.

Criticism, Belles Lettres and Scholarly Studies.—Few books of criticism were published in 1943, though many essays appeared in periodicals. Ellen Glasgow interpreted her ideals in writing in *A Certain Measure*, originally published as prefaces to her novels. Lionel Trilling's *E. M. Forster* and Edward Wagenknecht's *Cavalcade of the English Novel* were scholarly works. Alden Brooks in *Shaksper and the Dyer's Hand* presented the Elizabethan poet Dyer as his candidate for the authorship of Shakespeare's plays. More conservative was the approach of W. W. Greg in *The Editorial Problem in Shakespeare; a Survey of the Foundations of the Text* and Oscar James Campbell in *Shakespeare's Satire*. Edmund Wilson wrote a critical introduction for an anthology, *The Shock of Recognition;* and Max Lerner edited a collection called *The Mind and Faith of Justice Holmes*.

Romanticism and the Modern Ego by Jacques Barzun was a work of original thinking and forceful writing. Also an original contribution was *The World of Sholom Aleichem* by Maurice Samuel. Other scholarly publications included *Free Minds: John Morley and His Friends* by Frances Wentworth Knickerbocker; *Francis Bacon on Communication and Rhetoric* by Karl R. Wallace; *This Is Lorence*, an interpretation of Laurence Sterne by Lodwick Hartley; *The Great Age of Greek Literature* by Edith Hamilton. Critical analysis and interpretation of American phenomena were contained in *American Heroes and Hero Worship* by Gerald W. Johnson; *The Hero in History, a Study in Limitation and Possibility* by Sidney Hook; *Love in America* by David L. Cohn. Reinhold Niebuhr published the second volume of his *The Nature and Destiny of Man: A Christian Interpretation* and Jacques Maritain, now residing in the United States, published *The Rights of Man and Natural Law*. James Burnham presented new points of view in *The Machiavellians: Defenders of Freedom*. Unique in its field was Pál Kelemen's *Medieval American Art*, a two-volume survey of aboriginal culture, with many illustrations, which had been ten years in the making. The attention given Mark Van Doren's argument for a stronger classical basis of education in *Liberal Education* demonstrated the growing interest of the public. A conservative argument was also advanced by Jacques Maritain in *Education at the Crossroads.* Akin to this was *Science and Criticism; the Humanistic Tradition in Continental Thought* by Herbert J. Muller. Werner Jaeger, now of the Harvard faculty, published the second and third volumes of *Paideia: The Ideals of Greek Culture.* A new Biblical study was published by Edgar J. Goodspeed: *The Goodspeed Parallel New Testament,* giving the King James version and the American translation. The war did not interfere with the publication of *The Oxford Book of German Prose,* from Luther to Rilke, edited by H. G. Fiedler. And while Henry Hitch Adams wrote *English Domestic or Homilectic Tragedy, 1575 to 1642,* Barrett H. Clark exhumed thrillers by Bartley Campbell, Boucicault and Belasco in *Favorite American Plays of the Nineteenth Century.* A modern interpretation of 19th century fiction was to be found in *The Psychiatric Novels of Oliver Wendell Holmes* by Clarence B. Oberndorf.

Poetry.—Stephen Vincent Benét was writing a book-length poem about the rise of the American spirit when he died and his incomplete work, published as *Western Star, a Fragment,* showed how important the book would have been. *This Is My Beloved,* a book of love poems by Walter Benton, attained some popularity. Louis Untermeyer published a selection of poems by Robert Frost, with comment, in *Come In.* *Genesis* by Delmore Schwartz was the contribution of a younger man. In *Twelve Spanish-American Poets* H. R. Hays turned to the southern continent, while A. J. M. Smith edited a critical anthology called *The Book of Canadian Poetry.* Kenneth Fearing published *Afternoon of a Pawnbroker and Other Poems.* A selection of poems by Edna St. Vincent Millay was published as *Collected Lyrics.* Oscar Williams edited *New Poems, 1943,* an anthology of British and American verse. The Yale Younger Poets award went to Lieut. William Meredith for *Love Letters from an Impossible Land.*

Fiction.—Interest in American life overshadowed all other themes, including the historical. Conditions among the lowly were prominent in several distinguished first novels. Betty Smith (Mrs. Joseph Jones) portrayed many episodes in the life of a growing girl in *A Tree Grows in Brooklyn,* incorporating many bits of metropolitan folklore; it is revealing to know that she was attracted to her theme by reading Thomas Wolfe on Brooklyn life. Bucklin Moon, in *The Darker Brother,* succeeded in maintaining a proper balance between sympathy and curiosity in telling how a young Negro in Harlem is affected by white barriers. Ira Wolfert, war correspondent and author of *The Battle of the Solomons,* showed his knowledge of city exploiters in *Tucker's People,* which won a favourable critical press but no large sales. A writing talent of promise stands revealed in *Heaven Is a Sunswept Hill,* a novel about the stamina of settlers in the flooded districts of the Mississippi river; a tragic note intruded because its author, Earl Guy, was serving a long prison term. Another new novelist of promise is Alexander Saxton, who wrote *Grand Crossing.* None of these books, however, caught the turmoil of the human heart in wartime as well as a novel by a refugee, *Arrival and Departure* by Arthur Koestler, which caused much American discussion despite its lack of clarity.

Older writers were also interested in American social conditions. These were implicit in Wallace Stegner's story of a misfit American, *The Big Rock Candy Mountain,* which showed this author digging deeper for his material but failing to make his characters memorable, and in Robert Penn Warren's novel about a southern community, *At Heaven's Gate,* in which the story was handicapped by a confusing technique. *Lilly Crackell* by Caroline

Slade was practically a well-authenticated document of the effect of slum beginnings on a girl. James T. Farrell added another novel to his Chicago series in *My Days of Anger* and Erskine Caldwell repeated his familiar manner in *Georgia Boy.* American careers furnished the backgrounds for two semi-autobiographical novels, *Never Call Retreat* by Joseph Freeman, and *Journey in the Dark* by Martin Flavin, which won the Harper prize in fiction. *A Time to Live* by Michael Blankfort traced the career of a young liberal who found it impossible to trim his thinking to political expediency. Louis Bromfield added *Mrs. Parkington* to his gallery of resourceful women. Sinclair Lewis, returning to his early manner of treating an American institution ironically through one of its representatives, wrote only a minor novel in *Gideon Planish,* the story of a money-raising publicist. Writers exiled from their homelands and now living in the United States produced several novels with European backgrounds; Lion Feuchtwanger ridiculed Hitler's soothsayer in *Double, Double, Toil and Trouble* without writing a novel comparable with his early work, and Mark Aldanov wrote *The Fifth Seal,* which, because of the implied criticism of soviet diplomacy in Paris, caused a nine-day's protest from interested partisans in the United States; the novel, however, did not warrant unusual attention. Admirers of William Saroyan's writings found *The Human Comedy* filled with their favourite characters and the romantic warmth and good feeling displayed by no other author. Booth Tarkington painted the portrait of a kind woman in *Kate Fennigate;* Robert Nathan gave a touch of mysticism to the story of a farmer soldier in *But Gently Day;* Mary O'Hara added *Thunderhead,* the story of a stallion, to her widely acclaimed story of a boy and a horse, *My Friend Flicka,* of 1941. Pearl S. Buck's *The Promise* was deeply critical of the conduct of the Burma campaign. John Dos Passos described a cheerful and corrupt politician in *Number One.* Jesse Stuart described Kentucky hill life with characteristic humour in *Taps for Private Tussie,* which won the Thomas Jefferson southern fiction award.

The major interest of novel readers was John P. Marquand's *So Little Time,* a novel about the attempts of a middle-aged man, a veteran of World War I and the father of a son eligible for World War II, to bring his life into focus with the changing life about him. It was widely approved by readers of the hero's generation, who saw in his difficulties many of their own. Entertainingly written, it did not, however, measure up to *The Late George Apley,* the prototype of this and similar Marquand novels.

When Sholem Asch wrote *The Apostle,* a novel based on the life of Paul of Tarsus, he added fuel to the growing interest in books about religious characters. His earlier novel, *The Nazarene,* was in steady demand throughout 1943. In *The Apostle* Asch followed the New Testament chronicles much more closely than in the former book. This produced argument in Yiddish literary circles of New York city and in the Yiddish-language press to which Mr. Asch contributes; in his zeal to bring about a closer understanding between Christianity and Judaism he did not have the full support of all believers. The Lloyd Douglas novel of 1942, *The Robe,* sold in large quantities in 1943, as did Franz Werfel's *The Song of Bernadette,* giving support to the theory that the spiritual hunger of the reading public was growing. The welcome given Dr. Harry Emerson Fosdick's *On Being a Real Person,* a discussion intended to give anchorage to the distracted individual, was also considered a straw in the wind. But the religious tendency is not always shown in stories about religious characters; it appears in the hope and faith expressed by laymen in articles and commentaries. It is marked in the writings of men dealing with the postwar world, in which faith in honesty, justice and the good intentions of a common humanity is a necessity.

(*See also* English Literature.)   (H. Ha.)

American Medical Association.

In 1943, the American Medical association had more than 125,000 members out of about 155,000 doctors practising medicine in the United States, and 185,000 licensed to practise. The annual meeting of the house of delegates, in 1943, was in Chicago. The general session of the association was cancelled, but the 1944 session was scheduled during June in Chicago. The association had a gross income of approximately $2,000,000 annually. It is incorporated not for profit. The headquarters office is at 535 North Dearborn st., Chicago, Ill.

The association publishes the *Journal of the American Medical Association*, with a circulation of 107,000 weekly; *Hygeia*, with a circulation of more than 125,000 monthly, and medical journals in most of the medical specialties. The association also publishes the *Quarterly Cumulative Index Medicus*, which indexes regularly the contents of 1,400 medical periodicals, and a directory of United States physicians.

The library of the American Medical association conducts a package library service which sends articles and reprints to physicians to aid them in keeping up-to-date in medicine. Particularly requested in 1943 were articles on the sulfonamide drugs, penicillin, vitamins, industrial diseases, anaesthesia and the war.

Much of the work of the American Medical association is carried on by councils, including the council on pharmacy and chemistry which deals with drugs prescribed by doctors; the council on physical therapy which deals with physical apparatus, including eye glasses, hearing aids and devices for artificial respiration; the council on foods and nutrition which deals particularly with foods for special diets and foods for which medical claims are made; the council on industrial health which investigates industrial health service, standardizes health organizations, and advises on health problems in industry; the council on medical education and hospitals which investigates and rates medical schools and hospitals; the judicial council, which investigates charges of unethical conduct against physicians and medical organizations. Newly established in 1943 was the council on medical service and public relations, designed to analyze prepayment plans for medical service, group medical service and federal legislation relating to the medical profession, and to promote distribution of medical service and educate the public regarding medical service.

The bureaus of the American Medical association include the bureau of health education, which conducts radio programs, circulates pamphlets on health subjects and answers thousands of questions from the public; the bureau of legal medicine and legislation, which deals with standards of proposed federal and state legislation in the field of health, and analyzes court decisions on medical subjects; the bureau of medical economics, which makes available data on the economics of medical practice, makes surveys dealing with the distribution of physicians and prepayment medical service plans; the bureau of investigation, which studies quacks and nostrums; the bureau of exhibits, which provides exhibits for state and county medical societies, and national medical associations and many public agencies; the bureau of public relations, which distributes information regarding medical advancement and medical service to newspapers, magazines and other sources of information throughout the nation.

The association participated actively in the war effort through its committee on war participation, through the publication of the periodical called *War Medicine,* through the committee on postwar planning for medical service, and through membership of its executives on many advisory bodies in Washington, including the War Manpower commission, the division of medical sciences of the National Research council, National Roster of Scientific and Specialized Personnel, and the medical departments of the army and navy. In the headquarters office of the association an office of the War Manpower commission was maintained, charged with aiding in the procurement and assignment of physicians for the army, the navy, the public health service, industrial medicine and the civilian population.   (M. Fi.)

American National Red Cross: *see* RED CROSS.
American Samoa: *see* SAMOA, AMERICAN.
American Volunteer Group (Flying Tigers): *see* CHENNAULT, CLAIRE L.

Ames, Joseph Sweetman

(1864–1943), U.S. physicist and educator, was born July 3 in Manchester, Vt. Identified with Johns Hopkins university from his student days in 1883 until his retirement as president in 1935, Dr. Ames was best known for his aeronautical research. He was chairman of the National Advisory Committee for Aeronautics, 1927–39. He developed many safety and efficiency devices for aircraft, and in 1935 received the Langley gold medal of the Smithsonian institution, and the Sylvanus Reed award from the Institute of Aeronautical Sciences. He died in Baltimore, Md., June 24. (See *Encyclopædia Britannica*.)

Anaemia.

In 1943 much attention was directed to erythroblastosis, haemolytic syndromes and shock in relation to haemorrhage. The Rh factor in blood received much study both as a transfusion hazard and in its role in the production of erythroblastosis foetalis.

The discovery of the relationship between Rh agglutinins and the production of erythroblastosis foetalis stimulated the study of this factor. Many new examples were reported, the majority of the cases showing Rh positive foetuses with Rh negative mothers who developed anti-Rh agglutinins. While the incidence of Rh negative individuals was reported as similar in England and in the United States, among the Chinese it was found to be 21 times less frequent, and erythroblastosis was rare among Chinese infants. Erythroblastosis was successfully treated with transfusions with Rh negative blood. The disease was found in one of twins. The excretion of bilirubin and urobilinogen and the cell measurements were reported as characterizing the anaemia as a haemolytic process.

The haemolytic reactions resulting from iso-immunization following repeated transfusions of homologous blood developed according to a mechanism similar to that affecting the erythroblastic foetus, and endangered the life of transfused, anaemic mothers.

The haemolytic anaemias received extensive study. Additional data were published on acute haemolytic anaemias in fertilizer workers (metallic poisoning), following cross-country runs, after sulfathiazole, sulfadiazine, sulfapyridine or sulfanilamide, in blackwater fever, and in a patient with auto-agglutination and hyperglobulinaemia.

A number of new studies of chronic haemolytic anaemia with paroxysmal nocturnal haemoglobinuria (Marchiafava-Micheli syndrome) were reported. There was no significant change in the pH of the blood during the day or night.

The survival time of normal erythrocytes injected into patients with familial haemolytic anaemia was normal, but red blood cells from an individual with acholuric jaundice were completely destroyed in 19 days.

Several factors on the relation of diet and haemolytic anaemia were noted. The anaemia produced by a *p*-aminoazobenzene was prevented by a high protein diet. Increased erythrocyte destruction followed diets rich in fat. Rats fed high fat diets developed profound anaemia after trinitrotoluene poisoning, but not those on a high protein or high carbohydrate regime.

The blood volume was found to be low in chronic anaemia.

Dimorphic anaemia, a combination of deficiency of iron with a nutritional macrocytic anaemia, was described in Uganda. The anaemia of scurvy was found to be caused by generalized depression of erythropoiesis rather than a failure of maturation from a specific lack of vitamin C.

In hiatal hernia, 70% of the individuals showed some degree of hypochromic anaemia of haemorrhage, occasionally, however, of the pernicious anaemia type.

Aplastic types of anaemia were described after aspirin, antisyphilitic, sulfathiazole treatment, and from unknown causes.

Pyridoxine deficient diets produced a microcytic hyperregenerative anaemia in swine, corrected by pyridoxine administration. Vitamin B_6, a constituent of liver extract, cured anaemia of certain types in chicks. An erythropoietic substance developed in the serum of rabbits rendered anaemic by bleeding.

Surveys showed that the incidence of nutritional iron deficiency anaemia varied greatly in different communities (children, 1.5 to 85.0%; adults, 3.6 to 30.0%; pregnant women, 9.0 to 72.0%).

Haemorrhagic shock was found to be similar to shock from other causes. After a single, severe, non-fatal haemorrhage, haemodilution, with fall in the red blood cell volume, was most marked during the first hour but continued for 72 hours. The rate of haemoglobin regeneration with iron therapy after blood donation was found to decline gradually with successive haemorrhages until the rate was no more rapid than without iron. Bleeding, in thrombocytopenic conditions, was controlled by the oral use of pectin.

The use of concentrated red blood cell suspensions for transfusion in anaemia came into general use. A rise of approximately one gram of haemoglobin per 100 cc. followed the infusion of each 300 cc. of erythrocyte suspension, and the risk of a reaction from transfused iso-agglutinins was minimized. Universal group O cells suspended in pooled plasma reduced the number of reactions. Heparinized plasma was found to be the safest and most effective blood substitute, reducing the mortality from haemorrhage from 84 to 6%. The return of erythrocytes in animals so treated was not necessary for their survival.

BIBLIOGRAPHY.—R. R. Race, G. L. Taylor, D. F. Cappell and M. N. McFarlane, "Rh Factor and Erythroblastosis Fetalis: Investigation of 50 Families," *British Med. J.*, 2:289–293 (1943); H. R. Brown Jr. and P. Levine, "Rh Factor and Its Importance in Transfusion for Anemias of Erythroblastosis and Other Causes," *J. Pediatrics*, 23:290–296 (1943); E. D. Hoare, "Occurrence of Rh Antigen in Population: Notes on 5 Cases of Erythroblastosis Fetalis," *British Med. J.*, 2:297–298 (1943); A. S. Wiener and I. B. Wexler, "Transfusion Therapy of Acute Hemolytic Anemia of Newborn," *Am. J. Clin. Path.*, 13:393–401 (1943); D. R. Gilligan, M. D. Altschule and E. M. Katersky, "Physiological Intravascular Hemolysis of Exercise. Hemoglobinemia and Hemoglobinuria Following Cross Country Runs," *J. Clin. Invest.*, 22:859–869 (1943); M. I. Smith, R. D. Lillie and E. F. Stohlman, "The Toxicity and Histopathology of Azo Compounds as Influenced by Dietary Protein," *Publ. Health Rep.*, 58:304–317 (1943); V. Johnson, J. Longini and L. W. F. Freeman, "Destruction of Red Blood Cells After Fat Ingestion," *Science*, 97:400 (1943); A. Loewy, L. W. Freeman, A. Marchello and V. Johnson, "Increased Erythrocyte Destruction on High Fat Diet," *Am. J. Physiol.*, 138:230–235 (1943); A. P. Barer and W. M. Fowler, "The Effect of Iron on the Hemoglobin Regeneration in Blood Donors," *Am. J. Med. Sc.*, 205:9–16 (1943); R. Isaacs, "Effect of Pectin on the Coagulation of Blood in Thrombocytopenic Conditions," *J.A.M.A.*, 121:1306 (1943); Robert S. Evans, "The Use of Concentrated Red Cells as a Substitute for Whole Blood in the Transfusion Therapy of Anemia," *J.A.M.A.*, 122:793–796 (1943); H. A. Alt, "Red Cell Transfusions in the Treatment of Anemia," *J.A.M.A.*, 122:417–419 (1943); C. K. Murray, D. E. Hale and C. M. Shaar, "The Preparation and Use of Red Blood Cell Suspensions in Treatment of Anemia," *J.A.M.A.*, 122:1065–1067 (1943); L. L. Blum, "The Present-Day Status of Combined Blood-Plasma Bank with Reference to the Use of Concentrated Red Cell Suspensions," *J. Indiana S.M.A.*, 36:187–193 (1943); J. Litwins, "Universal O Blood Transfusion: Combination of Pooled Plasma and O Cells," *J.A.M.A.*, 123:630 (1943); A. C. Ivy, H. Greengard, I. F. Stein Jr., F. S. Grodins and D. F. Dutton, "The Effect of Various Blood Substitutes in Resuscitation after an Otherwise Fatal Hemorrhage," *Surg. Gyn. and Obst.*, 76:85–90 (1943). (R. Is.)

Anaesthesia. The extensive use of intravenous anaesthesia, particularly with pentothal sodium, not only by civilian anaesthetists but by experienced anaesthetists of the medical corps of the army and navy, established that procedure on a firm basis and settled the controversy that was raised because of the unsatisfactory results of anaesthesia with pentothal sodium on casualties at Pearl Harbor. Pentothal may be used for persons in shock; the preliminary use of morphine and atropine reduces the dose of pentothal sodium necessary. Above all, the skill of the anaesthetist with pentothal sodium is the deciding factor in whether it should be used in cases of shock. Furthermore, the dose employed for patients in shock is small in contrast to that for a robust patient. The administration of 50% oxygen

U.S. MEDICAL OFFICER demonstrating how to administer spinal anaesthesia, at the Tilton General hospital in Fort Dix, N.J. The army medical corps instituted training programs for medical officers and enlisted men to make up for the shortage of anaesthetists in 1943

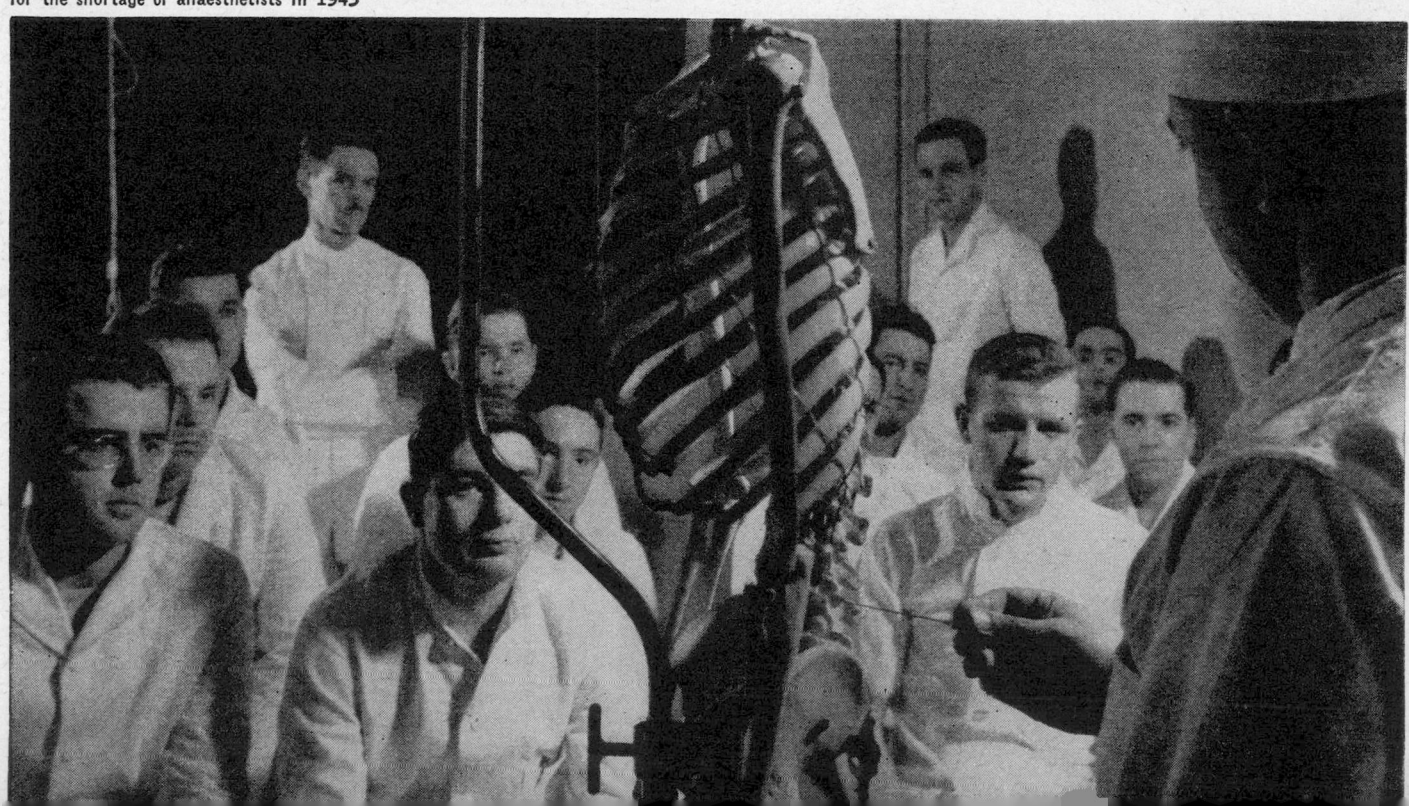

or 50% nitrous oxide combined with intravenous anaesthesia has furthered the use of this procedure.

Continuous caudal anaesthesia in obstetrics—the injection around the nerve roots at the lower end of the spine—suggested by R. A. Hingson and W. B. Edwards in Jan. 1942, was found not applicable to all women in labour; it depended for its success on the skill with which it was applied and a knowledge of the contraindications to its use. Infection had been one of the main hazards. Other hazards had been the production of spinal anaesthesia and the injection of the local anaesthetic agent into the blood stream. Needle breakage continued to occur and a small rubber catheter instead of a needle was one method suggested to prevent this. The introduction of continuous caudal anaesthesia, however, stirred everyone's interest in obstetric anaesthesia and much good should result from it in spite of the untoward results that were bound to occur owing to the unwise and unskilled use of this method in poorly selected cases.

In 1943 the army and navy of the United States and Canada continued courses of instruction in anaesthesiology for medical officers. The war demonstrated clearly the value of the physician anaesthetist. The usefulness of physician anaesthetists in providing supportive measures for patients in shock and their usefulness in connection with oxygen therapy and diagnostic and therapeutic blocks definitely established their importance in most military medical installations. The rosters of special societies for anaesthetists and the "Directory of Medical Specialists" in addition to the American Board of Anesthesiology, the subcommittee on anaesthesia of the National Research council and special societies were useful in the effort to distribute equitably the existing supply of trained anaesthetists between the military and civil practice. The co-operation of the senior consultants in anaesthesia of the allied forces resulted in a plan for the mutual collection of data that when compiled after the war should be extremely valuable.

In connection with the use of blood and plasma in the treatment of the anaesthetized patient in shock, the recognition of the Rh factor has been a most startling development.

In 1943 tentative plans were made for the allocation of anaesthetists to civil life at the termination of the war. The problem was not as great in this special field as it seemed to be in some of the other branches of medical practice. The scarcity of both physician and nurse anaesthetists was keenly felt in 1943, for never before had so much responsibility been assigned to the anaesthetist. (*See* also SURGERY.)

BIBLIOGRAPHY.—R. A. Hingson and W. B. Edwards "Continuous Caudal Analgesia; an Analysis of the First Ten Thousand Confinements thus Managed with the Report of the Authors' First Thousand Cases," *J.A.M.A.*, 123:538-546 (Oct. 30, 1943).   (J. S. L.)

Anderson, Sir John

(1882–), British cabinet member, was born July 8 in Scotland. He attended Edinburgh and Leipzig universities. He was first brought into public life by David Lloyd George and entered the British colonial office at the age of 23. He served as secretary of the important ministry of shipping, 1917–19. After World War I, he was a government "trouble-shooter" in Ireland and Bengal, where he employed strong measures to cope with unrest; he also served as chairman of the British board of inland revenue. He was permanent under-secretary of state for the home office, 1922–31, and governor of Bengal, 1932–37. Upon his return to England, he was elected to commons in 1938. With war impending, Anderson was made lord privy seal and minister of civilian defense, 1938, and was appointed secretary of state for home affairs, 1939. When Churchill became prime minister in 1940, he brought Sir John into his cabinet as head of the powerful home affairs committee, to which Churchill delegated responsibility for home

front activities. Anderson also acted as head of the reconstruction priorities committee, charged with recommending postwar plans to the prime minister. After the death of Sir Kingsley Wood, Sir John was named chancellor of the exchequer, Sept. 24, 1943.

Anderson, Sir Kenneth Arthur Noel

(1891–), British army officer, was born Dec. 25 and was educated at the Royal Military college, Sandhurst. Starting in the army as a 2nd lieutenant in the Seaforth Highlanders, 1911, he was wounded in World War I and was awarded the military cross. After the war, he advanced through the grades and was made major general in 1940.

In 1942 Gen. Dwight Eisenhower, U.S. commander of Allied forces in Africa, selected Gen. Anderson as one of his three task force commanders in French North Africa. Appointed acting lieutenant general, Gen. Anderson led the British 1st army to victory in the combined Allied campaign in North Africa, Nov. 1942 to May 1943. In July 1943 he was given the permanent rank of lieutenant general. A month later, in recognition of his services in the war, a knighthood was bestowed upon him. The United States also honoured him by making him a chief commander of the U.S. Legion of Merit.

Andrews, Charles McLean

(1863–1943), U.S. historian and educator, was born Feb. 22, in Wethersfield, Conn. Dr. Andrews had retired from Yale as professor emeritus of American history in 1931, after an active teaching career of 42 years, and resigned from the editorship of Yale's Historical Publications in 1933. He afterwards completed work on his monumental four-volume *Colonial Period of American History* (1934–38), the first volume of which was awarded the Pulitzer prize in 1935. He edited with his wife Jonathan Dickinson's *God's Protecting Providence* (1942). Dr. Andrews died in New Haven, Sept. 9. (See *Encyclopædia Britannica*.)

Andrews, Frank Maxwell

(1884–1943), U.S. army officer, was born Feb. 3 in Nashville, Tenn. He was graduated from West Point, 1906, became a cavalry lieutenant and was promoted through the grades to colonel in 1935. Gen. Andrews saw service in the Philippines, 1906–07, and in Hawaii, 1911–13. He was a major with the signal corps during World War I and served with the U.S. army of occupation in Germany, 1920–23. He was appointed temporary major general of the air corps in 1935 and major general commanding G.H.Q. air force, 1935–39. In Sept. 1941 he was promoted to the rank of lieutenant general and head of the Caribbean defense command and the Panama canal department. On Nov. 4, 1942, Gen. Andrews was given command of U.S. forces operating with the British in the middle east zone. On Feb. 5, 1943, he was named commander of all U.S. forces in the European theatre of operations, succeeding Gen. Eisenhower. An exponent of air power as an instrument of war equal in importance to land and sea power, Gen. Andrews was closely identified with the intensification of daylight raids on targets in occupied Europe by U.S. bombers. He was killed when a U.S. bomber in which he was a passenger crashed against a hillside in Iceland, May 3.

Angling.

Salt-water fishing in the United States was restricted to a considerable degree by coast guard regulations, but during the latter half of 1943 some areas were reopened, principally in Florida and on the Pacific coast.

The tackle shortage became acute by late summer, and stocks

of rods, reels, hooks and lines were practically exhausted. But interest in angling was maintained at almost a normal level, due in part to the emphasis laid on fish as a valuable contribution to wartime menus. The sale of fishing licenses dropped only about 5% under the 1942 figure.

In the tournament field, activities were further reduced, but the National Association of Angling and Casting Clubs held its 35th annual tournament in Chicago on Sept. 4, 5, and 6. New records in both bait and fly casting were established.

Four new world's records were broken, three of them in salt-water angling. On March 14, B. D. H. Ross took a 1,000-lb. mako shark at Mayor Island, N.Z. The largest wahoo ever to be caught by an angler was landed at Greer cay, Bahamas, on June 15. This specimen, taken by K. L. Ames, Jr., weighed $133\frac{1}{2}$ lb. A woman again made angling news by landing a huge channel bass weighing $67\frac{1}{2}$ lb. She was 16-year-old Lucia D. Cosby, and her prize fish, which broke the women's rod-and-reel record, was taken at Chesapeake Bay, Va., on Aug. 25. Conversely, another woman lost her record. In 1942, Hazel Griffin broke an eight-year record by landing a wall-eyed pike which weighed 19 lb. 12 oz. On May 26, Patrick Noon surpassed this mark with a walleye weighing 22 lb. 4 oz., taken from the Niagara river, Ont. (W. J. SH.)

Anglo-Egyptian Sudan.
A territory under the joint sovereignty of Great Britain and Egypt in northeastern Africa, south of Egypt (*q.v.*). Area 967,500 sq.mi.; pop. (est. 1941) 6,370,041. Chief towns (pop. est. 1941): Khartoum (incl. Khartoum North) (44,950); Omdurman (116,196); Port Sudan (26,255); Atbara (19,757); El Obeid (39,887). Governor general: Lt. Gen. Sir Hubert Huddleston; languages: English and Arabic; religion: Mohammedan.

History.—The political development of the Sudan registered an important advance in 1943. The earlier stages of this development may be recapitulated briefly. In 1922 had been enacted the first of a series of ordinances granting judicial powers to certain tribal heads. By 1932 by the Native Courts' ordinance this "devolution" policy had given the administration of civil and criminal justice to the local authorities. In 1937, by the Rural Areas ordinance, executive municipal and town councils were set up with administrative powers.

The government's 1943 legislation advanced a long step further. By its instrument provincial councils—partly nominated, partly elected—were advising provincial governors on important social and economic interests in the provinces.

Secondly, a central advisory council in Khartoum—again partly nominated, partly elected—was to be set up to advise the governor-general-in-council on matters affecting the government of the country as a whole.

Meanwhile, though the cost of living was about 170% above the 1939 figure, the economic situation of the country had been safeguarded. Additional wheat cultivation assured supplies guaranteeing self-support for the country without imports; while on the Gezira cotton plantations south of Khartoum land was made available for the production of increased maize supplies adequate to meet the requirements of the local population whose staple article of food it is. Nevertheless the Gezira cotton crop, harvested early in the year, was a bumper one and the treasury as well as the growers and the Sudan Plantations corporation all profited financially. (O. M. T.)

Education.—(Jan. 1, 1941) Government schools: elementary schools 137, scholars 17,184; intermediate schools 11, scholars 357; Gordon Memorial college, scholars 1,308; state-aided Koranic schools 501, scholars 23,000; scholars at non-government (mission) schools 12,925.

Banking and Finance.—Revenue (1942) £E9,114,809; ex-penditure (1942) £E8,626,425; public debt (Dec. 31, 1942) £E9,435,898.

Trade and Communication.—In 1942 imports were valued at £E8,105,900; the value of exported merchandise amounted to £E7,085,107. Communications: roads, suitable for motor traffic, all weather, *c.* 1,000 mi.; railways 1,991 route mi.; river service 2,325 mi.; motor vehicles licensed (1937) 4,354 cars, commercial vehicles and cycles; telephone subscribers (1938) 2,383.

Agriculture and Mineral Production.—(1938–39) Production (in short tons): cotton seed (1940–41) 98,435; ginned cotton (1940–41) 54,674; millet (1937–38) 347,225; sesamum 36,596; maize 11,354; wheat 9,039; ground-nuts 9,480; barley 1,768; gold (1938) 252 kg.

Angola: *see* PORTUGUESE COLONIAL EMPIRE.
Animal Fats: *see* VEGETABLE OILS AND ANIMAL FATS.
Animal Industry, Bureau of: *see* AGRICULTURAL RESEARCH ADMINISTRATION.
Annam: *see* FRENCH COLONIAL EMPIRE.
Anniversaries and Centennials: *see* CALENDAR, 1943, page xx.

Anthropology.
Anthropology during 1943 found increasing expression in war activities, though this did not prevent the maintenance of customary channels of communicating research findings, while certain gains of long-term value were registered.

The first of a new series of monographs published by the Viking fund appeared under the editorship of C. Osgood, and grants-in-aid for anthropological field work, offered by the same fund, of which P. Fejos was director of research, were announced. A new journal, *Acta Americana*, was launched under the editorship of R. Beals, as the organ of the Inter-American Society of Anthropology and Geography. The West China Frontier Research institute began a program of field studies under the direction of Li An-che; and an Institute of West African Arts, Industries and Social Science was made possible by a grant of £127,000 from the British treasury. It will be at Achimota, Gold Coast, and headed by M. Meyerowitz. Deering library, Northwestern university, acquired the library of the late Franz Boas, which was in 1943 installed as the Franz Boas Memorial Library and Anthropological Reprint Center.

A new program of African studies was initiated at Fisk university, and a Committee of African Studies instituted at the University of Pennsylvania. The South African journal *Bantu Studies*, which altered its title to *African Studies*, widened its scope. Anthropology in South Africa was further strengthened when Abbé Henri Breuil, distinguished French prehistorian, took up his duties as member of the Union's Bureau of Archaeology and honorary professor of archaeology at the University of the Witwatersrand. Activities of the International Institute for the Study of African Languages and Cultures, London, were resumed, and its journal, *Africa*, again began appearing regularly.

On Oct. 30, the Royal Anthropological institute held its centenary meeting. The work of the institute was outlined by Sir John Myres (who was knighted during 1943 for his services to scholarship), the place of anthropology in colonial development considered by Lord Hailey, and G. M. Morant, V. G. Childe, R. V. Sayce, and R. Firth discussed other aspects of the future development of the subject. The proceedings of the centenary meeting of the American Ethnological society, New York City, were published in the April-June issue of the *American Anthropologist*, with a bibliography of the society's publications. *The Journal of American Folklore*, appearing in a new format, included in the July number a comprehensive survey by W. D.

Hand of the organization and activities of North American folklore societies. As in 1942, only the Council of the American Anthropological association met; R. Redfield was named president for 1944.

The first number of the *American Journal of Physical Anthropology, New Series,* under the editorship of C. D. Stewart, published a group of studies on the anthropometry of Latin America. The changed policy of the new editor and his editorial board was reflected in an increased number of biometric papers. M. S. Goldstein's "Demographic and Bodily Changes in Descendants of Mexican Immigrants," in the *Publications* of the Institute of Latin American Studies, University of Texas, made available findings that confirm those of Boas and others on the plasticity of the human physical form, and W. A. Lessa, in his work "An Appraisal of Constitutional Types" (*Memoir 62,* American Anthropological association), presented a critical study of methods and findings in this field.

Understandably, little archaeological work was done outside the Americas. A report of the program of the Institute of Andean Research appeared in the second issue of *Acta Americana,* with a bibliography of its publications. An issue of *American Antiquity* was devoted to the results of excavations in Latin America. One theoretical paper in the same journal (Oct. 1943) by J. Bennett, "Recent Developments in the Functional Interpretation of Archaeological Data," made the point that undue stress had been laid on the material aspects of artefacts and indicated approaches toward analyzing the social behaviour of the peoples who used them. The Chicago Natural History museum, formerly the Field museum, Chicago, opened the first section of its Hall of New World Archaeology.

In the field of linguistics, there were to be noted the papers in *African Studies* dealing with Swahili, Lozi (a Barotseland *lingua franca* of Bantu base) and Thlaping, together with a report by C. M. Doke on the status of research into the native languages of South Africa. *Oceania* carried three instalments of T. G. H. Strehlow's "Aranda Grammar," as well as a number of other contributions to the study of native Australian tongues. In the U.S., two notable general papers and one monograph were inspired by the war: L. Bloomfield, *Outline Guide for the Practical Study of Foreign Languages,* B. Block and G. L. Trager, *Outline of Linguistic Analysis,* and R. A. Hall, *Melanesian Pidgin English* (all published by the Linguistic Society of America).

Contributions to the study of culture which appeared during the year included a paper on "The Future of Social Anthropology," by Lord Raglan, which engendered lively discussion by various members of the Royal Anthropological institute, according to abstracts published in *Man* (May-June 1943). L. A. White continued his studies in cultural evolution ("Energy and the Evolution of Culture," *American Anthropologist,* July-Sept. 1943), E. S. Goldfrank considered the problem of the relationship between historic change and social character (*ibid.,* Jan.-Mar. 1943), while in the field of social organization, M. Titiev's paper "The Influence of Common Residence on the Unilateral Classification of Kindred" (*ibid.,* Oct.-Dec. 1943) is to be remarked. The comprehensive study of the life of the Australian aborigines in the Ooldea region of western South Australia by R. and C. Berndt, which began in the 1941–42 volume of *Oceania,* was continued and, when complete, would materially extend our knowledge of native life on that continent. There were relatively few monographs, outside the standard series. Among the books of less restricted anthropological interest were *Alaska Diary* by the late A. Hrdlicka, *The Realm of the Rain-Queen, a Study of Lovedu Society* by E. J. and D. J. Krige, *Education and the Cultural Process,* by various authors (C. S. Johnson, editor), *The Irish Stone Age* by H. L. Movius, Jr. and *Keep Your Powder Dry* by M. Mead.

Memoir No. 61 of the American Anthropological association was issued as a memorial to Franz Boas. Essays covering the many aspects of his scientific activities and a definitive list of his publications are included to give a rounded picture of the man and his work. Obituary notices of Elsie Clews Parsons (*Journal of American Folklore,* Jan.-March; *American Anthropologist,* April-June) and of B. Malinowski (*Man,* Jan.-Feb.; *Oceania,* Sept. 1942; *American Anthropologist,* July-Sept.; *J. Am. Folklore,* July-Sept.), analyzing the influence of these figures in anthropological trends, constituted, with the Boas memoir, important additions to the literature on the history of anthropology.

War Activities.—Anthropologists were largely called upon to contribute their specialized knowledge to the war effort. The nature of the contacts they had established with native peoples the world over and the methods they had developed for understanding varied modes of life permitted them to give realistic aid to intelligence units, or to those carrying on economic and psychological warfare, and to advise concerning many types of postwar programs of rehabilitation.

One such contribution was the Intensive Language Training program, an outstanding educational achievement of the war effort, which was initiated and sponsored by the American Council of Learned Societies. The Army Area Training program, in most instances closely correlated with relevant language instruction, likewise drew heavily on the methods and information supplied by cultural anthropologists. The language-area method also figured largely in the training of civil affairs officers. The National Research council, through its division of anthropology and psychology, set up committees on oceanic and African anthropology, both of which were active in preparing memoranda and personnel lists, many of a restricted character.

The need to channel all these services, however, soon became apparent. The Ethnogeographic board was therefore established as a central clearing house under the joint sponsorship of the American Council of Learned Societies, the Social Science Research council, the National Research council and the Smithsonian institution and under the directorship of William D. Strong established headquarters in the Smithsonian institution. The manifold activities of the board and the large quantity of materials it made available to the services and civilian agencies amply demonstrated its value. Its staff aided importantly in bringing out the Smithsonian institution's *War Background Series,* and its *Survival on Land and Sea,* which was prepared at the request of the navy, was given wide distribution and was expected to be instrumental in saving many lives.   (M. J. Hs.)

Anti-Aircraft Guns: *see* MUNITIONS OF WAR.
Antigua: *see* WEST INDIES, BRITISH.
Antilles, Greater and Lesser: *see* WEST INDIES.

Antimony. Because of the large reserve accumulated, the use of antimony was relieved of allocation requirements and restrictions as of Jan. 1, 1943, after the War Production board had reported on the status of production, stocks and demand in 1943 and 1944.

In the past considerable amounts of low-grade ores had been imported from South America in order to build up the reserves, but such imports were expected to be heavily reduced in 1944. While 19,500 tons of metal were received in 1943 from South American ores, this was to be reduced to 1,250 tons in 1944 by the elimination of low-grade ores. Imports from Mexico were reported at 13,200 tons in 1943; (est.) 12,000 tons in 1944.

The Office of Price Administration established ceiling prices for antimony at 14.5 cents per lb., f.o.b. Laredo, Texas, for

U.S. Production, Stocks and Demand of Antimony, 1943 and 1944

	1943 Short tons	1944 Short tons
Stocks (Government and private)	22,066	36,090
Imports	32,700	13,250
Domestic production	5,124	4,000
Secondary recovery	18,000	12,000
Supply	77,890	65,340
Demand for		
Domestic primary.	23,500	24,000
Domestic secondary	18,000	12,000
Exports	300	500
Total	41,800	36,500
Reserve at December 31	36,090	28,840

99+% metal, and 15 cents for 99.8% metal   (G. A. Ro.)

GERMAN RAID on the ghetto in Warsaw. A bitter struggle between Warsaw Jews and nazi troops in April 1943 was reported to have resulted in the virtual extinction of the former

Anti-Saloon League of America.

The Anti-Saloon League of America, organized in 1895, is a nonpartisan, interdenominational, federated temperance organization. Its 32nd national convention was held in Washington, D.C., on May 16–17, 1943.

Nationally, the efforts of the league were directed during 1943 toward the prevention of the waste of manpower and materials involved in the manufacture and sale of alcoholic beverages during the war. Liquor control was characterized during the year by two principal developments: (1) Self-regulation by the liquor industry, such as rationing of existing liquor stocks; (2) Administrative restrictions imposed by the federal government as a conservation measure in aid of war production. The order requiring whisky distilleries to convert to the production of industrial alcohol remained in force throughout the year.

Several bills proposing restrictions by law upon the liquor traffic were pending in the 78th congress, such as H.R. 2082, the Bryson bill for war prohibition; S. 860, by Senator W. Lee O'Daniel, for the protection of the armed forces; S. 569, by Senator Arthur Capper, to prohibit the transportation of liquor advertising through the mediums of interstate commerce; and H.R. 2749, by Rep. Sam M. Russell, for prohibition in military camps and in zones around war production plants. No action was taken upon any of these measures.

The legislatures of nearly all of the states met in 1943. Measures relating to the liquor trade were considered in most of them, but few substantial changes were made in state laws. Liquor control authorities in many jurisdictions imposed severe rationing restrictions as a war measure, and in some instances decreased hours of sale.

The league continued its efforts to extend no-license areas by local option. The results showed gains in the number of places voting no-license.

On Nov. 16, 1943, Senator Frederick Van Nuys, from the committee on the judiciary, reported a resolution authorizing an investigation of the alcoholic beverage industry for alleged violations of ceiling prices, black market operations, profiteering, and monopolistic practices, on which hearings have been held.

The national headquarters were in 1943 at 131 B st. S.E., Washington 3, D.C. (*See* also LIQUORS, ALCOHOLIC.)

(E. B. Du.)

Anti-Semitism.

The policy of extermination of the Jews within all countries under the influence of national socialist Germany was continued in 1943 with increasing savagery. It was reported from reliable sources that by the end of 1943 all Jews living in Germany, Austria and Czechoslovakia had been either liquidated by assassination, starvation or concentration camps, or had been deported to Poland where an even more terrible fate awaited them. During 1943 the Jews of the Netherlands suffered a similar fate. Against the protests of the Dutch population, all Jews were deported to Poland. Their number was estimated at 180,000 persons. The official deportations from the Netherlands started in April 1943 and were carried through in three stages in the spring of 1943. In its official report of April 20, 1943 the Inter-Allied Information Committee on Occupied Countries in London estimated that at that time 2,000,000 Jews, men, women and children, had been annihilated by the Germans or under German influence and that 5,000,000 more were then in immediate danger of extermination. Sickening details of torture and massacre carried out by the Germans were given. Families were ruthlessly split up, all the goods and valuables in Jewish possession were appropriated by the Germans. Special extermination squads were trained for the liquidation of the Jews in Poland. These methods were applied wherever German influence spread.

During 1943 the situation of the Jews, which had been relatively still bearable in Vichy-controlled France and in fascist Italy, worsened rapidly when the Germans took over direct control of the country. In the formerly "non-occupied" zone of Vichy-France all the additional restrictive measures were introduced when the Germans occupied that part of France, and the policy of complete segregation and extermination was applied there as in other German occupied countries. The fall of fascism and of Mussolini's government in Italy in July 1943 brought with it the official abandonment of the racial legislation and the anti-Semitic measures introduced in Italy under German pressure in 1938. But when the Germans took over northern and central Italy in Sept. 1943, after the Italian government of Marshal Badoglio had concluded an armistice with the Allies, the situation of the Jews in Italy became much worse than under the fascist regime. In the southern part of Italy, occupied by Allied troops, anti-Semitic legislation was abolished, but in that part of Italy only an insignificant number of Jews live.

Denmark with its deeply ingrained democratic and humanitarian tradition maintained, even after the German occupation of April 1940, the complete equality of the Jews. But in 1943 the Germans, wishing to break the democratic spirit of the Danes, took over the administration of Denmark, and as a result began to introduce the German anti-Semitic measures there. Helped by the Danish population a large part of the 6,000 Danish Jews succeeded to escape into Sweden where they were received with exemplary hospitality by the Swedish government and people.

The systematic process of the liquidation of the Jews in Poland was interrupted by the heroic resistance which, in May 1943, the

Jews in the overcrowded ghetto of Warsaw put up when the Germans started the final liquidation of the ghetto. The Germans had to bring up artillery and tanks to suppress the rising. In the United States and in Great Britain many liberal and humanitarian circles and Jewish organizations demanded temporary measures to grant asylum to those Jews who could be saved from the German hell, in territories of the United Nations or in neutral countries until, after the victory of the United Nations and the restoration of civilized life and the rule of law in the German occupied countries, the Jews could return to their homelands and participate in their reconstruction.

In the countries liberated from fascist control by Allied advance, anti-Semitic legislature was everywhere abolished. In French North Africa General Henri Honoré Giraud cancelled on March 14 all anti-Semitic legislation introduced by Marshal Pétain's government since July 1940. While thus restoring the complete democratic equality of French Jews, General Giraud left the revocation of the Crémieux decree of 1870, which gave French citizenship to Algerian native Jews, in force. The French Committee of National Liberation restored the Crémieux decree of 1870 on Oct. 21, 1943. The official statement said: "The Committee, examining the situation of the Jews of Algeria, noted in view of existing texts—on the one hand, the abrogation of all acts discriminating against Jews, on the other hand, abrogation of the Crémieux decree effectively subordinated to the definition of conditions of application which were not issued—that the Crémieux decree is now in vigor." The number of Algerian Jews amounts to about 145,000. By this step the complete legal status of the Jews in liberated French territory was restored as it had been before the French capitulation in June 1940.

Anti-Semitic agitation in democratic countries like the United States and Great Britain was checked by the realization that all anti-Semitic propaganda played into the hands of the enemy. There was an increase of anti-Semitic hooliganism in Boston in the fall of 1943 which necessitated special measures on the part of the governor of the state. Anti-Semitic literature was generally coupled with seditious propaganda. But on the whole in the democratic countries anti-Semitism was everywhere on the decrease. It is characteristic that the new Argentine government under Ramirez, which came to power in June 1943 and which was sympathetic to fascism and hostile to the United States, condoned and even supported anti-Semitic propaganda, though the only open anti-Semitic official measure taken, the suppression of the Jewish press, was rescinded as a result of American protest. (*See* also FASCISM; JEWISH RELIGIOUS LIFE; REFUGEES.)

(H. Ko.)

Anti-Tank Guns: *see* MUNITIONS OF WAR.

Antoine, André (1851–1943), French actor-manager, founder of the Théâtre Libre and the Théâtre Antoine in Paris, was born Jan. 31 in Limoges. A report of his death was announced from Carteret, Brittany, according to a Berne dispatch of Oct. 21. (See *Encyclopædia Britannica*.)

Antonescu, Ion (1882–   ), Rumanian soldier and statesman, was born in Transylvania June 2 and fought with the Rumanian armies during World War I, after which he was promoted to the rank of colonel. He later became military attaché of Rumania in London and Rome, chief of the army's general staff and war minister. He was named prime minister by King Carol Sept. 5, 1940, in the midst of the disorders that followed the partition of Rumania. Antonescu's first act was to demand the abdication of Carol. The prime minister then assumed dictatorial powers and on Sept. 14, 1940, formally promul-

gated a totalitarian rule. He signed a pact with Germany, Nov. 23. In Jan. 1941, Antonescu subdued Iron Guardist anti-Semitic riots, and tightened his grip on the government, with German backing. On June 22, 1941, the day that Germany invaded Russia, Rumania also attacked, with Antonescu assuming title of generalissimo and commander of Rumanian armies in Bessarabia. The campaigns of the next two and a half years were most costly. In March 1942, Antonescu ordered drastic measures to curb antifascist unrest. As losses at the front mounted and the armies retreated, morale in Rumania fell. Antonescu's troubles in 1943 included a threatened invasion of Transylvania by Hungary, demands for aid by Hitler and revolt at home. He was said to have admitted loss of 500,000 men, including losses at Stalingrad.

Anzelevitz, Benjamin: *see* BERNIE, BEN.

Apples. The commercial apple crop in the United States in 1943 was estimated by the U.S. department of agriculture as about 31% smaller than the 1942 crop. Production of apples in 1943 was placed at 88,086,000 bu. compared with 128,273,000 bu. in 1942. The crop was about 28% of the eight-year average 1934–41. The decline in production was noted in the far west and eastern districts. The size and quality of the fruit was also not up to the average. Notwithstanding the shortage of labour the 1943 apple crop was more completely

HAULING APPLES from an orchard in New York state. The 1943 U.S. harvest was below average

harvested and utilized in all parts of the country. Apple prices in 1943 were from two and a half to three times the prices of

U.S. Apple Production in Leading States, 1943 and 1942

State	1943 bu.	1942 bu.	State	1943 bu.	1942 bu.
Washington . .	23,184,000	27,339,000	Colorado . . .	1,140,000	1,595,000
New York . .	12,250,000	18,997,000	Indiana	1,010,000	1,392,000
California . .	8,820,000	5,979,000	Missouri . . .	968,000	1,075,000
Michigan . .	6,144,000	9,234,000	Maryland . .	864,000	2,211,000
Virginia . . .	5,220,000	14,094,000	Connecticut. .	836,000	1,922,000
Pennsylvania .	5,070,000	10,031,000	New Hampshire	767,000	961,000
Illinois	2,790,000	3,410,000	Idaho	750,000	1,705,000
Oregon	2,664,000	2,652,000	Vermont . . .	722,000	731,000
Ohio	2,422,000	6,384,000	Maine	704,000	813,000
Massachusetts .	2,228,000	3,400,000	North Carolina	499,000	1,086,000
West Virginia .	2,046,000	4,686,000	Delaware . . .	499,000	940,000
New Jersey .	2,028,000	3,239,000	Kansas . . .	338,000	580,000

1942, and remained at the ceiling, bringing growers the largest returns in more than 20 years. The demand for fresh fruit was so great as to cause a shortage of small sized apples for processing into by-products. (J. C. Ms.)

Appleyard, Rollo

(1867–1943), British engineer, physicist and inventor, was born Jan. 1. He was educated at Dulwich college, and later was attached to the staff of the Royal Engineering college, 1885–92. He joined the London *Times* in 1905 as technical adviser and writer. Appleyard served with the navy during World War I as adviser on aeronautical instruments in the Air Service. Later, he was appointed to the War Staff's convoy section and edited *Convoy Instructions*. He invented the conductometer for measuring electrical conductivity and various instruments including some in the aeronautical field. His research covered dielectrics, alloys, thermometry and surface tension. Appleyard also is credited with designing the core of a section of the Pacific cable. He died in London, March 1.

Applied Chemistry: *see* CHEMISTRY.
Applied Psychology: *see* PSYCHOLOGY.
Appropriations and Expenditures: *see* BUDGET, NATIONAL.

Aquariums.

The aquarium in the Regents Park Zoological Garden, London, reopened on June 11, 1943, on a necessarily reduced scale, after having been closed for reasons of public safety, with the beginning of hostilities. No word was received of aquariums near active theatres of war, but undoubtedly such were closed, if not destroyed. During one of the German raids on England a bomb did actually hit the then closed London aquarium.

Aquariums in the United States retained a *status quo* for the year, there being no further closure of such public institutions, nor did any reopen during that period. All suffered from transportation and personnel difficulties and could do little more than attempt to hold their present status for the duration of the conflict. (C. M. BR.)

Aqueducts.

The Colorado river aqueduct, constructed by the Metropolitan Water District of Southern California, served a vital war need, providing a dependable supply of municipal and industrial water to Los Angeles and 12 neighbouring coast cities where there are major war industries. The aqueduct taps the Colorado river at Parker dam. The diversion is made possible through the regulation of the river by this dam and another larger dam, Boulder, situated 150 miles upstream, both erected by the federal bureau of reclamation. Construction of the pipeline and its distribution system, totalling 392 mi. in length, was completed on Aug. 18, 1941, at a cost of $200,000,000. The main aqueduct is 241 mi. long, extending from Parker dam to Cajalco reservoir, 12 mi. south of Riverside, California. The capacity of the system is 1,000,000,000 gal. per day.

Two miles of the 13.1-mi. Continental Divide tunnel of the bureau of reclamation's Colorado-Big Thompson project (Colorado) remained to be drilled. The entire length was planned to be lined with concrete. When completed the tunnel was expected to divert surplus water from the headwaters of the Colorado river on the western slope of the Rocky mountains to lands on the northeastern slope in northeastern Colorado to supplement an inadequate supply serving 615,000 acres of productive land.

Construction of the 40-mi. Salt Lake City aqueduct, 9 miles of which had been completed, was interrupted in Dec. 1942 by a stop-construction order issued by the War Production board to divert critical materials to other war uses. Approval was given in Oct. 1943, to install an additional 13,200 ft. of the 69-in. reinforced concrete pipe. The aqueduct has a capacity of 150 second feet. When completed it was expected to bring a supplemental supply of municipal and industrial water to Salt Lake City, Utah, where military and industrial activities increased the population by 50%.

Water brought to the irrigated lands of the Imperial valley, California, through the bureau of reclamation's All-American canal—the nation's greatest irrigation ditch—made possible in 1942 the production of crops valued at $38,163,000. This total is only slightly less than the construction cost—$38,500,000. The 80-mi. long structure brings water from the Colorado river at Imperial dam, near the Mexican border. Eighty-six and one-half miles of the 130-mi. Coachella branch of the All-American canal was completed and the War Production board in Oct. 1943, gave approval for the construction of an additional 27 mi. Ultimately 1,000,000 acres was planned to be served by the two canals.

Industries and towns in the upper San Francisco bay region (California) are served industrial and municipal water through the Contra Costa canal of the Central valley project. Thirty-eight miles of the 46-mi. waterway was completed by 1943. Completion of the Madera canal of this bureau of reclamation project, to bring water impounded by Friant dam to productive land in the San Joaquin valley, was authorized by the War Production board. Eight miles of the 37-mi.-long artificial waterway were built in 1941 before work was halted by the war.

Because of the war, construction on the 6-mi. Duchesne tunnel of the bureau of reclamation's Provo river project in Utah was stopped. The tunnel, 2.7 mi. of which had been completed, was to divert water for irrigation purposes from the Duchesne river on the Colorado river watershed to the Provo river for storage in the Deer Creek reservoir. (*See* also CANALS AND INLAND WATERWAYS; DAMS; TUNNELS.) (H. W. BA.)

ARA: *see* AGRICULTURAL RESEARCH ADMINISTRATION.

Arabia.

Total area (est.) 1,000,000 sq.mi. Total pop. (est. 1937) 9,300,000; Saudi Arabia 4,500,000; Yemen 3,500,000; Oman and Muscat 500,000; Kuwait 80,000; Trucial Sheikhs 80,000. Language: Arabic; religion: Mohammedan. Rulers: Saudi Arabia, King Abd-ul-Aziz ibn Sa'ud; Yemen, Imam Yahya ibn Muhammad ibn Hamid ad-din; Oman and Muscat, Sultan Sayyid Sa'id ibn Taimur; Kuwait, Sheikh Ahmad ibn Jabir as-Subah.

History.—There was no change in the international position of Saudi Arabia during 1943. King Abd-ul-Aziz ibn Sa'ud continued to be on friendly terms with the British government, and his relations with the U.S.A. were strengthened. Thus in April Alexander Kirk, the U.S. minister to Egypt and Saudi Arabia, visited the king in Riyadh; and in October two of the king's sons, the Emirs Feisal and Khalid, visited the United States at the invitation of President Roosevelt. During the year the American government

TWO SONS OF KING IBN SA'UD of Arabia—Prince Feisal (left) and Prince Khalid—toured the United States in the fall of 1943. They were greeted in Washington by Assistant Sec'y of State Adolf A. Berle, Jr. (left)

extended the application of the lend-lease act to Saudi Arabia. James S. Moose was made minister to Saudi Arabia in June.

The Saudi Arabian government was among the Arab governments to which the Egyptian prime minister, Nahas Pasha, sent invitations to take part in discussions on the question of Arab union. The king's views on the subject were expressed in a letter to Nahas Pasha; but, after a visit to Riyadh by a representative of Nahas Pasha in October, the king agreed to send a delegate to Cairo to discuss the matter further with the Egyptian prime minister.

Ibn Sa'ud's interest in Arab problems was also shown in an interview which he gave to a correspondent of the American periodical *Life* in May. He denied that the Jews had any right to Palestine. Their demands, he claimed, constituted an injustice to the Arabs and the Moslems in general and caused dissensions between the Moslems and their friends, the Allies. There were other countries more fertile and more suitable for Jewish settlement. The Arabs would safeguard the interests of the native Jewish population of Palestine, provided they committed no action that might lead to strife.

The government continued its efforts to improve the economic system. Agriculture was helped by subsidies, by the extension of the area under cultivation and by an increase in the settled population. The production of oil by American concessionary companies continued in spite of the lack of equipment.

In February the Imam of the Yemen interned the Germans and Italians in his territories. He too was invited by Nahas Pasha to take part in the discussions on Arab union; in reply he sent a letter asking for further details of Nahas Pasha's plans.

Finance.—Monetary unit, Indian rupee, and in Saudi Arabia the rial. Exchange rate in 1942: 1 rial=Rs. 1 (Indian)=U.S. cents 30.12.

Trade.—With India (1939–40): Oman and Muscat, imports Rs.24,55,362; exports Rs.35,71,387; other states of Arabia, imports Rs.9,89,030; exports Rs.73,18,701. With the United Kingdom (1938): Saudi Arabia and Yemen, imports £94,960; exports £28,871; Oman and Muscat, Trucial Sheikhs and Kuwait, imports £40,262; exports £18,354. Total trade of Oman and Muscat (1938–39): imports Rs.48,76,193; exports Rs.33,31,939; Kuwait (1937–38): imports £410,812; exports £174,006.

Archaeology.

Eastern Hemisphere.—As in the previous war years, the reports on archaeological discoveries in the year 1943 were brief and tardy. The following list cannot be assumed to be complete for 1943, and certain items of interest are mentioned which actually depend on excavations and explorations of several years ago. Information concerning the latter only came to hand in 1943. Planned excavations naturally were few. Moreover, reports from axis-occupied Europe were practically nonexistent.

There were two definite signs of planning for the future of archaeology, and a reconsideration of the role of archaeology in the postwar world—from the point of view of the archaeologist himself, and of his contribution to knowledge and human understanding. In August, the Institute of Archaeology of the University of London called a conference, which was attended by leading British archaeologists. The London conference considered the possible contributions which archaeology may make in the postwar world in Britain and overseas. The training of archaeologists, the means of permanent recording, and the place of the museum and of archaeological research in general education were also discussed. In July, a somewhat more specialized conference was convened in Jerusalem to consider the future of near eastern archaeology. The Jerusalem conference was somewhat more directly concerned with the legal status of an excavator and his finds in foreign states, but it also urged the establishment of international congresses, co-operation, planning and nomenclature. Preliminary discussions concerning the agenda of an American conference, to be called some time in the near future, were already under way.

Perhaps the outstanding archaeological events of the year 1943 were the publication of two different volumes, signed wholly or in part by Dr. Hallum L. Movius, Jr., of Harvard, which serve to distinguish him as one of the foremost American prehistorians. The first of these volumes, *Research on Early Man in Burma* (Trans. Am. Phil. Soc., n.s. vol. xxxii, pt. iii), Philadelphia: Am. Phil. Soc., 1943, is the work of Hellmut de Terra and Movius, with supplementary reports by E. H. Colbert and J. Bequaert. The second volume is Movius' *The Irish Stone Age* (Cambridge University press, 1942). Both volumes report for the first time work done previously to 1943, but their importance surpasses any available information on work accomplished within the last year. Word reached the Oriental institute of excavations carried on for the directorate of antiquities of the Iraq government by Seton Lloyd, which concerns the range of the earliest village horizons of northern Mesopotamia. This, also, is of extreme archaeological importance, but no details of the excavations were available in 1943. An important archaeological survey was carried on by Nelson Glueck in the Jordan valley. In addition, a remarkable chance find was made in the discovery of the tomb of the Emperor, Wang Chien, in China.

The Palaeolithic-Mesolithic Periods.—The Abbé Breuil (with collaborators) published a brief opinion on the crude pebble tool industries from the Atlantic coastal terraces of Portugal (*Proc. Prehist. Soc.*, viii). These shell-food collectors are said to have shown remarkably little industrial ingenuity from Abbevillian times to the Mesolithic, and Breuil suggests calling these industries "Lusitanian" to distinguish them from the more normal artifacts found in the interior.

Flint artifacts described as similar to the "Chellean," "early Acheulean," and "Acheulean IV" of east Africa, are reported from the five-metre gravels above the flood plain of the valley near the joining of the Blue and White Nile. "Late Acheulean" and "Levalloisian" artifacts appear as surface finds. The context is important, indicating that in this part of the Nile valley (Anglo-Egyptian Sudan), the river had nearly reached its present-day erosion level at the time the flints were produced.

Farther south in Africa, the materials from the Mumbwa caves of Northern Rhodesia were reworked in the consideration of new excavations, by J. D. Clark (*Trans. Roy. Soc. S. Africa*, xxix, pt. iii). No lower Palaeolithic material is accounted for, and the sequence indicates Rhodesian Stillbay, Northern Rhodesian Wilton, and then Iron Age. The previously discovered "furnace with iron slag" of the middle levels is found to have been a grave, with the "slag" not really slag, but a cemented sand and silt deposit.

In *Proc. Prehist. Soc.*, viii, Prof. Dorothy Garrod reported on the Levalloiso-Mousterian and the upper Natufian of Shukba cave in Palestine.

The above-mentioned *Research on Early Man in Burma* by de Terra and Movius considers materials collected in the Irrawaddy basin and in the northern Shan highlands. De Terra demonstrates that the Pleistocene geology of Burma closely resembles that of northern India, which he had studied so competently. Both areas are characterized by a tilted and folded lower Pleistocene series containing the Villafranchian fauna; this is followed unconformably by five successive terraces of similar composition, in the middle and upper Pleistocene. The same general sequence is shown by Teilhard de Chardin's scheme for south China, and a close correspondence is suggested between the Irrawaddy and the Yangtze terrace systems. There are also some features of the less-well-known Pleistocene of Malaya and Java which suggest the same sequence. De Terra offers an expanded tentative scheme of correlation of the Pleistocene sequences of the lowland regions, surrounding the mountain ranges of Eurasia. It would be highly desirable to have de Terra's studies extended to the eastern Mediterranean basin.

With the geological framework set, Movius discusses the artifacts recovered from the Burmese terraces. There are, briefly, two main ranges of chopper tools called early and late Anyathian (after *ān-ya-thā*, colloquial Burmese for an upper Burman). The early Anyathian may be subdivided (mainly on stratigraphic grounds) into three parts, the late Anyathian into two parts. Early Anyathian *1* artifacts are found *in situ*, but heavily abraded, in the highest terrace (middle Pleistocene); late Anyathian *2* artifacts appear in the gravels of terrace *4;* terrace *5* contains Neolithic materials.

There are only minor typological differences between the early and late Anyathian scraper and chopper tools. The tools are made in either silicified tuff or fossil wood; the tuff has working properties which are little inferior to flint, and Movius insists that the rather crude chopper tools were purposely so produced and do not depend on limitations imposed by the material.

In his conclusions, Movius gave the most useful synthesis available so far on the newly recognized chopper tool complex of southeastern Asia. It seemed clear that this area—China (including Choukoutien), Burma, Java, Malaya and India—supported a Palaeolithic population which produced rather heavy stone tools of a distinct chopper type. The general consistency of this tool type in the Asiatic area (*i.e.*, the area south of the Amur river) is also emphasized by the absence of the two main tool preparation traditions of the lower Palaeolithic in Europe and Africa, the true hand axes (bifaces) and the flake tools. The areas of distribution of the Asiatic chopper tools and of the European bifaces and flakes evidently overlap in India, and perhaps in east and south Africa. Taken with de Terra and Paterson's *Studies on the Ice Age in India,* this volume opens up vast new vistas in the prehistory of the old world.

In *Man*, xliii, 17 (March–April 1943), Prof. V. Gordon Childe considered evidence newly arrived from the Scandinavian countries to the effect that the classic Danish shell-mound or Ertebølle materials can no longer be considered as purely Mesolithic. Recent Danish work on the strand lines shows evidence of different Atlantic transgressions, and a rechecking of the excavations at Brabrand Sø, with an analysis of its pollen content, shows it to belong to a late Atlantic transgression comparable in date to Montelius' Neolithic III. There seems to be nothing to prevent the idea that an elemental Ertebølle actually appeared at the time of the early Atlantic transgression (*i.e.*, in the full Mesolithic range of time). On the other hand, such elements of the assemblage as pottery, *einkorn* grain, and ox bones were probably later and may be assumed as due to contact with nearby Neolithic groups.

Movius' *The Irish Stone Age* reported on the excavation of six Stone Age sites—one in County Waterford and five in Northern Ireland. The first part of the book is an intensive re-examination of the late glacial and postglacial chronology of northern and northwestern Europe, with emphasis on Great Britain and Ireland. The geochronological setting is necessary, since the available Stone Age range of Irish material does not immediately conform to the "classic industries" of western Europe. The assemblages in question are called early and late Larnian (from a concentration of the finds along the coast at Larne). The earlier material is fixed in time by overlying beds of Late Boreal-Early Atlantic peat (at least *c.* 6000 B.C.); the late Larnian assemblage was still being produced when the Neolithic peoples began to appear about 2000 B.C. The early Larnian flint tools include blades, scrapers and picks; superficially tanged points, choppers and a few axes are added in the late assemblage. The producers of the Larnian materials seem to have been hunters, food collectors and fishermen, whom Movius believes to have reached Ireland from northwestern Europe before the Litorina submergence. They seem to have been descendants of the final Upper Palaeolithic peoples of northwestern Europe, and, although later arrivals in Ireland pushed them into the interior, their basic stock is present in the Irish people of today.

In *Man*, xliii, 2 (Jan.–Feb. 1943), Prof. Childe concluded his series of syntheses of Russian investigations, this article being concerned with the range of materials from the Mesolithic to the Iron Age, in the forest zone.

The Near East.—Under Zaki Y. Saad, some 735 First Dynasty graves were cleared at Helwan, near Cairo, Egypt. The materials contained in the graves are in part shown in the *Illustrated London News* (May 1, 1943); they consist of pottery and stone vessels, part of an ivory boat model, and various beads and pendants of semiprecious stones. It is important to note that "scarabs" are mentioned as having been used as pendants in the necklaces, and one such object appears in a photograph. The proper Egyptian scarab does not appear until the latter half of the First Intermediate period, and to describe the elongated bug-shaped object shown in the photograph as a "scarab" is misleading, in view of the First Dynasty context claimed by the excavator. The graves also contained curved ivory wands with animal heads (described as "*objets d'art*") which are known from the reliefs to have been held by dancers, and probably beaten against one another as cymbals.

As regards Mesopotamia, it is unfortunate that the details of Seton Lloyd's new excavations (see above) were not available. The Oriental institute added to its growing list of publications of the Iraq expedition the volume on *More Sculpture from the Diyala Region* by Prof. Henri Frankfort.

Nelson Glueck carried on an important archaeological survey for the American School of Oriental Research and the Smithsonian institution, on the eastern side of the Jordan valley (Trans-Jordan). These explorations revealed the ruins of a large number of ancient sites, with a range of dates (on the basis of the potsherds collected) from the Chalcolithic to Byzantine periods. The sites of Biblical times were always built on easily fortified and usually isolated hills, which dominated perennial streams and strategic roads—sites which might guard the fertile irrigated plains and streams from which the inhabitants gained their sustenance. By a careful consideration of the geography of the Biblical narratives and by the various ranges of dates indicated by the pottery he collected, Glueck has suggested a number of identifications of these sites with towns of Biblical times. The identifications include Jabesh-Gilead, Zarethan, Soccoth and Zaphon. The survey also traversed the great dolmen fields of Trans-Jordan, from Tell el-Hammām to the Dead sea. Glueck describes the ruins of a stone house which he suspects was built by the dolmen builders; he follows Prof. Albright in suggesting a Neolithic (i.e., "Tahunian") date for the dolmens. In *Belleten*, vii, 26 (Türk Tarih Kumumu), there is a short report on the agora at Smyrna in Turkey, with plans, architectural photographs, and a sketch suggesting the original appearance of the basilica.

Some 30 tumuli were excavated on the island of Bahrein in the Persian gulf by P. B. Cornwell (*Asia*, April 1943, pp. 230 ff). Two types of tumuli are described, one of simple cairn-like rock mounds, and one composed of dirt and limestone chips which usually enclosed a tomb chamber or cist. The same types were noted in explorations in Saudi Arabia. One large Bahrein tomb contained the remains of beds, also pottery, bronzes, a circular ivory box fragment, ostrich shell fragments, and the skeletons of sheep. The human physical specimens recovered from the Bahrein tombs were mainly of adult males. An attempt is made to connect the Bahrein material to that of Mesopotamia, but this attempt is valid in only the most generalized sense.

In the *Geographical Journal*, ci, iii (1943), Major R. A. B. Hamilton describes different types of ruins he has observed in the Western Aden Protectorate of Arabia.

Europe.—Very little information is available on recent archaeological activities within Europe, although the *American Journal of Archaeology*, xlvii, 2 (April-June 1943) gives abstracts of notices contained in a mimeographed Swiss publication (*The New Pallas*, vi, 1942) which reached its editors. A number of the items noticed seem to refer to chance finds, although others (such as, that the Germans are undertaking research on the prehistoric cemeteries at Carnac, in Brittany) seem to imply planned archaeological operations. None of the notices seems particularly startling in an archaeological sense.

Two *Annuals* of the British School at Athens (vols. xxxviii and xxxix) appeared belatedly during 1943. The work of the late John Pendlebury in the plain of Lasithi, in east central Crete, and that of Miss Benton in a cave-sanctuary on Polis bay, Ithaca, were the only reports of excavations which the volumes contained. Miss Benton's work strengthens the case for the British school's belief that modern Ithaca is actually the Ithaca of Odysseus (the Germans believe otherwise).

In England, a fine group of ornaments was discovered in the graves of prosperous Anglo-Saxon peasants at Nassington near

DIGGING IN AN INDIAN CAVE in Bear Mountain-Harriman State park, N.Y., discovered by a Girl Scout in Aug. 1943. The material recovered included important remains dating back to the 12th century

Peterborough. The graves date to the 6th and 7th centuries, A.D., and the contents show evidence that the people were pagans and probably worshippers of Odin. Besides brooches, of which some circular examples bore swastikas, there were spear heads, shield bosses, needles, and beads of amber and glass, as well as incised and impressed decorated black burnished pottery. Most of these materials came from the graves of women.

An early Iron Age fort on an island in Loch Craignish, Argyll, Scotland, was investigated, as well as a hut circle inside a large stone-walled enclosure. A round-chambered cairn of early Bronze Age date, found at the north end of the lake, was also studied.

Africa.—In *Man*, xliii, 34 (May–June 1943), J. Joire gives an inventory of finds taken from 11 burial mounds on the Senegalese coast of Africa, some 122 mi. northeast of Dakar. The position of the bodies indicates a pre-Islamic date, and the excavator judges that the people may have been Serers. The finds consisted mainly of jewellery and weapons, and included one fine gold pectoral. The pectoral and some of the jewellery appear, in the opinion of the excavator, to be Mediterranean types, and trade is postulated as the means for their having reached this district.

Asia.—Workmen digging an air-raid shelter in Chengtu, Szechwan province, China, came upon the brick and stone tomb of Wang Chien, distinguished official and self-appointed emperor of China in the 10th century, A.D. (*A.J.A.*, xlvii, 3, p. 265). At the back of the tomb chamber was a throne on which stood a statue (presumably of the dead man); before this was a dragon-handled coffin, and cases which contained two sets of jade books. The text in these is a commentary on the reign of Wang Chien. The coffin and its contents had not been fully investigated.

Sources used in the preparation of this article, other than those specifically mentioned: *American Journal of Archaeology* (*A.J.A.*), *Antiquaries' Journal*, *Antiquity*, *Bulletin of the American Schools of Oriental Research* (*B.A.S.O.R.*), *Geological Magazine*, *Geographical Journal*, *Illustrated London News*, *Journal of Near Eastern Studies* (*J.N.E.S.*), *Man*, *Museum News*, *Nature*, the *New York Times*. (R. J. B.)

Western Hemisphere.—All professional archaeological explorations in the western hemisphere were terminated for the duration of World War II.

Archery.

The archery events of nationwide significance in 1943 were the various mail matches conducted by the National Archery association (N.A.A.), the annual championship tournament having been cancelled on account of the war. These mail matches included the 16th annual series of indoor matches of the Olympic Bowman league in February, the 14th annual Woman's Intercollegiate Archery tournament and a nationwide Clout shoot in May, a nationwide Target shoot in August and a nationwide Flight shoot in October.

In the indoor matches, first place in the men's division went to the Madison Archery club, Madison, Wis., and in the women's division, to a team from University of Connecticut, Storrs, Conn.

Although most colleges were operating on a revised and speeded-up schedule because of the war, there were 82 teams (8 archers to a team) representing 56 colleges taking part in the Intercollegiate event. This was won by Team 1 from University of Connecticut.

Nearly 400 archers competed in the Clout shoot, the men shooting 36 arrows at 180 yds. and the women and juniors shooting 36 arrows at 120 yds. A. L. Harrison, Altadena, Calif., won in the men's division (score 36–276). Mrs. H. A. Biltzenburger, Los Angeles, Calif., won in the women's division (score 36–314) and John Mahoney of San Diego, Calif., won in the junior division (score 36–290).

The nationwide Target shoot, which brought out an entry list of nearly 900, was won by C. J. Weese, Newark, N. J., in the men's division, Mrs. S. Robert Leaman, Bird-in-Hand, Pa., in the women's division, John Mahoney, San Diego, Calif., in the boys' division and Marilyn Reinecke, Chicago, Ill., in the girls' division. Mrs. Leaman turned in a record-breaking score of 72–604 in the Columbia Round.

The regular style event of the nationwide Flight shoot was won by E. Bud Pierson of Cincinnati, Ohio, with a shot of 522 yds. 5½ in., which betters the previous N.A.A. record by over 16 yds. The free style event was won by Mike Humbert of Springboro, Ohio, with a shot of 566 yds.

The National Field Archers association conducted a series of field archery events by mail.   (L. C. S.)

Architecture.

By 1943 practically all building of any consequence to the development of architecture had been arrested by the war. The controversies between modernism and traditionalism, the rise of national styles, the growth of regional characteristics were blotted out by more urgent problems confronting the peoples of the earth in their strife for freedom and existence.

Planning for the postwar period began in England and America. Building was considered an important factor in the absorption of manpower released by demobilization and termination of war production. The devastation caused by aerial bombing demanded reconstruction—the better life promised the people after the war required replanning of towns and regions. War-expanded industries began to concern themselves with postwar uses for their materials and production facilities. Out of these conditions arose new opportunities for architects, and architecture itself took on a new concept; it became a social function for the benefit of the community. These changes found expression in the publication of plans for towns and regions, in official reports, in literature, propaganda pamphlets, advertisements and in exhibitions.

In the practice of architecture a closer co-operation between designers and technicians was demanded. The increasing complexity of building operations coupled with the desire for greater efficiency and economy gave advantages to the larger organizations in which the talents of architects, engineers, cost estimators, and construction managers were combined. A large volume of planning and design was also carried out by public bureaus and the design offices or research laboratories of industries.

Planning and Design.—The plans for postwar building were aimed at social betterment. Architects and town planners directed their efforts toward the elimination of squalor, the avoidance of crowding and congestion in centres of population, the opening of built-up areas by parks and playgrounds, the infiltration of sunshine and healthy surroundings into the urban districts and through larger windows even into the buildings themselves. Where aerial warfare had brought destruction, reconstruction was combined with social improvement and modernization of the pattern of the communities. Here as well as in countries untouched by devastation, it was realized that the older towns and cities were ripe for reconstruction and that this work provided a large field of employment for the postwar period.

In the design of postwar communities and buildings a greater intermingling of society under more stringent economic conditions was anticipated. Government and municipality, it was thought, would have to provide more public facilities for the education, welfare, and recreation of the people. Housing, schools, nurseries, health clinics, hospitals and neighbourhood recreational centres were therefore the buildings to which emphasis was given.

The conflict between modern and traditional architecture remained undecided. Certain changes had, however, established themselves. The thinner walls and larger windows resulting from modern building technique produced a less massive appearance, the interiors were more open and allowed for greater flexibility in use, meaningless ornamental decoration was absent.

In British writings, attention was called to the charm and fine qualities of the traditional architecture of the past, the beauty of the landscape and its harmony with the mellow quali-

HOTEL STATLER, Washington, D.C. Holabird & Root, architects; A. R. Clas, assistant architect

ties of the old buildings. Simultaneously, and often by the same authors, it was considered probable that the modern movement through which design was passing during the interwar period would be continued after the war with increased tempo. In America it was predicted that the revolutionary changes in architecture which for so long had been only an intellectual ideal would come into existence as a technological necessity. The American Public Health association, through its committee on the hygiene of housing, had analyzed building requirements in the light of man's psychological and physiological needs and isolated the considerations that entered into the design of buildings for human needs. Scientific research was applied to the development of new building materials, construction methods and the design of building equipment. For example, the Pierce Foundation in New York carried out research and technical work "to the end that the general hygiene and comfort of human beings and their habitations may be advanced." Problems were here analyzed on the basis of human as well as economic requirements. Revere Copper and Brass, Inc., invited a group of well-known U.S. architects and designers to present in pamphlet form their conception of the buildings of the future.

Materials and Methods.—Three related forces presaged the coming of a revolutionary era in house technology: First, prefabrication and mass production of houses or components thereof; second, an immense progress in building technique as exemplified by modern construction, heating and air-conditioning, soundproofing, illumination and automatic control; third, the development of new materials, primarily plastics, plywood and light noncorroding metals. The war had given to prefabrication a fair volume of production in the demand for soldiers' huts and war workers' housing; in both cases the use was temporary and the living standards were consequently kept at a minimum. For postwar demands, standards were to be raised while costs were to be kept down. Multiple use of standardized sections, interchangeability of components of buildings similar to that of parts of the automobile, flexible and efficient planning, and reduction in field labour were the measures proposed for the accomplishment of these aims. An effort was made to arrive at a uniform basis or module to building dimensions. The function of every part of a residence was restudied in the light of social, economic and technological changes. Imaginative proposals stirred public interest. For example, it was suggested that the function of the kitchen be taken over by built-in equipment within the living or dining space; the tight shop-like kitchen which was the ideal of the prewar period was to disappear in favour of a more spacious room suitable for dining, living or children's play area. Sink, refrigerator and stove were all being considered for radical new design. Bathrooms were to be mass produced as one piece units composed of inter-connected fixtures completely piped and finished.

Building technique continued in its progress of supplying with ever increasing precision man's comfort within buildings. Interest continued to be focused on radiant heating (the warming of floors, walls or ceilings) and air-conditioning as a means to winter and summer comfort. Ultra-violet ray lamps were sometimes installed to kill germs. Eye fatigue was scientifically combatted in the design of illumination; the trend to increase the intensity of artificial lighting and to create brightness continued. Acoustic products and acoustic treatments were developed to prevent sound penetration between rooms and to provide for local absorption.

The demand for an increased speed of construction brought on by World War II combined with the high cost and relative inefficiency of labour at the building site had caused a movement away from natural materials toward the synthetic products.

MINISTRY OF EDUCATION AND HEALTH, Rio de Janeiro, Brazil. Lucio Costa, Oscar Niemeyer, Afonso Reidy, Carlos Leão, Jorge Moreira and Ernani Vasconcelos, architects; Le Corbusier, consultant

Increasingly stone and brick were substituted by cement products, plaster by wall boards, decorative clay tile by a variety of sheet materials, etc. Prominent among the new materials were plywood, plastics and light noncorroding metals for which the aeroplane demands of the war had created enlarged production facilities. New architectural uses for plastics products were investigated; pliable sheeting was developed for purposes of insulation and decorative covering; semirigid or rigid sheeting for wall boards and tiles; extruded products for mouldings, edgings, handrails, sunblinds, etc.; and finished moulded articles for structural functions, built-in fixtures and fittings, hardware, etc.

Examples of 1943 Architecture.—In the *United States,* the stringent control over materials enforced by the War Production board allowed only the building of essential war plants, housing for war workers, construction for military needs and the erection of buildings absolutely necessary to the safety and welfare of the public.

The housing for workers at the Ford bomber plant at Willow Run, Mich., was accomplished by the use of diverse types of structures: trailers, prefabricated single and multiple family houses and dormitories. Here as elsewhere the need for community centres to provide the eating, shopping, recreational and administrative facilities for the population was realized. Schools and nurseries for the children of war workers and infirmaries were also built. The firm of Eliel and Eero Saarinen and Robert F. Swanson was prominent among the architects for Willow Run.

The welfare building at the naval training station at Great Lakes, Ill., Skidmore, Owings and Merrill, architects, showed an ingenious use of laminated wood beams for the creation of long spans. Simplicity combined with unusual size gave impressive qualities to another naval training station on the east coast of

RESEARCH AND MANUFACTURING LABORATORIES of G. D. Searle & Co.,
Skokie, Ill. Herbert Banse, architect

the United States, Eggers and Higgins, architects.

The Statler hotel in Washington, Holabird and Root, A. R. Clas, associated architects, showed in the treatment of the guest rooms and public spaces the current trend of development in hotel design. The public lobby was broken up into a series of intimate spaces and segregated into the functions of lounging, the transaction of hotel business, and circulation. The guest rooms were furnished in the character of living rooms.

The house of John B. Nesbitt at Brentwood, Calif., Richard Neutra, architect, was indicative of a trend of departure from the severe character of the early functional style of architecture. Here as well as in the Weston Havens house at Berkeley, Calif., Harwell H. Harris, architect, a certain artistic freedom akin to poetry was reintroduced into modern architecture to create a play of form and of light and shade, and to add life to unadorned surfaces by the introduction of growing plants.

England's architectural activity was primarily devoted to plans for the rebuilding of Britain. The County of London plan prepared by J. H. Forshaw and P. Abercrombie at the request of Lord Reith, minister of works, proposed a 50-year program aimed at the repair of war damage combined with improvements to obsolescence, bad and unsuitable housing, inchoate communities, uncorrelated road systems, industrial congestion, a low level of urban design, inequality in the distribution of open spaces and increasing congestion. With an open mind to coming changes in architectural styles it advocated a liberal control of street architecture for harmony in aesthetic effect. The plan for the reconstruction of Coventry also aimed to create order and design out of disorder and destruction.

Housing, both temporary and permanent, and the few public buildings which were completed in wartime illustrate the development of British architecture. The estates for workers in the north of England designed by Arthur W. Kenyon combined the spirit of the modern age with the dignity of British brick architecture of the Georgian period. A temporary quality of design which war necessity gave to architecture was shown in a hostel for British war workers, F. R. S. Yorke, architect. The architecture of public buildings was exemplified in the Friern Barnet municipal offices in north London, Sir John Brown and A. E. Henson, architects. Here classic monumentality was expressed in motives somewhat influenced by Swedish architecture.

The architecture of *South America*, especially Brazil, came into prominence in the United States through an exhibition first held at the Museum of Modern Art in New York and later at the museums of other important cities. Lectureships and scholarships in architecture were exchanged between the countries of the Americas. (*See also* BUILDING AND CONSTRUCTION INDUSTRY.)

BIBLIOGRAPHY.—J. H. Forshaw, P. Abercrombie, *County of London Plan* (1943); Royal Institute of British Architects, *Rebuilding Britain* (1943); F. J. Osborn, ed., *Rebuilding Britain Series* (1941–43); Co-operative Permanent Building Society Series, *Design for Britain* (1942–43); R. Tubbs, *Living in Cities* (1942); J. M. Richards, *The Bombed Buildings of Britain* (1942); D. E. E. Gibson, *Plan for the New Coventry* (1941); Bournville Village Trust, *When We Build Again* (1941); American Public Health Association, *Housing For Health* (1941); J. M. Richards, *An Introduction to Modern Architecture* (1940); P. L. Goodwin and G. E. Kidder Smith, *Brazil Builds* (1943); Eliel Saarinen, *The City* (1943). Periodicals for the year 1943, *The Architectural Review* (London); *Journal of the R.I.B.A.* (London); *The Architectural Forum* (New York); *The Architectural Record* (New York); *The New Pencil Points* (New York).   (W. F. B.)

Archives, National.

The National Archives was established by an act of Congress approved June 19, 1934. Its primary objective is to make the experience of the American government and the American people as it is embodied in noncurrent records of the federal government available to guide and assist the government and the people in planning and conducting their activities. This is accomplished by selecting, assembling, preserving, organizing and making available for use the noncurrent records of the United States government that have permanent value.

There were on July 30, 1943, about 542,000 cu.ft. of records in the custody of the archivist of the United States. These included, in addition to the bulk of the older records, nearly all the records of emergency agencies of World War I, which have been extensively used in the planning and conduct of the present war. A 680 page *Handbook of Federal World War Agencies and their Records* was published in 1943.

A special function of The National Archives is the daily publication of the *Federal Register,* which contains all current administrative orders, rules and regulations issued by federal agencies that have general applicability and legal effect, including many documents on priorities, the selective service, export control and other phases of the war effort.

The Franklin D. Roosevelt Library at Hyde Park, which was dedicated in 1941, is administered by the archivist of the United States. The museum portions of the building are open to the public and the library is assembling and arranging the papers of the president and his associates.   (S. J. Bu.)

Areas and Populations of the Countries of the World.

The table that follows gives the area, population, and population per square mile for the various countries of the world. For many countries it was difficult under conditions of 1943 to secure population data which were entirely satisfactory. The latest available figures relate to different dates in different countries; and in some cases different dates connote different areas. The table gives figures for practically the entire world, however, with a minimum of overlap or similar complication and with a sufficient degree of accuracy to serve as a source of general information with respect to the relative importance of the several countries.

Name of State	Area (in Square Miles)	Population (000's omitted)	Population per Square Mile
Afghanistan	250,965	7,000	27·9
Albania	10,811	1,106	102·3
Andorra	193	6	31·1
Argentina	1,078,377	13,709	12·7
Australia, Commonwealth of	2,974,514	7,137	2·4
Australian colonies	188,818	1,019	5·4
Belgian colonial empire	922,234	14,204	15·4
Belgium	11,980	8,307	693·4
Bhutan	19,305	250	13·0
Bolivia (adjusted area)	420,849	3,472	8·2
Brazil	3,286,097	41,565	12·6
British colonial empire	3,448,552	72,288	21·0

Name of State	Area (in Square Miles)	Population (000's omitted)	Population per Square Mile
Bulgaria	42,741	6,676	156·2
Burma	233,591	16,824	72·0
Canada	3,694,591	11,507	3·1
Chile	286,486	5,024	17·5
China and dependencies (incl. Manchuria)	4,480,992	457,835	102·2
Colombia	439,768	9,388	21·3
Costa Rica	19,305	672	34·8
Cuba	44,015	4,232	96·1
Czechoslovakia (1937 area)	54,244	15,239	280·9
Denmark (exclusive of Greenland)	17,143	3,903	227·7
Dominican Republic	19,305	1,650	85·5
Ecuador (excl. of uninhabited territory)	175,676	3,000	17·1
Egypt (excl. of uninhabited territory)	386,100	16,783	43·5
Estonia	18,340	1,122	61·2
Ethiopia (Abyssinia)	347,490	9,300	26·8
Finland	134,324	3,675	27·4
France (incl. Alsace-Lorraine)	212,741	41,980	197·3
French colonial empire	4,703,013	72,086	15·3
Germany (1939 area: incl. Austria)	314,038	79,375	252·8
Great Britain and Northern Ireland, United Kingdom of	94,517	47,786	505·6
Greece	50,193	7,336	146·2
Greenland (Danish colony)	31,284	18	0·6
Guatemala	42,471	3,368	79·3
Haiti	10,039	2,600	259·0
Honduras	59,459	1,258	21·2
Hungary (1942 area)	61,892	13,644	220·4
Iceland	39,768	120	3·0
India (exclusive of Burma)	1,574,902	388,998	247·0
Iran (Persia)	634,362	15,000	23·6
Iraq	116,602	3,561	30·5
Ireland (Eire)	26,641	2,963	111·2
Italian colonial empire	1,240,147	4,651	3·1
Italy	124,015	44,533	359·1
Japan (proper)	147,490	73,114	495·7
Japanese empire	115,164	31,632	274·7
Latvia	25,405	1,951	76·8
Liberia	46,332	2,500	54·0
Liechtenstein	77	12	155·8
Lithuania	23,089	2,925	126·7
Luxembourg	1,004	301	299·8
Mexico	760,231	19,546	25·7
Nepal	54,054	5,600	103·6
Netherlands	12,741	9,076	712·3
Netherlands colonial empire	790,794	71,828	90·8
Newfoundland and Labrador	162,934	296	1·8
New Zealand	105,212	1,639	15·6
Nicaragua	49,421	1,380	27·9
Norway (including Svalbard)	149,035	2,953	19·8
Panama (exclusive of Canal Zone)	28,958	632	21·8
Paraguay (area adjusted)	153,282	1,015	6·6
Peru (revised area)	482,239	7,023	14·6
Poland (1938 area)	149,922	35,000	233·9
Portugal (inc. Azores and Madeira Isls.)	35,598	7,761	218·0
Portuguese colonial empire	803,638	10,831	13·5
Rumania (1941 area)	74,903	17,018	227·2
Salvador	13,127	1,830	139·4
San Marino	39	15	384·6
Saudi Arabia	1,003,860	7,000	7·0
South Africa, Union of	794,208	10,521	13·2
Spain (including Canary Isls.)	194,981	26,222	134·5
Spanish colonial empire	128,696	962	7·5
Sweden	173,359	6,458	37·3
Switzerland	15,830	4,284	270·6
Thailand (Siam)	200,000	15,717	78·6
Turkey	296,525	17,858	60·2
United States	3,022,387	135,646	44·9
United States territories and possessions	712,838	18,833	26·4
Uruguay	72,201	2,164	30·0
U.S.S.R. (1938 area)	8,176,054	172,000	21·0
Venezuela	352,123	3,653	10·4
Yugoslavia (1939 area)	91,428	15,920	174·1
World Total	51,762,069	2,209,376	42·7

Argentina.

A republic on the southeastern coast of South America, second largest state on the continent. Area: 1,079,965 sq.mi. The religion is Roman Catholic, the language, Spanish.

An official estimate of the population as of Dec. 31, 1943, was 13,709,238 persons (1941: 13,517,135). Argentine-born persons made up 76.9% of the total population (1940 est.), foreign-born (mainly Europeans) 19.9%, and mixed-bloods 3.2%. The basic stock is Spanish, with immigrants since 1860 estimated as 42% Italian, 33% Spanish, 8% Russian and Polish, 4% German and Austrian. The capital city is Buenos Aires (pop. est. 2,557,586 on March 31, 1943). Other major cities (with est. pop.) are Rosario (540,000); Avellaneda (a Buenos Aires suburb) (386,000); La Plata (248,000); Córdoba (273,852); Santa Fé (150,000); Tucumán (149,214); Bahía Blanca (114,148); Paraná (80,000). More than 50% of the population is classed as urban.

History.—In spite of powerful pressure from the United Nations, Argentina refused to sever diplomatic relations with the axis during 1943. At times in the year, notably shortly before President Ramón Castillo was displaced by a revolution (June 3-4), and in the first few days of the new administration then established, rumours indicated that a break might be impending, but control of foreign affairs remained in the hands of Argentineans who were determined to pursue an isolationist policy. In late 1942 a charge by the United States that active espionage was being carried on in Argentina had resulted in an investigation, as well as in some temporary restrictions on axis communications, and charges of espionage faced the German naval and air attaché, Capt. Otto Niebuhr, as a result. When he claimed diplomatic immunity, his recall was requested on Jan. 18, 1943. In the same period there was a sharp exchange of notes between the British and Argentine governments over the former's criticism

PRESIDENT PEDRO RAMÍREZ of Argentina (right) reviewing troops after his military coup d'état of June 4, 1943, which overthrew the regime of Pres. Ramón S. Castillo

of Argentine isolation. Argentina was pointedly ignored by Vice-President Wallace of the United States while on a South American visit in April, nor was it invited to be present at the United Nations Food conference held in the United States in May.

In internal politics the federal government retained emergency powers under the state of siege indefinitely extended Dec. 14, 1942. Much attention was focused upon political alignments in view of the presidential election due in 1945. Chief opponent of administration policy was former president Augustín P. Justo; his sudden death Jan. 10 removed one of the most powerful opponents of isolation. By June, President Castillo had broken Argentine precedent by coming out openly in favour of Robustiano Patrón Costas, with the administration coalition (the National Democrat and Radical Anti-Personalist parties) falling in line with the president. The plans and policies of the administration were aimed particularly at gaining the support of moderates. On the other hand, liberal Argentine parties found difficulty in settling former rivalries so that they could organize an effective opposition campaign.

On June 3–4 a comparatively bloodless revolution, headed by General Arturo Rawson and General Pedro P. Ramírez, deposed President Castillo and established a provisional administration (on June 18 it was officially decreed permanent). For two days the presidential office was held by General Rawson; he then resigned and was replaced by Ramírez.

Allied observers at first hoped that the new government would break with the axis, but cabinet and other appointments, as well as a vigorously nationalistic policy, soon made it apparent that the new government was even more conservative than that which it had displaced. Many of its leaders, including President Ramírez himself, had been associated with Argentine fascist groups. A rigorous proscription of pro-Allied newspapers followed a wave of criticism of the government's policy; in September alone more than 70 papers were suspended for varying periods of time, and some editors were jailed. When a federal interventor (Bruno Genta) discharged many liberal members of the staff of the great Litoral university of Entre Ríos, a serious student riot took place. In the last two months of 1943 there were additional disturbances among the students of other universities. The government suspended many pro-Allied organizations (including the *Junta Feminina de la Victoria,* a women's aid group not normally concerned with politics) on the charge that they were communist. Similar attempts against labour unions resulted in extensive strikes, with the government forced to modify its position in some cases. One of the most serious strikes started among the meat-packing employees of Avellaneda plants, in September, and lasted until Oct. 4, with a number of persons killed or injured during demonstrations. Late in November a general strike started in Mar del Plata over a new six-peso bicycle tax, and when police tried to punish strikers the action spread until some 30,000 workers had stopped work. The strike was not ended until Dec. 15, by which time arrested labour leaders had been released and the bicycle tax reduced to 50 centavos.

In the first week in September Foreign Minister Segundo Storni made an effort to secure lend-lease aid to be used to buy military supplies, but in response to the request the United States secretary of state, Cordell Hull, refused on the basis that Argentina was not co-operating with other American nations in maintaining hemisphere security. The interchange resulted in the resignation of Admiral Storni, but no change in general policy took place. Meanwhile, in the same month, General Rawson delayed in taking the post of ambassador to Brazil, to which he had been appointed, and instead toured the country making addresses in favour of a break with the axis powers. The administration finally had to order him to Rio de Janeiro, refusing to accept his tendered resignation.

Internal policies of the Ramírez administration included a number of measures designed to secure popular support: abolition of the official wine and grain boards, elimination of the hated Buenos Aires transportation monopoly, cuts in telephone, light and power rates, establishment of a national rental reduction measure, a reduction in the civil service for purposes of economy, an increase in pay for government employees, an increase in the minimum wage for farm labour, and an increase in farm loans to the amount of 20,000,000 pesos.

The most important international agreement made by Argentina during 1943 was the contract signed with Great Britain on Aug. 23 by which the entire exportable meat surplus of Argentina was put under contract for a period of two years from Oct. 1, 1942. The purchase was made by Great Britain for the United Nations. In November the same two nations entered into a price-fixing agreement on quebracho (tanbark). Other commercial treaties were signed with Chile and with Ecuador.

Argentina's favourable trade balance for the first nine months of 1943 was estimated at $73,500,000. In mid-September it was announced that £33,000,000 of the nation's £46,000,000 London-held bonds would be repatriated. In May the British-owned province of Buenos Aires waterworks was purchased by the government for 12,000,000 pesos, and in December the U.S.-owned street railway system of the city of Tucumán was purchased by the municipality. The greatest war-caused shortages felt in Argentina were in regard to fuel oils, with linseed oil and corn used in large quantities as a substitute, and in regard to rubber. Foodstuffs were generally plentiful.

Education.—Argentina provides free and compulsory education for its citizens. Elementary schools in 1941 numbered 14,059; secondary schools, 445 (in 1940). Enrolment in elementary schools was 2,005,462; in the secondary division, 75,903. Of the latter 42,000 students attended the 197 normal schools of the nation. There were in 1939 1,167 private schools with an enrolment of 139,917.

Finance.—The monetary unit is the peso, free value in 1943 25 cents U.S. (official type A exchange peso: 26.8 cents U.S.; type B exchange peso: 23.6 cents U.S.). The budget for 1943 placed expenditures at 1,204,000,000 pesos; in July it was estimated officially that the deficit for the year would amount to between 360,000,000 and 400,000,000 pesos (in 1942 expenditures had been 1,250,800,000 pesos; receipts: 1,001,700,000 pesos). Revenue for the first half of 1943 was 489,582,000 pesos; the largest sources of income were the income tax (133,793,000 pesos), excise duties (132,602,000 pesos) and customs (62,857,-000 pesos). The 1944 administrative budget (prepared before the revolution) estimated ordinary expenditures at 1,301,100,000 pesos; revenue at 1,107,300,000 pesos. The public debt as of Dec. 31, 1943, was 6,243,300,000 pesos (1941: 5,783,900,000 pesos). Gold and foreign exchange reserves in the Central bank on June 30, 1943, amounted to 2,580,200,000 pesos; notes in circulation were 1,691,960,000 pesos in value.

Trade and Communication.—In 1942 Argentina's trade totalled in value 3,063,319,700 pesos (exports: 1,788,958,100 pesos; imports: 1,274,361,600 pesos). Figures released for Jan. 1–June 30, 1943, valued the total foreign trade for the period at 1,323,-764,300 pesos (1942: 1,584,115,000 pesos). Exports were 880,135,-500 pesos in value, imports amounted to 443,628,800 pesos. Principal imports were: fuels and lubricants (1,160,500 short tons); stone, earth, glass and pottery (839,700 short tons); wood and manufactures (278,900 short tons); chemicals and drugs (104,170 short tons); iron and manufactures (106,800 short tons); foodstuffs (91,500 short tons); textiles (70,100 short tons); paper products (75,950 short tons). Leading exports for the first half-

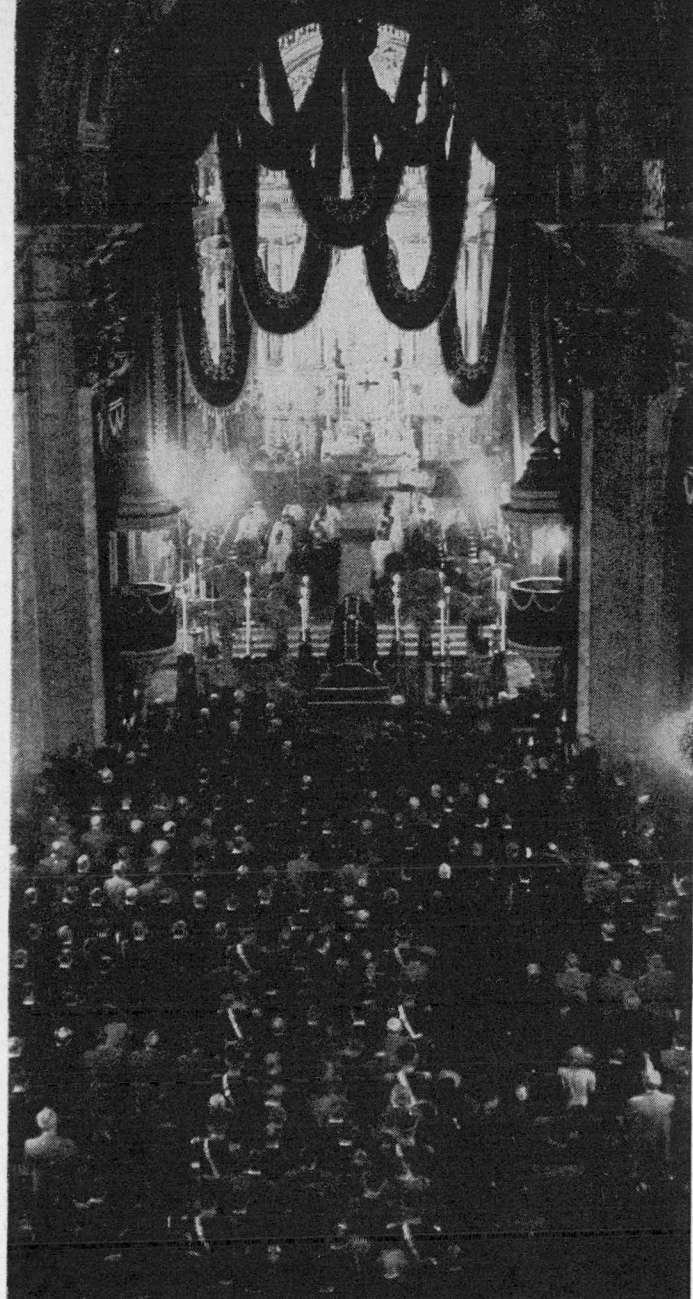

FUNERAL MASS at the cathedral of Buenos Aires June 12, 1943 for the 82 persons killed in Gen. Pedro Ramírez' coup d'état of June 4

year were (in short tons): meat (250,000); wheat (894,700); linseed (169,300); meat sundries (80,250); hides and skins (79,700); wool (60,950); quebracho products (68,100); maize (98,200); vegetable oils (56,550); minerals (51,250); oats (42,770).

In 1943 there were in operation 7,873 mi. of state-owned and 17,954 mi. of privately-owned railways. The national highway system approximated 36,600 mi., of which 11,224 mi. was listed as improved. Air transportation by Pan American gave service to all parts of America. The state merchant marine amounted to 38 vessels (approximately 200,000 gross tons).

Agriculture.—The chief resources of Argentina are agricultural and pastoral, with about 11% and 45% respectively of the total area of the country devoted to these activities in 1941.

Cereal production for the crop year 1942–43 was officially estimated as follows (in short tons): wheat (7,054,700); maize (2,138,500); oats (639,300); barley (358,800); rye (165,300); rice (111,300). Linseed production for 1942–43 was officially estimated at 1,681,000 short tons. Production (1941) of other oil-bearing seeds was (in short tons): rapeseed 53,391; peanuts

(shelled) 55,611; cottonseed 96,566; sunflower seed 442,803. Sugar production (1942) was 398,812 short tons; tobacco (official estimate 1942–43 year) 16,443 short tons.

Manufacturing.—Manufacturing became increasingly important in Argentina after 1936; the total value of industrial production (value added to that of raw materials) was estimated (1941) at approximately 3,400,000,000 pesos. Chief items of production were foodstuffs, textiles, forest products, paper products and chemicals. The number of industrial establishments in 1940 was estimated at 57,200; staff employed at 765,000 persons.

Mineral Production.—A total of 12,714,969 short tons of rocks and minerals was extracted in 1941, total value estimated at 183,051,000 pesos (increases of 4.3% and 7.4%, respectively, over 1940 figures). Metalliferous concentrates amounted to 122,033 short tons (value: 27,206,000 pesos); non-metalliferous (fuel, rock salts, etc.) totalled 12,592,935 short tons (value: 155,845,000 pesos); of this petroleum amounted to 3,857,782 short tons. (*See* also FASCISM.)   (D. RD.)

Arizona.

The "Apache state" lies in the southwestern part of the United States of America. It borders Mexico on the south; the Colorado river forms most of the western boundary. Area, 113,909 sq.mi. including 329 sq.mi. of water. Pop. (1940) 499,261, 65.2% rural and 34.8% urban. Native and foreign-born whites (including Mexicans) numbered 389,955 and 36,837 respectively; Negroes 14,993; other races (mostly Indians), 57,476. Estimated population of the state March 1, 1943 was 578,756. The capital is Phoenix with a population (1940) of 65,414; chief cities: Tucson (36,818); Douglas (8,623); Mesa (7,224); Globe (6,141); Prescott (6,018); Bisbee (5,853); Yuma (5,325) and Flagstaff (5,080).

History.—The state officials in 1943 were: chief justice, Archibald G. McAlister; governor, Sidney P. Osborn; secretary of state, Dan E. Garvey; attorney-general, Joe Conway; treasurer, James D. Brush. The state legislature of 1943 passed 96 acts. An act was passed authorizing the signing of a contract between the United States of America and Arizona providing for "delivery for use in this state of all such waters of the Colorado river as are available for use in this state." On Dec. 18, 1943 Utah withdrew objections to the contract for Arizona's participation in the Colorado river compact. On Dec. 21, California requested an oral hearing before approving.

Education.—According to the report of 1941–42 the net enrolment and the number of teachers in the public schools stood respectively as follows: elementary schools, 92,780 and 3,044; high schools, 23,650 and 937. In addition there were 58 private and parochial schools.

Public Welfare, Charities, Correction.—In Nov. 1943 there were 26,985 persons receiving assistance from the state department of social security and welfare. The total state appropriation to the department for 1943 was $1,856,200. Other state appropriations for 1943: industrial school $65,752; juvenile girl offenders $55,000; pioneer home $79,650; prison $182,195; state hospital for the insane $439,000.

Communication.—There was in 1943 a total of 3,678 mi. of highway in Arizona; improved state highway 2,800 mi.; unimproved state highway 877 mi. There were 2,165 mi. of railroads.

Banking and Finance.—National banks in 1943: deposits $169,881,098; loans and discounts $33,707,645; U.S. government securities $90,617,789; stocks, bonds and other securities $3,783,804. State banks: deposits $54,811,930; loans and discounts $9,772,061; U.S. government securities $26,333,411; stocks, bonds and other securities $3,077,201.

Agriculture.—To meet the labour shortage in 1943 many Indians from reservations were employed.

Leading Agricultural Products of Arizona, 1943 and 1942

Crop	1943 (est.)	1942
Wheat, bu.	462,000	575,000
Oats, bu.	203,000	252,000
Sorghum grain, bu.	1,728,000	1,190,000
Corn, bu.	402,000	396,000
Cotton lint, bales	139,000	193,000
Grapefruit, boxes	3,900,000	2,550,000
Oranges, boxes	850,000	700,000
Horses, head	73,000	74,000
Cattle and calves, head	911,000	980,000
Sheep and lambs, head	748,000	762,000

Manufacturing.—Less than 10% of the population was engaged in manufacturing. The most important industries were food, textile, metal and lumber products.

Mineral Production.—The mine production of copper for 1942 was 390,500 short tons. Production for 1943 was estimated to be higher than in the previous year.   (H. A. H.)

Arkansas.
Arkansas is an inland state in the south-central U.S.A., admitted to the union in 1836. Area 53,102 sq.mi., 377 of which are normally under water.

Pop. (1940) of 1,949,387 amounted to an increase for the decade between 1930 and 1940 of 94,905, or a gain of 5.1%. The average of inhabitants to the square mile is 37 persons. There are 53 towns and cities in the state having a total population of 431,910 urban and 1,517,477 rural. The Negro population was 506,770. Capital, Little Rock (pop. 1940, 88,039). Other cities: Fort Smith, 36,584; Hot Springs, 21,370; Pine Bluff, 21,290; North Little Rock, 21,137.

History.—The general assembly met in Jan. 1943 for its 54th regular session. Except for passage of the Abington bill, which outlawed the forcing of strikes by violence, controversial measures were significantly avoided.

The governor in 1943 was Homer M. Adkins, Democrat, re-elected in 1942. Other officers were J. L. Shaver, lieutenant governor; C. G. Hall, secretary of state; Guy E. Williams, attorney general; J. Oscar Humphrey, auditor; Earl Page, treasurer; and Claud A Rankin, land commissioner. The fiscal affairs of the state continued through 1943 on solid footing.

Education.—School attendance declined, as shown by the following comparison of state-wide attendance:

	White	Negro	Total
1941–42	344,285	109,704	453,989
1942–43	329,611	106,844	436,455

There were 7,292 white and 2,213 Negro teachers in the elementary schools in 1942–43, and 3,627 white and 468 Negro teachers in the high schools.

Public Welfare, Charities and Correction.—The state in 1943 maintained some 30 charitable and correctional institutions, including the state penitentiary farms, the state farm for women, girls' industrial school, boys' industrial school, Negro boys' industrial school, state hospital for nervous diseases, state's general hospital, tuberculosis sanatoriums, school for the blind, school for the deaf, Confederate veteran's home, children's home and hospital. The legislature of 1943 appropriated $4,000,000 for expenditure through the state department of public welfare in the fiscal year 1943–44.

Communication.—The highways, local, state and federal, totalled about 75,000 mi. in 1943. Of the state and federal system of nearly 10,000 mi., about 7,700 mi. were hard-surfaced with asphalt, concrete or gravel. There were about 5,000 mi. of railways in the state in 1943.

Banking and Finance.—On June 30, 1943, there were in Arkansas 161 state banks and trust companies, with combined resources of $204,492,580.95 and deposits of $190,153,515.75;

also eight building and loan associations, with resources of $3,456,944.32. There were 51 national banks, with assets of $252,354,000 and deposits of $245,961,000.

The total bonded debt of Arkansas on Dec. 31, 1943, stood at $142,218,016.67, a reduction for the year of $3,707,507.33. On that date, the state treasury had a cash balance, unhypothecated, of $17,700,000.

Agriculture.—Farming in Arkansas in 1943 was hit hard nearly everywhere by the worst drought in the history of the state. Cattle, hogs, sheep and work stock on Arkansas farms at the beginning of 1943 were valued at $118,147,000 There were approximately 216,000 separate farms in the state in 1943.

Table I.—Leading Agricultural Products of Arkansas, 1943 and 1942

Crop	Production	
	1943 (est.)	1942
Cotton, bales	1,090,000	1,485,000
Corn, bu.	23,508,000	37,110,000
Rice, bu.	12,690,000	13,515,000
Soybeans (for beans), bu.	2,168,000	3,585,000
Peaches, bu.	738,000	2,337,000

Manufacturing.—Lumber cut from Arkansas forests in 1943 measured in excess of 1,572,598,000 bd.ft. The output of manufactured lumber products was estimated at $100,000,000. The annual output of other industries was estimated in 1943 at $50,000,000, not including the manufacture of aluminum at two new plants built by the federal government at a cost of $70,000,000.

Table II.—Principal Mineral Products of Arkansas, 1942 and 1941

Mineral	1942		1941	
	Quantity	Value	Quantity	Value
Petroleum	26,577,852*	$25,970,935.17	26,250,274*	$24,210,971.75
Coal	1,899,844†	7,409,389.77	1,467,435†	4,930,579 92
Bauxite			956,617‡	4,783,085.90
Manganese	¶		7,157‡	143,738.54
Natural gas	29,559,502§	623,561.55	34,616,517§	739,371.95
Natural gasoline	31,445,961‖	1,082,435.02	24,867,370‖	984,033.97

*Barrels.   †Short tons.   ‡Long tons.   §Thousand cubic feet.   ‖Gallons
¶Not available for publication, at the request of the Office of War Censorship.

Mineral Production.—Mining operations in Arkansas in 1942 yielded products valued at $55,472,084.   (D. T. H.)

Armies of the World.
Because of the military need for censorship, no current data, official or otherwise, are available covering the statistics of this subject. The usual article is therefore omitted for the duration of the war. (For related topics see AIR FORCES OF THE WORLD; MUNITIONS OF WAR; SELECTIVE SERVICE, U.S.; WORLD WAR II.)

Armitage, Albert Borlase
(1864–1943), British explorer, was born July 2 at Balquhidder, Perthshire, Scotland. He was second in command of the Jackson-Harmsworth expedition to the north pole, 1894–97, and was navigator of the vessel "Discovery" during the British National Antarctic expedition, 1901–04. He served at sea throughout World War I, and was made commodore of the Peninsular and Oriental Steamship Line, 1923. He retired from the P. & O in 1924. Armitage, who had been given the rank of captain, retired, in the royal naval reserve in 1923, died Nov. 2.

Army, U.S.: see SELECTIVE SERVICE; UNITED STATES.

Arnim, Dietloff Juergen von
(1891?–   ), German army officer, was born of a wealthy and noble family. Little is known of his youth and early military career outside of Germany. An expert in tank

warfare, he had worked with Marshal Erwin Rommel before World War II and helped Hitler build up the wehrmacht. One of his first commands was as head of a panzer division. He later was transferred to the infantry and participated in the Polish campaign as commander of an infantry division. Early in the Tunisian campaign of 1942–43, there was considerable confusion as to the exact status of Arnim. In Jan. 1943, it was disclosed that he had been placed in command of axis armies in Tunisia, but later reports said that Marshal Rommel, Marshal Albert Kesselring and Gen. Walther von Nehring were also in command of part or all of axis forces in Tunisia. When Rommel returned to Germany in March 1943, for "reasons of health," Arnim was believed to have been given over-all command. On May 7, 1943, when the Allies took both Bizerte and Tunis, Arnim's units were driven back to the Cape Bon peninsula. On May 12, he indignantly branded Gen. Eisenhower's terms for unconditional surrender as "outrageous," but was compelled to accept them as his armies were shattered beyond repair. He was captured and taken prisoner to England.

Arnold, Henry H.

(1886–   ), U.S. army officer, was born June 25 in Gladwyn, Pa. He was graduated from West Point in 1907 and served in the Philippines until 1909. He set an altitude record in 1912, and was the first aviator to use radio in reporting artillery fire observed from a plane. During World War I he headed the information service of the signal corps's aviation division. Gen. Arnold led a round-trip flight of army bombers to Alaska in 1934. He was named major general, chief of the air corps, 1938. In Oct. 1940, he became the nation's first acting deputy chief of staff in charge of co-ordinating all matters pertaining to the air corps. In May 1941 Pres. Roosevelt made him a full-fledged deputy chief of staff, and on Dec. 15, 1941, the president named him for temporary promotion to the rank of lieutenant general.

In March 1942 Arnold was made commanding general of the army air force, which was put on an equal footing with the

ground forces. Just a year later, March 19, 1943, he was made a full general. He was present at the Churchill-Roosevelt conferences at Casablanca, Washington, Quebec, Cairo and Tehran.

Aronson, Naoum

(1872?–1943), Russian sculptor, was born in Kreslawka, Russia. In his youth he went to Paris, where he attended the École des Arts Decoratifs for a short time and then studied sculpture by himself. Among his subjects, Aronson prized his busts of Rasputin, Count Leo Tolstoy and Louis Pasteur, a study called "Aronson's Prophet" and a figure of a Jewish leader. He fled France after the nazi invasion and died in New York city, Sept. 30, 1943.

Arsenic.

There was almost no information on the subject of arsenic in 1943 beyond the fact that in the Material Substitution and Supply list issued by the War Production board on Oct. 1, 1943, arsenic and its derivatives were included among the materials the supply of which was not sufficient to meet current war and essential industrial demands.   (G. A. Ro.)

Art: *see* American Literature; Architecture; Painting; Sculpture; etc.

Art Exhibitions.

With the increased difficulties of transportation in wartime, museums had been curtailing their juried American exhibitions. The Pennsylvania Academy's annual and the Corcoran biennial in Washington were all invited for the first time. Chicago's Art Institute for the third consecutive year held an all-invitation annual and the Carnegie Institute of Pittsburgh followed suit after omitting their 1942 exhibition. Though closed since March 15, the Whitney museum opened its doors again for a well-selected November annual.

American art was featured in several important special exhibitions, such as Americans 1943—Realists and Magic Realists, and American Romantic Painters, both held at the Museum of Modern Art; Meet the Artist, a lively group of self-portraits assembled by the H. M. de Young museum in San Francisco; the Brooklyn museum's revival of The Eight and Art Begins at

UNDERGROUND MAZE of a shelter constructed for British art treasures in a Welsh mountain. Paintings are moved from one part to another in sealed cars along a 1,000-ft. tunnel

Home featured at the Addison Gallery of American Art in Andover, Mass. This inaugurated a new system whereby art patrons would buy pictures from the exhibition, use them in their homes for a period of time, then give them to the Addison gallery. A distinguished group of 18th century New England portraits was shown at the Worcester Art museum.

Notable one-man showings were the memorial exhibition of the sculpture of Gertrude Vanderbilt Whitney at the Whitney museum; the Alexander Calder retrospective at the Museum of Modern Art; Georgia O'Keeffe at the Art Institute of Chicago, where Edward Hopper was also accorded a room in their American annual; William Zorach at the Downtown gallery in New York; Everett Shinn at the Ferargil gallery; Marsden Hartley at Paul Rosenberg's.

Latin-American art came into even greater prominence with the opening of a series of South and Central American galleries at the Brooklyn museum and the featuring of recent purchases of Mexican and South American paintings at the Museum of Modern Art, which also organized and later circulated an important architectural show, Brazil Builds. Four Latin-American painters were featured by the San Francisco museum and Latin-American water colours were prominent in Brooklyn's and Chicago's International.

Boston's Institute of Modern Art featured Painting and Sculpture by American Negroes.

Two significant benefit exhibitions were held at the Wildenstein gallery in New York: Down the River Seine, a delightful group of French paintings shown for benefit of the *École Libre des Hautes Études,* and an outstanding Van Gogh exhibition for the benefit of the Queen Wilhelmina fund.

War themes were prominent in the year's schedule, as in the exhibition of 123 paintings of America at War commissioned for *Life* magazine, first shown at the National gallery in Washington and later circulated around the country. Airways to Peace at the Museum of Modern Art showed with maps, charts and globes the development of man's conquest of the air. Artists for Victory held a national print competition with the theme America in the War. A hundred prints were selected for showing throughout the country. The Fort Custer Army Illustrators exhibited a new group of lively water colours in the Art Institute of Chicago. A comprehensive exhibition held at the Portland (Oregon) Art museum told the dramatic story of shipbuilding in the northwest. Art of Our Allies was featured at the Boston Museum of Fine Arts.   (F. A. Sw.)

Art Galleries and Art Museums.

Announcement was made in January that the Whitney Museum of American Art was to combine with the Metropolitan museum. After the war a Whitney wing was to be built at the Metropolitan to house the 2,000 works of American art collected by Mrs. Whitney over a 25-year period and shown in the museum which she founded 12 years ago. For the time being the Whitney museum was to continue to function in its old quarters at 10 W. Eighth street.

Albert E. Gallatin removed his notable collection of 170 examples of abstract art from the Museum of Living Art at New York university and lent it to the Philadelphia museum. At his death it is to become their property. In this unusual collection are paintings by Arp, Klee, Duchamp, Miró's "Dog Barking at the Moon," Léger's "The City" and, perhaps most important of all, Picasso's "Three Musicians."

An anonymous donor provided for the setting up of the University of Arizona Gallery of Modern American Painting at Tucson and inaugurated the Arizona plan, whereby he would buy and present to the new gallery 12 paintings a year for a period of five years. The first selections were exhibited at the Metropolitan museum in April.

Another university gallery to buy contemporary Americans was the University of Nebraska, which continued its progressive policy and acquired distinguished works by Max Weber, Marsden Hartley, Julien Binford and Yasuo Kuniyoshi.

The Cleveland museum was fortunate in its recent acquisitions. They acquired a distinguished mature work of Francisco Goya, the "Portrait of Don Juan Antonio Cuervo," and a superb early work of Auguste Renoir, the portrait of Mlle. Romaine Lacaux executed in 1864. Even greater good fortune for Cleveland was the bequest of John L. Severance, which came to them at the close of 1942 but was exhibited as a feature of the year 1943. This collection is noted especially for its 18th century items and contains furniture and minor arts as well as paintings and oriental objects. A Boucher Beauvais tapestry and Nattier's "Madame Henriette" are notable.

Harvard university's Fogg museum received a wealth of material under the terms of the will of Grenville L. Winthrop. This collection of some four thousand items includes a variety of first quality oriental art, Rossetti's "Blessed Damozel," and other Pre-Raphaelite paintings, 52 water colours by William Blake, 40 drawings by Ingres, David's great portrait, "Girl in White Dress." The contents of the Winthrop collection were known to few people and placed the Fogg museum in a position of the greatest importance.

Among additions by the Joslyn Memorial in Omaha, Nebraska, were the "Young Man with a Pink," by Joos Van Cleve, a fine Flemish portrait of about 1520; and Goya's "Marquesa de Fontana."

Buffalo's Albright Art gallery made a notable purchase in Georges Seurat's "Le Chahut," painted in 1889. St. Louis acquired for its museum the "Portrait of Lady Gudeford" by Hans Holbein the Younger, dated in 1527 when the artist made his first visit to England. Murillo's "Virgin and Child," formerly in the collection of the Earl of Crawford, was secured for the Metropolitan museum, and a great Veronese altarpiece,

SALVADOR DALI explaining the details of one of his pictures at his one-man exhibit of portraits in New York city in April 1943

"Virgin and Child in Glory with Saints," has entered the collection of the Boston Museum of Fine Arts.

Mr. and Mrs. Chester Dale showed outstanding generosity to three museums. To the Art Institute of Chicago they sent on indefinite loan 50 20th century French canvases, including nine Picassos, among which are the famous "Family of the Saltimbanques" and "The Lovers," five works by Braque, Matisse's "Plumed Hat" and Modigliani's "Gypsy Woman with Baby."

To the Philadelphia museum the Dales lent an important group of both 19th and 20th century French and American paintings. Among these are Claude Monet's "Houses of Parliament," Henri Rousseau's "Boy on Rocks," and Toulouse-Lautrec's "Portrait of Jane Avril."

The National gallery in Washington, the third museum to benefit from the Dales's munificence, acquired, in addition to the outstanding loans already received, 11 old masters as a gift. In this group is an exquisite Boucher, "Venus Consoling Love," Zurbaran's "St. Lucy" and two paintings by Chardin.

The National gallery also received 63 American portraits as a gift from the Andrew W. Mellon educational and charitable trust. This notable group was formerly in the well-known Thomas B. Clarke collection and includes 19 Gilbert Stuarts, among which is the famous Vaughan "Portrait of George Washington."

The National gallery was also made the recipient of the superb Lessing J. Rosenwald collection of prints, drawings and manuscripts. Six thousand prints, hundreds of drawings and many rare books make up this wealth of material, which contains priceless 15th century prints, 230 Rembrandt etchings, 367 Whistlers.   (F. A. Sw.)

Arthritis.

The fundamental processes underlying the development of arthritis were studied in several ways. Five women with typical rheumatoid arthritis were placed under conditions which caused them to lose water from the body. This resulted in a decrease in their joint pains and swellings and an increase in the ability to move easily. These changes were reversed by causing the patients to accumulate body water. In some cases, at least, some of the symptoms of rheumatoid arthritis can be altered by variations in the amount of body water. Emotional stress is known to affect the onset and course of arthritis in many patients. In an attempt to elucidate the cause of this relationship a study was made on the skin temperatures under emotional stress in 25 arthritic and a like number of normal persons. Emotional stress was found to produce a drop in skin temperature indicative of a change in circulation. Comparatively little difference was noted in the two groups, however, and further work was indicated. Other studies showed that the heart and other organs than the joints are more frequently involved in rheumatoid arthritis than had been believed heretofore. This fits with the increasing emphasis on rheumatoid arthritis as a general disease.

According to Bauer and his colleagues the effect of the sulfonamide compounds represents the greatest advance ever made in the treatment of joint disease. These compounds exert dramatic and specific effect against certain of the so-called "specific" arthritides, particularly those caused by streptococci, gonococci, staphylococci, meningococci, colon bacillus and pneumococci. They were not found effective in rheumatic fever, rheumatoid arthritis or tuberculous arthritis. Freyberg evaluated carefully the proposed vitamin and endocrine treatments for chronic arthritis. In spite of favourable reports to the contrary he concluded that there was no vitamin or endocrine preparation which had a direct relationship to the common forms of rheumatic disease. Their value lay only in their effect on the general health. Good results

with several different kinds of gold compounds were reported as in previous years. In spite of extensive search a satisfactory nontoxic compound was not found. Although certain gold salts appeared to be of value for rheumatoid arthritis they should be taken only under experienced and competent medical supervision.

Surgeons reported some delicate and successful operations for the rehabilitation of joints already damaged by arthritis. This was not treatment in the strict sense, but was most important from the standpoint of restoring joint function. Industrial physicians recognized that arthritis varies in its ability to incapacitate all the way from mild joint pain to complete crippling. Satisfactory placement in industry for persons with arthritis is important and requires reason, sympathy and good common sense on the part of all concerned. Reports on the nature and frequency of arthritis among those in military service were not available but judging from previous military experiences it was almost certain that the problem of treatment and rehabilitation of service-acquired arthritis would be considerable.

BIBLIOGRAPHY.—M. N. Smith-Petersen, O. E. Aufranc, and C. B. Larson, "Useful Surgical Procedures for Rheumatoid Arthritis Involving Joints of the Upper Extremity," *Archives of Surgery* 46:764 (1943).   (E. P. J.)

Artillery: *see* MUNITIONS OF WAR; WORLD WAR II.

Art Sales.

Auction prices were up because of the closing of European markets and the prevalence of interested buyers, and auctioneers had an especially busy year. Parke-Bernet galleries did a $3,600,000 business during the 1942–43 season, the second highest for 10 years. Their top sale was the collection of Mr. and Mrs. Charles E. F. McCann, which brought $266,207. Many purchasers were foreign collectors in the United States for the duration. The Wadsworth Lewis collection of furniture, tapestries and Chinese art brought $187,238 A sale of unusual interest was Frank Crowninshield's modern French art, which totalled $131,365. In this sale Modigliani's "Madame Hebuterne" and Picasso's "Portrait of Braque" each brought $4,800, Forain's "Folies Bergère," $5,900 and Segonzac's "L'Église et La Marne, Champigny," $7,250.

Gimbel's, including the department in the Kende galleries at the Jay Gould mansion, concluded their 1942–43 season at $44,-225,000. Much of the material was from the Hearst collection; others were Stanley Bliss, Ewing Hill, and the stock of Marcus and Co., jewellers. They estimated 30,000 new collectors in the buying field.

A mild Bouguereau revival took place when Durand-Ruel acquired his 12-foot "Nymphs and Satyr" and sold it to a private collector at a reputed $12,000.

In London the salesrooms had the same brisk business as the New York auction houses and prices were maintained at a high level. Both Christie and Sotheby reported especially lively bidding in antique silver. L. W. Neeld's collection brought just under £8,000 for 15,000 ounces of silver. A George II salver brought £200. A record price was established when a single spoon dated 1481 brought the equivalent of $5,200. At Christie's sale of pictures belonging to the Countess of Oxford and Asquith, a Canaletto, "View of the Church of San Bartolomeo," brought $3,988. Morland's "A Winter's Morning" went for $924, indicating the continued popularity of the British school of painting on home soil.

A Bartolozzi coloured engraving of Lawrence's "Miss Farren" went for $1,932.

It was reported that sales continued to fetch high prices in Paris, Amsterdam and other continental centres under German domination. Since occupation money of questionable worth was used in these transactions, the sales could not be considered a valid measure of real values.   (F. A. Sw.)

Arts and Sciences, American Academy of: *see* AMERI-CAN ACADEMY OF ARTS AND SCIENCES.

Aruba: *see* CURAÇAO.

Asbestos.

Because of its position as a strategic mineral, no official data were published on asbestos output in any of the important producing countries for several years, and even the data on the small United States output was not reported for 1942. The Material Substitution and Supply list issued by the War Production board on Oct. 1, 1943, listed asbestos textiles as short in supply but cement sheets and short fibre were available in amounts in excess of current demand.

(G. A. Ro.)

ASCAP: *see* PERFORMING RIGHT SOCIETIES.
Ascension: *see* BRITISH WEST AFRICA.
Asia: *see* AFGHANISTAN; CHINA; INDIA; etc.

Asphalt.

The usual detailed statistics on petroleum asphalt production in 1942 were not made public, but a heavy increase in the United States was reported in the output of native asphalt, from 691,168 short tons in 1941 to 975,373 tons in 1942. The use of various types of petroleum asphalt in airport runway construction would indicate a marked increase in output.

(G. A. Ro.)

Assassinations.

The assassinations of 1943, actual or attempted, included the following:

Jan. 11. New York, N.Y. Carlo Tresca, anti-fascist leader and editor of Italian-language weekly, was shot and killed as he was leaving his office. His assailant escaped in a motor car.

Feb. 5. The Hague, Netherlands. Gen. Hendrik Alexander Seyffardt, pro-nazi army leader, was shot and mortally wounded outside his home.

Feb. 12. Netherlands. Reports reaching London said Dutch underground group known as "The Black Hand," shot and fatally wounded C. van Ravenzwaai, pro-nazi Netherlander who held portfolio as secretary for social affairs in Mussert cabinet.

April 15. Sofia, Bulgaria. Sotir Janeff, president of the Bulgarian parliament foreign affairs commission, editor of the semi-official *Slovo* and adviser to King Boris III, was shot and killed by two unidentified assassins, both of whom escaped. Janeff was a strong pro-nazi.

Aug. 28. Sofia, Bulgaria. Boris III, king of Bulgaria, died after a short illness. The official statement attributed his death to a heart attack, but it was widely rumoured that he died of a gunshot wound administered by an assassin.

Association for the Advancement of Science, American: *see* AMERICAN ASSOCIATION FOR THE ADVANCEMENT OF SCIENCE.

Association of Research Libraries.

The Association of Research Libraries is an association of 47 of the largest research libraries in the United States and Canada. Forty of the members are university libraries. Ordinarily there are two meetings a year, but in 1943 the only meeting was in Chicago on Jan. 31.

Most of the work of the association is done by committees. A committee on indexing and abstracting in 1943 was continuing an extensive study of the so-called "service basis" in selling indexing services. Other important committees were one on preventing postwar competition in book purchases, and one on filming of 19th century newspapers.

The most ambitious project of the association was the promotion of a printed book catalogue of the Library of Congress cards. A committee secured permission from the Library of Congress for the publication, made arrangement for its printing by the photo-offset process, and secured the necessary subscriptions. At the close of 1943, 53 of the proposed 160 volumes were published. The completed catalogue was expected to be one of the most important bibliographical tools in any research library, since it would list in alphabetical order all the books in the Library of Congress catalogued with printed cards and would reproduce all the bibliographical information on these cards.

The association also published *Doctoral Dissertations Accepted by American Universities, 1942–43,* completing ten years of such a classified list.

(P. N. R.)

Astronomy.

Solar System.—*The Sun.*—Both physicists and astronomers have long been interested in the chemical composition of the sun. Determination of which of the 92 chemical elements exist in the solar atmosphere is accomplished by a detailed study of the lines in the solar spectrum. The success of this study is dependent on the results of the laboratory studies of the spectra of various elements, as well as on theoretical investigations. During 1943, Charlotte E. Moore and A. S. King announced the identification in the solar spectrum of the lines of two elements not heretofore known to exist in the solar atmosphere—thorium and gold. Their detection raised to 66 the number of chemical elements identified. The presence of thorium in the sun is especially interesting, since it is the first radioactive element detected there. Failure of the remaining 26 of the 92 chemical elements to be detected in the solar spectrum does not necessarily mean that these elements are absent from the sun. For six of these elements the laboratory data on wave-lengths and intensities were inadequate in 1943. Of the remaining 20 elements, 11 have their strong spectral lines in an unobservable region of the solar spectrum, and five are radioactive elements of relatively short life. The other four elements have their strong lines in the observable region, and hence, if present, they must exist in such small amounts as to remain undetected.

Planetary System.—Five comets were discovered during 1943. Two of these proved to be rediscoveries of previously known comets, whereas the other three were observed for the first time. Two discovered by van Gent and by Diamaca were just below naked-eye brightness; the third, discovered by Miss Oterma, was of fifteenth magnitude.

Few observations of cometary spectra in the red beyond λ 5500 had heretofore been made. Swings, McKellar and R. Minkowski measured spectra of two bright comets in this region of wave-lengths, and compared these spectra with that of an oxy-ammonia flame. They found that some of the more prominent spectral features exhibit a behaviour to be expected from polyatomic molecules. Comparison with the oxyammonia flame led to tentative identification of several hitherto unidentified emission features in the cometary spectra as being due to a dissociation product of ammonia, probably to NH_2.

Observations of the surface features of the planets are exceedingly exacting, requiring both great skill and exceptional atmospheric conditions. M. Bernard Lyot and his associates at the Pic du Midi combined skill and excellent observing conditions to obtain some remarkable observations of Mars, and also of Jupiter, Saturn and Mercury. Their observations of the surface features of Mars showed a wealth of detail, and seemed to establish beyond question the semi-geometric nature of many of the surface markings on this planet. Of particular interest are their observations of surface features on the four bright satellites of Jupiter. Sufficient details of the surface features were observed to permit the preparation of maps for each of these satellites.

Stars.—*Special Stars and Stellar Structure.*—An extensive series of photographs of the visual double star 61 Cygni was obtained by Strand. From a study of these and other observations Strand found perturbations in the orbit of the visual components which are produced by a third and invisible body. These observed perturbations can only be explained satisfactorily if the third invisible body has the exceedingly small mass of 0.016 that of the sun, or 16 times the mass of the planet Jupiter. Since the smallest stellar mass previously known is 0.14 the sun's mass, this dark companion must have so little luminosity, if indeed it has any, that it can be considered a planetary object rather than a star. Thus for the first time in history a planet has been discovered outside the solar system. This planetary object moves about one of the visible components of the double star in a period of 4.9 years, the eccentricity of its orbit being 0.7. The semi-major axis of its orbit is 2.4 astronomical units, but due to the large eccentricity of its orbit, the planetary body comes within 0.7 astronomical units of its visible companion. The three body system of 61 Cygni is 11 light years away from us, making it one of the sun's nearest neighbours. The two visible components are red dwarf stars which revolve around their common centre of gravity in a period of 720 years. Strand's discovery of a planetary body outside the solar system was expected to affect profoundly the viewpoint of astronomers concerning the probability of the existence of other planetary systems.

The results of a study by Adams of interstellar lines in the spectra of 50 stars are of singular interest. The most prominent interstellar lines are those of calcium and hydrogen. In many of the spectra studied these lines are double or multiple, the different components being produced by interstellar clouds with differing radial velocities. The individual components of these interstellar spectral lines are sharp and narrow, indicating that the interstellar clouds of gas which produce them are discrete and have little internal motion. Adams found a general cloud in the direction of the bright stars in Perseus having a residual velocity of recession of 5 km./sec. In the direction of Orion, on the other hand, the clouds seem to be more broken and intermingled, and perhaps more turbulent than in most parts of the sky. Six stars in or close to the belt of Orion show the presence of two clouds, one with a velocity of recession of 7 km./sec. and the other with a velocity of approach of 15 km./sec. Some of the interstellar clouds observed show remarkably high radial velocities, higher than would be expected for these clouds. For example, a cloud in the direction of Sagittarius is receding at a velocity of 40 km./sec., and two clouds in the direction of Cygnus show velocities of recession of 41 km./sec., and 60 km./sec.

External Galaxies.—Hubble observed the direction of rotation in 15 spiral nebulae in which the spiral arms can be traced, and in which a general criterion for the tilt can be applied. By applying this general criterion to the 15 nebulae he found that all of them are rotating in the same direction. There still remained an ambiguity in regard to the tilt, so that although the fact of common rotational direction appeared to be established, the actual direction, *i.e.*, whether the arms were all trailing or all leading, remained uncertain. In the case of four of these spirals Hubble was able to apply a special criterion for tilt which was free from ambiguity, and he found that in these spirals the arms are trailing. Since he had already tentatively established that all 15 rotated in the same direction, it appears that we might assume, at least as a working hypothesis, that the arms of all spirals are trailing. This conclusion is of prime importance for attempts to explain the origin and development of the spiral arms.

Phenomena Visible in 1944.—*Jan. 25, 1944. Total Eclipse of the Sun.*—Visible in northern South America and northwestern Africa, with maximum duration in central Brazil. Partial phases visible in Florida and along the gulf coast of the United States near sunrise, and in Spain, southern France and the southern tip of England near sunset.

July 20, 1944. Annular Eclipse of the Sun. Visible in east central Africa, northern India, Burma and Indo-China, the southern Philippine Islands, along the north coast of New Guinea and on New Britain. Partial phases visible in the near east, southern Russia, China, Japan, Philippine Islands, the East Indies and Australia.

BIBLIOGRAPHY.—Harlow Shapley, *Galaxies* (1943); Leo Goldberg and Lawrence Aller, *Atoms, Stars and Nebulae* (1943). (N. L. P.)

ATC: *see* AIR TRANSPORT COMMAND.

Athletics: *see* TRACK AND FIELD SPORTS; etc.

Athlone, 1st Earl of

(ALEXANDER AUGUSTUS FREDERICK WILLIAM ALFRED GEORGE CAMBRIDGE) (1874–   ), British statesman, was born April 14 at Kensington palace, the third son of the 1st duke of Teck. Educated at Eton and the royal military college, Sandhurst, he served in Matabeleland, Southern Rhodesia, in 1896 and saw action during the Boer war. During World War I he was mentioned twice in dispatches, and in 1917 he was created 1st earl of Athlone. He was governor general of the Union of South Africa from 1923 to 1931. In 1936 he was appointed personal aide-de-camp to the king. He was appointed 16th governor general of Canada April 3, 1940, on the death of Lord Tweedsmuir. In a speech on Dec. 10, 1942, he defended Britain's imperial system, asserting that the independence of dominions was "a fact and not a fiction." In Aug. 1943, he gave a state dinner for Churchill and Roosevelt at Quebec. Subsequently, as acting chancellor for London university, he conferred an honorary degree on Roosevelt. In September he visited Alaska and inspected the new Alaskan highway.

Attu: *see* ALASKA; WORLD WAR II.

Auchinleck, Sir Claude John Eyre

(1884–   ), British army officer, was born in England, the son of Col. John Claude Auchinleck. He served in India in 1902, and was stationed in Egypt and Mesopotamia during World War I. In 1933 and 1935 he fought against native tribesmen on the northwest Indian frontier. In the spring of 1940 he was made commander of the Allied forces in northern Norway. He took Narvik but was forced to evacuate the city when the Allies failed to make additional landings in the south. In the summer of 1940, after the collapse of France, Auchinleck was appointed general officer commanding the English southern command, and he organized the first defenses of England to forestall the threatened German invasion. In Dec. 1940 he returned to India as commander in chief. In July 1941 he was made commander in chief of British middle east armies, succeeding Gen. Sir Archibald Percival Wavell. Auchinleck's armies in Libya launched an offensive Nov. 18, 1941, and advanced far into Libya, but were driven out in June 1942. Auchinleck then took over command of the British 8th army. On June 18, 1943, he was again made commander in chief in India. Responsibility for operations against Japan were at this time transferred from the Indian to the newly formed east Asia command.

Australia, Commonwealth of.

A self-governing member of the British Commonwealth of Nations, situated in the southern hemisphere between longitudes 113°9′ E. and 153°39′ E. and latitudes 10°41′ S. and 43°39′ S.; national flag, a blue ensign, with the Union flag in the quarter and six white stars in the field. Language, English;

AUSTRALIANS hauling gasoline cans away from a blazing fuel dump in New Guinea after Japanese bombers had scored a direct hit on the dump

religion, Christian (census 1933: Anglican, 2,565,118; Roman Catholic, 1,161,455; Presbyterian, 713,229; Methodist, 684,022; other Christians, 603,914). Ruler, King George VI; governor general (1943): the Rt. Hon. Lord Gowrie, V.C.; prime minister, Rt. Hon. John Curtin.

Area, 2,974,581 sq.mi.; pop. (est. Dec. 31, 1941) 7,137,221. Capital, Canberra. Chief cities (pop. Dec. 31, 1940): Canberra (11,000), Sydney (1,310,530), Melbourne (1,076,000), Adelaide (330,000), Brisbane (335,520), Perth (228,000), Hobart (66,-620), Newcastle (116,000).

History.—In accordance with the constitution it was necessary for a general election to be held at the latest in Nov. 1943. When John Curtin assumed office at the end of 1941 he was given full co-operation by the opposition parties under A. W. Fadden, but with the barest of majorities had but a precarious hold on office. The party truce virtually came to an end at the beginning of 1943 when Curtin introduced his militia bill. This bill empowered the government to use the militia for service beyond the confines of the commonwealth and its territories, but within an area (the S.W. Pacific) defined by the bill. The opposition had expected that such forces would be merged with the A.I.F. for service in any part of the world as strategy might require and felt that the government had broken its own promises at the dictate of the Labour caucus. As the year proceeded the opposition became increasingly critical of the prime minister's alleged weakness in dealing with labour unrest and accused him of introducing purely party legislation. In June the premier faced a censure motion, and though the government won by one vote—that of an independent—Mr. Curtin immediately announced his intention of seeking a dissolution. The election was held on Aug. 21 and resulted in the government's being returned with a net gain of 13 seats, losing only one seat—in Queensland. In the senate Labour won all 19 vacant seats, thus gaining a clear majority in both houses. The result was partly due to the lack of

cohesion and leadership in the opposition parties, but was in the main a tribute to the leadership of Mr. Curtin.

On Nov. 15, 1943, announcement was made in London that the duke of Gloucester had been appointed to succeed Lord Gowrie as governor-general of Australia.

In Nov. 1942 a special constitutional convention had met in Canberra to consider ways and means of transferring powers from the states to the commonwealth for the purposes of postwar reconstruction. It was agreed that state premiers should submit to their respective legislatures a draft bill listing 14 powers "to make laws in relation to postwar reconstruction" which should be referred to the commonwealth parliament for a period of five years to begin at the cessation of hostilities. During 1943 two states—New South Wales and Queensland—adopted the bill without qualification. Victoria, South Australia and Western Australia passed bills in a more or less mutilated form and in Tasmania the upper house twice rejected it altogether. The only solution of this urgent problem seemed to be for parliament to seek the necessary powers through an amendment to the constitution by means of a referendum which would probably be held early in 1944.

External Affairs.—The government decided that the war had demonstrated the desirability of Australia's developing a foreign diplomatic service of her own. In furtherance of this policy William Slater was appointed minister to the U.S.S.R. and took up his post at Kuibyshev in January. In October, Lt. Gen. Sir Iven Mackay was appointed first high commissioner in India and Thomas D'Alton became first high commissioner in New Zealand. On Nov. 5 Joseph Maloney, president of the New South Wales trades and labour council, was appointed to succeed William Slater as minister to the U.S.S.R. A diplomatic staff cadet system was introduced and a special training school was inaugurated.

In May the Australian legation at Kuibyshev took over the representation of Polish interests in the soviet union following the dispute between the soviet and Poland which resulted in the interruption of diplomatic representation.

During the year Herbert V. Evatt, the minister for external affairs, visited Washington and London to confer with President Roosevelt and Prime Minister Churchill, to discuss Pacific policy in relation to world strategy, and to strengthen the government's contacts with the Australian minister in Washington and the high commissioners in London and Ottawa. S. M. Bruce's appointment as high commissioner in London was extended for another year.

Public Finance and Economic Affairs.—During 1943 the economic life of the nation was subordinated to the overriding necessities of war. The government was faced with increased manpower requirements for the production of munitions of war, food, clothing and other essential supplies and services for their own and Allied forces and for defense construction works. The total working population was increased by bringing into industry people who were previously not engaged in work and it was estimated that the working population was 620,000 higher than before the war. Inevitably, however, the transfer of workers to the armed forces and munitions involved a great reduction in civilian goods and services and rationing was extended to a large number of commodities. Measures were introduced for the pooling of farm machinery and the planned production of foodstuffs which enabled primary production to be maintained in spite of 30% of the farm labour having been diverted to the services and munition works. To forestall inflationary tendencies the government placed a ceiling on all prices, to be held in the last resort by subsidies. The scheme came into operation in April and was working smoothly, the subsidies in the first year being estimated at £A.12,000,000. Further progress was made in the decentralization of industry and large sums were voted for the establishment of munition and other essential works in rural areas.

In February J. B. Chifley, the treasurer, submitted revised estimates which showed that war expenditure was likely to exceed the budget estimate of £A.390,000,000 by some £A.70,000,000. Concurrently he introduced increases in income tax on individuals estimated to produce £A.40,000,000 in a full year. He also announced the immediate establishment of a national welfare fund, to be financed out of revenue, of £A.30,000,000 per annum, or one-fourth of the total revenue collections from income tax on individuals, whichever were lower. Measures were introduced granting increased war pensions and repatriation benefits and a new maternity benefit of 25s. a week for six weeks and increased maternity allowances. The fund would ultimately finance sickness, unemployment, medical, hospital and dental services. In the meantime surpluses in the fund would be loaned to war expenditure. For the fiscal year ended June 30, 1943, total expenditure was £A.670,305,000, war expenditure accounting for £A.561,743,000, of which £A.158,891,000 was provided from revenue. Of the balance, £A.215,357,000 was raised by public loans and the sale of war savings certificates; temporary use of treasury balances provided £A.8,420,000; while £A.179,075,000 was financed by treasury bills discounted with the Commonwealth bank. Within a week of the opening of the new parliament in September, Chifley introduced his budget for the fiscal year 1943–44. Expenditure for purposes other than war was estimated at £A.144,526,000, an increase of £A.35,963,000 over the last year. Principal increases were: national welfare fund £A.29,750,000; increased war pensions £A.1,090,000; invalid and old age pensions £A.807,000; child endowment £A.595,000; widows' pensions £A.421,000. Expenditure from the national welfare fund would be less than £A.2,500,000 during the year, so that more than £A.27,000,000 would be available for war loans. War expenditure was estimated at £A.570,000,000 of which £A.403,000,000 not covered by revenue was to be financed by loans.

Education.—In 1939: state schools, 9,940; average attendance, 744,095; teachers employed, 31,199; private schools, 1,863; average attendance, 219,171; teachers, 11,496; technical schools, 94; total enrolment, 101,155; teachers, 3,276; business colleges, 122; total enrolment, 24,337; teachers, 727; universities, 8; total enrolment, 14,236.

Banking and Finance.—Revenue (actual 1942–43), £A.267,453,000; (est. 1943–44), £A.312,087,000; expenditure (actual 1942–43) ordinary, £A.108,563,000; defense, £A.561,743,000; (est. 1943–44) ordinary, £A.145,000,000; defense, £A.570,000,000; public debt (June 30, 1943) £A.2,006,000,000; notes issued April 26, 1943, £A.135,900,000; gold and sterling reserve (June 30, 1942), £A.35,141,000; exchange rate, £A.125 = £100 sterling (1£ = 403.5 cents U.S. in Dec. 1943).

Trade and Communication.—Overseas trade 1941–42 (merchandise): imports, £A.187,068,136; exports, £A.159,328,498. Communications and transport: 1940, roads, total mileage, *c.* 450,000; railways open to traffic (Dec. 1942) 27,159 mi.; airways (1942), distance flown, 7,666,000 mi.; passengers carried, 151,927; goods carried, 2,347,000 lb.; mails carried, 1,226,500 lb.; motor vehicle registrations (March 31, 1943): cars, 466,573; commercial vehicles, 255,379; cycles 48,286; wireless receiving set licences 1,393,872; telephones, number of lines, 537,702.

Agriculture, Manufacturing, Mineral Production.—Produc-

MRS. FRANKLIN D. ROOSEVELT arriving at the town hall in Sydney, Australia, during her five-week tour of the South Pacific in Aug. and Sept. 1943

WITHIN A HALF MILE of the fighting front, Australian troops in New Guinea cast their votes in the federal elections of 1943

tion, (in metric tons): wool (1942) 513,000; wheat (1942–43) 4,311,000; oats (1940–41) 185,000; barley (1940–41) 162,000; maize (1940–41) 233,000; rice (1941–42) 56,000; potatoes (1940–41) 462,000; cane sugar (1940–41) 820,000; wine (1940–41) 725,000 hectolitres; gold (1941) 35,960 kg.; coal (1941) 15,200,000; statistics for all other minerals not available for publication. Total value of production in £ Australian: (1940–41) pastoral and dairying 173,755,000; mineral 40,002,669; manufacturing 257,914,349. Labour and employment: employment in factories (1928–29 = 100) Feb. 1943, 170.0; number (March 1943) 736,000; unemployment, trade union returns (March 1943) 1.2%; total recorded material production (1940–41) £A.550,754,000. (See also NEW GUINEA.)   (W. D. MA.)

Australia, South: see SOUTH AUSTRALIA.
Autobiography: see AMERICAN LITERATURE; etc.
Automobile: see AUTOMOBILE INDUSTRY IN THE WAR.
Automobile Accidents: see ACCIDENTS; INSURANCE.

Automobile Industry in the War.
At the end of the second year of 100% war production, the automotive industry was operating at the rate of $10,500,000,000 a year. This was more than twice the industry's production in the previous peak year, 1941

The estimated aggregate value of war production by the automotive industry in the calendar year 1943 was $8,840,000,000 In addition, the industry produced essential replacement parts for motor vehicles valued at approximately $500,000,000 during 1943. The combined output of war articles and government authorized repair parts totalled $9,340,000,000.

In the third quarter of 1943, aircraft engines, airframes, propellers and aircraft subassemblies and parts comprised 40% of the automotive industry's war production; military vehicles and parts constituted 28%, tanks and parts 12%, guns of all types 7%, ammunition 4%, marine equipment 6%, and miscellaneous other war products 3%.

The annual rate of aircraft production by the automotive industry at the end of 1943 exceeded $4,000,000,000. This rate, for aircraft alone, was greater than the total dollar volume of

motor vehicles produced in the peak year 1941. Military vehicle production rate at the end of the year was 2½ times the 1941 actual volume of motor truck production.

The dollar volume of tanks and parts turned out by the automotive industry in the calendar year 1943 likewise exceeded the total dollar volume of motor truck production in the highest previous peacetime year.

The immensity of the volume of fighting equipment produced by the automotive industry may be more clearly visualized by translating the annual rate of $10,000,000,000 attained at the end of 1943 into physical units of bombers, fighter planes, tanks and vehicles. Converting the dollar volume of production in each of the major categories by dividing the average cost per unit into the aggregate dollar volume of each group, the following figures are obtained:

1. Aircraft, aircraft engines and parts equal in cost to 166 squadrons of aircraft each consisting of 15 heavy bombers, 30 medium bombers, and 90 fighter planes.
2. Military vehicles, tanks and parts equal in value to the cost of 110 armoured divisions of 3,314 vehicles each.
3. Marine equipment, equal in value to the cost of 100 submarines and 1,540 motor torpedo boats, and
4. $1,400,000,000 worth of cannon and machine guns of various sizes, ammunition of various sizes, and other war products.

Total war orders received by the industry during the period from Sept. 1, 1939, to Dec. 31, 1943, exceeded $29,000,000,000. Unfilled orders on hand at the year-end were approximately $14,700,000,000.

Specification changes, cancellations or "cutbacks" in orders became fairly numerous as the year progressed, but despite these handicaps the overall monthly totals of war product deliveries continued to climb throughout the year, with one exception.

As indicated above, the major production assignment given the industry consisted of aircraft products. Four complete planes, ready to fly, were in production Parts and subassemblies for many other types of combat craft were in production.

The huge volume of fighting equipment turned out by the industry was made possible by the practice of subcontracting, which was also a common practice prior to the war in the production of motor vehicles. An incomplete survey at the beginning of 1943 indicated that plants in 1,375 cities were engaged in the production of war products for former motor vehicle and parts manufacturers. These plants were scattered from coast to coast, and in 44 of the 48 states.

Fifty-six cents out of every dollar received by manufacturers in the industry were paid to subcontractors and vendors Most of the subcontractors and vendors were small firms employing only a few hundred workers; 35% of the firms employed from 100 to 500 employees, and 28% of the subcontractors and vendors employed less than 100 workers.

An analysis of 33 typical war products, including such items as tanks, machine guns, aircraft cannon, aircraft engines, bomber fuselages, aerial torpedoes, gyrocompasses, indicated that 33,182 parts out of a total of 50,880, or 65%, were furnished by subcontractors The percentage of parts subcontracted in certain items ranged as high as 98% or 99%. For example, an aerial torpedo with 5,112 parts included 4,999 parts which were furnished by subcontractors, or 98%. An aircraft cannon composed of 267 parts had 264 parts subcontracted, or 99%.

Engineers and production men trained in the mass production techniques of the motor industry of prewar years were able to devise shortcut methods, save materials and time in turning out the most intricate weapons of war. It was estimated that the dollar savings to the government and the taxpayers made by the special skills applied in the industry already amounted to more than $1,000,000,000. In particular instances the original cost of the product was cut in half.

During 1942 and the early part of 1943, materials shortages constituted the number one problem, aside from the main task of increasing the production and delivery of goods to the armed services. In the latter half of 1943, the number one problem became manpower. The industry undertook a number of steps to relieve the scarcity of qualified workers, and there already were indications that the problem was well on the way to solution.

Despite the drafting of an estimated 155,000 men from the former motor vehicle and body manufacturing plants into the army, employment continued to climb steadily throughout the year, reaching a total of 835,000 wage earners in December. This compares with a total of 636,000 in Dec. 1942, a gain of 31%. In Oct. 1943, 26.5% of all wage earners in the industry were women, as compared with 14.8% in January. Employment in former motor vehicle and body manufacturing plants in December was 63% above the prewar peak in June 1941. Average weekly wages per individual worker, and average hourly rates were also at the highest level in the history of the industry.

Keeping in mind that the subcontractors for a particular war product might be scattered from the east to the west coast, it can readily be seen how vital a role was played by transportation in serving as a virtual extension of the final assembly line. In cases of emergency, motor truck service was found especially useful in keeping the war plants in operation without the necessity of closing down for lack of parts or materials. The speed and flexibility of truck transportation was a lifesaver in thousands of war plants, when other means of transportation were not able to deliver in time. Besides the emergency situations where motor trucks came to the rescue, there were of course the regular day-to-day chores performed by motor trucks.

There were no records available on the totals in tonnage or ton miles of products transported by all types of motor trucks, but monthly indexes were compiled by the American Trucking association covering for-hire vehicles. These indexes indicated that for-hire trucks transported 28% more goods in 1943 than in 1941.

Transportation surveys made by state agricultural colleges in Missouri and Minnesota, covering 1,300 small firms in 15 counties, showed that 47.5% of all inbound freight was hauled by trucks and 49.6% of all outbound freight was shipped by trucks. In certain types of commodities, 100% of the inbound and outbound shipments moved over the highways.

During the period from Jan. 3, 1943, to Dec. 11, 1943, 76,071 motor trucks were released to civilian ration certificate holders and under government exemption permits. Total registrations of motor trucks at the end of 1943 decreased 3.7% below the preceding year, to approximately 4,500,000.

Despite gasoline shortages, private automobiles continued as the chief means of going to and from work. Surveys of 94 war plants by the war department indicated that 73.1% of the workers travelled by automobile, 13.2% by motor bus, 2.4% by other mass transportation methods, 1% by bicycle and motorcycle, and 10% walked; 56.5% of the total automobile mileage driven by these war plant workers consisted of driving to and from work, 14% in shopping, 14.3% in driving children to school, hauling products and business trips. Altogether, 84.8% of the mileage was for necessity purposes, while only 15.2% was for nonessential purposes.

Surveys by other organizations and in other places tended to corroborate the results of the survey in the 94 war plants indicating the automobile as the mainstay of worker transportation.

Intercity bus travel during 1943 increased approximately 150% above the average for 1941, while city bus and streetcar travel gained approximately 60% over 1941.

The best overall measure indicating the trend in total use of motor vehicles of all types was perhaps to be found in surveys by the U.S. Public Roads administration, compiled monthly. One of these indices consisted of counts of motor vehicles passing approximately 600 automatic traffic recorders, located at strategic points throughout the country. The average traffic in eastern states, where gasoline rationing began in May 1942, showed a decrease of 50% or more below the average of 1941. The average traffic in states where gasoline rationing began Dec. 1, 1942, reflected a decrease of 40% below the average of 1941.

Another general index compiled by the U.S. Public Roads administration on a monthly basis was developed from state gasoline tax collections. This index indicated a decrease of 39% in gasoline tax collections in those states where gasoline rationing began in May, and 28% in those states where gasoline rationing went into effect Dec. 1, 1942. The combined weighted average decline was approximately 33% below 1941.

Shortly after Pearl Harbor, leaders of the industry felt that the entire automotive industry, including former manufacturers of passenger cars, trucks, buses, taxicabs, and automotive replacement parts and accessories could do a much more effective job if they co-ordinated their efforts, so they organized the Automotive Council for War Production on Dec. 31, 1941.

Under the leadership of the board of directors and more than 50 committees on special subjects, the industry was able to produce and deliver nearly $13,000,000,000 worth of fighting equip-

THE "SEA MULE" tug, powered by a marine engine, was put to use by the U.S. armed forces in 1943 to push or tow barges or other cargo-carriers. Built in four sections at Detroit, it can be readily transported by truck, railroad or ship. One of its notable advantages is its shallow draft

ment to the armed services of the United Nations.

The 1943 production in terms of dollars was nearly six times as great as that of Dec. 1941.

Whenever a problem arose, a special committee was set up to aid in the solution. When conversion from peacetime to war work as rapidly as humanly possible was necessary, the council organized machine tool exchange and tooling information services which aided the manufacturers materially in locating the right machines and sources for the production of tools, dies, jigs and fixtures. Thousands of machines were loaned or sold to other manufacturers in the industry whenever the owner did not have any use for this equipment. Many machines were even shipped to Great Britain, Russia and China.

No sooner had the conversion and tooling-up problem been solved than shortages of materials developed. A committee of experts on materials was established to work closely with the War Production board and armed services in advising on the best procedures to be followed in the proper allocation and distribution of the steel, aluminum, copper and other vital sinews of war.

Although there were still shortages in certain kinds of materials in 1943 and a continued need for control to insure proper distribution to manufacturers of weapons in greatest need, there were indications that the materials bottlenecks were being broken.

The Automotive council committees most active in 1943 were those working on manpower problems. A committee on the supply of workers was working with national and local government agencies in developing new sources. Another committee on the utilization of labour conducted surveys and exchanged ideas on most effective ways of increasing production with the limited supply of workers available. Subcommittees on absenteeism, health, morale, all contributed their bit. From the beginning, other committees dealing with special war products such as aircraft engines, airframes, tanks, military vehicles, met at the council headquarters or in one another's plants to exchange technical information on ways of speeding up production, conserving materials, or developing shortcuts of various kinds.

A great many other problems were being handled by team work among the former competitors who now pooled their special knowledge for the benefit of soldiers on the fighting fronts throughout the world. (*See* also BUSINESS REVIEW.) (O. P. P.)

Automobile Insurance: *see* INSURANCE.

Aviation, Civil.

Military requirements dominated civil aviation activities throughout the world in 1943. During that year, as the aerial might of the United Nations achieved decisive supremacy over the air forces of the axis belligerents in all theatres of the war, the function of commercial air lines (for the most part operated by U.S. companies) was to transport strategic supplies, equipment and personnel between sources of raw materials, production centres and the fighting fronts. The emergence of air transport as an important cargo carrier in 1943 was one of the most significant developments in aviation.

Cargo Operations.—Movement of imported materials into the U.S. by air during 1943 amounted to approximately 41,000,-000 lb., valued at $116,209,000, or 5.83% of the total value of ocean cargo. The average unit shipped by air was valued at $2.85 per pound, or 81 times the average unit value of 3½ cents per pound for ship cargo. In terms of volume, the total shipments of 41,000,000 lb. represented .072% of the total 25,150,000 long-ton water-borne volume.

For each long ton shipped to the U.S. on the seas, 1.67 lb. of cargo were moved by air. On the average, during 1943, each unit of air cargo was 1,381 times smaller, 81 times as valuable, about

20 times as safe and moved more than 6 times as fast as cargo on ocean vessels.

U.S. foreign and domestic air lines, along with the army's air transport command and the naval air transport service, kept moving shipments of vital materials without which many war factories might have had to close down if air transport had not been available. Typical of such critical materials were mica, quartz crystals, industrial diamonds, tantalite, beryl and rare drugs. Some of these—tantalite, for example—are so rare that a nation at war could ill afford to have even the smallest shipment sunk at sea.

Summary of U.S. Air-line Activities.—The 18 domestic air lines and 3 international air lines of the U.S. in 1943 had more than doubled the volume of cargo carried in the last prewar year, 1941, and carried only 25% fewer passengers. This was accomplished with slightly more than half the equipment possessed by commercial air lines before the U.S. entered the war on Dec. 7, 1941. It was made possible by elimination of nonessential stops, standardization and better utilization of equipment, and a passenger priorities system which fully booked each plane for each flight.

The air lines' activities fell into two main categories: (a) transport operations, training programs, modification and maintenance of military equipment through contract with the army and navy and (b) continued operation of commercial air transport services.

In 1943 the world system of U.S. airways, in which military operations and commercial implications for the future are inextricably intermingled, passed the pioneer stage. Remote coral atolls and jungle rivers became seaplane bases. Airfields and air navigation aids were strung through tropical jungles, across desert wastes and uninhabited arctic regions. At the end of the year, almost any spot on the globe was within 60 hours' flying time of any sizable airport in the U.S.

Safety was a keynote in the vast expansion program, because of the extreme importance of the personnel and supplies carried. The air lines, in co-operation with the armed services, worked out many new devices and techniques to increase the safety of flight operations and improved existing ones. Most of the new developments remained on the secret list, but aviation authorities declared that their application to postwar aviation would bring about revolutionary changes.

International Air Transport.—Pan American Airways system in 1943 retained its leadership as the greatest international air line in the world.

With a fleet of 150 aircraft in operation at the end of 1943, Pan American Airways and its affiliate, Pan American-Grace Airways, had flown a total of 65,346,000 mi. as compared with 43,-939,744 mi. in 1942. The number of passengers carried was nearly double the figure for 1941: 606,700 as against 391,013; passenger-miles flown totalled 475,470,000 in 1943 as compared with 228,-630,621 in 1941. In 1943 the system carried 49,345,000 lb. of cargo, making a total of 72,735,000 ton-miles. A mail load of 14,465,400 lb. in 1943 was more than four times the 3,489,619 lb. carried in 1941.

In addition, a division of P.A.A. set up to carry out operations for the AAF's air transport command logged enough flying hours during 1943 to girdle the globe at the equator 4,560 times at 200 m.p.h. This division's services were scheduled over 15,570 foreign route miles to some 70 different locations in 31 countries and colonies on three continents. Its operations increased nearly five times over those of the preceding year. This division operated the largest fleet of aircraft in the system, flying 1,250,000 mi. a month carrying overseas cargo at the rate of 3,500,000 ton-miles every 30 days. The division had 117 flight crews of which

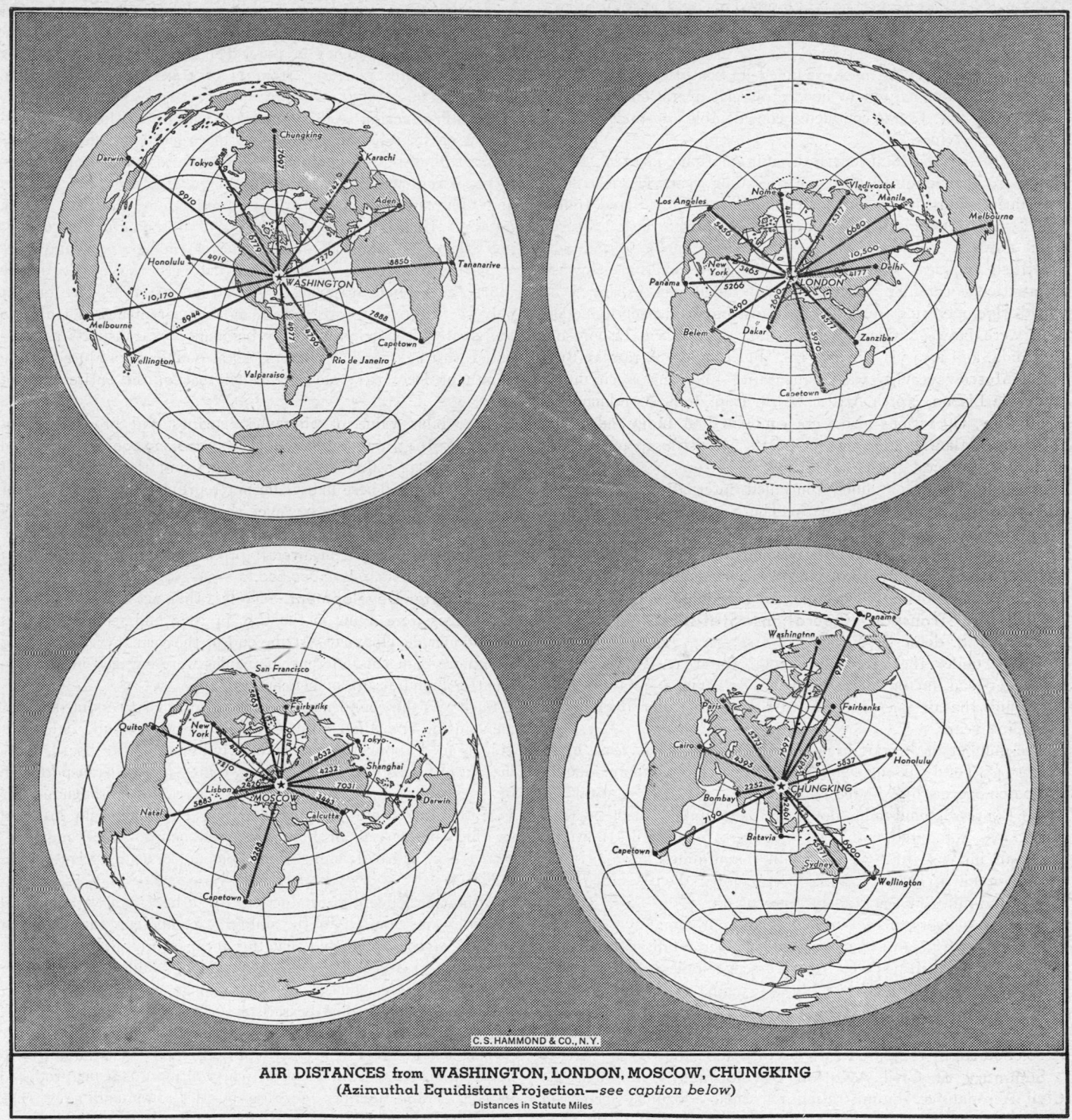

C. S. HAMMOND & CO., N.Y.

AIR DISTANCES from WASHINGTON, LONDON, MOSCOW, CHUNGKING
(Azimuthal Equidistant Projection—*see caption below*)
Distances in Statute Miles

AZIMUTHAL EQUIDISTANT PROJECTION showing air distances from the capitals of the principal four United Nations to other important cities. This type of map, ideal for computing air distances, is centred on a chosen spot (in each of the above four, the capital). A straight line on the map connecting the centre spot with any other spot on the map is the shortest distance between the two points, a great circle route

76 were expert in four-engine aircraft operation.

In Alaska, Pan American operations for the naval air transport service, and on civil routes, reached new levels in 1943 as military operations turned from the defensive to the offensive to drive the Japanese out of the strategic Aleutians. July was the climactic month in the campaign. During that month P.A.A. flew 477,440 plane-miles and 81,657 cargo ton-miles as compared with 88,190 plane-miles and 4,113 cargo ton-miles during the same month of the preceding year.

From Miami, over seven different routes to Mexico, the West Indies, the Caribbean area and the north and east coasts of South America to Buenos Aires, P.A.A.'s eastern division flew 12,146,294 plane-miles in 1943, an increase of 35% over the preceding year.

More than 125,000 passengers were flown 128,818,699 passenger-miles, which represented a 26% increase over 1942.

Early in 1943 the Civil Aeronautics board granted Pan American Airways a three-year temporary certificate to operate a new service between New Orleans, La., and Guatemala City in Central America, providing an additional connection with its network of Latin-American routes. The 1,075-mi. flight across the Gulf of Mexico was made in Boeing Stratoliners with accommodations for 33 passengers in pressurized cabins for high-altitude flying. This link reduced the time of travel from Chicago to the Canal Zone to approximately 21 hr.

American Export Airlines expanded its transoceanic operations during 1943. In addition to its commercial operation from New York to Foynes, Ire., it conducted considerable contract work for the armed services.

During 1943 the total length of civil aviation routes in Mexico had more than doubled over the preceding year. The expansion was due in part to wartime curtailment of water-borne traffic. Chicle, mineral concentrates and coffee comprised the chief cargo items flown.

British Overseas Airways, Great Britain's government-owned international commercial air line, continued and expanded its world-wide operations during 1943. Most important services operated were between Great Britain and America via Lisbon and Bermuda, and also via Foynes, Ire., and Canada. A regular Britain-to-Moscow service was inaugurated following a circuitous route via Lisbon, North Africa, Cairo, Iraq, Iran, Astrakhan and Kuibyshev. Operations also were conducted to India and across the South Atlantic, and to other points not disclosed for reasons of military secrecy.

Swedish A.B.A. air lines continued international operations chiefly to Britain and to Germany. The Netherlands K.L.M. lines maintained operations in the Caribbean area. International air operations of the axis nations, which had been fairly extensive at the start of the war, were virtually nonexistent in 1943. Germans continued operating commercial schedules to Lisbon, Port.

Civil Air Transport Operations Statistics.—Total miles flown by U.S. domestic air lines in 1943—93,122,000—was considerably under the 110,102,860 total for 1942. However, the passenger-load factor increased from 72.15 in 1942 to 91.4 in 1943, and the air lines actually carried more traffic than in the preceding year.

The number of aircraft in operation was 197, an increase of 18 over 1942. Total passenger-miles flown in 1943 was approximately 1,570,000,000, a 6% increase over the 1,481,976,329 total for 1942. Express pound-miles flown in 1943 totalled about 29,400,-000,000 as compared with 23,435,208,925 pound-miles flown in 1942, an increase of 25%. Air-mail pound-miles flown in 1943 were approximately 66,290,000,000, as compared with 40,096,554,-805 pound-miles in 1942, an increase of 65%.

Total passengers carried in 1943 were approximately 3,105,000, compared with 3,349,134 in 1942. Passenger fatalities numbered 23 in 1943 as against 55 in 1942. Passenger-miles flown per passenger fatality in 1943 were about 65,446,000, compared with 26,945,024 in 1942.

Gross income of domestic air lines reached a new high of $120,000,000, as compared with $108,000,000 for 1942.

Summary of Civil Aviation Development.—Although the Civil Aeronautics administration remained a civilian agency in 1943, most of its activities were devoted to projects serving the armed forces. The CAA conducted a $400,000,000 defense airport program. Landing fields suitable for transport aircraft were increased from 660 to 940 in 1943; total number of airports in all categories was approximately 3,000 at the end of the year.

There were 16,277,027 aircraft operations reported to CAA centres which controlled traffic on the federal airways, compared with 9,208,776 such operations in 1942.

During 1943 more than 10,000 transports and noncombat planes were inspected or flight-tested (sometimes both) at factories by CAA representatives. Airmen examined for certificates of competency included more than 18,000 would-be private pilots, 15,000 commercial pilots, 9,500 flight instructors and 9,000 engine mechanics.

The war training service branch of the CAA gave approximately 250,000 flight courses to army and navy cadets in 1943, as compared with 70,000 in 1942. The number of pilots holding CAA certificates increased from 110,510 in 1942 to 124,050 in 1943.

U.S. Production Achievement.—The American aircraft industry in 1943 set an all-time world's record in building 667,-000,000 lb. of military aeroplanes, exclusive of engines and equipment, which was nearly 2½ times the weight produced in 1942 and approximately 8 times 1941 production. Although 85,946 military planes were produced in 1943, the numerical total does not reflect the magnitude of the achievement because the average weight of each plane produced in that year was nearly double the average weight of planes produced in 1941. This was due not only to the trend toward larger and heavier planes, but also to the greater proportion of heavy bombers and transports as compared with fighters and trainers. Total poundage produced in the month of Dec. 1943 alone equalled that of the entire year of 1941.

The dollar value of airframes, engines and propellers produced in 1943 was estimated at $11,000,000,000 as compared with the 1942 value of $5,000,000,000 and the 1941 value of $1,750,000,000. These figures do not represent the total value of all aviation production, however, because many items such as armament, instruments and other equipment are not included.

Employees engaged in aircraft production at the end of 1943 totalled approximately 2,000,000.

Helicopter Development.—No less than six different helicopter designs were flying in the U.S. in 1943 and scores of others were under development. At the end of the year it was estimated that more than 100 different companies were engaged in development or manufacture of helicopters.

Such was the confidence in the helicopter's successful development in the immediate future that scores of companies and individuals filed applications with the Civil Aeronautics board, seeking authority to operate helicopter routes for the transportation of passengers, mail and express over routes throughout the U.S. totalling more than 100,000 mi. The applicants included existing commercial air lines, proposed new air-line companies, bus, truck, railroad and steamship operators and private individuals.

Although helicopter production for other than experimental purposes was limited to the military, competent authorities at the end of 1943 predicted that this form of aircraft had reached a satisfactory stage of development which would permit the construction of safe, efficient vehicles with a capacity of 12 to 14 passengers, which would be satisfactory for operation in shuttle, or bus-type, services.

The helicopter designed by Igor I. Sikorsky and built by Sikorsky division of United Aircraft corporation was being produced in considerable numbers for use by the army and navy. The Sikorsky design incorporates a single large three-blade rotor revolving in a horizontal plane above the fuselage of the craft, with a much smaller auxiliary tail rotor revolving in a vertical plane, which counteracts the torque induced by the main motor and is used also for steering. The engine is located in the fuselage under the main motor shaft, which it drives through suitable gearing and clutch mechanism. Provision for two occupants seated side by side is made in the enclosed cabin which forms the front of the fuselage.

Although most of the projects under way followed the basic arrangement described for the Sikorsky helicopter, many quite different designs also were being tested and flown. The Platt-LePage helicopter design utilized two rotors mounted on outriggers projecting from the sides of the craft a sufficient distance

PICKING UP A PACKAGE as a helicopter hovers several feet off the ground

AMPHIBIAN HELICOPTER with low-pressure pontoons

HOW A HELICOPTER can drop supplies to persons marooned in spots inaccessible except by air. Rescue of lost persons is also possible by means of a rope ladder

PASSENGER climbing aboard a U.S. army helicopter by means of a rope ladder dropped from the craft, which remains practically stationary in the air

THE HELICOPTER gave promise in 1943 of revolutionizing postwar civil aviation and providing a means of mass private transportation by air. Here a Sikorsky VS-300 is landing on a small flat roof

to permit their rotation in the same plane without interference. In this design the rotors revolved in opposite directions, thus equalizing the torque and eliminating the necessity for an auxiliary tail rotor. Steering was accomplished by causing one rotor to advance faster than the other.

Another design employed two rotors, one above the other, rotating in opposite directions around the same vertical axis. This was designed by the late Dr. George de Bothezat and manufactured by the Helicopter Corporation of America. Designated the GB-5, a most unusual feature of its design was the location of the engine between the counter-rotating blades and outside the cabin of the helicopter.

Again, since the two rotors revolved in opposite directions, thus cancelling out the torque, there was no need for an auxiliary tail rotor. Steering was accomplished by varying the pitch of one set of blades from the pitch of the blades on the other rotor, thus deliberately inducing torque which turned the cabin of the craft in the desired direction. This craft was test flown in 1943.

Late in 1943, a single-place 1,000-lb. helicopter designed and built by the P-V Engineering Forum was successfully flown. The arrangement and method of control was virtually the same as that described for the Sikorsky helicopter. It possessed a cruising speed of about 55 m.p.h. and a top speed of 90-100 m.p.h. (*See* also AIR FORCES OF THE WORLD; AIRPORTS AND FLYING FIELDS; MEDICINE; PETROLEUM; POST OFFICE.)   (C. B. F. M.)

Aviation, Military: *see* AIR FORCES OF THE WORLD; GLIDING; WORLD WAR II.

Avila Camacho, Manuel

(1897–   ), president of Mexico, was born at Teziutlan in the state of Puebla on April 24. After completing a course of commercial studies in his native town, he joined the successful revolution against Victoriano Huerta in 1914 and advanced to the rank of general of division. In the cabinet of President Rodriguez he was minister of war and navy. President Cárdenas later appointed him secretary of national defense and personally selected him as successor to the presidency. He was elected president July 7, 1940, by 2,476,641 votes to 151,101 for his opponent, Gen. Juan Andreu Almazán, according to tabulations of the Mexican congress. The new president was inaugurated Dec. 1, 1940.

During 1941 he negotiated a settlement of the oil-expropriation controversy with the United States. He consistently stressed hemispheric solidarity in defense and on May 22, 1942, three weeks after a German submarine had sunk a Mexican ship, Avila Camacho called for war against the axis. The congress unanimously approved his demand and on June 2 he signed the declaration of war against Germany, Italy and Japan (which was made retroactive to May 22) and Mexico joined the United Nations. A middle-of-the-roader keenly concerned with industrial development, Avila Camacho headed a vigorous program of Mexican war industry development, which supplied many minerals and other raw materials to U.S. factories during 1942 and 1943. (*See* also MEXICO.)

Azores, The: *see* PORTUGAL.

Bacon.

The statistics of bacon production in the United States were not separated from pork in general since the output of bacon varies in accordance with the changing cutting and trimming practices of the meat packers. These in turn are adjusted to the type of hog that predominates in the market. In 1943, when farmers were feeding hogs to the heavier weights because of the favourable price of pork compared to corn, the proportion of fat ran very heavy and led to a very fat type of bacon. This type was not desired for the military forces but lard and fat meats were wanted by the soviet army under lend-lease. The preferences of the British for a lean bacon, and the Russian desire for lard led to the trimming of meat cuts to suit the particular market to be served. The demand for bacon is fairly constant and varies little from month to month or year to year. With heavy pork production there is therefore no danger of shortages since in the general supply of hogs there is always enough of the bacon type to supply the demands. The price of bacon fluctuates with the price of pork in general and has no special market price of its own. (*See* also HOGS; MEAT.)   (J. C. Ms.)

Bacteriology.

Two classes of antibacterial therapeutic agents of direct application to wartime needs were being intensively investigated; the sulfonamides and the antibiotic substances derived from bacteria, actinomycetes and moulds.

The discovery and compounding of the various sulfonamides had been the work of chemists. The isolation of antibiotic substances, the testing of their activity and the solution of their modes of action against various bacteria were in the field of biochemical bacteriology and mycology.

Experimental medicine and clinical observation demonstrated the therapeutic usefulness of the sulfonamides and began to exploit the antibiotic substances.

The sulfonamides are a group of chemically related compounds but the antibiotic substances are less homogeneous, falling into seven chemical groups according to Selman A. Waksman: "1. lipoid bodies: pyocyanase and clavicin; 2. pigments: pyocyanin, prodigiosin, chrysogenin, chloraphin, toxoflavin and actinomycin; 3. polypeptides: gramicidin, tyrocidine, lysozyme and actinomycetin; 4. sulphur-bearing compounds: gliotoxin; 5. quinonelike compounds: citrinin, penicillic acid, fumigatin, possibly penicillin: 6. organic bases: streptothricin; 7. other agents: fumigacin, etc." Their action may be bacteriostatic, bactericidal or bacteriolytic. Of 200 species of fungi (mostly of *Penicillium* and *Aspergillus*) examined by W. H. Wilkins and G. C. M. Harris, 64 showed antibacterial activity.

Although the sulfonamides and the antibiotic substances of microbial origin differ as to origin and chemical nature, they were found to show some resemblance in their modes of action on bacterial cells, *i.e.,* by interference with essential metabolic processes. Many papers on bacterial metabolism appeared, among them an excellent review on "Factors Influencing the Enzymic Activities of Bacteria" by Ernest Frederick Gale. The reader is also referred to the address by Waksman on "The Microbe as a Biological System" in which it was stated of the antibiotic substances: "1. some act primarily upon bacteria, and others upon fungi; 2. some influence cell division, others affect respiration, still others interfere with the utilization of certain metabolites; 3. they are selective in their action, some being capable of acting upon a great number of organisms, and others upon only very few; 4. some act primarily *in vitro* and others act also *in vivo*; 5. they vary in their toxic effect upon the animal body, and in reactions upon the tissues; 6. some are hemolytic and others not; 7. some are water-soluble and others are only alcohol-soluble. Because of these properties, some can be used for general treatment, and others have only a local application." (*See* also EPIDEMICS AND PUBLIC HEALTH CONTROL.)

BIBLIOGRAPHY.—Ernest Frederick Gale, "Factors Influencing the Enzymic Activities of Bacteria," *Bact. Rev.*, 7: 139 (1943); Selman A. Waksman, "The Microbe as a Biological System," *J. Bact.*, 45: 1 (1943); Selman A. Waksman, "Nature and Mode of Action of Antibiotic Substances," *J. Bact.*, 45:64 (1943); W. H. Wilkins and G. C. M. Harris, "Investigation into the Production of Bacteriostatic Substances by Fungi. Preliminary Examination of a Second 100 Fungal Species," *Brit. J. Exp. Path.*, 24:141 (1943).
    (J. H. Bn)

Badminton. With David Guthrie Freeman, four-times national champion, in the army medical corps, badminton became more of a recreational than a competitive sport during 1943. No national championships were held, and what title play existed was restricted to sectional tournaments.

The middle Atlantic doubles tourney highlighted badminton in the east, with Carl Loveday and Cheever Lockwood of Montclair, N.J., winning the title with a 15–11, 15–10 decision over Frank Jasensky and Frank Williamson, New Rochelle, N.Y., in the final. The women's middle Atlantic championship went to Mrs. Roy Bergman and Helen Gibson of Westport, Conn., who defeated Mrs. Kenneth Davidson and Theresa Bellizzi, New Rochelle, in the final, 15–6, 15–1.

Richard Casey of St. Louis captured the midwest singles championship, downing Joe Tiberi of Chicago in the windup, 15–12, 15–2. Pearl Peterson of Detroit successfully defended her women's singles title with an 11–1, 11–4 victory over Eleanor Coambs of Chicago. Dean Foote and Jack Riday of West Allis, Wis., repeated as men's doubles champions, and Miss Coambs and Thelma Burdick of Chicago topped the women's doubles.

For southern California Helen Noble and LeRoy Erikson, both of Pasadena, were district singles champions. The New York metropolitan titles were won by Corporal Stig Larson and Theresa Bellizzi, both of New Rochelle. (M. P. W.)

Badoglio, Pietro (1871–   ), Italian army officer, was born at Grazzano Monferrato, Piedmont, on Sept. 28. He took part in the Eritrea campaign, 1896–97, saw service in World War I in 1915, and emerged as a general after the war ended in 1918. Elected a senator in 1919, he went to Brazil as ambassador in 1924 and returned to Rome in 1925 to assume the post of chief of the army general staff. He was created Marchese del Sabotino, 1928, was governor general of Libya, 1928–33. He participated in the Ethiopian campaign and was named viceroy of Abyssinia, 1936. He later resigned from the latter office and was created duke of Addis Ababa. When Mussolini declared war against the Allies in June 1940, Marshal Badoglio was in command of the Italian armies. While allegedly opposed to the Italian invasion of Greece in Oct. 1941, he nevertheless was made the scapegoat for its initial failures and resigned as chief of the general staff "at his own request," Dec. 6, 1941. For the next 18 months Badoglio shunned the limelight until his dramatic reappearance July 25, 1943. After a stormy cabinet session, Mussolini was ousted as premier and Badoglio was made his successor. On Sept. 3 the Italian marshal concluded a secret military armistice with Gen. Eisenhower and five days later, Sept. 8, 1943, Badoglio told the Italian people that he had signed unconditional surrender terms laid down by the Allies. The following day, Badoglio, in a letter to Hitler, explained that Italy was compelled to surrender to "avoid total ruin." After his installation as premier, Badoglio dissolved the fascist party, released many anti-fascist prisoners. On Oct. 13 he declared war against Germany and joined the Allies. Although he stubbornly refused to foreswear loyalty to King Victor Emmanuel III, the Italian general did promise, Oct. 20, that he would restore constitutional rule and step down as premier once Italy was liberated.

Bahamas. A group of some 3,000 islands, rocks and keys, north and northeast of Cuba. About 20 of the islands are inhabited, permanently or intermittently. Total area: 4,375 sq.mi.; pop. (1940 est.) 66,219 (1931 census: 59,828), with 15% white and the remainder Negro and mulatto. Capital, Nassau (pop. 19,756). The Bahamas form a British colony, with an appointed governor (in 1943, H.R.H. the Duke of Windsor) and legislative council, and an elected assembly.

History.—The war continued to affect the Bahamas during 1943, although financial conditions remained fairly satisfactory. Price control had been established in Dec. 1942; rationing of essential foodstuffs became necessary in July 1943. The prospective completion of war projects at Nassau caused the government to set up a special Out Islands department, designed to formulate work projects which would draw unemployed workers away from the capital. An arrangement made in May for the transportation of up to 6,000 Bahama labourers to Florida to fill labour demands there likewise helped with unemployment.

In July Sir Harry Oakes, the richest resident of the islands, was murdered; his son-in-law, Alfred de Marigny, was accused of the crime but won an acquittal in December.

Education.—In 1940 schools numbered 167 (46 denominational and private), with a total enrolment of 15,787 students.

Finance.—The monetary unit is the pound sterling (value in 1943 $4.03½ U.S.) Government revenues (1942) were estimated at £394,690; expenditures, £439,889.

Trade and Communication.—Trade figures for 1943 were not available; imports for 1942 totalled $6,129,000 (1941: $5,183,000), exports (exclusive of re-exports) $778,000 (1940: $528,000). The principal imports are foodstuffs and manufactures, largely from the United States, Canada and the United Kingdom. Exports of importance in 1943 were tomatoes (85,000 lugs, to

THE DUKE OF WINDSOR visited a camp of his subjects at Swedesboro, N.J., in May 1943. The Negroes had been sent from the Bahamas to help harvest an asparagus crop

Canada), crawfish (about 1,250,000 lb.) and other marine products, straw and shellwork, and wood products.

External communication is by air and boat, with schedules subject to war conditions. New Providence possesses good highways, and roads are under construction on other islands.

Resources.—The tourist trade is normally the most important single item in the colony's economy (tourist expenditure in 1941 est. $4,000,000), but was unimportant in 1943. Sponging, usually second in importance, remained practically suspended as in 1941 and 1942 because of disease in the sponge beds. To replace these industries, the Bahamas turned to sea food exports, sisal development (342 tons produced in 1941), spice, and straw and shellwork. The perfume industry declined due to lack of essential materials. (*See* also WEST INDIES, BRITISH.)

BIBLIOGRAPHY.—*West Indies Year Book, 1941–1942; Canada–West Indies Magazine* (Montreal. monthly); *Crown Colonist* (London, monthly); *Colonial Review* (London, quarterly).   (D. RD.)

Bahrein Islands: *see* BRITISH EMPIRE.
Baker Island: *see* PACIFIC ISLANDS, U.S.
Baltic States: *see* ESTONIA; LATVIA; LITHUANIA.

Baltimore.
Seventh largest city of the United States, Baltimore, Md. had a population by the 1940 federal census of 859,100. White population 692,705, non-white 166,395, mainly Negro, constituting 19.4% of total. Foreign-born white, 60,969, 7.1% of total. Area, 78.5 sq.mi., plus 13.35 sq.mi. of water.

Mayor Theodore R. McKeldin, Republican, elected May 4, 1943, took office May 18. His vote, 77,567, constituted a majority of 20,275 over the Democratic candidate, former Mayor Howard W. Jackson, running for a 5th term. McKeldin was the first Republican mayor elected since 1927. He received the largest majority ever given a Republican. Howard E. Crook, Democrat, was elected city comptroller. The council president, Thomas E. Conlon, Democrat, died in Oct., 1943, and the vacancy was filled by C. Markland Kelly. Democrats retained a solid membership in the city council during 1943.

Baltimore had a continued boom in 1943 as an important defense area, but at a less accelerated rate than in 1942. It continued to be a leading shipbuilding and plane manufacturing centre, and became a major producing centre of high octane gasoline with the erection of a $14,000,000 catalytic cracker at the Baltimore refining plant of the Standard Oil Co. of N.J.

Appropriations from tax levy were $56,498,601.71. Total appropriations, including approved expenditures from existing and tentative loans, were $68,540,157.71. The total taxable basis was $1,664,037,410. The tax rate, $2.85 per $100, increased 20 cents. Gross funded debt as of Aug. 31, 1943 was $161,727,-000; net general debt for 1943, $84,547,919.45. A bond issue of $12,500,000 was authorized for water supply during 1943.

(C. B. S.)

Bananas.
The exact amount of imports of bananas in 1943 was withheld as confidential information by the U.S. government. General trade sources indicated that imports were less than half the normal amounts. The scarcity of the fruit in the retail markets was sufficient proof of the scarcity. The problem of the banana trade continued to be transportation. Since about 80% of the imports were brought in by boat and particularly by the special banana-boats of the United Fruit company, the loss of these ships, which were taken over by the government, immediately stopped the normal trade. There were no railroad facilities to most of the banana areas except Mexico. The banana growers in Latin America were in great distress notwithstanding the aid given by the fruit companies and local

governments. The fruit companies experimented with dehydration and other methods of processing bananas without much success. The consumer prefers the natural fruit and the prospect of developing a new form in which to market bananas seemed remote in 1943. The efforts to shift the banana land to other uses was proceeding slowly in Central America since the natives were being trained in the growing of fibre plants such as abacá and hemp. These natives were hesitant to change, preferring to wait for the banana industry to recover.   (J. C. Ms.)

Bankers Association, American: *see* AMERICAN BANKERS ASSOCIATION.

Bank for International Settlements.
Though its functioning as a medium for financing international trade had been more or less stifled by the war, the Bank for International Settlements, located at Basle, Switzerland, continued in 1943 to render valuable service as banker for international Red Cross organizations. Also it continued to receive the co-operation of central banks and monetary institutions throughout the world.

Though the intensified warfare in Europe and the invasion of Italy by Allied forces placed a greater diplomatic strain upon the relationship of the bank to the nations involved, its board of directors carefully avoided implication in any transaction that might involve its policy of adherence to strict neutrality or give rise to a suspicion of serving the financial interests of one country to the disadvantage of another.

The balance sheet total at the end of the fiscal year, March 31, 1943, showed a gain of 6,736,527 Swiss gold francs, standing at 483,382,662 Swiss gold francs compared with 476,646,135 the previous year. The calendar year 1943 started with a balance of 479,214,390 Swiss gold francs and rose to a high of 486,491,650 on June 30. The balance sheet total on Sept. 30, 1943, stood at 484,371,943 Swiss gold francs.

A notable change in the asset account was the increase in "gold in bars" item, which stood at 80,066,994 Swiss gold francs on Sept. 30, 1943, compared with 42,082,396 on March 31, 1942. Among the liability items, short term and sight deposits in various currencies declined 5,401,077 Swiss gold francs at the end of the 1943 fiscal year compared with the previous year's close, but short term and sight deposits in gold showed an increase of 10,666,844 Swiss gold francs. Significant under "reserves" items was the disappearance, as of June 1943, of the dividend reserve fund, which prior to the 1943 fiscal year had been carried at more than 4,000,000 Swiss gold francs, but which in June 1942, had dropped to 1,626,940 Swiss gold francs.

In the distribution of its assets the bank paid particular attention to the maintenance of full liquidity in the markets where it had its commitments.

Banking.
A new peak in war production in 1943 found banking in the U.S. ready to assume its full responsibilities in the form of loans to war industries, purchase of government securities and assistance in the distribution of government bonds among individual and institutional purchasers. Deposits and investments increased to new high levels for all time, while the total of loans fell off slightly because of reduced

U. S. Banking, Deposits, Loans and Investments, 1942 and 1943
Total (in millions of dollars)

All banks	Deposits	Loans	Investments
1942—14,775	72,419	25,081	38,928
1943—14,618	96,329	22,241	65,640
Member banks			
1942—6,647	53,434	16,928	29,872
1943—6,703	73,465	14,823	52,332

civilian requirements, as shown on page 94 in the comparative table for years ending June 30.

The member banks of the federal reserve system (*q.v.*) assumed an increasing importance in the financing of the war, as is evidenced in the foregoing table. Excess reserves of member banks continued the decline of 1942, approaching the vanishing point in New York city and Chicago and reaching $1,020,000,000 for the entire country in July, the lowest point since 1937. This decline accompanied the remarkable growth in deposits, due to the absorption by the banking system of over $22,000,000,000 of additional U.S. government securities, and the continued growth in money in circulation, which stood at a record high of over $20,000,000,000 at the end of 1943—an increase of nearly $5,000,000,000.

The pressure on excess reserves was relieved by legislation which permitted banks to hold in war loan accounts the proceeds of U.S. government securities purchased for their own account or the account of customers without providing a reserve or paying Federal Deposit Insurance assessments on such deposits. Member banks were enabled to keep more fully invested by a practice inaugurated by the treasury of allotting in full at a fixed price to yield ⅜% all subscriptions to treasury bills in amounts not exceeding $100,000 while the Federal Reserve banks agreed to purchase all treasury bills offered at ⅜%, giving the purchaser an option to repurchase at any time prior to maturity at the same rate. Open market operations of the Federal Reserve banks also relieved the shortage of member bank reserves, their holdings of government securities reaching an all-time high of nearly $11,000,000,000 in Dec. 1943.

Although loans declined for 1943, a steady increase in volume marked the trend toward the year's end. Government guaranteed V-Loans were made available on a broader basis, to assure war contractors that their working capital invested in war production would not be frozen on contract terminations. Interest rates on loans were steady, with a rising tendency toward the end of the year. Bank earnings were aided by a substantial increase in the yield of short- and medium-term government securities, while long-term rates remained steady, aided by the support of the Federal Reserve banks. In addition to investing in large amounts of government bonds, the U.S. banks co-operated with investment bankers, brokers and others in intensive campaigns for the sale of government bonds to individuals, culminating in the Third War Loan drive in September, in which $18,943,000,000 in bonds were sold to nonbank investors. (See *Investment Banking*, below.)

Bank earnings increased substantially during 1943, although they were partly offset by increases in expenses, including taxes and salaries. For the first time in history, return on securities exceeded interest and discount on loans, because of expanded holdings of government securities. Service charges and trust department earnings again contributed substantially. Net profits were higher but dividends were down slightly, reflecting the need for building up surplus and capital funds in keeping with enlarged deposit liabilities. The war caused further drains on bank personnel, and in many banks women employees numbered more than half the clerical force. The banks organized and operated "ration banking" to facilitate the clearance of ration coupons between retailers and suppliers. (*See* also BUSINESS REVIEW; CONSUMER CREDIT; LAW; RATIONING.)

Canada.—Banking continued to serve the war needs of Canada during 1943, as production for war purposes resulted in an unprecedented increase in the industrialization of the dominion. There was a marked expansion in banking accounts, and deposits of the ten chartered banks increased nearly $500,000,000 to $4,085,000,000 on Sept. 30, 1943. The volume of loans and dis-

counts fluctuated in a narrow range, standing at $1,045,000,000 on that date. Holdings of securities increased by $502,000,000 to a total of $2,881,000,000, reflecting added purchases of dominion securities. Canadian banks were a large factor in the distribution of government securities to the public, which provided over 81% of funds borrowed, leaving only 18.5% to be absorbed by the banking system during the year ended Aug. 31, 1943.

Earnings were supplemented by new service charges, while bank taxation increased, with a wartime excess profits tax of 100% imposed, based on 1936–39 average earnings. More than 6,800 men and 150 women bank employees had enlisted in the armed forces. Many women were added to replace the men in the service, so that over half the employees were women. During the war, more than 200 branches had been closed to save manpower. On March 1 Canadian banks began to handle wartime consumer ration coupons for dealers in foodstuffs. The 3,200 Canadian branch banks accepted ration coupon deposits and handled coupon checks and ration transfers. They also continued to act for the government as licensed dealers in foreign exchange under the Foreign Exchange Control board.

The Bank of Canada increased its holdings of government securities by nearly $240,000,000 to $1,221,000,000 on Oct. 31, 1943. The note issue of the Bank of Canada rose to $836,000,000, an increase of $170,000,000, while the chartered bank note circulation declined from $69,000,000 to $46,000,000, as required by law.

Great Britain.—Banking in the United Kingdom continued to be entirely subject to the influence of total war. The 11 London clearing banks reported an increase in holdings of government obligations of £357,000,000 to £2,205,000,000 on Sept. 30, 1943, while loans were off somewhat to £741,000,000. Deposit liabilities reached a new high of £3,737,000,000, up more than £313,000,000 for the year. Interest rates remained stable under the control of government authorities. Note circulation of the Bank of England increased over £128,000,000 to £998,500,000 on Oct. 27. Due to the shortage of manpower, nonessential activities of all banks were reduced to a minimum. (*See* also BANK OF ENGLAND.)

Europe.—Germany continued to dominate banking on the continent, although gradually losing grip in Italy, which was invaded by the United Nations. Its influence also waned in neutral Spain and Switzerland as success attended the arms of the Allies. The deposits of the Reichsbank increased from 2,887,000,000 reichsmarks to 5,601,000,000 during the year ended Sept. 30, 1943. Note circulation increased from 22,600,000,000 reichsmarks to 30,099,000,000, not including a great volume of special paper marks used in occupied countries. There was a large expansion in treasury bill holdings from 24,641,000,000 reichsmarks to 35,010,000,000.

Note circulation of the Bank of France increased from 323,494,000,000 francs to 440,291,000,000, and government advances for German occupation costs increased from 180,999,000,000 francs to 271,371,000,000 at July 29, 1943. (*See* also BANK FOR INTERNATIONAL SETTLEMENTS.)

Investment Banking.—U.S. investment markets were completely dominated by government financing for the war, which raised the total national debt from $92,904,000,000 to $165,047,000,000 in the year ended Oct. 31, 1943. New corporate and municipal issues amounted to only $1,620,000,000 for the ten months ended Oct. 31, 1943, and of this total only $413,000,000 represented new capital, the balance being issued to refund outstanding securities, mainly for the purpose of taking advantage of interest rates at or near the lowest in history. Included in this total were new stock issues of $116,000,000, of which

$51,000,000 was for new capital and $65,000,000 for refunding. Corporations were not in the capital market to any great extent, as their needs for increased plants for war purposes were met largely by government financing, and materials and labour were not available for other purposes. States and municipalities raised only $145,000,000 of new capital, finding their needs reduced by full employment and satisfactory tax collections, while the lack of men and materials prevented new construction. The Securities and Exchange commission's rule requiring competitive bidding on new public utility security issues under their jurisdiction was under attack.

Municipal obligations advanced in price in 1943 as the supply of new issues dwindled and demand increased with higher income taxes. Tax collections were excellent because of increased industrial payrolls, and bonds of lower grade tended to advance more rapidly than those of proven quality. Life insurance companies, which benefited little from tax exemption, disposed of large blocks of municipals in a receptive market. Many railroads benefited from the market for their bonds by making large purchases for the retirement of debt out of wartime earnings. Yields of taxable government bonds of the longer maturities remained stable, while short-term governments were issued on a somewhat higher basis. Highest grade corporate bonds yielded slightly less, approaching government bond yields. The yield of lower grade corporate issues fell even further, narrowing the gap between issues of the various grades and prompting the flow of investment into the several offerings of government bonds designed to meet the requirements of all types of investors. Bankers and brokers devoted their organizations and extensive experience to promoting the two War Loan campaigns conducted during 1943 by the U.S. treasury. Particular stress was laid on obtaining subscriptions from individuals as a measure to take up excess purchasing power while providing the financial sinews of war. Both campaigns resulted in oversubscriptions, total sales amounting to $40,676,000,000. (*See* WAR BONDS.)   (E. B. L.)

Mutual Savings Banks.—Expenditures for war purposes increased rapidly after the United States became a belligerent nation and as a consequence there was more money available for deposit in savings banks, particularly in areas of great industrial activity. Total assets on July 1, 1943 were $12,436,067,000 and deposits credited to 15,552,095 accounts were $11,104,706,000, an increase of $758,333,000 in assets and of $750,174,000 in deposits during the year ended July 1, 1943. The combined surplus was $1,302,018,000 or 11.72% of deposits. Dividends averaged 1.87% in 1943, a slight decline from the average of 1.88% in 1942. The total number of mutual savings banks on July 1, 1943 was 535, the same as at the end of 1942.

Mutual savings banks continued to distribute large amounts of U.S. war savings bonds. In the 12 months ended Nov. 1, 1943 they distributed $490,494,225 par value of savings bonds and stamps. Of the total, $392,373,450 were series E, $12,837,798 were series F, $73,214,789 were series G and $12,068,188 were war savings stamps. After May 1, 1941 when the savings banks first became issuing agents for U.S. savings bonds, they distributed $1,139,217,844 par value of U.S. savings bonds and stamps, of which $913,359,720 were series E, $35,600,664 were series F, $166,363,027 were series G and $23,894,433 were war savings stamps.

During the three War Loan drives the mutual savings banks subscribed to Victory bonds for their own portfolios in the following amounts: First War Loan drive, Nov. 30, 1942–Dec. 23, 1942, $609,000,000; Second War Loan drive, April 12, 1943–May 1, 1943, $1,195,000,000; Third War Loan drive, Sept. 9, 1943–Oct. 2, 1943, $1,508,000,000.

Aside from U.S. government securities, the chief outlet for funds of savings banks in 1943 was insured mortgage loans of the Federal Housing administration. New York state banks were especially active in making these loans, because the New York state banking laws were amended to permit savings banks to make F.H.A. insured loans in states adjoining the state of New York, as well as in that state to which their lending was formerly confined. Uninsured loans in an adjoining state were legalized also, providing such loans were made on property within 25 mi. of the principal place of business of the lending bank. The New York law was further amended to permit savings banks to make uninsured loans not exceeding 80% of appraised value on real properties located not more than 50 mi. from the principal office of the savings bank and improved by single family, owner-occupied residences constructed not more than two years prior to the making of the loan. The previous limit was 66.6% of the appraised value.

On July 1, 1943 all the savings banks in New York state not previously admitted to the Federal Deposit Insurance corporation applied for membership in that corporation. Including these banks the total number of mutual savings banks in the Federal Deposit Insurance corporation on July 1, 1943 was 182, with deposits of $7,000,000,000 credited to 9,350,000 accounts. Following this action, the bank members of the Mutual Insurance fund, in existence since 1934, determined to liquidate that fund by returning its assets to the contributing banks. A first distribution of $37,695,000 was made Dec. 1, 1943.

In contrast to the action taken by the savings banks in New York, the Connecticut savings banks set up a new fund called the Savings Banks' Deposit Guaranty Fund of Connecticut, covering deposits of about $755,000,000 distributed among 900,000 accounts in 62 member banks. This organization took the place of the Mutual Savings Banks' Central fund organized ten years previously. An act passed by the general assembly had provided for the change in name and granted additional powers and duties, the most important of which was the absolute guarantee of all deposits in full in member banks.

Savings Bank Life Insurance.—On Oct. 31, 1943 there was a total of 204 banks in Connecticut, Massachusetts and New York having savings bank life insurance departments. Connecticut had eight issuing banks and ten agency banks; Massachusetts, 30 issuing banks and 112 agency banks and New York, 26 issuing banks and 18 agency banks. In Connecticut, the latest state as of 1943 to legalize savings bank life insurance, the total insurance in force on Oct. 31, 1943 was $2,060,177, representing 2,326 policies; an increase of $1,046,227 and 1,179 policies in the second year of operation. In Massachusetts the total in force on that date was $240,216,281 representing 296,635 policies; and in New York the total in force was $34,808,574, representing 38,901 policies.

British Savings Banks.—At the end of the fiscal year, Nov. 20, 1942, the Trustee Savings banks had total funds of £446,508,957; of which £264,577,260 were balances due depositors in the ordinary department, £113,918,096 were balances due depositors in the special investment department, £55,266,498 represented government stock held for depositors and £12,747,103 represented surplus funds. On Nov. 20, 1942 there were 91 Trustee Savings banks in the United Kingdom with 710 offices.

In the three-year period Nov. 21, 1939 to Nov. 30, 1942 the Trustee Savings banks made available £180,400,000 for war savings. Of this amount, increases in the balances due depositors in the ordinary department accounted for £116,100,000; sales of National Savings Certificates, sales of defense bonds and other war issues to depositors and investment of special investment department funds in treasury issues made up the remaining £64,300,000.   (HE. BR.)

Bank of England. During 1943 the bank note circulation continued to expand, the growth between Jan. 6 and Nov. 3 being from £920,000,000 to £1,005,000,000. The chief causes of the increase were greater industrial activity, a rise in the average earnings of workers, and to some extent the prevalence of hoarding. To provide this new currency the fiduciary issue was increased from £880,000,000 to £950,000,000 on Dec. 1, 1942, while there were further increases to £1,000,000,000 on April 13, and to £1,050,000,000 on Oct. 5, 1943. In April 1943 notes of £10 and upwards ceased to be issued, and it was announced that those already in issue would be withdrawn as opportunity offered. There was some evidence that these large-denomination notes were being used in undesirable transactions. A temporary check at this time to the growth in the note circulation was in part attributable to this withdrawal.

The bank continued its work in connection with the financing of the war. Loans by the banks to the government against treasury deposit receipts increased by about £350,000,000 during the year to the end of Sept. 1943, when their total was £1,114,500,-000. For a few weeks during October the weekly treasury bill issue was increased from £90,000,000 to £100,000,000. These extra bills were to mature in Jan. 1944, and so would put the banks in funds during the period of heavy tax collection.

On Aug. 31 the "tap" issue of 2½% national war bonds, 1951–53, was withdrawn and replaced by a new issue of 2½% bonds 1952–54.

The bank also assisted the dominions in the repayment out of their sterling balances of much of their long-term sterling debt. On Jan. 5 India 3½% stock, repayable in 1931 or any later year, was redeemed (£77,000,000 was outstanding when notice was given in Dec. 1941). In February and March vesting operations for five South African stocks (said to total about £42,000,000) and nine Indian railway sterling debenture stocks (said to total about £20,000,000) were carried through by the bank on behalf of the treasury.

During 1943 there were some relaxations of the exchange control procedure. "Sterling area" and "old" sterling accounts were abolished, and only one type of account was held by residents in the United States and Central America. In addition blocked sterling accounts were substantially reduced. The accumulation of sterling blocked in these accounts could now in most cases be remitted to the beneficiary, and further blocked sterling would be created only in the most exceptional circumstances. Dealings in sterling securities on behalf of non-residents were made much easier, and nonresidents could sell and reinvest the proceeds freely.

Remittances to evacuated children under the children's overseas reception board scheme were increased to a level which enabled most of the evacuees to maintain themselves without support from their hosts.

Following the expulsion of the enemy from French North Africa arrangements were made to specify French North and West African currencies, and to regulate payments between these territories and the sterling area.

Further releases of staff for national service were made during 1943. The bank retained only 53% of its male and 55% of its total prewar staff. The total clerical staff was 3,965, compared with 3,529 at the outbreak of war. This increase is accounted for by the formation of the wartime foreign exchange control, which employed 1,400 people at its peak in Oct. 1941, and employed 1,000 people by 1943. Much of the former London work of the bank had been evacuated to the country, and 1,500 men and women were employed at country premises. (N. E. C.)

Bankruptcy: *see* BUSINESS REVIEW; FEDERAL BUREAU OF INVESTIGATION.

Banks: *see* BANKING.

Baptist Church. The conventions of both Northern and Southern Baptists for 1943 were postponed one year. The Southern Baptists were to hold their 1944 convention in Atlanta, Ga. May 16–18—a much briefer period than hitherto allotted for the annual meeting. One of the urgent requirements for this assembly was the necessity of planning for their centennial celebration in 1945. Lacking the inspiration of their convention in 1943, the executive officers sought to bring enthusiasm and challenge to the local churches through extended use of the denominational press in each state and increased efforts of the state secretaries. One significant result was the final payment of a 20-year-old debt of some $18,500,000.

The Northern Baptists were to hold their 1944 convention in Atlantic City, N.J., May 23–26. In lieu of their 1943 convention, Parish day services were organized for meetings in the local churches. The main features of these programs were recorded addresses by officers of the convention and missionaries home from foreign fields. In this way reports of successful work at home and abroad were brought to the people in their own parishes.

During the convention year, May–April 1942–43, the Baptists of the north raised a World Emergency fund of $728,686.66, which was in addition to their normal gifts for all benevolent purposes. This fund was to be spent for emergencies arising chiefly from war conditions. For the year 1943–44 the goal of the emergency fund is $1,500,000. The total objective was $4,500,000, approximately 25% above the receipts for the year 1942–1943. (R. E. E. H.)

Bar Association, American: *see* AMERICAN BAR ASSOCIATION.

Barbados: *see* WEST INDIES, BRITISH.

Barbour, W. Warren (1888–1943), U.S. politician, was born July 31 at Monmouth Beach, N.J. He served several terms as mayor of Rumson, N.J., served as delegate-at-large to the Republican national convention that nominated Herbert Hoover, and in 1931 was appointed to fill a senate vacancy caused by the death of Dwight F. Morrow. A year later, he was elected to fill the unexpired term. Barbour was elected again in 1938 to fill a vacancy left by the resignation of Senator A. Harry Moore, and was re-elected to this seat in 1940. He died in Washington, Nov. 22.

Barclay, McClelland (1893–1943), U.S. illustrator, was born May 9 in St. Louis, Mo. He studied at the Corcoran School of Art in Washington, the Art Students' League in New York city and the Art Institute of Chicago. Barclay began as advertising illustrator in 1912, created the famous "Fisher Body Girl" and did other "pretty girl" covers

Bank of England
(£ million)

1943	Jan. 6	Apr. 14	June 30	Oct. 6	Nov. 3
Issue dept.					
Note circulation . .	920.0	943.5	946.3	991.3	1,005.1
Fiduciary issue . . .	950.0	1,000.0	1,000.0	1,050.0	1,050.0
Banking dept.					
Public deposits . . .	7.3	17.8	9.5	7.8	6.1
Bankers' deposits . .	157.6	131.9	238.1	150.2	152.8
Other deposits . . .	82.5	54.2	55.3	55.2	52.5
Govt. securities . . .	107.4	139.6	233.4	152.2	163.3
Discounts & advances	16.7	5.7	4.9	1.9	1.0
Other securities . . .	20.4	18.4	27.5	16.2	17.9
Reserve	30.8	57.8	54.8	60.5	46.9

for leading U.S. periodicals. He designed numerous patriotic posters during World War I and also had served as a camouflage expert for the navy. After the U.S. entry into World War II, he served in Australia and in New Guinea, where he recorded on canvas the fighting activity of U.S. forces. The navy department released a report on July 24 that he was missing in action.

Barium Minerals.
Production of crude barite in the United States decreased from 503,156 short tons in 1941 to 429,484 tons in 1942, a drop of 13%, as compared with an increase of 24% in 1941.   (G. A. Ro.)

Barker, Lewellys Franklin
(1867–1943), U.S. physician and educator, was born Sept. 16 in Norwich, Ont., Canada. He studied medicine at the University of Toronto, later completing his studies at the universities of Leipzig, Berlin and Munich. Dr. Barker joined Sir William Osler's staff at Johns Hopkins university, where he became resident pathologist in 1894 and later associate professor of anatomy and pathology. In 1900, he transferred to Rush Medical college as professor of anatomy and department head. When he returned to Johns Hopkins in 1905, he was named professor of medicine and chief physician of Johns Hopkins hospital, holding both posts until 1913, when he became professor emeritus and visiting physician at the hospital. In 1899, he was sent to the Philippines as medical commissioner to help fight the bubonic plague. He died in Baltimore, July 13.

Barley.
The 1943 barley crop of 322,187,000 bu., as estimated by the United States department of agriculture, fell one-fourth short of the record crop produced in 1942 but was almost a third above the average of 1932–41 of 243,373,000 bu. This was in accord with the 1943 goal, which called for less acreage than in 1942.

U.S. Production of Barley by Leading States, 1943 and 1942

State	1943 bu.	1942 bu.	State	1943 bu.	1942 bu.
North Dakota .	63,648,000	67,454,000	Texas	3,341,000	4,818,000
California . . .	36,372,000	43,819,000	Pennsylvania .	2,750,000	4,098,000
South Dakota .	35,343,000	59,364,000	Michigan . . .	2,558,000	7,293,000
Nebraska . . .	27,918,000	38,258,000	Missouri . . .	2,160,000	3,060,000
Minnesota . . .	22,718,000	50,327,000	Kentucky . . .	2,037,000	3,105,000
Colorado	17,616,000	15,816,000	Illinois	2,002,000	3,388,000
Montana . . .	15,939,000	12,330,000	Tennessee . . .	1,819,000	2,200,000
Kansas	15,540,000	16,646,000	Maryland . . .	1,748,000	2,365,000
Idaho	12,716,000	14,280,000	New York . . .	1,650,000	3,300,000
Washington . .	11,700,000	14,600,000	Arizona	1,612,000	1,856,000
Oregon	9,125,000	10,855,000	Virginia	1,575,000	2,120,000
Wisconsin . . .	9,022,000	15,174,000	Indiana	1,268,000	2,640,000
Utah	7,097,000	6,027,000	Iowa	1,102,000	4,158,000
Oklahoma . . .	3,750,000	10,625,000	North Carolina .	922,000	1,058,000
Wyoming . . .	3,392,000	2,600,000	Ohio	800,000	1,785,000

Barley acreage was expanded greatly in the Great Plains states but was grown on a much smaller acreage in the central states. The crop gave way to such war-emergency crops as flax, beans, soy beans and corn. In the western states yields were very good on irrigated land.   (J. C. Ms.)

Barr, Norman Burton
(1868–1943), U.S. welfare worker, was born Jan. 27 in Mount Palatine, Ill., and graduated from the University of Nebraska, 1893, and the Presbyterian Theological seminary, 1897. He was one of a group of notable welfare pioneers in Chicago, including Jane Addams and Graham Taylor. He founded the Olivet institute in a tenement district on Chicago's near north side in 1897 and was pastor of its church for 40 years. His small mission developed into a $750,000 institution. Dr. Barr maintained a free summer camp for mothers and children and also an "eviction house" which temporarily lodged evicted tenants. He retired from the institute in 1937, and died in Chicago, April 1, 1943.

Baruch, Bernard Mannes
(1870–), U.S. financier and government aide, was born Aug. 19 in Camden, S.C., the son of a Confederate surgeon. He moved to New York city at the age of 12 and later attended City college of New York. He entered Wall street, became a customer's man and speculator and by the age of 42 had amassed a fortune estimated at between $12,000,000 and $15,000,000. In 1916 President Wilson invited him to Washington, D.C., as a civilian member of the Advisory commission of the Council of National Defense. In March 1918 Baruch was made head of the War Industries board and was given virtually dictatorial authority over production. Under his guidance, U.S. industry functioned smoothly and poured war supplies overseas. He left his post in Jan. 1919 and went with President Wilson to the Versailles conference in the capacity of economic adviser.

During the early years of U.S. participation in World War II, Baruch headed a committee investigating the rubber crisis, and in Sept. 1942 he urged immediate measures to secure a new rubber supply, warning that failure to do so would cause a collapse on both the home and war fronts. He returned to government service in June 1943 as adviser on industrial production to OWM Director James Byrnes' personal staff, serving without title or salary. On Sept. 17, 1943, Baruch recommended a labour pool to meet the manpower crisis; he suggested that draft deferments be granted on grounds of occupation rather than on dependency. On Nov. 6, Byrnes named Baruch to head a new unit established within the OWM structure to deal with adjustments in war production and problems related to postwar conversion of the U.S. industrial war machine to a peacetime economy.

Basalt: see STONE.

Baseball.
In 1943, there were fewer leagues operating because a great fraction of peacetime professional players and turnstile spectators were wearing war uniforms in distant parts.* The 1943 world series play-by-play description, via short-wave, reached as far as Australia and Iceland to invisible audiences in camps and bases and even in units close to battle lines.

The 1943 world series, played by the same teams as in 1942, the New York Yankees, American league champions, and the St. Louis Cardinals, National league pennant-winners, set a new all-time high record of attendance for a 5-game series, 277,312, surpassing the record of 276,717, set in 1942. The third game of the 1943 series, played at Yankee stadium, New York, Oct. 7, hung up a new all-time attendance record for a single game, 69,990, exceeding the previous record of 69,902, made in the fourth game, 1942.

Total receipts for the series, $1,205,784 (including $100,000 for radio broadcasting privileges), also reached a new all-time high for a 5-game series, topping the former record, $1,205,249, made in the 1942 world series. More than one-fourth of this total, a sum of $308,373.48, representing the receipts of the third and fourth games, minus players' shares, and the total radio receipts, was donated to the Red Cross and the National War Fund, Inc., each receiving half.

These two agencies likewise divided equally the proceeds of the 16 special war games played by the major leagues on two special days, June 30 and July 28. Each of the eight clubs in each league played one war game at home and one away from home. The eight National league games produced $175,118.96 and the American league program turned over $151,439.88.

*As of Dec. 1, 1943, there were 347 major league players and 2,915 from the minors serving in the armed forces.

The Baseball Equipment fund, baseball's medium for supplying the armed forces with bats, baseballs and catching equipment, received $65,174, the proceeds of the annual All-Star game between picked teams from the two major leagues. The 1943 game was played in Philadelphia July 13, a night game. To this sum was added $25,000, the price of radio rights, a $20,000 donation from Commissioner Landis' office and $2,500 from each league treasury, making a total of $115,174 for the B.E.F. working capital.

The Baseball Equipment fund during 1943 continued its sending of "kits" containing bats, baseballs and catching equipment through army and navy headquarters to camps and bases in America and on overseas fronts. In 1943 no. 1 kits (bats and baseballs) were placed in 7,273 service units and 827 of the no. 2 kits (with catching equipment), totalling 8,100 kits as compared with 5,306 distributed in 1942. The report of the B.E.F. figured the 1943 output at 13,491 dozen baseballs, 40,473 bats, 26,982 rule books and 1,489 catching outfits (mitt, body protector, shinguards and mask). Through the B.E.F., the *Sporting News*, baseball's weekly newspaper, published by J. G. Taylor Spink, St. Louis, reached camp libraries, ships at seas, overseas units and U.S.O. clubs (about 4,000 weekly). Foul balls knocked into the stands at major league parks and returned by fans were shipped in lots of a dozen each for use in the armed services during recreation periods.

The Season.—The two major leagues played complete 154-game schedules, as in peace years, but the bookings of the teams were arranged to reduce travel to a minimum, in conformity with the program of the Office of Defense Transportation.

This was most prominent in the case of spring training. Instead of conditioning players in Florida, California and Texas, the 16 major league clubs pitched their training camps inside a boundary known popularly as "The Landis-Eastman Line," a marker prescribed by K. M. Landis, commissioner of baseball, after consultation with Joseph B. Eastman, director of the O.D.T. The southern limit of the training area was marked by the Potomac and Ohio rivers, the western by the Mississippi. The sole exception was the camp of the St. Louis Browns, of the American league, which was at Cape Girardeau, Mo. Both St. Louis clubs had the option of staying on their own side of the Mississippi, but the National league Cardinals nevertheless crossed over to do their training at Cairo, Ill.

In order to fit the round-the-clock working schedules of war-plants, shipyards, etc., starting times of ball games during 1943 were literally "all hours." On Aug. 11, 1943, there were major league games starting at the following ticks of the clock: 10:30 A.M., 12 noon and 1:30, 2:30, 3:30, 5:30, 5:45, 8:30 and 9:30, all P.M. Newark and Milwaukee had some 9:30 A.M. games. In the latter city the swing-shift fans entering the stands had their risibilities tickled at the sight of one of the veteran coaches of the home team pretending to be just finishing his night's sleep with home plate for his pillow.

Total attendance at big league games fell off about 13% from 1942, according to the Associated Press tabulation, in part attributable to the fact that in both leagues the pennant races became one-sided in their closing weeks. Five clubs showed gains over 1942, most notably the Philadelphia Nationals, who more than doubled their 1942 gate. The New York clubs were among those showing substantial losses; Brooklyn had a greater falling off than any of the other 15 clubs, but despite the drop of nearly 400,000, the Dodgers led both leagues in total home attendance.

How the 1943 attendance figures compare with 1942 may be noted in the first table in the next column.

In both leagues the pennant races were wide open at the finish. Reversing the trend of baseball fashions of modern times, the

Attendance figures, 1943 and 1942

NATIONAL LEAGUE			
	1943	1942	Difference
Brooklyn	688,633	1,087,860	− 399,227
St. Louis	545,019	571,297	− 26,278
Pittsburgh	542,211	500,000	+ 42,211
Chicago	510,000	590,972	− 80,972
New York	506,345	867,614	− 361,269
Philadelphia	466,876	230,183	+ 236,693
Cincinnati	395,748	470,582	− 74,834
Boston	312,923	346,249	− 33,326
Total	3,967,755	4,664,757	− 697,002

AMERICAN LEAGUE			
Detroit	620,135	580,087	+ 40,048
New York	618,798	922,011	− 303,213
Washington	580,000	403,000	+ 177,000
Chicago	508,962	426,874	+ 82,088
Cleveland	439,000	458,000	− 19,000
Philadelphia	400,000	423,000	− 23,000
Boston	364,691	741,026	− 376,335
St. Louis	215,295	256,000	− 40,705
Total	3,746,881	4,209,998	− 463,117
Grand total	7,714,636	8,874,755	−1,160,119

National league pennant-winner in 1943 had the wider margin of superiority over its contenders—the St. Louis Cardinals owning an 18-game advantage over the second-place Cincinnati Reds at the finish, while the New York Yankees stood 13½ ahead of the American league runner-up, the Washington Senators.

St. Louis, however, fell 1 victory short of equalling its 1942 total of 106. The Yankees were 5 games behind their 103 bag of 1942. The Cardinals' 18-game lead over second place was the largest in National league history since 1906, when the Chicago Cubs, winning 116 games for an all-time record, stood 20 games ahead of the second-place New York Giants at the finish.

NATIONAL LEAGUE
Final Standings

Club	St.L.	Cin.	Bkn.	Pitts.	Chi.	Bos.	Phila.	N.Y.	Won	Lost	Pct.	G.B.
St. Louis	—	12	15	15	13	19	13	18	105	49	.682	....
Cincinnati	10	—	9	9	13	11	19	16	87	67	.565	18
Brooklyn	7	13	—	11	10	9	17	14	81	72	.529	23½
Pittsburgh	7	13	11	—	14	10	12	13	80	74	.519	25
Chicago	9	9	12	8	—	14	10	12	74	79	.484	30½
Boston	3	11	12	12	8	—	11	11	68	85	.444	36½
Philadelphia	9	3	5	10	12	11	—	14	64	90	.416	41
New York	4	6	8	9	9	11	8	—	55	98	.359	49½

Ties.—Pittsburgh-St. Louis (2); New York-Cincinnati; St. Louis-Philadelphia; Pittsburgh-Philadelphia; New York-Philadelphia; Chicago-New York.

AMERICAN LEAGUE
Final Standings

Club	N.Y.	Wash.	Clev.	Chi.	Det.	St.L.	Bos.	Phila.	Won	Lost	Pct.	G.B.
New York	—	11	13	12	12	17	17	16	98	56	.636	....
Washington	11	—	13	8	9	14	12	17	84	69	.549	13½
Cleveland	9	8	—	15	15	9	10	16	82	71	.536	15½
Chicago	10	14	7	—	9	10	14	18	82	72	.532	16
Detroit	10	13	7	13	—	11	11	13	78	76	.506	20
St. Louis	5	8	13	12	11	—	9	14	72	80	.474	25
Boston	5	10	12	8	11	11	—	11	68	84	.447	29
Philadelphia	6	5	6	4	9	8	11	—	49	105	.318	49
Lost	56	69	71	72	76	80	84	105				

Ties.—New York-Boston; Boston-Detroit; St. Louis-Boston; Chicago-Philadelphia.

The World Series.—The 1943 world series, the second played since Pearl Harbor, brought together the same clubs which had competed in the 1942 post-season classic, though important players on both sides had joined the armed forces since the eventful October days of 1942.

War travel imperatives made changes in the world series schedule. In order to have only one mass excursion between New York and St. Louis, the first three games of the 1943 series were played at Yankee stadium. Peace schedules specify the first two games in one city, the next two in the other, then, if further play is necessary, a return to the first city for as many games as are required for one team to record four victories.

The Yankees, by winning the 1943 series, stretched the club's list of post-season inter-league championships to 10, twice as many as any other club has, and one-fourth of all the world

THE FREAK "BALLOON BALL" of Pitcher Truett Sewell of the Pittsburgh Pirates was largely responsible for his winning 21 games in 1943. The ball travels 25 ft. into the air and falls almost vertically across the plate. Circles indicate its path

series titles decided since competition began between the National and American leagues with the "unofficial" world series of 1903. The Boston and Philadelphia teams of the American league rate next best to the Yankees with five each. These three clubs have been responsible for 20 of the 25 world championships won by the American league of the 40 that have been contested.

Joe McCarthy, Yankees' manager, recorded his seventh world championship, placing him one notch further ahead of his nearest competitor for world series leadership honours, Connie Mack, who managed the Athletics of Philadelphia in their five series triumphs.

By defeating the Cardinals, 4 games to 1, the Yankees reversed the 1942 score. In 1942 the Yankees won the first game, the Cardinals the next four. In 1943 the first two games followed the 1942 pattern, the Yankees winning the first, the Cardinals the second. Then the picture changed, the Yankees sweeping on to take the next three.

Scores of the five games: First game: New York 4; St. Louis 2. Second game: St. Louis 4; New York 3. Third game: New York 6; St. Louis 2. Fourth game: New York 2; St. Louis 1. Fifth game: New York 2; St. Louis 0.

Another reverse of the 1942 picture was that the only Cardinal victory in the 1943 series was pitched by Morton Cooper, Cardinal ace, who in 1942, when he was named the National league's most valuable player, was defeated in the only game the Cardinals lost and batted out of the box in the other game he started. A sombre note was the sudden death of Robert Cooper, father of the Cardinals' brother battery, Morton and Walker Cooper, in the early morning of Oct. 6. Despite the shock of the news, the Cooper brothers carried through with their battery assignment that afternoon, Morton pitching and Walker catching the game which the Cardinals won, 4 to 3. The two-day recess between the third and fourth games made it possible for the brothers to attend their father's funeral on Saturday, Oct. 9, without being absent from the Cardinals' battle line. Morton appeared again as pitcher in the final game, striking out the first five Yankees who came to bat and losing an intense pitchers' battle with Spurgeon Chandler by the score of 2 to 0.

Walker Cooper, who was the Cardinals' field-captain, caught every inning of the series until he suffered a fracture of his right thumb in the 5th inning of the last game.

Though some of the brightest stars of the 1942 world series on both sides had entered the armed forces—Joe DiMaggio, Charley Ruffing, Phil Rizzuto and Buddy Hassett of the Yankees; Terry Moore, John Beazley, Enos Slaughter and Jimmy Brown of the Cardinals—the memory of 1942's thrills whetted the appetite of the baseball world for the 1943 replay.

The Yankees richly repaid the confidence of their admirers by winning in handy fashion. They played courageous and alert baseball, taking full advantage of every Cardinal lapse in fielding and brainwork. Spurgeon Chandler, the Yankee pitching ace, was every inch an ace in the world series. He held the Cardinals safe in the first game with 7 hits for a 4–2 decision; in the final game he scattered 10 St. Louis hits (all singles) for a 2–0 triumph to end the series and clinch the crown.

Bill Dickey, mighty catcher of the Yankees, smote a home run to the roof of the St. Louis right-field pavilion in the 6th inning of this final game with Keller on base to account for both the Yankee runs, and thereby placed his name in a bracket by itself in the all-time records. It was his eighth world series as a member of the Yankees. His winning homer made him the only man in history who has been on that many victorious world series teams. It climaxed an eventful year for the Yankee catcher in which he led the American league in batting with .351, although he was in only 85 games and did not amass as many as 400 times at bat, the necessary number to be awarded the league's batting championship.

Another outstanding Yankee hero was Marius Russo, southpaw who scored a notable victory over Brooklyn in the 1941 world series, but was not prominent in the Yankee picture in the ensuing two seasons because of muscular impairment of his pitching arm. His 1943 achievement was only a one-day performance, but that day he was the whole show. He went to the box in the opening St. Louis game, the 4th game of the world series. His team led in games won, 2 to 1, but the Cardinals were now in St. Louis for the first time in the world series schedule. Experts commenting on McCarthy's choice of Russo called it a "gamble," rather looking for a rout of the "lame-arm" southpaw and a Cardinal resurgence which would tie the series score and set the stage for a redhot climax on the home grounds of the 1942 world champions. Russo, however, had the Cardinals shut out for the first 6 innings. In the 4th the Yanks scored a run on a single by Dickey off Max Lanier, no. 1 St. Louis ace for the series as selected by the Cardinal manager, Billy Southworth, that is, starter of the first game in New York and again in this heavily important first game in St. Louis.

Dickey's single drove home Gordon and put Russo ahead 1 to 0. In the 7th inning a pair of Yankee infield errors allowed the Cardinals to tie the score with an unearned run, so that Russo, for all his fine pitching, stood on only even terms with his foemen with only two innings left to play. It was then that Russo stepped beyond his role of pitcher and "won his own game," as baseball phrases it when a pitcher does something notable as a batter. He came to bat first for the Yankees in the 8th. Batting right-handed against the Cardinal southpaw, Harry Brecheen, the Yankee pitcher drove a long 2-bagger to the extreme left-field foul line corner of the ball park. The next two Yankees did what was ordered, Stainback sacrificing Russo to third and Crosetti sending him home by sailing a long fly to centre on which Russo scored easily after the catch.

Russo then had to go to the box and suppress the Cardinals in their last two turns at bat. The Cardinals had two infield singles in the 8th but could not score. After Marion doubled with one out in the 9th, Russo retired the next two batters to consolidate the 2 to 1 score in his favour, which he built with his 7th-inning double.

Hero honours on the Yankee side went also to Frank Crosetti, veteran shortstop, whose all-around play was superb, Bill Johnson, the first-year third baseman, whose triple with the bases filled broke up the 3rd game and whose .300 batting average for the series was tops for the Yankees, and John Lindell, former pitcher converted into an outfielder by war exigencies, whose successful slide to third base was the turning-point in the 3rd game of the series, setting the stage for Johnson's base-clearing triple and the victory which put the Yankees ahead, 2 games to 1.

Palms were bestowed likewise on Joe Gordon, Yankee second baseman. Gordon proved a steady rock of strength for the Yankees in their 1943 series, hitting a home run in the first game to break a 1-1 tie score and setting three new fielding records. He handled 43 chances without any error, crossing off the record of 35 for a second baseman in a five-game series, which had stood since Eddie Collins of Philadelphia made it in 1910. Gordon's new record for most putouts, 20, topped the old one of 19, set by George Cutshaw of Brooklyn in 1916. His 23 assists erased the 21 first achieved by Germany Schaefer, of Detroit, in 1907, and equalled by Johnny Evers of Chicago in 1908.

On the Cardinal side, besides the pitching of Mort Cooper in the shadow of his family sorrow, the outstanding performer was Martin Marion, slim shortstop, who not only maintained his title to the no. 1 shortstop of his league but was the leading hitter of the series, both sides, with .357. His five hits included two doubles and a home run, his homer starting the scoring in the only game the Cardinals won. Ray Sanders, first baseman, also delivered a home run in this game and shared honours with Cooper and Marion in the Cardinals' brief taste of success.

The All-Star Game.—The annual All-Star game between picked teams of the two major leagues, played at Shibe park, Philadelphia, July 13, a night game, was an American league victory by the score of 5 to 3. The attendance was 31,938, about 5,000 below capacity.

Morton Cooper was the starting and losing pitcher in the All-Star game. A home run into the left-field pavilion with two on bases by Bobby Doerr, Boston Red Sox second baseman, sent across 3 runs in the 2nd inning. Ken Keltner's (Cleveland) double and Dick Wakefield's (Detroit) single added a fourth American league run off Cooper in the next inning.

Against the subsequent National league pitchers, John Vander-Meer, of Cincinnati, Truett Sewell, of Pittsburgh, and Alva Javery, of Boston, the American league stars were able to score only one run, an unearned run that counted when Billy Herman Brooklyn second baseman, threw wild to home plate on a double steal play.

But the trio of American league pitchers, Emil Leonard, Washington, Harold Newhouser, Detroit, and Tex Hughson, Boston, kept the National league's 10 hits so sparsely placed that they were good for only 3 runs, in three different innings. Vince DiMaggio, Pittsburgh, made the most impressive hits of the contest, a booming triple against the left-field wall in the 7th inning and a home run that landed in the upper left-field stand far over towards centre field in the 9th. In each case, DiMaggio was the first batter up in the inning and his power-drives, either one good enough to break up the game had there been men on bases, were worth only one run each.

The world series managers of 1942 and 1943 (Joe McCarthy and Billy Southworth) acted as managers of the rival All-Star teams. It was the 8th American league victory in 11 All-Star games played, starting at the Chicago World's Fair in 1933, giving the American league an even more impressive success score in All-Star game play than their 25–15 world series tabulation.

Individual Achievements.—The most-valuable-player honours for the year, as voted by the Baseball Writers' association, went to Spurgeon Chandler, Yankee pitching ace, and Stan Musial, St. Louis Cardinal outfielder, who achieved the National league batting championship in his second major league season. His hitting and all-around play contributed heavily to both the 1942 and 1943 pennant winning. Chandler led the American league pitchers in the W-L percentage with 20 victories against 4 defeats and in the earned-runs-allowed average with 1.64, the best figure recorded by a first-string major league pitcher since Walter Johnson, Washington, chalked up 1.49 in 1919. Chandler's two world series victories were the key games, the opening contest and the title-clinching 5th game.

League Leaders

BATTING
First Five in Each League

Player, club	G.	AB.	R.	H.	Pct.
Musial, Cardinals	157	617	108	220	.357
Herman, Dodgers	153	585	76	193	.330
Appling, White Sox	155	585	63	192	.328
Cooper, Cardinals	122	449	52	143	.319
Wakefield, Tigers	155	633	91	200	.316
Elliott, Pirates	156	581	82	183	.315
Witek, Giants	153	622	68	195	.314
Hodgin, White Sox	117	407	52	128	.314
Cramer, Tigers	140	606	79	182	.300
Case, Senators	141	613	102	180	.294

HOME RUNS

American League		National League	
York, Detroit	34	Nicholson, Chicago	29
Keller, New York	31	Ott, New York	18
Stephens, St. Louis	22	Northey, Philadelphia	16
Heath, Cleveland	18	Triplett, Philadelphia	15
Laabs, St. Louis	17	DiMaggio, Pittsburgh	15

RUNS BATTED IN

American League		National League	
York, Detroit	118	Nicholson, Chicago	128
Etten, New York	107	Elliott, Pittsburgh	101
Johnson, New York	94	Herman, Brooklyn	100
Stephens, St. Louis	91	DiMaggio, Pittsburgh	88
Spence, Washington	88	Musial, St. Louis	81
		Cooper, St. Louis	81

Musial's .357 batting average for 157 games was 27 points better than the runner-up for the National league batting title, the veteran Billy Herman, of Brooklyn. Musial led in total number of hits, in doubles and in triples. His hit-total, 220, made him the first National leaguer since 1939 to reach the 200-hit mark.

Luke Appling, Chicago White Sox shortstop, was the American league batting champion, the second time he achieved the crown, though his 1943 average of .328 was 60 points less than in 1936, his first championship year.

The home run champions in each league were also the top

THE WORLD SERIES of 1943 provided the annual relief from less pleasant news, noted Bishop of the *St. Louis Star-Times* in this cartoon, "Thanks for the Lift, Pal!"

run-drivers, Rudy York, Detroit first baseman, leading the American league with 34 homers and 118 runs-batted-in. Bill Nicholson, Chicago Cubs' right-fielder, had 29 homers to lead the National and 128 RBI.

The National league had no one pitcher outclassing his competition as did Chandler in the American and as Mort Cooper did in the senior circuit in 1942. Percentage honours for 1943 in the National went to Whitlow Wyatt, Brooklyn, with 14 wins against 5 losses. Howard Pollet, St. Louis southpaw, who joined the air force in mid-July, led the earned-run-averages with 1.75, the best in the National league since Carl Hubbell's 1.66 in 1933. Truett Sewell, Pittsburgh, and Elmer Riddle, Cincinnati, tied with Cooper, of the Cardinals, in total victories, each having 21. Cooper's percentage was the best of the trio, showing only 8 defeats.

The earned-runs-allowed tables in the National league indicated a remarkable superiority performance by the St. Louis pitchers. Pollet was the first of three Cardinal pitchers holding the first three places on the list of pitchers with 10 or more complete games to their credit, Lanier ranking second and Cooper third. Two other Card pitchers, Alpha Brazle and Harry Brecheen, led the secondary list, pitchers working 75 innings or more but not so many as 10 complete games. Four of the five are left-handers, Cooper being the only right-hand pitcher.

Ace Adams, New York Giants' bull-pen specialist, set a new 20th century record for number of games pitched, 70, surpassing the existing record of 61 which he wrote into the archives in 1942. Only one of his 1943 games was a complete contest, the rest being emergency work in relief of other pitchers.

Minor Leagues.—Nine minor leagues—three class AAs, one A-1, one A, two Bs and two Ds—operated in 1943, as compared with 26 that played full seasons in 1942, 41 in 1941 and 47 in the peak year of National Association history, 1912.

Eight of the nine active in 1943 held Shaughnessy post-season playoff rounds in which the first division teams met in an elimination series for the league championship. Lancaster, pennant-winner in the Inter-State league, was the only one of the eight pennant-winners victorious in a post-season playoff.

All three of the circuits which have composed class AA ever since that classification was instituted played full seasons. The Los Angeles Seraphs, Pacific Coast league pennant-winners, lost out in the playoffs, won by the San Francisco Seals, who finished second in the pennant race.

The Milwaukee Brewers, American association pennant-winners, had to yield to the third place Columbus Red Birds in the playoffs while the Syracuse Chiefs, International league third-placers, were victorious in the playoffs after the Toronto Maple Leafs won the pennant. Columbus defeated Syracuse, 4 games to 1, in the annual Junior world series between the playoff winners of these last two AA organizations. The Birds thus made Junior world series history, for it was their third straight victory in successive years. They defeated Montreal's Royals in 1941 and Syracuse in 1942. In the annals of the series, which has been played 26 times since its first meeting in 1904, no club before ever won three years in succession. It was the sixth time Columbus represented the association in the Junior series and its fifth successful title-quest. The Red Birds scored victories over the International league champions of 1933 and 1934, Buffalo and Toronto. Their only series defeat was in 1937, when they lost to the Newark Bears. The 1943 series adjusted itself to the war travel exigencies by playing the first three games in Syracuse, the last two in Columbus.

The Dixie series, played traditionally each year between the champions of the two class A-1 circuits, the Southern association and the Texas league, was absent from the baseball calendar because the Texas league did not operate in 1943. The Southern association, the only minor league extant which did not have Shaughnessy playoffs, returned to the split-season system of deciding its championship. Nashville's Vols, winners of the first half of the schedule, defeated New Orleans, second-half winners, in the playoff round for the title, 4 games to 1.

Adding together the two halves of the split-season, Nashville won 83 and lost 55 for a .601 percentage while New Orleans won 78 and lost 58 for .574, so that if played without splitting, the schedule still would have crowned Nashville pennant-winner. It was Nashville's fifth straight year to represent the Southern association in the Dixie series, had the series been played. They were victorious over the Texas league champions in 1940–41–42, the all-time record performance for a Southern association club.

In the only class A league that functioned, the Eastern, Elmira's Pioneers, after finishing second in the pennant race, won the playoffs, beating the pennant-winning Scranton Miners.

The third-place Norfolk Tars were first when the playoffs of the class B Piedmont league were concluded, the pennant-winning Portsmouth Cubs going down to defeat. Lancaster's Red Roses were both flag-winners and playoff winners in the other class B circuit, the Inter-State league.

The class D leagues alive were the Appalachian and the Pennsylvania-Ontario-New York. The Bristol Twins won the pennant and the runner-up Erwin Aces the playoffs in the Appalachian while the Pony league pennant-winners, the Lockport White Socks, had to give way to the Wellsville Yankees in the playoffs.

Minor league attendance statistics in the nine circuits which operated indicated that curtailment of night baseball and gasoline rationing regulations played a major role in the reduced total attendance at ball games during 1943.

The American association, comprising cities in the Mississippi and Ohio valleys mainly, Columbus, Louisville, Indianapolis, Toledo, Milwaukee, Minneapolis, St. Paul and Kansas City, reported a total of 1,359,059, an 8.2% increase over 1942's 1,247,320.

The other eight leagues ranged downward in comparative figures. The Eastern league—Elmira, Scranton, Albany, Hartford, Springfield, Mass., Utica, Wilkesbarre and Binghamton, cities located in a zone in which pleasure-driving was taboo during the summer months—showed a 32% drop, from 700,388 as of 1942 to 456,194.

The pleasure-driving ban was modified as the Eastern playoffs were starting, whereupon the 16 playoff games played to 66,461, the highest in the league's history since playoffs were instituted in 1937. One game, the 17-inning 3 to 3 tie between Elmira and Scranton at Elmira Sept. 26, set a new league record for a single game, 8,618.   (W. E. Bт.)

Basic English.
Basic English (British American Scientific International Commercial) is a system of 850 English words sufficient for the needs of ordinary conversation and written communication. The words were selected and the system developed between 1925 and 1932 by C. K. Ogden, M.A., of Magdalene college, Cambridge, England, editor of The International Library of Psychology, Philosophy and Scientific Method; and author of *Basic English, The System of Basic English,* etc.

The chief purposes of the system are:

1. To serve as an international auxiliary language for use throughout the world in general communication, commerce and science.
2. To provide a rational introduction to unlimited English; both as a first step, complete in itself, for those whose natural language is not English, and as a grammatical introduction, encouraging clarity of thought and expression, for English-speaking peoples at any stage of proficiency.

The vocabulary of Basic is made up of 400 general nouns, 150 adjectives, 100 "operators" (verbs, particles, pronouns, etc.) and 200 names of picturable things. All the Basic words are in common use but their selection was directed by their co-operative utility rather than by their frequency as determined by word counts. The syntax of Basic is that of normal English. There is accordingly nothing to be unlearned in passing from Basic to a more complete English.

The Basic word list was arrived at by:

1. The reduction of verbs to 16. Within the system this avoids the necessity of supplementing noun forms with corresponding verb forms.
2. The elimination: (a) of all words (with the exception of common objects) which can be defined in not more than ten other words in the Basic word list; (b) of words which, whether capable of definition within the set limit or not, are primarily emotive rather than referential; (c) of words which, though not capable of definition within the set limit have chiefly a literary or stylistic value; (d) of words which, whether capable of such definition or not, are used in context too abstruse for the level of general communication.

It need hardly be remarked that misapprehension may arise if the vocabulary is considered without reference to the principles on which it is based, and the specific recommendations as to word uses made in *The Basic Words* and *The ABC of Basic English.*

To its 600 nouns Basic English adds a list of 50 terms which, through world-wide diffusion, have already acquired international intelligibility (*e.g.*, passport, radio, etc.).

While the 850 words of the general Basic vocabulary are sufficient for the needs of ordinary communication, it is not claimed for them that they can express adequately the technicalities with which specialists alone are concerned. To this end further lists of words are appended—100 general science words and 50 words for each of the principal sciences (see *Basic for Science*, 1943). Similarly in the Basic version of the Bible 50 additional words (for verse reading) are used and 100 words of special Biblical significance. In practice it is found that native English speakers have little difficulty in learning to restrict themselves on occasion within the limits of Basic.

As a teaching system Basic was in extensive use before World War II in more than 30 different countries. The economy and wide utility of its vocabulary and its simplicity of construction (due to its treatment of the verb) enable the learner to make very rapid progress into its effective use in all forms of communication. Teaching texts include: *Basic Step by Step* (adapta-

DR. IVOR A. RICHARDS of Harvard university, foremost U.S. exponent of Basic English, examining a series of sketches for a film by Walt Disney on the simplified language of 850 words. Interest in Basic English became widespread in 1943 after a reference to it by Prime Minister Churchill at Harvard

OPERATIONS, ETC. 100	THINGS — 400 GENERAL				THINGS — 200 PICTURED		QUALITIES — 100 GENERAL		NO "VERBS"	
come	account	education	metal	sense	angle	knee	able	material	It	A
get	act	effect	middle	servant	ant	knife	acid	medical	is	week
give	addition	end	milk	sex	apple	knot	angry	military	possible	or
go	adjustment	error	mind	shade	arch	leaf	automatic	natural	to	two
keep	advertisement	event	mine	shake	arm	leg	beautiful	necessary	get	with
let	agreement	example	minute	shame	army	library	black	new	all	the
make	air	exchange	mist	shock	baby	line	boiling	normal	these	rules
put	amount	existence	money	side	bag	lip	bright	open	words	and
seem	amusement	expansion	month	sign	ball	lock	broken	parallel	on	the
take	animal	experience	morning	silk	band	map	brown	past	the	special
be	answer	expert	mother	silver	basin	match	cheap	physical	back	records
do	apparatus	fact	motion	sister	basket	monkey	chemical	political	of	gives
have	approval	fall	mountain	size	bath	moon	chief	poor	a	complete
say	argument	family	move	sky	bed	mouth	clean	possible	bit	knowledge
see	art	father	music	sleep	bee	muscle	clear	present	of	of
send	attack	fear	name	slip	bell	nail	common	private	notepaper	the
may	attempt	feeling	nation	slope	berry	neck	complex	probable	because	system
will	attention	fiction	need	smash	bird	needle	conscious	quick	there	for
about	attraction	field	news	smell	blade	nerve	cut	quiet	are	reading
across	authority	fight	night	smile	board	net	deep	ready	no	or
after	back	fire	noise	smoke	boat	nose	dependent	red	"verbs"	writing.
against	balance	flame	note	sneeze	bone	nut	early	regular	in	
among	base	flight	number	snow	book	office	elastic	responsible	Basic	
at	behaviour	flower	observation	soap	boot	orange	electric	right	English.	
before	belief	fold	offer	society	bottle	oven	equal	round		
between	birth	food	oil	son	box	parcel	fat	same		
by	bit	force	operation	song	boy	pen	fertile	second	**EXAMPLES OF**	
down	bite	form	opinion	sort	brain	pencil	first	separate	**WORD ORDER**	
from	blood	friend	order	sound	brake	picture	fixed	serious		
in	blow	front	organization	soup	branch	pig	flat	sharp		
off	body	fruit	ornament	space	brick	pin	free	smooth	The	We
on	brass	glass	owner	stage	bridge	pipe	frequent	sticky	camera	will
over	bread	gold	page	start	brush	plane	full	stiff	man	give
through	breath	government	pain	statement	bucket	plate	general	straight	who	simple
to	brother	grain	paint	steam	bulb	plough	good	strong	made	rules
under	building	grass	paper	steel	button	pocket	great	sudden	an	to
up	burn	grip	part	step	cake	pot	grey	sweet	attempt	you
with	burst	group	paste	stitch	camera	potato	hanging	tall	to	now.
as	business	growth	payment	stone	card	prison	happy	thick	take	
for	butter	guide	peace	stop	carriage	pump	hard	tight	a	
of	canvas	harbour	person	story	cart	rail	healthy	tired	moving	
till	care	harmony	place	stretch	cat	rat	high	true	picture	
than	cause	hate	plant	structure	chain	receipt	hollow	violent	of	
a	chalk	hearing	play	substance	cheese	ring	important	waiting	the	
the	chance	heat	pleasure	sugar	chest	rod	kind	warm	society	
all	change	help	point	suggestion	chin	roof	like	wet	women	
any	cloth	history	poison	summer	church	root	living	wide	before	
every	coal	hole	polish	support	circle	sail	long	wise	they	
no	colour	hope	porter	surprise	clock	school	male	yellow	got	
other	comfort	hour	position	swim	cloud	scissors	married	young	their	
some	committee	humour	powder	system	coat	screw			hats	
such	company	ice	power	talk	collar	seed	**50 OPPOSITES**		off	
that	comparison	idea	price	taste	comb	sheep			did	
this	competition	impulse	print	tax	cord	shelf	awake	left	not	
I	condition	increase	process	teaching	cow	ship	bad	loose	get	
he	connection	industry	produce	tendency	cup	shirt	bent	loud	off	
you	control	ink	profit	test	curtain	shoe	bitter	low	the	
who	cook	insect	property	theory	cushion	skin	blue	mixed	ship	
and	copper	instrument	prose	thing	dog	skirt	certain	narrow	till	
because	copy	insurance	protest	thought	door	snake	cold	old	he	
but	cork	interest	pull	thunder	drain	sock	complete	opposite	was	
or	cotton	invention	punishment	time	drawer	spade	cruel	public	questioned	
if	cough	iron	purpose	tin	dress	sponge	dark	rough	by	
though	country	jelly	push	top	drop	spoon	dead	sad	the	
while	cover	join	quality	touch	ear	spring	dear	safe	police.	
how	crack	journey	question	trade	egg	square	delicate	secret		
when	credit	judge	rain	transport	engine	stamp	different	short		
where	crime	jump	range	trick	eye	star	dirty	shut		
why	crush	kick	rate	trouble	face	station	dry	simple		
again	cry	kiss	ray	turn	farm	stem	false	slow		
ever	current	knowledge	reaction	twist	feather	stick	feeble	small		
far	curve	land	reading	unit	finger	stocking	female	soft		
forward	damage	language	reason	use	fish	stomach	foolish	solid		
here	danger	laugh	record	value	flag	store	future	special		
near	daughter	law	regret	verse	floor	street	green	strange		
now	day	lead	relation	vessel	fly	sun	ill	thin		
out	death	learning	religion	view	foot	table	last	white		
still	debt	leather	representative	voice	fork	tail	late	wrong		
then	decision	letter	request	walk	fowl	thread				
there	degree	level	respect	war	frame	throat	**RULES**			
together	design	lift	rest	wash	garden	thumb				
well	desire	light	reward	waste	girl	ticket	Addition of "s" to things	Questions by change of		
almost	destruction	limit	rhythm	water	glove	toe	when there is more	order and "do."		
enough	detail	linen	rice	wave	goat	tongue	than one.	Form-changes in names		
even	development	liquid	river	wax	gun	tooth	Endings in "er," "ing,"	of acts, and "that,"		
little	digestion	list	road	way	hair	town	"ed" from 300 names	"this," "I," "he,"		
much	direction	look	roll	weather	hammer	train	of things.	"you," "who," as in		
not	discovery	loss	room	week	hand	tray		normal English.		
only	discussion	love	rub	weight	hat	tree	"ly" forms from quali-	Measures numbers, days,		
quite	disease	machine	rule	wind	head	trousers	ties.	months and the inter-		
so	disgust	man	run	wine	heart	umbrella		national words in Eng-		
very	distance	manager	salt	winter	hook	wall	Degree with "more" and	lish form.		
tomorrow	distribution	mark	sand	woman	horn	watch	"most."			
yesterday	division	market	scale	wood	horse	wheel				
north	doubt	mass	science	wool	hospital	whip	**THE ORTHOLOGICAL INSTITUTE**			
south	drink	meal	sea	word	house	whistle	45 Gordon Square, London W. C. 1, England			
east	driving	measure	seat	work	island	window				
west	dust	meat	secretary	wound	jewel	wing				
please	earth	meeting	selection	writing	kettle	wire				
yes	edge	memory	self	year	key	worm				

tions are available for French, German, Spanish, Italian, Polish, Dutch, Norwegian, with others in preparation), *The Basic Way to English,* and *Learning the English Language* (designed for adult aliens in America). Special applications are its use for the deaf and dumb and for the blind. A point of general importance is the quantity of mature reading matter serving all interests which exists in Basic English.

The headquarters of Basic in 1943 were, in England, The Orthological Institute, 45 Gordon square, London W. C. 1; in America, The Harvard Commission on English Language Studies, Cambridge, Mass.

BIBLIOGRAPHY.—C. K. Ogden, *Basic English* (a general introduction) (London, 1938); Idem, *The ABC of Basic English* (London, 1939); Idem, *The Basic Words* (London, 1943), Idem, *Basic Step by Step* (London, 1939); Idem, *The System of Basic English* (New York, 1934); I. A. Richards, *Basic English and Its Uses* (contains selected bibliography) (New York, London, 1943); C. K. Ogden, ed., *The General Basic English Dictionary* (London, 1941). (I. A. Rs.)

Basketball. University of Illinois' famed "Whiz Kids" and Wyoming university shared honours in collegiate basketball during 1943. Illinois captured its second straight Big Ten championship with a starting team of juniors, and generally dominated the sport in the middle west. The Illini did not take part in postseason competition, and at the start of the 1943–44 season all of the "Whiz Kids" were in the armed services. Wyoming started its victorious campaign by winning the Rocky Mountain conference and went on to win the National Collegiate Athletic association tournament.

In a Red Cross benefit, Wyoming defeated St. John's college of Brooklyn, winner of the Madison Square Garden invitational, by a 52–47 score.

Dartmouth topped the Eastern league for the sixth straight year, while Duke held its title place in the south although menaced by George Washington. Rice and Texas shared honours in the southwest, while Tennessee and Kentucky dominated the Southeastern conference.

Washington replaced Stanford as the Pacific coast's No. 1 team, and Kansas and Creighton led the Big Six and Missouri Valley, respectively.

Phillips "66," made up largely of former Oklahoma A. & M. players, won the National A.A.U. championship with a 57–40 victory over the Denver Legion in the final. The annual tournament, held for the ninth successive time at Denver, Colo., attracted 34 teams. The two finalists placed two players each on the "All-American" A.A.U. team, Phillips with James McNatt, forward, and Gordon Carpenter, guard, and Denver Legion with Robert Gruenig, centre and Robert Doll, guard. Kenneth Sailors of Wyoming university earned the other forward position.

The American Institute of Commerce of Davenport, Ia., won the National Women's A.A.U. basketball championship with a 41–31 triumph over Des Moines in an all-Iowa final.

The Washington Bears won the U.S. professional basketball championship in the annual tournament at Chicago. The Oshkosh All-Stars were second and Fort Wayne, winner of the National Pro league title, was third. The Philadelphia Sphas won the American Professional league championship. The College All-Stars defeated the Washington Bears in the 1943–44 inaugural, 35 to 31. (M. P. W.)

Basutoland: see BRITISH SOUTH AFRICAN PROTECTORATES.
Battleships: see NAVIES OF THE WORLD.

Baur, Harry (1880?–1943), French actor, was born in Paris, the son of Alsatian parents. From the amateur stage in Marseilles, he worked his way to Paris and until World War I enjoyed moderate success in the capital's theatres. He was invalided out of the war and returned to the Paris stage, but soon received several motion picture contracts and quickly climbed to fame as one of the leading French character actors. His most successful roles were as Jean Valjean in *Les Misérables*, M. Lepic in *Poil de Carotte*, Ludwig van Beethoven in *The Life and Loves of Beethoven*, the mad emperor in *The Golem*, the police inspector in *Crime and Punishment* and the title role in *Rasputin*. According to a Stockholm report, he was arrested in Berlin in May 1942, for forging an "ahnpass," an Aryan ancestry certificate. A Vichy radio report of April 8 carried the news of his death in Paris.

Bauxite. No statistics were made public on bauxite output in any of the important producing countries after 1941, and of these many were rough estimates.

World Production of Bauxite
(Metric tons)

	1929	1938	1939	1940	1941
Br. Guiana . .	220,119	382,400	483,700	550,000	900,000
France	666,348	682,400	680,000	700,000	500,000
Greece	..	179,900	186,900	180,000	?
Hungary . . .	389,152	540,700	570,200	560,000	600,000
Italy	192,774	360,800	483,965	380,000	380,000
Neth. E. Indies	..	245,400	230,700	274,375	100,000
Surinam . . .	219,603	377,200	511,600	615,434	1,100,000
U.S.S.R. . . .	..	250,000?	250,000?	270,000?	?
United States .	371,648	315,900	381,300	445,958	900,000
Yugoslavia . .	103,366	396,400	318,800	260,000	400,000
World Total	2,185,000	3,850,000	4,370,000	4,500,000	5,500,000

In the United States the bureau of mines, assisted by the Geological Survey, carried on extensive exploratory programs in the southern states, and while the larger portion of the large tonnages that were developed was low-grade ore, sufficient commercial ore was found to help out materially in meeting the demand. To supplement the exploratory program for new ore bodies, extensive experimental work was also done on the development of methods of utilizing low-grade ores. However, late in 1943, when the supply of aluminum began to catch up with demand (*see* ALUMINUM) this work was sharply curtailed, in order that the funds and manpower involved might be utilized more effectively on materials, the supply of which was still short of current demand.
(G. A. Ro.)

Beans, Dry. A record crop of dry beans of 22,799,000 bags was harvested in 1943 according to estimates by the U.S. department of agriculture. This crop was 15% larger than the 1942 crop of 19,035,000 bags and 52% larger than the 10-year average 1932–41. An increased production of 55% was called for by the government to meet the greatly in-

U.S. Production of Dry Beans in Leading States, 1943 and 1942
(in 100 lb. bags)

State	1943	1942	State	1943	1942
Michigan . . .	5,797,000	5,284,000	New York . .	1,119,000	1,436,000
California . .	5,169,000	4,894,000	Colorado . . .	792,000	1,029,000
Idaho . . .	2,479,000	2,234,000	New Mexico . .	792,000	1,029,000
Wyoming . . .	1,378,000	1,024,000	Montana . . .	549,000	338,000

creased military, lend-lease and civilian requirements. The acreage was increased by growers 29% over 1942 but the average yield was below 1942 though above the 10-year average. A price-support program was operated by the government with ceiling prices to growers, who received, however, about 10% higher prices than in 1942. (J. C. Ms.)

Beatty, Sir Edward Wentworth (1877–1943), Canadian industrialist, was born Oct. 16 in Thorold, Ont. He studied law at Toronto university and joined the legal department of the Canadian Pacific Railway company in 1901, becoming vice-president in 1914. In 1918, he was made president and chairman of the road, and held both of these posts until 1942, when he resigned from the presidency because of illness. He was knighted in 1935 and was appointed Canadian representative of the British ministry of shipping in 1939. Sir Edward was chancellor of McGill university from 1921 until his death in Montreal, March 23, 1943.

Bechuanaland Protectorate: *see* BRITISH SOUTH AFRICAN PROTECTORATES.

Bee-keeping.

The 1943 crop of honey was estimated to be 189,000,000 lb. by the United States department of agriculture compared with a crop of 177,800,000 lb. produced in 1942 but lower than the average of other recent years. The number of colonies of bees was estimated to be 4,900,000 hives in 1943 which shows a decline for several years. This decline was attributed to the growing shortage of labour and the smaller number of skilled bee-keepers on farms, as well as to the sugar shortage. The cold wet spring was unfavourable for bees during blossoming time. A large proportion of the honey crop was used by the industries in baking, ice cream and syrup. The prices of honey to general consumers continued at near the levels of 1942 when they were about double the year 1941. A large part of the comb honey was sold locally near the point of production The price of the fine California white orange honey ranged much higher than that of clover and buckwheat honey. (J. C. Ms.)

Beer: *see* BREWING AND BEER.

Beers, Clifford Whittingham

(1876–1943), U.S. pioneer in the mental hygiene movement, was born March 30 in New Haven, Conn. He entered business after graduating from the Sheffield Scientific school, Yale, 1897, but suddenly at the age of 24, suffered from a delusion that he was developing a serious disease and leaped from a fourth-story window. He survived, was committed to a sanitarium and spent the next three years in asylums. He was pronounced cured and released in 1903 and immediately set about to improve conditions for the insane and mentally ill and launched a mental hygiene movement. His book, *A Mind That Found Itself* (1908), describing his bitter experiences during his confinement in institutions, reached its 24th edition in 1939. It resulted in institutional reforms throughout the world. He organized the Connecticut Society for Mental Hygiene, 1908, the first of its kind, and similar societies on a national and international scale. Beers died in Providence, R.I., July 9.

Belgian Colonial Empire.

The accompanying table gives material relative to the colonial and mandated territories administered by Belgium (*q.v.*). Total area 948,000 sq.mi.; total population (est. Dec. 31, 1939) 14,131,000.

History.—In Jan. 1943 the state department of the United States announced an agreement with the Belgian government which would bring Congo supplies to the United States under "Lease-Lend in reverse," with retrospective effect from June 1942.

The production drive continued under growing difficulties. Colonists feared that unless larger shipments of machinery spares and tools were forthcoming, output would drop. A less obvious need was better supplies of cheap goods for the native trade. When trading stations have little or nothing to offer the Negro labourer in exchange for his paper-money wages, he becomes suspicious and recalcitrant. Any serious labour trouble had to be avoided at all costs, to maintain the Congo's output of vital raw materials for war factories. The U.S. Economic mission under Hickman Price was grappling with this import problem.

Provisional output figures for 1942 included 5,500,000 carats diamonds (mainly industrial), and (in metric tons): 168,000 copper, 28,000 zinc concentrates, 27,000 manganese, 28,000 tin ore, 1,800 cobalt, 269 tungsten ore, 126 tantalo-colombite, 80,000 palm oil, 40,000 cotton.   (W. FOR.)

Belgian Congo: *see* BELGIAN COLONIAL EMPIRE.

Belgium.

A country of Europe, occupied by German troops in May 1940; area 11,775 sq.mi.; pop. (est. Dec. 31, 1939), 8,396,276; chief towns (pop. Dec 31, 1938): Brussels and suburbs (cap. 912,774); Antwerp (273,317); Ghent (162,858); Liége (162,229). Ruler: King Léopold III; prime minister (in exile): Hubert Pierlot; languages: French and Flemish; religion: Christian (mainly Roman Catholic).

History.—Forced deportation of Belgians to work in German factories continued during 1943, despite vigorous protests from the king, the clergy and the justices. There were no reliable statistics of the number deported, but it was certainly high in relation to the total population; estimates based only on admissions made by the Germans themselves in the Brüsseler Zeitung reached 430,000.

Sabotage was still widespread. Further evidence of the seriousness of the explosion which occurred in 1942 at the Tessenderloo chemical works came from Switzerland, where the underwriters paid out 2,045,000 Swiss francs. Savage reprisals follow every attack. Léon Degrelle, leader of the small Rexist (fascist) party, said in May 1943 that 518 "terrorist criminals" had been shot since the beginning of the year. No fewer than 151 secret newspapers were published, some in French, others in Flemish, representing every political opinion in the country from the Catholic party to the Communists.

The serious food shortage was favouring the spread of disease, the energy value of the official daily ration being only about 1,230 calories, against a minimum of 2,000 required to maintain health. The U.S. Board of Economic Warfare received information that a third of the 2,300,000 Belgian children under eighteen were consumptive.

Industrial activity generally was at a low ebb, owing to the deportation of skilled workers and also to an acute shortage of raw materials normally imported from overseas. This was true even where the Germans have pressed to restore output, as in

Belgian Colonial Empire

Colony and Area sq. miles (approx.)	Population (000's omitted) (est. Dec. 31, 1939)	Capital, Status, Governors, Premiers, etc.	Principal Products 1939 (in metric tons)	Imports and Exports 1939 (in thousand francs)	Road, Rail 1939	Revenue and Expenditure (in thousand francs)
BELGIAN CONGO, 927,000	10,356	Leopoldville, colony, *Governor General:* M. Pierre Ryckmans	copper ore (metal content) 122,600 gold (1940) 19,239 kg. coffee (1940) 24,000 coal 31,000	(1938) imp. 1,022,637 exp. 1,897,154	(1940) rds. open to traffic, 47,641 mi. rly. 3,106 mi.	(est. 1941) rev. 920,564 exp. 806,715
RUANDA and URUNDI, 21,200	3,775	Nianza (Ruanda), Kitega (Urundi), mandated territory united administratively with the Belgian Congo	coffee (export) 4,950 tons tin (export) 1,556 tons	imp. 55,041 exp. 83,855	roads open to traffic, 1,747 mi.	United administratively with the Belgian Congo

the locomotive and railway car works. Exceptions were electrical engineering, which was working at capacity under the eyes of German experts, and the rayon industry, into which German capital had been injected. Early in 1943 a new staple fibre factory near Ghent started work, using German beechwood as the chief raw material. Output was expected to reach 40 tons a day by the end of 1943.

The output of coking coal from the Campine field had been pushed up successfully to replace part of the former imports from England, but total output of all grades of coal appeared to be several million tons below pre-war level.

In Oct. 1943 the Belgian and Dutch governments (in London) made a currency agreement to promote postwar trade between the two countries. The rate of exchange was fixed at 16.52 francs (3.304 belgas) to the florin, and currency of either country would be made available to the other as required to finance imports.

(W. For.)

Education.—(1938) Primary schools 8,712; scholars 955,038; higher schools 273; scholars 86,279; universities (1937–38) 4; students 10,776.

Banking and Finance.—Revenue, ordinary (est. 1941) 12,-159,600,000 francs; expenditure, ordinary (est. 1941) 12,003,-000,000 francs; public debt (Dec. 31, 1939) 59,318,300,000 francs; notes in circulation (July 31, 1942) 58,537,000,000 francs; gold reserve (July 31, 1942) 21,677,000,000 francs; exchange rate (average 1940): belga=16.88 cents.

Trade and Communications.—External trade (merchandise): imports (1939) 19,426,000,000 francs; exports (1939) 21,580,000,000 francs.

Communication and Transport.—Roads, suitable for motor traffic (1939) 6,571 mi.; railways, open to traffic, main (1939) 3,190 mi.; airways (1938), distance travelled 1,457,050 mi.; passenger mileage 8,255,980 mi.; baggage mileage 156,762 ton mi.; mail mileage, 78,412 ton mi.; newspapers 52,504 ton mi.; shipping (July 1, 1939) 408,418 gross tons; tonnage launched (July 1938–June 1939) 27,600 gross tons; vessels entered, in net tons, (monthly average 1938) 2,497,000; (July 1939) 2,801,000; cleared (monthly average 1938) 2,502,000; (July 1939) 2,803,000; motor vehicles licensed (Dec. 31, 1938): 155,174 cars; 77,600 commercial; 67,016 cycles; wireless receiving set licenses (1938) 1,082,200; telephone subscribers, local (1938) 287,323.

Agriculture, Manufacturing, Mineral Production.—Production 1939 (in metric tons), wheat 349,000; oats 724,200; rye 349,400; potatoes 3,323,200; coal (1940) 25,605,000; pig iron and ferro alloys 3,059,000; steel 3,104,000; beet sugar (1940) 231,000; barley 51,000; butter 61,000; margarine 60,700; artificial silk 5,900. Industry and labour: industrial production (1929=100) average (1939) 83.3; (Jan. 1940) 79.1; number wholly unemployed (average 1939) 195,211; (March 1940) 163,598. (*See* also BELGIAN COLONIAL EMPIRE.)

Benefactions: *see* DONATIONS AND BEQUESTS.

Benét, Stephen Vincent

(1898–1943), U.S. poet and author, was born July 22 in Bethlehem, Pa., the younger brother of William Rose and Laura Benét, both well-known poets. When a freshman at Yale, he had his first book published, *Five Men and Pompey* (1915). After taking his M.A. from Yale in 1920, he went to live in France on a Guggenheim fellowship and there wrote his greatest epic, *John Brown's Body* (1928), a long narrative in verse of the Civil War, which won the Pulitzer prize as the best volume of verse for that year. More popularly known was his short story, *The Devil and Daniel Webster* (1937), a fantasy on the Faust theme, built around the life of the New England statesman. The story won

an O. Henry award, was dramatized and appeared in a screen version. At the outbreak of World War II, Benét abandoned work on another long epic poem, *Western Star,* to write anti-fascist propaganda for government agencies, including the *Prayer for United Nations.* In his poetry and fiction, he dealt mainly with the U.S. scene, writing with vigour, drama and humour. Benét died in New York city, March 13.

Benton, William

(1900–   ), U.S. educational administrator, was born April 1 in Minneapolis. Both of his parents were educators. After taking the A.B. degree at Yale university in 1921, he entered the advertising agency business. In 1929 he and Chester B. Bowles founded the Benton & Bowles advertising agency, which became in a few years one of the largest in the field. In 1936 Benton retired from the chairmanship of the agency, and in the following year became vice-president of the University of Chicago. At the university Benton had two main interests, one in economic problems, the other in the development of new instruments for education.

In 1943 Benton was vice-chairman of the board of trustees of the Committee for Economic Development, a group of business leaders who were studying ways and means of achieving maximum employment and productivity after the war and were encouraging business and businessmen throughout the nation to formulate postwar plans. In this capacity, Benton visited England in Aug. 1943 to discuss postwar business with British industrial and trade leaders. Benton was also associated with Nelson Rockefeller in the latter's work as Coordinator of Inter-American Affairs, and served as vice-chairman, under Eric Johnston, of the U.S. Commission of Inter-American Development.

As a result of his interest in the wider use of radio, motion pictures and publications in education, Benton was responsible for the policy and planning of the University of Chicago's two network radio programs, the Sunday "Round Table" on NBC, and "The Human Adventure" on the Mutual system Thursday evenings.

When the Sears, Roebuck Co. gave Encyclopædia Britannica, Inc., to the University of Chicago in 1943, Benton became chairman of the board of Britannica. At his instance the Britannica company in 1943 acquired from Western Electric Co. the largest producer of classroom motion pictures, Erpi Classroom Films, Inc., now known as Encyclopædia Britannica Films, of which he also became chairman. Benton also has business interests in New York.

Bentonite.

The production of bentonite in the United States increased from 354,028 short tons in 1941 to 374,-967 tons in 1942, of which 40% went into foundry and core sands, 31% in oil refining, and 13% in oil-well drilling. The Wyoming-South Dakota area accounted for 61% of the total tonnage and 76% of the total value. (*See* also FULLER'S EARTH; MICA.)

(G. A. Ro.)

Bequests, Philanthropic: *see* DONATIONS AND BEQUESTS.

Berlin.

The residence of Hohenzollern electors, kings and emperors from 1442 to 1918, and capital of the German reich after 1871, Berlin is the largest and most important city of Germany. Reorganized in 1920 to include several suburbs, greater Berlin in 1939 had an area of 332 sq.mi., and a population of 4,332,000. Its favourable situation in north Germany on the River Spree, between the Elbe and the Oder rivers, affords it cheap water transportation through Germany's wide-reaching system of rivers and canals. It is also the centre of Germany's network of railways, motor highways and commercial air lines.

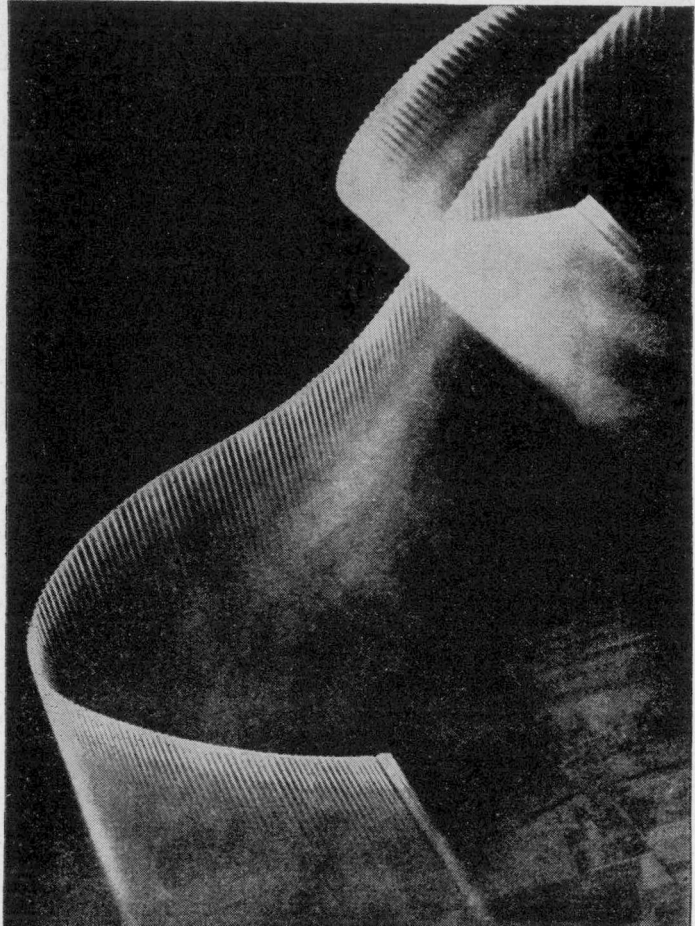

PATTERN OF GERMAN SEARCHLIGHTS during an Allied raid over Berlin in 1943. Each track of light is made up of little waves caused by the vibration of the plane

Politically important as the seat of the Prussian and German governments, it grew rapidly after 1860 as an industrial and banking centre. In World War II it became the focal point of the vast nazi organization for the economic exploitation of Europe.

During 1943 the capital was subjected to a score of devastating bombing raids by British and American planes which started large fires and destroyed a considerable part of the city. The central part where government offices and business houses are located and the industrial plants in the suburbs were especially severely attacked.   (S. B. F.)

Bermuda.   An island group and colony of Great Britain, 580 mi. off the North American coast at lat. 32° 15′ N. and long. 64° 50′ W. It has an appointed governor and elected representative assembly. Area: 19 sq.mi.; pop. 32,451 (official est. Dec. 31, 1941) not including military personnel of various types. The capital is Hamilton (pop. 3,217). In the first part of the year the governor was Viscount Knollys; he was replaced on Aug. 24 by Lord Burghley.

History.—While the war continued to affect Bermudian economy, increased shipping early in 1943 brought in large consignments of supplies, so much so that, on occasion, storage became something of a problem. Occasional shortages of items such as milk occurred. Rationing and price control remained in effect, with the latter being expanded. The financial condition of the colony remained satisfactory, but the prospective completion of defense construction foreshadowed a slump; as part of the tax program proposed to meet the decline in government income an income tax was introduced, but it was rejected by the assembly

in June. Some departures of civilian labourers were noted, also a growing scarcity of farm labour. In May a war refugee conference brought British and U.S. representatives to the islands; the short report made by the body, issued May 9, made some recommendations but held that the general problem of refugee aid must remain subordinated to the war effort. The first divorce law in the colony's history was enacted early in 1943.

Education.—At last report (1941) Bermuda had 29 government schools with an enrolment of 5,182. Small fees are charged and attendance is compulsory. During 1943 the assembly voted £20,000 for school construction.

Finance.—The monetary unit is the pound sterling (value in 1943, approx. $4.03½ U.S.). The yearly budget was balanced at £600,000; one item was a heavy increase in liquor taxes. By Oct. 31 it was estimated that the revenue for 1943 would approximate £742,816. Currency in circulation early in the year was £750,000 (prewar normal amount: £200,000) and there was concern over inflation. During the year an interest-free loan of £607,400 was floated for aid to Britain.

Trade and Resources.—Imports in 1942 were down, and consisted mainly of foodstuffs (value in 1941: £2,422,106; 1940: £1,469,504). The 1942 fish catch totalled 512,000 lb. (1941: 170,000 lb.), and 6,000 lobsters were caught as against 2,500 in 1941. Other 1942 production: potatoes, 101,000 bu. (85,000 bu. in 1941); miscellaneous vegetables, 255,000 bu. (200,000 bu. in 1941); eggs, 499,000 doz. (260,000 doz. in 1941); milk, 670,000 gal. (1941: 900,000 gal.); lily bulbs, 1,955,000 (1,500,000 in 1941). Tourist trade remained almost nonexistent, but transatlantic air travel continued heavy.

Communication.—A main station for transatlantic air travel, Bermuda found this activity so great in 1943 that in midyear an Airport board was created to govern traffic and supervise airports and equipment. The traditional Bermudian restriction to horse-drawn vehicles on the 120 mi. of island roads seemed doomed with the adoption, in the summer, of a legislative report favouring an increased use of motor vehicles after the war. Shortage of fodder was responsible for a reduction of the number of horses in the islands (1,300 in 1941; in 1942, 1,079).

BIBLIOGRAPHY.—*West Indies Year Book, 1941–1942; Crown Colonist* (London, monthly); *Colonial Review* (London, quarterly).   (D. RD.)

Bernie, Ben   (1891?–1943), U.S. orchestra leader and actor, was born Benjamin Anzelevitz in New York city. Son of a blacksmith and one of 11 children, he was given violin lessons and at the age of 15 made his debut at Carnegie hall. Later he toured the country playing in small vaudeville houses. In the "jazz era" which followed World War I, he acquired a dance band, called himself the "Old Maestro" and played to dance patrons in night clubs of New York city and Chicago. Bernie eventually became one of the highest paid entertainers in the United States. He died in Beverly Hills, Calif., Oct. 20.

Beryllium.   The United States output of 158 short tons of beryllium concentrates in 1941 was increased in 1942, but figures were not available for publication. Imports continued to be the main source of supply. War uses greatly increased the demand, and systematic efforts were being made to increase the domestic supply in order to reduce the necessity for imports from Brazil and Argentina. World production was reported at 4,014 short tons of ore in 1941 and 1,780 tons in the first half of 1942; Argentina and Brazil were the leading producers. Extensive exploratory work was being done in the United States to increase the small domestic output. Imports in 1942 were expected to be about double the 2,816 tons received in 1941.   (G. A. RO.)

Bessarabia: *see* RUMANIA.
Best Sellers: *see* PUBLISHING (BOOK).
Betatron: *see* RADIOLOGY.

Bevan, Arthur Dean

(1861–1943), U.S. surgeon, was born Aug. 9 in Chicago. He studied at the Sheffield Scientific school at Yale and took his M.D. degree from Rush Medical college, Chicago, in 1883. He joined the U.S. marine hospital service in 1883 and concurrently held a professorship in anatomy at Oregon State university. He later taught anatomy and surgery at Rush Medical college, and was named head of the college's surgical department in 1907. He was also professorial lecturer on surgery at the University of Chicago. Dr. Bevan was president of the American Medical association, 1917–18, and during World War I was director general of surgery in the U.S. surgeon general's office in Washington. He died in Lake Forest, Ill., June 10.

Beveridge Report: *see* SOCIAL SECURITY.
BEW: *see* FOREIGN ECONOMIC ADMINISTRATION.
Bible Society, American: *see* AMERICAN BIBLE SOCIETY.
Bicycling: *see* CYCLING.
"Big Inch" Line: see PETROLEUM.

Billiards.

Throughout 1943, billiards suffered from a wholesale lack of competition. There were only two championship contests. One was a challenge match between Willie Mosconi of Jackson, Mich., and Andrew Ponzi, Philadelphia veteran, who had twice previously held the title. Mosconi, who had annexed the crown in a tournament at Detroit the previous year, and Ponzi, the 1942 runner-up, clashed at Kansas City, Mo., in April. It was a 1,250-point struggle, and Ponzi dethroned the youthful Mosconi, 1,250–1,050.

In December at Rochester, N.Y., Ponzi again engaged in a challenge match for the championship, meeting Irving Crane of Livonia, N.Y., former titleholder. Ponzi emerged on top, defeating the challenger, 1,000–924, and thereby retaining the crown.

Otherwise, the sport was dormant. In the absence of competition, the three-cushion championship of the world remained in the possession of Willie Hoppe of New York, who finished on top the last two times the tournament was held. Hoppe devoted most of the year to a tour of service camps throughout the country, entertaining troops. (L. EF.)

Binyon, Laurence

(1869–1943), British poet and art historian, was born Aug. 10 at Lancaster. Best known for his ode *For the Fallen,* written during World War I, Binyon was the author of some 20 volumes of poetry. His last work was *The North Star and Other Poems* (1941). Long associated with the British museum, Binyon was widely recognized as an art historian and expert on Asiatic art. He was Norton professor of poetry at Harvard university, 1933–34, and Byron professor of poetry at the University of Athens, 1940. He died in Reading, England, March 10. (See *Encyclopædia Britannica.*)

Biochemistry.

Nutrition and Vitamins.—Among the ten "essential amino acids" previously found necessary for rat growth, two, namely histidine and arginine, were found to be unnecessary for maintenance of nitrogen equilibrium in man, while the other eight are necessary and sufficient. While this indicates that histidine and arginine may be unnecessary in human nutrition, this point cannot be considered proved as long as their importance for *growth* of humans, or for *nitrogen equilibrium* in rats remains unknown. For the maintenance of nitrogen equilibrium in dogs, histidine is less important than tryptophane.

Among the metabolic relations of vitamins, riboflavin, like pyridoxin and nicotinic acid, was found to be essential for haemoglobin formation in the dog. The nature of the anaemia of nicotinic acid deficiency was studied in detail. Pyridoxin deficiency has no effect on catalase activity of tissues. Studies on the effect of environmental temperature on the requirement of B vitamins showed that the requirement of thiamin is doubled, and that of choline is increased seven-fold by exposure to hot, moist (tropical) atmosphere, while the requirements of riboflavin, pyridoxin, inositol, para-aminobenzoic acid, and niacin remain unaltered. The inhibition of growth of rats caused by feeding poorly absorbed sulfonamides was traced to an inhibition of bacterial vitamin synthesis in the gut and was counteracted by liver concentrates, p-aminobenzoic acid, biotin, and folic acid concentrates. These sulfonamides have thus become an important tool in causing vitamin deficiencies in animals, and in distinguishing between vitamin synthesis by bacteria in the gut and vitamin synthesis in tissues of animals.

The value of urea as a partial substitute for food protein was demonstrated in dairy cattle. When quantities equal to 25% of the total nitrogen intake were fed as supplement to an otherwise inadequate diet, nitrogen balance, body weight and milk production were maintained in five of seven animals, while one animal showed no benefit from urea feeding.

Metabolism.—Studies with compounds containing stable and radioactive isotopes continued to provide new and fundamental information. The first evidence of the role of cholesterol as a precursor of other body steroids was found following the preparation of deutero-cholesterol. The biological conversion of this sterol to cholic acid was demonstrated and the fact that at least two thirds of the cholic acid has its origin in cholesterol, indicates that this may well be the sole source of this bile acid. The feeding of deutero-n-hexadecane in very small doses resulted in the recovery of fatty acids containing excess deuterium in the tissues; this showed that paraffin, to a minute extent at least, is a food.

Studies on the biological origin of purines and pyrimidines using various metabolites containing N^{15} showed that ammonia nitrogen is rapidly converted into purines and pyrimidines of the nucleic acids of tissues, and also of the uric acid and allantoin of urine. Accordingly, purines and pyrimidines belong to that large group of substances whose nitrogen is being rapidly replaced at all times. Among the three likely purine precursors, the imidazol group of histidine, the guanidine group of arginine, and urea, none is available for purine or pyrimidine synthesis. The synthesis of thyroxin by thyroid tissue was studied with the aid of radioactive iodine, I^{131}. It was found that the incorporation of I^{131} into thyroxin and diiodotyrosine by surviving thyroid tissue, is dependent upon the intactness of tissue structure (homogenization disrupts the process), upon adequate O_2 tension, and that it is inhibited by cyanide azide, CO, and other cytochrome-oxidase inhibitors. Studies on nitrogen fixation with the aid of N^{15} showed that this phenomenon is not so widely occurring as was formerly supposed. It is readily found for the free living nitrogen fixing bacterium, *Azotobacter vinelandii,* the blue green alga, *Nostoc muscorum,* the anaerobic bacterium, *Clostridium pasteurianum,* inoculated red clover plants, and excised root nodules of the pea plant; however, it could not be demonstrated for germinating peas, excised root nodules of leguminous plants, free living *Rhizobium,* and cell free preparations of *Azotobacter.*

The origin of urinary ammonia was traced to glutamine; urea and amino acids are excluded. A beginning was made toward an enzymatic interpretation of the effect of the adrenal hormones in carbohydrate and protein metabolism. Adrenalectomy, even more than hypophysectomy, causes a marked decrease in arginase activity of rat livers; while the administration of corticosterone and certain other ll-oxy adrenal steroids, but not desoxy-corticosterone, cause increases in liver arginase.

Penicillin.—In addition to the ether soluble, nitrogen containing, organic acid called penicillin A or notatin, a second, even more powerful and more widely effective antibacterial substance was separated, which is insoluble in organic solvents, and is designated penicillin B or penatin. It was shown to be a heat labile flavoprotein enzyme, which converts glucose plus oxygen into gluconic acid and hydrogen peroxide, and the liberation of this last substance was shown to be the basis of its antibacterial action. This enzymatic peroxide formation as a basis of bacterio-static action is a new idea.

Competitive Inhibition in Biochemical Processes.—Increasing attention was paid to biological inhibition by synthetic compounds which have structural similarity to natural compounds of great biological activity, like vitamins and hormones. Classical examples are the inhibition of succinic dehydrogenase by malonate, and the antagonism between sulfanilamide and p-aminobenzoic acid in the growth of bacteria. A more recent example is the production of thiamin deficiency by the feeding of a pyridine analogue of thiamin. From the structural similarity of local anaesthetics like cocaine, procaine, etc., to acetyl choline, a theory was advanced involving the idea of competition between these two kinds of compounds for the receptive substances in the nerve endings. A quantitative theory of synergism and antagonism among diverse inhibitors was developed, with special reference to the inhibition of bioluminescence by sulfanilamide, and to the antagonisms of this inhibition by urethane, p-aminobenzoic acid, glucose and other substances.

Cancer.—From Warburg's laboratory in Berlin-Dahlem came the report that the plasma of tumour rats contains about eight times as much zymo-hexase (2.3 μg per cc) as that of normals. This increase depends upon the presence of a tumour greater than 2% of the body weight. The plasma of pregnant rats has a normal zymo-hexase content. In human cancer the values were normal, perhaps because the tumours were not sufficiently large. Tumour tissue has a higher zymo-hexase content (87 μg per cc) than most other tissues, but muscle tissue (1460 μg per cc) has the highest, and it is thought that the most likely source of the increased zymo-hexase of the tumour plasma is some abnormality which liberates the enzyme from the muscle cells. (*See* also PHYSIOLOGY: VITAMINS.)

BIBLIOGRAPHY.—W. C. Rose, W. J. Harris, J. E. Johnson and D. T. Horner, "Further Experiments on the Role of the Amino Acids in Human Nutrition," *J. Biol. Chem.* 148:457-458 (1943); R. Elman, H. W. Davey and Y. Loo, "The Influence of Histidine on the Urinary Excretion of Nitrogen in Dogs Given Pure Amino Acids Intravenously," *Arch. Biochem.* 3:45-52 (1943); H. Spector, A. R. Maase, L. Michaud, C. A. Elvehjem and E. B. Hart, "The Role of Riboflavin in Blood Regeneration," *J. Biol. Chem.* 150:75-87 (1943); C. A. Mills, "Environmental Temperatures and B-Vitamin Requirements: Riboflavin and Pyridoxin," *Arch. Biochem.* 2:159-162 (1943); C. A. Elvehjem, "The Nutritional Significance of the Newer Members of the Vitamin B Complex," *Proc. Inst. Med. Chi.* 14:486-494 (1943); F. W. Barnes, Jr. and R. Schoenheimer, "On the Biological Synthesis of Purines and Pyrimidines," *J. Biol. Chem.* 151:123-139 (1943); M. E. Morton and I. L. Chaikoff, "The Formation in Vitro of Throxine and Diiodotyrosine by Thyroid Tissue with Radioactive Iodine as Indicator," *J. Biol. Chem.* 147:1-9 (1943); W. Kocholaty, "Purification and Properties of the Second Antibacterial Substance Produced by Penicillium Notatum," *Science* 97:186 (1943); E. C. Roberts, C. K. Cain, R. D. Muir, F. J. Reithel, W. L. Gaby, J. T. Van Bruggen, D. M. Homan, P. A. Katzman, L. R. Jones and E. A. Doisy, "Penicillin B, an Antibacterial Substance from Penicillium Notatum," *J. Biol. Chem.* 147:47-58 (1943); J. T. Van Bruggen, F. J. Reithel, C. K. Cain, P. A. Katzman, E. A. Doisy, R. D. Muir, E. C. Roberts, W. L. Gaby, D. M. Homan and L. R. Jones, "Penicillin B, Purification, and Mode of Action," *J. Biol. Chem.* 148:365-378 (1943); W. W. Kocholaty, "Purification and Properties of Penatin, The Second Antibacterial Substance Produced by Penicillium Notatum Westling," *Arch. Biochem.* 2:73-86 (1943); M. E. Hanke and Y. J. Katz, "An Electrolytic Method for Controlling Oxidation-Reduction Potential and Its Application in the Study of Anaerobiosis,"

Arch. Biochem. 2:183-200 (1943); K. V. Thimann, "On the Nature of Local Anesthesia," *Arch. Biochem.* 2:87-92 (1943).   (M. E. H.)

Biography: *see* AMERICAN LITERATURE; ENGLISH LITERATURE.
Biology: *see* MARINE BIOLOGY; ZOOLOGY.
Biotin: *see* BIOCHEMISTRY.

Birch, Reginald Bathurst (1856–1943), U.S. artist and illustrator, was born May 2 in London. He went to San Francisco in 1872 and worked with his father on theatrical posters. He later spent eight years studying at the Royal academy in Munich. When he returned to the U.S. his illustrations found an immediate sale in leading magazines. His fame, however, rested on one of his earliest creations, a golden-haired child in black velvet suit and white lace collar that he drew for Frances Eliza Hodgson Burnett's *Little Lord Fauntleroy* (1886). Years later, commenting on its fame, the artist said ruefully: "There is one of my early crimes for which I am still making expiation." Many of his illustrations appeared in a volume called *Reginald Birch—His Book* (1939), edited by Elisabeth B. Hamilton. He also produced many pen and ink drawings for the works of Frank Stockton, Ogden Nash, Mrs. Laura E. Richards and Louis Untermeyer. He died in the Bronx, N.Y., June 17.

Birth Control. The Planned Parenthood Federation of America, Inc., formerly the Birth Control Federation of America, Inc., made marked advances in 1943, concentrating on five programs of activity.

Public Health.—Five more states initiated co-operative efforts with the federation to include pregnancy spacing in their public health services—bringing the total number of states to eleven. The federation became a member of the National Health Council.

Clinical Service.—On Dec. 1, 1943, birth control services totalled 786; 211 in hospitals; 286 in public health quarters; 288 extra-mural; 372 of the total supported in whole or part by public funds. Services for treatment of sterility were listed in the federation's Clinic Directory.

Industrial Hygiene.—Absenteeism, due often to pregnancy or induced abortion, became an acute problem in many areas, as millions of women went into war work. The division of industrial hygiene, U.S.P.H. service, recommended, in an outline for use in industry, that "advice on the proper spacing of children, as a means of protecting the health of the mother and her children," be given married women workers, by counsellors in plants. Dr. Eva Dodge, the federation's assistant medical director, surveyed a number of plants, and, in co-operation with the Alabama state health department, assisted in preparing two pamphlets on this problem, for use by workers and management. A radio transcription, "Freedom From Fear," dealing with the problem of absenteeism, due to pregnancy, was produced by the federation for use of its state leagues.

Education. *Medical.*—Over 11,000 copies of Dr. Robert L. Dickinson's pamphlet, "Techniques of Conception Control," were sent on request to physicians, bringing the total to 56,000 issued on request to this group, and 17,000 were sent to registered nurses on request.

Birth control training institutes for public health nurses were held in Florida, Delaware and North Carolina.

Research.—Although no new discoveries were made during 1943, a special committee of the council on pharmacy and chemistry of the American Medical association continued research in chemical contraceptives, and the council on physical therapy initiated a co-operative program dealing with mechanical articles and devices. Reports appear in the *Journal of the American*

Medical Assn. for Dec. 18, 1943.

Social Work.—A new pamphlet, "The Case Worker and Family Planning," was sent upon request to 2,000 social workers. The federation participated, as a kindred group, in the National Conference of Social Work. A newly formed advisory committee directed work in this field.

Negro Program.—The division of Negro service, with its advisory council of 46, and sponsoring committee of 146 members, representing national professional, medical, religious and civic leadership, was strengthened, and a pamphlet, "Better Health for 13,000,000" published, reporting on the program of family planning for Negroes.

Religious.—The National Clergymen's Advisory council was organized with almost 1,000 members from 46 states. Organization of the council and election of officers were undertaken, and a pamphlet on "Marriage Counsel" for use of the clergy published.

Teaching in Medical Schools.—To stimulate better teaching of contraception in medical schools, Dr. W. E. Brown of Cincinnati Medical school visited 26 grade A colleges for the federation, finding some teaching of the subject in each. His teaching syllabus was distributed to grade A schools throughout the U.S., 45% of which were giving some instruction in 1943.

State Organizations.—In 9 affiliated states, Maryland, Delaware, West Virginia, Virginia, Florida, Iowa, Minnesota, Tennessee and Missouri, programs were broadened and strengthened by addition of professional staff members and executives. One more state, Ohio, became affiliated, bringing the total to 34.

Legal.—The U.S. supreme court refused to review the Tileston case involving the right of Connecticut doctors to advise contraceptives where life or health was threatened.

Massachusetts Referendum.—Although over 500,000 votes were cast in its favour, the referendum to amend the state law so that doctors might legally advise patients on contraception failed of passage.

International.—The war made organized work in occupied Europe impossible. In Great Britain educational work, clinical service and research were continued by the Family Planning association. In Australia the law passed in 1942 did not interfere with clinical work. Health boards in Bermuda planned wider dissemination of birth control information, to cope with the problem of overpopulation there.

Birth rates fell in most of Europe but were higher than in years in Great Britain. In the United States they were higher than for 20 years past. (*See* also BIRTH STATISTICS.)

BIBLIOGRAPHY.—J. H. J. Upham, "Teaching of Contraceptive Measures in Small Colleges," *Jl. Assn. Med. Coll.*, 18:307–312 (1943); Alabama State Health Dept., "The Molly Pitchers of This War," and "Employing the Married Woman Worker"; Planned Parenthood Federation, "Better Health for 13,000,000," and "The Case Worker and Family Planning"; Royal L. Brown and C. J. Gamble, "Studies of Spermicidal Times of Contraceptive Materials," *Human Fertility* 8:9–17 (1943); Leopold Z. Goldstein, "Jelly Alone as Contraceptive in Post-Partum Cases," *Human Fertility* 8:43–47 (1943); R. L. Brown, I. Levenstein and B. Bercker, "Spermicidal Times of Samples of Commercial Contraceptives Secured in 1942," *Human Fertility* 8:65–68 (1943); H. H. Ware, "The Physician's Responsibility in Planned Parenthood," *Va. Medical Monthly*, 70:238–242 (1943); C. C. Pierce, "Control of Conception as a Public Health Responsibility," *Mississippi Doctor*, 21:1–7 (1943); M. J. Bent, "Report of Sub-Committee on Birth Control," *Jl. Nat Med. Assn.*, 35:25–27 (1943). (M. SR.)

Birth Statistics.

According to provisional records, the number of births in the United States, Canada, and England and Wales was appreciably greater in 1943 than in 1942. For the United States and Canada, this established a rise for each year since the outbreak of the general war in 1939, while for England and Wales it marked the second year of successive increase. For the United States the provisional report showed that for the first nine months of 1943 there were

11.6% more births than for the same period of 1942. The gains were greatest in the Pacific coast and mountain states, the increases for these areas being 18.6% and 12.6% respectively; the west south central states had the smallest gain. During the entire calendar year 1942 there were recorded 2,807,445 births in the continental United States, with a birth rate of 20.9 per 1,000 total population. In Canada, cities of 10,000 or more had about 11% more births during the first nine months of 1943 as compared with the same period of 1942. During the entire year 1942 there were 271,981 births in Canada and the birth rate was 23.4 per 1,000 population. Births in London and the great towns of England and Wales were 9.4% more during the first nine months of 1943 than during the like period of 1942. There were altogether 654,039 births in England and Wales in 1942, the birth rate being 15.8 per 1,000 population.

While the United States, Canada, and England and Wales experienced increases in birth rates, the war adversely affected the rates of Germany and Italy. Thus, Germany had a birth rate of 20.4 per 1,000 in 1939, whereas the figure for 1942 was only 15.2. Over the same years, the birth rate for Italy fell from 23.5 to 20.2.

The rapid upswing in the birth rate of the United States in 1942 and 1943 radically altered the usual seasonal sequence in births. Ordinarily, births run to a minor peak in spring and a major peak in summer, with the low point for the year in December. During 1942 the peak for the year fell in October, with December the second highest point. These unusual peaks may possibly be related to the United States entry in the war in Dec. 1941, which undoubtedly hastened many contemplated marriages and also induced many already married to establish families. There were signs of a slackening in the rate of increase of births from 1942 to 1943. Although there was an 11.6% increase over the corresponding nine-month period ending in September, the increase for the month of September alone amounted only to 3.1%.

By virtue of the rise in the birth rate of the United States from its low point of 16.6 per 1,000 population in 1933, the country had an additional 2,000,000 babies born in the ten-year period since then. Of this total, the excess of the birth rate in 1941 over that of 1933 contributed about 280,000 babies, the excess of 1942 an additional 560,000, while the contribution for 1943 amounted to more than 650,000.

After an examination of existing literature bearing upon the question whether the ratio of males to females at birth increases in wartime, C. Panunzio in the *Milbank Memorial Fund Quarterly* (July 1943) concluded that there was some evidence, not wholly conclusive, indicative of such an increase.

In *Vital Statistics—Special Reports*, vol. 18, p. 324 (April 1943), the bureau of the census published the first of its studies on the completeness of birth registration in the United States. These studies are based upon a comparison of the census returns of infants on April 1, 1940, with the birth and death certificates filed during the four-month period from Dec. 1, 1939 and the census date. The report cited showed that during the test period, 92.5% of the actual births in the United States were duly registered. For white births, registration was 94.0% complete and for all other races it was 82.0%. In cities of 10,000 or more, the completeness of birth registration was 96.9%, while for smaller cities and rural areas, the figure was only 88.0%. On the whole, registration was most complete in the states of the northeast and on the Pacific coast, the poorest showing being made in the south central states.

Practically all births of white children in the United States are attended by a physician, but only half of the births of Negro children are so attended. Thus, in 1941, among white births,

65.7% were attended by a physician in a hospital, 31.2% by a physician elsewhere, 2.7% by a midwife, and only 0.4% otherwise. For Negro births, the corresponding percentages were 27.3, 23.4, 48.5 and 0.8.

An analysis of some social and psychological factors affecting fertility, based on the records of native white couples in Indianapolis, was presented by P. K. Whelpton and C. V. Kiser in the *Milbank Memorial Fund Quarterly*, July 1943. In summarizing the first results of the investigation, the authors found that fertility among Catholic couples was 18% greater than that among Protestants. On the other hand, mixed Protestant-Catholic unions were 10% less fertile than those of Protestants alone. Jewish couples were 25% less fertile than Protestants, but this finding is based upon a small sample. The authors also found confirmation of the usual relation that fertility decreases with advance in socio-economic status, whether measured in terms of rent paid (or the equivalent rental value for homeowners) or educational attainment of husband and wife. An exception noted in the upper rental brackets is accounted for by the greater fertility among homeowners, for fertility rates remain low among those in this bracket who rent their homes. The variation of fertility with socio-economic status was found to be much less marked among Catholic unions than among Protestants. There were definite indications that the excess of the fertility of Catholic couples over Protestant couples tends to become smaller with descent in socio-economic status. The authors announced their intention to present further reports on their findings. (*See also* Census, 1940.)

Bibliography.—A. J. Lotka, "Modern Trends in the Birth Rate," *Annals of the American Academy of Political and Social Science* (Nov. 1936); L. I. Dublin, "The Trend of the Birth Rate Yesterday, Today and Tomorrow," *Bulletin of the New York Academy of Medicine* (Aug. 1943); National Resources Board, "Problems of a Changing Population" (May 1938); W. S. Thompson, *Population Problems* (3rd ed., 1942); U.S. Bureau of the Census, *Vital Statistics—Special Reports and State Summaries* (issued irregularly), *Monthly Vital Statistics Bulletin, Annual Reports of Vital Statistics* and *Vital Statistics Rates, 1900–1940*; Metropolitan Life Insurance Company, *Statistical Bulletin* (issued monthly); Population Association of America, *Population Index* (issued quarterly at Princeton, N.J.). (A. J. Lo.)

Bismuth. The chief producers of bismuth are the United States, Peru, Mexico and Canada, but no specific information on current developments was received from any of these countries. The nearest approach to production statistics was a statement that the Peruvian exports in the first quarter of 1943 were about a half greater in value than in the same period of 1942. (*See also* Metallurgy.) (G. A. Ro.)

Black Markets. Black markets, the title bestowed upon those illicit areas of wartime commerce where articles are bought and sold in defiance of official price and rationing controls. The etymology of the term, as of the continental *marché noir* which already flourished in World War I, is doubtless to be sought in comparable expressions denoting forbidden activities carried on in dark secrecy to escape detection and punishment, *e.g.*, "black bourse," "black mass," "black hand." In the United States during 1943 the federal government conducted a large-scale public information campaign to heighten popular awareness of the evils of the "black market," which was defined as comprehending all types of illicit activity undermining wartime price and rationing restrictions. The term "black market" has thus come to have a very broad signification in the United States.

Black market activities in the United States antedated the country's entry into the war against the axis. During 1941, as the prewar defense program proceeded apace, shortages developed in essential industrial articles, notably fabricated iron and steel,

ALLEGED BLACK-MARKET MEAT SLAUGHTERHOUSE discovered near Chicago by government agents in the summer of 1943

machine tools and lumber; a thriving trade was carried on in such articles at double and triple the ceiling prices established under presidential order. The alarm occasioned in official quarters by these early but full-blown symptoms of an inflationary spiral, and the lack of statutory sanctions to curb this black market vanguard spurred the enactment of comprehensive legislation early in 1942 establishing nation-wide price and allocation (rationing) controls. Black markets sprang up in the train of new price ceiling regulations and rationing orders. Serious difficulties were experienced in the initial consumer-rationing programs—sugar, gasoline, coffee, fuel oil, rubber tires. Housewives foolishly allowed themselves to be stampeded into hoarding sugar and coffee; organized bands of professional criminals counterfeited gasoline and fuel oil ration stamps and cached precious stores of tires obtained by outright theft or overceiling cash payments. However, these troubles were dwarfed by those which followed the institution of comprehensive food controls, made possible for the first time after adoption of supplementary legislation in Oct. 1942.

The new controls were imposed at a time when growth of demand and reduction of civilian supply had resulted in extremely serious inflationary pressures. The crisis broke first in fresh meats. Enormous quantities of meat were unlawfully diverted by packers who disregarded official slaughtering quotas and by wholesalers and retailers who bought up supplies from these and other illicit sources. Early in 1943, as the U.S. began to seethe with alarm over the virtual disappearance of meat from many large population centres, and with the condition being widely misinterpreted by press reports and rumours as resulting from an infiltration of gangsters into the meat industry and a renascence of cattle rustlers in the west, vigorous enforcement steps were taken by the government. Within a period of three months more than 25,000 persons were investigated and some 1,000 prosecutions were brought against violators of both slaughtering quota restrictions and price controls. All but a very small number of these cases terminated in favour of the government. Because of an increased demand for poultry consequent upon the rationing of meat, a mushrooming of illicit poultry trade went hand in hand with the meat black market. Poultry quickly disappeared from many legitimate urban markets, and supplies normally purchased by the armed services became unobtainable in a number of eastern states. A nation-wide drive was carried out to end black market transactions in poultry by raisers and sellers and by itinerant hucksters who scoured the countryside for supplies. Some 350 prosecutions were instituted. Army officials obtained needed supplies by requisitioning at ceiling prices live poultry shipments seized by police officials on the open highways. As in the transference of black market activities from rationed meat to unrationed poultry, profiteers outdid themselves in fresh fruits and vegetables after canned and other processed foods were brought under control. A potato supply crisis in the spring of 1943 and later a similar onion shortage were aggravated by black market activities.

Official moves to stamp out particular black markets in the United States invariably succeeded whenever sufficient manpower could be concentrated for the purpose. The task of investigating violators and bringing them to justice demanded skilled and painstaking effort, particularly in the food and apparel industries where market structures were intricate and diversified. Unfortunately, in the United States the creation of an adequate professional enforcement organization met with serious budgetary handicaps. Late in 1943, as the immense administrative task of calculating simplified dollars-and-cents ceilings for thousands of consumers' articles was substantially advanced, as volunteer community enforcement panels were organized throughout the country, and as the statutory consumers' damage remedy won approval from high judicial authorities, it appeared that a significant strengthening of professional enforcement facilities at retail levels might come about. The national administration held to the view, however, that effective control of black markets both retail and wholesale could be accomplished only by combining adequate professional enforcement with the new program of community panels staffed by volunteers. (C. Bs.)

Blamey, Sir Thomas Albert

(1884–), Australian army officer, was born in Wagga Wagga, New South Wales, Jan. 24. He joined the commonwealth military forces in 1906. During World War I, he served as chief of staff for the Australian corps and was awarded the D.S.O. After the war, he was with the Australian imperial force, and in 1920 became deputy chief of the Australian general staff. As Australian defense representative, he was attached to the war office in London, 1922–24, later becoming 2nd chief of the general staff of the commonwealth military force. He was commander of the Victoria police, 1925–37. With the approach of World War II, he accepted an appointment as controller general of the recruiting secretariat, 1938, and assumed command of the Australian army corps, 1940. He was soon transferred to the Australian forces in the middle east, and in 1941 was elevated to the position of deputy commander in chief of the British middle east forces. In March 1942, when the Japanese were threatening the entire Southwest Pacific, Sir Thomas returned to Australia to take command of the Australian armies serving under Gen. Douglas MacArthur and played an important role in the New Guinea campaign, 1942–43. With the rank of lieutenant general, Sir Thomas held command of the Allied land forces in the Southwest Pacific, second in command to Gen. MacArthur. He was knighted in 1919.

Bledsoe, Julius (Jules) C.

(1898–1943), U.S. Negro singer and composer, was born Dec. 29, in Waco, Tex. He took his A.B. degree from Bishop college, Marshall, Tex., 1918, and later studied medicine at Columbia university. Gifted with a rich baritone voice, Jules Bledsoe was encouraged to further his musical training and consequently gave up his medical career to study voice in New York city, Chicago and Rome. Critics lauded his concert debut in New York in 1924, and in 1926 he was soloist in Boston concerts under the direction of Sergei Koussevitzky. He created the role of Tizan in the opera *Deep River* and reached nationwide popularity as a master of the spiritual style with his singing of *Ol' Man River* in *Show Boat* with the Ziegfeld company, 1927–29. He also appeared in the motion picture version of the same review. His compositions include the *African Suite* for violin and orchestra and several songs. He died in Hollywood, July 14.

Blockade: *see* SUBMARINE WARFARE.
Blood Pressure: *see* MEDICINE.
Board of Economic Warfare: *see* FOREIGN ECONOMIC ADMINISTRATION.

Bohemia and Moravia.

A protectorate of Germany in central Europe, formed in March 1939, after the dissolution and occupation of Czechoslovakia. Area, 19,058 sq.mi.; population, 7,000,000, almost completely Czech and Roman Catholic. President (1943): Dr. Emil Hácha. Capital: Praha (Prague). Chief cities: Praha (850,000), Brno (270,000), Moravská Ostrava (125,000), Plzeň (115,000).

History.—Little news penetrated from Bohemia and Moravia to the outside world in 1943. The Czech fascist movement, called Vlajka or The Flag, was disbanded and its property turned over to the German Red Cross. The movement had been founded in 1938 as a fascist party among the Czechs, but the German hopes of finding some support for a native fascist movement under the Czech population met with bitter disappointment. Under the Germans the Vlajka had been recognized as the only party allowed to hold public meetings, yet it failed to attract any support, and so had to be disbanded.

The German terror continued in Bohemia and Moravia during 1943. Most of the Jews were deported to eastern Poland or perished in concentration camps or were killed otherwise; the remainder, mostly old people, were all put into the small town of Terezín (Theresienstadt) which became the only recognized ghetto in Bohemia and Moravia and to which many Jews from Austria and Germany were also taken. The Czechs continued their movement of resistance and all their hopes were directed towards the Czechoslovak government established in London. (*See* also CZECHOSLOVAKIA; SLOVAKIA.) (H. Ko.)

Boisson, Pierre François

(1894–), French government official, began his career with the French colonial service in 1920 as an assistant administrator of colonies. His rise was rapid, and in 1939 he was sent to French Equatorial Africa as governor general. After the fall of France in 1940, Boisson decided to serve Vichy as governor general of the vast French possession in Africa, and forces under his command turned back a Free French and British expeditionary force that attempted to land at Dakar in Sept. 1940. Boisson, it was reported, ruthlessly suppressed pro-Allied groups in French West Africa, and at one time it was charged that he gave haven to German submarines at Dakar. Boisson ruled with an iron hand until the landings of U.S.-British forces in Morocco and Algeria in Nov. 1942 virtually isolated French West Africa from Vichy and weakened Boisson's strategical position. As a result he agreed on Jan. 7, 1943, to support the Allies and promised them the use of men and materials. Gen. Charles de Gaulle, however, regarded Boisson as an opportunist and pro-Vichyite and dismissed him from office on the following July 3. Boisson was subsequently called to appear before a purge commission of The French Committee of National Liberation and was arrested on charges of treason, Dec. 21, 1943.

Bolivia.

An inland republic of South America. Area: 419,470 sq.mi.; pop. (1941 est.) 3,457,000. The nominal capital is Sucre (est. pop. 32,000); the real seat of government is La Paz (est. pop. 280,000). Other cities (with est. pop.) are:

Cochabamba, 80,000; Oruro, 40,000; Potosí, 35,000; Santa Cruz de la Sierra, 30,000. Religion: Roman Catholic. President in 1943, until displaced by revolution on Dec. 20, 1943: General Enrique Peñaranda; president succeeding him: Major Gualberto Villarroel.

History.—Bolivia in 1943 became the second South American nation to declare war on the axis powers (Brazil was the first). The step was taken on April 7, while the vice-president of the United States, Henry Wallace, was in the country on a visit. The labourers of Bolivia had already been registered and had been given conscript status to the end that essential work in the mines and in agricultural enterprises would not suffer by loss of trained men to the army. In May, men in the professions were similarly listed. Censorship over all mediums of communication was established in the same month. Early in May President Peñaranda made a visit to the United States to further integrate the Bolivian effort with the inter-American war program; shortly after his arrival in the northern republic an announcement to the effect that economic co-operation between Bolivia and the United States would be intensified was issued. President Roosevelt also apologized for "excessive" rates charged Bolivia by U.S. bankers in the 1925–27 period. Other international developments during 1943 were an amicable agreement with Brazil for the exchange of raw materials (June 28) and a not-so-friendly interchange of comments with Chile over the perennial question of a Bolivian outlet to the Pacific.

Internal affairs were troubled throughout 1943. Serious controversy had been started by the use of military force in the suppression of a strike in the tin mines at Catavi in Dec. 1942, in which at least 20 miners were killed. Conditions in the mining area were investigated by a joint commission of U.S. and Bolivian experts, and reforms in regard to working conditions were recommended in its report. In succeeding months bitter attacks were made in the Bolivian congress on the administration of President Peñaranda for its policy in the Catavi strike. Both the National Revolutionary movement and the Leftist Revolutionary party opposed the administration. In September these charges forced the resignation of the cabinet.

On Dec. 20 a well planned revolution, led by Victor Paz Estenssoro of the National Revolutionary movement, overthrew the government and set up a new regime headed by Major Gualberto Villarroel. President Peñaranda was exiled. Although the new government announced that it would live up to all Bolivian commitments to the United Nations, the United States withheld recognition because of previous pro-nazi associations of the leaders of the revolution.

Education.—Bolivia had about 2,000 primary schools, with an estimated enrolment of more than 150,000, in 1941. The three universities have an unusually independent position. The 1942 budget allotted 125,420,000 bolivianos to education.

Finance.—The monetary unit is the boliviano, valued in 1943 at $2\frac{1}{4}$ cents U.S. ($.0236 U.S., controlled). National revenue (1942) was estimated at 1,104,518,300 bolivianos; expenditures at 672,402,400 bolivianos. Currency in circulation, on March 31, 1943, was stated as amounting to 1,737,400,000 bolivianos.

Trade and Communication.—Foreign trade (1941) amounted to: imports, 103,560,663 bolivianos; exports, 211,249,666 bolivianos (1940: 93,914,524 bs. and 174,181,877 bs., respectively). The United States took 60% of all exports in 1941 and supplied approximately 41% of all imports. The favourable trade balance of Bolivia with the United States for the first nine months of 1943 was $11,037,000 (merchandise and gold and silver). Imports from the United States were largely manufactures; exports to the United States were largely minerals; in 1942, however, Bolivia exported 1,486 tons of rubber, and on April 14, a rubber

agreement was signed with the Rubber Development corporation in order to push production of this item. Bolivia imports both foodstuffs and fuel from near-by countries.

There is external communication by rail to Chile, Peru and Argentina. Some parts of eastern Bolivia have outlets by river boat to the Amazon and La Plata systems. Bolivia has found air service particularly useful, with Panagra and Lloyd Aéreo Boliviano (leased to Pan American Airways) giving service to all important cities and with outside countries. Railway mileage (1941) was over 1,360 mi. Some 6,000 mi. of highways exist. In the 1943 budget funds for road construction were reduced 50% over 1942.

Minerals.—Mining is the chief Bolivian industry and minerals form over 95% of her exports. Tin amounts to about 80% of exports, and was estimated at 38,900 tons in 1942 (in 1941, 42,887 tons). Other minerals exported were (1941 figures): silver, 228,576 kg.; tungsten, 2,874 tons; lead, 15,654 tons; zinc, 6,067 tons (12,197 tons in 1940); copper, 7,274 tons; gold, 254 kg. Petroleum production approximates 114,300 bbl. per year.

(D. Rd.)

Bonaire: *see* CURAÇAO.
Bonds: *see* STOCKS AND BONDS.
Bonds, War: *see* WAR BONDS.

Book-collecting.
The rare book market enjoyed its biggest boom since the lean 1930s. The trend to higher prices affected even the ordinary second-hand and out-of-print items. It is significant that a copy of the Kelmscott Chaucer fetched £205 as against half that figure in 1941; it is even more significant that seven English county guides issued by the Shell Petroleum company (which can hardly be accused of trying to rig the book market), price half-a-crown each when new and in print, were knocked down to an unsentimental bookseller at 4s. 6d. a volume. The sharp falling-off in the number of American booksellers' catalogues reflected more than the concurrent shortages in labour and paper—books sold without the necessity for cataloguing them; it was essential simply for them to be on the shelves. Under a war regulation the British booktrade was required to charge home (not overseas) recipients of their catalogues an annual subscription price of one shilling. This seems to have kept up the quantity of British catalogues if not their physical quality. The London catalogues which, with their fine paper, wide margins, and superb plates once delighted hand and eye vanished for the duration.

Purchases by collectors from the occupied countries who went to America tended to broaden the base of the collecting pyramid. The incunabula market was livelier than in many years, and higher prices were recorded. But this condition was true in essence of every division of the printed book. Art and reference books soared, reflecting a collateral boom in the art market. The art and book collection of the late Condé Nast sold in New York for $118,406. A complete file of the *Burlington Magazine* (London, 1903-42) brought $525.

Unquestionably considerable buying was a hedge against inflation, and the *Times* (London) deplored the resurgence of "a kind of Stock Exchange mentality which does not serve the best interest of the rare book trade." On the other hand, much buying was by neophytes some of whom were undoubtedly drawn to books by the lack of consumer goods, and whose purchases were largely as unintelligent as they were uninspired—the phenomenon had been manifested before. A certain percentage of these newcomers was expected to remain within the fold, and some of them might well become the great collectors of tomorrow, so that the boom might turn out to have had its brighter aspects. Moreover it was not marked by the speculative insanity of the 1920s.

Bibliographical research continued to cover a diverse field, but the fruits were in large part not scheduled for immediate appearance. The late Anthony J. Russo's bibliography of James Whitcomb Riley, completed by Dorothy R. Russo, was in the printer's hands. Publication of Jacob Blanck's *Selective Bibliography of Nineteenth Century American Juvenile Books* was postponed until after the war. The Moscow State Publishing House issued a bibliography of Russian translations of classics in English and of Russian critical comment thereon; it disclosed the interesting fact that there have been four Russian editions of Chaucer's *Canterbury Tales.*

Sales.—Auction sales fell off in number, and no great libraries came under the hammer, although there were several important offerings of literary and historical manuscripts and letters. Owners of fine libraries which would in normal course have come on the market were obviously waiting for the graph of the price trend to define itself more sharply. The absorption of desirable books into permanent institutional collections continued, and had its persisting if indeterminate influence on values.

A complete series of plates for volume one of the original (1827) folio edition of John James Audubon's *Birds of America,* with some defects in the key wild-turkey reproduction, brought $3,900 at auction. Other representative figures (first editions unless otherwise noted) were as follows:

Audubon, *The Birds of America,* 1860 reissue of the elephant folio edition of 1827–38, $1,300; the same, first octavo edition, 1840–44, with one of 500 plates lacking, $350; T. E. Lawrence, *The Seven Pillars of Wisdom,* with autographs of Feisal and others associated with the desert revolt, $800; Jack London, *The Cruise of the Dazzler,* 1902, presentation copy, $175; R. L. Stevenson, *Travels with a Donkey in the Cevennes,* 1879, with the original drawing for the frontispiece, $400; Stevenson, *The South Seas,* 1890, one of 22 privately printed copies, $300; Stevenson, *The Beach at Falesa,* 1892, $425; Laurence Sterne, *A Sentimental Journey through France and Italy,* 1768, large paper, some defects, $190; Robert Burns, *Poems,* second (1788) American edition, George Washington's copy, with his autograph and bookplate, $1,100. (J. T. W.)

Books: *see* CHILDREN'S BOOKS; PUBLISHING (BOOK); *see also* under AMERICAN LITERATURE; ENGLISH LITERATURE; FRENCH LITERATURE; etc.
Book Sales: *see* BOOK-COLLECTING.
Boothe, Clare: *see* LUCE, CLARE BOOTHE.

Borates. The production of borates in the United States in 1942 dropped to 226,723 short tons, a decrease of 32% from 1940. Consumption in enamels was cut heavily by lack of steel for stoves, refrigerators, cabinets, etc., and use in pottery glazes also declined. Glass, the major essential use, took increased amounts. (G. A. Ro.)

Boris III (1894–1943), king of the Bulgarians, was born Jan. 30 at Sofia, the eldest son of Tsar Ferdinand I and Princess Marie Louise of Bourbon-Parma. Boris ascended to the throne in 1918 after his father's abdication, successfully weathered a series of political storms during the troubled postwar period and entrenched his authority by using his police force to "liquidate" political foes. Boris paid only lip-service to parliamentary government during his entire career. In 1934, he approved a military coup d'état engineered by the "palace guard," who suppressed the constitution, dissolved parliament and banned political parties. A year later, Boris established himself as dictator, paid frequent visits to Hitler and Mussolini and geared his foreign policy to that of the two axis chieftains. He was forced to give German armies the right of transit across Bulgarian territory in Nov. 1940, and to join Hitler and Mussolini in declaring war on the United States in Dec. 1941. Boris refused, however, to declare war on the U.S.S.R., aware of the great sentimental attachment of his subjects for "Mother Russia." Boris' popularity waned as the war continued. Rioting in Sofia on May day, 1943, was so serious that he was compelled to flee the capital for his own safety. His death in Sofia on Aug. 28 was both unexpected and mysterious. An official communiqué said the king had died after a brief illness. But some Hungarian sources in Berne said the king was assassinated by one of his own police bodyguards. His six-year-old son, Simeon II (*q.v.*), succeeded Boris to the throne.

Borneo: *see* BRITISH EMPIRE; NETHERLANDS COLONIAL EMPIRE; NETHERLANDS INDIES.

Boston. Ninth largest city of the United States, with a population of 770,816 by the federal census of 1940, Boston is a seaport at the head of Massachusetts bay and is the capital of the state of Massachusetts. Area, 43.9 sq.mi., comprising most of Suffolk county. Mayor (Jan. 1, 1944): Maurice J. Tobin.

Twenty-two councilmen and three school committeemen were elected in 1943. State Attorney-general Robert T. Bushnell conducted a vigorous campaign against gambling. State and city officials took measures to prevent the recurrence of a few acts of anti-Semitic violence which received nation-wide publicity. The School committee appointed Francis J. Daly to head the Office of Juvenile Adjustment, created to combat juvenile delinquency. The governor of Massachusetts appointed Thomas F. Sullivan police commissioner to succeed Joseph F. Timility, whose term expired Nov. 1.

The city council approved the modernized building code enacted by the state legislature in 1939. The state appropriated $4,700,000 to build three 7,000- and one 5,000-ft. runways at the General Edward L. Logan airport in East Boston. School registration was 101,320. Many pupils left school to take jobs.

Easing of dim-out regulations restored a normal appearance to the city streets. The influx of army and navy personnel combined with the taking over of many buildings to create a severe shortage in housing and hotels.

The shipyards of Boston continued to produce war and merchant ships in increasing numbers. On Oct. 1, 1943, metropolitan Boston was declared a Group II (labour stringency) area by the War Manpower commission. A six weeks' fisherman's strike was still unsettled Jan. 1.

Indices for Jan.–Oct. 1943 (average 1925–1927=100) were as follows: Manufacturing employment 150.3, a gain of 6.3%; manufacturers' payrolls 270, a gain of 24.7%; department store sales 83.8, a gain of 6.6%. Jan.–Oct. 1943 bank clearings increased 10.8%; bank debits increased 15.8%; building permits decreased 39.8%; gross postal receipts increased 4.5%; Boston elevated passengers increased 20%.

The 1943 tax rate remained at $41.00 on an assessed valuation (real and personal) of $1,445,668,300, a decline of $20,470,100. The 1943 budget totalled $74,929,808, a decline of $4,500,100, including provision for the following: city departments $12,118,-761, county departments $3,758,426, school department $16,145,-717, debt service $10,684,080, state tax $3,325,050. The net debt on Dec. 31, 1942 was $133,945,434, a decline of $5,761,144, including a general debt of $60,047,547, temporary loans of $75,245,672 and a public services debt of $40,539,339. The estimated debt reduction in 1943 was $6,000,000. (S. J. McK.)

Bosworth, Hobart Van Zandt

(1867–1943), U.S. motion picture actor, was born Aug. 11 in Marietta, O. In 1885 he played with a theatrical troupe in San Francisco, then joined the Augustin Daly stock company in New York. By the beginning of the 20th century, he had become widely known as a romantic actor and had been leading man to Minnie Maddern Fiske, Julia Marlowe and Henrietta Crosman. In 1909 he entered motion pictures and later headed the Bosworth company, which screened many of Jack London's stories. Bosworth himself was director and star in *The Sea Wolf*. In the early 1920s he was one of the best-known feature actors and stars. He died in Glendale, Calif., Dec. 30, 1943.

Botanical Gardens: *see* BOTANY.

Botany.

In *Pellia epiphylla* it had been assumed previously that the sperm swims by means of its two flagella from the antheridium to the archegonium. At the rate of swimming of the sperm, however, it would require, according to J. Walton (Univ. of Glasgow), several hours for the sperm to reach the archegonium. Walton found that the distance is traversed by the spermatocytes (each containing a single sperm) before the sperms are released. The spermatocytes are extruded by the antheridia into the water, rise to the surface, and are dispersed rapidly over the wet surface by surface tension forces. The sperm is not discharged from the spermatocyte until the archegonium is reached. The time required for the whole process is about 15 minutes.

A mutant obtained from *Neurospora* by X-radiation differed from the parent in having lost the capacity to form pyridoxin, and failed to maintain growth unless this substance was added to the culture medium. J. L. Stokes, J. W. Foster and C. R. Woodward, Jr. (Res. Lab. Merck and Co., Rahway, N.J.) demonstrated that this mutant could grow normally without the addition of pyridoxin provided that the pH of the medium was adjusted to the range from 6.0 to 7.3, and provided further that the nitrogen source in the medium was an ammonium compound, other forms of nitrogen being found to be ineffective.

By exposing germinating seed of *Crepis capillaris* and *Vicia faba* to X-rays, R. T. Brumfield (Harvard univ.) induced chromosome rearrangements in single cells in the young root tip. These chromosome characteristics, which served to identify such cells, *i.e.*, to "tag" them, were carried over into the cells resulting from the subsequent cell divisions, and permitted the author to determine what tissues were produced from these single cells. In this way evidence was obtained that the entire root develops from but a few cells, possibly as few as three, at the tip of the young root.

The effectiveness of X-rays in inducing chromosomal aberration was found by K. Sax (Harvard univ.) to be increased in tests with the microspores of *Tradescantia* by centrifuging the spores during the period of irradiation. The explanation given for this effect was that the stresses caused the broken ends of the chromosomes to separate and this favoured illegitimate unions between broken chromosomes.

Treatment by E. W. Newcomer (Univ. of North Carolina) of young cabbage plants with colchicine resulted in the production of an autotetraploid cabbage which differed from the parent type not only morphologically but also physiologically. The 4*n* cabbages were 25% to 50% higher than the diploids in reducing sugars, total sugars, acid-hydrolyzable substances, residual nitrogen (but not in soluble nitrogen) and vitamin C. The lower leaves of the tetraploid contained four times as much vitamin C as was found in the corresponding leaves of the diploid.

In at least nine genera of angiosperms, twin seedlings were found in which one of the pair had the normal diploid number of chromosomes, while the other had either the haploid, triploid, or tetraploid number. D. C. Cooper (Univ. of Wisconsin) found haploid-diploid twins in about 1% of the ovules of seven species of lilies. The haploid member of the twins was found to have been derived from the division of a synergid. Also, in a cross of *Nicotiana glutinosa* × *N. tabacum,* a haploid twin was found to have developed from a synergid. The role of synergids in the production of haploid plants is emphasized by these results.

In more than 50% of about 900 isolates of imperfect fungi, involving 3 orders, 29 genera and 35 species, it was found that the mycelium was composed of two culturally distinct types, one producing conidia in abundance, but with scant mycelium (designated as C), and the other producing an abundant mycelium but few conidia (designated as M). In subsequent work, H. H. Hansen and W. C. Snyder (Univ. of California), working with *Fusarium,* found that the M type was produced *de novo* from pure cultures of the C type, but the reverse change of M to C was not obtained. By means of crosses with *Hypomyces solani* f. *cucurbitae,* it was shown that M and C behave as allelomorphs, and further that M could function only as a male.

C. H. Meredith (Glenleigh Lab., Highgate, Jamaica, B.W.I.) found that a species of *Actinomyces* produced a substance that would dissolve the mycelium of *Fusarium oxysporum cubense.* The substance diffused through agar.

According to experiments by P. R. Burkholder (Yale univ.) extraordinarily large amounts of riboflavin (vitamin B₂) are formed by the yeast *Candida guilliermondia.* Most of the riboflavin accumulates in the medium.

H. L. Pearse (West. Prov. Fruit Research Inst., Stellenbosch, South Africa) grew grape vines (*Vitis vinifera*) in sand cultures maintained at various levels of nutritive capacity and found that better rooting of cuttings was obtained with cuttings taken from plants grown under semi-starvation conditions (with respect to both mineral and nitrogen components) than from plants grown under conditions of adequate or excessive nutrition. Furthermore, such cuttings responded more readily to treatment with the root-inducing chemical, indolebutyric acid.

By heating tryptophane, either in water or in solutions of NaOH (0.25 N to 0.00025 N), S. A. Gordon and S. G. Wildman (Univ. of Michigan) obtained a product which induced curvatures of the coleoptile of *Avena* in the manner of the natural auxins from plant tissue.

Crosses of certain soft red winter wheat varieties (*Triticum vulgare*) with Marquillo spring wheat in experiments by R. M. Caldwell and L. E. Compton (Purdue Univ. and U.S. Dept. of Agric.) resulted in the production of F₁ seedlings which uniformly developed normally until reaching the two-leaf stage, then all such plants died. The lethality was shown to be controlled by a pair of dominant complementary genes.

When W. S. Hale, S. Schwimmer, and E. G. Bayfield (U.S. Dept. of Agric. and Kansas Agr. Exp. Sta.) added ethylene to the storage space containing freshly-harvested high-moisture wheat seeds at the rate of one part of ethylene to 10,000 parts of air, they found that such treated wheat did not heat as rapidly or as much, furnished a better grade of grain, showed a higher percentage of germination, and gave a better baking performance than untreated wheat stored under identical conditions but without the addition of ethylene. (*See also* HORTICULTURE.)

BIBLIOGRAPHY.—Brumfield, *Amer. Jour. Bot.*, 30:101; Burkholder, *Arch. Biochem.*, 3:121 and *Proc. Nat. Acad. Sci.*, 29:166; Caldwell and Compton, *Jour. of Hered.*, 34:67; Cooper, *Amer. Jour. Bot.*, 30:408; Gordon and Wildman, *Jour. Biol. Chem.*, 147:389; Hale, Schwimmer and Bayfield, *Cereal Chem.*, 20:224; Hansen and Snyder, *Amer. Jour. Bot.*, 30:419; Meredith, *Phytopath.*, 33:403; Newcomer, *J. Eli. Mitchell Sci. Soc.*, 59:69; Pearse, *Ann. of Bot. n. s.*, 7:123, Sax, *Proc. Nat. Acad. Sci.*, 29:18; Stokes, Foster and Woodward, *Arch. Biochem.*, 2:235; Walton, *Nature*, 152:51.
(F. E. DE.)

RARE PLANTS, unknown to modern British botany, were discovered in the bomb craters and ruins of London in 1943. Here a botanist is examining a new flower which sprang up in a crater enriched with the nitrate of a bomb. No conclusive proof of the origin of these plants was advanced

Botanical Gardens.—Dr. E. D. Merrill of Harvard Botanical collections and Arnold arboretum finished a manual on *Emergency Food Plants and Poisonous Plants of the Islands of the Pacific* for use of U.S. forces in the Pacific area; a book of 150 pages, 113 illustrations, and a first printing of 125,000 copies. Under Dr. Merrill's direction a study was being made of the Harvard collection of plants from New Guinea and Solomon Islands. A plant survey of the Alcan highway was being made to furnish certain specific information needed by the engineers and military people for an interpretation of their aerial survey of the route. Dr. Merrill's group found a means of prolonging the life of cut branches used in camouflage. A number of members of the New York Botanical garden staff were being used as experts by the government and industrial organizations in the war effort.

The staff of the Brooklyn Botanic garden did much to aid the victory garden program in greater New York and neighbouring regions. Montreal Botanical garden extended its garden on medicinal plants, including not only those in medicinal use but many that were grown for medicine in Europe before the discovery of America, and certain plants used by the American Indian. This garden also directed 10,000 victory gardens in Montreal. Holden arboretum at Cleveland, O., devoted 100 ac. of its area to growing of garden and farm plants. University of Washington arboretum grew more than 100,000 units of a wide variety of deciduous species of plants for use as camouflage.

University of Wisconsin arboretum and Wild Life refuge increased the planting of wildflowers on the Wildflower trail,

planted 5,000 Tamaracks, initiated an extensive study of songbird nesting, started a survey of the parasitic fungi of the arboretum area, continued a study of effects of crowding on mixed fish populations in ponds, and began a study of life histories of native minnows to develop methods of artificial propagation. Morton arboretum continued its educational classes, and is writing a fern key. Cornell University arboretum added 400 ac. to its holdings to make possible an anticipated postwar expansion. Missouri Botanical garden issued the first two numbers of "Flora of Panama," a project under way for many years. They also acquired an additional tract of land of 160 ac., the last bit of virgin forest in the vicinity of St. Louis. Boyce Thompson Southwestern arboretum worked with commercial groups to develop the culture of jojoba nuts and the propagation and culture of cork oak. Jojoba nuts contain a wax that promised to substitute for the expensive carnauba wax. This wax could also be transformed into a rubber. (*See* also Horticulture.)   (W. C.)

Bougainville: *see* Solomon Islands.

Boutens, Peter Cornelis (1870–1943), Netherlands poet, was born Feb. 20 in Middelburg on the island of Walcheren, the Netherlands. He studied classical literature at Utrecht university and took his doctorate at that school in 1899. He was professor of classical languages at Noorthey institute in Voorschoten and later moved to The Hague, where he turned to writing. He translated into Dutch the works of the ancient Greek writers. Boutens' most famous work was *Beatrys* (1908), a mediaeval legend told in verse. His works were translated into English by Sir Herbert Grierson of Edinburgh university. The poet died at his home in The Hague, March 14.

Bowles, Chester (1901–   ), U.S. advertising executive and government official, was born in Springfield, Mass., Aug. 5. A graduate of Yale, 1924, he became an advertising copywriter and together with William Benton formed the advertising firm of Benton and Bowles, July 1929. Mr. Bowles was made chairman of the board of that company in 1936. In Jan. 1942, he took a leave of absence to work on a dollar-a-year job in Connecticut, later becoming OPA administrator for the state. On July 15, Prentiss M. Brown, then OPA national director, named Bowles as general manager of his agency. The latter, given full authority by Brown, reorganized the agency, simplified price and rationing regulations and encouraged establishment of advisory committees to deal with complaints of business and industry. As a result, congressional and press criticism of OPA methods subsided somewhat. On Oct. 25, 1943, Bowles succeeded Brown who had resigned four days earlier, as OPA administrator. While Bowles was reluctant to impose harsh measures, he nevertheless served notice on assuming his new post that he intended to hold cost-of-living prices to the levels of Sept. 1942. He stated bluntly that OPA would not be a doormat for "scheming" minority groups and warned against inflation.

Bowling. With bowling's two major championships—the American Bowling congress and Women's International Bowling congress—cancelled at the request of the Office of Defense Transportation, the pin-toppling interest of 1943 centred on the National Individual Match Game championship at Chicago. Ned Day of West Allis, Wis., after being voted "Bowler of the Year" by the Bowling Writers' association, went on to win the match game title with a 64-game average of better than 208 per game. Day outmatched a strong field which included: Paul Krumske of Chicago, second with 289.15 points to

Day's winning 315.21; Rudy Pugel of Milwaukee, third with 294.14; Buddy Bomar of Chicago, fourth with 294.30, and John Crimmins of Detroit, fifth with 294.11. Connie Schwoegler of Madison, Wis., the defending champion, finished ninth.

Deprived of its big classic during 1943, the A.B.C. continued to give recognition to its outstanding participants with a compilation of the year's outstanding scorers. Louis Foxie of Paterson, N.J., rolled the year's individual high of 824, which enabled his team to count a high 3,547 for team total and 1,286 for high team game.

In spite of the war hardships and a shortage of pin boys, bowling enjoyed one of its best years in 1943. An estimated 12,000,000 bowlers took part in the recreational phase of the game. Telegraphic bowling, a method by which scores sent by telegraph were compared and matches decided, became popular in view of limited transportation. High school bowling especially took to telegraphic play.

Although not made in regular A.B.C. competition, two team titles were claimed during 1943. The Detroit Strohs staked claim to the national team title, while Frank Mataya and Nelson Burton of St. Louis were regarded as the national doubles titlists. (M. P. W.)

Boxing.
Most of the ring champions were in the armed forces. Joe Louis, sergeant in the U.S. army, occupied himself exclusively with boxing exhibitions for the men in service. Billy Conn, outstanding challenger for the world heavyweight title, was a corporal in the army, stationed most of the year at Jefferson Barracks, Mo.

Championships in four divisions where possession was undisputed were frozen. In addition to Louis' heavyweight crown, they were the light-heavyweight, middleweight and welterweight championships. Gus Lesnevich, leader of the light-heavyweight, or 175-lb. class, was in the coast guard. Tony Zale, holder of the middleweight, or 160-lb. title, was in the navy. Freddie Cochrane, champion of the welterweight, or 147-lb. class, was in the navy.

Willie Pep, who shared the possession of the world featherweight title, made one defense of his crown, held the title, saw his remarkable streak of victories shattered after 62, and enlisted in the navy. This left only the lightweight and bantamweight classes untouched by the war. The flyweight class was dormant, as it has been for years. Little was heard of its world ruler, Jackie Patterson of Scotland.

Manuel Ortiz, Mexican resident of El Centro, Calif., ruler of the featherweight division, successfully defended his title no less than eight times, a record for championship defense in modern ring history. Starting on Jan. 2, he won a decision over Kenny Lindsay at Portland, Ore. On March 10, Ortiz knocked out Lou Salica in 11 rounds at Oakland, Calif. April 28 saw Ortiz knocking out Lupe Cordoza in six rounds at Fort Worth, Tex. On May 27, Ortiz won a decision over Joe Roberts at Long Beach, Calif. He followed this by knocking out Roberts in seven rounds at Seattle, Wash., July 13. In his sixth defense of the 126-lb. title Ortiz, on Sept. 5, knocked out Fileo Gonzalez in five rounds at Mexico City. On Oct. 2 he knocked out Leonardo Lopez in four rounds at Hollywood, Calif., and his amazing year concluded on Nov. 23 when he won a 15-round decision over the hitherto unbeaten Benny Goldberg of Detroit, at Los Angeles. Not even Joe Louis, most active of all the ring champions in modern history, could match this record of title defense.

Outstanding among the box-office attractions, however, was Beau Jack, who, under his real name, Sidney Walker, was originally a caddy and shoe-shine boy in his native Augusta, Ga. He not only contrived to lose and regain his world lightweight title

JOE LOUIS began a 14-week exhibition tour of U.S. army camps Aug. 30, 1943, with Sgt. George Nicholson, his old-time sparring partner. Here he is shown at Camp Edwards on the second day of the tour

in the states of New York, New Jersey and Pennsylvania, but he shared distinction for the year's largest gate receipts and established himself as the greatest box-office attraction active in the ring.

In six bouts Beau Jack drew a total of $481,415 to Madison Square Garden, where all his boxing was conducted, under the auspices of the Twentieth Century S.C., Mike Jacobs, promoter. His record gate for the year, which was also a new high for Beau Jack, was $104,976, for the bout in which he defeated Henry Armstrong, former triple champion of the ring, on the latter's return to action. It was held April 2, 1943, and attracted 19,986 persons.

Beau Jack drew $70,291 in a bout with Fritzie Zivic, former welterweight champion, Feb. 5. In a return bout against Zivic he drew $71,346, March 5. The Armstrong bout followed, and on March 21, Beau Jack drew $94,500 on a paid attendance of 18,343 persons, in a 15-round bout against Bob Montgomery, Philadelphia, in which Beau Jack lost his world lightweight title. Beau Jack lost a 10-round decision to Bobby Ruffin, Long Island City, on Oct. 4, in a bout that attracted receipts of $43,429. On

Nov. 19, he regained his lightweight honours in a title bout against Montgomery, winning a decision in 15 rounds before 17,866 persons who paid receipts of $96,873.

Sammy Angott, Washington, Pa., who voluntarily surrendered the world lightweight title late in 1942 to enter war work, returned to the ring early in 1943 and was indirectly responsible for the confusion surrounding the title as the year ended. The National Boxing association declined to recognize the tournament sanctioned by the New York State Athletic commission from which Beau Jack emerged the winner and champion. Instead, after Angott snapped Willie Pep's 62-straight winning streak, the N.B.A. sanctioned a bout between Slugger White, Baltimore, and Angott as for the title. Angott won the bout and gained recognition as champion in every boxing centre except New York, New Jersey and Pennsylvania.

Similar confusion surrounded the world featherweight title, a hold-over condition from 1942. Willie Pep, New York State Athletic commission champion, defended his title against Sal Bartolo in Boston, June 8, and joined the navy. Phil Terranova, Bronx, N.Y., conquered Jackie Callura, Hamilton, Ont., Aug. 16, and gained recognition as N.B.A. featherweight champion. Terranova knocked out Jackie Callura, in six rounds at New Orleans, Dec. 27.

Service boxers were conspicuous in the annual championships of the Amateur Athletic union, decided among an entry list of 89 boxers representing 16 district associations on April 12 and 13 in Boston. Though among the best tournaments on record in competition, the affair was a disappointment in receipts. Three army boxers gained the finals, but only one, Earl O'Neill, 118-lb. boxer from Fort Sill, Okla., won a title. Syracuse university won the Eastern Intercollegiate A.A. boxing championships held at Syracuse, March 6, with a record total of 30 points. Another record was supplied when Syracuse won six of the eight titles. A distinctive feature was the victory of Salvatore (Toots) Mirabito in the heavyweight division. He closed an outstanding college boxing career with his third such victory, as he registered his 30th straight college contest. He entered the army shortly afterward leaving behind a winning streak of 80 bouts in high school, prep and college competition. Boxers of the University of Wisconsin dominated the National Collegiate A.A. championships held at Madison, Wis., March 26. They clinched team honours, winning five individual titles. Michigan State's boxers won two and the other championship went to Washington State.

Boxing receipts at Madison Square Garden under direction of Promoter Mike Jacobs, reached an aggregate of $1,136,228 for 22 shows. The paid attendance was 322,512. The largest "gate" of the year was drawn by Beau Jack and Henry Armstrong on April 2 as stated above, and the largest crowd of the year was 21,240 attracted to the ten-round bout between Beau Jack and Fritzie Zivic, Feb. 5.   (J. P. D.)

Boy Scouts.
From the beginning of the war until the end of 1943, 47 different projects had been undertaken by scouts at the request of government agencies. They had collected scrap rubber, metal, tin cans, grease, books, musical instruments and nearly 500,000,000 lb. of waste paper. They had produced model planes and ships, served as civilian defense messengers, aeroplane spotters, fire watchers, assisted in making surveys for war housing agencies, in aiding rationing boards, selective service boards, community chests, war chests, foreign relief and in countless other ways helped in the war effort.

During 1943, especially, waste paper and scrap metal collections were carried on throughout the U.S. by scouts. Scouts also served as government dispatch bearers in the distribution of posters twice each month and the distribution of other government informational material throughout the nation. They assisted the Red Cross in the promotion of blood banks and aided the war housing program in 210 communities. The Food for Freedom program of the Boy Scouts of America was outstanding in the service projects.

A new pre-Ranger type of training was developed, designed to teach older boys skills which they might need if they entered the armed forces, to give them a variety of training, self-reliance and personal discipline and thus equip them for service if they should be called upon for military service.

In Feb. 1943, Dr. James E. West, who from the beginning of the organization had been chief scout executive, was promoted to the office of chief scout and Dr. Elbert K. Fretwell, former Professor of Education at Teachers' college, Columbia university, succeeded him as chief scout executive.

The new Aviation Merit badge pamphlets and the *Air Scout Manual* were issued and the air scout program attracted many boys. There was also a big increase in cubs, the program for younger boys. In spite of demands made by the various work projects, more scouts camped in their own troops in 1943 than in any previous year in scouting. The grand total membership of the Boy Scouts of America as of Dec. 31, 1943, was 1,613,783. Total troops and packs numbered 51,953.

Great Britain.—During 1943 British scouts carried on, as they had since the beginning of the war, by giving every possible assistance to the war effort. Scouts in England performed numerous war service jobs.

An example of the type of service scouts performed in 1943 was the account received of an entire Rover scout crew manning one of the leading ships of a British mine-sweeping flotilla in home waters. In the early days of the war, while still in their home town, this crew had sighted a U-boat and was able to direct destroyers to the spot to attack. They shared the record for their base of mines swept and carried out a number of special operations.

During 1943 a special war emergency section of the movement

U.S. BOY SCOUT learning to identify German planes from models

was introduced into British scouting under the name "War Service Patrols." On passing certain public service tests boys of 15 and over could be drafted into these special patrols and received advanced training in campaigning, health and endurance training, exploring, observation and other subjects of this kind.

(L. W. BA.)

Bracco, Roberto

(1861–1943), Italian dramatist, was born Nov. 10 in Naples. A protege of a Naples newspaper editor, Bracco at the age of 17 became a reporter. He worked on several newspapers and sometime later found his stride as dramatist and novelist. He became one of Italy's noted playwrights in the pre-fascist days, and aroused much interest in his psychological dramas. One of his plays, *Countess Coquette*, a Nazimova vehicle in 1907, established his reputation in the United States and was also received successfully in Paris. *The Little Saint* was produced in New York city in 1931. He wrote about 40 plays, including *The Right to Live, Phantasms, Madame President, One of the Honest Ones* and *Masks,* and about six volumes of stories. He fell into disrepute with the fascists in 1926 because of his Liberal views; his home was wrecked by a band of terrorists, and the remainder of his life was spent in obscurity. He died in Naples, April 21, according to a Swiss report.

Bracken, John

(1883–   ), Canadian political leader, was born at Ellisville, Ont., on June 22, and graduated from the Ontario Agricultural college, and the University of Illinois. After graduation Bracken went into the prairie provinces as a seed inspector for the Canadian government. He became professor of field husbandry at the University of Saskatchewan, and later president of the Agricultural college of Manitoba. It was while holding this post that in 1922 he was offered, and accepted, the leadership of the newly formed Agrarian or Progressive party in the province of Manitoba. He was returned to the legislature in a by-election held in Le Pas. In 1932 he headed a coalition government of Progressives and Liberals, and later the coalition principle was extended to include Conservatives, Co-operative Commonwealth Federationists, and Social Credit members. In Dec. 1942, he emerged as a national figure, when he was chosen national leader of the Conservative party by a nominating convention meeting at Winnipeg. In deference to his views, the name of the party was altered to Progressive Conservative.

During 1943, Bracken made an extensive tour of Canada, speaking in such centres as Quebec, Hamilton and Toronto. As Bracken did not attempt election to the house of commons, Gordon Graydon acted as Opposition leader.   (J. I. C.)

Bradley, Omar Nelson

(1893–   ), U.S. army officer, was born in Clark, Mo., on Feb. 12. He was graduated from the U.S. Military academy in 1915 and later from the Infantry school, the Command and General Staff school and the Army War college. Between 1929 and 1941 he served as chief of the weapons section at the Infantry school, commandant at West Point, and secretary of the general staff in Washington. Early in 1941 he was appointed commandant of the Infantry school. Two months after the U.S. entered World War II, Gen. Bradley was appointed to command the 82nd division, and in Feb. 1943, he was sent to North Africa. Near the end of the campaign there he was assigned to command the 2nd corps, which he led to victory at Bizerte and Tunis. Two days later the nazi commander surrendered 25,000 men to him. For this achievement he was made a lieutenant general and awarded the distinguished service medal. In Jan. 1944, it was announced that

Gen. Bradley would command the ground forces being massed in Britain for the invasion of Europe.

Brazil.

A republic in eastern and central South America and the largest independent country in the western hemisphere; language: Portuguese; capital: Rio de Janeiro (pop. 1940: 1,781,567); president in 1943 (since 1931): Dr. Getúlio Vargas.

Brazil is divided into 21 states and six territories. Five of these territories were created by presidential decree of Sept. 13, 1943 (effective Oct. 1). All frontier areas, they were separated, respectively, from Pará, Amazonas, Mato Grosso, Paraná and Santa Catarina states. They are: Amapá, adjoining Surinam and French Guiana; Rio Branco, adjoining British Guiana and Venezuela; Guaporé, on the Bolivian border; Ponta Pôra, north of Paraguay and east of the Paraguay river; Iguassú, between the Uruguay and Paraná rivers and north of the Argentine territory of Misiones.

The country has an area of 3,291,416 sq.mi. The population, according to the 1940 census (revised), was 41,565,083, an increase of 10,929,478 since 1930. In 1943 official sources estimated it at 43,500,000 as of the end of 1942.

The main concentrations of population are in the south and the east.[1] Four southern states, with less than 10% of the area, have 31.33% of the population (São Paulo 7,239,711; Rio Grande do Sul 3,350,120; Paraná 1,248,536; Santa Catarina 1,184,838). The five eastern states of Rio de Janeiro (1,862,900), Sergipe (545,962), Baía (3,938,909), Minas Gerais (6,798,647) and Espírito Santo (758,535), along with the Federal District (*i.e.,* Rio de Janeiro city, 1,781,567) occupy a seventh of the area and have 37.9% of the population. Another seventh of the area, the northeastern states of Maranhão (1,242,721), Piauí (826,320), Ceará (2,101,325), Rio Grande do Norte (774,464), Paraíba (1,432,618), Pernambuco (2,694,616) and Alagoas (957,628) has 24.13%. The Amazon valley states of Amazonas (453,233) and Pará (956,870) and Acre territory (81,326), with over three-eighths of the area have only 3.59% of the population. Interior Goiaz (661,140) and Mato Grosso (1,477,041) occupy a full quarter of the area but have only 3.05% of the population.

The capital and São Paulo city (pop. 1,318,000) between them have 7.4% of the population.

History.—World War II and its effects continued to dominate Brazil's history and development throughout 1943, its first full year as a belligerent. Her unstinted co-operation, coupled with the natural advantages of her strategic position, was of vital importance in expediting transport and communication between the North American arsenal of democracy and the Mediterranean war zone, while her economic contributions were of increasing consequence.

The axis submarine campaign in South Atlantic waters was only less intense than during 1942, and was at times far more active than in the North Atlantic. Between Brazil's entry into the war (Aug. 1942) and the close of 1943, 27 Brazilian merchant ships were lost. Against this, Brazilian forces alone had, by Aug. 31, chalked up a score of nine "sure" sinkings of axis submarines, as well as a number of probables.

In combatting subversive activities of enemy agents within the county, Brazil took vigorous steps to repress them. In July a presidential decree directed the liquidation of two of the largest and oldest German commercial firms in Brazil, with assets estimated at $6,000,000.

The war gave a tremendous stimulus to production and trade. Unemployment was at an all-time low, and the year's favourable

---

[1]Populations given for individual states include the territories segregated in 1943; see above.

trade balance was estimated to be in excess of $100,000,000. Foreign trade itself was marked by an increasing diversification of exports and featured by a sharp rise in export of manufactures. Continued prosperity and high export totals were assured by agreements with the United States for strategic materials and with Great Britain for purchase of all Brazilian meat exports for United Nations war needs. On Dec. 21 a further agreement was made with Great Britain and the United States under whose terms those two countries undertook to purchase the entire exportable excess of Brazil's 1943, 1944 and 1945 rice crops over and beyond 10,000 tons a year reserved for normal export demands.

Economic shortages and oversupplies arising from war conditions were in some instances acute. Industrial production as a substitute for importation of manufactured goods was stimulated. So, too, was the output of some critical and strategic war materials, although many of these were as yet only barely coming into production.

Continued acute gasoline shortage served to encourage the use of *gasogenios* (charcoal-burning equipment), and by the end of 1943 it was estimated that over 28,000 automobiles ($11\frac{1}{2}\%$ of Brazil's total) were thus equipped. Eight distilleries for fuel alcohol from mandioca were under construction. These, scheduled for completion in early 1944, would have a capacity of 4,500,000 gal., and an additional 12 distilleries were expected eventually to raise the capacity to 10,500,000 gal.

The war burden on the national transport system caused local shortages in some food commodities. At times meat and sugar were rationed in Rio de Janeiro and other large cities. To spread the wheat supply, it was required that 85% instead of 75% of the grain be used in the flour, thus conserving 100,000 tons of wheat. Sharp restrictions were put on the export of rice, which was limited to half the production in Rio Grande do Sul and a third in other states until the new crop came in.

The general prosperity, coupled with shortages in goods, brought a gradual rise in prices. Rents were frozen. Early policy was to avoid general price control. On Nov. 10, a country-wide raise in wages was imposed by government decree. As this in its turn threatened to precipitate price advances, a decree of Nov. 26 fixed ceiling prices as of Nov. 10 for all merchandise, wholesale and retail, and transportation rates.

Education.—At the end of 1941 Brazil had 47,601 schools of all types (59% more than in 1932); of these, 42,794 were primary. School enrolment totalled 3,791,500 (a 67% increase in nine years), including 3,350,737 in primary schools. As of Sept. 1942, there were 739 secondary schools. Over half of these were in two states and the Federal District. In addition there were a number of vocational and other specialized institutions.

Finance.—The monetary unit is the cruzeiro (value: approx. 5 cents U.S.), divided into 100 centavos. This supplanted the former unit, the milreis, in Nov. 1942.

The 1943 budget anticipated revenues of 4,777,700,000 cruzeiros and expenditures of 5,270,200,000 cruzeiros, aside from a balanced extraordinary budget of 600,000,000 cruzeiros for a public works program. The deficit in 1942 aggregated 1,166,200,000 cruzeiros against an anticipated 637,400,000, the excess being due primarily to war expenditures of 517,300,000 cruzeiros.

War costs are covered from taxes and by compulsory loans equal to the year's income tax payments (first half of 1943: approximately 323,369,129 cruzeiros).

On Dec. 31, 1942, the national debt aggregated 1,370,800,000 cruzeiros external and 8,895,900,000 internal. On Nov. 25, 1943, a readjustment of the external debt, which had been in default, was announced, under which service would be resumed with some

LOADING WILD BRAZILIAN RUBBER into a Pan American clipper at Manaus, far up the Amazon, for shipment to the United States in 1943

adjustment of interest.

Trade and Communication.—War conditions precluded publication of detailed data on foreign trade for 1942 and 1943. Those years, however, were marked by abnormal trends whose continuance is in many instances questionable and by wide fluctuations in monthly totals for individual commodities. These reflected war dislocations of trade, such as arbitrary routing of shipping for war purposes and temporary embargoes, or at least sharp restrictions, on export of commodities (as coffee), coupled with priorities for essential items.

In 1941, the last year for which complete totals were available, export aggregated 6,729,401,000 cruzeiros against 4,964,149,000 in 1940. The United States was overwhelmingly the greatest single purchaser of Brazilian goods in 1941, taking 56.9% (1940: 42.3%). Great Britain, 12.2% (1940: 17.3%), Argentina, 9.2% (7.2%), Japan, 4.0% (5.8%), Canada, 3.4% (2.1%), China 1.8% (3.1%) and Uruguay, 1.6% (1.5%) followed. Imports were supplied chiefly by the United States, 60.4% (1940: 51.9%), Argentina, 11.2% (10.8%), Great Britain, 5.7% (9.4%) and Curaçao, 4.4% (4.7%).

Raw materials made up 48.3% of 1941 exports, foodstuffs 46.2%, manufactures 5.5%. Imports comprised: manufactures

(52.3%), raw materials (33.3%), foodstuffs (13.6%), live animals (0.9%). The leading separate commodities were coffee (29.9%), raw cotton (15%), preserved and refrigerated meats (6.7%), cacao 4.7%, followed by hides and skins, carnauba wax, cotton cloth, vegetable oils (including cottonseed, oiticica, castor, copaiba, coconut, and babassu), castor oil seed, lumber, diamonds and quartz. Leading separate import commodity groups were machinery and apparatus, wheat, automobiles and accessories, iron and steel goods, coal, coke, etc., chemicals, gasoline, unrefined iron and steel, lubricating oils. During 1942 and 1943 sharp increases were registered in vegetable oil, rubber, minerals and other war commodities.

The outstanding feature of 1942 trade was the tremendous increase in value of exports and the decline of imports. Thus, export values reached 7,495,000,000 cruzeiros, an all-time high, eclipsing the previous 1941 record total by 11.4%, while imports declined 15.7% to 4,644,000,000 cruzeiros value. Approximately 70% of the 1942 exports went to other American countries (1941: 75.4%; 1940: 54.9%), who in turn supplied 84% of import values (1941: 83.4%; 1940: 74.3%). The increased exportation was the result of sharp increases in volume and value of vegetable oil, rubber, minerals and other war shipments, which continued through 1943.

In the first half of 1943 the "favourable trade balance" declined to a net of 631,277,000 cruzeiros, but rose later in the year so that unofficial sources estimated a total in excess of $100,000,000 (2,000,000,000 cruzeiros) for the full year. A feature of the first six months was the jump in exports to African countries (principally the Union of South Africa), which

THE HEALTH of Brazilian rubber workers was carefully watched by health officers to prevent the spread of tropical disease as the vast wild rubber lands of the interior were opened up in 1943. Here a doctor is taking the blood pressure of a worker

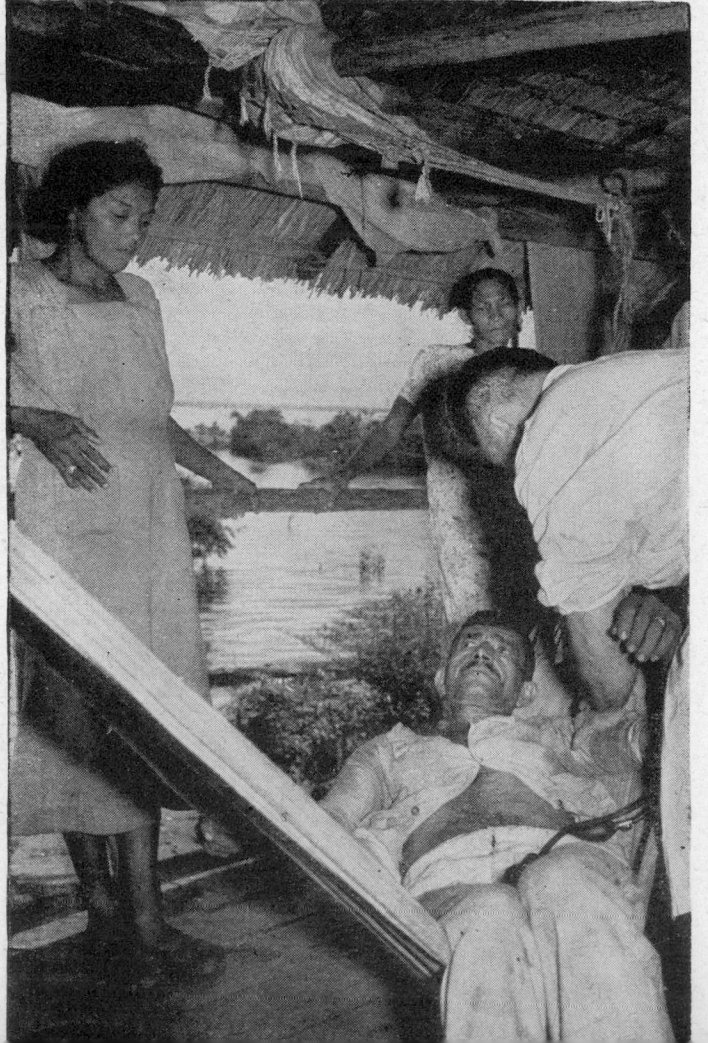

took 12% of all exports, against 1.8% in the first half of 1942 and a negligible quantity in 1941. In Nov. 1943 the total exportation during Brazil's first full year of war (Sept. 1942–Aug. 1943 inclusive) was officially reported as 7,943,918,000 cruzeiros, with the leading purchasers the United States, Great Britain, Argentina and South Africa. Of more lasting significance was the spectacular increase in the proportion of manufactured goods. United States purchases for 1943 were unofficially estimated to have increased some 35% over 1942 and sales even more.

External communications by air and by sea are normally good; during 1943, however, both were heavily taxed by war transport demands and subjected to the restrictions of war priorities. Too, shipping was harassed by the axis submarine campaign, although to a less degree than during 1942. Pan American Airways provides air transport north and south, with a transatlantic link from Natal to Africa and other parts of the eastern hemisphere, and a connection through Corumbá to the west coast of South America. In Dec. 1943 service on this last was increased from two to three flights weekly. In August, formal application was made in the United States by Eastern Air Lines for permission to inaugurate a service from that country due south by Venezuela through Manaus and Corumbá, thence by way of Asunción (Paraguay) to Buenos Aires.

Land communication with neighbouring countries is practically nonexistent except for rail connections with Uruguay and highway with Uruguay and Argentina.

Within Brazil, aviation is under control of the ministry of aviation. There is service to all parts of the country by Panair do Brasil (a Pan American Airways affiliate) and by Brazilian military planes. During 1943 the former began experimental night flights between Fortaleza and Natal. The Brazilian military planes maintain regular mail service over numerous economically unprofitable domestic routes and to Asunción, Paraguay. Air routes within the country total somewhat in excess of 125,000 mi. in length.

Rail and highway communications are generally inadequate. A national highway program was being formulated under a decree-law of July 1943. There are some 160,000 mi. of highway of all types. In 1941 the country had 242,995 motor vehicles, over half of them registered in São Paulo state and the Federal District. The rail system (20,906 mi.) is being extended.

Water routes play an important role in domestic communication, providing practically the only surface transportation in the Amazon basin and the major heavy freight link between northern and southern points. Under war conditions the needs of coastwise traffic, formerly met in considerable degree by foreign shipping, compelled the concentration of the Brazilian merchant marine in coast traffic. In 1942 this coastal trade carried 52% of the country's entire wartime shipping.

Agriculture.—Brazil is primarily an agricultural country. Coffee and cotton are the principal money crops, despite recent declines in their relative importance, but the country produces a wide variety of agricultural commodities.

Coffee is produced in 15 states, with an estimated 8,625,240 ac. devoted to its cultivation. São Paulo state accounts for 60% of production, Minas Gerais 20%, Espírito Santo and Paraná between them another 10%. Brazil is normally the world's third heaviest per capita consumer with 6.478 kgs. annually (Denmark 9.124 kgs.; United States 7.493 kgs.). Domestic consumption, however, accounts for but 4,500,000 to 5,000,000 bags. Export averaged 14,695,675 bags (of 132 lb. each) in the period 1925–39, but fell to 12,045,715 bags in 1940 and 11,052,484 in 1941. A large annual surplus necessitated systematic destruction. In 1943 some 2,300,000 bags were destroyed, bringing the total since 1931 to over 77,000,000. The Inter American Coffee Quota agreement of 1941, which allotted 9,300,000 bags (subsequently expanded) to Brazil as its quota for export to the United States, stabilized the coffee market; but unsatisfactory shipping conditions in 1942 so interfered with export that the total to all countries was only 7,259,658 bags. The United States, however, agreed to purchase for cash a minimum of 9,300,000 bags, regardless of shipping facilities, storing the excess. Although shipping conditions were materially improved, this system was continued through 1943. Actual export of coffee in the first eight months of 1943 totalled 6,863,282 bags, of which 85% went to the United States. During 1943 the Brazilian government made a gift of 400,000 bags to United Nations forces serving in combat areas.

Cotton is produced in a majority of the states, with São Paulo state accounting for nearly 70% of the total. Formerly over 50% of the cotton crop was exported; although export of raw cotton sharply declined because of war conditions and of increasing industrialization in Brazil, Brazilian cotton textiles were being increasingly exported.

Cacao is produced on a considerable scale in the tropical areas, but suffered heavily from world overproduction and from war conditions. Corn, rice, sugar, oranges, beans and mandioca are produced in important quantities for domestic consumption.

Rubber, indigenous to Brazil, grows wild in the Amazon valley. From early 1942 on, strenuous efforts were made to facilitate its gathering. The United States provided technical assistance and undertook to aid transportation and sanitation projects. The Brazilian government on its part furthered the migration of an estimated 80,000 labourers from other parts of the country to the rubber districts. Balata, close kin to rubber, used especially for machine belting and comparable purposes, is likewise found in quantity.

In 1939 Brazil had 40,564,839 head of cattle, 21,776,770 swine, 10,713,008 sheep, 6,579,536 horses, 6,037,202 goats, and 3,944,998 mules and asses. The cattle and swine industries are especially important in Minas Gerais and the southern states, sheep in Rio Grande do Sul. Approximately 4,500,000 cattle are slaughtered annually in the stockyards.

Meat products were exported in 1941 to the value of 523,718,-000 cruzeiros.

Manufacturing.—Manufacturing is primarily for domestic consumption. Exportation was greatly accelerated after 1939, so that in the first six months of 1943, manufactured goods represented 22.6% of all export values, against 11.9% in 1942, the previous high and 5½% in 1941. Exported manufactures are chiefly cotton textiles, chemical and pharmaceutical products and meat products.

During 1943 the huge steel plant at Volta Redonda (started in 1940 with United States financial aid) began partial production.

Mineral Production.—The great bulk of Brazilian mineral wealth lies in the eastern and southern portions and is only slightly exploited. Minas Gerais is the greatest centre of mineral resources. Coal, chrome and iron are in considerable quantity. Bauxite deposits are exploited in Minas Gerais; manganese is of growing importance. Some petroleum deposits in Baía state are being exploited. Production, however, is estimated at but 220 bbl. daily. (*See* also ARGENTINA.)

Bread and Bakery Products.
The newly formed Food Distribution administration of the War Food administration in its first order required that, beginning Jan. 18, 1943, all white bread in the United States must be made from enriched flour or have equivalent enrichment ingredients added to the dough. Economies were effected largely through prohibition of what was called consignment selling, whereby stale bread might be returned by the retailer, and through the establishment of maximum limits for the amounts of shortening, sugar and milk products used in the making of bread. There was a prohibition also at first against the slicing of bakers' bread, but because of consumer objections this requirement later was rescinded.

New and higher standards for levels of enrichment of flour, authorized by the Food and Drug administration as a result of recommendations made by the Food and Nutrition board of the National Research council, were put into effect beginning Oct. 1, 1943. Simultaneously, enriched bread was required to have higher levels of enrichment also, although the proposed standards of the Food and Drug administration had not up to the close of 1943 officially been put into effect. Enriched flour was required to have in each pound not less than 2.0 mg. of thiamin, 1.2 mg. of riboflavin, 16.0 mg. of niacin and 13.0 mg. of iron. Enriched bread was required to have not less than 1.1 mg. of thiamin, 0.7 mg. of riboflavin, 10.0 mg. of niacin or its amide and 8.0 mg. of iron to the pound. There were maximum levels of enrichment for both products and also standards for enrichment with calcium and vitamin D, but the addition of these dietary essentials was optional.

In line with recommendations of the Baking Industry Advisory committee to the War Food administration, an order was drawn up extending enrichment to all yeast-raised products and doughnuts, to the extent of their white flour content. The effective date of the order was to be May 1, 1944, when it was believed sufficient supplies of the necessary vitamins and minerals would be available.

It was estimated that approximately 12,000,000,000 loaves of commercial bread are baked annually, and the total flour consumption of the baking industry amounts to approximately 60,000,000 bbl. a year.

In Great Britain "national wheat meal" of 85% extraction continued to be used and this, of course, produced a brown loaf of bread. The British ministry of food required that seven ounces of calcium carbonate be added to each sack of flour, the idea being that this calcium would counteract the phosphorus bound in the form of phytic acid in the long extraction flour and would also contribute to the nutritive value of the product. Because of the need to conserve wheat which, of course, had to be imported, and in order to take advantage of the availability of home-grown potatoes, the British ministry of food in 1943 encouraged the consumption of potatoes as a substitute for bread. Through the ingenuity of British bakers considerable quantities of mashed potatoes or potato powder were used, especially in cake and confectionery products.

In Eire, where for two years all flour had been required to be 100% extraction, that is whole-wheat flour, it was decided late in 1943 to permit the use of 85% extraction flour, although whole wheat flour was still made available to those who wished to use it. (*See* FLOUR AND FLOUR MILLING.) (F. C. BG.)

Breadner, Lloyd Samuel
(1894–   ). Canadian airman, born July 14, at Carleton Place, Ont. He was educated at Ottawa. He had a distinguished record in World War I, becoming a flight sublieutenant in the royal naval air service in 1915. He later transferred to the royal air force, and by Nov. 1918 had attained the rank of major (equivalent to the present rank of squadron leader). From Oct. 1920, Air Marshal Breadner was associated with the royal Canadian air force, becoming certificate examiner to the air board. In 1922, he became director of civil aviation and had much to do with shaping civilian and commercial flying in Canada between the two world wars. From 1928 onward, however, he was drawn

into military aviation, serving as acting director of the R.C.A.F. till 1932. In 1936, he became air staff officer at National Defense headquarters, and in 1939 he accompanied Hon. J. A. Crearar to England to confer with the British government. In 1940, he was made air vice-marshal, and chief of air staff. He became air marshal in 1940 and on Nov. 11, 1943, was named air officer commanding the R.C.A.F. overseas.   (J. I. C.; S. LEA.)

Brereton, Lewis Hyde

(1890–   ), U.S. army officer, was born June 21 in Pittsburgh, Pa., and graduated from the naval academy at Annapolis, 1911. Two days after he was commissioned as an ensign he resigned to become a lieutenant in the army's coast artillery corps. He took flight training in 1912, served as a pilot in the Philippines and commanded one of the first U.S. flying units on the western front during World War I. A pioneer in the development of dive-bombing, he commanded in 1922 the first aviation attack group in the army air corps. He was in command of an airfield in the Canal Zone, 1931–35, and was transferred from his air command at the Tampa field in July 1941 to head the army air force in the Philippines. After fighting a losing battle against Japan's quantitative plane superiority there, he was made chief of U.S. air forces in India. Transferred to the middle east in July 1942, as U.S. air commander, he co-operated with the R.A.F. in joint attacks on axis military and supply bases. On Feb. 6, 1943, he succeeded Lieut. Gen. Frank M. Andrews as U.S. commander in the middle east. He was replaced by Maj. Gen. Ralph Royce in September on his appointment to an undisclosed post. The low-level U.S. bombing raid on the Ploesti refinery in Rumania was carried out at Gen. Brereton's order.

Brewing and Beer.

The generic word beer covers the malt beverage group, including beer, ale, porter, etc. Malt beverages are sold in all of the states of the U.S.A. under regulation and licence. They are taxed by the federal and state governments and in scattered cases local taxes are imposed. Aside from taxation, control is vested in the states, which generally treat beer apart from distilled liquors because of its low alcoholic content.

The industry's production and sales statistics are based on United States internal revenue reports of tax-paid withdrawals (sales) for the fiscal years ending June 30. As cited here, the reports cover the period after beer's relegalization by act of congress effective April 7, 1933 (which preceded the effective date of repeal of the prohibition amendment by eight months). On June 30, 1943 there were 470 breweries in the United States as compared with the peak of 750 in 1935.

Sales Records.—Following are the sales records in U.S. barrels (31 gal.) by fiscal years ending June 30: 1933 (85 days) 6,277,728; 1934, 32,266,039; 1935, 42,228,831; 1936, 48,759,840; 1937, 55,391,960; 1938, 53,926,018; 1939, 51,816,874; 1940, 53,014,230; 1941, 52,799,181; 1942, 60,856,219; 1943 (official but not audited), 68,491,045.

Per capita consumption was 15.5 gal. as compared with 14 gal. in 1942.

Package sales, considered significant of increased home use, continued to gain in 1943 when 60% of all beer was sold in bottles or cans (canned beer was available only for the armed forces overseas). In 1934 75% of all beer was sold in draught barrels.

Taxes.—Federal excise and special taxes on beer for the fiscal year 1943, ending June 30, totalled $458,872,516. Cumulative taxes after relegalization, April 7, 1933, totalled $2,905,952,782. The federal beer revenue is at the rate of $1,250,000 per day. State and local taxes and licence fees in 1943 were estimated at $150,000,000. After relegalization the combined public revenues from beer approximated $4,000,000,000.

War Conditions.—In addition to contributing to the war effort through payment of enormous taxes, aiding morale and in other ways, the beer industry used surplus farm crops not required for defense purposes and was virtually non-competitive with any defense activities. It required no imported raw materials and the export of beer and ale exceeded the imported finished product. Because of the war, world production and consumption reports for this industry were no longer available.

Industry features for 1943 were: 7% of available brewing malt was diverted for manufacture of industrial alcohol for munition needs; 15% of remaining malt supply was allocated, by government order, for brewing beer for the armed forces; purchase of new bottles was limited to 65% of 1942 orders; local and cross-country transportation of beer was voluntarily curtailed; an industry-wide program for equitable distribution had considerable success in meeting extraordinary problems of civilian requirements and population shifts to war production centres; brewers also co-operated with government agencies in eliminating black markets.

Valuable By-Products.—Wartime need for intensified conservation of food resulted in an industry campaign with government co-operation for the conservation and greater utilization of brewery by-products—chiefly brewers' yeast and brewers' spent grains. One-third, dry weight, of grains used by brewers was returned to the farmer as a concentrated protein-rich feed for livestock, particularly dairy cattle. Recovery was estimated at nearly 60 lb. (wet weight) per barrel of beer. In the calendar year 1943, it was estimated that an equivalent of 2,250,000 tons of wet grains were fed to stock throughout the United States. About a third was dried for long-distance transportation.

Because brewers' yeast is one of the richest natural sources of vitamins of the B complex group and is rich in nutritive proteins, the industry, in co-operation with U.S. War Food administration and the National Research council, set up a program for intensified processing and drying of this yeast for use as a concentrated food for the armed forces and war workers and for the Allies overseas.

Moderation and Law Observance.—The war and navy departments reiterated their policy of making mild beer available in the post exchanges and canteens at army and navy bases and opposed efforts to prohibit beer to the armed forces. The U.S. Office of War Information made a coast-to-coast survey of drinking conditions in and around army camps in 1943 and reported:

(1) There is not excessive drinking among troops, and drinking does not constitute a serious problem.
(2) Sale of 3.2 beer in post exchanges and training camps is a positive factor in army sobriety.
(3) No American army in all history has been so orderly.

The industry's army and navy co-operation program, initiated with the enactment of Selective Service in 1940, was intensified in 1943. Sponsored by the Brewing Industry foundation, the program enlisted the aid of brewers, wholesalers, retailers and their associations for co-operation with military and civil authorities in maintaining wholesome conditions where beer was sold, particularly in the vicinity of military posts. The war and navy departments officially advised commanding officers of posts and stations to make use of the program wherever conditions required it. (*See also* LIQUORS, ALCOHOLIC.)   (H. HY.)

Bricker, John William

(1893–   ), U.S. politician, was born Sept. 6 in Madison county, Pleasant township, O. He was graduated from Ohio State university, 1916, and took his law degree there in 1920. During World War I, he served as a 1st lieutenant in the U.S. army.

Upon his return to civilian life he entered public service as solicitor for Grandview Heights, O., 1920–28, and was assistant attorney general of Ohio, 1923–27. In 1929 he became a member of the public utilities commission, serving in that capacity until 1932; he was attorney general for Ohio, 1933–37. Elected governor of Ohio in 1939, he was twice re-elected to the same office. Bricker announced in Nov. 1943 his candidacy for the Republican nomination for president. At the same time he also declared that he did not intend to seek a fourth term as governor of Ohio.

Bridge, Contract: *see* CONTRACT BRIDGE.

Bridges.

The world's longest spans of the various types in 1943 are listed in the table.

World's Longest Spans

Type	Bridge	Location	Year	Span
Cable Suspension .	Golden Gate	San Francisco	1937	4,200 ft.
Eyebar Suspension	Florianópolis	Brazil	1926	1,114
Self-Anchored Suspension	Cologne-Mülheim	Germany	1929	1,033
Cantilever	Quebec	Canada	1917	1,800
Steel Arch	Kill van Kull	New York City	1931	1,652
Steel Fixed Arch . .	Rainbow	Niagara Falls	1941	950
Concrete Arch . .	Sando	Sweden	1943	866
Continuous Truss .	Duisburg	Germany	1935	839
Simple Truss . . .	Metropolis	Ohio river	1916	720
Wichert Truss . .	Homestead	Pittsburgh	1937	533½
Continuous Girder .	Mangfall	Germany	1935	354
Vertical Lift . . .	Cape Cod canal	Massachusetts	1935	544
Swing Span	Fort Madison	Mississippi river	1927	525
Bascule	Sault Ste. Marie	Michigan	1914	336
Masonry Arch . .	Plauen	Saxony	1905	295

The outstanding structural achievement of 1943 was the completion of the Sando bridge over the Angerman river in Sweden, with a span length of 866 ft., which makes it the world's greatest concrete arch span. (*See* table.) The previous record was held by the concrete arch bridge at Esla, Spain, with a span length of 645 ft., completed in 1940. The Sando bridge, commenced in 1938, collapsed in its initial construction stage in 1939, with the loss of 18 lives, due to failure of the falsework centring during pouring of the concrete. Finally completed, it was dedicated in July 1943, by the crown prince of Sweden.

The Peace River bridge on the new Alaska highway in British Columbia was dedicated on Aug. 30, 1943, by American and Canadian officials. It is a suspension bridge of 930 ft. main span, costing $1,500,000. The concreting for the main piers had to be executed at temperatures 40 degrees below zero. The work of erecting the main towers went forward on the ice, which was several feet thick, but had to be completed before the break-up of the ice in April. The structure was completed in a total construction time of eight months, fighting ice and snow, wind and floods. The bridge was built under the direction of army engineers for the U.S. government, and was then turned over to Canada.

A lift span that goes down instead of up is in Iraq, spanning the Shatt-al-Arab (River of the Arabs) formed by the confluence of the Tigris and Euphrates rivers a few miles above the Persian Gulf. It was conceived and built (1942–43) by the royal engineers of the British army. The span, accommodating both rail and road traffic, is 92 ft. long and weighs 35 tons. It is lowered 20 ft. below the surface of the water, instead of being raised above it to permit ships to pass. The span is balanced by counterweights passing over the towers and is raised or lowered by handoperated hoists, one at each corner, with several men working each hoist. This unique design was adopted for economy, in order to dispense with the high towers ordinarily required.

The new $6,500,000 high level toll bridge over the Thames river, connecting New London with Groton, Conn., was opened in Feb. 1943. The structure, of 5,926 ft. total length, has a central

THE PEACE RIVER BRIDGE of the Alaska highway in British Columbia was completed in the summer of 1943

cantilever section 1,240 ft. long with 352½ ft. anchor arms and a channel span of 540 ft. of which 216 ft. is a simple suspended truss. Balanced erection over the main piers was used, so as to require a minimum of falsework. Opened at a time of greatly reduced traffic, the bridge faced an immediate deficit in its first months of operation.

The city of Los Angeles completed in 1943 a $5,000,000 viaduct project, crossing the Los Angeles river at Aliso street. The channel span is a 222-ft. fixed, reinforced concrete arch with six ribs. The reinforced concrete viaduct includes a rigid-frame span which is continuous on each end with an 80-ft. anchor span, all of hollow box-girder construction; also 19 rigid-frame approach spans. This is the most notable of numerous crossings of the Los Angeles river channel, which traverses the city's industrial district. It was financed jointly by city, county, state, the three railroad companies, and the U.S. Work Projects administration.

The War Production board, in July 1943, ordered the city of Chicago to halt construction of a $1,100,000 bridge, a double-leaf bascule, spanning the south branch of the Chicago river at South Canal street. The stop-construction order was issued because it appeared that existing bridges could serve the area for the duration of the war and that use of critical materials required for completion of the project was unwarranted during the emergency.

The new Coastal highway in Georgia has a deck bridge 2,382 ft. long, under construction 1942–43 at a cost of $550,000, in the vicinity of Savannah. The main river crossing of this bridge has two sets of 91-150-91-ft. span continuous plate girders, flanked by simple girder spans and 36 reinforced concrete deck girder approach spans. The approaches to the structure are over soft material that had to be removed by dragline immediately ahead of a pumped fill and embankment.

During 1942 and 1943, no large steel bridges were undertaken in the U.S. The emphasis was on timber substitutes, because of the shortage of steel caused by war requirements.

In Pennsylvania, a highway bridge with six 129-ft. truss spans of timber with steel gusset plates was constructed over a channel of the Ohio river near Pittsburgh. The structure is supported on timber piers carried on piles and rock-filled cribs. The timber cribs to encase the wood piling were floated into place and sunk in a swift current. The timber trusses were assembled on barges and erected one at a time by a floating rig. This bridge illustrates how timber may be combined with a small amount of steel to produce a semi-permanent structure. The spans are designed to carry 13-ton trucks and 30-ton street cars.

In Portland, Ore., to save steel, a highway bridge built in 1942 has spandrel-braced three-hinged timber arches of 88-ft. span. The deck is of planking, surfaced with asphaltic concrete.

For salvage of the steel and the wire, the cables and the towers of the wrecked Tacoma Narrows bridge were taken down in 1943. The 232-ft. span of the Central viaduct spanning the Cuyahoga river at Cleveland was blasted to fall shoreward and to carry the bridge toward land for easy salvage of the steel.

During 1943, the methods of the bridge engineer, both in types of span and methods of erection, dominantly invaded the field of wartime structures wherever large roof spans were required. At the Lakehurst, N.J., naval air station, the methods and equipment used for steel erection were adapted to the construction of a timber arch hangar, of 246-ft. arch span, 170 ft. high and 1,000 ft. long, for the housing of blimps. Fireproofed wood was used. At two other locations, the U.S. navy built large blimp hangars of steel arch framing, using a large number of steel arch trusses of 328-ft. span and 185-ft. rise. The arches are all-welded, except for the field splices. Scarcity of steel resulted in the use of glued, laminated timber arches of 120-ft. span for a drill hall at a navy training centre in Maryland, and similar laminated timber arches of 70-ft. span for a recreational centre at a west coast navy yard. Timber bowstring trusses of 160-ft. span were built to support the roof of a hangar under construction 1942–43 near an eastern city for the U.S. army. The arched top chords of the timber roof trusses were built up of laminated, glued and spiked small members, and the bottom chords were heavy timbers spliced for tension.

The annual Artistic Bridge awards of the American Institute of Steel Construction, also the annual student competition in artistic bridge design, were suspended in 1943 for the duration of the war.   (D. B. S.)

Bridgman, George B.
(1864–1943), U.S. artist and art teacher, was born Nov. 5 in Bing, County of Monk, Canada, the son of a portrait painter. He studied painting in the United States and in academies in Paris and later taught art in Buffalo. His work, *Constructive Anatomy*, published in 1920, was regarded as an anatomical bible by thousands of U.S. artists. Bridgman taught at the Art Students league, New York city, 1899–1943. He died in New Rochelle, N.Y., Dec. 16.

Briquettes, Fuel: *see* FUEL BRIQUETTES.
British Borneo: *see* BRITISH EMPIRE.

British Columbia.
The most westerly province of Canada, bordering on the Pacific ocean. The crown colonies of Vancouver Island (1849) and of British Columbia (1858), after uniting in 1866, entered the Canadian confederation in 1871 to form the province. Area, 366,255 sq.mi., of which 6,976 sq.mi. are water. The total population of 817,861 (1941) was divided between 443,394 urban and 374,467 rural dwellers. Vancouver (275,353), Victoria, the capital (44,068) and New Westminster (21,967) lie in the southwestern corner—not far from the United States border. After the dominion census of 1941, the population status of many British Columbia centres changed, owing to increase of war industries. Based on ration book distributions, the population of Greater Victoria (including the municipalities of Sannich, Oak Bay and Esquimalt) was 82,390 in 1943; New Westminster (including parts of adjoining communities) 36,778; Vancouver city 306,167, and Prince Rupert 11,926.

History.—In Jan. 1943, the Hon. H. G. T. Perry, chairman of the postwar rehabilitation council, presented an interim report on work of that committee. John Hart, premier and minister of finance, in his budget address stated that provincial revenues during 1941–42 had established a new all-time record and amounted to $38,763,546, a sum $2,509,610 greater than that collected during the previous year. Expenditures amounted to $31,342,923. Estimated revenue collections amounting to $31,-987,537 and expenditures therefrom of $31,792,446 were antici-

Economic Activity in British Columbia, 1941-43

	Unit	1941	1942	1943 (est.)
Agriculture:				
Total value of production .	$	58,577,539	73,748,235	77,500,000
Livestock	$	7,472,000	9,324,000	10,000,000
Poultry products	$	6,085,000	8,806,000	9,500,000
Dairy products	$	16,209,733	17,662,371	18,000,000
Fruits and vegetables .	$	11,782,076	16,686,089	19,000,000
Field crops	$	14,552,000	18,137,000	18,500,000
Miscellaneous	$		3,132,775	2,500,000
Fisheries:				
Total value of production .	$	31,732,037	38,059,559	32,500,000
Pack of canned salmon	case	2,295,433	1,814,297	1,257,217
Forestry:				
Total value of production .	$	119,920,000	124,720,000	125,000,000
Timber scaled	M.B.M.	3,522,750	3,014,488	3,050,000
Paper production . .	ton	351,241	327,474	310,000
Mining:				
Total value of production .	$	78,479,719	75,551,093	65,000,000
Internal trade:				
Index of wholesale sales . .	1935-39=100	155.0	174.1	190.0
Index of retail department store sales	1935-39=100	134.8	159.5	161.0
Railway freight loaded . .	ton	9,139,480	9,500,400	9,200,000
Consumption of electric power	000 kw.hr.	2,407,480	2,565,905	2,610,000
Construction	$000	14,509	10,201	8,000
Bank debits	$000	2,427,200	2,841,100	3,300,000
Index of employment . . .	1926=100	135.6	164.8	190.0

pated for the fiscal year 1943–44. A reduction of $12,329,857 in the gross debt of the province for the fiscal year ended March 31, 1943, was also announced by Mr. Hart. The remaining members of the provincial cabinet in 1943 included: G. S. Pearson, provincial secretary, labour and fisheries; R. L. Maitland, attorney-general; A. W. Gray, lands and municipal affairs; E. C. Carson, mines and trade and industry; H. G. T. Perry, education; H. Anscomb, public works and railways; K. C. MacDonald, agriculture.

A rural electrification committee was formed to survey and report upon the extent and condition of electrical services in the province, with particular reference to the servicing of rural areas. The Public Utilities commission presented to the lieutenant-governor-in-council its report on the operation of the British Columbia Electric Railway Co., Ltd., The company provides electricity, gas and transportation services in Vancouver, the lower mainland of British Columbia and in Victoria, and electricity and water services in other parts of the province. Resulting from the report, and as a temporary war measure, an order was made providing for free electric service for one month in Vancouver and lower mainland areas, and two months in other parts of the province served by the company.

Education.—During the school year ending June 30, 1942, 118,405 students were enrolled in the elementary (78,221), junior high (14,758), superior (3,242) and high (22,184) schools of the province. Teaching staffs comprised 2,643 teachers in elementary, 540 in the junior high and 1,041 teachers in superior and high schools.

Communication.—Provincial highways in 1942 totalled 21,595 mi. and included 8,966 mi. of surfaced, 10,069 mi. of improved earth and 2,567 mi. of unimproved earth roads. Railway mileage amounted to 3,883 mi. of single track in the same year. The total number of telephones, 162,815, included 56,847 on automatic switchboards.

Manufacturing, Agriculture, Mineral Production.—Although affected by the growing shortage of manpower and rising production costs, business activity in British Columbia during 1943 maintained the relatively high level of 1942. Production in the basic industries reached an estimated net value of $472,000,-000 in 1942 compared with $379,925,005 in 1941. Salaries and wages paid to employees in the leading industries were estimated at $302,892,946 in 1942, an increase of approximately $63,367,487 over the estimated 1941 gross pay roll of $239,525,459.

According to preliminary provincial estimates the net value of production in 1943 amounted to $77,500,000 (1942, $73,748,235) in agriculture; $32,500,000 in fisheries (1942, $38,059,559);

$125,000,000 in forestry (1942, $124,720,000) and $65,000,000 in mining (1942, $75,551,093). (W. A. C.)

British East Africa.

Under this heading are grouped British colonial territories on the east coast of Africa, of which certain essential statistics are given in the table. *See* BRITISH EMPIRE for population, capital towns, status and governors. (*See also* RHODESIA.)

The East African governments in 1943 were mainly concerned with questions of manpower supply and production. The increasing prosperity of some sections of the population gave rise to fears of inflation. Native producers benefited from large sums paid regularly in allowances from thousands of Africans in military service. The cost of living had risen considerably for all sections of the community. East African troops were serving in Ceylon as well as in Africa and Madagascar, after taking a distinguished part in the victorious African campaigns. Owing to manpower shortage, recruiting for military service practically stopped.

Kenya.—The colonial office announced projects for development involving an expenditure of £20,000,000, all of which, with the exception of a loan of £500,000, would be in the form of grants under the Colonial Development and Welfare act. The scheme involved measures for soil conservation, African housing, water supplies, agricultural and educational projects, reafforestation and reclamation of tsetse fly areas. The colony in addition was preparing a five-year construction program to cost another £2,000,000 chiefly concerned with increased school and hospital accommodation. Kenya was now the world's principal source of pyrethrum seed; 20,000 lb. was sent to Russia to replant war-devastated Caucasian fields, 10,000 lb. to Brazil at the request of the U.S.A. Board of Economic Warfare. The British ministry of supply guaranteed to purchase the pyrethrum crop until 1947. Food rationing was introduced. Conscription of African labour was reintroduced for the sisal industry, after suspension when the food shortage was acute, and to supply labour for the pyrethrum

and rubber industries; and a system of rationing labour was under consideration to give priority to the war effort. European women aged 25 to 40 were being called up for national service.

Uganda.—The colony celebrated its 50th year of British rule. As in Kenya the war continued to bring prosperity to the native people. The British government agreed to buy the cotton crop until the end of the war.

Tanganyika.—The British ministry of supply sent a rubber expert to advise on the production of native rubber. Many old plantations were revived and research was undertaken at the Amani research station. An American naval sisal commission was sitting in Dar-es-Salaam and the U.S. authorities urged the need for greater production of this essential crop. The government undertook extensive measures for tsetse fly control. A survey of unworked coalfields was being carried out.

Zanzibar.—The clove industry again showed a record export. Zanzibar and also Mauritius sent students to be trained as social workers at the London school of economics.

Somaliland.—The military government undertook famine relief measures in the Gorama district with the aid of a specially recruited labour battalion and instituted searches for new water supplies. Good rains improved grazing in October. After a Durbar held by the governor, combatant tribes were reconciled and pardons granted to persons involved in extensive thefts of camels in 1941.

Nyasaland.—Restricted shipping facilities caused a set-back in trade. The shortage of imported goods considerably increased costs and offset the increased purchasing power of the African population. The production of plantation rubber and the collection of wild rubber increased.

Mauritius.—Over a third of the cultivated lands in the island were under food crops as a result of a drive, aided by Jewish refugees, to increase cultivation. Relatively large numbers of Mauritians were serving abroad with the armed forces.

Seychelles.—Coco-nut oil, a new export, was to be exported at the rate of five tons a month from October. (J. L. K.)

British East Africa

Territory and Area in sq.mi.	Principal Products	Imports and Exports Merchandise (in thousand £)	Road, Rail and Shipping	Revenue and Expenditure (in thousand £)	Education: Elementary and Secondary
KENYA 224,960	(1940 exports) coffee 165,974 cwt. (£406,283); sisal 23,748 tons; pyrethrum 97,720 cwt.; gold 104,015 oz.	(1941) imp. 8,085; exp. 4,739	(1937) rds. arterial, 3,160 mi.; rlys. 1,290 mi.; shpg. cleared 2,158,767 net tons	(1940) rev. 4,111; exp. 4,064	(1937) Europ.: schls., 35, schlrs., 2,091; African: schls., 52, schlrs., 4,593; Indian: schls., 7,635; mission schls. 100
MAURITIUS 720 (dependencies, 87)	(1939 metric tons) sugar 229,457; copra 1,600	(1940) imp. Rs. 37,932; exp. Rs. 32,833	(1939) rds. 700 mi.; rly. 141 mi.; shpg. cleared 776,454 net tons	(1940–41) rev. Rs. 18,342; exp. Rs. 18,816	(1938) schls., 126, schlrs., 39,952
NYASALAND 33,374	(1939 metric tons) tobacco 6,600; tea 5,100	(1941) imp. 968.3; exp. 1,296.8	(1939) rds. main, 1,852 mi.; rly. 289 mi.	(1940) rev. 909.7; exp. 1,002.0	(1939) elem.: Europ.: schls., 4, schlrs., 117; African: schls., 4,279, schlrs., 204,761
SEYCHELLES 156	(1939 metric tons) export: copra 4,700; cinnamon leaf oil 67.3	(1940) imp. Rs. 1,090; exp. Rs. 1,181	(1939) 60 mi. of 1st class cart rd.	(1940) rev. Rs. 694; exp. Rs. 712	(1939) elem. schls., 26, schlrs., 3,105; sec. schls., 3, schlrs., 415
BRITISH SOMALILAND 67,936	(1939) export: gums and resins, 10,861 cwt.; skins, number, 1,952,512	(1941–42) imp. 636; exp. 191	(1938) rds. for wheeled traffic, c. 2,000 mi.	(1941–42) rev. 216; exp. 189	(1938) elem.: govt. schls., 2, schlrs., 121; private-aided schls., 14, schlrs., 514
TANGANYIKA 342,706	(1941 exports) coffee 13,667 tons (£447,977); sisal 75,195 tons	(1941) imp. 3,656; exp. 5,680; re-exp. 664	(1939) rds. 2,927 mi.; rly. 1,377 mi.; shpg. cleared 3,077,951 net tons	(1941) rev. 2,675; exp. 2,550	(1938) elem.: Europ.: schls., 19, schlrs., 934; Indian: schls., 67, schlrs., 5,128; African: schls., 1,014, schlrs., 76,360
UGANDA 86,301	(1940 exports) coffee 343,016 cwt. (£469,495); cotton 54,206 tons (£3,760,109)	(1941) imp. 2,346; exp. 5,711	(1938) rds. 7,488 mi.; rly. 332 mi.	(1941) rev. 2,178; exp. 1,938	(1938) elem.: schls., 300, schlrs., 34,232; sec.: schls., 22, schlrs., 1,250
ZANZIBAR (640) and PEMBA (380)	(exports) cloves (1941) 329,823 cwt.; copra (1940) 184,890 cwt.	(1941) imp. 1,038; exp. 1,272; re-exp. 278	(1939) rds. (Z.) 151 mi.; (P.) 71 mi.	(1941) rev. 565; exp. 481	(1938) elem.: schlrs. (govt. schls.) 2,428, (private schls.) 2,930

British Empire. The governments of the British empire and the governors and premiers were as follows as of Dec. 31, 1943 (for British empire territories under military occupation during 1943 other than those indicated in the table, *see* WORLD WAR II and articles under individual territorial headings):

Country	Area Sq. miles (approx.)	Population (000's omitted) (est. Dec. 1939)	Capital	Status	Governors and Premiers
Europe					
Great Britain and Northern Ireland	93,991	47,735	London	Kingdom	George VI, King-Emperor. *Prime Minister* of Great Britain: Winston Churchill. Governor of Northern Ireland: The Duke of Abercorn. *Prime Minister* of Northern Ireland: Capt. Sir Basil Brooke.
Channel Islands	75	96	St. Helier / St. Peter Port	Kingdom of Great Britain and N. Ireland	*Jersey:* Under enemy occupation (German). *Guernsey:* Under enemy occupation (German).
Eire	26,601	2,963‡	Dublin	Dominion	*President:* Dr. Douglas Hyde. *Prime Minister:* Eamon de Valera.
Gibraltar	2	20	Gibraltar	Colony	Maj. Gen. Sir F. N. M. MacFarlane.
Isle of Man	227	49	Douglas	Kingdom of Great Britain and N. Ireland	Vice-Adm. Lord Granville.
Malta	122	270	Valletta	Colony	General Lord Gort.
Asia					
Aden, Perim, etc.	80	48	Aden	Colony	} Sir J. Hathorn Hall.
Aden Protectorate	112,000	600		Protectorate	
Bahrein Islands	213	120	Manama	Protectorate	Ruler: Sheikh Sir Hamad bin 'Isa al Khalifah.
Borneo:					
State of North Borneo	29,500	302	Sandakan	Protectorate	Under enemy occupation (Japanese)
Brunei	2,226	39	Brunei	Protectorate	" " "
Sarawak	50,000	c. 450	Kuching	Protectorate	Rajah: Sir Charles Vyner Brooke.
Burma	261,610	16,824†	Rangoon	Member of the British Commonwealth of Nations	Sir R. Dorman-Smith.
Ceylon	25,332	5,981*	Colombo	Colony	Sir A. Caldecott.
Cyprus	3,572	382*	Nicosia	Colony	Sir C. C. Woolley.
Hongkong	391	1,050	Victoria	Colony	Sir M. A. Young.
Indian Empire	1,575,187	388,800†	Delhi	Member of the British Commonwealth of Nations	Emperor of India: H.I.M. George VI. *Secretary of State:* L. S. Amery. *Viceroy and Governor General:* Field Marshal Lord Wavell.
Malaya:					
The Straits Settlements	1,357	1,435†	Singapore	Colony	Sir Shenton Thomas.
Federated Malay States	27,540	2,212†		Protectorates	The Rulers of Perak, Selangor, Negri Sembilan, and Pahang.
Unfederated Malay States	24,728	1,912§		Protectorates	The Rulers of Johore, Kedah, Perlis, Kelantan, Brunei, and Trengganu.
Palestine	10,100	1,545*	Jerusalem	Mandated territory	Sir H. A. MacMichael, High Commissioner.
Trans-Jordan	34,740	350	Amman	Mandated territory	Emir Abdullah ibn Hussein.
Africa					
Kenya Colony and Protectorate	224,960	3,500	Nairobi	Colony and protectorate	Sir Henry Moore.
Uganda Protectorate	93,981	3,830*	Entebbe	Protectorate	Sir Charles Dundas.
Zanzibar	1,020	250	Zanzibar	Colony and protectorate	Sir Henry Guy Pilling (Brit. Res.).
Mauritius	807	419	Port Louis	Colony	Sir Donald Mackenzie-Kennedy.
Nyasaland	47,949	1,680	Blantyre	Protectorate	Sir E. C. Richards.
St. Helena and Ascension	81	5	Jamestown	Colony	Major W. B. Gray.
Seychelles	156	32	Victoria	Colony	W. M. Logan.
Somaliland Protectorate	68,000	350	Berbera	Protectorate	Under military occupation (British).
Basutoland Protectorate	11,716	590	Maseru	Protectorate	Lord Harlech.
Bechuanaland Protectorate	275,000	275	Mafeking, in Cape Province	Protectorate	Lord Harlech.
Southern Rhodesia	150,333	1,434*	Salisbury	Self-governing colony	Hon. Sir E. Baring.
Northern Rhodesia	290,323	1,400	Lusaka	Colony	Sir John Waddington.
Swaziland	6,705	160	Mbabane	Protectorate	Lord Harlech.
Union of South Africa	472,550	10,521†	Seat of Government, Pretoria / Seat of Legislature, Cape Town	Dominion	M. J. de Wet. *Premier:* Field Marshal J. C. Smuts.
South-West Africa	323,000	321†	Windhoek	Mandated territory	Dr. D. G. Conradie, Administrator.
Nigeria, including British Cameroons	372,674	19,773	Lagos	Colony and protectorate and mandated territory	A. Richards.
Gambia	3,999	205	Bathurst	Colony	H. R. Blood.
Gold Coast, including British Togoland	91,843	3,572*	Accra	Colony and protectorate and mandated territory	Sir Alan Burns.
Sierra Leone and Protectorate	27,926	2,000	Freetown	Colony and protectorate	Major Sir H. C. Stevenson.
Anglo-Egyptian Sudan	967,500	6,362†	Khartoum	Condominium	Sir H. Huddleston.
Tanganyika Territory	374,000	5,284	Dar-es-Salaam	Mandated territory	Sir W. E. F. Jackson.
America					
Bahamas	4,404	66*	Nassau	Colony	H.R.H. the Duke of Windsor.
Barbados	167	198‡	Bridgetown	Colony	Sir H. Grattan Bushe.
Bermudas	19	32	Hamilton	Colony	Lord Burghley.
British Guiana	80,500	341	Georgetown	Colony	Sir G. J. Lethem.
British Honduras	8,598	59	Belize	Colony	Sir J. A. Hunter.
Canada	3,729,665	11,505†	Ottawa	Dominion	Earl of Athlone. *Premier:* W. L. Mackenzie King.

*Pop. est. 1940.   †Pop. est. 1941.   ‡Pop. est. 1942.   §Pop. est. 1940, excluding Brunei.   (Continued on next page)

Country	Area Sq. miles (approx.)	Population (000's omitted) (est. Dec. 1939)	Capital	Status	Governors and Premiers
America (Continued)					
Falkland Islands and Dependencies . .	4,618	3	Port Stanley	Colony	A. W. Cardinall.
Jamaica and Dependencies . .	4,846	1,198‡	Kingston	Colony	Sir John Huggins.
Leeward Islands	422	93‡	St. John (Antigua). . .	Colony	Sir D J. Jardine.
(Antigua, St. Kitts-Nevis, Montserrat, and the Virgin Islands)					
Newfoundland and Labrador .	c. 152,000	295	St. John's	Colony, Constitution suspended	Vice-Adm. Sir H. T. Walwyn.
Trinidad and Tobago	1,980	502‡	Port of Spain	Colony	Sir Bede Clifford.
Windward Islands	825	275‡	St. George's (Grenada) .	Colony	Sir Arthur Grimble.
(Grenada, Dominica, St. Vincent, and St. Lucia)					
Oceania					
Commonwealth of Australia . .	2,974,581	7,137†	Canberra	Dominion	Brig. Gen. Lord Gowrie. *Premier:* J. Curtin.
Fiji	7,055	215	Suva	Colony	Sir P. E. Mitchell.
New Zealand	103,415	1,640‖	Wellington	Dominion	Marshal of R. A. F. Sir Cyril Newall. *Premier:* Peter Fraser.
Papua	90,540	280	Port Moresby	Part of Commonwealth of Australia	H. L. Murray, Administrator.
Pacific Islands	c. 11,900	162		Colonies and Protectorate . .	Sir P. E. Mitchell.
New Hebrides	5,700	50	Vila	Condominium	Sir P. E. Mitchell.
New Guinea, Territory of . . .	93,000	675*	Rabaul	Mandated territory	Brig. Gen. W. Ramsay McNicoll.
Western Samoa	1,133	61*	Apia	Mandated territory	A. C. Turnbull, Act. Administrator.
Nauru	8	3		Mandated territory	Lt.-Col. F. R. Chalmers.

*Pop. est. 1940.   †Pop. est. 1941.   ‡Pop. est. 1942.   ‖Pop. est. 1943.

British Guiana.

A British crown colony in northeastern South America. Governor (1943): Sir Gordon Lethem. The area is 89,480 sq.mi. The population (1931 census: 310,933) was officially estimated at 354,219 as of Dec. 31, 1942. East Indians constituted the largest single population element (42.7%), being proportionately greater than in any other American area except Surinam and numerically more than in any except Trinidad. Negroes aggregated 38.2% and mixed races 12.3%.

The chief cities are Georgetown, the capital (pop. est. 71,160) and New Amsterdam (pop. est. 10,137). Under the "destroyer-base agreement" of 1940 the United States continued to maintain naval air and patrol bases in the colony in 1943.

History.—During 1943 British Guiana continued to feel the ill effects of wartime disruption of trade and shipping, although less so than her sister colonies in the West Indies. The situation was aggravated by prolonged rains and floods, with January-March rainfall the heaviest recorded since 1880. Offsetting this was an increasing attention to long-term and postwar development. Thus, imperial loans and grants were made for drainage and irrigation projects totalling £118,584, extension of the cattle industry, an airport at Georgetown, land settlement and other purposes. Moreover, the colonial office in London indicated that a "considerable number of large-scale proposals" for British Guiana development were under discussion. The drainage and irrigation development, involving an expenditure of £118,584, was expected to increase materially the colony's rice production.

Education.—There were 246 primary schools (enrolment 55,076), including 60 in remote areas, and seven government-aided secondary schools. In 1943 an imperial grant of £10,450 was made for the expansion and development of secondary education in the colony.

Finance.—The monetary unit, the British Guiana dollar, tied to sterling at 4.8665 to 1, is normally equivalent to the United States dollar (1943 exchange rate: approximately 83 cents U.S.). The colony's maximum income tax rate (25%) was exceeded in 1943 in only two other British American colonies.

Trade.—Under wartime conditions some statistical data on production and trade, particularly of strategic materials such as bauxite, were not made public or were delayed.

In 1941 export values totalled $19,585,033 (B.G. dollars), an increase of 28.6% over 1940 and 33.2% over 1939. Sugar and its derivatives made up 47.1% (1939: 55.3%), followed by rice, balata and timber; unlisted commodities (bauxite, diamonds, gold, etc.) together comprised 36%. Textiles, other manufactures, and foodstuffs were the leading imports.

Import values in 1941 were $17,191,692 (B.G. dollars), 21% more than in 1940 and 68% more than in 1939. The increases, however, reflected swollen unit values more than greater volume. Canada supplied 35.0% (1939: 18%), Great Britain 23.5% (1939: 39%), the United States 21.8% (1939: 14%). These same countries were the leading customers.

Communication.—External communication, maritime and air, is normally adequate. There is no practicable external communication by land, although a highway from Brazil was under study in 1943. Within the colony, railways (79½ mi.) are confined to the coastal area, as are most of the 322 mi. of highway. Communication with the interior in 1943 was mostly by trail and navigable rivers.

Agriculture and Forest Products.—Sugar is the colony's economic mainstay, and an estimated third of the population depend directly on it. It ordinarily provides the bulk of export values. Rice production, both for local consumption and for export was being stimulated in 1943. Forest products include balata (1941: 659,190 lb.) and various hardwoods, notably the greenheart, found only in British Guiana.

Mineral Production.—War demands for bauxite were unofficially estimated in 1943 to have more than doubled the 1939 production of 476,013 tons. Diamonds (1940: 33,351 carats) and gold (1940: 35,745 oz.) are also important.

BIBLIOGRAPHY.—*West Indies Year Book, 1943; Crown Colonist* (London, monthly); *Canada-West Indies magazine* (Montreal, monthly).

British Honduras.

A crown colony of Great Britain, located on the Atlantic side of Central America east of Guatemala, north of Honduras, and south of Yucatan (Mexico). Area: 8,598 sq.mi. A portion of the eastern boundary is still disputed by Guatemala although the claim has been suspended for the duration of the war. Pop. (1942 est.) 61,068; in the last census (1931) it was 51,347. The capital is

Belize (1931 pop., 16,687); other settlements are Corozal (2,700), Benque Viejo (1,500), El Cayo (1,500). Governor in 1943: Sir John Adams Hunter.

History.—During 1943 British Honduras was affected by the war largely through shortages in shipping. A foresighted policy of licensing imports, started in 1941, had enabled the government to bring about the importation of a stock of essential commodities, with the result that British Honduras was better supplied than most British Caribbean colonies as late as the summer of 1942. The cost of living steadily increased during 1943, and rationing of rice, a staple article in the diet of the poorer classes, was necessary. Limits on profits were also imposed.

Some shortage of labour occurred in the colony since more than 3,000 workers were employed at the Canal Zone, and an additional 600 were taken into the United Kingdom services.

Education.—There were about 80 church schools and half that many private schools in operation, with an enrolment of more than 10,000 students. Most schools receive financial aid from the government.

Finance.—The monetary unit is the British Honduras dollar, normally equivalent to the United States dollar (1943 exchange value 68 cents U.S.; this rate is nominal since the currency is restricted to the colony). It is tied to the pound sterling at 4.8665 to 1. The public debt in 1941 was $12,166,756. Government revenue in 1941 was $1,370,900, and expenditure $1,378,100.

Trade and Resources.—Exports for 1941 were valued at $3,357,546 (British Honduran currency); imports at $3,751,950, with a fourth of the imports re-exported. Imports are largely manufactured articles, textiles, foodstuffs and machinery, with the United States supplying about 43% in 1941. Exports are normally 80% forest products, the remainder agricultural; in 1941 about 63% of exports went to the United States. The mahogany cut for 1942 was estimated at 5,000,000 bd.ft. (1941: 7,000,000 bd.ft.). In 1941 there were 337,499 stems of bananas exported, 250 tons of sugar (1941-42 quota year), citrus fruits and fruit products to the amount of 11,526,000 lb., 2,444,508 coconuts, 362,811 lb. of copra and 1,564,337 lb. of chicle.

Communications.—In normal times Belize is connected with other ports by steamer service, and by air to Honduras and Mexico. Most transportation within the colony is by boat. Approximately 150 mi. of road exist; a former 25 mi. railway has been converted into a road. (*See also* WEST INDIES, BRITISH.)

BIBLIOGRAPHY.—*West Indies Year Book, 1941-1942*; *Crown Colonist* (London, monthly); *South American Handbook, 1943.*   (D. RD.)

British Isles: *see* GREAT BRITAIN & NORTHERN IRELAND, UNITED KINGDOM OF.

British Legion.
This national organization of men and women of all the fighting services drew into honorary membership 300,000 members of the forces serving in the British Isles or overseas in World War II. A hundred thousand of the new generation of sailors, soldiers and airmen discharged in the course of hostilities became full members and 1,750 of these were serving on branch committees. Working through the ministry of pensions advisory committee and its house of commons branch, the Legion had in 1943 succeeded in getting independent pensions appeal tribunals set up and won sub-

stantial improvements in pensions regulations. Its next objective was a preference in employment after the war for those who served, similar to the pledge given by the government after World War I. The Legion's rehabilitation work was extended during the year by the acquisition of Nayland Hall sanatorium and workshops, near Colchester, for women discharged from the women's auxiliary services suffering from tuberculosis. Its women's section, with the record number of 1,927 branches, opened a convalescent home at Knaresborough, near Harrogate. Brig.-General E. R. Fitzpatrick became chairman of the Legion and Lady Apsley M.P. was re-elected chairman of the women's section.

British Malaya: *see* FEDERATED MALAY STATES; STRAITS SETTLEMENTS; UNFEDERATED MALAY STATES; WORLD WAR II.

British Pacific Islands: *see* PACIFIC ISLANDS, BRITISH.

British Possessions in the Mediterranean: *see* MEDITERRANEAN, BRITISH POSSESSIONS IN THE.

British Somaliland: *see* BRITISH EAST AFRICA.

British South African Protectorates.
Under this heading are grouped the British protectorates in the south of Africa, of which certain essential statistics are given in the table. *See* BRITISH EMPIRE for population, capital towns, status and governors. For other territories of the British empire in the south of Africa, *see* SOUTH

British South African Protectorates

Territory and Area in sq.mi.	Principal Products (in metric tons)	Imports and Exports (in thousand £)	Road and Rail	Revenue and Expenditure (in thousand £)	Education: Elementary and Secondary
BASUTOLAND 11,716	(1938-1939) wheat, 33,100 maize, 68,800	(1940) imp. 938.3 exp. 461.7	rds. 502 mi.	(1939-40) rev. 392.9 exp. 368.2	(1939) Elem. schls.: native, 848; other schls., 69; total schlrs., 82,941
BECHUANALAND c. 275,000	gold (1940) 560 kg. silver (1938) 1,127 oz.	(1940) imp. 440.5 exp. 445.8	rds. 2,048 mi. rly. 396 mi.	(1939-40) rev. 188.0 exp. 225.5	(1940) Europ., schls., 11, scholars 189; native schls. 139, scholars 15,906
SWAZILAND 6,705	(1938) gold, 1,246 oz. tin, 174 tons maize, 5,900	In customs union with South Africa	rds. 654 mi.	(1939-40) rev. 109.8 exp. 159.8	(1940) Europ., schls., 10, schlrs., 377; native schls. 219, scholars 8,263

AFRICA, UNION OF.

History.—The protectorates had in 1943 more than 40,000 men in the Auxiliary Military Pioneer corps, many of them serving in the Mediterranean theatre of war. Large sums were subscribed by the native people for comforts for their serving men, and in Basutoland the native government imposed a war levy for this purpose of £5 a head on chiefs and 10s. on the ordinary taxpayer.

Chief Griffith of Basutoland died leaving a son, a minor, and was succeeded by his wife Chieftainess Mantseho as regent paramount.

The encouragement given by the Empire Cotton-Growing corporation to cotton growing in Swaziland produced successful results.

In Bechuanaland an irrigation scheme was completed and named after a local chief the Bathoen II irrigation dam. Its capacity is 390,000,000 gal.

Part of the production from the irrigated area was to provide a free meal daily for the school children of a large area. (J. L. K.)

British-U.S. War Boards.
Combined Food Board (United States, United Kingdom and Canada).—Acting jointly, the president of the United States and the prime minister of Great Britain on June 9, 1942, authorized the creation of the Combined Food board to obtain a planned and expeditious utilization of the food resources of

the United Nations. In Oct. 1943, Canadian Prime Minister Mac-Kenzie King accepted membership on behalf of the government of Canada.

The board was established to investigate and formulate plans with regard to any question relating to supply, production, transportation, disposal, allocation or distribution, in or to any part of the world, of foods, agricultural materials from which foods are derived and equipment and non-food materials ancillary to the production of such foods and agricultural materials

The chairman of the board in 1943 was U.S. Secretary of Agriculture Claude R. Wickard. The U.S. member was Marvin Jones, war food administrator; the United Kingdom member was R. H. Brand, head of the British food mission; the Canadian member, J. G. Gardiner, Canadian minister of agriculture.

Combined Production and Resources Board (United States, Great Britain and Canada).

—The creation of the Combined Production and Resources board was announced by President Roosevelt June 9, 1942. The board was established by the president of the United States and the prime minister of Great Britain in order to complete the organization needed for the most effective use of the combined resources of the United States and the United Kingdom for the prosecution of the war. On Nov. 10, 1942, the board was expanded to include a Canadian member. The board was to utilize the Joint War Production staff in London, the Combined Raw Materials board, the Joint Aircraft committee and other combined or national agencies for war production.

Members for the United States in 1943 were Donald M. Nelson, chairman of the War Production board; Charles E. Wilson, executive vice chairman of the WPB (deputy member); W. L. Batt, vice chairman, International Supply of WPB (deputy member); Fredrick M. Eaton, Solicitor of the WPB (executive officer) and Philip D Reed, London representative of the lend-lease coordinator. Members for Great Britain were Oliver Lyttelton, minister of production; Sir Henry Self, representative of the minister of production (deputy member); T. H. Brand, representative of the war cabinet secretariat in London (executive officer) and P. Hayward, representative of the ministry of production (secretary). Members for Canada were C. D. Howe, minister of munitions and supply; Edward P. Taylor, Canadian representative of the department of munitions and supply (deputy member) and Sydney D. Pierce, representative of the department of munitions and supply, Washington office (executive officer). W. M. Black was executive director of the combined staff.

Combined Raw Materials Board (United States and Great Britain).

—The establishment of the Combined Raw Materials board was announced Jan. 26, 1942. The board was given a comprehensive responsibility for the planning of the raw materials effort of the two countries and for collaborating with the other United Nations to provide for the most effective utilization of all raw material resources at their disposal.

The activities of the board were to include over-all review of the supply and requirements position of the United Nations for the major critical and essential raw materials, allocation of supplies of scarce raw materials among the United Nations when necessary, recommendations aimed at expanding supplies and conserving the use of raw materials in short supply and coordinating the purchasing activities of the United States and Great Britain in foreign raw material markets.

Members of this board in 1943 were William L. Batt, United States member; Fredrick M. Eaton, deputy member and United States executive secretary; George Archer, deputy member and United Kingdom executive secretary. The United Kingdom full membership was vacant as of Nov. 1943.

Combined Shipping Adjustment Board (United States and Great Britain).

—Creation of the Combined Shipping Adjustment board was announced Jan. 26, 1942. The function of the board was to co-ordinate the work of the British ministry of war transport and the War Shipping administration.

Members for the United States in 1943 were Rear Admiral Emory S. Land, chairman of the U.S. Maritime Commission and administrator of the War Shipping administration and David E. Scoll, assistant to the administrator of the War Shipping administration (executive officer). Members for Great Britain were Sir Arthur Salter, head of the British Shipping mission in the United States, W. O Hart, British executive officer and Lord Leathers, administrator of war transportation in London.

Munitions Assignments Board (United States and Great Britain).

—This board's establishment was also announced Jan. 26, 1942 The United States section of the board, working in close collaboration with the corresponding London organization, maintained full information of the entire munitions resources of Great Britain and the United States and translated such resources into terms of combat forces and their material reserves. It submitted such statements to the combined chiefs of staff, keeping the estimate up to date in the light of war developments and variations in production achievements and prospects. It kept the combined chiefs of staff informed and recommended measures necessary that planned requirements programs may be in line with strategic policy, changing operations conditions in their effect on war material and the realities of production. The United States section was responsible for making assignments of stocks and production of finished war material to the United States and Great Britain and to others of the United Nations.

Members for the United States in 1943 were Harry L. Hopkins, chairman; Admiral J. M. Reeves; Rear Admiral W. R. Purnell; Rear Admiral O. C. Badger; Lt. Gen. Brehon B. Somervell; Maj. Gen. B M. Giles; Brig. Gen P. H. Tansey; Maj. Gen. J. H. Burns, executive and Capt. W. S Gubelmann, secretary. Members for Great Britain: Admiral Sir Percy Noble; Lt. Gen. G. N. Macready; Air Marshal Sir William L. Welsh and Wing Comdr. T. E H. Birley, secretary. (See also CANADIAN —U.S. WAR COMMITTEES.)

British West Africa.

Under this heading are grouped the British colonial territories on the west coast of Africa, for which certain essential statistics are given in the accompanying table. See BRITISH EMPIRE for population, capital towns, status and governors.

With the immediate danger of war removed from West Africa in 1943 the colonial governments of the four colonies were pressing ahead with plans for social and economic development. Advisers for development (Noel Hall) and town planning (Maxwell Fry) were appointed to the staff of the resident minister. Colonel Oliver Frederick Stanley, the secretary of state for the colonies, visited all four colonies during 1943 and discussed local problems with leading Africans and Europeans. On his return, Colonel Stanley stated in the house of commons that he had asked each territory to prepare plans which could be put into operation when the war ended, and if necessary finance could be found under the Colonial Development and Welfare act.

A commission of inquiry into higher education in West Africa, with three African members to represent Nigeria, the Gold Coast and Sierra Leone, was appointed with Colonel Walter Elliot as chairman. The commission was to work in liaison with Sir Cyril Asquith's commission concerned with higher education throughout the colonial empire. The British council established an organization to cover British West Africa, with headquarters in the Gold Coast under the direction of W. H. Macmillan. The council was to establish cultural institutions in each of the colonies. An

British West Africa

Territory and Area in sq. mi.	Principal Products	Imports & Exports (in thousand £)	Road, Rail & Shipping	Revenue & Expenditure (in thousand £)	Education: Elementary & Secondary 1938
NIGERIA (including British Mandate of Cameroons) 372,674	(exports, 1940) (metric tons) palm kernels 107,600 groundnuts 245,800	(1940) imp. 7,479 exp. 11,604	(1939) rds. 20,990 mi. rlys. 1,901 mi. shpg. cleared 1,790,019 net tons	(actual 1939-40) rev. 6,113 exp. 6,499	elem. and middle schools 565; scholars 25,067
GOLD COAST (including Ashanti, Northern Territories and British Mandate of Togoland) 91,843	(1939) cocoa 200,000 metric tons; gold production (1940) 27,568 kg.	(1941) imp. 6,137 exp. 5,979	(1940) rds. 2,366 mi. rly. 500 mi. shpg. cleared (1941) 1,548,772 net tons	(1941-42) rev. 5,542 exp. 5,035	elem. schools 927; scholars 83,824; sec. and higher educ. scholars 2,078
ST. HELENA (47) and ASCENSION ISLANDS (34)	(1939) export flax fibre 834 tons; tow 512 tons	(1940) imp. 51 exp. 30	(1939) rds. 62 mi.	(1940) rev. 33.7 exp 33.4	(1939) 810 scholars
GAMBIA 3,999	(export 1940) (metric tons) groundnuts 43,700	(1941) imp. 503 exp. 290	rds.(1939)869mi. shpg. cleared (1940) 445,244 net tons	(1941) rev. 247 exp. 208	(1940) elem. schools 7, scholars 1,725; sec. schools 4, scholars 200
SIERRA LEONE 27,926	(1940 [value]) diamonds £780,770 iron ore £493,269	(1941) imp. 3,814 exp. 1,593	(1940) rds. 836 mi. rly. 311 mi. shpg. entered (1938) 2,725,573 tons	(1941) rev. 1,282 exp. 1,109	elem. schools 253; scholars 30,851

important political move was the appointment of unofficial members, including Africans, to the executive councils in Nigeria and the Gold Coast. Much attention was paid to production of all kinds to increase the contributions of minerals and tropical produce, including rubber, to the Allied war effort. West African troops were serving in India, including the West African frontier force which had won distinction in the East African campaigns against the Italians. This was the first time that a British West African force had served overseas.

Nigeria.—Sir Arthur Richards, formerly governor of Jamaica, in Dec. 1943 succeeded Sir Bernard Bourdillon as governor. A government committee recommended the appointment of Africans to the administrative service following the example set by the Gold Coast. A labour advisory board on which commercial employers and employees were represented was appointed to effect an improvement in rates of pay.

Gold Coast.—A grant of £127,000 under the Colonial Development and Welfare act made possible the formation of an institute of West African arts, industries and social science at Achimota college. The development of Achimota toward full university status was to be considered by the Elliot commission. Much attention was paid to the improvement of educational facilities, including the pay and pensions of teachers. A new town council for Accra was to have a majority of elected members. Sir Ofori Atta, a leading paramount chief, died, and was succeeded by Chief Opoku Akyeampong. Investigations were being carried out into cocoa diseases, particularly the "swollen root" disease.

Sierra Leone.—Freetown harbour played a vital part in the Allied war effort and the European population of the town increased from 200 before the war to several thousand. Transport and harbour facilities were improved, and higher grade iron ore was shipped at the rate of 8,000 tons a tide. Colonial development and welfare grants were made for women's education, for scholarships for students to Great Britain, and for the improvement of Fourah Bay college. A number of African women teachers were sent to England for training.

Gambia.—The sum of £30,000 was granted under the Colonial Development and Welfare act for the improvement of Bathurst harbour. The educational system was reviewed and substantial assistance provided to improve the conditions of service of teachers. The British government agreed to purchase the groundnut crops for 1943-44. A scheme whereby grain was marketed under government control greatly benefited the community as a

whole.

St. Helena.—Colonial development and welfare grants were made for the improvement of women's education and the establishment of a public library in Jamestown. The increased demand for local produce owing to restrictions on imports led to a larger area of land being cultivated with assistance from the agricultural department.

(J. L. K.)

British West Indies: *see* WEST INDIES, BRITISH.
Broadcasting: *see* RADIO.

Bromine. The series of increased outputs that prevailed after 1933 and brought the production of bromine in the United States in 1941 to 34,159 short tons, from 14 plants, was broken in 1942 by a decline to 32,940 tons. The production of bromine as a by-product of the recovery of magnesium in sea water was expected to contribute a further increase in 1943.

(G. A. Ro.)

Brooke, Sir Alan Francis (1883–), British army officer, was born at Baguères de Bigorre, France, on July 23, the son of Sir Victor Brooke. After completing his studies at the royal military academy, Woolwich, he joined the royal field artillery in 1902. He was stationed in Ireland from 1902 to 1906, then India. At the outbreak of war in 1914 he went to France. Advancing rapidly, he was soon recognized as an authority on artillery and was a general staff officer of the royal artillery at the time of the armistice. After the war he joined the staff college, Camberley, and the imperial defense college, and from 1929 to 1932 he was commandant of the school of artillery. After duty at various other military posts he was appointed in 1939 commander in chief of the anti-aircraft command. When Germany invaded the Low Countries on May 10, 1940, Brooke was commander of the B.E.F. 2nd corps in France. His guarding of the British retreat from Flanders was an important factor in the successful evacuation at Dunkirk. Back in England early in June, he hastily reassembled British military man power for the expected nazi invasion and prepared a formidable series of defense zones. For his work in Flanders he was knighted, and on July 19, 1940, he was appointed to succeed Sir Edmund Ironside as commander in chief of the home forces. On Nov. 18, 1941, Brooke succeeded Sir John Greer Dill as chief of the British imperial general staff. He accompanied Churchill to Washington in June 1942, to Moscow in Aug. 1942, and to conferences in Washington, Quebec, Cairo and Tehran in 1943.

Brooke, Sir Basil (1888–), British statesman, was born June 9, heir to a baronetcy established in 1822 and nephew to Gen. Sir Alan Brooke, who distinguished himself in both World Wars I and II. Educated at Winchester and Sandhurst, he entered the army and served throughout World War I, receiving the Military Cross and the Croix de Guerre with Palm. In 1929 he was elected to the Northern Ireland parliament, and in 1933 he became minister of agriculture and privy councillor. He resigned from the former post in 1941, when he became minister of commerce. On May 1, 1943, he succeeded John M. Andrews as prime minister of Northern Ireland, still retaining his commerce portfolio. Well known for his hostility to Irish Catholics, he announced soon after his appointment that Northern Ireland planned a program of closer cooperation with Great Britain in the war effort.

Brookings Institution.

The institution in 1943 conducted a program of research which was in large measure related to the war effort and postwar problems. Book-length studies included the following: *World Minerals and World Peace*, by C. K. Leith, J. W. Furness and Cleona Lewis, dealing with the distribution of essential minerals and its bearing on the maintenance of world order; *The New Philosophy of Public Debt*, by Harold G. Moulton, analyzing the belief that continuous deficit spending is essential to prosperity; and *Belgian Banking and Banking Theory*, by B. S. Chlepner, the development of Belgian banking in the light of modern theory The series, *Price Making in a Democracy*, by Edwin G. Nourse, was continued by the publication of four additional pamphlets. Other pamphlet studies included the following: *Is There Enough Manpower?* by Harold W Metz; *Collapse or Boom at the End of the War?* by H. G. Moulton and Karl T. Schlotterbeck; *Do We Want a Federal Sales Tax?* by Charles O. Hardy; *Rationing and Price Control in Great Britain*, by Jules Backman; *The Price Control and Subsidy Program in Canada*, by Jules Backman; *How Nazi Germany Has Controlled Business*, by L. Hamburger. Because of the war, the usual fellowships for advanced study were not granted.

(H. G Mo.)

Brown, Prentiss Marsh

(1889–   ), U.S. attorney and public administrator, was born June 18 at St. Ignace, Mich. He attended Albion college and the University of Illinois. Admitted to the Michigan bar in 1914, Brown embarked upon a career in law, business and politics. He ran as Democratic candidate for congress in 1924 and for the Michigan supreme court in 1928, although unsuccessfully on both occasions. Brown was elected to congress in 1933 and was elected to the senate for the 1937–43 term. While in the senate he became chairman of the democratic senatorial campaign committee and chairman of the special committee on taxation of governmental securities and salaries, 1938–40 He sponsored the important Price Control act of April 1942, and the Price Stabilization act of Oct. 1942. When he was defeated for re-election to the senate, he accepted President Roosevelt's request to succeed Leon Henderson as administrator of the Office of Price Administration in Jan. 1943. Brown warned the senate that federal subsidies were necessary to prevent price rises. After several months on the job, he was prevented by illness from actively guiding the OPA and resigned on Oct. 21, 1943.

Brozovich or Broz, Josip (Tito)

(1892–   ), Yugoslav guerrilla leader, was born near Zagreb in Croatia. He became a metal-worker, then served in the Austro-Hungarian army early in World War I In 1915 he went over to the Russians, along with thousands of his Slavic comrades. After the Russian revolution he fought in the Red army during the civil war. When he returned to Croatia in 1923, he became a labour leader and was soon imprisoned as a communist On his release he became leader of the underground labour movement, assuming the pseudonym of Tito.

After the German conquest of Yugoslavia in April 1941, Tito organized a band of guerrilla fighters. Many of the successes claimed by Col. Draja Mikhailovitch's (*q.v.*) guerrillas were

ANNOUNCEMENT OF GERMAN REWARD of 100,000 marks for the capture, dead or alive, of Josip Brozovich (Drug Tito), Yugoslav Partisan leader. It appeared in the Belgrade *Novo Vreme* July 21, 1943

said to have been won by Tito's partisans. Strong political differences led to discord and even armed conflict between the two groups. In an attempt to reconcile these factions, Allied aid was given to both. As the partisans increased in strength and ability to harass the enemy, a larger share of the supplies went to them. At the end of 1943 Tito was reputed to have a force of 250,000—more than ten times the size of Mikhailovitch's army.

Brunei: *see* BRITISH EMPIRE.

Bryn Mawr College.

A resident college for women at Bryn Mawr, Pa. President in 1943: Katharine E. McBride. Bryn Mawr, while carrying on its full academic program in 1943, placed special emphasis on three interdepartmental courses for the study of postwar problems: (1) international administration and reconstruction; (2) community organization and reconstruction; (3) language for reconstruction. All three included courses in history, languages, English composition, science, philosophy, economics, geography, international relief and administration and problems of the peace. The course in international administration also required advanced history, including research training on a special region, statistics, comparative government and international organization, public administration and accounting. The course in community organization included two years work in sociology, one in psychology and statistics and one summer of field work, and one spent in a language camp. The course in language for reconstruction, in addition to French, German and another language, with two years residence in one of the language houses on the campus, offered studies in either comparative government or international organization. For statistics of enrolment, faculty, library volumes, etc., *see* UNIVERSITIES AND COLLEGES.   (K. E. M.)

Bubonic Plague: *see* PLAGUE, BUBONIC AND PNEUMONIC.

Buckwheat.

Production of buckwheat in the United States in 1943 was estimated by the United States department of agriculture at 8,830,000 bu. compared with 6,636,000 bu. in 1942 and an average of 6,687,000 bu. for 1932–41. This was an increase of about 25% which resulted from an above-average

Estimated U.S. Production of Buckwheat in Leading States, 1943 and 1942

State	1943 bu.	1942 bu.	State	1943 bu.	1942 bu.
New York .	3,274,000	2,257,000	Wisconsin . .	261,000	210,000
Pennsylvania .	2,508,000	2,145,000	West Virginia .	209,000	209,000
Michigan . . .	800,000	391,000	Maine	140,000	119,000
Minnesota . .	442,000	420,000	Maryland . .	105,000	98,000
Ohio	350,000	216,000	Virginia. . . .	98,000	128,000

yield on a larger acreage. The principal buckwheat growing states, New York and Pennsylvania, harvested most of the increase, New York having particularly good yields. Frosts came late enough to allow the late-sown buckwheat to mature.

(J. C. Ms.)

Budget, National

On Jan. 13, 1944 President Roosevelt submitted his third war budget to congress, covering the fiscal year 1945. This budget was designated by the president as the outline of financial requirements for victory. It also outlined some of the measures which the president desired to assist in the reconversion of the economy to peacetime pursuits and to help military personnel and war workers find their way back into peacetime employment.

The budget estimates for the fiscal year 1945 were all based upon the assumption that the war would continue in the west as well as in the east throughout the fiscal year. This did not, of course, carry any implication as to the president's real expectations of the length of the war; it meant only that there was no other safe assumption upon which the government could plan its operations. Because of this assumption and because the scale of government operations in the fiscal year 1944 was already geared to an all-out war effort, there was little change shown in the expenditures' side of the government accounts.

The budget for the fiscal year 1945 anticipated a total of federal expenditures of approximately $100,000,000,000, only slightly more than the estimates for the fiscal year 1944. The anticipated expenditures for war activities of $88,200,000,000 were virtually the same as in the 1944 fiscal year, indicating that the government's war effort was already at about its maximum. Expenditures directly associated with the war completely dominated the entire budget, accounting for almost nine-tenths of total expenditures.

In explaining the war expenditures estimate for the fiscal year

CARTOON by Shoemaker In the *Chicago Daily News* inspired by President Roosevelt's budget message of Jan. 11, 1943: "The Poor Guy Who Tried to Figure Out How Much One Hundred and Nine Billion Is"

1945 the president submitted the data in Table I showing the growth and changing character of the war program. It may be seen that the entire war period was divided into four phases of which the final one, that of offensive war, had been reached. The striking thing about this analysis, in addition to the tremendous growth in the total outlays for war, was the sharp curtailment in the percentage accounted for by war construction and the growth in both munitions and upkeep of the armed forces. As the size of the armed forces was to reach its peak in the months ahead, the percentage of total war expenditures accounted for by pay and subsistence was expected to reach its maximum in the fiscal year 1945.

The magnitude of the total war program of the United States was brought out by the fact that appropriations, contract authorizations and government corporation commitments from June 1940 through Dec. 1943 totalled $344,000,000,000 and were expected to reach $397,000,000,000 in the course of the fiscal year 1945.

There were some interesting changes shown in the 1945 estimates from those of previous years. Because of the substantial rise in the national debt, the estimate for interest in the fiscal

Table I.—U.S. War Expenditures Estimate

Period	Average annual rate (in billions)	Per cent of total		
		Munitions, including ships	*Pay, subsistence	War construction
Preparedness: July 1940–Nov. 1941	$9.8	50	30	20
Defensive war: Dec. 1941–Oct. 1942	45.7	56	22	22
Aggressive deployment: Nov. 1942–Dec. 1943	83.5	59	28	13
Offensive war: **Jan. 1944–June 1944	97.0	64	30	6
July 1944–June, 1945 (fiscal year 1945). .	90.0	63	33	4

*Including also agricultural lend-lease and other civilian war activities.
**On basis of $92,000,000,000 for fiscal year 1944.

Table II.—*General Budget Summary of the United States*

Classification	Estimated 1945	Estimated 1944	Actual 1943
General and Special Accounts			
Receipts (based on present legislation):			
Direct taxes on individuals	$18,113,100,000	$19,422,600,000	$ 6,952,449,156
Direct taxes on corporations*	15,404,400,000	14,136,900,000	9,915,701,979
Excise taxes	4,251,510,000	4,273,810,000	3,776,956,397
Employment taxes	3,181,600,000	1,881,900,000	1,507,919,214
Customs	438,000,000	420,000,000	324,290,778
Miscellaneous receipts	2,036,770,000	2,442,900,000	907,327,977
Total receipts*	43,425,380,000	42,578,110,000	23,384,645,502
Deduct net appropriation for federal old-age and survivors' insurance trust fund	2,656,380,000	1,392,090,000	1,103,002,793
Net receipts, general and special accounts*	40,769,000,000	41,186,020,000	22,281,642,709
Expenditures:			
War activities (tentative estimate for 1945) (see also government corporations below)	88,200,000,000	88,500,000,000	72,108,862,204
Interest on the public debt	3,750,000,000	2,650,000,000	1,808,160,395
Other activities:			
Legislative establishment	29,549,800	28,756,500	26,694,653
The Judiciary	14,157,000	12,233,000	12,020,159
Executive office of the president	3,406,100	2,244,100	2,572,749
Civil departments and agencies	1,084,424,500	1,086,237,900	812,437,939
Post office deficiency		12,677,695	8,611,843
District of Columbia (Federal contribution)	6,000,000	6,000,000	6,000,000
General public works program	343,491,000	457,477,400	522,524,920
Veterans' pensions and benefits	1,252,179,000	865,389,000	599,777,891
Aids to agriculture	468,254,000	752,017,000	1,037,231,190
Aids to youth		20,000	17,914,849
Social security program	484,665,000	479,286,000	497,511,233
Work relief	2,325,000	43,273,700	317,385,759
Refunds	1,799,122,000	411,459,000	79,137,650
Retirement funds	471,663,500	473,957,600	322,041,800
Expenditures from anticipated supplemental appropriations	45,000,000	170,000,000	
Total, other activities	6,004,236,900	4,801,028,895	4,261,862,641
Total expenditures, general and special accounts, excluding statutory public debt retirement	97,954,236,900	95,951,028,895	78,178,885,240
Statutory public debt retirement			3,463,400
Total expenditures, general and special accounts	97,954,236,900	95,951,028,895	78,182,348,640
Excess of expenditures, general and special accounts	57,185,236,900	54,765,008,895	55,900,705,931
Checking Accounts of Government Corporations and Credit Agencies, etc., with the Treasurer of the United States			
Net expenditures from checking accounts:			
War activities	1,800,000,000	3,500,000,000	2,975,711,475
Other activities	15,000,000	**175,000,000	**1,475,772,673
Net expenditures from checking accounts, excluding redemption of obligations in the market	1,815,000,000	3,325,000,000	1,499,938,802
Redemption of obligations in the market (net)	1,346,000,000	2,770,000,000	693,746,663
Net expenditures, checking accounts of government corporations and credit agencies, etc.	3,161,000,000	6,095,000,000	2,193,685,465
Effect of Operations on the Public Debt			
Public debt at beginning of year	197,600,000,000	136,696,090,330	72,422,445,116
Increase in public debt during year:			
General and special accounts, excess of expenditures over receipts	57,185,236,900	54,765,008,895	55,900,705,931
Checking accounts of govt. corporations and credit agencies, etc., net expenditures	3,161,000,000	6,095,000,000	2,193,685,465
Trust accounts, excess of receipts over expenditures	−46,790,697	−2,121,340	−332,701,494
Statutory public debt retirement			−3,463,400
Adjustment for increase in treasury cash balance	100,553,797	46,022,115	6,515,418,710
Increase in public debt during year	60,400,000,000	60,903,909,670	64,273,645,213
Public debt at end of year	258,000,000,000	197,600,000,000	136,696,090,329

Expenditures shown in the above table are those made through the treasury. In addition, net expenditures through government corporations are estimated in the budget as follows: 1945, $1,815,000,000; 1944, $3,325,000,000; 1943, $1,499,938,802. Grand total treasury and government corporation expenditures: 1945, $99,769,236,900; 1944, $99,276,028,895; 1943, $79,682,287,422.
*Includes the following estimated amounts for excess profits taxes refundable in the postwar period: 1945, $624,000,000; 1944, $545,000,000, and 1943, $220,000.
**Excess of credits, deduct.

year 1945 was placed at $3,750,000,000 as against $2,650,000,000 in the fiscal year 1944. Average interest rates were less than 2% and interest received from all new government issues was fully taxable. As a result the net cost per dollar borrowed after Pearl Harbor was about one-third the cost of borrowings in World War I. The president anticipated gross interest payments of $5,000,000,000 annually on the debt as it would be at the end of the fiscal year 1945. He thought, however, that with a national income of $125,000,000,000 or more, that these payments need not prove oppressive and that by appropriate tax and other economic policies the payment of interest and the gradual repayment of principal during years of prosperity could be achieved without impairing the stability and growth of the national income.

The other major increase among the government expenditures was that anticipated for veterans' pensions and benefits. In addition to existing provisions of law, however, the president recommended a broad program to assist service men and women, meeting some of the problems they will face when discharged. His program included mustering-out pay and an educational and training program for those demobilized from the armed forces.

All of the items of expenditure which were to show a decline from the fiscal year 1944 to the fiscal year 1945 were those which had grown during the preceding years of economic depression. The largest cut suggested by the president was in aids to agriculture where the proposed expenditure for the fiscal year 1945 was almost $285,000,000 under that of the previous year. The decrease resulted largely from the omission of a recommendation for parity payments in agriculture and a reduction in the recommended appropriation for conservation and use of agricultural land resources. All in all, the total of government nonwar expenditures, excluding interest on the public debt, expenditures for veterans and provisions for tax refunds required by law, was expected to continue to decline as it had since 1939. It was expected that these items would amount to $2,953,000,000, a reduction of $571,000,000 below the figure for the fiscal year 1944.

On the receipts side of the budget little change was anticipated for 1945 from the estimates for 1944. Net receipts under legislation existing at the time the budget was submitted were estimated at $41,000,000,000 for the fiscal year 1944 and a little less than that figure for the fiscal year 1945. As compared with actual receipts in 1943 there was a substantial increase of $19,000,000,000 due to the Revenue act of 1942, the Current Tax Payment act of 1943, and the higher level of income and profits. While taxes on corporations were expected to yield somewhat higher revenues, taxes on individuals would decline because the receipts coincident with the transition to a current basis of individual income taxes were nonrecurrent.

With the volume of expenditures recommended at $100,000,000,000 and receipts from existing tax legislation estimated at $41,000,000,000, a deficit of $59,000,000,000 for the fiscal year 1945 was anticipated. This was virtually the same as the deficit for the fiscal year 1944. A deficit of this magnitude in the two years would raise the public debt to $197,600,000,000 by June 1944 and to $258,000,000,000 a year later.

In view of these prospective deficits the president again recommended the enactment of additional fiscal legislation. On the one

Table III.—Government Receipts and Expenditures—Great Britain

(£'000)

Receipts	Actual Receipts 1942-43	Estimate for 1943-44	Expenditures	Exchequer Issues 1942-43	Estimate 1943-44
Inland Revenue:			**Consolidated fund services:**		
Income tax	1,006,828	1,175,000	Interest and management of national debt	310,801	375,000
Surtax	75,358	80,000	Payments to N. Ireland	9,198	9,500
Estate duties	93,336	100,000	Other consolidated fund services . . .	7,389	7,500
Stamps	15,280	17,000			
National defense contribution	30,635			327,388	392,000
Excess profits tax	346,887	500,000			
Other inland revenue	950	1,000	**Supply services (excluding post office).**		
	1,569,274	1,873,000	Defense token votes	4	4
			Civil votes	437,658	444,652
Customs and Excise:			Revenue departments	18,118	19,458
Customs	459,489	525,320	Votes of credit	4,840,000	4,900,000
Excise	425,300	450,180			
	884,789	975,500		5,295,780	5,364,114
			Total ordinary expenditures	5,623,168	5,756,114
Motor vehicle duties	28,537	25,000	Sinking funds	14,199*	. . . .
Total tax receipts . . .	2,482,600	2,873,500	Total	5,637,367	5,756,114
Canadian government contribu-					
tion	224,719	. . . .			
Post office net receipt	12,377	400			
Wireless licences	4,560	4,700	*Self-balancing Revenue and Expenditure*		
Crown lands	1,000	800			
Sundry loans	4,062	4,100			
Miscellaneous	90,533	24,000			
Total ordinary revenue .	2,819,851	2,907,500	Post office	102,523	110,632

*Including supplementaries

hand, he urged the congress to retain the increase in social security rates tha were scheduled to become effective on March 1, 1944. On the other hand, he emphasized his support of the administration's revenue program calling for additional wartime taxes of $10,500,000,000. The president emphasized the fact that all the estimates presented in the budget were intimately related to the price stabilization program and that if general increases in wages, farm prices and profits were allowed federal expenditures would increase correspondingly. He therefore urged support for the stabilization program and retention of the legislation allowing renegotiation of war contracts for the purpose of preventing profiteering.

Besides covering possible contingencies associated with continuance of the war for the fiscal year 1945, the budget message discussed various problems of demobilization which were already arising and which would be intensified in the year ahead. The major problems of this character outlined in the budget message were those of contract termination, disposition of surplus property, industrial reconversion, manpower demobilization and reemployment, and veterans' legislation. In these fields the president stressed the need for the establishment of comprehensive and integrated policies as well as the need for guarding against any weakening of the administrative agencies established for carrying out these functions. As to reconversion policy in general the major aim of the government was stated to be the stimulation of private investment and employment. It was thought, however, that there would be urgent need for certain public works in the postwar period in connection with which careful planning was urged to assure priority for the projects of greatest need and for their timing in accordance with the requirements of the employment situation. In addition, the president recommended the broadening of the social security program as a fundamental means of easing the transition from a war to a peacetime economy. It was contemplated that this broadening of the program would include members of the armed forces as well as those employed in industry. (*See* also NATIONAL DEBT; NATIONAL INCOME AND NATIONAL PRODUCT; TAXATION; UNITED STATES.)

Great Britain.—Inasmuch as Great Britain reached virtually a full-war footing in the fiscal year 1942-43, the budget for the

fiscal year 1943-44 differed but little from the scale of expenditures and receipts attained in the previous year. Expenditures of the magnitude of £5,756,000,000 were proposed for the fiscal year 1943-44, little more than £100,000,000 above the total for the preceding year. Increases in expenditures for interest on the national debt and the prosecution of the war made up the bulk of the rise.

In his budget message the chancellor of the exchequer, Sir Kingsley Wood, stated that it was the objective of the government to limit the draft on capital to the same size as that of the fiscal year 1942-43. Accordingly, it was proposed that revenues be increased by roughly the same amount as the increase in expenditures, making total revenues amount to £2,907,500,000 for the fiscal year 1943-44. By way of emphasizing the financial burden on the British public, the chancellor pointed out that of the expenditures requiring domestic financing, more than 56% would be covered by current revenues.

The bulk of the new revenues were to be obtained by increasing taxes on beer and tobacco, although increases in the rates on other alcoholic beverages, entertainment and telephone services were also recommended. In addition the purchase tax on luxuries was to be increased from $66\frac{2}{3}\%$ to 100%, this increase coming on top of the doubling of the rate in the fiscal year 1942-43. Although the yield in this instance was not expected to be large, it was considered a desirable method of discouraging spending and the consequent utilization of manpower and materials. In the case of income and excess profits taxes which had already risen to very high levels, only minor changes in the interest of equity were recommended.

As in previous years, Sir Kingsley Wood used the budget message not only to review the purely fiscal situation of the government but to outline the status of the broader economic problem of war finance. He stressed the importance of lend-lease aid from both the United States and Canada and also pointed out that British reciprocal lend-lease aid had grown to large proportions. In two matters which had been made essential features of British wartime financial policy, a low level of interest rates and the avoidance of inflation, it was pointed out that a high measure of success had been achieved. Whereas the cost of living index rose only 28% between Sept. 1939 and March 1943, the advance during a comparable period in World War I had been 90%. (M. GT.)

Building and Construction Industry.

Construction in 1943 in the U.S. was confined to war needs—factories and camps, farm service buildings, homes for workers in war industries and military encampments. The tooling-up period had reached its peak by the end of 1942. Therefore, the volume of the building industry declined from $8,849,000,000 of work completed in the first eight months of 1942 to $5,826,000,000 in the same period of 1943.

The year was marked by experimentation with new methods of

Item	8 months 1943	8 months 1942	Percent change
New construction, total	5,826	8,849	−33.9
Private, total	1,011	2,168	−53.3
Residential building (nonfarm)	487	1,128	−56.8
Nonresidential building:			
Industrial	67	216	−69.0
All other	44	179	−75.4
Farm construction:			
Residential	34	85	−60.0
Nonresidential	45	61	−26.2
Public utility	334	496	−32.6
Public, total	4,815	6,676	−27.8
Residential	566	339	+67.0
Military and naval	2,190	3,202	−31.6
Nonresidential building:			
Industrial	1,659	2,205	−24.7
All other	24	113	−78.7
Highway	255	463	−44.9
Sewage disposal and water supply	40	78	−48.7
All other federal	65	237	−72.5
Miscellaneous public service enterprises	16	47	−66.0

construction, new materials, new ways of using old materials. The incentive to experiment was provided by: (1) the necessity of saving metal, lumber and certain plastics for the materials of war; (2) the importance of speed and quantity production; (3) the need to use a minimum of manpower and (4) the knowledge that a large postwar market would be attainable if the cost of production could be reduced.

The feasibility of prefabricating homes was a subject of considerable study. The term "prefabrication" was used loosely to cover three dissimilar processes, each using a different percentage of factory technique. The three methods included: (1) the fabrication of a complete house within a factory and the shipment of the entire house in large sections by rail, water or truck to various parts of the country, to be assembled at its destination; (2) the fabrication of parts of a house such as the kitchen, or bathroom, or the doors with fittings and frame, to be shipped to builders who have homes of their own specifications under construction; (3) the fabrication of a great many units at the building site by setting up a factory-like assembly line system.

Automobile methods of finance were advocated by some for the postwar building industry. Terms, such as "trade-in-house" were used without definition of the manner in which the trade could be effected. There was a deep conviction that it was desirable to reach the large potential market of people earning less than $2,000, not reached by new construction or rehabilitated old construction before the war. The buying and renting capacity of this income level spurred materials producers, architects and builders to predict the possibility of houses to sell as low as $1,000. However, blueprints did not specify the equipment of the house or reflect the cost of land and taxes upon the total cost of the house.

Because all building costing more than $6,000 per dwelling unit was stopped during the war, it was estimated that there would be a demand market in the future $6,000 to $10,000 home. Two pieces of legislation, the Wagner bill sponsored by the Urban Land institute and the Thomas bill sponsored by the National Planning association were dropped into the congressional hopper. Both bills would authorize the aid of federal funds to cities to buy up slum areas and redevelop them through private enterprise. They were widely discussed by technical groups throughout the country but achieved no popular or congressional attention.

BIBLIOGRAPHY.—*Survey of Current Business;* publications of the National Housing agency, the U.S. Department of Labor; the National Committee on Housing, Inc., F. U. Dodge Co., National Association of Housing Officials; *Architectural Forum.* (D. Rn.)

Great Britain.—Conditions in the industry remained fluid and work was spread over programs of national importance in the provinces and repair of war damaged property in the towns. New work was begun on some 3,000 cottages on a thousand sites, scattered over 38 rural districts.

The government announced its acceptance of the Scott and Uthwatt reports in principle, but its recommendations were still awaited. In anticipation of favourable decisions the minister of health approached local authorities with a request that they should, with other authorities concerned, secure a sufficiency of suitable sites for a one-year housing program and begin surveying and preparing the general lay-out.

Great interest was aroused in the government White Paper on training for the building industry. It sought to show that to attract the right type of people to this great industry some measure of security is essential and recommended the avoidance of casual labour, the guaranteed week and that the intake of labour at all stages be scaled nationally on expectation of work ahead. It proposed that the industry be built up to a ceiling of 1,250,000 workers (500,000 craftsmen) after the war for employment on a program estimated to last for 12 years. Half of the work outlined was for housing. Between 3,500,000 and 4,000,000 houses would be required.

After World War I, it took some 7 years to reach a production of 200,000 houses. To step up production, therefore, greater output per man-hour was expected to be required. It was estimated that prewar costs were made up of 60% material and 40% labour and that housing costs had gone up in 1943 approximately by 105% over prewar costs. This steep rise would seriously impede the industry and the question of economies would need to be thoroughly explored. If these were not to be secured at the expense of the operatives they would have to come from more efficient use of labour and material, through improved organization, standardization and prefabrication of building components, new methods, new materials and the thorough revision of local by-laws. (*See* also BUSINESS REVIEW; HOUSING; UNITED STATES.) (N. KE.)

Bulgaria.

A kingdom in the Balkan peninsula. Area (end of 1940) c. 42,796 sq.mi.; pop. (est. 1942) 8,700,000. Capital: Sofia. Chief cities: Sofia (est. 1942, 401,000), Plovdiv or Philippopolis (99,883), Varna (69,944), Russé or Ruschuk (49,447), Burgas (36,230), Plevna (31,520). Religion: mainly Greek Orthodox; about 1,000,000 Moslems; 50,000 Jews. King: Simeon II; premier (end of 1943) Dobri Boshiloff.

History.—Bulgaria's history in 1943 consisted of a long line of internal troubles, culminating in the death of the king. In 1941 Bulgaria had aligned itself fully on the side of the axis powers, and as a result of the alliance it occupied and annexed Greek Macedonia and western Thrace, and from Yugoslavia southern Serbia, territories of about 23,166 sq.mi., with about 3,000,000 inhabitants. Bulgaria continued in 1943 under a fascist royal dictatorship whose head was the king himself who ruled through puppet ministers of his own choice. The Bulgarian government participated in the war against Great Britain and the United States, yet the strong pro-Russian sympathies of the Bulgarian people and the pro-communist tendencies of the peasantry made it impossible for the government, in spite of strong German pressure, to participate in the war against the soviet union. Bulgaria and soviet Russia maintained diplomatic relations throughout 1942 and 1943.

On the whole, the Bulgarian government followed the nazi line in its domestic and foreign policies. Bulgarian anti-Semitism was as thorough, ruthless and barbaric as that practised in Germany and in other German satellites. There were many complaints from Greeks and Serbs in the newly annexed territories about the harshness and cruelty of Bulgarian rule. The pro-nazi Peter Gabrovsky was minister of the interior.

There was more and better organized protest against the policy of the government in Bulgaria than in any other German satellite country. Repeatedly in 1943 reports of open revolts of peasants, workers and students in many Bulgarian towns penetrated to the outside world.

At the end of March King Boris of Bulgaria visited Chancellor Hitler at his field headquarters. They tried to arrive at an even closer collaboration between the two countries. The king's return to Bulgaria provoked a crisis, for the Russian successes on the eastern front had strengthened the pro-Russian and anti-German sentiment of the people. The king found himself forced to assume *de facto* charge of foreign affairs, while Bogdan Philoff became under secretary of foreign affairs. In many of the larger towns a state of siege was proclaimed. But all these measures did not bring internal peace. Especially violent demonstrations were held throughout Bulgaria, in spite of many preventive arrests, on May 1, and Boris had to leave the capital in haste on the advice of his government. The unrest in Bulgaria frequently took the form of the assassination of prominent pro-axis personalities. Among them was Col. Athanas Panteff, former Bulgarian chief of police, whose national funeral services held on May 4 were followed by widespread rioting with a heavy death toll. Other prominent victims of Bulgarian patriots' terrorism were Sotir Janeff, a close personal friend of the king, president of the foreign affairs commission of the Bulgarian parliament and editor of the semiofficial *Slovo*, and Gen. Christo Lukoff, a former minister of war, both fervent friends of Germany and extreme Bulgarian nationalists. These assassinations were followed by that of Sapria Klevkoff, a member of parliament and, as it was reported, the 110th Bulgarian political supporter of Germany to die at the hands of terrorists.

King Boris III died on Aug. 28 in Sofia after four days of suffering of unexplained origin but which was reliably reported to have been caused by a shooting at a small railway station outside the capital, when the king was returning from a visit to Chancellor Hitler. His six-year-old son Prince Simeon of Tirnovo ascended the throne under the name of Simeon II. It was generally believed that Hitler had put before the king two urgent demands, one for full powers for the gestapo to repress Bul-

garian unrest and the other for fuller Bulgarian participation in the war. After the death of the king a regency council was appointed, consisting of Prince Cyril, Premier Philoff and Minister of War Gen. Nikola Michoff. The Bulgarian army, irrevocably committed to a pro-German policy, backed the continuation of a very determined pro-nazi policy in which Minister of the Interior Peter Gabrovsky was the strong man.

The unrest in Bulgaria in 1943 was increased by an expected Allied invasion of the Balkans. On Nov. 14 medium bombers of the 12th United States air force based in Italy bombed railway yards at Sofia, the first time that any target in Bulgaria had been bombed. Further attacks followed, among them on Dec. 10 a raid on Sofia which caused great destruction and killed many persons. The closer alliance of Turkey with the United Nations as expressed in the conference of Cairo on Dec. 5 and the growing strength of the pro-Russian partisan movement in Yugoslavia also caused concern.

Education.—Though elementary education is obligatory and free for children between the ages of 7 and 14, the census of 1934 showed 20.4% of the males and 42.8% of the females illiterate. In 1939 there were in Bulgaria 252 kindergartens, 4,743 elementary schools, 1,932 junior high schools and 112 senior high schools with 969,599 pupils. The university of Sofia had an enrolment of 4,377 men and 1,653 women.

Finance.—The revenue for 1941 was estimated at 10,160,000,-000 and the expenditure at 10,096,000,000 leva. On June 30, 1940, the total foreign debt amounted to 12,483,000,000 leva, the internal debt to 11,767,000,000 leva, of which 9,237,000,000 leva was not consolidated. The monetary unit is the lev, stabilized at 92 leva to one gram of fine gold (equal to .95 cent U.S. at the end of 1941). The note circulation on June 30, 1941 was 8,861,000,000 leva.

Trade and Communication.—Imports amounted in 1941 to 10,239,000,000 leva, most of which came from Germany, with Italy second. Exports for 1941 amounted to 9,215,000,000 leva, of which the largest part went to Germany. In 1939 machinery and war material, metal goods, textiles, vehicles and mineral oils were chiefly imported, and tobacco, fruit, eggs, wheat and hides exported. Bulgaria, though it has important ports at the Black sea and on the Danube, had in June 1939 a merchant

FUNERAL PROCESSION of King Boris III at Sofia, Bulgaria, Sept. 5, 1943

marine of only 14 ships of 17,476 tons. At the same time it had 2,211 mi. of railroad, 608 post offices, 798 telegraph offices and 772 telephone exchanges.

Agriculture and Mineral Production.—More than 80% of the population was engaged in agriculture in 1943. Fruit growing and the growing of tobacco and silkworm cocoons are highly developed. The chief crops are wheat, maize, barley, rye and oats. The country is poor in minerals, but rich in coal, yet industrial development has been very slow.　　　(H. Ko.)

Bumpus, Hermon Carey

(1862–1943), U.S. educator, was born May 5 at Buckfield, Me. A graduate of Brown university in 1884, he received his doctorate from Clark university in 1891. He taught zoology at Olivet college and at Clark and Brown universities. While a director of the American Museum of Natural History in New York city, 1902–11, he encountered constant friction with the trustees because of his insistence upon popularizing the various exhibits. After leaving the museum, he became business manager of Wisconsin university and was president of Tufts college, 1914–19. Dr. Bumpus was a member of the pure science faculty at Columbia, 1905–11, consulting director of the Buffalo Museum of Science, 1925–30, chairman of the committee on museums in national parks and chairman of the advisory board of the national park service, 1936–40. He died in Pasadena, Calif., June 21.

Bureau of Standards, National: *see* STANDARDS, NATIONAL BUREAU OF.

Burma.

A British province lying on the eastern side of the Bay of Bengal, between India and Thailand; occupied by Japan in 1942. Area 261,610 sq.mi.; pop. (1941) 16,823,798. Chief cities: Rangoon (cap. 501,219); Mandalay (est. 150,000); Moulmein (70,000). Religion: Buddhist (85%); governor: the Rt. Hon. Sir Reginald Dorman-Smith; ministerial adviser: the Hon. Sir Paw Tun; languages: Burmese and English.

History.—Japan set out to consolidate herself politically in Burma during 1943. All radio sets were called in for conversion to medium wave-length in order to prevent the Burmese owners from listening to British and U.S. propaganda. Schools were reorganized to inculcate the Greater East Asia spirit. The Japanese tried to win support with the slogan "Asia for the Asiatics." Books for instruction in the Japanese language were published in Burmese. Burmese students were sent to Japan on scholarships awarded by the Japanese government. A Japanese company published in Burmese a weekly pictorial edition of a Japanese newspaper.

In March Premier Hideki Tojo conferred with Dr. Ba Maw in Tokyo and declared that "Japan desired the creation of an independent Burmese state." In August the Japanese announced the abolition of their military administration. Dr. Ba Maw, as head of the Japanese-sponsored Burmese government, with the title of Adipadi, formally declared war on Britain and the U.S.A and signed a treaty of alliance with Japan.

In September Tokyo announced the signing of a treaty between Japan and Burma, incorporating into Burma Karenni, the Wa states and the Shan states, with the exception of Keng-tung and Mong-pan, which were incorporated into Thailand.

To be in readiness for the re-entry of the Allies into Burma, the governor, Sir Reginald Dorman-Smith, and his reconstruction department were building up an efficient civil affairs service to go back with the army and were working out plans for the physical reconstruction of Burma and for its future administration.

Education.—In 1940, total number of institutions 27,015, scholars 851,922; primary schools 5,679, scholars 384,060; middle

GEN. JUICHI TERAUCHI (in helmet), Japanese conqueror of Burma, paid a shoeless visit to the Dragon pagoda in Rangoon in 1943, accompanied by Dr. Ba Maw, Japan's native puppet (extreme left, barefooted). The picture was released through Portugal

1,018, scholars 139,190; high 399, scholars 94,353; special 1,172, scholars 19,190; unrecognized institutions 18,745, scholars 212,663; university (Rangoon) 2,365 students; arts college (Mandalay) 101.

Finance.—Revenue (est. 1941–42) Rs.17 crores 13 lakhs; expenditure (est. 1941–42) 18 crores 28 lakhs; public debt, (March 31, 1940) Rs.51 crores 22 lakhs; exchange rate: rupee (Rs.1) = 1s. 6d. One crore = 10,000,000 rupees; one lakh = 100,000 rupees.

Trade and Communication.—Overseas trade in merchandise (April-March 1940–41): imports Rs.29 crores 55 lakhs; exports, including re-exports Rs.55 crores 38 lakhs. Communication, 1940: roads suitable for motor traffic, all weather, 6,811 mi.; seasonal 5,661 mi.; railways open to traffic 2,060 mi.; inland waterways (approx.) 1,300 mi.

Agriculture.—Production (1940–41): rice 6,000,000 tons; groundnuts 160,000 tons; sesamum seed 72,000 tons; cotton 13,000 tons of lint; tobacco 106,869,600 lb.; teak 438,827 tons.

Mineral Production.—In 1939, petroleum 275,673,364 gal.; tin concentrates 5,441 tons; tungsten concentrates 4,342 tons; tin tungsten concentrates 5,593 tons; refined lead 76,000; antimonial lead 1,180 tons; zinc concentrates 59,347 tons; copper matte 7,935 tons; nickel speiss 2,896 tons; silver 6,175,000 troy oz.; gold 1,206 troy oz. (Ton = 2,240 lb.) (*See* also JAPAN; WORLD WAR II.)　　　(H. L.)

Burma Road: *see* ROADS AND HIGHWAYS.

Burns, John

(1858–1943), British politician, champion of the unemployed and of free speech, was born Oct. 20 in London. He retired from politics in 1918 after having served as Radical member of parliament and as cabinet minister. He was known throughout his life as "Honest John." Burns died in London, Jan. 24. (See *Encyclopædia Britannica*.)

Buses: *see* AUTOMOBILE INDUSTRY IN THE WAR; ELECTRIC TRANSPORTATION; MOTOR TRANSPORTATION.

Business Review.

Business and War.—The U.S. department of commerce estimated that 70% of the total output of American industry for 1943 was produced for war purposes. This figure afforded a reasonably accurate measure of the extent to which business and industry were working for the government. Although federal monthly expenditure reached its peak in June with a total of $8,300,000,000, the peak of war production was not reached until October. The War Production Board, taking the pre-Pearl Harbor month of Nov. 1941 as a base of 100, announced that in Nov. 1943 the index had risen to 648—6½ times the maximum for prewar months. By the end of the year the board announced that four production bottlenecks remained—landing .craft, trucks, electronics and heavy-duty tires. On Oct. 29, the navy cancelled contracts for 427 anti-submarine vessels, the largest single contract termination for the year, thereby substantially relieving pressure on basic war industries, and indirectly announcing the success of the antisubmarine campaign. In November the government began searching for buyers under the war surplus disposal plan. Thus the year 1943 marked the turning point in war production. (*See* also WAR PRODUCTION, U.S.)

Aircraft Industry.—The U.S. aircraft industry became the largest single manufacturing industry in the world, measured in terms of number of employees and size of pay rolls. For 1943, the value of products totalled $20,000,000,000, wages amounted to $2,700,000,000, with more than 1,000,000 workers employed. The total value of annual output for 1943 was more than 70 times greater than that of 1939, while pay rolls were 20 times greater. Notwithstanding this development, the industry failed to live up to expectations. On Jan. 2, 1943, the War Production board had set the 1943 goal at "about twice the number and about four times the weight of planes built in 1942." During the year plane production, all types, increased from 16,600 in the first quarter to 20,400 in the second quarter, rose to 22,500 in the third quarter and, at the October production rate, to 25,000 in the last quarter. A new record of heavy-bomber production was established in October after it had become clear that bomber production for heavy long distance attack was demanded on both the European and Pacific fronts. (*See* also AIR FORCES.)

Automotive Industry.—The automotive industry began the year with over $14,000,000,000 in unfilled orders. Aircraft products accounted for about 50%. The remaining half of the total backlog was broken down roughly as follows: military vehicles, covering about 60 different types, 20%; tanks and parts 15%; ammunition, artillery and small arms 9%; and other products 6%. The disclosure of the exact quantity of specific output was prohibited by the government as "information that would give aid and comfort to the enemy." The industry was able to reveal, however, that the unfilled orders in Nov. 1943 had exceeded those in January. By July the actual shipments surpassed those for the entire year 1942, and by mid-September the annual rate of production had mounted to $9,500,000,000. (*See* also AUTOMOBILE INDUSTRY IN THE WAR.)

Shipbuilding.—For three war years after 1939 the German submarines had been sinking tonnage faster than replacements could be made by the yards of the United Nations. The peak of the submarine wolf-pack tactics was reached in March 1943, but by midsummer the number of sinkings had grown negligible, while the destruction of submarines had expanded significantly, and precision bombing of German submarine bases and factories had gained in frequency and intensity. Shipping losses by Oct. 1943 subsided to the second lowest of any month during the war.

The U.S. Maritime commission began the construction of Liberty cargo ships in 1941. These vessels were designed for mass construction by subcontracting, subassembly, and prefabrication of hull and equipment. By Oct. 1943, 11 yards had delivered about 1,500 such vessels. Exceeding by 3,000,000 tons the original annual goal set by WPB, these shipyards had launched about 19,000,000 dead-weight tons by Dec. 1943.

By 1943 shipbuilding yards had become the chief customers of the steel industry, taking substantially more than the 16% of total steel shipments. Growing steadily, not only on both coasts but on the Great Lakes, shipbuilding became another billion-dollar industry. Perhaps the outstanding achievement of 1943 was the construction of tankers which not only relieved the oil shortage in the east with increased coastwise traffic, but also met the need for "oceans of oil" on the European and Pacific fronts. (*See* also SHIPBUILDING.)

Steel Industry.—Since steel had become the industrial giant that supplied the bone and sinew of mechanized warfare, that industry operated almost exclusively under the direction of the War Production board in 1943. WPB warned in April 1943 that the industry had not met its quota, in May the War Manpower commission demanded a 48-hr. week for steel workers, but in June a 26% deficiency still existed. The industry blamed the coal shortage, resulting from strikes by the United Mine Workers, for the closing of blast and open hearth furnaces. The first half of 1943 ended with a 43,800,000-ton production but in the second half, all-time monthly production records began to be broken in September, increased in October and November, operating in excess of 100% theoretical capacity—but by December open hearth production dropped for want of unfilled orders and because of labour unrest. The drop in lend-lease requirements, the contract cancellations of the war and navy departments with

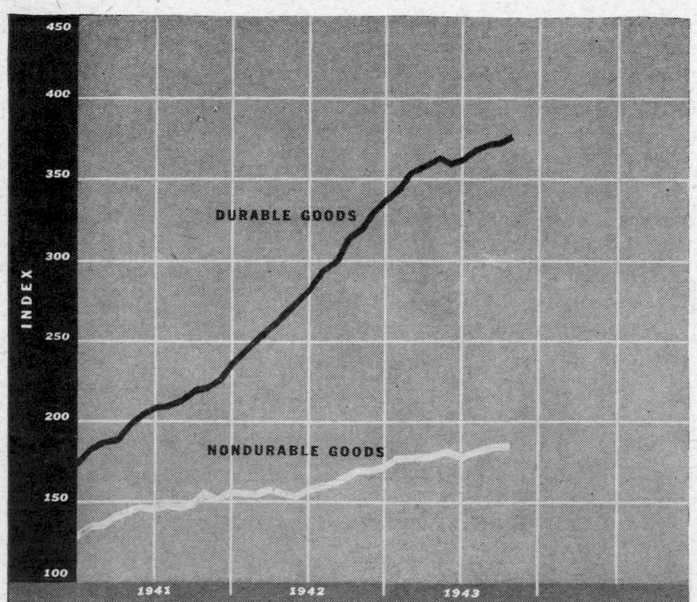

VOLUME OF MANUFACTURE of U.S. durable and nondurable goods, 1941–43, as estimated in The Federal Reserve *Bulletin* (1935–39=100)

Table I.—Indexes of U.S. Physical Production, Carloadings, Construction and Department Store Sales for 1943

Month of 1943	(1935-1939=100)				Freight car loadings	(1923-1925=100)			Department store sales (value)
	Industrial Production Physical Volume					Construction contracts awarded (value)			
	Total	Manufactures		Minerals		Total	Residential	All other	
		Durable	Nondurable						
Jan.	227	336	171	125	135	145	79	198	143
Feb.	232	344	174	131	139	102	56	140	168
March	235	351	174	132	138	85	42	119	136
April	237	356	175	131	136	63	33	87	128
May	238	359	176	129	135	52	31	68	125
June	236	358	177	117	127	45	32	55	129
July	239	359	176	135	141	60	36	80	142
Aug.	242	364	177	135	140	61	37	81	142
Sept.	244	366	177	137	139	65	35	89	132
Oct.	245*	369	178	135	140	51	36	63	140
Nov.	244	372	179	135	139	..	..	..	..
Dec.	..	372*	178*	..	..	..	..	..	..

Federal Reserve *Bulletin*.
*Estimated.

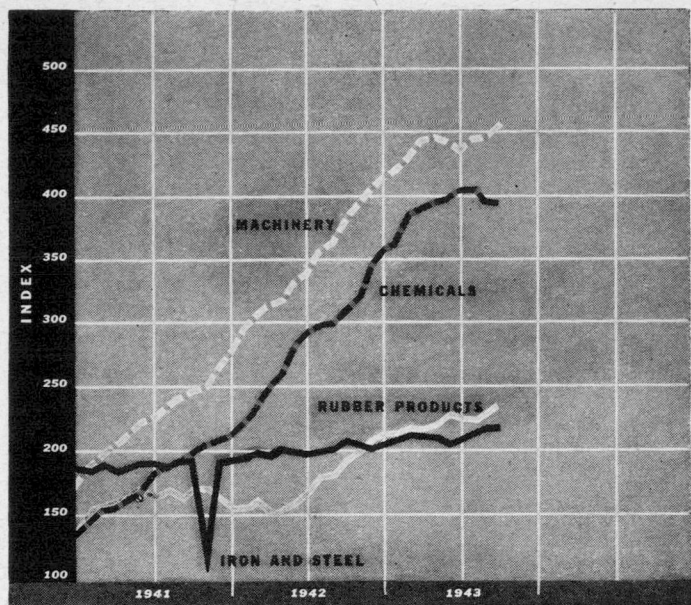

PHYSICAL PRODUCTION in leading U.S. war industries, 1941–43; Federal Reserve estimate corrected for seasonal variation (1935–39=100)

munitions plants and the increasing stock piles at mills allayed fears of inadequate output. (*See* also IRON AND STEEL.)

Critical Metals.—Strategic metals, including copper, lead, zinc, aluminum, magnesium, cobalt, molybdenum, vanadium, nickel and chrome, which WPB classified as "super-critical" in Aug. 1943 were available in ample supply for both direct and indirect war needs by December. Exact production figures were not available, but industrial sources reported that hundreds of millions of dollars worth of surplus metals were in federal and industrial stock piles. The sudden change in the fourth quarter from shortage to surplus was caused chiefly by the reduction of the armament program. Copper producers reported refined copper stock alone at around 400,000 tons, and some copper processors sought the consent of the Office of Civilian Supply to divert production to electric power companies, communication facilities and construction companies. (*See* also COPPER.)

Producers of aluminum (*q.v.*), like those of copper, had won the battle of production in 1943. Aluminum scrap, collected in nation-wide drives in 1942, had become a drug on the market, and by November processors began selling below ceiling prices, while high-cost producers sought subsidies to prevent shutdowns. Stock piles of primary aluminum—that made from bauxite ores, compared with secondary aluminum made from scrap—were estimated at 70,000,000 lb. at the close of 1943. In the autumn the government abandoned its plan to erect three aluminum-magnesium extrusion mills. During 1943 the astonishing increase in aluminum output, in the United States alone, turned the scales definitely in favour of Allied war plane production.

Production of magnesium (*q.v.*) for 1943 soared to around 500,000,000 lb., sufficient for all known military purposes. The year-end stock pile had fallen to 25,000,000 lb. despite earlier expectations of a larger supply, because the aircraft demand for this metal had grown abruptly with a better knowledge of the relative merits of magnesium and aluminum. The heaviest magnesium consumer, using about 60% of the total output, was the Chemical Warfare service.

Lead (*q.v.*) was the first metal to be removed from the critical list by WPB. The armed services had ordered a decrease in small arms ammunition production, but almost immediately the released lead was absorbed by batteries, cables and ethyl gasoline. The year 1943 ended with stock piles of the Metal Reserve

corporation of the government holding over 200,000 tons as a contingency against future emergencies.

Despite the wide use of tungsten (*q.v.*) in cutting tools, dies, drills, wires and electric light bulbs, Dec. 1943 found the producers of this metal with an almost normal supply on hand. About 60% had been imported from China and Latin America and 40% obtained from the mines scattered throughout Nevada, California, Idaho and Colorado. Marginal mines began to close down. Other hard-metals producers of molybdenum and vanadium had fulfilled production quotas and the ferro-alloy branch of WPB no longer recommended allocation to war production only. (*See* also STRATEGIC MINERAL SUPPLIES.)

Rubber.—One of the most crucial and unsolved production problems of 1943 was the development of the synthetic rubber industry. The third report of the Rubber director in 1943 placed the total existing supply at 751,000 tons, including 443,000 long tons of crude product, 275,000 long tons of synthetics, imports of 40,000 tons from South America and about 14,000 tons from Liberia with small shipments from Ceylon. Synthetic production was divided as follows: buna-S, 218,000 tons; buna-N, 17,000 tons; butyl, 11,000 tons; neoprene, 29,000 tons; and a negligible supply from thiokol. Dollar volume for the industry was well above that of 1942 primarily because OPA had allowed higher price ceilings on rubber goods sold to the government. (*See* also RUBBER.)

Oil and Gasoline.—The bureau of mines estimated motor fuel demands in the first quarter of 1943 at 18% below that for the same period of 1942, and the total oil demand at 9% less. By June, gasoline consumption had diminished 1% below the preceding year, and at the close of the third quarter the production of motor fuel, distillate fuel oil, residual fuel oil, kerosene and lubricants, plus changes in inventories, had increased reserves above the 1942 level by about 2%. Decreases in motor fuel use of 6% for the first three quarters were more than offset by the 8% increase in distillate and 11% increase in residual fuel oils. The bottleneck problem for the oil industry in 1943, like that in 1942, remained one of transportation despite heavier gas rations. (*See* also PETROLEUM; RATIONING.)

Railroad Transportation.—The U.S. railroads confronted the paradoxical situation of seeming to limit their own business by reducing civilian passenger travel. The explanation lay solely in troop movements. During the first 19 months of U.S. participation in the war, the railroads transported 21,754,305 soldiers (an average of more than 100,000 per day) in organized movements, compared with the 8,874,708 soldiers moved by rail for the entire duration of World War I. Although the strain on freight equipment also had become acute in 1942, the Class I roads carried approximately 15% more revenue ton-miles of traffic in the first ten months of 1943, about 55% more than for 1941 and 123% more than for the same period in 1939. (*See* also RAILROADS.)

Building.—Aggregate construction for 1943 fell below $8,000,-000,000, compared with $13,000,000,000 for 1942. According to the department of commerce, private construction fell below $1,600,000,000 and became "one of the most thoroughly deflated of all private businesses."

Construction indexes showed pronounced downward trends throughout the year, for value of building permits, dollar volume construction, number of dwelling units and nonresidential buildings. Two exceptions were shown, first, in the indexes of new residential buildings, which held unvaried throughout the year, and second, in expenditures for "additions, alterations and repairs," which showed a definite upward trend. Despite shortages in material and manpower, the actual dollar volume of 1943 construction exceeded that of the annual average from 1930 to

"THE USUAL FAMILY SQUABBLE," by Hutton of the *Philadelphia Inquirer*

1939. (*See* also BUILDING AND CONSTRUCTION INDUSTRY; HOUSING.)

Company Earnings.—The New York stock exchange survey of 494 listed companies showed that in the first three quarters of 1943, net earnings exceeded those of 1942 by 10%. The largest gain was found in the amusement industry, 48.2%; the largest loss in the building industry, 11%. Automobile makers gained 22.7%, petroleum companies 18.4% and food companies 14.6%. The aggregate return upon the combined capital of 275 leading industrial corporations reached 8.8%, compared with 8.1% in 1942 and 12.3% in 1941. Despite the large volume of business, stockholders did not share proportionately, as a lower margin of profit per sales dollar was obtained by the 73 largest manufacturing corporations whose sales volume had risen 34% above that of 1942. The 275 corporations paid 68% of their net income before taxes to the federal government, and although this proportion appeared abnormally high, it approximated the national average, since the president's annual budget message called for $108,000,000,000 out of a total national income of $145,000,000,000, thus requiring 74% of the national dividend for the federal treasury.

Confronting the uncertainties of a postwar reconversion period, many companies sought to build reserves out of earnings, but the treasury was averse to a policy that might become a refuge for tax avoidance. After allowing a deduction of a 10% credit for postwar refunds on excess profits taxes, the companies set aside reserves for federal income, excess profit and capital stock taxes, as well as certain state and foreign taxes.

Requirements of reconversion reserves varied widely. In the chemical industry peacetime production involved slight reconversion costs, whereas the automotive industry, which had practically abandoned the production of passenger cars for aircraft production, required substantial reconversion reserves. Corporate earnings were held in a state of uncertainty because renegotiation of contracts, hanging like the sword of Damocles, threatened every distribution of earnings. Certain companies that had enjoyed prewar monopolistic advantages suddenly confronted postwar competition from new substitutes, from foreign producers

subsidized by their governments and from postwar use of extensive plants erected by the government in wartime. They found it desirable to add to their contingency reserves. Still other corporations, laying postwar plans for the establishment of chain stores and outlets, withheld distribution of wartime earnings.

Retail and Wholesale Trade.—Notwithstanding price ceilings on retail goods, sales volume never fell below $5,000,000,000 per month in 1943, except for the first two months of the year—a showing well above the monthly average of $4,815,000,000 for 1942. Nondurable goods, as usual, took the lion's share of the consumer's dollar. The sales volume of nondurable goods, which customarily exceeded that of durable goods by two- or threefold, rose abruptly to seven- or eightfold. Fear of a shoe shortage struck the February retail market and sent total volume to an all-time peak, and when the second shoe ration stamp became available in June, total sales volume again soared, this time inducing a fear of clothing shortage. Beginning in June apparel inventories began a monthly decline, and when in September apparel sales reached $544,000,000, compared with $414,000,000 in January, the department of commerce considered the possibility of clothes rationing. As consumers' income rose, the proportion spent on women's wear increased, and that for men's wear declined. Table II shows the unmistakable increase in the monthly trends of retail trade sales for 1943.

Retail sales of durable goods continued the decline that had begun in May 1941. The average monthly sales stood at $1,035,000,000 in 1940, rose to $1,303,000,000 in 1941, dropped to $839,000,000 in 1942, and approximated $780,000,000 in 1943. Curtailment was heaviest in building materials, auto parts and accessories, home furnishings, farm implements and hardware. Despite this decline in durable goods sales, the dollar value of all retail sales was 62% higher than the annual average from 1935 to 1939, and since the cost of living had risen but 24%, there was ample evidence that consumers' standards of living were not falling and that, despite the economies of war, total civilian consumption had increased through a draft on increased physical production and inventories.

The curtailment of civilian production of durable goods had led to the belief that total retail inventories would almost disappear, but according to the bureau of foreign and domestic commerce, the Sept. 1943 total actually reached $27,800,000,000, because general merchandise and apparel stores had been able to add to their supplies of nondurable goods. While at no time did total inventories during 1943 attain the 1942 levels, they did approximate those for 1941.

Although about $1,000,000,000 in retail inventories had disappeared over the 12-month period, wholesale inventories maintained a remarkably steady position.

Combined sales of the 14 leading variety chains gained 7.5% over 1942 record sales. By Oct. 1943, when merchandise shortages had been predicted, these stores actually showed gains in sales volume. Sales were 33% greater in September than in

Table II.—*Indexes of U.S. Retail Trade, 1943* (1935–39 = 100).

Month of 1943	Chain store sales	Department store sales	Variety chain store sales	Mail order sales (2 companies) (in millions)	Durable goods sales	Nondurable goods sales
January . .	177	143	106	$96.6	82	155
February . .	194	167	125	99.3	90	170
March . . .	180	136	123	118.5	99	168
April	175	128	140	134.0	111	176
May	171	125	134	120.8	105	174
June	178	129	140	121.3	104	179
July	181	142	134	103.1	96	166
August . . .	184	142	132	111.0	95	169
September . .	179	132	138	133.4	98	184
October. . .	181	140	147	149.1	101	192
November . .	187	152	156	156.9	101	203
December . .	..	..	..	..	102*	201*

U.S. Department of Commerce; *Survey of Current Business.*
*Estimated.

January as consumers began extensive buying of luxury items. Department store sales ran about 60% cash sales, 5% instalment sales and 35% charge accounts. Inventories of these stores increased substantially in August and September, and unusually early holiday sales began in October.

Cost of Living.—The cost of living in 1943 was approximately 6% higher on the average than for 1942, according to estimates of the bureau of labor statistics. Using a different basis for computation, the National Industrial Conference board reported that by Oct. 1943 living costs were only 3.9% higher than for the same month in 1942. With trade union wages based upon the "little steel" formula, it became an important matter which index was used, but the War Labor board adhered to that of the bureau of labor statistics. U.S. earnings hit an all-time peak with a gross income of $103,000,000,000 in the first nine months of the year, and for the country as a whole the September dollar income was 20% higher than for the same month in 1942. The treasury reported in November that Americans were spending at the unprecedented rate of $91,000,000,000 annually, out of a total predicted national income of about $145,000,000,000. Wage earners attributed this increased spending to higher costs of living than were reflected in the indexes used for wage determination.

The department of commerce reported that during the fiscal year 1943, when per capita income payments rose at the most rapid rate since midsummer 1940, the cost of living index had risen only 2% per quarter compared with 3% per quarter in 1942. Largely as the result of price control, rationing and wage

Table III.—Disposition of Individual Incomes, 1940–1943
(in billions)

Income Disposition	1940	1941	1942	1943
Payments to individuals	$76.5	$92.2	$115.5	$142
Direct personal taxes	3.3	4.0	6.6	16
Disposable income	73.2	88.2	108.9	126
Spent for goods and services	67.5	74.6	82.0	90
Savings	7.5	13.6	26.9	36

U.S. Department of Commerce.

ceilings, the per capita expenditures of consumers dropped from 86% of income in 1940 to 66% for 1943, while net savings and personal taxes had grown from 14% to 34% of individual income. The disposition of individual incomes, 1940 to 1943, is shown in Table III.

The especially sharp rise in food prices in the first quarter of 1943 was attributed chiefly to an unprecedented rise in the price of fresh fruits and vegetables as the result of a late spring freeze and the lack of ceiling prices. The drop in food prices in June and July was attributed to the tremendous increase in victory gardens and to the roll-back of certain food prices under the regulations of the Office of Price Administration. In July came the first drop in meat prices, and the increased marketing of lambs, cattle and hogs, caused by the high prices of stock feed, further reduced meat prices in the last quarter. Consumers' organizations complained that although prices of canned goods remained fixed, the quality and quantity were lowered and that price control was meaningless without compulsory grade labelling. (*See* also PRICES.)

Clothing prices remained remarkably stable for the year. Throughout the years 1941 and 1942 consumer expenditures for wearing apparel kept in step with the rise of income, but during 1943 consumers spent proportionately much more, and by the fourth quarter, demands for luxury clothing swamped the retail clothing stores, especially in the fur trade. Jewelry and other luxury items, not included in the cost of living budget and not subject to price control, showed abrupt increases in total volume of holiday sales. Table IV shows the trend in the most important items entering into the cost of living.

Table IV.—Indexes of the U.S. Cost of Living, 1943 (1935–39 = 100)

Month of 1943	Combined cost of living	Food	Clothing	Housing	Fuel and light	Miscellaneous	Purchasing power of dollar measured by cost of living
January	120.7	133.0	126.0	108.0	107.3	113.2	82.9
February	121.0	133.6	126.2	108.0	107.2	113.6	82.6
March	122.8	137.4	127.6	108.0	107.5	114.9	81.4
April	124.1	140.6	127.9	108.0	107.5	114.9	80.6
May	125.1	143.0	127.9	108.0	107.6	115.3	79.9
June	124.8	141.9	127.9	108.0	107.7	115.7	80.1
July	123.9	139.0	129.1	108.0	107.6	116.1	80.7
August	123.4	137.2	129.6	108.0	107.7	116.5	81.2
September	123.9	137.4	132.5	108.0	107.7	117.0	80.7
October	124.1*	138.2	133.0	108.0	107.9	117.6	80.4
November	124.1	137.3	133.0	108.0	108.0	117.7	80.6
December	..	..	..	108.0*	108.3*	..	80.9*

U.S. Department of Commerce, *Survey of Current Business.*
*Estimated.

Fear that the cost of living could not be controlled was founded both on the rising prices of foodstuffs and on rising wages. Practically all wage adjustments came under the jurisdiction of the War Labor board, and only in exceptional instances were increases allowed above the 15% ceiling fixed by the "little steel" formula, and then chiefly as incentive wages related to increased output. Between May 1942 and July 1943, the cost of living had outdistanced hourly wage rates and was about 24% above the Jan. 1941 base, and collective bargains were for the most part written in terms of hourly wage rates. Management pointed to increases in average hourly earnings, which included bonuses, premiums and other incentive wage payments, showing that these had risen from 68.3 cents in January to 84.5 cents by June 1942 and to 95.9 cents by June 1943, and that concomitantly pay rolls had increased 140% above the 1941 base. Union leaders demanded wage increases because "take-home" pay had decreased, since wages were reduced 20% by the withholding method of collecting the income tax, 10% by reductions for war bonds and by the social security tax, group insurance charges and

UNO WHO, the common U.S. citizen of Cartoonist Manning of the *Arizona Republic* (Phoenix) was "thrown up for grabs" in 1943. Manning's cartoon is entitled "Inflation Squeeze"

check-off for union maintenance; but WLB related living costs to the contractual, not the "take-home," wage. The trend in income payments, wholesale prices, pay rolls, factory employment purchasing power of the dollar and prices of farm products gave a more exact explanation of the incomes used to defray costs of living. The data in Table V were combined from reports of the bureau of labor statistics, the Federal Reserve board, and the bureau of agricultural economics. (*See also* NATIONAL INCOME AND NATIONAL PRODUCT; WAGES AND HOURS.)

Table V.—*Trends in U.S. Income, 1943*

Month of 1943	Income payments (value) 1935–39= 100*	Wholesale prices 1926=100*	Factory pay rolls 1939= 100*	Factory employment 1939=100*	Purchasing power of dollar measured in farm prices 1935–39=100†	Prices of farm products †
Jan.	196.5	101.9	290.9	164.8	57.7	117.0
Feb.	200.6	102.5	297.5	166.4	59.1	119.0
March	204.4	103.4	304.5	167.6	57.7	122.8
April	207.3	103.7	309.7	167.7	56.9	123.9
May	208.7	104.1	313.5	167.2	56.2	125.7
June	211.3	103.8	317.1	167.8	55.3	126.2
July	213.8	103.2	315.1	169.6	55.9	125.0
Aug.	215.5	103.1	322.4	170.9	54.4	123.5
Sept.	217.7	103.1	328.3	170.4	54.4	123.6
Oct.	218.9	102.9	333.4	170.5	54.5	122.8
Nov.	221.4	102.6	270.9	170.7	55.7	122.0
Dec.		102.9‡			56.1‡	121.8‡

*Federal Reserve *Bulletin.*
†Department of Commerce, *Survey of Current Business.*
‡Estimated.

Securities.—Yields on all common stocks regularly traded on the New York stock exchange ended 1943 about twice as high as the yields of high grade corporation bonds. Listed industrial securities, according to the Dow-Jones average, rose from 125 in January to 136 in March and April, to 142 in May, levelled off in June and reached the high for the year in July at 146. August saw the market drop to 138, level off through November, and close the year slightly higher. The stock market justified none of the fears of those who had predicted runaway inflation. Approximately the same trends appeared for industrial, rail and public utility shares. The volume of trading for 1943 rose far above any year of the previous decade. New and refunding issues also increased with the latter accounting for three-fourths of the total volume.

In January congressional tolerance proved a bullish factor, and public interest was aroused in low-priced stocks. In March strike threats impaired price controls, forcing the market higher, but this was offset somewhat in April by demands for a 48-hr. week and more vigorous governmental controls. In August the unloading of war stocks turned the market downward. With congressional consideration of the treasury's ten-billion-dollar tax proposal, the market took a bearish turn in October, and congress reacted at once by shearing the tax bill to a two-billion-dollar levy. Except for tax loss sales, the market held its own in December. Following the recommendation of the treasury to use the period of high earnings to retire indebtedness, many industrial, railroad and public utility corporations substantially reduced their outstanding bonds. (*See also* STOCKS AND BONDS.)

Banking.—Money in circulation outside the treasury and the federal reserve banks in Jan. 1943 totalled $15,500,000,000 and exceeded $18,800,000,000 by October. By that time five-sixths of the money in use was in the form of paper currency, with $15,-100,000,000 in federal reserve notes. Bank deposits in February reached $54,800,000,000 and soared to $75,700,000,000 by September. In eight months bank deposits had risen about $21,000,-000,000, equal to the growth of both bank deposits and currency in circulation in 1942. The Federal Reserve board reported that of a total of $113,000,000,000 in deposits and currency outstanding at the end of August, over $40,000,000,000 belonged to business and $60,000,000,000 to individuals, trust funds and non-profit organizations, with the remaining $13,000,000,000 held in government accounts.

Excess reserves continued to decline throughout 1943. In Jan. they amounted to $2,300,000,000, and thereafter dropped irregularly until July 28, when they reached a low of $1,000,000,000. The U.S. securities that had stood at 109.8 in January had risen to 113.2 by September, giving substantial evidence that the "full faith and credit" of the federal government had been more than maintained during the year. (*See also* BANKING; NATIONAL DEBT.)

Bankruptcy.—Involuntary bankruptcies fell to a new low for seven years in 1943. For the first half of the year, about 167,000 business firms discontinued business for various reasons, such as shortage of inventory; army draft; difficulty in procuring materials, manpower or equipment; impairment of business profits by price controls and taxes; and disappearance of markets. It is important to distinguish business discontinuances from bankruptcies. According to Dun and Bradstreet 2,753 firms, compared with 7,641 for the year 1942, went bankrupt during the first three quarters of 1943, whereas the Small Business committee of the senate estimated that approximately 300,000 firms discontinued business for the year as a whole.

The drop in total liabilities of bankrupt firms was traceable chiefly to the decline in the number of firms failing. Retail trade failures from January through August 1943 were about one-third the number for the corresponding period of 1942. Declines in bankruptcies were most marked in general merchandise, furniture and automobile lines; the trend for bankruptcies in apparel shops and drug stores reached the average; while the number of monthly failures for hardware stores and restaurants was distinctly higher than the average. With the exception of two—one in steel and another in tool manufacture—all the manufacturing failures involved small scale enterprises. For the first three quarters, the percentage of discontinuances was four times as great for firms employing from one to three persons as for firms employing 50 or more. Both bankruptcies and discontinuances revealed that the smaller firms confronted in wartime greater dangers and business risks than larger firms.

Legislation.—The attitude of congress toward business was more favourable in 1943. In April, congress reduced the tax rate on corporate income recommended by the treasury and refused to raise the excess profits tax above 90%. Corporations were required, however, under the Current Tax Payment act, to investigate the family status, births and deaths of all employees for withholding income for tax purposes, and to estimate in advance payments to be made during the year as bonuses, premiums, commissions, fees and overtime wages. Thus business firms had become more and more, since the imposition of the social security tax, federal tax-collecting agencies. Moreover, wage deductions for war loan bond purchases had become an added governmental function imposed on business. Congress refused to levy the general retail sales tax supported by representatives of business and industry. In Oct. 1943, after the treasury had recommended a tax bill for $10,000,000,000, congress produced a revenue measure providing for about $2,000,000,000, and when the budget bureau's supplemental appropriation bill, usually accepted without any great dissent, was submitted, congress sheared 82% from that bill. Strenuous congressional efforts were made to reduce nonwar waste through reduction in longstanding expenditures. In August, the Office of War Information estimated that the treasury had saved $3,555,000,000 through renegotiation of contracts, and congress refused to make redress for the resulting uncertainty in business. (*See also* TAXATION.)

The administration of laws previously enacted gave rise to extensive management risks, such as the ever-increasing complexity of tax regulations, decisions and rulings; the extension and enforcement of price and wage controls; termination or partial cancellation of war contracts; alteration of priorities and allocation of producers' goods; and unexpected regulations and postwar plans issued by federal bureaus.

As a result of the attempts of the War Labor board and the Director of Economic Stabilization to prevent wage increases at a time of most acute manpower shortage, industry suffered the loss, through strikes, of 170,000 man-days in Feb. 1943; 230,000 in March; and 675,000 man-days in May. To enforce their rulings, the president, acting under the War Powers act, temporarily took over the coal mines May 1, released them in August, resumed control Oct. 27 and took over the railroads on Dec. 27. Upon order from the president to "hold the line" against inflation on April 8, the War Manpower commission froze 27,000,000 workers to their jobs in government, railroads, farm and industry, to ensure against wage increases and rising costs. Pursuant to rationing powers the number of commodities placed on rationed lists increased considerably, thereby placing more food industries under governmental surveillance. (*See* also LAW.)

Foreign Trade.—For the first time in the history of U.S. foreign trade, monthly exports exceeded $1,000,000,000, beginning in May, and reached a total of $10,278,000,000 for the first ten months. Lend-lease shipments accounted for more than $8,000,000,000, and exports sold for cash, $2,778,000,000. The Office of Lend-Lease administration reported that the distribution through June 30, 1943, had been made as follows: to the United Kingdom, $4,458,000,000; to the U.S.S.R., $2,444,000,000; to Africa and the Middle East $1,363,000,000; to the Far East and Oceania, $1,133,000,000; and to all other countries, $484,000,000; making a total value of $9,882,000,000 from the beginning of the lend-lease program. By far the greatest quantity of such exports was made in 1943 after the "arsenal of democracy" had begun to function. According to British authorities, the dollar value of lend-lease was not statistically accurate, nor ever could be, since "if the United States sends us aircraft for British crews to fly from British airfields, that is recorded as lend-lease. If they send such aircraft complete with American crews who fly from the same field, that is not reckoned as lend-lease." Moreover, the British noted, it was difficult ever to determine with statistical accuracy the difference between the American equipping of British men, and British manning of American equipment, nor could a commercial value be fixed on the pint of British blood plasma poured into American veins, or vice versa.

Export trade of 1943 accounted to no small extent for the nazi reverses on the Russian front. The U.S. exports to the U.S.S.R. were as follows: ordnance and ammunition, $316,000,000; aircraft and equipment, $522,000,000; industrial and naval supplies, $691,000,000; military vehicles and tanks, $372,000,000; and farm products, $416,000,000. According to the British information service, Britain had also exported, as of June 30, another $716,000,000.

Reverse lend-lease announced in the simultaneous reports by the United States and Britain in Nov. 1943 had taken place on an extensive scale during the year. The United Kingdom had rendered services and supplied materials valued at $871,000,000. Australia had supplied food and clothing amounting to $196,000,000; New Zealand had furnished about $51,000,000 in food, and India, $57,000,000; so that the total for reverse lend-lease approximated $1,171,000,000 during the year. According to these figures, American lend-lease exports exceeded imports by almost an eight-to-one ratio.

Table VI gives the exports and imports by months, showing the extent to which both exceeded those of 1942. The National Industrial Conference board differentiated the lend-lease and "cash" exports for the first nine months of the year. The totals

differed slightly because re-exports were included, but the preponderance of lend-lease monthly exports was outstanding. (*See* also INTERNATIONAL TRADE.)

Table VI.—*Comparative Trends in U.S. Exports and Imports for 1942 and 1943, Together with Relative Importance of Lend-Lease and "Cash" Exports for 1943*

Month	1943		1942		1943 Exports	
	Exports	Imports	Exports	Imports	Lend-Lease*	Cash*
Jan.	723	228	479	254	518	212
Feb.	710	233	478	254	522	198
March	977	249	611	272	754	238
April	970	257	695	234	839	141
May	1,075	280	525	191	838	247
June	997	302	619	220	792	211
July	1,242	300	629	214	1,021	230
Aug.	1,194	315	696	186	989	216
Sept.	1,216	280	725	196	..	..
Oct.	1,178	328	794	199	..	..
Nov.	1,024	317	780	168	..	..
Dec.	..	..	864	358	..	..

U.S. Department of Commerce, *Survey of Current Business.*
*National Industrial Conference Board: *The Record.*

Business Conditions in Other Countries.—*Great Britain.*—The financial structure of Great Britain sturdily withstood the strain of the fourth war year in 1943. The official price system remained remarkably stable. The cost of living index (July 1914 = 100) remained fixed at 165 each month during the first half of 1943, rose to 168 for July and October and continued firm through the last half year. No variation whatsoever occurred in the indexes for rents, fuel, light, iron and steel, nonferrous metals and cotton. Prices rose slightly for chemicals, oil, food and tobacco. The wage index of the London and Cambridge Economic service showed an increase from 139 in January to 143 in June, remaining thereafter at 144 (Dec. 1924 = 100).

War shackles on company earnings and profits were retained in 1943. Net profits for 515 companies dropped 6% below those of 1942, and 25% below prewar levels. The stock price index rose steadily until May, revived somewhat during the summer and levelled off at a lower point in the latter half year. The average rate of ordinary dividends rose from 8.3% to 11.9% between the second and third quarters, thus remaining at the same levels as 1942. Bank notes in circulation rose from £912,000,000 in January to £994,000,000 in October, while public deposits increased from £7,800,000 to £11,100,000. Indexes of gilt-edged securities, fixed interest investments, bank and insurance securities, all showed a steady and conservative tendency to rise throughout 1943. The chief obstacles to increasing physical production were labour shortages and strikes. (*See* also GREAT BRITAIN.)

Canada.—The phenomenal rate of industrial expansion began to abate in 1943. The official index of physical volume of business reached 236% of the 1935–39 average by September, falling below August and April but remaining 14% above the 1942 level. Output gains of 23% were recorded in manufacturing and 26% in mineral products. Production of newsprint and pulp dropped below the 1942 level early in the year, despite a high labour priority. Suspension of trading in wheat futures on the Winnipeg grain exchange in September facilitated national price controls. Since 1942 the controlled price of bread, the key item in the cost of living index to which wage payments were tied, had been preserved by subsidies to bakers covering the difference between flour costs and the market price of wheat, and in 1943 the Wheat board purchased wheat directly to regulate market flow.

More than $1,000,000,000 in mutual aid was given the United Kingdom. Huge wheat exports were sent to the U.S.S.R. on lend-lease accounts and to the United States for cheaper feed supplies for American livestock and dairy industries. These wheat exports substantially relieved the exchange pressure on the Canadian dollar. (*See* also CANADA.)

Germany.—Official statistical data continued unreliable in 1943 because they were issued by and for the propaganda ministry to show "the achievements of the defense year 1943." British estimates of bombing damage to war industries placed losses at 33%, Swedish estimates at 15%. Needle and shoe trade machines were moved out of some factories into homes. Shortages were especially acute in iron and steel, rubber, meats, clothing, shoes and oil despite conscription of millions from occupied territory. Closing of bank branches was extensive in preparation for complete nationalization of banks. The board of economic warfare estimated nazi loot and plunder as equivalent to $10,000,000,000 per year. According to nazi official data, stability dominated all prices, wages, loans, deposits, securities and incomes. In Sept. 1943, German armed forces commandeered all motor vehicles, mules, fuel, lubricants and tools in occupied Italy and conscripted labour for the service of the nazi army and industry. No trustworthy data were available showing the extent to which other occupied countries were impoverished by nazi officials and armies. (*See* also GERMANY.) (E. H. HE.)

Butter.

Total butter production in 1943 was estimated by the U.S. department of agriculture to be 2,138,000,000 lb.—about 1% more than was produced in 1942 and 1% below the 1935-39 average. The military and lend-lease needs took such a large share of the total that butter became scarce in many regions early in 1943, even with strict rationing and the production of a large quantity of substitute oleomargarine. The civilian consumption of butter declined steadily in 1943 and was only 13.3 lb. per capita compared to 17 lb. in 1940 and an average of 16.8 lb. for the five-year prewar period 1935-39. This was only 73% of the average while the consumption of margarine was 148% of the prewar period. The shortage of butter for civilians became so acute in October that the government announced that there would be no government buying of butter until April 1944 and that the entire production would be made available for civilian uses. The government requirements were stated to be 316,000,000 lb. for the military and 122,000,000 lb. for lend-lease, relief and other programs.

The goal for total milk production of 122,000,000,000 lb. for 1944 offered little hope for an increase in butter for civilian consumption due to the strong demand for fluid milk. The rationing of butter at 16 points per pound at the end of 1943 sharply reduced consumption in many areas. One important factor in the decline of butter production was the diversion of milk to fluid milk consumption because of the higher consumer buying power in the larger cities. Changes in food habits such as the increased consumption of quick lunches was an important factor.

The stocks of fluid cream in cold storage were very heavy, almost double the normal, and the excess was equivalent to about 9,000,000 lb. of butter. The heavy stocks in cold storage at the end of 1943 were held chiefly by the government to meet its needs until spring when buying for the government account is to be resumed. Consumers did not seem disposed to turn to butter-substitutes even at the high ceiling prices. (*See* also CHEESE; DAIRYING; MILK; OLEOMARGARINE.) (J. C. Ms.)

Byrnes, James F.

(1879–), U.S. official, was born May 2 in Charleston, S.C., of Irish parentage. At the age of 14 he left school to become office boy of a law firm. By studying stenography, he advanced to the position of court reporter. In 1910, he was elected to the house of representatives on the Democratic ticket and was re-elected six times, serving from 1911 to 1925. As a member of the deficiency committee during World War I, he formed a lasting friendship with Franklin D. Roosevelt, then an assistant secretary

of the navy. In 1930 he was elected to the U.S. senate and was re-elected in 1936. In June 1941 he was appointed associate justice of the U.S. supreme court. After serving 16 months on the supreme court bench, he was named by President Roosevelt to head the newly created Office of Economic Stabilization on Oct. 3, 1942. On May 28, 1943, he was moved into another newly created office, topping all other government agencies, the Office of War Mobilization. His job was to settle disputes between top administrators, bring about increased co-ordination between agencies and smooth out relations with congress. One of his first acts was to name Bernard M. Baruch his personal adviser. During the latter months of 1943, Byrnes took much of the responsibility for holding down wages and prices. He could not, however, hold congress in line.

Byron, Arthur William

(1872–1943), U.S. actor, was born April 3 in Brooklyn, N.Y. After a succession of stock company roles, he appeared in plays starring John Drew, Maude Adams, Mrs. Fiske, Maxine Elliott and Ethel Barrymore. His best performances were in *The Boomerang, The Lion and the Mouse* and *Tea for Three*. In 1936 he appeared with Katherine Cornell in *Saint Joan* and with John Gielgud in *Hamlet*. Celebrating his 50th anniversary on the stage, Byron in 1939 was seen in the Guild production of Stephan Zweig's *Jeremiah*. Byron, who also played character roles, was one of the founders of the Actors' Equity association and was elected as its president in 1938. He died in Hollywood, July 16.

Cabinet Members.

The following members of President Roosevelt's cabinet held office on Jan. 1, 1944:

Post	Name	State
Secretary of State	Cordell Hull	Tennessee
Secretary of the Treasury	Henry Morgenthau, Jr.	New York
Secretary of War	Henry L. Stimson	New York
Attorney-General	Francis Biddle	Pennsylvania
Postmaster General	Frank C. Walker	Pennsylvania
Secretary of the Navy	Frank Knox	Illinois
Secretary of the Interior	Harold L. Ickes	Illinois
Secretary of Agriculture	Claude R. Wickard	Indiana
Secretary of Commerce	Jesse H. Jones	Texas
Secretary of Labor	Frances Perkins	New York

Great Britain.—At the close of 1943 the war cabinet was composed as follows:

Post	Name	Party
Prime Minister, First Lord of the Treasury and Minister of Defense	Winston Churchill	Conservative
Lord President of the Council and Deputy Prime Minister	C. R. Attlee	Labour
Secretary of State for Foreign Affairs and Leader of the House of Commons	Anthony Eden	Conservative
Chancellor of the Exchequer	Sir John Anderson	Conservative
Minister of Labour and National Service	Ernest Bevin	Labour
Minister of Production	Oliver Lyttelton	Conservative
Home Secretary and Minister of Home Security	Herbert Morrison	Labour
Minister of Reconstruction	Lord Woolton	—
Minister of State (Cairo)	R. G. Casey	(from Australia)

For other ministers and members of the government, *see* GOVERNMENT DEPARTMENTS AND BUREAUS.

Cacao: *see* COCOA.

Cadmium.

The supply of cadmium in the United States continued to be well below demand. A survey by the War Production board for the third quarter of 1943 indicated a supply 25% short of requirements, and further restrictions were placed on uses of the metal in September.

In order to maintain a better control on distribution and use, sales to consumers were restricted until the usual consumers' stocks, equivalent to 8 to 12 months' requirements, were reduced to 2 to 3 months' requirements. The shortage was largely due to heavy consumption in aircraft (as electroplated parts), which was estimated to take about half of the total supply. While no official reports were made on production, world output in 1942 was unofficially estimated at 7,500 short tons, as compared with 4,200 tons in 1938   (G. A. Ro.)

Cady, Hamilton Perkins
(1874–1943), U.S. chemist and educator, was born May 2 in Camden, Kan. A graduate of the University of Kansas, 1897, he took graduate work at Cornell and received his Ph.D. from the University of Kansas in 1903. Dr. Cady joined the staff at Kansas in 1899 and was named professor of chemistry in 1911 He and another faculty member identified the presence of helium in natural gas produced in Dexter, Kan., in 1907, which eventually led to the establishment of a helium plant in that vicinity. Dr. Cady also invented scales to determine molecular weight of gases, fostered research in liquid ammonia and was co-author of several books on chemistry. He died in Lawrence, Kan., May 26.

Calendar of Events, 1943: *see* pages 1–15.

California.
A southwestern Pacific coast state of the United States (statehood granted Sept. 9, 1850). It is popularly called the "Golden state." Area, 158,693 sq.mi., including 1,890 sq.mi. of water; pop. (1940) 6,907,387, only 29% rural. A 1943 estimate, based on the issuance of War Ration Book No. 4, indicated that the population had risen to 7,814,676. Capital, Sacramento (105,958); other leading cities, Los Angeles (1,504,277); San Francisco (634,536); Oakland (302,163); San Diego (203,341); Long Beach (164,271); Berkeley (85,547); Glendale (82,582); Pasadena (81,864). Estimates for 1943 revealed substantial increases in population in each of these cities.

History.—On Jan. 4, 1943, Earl Warren was inaugurated as California's new Republican governor. His program, developed through action of the regular legislative session and a special one called on March 17, emphasized several changes from that of the previous administration. With the state income high, a tax reduction measure was drawn up by which it was estimated that taxes would be reduced in the next biennium by $65,000,000. A state guard program abolished the militia plan in force and substituted for it an organization based upon a community volunteer system. A State War council of about 100 persons (later reduced in size), representing the legislative and executive branches of the state government and also cities and counties of the state, was formed to co-ordinate defense plans with those of the armed services. A postwar planning council, particularly designed to cope with an expected tremendous postwar unemployment problem, and a food-and-fibre council, created to meet current agricultural harvest problems, were likewise set up. Governor Warren also backed an increase in the state old-age pension from $40 to $50 per month. During 1943 there was increasing mention of the governor as a vice-presidential possibility in the next national election.

A lessening of the danger of Japanese attack on the California coast resulted in changing the status of the aircraft warning service from an active to an alert basis on Oct. 16, and in lightening dimout restrictions substantially, effective Nov. 1.

Disturbances connected with war conditions occurred in two widely separated areas in the state during 1943. In Los Angeles, in June, fist-fights took place between service men and so-called (from extreme clothing styles) "zoot suit" gangs, many of whose members were of Mexican ancestry. In northern California, at Tulelake, a relocation camp used mainly for disloyal Japanese, the inmates rioted on Nov. 4 and held officials prisoner for several hours. The camp was then taken over from the War Relocation authority by the military.

Laxity in the enforcement of regulations in Folsom prison late in 1943 caused the removal of certain officials; a special session of the legislature was in prospect early in 1944 to consider changes in the state penal system.

In the economic field California took the lead over all other states in the U.S. in ship and plane production (9.9% of the total output). On Aug. 16 the first steel mill of the state (erected by Henry Kaiser at Fontana) started operation. Job stabilization started in the first month of the year. Occasional food shortages took place in congested areas, notably in milk products lines, and in all areas where defense plants operated or where military camps were located, serious housing shortages developed.

Education.—The amount assigned in 1943–44 to the public school system of the state was $78,914,772. Elementary schools, with an average daily attendance total of 689,876, were allotted $46,651,293 from state funds; secondary schools, with an average daily attendance of 348,371, were assigned $32,263,428.

Public Welfare, Charities, Correction.—State institutions numbered 19 in 1942: seven hospitals for the insane; two homes for the feeble-minded; three juvenile correctional schools; four prisons (three for men, one for women); two homes for war veterans; one home for the adult blind. The average population of these institutions (1941–42) was 36,347. Expenditures in 1942 for upkeep of institutions were $13,706,000. In the 1943–45 budget old-age pensions amounted to $96,733,000 of the total estimate.

Banking and Finance.—California state banks numbered 282 (82 departmental, 11 commercial, 13 savings, 10 trust companies, 166 branch banks). Deposits totalled $1,792,259,000 (1942: $1,469,844,000); total resources were $2,209,011,000. Property values in the state were assessed at $7,886,224,624. On Nov. 1 the state had $116,257,000 invested in war bonds. Receipts in the 1942–43 fiscal year amounted to $490,752,000 (1941–42: $345,443,602). Largest returns were derived from the unemployment insurance tax ($143,394,000; in 1941–42: $82,600,000). Other items were: bank and corporation tax, $18,433,765; liquor excise, $4,271,812; personal income tax, $10,312,343; motor and use tax, $1,412,828; retail sales tax, $3,060,602. The state budget for the 1943–45 biennium was $551,868,000. In the budget was included $43,750,000 for a postwar construction fund. Tax reductions over the previous biennium were estimated at $65,000,000. The state general fund showed a surplus of $84,200,000 on June 30, 1943 ($60,000,000 in 1942), which rose to $103,100,000 by Oct. 31.

Communication.—California in 1940 had 14,088 mi. of steam railway; 2,768 mi. electrified railway; approximately 900,000 mi. of public highway. During the 1941–43 biennium $82,093,000 was spent by the division of highways. Motor vehicles registered (Nov. 1) numbered 2,504,987 automobiles, 211,375 trucks, 18,930 motorcycles. In the first quarter of 1943, traffic deaths per million gallons of gasoline sold were 29.2 (in 1942: 24.3). In Sept. it was estimated that the state had 2,120,700 telephones (8% over 1942).

Agriculture.—The value of agricultural production in California in 1942 amounted to $769,722,000. Fruit and nut crops were valued at $325,539,000 (1941: $249,657,000); commercial vegetables at $154,539,000 (1941: $111,725,000); feed crops at $289,644,000 (1941: $218,433,000). Farm income in 1942 from livestock and livestock products was $294,136,000. The 1943 grape crop was estimated at $122,000,000 in value and 1,596,000 tons in weight (1942: 1,398,000 tons); wine grapes amounted to 531,000 tons; table grapes, 498,000 tons, raisin grapes (fresh), 109,000 tons; dried raisins, 368,000 tons. The cotton crop for 1943 was expected to amount to 360,000 bales; the bean crop to 277,900 tons.

Manufacturing.—In 1943 aircraft and shipbuilding contracts awarded to California plants were valued at $6,801,654,000 for the former, $2,979,497,000 for the latter. Labour statistics indicated the total number of industrial workers in the state (including clerical, etc.) to be 1,138,000 in November (1942: 608,000). Employees (industrial) in durable goods plants numbered 709,300; in nondurable, 179,600. Women workers amounted to approximately one-third of the total. Average weekly earnings in durable goods plants were $57.63; in nondurable goods plants, $43.48 (in 1942, $52.03 and $43.48, respectively). In 1943 manufacturing reached a peak in production in the summer and then leveled off.

Mineral Production.—Total output was valued at $419,536,000 for 1942 (official est.). Petroleum again accounted for the largest amount.

Production of Principal Minerals in California, 1942

Product	Quantity	Value
Gold	48,000 fine oz.	$ 5,180,000
Silver	610,000 fine oz.	434,000
Copper	17,950,000 lb.	2,333,000
Lead	11,656,000 lb.	862,000
Zinc	3,750,000 lb.	424,000
Other metals	..	16,381,000
Petroleum	283,660,000 bbl.	290,752,000
Natural gas	452,840,000 M.cu.ft.	28,076,000
Miscellaneous stone	..	15,000,000
Brick	..	6,000,000
Cement	18,460,000 bbl.	28,244,000
Salines	..	15,950,000

BIBLIOGRAPHY.—C. E. Chapman, *A History of California: The Spanish Period* (1921); R. G. Cleland, *A History of California: The American Period* (1922); R. D. Hunt and N. Sánchez, *A Short History of California* (1929); J. W. Caughey, *California* (1940).   (D. Rd.)

California, University of.
A state-supported, coeducational university, with headquarters at Berkeley, but with six other campuses, at Los Angeles, San Francisco, Davis, Riverside, Mt. Hamilton, and La Jolla. During 1943, the University of California considerably revised its program and undertook numerous new activities in order to effect more complete utilization of its resources in the interest of the nation. On July 1 the university introduced a wartime calendar, comprised of three full terms of 16 weeks each, as well as one summer session of six weeks concurrent with part of the summer term.

Facilities and training were provided for military and naval units on four of the university's campuses. In February the college of agriculture at Davis discontinued civilian teaching for the duration of the war, and turned over the greater part of its facilities to the United States signal corps. At both Berkeley and Los Angeles instruction was provided for trainees in the army specialized training programs and the naval V-12 program, as well as for pre-meteorology and meteorology units of the air corps and for selected groups sent for intensive, technical courses. At San Francisco instruction was provided for a large unit of the United States nurses cadet corps and for men in both dentistry and medicine for the army and navy.

Education and training continued for civilian students. Every undergraduate civilian student was required to fulfil the national service course requirement, either by following professional curricula of importance to the war effort or by selecting, in addition to his normal curriculum, a group of related courses designed to prepare him for useful service in connection with the war.

Through various faculty committees and such agencies as the Bureau of Public Administration and the Bureau of Business and Economic Research, the university began to prepare for the postwar period. For statistics of enrolment, faculty, library volumes, etc., see UNIVERSITIES AND COLLEGES.   (R. G. S.)

Camacho, Manuel Avila: see AVILA CAMACHO, MANUEL.
Cambodia: see FRENCH COLONIAL EMPIRE.

Cambridge University.
The number of matriculants in the academic year 1942–43 was 2,322, the second highest on record, as compared with 1,759 in 1941–42. The great majority of the 2,700 men undergraduates read scientific subjects, with resulting congestion in the laboratories. Science and engineering students who had passed the higher certificate with physics, mathematics, etc., might be allowed to complete a two-year or longer course, if their progress were satisfactory; but arts students were liable to be drafted to national service after reaching the age of 18 years.

There were 17 professorial vacancies. The following retired under the age limit: Professor Owen T. Jones (geology); Professor A. C. Pigou (political economy); Dr. P. H. Winfield (English law); Sir Frederick Gowland Hopkins (biochemistry); Dr. F. H. A. Marshall (reader in agricultural physiology); and Dr. John A. Ryle, the regius professor of physic, vacated his chair to take up a post at Oxford. The following chairs were filled: Dr. A. C. Chibnall (biochemistry); Dr. J. F. Baker (mechanical science); Dr. R. A. Fisher (genetics); Dr. W. B. R. King (geology); Henry A. Hollond (English law); Dr. W. W. Grave was appointed registrary on the sudden death of Ernest Harrison.

A bequest of £440,000 from the late R. R. Cory for the botanic garden was the largest single benefaction ever received. The Pitt Press assigned a sum of £44,000 to endow from the profits of the organization a chair in American history.

Among distinguished members of the faculty who died were John Hilton, professor of industrial relations, a well-known broadcaster; Francis M. Cornford, emeritus professor of ancient philosophy; and Terrot R. Glover, former public orator. Many generations of undergraduates also regretted the death of Stanley Brown, for 43 years chief clerk of the Union society.

BIBLIOGRAPHY.—*Cambridge University Reporter*, vol. 73; *Cambridge Review*, vol. 64.   (C. Fo.)

Cameroons: see BRITISH WEST AFRICA; FRENCH COLONIAL EMPIRE.

Camouflage.
Camouflage practises deception by concealing or disguising objects to render them unrecognizable to an enemy. For front-line fighting, available natural concealment provided the best camouflage. In the absence of

CAMOUFLAGED JAP PLANES at an airfield in the Wewak area, New Guinea, photographed during an Allied raid with parachute bombs in 1943

CAMOUFLAGE LESSON at West Point military academy. The cadets look at a model village through inverted binoculars; the effect is similar to viewing the earth from an altitude of 3,000 ft.

natural means, substitutes had to be devised. Netting, garnished with cloth strips, leaves and branches were draped to fuse a machine gunner and his weapon with the surrounding landscape or it might screen individual riflemen in advanced sharpshooting positions. Sacking might be coloured and shaped to imitate rocks, blending with stony soil or desert terrain. Net camouflage, properly trimmed and draped, transformed trucks, tractors and tanks into seemingly harmless haystacks. Another netting variation formed "flat tops" to screen antiaircraft guns emplaced for firing. If netting was not available, chicken wire, appropriately garnished, furnished suitable cover.

Men, horses, mules and inanimate objects were alike subject to camouflage. Soldiers appeared in dapple-painted clothing, ornamented with the foliage of their surroundings. In the tropics, vivid colours predominated in the soldier's individual camouflage; in the north, he dressed in white. If leaf or flower camouflage was used, the materials were kept fresh, since dead camouflage is worse than none at all. At the 1st service command camouflage school a "ragamuffin" suit was devised from coloured burlap garlands knotted together so that the outline of the soldier's body appeared in broken line and he easily melted into the immediate terrain.

Paints applied to battleships, trucks, tanks, jeeps or landing barges played a prominent part in camouflaging, haze-gray having the greatest disappearance value. Except where natural surroundings were particularly vivid, paint tones used were mostly neutral.

It was sometimes necessary to hide the location of industrial installations by elaborate flat-top camouflage. Whole factories disappeared under flats which, on their upper side, showed spying aviators only an innocent farm landscape with familiar barns, corn cribs, silos and rambling roads leading off into the distance.

One basic formula obtained whether camouflage was done in farm areas, cities or on battle lines, viz.: Either fuse the object with its immediate natural surroundings or bury it out of sight.

Military camouflage conceals, disguises or misleads by cleverly contrived means. Concealment might be used in mobilizing a striking force; location of important headquarters might be disguised to lose all of their military characteristics; and in the realm of misleading displays, phantom concentrations of dummy cannon, machine guns, antiaircraft guns and soldiers might be so arranged as to provoke a wasted enemy attack on an utterly worthless target. In Washington, D.C., the press carried headlines during 1943 concerning the presence of dummy aircraft guns and soldiers stationed on the roofs of government buildings.

In any case, good camouflage doesn't happen by chance. It is always carefully planned to be used in terrain which has been well studied in advance, and it is executed with the best possible natural or artificial media. The camoufleur, evaluating angles, light diffusion, colour and shadow factors, strives to have the attacking eye fail to see that which is protectively concealed. He always avoids harsh, straight lines, since they do not occur in nature.

All camouflage has two powerful enemies—the sharp eye of the low-flying reconnaissance aviator, and the exact, recording eye of the modern camera with its wide-angle lens, equipped with shutters synchronized to aeroplane flight. Camouflage which hoodwinks these two agents is indeed successful.

BIBLIOGRAPHY.—Robert P. Breckenridge, *Modern Camouflage* (1942); Herbert Friedmann, *The Natural-history Background of Camouflage*, Smithsonian Inst. (1942); *The Evening Star*, Washington (Oct. 18, 1943); Ralph Rodney Root, *Camouflage with Planting* (1942); Konrad F. Wittmann, *Industrial Camouflage Manual* (1942); Harper Goff, "Industrial Camouflage Experiments," *The Military Engineer* (March 1943); "Camouflage Do's and Don't's," *Military Review* (July 1943).

(R. S. T.)

Camp Fire Girls.

Besides achieving astonishing totals in pounds of waste fat and other salvage collected, war stamps and bonds sold (and bought), clerical and messenger service performed, supplies for hospital and U.S.O. recreation centres made, and other co-operation with war agencies, the Camp Fire Girls in 1943 did not neglect service to their communities.

Girls in the senior division of Camp Fire Girls (the Horizon clubs) trained themselves as child care, hospital and farm aides. With the two other leading national girls' organizations, Girl Scouts and Girl Reserves, standards of work and training were drawn up. A child care course was published by Camp Fire Girls, and many high school girls took this course and volunteered their service at day nurseries and child care centres where children of working mothers were cared for. The girls also proved themselves helpful and responsible in their services as junior hospital aides.

Farm Aides—A Guide for Group Leaders was published in 1943 by the three organizations jointly, the experience of the previous summer having indicated that supervision by trained adults, and preliminary training of the girls themselves, would add greatly to the efficiency of the work on farms and to the benefits of this work to the girls themselves.

The Horizon clubs (senior high school girls) carried out a

"World Horizons" project which led them to explore the possibilities of the coming air age and its implications in terms of "New Neighbours," "New Business," "New Careers."

With juvenile delinquency on the increase, particularly among the girls of early teen age, it became evident that membership in well-organized Camp Fire groups where girls enjoyed fun, friendship, guidance and service was one very effective way of offsetting this tendency, with the result that more women enlisted as volunteer leaders of Camp Fire groups, and the membership increased by 6%.

The recruiting, training and direction of these leaders was the major concern of the national and local Camp Fire councils, handicapped themselves by the draining off of their professional workers. The number of girls desiring membership far exceeded the trained leadership available.

At the meeting of the National Council of Camp Fire Girls held in Omaha, Neb., Oct. 19–22, 1943, Mrs. Quade C. Weld was re-elected national president. President Franklin D. Roosevelt was honorary president of Camp Fire girls in 1943 and Mrs. Roosevelt honorary chairman of the advisory committee. Miss Martha F. Allen was secretary and national executive and Earle W. Brailey treasurer. Lady (Walter) Hearn was president of British Camp Fire girls.   (C. F. Lo.)

Canada, Dominion of.
A dominion of the British Commonwealth of Nations (Statute of Westminster, 1931, 22. Geo. V.c.4.) covering all portions of North America north of the United States, except Newfoundland, Labrador and Alaska. The dominion is a federal union of nine provinces united under the terms of the (imperial) British North America Act of 1867—Ontario, Quebec, Nova Scotia and New Brunswick in 1867, Manitoba 1870, British Columbia 1871, Prince Edward Island 1873, Alberta and Saskatchewan 1905. Outside the provincial boundaries, the Yukon and Northwest Territories are under the dominion government. Area, 3,729,665 sq.mi.; pop. (1941) 11,505,898. Capital, Ottawa (pop. 154,585). Montreal is the largest city (city proper 890,234). Provincial capitals in the order of the provinces listed above are Toronto (city proper 657,612); Quebec (147,908); Halifax (69,326); Fredericton (9,905); Winnipeg (225,437); Victoria (42,507); Charlottetown (14,460); Edmonton (92,404); Regina (56,520). Other leading cities are Vancouver (271,597); Hamilton (167,830); St. John, N.B. (50,084); Kingston (29,545); Fort William (30,370); Port Arthur (24,217); Saskatoon (42,320).

The governor general in 1943 was the earl of Athlone; prime minister, William Lyon Mackenzie King.

History.—In the year 1943 the dominion government continued under the direction of Prime Minister Mackenzie King and the Liberal party, which had been re-elected on March 26, 1940. The Progressive Conservative party formed the official opposition with Gordon Graydon leading in the house of commons. John Bracken (q.v.), chosen Progressive Conservative leader at Winnipeg in Dec. 1942, had no seat in the dominion parliament at the close of the year 1943. The year was marked by the active appearance of two new political parties. *Le Bloc Populaire Canadien*, formed in Oct. 1942 by Maxime Raymond, had as the central themes of its program national independence, the frank acceptance of the federal principle, and the recognition of the family as the social and economic unit. On Aug. 22, 1943, at Toronto, the erstwhile Canadian Communist party formed the Labour Progressive party. The strength of these new parties was substantially shown when, on Aug. 5, they carried two of the four dominion by-elections, the Labour Progressives capturing Cartier (one of the Montreal ridings) and *le Bloc*, Stanstead, in rural Quebec.

In the provinces also was much political activity. On March 3 Mitchell Hepburn placed his resignation in the hands of Gordon Conant, the premier. Conant himself later resigned, owing to ill-health; his place was taken by Harry Nixon, leader of the Liberal party in Ontario. On Aug. 4 the provincial general elections were held, resulting in the total overthrow of the Liberal government. The Progressive Conservatives, led by George Drew (q.v.), captured the largest number of seats, 38, followed by the C.C.F., 34; the Liberals, 14; Labour, 2; Independent, 1. Drew was sworn in as premier. Coupled with the defeat of the late government was the dramatic rise of the C.C.F. to the position of second place in the legislature. In Prince Edward Island general elections were held in September. The Liberal party, which had come into office in 1938, was sustained with, however, a somewhat reduced majority. In the west the death of William Aberhart, the Social Credit premier of Alberta, was an event of considerable political significance. He was succeeded by Ernest Charles Manning and the ability of the government to carry the by-election in Red Deer might be regarded as an indication of its vigour under the new leadership. In spite, therefore, of the overwhelming absorption of the war, the year was marked by important and possibly far-reaching political changes.

On April 1, 1943 Anthony Eden, the secretary of state for foreign affairs of Great Britain, addressed a joint session of the Canadian parliament. Toward the end of May, Queen Wilhelmina of the Netherlands visited her daughter Princess Juliana at Ottawa. On June 16 Mme. Chiang Kai-shek addressed a joint parliamentary session in Ottawa, and also made a notable address at Montreal on China's role among the United Nations. In the middle of July, General Henri Giraud, chief of the French armies, was in Ottawa. Between Aug. 10 and 24 the Quebec conference brought to Canada President Roosevelt and Winston Churchill, the prime minister of Britain. At the conclusion of the conference, President Roosevelt visited Ottawa (Aug. 25), where he addressed a gigantic gathering of more than 30,000 persons before the parliament buildings.

The latter part of 1943 witnessed significant changes in Canada's diplomatic status. On Nov. 11 the Canadian and United States governments raised their legations to the rank of embassies. Ray Atherton became the first United States ambassador to Canada, while Leighton McCarthy became the first Canadian ambassador to the United States. A month later, Dec. 10, Canada elevated her legations in China, Brazil and the soviet union to embassies.

Forming the practical corollary to these diplomatic changes was close co-operation between Canada and the United States. On Aug. 21 a Canadian-United States Joint War Aid committee was set up to study the operation of the lend-lease and mutual aid legislation. At an earlier date, a joint economic committee discussed the opening of about 1,000,000 sq.mi. of territory in Alaska, the Yukon, British Columbia and the Northwest Territories. Immediate steps to assist the population were considered, as well as plans to increase the population by immigration. A highly interesting phase of mutual aid was the development by the United States war department of the petroleum fields at Fort Norman, Northwest Territories, in order to supply the Canada-Alaska highway. The scheme involved not only the exploitation of the petroleum fields proper, but the construction of a 500-mi. pipe line to White Horse, where the refineries and storage tanks were to be located. The whole plan encountered considerable criticism in the United States, and its further prosecution was problematical. In November Canada along with the United States and some 40 other nations signed at Washington, D.C., an agreement to feed, clothe and care for the civilian population of the axis-dominated countries, when they shall be liberated. The

United Nations' Relief and Rehabilitation administration, meeting in Atlantic City, N.J., assessed Canada's share of the $2,000,-000,000 to $2,500,000,000 program at $90,000,000, or its equivalent in supplies. Other forms of Canadian-United States cooperation, more closely connected with the military phases of the war, are considered in the section, *Canada at War.*

In the domestic field, the Canadian government throughout 1943 sought to combat inflation. The floating of two Victory Loans rather than one, was an attempt in this direction. In the late autumn it was clear that more drastic measures must be employed. After an extensive publicity campaign on the radio and in the press, on Dec. 5, Prime Minister King outlined his anti-inflationary program. He proposed controlling wages and farm prices, pledging an exhaustive review of wage and price standards in the event of the cost-of-living index rising 3% over a two-month period. On Dec. 8 the ban on wage increases became effective, except in cases of "gross inequality, or gross injustice." During the year 1943 there were 328 strikes, an emphatic commentary on domestic conditions.   (J. I. C.; S. LEA.)

Canada at War.—All information in regard to the operations and occurrences of the war which could be of service to the enemy was withheld by the government in 1943. The facts and figures here given are strictly confined to information disseminated by the government itself in the official monthly publication, *Canada at War,* and in departmental reports, bulletins and summaries.

In 1943 Canada entered on an increasingly active phase of its wartime role. Units of the Canadian navy and air force contributed to routing the enemy out of North Africa in the spring of the year. Throughout the summer, autumn and winter, the 1st Canadian division took an important share in the Sicilian and Italian campaigns. Thus Sept. 9, the fourth anniversary of Canada's declaration of war, witnessed all arms of the service in active and decisive operation. In Sicily, Canadian along with British troops broke the powerfully held Etna defense line, while in central Italy, Canadians maintained a steady advance in the face of determined resistance, inclement weather and difficult terrain. Canadian naval, air and land units, in co-operation with U.S. formations drove the Japanese out of Kiska in the Aleutian Islands, thus freeing the North American continent from fear of invasion.

The operations of the Canadian navy were diversified. Some units saw spectacular service in the Mediterranean and Pacific waters. The bulk of the Canadian navy, however, was concentrated in the North and Central Atlantic. There its duty was primarily that of convoy, and its chief enemy was the submarine. The type of duty to be performed emphatically conditioned the character of the Canadian fleet. It had in 1943 no ships larger than destroyers; the bulk of its 200 fighting vessels were escort ships of one kind and another. While the destroyers in commission in 1943 were acquired either from Britain or the United States, construction of vessels of this type in Canada had begun. In the year 1944 Canada planned to further increase its navy by adding medium cruisers and possibly aircraft carriers. As a result of its increasing naval power, Canada provided about one-half the protection for North Atlantic shipping. The cost in ships and men was heavy; 13 ships and more than 1,200 men were lost in the Mediterranean or in the Atlantic since the outbreak of war. The Canadian navy was thoroughly democratized through the "lower deck" system of advancement. Prospective officers were trained as ordinary seamen, proceeding through a year of practical experience before emerging in commissioned rank. Early in 1943 Rear Admiral L. W. Murray was appointed commander in chief, Canadian Northwest Atlantic. He was thus the first Canadian commander in chief to assume operational direction in a vital war area in which the enemy was actively engaged.

The royal Canadian air force saw world-wide service in 1943. Numbers of its personnel, attached to the British air force, engaged in the long-range bombing of German transportation and industrial centres. In October Canadian squadrons participated in all the raids on western Germany. Convoy patrol and anti-submarine operations in the Atlantic were increased, as it became possible to withdraw men and machines from the North Pacific theatre of war. The working of the British Commonwealth Air Training plan was expanded throughout the year. Canada carried about one-half the cost of the scheme, which totalled approximately $40,000,000 a month. In early 1943 the air crew graduates exceeded 50,000.

In August and September marked changes in the organization of the Canadian army were made. The 7th and 8th divisions and part of the 6th division, hitherto on duty in Canada, were broken out of their formations to provide reinforcements for troops in the field. Men considered unfit for active service were returned to civilian life. At the same time the number of training centres and, accordingly, the number of officers training, was reduced. In future a greater proportion of officers was to be drawn from men with overseas experience. By these means the Canadian home force was reduced by about 20,000 men. The Canadian overseas armies were composed of two corps of three infantry and two armoured divisions. In addition there was a large number of corps troops, engaged in transport, medical, forestry services, etc. The numerical strength of the Canadian army in November was officially stated to be 465,000 men. On Dec. 26 important changes were announced in the Canadian high command overseas. Lieut. Gen. Andrew McNaughton retired from the command of the Canadian army and his place was taken temporarily by Lieut. Gen. Kenneth Stuart. Lieut. Gen. Henry Crerar was appointed to the command of the newly formed Canadian corps in the Mediterranean area. The retirement of Gen. McNaughton was due to ill-health.

The increasing tempo of the war was reflected within Canada itself. This was best indicated by the intensive search for manpower. Responsibility for allocating manpower rested with the National Selective Service, under the department of labour. Beginning with April, six orders were issued transferring men from nonessential to such essential services as lumbering, farming, coal mining and munition manufacturing. In order to secure adequate labour for farm work, the unusual course was taken of releasing certain army personnel. On May 17 it was declared that a state of national emergency existed in respect to coal mining. Miners were prohibited from volunteering for the armed forces, were given automatic deferment from military training, or, if already enlisted, were given leave. In cities of more than 50,000 population, coal deliverymen were also "frozen" in their occupation. Competent university students were given deferment for one academic session only, unless they were enrolled in such courses as might be declared essential. Incompetent students were denied entrance, or if entered, were not allowed to remain at college. In order to meet the dangerous depletion of school staffs, teachers engaged in 1943 were retained in their profession. By these means, or by means of increased employment of women, attempts were made to meet the new wartime requirements.

Important financial adjustments were necessary in 1943. In March the fifth wartime budget was brought down. Of an estimated total expenditure of $5,500,000,000, considerably more than one-half was designated for war purposes, either for immediate national needs, or in the form of gifts of foodstuff or equipment for the United Nations. This vast sum of money was raised in part by taxation, but in larger measure by borrowing.

In fact, the budget brought only minor changes in taxation, usually in the form of adjustments in favour of certain groups in the armed services. The most important feature of the budget was the so-called "pay-as-you-owe" basis for income tax collection. Beginning with April, deductions were made at source on wages or salaries. Collections of other forms of income, *e.g.*, from investments, were put on a quarterly basis. The new tax scheme carried with it the wiping out of one-half of the tax on the 1942 income, except on invested income in excess of $3,000. For such, special provision was made. The adoption of the 1943 collection scheme seemed to have been dictated by administrative as well as political considerations, the number of taxpayers having expanded from about 250,000 in 1939 to over 2,000,000 in 1943. (For victory loans, etc., see *Finance*, below.) The drive for the sale of war savings certificates was maintained and even expanded in an effort to attract the small investor. The problem of war finance came, therefore, into increasing prominence. It contained such innovations as the instalment system of income tax collection and the tacit declaration on the part of the government of a new reliance on loans and borrowing, rather than on a "pay-as-you-go" basis of financing the war.

An important and integral part of wartime finance was price control. The agency most immediately concerned was the Wartime Prices and Trade board, which, under the minister of finance, dominated price control, consumer rationing and essential civilian supply. The activities of the board increased during the year 1943, when it became manifest that increased income, coupled with shortages in certain commodities, would cause a rapid rise in prices. In 1941 a price ceiling was established and a determined effort was made to hold, or at least to control, the prices of goods. As a result of the various control measures, food prices were kept relatively stable. In Jan. 1943 the prices of such commodities as tea, coffee and milk were actually reduced by means of subsidy, or by a reduction in import duty, as in the instance of oranges. The corollary of price control, wage control was politically dangerous. The National War Labour board, which administered wage control, had unfortunate difficulties with its personnel; L. J. Cohen, the original labour member, resigned. The numerous industrial disputes which marked the year 1943 may be regarded as indicative of the qualified functioning of the control measures. In an effort to offset inflation, the government throughout the autumn conducted a vigorous publicity campaign. In December the cost of living bonus was abandoned in favour of increases in the basic wage scale.

Closely associated with the conduct of the war on the home front were projects of postwar planning. The psychological value of such plans was recognized with the tabling of the Marsh report in March. The report took its popular designation from the name of its author, Leonard Marsh, research adviser to the Dominion Committee on Reconstruction. The report was a comprehensive document, embracing a study of contemporary social legislation, of principles underlying social security schemes and, finally, methods whereby such principles and experiences might be implemented. The Marsh report was, therefore, not a draft measure, but rather an initiation of the subject for discussion. Of more immediate effect were the provisions of the various rehabilitation plans for ex-servicemen. These covered a wide field ranging from clothing allowances to postgraduate courses at universities. In order to make these benefits more readily available, the ministry of pensions and health stationed welfare officers in the chief centres. To assist the welfare officers and to bring the task of rehabilitation close to everyday life, citizens' committees were established in practically every city.

Throughout 1943 various forms of civilian defense were maintained at a high level. Air Raid Precaution services had their headquarters at Ottawa, and established bodies across the country to study local conditions. The A.R.P. services were entirely voluntary and numbered in 1943 probably more than 80,000 persons in all branches. In the lower St. Lawrence valley, civilian defense organizations were carefully articulated with the protective system of the armed services in an effort to prevent a repetition of submarine raids on St. Lawrence shipping.

The fourth year of the war saw great advances in Canadian business. In spite of its small population, Canada reached the rank of third among the trading nations of the world. Canadian foods and Canadian munitions formed an important contribution to the armoury of the United Nations. The objective in food production was set very high, but it was not probable that all the objectives would be reached, because of shortages in farm labour and equipment and unfavourable weather conditions in central and eastern Canada. The processing and packing of meat was expected to exceed all previous records with 1,577,000,000 lb. packed during 1943. Extension in sheep breeding was undertaken in 1942 in order to increase both meat and wool supplies. Other foods destined largely for export were butter, cheese and powdered eggs; during the first eight months of 1943 nearly 10,000,000 lb. of dried eggs were shipped overseas. On the other hand, the wheat crop would probably be the lightest since 1937, in the neighbourhood of 300,000,000 bu. This was, of course, in response to direct government policy of reducing wheat acreage in favour of the acreage of feed grains. Significant experiments were undertaken in the course of the year looking to the production of peas, beans and oil crops suitable for supplying the liberated areas in Europe. In May a delegation of Canadian farm experts attended the United Nations Food conference at Hot Springs, Va. Problems relating to the production and distribution of food in the postwar period were discussed. The role of Canada with its considerable food-producing capacity was of great moment.

The production of munitions and ships in 1943 mirrored the new demands of war. The production of certain lines of equipment was reduced, while the production of other lines was accelerated. In the latter category stood naval vessels, guns, combat aircraft and radio location equipment. It was expected, therefore, that the change would be in kind, rather than in degree. A specific instance may be cited in the production of tanks, which would be discontinued largely in favour of engines and components for escort vessels, or self-propelling gun mounts. The production of instruments and communication sets for tanks, ships, planes and motorized vehicles was much accelerated. The manufacture of aeroplanes was likewise increased. In 1943 nine different types of aircraft were manufactured, and extended experiments conducted on other types, especially on cargo and transport planes. The aircraft industry employed more than 100,000 workers, about one quarter of whom were women. In view of the rapid expansion of this industry, it was expected that aircraft manufacturing would absorb workers from other programs which were curtailed.

The shipbuilding industry, which produced both cargo and war vessels, was expanded throughout 1943. Twenty yards were engaged in the merchant shipbuilding program, employing 43,000 men. In the second quarter of 1943 the rate of delivery was increased to one 10,000-ton ship every two days. Materials, like labour, were chiefly Canadian in origin. Cargo vessels were destined either for Canadian steamship firms, or for the ministry of war transport of the United Kingdom. After the war vessels chartered by the United Kingdom were to be returned to Canada and added to the Canadian merchant marine. The types of vessels chiefly constructed were 10,000 and 4,700 tonners, and oil tankers. The naval shipbuilding program was substantially increased. In the first half of 1943 contracts were let for 424

PRINCIPALS OF THE QUEBEC CONFERENCE on the citadel overlooking the Plains of Abraham in Aug. 1943. Front row, left to right: British Foreign Minister Anthony Eden; President Roosevelt; Princess Alice, wife of the earl of Athlone, governor-general of Canada; Prime Minister Winston Churchill. Rear row: earl of Athlone; Canadian Prime Minister Mackenzie King; Sir Alexander Cadogan, British permanent undersecretary of state for foreign affairs; Brendan Bracken, British minister of information

corvettes, frigates and steel minesweepers. Contracts were also let for wooden patrol vessels and minesweepers. The most considerable individual items of ship construction were two tribal class destroyers; in September one of these was launched. Eleven yards were engaged in warship building. The equipping of this rapidly growing fleet of war and merchant vessels was in the hands of 300 manufacturing firms which supplied everything from rivets to navigation instruments and marine engines.

The production of essential raw materials, timber, rubber, steel and nonferrous metals was much accelerated. Canada supplied Great Britain with 70% of its timber requirements, as well as providing 100,000,000 ft. to British commonwealth countries, and about 1,000,000,000 ft. to the United States. The production of rubber was increased with the opening of the Polymer corporation plant (a crown company) at Sarnia, Ont. It was expected that the plant would produce approximately 41,000 tons of synthetic rubber in the course of a year. As well as undertaking to meet its full war needs, Canada reduced its consumption of civilian rubber to 10% of what it was before the war. The reduction was still in progress by means of substitutes and reclaimed rubber.

The production of steel was placed at 5,000,000 tons for 1943. It was expected that more than 3,000,000 tons would be supplied by Canadian mills, the remainder coming from the United States. Canada manufactured all the necessary plate armour for her quota of tanks, armoured vehicles, gun shields and for certain naval purposes. Fine alloy steel for machine tools, armour and guns was produced in considerable quantities. Steel for shipbuild-

ing and for making shells was produced also; the latter in quantity of about 250,000 tons a year. As a result of war stimulus Canada advanced to the position of fourth among the steel-producing states of the United Nations.

In the field of base metals Canada maintained its position as the greatest exporting nation in the world. Canada provided about 40% of the war requirements of aluminum of the United Nations and 95% of the nickel. In order to further increase the output of aluminum the government and the Aluminium Company of Canada opened the hydroelectric power plant at Shipshaw in northern Quebec, in the spring of 1943. Certain metals, such as magnesium and mercury, formerly imported, were produced at home, actually leaving a surplus for export. Magnesium processing was developed from experiments conducted in the laboratories of the National Research council at Ottawa, by Walter Pidgeon. The year 1943 witnessed not only accelerated production in practically every line of industry, but great strides toward self-sufficiency in vital metal production.

In August the Quebec conference, the sixth meeting of President Roosevelt and Prime Minister Churchill, took place. Canada acted as the host of the conference. In addition, Canadian political and military leaders participated in the discussions. This was the second occasion at which Canadian chiefs of staff were present at a general war parley. The first occasion was in May during the United States-United Kingdom discussion at Washington, D.C. At Quebec there was a joint session of the war committee of the Canadian cabinet and the war cabinet of the United Kingdom. In order to assure continuous consultation, Canada maintained a joint staff mission in Washington, D.C., which was present, along with the British and United States staffs, whenever discussions were of direct interest to Canada.

Co-operation between Canada and the United States became

extremely close in the course of 1943. The armed forces of the two nations served together in driving the Japanese from the Aleutian Islands, as well as in Sicily and Italy. At home Canadian and United States formations made joint use of facilities for training parachute troops at Camp Shilo in Manitoba and at Fort Benning in Georgia. The two countries also formed a Special Service force, drawn from their respective armies, which would provide the nucleus for combined operations, probably in the Pacific. These evidences of co-operation in the military sphere may be regarded as earnest of the engagements entered into at Ogdensburg and Hyde Park in Aug. 1940 and April 1941 respectively. In economic matters a Joint Agricultural committee was set up in March. The duty of this committee was to review food production and distribution in Canada and in the United States. In order to further co-ordinate Canadian effort with that of the United States, the Canadian government created a food requirement committee which was intended to work in close harmony with the Combined Food board of the United States and Britain.

Throughout 1943 women played an increasingly important part in Canada's role as a belligerent. Women in the armed services numbered about 36,000, divided between army, navy and air force units. A much more substantial group of women, numbering over 250,000 were absorbed by war industry. There were 830,000 women engaged in the vital work of farming. Innumerable women served as volunteer workers, staffing day nurseries, checking prices and issuing ration books. In an effort to mitigate the burdens of national service, 26 day nurseries were established across Canada. At these nurseries children were cared for and provided with a hot meal. (*See* also BUSINESS REVIEW.)

Defense.—See *Canada at War,* above.

Finance.—For the fiscal year 1943–44 the expenditure of the Canadian government was estimated at $5,500,000,000. Of this sum, $2,890,000,000 was intended for Canadian war purposes, with an additional $1,000,000,000 given to the United Nations in war supplies, equipment and foodstuffs; $610,000,000 was set aside for ordinary government outlays. The estimated revenue for the same period was $2,752,200,000. As the fiscal year does not end till March 31, it is difficult to state how accurate such budgetary forecasts are. Figures available up to Nov. 30, 1943 showed that the ordinary revenue had reached a sum of $1,752,-456,426, while expenditure in the same period stood at $3,120,-838,024.

The borrowing operations of the government were highly successful. Two Victory Loans were floated in 1943 and both were heavily oversubscribed. The Fourth loan undertaken in the spring with an objective $1,100,000,000 brought in a sum of $1,308,985,-000; the Fifth loan, in the autumn, aiming at $1,000,000,000 actually netted $1,383,272,250. It was estimated that there were more than 3,000,000 cash subscribers to the Fifth Victory Loan. By means of the two loans, as well as treasury bills and two-year notes, the government provided itself with the sum of $3,227,260,750. The interest charges on such a sum were considerable, the interest on the public debt reaching $165,079,094. With any sharp decline in income a very serious situation might develop. In 1943 the national income was at a very high level ($8,500,000,000 estimated) and probably more widespread than ever before.

Trade and Communications.—In the interests of national security, it is impossible to give a complete outline of Canada's external trade in 1943. Information as to sailing directions and as to the character of goods exported was withheld. In the first ten months of 1943 exports of Canadian commodities were nearly 230% greater than in the same period of 1939. Of the grand total of $2,379,000,000, the sum of $837,000,000 represented ex-

ports to Great Britain and a sum of $911,000,000, exports to the United States. Thus it may be observed that World War II did not seriously alter the main outlets of Canadian trade. The war went far toward making Canada a creditor, not a debtor nation; likewise toward broadening the basis of its self-sufficiency.

Canadian transportation, as reflected in the reports of the Canadian National and Canadian Pacific railways, showed the stimulation of wartime business. The Canadian National anticipated a gross revenue of $440,000,000 for 1943, as compared with $375,000,000 for the year 1942. The Canadian Pacific reported increases of 70% in ton miles in freight and 250% in passenger miles over 1939. Yet these results were obtained with little increase in staffs, rolling stock or equipment. The most substantial advance in equipment was represented by the opening of the new Canadian National terminal in Montreal in July. This not only provided a thoroughly modern station, but further enabled the railway to consolidate its passenger traffic in the Montreal metropolitan region. The airlines of both the Canadian Pacific railway and the Dominion Department of Transport made notable advances during 1943. Preliminary figures showed that the Canadian Pacific Airways flew 70,000 passengers, 2,200,000 lb. of mail and 9,100,000 lb. of air cargo in 1943; comparable figures for the Trans-Canada Airways were 141,000 passengers, 3,900,000 lb. of mail and 840,000 lb. of express. Both railways gave increased attention to plans for the postwar period, and sections of the findings of the Canadian National railways were laid before the house of commons Committee on Rehabilitation and Reconstruction.

Agriculture.—The year 1943 was a difficult one for the Canadian farmer. As well as being faced with shortages in manpower and machinery, the direct consequences of the war, he was hindered by a late spring and an abnormally wet summer. Nevertheless, all demands for essential food commodities were successfully met.

Many Canadian farm products were destined for war export. The requirement of the British ministry of food for 675,000,000 lb. of bacon and pork products was satisfied. During the year about 7,000,000 lb. of butter and 16,800,000 one-pound tins of evaporated milk were shipped to the British food ministry. In the same period 10,080 short tons of dried egg powder (equivalent to 63,000,000 doz. eggs) were also dispatched to Britain. War demands caused the introduction of new crops, especially those producing vegetable oils. Hence, rape, linseed, flax and soybeans were grown extensively. They served industrial purposes, and some, like the soybean, had considerable food value. The grain crop in 1943 showed a marked decline, the wheat crop stood at 293,704,000 bu. Feed grains in the west were good and, with the free freight policy, farmers in eastern Canada and in British Columbia were assured sufficient food for their herds. The fruit and vegetable crop was light. Early in December a Dominion-Provincial Agricultural conference was held to map farm production for 1944. In most commodities the objectives for 1943 were called for again. To ease farming conditions more steel was to be released for the manufacture of agricultural machinery, 80% of the 1940 tonnage. At the same time National Selective Service policies applying to farm labour were more closely adjusted to meet the needs of this vital industry.

Manufacturing.—Throughout 1943 manufacturing was much quickened by governmental wartime expenditures. Munitions were turned out to the value of $55,000,000 a week. The output of army equipment reached its peak in the course of the year, and greater attention was directed toward the production of ships and aeroplanes. In November the 200th Canadian-built 10,000-ton merchant ship was delivered. Certain adjustments in the armament program were made necessary by the altering conditions of the war. Men and supplies thus released were absorbed in other war productions, or in the manufacture of certain lines of goods for civilian consumption. The proposed increase in the manufacture of farm machinery, mentioned above, may be cited as evidence of this. The year 1943 saw remarkable increases in the means of production. At the end of January the hydroelectric plant at Shipshaw, on the upper Saguenay, was opened. The peak production of the plant was set at 1,200,000 horsepower.

(J. I. C.)

Canadian Literature.

Outstanding novel in 1943 was Franklin Davey McDowell's *Forges of Freedom*, which crystallized 14th-century England at the time of the peasants' revolt. Frederick Niven wrote about the 1745 Jacobite rising in Scotland and called it *Under Which King?* Maida Parlow French turned to the Canadian scene with *Boughs Bend Over*, which described the founding of the United Empire Loyalist settlement in Matilda township on the St. Lawrence river. Evelyn Eaton added another historical romance to her list with *The Sea Is So Wide*, the setting still in Nova Scotia. Marius Barbeau produced a vigorous historical romance of fur trading along the Laird river in the northwest a century ago, under the title *Mountain Cloud*. Stephen Leacock added to his reputation as a humorist with a volume of deliciously *Happy Stories Just to Laugh at*.

Poetry.—There were five major collections of poetry. The perennial and major voice of E. J. Pratt was heard in *Still Life*, a collection of satirical and lyrical poems. In *Challenge to Time and Death* Audrey Alexandra Brown turned to war themes. *Tasting the Earth* by Mona Gould was the first book by a young poet anxious about the men and women of her generation at war, and the poems had a deep understanding of human experience. Amabel King's *New Crusaders, and Other Poems*, divided its pages between poems of war and poems of peace and was marked by facile phrase-making. The list of 1943 poetry chapbooks was long. Outstanding among them were Mary Elizabeth Colman's *For This Freedom Too*, the poems of which all treated war; Evelyn Eaton's *Birds Before Dawn*, a collection of extremely short, jewel-like poems; Ernest Fewster's *Litany Before the Dawn of Fire*, a mixture of short lyrics and long symbolic poems; Irene Chapman Benson's *Journey into Yesterday*, which contained striking poetic imagery.

Frederick B. Watt's *Who Dare to Live* was a long narrative poem about Canada's merchant marine. Wilmot B. Lane's *The Closed Book* was an epic of the soul's quest. John Coulter's *Transit Through Fire* was the libretto of an opera of that name which depicted the experiences of a 1942 varsity graduate. Frederick George Scott, beloved padre of World War I, published his *Collected Poems*. An oddity was the appearance of *At the Long Sault*, a number of new and hitherto unpublished poems of long-dead Archibald Lampman.

Nonfiction.—Wallace Reyburn's *Glorious Chapter* was the first eye-witness account of the famous Dieppe raid. Amea Willoughby's *I Was on Corregidor* was another eye-witness account of the war in the Pacific zone. *Free Trip to Berlin* by Isabel Guernsey reported the experiences of 15 months in a nazi concentration camp after the torpedoing of the "Zamzam." In *Malta Spitfire* Leslie Roberts told the first-person story of George ("Buzz") Beurling's air fighting. In *The War: Fourth Year* Edgar McInnis continued his indispensable chronology of the great conflict. In *Canada in World Affairs* R. MacGregor Dawson surveyed the international relationships of Canada during the 1939–41 period.

Other books on wartime (and postwar) themes included *Discharged* by Robert England, which studied exhaustively the problem of the civil re-establishment of war veterans in Canada; *Which Kind of Revolution?* by W. D. Herridge, which presented a plan for using Canada's resources to lift the people to prosperity; *The Dawn of Ampler Life* by Charlotte Whitton, in which she presented her own ideas on this theme and also analyzed the Beveridge and Marsh reports; *Social Security and Reconstruction in Canada* and *Public Health and Welfare Organization in Canada*, both by Harry M. Cassidy, the first of which gave the historical background of the subject and the second of which examined in detail one of the more difficult aspects of social security.

Biography.—Elsie M. Pomeroy published *Sir Charles G. D. Roberts*, a definitive life of the great Canadian who died in 1943. Another volume in the literary field was *The Autobiography of Oliver Goldsmith* by Wilfrid E. Myatt, who was grandnephew of the noted British writer and Canada's first native-born English-speaking poet. In the historical field, Arthur S. Morton's *Sir George Simpson* turned out to be a vivid pen picture; and R. F. Longley's *Sir Francis Hincks* was a full-length study of Canadian statesmen of pre-Confederation days.

Juveniles.—Roderick L. Haig-Brown presented *Starbuck Valley Winter*, a novel describing the adventures of running a trap line in British Columbia. Olive Knox appeared on the literary scene with a first book, *By Paddle and Saddle*, a novel of a trip across Canada in the early 19th century by a young Scottish lad. Helen Dickson Reynolds added *The Cruise of the Mamie L*, a novel of salmon fishing off the British Columbia coast, to her long list.

Literary Awards.—In 1943 the Canadian Authors' association, sponsors of the annual governor-general's literary awards, made two important changes. The three divisions were expanded by breaking the general nonfiction division into academic nonfiction and creative nonfiction; and the medals, formerly of bronze, were changed to silver. Winners in 1943 (for books published during 1942) were: fiction, G. Herbert Sallans for *Little Man*; poetry, Earle Birney for *David and Other Poems*; creative nonfiction, Bruce Hutchison, *The Unknown Country*; academic nonfiction, Edgar McInnis, *The Unguarded Frontier*.

(C. Cy.)

Canadian-U.S. War Committees.

After 1941, the following committees were set up for joint Canadian-U.S. operation in the fields of defense, economics and war production: Permanent Joint Board on Defense; Material Co-ordinating committee; Joint Economic committees; Joint War Production committee; Joint Agricultural committee and Joint War Aid committee.

The Canadian joint staff mission in Washington was represented when the British-United States combined chiefs of staff discussed material of direct concern to Canada. Canada also became a member of the Combined Production and Resources board with the United Kingdom and the United States and in Oct. 1943 was admitted to full membership on the Combined Food board of the United Kingdom and the United States. The United States War Production board established an office in Ottawa, and the Canadian Department of Munitions and Supply and Wartime Prices and Trade board sent representatives to Washington.

At Hyde Park, New York, on April 20, 1941, the prime minister of Canada and the president of the United States agreed "as a general principle that in mobilizing the resources of this continent, each country should provide the other with the defense articles which it is best able to produce, and above all, produce quickly, and that production programs should be co-ordinated to this end." In accordance with the Hyde Park declaration, the

United States agreed to buy enough Canadian war goods to enable Canada to pay for essential U.S. war materials. The contracts that the United States placed in Canada, after Hyde Park, not only took advantage of Canada's much earlier conversion to war production but at the same time contributed to the elimination of Canada's urgent need for U.S. dollars required to meet the cost of war purchases in the United States. Canada did not use lend-lease accommodations utilized by other United Nations.

Permanent Joint Board on Defense.—This board was set up by the United States and Canada in pursuance of a joint announcement by President Roosevelt and the prime minister of Canada, W. L. Mackenzie King, dated August 17, 1940, at Ogdensburg, New York, for the purpose of carrying out "studies relating to sea, land and air problems, including personnel and matériel," and to "consider, in the broad sense, the defense of the north half of the western hemisphere." Recommendations of the defense board resulted in the construction of a chain of air bases between Edmonton and Alaska and of the Alaska highway.

Material Co-ordinating Committee.—Establishment of this committee was announced May 1, 1941, shortly after the Hyde Park declaration. Through subcommittees on forest products, copper, zinc and ferro-alloys, the movement of primary materials between the two countries is promoted, available supplies are increased and information is exchanged on raw material stocks, production and consumption in both countries. In determining the allocation of critical war materials, the United States War Production board reviewed Canadian applications on the same basis as those from United States domestic industry. Canada, for its part, poured its resources of vital raw materials into the common pot.

Joint Economic Committees.—Establishment of these committees was announced June 17, 1941. The committees were instructed to study and report to their respective governments on the possibilities of "(1) effecting a more economic, more efficient and more co-ordinated utilization of the combined resources of the two countries in the production of defense requirements (to the extent that this is not covered by other committees and agencies) and (2) reducing the probable postwar economic dislocation consequent upon the changes which the economy in each country is presently undergoing." A large portion of the program under (1) had been fulfilled by 1943 as a result of joint recommendations of the committees. After the middle of 1942 most of their efforts were concentrated largely on postwar problems. At the end of Sept. 1942, the committees agreed to sponsor a study, to be known as the North Pacific Planning project, covering economic development of the area adjacent to the Alaska highway.

Joint War Production Committee.—This committee was first set up as the "Joint Defense Production committee" by President Roosevelt and Prime Minister W. L. Mackenzie King (announced November 5, 1941), pursuant to a recommendation of the Joint Economic committees of Sept. 19, 1941. The objective of this committee was to reduce duplication, arrange uniform specifications and quick exchange of supplies, break transportation bottlenecks and exchange information. Ten technical subcommittees were established. In an exchange of notes Nov. 30, 1942, Canada and the United States expressed their desire to continue in the postwar world their wartime co-operation.

Joint Agricultural Committee.—The organization of this committee was completed in March 1943. The purpose was to keep agricultural and food production and distribution in Canada and the United States under continuing review. To co-ordinate policies of food production, and to supervise the preparation of information on Canada's food position, the dominion government set up the Food Requirements committee to work closely with the Combined Food board of the United Kingdom and the United States.

Joint War Aid Committee.—The formation of this committee was announced Aug. 22, 1943, during the Quebec conference. Its stated purposes were to study problems arising out of operations of United States lend-lease and the Canadian mutual aid program and, where necessary, make recommendations to the proper authorities. (*See* also BRITISH-U.S. WAR BOARDS.)

(W. E. TH.)

Canals and Inland Waterways.

The principal canals and inland navigable waterways of the United States include the Great Lakes, the Mississippi river system, the Illinois waterway, the New York State Barge canal system, the Atlantic Intracoastal waterway extending from Trenton, N.J., to the Florida keys, the Gulf Intracoastal waterway extending from Apalachee bay, Fla., to the vicinity of the Mexican border, the San Joaquin-Sacramento river system in California, and the Columbia river system in the northwest. The Great Lakes have natural deep water except in the connecting channels which have been artificially deepened where necessary to accommodate deep-draught vessels. These connecting channels are the St. Mary's river and canal between Lake Superior and Lake Huron, the Straits of Mackinac connecting Lake Huron with Lake Michigan, the St. Clair river and lake and the Detroit river between Lake Huron and Lake Erie, the Welland canal joining Lake Erie and Lake Ontario, as improved by Canada, and the St. Lawrence river to the sea. The Mississippi river system embraces the river proper, the Red, Arkansas, Tennessee, Missouri, Illinois, Ohio, Monongahela, Allegheny and Kanawha rivers and other streams. The Mississippi river has a channel suitable for deep-draught, ocean-going vessels upstream to Baton Rouge, La., and thence a channel for modern barge navigation to Minneapolis, Minn., and in its principal tributaries which include the Ohio river and the Missouri river. The Illinois river and waterway to Lake Michigan has a barge channel which connects the Great Lakes with the Mississippi river system. An additional outlet from the Great Lakes to the sea is via the Oswego and Erie branches of the New York State Barge canal between Lake Ontario and the Hudson river. The Atlantic Intracoastal waterway and the Gulf Intracoastal waterway provide a protected channel for barge and other light-draught navigation following coastal sounds, bays, rivers and artificial channels. The San Joaquin-Sacramento river system, which has an outlet to the sea through San Francisco bay, provides a deep-draught channel to Stockton, Calif., on the San Joaquin river and a moderate-draught channel to Sacramento, Calif., on the Sacramento river and in addition other channel improvements. The Columbia river has a deep-draught channel to Portland, Ore., and to Vancouver, Wash., and depths suitable for commercial vessel traffic to the head of the pool formed by Bonneville dam and thence depths for barge navigation upstream to and including the Snake river.

Extensive dredging operations were executed on the Intracoastal waterway system, extending along the Atlantic and Gulf coasts, providing a more adequate channel for coastwise barge and other light-draught vessel traffic carrying petroleum products and other essential commodities. A channel of 12 ft. or more in depth heretofore authorized was made available throughout the Atlantic coast section of the waterway from Trenton, N.J., to Jacksonville, Fla. On the Gulf coast section of the waterway, work was actively prosecuted during the fiscal year 1943 on enlargement of the waterway between Carrabelle, Fla., and Corpus Christi, Tex., to provide a depth of 12 ft. in accordance with Public Law No. 675, 77th congress, approved July 23, 1942, which authorized such improvements from Apalachee bay, Fla., to the vicinity of the Mexican border. Funds were made available by the second Supplemental National Defense Appropriation act approved Oct. 26, 1942, and work was commenced promptly thereafter. When the scheduled work under way in 1943 is completed a continuous improved waterway having a least depth of 12 ft. would be available from Carrabelle, Fla., to Corpus Christi, Tex.

The Tombigbee waterway, which is one of many feeder channels of the Intracoastal waterway, extends from Mobile harbour, Ala., far inland through the Mobile, Tombigbee, Warrior and Black Warrior rivers. The Mississippi river inland waterway system connects with the Intracoastal system at Plaquemine and New Orleans, La. This interconnected network of improved waterways brings barge navigation within reach of many important industrial and farming centres. Other important canals of the United States include the Cape Cod canal, Massachusetts, and the Chesapeake and Delaware canal, Maryland and Delaware, which accommodate ocean-going vessels; and the Okeechobee-cross-Florida waterway which affords a light-draught barge channel across southern Florida. (E. Rd.)

Great Britain.—In 1943 a good deal was being done in the way of adapting inland waterways generally to meet the requirements of traffic as a relief to the pressure on railways and roads. The catchment boards who in 1943 had the control and administration of most of the rivers in England, were proceeding with river training and improvement works throughout the country. A good deal of discussion was taking place in connection with the issue in August of the third report of the Central Advisory Water committee, which dealt with a proposal to constitute new river authorities to take over the responsibility for most, if not all, the functions exercised by a variety of bodies associated with river control.

It is a complicated question involving many and diverse interests: land drainage, flood prevention, water supply, public health, irrigation and agriculture, fisheries, commerce, industry and navigation, as well as those associated with countryside amenities and recreation. It would be a difficult matter to reconcile all these different issues, and opposition was being manifested by navigation authorities (ports and canals) to a fusion of their own special sphere of operation with that of water administration for public uses.

Another noteworthy development was the passing of the Grand Union Canal bill, by which that company acquired powers to engage in shipping operations and, in fact, to take an active interest in all forms of transport whether by land, sea or air. This was the first occasion on which a canal company had been granted such powers by parliament, and considerable opposition was manifested by the shipping companies.

Notable, too, during the year was the closing down of two old canal undertakings: the Glamorganshire canal, 25 mi. long, from Merthyr to the sea, with a descent of 560 ft. through 50 locks, and the small local Monkland canal in the Glasgow area.

Interest was revived in a mid-Scotland ship canal and a small departmental committee of the ministry of war transport was set up to examine the project.

Europe.—Not much information could be gleaned about inland water developments on the continent of Europe and in enemy occupied countries generally, but a project was mooted for the construction of a canal to link the port of Venice with the town of Locarno on Lake Maggiore, and there was a report that Japanese engineers were planning a waterway to afford an inland passage from the Sea of Japan to the Pacific. It would link Tsuruga or Ohama on the Japanese sea with Osaka through Lake Biwa and would have a ten-mile tunnel. (B. Cu.)

Cancer. The most interesting contribution to the subject of cancer during 1943, at least from a theoretical aspect, was contained in a long report from the National Cancer institute which stated that at last it has been found possible to produce cancer in normal tissues growing in a fairly simple culture medium.

The failure of other workers in this field had probably been due to the fact that it had always been difficult to keep cultures of adult tissues alive over a long period, especially when exposed to relatively large quantities of the carcinogenic substances, and that too small doses of the cultures were injected into the mice which were employed to test the cultures for malignant cells. A highly inbred pure strain of mice was used, but even under exactly similar conditions some cultures produced large numbers of tumours and others very few. The quantities of the carcinogenic substance 20-methylcholanthrene used were very small, one-thousandth of a milligram to each cubic centimetre of culture medium. Some cultures gave rise to tumours after a relatively short exposure; others required months. One culture strain was exposed for 406 days but did not produce as many tumours as from cultures treated for only a week or two and then allowed to grow for many months without further treatment. The most interesting discovery was that of two untreated control strains. One gave rise to some 8% of tumours, while the other produced a greater number than any treated culture. The authors go into a very elaborate discussion of this fact, pointing out that the amounts of the 20-methylcholanthrene needed to produce cancer are extremely small, and they attempt to explain the production of tumours from untreated cells by the possibility of contamination of the cultures with very minute quantities of carcinogenic substances which by some accident were transferred to these cultures during the manipulations which took place in carrying them on. The tissues have to be replanted very frequently in fresh solution, usually every three to four weeks.

The writer does not agree with this explanation, but on the contrary thinks that this phenomenon explains admirably a series of random observations which were collected from about 1910 on, and were hitherto difficult to understand. For example, the repeated injection of the solution of an aniline dye listed under the trade name of Light Green F.S. produced a few sarcomata when injected subcutaneously into albino rats. Japanese workers obtained malignant tumours in mice by the injection of concentrated glucose solutions. Others noted that tumour production followed the injection of acids or alkalies, even common salt, into the tissues; others produced a few tumours in mice by injecting cholesterol which had been given large doses of X-rays, and these examples could be considerably multiplied where the injection of substances which had apparently no carcinogenic properties under ordinary circumstances produced an occasional tumour. One of the most interesting of these types was reported about 1931 following the insertion under the skin of guinea pigs of small sealed glass tubes containing a minute quantity of radium. After about a year tumours appeared at the site of the tubes. No direct chemical action is possible here. The only radiations which got through the glass were the gamma and beta rays from the radium, but there could be no leakage of radium salt from the tube. It may be suggested perhaps the tumours were produced by the activation of the cholesterol of the tissues. However, it is well known from the studies of Harrison S. Martland of a group of dial painters that radioactive material, when swallowed in very minute quantities, will produce a considerable variety of bone sarcomas in human beings. Martland showed conclusively that this was due to the deposition of the radium in the tissues, chiefly of the bone marrow, and other radiations of various types were given off which kept up a chronic inflammatory process, after a period of years followed by the appearance of tumour. Similar tumours have been produced in animals. Whether the authors' explanation of culture contamination is the correct one or not is not important, for it was generally believed in 1943 that the cancer process is due to a change in the quality of the normal cells of the body, a mutation perhaps, which renders them capable of growing indefinitely in their host. Hence cancer is frequently connected with chronic inflammatory processes or arises in tissues exposed for long periods to various irritating substances. The trend therefore on the whole has been away from the idea that there is any necessarily specific substance in the production of human cancer, though some of the hydrocarbons mentioned above, described originally by Ernest L. Kennaway and John W. Cook, were known in 1943 to occur in tar, soot and probably in certain lubricating oils and proved active generators of malignant growths in parts of the body which had been in contact with these oils for long periods. That soot is carcinogenic had been known for nearly 200 years. L. M. Shabad showed not only that the liver of persons who died of cancer contained a substance carcinogenic for mice, but lately found that the same is true of normal lungs of healthy persons, so that it is evident that in the body there are minute traces of substances which do not cause cancer in their healthy hosts, but do in the exceptionally sensitive reagent animal, the albino mouse, which has been so long employed in these studies.

Thus at last it was definitely shown that what had so frequently been assumed, that hereditary or other general susceptibility of the tissues of the body is necessary for the production of cancer, is not valid, and the results of the experiments just discussed also render it improbable that extraneous organisms, such as viruses, etc., play a necessary part in the inception of cancer.

From the diagnostic aspect of the cancer problem, an interesting series of publications appeared on the early diagnosis of cancer of the uterus by the microscopic examination of smears from the vaginal secretion. The original paper by George N. Papanicolaou and Herbert F. Traut appeared in the *American Journal of Obstetrics and Gynecology*, 42:193, Aug. 1941. Following that account, a well illustrated atlas of the microscopic appearances of the cancer cells seen in such smears was published by these authors, together with several papers by others confirming the results. A very considerable experience is required for this method, which is similar to the demonstration of cancer cells in abdominal and chest fluids, but the expert can render a correct opinion in a considerable percentage of cases of cancer. Obviously a positive diagnosis must be substantiated by examination of curettings before operation or radium treatment is undertaken. The importance of this study is that many patients can be diagnosed who will not submit to a surgical operation or removal of a biopsy specimen, and by this means the average time loss from the onset of symptoms may be considerably reduced from the usual six or seven months' lapse between the first symptoms and the application of the proper methods for cure.

The treatment of cancer of the prostate gland by orchidectomy has been carried on sufficiently long so as to judge roughly the relief period which this treatment offers. No one has assumed that such treatment will cure a malignant disease, but the occasional relief of symptoms was so prompt and complete that a little undue optimism was apparent in medical publications. It was by 1943 beginning to be recognized that while an occasional patient is completely relieved of symptoms for a time the procedure fails in a considerable proportion to be of any real benefit, and that sooner or later the disease again becomes active.

The real value of the procedure is that the favourable results afford the occasional patient complete relief of pain and confer ability to return to work for six months or even a year. In some instances the relief period was even longer, but these were few.

Cancer of the bladder has long been regarded as one of the most difficult types of cancer to treat. Very few of the patients appear in time for radical surgery, and many have to be satisfied with the destruction of the growth by means of electrocautery, in other words, a more or less palliative procedure. With the advent of 1,000,000-volt X-ray apparatus, it was hoped that a certain number of permanent cures could be obtained, and unquestionably an occasional patient will be cured with such treatment. Even with treatment by 200,000-volt radiation a considerable proportion may be relieved of all symptoms for a very considerable time, but reports appearing from institutions where 1,000,000-volt apparatus was available showed that while excellent palliation might be obtained for a very considerable time, sooner or later most of the patients had a recurrence of the tumour with the usual fatal termination. It was much too early to judge the final results.

Reports concerning the treatment of cancer with neutrons did not reveal any definite superiority to the results obtained with correctly applied roentgen rays or radium.

BIBLIOGRAPHY.—Wilton R. Earle, *Journal of the National Cancer Institute*, 3:555–558 (June 1943); Anderson Nettleship, *ibid*, 559–561; Earle, *ibid*, 4:164–213 (Oct. 1943); Earle, Nettleship and colleagues, *ibid*, 213–228 and 229–248.   (F. C. W.)

Candy. Of the 2,500,000,000 lb. of candy produced in 1943, about 20% was shipped to the armed forces in the United States and abroad. The army again included hard candy for Ration K, and the soldier's "last ditch" or extreme emergency food package, known as Ration D, contained a special type of chocolate and sugar, two of the most important candy ingredients. The Jersey City quartermaster depot and the candy industry developed in 1943 a chocolate bar which will remain solid up to 120° F. This bar, used by the armed forces in excessively warm climates, is made of sugar, skim milk powder, cocoa fat, oat flour, artificial flavouring and vitamin B. In addition, varieties of candies, particularly 5-cent and 10-cent bars, were purchased in large quantities for resale at post exchanges.

The industry's 1943 candy tonnage was produced by approximately 1,200 manufacturers in Chicago, Boston, Philadelphia, New York and other sections of the country, employing 50,000 persons, mostly women. The gain in volume over the 1942 figure was about 8% while the dollar value increase was approximately 20%. This was due to the fact that many candy manufacturers converted large portions of their output to higher priced candies, with the unit price of most items showing only a slight increase over 1942 prices. The average value of candy in 1943 was 19 cents per pound compared with 18 cents in 1942, 16 cents in 1940 and 14 cents in 1938.

However, instead of stressing the production of penny goods and five-cent bars, as they did in the years preceding World War II, candy manufacturers in 1943 went to higher priced goods, featuring fancy packages and other maximum priced units. Of the 2,500,000,000 lb. of candy made in 1943, the distribution was divided in approximately the following manner: penny goods, 10%, average value, 15 cents per lb.; bars (1-cent, 5-cent and others), 35%, average value, 22 cents per lb.; bulk candy, 20%, average value, 14 cents per lb.; 5-cent and 10-cent packages (other than bars), 12%, average value, 21 cents per lb.; plain packages, 15%, average value, 25 cents per lb., and fancy packages, 10%, average value, 75 cents per lb. In 1942, fancy packages amounted to only 1.2% of the entire tonnage while in 1939 it was less than 1%.

For the second year in its history, the candy industry in 1943 met sharp curtailment of ingredients. The sugar ration for most of 1943 was 80% of base period use. For the final quarter of the year, however, candy manufacturers, together with other industrial users, received a 10% "bonus" of sugar. This meant a 90% allotment of base period use. During the first six months of 1943, the candy industry received 60% of its chocolate requirements. On July 1, the War Food administration increased the quota to 70% of base period use while another 10% increase was granted the industry on October 1. The changed war picture and improved shipping were the factors responsible for these increases. Corn syrup and other corn products were not rationed in 1943 but, because of a corn shortage, refiners followed a "voluntary rationing" program. Candy manufacturers, however, received a minimum of 100% of base period use on all of their corn products. Many candy plants in 1943 continued to devote large portions of their facilities for the production of radio, plane, gasmask parts and other non-edible necessities.

Towards the end of the year, the industry with the aid of the U.S. department of agriculture launched a research development program, the purpose of which was to find greater use for soybeans, peanuts, cottonseed and other home-grown agricultural products in the production of candy.   (H. D. G.)

Cane Sugar: *see* SUGAR.

Canning Industry.

U.S. and territorial canned food production in 1943, including canned vegetables, fruits, fish, and milk, totalled about 420,000,000 cases as compared with 450,000,000 in 1942. Regular canned food items were packed in somewhat lower quantities than in 1942, because of difficulties resulting from delays in announcement of government policy, changes in regulations, shortages in manpower, and adverse climatic conditions in certain sections. Reductions were noted especially in the case of fruits and vegetables. Lesser reduction occurred in packs of specialty items, fish, and milk. There was a material increase in the pack of canned juices. At the beginning of 1944, statistics on the pack of meat products were incomplete. Considerable quantities of special rations were canned for the armed forces, but production statistics were not available.

Preliminary statistics for the major commodities in 1943, as compared with 1942, were:

	1942	1943
Fruits, cases	60,773,000	46,310,000
Vegetables, cases	229,023,000	208,881,000
Juices, cases	36,613,000	46,256,000
Specialties, fruit and vegetable, cases	32,428,000	29,000,000
Fish, cases	18,079,000	17,000,000
Milk, cases	77,318,000	72,965,000

For civilian consumption the 1943 pack of commercially canned food was supplemented by a record output of home-canned foods, estimated at about 260,000,000 cases.

Government restrictions on the use of tinplate were continued in 1943, governed by orders from the War Production board and War Food administration. There was an increased use of so-called "substitute" plates for cans, such as electrolytic plate having a weight of 0.5 lb. of tin per base box as compared with 1.25 lb. for the conventional "hot-dipped" plate, and "bonderized" plate which did not have tin coating but was chemically treated and enamelled to reduce corrosion. As a further measure in tin conservation there was increased use of lead-silver solder, which contained no tin. Extensive research was done by can manufacturers and the canning industry to determine the usefulness of substitute plates for the different classes of canned foods, and consideration was given to determine a proper balance between tin conservation and the "shelf-life" of the container.

ITALIAN WAR PRISONERS were placed to work in a cannery at Mount Morris, N.Y., in the fall of 1943 to help relieve the labour shortage

Late in 1942 the industry was urged to find a means of protecting the exterior of cans for army and navy overseas shipments. Such coating, to be practicable under 1943 production conditions, would have to be applied after the canning operation and possess the property of protecting the metal from rust and deterioration under extreme corrosion conditions. A study was undertaken jointly by the can manufacturing and canning industries and the properties of various coatings were investigated. The principal work was done with lacquers, paints, and waxes. The tests showed that adequate protection may be given by a number of coating materials and much of the 1943 and 1944 packs were to be coated for army and navy use.

The extensive nutrition studies begun in 1942 were continued and expanded in 1943 and were devoted exclusively to the study of nutrition values in heat-processed foods. This work, supported by the canning and can manufacturing industries, was planned first to determine the dietary factors as they existed, and later to study technological factors which affected these values. The work was carried on through financial grants to universities recognized for excellence in the field of nutrition and the findings of the research were made available to official agencies. In 1943 principal attention was given to determination of vitamin retentions in canning processes and a number of the more important canned foods were included.

Operations in the canning industry in 1943 were affected profoundly through applications of government decrees, delayed government policies, indecision as to future government plans, pricing methods, labelling, and related questions. The situation at the beginning of 1943 was indefinite through lack of facts from which the industry could make plans and this situation obtained at the beginning of 1944.

The rationing program brought canned foods under the point system in March 1943, on the basis of supplies then available, and point values were set to move supplies smoothly into consumption until the period of the next pack.   (E. J. C.)

Canol Oil Project: *see* NORTHWEST TERRITORIES; PETROLEUM.
Canton Island: *see* PACIFIC ISLANDS, U.S.
Cape Verde Islands: *see* PORTUGUESE COLONIAL EMPIRE.

Carlson, Evans Fordyce

(1896–   ), U.S. marine corps officer, was born Feb. 28 at Sidney, N.Y. He attended high school for a brief period, enlisted in the army when he was 16, and was honourably discharged in 1915 as a top sergeant. He was recalled at the time of the Mexican border troubles and later went overseas to France during World War I. He was mustered out in 1919 with the rank of captain, having received French and Italian decorations and a citation from General John J. Pershing. Carlson, however, chafed at the torpor of civilian life, and in 1922 he enlisted in the marines as a private. He was commissioned as a second lieutenant in 1923 and was assigned to duty in Central America and the orient. In 1937 he made a 2,000-mi. trip into China, observing the tactics employed by Chinese communist guerrillas in fighting the Japanese. Carlson subsequently resigned and revisited China in 1940 and 1941 as a civilian. Convinced that a U.S.-Japanese war was inevitable, he rejoined the marines and in May 1941 was returned to active duty as a major. In 1942 he was given command of a marine corps raiding unit. "Carlson's raiders," as they were later known, were thoroughly schooled in tactics similar to those employed by British commandos and Chinese guerrillas. In Aug. 1942 Carlson and his raiders staged a successful raid on Japanese-held Makin Island and later saw action on Guadalcanal. Carlson also participated in the invasion of the Gilbert Islands, Nov. 20–23 and after the battle declared: "Tarawa was the toughest job in marine history."

Carnegie Trusts.
Carnegie Corporation of New York, established by Andrew Carnegie in 1911 and endowed with $135,000,000, devotes its annual income to grants to institutions and agencies whose activities aim at the advancement and diffusion of knowledge and understanding among the people of the United States and of the British dominions and colonies.

During 1942–43, the corporation trustees appropriated a total of $2,562,900: library interests, $82,250; fine arts and museums, $38,500; research and publication $296,703; general educational purposes in schools, colleges, universities, etc., $2,145,447. The amount appropriated since 1911 totals $189,798,099.

The five other separately administered Carnegie organizations in the United States, which were founded by Mr. Carnegie for specific purposes before the establishment of the corporation, with endowments ranging in 1943 from $10,000,000 to $30,000,000, followed their established programs described regularly in their annual publications.

Carnegie Institute of Pittsburgh (1896), which comprises a museum of fine arts, a music hall, a museum of natural history, a public library, and an associated institute of technology with a library school, carried out its stated programs with modifications in staff and facilities caused by war conditions.

Carnegie Institution of Washington (1902), devoted to scientific research, has expended since its organization some $50,000,000 in its program of encouraging investigation, research and discovery, and the application of knowledge to the improvement of mankind, specifically by work in astronomy (Mt. Wilson observatory), terrestrial magnetism, geophysics, animal and plant biology, and historical research (especially in Yucatan). Most of its staff and a major part of its research facilities were engaged in services relating to the national emergency.

Carnegie Hero Fund Commission (1904), established to recognize heroic acts performed in the United States of America, the dominion of Canada, the colony of Newfoundland, and the waters thereof, by persons the nature of whose duties in following their regular vocations does not necessarily require them to perform such acts, announced that the list of its beneficiary aid showed a total of 3,292 medal awards and a total of $6,455,942 in pecuniary awards.

Carnegie Foundation for the Advancement of Teaching (1905), established to provide retiring pensions for teachers and to advance higher education, paid $1,931,238.72 in retiring allowances to retired college professors, or their widows, making a total of $44,424,603.59 paid for such purposes since its establishment. It also continued, chiefly from funds provided by the corporation, its program of educational research, including such activities as teacher-testing program, graduate examination study, etc.

Carnegie Endowment for International Peace (1910), established to serve the purpose indicated by its name, expended its income in research, study, and conferences on the causes of war and international misunderstanding. (R. M. LE.)

Caroline Islands: *see* PACIFIC ISLANDS, MANDATED.

Carver, George Washington
(*c.* 1864–1943), U.S. Negro chemurgist and agricultural expert, was born of slave parents near Diamond Grove, Mo. Dr. Carver, who was a member of the Tuskegee institute in Alabama from 1896 until his death, was appointed collaborator in the division of mycology and disease survey in the bureau of plant industry of the U.S. department of agriculture in 1935. His devotion to the improvement of farming conditions in the south and his development of hundreds of new synthetic products from peanuts, cotton and soybeans are world-famous. He was awarded the Spingarn medal in 1923 and the Roosevelt medal in 1939. Dr. Carver died in Tuskegee, Ala., Jan. 5. (See *Encyclopædia Britannica*.)

Casey, Richard Gardiner
(1890–), Australian politician, was born Aug. 29, and was educated at Melbourne university and at Trinity college, Cambridge. Casey served as liaison officer between the Australian government and the British foreign office for seven years, leaving this post in 1931 to enter the Australian house of representatives. During his nine-year tenure in the house, he acted as assistant federal treasurer, federal treasurer, minister in charge of development and minister for supply and development. His government sent him to London for the coronation and imperial conference in 1937, and in 1939 he again represented Australia at the London conference on the conduct of the war. Casey left the house of representatives in 1940 to accept the portfolio as Australian minister to the United States, where he remained for two years. Prime Minister Churchill recalled him in 1942 and placed him in the United Kingdom war cabinet as minister of state in the middle east. On Dec. 23, 1943, he was named governor of Bengal in what appeared to be a government move to alleviate the critical situation in that famine-ridden province.

Catastrophes: *see* DISASTERS.
Catholic Church: *see* ROMAN CATHOLIC CHURCH.

Catholic Community Service, National.
The National Catholic Community service is the agency designated by the Catholic Church in the United States to serve men and women in the armed forces and war workers in overburdened industrial communities. A member agency of the United Service Organizations, it provided in 1943 a wide variety of services designed to promote the spiritual, recreational, social and educational welfare of servicemen, servicewomen and war workers. It served also the wives and children of servicemen.

The N.C.C.S. was a development of the National Catholic War council, its counterpart in World War I. Like its predecessor, the N.C.C.S. was organized to serve men and women of every race and creed, but differed from other war service agencies in its special services for Catholics. As of Jan. 1944 it managed a total of 512 operations at home and abroad, 39 of which were supported by the N.C.C.S. independently of the U.S.O. and included clubs in Egypt, Hawaii, Australia, the Fiji Islands and England. (P. Dg.)

Catholic Library Association.

An international organization of librarians, educators and others interested in Catholic intellectual life, to promote Catholic literature and to develop and extend Catholic library work. The association was founded in 1921, as the library section of the Catholic Educational association: it became an independent body in 1931, and was incorporated under the laws of the state of Wisconsin in 1936.

The membership in Sept. 1943, was 1,086. Two new units, Galveston, Texas, and Boise City, Idaho, were added to the 18 local divisions. The regional and local units meet from two to six times annually, publish bulletins of professional and news interest, and bibliographies for elementary and high school libraries as well as for the general public.

The annual conference in 1943, scheduled for Buffalo, was cancelled because of travel restrictions.

The principal means by which the Catholic Library association attains its objectives are the publication of the official organ, the *Catholic Library World,* of the *Catholic Periodical Index,* and of the *Supplement* to the *Reading List for Catholics;* the maintenance of a central office for information, and of an agency for the bibliographical works of Rev. Stephen A. Brown, librarian in Dublin; and the promotion of National Catholic book week, which in 1943 was observed Nov. 7–13.

Publications during 1943 included the quarterly issues of the *Catholic Periodical Index* (publication of the four-and-one-half year cumulation, scheduled for Nov. 1943, was delayed because some European periodicals did not arrive); three additions to the bio-bibliographical series, *Contemporary Catholic Authors;* the *Catholic Library World* (1929–) published monthly from October to May. Officers for 1943–45 were Rev. Andrew L. Bouwhuis, S.J., Canisius College library, Buffalo, N.Y., president; Richard James Hurley, Library School, Catholic University of America, Washington, D.C., vice-president; Dorothy E. Lynn, University of Scranton, Scranton, Pa., secretary-treasurer. Official headquarters are at the office of the secretary-treasurer.

(A. L. Bs.)

Catholic Organizations for Youth.

Each of the 18,-976 Catholic parishes in the United States in 1943 promoted one or more organizations for youth. In 1940 the archbishops and bishops had established within the framework of the National Catholic Welfare conference (*q.v.*) a youth department charged with the responsibility of guiding and developing the Catholic youth apostolate and promoting, as the national, unifying and co-ordinating structure of all approved Catholic youth groups, the National Catholic Youth council.

The National Catholic Youth council is comprised of a diocesan section and a college and university section. The college and university section comprises two national student federations, the National Federation of Catholic College Students, uniting in 1943 the student bodies of some 90 Catholic colleges, and the Newman Club federation, uniting the Catholic student clubs in over 500 non-Catholic colleges. The diocesan section of the N.C.Y.C. is comprised of the diocesan youth councils, which in turn are made up of parish youth councils.

The constituent youth groups within the parish youth council continued in 1943 to receive program services from their parent bodies, such as the Sodality of Our Lady, the Mission Crusade,

and in some places the Catholic Youth Organization (C.Y.O.). Some of the larger of such groups in 1943 were: The Sodality of Our Lady, 3742 W. Pine blvd., St. Louis, Mo., with 9,626 units totalling 806,800 members; the Catholic Students Mission Crusade, Shattuc ave., Cincinnati, Ohio, with 2,978 units totalling 600 members; the Junior Catholic Daughters of America, 39 Manchester terrace, Mount Kisco, N.Y., with some 1,000 units totalling 15,000 members; the Columbian Squires, 45 Wall st., New Haven, Conn., with 408 units totalling 16,961 members; the Catholic Central Verein, 3835 Westminster place, St. Louis, Mo., with 25,000 members; and the Catholic Boy Scouts, with 4,385 troops under exclusively Catholic auspices. In 102 of the 116 dioceses of the United States the bishop had by 1943 appointed a Diocesan Youth director with the responsibility of guiding and directing all approved youth groups in the diocese.

(P. F. T.)

Catholic Rural Life Conference, National.

A national organization of bishops, priests and lay persons, founded in 1923 and dedicated to the economic, social and spiritual interests of the U.S. farmer. It functions as an educational and propaganda agency within the church for the application of the principles of Catholic philosophy to the sphere of agriculture.

Instead of the 21st annual convention a wartime meeting was held at Milwaukee, Wis., Oct. 9–13, 1943, attended by 400 delegates for the purpose of strengthening the work of the conference both during the war and in the postwar period. The conference went on record in favour of: (1) the farm co-operative movement to protect the family-type farm from economically powerful groups; (2) the government as custodian of the common good, seeking to achieve the widest possible distribution of land ownership; (3) the parity-price principle for agricultural products in relation to industrial products; (4) subsidies to farmers as a temporary, emergency measure.

The Most Rev. Aloysius J. Muench, bishop of Fargo, N. D., and president of the conference, presided at the conference's annual dinner.

The war activities of the conference were predominant in the rural-life schools of 1943, which were effective beyond expectation. The conference continued to work in co-operation with non-Catholic groups and governmental agencies, and entered into an understanding with the American Federation of Labor and the Congress of Industrial Organizations.

The Most Rev. Joseph H. Schlarman, bishop of Peoria, Ill., was elected president, and the Rt. Rev. L. G. Ligutti was reappointed executive secretary. *Land and Home,* a monthly, is the official publication. Permanent headquarters were at 3801 Grand ave., Des Moines 12, Ia. (J. LaF.)

Catholic Welfare Conference, National.

The conference was organized by the bishops of the United States in Sept. 1919, to unify, co-ordinate and organize the Catholic people of the United States in works of education, social welfare, immigrant aid and other activities.

The 25th annual meeting of the conference was held at Washington, D.C., Nov. 10–12, 1943, and was attended by 100 members of the hierarchy. Officers elected to the administrative board were: chairman of the administrative board, Most Rev. Edward Mooney, archbishop of Detroit, Mich.; vice-chairman and treasurer, Most Rev. Samuel A. Stritch, archbishop of Chicago, Ill.; secretary, Most Rev. Francis J. Spellman, archbishop of New York, N.Y. The Most Rev. John G. Murray, archbishop of St. Paul, Minn., and the Most Rev. James H. Ryan, bishop of

Omaha, Neb., were elected as new members of the board.

The assembled archbishops and bishops at Washington sent their traditional message of greeting to the Holy See, and confirmed their offering of $350,000 to the pope for distribution among the distressed peoples in the war zones. The hierarchy declared in a published statement that the Moscow conference had failed to dispel the fear that the ideals of the Atlantic Charter were compromised.

In the field of international relations, the preparation of material centring around the papal peace program, especially in its application to the postwar world, was the outstanding achievement. Spanish and Portuguese translations of the pamphlets on U.S. peace aims and the world society were issued.

The social-action department sponsored a conference on the religious and economic problems of Spanish-speaking groups in the United States, held during the week of July 19 in San Antonio, Tex. The report of the recommendations of the conference was widely distributed among clerical and lay leaders. The proposed National War Service act for drafting men and women into war industries was opposed by the administrative board in letters sent by the executive secretary to committees of the senate and house of representatives.

War relief services for morale and character for refugees, prisoners of war, and people in devastated areas were established, and operations were begun during 1943.

One of the most important works undertaken by the conference was the printing and distribution of the *Acta Apostolicae Sedis,* the official organ of the Holy See, which began publication in Sept. 1943, for many countries in which distribution of this official organ of papal documentation had ceased after Dec. 1940.

A new nationwide Catholic radio program, "The Hour of Faith," was inaugurated over the Blue network Oct. 19. The press department, through the N.C.W.C. news service, strengthened its coverage of Vatican news, and became the only source of reliable and complete information on Vatican wartime thought and activity. Publications subscribing to the news service increased to 204 in 32 countries. Subscribers to the Spanish-language news service increased considerably during 1943.

National offices are located at 1312 Massachusetts ave., N.W., Washington 5, D.C. The N.C.W.C. issues a monthly publication, *Catholic Action.* (J. LaF.)

Catholic Youth Organization: *see* CATHOLIC ORGANIZATIONS FOR YOUTH.

Catroux, Georges (1879–), French army officer, the son of a general, attended St. Cyr military academy and later served with the Foreign legion. He was appointed aide-de-camp to the governor general of Algeria, 1912, and went to the front in 1914 with the Algerian *tirailleurs.* Wounded and taken prisoner, he made several unsuccessful breaks for freedom, but did not obtain his release until the armistice was signed in 1918. He later became governor general of Damascus, where he served under Gen. Maxime Weygand during the campaign against the Druse tribesmen. Recalled to Morocco in 1926, he was put in charge of intelligence under the command of Gen. Henri Giraud during the Riff rebellion. In 1940, while he was governor general of Indo-China, his refusal to accede to Japanese demands to send troops into Indo-China led to his ouster by the Vichy government. He promptly went to England and joined the Free French. Gen. Charles de Gaulle named him commander in chief of Free French forces in the near east in July 1941. With the formation of the French Committee of National Liberation in June 1943, Catroux became a member of the committee as na-

tional commissioner without portfolio. In Nov. 1943 a crisis in Lebanon was precipitated when several Lebanese leaders were imprisoned for attempting to alter their constitution without the consent of the French. Catroux restored order by releasing the prisoners.

Cattani, Federico (1856–1943), Italian cardinal, was born April 17 in Marradi, Italy. He was ordained at the age of 23, served as vicar general in a diocese of his native province and was later called to Rome as counsellor to the Sacred Congregation of Sacraments. He became auditor of the Rota in 1909, later secretary of the supreme tribunal of the Segnatura, from which post he was elevated to cardinal deacon in 1935 by the late Pope Pius XI. He died in Rome, April 12, the third member of the sacred college to die within a month.

Cattle. The production of cattle and calves reached a new record in 1943 when the total number was 78,170,000 head as estimated by the United States department of agriculture. This compared to 75,162,000 head a year earlier and a 10-year average of 68,418,000 head for the period 1932–41. This record exceeded the previous high total in 1918 by over 5,000,000 head and the peak of 1934 by nearly 4,000,000 head. Compared with a year earlier there was an increase of nearly 1,000,000 head of dairy cattle, cows, heifers and heifer calves. The number of cattle being fed was of record proportions at the beginning of the year, amounting to an increase of 8% in the corn belt alone. Fewer cattle were on feed in the western states except California. During the early part of 1943 the federally inspected slaughter of cattle was much below the same period in 1942, amounting to 15% in the first 7 months. A much larger proportion of the cattle apparently went to non-inspected slaughter. Total slaughter was estimated at 28,300,000 head for 1943 compared to 27,100,000 head in 1942. This left an estimated total at the end of the year of 80,800,000 head of all cattle. The calf crop was estimated at 33,700,000 compared to 32,700,000 in 1942. The movement of cattle into corn belt feed lots was less than a year earlier, reflecting the influence of shorter supplies of feed and higher prices. Cattle feeding operations outside the corn belt were reported to be the smallest in five years. Since the numbers of cattle were at such high levels as to be excessive in relation to the feed and pasture resources of the country the War Food administration recommended that the goal for 1944 be set for a volume of slaughter about 19% larger than in 1943, which would decrease the total number of cattle on farms but not jeopardize a safe level of production. The production of beef in 1943 was estimated to be about 9,000,000,000 lb. or 325,000,000 lb. more than in 1942, and veal about 1,000,000,000 lb. or 62,000,000 lb. less than the previous year. The total requirements of beef and veal were estimated to be 11,280,000,000 lb. for 1944, about 10% more than was slaughtered in 1943. (*See* also LIVESTOCK.)

(J. C. Ms.)

Cazalet, Victor Alexander (1896–1943), British M.P., was born Dec. 27 and educated at Eton and Christ Church, Oxford. He served in World War I and won the military cross for gallantry. After the war he attended the Versailles conference and was a member of the British staff in Siberia, 1918–19. In addition to serving as Unionist M.P. from Chippenham, 1924–43, he had been parliamentary private secretary to the president of the board of trade. An authority on central European affairs, Col. Cazalet was appointed in 1940 as liaison officer to Gen. Sikorski, premier of the Polish government-in-exile. He was killed July 4 in the crash of a plane that was carrying Sikorski and his party back to England from a visit to Cairo.

CED: *see* Committee for Economic Development.
Celebes Islands: *see* Netherlands Colonial Empire; Netherlands Indies.
Cellulose Products: *see* Paper and Pulp Industry; Plastics Industry; Rayon and Other Synthetic Fibres.

Cement.

The war program, with its extensive military, industrial and housing construction, greatly increased the demand for cement, so that production increased 6% over the preceding year in 1940, 26% in 1941 and 11% in 1942, when the output included 182,781,184 bbl. of portland cement and 2,560,425 bbl. of special cements, a total of 185,341,609 bbl. Even with this heavy increase in output, demand continued to lead, and shipments for 1942 were 187,809,208 bbl. Consequently at the end of 1942 stocks had declined 14% to 21,206,022 bbl. (including 17,445,220 bbl. of finished cement, 3,509,336 bbl. of clinker and 251,466 bbl. of special cements) as compared with 24,738,811 bbl. in 1941. There was sufficient surplus capacity in the industry to cover any probable increase in demand, since the 166 plants contributing to the 1942 output were worked only at an average of 73.5%.

Normally the distribution of cement is highly seasonal, with shipments usually reaching a peak in midsummer, and a low in midwinter, with the peak as much as two to three times as great as the low. Because of the pressure for rapid completion of the work that characterized recent expansions in building construction, winter construction was increased, the low of Feb. 1942 being 8,293,000 bbl., as compared with 3,893,000 bbl. in Jan. 1940. The demand for speed in construction also manifested itself in the proportion of high-early-strength cement turned out, this type having increased by 39% in 1941 and 15% in 1942, with shipments of 7,065,700 bbl. (*See* also Gypsum.)   (G. A. Ro.)

Censorship.

Starting to build from the ground floor in Dec. 1941, a comprehensive censorship organization was created in the first twelve months after Pearl Harbor. Thereafter, the Office of Censorship, with a staff of about 13,000, continued to hold major responsibility, acting as an independent war agency responsible only to the president and in no way involved in the series of consolidations and reorganizations which so greatly changed the alignment of official Washington. For the fiscal year 1944, beginning July 1, 1943, congress without debate approved for the agency an appropriation of $27,800,000.

In 1943, the main problems of the office concerned improvement of technique, attainment of more efficient administration and efforts to make certain that increasing advantage was taken of the affirmative benefits flowing from the censoring process.

The purpose of censorship is to prevent important information from reaching the enemy, to attack the enemy's communications and to intercept all possible information regarding his plans. To attain those ends, the Office of Censorship was directed mainly along two lines: first, the censorship of all communications coming into or going out of the United States by mail, cable, radio or any other means; second, the supervision of a method of voluntary co-operation on the part of newspapers, magazines and other publications and radio stations in the United States to withhold from domestic circulation secret military information that might be of value to the enemy.

Control of the international mails, authorized by congress in the First War Powers act, was by far the largest physical task of the Office of Censorship. About 1,000,000 pieces of mail became available for examination daily at various Postal Censorship stations scattered about the rim of the country and at strategic points in the territories. Uniform treatment of these communications was essential, and schools of instruction were maintained for the constant training of personnel in the detailed regulations for handling international mail.

Further, to co-ordinate all censorship in this field, the various regulations drawn up in 1942 for postal, cable and radiotelephone communications were consolidated on Jan. 30, 1943, into a single handbook, entitled *U.S. Censorship Regulations.* The regulations prohibited all communication with enemy territory except by special license and gave notice that revealing references to such subjects as fortifications, ship and troop movements and secret military plans or weapons would be stricken out of all communications sent across the international boundaries. Copies of this handbook were made available to the public for guidance in writing letters, etc., to be sent abroad.

Nevertheless, it was necessary to establish a number of units for handling specialized communications. One such specially trained unit was created to handle letters going to and from prisoners of war, as provided by the Geneva convention. Another group of experts was set up to supervise censoring of trade, banking and shipping communications going out of or coming into the United States. Still another special unit dealt only with philatelic mail under instructions to prevent transmission of code messages or illegal transfer of funds in connection with shipments of stamps across international boundaries.

Batteries of translators also were created to make available language experts able to read some 200 different languages and dialects. Chemists were installed in laboratories at various stations to deal with secret ink messages. They worked in closest liaison with the intelligence agencies. In co-operation with the Bureau of Customs, units were established to examine all papers carried by international travellers at ports of entry and exit and to scrutinize all photographic prints and films, including motion pictures, which were presented for export or import. The Office of Censorship, however, did not examine mail to and from army and navy personnel overseas. That function was exercised by the armed services themselves.

Censorship of high speed news dispatches and other communications by cable, radio, telegraph, radiotelephone and land wire obviously involved a still greater degree of security. In addition, there was the desire for rapid handling of such communications in order to impose the least possible delay. A period of 24 hr. would be considered normal for handling of a letter through censorship, but in regard to high speed transmission of messages it was desired to reduce the censorship delay to a few minutes wherever possible and in many instances to less than a minute. In large part, this was achieved.

Highly expert staffs were on duty at the Cable Censorship stations 24 hr. a day. Extensive files of previous traffic and other pertinent information were kept readily accessible. As in postal censorship, specialists were assigned to the various classes of traffic. The handling of press dispatches alone, for instance, required the services of a sizeable staff recruited from the ranks of experienced newspapermen. It was against this particular operation that one of the few public criticisms of censorship in 1943 was directed. A number of British correspondents protested on several occasions, declaring that deletions from their dispatches, sent from New York to London, sometimes went beyond the requirements of security.

Toward the end of 1942, a minor controversy had arisen in congress over the application of censorship to communications between the continental United States and the territories. Some senators contended that there was no legal warrant for such censorship. At one time, legislation was proposed to legalize this operation specifically, but this proposal was not revived when the new congress met in Jan. 1943, and the controversy died out. Censorship of communications between the mainland and the territories continued.

Inside the United States, voluntary censorship of the press and of broadcasting continued under the supervision of the Office of Censorship and with the solid support of both industries. On Feb. 1, 1943, the Code of Wartime Practices for the American Press, and its companion piece, the Code of Wartime Practices for American Broadcasters, were revised. Some provisions were eliminated and others added, as dictated by experience. Another revision, relaxing the code, came in the closing months of the year because of an improved military situation and other factors. More complete weather reports were approved for newspapers. Weather news was broadcast by radio stations for the first time in almost two years. Virtually all remaining restrictions on information regarding war production, except in regard to secret models, were eliminated. The way was opened for greater publicity regarding the contribution of merchant shipping toward victory.

Both the Press and Broadcasting divisions, with very small staffs and no branch offices, continued to operate on the theory that every editor and broadcaster was his own censor and that the codes were his guide in hour-to-hour handling of the news. The percentage of violations was strikingly small. (*See* also NEWSPAPERS AND MAGAZINES; RADIO.)   (B. PR.)

Census, 1940.
The 1940 census of population in the United States covered a decidedly wider field than any earlier census. In spite of delays inevitably resulting from war conditions, reports were finally published in 1943 on many new topics, including the data on housing derived from the separate housing schedule, data on migration between 1935 and 1940, and data on families and fertility, these last mainly from sample tabulations. Departures in the way of geographic areas represented included selected housing data by city blocks, many tabulations for metropolitan districts (providing information heretofore available only for the central cities), and additional data for counties, townships and the smaller incorporated places. Persons who use in conjunction statistics from any of the reports based on a sample tabulation and statistics from the complete tabulation, will find slight differences in most of the items common to the two sources. The differences are in practically all cases too small, however, to detract from the usefulness of the data. The characteristics of each of the samples are discussed in the report presenting the data.

A selection from among the more significant of the published items is presented in the paragraphs that follow.

Growth of Total Population.—Estimates of the population of the United States as a whole have been made month by month on the basis of current records of births and deaths (corrected for under-registration) and net immigration. These estimates, which

are presented in Table I, make no allowance for postcensal movement of the armed forces away from continental United States. That is, they represent the *de jure* population, including men in military service abroad. (The estimates are presented to the last digit as computed instead of being rounded, not because they are assumed to be accurate to the last digit but for convenience in summation.)

The population of continental United States on Jan. 1, 1943, according to the estimates, was 135,645,969, which represents an increase of 1,692,744 over the population estimated for Jan. 1, 1942. The increase during the calendar year 1942 was thus almost twice as great as the average annual increase between 1930 and 1940. The rate of increase for 1942 was 1.3%, as compared with an average annual rate of 0.7% for the decade 1930 to 1940.

This recent acceleration of population growth results mainly from a very considerable rise in the birth rate. During the calendar year 1942 there were approximately 3,038,000 births, as compared with 2,717,000 births in 1941 and with an annual average of not quite 2,400,000 between 1930 and 1940. This increase in the birth rate has taken place since 1936, following an almost continuous decline since 1921, and is attributable mainly, in the first place, to the business prosperity induced by defense activities and, in the second place, to the anticipation of conscription and the entry of the United States into the war. A record marriage rate led to more first births and the number of children born to couples married earlier also increased. The number of deaths in 1942, however, was about the same as the annual average during the decade 1930 to 1940, the death rate in 1942 (based on registered deaths) being only 10.4, which is the lowest on record.

Net civilian immigration during 1942 amounted to 88,587, as compared with 41,162 in 1941 and with an average net emigration of about 5,000 per year during the preceding census period.

The number of births in the year 1943 seemed likely, on the basis of incomplete returns, to exceed very materially the number recorded in 1942. The numbers registered month by month for the first eight or nine months of the year exceeded the numbers registered during the corresponding months of 1942. The excess has been growing less, however, for several months and the number returned for October, the last month for which even preliminary data are available at this writing (Dec. 1943) is materially less than the number recorded for Oct. 1942. Thus, while the trend in the number of births has continued upward longer than was expected, it seems to have definitely passed the peak and begun a decline. The civilian death rate will probably not increase appreciably in 1944, but military mortality is likely to become a much more important factor. The rate of population growth is expected therefore to decline rather sharply as World War II continues.

Estimates of civilian population have been made for states and counties, on the basis of registrations for the various war ration books. The last of these estimates, based on the registration for war ration book 4, as of Nov. 1, 1943, distributes by states and counties an estimated total civilian population of about 127,261,000. It may be noted that this figure is less by 4,408,000, or 3.3%, than the total population returned in the 1940 census (which was 131,669,275). This means that inductions into military service have by so much exceeded the sum of natural increase and net immigration.

Educational Attainment.—A new measure of the educational

Table I.—*Estimated Population of Continental United States, by Six-Month Periods: July 1, 1940, to Jan. 1, 1943*

Date	Estimated population	Increase since last census		Increase in preceding 6 months		Gain or loss in preceding 6 months			
		Number	Per cent	Number	Per cent	Births	Deaths*	Excess of births over deaths	Net civilian immigration
Jan. 1, 1943	135,645,969	3,976,694	3.02	981,045	0.73	1,630,967	701,054	929,913	51,132
July 1, 1942	134,664,924	2,995,649	2.28	711,699	0.53	1,407,467	733,223	674,244	37,455
Jan. 1, 1942	133,953,225	2,283,950	1.73	750,352	0.56	1,400,533	681,971	718,562	31,790
July 1, 1941	133,202,873	1,533,598	1.16	564,940	0.43	1,316,685	761,117	555,568	9,372
Jan. 1, 1941	132,637,933	968,658	0.74	667,709	0.51	1,311,428	692,971	618,457	49,252
July 1, 1940	131,970,224	300,949	0.23	300,949†	0.23†	623,065†	353,212†	269,853†	31,096†
April 1, 1940 (census) . .	131,669,275	—	—	—	—	—	—	—	—

*Includes an estimate of military deaths and persons missing in action for the army, navy, marine corps, coast guard, and merchant marine. †Preceding three months only.

Table II.—*Population 20 Years Old and Over by Years of School Completed, by Colour: 1940*

(Percent based on number reporting grade completed)

Years of school completed	All classes		White	Nonwhite
	Number	Per cent		
Total	86,363,671	100.0	78,339,672	8,023,999
No school years completed	2,902,284	3.4	2,162,009	740,275
Grade school: 1 year	549,688	0.6	343,925	205,763
2 years	1,261,738	1.5	800,690	461,048
3 years	2,210,065	2.6	1,515,175	694,890
4 years	3,791,604	4.4	2,802,642	988,962
5 years	3,775,440	4.4	2,930,517	844,923
6 years	5,449,278	6.4	4,610,773	838,505
7 years	5,775,994	6.8	5,081,215	694,779
8 years	22,521,962	26.4	21,599,260	922,702
High school: 1 year	5,006,589	5.9	4,650,721	355,868
2 years	5,677,851	6.7	5,394,193	283,658
3 years	3,169,994	3.7	3,008,552	161,442
4 years	14,218,084	16.7	13,790,187	427,897
College: 1 year	1,799,165	2.1	1,744,115	55,050
2 years	2,321,509	2.7	2,239,869	81,640
3 years	1,010,848	1.2	979,184	31,664
4 years	2,833,359	3.3	2,751,303	82,056
5 or more	958,918	1.1	941,773	17,145
Not reported	1,129,301	—	993,569	135,732
Median years of school completed . .	8.8	—	8.9	6.0

attainment of the population is represented by the data on last (or highest) full grade of school completed, or, to use a somewhat more convenient expression, the number of years of school completed. The question on number of years of school completed was included in the 1940 census in place of the less comprehensive questions on illiteracy asked in previous censuses. The data for persons 20 years old and over, a group made up, for the most part, of persons whose formal education had been completed, are summarized in Table II.

Of the whole number of these persons who reported the amount of schooling they had completed, 2,902,284, or 3.4%, had never completed so much as one year of formal schooling, and an additional 4.7% had completed less than four years; 22,521,962, or 26.4%, had completed the eighth grade only; 14,218,084, or 16.7%, had completed four years of high school and an additional 16.3% had had one, two or three years of high school; 3,792,-277, or 4.4%, had completed four years (or more) in college and an additional 6.0% had had one, two or three years of college.

Figures representing the median number of years of school completed by various classes in the population are presented in Table III. The median is usually defined as that value, in a series of values arranged in ascending or descending order, which stands in the middle of the series, so that one-half of the items are greater than the median and one-half less. In order to understand clearly the relation between the frequency distribution presented in Table II and the medians presented in Table III, it is necessary to keep in mind the fact that the distribution is in terms of completed years, while the medians are expressed in decimals representing tenths of a year. For example, the number of persons shown as having completed 8 years of school includes not only those who have completed exactly 8 years but also all those who have completed in addition any fraction of a year. In other words, the range of the group is from 8 to 8.9 years. A median of 8.4, then, does not indicate a point beyond the limits of the 8-year group but rather a position within that group.

The median number of years of school completed by all persons 20 years old and over in the United States in 1940 was 8.8. Because of the more favourable educational opportunities in recent years there is a marked relationship between age and the amount of education, the educational attainment being progressively higher for the younger age groups. Thus, for the total population 20 to 24 years of age the median number of years of school completed was 11.2 (representing a position in the early

part of the third year of high school), while the median for persons 40 to 44 years old was only 8.6 years and for those 75 and over, 8.0 years. The medians for rural-farm areas are somewhat lower, age by age, than those for urban areas; and the medians for the nonwhite are decidedly lower than those for the white population.

Relative Ages of Husbands and Wives.—Of the 35,087,440 families in the United States in 1940, 26,605,800 were what has been termed normal families, that is, families including a husband and wife, with or without children. Among the tabulations made for these normal families was one showing the age of husband in combination with the age of wife. These figures are summarized for the United States in Table IV. (Because of mechanical limitations, the age of husband was tabulated in somewhat less detail than the age of wife, so that for comparison with the three columns representing husband's age from 35 to 64 it is necessary in each case to combine two lines to obtain the number of wives in the corresponding age group.)

On the basis of the figures in Table IV, two observations may be made: First, that in relatively few cases did the age of the wife materially exceed the age of the husband. About 9% of the wives of husbands under 25 years of age were returned as in the next higher age group, that is, 25 to 29 years; this does not necessarily mean, however, more than a year or two of difference in age. Considerably more than half of the married men under 25 years of age are either 23 or 24 years old, and the wife need be only 25 years old in order to be classified in the next higher age group. Likewise, only 6.7% of the wives of husbands aged 25 to 29 were 30 to 34 years old, and only 5.8% of the wives with husbands aged 30 to 34 were 35 to 39 years old.

The second observation is to the effect that a very large percentage of the wives were considerably younger than their husbands. For example, 44.5% of the wives with husbands 25 to 29 were under 25, and 53.1% of the wives with husbands 30 to 34 years old were under 30. In general, as the age of husbands increases, the proportion of wives who are considerably younger than their husbands also increases, mainly because of the tendency among men who marry late in life to choose wives considerably younger than themselves.

Relationship to Head of Household.—The term "private household," as used in the 1940 census, is defined as a group of persons including the head of the household, persons related to the head, and the unrelated lodgers, servants and hired hands, if any, who live in the same dwelling unit and share common household arrangements. The number of heads of private households is the same as the number of private households and is directly comparable with the number of private families. The number of private households in 1940 was 34,948,666, and the number of persons living in these private households was 128,427,069.

Table III.—*Median Years of School Completed by Persons 20 Years Old and Over, by Age, for the United States, by Colour and by Sex, and for Urban and Rural Areas: 1940*

Age	United States					Urban	Rural-non-farm	Rural-farm
	All classes			White	Non-white			
	Total	Male	Female					
Total, 20 and over	8.8	8.7	8.8	8.9	6.0	9.0	8.7	8.2
20 to 24 years . . .	11.2	10.9	11.5	11.7	7.4	12.0	10.7	8.8
25 to 29 years . . .	10.3	10.1	10.5	10.7	7.1	11.0	10.0	8.6
30 to 34 years . . .	9.5	9.2	9.9	10.0	6.7	10.3	9.3	8.4
35 to 39 years . . .	8.8	8.7	8.9	8.9	6.2	9.0	8.8	8.2
40 to 44 years . . .	8.6	8.6	8.7	8.7	5.8	8.8	8.6	8.2
45 to 49 years . . .	8.5	8.4	8.5	8.6	5.5	8.6	8.5	8.1
50 to 54 years . . .	8.4	8.3	8.4	8.4	5.0	8.5	8.4	8.0
55 to 59 years . . .	8.3	8.2	8.4	8.4	4.8	8.4	8.3	7.9
60 to 64 years . . .	8.3	8.2	8.3	8.3	4.4	8.4	8.3	7.7
65 to 69 years . . .	8.2	8.1	8.2	8.2	3.7	8.3	8.1	7.1
70 to 74 years . . .	8.1	8.0	8.1	8.2	2.9	8.3	8.1	7.0
75 and over	8.0	7.7	8.1	8.1	2.6	8.2	8.0	6.5

Table IV.—Age of Wife by Age of Husband, for the United States: 1940

(Figures based on a sample tabulation)

Age of wife	Total	Age of husband (years)							
		Under 25	25 to 29	30 to 34	35 to 44	45 to 54	55 to 64	65 and over
All ages . .	26,605,800	1,133,600	2,787,220	3,402,900	6,830,240	6,049,040	3,909,380	2,493,420
Under 20 years	466,600	304,840	114,800	27,820	13,540	3,320	1,580	700
20 to 24 years .	2,349,300	699,100	1,125,580	363,000	132,900	21,160	5,560	2,000
25 to 29 years .	3,584,560	103,500	1,320,920	1,415,280	648,940	77,360	14,560	4,000
30 to 34 years .	3,688,080	12,500	186,060	1,354,360	1,860,000	234,840	32,140	8,180
35 to 39 years .	3,552,520	3,560	24,780	196,700	2,523,580	705,860	81,100	16,940
40 to 44 years .	3,236,680	2,240	5,160	28,220	1,351,740	1,612,300	202,960	34,060
45 to 49 years .	2,923,600	1,620	1,780	6,460	225,620	2,084,120	529,220	74,780
50 to 54 years .	2,377,500	740	1,300	2,940	40,460	1,062,300	1,105,000	104,760
55 to 59 years .	1,760,020	1,060	1,000	1,360	11,760	178,460	1,226,440	339,940
60 to 64 years .	1,227,820	1,160	440	800	3,720	37,360	569,440	614,900
65 and over . .	1,439,120	3,280	5,400	5,960	17,980	31,960	141,380	1,233,160
Per cent. . .	100.0	100.0	100.0	100.0	100.0	100.0	100.0	100.0
Under 20 years	1.8	26.9	4.1	0.8	0.2	0.1	—	—
20 to 24 years .	8.8	61.7	40.4	10.7	1.9	0.3	0.1	0.1
25 to 29 years .	13.5	9.1	47.4	41.6	9.5	1.3	0.4	0.2
30 to 34 years .	13.9	1.1	6.7	39.8	27.2	3.9	0.8	0.3
35 to 39 years .	13.4	0.3	0.9	5.8	36.9	11.7	2.1	0.7
40 to 44 years .	12.2	0.2	0.2	0.8	19.8	26.7	5.2	1.4
45 to 49 years .	11.0	0.1	0.1	0.2	3.3	34.5	13.5	3.0
50 to 54 years .	8.9	0.1	0.1	0.1	0.6	17.6	28.3	6.6
55 to 59 years .	6.6	0.1	—	—	0.2	3.0	31.4	13.6
60 to 64 years .	4.6	0.1	—	—	0.1	0.6	14.6	24.7
65 and over . .	5.4	0.3	0.2	0.2	0.3	0.1	3.6	49.5

In addition to the private households, there were 80,122 quasi households (large lodging houses, hotels for transients, institutions, etc.) with 3,242,206 persons residing in them. The average number of persons per quasi household was 40.5, as compared with an average of 3.7 for private households.

The classification of the population in private households by relationship to head is shown in Table V. The first six classes, head, wife, child, grandchild, parent, and other relative, represent the population in private families. The two remaining categories, representing an aggregate of 5,496,378 people, represent the unrelated persons living in the private households, being mainly lodgers.

On the basis of the sex distribution, it may be noted that the heads of the families were dominantly male and that both the persons living outside private households and the lodgers living in such households showed a considerable excess of males, while the parents and the servants living in the households were largely females.

Table V.—Population in Private Households, by Relationship to Head, and Sex, and Population Outside Private Households, by Sex, for the United States: 1940

Relationship to head	Total		Male		Female		Males per 100 females
	Number	Per cent	Number	Per cent	Number	Per cent	
Total persons	131,669,275	100.0	66,061,592	100.0	65,607,683	100.0	100.7
In private households	128,427,069	97.5	64,039,104	96.9	64,387,965	98.1	99.5
Not in private households	3,242,206	2.5	2,022,488	3.1	1,219,718	1.9	165.8
Head (number of quasi households) . . .	80,122		49,800		30,322		
In private households	128,427,069	100.0	64,039,104	100.0	64,387,965	100.0	99.5
Head (number of private households)	34,948,666	27.2	29,679,718	46.3	5,268,948	8.2	563.3
Wife	26,570,502	20.7	—	—	26,570,502	41.3	—
Child	51,304,634	39.9	26,826,049	41.9	24,478,585	38.0	109.6
Grandchild	2,394,462	1.9	1,233,290	1.9	1,161,172	1.8	106.2
Parent	2,226,755	1.7	623,839	1.0	1,602,916	2.5	38.9
Other relative	5,485,672	4.3	2,711,422	4.2	2,774,250	4.3	97.7
Lodger	4,462,606	3.5	2,637,845	4.1	1,824,761	2.8	144.6
Servant or hired hand . .	1,033,772	0.8	326,941	0.5	706,831	1.1	46.3

Migration, 1935–40.—Among the new questions on the 1940 population schedule was one asking for the place of residence on April 1, 1935, of each person 5 years old and over, designed to give direct statistics on migration from one part of the United States to another. In the tabulations based on this question, migrants are defined as persons whose 1935 residence and 1940 residence were in different counties or who had moved to or from a city of 100,000 or more within the same county. Nonmigrants are persons who lived in the same county or city in 1935 and 1940 or in that portion of the same county outside a city of 100,000 or more.

In Table VI are presented migration data for heads of families which indicate for the migrants the movement between designated urban and rural areas. Of the whole number of families (heads of families) 87.0% were classified as nonmigrants, including 42.7% who in 1935 lived in the same house as in 1940 and 44.4% who lived in a different house but in the same county or city. The migrant families comprised 12.5% of the total, and for 0.4% migration status was not reported.

Of the 2,382,600 migrant families resident in urban places in 1940, 1,612,920 came from other urban places (that is, lived in other urban places in 1935), 399,260 came from rural-nonfarm areas, and 188,540 came from rural-farm areas. The figures therefore indicate for the period 1935 to 1940 a relatively small migration of families (family heads) from farms to cities.

Of the 1,227,540 migrant families living in rural-nonfarm areas in 1940, 646,060 came from urban places, 323,620 from rural-nonfarm areas in other counties, and 168,820 from rural-farm areas.

Of the 766,260 migrant families living in rural-farm areas in 1940, 195,300 (or a little more than the number of farm-city migrant families) came from urban places, 90,680 came from rural-nonfarm areas, and 408,280 from rural-farm areas in other counties.

Fertility.—The reports of the 1940 census contained the first statistics on the number of children ever born that the bureau of the census had ever published, though questions on this point were contained in the census schedules in 1890, 1900 and 1910 as well as in 1940. In the classification of women by number of children ever born, all children ever born alive to a woman dur-

Table VI.—Migration Status and 1935 Residence of Heads of Families, for the United States, Urban and Rural: 1940

(Figures based on a sample tabulation)

Status and 1935 residence	Total, 1940		Urban, 1940	Rural-nonfarm, 1940	Rural-farm, 1940
	Number	Per cent			
All heads of families	35,088,840*	100.0	20,735,200	7,211,120	7,142,520
Nonmigrant	30,555,400	87.0	18,271,700	5,944,940	6,338,760
1935 residence in—					
Same house as in 1940 . .	14,980,780	42.7	8,086,020	3,048,460	3,846,300
Different house (same county or city)	15,574,620	44.4	10,185,680	2,896,480	2,492,460
Migrant	4,376,400	12.5	2,382,600	1,227,540	766,260
From urban places:					
Total	2,454,280	7.0	1,612,920	646,060	195,300
Places of 100,000 or more . .	1,235,500	3.5	800,640	347,700	87,160
Places of 25,000 to 100,000 .	410,320	1.2	289,440	91,520	29,360
Places of 10,000 to 25,000 .	337,280	1.0	230,380	78,880	28,020
Places of less than 10,000 .	471,180	1.3	292,460	127,960	50,760
From rural areas:					
Total	1,750,460	5.0	646,900	549,200	554,360
Rural-nonfarm	813,560	2.3	399,260	323,620	90,680
Rural-farm	765,640	2.2	188,540	168,820	408,280
Rural, farm residence not reported	171,260	0.5	59,100	56,760	55,400
Urban-rural residence in 1935 not reported	171,660	0.5	122,780	32,280	16,600
Migration status not reported	157,040	0.4	80,900	38,640	37,500

*This figure differs from the corresponding figure presented in Table V because of sampling variation; the difference is, however, less than one-half of 1%.

ing her lifetime were counted, including children by any former marriage. The tabulations now published, including data for 1910 as well as for 1940, are summarized in Table VII.

Table VII.— Women 15 to 74 Years Old Who Were or Had Been Married, by Number of Children Ever Born, for the United States: 1940 and 1910
(Statistics based on a sample tabulation)

Number of children ever born	1940		1910	
	Number of women ever married	Per cent	Number of women ever married	Per cent
Total, 15 to 74 years	35,108,480	100.0	20,476,625	100.0
Reporting on children	30,648,780	87.3	18,911,838	92.4
Not reporting	4,459,700	12.7	1,564,787	7.6
Reporting on children	30,648,780	100.0	18,911,838	100.0
No children	6,223,960	20.3	2,570,074	13.6
1 child	6,606,120	21.6	3,187,739	16.9
2 children	5,990,700	19.5	2,964,832	15.7
3 children	3,943,240	12.9	2,338,236	12.4
4 children	2,586,240	8.4	1,857,260	9.8
5 children	1,707,040	5.6	1,451,787	7.7
6 children	1,164,140	3.8	1,173,150	6.2
7 children	779,000	2.5	913,581	4.8
8 children	580,120	1.9	744,884	3.9
9 children	384,860	1.3	558,800	3.0
10 or more	683,360	2.2	1,151,495	6.1

The figures indicate a decidedly lower fertility in 1940 than in 1910. Of the whole number of women 15 to 74 years old who were or had been married, as returned in 1940, 20.3% had never had any children, as compared with 13.6% of the corresponding group in 1910. Only 38.6% of the 1940 group reported 3 or more children, as compared with 53.9% of the 1910 group; and at the extreme end of the series, only 2.2% of the 1940 group reported 10 or more children, as compared with 6.1% of the 1910 group. To some extent these relations may be affected by differences in age distribution within the group comprising all ever-married women 15 to 74 years old. A more detailed tabulation providing data for women classified by age, however, shows the same relations, namely, a decidedly lower fertility for corresponding age groups in the more recent year. Of the women 50 to 54 years old, for example, in 1940, 15.2% reported no children ever born and 3.6% reported 10 or more, as compared with 8.9% reporting no children in 1910 and 12.3% reporting 10 or more.

Total Value and Rent of Dwelling Units.—One of the most interesting and useful of the tabulations of the 1940 housing census was one in which owner-occupied dwelling units were classified by value, and tenant-occupied units by monthly rent. On the basis of these classifications, total values (of all dwelling units including tenant-occupied) and total monthly rent (including estimated rent for owner-occupied units) have been computed. A summary of these estimates is presented in Table VIII.

Table VIII.—Total Monthly Rent and Estimated Value of Dwelling Units: 1940

Area	Number of dwelling units	Total monthly rent (dollars)	Average rent (dollars)	Total value (dollars)	Average value (dollars)
United States . . .	37,325,470	893,714,921	23.94	95,439,309,530	2,557
Urban	21,616,352	668,361,617	30.92	71,110,397,301	3,290
Rural-nonfarm . .	8,066,837	148,565,028	18.42	16,267,970,612	2,017
Rural-farm . . .	7,642,281	76,788,276	10.05	8,060,941,617	1,055
Northeastern States	10,312,732	350,651,248	34.00	37,178,472,623	3,605
North Central States	11,597,471	272,829,816	23.52	29,461,289,709	2,540
South	10,876,056	159,288,670	14.65	17,120,913,670	1,574
West	4,539,211	110,945,178	24.44	11,678,633,528	2,573

The total value of all dwelling units in the United States on the basis of these estimates was more than $95,000,000,000, and the average value per unit was $2,557. In making these estimates it was assumed that the value of the tenant-occupied and vacant units was 100 times the monthly rent.

The actual or estimated monthly rent of all dwelling units in the United States in 1940 was nearly $894,000,000 dollars,

or an average of $23.94 per unit. The annual total on this basis was something over $10,000,000,000. These figures are based on actual rentals reported for tenant-occupied nonfarm dwelling units, reported estimated rental values for all other dwelling units except owner-occupied farm homes, and monthly rentals for these latter estimated at the rate of 1% of the reported value.

The average value of urban dwelling units was $3,290, as compared with $1,055 for rural-farm units. The relation between urban and rural-farm rentals was practically the same. The average value of all dwelling units in the northeastern states was $3,605, of those in the north central states $2,540, of those in the south $1,574, and of those in the west $2,573, again with similar relations among the average monthly rentals.

Sixteenth Census Reports.—The major part of the material from the 1940 census is published in eight "volumes," most of the volumes containing several parts. Each volume has been made up by consolidating a series of state bulletins (in which form the data were first made public), including in each case a summary for the United States. There are four "volumes" presenting data specifically on population and four "volumes" presenting data on housing. In addition, there were available in 1943 20-odd supplementary reports, for the most part based on sample tabulations, covering subjects as follows:

The Labour Force (six reports), presenting detailed tabulations by occupation, industry, income, and personal and family characteristics
Nativity and Parentage of the White Population (three reports), including country of origin of the foreign stock and mother tongue of the entire population
Families (seven reports), including tenure, rent, family income, type of family, employment status and general characteristics
Education, Occupation, and Household Relationship of Males 18 to 44 Years Old
Characteristics of Persons Not in the Labour Force
Differential Fertility
Institutional Population
Characteristics of the Nonwhite Races
Internal Migration, 1935–40
Comparative Occupation Statistics, 1870–1940

More detailed statistics on educational attainment and relationship to head of household may be found in Volume IV of the reports on population. Additional data on the ages of husbands and wives and related topics appear in the report on Types of Families, and much additional detail on migration, including the numbers of migrants from each state to each other state, appears in the report on Internal Migration.

A circular describing all of the reports of the 1940 census may be obtained upon request from the bureau of the census, Washington 25, D.C. (*See* also ALIENS; BIRTH STATISTICS; HOUSING; IMMIGRATION AND EMIGRATION, U.S.; MARRIAGE AND DIVORCE; WAGES AND HOURS; WEALTH AND INCOME; U.S. DISTRIBUTION OF.)   (L. E. T.)

Centennials: *see* CALENDAR, 1944, page xx.

Central America.
That portion of the Americas lying between Mexico on the north and Colombia on the south, including the republics of Costa Rica, El Salvador, Guatemala, Honduras, Nicaragua and Panamá, and also the Panama Canal Zone and the colony of British Honduras. The total area is about 222,675 sq.mi. The population approximates 8,500,000, with by far the greater proportion living in the highlands of the western cordillera.

History.—No significant political changes took place in 1943, with the same administrations continuing in power during the off-election year and maintaining their policy of inter-American co-operation.

While shipping definitely improved during the year, shortages still were felt in Central America; lack of goods to be purchased was as serious as shortage of cargo space. Fuel oils continued scarce, and in one part of Honduras gas rationing was reported unnecessary for a time because of complete lack of gas. This factor, and lack of tires, decreased automobile traffic, including motor bus, by as much as 50%. Unemployment was nowhere reported as serious since export facilities had improved and projects, involving various new agricultural items of strategic significance (abacá, hemp, cinchona, rubber), were getting under way. Inter-American highway construction and work in the Canal Zone likewise absorbed labour.

The United States and Mexico became officially represented by embassies instead of ministries in all the Central American republics, during the year.

Trade and Communication.—Under war conditions detailed trade statistics for the year were not available. Trade of the republics with the United States, for the first nine months of 1943, showed balances favourable to the United States in the cases of Honduras ($644,000) and Panamá ($22,025,000); favourable to the republics in connection with Costa Rica ($143,000), Guatemala ($6,669,000), Nicaragua ($4,801,000) and El Salvador ($9,947,000). Values of exports increased, in proportion to volume.

External communication by sea improved as submarine action diminished, but shipping was still short of normal. Air service continued important. The TACA air line, active in Central America as well as in South America, was purchased by American capital during the year. Construction on the Inter-American pioneer road, completion of which had been scheduled for May 1943, was slowed by supply shortages because of shipping failures, and by construction difficulties caused by prolonged rainfall and the worst terrain south of Alaska. By the end of the year work on the road was reported halted since most goods were now going north by boat. (*See* articles on individual countries and HISPANIC AMERICA AND WORLD WAR II.)

BIBLIOGRAPHY.—Dana G. Munro, *The Five Republics of Central America* (1918); Chester Lloyd Jones, *The Caribbean Since 1900* (1936); C. D. Kepner, *Social Aspects of the Banana Industry* (1936).   (D. Rd.)

Cereals: *see* CORN; OATS; RICE; RYE; WHEAT.

Ceylon.
A British crown colony, lying off the southern extremity of India and approaching within 6° of the equator. Area 25,332 sq.mi.; pop. (est. Dec. 31, 1940) 5,981,000. Chief towns (pop. census 1931): Colombo (cap., 284,155); Jaffna (45,708); Galle (38,424); Kandy (37,147). Governor (1943): Sir Andrew Caldecott; languages, English, Sinhalese, Tamil; religions: Buddhism and Hinduism the chief.

History.—During 1943 Ceylon remained fully mobilized. The population contributed generously to the war effort: £75,000 was donated to war funds, and in a single savings week £2,750,000 was raised. Readers of the *Times* of Ceylon contributed £225,000 to their "send a plane" fund. To render the country self-supporting, rural schools undertook the cultivation of 30,000 ac. of crops.

After the fall of Malaya in 1942, Ceylon became the chief source of natural rubber in the British empire. A "grow more rubber" campaign was inaugurated and 20% of the trees were to be "slaughter tapped."

In order to stimulate social reform, village welfare societies were started in the rural districts. The island was administered by the governor, assisted by three ministers and an elected council of state. But Ceylon had been guaranteed full internal self-government as soon as possible after the war, and the board of ministers was asked to draw up its own schemes.

(H. G. RN.)

Education.—In 1940: Sinhalese and Tamil schools 3,175; scholars, 389,153 boys, 172,448 girls; English and bilingual schools 408; scholars, 71,536 boys, 30,702 girls. Total number of schools: 5,816; scholars 819,297.

Banking and Finance.—Revenue (1941–42) £9,384,400; (est.

TRAINED ELEPHANTS stacking timber in a Ceylon jungle after trees had been cleared for an R.A.F. airfield

1942–43) £11,133,333; expenditure (1941–42) £9,474,876; (est. 1942–43) £12,266,666; public dept (Sept. 30, 1940) £9,408,775 and Rs.45,270,000; currency Rs. 1 = 100 cents = 1s.6d. (30.3 cents U.S.) in 1943.

Trade and Communication.—Overseas trade, merchandise, 1941: imports Rs.259,510,454; exports (domestic) Rs.264,717,885. Communications and transport 1940: roads, motorable 5,633 mi.; railways (117 mi. narrow gauge) total 960 mi.; shipping, entered 6,489,322 net tons; motor vehicles licensed (Dec. 31, 1941), 20,092 motor cars and taxis; 4,394 trucks and vans; 2,486 omnibuses; 2,644 cycles; 66 tractors; 231 trailers; wireless receiving set licences (Dec. 31, 1940), 9,736; telephone instruments in use (1938), 10,424.

Agriculture.—Production, in metric tons: rice (1938–39) 300,000; copra (including coco-nut oil) (1939) 155,000; tea (1940) exports 112,000; rubber (1940) shipments 90,000.

Chain Stores: *see* BUSINESS REVIEW.

Chambers of Commerce.
The Chamber of Commerce of the United States, with headquarters in Washington, D.C., gave its attention during 1943 primarily to problems connected with the war and the postwar period. Participating in the work of the organization were 1,400 local chambers of commerce, 400 trade associations and an underlying membership of 1,000,000 business firms. Eric A. Johnston, of Spokane, Wash., was elected as president for a second year at the annual meeting in April 1943. Ralph Bradford was general manager.

A program of action for the 1943–44 year has been directed toward three major objectives: (1) Winning the war; (2) preparing for victory, including matters relating to a transition period and postwar reconstruction; and (3) long-range policies in line with the basic purpose to work for the preservation and strengthening of free enterprise and representative democracy.

Among activities in the legislative field were a broad campaign to stimulate businessmen and their organizations to make new contacts with their elected representatives in congress, the enlistment of state chambers in stimulating meetings and other congressional contacts, a wide dissemination of congressional district maps together with letters from divisional vice-presidents urging business participation in legislative affairs, a distribution of a state-by-state breakdown of roll call votes with a letter from President Johnston urging businessmen to know their congressmen, and an outline of chamber policies on taxation and renegotiation with an appeal to members to make acquaintance with congress.

Activities on postwar problems included a series of booklets sponsored by the chamber's committee on economic policy, a canvass of probable consumer demands after the war, and the promotion of local studies of possible employment conditions during the period of demobilization and reconstruction. The chamber also organized late in the year a special committee on international postwar problems. Through a special committee on international transport, the chamber offered recommendations for the future development of the American merchant marine and commercial aviation.

Channel Islands: *see* BRITISH EMPIRE.

Cheese.

Production of cheese in the U.S. continued to decline in 1943 from the high point in 1942. The total production of 1943 was estimated to be 914,000,000 lb. compared to 1,109,000,000 lb. in 1942 and 669,000,000 lb. as the average of 1935–39. This decline in cheese production was attributed to the large demand for fluid milk for consumption and raised the question of the possible control of whole milk late in the year 1943. As the demand for butter increased with the scarcity, many cheese factories shifted to butter making. The rationing of cheese continued through the year but did not operate to check the demand, only the absence of the product in the markets was effective. The estimated per capita consumption of cheese in 1943 was 4.9 lb. compared to 5.6 lb. as the average of 1935–39. (*See* also BUTTER; DAIRYING; MILK.)   (J. C. Ms.)

Chemical Therapy: *see* CHEMOTHERAPY.

Chemistry.

Any list of noteworthy chemical accomplishments of 1943 must include the vast industrial developments occasioned by the war, such as the new plants for the production of synthetic rubber, ammonia, chlorine, magnesium and other necessary commodities. The list should at least give passing mention to the large amount of government-subsidized research (Office of Scientific Research and Development) which cannot be discussed. In the same category is a large portion of privately sponsored research.

Many developments of the year can be mentioned, however, and of these none is more in the public eye than penicillin, a drug with phenomenal curative properties.

Penicillin.—The beneficial effects of certain kinds of bacterial products in combatting disease have long been known. Pasteur showed in 1877 that *Bacillus anthracis,* which causes the disease anthrax, can be repressed by other microorganisms. The French physician Felix Hubert d'Herelle in 1917 expanded the work of a British bacteriologist, F. W. Twort, and developed means of producing an active substance by bacterial growth which he named bacteriophage, a substance of low toxicity and of considerable commercial importance, but with the drawback of being too specific for general use.

It was Alexander Fleming of London, working with cultures of certain strains of staphylococci in 1929, who discovered that a certain green mould was able to destroy the colonies of staphylococcus on an agar plate culture. The green mould was found to be a species of fungus known as *Penicillium notatum.* The filtrates from the cultures of this mould were found to have strong germicidal activity, and Fleming named the material penicillin. Fleming's findings were reinvestigated and expanded in 1940 by an Oxford group of investigators headed by E. P. Abraham, E. Chain and H. W. Florey. Shortly thereafter, Florey visited America to interest the United States government and

several commercial laboratories in undertaking the commercial production of penicillin. His mission was successful and the year 1943 witnessed the building of new plants in at least 18 companies interested in this production. The new plant of the Commercial Solvents corporation of Terre Haute, Indiana, was nearly completed in 1943 and was equipped to be the largest producer of penicillin in America.

Of the two experimental approaches for the production of penicillin, namely, the bottle culture of the mould, and the deep culture technique, the second seemed best suited for large-scale production. Most of the smaller producers, however, were employing the bottle method.

Chemical studies showed that the bacteriostatic action of penicillin is not antagonized by pus, blood, hydrolytic products of proteins, or by products of tissue autolysis. After intravenous administration much of the active substance is recoverable in the urine. The material was shown to be particularly effective towards certain infections of the gas gangrene type, osteomyelitis, gonococcal infections, and many other types of infection. Some bacteria, notably *B. coli* and *B. influenzae* are not affected by it.

The structure of penicillin was not known in 1943, but considerable work was done on its chemistry. Penicillin seemed to contain 2 to 4% of nitrogen of a non-protein nature, and the preparations thus far prepared contained a pigment varying in colour from light yellow to dark brown. Possibly the nitrogen content and the pigmentation might be due to impurities. Penicillin is an acid. It is soluble in water and inorganic solvents such as ether, alcohol or acetone. It gives rise to salts such as the sodium, barium, or strontium salt, and also to ethyl, methyl and butyl esters. A methyl ester was prepared by Karl Meyer of Columbia university by the action of the free acid of penicillin and diazomethane. The esters were considerably less potent against haemolytic streptococci than penicillin itself. Work up to the close of 1943 was hindered by lack of an adequate supply of material and by lack of suitable criteria of ultimate purity. Many groups of workers were engaged in elucidating the chemistry of this material and in another 12 months it seemed certain great advances would be seen.

The Penny.—Shortage of materials caused problems in U.S. coinage, both the nickel and the penny having undergone change in alloy content. The traditional penny was made of 95% copper and 5% zinc and tin. During 1943 a zinc-coated steel penny was widely circulated, but it lacked popularity because of its silvery appearance when new.

Scheduled for production on Jan. 1, 1944 was a new copper penny which would contain 85–90% copper, and 10–15% zinc. The material for this new penny would be the small arms cartridge cases recovered from military authorities from proving grounds, firing ranges, and other training areas for troops. These cases contain 70% copper and 30% zinc, to which would be added sufficient copper to bring the content up to the required amount.

Fluorescein.—The organic dye, fluorescein, was given a new use. A quantity of the dye was cemented to an aviator's life jacket with a rip flap, so that if an aviator were forced to land in the ocean he might empty this packet of fluorescein into the ocean, with the result that a wide area of water would be converted into a visible yellow patch. In this way search for lost aviators would be made much easier.

Acrylonitrile.—In 10 years acrylonitrile changed from its status as a rare chemical to one which was produced in large quantities. Its two major uses were in the manufacture of methyl acrylate for the transparent plastic known as Plexiglas and in the production of Buna-N rubber.

Acrylonitrile itself, $CH_2=CHCN$, is made by dehydration of

2-hydroxyethyl cyanide, $HOCH_2CH_2CN$, which in turn is made from ethylene chlorohydrin, $HOCH_2CH_2Cl$, and sodium cyanide.

Its availability made it a logical compound to study, and H. A. Bruson of Rohm and Haas company and C. F. Koelsch of the University of Minnesota discovered that acrylonitrile was reactive toward a variety of compounds if an alkaline catalyst was present, such compounds including acetone and other ketones, ethyl alcohol and other alcohols, nitromethane and other nitroparaffins, and even such substances as indene, cyclopentadiene, oximes, mesityl oxide, malonic ester, and organic cyanides. These reactions all proceed by addition of the substance concerned across the double bond of acrylonitrile. If HX, H_2Y or H_3Z represent the substance, the reaction products, respectively, would have the formulas XCH_2CH_2CN, $Y(CH_2CH_2CN)_2$ and $Z(CH_2CH_2CN)_3$. Nitromethane, H_3CNO_2, for example, gives rise to triscyanoethylnitromethane, $NO_2C(CH_2CH_2CN)_3$. Yields of these preparations were high and usefulness for many of them is assured because of the polyfunctional nature of the substances formed.

Nitroparaffins.—Other experiments with nitroparaffins were reported by Kenneth Johnson and E. F. Degering of Purdue university. They discovered that 80–85% yields of propionaldehyde or butyraldehyde may be formed by adding the sodium salt of 1-nitropropane or 1-nitrobutane to cold, dilute sulphuric acid. Coupling of the nitroparaffins with aromatic diazo compounds produced azo dyes, one such being phenylazonitropropane, $C_6H_5N=NC(CH_3)_2NO_2$. Such substances dye wool or silk directly and are applicable to cotton if the coupling is performed on the fabric.

An ingenious method of analysis for mixtures of nitroparaffins by infrared spectroscopy was reported by J. R. Nielsen and D. C. Smith of the University of Oklahoma. The basis of the method was to find, from the spectra of the pure components (nitromethane, nitroethane, 2-nitropropane, 1-nitropropane) a set of wave lengths such that at each wave length only one component shows strong absorption while the others show weak absorption. For the four nitroparaffins mentioned, these bands were located, respectively, at 10.90, 10.06, 11.74, 8.15 microns. Only a few minutes were required for each analysis, and accuracy was within 0.1%. R. B. Barnes and co-workers of the American Cyanamide company have been active in developing infrared spectroscopy as a tool for the analysis and control of synthetic rubber.

Triptane or Trimethylbutane.—Improvement of motor fuel was an outstanding modern achievement of American chemists. The standard by which such fuels were evaluated was 2,2,4-trimethylpentane, an octane which is arbitrarily assigned a value of "100 octane" in the fuel-rating scale. Important milestones in this phase of petroleum technology were thermal cracking or pyrolysis, the use of tetraethyllead, catalytic cracking, and the "alkylation" by gaseous unsaturated hydrocarbons of paraffins such as isobutane or aromatic hydrocarbons such as benzene. The "alkylation" process may be illustrated by the formation of: (a) 2,2-dimethylbutane from ethylene and isobutane at 480° C. and 1,000 lb. per square inch; (b) isopropylbenzene from propylene and benzene, with suitable catalysts; (c) 2,2,3-trimethylpentane from 1-butene and isobutane, in the presence of concentrated sulphuric acid. Substances a, b, and c all were contributing to the relative excellence of aviation gasoline in 1943, since each possessed a rating of 90-98 octane or better.

The newest member of this group was trimethylbutane, $(CH_3)_3CCH(CH_3)_2$, one of the heptanes now marketed as "triptane." Trimethylbutane is not a new chemical. It had been known for years also that it possessed at least a 50% greater power output than 2,2,4-trimethylpentane but until 1943 it had

been impossible to acquire any sizeable quantity of it because of prohibitive costs. A new method was announced late in 1943 by V. N. Ipatieff and V. Haensel of the Universal Oil Products company which was claimed to bring its price below one dollar per gallon. This compound would result if propylene "alkylated" isobutane as outlined above. Conditions for this process were not revealed but it was demonstrated that liquid recoveries of over 90% were obtained of which over half is trimethylbutane.

Fluid Catalytic Cracking.—Reference should be made to a new type of powdered catalyst for converting gas-oil into unsaturated gaseous hydrocarbons used by the Standard Oil Company of New Jersey in their plant at Baton Rouge, La. The catalyst is so fine that it behaves like a fluid and the process is referred to as fluid catalytic cracking. Handling a solid in a manner similar to a fluid is a radical departure from previous industrial practice, and increased production of gasoline with less difficulty was achieved in 1943.

Mechanism of Organic Reactions.—In the so-called Arndt-Eistert reaction an organic acid, RCOOH, is converted to a higher acid, RCH_2COOH, by converting the original acid to its acid chloride, RCOCl, and treating the latter with diazomethane. It had been assumed that a ketene, $RCH=C=O$, is an intermediate in this process, hydration of which produces the final acid. Workers at the University of Minnesota (C. Huggett, R. T. Arnold, T. I. Taylor) demonstrated the essential correctness of this reaction by use of the isotope of carbon of mass 13, since from an original acid which contained 2.51% of C^{13}, the final acid contained 2.53% C^{13}.

Erwin Schwenk and Edith Bloch of Schering corporation (N.J.) made a substantial improvement in the Willgerodt reaction. In this reaction an aromatic ketone, $ArCOCH_3$, is heated under pressure with yellow ammonium sulphide to produce an amide, $ArCH_2CONH_2$. By use of morpholine and sulphur in place of ammonium sulphide the reaction has been carried out effectively without the use of sealed tubes.

The rearrangement of phenyl allyl ether to ortho allylphenol at 200° has been considered to proceed by transfer of the allyl group with an ortho phenol hydrogen. This mechanism was confirmed by use of a deuterium atom in place of the ortho hydrogen atom. In the final product the deuterium was found to be attached to the phenolic oxygen. This work was carried out by G. B. Kistiakowsky and R. L. Tichenor of Harvard university. Additional studies on the rearrangement of more complex allyl ethers were reported by W. N. Lauer, P. A. Saunders and Owen Moe of the University of Minnesota.

The use of diphosgene, CCl_3COCl, in carboxylation reactions was investigated by M. S. Kharasch and co-workers at the University of Chicago. By heating a mixture of diphosgene and diethylacetyl chloride, $Et_2CHCOCl$, for ten hours at 225° C., a 90% yield of diethylmalonyl chloride, $Et_2C(COCl)_2$, was obtained. They found that good yields could be obtained with many disubstituted acetyl chlorides, whereas poor yields were obtained with monosubstituted acetyl chlorides. For example, phenylacetyl chloride, $PhCH_2COCl$, gave rise to only 1.4% yield of phenylmalonyl chloride, $PhCH(COCl)_2$.

Structure of Vinyl Polymers.—Vinyl acetate, vinyl chloride and similar compounds of the structure, $CH_2=CHX$, are known to polymerize by opening of the double bond so that a chain of this nature is formed, $-CH_2-CHX-(CH_2-CHX-)_n-CH_2-CHX-$, in which n represents a large number. The end groups of these long polymer chains are usually not well understood, but the work of C. S. Marvel and G. E. Inskeep of the University of Illinois gave new information on the structure of the end group of polyvinyl alcohol. This polymeric alcohol is produced by alkaline hydrolysis of polyvinyl acetate. During this process

an irregular change was noted in the molecular weight of the polymer, which was explained by assuming that polyvinyl alcohol has one terminal aldehyde group, the structure of which may be visualized as $-(CH_2-CHOH)_n-CH_2CHO$. Under acid conditions this terminal aldehyde group can react with neighbouring hydroxyl groups, and under alkaline conditions the aldehyde function may condense with a similar function, giving rise to molecules of quite different molecular weight.

Aldol.—Two molecules of acetaldehyde condense in the presence of hydroxide to produce aldol, $CH_3-CHOH-CH_2-CHO$. This is a very old organic reaction, but the instability of aldol has made it difficult to study. Several groups of workers contributed to its understanding during 1943. Edward Connolly of the British Industrial Solvents and L. N. Owen reported data on the molecular weight of aldol in various solvents. Owen proved that the molecular weight increases with time for several hours. R. H. Saunders, M. J. Murray and F. F. Cleveland of the Illinois Institute of Technology, by Raman spectrum methods, showed the absence of an aldehyde group in freshly distilled aldol and suggested as a probable explanation the reaction of aldol with acetaldehyde to produce an unstable cyclic acetal:

$$CH_3CHOHCH_2CHO + CH_3CHO \rightarrow CH_3CH\underset{\underset{\textstyle O-CH(CH_3)-O}{|}}{}\! CH_2\underset{}{}CHOH$$

E. Spaeth and T. Meinhard of Germany proved that aldol could not be converted to a monoacetate by simple methods, but did succeed in preparing it indirectly. The substance which aldol changes to on standing was acetylated with acetic anhydride and pyridine. The resulting product was then decomposed thermally at about $210°$ C. and 50 mm. pressure to produce the desired acetate of aldol itself.

The Acetone-Formaldehyde Reaction.—Theodore White and R. N. Haward of Colemore Adhesives, England, unravelled part of the complex story that happens when acetone and formaldehyde react. Past workers obtained products which resinified on distillation, but the present investigators found that dilution with butyl phthalate permitted the product to be distilled without resinification, and to give rise to the formation of 4-hydroxy-

2-butanone, $CH_3COCH_2CH_2OH$. This substance was obtained in 28% yields by careful distillation and it was found to be fairly stable. If heated with concentrated phosphoric acid it underwent smooth dehydration into vinyl methyl ketone, a low boiling liquid which polymerized to a hard colourless resin. During the polymerization process it contracted 25% in volume, thereby changing in density from 0.84 to 1.12.

Alkaline condensation of formaldehyde with methyl ethyl ketone yielded a similar keto alcohol which, when treated with concentrated sulphuric acid, dehydrated to methyl propenyl ketone. The conversion of the latter to methacrylic acid was accomplished in 41% yield by treatment with sodium hypochlorite. This constitutes a new and interesting synthesis of methacrylic acid, the precursor of the important plastic Lucite.

Analogues of Pantothenic Acid.—Knowledge of the structure of the new vitamin, pantothenic acid, stimulated work on the preparation of compounds of analogous structure to see if they were also growth stimulators when tested on microorganisms. Pantothenic acid itself is made from β-alanine, $NH_2CH_2CH_2COOH$, and 2-hydroxy-3,3-dimethylbutyrolactone,

$$\underset{\underset{\textstyle CO}{|}}{HOCH}-CMe_2-\underset{\underset{\textstyle O}{|}}{CH_2}.$$

Jean Barnett and F. A. Robinson selected five other lactones, and they also substituted four other amino acids for β-alanine without being able to obtain a product in any case which would replace pantothenic acid as a growth stimulator. These workers, as well as another group of workers headed by R. Kuhn, obtained a reaction product between 2-hydroxy-3,3-dimethylbutyrolactone and taurine, which product was highly inhibitory to *Strep. hemolyticus*. This is the opposite effect to that shown by pantothenic acid. Taurine, $NH_2CH_2CH_2SO_3H$, differs from β-alanine by having a sulphonic acid group in place of a carboxylic acid group. In passing, it may be mentioned that A. A. Goldberg provided a new synthesis of taurine from 2-aminoethanol by conversion of it to 2-aminoethyl hydrogen sulphate, and reaction of the latter with hot aqueous sodium sulphite.

Separation of Rare Earths.—Joseph K. Marsh of Oxford reported that samarium might be separated from its neighbours, gadolinium or neodymium, by treatment of the acetates with sodium amalgam. Of these three elements samarium is the only one which is readily reduced to the metallic state. In a Sm-Nd mixture it was found possible to reduce the Nd-content from 70% to 0.01% in one step. Another common rare earth mixture which is easily purified by the sodium amalgam technique is that of ytterbium, lutecium and thulium. Only ytterbium acetate in a mixture of these three acetates reacts with sodium amalgam, hence its easy separation.

Traces of europium are often associated with ytterbium, and the work of P. W. Selwood provided a simple method of obtaining the europium content. If these compounds are reduced to the bivalent state, Selwood found that practically complete precipitation of europous sulphate, $EuSO_4$, could be obtained by coprecipitation with barium sulphate, after which the europous sulphate could be removed by washing the precipitate with hot concentrated nitric acid. In this manner pure specimens of europium may be obtained in days rather than years, which were required previously by the tedious fractional crystallizations. (*See* also VITAMINS.)   (C. D. Hu.)

Chemotherapy.
Many of the advances effected in chemotherapy during 1943 resulted from work intended to aid in the prosecution of the war effort by providing

THE BACTERIA-INHIBITING QUALITIES of penicillin are observable in this photograph of a staphylococcus culture. In the centre of the gray mass of the live culture, the penicillin excreted by the white mould has prevented the growth of staphylococcus colonies in the surrounding black ring

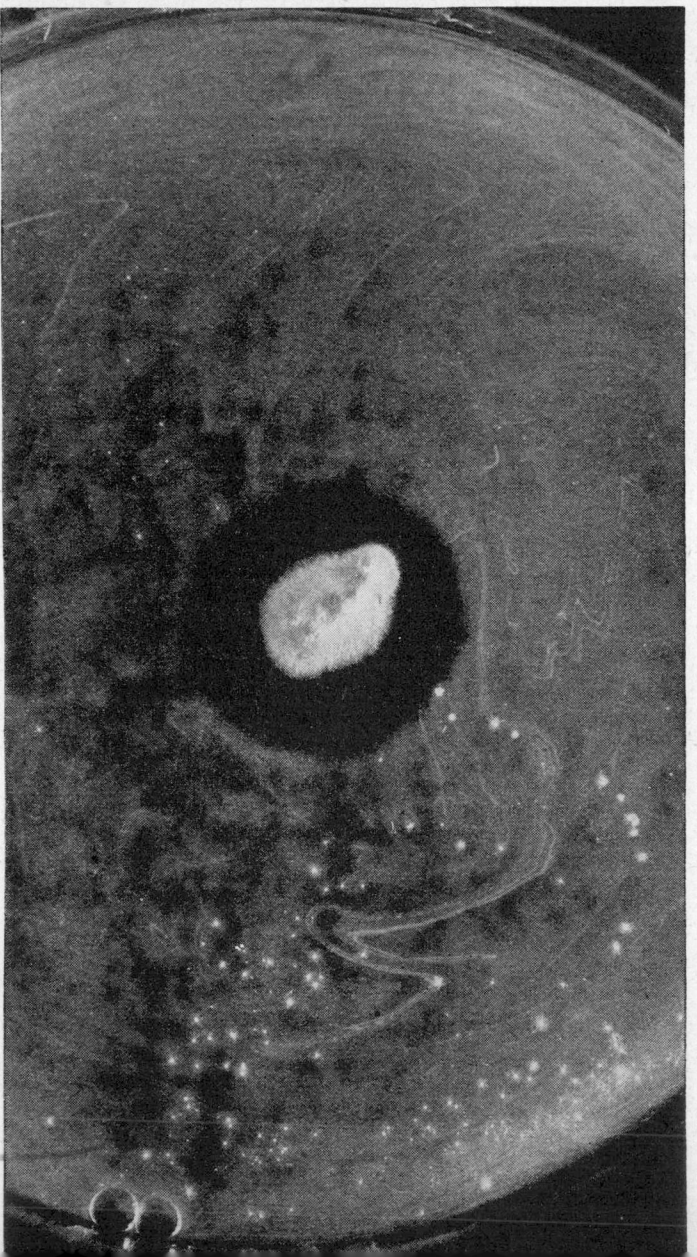

better medical treatment at the battle-front and in civilian life and by providing substitutes for scarce medicinal agents. Two of the outstanding advisory organizations that have continued to provide critical examination of the newer medicaments were the council on pharmacy and chemistry of the American Medical association and the division of medical sciences of the National Research council. Another office that was of much aid by providing funds for research was the Office of Scientific Research and Development. The Food and Drug administration contributed by initiating much research in its own laboratories and elsewhere and by enforcing the provisions of the Federal Food, Drug and Cosmetic act. Penicillin was used extensively for experimental purposes in the armed forces and in civilian practice. Because the supply was severely limited, it was allocated in measured amounts only after the case in which it was proposed as treatment was carefully considered by one or more authorities in this field. Even with careful husbanding of the supply, the drug could not be provided for all requests. It seemed unlikely that supplies would be ample for some time, although sufficient might be produced to permit more general distribution for civilian use by the middle of 1944. In 1943 penicillin was still extracted from the mould *Penicillium notatum*. It was believed that when its chemical structure is learned and synthetic manufacture is possible, there would be an unlimited supply.

Clinically, penicillin showed much promise in the treatment of osteomyelitis, pneumonia, gonorrhoea, syphilis and other infections. It was effective in infections resistant to the sulfonamides; it showed a low degree of toxicity. Its action was mainly bacteriostatic, occasionally bactericidal, and appeared even when the drug was present in minute dilutions provided the infection was caused by a susceptible organism. Experience during 1943 taught that penicillin must be given in infections such as osteomyelitis over a longer period of time than was formerly believed necessary; otherwise the infection will recur.

Other antibiotics (possibly 30) were investigated but none offered the practical promise of penicillin. One mould extract, patulin, was tried in England as a cure for colds but enthusiasm was short-lived, which meant that the public was yet without a "sure cure" or preventive for colds, vitamins and "cold vaccines" included.

The sulfonamides continued as objects of much investigation, partly for the development of new agents more active, absorbed more evenly and less toxic than the current ones, and partly for the development of ones which might affect tropical diseases. In 1943 malaria and dysentery were the only so-called tropical diseases which were believed to be affected to any degree by a sulfonamide. Included in the newer compounds that achieved clinical recognition were sulfamerazine and sulfapyrazine for pneumonia, etc. and phthalylsulfathiazole for the treatment of dysentery.

Diabetics were assured of one more active drug with certain advantages when globin insulin was made available. This insulin was claimed to produce fewer reactions and have a more even effect on the blood sugar.

Experimentally a vitamin (B_c) contained in a liver extract was found by one group to have a curative effect in the anaemia of chickens. Apparently this work was not repeated by other investigators and any clinical value in treating pernicious anaemia in humans remained to be proved.

Physicians were provided with an agent, thiourea, to treat the distressing forms of acute hyperthyroidism. It might save operating in a number of cases. Unlike hyperthyroidism, cancer remained without any drugs for its eradication; surgery and radium or x-ray radiation were the only means of combating this scourge.

Radioactive metals might in the near future be added to the medical armamentarium. In 1943, however, they were used chiefly in an experimental way, and then more for contributing to the knowledge of metabolism than in the treatment of disease. They provided a means of tracing the passage and storage of drugs and foods in the body.

While not strictly in the field of chemotherapy, mineral oil deserves mention, since its harmful possibilities when added to food were exposed. Of much importance is its interference with the absorption of carotene, the precursor of vitamin A, vitamins A, D and K, calcium and phosphorus. This should serve as ample warning to those who use much mineral oil as a laxative and as a salad dressing.

Another item worthy of mention, although not entirely in the field of chemotherapy, was the injection of local anaesthetics at the base of the spine to permit painless birth.

Although many mixtures were proposed for the treatment of burns, only the simplest agents, such as strips of petrolatum gauze, were favoured. Of course, concurrent treatment with serum, plasma and whole blood remained standard measures. Plasma was available in fluid and dry state, serum as whole serum and a concentrated part of the blood formed from the globulin fractions. This globulin fraction permitted certain emergency treatment with much reduction in bulk, an item of extreme importance in shipping. Other special agents investigated as blood substitutes were isinglass solution and a purified part of the haemoglobin of the blood.

In summary, further substantial inroads were made during 1943 in the treatment of diseases such as pneumonia, meningitis, osteomyelitis, gonorrhoea and syphilis, while afflictions such as cancer and colds remained essentially free of effect by chemotherapeutic agents. In addition to demonstrating the value of penicillin in syphilis, investigators studied further shortening of the treatment period by using excessive heat as an adjunct. Although several investigators claimed that sulfathiazole sprayed in the nose and throat would abate and cure a cold, sore throat and sinus infections, this work remained to be substantiated and in no case could such compounds be used freely by the public. No new practical agents were developed for the treatment of malaria and heart diseases, but globin insulin was accepted for the diabetic. In endocrinology major advances were only in refinements of treatment, although a few modifications, some minor in importance, of the more effective sex hormones were prepared. In this regard, some diabetics (those at the menopause) could be controlled simply with oestrogenic substances, although such cases had to be carefully chosen. No outstanding discoveries were made in vitaminology, although many advances were made in the technique of vitamin therapy. Of interest was evidence which seemed to prove that agents such as calcium pantothenate would not affect gray hair. For that matter, no one agent seemed to be effective unless there was a marked deficiency, of which graying hair was only one sign. (*See also* DENTISTRY; MEDICINE; PNEUMONIA; SURGERY; UROLOGY; VITAMINS.)

(A. E. SH.)

Chemurgy. The industrial uses of vegetable oils were sharply curtailed during 1943. The Food Distribution administration on Nov. 23 issued an order prohibiting the use of cottonseed, peanut, soybean and corn oils in the manufacture of soap, paint, varnish, lacquer, linoleum, oilcloth, printing inks and core oil. The prohibition, established because of the need of these oils in foodstuffs, had been in effect with various modifications through the entire year; the November order merely removed most of the modifications.

The needs of war thus suspended progress in increasing the nonfood consumption of these particular oils. It was estimated that if domestic farmers were able to produce the equivalent of the normal imports of oils and fats, more acres would be required for the purpose than in natural years were devoted to the production of cotton for export. The expansion of industrial uses was considered an important step in encouraging greater vegetable oil production. The latter in turn was viewed as a measure toward eventual alleviation of the long-standing problem of cotton surplus. The progress which was under way would undoubtedly be resumed with the establishment of peace.

Oilseed production in the United States in 1943 compared favourably with the record output of 1942. Soybeans at the end of the year were estimated at 206,000,000 bu., peanuts at 2,680,000 lb., cottonseed at 5,079,000 tons and flaxseed at 51,500,000 bu.

Milkweed floss received official recognition as an important and strategic raw material in the late summer. This came in the form of a series of orders, issued at navy and army request, to government agencies for the accumulation of a 10,000,000 lb. stock pile of the floss. The Commodity Credit corporation was instructed to obtain the floss, at the rate of 1,000,000 lb. in 1943, 3,000,000 lb. in 1944 and 6,000,000 lb. in 1945. This action was taken after exhaustive tests indicated the milkweed material to be superior to kapok for use in life preservers, life rafts and for other purposes. Kapok supplies from the orient were cut off, and those in hand were reported to be deteriorating in quality. The milkweed floss collections had to be made almost entirely from the wild plants, which grow abundantly in several areas, notably the northern lake region.

Government grants were made to enlarge the milkweed floss ginning capacity, already established by Boris Berkman's chemurgic research, at Petoskey, Mich., and also for the further prosecution of research at three different institutions.

The oil from milkweed seed has qualities virtually equivalent to those of soybean oil. The limited supply found a ready market. Other by-products from the plant were under investigation. The Soil Erosion service undertook thorough studies of milkweed as a soil binder, since it had an extensive root system.

Seed stocks of a new variety of corn, generally known as "waxey maize," were built up in 1943 to a point where commercial production was expected to be initiated in 1944. While the commercial varieties of corn were widely used for making cornstarch, none of them produced a starch suitable for certain adhesive uses and other industrial purposes, nor for tapioca. The U.S. source of these special starches was root crops of the tropics. "Waxey maize" has characteristics that enable it to meet these requirements. This might prove to be a second important instance of a crop being bred to meet industrial specifications; this already was done in Mississippi with cotton developed to meet the specifications of motor tire manufacturers.

Both corn and wheat were used in 1943, in unreported but extensive quantities, for the manufacture of alcohol for war purposes. Alcohols were required for butadiene necessary to the synthetic rubber program, for smokeless powder and plastics, for antifreeze solutions and in connection with other spectacular uses which might have important postwar consequences.

The shortages of rotenone, pyrethrum and other organic insecticides were sharply felt by farmers. Rotenone was obtained principally from South American plants, and pyrethrum from Japan and Kenya. They are toxic to insects but may be used without harm to animals or humans. Some relief for this shortage appeared in 1943 with the production of a spray material derived from the leaves and plants of Florida castor beans. The supply was marketed among citrus growers and potato producers. Potato producers took a particular interest in the material when they found that the substance apparently had a fertilizing as well as an insecticidal effect on their plants. This indication was being studied further in search of explanation.

Nicotine, it should be added, assumed new importance as a spray material in the absence of normal quantities of other substances. Studies were continued looking to a tobacco plant grown solely for this purpose.

Belladonna, digitalis and certain other pharmaceutical plants were produced domestically in the U.S. in 1943 in quantities sufficient for the national demand. This also was true of sage, which for the second year was grown on a large enough scale to meet U.S. needs.

Plans were formulated in late 1943 for a considerable increase in guayule production for rubber. The quayule plant, native to and grown only in the southwest, it was believed, could be grown at costs competitive with other sources of rubber. Research reduced the work necessary and improved the mechanical devices used.

No conclusive announcements appeared during 1943 with reference to expectations from *kok-sagyz*, the Russian dandelion, although experiments with its growth were conducted in most of the states. Another year's studies, at least, were expected before it could be indicated whether the plant might have economic possibilities.

Interest in chemurgy continued to rise, according to the National Farm Chemurgic council (50 West Broad Tower, Columbus, O.), the clearinghouse for information in this field. The demand for information and reports was beyond all previous years.

BIBLIOGRAPHY.—*The Chemurgic Digest*, published by the National Farm Chemurgic council; the *Agricultural Situation*, issued by the department of agriculture. Valuable general information on chemurgy is contained in *Pioneers of Plenty*, by Christy Borth, and in *Science Remakes Our World*, by James Stokley.   (W. McM.)

Chennault, Claire L. (1890–), U.S. army air officer,
was born Sept. 6 in Commerce, Tex. A school teacher during World War I, young Chennault was called up for service in 1917 and served in the aviation section of the signal reserve corps in the United States. After the war, he became an officer in the army air corps and commanded a pursuit squadron in Hawaii 1923–26. He retired from the army in 1937 and in the same year accepted General Chiang Kai-shek's offer to become aviation adviser to China; he then helped the Chinese to create an air force to fight the invading Japanese. In 1941, he founded the American Volunteer group of the Chinese army—a flying squadron of U.S. volunteer aviators who later became known as the "Flying Tigers." Though seriously hindered by inferior planes, the "Flying Tigers" reflected their superior training under Chennault by repeatedly repulsing Japanese air attacks on the Burma road—then China's lifeline. Chennault was called back to active duty with the U.S. army air force on April 16, 1942. He was promoted to brigadier general and in June 1942 was named commander in chief of the U.S. air task force in China. On July 4, his "Flying Tigers" were disbanded and its members were inducted into the regular U.S. army air corps. In 1943 he was promoted to major general and his force was expanded and reorganized into the 14th U.S. army air force. He returned to the U.S. in May to attend the Roosevelt-Churchill conference in Washington.

Chess. An "off" year in championship chess play, 1943 saw
few developments of major tournament importance. With neither the world nor the national championships contested, Dr. Alexander Alekhine continued his rule of globe-wide chess and Samuel Reshevsky carried on as U.S. national champion. Dr. Alekhine, the Franco-Russian master, was reported seriously ill in Europe.

Israel A. Horowitz of New York featured play in the United States by winning the open championship of the U.S. Chess federation and, at the same time, the New York state title. He and Anthony E. Santasiere, also of New York, were unbeaten in the tournament, but the latter lost out by having three draws to Horowitz' two. Their match, the final in the tournament, ended in a draw after 24 moves. In the same tournament, held at Syracuse, G. O. Christenson of Brooklyn was first in the expert's division and Louis Persinger of New York topped Class A.

Dr. Ariel Mengarini of Washington, D.C., succeeded Edward S. Jackson, Jr., as national amateur champion and holder of the Sturgis Stephens trophy. Reuben Fine, also of Washington, retained his national rapid transit championship, with Reshevsky again runner-up. Reshevsky won the metropolitan speed championship.

The United States Chess federation went on record as favourable to a postwar tournament with Russia. The soviet union was reported to have many more players than the United States, but few have competed in international tournaments and, consequently, the strength of Russian chess was relatively unknown.

(M. P. W.)

Chiang Kai-shek (1887–), Chinese statesman and
soldier, was born Oct. 31 at Feng-hwa, Chekiang. Chiang's popularity continued to grow in 1943 with his determination to resist Japan to the final end and to co-operate with the United Nations to establish a better world order. His power and prestige were further enhanced when he became president of the republic of China on the death of President Lin Sen, Aug. 2, 1943. In recognition of Chiang's brilliant leadership and statesmanship and China's magnificent defense, Chiang was awarded the Grand Cross of the Bath by Great Britain in April 1942, the Grand Cordon of the Aztec Eagle by Mexico on June 29, 1943, and the Legion of Merit in the Order of Commander-in-chief by the United States on July 7, 1943.

Under his heavy burden of responsibility Chiang had grown gray and austere but remained as vibrant and alert as ever. As president of the republic of China, commander in chief of all military forces, Tsung Tsai of the Kuomintang, chairman of the Supreme National Defense council, president of the combined national central banks, chairman of the Central Planning board and president of several educational and cultural institutions, Chiang became the centre of all political groups. Chiang's participation in the Cairo Conference November 22–26, 1943 was a diplomatic triumph for China.

Chiang studied military science in China and Japan from 1906–10 and in the U.S.S.R. in 1923, and became a faithful follower of Sun Yat-sen in 1910. In 1927 Chiang established the National government at Nanking and in 1937 he became the national leader and symbol of China's resistance. On July 7, 1943, the sixth anniversary of China's war of resistance, Chiang, rejoicing over his faith in the democracies and confidence in final victory, expressed the opinion that the time limit of Japan's defeat could not exceed two years.

BIBLIOGRAPHY.—Chiang Kai-shek, *Resistance and Reconstruction* (collected speeches 1937–1943); E. T. Clark, *The Chiangs of China*; R. Berkov, *Strong Man of China*; Hollington Tong, *Chiang Kai-shek*.

(H. T. Ch.)

Chiang Kai-shek, Madame (SOONG MEI-LING) (1898–), wife of General
Chiang Kai-shek, Chinese leader, was born in Shanghai, daughter of Charles Jones Soong of the wealthy Soong family. One of three famous sisters, she was educated in the United States and was graduated from Wellesley college in 1917. Returning to China, she served on the China Labour commission, the first woman ever appointed to this agency. She married Chiang in

1927. When her husband was kidnapped by Chinese rebels in 1936, she flew to their Sian stronghold, induced them to release Chiang and was instrumental in persuading him to forge a united front with the Chinese communists who wanted to halt Japanese encroachments in China. A strong and vivid personality, Mme. Chiang inspired Chinese fighters, aided thousands of orphans, re-settled refugees and established hospitals. In Nov. 1942 she trav-elled to New York to undergo medical treatment. After three months in a hospital, she visited the White House on Feb. 17, 1943, and addressed the congress on the 18th, being the first pri-vate citizen ever to do so. She asked for more help in the Pacific war, pointing out that Japan controlled more resources than Ger-many. Her travels and addresses in the United States and Canada during the ensuing four months were widely publicized. After a third visit to the White House on June 24, Madame Chiang made a 15,000-mile air trip back to Chungking, via Natal, Brazil, reach-ing home July 4. In Nov. 1943 she accompanied her husband to Cairo, serving as his interpreter in the conversations there with Churchill and Roosevelt.

Chicago.

Second largest U.S. city, a port of entry and the county seat of Cook county, Ill., at the southwest corner of Lake Michigan, Chicago is the largest centre of U.S. rail traffic and of long-distance air routes.

The population of the city proper by the federal census of 1940 was 3,396,808. The white population numbered 3,115,379; non-white, 281,429. The population of the 1,119 sq.mi. comprising the metropolitan district was 4,499,126. The census bureau in 1943 estimated a net decline of 32,113 in the civilian population of the metropolitan area.

The city's birth rate in 1943 continued the rise of 1942 but at a diminished tempo, the increase being 1.6 per 1,000 popula-tion in the first six months. Deaths from all causes in the first six months were 19,924 compared with 18,405 for the same period of 1942.

Mayor Edward J. Kelly, Dem., was re-elected for his fourth term, defeating George B. McKibbin, Rep., by a vote of 689,321 to 544,151. Democrats were elected to all minor offices.

Chicago's arms and munitions industry was virtually com-pleted in 1943, when new construction tapered off and pro-duction of matériel neared peak proportions. Factory and other industrial additions in 1943 cost $162,239,437, bringing the total of new facilities installed after June 1940 to a value of $980,894,-437 in the metropolitan area.

In 1943 Chicago's aluminum industry went into production, and the great Douglas cargo plane plant began delivery of planes. Total annual outlay of the government in the Chicago industrial area for supplies of all sorts was approximately $9,700,000,000, divided largely among 265 new war plants and 1,000 existing establishments expanded for war business. Prime war contracts totalled $5,321,000,000, subcontracts, $2,660,000,000, food for the armed forces, $1,000,000,000 and steel, $742,000,000.

Deep drafts upon the city's manpower brought orders late in 1943 from the War Manpower commission for the establishment of a 48-hour week in many industries. The number of persons on relief rolls dropped from 270,000 in June 1942 to 38,602 at the close of 1943, nearly all unemployables. The city's total relief expense in the seven years ending with 1943 was $185,000,000.

Crimes decreased by 16% in 1943 as compared with the 1942 total. Accidents were reduced by 4,033.

In an attempt to set up a tentative city budget for 1944, the city council in Dec. 1943 wrestled with proposals for drastic

EXCEPT FOR A FEW STEERS, the stockyard pens at Chicago were empty in early July 1943, as the U.S. meat shortage reached a crisis

175

increases in licence, inspection and permit fees to balance a loss of $2,000,000 in such revenue in 1943 caused by the closing of establishments and also to raise money for $4,500,000 in prospective salary increases. The proposed city budget for 1943 was $160,000,000, compared with $166,138,734 in 1942. At the close of 1943 the city's outstanding bonded debt stood at $65,000,000, compared with the peak of $140,500,000 in 1931, and all maturities of debt on Jan. 1, 1944 were met from funds on hand.

The first unit of the new subway system was opened for operation in October, a 4.73 mi. double track tube, mostly under State street, connecting the north side and south side elevated lines. Total cost of the section placed in operation was $34,119,189. Traffic increase of the elevated lines in the first month's operations after the subway opened was 15.83% over the same month of 1942. (L. H. L.)

Chicago, University of.

An institution of higher education and research in Chicago, Ill. Founded in 1891, the university is privately endowed, coeducational, and nonsectarian. In the academic year 1942–43, the university conferred 1,320 degrees, of which 692 were bachelor's (including 42 of the new bachelor's degrees for general education administered in the college), 363 were master's degrees in arts, literature and science, 143 were Ph.D. degrees, and 122 were professional degrees in business administration, divinity, law and medicine.

After exclusion of income from auxiliary enterprises and restricted expendable funds, as well as most of the income received and paid out on contracts (which were nonprofit) with the United States government for war purposes, the total income of the regular budget was $8,113,505, a decrease of $173,487 from the corresponding income for the 1941–42 year. The contracts with the government, for teaching, research, housing and messing, numbering 160, were with 19 different departments, bureaus, or agencies, and resulted in a gross income exceeding $5,000,000. Gifts for all purposes for the year 1942–43 totalled $1,148,550 and endowment funds at the end of the year amounted to $69,423,937. Book value of all university assets as of June 30, 1943, was $125,902,953. (For additional statistics of enrolment, faculty members, endowment, library volumes, etc., see UNIVERSITIES AND COLLEGES.)

Among the important developments of the year was the growth of the first two years of the college, established in 1942, which had a registration of 300 students. The University of Chicago press completed publication of *A Dictionary of American English,* preparation of which began in 1925. The divinity school of the university and three theological schools adjacent to the university and hitherto in loose affiliation with it—the Chicago Theological Seminary (Congregational), Disciples Divinity House and Meadville Theological Seminary (Unitarian)—organized the Federated Theological Faculty. Members of the academic staffs of all four schools form the Federated Faculty, which administers a common curriculum, except for a fraction reserved for denominational education, and degrees will be conferred by the university in co-operation with the schools. The schools retain their full independence.

The university devoted an increasingly large part of its efforts to war research and training during the year 1942–43, both in education and research. The number of civilian students declined to approximately half of normal enrolment, but registration of service students under such programs as meteorology and ASTP offset this decline. In addition to the large number of service students and the navy signal and radio schools on the quadrangles (personnel of which were not enrolled students), 1,629 special students completed noncredit war courses sponsored by the U.S. office of education under the ESMWT programs, and the university's Institute of Military Studies gave basic and specialized military training to 2,550 students, bringing the total so trained since 1940 to 9,500.

Chiefs of Staff, The Combined: see COMBINED CHIEFS OF STAFF, THE.

Child Labour: see CHILD WELFARE.

Children's Books.

More than in 1942, the books of 1943 were influenced by the war, in subject matter, in emphasis, in format and in quantity. The first eleven months of 1942 saw the publication of 831 children's books, while the same period in 1943 listed only 618 books, which resulted on the whole in a somewhat higher quality than in some earlier years. In appearance the books were remarkably attractive considering the restrictions under which they were made, involving narrower margins, poorer paper and greater simplicity of illustration. Many good books went out of print, especially among the less expensive reprints.

A great many books dealt directly with the war or activities which grew out of the war. There was much informational material about the various services, including the WACS and the WAVES, such as Mary Elting and Robert Weaver's *Soldiers, Sailors, Fliers and Marines* and Elizabeth Conger's *American Warplanes* for younger children, and for older boys and girls Keith Ayling's *Semper Fidelis,* Herbert Zim's *Air Navigation,* Kensil Bell's *Always Ready!,* and Douglas Coe's *Road to Alaska,* among many.

Fiction growing out of the war included adventure stories such as Stephen Meader's *The Sea Snake,* stories about children educated in nazi ideology such as Constance Savery's *Enemy Brothers* and Emma Sterne's *Incident in Yorkville,* stories about war industries and about living conditions in congested war industry centres. The number of vocational stories declined, but most of those published had to do with war activities, as Dorothy Deming's *Penny Marsh and Ginger Lee, Wartime Nurses.*

Indirectly connected with the war were the stories about the Allied countries, some just preceding the war, as Dola de Jong's story of Holland, *The Level Land,* and some with a war background, as Mollie Panter-Downes' *Watling Green* (England), Arkady Gaidar's *Timur and His Gang* (Russia) and Eleanor Lattimore's *Peach-blossom* (China).

Non-fiction about other countries increased in quantity and improved in quality with the publication of such books as Cornelia Spencer's *Made in China,* Ellen and Attilio Gatti's *Here is Africa,* Grace Hogarth's *Australia,* Mary Bonner's *Made in Canada,* Eric Kelly's *The Land of the Polish People,* Anne Peck's *The Pageant of Canadian History,* Mary Lucas' *Vast Horizons,* Helen Follett's *Islands on Guard* and Delia Goetz's *Half a Hemisphere,* while the United States and Alaska were well represented in Evelyn Stefansson's *Here Is Alaska,* James Dyett's *From Sea to Shining Sea,* Ann Hark's *The Story of the Pennsylvania Dutch* and May McNeer's *The Story of the Great Plains.*

Geography continued to be published in quantity and included men and women of many countries, times and interests. Nature books worth mentioning were Henry Kane's *The Tale of the Crow,* Jannette Lucas' *First the Flower, then the Fruit* and Dorothy Waugh's *Warm Earth.* Other books of special interest were Helen Dike's *Stories from the Great Metropolitan Operas,* Frank Henius' *Songs and Games of the Americas* and Opal Wheeler's *Sing for Christmas.*

Fiction included many stories of early American history, with emphasis on the fight for liberty and the ideals of democracy, stories of farm and family life which also portray American tradition and ideals, and stories of racial minorities as part of the national entity. Jim Kjelgaard's *Rebel Siege*, Elizabeth Yates's *Patterns on the Wall*, Valenti Angelo's *Look Out Yonder*, John Tunis' *Keystone Kids* and Florence Means's *Teresita of the Valley* were among the many of this group. Eleanor Estes added *Rufus M.* to her stories about the Moffats and Laura Wilder concluded her saga of the Ingalls family with *These Happy Golden Years*.

Other good fiction included Alice Dalgliesh's *The Little Angel*, Oskar Seidlin's *Green Wagons*, Pamela Travers' *Mary Poppins Opens the Door*, Katherine Pollock's *Sly Mongoose*, Patricia Gordon's *The Boy Jones*, Katharine Gibson's *Bow Bells*, Ruth Holberg's *Tibby's Venture*, Gertrude Newman's *Polly Poppingay, Milliner*, Catherine Coblentz's *The Beggars' Penny*, Robert Mc-Closkey's *Homer Price*, Phil Stong's *Missouri Canary*.

Julia Sauer's *Fog Magic* was one of the distinguished imaginative stories of the year. The outstanding collection of folk tales was *The Jack Tales*, compiled by Richard Chase; other good collections were Phyllis Fenner's *Giants and Witches* and Charles Gillham's *Beyond the Clapping Mountains*.

Stories of horses, dogs and other animals were found in abundance, notably Clarence Anderson's *Big Red*, Fairfax Downey's *Dog of War*, and Don Lang's *On the Dark of the Moon*.

The number of picture books was somewhat curtailed but among the best were *Don't Count Your Chicks* by the d'Aulaires, *Katy and the Big Snow* by Virginia Burton, *The 'Round and 'Round Horse* illustrated by Reginald Marsh, and Lee Kingman's *Pierre Pidgeon*. The number of preschool, nursery and toy books was, on the other hand, sharply increased and they were also of better quality than in earlier years.

Several well-known authors wrote outstanding first books for children, among them Esther Forbes, Manning Coles, Alfred Noyes, Antoine de Saint-Exupéry and James Thurber, while Sigrid Undset published her second, *Sigurd and His Brave Companions*.

There were new editions of Andersen's *Fairy Tales*, translated by Jean Hersholt, of Grimm's stories, illustrated by Wanda Gág, and several of selections from the Bible. (*See also* LITERARY PRIZES; PUBLISHING [BOOK].) (S. AN.)

Children's Bureau, United States: *see* CHILD WELFARE.

Child Welfare.

United States.—Although conditions for children in the United States remained highly favourable in comparison with those in countries suffering from invasion, air attack, occupation by enemy forces or widespread famine, many problems of child welfare, especially in relation to emotional and psychological development, were intensified in 1943. In general, existing health and welfare services for children were maintained approximately at existing levels in spite of shortages in medical, nursing and social-service personnel. Progress was made in providing for some of the most pressing wartime needs of mothers and children, such as programs for the prevention and control of juvenile delinquency, care for children of mothers employed in war industries, maternity and infant care for families of enlisted men in the armed forces and safeguards for young workers.

Juvenile Delinquency.—Children and adolescents were quick to feel the excitement and restlessness characteristic of a war period. For boys and girls who had insufficient parental supervision, whose schools were overtaxed or operating on a double shift, who had unaccustomed free time, spending money and little opportunity for wholesome recreation, it was easy to drift into delinquent behaviour. Those who came in conflict with the law represented a small minority even among wartime youth, but

they were a minority that caused increasing general concern.

An increase in juvenile delinquency—in the legal sense of an act or conduct that brings a child within the jurisdiction of the juvenile court—under wartime conditions in the United States is indicated clearly by the most comprehensive data available, *i.e.*, statistics reported to the children's bureau of the U.S. department of labour on delinquency cases disposed of by nearly 500 juvenile courts. For 83 of these courts serving areas of 100,000 or more population, a comparison between 1940 and 1942 shows a rise of 16% in delinquency cases in the 2-year period, from 65,000 to about 75,500.

This agrees very closely with the percentage increase shown by courts in 153 areas studied by the National Probation association.

Conditions characteristic of centres of war activity, where rapid influx of population overtaxed housing, schooling, hospital and recreation facilities, were apparently associated with a rise in juvenile delinquency. The percentage increase in delinquency cases disposed of by juvenile courts in areas of expanding population (41 of the 83 courts in the children's bureau series) was twice as great as the increase in cases disposed of by courts in areas of decreasing population.

The children's bureau commission on children in wartime at a meeting at the White House in Feb. 1943 gave special consideration to the problem of juvenile delinquency and recommended that the children's bureau issue a series of publications to aid families and communities in maintaining security in the lives of children and in dealing with behaviour problems.

One of these publications, *Controlling Juvenile Delinquency*, outlines a community program for the prevention and control of delinquency.

In view of the increase in the number of young girls arrested as prostitutes, especially where the May act, prohibiting prostitution in the vicinity of military establishments, was in force, and the high incidence of venereal diseases among these girls, the division of social protection of the Office of Community War Services and the children's bureau began work on plans for strengthening the juvenile services of police departments. At a conference held in Nov. 1943 and attended by members of these agencies and other federal bureaus and national private organizations in the fields of probation, juvenile delinquency, social work and education, the children's bureau was requested to explore the possibilities and to develop emergency and continuing programs for training policemen and policewomen dealing with juveniles.

Social Services for Children.—*Care for Children of Working Mothers.*—The increasing number of employed women with children under 14 (estimated at 5,500,000 in April 1943) was reflected in the growing need for day care and extended school services for children of preschool and school age. State and local committees on child care or on children in wartime, usually associated with defense councils, provided strong citizen leadership in some communities for the development of programs of child care. State and local welfare agencies and private social agencies took the lead in developing advisory and counselling services for mothers and foster-family day-care programs and group-care facilities for children of working mothers, as did state and local education departments in developing extended school services. But with some exceptions the development of child-care programs failed to keep pace with the growing demand for facilities.

The Federal Works agency continued to make funds available to local agencies for the construction and operation of child-care and nursery establishments under the Lanham ("Community Facilities") act. Nearly 2,000 of these units, with an enrolment of approximately 57,500 children, had been placed in operation by the end of Nov. 1943.

From Aug. 1942 until the end of June 1943, federal funds were available through the Office of Defense Health and Welfare Services from the president's emergency fund for the development of state plans for day care submitted by state welfare agencies and recommended for approval by the children's bureau and state plans for extended school services submitted by state education agencies and recommended for approval by the office of education.

Child-Welfare Services.—Programs for child-welfare services under the Social Security act (title V, part 3), were in operation during 1943 under plans approved by the children's bureau of the U.S. department of labour, in all 48 states, the District of Columbia, Alaska, Hawaii and Puerto Rico. The annual federal appropriation for grants to state welfare agencies administering these programs is $1,510,000. In spite of wartime demands for service, the number of children receiving case-work services under these programs declined from about 50,500 in May 1942 to 41,000 in May 1943, because of the shortage in trained personnel.

Aid to Dependent Children.—State programs for aid to dependent children as provided for in title IV of the Social Security act were in operation under plans approved by the Social Security board of the Federal Security agency in 45 states, the District of Columbia, Alaska and Hawaii, in Oct. 1943. A total of 690,418 children in 278,384 families were receiving allowances at that time; and payments to recipients during October totalled $11,291,506.

Allowances to Servicemen's Dependents.—In Oct. 1943, a liberalization of the benefits provided for in the Servicemen's Dependents Allowance Act of 1942 extended the allowances to apply to dependents of enlisted men in the first through the seventh grades instead of those in the four lowest grades only, and also to apply to dependents of enlisted women. The allowances were increased by increasing the amounts for children contributed by the government. The total allowance for a wife and one child was raised from $62 to $80 a month, and that for each additional child from $10 to $20 a month.

Child Health.—For the first 10 months of 1943 the birth rate was 22.1 per 1,000 estimated population, and the infant mortality rate was slightly under 40 per 1,000 live births, according to provisional figures from the U.S. bureau of the census. The infant mortality rate for each month was lower in 1943 than in 1942, although the rate established in 1942 (40 per 1,000 live births) was lower than that for any previous year on record. The maternal death rate in 1942, 26 per 10,000 live births, was also the lowest on record.

The incidence of the common communicable diseases of childhood, as reported to the U.S. public health service, during the first 6 months of 1943 ran about the same as or lower than during the corresponding period of 1942. During the summer and fall there was a widespread outbreak of poliomyelitis, however, which affected children in nearly every part of the country. The number of poliomyelitis cases reported reached 11,622 by Nov. 13 and exceeded the number reported in any year since 1931. Cases of measles and influenza also were above the median seasonal prevalence during the latter part of the year.

Emergency Maternity and Infant Care.—The outstanding development in the field of child-health services was the program authorized by congress for maternity and infant care for wives and infants of enlisted men in the four lowest pay grades of the armed forces. At the end of 1942, programs of limited extent were in operation in about half of the states; no federal funds had been provided except what could be set aside from the regular children's bureau appropriation for federal grants to

states for maternal and child-health services. The first special appropriation for this program, amounting to $1,200,000, became available in March 1943 for the remainder of the fiscal year 1943. For the fiscal year 1944 appropriations amounting to $23,000,000 were authorized by congress for grants to state health agencies for emergency maternity and infant care. By the end of 1943 plans approved by the children's bureau and involving the use of federal funds were in operation in every state and territory except North Dakota and Puerto Rico, and more than 161,000 cases had been approved for care.

Maternal and Child-Health Services.—The maternal and child-health programs provided for under the Social Security act (title V, part 1) continued in operation under plans approved by the children's bureau in all states and territories. The annual appropriation for grants to state health agencies for these services is $5,820,000. Wartime shortages in medical and nursing personnel and in hospital facilities were met so far as possible by reorganizing the programs with emphasis on preventive health measures that would enable available staffs to reach the greatest numbers of mothers and children.

Services for Crippled Children.—The crippled children's programs, for which the children's bureau receives an annual appropriation of $3,870,000 for grants to states under title V, part 2, of the Social Security act, also continued in operation in all states and territories, in spite of the intensification of wartime difficulties occasioned by the withdrawal of surgeons, nurses and physical therapists in large numbers for service with the armed forces, by lack of hospital facilities, by restrictions on transportation and by the scarcity of metal appliances. The number of children on state registers of crippled children on June 30, 1943, was approximately 354,000, an increase of some 13,000 in the course of a year. In Oct. 1943 a national conference on the development of state rheumatic-fever programs was held at the children's bureau. The number of states having programs for children with rheumatic fever included in their services for crippled children had reached 16 by the end of 1943.

School-Lunch Programs.—Lunches designed to maintain children's diets at an adequate level in spite of wartime food shortages and dislocations in home life were made available to some 5,000,000 school children under a new plan put into effect for the school year 1943–44 by the Food Distribution administration, department of agriculture, which was authorized to spend up to $50,000,000 for this purpose. Under this plan local sponsors of school-lunch programs may be reimbursed for the purchase of many nutritious foods up to a specified maximum that varies with the completeness of the meal served.

Child Labour and Youth Employment.—Wartime labour shortages in the United States brought about a large increase during 1942 and 1943 in the employment of boys and girls under 18 years of age—an increase intensified in 1943 with the drafting of 18- and 19-year-old boys into the armed forces.

A fair measure of the trend of employment of young workers in nonagricultural occupations is found in the number of employment or age certificates issued for minors going to work under the child-labour laws of the several states. More than twice as many young persons 14 through 17 years of age were issued certificates for full-time or part-time work in the first 6 months of 1943 as in the first 6 months of 1942; and almost four times as many in the entire year 1942 as in 1940.

The total of young workers 14 through 17 in all types of employment including agriculture reached a peak in July 1943, when an estimated 5,000,000 were at work. In Oct. 1943, after most schools had opened, the number had decreased by about 2,250,000; this left roughly 2,750,000 boys and girls working full-time or part-time—approximately 750,000, 14 and 15 years

CHILD WELFARE

of age and 2,000,000, 16 and 17 years of age. In other words, 1 in 6 of the population 14 and 15 years old, and 2 in 5 of the population 16 and 17 years old, were at work. These figures do not include children under 14 years of age, many of whom were known to be employed, the large majority in part-time jobs.

Federal and state agencies dealing with both youth employment and youth welfare problems felt considerable concern because health and accident risks were increasing for these young workers, as a result of new and untried conditions of employment; because thousands of boys and girls were cutting short their normal schooling to go to work; and because other thousands attending school and employed outside school hours, were working too long hours or late at night. At the same time, pressures to relax child-labour and compulsory-school-attendance laws resulted in some lowering of standards through state legislation and administrative action.

The child-labour provisions of the Fair Labor Standards act of 1938, which are enforced by the children's bureau of the U.S. department of labour, helped to protect the youth of the country against these pressures. This act provides a 16-year minimum age for employment of children in or about establishments producing goods for shipment in interstate or foreign commerce, and an 18-year minimum age for work in occupations found and declared by the chief of the children's bureau to be especially hazardous. Employment of children 14 and 15 years of age is permitted only in nonmanufacturing and nonmining occupations, outside school hours and only under conditions not detrimental to their health, schooling or well-being; the occupations and conditions permitted must be determined by the chief of the children's bureau.

The children's bureau developed, for certain industries and processes important to war production, advisory standards to meet the need for new standards for employment of youth in a wide variety of hazardous occupations. These advisory standards suggested the types of work in which minors might suitably be employed as well as those in which they should not be employed. They covered shipbuilding, lead and lead-using industries, employment involving exposure to carbon disulphide, employment involving exposure to chlorinated solvents, welding occupations, operation of metal-working machines and the aircraft industry.

The program of action adopted by the Tenth National Con-

ference on Labor Legislation, called by the secretary of labour in Dec. 1943, emphasized the importance of maintaining legal protections for safeguarding young workers, and not only recommended that plans be made for the revision upward of state child-labour standards as speedily as possible, but urged state labour commissioners and organized labour to give leadership and support to constructive programs for youth that would give full opportunity for the education and training needed to compensate for their premature withdrawal from school and to ensure their rightful place in the postwar world.

Inter-American Activities.—The predominant note in inter-American co-operation for child welfare in 1943 was the enlarging and strengthening of the work of the American International Institute for the Protection of Childhood, with headquarters at Montevideo, Uruguay. The proposals to this end, made by the Eighth Pan American Child Congress in 1942, were considered at a special meeting of the international council of the institute held in May 1943. At this meeting the council approved a resolution asking each government belonging to the institute to appoint as a technical member of the council a person experienced in directing child-welfare work. The council also decided to divide the institute into three departments—child health, education and welfare—as a means toward better co-ordination of the work. A plan for the further organization of these departments was later prepared by a committee and submitted to the members of the council. A technical advisory committee of 5 members was appointed by the council for 2 years to examine and pass on the programs of work presented by the three departments. The council also approved a resolution asking that, for better co-ordination of the work, the American republics be divided into four zones, with a technical member responsible for each zone.

In connection with the program of inter-American co-operation developed by an interdepartmental committee under the department of state of the United States, the children's bureau of the department of labour furnished consultation service on request of the respective governments to official agencies concerned with child health and welfare in Bolivia, Brazil, Chile, Costa Rica, the Dominican Republic, Ecuador, Mexico, Paraguay, Peru and Uruguay. Inter-American scholarships for professional study in fields affecting child welfare, such as public health, pediatrics, orthopedics, nursing, nutrition, social service, child guidance and education, were extended to students from other American re-

CHILDREN PLAYING in the child-care centre of a war plant in Buffalo, N.Y., in 1943 while their mothers are at work in the plant

publics in graduate schools and schools of social work in the United States and in some of these fields scholarships were given to an increasing extent for study in Latin-American countries, notably Argentina, Brazil and Chile.

American Republics.—In Chile services for mothers and children were reorganized and placed under the new national bureau for the protection of children and adolescents. The bureau, in the ministry of health, security and social assistance, has the following divisions: prenatal and maternal care, child health, care of children who are morally or physically neglected, wayward or delinquent, social services and foster-home placement, dental care and central files and co-ordination.

In Mexico the work of the federal department of public welfare and its bureau of child welfare, reorganized in 1942, continued to grow. A committee of physicians was appointed to investigate the activities of the child-health centres and to devise means of improvement.

In Peru the national service for the protection of mothers and children was established by a presidential decree of July 2, 1943. This service, under the national bureau of public health, was placed in charge of health and welfare work for mothers and children done by public and private agencies. The national institute of the child, official agency in charge of maternal and child-health work, and its branch institutes in several parts of the country were placed under the newly established service, which had the director of the institute as its head.

Developments in the field of nutrition included the meeting of the first national congress on nutrition in Havana, Cuba, Sept. 1943, and the establishment of a national institution of the science of nutrition in Mexico for the purpose of studying, among other problems, the state of nutrition of the Mexican people, and the nutritive value of the foods used by them, and participating in the work of other government departments for improving the people's food habits. The council of the American International Institute for the Protection of Childhood gave special attention at its meeting in May 1943 to the report of the nutrition committee and adopted proposals for nutrition studies to be made in several countries and for economic, administrative and educational measures to remedy undernutrition.

A new section to deal with the employment of women and children was established in the newly reorganized national department of labour in Brazil.

New developments in social insurance included a law enacted in Mexico in 1943, effective Jan. 1, 1944. This law, which applies to most employed persons, provides insurance for the contingencies of illness, accident, maternity, involuntary unemployment, invalidity, old age and death. Contributions are required from the insured, the employers and the government. Medical and surgical care, medicines and cash payments are provided for the insured in illness, pregnancy and childbirth. Their dependent wives and children are entitled to medical care and medicines. Emphasis is placed on preventive medical services.

In Panamá the previously enacted social-insurance law was revised by an act to take effect on July 1, 1943. The new act makes insurance compulsory for all public employees and for persons in private employment in specified parts of the country. In sickness the insured persons are to receive medical care at home or in a hospital, and medicine; in case of childbirth an insured woman is entitled to receive, in addition, one-half of her wages for 6 weeks preceding and 6 weeks following confinement.

In Paraguay a decree of April 13, 1943, laid down the principles for the organization of a system of social insurance for all employed persons under 60 years with an income below a specified amount.

National congresses especially devoted to child welfare were held in Peru and El Salvador during 1943. Child welfare also occupied an important place on the agenda of the first national congress of social welfare in Mexico.

Great Britain.—*Child Health.*—In Great Britain health conditions of children reflected the favourable effects of vigorous efforts to strengthen public-health measures and health services for mothers and children, according to the summary report of the ministry of health for the year ended March 31, 1943 (issued in Sept. 1943). Vital statistics for 1942 given in that report showed a live birth rate (15.8 per 1,000 population) higher than in any year since 1931, an infant mortality rate (provisional) of 49 per 1,000 live births compared with 59 in 1941, and a maternal mortality rate of 2.47 per 1,000 live births compared with 2.76 in 1941. The mortality rate for children 1 to 5 years of age continued to improve, being 2% lower than in 1941, and that for children 5 to 15 years of age regained the low level reached in 1939. Deaths from diphtheria reached a new low figure and deaths from tuberculosis, which had increased in 1940 and 1941, fell approximately to the prewar level.

One hundred and five emergency maternity homes with some 2,750 beds available were in operation in March 1943, together with 65 antenatal and 11 postnatal hostels. About 32,000 mothers evacuated from target areas were sent to the maternity homes during the year.

Orange juice and cod-liver oil, free or at low cost, were made available to all expectant mothers and all children under 5 years (previously under 2 years).

Child Welfare and Juvenile Delinquency.—Many additional nurseries for children of women workers were opened by the welfare authorities in Great Britain. At the end of March 1943, more than 1,000 of these were in operation and several hundred more were in preparation.

Because of the special need for its provisions, the British Adoption of Children (Regulation) act, 1939, which had remained inoperative because of the war emergency, was finally put into operation in June 1943. The act extends the existing responsibility of welfare authorities for the supervision of children placed by registered adoption societies to include children placed independently of these agencies.

Juvenile delinquency, which rose in Great Britain in the first two years of the war, began to decline in 1942, according to figures issued in July 1943 by the British Information Services.

Child Labour and Youth Employment.—As in previous war years, imperative production needs in Great Britain called into employment many boys and girls who might otherwise have continued in school beyond the legal school-leaving age (14 years). According to the British Information Services, 77% of the boys and 67% of the girls 14 through 17 years of age were engaged in full-time employment in 1943. Although under emergency orders, as in the past, "permissions" for relaxation of the standards for hours of work laid down in the Factories act were granted for employment of both minors and adults, the report of H. M. chief inspector of factories for the year 1942 (the latest available) stated that the tendency during that year was toward the reduction of the weekly hours, not only of young persons and of women subject to the act, but also of adult male workers.

The direct responsibility of the board of education for Youth Services for boys and girls 14 years of age and over who have left school, dating from the beginning of the war, continued. The Youth Advisory council which in 1942 succeeded the National Youth committee appointed in 1939, and on which are represented social-work agencies, youth-serving organizations, trade unions, the armed forces and organizations that carry on youth activities, gives advisory services to the board of education and offers suggestions on action that should be taken. Compulsory registration of boys and girls 16 and 17 years of age and subsequent interviews with them brought to light information as to how young persons used their leisure hours, the hours of employment, cases of double employment and wages, which became available to the committee.

British Dominions.—In Canada, as in the United States, wartime pressures increased the employment of children. Figures from the province of Quebec, for instance, showed that the number of age certificates issued for boys and girls 14 and 15 years of age going to work increased from 1,667 in the school year 1941–42 to 22,001 in 1942–43. Certain advances in standards, however, were made. In New Brunswick a 14-year minimum age for employment in factories was established for the first time, and in Quebec, the one Canadian province without compulsory-school-attendance requirements, a law was enacted, effective July 1, 1943, requiring children to attend school up to 14 years of age, with certain exemptions limited to a 6-weeks' period.

In New Zealand, which also faced an acute child-labour problem as the result of increasing employment opportunities and the growing shortage of manpower, the minister of education announced that the school-leaving age would be raised to 15 years by the beginning of 1944.

In Australia, the Maternity Allowance Act of 1912, amended in 1942, was again amended in 1943 by abolishing the means test and increasing the lump sum payable on the birth of each child.

Continental Europe.—The ravaging effects of the war on the health of children continued in German-occupied Europe. Malnutrition and undernourishment were widespread. Rickets, scurvy and contagious diseases, especially tuberculosis, diphtheria and malaria, were spreading to an extent considered disastrous, according to information available from Belgium, France, Greece, the Netherlands and parts of Poland. The most recent vital statistics available showed a fall in the birth rate in most of these countries:

in France the number of children born in 1942 was 28% below the 1937 figure; in Greece the number of births per month fell from 1,500 in the prewar period to fewer than 500 in Sept. 1942. In all these countries infant mortality increased.

Where educational systems were not entirely disrupted by the war, large numbers of children were prevented from attending school by lack of shoes and clothing. Because of their deteriorated physical condition, many children who continued to attend school did so irregularly, were unable to concentrate on their studies and sometimes fainted from hunger. The mental and physical development of children and their emotional state were affected by evacuation, deportation, forced labour and other conditions.

In the soviet union a government decree for the expansion of child-health work, dated late in 1942, called for the appointment of a specified number of physicians to the staffs of child-health centres and children's clinics in cities and of public-health nurses in rural districts. Provision was made for the appointment of a qualified pediatrician in each city, industrial settlement and provincial district, to organize and direct the medical treatment and preventive care given in child-health centres, children's clinics and other agencies to children of all ages.

The nation-wide program of compulsory industrial training of young people 14 to 17 years of age, introduced in the soviet union in Oct. 1940, was proceeding without interruption despite the war, according to *Pravda*, official Moscow newspaper. The number of schools providing this training increased from 1,550 at the end of 1940 to 1,700 in Sept. 1943. In that period more than 2,500,000 boys and girls entered these schools; 1,500,000 of them had completed their training by the end of Sept. 1943 and entered various industries.

New legislation on the treatment of juvenile delinquency went into effect in Finland in the beginning of 1943. The new law raised the minimum age of legal responsibility to 15 years (instead of 7 years as formerly), so that children under 15 are not brought before the courts. A special procedure is prescribed for dealing with young persons under 21. Their cases must be studied by the public-welfare agencies prior to a decision by the court. Children under 15 accused of punishable offenses and those between 15 and 18 accused of such offenses, but on whom no court sentence had been imposed, were to be placed in the care of public-welfare agencies. Probation and parole were permitted.

A law for compulsory sickness insurance was enacted in Spain in Dec. 1942. Some parts of the law were to become effective in the middle of 1943; others at the end of 1944. Insurance was to be required for all persons working for a living, whether for an employer or on their own account, with income below a specified amount.

International Co-operation.—Special significance for the children of the world lay in action taken at the United Nations Conference on Food and Agriculture in Hot Springs, Va., in May 1943. Ample evidence was introduced as to the malnutrition of children in many countries and as to the relationship between malnutrition and maternal, infant and childhood mortality. The obligation of governments was clearly recognized to meet the special needs of "vulnerable" groups, including infants, preschool and school children, adolescents, and expectant and nursing mothers.

At the first session of the council of the United Nations Relief and Rehabilitation administration, which met in Atlantic City, N.J. in Nov. 1943, further recognition was given to the needs of these vulnerable groups for medical care and health and welfare services. (*See also* BIRTH STATISTICS; CENSUS, 1940; CRIME; FEDERAL BUREAU OF INVESTIGATION; INFANT MORTALITY; MARRIAGE AND DIVORCE; SOCIAL SECURITY.)

BIBLIOGRAPHY—*United States: Controlling Juvenile Delinquency; a Community Program*, Children's Bureau Publication 301, U.S. Department of Labor; "Juvenile Court Statistics, 1940–42," Supplement to *The Child* (Dec. 1943); *Emergency Maternity and Infant Care for Wives and Infants of Enlisted Men in the Armed Forces*, Children's Bureau Folder 29, U.S. Department of Labor (1943); *Which Jobs for Young Workers?* Nos. 1–8, Children's Bureau, U.S. Department of Labor; *Guides to Successful Employment of Non-Farm Youth in Wartime Agriculture*, Children's Bureau Publication 290, U.S. Department of Labor (1943); *Annual Report of the Secretary of Labor, Fiscal Year Ended June 30, 1943*, U.S. Department of Labor (1944); *Resumé of the Proceedings of the Tenth National Conference on Labor Legislation, Kansas City, Mo., December 8–9, 1943*, Division of Labor Standards Bulletin 65, U.S. Department of Labor; *Behind the Child Labor Headlines*, annual report of the National Child Labor Committee for the year ending Sept. 30, 1943 (1943). Periodicals: *Public Health Reports*, U.S. Public Health Service, Federal Security Agency; *Monthly Labor Review*, Bureau of Labor Statistics, U.S. Department of Labor; *The Child*, Children's Bureau, U.S. Department of Labor; *Social Security Bulletin*, Social Security Board, Federal Security Agency; *Monthly Vital Statistics Bulletin*, Bureau of the Census, U.S. Department of Commerce.

Latin America: Dr. Guillermo Morales Beltramí, *Programa de trabajo, 1943* (Santiago, Chile, Feb. 1, 1943); *Le Reforma Médica*, July 15, 1943 (Lima, Peru); *Boletín Indigenista*, March 1943 (Mexico); *Memoria de Labores, 1942–43*, Secretaría del trabajo y previsión social (Mexico); *Diario Oficial*, Dec. 29, 1942 (Rio de Janeiro, Brazil); *El Popular*, Sept. 2, 1943 (Mexico); *International Labour Review*, June, July 1943 (Montreal).

Great Britain and British Dominions: Summary Report of the Ministry of Health for the Year Ended 31st March, 1943 (London, 1943); *Juvenile Delinquency in Britain During the War*, British Information Services (New York), I. D. 390, revised July 1943; *Annual Report of the Chief Inspector of Factories for the Year 1942* (London, 1943); *The Youth Service After the War*, Board of Education (London, Aug. 1943), *Educational Reconstruction*, Board of Education (London, July 1943); *The Labour Gazette*, Sept. 1943 (Ottawa); *International Labour Review*, July 1943 (Montreal).

Continental Europe: The Health of Children in Occupied Europe, International Labour Office (Montreal, 1943); *Pediatria*, No. 1, 1943 (Moscow); *Social Tidskrift*, No. 78, 1943 (Helsinki); *Revista de Trabajo*, No. 38, Dec. 1942 (Madrid); Press releases on statements submitted to the Subcommittee on Health and Medical Care at the first session of the Council of the United Nations Relief and Rehabilitation Administration, Nov. 1943.

(K. F. L.)

Chile. A republic on the Pacific coast of South America, extending from approximately 17° S. lat. some 2,800 mi. to Cape Horn. Area: 289,776 sq.mi. Pop. (1940 census) 5,023,539; official estimate 1942 5,122,665; over three-fourths of the population live in Chile's great central valley. The capital is Santiago (1940 pop., 639,546, without inclusion of suburbs). Other important cities (1940 census) are: Valparaíso (215,614); Concepción (92,364); Temuco (84,696); Viña del Mar (70,013); Osorno (62,106); Chillán (61,535); Valdivia (49,481); Puerto Montt (44,024); Talcahuano (41,536); Iquique (39,282); Rancagua (38,423); Linares (36,403); Curicó (35,270); La Serena (35,055); Nueva Imperial (33,361); Magallanes (Punta Arenas) (33,134). There is no established church, although a majority of Chileans are Roman Catholics. The language is Spanish. President in 1943: Juan Antonio Ríos.

History.—The long-expected rupture of Chilean diplomatic relations with the axis powers finally occurred on Jan. 20. The breakdown of Chilean isolation had been slow, and had been controlled by President Ríos until he considered that the proper moment had arrived. At the time of the severing of relations, it was estimated that about 20,000 Germans, 12,000 Italians, and 700 Japanese were resident in Chile. Shortly afterward news that Chilean representatives in Japan were being imprisoned resulted in confinement of Japanese diplomats in Chile. As a result of earlier conferences and of the new status of Chile in inter-American co-operative efforts, a lend-lease pact was signed with the United States on March 2, and in June an important new copper contract was concluded between Chile and the United States Metal Reserves corporation. By the latter, an earlier purchasing agreement was extended through July, 1944, with the prices paid for Chilean copper substantially increased. The United States also agreed to purchase reasonable amounts of gold and manganese to help out Chilean economy, and to aid in shipment of machinery and coal needed in Chilean industry. Chile likewise was represented at the United Nations Food conference held in the United States in May.

In spite of her abandonment of isolation, Chile maintained favourable relationships with Argentina. In April a ten-year contract was signed between the two countries by which Argentina purchased substantial quantities of nitrates. Late in August trade agreements were signed by which tariffs between the two

APPROVAL OF PRESIDENT RIOS' rupture of diplomatic relations with the axis Jan. 20, 1943, was expressed by Chileans with placards, flags and a great public demonstration

countries were greatly reduced, and basic plans for a projected customs union started, with hopes that other nearby states might eventually participate. Plans for improvement of trans-Andean roads were also laid.

The year's record involved much factionalism in Chilean internal politics. In the early months of the year the Socialist party was badly split by a difference of opinion between Marmaduque Grove and Salvador Allende, with the breach not healed until April, when the former became president of the party organization, the latter vice-president. In June Chile's 22 parties found hurried realignments necessary with the official dissolution of the world Communist organization. The Chilean Communist party, the strongest outside of Russia and the fifth strongest group in Chile itself, now attempted the organization of a powerful leftist coalition of the Communist, Socialist, Agrarian, and Socialist-Labour parties. Political manoeuvring so delayed constructive legislation that President Ríos in June formed a cabinet made up of experts rather than political personalities, and conditions caused him to postpone again a projected visit to the United States. The "ministry of experts" was dissolved in August, the administration including two members from the conservative Liberal party in its next cabinet (six of the "technical" ministers were retained).

In October a special session of the legislature was called to consider financial matters; a deficit of above 500,000,000 pesos was in prospect by 1944. Strikes in Chilean industries and ports caused trouble in succeeding weeks, and on November 16 congress finally granted emergency powers to President Ríos in the hope that executive action could improve Chilean conditions.

Various economic problems plagued Chile during 1943. One was a coal shortage; while Chile produces more coal than other South American countries, shipping was not available to move it. Many trains were not able to operate during the Chilean winter because of lack of fuel. High prices affected the volume of retail business, and shortages of some essential items were noticeable. Chilean workers were restive over wage levels which rose more slowly than prices and over the repeal of legislation which had guaranteed the single-shift day. Because of fuel shortages and tire shortages for motor cars of all types, the use of bicycles increased during the year.

Education.—Primary education is free and compulsory. In 1940 primary schools numbered 3,678, with an enrolment of 495,267; there were also 161 night schools with an enrolment of 9,784. Public secondary schools numbered 86, and private, 168, with enrolments of 30,420 and 16,356, respectively. In addition there were many special schools, and three universities had a registration of 7,904 students.

Finance.—The monetary unit of Chile is the peso, with a free value of approximately 3¼ cents U.S. in 1943 (its official value was $.0516, and the export draft price, $.04). Government revenue for 1942 was 2,953,800,000 pesos; expenditures, 3,052,000,000. The 1943 budget calculated ordinary revenue at 3,185,700,000 pesos, ordinary expenditures at 3,185,600,000 pesos; actual revenue in the first half of the year was announced as 1,227,300,000 pesos, and expenditures for the same period were 1,385,400,000. By November a deficit of over 570,000,000 pesos was expected. On June 30, 1943, money in circulation totalled 2,668,600,000 pesos (Dec. 1942: approx. 2,200,000,000 pesos).

Trade and Communication.—Exports for the first seven months of 1943 totalled approximately 512,500,000 gold pesos in value; imports, approximately 322,000,000 gold pesos (total trade for 1942 was: exports, 862,800,000 gold pesos; imports, 621,600,000 gold pesos). Exports in 1942 went mainly to the United States (80.3%); Europe (mainly Great Britain) received about 3.5% of exports, and other Latin American countries, 16%.

Goods from the United States formed 45.5% of total imports; from Europe (Great Britain and Sweden), 8.6%; from Latin American countries, 42.5%. Minerals formed the bulk of exports (in 1941, 79.8%, some 15% of which were nitrates and iodine). Copper was the largest single item of export. In the first three quarters of 1943, Chile built up a favourable trade balance with the United States amounting to $82,469,000.

Before the war Chile had extensive steamship connection with all parts of the world, partly under the Chilean flag (the three modern motorships of this line were purchased by the United States in July, 1943, leaving the Chilean company only six vessels available). Rail lines connect northern Chile with Bolivia, and combined rail and bus service, with Argentina. Reconstruction of the railway line across Uspallata pass, closed to rail service in 1934, was contemplated in agreements between Chile and Argentina. Air service to all parts of the Americas is supplied by Pan American Airways.

Internal communication is by highway, rail, air and coastal shipping. The railway system is 5,434 mi. in length, with the state owning 3,637 mi. There are 27,000 mi. of highway (approximately 16,500 mi. of this, unimproved dirt road). In 1941 the budget for highway construction amounted to 143,888,639 pesos. Internal air service is good.

Manufacturing.—Manufacturing establishments in Chile in 1941 numbered over 5,500, with nearly 300,000 employees. Production is largely textiles, leather goods, wood products and other items for domestic consumption. Production in 1942 was announced as 1.3% under that of 1941; in 1943 shortages of tools and machinery were reported.

Agriculture.—Agricultural production is large in value, but comparatively little of it is for export. Crop estimates for the 1942–43 season (in short tons) were: beans, 84,453; wheat, 940,955; forage barley, 44,161; malting barley, 34,003; oats, 84,969; rye, 6,921; chickpeas or garbanzas, 4,244; hemp, 22,587. Rice production was estimated at 128,275 short tons. In 1941 dried fruit exports amounted to 9,702 short tons. Wine production (1941) was 63,828,404 gal. The 1942–43 potato crop was officially estimated at 526,874 short tons. Lumber production in 1942 was 1,652,466 ft. (1941: 2,283,181 ft.).

Minerals.—Minerals comprise the greater part of Chilean exports. Coal production in 1942 was 2,370,992 short tons (in 1941: 2,272,469 short tons); gold, 12,844 lb. (1941: 17,694 lb.). Nitrate production (for the year ending June 30, 1942) was 1,502,392 short tons. Exports of other minerals were (1941 figures): copper, 499,923 short tons; manganese, 23,589 short tons; iron ore, 1,787,591 short tons; silver, 84,573 lb. (*See also* HISPANIC AMERICA AND WORLD WAR II.)

BIBLIOGRAPHY.—Luis Galdames, *A History of Chile* (1942; transl. by I. J. Cox); A. C. Wilgus (ed.), *Argentina, Brazil and Chile Since Independence* (1934).   (D. Rᴅ.)

China. China, a republic of Asia. Area, 4,480,992 sq.mi.; excluding Manchuria, Outer Mongolia and Tibet proper, 2,903,475 sq.mi. (more than 10% constituted occupied China). Estimated total population 450,000,000, with over 200,000,000 in occupied China. Wartime capital, Chungking (pop. 880,000, police census 1943). Cities over 1,000,000: Shanghai, Peiping, and Tientsin; cities close to 1,000,000: Nanking and Canton; cities over 500,000: Changsha and Chengtu; cities over 200,000: Kunming, Sian, Kweiyang, Foochow and Tsingtao; cities over 100,000 in population total about 100. President (1943): Chiang Kai-shek.

History.—Although a military stalemate continued to prevail in China, 1943 witnessed notable strides in the development of constitutional democracy and closer co-operation and amity between China and her allies.

China's hope for a brighter future rose with the signing of the

UNITED NATIONS DAY—June 14, 1943—was celebrated in Chungking with a parade of 10,000 people on Democracy road

Sino-American and British new treaties on Jan. 11, 1943, and ratification on May 10 which abolished extraterritoriality and related privileges. To undermine the effect of the new treaties Japan took similar steps in occupied China. China's faith in U.S. friendship was further augmented by the repeal of the Chinese exclusion law which passed the U.S. house of representatives on Oct. 21 and the Senate on Nov. 26. The improvement of China's relations with soviet Russia and Great Britain was demonstrated by the withdrawal of Russian troops from Sinkiang and repeated friendly and enthusiastic messages to Moscow by Chiang and by the reciprocal visit of the Chinese government mission to London in November.

The recall of the Chinese military mission to Washington on Dec. 31, 1942, was regarded as an indication of China's disappointment in Allied strategy. The meagre aid to her under the Lend-Lease arrangement (out of a total of lend-lease aid of

$8,253,000,000 to American Allies from March 1941 to Dec. 1942 China received only $156,738,000) prompted Madame Chiang to emphasize the importance of the China front and the tenacity of the Japanese in her addresses to the U.S. congress on Feb. 18, 1943. President Roosevelt's statement on Jan. 7 that "all the formidable obstacles to get the battle equipment into China" would be overcome and his pledge on Feb. 19 of rushing arms to China gave assurance to China.

Although China was not invited to the Casablanca conference, the announcement on Jan. 27, 1943, regarding the Allied objective of nothing less than unconditional surrender by the axis was welcomed by Chungking. On Feb. 5–7 General Henry H. Arnold and Field Marshal Sir John Dill discussed military actions against Japan with Chiang in Chungking. On Feb. 12, President Roosevelt said that great and decisive action would be taken to "drive the invaders from the soil of China." At the Quebec conference, which T. V. Soong joined on Aug. 22, the chiefs of staff turned their attention "very largely upon the war against Japan and the bringing of effective aid to China." The creation of a

CHINESE CASUALTIES being borne to the rear from the Salween river front in 1943

Southeast Asia command under Lord Louis Mountbatten by the Quebec conference, his subsequent conference in Chungking with Chiang, and assurances by British officials that Britain "will continue full military co-operation with the United States and China until Japan is defeated" gratified China. The Joint Four-Nation declaration of Nov. 1 at Moscow recognized China's position as one of the big four United Nations and frustrated Japan's hope for a negotiated peace. The Cairo conference solidified the four-power entente and vindicated China's territorial integrity and the justness of her cause by promising the restoration of all territory stolen from China by Japan since 1895.

Japan's military actions in China in 1943 were accompanied by repeated peace offers, one of which promised a return to the *status quo* of July 7, 1937. In an effort to force China out of the war before the Allies could launch a major offensive in the Pacific, Japan opened an offensive in western Hupeh and Hunan on May 11, aiming at Chungking and Changsha, which ended in a disastrous defeat in June. Early in November Japan renewed her attempt for the fifth time to capture Changsha in order to control the "rice bowl" and the railroad line to Canton, and see-saw battles developed around Changteh. With the support of the U.S. air force the Chinese routed the Japanese at Changteh toward the end of November. Japan's three-pronged drive up the Burma road in October was equally unsuccessful.

Following the death of Lin Sen on Aug. 2, Chiang became acting president and on Sept. 10 the Central Executive committee revised the organic law of the national government making the president chief executive and commander-in-chief of the military forces with three years' tenure. On Sept. 13 the committee unanimously elected Chiang president. On the same day Chiang stated that the Chinese communist problem was "a purely political problem and should be solved by political means." The committee resolved on Sept. 12 that a democratic constitutional government would be created within one year after the end of the war.

The Committee for the Establishment of Constitutional Government of 60 members, including two communists, was inaugurated on Nov. 12 to facilitate the establishment of constitutionalism.

China's serious domestic problem in 1943 was inflation; commodity prices rose to more than 100 times the prewar level.

Education.—The universities and technical colleges increased from 108 in 1937 to 133 in 1943 and the total enrolment in 1943 was 57,832 against 31,188 in 1937. About half of the 1943 students majored in science and technology. Of the 133 colleges, 51 were private institutions and 82 operated by the national and provincial governments. In 1940 appropriations from the national treasury to higher education and cultural institutions amounted to 44,130,000 yuan, 19,000,000 of which went to higher education.

The number of secondary educational institutions in Free China totalled 2,819 in 1942 (with an enrolment of over 600,000), against 3,264 in 1937; one-third of these were in areas occupied by Japan. In 1942 there were 232,145 primary schools with an enrolment of over 22,242,844 in Free China; the total number of persons between 5 and 15 was about 75,000,000. According to the ministry of education, about 48,000,000 of the 165,000,000 illiterates between the ages of 15 to 45 had been taught to read by 1943.

Defense.—In 1943 the army was estimated at 20,000,000, of which about 5,000,000 were front line troops. After the creation of the U.S. 14th army air force as a separate unit in China in March, Chinese air force pilots flew alongside their U.S. comrades. There were more trained Chinese pilots than planes, and those who received advance training in the United States amounted to several hundred.

Finance.—The official exchange rate of the national dollar was maintained at U.S.$5 for Chinese 100. Although no official figures were issued, the volume of note issue in 1943 was estimated at over 25,000,000,000 yuan—about four times that of 1940. The budget for 1943 was reported to be 45 times that of 1937,

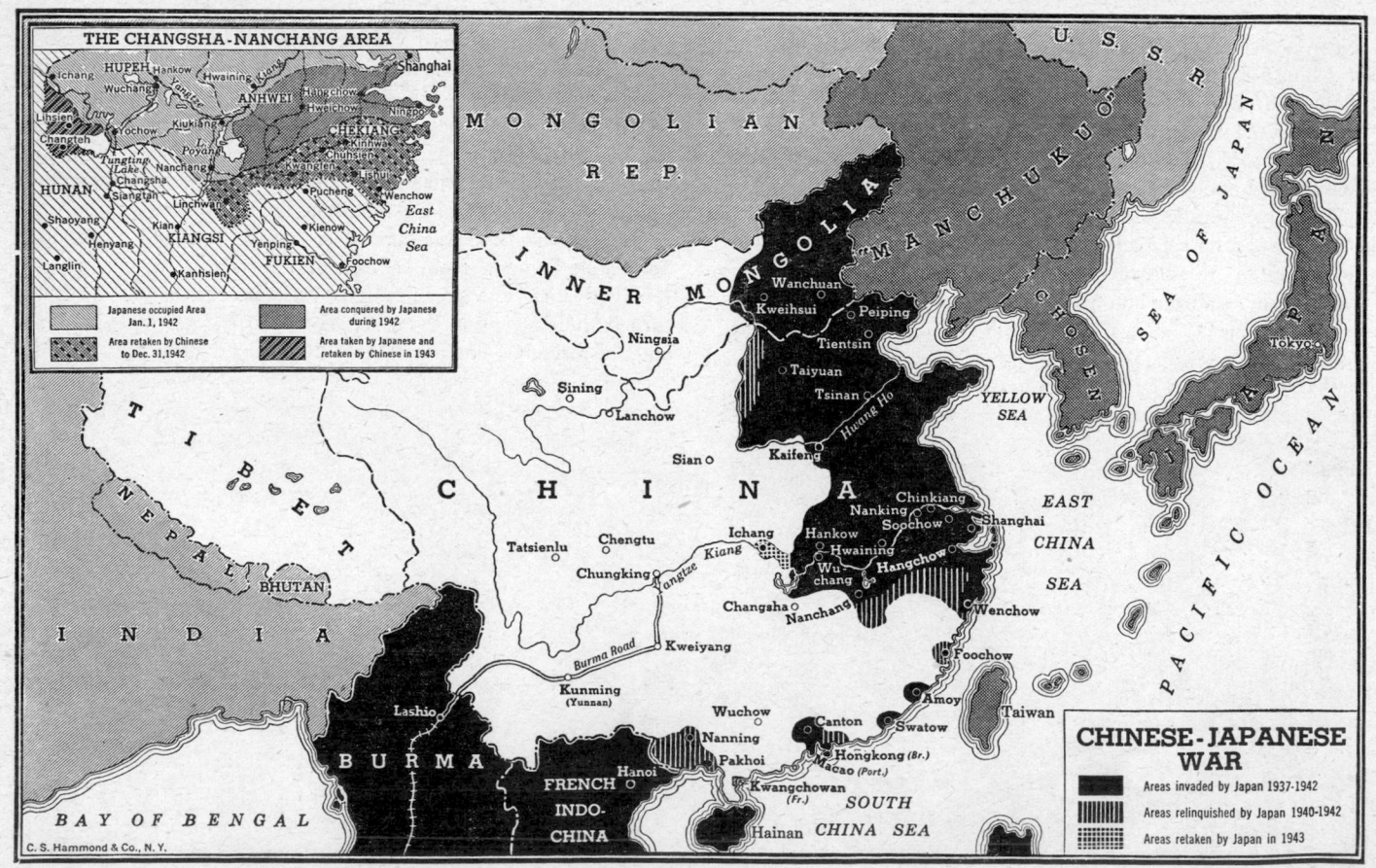

WELL-ENTRENCHED CHINESE MOUNTAIN TROOPS on the Salween river front. Here, near the Burmese border at China's "back door," the Chinese continued to stalemate Japanese attacks in 1943

which was slightly over 1,000,000,000 yuan. Before 1943 the total revenue constituted less than 30% of the total expenditures, but the financial authorities hoped to raise it to one-half in 1943. From 1937 to 1943 the total internal loans floated were 3,430,-000,000 yuan, 100,000,000 custom gold units, £20,000,000, and $300,000,000. The foreign loans extended to China from 1937 to Dec. 1942 amounted to $1,200,000,000, about half of which had not been used.

In July 1942 the right to use bank notes was centralized in the Central Bank of China. Government control over privately owned commercial banks was tightened; no new banks, except the county banks, were allowed to be formed. Besides the 300-odd modern and native banks, 175 county banks were established by May 1943.

Trade and Communication.—China's chief wartime exports were silk, bristle, coal, wood oil, tea and mineral products. Foodstuffs, principally rice, wheat and flour, were the chief imports. Due to the blockade China had to depend on the slender thread of air transport between India and Chungking as her international outlet.

Free China had 1,744 mi. of railroads, of which 1,000 were built during the war, and from Jan. to Aug. 1942 the railroads carried a total of about 17,000,000 passengers, 500,000 troops and 970,000 tons of freight. There were approximately 48,000 mi. of highway in Free China, and about 16,000 trucks aside from army trucks. A great part of all freight in Free China depended on stage and river transport. Free China had about 6,100 mi. of air routes with limited freight and passenger capacity. By the end of 1942 there were 41,175 mi. of telephone lines and 59,475 mi. of telegraph lines in Free China. Only 12 of the Free China cities had telephone service by the end of 1942. There were 10 large and 100 medium and small-sized broadcasting stations in Free China.

Agriculture.—Roughly 60% of the prewar agricultural and livestock production remained in Free China. The prewar aver-

age food harvest of the 15 interior provinces was about 1,670,-000,000 piculs on 635,000,000 mou of land, and the production and acreage showed slight change since 1937 (1 picul = 133⅓ lb.; 1 mou = 806.65 sq.yd.). In 1941 the total rice and wheat crops of Free China was 808,000,000 piculs. Livestock production had steadily declined since 1937. The collection of rice and wheat by tax payments in kind and by compulsory purchase proved successful, and the collection in 1942–43 was expected to increase from the 72,000,000 piculs of 1941–42 to 80,000,000, and the collection was more than enough to feed the army and public functionaries and their families.

Manufacturing and Mineral Production.—In 1942 the number of heavy industrial plants in Free China under the control of the national and provincial governments numbered about 100 each, while the privately owned factories totalled about 2,000, approximately 450 of which were concentrated in the Chungking area. In order of importance these private factories were: machinery, chemicals, textile and clothing, metallurgical, food, electrical equipment and printing. The production of important minerals in Free China in 1942 was approximately: coal, 6,000,000 tons; crude oil, including vegetable oils, 9,000,000 gal.; steel, 10,000 tons. In spite of the steady industrial progress the low volume of oil, iron and steel handicapped the program of making Free China self-sufficient even in the most essential industries. (*See also* WORLD WAR II.)

BIBLIOGRAPHY.—*China After Five Years of War,* Chinese News Service; *China Handbook 1937–1943,* Chinese Ministry of Information; G. B. Cressey, *China's Geographic Foundations;* H. D. Fong, *The Post-War Industrialization of China;* Hubert Freyn, *Free China's New Deal; Agrarian China,* Institute of Pacific Relations; Mme. Chiang Kai-shek, *China Shall Rise Again;* Paul Linebarger, *The China of Chiang Kai-shek;* Frank Price (ed.), *Wartime China as Seen by Westerners.* Periodicals: *Amerasia; Asia; Chinese Year Book; China at War; Contemporary China; Far Eastern Survey; Pacific Affairs; Voice of China.* (H. T. CH.)

Chinese-Japanese War: *see* WORLD WAR II.
Chinese Turkestan: *see* SINKIANG.

Chittenden, Russell Henry

(1856–1943), U.S. scientist and physiological chemist, was born Feb. 18 in New Haven, Conn. He was graduated from the Sheffield Scientific school (Yale university), 1875, with a Ph.B. degree and received his Ph.D. in 1880. Dr. Chittenden was an assistant instructor at Sheffield, 1875–77, professor of physiological chemistry, 1882–1922, and thereafter professor emeritus of that department. He was director of the Sheffield Scientific school, 1898–1922. An authority on nutrition, he was credited with the discovery of glycocoll and glycogen in the free amino acid of living tissue later known as protein. Among his works are *Studies in Physiological Chemistry,* four volumes (1884), *Physiological Economy in Nutrition* (1905), *Nutrition of Man* (1907) and *Development of Physiological Chemistry in the United States* (1930). He died in New Haven, Conn., Dec. 26.

Chosen

(KOREA). A part of the Japanese empire since 1910, Chosen is a peninsula extending southward from the northeastern side of the continent of Asia. It is bounded E. by the Sea of Japan, W. by the Yellow sea and N. by Manchuria and the maritime province of Siberia. Area, 85,206 sq.mi., including 1,018 adjacent islands; pop. (Oct. 1, 1940) 24,326,327. The population as of December 31, 1938, was 22,633,751, including 633,320 Japanese and 49,815 other foreigners. The capital is Seoul (Keijo), pop. (1938) 737,214. Other cities: Fusan (213,744); Phyong-yang (Heijo) (234,726); Taikyû (172,040). Buddhism, Confucianism and Taoism are prevalent forms of religion. There were 494,500 Chosenese and 5,800 Japanese Christians in Chosen in 1938. Chosen is ruled by a Japanese governor-general, appointed by the ministry of overseas affairs. The governor-general in 1943 was General Jiro Minami, appointed to this office in 1936.

History.—Chosen was not a theatre of hostilities during 1943 and little authentic news came out of the country. It was one of the decisions of the Cairo conference of President Roosevelt, Prime Minister Churchill and Generalissimo Chiang Kai-shek that Chosen should be freed from Japanese rule after the war and receive full independence "in due course." A leading representative of the Korean nationalists in the United States in 1943 was Dr. Syngman Rhee, who was chosen president of a Korean provisional government, formed in the French concession of Shanghai in 1919. In 1936 a working agreement had been reached between the middle class nationalist and communist groups working against Japanese rule.

Education.—Chosen in 1938 possessed 3,372 elementary schools, with 1,311,270 pupils. There were also 53 high schools, with 27,867 students, 57 girls' high schools, with 22,277 students, 226 technical schools, with 34,060 students, 10 normal schools, with 5,565 students, 18 special colleges (for medicine, dentistry, etc.) with 4,015 students. There was only one university, at Seoul, with 558 students, many of these Japanese. But there were 9,086 Korean students in Japan.

Finance.—The unit of currency is the Japanese yen (23.48 U.S. cents before outbreak of war in the Pacific). The Chosenese budget for 1942–43 was balanced at a figure of 1,012,577,000 yen. The national debt, as of 1941, was 593,646,215 yen and the amount of currency in circulation was 437,669,000 yen.

Trade and Communication.—Chosen's imports in 1939 were 1,388,448,284 yen, exports were 1,006,793,785 yen. For nine months of 1940 (after which period figures were no longer published) imports were 1,176,120,813 yen, exports 700,848,030 yen. There were 17,011 mi. of roads in 1939 and 2,619 mi. of government and 1,107 mi. of privately owned railways in 1940. There were 738 steamships of a total of 106,712 tons and 1,125 sailing ships of a total of 45,431 tons in Chosen in Dec. 1939. The length of telegraph and telephone lines in 1941 was respectively 5,406 mi. and 6,780 mi.

Agriculture, Manufacturing, Mineral Production.—Chosen is predominantly agricultural, with rice as its main crop. The rice crop was 106,775,869 bu. in 1940. There were 1,705,000 cattle, 1,400,000 pigs, 51,000 horses and 20,000 sheep in Chosen in 1939. Other important crops are barley, millet, apples, rye and soybeans.

The growth of industries important for war purposes is reflected in the following figures of value of output:

	1933	1938
Chemical products	51,992,000 yen	352,819,000 yen
Metals	29,238,000	91,966,000
Machine tools	3,010,000	26,798,000

The list of industries developed in Chosen includes cotton and rayon, cement, paper and pottery. Gold, iron, coal, wolfram and mica are important mineral resources.   (W. H. Ch.)

Christian X (1870–   ), king of Denmark, of whom a biographical account will be found in *Encyclopædia Britannica*. Nephew of Queen Alexandra of Great Britain, he succeeded his father, Frederick VIII, in 1912. Despite a serious fall from his horse in Oct. 1942, and ensuing pneumonia, the king remained the symbol and heart of Danish passive resistance to the nazis. When in Aug. 1943, opposition became open rebellion the Germans imprisoned Christian at Sorgenfri castle (Aug. 29). Even when nazi guards were removed, mail and telephone messages were still controlled, and the king, recognizing that he could not be a free agent, pledged himself to sign no call for a new government as long as the Germans remained in Denmark. His 73rd birthday, Sept. 26, was the occasion for

tens of thousands of greetings from a people who loved and admired him for his unyielding courage. On his way to Sorgenfri under "arrest" he had the opportunity to hear a group of Danes discussing earnestly among themselves, and said to them, "I am glad to hear that Danish is still spoken in my country. Keep it up." (*See* also DENMARK.)   (F. D. S.)

Christian Mission on World Order. A Christian Mission on World Order was opened on Oct. 28, 1943, at the Cathedral of St. John the Divine in New York city. It was followed by a series of meetings conducted by "teams" of ministers and laymen in 100 of the principal cities of the United States. Morning and afternoon study group meetings were held for over 20,000 persons. In the evening large massmeetings were held. The mission was initiated by the commission on a just and durable peace of the Federal Council of the Churches of Christ in America, and was sponsored by the Federal Council and by the Foreign Missions Conference of North America, the Home Missions Council of North America, the International Council of Religious Education, the Missionary Education Movement and the United Council of Church Women. All the activities were on an interdenominational basis.

The purpose of the mission was to seek to revive in the American people a sense of destiny in the performance of a great work of creation. That work of creation was portrayed as building a world fellowship, political expression of which would be as set out in the commission's statement "Six Pillars of Peace." Those were: (1) general collaboration between all nations; (2) particular collaboration on economic and financial matters of worldwide import; (3) international machinery to promote peaceful change as future conditions make necessary; (4) international organization to assure that the government of subject peoples is directed toward ultimate autonomy; (5) control of armaments; (6) an international bill of rights to assure intellectual and religious liberty.   (J. F. D.)

Christian Science. In 1943, the Christian Science Mother Church, The First Church of Christ, Scientist, in Boston, Massachusetts, through its Camp Welfare Activities supervised the work of 143 paid Christian Science Wartime Ministers and over 300 volunteer Christian Science Wartime Workers, who ministered to the spiritual needs of Christian Scientists and others in the armed forces in the United States and its territories, Canada, Great Britain and Northern Ireland, Australia, New Zealand and the Middle East.

These civilian workers serve with the approval and assistance of army and navy chaplains and commanding officers. They respond to calls for Christian Science help or healing, conduct Christian Science services, and provide Christian Science literature.

In 1943, there were 17 Christian Science chaplains in the United States Army and one in the United States Navy. Nine served in combat areas, and one was decorated by the French military authorities for unusual bravery during action in the Tunisian campaign.

During 1943, the Christian Science War Relief Committee, maintained by The Mother Church, shipped to England for free donation 256,887 pounds of clothing, valued at $256,887. Shipments of clothing to Russia for free distribution there amounted to 209,894 pounds, valued at $209,894. Donations of clothing were made to refugees of many nationalities in the United States, Canada, England and Russia, and to the Greeks in Egypt. In the fall, a shipment was sent to Malta.

The War Relief Committee distributed 173,963 knitted garments to men in the United States armed forces. The value of the yarn used in knitting these gifts was $153,856.

The healing and redemptive activities of the Church always have the primary place in Christian Science. *The Christian Science Journal,* official organ of the Church, contains a directory of branch churches, societies and authorized practitioners. Reading Rooms open to the public for study and meditation are also listed.

In September 1943, the Mutual Broadcasting System and the world-wide staff of *The Christian Science Monitor* joined facilities in a new type of integrated news programs with daily pick-ups from *Monitor* correspondents all over the world.

During 1943, *The Christian Science Monitor* received the F. Wayland Ayer Cup for excellence of typography, makeup and presswork, and a medal and citation awarded by the University of Missouri School of Journalism for fulfilment of the assignment given to it by Mary Baker Eddy "to injure no man, but to bless all mankind." (C. P. S.)

Christian Unity.

While the war prevented world gatherings of churches planned for 1943, the work of the World Council of Churches in formation went steadily forward. Regional meetings of its administrative committee were held; its secretaries officially visited nine countries, and frequent intercontinental visitation of leaders in behalf of the oecumenical movement took place between Europe, Australia, Asia and America. Seven additional churches joined the World Council during the year: Hungarian Lutheran, Presbyterian Church of Ireland, the Assyrian Church, the Anglican Church of New Zealand, the Cumberland Presbyterian Church of the United States and the Canadian Friends Yearly Meeting, also the General Convention of New Jerusalem.

Recently returned missionaries from North China reported that close federation of churches in that region developed quite apart from Japanese political pressure. An influential gathering in Chengtu of leaders representing thirteen denominations still operating in Free China, endorsed the idea of a united church for the postwar nation. On the other hand, the hope of final action approving the South India Scheme of Union was delayed by the unreadiness of certain elements in the existing United Church.

In Hungary the Reformed and Lutheran churches established an oecumenical council with view to collaboration with the World council. In England the committee on co-operation between the Free Churches issued an interim report which failed to recommend any specific action.

Baptists in Canada, divided into three regional groups, appointed committees to explore the possibility of union through a triennial general assembly. Arrangements for a Canadian Council of Churches went forward during the year.

Sharp division of opinion in the Commission on Approaches to Unity of the Protestant Episcopal Church caused the preparation of majority and minority reports with respect to relations with the Presbyterian Church in the United States of America. The minority report would have reconstituted the commission and virtually stopped active negotiations for organic union with the Presbyterians. Rather than face the possibility of an acrimonious discussion in the General convention, both parties finally agreed on a compromise resolution which was adopted, continuing the commission, with some change in personnel, under its present authorization to negotiate for organic union, but with agreement to refer the issue to the Lambeth Conference of Anglican Bishops before final consideration. No further action on this issue was taken by the Presbyterian Church in the United States of America during the year.

The committees negotiating the union of the Northern and Southern Presbyterian churches of the United States presented to their respective bodies for consideration and discussion a proposed constitution and directory of worship, but asked no immediate action upon them.

A committee representing the Northern Baptist convention and the Disciples of Christ met in Chicago in December to canvass the possibilities of closer relationships between these two denominations. Several points of possible co-operation were formulated which were later expected to be worked into the plan for submission to the two Churches. Their actual uniting was not, in 1943, under discussion.

Active discussion of full organic union, on terms formulated in 1943, continued in the Congregational Christian and Evangelical and Reformed Churches, paralleled by meetings for closer acquaintance and co-operative action in numerous centres. The proposed basis of union, revised in the light of these discussions, was to be put before the national bodies of the respective churches in 1944.

The biennial convention of the United Lutheran brotherhood, representing six synods, adopted resolutions calling for a nationwide study by laymen of the problems in Lutheran unity and urging leaders to intensify their efforts in this behalf. The monthly organ of the American Lutheran conference conducted a vigorous crusade for such unity in an elaborate series of editorials throughout the year.

The Federated Orthodox Greek Catholic Primary Jurisdictions in America was formally organized in December by the adoption of a constitution. This federation included the following Orthodox churches: Russian (one division), Serbian, Ukrainian, Carpatho-Russian, Rumanian and Syrian. It was constituted by action of their administrative authorities rather than by the canonical action of the church bodies themselves, but expected to create a united Orthodox front in America which might lead to many forms of co-operation.

It planned to develop a union school of theological education to be conducted in English, and applied for membership in the Federal Council of Churches. (H. P. D.)

Chromite.

World production and distribution of chromite was disorganized by the war in about every way possible. The United States is not normally a producer, but consumes half or more of the world output; because most of the sources of supply were in remote parts of the world shipping difficulties, shortage of bottoms and submarine losses seriously affected the supply from Africa, India and New Caledonia. Then approximately one-quarter of the potential output was lost by the occupation of Greece and Yugoslavia by Germany and of the Philippine Islands by Japan. The closing of the Mediterranean bottled up the Russian supply, and made it necessary to ship Indian and Turkish ore around the southern point of Africa. Besides, Turkey was not at war with Germany, and enormous diplomatic and economic pressure was put on the country to force it to ship chromite to Germany but without much success. Cuba was the only material producer from which supplies could be obtained without serious complications, but even in spite of these handicaps the United States supply was kept to a reasonably satisfactory level, from imports and from emergency domestic production, and by late in 1943 reserve stocks had been built up to a point where the production from marginal domestic mines was ordered discontinued. Production was developed in four areas in Canada, but output was far short of requirements. (G. A. Ro.)

Chronology: *see* CALENDAR OF EVENTS, 1943, PAGES 1–15.

Church, Samuel Harden

(1858–1943), U.S. industrialist, was born Jan. 24 in Hamilton, Caldwell Co., Mo. Compelled to give up school to help support his family, he found work as messenger boy with the Pennsylvania railroad, rose to superintendent of transportation of a branch office in Ohio and eventually became vice president of the railroad. Meanwhile, he continued his education and received degrees from Western university of Pennsylvania, Bethany college, W. Va., and Yale. He was made trustee of Carnegie institute when it was founded early in the 1900s, was its secretary until 1914 and was then named president—a post he held until his death. During both world wars he denounced Germany's wartime leaders and urged collective action against them. In 1914, shortly after the outbreak of war, he charged Germany with the "murder of civilization." Again, in 1940, he made international headlines with the announcement that he had been authorized to offer a $1,000,000 reward for the capture of Adolf Hitler, alive and unhurt, and his delivery to the League of Nations for trial. Church died in Pittsburgh, Oct. 11.

Churchill, Winston Leonard Spencer

(1874–   ), British statesman, was born at Blenheim palace, Oxfordshire, England, on Nov. 30, the elder son of Lord Randolph Churchill and Jennie, daughter of Leonard Jerome of New York city. For his biography and his political career during World War I, see *Encyclopædia Britannica*.

The outbreak of war on Sept. 3, 1939, was the occasion for Churchill's re-entry into the cabinet in his old office of first lord of the admiralty. On May 10, 1940, when the German drive on France began, Chamberlain resigned and Churchill became prime minister. Churchill emerged as a fighting leader and on June 4, 1940, after the evacuation of Dunkirk, he promised that Britain would fight on alone "whatever the cost may be."

The year 1943 was one of personal triumph for the British prime minister. Under his guidance England had been converted into a powerful military and air base. His arch-foe Hitler had been driven out of Africa and Sicily and was losing ground in Italy. Mussolini vanished as a political figure of importance, and at the end of the year Allied armies were preparing an invasion of western Europe from English bases. The planning and preparation that led to these successes were laid down, for the most part, in the six major conferences which Churchill attended in 1943. They were: (1) the Casablanca conference, Jan. 15–24, at which he and President Roosevelt agreed to demand unconditional surrender of the axis; (2) the Washington conferences, which started May 11, at which Churchill and Roosevelt decided on the strategy for the invasion of Sicily and Italy; (3) the Quebec parleys in August with Roosevelt, during which Churchill extended an invitation to Stalin to join a tripartite conference but bluntly declared that the Allies would not open a second front until it was militarily feasible; (4) the Cairo conference, Nov. 22–26, with Chiang Kai-shek and Roosevelt, in which agreement was reached to crush Japan; (5) the Tehran conference, Nov. 28–Dec. 1, with Stalin and Roosevelt, at which the conferees concerted plans for destruction of German military power and opening of second front; and (6) the second Cairo conference, Dec. 4–6, with Roosevelt and Turkish Premier Inönü, in which the "closest unity" of Turkish and Allied views was expressed.

With regard to postwar foreign policy, Churchill urged in an address at Harvard university on Sept. 6, 1943, intimate U.S.-British postwar co-operation, declaring no world peace system would be practicable without this unity. On plans for domestic reconstruction after the war, Churchill scolded critics for devoting too much discussion to postwar plans while the war was not yet

WINSTON CHURCHILL leaving Memorial hall, Harvard university, after receiving an honorary doctorate of laws Sept. 6, 1943

won. Churchill's speeches in 1943 sparkled with their customary literary power and vividness. Like a biblical prophet, he told commons on Feb. 12 that the Allies were resolved "to burn and bleed" Germany. On June 30 he made the famous prophecy of heavy fighting in Europe "before the leaves of autumn fall." On July 27, he warned Italy to surrender or be "seared and scarred and blackened." On May 19, addressing a joint session of the U.S. congress, he vowed that Britain would fight side by side with the U.S. against Japan "while there is breath in our bodies and while blood flows through our veins." In Dec. 1943, his health was taxed by his exertions, and he was taken seriously ill with pneumonia in the Middle East. By the end of 1943, however, he was well on the way to recovery.

Church Membership.

The following figures are from the 1943 edition of the *Yearbook of American Churches*, compiled under the auspices of the Federal Council of the Churches of Christ in America, summarizing the reports made by 256 religious bodies for the continental United States. The "inclusive membership" column gives the official records of the church bodies. The "13 years or over" column is given for use in comparisons and discussions of the relative numerical standing of the churches reported.

The total reported church membership in 1942 was 68,501,186. This was 51.1% of the total population of the continental United States, 133,953,225 persons, as estimated by the federal bureau of the census for Jan. 1, 1942. It was the highest proportion of church membership in the total population ever reported—a fact due partly to increase in church membership and partly to the incompleteness of former reports. Between 1926 and 1942, the reported church membership increased 25.5%, while the estimated population of the continental United States increased 14.3%.

Fifty-two religious bodies had 50,000 or more members each, and 97.2% of the church members of the nation belonged to these bodies. The remaining 2.8% were in 204 smaller bodies. Of the total reported church membership, 33.4% was Roman Catholic, 1.8% Old Catholic and Eastern Orthodox, 6.8% Jewish, and 58% Protestant.

Church Membership in the United States in 1942*

Body	Churches	Inclusive Membership	13 Years or Over
Adventists, Seventh Day	2,491	186,478	169,135
Assemblies of God	4,840	222,730	222,730
Baptist Bodies:			
American Baptist Association	1,064	115,022	93,955
Free Will Baptist	1,102	118,871	117,130
National Baptist Convention	24,575	3,911,612	3,619,451
National Baptist Ev. Assembly	176	55,897	49,749
Northern Baptist	7,365	1,538,871	1,461,027
Primitive Baptist	1,726	69,157	68,881
Southern Baptist	25,737	5,367,129	5,098,772
United American Free Will Baptist	1,712	60,000	52,694
Brethren (Dunkers)	1,019	179,843	175,416
Church of Christ, Scientist	2,113	268,915	268,915
Church of God (Anderson, Ind.)	1,412	83,875	71,293
Church of God (Cleveland, Tenn.)	1,686	82,462	72,154
Church of Jesus Christ of Latter Day Saints	1,598	816,774	668,667
Church of Jesus Christ of Latter Day Saints (Reorganized)	563	110,481	99,432
Church of the Nazarene	2,898	180,243	180,243
Churches of Christ	3,815	309,551	309,551
Congregational Christian	5,827	1,052,701	1,052,701
Disciples of Christ	7,919	1,655,580	1,489,995
Evangelical	1,983	248,475	238,379
Evangelical and Reformed	2,850	662,953	596,658
Four-square Gospel	408	250,000	250,000
Friends (Five Years Meeting)	508	69,832	58,258
Independent Fundamental	435	50,000	50,000
Lutheran Bodies:			
American Lutheran	1,826	547,812	388,072
Augustana Lutheran	1,126	352,571	267,172
Missouri Lutheran	4,326	1,320,510	930,791
Norwegian Lutheran	2,477	569,112	399,732
United Lutheran	4,046	1,709,290	1,223,222
Wisconsin Lutheran	745	315,560	188,447
Mennonite	445	51,879	50,000
Methodist Bodies:			
African M.E.	7,265	868,735	667,035
African M.E. Zion	2,252	414,244	332,376
Colored M.E.	4,200	380,000	320,000
Methodist	42,206	7,813,891	7,266,918
Presbyterian Bodies:			
Cumberland Presbyterian	1,088	72,591	50,811
Presbyterian, U.S. (South)	3,500	546,479	508,225
Presbyterian, U.S.A.	8,511	1,986,257	1,906,807
United Presbyterian	850	190,724	171,652
Protestant Episcopal	7,685	2,074,178	1,467,599
Reformed Bodies:			
Christian Reformed	306	126,293	69,980
Reformed Church in America	727	163,835	163,835
Salvation Army	1,515	220,307	96,961
Unitarian	365	61,600	61,600
United Brethren in Christ	2,788	425,337	382,804
Totals	204,071	37,878,717	33,449,228
Eastern Orthodox (11 bodies)	777	1,158,635	867,712
Jewish Congregations	3,728	4,641,184	3,341,652
Old Catholic (5 bodies)	256	80,586	65,436
Polish National Catholic	118	63,366	47,921
Roman Catholic	18,976	22,945,247	16,858,210
191 Smaller Religious Bodies	21,911	1,733,451	1,550,122
Totals	249,837	68,501,186	56,180,281

*Continental United States only.

(L. A. We.)

Church of England.

The year 1943 was an encouraging one in ecclesiastical history. The growth of the armed forces called for the release of more and more clergy from the already understaffed parishes to make good the shortage of navy, army and air force chaplains. In the religious life of the forces outstanding success attended the institution in many units of a kind of one-man religious "brains trust" known generally as "The Padre's Hour." Success also attended the work of the specially selected women who were assisting the chaplains in work among the women members of the forces.

In the more domestic life of the church four matters were outstanding: (1) The long and complicated education question reached a new stage with the publication of the government scheme. Speaking in the house of lords on Aug. 4 the archbishop of Canterbury (Dr. W. Temple) was able to give, with some qualifications, a cordial welcome to the first outline of this scheme and expressed the hope that the proposals would "secure and strengthen the religious foundation of education in all its stages."

(2) The cause of Christian reunion was furthered by a joint statement of Christian belief issued by the archbishop of Canterbury and the moderator of the Free Church Federal council on Jan. 4, and by a series of speeches and addresses by the archbishop of Canterbury. These included a memorable address to the joint synod of the convocation of Canterbury on May 25, in which he said that the divisions of Christians blunted the appeal to the general public at home or to the adherents of other religions abroad, and that "the obligation to attain to a real and organic unity of the church as the Holy Spirit may guide us, is urgent." In this connection the rather controversial problem of the scheme for church union in South India was the subject of prolonged discussion during the year.

(3) Interest in the problems of evangelism, including the presentation of the Gospel in terms of modern thought and the use of modern methods such as religious "brains trusts," broadcast and cinema services, etc., was stimulated by a debate in the summer session of the church assembly.

(4) Plans were also discussed for postwar reconstruction with a view to the more effective use of the available clerical manpower through the grouping of parishes and the adaptation of the parochial system to the situation created by enemy destruction of so many churches and the new needs of a population much shifted by war time movements of industry. Such plans should be facilitated by the Reorganization Areas measure introduced in the church assembly by the bishop of London. The better payment of the clergy should be facilitated by a new scheme ("Scheme K") issued by the ecclesiastical commissioners.

In the wider field of the Anglican communion the more notable events included the progress of the consideration of the South India scheme mentioned above; the appointment of the Ven. W. H. Stewart, archdeacon in Palestine, Syria and Trans-Jordan, to be bishop in Jerusalem; and last but not least, the flight of the archbishop of York to Moscow in September to convey a message of greeting to the patriarch of the Russian Orthodox Church from the archbishops of Canterbury and York in furtherance of "the friendly relationships" (in the words of the archbishop of Canterbury) "between the Church of England and the Orthodox Churches, including the Church of Russia."

(Ro. Sto.)

Church Reunion: see CHRISTIAN UNITY; RELIGION.
Cigars and Cigarettes: see TOBACCO.
Cinema Industry: see MOTION PICTURES.
C.I.O.: see CONGRESS OF INDUSTRIAL ORGANIZATIONS.

Citrine, Sir Walter McLennan

(1887–), British labour leader, was born in Liverpool Aug. 22, 1887, of working-class parents. After attending elementary schools, he found work as an electrician in Lancashire. He soon became active in the electricians' union and in 1914 became Mersey district secretary of the Electrical Trades union. In 1924 he was appointed assistant secretary to the Trades Union congress and acting secretary in Oct. 1925, after which he became the effective head of the British trade union organization. As such he has pursued a policy defined by himself as one of "opposing equally all dictatorships whether of the Right or of the Left." Citrine accepted a knighthood in 1935 and was made a member of the privy council in 1939. He was elected president of the International Federation of Trade Unions in 1928, and was a member of the government economic advisory council (1930–33) and of the B.B.C. general advisory committee. After the outbreak of World War II Citrine travelled widely as spokesman and delegate of the T.U.C., visiting France in 1939, Finland in 1940, the U.S.S.R. in Oct. 1941 and the U.S.A. in the winter of 1940–41. His diaries of the last three journeys are among his many publications.   (H. W. At.)

Citrus Fruits: *see* GRAPEFRUIT; LEMONS AND LIMES; ORANGES.
City Government: *see* MUNICIPAL GOVERNMENT.
Civil Aeronautics Administration: *see* AIRPORTS AND FLYING FIELDS.
Civil Air Patrol: *see* CIVILIAN DEFENSE.

Civilian Defense.

United States.—The United States Office of Civilian Defense was established May 20, 1941, to assure effective co-ordination of federal relations with state and local governments engaged in the furtherance of the various war programs; to provide for necessary co-operation with state and local governments with respect to measures for adequate protection of the civilian population in emergency periods; and to facilitate constructive civilian participation in the war program on the home front.

To carry out its functions, the Office of Civilian Defense has two principal divisions: the protection branch (which operates throughout the nation as the U.S. Citizens Defense corps), and the civilian war services branch (whose volunteers are members of the U.S. Citizens Service corps).

The operating unit in the local community was the defense council. In 1943, there were established throughout the U.S. 11,486 defense councils. On April 30, 1943, there were 5,510,000 men and women enrolled for training and service with the Citizens Defense corps. Trained to meet the hazards of enemy action, they utilized their training in innumerable natural disasters. They helped combat floods, fires, tornadoes, train wrecks and mine explosions. On Feb. 28, 1943, there were 3,371,000 men and women in the Citizens Service corps who worked in the fields of agriculture, consumer education, family and children's services, health, housing, manpower, nutrition, salvage, social protection, transportation, recreation and war savings.

Citizens Service Corps.—The civilian war services branch had the responsibility of assisting state and local governments in organizing defense councils to serve as the focal point for co-ordination of community resources in meeting local problems arising from the war.

Defense councils, with their committees and block organizations, engaged in many other programs: car sharing, vacant room surveys in war industry towns, explanation of point rationing, surveys of day-care needs for children of working mothers, securing donations for the blood plasma bank, victory gardens, scrap collection, tin can processing and collection, manpower and womanpower surveys for war industries, share-the-meat campaigns, the promotion of part-time and full-time aid for farmers, etc. These programs were carried out through the United States Citizens Service corps.

Co-operating with the U.S. department of agriculture, defense council committees during 1943 engaged in an over-all campaign to promote the production, sharing and scientific use of food. Defense councils helped mobilize townspeople for work on farms and in the planting of 20,000,000 victory gardens. Consumer committees co-operated in OPA's market basket and home-front pledge campaigns to combat the black market. Clothing clinics, "swap shops," courses in the care and repair of household equipment were sponsored. War price and rationing boards were aided by the efforts of consumer and other committees in the campaigns to increase community understanding and participation in the price control and rationing programs.

The children of an America at war required especial care and understanding. Over 1,000 child care committees were organized by defense councils to study the needs and to promote community programs for the children of mothers working in aviation, munition and other war plants. In 500 communities, federal funds amounting to more than $12,000,000 had been provided under the Lanham act to enable war impact areas to open nurseries and pre-school centres. Thousands of civilian defense volunteers worked in the nurseries, at recreation centres, playgrounds, schools, etc., and the scope of their activities was widened to include juvenile delinquency, child labour and other hazards affecting children in wartime.

The health of the home front was also a weapon in total war. In several states, civilian war services volunteers compiled complete rosters of all available nursing personnel and established these rosters on a county basis; registered nurses were placed in charge of all records and had the authority to call out nurses for special service in emergencies such as fires or train wrecks. Defense council health committees took part in the campaign to recruit men volunteers for work in hospitals to relieve the acute shortages of maintenance men and orderlies; this campaign was sponsored in co-operation with the American Hospital association.

Numerous important salvage campaigns were staged in 1943. In most communities, the salvage committees established by the War Production board were incorporated into the defense council structure. Scrap metals, fats, greases, silk and nylon hose, tin cans were combed out of the backyards, kitchens and homes of the United States and transformed into war goods. The conservation of private automobiles, tires and gasoline became the concern of civilian war services transportation committees working with the Office of Price Administration, Office of Defense Transportation and other agencies sponsoring car-sharing and conservation.

One of the most significant developments of 1943 was the establishment of the Junior Citizens Service corps by the national OCD. The JCSC officially recognized the war services of boys and girls under 16 and provided local defense councils with a mechanism for planning war service projects for organized and unaffiliated youth. In order to provide guidance to the JCSC, many states set up committees whose personnel represented youth interests on a state-wide basis. Typical war services being performed by the JCSC included: collection of scrap metals, fats, clothing, books for soldiers; assistance at child care centres, hospitals, war and rationing boards, recreation centres; participation in national war bond and stamp drives; the raising and conservation of food.

Citizens Defense Corps.—The protection branch developed comprehensive programs for training and organizing volunteers to safeguard the civilian population by such means as blackouts and other defense against air raids, camouflage and protective construction, defense from bombs and gases, decontamination of gassed areas, rescue of endangered persons and civilian casualties, evacuation and demolition of damaged structures and clearance of necessary thoroughfares, repair of disrupted utilities, auxiliary fire and police services, and many other "passive" defense measures. These programs were carried out through the United States Citizens Defense corps.

In each local community, the Citizens Defense corps was headed by a commander assisted by a staff. The operating units included: air raid wardens, fire guards, auxiliary firemen, auxiliary police, emergency medical services, rescue squads, emergency welfare services, messengers, control centre personnel, demolition and clearance, road repair, utility repair, etc.

During 1943, OCD's defense corps gave emergency service in floods, fires, war plant disasters, aviation accidents, etc. No region in the country escaped the shock of such emergencies. Floods in the midwest, fires in eastern factories and in western forests, explosions in southern mines were all tackled by volunteers trained to meet destructive forces. Many lives were saved and property damage was held to a minimum.

The well-organized and well-trained forces in the emergency medical services repeatedly gave aid in saving lives and in treating emergency casualties. These services included the administration of strategically based stocks of blood plasma, the functioning of mobile medical teams, the hospitalization and care of serious casualties and the use of life-saving procedures on the emergency scene. The medical division in co-operation with the U.S. public health service stored and distributed 158,290 units of plasma, liquid, dried and frozen in all important communities throughout the United States. Grants were made to 168 hospitals to enable them to establish plasma banks. In 20 coastal states, 321 institutions were designated as emergency base hospitals. Groups of physicians in more than 100 medical schools and hospitals responded to the invitation of OCD and the surgeon general of the U.S. public health service to form hospital units containing 15 doctors to the unit.

The war emergency radio service, a system of two-way communication for civilian defense inaugurated after specific authorization by the Federal Communications commission, was also used during 1943 in disasters, notably in the April and May floods in the middle west. Portable radios were used to route trucks, men, sand and equipment against the flood waters.

Communication via radio was paralleled with communication in the air. The Civil Air Patrol, organized a week before Pearl Harbor on the initiative of U.S. private flyers became an important unit of the protection branch. After organization and training by OCD, the CAP performed valuable services such as forest fire patrol, transporting blood plasma, reporting planes crashed on sea or land, etc. On April 29, 1943, the CAP was placed under the jurisdiction of the war department.

The former fire watchers service of the Citizens Defense corps was expanded and equipped to form the new and more effective fire guards. The national OCD also completed in 1943 the job of producing and delivering fire fighting equipment, including 7,000,000 ft. of hose, to the vital war areas. The volume of such equipment equalled approximately the volume of similar equipment produced in the previous 25 years.

In 1943, 124 cities and 2,260,000 people witnessed the demonstration "Action Overhead" which showed the nature and effects of enemy air raids. Staffed by members of the chemical warfare service, U.S. army, the demonstration resulted in widespread public education in the steps to be taken should raids occur. The education of the general public was one part of the over-all program. The system of schools and courses for the training of members of the Citizens Defense corps was revised in mid-year. The war department civilian protection schools were discontinued June 30. Revised standards of protection training were established by regulation, having been modified by British experience and the researches of OCD.

From its conception, OCD recognized British experience as the best available source of factual information for civilian protection in the United States. Commissions and individual representatives visited Great Britain. Reports were received from an attaché at the U.S. embassy in London. As of Oct. 20, 1943, 433 general reports and 116 medical reports had been received and consulted by selected staff members of the agency. On the basis of British experience, the rescue service was reconstituted and greatly enlarged. Two pilot schools for the training of instructors were held, one at the U.S. bureau of mines experiment station at Pittsburgh, Pa., the other at the University of California College of Mining, Berkeley, Calif.

The basic system of air raid signals was modified in Feb. 1943, by army regulations, concurred in by OCD, in order to provide intermediate audible public warnings between the confidential "Yellow" and the public "Red." Tests and exercises familiarized the public with these regulations and with the new signals. Exception was made for west coast communities which retained signals specified by the commanding general of the Western Defense Command. Extensive work was done to improve methods of blackout and dimout in coastal areas and important war centres. Dimout regulations were in effect along the coasts to reduce sky glow and to combat submarine sinkings. In addition, the protection branch worked with manufacturers to redesign warning devices and to make available sound machines capable of carrying warnings for great distances which would not require the use of critical materials.

The complex job of scientific and effective protection included the purchases not only of fire fighting equipment and medical supplies but of gas masks and other items. Those communities in critical areas unable to obtain equipment and supplies for themselves, were aided to protect themselves in the event of enemy attack. This job of distribution was virtually completed in 1943, including equipment for 5,400 medical field units and 1,500 casualty stations; gas masks produced were held in reserve at strategic locations for rapid shipment if needed.

The Emergency Welfare Service, organized during the year, brought together under one head five major functional services for use in emergencies or enemy attack: information and service centres; food and housing centres; central registry; clothing centres; rehousing and rehabilitation. Local Emergency Welfare Services operated jointly with state authorities and the American Red Cross in handling the emergencies and disasters of 1943.

A distinction was made, insofar as air raid hazard was concerned, between coastal areas and the interior of the country. In the latter case, a planned decrease in the protective forces was suggested to conform with the lessened danger of long range,

FIVE-MAN FIRE-FIGHTING CREW in a practice demonstration at a Flint, Mich., war plant in 1943

large-scale air attack. Dimout regulations were suspended by the army and navy in Oct. 1943 with a possibility of their return should the situation warrant it. (*See also* MUNICIPAL GOVERNMENT.)   (J. B. MN.)

Great Britain.—The year 1943 continued to show on the whole reduced activity by the German air force. No attacks of any real magnitude were launched, though there were a few short but sharp attacks made by long-range bombers. On the whole, activity was limited to raids by fighter bombers.

There were certain important developments during the year. A considerable expansion took place in the number of mobile columns, which had proved to be a valuable asset for reinforcing local authority services. The standard of training possible to achieve at these columns was very high, and they did some excellent work.

Another important development was the amalgamation of the first aid and rescue parties. This was effected partly on grounds of economy in manpower and partly on grounds of efficiency. It was found that, normally speaking, rescue work was required before first aid, and that during the time when casualties were being extracted from the débris, the first aid parties were standing by. Under the amalgamation it was made possible to deploy the parties in accordance with the needs of the situation, thereby effecting considerable additional efficiency.

The fire guard organization continued to expand, and an attempt was made during the year not only to combine in one document all the orders and regulations in regard to the administration of the fire guard plan, but also to set up all over the country an organization based on a detailed plan. In many cases the fire guard organization separated from the wardens' service and became a separate organization. Close linking up for operational purposes was effected with the national fire service. In addition, special courses for fire guard instructors were instituted at the ministry of home security schools at Falfield and Easingwold.

The civil defense staff college continued with a great variety of courses covering all aspects of civil defense, and proved of much value in stimulating thought and helping to maintain training and efficiency at a high level. The development of the housewives' section of the W.V.S. and similar organizations progressed rapidly, and proved in action to be a valuable adjunct to the civil defense services. (*See also* GREAT BRITAIN.)   (E. J. H.)

Civilian Requirements, Office of: *see* WAR PRODUCTION, U.S.

Civil Liberties. For developments of 1943 relating to civil liberties, *see* ALIENS; ANTI-SEMITISM; BIRTH CONTROL; EDUCATION; LAW; LYNCHINGS; NEGROES (AMERICAN); NEWSPAPERS AND MAGAZINES; RADIO.

Civil Service, U.S.
The civil services of governmental jurisdictions throughout the United States found 1943 a year in which war-fostered conditions combined to create an acute and all-pervading manpower shortage. Prime factors in this shortage were the mounting demands of the armed forces, war industry and agriculture on the fast dwindling labour reserves of the country. For public personnel agencies, the recruitment and retention of personnel to maintain the essential functions and services of government became their major contemporary problem.

Inductions of public employees into military service continued at a steadily quickening pace. Police and fire officials in many localities were concerned over the depletion in the ranks of their departments, made more acute by their inability to secure replacements. Following the lead of the national government, most state and local jurisdictions kept requests for military service de-

ferments of their employees to a minimum level; some refrained from making any such requests as a matter of general policy.

Varied devices to circumvent the manpower scarcity were initiated during the year. Civil service agencies turned to an increasing extent to the employment of women in jobs previously filled exclusively by men. Women operators and conductors appeared on several municipally owned streetcar lines; in Chicago, women lifeguards patrolled the city's public beaches. Teen-aged high school students in Birmingham, Michigan, were engaged to read the city's water meters. In the federal service, a concerted campaign to break down prejudices against the employment of physically handicapped workers resulted in the employment of more than 13,000 such workers in various government establishments. The work week of all federal employees was extended to 48 hours, and time-and-a-half pay for all work beyond 40 hr. per week was authorized, resulting in pay increases for most federal workers.

Rising living costs and the counter-attraction of high wages in war industry also caused numerous state and municipal governments to grant their employees pay increases during 1943. A noteworthy characteristic of this movement was the increased trend toward the adoption of schemes for gearing the rise and fall of public pay rates to corresponding fluctuations in living costs, particularly in the case of smaller city governments. Just prior to the beginning of the year, the National War Labor board modified its earlier stand by exempting state and local governments from previously established wage controls, as long as any increases made by them were not out of line with prevailing rates in their communities.

In June 1943, the number of paid civilian employees of the federal government within the continental limits of the United States reached an alltime peak of 3,002,453. Almost immediately, however, a sharp decline set in, and within three months the figure had decreased by approximately 200,000 employees. Congressional committees, bent on cutting federal expenditures, pressed for still further reductions and cited the need for closer control over future departmental requests for personnel. In state and local governments, less directly concerned with war activities, employment levels for the year remained relatively stable, showing a gradual decline as the effects of personnel shortages became felt.

Civil service reform scored added gains during the year, although at a slower rate than during peacetime years. Twelve cities and three counties adopted merit systems during 1943; in Georgia, three merit system agencies serving separate departments of the state service were combined. In Louisiana, on the basis of laws previously passed, merit systems became effective on Jan. 1 in the state service and in the New Orleans city service. Bills to establish civil service systems for state employment were introduced, but failed passage, in nine state legislatures. A recurring argument against them was that men in the armed forces would thereby be deprived of future employment opportunities. In the federal service, a congressional proposal that all positions paying more than $4,500 per year be subject to senate confirmation was defeated after sharp debate. Merit system supporters viewed the measure as a serious potential threat to the integrity of the federal civil service system.   (J. J. DN.)

Clair, Matthew Wesley
(1865–1943), U.S. Negro clergyman, was born Oct. 21 in Union, W.Va. He studied classics and theology at Morgan college, Baltimore, graduating in 1889. He continued his studies at Bennett college, Greensboro, N.C., receiving a Ph.B. degree, 1897, and a Ph.D. degree, 1901. Ordained a Methodist Episcopal minister in 1889, he led several congregations, 1889–97, and then served as presiding elder of the Washington district, 1897–

1902. He became pastor of the Asbury church, Washington, D.C., in 1902, and when he resigned from this post in 1919 he had the satisfaction of leaving behind an $80,000 church edifice which had been built under his leadership. After a year as superintendent of the Washington district, Dr. Clair was elected a bishop in 1920 and assigned to Monrovia, Liberia. While there he was appointed to the board of education by Liberian President C. D. B. King. He served several years as bishop of Liberia, later held position as presiding bishop of the Lexington, Ky., conference, and then retired. He died June 28 at his home in Covington, Ky.

Clark, Mark Wayne (1896–), U.S. army officer, was born May 1 at Madison Barracks, N.Y., where his father, Col. Charles C. Clark, was then stationed. A graduate of West Point in 1917, he saw service on the Western front in World War I and was wounded in June 1918. After the war, he was stationed with the army of occupation at Coblenz. He was graduated from the Command and General Staff school, 1935, and the Army War college, 1937. In Aug. 1942, he arrived in England to take over command of U.S. ground forces in the European theatre of operations, and in Nov. 1942, he was second in command of the U.S. forces that landed in North Africa. Three weeks before the invasion, General Clark and a group of U.S. officers were secretly landed on a coastal point in French North Africa. They established contact with French officers eager to co-operate with the United States and secured an agreement from these officers not to resist the American landings. He was awarded the distinguished service medal and the congressional medal of honour and promoted to a lieutenant general for his mission. He also headed negotiations with Adm. Jean Darlan for the cessation of all hostilities in Morocco and Algiers.

During 1943 he came more and more into prominence, as General Eisenhower's No. 1 U.S. field general. He commanded the U.S. fifth army in the invasion of Italy. In Dec. 1943, President Roosevelt, visiting Sicily on his return from Tehran, decorated him for "extraordinary heroism in action" at the landing at Salerno.

Clawson, Rudger (1857–1943), U.S. president of the Council of the Twelve Apostles of the Latter-Day Saints, was born March 12 in Salt Lake City. His father was an associate of Joseph Smith, founder of Mormonism. He studied at Deseret (now Utah) university and later served for 10 years as president of the Box Elder Stake at Brigham City. He was made a member of the Council of Twelve Apostles in 1898 and from 1910 to 1913 was head of the European mission. He was named president of the Council of Twelve Apostles in 1921. Clawson died in Salt Lake City, June 21.

Clays. There was a decrease of 13% in sales of kaolin in the United States in 1942, to 946,588 short tons, of which the paper industry used 59%. All major uses showed marked declines. Ball clay sales dropped 18% to 162,293 tons, of which 92% went into pottery and tile. Demand for industrial refractories led to an increase of 16% in the output of fire clay in 1942, to 4,839,332 tons, over 90% of which was used in refractories.

(G. A. Ro.)

Cleveland. Sixth largest city of the United States, Cleveland, O., had a population of 878,336 by the federal census of 1940. Area, 73.74 sq.mi. Mayor (Jan. 1, 1944): Frank J. Lausche.

Mayor Lausche was re-elected in Nov. 1943, by a record-breaking majority of 67,078, polling 113,032 votes while his Republican opponent, Edward C. Stanton, polled 45,954. His victory in the face of Republican gains elsewhere drew national attention to the Democratic mayor. At the same time there was elected to the city council a Democratic majority. Under the city charter Mayor Lausche began his new term Nov. 8, 1943.

Many municipal employees were granted pay increases to meet higher living costs. City council approved four salary ordinances which provided increases for hundreds of city employees. In Aug. 1943, the Cleveland board of education granted general pay increases to its employees, and in November the library board voted increases ranging from 6% to 8% to all Cleveland public library workers.

Manpower controls were tightened throughout 1943 in the Cleveland region as war industry expanded. In January the War Manpower commission through its Cleveland labour-management committee "froze" war workers to their jobs to prevent labour piracy. In May the minimum 48-hour work week went into effect and on Nov. 19 the War Manpower commission rated the city as an area of acute labour shortage.

Other events of 1943 included the following: Bishop Edward Francis Hoban on Jan. 21 became the first coadjutor in the history of the Catholic diocese of Cleveland. On May 20 the $20,000,000 aircraft engine research laboratory at Cleveland airport was dedicated. The Cleveland city council in June voted to change from eastern war time to the official state time, eastern standard time, beginning with the last Sunday in Sept. 1943, and to change back on the last Sunday of April 1944. In November the 1,700-bed United States general hospital in Parma Heights was completed. Births recorded in the city set an all-time high of 22,066 in 1943.

Products manufactured in Cleveland in 1943 were estimated to exceed $3,000,000,000 in value. Employment rose from 255,000 in 1942 to 287,000 in 1943. Arrivals of commercial vessels at the port of Cleveland totalled 3,217 in 1943, and of these 1,544 brought cargoes of iron ore.

The 1943 budget of Cleveland, prepared by Mayor Lausche, was $17,177,000, a reduction of $89,000 from 1942. County Auditor John A. Zangerle placed the valuation of land and buildings in Cleveland at $957,651,270 in 1943, compared with $923,-907,830 in 1942. The Cleveland tax rate was $3.13 per $100 value. Indebtedness as of Jan. 1, 1943, was $127,289,751.65. (P. By.)

Climate: *see* METEOROLOGY.

Clothing Industry. The clothing industry marked time in 1943 in the United States. Conservation measures and shortages affecting civilian wear were generally continued. Government regulation of manufacture became more stringent with ceiling prices and other price orders used to force manufacturers into low-priced production. Rising costs of labour and materials with fixed price ceilings caught many in a squeeze; such producers sought to find loopholes to avoid ceiling prices. Renegotiation affected many military garment manufacturers.

There were no style changes in civilian garments except for a great increase in pile-lined cotton outerwear. There were numerous improvements in army and navy utility garments—mainly dictated by reports from the field of action; navy jumpers were made six inches shorter and the colour of navy officers' uniforms was changed to slate gray. Tremendous numbers of cotton herringbone twill garments were made for the army. Great strides were made in the development of cold weather clothing, emphasizing multiple layers of light weight; this was achieved primarily by the U.S. air force research section and was the result of observing dress habits of Eskimos and other far northern people.

New commercial standards covering finished garment measurements were accepted by the various divisions of the industry. War developments of importance to postwar garment operations were flame, water and mildew proofing. Manufacturers considered postwar plans and consolidation of their position.

The Amalgamated Clothing Workers of America, largest union in the industry, established a labour insurance fund consisting of a 2% levy on the manufacturers' gross annual pay roll and a 2% fund for paid vacations. Many manufacturers offered employees group life insurance and set up pension plans.

Fabric, trimming and finding shortages hampered the industry. New plastic buttons replaced metal on military garments. New machinery was available only on priority—a black market on textiles, trimmings, findings and machines was budding. Rayon production increased tremendously but was still far short of demand. Thread deliveries were slow and there was a marked demand for new ready-wound paper bobbins. Manpower and womanpower shortages were felt; manufacturers paid marked attention to efficient methods of production. Girls were taught marking, cutting and other duties previously performed by men.

New machines included a faster overseamer, a detachable turntable cloth laying machine for all types of napped fabrics and special variety machines for small complicated sewing operations.

Greatest civilian shortages appeared in children's wear, men's shirts and pajamas. Apparel rationing was avoided.

Comparing the first ten months of 1943 with 1942, civilian production was off 14% and military production up 74% in the men's, youths' and boys' woollen field. In the cotton, leather and allied garment industry the same comparison showed a drop of 24% in civilian production and a rise of 85% in military production.

British clothing manufacturers were engaged in a most conservative civilian program; rationing continued, business profits were off. Australian clothing was rationed. Germany stopped almost all civilian garment manufacture. Delivery of U.S. 32-oz. kersey overcoating and overcoats to Russia helped to defeat the Germans on the cold eastern front.   (H. SN.)

Cloves: *see* SPICES.

Coal. **World Production.**—With no information available on coal production from any of the major producers except the United States, even estimates on world production for 1943 were impossible. It was thought that probably the reported output of 1,466,000,000 metric tons in 1939 had increased to something like 1,600,000,000 tons by 1941, but the figures were highly conjectural, and to attempt to extrapolate the conjectures to cover 1942 or 1943 seemed unwise. About all that could be said was that it was certain that all of the major producers, Germany, United Kingdom and the United States made the largest outputs that could be attained under the conditions prevailing. In Europe the only marked change in status during the year 1943 was the shift of Italy from the axis to the Allied Nations. As a partner in the axis, Italy received the necessary coal imports of some 1,000,000 tons monthly from German or German-controlled sources. It would now presumably fall to the United States to supply that portion of the country under Allied control with its fuel requirements, but since the major industrial areas of the country were still occupied by Germany, the bulk of the demand would still fall on Germany, if industrial production was to be maintained.

Table I.—*Coal Production of the World*
(Millions of metric tons—all grades)

	1929	1932	1937	1938	1939
Canada	15.87	10.65	14.37	12.97	14.08
United States	552.31	326.19	447.58	358.01	403.28
Belgium	26.93	21.42	29.86	29.58	29.85
Czechoslovakia	29.08	26.82	34.67	26.60	?
France	68.49	57.70	45.33	47.56	51.00
Germany	348.61	227.39	372.70	384.92	430.00
Netherlands	11.74	12.88	14.46	13.66	13.06
Poland	46.31	28.87	36.24	38.11	?
United Kingdom	262.05	212.08	244.27	230.66	236.70
U.S.S.R.	38.42	53.60	127.00	132.89	?
China	?	28.00	?	?	?
India	22.50	20.48	26.09	29.52	28.21
Japan	36.14	28.22	?	?	?
South Africa	13.02	9.92	15.49	16.28	16.89
Australasia	14.88	13.21	18.03	17.87	19.83
Total	1,559.00	1,124.00	1,550.00	1,469.00	1,466.00?

United States.—The coal output of the United States in 1942 included 580,000,000 tons of bituminous and 59,961,000 tons of anthracite, a total of 639,961,000 tons, and an increase of 12% over 1941. The bituminous total was a new record high, surpassing the former 1918 high by a small margin. Bituminous production was maintained throughout the year at an unusually

MINERS leaving a coal shaft on April 30, 1943, the dead line set by John L. Lewis for a general strike. On the following day, the U.S. government took over operation of the mines, and Lewis directed the miners to return to work

steady rate, varying little from a general average of 11,150,000 tons weekly, except at the end of June and at Christmas; anthracite output was somewhat less regular, with drops materially below the average in April, May, July and at the year-end. Consumption of bituminous coal increased 10% over 1941, to 540,726,000 tons, and stocks advanced 19% to 92,387,525 tons. Although the 1942 output was a marked increase over preceding years, it was still well under the potential full-time capacity of the mines, which is of the order of 685,000,000 tons, even on a five-day week basis, while a six-day week should give a potential output approximating 800,000,000 tons.

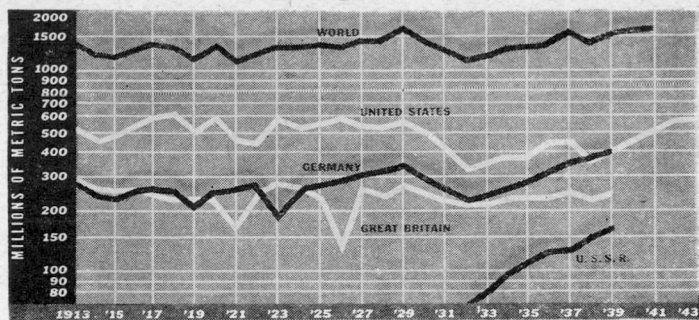

COAL PRODUCTION OF THE WORLD and the major producing countries, as compiled by *The Mineral Industry*

Table II.—*United States Production of Coal*
(Millions of Short Tons)

	1929	1938	1939	1940	1941	1942
Alabama	17.9	11.1	12.0	15.3	15.5	18.9
Colorado	9.9	5.7	5.9	6.6	6.9	8.0
Illinois	60.7	41.9	46.8	50.6	54.7	63.8
Indiana	18.3	14.8	16.9	18.9	22.5	25.5
Kentucky	60.5	38.5	42.6	49.1	53.7	60.0
Ohio	23.7	18.6	20.3	22.8	29.3	34.6
Pennsylvania	143.5	77.7	92.2	116.6	130.2	143.2
Tennessee	5.4	4.5	5.6	6.0	7.0	7.4
Utah	5.1	2.9	3.3	3.6	4.1	5.7
Virginia	12.7	12.3	13.5	15.3	18.4	19.9
West Virginia	138.5	93.3	108.4	126.4	140.3	156.8
Wyoming	6.7	5.2	5.4	5.8	6.6	8.0
Others	32.1	22.1	21.7	23.7	24.8	28.3
Total Bituminous	535.0	348.5	394.9	460.8	514.1	580.0
Anthracite	73.8	46.1	51.5	51.5	56.4	60.0
Grand Total	608.8	394.6	446.3	512.3	570.5	640.0

In 1943, both bituminous and anthracite were on a par at the end of November with the same period of 1942. Through the week ending Nov. 27, 1943, the bituminous total was 529,020,000 short tons and the anthracite total 54,937,000 tons, making a grand total of 583,957,000 tons, as compared with 583,813,000 in the same period of 1942. These figures indicate that production for the full year would not differ appreciably from the 1942 totals of 580,000,000 tons of bituminous and 59,961,000 tons of anthracite, but were likely to run slightly over these figures. Production during 1943 failed to keep pace with consumption, with the result that stocks were depleted to make up the deficit. By the end of September industrial and retail stocks had dropped from 85,889,000 tons to 72,866,000 tons, and those at Lake docks shrunk from 6,993,030 tons to 5,248,018 tons.

This unfavourable showing by the coal industry of the country during a year that should have produced the maximum output of which the mines were capable was the result of a recurring series of strikes in the industry. Some of these were "authorized" by union officials, and some were "unauthorized," but all were equally in violation of union pledges to refrain from strikes during the period of the war. Net results were, for the miners, an increase in pay to cover travel time, and overtime pay to cover the change from the five-day to a six-day week, and for the country a loss of coal output that was estimated by the Solid Fuels administration at 40,000,000 tons, which seems to be a rather conservative figure.

Coal requirements for 1943 had been estimated at 665,000,000 tons; production would be only about 640,000,000 tons; without the strikes the estimated requirements could have been met, and even exceeded, avoiding a shortage that had not only adversely affected industrial and munitions output, but also necessitated such stringent restrictions on domestic fuel that the householder who a year before converted his heating system from oil to coal stood a good chance of having a harder time to keep warm with coal than with oil. (*See* also FUEL BRIQUETTES.)

(G. A. RO.)

Great Britain.—During the autumn of 1942 there were widespread fears that a fuel crisis would develop during the late winter and early spring. Estimates by the ministry of fuel and power indicated that the consumption of coal would exceed production by 11,000,000 tons. The only factors that could save the position were mild weather, decreased consumption or increased output. Luckily the winter was mild because production in fact decreased though it exceeded the ministry's estimate by 3,000,000 tons. Increased efficiency in industrial consumption combined with economy to the point of hardship by the private householder sufficed and the gap was closed, the economies equalling 11,000,000 tons.

During 1943 production at the mines further declined and consumption increased in spite of greater efficiency in fuel consumption. In addition the liberation of North Africa, capture of the Italian islands and part of Italy itself created additional demands. How these were to be met without depriving Britain of power and warmth was the problem the ministry of fuel and power had to solve, either by increased manpower or increased output per man already employed.

Manpower can be divided into three categories—producers, transport hands and surface workers in approximately equal proportions. Of these the producers are on average the younger and more virile men, the very men who flocked into the army at the outbreak of war and after Dunkirk and who make excellent soldiers. Here was the greatest shortage. All through 1943 attempts to meet the annual wastage of some 20,000 men and especially to increase the number employed at the coalface were made by upgrading junior categories, by direction by the ministry of labour and by recalling men from civilian war work. It was found impossible to release more than a very limited number from the fighting services. Special efforts were made to recruit boys and youths by monetary inducements and the extension of pre-entry training schemes, but without any real success. At the close of 1943, the ministry of labour and national service decreed that any man, when called up for national service, could be directed *pari passu* either into the armed forces or the mines.

To effect increased output from the men already employed certain mines were closed and the employees directed to work in other mines where coal-getting conditions are better. It was expected that an additional 1,000,000 tons would be produced by this means. All the mines in the country were examined by officials and attempts were to be made where underground conditions are suitable to introduce American mechanical loading machinery. But this would mean the adoption of a method of mining which can only be used safely in a limited number of mines.

Some success was expected to meet the efforts of British mining engineers to produce loading machines suitable for established British mining methods. Mechanization had been carried to a high pitch already; nearly 70% of the coal produced was mechanically cut and conveyed but there was a gap in the complete mechanization cycle; all coal, after being broken mechanically, had to be loaded on to the conveyors or into trams by manual labour.

Opencast mining was progressing and over 2,000,000 tons were produced in 1943. In 1944 by means of additional machinery this amount was expected to be doubled or even trebled.

The bonus scheme based on output—that every man employed in every mine in a given coalfield gets a bonus of 3d. per shift for every 1% the coalfield output exceeds an agreed standard amount—had a full trial and did not prove the success hoped. The scheme, envisaging a whole coalfield, was too impersonal. It was therefore proposed to apply the scheme to individual mines.

On June 30 all coal became by purchase the property of the state and was vested in the Coal Commission, the purchase price being £66,666,000.

The British Coalowners association assisted by the department of scientific and industrial research decided to spend £200,000 per annum for five years on research with the object of increasing efficiency in the use of coal as a fuel and ultimately to find such uses for raw coal that it would cease to be regarded as a fuel and would be looked upon as a raw material for subsequent processing. (J. A. S. R.)

Minor Producers.—In Canada the coal production in 1942 was 18,707,100 short tons, as compared with 18,225,900 tons in 1941, and a new record figure. The value of the output, however, increased by 7%, against 2.6% rise in quantity. The total included 13,541,000 tons bituminous; 726,300 tons of sub-bituminous; and 4,439,800 tons of lignite. Imports of coal into Canada in 1942 included 20,807,005 tons of bituminous and 4,802,023 tons of anthracite, a total of 25,609,267 tons, an increase of 17% over 1941. Exports in 1942 were 815,585 tons, leaving a balance of 43,500,000 tons available for consumption. In order to develop the maximum output, subsidy payments were being made to mines requiring assistance in meeting increased costs of operation. Production during the first three quarters of 1943 was 13,126,656 tons, a decrease of 6% from the same period of 1942, but the drop was more than offset by imports of 20,432,551 tons, up 11% from 1942.

Chilean production amounted to 2,069,000 metric tons in 1942, and 704,000 tons in the first four months of 1943.

The Spanish output declined slightly, to 8,772,000 metric tons in 1942 as compared with 8,844,000 tons in 1941, but rose to 3,116,000 tons in the first four months of 1943. (G. A. Ro.)

Coast and Geodetic Survey, U. S.

Hydrographic surveys and charting of waters of the western Aleutian islands, together with geodetic control work in Alaska and Yukon territories, were the principal accomplishments of the U.S. coast and geodetic survey in 1943. Four ships of the survey's fleet were operated by the bureau to meet the immediate needs of the Alaskan sector command and one vessel was assigned directly to the commander of the north Pacific force. The work performed by the personnel of the survey ships contributed to the success of naval missions and the safe transportation of military personnel and equipment in these previously uncharted waters. A fifth survey vessel was engaged in southeast Alaska on the approaches to important base ports.

Through the co-operation of the U.S. coast guard, which furnished an amphibian plane and crew to fly the 9-lens camera, the coastal area of the Alaskan peninsula adjacent to Bristol bay was photographed for mapping. Later, all except two of the personnel of this party were killed while on an aerial photographic mission in the western Aleutians, when the plane crashed into Adak mountain and was destroyed. The accident, a major casualty attributed to war conditions, occurred shortly prior to the attack on Kiska island when survey work was being concentrated on the collection of data to assist in that action.

Geodetic control surveys were made from Seward peninsula along the shores of Bering sea to the lower Yukon river valley and from Tanana Crossing through Yukon Territory and British Columbia to southeast Alaska at the summit of White pass. The work included triangulation, levelling and astronomical observations of the first order of precision.

Within continental United States, survey ships were engaged on projects in coastal areas for naval purposes. Geodetic control was provided, and aerial photographic and ground surveys were made for military mapping. Tidal measurements were obtained and predictions of future tidal movements were prepared for military areas. The direction and velocity of currents in three restricted channels on the Atlantic coast were measured.

Analysis of geomagnetic observations and seismic records was continued. Isogonic lines were either determined from observations or extrapolated from available information for use on air maps of the hemisphere. Magnetic declinations were furnished for use on military quadrangles.

The production of nautical and aeronautical charts reached a new record at the close of the year. Naval operations and marine concentrations in all coastal waters required the issue of over 2,250,000 marine charts to navigators of ships of the United States. Training programs and domestic operations of the air forces and accelerated aviation activities were reflected in the issue of 15,000,000 aeronautical charts. (L. O. C.)

Coast Guard, U.S.

Characteristic of the U.S. coast guard's activity during 1943 was the continuance of its operational integration with the navy, of which it had been a part since Nov. 1, 1942. In 1943 the coast guard participated through its enlarged and more combatant operative arms with the other services on an unprecedented scale, collaterally maintaining all phases of its peacetime functions.

Most closely integrated with the navy were the larger coast guard vessels operating offshore as units of fleets, task forces and various sea-frontiers, performing duties as escorts of convoy and antisubmarine patrol in addition to continuing highly specialized work peculiar to the coast guard such as that in Greenland. Greatly determining the coast guard's operations in 1943 was the navy's landing craft and amphibious warfare program, in which the coast guard figured to a great degree, manning and operating numerous units of the amphibious fleets.

Not only were the warships of the coast guard engaged in 1943 in offensive actions but also they continued their traditional role of safeguarding lives at sea. During 1943 this consisted principally of rescue of personnel surviving hostile submarine action, although rescues were not confined strictly to deepwater, lifesaving in floods and other disasters far inland being examples.

The year 1943 saw the intensification of that part of the coast guard devoted to aids to navigation, including buoy tenders which worked in extremely close liaison with the navy in establishing and maintaining mine fields and navigational aids in waters surrounding newly established bases outside the continental limits, and lightships and district craft performing similar duties in domestic waters.

Units of the service ashore continued their preventive and remedial duties, with the effectiveness of lookout stations bolstered by especially trained beach patrols working with dogs and horses to facilitate the vital maintenance of security.

Coast guard air activities were enlarged in 1943, with emphasis placed on flying antisubmarine and personnel assistance and rescue sorties. Air field and base installations were also enlarged as part of the general policy of extending this activity's scope.

Enlargement of United States shipping fleets and maritime

WHEN THIS RUSSIAN FREIGHTER ran aground on the U.S. northwest coast early in April 1943, coast guardsmen made their way through miles of dense forest to reach the wrecked ship and rescue the crew. The rescue party is barely visible in the upper right centre of the picture

personnel in 1943 resulted in a like expansion of the coast guard's program for the administration of the bureau of marine inspection and navigation, most functions of which were transferred to the coast guard from the department of commerce. Within the year the coast guard fostered the widespread application of safety equipment aboard merchant vessels and the instruction of merchant seamen in the proper use thereof.

Connected with the huge logistics movements resulting from the prosecution of the war in 1943 was the coast guard's preoccupation with the exacting task of waterfront protection and maritime law enforcement. More fully than ever before the coast guard in 1943 was charged with the supervision of the loading of explosives and kindred cargoes, the safeguarding of waterfront, canal and important inland waterways from destruction, loss, sabotage and natural disasters. In 1943 the nation's largest firefighting fleet, operated and administered by the coast guard, practically and statistically proved its value.

Personnel expansion of the coast guard was consistent with the service's enormous material growth. At the start of 1943, 140,000 persons were enrolled in the regular and regular reserve establishments. At the end of the year this force had been enlarged to 165,000 officer and enlisted personnel. Subordinate commands included 34,000 members of the coast guard temporary reserve, augmenting the coast guard auxiliary and bringing the total of temporary reservists to 62,000 officers and men. At the end of 1943 the coast guard auxiliary police and the newly recruited coast guard volunteer port security force were playing important roles in maintaining security measures and also in releasing regular coast guardsmen for combatant duty.

To meet the exigencies and demands of coast guard fleets, new ratings and new ranks for officer and enlisted personnel were initiated, prompted also by the requirements of the enlarged military organization and especially by the necessity of manning the invasion landing craft.

For the first time, in 1943, voluntary enlistments in the coast guard were curtailed and then abolished. In lieu of traditional procedures, men were accepted for coast guard service after induction through the machinery of selective service. Receiving more emphasis than ever before, the policy of procuring officers from candidates in the enlisted ranks was inaugurated.

(R. R. W.)

Women's Reserve (Spars).—SPARS are members of the women's reserve of the United States coast guard reserve. The word SPAR was compounded from the coast guard motto "Semper Paratus" ("Always Ready"). SPARS were enlisted for the duration of World War II and six months thereafter, to take over coast guard jobs ashore so that more coast guardsmen might be released for sea duty.

The coast guard's women's reserve was originated by Public Law 773 of the 77th congress. Director of the SPARS in 1943 was Lieutenant Commander Dorothy C. Stratton, former dean of women and psychology professor at Purdue university.

The women's reserve may enlist up to 10,000 women under its 1944–45 program. To enlist, a woman must be an American citizen from 20 to 36 years old, with at least two years high school or business school education. If married, she may have no children under 18 years old, and her husband may not be in the coast guard. An applicant for officer training must fill the same qualifications with two exceptions. The officer age limit is extended to 50 years. Educational requirements specify a college degree or at least two years of college plus two years of business or professional experience. Officer candidates are trained at the Coast Guard academy, New London, Conn. They receive commissions after completing this course.

Enlisted SPARS train at the Coast Guard Training station, Palm Beach, Fla. They become seamen, second class, after a six-weeks basic training period. Those who successfully complete further training in specialty schools are assigned to duty as petty officers.

During 1943 approximately 6,000 enlisted SPARS and 500 officers were trained and placed on the job. Enlisted personnel served in the following specialty ratings: yeoman, storekeeper, cook and baker, pharmacist's mate, radioman, photographer's mate, coxswain, commissary steward, gunner's mate, quartermaster, bugler and carpenter's mate.   (D. C. Sn.)

Coates, Joseph Gordon

(1878–1943), New Zealand statesman, was born in Matakohe, N.Z. He had been active in public life for over 30 years, held various cabinet posts during that time and was premier from 1925 to 1928. He was named to the New Zealand war cabinet in 1940 and in that capacity went to Washington in the following year to organize the munitions supply for dominion defense. He became minister of armed forces and war co-ordination in July 1942. Mr. Coates died in Wellington, N.Z., May 27. (See *Encyclopædia Britannica*.)

Cobalt. Little was done in the way of cobalt production from domestic ores in the United States, aside from a small by-product recovery, but after 1940 the Belgian Congo residues were shipped to the United States for treatment, and there was in 1943 a moderate amount available from Canada. World output was unofficially estimated at 6,000 metric tons, mostly from Belgian Congo and Northern Rhodesia. The use of the metal in high-speed steels and permanent magnets has materially increased consumption during the war years.

(G. A. Ro.)

Cochin-China: *see* FRENCH COLONIAL EMPIRE.

Cocoa (CACAO). The supply of cocoa from Latin America and Africa appeared to be ample according to unofficial sources. The official statistics were held in confidence by the Combined Food board which had the responsibility of making allotments in 1943. Production of cocoa in West Africa was large and the surplus growing due to lack of shipping. There was said to be more than 300,000 tons available if ships could be had to transport it. The united supply came principally from Brazil which had a production for export of about 600,000 tons in 1942–43 and somewhat less in 1943–44. Next to Brazil in importance were the Dominican Republic, Ecuador and Venezuela. With the restricted manufacture of chocolate due to sugar control, the available supplies from Latin America plus about 150,-000 tons from Africa provided a sufficent quantity to build up supplies in 1943. The supplies of chocolate and other forms of cocoa in retail markets were maintained through 1943 at about the same level as in 1942. (J. C. Ms.)

Coco-Nuts. Imports of coco-nuts were limited to such supplies as could be shipped from Honduras in 1943 and some very small quantities from other sources. The official statistics on imports were held as confidential by the government. Lack of ships was the limiting factor. Supplies which formerly came from the Philippines and East Indies were practically exhausted. Production was encouraged in Latin America but increased very slowly and the increase was principally in Honduras. (J. C. Ms.)

Coffee. The end of coffee rationing in the United States in July 1943 was not followed by a rush to buy coffee as expected, since almost 90% of the requirements had been supplied under rationing. Consumers had developed more economical use of the product and also appeared to have saved stocks in anticipation of more severe rationing. According to figures released by the treasury department, census bureau, the amount of coffee imported for consumption from Oct. 1942 to Sept. 1943 inclusive was as follows: Brazil, 898,000,000 lb.; Colombia, 635,000,000 lb.; El Salvador, 120,000,000 lb.; Guatemala, 107,000,000 lb.; Mexico, 65,000,000 lb.; Costa Rica, 40,-000,000 lb.; Venezuela, 67,000,000 lb.; Haiti, 56,000,000 lb. and other Latin American countries about 90,000,000 lb. Brazil continued to produce heavily and found it necessary to continue to purchase and destroy much of the lower quality coffee to aid her producers. Shortage of shipping space was the only factor that prevented the United States having an ample supply at all times.

COFFEE BOY pouring a drink for an official of the Brazilian national coffee department at a warehouse in Ypiranga. Before rationing was removed in the United States July 1943, Brazil accumulated huge surpluses

With the improvement of shipping to Latin America in 1943 the imports under the coffee agreement were readjusted and a larger supply provided to meet the expected increase in consumption with the absence of rationing. The subsidy on the import of coffee was ended on Aug. 25, 1943. In the coffee trade the problem in late 1943 was to buy high quality coffee at ceiling prices, even with the large supplies available. Unofficial estimates of 1942–43 production was that the total crop of all countries accessible to the United States was about 1,308,160 short tons, including 660,800 tons from Brazil; 249,760 tons from Colombia; 56,000 tons from El Salvador and 53,760 tons from Guatemala as the largest producers. (*See* also BRAZIL; GUATEMALA; RATIONING.) (J. C. Ms.)

Coinage. The mint establishment of the United States, an instrumentality of the treasury department, during the calendar year 1943 found it necessary to continue the previous year's high rate of coin production in order to meet the augmented needs of the populace for fractional coins to implement exchanges occasioned by the great amount of business and war-effort activity. The three coinage mints, in Philadelphia, Pa., San Francisco, Calif., and Denver, Colo., were operated throughout the year on a three-daily-shift basis, with production of 2,023,898,270 pieces of domestic coin, having a value of $136,-237,136.70, and of 186,682,000 pieces of coin for foreign governments. This output was the largest during any calendar year of mint history. Domestic coin production by denominations, follows:

Half dollars	77,986,000 pieces
Quarter dollars	137,495,600 pieces
Dimes	324,059,000 pieces
Nickels	390,519,000 pieces
Cents	1,093,838,670 pieces

Coinage of the zinc-coated-steel one-cent piece was begun in Feb. 1943, and discontinued at the end of the calendar year. Arrangements were completed for it to be immediately succeeded by a copper coin made from 95% copper and 5% zinc, with a weight of 48 grains, but without other changes. The over-all output of the zinc-coated-steel cent was 1,093,838,670 pieces, having a value of $10,938,386.70.

The other mint service institutions consist of the assay office at New York with auxiliary silver bullion depository at West Point, N.Y., whose principal activities consist of receiving, valuing, refining, storing and issuing gold bullion and silver bullion, as affected by domestic production, import, export, and consumption of these metals; the assay office at Seattle, Wash., a bullion purchasing agency; and the gold depository at Fort Knox, Ky., a storage institution.

The augmented industrial role assigned to silver bullion resulted in use of considerable quantities of treasury silver, in lieu of copper, as bus bars for transmission of electric current, or otherwise, in plants engaged in war activities. Government-owned silver bullion in material quantities was sold or lend-leased for use in aiding the war effort, including the making of munitions of war and the supplying of industrial needs. The lend-leased bullion was to be returned, in kind, after the war's close.

An unusual activity of the year 1943 was the conversion, under legislation approved Dec. 18, 1942, of millions of worn and uncurrent silver dollar coins previously held in storage, to fractional silver coin for use in active circulation. This also conserved copper and silver, for use in war activities.   (N. T. R.)

Coke. The production of coke in the United States in 1942 increased by 8% over 1941, with 62,294,909 short tons of by-product coke and 8,274,035 tons of beehive coke, a total of 70,568,944 tons, besides 4,751,683 tons of breeze or screenings. This production of coke required 17% of the year's output of soft coal, the total charged into the ovens being 100,849,633 tons. During the year the number of ovens decreased from 31,685 to 29,598, with 1,327 additional ovens under construction at the end of the year. The capacity of the ovens in use at the end of the year was 74,963,567 tons per year. The largest consumer of the coke was the iron blast furnace, which took 79% of the total; domestic use took 9%, gas production 8% and foundries 4%.

Production during the first 10 months of 1943 totalled 59,411,000 tons, an increase of 2% over the same period of 1942. On this basis the total for the year was expected to be somewhere between 71,000,000 and 72,000,000 tons. Except for the series of coal strikes during the year, the 1943 total might have been expected to approach 73,000,000 tons.

No information was available from the other important coke-producing countries, which in order of importance were in 1942, Germany, Great Britain, U.S.S.R., France and Belgium.

(G. A. Ro.)

Cold, Common. Common colds occur in the United States with greatest frequency in three principal periods—January and February, April and May and September and October. The peak in January and February is the most serious as measured by absence from work and severe complications. The common cold is highly contagious and is responsible for an enormous amount of industrial absenteeism. Many measures were under investigation for the control of epidemics of this disease and to prevent its spread. Unfortunately cold vac-

cines whether given by injection, by mouth, or by inhalation failed to achieve general acceptance and satisfactory proof of the value of any of them was so far lacking. It was claimed by some that vitamins help to reduce the frequency and severity of colds but carefully controlled studies of this subject did not corroborate this view. Vitamins do not seem to prevent colds, shorten them or make them milder although they do have an effect on the general health. Some progress was made toward minimizing the complications of the common cold. Some of the drugs of the sulfonamide group when administered by spray or by mouth have been reported as exerting a definite effect on reducing the complications in some persons. It was not recommended that all persons with colds take sulfonamide drugs but those who are especially susceptible to late complications such as sinusitis might obtain favourable results. Considerable work was done in 1943 on the sterilization of air by various means so that the virus causing the common cold is not spread as readily or as rapidly. In a children's hospital ultraviolet radiation was found to be effective in cutting down the frequency of respiratory infections in the wards. A vapour made up of propylene glycol and other so-called aerosols also was found useful in reducing the incidence of respiratory infections in certain enclosed spaces such as hospital wards or air raid shelters. Further work along this line appeared highly promising and might reduce colds and other cross infections under certain circumstances.

BIBLIOGRAPHY.—Donald W. Cowan et al., "Vitamins for the Prevention of Colds," J.A.M.A. 120:1268–1271 (1942); Chester S. Keefer, "Control of Common Respiratory Infections," J.A.M.A. 121:802–806 (1943); Morris Siegel et al., "A Study on the Value of a Mixed Bacterial 'Oral Cold Vaccine,'" Am. J. Med. Sciences 205:687–692 (1943).   (E. P. J.)

Colleges and Universities: see UNIVERSITIES AND COLLEGES.

Colles, Henry Cope (1879–1943), British music critic and author, was born April 20 in Bridgnorth, Salop., England. He studied at the Royal College of Music, London, and at Worcester college, Oxford, receiving his B.A. degree in 1902 and his B.M. in 1903 from the latter school, where he was an organ scholar. He became a lecturer in musical history and taught music and criticism at the Royal College of Music. In 1924 he was made a member of the associated board of the Royal Academy of Music and the Royal College of Music. For over 30 years he was music critic of the London Times. Mr. Colles edited the third edition of Grove's Dictionary of Music and Musicians (1927) and the fourth edition with supplement in 1940. His other publications include Brahms (1908); The Growth of Music, Part I (1912), Part II (1913), Part III (1916); Voice and Verse (1928); The Chamber Music of Brahms (1933); and Oxford History of Music, vol. 7 (1934). He died in London, March 4.

Colombia. A republic of northwestern South America, lying between 12° 24′ N. lat. and 4° 17′ S. lat.; it is the only South American country with a littoral upon both the Caribbean and Pacific. Area: 439,714 sq.mi.; pop. (1938 census) 8,701,816. An estimated 7% of the population is Indian, 5% Negro, 68% mixed blood, 20% white. The bulk of the population lives in the great interior valleys and highlands. The capital is Bogotá (325,658); other cities are: Medellín (143,952), Barranquilla (150,395), Cali (88,366), Manizales (51,025), Cartagena (72,767), Ibagué (27,448), Cúcuta (37,323), Bucaramanga (41,714), Pasto (27,564), Santa Marta (25,113), Neiva (15,096), Popayán (18,292). Language: Spanish; religion: Roman Catholic. President in 1943: Dr. Alfonso López.

History.—The Liberal administration of President López maintained control of policy in 1943. In the March congressional elections the administration Liberals retained 60 seats in the house, the Conservatives held 50 and dissident Liberals 13. Since the Liberal forces won 13 of the 14 state elections, their position was much stronger in the senate. (Senators are chosen in Colombia by the state legislatures.) New cabinet appointments were made in August, shortly after the convening of congress, and in September and October the cabinet had to be reconstituted three times, largely because of inter-party quarrels over a future presidential candidate. In addition the administration was embarrassed by a serious transportation strike in the department of Caldas, which was accompanied by riots and which necessitated the declaration of martial law in the district, and likewise by a scandal in the Bogotá police department, involving high officials. On Nov. 16 President López requested a 90-day leave in order to take his wife to the United States for medical attention. He left Colombia on Nov. 24, with Vice-President Dario Echandia taking over the executive office in his absence.

Colombia finally joined the ranks of the belligerent Allied nations on Nov. 1, declaring war because of the sinking of a Colombian vessel by submarine attack. The new status involved no great change in policies already actively pro-Allied in sentiment.

In international affairs Colombia improved its relationships in two cases. At the start of 1943 a concordat with the Vatican was approved, by which Colombia will exercise the right of approval of episcopal appointments (which were limited to Colombian nationals), and by which church weddings are to be recognized by the state, but under provision of registration with the civil authorities. On Feb. 9 it was announced that Colombia was to resume diplomatic relations with Russia; in the summer Alfredo Michelson was named as Moscow representative for Colombia.

Inter-American co-operation, a definite part of the administration program, continued along lines inaugurated in 1942. The Ninth Inter-American conference, which was to have been held in Colombia late in 1943 (the last meeting was held in Peru, in 1938) was indefinitely postponed because of the war. An Inter-American School of Meteorology was opened in Medellín early in the year. In August the Colombian foreign office proposed that all South American states who had severed relations with the axis, but who had not yet entered the war, should enter into consultation to plan future relationships with the United Nations.

Effects of the war were felt in Colombia in 1943 in a continued rise in living costs and in shortages of manufactured items and some foodstuffs and raw materials. Abnormal accumulation of gold and foreign exchange took place, with a corresponding increase in note circulation (85,040,000 pesos in Aug. 1942 as against 108,488,000 a year later). On March 2 an economic plan was adopted, which embodied price control, particularly on food and drugs, an encouragement of co-operatives, a modification of the exchange control system, the establishment or reorganization of important government bureaus, and a plan for nationalization of foreign-owned properties of a public utility nature. This economic program supplemented an earlier one (Dec. 1942) which had inaugurated a plan of forced investment in government bonds. An $18,000,000 Export-Import bank loan was concluded during the summer, with $10,000,000 earmarked for stimulation of essential agricultural projects, and the remainder for highway construction. The government continued to favour co-operatives as a means of improving economic conditions; at the beginning of 1943 Colombia had approximately 200 of them, of all types, with a capital of over 10,000,000 pesos.

An unpopular law enacted in 1942, and requiring all foreign firms to retain a Colombian legal representative, was repealed in January.

Education.—The school system (1942) consisted of some 9,000 primary and 450 secondary schools, with a total enrolment of more than 700,000. The 1943 budget allotted 7,268,209 pesos to education (1942: 7,735,000 pesos).

Finance.—The monetary unit of Colombia is the peso (official value in Dec. 1943, 57 1/7 cents U.S.). Revenue for the first nine months of 1943 was 52,865,000 pesos (same period in 1942: 52,847,000 pesos). Expenditures for the same period were indicated as being 63,904,000 pesos, a deficit of 11,039,000 pesos. Total notes in circulation Sept. 30, 1943, amounted to 108,869,072 pesos.

Trade and Communication.—Colombian foreign trade for the first half of 1943 totalled 179,258,000 pesos (total trade for 1942 amounted to 296,884,000 pesos). Imports were valued at 66,537,000 pesos; exports at 112,721,000 pesos. Coffee exports for the period were valued at 88,285,000 pesos; petroleum at 4,663,000 pesos. No gold was exported. Colombian trade with leading countries for the first half of 1943 was as follows: United States, exports to: 77,320,000 pesos, imports from: 31,250,000 pesos; United Kingdom, exports: 250,000 pesos, imports: 3,460,000 pesos; Argentina, exports: 515,000 pesos, imports: 5,300,000 pesos; Brazil, exports: 1,600 pesos, imports: 4,050,000 pesos. The Colombian favourable trade balance with the United States amounted to $42,702,000.

Maritime communication improved in 1943. Railways cover 2,053 mi., and 7,700 mi. of improved highway, 35,450 mi. of unimproved highway aid in transportation. Boat service on Colombian rivers is important. Construction on a 512-mi. road designed to open rubber-producing areas near the headwaters of the Orinoco river was reported.

Agriculture.—Agriculture is the basic Colombian industry. Coffee is the principal item; 3,880,000 bags were exported in the 1942–43 quota year (18% over the previous year, but 17% under quota allowance). The Colombian quota was increased by 1,631,111 sacks in March 1943. Sugar production for 1942 (official estimate) was 71,800 short tons; rice production (1941) was 119,841,300 kgs., not enough for home consumption.

Mining.—Petroleum production in 1942 amounted to 10,590,000 bbl. (1941: 24,629,000 bbl.). The reduction in 1942 was largely due to the shortage in tankers. In the first eight months of 1943 petroleum output was 7,789,000 bbl. Other minerals produced (1942) were: gold, 596,618 fine oz.; platinum, 55,543 fine oz.; silver, 151,084 fine oz.; asphalt, 73,253 bbl.; salt, 40,490 short tons; cement, 229,050 short tons.

BIBLIOGRAPHY.—J. M. Henao and G. Arrubla, *A History of Colombia* (transl. by J. F. Rippy, 1938); *Foreign Commerce Weekly* (Washington).
(D. Rd.)

Colorado. A Rocky mountain state of the United States, in the west-central part; mean elevation above sea level, 6,800 ft. Admitted to the union in 1876 as the 38th state and known as the "Centennial state." Area 104,247 sq.mi., including 280 sq.mi. of water surface. Population (1940), 1,123,296; 52.6% urban, 47.4% rural; 93.6% native, 6.4% foreign born; white 98.5%, Negro 1.1%, other .4%; 102.6 males per 100 females. Capital and largest city, Denver (322,412). Other cities: Pueblo (52,162); Colorado Springs (36,789); Greeley (15,995).

History.—John C. Vivian (R.) was elected governor Nov. 3, 1942. Other officers elected were: lieutenant governor, William E. Higby (R.); secretary of state, Walter F. Morrison (R.); auditor, James L. Bradley (R.); treasurer, Leon E. Lavington (R.); attorney general, Gail L. Ireland (R.); superintendent of public instruction, Mrs. Inez Johnson Lewis (D.). Walter F. Morrison resigned in 1943 and L. J. Bennett was appointed to unexpired term as secretary of state.

Education.—In 1941–42 total elementary and secondary enrolment was 225,967; average attendance was 189,433 in public schools and 7,229 enrolled in parochial schools. Total number of teachers: public schools 9,488, parochial 479. Average salaries paid teachers were: elementary schools $1,133, junior high $1,902; senior high $1,590; average $1,390.

The legislature in 1943 provided for additional state aid to schools by earmarking 15% of the state income tax to be distributed to school districts in counties where matching funds were made available by special school district and county wide property tax mill levies. This aid provides for a minimum of $1,000 for each elementary classroom unit and $1,333 for each high school classroom unit. At the beginning of the fall term in 1943, there was a 10% shortage of teachers. This was alleviated somewhat by the granting of 1,200 war emergency teaching certificates and by the transportation of school children to other than their own districts.

Public Welfare, Charities, Correction.—Public welfare disbursements in 1942, including $9,627,590 in federal grants, amounted to $23,474,273. Pensions, 42,676 persons over 60, $18,-129,098; dependent children, 5,734, $1,585,631; blind, 637, $205,-939; direct relief, 9,657, $1,722,475; child welfare, 1,372, $44,-676; tuberculosis, 192, $92,697; of these amounts the state supplied 50%, federal 47%, and county 3%; unemployment insurance: 350,000 insured in 1942; 75,076 checks totalling $826,307 in benefits. There were four correctional institutions with 1,961 inmates and annual disbursements of $1,062,287; eight charitable institutions, with 6,314 inmates and annual disbursements of $2,307,085.

Communication.—The state highway system in 1943, including 3,995 mi. of federal aid primary, and 1,982 federal aid secondary roads, totalled 12,399 mi.; city streets, 3,491 mi.; county roads, 36,176 mi.; other local roads, 26,423 mi.; national forests, 788 mi.; toll, 8 mi.; total, 79,285 mi. Thirty railroads had 4,507 mi. of main line track. There were 37 airports and landing fields. Number of telephones, in excess of 270,000.

Banking and Finance.—As of Jan. 1943 there were 78 national and 62 state banks; total deposits, $564,101,579, assets, $593,903,986; 23 federal and 29 state savings, building and loan associations, with assets of $39,590,528.

The state property tax was reduced from 4.35 mills to 4.25 in 1941, to 4.00 in 1942 and to 3.85 in 1943. The biennial state budget for 1941–43 was $120,967,319; for 1943–5, $130,000,000. The surplus in state treasury Nov. 30, 1943, was $5,388,774; in state institutional postwar building funds $1,628,621.

Agriculture.—In 1943 acreage planted increased by 3.5% and acreage harvested by 5% over 1942. Farm crops were harvested from 6,111,000 ac., or 9% of the state area. Cattle, sheep, and hogs marketed increased by a substantial percentage. Total income from marketing of agricultural, livestock and livestock products was estimated at $330,000,000, of which slightly less than half represented agricultural products. The increase over 1942 was 40%. At the end of 1943 the number of cattle was 10% higher, sheep 5% and hogs 25% over Dec. 31, 1942.

Table I.—*Leading Agricultural Products of Colorado, 1943 and 1942*

Crop	Unit	1943 (est.)	1942
Wheat	bu.	31,540,000	27,406,000
Corn	"	14,430,000	18,228,000
Barley	"	17,616,000	15,816,000
Oats	"	5,355,000	5,647,000
Dry beans	100# bags	3,118,000	1,903,000
Sugar beets	tons	1,623,000	2,178,000
Tame hay	"	1,817,000	1,856,000
Potatoes.	bu.	18,705,000	17,020,000
Grain sorghums	"	1,707,000	1,744,000
Peaches	"	1,978,000	1,490,000
Apples	"	1,140,000	1,595,000

Manufacturing.—Total value of products manufactured in 1939 was $221,642,666, compared with $237,838,370 in 1937. Persons employed, 27,893 in 1939; 31,129 in 1937. Wages and salaries, $37,509,961 in 1939; $42,052,535 in 1937. Published figures on war production contracts alone totalled in 1941 in excess of $156,000,000; in 1942, $175,000,000.

Table II.—*Principal Industries of Colorado, 1939 and 1937*
(Exclusive of steel and rubber industries)

Industry	Value of Products	
	1939	1937
Meat packing.	$33,005,533	$39,805,939
Bakery products	8,422,889	11,844,068
Butter	6,627,153	8,394,917
Newspaper and publishing	9,567,285	9,471,535
Flour, etc.	6,916,494	10,229,567

Mineral Production.—Production of all minerals in 1943 was valued in excess of $80,000,000. Molybdenum continued in first

Table III.—*Principal Mineral Products of Colorado, 1942 and 1941*

Mineral	Value 1942	Value 1941
Gold	$ 9,597,420	$13,301,015
Coal.	21,972,500	18,416,460
Silver	2,185,344	5,192,318
Zinc.	5,082,000	2,358,300
Copper	289,200	1,592,528
Petroleum	2,520,000	2,337,533
Lead	2,095,644	1,433,436
Molybdenum.	27,750,000	25,883,000
Vanadium	1,500,000	1,300,000

place; vanadium and other nonprecious metals increased in relative importance. In 1943 Colorado produced in excess of 40,000,-000 lb. of elemental molybdenum, approximately 70% of U.S. and 65% of world output, and over 3,000,000 lb. of elemental vanadium, approximately 93.4% of U.S. and 48% of world output.   (E. NN.)

Colour Photography: *see* PHOTOGRAPHY.
Columbia, District of: *see* WASHINGTON, D.C.

Columbia University. An institution of higher learning in New York city. The budget appropriation for 1942–43 was $14,443,881.93. During 1943 the major portion of the university's activities continued to be devoted to the war effort. Since the proclamation of the national emergency, Columbia had signed 101 war contracts with the government, half of which had been concluded, the funds involved far exceeding the annual university budget. Columbia in 1943 provided housing, meals and lecture space for some 2,100 V-7 men in the naval reserve midshipmen's school; 546 men were enrolled in the V-12 unit in the college, engineering and medical schools and there was an additional group of 156 at the medical centre. For statistics of enrolment, faculty members, library volumes, etc., *see* UNIVERSITIES AND COLLEGES.   (M. H. T.)

Columbium. No information was available on the production of columbium in Nigeria, but it was reported that new alluvial deposits were discovered that materially increased the ore reserves.   (G. A. Ro.)

Combined Chiefs of Staff, The. The establishment of the combined chiefs of staff by the governments of the United States and Great Britain was announced on Feb. 6, 1942. The four United States members were known as the "Joint United States Chiefs of Staff" and consisted of the chief of staff to the commander in chief of the army and navy; the chief of staff, U.S. army; the commander in chief, U.S. fleet, and chief of naval operations, and the commanding general, army air forces. The four British members were known as "Representatives of the British Chiefs of Staff." They consisted of the head of the British joint staff mission in Washington and representatives of the first lord of the admiralty, the chief of the imperial general staff and the chief of the air staff.

Supporting committees were established to combine and co-ordinate all the factors of military intelligence, transportation, munitions, staff planning, meteorology and communications. A combined secretariat was set up to perform the necessary secretarial work for the combined chiefs of staff.

The combined chiefs of staff were charged under the direction of the president of the United States and the prime minister of Great Britain with collaborating in the formation and execution of policies and plans concerning the strategical conduct of the war, the broad program of war requirements and allotment of munitions resources and the requirements for overseas transportation for the fighting forces of the United Nations.　(F. B. R.)

Combined War Boards, British-U.S.: see BRITISH-U.S. WAR BOARDS.
Comintern: see UNION OF SOVIET SOCIALIST REPUBLICS.
Commerce, U.S. Department of: see GOVERNMENT DEPARTMENTS AND BUREAUS.
Commerce Commission, Interstate: see INTERSTATE COMMERCE COMMISSION.

Committee for Economic Development.

This committee was created in August 1942 as a private, non-governmental, nonprofit organization of U.S. businessmen. Its stated objectives were to stimulate, encourage and help individual companies in planning programs for products and markets that would enable them to reach and maintain high levels of productive employment in the postwar period and, through national research, to define conditions favourable for expansion of business enterprise when peace should come.

The CED's by-laws placed it under the general direction of a board of trustees, of which Paul G. Hoffman, president of the Studebaker (automobile) corporation, was named chairman, and William Benton, vice-president of the University of Chicago, vice-chairman.

Its Field Development committee, under the chairmanship of Marion B. Folsom, treasurer of the Eastman Kodak company, organized during the year 1943 more than 1100 community Committees for Economic Development in 47 of the 48 American states. These, following an approximately uniform procedure in their several communities, obtained and analyzed detailed information concerning current employment, employment in 1940 (America's most productive prewar year) and prospective employment in the postwar period. Guided by this knowledge, and by information concerning national business trends and various recommendations made available by the CED Research committee under the chairmanship of Ralph E. Flanders, president of the Jones & Lamson Machine company, they thereupon endeavoured to stimulate bold, sound planning, both by individual firms and by communities and districts, for expansion of postwar production and employment programs to levels in keeping with an anticipated increase in national productivity of 30% to 50% as compared with 1940.

The CED was founded in the belief that private enterprise could and should shoulder the chief responsibility for making the U.S. economy work at high levels of productivity; that the expected expansion in U.S. national income due to the technological stimulus of the war would find its chief market in abundant domestic employment; and that voluntary co-ordinated planning by business could, in large measure, achieve the desired result.　(P. G. H.)

Committee of National Liberation, French: see FRANCE
Commodity Prices: see BUSINESS REVIEW; PRICES.
Commons, Members of House of: see PARLIAMENT HOUSES OF.

Commonwealth Fund, The.

This endowment, established in 1918 by Mrs Stephen V. Harkness "to do something for the welfare of mankind" and later increased by gifts from the founder and from Edward S. Harkness, president of the fund from its inception until his death on Jan. 29, 1940, now amounts to approximately $48,000,000. In the year ending Sept. 30, 1943, the fund appropriated $1,503,124.35. Of this total considerably more than half was devoted to activities tending to promote or maintain physical and mental health. Public health activities, designed to raise standards of rural service, centred in Tennessee, Mississippi and Oklahoma. Fourteen rural community hospitals built or remodeled with aid from the fund were at work during the year. New construction was postponed till after the war. As means of strengthening teaching resources, fellowships were offered to instructors in medical schools and provision was made for visiting instructors, without restriction as to field; continued aid was given to departments of preventive medicine and psychiatry, to various forms of postgraduate medical education and to teaching arrangements designed to promote interplay between pediatrics and psychiatry. More than $324,000 was appropriated for medical research. The Commonwealth Fund fellowships for British graduate students at American universities were suspended during the war, but 18 fellowships for postgraduate study in medicine and public health were made available to Latin-Americans. The fund continued to aid child guidance enterprises in England, contributed to an advisory service for community mental hygiene clinics in the United States and published during the year seven books of educational significance in its fields of operation. Since the beginning of the war, the fund set aside nearly $1,250,000 for war relief and related purposes. The directors of the fund in 1943 were: Malcolm P. Aldrich (president), William E. Birdsall, Phil W. Bunnell, Adrian M. Massie, Lewis Perry, William E. Stevenson and Thomas D. Thacher.　(B. C. S.)

Communications Commission, Federal: see FEDERAL COMMUNICATIONS COMMISSION.

Communism,

or revolutionary Marxism, is a system of government evolved under the leadership of Lenin and Stalin in the soviet union, the former Russian empire. Originally, as envisaged by Lenin and his closest collaborators, communism was a world-wide revolutionary movement aiming at the creation of a world society in which everybody would contribute to the common weal according to his capacity and receive a reward according to his need. Russia was regarded only as the starting point, the transformation of Russia into a modern progressive and highly industrialized state was regarded not as an end in itself, but as a temporary measure. But the hope of communist or socialist revolutions outside Russia soon faded away: nowhere did communism become a real force; in many countries its most determined opponent, fascism, came to power and suppressed all communist agitation and organization. Thus for the last ten years communism in Russia has taken a different development from that foreseen by Lenin. It was replaced more and more by a national patriotic trend for which the transformation and strengthening of Russia was an end in itself.

Stalin had led this development. In the famous "purges" of 1937 he liquidated most of the old collaborators of Lenin, the devoted communists of the original revolutionary tendency. Stalin's own speeches, but even more the completely controlled literature, press and theatre of the soviet union stressed the glories of the Russian past and tried to instil a deeply nationalistic spirit in the soviet population and especially in the soviet youth. This trend which dominated all communist thought and propaganda in the last years became even more pronounced in 1943. A strong attachment to the Russian tradition expressed itself in the new relation to the Orthodox Church and in the reorganization of the Russian army as much as in the dissolution of the communist international, the Comintern, founded by Lenin in 1919 as an instrument of communist world revolution.

On May 22, 1943, the communist international was officially dissolved as having outlived its usefulness. It was recognized that "deep differences of the historic paths of development of various countries, differences in their character and contradictions in their social order, differences in the level and the tempo of their economic and political development," made every centralized international revolutionary action and direction impossible. World War II fundamentally affected the situation. The resolution proclaimed that in the countries fighting Germany it was "the sacred duty of the widest masses of the people and, in the first place, of the workers to aid by every means the military efforts of the governments of their countries." This dissolution of the communist international did not change the attitude of the communist parties outside Russia. From the moment that Germany had attacked the soviet union in June 1941, the communists in German occupied countries had become the most active supporters of the underground movement sabotaging and fighting the German occupation and influence in their countries, while the communist parties in Great Britain and the United States supported wholeheartedly the war effort of the governments of their countries, entirely subordinating the class struggle and all socialist demands to the most energetic prosecution of the war and the fullest aid to the soviet union.

The dissolution of the Comintern was followed in Sept. 1943 by the recognition of the Russian Orthodox Church. Metropolitan Sergius of Moscow came to Moscow from his semi-exile in a special train and was received by Stalin together with other high church dignitaries on Sept. 4. The next day all Russian newspapers gave front page prominence to the announcement that the government would place no obstacle in the way of a permanent organization of the church under a patriarch of all Russia and a re-established Holy Synod. Consequently Sergius was elected patriarch of all Russia and was installed on Sept. 12 in a brilliant ceremony in Moscow cathedral. All metropolitans and bishops of the Orthodox Church participated in the ceremony. The patriarch assured the government of the full support of the Russian Church for the war effort. This reconciliation of the Stalinist state with the Orthodox Church was only one of the many indications that the new Russia fully accepted and revalued all the Russian national and imperial traditions of the past which in the first years of the revolution had been violently denied and rejected.

This revival of Russian traditionalism and the new emphasis on Russian nationalism determined also the transformation of the communist army, diplomatic service and educational system. The change from the revolutionary attitude of Leninism to the emphasis on tradition was complete in all these fields. Stalin, who a few years ago had been simply comrade Stalin, assumed now the title of Marshal Stalin and dressed in a new ornate marshal's uniform. The Russian army tried to build up a strong traditional sense in the army officer corps. Generals of the czarist past, and great czars themselves, especially Peter the Great, were held up as examples. There was no stress put on revolutionary or working class heroes. As an American newspaper correspondent remarked, "perhaps as in no other land today, young Russian officers look back for guidance to the past. For Russians brought up after 1917, the rediscovery of national history is a new and exciting experience." The officers received back their massive gold shoulder epaulets of czarist time, distinguishing them more clearly from the rank and file than was done in the democratic armies, and generals were wearing again the striking red stripes on the sides of their trousers. Military discipline was strictly enforced, and the standard of saluting in the red army was unusually high. The former system of orderlies for officers was reintroduced, to take care of the officers' personal affairs, food, clothing and boots.

These changes in the army were paralleled by changes in the diplomatic service. Communist diplomats formerly appeared in simple dress. In 1943 they received ornate gold brocaded uniforms which they were wearing at the 26th anniversary celebration of the communist revolution. The new splendid formal attire again stressed the resemblance with czarist days. In the field of education coeducation was abolished in secondary and elementary schools, to take into account the different nature of the two sexes; the boys were to be trained for a stern soldier's life while the girls were regarded essentially as the future mothers. Military experts were to conduct drills for the premilitary age in the schools, and the teaching of Russian history and strict discipline of conduct were to be emphasized. This new stress put on the difference of the sexes, on motherhood, family and authority, was again a complete departure from the original communist attitude.

With the gradual abandonment of communist internationalism and the new stress on Russian nationalism, the ideas dominating the Russian empire of the czars began again to be stressed. Communist internationalism was replaced by Pan-Slavism. An all Slav committee was formed in Moscow and held its third meeting on May 9, 1943, with the participation of delegates of all Slav peoples. From Moscow all Slav peoples were summoned for the fight of Slavdom against the Germans. While the former organ of the communist international, the magazine, *Communist International*, which was founded in 1919, ceased its publication in July 1943, a new monthly called *Slavyane* or *Slavs* began its publication in Jan. 1943. The former slogan, "workers of all countries, unite," was replaced by the new slogan, "death to the German invaders." The old imperial Russian interest in the formerly Russian dominated territories on the Baltic sea and on the Black sea was revived, and Russian diplomacy seemed ready to resume an active forward policy in Iran and in the middle eastern countries as well as in the far east, thus resuming everywhere the traditional trends of Russian imperialism with a new vigour and strength.

BIBLIOGRAPHY.—David J. Dallin, *Soviet Russia's Foreign Policy 1939–1942* (1942); Maurice Hindus, *Mother Russia* (1943); William Henry Chamberlin, *The Russian Enigma* (1943); A. Yugow, *Russia's Economic Front for War and Peace* (London, 1943). (*See also* DEMOCRACY; FASCISM; SOCIALISM.) (H. Ko.)

Communist Party: *see* COMMUNISM.

Community Chest
is the name given to a local co-operative organization of citizens and social welfare agencies; also known as "community fund," "welfare fund" or "united fund." In most communities during 1942–43 the familiar peacetime community chest organization was enlarged and combined with the various appeals for war relief, changing its local name to "community war chest," "united war fund" or variants.

The new war chests differed in structure from place to place. However, in general, they combined the normal fund-raising activities of the community chest, in behalf of the community's voluntary health and welfare services, with responsibility for raising the community's contribution to foreign and domestic war relief causes. In general, the quotas of war relief funds adopted by the local war chests were arrived at through the budgeting of war relief appeals by a new wartime campaign organization, the National War fund, itself an extension of the fund-raising principle of the community chest. In many instances, the personnel of the community chest, with necessary supplementation, was responsible for administering the local war chest.

Fifteen and a half million contributions, making a total of $162,334,486, in 649 cities, were given to community chests and war chests to be used for voluntary social work and war relief activities during 1943. The average per capita raised for 1943 by 144 war chests which were included in an intensive study was $3.11, while 52 community chests which did not include war funds raised $1.40 per capita. Approximately one out of every four persons, in the 196 cities where the above community and war chests are located, made contributions for 1943.

On Oct. 1, 1943, 683 community chests were known to exist, 652 of them in continental United States, 27 in Canada, 2 in Hawaii, 2 in south Africa.

Community Chests and Councils, Inc., the national organization of community chests and councils of social agencies, was organized in 1918 as a clearing house of information for the 21 chests then organized. On Oct. 1, 1943, the number of member chests and councils, affiliated on a voluntary basis, was 459.

Officers for 1943–44 were: Gerard Swope, honorary president; Harry C. Knight, chairman of the board; E. A. Roberts, president; vice-presidents, Col. Robert Cutler, Harry P. Wareham; J. Herbert Case, treasurer; Lynn D. Mowat, secretary. Ralph H. Blanchard was executive director. The address of the association is 155 E. 44th st., New York 17, N.Y. (*See* also RELIEF.)

(A. T. B.)

Community Trusts.

The philanthropic resources of 76 community trusts and foundations in continental United States, Hawaii and Canada increased from $13,500,000 in 1925 and $45,000,000 in 1935 to $56,036,000 at the beginning of 1943. At the latter date the Chicago Community trust held charitable funds aggregating $10,600,000, and the resources of the New York Community trust totalled $10,036,487. Sizable community foundations were in operation also in Cleveland, Boston, Winnipeg and Indianapolis.

The New York Community trust led in volume of outpayments, disbursing $547,262, followed by Chicago Community trust, $242,941; Permanent Charity fund, Boston, $235,300, and Cleveland foundation, $222,450. Aggregate disbursements, exceeding $1,000,000 for the 12th consecutive year, totalled $1,725,095, compared with the $1,605,801 paid out by these agencies in 1941.

(R. Hs.)

Composers, Authors and Publishers, American Society of: see PERFORMING RIGHT SOCIETIES; MUSIC.
Confectionery: see CANDY.
Congo, Belgian: see BELGIAN COLONIAL EMPIRE.

Congregational Christian Churches.

The Congregational Christian denomination is the result of the merger (1931) of the Congregational Churches established in America in 1620 and of the Christian Churches formed in 1780 and the following years. In 1943 the combined churches had 5,921 churches and a total membership of 1,077,346. During the statistical year 1942, the denomination received 63,445 new members and made a net growth in membership of 10,657.

The denomination is governed by two cardinal principles: freedom of the local congregation in everything that concerns its life and work and fellowship of all the congregations in common enterprises. This freedom is not licence; it is a regulated freedom. The regulation comes from within, not from without. There is no power that can compel a congregation to do anything it does not wish to do. The slight measure of denominational control of a local church lies in the association to which the church belongs. This association is made up of official delegates of the churches that belong to it. It meets twice a year. The representatives of the churches make such reports of their life and work as they deem will be of interest, but there is no set form of report nor are there formal questions to be answered.

The denomination finds expression of its national life in the general council which meets biennially. The delegates to the council number 1,006 and are elected by the local associations and conferences. The council maintains a national office at 287 Fourth Avenue, New York, with a staff. It issues the *National Yearbook* and other publications for use of the churches and represents the churches in interdenominational relationships. Affiliated with the council are the Home and Foreign Mission boards and other denominational agencies.

The Congregational Churches are organized on the democratic basis. Every member has full right to discuss, to determine and to vote on all matters that concern the life and work of the churches.

The outstanding contribution of the Congregationalists to American life is the influence they exert in behalf of common democracy. The fathers held fast to the thought that God in His rule of the universe was guided always by absolute standards of righteousness. So the rulers of the local community representing Him tried to do their work in the same way. They drew their election from the people, but when an officer was elected he had more than the dignity conferred upon him by the free votes of the people, for he was also the representative of the higher power. This religious foundation of their civil government grew out of the close connection of the church with all phases of life. In such an atmosphere and with such ideas it was to be expected that the Bible should be the Great Book of Law.

The basis of membership in a Congregational Church is a statement of purpose rather than a statement of creed. Congregationalists hold that creeds, which are intellectual statements of religious experiences, represent landmarks along the pathway of religious thought. As experiences and intellectual capacities change, however, it is inevitable that creeds should change. Consequently, if the membership of a church is based upon the subscription of some particular historical creed, full opportunity for intellectual thought and intellectual freedom may not be supplied. No member is ever told that he must believe any specific religious tenet in order to be a good church member. So long as he shares in the common purpose and feels that through fellowship with other seekers after a genuine religious experience, he can best realize the development of his own life, he is worthy to be a member of the organization. This basis of membership naturally attracts to the Congregational fellowship those who are liberal and openminded in their attitude toward social, moral and religious questions. This basis of membership means that without controversy and difficulty, people of different shades of intellectual thought about religion work happily together in the Congregational fellowship.

(F. L. F.)

Congress, United States.

The 78th U.S. congress met for its second session Jan. 10 1944. It comprised the following members (as of Jan. 17, 1944):

United States Senate

Presiding Officer: Henry A. Wallace, Vice-President of the United States

Majority Leader: Alben W. Barkley, of Kentucky

Minority Leader: Charles L. McNary, of Oregon

State	Name	Party	Term Expires	Residence
Ala.	Bankhead, John H., 2nd	Dem.	1949	Jasper
	Hill, Lister	Dem.	1945	Montgomery
Ariz.	McFarland, Ernest W.	Dem.	1947	Florence
	Hayden, Carl	Dem.	1945	Phoenix
Ark.	Caraway, Hattie W.	Dem.	1945	Jonesboro
	McClellan, John L.	Dem.	1949	Camden
Calif.	Johnson, Hiram W.	Rep.	1947	San Francisco
	Downey, Sheridan	Dem.	1945	Atherton
Colo.	Millikin, Eugene D.	Rep.	1945	Denver
	Johnson, Edwin C.	Dem.	1949	Denver
Conn.	Danaher, John A.	Rep.	1945	Hartford
	Maloney, Francis T.	Dem.	1947	Meriden
Del.	Tunnell, James M.	Dem.	1947	Georgetown
	Buck, C. Douglass	Rep.	1949	Wilmington
Fla.	Pepper, Claude	Dem.	1945	Tallahassee
	Andrews, Charles O.	Dem.	1947	Orlando
Ga.	George, Walter F.	Dem.	1945	Vienna
	Russell, Richard B.	Dem.	1949	Winder
Ida.	Thomas, John	Rep.	1949	Gooding
	Clark, D. Worth	Dem.	1945	Pocatello
Ill.	Brooks, C. Wayland	Rep.	1949	Chicago
	Lucas, Scott W.	Dem.	1945	Havana
Ind.	[1]Jackson, Samuel D.	Dem.	1945	Fort Wayne
	Willis, Raymond E.	Rep.	1947	Angola
Iowa	Gillette, Guy M.	Dem.	1945	Cherokee
	Wilson, George A.	Rep.	1949	Des Moines
Kan.	Capper, Arthur	Rep.	1949	Topeka
	Reed, Clyde M.	Rep.	1945	Parsons
Ky.	Barkley, Alben W.	Dem.	1945	Paducah
	Chandler, A. B.	Dem.	1949	Versailles
La.	Overton, John H.	Dem.	1947	Alexandria
	Ellender, Allen J.	Dem.	1949	Houma
Me.	Brewster, Ralph O.	Rep.	1947	Dexter
	White, Wallace H., Jr.	Rep.	1949	Auburn
Md.	Tydings, Millard E.	Dem.	1945	Havre de Grace
	Radcliffe, George L.	Dem.	1947	Baltimore
Mass.	Walsh, David I.	Dem.	1947	Clinton
	Lodge, Henry C., Jr.	Rep.	1949	Beverly
Mich.	Vandenberg, Arthur H.	Rep.	1947	Grand Rapids
	Ferguson, Homer	Rep.	1949	Detroit
Minn.	Shipstead, Henrik	Rep.	1947	Miltona
	Ball, Joseph H.	Rep.	1949	St. Paul
Miss.	Eastland, James O.	Dem.	1949	Ruleville
	Bilbo, Theodore G.	Dem.	1947	Poplarville
Mo.	Clark, Bennett C.	Dem.	1945	St. Louis
	Truman, Harry S.	Dem.	1947	Independence
Mont.	Wheeler, Burton K.	Dem.	1947	Butte
	Murray, James E.	Dem.	1949	Butte
Neb.	Wherry, Kenneth S.	Rep.	1949	Pawnee City
	Butler, Hugh A.	Rep.	1947	Omaha
Nev.	Scrugham, James G.	Dem.	1947	Reno
	McCarran, Patrick A.	Dem.	1945	Reno
N.H.	Tobey, Charles W.	Rep.	1945	Temple
	Bridges, H. Styles	Rep.	1949	Concord
N.J.	Hawkes, Albert W.	Rep.	1949	Montclair
	[2]Walsh, Arthur	Dem.	1947	South Orange
N.M.	Hatch, Carl A.	Dem.	1949	Clovis
	Chavez, Dennis	Dem.	1947	Albuquerque
N.Y.	Mead, James M.	Dem.	1947	Buffalo
	Wagner, Robert F.	Dem.	1945	New York city
N.C.	Bailey, Josiah W.	Dem.	1949	Raleigh
	Reynolds, Robert R.	Dem.	1945	Asheville
N.D.	Langer, William	Rep.	1947	Bismarck
	Nye, Gerald P.	Rep.	1945	Cooperstown
Ohio	Taft, Robert A.	Rep.	1945	Cincinnati
	Burton, Harold H.	Rep.	1947	Cleveland
Okla.	Thomas, Elmer	Dem.	1945	Medicine Park
	Moore, E. H.	Rep.	1949	Tulsa
Ore.	McNary, Charles L.	Rep.	1949	Salem
	Holman, Rufus C.	Rep.	1945	Portland
Pa.	Davis, James J.	Rep.	1945	Pittsburgh
	Guffey, Joseph F.	Dem.	1947	Pittsburgh
R.I.	Gerry, Peter G.	Dem.	1947	Warwick
	Green, Theodore F.	Dem.	1949	Providence
S.C.	Smith, Ellison DuR.	Dem.	1945	Lynchburg
	Maybank, Burnet R.	Dem.	1949	Charleston
S.D.	Bushfield, Harlan J.	Rep.	1949	Miller
	Gurney, Chan	Rep.	1945	Yankton
Tenn.	McKellar, Kenneth	Dem.	1947	Memphis
	Stewart, Tom	Dem.	1949	Winchester
Tex.	O'Daniel, W. Lee	Dem.	1949	Ft. Worth
	Connally, Tom	Dem.	1947	Marlin
Utah	Murdock, Abe	Dem.	1947	Beaver
	Thomas, Elbert D.	Dem.	1945	Salt Lake City
Vt.	Austin, Warren R.	Rep.	1947	Burlington
	Aiken, George D.	Rep.	1945	Putney
Va.	Glass, Carter	Dem.	1949	Lynchburg
	Byrd, Harry F.	Dem.	1947	Berryville
Wash.	Bone, Homer T.	Dem.	1945	Tacoma
	Wallgren, Mon C.	Dem.	1947	Everett
W.Va.	Revercomb, Chapman	Rep.	1949	Charleston
	Kilgore, Harley M.	Dem.	1947	Beckley
Wis.	LaFollette, Robert M., Jr.	Pro.	1947	Madison
	Wiley, Alexander	Rep.	1945	Chippewa Falls
Wyo.	O'Mahoney, Joseph C.	Dem.	1947	Cheyenne
	Robertson, Edward V.	Rep.	1949	Cody

[1]Appointed Jan. 28, 1944, to fill vacancy caused by the death of Frederick Van Nuys, Jan. 25, 1944.

[2]Appointed Nov. 26, 1943, to fill vacancy caused by the death of W. Warren Barbour, Nov. 22, 1943.

United States House of Representatives (*served in 77th Congress)

Speaker: Sam Rayburn, of Texas

Majority Leader: John W. McCormack, of Massachusetts

Minority Leader: Joseph W. Martin, Jr., of Massachusetts

State	Dist.	Name	Party	Residence
Ala.	1	*Boykin, Frank W.	Dem.	Mobile
	2	*Grant, George M.	Dem.	Troy
	3	Vacant		
	4	*Hobbs, Sam	Dem.	Selma
	5	*Starnes, Joe	Dem.	Guntersville
	6	*Jarman, Pete	Dem.	Livingston
	7	*Manasco, Carter	Dem.	Jasper
	8	*Sparkman, John J.	Dem.	Huntsville
	9	Newsome, John P.	Dem.	Birmingham
Ariz.		*Murdock, John R.	Dem.	Tempe
		Harless, Richard F.	Dem.	Phoenix
Ark.	1	*Gathings, E. C.	Dem.	West Memphis
	2	*Mills, Wilbur D.	Dem.	Kensett
	3	Fulbright, J. W.	Dem.	Fayetteville
	4	*Cravens, Fadjo	Dem.	Fort Smith
	5	Hays, Brooks	Dem.	Little Rock
	6	*Norrell, W. F.	Dem.	Monticello
	7	*Harris, Oren	Dem.	El Dorado
Calif.	1	*Lea, Clarence F.	Dem.	Santa Rosa
	2	Engle, Clair	Dem.	Red Bluff
	3	Johnson, J. Leroy	Rep.	Stockton
	4	*Rolph, Thomas	Rep.	San Francisco
	5	*Welch, Richard J.	Rep.	San Francisco
	6	*Carter, Albert E.	Rep.	Oakland
	7	*Tolan, John H.	Dem.	Oakland
	8	*Anderson, John Z.	Rep.	San Juan Bautista
	9	*Gearhart, Bertrand W.	Rep.	Fresno
	10	*Elliott, Alfred J.	Dem.	Tulare
	11	Outland, George E.	Dem.	Santa Barbara
	12	*Voorhis, Jerry	Dem.	San Dimas
	13	Poulson, Norris	Rep.	Los Angeles
	14	*Ford, Thomas F.	Dem.	Los Angeles
	15	*Costello, John M.	Dem.	Hollywood
	16	Rogers, Will, Jr.	Dem.	Culver City
	17	*King, Cecil R.	Dem.	Los Angeles
	18	*Johnson, Ward	Rep.	Long Beach
	19	Holifield, Chet	Dem.	Montebello
	20	*Hinshaw, Carl	Rep.	Pasadena
	21	*Sheppard, Harry R.	Dem.	Yucaipa
	22	Phillips, John	Rep.	Banning
	23	*Izac, Edouard V. M.	Dem.	San Diego
Colo.	1	Vacant		
	2	*Hill, William S.	Rep.	Fort Collins
	3	*Chenoweth, J. Edgar	Rep.	Trinidad
	4	*Rockwell, Robert F.	Rep.	Paonia
Conn.		Monkiewicz, B. J.	Rep.	New Britain
	1	Miller, William J.	Rep.	Wethersfield
	2	McWilliams, John D.	Rep.	Norwich
	3	Compton, Ranulf	Rep.	Madison
	4	Luce, Clare Boothe	Rep.	Greenwich
	5	*Talbot, Joseph E.	Rep.	Naugatuck
Del.		Willey, Earle D.	Rep.	Dover
Fla.		*Green, Lex	Dem.	Starke
	1	*Peterson, J. Hardin	Dem.	Lakeland
	2	Price, Emory H.	Dem.	Jacksonville
	3	*Sikes, Robert L. F.	Dem.	Crestview
	4	*Cannon, Pat	Dem.	Miami
	5	*Hendricks, Joe	Dem.	De Land
Ga.	1	*Peterson, Hugh	Dem.	Ailey
	2	*Cox, Edward E.	Dem.	Camilla
	3	*Pace, Stephen	Dem.	Americus
	4	*Camp, Albert S.	Dem.	Newnan
	5	*Ramspeck, Robert	Dem.	Atlanta
	6	*Vinson, Carl	Dem.	Milledgeville
	7	*Tarver, Malcolm C.	Dem.	Dalton
	8	*Gibson, John S.	Dem.	Douglas
	9	*Whelchel, B. Frank	Dem.	Gainesville
	10	*Brown, Paul	Dem.	Elberton
Ida.	1	*White, Compton I.	Dem.	Clark Fork
	2	*Dworshak, Henry C.	Rep.	Burley
Ill.		*Day, Stephen A.	Rep.	Chicago
	1	Dawson, William L.	Dem.	Chicago
	2	Rowan, William A.	Dem.	Chicago
	3	Busbey, Fred E.	Rep.	Chicago

State	Dist.	Name	Party	Residence
Ill.	4	Gorski, Martin	Dem.	Chicago
	5	*Sabath, Adolph J.	Dem.	Chicago
	6	O'Brien, Thomas J.	Dem.	Chicago
	7	*Schuetz, Leonard W.	Dem.	Chicago
	8	Gordon, Thomas S.	Dem.	Chicago
	9	*Dewey, Charles S.	Rep.	Chicago
	10	Church, Ralph E.	Rep.	Evanston
	11	*Reed, Chauncey W.	Rep.	West Chicago
	12	*Mason, Noah M.	Rep.	Oglesby
	13	*Allen, Leo E.	Rep.	Galena
	14	Johnson, Anton J.	Rep.	Macomb
	15	*Chiperfield, Robert B.	Rep.	Canton
	16	*Dirksen, Everett McK.	Rep.	Pekin
	17	*Arends, Leslie C.	Rep.	Melvin
	18	*Sumner, Jessie	Rep.	Milford
	19	*Vacant*		
	20	Simpson, Sid	Rep.	Carrollton
	21	*Howell, Evan	Rep.	Springfield
	22	Johnson, Calvin D.	Rep.	Belleville
	23	Vursell, Charles W.	Rep.	Salem
	24	*Heidinger, James V.	Rep.	Fairfield
	25	*Bishop, C. W.	Rep.	Carterville
Ind.	1	Madden, Ray J.	Dem.	Gary
	2	*Halleck, Charles A.	Rep.	Rensselaer
	3	*Grant, Robert A.	Rep.	South Bend
	4	*Gillie, George W.	Rep.	Fort Wayne
	5	*Harness, Forest A.	Rep.	Kokomo
	6	*Johnson, Noble J.	Rep.	Terre Haute
	7	*Landis, Gerald W.	Rep.	Linton
	8	LaFollette, Charles M.	Rep.	Evansville
	9	*Wilson, Earl	Rep.	Huron
	10	*Springer, Raymond S.	Rep.	Connersville
	11	*Ludlow, Louis	Dem.	Indianapolis
Iowa	1	*Martin, Thomas E.	Rep.	Iowa City
	2	*Talle, Henry O.	Rep.	Decorah
	3	*Gwynne, John W.	Rep.	Waterloo
	4	*LeCompte, Karl M.	Rep.	Corydon
	5	*Cunningham, Paul	Rep.	Des Moines
	6	*Gilchrist, Fred C.	Rep.	Laurens
	7	*Jensen, Ben F.	Rep.	Exira
	8	Hoeven, Charles B.	Rep.	Alton
Kan.	1	*Lambertson, William P.	Rep.	Fairview
	2	Scrivner, Errett P.	Rep.	Kansas City
	3	*Winter, Thomas D.	Rep.	Girard
	4	*Rees, Edward H.	Rep.	Emporia
	5	*Hope, Clifford R.	Rep.	Garden City
	6	*Carlson, Frank	Rep.	Concordia
Ky.	1	*Gregory, Noble J.	Dem.	Mayfield
	2	*Vincent, Beverly M.	Dem.	Brownsville
	3	*O'Neal, Emmet	Dem.	Louisville
	4	Carrier, Chester O.	Rep.	Leitchfield
	5	Spence, Brent	Dem.	Fort Thomas
	6	*Chapman, Virgil	Dem.	Paris
	7	*May, Andrew J.	Dem.	Prestonsburg
	8	*Bates, Joe B.	Dem.	Greenup
	9	*Robsion, John M.	Rep.	Barbourville
La.	1	*Hébert, F. Edward	Dem.	New Orleans
	2	Maloney, Paul H.	Dem.	New Orleans
	3	*Domengeaux, James	Dem.	Lafayette
	4	*Brooks, Overton	Dem.	Shreveport
	5	McKenzie, Charles E.	Dem.	Monroe
	6	Morrison, James H.	Dem.	Hammond
	7	Larcade, Henry D., Jr.	Dem.	Opelousas
	8	*Allen, A. Leonard	Dem.	Winnfield
Me.	1	Hale, Robert	Rep.	Portland
	2	*Smith, Margaret Chase	Rep.	Skowhegan
	3	*Fellows, Frank	Rep.	Bangor
Md.	1	*Ward, David J.	Dem.	Salisbury
	2	Baldwin, H. Streett	Dem.	Hydes
	3	*D'Alesandro, Thomas, Jr.	Dem.	Baltimore
	4	Ellison, Daniel	Rep.	Baltimore
	5	*Sasscer, Lansdale G.	Dem.	Upper Marlboro
	6	Beall, J. Glenn	Rep.	Frostburg
Mass.	1	*Treadway, Allen T.	Rep.	Stockbridge
	2	*Clason, Charles R.	Rep.	Springfield
	3	Philbin, Philip J.	Dem.	Clinton
	4	*Holmes, Pehr G.	Rep.	Worcester
	5	*Rogers, Edith N.	Rep.	Lowell
	6	*Bates, George J.	Rep.	Salem
	7	*Lane, Thomas J.	Dem.	Lawrence
	8	Goodwin, Angier L.	Rep.	Melrose
	9	*Gifford, Charles L.	Rep.	Cotuit
	10	Herter, Christian A.	Rep.	Boston
	11	Curley, James M.	Dem.	Boston
	12	*McCormack, John W.	Dem.	Dorchester
	13	*Wigglesworth, Richard B.	Rep.	Milton
	14	*Martin, Joseph W., Jr.	Rep.	North Attleboro
Mich.	1	Sadowski, George G.	Dem.	Detroit
	2	*Michener, Earl C.	Rep.	Adrian
	3	*Shafer, Paul W.	Rep.	Battle Creek
	4	*Hoffman, Clare E.	Rep.	Allegan
	5	*Jonkman, Bartel J.	Rep.	Grand Rapids
	6	*Blackney, William W.	Rep.	Flint
	7	*Wolcott, Jesse P.	Rep.	Port Huron
	8	*Crawford, Fred L.	Rep.	Saginaw
	9	*Engel, Albert J.	Rep.	Muskegon
	10	*Woodruff, Roy O.	Rep.	Bay City
	11	*Bradley, Fred	Rep.	Rogers City
	12	Bennett, John B.	Rep.	Ontonagon
Mich.	13	*O'Brien, George D.	Dem.	Detroit
	14	*Rabaut, Louis C.	Dem.	Grosse Pointe Park
	15	*Dingell, John D.	Dem.	Detroit
	16	*Lesinski, John	Dem.	Dearborn
	17	*Dondero, George A.	Rep.	Royal Oak
Minn.	1	*Andresen, August H.	Rep.	Red Wing
	2	*O'Hara, Joseph P.	Rep.	Glencoe
	3	*Gale, Richard P.	Rep.	Mound
	4	*Maas, Melvin J.	Rep.	St. Paul
	5	Judd, Walter H.	Rep.	Minneapolis
	6	*Knutson, Harold	Rep.	St. Cloud
	7	*Andersen, H. Carl	Rep.	Tyler
	8	*Pittenger, William A.	Rep.	Duluth
	9	Hagen, Harold C.	F.L.	Crookston
Miss.	1	*Rankin, John E.	Dem.	Tupelo
	2	*Whitten, Jamie L.	Dem.	Charleston
	3	*Whittington, William M.	Dem.	Greenwood
	4	Abernethy, Thomas G.	Dem.	Okolona
	5	Winstead, Arthur	Dem.	Philadelphia
	6	*Colmer, William M.	Dem.	Pascagoula
	7	*McGehee, Dan R.	Dem.	Meadville
Mo.	1	Arnold, Wat	Rep.	Kirksville
	2	Schwabe, Max	Rep.	Columbia
	3	Cole, William C.	Rep.	St. Joseph
	4	*Bell, C. Jasper	Dem.	Blue Springs
	5	Slaughter, Roger C.	Dem.	Kansas City
	6	Bennett, Marion T.	Rep.	Springfield
	7	*Short, Dewey	Rep.	Galena
	8	Elmer, William P.	Rep.	Salem
	9	*Cannon, Clarence	Dem.	Elsberry
	10	*Zimmerman, Orville	Dem.	Kennett
	11	Miller, Louis E.	Rep.	St. Louis
	12	*Ploeser, Walter C.	Rep.	St. Louis
	13	*Cochran, John J.	Dem.	St. Louis
Mont.	1	Mansfield, Mike	Dem.	Missoula
	2	*O'Connor, James F.	Dem.	Livingston
Neb.	1	*Curtis, Carl T.	Rep.	Minden
	2	Buffett, Howard H.	Rep.	Omaha
	3	*Stefan, Karl	Rep.	Norfolk
	4	Miller, A. L.	Rep.	Kimball
Nev.		Sullivan, Maurice J.	Dem.	Reno
N.H.	1	Merrow, Chester E.	Rep.	Center Ossipee
	2	*Stearns, Foster	Rep.	Hancock
N.J.	1	*Wolverton, Charles A.	Rep.	Merchantville
	2	*Wene, Elmer H.	Dem.	Vineland
	3	Auchincloss, James C.	Rep.	Rumson
	4	*Powers, D. Lane	Rep.	Trenton
	5	*Eaton, Charles A.	Rep.	Watchung
	6	*McLean, Donald H.	Rep.	Elizabeth
	7	*Thomas, J. Parnell	Rep.	Allendale
	8	*Canfield, Gordon	Rep.	Paterson
	9	Towe, Harry L.	Rep.	Rutherford
	10	*Hartley, Fred A., Jr.	Rep.	Kearny
	11	Sundstrom, Frank L.	Rep.	East Orange
	12	*Kean, Robert W.	Rep.	Livingston
	13	*Norton, Mary T.	Dem.	Jersey City
	14	*Hart, Edward J.	Dem.	Jersey City
N.M.		Anderson, Clinton P.	Dem.	Albuquerque
		Fernandez, Antonio M.	Dem.	Santa Fe
N.Y.		*Merritt, Matthew J.	Dem.	Flushing
		Stanley, Winifred C.	Rep.	Buffalo
	1	*Hall, Leonard W.	Rep.	Oyster Bay
	2	*Barry, William B.	Dem.	St. Albans
	3	*Pfeifer, Joseph L.	Dem.	Brooklyn
	4	*Cullen, Thomas H.	Dem.	Brooklyn
	5	*Heffernan, James J.	Dem.	Brooklyn
	6	*Somers, Andrew L.	Dem.	Brooklyn
	7	*Delaney, John J.	Dem.	Brooklyn
	8	*O'Toole, Donald L.	Dem.	Brooklyn
	9	*Keogh, Eugene J.	Dem.	Brooklyn
	10	*Celler, Emanuel	Dem.	Brooklyn
	11	*O'Leary, James A.	Dem.	W. New Brighton
	12	*Dickstein, Samuel	Dem.	New York city
	13	*Capozzoli, Louis J.	Dem.	New York city
	14	*Klein, Arthur G.	Dem.	New York city
	15	Burchill, Thomas F.	Dem.	New York city
	16	Fay, James H.	Dem.	New York city
	17	Baldwin, Joseph C.	Rep.	New York city
	18	*Kennedy, Martin J.	Dem.	New York city
	19	*Bloom, Sol	Dem.	New York city
	20	*Marcantonio, Vito	Am.Lab.	New York city
	21	*Vacant*		
	22	*Lynch, Walter A.	Dem.	New York city
	23	*Buckley, Charles A.	Dem.	New York city
	24	*Fitzpatrick, James M.	Dem.	New York city
	25	*Gamble, Ralph A.	Rep.	Larchmont
	26	*Fish, Hamilton	Rep.	Newburgh
	27	Le Fevre, Jay	Rep.	New Paltz
	28	*Byrne, William T.	Dem.	Loudonville
	29	Taylor, Dean P.	Rep.	Troy
	30	Kearney, Bernard W.	Rep.	Gloversville
	31	*Kilburn, Clarence E.	Rep.	Malone
	32	Fuller, Hadwen C.	Rep.	Parish
	33	*Douglas, Fred J.	Rep.	Utica
	34	*Hall, Edwin A.	Rep.	Binghamton
	35	*Hancock, Clarence E.	Rep.	Syracuse
	36	*Taber, John	Rep.	Auburn
	37	Cole, W. Sterling	Rep.	Bath
	38	*O'Brien, Joseph J.	Rep.	East Rochester

State	Dist.	Name	Party	Residence
N.Y.	39	*Wadsworth, James W.	Rep.	Geneseo
	40	*Andrews, Walter G.	Rep.	Buffalo
	41	Mruk, Joseph	Rep.	Buffalo
	42	*Butler, John C.	Rep.	Buffalo
	43	*Reed, Daniel A.	Rep.	Dunkirk
N.C.	1	*Bonner, Herbert C.	Dem.	Washington
	2	*Kerr, John H.	Dem.	Warrenton
	3	*Barden, Graham A.	Dem.	New Bern
	4	*Cooley, Harold D.	Dem.	Nashville
	5	*Folger, John H.	Dem.	Mount Airy
	6	*Durham, Carl T.	Dem.	Chapel Hill
	7	*Clark, J. Bayard	Dem.	Fayetteville
	8	*Burgin, William O.	Dem.	Lexington
	9	*Doughton, Robert L.	Dem.	Laurel Springs
	10	Morrison, Cameron	Dem.	Charlotte
	11	*Bulwinkle, Alfred L.	Dem.	Gastonia
	12	*Weaver, Zebulon	Dem.	Asheville
N.D.		*Burdick, Usher L.	Rep.	Williston
		Lemke, William	Rep.	Fargo
Ohio		*Bender, George H.	Rep.	Cleveland Heights
	1	*Elston, Charles H.	Rep.	Cincinnati
	2	*Hess, William E.	Rep.	Cincinnati
	3	Jeffrey, Harry P.	Rep.	Dayton
	4	*Jones, Robert F.	Rep.	Lima
	5	*Clevenger, Cliff	Rep.	Bryan
	6	McCowen, Edward O.	Rep.	Wheelersburg
	7	*Brown, Clarence J.	Rep.	Blanchester
	8	*Smith, Frederick C.	Rep.	Marion
	9	Ramey, Homer A.	Rep.	Toledo
	10	*Jenkins, Thomas A.	Rep.	Ironton
	11	Brehm, Walter E.	Rep.	Logan
	12	*Vorys, John M.	Rep.	Columbus
	13	Weichel, Alvin F.	Rep.	Sandusky
	14	Rowe, Ed.	Rep.	Akron
	15	Griffiths, P. W.	Rep.	Marietta
	16	Carson, Henderson H.	Rep.	Canton
	17	*McGregor, J. Harry	Rep.	West Lafayette
	18	Lewis, Earl R.	Rep.	St. Clairsville
	19	*Kirwan, Michael J.	Dem.	Youngstown
	20	Feighan, Michael A.	Dem.	Cleveland
	21	*Crosser, Robert	Dem.	Cleveland
	22	*Bolton, Frances P.	Rep.	Lyndhurst
Okla.	1	*Disney, Wesley E.	Dem.	Tulsa
	2	*Vacant*		
	3	Stewart, Paul	Dem.	Antlers
	4	*Boren, Lyle H.	Dem.	Seminole
	5	*Monroney, Mike	Dem.	Oklahoma City
	6	*Johnson, Jed	Dem.	Anadarko
	7	*Wickersham, Victor	Dem.	Mangum
	8	*Rizley, Ross	Rep.	Guymon
Ore.	1	*Mott, James W.	Rep.	Salem
	2	Stockman, Lowell	Rep.	Pendleton
	3	*Angell, Homer D.	Rep.	Portland
	4	Ellsworth, Harris	Rep.	Roseburg
Pa.		Troutman, William I.	Rep.	Shamokin
	1	Gallagher, James, Sr.	Rep.	Philadelphia
	2	*Vacant*		
	3	*Bradley, Michael J.	Dem.	Philadelphia
	4	*Sheridan, John E.	Dem.	Philadelphia
	5	Pracht, C. Frederick	Rep.	Philadelphia
	6	*Myers, Francis J.	Dem.	Philadelphia
	7	*Scott, Hugh D., Jr.	Rep.	Philadelphia
	8	*Wolfenden, James	Rep.	Upper Darby
	9	*Gerlach, Charles L.	Rep.	Allentown
	10	*Kinzer, J. Roland	Rep.	Lancaster
	11	Murphy, John W.	Dem.	Dunmore
	12	*Miller, Thomas B.	Rep.	Plymouth
	13	*Fenton, Ivor D.	Rep.	Mahanoy City
	14	Hoch, Daniel K.	Dem.	Reading
	15	*Gillette, Wilson D.	Rep.	Towanda
	16	*Scanlon, Thomas E.	Dem.	Pittsburgh
	17	*Vacant*		
	18	*Simpson, Richard M.	Rep.	Huntingdon
	19	*Kunkel, John C.	Rep.	Harrisburg
	20	Gavin, Leon H.	Rep.	Oil City
	21	*Walter, Francis E.	Dem.	Easton
	22	Gross, Chester H.	Rep.	Manchester
	23	Brumbaugh, D. Emmert	Rep.	Claysburg
	24	*Snyder, J. Buell	Dem.	Perryopolis
	25	Furlong, Grant	Dem.	Donora
	26	*Graham, Louis E.	Rep.	Beaver
	27	*Tibbott, Harve	Rep.	Ebensburg
	28	*Kelley, Augustine B.	Dem.	Greensburg
	29	*Rodgers, Robert L.	Rep.	Erie
	30	*Weiss, Samuel A.	Dem.	Glassport
	31	*Eberharter, Herman P.	Dem.	Pittsburgh
	32	*Wright, James A.	Dem.	Pittsburgh
R.I.	1	*Forand, Aime J.	Dem.	Cumberland
	2	*Fogarty, John E.	Dem.	Harmony
S.C.	1	*Rivers, L. Mendel	Dem.	North Charleston
	2	*Fulmer, Hampton P.	Dem.	Orangeburg
	3	*Hare, Butler B.	Dem.	Saluda
	4	*Bryson, Joseph R.	Dem.	Greenville
	5	*Richards, James P.	Dem.	Lancaster
	6	*McMillan, John L.	Dem.	Florence
S.D.	1	*Mundt, Karl E.	Rep.	Madison
	2	*Case, Francis	Rep.	Custer
Tenn.	1	*Reece, B. Carroll	Rep.	Johnson City
	2	*Jennings, John, Jr.	Rep.	Knoxville
Tenn.	3	*Kefauver, Estes	Dem.	Chattanooga
	4	*Gore, Albert	Dem.	Carthage
	5	McCord, Jim	Dem.	Lewisburg
	6	*Priest, J. Percy	Dem.	Nashville
	7	*Courtney, Wirt	Dem.	Franklin
	8	Murray, Tom	Dem.	Jackson
	9	*Cooper, Jere	Dem.	Dyersburg
	10	*Davis, Clifford	Dem.	Memphis
Tex.	1	*Patman, Wright	Dem.	Texarkana
	2	Dies, Martin	Dem.	Orange
	3	*Beckworth, Lindley	Dem.	Gilmer
	4	*Rayburn, Sam	Dem.	Bonham
	5	Sumners, Hatton W.	Dem.	Dallas
	6	*Johnson, Luther A.	Dem.	Corsicana
	7	*Patton, Nat	Dem.	Crockett
	8	*Thomas, Albert	Dem.	Houston
	9	*Mansfield, Joseph J.	Dem.	Columbus
	10	*Johnson, Lyndon B.	Dem.	Johnson City
	11	*Poage, William R.	Dem.	Waco
	12	*Lanham, Fritz G.	Dem.	Fort Worth
	13	*Gossett, Ed.	Dem.	Wichita Falls
	14	*Kleberg, Richard M.	Dem.	Corpus Christi
	15	*West, Milton H.	Dem.	Brownsville
	16	*Thomason, R. Ewing	Dem.	El Paso
	17	Russell, Sam M.	Dem.	Stephenville
	18	*Worley, Eugene	Dem.	Shamrock
	19	*Mahon, George H.	Dem.	Colorado City
	20	*Kilday, Paul J.	Dem.	San Antonio
	21	Fisher, O. C.	Dem.	San Angelo
Utah	1	*Granger, Walter K.	Dem.	Cedar City
	2	*Robinson, J. Will	Dem.	Provo
Vt.		*Plumley, Charles A.	Rep.	Northfield
Va.	1	*Bland, Schuyler O.	Dem.	Newport News
	2	*Harris, Winder R.	Dem.	Norfolk
	3	*Satterfield, Dave E., Jr.	Dem.	Richmond
	4	*Drewry, Patrick H.	Dem.	Petersburg
	5	*Burch, Thomas G.	Dem.	Martinsville
	6	*Woodrum, Clifton A.	Dem.	Roanoke
	7	*Robertson, A. Willis	Dem.	Lexington
	8	*Smith, Howard W.	Dem.	Alexandria
	9	*Flannagan, John W., Jr.	Dem.	Bristol
Wash.	1	*Magnuson, Warren G.	Dem.	Seattle
	2	*Jackson, Henry M.	Dem.	Everett
	3	Norman, Fred	Rep.	Raymond
	4	Holmes, Hal	Rep.	Ellensburg
	5	Horan, Walter F.	Rep.	Wenatchee
	6	*Coffee, John M.	Dem.	Tacoma
W.Va.	1	Schiffler, Andrew C.	Rep.	Wheeling
	2	*Randolph, Jennings	Dem.	Elkins
	3	Rohrbough, Edward G.	Rep.	Glenville
	4	Ellis, Hubert S.	Rep.	Huntington
	5	*Kee, John	Dem.	Bluefield
	6	*Smith, Joe L.	Dem.	Beckley
Wis.	1	*Smith, Lawrence H.	Rep.	Racine
	2	Sauthoff, Harry	Pro.	Madison
	3	*Stevenson, William H.	Rep.	La Crosse
	4	*Wasielewski, Thad F.	Dem.	Milwaukee
	5	McMurray, Howard J.	Dem.	Milwaukee
	6	*Keefe, Frank B.	Rep.	Oshkosh
	7	*Murray, Reid F.	Rep.	Ogdensburg
	8	Dilweg, La Vern R.	Dem.	Green Bay
	9	*Hull, Merlin	Pro.	Black River Falls
	10	O'Konski, Alvin E.	Rep.	Mercer
Wyo.		Barrett, Frank A.	Rep.	Lusk

Congress of Industrial Organizations.

During 1943, C.I.O.'s membership totalled 5,600,000. Through the activities of various C.I.O. affiliates and about 3,500 labour management committees new plans were adopted which increased war production. This won for hundreds of C.I.O. plants and thousands of C.I.O. members official recognition for their contributions to increased output. The C.I.O. raised more than $22,000,000 for war relief; more than 2,000 C.I.O. members were active on governing boards of community social agencies.

The wave of anti-labour legislation, climaxed by the Smith-Connally bill, also prohibiting political contributions by unions, resulted in an increase in C.I.O. political action. In addition to political pressure for price control, anti-poll tax legislation, the Wagner-Murray-Dingell bill, centralization and co-ordination of war planning, and a progressive tax program, the C.I.O. established a Committee on Political Action. Its purpose was to achieve united action in the political field with all organized labour.

The C.I.O. planned to attend the World Labor congress in London during June 1944.

In 1943, Philip Murray was re-elected C.I.O. president, and James B. Carey secretary-treasurer. (*See also* AMERICAN FEDER-

ATION OF LABOR; LABOUR UNIONS; STRIKES AND LOCK-OUTS; UNITED STATES.) (P. MY.)

Coningham, Sir Arthur

(1895–), British air force officer, was born in Brisbane, Australia, and educated in New Zealand. He joined the New Zealand infantry in 1914 and served for two years in Samoa and Egypt. Transferring to the royal flying corps in 1916, he became one of the outstanding British airmen of World War I, receiving the military cross, the D.S.O. and the D.F.C. His flight from Cairo to Kano in Oct. 1925, won him the air force cross. In 1941 Coningham was knighted as companion of the bath. As Northwest African tactical air force commander, Coningham worked in close co-operation with Gen. Bernard Montgomery in chasing the Afrika Korps out of Libya, 1942–43. Air Marshal Coningham continued to participate in the campaign which drove the axis from Tunisia, serving under Gen. Dwight Eisenhower in the Sicilian campaign during July and August of 1943.

Connecticut.

The next to the smallest of the New England states, Connecticut is one of the thirteen original states, commonly known as the "Nutmeg state," the "Constitution state," or the "Land of Steady Habits"; area, 5,004 sq.mi. (incl. 125 sq.mi. water); population (1940), 1,709,242, or 348.91 persons to the sq.mi.; capital and largest city, Hartford (166,267). Other large cities with 1940 population figures: New Haven (160,605); Bridgeport (147,121); Waterbury (99,314); New Britain (68,685); Stamford (60,996). Hartford and Bridgeport, on account of the great influx of war workers, each claimed populations of 200,000 by 1943.

History.—The state officers during 1943 were all Republicans: governor, Raymond E. Baldwin; lieutenant governor, William E. Hadden; secretary of state, Frances B. Redick; treasurer, Carl Sharpe; comptroller, Fred R. Zeller; attorney general, Francis A. Pallotti. The United States senators were John A. Danaher (Republican), term expiring 1945; Francis T. Maloney (Democrat), term expiring 1947.

During the regular session of the general assembly (Jan. 6 to May 19), there was a Republican majority of 14 in the senate and one of 132 in the house, which enabled the administration to carry out most of its legislative program. Important measures enacted: the governor was empowered to suspend or modify any law which in his opinion conflicted with the war effort; the public works department was abolished and most of its duties transferred to the comptroller; a postwar planning commission was established; the commission on forests and wildlife allotted $400,000 to purchase additional land; maximum payments for workmen's compensation were increased from $25 to $30 per week; the state defense council was replaced by a war council with greater powers.

Local elections in 143 towns in October resulted in a Republican gain of four. In the November local elections, Republicans regained control in Hartford for the first time in ten years, and although Democrats retained control in New Haven and Waterbury, it was with sharply reduced pluralities. Bridgeport remained in the Socialist column. In these elections no federal questions were involved.

Education.—In 1941–42 the 841 elementary schools of the state had 171,612 pupils and 5,205 teachers; the 45 junior high schools had 23,540 pupils and 748 teachers; and the 94 high schools had 74,178 pupils and 3,163 teachers—a total of 980 schools, 269,330 pupils and 9,116 teachers. These were all decreases from the year 1940–41. Total expenditures of the state for education, however, were $30,415,656, an increase of $1,207,900.

Public Welfare, Charities, Correction.—During June 1943,

there were 44,473 persons in the state receiving some kind of public assistance. This was a reduction of 28½% from June 1942. The amount paid to these people in June 1943 was $1,212,720, a reduction of 26.8% from the year before. Public assistance in the categories of agricultural commodities, Civilian Conservation corps and Work Projects administration disappeared entirely; even the number of those receiving old age assistance, 15,632, was a decrease of 11% over 1942. The only category showing an increase was aid to dependent children which, with 6,835 cases, was 11% higher.

As of June 30, 1943, there were 3 state hospitals for the mentally ill, with 7,527 patients, 2 institutions for the feeble-minded, with 2,124 inmates, 2 institutions for 86 blind persons, and 1 institution for 140 deaf persons. The state maintained 15 correctional institutions.

Communication.—For the first 10 months of 1943, there were registered 518,468 motor vehicles, being a reduction of only 7.4% compared with 1942; operators' licenses declined 4.7% to 596,556. As of June 30, 1943, the state aid and trunk line highway system totalled 2,918 mi., of which 786 were concrete and 2,132 other kinds of improved roads. New highway construction was practically nil. In February the new New London-Groton bridge on U.S. highway No. 1 was opened for traffic. The state was served by 3 railroad companies with mileage of 875; 47 bus companies, and 114 taxicab companies. As of June 30, 1943, there were 468,177 telephone outlets.

Banking and Finance.—On Sept. 30, 1943, deposits in 72 savings banks were $859,483,124, an increase of $71,000,000 over 1942; the assets of 64 state banks and trust companies were $636,336,321, an increase of $133,000,000; the assets of 51 (a decrease of 1) national banks, on June 30, 1943, were $641,-948,000, an increase of $161,000,000. There were 34 building and loan associations.

Total cash receipts of the state for the year ending June 30, 1943, were $103,097,008; disbursements were only $73,636,299. The budget adopted by the general assembly for the biennium 1943–45 was $118,430,421. The total of all state bonds outstanding July 1, 1943, was $26,507,000, against which a retirement fund of $15,741,189 had been set up, making a net state debt of $10,765,811.

Agriculture.—While Connecticut is not primarily an agricultural state, the cash farm income for 1942 was reported by the department of agriculture as $75,075,000, an increase of almost $10,000,000 over 1941. Livestock and livestock products, as usual, accounted for over half the total, the balance being made up by crops, which, in order of importance, were tobacco, truck crops, potatoes and apples.

Table I.—*Leading Agricultural Products of Connecticut, 1943 and 1942*

Crop	1943 (est.)	1942
Tobacco, lb.	18,640,000	18,577,000
Potatoes, bu.	3,536,000	2,942,000
Corn, bu.	2,050,000	2,058,000
Apples, bu.	858,000	1,992,000

Manufacturing.—The index of business activity in the state rose in April 1943 to 227.2 (monthly average in 1939=100), the highest point ever attained. In June it had declined to 219.7. Several areas in the state were declared "labour shortage areas" by the War Manpower commission, with the result that contracts which would have been awarded to Connecticut were allocated elsewhere. In 1943 there were 3,688 manufacturing plants in the state employing 544,611 persons, of which 349,435 were men and 195,176 women. Production figures were undisclosed, but Connecticut received nearly 4% of all federal war contracts awarded between June 1940 and June 1943.

Mineral Production.—The state's production of minerals is very small; for many years the cost of mining iron and copper has been prohibitive. Search for strategic materials disclosed mica deposits, which were being worked, and in 1943 a deposit of the rare element beryllium was discovered.   (J. BR.)

Conscientious Objectors: see FRIENDS, RELIGIOUS SOCIETY OF; PACIFISM.
Conscription: see SELECTIVE SERVICE, U.S.
Conservation, Soil: see SOIL EROSION AND SOIL CONSERVATION.

Conservative Party, Great Britain.

eral Reserve board of Regulation W, which prescribed minimum down-payments and maximum payment-periods for instalment sales and loan contracts. The liquidation was gradual at first, but it was accelerated in 1942, first by the stoppage of production of consumers' durable goods that had been sold largely on credit terms and then by the tightening of the instalment credit requirements of the regulation and the broadening of its scope to cover instalment sales of additional goods, charge-accounts and single-payment loans.

Throughout the past year sales of consumers' durable goods have remained relatively constant and there has been no significant tightening of credit terms under Regulation W. Hence the slowing down of the rate of liquidation. But even if credit terms were further restricted the resulting decline in outstandings would be small. By the close of 1943, the outstanding amount of consumer credit had been reduced to about 45% of its prewar level of $10,000,000,000. As the solid core is approached further liquidation will be more and more difficult. It seems probable, therefore, that the liquidation of consumer credit which has contributed during the last two years a significant anti-inflationary force will come to an end early in 1944. The pattern of liquidation is indicated by the following figures:

| | Average Monthly Liquidation (Adjusted for seasonal) | |
	Million dollars	Per cent of outstandings
Last quarter of 1941	120	1.2
First half of 1942	320	3.8
Second half of 1942	245	3.5
	180	3.1
	100*	2.3

IMPORTANT

THIS SHIPMENT CONTAINS A VERY VALUABLE WORK— VOLUMES 13-24 OF A 24 VOLUME SET OF THE ENCYCLOPAEDIA BRITANNICA

VOLUMES 1-12 ARE CONTAINED IN SEPARATE CARTON.

EVERY PRECAUTION HAS BEEN TAKEN TO HAVE THESE BOOKS REACH YOU IN PERFECT CONDITION. SHOULD YOU HAVE OCCASION TO REPORT DAMAGE OR DEFECTS BE SURE TO RETURN THIS IDENTIFICATION SLIP.

C. S. 11

Job Number 66432
Gathered by 6013
Packed by 6022
Nailed by 3233

disappearance of consumer credit as the Office of Price Administration developed a plan of instalment selling for postwar to divert purchasing power from create a backlog of prepaid orders for produce an orderly postwar market for goods that have disappeared for the duration by determining the order of priority to these goods when they again become available. The plan was opposed by the treasury department on the ground that postwar delivery sales would interfere with sales of bonds and by the National Automobile Dealers' association around that it would extend government control into the postwar period. Nevertheless, a number of enterprises put into effect somewhat similar plans for the sale of household electrical appliances, motion picture theatre equipment, printing presses and similar goods.

The year witnessed the beginnings of what is likely to become an increasingly heated debate on the desirability of continuing federal control of consumer credit into the postwar period. One group of instalment sellers who use liberal credit terms as a is organized to attack Regulation W as an inequitable restraint on freedom of contract. On the other hand, a number of other merchants, notably department store officials, drew attention to the beneficial effects of federal regulation both and called to the necessity of restraining demand for consumers' durable goods immediately following the war and urged the continuation of the Federal Reserve board's controls.

In the field of state legislation to correct social evils in consumer credit granting, some progress was made during the year. Three additional states—Idaho, Nevada and Colorado—enacted

Consumer Credit. which had been in progress since Sept. 1941, continued through 1943, but the rate of liquidation declined.

The downward trend began with the promulgation by the Fed-

statutes based upon the Uniform Small Loan law, and Ohio and Nebraska replaced out-moded regulatory statutes with modern ones based upon the model law. Publication by the Russell Sage foundation of a tentative draft of a model law to authorize and to regulate the making of personal instalment loans by banks led to a vigorous debate in banking circles on the merits of a provision requiring banks to state and to compute their personal-loan charges in simple interest. Although banks in some states violently opposed this requirement, the state bankers' association and state banking department in Nebraska supported a bill based upon the foundation's recommendation, which became law.

(R. Nt.)

Contract Bridge.
The only changes in contract bridge during 1943 were in the Official Laws. These were revised for the first time since 1935 by a committee representing the foremost American bridge bodies, namely, the Whist Club of New York and the National Laws Commission of the American Contract Bridge league. No sweeping or significant changes were promulgated—none that would affect standard techniques of bidding or play. A bonus of 50 points was authorized for fulfilling a doubled or redoubled contract (irrespective of vulnerability), but aside from this the new code was aimed largely at clearer and more equitable definition of law violation and penalties therefor.

Despite the war, tournament bridge continued to flourish. The results in the three most important American tournaments during 1943 were as follows:

Eastern States Tournament.—Open Pairs: won by A. Goldstein and Jules Tilles, New York city; Open Teams-of-Four: won by Mrs. A. M. Sobel, Howard Schenken, Peter Leventritt, New York city, and Charles H. Goren and Sidney Silodor, Philadelphia; Women's Pairs: won by M . A. M. Sobel and Miss Ruth Sherman, New York city; Mixed Pairs: won by Mrs. A. M. Sobel and Edward Hymes, Jr., New York city; Nonmaster Pairs: won by Louis Kelner and Pvt. Martin J. Dupraw, New York city.

Summer National Tournament.—Masters' Pair Championship: won by Howard Schenken, New York city, and John R. Crawford, Philadelphia; Masters' Team-of-Four Championship: won by Howard Schenken and Edward Hymes, Jr., New York city, and Sidney Silodor, Charles H. Goren and John R. Crawford, Philadelphia; National Men's Pair Championship: won by Charles Solomon and Charles H. Goren, Philadelphia; National Women's Pair Championship: won by Mrs. Mae Rosen and Mrs. E. J. Seligman, New York city; Mixed Team-of-Four Championship: won by Mrs. A. M. Sobel, New York city, and Mrs. Olive Peterson, Charles H. Goren and Sidney Silodor, Philadelphia; Nonmasters' Pairs Championship: won by A. J. Mill and Robert S. Tyson, New York city; Amateur Team-of-Four Championship: won by Mrs. A. P. Hess, Mrs. Ruth Rice, Fred Slater and Harold Frankenheimer, New York city.

Winter National Tournament.—Open Pairs: won by Mrs. E. J. Seligman and Mrs. Ruth Chase Goldberg, New York city; Women's Team-of-Four: won by Mrs. R. C. Young, Bywood, Pa., Mrs. J. E. Folline, Richmond, Mrs. Wilkinson Wagar, Atlanta, and Mrs. A. M. Sobel, New York city; Mixed Pairs: won by Mrs. Olive Peterson and Charles H. Goren, Philadelphia; Open Teams-of-Four: won by Mrs. A. M. Sobel and B. J. Becker, New York city, Sidney Silodor and Charles H. Goren, Philadelphia; Amateur Pairs: won by Herbert Stein, Hempstead, N.Y., and Dr. Maxwell Mitchell, Baldwin, N.Y. (E. Cul.)

Contract Renegotiation: *see* Business Review.
Controlled Materials Plan: *see* Priorities and Alloca-

tions; War Production, U.S.
Convoys: *see* Submarine Warfare.
Coordinator of Inter-American Affairs: *see* Inter-American Affairs, Office of the Coordinator of.

Copper.
No production figures were received for 1942 except for the United States, so no column for that year could be added to the world production table.

Table I.—World Production of Copper
(In thousands of metric tons)

	1937	1938	1939	1940	1941
Belgian Congo . .	150.6	124.0	121.5	148.6	165
Canada	238.1	263.3	281.5	281	?
Chile	412.9	351.4	339.2	352.4	453.6
Japan	75.9	77.0	77.0	113	?
Mexico	46.8	41.4	48.8	40.9	51.6
Peru	35.7	37.5	35.4	36.4	37.7
Rhodesia	212.7	215.3	216.0	231.3	?
U. S. S. R. . . .	92.5	114.5	144.0	151	?
United States . .	757.4	505.0	666.8	824.7	876.4
World Total . .	2,271.6	1,984.1	2,161.5	2,346.3	2,550
Ex. U. S. . . .	1,514.2	1,479.1	1,494.7	1,521.6	1,674

In the United States mine production increased from 958,149 short tons of recoverable metal in 1941 to 1,072,003 tons in 1942, an increase of 12% and a new record high. The leading producing states, Arizona, Utah, Montana, New Mexico and Nevada, furnished most of the increase, and such small declines as there were were confined to the minor producing areas. Table II shows the distribution of the production by states.

Table II.—Mine Production of Copper in the United States
(Thousands of short tons)

	1936	1937	1938	1939	1940	1941	1942
Alaska	18.9	17.3	14.5	0.1	0.1	—0.1	—0.1
Arizona	211.3	288.5	210.8	262.1	281.2	326.3	390.5
California . . .	4.4	5.3	0.8	4.2	6.4	3.9	0.9
Colorado . . .	8.9	10.9	14.2	13.2	12.2	6.7	1.2
Idaho	1.5	2.2	2.1	2.5	3.3	3.6	3.6
Michigan . . .	48.0	47.5	46.7	44.0	45.2	46.4	45.5
Montana . . .	109.5	144.5	77.2	97.8	126.4	128.0	139.5
Nevada	70.7	74.6	46.2	66.6	78.5	78.9	80.7
New Mexico . .	3.2	32.1	20.4	46.1	69.8	73.5	79.4
Utah	126.2	206.0	108.1	171.9	231.9	266.8	307.1
Washington . .	0.1	0.1	6.0	9.0	9.6	8.7	8.1
Others	13.2	13.0	10.8	10.8	13.5	14.9	15.6
Total . . .	614.5	842.0	557.8	728.3	878.1	958.1	1 072.0

Table III shows a statement of estimated copper supply in 1942 and 1943 made public about midyear of 1943, the figures being short tons.

Table III.—Estimated Copper Supply in U.S.
(Short tons)

	1942	1943
Domestic primary	1,098,007	1,200,000
secondary	54,337	70,000
Total	1,152,344	1,270,000
Imports	667,636	680,000
Brass mill scrap	435,000	483,000
Other scrap	612,000	645,000
Total supply	2,866,980	3,078,000

The following data were released from censorship late in Dec. 1943, covering operations during the past three years, in short tons:

	Smelter Output	Refinery Output	Consumption
1941	1,016,996	1,065,667	1,557,765
1942	1,152,344	1,135,708	1,517,983
1943, 11 mo.	1,095,956	1,102,227	1,579,427
1943, rate for year	1,195,584	1,202,430	1,723,008

The first and second columns cover domestic output only, while the third includes imported copper. It would appear from these

REMOVING ORE from an open-pit copper mine in Chile

figures that the performance during the year checks quite closely with that anticipated, as shown in the preceding estimate.

According to reports issued by the War Production board the output of brass-mill products increased from 1,201,491 tons in the first half of 1942 to 1,410,444 tons in the first half of 1943. Another announcement stated that since the Copper Recovery corporation had substantially completed the work for which it had been established, namely the recovery of idle and excess inventory stocks for use in the war program, it would be disbanded at the end of the year.

Late in 1943 it was reported that the supply position in the United States had been considerably improved, and that demand was approximately balanced by supply.

No reports whatever were received on production in 1943 in countries outside of the United States, and reports covering 1942 were scanty. A press report gave the 1942 output of Canada as 270,000 short tons, which is lower than had been expected. Belgian Congo was credited with 168,000 metric tons, a moderate increase over 1941. Exports from Peru were 35,139 tons in 1942, against 35,325 tons in 1941. Publication of output was discontinued in Chile, but the rate in the first quarter of 1942 was somewhat ahead of that for 1941.

A combined copper committee for the United States, United Kingdom and Canada was established in Feb. 1943. The object of this committee, as stated in the official announcement of the appointments, was to take over "the primary responsibility for assembling and reviewing data relating to supply requirements, inventory and consumption of copper in order that the copper supply available to the three countries may be utilized to the best advantage in war production." The formation of the committee followed an investigation which showed that there was need for more comprehensive and better-integrated information on the respective programs involving the use of copper, and the require-

ments and supplies available to meet them.

It is interesting to note that the figures presented above for the copper supply of the United States in 1942, a total of 2,866,980 short tons, including secondary copper, was about 2% larger than the estimated figure for world production of new copper in 1941. If we may assume that the same condition would hold true for the succeeding years, we have a basis for an estimate of world production in 1942 at about 3,000,000 short tons, or 2,720,000 metric tons; this may prove not to be well founded, but it is the first data to become available as a basis for such an estimate. (*See* also BUSINESS REVIEW; MINERAL AND METAL PRODUCTION AND PRICES; STRATEGIC MINERAL SUPPLIES.)   (G. A. RO.)

Copra: *see* COCO-NUTS.

Copyright. During the year 1943 no new copyright legislation was enacted although several amendatory bills were introduced in congress. The main proposals were a revival of efforts to amend the Copyright Act of 1909 to encompass transcriptions and recordings of every character, involving commercial public performance. Because of the exigency of other matters, however, no action was taken by congress in relation to these bills.

From the beginning of 1943 there was a steady falling off in the number of copyright registrations, amounting to 11.7%, particularly in relation to foreign works published abroad, with a resulting decline in gross receipts. This general decrease was noticeable in registrations for all classes of works but was least felt in the class of musical compositions.

The copyright law in force requires, as one of the conditions precedent to the registration of a claim to copyright in any work, the deposit of two copies of American books and one copy of foreign books, for the enrichment of the Library of Congress. During the fiscal year 1943, 252,123 books and other articles were deposited for copyright registration, including 17,316 printed volumes, 55,116 pamphlets and leaflets, 85,990 periodicals, 4,190 dramas, 57,343 pieces of music, 1,462 maps, 1,655 photographs, 15,329 prints, labels and pictorial illustrations, 3,484 motion pictures and 5,368 works of art and drawings. These were all produced in the United States. From abroad there were received 156 books in foreign languages and 517 books in English. Of this great collection of copyrighted works, 161,281 were transferred to the permanent collections of the Library of Congress; 1,653 were sent to other governmental libraries and 3,392 were returned to the claimants of copyright.

(C. L. B.)

Corn (MAIZE). A second record crop of corn was harvested in 1943 as estimated by the United States department of agriculture at 3,077,159,000 bu. This is about 55,000,000 bu. below the all-time record crop of 1942 of 3,131,518,000 bu., but it is 727,000,000 above the 10-year average 1932–41 of 2,349,276,000 bu. The acreage in 1943 was about 6% above 1942, 94,267,000 acres compared to 89,484,000 but less than the 10-year average of 94,511,000 acres. The average yield in 1943 was 32.7 bu. compared to 35.5 bu. in 1942 and a 24.9 bu. average in 1932–41. The favourable returns were due to good weather in the fall which permitted the late planted grain to reach maturity. More than half of the corn acreage grown in 1943 was grown from hybrid seed. In most of the corn belt states more than 90% was grown from hybrid seed, and it was gaining rapidly in surrounding areas. The acreage harvested for grain was the largest after 1933, yet the percentage of the crop harvested was smaller than either 1941 or 1942. The use of mechanical pickers was widespread.

U.S. Corn Production by States, 1943 and 1942

State	1943 bu.	1942 bu.	State	1943 bu.	1942 bu.
Iowa	640,740,000	574,080,000	Louisiana	23,018,000	24,412,000
Illinois	426,600,000	416,934,000	South Carolina	24,720,000	21,330,000
Nebraska	216,632,000	242,708,000	Colorado	14,430,000	18,228,000
Indiana	210,406,000	216,702,000	Maryland	11,804,000	16,344,000
Minnesota	215,468,000	207,190,000	West Virginia	14,042,000	13,770,000
Ohio	174,042,000	185,752,000	New Jersey	6,086,000	8,370,000
Missouri	139,810,000	146,899,000	Florida	8,151,000	7,413,000
Wisconsin	108,924,000	103,544,000	Delaware	3,225,000	4,092,000
South Dakota	79,718,000	101,673,000	Montana	3,230,000	3,800,000
Kansas	84,318,000	90,063,000	New Mexico	2,930,000	3,792,000
Kentucky	75,350,000	82,200,000	Vermont	2,432,000	2,800,000
Texas	88,416,000	78,561,000	California	2,516,000	2,574,000
Tennessee	65,964,000	75,924,000	Idaho	1,683,000	2,444,000
Michigan	52,904,000	69,703,000	Connecticut	1,920,000	2,058,000
Pennsylvania	49,172,000	54,567,000	Wyoming	1,243,000	2,013,000
Mississippi	43,508,000	49,198,000	Massachusetts	1,722,000	1,804,000
North Carolina	51,018,000	47,068,000	Oregon	1,862,000	1,742,000
Alabama	48,510,000	43,960,000	Washington	1,457,000	1,353,000
Georgia	45,288,000	39,160,000	Utah	882,000	792,000
Arkansas	25,262,000	37,116,000	Maine	640,000	672,000
Oklahoma	23,350,000	35,631,000	New Hampshire	615,000	630,000
Virginia	33,275,000	35,586,000	Arizona	402,000	396,000
North Dakota	25,335,000	28,425,000	Rhode Island	304,000	328,000
New York	22,715,000	27,600,000	Nevada	120,000	120,000

The great need for feed for the large number of livestock on farms led the War Food administration to suggest for 1944 a 100,000,000 acreage for corn. The largest increases were suggested for the northwestern region where feed must be shipped in and where it was very short in 1943 and caused much livestock to be moved to market early. Increased acreage was also asked for in the north central region where corn usually yields more feed units per acre than any other feed grain. Corn usually furnishes two and a half times as much grain for livestock as do oats, barley and grain sorghums combined. It was expected that the additional fertilizer required would be available.

Corn prices advanced during 1943 but because of the greater returns received from corn by feeding it to hogs than selling it at ceiling prices, relatively little corn was moved from farms, causing shortages in processing and feed-mixing plants and in areas where corn is usually purchased. Special efforts were made to move corn to the deficit areas by the War Food administration by purchasing corn in July and August and assuring sellers that they would receive any rise in price before October 31. These purchases were sold to processing plants and livestock feeders. The average price of corn was about $1.09 per bu. in the fall of 1943 compared to a 5-year average of 83 cents per bu. in 1935–39. At the same time hogs were about 14 cents per lb. compared to 8.38 cents per lb. in the 5-year prewar period.

(J. C. Ms.)

Cornell University.

An institution of higher learning, nonsectarian and co-educational, at Ithaca, N. Y., founded in 1865 and incorporated as a land-grant college under the Morrill act of 1862. The university comprises the endowed schools and colleges of arts and sciences, engineering, architecture, law, medicine and nursing and the state-supported colleges of agriculture, home economics and veterinary medicine. The divisions of medicine and nursing are in New York city and are operated in conjunction with the New York Hospital. Two experiment stations, at Geneva and Farmingdale, N. Y., are operated in connection with the college of agriculture. Degrees for advanced study other than professional are awarded through a graduate school.

The foremost development in organization during 1943 was the affiliation of the New York Hospital school of nursing as an integral part of the university, offering the degree of bachelor of science in nursing. Special wartime developments were the assignment of large contingents of army personnel to the campus and great expansion of the naval training school, the government-sponsored war research program, and war training courses offered in co-operation with the U.S. office of education. For statistics of the faculty, student enrolment, library, endowment, etc., see UNIVERSITIES AND COLLEGES. President, Edmund Ezra Day, Ph.D., LL.D.

(E. E. D.)

Cornhusking.

With farmers busy with the harvest and many of the contenders in the armed forces, no national and but few state championships were held in cornhusking during 1943. It marked the second straight year in which the national meet was postponed. Floyd Wise of Prairie Center, Ill., in 1943 a member of the U.S. armed forces, continued to be regarded the country's champion cornhusker, having won the last national event in 1941.

(M. P. W.)

Corundum: see ABRASIVES.
Cosmetics: see SOAP, PERFUMERY AND COSMETICS.
Cosmic Rays: see PHYSICS.

Costa Rica.

A Central American republic, north of Panamá and south of Nicaragua. Area: 23,000 sq.mi.; pop. (1940 est.) 656,129. The population is predominantly white (approximately 80%); an estimated 3% are Negroes, living in the Caribbean coastal area. The bulk of the population lives on the Meseta Central, or central plateau area. Capital: San José (68,465); other cities are Heredia (9,610); Alajuela (9,232); Limón (9,129); Puntarenas (7,722); Cartago (8,786). Language: Spanish. President in 1943: Dr. Rafael Angel Calderón Guardia.

History.—Costa Rican co-operation in the United Nations war effort was continued during 1943, the most significant single development being the arrangement in March of an agreement by which the United States was given a 25-year lease on 10,000 ac. of land for the production of cinchona. The United States also planned to purchase all suitable balsa wood that Costa Rica could produce, with a formal agreement pending signature in October.

Certain constitutional guarantees remained suspended, as in 1942. Much interest developed during the year in political alignments being made in prospect of the presidential election due in 1944. Leading candidates were a former president, León Cortez, and Teodoro Picado, the latter the present choice of the National Republican party (now in power) and also backed by the Vanguardia Popular, the former Communist party. Electoral reforms proposed in the spring raised objection on the ground that one candidate would be favoured, and by June the proposed laws were withdrawn. In the same month Archbishop Sanbria announced that Catholic workers could hold membership in the former Communist party, but not in fascist or nazi organizations.

A new labour code introduced in April was opposed by conservatives, but was passed by the legislature in November.

Serious advances in prices in the early months of the year resulted in a drastic decree designed to curb profiteering; for profit-taking of over 20% penalties ranged up to six months in prison. Shortages in many items were noted. In the latter half of the year conditions improved, and by September price levels had dropped slightly. Private automobiles were allowed three gallons of gas in May where none had been allowed in April.

Both Mexico and the United States raised the rank of their official representative from minister to ambassador.

Education.—In 1942 Costa Rica had 697 schools, with an estimated attendance of 73,320. Private schools numbered 61, with 3,889 students. The literacy rate (76%) is the best in Central America.

Finance.—The monetary unit is the gold colón, valued at 17.7 cents U.S. in 1943. It has been withdrawn from ordinary circulation. The 1943 budget was balanced at 44,454,839 colones, but a deficit was expected for the year. The public debt (Dec. 31, 1941) was 149,195,010 colones (105,175,023 external; 44,019,987 internal). Notes in circulation (1941) totalled 66,900,000 colones.

Trade and Communication.—No 1943 figures on trade were available; in 1941 imports were valued at $17,754,186; exports, $10,053,257. The favourable trade balance with the United States for 9 months of 1943 was $143,000. Costa Rica has some 450 mi. of railway, and about 300 mi. of roads.

Agriculture.—The coffee crop for the year 1942–43 was estimated at 57,485,960 lb. Cocoa exports (1942) amounted to 12,176,178 lb., banana exports (1942) to 2,144,400 stems, sugar production (1942) to 23,000 short tons.

BIBLIOGRAPHY.—Dana G. Munro, *The Five Republics of Central America* (1918); Chester Lloyd Jones, *The Caribbean since 1900* (1936); *The Inter-American Monthly* (Washington); *The Foreign Commerce Weekly* (Washington). (D. Rd.)

Cost of Living: *see* BUSINESS REVIEW.

Cotton.

Cotton Manufacture.—All the demands for cottons for military use were met promptly. The main problem facing the industry in the U.S. was that of meeting demands for essential civilian requirements, and also for lend-lease and rehabilitation.

The year 1944 loomed large as possibly the strategic year in the determination of future trends in the cotton industry. Some time or other the sellers' market was expected to give way to a buyers' market. In 1943, the prospect of demand for lend-lease and rehabilitation, the possible void existing in some households, although this is exaggerated, and the reclothing of returned service men, were all on the bullish side. On the other hand, the fact that a very much higher production level was built up than existed before World War II, coupled with possible buyer resistance as the tax burden became more and more acute, indicated that the continued activity was not likely to be maintained indefinitely. The turn in demand could easily come during 1944, or shortly thereafter. For that reason, the industry became more and more impressed with the need for research: particularly research of a type which would enable manufacturers to make a profit no matter what the future course of demand might be, nor what happened to the various raw materials. On the latter point, there was a growing feeling that the so-called "battle of the fibres" had developed to a point where it was not a battle at all but rather a question of which fibres best served to produce a specific end-product. Those were the fibres which would eventually win out, and consequently that was why research—both technical research and product research—was so important in 1943. (*See* also LINEN AND FLAX; RAYON AND OTHER SYNTHETIC FIBRES; TEXTILE INDUSTRY; WOOL.) (D. G. Wo.)

Cotton Production.—The 1943 cotton crop of the United States was estimated by the United States department of agriculture in December at 11,478,000 bales of 500 lb. gross weight. This compared with a crop of 12,817,000 bales produced in 1942 and a 10-year average of 12,474,000 for 1932–41. The acreage in 1943 was 21,874,000 acres compared to 22,602,000 acres in 1942 and 27,718,000 acres average for the 10 years 1932–41. The relatively high yield per acre in 1943 of 252 lb. was only 20 lb. below the record high yield of 1942 but was 35 lb. above the average and was exceeded in only two other years of record. The acreage, on the contrary, was the smallest of any year since 1900.

The production of American Egyptian cotton was estimated at 68,300 bales compared to 75,300 bales produced in 1942. The production of Sea Island cotton was estimated at only 300 bales compared to 800 bales in 1942. The production of cottonseed from the 1943 crop was forecast at 5,116,000 tons, compared to 5,717,000 tons in 1942 and 5,549,000 tons on the 10-year

average. This production is computed by taking 65 lb. seed for each 35 lb. net of lint. Most of the cottonseed goes to oil-mills for crushing to secure the vegetable oil. From the 5,717,000 tons of seed produced in 1942, 4,514,728 tons were delivered to mills for crushing, according to the bureau of the census.

U.S. Production of Cotton by States, 1943 and 1942

State	1943 bales	1942 bales
Texas	2,860,000	3,038,000
Mississippi	1,840,000	1,968,000
Arkansas	1,110,000	1,485,000
Alabama	955,000	925,000
Georgia	850,000	855,000
North Carolina	595,000	727,000
Oklahoma	385,000	708,000
South Carolina	695,000	699,000
Tennessee	490,000	625,000
Louisiana	735,000	593,000
California	360,000	402,000
Missouri	295,000	417,000
New Mexico	111,000	111,000
Virginia	25,000	34,000
Florida	17,000	16,000
All others	16,000	21,000

World Cotton Production.—Total world production of cotton, United States and foreign, reached a high record of 36,745,000 bales in 1937 and then began to decline. The total for 1942 was 26,483,000 bales, which is about the average since the year 1924. Foreign production increased during the first full war year 1940 to 16,289,000 bales and then began to decline, being only 13,850,000 bales in 1942 and probably the crop for 1943 would show a small increase, if any. At the same time the world carryover of foreign cotton increased from 7,501,000 bales, or a 5.2 months' supply in 1939 to 12,445,000 bales in 1943 or about a 12 months' supply. This represented 52% of the world's carryover cotton in 1943 compared to only 35% in 1939.

Consumption of foreign-grown cotton was about 17,258,000 bales in 1938–39 but declined steadily thereafter to 12,700,000 bales in 1942–43, a reduction of 28% in four years. At the same time the consumption of American cotton declined only slightly from 12,876,000 bales in 1939 to 12,140,000 bales in 1942. Mill consumption increased in the United States during this period from 7,784,000 bales in 1939 to 11,100,000 in 1942. The labour situation in cotton mills threatened to bring about a decline in spinning late in 1943. With total world carryover of cotton at the high level of 23,900,000 bales and production being maintained the outlook was for an abundant supply when peace comes.

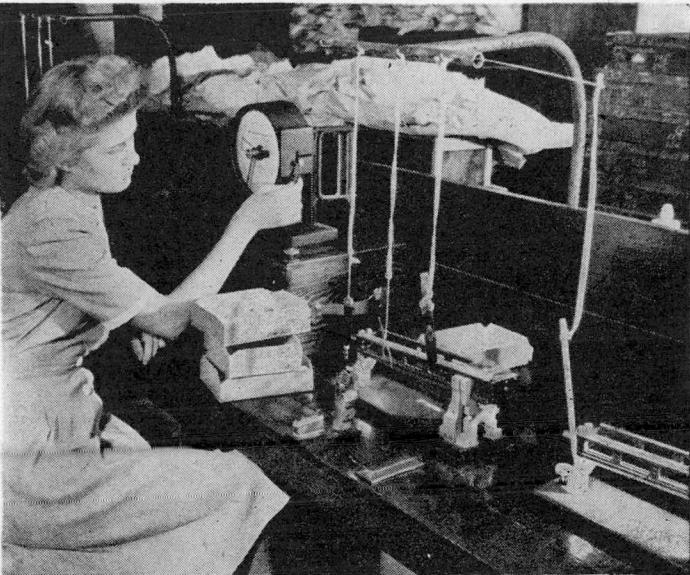

TESTING THE BREAKING STRENGTH of cotton fibres at a U.S. department of agriculture laboratory, Stoneville, Miss., in 1943

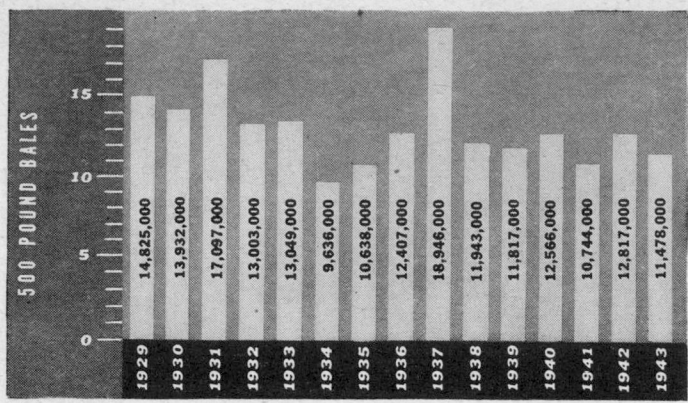

COTTON CROP in the United States. The figure for 1943 is the department of agriculture's estimate of Dec. 1

Foreign cotton being available at lower prices than American cotton was expected to direct consumption to the foreign stocks. Under the "Steagall amendment" the price of American cotton would continue to be supported for two years after World War II by means of a loan amounting to 90% of parity. While growers were receiving the highest prices in many years (20.20 cents in September, the highest since 1928), the total income to cotton growers was estimated to be about $1,301,000,000 for 1943. In 1942 this total was put at $1,426,000,000, the highest after 1929. A shift to the use of foreign-grown cotton was particularly evident in 1942, however. Canada began to use Brazilian cotton which sold delivered in Canada at several cents a pound under U.S. prices until the shipping situation became so tight as to cause a return to the use of U.S. cotton.

Cotton production in foreign countries in 1943 did not reflect an effort toward expansion. Southern Brazil reported a small increase for 1942–43 production, bringing the total for Brazil to about 2,081,000 bales. Egypt forecast for 1943 the lowest production since 1895, or only 708,000 bales. This change was due to the adjustment of Egyptian agriculture to the need for food crops and to avoid further increase in stocks. A record crop for Argentina was reported, but the total was not important, amounting to only about 500,000 bales. Reports from smaller producing countries were almost all toward a decline in production. What Japan was able to accomplish in the far east was unknown. Russia was unable to make important expansion of acreage because of the need for food crops.   (J. C. Ms.)

Cottonseed Oil: *see* Vegetable Oils and Animal Fats.
Countries of the World, Areas and Populations of the: *see* Areas and Populations of the Countries of the World.
Credit, Consumer: *see* Consumer Credit.

Cremonesi, Carlo, Cardinal (1866–1943), Italian ecclesiast, was born Nov. 4 in Rome. He studied at the Roman seminary, taught at the Pontifical college for the Propagation of the Faith for 20 years, and was a prelate of the Holy See, 1910. In 1921, he was named titular archbishop of Nicodemia and subsequently held other important administrative posts in the Holy See. He was papal secret chamberlain under Leo XIII and Pius X and was created cardinal, Dec. 16, 1935. He died on Nov. 25, according to a Vatican city broadcast.

Cricket. By the end of the season 1943 in Great Britain, it was plain that those who favoured the one-day match in the first class county championship, though they might be many in number and insistent of voice, were found but rarely among the members of the respective country clubs, to whose

advice, as expressed by their committees, the Marylebone club turned in this matter. In July the Advisory County Cricket committee met at Lord's, and discussed the feasibility of the two-day match. On that, and on other kindred topics, the Marylebone club were to receive the advice of a sub-committee towards the end of 1943. A minority of the counties favoured the two-day scheme, as suggested by Sussex and Lancashire. The equable solution would seem to rest in one season of experiment at the end of the war.

Interest in the charity matches—chiefly for the Red Cross—at Lord's was greater even than in 1942 and reached its climax in a particularly fine game in early August when an England 11 beat a team from the dominions by 8 runs. The dominions had been set to make 360 to win in 4½ hr. A glorious century by the New Zealander, Lieut. C. S. Dempster, set them on their way; but defeat seemed near when C. B. Clarke, West Indies, joined Flying Officer S. Sismey, Australia. These two, adding 108, narrowly failed to achieve victory.

Oxford just saved the game against a stronger Cambridge team. The Eton v. Harrow match, played at Eton and confined to one day, was spoiled by rain, Harrow making 88 for 3 wickets. Among other matches between young cricketers, "The Rest" played a drawn game with "The Lord's Schools." In this match, very fine form was shown as a batsman by W. H. H. Sutcliffe, son of the noted England and Yorkshire player, Herbert Sutcliffe.

For concentrated excitement, perhaps the best cricket was to be found in the Saturday-afternoon league matches round Birmingham, in Lancashire, in Yorkshire and in North Staffs. In these matches were to be seen many of the cricketers, now serving in His Majesty's forces, whose names were familiar and established in days of peace. Of less technical excellence, but of perhaps more historic interest, were a few matches played between teams of United States troops stationed in England. Everywhere the game flourished, with an enjoyment all the keener for the thought of what might have been lost.

A tribute must be paid to the honoured memory of the world's greatest slow left-hand bowler, Capt. Hedley Verity of Yorkshire, who died of wounds as a prisoner of war in Italy. He was great, both as a man and as a cricketer.   (R. C. R-G.)

Crile, George Washington (1864–1943), U.S. surgeon and scientist, was born Nov. 11 in Chili, Ohio. Early in his career as a surgeon, Dr. Crile developed the nerve-block system of anaesthesia and was believed to have been one of the first doctors to perform a direct blood transfusion. He established the Cleveland clinic in 1921, which was destroyed by fire eight years later. Dr. Crile's works included *The Surgical Treatment of Hypertension* (1938) and *Intelligence Power and Personality* (1941). He died in Cleveland, Jan. 7. (See *Encyclopædia Britannica*.)

Crime. By the midyear point of 1943, the temporary effects of World War II upon crime rates in the United States were becoming more clearly evident. The first year of the war (1942) saw an increase in murder, manslaughter, rape and aggravated assault, and declines in the number of robberies, burglaries, auto thefts and larcenies generally. Thus crimes against the person increased, while crimes against property showed a marked drop. Since crimes against property are many times more numerous than those committed against the person, the net effect of these divergent shifts was to reduce the general crime rate.

The tendencies noted during the first year of the war were extended into the second year—at least so far as June 30, 1943. Comparing the first six months of 1943 with the corresponding period of 1942 (Table I), it is apparent that crimes against property were still declining, while the rise previously noted for murder and manslaughter was offset by a drop in 1943. Hence the general result of the war appears to have been to reduce the

Table I.—*Crimes in 1939-43*
(In 318 U.S. Cities of over 25,000 population)

Offense	Average 1939-1941	1942	January to June	
			1942	1943
Murder and Non-Negligent Manslaughter	2,632	2,673	1,264	1,183
Negligent Manslaughter	1,978	2,003	973	802
Rape	4,286	4,764	2,300	2,673
Robbery	26,965	24,370	12,821	11,836
Aggravated Assault	21,864	23,533	11,042	11,585
Burglary—Breaking or Entering	143,313	124,428	66,933	63,015
Larceny—Theft	388,309	377,105	196,473	160,025
Auto Theft	84,293	79,713	41,068	38,211

number of crimes in most categories, while marking up an increase for rape and aggravated assault.

On the basis of a large sample of crime returns in both urban and rural areas, the estimated total of "reportable offenses" (listed in Table I) for the entire United States in 1942 was 1,436,748. During an average day in that year 31 persons were feloniously killed, 27 were raped and 142 were attacked with a deadly weapon. Robberies averaged 129 per day, burglaries 729 and other thefts 2,416. In addition, 459 automobiles were stolen in the average 24-hour period. The estimated total of these crimes was 6.2 less in 1942 than in 1941.

Such offenses are not evenly distributed with reference to population. On the contrary, the New England, middle Atlantic and north central states consistently show lower crime rates than those for the rest of the country. The first half of 1943 was no exception to this general rule (Table II). As noted by many com-

Table II.—*Regional Distribution of Crime, January to June, 1943*
(Number per 100,000 inhabitants)

Geographic Divisions	Murder and Non-Negligent Manslaughter	Robbery	Aggravated Assault	Burglary—Breaking or Entering	Larceny—Theft	Auto Theft
New England	0.54	7.3	4.9	115.8	235.2	68.6
Middle Atlantic	1.30	9.9	14.5	92.0	182.0	44.2
East North Central	1.82	31.5	20.1	137.9	350.5	65.6
West North Central	1.66	10.4	12.0	113.4	318.5	56.8
South Atlantic	6.64	33.7	77.7	188.2	533.1	98.8
East South Central	8.20	32.5	52.3	201.1	441.6	91.9
West South Central	6.62	25.5	25.7	173.4	540.5	90.0
Mountain	2.08	31.8	15.9	223.6	702.9	119.7
Pacific	1.82	47.9	24.8	236.2	727.8	232.8

mentators, the persistently high crime rates of the southern tier of states are attributable largely, if not wholly, to the numerous crimes committed by and against Negroes in that area.

There is a pronounced tendency toward higher crime rates in the larger cities, as illustrated in Table III. Recent years, however, have shown what appeared to be a trend toward higher rates among Group II cities (between 100,000 and 250,000 population) than in Group I cities (over 250,000 population). A simi-

Table III.—*Distribution of Crime Rates by Size of Cities*
(January to June, 1943)

Offense	Population Groups of Cities (000 omitted)						
	I Over 250	II 100–250	III 50–100	IV 25–50	V 10–25	VI under 10	Gen'l Rate
Murder and Non-Negligent Manslaughter	2.86	2.82	2.67	2.01	1.39	1.89	2.48
Manslaughter by Negligence	1.74	2.26	1.49	1.46	0.74	0.79	1.53
Rape	6.67	5.60	4.69	3.89	4.25	3.48	5.46
Robbery	31.9	24.2	20.8	12.6	8.6	9.0	22.9
Aggravated Assault	27.2	28.1	29.4	26.8	14.5	13.3	24.6
Burglary—Breaking or Entering	167.2	193.7	150.7	134.0	111.7	92.8	148.6
Larceny—Theft	385.7	479.5	450.0	449.1	361.8	232.8	392.7
Auto Theft	86.5	111.7	81.5	73.2	62.0	48.2	80.9

lar pattern is traced for the first six months of 1943, with Group II cities in a leading position with respect to negligent manslaughter, burglary, auto theft and larcenies generally. In 1943, Group III cities (between 50,000 and 100,000 population) recorded the highest rates as to only one of the eight crime categories and were in second place as to another. Whereas in 1942 it appeared as though the Group III cities might be tending toward a higher status in the matter of crime frequency, the indications for 1943 are that this change in relative status will be delayed, if it has not already been offset.

The average loss, in terms of dollar value of property stolen, greatly increased in 1943 as to burglaries and larcenies (10.2% and 27.1%, respectively), but declined as to robberies (6.7%) and was virtually unchanged as to auto thefts. Net effect was that despite the decline in the number of crimes against property, the losses for 1943 were about as high for the first half of 1943 as for the corresponding period of 1942.

Robberies of oil stations and of banks greatly declined in number in 1943 (76.9% and 50.0%, respectively) while pocket-picking and purse-snatching markedly increased (26.2% and 19.9%, respectively). Forcible rape showed an increase of 14.4% during the first six months of 1943, as compared with the first half of 1942. The per cent of stolen cars recovered was 97.8 in 1943, as compared with 97.5 in 1942.

The *Uniform Crime Reports* entered their 14th year in 1943. In 1943, they included reports from 2,100 cities, towns and villages, having a combined population of 65,064,727. (*See also* CHILD WELFARE; FEDERAL BUREAU OF INVESTIGATION; KIDNAPPING; LAW; POLICE; SECRET SERVICE, U.S.)

BIBLIOGRAPHY.—*Uniform Crime Reports* (semiannual bulletins) for 1942 and for the first half of 1943, Federal Bureau of Investigation; *Judicial Criminal Statistics, 1941*, U.S. Bureau of the Census (1943); *Prisoners in State and Federal Prisons and Reformatories, 1940*, U.S. Bureau of the Census (1943). (BR. S.)

Great Britain.—No precise survey of crime in Great Britain in wartime was possible owing to the withholding of official statistics, but it was known that the amount of crime during 1943 was one of the smallest on record. Some police and penology authorities attributed this mainly to the all-compelling demands of men for the armed services and full employment throughout war industries.

Murders were no more than during peace years. Cases of housebreaking dropped by a fifth. Those of armed hold-up, robbery with violence, "smash-and-grab" raids on shop windows, bag-snatching and assaults during blackout hours were far fewer than anticipated. Bigamy increased, defendants being mostly service men.

Rigorous official action in detection was believed to have broken the back of serious "black market" trading. Magistrates were empowered to increase sentences in cases of summary jurisdiction of "black-marketing" offenses from a maximum of 6 months to 12 months.

During 1943, juvenile delinquency in London rose at one period to 25% above 1938 figures. Figures for the metropolitan police area disclosed that 8 out of every 1,000 children between the ages of 8 and 17 were guilty of offenses. Over the country as a whole juvenile crime decreased, one Welsh county reporting a decline of 40% within 12 months.

There was no notable change in penal policy. An official effort was made to secure a younger magistracy for juvenile courts. Irregularities at one of these courts at Hereford, which led to the birching of a boy before an appeal against the sentence could be lodged, impelled an official inquiry and aroused a new public interest in the procedure of such courts and in birching as a punishment.

A movement arose among magistrates to extend the system of

releasing prisoners on probation to cover periods up to three years. (*See also* PRISONS.) (P. BN.)

Croatia.

A "kingdom" formed from Yugoslavia in the north-western part of the Balkan peninsula after the German aggression of April 1941, when Croats of the fascist terrorist organization "Ustasha" set up in Zagreb, the capital of Croatia, an "independent" Croat regime with Dr. Ante Pavelitch as head of the new state and as poglavnik (leader) of the Croat fascists. On May 17, 1941, the Italian prince Aimone was elected king of Croatia, yet he never dared to set foot on the soil of his new kingdom.

Croatia has an area of 44,453 sq.mi. with about 7,000,000 inhabitants, of whom about 5,000,000 are Catholic Croats. The Mohammedan minority in Bosnia enjoyed a privileged position.

The cruelty and lawlessness of the Croat regime continued to provoke incessant internal disorders and uprisings in 1943. During long periods whole regions of Croatia were held by guerrilla forces, especially those organized by General Tito (Josip Brozovich), who for some time had his headquarters in northwestern Bosnia, not many miles south of Zagreb. The surrender of Italy in Sept. 1943 made conditions worse. King Aimone was officially deprived of his throne by a proclamation of Ante Pavelitch on Sept. 10, and Croatia became a republic under German protectorate instead of a kingdom under Italian protectorate. Nikola Manditch, a Bosnian lawyer from Sarajevo, was appointed premier of the Croat government. The Croat troops fighting in Russia were brought home to fight the patriots. The Ustasha secret police was reformed, after a visit of Heinrich Himmler, under German leadership. The economic situation was far from satisfactory, food prices went up to fantastic heights and the black market flourished. Efforts to win over the former Croat peasant party and its leader, Dr. Vlatko Matchek, failed. (*See also* DALMATIA; MONTENEGRO; YUGOSLAVIA.) (H. KO.)

Crop Insurance: *see* AGRICULTURE.

Crowley, Leo Thomas

(1890?–), U.S. government official, was born in Milton Junction, Wis. He attended the University of Wisconsin for a brief time, became salesman for a paper company at the age of 20 and president of the organization at 23. He subsequently held positions of importance in several financial institutions. He was called in to advise Secretary of the Treasury Henry Morgenthau when the Farm Credit administration was in the process of organization. He became regional administrator for FCA at St. Paul and was then chairman of the Federal Deposit Insurance corporation in Washington, 1934–39. Although he wished to leave to assume an executive post with a utilities firm, he heeded President Roosevelt's request to continue with the FDIC but received no salary for his work with the government. In March 1942, he also became Alien Property Custodian. This office, first instituted by President Wilson during World War I, had lain dormant in the department of justice for eight years before it was revived in 1942. An administration "trouble-shooter," Crowley came into the limelight in 1943 as a result of the quarrel between Vice-President Henry Wallace and Secretary of Commerce Jesse H. Jones. After President Roosevelt had chastised both members of his administrative family for airing their row, he removed agencies dealing with foreign economic operations from their control. Roosevelt then created a new superagency, the Office of Foreign Economic Warfare, and appointed Crowley administrator of this bureau in Sept. 1943.

Cruisers: *see* NAVIES OF THE WORLD.

Crumit, Frank

(1889–1943), U.S. stage and radio star. After graduating from Ohio university he went into vaudeville. His informal act, featuring song and ukelele-strumming made him a star almost overnight. He appeared in a succession of musical comedies and played leading man to Julia Sanderson, whom he later married. The Crumits entered the radio field in 1928 and won nation-wide popularity as the "Singing Sweethearts of the Air." They inaugurated the "Battle of the Sexes" quiz program in 1930. Crumit died in New York city, Sept. 7.

Crushed Stone: *see* STONE.

Cryolite.

No specific information was made public on cryolite after the occupation of Denmark by Germany and of Greenland by the United States, but apparently adequate amounts were being obtained from Greenland, since the supply was officially reported as sufficient to meet current war demands and essential industrial requirements. (G. A. RO.)

Cuba.

A West Indian republic including the island of the same name, the Isle of Pines and other minor islands in its limits; total area: 44,164 sq. mi. Population (unofficial est., 1942), 4,420,000; a census was started in July, 1943, in preparation for the 1944 presidential election, but no reports were available at the close of 1943. The capital is Havana (pop. est., including suburbs, 783,000); other large cities (with est. pop.) are: Santiago, 152,000; Camagüey, 138,295; Cienfuegos, 92,258; Santa Clara, 99,509; Sancti Spiritus, 92,000; Guantánamo, 68,000. President in 1943: Colonel Fulgencio Batista.

History.—In the winter of 1942–43, Cuba was greatly concerned over sugar prospects. The 1942 sugar contract with the United States had been for 4,000,000 short tons, a good percentage of the normal crop of prewar years. Unfortunately, lack of shipping had resulted in a failure to move the entire amount, and Cuban warehouses still held 1,500,000 tons. One of the reasons for concern was uncertainty as to whether the United States would await delivery before making payment, or not; this worry was removed in Dec. 1942, by an agreement by which Cuba was given 95% of the value of the unshipped sugar. Another problem in the situation was the fact that not only would the U.S. have the stored sugar to draw upon in 1943, but the same sugar would substantially reduce storage space available. In February the two countries finally came to an agreement for the season's production, setting it at a total of 3,225,000 short tons of which the United States was to absorb 2,700,000 tons. The amount was well under that of 1942, but as liberal as could be expected under the circumstances.

In the first half of 1942, shipping conditions improved steadily and when Cuban representatives went to Washington for early negotiations over 1944 production, it appeared probable that most of the 1943 crop would be moved by the end of the year. In August an agreement was concluded whereby the United States contracted for 4,000,000 short tons. Cuba had desired an increase in price, in view of generally increasing price levels in wages and in living costs, but the price fixed was the same as that for the previous years ($2.65 per 100 lb.). It was agreed, however, that if prices of sugar should increase in the U.S., a percentage of such increase should go to Cuba. Attempts to dispose of 100,000,000 gallons of molasses were less successful as late as November, since prices obtainable were lower than Cuba was willing to accept. It was expected, however, that most of this product could be converted into gin for new markets opened by the liquor shortage developing in the U.S.

In the domestic political field, there was definite activity as Cuban parties began preparations for the presidential election

PRESIDENT FULGENCIO BATISTA of Cuba (centre, with arm extended) examining U.S. motorized equipment sent to the island in 1943

campaign of 1944. Under the Cuban constitution, President Batista would be ineligible (no president may hold more than four consecutive terms), and early in the year he announced that he was not a candidate. Cabinet reorganizations took place in March and April; in the ministry set up in March two parties (the ABC and Communist), formerly in opposition to the administration, were given representation. Some weakening of the government coalition developed in May, when Vice-President Gustavo Cuero Rubio resigned in order to head a newly formed party. Other leading candidates were Carlos Saladrigas, former premier and most likely administration candidate, and Ramón Grau San Martín, leader of the *Auténticos*, the strongest opposition party. The campaign promised to develop largely on personalities (frequently the case in Cuba) and on a few domestic issues.

Diplomatic relations between Cuba and Spain, somewhat strained in 1942, were improved in midsummer of 1943 by the arrangement of a convention looking toward the release of frozen credits dating back to the Spanish Civil War. The agreement promised to restore needed Cuban markets, notably for tobacco. Other diplomatic enterprises involved a new military and naval pact with the United States (Feb. 1) by which the two nations continued the co-operation of previous months. In this connection the two states agreed upon a mutual military conscription program. One of the reasons for a special legislative session in January was the arrangement of a treaty of amity with China. In March friendship of a closer neighbour was signified in the visit of President Rafael Calderón Guardia of Costa Rica.

Cuba's new military training program got under way in 1943. With registration in April, it was expected that 8,000 inductees would go into the army every four months. Earlier, because of shortage of officer material, President Batista had ordered recalled 48 former Cuban army officers who had gone into exile in 1933. The conscript army was not liable for service outside Cuba, and the administration emphasized the enlistment of several thousand volunteers who might serve in a possible expeditionary force.

War conditions still affected the island economy in 1943, in spite of an eased shipping situation. Price ceilings were set in July on various food items and on utility charges. A board of economic warfare was established in June, and censorship of all types of communication, in April. In August a postwar planning group was organized; Cuba's experience after World War I, when the bottom had dropped out of sugar prices, was a sore memory. In line with the advice of economic advisers, the

government in October ordered the big Tinguaro sugar mill, damaged by fire and not repaired, put in operation at once under penalty of intervention by the government itself.

A national food congress was held in Havana in September, and Cubans interested in stimulation of diversified agriculture continued a program calling for the erection of refrigerator warehouses and dehydration plants. In July export of meat and charcoal was prohibited for a time, with the ban later partially relaxed. The widespread shortage of fuels and of rubber and manufactured articles affected transportation and the volume of retail sales.

Education.—In 1942, urban and semi-urban elementary schools numbered 4,227 lower primary schools, with 437,965 students, and 37 higher primary schools, with 7,741 pupils. Civic-rural schools (elementary level) numbered 1,113; enrolment, 57,050 pupils. There were 24 secondary schools with 18,664 students, and 4 arts and trades schools. The National university, at Havana, had an enrolment of 13,949.

Finance.—The Cuban monetary unit is the peso, officially set at par with the United States dollar. Revenue for 1942 was 95,724,000 pesos; expenditures 104,810,000 (with an additional appropriation of 16,000,000 pesos made to cover the deficit). The budget for 1943 was balanced at 89,993,595 pesos. The public debt (Jan. 1, 1943) was 118,416,000 pesos (111,099,000 external; 7,317,000 internal), not including a floating debt of over 50,000,000 pesos. In Oct. 1943, U.S. currency in Cuba totalled $164,016,729, and Cuban currency amounted to 121,847,112 pesos.

In January, the government was authorized to purchase $15,-000,000 worth of gold from the United States as a reserve (plus $5,000,000 U.S. currency) for a new issue (20,408,000 pesos) of Cuban silver certificates. In March an additional 5,102,000 pesos of silver certificates were issued.

Trade and Communication.—No recent trade figures were available (1941 total value was $345,397,728), but statements issued indicated that imports for the first half of 1943 were 13% greater than in a similar period for 1942, and exports were up 26.4%. The Cuban trade balance with the United States for the first three quarters of 1943 was favourable in the amount of $103,518,000. Between 80% and 90% of Cuban trade is with the United States.

Cuba has extensive service with outside countries by sea and air. For the first half of 1943, air traffic with Miami, Fla., decreased, but inter-island traffic increased. A new air mail service to Mexico was started Jan. 1, 1943. Air express shipments (1942) amounted to 760,027 lb.; air mail to 119,227 lb. The railway system is 3,850 mi. in length (1942); the highway system amounted to 2,390 mi. improved roads and approximately 2,000 mi. unimproved. The highway maintenance appropriation for the 1942–43 fiscal year was 95,000 pesos, with 425,000 pesos available for construction. Lack of motor fuels affected transportation; by law, cars must use a mixture of 75% alcohol and 25% gasoline.

Agriculture.—The dominant crop is sugar and sugar derivatives. The 1943 crop was set at 3,225,000 short tons (1942: 4,016,000 short tons), of which 2,700,000 tons were taken by the U.S., 300,000 tons went to other export markets, and 225,000 tons reserved for domestic use. Tobacco production for 1942 was estimated at 51,400,115 lb., and it was expected that the 1943 crop would be about 16% above this figure. The 1943 banana export crop was estimated at 1,800,000 stems (1942: 2,245,000 stems), with disease affecting production. In 1942 Cuba produced 500,000 loofah (gourd) sponges.

An early season drought affected butter production (in 1942 butter exports had been 648,000 lb.; cheese exports, 959,000 lb.).

Minerals.—Cuban mineral exports for 1941 showed values of:

copper $1,329,346; manganese $6,510,131; iron ores $209,924; chromium ores $1,329,496. (*See also* WEST INDIES.)

BIBLIOGRAPHY.—Charles Edward Chapman, *A History of the Cuban Republic* (1927); Russell H. Fitzgibbon, *Cuba and the United States 1900–1935* (1935).   (D. RD.)

Cudahy, John

(1887–1943), U.S. businessman and diplomat, was born Dec. 10 in Milwaukee, Wis., member of a wealthy U.S. packing family. He was graduated from Harvard in 1910 and took his law degree at the University of Wisconsin, 1913. He practised law in Wisconsin until the U.S. entered World War I and then served with the A.E.F. in France. After the war, he resumed his law work and entered politics. He ran unsuccessfully for governor of Wisconsin, 1916, on the Democratic ticket, and was later a substantial contributor to the Democratic presidential campaign fund. After Franklin D. Roosevelt's election in 1932, Cudahy served successively as U.S. envoy to Poland, Ireland, Belgium and Luxembourg. He remained at his post in Brussels during the German invasion of the Low Countries, 1940, and later became an apologist for King Leopold III, whose capitulation evoked sharp criticism from Allied nations. Cudahy was killed Sept. 6, during a riding accident on his estate near Milwaukee, when he was thrown from his horse.

Cunningham, Sir Andrew Browne

(1883–   ), British naval officer, commander of the British Mediterranean fleet after 1939, was born in Bishop's Waltham, Hants., England. He entered the royal navy in 1898. During World War I, Sir Andrew commanded the destroyer "Scorpion" and staged daring raids against enemy shipping in the Mediterranean. He was a rear admiral in 1933–36, and was made a vice-admiral commanding a battle cruiser squadron in 1937. He was also lord commissioner of the admiralty and deputy chief of the naval staff, 1938–39. In April 1940, Sir Andrew, aboard his flagship "Warspite," led a destroyer flotilla into Narvik fjord and sank seven German destroyers. Except for the Narvik battle, he had most of his naval experience in the Mediterranean, of which he was said to know every bay and inlet. At the outbreak of war in 1939, he was made commander in chief of the Mediterranean fleet, which played an important part in the North African and Italian victories. In June 1942, he was made a baronet, and in January 1943, he was promoted to the rank of admiral of the fleet. He succeeded Admiral Sir Dudley Pound as first sea lord and naval chief of staff in Oct. 1943, being replaced in the Mediterranean by Sir John H. D. Cunningham.

Curaçao.

A Caribbean colony of the Netherlands, composed of the islands of Curaçao (210 sq.mi.), Bonaire (95 sq.mi.), and Aruba (69 sq.mi.) in the Leeward group some 40 mi. off the coast of Venezuela, and in the Windward Islands, St. Eustatius (7 sq.mi.), Saba (5 sq.mi.) and the southern portion of St. Martin (17 sq.mi.). The total area is 436 sq.mi. The total pop. (1941 official est.) is 109,592 (Curaçao Island, 68,217; Aruba, 31,522; Bonaire, 5,556; St. Eustatius, 1,146; Saba, 1,213; St. Martin, 1,938). The official language is Dutch; the majority of the inhabitants are Roman Catholics. Willemstad (pop., 1939 est., 31,264), on the island of Curaçao, is the capital. The colony is administered by an appointed governor and a majority-elected council. The governor in 1943 was Dr. Pieter A. Kasteel.

History.—Curaçao continued to be important in the war effort because of petroleum production, and an expansion of refining facilities took place during 1943. The colony was still affected by shipping shortages, and scarcity of some items was reported as well as a 50% increase in price levels. Maximum prices were set on essentials early in the year, and by March food cards had

DUTCH MARINES in Curaçao

been issued in prospect of later food rationing. Due to the rise in living costs, government and refinery employees on Aug. 31 were given a 30% wage increase, retroactive to July 1, 1943.

Venezuela military observers, sent under mutual agreement with the colonial administration, arrived in Curaçao in March.

Education.—The school system possessed 49 elementary schools (1938) with an enrolment of 11,044.

Finance.—The monetary unit is the guilder (value in 1943 approximately 54 cents U.S.). After Jan. 1, 1943, a new currency went into use and United States paper currency was no longer allowed in circulation. The new coinage was minted in the United States. The 1944 budget estimated ordinary revenue at 17,748,417 guilders, and extraordinary revenue at 7,166,084 guilders; current expenditures at 13,220,793 guilders, and extraordinary expenditures at 7,690,240 guilders.

Trade and Resources.—The main resource of the colony is the refining of crude petroleum (primarily from Venezuela) on Aruba and Curaçao, with the large refineries further expanded during the year. This industry accounts for practically the entire export trade of the islands, and most of the import trade. No wartime statistics were made public; in 1938 petroleum product exports were valued at 151,026,135 guilders, petroleum imports at 138,740,326 guilders. Other imports are largely foodstuffs and manufactured items, with most articles (except meats from Argentina) coming from the United States in 1943. Phosphate mining was at a standstill, since supplies on hand were sufficient to meet demand for some time to come. Because of labour shortage the harvesting of aloes ceased in September with only 75% of the crop gathered (approximately 3,000 cases). In normal times there are small exports of hides and skins, Panama hats, crude salt, orange peel and divi-divi for tanning.

Communication.—Both Aruba and Curaçao have good connections with the outside world by air and steamer lines. Communication with the other islands is largely by small vessels. On Dec. 3 an air line from Curaçao to St. Martin was opened; on

Dec. 20 the first direct radio-telephone line to the United States went into operation. (*See* also HISPANIC AMERICA AND WORLD WAR II.)

BIBLIOGRAPHY.—*Netherlands News,* Netherlands Information Bureau (New York, bi-weekly); J. K. Wright and William van Royen, *The Netherlands West Indies: Curaçao and Surinam* (1941). (D. RD.)

Curling. Skipped by novelist Ben Ames Williams, the Country club of Brookline, Mass., won both the Mitchell and Allen medals in the Grand National Curling club tournament. It marked the first time in 12 years that one rink had won both medals, a Brookline entry having last scored a double in 1931. Novelist Williams' curlers defeated another Brookline rink, 15–10, to win the Mitchell medal, and out-stoned Utica, N.Y., 14–9, for the Allen medal. The Country club of Brookline added further to its curling honours by winning the Dykes trophy, awarded to the winner of the junior rink event. Brookline defeated Utica, 17–5, in the Dykes final. Junior curlers are those who have not competed regularly in the Grand National. In the annual competition between the United States and Canada, the latter won the Gordon International medal. Detroit won the Waterloo trophy in the annual Ontario bonspiel at Toronto, defeating the Hamilton Victoria rink, 17–13, in the final.

(M. P. W.)

Currency: *see* COINAGE.

Curtin, John (1885–   ), Australian statesman, born Jan. 8 at Creswick, Victoria, Australia. Educated in the state schools, Curtin later became actively engaged in politics and labour journalism. As general secretary of the Victorian Timber Workers' union, 1911–15, and editor of the *Westralian Worker,* 1917–28, he became an exponent of the Australian Labour party's dual traditions of nationalism and theoretical socialism. During World War I, he was secretary of the anticonscription campaign. He was a member of the Australian house of representatives, serving from 1928 to 1931 and again from 1934 to 1941. During the latter period he was leader of the Federal Labour party and the parliamentary opposition. He succeeded Arthur Fadden as prime minister of Australia Oct. 3, 1941.

Throughout 1942 and early 1943 Curtin stressed the danger of invasion and warned the Allies against underestimating Japanese power. To prevent such an invasion by carrying the war to the enemy he sponsored a bill allowing conscripted troops to be sent outside Australian territory. The bill was passed in the senate Feb. 18, 1943, but was later defeated in the house. On June 7, Curtin announced his belief that the danger had passed. On June 24 a vote of nonconfidence in the ministry was defeated, and on Aug. 21 the party was re-elected.

In a speech made at Adelaide Aug. 14, Curtin proposed that an empire council be established to discuss matters of empire policy.

Cycling. With bicycles on the war ration list and with most of the riders in the service of their respective countries, cycling activity was reduced to a minimum for the year 1943, and for the second year, the names of existing champions based on the last year of competition (1941) were kept on the record books. For the fourth year the colourful and popular international six-day bicycle race was called off. Similarly there was no competition for world titles and cycling organizations such as the American Bicycling league of America, the National Cycling association and the Century Road club were without competition. However, an encouraging announcement was made by Cy Panitch, president of the Bicycle Club of America, who said that membership in that organization had increased 25% in 1943.

Furman Kugler, second ranking rider in America, won the New Jersey state cycling championship, in one of the rare title events, with a total of 16 points, having finished first in the 5-mi. and 10-mi. races sponsored by the Amateur Bicycle league of America.

A summary of the 1941 records, which still stood in 1943, follows:

The N.C.A. sprint championship was won by Tom Saetta of Brooklyn, while Mike DeFilipo of Newark won the paced title. The A.B.L. senior road championship was won by Marvin Thompson of Chicago, and the junior title went to Andrew Bernadsky of San Francisco. The girls' champion was Jean Michels of Chicago.

The track championships of the A.B.L. were won by Bob Stauffacher of San Francisco, who triumphed in the senior class, and Chuck Edwards of Chicago, winner among the juniors. Stauffacher also captured the Century Road club's senior title.

The A.B.L. of America selected an all-American cycling group as shown in the table.

Name	City	Points
George Hurlburt, Jr.	Buffalo	275
Furman Kugler	Somerville, N.J.	195
Jerry Kandler	Milwaukee	190
Iggy Gronkowski, Jr.	Buffalo	115
George Woof	San Francisco	98
Johnny Weber	Milwaukee	85
James Dolle	Irvington, Ind.	84
Isamer Fiyuyama	Honolulu	79
George Edge	Philadelphia	74
Harry Naismyth	Somerville, N.J.	67
Bruce Burgess	Irvington, Ind.	65
Francis McCabe	Honolulu	64

Other events in 1941, the last of their kind to be held for the duration, included an international bike race over the Inter-American highway from Tegucigalpa, Honduras, to Guatemala City. The Guatemala team won with Fraterno Vila, 18-year-old star, pedalling at the rate of 15 m.p.h. Tommy Hayes of Dallas, Texas, won the seventh annual national 100-mi. motorcycling championship, winning in the amazing time of 1:15:46.51. Also, the six-day bike race which was held in Montreal, Canada, was won by the team of Angelo DeBacco of Newark, N.J., and René Cyr of Montreal. Second place was taken by the popular team of Jules Audy of Montreal and Cecil Yates of Chicago.

(T. J. D.)

C.Y.O.: *see* CATHOLIC ORGANIZATIONS FOR YOUTH.

Cyprus: *see* MEDITERRANEAN, BRITISH POSSESSIONS IN THE.

Czechoslovakia. Czechoslovakia, a republic in central Europe, was dismembered in 1938–39 as a result of axis aggression (*see* BOHEMIA AND MORAVIA; SLOVAKIA). The area of Czechoslovakia was 54,244 sq.mi., the pop. (1930 census) 14,729,536. The Czechoslovak government was reconstituted in 1940 in England and recognized by all the Allies as a member of the United Nations. President (1943) Dr. Eduard Beneš; prime minister, Msgr. Jan Šramek.

History.—During 1943 the Czechs and Slovaks in their homeland continued the struggle for national liberation. Their hopes there were concentrated upon their government in England, upon the Czechoslovak army trained in Great Britain, and upon the reconstitution of the democratic Czechoslovak republic through the defeat of Germany. On Aug. 5, 1942, the British government officially repudiated the Munich agreement of Sept. 1938, and thus recognized Czechoslovakia's frontiers as of before Sept. 1938. The soviet union took the same line.

The Czechoslovak government in London represented all the different elements of the republic—Czechs, Slovaks and the Carpatho-Russians of Ruthenia. The latter were represented by two members in the Czechoslovak state council, Dr. Pavel Cibere and Ivan Petruščak, an active trade union journalist. Though Ruthenia is inhabited by a population related to the Ukrainians and Russians, the soviet government officially recognized Ruthenia as part of Czechoslovakia. The soviet union raised its minister to Czechoslovakia to the rank of ambassador, and on Jan. 29, 1943, the soviet ambassador Alexander Bogomolov presented his credentials to President Beneš, accompanied by two counsellors and the military attaché of the embassy.

Throughout the year Czechoslovakia maintained the most cordial relations with all the leading United Nations. Msgr. Jan Šramek, the premier of the government, broadcast on Sept. 2, the fourth anniversary of the war, a message to Czechoslovakia in which he said: "We wish to deepen our bond of alliance with Great Britain, the United States, and with France, whose return to the ranks of the great European powers we consider absolutely essential. We also wish to continue in our close collaboration with the soviet union and we believe it unconditionally necessary for Russia to take a permanent part in the European politics."

The wise and moderate policy of the Czechoslovak government strengthened Czechoslovakia's diplomatic position and prestige among the United Nations. In pursuance of this policy President Beneš arrived on Dec. 11, 1943, in Moscow to sign a treaty of friendship between Czechoslovakia and the soviet union. He was received with extraordinary honours, and the soviet government made clear the great importance which it attached to its relations with Czechoslovakia, thus cementing the long-lasting friendship between the two countries. On Dec. 12 Foreign Commissar Molotov on behalf of the soviet union, and the Czechoslovak ambassador Zdeněk Fierlinger on behalf of his republic, signed a treaty of friendship, mutual assistance and postwar collaboration between the two countries. Like the British-soviet treaty of 1941, the agreement was concluded for 20 years, and for additional periods of five years if not renounced by one of the parties 12 months before expiration.

The two powers promised mutual assistance in the war against Germany and her satellites, as well as postwar collaboration. They pledged not to enter into negotiations with any German government which did not renounce aggression explicitly, and in the postwar period to render mutual military assistance in case Germany resumed the *Drang nach Osten* policy. Both countries promised noninterference in the internal affairs of the other state.

It was of highest importance that the two countries declared the treaty open for a third power, bordering on the two states and an object of German aggression, to join the treaty, thus making it a tripartite agreement. This invitation was aimed at Poland, with whom Czechoslovakia had entered into an agreement on Jan. 23, 1942, and with whom the Czechoslovaks wished to establish the most favourable relationship. Upon leaving Moscow Dec. 22, President Beneš told the press that his government and the soviet union hoped to reach an agreement with Poland concerning a stable peace and steps to prevent future aggression by Germany.

BIBLIOGRAPHY.—Czechoslovak Ministry of Foreign Affairs, *Four Fighting Years* (London, 1943); Cecily Mackworth, *Czechoslovakia Fights Back* (London, 1943).   (H. Ko.)

Dafoe, Allan Roy

(1883-1943), Canadian physician, was born May 29 at Madoc, Ont., the son of a country doctor. He took his degree in medicine at the medical school of the University of Toronto in 1907 and practised in several Canadian mining towns before settling in Callander, an Ontario lumbering community. On the morning of May 28, 1934, he was called to the farmhouse of Oliva Dionne, a French Canadian farmer, to attend a childbirth. In the short space of an hour, Dr. Dafoe delivered five baby girls to Mme. Dionne Convinced that the infants could not live, he baptized them sep-

arately. The children, however, did survive, and then Dr. Dafoe realized that in delivering quintuplets, he had made medical history. He became legal guardian of the five Dionne babies, but resigned in 1939 because of friction with the parents of the children. Thereafter, Dr. Dafoe devoted most of his time to the children in his capacity as a personal physician. He became nearly as famous as his five protégées and his life was fictionalized in moving pictures. He died of pneumonia in a hospital at North Bay, Ont., June 2.

Dahomey: *see* FRENCH COLONIAL EMPIRE.
Dairy Industry, Bureau of: *see* AGRICULTURAL RESEARCH ADMINISTRATION.

Dairying.

The number of milk cows in the United States at the beginning of 1943 was estimated by the U.S. department of agriculture to be 26,946,000 head compared to 26,398,000 head in 1942 and a 10-year average of 25,316,000 head. The number in 1943 set a new record but only a little more than equal to the high point reached in 1934. The increasing demand for dairy products caused an improvement in the breeding and feeding of the dairy cattle, thereby increasing production more than merely by the increase of numbers. An increased number of heifer calves were being kept for cows, indicating a continued increase through the year. The severe shortage of dairy feeds, particularly in the greater dairy states, caused the marketing of a large number of cows and calves. The feed shortage also reduced the milk production per cow toward the end of 1943. The amount of the more concentrated feeds used was less than in 1942 because of the great difficulty in buying these feeds in the New England states. In the corn belt, heavy feeding was practised though the amount of milk produced was not equal to that of 1942.

The milk production of 1943 was about the same as in 1942, being estimated at 118,000,000,000 lb. compared to 119,240,000,000 lb. in 1942 and the 1937-41 average of 107,903,000,000 lb. The expansion of fluid milk consumption caused a reduction in the manufacture of cheese and dried and evaporated milk in 1943. Consumption of fluid milk in large cities was estimated to be 15% above the 1942 level and 34% above the 1935-39 average. The War Food administration asked the dairymen for a production of 122,000,000,000 lb. of milk in 1944, which would require 2% increase in the number of cows and better feeding in order to produce at least 50 lb. more of milk per cow. (*See* also BUTTER; CHEESE; MILK.)   (J. C. Ms.)

Dalmatia.

A Yugoslav province, formerly a part of Austria, on the northeastern shore of the Adriatic sea, inhabited by Croats. When Yugoslavia collapsed under German aggression in April 1941, part of the Dalmatian coast, including the important naval ports of Cattaro and Spalato, was directly annexed by Italy, while a smaller part, including Ragusa, became officially part of Croatia, but was put under Italian military control.

This Italian military control came to a sudden end in 1943, when Italy surrendered to the Allies. A small part of the Italian army joined the Yugoslav patriot forces, the arms and supplies of some Italian divisions fell into the hands of the Yugoslav guerrillas, while the occupation of the country was taken over by the German army. The incessant warfare which Serb and Croat patriots had formerly waged against the Italian forces of occupation were now resumed against the German forces of occupation. The Partisan army under General Tito (Josip Brozovich) succeeded even in capturing for a short time Spalato and other important cities of the Dalmatian coast, but had to abandon them

DOUGLAS DAM of the Tennessee Valley authority on the French Broad river in eastern Tennessee, was placed in operation in March 1943 after a record-breaking construction period of 12 months and 19 days. The dam is 161 feet high and 1,682 feet long and was built at a cost of $36,500,000

under increased German pressure. (*See* also CROATIA; MONTENEGRO; YUGOSLAVIA.)   (H. KO.)

Dams. On May 17, 1943, the royal air force attacked and severely damaged the Möhne, Sorpe and Eder dams in Germany, releasing at least 75% of the stored water and causing the most severe floods on record in the Ruhr valley and along the Rhine river below Duisburg-Ruhrort.

Several 1,500 lb. mines were dropped against the upstream face of the dams from planes flying over them at altitudes of less than 100 ft. to enable accurate placing of the explosives. After repeated attacks for more than an hour, in the face of heavy anti-aircraft fire from gun emplacements on the dam itself, a breach about 100 yd. wide was made in the centre of the Möhne dam. The Eder dam was broken down in two places, making a breach almost as wide as at the Möhne dam. The Sorpe dam was also breached.

The Möhne dam, a curved gravity structure of stone masonry, 131 ft. high and 2,132 ft. long, was built in 1913, creating a reservoir of 110,255 ac.ft. capacity. The Sorpe dam, 197 ft. high, created a reservoir of 65,666 ac.ft. capacity. Together, the Möhne and Sorpe dams controlled almost three-fourths of the Ruhr river watershed and about two-thirds of the water storage in the industrial area of the Ruhr.

The Eder dam, a curved gravity concrete structure, 157 ft. high and 1,312 ft. long, was built in 1914, creating the largest reservoir in Europe with a capacity of 163,760 ac.ft. It controlled the flow of the Weser river for navigation and flood protection. This reservoir was completely emptied through the breach.

Besides the damage caused by the flooding of industrial plants and the sweeping away of bridges and railway embankments, the loss of this tremendous amount of storage seriously affected some 300 waterworks and pumping stations, extensive canal systems for navigation, and many hydroelectric plants, the backbone of this great industrial region of Germany.

In the United States, at the Central valley project in California, construction of Shasta dam, second largest concrete dam in the world, was over 80% complete by April 1943, with 5,000,000 cu.yd. of concrete in place.

In the Tennessee valley, construction of Fontana dam, largest and highest concrete dam east of the Rocky mountains and world's fourth largest concrete dam, was over 50% complete on Nov. 1, 1943, with 1,500,000 cu.yd. of concrete in place and construction proceeding at the rate of 200,000 cu.yd. of concrete per month.

Douglas dam, also in the Tennessee valley, was closed and filling of the reservoir started by Feb. 1943, 13 months after authorization of construction. This remarkable accomplishment was made possible by the fact that Douglas dam was almost an exact duplicate of the concrete section of Cherokee dam, completed in 1942, and it was possible to use the same plans and

Chief Dams Completed or Under Construction During 1943

Name of Dam	River	Place	Type	Maximum Height, Feet	Crest Length, Feet	Volume (Cu. yd.)	Purpose*	Built by	Progress*
Anderson Ranch	Boise, S. Fork	Idaho, U.S.	Earthfill	330	1,350	9,500,000	I, F, P	U.S. Reclamation Bureau	U
Apalachia	Hiwassee	North Carolina, U.S.	Concrete, straight gravity	150	1,250	450,000	P	Tennessee Valley Authority	C
Bluestone	New	West Virginia, U.S.	Concrete, gravity	180	2,060	950,000	F	U.S. Army Engineers	U
Davis	Colorado	Arizona, U.S.	Earth and rockfill	138	1,600	4,230,000	P	U.S. Reclamation Bureau	U
Denison	Red	Texas, U.S.	Earthfill	165	14,000	17,370,000	F, P	U.S. Army Engineers	U
Dique la Vina		Argentina	Concrete arch	345	.	223,000	I, P	Province of Córdoba	U
Douglas	French Broad	Tennessee, U.S.	Earthfill and concrete gravity	160	1,682	1,000,000 (earth) 536,000 (conc.)	P	Tennessee Valley Authority	C
El Azucar	San Juan	Mexico	Earthfill	142	18,900	5,677,031	I	Mexican National Commission of Irrigation	C
El Palmito	Nazas	Mexico	Earthfill	295	1,005	6,632,348	I, P	Mexican National Commission of Irrigation	U
Fontana	Little Tennessee	North Carolina, U.S.	Concrete, straight gravity	470	1,750	2,600,000	P	Tennessee Valley Authority	U
Fuihodo	Yalu	Manchuria		298	2,730	3,530,000	P	Yalu River Hydro-Electric Co.	U
Green Mountain	Blue	Colorado, U.S.	Earth and rockfill	285	1,300	4,861,000	I, P	U.S. Reclamation Bureau	U
John Martin	Arkansas	Colorado, U.S.	Earthfill and concrete gravity	130	14,000	5,915,000 (earth) 220,000 (conc.)	F	U.S. Army Engineers	U
Kanopolis	Smoky Hill	Kansas, U.S.	Earthfill	120	15,400	14,700,000	F	U.S. Army Engineers	U
Merriman	Rondout	New York, U.S.	Earthfill	200	2,500	6,600,000	W	N.Y. Board of Water Supply	U
Norfork	North Fork	Arkansas, U.S.	Concrete, straight gravity	220	2,624	1,470,000	F, P	U.S. Army Engineers	U
Santa Fe	San Gabriel	California, U.S.	Earthfill	92	24,100	12,000,000	F, W	U.S. Army Engineers	C
San Vicente	San Vicente	California, U.S.	Concrete, straight gravity	199	980	2,000,000	W	City of San Diego	U
Shasta	Sacramento	California, U.S.	Concrete, straight gravity	560	3,500	5,400,000	I, F, P	U.S. Reclamation Bureau	U
Wolf Creek	Cumberland	Kentucky, U.S.	Earthfill and concrete gravity	242	5,730	11,500,000 (earth) 1,250,000 (conc.)	F, P	U.S. Army Engineers	U

*I—Irrigation, C—Completed in 1943, U—Under construction, F—Flood control, W—Water supply, P—Power.

222

DANCE

construction equipment with only slight changes.

The Mexican national commission of irrigation completed work in 1943 on the main structure of El Azucar dam, an earthfill four miles long on the San Juan river. Much work remained, however, on the spillway which has a capacity of 706,000 cu.ft. per sec. In Argentina, the Medrano dam, a low diversion dam on the Tunuyan river, was replaced by the Tiburcio Benegas dam to irrigate 132,145 ac. The Kariba dam, proposed as a postwar project by the government of Southern Rhodesia, was to be built in Kariba gorge of the Zambesi river, 200 mi. below Victoria falls, to provide hydroelectric power and water for irrigation.

The table on page 221 includes 20 of the many important dams of the world completed or under construction during 1943. (*See* also AQUEDUCTS; IRRIGATION; TENNESSEE VALLEY AUTHORITY.)

(B. O. M.)

Dance. Ballroom.—In 1943, schools throughout the U.S. reported heavy enrolments in social dancing, far exceeding those of the "dance-boom years" prior to and during World War I.

People always dance more in wartime than in peacetime. It's the natural reaction to tense times. But never before had the urge to do a little plain and fancy rug-cutting been so widespread as in 1943. It was a year in which ballroom dancing stepped far beyond its former role of social pastime and became many things to many people.

In 1943, people who had never taken a rhythmic step before in their lives turned to the dance floor. Staid civilians, heretofore content to fill spectator roles, took up dancing—for relaxation, for escape, as a panacea for war nerves and a release for pent-up emotions. The U.S.O. halls, canteens, and various centres where service men gathered accented dancing as a means of recreation and fun. Defense plants all over the country discovered in music and dancing an antidote for clock-watching, fatigue, absenteeism.

In a recent survey of defense plants—where the debutante worked side by side with ex-stenographers and home girls—it was found that music and dancing speeded up production at least 8%. The workers danced during rest periods and lunch hours, and by the end of 1943 there were approximately 2,000 plants in the U.S. fully equipped with special floors, recorded music, loudspeakers and various other "ballroom" facilities.

The urge to dance came from the workers themselves. It was a way of expression the initiated saw coming long before U.S. entry into the war. At that time emphasis was placed on participation or group dances which were later to become favourites in U.S.O. centres and other gathering places frequented by service men. The participation dances are conducive to "mixing," and are therefore infallible ice-breakers. They were favourites in both civilian and military circles and bade fair to remain popular for the duration.

The war brought this development in the modern dance: a tempo either very slow or very fast. There was no middleground—the medium tempo was in 1943 practically extinct. Examples of this trend were the fast fox trot, danced to the rousing, swashbuckling "Pistol-Packin' Mama," and the slow fox trot, timed to the dreamy and sentimental "People Will Say We're in Love." It remained for Salt Lake City to coin the most amusing name for the slow-motion fox trot: "Holy Kiss Dance."

Perhaps because the fox trot is an adaptable step which can fit into either fast or slow tempo, it stood out as the most popular modern dance in 1943. There were flares of interest in the tango and the polka during 1943, but these dances seemed definitely on the wane. The once-popular conga was scarcely more than a vague prewar memory.

The rumba continued to gain adherents, especially among younger dancers. The radio and the movies carried the lilting rumba rhythms far into the hinterlands, and the dance became nationally known and generally popular. The tango, introduced by the Vernon Castles shortly before World War I, had no such means of exploitation—and never won such widespread popularity. Sharing favour with the rumba was that lively, challenging newcomer, the samba. The samba, a product of Brazil, gained new impetus after it had been nationally exhibited in a Walt Disney short.

Perhaps one reason why the samba and the rumba continued to hold the affection of dancers was that they allowed for much originality among individual couples.

The year 1943 saw a renewed interest in that most romantic of all dances, the waltz. This dance, which only a few years before was monopolized by the older generation, found increasing favour with the young. People of all ages were waltzing in 1943. The cause was not hard to find. Never before had there been such a wealth of romantic tunes, or such a wholesale revival of the old familiar waltz melodies. People like to hear the old familiar songs, and to dance the old familiar steps.

But the rumba and the waltz were, after all, created in other countries. The American spirit of nationalism still stood firmly behind the appeal of the jitterbug steps that originated on native soil. So strong was that appeal that *Life* magazine in Nov. 1943, devoted its front cover and nine full pages to the jitterbug, hailing the "Lindy Hop" as "the true national folk dance of America." Because of its strenuous routine, this type of dance was usually indulged in by the young, whose exuberance it expressed so well.

For many seasons it was possible to tell from what section of the country a "rug-cutter" came, simply by the step he did and the name he called it. There were any number of picturesque versions of the "Lindy Hop," which is the basic, nationally known jitterbug routine. Each section had its own pet steps. In Los Angeles there was the "Balboa," and in various parts of the country there were jive dances bearing such provocative titles as "Jersey Jump," "Flea Hop," "Jig Walk," etc.

But, with the war, New Yorkers suddenly found themselves in military camps and defense centres all over the country. Girls and boys from small communities invaded large cities by the hundreds of thousands. On bleak plains and in barren spots, mushroom cities surrounding defense plants sprang up overnight. There was no time for sectional differences. The Jitterbug steps done in Manhattan were learned and adapted by young people

YOUNG MALE AND FEMALE REACTIONS to the "jive" dance music of Harry James during a concert in a New York theatre in April 1943. James was the year's favourite bandleader of the nation's "jitterbugs"

from every state in the union—and they, in turn, gave out steps of their own improvisation.

The result was a surprising standardization of a dance whose chief characteristic had been diversity. The jitterbug, still in a stage of transition, began to fall into a definite pattern. It was no strange thing in 1943 to see a girl from Indiana or Texas dance with a boy just arrived from New York and never miss a step.

Arthur Murray, at the request of the Office of War Information, created two special participation dances. One of these, "The Victory Walk," is danced to marching tempo. The other, created for the tune, "Praise the Lord and Pass the Ammunition," is equally lively and gay. Despite the fact that these dances won national approval, they did not sweep the country off its feet. Nor was this surprising. It is an established fact that dances born in wartime are shortlived. Steps popular before the war continued in favour. Before World War I the Vernon Castles popularized the "animal" dances, such as the "Bunny Hug," "Lame Duck," "Turkey Trot," etc. It was not until 1919 that new rhythms and steps made their appearance.   (A. Mu.)

Ballet.—U.S.O. shows used all types of dancing and dancers, and found the men in the service highly appreciative of the best. At the performance of the Ballet Russe de Monte Carlo at Fort Monmouth, Fort Hancock, etc., the dancers were received with the greatest enthusiasm by the soldiers. At the New York City American Theatre Wing canteen, alone, at least 520 dancers appeared.

The department of agriculture in its 1943 educational drive for food conservation and against the black market, used the dancer, Tamiris, in a principal role in its dance-play, "It's Up To You."

In the defense plants, the "Lunchtime Follies," directed by Lil Liandre, relaxed, delighted and educated the workers with popular and serious dance acts.

Throughout the country local dancing teachers organized their advanced pupils into performing groups and sent them to nearby camps, canteens, soldiers' hospitals and war benefits. Hundreds of schools gave at least one performance every week as their contribution to morale.

In the entertainment world of theatre, movie and concert, dance also became more popular through the need of lively, colourful, dynamic entertainment. Almost every Broadway show had a featured dance attraction and many had full fledged ballets by leading choreographers. To mention just a few such "hits": (1) *Carmen Jones*, ballet by Eugene Loring; (2) *Early to Bed*, premier dancer Jane Deering playing leading ingenue and dancing role; (3) *Oklahoma!* ballet by Agnes de Mille; (4) *One Touch of Venus,* ballet by de Mille; (5) *Rosalinda,* ballet by William Dollar; (6) *The Merry Widow,* choreographed by Balanchine with incidental dances by leading ballet stars.

In rehearsal for 1944 were shows with ballets by Massine, Arthur Mahoney, Tamiris, Catherine Littlefield, Charles Weidman and others.

The Metropolitan Opera company faced the criticism of long standing at the historic Opera Guild's Round Table discussion headed by Mrs. John de Witt Peltz. Agnes de Mille, Anton Dolin, La Meri and Alexis Dolinoff helped to point out the causes of criticism of the ballet at the "Met." One admirable outcome of the discussion was that Marina Svetlova, a real prima ballerina, was acquired by the "Met."

Touring dance companies did a sell-out business but suffered considerably from travel conditions. The Ballet Russe de Monte Carlo started its season on the road without a New York opening. It presented four new ballets including *The Red Poppy* by Schwezoff, *The Cuckold's Fair* by Pilar Lopez, *Etude* by Nijinska

and *Ancient Russia* by Nijinska. Lubov Roudenko and M. Mladova left the company to be featured in Broadway attractions.

Ballet Theatre had its usual opening season at the Metropolitan Opera House, presenting the following new ballets: *Fair of Sorochinsk* with choreography by Lichine, *Dim Lustre* with choreography by Tudor, *Pictures of Goya* with choreography by Argentinita, and *Mademoiselle Angot* with choreography by Massine. The most noteworthy of these was the one by Argentinita, adding as it did a brilliant, varied and artistic episode in the best Spanish manner.

The illness of Alicia Markova gave opportunity to Alicia Alonzo to play the leading role in *Giselle*; to Nora Kaye in *Romeo and Juliet*; and to Rosella Hightower as the Swan Queen in *Swan Lake*. After the New York season was over, Nana Gollner with her husband, Paul Petroff, joined the company from South America. Irina Baronova took a leave of absence from the company in the spring but did not return in the fall. Karen Conrad and Sono Osato also left the company for Broadway contracts.

Colonel W. de Basil's Original Ballet Russe was practically disbanded when Colonel de Basil made an arrangement with the Teatro de Colon in Buenos Aires, Arg., to become its director and retain only about a dozen members of the company as a resident ballet.

Mia Slavenska, erstwhile ballerina of the Ballet Russe de Monte Carlo, started her own dance ensemble and opened her cross-country tour of 70 bookings the last week in 1943. Her program consisted of divertissement, classic, character and modern with a new 30-minute ballet, *Belle Starr*. Slavenska's partner was the young American dancer and choreographer, David Tihmar. Slavenska and Tihmar shared honours not only as soloists but as choreographers of the company. Other members of the company were Jack Gansert, Norma Vaslavina and Audrey Keane.

Another new company to make its debut late in the year was the American Concert ballet, a group of young dancers and choreographers who banded together in a co-operative enterprise to produce an outstanding program of four ballets: *The Five Gifts of Life* by William Dollar, *Mother Goose Suite* by Todd Bolender and *Sailor Bar* by Mary Jane Shea. Balanchine lent the company his blessing and his ballet *Concerte Baroco* to Bach music.

Edwin Strawbridge's *America Dances,* a ballet on American history, started on tour for young audiences in December. Miriam Marmein continued her yearly coast to coast tour presenting drama dances. Angna Enters continued to paint, write books and give recitals. La Meri moved to larger quarters and opened an intimate theatre where she continued her fortnightly performances of the ethnologic dance. Martha Graham gave a Broadway recital after two years' absence. Ruth St. Denis worked in an aeroplane plant for a while in Los Angeles "to do her bit," but later devoted her entire time to teaching classes in "temple dancing." Ted Shawn conducted his summer school at Jacob's Pillow with a faculty representing many phases of the dance. The Duncan Guild continued to grow and present conferences and recitals on the work of Isadora Duncan. Many schools and colleges ran special dance sessions with special dance faculties. National Dance week was celebrated for the ninth consecutive year throughout the U.S

In soviet Russia the soldiers continued to dance behind the lines to keep up their health, spirits and courage. The soviet government considered dancing so important that it frequently sent lengthy cablegrams to the American press about its new ballets and their dance artists. The periodic dance festivals were observed under any and all conditions. The leading dancers went to the front continually to entertain the soldiers and the famous tripartite conference took time out to see the soviet ballet dance "Swan Lake."

The Sadler's Wells ballet carried on in London and in the provinces with the biggest audiences ever known. New ballets were added and the prewar favourites continued. The Ballet Rambert carried the dance to the defense workers with signal success. The Jooss ballet, with a company of 26, established themselves in a new headquarters in the Arts theatre at Cambridge, and from there toured the country with two new ballets as well as old favourites redone with their erstwhile brilliance. Ballroom and folk dancing continued to flourish in England and the London *Dancing Times* reached America regularly each month.

In the United States, *Dance Magazine*, published by Rudolf Orthwine, who took over the *American Dancer* and *Dance* and made them into a new magazine in 1942, continued its policy of representing the whole field of the dance. It added a Teachers' edition that dealt with technical information for the professional and a Skating department edited by Alan E. Murray, the skater who first translated Cecchetti to the skating world.

Certainly skating was slowly but surely becoming the dance on ice. What is more, Gloria Nord, lead in the Roller Skating show, was an erstwhile dancer and referred to as the rollerina and ballerina on wheels.

Catherine Littlefield, ballet dancer and choreographer, officiated in 1943 at the Center Theatre Ice show and Sonja Henie's yearly extravaganza. Dance producer Chester Hale choreographed the "Ice Capades" and dancer Harry Losee the movie version.

There were functioning versions of local civic dance groups of varying sizes and excellence from the full time performance San Francisco Ballet company to the creative children's ballet companies that gave one or two performances a year. In 1943, the Dancing Masters of America under the leadership of Anna M. Greene gave the movement new impetus by sponsoring the organization of civic ballet by its local clubs throughout the country. (L. MH.)

Danchenko, Vladimir Nemirovich

(1858?–1943), Russian dramatist and director of the Moscow Art theatre, was born in Tiflis. A successful writer of novels and drama, he appeared frequently on the amateur stage and in 1891 was put in charge of the Moscow Philharmonic school's drama department. With the late Stanislavsky, noted Russian actor and producer, he founded the Moscow Art theatre in 1898 in a move to lift the national theatre from its artificiality and stagnation. They introduced plays by the younger generation of Russian writers and brought a spirit of realism and vitality to the stage. The Moscow Art theatre achieved a world-wide reputation, toured the continent with great success and in 1926 made a 26-week road tour of the United States. His last production, *Last Days of Pushkin* by Bulgakov, had its première only two weeks before his death. He published *My Life in the Russian Theatre* (1936), and shortly before his death received a state premium for war services awarded him by Stalin. He died in Moscow, April 25.

Dartmouth College.

An institution wholly undergraduate, for men, at Hanover, N.H. Civilian enrolment of 361 during the summer 1943 term was lowest since 1894. Normal enrolment was maintained, however, with assignment to Dartmouth of the largest navy V-12 unit in the U.S., totalling 2,000 navy and marine trainees in the Navy College Training program. The college provided all instruction, housing and messing for the unit. New freshmen trainees were received every four months. The majority of military students followed prescribed curricula for a total of four 16-week terms preparing for midshipmen's schools and commissions as deck officers, or marine officer training schools and commissions in the marine corps. Other trainees at Dartmouth were preparing for medical, engineering, supply and aviation commissions. President Hopkins announced that Dartmouth would continue to offer its liberal arts curriculum to all civilian students qualifying for admission even though this number became steadily smaller. For statistics of enrolment, faculty, endowment, library volumes, etc., *see* UNIVERSITIES AND COLLEGES. (S. C. HA.)

Darwin, Leonard

(1850–1943), British economist and eugenist, fourth son of Charles Robert Darwin, was born Jan. 15. He attended Woolwich Royal Military academy, and was later instructor at the school of military engineering in Chatham, 1877–82. He served on the intelligence staff in the war office, 1885–90 and left the army in the latter year with the rank of major. In 1892 he became liberal unionist member of parliament for the Lichfield division of Staffordshire. He was president of the Royal Geographic society, 1908–11, and of the Eugenics Education society, 1911–28. He also held the post of chairman of the Bedford College for Women, University of London, 1913–20. He wrote several books on economics and eugenics, among which were *Bimetallism* (1898), *Municipal Trade* (1903) and *The Need for Eugenic Reform* (1926). He died in Sussex, March 21.

Dashwood, Mrs. Elizabeth M.: *see* DELAFIELD, E. M.

Daughters of the American Revolution, National Society of.

The National Society of Daughters of the American Revolution was founded in 1890 for historical, educational and patriotic purposes. Membership: about 145,000 in 2,570 chapters. President general: Mrs. William H. Pouch. Headquarters: Administration Building, 1720 D St. N.W., Washington, D.C.

The society adopted as its principal war project the D.A.R. war project fund, resulting from voluntary contributions of $1 or more from members, to be used to further the blood plasma program and to purchase surgical and medical life-saving equipment. In Oct. 1943 this fund totalled $162,000, from which purchases have been made through the American Red Cross of 33 mobile blood donor units, 17 stationary blood donor centres, 8 station wagons, 2 Buick sedans and 1 truck. Over $33,000,000 in war bonds and stamps were subscribed by members and thousands of buddy bags were sent to members of the armed forces.

During 1943, gifts totalling $77,000 for 14 approved schools for foreign-born and southern mountaineers were approved. Regular activities included instruction in the right use of leisure and respect for rights of others to 235,000 children in 7,200 Junior American Citizens clubs, which in one Pennsylvania city invested $65,000 in war stamps; and distribution of 300,000 manuals for citizenship in 16 languages, to aid in naturalization. High school seniors from every state, winners of the Good Citizenship contest, were given a war bond in lieu of the regular award of a trip to Washington, since the society now holds its annual congresses outside of Washington city during the war period. About 53,900 copies of the *National Defense News* were distributed, as well as hundreds of thousands of Flag Codes and copies of other patriotic and educational literature. Through 118 clubs the society furthered its educational endeavours in training girls in homemaking. A student loan fund is maintained to assist worthy young persons in the pursuit of education.   (H. R. P.)

Davies, Joseph Edward

(1876–   ), U.S. lawyer and diplomat, was born Nov. 29 in Watertown, Wis. He was graduated from the University of Wisconsin, 1898, and received his law degree from the same school in 1901. Admitted to the Wisconsin bar in the latter year, he practised law until 1913. During this period he also held office as state's attorney from 1902 to 1906. He was associated with the federal trade commission, 1914–18, and after an unsuccessful candidacy for the senate in 1918, he established a law practice in Washington. In 1936, President Roosevelt asked him to become U.S. ambassador to the soviet union. The assignment was accepted eagerly and on Nov. 16 became official. The next two years were spent in carrying out the famous "mission to Moscow." Davies was extremely popular with the Russians and was largely responsible for the excellent relationship that developed between the U.S. and the U.S.S.R. He left the soviet union in 1938 and was named ambassador to Belgium. He was recalled to Washington in Jan. 1940 to serve as a special assistant to Secretary of State Cordell Hull. After his return to the U.S., Davies emphasized the necessity for mutual confidence and the closest co-operation with the soviet union. In May 1943, he carried a personal message from President Roosevelt to Premier Stalin. In the light of subsequent events, it was surmised that Davies had laid the groundwork for the Moscow and Tehran conferences, held at the end of 1943. He wrote *Mission to Moscow* (1941), an "inside" story of Russia which was later made into a motion picture.

Davis, Chester Charles

(1887–   ), U.S. government official, was born Nov. 17 near Linden, Dallas Co., Iowa. He was graduated with a bachelor's degree from Grinnell college, Iowa, 1911, and upon leaving school was associated with several journalistic enterprises in South Dakota and Montana. In 1921 he became commissioner of agriculture and labour for the state of Montana; four years later he was director of grain marketing for the Illinois Agricultural association, and he was associated with farm organizations from 1926 to 1928. From 1929 to 1933 he was engaged in the processing business. At this period of the economic depression, the new Roosevelt administration sought to alleviate the plight of the farmer through the medium of the Agricultural Adjustment administration. Davis was chosen administrator of the AAA in 1933 and continued in this capacity until 1936. He also served with the Export-Import Bank of Washington and the Commodity Credit corporation. From 1936 to 1943, Davis was affiliated with the federal reserve system, first as a member of the board of governors and later as president of the Federal Reserve Bank of St. Louis. In March 1943 President Roosevelt named Davis food administrator. Davis soon came into conflict with the OPA, however, and resigned on June 28. In accepting his resignation, President Roosevelt criticized Davis for failure to co-operate in the system of "co-ordinated controls."

Davis, Elmer

(1890–   ), U.S. journalist, radio news analyst and government official, was born Jan. 13 in Aurora, Ind. A graduate of Franklin college, he was a Rhodes scholar at Queens college, Oxford university, completing his studies there in 1912. Davis was a reporter and editorial writer on the *New York Times,* 1914–24, wrote a dozen books, including essays, short stories and satires, and reached the top rung of radio fame in 1939 as a news analyst for the Columbia Broadcasting system. On June 13, 1942, President Roosevelt announced his decision to fuse the various overlapping government information services into a single centralized organization and appointed Davis to head the new organization, known as the OWI (Office of War Information, *q.v.*). Davis had the delicate task of co-ordinating the government's war publicity and propaganda, both at home and abroad. His work was complicated by army and navy censorship and by the reluctance of high officials to consult him before talking to the press. Under his direction OWI took a frank view of the war, consistently warning the American people that the conflict would be long and hard. During 1943 Davis and the OWI had a rough year. They were under constant attack. Late in the year there was much criticism from professional newspaper sources, when the British released news of the Cairo conference, and the Russians of the Tehran conference, before OWI permitted American papers to use it. On Sept. 18, the OWI reorganized its overseas activities, separating propaganda and information.

Deafness.

The development of such drugs as the sulfonamides and penicillin was expected to have a great effect in reducing the total amount of deafness in the United States by the extent to which the use of these drugs in meningitis, scarlet fever and similar infections prevents the complications related to hearing. The deaf benefit greatly by the extension of funds to welfare agencies charged with instruction and care of the hard of hearing. Organizations such as the Federation of Organizations for the Hard of Hearing do a great deal to extend education in lip reading and in other techniques of communication.

Statistics assembled by Harry Best indicated something over 60,000 cases of deafness in the U.S. in 1940. He also provided a complete list of schools for the deaf in the U.S. The problem of the completely deaf is modified by partial loss of hearing coming with advanced years. Important studies were made dealing with the measurement of air and bone conduction in hearing and the changes that take place in the tissues with progressive hardness of hearing.

In 1,000 cases of otosclerosis, 50% began between the 16th and 30th year of age and 14% in those younger than 16. If fixed changes occurred in the hearing before adulthood, there was not much that could be done to increase hearing.

During 1943 there was continued progress with the fenestration or window operation for loss of hearing. Operative success occurs when the opening into the semicircular canal is not refilled by bony tissue. In 1943 it was said that two factors retarded the use of hearing aids—first, sensitiveness of patients in admitting deafness by wearing hearing aids and, second, their high cost. At the end of 1943 a new hearing aid was developed which could be purchased for $40, the purchase price including the service. The result of the introduction of this hearing aid was to bring about a lowering in cost of similar devices and a wide extension in the use of such hearing aids.

BIBLIOGRAPHY.—Harry Best, *Deafness and the Deaf in the United States: Considered Primarily in Relation to Those Sometimes More or Less Erroneously Known as "Deaf-Mutes"* (1943); Edward J. Stieglitz, ed., *Geriatric Medicine: Diagnosis and Management of Disease in the Aging and in the Aged* (1943).   (M. FI.)

Deaths (of prominent persons in 1943): *see* OBITUARIES.

Death Statistics.

Judging from mortality reports, health conditions in the United States and Canada during 1943 were not as good as in 1942. England and Wales, on the other hand, had an improvement. Provisional reports for the United States covering the first nine months of 1943 showed an increase of 4.9% in the death rate over the same period of 1942. The largest increases were reported in the New England, Middle Atlantic and Pacific Coast areas, while the increases were smallest in the states of the south. According to reports for the United States as a whole, there were 1,385,033 deaths during 1942, the death rate being 10.4 per 1,000 total population. Canadian cities and towns of 10,000 or more people had 6% more deaths during the first nine months of 1943 than during the corresponding period of 1942. Total deaths in Canada during 1942 numbered 112,864, with a death rate of 9.7 per 1,000 population. London and the great towns of England and Wales experienced 2.3% fewer deaths through the first nine months of 1943 than the same period of 1942. During 1942 as a whole, there were 480,131 deaths in England and Wales, with a corresponding death rate of 11.6 per 1,000 population. Civilian air-raid deaths in that country for the four-year period of war ending in Sept. 1943 totalled 49,130. Of this number, there were 23,265 up to the end of 1940; in 1941, there were 20,520 deaths, 3,235 in 1942, and 2,110 through September of 1943.

Official figures issued by the United States as of Nov. 11, 1943, reported a total of 121,319 casualties in the armed services. These were classified as follows: dead—army 12,841, navy, 12,883; wounded—army 30,263, navy 5,640; missing—army 23,954, navy 8,918; prisoners of war—army 22,592, navy 4,228. The 25,724 dead so far in this war may be compared with the 50,510 Americans killed or died of wounds in World War I, 1,704 in the Spanish-American War, 110,070 Union soldiers and 74,524 Confederates in the Civil War, 1,549 in the Mexican War, 1,956 in the War of 1812 and 4,044 in the Revolutionary War. American experience with fatalities from wounds in World War II seemed remarkably good, as compared with experiences in previous wars. Factors contributing to the improvement were the use of sulfa drugs, blood plasma, new anaesthetics, and also the efficient organization of the medical services of the armed forces at every stage from the field to the hospitals in the United States.

For the calendar year 1942, the death rates per 100,000 population for the ten leading causes were: diseases of the heart 295; cancer 122; intracranial lesions of vascular origin including cerebral haemorrhage 90; nephritis 72; influenza and pneumonia 56; tuberculosis 43; premature birth 26; diabetes mellitus 25; motor vehicle accidents 21; and syphilis 12.

The most detailed and current account of the trend of the death rates from the leading causes was available from the records of the many millions of industrial policyholders of the Metropolitan Life Insurance company. According to this experience for the first ten months of 1943, the death rates were appreciably higher than during the like period of 1942 for the following of the more important causes of death: whooping cough, diphtheria, influenza, pneumonia, cerebral haemorrhage, diseases of the coronary arteries, chronic heart diseases and war deaths by enemy action. Decreases in death rates were recorded for tuberculosis, syphilis, suicides, homicides, occupational accidents and motor vehicle accidents.

Beginning with 1943, the United States bureau of the census issued a monthly report on "Current Mortality Analysis" based on a study of a sample of death certificates received. This report was prepared principally in order that, during the war, health officers might watch the current trend of a number of diseases and thus note significant departures that might cause concern. A complete account of this innovation is given in *Vital Statistics—Special Reports,* vol. 17, no. 26, issued by the bureau of the census, June 18, 1943. The report for August indicated that poliomyelitis reached epidemic proportions that month. The report also noted a continuation of the unusually high death rate from cerebrospinal meningitis which first showed itself late in 1942;

a prognostication is made that the rates would remain high through the spring of 1944. This high mortality, which is attributed, in part, to the crowded conditions of the population during the war, was previously noted as a wartime phenomenon, although many epidemics have been experienced in time of peace. Case fatality from cerebrospinal meningitis was radically reduced by the use of sulfa drugs.

Several interesting observations were made in a study of mortality according to marital status which compared the situation in 1929-31 with that in 1939-41. The data related to the population of New York state, exclusive of New York city. It is generally established that the death rates are lower for the married than for the single, much more so among men than among women. Widows and widowers generally have the highest death rates. During the decade under review, the death rates fell somewhat faster among the married than among the single under age 40. The result has been to add to the relative advantage of the married at these ages. Among men, the difference in trend between the single and the married was very slight. Among women, the improvement was much more rapid for the married, due in large measure to the marked decreases in mortality from the conditions associated with childbearing. At ages 40 and over, the decline in mortality was more rapid among the single, so that the difference in the death rates between the single and married at these ages was reduced. Mortality of widowers during the decade under review did not improve as rapidly as that of either married or single men; the situation among widows was not as clear.

It was estimated that at least three workers in the United States are killed in accidents while off their jobs for every two who are fatally hurt while on the job. This conclusion was based upon the records of white male industrial policyholders of the Metropolitan Life Insurance company who died in accidents during 1937-39. Among the occupations practically free from special hazards were clothing factory operatives, cotton and woollen mill operatives, store clerks and salesmen, office workers and printers. Fatal accidents of nonoccupational origin were relatively more frequent than those of occupational origin even in such vocations as machinists, farmers and farm labourers, mechanics, and iron and steel mill workers. Among the occupations in which fatalities from injuries suffered on the job were relatively more frequent than those off the job are electric light and power linemen, coal miners, structural iron workers and railroad trainmen.

Some idea of the differentials in longevity according to social class is provided in "Life Tables for Social Classes in England" by C. Tietze, published in the Milbank Fund *Quarterly,* April 1943. The data reflect conditions in 1931. The professional and allied classes had an average length of life of 63.1 years; skilled workers, 60.0 years; and unskilled workers, 55.7 years.

In 1943, the United States bureau of the census published life tables for urban and rural areas in various regions of the

Average Duration of Life in Years in the United States According to Place of Residence, Based on 1939 Mortality

Sex and Place of Residence	White Persons				Nonwhite Persons			
	All Areas	The North	The South	The West	All Areas	The North	The South	The West
Males								
Cities of 100,000 or more	61.6	62.1	59.7	60.7	51.0	51.8	48.9	58.4
Other urban places	61.4	62.9	57.0	61.3	46.9	52.8	45.2	52.2
Rural territory	64.1	64.7	64.0	62.5	55.2	49.3	55.9	48.3
Females								
Cities of 100,000 or more	66.3	66.4	65.7	66.2	54.6	55.3	53.0	62.4
Other urban places	66.2	66.8	63.4	67.9	51.1	56.1	49.6	50.9
Rural territory	67.5	67.7	67.5	67.0	57.2	50.7	57.9	48.9

country. The findings were based on mortality in 1939. The table on page 226 presents the figures for average length of life from this study. On the whole, longevity is greater in the rural territory than in urban places. The south generally made the poorest showing and the north the best.

For the United States as a whole, the average length of life corresponding to the mortality statistics for 1941 was 64.36 years. The figures according to colour and sex are: white males 63.39 years; white females 68.08 years; coloured males 53.48 years; and coloured females 56.77 years. Compared with 1900–02, these represent gains of 15.16 years for white males; 17.00 years for white females; 20.94 years for coloured males; and 21.73 years for coloured females. (*See* also ACCIDENTS; CENSUS, 1940; INFANT MORTALITY; SUICIDE STATISTICS.)

BIBLIOGRAPHY.—W. F. Wilcox, *Introduction to the Vital Statistics of the United States,* Bureau of the Census (1933); L. I. Dublin and A. J. Lotka, *Length of Life* (1936); L. I. Dublin and A. J. Lotka, *Twenty-five Years of Health Progress,* Metropolitan Life Insurance Co. (1937); U.S. Public Health Service, *Public Health Reports* (issued weekly); U.S. Bureau of the Census, *Vital Statistics—Special Reports and State Summaries* (issued irregularly), *Monthly Vital Statistics Bulletin, Current Mortality Analysis* (issued monthly), *Annual Reports of Vital Statistics,* and *Vital Statistics Rates, 1900–1940;* Metropolitan Life Insurance Company, *Statistical Bulletin* (issued monthly); Population Association of America, *Population Index* (issued quarterly at Princeton, N.J.). (A. J. Lo.)

Debts, Government: *see* NATIONAL DEBT.

Decorations, Military and Naval.

During World War II it was announced by the United States that there had been created a legion of merit in four degrees, something new in the history of the United States decorations. There was also created the medal for merit, a decoration for award to civilians—again a departure from previous practices. Both of these decorations can be awarded to foreigners, in fact the grade of chief commander, commander and officer of the legion of merit may only be awarded to officers of foreign friendly nations. Presidential naval unit citations and army distinguished unit badges have been awarded to whole organizations for collective recognition of outstanding performance in the face of the enemy.

The air medal, a popular decoration in the air forces of the army and navy was completed during 1943. The navy, following the lead of the army, created the navy and marine corps medal for noncombat service, which is similar to the conditions of award of the army soldier's medal. The navy also adopted the use of the army's silver star and Purple Heart.

Silver oak leaf clusters were authorized by the army to represent five additional awards of any army decorations. The army, following the example of the navy, coast guard and marine corps created a good conduct medal to be known as the army good conduct medal.

The merchant marine distinguished service medal was authorized April 11, 1943, and is awarded by the U.S. maritime commission to any person in the merchant marine who on or after Sept. 3, 1939, distinguishes himself in the line of duty.

Merchant marine combat bar is issued to all crew members of merchant ships attacked. A crew member forced to abandon his vessel is awarded a silver star for attachment of the bar. American Typhus commission medal was authorized Dec. 24, 1942; the ribbon consists of a maroon background with a yellow central stripe—the medal had not been struck at the close of the year.

Army of Occupation of Germany medal (1918–23) was authorized Nov. 21, 1941, for those who served in Germany or Austria-Hungary from Nov. 12, 1918, to July 11, 1923, also to members of the naval service detached from ships for shore duty. This medal was to be issued after World War II.

The American defense service medal was authorized June 28, 1941—for those of the army who were outside the continental United States a clasp "Foreign Service," and those of the navy "Fleet" for service on high seas, and "Base" for service on shore outside continental United States will be issued.

There was also authorized a women's army corps medal for award to those women who were formerly in the women's army auxiliary corps and who re-enlisted in the WAC. This was the first time a medal was created exclusively for women.

CAPT. JOSEPH J. FOSS of the U.S. marines receiving the congressional medal of honour from President Roosevelt May 18, 1943, for shooting down 26 Japanese planes. With him are his mother (left) and wife

The world was divided into three parts for the award of World War II campaign medals—American campaign; European-African-Middle Eastern campaign; and Asiatic-Pacific campaign. Clasps were to be announced as the campaigns closed. The medals were to be furnished after the war but the ribbons were worn immediately.

Silver battle stars were authorized by the army to represent five battle engagements; previously bronze battle stars only were used.

Civilian government employees of the war department were given recognition on Dec. 8, 1943, when the initial awards of ribbons (no medals to accompany these awards) were made to those employees who had performed faithful service—civilian service; meritorious civilian service or exceptional civilian service.

There were numerous foreign decorations created but these awards would not be generally known until after World War II.

(A. E. Du.)

Defense, Civilian: see CIVILIAN DEFENSE.

Defense, National (U.S.): see AIR FORCES OF THE WORLD; WAR PRODUCTION, U.S.

Defense Board, Economic: see FOREIGN ECONOMIC ADMINISTRATION.

Defense Communications Board: see WAR COMMUNICATIONS, BOARD OF.

Defense Transportation, Office of.

The Office of Defense Transportation was created by executive order on Dec. 18, 1941, to "assure maximum utilization of the domestic transportation facilities of the nation for the successful prosecution of the war." Joseph B. Eastman, chairman of the Interstate Commerce commission, was appointed director of the agency.

During 1943 the Office of Defense Transportation continued to exercise supervisory powers over the various branches of domestic transportation under broad programs developed in 1942. Certain orders of the agency were revised to meet changed conditions, and new controls were established as need arose. While expanding war traffic exerted increasing pressure on all types of domestic transportation, no serious failures or interruptions of service occurred.

Steps were taken early in 1943 to avert threatened congestion of rail freight movement on the western transcontinental lines. The associate director of the Office of Defense Transportation's division of railway transport, in charge of the western region, was vested with Interstate Commerce commission powers to divert traffic from heavily burdened to less crowded routes. Similar arrangements subsequently were made for traffic diversion in the eastern and southern regions.

Deliveries of petroleum products transported to the east coast in solid trains of tank cars, operated under the supervision of the Office of Defense Transportation, reached a peak of over 1,000,-000 barrels a day in July 1943. Shortages of various types of freight cars were experienced occasionally in certain regions, but the car-supply situation was kept generally under control by the heavier loading required under general orders ODT 1 and 18, by utilization of refrigerator cars for carriage of general freight in the direction of the normal empty movement, and by other measures to increase efficiency of operations.

Railroad passenger travel in 1943, including organized troop movements, rose more than 65% over the record total of the previous year. The increased traffic had to be handled by the carriers without any significant additions to the supply of passenger equipment. The Office of Defense Transportation helped to alleviate crowded travel conditions, and assure space on regular trains and on intercity buses for the large volume of furlough and essential civilian business traffic, by conducting a continuing campaign to curb unnecessary civilian travel.

Conservation measures in the fields of motor transport and local transport were intensified throughout the year. Many joint action plans for pooling use of truck, bus, or taxicab facilities were put into effect. Development of an acute gasoline shortage in the northeast in May 1943, caused the agency to order sharp emergency reductions in commercial motor vehicle mileage and restriction of all wholesale and retail deliveries in that region. While the order cutting bus and taxicab mileage was revoked in August, the restrictions on deliveries were extended to the whole country in October.

The Office of Defense Transportation in mid-June 1943, broadened its permit system for control of Great Lakes shipping. Late opening of the navigation season in 1943 made it impossible to match the high 1942 record for movement of iron ore down the Lakes, but the grain movement surpassed the total of the previous year.

After the beginning of 1943, the Office of Defense Transportation acted as claimant agency for domestic transportation under the Controlled Materials plan of the War Production board. The agency functioned also as claimant for gasoline and rubber for highway use. In May 1943, as the result of a labour dispute, the Office of Defense Transportation took over operation of the American Railroad of Puerto Rico. A regional office was established in Hawaii in the summer of 1943. (See also ELECTRIC TRANSPORTATION; MOTOR TRANSPORTATION; RAILROADS.)

(J. B. E.)

De Gaulle, Charles: see GAULLE, CHARLES DE.

De Geer, Gerard (Jakob),

BARON (1858–1943), Swedish geologist, was born Oct. 2. A professor of geology at Stockholm university, 1897–1924, he was also founder and head of the Geochronological institute in that city. From his study of various sediments in earth layers, he was able to calculate the duration of the different stages of prehistoric eras—a branch of geology known as geochronology—and was also able to compute a climatic calendar that embraces a 16,000-year period in world history. Though he devoted most of his research to Sweden's geological and geographical changes, he also made scientific investigations in Canada and the U.S. and found a similarity in soil cross sections of both continents. He was the author of numerous scientific works on glacial and postglacial phenomena and was a member of a score of learned societies. He died in Stockholm, July 23, according to an American-Swedish news agency report.

Delafield, E. M.

(MRS. ELIZABETH M. DASHWOOD) (1891–1943), British novelist who specialized in gentle and restrained satire of the English middle class and excelled in the employment of the psychoanalytic technique in baring the motives of her principal characters. Among her best known works are: *Challenge to Clarissa* (1931), *Diary of a Provincial Lady* (1931), *The Provincial Lady Goes Further* (1932), *The Provincial Lady in America* (1934), *Straws Without Bricks* (1937), *The Brontes* (1938), *The Provincial Lady in Wartime* (1940) and *No One Will Know,* a three-act comedy (1941). Mrs. Delafield, who worked with the British Ministry of National Service during World War I, also served as a speaker for the British Ministry of Information in World War II. She died Dec. 2 at her home in Cullompton, Devonshire, England.

Delaware.

Delaware, nicknamed the "Diamond state," is located on the middle Atlantic seaboard of the U.S.A. and was the first to ratify the federal constitution on Dec.

7, 1787. Area 2,057 sq.mi. (land, 1,978; inland water, 79). Pop. (1940), 266,505, of whom 139,432 were urban and 127,073 rural. Native white numbered 215,695; foreign, 14,913; Negro, 35,820. Estimated population for 1943 was 273,778, of whom 187,680 were in New Castle county. Capital, Dover (5,517). Wilmington is the only larger city (112,504 in 1940).

History.—Civilian defense activities in Delaware reached their peak during 1943 with the training of gas detection, plant protection and bomb reconnaissance personnel. Air spotter programs were later reduced from 24 hours a day to one day a week, and the closely enforced dim-out along the coast was eased. The factories of the state, especially in the Wilmington area, continued their high rate of production of war materials. The estimated increase of retail and wholesale business during 1943 was not more than 15%.

The state legislature met in session on Jan. 4, 1943, and continued until April 9. Outstanding legislation included the creation of a state guard, the conferring of emergency powers upon the governor, enactment of a building code for New Castle county, and the establishment of a State Soil Conservation commission. The governor in 1943 was Walter W. Bacon; secretary of state, William J. Storey; adjutant general, Paul R. Rinard; attorney general, Clair J. Killoran.

Education.—There were 165 elementary and 44 secondary schools in 1943 with a total enrolment of 42,641 pupils and a teaching staff of 1,679. Although the loss of teachers was great, no schools were closed and only some agricultural and manual training courses had to be omitted.

Public Welfare.—The public assistance costs for the fiscal year ending June 30, 1943 were $607,740.90. In July 1942 the total case load was 3,279, but by the end of the fiscal year 1943 it had experienced a 23% decrease to 2,533. During the same period, 15 welfare institutions had case loads of 8,274 at the beginning of the fiscal year and 7,651 when the year was finished. Statistics were not available for the number of inmates in each of the county prisons.

Communication.—In 1943 there were 3,939 miles of highways under state control. All new construction ceased because of the war, and the resources of the State Highway commission were devoted toward the maintenance of the existing highways. Highway expenditures during 1943 were $2,594,961.90 as compared with $4,088,515.85 for the previous year. The Federal Aid expenditure in 1943 was $191,662.89 as compared with $708,-532.52 for the foregoing year. Railroad mileage (1938) 297. The waterborne commerce for 11 months of 1943 was 153,938 tons. The 10 airfields of the state were either under the control of the army or closed to civilian traffic. There were approximately 70,000 telephones as of Oct. 31, 1943.

Banking and Finance.—There were, in 1943, 30 state banks with resources of $413,278,677.77 and deposits of $357,855,263.90. The 13 national banks had resources of $28,107,837.88 and deposits of $23,254,597.07. The resources of the 42 building and loan associations were $14,595,983.23. The state budget (fiscal year 1942-1943) was $10,967,338.14, the receipts $12,139,712.63, and the expenditures $10,111,194.22. The state's gross debt was $4,943,300 and the net debt was $4,867,845.41.

Agriculture.—The total value of agricultural production in

Table I.—*Leading Agricultural Products of Delaware, 1943 and 1942*

Crop	1943	1942
Corn, bu.	3,226,000	4,092,000
Apples, bu.	499,000	940,000
Hay, tons	95,000	92,000
Wheat, bu.	1,008,000	1,380,000
Tomatoes, tons	5,500,000	5,500,000
Strawberries, crates	69,000	110,000
Lima beans, tons	5,700,000	8,910,000

1943 (Jan.–Sept.) was $63,612,000. The cash income from crops was $11,016,000 and from livestock $52,596,000. A serious drought reduced the crop yields to a low level for most crops, except those harvested before the drought began on June 13.

Manufacturing.—The estimated total value of manufactures as of Nov. 1, 1943 was $171,299,798.05.

Table II.—*Principal Industries of Delaware, 1943 and 1942*

Industry	Value of Products	
	1943	1942
Chemicals	$22,333,203.62	$17,627,502.30
Shipbuilding	57,213,700.04	17,652,483.42
Foundries, machine shops, tools.	35,454,394.14	38,759,988.04
Leather	8,510,131.61	7,469,668.74
Fibre	2,988,317.81	16,362,262.83
Textiles	35,070,462.60	15,641,112.39
Canning and packing	9,216,774.15	2,842,834.80

Mineral Production.—The chief products, granite, building stone, brick and clay products, had a total value of $172,277.96 (Nov. 1, 1943). The decrease from $325,673.19 for the same period of the previous year was largely due to the curtailment of building.

BIBLIOGRAPHY.—C. A. Weslager, *Delaware's Forgotten Folks* (1943); Gilbert Byron, *Delaware Poems* (1943); *Delaware Cases 1792–1830*, edited by Daniel J. Boorstin, (1943). (L. D. V.)

De Marigny, Alfred: *see* OAKES, SIR HARRY.

Democracy is not only a technique of government, based upon freely elected representative institutions, and upon an executive responsible to the people; it is based upon the belief of the equality of all individuals and of the equal right of all to life, liberty (including the liberty of thought and expression) and the pursuit of happiness. The denial of this equality and of individual liberty, the proclamation of authoritarianism and of the inequality of men and races as a "new order," is characteristic of fascism, which arose as a conscious and aggressive world-wide opponent of democracy.

The year 1943 saw democracy for the first time in many years again on the offensive, not only holding its own, but also beginning to defeat fascism. The advance of democracy was twofold, in the field of war strategy and in the field of ideology. In the war the tide turned definitely against the fascist aggressors. In 1940 German aggression against France and in 1941 against soviet Russia, as well as Japanese aggression against America at the beginning of 1942 had convinced many of the inferiority of democracy in the field of war and industrial mobilization: the splendid achievements of British and American industry and war strategy in 1943 proved that within a short time democracy did mobilize better than fascism could in many years of preparation and of totalitarian organization. These successes of democracy in proving its superior efficiency brought also in the ideological field a reassertion of the faith in democracy. The ignominious collapse of Mussolini, the father of fascism, and of fascist Italy in the summer of 1943 convinced many that fascism did not strengthen nations but undermined their moral fibre.

In the democratic countries the democratic liberties were everywhere maintained in spite of the war and, in many fields, even broadened. The anti-democratic movements in the United States and in Great Britain were discredited and weakened. In the western hemisphere only Argentina adopted during 1943 a strictly anti-democratic trend, yet even there the majority of the population opposed the pro-fascist policy of the authoritarian government.

The few neutral countries of Europe reflected in 1943 the growing faith in the victory of democracy. In spite of the strong German pressure the Danish people, under German occupation, gave a smashing demonstration for democracy in their parliamentary elections in March 1943. More than 90% of the electorate voted, and the five democratic parties polled 362,000 more votes than in the elections of 1939. The greatest gain was shown by the Social Democrats, the strongest single party, and by the violently anti-nazi conservative party whose political leader was in Great Britain leading the fight against Germany. The two non-democratic parties, the Danish nazis and the Farmers' party, received together only 68,000 votes out of a total of almost 2,000,000. Thus the elections became a heavy blow to the prestige of German fascism and forced the Germans to take over the administration in Denmark.

A similar success for democracy was achieved in Switzerland where the elections in the fall of 1943 brought a great gain to the Social Democrats who for the first time became the strongest political party in the National council having almost 25% more seats than in 1939. The two leading fascist organizations in Switzerland, the Nationale Gemeinschaft and the Rassemblement Federal, were dissolved in July 1943 and their newspapers suppressed.

Of even greater importance as an indication of a swelling world-trend in favour of democracy were the elections held in July 1943 in the Union of South Africa. The democratic parties, which had supported the war from the beginning, received under the leadership of Field Marshal Jan Christiaan Smuts 107 seats while the pro-fascist opposition, which had opposed South Africa's participation in the war, received only 43 seats. While the democratic and pro-war parties had had in the last parliament a majority of only 18, they gained in 1943 a majority of 64. All cabinet ministers were re-elected, some with record majorities The number of voters was unusually large. (*See also* COMMUNISM; EDUCATION; FASCISM; GREAT BRITAIN; UNION OF SOVIET SOCIALIST REPUBLICS; UNITED STATES.)

BIBLIOGRAPHY.—Basil Mathews, *United We Stand* (1943), Ernest Jaekh, *The War for Man's Soul* (1943).　　(H. Ko.)

Democratic Party.

The Democrats retained control of both the house of representatives and the senate through 1943, but their majority was so slight that they suffered many reverses on the domestic front. Teaming with the Republicans, conservative members of the dominant party staged numerous rebellions against the congressional leadership and the administration.

Capitol hill recalcitrancy became more marked as the result of a July-August recess spent among the home folks. Constituents criticized chiefly the "bureaucrats," especially the Office of Price Administration, the administration's alleged coddling of labour and huge expenditures of money. It was this accumulation of complaints which inspired an unprecedented display of bipartisan bitterness toward the executive branch.

As the year ended, 40 or 50 Democrats, principally southerners, were voting with the Republicans on many controversial domestic policies. With the majority having only a few more seats than the opposition—219 to 208 in the house and 58 to 37 in the senate—the Democrats were fortunate that they did not receive more rebuffs. The Republicans, however, exercised unusual restraint in many instances lest they be accused of hampering the war effort.

Almost every major measure considered or enacted into law concerned the war effort and domestic problems arising from the conflict.

Appropriations voted by the first session of the 78th congress totalled $114,500,000,000, and of this amount only $11,000,000,-000 was allocated for financing the civilian establishments and the public debt. The balance was for war purposes. This sum brought the amount of money voted for military or naval or associated activities since July of 1940 to approximately $350,-000,000,000.

The lend-lease act was extended for another year, or until March 11, 1944, and an additional $6,273,629,000 was set aside for this account. Since the original passage of the measure on March 11, 1941, lend-lease money and departmental sums made available to the Allies amounted to $60,653,629,000 by the end of 1943.

These extraordinary financial demands necessitated raising the debt limit from $125,000,000,000 to $210,000,000,000, which was voted without opposition.

Two new revenue acts were passed during 1943. The first one, which became law on June 9, 1943, provided for a modified pay-as-you-go plan under which partial collections are withheld at the source by the employer. In the second taxation program submitted in September, the treasury asked for an additional $10,500,000,000 in new levies, but the house responded with only $2,140,000,000. The senate increased the amount to $2,275,000,-000, but the measure had not been acted on by that body when congress adjourned on Dec. 23, 1943.

Robert L. Doughton, chairman of the house Ways and Means committee, estimated that these two measures would raise an additional $43,000,000,000 in a full year of operation, as against federal receipts of only $5,700,000,000 from all sources in the prewar year of 1939.

The authority to negotiate reciprocal trade agreements was extended for two years, or until June 12, 1945. The administration had asked for a three-year renewal. Only a personal appeal by Cordell Hull, secretary of state, prevented the congress from scrapping this legislation on the theory that economic disturbances caused by the war had outmoded it.

Sporadic strikes, and especially a walkout by 600,000 United Mine Workers in the spring, led to passage of the Connally Antistrike bill, as it is generally known. This empowers the government to take over and operate any kind of property where production of articles necessary to the war effort is impeded by strikes or other causes.

Differences over methods for preventing inflation precipitated the most serious struggles between the congress and the White House Under pressure from their constituents, the legislators rebelled against executive controls on prices and wages

In July the president vetoed a measure continuing the Commodity Credit corporation, which finances subsidy payments designed to keep down the cost of living, on the ground that it was "inflationary." In October Mr. Roosevelt asked again for renewal of this agency's life and for further power to use federal funds to check price rises by supporting farm income levels.

Congress, however, rejected the subsidy scheme. It voted to extend the CCC to June 30, 1945, but it prohibited the use of consumer subsidies after Dec. 31, 1943

Soldiers' legislation provoked extended debate. A proposal to set up a federal commission to supervise armed service balloting in the national elections was defeated by a coalition of "states rights" southern Democrats, who contended that the scheme invaded the 48 commonwealths' prerogatives, and Republicans. A bill providing for the draft of pre-Pearl Harbor fathers was amended so as to place the benedicts at the bottom of all selective service lists.

The Democratic leadership of congress remained unchanged during 1943. Vice President Henry A. Wallace of Iowa presided over the senate, and Senator Alben W. Barkley of Kentucky served as majority leader. Sam Rayburn of Texas held office as speaker, and Representative John W. McCormack of Massachusetts as house floor leader

Edward J. Flynn of New York resigned as Democratic national chairman in January of 1943. He was subsequently appointed minister to Australia, but he asked the president to withdraw his name when it appeared that he could not be confirmed by the senate.

Postmaster General Frank C. Walker of Pennsylvania supplanted Mr. Flynn as national chairman. Representative Patrick Henry Drewry of Virginia continued as chairman of the Democratic Congressional committee, and Senator Joseph F. Guffey of Pennsylvania as head of the Democratic Senatorial committee. (*See also* UNITED STATES.) (R. TU.)

Denmark.
A monarchy of north central Europe. Area, 16,575 sq.mi.; pop. (est. 1940) 3,844,312. Capital: Copenhagen (890,130). Other principal cities: Aarhus (99,881); Odense (85,521); Aalborg (55,652). Religion: Lutheran Christian. Ruler in 1943: King Christian X (*q.v.*); prime minister: Erik Scavenius, Nov. 8, 1942 to Aug. 29, 1943, after which there was no government except the illegal regime of the occupying Germans; Dr. Werner Best was "minister" and General Hermann von Hanneken military commander.

History.—Before the end of 1942 it was amply clear that the nazis had failed utterly to win over the Danes, their neighbours and their "racial brethren," or to make of Denmark the model collaborationist community which they had promised the world. The Danish army at last had to give up 100,000 rifles to the Germans, but its 3,000 horses were kept for farm work. The mounting encroachments against Danish sovereignty led to mounting resistance.

The underground press continued to flourish, despite the elimination by the gestapo of all but one of the staff of the largest paper, *De Frie Danske.* The number of police was approximately tripled. Parachutes brought powerful explosives from planes prepared in England. "Para-Danes" committed well-planned acts of destruction and trained thousands in the art of sabotage. The power station at the Recoil-Rifel syndicate's plant in Copenhagen was blown up; a building made over into a hospital for the nazis was burned down just after 500 new beds had been installed; locomotives exploded; bridges were blown up; tracks were torn up; switch towers were ruined; roads were mined; metal and machine shops were destroyed by bombs; shipyards were swept by fire; tunnels to Jutland were dynamited.

In Jan. 1943 the Germans announced that the Danish elections scheduled for March 23 could not be held; then for some reason they changed their minds, and two weeks prior to the date set the elections were permitted. The largest parties quickly combined in common newspaper advertisements appealing to the citizens to vote for any one of them as an expression of their Danism and their democracy. The coalition parties polled 363,-000 more votes than in 1939. "Dansk Samling," which had only 8,553 votes in 1939, was not in the coalition, and stood for direct protest against German occupation; this party increased its vote fivefold to 43,257. The Danish nazis polled only 43,277 votes against the combined total of 2,009,295 who spoke out for Denmark versus Germany. The claims of democratic Danes that 98% of the people were with them were spectacularly confirmed.

This evidence of unity among themselves, coupled with the successes of the Russians and the Allied armies in Italy, led to increased sabotage and an inevitable German crackdown. The occasion came with the Swedish restrictions on German traffic and transit through Sweden to Norway (Aug. 15 and 20). This heightened the importance of routes through Denmark, and made more serious the general strikes at Esbjerg and Aalborg. An aluminum plant was wrecked, "unpopular persons" were thrown into canals, and a clash between Danish and German soldiers led to a declaration of "state of emergency" on Fyn (Aug. 20). Premier Scavenius tried to resign, and the nazis demanded that

GERMAN TROOPS chasing Danish patriots in Axeltory square, Copenhagen, during the anti-nazi uprisings in Aug. 1943

the death penalty be decreed for sabotage. Rapidly disturbances spread until strikes and riots tied up nine cities. The king broadcast an appeal for cessation of violence, but refused the German request to declare martial law.

The crescendo of German impatience and Danish wrath rose to its finale on Aug. 28, 1943. In the early morning of Aug. 29 the Germans took the final step, and the irretrievable break was made. Scavenius and his cabinet were out, the king was taken a prisoner to Sorgenfri ("Without-Care") Castle; and the German army was sole master in Denmark. Many labour leaders, editors, professors and army officers were arrested.

Vice Admiral H. A. Vedel rose early in the morning to get to Naval Headquarters, and sent a message to the fleet: "Now or never. Proceed to Sweden or scuttle the ships." Nine small warships raced successfully to the Swedish shore; one light cruiser, the *Niels Juel,* was sunk by German torpedo planes in the attempt; 45 other vessels were blown up in harbour, along with ammunition dumps and harbour installations. The king pledged that he would not authorize any new Danish government while Germans remained in Denmark. (Frits Clausen had disappeared in disgrace, having reportedly embezzled funds.) In Denmark government was suspended.

Repeatedly the nazis had demanded the application in Denmark of the Nuremberg laws against the Jews. The king had said that if the yellow "J" was required in Denmark he would wear one himself. In Sept. 1943 Curt Daluege, right hand man to the late "Hangman" Heydrich, came to Denmark and on Sept. 30 a general search for Jews began, synagogues were burned and arrests were made. About 1,100 were taken to a camp at Maria Theresien Stadt in Czechoslovakia; 143 communists were sent to Stutthof, near Danzig. But Sweden protested and offered asylum, and some 8,000 Danes fled across the sound (of whom about 5,000 were Jews).

German demands for forced labour continued, 35,000 men being called for in November. This number was reportedly reduced later to 7,000. Fines for violence were levied on Odense (1,000,000 kroner) and on Copenhagen (5,000,000 kroner). Farms and houses were requisitioned for bombed-out German families. Food and other supplies were taken at an increasing rate, and goods (such as coal) in return amounted to only about one-fifth of the "exports." The National bank showed a German debt to Denmark of about 3,500,000,000 kroner—a figure about six times the total revenue of the Danish state in 1937–38.

Denmark was a potential landing point in 1943 for a continental invasion, hence the Germans busied themselves with defense works—guns, mines, fortifications, airfields, tank traps. General von Hanneken moved his headquarters from Copenhagen to Silkeborg, then to Holsted, and Minister Best was reported likewise to have moved with all his property to Jutland. Troops were increased to 10–15 divisions.

Education.—In 1940 there were 407,355 students in the elementary schools and 67,064 in the middle and secondary schools. In the two Danish universities 6,474 students were enrolled.

Economic and Financial Conditions.—Denmark, a rich agricultural country, was not starving in 1943. Lack of fodder and slaughter of livestock, however, were beginning to show serious effects. Coal was unobtainable in needed quantity from Germany, and 40,000–50,000 men were put to work cutting peat. Sabotage threw thousands of workers out of normal employment and destroyed productive establishments.   (F. D. S.)

Dennis, Charles Henry

(1860–1943), U.S. newspaper editor, was born Feb. 8 on a farm near Decatur, Ill. After graduating from the University of Illinois in 1881, he worked on a local paper, the Champaign *County Gazette.* Subsequently he went to Chicago, where he was hired by Victor Lawson in 1882 as reporter on the Chicago *Daily News,* then an enterprising six-year-old newspaper. He worked for the paper 61 years, rising from reporter to editor, 1925–34. He retired in the latter year as editor emeritus but continued to write a feature column on the editorial page. He was the author of *Eugene Field's Creative Years* (1924) and *Victor Lawson* (1935). Dennis died in Evanston, Ill., Sept. 25.

Dentistry.

Schour and Sarnat described some of the oral manifestations of occupational origin. These manifestations, which are reactions to noxious agents, chemical, physical or bacterial, take one or more of the following forms—abrasion, decalcification of the teeth, inflammation and circulatory disturbances of the mucous membranes. Of particular interest was the observation that munition workers exposed to acids often show decalcification of the teeth; metal workers develop enamel pigmentations. Gingival haemorrhage and ulceration and necrosis of the mandible were reported among those exposed to benzine, such as coke-oven and smokeless-powder workers. These developments naturally stimulated employers of labour to develop dental programs and dental care in their plants.

Thomas, in a paper on "Mouth Infection in Industrial Workers" pointed out the importance of maintaining oral health as a means of preventing enormous loss of man hours and of increasing production. Hooper, dental consultant for the Chicago, Milwaukee, St. Paul and Pacific railroad, stated in a paper on "Dental Services in Industry," that, "No student of the problem of employee absenteeism resulting from non-occupational illnesses, can come to any other conclusion than that oral sepsis is a major, if not the major, underlying 'root' cause of an astonishing proportion of it. The industrial executive . . . the president, or the operating vice-president must consider what oral antisepsis, insisted upon and maintained among his employees, would mean in more production. If he will give this the same kind of businesslike analysis that he gives his other production problems, there will be a great and sudden increase in the number of dental clinics set up in industry."

A recognition of the importance of these conditions resulted in the council on dental health of the American Dental association making a study of the problems of industrial workers. In fact, industries developed dental service with the employment of dentists in their plants, so that an organization of industrial dentists was formed during 1943.

The problem of loss of manpower in the war services through dental disease, was of equal importance with loss of manpower in industry, and the dental corps of the army had a large expansion during 1943, to take care of the dental conditions of the armed forces. A completely healthy dental apparatus, from every point of view, is of especial importance, it was found, among men in the Aviation corps. Flight surgeons studied this problem carefully. Joseph and his colleagues pointed out that of the men exposed to simulated altitude runs in low pressure chambers, 1.2% experienced toothache. The pain was due to (1) reaction of vital pulps of carious teeth to lowered atmospheric pressure; (2) reaction of degenerated pulps to lowered pressure; (3) the presence of inlays with residual air spaces beneath them. Expansion of the air trapped beneath the inlay may cause pain or expulsion of the filling. The histologic structures allow little compensation for changes in circulatory or gaseous volume within the confined area of the pulp chamber, root canal or apical alveolar structure; therefore, pathological conditions may become apparent in the low pressure chamber.

War accidents to face and jaws stimulated the study of methods to improve the treatment of fractured jaws. The method most commonly used in fracture of the lower jaw was the wiring of the teeth of the lower jaw to those of the upper, using the upper teeth as a splint. This made it impossible for the patient to open the jaw or to eat solids during the period of bone repair, and patients had to live on fluids. A new method of "skeletal fixation," which made possible the use of the jaw while the fracture was healing, had a remarkable development in use and popularity during 1943. Winter reviews 50 cases of the use of the Roger Anderson skeletal fixation appliance in mandibular fracture. Pins are inserted in the bone on either side of the fracture, the fragments are brought in proper alignment and the clamps attached to the pins are tightened on a connecting rod which holds the fractured fragments firmly in position. The advantages of this appliance were its ease of application, complete functioning of the mandible, minimum of nursing care, and no feeding problem. Similar types of appliances are in use, and many articles appeared in the literature during 1943 describing the results of this type of treatment, most of which were favourable.

Dental caries is a hardy perennial, and every year many articles are devoted to this subject. Fluorine as a protective against dental caries continued to attract the centre of attention. The low incidence of dental caries among persons living in areas supplied by waters containing fluorides, was reported from many sections of the world. Dean reported that less than 0.5 parts per million of fluorine in drinking water brings high caries experience, while in 0.5 parts per million of fluorine or more, there is low caries experience. The addition of fluorine to drinking water supplies as a mass means of controlling dental caries is alluring. Dean commented that, "Viewing the domestic water problem in this light, one might with justification expect that the community's public water supply is destined to play an important role in communal dental health."

BIBLIOGRAPHY.—Schour and Sarnat, "Oral Manifestations of Occupational Origin," *J.A.M.A.* 120:1197–1207 (Dec. 12, 1942); Earle H. Thomas, "Mouth Infection in Industrial Workers; Serious Menace to General Health; Resultant Loss to War Production," *Jour. A.D.A.* 30:1249–1262 (Aug. 1, 1943); T. V. Joseph *et al.,* "Toothache and the Aviator; Study of Tooth Pain Provoked by Simulated High Altitude Runs in Low Pressure Chamber," *U.S. Nav. M. Bull.* 41:643–646 (May 1943); Leo Winter, "Fractures of Mandible; Report of 50 Applications of Roger Anderson Skeletal Fixation Appliance," *Am. J. Surg.* 41:367 (Sept. 1943); David B. Ast, "Caries—Fluorine Hypothesis and Suggested Study to Test Its Application," *Public Health Reports* 58:857–879 (June 4, 1943); H. Trendley Dean, "Domestic Water and Dental Caries," *Jour. Am. Water Works Assoc.* vol. 35, no. 9 (Sept. 1943).   (L. M. S. M.)

Deposit Insurance Corporation, Federal: *see* FEDERAL DEPOSIT INSURANCE CORPORATION.

Dermatology. Interest in tropical medicine stimulated a symposium on tropical diseases of the skin. The following subjects were included: "Tropical Mycoses" by L. McCarthy; "Medical Entomology in Relation to Tropical Dermatoses" by M. E. Obermayer; "Yaws, Cutaneous Leishmaniasis and Pinta" by H. Fox; "Tropical Lymphangitis and Abscesses" by A. W. Grace; and "Leprosy" by C. N. Frazier.

Dermatitis due to contact with the manzanillo tree (beach apple) was reported by Satulsky and Wirts in a detachment of soldiers on the Canal Zone. Sixty men were affected, half of whom had temporary blindness from conjunctivitis and oedema of the eyelids. The cutaneous eruption was erythematous, often with vesicles or even large bullae. All recovered without sequelae in a week.

Under the title of "Dhobie Mark Dermatitis," Livingood, Rogers and Fitz-Hugh reported 52 cases in one military organization of an eruption due to marking clothes by native "dhobies" (laundrymen). The eruption varied from a mild erythematous to a bullous one, and was caused by the juice of nuts of a native tree. The authors thought it unlikely that fungous infections of the skin were due to laundering by dhobies.

Two cases of Calabar swelling (filariasis due to Loa Loa) were reported by Guy, Cohen and Jacob. The patients were missionaries returned from the French Cameroons in West Central Africa. Microfilariae were demonstrated in the blood and two adult worms were removed under local anaesthesia from the palpebral conjunctiva.

The histamine test was performed by Pardo-Castello and Tiant in approximately 300 cases of leprosy. It was reliable in delimiting areas of anaesthesia, particularly in maculo-anaesthetic lesions of the tuberculoid and nonspecific types. A reaction on normal skin consisted of a wheal with a surrounding erythema. In anaesthetic areas of leprosy, the erythema was always absent. The test was of no value in Negroes.

Among 20,000 men examined for induction into the army, Bereston and Ceccolini found 27 cutaneous entities, comprising 733 cases of dermatoses or syphilis. The commonest diseases of the skin in the order of frequency were acne vulgaris, psoriasis, pyoderma, tinea, varicose eczema, disseminated neurodermatitis, lipoma, sebaceous cyst, seborrhoeic dermatitis and nevus flammeus. Generalized psoriasis was the commonest cause of rejection, with disseminated neurodermatitis second, and neurofibromatosis third.

In view of the extensive use of sulfonamide drugs locally as well as internally, attention was called to the possible danger of sensitization by topical applications by Shaffer, Lentz and McGuire. Cohen, Thomas and Kalisch thought that sulfathiazole was potentially too dangerous a drug to use indiscriminately in mild ointments and that its intermittent use might produce dangerous reactions. Weiner considered that the incidence of sensitivity was low. Following the report by Bloom of two severe cutaneous reactions (one fatal) to sulfonamides, the section on dermatology at the annual meeting of the New York State Medical society voted unanimously to condemn the indiscriminate use of sulfonamides for relatively harmless diseases of the skin, and also the use of prepared dressings containing sulfonamide drugs, which are sold promiscuously to the laity.

Schwartz reported an outbreak of "cable rash" among electricians who were installing heat and flame proof cables in ships. The eruption which he had first described in 1935, was due to constant handling of cables in which halowax was flaked off upon the skin. The eruption occurred on the exposed parts, chiefly the face, and consisted of pinhead to pea-sized, straw-coloured cysts, due to plugging of the pilosebaceous follicles.

The histochemistry of lesions of pemphigus with special reference to bullous formation was studied by MacCardle, Baumberger and Herold. They concluded that hydrostatic pressure was not the prime factor in forming the bullae; that cohesion in pemphigus was good in spite of the Nikolsky sign; that polarographic studies showed no changes in bullous fluid as compared with normal serums. They found that the entire skin in pemphigus vulgaris contained increased amounts of silicon, iron, manganese and selenium.

What was apparently the first epidemic of erythema infectiosum in New York city was described by Chargin, Sobel and Goldstein. It affected 80 of 137 children in an orphanage. The incubation period varied from 1 to 12 days. The characteristic erythema of the cheeks was associated with mild constitutional symptoms and followed by frequent relapses, but no sequelae. Laboratory and epidemiologic studies failed to give any clue as to the causation.

Swartz and Lever treated 13 patients with dermatitis herpetiformis during the past two and one-half years with various sulfonamide compounds. Sulfapyridine controlled the eruption only as long as the drug was administered. Sulfanilamide was less effective even in larger doses. Sulfathiazole was of little value, while sulfaguanidine and sulfadiazine had no effect. No damage to the haemopoietic system was observed in any case. (*See also* MEDICINE.)

BIBLIOGRAPHY.—E. M. Satulsky and C. A. Wirts, "Dermatitis Venenata Caused by the Manzanillo Tree," *Arch. Dermat. & Syph.*, 47:797–798 (1943); C. S. Livingood, A. M. Rogers and T. Fitz-Hugh, Jr., "Dhobie Mark Dermatitis," *J.A.M.A.*, 123:23–26 (1943); W. H. Guy, M. Cohen and F. M. Jacob, "Infection with Loa Loa," *Arch. Dermat. & Syph.*, 47:763–767 (1943); V. Pardo-Castello and F. R. Tiant, "The Histamine Test: With Particular Reference to the Diagnosis of Leprosy," *Arch. Dermat. & Syph.*, 47:826–829 (1943); E. S. Bereston and E. M. Ceccolini, "Incidence of Dermatoses in Twenty Thousand Army Induction Examinations," *Arch. Dermat. & Syph.*, 47:844–848 (1943); B. Shaffer, J. W. Lentz and J. A. McGuire, "Sulfathiazole Eruptions: Sensitivity Induced by Local Therapy and Elicited by Oral Administration," *J.A.M.A.*, 123:17–23 (1943); L. Schwartz, "An Outbreak of Halowax Acne ('Cable Rash') Among Electricians," *J.A.M.A.*, 122:158–161 (1943); R. C. MacCardle, J. P. Baumberger and W. C. Herold, "Histochemistry of Pemphigus Lesions: With Special Reference to Bullous Formation," *Arch. Dermat. & Syph.*, 47:517–545 (1943); L. Chargin, N. Sobel and H. Goldstein, "Erythema Infectiosum," *Arch. Dermat. & Syph.*, 47:467–477 (1943); J. H. Swartz and W. F. Lever, "Dermatitis Herpetiformis: Immunologic and Therapeutic Considerations," *Arch. Dermat. & Syph.*, 47: 680–693 (1943). (H. Fx.)

Destroyers: *see* NAVIES OF THE WORLD.

Detroit. Fourth largest city of the U.S.A., Detroit is the centre of the large industrial area of southeastern Michigan. Area, 137.9 sq.mi.; pop. (1940) 1,623,452; estimated (Dec. 1, 1943), 1,875,000. Foreign-born white, 320,664, of whom 110,698 were British and Canadian; 52,235 Polish, ranking second. Assessed value as of July 1, 1943, $2,794,425,810; gross bonded debt as of Dec. 31, 1942, $347,022,739, which included $91,788,739 of utility debt; net debt, $246,308,889 excluding all utilities; gross city appropriation, fiscal year ending June 30, 1944, $182,989,931 including utilities; tax levy, city and school purposes, $78,319,372; combined tax rate $28.03. Mayor, Jan. 1, 1944: Edward J. Jeffries, Jr.

The outstanding event of 1943 in the civic life of Detroit was the race riot of June 19 and 20. The affair had its roots in the large increase in Negro population (from 40,858 in 1920 to 149,119 in 1940 with later increases) and the resulting housing congestion, discrimination in certain war plants, unsatisfactory social conditions, and resentment on the part of some whites at the taking over of public recreation facilities by Negroes. The immediate cost was the loss of 34 lives, 1,000 persons injured, and $2,000,000 in property destroyed, with incidental financial losses due to absenteeism and extra-governmental costs (*see* RACE RIOTS).

There was the usual political aftermath to this unfortunate

affair. Mayor Edward J. Jeffries and his administration were accused by some whites of coddling the Negroes and of laxity in police activity. The Negroes in turn charged the police with unnecessary harshness and the administration with neglect and discrimination. In consequence, the Negroes joined with organized labour (both C.I.O. and A.F. of L.), and the Democratic organization in an effort to elect a "labour" ticket.

As a city whose industrial life depended originally on the automobile and then upon arms production, the problem of transition from war back to peace had much official and civic attention in 1943. The city government proposed to cope with the possibly resulting unemployment situation by extensive public works for which detailed plans were being drafted. To meet the costs, an appropriation of $6,000,000 a year was being accumulated. Effort was also made to supplement this fund by heavy taxes on the gross income of certain privately owned utilities, a tax on racing and much increased state-aid.

The graft inquiry begun in 1941 was brought to final and successful conclusion with the denial of appeals to some of the more prominent accused. In addition to numerous police officials, a prosecutor and sheriff were incarcerated.　　　(L. D. U.)

Devers, Jacob L. (1887–), U.S. army officer, was born Sept. 8 in York, Pa. On his graduation from West Point in 1909 he was commissioned a second lieutenant in the field artillery. During World War I he served at Fort Sill, Okla., first as an artillery instructor and later as executive officer. He later spent five years as instructor of military tactics at the U.S. Military academy. As a division commander under Maj. Gen. Adna R. Chaffee, who built up the armoured force, he became experienced in the problems of mechanization, and in 1939 he was sent to Panamá as chief of staff in charge of mechanization of the Panama canal defenses. The next year he was recalled to direct the construction of Ft. Bragg. On Gen. Chaffee's resignation in 1941, Gen. Devers was appointed to fill his post as commander of the armoured force at Ft. Knox, Ky., and in Sept. 1942 he was advanced to the rank of lieutenant general. He remained at Ft. Bragg until May 1943, when he was named to succeed Lieut. Gen. Frank M. Andrews, killed in a plane crash, as commander of U.S. forces in the European war theatre. On Dec. 28, President Roosevelt announced the appointment of Gen. Devers as deputy commander in the Mediterranean theatre under Gen. Sir Henry Maitland Wilson.

Diabetes. A discovery which eventually might lead to the heart of the diabetic problem occurred in 1943 when J. S. Dunn, H. L. Sheehan and N. G. B. McLetchie produced necrosis or destruction in the islands of Langerhans of a rabbit's pancreas with alloxan.

The pancreas has been known to be the seat of diabetes since its removal by Joseph von Mering and Oscar Minkowski in 1889 was followed by that disease. Twelve years later E. L. Opie and L. W. Ssobolew localized the carbohydrate controlling function in groups of cells, constituting a 20th of the gland by weight, named the islands of Langerhans and from which in 1921 Frederick G. Banting and C. H. Best extracted insulin. Later in 1937 the experimental production of diabetes by repeated injections of anterior pituitary extract by F. G. Young was accompanied by the degeneration of the islands. When Dunn *et al.* injected alloxan into rabbits intravenously in the strength of 200 milligrams per kilogram weight, the animals died in 14 to 48 hours and save for slight involvement of other organs, the only pathological lesion found was a selective necrosis of the islands of Langerhans. The rabbits at first exhibited a temporary rise of blood sugar and then a fall to low levels of sugar such as is observed after an overdose

of insulin. Arguing that since the islands were destroyed, if the animals could be kept alive during the hypoglycaemic phase, they should eventually develop diabetes, C. C. Bailey and O. T. Bailey protected and revived the rabbits with intravenous injections of 50% glucose and were rewarded by the appearance of hyperglycaemia, glycosuria and full-fledged diabetes the next day. J. S. Dunn and co-workers in Glasgow, C. C. and O. T. Bailey in Boston, and M. G. Goldner and G. Gomori in Chicago confirmed and extended the original experiments with rats and dogs thus establishing a third method whereby diabetes can be produced, the first by means of a chemical.

Alloxan at the close of 1943 had not been recognized in pure form in the body, but its structure is such that it is easy to believe it might play a significant role in man's daily metabolism. It is the ureide of mesoxalic acid and a powerful oxidizing agent. It can be produced by the oxidation of uric acid, the end product of purine metabolism in man. A satisfactory test for alloxan in body fluids had not been devised by the close of the year.

The diabetes of the alloxan rabbit or rat extraordinarily resembles that of the human subject. One of the Baileys' rabbits weighing 1,520 grams showed polydipsia and polyuria with water intake ranging between 350 and 700 cc., and urinary output between 160 and 470 cc. daily. The blood sugar rose to 640 milligrams per 100 cc. and in another rabbit not given insulin the blood sugar reached 700 milligrams, the lipaemia 8,412 milligrams and total acetone bodies expressed as acetone 144 milligrams per 100 cc. In a rat typical symptoms of diabetic coma, including Kussmaul respiration, developed. That rat died, but another with similar acidosis recovered with insulin. All five rabbits with alloxan diabetes under observation for two and a half months to five months developed cataracts and cataracts were also seen in an alloxan rat. Transitory diabetes was brought on when repeated small doses of alloxan, not less than 40 milligrams per kilogram body weight, were injected instead of the customary 200 milligrams per kilogram.

The ease with which alloxan diabetes can be produced in rabbits and rats and its close similarity to that in man furnish opportunities for the study of the disease and its complications both with and without treatment under conditions not hitherto so easily available and also the possibility of penetrating further than before into the causation of the disease.

The average duration of life of a diabetic at the beginning of the 20th century was 4.9 years, but by 1938–40 had reached 14.1 years. Based upon life expectancy as calculated by the Metropolitan Life Insurance company for one large clinic, the expectancy for different age groups approximated two-thirds of the corresponding population as a whole. This period of duration is far too short.

Diabetic coma caused two-thirds of all diabetic deaths in large diabetic clinics both in Germany and the U.S. up to 1914. Treatment was hopeless. From then until 1922 the rate fell to 40% among the clientele of one large clinic as a result of J. G. Allen's introduction of undernutrition and the better education of the patient. Insulin lowered the mortality still more rapidly and between 1922 and 1925 it fell to 20%. The downward trend was accelerated in 1936 by the discovery of H. C. Hagedorn's protamine and D. A. Scott and A. M. Fisher's protamine zinc insulin when only 3.6% of 929 diabetics after discharge from one clinic succumbed to this needless complication. Treatment of the actual coma state also progressed, but even in 1943 the treatment of coma was often unsuccessful. It is therefore worthy of mention that in one recent series of 104 successive diabetic coma cases death occurred in but one instance. Success in this series was attributed to the preliminary organization of the clinic for emergency admissions, available help from the laboratory day and night, Sundays and holidays, and the prompt and detailed clinical and nursing care of such cases by physicians of wide diabetic experience, the use of insulin in adequate dosage, the alleviation of dehydration with salt solution and especially to the avoidance of confusing or obscuring the blood picture by the employment of glucose or alkalies. No diabetic should die of diabetic coma.

BIBLIOGRAPHY.—J. S. Dunn, N. G. B. McLetchie, and H. L. Sheehan, "Necrosis of Islets of Langerhans Produced Experimentally," *Lancet* 1:484–487 (1943); J. S. Dunn and N. G. B. McLetchie, "Experimental Alloxan Diabetes in the Rat," *Lancet* 245:384–387 (1943); J. S. Dunn, J. Kirkpatrick, N. G. B. McLetchie and S. V. Telfer, "Necrosis of the Islets of Langerhans Produced Experimentally," *Jour. Path. and Bact.* 55:245–257 (1943); A. Braunschwig, J. G. Allen, M. G. Goldner and G. Gomori, "Alloxan," *J.A.M.A.,* 122:966 (1943); C. C. Bailey and O. T. Bailey, "The Production of Diabetes Mellitus in Rabbits with Alloxan," *J.A.M.A.* 122:1165–1166 (1943); M. G. Goldner and G. Gomori, "Alloxan Diabetes in the Dog," *Endocrinology* 33:297–308 (1943).   (E. P. Jo.)

Diamonds.

World production of diamonds is shown in the accompanying table; official figures on output are lacking in many cases and the data for the war years are those of S. H. Ball.

World Production of Diamonds
(Thousands of carats)

	1938	1939	1940	1941	1942
Angola	651	690	784	787	792*
Belgian Congo	7,206	8,360	9,603	5,866	6,018
Gold Coast	1,297	1,088	825*	1,000	1,000*
Sierra Leone	690	600*	750	850	850*
South Africa	1,238	1,250	543	112	106
South West Africa . . .	155	35	30	47	60
Brazil	235	350*	325	325	300
Others	148	127*	152*	118	128
Total	11,620	12,500	13,012	9,105	9,254

*Estimated.

Production in 1942 was thought to have improved slightly over 1941, though outputs in most of the major producing countries were far below their usual levels. With Congo, Gold Coast, Sierra Leone and Angola producing 93% of the total output, there was a higher percentage than ever of industrial stones in the total, but so long as war demand lasted, industrials would be of more importance than gem stones. It was estimated that sales of industrial stones were in 1943 approaching in value the sales of gem stones. There were three reasons for this shift in the relative position:

1. Gem stones were a luxury, the sale of which was not greatly encouraged, while industrial stones were essentials in the war program.
2. War production heavily increased the already rapidly growing uses for industrial stones.
3. While gem sales served to increase an ever-growing pool of stones in the hands of the buying public, from which there were no deductions except irretrievable losses and such small amounts as were involved in recutting old gems, industrial stones were subject to such heavy wear that the average life in constant use was about two years.

The scale on which industrial diamonds were in use was not known, but it was quite possible that replacement of wear alone, without considering additions for new uses, might be of the order of two or three million

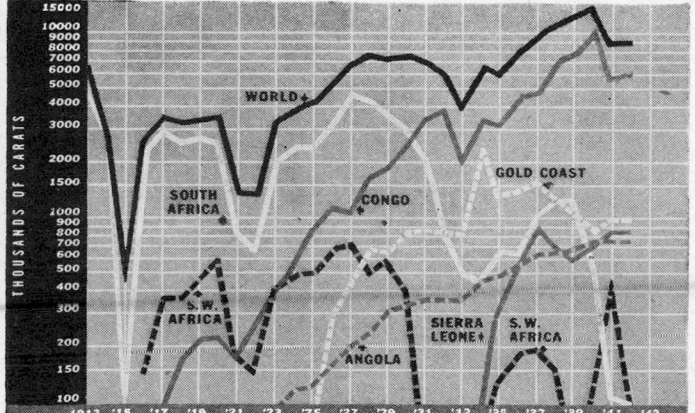

DIAMOND PRODUCTION OF THE WORLD and the major producing countries as computed by *The Mineral Industry*

carats a year, and possibly even more.

Sales of diamonds by the Diamond Trading company increased from about £7,000,000 in 1941 to £10,500,000 in 1942, and were expected to exceed £17,000,000 in 1943, with most of the increase in industrial stones.

Belgium and the Netherlands were no longer factors to be considered in the cutting trade, which was in 1943 carried on chiefly in Palestine, United States, South Africa, Great Britain, Puerto Rico, Cuba and Brazil. The number of cutters available was only a fraction of the number formerly working in the Low Countries, and many of these, especially in the United States and Great Britain, were engaged in the preparation of industrial stones, rather than in the cutting of gems.

In Nov. 1943, it was reported that a 530-carat diamond had been discovered in Sierra Leone. This would rank about eighth in size among the large stones on record.   (G. A. Ro.)

Diatomite.

Production was not reported in the United States, where about one-third of the world's output is made; production was estimated at 114,300 long tons in 1941, and presumably increased somewhat after that year, since many of the uses were enlarged by war demands.   (G. A. Ro.)

Dickinson, Luren Dudley

(1859–1943), U.S. politician, was born April 15 in Niagara county, N.Y. He was educated in Michigan's public schools and taught rural school for 19 years before entering the political arena. He was state representative for three terms between 1897 and 1908, state senator for one term and was seven times elected lieutenant governor of Michigan. In March 1939, he succeeded to the governorship after the death of Gov. Frank D. Fitzgerald but lost his seat in the 1940 elections. Shortly after he took over the executive office, Mr. Dickinson gained national prominence as a crusader against "high life in high places." He died at his farm near Charlotte, Mich., April 22.

Dickinson, Willoughby Hyett Dickinson,

1ST BARON (1859–1943), British statesman, politician and pacifist, was born April 9, the son of a British parliamentarian. He attended Eton and Trinity college, Cambridge, studied law and was called to the bar in 1884. He served on the London county council, 1889–1907, and was its chairman in 1899. He was chairman of the London Liberal federation, 1896–1918, was made a privy councillor in 1914. He was created first Baron Dickinson of Painswick in 1930 and joined the Labour party the same year. Lord Dickinson, who was chairman of the League of Nations society, 1915–18, was widely credited with being the originator of the League of Nations. In 1923, he was substitute delegate to the Geneva assembly. He was also life president of the World Alliance for Promoting International Friendship Through the Churches. He died at his home in Painswick, England, June 1.

Dictatorships: *see* COMMUNISM; FASCISM; GERMANY; JAPAN; RUMANIA; SPAIN; UNION OF SOVIET SOCIALIST REPUBLICS.

Dietetics.

The Food and Nutrition board of the National Research council reported on dehydrated fruits and vegetables, on fats, on milk, and on the nation's protein supply. One group sponsored a survey of dental caries, another the nutritional aspects of ageing, while a different group reported on early recognition of dietary deficiencies. The recommended dietary allowances formulated by the Food and Nutrition board in 1941 were used to guide the planning and appraisal of peace and wartime dietaries. Studies indicated that adults may be maintained on diets somewhat lower in thiamin and riboflavin than the figures given in the dietary allowances. Additional recommendations were made by the Food and Nutrition board relative to iodine, copper and vitamin K.

Further investigations were reported on the essential amino acid requirements of humans, and on the amino acid composition of foods. Tools were thus provided to construct a program for supplying an adequate protein intake with the use of supplementary vegetable proteins where there is a shortage of animal proteins.

The Committee on Food Composition appointed by the Food and Nutrition board of the National Research council assembled, co-ordinated and appraised these recent data. Data were assembled to meet the need for information concerning the composition of commercially produced dehydrated vegetables and soups. As a supplement to this survey comparison was made of various special methods of dehydration; it was found that the use of heated, natural gas as the dehydration atmosphere resulted in high vitamin C retention in certain vegetables. The committee also correlated and planned experiments to determine losses of nutrients during the processing, preparation and storage of foods.

Further appraisals of the dietary intake of certain population groups in terms of currently accepted standards indicated a need for continued efforts to raise the level of intake of various nutrients. The use of foods of high nutritive potency provides one of the most effective means of bringing about a quantitatively significant increase in intake. In the large-scale feeding of industrial workers, dried yeast was incorporated in various dishes with considerable success. The tremendous expansion in the production of soya products permitted United States civilians to use large quantities of these high protein products. In 1943, 300,000,000 lb. of soya products were made available, representing 140,000,000 lb. of high-quality and low-cost protein, as well as substantial amounts of vitamins of the B complex, and iron, phosphorus and calcium. This offered enough protein for a full year's requirement for more than 2,000,000 people. The Office of Foreign Relief and Rehabilitation Operations developed food products of high nutritive potency such as spaghetti to which dried egg and soybean flour were added; and dehydrated soup powder which contained split peas, soybeans, dried skim milk, brewer's yeast and seasoning. Since these products were for foreign consumption, each of the processed foods was subjected to acceptability testing with nationality groups. The Committee on Food Habits of the National Research council assumed responsibility for this project. Flour enrichment in the United States was further modified. Riboflavin limits were not less than 1.2 or more than 1.5 mg. per pound of flour, while thiamin was from 2.0 to 2.5 mg. per pound of flour. The lower and higher limits for niacin were 16.0 and 20.0 mg. per pound of flour, while iron was not less than 13.0 or more than 16.5 mg.

The nutritional analysis of the estimated civilian food supply in the United States for the full year 1943 indicated that the per capita consumption of most nutrients would be slightly higher than the yearly average during 1935–39. The increases in the consumption of calcium, riboflavin and thiamin were a result of the further enrichment of white flour and the increased consumption of fluid milk. With rationing of the more important foods and with greater purchasing power, more people received a fairer share of the total nutrients in 1943 than in the prewar period. According to V. P. Sydenstricker, this seemed to be the situation in England also. (See also FOOD RESEARCH; VITAMINS.)

BIBLIOGRAPHY.—United Nations Conference on Food and Agriculture. Final Act and Section Reports. Department of State Publication 1948.

Conference Series 52 (1943); F. L. Gunderson, "Peacetime and Wartime Functions of the Food and Nutrition Board, National Research Council," *Nutrition Reviews*, 1: 161-164 (1943); C. A. Elvehjem, "Newer Findings in Vitamin Research," *J. Am. Dietet. Assn.*, 19: 743-745 (1943); Food and Nutrition Board, National Research Council, "Recommended Dietary Allowances," Reprint and Circular Series, No. 115 (1943); W. C. Rose *et al.*, "Further Experiments on the Role of the Amino Acids in Human Nutrition," *J. Biol. Chem.*, 148: 457-458 (1943); R. C. Clouse, "Compilation of Recent Data on Mineral and Vitamin Values of Foods," *J. Am. Dietet. Assn.*, 19: 496-504, 746-755 (1943); V. Cheldelin and R. R. Williams, "Studies of the Average American Diet," *J. Nutrition*, 26: 417-430 (1943); H. T. Kelly and M. Sheppard, "Nutritional Failure Among Private Patients," *J. Am. Dietet. Assn.*, 19: 346-348 (1943); C. A. Heller, C. M. McCay and C. B. Lyon, "Adequacy of the Industrial Lunch and the Use of Brewer's Yeast as a Supplement," *J. Nutrition*, 26: 385-390 (1943); B. G. Leaming, "Soya Products—Availability, Nutritional Values, and Utilization," *J. Am. Dietet. Assn.*, 19: 824-827 (1943); Bureau of Agricultural Economics, U.S. Dept. of Agri., "The National Food Situation," Release NFS-7 (1943); V. P. Sydenstricker, "Nutrition Under Wartime Conditions," *Bulletin of the New York Academy of Medicine*, 19: 749-765 (1943).   (D. F. TR.)

Dimension Stone: *see* STONE.

Diplomatic Services: *see* AMBASSADORS AND ENVOYS.

Disasters.

During 1943 loss of life and property in accidents included the following:

Aviation

Jan. 15	Near Paramaribo, Dutch Guiana. Maj. Eric Knight, novelist, was among 35 persons killed when transport plane crashed in jungle.
Jan. 22	Pacific ocean. U.S. navy reported that transport seaplane carrying crew of 9 and 10 naval officers was more than 24 hrs. overdue on flight from Pearl Harbor to San Francisco.
Jan. 26	Near Flomaton, Ala. Brig. Gen. Carlyle H. Walsh and nine others were killed in crash of army transport plane.
Feb. 9	Newfoundland. Ferry-command plane crashed, killing 13 passengers and crew of 6.
Feb. 18	Seattle, Wash. Fourteen persons were killed, 13 others were injured when bomber crashed into packing plant. Twenty employees in plant were reported missing.
Feb. 22	Lisbon, Portugal. Four persons were killed and about 20 others were missing after a Clipper flying boat crashed in landing on Tagus river.
May 3	Iceland. Lt. Gen. Frank M. Andrews, Bishop Adna W. Leonard and 12 others were killed in crash.
May 13	Near El Paso, Tex. Fifteen men were killed when two army bombers collided at army field.
May 20	Chicago. Twelve persons aboard army bomber met death when plane crashed into giant gas storage tank and set aflame 18,000,000 cu.ft. of gas.
June 6	Near Austin, Nev. Bodies of 15 persons were found in wreckage of army plane; plane had been missing for 6 days.
July 4	Gibraltar. Premier Wladislaw Sikorski of Polish government-in-exile, his daughter, Mme. Sophia Lesniowska, and 14 others were killed in crash of plane soon after taking off from Gibraltar.
July 28	Near Bowling Green, Ky. Twenty persons were burned to death when air liner crashed and exploded.
Aug. 1	St. Louis, Mo. Ten persons, including Mayor William D. Becker of St. Louis, were killed in crash of army troop glider.
Aug. 26	Rio de Janeiro. Crash of air liner into Rio de Janeiro bay brought death to 18 of 21 persons aboard plane.
Sept. 20	Maxton, N.C. Crash of army transport plane at Laurinburg-Maxton airfield resulted in death of 25 persons aboard craft.

Fires and Explosions

Jan. 31	Near Seattle, Wash. Twenty-eight patients were burned to death in fire that swept through sanatorium for aged invalids.
March 24	Ravenna, Ohio. Ten workers were killed and two others were injured in explosion at government ordnance plant.
March 28	Naples, Italy. At least 79 persons were killed and 1,179 were injured when an ammunition dump in port area blew up. (Berne dispatches said at least 400 were killed and 2,000 injured.)
May 4	Elkton, Md. Munitions plant blast took toll of 13 known dead.
May 5	La Follette, Tenn. Ten miners were trapped and killed in coal mine explosion.
July 9	Chicago. Seven firemen were killed and two others severely injured in collapse of flame weakened roof and walls of four-story structure.
July 12	Eglin Field, Fla. Seventeen officers and men were killed and 51 others injured in accidental explosion at army air base.
Aug. 19	Kearny, N.J. Thirteen persons were killed in explosion that destroyed war plant.
Aug. 28	Birmingham, Ala. Nineteen persons were killed and 25 others injured when two gas explosions sealed coal mine tunnel.
Sept. 7	Houston, Tex. Forty-five men died in fire that swept old hotel in Houston's midtown section.
Sept. 12	Philadelphia. Fire swept through Broad Street station and adjacent buildings, destroying large part of terminal, and causing damage estimated at $250,000.
Sept. 17	Norfolk, Va. Twenty-four persons were killed and 250 others injured when "ammunition in transit" at Norfolk naval air station blew up.
Dec. 24	New York city. At least 17 persons were burned to death when flames razed dilapidated lodging house.
Dec. 25	Wildwood, N.J. Fire that started on ocean pier destroyed three theatres, two hotels, an amusement pier, 25 stores and nine homes.

A BURNED-OUT JOURNAL BOX on a coach caused the worst U.S. train wreck in 25 years Sept. 6, 1943, at Philadelphia, Pa. Seventy-nine passengers of the Pennsylvania's "Congressional Limited," bound from Washington to New York city, were killed

Above: LOCOMOTIVE AND TENDER of the "Twentieth Century Limited" lying on an embankment after the locomotive boiler exploded Sept. 7, 1943, near Canastota, N.Y., killing three crewmen and derailing the train

Right: WITH ITS RIGHT WING SHATTERED, this glider plunged to earth Aug. 1, 1943, at the St. Louis, Mo., airport, carrying ten men to their death, including the mayor of St. Louis. A faulty wing connection caused the crash

Below: THE PENNSYLVANIA RAILROAD'S Broad Street station in Philadelphia was partially destroyed by fire Sept. 12, 1943. Damage was estimated at $250,000

Marine

March 5   Near Carrabelle, Fla. Fourteen soldiers were believed drowned during manoeuvres in Gulf of Mexico off Florida when landing ramp of their army barge was accidentally lowered.

April 19   Near Sayville, N.Y. Seven sea scouts were drowned and three others were lost when their cabin cruiser capsized near shores of Sayville.

June 6   Near Norfolk, Va. Eighty-four men were killed in explosion that followed collision between ammunition ship and oil tanker off east coast of U.S.

Aug. 31   Near east coast Canadian port. Death of 30 seamen in collision of two Allied merchantmen off eastern seaboard was disclosed.

Oct. 20   Off Florida coast. Eighty-eight men died when two blacked-out tankers, one of which carried thousands of tons of aviation gasoline, collided and exploded off the Florida coast.

Natural Disasters

Jan. 1   Point Pleasant, W.Va. Ohio river flood waters caused estimated damage of $1,500,000, left about 17,000 homeless in northern West Virginia communities and temporarily halted industry in war plants.

Nov. 26   Ankara, Turkey. About 1,800 persons were killed and 2,000 others were injured in series of quakes that rocked northern Turkey, Ankara dispatches reported.

Railroad

May 23   Near Delair, N.J. Fourteen persons were killed and more than 100 were injured when passenger train crowded with week-end tourists jumped tracks.

June 4   Bombay. Fifty-two persons were killed and 100 were injured when Bombay-Calcutta mail train crashed.

Aug. 30   Wayland, N.Y. At least 27 persons were killed when freight engine moving from siding crashed into locomotive of crack express train.

Sept. 6   Philadelphia. Seventy-nine persons were killed and more than 100 others were injured when over-heated journal on end of car axle broke, derailing Congressional Limited as it was rounding curve within city.

Sept. 7   Near Canastota, N.Y. Three persons were killed and seven were injured when 20th Century Limited jumped tracks near Wampsville crossing.

Dec. 16   Near Rennert, N.C. Seventy-two persons were killed and scores injured when three coaches of a southbound train were derailed and fell on adjoining tracks directly in path of speeding northbound express.

Miscellaneous

March 4   London. 178 persons were killed and 60 others were injured when woman carrying baby tripped on stairs, causing panic at entrance of air raid shelter during German air attack.

(*See* also ACCIDENTS.)

Disciples of Christ.
Statistics as of June 30, 1943, showed a total membership of 1,679,012 in the United States and Canada (Canada 9,341). This was a net gain of 14,069 for the year—a slight offset to a net loss of 107,023 for the previous year. Reported additions were about normal—46,760 by baptism, 43,827 otherwise, or 2,861 less than in 1942. (Actual additions must be more than reported, to balance losses by death and provide even a slight increase.) In 1943, there were 8,050 churches in the United States and Canada (a gain of 48), and 7,801 ministers (a gain of 108). Chaplains in service increased from 203 in 1942 to 339 in 1943. Disciples had churches in 39 other countries, most of which were not mission fields. There were 13,030 members in Great Britain, 30,605 in Australia, 4,222 in New Zealand (losses of 415, 455 and 309, respectively). There was no report in 1943 from Poland, previously listed as having 65 churches and (estimated) 40,000 members. The world membership in 1943 was 1,842,123—a gain of 15,689, or nearly double the loss in 1942. Receipts and expenditures increased: for local church maintenance in the United States and Canada to $15,109,797 (gain $1,629,423); for missions and benevolences, almost tripled, to $5,505,779 (gain $3,482,165). Collection of the Emergency Million, subscribed in 1942, was completed in 1943, liquidating the long-standing debt of the United Christian Missionary society and furnishing funds for special war projects. The foreign missionary agency was able to continue its work in all fields except Japan and the Philippines. The missionary magazine, *World Call*, increased its monthly circulation to 46,154 (gain 6,604, after a gain of 3,953 the year before). The latest international convention of Disciples of Christ (U.S. and Canada) met at Grand Rapids, Mich., July 28–Aug. 2, 1942. The next, scheduled for May 1944, was expected to be postponed until October. Its president in 1943 was the Rev. C. E. Lemmon of Columbia, Mo.

(W. E. GA.)

District of Columbia: *see* WASHINGTON, D.C.

Ditter, J. William
(1888–1943), U.S. congressman, was born Sept. 5 in Philadelphia, Pa. He received a law degree from Temple university law school in 1913, and was admitted to the Pennsylvania bar the same year. In 1921 he taught history and commerce in Philadelphia high schools, and in 1925 he established a private law practice. He was elected on the Republican ticket to the national house of representatives by the 17th Pennsylvania district in 1933, and served in that capacity until his death. While in congress, Ditter was chairman of the Republican congressional committee and a member of the powerful house appropriations committee. As ranking minority member of the appropriations subcommittee on naval affairs he maintained a close working relationship with the navy department. He was killed when the naval plane in which he was flying from Massachusetts to Philadelphia crashed on the night of Nov. 22.

Divorce: *see* MARRIAGE AND DIVORCE.
Dodecanese: *see* ITALIAN COLONIAL EMPIRE.

Doenitz, Karl
(1892–   ), German naval officer, was born in Mecklenburg province. He was commissioned an ensign in the Imperial German navy in 1913 and served in the submarine division during World War I. Taken prisoner by the British in 1918, he was subsequently committed to a Manchester asylum for the insane. His repatriation followed in 1919, but the suspicion existed that he had feigned insanity to hasten his release. After the war, he resumed his service with the German navy and was associated with the U-boat service. In 1933, Doenitz was believed engaged in building submarines in hidden shops and in training the crews to man them, in violation of the Versailles treaty. By Oct. 1935 the first flotilla was afloat, and in 1936 Doenitz was linked publicly with the nazis when he was named commander of the 1st submarine flotilla. His rise was swift. A commodore when World War II started, he was promoted to the rank of rear admiral in Nov. 1939, and in Jan. 1943 he replaced Grand Admiral Erich Raeder as commander in chief of the German navy. His appointment gave strength to the belief that the Germans were putting more reliance on U-boat campaigns to halt the flow of U.S. supplies to Europe. Employing his "wolf-pack" method of attack, Doenitz inflicted grave losses upon Allied shipping. However, improved escort technique and constant patrol, both by sea and air, enabled the Allies to overcome the U-boat menace.

Dog Racing.
Boston again proved the capital of dog racing during 1943, with the Wonderland track setting records in crowd and pari-mutuel handle. Because of the transportation problem, the Massachusetts Racing commission refused licences to Massoit and Taunton tracks but the sport still managed to hold up with the usual dozen tracks in operation throughout the nation. Although attendance at Florida tracks fell off as much as 30%, betting held fairly close to the 1942 season and the handle at Miami Beach, Jacksonville and Tampa was each over that of the previous year. Fern Nature was recognized as the champion racer of Florida, winning the Flagler derby and other stakes. Gypsy Band and Hetty Andrews featured the racing at Boston.

(M. P. W.)

Dog Shows: *see* Shows.
Dominica: *see* West Indies, British.

Dominican Republic.
A West Indian republic occupying the eastern two-thirds of the island of Hispaniola or Haiti. Area, 19,326 sq.mi.; pop. (1939 est.) 1,654,993. The greater part of the population is concentrated in two areas: the Cibao lowlands in the north, and around Ciudad Trujillo in the south. At least 75% of the population is of mixed blood. Capital city: Ciudad Trujillo (formerly Santo Domingo) (pop. *c.* 100,000); other cities are: Santiago de los Caballeros (33,919) and Puerto Plata (11,777). Religion: Roman Catholic; language: Spanish. President in 1943: General Rafael Leonidas Trujillo Molina.

History.—No change in the administration policy of co-operation in hemisphere defense took place in 1943. Official censorship of all mediums of communication was established April 16. United States representation, and that of Peru, was changed to the status of embassy during the year.

While shipping operations improved, war conditions continued to cause shortage in the Dominican Republic, as everywhere, of such items as gasoline, iron and steel, and electrical appliances. Due to the lack of tires in particular, truck operation was reported as reduced by 60%, with horse-drawn vehicles used wherever available. Control commissions were set up for several commodities, such as textiles and nails, and in spite of price-fixing legislation, the cost of living steadily increased. Thanks to an agricultural diversification program started about a decade ago, basic food conditions were much better than in some other Caribbean states, and some foodstuffs were available for export.

Crops for 1943 were generally good. The cocoa harvest was unofficially estimated at 240,000 bags, and exports for the season were 50% over 1942. Sugar production, estimated at 473,000 tons, lower than the 530,000 tons of 1942, was not a serious problem since much of the previous year's crop had not been moved. Little unemployment was reported, largely due to a government building program in preparation for a centennial celebration in 1944.

The coffee quota of the republic for the 1942–43 year, under the inter-American coffee agreement, was increased from 132,554 bags to 194,691 bags.

Education.—In 1941 the educational system of the republic had schools and enrolments as follows: 616 basic primary, with 77,049 students; 147 graduate primary, with 46,592 students; 16 secondary, 3,133 pupils; 57 vocational, 3,702 students; 5 adult night, 584 students. The budget (1941) was set at 1,330,168 pesos for education; local governments contributed an additional 56,561 pesos.

Finance.—The monetary unit is the peso, equal in value to the United States dollar. Revenue in 1942 was 14,943,061 pesos; expenditures, 12,788,925 pesos. The external debt (Dec. 31, 1941) was officially indicated as 14,430,000 pesos; it was unofficially estimated as having been reduced to approximately 10,000,000 pesos by the end of 1943.

Trade and Communication.—Trade figures for 1941, the latest year available, showed a total of 28,862,968 pesos for the year (1940: 28,812,789). Imports were valued at 11,739,031 pesos (up 11%); exports at 17,739,031 pesos (down 6.4%). Raw sugar is the largest item of export; others are molasses, cacao, coffee, rice, cattle, gold. Principal imports are cotton and manufactures, chemicals and pharmaceuticals, machinery and paper products. In 1941 the United States took 51% of Dominican exports. The republic had a favourable trade balance with the United States of $362,000 in Sept. 1943.

The republic has 163 mi. of public railway and 622 mi. on sugar plantations. There were approximately 1,190 mi. of first-class highway, 2,150 mi. of unimproved; the highway appropriation was set at $461,650. During the year four schooners were built for inter-island trade.

Manufacturing.—A total of 1,829 manufacturing establishments listed for 1941 had a capital investment of 75,969,535 pesos; the total number of workers was approximately 38,000.

(D. Rd.)

Donations and Bequests.
Giving away of money by the American people surged to an all-time high in 1943, with individual and institutional contributions estimated at more than $2,000,000,000.

Increased national income and multiplying war-charity appeals were probably the obvious causes for the diversion of this vast amount of money to philanthropic causes, but it was also true that the lowering of income tax exemptions, which caused more persons to file returns, brought to light deductions for philanthropic purposes by those persons in the lower income brackets who, heretofore, had been the unknown quantity in giving.

In 1941, the total contributions to philanthropic funds amounted to $1,465,024,000 from all sources and, of this amount, $1,236,711,000 was reported to the government as contributions of individuals. In 1942, this amount jumped to $1,916,098,000, of which $1,669,541,000 came from individuals.

It is on the basis of these figures, and the still further lowering of income tax exemptions, that the estimate is made that American philanthropic funds would stand at well over $2,000,000,000 for 1943.

The continued study by The John Price Jones corporation of New York of publicly announced gifts of $1,000 and more in eight large cities (New York, Chicago, Washington, Philadelphia, Baltimore, St. Louis, Boston and San Francisco) presented a gauge of the trend in American giving for the year 1943. The total of gifts in these cities for 1943 was $135,203,402 compared with $78,269,358 for 1942. This study showed that the most popular types of philanthropy were American war organizations, such as the Red Cross and National War Fund, which received $36,521,930; community war chests, that is, community chests which included in their quotas funds for war emergency work, $71,976,602; and foreign relief, $10,157,072.

It is interesting that, although most of the philanthropic funds for 1943 went to these organizations, giving to other types of organized philanthropy, in most cases, showed gains over 1942.

The study of bequests for 1943 in these eight cities showed that $40,710,881 was willed for charitable purposes. In the case of bequests, the trend was as in other years, $16,925,831 going to educational institutions, $7,780,926 for health purposes, $5,253,126 to fine arts and $4,820,876 to religious organizations.

New York continued to be the most generous city with philanthropic gifts of $51,044,470 and bequests of $29,660,303. (*See also* Carnegie Trusts; Commonwealth Fund, The; Community Chest; Falk Foundation, The Maurice and Laura; Rockefeller Foundation; Rosenwald Fund, The Julius; Russell Sage Foundation; War Relief, U.S.)   (J. P. J.)

Doolittle, James
(1896–   ), U.S. army air officer, was born Dec. 14 at Alameda, Calif. He joined the army as a flying cadet during World War I and became an officer, but the army refused to let him go overseas, declaring he was too valuable as an instructor. After the war, he studied engineering, graduating from Massachusetts Institute of Technology in 1925 with a doctor of science degree. An expert pilot, he toured European and South American capitals, thrilling crowds with stunt flights. In 1930, he won the Harmon trophy

for his experimental flights; in 1931, he won the Bendix trophy race from Burbank to Cleveland; in 1933, he won the Thompson trophy. He then retired from racing to join the army board studying reorganization of the air corps. In July 1940, he was ordered back to active duty as a major in the air corps reserve and in Jan. 1942, he was promoted to lieutenant colonel in the air corps. On April 18, 1942, Doolittle electrified the world by leading a U.S. bomber squadron in a spectacular daylight raid over Tokyo. For this exploit, he was awarded the congressional medal of honour by President Roosevelt and was promoted to the rank of brigadier general. He was sent to Africa with Gen. Dwight D. Eisenhower, and on Nov. 21 was promoted to major general. On Feb. 26, 1943, he became head of the bomber command in the Northwest Africa air forces under Maj. Gen. Carl W. Spaatz and British Air Marshal Sir Arthur Tedder. A few days after Eisenhower was named invasion commander, Doolittle was appointed (Dec. 28, 1943) to head the 8th U.S. air force, which included all U.S. air units in Britain.

Draft: *see* SELECTIVE SERVICE, U.S.
Drama: *see* THEATRE.
Dress: *see* FASHION AND DRESS.

Drew, George Alexander

(1894–   ), Canadian politician, and premier of Ontario. He was born at Guelph, Ont., May 7, and received his education at the Collegiate institute of Guelph, Upper Canada college, and the University of Toronto. His military career began in 1910 when he joined the 16th battery Canadian artillery at Guelph. He had a distinguished record in World War I going overseas in 1915. Wounded in 1916, he was invalided home, but was not discharged till June 1919. Among Drew's writings are *Canada's Fighting Airmen, The Truth about the War,* etc. Admitted to the bar in 1920, he practised in Guelph till 1925, and then in Toronto. Entering the provincial legislature, he became the leader of the Progressive Conservative opposition. In 1942, Drew denounced the Canadian government's action in despatching troops to Hongkong. Proceedings were initiated against him, but were later dropped. After the formation of the Progressive Conservative party at the Winnipeg convention, Dec. 1942, Drew returned to organize the party's forces in Ontario. In the general provincial elections, Aug. 4, his party was successful in securing the largest number of seats; Drew became premier, assuming the portfolio of education.   (J. I. C.; S. LEA.)

Drought.

The year 1943 as a whole did not have notably deficient moisture in any of the important agricultural regions of the world.

In the Pacific, Asiatic and Australian theatres of war no important drought conditions were reported, although because of war restrictions the information coming from these areas was very meagre. In Europe, the latter half of the year 1943 appeared to have been more or less dry in the northern portions and wet in the Mediterranean region. During a long period in autumn, abnormally high pressures existed over the British Isles and neighbouring regions, producing a drought which in some localities reached serious proportions. The winter grasses and cereals were retarded in their growth during that portion of the year. In Italy, on the other hand, troops at this time were fighting through rain and mud.

In the United States, the conditions were favourable during the growing season in most localities, but a fall drought similar to one which occurred in 1939 affected some of the more important agricultural areas. In the winter wheat areas where the plants are supposed to germinate and begin their growth in the fall, the prospective crops were seriously reduced. In the great winter wheat region of Kansas, the November precipitation was only 17% of the normal for that month over the state as a whole, and the ample rains which finally came in December were, in some localities, too late to restore the wheat to its proper condition. In Oklahoma, Arkansas and parts of Kansas, November was the driest on record since 1910. The drought was accompanied by numerous dust storms. Many farmers planted wheat in the dust, expecting rain to come. Considerable quantities failed to germinate or dried after germination.

The region of autumn drought extended from Colorado through the Dakotas to the Great Lakes region and southward to northern Tennessee, Arkansas and northern Texas. Thus, approximately 17 states were more or less seriously affected by the drought. Throughout the entire region the water shortage affected the condition of pastures and necessitated stall or yard feeding of stock. Water had to be hauled for cattle. The drought conditions also extended through West Virginia and into North and South Carolina, parts of Georgia and Alabama. During the three fall months of September, October and November the following percentages of the normal precipitation were measured in the various states: North Dakota 55%; South Dakota 92%; Nebraska 56%; Kansas 72%; Oklahoma 75%; Iowa 64%; Illinois 71%; Ohio 59%; Kentucky 63%; West Virginia 64%; North Carolina 55%; South Carolina 57%.

Late summer and early fall drought conditions occurred in certain eastern states, particularly Pennsylvania, New Jersey, Delaware and Maryland. The drought in the Carolinas, parts of Georgia and Alabama started in late summer. In Pennsylvania, September was the driest ever recorded. July and August were also dry. Water had to be hauled and special feeding had to be employed for livestock. Many wells, previously dependable, dried up and streams dwindled until special sanitary precautions had to be taken. Crops were, of course, extremely poor. The planting of winter grains was delayed and fall plowing was impossible in the hard, dry soil. In New Jersey, August was extremely dry, and important truck crops in the southern part of the state were greatly curtailed. In some sections the second cutting of alfalfa was almost a complete failure. In Maryland, the summer drought ended with ample rains on Sept. 30, only after about 50% failures of most crops. Dairying suffered through lack of adequate pasturage.

Dust storms which usually have their maximum occurrence during the spring months were more commonly observed in the autumn of 1943. In South Dakota, several severe but somewhat localized dust storms were observed in October, while dust storms and wind erosion of the bare soil occurred through extensive areas of Kansas, Nebraska and Oklahoma. In some cases in these sections, the small quantity of winter grains which penetrated through the dry soil later had the soil blown from the roots in dust storms.

In addition to dust there were numerous prairie and forest fires. The forest fire conditions were particularly noted in Arkansas where large stands of timber, rendered inflammable by the drought, were destroyed by fire.

South America during 1943 appeared to enjoy more than ample rains throughout. (*See* also AGRICULTURE; IRRIGATION; METEOROLOGY; SOIL EROSION AND SOIL CONSERVATION.)

     (H. R. B.)

Drugs and Drug Traffic.

The drug industry in the U.S. was called upon to increase its output of essential items while facing wartime disruptions resulting from shortages in skilled manpower, in basic raw materials, and in equipment. To safeguard consumers from the violations such conditions might foster, the Food and Drug administration gave increased regulatory attention to possible breakdowns of control in the manufacturing and packaging of drug products and to unauthorized substitutions for scarce ingredients. During the shortage of physicians for civilians, public safety required intensified surveillance over the directions, warnings and therapeutic claims on the labels of preparations with which persons might attempt self-medication.

In the fiscal year 1943, attention was given to the output of 2,738 manufacturers of drugs, therapeutic devices and vitamin preparations destined for both civilian and military use. Seizure

CINCHONA SEEDLINGS in a greenhouse of the U.S. department of agriculture at Glenn Dale, Md. Plantings were made in quantity during 1943 to replace the supply of quinine from the Netherlands Indies cut off by the Japanese in 1942. The bark of the cinchona tree yields quinine in about ten years

of 287 violative shipments was effected. The consignments thus removed from consumer channels comprised 16 preparations alleged to be dangerous to health; 107 bearing false and misleading claims, inadequate directions and warnings, or without mandatory label statements; 111 items differing from required standards of potency; 3 containing filth and decomposition; and 50 that were short in contents or otherwise constituted economic cheats. Fewer drug products containing dangerous ingredients or mixtures were seized than in 1942; the number of substandard-drug seizures almost doubled. Permission was given for the introduction of 148 new drugs into interstate commerce after the filing with the federal security administrator of applications establishing their safety for use.

Court decisions rendered in the 1943 fiscal year affecting public protection under the federal drug laws included an appeals court ruling that an article may be misbranded by the addition of false and misleading circulars after shipment, while it is being held for sale. (W. G. CA.)

League of Nations.—The opium section of the League of Nations continued to function despite difficulties of communication. The Permanent Central Opium board discharged its duties even though seriously impeded by current conditions. Statistical returns were received from 50 governments out of 66 contracting parties and from 62 out of 99 dependencies and colonies. No government denounced the conventions. There were three accessions to the conventions since the outbreak of the war. International control continued and was likely to be operative over a considerable part of the world. Its complete re-establishment would be a matter of utmost urgency on cessation of hostilities. In all belligerent territories, with the exception of Japan, the system of import and export certificates for narcotic drugs continued in force.

Leaks developed. Much Iranian opium manufactured by the government monopoly found its way into the illicit traffic. Clandestine production of opium in Mexico continued on a large scale. The Mexican government took stringent measures to stamp out this traffic.

Opium supplies, in contrast to other strategic materials, appeared to be satisfactory in all territories. Several South American countries started opium production on a small scale.

A substitute for morphine, known as demerol in the United States and dolantin in Europe and South America, appeared on world markets. It was placed under anti-opium legislation in

every country where it was consumed. A recommendation was to be made to place it under Article 10 of the Geneva Narcotic convention of 1925.

On Sept. 21, 1943, the United States government addressed aide-memoire to the British, Netherlands and other interested governments in regard to the suppression of the nonmedical use of narcotic drugs in areas in the far east occupied by Japanese forces when such areas would be reoccupied by the armed forces of the United Nations.

The British and the Netherlands governments announced in November that they had decided to prohibit the use of opium for smoking and to abolish opium monopolies in their territories when those territories were freed from Japanese occupation.

BIBLIOGRAPHY.—"Traffic in Opium and Other Dangerous Drugs for the Year Ended December 31, 1942," U.S. Treasury dept., Bureau of Narcotics, Washington, D.C.; Statement of Acting Secretary of State, Department of State Press Release No. 473 dated November 10, 1943. (H. J. A.)

Drunkenness: *see* INTOXICATION, ALCOHOLIC.

Duncan, Sir Patrick

(1870–1943), British politician, was born Dec. 21. He attended Balliol college, Oxford, and entered the colonial service in 1894. He was made treasurer of the Transvaal colony in 1901, succeeded to the post of colonial secretary, 1903–06, and was acting lieutenant governor in 1906. Sir Patrick held the interior, public health and education ministries, 1921–24, and was minister of mines, 1933–36. He assumed the office of governor general of the Union of South Africa in 1938, the first South African resident to become a representative of the king in the dominion. It was during his governorship that Premier Hertzog sought to prevent a declaration of war against Germany at the outbreak of World War II, a measure which Sir Patrick helped to defeat. As a result Hertzog resigned. Sir Patrick died in Pretoria, Union of South Africa, July 17.

Du Pont, Richard Chichester

(1911–1943), U.S. glider champion, was born Jan. 2 in Wilmington, Del. He learned to fly in 1930 and was National Soaring champion in 1934, 1935 and 1937. He established a U.S. soaring distance record of 158 mi. in 1934 and a

U.S. altitude record of 7,200 ft. in 1938. As special assistant to Gen. Henry H. Arnold, chief of the U.S. air forces, he was sent on a mission to Sicily in 1943 to observe glider forces in operation. Less than a week after his return to the United States, he was killed in the crash of a glider at March field, Calif., Sept. 11.

Dust Storms: *see* DROUGHT.
Dutch Borneo: *see* NETHERLANDS COLONIAL EMPIRE.
Dutch Colonial Empire: *see* NETHERLANDS COLONIAL EMPIRE; NETHERLANDS INDIES.
Dutch East Indies: *see* NETHERLANDS INDIES.
Dutch Guiana: *see* SURINAM.

Dyestuffs. The paramount task facing the organic chemicals industry in 1943 was no different from that of the previous year and consisted primarily of satisfying the greatly expanded demands of the army and navy. The War Production Board Conservation Order M-103 which was in effect from April 1, 1942 on proved its workability. Quotas were set quarterly and were determined by the supply of raw material available for the manufacture of dyestuffs. Military and civilian requirements were considered, and the production of specific dyes or groups of dyes was controlled and regulated to provide a regular flow of colouring material in sufficient quantities to satisfy essential needs. Order M-103 was revised on Oct. 23, increasing the sale and delivery of certain classes of dyes for civilian consumption from 15% to $17\frac{1}{2}$% per calendar quarter. The augmented allotments for civilian use were made possible by smaller military requirements for certain types of dyes due to reduction in purchases of woollen and worsted fabrics. Export quotas were increased also from 15 to 17%. These were set up after a study of past shipments and potential demands and, unlike the American civilian quotas which were based on past use, the export quotas were based on production. They were applicable to friendly nations who were no longer able to obtain their supplies of dyestuffs from Europe and were dependent upon the United States.

The policy of the War Production board was to make available dyes of high quality and performance in order to maintain the standards of civilian war textiles as close as possible to the desirable properties of fabrics processed during peace. The shortage of fibres of different kinds compelled the textile manufacturers to use their ingenuity in developing fabrics from available materials. Old-staple fibres were blended with newer synthetics and the resulting mixtures presented technical problems in colour application. Scientific research in the further development of dyes and dyeing processes to colour these complex textiles was actively carried out in the laboratories of dyestuff manufacturers. High-speed methods were developed which had previously been thought impossible. An outstanding contribution by dyestuffs technicians was a procedure for the continuous dyeing of indigo on navy wool flannel, effecting savings in time and operating cost.

Production of coal-tar dyestuffs in 1942 amounted to 151,878,-000 lb., which was 17,000,000 lb. less than the peak output for 1941. Sales were 144,847,000 lb., and valued at $99,431,000. Vat-colour production, exclusive of indigo, was 27,432,000 lb., 3% higher than in 1941, and accounted for a slightly larger portion of the 1942 production, although, in general, little change occurred in the relative importance of the dyes by class of application. The principal colours manufactured were vat, direct, sulphur and acid, which accounted for approximately 78% of the total. The quantity of unclassified dyes listed by the U.S. tariff commission, including the more important military dyes, increased by 2,600,-000 lb. and that of the classified dyes decreased by 19,000,000 lb. Figures for 1943 production and sales were not available.

(A. G. BN.)

EAC: *see* EUROPEAN ADVISORY COMMISSION.

Eaker, Ira C. (1896–   ), U.S. army air officer, was born April 13 in Field Creek, Tex. He studied at the University of the Philippines, Columbia and Southern California universities and was commissioned as second lieutenant in the infantry reserve in 1917. Transferred to the Philippines in 1919, he served in the air corps and later was given command of the Manila air depot. In 1929, he was co-pilot in an army plane which established an endurance flight record of 150 hr. and 40 min., and some years later he made a cross-continent "blind flight." He served as executive officer in the air corps headquarters in Washington, 1937–40, and by Jan. 1942, he had become a brigadier general. He was made chief of the U.S. bomber command in the European theatre of war in the summer of 1942. Upon the transfer of Maj. Gen. Carl Spaatz to North Africa in Dec. 1942, Eaker succeeded him as commander of the 8th U.S. air force on Feb. 15, having been advanced to rank of major general. His force was doubled by summer and greatly increased again by October, when it had assumed full partnership with the R.A.F. in bombing the axis. Promoted to lieutenant general, Eaker stated in October that the task of the air force for the winter would be to destroy Germany's production and transportation facilities so that invasion could be carried out with fewer casualties. On Dec. 28, 1943, Gen. Eaker was appointed commander of all Allied air units in the Mediterranean theatre. He was succeeded as commander of the 8th air force by Maj. Gen. James H. Doolittle.

Ear, Nose and Throat, Diseases of. From the point of view of the otolaryngologist, it is imperative that a flier should possess normal nasal function, average ears and hearing, eustachian tubes and sinuses without obstruction, normal balancing mechanisms and no vertiginous episodes. He must be free of cold or acute respiratory infection.

On descent, most individuals can equalize the relative negative pressure of the middle ear pneumatic system through swallowing, yawning or making some movements of the lower jaw. If some obstruction is present in the eustachian tubes secondary to a pharyngitis or an acute head cold, aeration of the middle ear cavity is interfered with so that a cycle of events takes place that brings about aero-otitis media. When the negative pressure inside the middle ear reaches 100–120 mm. Hg (mercury), pain is severe and a moderate amount of hearing loss takes place in the low tone range. The drum membrane becomes sharply retracted, the blood vessels of the handle of the malleus are congested, later ecchymosis in the flaccid membrane develops, and after some hours, depending upon the differential negative pressure, sero-sanguineous fluid and bubbles form in the middle ear. The fluid elements in the middle ear cavity constitute a recovery cycle, as the relative negative pressure is reduced proportionately to the amount of fluid formed. In time, however, pressure is equalized. It takes from 3 days to 3 weeks for recovery from aero-otitis media; very few cases become infected, and politzerization and catheterization of the eustachian tubes when performed immediately is effective, though not so efficient as one would wish.

The best treatment is to return to the level at which block of the eustachian tube and middle ear cavity took place, either in actual flight or in a pressure chamber, and to descend to ground level slowly, swallowing frequently. In this manner, the pressure outside the drumhead and that of the air passing through the eustachian tube are altered simultaneously, whereas in catheterization and politzerization only that entering the eustachian tube is altered. If aero-otitis is present for a few days, heat causes an increase in fluid production in the middle ear, analgesics relieve pain and a shrinking solution to the orifice of the eustachian tube mouths decongests the swollen mucosa. All of these measures afford considerable relief to the unbalanced state of affairs present. Opening of the drumhead (myringotomy) is best avoided.

Aerosinusitis is a similar cycle of events taking place in the accessory sinuses of the nose and has increased in frequency as greater altitudes and speeds of ascent have been achieved. On ascent, the pressure inside an obstructed sinus becomes greater than that outside with consequent expansion to the limit of the elasticity of its walls or structures. Pain results.

During descent, the opposite effect is present. Redundant tissue or polyps may then form a ball valve over an ostium, or pus flowing over an ostium can be drawn into a sinus which may have been empty and sterile. If the relative negative pressure inside a sinus becomes great enough, the mucous membrane may be torn away from its walls. Haemorrhage in the cavity or haematoma beneath the mucosa is not rare. The best treatment for aerosinusitis is to carry out the general suggestions outlined under the treatment for aero-otitis media, namely, to provide conditions for the equalization of pressure as quickly as possible as well as to relieve pain and discomfort.

BIBLIOGRAPHY.—*Year Book of Eye, Ear, Nose and Throat, 1942* (Bothman-Crowe).   (G. M. C.)

Earnings, Company: *see* BUSINESS REVIEW.
Earthquakes: *see* DISASTERS; SEISMOLOGY.
East Africa, British: *see* BRITISH EAST AFRICA.
East Indies, Dutch: *see* NETHERLANDS INDIES.

Eastman, Joseph B.

(1882–   ), U.S. government official, was born June 26 in Katonah, N.Y. He was graduated from Amherst college in 1904 and studied law at Boston university. He was appointed to the Interstate Commerce commission by President Wilson in 1919 and was reappointed by succeeding presidents until 1933, when he served as President Roosevelt's federal co-ordinator of transportation. During his 14-year tenure on the ICC, Eastman was considered a "government-ownership" man by many railroad presidents because he fought to lower freight rates and executive salaries. He denounced the unnecessary duplication of services and sought to outlaw dummy corporations and holding companies. In 1936, he returned to the ICC and in Dec. 1941, Mr. Eastman, then chairman, was appointed by President Roosevelt as director of the newly-established Office of Defense Transportation (ODT), designed to co-ordinate federal and private transportation policies. During 1942 and 1943, he curbed civilian use of motor cars, trucks, buses and trains in a variety of ways to save fuel and to make possible constantly increasing traffic in war materials.

Eclipses of Sun, 1944: *see* ASTRONOMY.
Economic Association, American: *see* AMERICAN ECONOMIC ASSOCIATION.
Economic Defense Board: *see* FOREIGN ECONOMIC ADMINISTRATION.
Economic Development, Committee for: *see* COMMITTEE FOR ECONOMIC DEVELOPMENT.

Economics.

Contributions to applied economics were more significant than to theoretical economics during 1943. In May about 675,000 man-days were lost through strikes because labour leaders questioned the validity of the War Labor board decision to restrict wage increases to the cost of living index of the bureau of labor statistics. They charged that it did not give proper weights to items in family wartime budgets, so an impartial committee of experts known as the Mills committee was set up to investigate and in October reported that the index "defined with satisfactory accuracy" the changes in living costs, and that it was the purpose of the index to measure changes in prices, not changes in standards of living, as labour leaders had urged. Had this index been found wanting the "little steel" formula used as a model for wage stabilization would have been abandoned and governmental price controls definitely endangered.

Sir John Maynard Keynes submitted a plan for a postwar international clearing union of the United Nations designed to stabilize foreign exchange based upon assigned "bancor" quotas for member countries. Under this plan, gold possessed only "great psychological value," although the clearing union would not dispense with it immediately but would supplant it eventually with credits for international settlements. Simultaneously, the federal treasury submitted the White plan for an international currency in "unitas," not dollars, designed to maintain stability with a gold stabilization fund. Preliminary conferences were held and both plans given widespread professional consideration pending the call of a conference of representatives of the United Nations to consider the problem of international monetary stability in the postwar period.

The Brookings institution published a brief appraisal of the theories underlying federal debts, unbalanced budgets, postwar deficits, employment and inflation. The conclusions were critical of prolonged deficits and continued spending. The Conference on Research in Income and Wealth of the National Bureau of Economic Research published significant findings on income size distributions within the United States, conceding that much statistical groundwork remained to be done.

Among government publications, perhaps the reports of the National Resources Planning board, submitted to congress by the president in March, required the most careful scrutiny. These reports recommended a postwar readjustment period with extended wartime controls to prevent booms and depressions; gradual demobilization of the armed forces co-ordinated with re-employment; guarantees of right to work, to fair pay and to an adequate living; enterprise free from arbitrary public and private authority; a cabinet post for social security, education and youth programs; maintenance of national income at a level of $125,000,000,000 annually; and higher income and lower consumption taxes. Among the most important fields of private research were those dealing with war contract termination problems, the government surplus disposal program, postwar re-employment, lend-lease, international settlements, removal of trade barriers, taxation and fiscal policy.

Graduate study and research in economics in the universities came almost to a standstill. Many courses emphasized contemporary and postwar problems. Some teachers were drawn into the armed services. Others entered civil service, holding strategic positions, and congress launched attacks against "Washington economists," primarily those whose academic training had been in the field of pure theory, or whose civil service classification designated them as "economic analysts" regardless of their lack of professional training. Research organizations, private industry and law firms added large numbers of professionally trained economists to their full-time staffs during the year. (E. H. HE.)

Economic Stabilization, Office of.

The function of the Office of Economic Stabilization is to provide over-all direction and co-ordination for the government's program of stabilizing wages and living costs. The director is assisted by a board composed of the heads of agencies concerned with price and wage control and representatives of labour, management and farmers appointed by the president. Because it is concerned primarily with policy-making, the Office of Economic Stabilization operates with a very small staff.

The office was established on Oct. 6, 1942, by executive order, with former Justice James E. Byrnes of the supreme court as director. On May 29, 1943, Mr. Byrnes resigned to become director of the Office of War Mobilization, and Fred M. Vinson, who had been associate justice of the federal court of appeals for the District of Columbia and chief judge of the emergency court of appeals, was appointed to succeed him.   (F. M. V.)

Economic Warfare, Office of: *see* FOREIGN ECONOMIC ADMINISTRATION.

Ecuador. A Pacific coast republic of South America, located astride the equator. The area of Ecuador was claimed to be 337,392 sq.mi. (including the 2,400 sq.mi. of the Galápagos Islands) previous to the settlement of a boundary dispute with Peru in 1942. Pop. (1942 census): 3,085,871; of this figure 28% are estimated as white, 30% as Indian, 40% as mestizo. The capital is Quito (pop. 150,347); other cities are: Guayaquil (159,940); Cuenca (45,000); Riobamba (24,000); Latacunga (18,000); Loja (18,000). President in 1943: Dr. Carlos Arroyo del Río.

History.—During 1943 there was no change in Ecuadorian co-operation in inter-American policy. On March 26, publication of news on hemisphere defense or local military developments was prohibited. In May all communication with axis countries was terminated, and property of axis nationals was taken over by the government. All vessels of over 20 tons were placed under national control. On Feb. 23, arrangements were made whereby the United States was to purchase all Ecuadorian quinine available for export, and in June the same nation extended a $5,000,000 stabilization fund agreement for an additional year. In November the extraordinary powers which had been granted to the executive because of world conditions were continued in force until Aug. 1944.

Ecuadorian internal politics were marked by preparation for the 1944 presidential election. At least six candidates were reported as in the field in May, one of them being Former President Ibarra. In February several Liberal party candidates for congress were arrested on a charge of political conspiracy, and a minor revolt, in August, was easily suppressed.

In the economic field, conditions in Ecuador generally improved through the year, although a flour shortage occurred in May. Most serious was an increased cost of living, estimated as over 50% higher than in 1939. Price control was not altogether effective. Late in April, after the visit of Henry Wallace, the U.S. promised to send urgently needed locomotives and railway equipment, and a comprehensive social and sanitary improvement program was outlined. Defense construction at Salinas (90 mi. from Guayaquil) and in the Galápagos Islands by the United States gave employment, and demands for balsa and rubber, in addition to usual agricultural work, absorbed all available labour. The coffee, cacao and rice crops (the latter important in Ecuadorean domestic economy as the staple food of the masses) were all estimated as heavier than in 1942; sugar, and probably cotton, production was expected to be under the previous year. On Oct. 6, a National Bank of Provincial Development (capital: 100,-000,000 sucres) was established with the purpose of furthering the agricultural program and other projects.

Platinum exports were prohibited in November.

Education.—The school system in 1941 had 3,140 primary schools, with 6,076 teachers and an enrolment of 248,905 pupils; 23 public secondary colleges, with 9,137 students; 12 vocational schools, with 1,288 students; 4 universities, with 1,755 enrolled. The 1943 budget allowance for education was 24,647,000 sucres (14% of the total).

Finance.—The monetary unit is the sucre, value in 1943 approximately 7 cents U.S. The ordinary budget for 1943 was balanced at 159,383,000 sucres (1942: 119,567,000 sucres). The 1944 budget was set at 198,260,000 sucres. The circulating medium totalled 437,592,502 sucres in April 1943. The public debt in 1941 was 47,062,645 sucres.

Trade and Communication.—Foreign trade in 1942 was valued at 498,405,000 sucres (exports: 298,690,000 sucres; imports: 199,715,000 sucres). The United States normally leads in Ecuadorian trade (Ecuador's favourable trade balance in Sept. 1943, was $5,759,000). In at least one month in 1943 (April), Argentina supplied more goods to Ecuador than the United States.

Major Exports of Ecuador, 1942 and 1941

Product	Value, 1942	Value, 1941
Rice	59,214,841 sucres	24,041,646 sucres
Cacao	40,326,499	34,364,452
Rubber	35,481,212	6,978,249
Panama hats	22,121,127	16,230,669
Balsa	25,613,454	8,638,814
Coffee	17,277,646	23,827,134
Tagua	7,042,289	6,120,478
Hides and skins	3,886,330	3,563,233
Bananas	3,106,860	4,658,297
Mineral concentrates	25,374,413	29,425,725
Crude petroleum	24,820,362	13,425,462
Copper and lead	13,492,992	17,658,510

The principal manufacturing industry is in textiles, with approximately 20 cotton mills in operation in 1941, with 3,500 employees, and 10 mills producing other textiles.

External communication is by sea and air; nearly all traffic is through Guayaquil. Ecuador possesses about 600 mi. of railways, and 4,231 mi. of highway, of which approximately one-sixth is paved. The highway appropriation for the fiscal year ending March 30, 1943, was for 7,140,000 sucres, with half to be spent on new construction. Domestic airlines and the Guayas river afford additional means of communication. (*See* also HISPANIC AMERICA AND WORLD WAR II.)   (D. RD.)

Eden, (Robert) Anthony (1897–   ), British statesman, was born June 12 and was educated at Eton and at Christ Church, Oxford. After service in World War I from 1915 to 1918, he contested the Spennymoor division of Durham in 1922, and in the following year he was elected for Warwick and Leamington, which he thereafter continued to represent. He was lord privy seal and a privy councillor, 1934, and in 1935 he entered the cabinet as minister without portfolio for League of Nations Affairs, holding this post until the following December, when he became foreign minister. Disagreement with Prime Minister Chamberlain over the latter's policy of "appeasing" Germany and Italy led to his resignation Feb. 20, 1938. Upon the outbreak of war Sept. 3, 1939, he re-entered Chamberlain's cabinet as dominions secretary. On May 11, 1940, he was named secretary of state for war in Churchill's cabinet, and on Dec. 23, 1940, he was appointed to the foreign ministry again.

On Nov. 22, 1942, Eden replaced Sir Stafford Cripps as leader of the house of commons, although he still retained his post as foreign secretary. During 1943 he participated in a number of international conferences, notably the parleys with Stalin at Moscow and Tehran and the Cairo conferences with Chiang Kai-shek and President Ismet Inönü of Turkey.

Education. The chief issues which occupied the attention of educators in the United States in 1943 were the continued and mounting shortage of teachers, the large number of boys and girls who, lured by wage-earning opportunities, left school without completing their courses, and the problem of providing financial support for education. At the level of higher education the difficulties of adjusting the relations between the colleges and the armed services were removed but a new issue, the future of the college curriculum, arose. Finally, active attention was devoted to the problem of training men and women when hostilities cease.

The Shortage of Teachers.—The shortage of teachers, which had already begun to make itself felt in 1942, increased during 1943, when it was estimated that more than 100,000 teachers had left the profession to join the armed forces or to enter defense industries. It was anticipated that this number would continue to grow, particularly since steps were not taken immediately to adjust teachers' salaries to the increasing cost of living. With 40% of the teachers receiving less than $1,200 a year and 8% less than $600 a year, the temptation to enter well-paid positions in defense industries could not be resisted. The exodus of teachers was in the main from rural and village schools; teachers who left the urban schools were chiefly those whose special training was needed in defense industries and by the armed forces. The effect on all schools—rural and urban—was serious. In rural schools it was estimated that about 6,000,000 pupils would be taught by inexperienced teachers, assuming that the schools were opened at all. In urban schools serious difficulties were encountered in replacing teachers of mathematics, chemistry, physics and industrial and physical education. The War Manpower commission, as a result of pressure brought to bear upon it by school officials and educational associations, declared teaching an essential occupation and sought, under its stabilization plan, to regulate the transfer of teachers from one position to another for increased pay. Nevertheless, the turnover of teachers was nearly double that in any normal year (189,000 as contrasted with 95,000).

In an effort to check the migration from the profession a variety of schemes was tried. Attention was directed to the importance of education in a democracy; parent-teacher associations conducted publicity campaigns among the public and among teachers; promises of better conditions of service, tenure and old-age security were made; promising candidates were encouraged to enter the profession; and emergency training courses were established for inexperienced teachers or for those who had been out of the profession for some time and wished to help during the emergency. In many localities the services of citizens were secured to give part-time instruction in such subjects as music, art and physical education. Courses were also offered to experienced teachers who were ready to change from their own fields of specialization to those in which there were serious shortages. Many of the teacher-training institutions offered accelerated courses to meet the situation. Among the methods of publicity employed to recruit teachers were such pamphlets as that issued by the Michigan state department of education under the title "Should I Consider Teaching? Is It the Career for Me?" or such posters as that distributed to the high schools in Washington, "You Are Needed to Teach." In one field—physical education—a national committee on meeting teacher shortage in wartime physical education was formed.

To meet the emergency created by the teacher shortage President Roosevelt submitted a proposal to congress to provide a fund of $3,900,000 to assist colleges and universities, including junior colleges and normal schools, in offering short training courses for rural- and elementary-school teachers and teachers of vocational subjects, physical science, mathematics and such other subjects as might be essential to meet wartime needs as determined by the chairman of the War Manpower commission. (See *Journal of the National Education Association* and *Education for Victory*, bi-weekly of the U.S. office of education.)

The Exodus from School.—It was estimated by the middle of 1943 that 2,000,000 boys and girls between the ages of 14 and 18 had left school to enter wage-earning occupations, and that of these 25% were under 15. This was a consequence of the labour shortage and the high wages which could be earned after a very short period of training. To some extent the disruption of school organization through the shortage of teachers and lax enforcement of compulsory attendance laws may have exercised some influence. The situation became sufficiently serious for the War Manpower commission, the children's bureau of the department of labour, and the U.S. office of education to issue an announcement to urban communities stating that "The first obligation of school youth is to take advantage of their educational opportunities in order that they may be prepared for citizenship and for service to the Nation. . . . School authorities, employers, parents and other interested groups should recognize the obligation to safeguard the physical and intellectual development of youth." The educational policies commission of the National Education association issued a similar recommendation: "School attendance until graduation is the best contribution to the war effort which school-age youth can make." Both groups urged that arrangements be made to combine part-time work in war occupations with the continuation of regular schooling until high-school graduation. Not only was the academic education of youth being sabotaged but young workers were being exploited and were not being paid the "wages paid to adult workers for similar job performances"—the policy of the War Manpower commission. (See *Education for Victory*, official bi-weekly of the U.S. office of education, especially the issue for Sept. 15, 1943.)

Juvenile Delinquency.—The increase in juvenile delinquency which was noted during the year was found among wage-earning adolescents as well as among younger children who were left without supervision when their mothers entered defense industries. The increase of 10% in juvenile delinquency in 1941 grew to 25% or more in 1942 and continued to grow in 1943, creating serious problems for child-care agencies, educational institutions and juvenile courts.

Schoolwork and the War.—The work of the elementary schools was not seriously affected by the course of the war. Such adjustments as were necessary were made. Largely through the efforts of a number of educators working in co-operation with the Civil Aeronautics administration, courses and textbooks dealing with aviation were made available as part of a program to make children air conscious.

In the high schools a definite shift of emphasis was noted from the humanities, especially foreign languages, to such subjects as mathematics, physics, chemistry, flight aviation, physical education and vocational education. This was due in part to the introduction of preinduction courses, prepared by the preinduction training section, headquarters services of supply of the war department and the U.S. office of education. Outlines and textbooks were provided in electricity, radio, shopwork, machines and automotive mechanics. In some schools courses on postwar planning were introduced. The general trend to practical or wartime subjects stimulated teachers and organizations interested in foreign languages to engage in active campaigns to maintain and encourage their study.

The chief emphasis at the high-school level was on vocational training. The enrolments in federally aided vocational schools and classes showed an increase from 2,434,641 in 1942 to 2,630,097 in 1943, distributed in vocational agriculture, trade and industrial, home economics and distributive education classes.

The Study of United States History.—The New York *Times*, which in 1942 had published the results of an investigation into the place of the history of the United States in high schools, carried the investigation further, into the college. Considerable interest and controversy were aroused when the results of a test in the subject, given to 7,000 students in 36 colleges and universities, were published. The report of the survey seemed to point to neglect of the subject and a great amount of ignorance of American history among college students. The challenge was taken up throughout the country; by some the test itself was criticized from the technical point of view; others alleged that the students had not taken the test seriously; others, again, attributed their failure to show an adequate knowledge to the gradual substitution of "social studies" for the study of history in high schools.

The senate committee on education and labour discussed the report of the survey and considered a proposal to promote the study of American history in schools and colleges by means of federal aid. The New York *Times* report of the survey was ordered by the senate to be published as a senate document. The subject was one which was definitely included in the army and navy courses given in colleges under the scheme adopted for training of army and navy personnel, and it was urged that the subject be included in the high-school victory courses sponsored by the U.S. office of education.

The American Legion at its annual meeting passed a resolution stressing the importance of the teaching of United States history. In Illinois a law was enacted requiring publicly supported institutions of education to teach American history and the principles of American government. Similar action was proposed in other states.

Nor was the challenge ignored by professional organizations more closely concerned with the status of the teaching of history in schools and colleges. The American Historical association, the Mississippi Historical association, and the National Council for the Social Studies appointed a committee to undertake a comprehensive survey to promote the improvement of the teaching of history, to investigate both the teaching and textbooks in the subject and to investigate the number of pupils in elementary and high schools who study the subject. The committee, of which Prof. Edgar B. Wesley of the University of Minnesota is chairman, was expected to publish the results of its survey early in 1944.

Civil Liberties and Salute to the Flag.—The litigation arising from the refusal of parents belonging to Jehovah's Witnesses to allow their children to salute the flag in school exercises, which had resulted in their prosecution, finally reached the supreme court. In a significant decision the court ruled that children whose parents are opposed to the practice of salute to the flag in schools cannot be compelled to participate in the exercise as a condition of attending a public school. The decision was widely approved as a guarantee of civil liberties and as an illustration of continued respect for the Bill of Rights even in time of war and of the sincerity of American faith in the "Four Freedoms."

Higher Education.—The specialized training programs for army and navy personnel were launched in the spring of the year in some 500 colleges and universities of the country. The institutions were approved after inspection and received contracts to carry out the programs which they were best equipped to give. The programs for specialized training covered the following types of activities: engineers, aviation cadets, WACs, basic training, personnel psychology, area and language training, premedical and medical training, dental training, veterinary medicine, meteorology, chemical warfare, etc., in accordance with the needs of the army and navy respectively.

The selection of suitable candidates for admission to the colleges and universities for the specialized courses of training was carried out by classification and unit personnel officers, following

STUDENTS in a class in communications at Duke university, offered in collaboration with the U.S. Office of Education's program for college training of war workers. The 1943 program included World War II veterans discharged from the army

uniform standards and procedures adopted for the whole country. In the case of the army specialized training program (ASTP) enlisted men were assigned to the selected institutions as privates and were provided with free quarters, mess, clothing, equipment and instruction. All were required to follow a basic program in English and history, mathematics, physics and chemistry, after which they might be recommended for admission to officer candidate schools, or for immediate service with combat troops or for participation in an advanced program in accordance with their special aptitudes. A corresponding program was developed for the training of naval personnel. While the objectives to be attained were formulated by the army and navy authorities, the methods of attaining them were left to each institution.

During the year the army specialized training reserve program was introduced, under which qualified 17-year-old men could receive academic instruction preparatory to army specialized training. For this program 17-year-old high-school graduates were required to take a test administered jointly by the army and navy. If selected they pursued three 12-week courses in English, geography, history, sciences and mathematics. They enjoyed an inactive status and were not in uniform but received instruction, room and board and medical service. At the end of the term in which they became 18 they were placed on active military duty and sent to army training centres for military training, on completion of which a further selection took place for continuation in the army specialized training program.

Although the uncertainties about the immediate future of institutions of higher education were removed by the settlement of the status of selectees, enrolments in general inevitably showed a decrease. In the men's colleges the undergraduates were either below the draft age or in deferred occupations, or else were deferred, together with graduate students, under a liberal policy of the Selective Service bureau, if they were engaged in preprofessional or professional studies, agriculture, forestry, pharmacy, optometry or as internes. Deferment was granted in this way in some 20 scientific and specialized fields to full-time students, if the institution attended certified to their competence and promise of completing their studies successfully by July 1, 1945.

Statistics of enrolment for the academic year beginning in the fall of 1943 were not available for the whole country, chiefly because the academic year was completely disrupted. Reports from 497 institutions showed that there had been a decrease in enrolments of 11.6% among men and 3.5% among women during the year. Colleges now admit students at different times of the year and those which were on a semester basis fell into line with the army or navy programs and adopted 4 terms of 12 weeks each. It seemed not improbable that the accelerated programs adopted practically throughout the country might remain permanent, provided that the necessary adjustments could be made for faculty members and means of support could be found for students who in the past had earned money for their education during the long vacations. "Class" lines as such began to disappear and commencements were held at different times of the year.

So far as aid to students was concerned the possibility of restoring the system administered by the National Youth administration, which was abandoned when congress refused its request for a new appropriation, was suggested as a permanent policy of the federal government. The work of the National Youth administration was referred to as a "most acceptable experience," which combined both work and education as a condition of student aid. The national examinations given under the joint auspices of the army and navy would serve as a guide to the selection of promising high-school students for aid to assist them in continuing their education in college.

The Future of Higher Education.—The future of the liberal arts college occupied the attention of many educators. The shortage of specialists for war needs directed attention to certain defects which would require correction. The shortage of language specialists stimulated experiments in the teaching of languages. The whole approach was broadened to include not only the language but every cultural aspect of the country in which it is spoken; the methods and scope of the "language-area studies," as they have come to be known, would have an important influence on the teaching of all foreign languages. The report of the first year of the experiment, published by the American Council of Learned Societies, testified to its success in the teaching not only of the languages usually taught in schools and colleges but in a vast array of the lesser-known languages.

The emphasis placed by the army and navy specialized programs on technical and scientific studies aroused great concern about the future of the humanities. At the beginning of the year Wendell Willkie, in an address at Duke university on "Freedom and the Liberal Arts," directed attention to the seriousness of the situation. The American Council of Learned Societies and some of the educational foundations organized discussions and research into the future of the humanities and of the liberal arts in general. The Association of American Colleges published an important report of its committee on "The Restatement of the Nature and Aims of Liberal Education." The report recommended a program of liberal education adapted to the needs of the modern world, in which enduring human values would be definitely included. Among other matters the report suggested more flexible methods of admission to college, particularly for demobilized members of the armed forces, more individual instruction and less lecture methods, reform of examination procedures and effective guidance of students.

In addition to many articles in general and professional journals a number of books began to appear on the subject of the college and school curriculum. Among these were Robert M. Hutchins' *Education for Freedom* (Louisiana State University Press, Baton Rouge, La.), Jacques Maritain's *Education at the Crossroads* (Yale University Press, New Haven, Conn.) and Mark Van Doren's *Liberal Education* (Henry Holt and Company, New York).

Postwar Education of Service Men and Women.—Plans were developed during 1943 to provide for the postwar education of service men and women. These plans concerned two groups in particular: (1) the great majority of ex-service men who require short periods of training and (2) others, including those whose education was interrupted by the period of service and those specially qualified who could benefit by a more extended program of general, technical or professional education.

In October President Roosevelt sent a message on the subject to congress urging immediate planning and action so that service men and women might be demobilized into a sound and prosperous economy with a minimum of unemployment and dislocation and that with the assistance of the government they might be given an opportunity to find jobs for which they are fitted and trained, with special training and education for those who desire it. He urged federal assistance to make such training possible for such periods as were needed by individuals according to ability. The federal government would provide the necessary funds and supervise their expenditure under generally accepted standards, but the control of education and certification of trainees and students would be left to the states and localities. Special provision would be made for the rehabilitation of disabled veterans.

The president's address was based on the report of a committee appointed in 1942 and reporting in Aug. 1943. The committee distinguished between the two groups mentioned by the president. For those in the second group—those qualified for advanced and professional and technical education—the committee recommended selection on a competitive basis, and that the award of scholarships, carrying with them reasonable maintenance allowances, should be determined by the needs of technical and professional occupations in which shortages of adequately trained personnel exist. Scholarships should be tenable for a period not to exceed four years, their continuation depending on the academic and general progress of the students.

In a bill introduced by Senator Claude Pepper and intended to provide loans to personnel in the armed forces and to merchant seamen, provision was made to grant loans up to $4,800, the estimated cost of four years of education, including living expenses, tuition, books and supplies as well as living expenses for dependents. If the student "showed good faith and diligence in his or her work" on certificate from the institution attended, only half of the loan would have to be repaid at 1% interest and in 10 instalments, if necessary.

It was expected that some provision would also be made for the re-education of men and women working in war industries to equip them for the changed occupations in peacetime industries.

National Scholarships for Girls.—Seven women's colleges—Barnard, Bryn Mawr, Mount Holyoke, Radcliffe, Smith, Vassar and Wellesley—informally associated in the Seven College conference planned to award 21 scholarships to incoming freshmen. The plan, which was to go into effect in May, 1944, was intended to encourage students of exceptional promise to come to these colleges from distant parts of the country. A prize of $100 was to be awarded to each successful candidate with additional amounts on the basis of need, to cover the cost of tuition, board and room in whole or in part. Scholarships would be renewable for the full college course, if the winner maintained a high honour record. The executive secretary of the conference in 1943 was Mrs. F. Murray Forbes, Jr., 21 Beaver Pl., Boston. (For statistics of institutions *see* UNIVERSITIES AND COLLEGES.)

Federal Aid for Education.—The effort to secure federal aid for education, which began during World War I, was continued during 1943 but was again defeated. Since 1917 the need for federal aid to implement the American ideal of equality of educational opportunity was believed by some educators to be greater than ever. The war revealed the differences in educational provisions in the country as never before. Under the selective draft system large numbers of draftees were shown to be wholly or functionally illiterate, and another large number were rejected on physical grounds. The shortage of teachers revealed the low standards of remuneration which prevailed in the country.

In June 1943, the Thomas-Hill bill (S. 637) was approved by the senate committee on education and labour. The bill provided for the allocation of $200,000,000 a year to the states during the war "for payment of increased teachers' salaries and other unusual expenditures" arising out of the emergency, and a continuing postwar appropriation of $100,000,000 a year to be used for the equalization of opportunities among and within the states for public elementary and secondary education, including kindergarten and nursery schools and education through the 14th grade (*i.e.*, junior colleges).

The fund for emergency purposes was to be provided: (1) to keep schools open and to pay teachers' salaries; (2) to employ additional teachers in order to reduce the size of the larger classes; (3) to raise substandard salaries; and (4) to adjust salaries to meet the increased cost of living. The average number of pupils in average daily attendance was to be employed as the basis for distributing appropriations to the states.

The basis for the distribution of the equalization fund was to be the number of persons 5 to 17 years of age and the total income payments in each state; the larger amount of aid would

under this formula go to the poorer states which had the larger number of children and the lower income payments.

The index of need in the states was, according to the bill, to be computed by the U.S. commissioner of education, in whom the administration of the bill's provisions was to be vested. The control of education was to be left to the state and local school authorities. The distribution of the federal funds was to be made by the state authority in each state. To prevent the use of federal funds to replace or reduce state funds for education each state would, according to the bill, be required to continue to spend as much for education as it had in 1941 in order to qualify for federal aid. A similar safeguard against the reduction or replacement of state or local funds by federal aid was provided in the special aid to be given to maintain schools for minority races on the basis of their proportion to the total population.

The bill came before the senate in October but was defeated on the following amendment: "Provided that there shall be no discrimination in the administration of the benefits and appropriations under the respective provisions of this act or in the state funds supplemented thereby on account of race, creed or color." The bill was referred back for further action to the senate committee on education and labour. The corresponding bill, H.R. 2849, was still scheduled to be discussed in the house of representatives.

In view of the continued need of labour, it was estimated that if care were provided for the children of working mothers, the number of women engaged in defense industries—about 18,000,-000—could be increased. Under the Lanham act, 1942, provision had been made for the care of children and for other emergency needs. Funds had already been made available to the extent of $300,000,000 up to June 30, 1943, for the construction, maintenance and operation of community facilities, including schools. An additional amount of $200,000,000 was authorized by congress to be used until the War-area Child Care act of 1943 should become effective. Under the latter act the administration of provisions for the care of children was transferred from the Federal Works agency to the children's bureau and the U.S. office of education. Care was provided in 1943 for 320,000 children, of whom 60,000 were between the ages of two and five. Guidance in the organization of wartime child-care programs and state and local programs of child welfare, nursery schools and extended school services was given by the director of community war services of the Federal Security agency.

Educational Needs of the Future.—The National Resources Planning board in its recommendations outlined the financial needs of American education in the postwar era. On the basis of the total expenditures for education of $2,817,000,000 in 1940, the board recommended an expenditure of $6,100,000,000. Among the items to be included were the following: For preschools, elementary and high schools, $3,000,000,000; for junior colleges, $400,000,000; for colleges, universities, professional and technical institutions, $1,000,000,000; for adult education, $300,000,000; for student aid, $300,000,000; and for public libraries, $200,000,-000. For the five-year period immediately following the war the board recommended an expenditure of $2,380,000,000 to eliminate building deficiencies in education (the cost in 1940 was $382,000,000).

The board included in its program of education increased attention to education for health and safety, vocational training, leisure education, education in home and family living, training for national security and citizenship, social and economic education, retraining of men and women demobilized from the armed forces and defense industries and provision of opportunities for those whose education had been interrupted by the war. In order to equalize the educational opportunities throughout the country the board urged the provision of adequate funds by the federal government. The board also recommended that the functions of the U.S. office of education should be enlarged so that it might become "the major instrument in educational research and planning."

International Relations in Education.—Considerable attention was devoted during 1943, both in Great Britain and in the United States, to the future of education, the rehabilitation of education in Germany and to the creation of an international agency for education. In the United States the division of cultural relations of the state department and the Office of the Coordinator of Inter-American Affairs continued their activities in promoting relations between the United States and the republics of Latin America, and plans were considered by the former for the extension of its sphere of work to other parts of the world.

The third report of the Commission to Study the Organization of Peace, issued in Feb. 1943, contained a paper by I. L. Kandel on "Education and the Postwar Settlement" in which were discussed such topics as "Education an International Concern," "Need of an International Educational Organization," "The Pattern of Educational Reconstruction," "Educational and Intellectual Rehabilitation" and "International Centers for the Study of Education."

In May 1943, the educational policies commission of the National Education association issued a report on *Education and the People's Peace.* After reviewing the international status of education in the period between the two wars and the opportunity offered for correcting past mistakes the report urged: (1) the importance of developing public opinion in the United States on the issues of peace and international organization; (2) the necessity of creating a council of education for the United Nations; and (3) the need of a permanent international agency for education related to other parts of the emergent world organization. The function of an international agency for education would be "to keep constantly in touch with educational procedures throughout the world, and to report its findings publicly." (National Education Association, Washington, D.C.)

The Universities Committee on Post-War International Problems issued a pamphlet on *Education and World Peace,* prepared by members of the faculty and students of the graduate school of education, Harvard university. In this pamphlet the major problem indicated in the title was broken down into the more specific questions implicit in it, and the more important arguments for and against the principal current answers were formulated. Among the questions discussed were the following: the relation of education to world organization for international peace and order; the creation of a permanent international office of education; the establishment of an international university; and the formation of an international education association. (Published by the World Peace Foundation, Boston.)

In September an international education assembly met at Harper's Ferry, Va., under the auspices of the Liaison Committee for International Education, which consists of representatives of various educational organizations in the United States. The assembly voted in favour of the establishment of an international commission for education to co-operate with governments in rebuilding educational and cultural programs in war-devastated countries, to assist new governments in axis countries in reconstructing their educational systems in harmony with peace aims, to eliminate educational and cultural activities that threaten peaceful relations among nations, to encourage the provision of equality of opportunity in education, to assist in the elimination of illiteracy and to encourage the establishment of international institutions for the training of educational and cultural leaders.

EXHIBITION OF RUSSIAN CHILDREN'S WORK at the Palace of Young Pioneers, Leningrad, in June 1943

The assembly unanimously voted for the establishment of an international education office.

In England the Joint Commission of the Council for Education in World Citizenship and the London International assembly issued a report on *Education and the United Nations* (reprinted by the American Council on Public Affairs, Washington, D.C.). The London International assembly is an unofficial assembly of members, lay and professional, representing all the United Nations, together with representatives of some of the Allied governments and ministries of education in London. The report dealt with the status of education in nazi-occupied countries and with the future of education in the enemy countries, especially Germany, and in the United Nations and proposed the establishment of an international authority for education. The report recommended that (1) since education would be one of the chief responsibilities of the United Nations, a United Nations bureau of educational reconstruction be established at once; (2) during the occupation of Germany education should be under the control of a high commissioner to insure that nazi and militarist influences are eradicated and to supervise the re-education of the German people; (3) an international organization of education be created as soon as practicable for the advancement of education and the promotion of education in world citizenship—such an organization to be one of the principal parts of any new international authority that might be established and to consist of representatives of governments, education authorities and associations of teachers, parents and students; and (4) in order to keep the United Nations united by a dominating motive to build a better world and to educate in principles of world citizenship educational facilities be extended, with financial aid if necessary, from the community of nations.

Education in the Occupied Countries.—An inter-Allied bureau was established in London to consider measures needed to restore the educational services in the occupied countries. The bureau was the result of conferences held by ministers of education of the governments-in-exile in co-operation with the president of the English board of education. The United States was represented at these conferences by an unofficial observer. The chairman of the bureau in 1943 was Jules Hoste, Belgian undersecretary for education. The bureau's work would include the purchase and distribution of books and periodicals, the preparation of films and other visual aids and the collection of scientific equipment. Plans for the financial support of education when re-established in the occupied countries were also the subject of discussion.

Soviet Union.—During the summer of 1943 it was announced that coeducation, which had been introduced in the early years of the revolution, would be abolished in the secondary schools of the soviet union. The measure had already been proposed in 1940 but was delayed by the outbreak of war. The reasons put forward for the separation of boys and girls were that the needs of the two sexes were different and that each should be given that education which would best equip them for their future lifework. The emphasis in the education of boys would be on technical and military training and in that of girls on handicrafts, domestic science, hygiene and child care. Girls would continue to enjoy equal opportunities with boys to enter the universities.

Academic Freedom.—It is interesting to note that there were no cases during World War II of dismissal of academic personnel on charges of disloyalty. This is in striking contrast with the dismissal of a small number of professors for disloyalty at the outbreak of World War I, including the *cause célèbre* of the late Dr. James McKeen Cattell. The situation in 1941–43 was due in part to the hostile attitude already engendered against the nazis for their persecution of intellectuals and institutions of learning generally and against the Japanese for their insidious attack on Pearl Harbor. In part it was also due to the fact that strong professional organizations were developed after World War I for the protection of academic freedom.

The uncertainty of the future of colleges and universities after Pearl Harbor, when there was pressure for financial retrenchment in these institutions, created a feeling of insecurity among faculty members. The difficulties were overcome, however, by the absorption of specialists in public services and war industries, by the selective draft and enlistments and by the adoption of many institutions for the training of army and navy personnel. Although some institutions were compelled by circumstances to retire members of their staffs, the retirements did not constitute cases of violation of tenure principles.

In a report published in the February issue of the *Bulletin* of the American Association of University Professors, it was stated that 149 cases had been considered by its committee A on academic freedom and tenure in 1942. Of these, 80 had been closed at the end of that year. The majority of the cases concerned wrongful dismissals, violating the principles adopted by the association in 1915, 1925 and 1940 and reprinted in the February issue of the *Bulletin*. The December issue of the *Bulletin* of the association contained a list of 12 "censured administrations," that

is, administrations of institutions "not observing the generally recognized principles of academic freedom and tenure, endorsed by this Association, the Association of American Colleges, the Association of American Law Schools, and the American Association of Teachers Colleges." (I. L. K.)

Great Britain.—*Reform Proposals.*—On July 16, following more than two years' discussion and negotiation with parties concerned, the president of the board of education, R. A. Butler, presented to parliament a White Paper (*Educational Reconstruction*, Cmd. 6458) outlining the government's policy for postwar reform of the education service.

The changes proposed demanding legislation included a complete recasting of the public system of education, to comprise three successive stages—primary, secondary and further education; the laying of a statutory duty upon the local education authorities to secure "the provision of efficient education throughout those stages for all persons capable of profiting thereby"; the laying of a statutory duty upon the parent "to cause his child to receive efficient full-time education suitable to the child's age and aptitudes"; provision where needed of nursery schools for children below compulsory school age; raising of the age of compulsory full-time attendance at school from 14 to 15, and later to 16; institution of a system of compulsory part-time education for all young persons between leaving school and the age of 18; completion of the reorganization of the existing public elementary schools to make available well-designed and -equipped primary schools for all children up to the age of 11, and secondary schools with varied facilities for advanced work for all children over that age; provision of adequate and co-ordinated facilities for technical and adult education; expansion of the school medical service to include treatment as well as inspection and its extension to cover the system of part-time education; transformation of the power to provide meals, milk and other refreshment at school into a duty; the laying of a statutory duty upon all primary and secondary schools to begin each school day with a corporate act of worship and to give religious instruction; more complete maintenance and a 50% grant toward the cost of any required alterations of premises, on conditions, to managers or governors of voluntary schools; retention of county councils and county borough councils only as local education authorities, the county authorities to be assisted in their areas by district committees to which powers might be delegated if desired; and registration and inspection of private schools.

Administrative changes proposed included a progressive decrease in the size of classes in primary schools; abolition of the special place examination deciding entry to secondary schools; a common code of regulations for all secondary schools; remodelling of the secondary school curriculum; expansion of the Service of Youth; improvement of the facilities for enabling poor students to go to the universities; and reform of the methods of recruitment and training of teachers. The ultimate additional cost of the reforms was estimated at £67,400,000; and to ease the burden on local rates it was proposed to increase the aggregate exchequer grant from 49.36% to 55%.

The White Paper proposals as a whole were warmly welcomed by parliament, press and public, but several criticisms were widely made: The timetable for bringing the reforms into operation was considered dilatory, the financial allocation to technical and adult education too small. The total extinction of the smaller local education authorities was condemned. A definite date for the raising of the school age to 16 was demanded. The proposals concerning the voluntary schools and religious instruction were variously criticized along familiar lines.

After further consultations Mr. Butler introduced an education bill into parliament on Dec. 15. This included all the legislative

CLASSROOM of Japanese evacuee school children at a U.S. relocation centre in 1943

changes proposed in the White Paper, with some modifications in deference to public criticism. The timetable was speeded up and April 1, 1945, appointed for raising the school age to 15—a delay of two years being permitted if exceptional circumstances demanded. The age was further to be raised to 16 by order in council as soon as the minister deemed it practicable. The financial allocation to technical and adult education was more than trebled. The proposal for district committees was dropped in favour of one for "divisional executives" with statutorily delegated powers, while boroughs and urban district councils having populations of 60,000 or a school population of 7,000 were given the right to frame their own scheme of delegation. Some slight concessions were made to the voluntary bodies.

Important new proposals included the translation of the board of education into a ministry and the investing of the minister with appropriate powers (the old style and title being retained in both cases); and the setting up of two central advisory councils for education, one for England, the other for Wales and Monmouthshire, with the duty of taking the initiative in offering advice to the president. (*See* also CAMBRIDGE UNIVERSITY; LONDON UNIVERSITY; OXFORD UNIVERSITY.) (H. C. D.)

Education, U.S. Office of: *see* EDUCATION; FEDERAL SECURITY AGENCY.

Education Association, National: *see* NATIONAL EDUCATION ASSOCIATION.

Eggs. The production of eggs in the United States in 1943 reached a new high record of nearly 5,000,000,000 dozen, more than the goal set for the year. This amount is about 50% above the average from 1933 on. After 1926 the total crop of eggs produced ranged from about 2,800,000,000 dozen to 3,220,000,000 dozen. The manner in which poultry raisers responded to the war need was much beyond the expectation of those who were planning the goals. While this high rate of production was not likely to be maintained in 1944 the surplus of 1943 was expected to go a great way to meet the large requirements for military, lend-lease and other special uses. There were about 32% more laying hens in farm flocks at the end of the year 1943 than the 10-year averages and also a large increase in the number of pullets not yet of laying age. This increase resulted from a heavy late hatch in the early summer. The factors that favored this heavy egg production were the high price of eggs and the large number of layers on farms. The total income from chickens and eggs in 1943 was estimated to total over $2,000,000,000, compared to $1,300,000,000 in 1942. This increase resulted from both higher prices and a larger volume of production. Cash income from poultry in 1943 was about 13% of total farm cash income, having increased more than the over-all livestock or crop production.

The goal for 1944 was set at the high total of 5,000,000,000 dozen eggs, but the shortage of feed in late 1943 threatened to reduce production sharply in some areas. A campaign to cull flocks 10% was proposed to save feed and the goals for poultry meat were reduced.

The demand for eggs for military, lend-lease and other uses continued to increase through 1943. Dried egg production was about 275,000,000 lb. in 1943 compared with 236,000,000 lb. in 1942. Egg-drying facilities were expanded several times after 1941 and could produce about 420,000,000 lb. annually if operated to full capacity at all times. Dried egg production increased rapidly during the first half of 1943 but slowed down later in the year when the prices of shell eggs rose in relation to eggs for drying. A total of 800,000,000 dozen eggs was estimated to be the total requirement for 1943 to meet the schedule of deliveries to war agencies. This was about 16% of United States egg

EGG POWDER on a packing line after dehydration

production compared with less than 1% so used prior to 1941. All the dried product was reserved for government uses. (*See* also POULTRY.) (J. C. Ms.)

Egypt. An independent kingdom of northeast Africa; bounded N. by the Mediterranean, S. by the Anglo-Egyptian Sudan, N.E. by Palestine, E. by the Red sea, W. by Libya and the Sahara. Area *c.* 383,000 sq.mi. (arable land 13,600 sq.mi.); pop. (est. Dec. 31, 1939), 16,680,000. Chief towns (pop. 1937): Cairo (cap. 1,307,422); Alexandria (682,101); Port Said (126,907); Tanta (94,421); Mansura (68,637); Damanhur (61,791); Assuit (59,925). Ruler, King Farouk I; premier, Mustapha Pasha Nahas (Feb. 5, 1942); language, Arabic; religion, Mohammedan 91%; Copt 7%.

History.—The war receded from Egypt's borders as the Allied armies pursued and finally annihilated the German Afrika Korps. The Mediterranean ceased to be "closed" and at the end of the year convoys were beginning to arrive regularly from the west. Finally, domestic politics were unruffled by ministerial crises and Nahas Pasha remained firmly in power as prime minister. In the early summer the premier made some important changes in his cabinet, an outstanding new-comer being Amin Osman Pasha as minister of finance.

Egypt's economic problem was a serious government preoccupation throughout the year. Her position as the great war-entrepôt of the whole middle east brought money into the country where opportunities for sound investment were scanty. This led to ill-advised local speculation. At the same time, owing to the war shortage of shipping, the normal import of goods and commodities was so curtailed that supplies fell far short of public demand. The result was hoarding and black market speculation.

Amin Osman Pasha's program to control prices and check profiteering was only moderately successful. Energetic police action was taken sporadically against profiteers; but conditions in Egypt did not lend themselves to rationing control on normal lines, and by the end of the year the cost of living figure stood at 250%

above the 1939 index.

But the finance minister's handling of the problem of the surplus and idle accumulations of private money was an outstanding success. Between October and the end of the year the Egyptian government issued five loans—long and short—totalling about £E80,000,000. The public response was excellent and on each occasion the lists were closed as fully subscribed on the day of issue. The greater amount was to be applied as national loans to convert in Jan. 1944 the whole of the existing unified and preference loans which were long-standing international obligations on the country.

Simultaneously, to ease the local economic situation, the government maintained the previous restrictions on cotton cultivation so as to keep sufficient land for food production to meet the war shortage in wheat importations, etc. Again, to assist the agricultural population, and to prevent speculation in land, the rents of farms were frozen on the existing 1943 level.

During the year three historic war conferences were staged in Cairo. In January, Winston Churchill visited the middle east command in connection with the Allied operations in North Africa. In November, he and President Roosevelt and Generalissimo Chiang Kai-shek conferred on the far eastern campaign. In December, the president of the Turkish republic discussed the position of Turkey with the British prime minister and President Roosevelt.

In the summer, in response to an Egyptian appeal for funds to commemorate the El Alamein victory of Oct. 1942, upwards of £80,000 was subscribed by Egyptians of all grades. A sports club for British soldiers was opened in Cairo and steps were being taken to equip a rest hostel in England for the lasting benefit of troops of the British 8th army. In December a third daughter was born to King Farouk and Queen Farida.   (O. M. T.)

Education.—(1938–39): Elementary and secondary schools 4,065; scholars 1,064,209; colleges 8; scholars 1,980; Fuad I university: scholars male 8,393; female 7,043; foreign schools (1936–37) 410; scholars 76,750.

Banking and Finance.—Revenue (est. 1942–43) £E53,526,-000; expenditure (est. 1942–43) £E53,526,000; public debt (May 1, 1941) £E93,363,680; notes in circulation (Jan. 31, 1943) £E74,500,000; gold reserve (Jan. 31, 1943) £E6,300,000; foreign assets reserve £E76,400,000; exchange rate (£E1 = 100 piastres): (average 1942) £E1 = 413.8 cents; (May 1943) £E1 = 413.8 cents.

Trade and Communication.—External trade (merchandise): imports (1940) £E31,600,000; exports (1940) £E62,000,000. Communications and transport, 1938: roads, main 1,240 mi.; secondary 3,430 mi.; railways (1939), state 3,550 mi.; agricultural 879 mi.; shipping (1939) 110,000 tons gross; entered ports 35,-390,325 tons gross; passed through Suez canal 25,827,977 tons gross; motor vehicles licensed (Dec. 31, 1938): cars 29,382; commercial 4,074; cycles 2,051; wireless receiving set licences (Dec. 31, 1938) 78,823; telephone instruments in use (April 30, 1938) 59,922.

Aerial Navigation (1938)

	Misr Airways Company	Imperial Airways Ltd.	"K.L.M." Royal Dutch Air Lines
Passengers	18,559	6,056	2,450
Freight and baggage (Kg.)	63,828	114,189	45,140
Mails (Kg.)	16,435	1,482,130	131,851
Miles flown	1,011,104	6,967,035	2,795,180
Regularity of service	98.1%	99.9%	98.2%

Agriculture and Minerals.—Production (1940) (in short tons): cotton, ginned 454,148; maize 1,685,967; wheat 1,499,789; rice 727,298; petroleum 1,024,037; natural phosphates 201,721; cane sugar, refined 191,800; barley 265,765; ground-nuts 17,967. (*See also* ANGLO-EGYPTIAN SUDAN.)

LIEUT. GEN. ROBERT L. EICHELBERGER at a front-line gun position near Buna village, New Guinea, before Japan's total defeat there in the first week of Jan. 1943

Eichelberger, Robert Lawrence (1886–   ), U.S. army officer, was born March 9 in Urbana, Ohio. A graduate of West Point, he was commissioned a 2nd lieutenant in 1909, saw service on the Mexican border and the Panama Canal Zone and in 1918 was awarded the D.S.C. and D.S.M. while serving with the army of occupation in eastern Siberia. In addition, three decorations were bestowed upon him by the Japanese government. After World War I, he was stationed in the orient. On returning to the United States, Eichelberger was attached to the general staff for several years in the early 1920s. He returned to West Point, where he held the post of adjutant, 1931–35. He was then transferred to Washington, where he acted as secretary to the general staff in the years preceding the outbreak of World War II. In 1940, Eichelberger was re-assigned to West Point, where he streamlined the entire curriculum of training. During his 14 months as superintendent of the academy, he introduced an air training course which enabled cadets to qualify for commissions in the air force. Made a brigadier general in 1940, Eichelberger was promoted to the rank of major general in Oct. 1942, and in Jan. 1943, Gen. Douglas MacArthur revealed that Eichelberger had been placed in command of U.S. troops in Papua. For his participation in this campaign, he was awarded the distinguished service cross for the second time.

Eire. Eire is the southern portion of an island to the west of Great Britain, extending from 51° 26′ to 51° 21′ N., and from 5° 25′ to 10° 30′ W. Under the constitution, operative since Dec. 29, 1937, the name "Irish Free State" given by the treaty of 1921 to the 26 counties and four of the county boroughs of southern Ireland was replaced by that of "Eire," or Ireland. President: Dr. Douglas Hyde (*de h-Ide*). National flag: the tricolour of green, white and orange.

Area 26,601 sq.mi.; pop. (est. June 30, 1942) 2,963,000. Chief towns (pop. register 1941): Dublin (cap., 489,276); Cork (76,758); Limerick (42,522); Dun Laoghaire (41,924); Waterford (28,481). Languages: Irish and English; religion: Christian (Roman Catholic 93%).

History.—The chief interest of the year 1943 centred in the general election (June 22). In April the government introduced two bills to amend the electoral law. The General Election (emergency provisions) bill, which was passed, provided for the continuance in office of the existing Oireachtas until a new one had been elected. The Elections (Duration of Dáil Eireann) bill, which was withdrawn after second reading, provided for the extension of the life of future parliaments from five to six years.

External affairs played practically no part in the election campaign. In his speeches Eamon de Valera reiterated his assurance that since the agreement of 1938 the only problem outstanding between Eire and Great Britain was that of partition. William Cosgrave gave a special turn to the campaign by his promise, if given a majority, to form a "national government" representing all parties. This promise was ridiculed by de Valera, who referred to the proposed government as a "mixus-gatherum."

The result of the election was highly disappointing to both the principal parties. In the old Dáil, de Valera, with 77 deputies, had a majority of 16 over all other parties combined. The figures for the new Dáil were: Fianna Fáil, 67; Fine Gael, 32; Labour, 17; Farmers, 14; Independents, 8. Fianna Fáil had thus lost ten seats, but Fine Gael (Cosgrave's party) had gained no advantage, having itself fallen from 45 to 32, and having lost three of its leaders—General Richard James Mulcahy, Professor John Marcus O'Sullivan and John Costello. The chief surprise of the election was the re-emergence of the Farmer's party, which in the previous Dáil was virtually nonexistent. The new party was in effect a coalition between disparate groups, and its stability was by no means assured.

On July 1 de Valera was again elected Taoiseach by 67 votes to Cosgrave's 37, Labour and Farmers having abstained from voting. On July 2 he announced the names of his ministers; the only change was the addition of Seán Moylan as minister for lands. An election for the senate took place on Aug. 25 on a complicated and much-criticized system. Prominent new senators were General Mulcahy, Professor Fearon of Trinity college, Dublin, and Donal O'Sullivan, who was clerk of the senate abolished by de Valera in 1938.

In March the office of Ulster king-of-arms, created in 1552, was abolished, and its functions transferred to the National library. In England the Ulster title was added to that of the Norroy king-of-arms.

While efforts to make Eire self-sufficient in home-grown wheat had given satisfactory results, the 1943 harvest, largely because of wet weather, did not entirely come up to expectations. An increase in the compulsory tillage area and a rise in the price of wheat from 50s. to 55s. per barrel was announced for 1944. Owing to the growing shortage of pork and bacon, it was found necessary to discontinue the maximum price for live pigs.

(M. T.)

Education.—In 1940–41: elementary schools 5,076; scholars 462,245; secondary schools 352; scholars 38,713; universities, National, 4,039 students; Trinity college, Dublin, 1,391.

Banking and Finance.—Revenue, ordinary (1941–42) £36,-980,000; expenditure, ordinary (1941–42) £40,625,000; revenue (est. 1942–43) £38,365,000; expenditure (est. 1942–43) £44,270,-000; public debt (March 31, 1942) total, £55,684,675; notes in circulation (April 30, 1943) £29,200,000; reserve, gold (April 30, 1943) £2,601,685; securities reserve £20,600,000; exchange rate (Dec. 1943) £1 = $4.035 U.S.

Trade and Communication.—Foreign trade (merchandise): imports (1942) £34,692,000; exports and re-exports (1942) £32,616,000; roads, main (1940–41) 10,000 mi.; secondary,

39,000 mi.; railways, total track mileage (1941) 2,492 mi.; shipping (1941): vessels 505; net tonnage 37,272; motor vehicles licensed (Aug. 1942): private cars 7,991; other vehicles 23,508; wireless receiving set licences (1940–41) 183,578; telephones, installations (1940–41) 27,870.

Agriculture, Manufacturing, Mineral Production.—Production (1941) in metric tons: oats 695,400; wheat 442,400; potatoes 3,748,600; barley 145,200; beet sugar 97,000; coal 155,000; wool 7,421. Livestock, number (June 1, 1940): cattle 4,023,027; sheep 3,070,588; pigs 1,049,089. Agriculture and fisheries, net output (1940–41) £55,048,000. Number of insured workers (1940–41) average 440,756; number of unemployed, average (1941) 74,656; (July 31, 1942) 55,000.

Eisenhower, Dwight D.

(1890–   ), U.S. army officer, was born Oct. 14 at Denison, Tex. He was admitted to West Point, graduating in 1915, and during World War I was an instructor at several U.S. army camps. After graduating from the Army War college, he served in the office of the chief of staff in Washington. In 1935, he went to the Philippines as Gen. MacArthur's chief of staff and helped plan the commonwealth's defenses. In June 1942, Gen. Eisenhower was given command of the newly established U.S. headquarters in England for the European theatre of operations and was promoted to the rank of lieutenant general. On Nov. 8, 1942, he led a huge force of U.S. troops which landed in French North Africa. He subsequently concluded a politico-military arrangement with Adm. Jean Darlan to join the Allied cause.

On Feb. 6, 1943, Eisenhower was named commander of all Allied forces in the North African theatre of war and was appointed to the rank of full general five days later. Under his command the Allied forces chased the axis armies out of Tunisia and on July 10, 1943, they invaded Sicily, completely overrunning the island by Aug. 17. Eisenhower then launched the invasion of Italy on Sept. 3. Five days later he announced the Italians' unconditional surrender. On Dec. 24, 1943, Pres. Roosevelt announced that Eisenhower had been named to command the Allied armies scheduled to invade western Europe in 1944. Several days later, Eisenhower predicted that Germany would be defeated completely sometime in 1944.

Elections.

The 1943, off-year elections, although few and scattered, were highly significant. As the first to be held since the United Nations began to achieve large-scale victories in North Africa, Italy the southwestern Pacific and in the skies over Germany, they furnished an index to the nation's mood under changing conditions and the people's response to new issues and problems born of the war. The Republicans scored heavily in all major tests. Their triumphs marked their greatest resurgence since their national and state crackup in 1934 and 1936.

In New York state the G.O.P. nominee for Lieutenant Governor, Joe R. Hanley, president of the state senate, defeated Lieutenant General William N. Haskell (retired) by a majority of 347,960. Hanley captured 55.2% of the total vote. Governor Thomas E. Dewey's lead over John J. Bennett, Jr. in 1942 was 630,000.

The American Labor party, which supported General Haskell, polled 324,550 ballots as against more than 400,000 when it nominated a separate candidate, Dean Alfange, in the 1942 gubernatorial contest; 288,508 of the A.L.P. ballots were cast in New York city.

The New York struggle commanded most interest for obvious reasons, including the fact that it is President Roosevelt's home state. Observers regarded the outcome as popular endorsement of Governor Dewey's ten-month-old administration at Albany.

It also meant that if Governor Dewey should leave the gubernatorial chair before the expiration of his term on January 1, 1947, the nation's greatest state would remain in Republican hands—a distinct political asset.

In New Jersey Walter E. Edge, former United States senator and Herbert Hoover's ambassador to France, won the governorship contest over Vincent J. Murphy, Democrat, by 128,008. Mr. Murphy was mayor of Newark and secretary of the state Federation of Labor. The percentage of the vote given the winner was 55.6. The Republicans retained control of the legislature by a heavy margin.

The surprise outcome occurred in normally Democratic Kentucky, where former Judge Simeon S. Willis, Republican, nosed out J. Lyter Donaldson, former highway commissioner, by 8,303 votes for governor, with a percentage total of 50.8. The Willis victory also contributed to the election of seven Republicans to important state offices. The Democrats held the legislature, but by reduced margins.

An unusual feature of this election was the fact that 4,180 more people went to the polls than in the regular 1942 contest. The increased vote was especially surprising in view of the fact that many young men had left the district to enter the armed services or to seek more lucrative employment in industrial centres. Save for a few small distilleries, the 4th district is strictly rural.

The Republicans also came out ahead in most of the mayoralty and township contests, regaining many cities which had been under Democratic rule for 10 and 15 years. Most notable struggle for city hall control was in Philadelphia, where Acting Mayor Bernard Samuel got a 63,339 majority over William C. Bullitt, former ambassador to Russia and France by appointment of Franklin D. Roosevelt.

The G.O.P. achieved an even more spectacular success in a special congressional election in the 4th Kentucky district, which had been a Democratic stronghold for years. On December 2, 1943, Chester O. Carrier, Republican, led his opponent, J. Dan Talbott, by 12,568. President Roosevelt carried this district by 10,000 in 1940, and Ed W. Creal, the Democratic incumbent whose death necessitated the election, won by 4,866 in November of 1942.

These results merely pointed up a trend which had been in effect for several years. The Republicans won or made the more impressive showing in every trial since the regular elections in 1942. In the 6th Missouri district Marion Bennett, Republican, was elected to the house by 62.9% of the vote in the spring of 1943. His late father got only 54.5% in November of 1942.

In the 2nd California district the Democratic candidate for a house vacancy was elected, but only because the opposition was divided. The two G.O.P. entries polled 60.3% of the total vote. In the 2nd Kansas district a special congressional election held on Sept. 4, 1943, gave Erret P. Scrivner, Republican, a percentage of 69.8 as against 59.2 for the G.O.P. winner in Nov. of 1942—the late U. S. Guyer.

The election results and deaths during 1943 changed the complexion of congress only slightly. At the opening of the session in Jan. 1943, there were 222 Democrats, 208 Republicans, 2 Farmer-Labor members, 1 American Labor representative, 1 Progressive and 1 vacancy. As the year closed, there were 218 Democrats, 208 Republicans, 2 Farmer-Laborites, 1 American Labor member, 1 Progressive and 5 vacancies.

In the senate the Republicans lost a seat through the death of W. Warren Barbour of New Jersey. By appointment of the then governor, Charles Edison, Arthur Walsh, a Democrat, took Mr. Barbour's place. Mr. Walsh was executive vice president of the Thomas A. Edison, Inc. industries, and formerly served as assist-

ant administrator of the national housing administration. He must stand for election in Nov. of 1944.

The senate membership at the end of the year consisted of 58 Democrats, 37 Republicans and 1 Progressive, Robert Marion La Follette, Jr., of Wisconsin.

Other statistics reflect the extent of the Republican comeback that was climaxed on Nov. 2, 1943. The minority in 1943 had 26 governors in the 38 states outside the solid south; the comparative figure was 9 in 1936. The only governorship above the Mason and Dixon line and east of the Mississippi river held by the Democrats was in Indiana.

In those same 38 commonwealths the Republicans controlled both houses in 28 legislatures, the Democrats dominated 8 in the same manner and 2 were split. The 26 states where G.O.P. adherents sat in the gubernatorial chair in 1943 had a population of 85,000,000 and 339 votes in the electoral college.

Since all the victorious and defeated candidates in the 1943 contests urged full support of the war effort, that issue was not directly involved. Republicans argued, however, and many Democrats agreed, that the outcome registered popular dissatisfaction with the administration's handling of the home front.

The G.O.P. spokesmen also noted that Senate Majority Leader Alben W. Barkley, in campaigning for Mr. Donaldson in Kentucky, declared that a vote for Mr. Willis amounted to a repudiation of the president. Mr. Roosevelt journeyed to Hyde Park to cast his ballot for General Haskell, an old friend, and wrote a letter praising another old acquaintance, Mr. Bullitt, during the Philadelphia mayoralty fight.

Irritations and pressures associated with the global conflict were generally regarded as basic factors for the Democratic defeats. The electorate apparently manifested its discontent over heavier taxes, rationing of food, gasoline and other necessities, shortages of commodities, discomforts and inconveniences burdening their daily lives, conflicting rulings by the "bureaucrats," the administration's handling of labour and strikes.

The elections were held in the midst of clashes involving President Roosevelt's aides, War Mobilization Director James F. Byrnes and Economic Adviser Fred M. Vinson, the farmers and powerful labour groups. The people went to the polls at a time when the administration was insisting on subsidies to hold down food costs, while the agricultural bloc on Capitol hill was demanding price increases.

Wage disputes affecting 1,000,000 nonoperating railroad workers and 600,000 members of the United Mine Workers were still unsolved on election day, with Byrnes and Vinson maintaining that acquiescence to the demands of all these groups would precipitate inflation.

As the party in power, the Democrats naturally felt the full impact of this accumulation of grievances.

Ballot-box statistics also indicated that many influential elements once loyal to the New Deal turned against it on Nov. 2, 1943. These included farmers, organized and unorganized labour, the white-collar class, small business men, harassed housewives and the Negro vote.

There was distinct evidence that the Negro vote, traditionally Republican, deserted the Democrats. Republican candidates swept wards in New York city's Harlem, in Philadelphia and in Louisville where the Negroes had been returning Democratic candidates for more than a decade. Negro leaders attributed the defection to alleged Army-Navy discrimination against members of their race.

Historically, the administration suffered the normal vicissitudes which befall a party that has been in power for long. Assuming that Samuel J. Tilden did defeat Rutherford B. Hayes in 1876, the only period since the Civil War when one party enjoyed a four-term tenure was from 1897 to 1913, encompassing the regimes of William McKinley, Theodore Roosevelt and William Howard Taft.

When President Roosevelt was asked for comment on the Nov. 2 returns, he replied that he was more interested in the news from the Solomon islands and the Italian battlefront. Wendell Willkie interpreted the results as a rebuke to Washington, but Governor Dewey said that the Republican victory in his state had no national import.

Postmaster General Frank C. Walker, who doubles as Democratic national chairman, attributed the outcome to local conditions and prejudices. Harrison E. Spangler, the Republican national chairman, said: "The Republican party is now the resurgent, dominant, victorious party of the United States. It is a unified party looking to the future."   (R. Tu.)

Electrical Industries.

In the United States, electrical manufacturing, which in the previous year had increased its production by 50%, in 1943 increased another third and its index of production stood at 553, based upon 1925 equaling 100. It was estimated that the value of the output stood somewhere close to $10,000,000,000.

Using the same basing period, the federal reserve board index of production for all manufacturing reached in 1943 the record height of 267. This affords a measure of comparison for the electrical manufacturing industry performance.

The great increase naturally came in industrial equipment, the index for which reached a high of 636. Production of civilian equipment, on the other hand, reached almost the vanishing point, standing at index 9 for electrical appliances.

The production figures are further indication of the fact that the preparation for war production was coming to a close. Equipment for transmitting and distributing electricity, for instance, was down to index 167 from a high in 1942 of 213. Insulated wire and cable, which is some measure of non-utility construction, was off from index 155 to 129.

The manufacturing production continued to expand during the year despite the fact that new orders were around 5% below those for 1942. Backlog figures were not available but they were down and, with further war order cutbacks, should melt very fast.

Because so much of the industry produced for war, virtually the same products as for peace, there was not a large reconversion problem. The appliance manufacturers, which represent the bulk of the non-electrical war material production, expected to reconvert in less than six months at the outside, mostly less than three months, once labour and materials were made available.

The electric power industry was expected to have no reconversion problem. It didn't have to convert for war and therefore would not need to change back for peacetime operations. However, its operations showed the full impact of war.

In 1943, for the first time, the energy output exceeded 200,000,000,000 kw.hr., reaching the total of 221,000,000,000, an increase of 17%. The first 100,000,000,000 mark was passed in 1936. The first two war years combined (1942 and 1943) showed an increase of more than 50,000,000,000.

Approximately one-third (74,400,000,000) was produced from water power and the remainder (146,600,000,000) from fuel power. These percentages did not vary perceptibly from the previous year. Imports from Canada increased about 100,000,000 kw.hr., bringing the total for the year up to 1,540,000,000. This was about two-thirds greater than in the years when Canada was in the war but the U.S. was not—1940 and 1941—but was still a third less than 1939.

Output from publicly owned plants increased faster during the year than from private plants. In 1943, publicly owned plants accounted for 18% of the total generation, whereas in 1942 the percentage was but 15. The total output from federal and locally owned systems including rural co-operatives was 39,640,000,000 kw.hr. and for privately owned, 181,360,000,000. Federal participation in power production in 1933 was less than 500,000,000 kw.hr.; in 1943, it was in excess of 24,000,000,000. Local publicly owned generation was 15,300,000,000 kw.hr.

The load on the utility systems gained rapidly throughout the year, reaching an aggregate of non-coincident peaks in December of 37,130,000 kw., or 4,200,000 kw. more than in 1942. To meet this increased demand the utilities installed, in 1943, 2,900,000 kw. new generating capacity; nevertheless the net dependable reserve was reduced from 20.4% in 1942 to 14.7% in 1943. There was more than 7,000,000 kw. additional capacity available but because its availability was not assured 365 days in the year it was not included in the dependable capacity total.

Of the new capacity added in 1943, 1,100,000 kw. was hydro and 1,800,000 kw. was fuel power. Private companies were responsible for 1,700,000 kw. and municipal and federal for the other 1,200,000 kw.

The amount of new generating capacity scheduled for addition in 1944 was approximately half of the 1943 additions, 1,465,900 kw and for 1945, 287,500 kw. The additions for 1944 reversed the order of capacity addition for the first time, with federal and municipal being larger than private companies by a small margin.

By the end of the year, power utility capacity had grown to almost 50,000,000 kw., the actual total being 49,442,000 kw. The increases in fuel and hydro capacity followed approximately the same pattern as the previous year. There was a marked change, however, in the percentage of ownership. Government bodies, federal and local, in 1943 owned 19.4% of all utility generating capacity, an increase from 17.5% in 1942. The increase of more than 1,000,000 kw. of federally owned capacity created the sharpest gain ever in this type of ownership.

Since the added generating capacity in itself was not sufficient to turn out the increased demand for energy, it was necessary to work existing equipment longer hours. The average hours use per kilowatt passed for the first time half the number of hours in the year with a performance of 4,611 hours. Fuel capacity passed 3,000 average hours use for the first time and hydro went to 5,483 or a use factor of nearly two-thirds.

Coal consumed during 1943 amounted to 76,950,000 tons, oil to 15,280,000 bbl. and gas to 287,940,000,000 cu.ft. The oil consumption did not increase, but gas consumption was up 20% and coal 12.4%. For the first time the fuel efficiency of power generation was poorer. It was 1.34 lb. of coal per kw.hr. in 1943 against 1.31 lb. the previous year.

Fuel was a major problem in 1943. At the beginning of the year utility stock piles averaged 101 days supply. By the end of November this coal pile had dropped to 69 days.

Customer statistics showed the restrictive effect of war upon civilian economy. Fewer than 200,000 additional residential customers indicated the near cessation of home construction, while a loss of 80,000 commercial and industrial customers gave evidence of the inability to do business as usual. At the end of the year the total number of customers was 32,395,000.

These customers purchased a total of 186,000,000,000 kw.hr., with large light and power customers (industrials) exceeding for the first time a usage of over 100,000,000,000 kw.hr. Totals for the several groups were as follows: Rural, 2,875,000,000; residential, 28,775,000,000; small light and power, 29,100,000,000; large light and power, 106,050,000,000; electric railways, 4,675,000,000; street and highway lighting, 2,150,000,000; electrified rail-

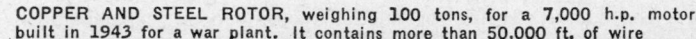

FOURTEEN-FOOT FLYWHEEL, part of an electric motor-generator set built in 1943 for the Kaiser steel plant at Fontana, Calif. The manufacturers estimated that the flywheel contained "more than enough energy to yank the battleship 'North Carolina' a foot in the air in one second"

WELDERS sealing the joints of a frame for a turbo-generator to be used in a U.S. war plant. Power generation continued to increase in the United States in 1943

CHICAGO'S FIRST SUBWAY, 4½ mi. long, was opened to the public Oct. 17, 1943

COPPER AND STEEL ROTOR, weighing 100 tons, for a 7,000 h.p. motor built in 1943 for a war plant. It contains more than 50,000 ft. of wire

roads, 2,575,000,000; municipal and miscellaneous, 9,800,000,000.

Although virtually no appliances were available all year, the residential usage increased from 1,012 to 1,073 kw.hr. in 1943.

In 1943, revenue passed the $3,000,000,000 mark for the first time, reaching a total of $3,096,600,000. With the exception of 1938, revenue increased from 1933 on, at approximately the same rate as during the '20s. Average revenue per residential kilowatt-hour continued its unbroken downward path to $3.64 in 1943.

Operating expenses, on the other hand, rose 12.1% resulting in an operating ratio before taxes of 40.3%. Taxes did not advance as sharply as in the two previous years but enough to take more than 25 cents out of every dollar of gross revenue.

Holding company divestments as the result of the operations of the Holding Company act numbered 32 in 1943, of which nine were sales to cities, PUD's (public utility districts) or rural co-ops. The remaining 70% remained in private ownership.

The fear that dismemberment of holding companies would result in many purchases by cities was not borne out. In fact, the whole public ownership program was quiet. In all, 12 elections were reported, the smallest number since the New Deal came in. Three were for and nine against municipal ownership.

There were few additional new REA lines because of material restriction but a number of farms along already built lines were connected, bringing the total consumers up to 1,080,000. Total energy input into REA systems exceeded 2,000,000,000 kw.hr. for the first time, 90% of which was purchased at an average cost of 8.5 mills per kw.hr.

To handle war regulation of utilities there was created within the War Production board the Office of War Utilities. Inventory control was tightened and exchange of excess stocks made mandatory. By the end of the year $25,000,000 in excess inventory had been distributed. As the year 1943 progressed, restrictions on materials were modified gradually.

War time was revoked in Michigan, Ohio and Georgia and on November 1 dimout regulations on Atlantic and Pacific coasts were cancelled. Because of coal shortages and transportation problems, a mandatory conservation program was scheduled for the middle of the year but was dropped in favour of a voluntary program which started on September 15.

Federal Power commission invoked the president's directive for supplying cheapest power to war loads over another's lines, known as the common carrier principle, against Washington Water Power in favour of Bonneville administration, but later, because loads were too small, withdrew the order. Renegotiation of power contracts was reported by the army to have returned $4,000,000 in the first fiscal year.

Rate reductions were numerous and those reported totaled about $6,000,000. Detroit, failing through the state commission and the courts to force a return to customers of taxable excess profits, levied a 20% excise tax against local utilities. OPA ruled out fuel and other automatic rate adjustments, because it considered them inflationary. The New York commission ruled 5½% return to be fair, while Pennsylvania allowed over 6% because of postwar equipment needs.

National Association of Railroad and Utilities Commissioners intervened in an Arkansas aluminum rate case where states rights were being challenged. As a result of the Jersey Central supreme court decision it voted to ask congress to amend the Federal Power act to prevent FPC encroachment on state jurisdiction.

Several bills were introduced during the year to tax public power. One was passed in Georgia but vetoed by the governor. There was also a large amount of investigation of public power, including REA, Columbia river, Shipshaw and Grand river flood control. Texas investigated all public power activities in the state.

The supreme court in the Jersey Central case extended federal

GLASS GLOBE which is lighted electronically by a high frequency radio beam, without wires. The inside of the globe is coated with phosphors

jurisdiction to intrastate utilities connected to interstate lines, even though they had no control over interstate delivery. Because so many justices disqualified themselves, it was impossible to get a quorum to review the "death sentence" decision of a lower court in upholding Section 11(b)(1) of the Holding Company act.

Lighting.—Changes in lighting equipment design were limited in 1943 to substitutes to meet limitation orders of WPB and to equipments for some special war purpose. Many of these, however, were expected to find their way into peacetime use after the war. Half the previous types of lamps were permitted and the seven normal voltages were restricted to three, 115, 120 and 125 volts. Fluorescent lamp manufacture was restricted to white and daylight.

A number of special war application lamps, especially for aeroplanes, were developed. Sealed-in reflector type lamps in many new forms were introduced. Lime glass was used in place of lead in fluorescent tubes and a plastic base was found. Considerable headway was made in starterless fluorescent lighting, although the material situation was responsible for holding up some work. Material savings also gave impetus to the use of higher voltages with fluorescent lighting. The final limitation order on fluorescent fixtures limited metal to three pounds per fixture exclusive of ballast. Some modifications were made as the year came to an end.

Plastic reflectors were developed for industrial incandescent lighting. Portable extension fluorescent lighting was more common, especially for aeroplane assembly and servicing. Use of fluorescent tubes was extended to explosion-proof fixtures.

Lighting glassware was developed to withstand hydrostatic pressures up to 375 lb. per square inch, thermal shock from 302° F. dry to 41° F. in water in 15 seconds, and for airport practice a dead weight of 300,000 lb. without fracture.

Indirect lighting of large high bay industrial areas with a mixture of 3 kw. mercury vapor and incandescent lamps was tried out satisfactorily.

Battery lighting for military emergency purposes found several applications, such as markers for supplies dropped by parachute and floating lanterns without oil ignition hazard for use with shipwrecks. Cold cathode found an enlarged field of application. Considerable research work in this type of lighting was started. At the year's close, the Illuminating Engineering society voted to set up an independent research foundation to engage broadly in lighting research. (*See* also PUBLIC UTILITIES; TENNESSEE VALLEY AUTHORITY.)   (S. B. W.)

Electric Lighting: *see* ELECTRICAL INDUSTRIES.
Electric Transmission and Distribution: *see* ELECTRICAL INDUSTRIES.

Electric Transportation.

All forms of electric transportation in the United States and Canada were called upon to render tremendously increased service in 1943. Shortages of rubber and gasoline sharply curtailed the use of private automobiles and thereby placed a heavy added burden on public transportation. The motor bus, which had made big inroads on the business of electric transportation before the war, was unable to take care of the increased demand. Motor bus operations were, in fact, somewhat reduced for a time on account of the gasoline shortage.

Street cars showed the largest increase in traffic of all forms of electric transportation, having a gain estimated at about 2,000,000,000 passengers. Rapid transit—subway and elevated railway services—showed only a small gain in patronage. This was due to the fact that the great bulk of the rapid transit riding is in the city of New York, where the use of private automobiles has always been relatively low and there has been comparatively little expansion of industry due to the war. As a consequence there was not the same increase in demand for public transportation as in many other cities. Riding on electric trolley buses showed a big percentage increase, but this form of electric transportation was not developed to a point where it was very important numerically from the standpoint of passengers carried. Because the electric operations of the trunk line railroads were considered as part of their general operations, no exact figures were available as to the extent of their increase in traffic. Indications were that the gain in electric suburban traffic was approximately 10%. The main line traffic gains of electrified railroads

Table I.—Passengers, Vehicle Miles and Revenue

	1943	1942	Percent Increase
Passengers Carried			
Street car	9,100 million	7,188 million	26.6
Rapid transit	2,700 ,,	2,580 ,,	4.7
Electric coach	1,300 ,,	979 ,,	32.8
Total	13,100 ,,	10,747 ,,	21.8
Vehicle Miles			
Street car	963 million	844 million	14.0
Rapid transit	458 ,,	465 ,,	−1.5
Electric coach	164 ,,	145 ,,	13.1
Total	1,585 ,,	1,454 ,,	9.0
Revenue			
Street car	$522 million	$402 million	29.8
Rapid transit	152 ,,	144 ,,	5.2
Electric coach	70 ,,	53 ,,	33.4
Total	$744 ,,	$599 ,,	24.0

(Data from American Transit Association)

Table II.—Ten-Year Record of Passengers Carried

Calendar Year	Surface Railway	Rapid Transit	Trolley Coach	Total
1933	7,074,000,000	2,133,000,000	45,000,000	9,252,000,000
1934	7,394,000,000	2,206,000,000	68,000,000	9,668,000,000
1935	7,276,000,000	2,236,000,000	96,000,000	9,608,000,000
1936	7,501,000,000	2,323,000,000	143,000,000	9,967,000,000
1937	7,161,000,000	2,307,000,000	289,000,000	9,757,000,000
1938	6,545,000,000	2,236,000,000	389,000,000	9,170,000,000
1939	6,171,000,000	2,368,000,000	445,000,000	8,984,000,000
1940	5,943,000,000	2,382,000,000	534,000,000	8,859,000,000
1941	6,074,000,000	2,410,000,000	641,000,000	9,125,000,000
1942	7,188,000,000	2,580,000,000	979,000,000	10,747,000,000

(Data from American Transit Association)

such as the Pennsylvania, New Haven and others followed the general trend of railroad traffic.

The 1943 riding on all forms of electric transportation services far exceeded the figures for any of the 10 previous years. For the electric trolley coaches they reached an all-time peak. For the subway and elevated railway lines they were close to peak levels. For the street railways, however, the number of passengers amounted to only about three-fourths of the number carried in the 1920's, when the extent of the surface electric railway systems was much greater than at present. Table I, accompanying, gives the details of changes in traffic, vehicle miles and revenue in 1943 as compared with 1942. Table II presents the traffic record for the previous 10 years.

Trackage.—Exact statistics were not available concerning the changes that took place in electric railway track mileage and trolley bus route in 1943. Street railway service was resumed on a number of lines where it had previously been abandoned, but the mileage involved was not great. The general purpose of these extensions was to release motor buses for service to war plants to which rail service was not available. A few minor extensions were made to trolley bus routes, but again the mileage involved was relatively slight. Rapid transit trackage showed practically no change.

Lack of changes in the extent of electric transportation systems was due principally to the policy established by the local transport division of the office of defense transportation, which, broadly speaking, ruled against either extensions or abandonments of electric transportation systems. Much the same condition prevailed in 1942. As a result the situation in 1943 was approximately the same as that existing at the beginning of 1942 when there were some 15,000 mi. of surface electric railway track in the United States, about 1,200 mi. of rapid transit track and 2,000 mi. of trolley bus route.

Equipment.—The large increase which took place in riding created a serious problem with respect to equipment. At the beginning of 1943 the electric transportation systems, not including the electrified suburban railroads, had a total of only 40,871 vehicles as compared with more than 58,000 10 years earlier when the traffic demands were considerably less. Table III shows the amount and distribution of this equipment. Energetic efforts were made to secure additional vehicles but war conditions made it almost impossible to do so. The war production board authorized the construction of only 270 new street cars and 75 electric trolley buses during 1943. No new rapid transit cars were authorized. This was only about half of the number of vehicles authorized in 1942. The 1943 total was far below normal replacement requirements. As a result the electric transportation systems were hard pressed to meet the demands placed upon them. A considerable number of old vehicles were taken out of storage and rehabilitated, but this was only a minor help in solving the problem. A further problem was created by the shortage of replacement parts, which made it impossible to keep the full complement of vehicles in regular operation. Despite these handicaps, the electric transportation lines, generally speaking, accepted the

…reatly increased loads that were thrust upon them and handled …em safely and efficiently.

Table III.—*Electric Transportation Equipment as of Jan. 1, 1943*

Population of Cities	Passenger Cars		Trolley Buses	Total
	Surface Railways	Rapid Transit		
Over 500,000	15,993	10,278	671	26,942
100,000 to 500,000	6,916	—	2,209	9,125
50,000 to 100,000	1,644	—	292	1,936
Less than 50,000	896	—	191	1,087
Suburban Areas	1,781	—	—	1,781
Total for U.S.	27,230	10,278	3,363	40,871

(Data from American Transit Association)

(J. A. Mi.)

Electrification, Rural: see RURAL ELECTRIFICATION.
Electron Microscope: see PHOTOGRAPHY.
Elementary Education: see EDUCATION.

Elks, Benevolent and Protective Order of.

This fraternal order was organized in 1868 in New York city for the purposes of practising charity, justice, brotherly love and fidelity; promoting the welfare and enhancing the happiness of its members; quickening the spirit of American patriotism and cultivating good fellowship. Membership was limited by statute to white male citizens of the United States, 21 yr. of age, or over. In 1943 there were 1400 lodges in the order, with a membership of 575,000. Charitable expenditures for 1942–43 amounted to more than $2,250,000. *The Elks Magazine*, the official organ, was instituted in 1922. A home for aged and indigent members was established in Bedford, Va., in 1902; and, in 1926, in Chicago, Ill., a superb memorial building was dedicated to members who served in World War I. The order created the Elks National Foundation fund in 1928, to finance scholarships for deserving students and the care of crippled children and tubercular patients.

An Elks War commission was appointed in 1942, to co-operate fully with the United States government in the prosecution of the war.   (J. E. Ms.)

Ellice Islands: see PACIFIC ISLANDS, BRITISH.
El Salvador: see SALVADOR, EL.

Ely, Richard Theodore

(1854–1943), U.S. economist, was born April 13 on a farm at Ripley, Chautauqua county, N.Y. After studying at Columbia university, he went to Germany on a fellowship in letters, took his Ph.D. at Heidelberg, 1879, and completed his studies at Halle, Geneva and at the Royal Statistical Bureau in Berlin. On his return to the United States, he was named professor of political economy at Johns Hopkins, 1881. His advocacy of greater academic freedom and his then controversial history of the labour movement in America aroused widespread indignation among conservative elements. Their clamours for his dismissal led to his resignation in 1892. Dr. Ely then went to the University of Wisconsin as head of the department of political economy, and later established the Institute for Research in Land and Public Utility Economics, which was subsequently transferred to Northwestern university in 1925, when he became research professor at that school.

Dr. Ely, who stayed at this post until 1933, died in Old Lyme, Conn., Oct. 4.

Embassies, Great Britain: see AMBASSADORS AND ENVOYS.
Embassies, United States: see AMBASSADORS AND ENVOYS.

Emergency Management, Office for.

On May 25, 1940, President Roosevelt, in an administrative order issued "in pursuance of Part I of Executive Order No. 8248 of September 8, 1939," found the existence of a threatened national emergency and established, in the executive office of the president, the Office for Emergency Management. Thus, the Office for Emergency Management (OEM) was created a few days prior to the establishment of the Advisory Commission to the Council of National Defense on May 29, 1940.

On Jan. 7, 1941, the president issued Executive Order No. 8269 establishing the Office of Production Management within the Office for Emergency Management. This was a significant step, in that the Office for Emergency Management replaced the Advisory Commission to the Council of National Defense as the over-all co-ordinating defense organization.

In Aug. 1943, the following agencies were within the framework of the Office for Emergency Management:

Board of War Communications (*q.v.*); National War Labor board (*q.v.*); Office of Alien Property Custodian; Office of Civilian Defense (*q.v.*); Office of the Coordinator of Inter-American Affairs (*q.v.*); Office of Defense Transportation (*q.v.*); Office of Lend-Lease Administration; Office of Scientific Research and Development (*q.v.*); Office of War Information (*q.v.*); War Manpower commission (*q.v.*); War Production board (including the Office of Rubber Director) (*q.v.*); War Relocation Authority (*q.v.*); War Shipping administration; Office of Economic Warfare; Office of Economic Stabilization (*q.v.*); Office of War Mobilization (*q.v.*); the Committee on Fair Employment Practice and the Division of Central Administrative Services.

The Emergency Price Control Act of 1942, approved by the president on Jan. 30, 1942, created the Office of Price Administration (*q.v.*) as an independent agency under the direction of a price administrator, outside the boundaries of OEM, wherein it had previously been lodged. The functions of the Office of Defense Health and Welfare Services were transferred to the Federal Security agency April 29, 1943. The Civil Air patrol was transferred to the War department April 29, 1943.

The administrative order of May 25, 1940, provided that OEM "shall be under the direction of one of the Administrative Assistants to the President, to be designated by the President." An administrative order of Jan. 7, 1941, which further defined the functions of OEM, provided that "Provision may be made . . . for the maintenance of routine office services required in the conduct of the work and activities of the agencies coordinated through or established in the Office for Emergency Management." W. H. McReynolds was the first liaison officer for Emergency Management. In April 1941 he was succeeded by Wayne Coy, who was liaison officer in addition to being assistant director of the Bureau of the Budget. On June 8, 1943, James F. Byrnes, Director of War Mobilization, succeeded Mr. Coy as liaison officer. On July 29, 1943, the functions of the liaison officer with respect to the Division of Central Administrative Services were vested in the director of the division.   (J. F. B.)

Emery: see ABRASIVES.
Emigration: see IMMIGRATION AND EMIGRATION, U.S.

Employment.

Steady spread of war and the increased significance of industrial production of almost all kinds in the global war after 1939 resulted in an expanding tempo of world economic activity through 1943. Employment increased to maximum levels in practically all countries, although some suffered economically because of isolation by naval blockades. In others, for instance those countries conquered by Germany, there was plenty of work but very little livelihood for large masses of people.

One cannot have complete confidence in the employment statistics of many nations. The war diverted attention and funds from the task of gathering statistics. The general picture derived from the data reported by the various nations to the International Labour Office is undoubtedly correct; but, with the exception of the figures on Great Britain, Canada, the United States, Sweden and Union of South Africa, all figures were in 1943 incomplete or of doubtful validity. One would not be justified in basing calculations and comparisons upon the figures available for countries other than those mentioned above.

The published figures are of two principal kinds and were gathered in several different ways: statistics of employment, i.e., the number of persons in paid employment, and statistics of the number of persons unemployed or of the number applying for work at the employment exchanges.

The employment statistics are derived from establishment reports collected by mail or through field agents or inspectors. Unemployment statistics are obtained from the number of applications for work on file at the employment exchanges, the number of applications for benefits at the offices of unemployment insurance agencies, and also from unemployment relief records, reports of trade union secretaries and special censuses of unemployment.

United States.—Employment reached an all-time high in the United States in 1943, with 55,500,000 persons reported by the United States bureau of labor statistics as being employed in July 1943. This did not include the 9,300,000 in the armed forces.

The manufacturing employment index in Sept. 1943 was 160.5 (using 1929 base). On the new base (1939=100), the index figure for Sept. 1943, was 170.2. The index of employment in the durable goods industries (1939=100) was 230.7 in Sept. 1943. It was 122.6 in the nondurable goods industries.

The U.S. census bureau's estimate of expected growth of the female labour force between April 1940 and Aug. 1943 (based upon the trend from 1930 to 1940) was 900,000, whereas the actual increase was about 4,000,000, indicating an increase in female employment of 3,100,000 directly attributable to the war. From the time the United States entered the war up to Aug. 1943, women between the ages of 35 and 54 in the labour force increased by 1,400,000, or about 1,100,000 more than the growth which would normally have occurred under peacetime conditions. A large proportion of these were older, married women who had no children or whose children no longer required their care.

The number of women employed in agriculture was more than three times as large in August, 1943 as in April, 1940. Of the 3,100,000 women who entered employment after 1940, about 1,300,000 were working on farms.

Great Britain.—Of the 16,000,000 men in Great Britain between 14 and 64 years of age, more than 15,000,000 were either in the armed services or in paid employment in 1943. Of the 17,000,000 women between 14 and 64 years of age, 7,750,000 were in paid employment or in military services. Of the single women between 18 and 40 years of age, 91% were in paid work; and of the married women without children in the same age group, 80% were employed in some capacity in the war effort. More than 1,000,000 men and women over 64 years of age were in paid employment.

After the outbreak of the war, 800,000 women between the ages of 40 and 60 entered industrial employment, thereby doubling the number of paid women workers in this age group. In 1939 the British Employment exchange statistics showed an average of 1,297,801 persons wholly out of work. In 1942 the corresponding figure was 117,244 and in July 1943, 72,140.

This represented, probably, as high a percentage of a total population actually employed as it was practicable to achieve. It was more complete employment of the population than obtained in the United States or Canada in 1943.

Canada.—The Canadian industrial employment index (1929

=100) was 193.9 in July 1943, indicating a somewhat large drift of population from rural to urban employment than in th United States. The index of general employment in Canada (a in the United States) did not go as high as the index of industria employment. It stood at 156.2 in July 1943 (1929=100).

South Africa and Australia.—The Union of South Afric employment index stood at 160.7 (1929=100) in June 194 which was approximately the same level of employment whic had existed since 1941. Australia's figures were incomplete an provisional but indicated for the first quarter of 1943 approxi mately the same level of employment which had obtaine throughout 1942. The indexes were approximately 35% abov 1933, which is the base year for Australia.

South America.—Argentina's statistics showed that industria employment had been gradually rising from 1940 on, and th index in July 1943 was 129.2 (1937=100). Very little chang occurred in the index of Argentinian employment throughou 1942–43. The index for Chile was 128.0 in April 1943 (1937= 100). Employment had remained at approximately that leve since 1941.

Japan.—Japan published provisional figures showing industria employment in 1943 approximately double that of 1929. The in dex for May 1943 was 206.0 (1929=100) but all of the Japanes figures for 1943 were published as "provisional figures." If cor rect, they would indicate that industrial employment in Japan ha risen more than in most of the countries of the world. This woul not be surprising, in view of the large increase in raw material and supplies available to the Japanese.

Sweden.—The Swedish index of employment, contrary t those of other countries, showed lower employment in 1942–4 than obtained from 1935 through 1939. The index stood at 110. in 1938, 112.7 in 1939 and 109.2 in 1940 (1929=100) bu throughout 1942 and 1943 the index fluctuated between 96 an 90, and in Aug. 1943, was only 90. This may have resulted from the cutting off of foreign trade to some extent by Allied blockade. intended to prevent Swedish products from reaching Germany and German closure of access to the Atlantic.

None of the other countries published employment statistics i 1943, and it was impossible to determine from the figures pub lished for previous years what the trends of employment woul be in the respective countries during 1943. Many of them wer in the war zone and their employment situation was directl affected by the war; e.g., Norway, the Netherlands, Poland, Ru mania, Switzerland, Russia, Germany, Denmark, Finland, France Czechoslovakia and Hungary.   (D. D. L.)

Enderbury Island: *see* PACIFIC ISLANDS, U.S.

Endocrinology.
Relatively simple chemical compounds apparently may be used to depress the activity of certain glands in a specific manner. Thiourea and its derivatives exert this effect upon the thyroid gland; alloxan depresses the insulin-secreting cells of the pancreas. These discoveries may lead the way to further advances in physiological knowledge and to the development of chemotherapy in the treatment of glandular disorders.

Anterior Pituitary Gland.—There was further separation and purification of the anterior pituitary hormones. The work of Fraenkel-Conrat and others in the laboratories of H. M. Evans established more firmly that the following hormones are separate entities: lactogenic, interstitial-cell stimulating (ICSH), follicle stimulating, growth, thyrotropic and adrenocorticotropic. The gentleness of the chemical methods which were used deprecated the possibility that the active fractions might be decomposition products of an original single large molecule.

While the anterior pituitary gland is essential to true growth (increase in length), it is not essential to the formation and deposition of adipose tissue (increase in weight). Hetherington further demonstrated that hypothalamic injury could lead to obesity even in animals which had been hypophysectomized for a long enough period to induce thyroid and adrenocortical atrophy. The latter glands are therefore also nonessential as regards weight gain by fat deposition.

As regards the influence of the anterior pituitary on growth, Evans *et al.* demonstrated that the action of growth hormone was antagonized by the simultaneous administration of adrenotropic hormone. This is in accord with the opposing effects of the anterior pituitary and the adrenal cortex on nitrogen retention, but it complicates our understanding of the regulation of growth by the anterior pituitary gland.

The level of thyrotropic hormone in the blood is low in hyperthyroidism and high in hypothyroidism. This seemed to indicate that the anterior pituitary could not be a primary aetiological factor in these thyroid disturbances, and that the variations in thyrotropic hormone might be an attempt at compensation. A new light was shed on this problem when it was discovered that thyrotropic hormone was inactivated by incubation with slices of thyroid tissue. Rawson *et al.* reported further work to show that hyperplastic and hyperfunctioning thyroid tissue had a greater inhibitory action, while hypofunctioning thyroid tissue had practically no inhibitory effect upon thyrotropic hormone in vitro They also found that the inactivation depended upon an oxidation, probably of a sulfhydryl to a disulfide configuration, and that the inactivated thyrotropic hormone could be reactivated by suitable chemical measures. This work indicated the necessity for a re-investigation of anterior pituitary-thyroid regulation, using the total thyrotropic content (active plus reactivated) of blood and urine as an index of the regulatory activity of the pituitary.

A new aspect in the picture of anterior pituitary-thyroid regulation appeared in the observations of Reforzo-Membrives on the existence of a thyroid-inhibiting factor in the pituitary. He found that the administration of preparations of pituitary glands taken from animals previously treated with thyroid extract resulted in a depression of thyroid activity in the recipient animals. This was evidenced by the basal metabolism of the whole animal, and by the histology and respiratory capacity of its isolated thyroid tissue.

Thyroid.—Having previously investigated the thyroid hormone activity of casein which had been iodinated to varying extents, Reinecke and co-workers reported the production of other iodinated proteins which exhibited thyroid activities as much as four times that of natural thyroglobulin. Hydrolysis of these compounds yielded 80 times as much l-thyroxine as can be prepared from equal amounts of desiccated thyroid glands.

The possibility of thyroid hormone production in tissues of the living organism other than the thyroid gland was substantiated by Chaikoff and co-workers. They demonstrated the production of both diiodotyrosine and thyroxine not only in thyroidectomized rats, but also in rats from which both the thyroid and the hypophysis had been removed. This, and previous related work, invited a reasonable speculation of a general nature, namely, that the endocrine glands may not be the sole sites of hormone production in the body but may be merely collections of specialized cells which can produce the hormones more efficiently than other cells.

Previous observations on the production in experimental animals of hyperplastic thyroid enlargement accompanied by evidences of decreased rather than increased thyroid function, led during 1943 to the therapeutic use of thiourea and thiouracil in human hyperthyroidism. Kennedy had reported experimentally

produced goiters in animals fed on rape seed. Mackenzie and Mackenzie described a similar syndrome as a result of sulfanilamide treatment, and Richter obtained identical results with thiourea. The Mackenzies and Astwood further reported that thiourea and its derivatives did not produce hypothyroidism by antagonizing the action of thyroid hormone but rather by preventing the gland from producing it. The hyperplasia of the thyroid did not occur in the absence of the pituitary gland, nor did it develop when thyroid extract was administered simultaneously with the thiourea. All these results support the following hypothesis: Thiourea (and sulfanilamides) interfere with the formation of thyroid hormone from its precursors. The lowered level of thyroid hormone in the blood leads to a counter-regulatory action on the part of the pituitary gland as a result of which there is thyroid hyperplasia. In the presence of the thiourea the hyperplastic tissue is impotent as regards the production of thyroid hormone so that functional hypothyroidism persists.

The successful treatment of hyperthyroidism by thiourea and thiouracil, including reduction of the goiter, was reported in some 15 human cases by Astwood, Williams and Himsworth.

Pancreas.—Jacobs had previously found that the administration of alloxan caused hypoglycaemia in rabbits. Using the drug for another purpose Dunn and co-workers confirmed Jacobs' observation and (among other pathological findings at post-mortem examination) discovered a necrosis of the insulin-producing cells of the pancreas. Some of their animals which survived the initial effect of the drug later developed a permanent diabetes. By varying the dose of alloxan so as to avoid death from hypoglycaemia and damage to tissues other than the pancreas, Goldner and Bailey and Bailey were able to produce diabetes practically at will in rats, guinea-pigs, rabbits and dogs. In the latter experiments kidney and liver damage seemed to be at a minimum, the acinar tissue of the pancreas and the α-cells of the islands of Langerhans appeared to be entirely unaffected, while the β-cells of the islands were completely destroyed. These observations offered a new tool for the investigation of the diabetic syndrome and perhaps also of the separate functions of the component cells of the islands of Langerhans. The possibility of the use of alloxan for the treatment of spontaneous hyperinsulinism also emerged. (*See also* PHYSIOLOGY; ZOOLOGY.)

BIBLIOGRAPHY.—H. Fraenkel-Conrat, "The Chemistry of the Hormones," *Annual Review of Biochemistry,* 12:273 (1943); A. W. Hetherington, "The Production of Hypothalamic Obesity in Rats already Displaying Chronic Hypopituitarism," *Am. Journal of Physiology,* 140:89 (1943); W. Marx, M. E. Simpson, C. H. Li and H. M. Evans, "Antagonism of Pituitary Adrenocorticotropic Hormone to Growth Hormone in Hypophysectomized Rats," *Endocrinology,* 33:102 (1943); R. W. Rawson, R. M. Graham and C. B. Riddell, "The Effect of Normal and Pathological Human Thyroid Tissues on the Activity of the Thyroid-Stimulating Hormone," *Annals of Internal Medicine,* 19:405 (1943); J. Reforzo-Membrives, "Thyroid-Inhibiting Action of the Hypophyses of Rats Fed with Thyroid," *Endocrinology,* 32:263 (1943); E. P. Reinecke and C. W. Turner, "The Recovery of l-Thyroxine from Iodinated Casein by Direct Hydrolysis with Acid," *J. Biological Chemistry,* 149:563 (1943); M. E. Morton, J. L. Chaikoff, W. O. Reinhardt and E. Anderson, "The Formation of Thyroxine and Diiodotyrosine by the Completely Thyroidectomized Animal," *Journal Biological Chemistry,* 147:757 (1943); T. H. Kennedy, "Thioureas as Goitrogenic Substances," *Nature,* 150:233 (1942); C. G. Mackenzie and J. B. Mackenzie, "Effect of Sulphonamides and Thioureas on Thyroid Gland and Basal Metabolism," *Endocrinology,* 32:185 (1943); E. B. Astwood, J. Sullivan, A. Bissell and R. Tyslowitz, "Action of Sulfonamides and of Thiourea upon Function of Thyroid Gland of Rat," *Endocrinology,* 32:210 (1943); E. B. Astwood, "Treatment of Hyperthyroidism with Thiourea and Thiouracil," *J.A.M.A.,* 122:78 (1943); R. H. Williams and G. W. Bissell, "Thiouracil in the Treatment of Thyrotoxicosis," *New England Journal of Medicine,* 229:98 (1943); H. P. Himsworth, "Thyrotoxicosis Treated with Thiourea," *Lancet,* 245(2):465 (1943); H. Jacobs, "Hypoglycemic Action of Alloxan," *Proceedings Society for Experimental Biology and Medicine,* 37:407 (1937); J. S. Dunn, N. B. McLechie and H. L. Sheehan, "Necrosis of Islets of Langerhans Produced Experimentally," *Lancet,* 245(1):484 (1943); C. C. Bailey and O. T. Bailey, "The Production of Diabetes Mellitus in Rabbits with Alloxan," *J.A.M.A.,* 122:1165 (1943); M. E. Goldner and G. Gomori, "Alloxan Diabetes in the Dog," *Endocrinology,* 33:297 (1943). (S. So.)

England: *see* GREAT BRITAIN AND NORTHERN IRELAND, UNITED KINGDOM OF.

English Literature. All things considered—and how much that is utterly antagonistic to letters is contained in that word "all"—English literature in its varied branches made a surprisingly good showing in the year 1943. The war, it is perhaps safe to say, inspired directly no book of permanent value, either in verse or prose; and the book which possibly came nearest to interpreting its deeper significance in a lasting form, Richard Church's *Twentieth-century Psalter,* is, understandably enough, the work of an older poet, not immediately involved in the military conflict. Great poetry springs from action and contemplation, and the stress of action which has most younger writers by the throat leaves no leisure for distilling experience. Such war poets, therefore, as John Pudney in *Beyond This Disregard,* Alan Rook in *These Are My Comrades* or the contributors to the anthology, *More Poems From the Forces,* though by no means mere impressionists, more often reflected sensitively or graphically on particular incidents of war or war-training than crystallized something memorable. An exception might be made in prose for M. Saint-Exupéry's *Flight to Arras,* which did translate action into dramatic spiritual experience. But the best war books were like A. B. Austin's account of the Dieppe raid, *We Landed at Dawn,* vivid and accurate journalism. And the best poetry of the year, though it assimilated something of the agony through which humanity is passing, was not immediately concerned with the war. Mentioned particularly should be Kathleen Raine's *Stone and Flower, The Angry Summer* by Idris Davies, Edwin Muir's *The Narrow Place,* Cecil Day Lewis' *Word Over All* and Lawrence Durrell's *A Private Country.* Edith Sitwell's *A Poet's Notebook* also deserves special mention as a book of lasting value for all who would study the meaning of the poetic in art and life.

The year produced three particularly good books of criticism, David Cecil's *Hardy the Novelist,* C. M. Bowra's *The Heritage of Symbolism* and Charles Williams' *The Figure of Beatrice.* So cultivated a critic as Lord David Cecil might easily have been more alive to Hardy's artistic defects than to his profound poetic qualities. But by basing his appreciation on the latter, he composed a book which is a model of wise imaginative appraisement. C. M. Bowra covered a wide field in studies of Valéry, Rilke, Stefan George, Blok and Yeats. But through the diversity of his subject matter he found a common aim in the effort of these poets to find a new way to the reality which orthodox religion has ceased to possess. Charles Williams' study of Dante also broke new human ground but within the spiritual realm of orthodoxy. Other critical books deserving mention are E. M. W. Tillyard's *The Elizabethan World Picture,* Evelyn Hardy's *Donne: A Spirit in Conflict,* Janko Lavrin's *Dostoevsky* and F. A. Lea's *Carlyle: Prophet of Today.*

Perhaps the most notable biography of the year was Catherine M. Maclean's *Born Under Saturn,* a life of Hazlitt so industriously and understandingly complete that it is unlikely to be superseded. The Countess of Birkenhead's life of Joseph Severn, *Against Oblivion,* was pleasantly done as was J. A. Lloyd's *Ivan Turgenev.* Georgina Battiscombe's *Charlotte Mary Yonge* was an appreciative biography of a Victorian novelist, who, despite her sheltered religious respectability, is still read, and a trusty guide to her many novels. Of timely interest was Hampden Jackson's *Jean Jaurès,* a biography of the French socialist, and Lord Rayleigh's *Life of Sir J. J. Thomson,* the scientist.

Fiction continued to show few surprises. There was plenty of able story-telling and much of it provided a good journalistic picture of war conditions, the most notable of this kind being J. B. Priestley's documentary *Daylight on Saturday.* But of really creative work there was little. C. S. Lewis' *Perelandia* was an imaginatively ingenious picture of life on the "unfallen" planet

HILARY ST. GEORGE SAUNDERS, popular British novelist of World War II, at his desk in the parliament library. His *Combined Operations,* published in 1943, tells the story of the spectacular British Commando raid on St. Nazaire, France, in March 1942

Venus. Robert Graves's *Wife to Milton* was a clever period reconstruction, but far from fair to Milton. James Hanley's *No Directions* and Neil M. Gunn's *The Serpent* had the compelling quality to be expected of their authors, and *Saturnine* by Rayner Heppenstall was at least experimental, if not to many people's taste. Virginia Woolf's collected short stories, *A Haunted House,* were, it need hardly be said, of exceptional distinction.

It remains only to mention one or two books of religious, philosophical or political interest. Christopher Dawson's *The Judgement of the Nations* was a brilliant plea for a new cultural unity of Europe based on the common Christian tradition. Gerald Heard in *Man the Master* searchingly analyzed the diseased condition of modern man and looked to a caste of new Brahmins to effect a cure. Charles Raven wrote suggestively of *Science, Religion and the Future,* Herbert Read of *The Politics of the Unpolitical,* H. J. Massingham in *The Tree of Life* traced the kinship, so lamentably lost, of a true love of nature and a true Christianity, and Victoria Sackville West in *The Eagle and the Dove* discussed two famous saints, St. Teresa of Avila and St. Thérèse of Lisieux. (*See also* AMERICAN LITERATURE; PUBLISHING [BOOK].)   (H. I'A. F.)

Entomology. The war is having a marked influence on entomology as a science and a profession. There has been great need for trained men in the medical and sanitary work, especially in connection with the control of mosquitoes and the elimination of malaria, yellow fever and dengue fever; the elimination of lice and fleas to prevent typhus fever; as well as all other insect-borne diseases. The men most suitably trained for this service are the entomologists. Those students who had completed the regular university courses were accepted by the armed forces—many of them were given commissions, while those having a Ph.D. degree or who had several years' experience after graduation were given commissions. These men were placed very largely in charge of making mosquito surveys, in identifying the mosquitoes and preparing keys, handbooks and manuals and in conducting campaigns for the extermination and control of these pestiferous and dangerous insects at home and abroad. In 1943 it was estimated that there were between 1,000 and 2,000 such men in the armed forces; 104 graduates in entomology at the University of California were in 1943 in the service of the U.S. and a similar situation undoubtedly held true for other universities and colleges throughout the entire country.

The insect control problems arising from the 2,000,000 victory gardens throughout the United States did much to make the nation entomology-conscious. The interest of all professional men, labourers and other classes would do much to emphasize the importance of insects to agriculture and might result in far greater support for this science in relation to public health, to agriculture and as an interesting and instructive field in biology. During this war period professional entomology advanced farther than in any previous period of 50 years.

Some New Insecticides.—A dichloroethyl ether sodium sulphate solution was used successfully by W. H. Lange, Jr. (1943) for the control of the cabbage maggot, *Chortophila brassicae,* in the Salinas valley, Calif. It was prepared by mixing 20 cc. of the former with 0.4 cc. of the latter, designated as Tergitol 7, in 1 gal. of water.

A propylene dichloride emulsion proved to be as effective as ethylene dichloride and more efficient than paradichlorobenzene for the control of the peach borer, *Conopia exitiosa,* in eastern United States (Snapp, 1943).

A commercial preparation, "Tritox" (trichloracetonitrile), is a clear, volatile, noninflammable liquid, the vapour of which has a great penetrating power and is quite toxic to insects and relatively harmless to man. Good results were obtained by H. Kemper (1941) with it in killing the adults of the granary weevil, *Sitophilus granarius,* the drugstore beetle, *Sitodrepa panicea,* the bean weevil, *Acanthoscelides obtectus,* and the larvae of the mealworm, *Tenebrio molitor,* and the Mediterranean flour moth, *Ephestia kühniella.*

Quartz dust at 1 to 2% mixed with stored grain to prevent infestation and destruction by the granary weevil, *Sitophilus granarius,* in Europe was found to cause silicosis and its use was prohibited in Germany in 1941.

The use of rotenone dusts for the control of the pea weevil, *Laria pisorum,* on field peas was prohibited in order to conserve this important insecticide for the protection of more essential food crops. The application of this insecticide to edible peas for drying, when just flowering, in Washington did not give complete control, so that it was necessary to fumigate all dry peas at harvest to insure complete protection from this weevil (Webster, *et al.,* 1943).

Cryolite in light medium oil sprays gave control of the codling moth equal to arsenate of lead sprays in Washington during 1941–1942. Very light oil sprays killed from 79.7 to 89.6% of codling moth eggs. Micronized phenothiazine and xanthone gave satisfactory control of this important apple insect but also caused injury to the calyx or the fruit (Webster, *et al.,* 1943).

Adding proprietary thiocyanates to cubé dusts improved the control of pea aphis, *Macrosiphum onobrychis* (Wilson and Campau).

Aerosols are air or gaseous suspensions of atomized or finely divided particles of nonvolatile insecticides, certain types of which are also designated as air suspensions and as insecticidal smokes. According to Roark (1942) aerosols are formed by dis-

persing nonvolatile insecticides in the air or by enhancing the efficacy of fumigants of low volatility by dispersing a liquid or solid in the air in colloidal form, thus creating a mist or smoke. Certain types were formed by spraying the insecticide against a hot plate, by evaporating a low melting solid such as naphthalene by means of an electric heater and by spraying solutions in liquefied gases.

In the former case the materials were sprayed directly on a plate heated to 400 C. (752° F.) and the dispersing particles carried through a venturi tube into a cylinder or other container by a strong air blast. In this manner orthodichlorobenzene containing 5% lauric acid used at the rate of 1½ lb. per 1,100 cu.ft. of air space completely killed all specimens of the American cockroach, *Periplaneta americana,* German cockroach, *Blatella germanica,* the bedbug, *Cimex lectularius,* and the confused flour beetle, *Tribolium confusum.*

Orthodichlorobenzene with oleic acid gave good control of the housefly, *Musca domestica.* Orthodichlorobenzene is also a good activator and solvent of other insecticides (Goodhue and Sullivan, 1941). Other investigations by Goodhue (1942) resulted in the formation of aerosols without heat. The insecticide is dissolved in a liquefied gas in a closed container and afterward released through a spray nozzle by its own pressure. The solvent forms the aerosol by rapid evaporation, the heat of evaporation being supplied by the atmosphere. The solvent must be gaseous at temperatures considerably lower than when the insecticide is to be used as a spray or aerosol and the preparation must therefore be made at temperatures considerably lower than those occurring normally indoors or outside where the materials are to be used. An example of very effective aerosol extensively employed in 1943 in the control of mosquitoes and houseflies indoors where the insecticidal vapour can be held is prepared by incorporating 0.4% pyrethrins in 1% sesame oil, and mixing them with dichlorodifluoromethane which acts as a solvent and expelling gas. A dosage of 5 mg. pyrethrins and 10 mg. sesame oil in the solvent expelled under pressure caused by room temperature is sufficient to kill mosquitoes in 1,000 cu.ft. of air space. This and similar aerosols are prepared in convenient-sized bombs for treating rooms, buildings, tents and other enclosures and have proved to be a marvelous means of reducing malaria, yellow fever and other mosquito-borne diseases in temperate and more particularly in the tropical regions where these diseases are among the most important hazards in modern warfare.

Vapour sprays are similar to aerosols in that they consist of very finely divided particles of insecticides suspended in air. This condition is brought about by selecting an oil-soluble insecticide such as pyrethrum and forcing it under great pressure through a fine nozzle and a venturi tube in sufficient quantities to form a cloud which may be directed to envelope a vine or a tree in a very fine mist or a coarser spray if desired. Insects are killed by direct contact with the chemicals. Light, highly refined oils are used so as to avoid injury to the plants. The insecticides are applied with hand atomizers for small gardens and specially constructed power machines that make it possible to cover large acreages of field crops and orchards in a short time. These vapour sprays have been most useful in the control of small insects and mites such as thrips, aphides, scale insects, leafhoppers, orchard red spiders and similar mites. They are also applied by aeroplane. They might be said to be the forerunners of modern fly sprays and aerosols. Both have the great advantages of ease of application and small labour requirements in the treatment of insect pests. They are most successfully used when there is a minimum of wind or air movement.

Rotenone is a crystalline chemical compound ($C_{23}H_{22}O_6$) and a poisonous principal derived from certain leguminous plants

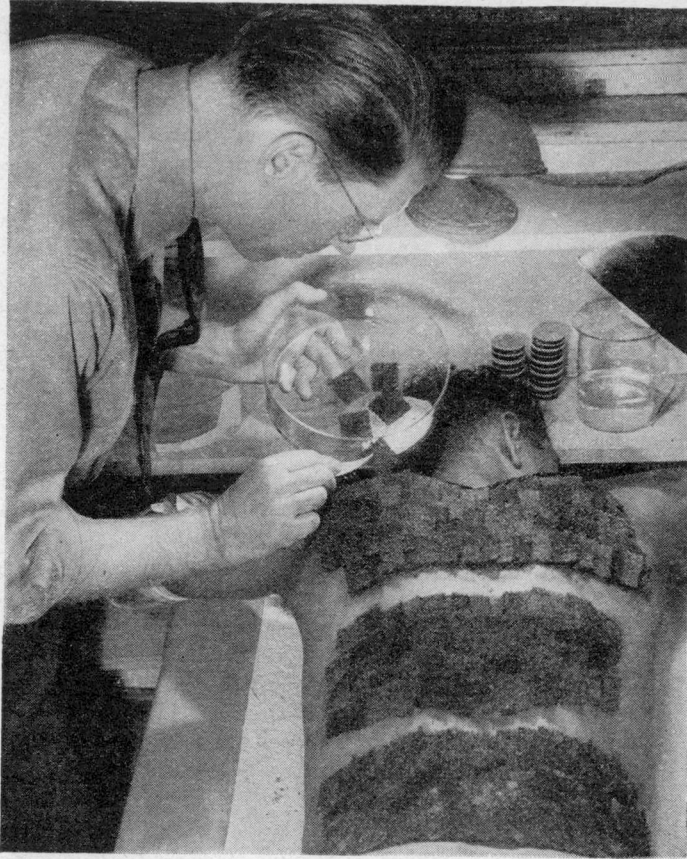

LICE feeding on the back of a volunteer in the laboratories of the U.S. department of agriculture in 1943. The lice are placed on the host's back by means of cloth squares. This method is used to maintain a supply of lice to be used in testing new insecticides for the armed forces

which has long been used by the natives of various countries as a fish poison. It is obtained chiefly from the roots of *Derris elliptica, D. uliginosa* and *D. malaccensis,* which furnish the derris-root of commerce produced in the Malay states and the East Indies. A secondary and growing source is obtained from roots of cubé or timbo, the source of which is *Lonchocarpus urucu* and *L. utilis* and *L. chrysophyllus* of tropical South America, the latter also being cultivated in the Federated Malay states; and still another source is from *Tephrosia toxicaria* of tropical South America and *T. vogalii* of tropical Africa and many other species. A possible commercial source may be available from *T. virginiana* of North America. Still other sources are *Mundulea sularosa* of tropical east Africa, Madagascar, India and Ceylon; and *Millettia* spp. (closely related to *Wisteria* spp.) of China, Formosa and India.

Because of its high toxicity to insects and its low toxicity to man rotenone is specially useful on vegetables and leafy crops consumed in the green or fresh condition. However, it has great value in controlling certain specific insects and much of the available material was either taken over by the army or placed on strict rationing bases for agricultural necessities.

A tremendous amount of investigation work throughout the world was done testing the effects of rotenone products on a great many species of insects. References to a number of published accounts of these researches were collected and published (mimeographed) in the "E" series of the bureau of entomology and plant quarantine, United States department of agriculture by R. C. Roark. These refer to the following orders of insects: Part I Collembola, Orthoptera, Dermaptera, Odonata, Isoptera, Corrodentia and Mallophaga. Part II, Thysanoptera. Part III Hemiptera, Homoptera. Part IV Hemiptera, Heteroptera. Part V Anoplura. Part VI Coleoptera.

Insect Resistance to Insecticides.—Economic entomologists have been interested in the resistance of certain insects to the continued use of the specified insecticides. This condition was first reported by A. L. Melander in connection with the resistance of the San Jose scale, *Quadrapidiotus perniciosus,* to lime-sulphur sprays in the apple region of the state of Washington in 1914. From then on, many other insects were thought to be resistant to insecticides. Up to 1943 there appeared to be experimental proof of such resistance in the following cases:

1.—San Jose scale, *Quadrapidiotus perniciosus,* to lime-sulphur sprays.
2.—Red scale, *Aonidiella aurantii,* to HCN fumigation.
3.—Black scale, *Saissetia oleae,* to HCN fumigation.
4.—Citricola scale, *Coccus pseudomagnoliarum,* to HCN fumigation.
5.—Citrus thrips, *Scirtothrips citri,* to tartar emetic-sucrose sprays.
6.—Codling moth, *Carpocapsa pomonella,* young larvae to arsenical and other sprays.
7.—Screwworm, *Cochliomyia americanum,* primary larvae to phenothiazine.

Codling Moth Investigations.—While most insects are more or less sporadic in their appearance in destructive numbers and require only occasional treatment, the codling moth maintains a remarkably even level and requires a regular control program every year. For many years lead arsenate was the standard insecticide used for its control. This routine was greatly disturbed because of the presence of arsenate of lead residue on the outside of the fruits. Then began a thorough and extensive search for insecticidal substitutes for lead arsenate. These investigations resulted in many attempts to substitute organic compounds like nicotine, rotenone, pyrethrum and other plant products for the inorganic compounds or the heavy metals. Some of these new organics proved quite successful and were being used to great advantage during World War II when arsenical compounds had not always been readily available for pest control purposes.

Cattle Grubs.—Estimates by the United States department of agriculture placed the losses due to the cattle industry by grubs in the United States at $50,000,000 while the University of Idaho believed the losses to be twice as much. The grubs seriously affect the living animals and spoil much of the hides for leather. A very effective control was perfected which consists of a mixture composed of one part of ground derris or cubé, 5% rotenone content and three parts of tripoli earth or pyrophyllite. This dust is applied at the rate of 3 oz. to the animal by means of a hand shaker-top can. Two men work on opposite sides of the same animal—each applying the dust with one hand and rubbing it into the hair with the other hand. In this way two men may treat as many as 100 head of cattle a day.

Wood Preservatives for Control of Termites.—According to Snyder (1943) there are three general classes of wood preservatives employed in preventing the attacks of termites: (1) oils such as creosotes and combinations of petroleum or tar. These are specially recommended for treatment of timbers which may be used in contact with the ground. (2) Water-soluble salts such as zinc chloride—chromated zinc chloride, and (3) a number of proprietary preservatives.

Pierce's Virus Disease Carried by Leafhoppers.—One of the most serious of virus diseases was found to be the cause of the Anaheim disease of the grape which practically annihilated the wine grape industry in Orange county in California around the turn of the century. At that time the cause of the disease was unknown. Later the virus was discovered to be the cause of this disease and the disease was called Pierce's disease. Even after the virus was discovered there remained to be found the sources or vectors responsible for transmitting the disease to the grapevines. This was accomplished and at least three leafhoppers were known in 1943 to be vectors of the disease: the green sharpshooter, *Draeculacephala minerva,* the red-headed sharpshooter, *Carneocephala fulgida,* and the blue sharpshooter,

Cicadella circellata. Another leafhopper, *Helochara delta*, was suspected as a carrier.

C. V. Riley Centennial.—In Sept. 1943 the centennial celebration of the birth of C. V. Riley, which occurred at Chelsea, England in 1843, was held at the museum of the Jefferson National Exposition Memorial exhibit at St. Louis. C. V. Riley (1843–1895) became in many respects the most eminent economic entomologist in the United States and the first entomologist of the United States department of agriculture. He was a systematic entomologist at first. After serving some time as an entomological contributor to the *Prairie Farmer* of Chicago he became state entomologist of Missouri (1868–1877); chairman of the United States Entomological commission (1877–1880); first entomologist of the United States department of agriculture (1878); and founder of the division of entomology, now the bureau of entomology and plant quarantine, United States department of agriculture. He also was responsible for the beginning of the insect collections in the United States National museum by presenting to that institution his own collection as a nucleus. He organized the economic entomologists in North America and was their most prominent and important leader during his lifetime. (E. O. E.)

Entomology and Plant Quarantine, Bureau of: *see* AGRICULTURAL RESEARCH ADMINISTRATION.
Enzymes: *see* BIOCHEMISTRY.

Epidemics and Public Health Control.

Venereal Disease.—In a report on the activities and objectives of the Chicago Intensive Treatment Center, the authors outlined their case finding methods, and their methods of treating both active and latent cases of syphilis and gonorrhoea. Cases were found by: (1) thorough search for and complete examination of all known contacts of military personnel; (2) routine examination of all groups, such as selective service registrants and court cases; and (3) complete co-operation of the majority of taverns, hotels and industrial groups in searching out, for the health department, suspects of venereal disease.

Treatment of syphilis consisted of: (1) Modified Simpson-Kendell-Rose method, called by them the "Fever-chemotherapy" method. (2) Modified Schoch-Alexander method, called the "Intensive Chemotherapy" method. (3) Modified Eagle-Hogan method, called the "Long Term Intensive Chemotherapy." Mapharsen and bismuth were used.

Gonorrhoea was treated by the sulfonamide method (sulfathiazole for both males and females) and the artificial fever plus sulfonamide method (sulfonamide-resistant methods).

The report was a preliminary one but it outlined the safeguards and precautions to be observed.

Malaria.—Sisk believed there would be an almost certain possibility that troops infected with malaria would return to all sections of the United States. There was expected to be numerous infectious relapses among these men. He showed the need for a resurvey for the potential malaria-spreading mosquito and advised search for both adults and larvae of the Anopheles mosquito by experts.

Talbot advised all military personnel in areas of endemic malaria be examined monthly, using a thick blood smear, and treated vigorously even if there are no symptoms. In general, he treated all men only after symptoms occurred, except those who were in combat zones where all persons who were ill were advised to have prophylactic therapy. He further stated that malaria, like syphilis, might cause symptoms in any part of the body. A positive Wassermann or Kahn test is no criterion of the absence of malaria.

Epidemic Meningitis.—Kuhns, *et al.*, gave 2 to 3 gr. of sulfadiazine daily for 2 to 3 days to some 15,000 soldiers in an outbreak of meningitis. They materially lowered the incidence of the disease. The carrier rate was also lowered.

Epidemic Diarrhoea of the Newborn.—Twyman and Horton reported the use of succinyl sulfathiazole as a specific measure in the treatment of this disease. When combined with opiates, the results were even better. Lembcke, *et al.*, reported on two outbreaks in Syracuse, New York, and advised laboratory controlled methods for sterilizing nipples and formula, good nursing technique, reporting and isolation of cases and immediate epidemiological investigation by a competent person, which usually means an epidemiologist connected with a public health department. (*See* also BACTERIOLOGY; ENTOMOLOGY.)

BIBLIOGRAPHY.—"Intensive Treatment of Gonorrhea and Syphilis," Chicago Intensive Treatment Center, *J.A.M.A.* (Nov. 27, 1943); Wilfred N. Sisk, "Post War Malaria Prevention by the County Health Department," *American Journal of Public Health* (Nov. 1943); David R. Talbot, "New Aspects of Malaria," *J.A.M.A.* (Sept. 25, 1943); Dwight M. Kuhns, Carl T. Nelson, Harry A. Feldman, L. Roland Kuhn, "Prophylactic Value of Sulfadiazine in the Control of Meningococcic Meningitis," *ibid.* (Oct. 9, 1943); Allan H. Twyman and George R. Horton, "Treatment of Epidemic Neonatal Diarrhea with Succinyl Sulfathiazole," *ibid.* (Sept. 18, 1943); Paul A. Lembcke, James J. Quinlivan and Norris G. Orchard, "Epidemic Diarrhea of the Newborn," *Amer. Jour. of Public Health* (Oct. 1943).
(H. BU.)

Episcopal Church: *see* PROTESTANT EPISCOPAL CHURCH.
Eritrea: *see* ITALIAN COLONIAL EMPIRE.
Espionage: *see* FEDERAL BUREAU OF INVESTIGATION.

Estonia. One of the Baltic states of northeastern Europe, north of Latvia, south of Finland, formerly a republic; became part of Germany's "Ostland" (*q.v.*) in 1941. Area, 18,371 sq.mi.; pop. (est. 1939) 1,122,000. Chief towns: Tallinn (capital 146,400); Tartu (60,100); Narva (24,200); Nomme (19,700); Pärnu (21,500). Language, Estonian (a Finno-Ugrian tongue). Religion, Christian (Lutheran 78%, Greek Orthodox 19%). Ruler in 1943: the German reich through Reichscommissar H. Lohse of the Ostland and Commissioner-General Karl Sigismund Litzmann for Estonia. Dr. E. Mae headed a five-man state council.

History.—Estonia's long-feared troubles began with the German invasion of Poland in 1939. In one of her early countermoves, the U.S.S.R. had persuaded Estonia to sign a "treaty of mutual assistance," Sept. 29, 1939. In June of 1940 the Russians occupied the country, in July the people voted to join the soviets, and in Aug. 1940, Estonia became the 16th soviet republic. A tense year of readjustment followed, in which many Estonian leaders were killed or exiled. Then came the German attack on Russia, June 22, 1941, and in the following months the slow nazi conquest of the Baltic. Estonian subjugation was completed only at the very end of 1941. Thereafter only vague and contradictory reports reached the west.

Seemingly the German Balts who were moved out of the country in late 1939 were being returned very slowly, and land re-allotments probably were held in reserve as bribes for aid. Even some of the Russian collectivization was apparently let alone—the soviet reorganization itself had of course but barely got under way. In some cases the German state simply became the collective owner and took for its use crops intended to be distributed among the workers.

Disillusionment and unrest, if not despair, evidently continued to pervade the unfortunate little country in 1943. Libraries were partially destroyed and thoroughly Germanized. Schools and universities were closed or nazified. Brother fought brother, as the Russians announced the noble struggle of their Estonian cohorts and the Germans drafted men of 17 to 45 into Waffen-SS battalions. Rumours came of sabotage and terrorism, mass arrests and executions. But for what should the Estonian fight? Russian rule had been disappointing; German domination had been devastating. Could this land of one million people dare hope for autonomy? Perhaps the Germans would help Estonia in a new declaration of independence if they themselves were driven out—but obviously only in that case. As for the Russian attitude it became increasingly clear during 1943 that Stalin and his colleagues would demand control of the Baltic littoral as a defense against any future threat from the west. The Moscow and Tehran conferences seemed to give silent confirmation of this decision.

Abroad the Estonians were less vocal than their neighbour peoples, except possibly in Moscow, where each nation was represented by a government-in-exile. Indisputably most things both present and future depended on the outcome of the military conflict raging on all sides of the land. At the close of the year the Russian advances to the south indicated the possibility of a German withdrawal from Estonia.

At the end of 1943 the only available statistics which could give a fair picture were mostly for the period preceding the invasions.

Education.—In 1937–38 there were 1,224 elementary schools, 58 middle schools, 39 technical schools and 30 agricultural schools. Tartu (Dorpat) university had 3,219 students and 217 professors in 1938.

Finance.—The monetary unit is the kroon (26.7 U.S. cents at par). Effects of German monetary changes in 1941–43 were uncertain. Revenue (est. 1939–40) 99,293,000 kroons; expenditure 99,293,000 kroons.

Trade and Communication.—Imports in 1939 totalled 101,-351,000 kroons; exports, 118,217,000 kroons. Principal imports were raw cotton, sugar, woollen yarns and thread, iron and steel. Principal exports were butter, wood and paper, cotton goods, cellulose, flax and tow, meat products and eggs. Imports were chiefly from Germany, Great Britain, Sweden, the United States and the U.S.S.R. Exports were chiefly to Great Britain, Germany, Finland, the United States and Sweden. In 1942–43 what trade existed was confined largely to Germany and her satellites, even Sweden being largely cut off.

Agriculture.—Production (in short tons) of the leading crops in 1939 was as follows: rye 250,994, potatoes 963,741, oats 164,684, barley 99,207 and wheat 94,026. Estonia in 1938 had 660,890 cattle, 649,730 sheep, 384,580 pigs, 219,020 horses and 1,596,570 chickens.

Manufacturing and Mineral Production.—Manufacturing production was valued at 166,238,000 kroons in 1937. One of the larger cotton mills in Europe is at Narva, where textile manufactures in 1937 were valued at 47,425,000 kroons. Other important industries are paper and wood, food products, cement, flax, leather. Shale oil production rose rapidly to 209,437 short tons in 1939. Approximately 60,000 people were employed in industry in 1938.

BIBLIOGRAPHY.—Gregory Meiksins, *The Baltic Riddle* (1943); Joachim Joesten, "German Rule in Ostland," *Foreign Affairs*, XXII, No. 1 (Oct. 1943), pp. 143–147.   (F. D. S.)

Etching. Within the borders of the countries conquered by nazi Germany, all healthy art growth ceased. Alone among the warring nations of Europe, England carried on. British art organizations held their exhibitions as usual, contributed to by British artists and widely attended by the British public. The Royal Society of Painter-Etchers and Engravers held its annual show in January and, somehow, most of the better-known British printmakers managed to send to it. The same may be said of the graphic arts section of the annual exhibition of the royal academy. Sales were above average.

Turning to the western hemisphere, etching as an independent art medium flourished in the United States. In spite of the fact that many of the best-known etchers were in active military service or in some form of war industry, the work of many of these appeared somewhere in the countless exhibitions held all over the country in 1943. The veteran Frank W. Benson no longer worked in the medium, nor did Harry Wickey nor Kenneth Hayes Miller, to mention two who had outstanding accomplishment to their credit. Franklin T. Wood laid aside his needle, Arthur William Heintzelman's preoccupation with his duties as curator of a great print collection deprived the world of new plates from his hands, and that brilliant performer, John W. Winkler, remained in persistent retirement. Samuel Chamberlain was in military service overseas, Louis C. Rosenberg returned to his first love, architecture, James E. Allen was working largely in the commercial field, and Kerr Eby, as a war correspondent, was drawing the life of the U.S. marines in the Pacific theatre of war. Ill health restricted the output of the veteran etcher and master draughtsman, Mahonri M. Young, and nothing was heard of that other veteran, Herman A. Webster, who made his home in Paris. Sears Gallagher published no new plates in 1943, nor did that exquisite landscapist of the northwest, Helen A. Loggie. But except for these, the better-known names in contemporary American etching carried on. Paul F. Berdanier, Isabel Bishop, Cornelis Botke, John E. Costigan, Ralph Fabri, Eugene Higgins, Robert Fulton Logan, Luigi Lucioni, Roi Partridge, Martin Petersen, Grant Reynard, Ernest D. Roth and George Wright all published new plates in 1943. Among newer names in the field, Theodore Brenson, Kathrin Cawein, Minna Citron, Frank T. Fellner, Isac Friedlander, Harold C. Geyer, Platt Hubbard, Lino S. Lipinsky, Joseph Margulies, Helen Miller, Henry O'Connor and Reynold H. Weidenaar were all active, while of the newest comers must be mentioned the accomplished artists Pasquale Masiello, Stephen Csoka, Karl M. Schultheiss and Helen King Boyer. In the hands of all of these the now well-established tradition of American etching seemed to be safe.

The three oldest print societies, and most influential, continued to be the Society of American Etchers, with headquarters in New York city, the Chicago Society of Etchers, in the middle west, and the Print Makers Society of California, on the west coast. Each of these holds a regular annual exhibition, of national scope, and various travelling exhibitions throughout the year. In addition, the National Academy of Design, in New York city, conducts a great national print show in connection with its annual. The most comprehensive and representative exhibition of contemporary American prints ever brought together, numbering nearly 600 items and covering every branch of the printmaker's art, took place at the Metropolitan museum in New York city early in the year, organized and sponsored by Artists for Victory, Inc., a war emergency organization of artists. The same group was in the closing weeks of the year bringing together by invitation a collection of 50 prints by 50 living American printmakers, to be sent to England in exchange for a corresponding exhibition of British prints to visit this country in 1944.

Meanwhile the etchers and other printmakers of Canada, comprising a comparatively small but active and able group, continued to produce work and hold exhibitions in the face of all the difficulties attendant upon wartime conditions. The Society of Canadian Painter-Etchers continued to be their leading print organization. Central and South American etchers were probably less affected by the war than were those of any other country in the world. But neither in Mexico nor in South America did the copper plate medium attain the degree of development and excellence achieved by lithography and woodcut.   (J. T. Ar.)

Ethical Culture Movement.

A movement in religion started in 1876 by Felix Adler in New York city, and established ten years later in London by Stanton Coit. Societies were active in 1943 in New York city, Brooklyn, Philadelphia, St. Louis and Chicago, and there were four in London, England. The purpose of this innovation was to provide spiritual homes for people of different religious antecedents to whom the profession of traditional creeds was incompatible with intellectual honesty, and to act as a liberalizing influence on other religious bodies by inducing them to accord greater mental liberty to their adherents, and to place the development of ethical knowledge and practice above the study of theological tenets. The principle most emphasized was that of "the independence of ethics," which was cardinal in the Platonic and Aristotelian traditions but had been lost to view during much of the Christian period, although great theologians had at times reasserted it.

The Ethical Culture societies conduct Sunday and week-day services and a variety of educational and social welfare activities. The first social settlement in the United States (the University Settlement in New York city) was an enterprise of the movement, which also originated, in New York and Chicago, the Visiting Nurse associations and the societies providing legal aid for the poor. A considerable literature devoted to vindicating the spiritual nature and dignity of man against the doctrine of human animality has been produced. The movement is experimental and pragmatic in action, though the founder and the majority of the leaders offered reasoned rejections of the pragmatist doctrine in metaphysics. Enterprises of the societies in England and America included sustained efforts for the relief of refugees from European persecution, and their re-education and integration into English-speaking society; also, in 1943, full participation in wartime service activities. The formerly flourishing branches of the movement in Germany and Austria were suppressed by the nazis.

The Standard, edited by George E. O'Dell, is published each month at 2 W. 64th st., New York city. An authoritative exposition of the movement's principles is to be found in two volumes by Felix Adler, *An Ethical Philosophy of Life* and *The Reconstruction of the Spiritual Ideal*. The English Ethical union (president, Lord Snell) had offices in 1943 at Chandos House, Palmer Street, London, S.W.1.   (Ho. J. B.)

Ethiopia.

A kingdom of northeast Africa. Area, c. 350,000 sq.mi.; pop. (est. Dec. 31, 1939) 9,500,000; cap. Addis Ababa; religions: Christian (Copt) and Mohammedan; languages: Amharic and Arabic; ruler: Emperor Haile Selassie.

History.—The emperor's announcement that his country had decided to join the war effort of the United Nations was welcomed by the Allies. The United States extended lend-lease aid to the emperor's government.

The revenue of the empire raised under great postwar difficulties was slender, and export trade was hampered by war conditions abroad. The land tax was halved. Under the agreement and military convention with Great Britain, financial help was provided in the form of quarterly grants over a period of four years. British officers were appointed to the administration as commissioner of police, judges, magistrates, army officers and in leading posts. The educational system was also being reorganized with British assistance, but difficulties were experienced owing to lack of supplies.

The British council opened cultural institutions in Addis Ababa and elsewhere. The council conducted classes and loaned workers to assist in educational work. The Friends ambulance unit, although primarily engaged in medical work in isolated stations, also assisted in educational activities. Plans were being made to deal with the rehabilitation of destitute children and unemployed adults by means of agricultural communities, and the training of boys in units attached to the Ethiopian army. An Ethiopian society entitled Yageur Fekir assisted distressed youths. An industrial school for boys was set up. Medical services under a British director were improving in spite of the shortage of materials and personnel. The social and economic progress of Ethiopia was much hampered by a lack of trained personnel in all the technical services. The internal situation of the country was satisfactory. The British troops had been withdrawn except in places defined in the agreement with Great Britain. The emperor's government set itself the task of reconciling tribal differences. Provincial governors were appointed by the emperor, and ecclesiastical preferments and finance were subject to state control. The emperor's government co-operated with neighbouring territories in an extensive locust campaign.   (J. L. K.)

Trade and Communication.—Chief exports: hides and skins, coffee (14,330 short tons in 1937–38) and gold. Roads (1940) c. 4,340 mi.; railways (Addis Ababa to Jibuti in French Somaliland) 486 mi.

European Advisory Commission.

The establishment of the European Advisory commission was announced in the joint communiqué of the Tripartite conference at Moscow which was published on Nov. 1, 1943. The communiqué stated in this regard "the conference agreed to set up machinery for ensuring the closest co-operation between the three governments in the examination of European questions arising as the war develops. For this purpose the conference decided to establish in London a European Advisory commission to study these questions and to make joint recommendations to the three governments."

The joint communiqué went on to point out that provision was made for continuing when necessary the tripartite consultations of representatives of the three governments in the respective capitals through the existing diplomatic channels. It also announced the establishment of another organization, the Advisory council for matters relating to Italy, to deal "with day to day questions other than military preparations" and to make "recommendations designed to co-ordinate allied policy with regard to Italy."

The European Advisory commission met for the first time on Dec. 15, 1943 at Lancaster House, St. James' Palace, London. The U.S. representative on the commission was Ambassador John G. Winant. The soviet representative was Ambassador Foydor Gousev. The British representative was Sir William Strang, who was until this appointment assistant under secretary of state for foreign affairs of the British foreign office.

Each of the representatives on the commission was assisted by a staff supplied by his own government, and there was to be a joint secretariat made up of personnel designated by the three governments.   (H. F. Ms.)

European War: *see* WORLD WAR II.
Events of the Year: *see* CALENDAR OF EVENTS, 1943, pages 1–15.

Ewing, James

(1866–1943), U.S. pathologist, was born Dec. 25 in Pittsburgh. He took his A.B., 1888, and his A.M., 1891, from Amherst college and was graduated from the College of Physicians and Surgeons of Columbia university in 1891. He received his early apprenticeship in pathology under American and European authorities and from 1899 to 1932 was professor of pathology at Cornell university medical college. Dr. Ewing was in the forefront of medical specialists who developed the use of radium in the treatment of cancer. With Dr. James Douglas, he used the Memorial hospital in New York city as a testing ground for his work and was director of the hospital from 1913 to 1939. One of his notable contributions to the literature of cancer was his treatise on tumours, *Neoplastic Diseases*. He was professor of oncology at Cornell medical college, 1932–43, and consulting pathologist at several New York hospitals. He died in New York city, May 16.

Exchange Control and Exchange Rates.

The requirements of economic warfare, not currency defense, shaped the pattern of exchange control in the United States. The general program of foreign funds control changed little during 1943. The assets of all continental European states, China, Japan, Japanese occupied areas and certain individuals and institutions in Latin America remained frozen, and the general and special licensing system for the selected release of these funds was maintained. Only the currencies of Sweden, Switzerland, six sterling countries and Latin-American nations were actively quoted in New York, and most of these were regulated in the home countries. The year 1943, however, marked the development of a financial program in liberated areas, North Africa and Italy, and a modification of the system regulating the real movement of trade by the Foreign Economic administration (formerly Board of Economic Warfare).

The exchange control system of the United States was geared, first, to prevent the enemy from using dollar assets potentially or actually under his control. Even the funds of European neutrals were thus placed under protective freezing. About $8,500,000,000 of blocked funds were held in the U.S. and during 1943 (fiscal year) the treasury received some 238,000 applications for release of assets totalling almost $4,900,000,000, 20% of which were approved. Compared with former years, fewer applications were filed during 1943 and a larger proportion denied.

Second, exchange control was aimed at preventing axis nations from realizing profits on war loot. Hence, the importation of securities and currency was steadily regulated. In the summer of 1943, a further prohibition, effective Aug. 25, 1943, was placed on the importation of checks, bills of exchange and promissory notes from all blocked countries excepting China. The exportation of checks, bills of exchange and currency to these countries was also prohibited in 1943; but the ban on the transfer of foreign-owned property held in the United States, which had been progressively eased since 1942, was further liberalized.

To prevent traffic with the enemy, the treasury also regulated transactions of nationals with individuals and companies included on the "Proclaimed List of Certain Blocked Nationals," and on the unpublished list of "Special Blocked Nationals." Late in 1943, the Banco de la Nacion and the Banco de la Provincia de Buenos Aires, two important semipublic banks in Argentina, were appended to the latter list; shortly thereafter the Argentine government formally announced its intention to repatriate earmarked gold held in the United States.

The military occupation of territories in North Africa and Italy brought new financial responsibilities to the Allied governments in 1943. Controls over finance, property and foreign exchange in liberated areas were found necessary. North African officials, after long negotiations, passed a trading with the enemy ordinance, which introduced a system of selective controls resembling the U.S. program. To guard against the use of frozen dollar assets by collaborationist institutions, a new licensing system was devised for the release of holdings of liberated-areas nationals.

The immediate currency needs of the American and British forces in liberated areas were supplied by the issue of spearhead currencies upon invasion, for which a new, unified occupation money was later substituted. The spearhead currency of the United States, first employed in North Africa in 1942, and during 1943 in the Italian theatre, was the yellow-seal dollar in denominations of $1, $5 and $10 It duplicated the design of the home currency, but a yellow seal was affixed instead of a blue. The British military authorities concurrently issued a special spearhead pound note. The same conversion rates for the yellow-seal dollar and the B.M.A. note were applied in North Africa and Italy, $4=£1.

The use of the familiar local currencies, as soon as military conditions permitted, was preferable. Consequently in 1943 to supplement existing supplies and counteract local shortages or surpluses, a new Allied military lira was jointly issued as legal tender and circulated at par with the local lira. This amlira was to serve primarily as a pocket money currency, and of the eight denominations issued, the maximum had a value equivalent of only $10. Both the amlira and the Italian lira exchanged for the dollar at the official rate of 100 lira=$1 (400 lira=£1). The North African franc, which had been valued in 1942 at 75 fr.=$1 (300 fr.=£1), was appreciated by a half on Feb. 2, 1943 to 50 fr.=$1 (200 fr. =£1). The French Equatorial African franc and that of all colonies under de Gaulle control had previously been valued at the prewar level of 176.6 fr.=£1; thus during 1943 two conflicting franc rates were current in Africa.

Continental Europe.—The Central Clearing office in Berlin and the needs of the nazi war machine continued to dominate the flow of trade and foreign payments on the European continent in 1943. Germany's clearing debts to occupied or controlled countries grew steadily; and mounting pressure by satellite states and European neutrals for a reduction of these debts, coupled with some increase in neutral trading *inter se*, characterized the year.

The major part of satellite states' total trade was transacted with Germany, the remainder with other nations in the nazi orbit, and with the possible exception of Finland, Norway and Slovakia, exports to Germany exceeded imports. Most of the trade and clearing agreements prevailing in 1942 among the 20 states associated with the new order economic system were renewed with minor modifications during the first half of 1943. Seventeen of these countries utilized the Central Clearing office in Berlin for most of their international payments, the exceptions being Spain, Portugal and Turkey. France dealt with Belgium, the Netherlands and Norway through Berlin but concluded transactions with all other countries directly. Norway dealt directly with only Sweden and Denmark; and even the two unoccupied countries, Bulgaria and Rumania, cleared mutual payments through the Berlin central office.

Germany, unlike Japan, maintained stable exchange rates for most foreign currencies during the year, the last rates fixed in 1942 prevailing in 1943. Apart from direct confiscation, Germany managed to finance the large volume of excess foreign purchases and maintain stable rates, primarily by accumulating clearing debts in exporting countries. These debts were offset somewhat by limited exports of German goods. The occupation-costs levy was another device for securing additional local credit, since occupation charges were generally met by advances from the central bank in the occupied country.

The Kassenscheine, a military currency, which was issued by the Reich Credit offices for army purchases, exchanging for local currencies at fixed rates, during 1943, circulated in certain occupied areas of the U.S.S.R. and in northern Italy, where the lira rate was depreciated from 7.6 lire=1 r.m. to 10 lire=1 r.m. The yen-lira rate was similarly revised from 22.35 yen=100 lire to

17 yen=100 lire.

Pressure for the reduction of Germany's swollen clearing deficits gave rise to several schemes for partial repayment. In the spring of 1943, Hungary's debts in France were assumed by Germany, an equivalent amount being charged off the nazi clearing deficit. Rumania repatriated part of its public debt with a portion of its Berlin clearing claim. Most countries associated with the nazi clearing system provided local facilities for the rediscount of exporters' frozen claims. Export trade was made somewhat less attractive in Belgium with a new regulation that 30% of all commodity-accounts claims were to be paid in blocked treasury bills.

Among the neutral countries, Turkey during 1943 was the smallest participant in German Europe's trade. Agreements concluded with the nazi family of nations were little more than isolated barter pledges, generally providing for the shipment of German goods prior to the execution of Turkish sales. Controls over income to foreigners from Turkish property were tightened.

Spain and Portugal, exporters of products sought by both groups of belligerents, were also able to exact more favourable terms of payment from Germany. Germany, followed by the United Kingdom and Switzerland, was the largest participant in Spain's foreign trade; nevertheless, Spain's clearing claim on Berlin was relatively small. In March 1943, the Spanish system of foreign trade control was revised; the Banco Exterieur de España was granted a monopoly on the issue of all import or export permits, the government being assigned a portion of the profits arising therefrom. During February, Portugal and Spain concluded new bilateral trade and payments agreements aiming at a higher degree of self-sufficiency for the Iberian peninsula.

Both Sweden and Switzerland, during 1943, had close dealings with the nazi clearing sphere. German shipments to Sweden fell short of expectations; the Swedish government therewith limited the granting of credit guarantees on frozen claims to exporters. Moreover, Sweden refused to accept German gold and in negotiating 1944 agreements, made demands for anticipatory payments. Switzerland's clearing agreement with Germany expired on Jan. 15, 1943, and only after long negotiations was renewed late in the year. In the interim, a *de facto* clearing system for a limited volume of trade was maintained, and the federal guarantee on clearing claims lapsed. The standstill credit agreement with Germany was renewed for June 11, 1943–May 31, 1944, with new provisions for the progressive liquidation of arrears; and a trade agreement which more closely approached bilaterally balanced exchange was ultimately concluded for the period of Oct. 11 to Dec. 31, 1943. New or revised trade and payments treaties were also made with Spain, Portugal, Hungary and Bulgaria.

Latin America.—Almost every Latin-American country during 1943 was exporting more than it could import, facing serious inflationary problems and accumulating large foreign balances. Argentina's balance of trade and payments positions were extremely favourable, and large volumes of refugee funds exaggerated the size of the capital inflow. Consequently, by April 20, after three weeks of violent fluctuation, the free peso rate in Buenos Aires rose to $.2506, the highest level in more than four years. Moreover, the central bank simultaneously lowered its official buying rate for exchange arising from nonregular exports from 4.2182 to 3.9702 pesos to the dollar. The decree of April 20 empowered the ministry of finance to control all foreign capital movements and prohibited the inflow of floating funds seeking temporary refuge in Argentina. Productive capital for genuine long-term investment was granted entrance. The decree of Sept. 17 provided for the repatriation of a large block of sterling obligations, about £33,000,000 out of a total sterling indebtedness of some £39,000,000.

In Brazil, the mounting accumulation of dollar and sterling assets, because of a favourable balance of trade, provided the basis for a compensation agreement with the United Kingdom with respect to blocked cruzeiro balances—frozen liabilities which had been contracted under the milreis monetary regime. Under a new agreement, during November, with foreign owners of public obligations, it was possible for the Brazilian government to grant more favourable terms to creditors than in the previous debt plan (expiring March 1944). To prevent entry of axis funds, the

Latin-American Exchange Rates*

Averages are based on actual selling rates for sight drafts on New York, in units of the foreign currency per dollar, with the following exception: Cuba—United States dollars to the peso. The peso of the Dominican Republic, the Guatemalan quetzal and the Panamanian balboa are linked to the dollar at 1 to 1; the Haitian gourde is fixed at 5 gourdes to the dollar.

Country	Unit quoted	Type of exchange	Annual average rate 1941	Annual average rate 1942	Jan.	Feb.	March	April	May	June	July	Aug.	Sept.	Oct.	Latest rate	Latest date
Argentina†	Paper peso	Official A	3.73	3.73	3.73	3.73	3.73	3.73	3.73	3.73	3.73	3.73	3.73	3.73	3.73	Nov. 13
		Official B	4.23	4.23	4.23	4.23	4.23	4.23	4.23	4.23	4.23	4.23	4.23	4.23	4.23	,,
		Bid	4.88	4.94	4.94	4.94	4.94	4.94	4.94	4.94	4.94	4.94	4.94	4.94		,,
		Free market	4.24		4.24	4.23	4.20	4.10	4.00	3.98	3.99	4.00	4.00	4.00		
Bolivia	Boliviano	Controlled	43.38	46.46	46.46	46.46	42.42	42.42	42.42	42.42	42.42	42.42	42.42	42.42	42.42	Nov. 22
		Curb	54.02	49.66	50.00	48.67	46.00	46.00	45.30	43.30	43.09	44.00	44.50	44.50	44.50	,,
Brazil	Cruzeiro‡	Official	16.50	16.50	16.50	16.50	16.50	16.50	16.50	16.50	16.50	16.50	16.50	16.50	16.50	Nov. 18
		Free market	19.72	19.64	19.63	19.63	19.63	19.63	19.63	19.63	19.63	19.63	19.63	19.63	19.63	,,
		Special free market	20.68	20.50	20.50	20.50	20.50	20.50	20.50	20.50	20.50	20.50	20.30	20.30	20.30	,,
Chile	Peso	Official	19.37	19.37	19.37	19.37	19.37	19.37	19.37	19.37	19.37	19.37	19.37	19.37	19.37	Nov. 20
		Export draft	25.00	25.00	25.00	25.00	25.00	25.00	25.00	25.00	25.00	25.00	25.00	25.00	25.00	,,
		Curb market	31.78	31.75	34.16	33.55	33.81	33.00	30.97	31.48	31.88	31.26	31.70	31.64	32.50	,,
		Free	31.15	31.13	31.00	31.00	31.00	31.00	31.00	31.00	31.00	31.00	31.00	31.00	31.00	,,
		Gold exchange	31.15	31.13	31.00	31.00	31.00	31.00	31.00	31.00	31.00	31.00	31.00	31.00	31.00	,,
		Mining dollar	31.35	31.13	31.00	31.00	31.00	31.00	31.00	31.00	31.00	31.00	31.00	31.00	31.00	,,
		Agricultural dollar	31.15§	31.13	31.00	31.00	31.00	31.00	31.00	31.00	31.00	31.00	31.00	31.00	31.00	,,
Colombia	Peso	Controlled	1.75	1.75	1.75	1.75	1.75	1.75	1.75	1.75	1.75	1.75	1.75	1.75	1.75	Nov. 27
		Bank of Republic Stabilization fund‖	1.76	1.76	1.76	1.76	1.76	1.76	1.76	1.76	1.76	1.76	1.76	1.76	1.76	,,
		Curb	1.86	1.77	1.77	1.77	1.77	1.77	1.77	1.75	1.75	1.75	1.75	1.75	1.75	,,
Costa Rica	Colon	Uncontrolled	5.85	5.71	5.64	5.66	5.65	5.66	¶	5.67	5.64	5.64	5.63	5.65	5.65	Oct. 30
		Controlled	5.62	5.62	5.62	5.62	5.62	5.62	5.62	5.62	5.62	5.62	5.62	5.62	5.62	,,
Cuba	Peso	Free	.98	1.00	1.00	1.00	1.00	1.00	1.00	1.00	1.00	1.00	1.00	1.00	1.00	Nov. 6
Ecuador	Sucre	Central bank (Official)	15.00	14.39	14.10	14.10	14.10	14.10	14.10	14.10	14.10	14.10	14.10	14.10	14.10	Nov. 17
Honduras	Lempira	Official	2.04	2.04	2.04	2.04	2.04	2.04	2.04	2.04	2.04	2.04	2.04	2.04	2.04	,,
Mexico	Peso	Free	4.86	4.85	4.85	4.85	4.85	4.85	4.85	4.85	4.85	4.85	4.85	4.85	4.85	Nov. 15
Nicaragua	Cordoba	Official	5.00	5.00	5.00	5.00	5.00	5.00	5.00	5.00	5.00	5.00	5.00	5.00	5.00	Nov. 13
		Curb	5.93		5.05	5.00	5.00	5.01	5.11	5.26	5.24	5.30				
Paraguay	Paper peso	Official		333.00	333.00	333.00	333.00	333.00	333.00	333.00	333.00	333.00	333.00	333.00	333.00	Oct. 30
Peru	Sol	Free	6.50	6.50	6.50	6.50	6.50	6.50	6.50	6.50	6.50	6.50	6.50	6.50	6.50	Nov. 27
Salvador	Colon	Free	2.50	2.50	2.50	2.50	2.50	2.50	2.50	2.50	2.50	2.50	2.50	2.50	2.50	,,
Uruguay	Peso	Controlled	1.90	1.90	1.90	1.90	1.90	1.90	1.90	1.90	1.90	1.90	1.90	1.90	1.90	,,
		Free	2.31	1.90	1.90	1.90	1.90	1.90	1.90	1.90	1.90	1.90	1.90	1.90	1.90	,,
Venezuela	Bolivar	Controlled	3.26	3.35	3.35	3.35	3.35	3.35	3.35	3.35	3.35	3.35	3.35	3.35	3.35	Nov. 15
		Free	3.76?	3.45	3.35	3.35	3.35	3.35	3.35	3.35	3.35	3.35	3.35	3.35		

*Source: U.S. Department of Commerce, *Foreign Commerce Weekly*, Oct. 30, Dec. 4, Dec. 18, 1943. †Special rates apply to automotive equipment and agricultural machinery imported from the United States into Argentina. ‡After Nov. 1, 1942, exchange quotations have been expressed in terms of cruzeiros and centavos to the dollar, which under the Brazilian law of Oct. 6, 1942, replaced the milreis as the official monetary unit. §Established Mar. 25. ‖In 1941 and 1942, for Class 2 merchandise, 1.795; Class 3, 1.875; Class 4, 1.195. During 1943, for Class 2 merchandise, 1.765; Class 3, 1.775; Class 4, 1.785. ¶Data not received. ?July 24–Dec. 31.

Bank of Brazil under its exchange control authority imposed new, rigid restrictions on the import and export of paper currency, prohibiting all unauthorized movement. In September, the special free rate for dollars was reduced to 20.30 cruzeiros.

At the close of 1942, the Colombian Office of Exchange and Export Control set up a new semiflexible procedure for the discount of foreign drafts by the Bank of the Republic whereby exchange originating in certain transactions was partially purchased with national economic defense bonds, and not entirely with cash. To stabilize the prevailing exchange rate and to curb inflation, the central bank was also authorized in June, 1943, to sell nonnegotiable certificates of deposit bearing a two-year maturity and an optional backing of gold or dollars. The ministry of finance was required to authorize any new capital imports. On April 7, the export control office lowered the rates applicable to import payments made through the Stabilization fund. (*See* table, footnote II.)

Mexico also recorded a net export surplus in 1943 and, in contrast with former years, a great influx of foreign capital. With inflation and expanded currency needs, Mexico suspended silver sales abroad early in the year and even suggested a possible lend-lease silver grant. On Aug. 16, however, the finance ministry announced the projected renewal of shipments in April 1944. The government, in July, launched a new $40,000,000 defense loan to finance the acquisition of exchange from the central bank for the redemption of foreign obligations.

In Paraguay, the Exchange Control law of 1941 was revised; the new law of Feb. 18, 1943, tightened controls governing the possession of foreign exchange. It also set up an exchange fund to finance the repurchase of foreign-owned enterprises in Paraguay and established two selling rates for foreign drafts, distinguishing between necessary and nonessential imports. Formally unable to convert foreign exchange holdings into a true gold reserve, the Bank of the Republic on Sept. 13 was empowered to buy and sell gold bullion or coin. A new currency, the guarani, was established on Oct. 5, gradually replacing the former paper peso at the rate of 1 guarani = 100 pesos. An innovation in monetary standards, its value was not set in terms of gold or of dollars exclusively but rather linked to the several currencies of the countries important in its balance of payments.

Unlike most other Latin-American countries, Uruguay evidenced a shortage of foreign exchange early in 1943; in later months, however, the balance of payments shifted and pressure on prevailing rates was eased. In September, after the political upheaval in Argentina, some "scare" capital flowed into Uruguay. The dollar-buying rate of the central bank of Ecuador was lowered to 13.50 sucres in July; the curb rate in Chile dropped markedly in the middle of the year and in Bolivia declined steadily throughout the year. At the end of March, to relieve a coin shortage, Honduras utilized dollar exchange for the purchase of some $1,500,000 in 50- and 10-cent pieces from the United States; Cuba bought gold as backing for a new currency.

United Kingdom.—Although no major change was introduced during 1943 into the United Kingdom's exchange control system, the program was somewhat liberalized to simplify administration and to reduce the volume of accumulated debts. Four major types of accounts for foreign creditors—registered, special, sterling area and Central American—were maintained. Early in 1943, however, the regulations governing the sterling holdings of U.S. residents were simplified. Since July 1940, most U.S. funds had been held in three categories of accounts: registered, representing sterling freely convertible into dollars at the official rate and applying principally to new money held on behalf of American banks; sterling area accounts, held for individuals having certain periodic payments to make to the United Kingdom; and, least

common, old or free prewar accounts, which were in existence prior to the institution of controls in 1940 and used for discharging equally old obligations, convertible at the free market rate. On Feb. 2, all categories were merged under the heading registered accounts. A similar ruling applicable to the holdings of Central American residents was also issued; on Aug. 25, old sterling accounts for this area were redesignated Central American accounts.

Unaffected by these regulations were the blocked funds of American film companies held in a special account and blocked accounts maintained for U.S. residents representing the proceeds of the liquidation of certain capital assets. However, all special restrictions on the remittance of film royalties were removed in May (retroactive to Oct. 25, 1942); thereafter, such transactions were subject only to customary regulations on all transfers abroad. Measures relating to the accumulation and use of funds arising from capital transactions and held on blocked account were also liberalized. In fact, a major portion of these realized capital balances, frozen since Nov. 1940, were by a retroactive order in October released for transfer. The United States was the principal beneficiary under this new ruling, since the release was not extended to the funds of Canada, Newfoundland, Switzerland and Argentina. In addition, a more lenient policy was adopted on the sale and purchase of sterling securities by nonresidents; the ban on the acquisition of bearer securities was also lifted.

Among the other developments in 1943, three franc currencies —Algerian, French Moroccan, French West African—were added to the designated list of currencies which residents were required to offer to the Bank of England. The list released at that time also included the currencies of eight countries in the western hemisphere and three in Europe. Procedure on interest and dividend payments and capital repayments credited to Sweden or Switzerland was tightened. The Anglo-Italian payments system was revised on Oct. 8; use of the Anglo-Italian Clearing office was thereafter reserved for debts contracted prior to that date. Lastly, the United Kingdom participated with the United States in exchange control and monetary programs in liberated areas and other areas.

Other Areas.—Even at the beginning of 1943, the sterling assets of British empire and other sterling bloc countries had reached nearly £600,000,000. India was probably the largest creditor despite repatriations of sterling loans during 1943 with part of these funds. Inflation was rampant in India, Egypt and other Middle East countries, and gold was imported in a partial attempt to mop up excess purchasing power resulting from Allied expenditures. At the request of the Egyptian government, gold was supplied by Britain and sold to the public in the form of small 18.69 dirhem bars (about 2 oz.) of .996 fineness at 177.3 piastres per dirhem. On April 11, the following exchange rates were set: 100 Egyptian pounds = 5.524 Norwegian crowns, 12.948 Dutch florins, .815 Belgian francs, .552 French francs, .186 Greek drachmas. These rates were applied to pre-occupation obligations which cleared through the Office of Occupied or Controlled Territories. In May, all foreign exchange transactions in Afghanistan were centralized in the Bank of Afghanistan (Bank Shahi). By December, the influx of Indian funds had risen so greatly that the bank reduced its official rupee-buying rate. The dollar rate was lowered on Oct. 13 from $1 = 13.0472 afghanis to $1 = 11.5528 but soon after returned to its former value.

Australian sterling holdings were high, about £60,000,000 at the beginning of 1943, and dollar funds from the expenditure of American troops in the Pacific also plentiful. The commonwealth, however, maintained only a small dollar reserve, remitting the remainder to Britain. The prohibition on the unlicensed import of gold into Canada was extended to the end of the year. The Canadian Foreign Exchange Control board was granted the power to declare bankrupt nonresident persons or firms attempting to evade prosecution or investigation under the Foreign Exchange Control order. All gifts under $25, however, were freed from exchange restrictions.

Exchange conditions in the orient during 1943 were chaotic, under the reign of the twin devils inflation and depreciation. Prices and note circulation had risen tremendously in China; nevertheless the official rate, Ch. $20=U.S. $1, was maintained with a special rate of 30=1 for diplomatic, educational, missionary and certain other transfers. From all indications, including the black market rate of U.S. $1=Ch. $80-$90, with unpegged exchange, the currency would have fallen precipitously. In May, to check the efflux of precious metals, unlicensed exports of gold and silver were prohibited. A month later a ruling permitting private trading in gold was issued. Ostensibly to bolster the falling currency, $200,000,000 in gold bullion was purchased from the United States with part of the $500,000,000 stabilization loan granted China in 1942. The Bank of Japan remained the central clearing agency in the Japanese sphere and the military yen the dominant currency. Japan had depreciated the currencies of occupied territories, mostly to parity with the yen. Unlike Germany, Tokyo made no attempt or even promises to nominally stabilize rates in most areas, and by 1943 satellite currencies had fallen relatively lower than in continental Europe. (*See* also GOLD.)

BIBLIOGRAPHY.—*The Economist* (London); U.S. Department of Commerce, *Foreign Commerce Weekly;* U.S. Treasury, *Press Releases;* Foreign Economic Administration, *Press Releases;* The *New York Times;* The *Times* (London).   (D. B. B.)

Exchange Rates: *see* EXCHANGE CONTROL AND EXCHANGE RATES.

Exchange Stabilization Funds.

Exchange stabilization funds during 1943 were relatively inactive. In Europe, war and strict economic controls completely paralyzed the operations of such funds. In most Latin-American countries, surplus exchange holdings limited the need for a vigorous stabilization policy to support currencies.

The role of the U.S. Stabilization fund in controlling foreign exchange values was diminished in 1943. However, several agreements with small nations for the purpose of stabilizing exchange rates were renewed. The agreement in which the United States undertook to sell gold to Cuba in maximum installments of $5,000,000 was extended to June 30, 1945. In the first half of 1943, a credit slightly exceeding $5,000,000 was granted Cuba by the U.S. Stabilization fund. During the same period, the fund increased its holdings of Swiss francs by more than $500,000. On June 30, stabilization agreements with Ecuador and Iceland were renewed for one year and the Mexican accord extended for two years. The maximum sums which the United States was obliged to purchase were: $5,000,000 in Ecuadoran sucres; $2,000,000 in Icelandic krónur; $40,000,000 in Mexican pesos. Later in the year, an agreement with Brazil, like the Cuban accord, specifically endorsed the sale of gold. Perhaps the most outstanding event of 1943 was the passage of a bill in April extending the life of the $2,000,000,000 Stabilization fund to June 30, 1945. At the same time, the president's power to devalue the gold content of the dollar was revoked, and the act specifically forbade the transfer of the gold holdings to any international stabilization fund without the consent of congress.

In April, draft outlines of proposals for an international stabilization fund and an international clearing union were made public by treasury experts in the United States and the United Kingdom, respectively. The Canadian ministry of finance released another proposal for an international exchange union in July. Experts from various countries participated in discussions relative to these plans throughout the year; the U.S. treasury officials conferred with representatives of approximately 30 nations. The future establishment of any such international stabilization or clearing system would, in all likelihood, strip the national stabilization funds of their functions. (*See* also EXCHANGE CONTROL AND EXCHANGE RATES; GOLD.)   (D. B. B.)

Expenditure, Government: *see* BUDGET, NATIONAL.

Export-Import Bank of Washington.

The Export-Import Bank of Washington, an agency of the United States, was established on Feb. 12, 1934, for the purpose of financing and facilitating trade relations between the United States, its territories, insular possessions and foreign countries. By an act of congress approved Sept. 26, 1940, the Export-Import bank was to continue as an agency of the United States until Jan. 22, 1947, or such earlier date as might be fixed by the president by executive order. By this act it was also granted specific authority to make loans which would assist in the development of the resources, in the stabilization of the economies, and in the orderly marketing of the products of the countries of the western hemisphere.

The bank in 1943 had lending authority of $700,000,000. Its capital consisted of $1,000,000 of common stock and $174,000,000 of preferred stock. All common stock, except 11 shares standing in the respective names of the trustees, was held jointly by the secretaries of state and commerce in their official capacities. All of the preferred stock was purchased by the Reconstruction Finance corporation. Its governing body was a board of 11 trustees of which the chairman was the foreign economic administrator and on which were represented the departments of state, treasury, commerce and agriculture and the Reconstruction Finance corporation.

From its creation to the end of 1943, the bank had authorized $1,164,948,061 of loans compared with $1,101,761,946 at the close of 1942. During the year 1943, disbursements amounted to $55,687,885 and repayments to $32,250,352. As a result, outstanding loans at the end of 1943 were $204,937,874 compared with $181,500,341 at the end of the previous year.

Although the operations of the bank in behalf of United States foreign trade had been world-wide, circumstances restricted them following the outbreak of World War II almost entirely to the western hemisphere, and particularly to the making of loans to develop resources vital to the war effort. Because of transportation difficulties and other wartime impediments to foreign trade, the bank also continued during 1943 its plan for underwriting letters of credit of approved foreign banks which were opened in the United States by U.S. commercial banks, thus helping to preserve long-established markets and trade channels to the extent possible under wartime conditions.   (W. L. PI.)

Exports: *see* AGRICULTURE; INTERNATIONAL TRADE.

Eye, Diseases of.

Experiments conducted by Bellows and Gutmann with the use of sulfonamides in treatment of intraocular inflammation resulted in a simple method of obtaining chemotherapeutically effective levels of the sulfonamide compounds for combating infection of the anterior segment of the eyeball by the application of the drug in the presence of a suitable wetting agent.

It was shown that the sulfonamide compounds, with the exception of sulfanilamide, penetrate the cornea poorly. Further, the concentrations reached in the ocular tissues and fluids when other of the sulfonamides are administered orally or locally fall short of the values necessary for therapeutic effectiveness.

A wetting agent is defined as a substance which, by lowering interfacial tension, increases penetration and acts as a detergent or emulsifying agent, bringing about an increased penetration of both the wetting agent and other substances which by themselves would not penetrate readily. The sulfonamide compounds employed were sulfanilamide, sulfathiazole, sulfadiazine and sulfapyridine. The wetting agents used were:

Aerosol OT	Tergital O8	Sodium lauryl sulfate
Aerosol OS	Ocenol KD	Zephiran
Tergital 4, 7		

All the wetting agents caused a definite increase in the concentration of the sulfonamide compounds in the aqueous humor, so that they reached a point above that considered necessary for chemotherapeutic effectiveness. By application of heat the concentration of the drug in the aqueous humor of the eyes was increased threefold.

The sulfonamide compounds, however, have an unfavourable effect on actively growing epithelium, as shown by a greater than twofold increase in the time required for epithelial regeneration. They increase the amount of scarring. Therefore, the local use of these drugs should be avoided in the treatment of injuries of the face or cornea.

Industrial Hazards.—The eyes of welders are, supposedly, fully protected from the dangerous actinic rays of either gas flame or electric arc. Is there, in spite of this protection, a depletion of visual purple that might retard adaptation to differences in brightness?

Sixty-one welders were given tests for speed of dark adaptation before and after a day's work. Thirty-nine were on the day shift and 22 on the night shift. Half the welders (31) each received 10,000 units of vitamin A before starting work and again in the middle of the shift. Other welders received a placebo at the same time. There was in 1943 no evidence of a general lack of dark adaptation among welders and no evidence of any decrement in this function during an 8-hour shift. Individual differences in age, domicile, type of goggles and food showed no relation to differences in gain or loss of speed of dark adaptation during an 8-hour shift. The clinical conclusion was that the excessive number of complaints among welders was due to inadequate protective equipment or carelessness in its use. (*See* also VITAMINS.)

BIBLIOGRAPHY.—Hedwig S. Kuhn and Ernest C. Willie, Jr., "Are Welders Subject to Depletion of Visual Purple While at Work?" *American Journal of Ophthalmology* (Jan. 1943); John G. Bellows and Martin Gutmann, "Application of Wetting Agents in Ophthalmology," *Archives of Ophthalmology* (Sept. 1943); John G. Bellows, "Local Effect of Sulfanilamide and Some of its Derivatives," *ibid.* (July 1943).

(W. L. Be.)

Fair Labor Standards Act: *see* CHILD WELFARE.

Fairs, State: *see* SHOWS.

Falange: *see* FASCISM.

Falk Foundation, The Maurice and Laura,

of Pittsburgh, Pa. continued during 1943 to devote its funds to the financing of definitive research investigations of specific economic problems basic to the development of U.S. industry, trade and finance, but with special emphasis on problems of postwar readjustment and economic reconstruction. Grants voted in 1943 totalled $152,166.67 and included $75,000 to the Brookings institution, Washington, D.C. for sequential studies to analyses of economic problems made under the foundation's grants of previous years. Special wartime out-of-program grants included $16,500 to the United War fund and $4,000 to the American Red

Cross. Payments in 1943 on grants made in 1943 and earlier years totalled $177,166.67 and included $30,000 to the Brookings institution, for studies of demobilization and economic reconstruction; $22,500 to the National Bureau of Economic Research, New York, for statistical analyses of trends in the service industries; and $50,000 to the Carnegie Institute of Technology on a $300,000 endowment grant for the Maurice Falk Professorship of Social Relations.

In 1943 the following publications were issued as reports on studies made under the foundation's grants: *Collapse or Boom at the End of the War?* (Brookings Institution); *Do We Want a Federal Sales Tax?* (Brookings Institution); *The New Philosophy of Public Debt* (Brookings Institution); *Basic Criteria of Price Policy* (Brookings Institution); *American Agriculture, 1899–1939* (National Bureau of Economic Research); and *Employment in Manufacturing, 1899–1939* (National Bureau of Economic Research).

(J. S. G.)

Falkland Islands: *see* BRITISH EMPIRE.

Famines.

The famine in Bengal, India was the most severe in 1943 with the other in China of almost equal proportions. Both of these disasters were to some extent due to conditions caused by World War II, partly the result of crop failure, inadequate transportation and changing government policies.

In Bengal, the food shortage had been growing steadily with the increase of population without a corresponding increase in food production. During the period 1933–43, population increased about 50,000,000 while at the same time the per capita yield of rice declined and the pressure on the land increased in the same proportion. In some districts there were over 2,000 persons per square mile in rural villages, most of them living on the extreme margin of subsistence. In 1942, the rice crop of Bengal was seriously damaged by a cyclone and floods and an unusual scarcity could be foreseen. Prices began to rise because of a fear of Japanese invasion. Peasants who grew a surplus for market found themselves able to meet their obligations with a smaller part of their crop and began hoarding the remainder through fear of the future. This aggravated the shortage in the cities and villages and the poor classes, already living on a subsistence margin with shrinking income, were rendered destitute. Statistics of agriculture and health are very inadequate in India; official estimates placed the number affected at about 7,000,000 but reliable data on the actual number of deaths were not available at the end of the year. Estimates ranged from 250,000 to 1,000,000 for Bengal alone. In Calcutta alone, more than 150,000 were reported destitute.

The Central India government made special efforts to increase the 1942–43 rice crop and the area was reported to be the largest of the period 1933–43. A low yield of 24.5 bu. per acre resulted from drought in parts of the country, bringing the 1943 crop to 1,834,000,000 bu. compared with 1,895,000,000 in 1942.

While the second largest rice producer, India was usually the largest importer, bringing in about 3,000,000,000 lb. yearly, 80% of it from Burma and the rest from Thailand and Indo-China. With these sources cut off by the Japanese invasion the shortage had to be made up by other grains, principally wheat from Australia.

The Central government of India as well as the Bengal government increased shipments of rice and other grains to the stricken regions. In six months about 475,000 tons were shipped to Bengal alone. In Bengal, 5,500 free food kitchens were set up by the government and served over 2,000,000 persons daily. Sufficient supplies were said to be in sight to carry through until the new rice crop became available in December. To prevent a repetition of the famine in 1944, the government sought ships with which to bring wheat from Australia. At the All India Food conference plans were made by the government to introduce rationing in Punjab, the bread basket of India, to make available larger quantities of grains to be shipped to the provinces of shortages. The food conference agreed to a general supervision of the distribution of grains and other foodstuffs.

In China, the suffering was most acute in those provinces, Kwangtung and Honan, which formerly depended on rice from Thailand, Indo-China and Burma which were, in 1943, cut off. The invasion by the Japanese of the "rice bowl" area around Tungting lake produced another serious shortage. Late in 1943, however, the Chinese armies had successes in this region and regained much of the best producing area.

The 1942 and 1943 rice crops in Free China, which represented about two-thirds of total Chinese production, were about normal but little surplus was available for distribution to areas where the 1943 crop was short. Several areas harvested poor crops in 1943 and therefore faced famine or near-famine conditions. Lack of transportation facilities and the prior claims of military needs were the principal factors handicapping relief efforts. Official figures were not available for China but best estimates put the total of the Chinese crop in prewar 1930–35 at 2,300,000,000 bu., which was about 500,000,000 bu. more than the production of India and about one-third of the world's total.

(J. C. Ms.)

Farm Co-operatives: *see* FARM CREDIT ADMINISTRATION.
Farm Credit: *see* FARM CREDIT ADMINISTRATION.

Farm Credit Administration.

Highlighting the Farm Credit administration's activities in 1943 were an accelerated demand for production credit, an increased amount of credit extended to finance the war-expanded operations of farmers' co-operatives, and large repayments on the principal of outstanding farm mortgage loans.

Credit extended to farmers and their co-operative associations through the facilities of the Farm Credit administration totalled $1,186,092,658 in 1943, compared to $964,552,979 in 1942.

About 50% of this amount, or $593,735,184, was short-term credit used to finance the production of crops and livestock, including a number of new crops.

Short-term production credit totalling $501,211,688 was extended by 529 production credit associations, $19,269,945 by the 11 emergency crop and feed loan offices, and $73,253,551 by the Regional Agricultural Credit corporation of Washington, D.C. RACC loans were authorized early in 1943 to finance farmers producing needed war food, fibre and oil-bearing crops.

Farmers' co-operatives used credit from the 13 banks for co-operatives amounting to $398,581,320, an increase of 58% over 1942. Much of this credit was used in processing and preparing for shipment food vital to the war effort.

The loans and discounts for the 12 federal intermediate credit banks totalled $927,435,580 for 1943. While not loaning directly to farmers, these banks provided loan funds for 529 production credit associations, advanced funds to the banks for co-operatives to carry the major part of their commodity loans, made agricultural loans to and discounted loans for privately capitalized financing institutions, and made direct loans to co-operatives.

Long-term farm mortgage loans closed by the 12 federal land banks and the Federal Farm Mortgage corporation in 1943 amounted to $92,397,244 compared to $82,508,218 in 1942. Despite an increase in the amount of new credit extended loans outstanding continued to decline because of large principal repay-

ments. On Dec. 31, 1943, outstanding loans totalled $1,764,127,623 compared to $2,115,043,460 on the same date in 1942.

The Farm Credit administration through its 12 district offices and local associations continued to urge farmer-borrowers to use their increased income to buy war bonds, to pay off debts, or to make provision for future instalments of Federal land bank and Commissioner loans by putting money in the Future Payment funds of the 12 land banks and Federal Farm Mortgage corporation. Money in these funds amounted to $25,723,247 on Dec. 31, 1943, compared to $17,701,767 in 1942. Repayments on the principal of Federal land bank and Commissioner loans totalled $427,119,112, or 41% more than in 1942.

(A. G. BL.)

Farm Income: *see* AGRICULTURE.
Farm Machinery: *see* AGRICULTURE.
Farm Mortgages: *see* FARM CREDIT ADMINISTRATION.

Fascism.

The year of 1943 marked definitely the turning point in the fortunes of fascism as a movement of international importance and in all probability sealed its world-wide decline. In Oct. 1942 fascism had celebrated the 20th anniversary of its triumphant coming to power in Italy under Mussolini's leadership. In these 20 years fascism had established itself in Germany, Japan, Spain, France, Hungary, Rumania, Bulgaria, Slovakia, Croatia and had exercised its influence in some Latin American countries, especially in Argentina, and before World War II also in Poland and Greece. Fascism had always boasted of its superiority compared with "obsolete" and "decadent" democracy, of its higher efficiency and military invincibility. The events of 1943 proved definitely that, in spite of its many years of preparation and its supreme efforts at total mobilization, fascism was surpassed in the course of only a few years by the democracies in the field of industrial efficiency and war strategy. In 1943 fascism was put everywhere on the defensive. The only point on the globe where it made definite gains was Argentina.

The greatest blow to the prestige and influence of fascism was delivered on July 25, 1943, when in the land of its first triumph the king of Italy dismissed Benito Mussolini and appointed Marshal Pietro Badoglio as prime minister. The whole structure of fascism collapsed with incredible ease and speed. On July 28 the dissolution of the fascist party and the abolition of the special fascist tribunals for the defense of the state were decreed. The official announcement over the Italian radio declared that "Italy has found it necessary to rid herself of a political system that she found harmful to the nation; this political system has been done away with. Fascism in Italy is over, forever." The overthrow of fascism in Italy was the result of a revolt within the highest ranks of the fascist party against the leadership of Mussolini. The difficult and almost chaotic situation in which Italy found herself as a result of 20 years of fascist administration and of fascist aggression was made clear already at the beginning of July, when against widespread criticism and unrest Mussolini declared that Italy must stand with the fascist axis or sink to the rank of an insignificant power. He warned then already that the Italians must not make scapegoats of the fascist bureaucracy and threatened the most draconic measures against all who would undermine fascist and Italian morale. But this morale had been destroyed and corrupted by 20 years of fascist regime, and thus the end of fascism in Italy was joyously welcomed by the Italian people and the promise of a clean sweep of the Italian national life from all traces of the fascist regime was given by the new Italian government.

The Germans, in occupying northern and central Italy, succeeded in rescuing Mussolini who had been imprisoned by the Italian government. On Sept. 15, 1943 Mussolini again "assumed the supreme leadership of fascism in Italy." He appointed Alessandro Pavolini provisional secretary of the fascist national party, which was now renamed Republican Fascist party, thus expressing the party's new hostility to the king and the House of Savoy. A new fascist Italian cabinet was set up, but this new cabinet never exercised any actual authority which was entirely in the hands of the German army of occupation.

The downfall of fascism in Italy made a great impression in the smaller fascist satellite nations, in Hungary, Bulgaria, Rumania, Slovakia and Croatia. In all these countries the opposition to fascism grew, and the governmental circles themselves were reported reliably to be on the lookout for some form of compromise to avoid the debacle involved in the expected victory of the democracies. It was only in Spain that the fascist regime of General Franco, backed by the fascist party, the Falange, showed no sign of weakening. The Falange was active in promoting fascist ideas in Latin America, where they found a fertile field in Argentina. The new government of General Ramirez, who came to power in June 1943 as a result of an army revolt, not only refused to break Argentina's ties with the axis, but went much further than its predecessor in the suppression of all democratic liberty in the country. The policy of the government was anti-American, and Argentina tried to win over neighbouring Latin American republics for a common pro-Fascist policy. While thus the influence of fascism grew in South America and came daringly more into the open, fascism suffered a definite set-back in South Africa. The very strong fascist groups, which from the beginning had opposed South African participation in the war and were violently hostile to Britain, united under Dr. D. F. Malan, but were heavily defeated in the elections of July 1943, when the democratic parties under the leadership of Fieldmarshal Jan Christian Smuts gained in "the most spectacular victory in the history of South Africa" a majority of 64 seats as against 13 voices with which Smuts had carried in Sept. 1939 his declaration of war against the then much stronger pro-fascist opposition. This defeat of the fascist party in South Africa, perhaps the strongest and most effective fascist party in any democracy, coming only a very few days after Mussolini's downfall and the liquidation of fascism in Italy, confirmed the general trend towards democracy in the world, to which Argentina formed the only exception.

In the great democracies fascist propaganda tried to carry on ceaselessly its activities for undermining the democratic powers. The main lines of this propaganda remained unchanged: they played in America upon prejudices against the British Empire and in Britain upon the apprehension of an expanding American imperialism, in both countries upon the fear of communism and especially upon the dislike of Jews. By a dexterous use of insinuations, distortions and emotional appeal to prejudices fascist propaganda was to a certain degree successful in its efforts to confuse and disunite the democracies. In Great Britain its influence was, however, so much on the decline that the government could release from prison in Nov. 1943 the British fascist leader, Sir Oswald Mosley. Mosley, who had been confined since 1940, was freed because of ill health. His release provoked widespread protests on the part of labour. (*See also* ANTI-SEMITISM; ARGENTINA; COMMUNISM; DEMOCRACY; GERMANY; ITALY; JAPAN; RUMANIA; SPAIN.)

BIBLIOGRAPHY.—John Roy Carlson, *Under Cover* (1943); Ernest Jaekh, *The War for Man's Soul* (1943); Basil Mathews, *United We Stand* (1943); Herbert L. Matthews, *The Fruits of Fascism* (1943).   (H. Ko.)

Fashion and Dress.
During 1943, American fashion began to show a momentum of its own, an honest freedom from the great tradition of Paris on which it had leaned so heavily, so long. Clothes were at once less cautious and less tricky. Still marked by the simplicity that wartime fabric shortages and the wartime work and psychology of women demanded, the simplicity was tempered by inventiveness of cut, a genuine suppleness of line.

Two very distinct silhouettes emerged over the year. One was tubular, slim, reedy, exemplified in straight chemise dresses cinched in at the waist by belt, not fit; in knitted dresses that pulled on over the figure like knee-length sweaters. The other silhouette was chunky, bulky, giving the effect of fullness without gathers—robust boxcoats in wool or fur, or wool lined in fur; wool dresses cut with the generosity of officers' greatcoats, then decisively belted in.

With either silhouette, the look of the head was decidedly neat and small, the hair folded up off the ears and moored on top of the head, netted neatly at the back of the neck, or twisted in tight neat braids. Hats fitted close to the skull—little felt caps, coifs bound tight around the hairline, wide bands of material (called "curvettes") worn over the top of the head and tied under the hair in back with strings of felt or velvet ribbon. This curvette was the most popular headpiece (it could scarcely be called a hat) of the young. It was seen in every material—felt, fur, crocheted wool flecked with coloured sequins for the evening. Many secured their hair in simple snoods of veiling anchored on the head by a band of ribbon.

Suits, still the most popular single fashion because of their enormous versatility, grew sophisticated, even flippant, in cut at no sacrifice of functional usefulness. The straight, spare skirt was broken across the front by soft trouser pleats, and a new hike-back skirt appeared—still straight in front, but hiked up slightly in back to make it swing out gracefully behind. The suit jacket grew shorter—and niftier. Three jackets in particular marked a development: (a) the short, fitted jacket, nipped in snugly at the waist, slightly flared out over the hipbones; (b) the bolero, fitted close to the lines of the figure after the authentic Spanish fashion; (c) the box jacket, extremely young and casual, its squared-off, sawed-off lines accentuating the slimness of the skirt.

Long coats adapted from officers' greatcoats, and short coats adapted from seamen's jackets, were seen everywhere—practical, dashing, adaptable; but it was the fur-lined coat, launched in the autumn, that became the big news of winter. Simple tweed reefers, loose box coats, slim mid-length tuxedo coats all wore fur linings. Even the raincoat made a welcome fur-lined appearance, gave women an opportunity to be warm in any weather.

The younger generation made almost a uniform of the pinafore or jumper dress, perfect in cottons for summer; and—in gray flannel, checked tweed, or bright wool jersey—a wonderful campus costume worn with any of many shirts and blouses. A few of the more daring began to couple the pinafore with an adaptation of the ballet dancer's leotard: waist-length tights and a separate crew-neck shirt of striped or figured wool jersey. This basic outfit dispensed with stockings and most underclothing, and over it a pinafore or simple wrap-on skirt completed a whole costume.

After several years of covered-up necklines for both day and evening, décolletage came back in fashion. It was first seen during the summer in gingham beach dresses with shoulder-strap tops, and in printed silk town dresses with matching jackets to cover their backless, sleeveless nakedness on the street. By winter, 1943, the covered-up, short-skirted dinner dress of 1942 had become a full-fledged, décolleté evening dress: short black slipper satin dresses with ribbons of satin over bare shoulders; halter tops of white satin and sequins barbarically strapping naked backs above simple short black crepe skirts; short black crepe dresses with deep oval décolletage and tiny cap sleeves (a fashion stemming from the blouse of Mexican women) dangerously edged in black lace. Almost all these décolleté dresses

SEAMAN JACKETS with handjamming pockets were favourite coats of U.S. girls in 1943

BLACK WOOL PINAFORE, similar to a sleeveless, calf-length, pull-on sweater

SHORT-SKIRTED, décolleté evening dress —a radical departure in 1943 from the evening clothes of the preceding decade

WOOL FLEECE COAT lined in ocelot. The fur-lined greatcoat for all occasions was the most important coat of the fall of 1943 in the United States

had tailored black silk jackets to turn them into modest suits for restaurants and theatres.

The deep oval décolletage with its little cap sleeves proved so becoming to so many women, and such a relief from high-neck, long-sleeve fashions that it spread to clothes of every description . . . dresses of pastel wool, of stiff brown moiré, of soft crepe in black or lively colours. Both the oval and the halter neckline were uppermost also in a new genre of playdress for the south . . . a casual, feminine type of dress, made in coarse colourful cottons from Mexico and Guatemala, that threatened to supplant the shirtwaist dress, to banish the ubiquitous slacks from the beach and relegate them forever to fields in which they have a real function—factories, decks of boats, western plains, backwoods' camps. (*See also* FURS.)   (C. SN.)

FBI: *see* FEDERAL BUREAU OF INVESTIGATION.
FCA: *see* FARM CREDIT ADMINISTRATION.
FCC: *see* FEDERAL COMMUNICATIONS COMMISSION.
FDIC: *see* FEDERAL DEPOSIT INSURANCE CORPORATION.

Federal Bureau of Investigation.
Faced with the greatest responsibilities in its history, the Federal Bureau of Investigation accomplished its greatest results during the fiscal year 1943.

Eight German sabotage agents, fresh from the sabotage schools of Germany, landed on the eastern coast. They were brought near the shore by submarines. Four of them landed near Amagansett, Long Island, N.Y., and the other four landed near Jacksonville, Fla. They were apprehended by the FBI, and after trial before a military tribunal, six received death sentences and the other two were sentenced to life and 30 years, respectively.

During the fiscal year 1943, 10,294 convictions resulted from FBI investigative activity with sentences imposed totalling 7 death, 3 life, 24,624 years, 3 months and 6 days. These figures indicate a marked increase over those of the preceding fiscal year. Of the cases investigated by the FBI which were brought to trial, convictions were obtained in 95.8% of these cases.

During the year 8,367 federal fugitives from justice were located by special agents of the FBI. A total of 11,976 fugitives were located for state, county and municipal law enforcement agencies when their fingerprints were sought through the files of the identification division of the FBI. Fines imposed, savings effected and recoveries resulting from the bureau's work during the fiscal year totalled $29,229,750.91.

Espionage.—There were 28 convictions during the fiscal year for espionage or for failure to register as foreign agents, with the imposition of sentences totalling 255 years.

The counterespionage program of the FBI brought enemy espionage within the United States under control. Liaison established with United Nations intelligence agencies resulted in co-operation on security matters. As a result of work done over the years it was possible in many instances to render negative many enemy agents before they were even able to start their particular assignments.

Sabotage.—During the fiscal year 90 convictions resulted from prosecutions in federal courts in sabotage cases investigated by the FBI. Sentences imposed totalled 6 death, 1 life, 287 years and 6 months, with fines of $31,004. Savings and recoveries in these cases realized $174,940.62.

Although there was a substantial increase in the number of cases of suspected sabotage reported during 1943, there was no evidence of any foreign-directed acts of destruction. In almost all instances the sabotage was committed by individuals acting on their own initiative because of maliciousness, spite or as a prank.

From the inception of the emergency until the end of the fiscal year 1943, a total of 10,371 cases of suspected sabotage were investigated by the FBI. Technical sabotage in some form was found in 943 instances and 466 convictions resulted from prosecutions in state and federal courts. Sentences totalled 6 death, 1 life, 1,051 years, 8 months and 16 days, while fines, savings and recoveries amounted to $216,969.62.

FBI Laboratory.—Closely related to espionage, sabotage and other security matters is the work of the FBI technical laboratory, since many investigations depend a great deal upon the results obtained in the technical laboratory for a successful conclusion of the case. The achievements of the FBI laboratory for the fiscal year ending June 30, 1943, far surpassed those of any prior year. A total of 193,371 examinations involving 247,886 individual specimens of evidence were conducted by laboratory technicians as compared with 51,475 examinations during 1942 and 14,589 during 1941.

A great portion of the year's activities was directly concerned with the war effort.

Female technicians came into their own during 1943 in the FBI laboratory as a result of the extreme shortage of male personnel and the necessity of placing every possible male agent in the investigative field. It was necessary to train women in practically every phase of the FBI laboratory's work. Women were found to be particularly adept in document examinations, cryptographic work, photography and spectrographic analyses.

Assistance was rendered to other agencies of the federal government in 532 instances, and the technicians aided state, county and municipal law enforcement agencies in 982 cases. This particular aspect of the FBI's work is made as a co-operative gesture, and all of the work done for other agencies in the laboratory is performed free of charge. FBI technicians testify in state, county and local courts throughout the entire nation each year.

As the fiscal year 1943 ended a total of 14,432 enemy aliens had been apprehended since the outbreak of the war on Dec. 7, 1941, consisting of 5,234 Japanese, 5,685 Germans, 3,490 Italians, 11 Hungarians, 11 Rumanians and 1 Bulgarian. Those not immediately released were held for hearings before the enemy alien hearing board, which makes recommendations to the attorney general as to whether the alien should be interned, released or parolled. With reference to the 14,432 enemy aliens arrested from Dec. 7, 1941, to June 30, 1943, 4,150 were released after submitting convincing proof of their patriotism and explaining their suspicious activities to the satisfaction of the United States attorneys or to the various enemy alien hearing boards; 5,833 were interned; 3,869 parolled; 42 were repatriated; 22 had died; and 516 cases were pending.

Large amounts of prohibited material were seized in searches of the homes of enemy aliens. From the outbreak of the war until the end of the fiscal year, 24,662 premises of enemy aliens were searched for contraband materials by the FBI and co-operating local law enforcement agencies. Some of the items seized were as follows: 4,401 guns of various types, 303,547 rounds of ammunition, 3,125 short-wave radio receiving sets, 15 short-wave radio transmitting sets, 874 other signalling devices, 4,048 cameras, 2,320 sticks of dynamite, 2,828 dynamite caps and 3,787 ft. of dynamite fuse.

Sedition.—During 1943 there were 29 convictions under the sedition statutes, with sentences aggregating 146 years and 1 day. Fines imposed amounted to $17,250. A total of 1,094 cases were investigated by the FBI and as the year ended, 42 individuals and 1 corporation were under indictment awaiting trial.

Selective Training and Service Act.—In the enforcement of the criminal provisions of the Selective Training and Service act the FBI meticulously avoided the policy of making mass arrests and "slacker raids." Each case submitted to the FBI was handled individually, and a substantial portion of the investigations were terminated when compliance with the law was secured. A total of 204,519 cases were closed in matters involving reported violations of the Selective Training and Service act. Convictions for the fiscal year 1943 totalled 3,071, while sentences aggregated 7,542 years, 2 months and 29 days. In addition, fines amounting to $478,001.04 were imposed. Since Oct. 16, 1940, the first registration date, a total of 4,380 convictions have resulted from investigations made by the FBI.

War Frauds.—With the rapidly rising war production a marked increase in the number of cases involving war frauds of various types was noted. Continuous and preferred attention was afforded investigations of this type by the FBI. There were 66 convictions during the year, with sentences of 93 years, 8 months and 2 days and fines, savings and recoveries amounting to $164,484.45. Numerous prosecutions were pending on June 30, 1943.

In the year ending June 30, 1943, the FBI's personnel continued to expand to meet the ever-increasing responsibilities brought on by the war. A total of 390,805 national security matters were reported to the FBI for investigative attention during the fiscal period as compared with 218,734 during the year 1942, 68,368 during 1941, 16,885 during 1940, 1,651 during 1939 and 250 during 1938.

At the request of the war and navy departments special inquiries concerning the loyalty of designated aliens employed on war contracts were conducted by the FBI, and although the responsibility for these inquiries was transferred to the office of the provost marshal general of the war department, name searches on aliens employed on war contracts were being made at the request of the war and navy departments. During the fiscal year 77,472 searches of this type were made through the FBI files.

Federal Bank Robbery Act.—Sixty-one fugitive bank robbers were located, among them several sought for many years. There were 92 convictions in federal courts for bank robbery, larceny and burglary, resulting in total sentences of 725 years, 2 months and 10 days.

From the passage of the Federal Bank Robbery act in 1934 to June 30, 1943, there were 970 bank robberies coming within the jurisdiction of the FBI. Convictions in federal courts totalled 699, with sentences imposed consisting of 2 death, 14 life, 11,384 years, 3 months and 24 days, with fines and recoveries amounting to $351,100.08. Four bank bandits were killed resisting arrest, 3 committed suicide and 1 was adjudged insane. As a result of the FBI's activity in this field, bank robbery declined more than 92% since the peak year 1932.

Extortion.—From the passage of the Federal Extortion act on July 8, 1932, to June 30, 1943, 890 convictions in federal courts resulted from investigations of this character. Sentences totalled 3,775 years, 5 months and 5 days. In addition, 4 extortioners were killed during that period while resisting arrest, 2 others committed suicide and 33 were found insane.

In the fiscal year 1943, there were 71 convictions from prosecutions in federal courts, with sentences totalling 218 years, 10 months and 10 days. Fines of $2,430 were imposed and 22 fugitives from justice were located.

Kidnapping.—During the fiscal year 1943, 29 kidnapping cases occurred and all of these were solved. Forty-seven convictions were obtained as a result of the work of the FBI, with sentences totalling 461 years, 10 months and 3 days. Thirty-four fugitives sought for this violation were located during the year.

From the passage of the Federal Kidnapping act on June 22, 1932, to the close of the fiscal year June 30, 1943, 254 cases of kidnapping and conspiracy to kidnap were investigated by the FBI. Of these, 252 were solved and the remaining two were still under the act of investigation as the year ended. There were 496 convictions in federal and state courts, with sentences of 5,482 years, 6 months and 20 days, and fines of $34,270.80. In addition, there were 12 death sentences and 44 life sentences. Eight kidnappers were killed during this period while resisting arrest, 7 were murdered by other gang members, 9 committed suicide, 2 were lynched and 1 was declared insane.

Illegal Wearing of Uniform.—Violations of this type increased manyfold during 1943, and 428 convictions with sentences of 385 years, 6 months and 2 days resulted from the investigative efforts of the FBI. Fines of $5,020 were imposed.

National Bank and Federal Reserve Acts.—During the fiscal year 1943, irregularities in national banks, member banks of the federal reserve system and banks insured by the Federal Deposit Insurance corporation exceeding $3,700,000 were reported to the FBI for investigation. A total of 16,924 banks, or 94% of all banking institutions, were covered by the FBI's jurisdiction. Two hundred and twenty-two convictions resulted from prosecutions in federal courts. Sentences imposed totalled 781 years, 8 months and 2 days, while fines and recoveries amounted to $334,514.95. Twenty-six fugitives from justice were located in connection with this particular type of violation.

National Bankruptcy Act.—Twenty-four fugitives from justice were located in cases of this type during the year 1943, while prosecutions for violations of this act resulted in 72 convictions. Sentences totalled 135 years, 9 months and 21 days, while fines of $23,862.79 were imposed and concealed assets valued at $108,894.59 were recovered through investigative activity.

National Motor Vehicle Theft Act.—Since the enactment of this law in 1919 making it a federal offense to transport a stolen vehicle in interstate commerce, 72,106 motor vehicles valued at more than $40,000,000 have been recovered in cases investigated by the FBI through June 30, 1943. During the fiscal year 1943, 5,717 stolen motor vehicles valued at $3,227,-120.83 were recovered in cases involving violations of this statute. A total of 2,171 convictions resulted from prosecutions in federal courts, with sentences aggregating 6,410 years, 3 months and 27 days. Fines amounting to $8,671.02 were imposed and 745 fugitives from justice were located.

National Stolen Property Act.—Fifty-three convictions resulted during 1943 in cases involving violations of this statute, which prohibits the interstate transportation of property or money valued at more than $5,000 which has been stolen, embezzled or otherwise taken feloniously. Sentences imposed totalled 261 years, 10 months and 2 days, while fines, savings and recoveries amounted to $25,385. Seventy-three fugitives from justice were located.

Theft, Embezzlement and Illegal Possession of Government Property.—A total of 634 convictions resulted from prosecutions in federal courts during the year 1943. In violations of this type sentences totalled 1,139 years, 2 months and 9 days, while fines, savings and recoveries amounted to $67,099.47. Eighty fugitives from justice were located.

White Slave Traffic Act.—The fiscal year 1943 witnessed a rather substantial increase in convictions under this law, there being 533 successful prosecutions as compared with 384 during the preceding fiscal period. Sentences imposed during the year ending June 30, 1943, totalled 1,510 years, 4 months and 23 days, while fines amounted to $94,252.01. Two hundred $67,099.47. Eighty fugitives from justice were located.

Identification Division.—The fiscal year 1943 witnessed the greatest growth of the identification division in its history, and during this period of time this division rendered its greatest service to law enforcement agencies, the armed services, war industries, other government organizations and law-abiding citizens. The identification of mangled bodies in aeroplane crashes, drowned seamen washed ashore and victims of other catastrophes demonstrated the infallibility of fingerprinting as a means of identification.

At the end of the fiscal year June 30, 1943, there were 69,644,540 fingerprint cards on file in the FBI's identification division, an increase of 26,770,462 over the total in file on June 30, 1942. During the year an average of 93,540 sets of fingerprint cards were received each day, and this rapid expansion of the FBI fingerprint files made it necessary to transfer the entire identification division from the department of justice building to larger quarters in the National Guard armory in Washington, D.C.

The value of the civil section of the identification division to law-abiding citizens was increasingly recognized during the year. As of June 30, 1943, 4,943,645 personal identification cards were on file, an increase of 1,819,374 over the total on file one year before.

The record number of 11,976 fugitives was identified during the year by searching incoming arrest cards through the fingerprint files. As the year ended, wanted notices on 58,114 fugitives, including 8,691 parole violators and 1,030 probation violators, were posted in the fingerprint files of the identification division.

More than 20,000,000 fingerprint cards representing applicants in war industries were submitted during the fiscal year. The percentage of identifications of this type of fingerprint card was 5.35, and criminal records located were made available only to the armed services. In many instances individuals seeking positions of trust and responsibility were identified with prior criminal activity making them unfit for the places sought.

Despite the war 42 foreign countries and territorial possessions of the United States co-operated in the international exchange of fingerprint cards in the fiscal year 1943. A total of 1,325 fingerprint cards was transmitted to other countries in international exchange and these resulted in 125 identifications by the end of the fiscal year. A total of 177,326 sets of fingerprints was submitted to the FBI during this period; of these, 15,751 were identified through the files of the FBI.

National Police Academy.—Three sessions of the FBI National Police academy were held during the year and 113 police officers from various parts of the country and Canada were added to the list of graduates, totalling 740 at the end of 1943.

Uniform Crime Reporting.—Monthly crime reports received during the calendar years of 1941 and 1942 from the police in over 2,100 cities having a combined population exceeding 65,000,000 made possible the preparation of various crime statistics which are of inestimable value to law enforcement agencies and public officials throughout the United States.

Juvenile Delinquency.—These statistics reflected that significant and substantial increases were registered in the field of juvenile delinquency during the year, and arrests of girls under voting age increased from 9,675 in 1941 to 15,068 in 1942, or 55.7%. Arrests of girls under 21 for prostitution and commercialized vice showed a 64.8% increase, while for other sex offenses during the same period there was an upswing of 104.7%. Arrests for vagrancy increased 124.3%, while drunkenness and disorderly conduct registered increases of 39.9% and 69.6% respectively. These figures are based on the calendar year 1942 in comparison with the calendar year 1941.

Arrests for rape increased 10.6%, while disorderly conduct and drunkenness among boys under 21 increased 26.2% and 30.3% respectively, according to the arrest records of the calendar year 1942 over those arrested during the calendar year 1941. (See also CHILD WELFARE; CRIME; KIDNAPPING; POLICE; SECRET SERVICE.)　　　　(J. E. H.)

Federal Communications Commission. The agency of the United States government charged with regulation of interstate communications by wire and radio devoted an increasing proportion of its time during 1943 to communications problems arising out of war.

At the end of 1943 the FCC's Foreign Broadcast Intelligence service—which was set up to monitor foreign broadcasts and relay significant items to government war agencies as an aid in countering enemy propaganda and mapping foreign policy—was surveying 2,500,000 words a day of foreign broadcast material in 35 languages and dialects. Co-operative arrangements were completed with the Office of War Information, British Ministry of Information, British Broadcasting corporation and listening posts of other friendly nations for coverage and transmission to FBIS of broadcasts not well heard in the United States.

An important war service was performed by the Radio Intelligence division in maintaining a round-the-clock patrol of the spectrum to guard against illegal or enemy radio transmissions, trace sources of interference to military and commercial radio broadcasts, and through radio direction-finding equipment assist ships and planes in distress. RID investigated 3,960 cases of illegal radio operation during the fiscal year 1942-43.

To conserve broadcast equipment without impairing quality of service, the FCC in Nov. 1942 required readjustments of broadcast transmitters, decreasing radiated power by one decibel. A voluntary reduction in time of operation of standard broadcast station from 12 hr., in the case of unlimited time stations, to 6 hr. a day was authorized. In Aug. 1943, the commission announced it would authorize civilian construction involving the use of idle equipment to increase power of 100-watt local channel standard broadcast stations to 250 watts and for new local channel stations in communities where no station was located (excluding communities within metropolitan areas with radio service). Multiple ownership of standard broadcast stations serving substantially the same area was banned (Nov. 1943) and in December the licence periods of standard stations were extended from two to three years, maximum statutory limit.

The largest telephone rate investigation of the year ended Jan. 1943 when the FCC announced that the American Telephone & Telegraph Co. Long Lines department had agreed to overall rate reductions to the public (in overtime charges on toll calls, and in rates charged for private line telephone and telegraph and radio program transmission) totalling about $34,700,000 annually.

Another important development was the merger of Western Union and Postal Telegraph, Inc., the two major domestic competing telegraph carriers—authorized in permissive legislation by congress in March 1943 and approved by the FCC Sept. 27, 1943.

The supreme court handed down two significant decisions in the radio field: *National Broadcasting Company* v. *United States* and the *Columbia Broadcasting System* v. *United States*, both of which were decided in favour of the FCC (May 10, 1943) and its chain broadcasting regulations, designed to foster competition in network broadcasting and expand the listening opportunities of radio audiences. In *Federal Communications Commission* v.

National Broadcasting Company (KOA) the supreme court (May 17, 1943) affirmed the district court of appeals' decision favouring KOA, holding that a Class I radio station has a right to intervene in proceedings on an application which involves the nighttime operation of another station on the channel already occupied by the Class I licensee.

During the year two bills were introduced, one in the senate (S. 814) and one in the house (H.R. 1490) to amend the Communications act of 1934, under which the FCC was established. Hearings on the senate bill were held in Nov. and Dec. 1943.

No hearings had been called on the house bill at the end of the year.

Members of the commission in 1943 were James Lawrence Fly, chairman; Paul A. Walker, Norman S. Case, T. A. M. Craven, Ray C. Wakefield and Clifford J. Durr. There was one vacancy. (*See* also RADIO; WAR COMMUNICATIONS, BOARD OF.)

(J. L. FY.)

Federal Council of the Churches of Christ in America.

In 1943 the council consisted of 25 national denominations. The member denominations included most of the major Protestant bodies and two churches of the eastern Catholic group (the Syrian Orthodox and the Ukrainian Orthodox).

The total membership of the constituent denominations in 1943 was 25,551,560 with local congregations of more than 140,000.

Through the general commission on army and navy chaplains the recruiting of Protestant ministers for religious work in the army and navy was carried on. The chairman of the commission, Dr. William B. Pugh, made a visitation to the chaplains in all the overseas theatres of military operations. Through the Christian commission for camp and defense communities guidance was given to local churches facing new responsibilities because of their proximity to camps or wartime communities. A program for securing the co-operation of local churches in the resettlement of Japanese Americans as they were released from the government camps was developed to the point at which assistance had been given in the relocation of 17,000. The committee on foreign relief appeals continued its work in co-ordinating the work of the churches in securing support for refugees, prisoners of war, China relief, missionaries cut off from their normal bases of support and other wartime works of mercy. A new committee on overseas relief and reconstruction began plans for assistance to European churches after the war.

The commission on a just and durable peace promulgated a platform for postwar reconstruction known as "Six Pillars of Peace."

The commission also conducted regional conferences in 100 different cities in the month of November. A new commission on the church and minority peoples began its work of making a co-operative approach to racial problems in the light of the experience of the war.

A plan for uniting the federal council and seven interdenominational agencies working in more specialized fields, such as the Foreign Missions Conference of North America and the Home Missions Council of North America, was carried further toward completion.

The council continued its work in the fields of evangelism, worship, family life and social service. A major feature was the holding of "Christian Missions," each a week in duration, in military and naval camps.

Ten religious programs over national radio networks were presented each week throughout the year. The *Federal Council Bulletin* (monthly) and *Information Service* (weekly) continued

to be published.

(S. McC. C.)

Federal Deposit Insurance Corporation.

During the year 1943 the beneficial effects of the protection and influence of the Federal Deposit Insurance corporation, with regard to banking institutions as well as depositors, continued to be manifested in ever-growing soundness of banking in general and also in vast increases in savings by the people.

Capital and surplus of the insurance corporation increased about $100,000,000 during 1943, standing at $700,000,000 at the end of the year, or nearly two and one-half times the amount of capital available at the beginning of its operations in 1933. During 1943 only five insured banks were closed or merged with financial assistance from FDIC, affecting about 50,000 depositors with total deposits of less than $10,000,000. This was the smallest number of bank closings recorded in any calendar year during the ten years of FDIC operation.

Outlays in 1943 on account of banks in difficulties were $7,000,000, about 80% of which was recoverable.

Fewer than one-fifth of 1% of depositors in participating banks held accounts in excess of $5,000, the maximum amount fully covered by federal insurance. As of Dec. 31, 1943, deposits of insured banks amounted to $113,000,000,000 and their total assets were $122,000,000,000. Three-fourths of the assets were in United States government obligations, cash, and balance with other banks included in the federal reserve system. Of the remaining assets, only 5% were criticized in 1943 by federal bank examiners. Assessments during the year exceeded $70,000,000, and income from investments approximated $14,000,000.

The only legislation in 1943 directly affecting FDIC was an act passed April 13, permitting the deduction of war loan accounts from total deposit liabilities in calculating the base for FDIC assessments. (*See* also BANKING.)

(C. A. SR.)

Federal Home Loan Bank: *see* NATIONAL HOUSING AGENCY.
Federal Housing Administration: *see* NATIONAL HOUSING AGENCY.

Federal Land Banks: *see* FARM CREDIT ADMINISTRATION.

Federal Power Commission.

The most important of the court cases in 1943 was the decision of the supreme court of the United States in the case of *Federal Power Commission* v. *Hope Natural Gas Company*, upholding an order of the commission for a reduction in rates based upon the "actual legitimate cost" of, or "prudent investment" in, the company's property as a rate base. This decision taken in conjunction with the previous opinion in the case of *Federal Power Commission* v. *Natural Gas Pipeline Company* was generally considered to inaugurate a new era in public utility rate making for both federal and state regulatory authorities, by establishing "actual legitimate cost" or "prudent investment" as a basis for rate making and discarding the so-called "fair value" rule of *Smyth* v. *Ames* (decided in 1898) which prescribed a complex set of factors, including "reproduction cost," for determination of a rate base.

Other notable court cases sustaining the commission included the decision upholding the commission's determination of the actual legitimate original cost of the Niagara Falls Power company project 16, located near Niagara Falls, N.Y., as $27,910,538.73, disallowing claimed project costs amounting to $16,543,329.95. This, beside deciding important questions relative to the commission's authority, marked the end of a controversy covering a period of 20 years. In a series of decisions during the year the courts also upheld other orders of the commission determining the actual legitimate original cost of other projects licensed under part I of the Federal Power act and the charging off of write-ups and other inflationary items.

The courts also upheld similar action of the commission in reclassifying the accounts of public utilities under part II of the Federal Power act and of natural gas companies under the Natural Gas act, sustaining comprehensive authority in the commission over the accounts of public utilities and natural gas companies.

The war activities of the commission during 1943 included continued co-operation with the War Production board in the handling of power and gas problems relating to the war; the collection and analysis of power statistics related to the war for all federal agencies; supervision of a nation-wide electric and gas plant protection program in co-operation with the war department; the negotiation, in co-operation with federal procurement agencies, of war power contracts with a view to assuring government a supply of power for its war activities at reasonable rates; and the ordering of temporary emergency interconnections for war purposes. The commission in 1943 also passed upon applications for certificates of public convenience and necessity for a wide range of additional natural gas pipe line facilities used in war production, both major long-distance pipe lines and shorter connections. The largest natural gas pipe line authorized by the commission was planned to extend approximately 1,200 mi. from Texas to West Virginia. Another natural gas pipe line of major importance, authorized by the commission, was to extend a distance of 237 mi. from Oklahoma to the mid-continent area.

The commission also was active in rate cases, particularly natural gas cases, and by the end of 1943 had ordered rate reductions aggregating nearly $35,000,000 per year in wholesale rates. Nearly $10,000,000 in rate reductions for natural gas were effected without formal hearings, following conferences with company representatives, and, in some cases, without either hearing or field investigation.   (L. O.)

Federal Public Housing Authority: *see* NATIONAL HOUSING AGENCY.

Federal Reserve System.
The burden of expediting the financing of war activities not only of the United States but to a considerable degree those of allied nations—and at the same time maintaining a stiff resistance to the inflationary repercussions of such prodigal expenditures as incurred in total war—taxed the resourcefulness of the federal reserve system of the United States in 1943. The inflationary potential was apparent in the fact that the monetary cost of the United Nations' war effort to the end of 1943, estimated at $450,-000,000,000, was more than three times the total amount spent by the Allied powers during the entire World War I. Nevertheless, the restrictive measures enforced in the United States kept the nation's economy on a fairly even keel.

In an effort to reduce the proportion of new federal debt absorbed by the banking system, and thereby relieve the inflationary pressure exerted by bank deposits created by holdings of government securities, sales to commercial banks were limited to $5,000,000,000 in the Second War Loan drive of April 1943, and to $3,200,000,000 after the conclusion of the Third War Loan drive in October. During the year the banking system absorbed approximately 45% of the total increase in the interest-bearing and guaranteed debt of the United States, this increase amounting to nearly $60,000,000,000. This was regarded as a more favourable showing than in 1942, when the banks purchased one-half of all new government obligations.

The federal reserve system aided the treasury in its efforts to borrow directly from the people the largest possible sums of money, but since it continued to be necessary also to borrow from the banks, the system took further steps to assure adequate reserves to permit bank purchases of all securities not sold elsewhere. This was accomplished through purchases by the reserve banks in the open market and directly from banks short of reserves, at a rate of $\frac{3}{8}$ of 1%, with a repurchase option available to sellers, in continuation of a policy formulated in 1942 by the Federal Open Market committee. Federal reserve banks increased their holdings of government securities in 1943 by approximately $5,000,000,000, mostly in relatively short-term issues. Bank holdings of long-term securities declined. Also instrumental in maintaining excess reserves was an amendment in April to the Federal Reserve act, suspending the requirement that member banks hold reserves against treasury balances arising as a result of subscriptions for government securities.

Under operation of Reserve Board Regulation V, issued in 1942 to permit the war and navy departments and maritime commission to guarantee loans made to expedite war production, total V loans outstanding on Sept. 30, 1943, amounted to $1,708,000,000, of which $1,413,000,000 was guaranteed. A broadened program for granting VT loans was announced in September, designed to provide contractors additional funds as a means of freeing their working capital invested in war production in the event of contract terminations.

Bank deposits in the United States reached a total of approximately $105,000,000,000 by the end of 1943, compared with $85,-800,000,000 on Dec. 31, 1942. While a large portion of the accumulation of demand deposits was in business holdings, the bulk was in cash holdings of individuals, who held the major portion of currency outside the banks and the $32,000,000,000 of time deposits in commercial and savings banks. The alarming increase in currency in circulation that had characterized the two or three years preceding 1943 continued at a rate that brought the total to more than $20,000,000,000 by the end of the year, compared with $11,200,000,000 on Dec. 31, 1941. With national income, employment and industrial production at all-time high levels, it was regarded as probable that a large portion of the increase in money in circulation was attributable to the rapidly expanding wage and salary payments and other transaction needs. The existence of currency "hoarding" was conceded, however, as a natural concomitant of vastly larger incomes of the lower and middle-income groups, which are historically not inclined to patronize banks. Other contributing factors to the preference for currency over deposits were believed to be wartime population shifts and bank service charges.

Due to the policy of regulating consumer credit, the total amount of such credit outstanding in the second half of 1943 was $4,750,000,000, about one-half the peak of $9,500,000,000 outstanding in 1941.

Steadily rising currency demands and an increasing tendency on the part of banks to invest their reserves more fully, were influential factors in the continued decline of excess reserves of member banks. From a peak of $7,000,000,000 at the beginning of 1941, excess reserves declined to about $2,000,000,000 by the first of 1943, and in the later months of the year were hovering around $1,000,000,000. Also contributing to the decrease in excess bank reserves was the $700,000,000 decline early in 1943 in the monetary gold stock, which had remained steady at $22,750,000,-000 since 1941. As in 1942, the heaviest drains on bank reserves were felt in New York, where the treasury continued to raise more funds by borrowing and taxes than it spent, resulting in a net outflow to other parts of the country.

Commercial loans, which had continued their 1942 decline through the first half of 1943, rose rapidly in the autumn and regained about one-half their losses of the previous year. Loans for purchasing and carrying securities increased slightly in 1943.

The board of governors in 1943 was composed of Marriner S. Eccles, chairman; Ronald Ransom, vice-chairman; M. S. Szymczak, John K. McKee, Ernest G. Draper and R. M. Evans. (*See* also BANKING; CONSUMER CREDIT.)

Federal Savings and Loan Insurance Corporation: *see* NATIONAL HOUSING AGENCY.

Federal Security Agency.

The purpose of the U.S. Federal Security agency, as stated in the authorization under which it was established in 1939, is "to promote social and economic security, educational opportunity and the health of the citizens of the Nation." To that end, and in the interests of efficient and effective public service, it administers a broad range of related programs in these fields. Its constituent units are: the Social Security board, the public health service, the Food and Drug administration, the office of education, the office of vocational rehabilitation and St. Elizabeth's hospital. The Civilian Conservation corps and the National Youth administration, two former units whose activities were terminated by congressional action, were under liquidation during the year 1943 and their facilities transferred to other war agencies, particularly the war department. The Federal Security agency also represents the federal government's interest in Howard university, the Columbia Institution for the Deaf and the American Printing House for the Blind.

Over-all correlation of activities and programs throughout the agency is carried on through the office of the administrator, which includes, in addition to the administrative officers, a committee on physical fitness and the office of community war services.

The agency and its constituent units, during the year 1943, carried on many activities arising from and directly connected with the war, along with their continuing responsibilities. The public health service carried on special health protection, disease control and research programs directed toward maintaining conditions conducive to health for the armed forces and civilian workers.

The office of education helped the educational institutions and groups of the country adapt their programs to war needs. It administered the training of thousands for jobs in war industry and assisted the war and navy departments in setting up training courses for the military services.

War production greatly increased the number of persons in jobs covered under the Social Security act, both for old-age and survivors insurance and unemployment compensation. For the same reason, the number of persons on state-federal public assistance rolls decreased. In addition to these continuing programs, the Social Security board was responsible for administering emergency programs for civilian war benefits, civilian war assistance and aid to enemy aliens and others affected by restrictive government action.

The Food and Drug administration intensified its efforts to maintain the integrity of the nation's food and drug supply in the face of wartime factors, such as rapidly increased production, restriction of transportation and shortage of materials and skilled employees, which endanger this supply. At the request of the military services, food and drugs purchased for the U.S. armed forces and for the Allies also were inspected and tested by the Food and Drug administration.

An office of vocational rehabilitation was created to discharge the federal responsibility in connection with the vocational rehabilitation amendments of 1943. These amendments provided the necessary framework within which a peacetime as well as a wartime program of rehabilitation would be administered. The scope of services available to disabled persons under this federal-state program was broadened to include any services necessary to render them capable of engaging in remunerative employment or to render them more advantageously employable. Sole responsibility for the administration, supervision and control of this program rested with the state boards of vocational education. Responsibility for certification of federal funds and establishing standards rested with the Federal Security agency.

The office of community war services operated as the war arm of the Federal Security agency. Because of the close relationship between the emergency needs for health, welfare, recreation, education and related services and the continuing programs of the Federal Security agency this office was given the task of bringing into common action the services of interested federal-state and local public and private agencies, to help states and communities meet these needs. For recreation, social protection and, during a limited period, for services to children of working mothers, fields where national war programs were needed, the office of community war services assumed direct responsibility. Through these programs it helped hard-pressed communities in war areas to develop effective local services.   (P. V. M.)

Federal Trade Commission.

The Federal Trade commission in 1943 conducted numerous special investigations and studies in support of the U.S. war effort as well as administering the laws under its jurisdiction, namely, the Federal Trade Commission act, certain sections of the Clayton act, the Wool Products Labeling act, and the Export Trade act.

Designated by the War Production board to investigate compliance by industries with the board's orders relative to the allocation of the supply and the priorities of delivery of critical war materials, the commission conducted such inquiries in the glycerine, capital equipment, electric lamp, electric fuse, silverware, costume jewellery, cotton textile, and paint, varnish and lacquer industries.

Other investigations undertaken for government war agencies, including the Office of Price Administration and the Office of Economic Stabilization, related to (1) costs, prices and profits in the bread-baking, flour-milling, biscuit and cracker, steel-producing and fertilizer industries; (2) methods and costs of distributing principal consumer commodities, including food, wearing apparel, carpets, building materials, petroleum products, automobiles, tires and tubes and electrical household appliances; and (3) 1940 financial operations of 86 industrial corporation groups. The reports on studies of costs, prices and profits provided the government with factual background for its price stabilization functions.

In connection with its work of surveying radio and periodical advertising, the commission analyzed for and reported to various war agencies such advertisements as contained pertinent references to war production, price rises and trends, rationing, priorities and other war-related subjects. Advertisements found to contain possible violations of the Office of Censorship's wartime codes of practices for the press and radio were transferred to that agency for appropriate action.

During the year the commission issued 224 formal complaints alleging violations of the laws administered by it, entered 132 orders to cease and desist from such violations, and accepted 279 stipulations to discontinue unlawful practices. These legal proceedings were directed to promoting free and fair competition in interstate trade in the interest of the public through the prevention of price-fixing agreements, restraint-of-trade combinations, boycotts, unlawful price discriminations, and other unfair methods of competition and unfair or deceptive acts or practices, and to safeguarding the health of the consuming public by preventing the dissemination of false advertisements of food, drugs, devices and cosmetics which might be injurious to health.

The commission also administered fair trade practice rules for more than 150 industries. (G. S. F.)

Federal Works Agency.
In 1943 virtually all activities of the Federal Works agency and its constituent administrations, including the Public Roads administration and the Public Buildings administration, were devoted to the war effort.

Communities which had experienced abnormal population increases because of war activities and which were financially unable to meet the exigencies thus created, were assisted in building, and in some instances in maintaining and operating, such facilities as schools, hospitals, water systems and sewage disposal systems, and in providing additional police and fire protection. War nurseries and child care centres were established in cooperation with local agencies for the care of children of working mothers. Recreation centres were provided for servicemen. Roads were constructed where necessary to the war effort.

As of June 30, 1943, the president had approved 2,480 construction projects with an estimated cost of $322,770,915, under Title II of the Lanham act. Contracts had been awarded for 2,049 projects, construction had been substantially completed on 1,339, and 1,262 were entirely completed. As of the same date 1,027 war public service projects had been initiated to cost $25,463,574. On Nov. 24, 1943, approximately 58,000 children of working mothers were enrolled in 1,915 war nurseries and child care centres operated with Federal Works agency assistance.

The Public Roads administration completed, at a cost of $274,701,799 (of which 72% was furnished by the government), 8,445 mi. of highways of all classes and eliminated 187 highway-railroad grade crossings. The road mileage completed included 2,836 mi. of access roads to war industries and military and naval establishments. Practically all the projects completed were urgently needed in the war effort in 1943. The administration continued its part of the construction of the Alaska highway and of the Inter-American highway. More than a score of flight strips were completed to provide emergency landing and take-off facilities for military aircraft.

The Public Buildings administration, under assignment from the Federal Public Housing authority, erected and managed 16 buildings at four separate residence hall projects in or near the District of Columbia, having accommodations for 9,000 women employees of the federal government and personnel of the WAVES. The administration also handled the maintenance, repair, alteration, improvement and preservation of more than 3,500 buildings throughout the United States; directed wartime emergency measures to protect government buildings and other property against sabotage and enemy attack; and handled the decentralization of numerous government agencies from crowded Washington to other cities.

The Work Projects administration, which since its establishment in 1935 had provided jobs for more than 8,500,000 citizens, passed out of existence June 30, 1943, under an executive order issued Dec. 4, 1942. Projects throughout the country were terminated as quickly as possible and there reverted to the treasury in excess of $106,000,000 of WPA's final appropriation. Details of liquidation carrying over after June 30 were left to FWA.

The Public Works administration proceeded with its liquidation under the direction of the Federal Works administrator. Grand River dam, in Oklahoma, completed as a PWA project, was transferred by executive order to the jurisdiction of the secretary of the interior. (*See also* NATIONAL HOUSING AGENCY.) (P. B. F.)

Federated Malay States.
One of the three principal administrative divisions of British Malaya, the other two being the Straits Settlements and the Unfederated Malay States (*qq.v.*). There are four of the Federated States—Perak, Selangor, Negri Sembilan and Pahang, of which the first three are on the west coast of the Malay peninsula, while Pahang is on the east coast. Area, 27,540 sq.mi.; pop. (est. 1941) 2,193,605, distributed as follows: Perak, 984,464; Selangor, 696,173; Negri Sembilan, 293,510; Pahang, 219,458. The capital and largest city is Kuala Lumpur (Selangor), pop. (1939) 138,425. Racially the population was divided as follows (est. 1941): Europeans, 11,019; Eurasians, 5,226; Malays, 713,679; Chinese, 978,208; Indians, 468,029; others, 17,444.

Before the Japanese occupation in 1941–42 the nominal ruler of each state was a native sultan, who received political advice from a British resident, himself under the authority of the high commissioner, who was also governor of the Straits Settlements. This joint office, until the Japanese invasion, was held by Sir Thomas Shenton Whitelegge Thomas (appointed in 1934). Information about conditions in the states after the Japanese occupation was scanty; but it seems that the sultans remained in their old capacity as nominal rulers, taking "advice" from Japanese military officers. Malaya was included in the Japanese idea of "Greater East Asia" and was combed for raw materials useful to the Japanese war effort, notably rubber, tin and iron.

Education.—Expenditure on education in 1940 was £437,796. There were 35 English schools for boys (13,564 pupils) and 14 English schools for girls (5,941 pupils). There were 582 Malay schools (63,638 pupils) and 572 Chinese schools (58,227 pupils). There were 580 schools in Tamil (the Indian dialect spoken by many Indians in Malaya), with 23,527 pupils.

Finance.—Revenue in 1940 was £11,493,060, expenditure was £9,166,303. Public debt at the end of 1940 was £9,950,000.

Agriculture and Mineral Production.—Rubber and tin are the most important products of the Federated Malay States. There were 1,699,459 ac. of rubber plantations in 1940, 251,960 ac. in coco-nut groves, 186,310 ac. in rice-paddies, 40,629 ac. of oil-bearing palms. Mineral production in that year was as follows: tin 35,689 tons; gold 81,633 oz.; tungsten 90 tons; coal 781,508 tons. There were 90,145 miners, mostly Chinese, while the labourers on rubber plantations were mostly Indians. (*See* also JAPAN.) (W. H. CH.)

Federation of Labor, American: *see* AMERICAN FEDERATION OF LABOR.

Feldspar.
Sales of feldspar in the United States declined from 338,860 long tons in 1941 to 307,823 tons in 1942, largely because of decreased use in enamel and porcelain coatings on steel. Consumption in plate glass declined, but this was more than offset by increased demand for glass containers. Canadian production was 20,288 short tons in 1942, as compared with 26,040 tons in 1941. Production through August 1943 was 15% of the same period of 1942. (G. A. Ro.)

Fencing.
In spite of a greatly curtailed schedule in all sections of the United States most of the older established fencing groups carried on with better than average results. The National Collegiate A.A. championships and the Mid-West Division championships of the Amateur Fencers League of America were omitted in 1943. Much emphasis was placed on the national championships. In the foil Warren Dow of the New York Athletic club again placed first with Alfred Snyder (Salle Santelli) and Robert Kaplan (N.Y. university) second and third respectively. In the épée Robert Driscoll (Fencers' club), Greg-

CONTESTANTS practising for the 50th annual Intercollegiate Fencing Association championships in New York city in March 1943

ory Flynn (Michigan division) and August von Munchhausen (Saltus club) finished first, second and third in the order named. Norman Armitage (Fencers' club) again won the national sabre title with Tibor Nyilas and George Worth both of the Salle Santelli finishing second and third. In the National Women's championship Miss Helena Mroczkowska (Fencers' club) placed first, Miss Ruth Maxwell (Fencers' club) second and Miss Maria Cerra (Salle Santelli) third.

The Big Ten conference operating on a very reduced schedule held the annual conference meet at the University of Chicago. The team championship was won by the University of Illinois. In the individual championships Arthur Cohen (University of Chicago) placed first in foil, Robert O'Donnell (University of Chicago) first in épée and Ray Siever (University of Chicago) first in sabre.

The Michigan, California and New York divisions of the Amateur Fencers League of America were the most active of all the 29 divisions. In the New York division in the Metropolitan championships John R. Huffman won the foil, Tibor Nyilas the sabre and Al Schrobisch the épée. Ambitious schedules were successfully followed and new names appeared among the older and familiar ones in the championships. The Texas, Philadelphia, St. Louis, Illinois and Northern Ohio divisions suffered due to the loss of men to the armed forces. Competitions were held, however, in schools and colleges and fencing in these areas was far from extinct. The remaining 20 divisions scattered about the United States were largely inactive as far as formal competition was concerned. (H. J. Z.)

Fertilizers.
The international fertilizer situation was materially changed in 1943 by the shifting of control in the Mediterranean and by the reduction of the submarine menace. North African countries normally produced annually about 4,000,000 tons of phosphate rock, most of which was exported to Europe including the British Isles. In 1941 and 1942 the axis powers controlled and absorbed whatever tonnage was produced, and Great Britain was completely cut off. In 1939 Palestine produced 635,000 tons of potassium chloride which went largely to Great Britain. These sources of supply were again open for shipment to the Allied Nations.

The loss of phosphate raw material seriously affected axis food production, as well as their munitions program. Their domestic resources were small and difficult to operate. Nauru and Ocean island in the South Pacific produced in 1941 approximately 1,000,-000 tons of phosphate rock, most of which went to Australia and

New Zealand. After Dec. 1941, these islands were under Japanese control and no doubt were utilized to the utmost to furnish Japan with much needed phosphates. Bombing attacks by Allied Nations late in 1943 were reported to have damaged operating facilities severely.

Movement of Russian potash and phosphates and Spanish potash to Allied Nations became possible in late 1943, whereas practically no shipments had so moved after 1940. As shipments were resumed from these sources, the call for shipments from the United States would be lessened and adequate supplies for American agriculture would be available.

The demand for increased food, feed and fibre production in the United States to supply the armed forces, to fulfil lend-lease commitments, to help feed the peoples of reoccupied countries, and to meet domestic civilian needs greatly increased the demand for fertilizers. Requirements for nitrogen for the manufacture of explosives and other munitions caused a definite shortage of that material in 1943 for use by agriculture. The construction of new synthetic nitrogen plants and changes in the munitions program greatly relieved the nitrogen shortage. Approximately 625,000 tons of nitrogen were expected to be available to American agriculture for the crop-planting year ending June 30, 1944, as compared to 460,000 tons the previous year. Demand for increased supplies of phosphates were met by speeding up production in all operating plants and constructing a few new ones. Production for the year ending June 30, 1944, was expected to approach 7,000,000 tons as compared to 5,144,000 tons produced in the 1942 calendar year. American production of potash in the year ending June 30, 1944, was expected to be about 700,000 tons expressed in terms of K_2O. Requirements for war chemicals and lend-lease left about 540,000 tons for agriculture, not enough to meet all demands but as much as was used any year except in 1942. Total fertilizer consumption in the United States in the 1943–44 year was expected to exceed 11,000,000 tons. (C. J. Br.)

FHA: *see* NATIONAL HOUSING AGENCY.
FHLB: *see* NATIONAL HOUSING AGENCY.
Fiction: *see* AMERICAN LITERATURE; CANADIAN LITERATURE; ENGLISH LITERATURE; FRENCH LITERATURE; ITALIAN LITERATURE; RUSSIAN LITERATURE; SPANISH-AMERICAN LITERATURE; SPANISH LITERATURE.
Fighting France (Free France): *see* FRANCE; FRENCH COLONIAL EMPIRE.
Fiji: *see* PACIFIC ISLANDS, BRITISH.
Financial Review: *see* BUSINESS REVIEW.

Finland.
An independent republic of northern Europe. Area, 134,000 sq.mi. (land area, 121,000 sq.mi.), after cession of 13,500 sq.mi. to the U.S.S.R. in 1940. The boundary in 1943 was somewhat expanded. Pop. (census of 1940) 3,887,217. Capital, Helsinki; pop. (est. Jan. 1, 1939), 304,965. Other principal cities: Turku (74,315); Tampere (76,730); Viipuri (74,247). Language and nationality, 90% Finnish, about 10% Swedish. Religion, Lutheran Christian. President in 1943: Risto Ryti (re-elected in Feb. 1943, and re-inaugurated on March 1); Prime Minister, Edwin Linkomies.

History.—Finland's position grew more desperate as 1943 progressed. The fiction of a separate war in the north could no longer be argued seriously. Finland was caught in the German vise.

Rumours of Finnish devices for peace and of the issuance of "feelers" were rife almost throughout the year. Russia was reported (probably falsely) to have made a peace offer to Finland in Jan. 1943. U.S. Under-Secretary of State Sumner Welles in February appealed to the Finnish people to pull out of the war.

Also in February Björn Prytz, Swedish minister in London, journeyed hastily to Stockholm, and rumours flew that he was to be intermediary in a Finnish-Russian peace move. Through March and April the rumours gradually died out, and in May a group of U.S. leaders signed a petition for a U.S. declaration of war on Finland. In April all but one U.S. diplomatic officer were removed from Helsinki, and only this token representation was maintained as chargé d'affaires (Robert McClintock until mid-November, succeeded by George L. West, Jr.). In Aug. 1943 some 33 Finnish politicians sent to the government a request for peace. At approximately the same time Eero Vuori, chief of the Finnish Trade Union congress, met in Stockholm with Arthur Deakin, official of the British Transport and General Workers union; peace was the issue, but no results showed. Through September and October suggestions of peace proposals continued. Premier Linkomies in September expressed regret at being at war with Great Britain and hoped that Finland could withdraw from the war with the U.S.S.R. Vaino Tanner, finance minister and ardently anti-soviet, made a radio address urging that Finland be realistic and make a "reasonable" peace with Russia. But 1943 passed with no agreement, and all that was really sure was that Russia and Finland had not agreed on what was reasonable. Russian propaganda continued to be as harsh toward the Finns as toward the Germans and pointed out that the Finns, while winning, had seemed quite eager to participate in the results of a Hitler New Order.

From a purely military standpoint the war in the north remained a stalemate, with only minor border forays and slight movement. Perhaps Col.-General Eduard Dietl and the German forces were concerned largely with their relations with the Finns; and certainly the Finns were not eager to risk increased casualties for futile conquests.

The food situation was bad, but good harvests and 30,000 tons of grain from Germany gave Finland about a six-month supply. Nevertheless, dependence on Germany for supplies may have been the chief factor holding the country to an allegiance of which it had completely sickened. Industrial production dropped, according to Moscow reports, to 35% of normal. Some trade was still carried on with Sweden, and in Dec. 1943 an agreement was signed for the first 6 months of 1944, providing a Swedish credit of 5,000,000 kronor to Finland for purchases in Sweden. Trade agreements were also negotiated with Germany, Denmark and Spain.

Payment of the much-discussed debt to the U.S. was resumed in June 1943, and in October Finland agreed to a plan to repay the instalments missed in 1941 and 1942 over a period of ten years.

At least 11,000 Ingermans, descendants of Finns who moved some 250 years ago to the region southeast of Leningrad, were sent to Finland in 1943 by the Germans, and about 25,000 more were expected. Starvation and hardship had played havoc with these people, but the Finns were glad to welcome their distant kinsfolk.

A presidential election was held on Feb. 15, 1943, resulting in the re-election of Risto Ryti by 269 votes out of 300. On his re-inauguration on March 1, the first time any Finnish president had succeeded himself, the cabinet resigned according to custom. The reshuffling, after some delay, brought in as prime minister Edwin Linkomies, Conservative leader, chairman of the editorial board of the *Uusi Suomi,* and professor at the university. Sir Henrik Ramsay, Finn of Scotch descent, became foreign minister. The former holders of these key posts, J. W. Rangell and Rolf Witting, were probably the strongest pro-nazis in the cabinet. Marshal Mannerheim remained, at 75 years of age, head of the armies.

Few statistics of agriculture, finance, manufacturing, etc.,

reached the outside world after the first Finnish-Soviet "winter war" of 1939–40, and figures available at the end of 1943 still pertained mostly to 1938 and 1939.

Education.—In 1939 there were some 11,200 elementary schools, with 411,000 students and 13,500 teachers; 383 professional schools in 1937 with 20,583 students, 68 middle schools with 8,546 students, and 150 lyceums with 42,034 students. There were five universities, of which that at Helsinki was the largest (enrolment, 6,461 in 1938).

Finance.—The monetary unit is the Finnish markka (= 2 U.S. cents approximately; at the last free quotation in 1939, 49 FM = $1). Foreign debt (Sept. 1939), 1,040,000,000 FM; internal debt (Sept. 1939), 2,810,000,000 FM; note circulation (April 1, 1941), 5,720,000,000 FM.

Trade.—Exports (1938) totalled 8,431,111,000 FM; (1940) 2,870,000,000 FM; imports (1938) 8,612,283,000 FM; (1940) 5,180,000,000 FM. Major export commodities, with their values in 1940 were as follows: pulp, paper, etc. 950,000,000 FM; timber and wood 1,200,000,000 FM; foods of animal origin 70,000,000 FM; metals and metal goods 200,000,000 FM; hides, skins, etc. 90,000,000 FM; minerals 80,000,000 FM. Major import commodities with values in 1938: metals and metal goods 1,420,500,-000 FM; machinery and apparatus 1,120,300,000 FM; minerals 661,100,000 FM; colonial products 585,500,000 FM; oils, fats, waxes 503,300,000 FM; transportation equipment 482,900,000 FM. Great Britain, Germany and the United States were the leading importers of Finnish products, while the same three countries plus Sweden supplied most of Finland's imports.

Communication.—Railways (1938) totalled 3,530 mi. and carried 21,200,000 passengers and 15,710,000 tons of freight in 1937. Buses in operation numbered 2,500 in 1937; 20,300 mi. of main highways were maintained by the state. In 1938 there were 185,456 telephones in operation, 1,593 mi. of telegraph lines, 18 broadcasting stations and 293,790 radio sets.

Agriculture.—The chief crops in 1939, with their yields in short tons, were as follows: oats 879,635; wheat 250,222; barley 211,642; rye 364,861; potatoes 1,715,179. Livestock in 1937: 380,038 horses; 1,925,078 cattle; 1,072,307 sheep; 10,372 goats; 504,164 pigs; 100,356 reindeer; 2,814,960 poultry; 18,374 beehives.

Manufacturing.—In 1937 there were 4,264 establishments which employed 207,506 workers and produced goods valued at 21,076,045,000 FM. The chief products and their values were as follows: wood and paper 9,428,919,000 FM; food and luxuries 3,453,956,000 FM; textiles 2,264,267,000 FM; machinery 2,113,-012,000 FM; metal 1,767,424,000 FM; leather and rubber 946,-071,000 FM.

In 1940, after the winter war, there remained to Finland 3,896 industrial establishments and 175,622 workers. Total industrial production was valued at 19,915,000,000 FM.

Mineral Production.—Following are the chief mineral products of Finland and their output in 1938: pyrite ores 113,514 tons; pyrites (sulphur content) 48,811 tons; copper ore 15,542 tons; copper 13,483 tons; gold 3,858 oz.; and silver 57,900 oz.

(F. D. S.)

Fire Insurance: *see* INSURANCE.

Fires and Fire Losses.
The losses by fire, including lightning, in the United States as compiled by the National Board of Fire Underwriters for 1943 amounted to $380,235,000. This was an appreciable advance and probably was due to the pressure caused by war work. For approximately three years the manufacturing plants were taxed heavily, because they were operating not 8 hours per day as in

peacetime but 16 and in most instances 24 hours. This continual strain on machinery had its effect not only in starting fires but in spreading the damage once the fire started. Again, the changing personnel to be trained had to be taken into consideration, together with the changes in materials used in making the same form of product. Finally, another consideration was the change in the form of the product itself. The business is one in which inspection service, to see that all properties are kept in good order, plays a fundamental part. It suffered as much, if not more than most businesses, because skilled inspectors had been drawn from it into government work. (*See also* DISASTERS.)   (E. R. H.)

Fires and Fire Prevention: *see* WARFARE, INCENDIARY.

Fish, Bert (1875-1943), U.S. foreign service official, was born Oct. 8 at Bedford, Ind. He studied law at the John B. Stetson university in Florida, was admitted to the bar in 1902 and practised in De Land, Fla., until 1926, when he became judge of the criminal court of Volusia county. He was appointed minister to Egypt, 1933, to Saudi Arabia, 1939, and to Portugal, 1941. Fish was chairman of the American delegation to the Capitulations conference held in Montreux, Switzerland, in 1937. He died at his post in Lisbon, July 21.

Fish and Wildlife Service: *see* WILD LIFE CONSERVATION.

Fisheries. The fisheries of the world, in normal times, annually yield about 17,500,000 tons of 2,000 lb. each, of food and industrial products, with a value of about $762,000,000. The fisheries conducted in the North Atlantic area by bordering countries produce 7,550,000 tons, valued at $374,000,000; with the production by eastern North Atlantic countries amounting to 6,100,000 tons, valued at $310,000,000, and by western North Atlantic countries to 1,450,000 tons, valued at $64,000,000. In 1943 as in 1942 the catch was below normal because of the difficulty of operating under war conditions. Prices, however, continued to advance sharply and fishermen received a high return for their catches. The species of importance in the North Atlantic area include herring, cod, haddock, mackerel, halibut, rosefish, swordfish, crabs, shrimp and oysters. In some of the warring countries conservation regulations continued to be relaxed in an effort to increase fish production, without regard to the effect of unrestricted operations on the maintenance of fish supplies in the sea.

As a result of the war, generally, operations by warring nations were considerably curtailed due largely to the loss of fishing craft to military forces. The remainder of the fleet found it difficult to conduct fishing on the usual banks. In order to make up for the deficiency of its domestic fisheries, Great Britain placed considerable dependence on supplies of salted, frozen and canned fish from Newfoundland and Canada; salted, fresh and frozen fish from Iceland; and canned salmon, sardines, mackerel and sea herring from Alaska, California and Maine. Because of difficulties in securing refrigerated cargo space on transports and of holding chilled fish in cold storage in England, the importation of frozen fish was retarded. Price orders and zoning systems of distribution continued in effect in England for most items of fresh and frozen fish.

While the situation in many sections of the world was not conducive to normal fishing operations during 1943, many countries took renewed interest in exploiting the fishery resources. For instance, New Zealand fish canners expanded the canning of mullet, kingfish and trevally. The Australian government continued its research program to increase the production of marine foodstuffs which were urgently needed to replace the former imports of

these items, and a comptroller of fisheries was appointed to promote the more orderly marketing of fish.

The shrimp and shark fisheries on the west coast of Mexico continued to expand. Livers from the sharks were exported to the United States where they were used in the manufacture of vitamin A fish-liver oils. The fisheries of Peru expanded at a greatly accelerated rate, especially in the production of canned fish and fish livers. Quantities of salted fish were exported. Chile conducted a sizable fishery, a considerable portion of the catch being canned and marketed in other South American countries. A number of fishing boats were under construction in Chile and Peru. In Uruguay the fisheries continued at a lively rate. The government of Venezuela furthered its broad program to develop the food industries of the republic and the production of canned fishery products increased during the year. As in many countries of the world, the fish canning industry of Venezuela was seriously hampered by a scarcity of tin-plate from which to make cans; therefore steps were taken to provide methods of preserving the catch by salting.

Limited fishing activities were conducted in Germany and Italy, and in the axis-dominated countries of Norway, Denmark, Finland, the Netherlands, Belgium and France. Except in Italy, and possibly France, any exportable surpluses in the various countries were shipped to Germany. Even then consumption of fish in Germany was only about one-half of prewar levels.

The fisheries of North America, which normally yield over 3,000,000 tons on both coasts and in the interior waters, were prosecuted a little more extensively in 1943 than in the previous year, but still under 1941. The catch of fishery products in the United States and Alaska was estimated to have totalled about 1,875,000 tons compared with the record yield of about 2,400,000 tons in 1941. Declines in the catch were attributed to the requisitioning of fishing vessels by the armed forces, restrictions on the operation of fishing craft, and a shortage of fishermen and shore workers. In Newfoundland the catch of codfish was retarded because of adverse weather conditions early in the summer. In Canada the 1943 pack of salmon in British Columbia amounted to about 1,250,000 cases, a decrease of about 550,000 cases, compared with the previous year. Most of the pack was sent to the British Isles. Large shipments of canned herring were also sent to Great Britain from Canada.

In Newfoundland the export market for salt cod, which is the main outlet for this product, continued good and no difficulty was experienced in finding buyers for the production. The exports of salted cod from Newfoundland, as well as Canada, were made in conformity with international action taken through the Combined Food board. A large portion of the 1943 production of salted cod from Newfoundland was marketed to Spanish, Portuguese and Puerto Rican buyers.

The position of the fishing industry in the United States improved materially during 1943, brought about by a higher price structure. During the year the United States government continued the purchasing or chartering of fishing vessels for conversion into naval craft, some of which were replaced or returned.

Sealing operations on the Pribilof Islands in Alaska were greatly expanded, the take amounting to 117,000 seal skins, which was the largest for many years.

The production of canned salmon in Alaska was larger in 1943 than in the previous year, amounting to about 5,405,000 cases. A large portion of the pack was purchased by the government for military and lend-lease purposes. The total pack of canned salmon in North America (Alaska, British Columbia, Pacific coast states) amounted to 7,025,000 cases in 1943, compared with 7,644,000 cases in 1942. The total pack of canned fishery products in the United States and Alaska in 1943 totalled about 636,000,000 lb.,

FISHERMEN'S CRAFT at a cannery wharf in Vancouver, B.C. Wartime food demands spurred salmon fishermen to record hauls in 1943

compared with 660,646,000 lb. in the previous year. Supplies of canned fish available to United States civilians were far below normal because of heavy government purchases of salmon, sardines and mackerel for the armed forces and for shipment to the United Nations.

In order to conserve critical material and manpower, the Alaska salmon industry and the California sardine industry operated under a concentration plan of the co-ordinator of fisheries of the department of the interior.

In various countries of South and Central America further interest was shown in exploiting local fishery resources. Attention was directed mainly toward producing marine products for domestic consumption to replace foods from abroad. Under the U.S. government's program for co-operation with other American republics several were assisted in fishery matters.

Vitamins.—During 1943 interest was continued by various countries in securing an adequate supply of fish oils potent in vitamins A and D. In the United States the production of vitamin A from fish oils for the 12-month period ending Oct. 31, 1943 was estimated at 86.6 trillion units. The holdings in the U.S. as of Oct. 31 amounted to 54.7 trillion. Manufacturers of vitamin fish oils in the United States continued to exert efforts to augment supplies from domestic and foreign sources. The fishery on the Pacific coast for soupfin sharks, the liver of which is potent in vitamin A, was prosecuted intensively and large quantities of the meat were marketed commercially. Efforts were continued during the year to locate sources of vitamin-bearing fish oils in other American republics, in India, in the South Pacific and in West and South Africa.

Whaling.—During the two decades from 1920 to 1940 the whale fisheries of the world were prosecuted with renewed vigour. Operations were centred almost entirely in the Antarctic. Previously, little whale fishing was done in this area because of dangerous weather and ice conditions. In recent years, however, such adverse conditions were no obstacle to the staunchly-built factory ships and killer boats. The take was enormous. During the period from the season 1919–20 (the inception of the fishery on a large scale in the Antarctic) to the 1938–39 season, inclusive, 421,708 whales were captured in this region, from which 32,741,897 bbl. of oil were produced.

Because of war conditions complete data were not available on the whole production during the seasons 1939–43. (*See also* MARINE BIOLOGY.)   (R. H. F.)

Fitzroy, Edward Algernon

(1869–1943), British politician, was born July 24. He attended Eton and Sandhurst military academy and served in World War I with the First Life Guards. He was Conservative member of Parliament from south Northamptonshire (now Daventry division) almost continuously from 1900 to 1943 and was deputy chairman of committees in the commons, 1922–28. As speaker of the house from 1928 until his death, he directed the house sessions through some of the most troubled years in the empire's history.

A London dispatch of March 3 carried the report of his death.

Flax: *see* LINEN AND FLAX.
Flint: *see* ABRASIVES.

Floods and Flood Control.

General flood control legislation provided, up to December 1943, authorizations totalling $930,400,000 for the construction of nearly 500 reservoirs and local protection projects widely dispersed throughout the United States, exclusive of the large project authorized separately for the alluvial valley of the Mississippi river.

The projects were integral parts of comprehensive and co-ordinated plans for the beneficial development of the water resources of the United States, and they provided economic flood protection for a large number of centres of population and for many thousands of acres of rich agricultural lands. Many of the reservoirs are suitable for advantageous development of multiple-purpose projects for flood control in combination with hydroelectric power and other water uses.

Work under the federal program for national flood control was started in 1937, when the first funds for that purpose were appropriated by congress.

By the end of 1943, 44 reservoirs and 101 local protection projects were placed in operation.

The program was thoroughly co-ordinated with the war effort of the United States. Although all flood control projects, being directly beneficial to the national economy, were directly or indirectly related to the war effort, the only new work initiated in 1943 was three projects determined to have direct value to the prosecution of the war. One of these was a multiple-purpose dam and reservoir project to provide flood protection and increased water supply for an important steel producing region, and the other two were local protection projects to give direct flood protection to industries supplying material to the army and navy. In 1943, work was continued on two multiple-purpose dam and reservoir projects, which were determined necessary to supply additional power for war industries.

Complying with existing federal policy, which required curtailment of public works not essential to the war, all projects under way prior to the announcement of this policy were or were being brought to completion or to a safe point of suspension. In many instances, completed portions of suspended projects afforded substantial amounts of flood protection.

An act of congress approved July 12, 1943, authorized the expenditure of $10,000,000 for emergency flood control work made necessary by floods which occurred in the spring of 1943. Work accomplished under the authority of the emergency act included repair, restoration and strengthening of existing levees and other flood control structures which were threatened or destroyed by floods in numerous localities of the country.

SUBMERGED FARMLAND on the Illinois side of the Wabash river west of Vincennes, Ind., in May 1943. Of the midwestern states, Illinois suffered the heaviest damages from the record spring floods

Work was being carried on as rapidly as practicable to complete plans and designs for the remaining portions of the suspended projects and for many additional authorized project, in order that a large-scale program of actual construction operations might be ready for initiation without delay at the end of the war. This backlog of economically justified projects was to be available to assist in the transition from war activities to a normal peacetime economy. (*See* also DAMS; FORESTS; IRRIGATION; METEOROLOGY; SOIL EROSION AND SOIL CONSERVATION.)   (E. RD.)

Florida.

An extreme southeastern state of the United States, called the "Peninsula state" because of its peculiar outline. Its coast line is greater than that of any other state, extending 472 mi. along the Atlantic and 674 mi. along the Gulf of Mexico. Area, 58,560 sq.mi., of which 4,298 sq.mi. are water surface; pop. (1940) 1,897,414, of which 1,045,791 were urban and 851,623 were rural; 1,384,365 white and 513,049 Negroes. Only about 60,000 were foreign born. Capital, Tallahassee (16,240). The larger cities are Jacksonville (173,065), Miami (172,172) and Tampa (108,391).

Florida in the census of 1940 gained an additional representative, who was chosen from the state at large in 1942, the state at that time not having been redistricted.

The state elective administrative officers, whose terms expire in Jan. 1945 are as follows: Spessard L. Holland, governor; R. A. Gray, secretary of state; J. Thomas Watson, attorney-general; J. M. Lee, comptroller; J. Ed. Larson, state treasurer; Colin English, superintendent of public instruction; and Nathan Mayo, commissioner of agriculture.

Education.—The biennial report of the state superintendent of public instruction, 1941–42, showed enrolment in the public schools through grade 12 as follows: white 282,629; Negro 104,260; total 386,889. There were 1,864 elementary and 708 secondary public schools in the state, with instructional staffs totalling 13,721 teachers, of whom 10,320 taught in the schools for whites and 3,401 in the schools for Negroes.

Public Welfare, Charities, Correction.—Florida disbursed for pensions, benefits and public welfare $13,470,878.91 in 1942–43. From grants by the federal government, the state received in 1942–43, for old-age pensions $3,875,922.36; for dependent children $726,954.79, and for pensions for the blind $277,322.81. The unemployment compensation benefit receipts were $2,210,000.00, with benefit disbursements of $2,365,747.69. Disbursements for

old-age assistance were $7,319,077.17.

Florida has no state penitentiary, but in 1943 maintained a prison farm at Raiford, an Industrial School for Boys at Marianna and an Industrial School for Girls at Ocala. The appropriation for these institutions for 1942–43 carried the sums of $665,394.82, $240,943.17 and $87,587.68 respectively. The state also supported a state hospital for the insane, the Florida Farm colony for the feeble minded and the Florida School for the Deaf and Blind. The total disbursements for charities, correction and hospitals for 1942–43 were $2,761,028.56.

Communication.—The total highway mileage in the state in 1942, exclusive of roads built for military purposes for which no figures are obtainable for publication, was 13,400 mi. approximately, of which about 8,000 mi. were paved or hard-surfaced. In 1942–43 disbursements by the state road department, including federal aid, were $10,711,185.28. Florida in 1943 had about 6,000 mi. of railroads.

Banking and Finance.—On June 30, 1943, there was a total balance in the treasury of $16,534,595.31. The state is constitutionally forbidden to incur a debt by borrowing except to put down rebellion or repel invasion. The constitution also inhibits the legislature from levying an income tax, and a constitutional amendment forbids any state *ad valorem* tax on real estate. Homesteads are constitutionally exempted from taxation by local taxing units up to the value of $5,000.

On June 30, 1943, there were within the state 54 national banks with deposits amounting to $722,423,000 and 113 state banks and trust companies with deposits of $250,251,000, representing total deposits of $972,674,000, a gain in deposits of $388,442,000 in the fiscal year.

Agriculture.—In 1940 the U.S. census showed that there were 62,248 farms with a total acreage of 8,337,708 ac., of which 1,751,275 were in crops, 462,248 were idle (fallow), 2,643,065 were in pasture, 1,649,960 were in farm woodland and the rest mainly in fruit.

Principal Agricultural Products of Florida, 1943 and 1942

Crop	1943	1942
Corn, bu.	8,151,000	7,413,000
Tobacco, lb.	14,810,000	14,778,000
Potatoes, bu.	3,703,000	4,116,000
Sugar cane, short tons	990,000	663,000

The citrus production for the season 1942–43 and the estimates for 1943–44 were as follows: oranges (including tangerines) 41,400,000 boxes and 42,700,000 boxes; grapefruit 27,300,000 boxes and 25,000,000 boxes.

On Jan. 1, 1943, the livestock resources of the state were as follows: 1,042,000 beef cattle, 123,000 milch cows, 608,000 swine, 23,000 sheep, 20,000 horses, 35,000 mules.

Manufacturing.—The more important manufactures of the state in 1943 were lumber, naval stores (turpentine and rosin) and cigars. Shipbuilding developed greatly after 1940.

The cigars manufactured in Florida are valued at around $21,-000,000 annually. Tampa and Jacksonville are the leading cities in this industry. Tung oil and the production of paper pulp and the manufacture of paper and paper board are also important industries. Most of the wood pulp and of the wood pulp products now being produced in Florida are being used in the war effort.

In 1939, according to the U.S. census figures (1940), the state had 2,083 manufacturing establishments, paying $37,823,204 to 52,728 workers and producing $241,238,534 worth of goods.

Mineral Production.—Florida has only limited resources in minerals, but has large and rich deposits of phosphates, lime and limestone and less extensive, though highly valuable, deposits of kaolin and fuller's earth. The mineral products of the state in 1943 were worth about $14,000,000.   (J. M. L.)

Flour and Flour Milling.
The food parley held at Hot Springs, Va. during May 1943 discussed and approved the maximum use of flour in feeding civilian populations during the war and for relief programs after the war.

The civilian consumption of wheat for 1943 by the United States was placed at 240.8 lb. per capita as compared with 224.4 lb. in 1942; 220.1 lb. in 1941; 219.1 lb. in 1940 and the 1935–39 average of 222.4 lb. The consumption of rye, oats and barley was also increased for 1943.

The increase in flour produced in 1943 was 16,834,350 bbl. and this was produced in mills having a reduced capacity as compared with the census capacity reporting in 1928, 15 years before. While the production of flour in 1942 in the United States was 108,631,604 bbl. the output for 1943 was expected to exceed 125,000,000 bbl.

Outstanding developments in the technology of the processing of wheat occurred in the industrial utilization of grains and the by-products of milling. A number of millers were grinding wheat used in the manufacture of industrial alcohol and there were good technological grounds for believing that after the war these alcohols would be derived competitively from petroleum and the grains.

Although the diversion of essential bread grains to other uses such as the production of alcohol and the diversion of wheat to animal feeding trespassed on bread reserves the supply of wheat for bread production was adequate for 1943.

The milling industry was concerned with the cost of blending in the flour as milled, thiamin, niacin, riboflavin and iron and pointed out that the cost of these materials would be 15.19 cents for 100 lb. of flour. New bread enrichment levels became effective on Oct. 1, 1943.

The new basis made numerous changes from the old enrichment levels and increased enrichment costs considerably. Beginning Oct. 1 all bread conformed to the following enrichment standard in milligrams per pound of bread:

	Minimum	Maximum
Vitamin B₁	1.1	1.6
Riboflavin	0.7	1.6
Niacin	10.0	15.0
Iron	8.0	12.5

Optional ingredients were calcium and vitamin D. The minimum standard for calcium was 300 milligrams and the maximum 800 milligrams. The minimum standard for vitamin D was 150 U.S.P. units and the maximum 750 U.S.P. units.

A major revolution in the conduct of the milling business took place when the time-honoured 196-lb. barrel was put aside as the common unit of transactions in flour. In its stead a new 100-lb. unit brought about by the War Production board's order became effective on May 1, 1943. The usual practice of packaging flour was modified by compressing it under approximately 2,000 lb. pressure. Progress was made in milling technique so that nothing but the flinty bran was removed and practically all of the vitamins present in the grain were retained in the milled flour.

Sealock and Livermore (*J. Nutrition,* 25:265 [1943]) investigated the merits of a new type of whole wheat bread. The wheat from which this bread was made was produced by the new "flotation process of Earle" and was known as "peeled wheat." It contained 98% of the original weight of the wheat kernel since only the thin epidermis or "beewing" was removed. The peeled wheat bread furnished thiamin, riboflavin and nicotinic acid in amounts equal to the upper level recommended by the Food and Nutrition board of the National Research council.

All bread and flour sold in the states of South Carolina, Louisiana and Texas had to be made from enriched flour.

Direct evidence of the value of the enrichment of flour was provided by Williams, Mason and Wilder (*J.A.M.A.,* 121:943 [1943]) Their results showed that the ingestion of a diet which provided only 0.22 mg. of thiamin for each 1,000 calories results after some months in mild thiamin deficiency, whereas the substitution of enriched white flour or whole wheat flour provided 0.45 mg. of thiamin for each 1,000 calories and in large measure prevents the development of deficiency signs and symptoms. (*See* also BREAD AND BAKERY PRODUCTS; VITAMINS.)

(H. E. BA.)

Fluorspar.
Shipments of fluorspar in the U.S. increased from 320,669 short tons in 1941 to 360,316 tons in 1942, while consumption increased from 303,600 tons to 360,800 tons. Labour shortage cut production of metallurgical grade fluorspar toward the end of 1942, but at least five new producers were scheduled to start operation during 1943.

The normal world production is about 500,000 metric tons, of which the United States supplies one-third, Germany slightly less, with most of the remainder from U.S.S.R., France and Great Britain, but no current data were available from any of these except the United States. The normally small output of Canada was enlarged after 1939, mostly in the Madoc district of Ontario.

(G. A. Ro.)

"Flying Tigers": *see* CHENNAULT, CLAIRE L.
Food and Drug Administration: *see* DRUGS AND DRUG TRAFFIC; FEDERAL SECURITY AGENCY.

Food Research.
Food research in 1943 was motivated by the needs imposed by war; many findings were used immediately to serve mankind. For the first time in the United States, the food research needed by the quartermaster corps of the army and by the bureau of supplies and accounts of the navy was correlated with civilian research in one unit, the Agricultural Research administration. Unprecedented advances were made in food preservation, particularly in dehydration. Special emphasis was placed on improving the culinary and nutritive quality of dehydrated products.

Dehydrated Foods.—Methods of assessing quality in spray-dried whole eggs, now the principal dried-egg product, were evaluated by M. W. Thistle *et al.,* primarily because of the need for eggs in Britain. Moisture content, bacterial count and either fluorescence measurements or potassium chloride values seemed necessary for control purposes; the two latter tests closely checked palatability ratings. Because W. H. White and Thistle found that dried eggs deteriorated at 95° F. but changed little at 80° F., it was required that all

HOMEMADE FOOD DEHYDRATOR with electric-light bulbs for heating and electric fan at rear to circulate air. Thousands of U.S. housewives used this method of preservation for the first time in 1943

Canadian egg powders exported to England be cooled to 80° F. or lower within one hour from the time of preparation. The investigators later showed that for high quality, dried eggs should be stored at 60° F.; moisture content should be less than 2%, a limit not practical commercially in 1943. Packing in carbon dioxide had a preservative effect; compression had no effect. With moisture levels of from 0.5 to 1% and pH adjusted to 6.5, G. F. Stewart et al. obtained dried eggs of superior keeping qualities; storage temperatures above 68° F. were detrimental. Good-quality dehydrated eggs were obtained by H. E. Gorseline et al. only from good-quality fresh eggs, hygienically handled throughout dehydration. That the British organoleptic method of scoring the palatability of eggs numerically is reliable, was established statistically by G. Levin. A. H. Steffen et al. developed a chemical method of scoring by using the colour density of silver sulphide spots. Correlation with subjective scores was high. In home cooking, R. Jordan and M. S. Sisson made muffins with spray-dried whole egg equal in quality to those made with fresh eggs. Custards, though good, did not equal in flavour and texture those made with fresh eggs.

A dried-milk powder that had keeping qualities superior to those of whole dried milk, was produced by C. D. Dahle and D. V. Josephson. Fresh milk was separated into skim milk and cream; the skim milk and the butter fat from the cream were treated to reduce lecithin content, then combined, pasteurized, homogenized and dried. Nitrogen storage improved the keeping quality. In December 1943 C. C. Van Leer gave what he believed to be the first American report on the "Niro" method of milk drying, developed in 1937 in Denmark and adopted commercially on the continent. In this method, milk is separated into cream and skim milk which are treated separately, remixed and spray-dried.

The experimental dehydration of precooked meats and unblanched vegetables was accomplished by F. M. Tiller et al. with infra-red radiation in the relatively short times of from 5 to 30 minutes. Dehydrated beef and pork, packed tightly in hermetically sealed, air- and moisture-resistant packages by H. R. Kraybill, did not become rancid or bacteriologically contaminated for long periods. Dried, slightly precooked meat, when cooked, was found by E. C. Bate-Smith et al. to be practically indistinguishable from cooked, fresh minced meat. The dried raw product on cooking had a slight "twice-cooked" flavour but was satisfactory. Compression decreased the development of rancidity during storage. Antioxidants of recognized value in delaying rancidity in fats and fatty foods were reviewed by H. S. Mitchell and H. C. Black, who found gum guaiac to be an effective antioxidant for lard, food fats, dehydrated pork and, probably, dehydrated beef.

On the basis of microscopical studies on many samples of dehydrated vegetables, R. M. Reeve reported the presence of two protective mechanisms: the solution of carotene in oils liberated by heat and the sealing of the tissues against oxidation by the drying of starch which has undergone gelation. For vegetables that contained little starch, a pectin dip was suggested; blanching was recommended for all. M. E. Davis and L. B. Howard measured some rehydration changes in vegetables quantitatively, and evaluated texture organoleptically. Rehydration was affected by size and shape of pieces, variations in drying process, conditions and time of storage, and soaking previous to cooking. The palatability of several cooked dehydrated vegetables decreased as the time of soaking previous to cooking was in-

creased, according to F. Fenton and H. Gift. Storage temperature had little effect on the flavour of cooked beets and rutabagas, but the flavour of cabbage, commercially dehydrated without blanching and stored for five months at 57° F. or above, was weak and unacceptable. Many varieties of cabbage scalded (blanched) in sodium sulphite solution, then dehydrated by R. J. L. Allen et al., gave cooked products with good flavour and texture, and with a colour closely resembling the fresh product. Cabbage dried without scalding was unsatisfactory. Similar results with dehydrated carrots and cabbage were reported by G. Mackinney et al.; the sulphite dip was used after blanching. About half of 62 varieties of peaches dehydrated by J. S. Caldwell et al. gave excellent to good products when cooked.

Frozen Foods.—Frozen beefsteaks and pork roasts, thawed at oven temperature and then cooked, were observed by G. E. Vail et al. to be only slightly less tender than paired cuts thawed at room or refrigerator temperature. C. W. Du Bois and D. K. Tressler reported that the development of rancidity in frozen ground pork and beef was retarded by sage, mace and ginger, but was hastened by table salt and by holding meat unfrozen after slaughter. The development of off-odours and flavours in undrawn poultry was prevented by prompt freezing by G. F. Stewart et al. Prompt quick freezing of dressed birds, to be eviscerated and refrozen at a later date, offered the possibility of running an evisceration plant the year round. The skins of some peas toughened when they were held after vining and before freezing, were bruised, or were held in freezing storage for six months; thawing previous to cooking caused no toughening, according to objective tests by M. M. Boggs et al.

Brined Vegetables.—Unshelled and uncut green beans, lima beans and peas, brined by merely covering them with a suitable salt solution, kept nine months without spoilage when stored in open containers in unsheltered places according to J. L. Etchells and I. D. Jones. Beans of superior flavour that occupied half the space were obtained by dry-salting, compressing and storing in closed containers. Peas and green lima beans (presumably removed from the pods) could not be satisfactorily brined by F. W. Fabian and H. B. Blum because of rapid spoilage, but green beans, corn and okra brined well. The addition of some of the sugars and of vegetable acids lost during brining improved the flavour.

Canned Vegetables.—Canning peas by a specified alkalizing treatment and processing at 260° F., gave a normal canned-pea texture while elevating the pH enough to protect the green colouring considerably, according to J. S. Blair and T. B. Ayres. They believed that the lowering in pH that accompanies the conventional canning of most vegetables might be a causative factor in producing unfavourable flavour changes.

Sulphited Fruits.—Unable, because of war, to import from Holland strawberries preserved in sulphur dioxide solution, English jam manufacturers sought the fruit in Canada and the U.S. Five of 12 U.S. varieties of strawberries made into jam from sulphited fruit according to English methods were considered by C. W. Culpepper and Caldwell to be excellent or very good. Suitable concentrations of calcium carbonate insured satisfactory firmness. Frequently the long cooking needed to reduce the sulphur dioxide content to the level permitted by British food regulations caused an undesirable loss of volatile constituents. J. G. Woodroof and S. R. Cecil, studying the preservation of peaches with sulphur dioxide and the subsequent use of the fruit, obtained peach jams and preserves superior to those made from dehydrated fruit, and at least equal in palatability and colour to those made from frozen peaches.

Foods, Not Preserved.—A detailed study by F. W. Fabian and H. B. Blum as to the influence of saltiness, sourness and sweetness on one another contributed much to an understanding of food tastes. The quality of coffee was not impaired when the vapours were continuously removed for 55 days, according to a method used by A. C. Shuman and L. W. Elder. Staling appeared to be due to oxidation products that were volatile or were formed in the vapour phase. Wheat-germ oil fortified with citric acid, according to Lips and McFarlane, was an effective and practical anti-oxidant for a blend of meat-food fats and vegetable oils and for lard. The shortening value of fat used in pastry was closely related to the "worked consistency" of the fat as determined by L. R. Hornstein et al. The "worked consistency" was obtained by repeatedly cutting fats with fine wires; it is probably a measure of plasticity and can be measured by a penetrometer. Fats that became softest (were most plastic) during incorporation into a dough usually made the most tender pastries. The theory that unsaturation, as such, plays a deciding factor in determining shortening power might be invalidated; more research was necessary. Within limits, enrichment with steeped wheat germ or its extract improved the bread-making properties of dough, according to E. Grewe and J. A. Le Clerc. Beef roasts oven-cooked at 176° F. by S. Cover were more tender than paired roasts cooked at 257° F.; the flesh was mealy. Desirable qualities in shell eggs were stabilized by E. M. Funk who immersed whole eggs in agitated liquids at about 140° F. Treated eggs were superior to untreated ones for cooking. Pasteurization of the shell eggs reduced bacterial spoilage. Application of the process could be a means of reducing bacterial content in frozen and dried eggs. L. S. Stuart and E. H. McNally found that bacteria penetrated to the shell membrane of eggs almost instantaneously but that the membrane itself possessed limited bactericidal activity.

Objective Tests.—A specially adapted hydraulic laboratory press was developed by B. Tannor et al. to determine juiciness in cooked meat. A simple and inexpensive line-spread device, used by E. A. Grawemeyer and M. C. Pfund, to measure consistency in applesauces and cream fillings, gave values fully as significant as penetration and viscosity measurements. The amount of substances insoluble in 80% alcohol was found by F. A. Lee to be a measure of toughness in frozen asparagus.

Some Reviews and Books.—The recent literature on bacterial food poisoning was reviewed by C. E. Dolman. The customary annual review of the literature on fats was prepared by Piskur for 1942. Up-to-date discussions and excellent research bibliographies on experimental cookery, food preparation, freezing and dough were given in books by B. Lowe, M. D. Sweetman, D. K. Tressler and C. O. Swanson, respectively. (See also DIETETICS.)

BIBLIOGRAPHY.—(All references are for 1943) M. W. Thistle, J. A. Pearce and N. E. Gibbons, "Dried Whole Egg Powder, I. Methods of Assessing Quality," *Can. J. Research*, D, 21:1–7; W. H. White and M. W. Thistle, "Dried Whole Egg Powder, II. Effect of Heat Treatment on Quality" and

"IV. Effect of Moisture Content on Keeping Quality," *ibid.*, D, 21:194–202, 211–22; W. H. White, M. W. Thistle and M. Reid, "Dried Whole Egg Powder, VI. Effect of Storage Temperature and Gas Packing on Keeping Quality," *ibid.*, D, 21:271–76; G. F. Stewart, L. R. Best and B. Lowe, "Study of Some Factors Affecting the Storage Changes in Spray-Dried Egg Products," *Proc. Inst. of Food Technologists*, 77–89; H. E. Gorseline, L. S. Stuart and V. H. McFarlane, "Sanitation Pays Dividends to the Egg Dehydrator," *Food Industries*, 15, No. 7:90–1, 140; G. Levin, "Taste Scoring Tests on Dried Whole Eggs," *Egg and Poultry Mag.*, 49:371, 375–77; A. H. Steffen, E. W. Hopkins, R. W. Kline and G. H. Whetzell, "A Chemical Method for Scoring Dried Whole Eggs," *ibid.*, 49:308–10, 334–36; R. Jordan and M. S. Sisson, "Use of Spray-dried Whole Eggs in Muffins" and "Use of Spray-dried Whole Eggs in Baked Custards," *ibid.*, 49:218–21 and 266–69, 87–88; C. D. Dahle and D. V. Josephson, "Removal of Oxidizing Factors Makes Whole Dry Milk Keep," *Food Industries*, 15, No. 11:76–7; C. C. Van Leer, Jr., "First American Report on 'Niro' Milk Drying," *Quick Frozen Foods*, 6, No. 5:62; F. M. Tiller, E. E. Litkenhous and W. Turbeville, "Infrared Dehydration of Meats and Vegetables Tested," *Food Industries*, 15:77–9, 121; H. R. Kraybill, "The Dehydration of Meat," *Proc. Inst. of Food Technologists*, 90–4; E. C. Bate-Smith, C. H. Lea and J. G. Sharp, "Dried Meat. I.," *J. Soc. Chem. Ind.*, 62:100–4; H. S. Mitchell and H. C. Black, "Stabilization of Fats and Fatty Foods," *Ind. and Eng. Chem.*, 35:50–2; R. M. Reeve, "A Microscopic Study of the Physical Changes in Carrots and Potatoes During Hydration," and related papers, *Food Research*, 8:128–36, 137–45 and 146–55; M. E. Davis and L. B. Howard, "Effects of Varying Conditions on the Reconstitution of Dehydrated Vegetables," *Proc. Inst. of Food Technologists*, 143–55; F. Fenton and H. Gift, "Palatability Studies of Commercially Dehydrated Vegetables," *Food Research*, 8:364–76; R. J. L. Allen, J. Barker and L. W. Mapson, "The Drying of Vegetables. I. Cabbage," *J. Soc. Chem. Ind.*, 62:145–60; G. Mackinney, H. F. Friar and E. Balog, "Sulfured Dehydrated Vegetables," *Fruit Products J.*, 22:294, 315; J. S. Caldwell, C. W. Culpepper and D. H. Scott, "Varietal Suitability for Dehydration in Eastern Freestone Peaches," *ibid.*, 23:68–71, 89, 101–6; G. E. Vail, M. Jeffery, H. Forney and C. Wiley, "Effect of Method of Thawing Upon Losses, Shear, and Press Fluid of Frozen Beefsteaks and Pork Roasts," *Food Research*, 8:337–42; C. W. Du Bois and D. K. Tressler, "Seasonings, Their Effect on Maintenance of Quality in Storage of Frozen Ground Pork and Beef," *Proc. Inst. of Food Technologists*, 202–7; G. F. Stewart, H. L. Hanson and B. Lowe, "Palatability Studies on Poultry: A Comparison of Three Methods for Handling Poultry Prior to Evisceration," *Food Research*, 8:202–11; M. M. Boggs, H. Campbell and C. D. Schwartze, "Factors Influencing Texture of Peas Preserved by Freezing," *ibid.*, 8:502–15; J. L. Etchells and I. D. Jones, "Commercial Brine Preservation of Vegetables," *Fruit Products J.*, 22:242–46, 251, 253; F. W. Fabian and H. B. Blum, "Preserving Vegetables by Salting," *ibid.*, 22:228–36; J. S. Blair and T. B. Ayres, "Protection of Natural Green Pigment in the Canning of Peas," *Ind. Eng. Chem.*, 35:85–95; C. W. Culpepper and J. S. Caldwell, "Varietal Adaptability of Strawberries to the Preservation in Sulphur Dioxide-Calcium Solution," *Fruit Products J.*, 23:5–9, 25, 27, 29, 46–51; J. G. Woodroof and S. R. Cecil, "Preserving Fruits with Sulphur Dioxide Solution," *ibid.*, 22:132–35, 155, 166–69, 187, 202–5, 219, 221, 237–41, 253; F. W. Fabian and H. B. Blum, "Relative Taste Potency of Some Basic Food Constituents and Their Competitive and Compensatory Action," *Food Research*, 8:179–93; A. C. Shuman and L. W. Elder, Jr., "Staling *vs.* Rancidity in Roasted Coffee," *Ind. and Eng. Chem.*, 35:778–81; A. Lips and W. D. McFarlane, "The Development of a Practical Antioxidant for Lard and Shortening," *Oil and Soap*, 20:193–6; L. R. Hornstein, F. B. King and F. Benedict, "Comparative Shortening Value of Some Commercial Fats," *Food Research*, 8:1–12; E. Grewe and J. A. Le Clerc, "Wheat Germ in Bread Making," *Cereal Chem.*, 20:434–47; S. Cover, "Effect of Extremely Low Rates of Heat Penetration on Tendering of Beef," *Food Research*, 8:388–94; E. M. Funk, "Stabilizing Quality in and Pasteurization of Shell Eggs," *Missouri Agr. Exp. Sta. Research Bull.*, 362 and 364; L. S. Stuart and E. H. McNally, "Bacteriological Studies on the Egg Shell," *Egg and Poultry Mag.*, 49:28–31, 45–7; B. Tannor, N. G.

Clark and O. G. Hankins, "Mechanical Determination of the Juiciness of Meat," *Agr. Research*, 66:403–12; E. A. Grawemeyer and M. C. Pfund "Line-Spread as an Objective Test for Consistency," *Food Research*, 8:105–8; F. A. Lee, "Determination of Toughness of Frozen Asparagus," *ibid.*, 8:249–53; C. E. Dolman, "Bacterial Food Poisoning," *Can. J. Pub. Health*, 34:97–111, 205–35; M. M. Piskur, "Review of Literature on Fats, Oils and Soap for 1942—Part 2," *Oil and Soap*, 20:58–9 and 62–7; B. Lowe, *Experimental Cookery*; M. D. Sweetman, *Food Selection and Preparation*; D. K. Tressler and C. F. Evers, *The Freezing Preservation of Foods*; C. O. Swanson, *Physical Properties of Dough*.   (M. C. P.)

Football.

The navy department granted permission to its cadets in training in the colleges and universities of the U.S. to participate in varsity sports. With few exceptions, the teams were composed predominantly of such trainees in the V-12 and V-5 programs. Intercollegiate football enjoyed a full season of play that was highly prosperous for many, although there was a general falling off in attendance of 18%.

The army declined to grant such permission to its college trainees, holding that their work program was too heavy to permit them time for varsity competition. As a consequence, the great majority of the colleges with army training units abandoned intercollegiate football for the duration of the war.

Among these were Alabama, Tennessee, Florida, Mississippi, Mississippi State, Fordham, Syracuse, Georgetown, Stanford, Santa Clara, Oregon, Oregon State and Washington State. A few colleges carried on informally on a minor scale, cancelling their regular schedules.

These included Boston college, Vanderbilt and Harvard. Harvard had a navy unit but elected to play informally against service and small college elevens.

A number of colleges continued to carry on as in peacetime with civilian players under the draft age or classified as IV-F. In almost every instance they suffered defeat after defeat. They included Ohio State, ranked the top team of 1942, Pittsburgh, Nebraska, Georgia, Louisiana State and Indiana. Minnesota, annually one of the best teams in the country, and Wisconsin, one of the strongest in 1942, both had weak elevens, because their best players performed for other teams or on the fighting fronts.

It was the colleges with veteran players in the navy and marine training units that had the strong teams. Adding to the interest in the season was the fact that many of these players were transferred to other colleges and in numerous instances competed against their former alma maters. In the middle of the season some of them were shipped to other training centres, and there were instances where a player competed against the same opponent a second time after being ordered to another college. As a consequence some teams were considerably weaker in November than they were in October and others were strengthened by new-

STEVE FILIPOWICZ, fullback for the college All Stars, tackled by George Smith of the Washington Redskins in the annual collegiate-professional night game Aug. 25, 1943, at Evanston, Ill. The college team won, 27 to 7

comers in the latter half of the season.

The most celebrated player to be transferred in midseason was Angelo Bertelli. He was the master mind and hand in running the Notre Dame T formation and one of the finest passers football has known. Bertelli was sent by the marines to the boot camp at Parris Island, S.C., before Notre Dame met Army in New York. He was voted the Heisman trophy as the outstanding player of the year.

Notre Dame was rated as one of the great teams of all time since it routed some of the strongest elevens in the country. Michigan, Georgia Tech, Navy, Army and Northwestern, all powerful clubs, were numbered among its victims.

. In its next to last game it barely managed to win by a point, 14–13, from the Iowa Naval Pre-Flight Seahawks. Composed of former professional and Western Conference stars, the Seahawks clearly outplayed Notre Dame in the first half but the latter showed its mettle by pulling out the victory in the second half.

In the final game, with the Great Lakes Naval Training station eleven, Notre Dame was defeated in the last 30 sec. of play by an opponent that had been beaten twice. A 46-yard touchdown pass finally defeated Frank Leahy's eleven and ruined its hopes of being the first Notre Dame team since 1930 to win every game. Great Lakes tied Notre Dame in 1942 and also during World War I in 1918.

Despite its sensational defeat, Notre Dame was still ranked No. 1 in the final country-wide poll of the Associated Press. Next in order were rated Iowa Pre-Flight, Michigan, Navy, Purdue, Great Lakes, Duke, Del Monte Pre-Flight, Northwestern and March Field. Army, which had been ranked high all season, dropped to eleventh position in the final vote after losing to Navy by 13–0, for the fifth successive year, in their first meeting at West Point since 1892.

Navy was voted the No. 1 team of the east. Duke was champion of the Southern conference, Georgia Tech of the Southeastern conference, Texas of the Southwestern conference, Tulsa of the Missouri Valley, Oklahoma of the Big Six and Colorado college of the Rocky Mountain conference.

The Pacific Coast conference title was decided by the meeting in the Rose Bowl between Southern California and Washington, representing the southern and northern divisions of the group. Southern California won by the score of 29–0 from its heavily favoured opponent.

In the Sugar Bowl, Georgia Tech played Tulsa, the former winning by 20–18. Louisiana State and Texas A. & M. met in the Orange Bowl, victory going to State, 19–14. In the Cotton Bowl, Texas and Randolph Field were matched and a 7–7 tie resulted. The East-West Shrine game also resulted in a 13–13 draw.

In addition to Bertelli, the most famous players of the year were Bob Odell of Penn, Otto Graham of Northwestern, Eddie Prokop of Georgia Tech, and Creighton Miller and Jim White of Notre Dame.

Notre Dame drew close to 500,000 spectators to its ten games. All-time records were set for the Michigan game at Ann Arbor (86,000), for the Navy game at Cleveland (82,000) and for the Northwestern game at Evanston (49,000).

Southern California and College of the Pacific drew 75,000 to their meeting at Los Angeles. Pennsylvania played to 200,000 in three games with Army, Navy and Cornell, and Army and Notre Dame drew the usual 76,000 in New York. Only 15,000 saw the Army-Navy game, restricted to residents within a ten-mile radius of West Point.

Amos Alonzo Stagg, 81-year-old coach of Pacific, was voted coach of the year by his colleagues in a national poll and was also named football's "man of the year" in a football writers' poll.

Professional Football.—With many of the players in service the National Football league continued to operate, all but one club, the Cleveland Rams, putting teams on the field. It was a highly successful season, the attendance averaging 36% per game over 1942. The quality of the football was not as good, but such stars as Sid Luckman of the Chicago Bears, Sammy Baugh of the Washington Redskins and Don Hutson of the Green Bay Packers were the usual magnets in the big cities, where money was plentiful.

The results of the games were bewildering. The Chicago Bears, with a line inferior to standard, overwhelmed the New York Giants, 56–7. The following week they were soundly thrashed by the Redskins, 21–7. Then along came the Giants to beat the Redskins, 14–10, after the latter had lost their first game of the season to the Philadelphia-Pittsburgh Steagles.

A week later the Giants, in the final game of the schedule, thrashed the Redskins decisively, and a tie for first place resulted in the Eastern division. In the play-off, the Redskins turned about and administered an even more crushing defeat to the Giants, 28–0. Baugh, Washington's great passer, ruined the day for the New Yorkers with one of his finest all-round exhibitions, completing 16 of 21 passes for 199 yards.

The Bears won the championship of the Western division. In the play-off for the league championship, the Bears avenged their earlier humiliation with a smashing 41–21 victory over the Redskins. Luckman, the Chicago quarterback, turned in a brilliant farewell performance before joining the merchant marine, setting a league play-off record with five touchdown passes. Baugh was hurt almost at the start of the game when he tackled Luckman and did not return until the second half, when he launched two passes for touchdowns.

Canada.—As in 1942, football in the dominion had a decided military tinge. All branches of the service had teams and football was introduced into the maritimes, which previously had seen only English rugger. The quality of the play was not up to peacetime standards but there was a lot of activity. The East-West play-off for the Grey cup and the Canadian championship resulted in a clear-cut, 23–14 victory for the Hamilton Flying Wildcats over the Winnipeg R.C.A.F. Bombers at Toronto. In 1942 the Bombers lost to the Toronto R.C.A.F. Hurricanes. The Wildcats had nine or ten air force men in their line-up and Winnipeg had so many airmen that the team was sponsored by the R.C.A.F. Hamilton had qualified to represent the East by defeating the Lachine R.C.A.F. team, composed entirely of men in the air force, 7 to 6.

Lachine won the championship of the Quebec Rugby Football union. Hamilton played in the Ontario Rugby Football union with two Toronto service teams, the R.C.A.F. and the Navy, and Balmy Beach, a civilian team.

In the Quebec league, both Army and Navy had teams, along with the Verdun Grads and McGill. The Western Canada league included the Regina All Services Rough Riders and the Winnipeg United Services team, besides the Winnipeg R.C.A.F. Bombers.

Possibly the best team in Canada was Halifax Navy, which easily defeated teams from Ontario and Quebec in exhibition games. Hamilton turned down Halifax's challenge.

The outstanding player was Joe Krol, Hamilton's triple-threat back, who led the Flying Wildcats to victory over the Bombers. Krol, a civilian, was offered a contract by the Detroit Lions to turn professional before the season started. (A. DA.)

Great Britain.—The Rugby union game again provided some excellent football, especially in the inter-services matches and the "service" internationals. (The players were drawn from the Rugby union and the Rugby league, but the matches were played under Rugby union rules). Wales beat England twice, at Swansea and at Gloucester. England, however, made amends by beating Scotland at Edinburgh and at Leicester. The Army and the R.A.F. met at Richmond and at Leicester, each winning once. Air Commodore G. A. Walker, who captained the R.A.F. at Richmond, very shortly afterwards met with a serious accident while on active service so that spectators saw the last of this brilliant little halfback, as a player. R. E. Prescott captained the Army and the "England" sides in all the matches. The Rugby League challenge cup was won by Dewsbury. An interesting match was played at Leeds, between Rugby union and Rugby league players attached to the Northern Command. The league side won by 18–11, the game being played under the Rugby union rules.

Five international association matches were played, three between England and Wales, and two between England and Scotland. Honours were even between England and Wales, each side winning a match and one being drawn. Against Scotland, however, England did better, drawing the first (at Wembley), but beating Scotland decisively in the second (at Glasgow) by 4–0. Blackpool won the northern cup, the Arsenal the southern cup, and the Rangers the Scottish cup. In a friendly match, Blackpool then beat the Arsenal by 4–0 at Chelsea.

Midway through the season, E. Hapgood, the veteran England and Arsenal back, retired from the game after a magnificent record. The outstanding player was once more Stanley Matthews, formerly of Stoke and in 1943 with Blackpool, and he was at his elusive best in the game at Chelsea.   (D. R. G.)

Ford, Edsel Bryant

(1893–1943), U.S. automobile manufacturer, was born Nov. 6 in Bagley, Mich., now the heart of downtown Detroit. The only child of Henry Ford, he studied at the Detroit university school and then entered his father's plant, at the age of 19. He completed several years of training in the shops, advancing from workman to designer, and then was made an executive in the firm. He became vice-president of the Ford Motor company in 1918, and after the Ford family bought out all the minority stockholders he was made president in 1919. He was also named treasurer in 1921. Though overshadowed by the stature of his father in the automobile field, young Ford was regarded as one of the outstanding industrial leaders in the country. He carried Ford production beyond the early Model T, introduced the Model A with conventional gearshift, streamlined the ancient Ford chassis and developed the Mercury automobile. The expansion of the Ford Motor company, which paralleled the industrial progress in the U.S. following World War I, was attributed in large part to the executive skill of the younger Ford. He died at his home in Grosse Pointe Shores, Mich., a suburb of Detroit, on May 26.

Foreign Economic Administration.

In a determined step to establish more orderly methods of procedure and to put an end to bickering among officials engaged in various phases of United States economic operations with relation to foreign countries, President Roosevelt on Sept. 25, 1943, effected a consolidation of the several agencies involved by creating the Foreign Economic administration, with Leo T. Crowley as administrator. Into this new wartime authority went the Office of Economic Warfare (successor to the BEW), the Office of Lend-Lease Administration, the Office of Foreign Relief and Rehabilitation Operations, and the economic operations of the Office of Foreign Economic Coordination. Soon to follow as part of the new set-up were certain functions of the War Food administration and the Commodity Credit corporation, which were transferred to FEA by executive order of Oct. 6, 1943. The functions of these two agencies placed under the Crowley administration were those having to do with the development of food and food facilities in foreign countries.

The administrative organization of FEA was rather pretentious, including two deputy administrators with staffs of assistants, advisors and consultants. Six staff offices, headed by a general counsel and five assistant administrators, reported directly to the office of the administrator. Highly important in the organization were the bureau of areas and the bureau of supplies. These two bureaus were designed to work in closest co-operation.

The bureau of areas, consisting of Pan-American, liberated, and general and special areas, was set up to decide upon and co-ordinate programs affecting operations in all areas; to analyze foreign requirements with reference to area considerations; to supervise economic intelligence and analysis work and preclusive buying; and to oversee field work in general.

The bureau of supplies was made up of the requirements and supply branch, the foreign procurement and development branch, the transportation and storage branch, engineering service, trade relations staff, statistics and reports service and related consolidated commodity divisions. Among its duties were the analysis of foreign requirements and requisitions with reference to availability of supplies; regulation of the flow of commercial exports, and planning for transportation, warehousing and redistribution of commodities and materials.

Economic Warfare Agency.—Ante-dating by less than two-and-a-half months the sweeping reorganization of foreign economic activities of the United States under the Foreign Economic administration, the Office of Economic Warfare came into being through drastic action by President Roosevelt, precipitated by a spectacular public quarrel between Vice-President Wallace as chairman of the Board of Economic Warfare, and Secretary of Commerce Jesse H. Jones as chairman of the Reconstruction Finance corporation. The president, by executive order of July 15, 1943, abolished BEW and created in its place the Office of Economic Warfare under the direction of Leo T. Crowley, then alien property custodian and chairman of the Federal Deposit Insurance corporation. At the same time the president deprived Secretary Jones of his power over foreign financial operations and restored to Secretary of State Hull complete authority in foreign affairs.

A contributing factor in the summary action of the president was an acute dispute between field representatives of several United States agencies in North Africa that brought threats of army intervention.

Functions of the Office of Economic Warfare—carried on by BEW before it was superseded by OEW in July—constituted one of the most important phases of the war. By devious means, information was obtained regarding needs of the enemy and ways were devised to deprive him of such materials and commodities so far as possible. At the same time new sources of supply were developed for many raw materials that in normal times came from areas overrun by enemy troops.

At the close of the fiscal year 1943, the volume of development and procurement operations exceeded $1,500,000,000, a large majority of which was handled through regular commercial import channels.

The economic warfare policy was administered by three offices—imports, exports and economic warfare analysis. The office of imports directed about 100 purchase programs, involving many individual items from 40 different countries. The office of exports directed necessary controls over shipments, through a licensing system, to protect U.S. supplies of strategic materials, at the same time allowing friendly nations as much as possible. Export controls were applied to 2,500 commodities, flowing from about 16,000 export concerns to more than 140 different country designations and thousands of individual consignees, all of whom were screened against the "blacklist" of axis suspects. The office of economic warfare analysis was of great strategic value to army and navy through providing accurate information regarding economic conditions in all countries, especially those of the enemy.

Lend-Lease Program.—Two outstanding trends in 1943 in the vast operations conducted under the Lend-Lease administration were the development of formidable reverse lend-lease and the stepping-up of shipments of food and munitions of war by the United States, especially to Russia. Both of these developments were attributable to the favourable turn of events in the Atlantic and European war areas, aided by greater productive capacity of the United States and Allied nations. Reduction of the U-boat menace in the Atlantic expedited delivery of munitions and machinery to Russia and also the transport of U.S. troops and matériel to England and North Africa. British reverse lend-lease immediately began to mount with the wide variety of goods and services provided without charge to United States forces in England and the Mediterranean area.

Upon the merging of lend-lease activities with other agencies under the Foreign Economic administration, Edward R. Stettinius, Jr., who was appointed lend-lease administrator Oct. 28, 1941, was transferred to the state department as under secretary of state.

During 1943, increasing concern was manifested by congress over the uses to which lend-lease funds were put, and appropriations were reduced below amounts requested. Up to Dec. 1, 1943, more than $60,000,000,000 had been authorized by congress for lend-lease purposes since the act was passed March 11, 1941. Of this total, $24,670,000,000 had been appropriated to the president to provide goods and services to those countries whose defense he deemed vital to the defense of the United States. The remainder—$35,970,000,000—represented authorized transfer of military goods and services procured with appropriations to the army, navy and maritime commission. Lend-lease aid had accounted for about 13.5% of total U.S. war expenditures up to Oct. 31, 1943. Goods transferred and services rendered were valued at $17,533,000,000.

Of this amount, $9,280,000,000 was credited to the first ten months in 1943. War goods transferred to the Allies during June 1943 totalled $1,030,000,000, exceeding $1,000,000,000 in one month for the first time.

In addition to the British commonwealth of nations, comprising the United Kingdom, Australia, New Zealand and India, 39 other countries were declared by President Roosevelt as eligible for lend-lease aid, up to Dec. 1, 1943. They were:

Argentina	El Salvador	Netherlands
Belgium	Ethiopia	Nicaragua
Bolivia	Fighting France	Norway
Brazil	French N. & W.Africa	Panamá
Chile	Greece	Paraguay
China	Guatemala	Peru
Colombia	Haiti	Poland
Costa Rica	Honduras	Saudi Arabia
Cuba	Iceland	Turkey
Czechoslovakia	Iran	U.S.S.R.
Dominican Republic	Iraq	Uruguay
Ecuador	Liberia	Venezuela
Egypt	Mexico	Yugoslavia

To Nov. 1, 1943, about 40% of total lend-lease shipments to the United Kingdom consisted of munitions, 26% industrial material for the fabrication of military goods, 34% foodstuffs. In contrast, the shipment of munitions to Russia comprised 56% of total lend-lease exports to that country, with foodstuffs reaching only 17% and industrial items 27%. During the year several industrial plants in the United States were dismantled and the machinery transported to Russia.

Reverse lend-lease loomed larger toward the end of 1943. As of July 1, the British reverse lend-lease totalled $1,171,000,000, and the current expenditures were estimated to be at the rate of about $1,250,000,000 a year, exclusive of supplies to U.S. forces in colonial theatres of war and important raw materials provided under reverse lend-lease.

Australia and New Zealand supplied United States troops in the Southwest Pacific with 90% of their food requirements, as well as other facilities.

Reverse lend-lease aid also was provided in the middle east, Russia, China and other countries.

Foreign Relief and Rehabilitation Operations.—In its first year the work of the Office of Foreign Relief and Rehabilitation Operations, under the direction of Herbert H. Lehman, was more one of planning than of giving relief. The organization occupied itself principally with training and building its staff, with gathering data on the needs in the various occupied countries, with making general preparations for the work ahead, and stock-piling. Fortified supplemental foods, packaged medical units and economical relief clothing were developed. In attempting to determine a basic ration, OFRRO co-operated closely with the inter-Allied committee on postwar requirements (Leith-Ross committee). There was very general agreement that an attempt should be made to provide for absolute necessities for as many people as possible and that more liberal allowances should be given as soon as production and shipping facilities permit. A bare subsistence ration of 2,000 calories a day was determined. The committee on health and medical care in the OFRRO laboured to gather and analyze available information concerning disease prevalence and important health problems in areas which might be reoccupied by Allied armed forces; to appraise the epidemic and other disease conditions which were likely to be an important part of relief and rehabilitation; and to estimate the amount and kinds of essential health and medical supplies and equipment which would have to be provided.

The principal theatre of field operations in 1943 was North Africa. There a survey revealed that milk for the children was the immediate need. Distribution of milk was begun, and some 200,000 children received slightly under a pint of milk a day. Besides this and similar work of emergency and special relief, members of the OFRRO field mission engaged in the liberation of refugees from the internment camps of Algiers and French Morocco.

In Tunisia distribution of essential supplies to distressed civilians—for the most part not gratis but by sale through the normal channels of trade—was executed close on the heels of Allied military operations.

On Sept. 25, the duties and responsibilities of OFRRO were absorbed by the Foreign Economic administration. On Nov. 9, the United Nations Relief and Rehabilitation administration was created when 44 nations united and associated in the war signed an agreement at the White House in Washington. Under this agreement and in the light of the policies established by UNRRA at its conference in Atlantic City, the organization will carry on relief and rehabilitation in the areas liberated from the enemy.

Foreign Exchange: *see* EXCHANGE CONTROL AND EXCHANGE RATES.

Foreign Investments in the United States.

The value of foreign holdings of United States stocks, bonds, cash balances and other dollar assets, excluding gold, estimated at $9,019,000,000 at the end of 1941, probably increased by $1,125,000,000 during 1942 and 1943, despite the seizure by the United States of certain enemy properties. The growth in short-term assets exceeded this increase by about the value of the seized properties.

Among the interesting developments in this field between 1941 and 1943 was the cessation of large-scale liquidations of British investments in the United States after about the middle of 1941 when the operation of the Lend-Lease act eased Great Britain's burden of payments for future purchases. During 1943 Canadian distilleries made further purchases of leading American liquor-producing companies, and Guatemala and Haiti announced purchases of United States government bonds as part of their contribution to the war effort. The actions of the treasury department and of the office of alien property custodian concerning enemy-controlled properties were of particular interest.

The administration of controls over foreign property in the United States from 1940 to 1943 was in general focused on enemy and enemy-controlled properties and the property of neutrals whose relations to the axis were suspect. Legislation and executive orders gave the treasury department and the alien property custodian the primary responsibility for the control of these properties.

The treasury's general jurisdiction covered:

1. Dollar balances, bullion and securities of governments or nationals, except those businesses under the jurisdiction of the alien property custodian.
2. All property of the occupied and neutral countries and their nationals except those particular business enterprises where the alien property custodian determined that it was in the national interest that he assume control.
3. All transactions or business dealings with countries blocked under freezing orders including the control of trade and commercial communications with the enemy and enemy-controlled countries.

The alien property custodian, in general, had jurisdiction of the following:

1. Enemy-owned or controlled business enterprises, whether controlled directly, through neutrals, or by virtue of the occupation of invaded countries. This jurisdiction extended to the dollar balances and other assets of such businesses.
2. All other types of enemy property, except dollar balances, bullion and securities. These included estates, trusts, properties in receivership proceedings, real estate, mortgages, personal property, etc.
3. All foreign-owned patents, copyrights, trade marks and ships.
4. The interests in other business enterprises of all foreign nationals when the custodian certified to the secretary of the treasury that it was in the national interest for him to assume control.

Executive orders in 1940 and 1941 immobilized the assets in the United States of the axis and invaded countries. This served as formal notice that any attempt to secure control of the dollar assets of invaded countries or of their nationals by duress would be blocked, while the requirement that all foreign assets in the United States be registered laid the basis for effective control. Even prior to Dec. 7, 1941, control had definitely shifted from a passive measure to a valuable weapon of economic warfare.

The office of alien property custodian and the treasury strove toward the following objectives:

1. The complete severance of all financial and commercial intercourse, trade and communication, direct and indirect, between the United States and the other American republics on the one hand, and axis or axis-dominated countries on the other.
2. Control over the following potentially dangerous use of enemy property:
   a. The use of assets to finance propaganda, espionage, and sabotage in the United States, or in other United Nations countries.
   b. The acquisition of stocks of strategic materials in United Nations countries even though such materials were of no direct use to the enemy, but were diverted from the war effort of the United States.
   c. The mismanagement of plant and equipment either through failure to convert to wartime production or through less than full utilization with the specific objective of retarding maximum wartime production.
   d. The mismanagement of properties and goods by permitting them to deteriorate.
   e. Limitations on the use of important techniques and processes through the control of patents, patent applications and copyrights.
3. To promote the war effort of the United States by making available enemy-controlled productive enterprises.

The first of these objectives was aided by the treasury's procedure of licensing foreign transactions in the United States, a system of export control, and the publication of a list of persons and enterprises in Latin America and in the eastern hemisphere who were friendly to the enemy. This list, known as "The Proclaimed List of Certain Blocked Nationals," contained over

Estimated Foreign Investments in the United States by Principal Countries and Areas, End of 1941
(in millions of dollars)

Country	Long term*	Short term	Total
Canada	992	375	1,367
Belgium	140	119	259
France	292	455	747
Germany	86	7	93
Italy	37	15	52
Netherlands	815	187	1,002
Switzerland	697	349	1,046
United Kingdom	1,711	403	2,114
Other Europe	169	492	661
Total Europe	3,947	2,027	5,974
Latin America	120	426	546
Rest of World	142	890	1,032
Grand Total	5,301†	3,718	9,019†

*Stocks, bonds, business enterprises, estates, trusts, real estate and mortgages.
†Includes estimated holdings of $100,000,000 of government securities not allocated geographically.
Sources: Long-term data from International Economics and Statistics Unit, Bureau of Foreign and Domestic Commerce, United States Department of Commerce; Short-term data from Bulletin of the United States Treasury Department for March 1942, as adjusted by the United States Department of Commerce.

11,000 names at the end of 1942, and served the other American republics in controlling anti-United Nations activities.

To obtain their objectives the treasury and the alien property custodian also took control of a number of enemy properties in the United States. Both agencies were reported to have liquidated more than 500 enterprises by May 1943, and were in the process of liquidating others. It had previously been determined that these were nonessential to the war effort and that the national interest would be best served by making their productive assets and labour available to other producers. The shares of a number of concerns important to the war production were vested (the outright transfer of title to property from the foreign owner to the custodian). The custodian, where necessary, replaced the management and other personnel by loyal, competent persons. In 1943, he announced his intention to offer enemy properties at public sale. Significant proportions of vested German and Japanese assets were in chemical and insurance companies, respectively. Italian interests, except for ships, were relatively small and scattered. Rumanian, Hungarian and Bulgarian nationals had little property in the U.S.

Almost 1,800 vesting orders were issued between March 1942, and July 1943. About half of the 318 vested business enterprises were German-owned and 40% were Japanese. Of the 72,000 copyrights vested in 63 orders, 70,000 were almost equally divided between French and Italian music publishers. German-owned copyrights, although concentrated in scientific and technical works, were a relatively small part of the total. More than 41,000 patents and patent applications were vested; over 25,000 of these were German-owned. About three-fourths of the 861 orders vesting estates and trusts pertained to German interests. The proceeds of properties sold and liquidated by the custodian and royalties collected on patents and copyrights were being held by him pending ultimate congressional disposition of enemy property in the United States. (*See* also EXCHANGE CONTROL AND EXCHANGE RATES.) (M. AB.)

Foreign Relief and Rehabilitation Operations, Office of: *see* FOREIGN ECONOMIC ADMINISTRATION.
Foreign Trade: *see* INTERNATIONAL TRADE.

Forests. Early in 1943 Lyle F. Watts was appointed chief of the forest service, United States department of agriculture, succeeding Earle H. Clapp, who had been acting chief after the death of Ferdinand Silcox in 1939. In transmitting his first annual report to the secretary of agriculture, Mr. Watts said, "There is reason for concern that wartime demands have unnecessarily accentuated forest problems urgently in need of solution before the war." Pointing out "that we cannot continue indefinitely to cut more than we grow," Mr. Watts urged public regulation of forest practices on privately owned lands. He declared that nationwide action on such a vital issue could not be effective if left to the states with no more than financial aid from the federal government. He suggested comprehensive federal legislation in which regulation of forest practices would be "supported by an expanded and accelerated program of public acquisition of forest lands to relieve private ownership of responsibility where conditions make this equitable or prudent," and would be "supplemented by better protection and by various aids to private owners."

Public regulation of forest practices was considered by the legislatures in 15 states during 1943. California, Maryland and Minnesota adopted regulatory laws. Seven other states had previously enacted such legislation, although only Oregon and Virginia had attempted enforcement. The Eastern States Conservation conference sponsored by the Council of State Governments approved a model bill for forest regulation by the states after a year's study of the problem.

Maintaining the output of lumber and other forest products continued to present a major wartime problem. No sooner was wood called upon to replace critical metals in many fields than wood itself became a critical material. In spite of all efforts to stimulate output, lumber cut during 1942, amounting to some 36,400,000,000 bd.ft., fell some 6,000,000,000 bd.ft. short of consumption.

With stocks on hand at a critical low and dwindling rapidly, the War Production board called upon the forest service to utilize its field organization to facilitate the output of lumber and pulpwood in the eastern states. Although the shortage of manpower was fully recognized, there was need for special service, particularly to small operators, in meeting the many inevitable procedures incident to war, in providing technical guidance for forest cutting practices and in obtaining a log supply for mills not adequately provided with standing timber.

Production from farm woodlands for war needs was also stimulated by the assignment of 76 foresters by the forest service in co-operation with the states to marketing projects involving 285 counties in the eastern states under the Norris-Doxey Farm Forestry act.

The national forests contributed to national needs as never before. The cut of timber from the national forests in the fiscal year ending June 30, 1943, again established an all-time high of 2,359,473,000 bd.ft. Of special importance was the program for obtaining Sitka spruce from the national forests of Alaska. Working under the most difficult winter conditions, contractors engaged by the forest service delivered the first raft of logs to Puget sound in Jan. 1943. The yield of aircraft quality lumber from the Alaskan logs exceeded all expectations. During the summer logs were arriving at a rate of 5,000,000 bd.ft. a month.

Forest service research furnished a partial solution to the problem of labour shortage in the production of turpentine and rosin. Chemical treatments applied in the woods make it possible to double the interval between successive chippings without reducing the yield of gum. Looking to the future, substantial progress was made in selecting and propagating strains of pine giving unusually high yields of gum. Individual trees yielding between two and three times as much gum as their associates of the same size and vigour were segregated.

Indicative of the potential disruption and damage to war industries and transportation which forest fires may cause, as well as of the importance of wood in the war, is the record of two

WYOMING'S most disastrous forest fire, set by lightning on July 31, 1943, in the Big Horn national forest, destroyed thousands of acres of timberland. Soldiers joined with forest rangers and civilians in attempting to control the spread of the flames

incendiary bombings by Japanese which occurred in the forests of western Oregon. Fortunately neither resulted in a serious outbreak.

Because of the importance of more intensive forest fire protection in wartime, congress again supplemented regular appropriations with emergency funds. The $12,212,000 made available in the fiscal year ending June 30, 1943, served to protect the zones of greatest danger, but left unprotected, as in previous years, about a third of the entire area needing organized protection, mostly in the south. And fires in the south were particularly widespread during the spring of 1943.

The fire protective agencies were handicapped by loss of experienced men to military service and war industries. Liquidation of the Civilian Conservation corps was offset in a limited way by the availability of some 2,000 conscientious objectors assigned to the forest service for work of national importance under civilian direction. Sixty of these men volunteered as "smoke-jumpers" in the Pacific northwest and northern Rocky Mountain regions, thus permitting an expansion of the use of parachutes to drop men and supplies from aeroplanes for prompt attack on fires in remote and inaccessible areas.

When the Japanese invasion of the Netherlands Indies and shipping difficulties cut off the supply of imported rubber, the United States undertook the development of native sources as well as the manufacture of synthetic rubber. For many years natural rubber was produced commercially but in limited volume from guayule, a desert plant native to parts of northern Mexico and southern Texas. Production in the United States was limited to one concern with several hundred acres of plantations and a small extraction plant in California. Expansion of plantations and other facilities for the production of guayule rubber was assigned to the forest service.

By June 30, 1943, 23,470 ac. had been planted with guayule. Seven nurseries, aggregating over 3,400 ac., were established in California, Arizona, New Mexico and Texas. Sufficient stock was available in these nurseries for the additional planting requested by the rubber director for the 1943–44 season. From mature cultivated shrub 440 tons of high quality rubber were extracted.

A pilot plant was erected to gain experience with a process extensively used in Germany for the production of ethyl alcohol or high protein livestock feed from wood waste or low quality timber. By this process sawmill waste was successfully used for the manufacture of synthetic rubber. (C. E. B.)

British Empire.—For yet another year the main effort on the part of empire foresters was in the supply of timber and other forest products required either for munitions of war or to replace timber previously imported from other countries. There was also an increased concentration of thought on postwar planning. The British Forestry commission produced an important note on postwar forest policy, the main aim of which would be to ensure at least 5,000,000 ac. of effective woodland which would be secured from 2,000,000 ac. of existing woodlands and 3,000,000 ac. to be obtained from afforestation of bare lands. The note also proposed the dedication of existing private woodlands in return for state assistance. At the close of the year discussion was continuing. The Canadian Society of Forest Engineers issued a statement of the forest policy they considered suitable for Canada. Proposals for largely increasing the area to be planted by the state in the Union of South Africa were also put forward. Other forest departments of the empire were engaged in postwar planning, often in collaboration with other authorities such as agricultural and veterinary departments.

It was being realized that the many new uses for timber introduced during the war, as well as the improved methods of using timber and its main bases, cellulose and lignin, must result to some extent in a change in the chief objects of forest management. The old demand for large sizes of lumber was to a great extent replaced by a demand for veneers and the building up of laminated wood structures. It seemed possible, therefore, that forests would have to be managed to produce the maximum quantity of wood rather than the smaller quantity of superfine large timber. (*See also* LUMBER.) (H. R. BD.)

Formosa (TAIWAN), Japanese colony, ceded to Japan by China after the war of 1894-95, a large island in the western Pacific, separated from China to the west by the Taiwan straits and from the Philippines to the south by the Bashi and Balintang channels. The Pescadores (Bōkotō) and other outlying islands form a political division of the Taiwan government-general. Area 13,429 sq.mi.; pop. (1938) 5,746,959, of whom 308,845 were Japanese and about 150,000 aboriginal tribesmen in the mountainous interior. The majority of the Formosans are of Chinese stock, and restitution of the island to China was one of the decisions of the Cairo conference of President Roosevelt, Prime Minister Churchill and Generalissimo Chiang Kai-shek in the last days of Nov. 1943. Capital, Taihoku. Governor-general in 1943, Admiral Kiyoshi Hasegawa. There is a large naval base at Mako, in the Pescadores.

Education, Trade, Agriculture, Mining, Industries.—In 1937 there were 143 primary schools, with 1,108 teachers and 43,671 pupils, for the Japanese, and 788 schools, with 7,242 teachers and 445,396 pupils, for the natives. The unit of currency is the Japanese yen, valued at 23.48 U.S. cents before the outbreak of war in the Pacific. The Formosan budget was 183,014,971 yen in 1938-39, 260,530,226 yen in 1939-40. Overseas trade, overwhelmingly with Japan and its territories, amounted to 592,938,000 yen (exports) and 408,650,000 yen (imports) in 1939. Formosa is one of the world's largest producers of camphor, and there is a government monopoly of this product, and also of salt, opium and tobacco. The soil and climate of Formosa have proved favourable to the cultivation of sugar, and there was a sharp increase in the output of sugar to 2,364,550,976 *kin* in 1939, as compared with 1,650,266,812 *kin* in 1938. (The

kin is about one and one-third U.S. pounds). The output of rice increased from about 330,000 tons in 1899 to about 1,600,000 tons in 1938. More than half the annual rice crop is exported to Japan. The island contains limited deposits of gold and iron and is a producer of tea and jute. There were 646 mi. of government and 317 mi. of privately owned railways in Formosa in 1937, besides 1,246 mi. of railways designed for the use of private firms, mostly sugar companies. There were 217 telegraph offices in the island, with 734 mi. of line. There were 2,946 mi. of telephone lines. There were 633,053 savings bank depositors in the island in 1937, and deposits in savings banks amounted to 27,136,748 yen. (W. H. CH.)

Foundations: *see* DONATIONS AND BEQUESTS and foundations under their specific names.

Four-H Clubs. Approximately 1,690,000 rural girls and boys between the ages of 10 and 21 enrolled as 4-H club members in 1943.

The 4-H members produced about 5,000,000 bushels of garden products during the year; produced and cared for 9,000,000 chickens and other poultry; cared for and managed 90,000 head of dairy cattle and 600,000 head of other livestock; grew 12,000,000 pounds of soybeans, peanuts and other legumes; and canned 15,000,000 jars of vegetables, fruits and meats. They collected more than 300,000,000 pounds of metal scrap and purchased or sold to others over $25,000,000 worth of war bonds and stamps. Some 800,000 members helped to safeguard their own health and that of their families and communities by having periodic health examinations, checking food and health habits, taking first aid and home nursing courses, and removing farm and home accident hazards. There was a marked increase in the number of 4-H members who helped care for and repair farm and home equipment, who repaired and remade their own and frequently their families' clothing, who helped provide farm fuel supplies, and participated in fire prevention activities. In addition, 4-H members worked many hours on home and neighbouring farms to help relieve the shortage in farm labour.

Because of wartime conditions only one national 4-H event was held in 1943, the 22nd annual National 4-H Club congress. This was held in Chicago, Ill., Nov. 28 to Dec. 1, with an attendance of approximately 800 rural girls and boys accompanied by their state 4-H leaders. Forty-six states and two provinces of Canada were represented. A national 4-H Mobilization week was observed Feb. 6-13 and a national 4-H Achievement week Nov. 6-13.

The 4-H clubs are conducted by county agricultural and home economics extension agents co-operatively employed by the U.S. department of agriculture, the state land-grant colleges, and the counties in which they work. There is a supervisory staff located at the state land-grant colleges and the U.S. department of agriculture. Assisting the county agents in conducting the 4-H clubs are volunteer local leaders (157,726 in 1943). In 1943 there were about 93,000 clubs representing practically every county in the 48 states and Alaska, Hawaii and Puerto Rico. (M. L. W.)

France. An occupied state situated in the west of Europe; bordered N. by Belgium and Luxembourg, N.E. by Germany, E. by Germany and Switzerland, S.E. by Italy, S. by Spain, with the Mediterranean sea on its southeast coast, the Atlantic ocean on the west, and the English channel and the North sea to the north. Area, 212,736 sq.mi.; pop. census (1936) 41,907,056; estimate (April 1, 1941) 39,302,511, exclusive of war prisoners; provisional capital, Vichy; chief of state in 1943 (since 1940): Marshal Henri Philippe Pétain. By the armistice

JOYOUS FRENCHMEN turned out in droves to welcome the British 1st army as it entered Tunis May 7, 1943

of June 22, 1940, France was divided into two zones: the occupied and the unoccupied (*c*. 85,000 sq.mi.). Although the Germans in Nov. 1942 occupied the whole of France (save portions of Savoy and the Riviera occupied by the Italians) the line of demarcation was maintained until March 1, 1943, when it was abolished, and postal communication and unlimited travel between the two zones was restored except for Jews. After the Italians surrendered to the Allies on Sept. 3, 1943, the portions of French territory occupied by them were taken over by the Germans.

Language: French; religion: Roman Catholic; *c*. 1,000,000 Protestants.

History.—The history of France in 1943 must be studied under two different heads—that of totally occupied metropolitan France and that of the gradually-liberated French colonies and protectorates.

Occupied France.—The year 1943 was one of hardship for metropolitan France. On Jan. 4, 1943, as a reply to the North African campaign of the Allies, the Germans created a closed military zone along the French Mediterranean coast, from Menton to the Pyrénées, and rushed fortifications in order to ward off a possible Allied attack. By the end of March, having decided to expand these fortifications along the whole South European coast, they demanded 100,000 French workers to help construct a "Mediterranean wall."

In all, German demands for French workers during the year amounted to over 1,000,000 men: on February 21, they asked for 250,000 workers to supplement 130,000 already there, promising to release only 50,000 war prisoners in exchange; on April 12, Vichy announced that "250,000 French prisoners would become 'free labourers' in German war plants on 'captivity furlough',", and on April 15, Madrid reported that Pierre Laval, Pétain's chief of government, had turned over to the German Labour corps all of the 1,250,000 French war prisoners. Still, in May, 400,000 more workers were sent to Germany by Laval, and on June 5, he broadcast from Paris the order to mobilize the 1942 military class for work in Germany, whereby 200,000 were to go without delay.

Fearing a possible vengeance of French patriots, Laval on Jan. 30, organized a "French militia," dressed in brown shirts, as his own elite guard. The French chief of government seemed to have foreseen that he would need protection, as once again there was an attempt on his life; while he and his finance secretary, Pierre Cathala, were returning from a conference with Adolf Hitler (April 29) they were wounded by a time bomb, although Vichy officially denied the attack. There were also two more assaults on the life of the notorious collaborationist, Marcel Déat. For the first attempt in Tours, seven patriots were executed by the Germans on Jan. 13; the second took place near Paris, on March 10, but Déat escaped unharmed.

On the whole, 1943 was the most fertile year yet in sabotage, assaults on the occupying authorities as well as on French Quislings, and in open revolts. On March 7, 200 persons were arrested for blocking trains transporting conscripted workers from Marseilles and Lyon. On March 8, 23 nazis were killed in Lille, and on March 10, 12 were assassinated in Lyon. The same day, a munition train was blown up between Valence and Vienne. On March 13, Swiss dispatches stated that French guerrillas (mostly fugitive conscripted workers) under the command of General Cartier and supplied with arms by Allied planes, were battling Italians in the Haute-Savoie. However, on March 17, aided by French police forces, the Germans blockaded the fighters and put a momentary end to the revolt. After a short pause, riots again took place in various French towns, and on May 18, martial law was declared in Clermont-Ferrand. The Swiss press stated that 150 persons, including many government officials, were arrested for plotting against Laval, when in his effort to collaborate at any price, he agreed to send 400,000 more French workers to Germany. The underground's answer was the assassination in Marseilles of Jean Bouisson, propaganda chief of Pierre Laval's militia (May 30). On June 27, the Berlin radio announced that Fritz Schmidt, nazi party chief in Holland, engaged in conscripting workers, "met with a fatal accident during a tour of France." In August, street fights broke out in Paris and its suburbs, and throughout the country patriots revolted and killed nazis, German casualties amounting to thousands of men.

While Laval forced France into a still closer collaboration with

Germany and, besides his "labour levy," applied drastic measures against the Jews (he denaturalized 100,000 Jews and authorized that several thousands be taken as hostages, shot or deported to the east), Pétain tried to maintain the Vichy regime by pursuing the policy of his much publicized "national revolution." On May day, 1943, he asserted that France was "on the right road" to revival, and asked the people to "smash the lies which aim at seducing you." However, the Vichy home intrigues developed into a new crisis, when suddenly, on Nov. 18, Pétain's resignation was reported by Berne. He was said to have resigned because he was not permitted to make a broadcast on Nov. 13, convoking the chamber of deputies to choose his successor and establish a parliamentary government; but soon the crisis seemed to dissolve, and little news leaked out about the incident. The Swiss press explained that all had been staged by the old marshal himself in an attempt to prevent Laval from succeeding him after his death.

During the fourth year of occupation, the population of France saw itself deprived of most of the natural resources and manufactured goods. The breadlines became each day longer; on February 27, the people were faced with the necessity of living one whole month of 1943 without bread.

The tragic situation of the French people was further aggravated during 1943 by the intensive air raids of the Allied air forces. Frequent, devastating attacks were carried out over the French channel ports (especially towards the end of the year, when the Germans installed rocket guns there), industrial centres, railroad junctions, airfields, power stations, etc. Towns like Lille, Abbeville, Le Havre, Brest, Lorient, St. Nazaire, Le Creusot, Lyon, Marseilles, as well as the industrial suburbs of Paris, were systematically blasted from the sky; Renault, Citroën, Potez and other plants which were doing high-speed work for the German war industry, if not entirely put out of production, were at least extremely damaged, and their production power was considerably diminished.

Underground Movement.—The efforts of the underground movement in 1943 were particularly concentrated on: (1) preventing the French workers from going to Germany; (2) forming of organized resistance to the Germans, and (3) helping political prisoners escape to England and Africa. The French clandestine press served actively those purposes. In the summer of 1940, there were only three underground newspapers; by the summer of 1943, the number had increased to 70, with a total circulation of 800,000 a month, the chief publications being: *Combat, Libération, Défense de la France, La France, L'Humanité, La Vie Ouvrière, Résistance, Cahier français du témoignage chrétien, Le Populaire, Franc Tireur.*

Fearing the interference of the underground, the Germans transferred their most valuable prisoners to Germany, and, on April 4, it was announced that the former French political leaders, Léon Blum, Edouard Daladier, Paul Reynaud and Georges Mandel, and General Maurice Gamelin, were interned somewhere in Germany.

Finance.—The 1943 French budget, as reported in Switzerland, listed for the year expenditures of 128,000,000,000 francs (about $2,560,000,000) and revenues of 102,000,000,000 francs (about $2,040,000,000). It did not mention the government's debt of 201,000,000,000 francs to the Bank of France to meet German occupation costs, which in 1943 amounted to 300,000,000 francs a day, while 125,000,000 francs would have been sufficient to cover the expenses. On the black bourse of neutral countries, the value of the franc varied from 250 to 350 to the dollar, while the official rate remained 43.50. So far, World War II had cost France $10,100,000,000, according to an estimate of the department of commerce, Washington, Feb. 5, 1943.

Liberated France.—Meanwhile, in North Africa, the military operations of the Allies progressed steadily—operations in which French troops took a prominent part (*see* WORLD WAR II).

The political situation in North Africa, complicated by the assassination of Admiral Jean Darlan on Christmas eve, 1942, suffered several serious crises in 1943. The disagreement between Generals Charles de Gaulle and Henri Honoré Giraud increased when a spokesman of de Gaulle, broadcasting from London, on Jan. 1, 1943, demanded that the "Vichy-packed" French Imperial council in Algiers be eliminated, before de Gaulle would join with Giraud. De Gaulle's forces were further irked by the report that Marcel Peyrouton, former Vichy minister of the interior and ambassador to Argentina, had been appointed governor general of Algeria Jan. 19, 1943.

At the end of the historic meeting of Casablanca (Jan. 10–24, 1943) between President Roosevelt, Prime Minister Winston Churchill, de Gaulle and Giraud, the latter two announced: "We have met. We have talked. We have registered our entire agreement on the end to be achieved, which is the liberation of France and the triumph of human liberties by the total defeat of the enemy. This end will be attained by a union in war of all Frenchmen fighting side by side with all their Allies." It must be pointed out, however, that the understanding at Casablanca was of a purely military nature; the political situation continued as before. On Feb. 9, Peyrouton created a Permanent Council of War Economy, of 39 members, headed by Gen. Jean M. J. Bergeret, former Vichy air minister, and a few days later, he appointed Antoine Gardel, former aide to General Maxime Weygand, director of Press and Information services. At the same time, de Gaulle, demanding the restoration of the laws of the republic, told a press conference in London that if freedom of the press, individual liberty and the right to peaceful assembly were restored in French North Africa, the differences between him and the regime of Gen. Giraud would soon disappear. On Feb. 8, Gen. Georges Catroux, Fighting French delegate and commander in chief in Syria, arrived in Algiers to represent General de Gaulle in conferences with General Giraud. From that time on General Catroux was the constant mediator between the two generals.

Negotiations leading to the formation of the French Committee of National Liberation were made public on April 19, 1943, by the French military mission in Washington. At first, Gen. Giraud proposed to Gen. de Gaulle the creation of a "French Council of Overseas Territories," which would exercise French sovereignty until the creation of a provisional government. In his answer to this proposal, made public in Washington on April 21, Gen. de Gaulle urged representation of the French underground movement, curbing of the military commander's authority and removal of Vichyites from important posts in North Africa. On April 27, Gen. Giraud offered through Gen. Catroux to meet de Gaulle, but, almost simultaneously he accepted the services of Vice Admiral Emile Henri Muselier, former naval chief to Gen. de Gaulle, who had been dismissed by the latter. On May 10, however, Gen. Giraud made again unity proposals to Gen. de Gaulle, who finally accepted the principle of a seven-man council and announced on May 24, 1943, that he would soon leave for Algiers with René Massigli, foreign affairs commissioner and André Philip, interior commissioner; Gen. Catroux was to precede them.

French Committee of National Liberation.—Generals de Gaulle and Giraud met in Algiers on May 30, 1943, and on the following day the French Committee of National Liberation was formed as follows: the two generals became co-presidents; the Giraud appointees were Jean Monnet and Gen. Alphonse-Joseph Georges, who had just escaped from France; the de Gaulle appointees were Gen. Catroux, René Massigli and André Philip, who was elected by the other six. On June 7, the French Committee of National

Liberation appointed a cabinet of 14 and subsequently it was recognized by 25 countries. The United States, Great Britain, Canada and the U.S.S.R. recognized it on Aug. 26. As an immediate consequence to the committee's creation, there were several resignations of high officials, as for instance those of Marcel Peyrouton and Gen. Charles Noguès, resident general of Morocco, who was replaced by Gabriel Puaux, on June 7. But, far from being satisfied by this state of affairs, Gen. de Gaulle, on June 11, threatened to resign from the Committee of Liberation unless it would agree to the elimination of Vichyite officers from the army. He also opposed Gen. Giraud as national defense minister while still army commander and urged the dismissal of Pierre Boisson, Vichyite French West Africa governor general and the elimination of Vice Admiral Muselier. A new compromise was reached, however, on June 22, under which Gen. Giraud was to retain command of the French armies in Morocco, Algeria, Tunisia and French West Africa, while Gen. de Gaulle was to continue as commander of all forces in the rest of the empire. An eight-man committee, including the two generals, was set up to reorganize the French army. In the summer of 1943, following an invitation issued a long time before by President Roosevelt, Gen. Giraud visited the United States. He arrived in Washington on July 7, and conferred with Roosevelt and his military leaders, about the rearmament of 300,000 French soldiers with U.S. equipment.

After a trip to Canada, Giraud returned to Algiers via London where he saw Prime Minister Winston Churchill. Upon his arrival in Algiers on July 22, he was faced with a new crisis, and on July 31, the Committee of Liberation proceeded to an important reorganization by a new distribution of roles. Gen. de Gaulle was named head of a newly formed National Defense committee which made him civil leader; Gen. Giraud was named military commander subject to committee decisions. Information Commissioner Henri Bonnet declared that complete unity had been achieved. On Aug. 12, a Commission of Purification was set up in Algiers by the Committee of Liberation to eliminate advocates of collaboration from public posts. These measures met with the approval of the French Council of Resistance (union of underground groups in occupied France) who, on July 25, had asked the Liberation committee "to finish once and for all with the survivals of Vichy," and to "remain faithful to General de Gaulle." The Commission of Purification proceeded to arrest leading collaborationists, accused of treason by the Committee of Liberation, including Pierre Pucheu, former Vichy minister of interior; Gen. Jean Bergeret; former Premier Pierre-Etienne Flandin; Marcel Peyrouton; Pierre Tixier-Vignancourt, former Vichy secretary of information; Pierre Boisson, former governor general of French West Africa; former deputy André Albert; former director of the state bank in Casablanca, Desoubry and numerous other well-known personalities. On the other hand, the question of the political prisoners interned in North Africa by the Vichy regime, was finally solved; on Oct. 14, Algiers announced that 7,100 men and women had been freed. On Oct. 21 the Crémieux decree (see ANTI-SEMITISM) was reinstated in Algeria, and towards the end of 1943 the Committee of Liberation decided to grant "full citizenship rights" to French Moslems there and to increase their proportion in political offices.

On Sept. 25, 1943, the United States signed a lend-lease agreement with the Committee of Liberation, formalizing an aid program in effect since the Casablanca conference. On Oct. 19, Algiers reported that Gen. de Gaulle had conferred with British Foreign Minister Anthony Eden and U.S. Secretary of State Cordell Hull, when they stopped in Africa on their way to Moscow, and that "substantial unanimity" on future programs had been reached. There was a certain discontent at Algiers, as France had not been invited to the Moscow and Tehran conferences.

On Nov. 3, a Provisional Consultative assembly composed of 84 members, including numerous former deputies and delegates of the resistance, met in Algiers and functioned as a kind of an advisory body without legislative power. Gen. de Gaulle described it as the "voice of the nation rising from the dungeon." On Nov. 25, it was announced by the Committee of Liberation that the membership of the assembly would be raised to 102 to include 18 more members of the underground. On account of certain disagreements, Gen. Giraud and four of his supporters resigned on Nov. 9 from the Committee of Liberation, but he remained head of the French army. And on Nov. 30, Commissioner of Justice François de Menthon declared that Gen. Charles de Gaulle and all members of the French Committee of National Liberation would resign "to the president of a provisionally elected French assembly after liberation." (*See* also FRENCH COLONIAL EMPIRE; INTERNATIONAL LAW; WORLD WAR II.)

BIBLIOGRAPHY.—Vercors, *Les Silences de la Mer* (only underground book published in France in 1943); André Labarthe, *Retour au Feu* (1943) (Tunisian campaign).

France, Free (Fighting France): *see* FRANCE; FRENCH COLONIAL EMPIRE.

Franco, Francisco

(1892–), Spanish soldier and statesman, was born in Galicia. After military service in Morocco, he became a colonel in 1926, and served under the Spanish republic of 1931 in the Balearic Islands, being later transferred to Morocco again. In 1935, he was made chief of staff. On the outbreak of the civil war in June 1936, he flew to Tetuan, in Spanish Morocco, and there organized the transport of Foreign Legionaries and Moorish troops to the Spanish mainland, whither he soon followed. Upon the death of Gen. Sanjurjo, Gen. Franco became military leader of the insurgents. After his victorious conclusion of the civil war in 1939 he added the title of prime minister to the others he possessed, organized his cabinet, and began the task of reconstruction. Franco issued a declaration of "strictest neutrality" in Sept. 1939.

Franco's position in 1942–43 was unenviable. Successive Allied victories led him to water down his pro-axis sentiments and hew closely to the line of neutrality. He tried the role of peacemaker on May 10, 1943, urging both the Allies and axis powers to cease fighting because, he asserted, a deadlock had been reached. His appeal was ignored by the Allies, since it was presumed that Germany was using him as a mouthpiece to sound out Allied sentiments regarding a negotiated peace. Within Spain, opposition to his rule grew during 1943, with the monarchists purportedly seeking to oust him from power; on July 18, he warned the monarchists that he would not tolerate continued plotting for his overthrow. (*See* also SPAIN.)

Fredendall, Lloyd R.

(1883–), U.S. army officer, was born Dec. 28 in Wyoming. A cadet at the U.S. Military academy, 1901–02 and 1902–03, he was commissioned a second lieutenant of infantry in 1907. He graduated from the Army Signal school in 1914, took a field officers' course in 1922, graduated from the Command and General Staff school with honours in 1923, and completed studies at the Army War college in 1925. During World War I, he served as General Pershing's staff assistant. From his post as chief of an army corps at Chicago, he went into active duty in 1942. He commanded the U.S. army corps in North Africa until he was replaced by General George Patton during the Tunisian campaign. On his return to the United States he was made commander of the second army at Memphis, Tenn., replacing Gen. Ben Lear, who was retiring. On May 27, 1943, Fredendall was promoted to the rank of lieutenant general.

Free France (Fighting France): *see* FRANCE; FRENCH COLONIAL EMPIRE.

Freeman, James Edward

(1866–1943), U.S. clergyman, was born July 24 in New York city. After finishing his public school education, he worked for 15 years in the legal and accounting departments of the Long Island and New York Central railroads. He was well on the way to a successful business career when Bishop Henry C. Potter induced him to study for the ministry. He was ordained as Episcopal deacon in 1894. During the years that followed he built large congregations in Yonkers, Minneapolis and Washington and founded numerous community centres. He went to Washington as rector of the Church of the Epiphany in 1921 and was elected the third Protestant Episcopal bishop of Washington in 1923. Soon after he became bishop he revived a 40-year-old plan to construct the National cathedral in Washington, a national shrine similar to Westminster abbey. He raised enough funds to get construction under way and open the partially completed structure for worship in 1932. He died in Washington, June 6.

Freeman, Richard Austin

(1862–1943), British author, first served in the Gold Coast colony as assistant colonial surgeon. At the turn of the century he became acting deputy medical officer at the Holloway prison and in 1904 acting assistant medical officer of the Port of London. His wide medical background gave credence to the exploits of his chief mystery story hero, detective-pathologist Dr. Thorndyke. His works include: *The Red Thumb Mark* (1907), *The Eye of Osiris* (1911), *The Singing Bone* (1912), *The Cat's Eye* (1923), *The Stoneware Monkey* (1938), *Dr. Thorndyke's Crime File* (1941), an omnibus of Dr. Thorndyke stories, and *The Jacob Street Mystery* (1942). Dr. Freeman died at Gravesend, England, Sept. 30.

Freer Gallery of Art: *see* SMITHSONIAN INSTITUTION.

French Colonial Empire.

Total area (excluding Syria and Lebanon) (approx.) 4,579,000 sq.mi.; total pop. (est. Dec. 1939) 67,591,000. Certain essential information on the French colonies, protectorates and mandates is given in the table.

The year 1943 saw the extension of the authority of the French Committee for National Liberation over all French colonial possessions, with the exception of Indo-China which remained under Japanese control.

French North Africa.—Relief measures, following on military operations, necessitated the establishment of an Anglo-American North African economic board to supervise the supply of civilian goods and restore normal economic conditions. By May 31, 170,-000 tons of lend-lease goods had been received and, in exchange, 50,000 tons of raw materials were exported to the United Kingdom and the United States, including manganese, cobalt ore, cork, tanbark, red squill, iron ore and phosphate rock. In March, a rationing system for clothes was announced. On May 18, the Vichy press laws were abrogated. An order of Feb. 17 allowed Jews to enlist in combatant units and in March it was reported that the Jewish Affairs bureau had been liquidated. An economic high council was set up on Feb. 5 on which each country of French Africa was represented. The exchange rate was changed from 75 francs to the dollar and 300 francs to the £ to 50 francs to the dollar and 200 francs to the £. Transfer of funds between territories under the control of Generals de Gaulle and Giraud was allowed in May.

Algeria.—Marcel Peyrouton, who was appointed governor-general in January, ordered the reinstatement of municipal officers who were in office on June 22, 1940, and the return of public officials and members of the administration dismissed by Vichy laws. The Délégations Financières and Conseil Supérieur were reestablished in February and a Conseil Permanent de l'Economie de Guerre was created the same month. In April municipal councils were reinstated.

On June 3 General Georges Catroux was nominated governor-general in place of Peyrouton who resigned.

In the autumn M. Walet, attorney-general at the court of appeal, was dismissed on the recommendation of the "Purge Commission."

General de Gaulle announced on Dec. 12 that French citizenship

French Colonial Empire
(as at Dec. 14, 1943)

COUNTRY AND AREA sq. miles (approx.)	POPULATION (est. Dec. 31, 1939) (000's omitted)	CAPITAL, STATUS, GOVERNORS, PREMIERS, ETC.
AFRICA		
FRENCH EQUATORIAL AFRICA, 867,700. . .	3,500	Brazzaville, *Governor-General:* M. Eboué.
GABON, 106,500. . .	410*	Libreville, colony, *Governor:* M. Servel
MIDDLE CONGO, 159,700	747*	Brazzaville, colony, *Governor:* M. Fortuné.
OUBANGUI-CHARI, 214,600 . . .	834*	Bangui, colony, *Governor:* M. Sautot.
CHAD, 386,900 . . .	1,432*	Fort Lamy, colony, *Governor:* M. Rogue.
CAMEROONS, 161,200 . .	2,609	Yaoundé, mandated territory, *Commissioner:* M. Carras.
ALGERIA, 845,400 . . .	7,600	Algiers, colony, under jurisdiction of the Minister of the Interior, *Governor-General:* General Catroux.
MOROCCO (F.), 165,800	6,600	Rabat, protectorate, under the Minister of Foreign Affairs, *Sultan:* Sidi Mohammed, *Resident-General:* M. Puax.
TUNISIA, 48,800 . . .	2,730	Tunis, protectorate, under the Minister of Foreign Affairs, *Bey:* Sidi Mohammed el Tahar. *Resident-General:* General Mast.
FRENCH WEST AFRICA, 1,807,060.	14,800	Dakar, *Governor-General:* M. Cournarie.
SENEGAL, 77,000 . .	1,790*	St. Louis, colony, *Governor:* M. Deschamps.
MAURITANIA, 330,000	383*	St. Louis, colony, *Governor:* M. Chalvet.
FRENCH GUINEA, 97,000 . . .	2,011*	Conakry, colony, *Governor:* M. Croccichia.
IVORY COAST, 183,000	3,851*	Abidjan, colony, *Governor:* M. Latrille.
DAHOMEY, 43,000 . .	1,352*	Porto Novo, colony, *Governor:* M. d'Astier de Pompignan.
FRENCH SUDAN, 577,000	3,569*	Koulouba (Bamako), colony, *Governor:* M. Calvel.
NIGER, 500,000 . . .	1,747*	Niamey, colony, *Governor:* M. Toby.
DAKAR AND DEPENDENCIES, 60	126,129*	Dakar, colony, *Governor:* M. Bienés.
TOGOLAND, 20,000. . .	781	Lomé, mandated territory, *Commissioner:* M. Noutary.
FRENCH SOMALILAND, 8,380 . . .	50	Jibuti, colony, *Governor:* M. Saller.
MADAGASCAR AND DEPENDENCIES, 236,900	3,900	Antananarivo, colony, *Governor-General:* M. de Saint-Mart.
RÉUNION, 920	210	St. Denis, colony, *Governor:* M. Capagorry.
AMERICA		
ST. PIERRE AND MIQUELON, 93	4	St. Pierre, colony, *Administrator:* M. Garrouste.
FRENCH GUIANA, including Inini, 34,740 . .	37	Cayenne, colony, *Governor:* M. Rapenne.
GUADELOUPE, 690 . .	310	Basse-Terre, colony, *Governor:* M. Bertaut.
MARTINIQUE, 386 . . .	260	Fort-de-France, colony, *Governor:* M. Ponton
ASIA		
FRENCH INDIA, 190 . .	300	Pondicherry, colony, *Governor:* M. Bonvin.
FRENCH INDO-CHINA, 283,000 . . .	23,700	Saigon, *Governor-General:* Admiral Decoux.
ANNAM, 55,800 . . .	5,656*	Hué, protectorate, *Resident-Superior:* ?
CAMBODIA, 69,200 . .	3,046*	Pnom-Penh, protectorate, *Resident-Superior:* ?
COCHIN-CHINA,25,400	4,616*	Saigon, colony, *Governor:* ?
LAOS, 88,800 . . .	1,012*	Vientiane, colony. ?
TONGKING 43,800 . .	8,700*	Hanoi, protectorate, *Resident-Superior:* ?
KWANGCHOW WAN, 310	250	Fort Bayard, territory (leased from China), *Administrator:* ?
OCEANIA		
FRENCH TERRITORIES IN THE PACIFIC	. .	*Commissioner General in the Pacific:* M. Tallec.
NEW CALEDONIA AND DEPENDENCIES, 7,310	55	Nouméa, colony, *Governor:* M. Tallec.
NEW HEBRIDES, 5,700 .	50	Vila, Franco-British condominium, *High Commissioner:* M. Tallec.
PACIFIC ISLANDS, including Society Is., Tuamotu Is., Tubuai Archipelagos,etc.1,540	45	Papeete, colony, *Governor:* Colonel Orselli.

*Population 1936 census.

RAVAGED PORT OF TUNIS after its capture by Allied forces May 7, 1943

was to be accorded to Moslem élite in Algeria; the proportion of Moslems in local assemblies was to be increased and more administrative posts were to be opened to them.

Tunisia.—Approximately 8,000 refugees were given clothes and employment; markets in essential commodities reopened under Allied supervision; food was imported at the rate of 140 tons daily and the whole railway network was restored by the end of May. The Sultan Mohammed el Moncef was deposed in May and succeeded by Sidi Alim Pasha who resigned in July.

General Charles Mast was appointed resident-general on May 7 and took up his duties on June 25, General Alphonse Juin holding temporary office until his arrival. M. Joppe, attorney-general, was suspended and replaced by M. Verin.

French Morocco.—Gabriel Puaux was nominated resident-general on June 3 to replace General Charles Noguès, M. Meyrier acting as resident-general until Puaux's arrival on June 21.

By September no high official retained the post he held at the time of Puaux's appointment. Under Noguès the municipal councils were reinstated in April and Colonel Maurice Herviot was replaced by Colonel Ferdinand Taillardat as director of public security in the Morocco provisional government.

French West Africa.—Pierre Boisson's resignation as governor was announced on June 29. French reservists demobilized in 1940 were ordered to return to their units by Jan. 15. The appointment of Admiral William A. Glassford, Jr., head of the U.S. mission to Dakar, as President Roosevelt's personal representative in French West Africa was announced on May 28.

Elected municipal councils were restored in March. An economic council was set up which reported a decrease in the production of ground-nuts and the export to the Allies of oil seeds, rubber and mahogany.

French Equatorial Africa.—General de Gaulle and René Pleven arrived in Brazzaville on Aug. 28 on a visit.

French Somaliland.—Jibuti adhered to General de Gaulle on Dec. 28, 1942.

Madagascar and Réunion.—General Paul Louis Legentil-

homme, high commissioner, landed on Jan. 7. The British were continuing improvements at Diego Suarez on the basis of French prewar plans, and the British government had paid £10,000 in compensation to civilians for damage done by British troops. On Sept. 25 it was announced that General Albert Lelong had been appointed to command French troops in Madagascar.

Martinique, Guadeloupe and French Guiana.—See *French Possessions in America.*

St. Pierre and Miquelon.—See *French Possessions in America.*

French India.—In January the governor, Louis Bonvin, stated that the colony was still governed by the laws of the Third Republic.

French Oceania.—It was announced on Oct. 15 that Christian Maigret had been appointed temporary governor. In November, Jacques Tallec was appointed commissioner general in the Pacific, governor of New Caledonia and high commissioner of France in the New Hebrides.

French Indo-China.—An agreement was reported to have been signed with Japan for the export of grain. (*See also* LEBANON; PACIFIC ISLANDS, FRENCH; SYRIA.)   (X.)

French Possessions in America.—The French colonies in America are in three regional groupings: two small islands at the mouth of the Gulf of St. Lawrence, St. Pierre and Miquelon (area: 93 sq.mi.; pop. 4,000); French Guiana and Inini, on the east coast of South America north of the Amazon river (area: c. 34,700 sq.mi.; pop.: c. 36,000); some half-dozen islands in the Lesser Antilles, of which the most important are Martinique (area: 386 sq.mi.; pop.: 255,000) and Guadeloupe (area: 583 sq.mi.; pop.: 304,250). The total area of the remaining islands is 104 sq.mi.; pop.: approx. 33,000. About 95% of the pop. is Negro or mulatto.

The opening months of 1943 found the southern French possessions in serious circumstances. While the French West Indies had officially announced independent action in relation to Vichy France, the administration had remained loyal to that government and had refused to co-operate with the American nations. For this reason the United States had cut off diplomatic and commercial relations in Nov. 1942, and no vessels arrived in the

French colonies with supplies. Stocks of supplies had already been short, and real hardship followed.

On March 16 a bloodless coup by army officers, supported by the populace, seized control in French Guiana and declared adherence to the Free French cause. Jean Rapenne was appointed governor of the colony by General Giraud. Brazilian and United States military observers arrived at Cayenne at the end of the month, and much-needed supplies followed with a consequent improvement in conditions.

In the Antilles the governor, Admiral Georges Robert, held out until June 29 when he requested that United States plenipotentiaries be sent to discuss a transfer of authority. After a conference, Henri-Etienne Hoppenot was named high commissioner of the Antilles by the French Committee of National Liberation. Admiral Robert resigned July 13, and by August was on his way to Vichy. United States shipments to the islands were then resumed with an improvement in conditions, but strict control over profits was retained, and sale of autos, tires and tubes was carefully rationed.

In St. Pierre and Miquelon a Council of Fisheries was established, replacing a former consultative commission. Prohibition of the export of postage stamps was ordered April 29.

Trade and Resources.—Trade statistics were not available; the shipping shortage and the political situation reduced the trade of the southern French colonies to a standstill in the early part of the year. St. Pierre and Miquelon in 1942 exported dried fish to the amount of 50,596 short tons (the total codfish catch was 88,690 tons; in 1941 it had been 83,683 tons). Cod-liver oil production for 1942 amounted to 2,475 gal. common, and 3,200 gal. steam process, oil. In 1942 the production of silver and platinum fox skins was 306.

In normal times French Guiana exports gold, cabinet woods, fish glue, rum and cacao. The French West Indian islands produce mainly sugar, rum and bananas for export, with lesser output of cacao, coffee and vanilla. Both areas depend on imports for the greater part of food requirements, and all nonfood needs.

(D. Rd.)

French Committee of National Liberation: *see* FRANCE.
French Congo: *see* FRENCH COLONIAL EMPIRE.
French Equatorial Africa: *see* FRENCH COLONIAL EMPIRE.
French Guiana: *see* FRENCH COLONIAL EMPIRE.
French Guinea: *see* FRENCH COLONIAL EMPIRE.
French Indo-China: *see* FRENCH COLONIAL EMPIRE.

French Literature.

After the occupation of all metropolitan France by the German troops in Nov. 1942, the only books or news of books that seeped across French frontiers were brought by underground representatives or by occasional refugees, with the result that only the most fragmentary information was available.

Two new elements would appear to have characterized the literary scene inside France during 1943: namely, the appearance of an organized underground literature functioning in defiance of the nazis (*Editions de Minuit, Cahiers de la Libération, Lettres Françaises*—not to be confused with the review of the same name in Buenos Aires—etc.) and the final withdrawal into silence of most of the established prose writers after the disappearance of the so-called "unoccupied" zone.

The poetic renaissance, already noted in 1942, gained in momentum during 1943. Foremost among the participants in this attempt to forge a secret language of communication through the medium of poetry were the former Surrealist poets, Aragon and Eluard, both of whom furnished brilliant examples of the poetry of resistance through allusion (see *Les Yeux d'Elsa*, by Louis Aragon, *Un Seul Nom*, by Eluard). Henri Michaux, Alain Bousquet, Pierre Emmanuel, Jacques Destaing, Maurice Hervent, Armand Robin, Lanza del Vasto and others figured among those taking part in this poetic conspiracy.

After three years of "collaborationist" direction under the editorship of Pierre Drieu la Rochelle, and an unsuccessful attempt to return it to its former editor, Jean Paulhan, the famous *Nouvelle Revue Française* died an ignominious death in the summer of 1943. This fact, along with a few others such as the incarceration of André Malraux, the execution by the nazis of Jacques Decour, editor of the clandestine *Lettres Françaises,* suffice to describe the condition of writers inside France during this year of terror and suffering. The only ones, apparently, who were able to make themselves heard were the "collaborators"—among whom were Henry de Montherlant, Pierre Drieu la Rochelle, Louis Ferdinand Céline, Alphonse de Chateaubriant, Fernandez, Abel Bonnard, Jacques Chardonne, Abel Hermant, Paul Morand, Henry Bordeaux, Jean Giono—every means of modern publicity having been put at their disposal by the occupation authorities. This list is not long if it is recalled that France counted at least 100 outstanding names and fully five times as many talented, if less known, writers. The others either worked in silence on manuscripts that could only appear in a liberated France, contributed anonymously to the clandestine press, or were content to publish barbed literary criticism, historical essays, etc. which permitted them to define their attitude.

The majority were said to be living in circumstances of great material distress.

PRESIDENT ROOSEVELT rode in a jeep down the troop-lined streets of Casablanca during the military conference there Jan. 14–24, 1943

In Switzerland the *Cahiers du Rhône* (Albert Béguin, director) which edited Aragon's *Les Yeux d'Elsa,* published a discussion of *Le Génie de la France,* in which Aragon, Thierry Maulnier, Stanislas Fumet, A. Rousseau, G. Cattani and others participated. These texts could not be consulted in the United States. In all, some 40-odd volumes by French writers were brought out in Switzerland, in Neuchâtel, Lausanne, Geneva, Fribourg: a novel by Edmond Jaloux, *Le Culte Secret, Le Théâtre des Esprits,* by Marcel Brion, *Un Homme Pressé,* by Paul Morand, several volumes of poetry and a miscellany of novels, literary criticism, historical essays, etc.

Across the Mediterranean, in Algiers, the literary event of 1943 was the liberation of André Gide which resulted from the Allied occupation of Tunis, where Gide had been as much a prisoner of the nazis as he would have been in France. His description of the Allied victory in Tunis was published in book form together with a collection of *Interviews Imaginaires,* which, in stressing the importance of conserving the integrity of the French language, managed to convey subtly and with his accustomed artistry, the undying French love of liberty. Although André Gide was in 1943 over 70 years old, he was said to be planning the publication of a review, *Arches,* in collaboration with Robert Aaron (formerly of the N.R.F.) to appear in Algiers. The brilliant Algerian review, *Fontaine,* continued to appear regularly and published one number that was entirely devoted to the literature of the U.S.A. A long poem by Philippe Soupault, written in his best vein, "Ode à Londres," was published by *Fontaine* after the author's liberation from a Tunisian prison.

Mention should be made of the continued appearance of *La France Libre* in London, a review which although not primarily concerned with literary matters, nevertheless maintained its usual high literary standard and rendered important service by publishing extracts from such clandestine French papers as *L'Art Français, L'Université Libre, Les Lettres Françaises,* etc. An anonymous novelette from France, *La Patrie Secrète,* appeared in serial form. A series of articles by René Avord on *La Pensée Française en Exil* furnished an interesting analysis of the works of Jacques Maritain and Georges Bernanos, among others. After the 1943 fall issue, the editor of *La France Libre,* André Labarthe, transferred his own activities and those of the review to the United States. Further French literary events in London were the reprinting of books smuggled from France: *Silence de la Mer, Les Yeux d'Elsa* (Horizon-France Libre), and the publication of leaflets to be dropped on France by the R.A.F., *La Revue du Monde Libre,* with contributions by Paul Eluard, Rebecca West, René Avord, Salvador de Madariaga and others.

The new world witnessed a great increase in the publication of French books, reviews, pamphlets and newspapers, both in North and South America. A new weekly, *France-Amérique,* appeared in New York under the editorship of Henri Torrès and Emil Buré, and to the list of French publishers in that city was added that of Jacques Schiffrin (former director of the *Editions de la Pléiade,* Paris) who inaugurated his activities with André Gide's *Interviews Imaginaires,* and reprints from clandestine French editions. Although a generally excellent literary standard characterized the 100 or so French books published in the western hemisphere during 1943, it is scarcely an exaggeration to say that except for many notable reprints, at least four out of five were inspired by events after 1940 and were either historical, economic or political —very often political—in character. In addition to the Gide volume, a few scientific books, such as Dr. Paul Rivet's *Les Origines de l'Homme Américain* (Collection France Forever, Editions de l'Arbre, Montreal); a number of war diaries, the most outstanding of which were those of Jean Hélion and Jean Malaquais; an important contribution to the history of the French tragedy by the

great French journalist, Pertinax, entitled *Les Fossoyeurs;* Vladimir Pozner's novel of occupied France, *Gens du Pays;* Roger Caillois's brilliant collection of essays entitled *Communion des Forts;* André Labarthe's *Retour au Feu,* a moving account of the French participation in the battle of North Africa; a children's book by Antoine de St. Exupéry, *Le Petit Prince;* a new volume on Byzance by the great orientalist, Professor Henri Grégoire— constituted the more important prose works published in the Americas during 1943, in book form. A long poem by André Breton, the right to publish which was denied him by Vichy in 1940, appeared under the imprimatur of "Sur," in Buenos Aires.

To the list of existing reviews: *VVV* (Surréaliste, New York), *Dyn* (dissident-Surréaliste, Mexico), *La Nouvelle Releve* (Catholic, Montreal), *Amerique-Française* (Montreal), *Lettres Françaises* (Buenos-Aires), were added *Hemispheres* (New York, editor Yvan Goll), a bilingual poetry review; *Gants du Ciel* (Montreal), a well printed review of apparent new-comers; and *Renaissance,* the official review of the École Libre des Hautes Études, New York, edited by Henri Grégoire and Alexander Koyré. Of these reviews, more or less unequal in quality, it may be said that *Lettres Françaises* (edited by Roger Caillois) maintained its high literary standard and gave a more exact, more penetrating account of French letters throughout the world than did the others. It was in *Lettres Françaises* that St. Jean Perse published his most recent work, a long poem in nine parts, entitled, "Pluies." (*See* the Oct. 1943 number.)   (E. Js.)

French North Africa: *see* FRENCH COLONIAL EMPIRE.
French Pacific Islands: *see* PACIFIC ISLANDS, FRENCH.
French Somaliland: *see* FRENCH COLONIAL EMPIRE.
French Sudan: *see* FRENCH COLONIAL EMPIRE.
French West Africa: *see* FRENCH COLONIAL EMPIRE.
Frequency Modulation: *see* RADIO.

Friends, Religious Society of.

The Religious Society of Friends was in 1943 composed of 54 yearly meetings and annual conference groups with an approximate membership of 164,000, representing 30 different countries. In the United States and Canada there were 113,857 members in 1943 and they comprised 29 yearly meetings. The Friends general conference was composed of six of these yearly meetings with a membership of 17,202, with headquarters at 1515 Cherry st., Philadelphia, Pa. The Five Years meeting had its headquarters at 101 S. 8th St., Richmond, Ind., and had a membership of 69,747. The other remaining yearly meetings were Conservative and Independent associations and had a membership of approximately 26,908.

Schools, hospitals and meetings were conducted in Palestine, Africa, Cuba, Mexico and Jamaica by the board of missions of the Five Years meeting. The mission stations in Bolivia, Honduras, Guatemala and Alaska were continued under the care of Oregon and California Friends. In Denmark, France, Germany, Holland, Norway, Sweden and Switzerland, the yearly meetings of Friends continued to be active. There were also organized meetings in China, India, Syria and Palestine, Africa, Australia and New Zealand. The yearly meeting in Japan was discontinued due to the formation of the national church in Japan.

A new directory of all meetings for worship in the United States and Canada was published by the American section of the Friends World Committee for Consultation with headquarters at 20 S. 12th St., Philadelphia.

The American Friends Service committee in the United States co-operated with the Friends' Service council in England in humanitarian services of relief, child feeding, assistance to refugees, Japanese relocation, social industrial rehabilitation, peace education and civilian public service.

The American Quaker Workers had to leave France and were interned at Baden-Baden, Germany. The European staff members carried on under the organizational name "Secours Quaker" and were responsible for 350 children in colonies, distributed milk daily to 4,000 babies and extra food ration to 2,500 children in public schools. Four workers were active in North Africa assisting in the liberation of refugees still in internment camps.

The American Friends Service committee co-operating with the National Japanese Student Relocation council assisted in locating 2,000 American-born Japanese students in colleges outside the Japanese internment camps. Hostels were established in Chicago, Ill., Cincinnati, Ohio, and Des Moines, Iowa, where Japanese were assisted in finding new work.

The summer projects of the peace section included two International Service seminars. One was held at Guilford college, North Carolina, and was composed largely of students from Latin American countries. The seminar at Camp Kanesatake, Pennsylvania, was made up of students from Europe and the orient. Three groups of young people worked on projects of rural rehabilitation in Mexico.

The social-industrial section of the service committee conducted eight work camps for college and high school students. The camps were located to serve a fishing community in Vinal Haven, Maine; a migrant labour camp in New Jersey; a marginal farming community in Missouri; Negro neighbourhoods in Chicago, Ill., and Indianapolis, Ind.

Civilian public service continued as an alternative to military service provided for conscientious objectors by the National Selective Service act. The Society of Friends in co-operation with the Brethren and Mennonites operated the C.P.S. camps where men carried on work of national importance. Nearly 7,000 men were in these C.P.S. camps. About 28% of the men received maintenance for the services they rendered in mental hospitals, dairy farms, agricultural experiment stations, and in coast and geodetic service. The others, or 72%, paid their own maintenance and worked on projects of forest service, soil conservation, park service and farm security. A unit of 70 men prepared to go to China to work with the Friends ambulance unit in transporting medical supplies and nearly 200 men entered colleges for special courses on postwar reconstruction, but both of these projects were made void by an act of congress in July 1943.

The Religious Society of Friends is a spiritual movement which was started in England over 250 years ago. The founder, George Fox, emphasized the dignity and worth of the individual as having direct access to God. Quakerism, as the spiritual movement is often called, is known as a Way of Life which recognizes the divine nature of human beings, believes in the equality of all races, encourages simplicity and naturalness in thought and action, and maintains a pacifist testimony. The meetings for worship are conducted in an atmosphere of quiet reverent waiting in which any of the members may participate in vocal ministry as led by the Holy Spirit.   (L. D. SH).

Fruit: *see* AGRICULTURE; APPLES; BANANAS; GRAPEFRUIT; GRAPES; LEMONS AND LIMES; ORANGES; PEACHES; PEARS; PLUMS AND PRUNES.

FSLIC: *see* NATIONAL HOUSING AGENCY.

FTC: *see* FEDERAL TRADE COMMISSION.

Fuel Briquettes. Although the United States is only a minor producer of fuel briquettes, it was the only country from which data were received. Production increased from 1,298,606 short tons in 1941 to 1,748,300 tons in 1942, with 30 plants in operation in 14 states.   (G. A. Ro.)

Fuel Oil: *see* BUSINESS REVIEW; PETROLEUM; RATIONING.

Fuller's Earth. In 1941 the production of fuller's earth in the U.S. broke the decline that had been under way for more than a decade, and increased to 207,446 short tons, 43% over 1940, though some of this increase was due to the inclusion in the figures of considerable tonnages of Texan material which had not heretofore been classed as fuller's earth. In 1942 the output dropped to 204,244 tons.   (G. A. Ro.)

Fuqua, Stephen Ogden (1874–1943), U.S. army officer, was born Dec. 25 in Baton Rouge, La. A student at West Point, 1892–93, he was an infantry captain with the U.S. volunteer army during the Spanish-American War and served in the Mexican expedition in 1914. During World War I he served in France on the operations section of the staff of the First Army and as chief of staff of the First Division, with rank of temporary colonel. He was made chief of infantry in 1929 with rank of major general, a promotion which skipped him over the heads of 165 colonels and brought about considerable opposition in army circles. He held that post until 1932, when he was named military attaché to Spain. He returned to the United States in the fall of 1938 and retired from the army at the end of that year. He afterward became military affairs editor for *Newsweek* magazine. He died in New York city May 11.

Furniture Industry. All production records for the furniture industry in the United States were broken during 1943 when approximately $1,000,000,000 worth of wooden household furniture, army and navy furniture, defense housing furniture, aeroplane parts, boat hulls, and other war equipment were produced by the 2,250 factories comprising the industry. Of the 2,250 factories, approximately 750 were engaged entirely in war work; of the remaining 1,500, approximately half were devoting about 50% of their productive capacity to war contracts but producing also some civilian furniture.

Despite the great shift during 1942 from peacetime to wartime production, the industry shipped in 1943, $550,000,000 worth of household furniture to merchants, a drop of only 18% below 1942 shipments of $630,000,000.

At the close of 1943, WPB issued an order limiting furniture manufacturers to 84% of the hardwood lumber they had used in making civilian furniture during 1943 and banned the production of such "non-essentials" as home bars, cellarettes, magazine racks, tea wagons, curio cabinets, pier cabinets, what-nots, chaise longues, record cabinets, Lazy Susans, bird cages and stands, ferneries, towel racks and juvenile bookcases, chiffoniers, wardrobes and toy chests. These ordinarily account for but 2% of the industry's output.

At the same time, WPB placed restrictions upon the use of seven critical hardwoods by the industry: ash, beech, yellow birch, hickory, hard maple, oak and rock elm. Since these woods were scarce for six months, few factories used them except for war work and government housing projects.

Few furniture plants ceased operations during 1943 and these were upholstering firms that refused to continue production when the use of spring wire was denied the industry. After shipping all the furniture with springs they were able to complete before the government deadline, about 25 factories discontinued operations for the duration. All others adopted wooden springs or padded construction or secured government contracts to maintain operations.

Furniture markets were discontinued in High Point, N.C., and Los Angeles during 1943 because the exhibition buildings formerly devoted to home furnishings were taken over by government agencies. Markets continued to be held, however, in New York, Chicago, Grand Rapids and Jamestown, N.Y., although on a limited scale compared with normal times.

The manpower shortage was being partially relieved by the use of women. Government reports showed 25,000 employed in 1943 in furniture plants, representing about 20% of factory personnel. While the number of employees dropped 20% during the year, pay rolls were down only 8%, due to overtime, etc.

No reports were available regarding furniture production outside of the United States. (*See* also INTERIOR DECORATION.)

(J. A. G.)

Furs. The year 1943 brought a very large volume of business to the American fur industry. Based on U.S. treasury department tax figures, the cash turnover of furs in retail stores totalled approximately $450,000,000. The revenue derived by the government from the 10% tax on fur apparel was therefore approximately $45,000,000. All branches of the industry shared profitably in this turnover. Prices were higher than in 1942, but were prevented from going to extreme levels by the restraining influence of the OPA regulation which attempted to establish ceilings on fur skins and manufactured garments. Business in furs increased steadily month after month and since there were no strikes or labour difficulties, other than a growing shortage of skilled workers, production was maintained at a steady pace throughout the year instead of being concentrated in the summer months, as in previous years. The manufacturing branch of the industry benefited by this spreading out of the manufacturing season and the consequent elimination of the customary slack period, which was usually accompanied by unemployment. The industry, for the first time in a decade, ended the year without a surplus of merchandise since demand managed to keep ahead of supply throughout the 12 months.

The supply of American and Canadian raw furs was somewhat less than in 1942, especially of the farm-bred furs such as mink and silver fox. It was one of the biggest years for mink fur in the history of the trade. Prices on this fur, because of a large carry-over of mink skins from 1942, enabled manufacturers to buy mink at very reasonable prices and supply the public with good mink coats at comparatively low prices. This fur sold freely and by October of 1943 the supply was pretty well exhausted. There was an exceptional demand for scarfs and neckpieces made from mink.

Muskrat was the most popular fur of the year, and was dyed and worked to resemble mink. The next most popular fur was Persian lamb, which was in very good supply through shipments from Russia, Afghanistan and southwest Africa. The trade drew its largest supply of lambskins from Africa and shipping space, in spite of restrictions, was found on ships returning from Cape Town. Silver fox, beaver, nutria, red fox, skunk, raccoon and opossum were all furs in great demand. The favourite coat style of the year was the tuxedo front fashion. Canada was the largest source of so-called foreign furs, but the United States also imported nutria, viscacha, pony, kidskin, skunk, fox, lambskins and spotted cat from the Central and South American countries. The United States did not receive any furs from India or the far east, but imported quantities of rabbitskins, opossum, wallaby and fox from Australia and New Zealand. Actual import figures were not issued by the government.

The trade complained constantly to the OPA about the inequalities and the impractical provisions of regulation No. 178, which governed fur prices. OPA finally agreed to hold hearings and, after months of consultations with different branches of the trade, decided to revise the regulation and announced that the new regulation would be ready in November. The fur trade

waited for the OPA announcement, but finally was forced to go ahead and operate under the old regulation. Up to the end of the year there had been no further word from the OPA. It was expected, however, that the new regulation would go into effect by the spring of 1944. This regulation would attempt to hold fur prices at the same levels as prevailed in 1942.

Up to the end of Nov. 1943 there were 81 failures in the American fur industry, with total liabilities of $1,387,758, according to the American Fur Merchants association of New York. Most of these failures were in the New York trade and were fewer than at any time from 1938 to 1943. Out-of-town firms transacted anywhere from 50% to 100% more business than they did in the previous year and hundreds of thousands of new consumers were found in areas which gave employment to millions of workers in war industries. War workers brought about a demand for a somewhat better type of garment than in former years. The most popular price range was between $200 and $300 for a coat. Manufacturers and retailers ended the year in a strong financial condition and with only limited stocks of merchandise to carry them into the new year, with the possible exception of some of the higher priced luxury garments. The raw fur season of 1943 which began in November found the fur markets greatly in need of fresh pelts. Prices paid to trappers and fur farmers were up about 50%, on the average, as compared with the opening prices in 1942. There appeared to be a somewhat short catch and a disregard in the country collecting points for OPA ceiling prices.

The fur industry provided the American and Allied merchant seamen with fur-lined vests free of cost through the fur vest projects in New York, Chicago, Los Angeles, San Francisco, Milwaukee and other cities. Both labour and management provided the time, the material, and the labour-hours, in co-operation with the member workers of the International Fur and Leather Workers union.

(W. J. Bt.)

FWA: *see* FEDERAL WORKS AGENCY.

Gager, Charles Stuart (1872–1943), U.S. botanist, was born Dec. 23 in Norwich, N.Y. (For his early career, see *Encyclopædia Britannica*.) In 1910 he became director of the Brooklyn Botanic garden, a position which he held until the time of his death. Dr. Gager engaged in a large variety of scientific enterprises. He edited the *Brooklyn Botanic Record*, beginning in 1912, and was business manager of the *American Journal of Botany*, 1914–35. He also became business manager of *Ecology* in 1920, and of *Genetics* in 1922. He wrote widely in scientific and educational journals and published, in addition to several earlier works, *The Plant World* (1931). Dr. Gager served on several committees of the National Research council, and was a member of the botanical committees for the Chicago and New York world fairs. On June 4, 1941, Swarthmore college honoured him with the Arthur Hoyt Scott Garden and Horticultural award. He was president of the Botanical Society of America in 1936. In 1941 he was elected an honorary member of the Royal Agricultural and Horticultural Society of India. He died on Aug. 9.

Galway, George Vere Arundell Monckton-Arundell, 8TH VISCOUNT, (1882–1943), Irish peer, was born March 24. He was educated at Eton and at Christ Church, Oxford, where he received his B.A. and M.A. degrees. He served in World War I and was in command of the Life Guards when he retired from the army in 1929. He succeeded to the title in 1931. Viscount Galway served as governor general of New Zealand, 1935–41. He died March 27.

Gambia: *see* BRITISH WEST AFRICA.

Gandhi, Mohandas Karamchand

(1869–   ), Hindu nationalist leader, was born at Porbandar (Kathiawar), India. For his biography, see *Encyclopædia Britannica*. On Jan. 22, 1937, Gandhi announced his retirement from active Indian politics, but by 1940 he was as prominent as ever in Indian affairs of state. The All-India congress on March 20, 1940, delegated to him the direction of negotiations with Great Britain for national independence. On Sept. 17, 1940, the congress committee elected Gandhi its leader. In April 1941, he announced that the congress had temporarily abandoned its aim of independence for India, but he reaffirmed his personal policy of nonviolence. On Dec. 30, 1941, Gandhi resigned from its leadership.

On March 27, 1942, Gandhi conferred with Sir Stafford Cripps; later he rejected the latter's proposals for Indian postwar independence. On Aug. 9, after the All-India Congress party had approved his proposals for a civil disobedience campaign, Gandhi was arrested with 200 other Indian leaders and was held as a political prisoner in the Aga Khan's palace in Poona. On Feb. 10, 1943, he began a 21-day fast, precipitating renewed strikes and demonstrations among his followers. As the fast continued, small hope was held out for Gandhi's recovery, but in spite of world-wide pleas for his release he remained a prisoner, the government looking on his fast as "political blackmail." Toward the end of the month he rallied, and on March 3 he ended his fast. At the end of 1943 he was still a prisoner. (*See also* INDIA.)

Garnet: *see* ABRASIVES.

Gas, Natural.

The total production of natural gas in the United States in 1941 was estimated at 4,104,000,000,000 cu.ft.; after deducting losses of 630,000,000,000, 16,000,000,000 pumped back into the ground for storage and 644,000,000,000 for repressuring the field, the marketed total amounted to 2,813,000,000,000, an increase of 22% over 1940. In 1942 the marketed production increased 9% to 3,055,000,000,000 cu.ft., of which the various leading uses took the following percentages: light, fuel and power in the producing field 22%; domestic use 16%; carbon black plants 11%; electric power and public utility plants 7%; petroleum refineries and commercial uses each 6%; the remaining 32% included a wide variety of minor industrial uses and a small amount exported, mainly to Mexico. Natural gas was piped to and sold in the following states, in addition to the 26 states in which it is produced: Alabama, Arizona, District of Columbia, Florida, Georgia, Iowa, Maryland, Minnesota and Nebraska.

In 1942 a total of 3,000,000,000,000 cu.ft. of natural gas was treated for the recovery of natural gasoline vapours, resulting in the production of approximately 1 gal. of natural gasoline for each 1,000 cu.ft. of gas treated.

Canadian production in 1942 was 42,700,000,000 cu.ft., a reduction of 2% from 1941. (G. A. RO.)

Gasoline: *see* PETROLEUM; RATIONING.

Gaulle, Charles de

(1890–   ), French soldier and leader of the forces of Fighting France after the armistices of June 22–24, 1940, graduated from St. Cyr military college at Paris shortly before the German invasion of France in 1914. Wounded three times during World War I, he was captured by German troops at Verdun in 1916, but escaped and saw further action on the western front and in the near east. Foreseeing the future tactical importance of tanks and combat cars, he waged a one-man campaign to persuade France to mechanize her infantry after 1918, but army officers preferred to place their trust in such measures of immobile defense as the Maginot line. The first several days of Germany's lightning thrust through Belgium and the Netherlands in May 1940 proved the correctness of de Gaulle's theories, and he was belatedly made undersecretary of war in Reynaud's cabinet. He parted ways with Marshal Pétain's government when it elected to surrender, and he fled to London. There on June 23, 1940, he announced formation of the French National committee, an expatriate military and political organization. Many French possessions in Africa, Asia, Oceania and the Americas rallied to de Gaulle's banner. His attempt to seize Dakar, with British aid, in Sept. 1940 was repelled by Vichy-controlled forces, but in 1941 Syria, Lebanon, St. Pierre and Miquelon joined his movement. In September of that year the Free French National council was formed with de Gaulle as its president. He aligned his policy with that of the U.S. and Britain, concluded a politico-military alliance with the U.S.S.R. and declared his council at war with Japan, Dec. 8, 1941. During 1942, the French underground factions united and accepted de Gaulle's leadership in the struggle against the axis. After Adm. Jean Darlan's assassination in Dec. 1942, de Gaulle made repeated efforts to meet with Gen. Henri Giraud, the admiral's successor but was snubbed by the French general. Angered by Giraud's attitude, de Gaulle in early 1943 called Giraud's regime "baseless and artificial." Giraud was finally compelled to confer with the Fighting French leader, who was supported by the majority of Frenchmen in North Africa as well as France. The two leaders met in Algiers and on June 3, 1943, announced formation of the French Committee of National Liberation, a trustee government to administer French interests until the Germans were driven out of metropolitan France. On Nov. 9, 1943, de Gaulle assumed full control of the French committee, and Giraud resigned as co-president.

Gems and Precious Stones.

With Burma, Thailand, and Indo-China in Japanese hands, access was lost to an area that previously had supplied a large portion of the demand for precious and semiprecious stones other than diamonds, and in other areas, such as India, Ceylon and Australia production was hampered. Increased trade in South America brought to the United States greater supplies of many semiprecious stones, and domestic production supplied a fair amount, though considerably less in 1942 than in previous years. The only precious stone mined in the United States is the sapphire, of which about 50,000 oz. was produced in 1942; some of this was of gem quality but the bulk of the output was for instrument jewels. The value of crude gem stones produced in the United States in 1942 was estimated by the U.S. bureau of mines at $150,000 as compared with $240,000 in 1941; when cut, these values were increased to $400,000 and $770,000 respectively. Sapphires represented 31% of the total, turquoise 21% and various quartz minerals 20%. Producing states, in decreasing order of importance were Montana, Nevada, Oregon and Wyoming. (*See also* MINERALOGY.) (G. A. RO.)

General Education Board: *see* ROCKEFELLER FOUNDATION.
General Federation of Women's Clubs: *see* WOMEN'S CLUBS, GENERAL FEDERATION OF.

Genetics.

The work of Lindegren and Lindegren on the genetics of commercial yeasts made available an important new source of high protein- and vitamin-rich foods at low cost. They isolated rapidly growing strains with different taste qualities which might be used in the production of nutritious and palatable synthetic foods, grown rapidly on inexpensive substrates.

Serological Genetics.—Wiener and Sonn studied the linkage of the Rhesus factor first reported by Landsteiner and Wiener as a dominant which, when present in the human foetus of a recessive, rh-negative mother, may lead to the highly fatal condition, erythroblastosis foetalis. They found that the Rh-rh factors are not linked to the blood group genes, A, B, O or to the M, N blood factors. Thus three pairs of human chromosomes in addition to the sex-chromosomes were known in 1943 to carry genetic markers usable in further linkage studies through the wide distribution of contrasting alleles in human populations. Neel and Valentine showed that the rare blood disease, thalassemia or Cooley's anaemia, fatal in infants, is due to an incomplete recessive. They reported on the abnormal blood picture of the heterozygotes. This was the first case in which the carriers of a condition of medical importance could be certainly recognized.

In mice, Gowen and Calhoun separated strains with differential resistance to mouse typhoid and showed that these differ in the numbers of leucocytes. Gruneberg found that the recessive gene for flexed tail in mice also produces an anaemia characterized by development of erythrocytes, deficient in haemoglobin and rich in detachable iron, over a long period of embryonic life. Sawin and Glick discovered that an atropine hydrolyzing enzyme in the blood of rabbits is conditioned by an incompletely dominant gene, with higher incidence in some rabbit strains than in others. Irwin and collaborators continued the genetic analysis of cellular antigens in species crosses of pigeons and doves.

Physiological Genetics.—Waddington traced the development of several leg mutants in *Drosophila* in prepupal and pupal stages. Goldschmidt reported on a series of wing shape alleles at two loci in *Drosophila* and found one case of interaction between alleles at these loci which represents a threshold condition where lines differing in genetic modifiers may be isolated, giving symmetrical and asymmetrical expressions of wing characters. Stern showed that the factor, cubitus interruptus, in *Drosophila* has an effect cumulative toward the wild-type character in haploid, diploid and triploid doses. From reactions of the ci alleles in these combinations and in heterozygous combinations with wild-type alleles at this locus he has proposed a theory of gene action based on (a) presence of and amount of a substrate in the cell; (b) combining action of gene with substrate; (c) efficiency of gene in utilizing substrate. Mampell described a dominant "mutator" gene in *Drosophila pseudo-obscura* which increases normal mutation rate 34 times in the heterozygote and 70 times when homozygous.

Radiation Genetics.—Radiation experiments on plants and animals showed that neutron radiation and X-ray radiation in equivalent doses as regards ionization behave differently in inducing chromosome breaks and gene mutations. Neutrons produce more chromosome breaks; X-rays induce more point mutations. Eberhardt found more breaks in the fourth chromosome of *Drosophila* after neutron radiation. Giles found higher breakage from neutrons in the plant, Tradescantia; higher lethal mutation rate in *Drosophila* from X-rays. Lea and Catcheside decided that breaks in Tradescantia chromatids are produced by not less than 17 ionizations per chromatid. They considered that dense ionization along neutron paths explains their effectiveness in causing breaks. Conversely, only as a fast electron slows up (tail of the path) is the ionization dense enough to produce breakage.

Genetics and Evolution.—The book of 1943 in this field is by Julian Huxley (see *Bibliography*). Many genetic and cytogenetic studies on speciation, particularly in plants, appeared. Faberge reported on extensive eco-genetic work on populations of Iceland and Alpine poppies. He established that many taxonomic characters in this group are due to single genes or com-

binations of two genes. Charles and Goodwin analyzed the minimum gene differences for leaf characters in two species of goldenrod which hybridize. Moore crossed the dominant non-spotting mutation in the frog, *Rana pipiens*, to two other species and proved it dominant in them. Wharton published a comparative study of the metaphase and salivary chromosomes of 86 species and subspecies of *Drosophila*. She concluded that chromosome configuration *per se* is less important in speciation than was formerly supposed. Dobzhansky and Wright continued the analysis of the genetic structure of natural populations, based on field-laboratory studies of *Drosophila pseudo-obscura* and the desert plant, Linanthus. They found that *Drosophila* populations vary seasonally in gene structure, apparently in adaptive response to environmental factors through natural selection.

BIBLIOGRAPHY.—*Genetics*, vol. 28 (1943); *Journal of Genetics*, vol. 44 (1943); *Journal of Heredity*, vol. 34 (1943); Julian Huxley, *Evolution, The Modern Synthesis* (1943).   (W. P. S.)

Geographical Society, American: *see* AMERICAN GEOGRAPHICAL SOCIETY.

Geography.

War in foreign lands inevitably gives rise to a demand for geographic information out of all proportion to the interest shown in peacetime. This effect, though important also in other fields, is probably more striking in the case of geography than that of any other profession, other than the military professions themselves. It is particularly marked in the United States, a country whose people have been accustomed to think of foreign lands as remote and of minor importance to them but in 1943 found the specific beach characteristics of tiny Pacific islands half way round the world of vital importance to their sons. In World War I, which was concerned primarily with Europe and in which Americans fought chiefly in France and Italy, U.S. geographers were called upon in considerable numbers to assist the government as well as to furnish

GIRL OPERATORS putting together a maze of slotted templates to serve as a base for a map compilation from aerial photographs. Each strip represents the flight line of a plane; the intersections of the template arms locate the prominent features that will serve as landmarks

information for the public. In World War II, the demands were vastly greater for the issues were world-wide. Americans have fought in Africa, Europe, Asia and the islands of the Pacific, and the use of air transport caused areas previously isolated from U.S. concern to be of critical importance for the maintenance of connections to and from the battle fronts.

The effects on the use and development of geography are to be found in three major fields: (a) popular interest in information concerning battle areas; (b) the demand for precise geographic information concerning almost all foreign areas by the federal government, primarily for the military services, the other war agencies and the state department; (c) the requirements for geographic training of selected military personnel in the army and navy training courses in hundreds of colleges and universities.

Popular Interest.—The reaction of the press to public interest in the geography of war areas was immediate. The most obvious measure was the great increase in use of maps in newspapers and magazines. In some of the latter, professional geographers introduced marked innovations in cartographic art, in many cases with notable success. The U.S. public was acquiring an education in the geography of the world such as it never had before. The comparative ease with which small handfuls of leaders could be transported across oceans and continents almost overnight, in contrast with what appeared as the pedestrian pace of troops shipped in convoys, stimulated imaginative predictions of a new world to come. If some of these publications in serious magazines, and even in book form, appeared to be influenced by the example of Superman and deserved place only in Sunday supplements, they were nevertheless symptoms of a stirring of the national thought toward a truer appraisal of the kind of world in which it lives.

Geography in War Agencies.—Whereas the federal government during the 1930s had increasingly utilized geographers in the study of domestic problems, practically none, except for a small unit in the state department, were engaged in study of the geography of foreign lands. Major steps to remedy this situation were taken, as a result of the wars in Europe and Asia, some months before Pearl Harbor. The army brought professional geographers who held commissions in the reserve corps to do intelligence work in Washington; the office of geographer in the state department was expanded, and the new Office of Strategic Services (at that time called the Coordinator of Information) set up a geography division; several geographers were added to the staff of what shortly became the Board of Economic Warfare (now included in the Foreign Economic administration).

After Pearl Harbor, all of these were rapidly expanded and various other agencies concerned with the war called upon geographers to supply expert services. By the end of 1943 more than 200 professional geographers were employed in government agencies in Washington, or nearly 5 times as many as in peacetime. In research and analysis of geographic information, as well as in the compilation and construction of maps, they performed one major part of the intelligence service provided by the military intelligence division of the army and the Office of Strategic Services, as well as the army map service and the board of geographic names. Geographers contributed detailed specific information on the terrain, climate, transport routes, food and industrial resources of each area to which U.S. troops had been sent. Geographers who were specialists in maps were included in the working staffs taken to the conferences at Quebec and Cairo. By the end of the year, geographers were at work at outposts near the battlefronts, at London, in North Africa and in the far east.

EDITING the final details on a huge map base of an army air force aeronautical chart of a section of North Africa

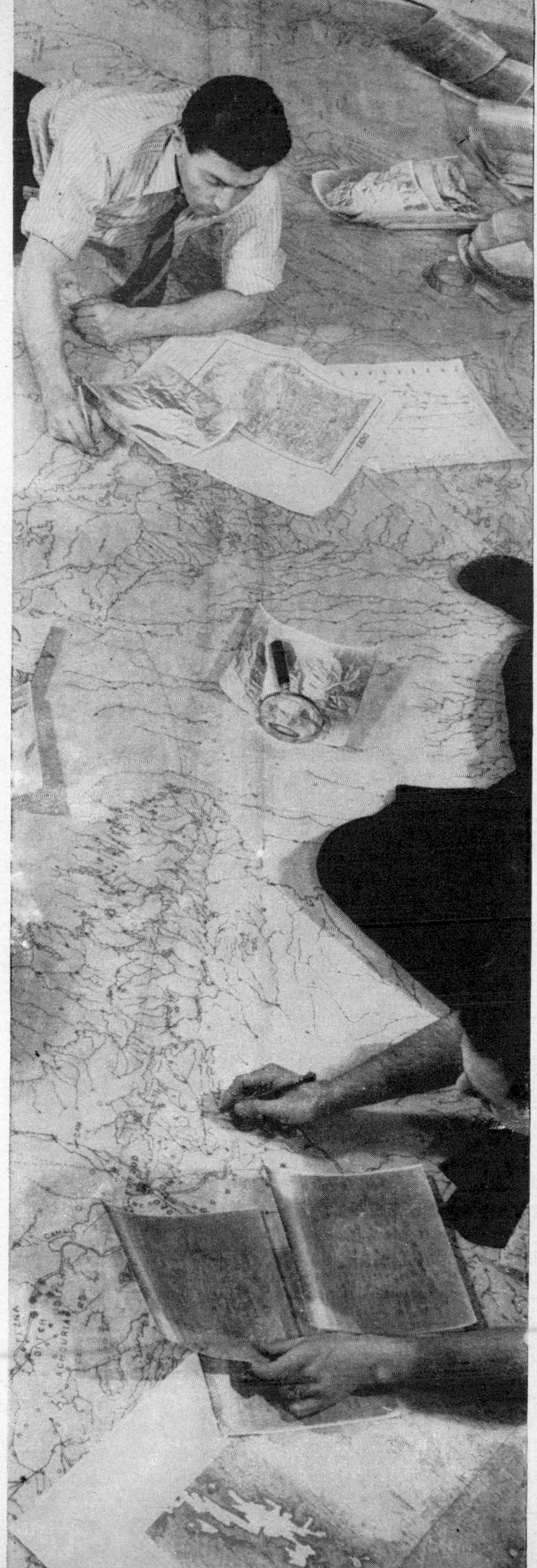

Whereas the first demand for geographic information had been for purposes of planning combat activities and supply routes, successful advance of U.S. troops in any area led immediately to problems of military government in occupied areas; in various of these agencies geographers were at work supplying background information needed by the authorities who had to organize the reconstruction of agriculture, industry, utilities and transport and the reorganization of civil life.

Training Courses.—In the various training courses organized in U.S. colleges and universities for the army and navy, geography played an important role. The course programs in meteorology for aviators included general surveys of world geography, and the area programs designed for officers in military government naturally required basic courses in the geography of the areas concerned. This presented almost every college in the land with a serious difficulty; those in which the study of geography had been well developed had in most cases previously lent some of their best personnel to government service for the duration. Many colleges unfortunately had not previously included the subject in their curriculum but now suddenly had its importance thrust upon them. As a result it was necessary in many institutions to draft men from related departments, from geology, or history, or from wherever, and assign them to teach with whatever preparation could be provided them almost overnight. Unfortunately, lack of national planning for this particular emergency had permitted the induction into the army of large numbers of young graduate students in the field who would otherwise have been available for this specialized service. (*See also* AMERICAN GEOGRAPHICAL SOCIETY; NATIONAL GEOGRAPHIC SOCIETY.)

(R. HAR.)

Geology. Research and writing in pure geology were at a low ebb. A number of foreign journals and at least one domestic one (*The Journal of Geomorphology*) were discontinued for the duration of World War II. European geological publications either were not reaching the United States or were greatly delayed in their appearance.

Many strategic areas in America were being mapped topographically for the first time on the basis of aeroplane photographs. This new method is three to five times faster than required by former techniques. The new system augured well for the future since less than half of the United States was carefully mapped. The new book *Aerial Photographs and Their Applications* by H. T. U. Smith is of interest in this connection.

The demands of the world conflict upon the mineral industry apparently reached their peak only in the metalliferous branch.

The need for well-trained applied geologists and geophysicists was greater than ever before as a result of the greater tempo of mineral exploration and development; yet the number of students preparing for these fields in the colleges and universities fell to a new low since the widespread application of highly specialized techniques in prospecting.

The Office of Scientific Personnel of the National Research council co-operated in an effort to alleviate the wartime personnel problem in geology by (1) assisting in placing qualified workers in positions connected with the war effort and (2) taking steps to secure deferment of those vitally needed in the mineral industry because of their special skills.

The opinion prevailed among geologists that the full potentialities of the science were not being utilized by the military authorities of the Allied nations, and that the profession was not adequately appreciated by laymen. For these and other reasons steps were taken to organize an association of geological societies

CAVE 40 FT. HIGH, discovered in the Rock of Gibraltar during military tunnelling operations. Sealed 20,000 years ago, the chamber contains a freshwater lake 40 yd. long

which might wield a greater national influence.

Geomorphology.—Of interest in this field are the books by R. A. Daly, *The Floor of the Ocean,* and C. A. Cotton, *Climatic Accidents in Landscape-making.*

Historical Geology.—A noteworthy contribution was G. G. Simpson's "Mammals and the Nature of Continents," which appeared in the *American Journal of Science* for January. This study supports the hypothesis that the continents were essentially stable throughout the period involved in mammalian history.

The March issue of the same journal carried an interesting article on paleopedology (the study of fossil soils) by C. C. Nikifovoff.

Sedimentation.—Vol. 5 of *The Report of the Great Barrier Reef Committee on Great Barrier Reef Bores* should be of interest to workers in this field. The mollusks contained in the reef are reported to be of recent age, thus indicating an extraordinarily rapid rate of deposition of the reef limestone.

The book entitled *Micromeritics, The Technology of Fine Particles* by J. M. Dalla Valle should be of special interest to metallurgists and engineers as well as to geologists.

Petrology.—A semi-popular treatise, *Minerals and Rocks— Their Nature, Occurrence and Uses,* came from the pen of R. D. George. An intriguing article entitled "Some Petrological Concepts and the Interior of the Earth" by A. F. Buddington appeared in the March issue of the *American Mineralogist.*

The report by E. B. Sandell and S. S. Goldich on "The Rarer Metallic Constituents of Some American Igneous Rocks" published in the *Journal of Geology* deals with the distribution of minor elements and gives estimates of the probable abundance of these in the earth's crust.

Vulcanology.—Attention is called to the unusual outbreak and development during 1943 of the Mexican volcano Paricutin, which arose in February from a cornfield some 200 mi. west of Mexico City. By late September Paricutin had reached a height of 1,500 ft. This is the first volcanic outbreak whose entire early history has been observed and recorded by man. It was described by P. D. Trask in *Science.*

Structural Geology.—Two books in the field of structural geology may be mentioned: *The Dynamics of Faulting and Dyke Formation with Applications to Britain* by E. M. Anderson and *Structural Petrology of Deformed Rocks* by H. W. Fairbain.

Economic Geology.—Considerable interest was shown in the subject of the political control of mineral resources. This was exemplified by the appearance of *Minerals in World Affairs* by T. S. Lovering; *World Minerals and World Peace* by C. K. Leith, J. W. Furness and Cleona Lewis; and *Strategic Materials and National Strength* by H. N. Holmes.

Much attention was given to the world's petroleum resources as a result of dwindling petroleum reserves and the expanding industrial uses for petroleum and its products. These and related problems were considered in an article in *Science,* "Petroleum—Past, Present and Future," by P. K. Frolich.

An innovation in petroleum geology was the initiation of an annual review of the science by the members of the staffs of the departments of geology, geophysics and petroleum engineering of the Colorado school of mines under the sponsorship of the Research committee of the American Association of Petroleum Geologists.

Military Geology.—The increased interest in this field was manifested by the appearance of the authoritative work on *Map Interpretation with Military Applications* by W. C. Putnam and an article by C. E. Erdmann, "Application of Geology to the Principles of War," in the *Bulletin of the Geological Society of America.* A bibliography on military geology and geography prepared by Marie Siegrist and Elizabeth Platt was issued by the division of geology and geography of the National Research council. (*See also* MINERALOGY; PALEONTOLOGY; SEISMOLOGY.)

(F. M. V. T.; B. H. P.)

George, Harold Lee (1895–   ), U.S. army officer, was born July 19 in Somerville, Mass. Educated at George Washington university and the National university of Washington, he was appointed as secretary to the U.S. comptroller of currency in 1917. He soon left this post, however, to join the army and was commissioned a 2nd lieutenant in the air force the same year. Remaining in the army after the war, he was closely associated with Gen. "Billy" Mitchell, the prophet of air power. When Gen. Mitchell was given the opportunity to demonstrate the value of aerial bombardment in 1921, George piloted one of the six Martin bombers which sank the ex-German battleship "Ostfriesland" during an experimental raid. He also served as a defense witness for Mitchell when the general was tried for insubordination. George engaged in experimental work in developing aerial armament and bombs at the Aberdeen Proving grounds, 1921–25, and was head of the bombardment section in the office of the chief of the air corps for the next four years. In 1940, he became commanding officer of the 2nd bombardment squadron, the first organization to be equipped with four-engined Flying Fortresses. The following year, he was named assistant chief of air staff for war plans. In March 1942, George became the commanding general of the air ferrying command, later known as the Air Transport command.

George VI. A visit by air in 1943 to all his fighting services in North Africa and the Mediterranean was the outstanding event in the king's year, most of which was otherwise spent in or near London, in close contact with his ministers and in holding investitures. Twice in September the king dined with

KING GEORGE VI (right) enjoying the antics of comedians at a vaudeville show for the British home fleet in April 1943

the prime minister in Downing St., and in November he entertained the visiting regent of Iraq for two days at Buckingham palace. His gift of a jewelled sword of honour in token of British "homage to the steel-hearted citizens of Stalingrad" followed an exchange of messages with President Kalinin of the U.S.S.R., after the great victory there in February. On the fourth anniversary of the war the king ordained a national day of prayer on September 3 and on September 12 a day of thanksgiving for the unconditional surrender of Italy.

The king's only previous visit to the front was in Dec. 1939, when the British army was still in France. The African journey, lasting a fortnight, began on June 11, 1943, and was made in a four-engined bomber, piloted by Group Captain Fielden. With the king were the secretaries of state for war (Sir James Grigg) and air (Sir Archibald Sinclair). Reaching Algiers on June 12 the king was received by General Dwight Eisenhower, Allied commander-in-chief, General Sir Harold Alexander, commander in the field, Harold Macmillan, resident minister, and Robert Murphy, President Roosevelt's personal representative. June 14 was spent with General Mark Clark's 5th American army. On June 16, attended by Admiral Sir Andrew Cunningham, Allied naval commander-in-chief, the king visited the Allied fleet, boarding, among other vessels, a U.S. battleship to be received by Vice Admiral Hewitt, U.S.N. Back in Africa the king, on June 17, saw a U.S. air headquarters and the 1st British army under General Kenneth A. N. Anderson. In Tunis on June 18 he visited General Louis Jacques Barré of the Free French and General Bernard L. Montgomery's 8th British army. Next day on the cruiser "Aurora" he reached Malta to tour war-scarred Valletta with the governor, Viscount Gort, and the council. June 21 was spent in Tripoli. Before returning to England, reached on June 25, the king invested General Eisenhower with the G.C.B., knighted Generals Montgomery and Henry Maitland Wilson (commanding in the near East) and instituted the Africa Star and the 1939–1943 Star, for hard fighting on all fronts. (L. Du.)

George of Bavaria, Prince

(1880–1943) was born April 2, the grandson of Emperor Franz Josef of Austria-Hungary and eldest son of Prince Leopold of Bavaria. In 1912, amid regal pomp and splendour, he was married at the Schoenbrunn palace to the Archduchess Isabelle Marie of Austria. The alliance was not a happy one, however, and the marriage was annulled a year later. In 1919, Prince George entered a Jesuit monastery at Innsbruck, was ordained in 1921 and subsequently became dean of the chapter of St. Peter. His death, according to a Berlin radio broadcast of June 1, was announced by the Vatican.

Georgia.

A southern state, one of the original states of the United States; popularly known as the "Empire State of the South." Area 58,876 sq.mi. (including 358 sq.mi. of inland water); pop. (1940) 3,123,723; urban 1,073,808 (34.4%); rural 2,049,915 (65.6%); native white 2,026,362 (64.9%); Negro 1,084,927 (34.7%); foreign born white 11,916 (.4%); other races 518. Capital, Atlanta (302,288); the next largest cities are Savannah (95,996), Augusta (65,919), Macon (57,865).

History.—Ellis G. Arnall was inaugurated governor on Jan. 12, 1943. The general assembly was in regular session from Jan. 11 to March 18. Among the many important legislative reforms enacted in this session were: a reorganization of the board of regents of the university system to provide for appointment of the members of the board by the governor subject to senate approval, to remove the governor from membership on the board and to secure a restoration of the accredited rating of the state's university system; the proposal as a constitutional amendment

of a retirement plan for the state's 23,500 teachers; abolition of the power of the governor to grant pardons and paroles and the vesting of this power in a three-man commission; abolition of the system of allocating all incomes from certain taxes and fees to certain departments; requirement that physicians test expectant mothers for venereal disease; provision for the election of the state auditor by the legislature (previously he had been appointed by the governor); placing the state on Central War Time (some localities refused to adopt the change and remained on Eastern War Time).

On Aug. 3, 1943, these actions and proposals of the general assembly, among others, were ratified as constitutional amendments in a special election: reorganization of the board of regents; establishment of the Pardon and Parole board; teachers' retirement act; reduction of the legal age of voting in state and national elections from 21 to 18; authorization of the appointment of an interim commission to draft a new constitution for presentation to the general assembly (to meet in Jan. 1945) for approval and submission to the people; exemption of out-of-state subsidiaries of Georgia corporations from the state's ad valorem and intangible taxes; granting all war veterans uniform civil service preference in state and local government jobs coming under merit employment systems.

An extra session of the general assembly met Sept. 27 to Oct. 1, 1943 to enact prison reform measures. The session abolished the state Board of Prisons and created the office of director of corrections. The three-man Board of Prisons was retained in an advisory capacity until Jan. 1. Gov. Arnall appointed Wiley Moore director of corrections, without pay, to reorganize the penal system.

Chief state officers for 1943 were: governor, Ellis Arnall; attorney-general, T. Grady Head; secretary of state, John B. Wilson; treasurer, George B. Hamilton; comptroller general, Homer Parker; chief justice, Charles S. Reid; superintendent of schools, M. D. Collins.

Education.—There were 3,727 elementary schools in Georgia and 1,494 schools having high school grades, according to figures released in 1942. Enrolment (1942–43) was: elementary schools 619,068 (374,875 white; 244,193, Negro); high schools 144,156 (117,298 white; 26,858 Negro). During the 1941–42 session there were 16,822 teachers in the elementary schools of Georgia (10,912 white; 5,910 Negro) and 5,957 in the secondary schools (5,067 white; 890 Negro).

Communication.—On Aug. 31, 1943, there were 99,074.96 mi. of highways in Georgia (13,995.02 state, 85,079.94 county). During the fiscal year ending June 30, 1943, total expenditures of state funds by the highway department amounted to $11,118,-524.46 (including $2,666,790.93 paid to counties on refunding certificates and $8,451,733.53 for actual operations). As of Dec. 31, 1942, steam railways in Georgia owned 6,215 mi. of road (first main track).

Airports in the state included: municipal 30; commercial 5; intermediate 12. There were 276,519 telephones of the Southern Bell Co. and 28,268 independent telephones in operation as of Nov. 1, 1943.

Banking and Finance.—On June 30, 1943, there were 245 state banks in Georgia with deposits (exclusive of interbank deposits) amounting to $340,120,000; loans $97,728,000; investments $160,622,000. There were 47 national banks with deposits (exclusive of interbank deposits) amounting to $531,-954,000; loans, $122,331,000; and investments, $352,433,000. Total state treasury income for the year ending June 30, 1943, amounted to $58,183,496.83; total payments from the treasury on appropriations amounted to $55,189,124.02. The fixed debt on June 30, 1943, stood at $19,759,784.03; the net fixed debt as of that date was $14,081,790.93.

Agriculture.—Total value of agricultural production in Georgia for 1943 amounted to $368,930,000, the second highest in the state's history.

It was exceeded only by the record valuation of $578,000,000 in 1919.

Higher prices and increased production over 1942 accounted for the increase.

Table I.—*Leading Agricultural Products of Georgia, 1943 and 1942*

Crop	1943 (est.)	1942
Cotton, bales	850,000	855,000
Cottonseed, tons	379,000	382,000
Corn, bu.	45,288,000	39,160,000
Oats, bu.	10,120,000	10,152,000
Potatoes, sweet, bu.	9,375,000	8,000,000
Tobacco, lb.	65,004,000	59,710,000
Hay, tons	897,000	815,000
Peanuts, lb.	910,080,000	627,690,000
Velvet beans, tons	422,000	400,000
Peaches, bu.	1,593,000	6,177,000

Manufacturing.—No census of manufactures had been compiled since the federal census of 1939. There were, in 1939, 3,150 manufacturing establishments in Georgia that produced goods valued at $677,402,657, employed 170,165 persons and paid in salaries and wages $132,188,496.

Unemployment benefits paid from Jan. 1 to Dec. 20, 1943, amounted to $963,701.10.

Mineral Production.—Total value of mineral production for

Table II.—*Principal Mineral Products of Georgia, 1942 and 1941*

Mineral	Value of Products	
	1942	1941
Clay:		
Products other than pottery and refractories	*	$2,689,000
Raw	*	2,609,605
China or paper clay		
Refractory kaolin	$6,854,334	*
Miscellaneous		
Fuller's earth		
Stone:		
(Granite, marble, sandstone, limestone, misc. stone)	7,372,810	5,809,755

*No comparable figures.

1942 was $20,075,924 and for 1941, $21,049,261.   (E. C. GR.)

German Literature.

Literature is more inseparably linked with social and political history in Germany than is the case in any other country. This was particularly true of the latest period of national socialist totalitarian domination. All authors must be members of the nazi writers' association, must submit their books for approval to nazi authorities before they are printed, and must conform strictly to nazi ideology.

This situation, together with the fact that virtually all persons were forced into military service or war work, explains why few notable works of literature were being produced in Germany.

It was therefore to the refugees outside the reich that one looked for German literature today.

Many of them sought to explain the rise of national socialism in Germany or conditions there. Four of these were *The World of Yesterday*, an informal autobiography and cultural history of his times by Stefan Zweig; *The War for Man's Soul*, by Ernest Jaeckh, a liberal scholar and expert on Turkey who in 1920 founded the Hochschule fuer Politik in Berlin; *Flight from Terror*, by Otto Strasser and Michael Stern; and, in lighter vein, *Blood and Banquets*, by Bella Fromm, who gives a kind of social diary describing the celebrities whom she met at dinners and cocktail parties. *The Other Germany*, by Heinrich Fraenkel, attempts to demonstrate the existence of a large liberal anti-nazi population in Germany who are ready to co-operate in establishing democratic government. *The Passing of the European Age*,

by Eric Fischer, an Austrian refugee, is an interesting and scholarly study of civilization at the centre and at the periphery, that is, of the transfer of European culture by emigrants to colonial lands, its development under new frontier conditions, and its later reflex influence upon the mother-countries from which the emigrants came.

Notable in fiction are two short novels contributed by Thomas Mann and Franz Werfel to *The Ten Commandments*, a collection of ten short stories edited by Armin L. Robinson which reflect on the nazi disregard of the Mosaic law.

The *Frankfurter Zeitung*, founded in 1856, one of Germany's oldest and most distinguished newspapers, known for its able financial and literary articles, was compelled to suspend publication on Sept. 1, 1943. *The Rise and Fall of the House of Ullstein*, by Herman Ullstein, tells well the half-century story of another of Germany's greatest newspaper and publishing businesses.   (S. B. F.)

Germany.

A totalitarian state or dictatorship, known as the "third reich," in central Europe south of the North and Baltic seas and north of the Alps, Italy and the Balkans. Flag, black hooked cross (swastika) in a round white centre on a red background. Capital, Berlin (*q.v.*). Chief cities (1939 census): Berlin (4,338,767); Vienna (1,920,390); Hamburg (1,712,843); Munich (828,938); Cologne (769,437); Leipzig (707,578); Essen (667,004); Dresden (630,664); Breslau (630,041); Frankfurt-on-Main (553,462); Duesseldorf (541,625); Dortmund (539,682). Religion (1933): Protestants 62.7%; Catholics 32.5%; Jews 0.7%; others 4.1%. Reich chancellor and leader (fuehrer), Adolf Hitler (*q.v.*).

Area and Population.—The area of the old reich was 181,742 sq.mi.; population (census of May 17, 1939), 69,316,465. The area of "Greater Germany," prior to the annexations of 1939–42, was 225,199 sq.mi. and the population 79,364,408, including the populations of the following *Länder:* Prussia 41,684,788; Bavaria 8,224,541; Württemberg 2,898,888; Mecklenburg 900,589; Baden 2,503,225; Saxony 5,232,929; Thuringia 1,744,323; Hesse 1,468,468; Oldenburg 576,951; Brunswick 583,922; Anhalt 431,686; Lippe 187,281; Hamburg 1,712,843; Schaumburg-Lippe 53,277;

"BEGINNING TO HEAR THE BIRDIES SING." A cartoon of 1943 by Orr in the *Chicago Tribune*

Bremen 413,759; Saarland 842,420; Austria 6,638,364; Sudetenland 2,944,279.

The population of "Greater Germany" in 1943 was approximately 98,582,000 as a result of the annexation during 1939–42 of the following territories: Bohemia-Moravia (6,805,000); Memel (153,000), Eupen-Malmédy (60,000); Polish lands (Danzig, Polish Corridor, Silesian border districts, totalling about 10,000,-000); Alsace-Lorraine (1,900,000); and Luxembourg (301,000). This figure of 98,582,000, however, made no allowance for decreases in population caused by Germans killed in war, Poles expelled or killed, and Jews deported or exterminated, or for the increase from prisoners of war and imported foreign workers.

Outside "Greater Germany," Hitler also controlled millions of people in lands which were conquered and occupied by his armies, but which were not directly annexed to the reich: the Gouvernement General of Poland (15,000,000) under the administration of Hans Frank; Denmark (3,777,000); Norway (2,900,000); Netherlands (8,640,000); Belgium (8,386,000) and France (40,-000,000), the northern three-fifths of which was "occupied" in June 1940, and the remainder in Nov. 1942, after the Anglo-American occupation of French North Africa. Alsace-Lorraine (1,900,000) was incorporated directly into the reich on Nov. 30, 1940. In addition, by the infiltration of German troops and secret agents, Germany gradually acquired domination over Slovakia (2,653,564) in 1939, and over Hungary (12,708,439), Rumania (19,934,000) and Bulgaria (6,078,000) in the winter of 1940–41. In April 1940 a blitzkrieg brought Yugoslavia (15,703,000) and Greece (7,109,000) under nazi domination. This brought the total population under German domination, both in "Greater Germany" and the occupied lands, to more than 240,000,000. Even this figure did not include the indeterminate population in the regions of the U.S.S.R. which Hitler conquered in 1941–42 but had lost in large part by the end of 1943.

History.—The chief events during 1943 were: the intense Allied bombing of German cities; the rolling back of the nazi armies in Africa, Italy and the U.S.S.R.; the failure of the German submarine campaign; and the increased resistance and sabotage in the conquered countries. All this led to a decline in German civilian morale and to a stiffer attitude toward Germany in the neutral countries of Sweden, Switzerland, Turkey and Portugal.

During 1943 giant British and U.S. bombers rained down about

150,000 tons of explosive and incendiary bombs on Germany 21 largest industrial centres. As a result, in the eight mont from April 1 to Dec. 5, according to German official figure 124,630 persons were killed and 30,000 missing. The homes 2,580,000 persons and the places of employment of 1,960,0 workers were destroyed. The casualties for the hardest-hit citi were: Hamburg 28,390; Berlin 16,639; Cologne 8,251; Dortmur 7,106; Hanover 6,518; Duesseldorf 6,207; Bochum 4,90 Wuppertal 4,632; Mannheim 4,367; Nürnberg 3,674; Frankfu 3,486; Kassel 3,532.

These official German figures, however, were probably a understatement. Swedish and Swiss eyewitnesses and travelle gave much higher estimates. Also the German figures did n include the last four weeks of the year, when the raids we heaviest and most frequent, including further devastating blov on Berlin, Bremen, Leipzig, Frankfurt and Mannheim. Probabl 6,000,000 people—nearly a tenth of Germany's prewar popul tion—were driven from their homes and forced to seek shelte with others or to wander to less dangerous areas in easter Germany or western Poland.

In carrying out these devastating mass raids the Allies ha many aims in view: the direct destruction of factories engage in war production; the disruption of the German transportatio system; the weakening of German morale; and the general sof ening up of nazi strength preparatory to an Allied invasion c western Europe which would create the real "second front" fo which the Russians had long been clamouring. How far these aim were achieved it is impossible to say definitely. Probably Ger man production was slowed down as much as 20%. Transporta tion difficulties were greatly increased. The failure of the Germa submarine campaign was also partly a result of the blows at th German ports of Kiel, Hamburg, Bremen, Emden and elsewher as well as to inland plants which fabricated submarine parts an machinery. The failure of the German luftwaffe to give adequat coverage on the eastern front and at the same time to preven the raids on Germany from Britain and from the new Allied base in Africa and Italy was partly due to the bombing of aircraf factories, synthetic gasoline plants and the Rumanian oil field at Ploesti.

(For the various German campaigns of 1943, *see* WORLD WAI II.)

Education.—In the old reich in 1938 there were 51,118 public elementary schools (*grundschule*) with 7,596,437 pupils; 1,563

FOUR-MOTORED "LIBERATORS" of the U.S. army air force over the German naval base at Kiel May 14, 1943

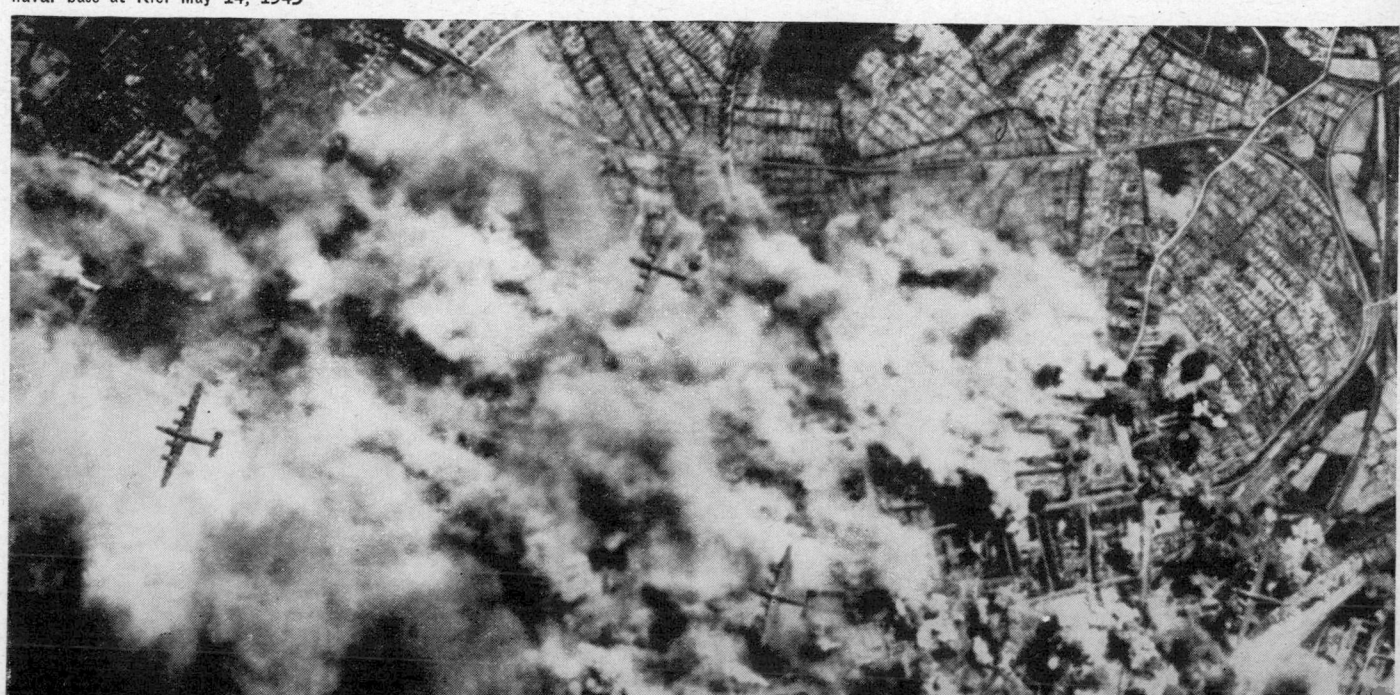

THE HOLLOW RUINS OF DUESSELDORF, photographed after the 56th R.A.F. bombing of the German industrial centre on the night of June 11, 1943

elementary "middle schools" teaching English and French with 272,635 pupils; 2,282 secondary schools with 670,895 pupils; 10 technical high schools with 9,554 students; and 25 universities with 48,139 students. The nazis established many special schools for training "leaders," with emphasis on comradeship, sports, nazi ideology and leadership.

Defense.—After 1935 the German army was based on the principle of universal military training for two years, in addition to semimilitary training in the Hitler Youth (eight years) and Labour corps (six months). The army in 1943 consisted of more than 300 divisions of 12,000–14,000 men each if at full strength, but by Dec. 31 many divisions had become skeletal because of very heavy losses in the U.S.S.R., the Balkans, North Africa, Sicily and Italy. These probably amounted to more than 1,000,000 men in 1943, in addition to more than 700,000 killed and missing and 1,500,000 wounded earlier in the war.

In addition to the German armies, Hitler had had Italian, Rumanian, Hungarian and other troops fighting his battles, but these began to disintegrate or return home as the tide of war turned against Germany in 1943. The Italian army disintegrated completely after the collapse of the Mussolini regime in July, and many of the Falangist Blue division had returned to Spain by the end of 1943.

The navy in 1943 consisted of the 35,000-ton battleship "Tirpitz," two 26,000-ton battleships, two 10,000-ton pocket battleships, 11 cruisers, about 50 destroyers, probably 400 submarines and perhaps two incomplete aircraft carriers. Germany acquired in addition a few French naval units when she seized Toulon in Nov. 1942, and a few Italian naval units in the summer of 1943. The "Tirpitz," however, was reported badly damaged in a northern Norwegian fiord by three British midget submarines, and the 26,000-ton "Scharnhorst" was sunk in a naval battle in the Arctic circle on Dec. 26. Sixty German submarines were destroyed in the three months September-November, 1943. Submarine losses were heavy throughout the year owing to increased Allied air protection, aided by planes based on the Portuguese Azores and by the activity of Allied patrol boats. New submarine construction was seriously handicapped by intense Allied air raids on Hamburg, Bremen, Emden and other ports and on German industrial centres.

Total figures for the German air force were not available. But production of German planes, as a result of the bombing of the Messerschmitt plant at Wiener-Neustadt near Vienna, the ball-bearing factory at Schweinfurt and other factories, was believed to have been cut down to 2,500 planes a month by the end of 1943, while plane production in the United States alone soared to more than 8,000 a month. German plane production was insufficient to offset the heavy losses in Germany, the U.S.S.R. and Italy. Allied air superiority became evident as Germany was less and less able to meet the double task of protecting its eastern front and of stopping Allied mass raids on cities within the reich.

Finance.—The unit of currency is the German mark, nominally equivalent to 40.3325 U.S. cents. The Germans also issued special paper marks (*reichskassenscheine*) of varying value for use in the occupied territories. Revenues and expenditures had not been published since 1935. The total amount levied by Germany on the occupied countries of Europe up to Sept. 1943 was estimated at 42,800,000,000 marks and the annual rate in 1943 was 15,850,-000,000 marks. In addition, the amount due to the occupied countries through Germany's blocked-mark system of not paying for imports was estimated in Sept. at 17,500,000,000 marks, and was increasing in 1943 at the annual rate of 6,700,000,000 marks. The reich debt at the end of 1943 was estimated at more than 200,000,000,000 marks, and the note circulation at 28,050,000,000 marks in Sept. 1943.

Trade and Communications.—As a result of the war, Germany was cut off from world trade and was confined to trade with the occupied countries in Europe and a few neutrals like

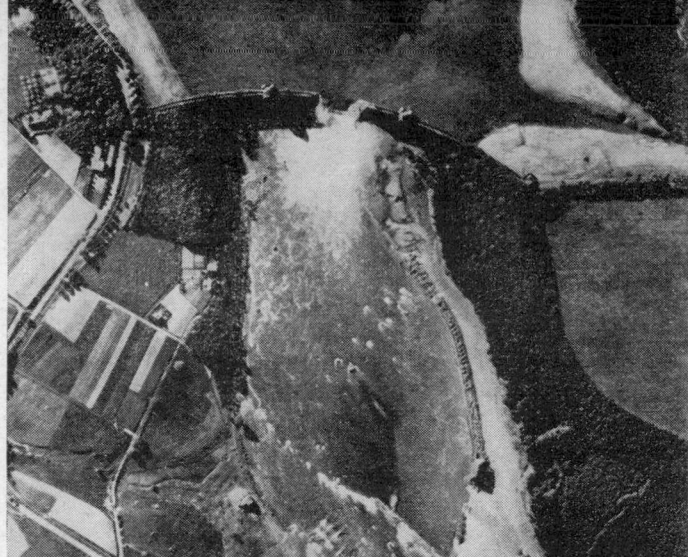

BREACH IN THE MOEHNE DAM, Germany, after British bombers dropped 1,500-lb. mines on and near the structure May 16, 1943. The Ruhr valley was flooded as a result of this raid

Sweden, Switzerland and Turkey.

Her prewar trade, for which alone figures were available in 1943, is given in Table I.

The German state railway (*reichsbahn*) in 1938 included 53,330 km. (33,076 mi.) of standard-gauge lines and 879 km. (546 mi.) of narrow-gauge lines. Privately owned lines included 3,732 km. (2,313 mi.) of standard and 752 km. (476 mi.) of narrow gauge. In spite of Germany's stripping the conquered territories of much of their rolling stock, the German railways during the war were put under a very heavy strain and in 1943 were in worse condition than in 1939. On the Russian front the Germans lost 700 locomotives and 17,000 freight cars in 1943, in addition to many locomotives and trains which were destroyed by Allied planes in western Europe. The bombing of the Moehne and Eder dams on May 16 disrupted the Ruhr area canal system and inundated Kassel, where Germany's most important locomotive works were located.

In 1938 there were 132,094 mi. of road in Germany, and by the middle of 1939, 2,264 mi. of the new concrete automobile highway network (*reichsautobahn*) were opened to traffic. This new highway had been partly designed for strategic purposes, but owing to lack of fuel for trucks was of little military value in 1943.

Agriculture, Manufactures and Mineral Production.—Germany's prewar agricultural and mineral productions are shown in Tables II and III.

Germany's harvests in 1943 were generally better than in 1941 and 1942. The wheat harvest, according to Herbert Backe, secretary of state for agriculture, would reach 4,200,000 metric tons, which, however, was less than the prewar average. The mirage of vast grain supplies from the Ukraine vanished as the nazis were swept west of the Dnieper river by Stalin's armies in the autumn of 1943. As the Germans continued to drain agricultural supplies from the other conquered territories the food situation did not become acute for the nazi "master race" in

Table II.—Agricultural Production from 1932 to 1939
(In thousands of metric tons)

	Rye	Wheat	Barley	Oats	Potatoes	Sugar Beets	Fodder Beets
1932 . . .	8,363	5,003	3,214	6,650	47,016	7,875	34,486
1933 . . .	8,727	5,604	3,468	6,952	44,071	8,578	30,716
1934 . . .	7,607	4,532	3,203	5,452	46,780	10,394	33,804
1935 . . .	7,478	4,667	3,387	5,385	41,015	10,567	34,711
1936 . . .	7,386	4,426	3,399	5,618	46,323	12,095	37,826
1937 . . .	6,920	4,580	3,640	5,920	53,600	15,701	40,538
1938 . . .	8,463	5,502	4,177	6,274	48,700	17,200	41,700
1939 . . .					54,540	17,400	39,500

*Figures for 1939 are estimated. The total grain harvest was estimated at 27,430,000 metric tons, *i.e.*, 6.4% more than the total for 1938.

1943, though the subject populations suffered severely from inadequate rations or from lack of food of their own.

Manufactures were subjected to a still tighter strait jacket in 1943 in order to increase the production of war materials. Many small plants were closed and all factories had to manufacture exactly what they were told to make. War goods superseded consumers' goods even more completely than hitherto. By the end of 1943 new clothing, household utensils and new housing were almost unobtainable. After Sept. 8 complete control over all production was given to Albert Speer, the minister of munitions and armaments. This 39-year-old favourite architect of Hitler thus became "economic czar" for the duration of the war, with even more power than Hermann Goering.

Due to the recruiting of men from fields and factories for the army and to the demands for increased production caused by the war, and also to the greater amount of labour required to produce substitute (*ersatz*) instead of natural products, Germany suffered an increasingly severe labour shortage during 1943. This was partly met by employing more women and children, women being conscripted for work up to the age of 60. The labour shortage was also partly met by renewed efforts, not very successful, to induce more French, Italian and other foreign

Table III.—Production of Minerals and Manufactured Products, 1933–37
(In metric tons)

	1933	1934	1935	1936	1937
Coal . . .	109,532,600	125,405,600	143,491,300	159,756,600	184,500,000
Lignite . .	126,756,600	137,223,400	147,162,100	161,426,900	184,700,000
Iron ore . .	2,592,000	4,343,000	6,044,000	7,570,000	9,792,000
Lead . . .	91,000	98,400	122,300	139,000	158,500
Zinc . . .	162,000	212,800	205,000	207,700	194,300
Rock salt . .	1,841,300	2,024,200	2,077,200	2,383,800	2,707,000
Potash . .	7,362,800	9,616,700	11,672,500	11,764,600	14,460,000
Pig iron . .	5,246,500	8,716,700	12,846,200	15,302,500	15,960,000
Steel . . .	7,393,200	11,601,700	16,013,500	18,590,900	19,387,000

workers to accept employment in Germany. These "slave workers" often had no alternative except starvation, since the nazis closed down the home factories where they had been employed. The total number of war prisoners and foreign workers who were forced to work in Germany at the end of 1943 was estimated at more than 10,000,000.

These foreign workers included about 3,000,000 Russians, carefully guarded and feared by the Germans; 2,500,000 Frenchmen; 1,800,000 Poles, 1,000,000 Italians; 1,000,000 Czechs; 700,000 Belgians; and numerous Dutch, Scandinavians, Balts, and Balkan nationalities. They were housed separately, kept in control by the threat to withhold their meagre food rations, and carefully watched by armed German foremen and gestapo officials. During the frequent Allied bombings of industrial centres, in which factory records were destroyed, many of the slave workers managed to escape and return home secretly.

(*See* also ANTI-SEMITISM; BUSINESS REVIEW; FASCISM; ROMAN CATHOLIC CHURCH; WORLD WAR II.)

BIBLIOGRAPHY.—See *Statistisches Jahrbuch für das Deutsche Reich* (annual, to 1939); *Target: Germany* (1943); Hauptmann Hermann (pseud.), *The Luftwaffe: Its Rise and Fall* (1943); T. H. Minshall, *Future Germany* (1943); P. Schwarz, *This Man Ribbentrop* (1943); R. G. Swing, *Preview of History* (1943).   (S. B. F.)

Table I.—Imports, Exports and Balance of Trade, 1932–39

	Total Yearly			Monthly Average		
	Imports Million marks	Exports Million marks	Balance Million marks	Imports Million marks	Exports Million marks	Balance Million marks
1932 . . .	4,667	5,739	+1,072	389	478	+89
1933 . . .	4,204	4,871	+ 667	350	406	+56
1934 . . .	4,451	4,167	− 284	371	347	−24
1935 . . .	4,159	4,270	+ 111	347	356	+9
1936 . . .	4,218	4,768	+ 550	352	397	+46
1937 . . .	5,468	5,911	+ 443	456	493	+37
1938* . . .	6,052	5,620	− 432	504	468	−36
1939† . . .	2,755	2,814	+ 59	458	468	+10

*Figures do not include Austria and Sudeten area.
†Figures are for the first six months of 1939 only

Gibraltar: *see* MEDITERRANEAN, BRITISH POSSESSIONS IN THE

Gilbert and Ellice Islands Colony: *see* PACIFIC ISLANDS, BRITISH.

Ginger: *see* SPICES.

Giraud, Henri Honoré

(1879–   ), French army officer, was born Jan. 18 in Paris and attended St. Cyr Military academy and the École Supérieure de Guerre. Early in World War I, he was wounded and captured by the Germans, but escaped in 1915 and returned to the front. Toward the end of the war he was chief of staff of a Moroccan division and he participated in the Riff campaign. After the German break-through at Sedan in May 1940, General Giraud took command of the Allied armies in northern France; but he was captured and interned in Koenigstein prison, Saxony. In April 1942, Giraud staged another daring prison break and escaped to Vichy via Switzerland. He then fled Vichy and offered his services to the U.S. armies at the start of the North African campaign. On Nov. 15, 1942, Admiral Darlan named Giraud commander of all French armed forces in North Africa. After Darlan's assassination, Giraud was named high commissioner of French North Africa, Dec. 27. In Jan. 1943, a bitter feud broke out between Giraud and Gen. Charles de Gaulle. On Feb. 6, Giraud assumed the title of French civil and military commander-in-chief in North Africa; the following month he formally severed all ties with Vichy and pledged restoration of free republican rule in France after the war. In the summer of 1943, Giraud's popularity ebbed. He had the backing of the U.S. state department and Great Britain, but the majority of Frenchmen in North Africa supported de Gaulle. Giraud finally invited his rival to Algiers and on June 3 a new governing body for France was created with Giraud and de Gaulle serving as co-presidents. Subsequently, Giraud lost ground to de Gaulle and on Nov. 9, 1943, the former resigned as co-president of the French Committee of National Liberation, but retained his post as commander-in-chief of French forces. (*See also* FRANCE.)

Girl Scouts.

In 1943 the Girl Scouts worked closely with other organizations in order to bring the citizenship training of scouting to more of the girls who were asking for it. Protestant, Roman Catholic, and Jewish advisers or advisory committees were appointed to work with the Girl Scout national organization. A committee of leading educators and one representing the National Congress of Parents and Teachers were also appointed. The General Federation of Women's Clubs and the men's and women's civic clubs such as Rotary, International and Zonta worked out plans for closer co-operation.

Planning with the whole community to meet the needs of youth in wartime, Girl Scouts in many towns opened their day camps to all neighbourhood children who wished to come. Troops were organized in war workers' trailer camps and in mushrooming boom towns. By the end of 1943, the total membership was 817,000, an increase of 100,000 over 1942.

Girl Scouting put special emphasis on projects that would not only enable girls to contribute to the war effort but also prepare them for intelligent citizenship later. For example: Senior Girl Scout hospital aides helped to relieve the shortage of nurses by serving in children's wards, linen rooms, laboratories, and kitchens. Wing Scouting, founded in 1942, became the fastest growing section of the older girls' program and began to prepare many girls for future service in aviation.

Through the Juliette Low World Friendship fund (formerly the Juliette Low Memorial fund) aid was sent to the British Guides for their relief work, to the Guides of Malta, and to the children of Greece, Russia, and China. Foreign students were also given scholarships for training in Girl Scout leadership so that they might help to develop or re-establish Girl Scouting in their own countries.   (C. M. R.)

Glands: *see* ENDOCRINOLOGY; MEDICINE.

Glass.

The major effect of the war upon the U.S. glass industry in 1943 was the stimulation of production of bottles, jars and containers. The increased volume of these items became necessary because of the greater amount of food preservation, both commercial and domestic. The total value of glassware made in the U.S. exceeded $500,000,000, for the first time in history. Much more than half of this value came from bottles and containers, which replaced many articles formerly made from tin plate and other metals. The new record in production of these items exceeded 90,000,000 gross.

Plate glass, made chiefly for military purposes, showed a slightly higher production than in 1942, exceeding 65,000,000 sq.ft. Bullet-resistant glass, made by joining tempered sheets

TESTING IMPACT-RESISTANT GLASS for aeroplane windshields, developed by the Civil Aeronautics administration to prevent injury to pilots in mid-air collisions with birds. Freshly-killed chickens and turkeys are fired at the windshields at a velocity of 300 m.p.h.

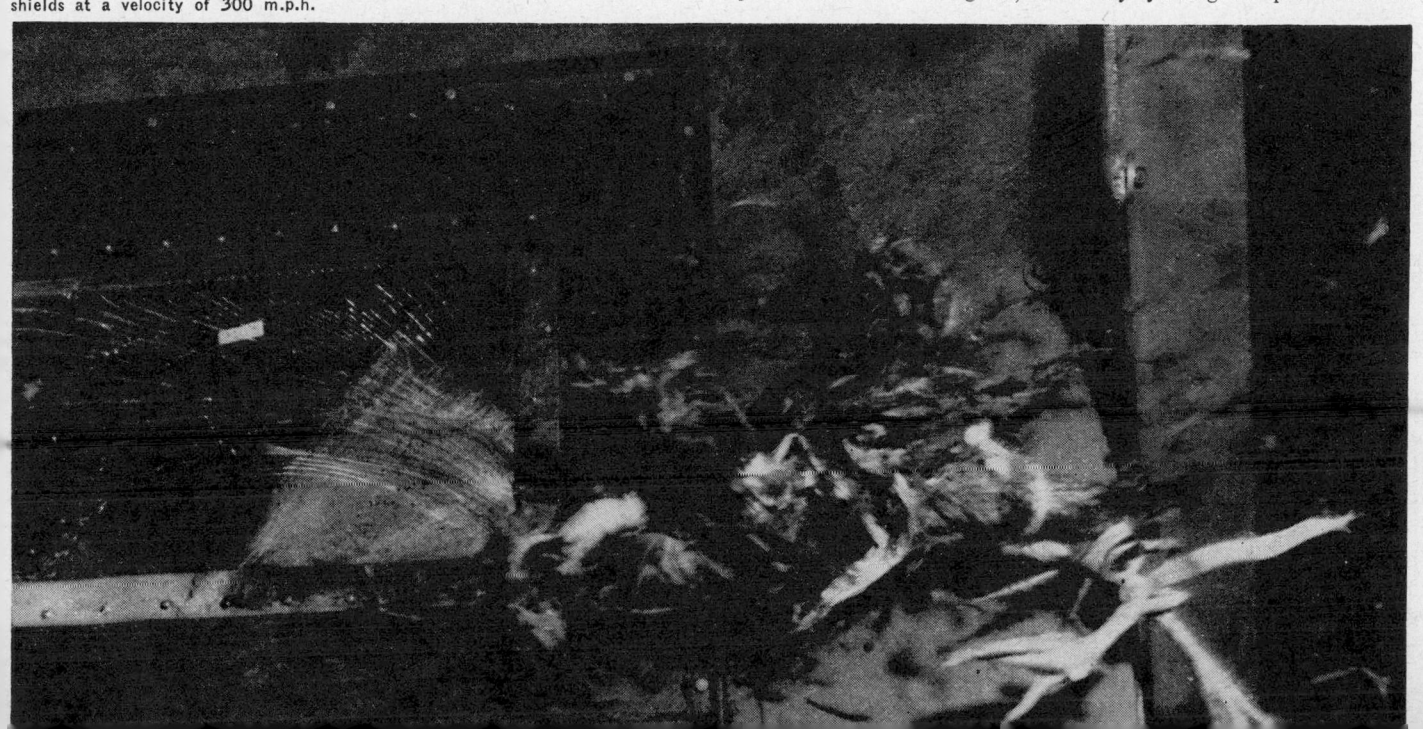

with plastic intermediate layers, bent into suitable curvatures, was successfully installed in the noses and cockpits of military planes. Data on window glass were not available, but the quantity made was relatively small on account of so little new construction.

The production of optical glass and the manufacture of lenses and prisms continued at unprecedented rates. Research developed new techniques for the heat-treatment of optical glass.

Operating conditions continued to be difficult on account of labour shortage, lack of kraft paper for shipping cartons and more severe restrictions upon raw materials, including nitrates.

Tiny insulators and other small parts hitherto not readily fabricated from glass were produced by the Corning Glass Works by a new process. In this method, powdered glass is mixed with a binder, high pressure is applied, and subsequent heating welds the glass particles together and drives off the volatile binder. A new development in the fibre glass field consisted in reinforcing plastic sheets with matted glass fibres so that they developed tensile strengths as high as 80,000 lb. per sq.in. Precision gauges made entirely of glass were found superior to metal gauges in permanent accuracy and low cost. Glass piping and other forms were successfully welded electrically.

The Federal Trade commission ordered that the word "glass" could not be used as part of the trade names of certain products made of organic plastics. (S. R. S.)

Glassford, William Alexander, II
(1886–   ), U.S. naval officer, was born June 6 in San Francisco. He was graduated from the U.S. Naval academy in 1906 and during World War I, he was a gunnery officer on a destroyer and later an executive officer on a destroyer tender. He won the D.S.M. for bringing the destroyer Shaw, of which he was commander, safely into port after a collision with a British vessel. During the period from 1924 to 1935, he was assistant director of naval communications, staff member of the Naval War college, commander of the battle force and commander-in-chief of the U.S. fleet. After Japan attacked Pearl Harbor, Glassford, who was commander of the Yangtze patrol, was placed at the head of the newly organized Southwest Pacific naval command, Feb. 1942. Later that month, he participated with the Dutch fleet in the battle of the Java sea. He was then given the post of commandant of the sixth naval district and Charleston navy yard. On May 24, 1943, President Roosevelt nominated him for promotion to vice-admiral; two days later, Adm. Glassford, who had been decorated for negotiating the agreement whereby French authorities opened Dakar to U.S. naval forces, was made President Roosevelt's personal representative, with the rank of minister, to French West Africa.

Gliding.
On July 9, 1943, in the invasion of Sicily, the U.S. army used gliders for the first time as a major tactical weapon. The success of this venture was reflected in renewed orders for 15 place transport gliders, and orders for still larger transport gliders.

In 1943, two of the most outstanding personalities in the field of gliding lost their lives in the service of the nation. On January 24 Major Lewin B. Barringer, chief of the glider section of the army air forces, was lost on a routine flight over the sea. In the capacity of special civilian assistant to the commanding general of the army air forces, Richard C. du Pont was killed while testing a giant transport glider on Sept. 11.

Prior to the war, Mr. du Pont as president and director, and Major Barringer as manager and director of the Soaring Society of America, were largely responsible for the existence of the nucleus of trained glider pilots with which the army started its

glider program.

Civilian gliding activities included:

The establishment of a new national altitude record of 19,434 ft. above point of release for single place gliders, by Capt. J. Shelly Charles at Atlanta, Georgia on July 18.

Two new Civil Aeronautics administration approved, single place, all wood training glider designs, suitable for the high school gliding program. They are the "Denver Pioneer" by the University of Denver and the "Cadet" by Cadet Aeronautics, Inc.

A major soaring contest was held at Bishop, Calif. on Sept. 4, 5 and 6 under the sanction of the Soaring Society of America.
(B. Sk.)

Glyn, Elinor
(1864–1943), British author, was born Oct. 17 in Jersey, the Channel islands. Daughter of a British civil engineer, she married in 1892 and wrote a few novels to bolster the family finances. Her early works, lightly garnished with sentiment and romance, were "reliable" light reading. But in 1906, Mrs. Glyn, determined to make romance pay, created *Three Weeks*, written in six weeks. Published in 1907, this novel was an immediate success, but it was considered "shocking" by ecclesiasts and lay authorities and was banned for a time in Britain and the United States. During the 1920s, Mrs. Glyn was regarded as a daring "love analyst." She went to Hollywood, where she advised silent screen directors on love scenes. In 1927, she published another best-seller, *It*. Although it was frequently asserted that Mrs. Glyn glamourized the pronoun "it" and made it synonymous with sex appeal, Mrs. Glyn herself modestly declined to accept this honour. Her later works included *The Flirt and the Flapper* (1930) and *Romantic Adventure* (1936). Mrs. Glyn died in London, Sept. 23.

G-Men: *see* FEDERAL BUREAU OF INVESTIGATION.

Goering, Hermann Wilhelm
(1893–   ), German reichsmarshal and statesman, was born at Rosenheim, Bavaria, on Jan. 12 and was commander of the famed Richthofen squadron in the German air force during World War I after Richthofen's death. Goering was an early member of the nazi party and became air minister and minister of the interior in 1933 upon Hitler's accession to the chancellorship. (See *Encyclopædia Britannica*.) On July 19, 1940 Hitler conferred the newly created title of marshal of the reich on Goering. As head of the economics general staff, he had supreme control over Germany's economic life. Goering was generally regarded as second man in Germany during World War II. His prediction in 1941 that the luftwaffe could do one hundred to one thousand times more damage than the R.A.F. was a sorry one, but his position as leader remained intact. Late in 1942 he told his countrymen, fearful of another Russian winter campaign, that they would be fed if necessary at the expense of conquered nations. On April 20, 1943, Hitler's 54th birthday, Goering proclaimed that the issue of the war had become one of "victory or destruction." In August, following meetings at Adolf Hitler's headquarters, it was reported that Goering had been given still further powers "of enormous magnitude."

Gold.
With respect to gold, the year 1943 was conspicuous chiefly for an acceleration of two major trends which had set in during 1942. These were: (1) a reversal of the steady rise in world gold production which, until 1942, had endured for 19 years (see *Production*, below), and (2) a turning of the tide in the most spectacular international gold movement in history—the so-called "flight to the dollar," which between 1933 and 1941 produced a rise in U.S. holdings of monetary gold from roughly

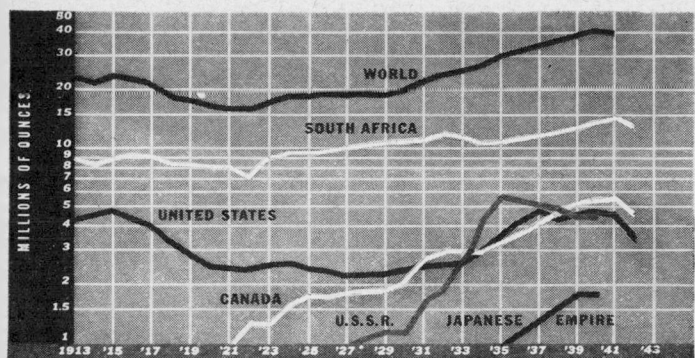

GOLD PRODUCTION: world total and output of the principal producing countries, as compiled by *The Mineral Industry*

$4,000,000,000 to almost $23,000,000,000.

In some ways even more striking than the decline in world gold output was the change in direction of the world gold movement. Whereas 1942 represented the ending of the flood tide of gold to the United States, 1943 brought a real ebb tide in this movement. As seen in Table I, in the first ten months of 1943, gold stocks declined by more than $610,000,000, which was far and away the largest loss by the United States in its history.

Table I.—*Analysis of Changes In Gold Stock of the United States*
(In millions of dollars)

Period	Gold stock at end of period	Increase in gold stock	Net gold import	Ear-marked gold	Domestic gold production
1934*	8,238	4,202	1,134	+ 83	93
1935	10,125	1,887	1,739	− 86	111
1936	11,258†	1,133	1,117	− 200	132
1937	12,760†	1,503	1,586	− 334	144
1938	14,512	1,752	1,974	− 534	149
1939	17,644	3,132	3,574	− 645	162
1940	21,995	4,351	4,745	− 408	170
1941	22,737	742	982	− 458.4	169
1942	22,726	− 10.3	‡	− 76.1	125.4
1943:					
Jan.	22,683	− 43.3	.	− 63.4	4.7
Feb.	22,644	− 39.3	.	− 59.0	4.1
March	22,576	− 68.0	.	−101.0	4.5
April	22,473	−103.1	.	− 45.1	4.9
May	22,426	− 46.3	.	− 51.7	4.1
June	22,388	− 38.9	.	− 63.7	3.9
July	22,335	− 52.7	.	− 91.3	3.9
Aug.	22,243	− 92.0	.	− 80.6	3.6
Sept.	22,175	− 67.8	.	− 40.6	3.3
Oct.	22,116	− 59.3	.		3.3
Jan.-Oct.	22,116	−610.5	.	−672.5§	40.4‖

*Figures based on rate of $20.67 a fine ounce in Jan., 1934, and $35 a fine ounce thereafter.
†Includes gold in the inactive account.
‡Net gold import figures have not been released for months subsequent to Dec. 1941.
§Gold under earmark at Federal Reserve banks for foreign account amounted to $3,346.3 millions on Oct. 30, 1943.
‖Preliminary.

For the most part this "loss" of gold was not a physical loss. As a matter of fact, the U.S. showed a net import balance of about $22,000,000 on the actual movement of gold into and out of the country. The decline in gold stocks was the direct result of gold earmarking in the U.S. for foreign account. Aside from its lend-lease activities, the foreign trade of the United States showed an "unfavourable" balance in 1943, chiefly because countries (particularly in Latin America) were unable to offset their exports to the United States with merchandise which they ordinarily would have imported. This enabled them to build up large bank balances in the United States.

Wherever free markets existed for gold in 1943 it sold at a premium, that premium ranging from 10% in the case of Latin American countries to as much as 100% in inflation-ridden India and Egypt, where the governments resorted to official sales of the metal to the public as a means of absorbing excess purchasing power. And finally there was the fact that the nation which was the chief advocate of managed exchanges—Germany—stood in the shadow of military defeat, while the three major powers among

the United Nations—Great Britain, U.S.S.R. and the United States—were the three powers which had the largest stakes in the perpetuation of gold, in one form or another, as the basic money of international exchange. (*See also* EXCHANGE CONTROL AND EXCHANGE RATES; FEDERAL RESERVE SYSTEM.)

(E. H. Co.)

Production.—There was a very definite decline in world production of gold in 1942, amounting to about 11% as compared with 1941. While the available data were still so incomplete in 1943 that no very accurate estimate could be made of the total, it was probably around 35,000,000 or 36,000,000 oz. Declines were registered for every country for which comparable data were received covering 1941 and 1942.

Some of the more important decreases, in order of decreasing size, were: United States, 27%; Canada, 10%; Australia, 23%; South Africa, 2%; Colombia, 9%; Southern Rhodesia, 4%. The decreases in most cases were due to shortage of manpower, which was needed more for other metals than for gold.

Table II.—*Value of Gold Produced, 1900-43*
(In millions of old dollars, $20.67 an oz.)

Year	South Africa	Russia	Canada	U.S.A.	Australia	All others	Total
1900	6	20	28	79	73	48	254
1910	155	35	10	96	65	93	454
1915	186	27	19	99	48	89	468
1922	144	3	27	48	18	78	317
1929	215	21	40	46	12	71	403
1933	227	54	61	45	16	120	523
(In millions of new dollars, $35 an oz.)							
1934	367	135	104	94	30	228	958
1935	377	158	115	110	31	249	1,040
1936	396	185	131	130	40	275	1,157
1937	410	180	143	143	47	298	1,221
1938	425	184	165	151	54	337	1,316
1939	448	190	178	165	56	358	1,395
1940	492	140	186	210	56	335	1,419
1941	504	150	187	209	51	334	1,435
1942	494	.	169	131*	43	303	1,140†
1943‡	450	.	130	48*	27	220	875†

*Exclusive of Philippines.
†Exclusive of Russia, for which no official figures are available later than 1941.
‡Estimated.

Mine production of gold in the continental United States dropped from 4,750,865 oz. in 1941 to 3,457,110 oz. in 1942, a decline of 27%, the result of a shift of manpower to work of greater strategic importance or better pay; also in Oct. 1942 the War Production board ruling closed all primary gold mines, so that most of the gold produced in the last quarter of 1942 and in 1943 was a by-product of operations carried on primarily for nonferrous metals. As a result, the only important producing state to show an increase in output was Utah. The percentages of decline in the major producing states, in decreasing order of actual output, were as follows: California, 40%; Alaska 26%; Colorado, 28%; Montana, 41%; South Dakota, 13%; Nevada, 19%; Arizona, 22%; Idaho, 39%; and Oregon, 51%.

Nothing whatever was known of the status of gold production in the Philippine Islands after Japanese occupation, but mint and refinery receipts in the United States in 1942 dropped to 140,330 oz., as compared with 1,130,933 oz. in 1941.

The decline in United States output was even more pronounced in 1943 than in 1942. The total for the first three quarters of the year was 1,165,000 oz., with about 1,465,000 oz. expected for the year's total—a decline of 58% from 1942 and 69% from 1941. There was an almost continuous decline in output throughout 1943, the trend of which is best shown by the following daily average outputs in fine ounces for the periods indicated:

U.S. Daily Average Output

Year 1941	13,016	May	3,998
January 1942	10,168	June	3,772
Year 1942	9,590	July	3,493
January 1943	4,315	August	3,355
February	3,979	September	3,133
March	4,217	October	3,516
April	4,529		

Canadian production declined from 5,345,179 oz. in 1941 to 4,841,306 oz. in 1942. In Quebec and Saskatchewan, increases in by-product gold from copper and other nonferrous ores more than offset declines in primary gold output, but in most of the other provinces there were declines in output. During the first three quarters of 1943, the output totalled 2,842,122 oz., as compared with 3,727,457 oz. in the same period of 1942, a decline of 24%, against a drop of less than 10% in 1942 as compared with 1941.

The South African output showed a comparatively small decline in 1942, standing at 14,120,617 oz., as compared with 14,386,361 oz. in 1941. The production rate declined still further in 1943, equivalent to 12,850,000 oz. as estimated from the returns of the first three quarters, which totalled 9,637,000 oz.

After the United States and Canada, the next largest decline was in Australia, from 1,570,000 oz. in 1941 to 1,180,000 oz. in 1942. Production during the first half of 1943 averaged only about 72,000 oz. monthly, against 98,000 oz. in 1942.

The 1942 decline in Southern Rhodesia was 30,000 oz. to 760,000 oz. and with returns for nine months of 1943 at 500,000 oz. and dropping almost every month, the 1943 total was likely to be about 100,000 oz. less than that of 1942. India also had a 30,000-oz. drop in 1942, to 257,000 oz., and returns of 192,000 oz. for the first nine months of 1942 were at about the same rate. Gold Coast declined 100,000 oz. in 1942, to an estimated 785,000 oz.; specific figures were not at hand for 1943 at the end of that year, but apparently the decline continued. The 1942 output in Mexico was little different from the 800,000 oz. in 1941. In 1942 Colombia dropped about 50,000 oz. below the 656,000 reported in 1941, and with returns of 438,000 oz. through Sept. 1943, apparently showed another decline for the year. (*See* also MINERAL AND METAL PRODUCTION AND PRICES.)

(G. A. Ro.)

Gold Coast: *see* BRITISH WEST AFRICA.

Golf. It is a significant fact, that, of the 12 players whose names were inscribed as winners of the U.S. Amateur Championship over a period of 15 years, from 1927 through 1941, 10 were in uniform by 1943. So were hundreds of other golfers less well-known. Among professional ranks, approximately 20% of the Professional Golfers' association membership were giving military service.

Meantime, golfing organizations turned their attention almost entirely to the support of war work. The United States Golf association continued on a definite program of encouraging members' clubs to carry on organized support of fund-raising programs for patriotic purposes and the sale of war bonds. Special tournaments on national holiday dates were a part of the program. The association also sponsored the growing of victory gardens by club members on club property. It urged member clubs to give preference to disabled ex-service men, when employing new help.

The Professional Golfers' association arranged benefit matches and collected funds for service benefits in all tournaments played. Most notable among these was a team match at the Plum Hollow club of Detroit, in which the war-orphaned Ryder Cup team captained by Craig Wood defeated a team captained by Walter Hagen. The sum of $36,000 was realized. This went to purchasing golf equipment for American forces on the far-flung battle fronts.

Club tournaments continued on a greatly reduced schedule, with a few district and state championships. All of course missed the presence of popular favorites now in service. Among professional ranks, more "name" players were available even

with such notables as Sam Snead, Ben Hogan, Horton Smith, Jimmy Thompson, Paul Runyan, Victor Ghezzi, E. J. "Dutch" Harrison, Clayton Heafner, Jim Turnesa and others in uniform. A few competitive events of interest were staged, notably in the middle west.

The Tam O'Shanter Country club of Chicago was the scene of one such event in which there were competitions for amateurs, women and an open contest. Harold "Jug" McSpaden emerged as the winner of the open tournament. At the end of 72 holes of play he was tied with William "Buck" White, competing in his first big tournament, at 282. In the play-off McSpaden won with a card of 71 against White's 72.

Dale Morey of Martinsville, Ind., former captain of Louisiana State university team, won the amateur event, defeating Robert Cochran of St. Louis 4 and 3. Miss Patty Berg of Minneapolis, former U.S. Women's champion, won the event for women, with a total of 307 for 72 holes of play. Miss Elizabeth Hicks of California was runner-up with 312. Miss Hicks wears the uniform of the SPARS. Miss Berg was sworn in as a member of the Marines the day after she won. Earlier in the year she had won the Women's Western Open title, defeating Miss Dorothy Kirby of Atlanta in the final match. This was Miss Berg's first tournament appearance following an injury to a knee sustained in an automobile accident 18 months earlier.

The Golden Valley Country club of Minneapolis was the scene of a round-robin team match, involving eight teams of well-known professionals. Craig Wood and Jimmy Demaret proved the winning combination, finishing the 126 holes of play with a total of plus 12. Next in line were Byron Nelson and Harold McSpaden scoring plus 9. The latter pair led from the first round through the sixth and were again leading at the end of nine holes of the last round. On the last nine they were the victims of great golf by Willie Goggin and Tony Penna, who beat par on six of the nine holes, winning four of the six.

Wallace Ulrich of Carleton college won the individual intercollegiate title from 74 other college golfers who competed at the Olympia Fields Country club near Chicago, defeating William Roden of the University of Texas in the final match by 4 and 2. Team honors went to Yale university with a score of 614 for a four-man team over 18 holes. Michigan was second with 618.

The year saw the passing of a notable figure in golf, Ted Ray, famous British professional, who won the United States Open championship in 1920. Twice a visitor to the U.S., Ray was a familiar figure to golfers. He first came into prominence in 1913, when he and his compatriot, Harry Vardon, finished in a tie for the U.S. Open at Brookline, Mass., only to be beaten by Ouimet in the play-off. A giant of a man, he was known in his heyday as one of the longest hitters in golf.   (I. BN.)

Golikov, Filip Ivanovich (1900–   ), Russian army officer, joined the Red army in 1918. An able tactician, his talents were recognized and he was awarded a military scholarship to the famous Frunze Military academy. One of the young generals of the soviet union, he was rapidly promoted and was made deputy chief of the general staff. Regarded as one of Russia's principal tank experts, he was decorated for his work in the Russo-Finnish campaign, 1939–40, which provided him with an opportunity to test his theories on mechanized warfare. In July 1941, he left the soviet union to lead a military mission to Great Britain. Following these conferences, he visited the United States to discuss lend-lease arrangements. The end of 1941 found him back in the field of operations, leading one of the seven armies which turned back the nazi tide during the titanic battle before Moscow in the winter of 1941–42.

At the beginning of 1943, Stalin promoted Golikov from army commander to commander of the Voronezh front in the Ukraine. He led the forces that recaptured Kursk, Rostov and Kharkov, in Feb. 1943.

Gonorrhoea: *see* VENEREAL DISEASES.

Göring, Hermann Wilhelm: *see* GOERING, HERMANN WILHELM.

Government Departments and Bureaus.

The following are the leading officers of the more important government departments and bureaus of the United States. The date for the information is Jan. 1, 1944.

Department or Bureau	Name	Post
Department of State	*Hull, Cordell	Secretary
	*Stettinius, Edward R., Jr.	Under-Sec'y
Department of the Treasury	Morgenthau, Henry, Jr.	Secretary
	Bell, Daniel W.	Under-Sec'y
Bureau of Comptroller of Currency	Delano, Preston	Comptroller
Treasurer of the U.S.	Julian, William A.	Treasurer
Bureau of Customs	Johnson, W. R.	Commissioner
Bureau of Internal Revenue	Hannegan, Robert E.	Commissioner
War Department	*Stimson, Henry L.	Secretary
	*Patterson, Robert P.	Under-Sec'y
General Staff	*Marshall, George C., Gen.	Chief of Staff
Army Service Forces	*Somervell, Brehon, Lt. Gen.	Comm'd'g Gen.
Army Ground Forces	*McNair, Lesley J., Lt. Gen.	Comm'd'g Gen.
Army Air Forces	*Arnold, Henry H., Gen.	Comm'd'g Gen.
Department of Justice	Biddle, Francis	Att'y-Gen.
Solicitor General	Fahy, Charles	Solic. Gen.
*Federal Bureau of Investigation	Hoover, J. Edgar	Director
Bureau of Prisons	Bennett, James V.	Director
Immigration and Naturalization Service	Harrison, Earl G.	Commissioner
*Post Office Department	Walker, Frank C.	Postm'r Gen.
Department of the Navy	*Knox, Franklin	Secretary
	Forrestal, James V.	Under-Sec'y
Office of Commander in Chief, U.S. Fleet, and Chief of Naval Operations	*King, Ernest J., Adm.	Commander in Chief, U.S. Fleet, and Chief of Naval Operations
Bureau of Naval Personnel	Jacobs, Randall, Rear Adm.	Chief
Bureau of Ordnance	Hussey, George F., Jr., Rear Adm.	Chief
*U.S. Marine Corps Headquarters	*Vandegrift, Alexander A., Lieutenant Gen.	Commandant
*U.S. Coast Guard	Waesche, Russell R., Vice Adm.	Commandant
Department of the Interior	Ickes, Harold L.	Secretary
	Fortas, Abe¹	Under-Sec'y
General Land Office	Johnson, Fred W.	Commissioner
Office of Indian Affairs	Collier, John	Commissioner
Solid Fuels Administration for War	Ickes, Harold L.	Administrator
Office of Fishery Coordination	Ickes, Harold L.	Fishery Co-ordinator
Geological Survey	Wrather, William E.	Director
*Fish and Wildlife Service	Gabrielson, Ira N.	Director
Bureau of Reclamation	Bashore, Harry W.	Commissioner
National Park Service	Drury, Newton B.	Director
Bureau of Mines	Sayers, Royd R.	Director
Division of Territories and Island Possessions	Thoron, Benjamin W.	Director
Department of Agriculture	*Wickard, Claude R.	Secretary
	Appleby, Paul H.	Under-Sec'y
*Agricultural Research Administration	Auchter, E. C.	Administrator
Bureau of Animal Industry	Miller, Arthur W.	Chief
Bureau of Agricultural and Industrial Chemistry	Skinner, W. W.	Acting Chief
Bureau of Dairy Industry	Reed, Ollie E.	Chief
Bureau of Entomology and Plant Quarantine	Annand, P. N.	Chief
Office of Experiment Stations	Jardine, James T.	Chief
Bureau of Plant Industry, Soils, and Agricultural Engineering	Salter, R. M.	Chief
Bureau of Human Nutrition and Home Economics	Sherman, Henry C.	Chief
Bureau of Agricultural Economics	Tolley, Howard R.	Chief
War Meat Board	Reed, Harry E.	Chairman
*War Food Administration	*Jones, Marvin	Administrator
Commodity Credit Corporation	Hutson, J. B.	President
Food Distribution Administration	Hendrickson, Roy F.	Director
Agricultural Extension Service	Wilson, M. L.	Director
Office of Labor	Bruton, Philip G., Col.	Director
Food Production Administration	Hutson, J. B.	Director
Agricultural Adjustment Agency	Dodd, N. E.	Chief
Soil Conservation Service	Bennett, Hugh H.	Chief
Federal Crop Insurance Corporation	Wright, J. Carl	Acting Manager
Farm Security Administration	Hancock, Frank	Chief
*Farm Credit Administration	Black, Albert G.	Governor
Forest Service	Lyle, F. Watts	Chief
Office of Foreign Agricultural Relations	Wheeler, L. A.	Director
Rural Electrification Administration	Slattery, Harry	Administrator
Department of Commerce	*Jones, Jesse H.	Secretary
	Taylor, Wayne C.	Under-Sec'y
Bureau of the Census	Capt, James C.	Director

Department or Bureau	Name	Post
Bureau of Foreign and Domestic Commerce	Taylor, Amos E.	Director
*National Bureau of Standards	Briggs, Lyman J.	Director
*Coast and Geodetic Survey	Colbert, Leo O.	Director
Civil Aeronautics Board	Pogue, L. Welch	Chairman
*Reconstruction Finance Corporation	Henderson, Charles B.	Chairman
War Damage Corporation	Clayton, W. L.	President
Patent Office	Coe, Conway P.	Commissioner
Weather Bureau	Reichelderfer, F. W.	Chief
Department of Labor	Perkins, Frances	Secretary
	Tracy, D. W.	Asst. Sec'y
U.S. Conciliation Service	Steelman, J. R.	Director
Bureau of Labor Statistics	Hinrichs, A. F.	Acting Commissioner
Children's Bureau	Lenroot, Katharine F.	Chief
Women's Bureau	Anderson, Mary	Chief
Wage and Hour and Public Contracts Divisions	Walling, L. Metcalfe	Administrator
*Federal Security Agency	*McNutt, Paul V.	Administrator
Office of Education	Studebaker, John W.	Commissioner
Public Health Service	Parran, Dr. Thomas	Surgeon Gen.
Social Security Board	Altmeyer, Arthur J.	Chairman
Food and Drug Administration	Campbell, W. G.	Commissioner
Office of Community War Services	McCloskey, Mark A.	Director
*Federal Works Agency	Fleming, Philip B., Major Gen.	Administrator
Public Buildings Administration	Reynolds, W. E.	Commissioner
Public Roads Administration	MacDonald, Thomas H.	Commissioner
War Public Works	Snyder, Baird	Director
War Public Services	Kerr, Mrs. Florence	Director
Independent Offices		
*Federal Communications Commission	Fly, James L.	Chairman
*Federal Deposit Insurance Corporation	*Crowley, Leo T.	Chairman
*Federal Power Commission	Olds, Leland	Chairman
*Federal Reserve System, Board of Governors of the	Eccles, Marriner S.	Chairman
*Federal Trade Commission	Freer, Robert E.	Chairman
*Government Printing Office	Giegengack, A. E.	Public Printer
*Interstate Commerce Commission	Patterson, Wm. J.	Chairman
Library of Congress	MacLeish, Archibald	Librarian of Congress
National Advisory Committee for Aeronautics	Hunsaker, Dr. Jerome C.	Chairman
National Capital Park and Planning Commission	Grant, U. S., III, Major Gen.	Chairman
*National Labor Relations Board	Millis, Harry Alvin	Chairman
*National Mediation Board	Leiserson, William A.	Chairman
Railroad Retirement Board	Latimer, Murray W.	Chairman
*Securities and Exchange Commission	Purcell, Ganson	Chairman
Tax Court of the United States	Murdock, J. Edgar	Presiding Judge
*Smithsonian Institution	Abbot, C. G.	Secretary
*Tennessee Valley Authority	Lillienthal, David E.	Chairman
*The National Archives	Buck, Solon J.	Archivist
U. S. Civil Service Commission	Mitchell, Harry B.	President
U. S. Employees' Compensation Commission	Swofford, Mrs. Jewell W.	Chairman
U.S. Maritime Commission	*Land, E. S., Rear Adm.	Chairman
U.S. Tariff Commission	Ryder, Oscar B.	Chairman
*Veterans' Administration	Hines, F. T., Brig. Gen.	Administrator
Executive Office of the President		
Bureau of the Budget	Smith, Harold D.	Director
Emergency War Agencies		
*Office for Emergency Management		....
*Office of War Mobilization	*Byrnes, James F.	Director
*National War Labor Board	Davis, William H.	Chairman
Office of Alien Property Custodian	*Crowley, Leo T.	Custodian
Office of Civilian Defense	Martin, John B.	Acting Director
*Office of the Coordinator of Inter-American Affairs	Rockefeller, Nelson A.	Coordinator
*Office of Defense Transportation	*Eastman, Joseph B.	Director
*Office of Economic Stabilization	*Vinson, Fred M.	Director
*Office of Scientific Research and Development	Bush, Dr. Vannevar	Director
*Office of War Information	*Davis, Elmer	Director
*War Manpower Commission	*McNutt, Paul V.	Chairman
*War Production Board	*Nelson, Donald M.	Chairman
	*Wilson, Charles E.	Executive Vice Chairman
	Krug, J. A.	Program Vice Chairman
	Boulware, Lemuel R.	Operations Vice Chairman
	Whiteside, Arthur D.	Vice Chairman for Civilian Requirements
	Golden, Clinton S.	Vice Chairman for Manpower Requirements
	Keenan, Joseph D.	Vice Chairman of Labor Production
	Batt, William L.	Vice Chairman (International Supply)
	Davis, Donald D.	Vice Chairman
Office of Production Research and Development	Davis, Harvey N.	Director
Office of Rubber Director	Dewey, Bradley, Col.	Director
Office of War Utilities	Krug, J. A.	Director
Smaller War Plants Corporation	Maverick, Maury²	Chairman
*War Relocation Authority	Myer, Dillon S.	Director
*War Shipping Administration	*Land, E. S., Rear Adm.	Administrator
*Foreign Economic Administration	*Crowley, Leo T.	Administrator
*Export-Import Bank of Washington	Pierson, Warren L.	President

Department or Bureau	Name	Post
Committee on Fair Employment Practice	Ross, Malcolm	Chairman
*National Housing Agency	Blandford, John B., Jr.	Administrator
Federal Home Loan Bank Administration	Fahey, John H.	Commissioner
Home Owners' Loan Corporation	Cotter, Charles F.	General Manager
Federal Housing Administration	Ferguson, Abner H.	Commissioner
Federal Public Housing Authority	Emmerich, Herbert	Commissioner
Office of Censorship	Price, Byron	Director
*Office of Price Administration	*Bowles, Chester	Administrator
Petroleum Administration for War	Ickes, Harold L.	Administrator
	Davies, Ralph K.	Deputy Administrator
President's War Relief Control Board	*Davies, Joseph E.	Chairman
*United Nations Relief and Rehabilitation Administration	*Lehman, Herbert H.	Director General
*Board of War Communications	Fly, James L.	Chairman
Selective Service System	*Hershey, Lewis B., Maj. Gen.	Director
Quasi-Official Agencies		
*American National Red Cross	Davis, Norman H.	Chairman
*Pan American Union	Rowe, L. S.	Director General
*National Academy of Sciences and National Research Council	Jewett, Frank B.	President, National Academy of Sciences
	Harrison, Ross G.	Chairman, National Research Council

*See separate article.
[1]Discharged from the navy, Dec. 13, 1943. Renominated by Pres. Roosevelt.
[2]Appointed Jan. 8, 1944.

Great Britain.—The following were His Majesty's chief officers of state and the permanent officials of the more important of the government departments of Great Britain at the close of 1943:

Ministry or Department	Name	Post
Admiralty, The Board of	A. V. Alexander	First Lord
	Sir Henry V. Markham	Permanent Secretary
Agriculture and Fisheries, Ministry of	R. S. Hudson	Minister
	Sir Donald Fergusson	Permanent Secretary
Aircraft Production	Sir Stafford Cripps	Minister
	Sir Harold Scott	Permanent Secretary
Air Ministry	*Sir Archibald Sinclair	Secretary of State
	Sir Arthur Street	Perm'nt Under-sec'y
Assistance Board	Lord Soulbury	Chairman
	Sir George T. Reid	Secretary
Burma Office	L. S. Amery	Secretary of State
	Sir David T. Monteath	Perm'nt Under-sec'y
Cabinet Office	Sir Edward Bridges	Perm'nt Sec'y and Sec'y of the War Cabinet
Civil Service Commission	A. P. Waterfield	1st Commissioner
Colonial Office	*Oliver Stanley	Secretary of State
	Sir George Gater	Perm'nt Under-sec'y
Commissioners of Crown Lands	The Minister of Agriculture and Fisheries (ex-officio)	Commissioner
	O. S. Cleverly	Perm'nt Commissioner
Crown Agents for the Colonies	J. A. Calder / H. F. Downie	Crown Agents
Customs and Excise, Board of	Sir Archibald Carter	Chairman
Dominions Office	Viscount Cranborne	Secretary of State
	Sir Eric Machtig	Perm'nt Under-sec'y
Duchy of Lancaster	Ernest Brown	Chancellor
Economic Warfare, Ministry of	Earl of Selborne	Minister
	Earl of Drogheda	Director-General
Education, Board of	R. A. Butler	President
	Sir Maurice Holmes	Permanent Secretary
Food, Ministry of	Col. J. J. Llewellin	Minister
	Sir Henry L. French	Permanent Secretary
Foreign Office	*Anthony Eden	Secretary of State
	Sir Alexander Cadogan	Perm'nt Under-sec'y
Fuel and Power, Ministry of	Major Gwilym Lloyd George	Minister
	Sir Frank N. Tribe	Secretary
Health, Ministry of	H. U. Willink	Minister
	Sir John Maude	Secretary
Home Office and Ministry of Home Security	*Herbert Morrison	Minister
	Sir Alexander Maxwell	Perm'nt Under-sec'y, Home Office
	Sir William B. Brown	Secretary, Ministry of Home Security
India Office	L. S. Amery	Secretary of State
	Sir David T. Monteath	Perm'nt Under-sec'y
Information, Ministry of	Brendan Bracken	Minister
	C. J. Radcliffe	Director-General
Inland Revenue, Board of	Sir Cornelius J. Gregg	Chairman
Labour and National Service, Ministry of	Ernest Bevin	Minister
	Sir Thomas W. Phillips	Secretary
Lord Chancellor	Viscount Simon	
Lord Privy Seal	Lord Beaverbrook	
Minister without Portfolio	Sir William Jowitt	(Dealing with postwar reconstruction)
Minister of State	R. K. Law	
Minister of State (Cairo)	*R. G. Casey	
Deputy Minister of State (Cairo)	Lord Moyne	
Minister Resident in W. Africa	Viscount Swinton	
Minister Resident in N.W. Africa	Harold Macmillan	
Minister Resident in Washington for Supply	Ben Smith	

Ministry or Department	Name	Post
Paymaster-General's Office	Lord Cherwell	Paymaster-General
	L. Cuthbertson	Asst. Paymaster-Gen.
Pensions, Ministry of	Sir Walter Womersley	Minister
	Sir Alexander Cunnison	Permanent Secretary
*Post Office	Capt. Harry Crookshank	Postmaster-General
	Sir Thomas Gardiner	Director-General
Privy Council Office	C. R. Attlee	Lord President
	E. C. E. Leadbitter	Clerk of the Council
Production, Ministry of	*Oliver Lyttelton	Minister
	J. H. E. Woods	Permanent Secretary
Reconstruction, Ministry of	Lord Woolton	Minister
	Norman Brook	Secretary
Scottish Office	Thomas Johnston	Secretary of State
	Sir Horace P. Hamilton	Permanent Under-sec'y of State
Supply, Ministry of	Sir Andrew Rae Duncan	Minister
	Sir William Douglas	Permanent Secretary
Town and Country Planning, Ministry of	W. S. Morrison	Minister
	Sir Geoffrey Whiskard	Permanent Secretary
Trade, Board of	Hugh Dalton	President
	Sir Frederick Leith-Ross	Chief Economic Adviser to H. M. Govt.
	Sir Arnold E. Overton	Permanent Secretary
Treasury	*Winston Churchill	Prime Minister, First Lord and Minister of Defense
	*Sir John Anderson	Chancellor of the Exchequer
	Sir Richard V. N. Hopkins	Permanent Secretary and Head of H.M. Civil Service
War Office	Sir James Grigg	Secretary of State
	Sir Frederick C. Bovenschen)	Joint Perm'nt
	Sir Eric Speed	Under-sec'ies
War Transport, Ministry of	Lord Leathers	Minister
	Sir Cyril W. Hurcomb	Director-General
Works, Ministry of	Lord Portal	Minister
	F. P. Robinson	Permanent Secretary

*See separate article.

Government Expenditures: see BUDGET, NATIONAL.
Government Printing Office: see PRINTING OFFICE, U.S. GOVERNMENT.
Government Receipts: see BUDGET, NATIONAL.
Governors and Premiers, British: see BRITISH EMPIRE.
Grain: see BARLEY; CORN; OATS; RICE; RYE; WHEAT.
Granite: see STONE.

Grapefruit. The total grapefruit crop of 1943 was estimated by the U.S. department of agriculture to be 49,187,000 boxes or 3% less than the 1942 crop, but 2% more than was produced in 1941. Florida produced 25,000,000 boxes compared to 27,300,000 in 1942. The Texas crop was estimated at 17,200,000 boxes, a decline of 2% from the previous year. A strong demand kept prices of all citrus fruits at high levels, and

U.S. Production of Grapefruit by States, 1943 and 1942

State	1943 boxes*	1942 boxes*	State	1943 boxes*	1942 boxes*
Florida			California		
Seedless	11,500,000	10,300,000	Desert Valleys	1,316,000	1,254,000
Other varieties	13,500,000	17,000,000	Other varieties	1,771,000	1,817,000
Texas	17,200,000	17,510,000	Arizona	3,900,000	2,600,000

*Net contents of boxes of grapefruit are 60 lb. in California; in Florida and other states, 80 lb.

grapefruit sold at prices more than one-third higher than in 1942. There was a particularly strong demand for fruit juices for the armed forces, lend-lease and civilian consumption.

(J. C. Ms.)

Grapes. The total grape crop of the United States in 1943 was estimated by the U.S. department of agriculture at 2,789,900 tons, 16% more than the 2,402,000 tons produced in 1942 and 18% above the 10-year average 1932–41. This was, up to Jan. 1, 1944, the largest crop on record of this rapidly-increasing fruit. The expansion was chiefly in California where more than 90% of the total production is grown. The California crop in 1943 was estimated to be 2,610,000 tons and 21% higher than the previous year, while production in other states was about the same percentage smaller. The raisin varieties increased 24% and a raisin pack of more than 368,000 tons was expected. Shipments of grapes for the fresh fruit market were restricted and forced

State	1943 tons	1942 tons	State	1943 tons	1942 tons
California	2,610,000	2,160,000	New Jersey	2,100	2,600
Michigan	42,400	46,000	Tennessee	2,000	2,700
New York	36,000	69,600	Kentucky	1,800	2,000
Ohio	17,900	22,400	Oregon	1,800	1,800
Pennsylvania	15,300	21,500	Georgia	1,700	2,100
Washington	14,300	14,900	Virginia	1,100	1,900
Arkansas	7,300	8,400	Alabama	1,100	1,400
Missouri	5,200	7,200	South Carolina	1,100	1,400
North Carolina	5,200	6,400	Arizona	1,100	700
Illinois	2,900	4,300	Delaware	1,000	1,200
Iowa	2,900	3,200	New Mexico	900	900
Oklahoma	2,300	3,100	West Virginia	800	1,400
Kansas	2,200	3,600	Utah	800	700
Texas	2,200	2,200	Connecticut	700	1,100
Indiana	2,100	2,800	Florida	450	600

into raisins because of the large wartime demand. To assure the production of much-needed supplies of jams, jellies and lades, the War Food administration placed restrictions on the sale of grapes for fresh consumption in the principal areas of New York, Pennsylvania, Michigan, Ohio and Washington. Price ceilings were above the level of 1942 prices and auction sales at New York ranged from 42% to 85% higher than for the previous year. Ceiling prices of raisins were held to 1942 levels to civilians by the government purchase and resale program. Growers received prices about 40% higher than in 1942.

(J. C. Ms.)

Graphite. There were three graphite plants in operation in Alabama, one in Pennsylvania and one in Texas, and possibly some others, supplying their output for the Metals Reserve Co. stock pile. With this supply, and that of Madagascar again available, stocks were built up to a point where flake graphite was removed from the list of materials short in supply and placed in that in which supply and essential demands were balanced, while amorphous graphite was transferred to the surplus list. Stock-piling was to be discontinued and the mines put in a stand-by condition.

Shipments from Ceylon through Sept. 1943 totalled 298,889 cwt., against 433,367 cwt. in the same period of 1942.

(G. A. Ro.)

Gravel: *see* SAND AND GRAVEL.

Gray, George Kruger

(1880–1943), British painter and sculptor, was born Dec. 25 in Kensington and studied at the Royal College of Art. In addition to his sculpture and his landscape and portrait painting, he designed and painted stained glass windows, created numerous ecclesiastical works including altar pieces, war memorials, seals, medals, coins and heraldic works. He designed the coinage and official seals for the Union of South Africa, coins for Australia, Canada, Southern Rhodesia, New Zealand and the new Great Seal of George VI, as well as the Imperial silver coinages of George V and George VI. A London dispatch of May 4 carried the news of his death.

Great Britain & Northern Ireland, United Kingdom of.

This comprises the main island of Great Britain, with numerous smaller islands off the English and Scottish coasts, and the six northeastern counties of Ireland. It is a constitutional monarchy, with a king and a parliament of two houses: the house of lords consisting of about 670 hereditary peers, 24 spiritual peers, 16 Scottish representative peers, a number of Irish representative peers (in 1940, 14; vacancies are no longer filled) and a few life peers who have held high judicial office; and the house of commons,

VEGETABLE GARDENS began to appear in London in 1943 where gaping craters and demolished buildings had lain since the German air raids of 1940. This garden is in London's East End, with St. Paul's cathedral in the background

numbering 615 members, elected by a practically universal suffrage. Flag, the Union Jack, consisting of a red cross on a white field (for England), surcharged on a diagonal white field (for Ireland), surcharged in turn on a diagonal white cross on a blue field (for Scotland). Ruler: King George VI (*q.v.*); premier: Winston S. Churchill, (*q.v.*); established church: Protestant Episcopal.

Area and Population.—Area 93,991 sq.mi.; pop. (est. Dec. 31, 1939) 47,735,000 (England and Wales 41,417,000). Chief towns (pop. est. June 30, 1938): London (cap.), city and metropolitan police districts, 8,700,000; city and metropolitan boroughs only, 4,062,800; Glasgow (June 30, 1939), 1,131,500; Birmingham, 1,041,000; Manchester (including Salford), 932,300; Liverpool, 827,400; Sheffield, 520,000; Leeds, 494,000; Edinburgh (June 30, 1939), 473,200; Belfast (Jan. 1, 1939), 443,500; Bristol, 415,000; Hull, 318,700.

History.—As in 1942 the domestic history of the United Kingdom in 1943 was largely a record of industrial and agricultural production. The mobilization of men and materials reached a new high level. Out of 15,900,000 males between the ages of 16 and 64, 15,200,000 were, in the summer, either in the forces or in full-time employment; the remaining 700,000 included schoolboys and the disabled. Out of 17,230,000 women between the same ages, 7,100,000 were in the services or on full-time work. The remaining 10,130,000 included schoolgirls, 650,000 women in part-time employment, and millions of housewives fully occupied in their homes and with voluntary work. No less than 40% of the aircraft industry's workers consisted of women. In industry hours of labour were appreciably lengthened, in many cases by much more than the average of about 10%. The total production of munitions rose from an index number of 100 in the first half of 1940 to about 300 in the first half of 1943.

The comparative figures of aircraft production were as follows:

	First half of			
	1940	1941	1942	1943
Structural weight	100	161	·244	364
Engine horse-power	100	179	373	486

The enormous increase in munitions production, moreover, was achieved in spite of the dislocation involved in the policy of changing over from the production of defensive to offensive weapons which was decided upon at the beginning of 1943, when for the first time the Allies secured the strategical initiative. The production of weapons and equipment which had become obsolete, which were primarily needed for desert warfare, or of which abundant supplies were in reserve, was stopped or curtailed, and production was concentrated on the most modern and offensive types of weapons. Emphasis was laid on the production of aircraft, naval craft specially designed to combat the U-boats, radio equipment, and scientific instruments used in naval warfare.

The concentration of industry, which alone made possible the achievement of the government's vast program of production, was virtually completed during 1943, the only industries from which considerable numbers of workers could still be released being clothing and printing. In this process of concentration some 2,800 establishments were closed down, releasing nearly 250,000 workers for the services or for work in other more vital industries.

Since the wartime demand for labour could never be satisfied, the fall in unemployment continued in 1943. In January, April and October the respective numbers of unemployed in Great Britain were 99,000, 80,000 and 74,000, compared with 136,000 in March 1942.

This mobilization of the country's manpower for war purposes was accomplished without serious opposition either in parliament or elsewhere, though Ernest Bevin's announcement that women up to the age of 51 were to be called up for national service met with some criticism in the house of commons. The government's success in stabilizing the cost of living at 100% above the July 1914 level, the high level of earnings in industry as a whole, and improved industrial relations had largely contributed to the absence of serious labour troubles since 1939. In 1943, however, industrial unrest was becoming more pronounced, though it never assumed really serious proportions. There were many strikes in local aircraft factories, among the miners, the bus workers and the engineers, one or two stoppages (at Nottingham and in a London district) in the railway industry, and dock strikes at Liverpool and in London. The trade unions were pledged by law and agreement not to strike without due notice and previous arbitration procedure, and since 1939 there had been no authorized strike. "Unofficial" strikes, however, were becoming a habit, and the union officials seemed to be powerless to avert them. The main grievances were not the general level of wages, for the average rise in earnings between Oct. 1938 and Jan. 1943 was 65%. On the other hand, workers were sometimes compulsorily moved from higher- to lower-paid work, and the average earnings of miners were considerably less than those of munition workers.

Serious trouble of another kind threatened in the summer of 1943, when the union of post office workers sought affiliation with the Trade Union Congress, in defiance of the Trades Dispute act of 1927. In the end the workers decided to shelve the matter until after the war: had they persisted in their original intention of defying the law, they would have been disqualified from the civil service establishment and would have forfeited their pension rights.

The defense regulations gave the government extensive power over capital as well as labour. Early in 1943 the minister of aircraft production decided compulsorily to purchase the shares of Short Brothers, as a means of changing the board of directors and without an undertaking to resell the shares to the proprietor after the war. Unsatisfactory production figures caused this drastic step to be taken: it was said that at one time the firm was taking three times as many man-hours as another firm to produce a comparable aircraft. But Sir Stafford Cripps found the position of the aircraft industry in general satisfactory, and in January he spoke of the valuable contribution which the joint production committees (started in the engineering industry in 1942) were making towards improving factory production.

The Food Situation.—The cost of living was kept stable in 1943, chiefly by means of food subsidies—costing about £70,000,000 in 1940, £145,000,000 in 1942, and £210,000,000 (estimate) in 1943.

The year saw no important changes in rationing or food policy. It was announced in January that a bread-rationing scheme was ready for immediate introduction should such a step become necessary; but Lord Woolton preferred to rely on voluntary restriction of consumption. The potato, he said, was "the key to the food problem," and reiterated appeals were made to eat less bread and more potatoes. During the year, home-grown oats, barley and potato-flour were added to the national loaf, and the system of "points" rationing was extended.

In agricultural as in industrial production, labour was the chief bottleneck, and the Women's Land army (52,000 strong in Jan. 1943) was further increased during the year to take the place of men called to the forces. The farmers again made heroic efforts to increase food production and so relieve the strain on shipping. In 1943 the arable area in the United Kingdom approached 18,000,000 ac., compared with nearly 13,000,000 ac. in 1939. Still more grassland was plowed up. It was estimated that 1,000,000 tons more bread corn were produced than in 1942, and an additional 250,000 tons of potatoes, thus liberating enough shipping to transport overseas eight or ten divisions with their equipment. (*See* AGRICULTURE.)

To relieve the housing shortage in certain rural districts, the ministry of health made plans early in 1943 for the construction of 3,000 new cottages exclusively for rural workers. But by the end of 1943 little had been accomplished, because of the shortage of labour and materials. Building costs had risen by 105% since 1939, and the least expensive of the first 54 houses for which tenders were approved was to cost about £850. (*See* HOUSING.)

Repeated requests for further preferential treatment so far as food rations were concerned, for workers in "heavy" industries, were not conceded, though the provision of works canteens went on. There were in 1943 more than 7,500 works canteens, where at least one cheap and nourishing meal a day could be obtained without the surrender of coupons.

Civilian Casualties.—The number of civilian casualties in air raids on Britain during the first ten months of 1943 was lower than that in any comparable period since the beginning of large-scale air attack; 2,228 people were killed during this period, the figures for the whole of 1941 and 1942 being 20,863 and 3,221 respectively. The number of civilians injured and detained in hospitals to the end of Oct. 1943, was 3,183, the figures for the whole of 1941 and 1942 being 21,839 and 4,149 respectively. The coastal districts of the south and east were the chief sufferers. London's remarkable new gun barrage was heard for the first time at the beginning of March, when there was an ineffective attack on the capital, apparently in retaliation for the R.A.F.'s heavy assault on Berlin two nights earlier. Damage and casualties were slight, but on this occasion there was a serious accident at one tube station shelter in an East End district. Bad lighting and the lack of sufficient hand-rails and of police supervision caused the deaths from suffocation of 173 people and serious injuries to 62 others, at the beginning of the rush for the shelter.

The cessation of large-scale air raids on Britain caused the government in March to reduce the rates of premium payable on the voluntary "private chattels" scheme for the insurance of furniture and personal belongings, and on the compulsory "business" scheme for the insurance of plant, machinery and business equipment.

Civilian Defense and Rationing.—During the 12 months ended June 1943, the whole-time personnel of the civil defense services was reduced by about one-third, and, though these services continued to be maintained at a high level of preparedness in view of the possibility of large-scale German reprisals for the increasing weight of the R.A.F.'s assault, it was nevertheless found possible to make a further substantial cut in these services in the less vulnerable areas. (*See* CIVILIAN DEFENSE.)

Supplies of goods for civilian consumption had already, at the beginning of the year, been cut to the bone, and the board of trade imposed a ban on the usual January sales, except for the disposal of "oddments." The retail trade in merchandise other than food fell from a monthly average of 102 in 1942 (1937=100) to 89 for the first seven months of 1943. Nearly all clothing would ultimately be "utility"; only "utility" furniture was manufactured after Nov. 1942, and it could be bought only by persons setting up a home on marriage, or in anticipation of the birth of a child, or by persons who had lost their homes through air raids.

The battle for fuel, which began in the summer of 1942, was waged with greater intensity in 1943. Coal rationing was nominally avoided, but supplies nevertheless were severely restricted. The exceptionally mild winter of 1942–43 tended to obscure the growing seriousness of the coal position. Production continued to fall below the corresponding figures for 1942. There was a shortage of young recruits to the industry, the best men were in the forces, the district output bonus scheme was a failure. Pits nearing exhaustion continued to be worked; there was a shortage of machinery for coal cutting; the miners were dissatisfied with their working conditions; and there was much absenteeism. Moreover, from the beginning of July 1943, till mid-November, strikes caused the loss of over 500,000 tons of coal, all the 421 stoppages being unauthorized by the Mineworkers' federation. The failure of voluntary recruitment caused the government in December to decide on a policy of conscription. To the end of September the number of men who, having chosen coal mining as an alternative to the services, had been placed in the mines was only 3,366 (about one-tenth of the total required to offset the annual wastage through death, accident and retirement). A total of 30,000 men between the ages of 18 and 25, it was announced in December, were to be drafted into the mines by the end of April 1944, the men to be chosen by ballot. (*See* also COAL.)

OPERATIONS ROOM of the British navy's command of the western approaches. Here Admiral Sir Max Horton (second from right, near ladder) directed the successful antisubmarine campaign of 1943 in the north Atlantic

Taxation.—The 1943 budget was the largest in British history, the chancellor proposing to spend £5,756,000,000 (more than the whole national income as recently as 1940). He intended to raise £2,908,000,000 in revenue (51% of the total expenditure), representing about £100,000,000 of additional taxation, the increased burden being placed on "voluntary" expenditure on tobacco, alcohol, entertainments and luxury goods, the purchase tax on which was raised to 100%. But the purchase tax was removed from utility cloth and other "utility" textiles. £2,848,-000,000 were to be borrowed. When, at the beginning of Sept. 1943, the country entered the fifth year of the war, national expenditure had exceeded £18,000,000,000 and revenue £8,000,-000,000, so that about £10,000,000,000 had been added to the national debt, making a total of £18,230,000,000. Sir Kingsley Wood announced the government's intention of maintaining its policy of cheap money after the war, and said that the basic objective to which monetary and economic policy must be subordinated was "active employment for our people."

Hitherto, the amount of a person's income tax had been based on the earnings of the preceding year. In the case of weekly wage-earners (and war taxation greatly increased the number of income-tax payers) the time-lag between money earned and tax paid was ten months: this situation, it was felt, might create hardship whenever earnings either fluctuated considerably, declined, or, through unemployment or old age, ceased. The new chancellor, Sir John Anderson (Sir Kingsley Wood died suddenly in September), decided to apply, as from April 1944, the principle of "pay-as-you-earn," not only to weekly wage-earners, but to all salaried incomes up to £600 a year. Subsequently, in November, he undertook to extend the concession to all Schedule E incomes later in 1944. The weekly tax payment, therefore, would in future be based on the same week's earnings.

Reverse Lend-Lease.—In November the government issued as a *White Paper* a report on "mutual aid," which described Britain's contribution to the war effort of the United Nations. Much of this effort, consisting of services rendered, was incapable of monetary valuation, as the figures were necessarily incomplete. The main items were:

	Millions
Aid given to U.S. forces in Britain (in yr. ending June 1943)	£ 216
Aid to the U.S.S.R.	179
Aid to other Allies (to the beginning of 1943)	186
British expenditure in overseas territories, to June 1943	2,250
	£2,831

Legislation.—The output of legislation during the parliamentary session ending in Nov. 1943 was neither large nor important. The commons found the Catering Wages bill exceptionally controversial, the opposition to it coming from all sections of the trade, from the hotels and restaurants association to the coffee stall keepers and the eel and pie traders. The act was designed to secure adequate wages and decent working conditions in the catering industry.

British public opinion in 1943 became increasingly concerned with the problems of peace and reconstruction. In his Mansion House speech in Nov. 1943, the prime minister defined the government's task as that of providing food, work and homes for all, in the immediate postwar years. He proceeded to appoint Lord Woolton minister of reconstruction, with a seat in the war cabinet. At the ninth session of the existing parliament which the king opened on Nov. 24, the speech from the throne foreshadowed the introduction of bills to provide for the reinstatement of ex-servicemen in civil employment; to make further provision for the training and employment of disabled persons; and to reconstruct the national system of education. Further legislation was contemplated, providing for an enlarged and unified system of social insurance and a comprehensive health serv-

ice, and the reform of workmen's compensation.   (A. AL.)

Education.—In 1937–38: elementary, England and Wales—departments under separate head teachers, 29,988, scholars on register 5,150,874; elementary, Scotland—schools 2,895, scholars 617,047; elementary, Northern Ireland—schools 1,700, scholars 191,862; secondary, England and Wales—grant-aided schools 1,398, scholars 470,003; secondary, Scotland—grant-aided schools 252, scholars 156,645; secondary, Northern Ireland—grant-aided schools 75, scholars 14,557; universities, students: England 41,-707 (full time, 36,378); Wales 3,089 (full time, 2,970); Scotland 10,384 (full time, 9,841); Northern Ireland 1,590 full-time students.

Banking and Finance.—Revenue, ordinary (est. 1943–44) £2,907,500,000. Expenditure, ordinary (est. 1943–44) £5,756,-114,000. Revenue, ordinary (actual 1942–43) £2,922,400,000. Expenditure, ordinary (actual 1942–43) £5,740,300,000. Notes in circulation (Nov. 17, 1943) £1,013,682,527. Public debt (national) March 31, 1943, £15,565,718,000. Exchange rate 1943, £1=403.5 cents.

Table I.—*Estimated Revenue and Expenditure 1943-1944*
ESTIMATED REVENUE 1943–44

	£	£
Income Tax	1,175,000,000	
Surtax	80,000,000	
Estate Duties	100,000,000	
Stamps	17,000,000	
National Defense Contribution and Excess Profits Tax	500,000,000	
Other Inland Revenue Duties	1,000,000	
Total Inland Revenue		1,873,000,000
Customs	525,320,000	
Excise	450,180,000	
Total Customs and Excise		975,500,000
Motor Vehicle Duties		25,000,000
Post Office (net receipt)		400,000
Crown Lands		800,000
Wireless Licences		4,700,000
Receipts from Sundry Loans		4,100,000
Miscellaneous		24,000,000
Total Ordinary Revenue		£2,907,500,000

ESTIMATED EXPENDITURE 1943–44

	£
Interest and Management of National Debt	375,000,000
Payments to Northern Ireland	9,500,000
Miscellaneous Consolidated Fund Services	7,500,000
Total	392,000,000
Supply Services	
Defense (token votes*)	4,000
Civil	
Central Government and Finance	3,209,000
Foreign and Imperial	15,520,000
Home Department, Law and Justice	20,617,000
Education and Broadcasting	82,028,000
Health, Labour, Insurance (inc. Old Age and Widows' Pensions)	198,876,000
Trade, Industry and Transport	17,861,000
Works, Stationery, etc.	14,547,000
War Pensions 1914–18, and Civil Pensions	39,219,000
Exchequer Contributions to Local Revenues	52,773,000
War Services (token votes*)	2,000
	444,652,000
Votes of Credit	4,900,000,000†
Tax Collection—Customs and Excise and Inland Revenue votes (inc. Pensions £1,469,000)	19,458,000
	£5,364,114,000
Total Ordinary Expenditure	£5,756,114,000

*Substantive cost to be met from votes of credit.
†Excluding value of supplies in kind under lend-lease and similar arrangements.

Trade and Communication.—Overseas trade in million £: imports, merchandise (1939) £885.5; (1940) £1,099.9; exports, domestic (1939) £439.6; (1940) £413.1; re-exports (1939) £46.0; (1940) £26.2.

Table II.—*Overseas Trade, Showing the Variations in the First Eight Months (Jan. 1–Aug. 31) of Each of the Years 1937–40*
(in million £)

	1937	1938	1939	1940
Imports	654.4	616.5	605.9	792.9
Exports	341.4	306.9	313.6	312.6
Re-exports	54.2	42.4	36.3	22.6
Total Exports	395.6	349.3	349.9	335.2

Communication.—Roads (March 31, 1938): England and Wales (class I) 20,627 mi.; (Class II) 13,070 mi.; Scotland (class I) 6,632 mi.; (class II) 3,967 mi.; Northern Ireland (class I) 1,273 mi.; (class II) 1,933 mi. Railways (Dec. 31, 1938): Great Britain, track open to traffic, excluding sidings, 20,007 mi.; Northern Ireland, standard gauge 633 mi.; narrow gauge 121 mi. Airways (1938): distance flown 14,331,000 mi.; passengers carried 222,200; mail carried 3,453 tons; freight carried 2,527 tons. Empire services (airways), traffic ton miles including passenger ton miles (1937–38) 7,153,767; (1938–39) 13,734,899; passengers carried (1939) 12,614. Shipping, excluding vessels under 100 tons (July 1, 1939) 17,984,158 gross tons; under construction (July 1, 1939) 791,500 gross tons; shipping (net tonnage with cargo), entered (monthly average 1938) 5,698,000; cleared (monthly average 1938) 4,907,000; entered (Aug. 1939) 6,617,000; cleared (Aug. 1939) 5,525,000. Motor vehicles licensed (Sept. 30, 1938): cars 1,944,394; hackney vehicles (taxis, buses, coaches, etc.) 87,730; commercial vehicles 590,397; motorcycles 462,375; total 3,084,896. Wireless receiving set licences (Sept. 30, 1939) 9,085,050; telephones (Dec. 31, 1939): number of stations (including public and private lines, call boxes, etc.) 3,235,500.

The British railways in 1943 carried the greatest volume of traffic in their history. During the first four years of the war they moved over 1,000,000,000 tons of freight, and ran 180,000 special trains for the transport of troops and equipment. In the summer of 1943 the equivalent of 30 divisions a week was being carried in special trains. Transport restrictions operated all over the country, a 9 P.M. curfew for buses being the general rule.

Agriculture, Manufacturing, Mineral Production.—Production in 1939 (in metric tons): wheat 1,680,000; oats 1,760,800; barley 903,300; potatoes (1938) 5,197,100; beet sugar (1940) 470,000; hops (1938) 131,000; coal (1938) 230,658,000; iron ore (metal content) (1938) 3,615,000; pig iron and ferro-alloys (1938) 6,870,000; steel (1938) 10,565,000; sea fisheries (wet fish only) (1938) 1,062,665; whale oil (1938) 221,100; benzol (1938) 218,800; shale oil (1938) 131,000; beef and veal (1937–38) 688,000; pig meat (1937–38) 415,200; mutton and lamb (1937–38) 257,000; wool (1938) 50,300; wood pulp (1938) 270,000; silk, artificial (1940) 45,360; margarine (1938) 211,600; butter (1938) 47,000; cheese (1938) 44,100; flax (fibre) (Northern Ireland) (1938) 4,100; rye (1938) 10,900; lead ore (metal content) (1938) 30,200; aluminum (smelter production) (1940) 35,000; super-phosphates of lime (1937) 449,000; tin ore (metal content) (1939) 1,700.

Table III.—*Agricultural Production, in Thousands of Metric Tons,* and Acreage, England and Wales, 1938 and 1939*

Crops	1938 Thous. met. tons	1938 Acres	1939 Thous. met. tons	1939 Acres
Wheat	1,855	1,830,261	1,555	1,682,616
Barley	803	885,499	794	910,073
Oats	1,069	1,300,530	1,119	1,358,008
Mixed Corn	74	92,240	72	82,781
Seeds hay	1,281	1,184,082	1,700	1,302,858
Meadow hay	3,131	4,229,308	4,535	4,611,564
Beans (for stock-feeding or seed)	106	129,817	109	132,968
Peas (for stock-feeding or seed)	30	38,153	23	36,800
Potatoes	3,486	474,786	3,312	453,976
Turnips and Swedes	5,081	421,190	4,947	394,249
Mangolds	3,599	212,531	3,938	208,891

*One metric ton = .98421 English ton.

Industry and Labour.—Index of industrial production (1929 = 100) av. (1938) 115.5; av. (Jan.–June 1939) 123.1; index of employment (1929 = 100) av. (1939) 113.0. Industrial population, insured (July 1939) 14,838,000; unemployed, wholly, av. (1940) 802,921; temporary av. (1940) 159,782; wholly av. (1941) 292,000. (*See also* BUSINESS REVIEW; WORLD WAR II.)

Great Lakes Traffic: *see* CANALS AND INLAND WATERWAYS.

Greece. A kingdom in the southern part of the Balkan peninsula, in 1943 under German and Bulgarian occupation, while the Italian influence ended with Italy's surrender to the Allies in Sept. 1943. Area 50,147 sq.mi., of which 41,328 are mainland; pop. (census May 16, 1928) 6,204,684; (estimated, 1940) 7,150,000. Capital, Athens (392,781). Chief cities: Thessaloniki (236,524), Patras (61,278), Cavalla (49,980), Candia (33,404), Corfu (32,221). Religion: mostly Greek Orthodox; 126,017 Mohammedans; 72,791 Jews. King: George II; prime minister (1943): Emmanuel Tsouderos.

History.—The Greek government-in-exile under King George II moved its seat in March 1943 from London to Cairo. The king was not popular with the large republican group in his country, though his new government-in-exile represented all Greek shades. Premier Tsouderos remained in office throughout the year. Vice-Premier Panayotis Kannelopoulos resigned on March 10 and the premier took over the ministry of defense. Vice-Admiral Petros Voulgaris was appointed Greek minister for aviation on May 21.

As in Yugoslavia, the Greek people in the homeland were torn by a violent strife among different factions, royalist, republican and communist. On July 4 the king broadcast from Cairo and appealed for political unity. He promised that as soon as the seat of government could be transferred to Greek soil, its members would resign so that a government fully representative of all parties could be composed. In a letter to Premier Tsouderos made public in December King George declared he would return to Greece only in conformity with the wish of the nation.

The Germans fortified the Greek coast during 1943 against the danger of an Allied invasion, and Allied air forces repeatedly bombed Greek ports and airfields in the fall.

The Greek guerrillas or Andartes were first organized as a national movement on May 20, 1942 and harassed the forces of occupation in spite of savage reprisals by the Germans, under the command of Col. Gen. Alexander Loehr. But the effectiveness of the guerrillas was diminished in 1943 by their split into three warring factions. On the one side was the Greek National Liberation front or E.A.M. with the Popular Liberation army or E.L.A.S., under communist leadership and strongly leftist in its political views. Opposed to it was the Greek National Democratic army or E.D.E.S. under General Napoleon Zarvas. A third group was the National Social Liberation army or E.K.K.A. British liaison officers brought about an agreement among the guerrilla leaders to act together against the Germans, but in the fall of 1943 the Greeks disregarded this agreement and fought more savagely among themselves than against the German invaders.

Education.—Education was compulsory for all children between the ages of 7 and 12. In 1938 Greece had 743 kindergartens with 38,338 pupils, 8,339 primary schools with 985,018 pupils and 407 high schools with 92,687 pupils. There were 3 universities with 7,230 students, an institute of technology with 521 students and a school of fine arts.

Finance.—The monetary unit was the drachma, stabilized in 1928 at 77.02 to the dollar; the stabilization was suspended in April 1932. For the year 1939–40, the revenue was estimated at 14,014,000,000 and expenditure at 14,653,000,000 drachmai. On Dec. 31, 1938, the public debt amounted to 52,140,000,000 drachmai.

Communication and Trade.—Greece had an important merchant marine which consisted on June 30, 1939, of 589 steam and motor ships of 1,812,723 tons and 710 sailing vessels. In 1939 there were 1,668 mi. of railroad and 42 telephone exchanges with 38,427 subscribers.

In 1940 the value of imports amounted to 12,215,000,000, the value of exports to 9,079,000,000 drachmai. Germany was first and the United States second in both imports and exports. The chief imports were cotton piece goods, woollen goods and machinery; the chief exports, currants, raisins and tobacco.

Agriculture and Mineral Production.—Greece is chiefly an agricultural country, though the mountainous character allows only one-fifth of the area to be cultivated. Olive and fruit, tobacco and currants are ordinarily produced in great quantities and good quality. Breeding of sheep and goats is important. Iron ore and pyrites, magnesite, lignites, chromites, lead and emery are found. Industrial development is insignificant, but was growing before the German invasion of 1941.

BIBLIOGRAPHY.—Stephen Lavra, *The Greek Miracle* (1943); Betty Wason, *Miracle in Hellas* (1943); Amyntor, *Victors in Chain* (London, 1943). (H. Ko.)

Greenland. The world's largest island (736,518 sq.mi., some 705,000 covered by glacier), in the North Atlantic ocean, N.W. of Iceland. A Danish possession, it came under United States protection in 1941. Capital, Godthaab. A population of about 18,000 (est. 1941) is scattered in small settlements on the west coast, and 1,000 on the east coast, about 600 in all being Danes, the rest native Greenlanders. Seats of the governors are Godhavn in the north and Godthaab in the south.

History.—Through 1943 Greenland continued under the regime established by the agreement of April 9, 1941, between the Danish minister in Washington, Henrik de Kauffmann, and Secretary of State Cordell Hull. The continuance of Danish sovereignty was recognized; the United States obtained the right to build bases for planes, radio and weather stations, and to maintain them by "any and all things necessary"; the agreement to stand "until the present dangers to the American continent have passed." Actual administration in Greenland remained in Danish hands as before.

Greenland's cryolite, vital for the manufacture of aluminum, continued to move to Canada and the U.S. during 1943. Trade relations were largely with the U.S. because of the continued closure of the old-established monopolistic connections with Denmark.

One of the small but important actions of the war took place in 1943 off Greenland's east coast, where for the second time in two years a German weather station was demolished. Reports of weather conditions from Greenland had become essential for accurate forecasting in the North Atlantic and even in western European regions. Hence when the U.S. army sledge patrol spotted the new nazi base on an island off the coast the Germans knew they would be attacked. They captured two of the patrol, however, and killed the third man. Then they attacked a hunting and weather station to the north operated by Danes, most of whom escaped in the darkness. One, made prisoner, was forced to guide the German lieutenant on an exploring trip; he watched for an opportunity, overpowered the nazi, and after a 40-day sledge trip handed him over to army custody. Two coast guard cutters forced their way slowly through the ice toward the base, and planes bombed the installations as early as May. The bombings destroyed all but one of the carefully built structures of the post, and sank the German supply ship. When the coast guard force arrived no Germans were left, though at other points the Americans took two prisoners. Presumably the rest of the force had been evacuated by plane.

Trade and Finance.—Exports (largely fish and fish products) in 1939 totalled 1,847,000 kroner (1 krón = 18¢ U.S. in 1939), exclusive of export of 56,455,300 kg. of cryolite. Imports in 1939 totalled 4,149,000 kr. and consisted chiefly of foodstuffs (607,000 kr.), wood (468,000 kr.), manufactures (451,000 kr.), fruits and

other colonial wares (389,000 kr.), meat (253,000 kr.).

The government budget for 1939–40 was balanced at 6,035,000 kr.

BIBLIOGRAPHY.—Austin H. Clark, *Iceland and Greenland*, Smithsonian Institution War Background Studies No. 15 (Washington, 1943). (F. D. S.)

Gregory, Jackson (1882–1943), U.S. author, was born March 12 at Salinas, Calif. He became a high school principal but soon forsook his academic career for newspaper reporting. Beginning in 1914 he wrote more than a score of books, mainly western adventure tales, including *Wolf Breed* (1917), *Judith of Blue Lake Ranch* (1919), *Redwood and Gold* (1928), *Sudden Bill Dorn* (1937) and *Ace in the Hole* (1941). He completed his last book, *The Hermit of Thunder King*, shortly before his death in Auburn, Calif., June 12.

Grenada: *see* WEST INDIES, BRITISH.
Grindstones: *see* ABRASIVES.

Gromyko, Andrei A. (1909–), Russian diplomat, was born July 5 in the village of Stayre Gromyki in the Gomel region of the U.S.S.R. After his graduation from the Minsk Institute of Agricultural Economics in 1934, he became a member of the scientific staff of the Institute of Economics of the Academy of Science of the U.S.S.R. He remained in the post until May 1939, when he was made chief of the division of American countries in the people's commissariat of foreign affairs. Only a few months later he again resigned to become counsellor of the U.S.S.R. embassy in Washington. He served in this capacity under Ambassador Constantine Oumansky until 1941, then under Ambassador Maxim Litvinov. On Aug. 21, 1943, diplomatic circles were startled to learn that Ambassador Litvinov had been recalled and Gromyko appointed ambassador in his stead. This was the second change in Russian diplomatic personnel to be made within a short time, for Ivan Maisky, ambassador to London had been recalled the preceding month. Speculation on the significance of these changes was widespread, especially in view of the forthcoming conference at Moscow. On Sept. 2 it was announced that Gromyko had also been appointed to succeed Litvinov as ambassador to Cuba.

Guadalcanal: *see* SOLOMON ISLANDS; WORLD WAR II.
Guadeloupe: *see* FRENCH COLONIAL EMPIRE.

Guam. Guam is the largest and most populous of the Mariana group of islands in the North Pacific, is in 13° 26' N. lat. and 144° 39' E. long., and is located about 1,823 mi. S.E. of Hongkong, about 1,506 mi. E. of Manila and 5,053 mi. S.W. of San Francisco. Pop. (1940) 22,290; area 206 sq.mi. Capital Agana (10,004).

History.—The question of fortifying Guam had been discussed in naval circles as U.S.-Japanese relations became more tense in the later 1930s. The naval appropriations bill of 1939 contained an item of $5,000,000 "to establish, develop or increase naval aviation facilities" in Guam, to improve harbour facilities and "for other purposes." However, the item relating to Guam was struck out of the bill before it reached the senate. Subsequently, however, the government initiated construction operations on Guam, and a number of building workers were caught when the island was attacked by the Japanese immediately after Pearl Harbor. A Japanese statement of Dec. 12, 1941, claimed the occupation of Guam and the capture of 300 Americans, including the governor of the island, Capt. G. G. McMillin. The navy department confirmed the loss of the island the next day.

After that time Guam was out of the news. It was so far within the Japanese naval defense lines that it had not yet been attacked by U.S. naval or air forces up to the end of 1943.

Government.—Under U.S. administration the governor of Guam was a navy officer with the rank of captain. The governor was also commandant of the naval station. There was a native congress with advisory powers, but the governor possessed final authority. The natives of Guam are of Chamorro stock, with a strong intermixture of Spaniards and Filipinos. The language is a Malay dialect, corrupted by Tagal (a Filipino dialect) and Spanish.

Industry and Trade.—The economy of Guam is predominantly agricultural. Production is almost entirely for local consumption and includes corn, rice, sweet potatoes, coffee, bananas, pineapples, citrus fruits, limes, breadfruit, mangoes, yams, tobacco, alligator pears, sugar cane and timber. The only export product of any consequence is copra, the normal crop being about 2,000 tons. Imports and exports for the year ending June 30, 1940, were $642,936 and $102,575, respectively. Most of the imports were for the benefit of the naval and marine forces.

Finance and Education.—The revenues for the fiscal year 1940 were $283,619 and expenditures were $259,626. The only banking institution was the Bank of Guam, established by the naval government in 1915 for general banking business and as a depository of the naval government of Guam. Education under U.S. administration was compulsory between the ages of 7 and 12. In 1940 there were 23 primary schools, 5 industrial schools, one high school, one private school and one school for Americans. Average enrolment was 4,694.   (W. H. Ch.)

Guariglia, Raffaele
(1889–   ), Italian diplomat, a doctor of laws from the University of Naples, served from 1910 to 1919 in various embassy offices: Paris, London, St. Petersburg (now Leningrad), Brussels. In 1920 he became chief of the oriental bureau of the Italian foreign office, retaining the position until 1926, notwithstanding the fascist upheaval of 1922. In 1926 Guariglia became director general of political affairs for the Italian foreign office. From 1932–35 he was ambassador to Spain, returning to Italy to take charge of Ethiopian affairs. In 1937 he became ambassador to Argentina; in 1938 to France, where he remained until Italy's declaration of war. In Feb. 1943, Guariglia was sent to Turkey as ambassador. He was secretary of foreign affairs in the cabinet formed by Marshal Pietro Badoglio, July 26, upon Mussolini's downfall. A period of intense activity followed. Guariglia sought first Turkish, then Vatican, aid in negotiating a peace. He conferred with Ribbentrop in Italy on Aug. 6, but was unable to get the Germans to withdraw peaceably from Italy. On Sept. 15, German sources reported that Guariglia had been placed under arrest at the order of the German puppet governor of Rome.

Guatemala.
A republic of Central America, bounded by Mexico, British Honduras, Honduras and El Salvador. Area, 42,364 sq.mi. (a boundary dispute with British Honduras was suspended for the duration). Pop. (1940 census), 3,284,269, of whom two-thirds are Indian. Capital: Guatemala City (163,826); other cities: Zacapa (14,443); Quetzaltenango (33,538); Cobán (8,001); Chiquimula (10,868); Puerto Barrios (15,784); Totonicapán (5,623). Religion: Roman Catholic. President in 1943: General Jorge Ubico.

History.—Affairs in Guatemala were quiet during 1943, with little change in policies or general conditions. The main effects of the war were felt in rising living costs, estimated at as much as 40% over 1941. Factors causing the rise were on the one hand due to an augmented income because of a profitable coffee year

REVIEW OF CADETS at the Guatemalan military academy in 1943

and the export of foodstuffs to the Canal Zone, also the high wages paid on various war construction projects, and on the other hand to the diminishing supply of consumer goods. Various types of regulatory control remained in effect, such as the freezing of rents and of certain imported items, a moratorium on car payments, gasoline rationing and the prohibition of export for some items (cattle export was forbidden May 6).

Education.—Schools in 1942 numbered 2,691. Enrolments were as follows: infant schools 9,680; primary schools 130,802; adult schools 4,503; normal schools 1,039; vocational schools 3,236; secondary schools 1,006. Enrolment in the National university was 576.

Finance.—The monetary unit is the quetzal, maintained at parity with the United States dollar. The internal debt of Guatemala (1942) was 3,877,134 quetzales; the external debt, 1,520,432. The circulating medium averaged (1942) 27,991,482 quetzales. Revenue for the first quarter of 1943 was 5,075,000 quetzales; expenditures, 3,504,000 quetzales.

Trade and Communication.—No complete trade figures were available; in 1941 exports were valued at $14,502,803; imports at $16,098,907. The trade balance with the United States for nine months of 1943 was favourable to the extent of $6,669,000.

Agriculture is the main industry of Guatemala. Coffee exports for the 1942–43 coffee season (Oct.-June) were 678,941 bags of 132 lb. each. Banana exports (1942) amounted to 4,639,888 stems (1941: 7,151,593 stems). Chicle exports amounted to 3,538,000 lbs. (1941: 2,878,000 lb.). The 1942–43 sugar crop estimate was 22,800 tons; cotton (1941–42), 1,914,957 lb.; wool (1941–42), 376,761 lb. Milk, butter, and cheese (1941–42) were produced in the amounts of 12,727,585 gal., 1,168,238 lb., and 3,027,590 lb., respectively. Fibre production (1942) was: maguey, 768 tons; hehequen, 85 tons; yucca, 12,552 tons.

The total highway mileage is 3,998 mi.; the federal system amounts to 1,806 mi. (with 427 additional mi. under construction); the remainder is departmental highway. In 1941–43 road-building machinery shipped from the United States was valued at $145,270. Railway mileage is 600 mi. public road, 280 mi. private. External and internal air service is extensive. (*See* also BRITISH HONDURAS.)

BIBLIOGRAPHY.—Dana G. Munro, *The Five Republics of Central America* (1918); Chester Lloyd Jones, *The Caribbean since 1900* (1936), *Guatemala Past and Present* (1940).   (D. Rd.)

Guayule: *see* CHEMURGY; RUBBER.

Guggenheim Memorial Foundation.

The John Simon Guggenheim Memorial foundation granted 79 fellowships, with stipends totalling about $205,000, for the year 1943–44. Of these awards, 59 went to the fellowship program of the United States, 5 to that of Canada, and 15 to the program of Latin America. Since its establishment in 1925 by Simon Guggenheim and his wife, the foundation had, by 1943, contributed about $2,692,000 in the form of 1,304 fellowships to the advancement of research in all fields of knowledge and creative work in the arts.

At the time of the death of Guggenheim in 1941, the foundation, already having an endowment of $8,415,131, became the residuary legatee of almost his entire estate. All contributions had been made by the co-founders. Headquarters of the foundation are at 551 Fifth avenue, New York city.

Guiana, British: *see* BRITISH GUIANA.
Guiana, Dutch: *see* SURINAM.
Guiana, French: *see* FRENCH COLONIAL EMPIRE.
Guinea: *see* FRENCH COLONIAL EMPIRE; PORTUGUESE COLONIAL EMPIRE; SPANISH COLONIAL EMPIRE.
Guinea, New: *see* NEW GUINEA.

Gustavus V

(1858–   ), king of Sweden, of whom a biographical account will be found in the *Encyclopædia Britannica,* ascended the throne in 1907, and years before 1943 had attained the rank of Europe's oldest living monarch.

The eighty-five year old sovereign continued in 1943 as leader of his nation's neutrality, a personification to his people and to the world of the strict and persistent policy which held Sweden to peace. Firmly and honestly he attempted to fulfill his chosen motto: "With the people for the fatherland." **(F. D. S.)**

Gymnastics.

Arthur E. Pitt of Union City, N.Y., continued his dominance of the National A.A.U. gymnastic championships during 1943 to capture the all-around title and place his Swiss Gymnasium society second in the team standings. Pitt repeated his all-around conquest with firsts in calisthenics, side horse and horizontal bar, scoring 295.1 points to 275.8 for Ensign Newton Loken of the Iowa Pre-Flight school. Although Penn State college won only one individual title, its accumulation of seconds and thirds brought the collegians the team title with 64 points to 41½ for the Swiss Gym society.

After a year's lapse, the women's nationals were held in conjunction with the men's at New York and resulted in the Philadelphia Turners easily winning the team title. Pearl Nightingale of the Philadelphia team won the all-around women's championship with firsts in the side horse vault, flying rings and parallel bars. **(M. P. W.)**

Gynaecology and Obstetrics.

William P. Healy re-emphasized the importance of periodic examinations to ensure early diagnosis of the "silent disease," cancer of the genital organs; he recommended further investigation of the possible influence of endocrine glands on cancer. H. E. Schmitz and his coworkers offered noteworthy contributions on the effect of preoperative irradiation of adenocarcinoma of the uterus, using progressively increasing dosage with radium augmented by deep X-ray therapy. Results in general from treatment of cancer of the female pelvic organs seemed to be slowly but only slightly improving.

Emil Novak stated that recent studies have not added much to our knowledge of the physiology of endocrine glands in pregnancy, lactation and the puerperium, whereas progress has been made in the treatment of such conditions as amenorrhoea and sterility, primary dysmenorrhoea, functional bleeding, and disturbances of the menopause.

The treatment of acute gonorrhoeal infection by sulfanilamide and sulfathiazole was in 1943 firmly established. One of the latest and largest series of salpingitis (214 cases) to be so treated was described by D. N. Barrows and J. S. Labate. They found that this chemotherapy was remarkably and quickly effective for both gonorrhoeal salpingitis and associated vaginitis. They stated that the earlier it is possible for the treatment to be begun the more rapid is the subsidence of the masses and the disappearance of symptoms.

In the field of sterility studies, that is, of "barren marriages," interest was aroused by accounts of success from artificial insemination. Briefly, this consisted in the use of seminal fluid from professional donors, unknown to the sterile couple, for artificial injection into the uterus of the wife when the husband had been proven sterile. Scientifically this might be acceptable but, as said by George W. Kosmak, "whether ethical considerations should be subordinated to those of a material character to relieve sterility is more than an academic problem . . . to place (human relationships) on a level with the propagation of animal life undertaken for convenience and gain."

Claire E. Folsome, of New York, where most of this agitation to apply "experiences of veterinary practice to the human subject" (Kosmak) were current, analyzed some of the extravagant claims and statistics of advocates of the procedure. Folsome's study showed it to be a "medical procedure valuable only as a final answer in certain carefully selected and thoroughly studied cases." Even then the "results obtained . . . have been little more than mediocre." Folsome's review was "to place on record a protest against publication of such extreme claims on the subject of human sterility until these are checked and verified."

In obstetrics, the year 1943 saw as one outstanding contribution the establishment of continuous caudal analgesia as an accepted procedure for relief of pain during labour and delivery. It was promulgated by W. B. Edwards and R. A. Hingson, and is spectacularly effective as well as apparently safe, when given by skilled individuals. Otherwise, of course, it has risks as does any anaesthetic unskilfully administered. The method consists in injection of an anaesthetic mixture (procaine or "metycaine") into the caudal canal at the lower end of the sacrum but outside the spinal canal itself. Thus these low-lying nerves and their ganglia are anaesthetized so that the patient feels no pain, repeated injections being given at intervals through the needle left *in situ* in order to maintain this state of analgesia or local anaesthesia. The patient remains conscious, the infant is unaffected, and the maternal soft parts, often resistant, are more relaxed than usual thus facilitating labour and delivery. The method is safe provided the person administering the analgesia is trained and experienced in the method. The authors of the method completed a comprehensive monograph on the subject to be published early in 1944.

Many instances of thrombophlebitis result, according to Alton Ochsner and Michael E. de Bakey, from a spasm of the blood vessels of neurogenic origin. They demonstrated that the pain and swelling, as well as much of the interference with venous circulation, could be promptly relieved by an injection of the meninges of the spinal cord at proper sites, using an anaesthetic mixture usually procaine hydrochloride. This suggestion gained wider acceptance during 1943 when Edwards and Hingson found their method of analgesia described for labour and delivery particularly efficacious for thrombophlebitis. This did not replace the use of heparin.

World War II had its influence on obstetric care. E. J. Krahulik and W. B. Thompson advocated what many have had to practise, namely the conclusion that greater service could be offered to the community by hospitals if a larger number are given hospital delivery through abbreviated periods of postpartum care in the hospitals. They recommended that patients stay only 8 to 10 days, and then depend upon help from neighbours and relatives at home. H. A. Stephenson amplified this plan by suggesting less frequent antenatal office visits and relegation of office routine to the nurse on account of the physician shortage.

Legislation for federal aid in obstetrics and pediatrics for families of enlisted service men under the children's bureau of the department of labor was enacted. This provided money grants to pay $50 as the doctor's fee for confinement, and sufficient additional to give the patient a limited period of hospitalization of the "semi-private" room type. This was received with mixed reactions by the medical profession. Some endorsed it, but others looked upon it as a trial attempt at socialization of medicine under government control.

BIBLIOGRAPHY.—William P. Healy, "Role of Gynaecologist in Field of Cancer," Janeway lecture, *Am. J. Roentgenol.*, 49:1–10 (1943); H. E. Schmitz, J. F. Sheehan and J. Towne, "Effect of Preoperative Irradiation on Adenocarcinoma of Uterus," *Am. J. Obst. and Gynec.*, 45:377–390 (1943); Emil Novak, "Present Status of Gynecological Organotherapy," *South M. J.*, 36:145–152 (1943); *Idem*, "Physiology of Endocrines in Pregnancy, Lactation and Puerperium," *J. Clin. Endocrinol*; 3:274–280 (1943); D. N. Barrows and J. S. Labate, "Sulfanilamide and Sulfathiazole Therapy in Acute Salpingitis," *Am. J. Obst. and Gynec.*, 45:82–88 (1943); George W. Kosmak, editorial, "Artificial Insemination," *ibid.*, 45:1066–1067 (1943); Claire E. Folsome, "Status of Artificial Insemination; a Critical Review," *ibid.*, 45:915–927 (1943); W. B. Edwards and R. A. Hingson, "Continuous Caudal Analgesia in Obstetrics," *J.A.M.A.*, 121:225–229 (1943); E. J. Krahulik and W. B. Thompson, "Influences of War on Obstetrical Hospitalization," *West. J. Surg.*, 51:52–55 (1943); H. A. Stephenson, "Obstetrics as Affected by Problems of War with Particular Reference to Office Procedure," *West. J. Surg.*, 51:60–61 (1943).   (P. T.)

Gypsum.

Mine production of gypsum in the United States decreased by 2% in 1942, to 4,697,568 short tons, and production of calcined gypsum was still lower. Production of crude and calcined gypsum was respectively 17% and 20% lower in the first three quarters of 1943 than in the same period of 1942. The main losses were in uses in building construction; while several minor uses showed gains, the tonnages involved were small, and the only important use showing an increase was agricultural gypsum.

Canada showed a heavy drop in gypsum production in 1942, with 580,575 short tons, a 64% decrease from the record high made in 1941. The decline was mainly due to lack of shipping facilities, the bulk of the Canadian output being normally exported to the United States. The decrease continued in 1943, output through August being 48% less than that of the same period of 1942.   (G. A. Ro.)

Haakon VII

(1872–   ), king of Norway, of whom a biographical account will be found in *Encyclopædia Britannica,* was born Prince Charles of Denmark, second son of Frederick VIII (and brother of Christian X). Upon the separation of Norway from Sweden he was elected king by the Norwegian Storting (Nov. 18, 1905), and took the old Norse name of Haakon, and that of Olav for his son, the crown prince. Haakon married Maud (1869–1938), youngest daughter of King Edward VII of England.

The unanimous loyalty of Norwegians to their exiled king after 1940 was more than a sign that their land was in trouble. Haakon's personal bravery and uprightness, his nonpartisan nationalism, his zealous industry, his dignified acceptance of necessity while fighting vigorously for the independence of his people, all gave rich meaning to the motto he had chosen in 1905: "All

for Norway." Through disillusionment, bitterness, distress from 1940 through 1943, the Norwegian people both at home and abroad, on land and sea, had one rallying point. In 1943 hopes brightened for both the king and his people as he, in London, guided and personified Norwegian resistance. (*See also* NORWAY.)
     (F. D. S.)

Haiti.

A West Indian republic occupying the western third of the island of Hispaniola (also known as Haiti). Area: 10,748 sq.mi. Pop. estimates vary from 2,600,000 to 3,000,000, with the latter figure usually quoted. The population is almost entirely Negro. The capital is Port-au-Prince (pop. 125,000); other cities are: Les Cayes (15,000); Cap Haitien (20,000); Gonaïves (20,000); Jacmel (10,000). Official language: French; official religion: Roman Catholic, with the lower classes practising the folk religion of vodun or voodoo. President in 1943: Elie Lescot.

History.—Haiti continued during 1943 policies in inter-American co-operation as they had been laid down in the previous two years. Much interest was centred on the work of SHADA (the Société Haitiano-Américaine de Developpement Agricole), notably in the production of rubber. By the end of 1943 it was estimated that the agency would have between 60,000 and 85,000 acres planted to cryptostegia, harvesting about 3,000 lb. of rubber therefrom in the following year and possibly 12,000 tons in 1945. SHADA also produced some sisal, lumber, oils, cacao, fruits and spices. Some Haitians feared that the emphasis on rubber production would lead to serious problems after the war; after a visit of President Lescot to the United States this aspect of Haitian economy was covered by a Washington announcement in November that a study of postwar possibilities for small industry would be made, that an additional $9,600,000 would be spent on the rubber project, and that United States experts would be available for solution of island problems.

Shipping to Haiti increased during 1943 over the previous year, and general economic conditions were better. Nevertheless, war shortages were felt. Little newsprint was available for Haiti's 52 publications, and most newspapers were reduced to two pages. In March goods were ordered moved by boat whenever possible. Export of staple domestic foodstuffs was also prohibited in March.

Education.—Haiti was estimated (1941) to have 176 urban

ELIE LESCOT (right), president of Haiti, being welcomed at Washington Oct. 14, 1943 by President Roosevelt and Representative Sol Bloom (left), chairman of the house foreign affairs committee. Mrs. Roosevelt is in the background

primary schools, enrolment approx. 40,000; 459 rural elementary schools, enrolment 33,246; 200 Catholic parochial schools (elementary), enrolment approx. 12,000. There were 10 vocational schools, with 1,368 pupils; 17 secondary schools, with 4,000 students. Statistics are questionable, since enrollment does not necessarily mean attendance. The illiteracy rate approximated 90%. English was being introduced into all grades above the fourth; in March seven teachers were reported sent from the United States to launch the program.

Finance.—The monetary unit is the gourde, fixed by law at 20 cents U.S. Revenue (for the fiscal year Oct. 1, 1942–Sept. 30, 1943) was $6,545,817 (1942: $5,119,851); expenditures were $5,605,906 (1942: $5,545,232). The public debt on Sept. 30, 1943, was $13,226,609 (1942: $14,117,850).

Trade and Resources.—Haitian trade for 1942–43 totalled 94,320,000 gourdes (imports: 44,883,000 gourdes; exports: 49,437,000 gourdes). Haiti's favourable export balance with the United States on Sept. 30 was $1,276,000. The United States took approx. 81% of exports, and supplied 75% of imports. Haitian products are almost entirely agricultural, and are indicated in the following table:

Haitian Exports, 1941-42 and 1942-43 (11-month period)

Product	1942-43	1941-42
Coffee	25,003,520 kilos	15,810,820 kilos
Cacao	1,670,949	1,246,822
Logwood	2,917,000	2,493,000
Cotton	1,559,746	2,289,536
Sisal	9,538,388	9,380,919
Raw sugar	11,534,422	6,580,543
Bananas	442,828 stems	1,930,934 stems

Communication.—External communication is by sea and air; shipping increased in 1943. Highway mileage is 2,937 km. improved road, 43,987 km. unimproved. Motor traffic was seriously curtailed by lack of fuel and equipment. The 1941–42 allowance for highways was 626,089 gourdes. Haiti has about 160 mi. of railroad.

BIBLIOGRAPHY.—Harold Palmer Davis, *Black Democracy* (1929); James Graham Leyburn, *The Haitian People* (1941); Chester Lloyd Jones, *The Caribbean since 1900* (1936). (D. RD.)

Hall, Radclyffe

(1886?–1943), British novelist and poet, was born in Bournemouth, Hampshire, England, and was educated at King's college, London, and in Germany. Her best-selling novel, *The Well of Loneliness*, published in 1928 caused a furore in England and the United States and was the subject of court disputes in both countries to determine whether or not the work was immoral in subject and tone. Miss Hall's other works include the following novels: *The Forge, The Unlit Lamp* (1924), *A Saturday Life* (1925), *Adam's Breed* (1926), which won several prizes as the best book of that year and the gold medal of Eichelbergher Humane Award in 1930, *The Master of the House* (1932) and *Sixth Beatitude* (1936); a collection of short stories, *Miss Ogilvy Finds Herself* (1934) and numerous poems set to music. An uncompleted novel at which she was working at the time of her death was destroyed according to her wishes. She died in London, Oct. 7.

Hall, Sir (William) Reginald

(1870–1943), British intelligence officer, was born June 28. His genius for code deciphering and spy-trapping came to the fore during World War I when he was made director of naval intelligence. In 1914, he devised the system of false messages that lured a German naval squadron into a fatal trap near the Falkland Islands, where it was set upon by British warships and ultimately destroyed. Sir Reginald also used trick messages to entice the unsuspecting Franz von Rintelen, chief of German espionage in the United States in World War I, back to Europe, where he was captured off Ramsgate in August 1915 while he was enroute to the reich. Another of Sir Reginald's accomplishments was the interception of the historic Bernstorff letter inviting Mexico to join with Germany against the United States during the first world conflict. After the war, he returned to "shore duty" and was an M.P., 1919–29. Sir Reginald, who was knighted in 1918, retired from the navy in 1926 with the rank of admiral. He died in London, Oct. 22.

Halsey, William Frederick, Jr.

(1882–   ), U.S. naval officer, was born Oct. 30 in Elizabeth, N.J. An Annapolis graduate, he commanded a destroyer patrol force in World War I. Subsequently he was commander of the aircraft carrier "Saratoga," commandant of the Pensacola naval air station, and, in 1938, commander of a carrier division including the "Yorktown" and "Enterprise." Vice-Admiral Halsey led the attack against Japanese bases on the Marshall and Gilbert Islands, Jan. 31 and Feb. 1, 1942. On Oct. 24 he replaced Vice-Admiral Robert Lee Ghormley as commander of U.S. naval forces in the South Pacific. Three weeks later Halsey engaged a large Japanese force off the Solomon Islands in a three-day battle. Although outnumbered, his fleet was victorious, sinking 28 Japanese ships. In recognition of this achievement, Halsey was made a full admiral and awarded the congressional medal of honour. In 1943 he continued his aggressive naval warfare, demonstrating further what Admiral Chester W. Nimitz called his "rare combination of intellectual capacity and military audacity." He conferred with General MacArthur in May, and, on July 2, his force was put under MacArthur's command. Further victories in the Solomons followed. In a battle off Bougainville shortly after the initial landings on Nov. 1, Halsey's fleet sank five Japanese ships and damaged four.

Hammerstein-Equord, Kurt von,

BARON (1878–1943), German army officer, was born Sept. 16 in Hinrichshagen, Mecklenburg-Strelitz, of a Junker family. He joined the army in his youth and during World War I was major on the general staff. Hammerstein-Equord was involved in the postwar Kapp *putsch*, a conspiracy of the German army to seize control of the government. In this plot, his father-in-law, Gen. Walther von Luettwitz, an extremist leader, marched his troops into Berlin in 1920 and with Wolfgang Kapp established a short-lived government. Hammerstein-Equord was promoted to commander in 1929 and was named to the army command in 1930. He resigned, however, in 1933 with rank of general, shortly after Hitler came to power and was replaced by Col. Gen. Werner von Fritsch. It was rumoured at that time that he was out of sympathy with the new regime, a report that seemed to be substantiated by his continued retirement during the years when the army reached its greatest period of expansion. A notice of his death appeared in a Berlin newspaper, April 24.

Hammer Throw: *see* TRACK AND FIELD SPORTS.

Hand-ball.

The continuance of the war seriously curtailed competitive activity of this sport with the result that in 1943 only one national tournament was held. This was the annual classic of the four-wall championships, held at the Olympic club of San Francisco. The winner in the singles was Joseph P. Platak of Chicago, serving with the U.S. navy, who regained the title he was forced to vacate the previous year because of his inability to obtain the necessary furlough. Platak had previously won the championship for seven years in succession and his 1943 victory made it his eighth triumph and gained for him third place in the country among the outstanding athletes of the year.

National Four-Wall Rankings for 1943

Singles	Doubles
1. Joseph P. Platak, Chicago	1. Joe Gordon and H. Smith, Long Beach, Calif.
2. Abe Smith, Oakland, Calif.	2. Al Cram and B. Hackney, Long Beach, Calif.
3. Angelo Tocchini, Oakland, Calif.	3. R. Leu and M. De La Pena, San Francisco, Calif.

(FR. RO.)

Harbours: see RIVERS AND HARBOURS.

Harper, Samuel Northrup

(1882–1943), U.S. educator and son of William Rainey Harper, first president of the University of Chicago, was born April 9 in Chicago. After receiving his A.B. degree in 1902, he studied at the École des Langues Orientales Vivantes in Paris and at Columbia university. One of the leading U.S. authorities on Russian life and language, he made 18 trips to Russia to study the tsarist and soviet regimes. He joined the faculty of the University of Chicago in 1905 as assistant professor of Russian language and institutions and was named head of the department in 1930. Professor Harper served as special attaché to the Russian division of the state department in the first years of the soviet union and was the author of numerous works in his field. He died in Chicago, Jan. 18.

Harriman, W. Averell

(1891–), U.S. diplomatic representative, was born Nov. 15, son of E. H. Harriman, railroad magnate. On his graduation from Yale university in 1913 he carried on in his father's enterprises, becoming chairman eventually of the Illinois Central and Union Pacific railroads, as well as a partner in Brown Brothers, Harriman and company. Entering government service during President Roosevelt's first term of office, he served as an NRA administrator, a member of the business advisory council of the department of commerce and director of the raw materials division of the Office of Production Management. In March 1941, he was sent to Great Britain as lend-lease representative, with the rank of minister. In Sept. he headed the American delegation of a U.S.-British joint mission to Moscow. In Aug. 1942, he visited Moscow again at the time of the Stalin-Churchill conferences. On Oct. 1, 1943, Pres. Roosevelt named Harriman ambassador to the U.S.S.R., succeeding Adm. William H. Standley. He was escorted to Moscow by Secretary of State Cordell Hull and there participated in the tripartite conferences.

Harris, Sir Arthur T.

(1892–), British air officer, was born April 13 in Cheltenham, England. Educated in English public schools, he enlisted during World War I and joined the royal flying corps in 1915. He commanded several squadrons on the western front and was decorated with the air force cross in 1918. Made an air commodore in 1937, he was named air vice-marshal in 1939 and rose to commander in chief of the R.A.F. bomber command in Feb. 1942. A firm believer in mass raids, Air Marshal Harris developed the "saturation" technique of mass bombing—that of concentrating clouds of bombers in a giant raid on a single city with the object of completely demolishing it. He applied this method with great destructive effect on axis-occupied Europe beginning in 1942 and continuing throughout 1943.

Hart, Albert Bushnell

(1854–1943), U.S. educator, was born July 1 at Clarksville, Pa. He was connected with the faculty of Harvard university for 43 years before retiring in 1926 as professor emeritus of the science of government. After his retirement, he maintained quarters above Widener library and continued his writings. He was named editor of the Roosevelt Encyclopaedia in 1927 and was the author, joint author or editor of about 100 volumes. An outstanding authority on George Washington, he was chosen a member and historian of the U.S. commission for the celebration of the 200th anniversary of the birth of Washington, a task which was in preparation for six years before the 1932 countrywide festivities. Dr. Hart died in Boston, June 16. (See Encyclopædia Britannica.)

Hart, Lorenz

(LARRY) (1895–1943), U.S. song-writer and musician, was born in New York city May 2. While a student at Columbia university, he met Richard Rodgers, then a freshman. Both were aspiring musicians, and they pooled their talents to produce the Columbia Varsity Show of 1920. This first effort was successful and gave birth to the famous Rodgers-and-Hart combination. Generally, Hart wrote the lyrics while Rodgers composed the music, but both were gifted in either specialty. They wrote the lyrics and music for more than 25 Broadway shows and for a number of motion pictures. Among their more prominent successes were: *Babes in Arms* (1937), *I'd Rather Be Right* (1937), *The Boys from Syracuse* (1938) and *I Married an Angel* (1938). Hart died in New York city Nov. 22.

Hartley, Marsden

(1877–1943), U.S. painter, was born Jan. 4 in Lewiston, Me. He studied art at the National academy in New York city and later in Europe. Best known of his paintings are his landscapes and marines, "Fox Island, Me.," "The Spent Wave" and "Evening Storm, Schoodic, Me." After a period in the west painting rugged landscapes, he returned to Maine to do a series of church pictures, fishing scenes and other outdoor subjects. He spent a year in Mexico in 1930 on a Guggenheim fellowship and later did a series of mountain studies along architectural lines in New Mexico. Hartley died in Ellsworth, Me., Sept. 2.

Harvard University.

Founded in 1636, Harvard is the oldest institution for higher education in the United States. Gifts during the academic year 1942–43 were $5,244,255. Scholarships and other student aids totalled

AFTER RECEIVING an honorary LL.D. at Harvard university Sept. 6, 1943, Winston Churchill delivered an extemporaneous address to 6,000 U.S. soldiers and sailors enrolled at the university

$779,731, exclusive of student loans. At the beginning of the academic year, July 1, 1943, the civilian student enrolment had fallen to less than 25% of the peace-time normal, but the university's facilities were fully occupied by more than 6,000 army and navy men sent to Harvard for specialized training in 11 different service schools. A great deal of wartime research was being conducted in the university laboratories. All departments of the university operated on a new intensified 12-month, 3-semester schedule. A notable event of the year was the conferring of an honorary degree on British Prime Minister Winston Churchill.

For statistics of student enrolment, faculty members, endowment, library volumes, etc., *see* UNIVERSITIES AND COLLEGES.

Hassani, Mohamed Tageddine el

SHIEK (1886–1943), Syrian jurist and politician, received his education in Damascus and Cairo. He gave up teaching for politics, entered the Syrian congress in 1919, became sheik of the Ulemas the next year and served as councillor of state and at the court of cassation, 1921–23. He was caliph of Damascus, 1924–28, deputy to the constituent assembly, 1928, and president of the council of ministers and minister of the interior, 1928–31 and 1934–36. He was proclaimed president of Syria in Sept. 1941, when the former French mandate was declared independent by agreement with the Fighting French. He died Jan. 17, according to a report from Beirut, Lebanon.

Hawaii.

The territory of Hawaii consists of a group of eight larger islands and numerous islets in the Pacific ocean between latitudes 18°55′ and 22°15′ N. and between 154°50′ and 160°30′ W. longitude. Their total area is 6,438 sq.mi. The islands are of volcanic origin. From southeast to northwest, they are Hawaii, Kahoolawe, Maui, Lanai, Molokai, Oahu, Kauai, Niihau. In addition, stretching northwestward beyond Niihau over 1,100 mi. is an archipelago of rocks, reefs and shoals which includes Midway (longitude 177°22′ W.). Likewise, 960 mi. south of Honolulu and a part of the city and county of Honolulu lies Palmyra, a coral atoll consisting of 55 islets, five miles long and two and a half miles wide. The youngest island, geologically, and the largest in the group is Hawaii, with an area of 4,030 sq.mi. The capital of the territory is Honolulu, situated on the island of Oahu. It is a completely modern city with a population (1940 census) of 180,986. The population of the territory (1940) was 423,330. The racial origin of this population, in addition to the native Hawaiians and Caucasians from the mainland, is Japanese, Chinese, Korean, Filipino, Portuguese. However, 82% of the population is native born.

History.—Ingram M. Stainback took office as governor on Aug. 24, 1942, succeeding Joseph B. Poindexter. Joseph R. Farrington was territorial delegate in congress in 1943. Territorial tax collections on business and otherwise for the fiscal year ending June 30, 1943, amounted to $35,827,659, as compared to $27,215,950 for the previous year. Cash on hand and in banks increased by over 48%, while federal internal revenue collections increased from $32,067,927 in the fiscal year 1942 to $75,996,558 in the fiscal year 1943. This increase in federal collections was due to increased rates of taxation.

Agriculture.—Hawaii's chief crops are sugar and pineapples. Expert management, scientific methods and costly irrigation works raised the sugar production to a maximum of 1,035,548 tons in 1933 with a value of $66,482,181. Production of sugar in 1942 amounted to 870,109 tons. The pineapple industry, next in importance, produced approximately 21,190,000 cases of canned pineapple and pineapple juice for the year ending May 31, 1943.

Because of the shipping situation brought about by the war, an extensive program of production of food crops for local consumption was under way.   (B. W. T.)

Hawkes, Herbert Edwin

(1872–1943), U.S. educator, was born Dec. 6, in Templeton, Mass. He graduated from Yale in 1896, took his Ph.D. there in 1900, and later studied at Goettingen university. He became instructor in mathematics at Yale in 1898 and advanced to assistant professor in 1903. Dr. Hawkes was appointed mathematics professor at Columbia in 1910 and was named dean in 1918—a post he held until his death in New York city, May 4, 1943.

Hay.

The 1943 crop of hay in the United States was the second largest on record, only 5% smaller than the record 1942 crop. The 1943 crop was estimated by the U.S. department of agriculture at 99,543,000 tons compared to 105,295,000 tons in 1942 and a ten-year average of 82,952,000 tons. This total was divided as follows: tame hay 87,000,000 tons, including 32,000,000 tons of alfalfa, 29,000,000 tons of clover-timothy, 7,000,000 tons of annual legumes and 6,000,000 tons of lespedeza. These were about the usual proportions of each class. Wild hay yields were below those of 1942 and offset the increase in acreage cut. Total wild hay production was 12,279,000 tons compared to 13,088,000 tons in 1942 and a ten-year average of 9,675,000 tons. Alfalfa production for hay was 11% off from 1942 due to a reduction in the number of acres harvested. Clover-timothy hay increased in 1943 over 1942 by 2% and production was 25% above the ten-year average. Sweet clover hay, three-fourths of which is produced in the north central states, declined in acreage and production in 1943 by about one-third. Lespedeza hay was also below the record production of 1942. Pea, bean and peanut hays were increased by 400,000 to a total of 7,100,000 tons. Yields of both soybean and cowpea hay were below those of 1942 in all sections of the country. Other grain hays were increased about 5%. A production of 8,000,000 tons of millet, sudan and other minor hay crops represented a decrease of 4% compared to 1942.

Hayseed.—The total acreage of hays grown for seed in 1943 exceeded the area of 1942 by 7%. This was due to the price-supporting program, good weather and the fact that less labour is needed for harvesting seed than hay. But 1943 was not a good seed year and the dry summer in some localities held down yields below average. The high price of seeds encouraged growers to harvest some fields of low yields that would not have been saved under normal conditions.

The production of the principal kinds of hayseed was about 3% smaller than 1942 but 6% above the average. Alfalfa seed at 1,114,900 bu. was 15% larger than 1942 but below the ten-year average; red clover also yielded an increase over the past year, 1,142,900 bu. or 11% more than in 1942. This was chiefly due to 15% increase in acreage. Alsike at 238,900 bu. was 5% below 1942 and 25% below the average. Sweet clover produced the smallest crop since 1922 and only one-half the average. Timothy seed was 11% below 1942 estimated at 1,499,000 bu. and 6% below the ten-year average. Lespedeza was 6% below 1942 but 67% above the average. The total 1943 crop was 159,920,000 lb. compared with an average of 95,564,000 lb. (*See also* ALFALFA; SOYBEANS.)   (J. C. Ms.)

Hayashi, Senjuro

(1876–1943), Japanese army officer and politician, was born Feb. 23 at Ishikawa-Ken. He was a graduate of the Military academy, 1896, and the Military Staff college, 1903. He was later director of both schools. At the outbreak of the Manchurian "incident" in 1931, Hayashi, then commander of Japanese forces in Chosen, marched his troops into Manchuria without waiting for authority from headquarters in Tokyo; a year later he was promoted to full general. In 1934 he was appointed war minister and made efforts to check the growing power of the clique that supported his predecessor, Gen. Sadao Araki, then scored for his fascist leanings. Gen. Hayashi retired from the war ministry in 1935 and was subsequently named to the supreme war council, but resigned early in 1936 after the assassination of Viscount Makoto Saito and other prominent statesmen by a mutinous band of junior army officers. He was premier from February to May 1937; the short life of his premiership was a sign of the growing ferment on the Japanese political stage. A Tokyo dispatch broadcast from Berlin, Feb. 4, reported his death.

Health, Industrial: *see* INDUSTRIAL HEALTH.
Hearing Aids: *see* DEAFNESS.

Heart and Heart Diseases.

Interest was focused largely on (1) cardiovascular examination for military service with an attempt to define more accurately the criteria for admission to army and navy than had previously been done, and (2) diagnosis and disposition of cardiacs found in the service. One of the most interesting of the studies of 1943 was that of the re-examination of cardiovascular rejectees in five of the larger cities of the country. A group of approximately 5,000 men who had been rejected in 1942 because of a diagnosis of cardiovascular disease were re-examined, 1,000 each in Boston, Chicago, New York, Philadelphia and San Francisco. The aim of the examination was threefold:

1. To determine the percentage of possible salvage.
2. To compare the results of examination by doctors of the local boards and induction stations with those of cardiovascular specialists.
3. To identify and to study the particular problems that concerned all these groups.

Of the total of 4,994 cardiovascular rejectees examined, 863 or 17.3% were resubmitted as 1-A—18.8% in Boston, 3.9% in Chicago, 19.2% in New York, 16.5% in Philadelphia, and 28.6% in San Francisco. Chicago's yield was the least because of the fact, apparently, that cardiovascular experts had already been used freely in the initial examinations. San Francisco's was the highest because of the inclusion of a good many borderline cases, recognized as such. In Boston there was a large borderline group, of 11.4%, thought to be normal but not fitting the current criteria of the army manual of mobilization regulations. These borderline groups in particular, as well as the individuals resubmitted as 1-A, were to be the subject of follow-up study in future years.

The chief cause for rejection was rheumatic heart disease, making up about 60% of the final 4-F group. The second most common cause for final rejection was hypertension, making up 26% of the 4-F cases. The third cause of rejection was neurocirculatory asthenia, making up 5% of those labelled 4-F. The fourth condition responsible was sinus tachycardia with 4.5% of the final 4-F cases, and the fifth was congenital heart disease with a fraction less than in the tachycardia group. Other causes for rejection were few in number and included cardiac enlargement as discovered by X-ray enlargement alone, arrhythmias, cardiovascular syphilis (in only 17 cases), and coronary heart disease (in only 6 cases).

A review of the re-examination of these cardiovascular rejectees revealed eight problems of particular interest:

1. The interpretation of apical systolic murmurs.
2. The upper limits of blood pressure.
3. The limits of the normal pulse rate.
4. The heart size.
5. The electrocardiogram.
6. Neurocirculatory asthenia.
7. Recent rheumatic fever.
8. Exercise tests.

In brief, apical systolic murmurs may, if very slight or even slight, in the absence of any other abnormality, doubtful findings, or an authenticated history of rheumatic fever, be considered acceptable for service. The upper limits of normal blood pressure were listed as 160 systolic and 90 diastolic. The limits of the normal pulse rate were extended to 40 as the low and 120 as the high. It was also felt that heart size might be given a wider range, especially according to body build, and that minor variations of the electrocardiogram should not be cause for rejection. Neurocirculatory asthenia, on the other hand, even if very slight, was viewed as a cause for immediate rejection, and recent rheumatic fever too. Exercise tests were not found of much value.

One of the important problems that faced the army and navy during 1943 was the frequent occurrence of rheumatic fever in army camps and in naval stations where large numbers of young men were crowded together and exposed to haemolytic streptococcus infections. A small percentage of such men were practically certain to come down with rheumatic fever; although this figure was small so far as percentage was concerned, the absolute numbers of such men might be considerable. It was a real problem since rheumatic fever puts patients to bed usually for months at a time and is very likely to damage the heart. Whether or not to discharge cases of rheumatic fever from the service after recovery in the absence of heart disease was also a problem that concerned the medical services. Generally the custom was to discharge such patients, largely because of the threat of recurrent trouble in the future. It was also thought wise not to admit any man into the army who had an authenticated history of rheumatic fever within five years of the time of examination.

Advances in civilian medicine were somewhat retarded by the war but two or three important contributions should be mentioned. Lumbodorsal splanchnic sympathectomy for hypertension became established as by far the most promising therapeutic measure for serious hypertension in young and middle-aged persons that had been introduced. R. H. Smithwick's success in over 60% of the cases (followed now for from one to five years) quadrupled the success of the older procedures along this line. On occasion patients already showing effects of serious strain on heart, kidneys and arteries can be rescued, at least for the time being. The procedure is applicable in particular to those with high diastolic pressures, relatively small pulse pressures, and marked reaction to sedation, posture and cold.

Another comforting discovery during 1943 was the doubling of the expectation of life after the first attack of angina pectoris which resulted from a more adequate follow-up study than had ever been carried out before. A series of 497 patients who were seen for angina pectoris between 1920 and 1930 were reviewed in 1943. Fifty-two of these were still living with an average duration of life of 18 years after the first attack; 445 had succumbed with an average duration of life of 8 years. Including both living and dead cases, the average duration of life of the whole series was 9 years and this was expected to be increased a bit more before the conclusion of the follow-up study. This average prognosis, therefore, of 9 to 10 years was announced as an encouraging revision of the current statements of the average duration of life after the first attack of angina pectoris recorded as $4\frac{1}{2}$ to 5 years in the medical textbooks.

BIBLIOGRAPHY.—R. L. Levy, W. D. Stroud, and P. D. White, "Report of the Re-examination of 4,994 Men Disqualified for General Military Service Because of the Diagnosis of Cardiovascular Defects. A Combined Study Made by Special Medical Advisory Boards in Boston, Chicago, New York, Philadelphia and San Francisco," *J.A.M.A.*, 123:937–942 (Dec. 11, 1943); A. F. Coburn, "Management of Navy Personnel with Rheumatic Fever," *U.S. Naval Med. Bull.*, 41:1324–1328 (Sept. 1943); A. M. Master, "Rheumatic Fever in the Navy," *U.S. Naval Med. Bull.*, 41:1019–1021 (July 1943); Reginald H. Smithwick, Personal communication (1943);

P. D. White, E. F. Bland, and E. W. Miskall, "The Prognosis of Angina Pectoris: A Long Time Follow-up of 497 Cases, Including a Note on 75 Additional Cases of Angina Pectoris Decubitus," *J.A.M.A.*, 123:801–804 (Nov. 1943).   (P. D. W.)

Helicopter: *see* AVIATION, CIVIL.

Helium.

Extensive additions were made to the helium production capacity of the United States, and it was known that reserves were adequate, but no specific information was made public because of the importance of the product in aviation with craft lighter than air.   (G. A. Ro.)

Hemp.

The 1943 crop of hemp for fibre in the United States was ten times larger than in 1942, amounting to 134,251,000 lb. compared to 13,922,000 lb. produced in 1942 and 2,901,000 lb. as the average for the ten years 1932–41. Prior to World War II only Wisconsin and Kentucky produced hemp in any quantity. The season of 1943 was unfavourable to hemp culture in Minnesota and Indiana where floods caused the abandonment of about 18% of the acreage.

The growing of hemp for the seed is chiefly confined to Kentucky and Tennessee. The acreage planted in 1943 was 57,700 ac., nearly 60% more than the 36,300 ac. of 1942. The total crop of seed in 1943 was estimated by the United States department of agriculture at 19,223,000 lb. or nearly twice the crop for 1942. The entire crop is under the control of War Hemp Industries, Inc.   (J. C. Ms.)

Henderson, Leon

(1895–   ), U.S. economist, was born in Millville, N.J. on May 26. In 1917 he entered the U.S. army as a private, attaining the rank of captain of ordnance by 1919. In 1920 Henderson returned to Swarthmore college, where he received his B.A. degree. During the early New Deal era, he served as consulting economist to the Work Projects administration. In 1939 he was appointed to the Securities and Exchange commission.

On April 11, 1941, President Roosevelt created the Office of Price Administration and Civilian Supply (later renamed the Office of Price Administration, *q.v.*) and placed Henderson at its head as price administrator. Henderson accepted the appointment and in July 1941 resigned his post with the SEC. In Jan. 1942 he was made head of the civilian supply division of the War Production board.

Henderson predicted that his efforts to impose rationing and other restrictions on Americans would make him the most unpopular man in the United States. In Dec. 1942, as his prophecy seemed to be approaching fulfilment, he resigned from both the WPB and the OPA. The latter resignation was to take effect upon the appointment of a successor; on Jan. 18, 1943, Prentiss M. Brown was named to succeed him, and on Jan. 20 he turned over his duties to Brown. On May 12, 1943, he joined the Research Institute of America as chairman of the board of editors.

Heward, Leslie Hays

(1897–1943), British musician and composer, was born Dec. 8 in Liversedge, Yorkshire. An infant prodigy, he was a church organist at the age of eight and assistant organist at the Manchester cathedral at 18. He won a composition scholarship at the Royal College of Music in 1917, was made music master at Eton college in the same year, and later became music director of Westminster school. He was named conductor of the British National Opera company in 1922 and two years later went to South Africa to direct the Cape Town Municipal Orchestra and the Cape Peninsula Broadcasting association. When he returned to England in 1927, he resumed his former post with the British National Opera but a few years later joined the City of Birmingham Orchestra, also as conductor, a post he held until his death. Heward died in Birmingham, May 3.

Hewitt, Henry Kent

(1887–   ), U.S. naval officer, was born Feb. 11 in Hackensack, N.J. A graduate of the U.S. Naval academy, 1906, he was commissioned an ensign in 1908. He won the naval cross for distinguished service in World War I, and later served as commander of a destroyer division. He was inspector of ordnance in charge of the naval ammunition depot at Puget sound and commanded the cruiser "Indianapolis," on board which President Roosevelt sailed for South America in 1936. He was promoted to rear admiral in Dec. 1940.

Adm. Hewitt was named to command the U.S. naval units in the huge Allied fleet that protected the U.S. landings in North Africa Nov. 8, 1942. Shortly after these landings Adm. Hewitt commanded the naval engagement that helped force the surrender of Casablanca. In recognition of his services in North Africa he was made a vice-admiral in Nov. 1942.

Adm. Hewitt's fleet also played its part in the Sicilian campaign in 1943 and in the attack on the Italian mainland, particularly the landings at Salerno.

Highways: *see* ROADS AND HIGHWAYS.
Highway to Alaska: *see* ROADS AND HIGHWAYS.

Hilbert, David

(1862–1943), German mathematician, was born Jan. 23 in Koenigsberg. He studied at the Universities of Koenigsberg, Heidelberg, Leipzig and Paris and in 1895 began his life-long association with the University of Goettingen as professor of mathematics. He made basic investigations in all the major branches of pure mathematics, among which were his geometric spaces of infinitely many dimensions, his algebraic basis theorem, and his minimum condition in the calculus of variations. He was also the leader of the formalist school in mathematical logic which believes that all mathematics can be developed from sets of axioms. Hilbert's work on infinitely many dimensional spaces was applied by others to quantum mechanics. He died in Goettingen, according to a Berne dispatch of Feb. 19.

Himmler, Heinrich

(1900–   ), head of the German police and founder of the *Schutzstaffel*, was born Nov. 7 at Munich. At the University of Munich, he specialized in agriculture. In later life he became a member of the Academy of German Law. From an insignificant beginning he rose steadily to power in the Hitler political revolution. Although a participant in the abortive Munich beer hall putsch in 1923, he escaped imprisonment. In 1927 he became deputy leader of the German S.S. (Black Shirts), expanded to offset the power of the Brown Shirt troops, and was made leader in 1929. The fuehrer never had a more loyal or ruthless devotee. Himmler served as reich director of propaganda from 1926 to 1930, became a member of the reichstag and the Prussian state council in 1933, commander of the united German police forces in 1936 and deputy head of the reich administration in 1939. During 1942 he was sent by Hitler to various occupied countries to quell anti-nazi resistance, working closely with his pupil and lieutenant, Reinhard Heydrich, later assassinated in carrying out a program of wholesale executions among subjugated peoples. In 1943, Allied successes engendered defeatism on the home front and led to increased activity by resistance groups in the occupied countries. Himmler's reply to growing anti-naziism at home and in the conquered areas was more executions. Determined to crush all opposition to his regime, Hitler named Himmler minister of the interior, Aug. 24. The Gestapo chief attempted to brace German morale by execution of civilians for "defeatist utterances," and used customary terror technique to stamp out revolt in the occupied countries.

Hinsley, Arthur

(1865–1943), British cardinal, was born Aug. 25 in Selby, Yorkshire, England. Educated at Ushaw and at the English college, Rome, he taught school and was rector of a London parish until 1926, when he was consecrated bishop. He was sent to Africa as Visitor Apostolic to Catholic missions and there contracted paratyphoid which seriously affected his vision and hearing. He retired in 1934, but the death the following year of the incumbent archbishop of Westminster left England's Catholics without a ruling prelate for the jubilee of King George V. Consequently Hinsley was called out of retirement and named archbishop of Westminster; in 1937 he was made cardinal. Outspoken on political matters, he criticized the negative stand of Pope Pius XI on the Ethiopian invasion. He despised Germany's national-socialism, denounced the Hitler party as "pagan upstarts" and, although no friend of communism, paid frequent tribute to the Russian people for their defense of their homeland. Cardinal Hinsley died in Hertfordshire, March 17.

Hispanic America:

see ARGENTINA; BOLIVIA; BRAZIL; BRITISH GUIANA; BRITISH HONDURAS; CHILE; COLOMBIA; COSTA RICA; ECUADOR; FRENCH COLONIAL EMPIRE; GUATEMALA; HONDURAS; NICARAGUA; PANAMA; PARAGUAY; PERU; SALVADOR, EL; SURINAM; URUGUAY; VENEZUELA.

Hispanic America and World War II.

The record of 1943 showed two additional Hispanic American countries added to the list of those at war with the axis powers. Bolivia entered the war on April 7, 1943, mainly as a gesture showing solidarity of the current administration with United Nations policies. The move also made logical the mobilization of labour in the production of tin and other strategic materials. The other nation to declare war on Germany was Colombia, which took the step on Nov. 27, following the sinking of a Colombian vessel by a submarine (the second incident of this kind). In both cases the war declaration was followed by the usual sequestration of axis-owned funds and property and detention of enemy aliens, and beyond this occasioned little change in policy.

Greater interest was concentrated on the development of affairs in Chile and in Argentina, at the beginning of 1943 the only two states in the western hemisphere which had not yet broken off relations with the axis. Definite pressure toward the severance of relations had been maintained throughout 1942 by the United States, and in Chile there had been a steady trend in this direction. President Juan Antonio Ríos had moved cautiously, however, and not until Jan. 20, 1943, did he consider that the time for rupture of relations had arrived. Following the break, a report that Chilean diplomatic representatives in the far east were being improperly treated resulted in confinement for a time of Japanese representatives in Chile. The abandonment of isolation by Chile was shortly followed by new lend-lease arrangements (March 2), and in June by a new copper purchase agreement with the United States.

In Argentina the Castillo administration stubbornly refused to abandon neutrality, in spite of charges of axis espionage which led to the requested recall of the German military and naval attaché and a brief suspension of communication with axis countries. During the spring the administration began preparations for the next election, with some trend away from the conservative and toward the moderate, liberal body of public opinion. On June 4-5 a well organized revolution, headed by Generals Arturo Rawson and Pedro P. Ramírez, deposed President Ramón Castillo and took over control. Apparently under the impression that a breakaway from isolation would follow, the new administration was promptly recognized by the United States and other United Nations powers, but the new government proved for the time being even more nationalistic than the preceding one. General Rawson, who favoured a break with the axis, was replaced by General Ramírez, and strict censorship over every expression in the press of pro-Allied sentiment was established. The new government inaugurated a program designed to win internal support (see ARGENTINA), but had serious difficulties with labour, student groups, and, eventually, financial interests. One attempt was made to gain lend-lease assistance from the United States, but it was promptly refused on the ground that Argentina was not co-operating properly in maintaining hemisphere safety. By the end of 1943 the Ramírez administration was faced with the alternatives of continuing isolation, with an increasing commercial and diplomatic pressure from the United Nations and a possible revolt at home, or of finally breaking with the axis.

In one other case in the Americas pressure was applied by the United States toward removal of a danger spot. In the French colonies in America the administration, while nominally independent, was still loyal to Vichy France. In Nov. 1942, the United States broke off diplomatic and commercial relations with Martinique and French Guiana, and the areas were thus deprived of foodstuffs and other needed resources. In March a revolution placed French Guiana on the side of the French authorities opposed to the axis, and in June Admiral Georges Robert retired as governor of Martinique, to be replaced by an appointee of General Henri Giraud (Henri Etienne Hoppenot).

In general during 1943, administrations in power in Hispanic America remained in control. One break in the ranks occurred. On Dec. 20, 1943, the administration of President Enrique Peñaranda of Bolivia was unseated by a revolution headed by

THE ONLY "PAN-AMERICAN RAT HOLE" in 1943, according to Bishop of the *St. Louis Star-Times*

Victor Paz Estenssoro and supported by parties which had a pro-fascist reputation. All through the year attacks in the Bolivian congress on the administration had been frequent and bitter, the most serious charges being connected with the use of military force in repressing strikes in the tin industry in Dec. 1942 (an investigation in the spring of 1943, made by a joint Bolivian-United States commission, indicated that conditions in the industry did need some attention). While the new administration (under President Gualberto Villarroel) pledged support of all commitments made by Bolivia to the United Nations program, the previous allegiances of the leaders of the revolution, and a suspected connection with the reactionary Ramírez group in Argentina caused the United States and other American states to withhold recognition of the new government.

In other respects the general program of inter-American defense was carried out along lines already laid down. The construction of naval and air bases from Ecuador to the Bahamas moved toward completion, in some cases causing concern over unemployment when the special construction ceased. Two of the nations at war gave indications that they were seriously considering actual participation in military campaigns. Brazil, already doing a workmanlike job of patrolling offshore waters, and with at least a half dozen submarines credited to its air service, officially planned sending an expeditionary force to the European sector, and news reports stated that Brazilian officers were in the field gaining experience. Cuba likewise was organizing a volunteer corps for overseas duty (its conscripts are liable only for service in Cuba). At least one press report hinted at possible Mexican participation in the future, along similar lines. Control of communications and some supervision of war items in news publications were also exercised through 1943. In a few cases, as in Ecuador, import quotas were used to direct the flow of essential goods.

The year saw fewer western hemisphere conferences than in 1942. The regular International American (Pan American) conference, scheduled to meet in Colombia late in the year, was indefinitely postponed; this followed the precedent set in World War I, and in any case the machinery of co-operation between American nations was well enough organized to function without the formal meeting. Some visiting by prominent persons occurred, as when Vice-President Wallace of the United States made a South American trip in April, and when the presidents of Bolivia, Paraguay, Haiti and Colombia visited the United States. The chief executive of Costa Rica visited several neighbouring states, and other contacts were made in hemisphere relations by military leaders, executives, experts and diplomatic representatives. Some inter-Hispanic American commercial agreements were signed; probably the most important of these was a set of conventions arranged between Chile and Argentina which it was hoped would be the basis for a future customs union taking in several nations in the area. The United States was a party to a number of inter-American conventions; in three cases these concerned the continuation of currency stabilization funds (Mexico, Cuba and Ecuador). In June a new copper contract was signed with Chile, and other agreements concerning the purchase or development of production of strategic materials were either continued or established (at least three were worked out with Brazil alone). Economic planning was undertaken as in the setting up of a joint United States-Mexican Economic commission (announced in April), and the inauguration of a Bolivian Development commission and of an Economic Defense plan in Colombia. The comprehensive food production program for the Caribbean, under the general direction of the United States Board of Economic Warfare, was carried ahead.

As the year passed, postwar planning received increased at-tention.

In internal politics 1943 was generally quiet, except in those cases already noted. The year was not a presidential election year, although in several states, such as Cuba, Costa Rica and Ecuador, parties were active in preparation for 1944. In Panamá the chief executive was continued in office without election because of war conditions. Chief executives in most cases continued to exercise extraordinary powers, either by virtue of special legislation or by continuation of a state of siege. The dissolution of the World Communist party, in June, caused some reorganization of national Communist parties in those states where these had strength (notably Chile and Costa Rica). A trend toward nationalization of foreign-owned corporations, particularly where concerned with utilities, was apparent with the opportunity toward purchase offered by a favourable exchange situation.

Throughout Hispanic America there was a definite increase in the cost of living during 1943. The generally favourable export situation, combined with a shortage of consumer goods, forced up price levels, and price controls were not always too effective. Rationing of at least some items was in effect in most Hispanic American states. The shipping situation was definitely improved over 1942, which offered some relief, but some goods, such as fuel, some types of machine parts and certain manufactured articles, were simply not available. In some sections there was much concern over inflation. In the field of trade there was a notable increase in the net export balance of the American republics in their trade with the United States. The total for both merchandise and gold and silver, through September, amounted to $404,372,000; where favourable balances existed, they ranged from $143,000 for Costa Rica to $103,518,000 for Cuba. Only with Panamá, Honduras and Venezuela did the United States itself have a favourable balance. The volume of Mexican trade was estimated at 259% compared with 1942 (Nicaragua 225%, Haiti 175% and several above 100%). Hispanic American bonds likewise rose in value, with a tendency toward resumption of bond service where this had been discontinued. Credit and collections were generally rated as good. Currencies were strong in most states; one new unit appeared with the establishment of the "guarani" in Paraguay, replacing the peso.

Few areas suffered from unemployment, because of war demands, and both Mexico and the Bahamas sent labourers to the United States.

(*See* articles on individual countries.)

(*See* also INTER-AMERICAN AFFAIRS, OFFICE OF THE COORDINATOR OF; PAN AMERICAN UNION; WORLD WAR II.)

Net Balance of Trade in Merchandise and Gold and Silver with the Hispanic American Republics, Jan.-Sept., 1943 and 1942

Country	1943 (9 mo.)	1942 (9 mo.)
Costa Rica	− $143,000	+ $222,000
Guatemala	− 6,669,000	− 7,665,000
Honduras	+ 644,000	− 1,735,000
Nicaragua	− 4,801,000	− 7,628,000
Panamá, Republic of	+ 22,025,000	+ 16,318,000
El Salvador	− 9,947,000	− 8,593,000
Mexico	− 19,031,000	− 32,932,000
Cuba	− 103,518,000	− 31,926,000
Dominican Republic	− 362,000	− 513,000
Haiti	− 1,276,000	+ 340,000
Argentina	− 73,485,000	− 66,096,000
Bolivia	− 11,037,000	− 10,135,000
Brazil	− 50,774,000	− 51,584,000
Chile	− 82,469,000	− 64,093,000
Colombia	− 42,702,000	− 47,725,000
Ecuador	− 5,759,000	− 819,000
Peru	− 4,779,000	− 5,528,000
Paraguay	− 1,554,000	− 1,753,000
Uruguay	− 27,370,000	− 6,620,000
Venezuela	+ 19,235,000	+ 16,453,000
Total	−404,372,000	−312,012,000

Source: *Foreign Commerce Weekly*, Dec. 4, 1943.

BIBLIOGRAPHY.—Foreign Policy Association *Reports* (semi-monthly); *Foreign Commerce Weekly; Inter-American Monthly; Bulletin of the Pan American Union* (monthly). (D. RD.)

Hispaniola: *see* DOMINICAN REPUBLIC; HAITI; WEST INDIES.

Hitler, Adolf

(1889–   ), German statesman, was born at Braunau on the Inn, Austria, April 20. For his career prior to 1943 see his biography in *Encyclopædia Britannica*.

Fear that the German home front was cracking at the seams impelled Hitler in 1943 to alter his propaganda tack, substituting for the customary promises of a short war and *lebensraum*, the grim alternative of "win or die." He boasted on March 30 that his armies would fight on until "unequivocal victory" had been won, but warned the Germans that they would become "red slaves" if they lost. The German victories at Kharkov and Belgorod in March established the basis for his declaration on March 21 that the crisis on the Russian front had been overcome; he also spoke of measures that would guarantee "final victory." But in April, he was faced with a new crisis—the impending collapse of axis armies in Africa—and he conferred with Mussolini, presumably on measures to salvage what they could from Africa and prepare to meet new Allied blows. The two dictators conferred again on July 19; six days later Mussolini was overthrown. By September, Italy had surrendered to the Allies and Hitler complained, Sept. 10, that he was a victim of Italian "deception" and vowed vengeance on Pietro Badoglio, Mussolini's successor, for his "treachery." In the autumn of 1943, German cities were being scourged from the air, and German soldiers were again in retreat on the Russian front. On Oct. 8, Hitler appealed to his people not to be discouraged by these reverses. But defeatism was growing on the home front and, a month later, the fuehrer warned that he would resort to mass executions to prevent an internal collapse. His last two speeches of 1943, on Nov. 29 and Dec. 31, were gloomy and desperate. His strident boasting could no longer conceal a subconscious and gnawing premonition that Germany was facing disaster, and again he warned that Germany must win or face total destruction. Throughout 1943, there were recurring reports that the German generals were awaiting the opportune moment to overthrow the fuehrer and seek a negotiated peace with the Allies. (*See also* GERMANY.)

Hobby, Oveta Culp

(1905–   ), U.S. director of the Women's Army corps (WAC) (*q.v.*), was born Jan. 19 in Killeen, Tex. A graduate of the University of Texas Law school, she was successively a member of the Texas legislature, assistant city attorney of Houston and a bank director. She also helped codify Texas banking laws and was the author of a text on parliamentary law. In 1931, she married William Pettus Hobby, former governor of Texas, and took an active interest in his newspaper, the *Houston Post*, becoming executive vice-president. In 1941, Mrs. Hobby was called to Washington on a dollar-a-year job as chief of the women's interests section of the war department's public relations bureau. At the behest of General Marshall, she drafted plans for a women's army and on May 16, 1942, she was sworn in as director of the first force of this kind in United States history, with a rank equivalent to that of a major. Starting with a goal of 12,200 women in uniform, the corps was subsequently authorized to expand to 150,000, in order to release more men for service on fighting fronts. At the end of the first year, members were serving in 225 army posts. In July 1943, WAAC became WAC; the word "Auxiliary" was dropped and the corps became an integral part of the army. Mrs. Hobby, as colonel, continued in command.

Hockey: *see* ICE HOCKEY.

Hoffman, Paul Gray

(1891–   ), U.S. industrialist, was born Apr. 26 in Chicago. He attended the University of Chicago, 1908–09, and went to Los Angeles in 1911, where he worked as an automobile salesman for the Studebaker corporation. During World War I he was a lieutenant in the field artillery, and after he was mustered out he returned to Los Angeles and founded the Paul G. Hoffman company, a motorcar distributing agency. He was Studebaker's vice-president in charge of sales, 1925–31, and was named president of the Studebaker Sales Corporation of America, 1931. During the depression years the big auto plant went into receivership. It was reorganized, and in 1935 Hoffman was made president of the firm. Under his guidance Studebaker not only was put back on a solid financial basis but was competing successfully with the giant auto combines in Detroit in producing medium-priced motorcars.

In 1937 he was elected to the board of trustees of the University of Chicago. In 1942 he became a federal reserve bank director. Hoffman was the leading spirit in the organizing in Sept. 1942 of the Committee for Economic Development (*q.v.*), of which he became chairman. In June 1943 he became a director of United Air Lines and of *Encyclopædia Britannica*.

"THAT FORTRESS OF EUROPE," pictured in 1943 by Russell of the *Los Angeles Times*

Hogs.

The year 1943 began with an all-time record number of hogs on farms. The total of 73,660,000 head on Jan. 1, as estimated by the United States department of agriculture, was 22% or 13,283,000 head more than in 1942 and 4,356,000 head more than the previous high record of 1923. The average for the ten-year period 1932–41 was 51,508,000 head. The spring pig crop was estimated at 74,000,000, which was 22%

larger than the 1942 spring farrowings. The fall pig crop was forecast to be 53,000,000 head, making a total of 127,000,000 head compared to 105,000,000 head in 1942 and 73,148,000 head as the ten-year average. These pigs were fed to heavy weights and brought a large increase in pork and lard to set a new record. The large spring pig crop resulted in a heavy utilization of feed, particularly corn, because the price of corn and hogs made it greatly to the farmers' advantage to feed corn to hogs rather than to market it as corn. This also led to the feeding of hogs to the maximum weights and also created a scarcity of corn for industrial uses and for purchase by livestock feeders outside the corn belt.

The slaughter of hogs in 1943 was estimated to be 93,200,000 head, compared to 77,900,000 head in 1942. Since the fall pigs and part of the spring pigs are marketed in the following year, the full increase in the fall pig crop of 1943 was not shown in the slaughter figures, but would be reflected in market receipts in 1944. The total hog slaughter was the highest on record, though the peaks of 1923 and 1933 were near the total of 1942. The capacity of the packing plants was taxed to the limit and at many markets receipts of hogs during the late months of 1943 made embargoes necessary since the packing plants could not handle the large numbers offered for sale. Hog prices remained quite steady through the year until the early fall when receipts at the markets became heavy. The government issued several appeals to farmers to hold hogs on the farms until the stockyards could be cleared. The War Food administration stated that the demand for pork exceeded the supply and that the government would purchase for lend-lease and other uses at prices that would reflect $13.75 per 100 lb. at Chicago.

The shortage of feed in prospect led the government to plan goals for 1944 on a somewhat reduced scale. A spring pig crop of 62,000,000 head and a fall crop of 43,000,000 head, or a total of 105,000,000 head was recommended. This number was expected to meet the food requirements of 14,790,000,000 lb. of pork and lard, of which 7,320,000,000 lb. was for civilians and 5,170,000,000 lb. for noncivilians, with 2,300,000,000 lb. as reserve and carry-over to the next year. (*See* also MEAT.)

(J. C. Ms.)

HOLC: *see* NATIONAL HOUSING AGENCY.
Holland: *see* NETHERLANDS.
Home Building, Federal: *see* NATIONAL HOUSING AGENCY.

Home Economics.

Home economics activities in the United States were centred in national organizations and in federal agencies. During 1942–43 the work of all was focused on wartime needs.

The American Home Economics association, at a wartime institute held in lieu of an annual meeting, considered how home economists might help families to strengthen homes in war and postwar periods. Three problems were discussed: managing finances in a war and postwar period, mobilizing human and material resources, and maintaining and creating values for families.

Representatives of the division of family relations and child development of the association worked on plans that might induce states, and through them smaller localities and communities, to help families readjust to wholesome relationships in the postwar period. During the war year of 1943, the major emphasis was to see that child care centres were provided.

The Association of Land-Grant Colleges and Universities reported that wartime adjustments made in home economics college programs included: modification of courses, with increased attention to the conservation of food, clothing, furniture and equipment, methods of saving time and energy, and problems created by working mothers and broken homes; accelerated programs

and refresher courses, particularly in nutrition; help with local and state programs; and the redirection of research, with emphasis on nutritive value and food preservation. The demand for home-economics-trained women far exceeded the supply.

The home economics education service (U.S. office of education, Federal Security agency) listed among the changes brought about by the war in the grade and high school programs: more emphasis on food conservation; the training of child-care aides; more instruction in home nursing and first aid; education in rationing and price ceilings; inclusion of nutrition in the elementary program; and less formal teaching in adult classes.

About $5,000,000 of federal funds were expended for the promotion and development of education for the vocation of home making. Approximately 18,000 high schools, about half of them federally reimbursed, offered instruction in home economics; approximately 350 teacher-training institutions, about one-third of them federally reimbursed, prepared home economics teachers.

The co-operative extension work in agriculture and home economics (War Food administration), a co-operative educational undertaking of the U.S. department of agriculture, the land-grant colleges and county governing bodies, was made a part of the War Food administration. This bureau was given the responsibility for educational programs dealing with war food production and conservation. More than 7,500,000 rural women enrolled in this program. The American Institute of Public Opinion reported that in the U.S.A. 24,800,000 families, or 75%, did some canning and put up 4,100,000,000 containers of all sizes; this is about 165 containers per family.

The bureau of human nutrition and home economics (Agricultural Research administration, U.S. department of agriculture) in its home economics research, investigated more problems in food and nutrition than in other fields. Many of the scientific data were interpreted in popular publications to help homemakers adjust to wartime supplies and shortages. There were pamphlets on meat; food preservation and waste; vitamins; fats and vegetables in wartime meals; and on the care of equipment, clothing, household textiles and rubber goods. Of the 113 available publications, more than 28,000,000 copies were distributed directly.

The office of experiment stations (Agricultural Research administration, U.S. department of agriculture) administers specified federal grants assigned to agricultural experiment stations for research, which may include home economics. In 1943–44, 39 states received federal support for 161 home economics projects, of which 134 were in food and nutrition. Forty-six stations and two other agencies participated in the national co-operative project, conservation of nutritive values of foods. Home economics took the lead, with representatives from 38 states.

The stations continued and extended studies on the standard allowances of nutrients established by the National Research council. Home economists made use of their strategic positions in land-grant institutions to work on nutrition problems requiring human beings as subjects. (*See* also DIETETICS; FOOD RESEARCH.)

BIBLIOGRAPHY.—"The Wartime Institute; a Series of Talks," *J. of Home Econ.*, 35:393–434 (1943); *Report* of the Committee on Instruction in Home Economics, Association of Land-Grant Colleges and Universities, Oct. 1943; Report from the Home Economics Education Service, U.S. Office of Education, Federal Security Agency, Dec. 1943 (typed; personal communication); *Report* of Cooperative Extension Work in Agriculture and Home Economics, 1943, U.S. Department of Agriculture, War Food Administration, Extension Service; *Report* of the Chief of the Bureau of Human Nutrition and Home Economics, 1943, Agricultural Research Administration, U.S. Department of Agriculture (in press); *Wartime Research in Home Economics at the State Agricultural Experiment Stations*, Office of Experiment Stations, Agricultural Research Administration; typed report sent to the Secretary for inclusion, in abstract form, in the *Proceedings* of the Association of Land-Grant Colleges and Universities, 1943, (in press); B. R. Andrews, "Sarah Louise Arnold, 1859–1943," *J. of Home Econ.*, 35:339–40; N. K. Jones, "Abby L. Marlatt," *ibid.*, 35:483–4 (1943).

(M. C. P.)

Home Loan Bank, Federal: *see* NATIONAL HOUSING AGENCY.

Home Owners' Loan Corporation: *see* NATIONAL HOUSING AGENCY.

Honduras. A republic of Central America, bounded by Guatemala, El Salvador and Nicaragua. Area 59,145 sq.mi.; pop. (1940 census) 1,107,859. The 1940 census listed 20,327 persons as white, 105,752 as Indian, 957,135 as mestizo and 24,200 as Negro. Most of the population is classed as rural (71%). Capital: Tegucigalpa (47,223); other cities: San Pedro Sula (20,392); La Ceiba (11,293); Choluteca (5,057). Religion: Roman Catholic; language: Spanish. President in 1943: General Tiburcio Carías Andino.

History.—In 1943 the war continued to be felt more seriously in Honduras than in any other Central American country. The banana industry, furnishing ordinarily 65% of Honduran exports and a great part of government income, remained at about one-fourth of normal output, with resulting unemployment and financial shortages. In the latter part of the year six vessels were added to the banana fleet, with some improvement of conditions. The United Fruit company planned hemp plantings as a substitute crop and also established an agricultural school to study the problem. One firm, producing dehydrated banana products, increased its output to full capacity. Work on the Inter-American highway project and other strategic roads eased unemployment to some extent. In June a financial mission was sent from the United States to aid in solution of Honduran problems.

Transportation difficulties became greater during the year, because of shortages of fuel, tires and equipment. Freight cars were added to passenger trains to conserve fuel, and bus and truck facilities were reported as 50% below normal. At one time on the north coast there was complete lack of gasoline.

By July 1943 Honduras had sent 25,191 lb. of rubber to the United States to aid in the war effort.

Education.—Elementary schools in 1940 numbered possibly 1,000, with an enrolment of 51,900. Secondary schools numbered 11, with an enrolment of approximately 2,300. The National university at Tegucigalpa had an enrolment of 300. In the 1942–43 budget, education received 918,000 lempiras (1941–42: 761,000 lempiras).

Finance.—The monetary unit is the lempira (value in 1943 approximately 49 cents U.S.). In the 1942–43 budget expenses were estimated at 12,222,000 lempiras; revenue at 12,542,000 lempiras (revenue in 1941–42 was 11,499,000 lempiras; expenses: 11,647,000 lempiras). Importation and use of $1,500,000 in U.S. currency was authorized March 18.

Trade.—No late figures on Honduran trade were available. Banana export (normally 65% of all exports, and 13,438,935 stems in 1940–41) remained low, although increased toward the end of the year. Silver is second in export (1940–41: 3,037,559 kgs.). In the first half of 1943, export of precious metals (silver and gold) was valued at $1,104,672. Other items in normal Honduran trade are coco-nuts, coffee, tobacco, cattle.

Communication.—Railway mileage is 903.4 mi., with 839.9 mi. of fruit company road. Motor roads amount to some 500 mi. Internal air service is well-organized, and there is connection with the outside world by air and steamer.   (D. RD.)

Honduras, British: *see* BRITISH HONDURAS.
Honey: *see* BEE-KEEPING.
Hongkong: *see* BRITISH EMPIRE.

Hopkins, Harry L. (1890–   ), U.S. politician, was born Aug. 17 in Sioux City, Ia. After graduating from Grinnel college in 1912, he went to New York city to engage in social service work. He later became a fast friend of Franklin Delano Roosevelt, then governor of New York, who in 1933 appointed him federal administrator of emergency relief. From 1935 to 1938 he was administrator of the Works Progress administration. He was appointed secretary of commerce in 1938 but resigned in Aug. 1940 because of ill health. In Jan. 1941, he was sent to London as President Roosevelt's personal emissary to study the war situation at first-hand. On March 27, 1941, the president named him lend-lease co-ordinator. He went to London on a second mission in July 1941, going thence to Moscow. The next month he retired as lend-lease administrator, being succeeded by Edward R. Stettinius, Jr.

On Jan. 10, 1943, President Roosevelt appointed Hopkins head of the newly formed Russian Protocol committee. In May Hopkins was appointed to the advisory committee of the Office of War Mobilization. He accompanied Roosevelt to the international conferences at Casablanca, Quebec, Cairo and Tehran.

Hops. The production of hops in the United States as estimated by the United States department of agriculture was 42,297,000 lb. in 1943, compared to 35,153,000 lb. in 1942 and above the ten-year average of 1932–41, 37,992,000 lb. In Washington the crop of 15,207,000 lb. was the largest on record. Because of a decrease in acreage the Oregon crop was below average while in California the crop was above last year's as well as above the average. Favourable weather for harvest aided the pickers and few hops were left unpicked. A large part of the crop was harvested by machines this year. Yields were better than expected and quality was good.

U.S. Production of Hops by States, 1943, 1942 and 10-yr. Average

State	1943 lb.	1942 lb.	10-yr. average lb.
Washington	15,207,000	11,788,000	9,594,000
Oregon	14,450,000	13,124,000	18,763,000
California	12,640,000	10,241,000	9,635,000

(J.C.Ms.)

Hormones: *see* ENDOCRINOLOGY.

Horse Racing. Racing in the United States in 1943 reflected the general conditions surrounding it. The immensely increased circulation of money caused by the

FLIERS OF HONDURAS were on daily patrol of the republic's Atlantic coastline in 1943, in co-operation with the U.S. anti-submarine forces

START OF THE 1943 KENTUCKY DERBY at Churchill Downs, Louisville, Ky., May 1. Count Fleet was the winner

war effort, combined with a public living under high tension and avid for excitement sent greater throngs of people to the race tracks than ever before. Despite the ban on pleasure driving, not relaxed until well into the summer, and in some sections, the fall, the national attendance was record-breaking, while the wagering reached figures described as "astronomical." As high as $2,926,-702 was bet on a single day at one of the New York tracks, the great centre of the sport. The national total for the year approximated $700,000,000, as a result of which a taxation revenue accrued to some 15 different states of about $35,000,000—in New York alone the amount exceeded $19,000,000. This led to the distribution, in stakes and purses, of the largest amount ever raced for in a single year, $18,547,635, as against the previous record of $18,136,118 in 1942.

The richest single race run was the Kentucky Derby, which netted the winner, Count Fleet, $60,725. This three-year-old colt at the close of the season was unanimously voted the "horse of the year." Bred and owned by Mrs. John D. Hertz and a son of Reigh Count (Kentucky Derby winner in 1928) and Quickly, by Haste, he was undefeated in six races, all his starts, and earned $174,055. His victories included the "Triple Crown" of Kentucky Derby, Preakness and Belmont stakes, all won in effortless style. Otherwise the honours and the money were much more widely scattered than usual, there being a lack of really dominant horses in the other divisions.

The champion two-year-old, Occupy, bred and owned by John Marsch and by Bull Dog—Miss Bunting, by Bunting, won $112,-949. The leading money-winner among the older horses was the four-year-old Thumbs Up, by Blenheim 2d—Gas Bag, by Man o'War, whose credit was $97,100. These figures are in sharp contrast to those for 1942, when three different horses each won over $200,000. The same condition extended over into the domain of speed. Not a single time record of importance was either beaten or equalled during the entire year and it was the general remark that the horses, as a lot, were slower than usual.

Among the winning stables, that of Calumet Farm (Warren Wright) took the honours with 73 races and $267,915; its trainer, Ben Jones, thereby taking the lead in his department, from the money standpoint. But from that of number of races won, the title once again went to Hirsch Jacobs with 128, this being the tenth time in the past 11 years that he has held the lead. The leading race-winning jockey was Johnny Adams with 228, he having also led in 1942 with 245. Among the money-winning jockeys the leader was Johnny Longden, whose mounts accounted for $573,276 in stakes and purses. The leading money-winning sire was the stallion Bull Dog, whose get won $367,771.

One of the features of the year was the great upturn in thoroughbred values as shown by the yearling sales, where an average of $1,868 was registered, as against but $636 in 1942; with the highest price paid $66,000 as against but $9,000 in 1942. A grand total of $2,074,736 was paid for 1,370 animals of all ages

sold at auction, with an average of $1,514, as against one of but $489 for 1,914 sold in 1942. The stimulus to breeding as well as racing was, therefore, equally great. On the harness racing side governmental restriction worked greater hardships than on the thoroughbred, as before causing the cancelling of many of the most important meetings. Otherwise the season was one of unusual success at both the major and the minor tracks. The big winner of the year was the three-year-old Volo Song, by Volomite-Evensong, by Nelson Dillon, who took the annual Hambletonian stake, worth $42,298; his best heat being in 2:02½ (one mile). He was owned by W. H. Strang, Jr., and trained and driven by Ben White. Values for trotters took a big upward turn and a new record of $15,500 for a Standard-bred yearling was established at the annual sale of Walnut Hall Farm, where Volo Song was bred. (J. L. HE.)

Great Britain.—Horse racing in 1943 was again severely restricted on account of transport difficulties, Ascot, Windsor and Salisbury in the south and Stockton and Pontefract in the north, in addition to Newmarket, being the only racecourses used. The wartime classic races were all run at Newmarket and proved that the three-year-old fillies were better than the colts. Lord Derby's filly Herringbone, by King Salmon—Schiaparelli, trained by W. Earl and ridden on each occasion by H. Wragg, won the One Thousand Guineas and the St. Leger, and J. V. Rank's filly Why Hurry, by Precipitation—Cybiane, trained by N. Cannon and ridden by C. Elliott, was successful in the Oaks. Lord Rosebery's filly, Ribbon, was narrowly beaten in each of these three races. The Hon. Dorothy Paget won the Derby with Straight Deal, a colt by Solario—Good Deal, who was trained by W. Nightingall and ridden by T. Carey, and also owned the best two-year-old of the season in Orestes, a colt by Donatella II—Orison, who was unbeaten. Kingsway, by Fairway—Yerna, owned by A. E. Saunders and trained by J. Lawson, won the Two Thousand Guineas, in which he was ridden by S. Wragg. The best of the older horses were Ujiji, winner of the Gold Cup, and Shahpoor, who won the Jockey Club Cup. Linklater proved himself the best sprinter of the year when he again won the Nunthorpe Stakes at Newmarket. G. Richards was once again champion jockey with 65 victories, and during the season he beat F. Archer's record of 2,749 winners that had stood since 1886. Miss D. Paget headed the winning owners with £13,145 won in stake money, and W. Nightingall was the most successful trainer. (A. K. B.)

Horses. The number of horses and colts on United States farms declined about 2% in 1942, a continuation of the steady decline since 1915. The total number was estimated by the department of agriculture on Jan. 1, 1943 at 9,678,000 head compared with 9,907,000 head in 1942 and 11,409,000 head as the average for 1932–41. The record number in 1915 was 21,-431,000 head before the widespread use of autos and tractors began on farms. There was a sharp drop in the number of horse colts raised on farms in 1942 the total being the smallest in 24 years of record. The decline was most noticeable in the central states Indiana, Illinois, Ohio, Iowa, and Michigan where farm power machines are most universally used. In New England, the southeast and far west there was little change. Gasoline rationing was expected to stimulate the return of the horse but there was no evidence that it had much effect. The scarcity of horse drawn vehicles was a retarding factor as well as the lack of facilities to take care of horses in cities, and moreover the slow speed of horse travel. Light horses for riding and showing showed little change since the interest of the people was so fully taken by other activities.

The army's requirements for horses were smaller than expected and were quickly supplied by the western range breeding farms. Range bred animals were plentiful and best suited to this work. The average value of horses increased slightly in 1942 to $79.97 per head as the average on Jan. 1, 1943 from $64.75 per head on Jan. 1, 1942, and the record of $99.18 per head in 1937. The total value of horses was $773,917,000 in 1943 compared to the record low value of $641,520,000 in 1942.

The use of horse meat was limited to the making of special foods for dogs and other pets. The use of horse meat for human food had always been very limited in the United States and showed no signs of increasing after the war began. From 15,000 to 30,000 animals were slaughtered each year from 1933 to 1943 and the higher price of feed caused the marketing of more than 40,000 in 1943.

Mules.—The number of mules declined 3% in 1942. The estimated total number of mules on farms was 3,712,000 head on Jan. 1, 1943, compared with an average of 4,542,000 head in the period 1932–41. The value of mules per head increased in 1942 to $127.46 compared with $107.51 a year earlier. Most of the mules are raised in the south central states with Texas producing more than twice as many as any other state. Next in importance as mule raising states are Mississippi, Georgia, Alabama, North Carolina, Tennessee, Arkansas and Kentucky. The army demand for mules dropped off as the needs for foreign campaigns were supplied by purchases in the localities abroad. The increase in prices of mules was attributed more to expansion of the cotton acreage than to the demand for animals for the army or other war activities. (*See* also SHOWS.)   (J. C. Ms.)

Horse Shows: *see* SHOWS.

Horticulture.
Horticulture throughout the world in 1943 saw greatly restricted flower production and greatly expanded production of food. In the United States the restrictions caused florists to devote some of their greenhouse area to vegetables instead of ornamental plants. Shorter hours went into force and there was doubling up in deliveries. At the same time, prices were increased to a degree not known for many years. On the whole, therefore, florists had an unusual measure of prosperity. However, leading florists made efforts to see that prices did not reach excessively high points.

The growing of ornamentals in the British Isles was permitted to continue at about the same rate as in 1942 and shipments of tulip bulbs to the United States were made. Large vegetable and flower shows were held by the Royal Horticultural society in London, and attended by throngs. Canada bought a reasonable number of bulbs from England and the United States. The European bulb industry shrank to very small proportions, although the Netherlands sold some bulbs to Germany. The Netherlands growers were reported to have given up much of their bulb acreage to the growing of vegetables, but to have preserved strains of their best tulips and narcissi, hoping to resume business on a large scale at the end of the war.

The seed business continued to reverse former conditions. Such seeds as were, at one time, purchased in great quantities abroad were being shipped from the United States to the very lands from which they were once brought. Well over 100,000,000 lb. of vegetable and field seeds were sent by ship and plane to the Allied forces overseas. Shipments made to the U.S.S.R. were particularly heavy and victory gardens were planted in Stalingrad and Leningrad. Late in the year, however, large consignments of field seeds to Russia were held up by lack of shipping accommodations. Many seeds were sent to North Africa, where efforts were made to induce food production by refugees from Europe and Italian prisoners. Large shipments of vegetable seeds were made to the British Isles, where 8,000,000 ac. of new land were being cultivated. Both vegetable seeds and canning equipment were sent to Australia.

In the United States great stress was placed on home gardens and community gardens under the general name of victory gardens, of which some 20,000,000 were listed. Late in the year the department of agriculture in Washington expressed the wish that this number be increased to 22,000,000 in 1944, and that larger gardens be made where possible. A Victory Garden institute, supported by industrial corporations, was organized in New York city. The 1943 victory gardens produced 8,000,000 tons of food, with an estimated value of $1,000,000,000.

The use of fertilizers and insecticides was restricted and a shortage of tools began to develop. Pyrethrum flowers used for an insecticide grow in territory controlled by the Japanese. They also grow to some extent in North Africa, but the natives lagged in the work of harvesting the flowers.

The cultivation of rotenone, which is even more important as an insecticide, gained ground in Brazil and Peru. Planting stocks of derris, from which it comes, were distributed to growers in Central America, Colombia and Ecuador. Plantings in Ecuador increased so fast in 1943 that more than 2,000 ac. were promised by 1945. The government completed arrangements for planting 100,000 cuttings in Haiti.

Efforts were being made to increase the production in South America of other economic plants, formerly imported from the far east. Among them was the cinchona tree, from the bark of which quinine is made. Before the war 95% of the world's supply was produced in the Netherlands Indies. In 1943, agreements were made to provide thousands of acres for growing cinchona trees in Guatemala, Colombia, Brazil and other Latin American countries. Large plantings were also made of abacá a banana-like tropical plant from which comes hemp for making rope. Progress was made in establishing various food materials like vanilla, ginger, black pepper and nutmeg in the Latin Americas on a commercial basis.

Lack of manpower was keenly felt by fruit growers and market gardeners as well as general farmers throughout the United States. Thousands of Mexicans and natives from islands off the Atlantic coast were imported to help in this work. Labourers were sent from the southern states to Maine in the autumn to help harvest a record-breaking potato crop. In some sections soldiers were used to pick apples, but the apple crop was considerably smaller than in 1942. The peach crop was greatly reduced by late frosts in the spring.

Buying of seeds for planting the crops of 1944 began early in the fall of 1943, but the indications were that there would be sufficient seeds to meet all demands, although some varieties might not be available. Production of 22 kinds of food crop seeds was estimated late in the year to total 214,651,000 lb., this being about 15% larger than the 1942 production. The largest increases were in lettuce, carrots, onions, winter squash, cucumbers, sweet corn and certain beets. There was a decline in cabbage, turnips and romaine lettuce.

Greatly increased interest in soybeans as a food product was shown by amateurs and increased plantings seemed likely in the future. Certain varieties proved to be excellent for home use, although the pods were small and difficulty in shelling was encountered.

Late in the year the George Robert White medal of honour, the outstanding horticultural award of the United States was given to Richardson Wright, editor of House and Garden, New York. (*See* also BOTANY.)　　　(E. I. F.)

Hospitalization Insurance: *see* INSURANCE.

Hospitals.
Many factors contributed to increase the number of people seeking hospital care in 1943. Even in established communities there was a "doubling up" of families which left less opportunity for the sick to be cared for at home. Many new industrial communities mushroomed far beyond the ability of available hospital beds to meet their needs. Improved economic conditions enabled more persons to pay for hospital care. Births increased as much as 30% in many large areas. The proportion of mothers seeking the hospital for maternity care continued its rapid increase. The movement of one-third of the most active physicians and nurses into the armed services threw such a load on the remainder that people simply could not get the home care they needed and could get in peacetime.

This movement of physicians and nurses into the armed services reduced the professional staffs of hospitals by as much as 40% in some instances. But the hospital is a self-contained unit and its lay force in dietary, mechanical, housekeeping and similar departments is quite as necessary as is its professional personnel. This group was even more seriously depleted both by entrance into the armed services and by the lure of high wages paid in the defense industries.

The problem was met by stripping every procedure of as many of its niceties as possible without detriment to the patient, by

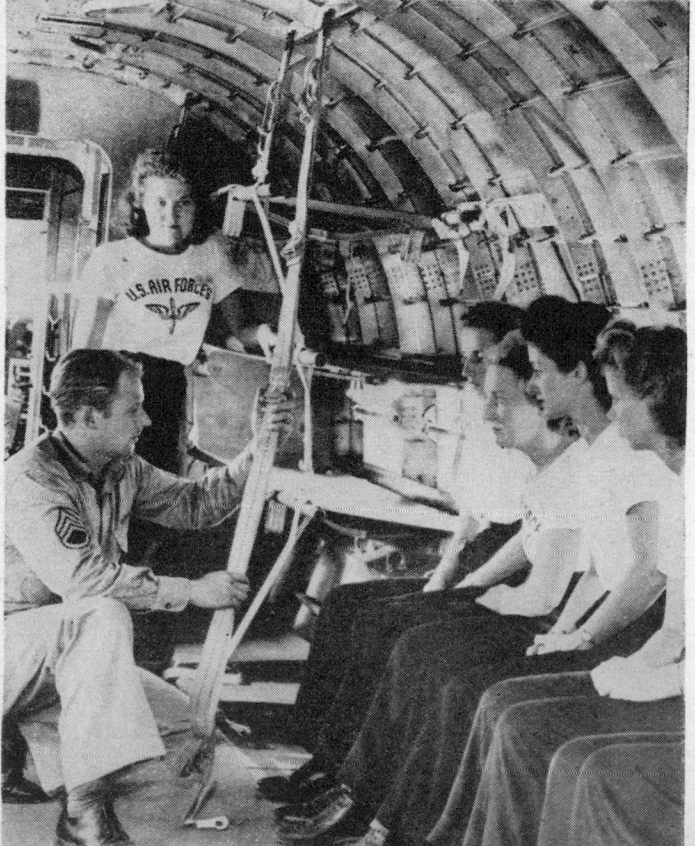

FLIGHT NURSES at Bowman Field, Kentucky, learning how to set up a "flying hospital" in eight minutes. Many such U.S. air ambulances were in operation on all fronts in 1943

calling personnel from retirement back into service, by the wide use of volunteer and other part-time workers, by limiting admission of patients to those in most acute need, and by discharging them at the earliest possible moment to spend their convalescence at home.

A more permanent problem for hospitals was the threat of new social security legislation which proposed to make some form of insurance for the payment of hospital bills compulsory and under governmental auspices. The 15,000,000 people enjoying the protection of the existing voluntary hospital insurance plans fostered by the voluntary hospitals of the United States proved that the unpredictable cost of hospitalization could be carried by the wage earner at moderate cost. The extension of protection by compulsion and to those who do not need protection was being combated by hospitals in the fear that such governmental control would rob the hospital of its initiative, the individual of his independence, and both the hospital and the medical profession of the incentives which gave them the medical leadership of the world and the American people the best medical care of any people in the world.

BIBLIOGRAPHY.—Ellis Kellert, "Laboratory Burden Can Be Cut in Half," *Hospitals*, 17:90–92 (Oct. 1943); Oliver G. Pratt, Donald S. Smith, James E. Moore, H. J. Stander, "Conserving the Medical Staff," *Hospitals*, 17:43–50 (Nov. 1943); (No author) "Maternity Facilities," *Hospitals*, 17:116–118 (April 1943); Alfred E. Maffly, "This Is No Time to Hoard Beds," *Modern Hospital*, 61:68–70 (Nov. 1943); Mildred Stewart Tucker and others, "Volunteers," *Modern Hospital*, 61:57–96 (Nov. 1943); A. J. Altmeyer, "One Health Insurance Agency: The Government," *Hospitals*, 17:37–40 (Oct. 1943); E. A. Van Steenwyk, "Let Government Help Not Kill Voluntary Plan," *Hospitals*, 17:41–44 (Oct. 1943).　　　(W. P. Mi.)

Housing.
Manpower and metals were needed for war purposes in 1943 as in 1942. Therefore, new housing construction was limited to the 820 localities in which there was a shortage of homes for in-migrating war workers and families of military personnel. It was estimated by the National Housing agency that 3,533,721 living units were provided from the inception of the war housing program on July 1, 1940, to July 31, 1943. These were made available in the following manner:

One million eight hundred thousand rooms, apartments or individual homes were found in existing buildings that required no structural change. Private industry built 764,402 new units and converted 204,300 units in existing structures. Most of the financing was guaranteed by the government through NHA's Federal Housing administration. NHA's Federal Public Housing authority financed, with public funds, 700,426 new units (mostly temporary construction to be removed when the war is over) and 64,593 conversions. These units were built by private construction firms, but turned over to the government for management when completed.

In the first eight months of 1943, despite the labour shortage, housing production nearly doubled that completed in the same period of 1942. The 370,837 units built exceeded 1942 production by 197,749. This resulted from the co-ordinated team work of the housing agencies united under NHA in Feb. 1942. Besides uniting many of the operations of its 16 entities, NHA had effected cordial working relationships with the War Manpower commission, the War Production board, the army and navy, and the congress. Therefore, it was possible to turn out in 1943's first eight months, 99,640 privately financed units, 267,107 publicly financed new units, and 4,090 publicly financed conversions of existing structures. At the end of September, 84,291 new privately financed family dwellings were under construction, 13,479 publicly financed conversions, 115,341 publicly financed family units, 30,387 dormitory units, and 8,901 trailers.

On May 13, 1943, the president sent a message to the congress calling attention to an estimated in-migration of 1,100,000 to war production centres during the fiscal year 1944. This estimate was revised to 1,200,000 in Sept. 1943, requiring 925,295 added housing accommodations, 560,000 to be provided in existing structures. Congress, which had appropriated $915,000,000 in 1942 for the construction of war housing, and another $100,000,000 in July 1943, was asked in September to appropriate for the use of FPHA, an additional $200,000,000 to provide 164,095 more units of temporary construction. On March 23, 1943, it increased the authority of FHA to issue mortgages on privately financed war housing from $800,000,000 to $1,200,000,000, and from $1,200,-000,000 to $1,600,000,000 on Oct. 15, 1943.

Every effort was made to have private enterprise finance and build wherever it was economically feasible. Publicly financed housing was programmed wherever there was uncertainty concerning the future need of the structures in the community at the close of the war.

Construction agencies started in 1941 to battle with the problems of cutting down the amount of critical material contained in each house, and with methods of housing workers so that a minimum of houses might be built. Temporary family dwellings were built with less than 2,000 lb. of critical metals per unit, as compared with the prewar permanent units which contained about 9,000 lb. To save materials, much emphasis was placed upon dormitories. But in many localities they proved unacceptable to workers. Consequently, relatively more family units were programmed in the latter part of 1943 and fewer dormitories. In Sept. 1943, the estimate of family units required was raised from 260,000 to 340,000 and the dormitory program cut from 70,000 to 25,000.

Since war housing was constructed to shelter war workers, the size and cost was restricted to meet the income of the war worker, and to use a minimum of critical materials. Private construction was topped at $6,000 per unit, public, consisting mainly of temporary dwellings, averaged $3,000 per family unit.

The Negro war worker, as the Negro in prewar days, was found to be living in intolerable conditions. It was difficult to find accommodations in areas not already established for Negroes. Consequently, they were forced into already overcrowded, insanitary quarters. In Detroit, Baltimore, Washington, Los Angeles and other cities, grave situations arose. Special emphasis was placed upon finding accommodations for Negroes. Many builders realized for the first time that there was a large ready market for Negro purchasers or renters. Many sought to supply the market, but it was difficult to interest mortgage money, and there was also great community resistance. Some progress, however, was made.

Great popular interest was aroused in the question of construction of homes for the postwar period. Several cities—Buffalo, Syracuse, Boston, Chicago—began to measure the future housing needs of their population. The national market was estimated to be from 620,000 to 2,000,000 a year for ten years following the war. The greatest market was said to be in the house costing less than $4,000, but a sizable demand was predicted for the $6,000 to $10,000 home. To prepare for the postwar period, chambers of commerce, real estate and civic associations studied methods of rebuilding slum and blighted areas. (*See also* BUILDING AND CONSTRUCTION INDUSTRY; BUSINESS REVIEW; CENSUS, 1940; FEDERAL WORKS AGENCY; MUNICIPAL GOVERNMENT; NATIONAL HOUSING AGENCY; WASHINGTON, D.C.)

BIBLIOGRAPHY.—Publications of the National Housing Agency, The National Committee on Housing, Inc., The Architectural Forum, F. W. Dodge Corporation, National Association of Housing Officials.   (D. RN.)

Great Britain.—The findings of the advisory committee set up by the ministry of health to recommend standards for postwar housing had not been published but it was anticipated that they would make some revolutionary recommendations as a result of the evidence which they received from all sorts of societies and organizations concerned. The only outstanding event in connection with housing generally in 1943 was the scheme of the ministry to produce 3,000 houses for rural workers; many regarded this number of houses to be built immediately as by no means large enough. It may be assumed that the scheme was in the nature of an experiment and a purely emergency measure. Costs had risen over 100% on prewar figures but it was expected that they would drop again considerably with the passing of wartime conditions. Nevertheless the costs of the postwar house were likely to be much higher than prewar although the higher costs should not prevent the introduction of a higher standard of housing.

A few houses experimenting with new methods of construction and use of materials were erected by various interests, although anything approaching the final and acceptable prefabricated house had not yet appeared. Much was being done by manufacturers of the components for houses, such as windows, doors, and so on, and more particularly in connection with standardization of equipment for cooking, heating, refrigeration, etc. It may be taken that even though the structure of the small house would probably be carried out largely on traditional lines, there would be available and generally used a standard of mass-produced equipment of every kind.

The work of the board of trade in producing utility furniture for those who had lost their homes through enemy action and for the newly married had undoubtedly set a standard in simplicity which would have its influence.

The services of the most eminent designers were secured for this furniture, resulting in the best possible use being made of such materials as were available. The furniture was well received and something like 140,000 people had been supplied. (F. R. Y.)

Housing Administration, Federal: *see* NATIONAL HOUSING AGENCY.

Housing Agency, National: *see* NATIONAL HOUSING AGENCY.

Housing Authority, U.S.: *see* NATIONAL HOUSING AGENCY.

Howard, Leslie

(1893–1943), British actor and director and producer of motion pictures, was born Leslie Stainer on April 3 in London. The son of a stockbroker, he worked as a bank clerk until the outbreak of World War I, when he joined the British army. Invalided out of the army in 1917, he became an actor, changed his last name to Howard and appeared in a number of plays in London and New York city. His first movie, *Outward Bound,* was an immediate success. Outstanding pictures in which he appeared included *The Cardboard Lover, Berkeley Square, The Animal Kingdom, Of Human Bondage, British Agent, The Scarlet Pimpernel, The Petrified Forest, Pygmalion, Gone with the Wind* and *The Invaders.* After the outbreak of World War II, he returned to England to make a series of war pictures for the British government. In April 1943, he undertook an extensive lecture tour of Spain and Portugal under the sponsorship of the British council. While flying en route to London, the British transport plane in which he was a passenger was shot down by an enemy plane on June 1 and all passengers aboard were presumed lost. Howard's last picture was *Spitfire* (1943), which portrayed the life of Reginald Joseph Mitchell, designer of the British Spitfire fighter plane.

Howland Island: *see* PACIFIC ISLANDS, U.S.

Hrdlicka, Ales

(1869–1943), U.S. anthropologist, was born March 29 at Humpolec, Bohemia. Dr. Hrdlicka travelled the world over for 40 years in search of data that would shed new light on the origin of the human race and explain the phenomenon of prehistoric migration. Although Dr. Hrdlicka calibrated many human and anthropoid skulls in his research, he was immune to the "missing link" theory. He contended that human life did not exist on the American continent in prehistoric times and that man migrated from Asia by way of Alaska at a comparatively late period. To prove his view, he presented his findings, accumulated after painstaking research in Siberia and the Aleutians, in scores of articles in scientific journals. He retired from the National Museum of the Smithsonian institution, Washington, in 1942, but was later restored to active service. His later works include *The Peoples of the Soviet Union* (1942) and *Alaska Diary, 1926–31* (1943). Dr. Hrdlicka died in Washington, D.C., Sept. 5. (See *Encyclopædia Britannica*.)

Hull, Cordell

(1871–   ), U.S. statesman, was born Oct. 2 in Overton (now Pickett) county, Tenn. He was graduated from the Cumberland university law school in 1891 and served as a captain in the Spanish-American War. He served in congress from 1907 to 1933, except for one brief interval, 1921–23. He was elected to the senate in 1931 but resigned in 1933 to become President Roosevelt's secretary of state. Internationally, his name became closely associated with the "good neighbour" policy in South America and elsewhere; he was a consistent foe of aggression in settling disputes. He roundly denounced the Japanese attack on the Philippines and Pearl Harbor on Dec. 7, 1941, as a "treacherous and utterly unprovoked attack."

On April 8, 1943, Secretary Hull signed a reciprocal trade agreement with Iran, the 27th of a series of such pacts made by the United States and the 7th since the beginning of World War II. In a speech on foreign policy (Sept. 12), he stressed the necessity of postwar co-operation between nations. In August Hull accompanied President Roosevelt to Quebec, where he participated in the British-Canadian-American conferences. Two months later he travelled to Moscow to confer with Anthony Eden, British foreign secretary, and Vyacheslav Molotov, soviet

SECRETARY HULL and Foreign Commissar Molotov at the Moscow airport shortly after Hull's arrival to take part in the Allied conference which resulted in the Pact of Moscow, announced Nov. 1, 1943

foreign commissar. This, the first meeting between statesmen of the three countries, foreshadowed the later conference between the heads of the states themselves at Tehran.

Hungary.

A kingdom in central Europe. Area (1940) 61,728 sq.mi.; pop. (1940) 12,708,439. Capital: Budapest. Chief cities: Budapest (1,115,877); Szeged (131,893); Debreczen (122,517); Kolozsvár (100,844); Kecskemét (83,732). According to official figures published in 1942, the territory acquired by Hungary from Yugoslavia in 1941 and called officially "Southland," contained 339 towns with a population of 1,024,876. As a result of this expansion, the population of Hungary in 1942 was officially estimated at 14,733,000 in an area of 66,409 sq.mi. Religion: the majority are Roman Catholics, with strong Protestant and small Jewish and Greek minorities. King: throne vacant since 1918, royal functions exercised by regent Nicholas Horthy de Nagybánya. Premier (1943): Nicholas von Kallay.

History.—During 1943 Hungary continued as an ally of Germany in the axis war against Great Britain, the soviet union and the United States. As a result of its co-operation with Germany, Hungary had gained large territories from Czechoslovakia (Ruthenia and eastern Slovakia) and from Rumania (northern Transylvania). When Yugoslavia collapsed after German aggression in April 1941, Hungary occupied and formally annexed fertile Yugoslav provinces north of the Danube. In its desire to keep the territories acquired between 1938 and 1941, Hungary was determined to fight on the side of Germany. But the rapid advance of the Russian troops in 1943 toward the Carpathian mountains filled the strongly anti-communist and pro-fascist government of Hungary with deep apprehensions. On the whole the Hungarian government continued to follow the nazi line in its foreign and domestic policies in 1943, yet of all the satellites of Germany it retained the greatest independence and even kept the traditionally parliamentary forms of the Hungarian constitution.

The anti-Semitic legislation, though theoretically as thorough as in Germany, was not applied with the same ferocious ruthlessness as in other German satellite states.

Admiral Nicholas Horthy, the regent of Hungary, visited Chancellor Adolf Hitler in April 1943. Their conversations may have dealt with the questions of Hungary's active participation in the war against the soviet union where Hungarian troops had suffered heavy losses. The troops in Russia had been under the command of Col. Gen. Vitez Gusztav Jany, who was wounded and succeeded by Col. Gen. Ludwig von Csata, commander of the 5th Hungarian army corps in Russia. When Col. Gen. William Nagy resigned as Hungarian war minister in June 1943, Col. Gen. Ludwig von Csata was appointed to succeed him.

The Hungarian government found itself in a difficult situation. There was a rising demand for a *rapprochement* with the Allies if that could be done without incurring German measures of retaliation, and at the same time with Hungary keeping as much as possible of its territorial gains of the previous five or six years. On the other hand there was a strong pro-nazi minority represented by the party led by the former prime minister, Bela Imrédy, and the numerous German minority in Hungary. This opposition demanded an even closer association with Germany and the complete nazification of the country. Fortunately for the government the Hungarian nazis were torn by internal strife and rival leadership. Thus while German-Hungarian relations were more strained than those between Germany and any other of the satellites, Hungary sought some backing in its close friendship with Italy. In June 1943 the Italian minister of national education visited Budapest for the opening of new offices of the Italian Institute of Culture. This effort at a backing by Italy received a rude shock in July 1943 with the collapse of the Italian fascist regime.

Some of the opposition to the pro-nazi legislation of the government in 1943 came from the Catholic primate of the country, Justinian Cardinal Serédi, who declared that "Christ's teachings do not acknowledge difference between men and men and do not know prerogatives which would entitle a man or a nation to oppress another man or nation on racial or national grounds. Human freedom is the greatest among human rights and for it humanity has fought out innumerable battles; such a battle is going on also today and it will continue until freedom will have become such a natural need for people as air." Nothing definite was known about the strength of the underground movement in Hungary in 1943. The social democratic party still was allowed to function but remained strictly within legal bounds. In the United States a Committee for a New Democratic Hungary was formed under the chairmanship of Professor Rustem Vambery.

Education.—Education is compulsory for children between 6 and 12, while for three more years they have to visit continuation schools or courses, many of them specialized agricultural schools. Besides these continuation schools and a relatively large number of special schools, Hungary had, in 1939, 8,103 elementary schools with 23,215 teachers and 1,104,916 pupils. In the cities there existed 418 primary schools with 4,619 teachers and 105,466 pupils. High schools of different kinds numbered 263, with 4,709 teachers and 79,435 students. There were four universities, Budapest, Pécs (Fünfkirchen), Debreczen and in the newly acquired Transylvanian territory Kolozsvár (Cluj or Klausenburg). These universities had a total of 7,032 students, including 1,011 women.

Finance.—The monetary unit is the pengö, containing 0.263158 grams of fine gold, equal to 19.77 cents U.S. in March 1941. The revenue for 1943 was estimated at 4,047,000,000, the expenditure at 4,247,000,000 pengös. The public debt amounted on Sept. 30, 1942 to 4,869,000,000 pengös, bank notes in circulation on Sept. 30, 1942 to 2,470,000,000 pengös. As against this circulation, the national bank of Hungary had a metal reserve, including foreign exchange, of 166,000,000 pengös.

Trade and Communication.—Hungary imported, in 1941, goods valued at 730,000,000 pengös and exported to a value of 791,000,000 pengös. Of the imports in 1939 almost half of the value came from Germany and half the exports went there. Italy held the second, Great Britain the third place.

In 1939 Hungary had 6,307 mi. of railroad, 2,898 post offices, 6,902 mi. of telegraph lines and 20,976 mi. of telephone lines.

Agriculture, Manufacturing, Mineral Production.—Hungary's main production is agriculture. In the fertile plains of the Danubian basin potatoes, maize, wheat, sugar beets, rye, barley and grapes are grown. Hungary is rich in forests, pigs and cattle. It has a wealth of good coal and important bauxite deposits. Most of the industry is connected with agriculture. Hungary produced in 1939, 10,625,452 tons of coal, 500,193 tons of bauxite, 409,292 tons of pig iron and 732,615 tons of steel.

(*See* also RUMANIA; WORLD WAR II.)　　　(H. Ko.)

Hurdling: *see* TRACK AND FIELD SPORTS.
Hygiene, Industrial: *see* INDUSTRIAL HEALTH.
ICC: *see* INTERSTATE COMMERCE COMMISSION.

Ice Hockey. The Detroit Red Wings were dominant in professional hockey during the 1942–43 season, first winning the National Hockey league championship and then taking the Stanley cup playoff. Detroit finished four points ahead of the Boston Bruins in league play and swamped the same Bruins, four straight, in the cup final. Goalie John Mowers keynoted the Red Wings' triumph in the Stanley cup series by blanking Boston in two of the cup matches.

Although many outstanding players from Canada and the United States were taken into the armed forces, hockey enjoyed another successful season. The N.H.L. operated with only six teams instead of the usual seven, but nevertheless drew 1,446,747 fans. It marked an increase of 17,544 spectators per team over the 1941–42 season.

Minor league hockey was hard hit during 1942–43. The American Hockey association, a midwestern league, disbanded and the American league in the east was cut from ten to eight teams. The American association also failed to open at the start of the 1943–44 season, while the American league dropped further to six teams and split into two divisions—Providence, R.I., Hershey, Pa., and Buffalo, N.Y., in the east; Indianapolis, Ind., Cleveland, O., and Pittsburgh, Pa., in the west.

Buffalo won the American league hockey championship, while the Eastern league amateur crown went to the Curtis Bay Coast Guard Cutters. The Ottawa Commandos captured the Allen cup, emblematic of Canadian Amateur Hockey supremacy. Dartmouth was unbeaten in U.S. college competition to retain the Pentagonal championship.

Centre Bill Cowley of Boston was awarded the Hart trophy as the most valuable player in the National Hockey league. The George Vizina cup for the outstanding goal-guarding job went to Detroit's Mowers. Gay Stewart of Toronto was judged the outstanding rookie, while Max Bentley of Chicago won the Lady Byng trophy as the player with the best conduct on the ice. Doug Bentley, also of Chicago, led the league scoring with 73 points to tie Cooney Weiland's record, made during the 1929–30 season while with Boston. Doug Bentley and Cowley were placed on the league's all-star team, along with Frank Brimsek, Boston goalie; Earl Seibert of Chicago and Jack Stewart of Detroit, defensemen, and Joe Benoit, Canadiens, right wing. Jack Adams, who during 1942–43 piloted Detroit to its fourth league title and third Stanley cup, was named manager.　　(M. P. W.)

Iceland. An island state of the North Atlantic. Area, 39,709 sq.mi.; pop. (est. 1939) 120,264. Capital, Reykjavik, the only large town (pop. in 1939, 38,219). Religion, Lutheran Christian. Hereditarily united with Denmark, Iceland became an independent state Dec. 1, 1918, legally united with Denmark only by recognition of a common king. After April 9, 1940, the executive power was wielded by the Icelandic ministry, with a regent, Sweinn Björnsson. The chief minister in 1943 was Dr. Björn Thordarson, who formed a nonpartisan government on Dec. 16, 1942.

History.—Through 1943 the United States military occupation of Iceland continued, and the island continued to be an important Atlantic mid-station in the world-wide war. Major General William S. Key took command of the U.S. garrison in June.

Independence was the most important political question of 1943, but it was hardly a "question." By the agreement with Denmark of Dec. 1, 1918, Iceland might sever all ties with Denmark after Jan. 1, 1944. On May 17, 1942 the Althing resolved that Iceland did not intend to continue the union after the date set, and on Dec. 1, 1943 the three major parties in the Althing (Progressive, Independence and Socialist Labour [Communist], with 45 of the 52 total seats) issued a statement announcing their agreement that an Icelandic republic should be established not later than June 17, 1944.

The cost of living index, based on 100 for 1939, soared to 272 in Dec. 1942, but by Aug. 1943 had dropped to 247. The feared runaway inflation was averted, at least for a time, through strong governmental action including price fixing and subsidies.

THE WINTER OF 1942-43 was a bleak one for U.S. soldiers stationed in Iceland, but winterized tents and large stoves kept them warm

Commercially the most notable thing was the shift of trade from Britain to the U.S. (See *Trade,* below.)

The Roman Catholic Church appointed Jóhannes Gunnarsson Bishop of Iceland—the second Catholic bishop since Lutheranism became the state religion in 1550.

A dream of years approached realization despite wartime obstacles and delays: the hot springs were being connected by pipe lines with the homes of Reykjavik to supply steady heat for houses, heat and water for private greenhouse vegetable gardens, and water for health baths.

Finance.—Monetary unit: krón = 18 U.S. cents (1939), about 15.5 U.S. cents in 1942; in 1939 government revenues were 19,-930,879 krónur (and estimated for 1943 at 33,736,100 kr.); expenditures, 19,378,318 kr. (and estimated for 1943 at 28,333,238 kr.); national debt (1939), 56,648,000 kr.; notes in circulation, 14,000,000 kr.; gold reserve, 5,762,000 kr.; bank capital and reserves, 17,577,000 kr.; bank deposits, 76,720,000 kr.; total bank funds, 48,997,000 kr. Bank deposits were 452,421,000 in July 1943. Note circulation jumped from 24,580,000 kr. in Jan. 1941

to 123,810,000 kr. in Aug. 1943; loans in the same period, from 92,137,000 kr. to 170,594,000 kr. Gold reserves and bank capital remained practically at the 1939 figures.

Trade.—Exports in 1939 totalled 69,654,000 kr.; chief articles of export were fish and fish products. Imports in 1939 totalled 61,639,000 kr. The chief imports were gasoline, textiles, metal wares, wood and machines. Great Britain took most of Iceland's exports in 1939 (11,794,000 kr.), followed by Sweden (8,517,000 kr.); Denmark (7,708,000 kr.); Germany (7,488,000 kr.) and the United States (7,378,000 kr.). Great Britain also was first in supplying Iceland's imports, with goods valued at 13,785,000 kr. Denmark was second (12,684,000 kr.) and Germany was third (10,125,000 kr.).

The years 1941 and 1942 show some significant contrasts with the peacetime balance depicted in the above paragraph. Exports rose steeply in value: 188,504,000 kr. in 1941, about two and one-half times the value of 1939; in 1942 the figure was 200,433,-000 kr. In 1941 a large credit balance was allowed to accumulate, but in 1942 Iceland imported more than she exported, and continued to do so in 1943. Iceland sold her fish to Great Britain, amounting in the first seven months of 1943 to about the same as in 1942, and simultaneously she increased exports to the U.S. Her purchases, however, showed a startling reversal from a British trade double the American to an American more than double the British. Unemployment was nonexistent.

Communication.—Highways (1936) totalled 2,728 mi., of which 1,736 mi. were improved and 992 mi. were unimproved. Miles of telegraph lines (1939): 9,700. Military occupation led to unrevealed new construction.

Agriculture.—In 1938 the chief products with their yields in tons were as follows: hay (269,024), potatoes (13,160), turnips (2,856).

BIBLIOGRAPHY.—Austin H. Clark, *Iceland and Greenland,* Smithsonian Institution War Background Studies No. 15 (1943).   (F. D. S.)

Ice Skating.

Of the two competitive phases of ice skating, only figure skating held a national championship during 1943. The war forced cancellation of the National speed championships, but minor tournaments were held both on the east coast and in the middle west.

Gretchen Merrill, a 17-year-old member of the Skating club of Boston, won the women's senior figure skating championship of the United States, having placed as runner-up the two previous years. The national men's senior title went to Arthur R. Vaughn, Jr., of Philadelphia. Vaughn, who placed third in the senior event in 1942, is a brother of Mrs. Jane Vaughn Sullivan, the 1942 senior women's champion who did not defend her title in 1943.

With Ken Bartholomew, the '42 national champion, in the armed services, Dick Werner of Patterson, N.J., dominated men's speed skating. Werner won the Middle Atlantic, New York State and Eastern championships. Carmelita Landry of Fitchburg, Mass., continued her rule of women's speed skating by winning the Middle Atlantic and New York State titles. Miss Landry won both the National and North American crowns in 1942.

Musical ice shows continued their upward trend in popularity, with three major shows touring the country. Forty performances in New York's Madison Square Garden alone attracted 385,000 spectators.   (M. P. W.)

Idaho.

One of the far northwestern states of the U.S. belonging to the group regionally designated as the Pacific northwest. Idaho was admitted to the union on July 3, 1890, and is popularly known as the "Gem state." Area, 83,888 sq.mi., pop. (1940) 524,873, of which 66.3% was rural, 33.7% urban. There were 3,638 Indians in the state. Principal cities are Boise, the capital (26,130), Pocatello (18,133), Idaho Falls (15,024), Nampa, (12,149) and Twin Falls (11,851).

History.—There was no general election in 1943. State officers elected Nov. 3, 1942 were as follows: governor, C. A. Bottolfsen (Rep.); lieutenant governor, Edward Nelson (Rep.); secretary of state, George H. Curtis (Dem.); attorney general, Bert H. Miller (Dem.); auditor, Calvin E. Wright (Dem.); superintendent of public instruction, C. E. Roberts, (Dem.); mine inspector, Arthur Campbell, (Dem.); state treasurer, Mrs. Myrtle Enking Beatty (Dem.). The legislature elected in Nov. 1942, convened in Jan. 1943: both houses were Republican. The principal subject of controversy was the Old Age Pension act adopted by a safe majority in 1942 on an initiative vote. Within ten days after the election Chase A. Clark, then governor, declared the act a "law in full force and effect." The legislature "repealed" the act and Governor Bottolfsen signed the repeal. Pension advocates immediately started a movement for the recall of the governor and of all legislative members who had supported the repeal. Up to the close of 1943 a sufficient number of signers had not been secured.

Education.—The school population in 1942–43 was 118,000. There were 80,572 pupils and 3,802 teachers in 1,005 elementary schools. High school enrolment was 28,007 pupils with 1,326 teachers in 176 high schools. Enrolment in other educational institutions was as follows: state university (Moscow), 871; southern branch (Pocatello), 760; normal school (Lewiston), 241; normal school (Albion), 78; junior college (Boise), 496; junior college (Coeur d'Alene), 51.

Charities and Correction.—There were two institutions for the insane, one at Blackfoot and one at Orofino, as well as a home for the feeble-minded at Nampa. The penitentiary at Boise had 148 inmates at the close of 1943; it has a capacity of 400. The reform school, known as the "state industrial school," located at St. Anthony, has a fairly constant population of 250.

Communication.—There were 4,910 mi. of state highway and approximately 33,000 mi. of county and forest roads at the close of 1942, with very little construction of other than military roads in 1943. The state had 2,890 mi. of railroad in 1942. Eight major airports were under government control and there were, in addition, a large number of emergency and forest landing fields. There was a very large growth in telephone service during 1943, because of military requirements. The number of instruments in use was estimated at 90,000 with approximately 160,000 mi. of wire. Telegraph mileage was approximately 9,000 mi.

Banking and Finance.—On Dec. 31, 1943 there were 33 state banks with capital of $1,250,000 and surplus of $1,005,500. As of Oct. 18, 1943, there were 54 national banks with capital of $3,510,000 and surplus of $2,788,050. Assessed valuation of the state in 1943 was $408,549,711. State treasurer's receipts were $45,665,550; disbursements $41,352,960. Bonded debt of state government was $1,390,600 and will be cancelled by Dec. 31, 1944.

Agriculture.—Total value of all farm crops in 1943 was $185,-

Table I.—*Principal Agricultural Products of Idaho, 1943 and 1942*

Crop	1943	1942
Wheat, bu.	22,720,000	20,770,000
Corn, bu.	1,683,000	2,444,000
Oats, bu.	7,400,000	7,898,000
Barley, bu.	12,716,000	14,280,000
Sugar beets, short tons	608,000 (est.)	1,076,000
Dry beans, cwt.	2,479,000	2,234,000
Dry peas, bu.	3,326,000	1,775,000
Hay (tame), tons	2,189,000	2,141,000
Potatoes, bu.	43,470,000	30,590,000

271,000; in 1942, $134,660,000. Both figures exclude statistics for sugar beets.

Manufacturing.—Defense and war-material manufacturing took over the state's manufacturing activities to such an extent that no statistics were available for 1943. In 1940 there were 533 plants with 12,797 workers and payrolls aggregating $16,249,685.

Mineral Production.—Total value of mineral production in 1943 for the five leading metals was $43,910,180 as compared

Table II.—*Principal Mineral Products of Idaho, 1943 and 1942*

Mineral	Value, 1943	Value, 1942
Gold	$ 1,120,000	$ 3,325,700
Silver	8,298,880	10,414,144
Copper	663,000	830,060
Lead	14,222,800	15,263,806
Zinc	19,605,500	16,229,616

with $46,063,326 in 1942. The production of zinc in 1943 was the largest in the history of the state.

(B. DE.)

Illinois. A north central state of the United States, admitted to the union in 1818, nicknamed the "Sucker state," sometimes called the "Prairie state." Total area, 56,400 sq.mi. of which 55,947 sq.mi. are land. Pop. (1940) 7,897,241, including 3,967,481 males and 3,929,760 females; 7,503,987 white, 393,254 nonwhite. Population classed as urban was 5,809,650, rural not on farms 1,121,823, rural farm 965,768. The census bureau estimated the 1942 population at 8,008,067. Springfield, the state capital, with a population of 75,503, is the fifth Illinois city in size. Chicago (3,396,808) is the largest Illinois city, followed by Peoria (105,087); Rockford (84,637); East St. Louis (75,609).

History.—Intense effort in war industry and agriculture, despite the absence of 750,000 residents in the armed forces, featured Illinois life in 1943. The state stood sixth in the union in war expenditures. Up to Oct. 1, 1943, supply contracts and capital investments in plant and facilities totalled $9,015,490,000, excluding subcontracts and prime contracts of less than $50,000.

Of this amount $1,482,069,000 was for aircraft, $197,840,000 for ships and boats, $2,928,678,000 for ordnance and $3,140,589 for all other supply contracts. The total amount of facility contracts, principally industrial installations, was $1,266,314,000.

More than 800 Illinois plants were engaged in the manufacture of aircraft and parts. The four great ordnance plants erected in the state neared the saturation point of production, as was the case with tank and artillery plants. Production of landing barges and similar watercraft was stepped up throughout 1943.

Dwight H. Green was governor of Illinois in 1943; Hugh W. Cross, lieutenant governor; Edward J. Hughes, lone Democrat official, secretary of state; Arthur C. Lueder, state auditor; William G. Stratton, state treasurer; and George F. Barrett, attorney general.

Education.—Latest available statistics in 1943 placed enrolment in the approximately 12,000 school districts of Illinois at 1,281,854, with private and parochial school enrolment at 252,-504. The state superintendent's estimate of total 1943 enrolment was 1,500,000. The decline of enrolment in 1943 was estimated at 7.5% for high schools and 6% for grade schools. Teachers in public schools numbered 45,438. Total expenditures by the state government for education in the fiscal year ended June 30, 1943, were $30,531,905.

Public Welfare, Charities, Correction.—Decline of the relief load in 1943 caused the return to the state treasury of $10,428,463 of unspent relief funds. Recipients of old-age assistance declined by 3,335. At midyear, the total receiving old-age assistance was 147,637, and dependent children receiving aid numbered 60,965. Payment of unemployment benefits decreased by 82% under the 1942 payments in the first half of the year. There were 30,899 in the state's nine hospitals for mental patients. The total population of welfare institutions was 42,778 on June 30, 1943. The population of Illinois's three main prisons and the state prison farm had declined by 880 by Aug. 10, the lowest figure in 13 years.

Communication.—The network of high-type highways in Illinois comprised 13,683 mi. in 1942, connected to about 56,000 mi. of lower-type road. State government expenditures on roads in the fiscal year ending June 30, 1943, were $50,798,801, both direct and in aid of localities. Illinois railroad mileage approximated 11,500.

Banking and Finance.—As of June 30, 1943, Illinois had 813 banks, of which 340 were national banks, 120 state institutions with memberships in the federal reserve system and 353 nonmembers. Total deposits were $7,826,735,000, total investments, $5,079,589,000.

Total appropriations by the state legislature for the biennial period July 1, 1943–June 30, 1945, were $503,847,000. Receipts for the fiscal year ending June 30, 1943, were $256,399,299. State trust funds and surplus included $98,000,000 invested in war bonds. The state had a bonded debt of $149,461,500.

Agriculture.—Major state crops harvested in 1943 had a value of $770,171,000, the highest since 1919, and $140,381,000 greater than in 1942. Hog production in 1943, 11,009,000 head, was the largest on record. Higher prices accounted for the gain in crop income, as the actual quantity of produce was a fraction of one per cent less than in 1942.

Table I.—*Leading Agricultural Products of Illinois, 1943 and 1942*

Crop	1943 (est.)	1942
Corn, bu.	446,148,000	433,438,000
Soybeans, bu.	75,250,000	73,794,000
Oats, bu.	113,632,000	141,320,000
Wheat, bu.	17,330,000	12,818,000
Tame hay, tons	3,261,000	3,942,000

Manufacturing.—The value of products manufactured in Illinois in 1939, according to the U.S. biennial census (last before World War II), was $4,794,860,733; the number employed was 688,800; total wages and salaries were $988,453,881. The principal industries and the value of their products were as follows: meat packing, $479,501,224; steelworks and rolling mills, $207,301,815; petroleum refining $122,933,528; tractors, $121,550,621.

Mineral Production.—The total value of minerals produced

Table II.—*Production of Coal and Petroleum in Illinois, 1940 and 1939*

	1940	1939
Bituminous coal, tons	45,977,479	47,627,454
Petroleum, bbl.	146,788,000	94,912,000

in Illinois in 1939 was $210,295,738. (L. H. L.)

Illinois, University of.

On March 2, 1943, the University of Illinois observed the 75th anniversary of its opening. More than 600 faculty and staff members were on leave in 1943 for war service. Teaching was on a year-around schedule, eliminating the usual summer let-up. Teaching of civilian students continued without curtailment and with 32 special courses added and the wartime and postwar values of all courses emphasized.

In May 1942, a Naval Training station was located on the campus, training signalmen and diesel-enginemen. Nearly 2,000 men were assigned to the station, with the personnel changing periodically as courses were completed. Under the army specialized training program and the navy V-12 program, an initial quota of 2,800 soldiers and sailors was assigned to the university for college training both in basic subjects and in various specialized fields including medicine and dentistry. Hundreds of others were examined at the university as an army specialized training and reclassification centre.

Under the engineering, science and management war training program 23,000 persons in 55 war-factory centres of Illinois were instructed through the division of university extension. Agricultural extension activities turned to intensive drives to increase farm production, to educate consumers in the conservation of foods and materials, and to promote victory gardens.

In the university's laboratories, the "down-draft coking principle" was built into a "furnace of the future," and a conversion burner for existing home furnaces was tested and made ready for postwar production, both promising a 25% fuel saving and smokeless burning of soft coal—goals long sought to benefit health and cleanliness in U.S. cities.

The operating budget for 1943–44 was $13,114,348, of which $7,304,962 was from state tax revenues. For statistics of enrolment, endowment, library volumes, etc., see UNIVERSITIES AND COLLEGES.

Illumination: *see* ELECTRICAL INDUSTRIES.

I.L.O.: *see* INTERNATIONAL LABOUR ORGANIZATION.

Immigration and Emigration, U.S.

The immigration and emigration of aliens are controlled in the United States by laws and treaties and by regulations based thereon, and are under the direction of the commissioner of immigration and naturalization in the department of justice. Aliens seeking to enter the United States for permanent residence are limited as to quality by the act of Feb. 5, 1917, which requires that they meet certain standards, mentally, physically, morally and economically. The Quota act passed on May 26, 1924, limits the number that may enter for permanent residence from certain countries.

During the fiscal year ended June 30, 1943, officers of the immigration and naturalization service passed upon 41,848,384 persons' entries into the United States. Of these 40,717,372 were across land borders, including 5,623,592 alien entries and 9,182,720 citizen entries from Canada, and 14,754,846 alien entries and 11,156,214 citizen entries from Mexico (making a total of 20,378,438 aliens and 20,338,934 citizen entries across both land borders). Alien entries for permanent residence numbered only 23,725 for the fiscal year ended June 30, 1943, a decrease of 5,056 from the fiscal year 1942 and the second lowest number to take up permanent residence in the United States for any fiscal year since 1831.

Quota immigrants numbered only 9,045, although under the law, 153,774 quota immigrants could have been admitted. Only 5,107 emigrant departures occurred during the fiscal year of 1943, the lowest number since 1908 when records of departure were first made. Immigration of permanent residents exceeded emigration by only 18,618.

During the period 1,495 aliens were excluded. There were 35,738 vessels boarded and 961,142 alien and citizen seamen inspected. The immigration border patrol officers patrolled 10,276,454 mi., examined 8,874,998 conveyances and questioned 24,598,186 persons, which resulted in the apprehension of 16,330 persons and the seizure of 147 conveyances. During this period 4,207 aliens were deported from the United States and 11,947 who had been adjudged deportable were allowed to depart at their own expense without warrants of deportation. (*See also* ALIENS; CENSUS, 1940; REFUGEES.) (E. G. H.)

Imports: *see* INTERNATIONAL TRADE.

Incendiary Warfare: *see* WARFARE, INCENDIARY.

Income, U.S. Distribution of: *see* WEALTH AND INCOME, U.S. DISTRIBUTION OF.

Income Tax: *see* TAXATION.

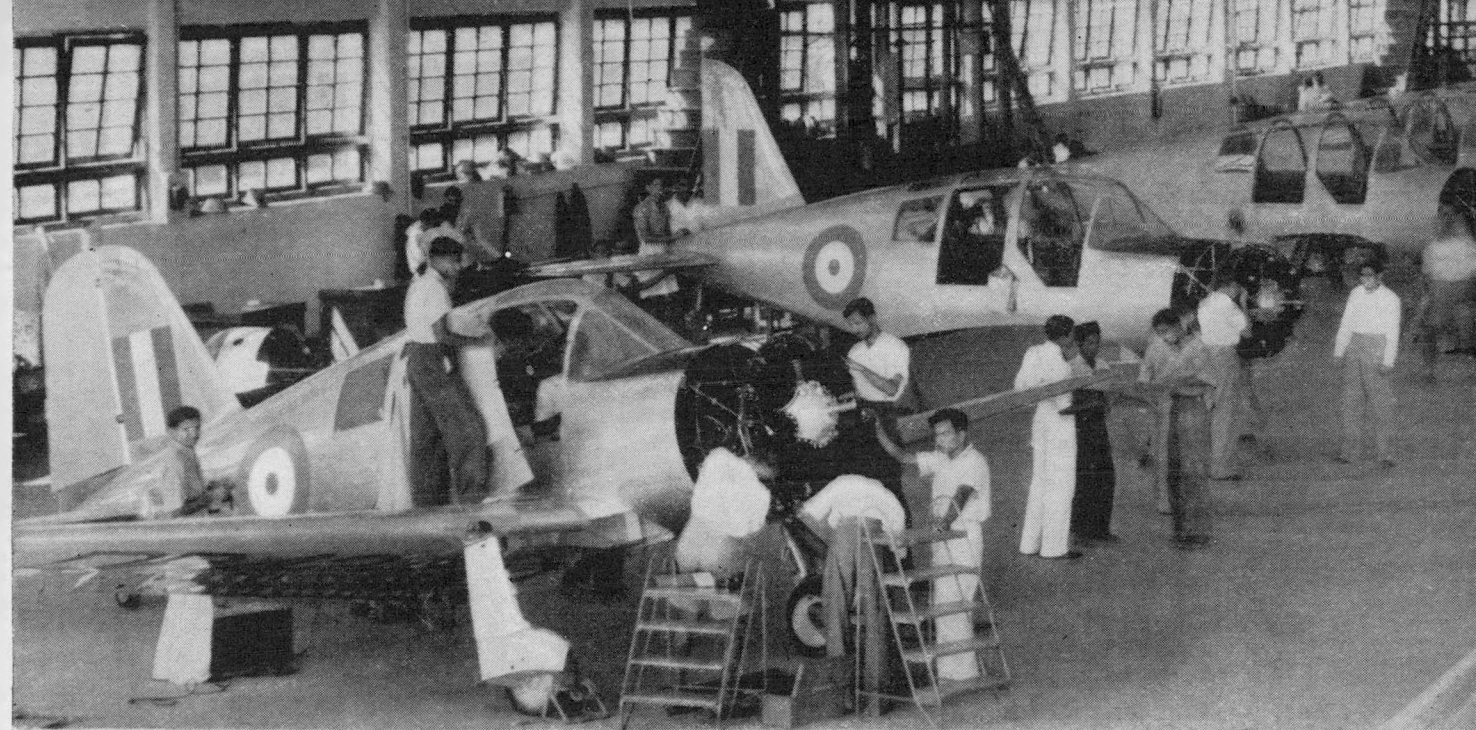

R.A.F. TRAINERS on an assembly line near Bangalore, India. This aircraft factory was established by an American, William D. Pawley

India.

A sub-continent projecting from the mainland of Asia, India lies between the 8th and the 37th degrees of north latitude. It comprises 11 major or "autonomous" provinces, five minor areas directly administered by the central British government and a large number (between 500 and 600) of states under Indian rulers. The latter are scattered about the sub-continent and vary greatly in size and importance, as well as in the powers enjoyed by their chiefs. British India (the 16 major provinces and minor areas) has its capital at New Delhi and is under a viceroy and governor-general (Field Marshal Viscount Wavell, appointed in June 1943), who is also the representative of the crown in its relations with the native states. The total area is 1,575,187 sq.mi., of which the native states and agencies total 712,508 sq.mi.; pop. (est. 1941 census) 388,800,000. Chief cities (pop. census 1931): Calcutta (1,485,582); Bombay (1,161,383); Madras (647,230); Hyderabad (466,894); Delhi (447,442); Lahore (429,747). Languages: Hindi, Tamil and Urdu the most important; religions: Hinduism (approx. two-thirds), Mohammedan (approx. one-fifth). Ruler, George VI, emperor.

History.—The year 1943 appeared to dawn more prosperously after the troubles and anxieties of 1942. The campaign of violence inaugurated by the Indian National congress had collapsed, and its leaders were under arrest. The Japanese invasion had been halted on the frontier, and air attack on Indian towns had proved less formidable than had been feared. In three raids on Calcutta at the end of 1942, only 23 were killed and 100 wounded. There was no panic and the A.R.P. services acquitted themselves well.

Financially, India was prospering as a result of the war. The great "steel cities" at Jamshedpur and Khumbarbhudi and the government ordnance factories were working at top speed. India was the centre of the South Eastern Supply Group, and the mills at Cawnpore and other places turned out vast quantities of khaki cloth, boots, equipment and tents. War orders were placed at the rate of over £15,000,000 per month. Under the Bevin scheme, skilled Indian workmen were sent in batches to England for training, and it was found possible to spare considerable supplies for the U.S.S.R. and China. The Bombay dockyards were busy night and day.

Still more significant was the effect of the war on India's external position. Before the war, the sterling debt of the government of India was roughly £360,000,000; in 1943 it was down to £12,500,000.

Ever since his internment in the Aga Khan's palace at Poona, Mohandas Gandhi had maintained a personal correspondence with the viceroy on the subject. When it was pointed out that his conduct had resulted in serious outbreaks, involving great destruction of property and loss of life, he replied that these were not the work of congressmen, or alternatively, that they had been provoked by the "leonine violence" of the British government. Finally he declared his intention, unless he and his colleagues were unconditionally released, of starting on Feb. 9 a three-weeks' fast on lime juice and water. This was the ninth occasion upon which Gandhi had resorted to this time-honoured Indian method of coercing a recalcitrant opponent. His most successful one was in Sept. 1932, when by a threat of "a fast unto death," he had in seven days induced Ramsay MacDonald to abandon the "communal award," which gave separate electorates to the untouchable Hindu castes under the new constitution.

Lord Linlithgow, however, stigmatized the 1943 fast as "political blackmail," and warned Gandhi that he alone was responsible for the result. He was willing to release Gandhi if he repudiated or dissociated himself from the resolution of Aug. 8, and the policy which that resolution represented, but neither Gandhi nor the congress was prepared for this repudiation. The viceroy offered, moreover, to allow him to perform his feat in a friend's house, and relaxed to a limited extent the embargo on receiving visitors. Gandhi refused the offer of release unless it was unconditional, and the fast duly began. He was 73 and there was considerable anxiety when it was announced that he was seriously ill. Madhao S. Aney and C. R. Rajagopalachari visited him and tried to induce him to abandon his intention, and appeals were addressed to the viceroy and Winston Churchill. Gandhi later rallied and emerged from his fast on March 3, apparently little the worse for his ordeal.

One of the results of the fast was a distinct exacerbation of communal tension. Mohammed Ali Jinnah and members of the Muslim league watched closely for any signs of yielding to congress demands on the part of the government of India. About 1922, in the days of the Khilafat movement, there had seemed to be strong hopes of a Hindu-Muslim *rapprochement*. Under the leadership of Abdul Ghaffar Khan, the Red Shirt leader, the Pathans of the North West Frontier province had gone over almost en masse, and, as a result of the elections of 1935, they had returned a congress government to office. But experience of the treatment they received from Hindu congress ministries between 1937 and 1939, especially in the United provinces, brought a sad disillusionment. None of the congress prime ministers formed coalition cabinets; government posts went to Hindus, and children attending government schools were reported to have been compelled to sing the Hindu national anthem, *Bande Mataram*, bow to Gandhi's portrait, and submit to other observances deeply repugnant to the Muslim conscience.

Although the president of the Indian National congress was Moulana A. K. Azad, a distinguished Mohammedan theologian, it was felt that this really counted for little; congress rule meant the restoration of the Hindu raj. The proposal put forward by Sir Stafford Cripps in 1942, that after the war the new constitution would be drawn up by a constituent assembly, caused deep disquiet, for such a body would naturally be preponderantly Hindu in its composition. By 1943 there were Muslim ministries in all the provinces excluding those taken over by the governors when the congress ministries were withdrawn at the outbreak of war. Efforts to bring about an understanding between the Hindus and the Muslim league on the part of Sir Tej Bahadur Sapru, the Liberal leader, and Rajagopalachari, the ex-premier of Madras, proved abortive. Jinnah had declared that India is "two nations": there had to be two Mohammedan national states, Pakistan and North Eastern India. Muslims would never collaborate in a federation in which they were placed in a permanent minority. Meanwhile matters remained at a deadlock, and Rajagopalachari was not the only politician who now regretted that the Cripps proposals were so summarily rejected.

Lord Linlithgow was due to retire in the autumn, and speculation was rife about the new viceroy when on June 19 it was announced that the commander in chief, Sir Archibald Wavell, had been appointed, with the title of viscount. He was to be succeeded by Sir Claude Auchinleck. At the same time, in order to relieve the commander in chief of the responsibility for the conduct of operations against Japan, a separate East India command was set up, and subsequently Lord Louis Mountbatten, famous as organizer of commando raids, was given the post. Never before had the office of viceroy been held by a serving soldier. Lord Wavell had had the unique advantage of two years' previous experience in the government of India before assuming office, and he had won the enthusiastic admiration of the Indian troops by his conduct of the African campaign.

Lord Linlithgow retired on Oct. 18. He had been viceroy and governor-general for the unprecedented period of seven and a half years, and none of his predecessors since Lord Canning had been confronted with equally grave anxieties. It was especially disappointing for him that the Act of 1935, in the framing of which he had taken so prominent a part, had never been given a chance of working.

The closing months of Lord Linlithgow's Indian career were darkened by the outbreak of famine in Bengal; the first for over 40 years. Famines are really endemic in India, where the staple foods are rice, millet and wheat, and the crops depend on the monsoon. It had been hoped that the peril had been permanently averted by the erection of extensive irrigation works like the Sukkur Barrage on the Indus, but the large increase in the population, over 60,000,000 in the preceding decade, had more than counterbalanced any advantage derived from this.

Economically, the year 1942 had been disastrous for eastern India. About 650,000 tons of grain had gone abroad to feed the Indian troops, and in October a cyclone and tidal wave had swept over the normally surplus district of Midnapur. Eleven thousand people lost their lives, and 75% of the cattle were drowned. Not

only were the crops and stores of grain totally destroyed, but the fertility of the soil was permanently affected. This was followed by a serious outbreak of rice disease in eastern Bengal. The supply of Burmese rice was entirely cut off, and fears of a Japanese invasion led to extensive hoarding. The cumulative effect can be imagined when we realize that in a country of the size of India an increase of an ounce of food a day *per capita* means an additional 4,000,000 tons per annum. The government of India was censured for not taking prompter and more resolute action; but the provinces with a surplus were naturally reluctant to part with it, and the Bengal ministry was confident that it could cope with the situation unassisted.

Matters assumed a serious aspect by August. Crowds of destitutes were invading Calcutta in search of food, and it became an everyday occurrence to find corpses lying in the streets. Between Aug. 15 and Oct. 15, the mortality in the capital alone rose to 8,000. Voluntary societies worked heroically, but were handicapped by a shortage of supplies, and an outbreak of cholera or smallpox was apprehended.

On assuming office, Lord Wavell at once visited the spot, and enlisted the co-operation of the military authorities. All the troops not required for operations against the Japanese were detailed for relief work. Rest camps and hospitals had been established outside the city, and the sick and starving were removed to them. Over 5,000 free kitchens were opened, and 2,000,000 people were fed daily. Considerable supplies of grain, milk products and drugs arrived by sea, and the peak of the danger was apparently past. But it would take months to restore normal conditions; one of the greatest difficulties was that of food distribution in rural areas away from the beaten track. (*See* also FAMINES.)

Lord Wavell was faced with a threefold task—the defeat of Japan, the economic rehabilitation of Bengal, and the political settlement. (*See* also BURMA; WORLD WAR II.)   (H. G. RN.)

Education.—(1938-39): Number of recognized institutions in British India (excluding Burma) 211,192; scholars in recognized institutions: primary, males 9,407,782; females 1,462,263; middle, males 1,150,272; females 179,506; high, males 1,059,909; females 115,341. Unrecognized institutions, 19,354. Universities, British India 15, native states 3; total number of students, 140,461.

Finance.—Revenue, central government (est. 1942-43) rupees 191,48,07,000; expenditure, central government (est. 1942-43) Rs.226,54,91,000; public debt (March 31, 1940): in India Rs.450,23,00,000; in England £280,100,000; notes in circulation (April 30, 1943) Rs.669,40,00,000; reserve (April 16, 1943) gold Rs.44,40,00,000, silver rupee coins Rs.13,70,00,000, sterling securities Rs.568,10,00,000. Currency: 1 rupee (Rs.1); Rs.100,-000=1 lakh, written Rs.1,00,000; Rs.10,000,000=1 crore=100 lakhs, written Rs.1,00,00,000; one hundred crores is written Rs.100,00,00,000. Exchange rate (average 1941) Rs.1=1s. 6d.= 30.14 cents U.S.; (July 1943) Rs.1=30.12 cents.

Trade and Communication.—Overseas trade (1942-43): imports, merchandise Rs.110,44,82,618; exports, Indian merchandise Rs.187,60,10,948; re-exports, merchandise, Rs.6,95,22,253; gold coin and bullion (1939-40), imports Rs.1,32,72,707; exports, Rs.36,00,26,302; imports of Afghan merchandise (1939-40) Rs.3,97,06,671; exports of Indian produce to Afghanistan (1939-40) Rs.72,79,399.

Indian Imports and Exports 1942-43

	Imports from Rs.	Exports to Rs.
U.K.	29,53,43,000	57,34,26,000
Burma	...	...
Japan	...	...
U.S.A.	19,00,08,000	27,79,34,000

Communication.—Roads (March 31, 1938) British India only, 83,612 mi. motorable roads, 201,701 unsurfaced. Railways

(March 31, 1940) route mileage: broad gauge 21,154 mi.; metre gauge 15,899 mi.; narrow gauge 4,103 mi. Shipping, tonnage entered (monthly average 1939) 924,200; tonnage cleared (monthly average 1939) 917,500. Motor vehicles licensed (March 31, 1940): British India 94,788 cars and taxis; 43,187 commercial vehicles; 8,602 motorcycles. Wireless receiving set licences, all India (Jan. 1941) 121,534. Telephones (March 31, 1940): 86,219 straight-line connections, 626 exchanges.

Agriculture, Manufacturing, Mineral Production.—Production (in metric tons): rice (1940–41) 33,332,800; wheat (1940–41) 10,957,100; cane sugar, raw (1939–40) 2,770,000; maize (1937–38) 2,080,800; barley (1938–39) 2,119,500; jute (1940) 2,280,000; coal (1940) (British India) 26,496,000; iron ore (metal content) (1939) 1,994,000; pig iron and ferro-alloys (1939) 1,785,000; steel (1939) 1,035,000; petroleum, crude (1940) 325,000; cotton, ginned (1940–41) 1,049,600; groundnuts (1940–41) 3,528,700; tobacco (1939–40) 495,800; tea (1940) 174,800; manganese ore (metal content) (1939) 430,000; linseed (1940–41) 473,500; gold (1940) 9,000 kg.; bauxite (1939) 9,100; chrome ore (chromic oxide content) (1939) 25,-000; rape seed (1940–41) 1,135,900; sesamum (1940–41) 408,-200. Industry (excluding Burma): cotton (1939–40) yarn spun 1,233,686,576 lb.; woven goods 4,012,529,025 yards; number of mills 388; average number employed 430,165. Jute (1937–38): mills 105; average number employed 309,000. Total number of factories (1939) 10,466; average daily number employed (1939) 1,751,137.

Indiana.

A north central state with the popular name "Hoosier," Indiana became the 19th state in the union Dec. 11, 1816. The total area of the state is 36,555 sq.mi., of which approximately 510 sq.mi. are water. The population, according to the census of 1940, was 3,427,796; 1,887,712, or 55.1%, were urban; 1,540,084, or 44.9%, rural. Of the total, 93.2% were native white, 3.2% foreign-born white, and 3.6% Negro. Capital, Indianapolis (pop. 1940, 386,972), the largest city. Other cities: Fort Wayne (118,410); Gary (111,719); South Bend (101,268); Evansville (97,062); Hammond (70,184); Terre Haute (62,693); East Chicago (54,637); Muncie (49,720); Anderson (41,572).

History.—The 83rd general assembly, in session Jan. 7–March 8, 1943, though strongly Republican, developed little friction with the governor, a Democrat. Notable was the number of interim commissions (12) created to investigate conditions, codify laws, and locate institutions, and to report to the next general assembly. An act identical with one passed by the Kentucky legislature and enacted later by congress defined the state boundary along the Ohio river southeast of Evansville so as to include in Indiana a strip of land containing the Evansville water works, which Kentucky had claimed and against which it had levied taxes.

Perhaps the most important act was that fixing financial responsibility for operators of motor vehicles.

Much needed regulation was instituted for nursing homes for the aged, many of which sprang up after the establishment of old age pensions; they were required to secure licences and to comply with reasonable specifications. Improvement was made in the investment of the common school fund, which was formerly handled by the counties and for the most part put into mortgage loans. The state personnel board, established in 1941 by an act which put a number of Indiana state departments and institutions upon the merit basis, was abolished and substantially the same act was re-enacted with the sole object of changing the membership of the board—the board had been at odds with various state officers and institutions in the two years of its existence.

A most unusual circumstance was the delay in the printing of the acts of the general assembly. In Indiana, acts without an emergency clause become effective only upon proclamation of the governor reciting the fact that printed copies of the acts have been received by all the county clerks of the state. This process has usually been completed in May or June, but in 1943 it was not completed until Nov. 3. The delay caused embarrassments; some of the most important laws required action on or before July 1.

Officers of the state in 1943 were: Henry F. Schricker, governor; Charles M. Dawson, lieutenant governor; Rue J. Alexander, secretary of state; James M. Givens, treasurer; Richard T. James, auditor; James A. Emmert, attorney general; Clement T. Malan, superintendent of public instruction.

Education.—The number of elementary or common schools in the state in 1942–43 was 2,793. Pupils enrolled in them numbered 464,190; there were 11,844 elementary teachers. There were 866 high schools, with 183,189 pupils and 7,843 teachers (these are teachers in senior high schools; there were 1,103 junior high school teachers, for the most part counted as teachers in elementary schools). There was a total of 25,871 teachers in the state.

Public Welfare, Charities, Correction.—The state expended no money on relief in 1943. The amount spent by the townships of the state was much less than in 1942 but the statistics were not available at the end of the year. Receipts of the state for unemployment insurance in the fiscal year 1942–43 were $33,032,-123; benefit payments were $3,815,086; administrative expenses of the system were $1,078,098. The state in 1943 maintained eight institutions for mental cases, including epileptics, nine homes, hospitals, and schools, three university hospitals, a school for the blind, a school for the deaf, and six penal and correctional institutions.

Communication.—Railway mileage in 1941 was 6,928; this figure remained approximately the same in 1942 and 1943. In 1942 there were approximately 10,210 mi. of highways in the state highway system and 70,610 mi. of county roads. Telephones in use numbered 564,794 in 1942.

Banking and Finance.—The total revenue of the state to meet the 1942–43 budget (July 1–June 30) was $48,836,701. The estimate of state revenues for 1943–44 was $36,000,000. Appropriations for 1942–43 amounted to $41,298,161; disbursements for the year amounted to $39,766,619. Appropriations amounting to $46,758,342 were made for the year 1943–44. On June 30, 1943, there was no state indebtedness (there is a constitutional provision strictly limiting state borrowing).

There was a balance of unappropriated surplus in the treasury of $26,977,988.

Two new state banks were organized, the first in more than five years; on June 30, 1943, there were 376 banks, three less than the year before. The state banks had total loans and discounts of $161,195,000; deposits amounted to $802,710,000; total capital was $64,261,000; total surplus amounted to $19,533,-000. State Building and Loan associations numbered 179, with assets of $96,632,000. Credit unions reported to the State Department of Financial Institutions, 135, with assets of $4,007,000. On Oct. 18, 1943, there were in Indiana 221 banks (state and national) members of the federal reserve system. They had total assets of $1,521,591,000, including $782,250,000 in United States government direct and guaranteed obligations, $202,853,000 in loans and $31,153,000 cash in vault. Excluding reciprocal bank balances, they had total deposits of $1,434,659,000 (total liabilities, $1,436,686,000).

Agriculture.—Conditions were not so favourable for agricultural production in 1943 as in 1942, and the (estimated) produc-

Leading Agricultural Products of Indiana, 1943 and 1942

Crop	1943 (est.)	1942
Corn, bu.	200,136,000	216,702,000
Wheat, bu.	15,062,000	13,865,000
Oats, bu.	33,396,000	53,428,000
Soybeans (for beans), bu.	27,702,000	29,757,000
Rye, bu.	1,560,000	1,944,000
White potatoes, bu.	5,100,000	6,480,000
Barley, bu.	1,620,000	2,256,000
All tame hay, tons	2,602,000	2,809,000

tion was somewhat smaller. There was a shortage of rainfall in most parts of the state (6.48 in. at Indianapolis), though planting was late in many parts of the state owing to rainfall in the planting season. There was little damage from frost; damage to the corn crop by the European corn borer was estimated at about $8,000,000.

Manufacturing.—Practically all the manufacturing plants in the state were given over, in whole or in part, to production for the war. The munitions plants and plants erected for the manufacture of war machinery reached full production during 1943; the one exception was the munitions plant in Vermillion county, near Terre Haute, work on which was abandoned before the plant was completed. The total production of manufacturing plants of all kinds during 1943 was the greatest in the history of the state. Among the largest and most important products were munitions, aeroplane engines, propellers and other parts, bomb sights, landing barges, brass and rubber articles, fabricated aluminum, high octane gasoline, and medicines.

Mineral Production.—During the years ending June 30, 1943 and June 30, 1942, respectively, 10,508,027 (9,565,037) tons of coal were mined in Indiana; $10,847,020 ($9,127,060) were paid in wages to a total of 5,678 (5,420) miners; there were 21 (12) fatal accidents in the 51 mines reporting; "strip" mines are not included in these figures; these have a substantial product.

In the first 11 months of 1943, 247 oil and gas wells were completed; the total production of oil was 4,866,500 bbl. (in the year 1942, it was 6,609,000 bbl.).   (C. B. C.)

Indians, American.

Indian claims against the federal government for its failure to make adequate compensation for ceded Indian lands had been a long continuing problem. In some cases Indian lands were relinquished as a result of treaties officially negotiated, but never ratified by the senate. In other cases, treaties were ratified, but their terms were not fully carried out by the government. Sometimes there were errors in the surveys; sometimes whites were given title to lands which the Indians had never relinquished.

On Nov. 12, 1943, Secretary of the Interior Ickes ordered the restoration of more than 1,000,000 ac. of land within the ceded portion of the Wind River reservation in Wyoming—land which had never been sold even though the Indians had been deprived of its use. The court of claims rendered a decision on Aug. 4, 1943 affirming the right of the Confederated Ute tribes to more than 4,000,000 ac. of previously ceded but unsold lands in western Colorado.

For many years, the California Indians had a substantial claim against the government for lands confiscated in the 1850s as the result of treaties which were never ratified by the senate. In 1928, congress passed a bill permitting suit in the court of claims. Such suit was delayed until the accumulated offsets as the result of gratuity appropriations on behalf of the California Indians almost equal the claim. A bill was pending in congress in 1943 to provide an outright appropriation to the California Indians to right this long standing wrong.

On April 19, 1943, the United States supreme court confirmed the earlier decision of the court of claims, rejecting the claims of the Sioux Indians to the Black Hills of the Dakotas, formerly part of the Sioux reservations.

On June 11, 1943, a sub-committee of the Senate Committee of Indian Affairs issued a report (No. 310) recommending that the Indian bureau be abolished. Thirty-three separate recommendations were made, ranging from the disposal of the Indian Bureau library, the immediate closing of all Indian boarding schools, the elimination of the revolving credit fund, and the transfer of all Indian hospitals to the Public Health service, to the termination of federal trusteeship over Indian lands, and the immediate disbursement of individual and tribal funds of almost $70,000,000 dollars on deposit with the U.S. treasury. The most obvious aim of the report was to transfer the expenses of Indian administration from the federal government to the respective states and to open the Indian estate to dissolution. There was little evidence that the report would be implemented by congressional action.

On Sept. 7, 1942 the attorney general of Alaska issued an opinion to the effect that all children born in the territory of Alaska are eligible to attend the territorial schools without discrimination. He stated that while the federal government operated a number of schools for native children, this was a gratuitous service which the territory of Alaska could not demand as a right. This was a much needed interpretation of the Alaska statutes, for until recently the schools of the territory refused to admit full blood native children, although accepting without discrimination the children of mixed parentage. The attorney general further held that determination as to which of two schools, territorial or federal, a child shall attend is a matter of election by the parent and not by the school authorities.

Since all Indians of the United States were given full citizenship in 1924 they were subject to the draft as were all other citizens. However, a large percentage of young Indian men volunteered. Almost 20,000 Indian men and women were in the military service in 1943. All of the armed forces accepted Indians without discrimination, and they were to be found on every front. Through merit they won admission to officers' training schools and many held commissions. Indians constituted a large proportion of the infantry which fought with MacArthur in Bataan, and the 45th division which was in the van of the Sicilian invasion numbers more than 1,500 Indians. Almost every type of award for distinguished services in the army, navy or marine corps was won by Indians.

Despite the fact that they were among the poorest group economically in the United States, individual Indians purchased more than $1,164,000 in treasury and war bonds during 1943 and more than $2,000,000 of tribal funds was similarly invested. More Indians than ever before left the reservations to engage in war work.

In November, the department of the interior signed an agreement with the state of South Carolina and the Catawba Indians providing for the rehabilitation of the tribe. The state agreed to furnish funds for land purchase and improvement and to admit Indian children to public schools and state institutions of higher learning. The Indian service would furnish supervision and guidance.

After the purchase of Alaska, the natives opposed the establishment of reservations in the fear that this might endanger their citizenship rights. However, they found that the General Land office classified as public domain all land in Alaska which had not been either homesteaded or reserved, with the result that native villages, fishing sites and hunting grounds are in the public domain and subject to filing. As a result, numerous requests were being filed for the establishment of reserves to protect these native rights, which are of prehistoric occupancy.

Within the year, eight reserves of varying sizes were declared by the secretary of the interior under the terms of the Alaska act.

(W. W. B.)

Indo-China, French: see FRENCH COLONIAL EMPIRE.

Industrial Health.

Events during 1943 convinced physicians in industry that rehabilitation and re-employment of the disabled were certain to occupy a large share of attention for years to come. The rate of discharges from the armed forces became sufficiently great to provide good insight into the general nature of these problems. Many physical defects unacceptable to the army or navy were found not to interfere in any way with very acceptable work ability. Through well-conducted programs of physical examination and job analysis, industrial physicians were finding it possible to match occupation and restricted physical or mental ability with excellent results. Veterans with a degree of disability which necessitated vocational retraining would obtain these services from the Veterans Bureau. Congress passed the Borden-LaFollette bill, assigning responsibility for rehabilitating nonservice connected disability to the Federal Security agency, using the established state rehabilitation services as major agencies of administration. Legal obstacles to employment of the handicapped were a source of concern to employers and physicians and interest was revived in securing proper relief through amendment of workmen's compensation laws.

The Chamber of Commerce of the United States appointed an advisory health council, one of whose subdivisions was to concern itself with extension of industrial health services. A vigorous attempt was made in Philadelphia jointly by the local chamber of commerce and the county medical society to bring good medical service widely to small plants in that area. A number of experiments in the provision of general medical coverage for workers in addition to necessary medical and hospital attention for compensable disability aroused considerable interest. These steps were necessary in many instances because isolated location or sizeable shifts in industrial population made dependable medical and health facilities in sufficient quantity unavailable. Considerable acceleration in industrial health activity by workers' organizations was noted, due in great part to freezing of wages and hours. The United Automobile Workers established a medical research institute to arrange for physical examination of workers, to investigate industrial environment, to provide health education and to assist in rehabilitation. Union health councils were being advocated as an expression of the workers' increasing interest in their own health.

In one instance, health and safety clauses were included in a proposed employment contract which called for joint labour-management control over industrial health services as well as general medical and hospitalization activities.

A laboratory of industrial hygiene was organized in the army, under the occupational hygiene branch of the surgeon general's office, to facilitate investigation and control over working conditions in arsenals, depots and ordnance plants.

Industrial Hygiene and Toxicology.—Industrial hygienists were still unable to keep pace with the industrial processes and materials that were being introduced, many without suitable toxicologic investigation. Some of the rarer metals came under scrutiny, such as selenium, tellurium and beryllium, and attention was called to potential risks. Warnings were also issued regarding the necessity for suitable safeguards against radium exposures in the currently important dial painting industry. In most respects, however, the bulk of control measures were, of necessity, directed at old offenders.

Industrial Medicine and Surgery.—Maintaining the work force at maximum health and efficiency was complicated mainly by shortages in trained personnel and continued influx of inexperienced or substandard workers into employment. Both of these factors were regarded as substantial contributing causes to increased lost time from accidents and occupational disease. Women in industry continued to present special medical and health problems which were the subject of several investigations. The greatest amount of lost time was found to occur in married women with associated home responsibilities, especially young children. Maintenance of day nurseries proved to be the best immediate solution, although they, in turn, served to produce their own health problems. Elsewhere it was advocated that employment of mothers with children under 14 be prohibited.

The techniques of tuberculosis case-finding in industry were vastly extended. Significant findings were uncovered in 1% to 2% of those examined.

The effects of aluminum dust on disabling silicosis were still under close and expectant observation. Inhalations of this dust were described as producing considerable symptomatic relief. No other essentially new therapeutic principles emerged in the medical and surgical management of industrial disability. Evidence began to accumulate that the X-ray appearance of certain welders' lungs was caused by depositions of iron which produce no functional impairment.

As in other years, personal illnesses not associated with work as a cause were still the most prolific cause of industrial absenteeism.

New occupational disease compensation laws were enacted in Arizona and Oregon. Kansas, Nevada, New Jersey and West Virginia authorized legislative commissions to survey occupational disease and the need for special remedial legislation. (See also ACCIDENTS; DERMATOLOGY; MEDICINE.) (C. M. PN.)

Industrial Production: see BUSINESS REVIEW; WAR PRODUCTION, U.S.

Infantile Paralysis.

During 1943, major outbreaks of infantile paralysis occurred in many parts of the United States. There were over 12,000 cases reported —the largest number since 1931—exceeded in magnitude only by the outbreaks of that year and 1916.

Through assistance from the National Foundation for Infantile Paralysis, Yale university, The Johns Hopkins university, the University of Michigan, the University of California, and the University of Southern California carried on epidemiological field work in the epidemic areas on a basis heretofore impossible. These studies gave added confirmation to the fact that the virus apparently is widespread in nature, being excreted through the intestine of both patients and healthy contact carriers. The virus was again demonstrated in sewage of large cities with serious outbreaks. It was also shown that cases diagnosed as infantile paralysis which occurred in the winter not only suffered from typical symptoms but were proven to be true poliomyelitis by recovery of the virus from the stools.

Many studies aimed at improvement of accurate diagnosis by use of laboratory methods were negative. No real progress in the production of induced immunity was reported during 1943. Several workers reported that in the experimental animal, resistance to artificially produced infection was increased when the nutritional state of the animal was markedly lowered. A significantly greater number of animals with good nutrition were paralyzed within a shorter incubation period than in those groups maintained in the poorer nutrition.

Laboratory studies showed that ozone was an efficacious virucidal agent. It was also shown that the activated sludge process of treatment of sewage effectively inhibited or destroyed virus contaminated material. Improved techniques in the use of the ultracentrifuge allowed for accumulation of great quantities of highly concentrated virus. Histological study of poliomyelitis in the experimental animal demonstrated a heretofore described degeneration of the motor end plates of paralyzed muscles.

The outbreaks of 1943 afforded the first opportunity to apply on a large scale basis the method of treatment advocated by Sister Kenny of Australia. Most workers believed that the application of heat during the acute stages coupled with the earliest possible use of specialized physical therapy in an intensive manner lessened both the severity and duration of pain and contributed materially to the recovery of function with a minimum of structural deformities. (*See* also NERVOUS SYSTEM.)

BIBLIOGRAPHY.—Herman Kabat and Miland E. Knapp, "The Use of Prostigmine in the Treatment of Poliomyelitis," *J.A.M.A.*, 122:989–995 (1943); H. M. Hines, B. Lazere, J. D. Thomson and C. H. Cretzmeyer, "Role of Vitamin E in Neuromuscular Atrophy and Regeneration," *Am. J. of Physiology*, 139:2 (1943); Harve J. Carlson, Gerald M. Ridenour and Charles F. McKhann, "Effect of Activated Sludge Process of Sewage Treatment on Poliomyelitis Virus," *Am. J. Pub. Health*, 33:9 (1943); Raymond E. Lenhard, "The Results of Poliomyelitis in Baltimore," *J. of Bone & Joint Surg.*, XXV:1 (1943); George Y. McClure, "Study of Sensory Ganglia in Macaca Mulatta after Gastrointestinal Administration of Poliomyelitis Virus," *Am. J. of Path.*, XIX:4 (1943); Joseph Moldaver, "Physiopathologic Aspect of the Disorders of Muscles in Infantile Paralysis. Preliminary Report," *J.A.M.A.*, 123:74–77 (1943); Joseph L. Melnick and John R. Paul, "Susceptibility of Cebus Capucina (The South American Ringtail Monkey) and Cercopithecus Cephus (The African Mustache Monkey) to Poliomyelitis Virus," *J. of Exper. Med.*, 78:4 (1943); James H. Peers, "The Pathology of Convalescent Poliomyelitis in Man," *Am. J. of Path.*, XIX:4 (1943); Arthur L. Watkins, Mary A. B. Brazier and Robert S. Schwab, "Concepts of Muscle Dysfunction in Poliomyelitis Based on Electromyographic Studies," *J.A.M.A.*, 123:188–192 (1943); Aladan Farkas, "Paralytic Scoliosis," *J. of Bone & Joint Surg.*, XXV:3 (1943); Thomas B. Turner and Lawrence E. Young, "The Mouse-Adapted Lansing Strain of Poliomyelitis Virus. I. A Study of Neutralizing Antibodies in Acute and Convalescent Serum of Poliomyelitis Patients," *Am. J. of Hygiene*, 37:1 (1943).   (D. W. G.)

Infant Mortality.

Provisional reports of births and deaths in the first year of life indicate that infant mortality in the United States, Canada, and England and Wales for 1943 was the best on record. For the first time, the infant mortality rate for the United States fell below the level of 40 per 1,000 live births. In 1942, the last year of complete record, there were reported 113,418 deaths under one year of age and 2,807,445 births, so that the infant mortality rate was 40.4 per 1,000 live births. Records covering the first nine months of 1943 show a 7% decrease from the same months of the year before. Canada, in 1942, had 14,637 infant deaths and 271,981 births, so that the infant mortality rate was 54 per 1,000 live births. In London and the great towns of England and Wales, infant mortality for the first nine months of 1943 was 3% lower than for the same period of 1942. Deaths under one year of age in England and Wales as a whole in 1942 totalled 32,260; with 654,039 births, the infant mortality rate was 49 per 1,000 live births.

In 1942, Germany had an infant mortality rate of 66 per 1,000 live births, compared to 59 in 1941.

An analysis of infant mortality according to month of birth showed that the chances of survivorship to their first birthday anniversary are best for babies born in summer, which is also the season when most babies are born. The study was based on data for the United States covering the period 1935 to 1937, the latest years for which the pertinent records were available (Statistical Bulletin of the Metropolitan Life Insurance company, June 1943). Among babies born during the summer months, mortality from conditions largely congenital in nature, such as stillbirth, premature birth, congenital debility, and congenital malformation, was at a minimum. This was taken to indicate that summer babies are constitutionally stronger against the hazards

of early infancy than babies born in other seasons. But, in addition, the study indicated that the summer is the best time for a baby to be born. This conclusion was based upon the variation in mortality from environmental causes (all other than those specified above) according to month of birth; this also tended to have its low point for babies born during the summer.

Although it was commonly believed that health conditions are better in rural sections than in urban communities, the contrary situation was found in a study of infant mortality in which both births and deaths were duly allocated to the regular place of residence of the mother. Thus, it was observed that in 1941 the infant mortality rate among the white population in cities of 100,000 or more was, on an average, 33.7 per 1,000 live births. In cities of 10,000 to 100,000, the average rate was noticeably higher, namely 40.3 per 1,000, while the poorest showing was made by the aggregate of towns and villages of 2,500 to 10,000, the rate being 46.6 per 1,000; the rural sections, as a whole, had a rate of 45.0 per 1,000. The better showing of the large cities may be attributed to the accessibility of maternity hospitals and facilities especially designed for the care of pregnant women and newborn children, to the ready presence of specialized physicians, and to the availability of nursing services. In order to improve the situation in rural sections, the states were being encouraged to develop and expand maternity centres in the less densely populated areas. The initial step in this direction was provided for in the Social Security Act of 1935; another important step was taken when the congress appropriated funds, in 1943, to provide medical, hospital and nursing care for the wives and babies of men in the lower ranks of the armed services.

Considered according to race, the infant mortality rates per 1,000 live births in the United States for 1941, the latest year with data available, were: white 41.2; Negro, 74.1. The recorded stillbirth rates per 1,000 live births were: white, 26.5; Negro, 55.4. The proportion of stillbirths not attended by a physician were: white, 2.7%; Negro, 39.9%. In 1941, there were 40.9 illegitimate births per 1,000 live births, the figure for the white population being 19.0 and that for all other races, 176.2.

A study of stillbirths in relation to age of mother and order of child at birth showed that the hazard of stillbirth is least among young women of ages 20 to 29 who are bearing their second child (*Statistical Bulletin* of the Metropolitan Life Insurance company, Oct., 1943). The chances of a stillbirth rise markedly with the age of the mother, particularly so in the case of first births.

A high frequency of stillbirths is also observed among women with large families.

Infant mortality rates per 1,000 live births for the principal causes of death in the United States in 1941 were as follows (the first figure relates to the white population and the second to all other races): premature birth, 12.6, 17.9; influenza and pneumonia, 5.6, 14.0; congenital malformations, 5.0, 2.5; injury at birth, 4.4, 3.5; diarrhoea and enteritis, 3.2, 7.1; other causes, 10.3, 29.8.

BIBLIOGRAPHY.—L. I. Dublin and M. Spiegelman, "The Control of Disease and Death in Infancy and Childhood," *Record of the American Institute of Actuaries* (June 1941); U. S. Public Health Service, *Public Health Reports* (issued weekly); U.S. Bureau of the Census, *Vital Statistics —Special Reports and State Summaries* (issued irregularly), *Monthly Vital Statistics Bulletin Current Mortality Analysis* (issued monthly), *Annual Reports of Vital Statistics*, and *Vital Statistics Rates, 1900–1940*; Population Association of America, *Population Index* (issued quarterly at Princeton, N.J.).   (A. J. Lo.)

Infantry: *see* MUNITIONS OF WAR; WORLD WAR II.

Inflation: *see* BUSINESS REVIEW; CONSUMER CREDIT; PRICES; UNITED STATES.

Information Board, United Nations: *see* UNITED NATIONS INFORMATION BOARD.

Ingersoll, Royal Eason

(1883–), U.S. naval officer, was born June 20 in Washington, D.C., the son of Rear Adm. Royal Rodney Ingersoll. He was appointed to the Naval academy from Indiana, 1901, and after graduation was assigned to several U.S. warships. He was on duty at the Naval academy, 1911–13, when he received orders to join the Asiatic fleet. He went to the office of naval operations in 1916, and during World War I received the navy cross for his services in organizing, developing and directing the communications office of the navy department. Pres. Roosevelt in 1938 nominated him rear admiral, jumping him over the heads of a dozen senior officers. On Dec. 20, 1941, Secretary of Navy Knox appointed him commander of the Atlantic fleet to succeed Adm. Ernest J. King, who was designated commander in chief of the U.S. fleet. Under his command, in 1942 and 1943, the Atlantic fleet not only did extensive convoy duty but also played an important part in the invasion of North Africa, Sicily and Italy. On July 3, 1942, Pres. Roosevelt named Ingersoll for promotion to full admiral.

Ingram, William ("Navy Bill")

(1897?–1943), U.S. marine officer and football coach, was graduated from the United States Naval academy in 1920. A star football player, he joined the navy after graduation, but resigned in 1922 to become coach of William and Mary college, Williamsburg, Va. He then accepted a contract as football coach at the University of Indiana in 1923, remaining there until 1925; in January 1926 he returned to his alma mater as football coach, a post he held for five years. He was then coach at California, 1931–34. In 1935, "Navy Bill" quit coaching, became an executive in a grocery chain and was sworn into the marine corps in Jan. 1943 as a major in the procurement division.

He died in Los Gatos, Calif., June 2.

Inland Waterways: see CANALS AND INLAND WATERWAYS.
Inner Mongolia: see MONGOLIA.

Inönü, Ismet

(ISMET PASHA) (1884–), Turkish statesman, was born in Smyrna (Izmir) on Sept. 24. At the age of 12, he entered an artillery school in Constantinople, later studied at the General Staff college, and had risen to the rank of a full general in 1926. During World War I, he saw action in Palestine against the British and was Kemal Ataturk's chief of staff during the campaign against the Russians in eastern Turkey. When the Greeks invaded Turkey in 1921, Inönü again acted as Ataturk's chief of staff. He defeated the Greeks twice at Inönü and took the name of the battlefield after Ataturk decreed that all Turks must have last names. When the Turkish republic was proclaimed on Oct. 29, 1923, Ataturk became president and Inönü was made premier. Although Inönü approved Ataturk's radical measures to westernize Turkey, he himself was more conservative and disagreed frequently with his chief. Inönü resigned unexpectedly in 1937, but after Ataturk's death in 1938, he was unanimously chosen president by the Grand National assembly.

During the early part of World War II, he carefully avoided offending either Germany or the U.S.S.R. In late 1943, he went to Cairo to confer with President Roosevelt and Prime Minister Churchill and on Dec. 7, the three leaders proclaimed the "closest unity" of Turkey with the United Nations.

Insects: see ENTOMOLOGY.
Instalment Selling: see CONSUMER CREDIT.
Insulin: see DIABETES.

Insurance.

Accident and Health.—Accident and health insurance continued to show substantial gains in the United States in 1943, with an estimated 10 to 12% increase in premium income, bringing the total to approximately $400,000,-000. About 55% of employed persons had some form of accident and health coverage, compared to 20% in 1934.

Group and payroll deduction coverages continued to show a marked increase, although the rate of personnel expansion in war plants was more stabilized. There was a great increase in insurance on employed women. Railroad ticket accident business showed a 35% increase to approximately $2,500,000 in premiums.

Caution in underwriting war workers and employed women was shown because of a probable decline in postwar earnings. Some advocated restricting indemnity in such cases to 50 to 60% instead of the usual 80%. In view of satisfactory experience on servicemen while still in the U.S., companies continued their liberal attitude in keeping policies of servicemen in force as long as they remained in the country. Plans were made for liberal reinstatement provisions without penalty for servicemen returning to civilian life. (C. D. Sp.)

Great Britain.—Some contraction in the volume of accident and miscellaneous insurance continued during 1943, largely because of the drop in motor premiums caused by the laying-up of motor vehicles, and the operation of the 20% rebate allowed off private car premiums. This was accompanied by an improvement in the experience, and the accident results disclosed during the year were uniformly favourable. Road accidents tended to decline through smaller traffic and greater familiarity with blackout conditions. Workmen's compensation insurance expanded especially in the heavier industries, where the war effort required the payment of increased wages upon which insurance premiums were based. Periods of incapacity tended to be shorter in wartime with a consequent relief on the claim strain. Personal accident insurance was in demand in connection with certain classes of war work, but the ordinary business of this class was not in so great demand. (C. E. G.)

Automobile.—Automobile insurance premium volume in the United States was down about 20% in 1943. Most of this reduction was chargeable to the eastern territory, where severe gasoline rationing caused many private automobiles to be retired from service. In addition, further reductions in national rates meant less premium per unit insured.

The frequency of accidents continued to decline during 1943, as did the number of fatalities, but a marked increase in the number of persons injured per accident partially offset this reduction. There was also a definite increase in the cost per liability claim because of inflationary tendencies, and higher repair costs and automobile values had the same effect on property damage, fire and collision losses. In spite of these factors, the companies continued to show favourable underwriting results. (G. E. Ho.)

Fire.—There were two outstanding events in regard to U.S. fire insurance in the year 1943. The first was in regard to the War Damage corporation (*see* below). At the close of its first year, July 1, 1943, so few losses had been sustained that it was suggested that no premiums be charged for the next year; but this plan was not adopted. No serious losses occurred until Jan. 3, 1944, when the United States steamer "Turner" exploded, broke in two and sank off the northern part of the New Jersey coast. The explosion was so great that there was considerable damage to glass on the Jersey coast. Within a week public announcement was made in the press that the War Damage corporation would assume liability.

The second event was the adoption of the standard fire insurance policy effective July 1, 1943. This action occurred in the state of New York but the new policy, because of its simplicity and its broader coverage, appealed to other states so quickly that at the close of 1943 it had been adopted by some thirty.

According to the *Insurance Year Book, 1943*, published by the Spectator company, premium receipts during 1942—the last year for which complete statistics were available—from all forms of underwriting—stock, mutual, Lloyds and reciprocal—amounted to $1,396,000,000. The total income including interest, rents, etc., amounted to $1,534,000,000. The losses paid amounted to $727,000,000 and the total disbursements, including all forms of expenses, amounted to $1,424,000,000. (*See* also FIRES AND FIRE LOSSES.)   (E. R. H.)

Hospitalization.—Membership in nonprofit Blue Cross hospital service plans passed 13,000,000 by the end of 1943, enrolled in 77 plans in 36 states of the U.S.A. and 3 Canadian provinces. Enrolment of 500,000 new members during the third quarter of 1943 was greater than for any quarter in Blue Cross history.

The year 1943 was marked by a trend toward consolidation of plans to cover state-wide areas; by absorption of "single-hospital" plans in community-wide programs; and by extension of the movement toward uniform rates and benefits among plans.

(A. G. S.)

Life.—During 1943, the legal reserve life insurance companies of the United States and Canada increased their investments in government bonds by about $3,000,000,000, an amount greater than the increase for the year in the companies' total assets. At the end of 1943, the total life insurance (excluding reinsurance) in force in these legal reserve companies was estimated at more than $146,000,000,000, about 7% greater than the amount outstanding at the end of 1942. New paid-for coverage issued during 1943 amounted to over $13,000,000,000. The assets of the companies at the end of 1943 reached an estimated total of more than $40,000,000,000, after paying or crediting to policyholders and beneficiaries about $2,600,000,000 during 1943.

The mortality experienced in the United States and Canada during 1943 continued favourable, although it was not quite as low as in 1942. War deaths resulting directly from enemy action comprised less than 2% of total deaths among ordinary policyholders during 1943, and a considerably smaller proportion among industrial policyholders. An increase in the mortality from pneumonia during 1943 marked a reversal of the sharp downward trend which had been in evidence each year since the introduction of serums and sulfa drugs in the treatment of this disease. The record for tuberculosis continued to be generally favourable. In spite of the increased industrial activity in connection with the war production program, the death rate from occupational accidents remained relatively stable.

The interest rate earned during 1943 on the aggregate of life insurance companies' assets followed the downward trend characteristic of preceding years. This reflected to a marked degree the low yield obtainable on government bonds, in which as much as one-third of the assets of the companies had been invested.

The year 1943 witnessed a legislative development of great significance to U.S. life insurance, in the enactment by some 14 states—as part of a nation-wide legislative program—of new standard valuation and nonforfeiture benefit bills. The proposed legislation was recommended by the National Association of Insurance Commissioners and endorsed by many insurance organizations. It provided for the use of modern mortality tables, and dissociated to a greater extent than did current laws, the minimum nonforfeiture value requirements from the policy valuation basis. It also provided a new method of determining minimum nonforfeiture values under which such values were more nearly related to the real equities of the policyholder at the time of default than had been true under existing nonforfeiture legislation.

The war was directly responsible for the incorporation of war risk provisions limiting the insurance company's liability in event of death while in military service. Prior to the entry of the United States into World War II, only a very small proportion of life insurance policies in force on citizens of the U.S. contained or retained any limitation of the life insurance benefits on account of war service or required the payment of extra premiums in such event. While the companies were therefore absorbing the war risk on practically all of their existing policyholders in 1943, the safety of the insurance of the general body of policyholders demanded that the companies take the necessary precautionary measures in respect to new insurance.

BIBLIOGRAPHY.—*The Spectator (Life) Insurance Year Book* (1943); *Report* of the Superintendent of Insurance of the Dominion of Canada, for 1943, vol. ii (Life Insurance Companies, Ottawa, Ont.)   (L. A. L.)

Marine and War Risk.—The war continued to be the most important factor in marine insurance during 1943. Many new ideas were adopted to enable underwriters to meet the needs of importers and exporters trading in wartime. One was the war risk extension clause which involved amending the terms of the war risk coverage to permit cargoes to be covered against war risk on shore at transshipping ports beyond the 15-day period originally allowed. Frequently ships were diverted from their expected routes and cargo was discharged for transshipment. If the goods were kept on docks or in a warehouse over 15 days before being loaded on an on-carrying steamer, the war risk insurance lapsed. All this might be without any knowledge of the owners, who automatically lost their insurance protection. To enable a shipper to have a war and marine risk cover that would be continuously in force from the start to finish of a voyage regardless of interruptions or transshipments, extension clauses were agreed upon and shippers acquired continuous protection. New rate schedules were adopted, combining in one additional rate the surcharge for the additional marine risks due to war conditions and the charge for the extended coverage at transshipping points. There was also issued a schedule of charges for the extended war risk insurance coverage, so that the shipper knew in advance exactly what his continuous cover would cost, regardless of all delays on the voyage.

Changes were made in the f.c. and s. clause in both the United States and Great Britain. The standard f.c. and s. clause in use throughout the world for many years read in part "Warranted free of capture, seizure . . . also from the consequences of hostilities or warlike operations." A number of disputes arose as to what was intended by the words "consequences of hostilities or warlike operations." Several types of losses, such as a collision in a convoy at night due to the ships running without lights, were capable of being interpreted either as war or marine losses. In the early part of 1943 the British Government War Risk bureau and British commercial underwriters agreed on a war coverage and a corresponding f.c. and s. clause for marine policies whereby all these borderline cases were to be considered as coming under marine policies and the war risk cover was limited to losses actually caused directly by a hostile act by or against a belligerent power.

The War Shipping administration and commercial underwriters in the United States were invited to agree to the new clauses, but the WSA, after consultation with the Office of Price Administration, declined to do this, as they feared it might result in higher marine rates on certain imported essential commodities on which they were endeavouring to keep prices down. Therefore, the WSA proposed a new definition of "consequences of hostilities" under which all these borderline cases would be considered war losses. This was the first instance in years where there was a difference in conditions in the ocean cargo policies issued in the United States and Great Britain.

Because war losses in the Atlantic on account of submarines decreased steadily during 1943, war risk rates also decreased. Cargo underwriters showed a profit on their war risk business, on which they had a heavy loss in 1942. Hull underwriters, however, had a poor year, largely because of the unprecedented number of collisions. Rates on renewals were increased, but did not keep pace with the increased losses due to operating under wartime conditions. A series of discussions between the War Shipping administration and the hull syndicate resulted in the "Wartime-hull Insurance Agreement (1943)," under which the syndicate agreed to insure U.S. privately-owned, ocean-going vessels, without any navigating limits or trading warranties, but subject to the new f.c. and s. clause excluding the so-called borderline cases.

(S. D. McC.)

War Damage.—By act of U.S. Congress approved March 27, 1942, Reconstruction Finance corporation had been authorized to supply War Damage corporation with funds in an aggregate amount not exceeding $1,000,000,000, for the purpose of providing through insurance reasonable protection against loss of or damage to property resulting from enemy attack or from the action of the military, naval or air forces of the United States in resisting enemy attack. To avoid the necessity of creating a complete governmental organization to handle the program, the corporation entered into separate agreements with 546 fire insurance companies pursuant to which such companies agreed to act as "fiduciary agents" for the corporation in receiving applications and premiums, issuing policies and otherwise handling the program. The participating companies had a 10% interest in the operating profits or losses of the program, subject to a limit of $20,000,000. As of June 30, 1943, premiums collected aggregated approximately $132,200,000, and it was estimated that approximately $136,700,000,000 of War Damage corporation insurance was in force on that date. In excess of 5,000,000 policies had been issued by the corporation.

Effective Dec. 21, 1942, the corporation had made available insurance on money and securities through the facilities of 88 casualty and surety insurance companies likewise acting as "fiduciary agents" of War Damage corporation. As of June 30, 1943, premiums from the money and securities program aggregated approximately $600,000, and it was estimated that approximately $3,200,000,000 of War Damage corporation insurance covering money and securities was in force under approximately 3,000 policies.

War Damage corporation was also authorized to compensate for loss or damage to property sustained during the period from Dec. 6, 1941 to July 1, 1942, without premium or other charge, subject to the limitations prescribed in the act. The corporation by 1943 had investigated and adjusted claims for loss sustained during this period as a result of enemy attack or action of the military, naval or air forces of the United States in resisting enemy attack in the Hawaiian Islands, Alaska and certain other areas within the geographical purview of the act. Practically all of the Hawaiian eligible claims had been paid by the end of 1943. The Alaskan claims were in process of adjustment and payment, as were certain marine claims. As of Dec. 18, 1943, $255,581.97 had been paid to compensate for loss sustained during the period from Dec. 6, 1941 to July 1, 1942. (W. L. C.)

Great Britain.—The various forms of insurance against loss or damage due to war risks were transacted during 1943 without any alteration in scope, but with certain revisions in premium rating. These revisions were mostly in a downward direction, because the course of the experience was much more favourable than during 1940 and 1941, when these insurance schemes first came into operation. The insurance of vessels or cargoes at sea, carried on partly by the War Risks Insurance office and partly by private insurers was rated according to a schedule, with varying rates according to the voyage. This schedule was revised several times during 1943, following the improved course of the war, and some substantial reductions were possible in rates for Mediterranean voyages and also in some parts of the far east. Atlantic voyages too could be covered at moderate rates.

Rates of premium for war risk insurance on land were made for set periods and fluctuated less often. Under the commodity scheme the rate of 5s.% per month, fixed on April 3, 1942, was reduced to 2s. 6d.% per month from March 3, 1943. After Dec. 3, 1942, policies could be obtained for three-monthly periods. Under the business scheme applying to trade plant, machinery and fixtures, policies were issued for six-monthly periods. The rate of 10s.% for the period fixed on Oct. 1, 1942, was reduced to 5s.% on April 1, 1943. Private chattel insurances ran for 12 months from any date, and in March 1943 the rates were fixed at 10s.% per annum on the first £2000, 15s.% on the next £1000 and 20s.% on the next £7000, being one-half of the rates previously in force. (*See also* VETERANS' ADMINISTRATION.)

(C. E. G.)

Insurance, Crop: *see* AGRICULTURE.
Insurance, Old Age: *see* SOCIAL SECURITY.

Inter-American Affairs, Office of the Coordinator of.

Operations of the U.S. Office of the Coordinator of Inter-American Affairs for 1943 group themselves into two broad classifications—wartime economic development work with related health, sanitation and food supply programs, and informational activities involving the press, radio, motion pictures and education.

A basic program was formulated to protect the health of armed forces at bases throughout the hemisphere, as well as that of war and agricultural workers in certain strategic regions of the American republics. Health and sanitation projects, developed by the United States jointly with the governments of 18 other American republics, included control of malaria and other tropical diseases, drinking water and sewage disposal projects, and programs for training medical and nursing personnel.

The food supply program for 1943 centred in regions of the hemisphere where the war made large military concentrations necessary. Migrations of workers to areas of strategic material production further aggravated food shortages. Agricultural experts, crop specialists and technicians were loaned by the U.S. to some of the other American republics.

Another important economic activity concerned hemisphere transportation problems, created largely by war disruptions. Cooperative projects were undertaken to solve these problems as well as those arising from greatly increased shipments of war materials.

The informational activities of the Coordinator's office furthered the exchange of all types of knowledge and information to aid mutual understanding and unity among the American republics. Wide distribution was given to news of inter-American significance. An illustrated magazine, *En Guardia,* was distributed in Spanish and Portuguese to a selected list of 500,000 subscribers in Central and South America, and a quarterly edition of this magazine was distributed in French in Haiti.

Radio coverage was also extensive. Besides news broadcasts—for which a special inter-American news report was provided 24 hours daily, seven days a week, other programs were broadcast or transcribed for rebroadcast. Special scripts dealing with the history, culture, resources, and war activities of Central and South American republics were furnished weekly during 1943 to more than 500 radio stations in the hemisphere. Wide use of motion pictures was also made during 1943, particularly of 16 mm. educational and documentary films.

During 1943, the Inter-American Educational foundation was organized by the Coordinator's office to develop a program of hemisphere education. Co-operation was effected through the various ministries of education and through existing educational organizations.

A wide variety of inter-American activities were sponsored in the United States during the year through the establishment of Inter-American centres in strategic regional cities. Here reliable informational materials—pamphlets, motion pictures, graphic materials, exhibits and speakers—were made available for individuals and groups.   (N. A. R.)

Inter-American Defense Board.
The Inter - American Defense board represents a significant and definitely objective step in the evolution of inter-American co-operation, being the first attempt at collaboration in the military field through a body of representatives of all the American republics.

The board was established on March 30, 1942, pursuant to Resolution XXXIX of the Third Meeting of the Ministers of Foreign Affairs of the American Republics at Rio de Janeiro, Jan. 15–28, 1942, which recommended "the immediate meeting in Washington of a commission composed of military and naval technicians appointed by each of the Governments to study and recommend to them the measures necessary for the defense of the Continent."

The membership of the board is composed of distinguished army, navy and air officers, carefully chosen for their military and diplomatic experience. Numbered among the delegates are former chiefs of staff and former cabinet members. The headquarters of the board are in the Federal Reserve building in Washington, and it operates under the auspices of the Pan American union. The board holds its regular meetings on the second and fourth Tuesdays of each month, in addition to numerous meetings of its various committees. Its recommendations are transmitted in the form of resolutions to the governments of the American republics.

The organization and functions of the board are outlined in its regulations. Under these regulations, the chief of the delegation of the country in which the board is located is *ex officio* the chairman of the board. Provision is also made for a co-ordinator and a secretary general. Officers of the board in 1943 were: Lieut. Gen. Stanley D. Embick, U.S.A., chairman; Maj. Gen. Blanton Winship, U.S.A., co-ordinator, and Col. Edward H. Porter, U.S.A., secretary general.   (B. Wp.)

Inter-American Highway: *see* ROADS AND HIGHWAYS.
Interior, U.S. Department of: *see* GOVERNMENT DEPARTMENTS AND BUREAUS.

Interior Decoration.
The field of interior design was limited in many ways during 1943 because of shortages and wartime restrictions. Building was still at a standstill, but the designing of interiors continued and showed considerable originality, with the trend more and more away from copying the traditional and toward original contemporary design. Restrictions on the manufacturing of furniture per se, that is, the general type, gave impetus to designers to break away from the usual and create new designs more suitable to the times. An outstanding influence was the influx of low cost war workers' homes which necessitated the designing of simple, easily constructed and inexpensive furniture.

The outstanding motive behind decoration was to create an

U.S. SOUTHWEST DESIGN was a new trend in interior decoration in 1943. The table in this dining room is of native New Mexican pine, the banquettes of yellow satin and the chandelier of wrought iron. The Navajo rug has brown, yellow and black shades

atmosphere suitable for present day living, from which emanated a style that was comfortable, convenient and pleasing to the eye. For a more detailed description of the trend some of the important features of interior decoration are outlined below.

Wall Treatment, Interior Trim and Floors.—Walls were most frequently painted or papered though wood panelling, and prefabricated wood veneers on wallboard were increasingly popular. Woodwork was either painted or of the same material as the walls. Various hardwood and tile flooring continued to be used extensively.

Floor Coverings.—Carpets and rugs were predominantly plain. Selection of material and colour was very limited, the colours running to the lighter shades, and cotton textures were more accessible than the ever popular wool floor coverings. Textured weaves continued to be most popular.

Window Treatment.—Windows were treated simply, the object being to make them harmonious with the room. A draw curtain usually covering the entire wall where windows occurred was a satisfactory treatment as it could be drawn aside to allow full benefit of light and air or when closed give a continuous line around the room. With a strip of fluorescent lights concealed above the curtains a soft, diffused light gave an interesting effect when the curtain was drawn at night. Materials were generally plain light weight, often textured, cottons or cotton and artificial silk mixtures in colours blending with the walls. Printed chintzes and cottons were still seen though not so frequently as in former years. Venetian blinds were still popular though they began to be supplanted to some extent by the draw curtain.

Furniture.—Furniture designed to fit the needs of contemporary living was increasingly evident. Simple functional pieces formed the setting of most interiors with units built in where convenient, allowing more space and creating unity between furnishings and architecture. The scale of furniture was lighter and less massive than that of former years. Light wood finishes such as pine, birch, bleached walnut and mahogany were the most popular.

Furniture Coverings.—Fabrics were affected by wartime restrictions in many ways, thereby limiting the field somewhat.

Colours were limited and new designs were infrequent as the materials themselves were so difficult to obtain. There were few new upholstery fabrics. Plain, textured weaves and bright floral prints continued to be seen most often.

Decorative Accents.—Lamps and other decorative accessories followed the trend of the time and remained simple and functional. Unexaggerated forms and clear, bright colours gained importance over the more elaborate, intricate bric-a-brac seen so often in previous years. Old Chinese pottery fitted in well with the simple contemporary interiors, and a Chinese influence was often felt in their decoration. Various types of plants, such as large tropical varieties, played an important part in giving an interesting, livable atmosphere to homes. (G. M. J.)

International Labour Conference: *see* INTERNATIONAL LABOUR ORGANIZATION.

International Labour Organization.
Temporary headquarters of the I.L.O. continued to be at Montreal.

Merchant Seamen and the War (Studies and Reports, series P., no. 5, pp. 154) made public for the first time the proceedings of a session of the Joint Maritime commission—the 12th, London, 1942, at which this body of shipowners and seamen adopted a set of proposals for safety measures for seamen in wartime, many of which were put into force by the governments of the United States and Great Britain. It brought a step nearer the realization of an international maritime charter to be embodied in and enforced as an I.L.O. convention. Much work was done by the I.L.O. at the request of the Joint Maritime commission to secure wider ratification of the I.L.O. maritime conventions.

The consultative subcommittee of the J.M.C. met in London in May and urged more rapid implementation of the resolutions of the J.M.C. affecting the life and work of merchant seamen. The governing body and the office agreed to press for further ratifications and to study the possibility of ratifications on the basis of collective agreements, to continue collection of information on the development of safety measures in wartime, to urge representation of the shipping industry, along with the I.L.O., at the peace conference, and in every way to carrying out the resolutions of the J.M.C. They brought to the attention of the governments of member states the resolutions of the J.M.C. and asked for detailed information on the measures taken or contemplated on ensuring equality of treatment between seafarers, and on the subject matter of other resolutions. The governing body decided to convene the next session of the J.M.C. in 1944.

Other meetings of importance held in 1943 by or with the active participation of the I.L.O. included: (1) The 7th Canada-U.S. meeting on labour supply, New York, Feb. 13–14, at which manpower development and labour-management were discussed on the basis of another important publication of the year, *Joint Production Committees in Great Britain* (S. and R., ser. A, no. 42, p. 74 and chart); (2) Conference of the Joint Canadian-American Women's Committee on International Relations, Montreal, May 15–17; (3) First Inter-American Population Congress, Mexico City, Oct. 12–21, at which Pierre Waelbroeck, chief of the labour conditions, employment and migration section, represented the I.L.O. and presented two papers: (a) "Migration Problems of Postwar Europe," based on *The Displacement of Population in Europe*, by Eugene M. Kulischer (S. and R., series O, no. 8, pp. 171) which had been prepared for, and edited by Waelbroeck's section, and published by the I.L.O. in Sept.; (b) "The Organization of Migration in Relation to Postwar Reconstruction"; (4) At a public hearing (June 11) of the enquiry into industrial relations and wage conditions, upon invitation of the Canadian Na-

tional War Labour board, the I.L.O. presented a memorandum on the experience of other countries in regard to legal regulation of collective agreements, conciliation in labour disputes, the right to strike, etc.

The I.L.O. was represented by Acting Director Phelan at the first session of the council of the United Nations Relief and Rehabilitation administration at Atlantic City, N.J., in November at the invitation of Dean Acheson, its chairman.

In addition to the publications already cited, Studies and Reports issued in 1943 were: *Labor Conditions in War Contracts* (ser. D, no. 23, pp. 74) in revised edition; *International Standardization of Labor Statistics*, (ser. N, no. 25, pp. 169). Other important publications were: the first two issues of a new series of pamphlets on postwar reconstruction, *The Health of Children in Occupied Europe* (43 pp.); *Manpower Mobilization for Peace* (78 pp.); *The Co-operative Movement in the Americas* (59 pp.); *Labor Problems in Bolivia* (Report of the Joint Bolivian-U.S. Labor commission, Spanish and English texts, 96 pp.); and *Year Book of Labor Statistics* (1942, 7th year, 222 pp.); *Intergovernmental Commodity Control Agreements* (221 pp.).

The serials, the *International Labour Review* (monthly), and the *Industrial Safety Survey*, and the *Legislative Series* (about 900 pp. in 1943), both quarterlies, were continued at peak output, and reprints of many important articles in all three were widely circulated.

Great Britain ratified two conventions: No. 64, Contracts of Employment, and No. 65, Penal Sanctions, both relating to indigenous workers. This made the total number of ratifications on Nov. 30, 886.

The governing body of the I.L.O. held its 91st session in London, Dec. 16–20. After taking action on the tripartite basis on many of the far-flung services of the office in wartime it voted to convene the 26th session of the International Labour conference in Philadelphia on April 20, 1944, with the following agenda:

1. Future Policy, Program and Status of the I.L.O.
2. Recommendations to the United Nations for Present and Postwar Social Policy.
3. Organization of Employment in the Transition from War to Peace.
4. Social Security: Principles and Problems Arising out of War.
5. Minimum Standards of Social Policy in Dependent Territories.

Also significant was the maintenance of the continuity of French membership. The commissioner of labour for the French Committee of National Liberation, Adrien Tixier, a former assistant director of the I.L.O., occupied at this meeting the French seat on the governing body. The president of Haiti took steps to retain Haitian membership in the I.L.O. when its resignation of membership in the League of Nations would become effective. (*See* also CHILD WELFARE; LEAGUE OF NATIONS; REFUGEES.) (S. McC. L.)

International Law.
The problems of international law arising during 1943 revolved mainly about the development of economic war, which reached a point never heretofore known. Not only did this form of warfare impair many old conceptions concerning international law, but its results threatened to carry over into peacetime, and thus to make a restoration of friendly relations or economic peace difficult or doubtful. This process began in World War I. But in comparing the two wars, law, both between belligerents and between belligerents and neutrals, was then far more respected than it was in 1943.

The Connally resolution and those adopted at Moscow, Cairo and Tehran, also raised doubts about the future. While assuring unity of action during World War II, they promised "peace and security" after the war, to be obtained by the united force of the victors against "aggressors." "Aggressor" is a political, not a legal term, and is usually identified with the dissatisfied. The attempt to produce peace by force, the "hue and cry" theory, undid the League of Nations. Russia, Great Britain and the United States seemed again to be subscribing to a theory which had demonstrated its war-provoking tendencies.

Economic War.—In the United States economic war began by the freezing of the bank accounts of citizens of Norway and Denmark (5 Fed. Reg. 1400) and then of all the European countries—except Turkey—after Germany overran and occupied much of Europe. Control was tightened by requiring reports covering all funds owned by aliens, resident or nonresident (T.F.R. 300). More than $7,000,000,000 was reported as owned by nationals of "blocked" countries. This "freezing" was designed to prevent American-controlled funds from reaching the axis powers, the military occupants of several countries, but also served to deprive the owners of access to their funds. This was even applied to residents of neutral countries, like Sweden and Switzerland—and, if proclaimed, residents of the United States—but was ameliorated by the extension of licences from the treasury. In March 1941, the so-called Lend-Lease act extended American governmental aid to countries fighting the axis, assistance amounting to over $18,000,000,000 at the end of Nov. 1943. In July 1941, the freezing of funds was extended to Japan and its nationals.

After the United States entered the war, the alien property custodian took over German, Japanese and Italian direct investments, amounting near the end of 1943 to some $130,000,000. In July 1942, an Inter-American Conference on Systems of Economic and Financial Control recommended to all the countries of this continent the liquidation of all local businesses friendly to the axis. At the same time, long blacklists of citizens or firms of nonenemy countries were prepared in the United States and Great Britain, by which nationals of those countries were prohibited from entering into any trade relations with the citizens or firms on the blacklist. In Britain, for example, 1,164 Swiss firms were blacklisted up to the end of 1943. These measures were independent of the so-called "blockade," designed to keep any commodities out of the hands of the axis powers. Resident enemy nationals might by proclamation of the president be interned for the duration of World War II.

These measures were directed not merely against enemy nationals or persons domiciled in enemy countries, but under the first and second war powers act were directed against those who were thought not to manifest "loyalty" to the Allied cause. (Americans of Japanese origin were evacuated from the west coast and subjected to restrictions.) It was a form of "boycott" which cut across national lines and might even affect citizens of the boycotting countries. How far the Latin American countries had acted upon the recommendation of the Inter-American Conference on Systems of Economic and Financial Control was not known at the end of 1943.

These measures irritated neutral countries considerably. The restrictions on the axis necessarily involved, as in World War I, restrictions on the importations allowed to neutrals. Sweden, Switzerland, Spain and Turkey were in continuous negotiation with both belligerents for permission to import needed materials, against an assurance that these materials would not reach the enemy. Switzerland was especially irritated at the Allied effort to limit closely the trade between Switzerland and Germany, which she contended was within her legal right and necessary to Swiss economic life. By penalizing Swiss firms for undertaking this normally privileged trade, Switzerland claimed that her independence was impaired. Since only a few countries in the world possessing overseas transportation facilities were in a position to apply blacklists and thus regulate to some extent the trade of neutrals, the question was raised as to the future of the small state, and whether its independence in time of war is more than nominal.

The fate of the sequestrated investments, direct and indirect, could not be determined in 1943. Probably all the belligerents seized or controlled enemy-owned property, giving an expanded definition to the concept "enemy." Few countries seemed to have confiscated the property. A newspaper report stated that Colombia nationalized axis trademarks, and the alien property custodian undertook to license to Americans patents owned by enemies and nationals of countries occupied by the enemy. Congress did not indicate a confiscatory policy. The Gearhart bill proposed confiscation while purporting to avoid that conclusion, by providing, as did Article 297 of the treaty of Versailles, that the enemy countries would compensate their own nationals for their losses. The author of the provision, ex-solicitor Nielsen of the department of state, doubted whether it ameliorated the obloquy of confiscation. Confiscation would impair, as Cordell Hull remarked, the interests of American citizens and the future of foreign investment (letter to Senator Capper, 31 *A.J.I.L.* 680).

Nonbelligerency.—This term has come into common parlance without any clear appreciation of its meaning. It seems designed to indicate a neutral's status of favouritism toward one belligerent while yet avoiding participation in the war. For example, a neutral country, like some South American countries, undertakes to extend facilities to one belligerent, like the United States, which the law of neutrality would foreclose. The term received currency when Germany and Italy intervened in the Spanish civil war to help Franco defeat the loyalists. In itself it does not indicate what measures the nonbelligerent may adopt to express his favouritism. It is, therefore, not a legal but a political term. It beclouds the clarity which international law was designed to afford as to the status of any country in time of war. The unneutral acts committed in the name of nonbelligerency expose the nonbelligerent to the dangers of war. It is used to justify departures from neutrality and breaches of the law. If it conveys the impression that such breaches are privileged or lawful, it is deceptive. It is a further impairment of law.

The Doctrine of Nonrecognition.—The refusal to recognize facts, which bulks large in the philosophy of the new theory of identifying peace with the maintenance of the *status quo*, operated strangely in numerous American cases decided during the period 1940–43, in connection with the refusal of the United States to recognize the absorption by soviet Russia in 1940 of the Baltic countries of Estonia, Latvia and Lithuania, later militarily occupied by Germany. Numerous ships belonging to citizens of the Baltic countries were located in American ports. The soviet government, under its established principles, undertook to confiscate or nationalize these ships. Then commenced a series of suits by the old owners or, as their representatives, the consul of Estonia, Latvia or Lithuania, still recognized by the United States, as against some agent of the soviet government, both claiming title. Since the annexation was not recognized by the United States, the courts found one reason or another for refusing to recognize the title of the soviet agent. Since the old owner had nevertheless been in fact displaced, they declined to recognize him as the entitled claimant, either because he had failed to prove ownership or because letters rogatory would not be issued to the soviet supreme court, making inquiry into the fact of ownership. Sometimes the libellant was an agent of the soviet government whom the courts regarded as not the real party in interest. It might have been easier to refuse to recognize the soviet title to property in American waters on the simple ground that confiscatory decrees, even of a recognized government, operating on property in the United States, are contrary to American public policy. Even this established doctrine is beclouded by *United States* v. *Pink*, 315 U.S. 203. The confusion entailed in American courts by the refusal of the U.S. government to recognize the soviet government down to 1933 was perpetuated by the cases arising out of the refusal to recognize the annexation by the U.S.S.R. of the Baltic republics. *See* H. W. Briggs, "Non-Recognition in the Courts: The Ships of the Baltic Republics," 37 *A.J.I.L.* 585.

Enemy "Native, Citizen, Denizen or Subject."—On Aug. 18, 1943, the United States court of appeals for the second circuit decided three cases interpreting the term "native, citizen, denizen or subject" of Germany under the Alien act of July 6, 1798, and clarified some of the legal conditions attaching to collective naturalization. Without stating the full facts of the cases, discussed in the opinions and in 37 *A.J.I.L.* 634, the court held that the annexation of Austria by Germany in 1938 could not extend German citizenship to a citizen of Austria who had left that country prior to the annexation and was a permanent resident of the United States. *United States* ex rel. *Schwarzkopf* v. *Uhl, District Director of Immigration*, 137 F. (2d) 898. They reiterated the oft-repeated doctrine, both of American and of international law, that personal election plays an important part in the effect of annexation on citizenship, and that departure from the country prior to annexation manifests an election not to be considered an "inhabitant" or to "remain" in the country. In another case, *United States* ex rel. *Zdunic* v. *Uhl*, 137 F. (2d) 858, a citizen of Yugoslavia, residing in Austria from 1922 until 1939, was apparently deemed not a "denizen" of Austria. That was a term of art known only in English law. In another case, *United States* ex rel. *Wakler D'Esquiva* v. *Uhl*, 137 F. (2d) 903, a person born in Vienna, though having left Austria in 1919, was deemed a "native" of Germany if, on proof, the United States was deemed to "recognize" the absorption of Austria into Germany. Since the department had both recognized and refused to recognize that absorption, it might be difficult for the district court to decide the issue on the criterion of recognition.

Provision was made by executive order 9372 of Aug. 27, 1943, exempting from the classification "alien enemy" all enemy nationals certified by the attorney general or the commissioner of immigration as persons loyal to the United States (*Bull.* D. S., Sept. 4, p. 155). At an earlier date, nationals of Austria and Italy were excused from registering as enemy aliens (M. Domke, *Trading with the Enemy in World War II*, p. 70).

Among the notable events of the year 1943 were:

The reciprocal exchange of patents between the United States and Great Britain, by which each country agreed to make nationally registered patents available to the other, for the duration of the war.

The German attacks upon Swedish vessels and deposit of anchored mines in Swedish territorial waters.

The exchange of notes by which the United States agreed with the United Kingdom and various dominions, including India, that each country may bring its prizes into and take prizes in the territorial waters of the other (*Bull.* D. S., Feb. 6, p. 133).

The agreement (*Bull.* D.S., Aug. 14, p. 96) by which, under reverse lend-lease, the British government undertook to compensate private owners for private property expropriated to build the naval bases leased to the United States on British islands off the American coast.

The agreement (*Bull.* D. S., Oct. 2, p. 230) by which Mexico agreed to make specific payments in execution of the award compensating American oil companies for properties expropriated by Mexico, an award which significantly left unmentioned the bases on which it was reached, including the crucial question of compensation for subsoil petroleum.

The declaration of the United Nations of Jan. 5, 1943 (*Bull.* D. S., Jan. 9, p. 21) by which the Allied governments agreed to regard as null and void all transfers of property made by nationals or residents of occupied countries to German nationals, a transfer which led Dr. Frank Munk to propose that the six great trusts organized by Germany from German and transferred property be left unimpaired, but stock ownership be vested proportionately in the countries whose nationals were thus expropriated or who voluntarily parted with their assets.

The warning of Sept. 21 from the department of state (*Bull.* D.S., Sept. 25, p. 207) to neutral countries against the acquisition of Italian properties or enemy-owned shares in Italian companies, which the United States and the United Kingdom reserved the right to treat as void.

The refusal of a New York court to permit a French national to replevin his securities from a New York bank, held in the name of the French branch, since there was no French government in existence after the German occupation to which application could be made for release of the securities (*Bercholz* v. *Guaranty Trust Co.*, 44 N.Y.S. [2d] 148 [1943]). The New York courts had previously held (*Bollack* v. *Société Generale . . .*, 263 App. Div. 601 [1942]) that they would not give effect to a French confiscatory decree purporting to confiscate the bank deposits in New York of French nationals who fled the country in 1940.

The treaty signed Jan. 11, 1943, by which the United States abandoned extraterritorial rights in China, including rights under the "Boxer Protocol" of 1901 (*Bull.* D. S., Jan. 16, p. 59). This policy has since been implemented by a statute repealing Chinese exclusion (Nov. 1943).

The decision of the house of lords in the case of the soviet corporation *Sovfracht* v. *Van Udens Bros.*, (1943) 1 All. Eng. Rep. 76, that a Dutch company of shipowners having an arbitration agreement with the charterers of their vessel, a Russian company, could not pursue the arbitration in England since, being domiciled in Holland, enemy-occupied territory, they were themselves deemed to have "enemy character," which was a question of domicile and not one of nationality or patriotic sentiment.

The decision of the probate divorce and admiralty division in the case of the *Lubrafol* v. *Owners of the Steamship Pamia*, (1943) 1 All Eng. Rep. 269, that when the plaintiff Belgian company removed its domicile to Pittsburgh under authority of a Belgian order in council three months before the invasion of Belgium, they had a commercial domicile in the United States and could not be charged with "enemy character," thus distinguishing the case from the *Sovfracht*. A somewhat similar decision was made by Conger, J. in *Chemacid* v. *Ferrotar Corp.*, 51 F. Supp. 756 (S.D. N.Y. 1943).

The trial of "war criminals" for atrocities committed was considerably agitated during 1943. The warning to neutral countries to refuse them asylum was not hospitably received. There is much critical literature on the subject, questioning the wisdom of such trials, on the argument that the trials might not be genuine, that executions by Allied or international courts might introduce a dangerous precedent, that execution or other sanctions might martyrize the accused, that it would psychologically do harm both to victor and defeated countries, and that it would make difficult a restoration of peace (*Cf.* C. Arnold Anderson, in [Dec. 1943] 37 *Am. Pol. Sci. Rev.* 1081). (*See* also PRISONERS OF WAR.) (E. BD.)

International Trade. International trade in 1943 was predominantly war trade carried on within three groups of countries almost completely insulated from each other by blockade and counterblockade. The first of these groups included the United States, Canada and the countries in the Latin American area, the United Kingdom and British countries outside of the western hemisphere, the U.S.S.R., the European neutrals and their possessions, the countries of the middle east, and Free China. The second comprised Germany, Italy, the European countries under axis domination, and the European neutrals. The third consisted of Japan and the countries under Japanese occupation. The European neutrals, which maintained trade relations on some basis both with the rest of continental Europe and with the countries outside the German and Japanese spheres, appeared in two of the groups; otherwise they were mutually exclusive trading areas. The oversea trade of Sweden, which had been conducted on a very limited scale through the port of Göteborg under British-United States and German surveillance, was interrupted in Oct. 1943, as a result of the denial by Germany to Swedish vessels of transit through the Skagerrak in retaliation for the withdrawal by Sweden of transit privileges for German troops and supplies through Sweden.

Very little was publicly known about trade within the areas under German and Japanese control in 1943. The trade of Germany with other European countries and their trade with each other was carried on under the terms of comprehensive trade agreements, payment being made through clearing accounts. There was considerable evidence that Germany was experiencing increasing difficulty during 1943 in meeting export commitments under these agreements. As a result, imports into Germany were curtailed in some instances, and large clearing balances against the reich were accumulated. The major development in 1943 affecting trade within the area dominated by Japan was the growing shortage of shipping. Because of the lack of transportation, the movement of strategic materials and foodstuffs was curtailed even where supplies were available. Output within the area was undoubtedly reduced also as a consequence of Japan's inability to transport materials and equipment to points of production.

The broad features of the foreign trade of the United States, Canada and the Latin American countries in 1943 were made public and provided considerable information regarding the international trade of the United Nations group of countries, even though foreign trade statistics for many of them were not available.

United States foreign trade in 1943 was dominated by lend-lease shipments, which comprised approximately 80% of total exports, as shown in the accompanying table.

Total shipments in 1943 were nearly $13,000,000,000. The value of exports, which were exclusive of supplies destined for the armed forces of the United States in foreign countries, was 60% greater than the 1942 total and constituted a volume of shipments unparalleled in the history of international trade. Lend-lease shipments exceeded $10,000,000,000 during the year and other exports amounted to approximately $2,600,000,000, as compared with $4,900,000,000 and $3,100,000,000, respectively, in 1942. The reports of the president to congress on lend-lease operations indicated that an increased proportion of total exports from the United States in 1943 consisted of military items, although shipments of industrial materials and equipment and of foodstuffs continued very heavy.

The value of imports into the United States in 1943, amounting to approximately $3,400,000,000, equalled or surpassed the highest levels since 1929 despite the severance of trade with areas formerly furnishing almost half of total imports into the country. Exports for cash, i.e., exports other than lend-lease shipments, were exceeded by imports during the year by approximately $750,000,000.

United States exports to countries outside the western hemisphere in 1943 consisted almost entirely of lend-lease shipments. By the same token, cash-purchase or commercial exports were concentrated almost entirely in trade with Canada and with Latin America. Judging from published records for the first ten months of the year, more than one-third of total exports in 1943 went to the United Kingdom and more than 20% to the U.S.S.R. Shipments to Africa, the middle east, and the Mediterranean area accounted for more than 10% of the total and those to China, India, Australia and New Zealand for somewhat less than 10%.

Exports to Canada (as shown in Canadian import statistics) accounted for another 10% or more.

Exports from Canada reached unprecedented levels in 1943, partly as a result of a greatly expanded war trade with the United

exceeded imports by a margin without parallel in the history of Canadian foreign trade. Much of the export surplus was accounted for, however, by shipments to the United Kingdom financed under Canada's provision of $1,000,000,000 for mutual aid to the United Nations or in other ways not requiring immediate payment. Trade with the United States resulted in an apparent excess of imports, partly as the result of the inclusion of lend-lease deliveries to Canada by the United States for other than Canadian account.

The trade of the Latin American countries was maintained at high levels in 1943 despite an acute shortage of shipping which affected most of the area during the early part of the year. Exports, estimated at $2,400,000,000, were higher than in preceding years, largely as a result of the extraordinary volume of shipments to the United States, placed at $1,300,000,000 as compared with $1,100,000,000 in 1942 and an average of $600,000,000 in 1938-39. Aggregate imports into the Latin American countries, estimated at approximately $1,400,000,000, were at about the level of preceding years on a value basis. Of this total, $800,000,000 represented imports from the United States. Perhaps the most notable development of 1943 was the continued accumulation by the Latin American countries of gold and foreign exchange, estimated privately to have reached a total of $2,000,000,000 by the end of 1943. The balance of exports, which was the principal factor involved, was roughly $900,000,000. Of this amount, more than $500,000,000 was accounted for by the excess of exports over imports in trade with the United States.

Not even the totals of British foreign trade in 1943 were publicly known. It was apparent from available records of United States, Canadian and Latin American exports, however, that imports into the United Kingdom from these sources in 1943 exceeded imports from all sources in prewar years on a value basis. A high proportion of these imports consisted of military supplies, as indicated by data on lend-lease shipments from the United States. What the comparative levels of imports of civilian-type goods may have been could not be determined on the basis of publicly available information. Other evidence, especially the continued severity of rationing restrictions on food, indicate that imports of this character were below normal requirements.

British exports in 1943 were probably only a fraction of their prewar volume, although no definite figures are available. What must have been an enormous excess of imports over exports was financed by: (1) Lend-lease aid from the United States; (2) mutual aid from Canada; (3) further liquidation of British investments in certain countries; and (4) the accumulation of blocked sterling balances. It was estimated that blocked sterling balances were somewhere between £1,000,000,000 and £1,300,000,000 at the end of the year. (*See also* BUSINESS REVIEW; FOREIGN ECONOMIC ADMINISTRATION.) (A. MY.)

U.S. Trade Agreements.—On June 7, 1943, President Roosevelt signed a joint resolution extending for a period of two years from June 12, 1943, the authority to enter into trade agreements with foreign countries. During 1943 reciprocal trade agreements were signed with Iran, on April 8, and with Iceland, on Aug. 27. Conclusion of these two agreements increased to 28 the number of countries with which trade agreements have been concluded under authority of the Trade Agreements act. The 28 countries, in the order in which the agreements were signed, were: Cuba, Brazil, Belgium and Luxembourg, Haiti, Sweden, Colombia, Canada, Honduras, The Netherlands, Switzerland, Nicaragua, Guatemala, France, Finland, Costa Rica, El Salvador, Czechoslovakia, Ecuador, United Kingdom, Turkey, Venezuela, Argentina, Peru, Uruguay, Mexico, Iran and Iceland. On June 23, public notice was given of intention to negotiate an agreement with Paraguay. Negotiations with Bolivia continued. (D. AN.)

United States Foreign Trade, 1939–43*
(In millions of dollars)

	General imports	Total exports	Lend-Lease shipments	Exports exclusive of Lend-Lease shipments	Balance of exports (+) or imports (−) exclusive of Lend-Lease shipments
1939	2,318	3,177	—	3,177	+859
1940	2,625	4,021	—	4,021	+1,396
1941	3,345	5,147	741	4,406	+1,061
1942	2,742	8,035	4,895	3,140	+398
1943:					
January .	228	730	535	195	−33
February .	234	719	529	190	−44
March . .	249	988	777	211	−38
April . .	258	980	775	205	−53
May . .	281	1,085	848	237	−44
June . .	295	1,002	791	211	−85
July . .	300	1,262	1,021	241	−59
August . .	315	1,204	989	215	−101
September	285	1,233	1,001	232	−53
October .	329	1,193	950	243	−86
November	317	1,074	858	216	−101
December	274	1,249	1,027	222	−52
Total . .	3,365	12,717	10,101	2,616	−749

*Exclusive of trade in gold and silver.
Source: U.S. Department of Commerce.

States and partly as a result of heavy shipments, largely without immediate payment, to the United Kingdom. Imports into Canada, of which approximately four-fifths were supplied by the United States, were also at record levels. Exports during 1943

Interstate Commerce Commission.

The Interstate Commerce commission, established Feb. 4, 1887, for the regulation of carriers engaged in U.S. interstate commerce on land and water, consists of 11 members appointed by the president. From its membership the commission selects its chairman (J. Haden Alldredge in 1943). On a virtual leave of absence as commissioner in 1943, Joseph B. Eastman was serving as director of the Office of Defense Transportation (q.v.) and Commissioner John L. Rogers was assistant director of that office, which also utilized the services of many of the commission's employees.

In 1943 the carriers subject to the commission's jurisdiction were called upon to carry an increasing burden of wartime transportation, and many changes in normal modes of operation and routing of traffic were necessary. Railroad freight traffic reached a new high record, and passenger travel also increased. Motor-truck and bus traffic continued to be very heavy. A number of motor-carrier freight lines adopted plans for co-ordination of their operations in order to save rubber, gasoline and manpower by avoiding duplications in service. Many motor carriers and a few water carriers were granted temporary operating authority to meet urgent needs for transportation service which could not be furnished by other means.

The commission's emergency powers with respect to railroad service proved to be of the utmost importance in 1943. The number of orders issued in the exercise of these powers exceeded that for any previous year. These orders were instrumental in preventing any serious or long-continued shortages of railroad transportation.

In the early part of 1943 the commission reopened for further hearing the proceeding in which it had authorized certain general increases in railroad freight rates in 1942. After further hearing it found that the increased rates were no longer necessary under current conditions. Accordingly the increases in rates were suspended until July 1, 1944. Moderate general rate increases for motor carriers in certain sections of the country were authorized in 1943. Hearings in the comprehensive proceedings relating to class rates and the basic classifications were completed in 1943.

Further progress in the financial reorganization of railroads under the Bankruptcy act was made during the year. In this way and by other means the railroads continued to reduce their funded debt and lighten their burden of fixed interest charges. A revised and simplified edition of the commission's accounting rules for steam railroads was issued in 1943.   (J. H. A.)

Intestinal Disorders: see ALIMENTARY SYSTEM, DISORDERS OF.

Intoxication, Alcoholic.

There is a growing volume of evidence that chronic alcoholic intoxication is the expression of a particular kind of neuroses, that the problem falls within the purview of the student of personality, and that treatment is essentially and finally a personal matter.

The medical writings for 1943 contained no new contributions for a better understanding or specific solution of chronic alcoholism. Contributions on the conditioned reflex treatment of chronic alcoholism continued to occupy attention. This treatment consisted of establishing, under institutional supervision, a reflex aversion to the sight, smell, taste and thought of alcoholic beverages, by means of chemically induced emesis.

The controversy of ambulant versus institutional treatment was revived. The former involved the use of benzedrine sulphate, the value of which was not fully established, and, also the activities of "Alcoholics Anonymous" that sought to engage the alcoholic in social activities in a nondrinking environment, and offered constructive ways of employing vocational abilities and leisure time through the advantage of mutual understanding and past experience. Alcoholism as a disciplinary problem in the military forces was the subject of comment.

Chemical tests for the presence of alcohol in the blood, as a diagnostic criterion of drunkenness, in connection with the prosecution of motor traffic violation, seemed to have passed the twilight zone of experiment and to have entered the realm of scientific dependability. Some courts of law still refused the admissibility of such evidence where there is absence of consent in submitting to such tests. Three states recognized by law the reliability of chemical tests for intoxication and their admissibility in evidence. Other courts, in the absence of specific legislation, admitted these results in evidence, and ways and means were being considered to make such tests compulsory. The supreme court of one state ruled that the test of intoxication is not the amount of liquor consumed, but the amount of alcohol in the blood. (See also LIQUORS, ALCOHOLIC; PSYCHIATRY.)

BIBLIOGRAPHY.—Merrill Moore, "A Didactic Note on Alcoholism," *Jour. of Nervous and Mental Disease,* 97:1–5 (1943); S. Alan Challman, and Merrill Moore, "The Soldier Who Drinks Too Much," *Military Surgeon,* 91:648–650 (1942); "Scientific Tests for Intoxication," *J.A.M.A.,* 121: 1377 (1943).   (W. L. T.)

Inventions: see PATENTS.
Investment Banking: see BANKING.

Iodine.

No information was available on iodine in 1943, beyond the fact that the supply was sufficient to cover immediate needs for both war and essential industrial uses. The United States output was not reported after 1937, but it was known to have increased materially over the approximately 300,-000 lb. reported in that year.   (G. A. Ro.)

Iowa.

A north central state of the United States, admitted as the 29th state on Dec. 28, 1846; popularly known as the "Hawkeye state." Area, 56,280 sq.mi., of which 294 sq.mi. are water. The population in 1940 was 2,538,268 with 1,084,231 listed as urban and 1,454,037 as rural. Native whites numbered 2,403,446, foreign-born whites, 117,245, Negroes 16,694 and other non-whites, 883. The bureau of the census estimated the population of Iowa on March 1, 1943, at 2,308,748, a decrease of 228,-260. Capital, Des Moines (159,819 in 1940). Other principal cities: Sioux City (82,364), Davenport (66,039), Cedar Rapids (62,120), Waterloo (51,743) and Dubuque (43,892).

History.—There was no state election in 1943. Officers elected Nov. 3, 1942, all Republicans, continued in office during 1943: governor, Bourke B. Hickenlooper; lieutenant governor, Robert D. Blue; auditor, C. B. Akers; secretary of state, Wayne M. Ropes; secretary of agriculture, Harry D. Linn; attorney general, John M. Rankin; and superintendent of public instruction, Jessie M. Parker. John M. Grimes was appointed treasurer on Oct. 21, 1943, to fill the vacancy caused by the death of W. G. C. Bagley. The general assembly was in session from Jan. 11 to April 8, 1943. Among the acts passed was one providing "rules of civil procedure."

Education.—For the school year 1941–42 there were 357,049 pupils enrolled in the 10,204 public elementary schools, 133,885 pupils in the 1,006 public high schools and 1,918 students in the 27 junior colleges. There were 24,808 teachers in the public schools. The property tax levy for schools in the local districts for the year 1939–40 was $41,711,546.

Public Welfare, Charities, Correction.—The state appropriation for the year 1943–44 included $8,500,000 for old-age assistance, $500,000 for state emergency relief and $260,000 for child welfare and aid to the blind. The state maintained five penal and correctional institutions with a total of 2,665 inmates and ten eleemosynary institutions with 11,130 inmates, as of July 1, 1943.

Communication.—As of July 1, 1943, there were 5,488.5 mi. of paved primary roads in Iowa and 3,092.7 mi. gravelled or otherwise surfaced. Construction work on primary roads for the fiscal year 1942–43 totalled $3,654,242 and maintenance $4,063,-255. Of the secondary roads 46,967 mi. had been gravelled. At the close of 1942 there were 9,351.84 mi. of steam railroads in Iowa and 435.1 mi. of electric interurban tracks. Iowa has approximately 10,297 mi. of telegraph lines and 90,335 mi. of telephone lines, with 594,759 telephones.

Banking and Finance.—There were 102 national banks in Iowa on June 30, 1943, with deposits of $485,790,000 and resources of $515,517,000. The 542 state banks had deposits of $787,765,327 and resources of $845,261,046. The income of the state government for 1942–43 was $33,536,537 of which $19,475,-960 came from a retail sales tax and $7,781,985 from the income tax.

Agriculture.—There were 208,870 farms in Iowa in 1943 with 34,650,845 ac. For the first eight months of 1943 Iowa farmers received a cash income of $1,021,898,000, an increase of approximately one-third over that for the same period of 1942.

On Jan. 1, 1943 there were 13,028,000 hogs on Iowa farms, 1,866,000 sheep, 5,422,000 cattle, 658,000 horses and 39,000 mules.

Table I.—*Leading Agricultural Products of Iowa, 1943 and 1942*

Crop	1943 (est.)	1942
Corn, bu.	641,212,000	574,080,000
Oats, bu.	189,345,000	196,270,000
Hay, tame, tons.	4,855,000	6,683,000
Soybeans (grain), bu.	39,300,000	35,451,000
Soybeans (hay), tons	144,000	212,000
Barley, bu.	1,035,000	4,158,000
Wheat, bu.	3,025,000	4,193,000
Potatoes, bu.	5,529,000	6,600,000
Rye, bu.	202,000	279,000

Manufacturing.—The total value of products manufactured in Iowa in 1939 was $718,531,801. There were 2,670 manufacturing establishments with 11,501 salaried employees who received $23,535,779 and 65,314 wage earners who received $73,466,119. Meat packing and butter headed the list of industries. War industries were built up at Burlington, Ankeny, Cedar Rapids and other centres.

Mineral Production.—In 1942 Iowa ranked 31st among the

Table II.—*Principal Mineral Products of Iowa, 1940 and 1939*

	Production, 1940	Value, 1940	Value, 1939
Cement	4,605,886 bbl.	$7,641,163	$7,771,503
Coal	3,231,177 tons	8,045,630	7,503,000
Gypsum	487,379 tons	587,223	510,120
Sand and gravel	3,464,803 tons	1,852,285	1,299,449
Stone	4,013,740 tons	3,832,070	4,385,234

states in the value of mineral products.   (R. A. GA.)

Iowa, State University of.

An institution of higher education at Iowa City, Ia., established Feb. 25, 1847. It was the first state university to admit women on equal standing with men. In March 1943, the university began training of army air force pre-meteorology students and in May the first of some 1,300 army specialized training cadets arrived for work in six fields. Civilian campus enrolment continued to decline, but with the specialized army units university faculty members gave instruction to some 4,700 persons. The U.S. navy continued to train cadets in a pre-flight program with a constant total average of 1,800, using facilities of two men's dormitories, the field house and sports fields. More than 100 men of professorial rank entered government war service and

6,600 alumni and former students in December were listed in the armed forces. For statistics of enrolment, faculty, literary volumes, etc., *see* UNIVERSITIES AND COLLEGES.

Iowa State College.

Service to the armed forces and for the war effort continued and expanded at this land-grant college during 1943. In addition to carrying on regular undergraduate and graduate instruction in agriculture, engineering, home economics, science and veterinary medicine, the college had in training some 3,400 men in uniform at one time. New contingents added during the year included the navy specialized training program, the second stage of navy aviation training and the army specialized training program. The quota of sailors in the navy electrical, diesel and cooks and bakers schools was increased. The college also trained 90 young women in engineering for the Curtiss-Wright corporation. (For statistics of enrolment, faculty, library, volumes, etc., *see* UNIVERSITIES AND COLLEGES.)

Iran.

Known before March 1935 as Persia, a country of western Asia bounded on the east by India and Afghanistan, on the north by the U.S.S.R., on the west by Iraq and Turkey, and on the southwest and south by the Persian gulf and Arabian sea; ruled after 1926 as a constitutional kingdom. Ruler: Shah Mohammed Reza Pahlavi; premier (1943): Ali Suhaili. Area, *c.* 628,000 sq.mi.; pop. (est.), 15,000,000. Chief towns: Tehran (cap., 360,000), Tabriz (220,000), Meshed (140,000), Shiraz (120,000), Isfahan (100,000). Language, Persian; religion, Mohammedan.

History.—Tribal unrest in southern Iran provided an opportunity for German agents, who tried to direct it toward the sabotage of the lines of communication between the Persian gulf and the U.S.S.R. In August the government offered a substantial reward for the capture of any Germans living without permission in Iran, and early in the following month ordered the arrest of a number of Iranians believed to be conspiring with these agents. A few days later, on Sept. 9, Iran declared war on Germany.

Meanwhile the country had been assisted by the United States and Great Britain to play its important part in the war by providing a route for supplies to the soviet union. The United States army became, during 1943, the leading partner in the organization of transit across Iran, assuming responsibility for the operation of the Trans-Iranian railway from the gulf as far as the Russian-occupied zone, and supplementing with its own convoys the road service organized in 1941 by the United Kingdom Commercial corporation.

Internally, the rising cost of living and the recurrent local shortages of food still presented grave problems. There had been a bread riot in Tehran at the end of 1942, but the situation in the capital was subsequently eased by the creation of a single state bakery, distributing 160,000 loaves daily through 28 government shops. The Allies also supplied a quantity of grain, and the harvest promised well. The problems of inflation and of the unbalanced budget were tackled by Dr. Arthur C. Millspaugh, who returned to Iran in January as financial adviser, and who was empowered to make regulations having the force of law.

Qavam es-Saltaneh resigned the premiership in Feb. 1943 and was succeeded by Ali Suhaili, who continued in office until the autumn elections.

Two economic agreements were concluded during 1943 by the Iranian government—a reciprocal trade agreement with the United States, and a settlement of the royalties to be paid by the Anglo-Iranian Oil company at £4,000,000 a year for the duration of the war. The company's net profits for 1942 were more than double those of 1941.

At the end of November Tehran was the scene of the first three-cornered conversations between President Roosevelt, Marshal Stalin, and Mr. Churchill. These were followed, on Dec. 1, by a joint declaration of the three leaders which associated the United States with the assurances given to Iran by Great Britain and the U.S.S.R. in Jan. 1942. (For the text of the declaration, *see* UNITED STATES OF AMERICA.)

Education.—(1937) 4,939 schools; 273,600 scholars; one university at Tehran.

Banking and Finance.—Revenue, ordinary (1942–43) 3,137,-366,000 rials; expenditure, ordinary (1942–43) 3,137,695,000 rials; foreign loan (Dec. 31, 1941) £930,541; public debt (Dec. 31, 1938) 98,900,000 rials; note circulation (Nov. 30, 1942) 2,554,000,000 rials; gold reserve (Nov. 30, 1942) 310,949,000 rials; exchange rate (May 31, 1943) 1 rial = 3.077 cents U.S.

Trade and Communication.—Foreign trade (merchandise) 1941–42: imports 1,802,400,000 rials; exports 3,405,600,000 rials. Communications 1938: roads fit for wheeled traffic, c. 8,700 mi.; railways open to traffic, 1,072 mi.

Agriculture and Mineral Production.—Production, est. 1937–38 (in metric tons): petroleum, crude (1940) 10,426,000; wheat 1,942,300; barley 706,900; rice 382,100; cotton (1940–41) 50,000; wool (1940) 15,500; beet sugar (1939–40) 25,200; tobacco (1940–41) 12,700.

Iraq. An Arab state of the near east, between Iran, Syria and Arabia, watered by the Tigris and Euphrates; an independent kingdom after 1932, when the British mandate was terminated. Area, 116,000 sq.mi.; pop. (census Oct. 1934) 3,561,-000 (est. Dec. 31, 1939), 3,700,000. Chief towns: Baghdad (cap. 400,000), Mosul (260,000), Basra (180,000). Ruler: King Feisal II; regent: Prince Abdul-Ilah; premier (1943): General Nuri es-Sa'id; language: Arabic; religion: Mohammedan.

History.—Throughout 1943 Iraq continued to be ruled by the government which Nuri Pasha Sa'id had formed in Oct. 1942. The government remained substantially unchanged in personnel.

The most important of the government's acts was its declaration of war on the axis powers (Jan. 16). In its official statement, the government accused the axis of a hostile attitude toward Iraq over a long period and of having tried to destroy the legitimate government and promote disunity. For this reason and also because it was in the interests of Iraq and of the Arabs

IRAQI "QUISLINGS" in Germany—the Mufti of Jerusalem and former Premier Rashid Ali el-Gailani—appearing in public on the second anniversary of the British occupation of Iraq in May 1943. The photograph was sent to the United States through neutral sources

to adhere to the declaration of the United Nations, the Iraqi government considered itself in a state of war with the axis.

The other important political activity of 1943 was the establishment of closer ties with other Arabic-speaking countries, and especially with Egypt. In January the regent and prime minister and in March the king paid official visits to Cairo. In July the prime minister went once more in order to discuss with Nahas Pasha, the Egyptian prime minister, the question of union between the Arab peoples; he subsequently described the discussions as having had "important results." On the same trip he also visited Palestine, Trans-Jordan, Syria, and Lebanon, to discuss the same subject with the authorities, and made statements in support of the idea of a greater Syrian state.

In internal politics, 1943 saw a revision of the constitution designed to make possible more stable governments. This received the approval of parliament in June. Shortly afterward the chamber was dissolved, and a general election was held in October

The economic situation gave some cause for anxiety. There were inflationary tendencies, and wartime control of supplies was made difficult by the existence of a well-organized "black market." The government took severe steps to fight these evils; for example it drew up a "law for the reorganization of economic life," which set up a higher committee on economic life.

Education.—In 1938: elementary schools, government, 741; scholars 94,368; new schools opened 1938–39, 22; secondary schools 14; scholars 1,904; intermediate schools 48; scholars 10,611.

Finance.—Revenue, ordinary (est. 1941–42) 6,800,000 dinars; expenditure, ordinary (est. 1941–42) 6,700,000 dinars; notes in circulation (Jan. 31, 1943) 21,900,000 dinars; foreign assets reserves (Jan. 31, 1943) 23,400,000 dinars; exchange rate (1943) (currency based on sterling): 1 dinar = £1 sterling = approx. 403.5 cents U.S.

Trade and Communication.—Foreign trade, 1941 (merchandise): imports 6,948,000 dinars; exports, domestic (excluding crude petroleum) 3,906,000 dinars. Communication: roads open to traffic (1940), c. 4,000 mi.; railways open to traffic (June 1940), 947 mi.

Agriculture and Mineral Production.—Production 1938–39 (in metric tons): petroleum, crude (1940), 3,438,000; wheat 600,000; rice 360,000; barley 1,138,400; tobacco 4,000; wool (1938) 8,300; cotton (1940–41) 3,600; cotton seed (1940–41) 8,500.

Ireland: *see* EIRE.

Ireland, Northern. Northern Ireland forms part of the United Kingdom of Great Britain and Northern Ireland but (since 1920) has its own parliament and executive, with limited powers for local purposes, though also represented in the imperial parliament by 13 members. Area 5,238 sq.mi.; pop. (June 1939) 1,295,000. Chief cities (pop. census 1937): Belfast (cap. 438,086), Londonderry (47,813). Language: English; religion: Christian (Roman Catholic, 33.75%; Presbyterian, 31.4%; Episcopalian, 27%). Ruler and national flag, as for Great Britain. Governor: the duke of Abercorn; premier (1943): Sir Basil Brooke.

History.—In spite of some labour unrest at the beginning of the year, the war effort of Northern Ireland developed rapidly during 1943. The number of registered unemployed persistently declined, reaching a record low level of 12,500 by mid-October.

On May 1 Prime Minister J. M. Andrews yielded to the pressure of malcontents within his own party and resigned his office. His place was taken by Sir Basil Brooke, who retained his former position as minister of commerce and production. The cabinet was reconstituted as follows: minister of finance, Major J. M. Sinclair; minister of home affairs, William Lowry, K.C.; minister of labour, William Grant; minister of education, the Rev. Professor Corkey; minister of agriculture, the Rev. Robert Moore; minister of public security, H. C. Midgley. Only the attorney general (J. C. MacDermott, K.C.), the parliamentary secretary to the ministry of education (Mrs. Parker), the chief whip (Sir Norman Strong), and the parliamentary secretary to the prime minister (Sir J. Davidson) retained their former positions in the government.

Two Northern Ireland seats in the British House of Commons were filled in the course of the year. J. Beattie (West Belfast) became the first Labour M.P. to represent an Ulster constituency at Westminster, and V. Dermot Campbell retained the County Antrim seat for the Unionist party.

It was announced that the Belfast city administrators, appointed by virtue of the Belfast County Borough Administration act (1942), would shortly cease to hold office.

Considerable progress was made in the preparation of plans for postwar reconstruction. The Northern Ireland planning advisory board continued its investigations into postwar problems and in some fields the drafting of tentative plans was reported to be well advanced. On the initiative of the board, the ministry of home affairs began a detailed survey of housing conditions in the province. The planning commission (a body of experts mainly concerned with the more technical aspects of physical reconstruction) was reported to have prepared a master plan for the whole of Northern Ireland into which local authorities would be invited to fit their detailed plans for postwar building and redevelopment. Committees to consider the future of the linen industry and agriculture were also set up by the ministries concerned.

There was considerable public agitation during the year concerning the serious housing situation, particularly in Belfast. In spite of the fact that more than 44,000 war-damaged houses had been made habitable, the shortage of housing accommodation remained acute. In November the government offered a subsidy of £390 per house for the immediate erection of 750 houses in Belfast. (AR. B.)

Education.—In 1941-42: elementary schools 1,681; scholars 183,872; secondary schools 75; scholars 14,772; university students 1,626; technical schools 60; students 20,462.

Finance.—Revenue (est. 1943-44) £51,825,000; expenditure (est. 1943-44) (including £31,800,000 imperial contribution, and surplus £111,000) £51,825,000; 1942-43, estimated revenue, £41,797,000; estimated expenditure (including £21,300,000 imperial contribution, and surplus £84,000) £41,797,000; exchange rate (1943) £1 = 403.5 cents U.S.

Trade and Communication.—External trade 1938: imports, £54,385,000; exports, £51,061,000. Communication 1939: roads fit for motor traffic, 13,043 mi.; railways, standard gauge 741 mi., narrow 121 mi.; canals 180 mi. Shipbuilding, tonnage launched (1938) 79,468; value of linen goods exported (1938) £5,480,000.

Agriculture.—Total area under crops 1942, 1,263,131 ac.; including 522,050 ac. cereal crops, 187,320 potatoes, 72,996 flax, and 435,429 ac. hay. Cattle 826,651; sheep 741,601; pigs 271,-227; poultry 13,339,558. In 1941-42, cattle and sheep to value of £2,820,000, bacon and pigs to value of £2,480,000, eggs £3,500,-000, potatoes £850,000, and fruit more than £500,000 were shipped from Northern Ireland to Great Britain.

Irish Free State: see EIRE.

Iron and Steel.

For convenience in coverage, this subject is subdivided into three heads—iron ore,

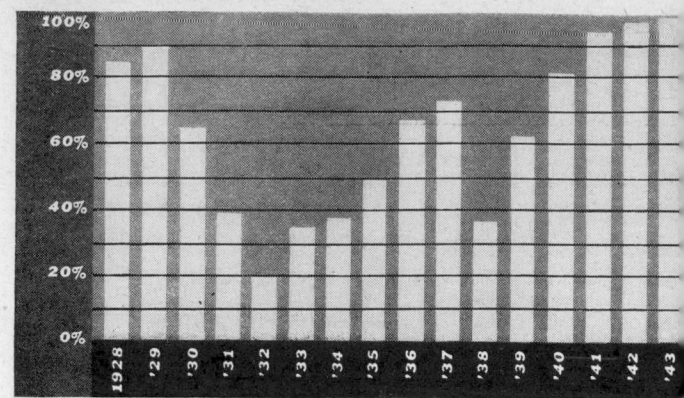

STEEL PRODUCTION in the United States; monthly average percentage capacity (figures compiled by American Iron and Steel Institute)

pig iron and steel. Production data were suppressed by all of th[e] major producers except the United States.

Iron Ore.—Such information as was available in 1943 on worl[d] iron ore production is shown in Table I.

Production of usable iron ore in the United States in 1942 ros[e] to 118,189,336 short tons, from 141,710,416 tons of crude ore[,] an increase of about 14% over 1941. The Lake Superior distric[t] accounted for about 90% of the total ore shipped. Productio[n] for the first three quarters of 1943 totalled about 90,000,000 ton[s] of usable ore, of which the Lake Superior district supplie[d] about 86%.

Lake shipments were hampered in the spring of 1943 by late clearance of ice from the lakes, and again in the winter b[y] early freezes. The November shipments were down to 6,940,50[0] tons, from 11,612,542 tons in the same period of 1942. Tota[l] shipments for the 1942 season, at 102,596,379 tons, cannot b[e] duplicated in 1943, though ore consumption has been materiall[y] greater than in 1942, and the deficit has had to be supplied fro[m] other sources.

Although Canada is not normally a producer of iron ore, be[-] cause of the ready accessibility of rich ores from the Unite[d] States and Newfoundland, war demand led to several rathe[r] extensive new developments in Ontario, Quebec and Britis[h] Columbia. All three provinces were paying bounties on iron ore

Table I.—World Production of Iron Ore
(In millions of long tons)

	1929	1932	1937	1938	1939	1940
North America—						
Newfoundland	1.5	0.1	1.6	1.7	1.7	1.4
United States	73.0	9.8	72.1	28.4	51.7	73.8
South America—						
Chile	1.8	0.2	1.5	1.6	1.6	1.7
Europe—						
Austria	1.9	0.3	1.9	2.6	?	?
Czechoslovakia	1.8	0.6	1.8	?	?	?
France	49.9	27.2	37.3	32.6	?	?
Germany	6.3	1.3	9.4	10.8	?	?
Luxembourg	7.5	3.2	7.6	5.0	2.3	?
Spain	6.4	1.7	1.0	2.5	2.2	2.8
Sweden	11.3	3.2	14.7	13.7	13.6	?
U.S.S.R.	6.9	12.0	27.6	26.0	?	?
United Kingdom	13.2	7.3	14.2	11.9	?	?
Asia—						
China	2.6	2.2	?	?	?	?
India	2.4	1.8	2.9	2.8	3.1	?
Malaya	0.8	0.7	1.7	1.7	2.0	?
Africa—						
Algeria	2.2	0.5	2.3	3.0	2.7	?
Morocco (Span.)	1.2	0.2	1.4	1.3	1.0	0.4
Australia	0.9	0.6	1.9	2.3	2.6	?
World Total	200.0	75.0	214.0	161.0	200?	208?
Ex. U.S.A.	127.0	65.2	142.0	132.6	141?	134?
Ex. British	191.1	64.3	191.6	139.5	?	?
Brit. Empire	18.9	10.7	23.4	21.5	?	?

Table II.—World Production of Pig Iron
(In millions of long tons)

	1929	1932	1938	1939	1940
North America—					
Canada	1.2	0.2	0.7	0.8	1.0
United States . .	42.6	8.8	19.2	31.8	42.4
Europe—					
Belgium	4.0	2.7	2.4	3.0	2.2
Czechoslovakia .	1.6	0.4	1.2	0.3	. . .
France	12.3	6.8	6.0	7.8	4.6
Germany . . .	13.2	3.9	18.2	21.7	20.6
Luxembourg . .	2.9	1.9	1.5	1.8	1.1
U.S.S.R.	4.0	6.3	14.8	15.0	15.3
United Kingdom	7.6	3.6	6.8	8.2	8.3
Asia—					
India	1.4	0.9	1.5	1.8	?
Japan	1.5	1.5	3.1	3.3	3.0
World Total. .	97.2	39.2	80.5	100.0	104.0
Ex. U.S.A. . .	54.6	30.4	61.2	68.2	61.6
Ex. British . .	86.7	34.3	70.3	88.5	91.6
Brit. Empire .	10.5	4.9	10.2	11.5	12.4

to promote output.

Ore production of the Wabana mines in Newfoundland increased from 950,000 tons in 1941 to 1,200,000 tons in 1942, but exports declined from 1,235,000 tons to 980,000 tons, and the mine was closed for several months early in 1943 because of accumulated stocks.

Pig Iron.—In addition to the record of earlier years, as shown in Table II, the following text presents such later information as was available in 1943. The output of blast furnaces in the United States rose from 56,686,604 short tons in 1941 to 60,903,304 tons in 1942, including 59,077,544 tons of pig iron and 1,827,360 tons of ferroalloys. Ore consumption was 110,424,000 tons. The expansion program for new blast furnace capacity was about complete, 9 out of 10 furnaces under construction being scheduled to start operation before January 1, 1944.

Canadian production in 1942 included 1,975,015 short tons of pig iron and 213,636 tons of ferroalloys, a total of 2,188,651 tons. Through October 1943, Canadian furnaces with an annual capacity of 2,756,160 tons turned out 1,478,760 tons of pig iron and 185,480 tons of ferroalloys, a total of 1,664,240 tons, against 1,817,391 tons in the same period of 1942.

Spanish production was declining slightly, having been 580,771 metric tons in 1940, 536,865 tons in 1941 and 528,417 tons in 1942, and at a rate of 524,000 tons during the first quarter of 1943.

Steel.—As with pig iron, Table III shows past performance, and the text gives whatever later information was received.

Table III.—World Production of Steel
(In millions of long tons)

	1929	1932	1938	1939	1940
North America—					
Canada	1.4	0.3	1.1	1.3	2.0
United States . .	56.4	13.7	28.7	47.7	60.2
Europe—					
Belgium	4.0	2.7	2.2	3.0	2.2
Czechoslovakia .	2.2	0.7	1.7	0.4	. . .
France	11.7	6.9	6.1	8.4	5.4
Germany . . .	16.0	5.7	22.9	26.4	25.1
Italy	2.1	1.4	2.3	2.7	2.5
Luxembourg . .	2.7	1.9	1.4	1.8	1.3
Poland	1.4	0.5	1.5	1.6	?
Sweden	0.7	0.5	1.0	1.1	0.9
U.S.S.R. . . .	4.6	5.7	18.2	18.5	19.5
United Kingdom.	9.6	5.3	10.4	13.5	13.4
Asia—					
Japan	2.3	2.4	5.9	6.3	6.3
World Total. .	118.1	49.9	107.1	134.6	159.8
Ex. U.S.A. . .	61.7	36.2	78.8	86.9	99.6
Ex. British . .	106.1	6.4	93.0	117.3	141.3
Brit. Empire .	12.0	43.5	14.1	17.3	18.5

Steel production in the United States in 1942 reached a total of 86,029,921 short tons, an increase of 4% over 1941. Plant operation averaged 96.8% of capacity for the year, with a high of 101.3% in October. The production goal for 1943 was 91,500,000 tons but this could not be attained, since the total through November was 81,589,202 tons, with a probable total of 89,000,000 tons for the full year. The chief reason for the failure to reach the desired total was the succession of four coal strikes during the year, as a result of which blast furnaces in several areas had to be banked during the strike periods due to shortage of coke. To a lesser degree, shortage of scrap was also a contributing factor, particularly during the latter half of the year. Purchased scrap constituted 45% of the total scrap consumed in 1942, but only 42% in August 1943. In an effort to remedy this shortage, an intensive drive for the collection of scrap was carried on during the last quarter of the year.

Steel production in Canada failed in 1943 to show the marked increase that had been made in 1942; production through Oct. 1943 totaled 2,509,712 short tons (a rate of 3,012,000 tons for the full year), in comparison with 3,121,361 tons in 1942. Scrap was more plentiful in Canada than in the United States, the scrap content of the furnace charge running better than 54%, against less than 50% in the United States. (*See also* BUSINESS REVIEW; METALLURGY.) (G. A. Ro.)

Iron and Steel Institute, American: *see* AMERICAN IRON AND STEEL INSTITUTE.

Irrigation.
United States.—Snow surveys made by the U.S. department of agriculture throughout the 11 western states at predetermined intervals resulted in irrigation water supply forecasts for the several basins of this area. These forecasts promised an abundant water supply for the entire irrigated west with the exception of southern Utah, Arizona and eastern New Mexico, where no serious shortage was forecast, but conservation was recommended. These forecasts proved to be very accurate, so that there was neither a reduction nor loss of irrigated crops.

War activities in the United States, as in all other countries of the civilized world, caused retrenchment or complete cessation of most civil improvements during 1943. Only such construction of new works or expansion of irrigated areas as were necessary to produce more food or fibre were undertaken.

On other than federal irrigation projects, the Imperial Valley Irrigation district led in major activities, although here, too, all operations were very seriously handicapped and had to be curtailed by reason of shortage of labour. This shortage affected all departments of this 500,000-ac. district but was especially serious in canal-maintenance work and drainage construction. The All-American canal continued to function satisfactorily except for the lower end. It was operated by the U.S. bureau of reclamation, since there remained minor construction work before the operation could be turned over to the district. For the power system of the district, there was a gradual increase in both power load and power sales during the year. Following negotiations of more than 12 months, the district took over ownership of the electric properties of the California Electric Power company as the result of a $6,000,000 issue of revenue bonds voted by the district. This was expected to greatly increase the efficiency of the district's power distribution system.

In general, the crop situation was quite satisfactory. Yields were good and prices above average. Some difficulty was experienced with farm labour, there being a serious shortage at times However, all crops were harvested with little if any loss from lack of labour. The co-operation of the Mexican government with the government of the United States in supplying Mexican farm labour was very helpful. The total acreage of crops was about the same as for 1942. However, some shift was made from alfalfa and vegetables to flax. The area given over to the various crops in 1943 was as follows: Flax 144,618 ac.; alfalfa 114,085 ac.; garden crops 53,738 ac.; barley 32,848 ac.; rice 7,701 ac. All other crops, including sugar beets and citrus totalled 31,909 ac., making a grand total of 384,899 ac. farmed and irrigated within the boundaries of the district.

In central California the Nevada Irrigation district voted new bonds in the amount of $1,500,000, part of which was to be used to complete purchase of irrigation works and for the enlargement of the Bear River canal. The balance of the funds was for construction of Scotts Flat dam on Deer creek, extension of the Deer Creek South canal, and construction of the Combe-Ophir canal. Preliminary work was undertaken at the Scotts Flat dam —clearing the reservoir site and drilling the outlet tunnel, but actual construction was not to be undertaken until the conclusion of the war.

Federal irrigation activities continued to remain under the U.S. bureau of reclamation. As a result of the efforts of that bureau to bring about increased war-food production, the war board in 1943 lifted stop-construction orders on 13 of the bureau's irrigation projects on which the board had previously halted work in the fall of 1942, in order to save labour and strategic materials for strictly war purposes. The extensions of irrigation service on these developments, scattered over eight western states, were designed to provide water for 200,000 additional acres of land in 1944, 793,000 ac. by 1945, and a total of more than 1,000,000 ac. by 1946.

Work was halted in the fall of 1942 on practically all irrigation construction on bureau of reclamation projects. The War Food administration, which recommended the resumption of construction on the majority of the 13 projects approved, also made favourable recommendations on 13 additional projects and had under consideration about 50 others. From the 4,000,000 ac. already irrigated by the bureau of reclamation, crops valued at $272,000,000 were harvested in 1942. A crop value of at least that much was expected for the 1943 harvest. The bureau had 71 projects in operation, under construction or authorized, 52 of which were generating power or supplying water for irrigation or other beneficial uses. The storage capacity of 81 of its reservoirs in 1943 reached a new high of more than 64,000,000 ac.-ft.

Shasta dam on the Sacramento river, key structure of the vast Central Valley project (California), was about 90% complete. This structure was to contain 5,556,700 cu.yd. of concrete, and ultimately will be more massive than Boulder dam and higher than Grand Coulee. Two of five generators, each rated at more than 70,000 kw., were being installed.

The Green Mountain dam of the Colorado-Big Thompson project (Colorado), with its power plant of more than 20,000 kw., was completed early in 1943. Construction to increase the height of the Altus dam (Lugert-Altus project, Oklahoma) to supply additional water, was completed.

Other dams under construction in 1943 by the bureau of reclamation included Keswick dam (Central Valley project, Calif.), Wickiup dam (Deschutes project, Oregon), Anderson Ranch dam (Idaho), Deerfield dam (South Dakota), Jackson Gulch dam (Colorado) and the Newton dam and Scofield dam (Utah). In addition there were many smaller structures, including canals and aqueducts, under construction.

Argentina.—Irrigation systems are under federal and provincial control. In the most important and productive provinces the distribution works were constructed by the irrigators with some aid from the provincial government and in some cases from

the federal government. In other provinces and in national territories, the federal government was the principal builder of irrigation works—in many cases to promote settlement in remote regions of the country.

A marked interest arose in all of the country in the construction of reservoirs for conservation and flood control, and new appropriations were authorized for construction of large dams. During 1942, construction of the Nihuil dam across the Atuel river in Mendoza province was started and continued into 1943. This structure was to extend and improve service to 172,-900 ac. of land already partly irrigated. In the province of Córdoba, the San Roque, La Viña and Cruz del Eje dams were completed.

These dams are for irrigation, flood control and hydroelectric power.

During 1943 the national government also started construction on Cadillal dam (145,985 ac.-ft. capacity) and the Escaba dam (102,190 ac.-ft.), both in the province of Tucumán. These reservoirs were expected to permit the improvement and extension of the present irrigated area to a total of 172,900 ac. of sugar cane, tobacco and citrus in this sub-tropical zone.

Canada.—In 1935 there was set up in the dominion of Canada, a federal agency known as the Canadian Prairie Farm Rehabilitation administration, which had headquarters in Regina, Saskatchewan. This agency developed a water program for postwar years, to cost more than $100,000,000 and to involve reclamation work on the Canadian prairies. It was to include an enormous amount of dam construction and ditch-digging, affording employment for thousands of men and many contractors. Eight irrigation projects costing $17,000,000 were in 1943 ready for immediate construction after the war ends, while six more, to cost about $1,500,000, were virtually ready. Twelve more projects to cost an estimated $48,000,000 were in preliminary stage of development, while an additional six with an estimated cost of $15,000,000 were yet unsurveyed. The agency had in mind the development of another group for power and irrigation, which when completed would cost about $30,000,000.

Mexico.—After the creation of the Mexican Commission of Irrigation in 1926, it did much to promote irrigation agriculture in that country. During the period 1941 to 1946 it was planning new irrigation works to serve approximately 1,750,000 ac. This would bring the total to 2,500,000 irrigated acres, which it was estimated would affect a total population of over 1,000,000 people by the close of 1946.

As in the United States, the irrigated regions of Mexico were the only agricultural zones where it was relatively easy to balance agricultural production. It was intended, therefore, that these regions would serve as a central nucleus when agriculture in the postwar period would be co-ordinated with the economies of all the countries of the world and especially the Americas. There was evident a well-formed plan of development by the Mexican government to raise the living standards of the Mexican rural population.

Peru.—The Peruvian government approved plans for an irrigation project to cost $15,000,000. This project compared favourably in size with any in the South American countries, involving about 250,000 ac. Approximately half of this acreage was in 1943 only partially or inadequately irrigated and the balance in desert. The project was located just north of the Chimbote bay region on the western slope of the Andes. In the irrigation program there was to be also hydroelectric development of about 100,000 kw. from the flow of the Santa river. The development was expected to extend over a period of about 3 to 8 years.

Venezuela.—The government of Venezuela undertook from 1941 on a program of irrigation development. Five small proj-cts completed would furnish irrigation water for about 29,640 c., and it had under study and fairly well advanced in preliminary surveys, another group of projects totalling about 434,-20 ac.

During 1942, Venezuela enacted a reclamation law which proided for the granting of concessions for use of water occurring n public lands under specified time-limiting conditions. Certain rovisions also governed development and appropriation of round water for use in irrigation. Reclamation was governed and irected by a Federal Water commission created by the 1942 Reclamation act.

(*See* also DAMS; DROUGHT; SOIL EROSION AND SOIL CONSERVATION.)

BIBLIOGRAPHY.—M. R. Lewis, "Practical Irrigation," U.S. Department f Agriculture *Farmers' Bulletin No. 1922* (1943); Carl Rohwer, "Design nd Operation of Small Irrigation Pumping Plants," U.S. Department of griculture *Circular No. 678* (1943); F. J. Veihmeyer and A. H. Hendrickon, "Essentials of Irrigation and Cultivation of Orchards," California Agriultural Extension Service *Circular No. 50* (rev. 1943).   (A. T. M.)

slam.

The Islamic world after 1939 was affected by the war in common with the rest of the world. The figure for on-Arabian pilgrims at Mecca in 1942 fell to about 25,000 19,000 in 1941), compared with nearly 60,000 in 1939. This was ccounted for not only by the scarcity of shipping but by the nsettled political conditions in overseas countries. On the other and, the progress of modernity in Islam was evidenced not only n Turkey but in India, Egypt, and North Africa generally. During 1943 the Moslem league in India greatly strengthened ts position and extended its influence. El Azhar university in gypt was exploring modern ideas and modern methods more nd more and under the influence of its progressive leader, the heikh al-Maraghi, was finding considerable points of contact in Moslem theology with modern movements. The modern Arabic ress was developing a technique of its own, and serving as a aluable link between historic traditions and modern needs. The ntellectual confusion in France was helping in the emancipation f Moslem ideas in North Africa, which hitherto had been under rench hegemony. The social services under the ministry of ealth in Turkey were proceeding actively with a ten-year plan vhich would give the lead to other Islamic countries. There vere no notable literary developments of the ideas of modern slam during 1943, but the Moslem press in Egypt and India coninued to give support to reasonable progressive views about nity and inter-communications in the Moslem world.

(A. Y. A.)

sle of Man: *see* BRITISH EMPIRE.

Italian Colonial Empire.

The accompanying table gives essential information relating to the so-called Italian colonial empire. The year 1943 confirmed the virtual disappearance of the Italian colonial empire as such. Italian forces were driven out of Libya by the end of January and a British military government under Brigadier Lush was set up. Military courts were established to deal with espionage, looting, and violence, and all fascist organizations, both political and educational, were dissolved. The Italian civil and criminal courts were allowed to continue, and in Tripolitania, though some 4,000 prominent fascists had fled, enough Italians were left to staff the administration under British control. Food shortage was a considerable problem at first in Tripolitania owing to previous German looting, but the Italian colonists soon returned to their farms. In Cyrenaica the administrative problem was simplified by the evacuation of the whole Italian civil population with the retreating axis armies, and the farms there were worked by Arabs. The lira continued to circulate, together with the British military currency at the rate of 480 lire to the £.

In Albania, the conquest of which in 1939 had not been recognized by the United States and Great Britain, there were many cabinet changes during the first half of 1943, indicating the uneasy situation there. On Jan. 19 the Kruja cabinet resigned and Ekrem Libohova, a former foreign minister, formed a government; on Feb. 13 he was succeeded by Maliq Bushati (foreign minister 1939–41), but on May 12 Libohova resumed the premiership. On March 17 General Alberto Pariani became governor-general in succession to Jacomini. After the surrender of Italy in Sept. 1943, the Germans announced that Italian troops in the Balkans were being disarmed and that Albania and the whole Dalmatian coast were under the control of German and Croat troops. Throughout 1943 there were constant acts of sabotage and violence against the occupying authorities, and guerrilla fighting, in which Italians often assisted the Albanians, increased after the assumption of control by the Germans.

The Italian surrender also had grave repercussions in the Dodecanese. The garrison at Rhodes surrendered immediately to the Germans and, in spite of Allied landings during September and October on Leros, Cos, Castelorizzo and Kalymnos, the Germans gradually took over all the islands. At the beginning of October the Germans captured Cos and Stampalia, on Nov. 16 Leros was recaptured from the Allies, and on Nov. 19 they reported the capture from the Italians of Patmos, Lipso and Nicaria. (*See* WORLD WAR II.)

On Oct. 13 it was announced in the British parliament that an assurance had been received from the Badoglio government

*Italian Colonial Empire**

Country and Area Square miles (approx.)	Population (000's omitted) (est. Dec. 1939)	Capital, Status, Governors, Premiers, etc.	Principal Products (in metric tons)	Imports and Exports 1938 (in lire, 000's omitted)	Road, Rail and Shipping 1938	Revenue and Expenditure (in lire, 000's omitted)
AFRICA Italian provinces of LIBYA, 213,821	800†	Tripoli; included in the national territory of Italy: under British military occupation.	(1939) barley 22,600 wheat 20,700	imp. 882,057 exp. 108,961	rds. 3,250 mi. rly. 271 mi. shpg.: passengers arrived 127,458 departed 122,521	(est. 1939–40) rev. and exp. 600,115
LIBYAN SAHARA, 465,362 . . .	49†	Homs; colony, under British military authority.				
ERITREA, 86,166	1,000	Asmara; colony, under British military occupation.	salt (1937) 156,000 barley (1937) 19,000	No separate figures	rly. 215 mi.	No separate figures
SOMALILAND, ITALIAN, 270,972 .	1,300	Mogadiscio; colony, under British military occupation.	maize (1938) 25,000	No separate figures	rly. 70 mi.	No separate figures
ASIA Italian islands of the Aegean sea, 1,035	122	Rhodes; colony: in German occupation	barley (1939) 2,200; olive oil (1940) 400; wine (1939) 33,000 hectolitres	imp. 157,421 exp. 21,851	rds. 382 mi.	(1934–35) rev. and exp. 48,000

*See the first paragraph of the accompanying article.
†Libyan population census 1936, Italians excepted; the latter (approx. 150,000) being included in Italy.

that the king would in future be referred to only as the king of Italy. (*See* also ALBANIA; ETHIOPIA; YUGOSLAVIA.)

(C. M. CL.)

Italian East Africa: *see* ITALIAN COLONIAL EMPIRE.

Italian Literature.

Italy's emergence as a major theatre of war dwarfed by comparison every manifestation of the country's cultural activity. The bombing of Italian cities, the invasion of the peninsula, the downfall of the fascist government and the ensuing dislocation of the country's life made it virtually impossible to garner material sufficient for a fair estimate of the Italian literary output for 1943. However, from what little is known, it appears that nothing of distinction or importance appeared either in the field of drama or fiction. New editions of old novels, dating back to 60 years, served perforce as substitutes for the reading public. On the other hand, literary and historical research continued to hold a prominent place. The Regio Istituto di Studi Romani published Ciaceri's *Opera di Tito Livio e la Moderna Critica Storica*, besides a series of studies on the influence of Rome, over Greece, Rumania and other Latin countries. The Istituto di Studi Filosofici initiated publication of the *Edizione Nazionale dei Classici del Pensiero*, with A. Giuliano and E. Castelli as editors. This collection was to include rare and inedited works by outstanding Italian thinkers from the middle ages to our day. Under the title *Biblioteca Universale "La Meridiana,"* Sansoni brought out in various languages the first ten volumes of an ambitious series of the most distinguished contributions to art and science. V. De Bartholomaeis' compilation of religious plays of the 15th and 16th centuries, *Laudi Drammatiche e Rappresentazioni Sacre*, was published by Le Monnier. The Centro Di Studi Manzoniani sponsored M. Parenti's *Immagini della vita e dei tempi di A. Manzoni*. A. Bruers assembled in a single volume (Zanichelli) his scattered essays on literary criticism. An analysis of the personality and works of L. Chiarelli was published by M. Lo Vecchio Musti (Cenacolo).

The most significant works by Italian writers in exile included *What To Do With Italy* by Gaetano Salvemini and G. La Piana (New York); G. A. Borgese's *Common Cause* (New York); L. Weiczen-Giuliani's *Historia del Socialismo en el Siglo XX* (Mexico) and volume III of *Quaderni Italiani* (New York), devoted in great part to the role played by the Italian anti-fascists and the Vatican in the Spanish Civil War.

The meagre information which filtered through the press revealed that a strong reaction had set in against the young Italian writers who poured out the pent-up anguish of their turbulent adolescence in their books.

Still more vocal was the revulsion against the very pillars of the dictatorship: "propaganda, rhetoric, superficiality and confusion."

These healthy symptoms, together with the undercurrents perceptible in Italian literature after World War I, the return to militant liberalism by such men as the philosopher Benedetto Croce and Professor Adolfo Omodeo, President of Naples university, and the spirit which imbued the works of Italian writers in exile, were heartening portents of the revival which we may expect in Italian letters.

Fascism, during its 20 years of power, could not boast of a single outstanding fascist writer and did not succeed in leaving behind it a single literary work worth remembering and it was to the credit of the young Italian writers who preferred escapism or silence to the dictator's prizes and laurels. (M. F. C.)

Italian Somaliland: *see* ITALIAN COLONIAL EMPIRE.

COLUMN OF U.S. JEEPS heading inland after the initial Allied beachhead had been established near Salerno, Italy, Sept. 9, 1943

Italy.

A kingdom consisting mainly of the peninsula projecting south into the Mediterranean from the mass of central Europe. The land boundaries, which reach as far north as 46°40′, are formed by France, Switzerland, Germany and Yugoslavia. Capital, Rome. Ruler: King Victor Emmanuel III. National flag: green, white and red in vertical stripes, with the arms in the white stripe.

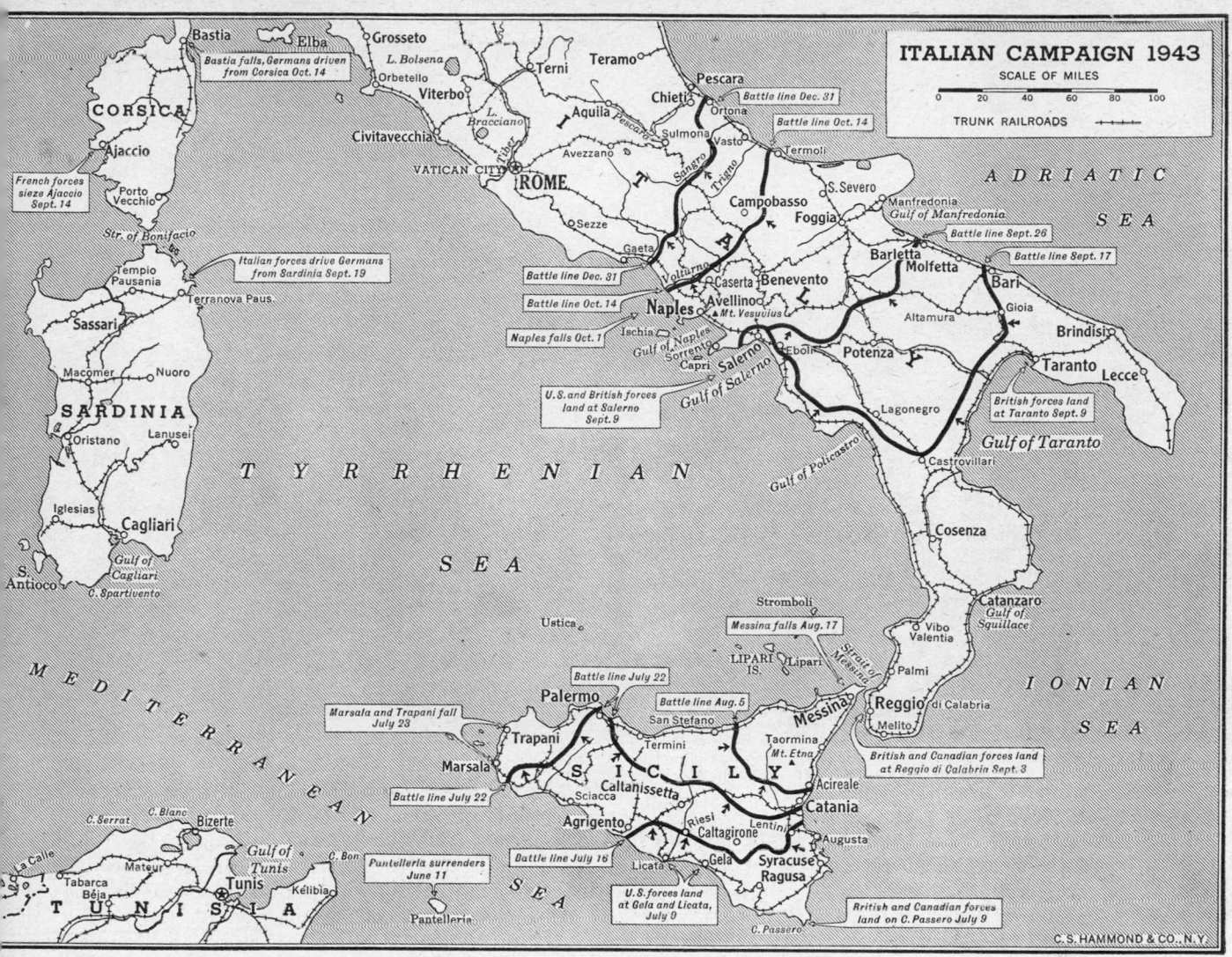

ITALIAN CAMPAIGN 1943
SCALE OF MILES
0   20   40   60   80   100
TRUNK RAILROADS

C. S. HAMMOND & CO., N.Y.

Area and Population.—Excluding Libya: area 119,764 sq.mi.; pop. (est. Jan. 1, 1940) 44,815,000. Chief cities (pop. 1936): Rome (1,155,722), Milan (1,115,848), Naples (865,913), Genoa (634,646), Turin (629,115). Language, Italian; religion, Roman Catholic.

History.—By Jan. 1943, the Italian people had become thoroughly apathetic toward the war. Nothing that Mussolini did or said could make them otherwise. On Feb. 5 the duce forced the resignation of twelve members of his cabinet, including his own son-in-law, Count Ciano, and two days later he reorganized his entire administration. But no change in personnel could help now. The bread ration of his countrymen had fallen to one third below the lowest figure quoted for World War I; a swarm of British bombers constantly blasted Turin, Milan, and Genoa; Russian victories in the east decimated Italian divisions brigaded with Nazi armies; and finally in May it was evident that the conquest of Libya and Tunisia by the Anglo-French-American forces during the first five months of 1943 had ended Italy's African empire.

By the end of spring invasion from Africa seemed imminent. But before Italy and Sicily could be attacked, it was first necessary to subdue the islet of Pantelleria, 40 mi. from Tunis, 65 from Sicily. This was accomplished, and exclusively by air assault, on June 11. One month later, July 10, the Americans and British invaded Sicily, which fell 38 days later.

Quite as important as this feat of arms was the deposition of Mussolini on July 25. The duce, it seems, at last demanded too

many sacrifices for even the fascist grand council to accept, and by a sudden *coup d'état*, Marshal Pietro Badoglio arrested fascism's founder in the name of the king and spirited him away into captivity. Badoglio made a pretense of continuing the fighting, but soon agreed to unconditional surrender. When this was announced the first week in September, the enraged Germans occupied Naples, Rome, Milan, Turin and other cities. Riots promptly broke out everywhere in northern Italy but quickly were suppressed. Badoglio's government declared war on Germany but Mussolini, rescued by the German luftwaffe and backed by German bayonets, reappeared in Italy once more, claiming that he stood for an Italian republic. Italian soldiers in Croatia, Albania, Greece, and in the Dodecanese Islands were disarmed by angry German detachments. The Italian fleet steamed to Malta, losing one battleship en route by German bombing.

On Sept. 3 the invasion of the Italian mainland commenced as the British 8th army crossed from Sicily to the toe of Italy. The following week the American 5th army under Gen. Mark Clark landed at Salerno. The Americans had grave difficulty in securing their beachhead; the Germans, indeed, were so confident of victory that they announced that the Americans had been driven into the sea, and as a matter of fact this almost happened. It was a good ten days before Clark's 5th army could be considered firmly established on shore, and not until Sept. 17 did it make contact with the British 8th army marching up from the south against little opposition. The Germans retreated promptly to the north, making a shambles of Naples as they did so. That city

SHIPS BURNING in Palermo harbour, Sicily, during a German air raid which followed U.S. occupation of the city July 22, 1943. The hulks in the foreground are of axis ships sunk previously by Allied bombers

was the American objective, but so high were the mountains that stood between it and Salerno, that it was Oct. 1 before American troops occupied the important port. They found a wrecked city, the harbour junked with dynamited ships, water and lighting facilities ruined and a population starving, drawing its drinking water from the sewers. Even the library of the University of Naples was looted and ruined by the Germans, who also set time bombs in hotels and in the post office so that the maximum number of Italian and American lives might be taken even after the city was evacuated.

Meanwhile on Sept. 30 a conference took place on a British battleship between Gen. Dwight Eisenhower, Allied commander-in-chief, and Marshal Badoglio.

During the last quarter of 1943 the political question of what should be done to Italy and who should govern Italy attracted almost as much attention as the continuance of the war. Scarcely any Italians wanted Victor Emmanuel to remain as king, but some did believe that a liberal and anti-fascist monarchy under his son, or perhaps a regency for his grandson, would be the best solution for their country. This seemed to be the opinion of Count Carlo Sforza, Italy's foremost anti-fascist exile, who expressed himself as willing to collaborate with the monarchy but not with Badoglio. Other Italians, however, made it quite evident by mass meetings, or by attempted mass meetings (one of which was forbidden by the Allied military government in Naples), that not only Badoglio but the house of Savoy must be eliminated. Roosevelt meanwhile assured the Italian people that they would ultimately determine entirely for themselves their own form of government, and with this pledge even Stalin apparently was content, for the U.S.S.R. associated herself with Britain and the United States in a joint resolution to the effect that complete guarantees concerning freedom of speech, assembly, and the press, together with the final elimination of all

traces of the fascist regime, must for the time being be considered subordinate to military objectives.

Those objectives soon became apparent as the British 8th army advanced up the eastern coast of Italy, securing after desperate German resistance the great Foggia air base on Sept. 28 and coming abreast of the American 5th army, which, with several British divisions attached to it, was pushing northward toward Rome.

Three months of steady fighting during October, November, and December brought both armies nearer their goal, but progress was slow. Torrential rains bogged down the invaders and the terrain was mountainous. As 1943 ended the Allies were still 75 to 80 mi. from Rome. (See WORLD WAR II.)

Education.—Public elementary schools in 1937-38, 131,580; pupils, 5,411,596. Students in secondary schools, 647,505; in universities, 77,429. A special school charter of 1939 required all education in Italy to have a fascist stamp.

Finance.—Estimates for year ending June 30, 1940: revenue, 24,560,000,000 lire; expenditure, 29,316,000,000 lire. Lira quoted Dec. 1939 at 5 cents; in June 1941, 5.262 cents.

Trade and Communication.—In 1939: imports, 11,061,000,-000 lire; exports, 8,007,000,000 lire. Railways, 17,824 mi. Shipping: 2,301 sailing vessels, 1,057 steamships, 293 motorships. Total more than 2,200,000 short tons.

Agriculture, Manufacture and Minerals.—Livestock in 1938: horses, 791,120; asses, 791,390; mules, 431,150; cattle, 7,666,890; pigs, 2,940,440; sheep, 9,467,400; goats, 1,828,070. In short tons: wheat 1,369,000,000; maize 410,000,000; beans 179,000,000; olives 225,000,000.

Most important industry, textiles, with 938 factories in 1938. In minerals, sulphur continued to lead, there being mined, in 1938, 2,604,735 short tons, to 930,000 tons of iron pyrites, next competing mineral. (See also ALBANIA; ANTI-SEMITISM; FASCISM; ITALIAN COLONIAL EMPIRE; NAVIES OF THE WORLD.)

BIBLIOGRAPHY.—R. G. Woolbert, *Italy's Role in the European Conflict.*

Foreign Policy Association reports (May 1940); L. E. Frechtling, *ibid.* (Feb. 1941). G. and F. Nicotri, *Freedom for Italy* (1942); C. Sforza, *The Real Italians* (1942); H. L. Matthews, *The Fruits of Fascism* (1943).

(W. P. Hl.)

Ivory Coast: *see* French Colonial Empire.

Jacobs, William Wymark ("W. W.")

(1863–1943), British author, was born Sept. 8, at Wapping, east London. He attended private school and for 16 years held a civil service post in a savings bank department. His books on seafaring men and dockyard hands, speaking through their characters, displayed a gentle humour and economy of style. Though his seamen were rarely at sea, their adventures or misadventures ashore provided many a thrilling tale. His first volume of short stories, *Many Cargoes* (1896), had an immediate success and was followed by two similar volumes, *The Skipper's Wooing* (1897) and *Sea Urchins* (1898). One of his most famous short stories, *The Monkey's Paw,* came to be regarded as a "horror" classic and was dramatized for the screen, stage and radio. An omnibus, *Snug Harbour,* containing some 17 volumes of his work, was published in 1931. Jacobs died in London, Sept. 1.

Jamaica: *see* West Indies, British.

Japan.

An empire, consisting of a chain of islands in the western Pacific, stretching from South Sakhalin (Karafuto) (50° latitude) to the South Seas mandated islands, which extend over a great expanse of the Pacific, some being located near the equator. The Japanese empire includes Chosen (*q.v.*) on the mainland of Asia and the small Kwantung leased territory, with the city of Dairen, at the tip of the Liaotung peninsula. Chosen, Formosa (Taiwan) (*q.v.*) and South Sakhalin, together with the South Seas islands, are administered as colonies. The area of the Japanese empire is 263,359 sq.mi., of Japan proper (the four large islands, Honshu, Hokkaido, Shikoku and Kyushu, with many adjacent smaller islands) 148,756 sq.mi. Population of the empire (census of 1935) was 97,697,555, of Japan proper, 69,254,148. An estimate of the Cabinet Statistics bureau placed the population of the empire at 103,087,100 on Dec. 1, 1937. The same source estimated the population of Japan proper at 72,875,800, as of Oct. 1, 1939.

Capital, Tokyo (*q.v.*). Japan's six largest cities are Tokyo (pop. 5,875,667, census of 1935; 6,581,100, estimate of 1939); Osaka (pop. 2,989,874, census; 3,394,200, estimate), Nagoya (pop. 1,082,816, census; 1,249,100, estimate), Kyoto (pop. 1,080,593, census; 1,177,200, estimate), Kobe (912,179, census; 1,006,100, estimate) and Yokohama (704,290, census; 866,200, estimate). Buddhism is the most prevalent religion, followed by Shintoism, the indigenous faith of Japan. There were 41,127,307 Buddhists in Japan in 1936, 16,525,840 Shintoists, 215,166 Japanese Christians of Protestant denominations, 111,856 Roman Catholics and 41,251 Greek Orthodox believers in 1938. U.S. and British missionary work was suspended after the outbreak of the war, but Japanese Christians remained free to profess their faith.

The Japanese sovereign is Emperor Hirohito. The prime minister during 1943 was Gen. Hideki Tojo.

History.—The second year of Japan's war against the western powers, which began with the attack on Pearl Harbor on Dec. 7, 1941, differed appreciably in strategic outline from the first. During 1943 Japan was entirely on the defensive. No major Japanese offensive was launched in any direction. The Japanese forces which had occupied Attu, in the Aleutians, were destroyed and a larger force, which had established itself on Kiska, in the

same region, slipped away under cover of fog. Gen. Douglas MacArthur's campaign in northeastern New Guinea moved ahead. There were successful landing operations in New Britain, directed against the main advanced Japanese base of Rabaul. The last Japanese centre of resistance in the New Georgia group, Bairoka Harbor, was evacuated by the Japanese. The Americans occupied Vila, on Kolombongara Island, and effected landings on Bougainville, northernmost of the larger islands of the Solomon group.

An offensive from another direction was launched when a marine force late in November occupied the small Gilbert group of islands.

The balance of naval force in the Pacific during 1943 shifted so much in favour of the United States that it became a part of American naval strategy to tempt or provoke the Japanese main fleet into a decisive engagement by sending task forces to attack points well within the range of Japanese naval power.

Except for some stiffening of U.S. air support, there was no major change in the military situation in China during 1943. Japanese local attacks in the "rice bowl" area of China, in Hunan province, south of the Yangtze river, and in the rugged Salween river region of Yunnan led to no important results. No important city changed hands. The so-called Ledo road, being pushed into China from northern Assam under the direction of a U.S. engineering force, made further progress. American public opin-

THE SLOGAN "AAA" (Asia for the Asiatics) appeared throughout Japanese conquered territories in 1943

ion was shocked by the news in April that some of the aviators who had taken part in the Doolittle raid on Tokyo in April 1942 had been put to death after some kind of trial by the Japanese authorities.

While the territorial results of 1943 were much less favourable for Japan than those of 1942, Japan remained in possession of all its major conquests of the first months of the war. The Japanese hold on Burma was harassed by periodic air bombing, but there was no direct disturbance of the Japanese rule and exploitation in Malaya, the Netherlands Indies and the Philippines. The U.S. offensives were still on the outer periphery of Japan's enormously enlarged empire. Much more serious, from the Japanese standpoint, than the comparatively small territorial losses of 1943 were the severe losses in shipping as a result of activity of U.S. submarines and the increasingly unfavourable balance sheet of losses in air combat. (*See also* WORLD WAR II.)

Policy in Conquered Countries.—The apparent Japanese military decision to concentrate on holding what had been conquered rather than to launch new offensives was accompanied during 1943 by interesting political and economic moves in the vast area of southeastern Asia and adjacent archipelagoes which had fallen under Japanese military control. Japanese policy aimed at two main objectives: to make political capital by granting the show of independence and sovereignty to some of the countries which had been occupied and to draw as effectively as possible on the rich stores of strategic raw materials in which this part of Asia abounds.

Formal independence was granted to Burma on August 1 under a native government headed by a political leader named Ba Maw. There was a similar grant of independence to the Philippine puppet government headed by José P. Laurel in October. In neither case was there, of course, any withdrawal of Japanese troops or of Japanese supervision and control in all important matters. But the setting up of native governments in Burma and the Philippines may have relieved the Japanese army of some of its policing tasks. Both in Burma and in the Philippines armed native units, the numbers and military value of which were difficult to gauge, were created. Japanese influence in these countries found expression in native parties, the Kalibapi in the Philippines and the Dabama Sinyetha in Burma. Thailand was rewarded for co-operation with Japan by a grant of additional territory, the four Unfederated Malay States (*q.v.*), Perlis, Kedah, Kelantan and Trengganu in northern Malaya and the Shan States in southeastern Burma. Here the motive was probably twofold. There was an attempt to appeal to Thai nationalism (Thailand, with Japanese collaboration, had already enlarged its territory at the expense of French Indo-China) and to give the Thai government an interest in resisting the reoccupation of this territory by United Nations forces.

No governments were set up in the Netherlands Indies or in Malaya; but Malay local councils were set up in these regions and a so-called all-Java cultural movement was launched under Japanese inspiration. A treaty of alliance was concluded with the Nanking government, headed by Wang Ching-Wei and, in an effort to split Chinese nationalist sentiment, the foreign concessions were formally returned to the authority of this regime, although Japanese military control remained unrelaxed. A further Pan-Asian move was the setting up in Singapore of a "provisional government of Free India," headed by the irreconcilable Bengal enemy of British rule, Subhas Chandra Bose.

Japan had set up a ministry of Greater East Asia, headed by Razuo Aoki, in Nov. 1942. Its task was to exert a centralizing and co-ordinating influence on the economic development of the occupied regions in the south. The Southern Development bank was created for financial operations in these regions and it was

U.S. AIRMAN, believed to be one of the Tokyo raiders, being escorted from a plane by Japanese after his capture. This picture was released by the Japanese through a neutral source in 1943 after their announcement that some of the captured U.S. airmen who participated in the Doolittle raid had been executed

stated that this bank would lend 3,300,000,000 yen for the needs of the military budget in 1943–44. This probably represented the value of the material which Japan planned to obtain in southeast Asia during the year in question.

While this part of the world is rich in many raw materials (rubber, tin, oil, quinine, sugar, to mention a few of the more important), lack of shipping and of adequate land transportation handicapped Japanese exploitation to a considerable extent. Japan by 1943 had not invested much capital in industrial development in the south, because the military hold on these new conquests was somewhat precarious, and the government's economic policy was to concentrate war industries within what might be called the inner ring of Japan's defenses, in Japan proper, Chosen, and Manchuria.

Internal Developments.—There were no drastic changes in the Japanese internal political set-up as a result of the great expansion of the war. Hideki Tojo remained head of the cabinet; a veteran diplomat and former ambassador to Great Britain and to the soviet union, Mamoru Shigemitsu, took over the portfolio of minister of foreign affairs in April 1943.

Besides the regular annual session of the diet, ending in March, there were two brief extraordinary sessions, in June and October, apparently designed to communicate to the deputies and through them to the people a sense of the gravity of the war situation and also to thresh out the details of a new system of government regulation of the major war industries. Plans for fire prevention and for the evacuation of the larger Japanese cities in the event of air raids were announced, and Prime Minister Tojo told the October session of the diet that Japan had built "an invincible fortification against invasion."

An Ordinance for Wartime Administrative Authority to Act was passed by the diet on March 17, 1943, and conferred on Tojo virtually dictatorial powers over production in the following key industries: aircraft, shipping, iron and steel, coal, light metals. Perhaps as a counterbalance to this extension of government control over business, seven representatives of big industrial and commercial firms were given *shinnin* rank (the first category in the civil service) and were appointed as cabinet advisers. This move was apparently designed to facilitate discussion at the top level between government and big business on vital issues of economic war mobilization.

A second exchange of interned civilians was arranged between Japan on one side and the United States, Great Britain, and Canada on the other, after some difficulty and delay; and the Swedish ship "Gripsholm" brought a considerable number of repatriates back to the United States in Dec. 1943.

Education.—There were 48,637 schools of all types in Japan in 1938, with 15,638,780 pupils. There were 563 middle schools (the equivalent of U.S. high schools), with 364,486 students, and 45 universities, with 6,385 professors and 72,968 students.

Finance.—The unit of currency is the yen (officially valued at 23.48 U.S. cents before the outbreak of war in the Pacific). The budget for 1942–43 plainly reflected the tremendous strain of the war against the west. It called for expenditures of 30,000,000,000 yen and revenue receipts of 8,000,000,000 yen. The 1941–42 budget was set at 13,875,000,000 yen, of which 7,574,000,000 yen was raised through loans. The national debt was growing at a dizzy pace and at the end of 1943 must have been well in excess of the national income, estimated at 45,000,000,000 yen in 1942. Currency in circulation on Sept. 30, 1941: 4,619,000,000 yen.

The Bank of Japan is the central bank of note-issue. The Yokohama Specie bank is in charge of foreign exchange transactions (almost nonexistent after the outbreak of war with the west) and finances foreign trade. Commercial banking is mostly in the hands of seven large banks, which are closely tied in with the big Japanese trusts and cartels: the Mitsui, Mitsubishi, Dai-ichi, Sumitomo, Yasuda, Dai Hyaku, and Sanwa.

Trade and Communication.—Trade figures for Japan proper, excluding its colonies, were as follows:

	1939 (yen)	1940 (yen)
Imports	2,917,000,000	3,709,035,000
Exports	3,576,000,000	3,972,400,000

After 1940 there was no publication of detailed trade figures and after July 1941, there was almost no foreign trade, in the normal sense of the term. At that time the United States, Great Britain, and the Netherlands Indies adopted retaliatory economic measures, following the Japanese occupation of southern Indo-China, that brought Japan's trade with those countries to a standstill. Following Pearl Harbor Japan's commercial exchanges were almost entirely with countries under its direct or indirect military control. The only exceptions were a small trade with the soviet union, occasional exchanges of blockade-running cargoes with Germany and a trickle of trade with Free China across the loosely held front.

There were 16,549 mi. of state and private railways in Japan in 1938, 3,176 mi. in Chosen and 209 in South Sakhalin. The completion in 1942 of an undersea railway tunnel beneath the Kwannon strait, between the cities of Shimonoseki, in Honshu, and Moji, in Kyushu, eliminated the necessity of transshipment of troops and supplies across this narrow body of water.

At the end of 1939 Japan possessed 4,084 ships of over 100 tons, with an aggregate tonnage of 5,728,779 tons. As of Sept. 30, 1938, there were 17,791 sailing ships, average tonnage 1,046,476. U.S. naval sources estimated Japanese merchant shipping losses during the first two years of the war at 2,000,000 to 2,500,000 tons. No figures of Japanese ship construction were available after 1936, when 295,000 tons of shipping were turned out.

Commercial aviation continued in the hands of a semi-governmental monopoly, the Japan Airways Co., established in 1939 and capitalized at 100,000,000 yen. The length of its routes in 1938–39 was about 10,000 mi. The number of flights was 17,144, the aggregate length of flights 3,788,023 mi., the number of passengers carried 69,268, the quantity of goods conveyed 328 tons, the amount of mail carried 903 tons.

There were 13,648 telegraph stations in Japan proper in 1939, and 75,838,875 domestic and 1,261,295 foreign messages were handled in the year 1938–39. The length of the inland telegraph lines was 259,709 mi. in 1938. There were 6,197 telephone exchanges in Japan on Sept. 30, 1939, and 1,006,498 subscribers to telephone service.

Agricultural Production in Japan, 1940

	Cultivated area (acres)	Yield (tons)
Rice	7,837,888	9,999,308
Wheat	2,078,023	1,415,581
Barley	840,941	829,508
Rye	999,599	690,297

Agriculture.—Because of the pressure of population on the limited amount of arable land, Japan is a country of small rice and silk farms and fishing villages, with almost no large-scale farming with modern machinery and a minimum of animal husbandry. There were 5,519,480 farm households in 1938, and the amount of land under cultivation was about 15,000,000 ac., the average size of the holding thus being less than three acres. For several years before 1938 there had been a slight declining tendency in the number of farms; the cultivated area remained almost stationary. Rice has always been Japan's largest crop and represented about half the reported value of the country's agricultural produce in 1939. The total reported value, excluding meat, milk, and eggs, on which no data were given and which do not figure largely in Japanese farm output, was 5,614,000,000 yen. The value of rice produced in that year was 2,874,000,000 yen. The value of silk cocoons produced in 1939 was 883,000,000 yen. There were 1,894,261 cattle, 1,140,479 swine, 114,000 sheep, and 281,741 goats in Japan in 1938. There were 1,431,920 horses in 1936.

Manufacturing.—There were 112,332 factories employing more than five persons each in Japan in 1938, with 3,604,283 workers and an output valued at 19,667,219,686 yen. This was an increase of almost 20% over the value of production in 1937 and reflected the stimulation of the war industries because of the hostilities in China. The most important industries, and the value of their output in 1938, were as follows: metal (4,687,166,-000 yen); spinning and weaving (3,984,829,000 yen); machinery and tools (3,821,881,000 yen); chemicals (3,460,581,000 yen); foodstuffs (1,786,275,000 yen); 1,442,713 persons were engaged in fishing in 1938.

Mineral Production.—Japan is poor in natural resources. Its principal minerals are coal (41,803,000 tons, valued at 305,537,-000 yen); gold (784,308 oz., valued at 74,828,000 yen); copper (85,950 tons, valued at 66,617,000 yen). These figures are for 1936, since the publication of statistics of mineral output was forbidden after that year. On a percentage basis, mineral output in 1939 was about 20% higher than in 1936. Oil is a conspicuous deficiency in Japan's economy, although this was at least temporarily remedied by the conquest of the Netherlands Indies and Burma. There was a limited amount of oil in the northern prefectures of Honshu and experiments were conducted in manufacturing oil from coal in South Sakhalin and in extracting oil from shale in Manchuria. (*See* also FASCISM; UNITED STATES; WORLD WAR II.)

BIBLIOGRAPHY.—Sir George Sansom, *Japan: A Cultural History;* annual issue of *The Japan Year Book* and *The Japan-Manchoukuo Year Book;* E. B. Schumpeter and others, *The Industrialization of Japan and Manchoukuo, 1930–1940;* T. Yano and K. Shirasaki, *Nippon: A Charted Survey of Japan;* The Mitsubishi Economic Research Bureau, *Japanese Trade and Industry: Present and Future;* Hugh Byas, *Government by Assassination;* Otto D. Tolischus, *Tokyo Record.*   (W. H. CH.)

Japanese Relocation, U.S.: *see* ALIENS.
Jarvis Island: *see* PACIFIC ISLANDS, U.S.
Java: *see* NETHERLANDS COLONIAL EMPIRE; NETHERLANDS INDIES.

Jeffers, William M.

(1876–   ), U.S. railroad executive, was born Jan. 2 in North Platte, Neb. He started work with the Union Pacific railroad in 1890 as an office boy. He was then telegrapher, clerk, dispatcher, trainmaster, superintendent and vice-president and, by Oct. 1937, president of the road. On Sept. 15, 1942, Donald Nelson, WPB chairman, made Jeffers head of the rubber administration and gave him the task of executing the Baruch committee's proposals for tire conservation, gasoline rationing and expansion of synthetic rubber production. Ten days after he took over, he ordered nation-wide gas rationing to save tires, effective Dec. 1. His whole background as a hard-hitting railroader made it easy for him to take literally the recommendation of Bernard Baruch that the rubber program "should be bulled through." He did exactly that. His directness, bluntness and force enabled him to do unpopular things with impunity. He battled army, navy, Sec. Ickes and others for priorities on equipment needed to make new plants—and got the priorities.

In May, Under Secretary of War Robert P. Patterson and Jeffers declared a truce in their high-octane gasoline v. rubber war and the two men formed part of a committee to tour U.S. war plants to speed production of critical materials and commodities.

Jeffers resigned on Sept. 4, saying that "the big job is done" and that he could serve the country better by returning to his old work as president of Union Pacific.

That month synthetic rubber production was 30,000 tons, about half the prewar consumption.

Jespersen, Jens Otto Harry

(1860–1943), Danish philologist and educator, was born July 16 at Randers, Denmark. One of the world's outstanding authorities on English grammar, he was professor of English at Copenhagen university, 1893–1925, and lecturer at Columbia university, 1909–10. He devised an "interlanguage," Novial, in collaboration with the International Language association, which he explained in his book, *An International Language* (1929). He was the author of numerous books on language, its history and growth, and on English grammar, the most complete of which was his *Modern English Grammar* in four volumes. He died April 30 after an operation in Roskilde, Denmark, according to information received in New York city, May 15. (See *Encyclopædia Britannica*.)

Jesschonnek, Hans

(1898–1943), German army officer, was born Dec. 10. A veteran of World War I, Jesschonnek served in the formidable German blitzkrieg armies of World War II and rose quickly to the rank of a colonel general. He was credited with organizing the Luftwaffe for the short Polish campaign in 1939 and was regarded with some fondness by Hitler. But an official German announcement in Dec. 1942 that Jesschonnek had been serving as chief of staff of the German air force since 1939 came as a complete surprise to Allied leaders. He had been little known and until this disclosure he was not regarded as a prominent figure in the German military. News of Jesschonnek's position came at a time when Hitler was reshuffling his army command because of the failure of his Russian campaign. The next heard of Jesschonnek was a Berlin radio announcement on August 20 which said that he had died "of a serious illness" at the headquarters of Marshal Hermann Goering.

Jewish Religious Life.

The year 1943 brought to the Jew and Judaism a continued crescendo of horror. In the slaughterhouse of Europe, the struggle of a remnant of Jewry for sheer physical survival left little room for cultivation of Judaism after synagogues and Jewish communities were destroyed and the nazi's "extermination commissions" had annihilated an estimated 4,000,000 Jews.

Yet Jewish refugees were found in mountain caves with their scrolls of the Torah and religious books. Jewish religious life fell a sacrifice in countries such as Holland, Denmark and Italy.

The free Christian world, and even more strikingly Christian prelates and laity in axis-occupied lands, reacted not only in brave words of protest and denunciation, but also in action, such as in opening monasteries and religious organizations to shelter Jews. The Federal Council of Churches of Christ in the United States set a special day of compassion and prayer for the Jews of Europe, while American Jewry took on itself a six-week period of mourning and intercession. On the favourable side of the ledger the relaxation of the soviet's proscription of religion and the influx from Poland into Russia of traditional Talmudic and Zionist Jewish refugees opened up a new chapter in the story of Judaism in Russia.

Outside of Europe, Judaism suffered numerous setbacks. Sporadically in the United States synagogues were defaced with swastikas and cemeteries violated. The Quebec city council which for more than a decade opposed the building of a synagogue in the city, expropriated a site on which the foundations of a syna-

EXECUTIVES of the Jewish Agency for Palestine—rulers of all Jews in the mandate—in their headquarters at Jerusalem. At the extreme right is the chairman, David Ben-Gurion, a Pole

gogue were being laid. Jewish life in Argentina felt the government's repressive hand. The war continued to take men from synagogues, teachers from religious schools, rabbis from their pulpits. In the United States more than 200 Jewish chaplains were in the armed services.

Within the Jewish community there was warm discussion about such problems as the type of religious education to be given to the refugee children reaching Palestine, and the creation of the American Council for Judaism. This organization stressing Reform Judaism as a spiritual force to the exclusion of Zionist and other traditional and historico-cultural aspects of Jewish life, was denounced by the overwhelming majority of the rabbinate of the United States and was asked by the organized Reform rabbinate to disband.

Even in a world of war the Torah was still going forth from Zion, and from Palestine came the news of a projected new edition of the Hebrew Bible under the auspices of the Hebrew university, an encyclopaedia of the Scriptures and a new edition of the Talmud. Everywhere Jewish groups stressed the spiritual values which must come to expression in the postwar world if there is to be enduring peace. Thus the American Jewish conference, representing the totality of American Jewish life called "upon the members of the American Jewish community to strengthen their commitments to the synagogue and the agencies of Jewish culture in an effort to revive the broken spirits of our stricken brethren in Europe, to compensate for the destruction of their organized religious life, as well as to remain true to our historical heritage as a people. We call upon the members of the Christian communions in the United States to employ the immeasurable power of their faith to restore the presence of God in a world that has almost been destroyed by the agencies of evil." (*See* also ANTI-SEMITISM.)

BIBLIOGRAPHY.—*The Contemporary Jewish Record* (1943); *American Jewish Year Book* (1942–43).   (D. DE S. P.)

Jewish Welfare Board, National.

Organized in 1917, the National Jewish Welfare Board is the sole organization authorized to serve the special religious, cultural and hospitality needs of the Jewish members of the armed forces of the United States. Authorization for its work with the military comes from two sources: from the war and navy departments of the United States government; and from 37 national Jewish organizations, representing every phase of Jewish life in the United States.

The board is the Jewish member of the United Service Organizations, Inc. (U.S.O.) and serves wholly or in part in 206 U.S.O. recreational facilities in the United States. The board also serves special needs of Jewish soldiers overseas. It enlists rabbis to serve as Jewish chaplains in the army and navy and grants them ecclesiastical endorsement. Other activities of the board include service to Jewish youth on college campuses; rehabilitation work to veterans of the American armed forces; special services to wounded soldiers and sailors in general hospitals.

In 1943 there was a professional staff of 297 serving at home and abroad. The program for the armed forces in 1943 was supported and amplified by army and navy committees in 480 cities in the United States and 27 communities overseas.

In 1943 there were 209 Jewish chaplains serving with the armed forces. These were helped by 297 J.W.B. field workers, by 200 civilian rabbis recruited by the board, and innumerable Christian chaplains. During the High Holy Days of 1943, they conducted 2,000 religious services in 34 countries, reaching more than 200,000 Jewish soldiers and sailors.

Other interests of the board are the National Association of Y.M.H.A.s, Y.W.H.A.s and Jewish community centres of the United States and Canada. Affiliated with the board in 1943 were 315 such organizations, with a total membership of 410,000 men, women, young people and children.

The Jewish Welfare board assists these organizations to provide wholesome recreation, informal educational activities, opportunities for self-improvement through participation in a variety of Jewish and general cultural pursuits. The affiliation of the J.W.B. with Associated Youth Serving Organizations (A.Y.S.O.) is in line with its interest in the welfare of children and youth.

Annual meetings of the board were suspended for the duration of World War II. Officers in 1943 were: Frank L. Weil, New York, president; Walter Rothschild, New York, chairman National Army and Navy committee; Mrs. Samuel Glogower, Detroit, chairman Jewish Center division; Mrs. Alfred R. Bachrach, chairman Women's division; Louis Kraft, executive director. Offices are at 220 Fifth ave., New York city.   (F. L. W.)

Johns Hopkins University.

An institution of higher education at Baltimore, Md.; president, Isaiah Bowman. During 1943 the university's wartime activities took a new turn with the introduction of the Army Specialized Training program, under which 500 army trainees were assigned for studies in the engineering and area and language curricula. In addition, about 75% of the student body of the medical school were inducted into army or navy and continued their medical studies as members of the armed forces. Wartime research under the Office of Scientific Research and Development was expanded during the year, and the Engineering Science Management War Training program was continued. The School of Medicine and the School of Hygiene and Public Health joined in offering a series of short refresher courses in medical and surgical specialties for commissioned personnel in the armed services. For statistics of enrolment, endowment, library volumes, etc., *see* UNIVERSITIES AND COLLEGES. (I. Bo.)

Johnston, Eric A.

(1896–), U.S. industrialist, was born Dec. 21 in Washington, D.C. After working his way through the University of Washington, where he received the LL.B. degree in 1917, he served as a captain in the marine corps from 1917 to 1922. On receiving a medical discharge because of an injury suffered in China, he returned to Spokane. The next year he organized the Brown-Johnston company, an electrical manufacturing firm, and became its president. Ten years later he organized and became president of the Columbia Electric company. He also achieved controlling positions and directorates in several other firms in Spokane and Seattle. In 1931 Johnston was elected president of the Spokane Chamber of Commerce, and from 1934 to 1941 he was a director of the Chamber of Commerce of the U.S. He was elected president of this organization in April 1942 and was re-elected in 1943. In February and March 1943, in his role as chairman of the U.S. Commission of Inter-American Development, Johnston made a 20,000-mi. aeroplane trip through seven countries of South America, conferring with government leaders and businessmen on plans for postwar economic co-operation. He indicated that surplus war plants might be dismantled and sent to South America after the war. On his return to the U.S. he emphasized the importance of sending U.S. money and skill "down the broad avenues of exploration and not the blind alleys of exploitation." In August, at the invitation of Lord Halifax, he visited England, where he urged that postwar world trade be based to the maximum extent on free competitive enterprise. He is a member of the Economic Stabilization board; is on the Economic Advisory committee of the state department; is on the board of trustees of the Committee for Economic Development, and serves on numerous committees in Washington as a representative of American business.

Johnston Island: *see* PACIFIC ISLANDS, U.S.
Joint War Committees (U.S. and Canada): *see* CANADIAN-U.S. WAR COMMITTEES.

Jones, Jesse Holman

(1874–   ), U.S. secretary of commerce, was born in Robertson county, Tenn., on April 5. At Dallas, Tex., in 1895 he became manager of a lumber company and seven years later organized his own firm. He engaged in extensive real estate operations and bought control of the Houston *Chronicle*, of which he is publisher. President Hoover appointed him a director of the Reconstruction Finance corporation in 1932 and he became chairman the following year. In July 1939 Jones was appointed administrator of the Federal Loan agency. On Sept. 13, 1940 President Roosevelt nominated him secretary of commerce. His position in the

END OF THE WALLACE-JONES FEUD in July 1943, cartooned by Seibel in the *Richmond Times-Dispatch* with the title "Right Out Where the Neighbors Can See"

defense program, which started in 1940, was a key one. His agencies provided the money for new plants, as well as for building up stockpiles of critical raw materials. Jones came under fire in 1942 when the Truman committee of the senate blamed him for much of the rubber shortage. On June 29, 1943, Vice-President Henry A. Wallace, chairman of the Board of Economic Warfare, attacked Jones violently for alleged failures to supply funds to acquire critical materials. Jones retaliated by charging Wallace with "malice, innuendo, half-truths and no truths at all." The president then eliminated the Board of Economic Warfare and rebuked both Wallace and Jones for their "acrimonious public debate."

Jones, Marvin

(1886–   ), U.S. jurist and politician, was born near Valley View, in Cooke county, Tex., Feb. 26. He was graduated from Southwestern university, 1905, received his law degree from the University of Texas and was admitted to the Texas bar in 1907. He established a private practice of law in Amarillo, Tex., and in 1913 was appointed chairman of the board of legal examiners in the 7th supreme judicial district of Texas. He was elected to the house of representatives in 1917, where he served continuously for 24 years. While in congress, he was chairman of the house committee on agriculture for a number of years. On Nov. 20, 1940, he resigned from the house to accept an appointment as judge of the U.S. court of claims. Jones acted as principal adviser to director of economic stabilization James F. Byrnes on food problems, and was appointed head of the war food administration on June 28, 1943, when Chester C. Davis resigned from that post. Judge Jones had previously served as conference president and chairman of the U.S. delegation to the United Nations parley on food and agriculture at Hot Springs, Va.

Jordana y Souza, Francisco Gómez

(1876–   ), Spanish army officer and politician, received his education at the Military academy and Staff college. He saw service in Cuba early in his career. In 1903, with the rank of captain, he was attached to the general staff. Later, he became an instructor at the Escuela Superior de Guerra. Promoted to the rank of brigadier general in 1920, he was placed in charge of Moroccan affairs in the Primo de Rivera government. In 1928, with the rank of lieutenant general, he was appointed high commissioner of Morocco. Jordana supported the rebel uprising against the Spanish republican government and subsequently held a number of important posts in the Franco dictatorship. Vice-president and minister of foreign affairs in 1938, he became president of the council of state the following year. He held this post until Sept. 3, 1942, when he again became foreign minister, succeeding Gen. Francisco Franco's brother-in-law, Ramon Serrano y Suñer. In April 1943, Jordana launched an appeal for peace, declaring that the nations engaged in the struggle were too powerful for either side to achieve total victory. His statement, regarded as a peace feeler made at Germany's request, was abruptly dismissed by U.S. Secretary of State Hull with a reiteration that unconditional surrender of the axis was still the sole objective of the Allies.

Judaism: *see* JEWISH RELIGIOUS LIFE.
Jugoslavia: *see* YUGOSLAVIA.

Juin, Alphonse Pierre

(1888?–   ), French army officer, was born in Bone, Algeria, the son of a policeman. He was educated at St. Cyr, French military academy. During World War I, he served as captain with Moroccan forces, and later became chief of staff to Marshal Lyautey. A divisional commander during the battle of France, June 1940, he was taken prisoner by the nazis and was released a year later. There were indications that Pierre Laval had arranged for Juin's release from the nazis in order to have him supplant Gen. Maxime Weygand. On Nov. 20, 1941, Weygand "retired" and Juin was named commander-in-chief of the French forces in North Africa. At the time of the Allied landings in North Africa in Nov. 1942, Darlan and Juin agreed to surrender Algiers after 16 hours of hostilities. Captured by the Allies, Juin carried on negotiations with them and concluded an armistice, acting under Adm. Jean Darlan's authority. After the latter's assassination, Gen. Giraud, who became high commissioner of North Africa, appointed Juin commander-in-chief of French forces in North

Africa, Dec. 29, 1942. Although he was unpopular with the de Gaullists, the French Committee of National Liberation approved Juin's nomination as commander-in-chief of Giraud's forces in June 1943. Juin led French armies in Tunisia, and was in command of French units on the Italian front, Dec. 1943.

Juke-Boxes: *see* Performing Right Societies.
Julius Rosenwald Fund: *see* Rosenwald Fund, The Julius.
Jumping: *see* Track and Field Sports.
Justice, U.S. Department of: *see* Government Departments and Bureaus.

Justo, Agustín P.

(1876–1943), Argentine statesman, was born Feb. 26 in Concepción del Uruguay, province of Entre Rios, Argentina. After studying at military academies, he became professor of military science at the Officers' Training school, 1903. Later, he taught civil engineering at the University of Buenos Aires and mathematics at the San Martín Military college. He rose to rank of general and for a brief period after the revolution of 1930 served as army commander-in-chief. Gen. Justo held the portfolios of war, agriculture and public works and climaxed his political career with election to the presidency in Nov. 1931, on a conservative coalition ticket. During the early years of his presidency, he was faced with the political and economic reconstruction of his country, weakened by revolution and the world economic depression. His tenure of office, 1932–38, was marked by his inauguration of what was tantamount to a "police state," though his presidential acts were considered more moderate than those of his predecessor, President Uriburu. A vigorous opponent of President Castillo's neutrality stand during World War II, Justo urged his countrymen to declare war on the axis powers. After Brazil declared war on the axis, he accepted a commission as a general in the Brazilian army. His death in Buenos Aires on Jan. 10 removed Castillo's most formidable foe from the Argentine political arena.

Jute.

The supply of jute for bagging in the United States continued to be fairly adequate in 1943 due to the application of vigorous control measures. Although 83% of the jute comes from the province of Bengal, India, through Calcutta, considerable supplies came through in 1943. All imports and distribution were under control of the War Production board. Stocks were sufficient at the end of the year to meet all of the most vital needs and retain a small stock pile. Efforts to extend the use of substitute fibres and to mix cotton and other fibres with jute were continued with some success. Paper and cotton bags were being used to a larger extent in many industries. The crop of jute in India was above the average and shipping improvements gave some prospect that imports might increase in 1944. Special efforts were continued to get larger supplies of abacá, sisal, henequen, etc., from Latin America. (J. C. Ms.)

Juvenile Delinquency: *see* Child Welfare; Crime.

Kaiser, Henry J.

(1882–   ), U.S. construction expert, was born May 9 in Canajoharie, N.Y. After 16 years with road construction projects in Canada, California and Cuba, 1914–30, he entered the dam construction field and by 1933, became head of Six Companies, Inc.—the organization that built Boulder and Parker dams. Kaiser, who was famous for completing construction jobs ahead of schedule, entered shipbuilding in Jan. 1941. In 1942, he obtained control of four large shipyards on the west coast. He revolutionized shipbuilding by prefabricating ship sections. On Nov. 18, his yard in Vancouver, Wash., assembled and launched a 10,500-ton Liberty ship in 3 days, 23 hours and 40 minutes. The year brought troubles too. On Jan. 17, the Kaiser-built 16,500-ton tanker *"Schenectady"* broke in two and sank. Labour troubles, with inter-union disputes, disrupted the Portland, Ore., yards. Before these difficulties had been disposed of, Kaiser, seeking a new field to conquer in aeroplane building, became involved in Brewster Aeronautical corporation's difficulties. He was made chairman on March 16, and president on Oct. 7. Kaiser arranged to get out of the bomber business, and to concentrate on Corsair fighters, promising 150 a month by May 1944.

Kameroons: *see* British West Africa; French Colonial Empire.

Kansas.

A central state of the United States, admitted Jan. 29, 1861; popularly known as the "Sunflower state." Total area, 82,276 sq.mi., of which 82,113 sq.mi. are land; pop. (1940) 1,801,028, a decrease of 79,971 or 4.3% from 1930. Capital, Topeka (67,833). The two larger cities were Kansas City (121,458) and Wichita (114,966). Of the state's population in 1940, 753,941 were urban, or 41.9%; 96.3% were white, 3.7% Negro and other races, 2.9% foreign born. Wartime population changes were important. The state census as of March 1, 1943, gave a total population of 1,803,201, a gain of 58,752 over 1942. Wichita became the largest city with 184,115, a gain of 50,971 for the year. Kansas City became the second city with 125,520 and Topeka third, 73,764.

History.—The executive officers in 1943 were: Andrew F. Schoeppel, governor; J. C. Denious, lieutenant governor; Frank J. Ryan, secretary of state; George Robb, auditor; Walter E. Wilson, treasurer; A. B. Mitchell, attorney-general; George L. McClenny, superintendent of public instruction; Charles F. Hobbs, commissioner of insurance; William C. Austin, state printer.

The legislature of 1943 passed little important legislation of a more permanent character, but enacted a number of laws growing out of war requirements. A new version of the Republican river compact with Nebraska and Colorado was signed Dec. 31, 1942, and ratified by the Kansas legislature. The long-standing problem of taxing transient cattle from the southwest, fattening in the Bluestem pastures on summer grass, was given a new adjustment by offering reciprocity treatment and tax levies proportional to the time spent in the state.

Education.—Enrolment in the public elementary and secondary schools declined from 460,036 in 1930 to 365,970 in 1940 and the number of teachers from 19,141 to 18,944. The high school enrolment in 1940 was 111,953. In 1937 there were 83,001 pupils enrolled in one-teacher rural schools, reduced in 1939 to 69,335. During the school year 1941–42, 219 small school districts were closed and other opportunity was provided.

Communication.—Kansas had 9,349 mi. of primary and 9,862 mi. of rural highways in 1939. In that year there were 8,667 mi. of railroads and 342,277 telephones.

Banking and Finance.—As of June 30, 1941, there were 660 active banks, 180 of which were national, with total deposits of $463,000,000. Savings banks held $79,800,000 of deposits. The budget estimates recommended to the legislature of 1943 were $19,067,365 for the biennium 1943–45, slightly less than the preceding period. In 1940 the state debt was $18,156,000 and debts of local governments, $98,493,000.

Agriculture.—The 1943 production of Kansas crops was 18% less than 1942, but, with the exception of 1941 and 1942, was greater than any year since 1932. The acreage was 3.5% above 1942 and the largest since 1932. Subsoil moisture was good and the wheat crop matured in spite of rainfall shortage, but floods and drought injured later maturing crops.

Leading Agricultural Products of Kansas, 1943 and 1942

Crop	1943 (est.)	1942	Crop	1943 (est.)	1942
Wheat, bu.. .	150,657,000	206,775,000	Potatoes, bu..	2,047,000	2,300,000
Corn, bu.. .	71,610,000	90,060,000	Barley, bu.. .	1,342,000	1,287,000
Oats, bu.. .	45,766,000	46,232,000	Tame hay, tons	1,719,000	2,059,000

An unusual number of cattle and sheep were wintered on wheat pasture and other feeds in western Kansas during the winter of 1942–43. The spring cattle movement from the southwest into the Bluestem pastures was about 13% larger than the previous year—229,000 compared with 202,000 and a 10-year average of 190,000. The pastures were fully stocked, with the largest supply of local and wintered-over cattle in years.

Manufacturing and Mineral Production.—For military reasons reliable figures for 1943 on these items were not available.

Principal Mineral Products of Kansas, 1939 and 1938

Mineral	Value, 1939	Value, 1938
Petroleum	$63,100,000	$72,100,000
Natural gas	29,356,000	27,485,000
Zinc	7,172,984	7,010,304
Cement	5,614,112	4,949,018
Coal	5,490,000	5,263,000
Stone	4,550,000	4,958,723

(J. C. Mn.)

Keitel, Wilhelm

(1882–   ), German army officer, born Sept. 22, was a commander of artillery during World War I. On April 1, 1934, he was promoted to major general and the following year, when Germany introduced conscription, he took charge of the personnel section (*Wehrmachtsamt*) in the war ministry, and was thus connected to a certain extent with the reoccupation of the Rhineland in 1936, and with the dispatch of German reinforcements to nationalist Spain. In Feb. 1938, during Hitler's "army purge" of Gen. von Blomberg and other conservative members of the high command, Gen. Keitel was appointed chief of the supreme command of the German armed forces. He thus directed operations against Poland, Norway, the Netherlands, Belgium, France and Britain in 1939 and 1940. On June 22, 1940, he signed the German-French armistice and on July 19 he was created field marshal by Adolf Hitler. Of the nazi high command triumvirate at the start of World War II—Brauchitsch, Halder, Keitel—only Keitel survived the 1941–42 purges. In 1943, as army chief of staff, he participated with Hitler in several important conferences with leaders of Italy, Rumania and other satellites.

Kelly, Howard Atwood

(1858–1943), U.S. gynaecologist and radiologist, was born Feb. 20 in Camden, N.J. One of the original members of the faculty of Johns Hopkins Medical school, Dr. Kelly was a member of the school's "big four"; the others were Dr. William H. Welch, Sir William Osler and Dr. Henry T. Halstead. After his retirement in 1919, Dr. Kelly remained consulting gynaecologist at Johns Hopkins hospital. He was a pioneer in the use of radium treatment for cancer. His last published work was *Electrosurgery*, written in collaboration with Grant E. Ward (1932). He died in Baltimore, Jan. 12. (See *Encyclopædia Britannica*.)

Kenney, George Churchill

(1889–   ), U.S. army officer, was born Aug. 6 in Yarmouth, Nova Scotia, the son of U.S. citizens. He attended the Massachusetts Institute of Technology for three years, but left in 1911 and later worked at civil engineering. In June 1917, he enlisted as a flying cadet in the U.S. signal corps reserve's aviation section and was commissioned as a first lieutenant in Nov. 1917. He saw active duty in France and was awarded the

D.S.C. for extraordinary heroism in action. He was shot down twice. At the end of the war, he held the rank of captain. Kenney attended the Command and General Staff school, 1927, and the Army War college, 1933. In 1940, he irritated ranking U.S. military officials with the statement that the U.S. air force could be "thrown into the ash can" because it was too antiquated for the kind of war the Germans were planning. He was promoted to the rank of brigadier general, Jan. 1941, and became a major general, Feb. 1942. In command of the Fourth air force at San Francisco, he was later transferred, Sept. 1942, to the Southwest Pacific. There, under Gen. Douglas MacArthur, he was placed in command of Allied air forces. His fliers soon gained air supremacy over New Guinea and Kenney, co-operating with Gen. Sir Thomas Blamey's ground forces, sped supplies to Allied troops in the Buna area entirely by air. Kenney's ingenuity in devising new methods of aerial attack was recognized by the war department, which credited him with the origin of the accurate and deadly skip bombing technique. He was decorated by MacArthur for meritorious service in inventing a new fragmentation bomb dropped by parachute. Holding the rank of lieutenant general, Kenney headed a military commission to Washington from MacArthur in March 1943, presumably to request increased air aid. He returned to New Guinea the following month.

Kenny Treatment: *see* INFANTILE PARALYSIS.

Kent, Raymond Asa

(1883–1943), U.S. college president, was born July 21 in Plymouth, Ia. He received his A.B. degree from Cornell college, Mount Vernon, Ia., and his A.M., 1910, and Ph.D., 1917, from Columbia university. He was professor of education at the University of Kansas, 1916–20, and dean of the College of Liberal Arts and professor of education at Northwestern university, 1923–29. He served as president of the University of Louisville, 1929–43. Dr. Kent was active on governmental educational boards and commissions and in 1942 was named by the navy to a board of curriculum policy consultants. He died while on a train en route from Washington, Feb. 26.

Kentucky.

An east south central state of the United States, admitted June 1, 1792, popularly known as the "Blue Grass state." Area, 40,598 sq.mi., of which 489 sq.mi. constitute water. Pop. (1940) 2,845,627, of which 1,996,300 or 70.2% was rural and 849,327 or 29.8% urban. Negroes constituted 214,031 or 7.5%; and 15,631 were of foreign birth. Capital, Frankfort (11,492); largest city, Louisville (319,077). Other cities: Covington (62,018); Lexington (49,304); Owensboro (30,245); Paducah (33,765); Ashland (29,537). The U.S. census bureau estimated that war and war industries reduced the population in 1943 by 8.8% or 251,504.

History.—In the state election Nov. 2, 1943, Simeon S. Willis (R.) defeated J. Lyter Donaldson (D.) 279,144 votes to 270,525 for the governorship. The Republicans also elected Kenneth H. Tuggle, lieutenant governor; Eldon S. Dummit, attorney-general; Irvin Ross, auditor; Thomas W. Vinson, treasurer; John Fred Williams, state superintendent of public instruction; and Elliott Robertson, commissioner of agriculture. The Democrats elected the secretary of state, Charles K. O'Connell, with a plurality of 114 votes over his opponent. The general assembly remained Democratic in both branches—56 to 34 seats in the house, 22 to 15 in the senate. In a special congressional election Chester O. Carrier (R.) defeated J. Dan Talbot (D.) by 12,000 votes in the Fourth district Nov. 30, 1943. Two proposed amendments to the state constitution were rejected: No. 1 (to extend workmen's compensation) by 82,305 votes to 78,466; No. 2 (to raise the constitutional limitation of salaries) by 121,997 votes to 44,765.

Education.—The elementary schools of the state in 1943 enrolled 561,844 pupils; and 697 high schools had 133,657 pupils. The total number of teachers in the public schools exceeded 19,000 in 1942.

Public Welfare, Charities, Correction.—Public assistance gradually consumed a larger amount of public funds. In 1939 recipients of state aid numbered 45,000; in 1943 the total was 54,000. These figures included the needy blind group. The correctional institutions in 1943 were the LaGrange reformatory; Eddyville penitentiary; and the reform school. County votes during the year increased the "dry" area of the state to 75 counties.

Communication.—The state in 1943 maintained directly nearly 10,000 mi. of highways of all types. There were 26 electric co-operatives serving 40,000 rural homes, chiefly in Tennessee Valley authority areas.

SIMEON S. WILLIS, Republican, elected governor of Kentucky Nov. 2, 1943 in a close contest

Banking and Finance.—The general budget for 1943–44 was $28,774,207. The budget did not include road and bridge projects separately maintained by fees and sales of fuel. Sources of the general fund in the fiscal year 1942–3 were: alcoholic beverage taxes $6,647,369; income taxes from corporations and individuals $9,225,000; property $6,984,970; excise taxes $6,871,409; licences of various sorts $1,862,424. The motor and road revenues exceeded $16,000,000. There were 302 state banks and trust companies in 1943 with total resources of $477,000,000.

Agriculture.—The leading agricultural crops for two years were as reported in the accompanying table.

Leading Agricultural Products of Kentucky, 1943 and 1942

Crop	1943 (est.)	1942
Wheat, bu.	3,902,000	5,194,000
Corn, bu.	75,350,000	82,200,000
Oats, bu.	1,760,000	1,760,000
Tobacco (all types), lb.	328,811,000	284,773,000
Tame Hay, tons	2,172,000	2,170,000
Irish Potatoes, bu.	4,664,000	4,560,000

Mineral Production.—In 1942 there were 63,463,700 tons of coal mined; the production of oil amounted to 4,250,000 bbl. Natural gas was not reported officially. There were 159 fatalities in the coal mines. (E. T.)

Kenya: *see* BRITISH EAST AFRICA.

Keppel, Frederick Paul

(1875–1943), U.S. educator, was born July 2 on Staten Island, N.Y. After receiving his A.B. degree from Columbia university in 1898, he joined the faculty of that school, later becoming dean of Columbia college, 1910–18. He resigned to become an aide in the war department on a dollar-a-year basis. He subsequently became director of the American Red Cross

foreign operations, 1919–20, executive secretary of the Russell Sage foundation and president of Carnegie corporation, 1923–41. In 1941, he was again called to serve the government as a member of the board of appeals on alien cases. He was also a director of Columbia Broadcasting system at the time of his death in New York city, Sept. 8.

Kesselring, Albert

(1887–   ), German army officer, began his career as an aviator in World War I. His friendship with Reichsmarshal Hermann Goering aided his rise in German military circles, and in 1936, he was appointed first chief of the luftwaffe's general staff but later resigned because his technique of air operations met with disapproval. The shakeup in the German high command in Feb. 1939 brought Kesselring back to favour and he directed air operations between Danzig and Brest-Litovsk during the Polish campaign in Sept. 1939. As commander of Air Fleet II, he guided the air attack upon the Netherlands, Belgium and France in May 1940. Kesselring was then promoted by Hitler to the rank of general field marshal. He participated in the battle of Britain, commanded a German aviation unit on the Russian front, 1941–42, and served as chief of the luftwaffe in Italy, Feb. 1942. In the winter of 1942–43, when the axis forces in North Africa were being hard pressed, Kesselring attempted unsuccessfully to transport troops to Marshal Erwin Rommel. The latter complained that he was not receiving proper air support, and on Dec. 29, 1942, a London dispatch announced that Kesselring had been shifted from the Mediterranean to the Don front in Russia. In early 1943, he returned to the Mediterranean and in Sept. 1943, he was placed in command of the central Italian front. Rommel was reported to have clashed with Kesselring again in Oct. 1943, and was said to have assumed command of the axis forces in Italy, with Kesselring once more being shuttled back to the Russian front.

Kidnapping.

Most notable feature of kidnappings in 1943 was their virtual disappearance in connection with gang warfare. The gradual subsidence of the gangs themselves apparently removed the occasion for the use of kidnapping as a side-line of their operations. As in previous years, kidnappings were most frequent in the United States, though the far east, long a centre for such crimes, and western Europe, both reported isolated cases.

World War II provided the setting for three kidnapping episodes. In May, the daughter of A. Seyss-Inquart was reported held as a hostage by Netherlands patriots, and in October there was a Japanese attempt to kidnap the British consul at Macao. In June, the Reverend W. A. Green was kidnapped and robbed at Atlantic City, N.J. Five U.S. soldiers were arrested and indicted for the crime.

There was little kidnapping for the purpose of extorting ransom, but several instances in connection with major burglaries. In April, the manager of a night club in New York was taken from his home, forced to open a safe, and then was left bound; the kidnappers escaped. In August, bandits took K. M. Rowe, president of the Arkansas Valley State bank from his home and forced him to open the bank vault; the perpetrators were apprehended. The following month, W. P. Forshee, branch manager of the Royal Bank of Canada at Wheatley, Ontario, was forced to leave his home and to open the bank vault. The six bandits fled after looting the bank.

Fugitives from institutions also employed kidnapping as an aid to their escape. Three convicts escaping from the Mississippi State penitentiary kidnapped a woman and later released her at Memphis, Tenn. Similarly, E. Caster, fleeing from the Pennsylvania Hospital for the Criminal Insane, abducted C. M. Murray at Fairview, Ohio.

Most striking of the kidnappings motivated by robbery, was that of J. Muldoon, who was taken and later drugged, in connection with a liquor truck holdup. Three men suspected of the crime were arrested by New York city police.

Infant kidnappings were relatively frequent, as in previous years. Two similar cases were those of the Serdinia and Zabinsky babies, who were kidnapped, and later abandoned and recovered, in New York city. On July 4, James DiMaggio, three years old, was reported missing. He was later found by New York city police. Mrs. M. P. Tilove admitted the abduction and was committed to Bellevue hospital for psychological examination. On Aug. 28, she was declared sane and was indicted by a federal grand jury ("Lindbergh law"). Upon admission to bail, Mrs. Tilove cited worry and despair occasioned by divorce proceedings as the reason for her act. At her trial on Oct. 27, her former husband testified that she had tried to convince him that the DiMaggio baby was his own child.

Despite the burdens imposed by war activities, the Federal Bureau of Investigation (U.S.) continued to be the world's outstanding police agency in kidnapping cases. From June 1932, when it was granted an effective jurisdiction in kidnappings, the FBI had solved 99% of the cases it investigated.

During 1943 a Mexican decree placed kidnapping in the category of capital offenses. (*See* also FEDERAL BUREAU OF INVESTIGATION.)   (BR. S.)

King, Ernest Joseph

(1878–), U.S. naval officer, was born Nov. 23 in Lorain, O. He left Annapolis to serve in the Spanish-American War, returning to the naval academy to graduate in 1901. During World War I he was assistant to the chief of staff of the commander in chief of the U.S. fleet. In 1933 he was promoted to rear admiral and he was vice-admiral in command of the fleet's aircraft battle force, 1938–39.

On Feb. 1, 1941, Adm. King was made commander of the Atlantic fleet and on Dec. 20, 1941, 13 days after the Japanese attack on U.S. possessions in the Pacific, he was designated commander in chief of the U.S. fleet, in what was apparently a shakeup in navy organization as well as personnel. On March 9, 1942, he took over the post of Adm. Harold R. Stark, chief of naval operations, in addition to the office of commander in chief of the U.S. fleet.

Throughout 1943 U.S. naval strategy was closely linked with that of Great Britain, and Adm. King took part in several military and naval conferences. In September he appeared before the Senate-House Military Affairs committee to urge the drafting of fathers rather than a lowering of physical standards for army and navy.

King, William Lyon Mackenzie

(1874–), Canadian politician, was born at Berlin (now Kitchener), Ont., Dec. 17. His grandfather, William Lyon Mackenzie, had been prominent in the struggle for political freedom in 1837. King entered parliament in 1908, became leader of the Federal Liberal party in 1919, and was returned to office as prime minister for the third time on Oct. 23, 1935. Shortly after Canada entered World War II, King's foes charged him with negligence and incompetence in handling the war effort. But the country did not support this view, and in March 1940 his party won a landslide election, adding 25 seats to its parliamentary majority. In Aug. 1940, when a nazi invasion of Britain appeared imminent, the Canadian prime minister and President Roosevelt agreed to set up a permanent joint board of defense to study common defense problems. The fruit of another parley with President Roosevelt on April 20, 1941, was a U.S.-Canada pact for co-operation in producing war materials for Britain.

In April 1942 King asked for a plebiscite giving authority to send conscripted soldiers overseas and won an overwhelming majority. During 1942 and 1943 he attended sessions of the Pacific war council and several Churchill-Roosevelt conferences in Washington and Quebec. On April 23, 1943, he indicated that air concessions over Canada would end with the war, saying that Canada intended "to press vigorously for a place in international air transportation."

In June 1943 Columbia university conferred upon King an honorary degree of doctor of laws.

Kingman Island: *see* PACIFIC ISLANDS, U.S.

Kinnick, Nile Clarke, Jr.

(1919?–1943), U.S. football star, was all-American halfback of 1939 at the University of Iowa and 1939 "athlete of the year." Besides his outstanding record in sports, he was a brilliant student and had been elected to Phi Beta Kappa. After his graduation, he returned to Iowa to study law but left school to enlist in the naval air corps in Sept. 1941. He received his naval training at Corpus Christi, Tex., and Pensacola, Fla., and was later commissioned as ensign. Assigned to an aircraft carrier, he was reported lost by the navy department on June 2 when his plane made a forced landing at sea.

Kisch, Frederick Hermann

(1888–1943), British army officer, was born in August in Darjeeling, India. He attended the Royal Military academy at Woolwich and joined the Royal Engineer corps in 1909. He saw service in France and Mesopotamia during World War I and was decorated for bravery. In 1919, he was sent as delegate to the Versailles peace conference. Kisch retired from the army in 1922 and went to Palestine as a member of the Zionist Executive in Jerusalem, an organization which acted as a link between the British authorities and the Jewish population. He rejoined the Royal Engineers in 1939 and was named chief engineer of the British 8th army. Brigadier Kisch was credited with construction of the fortifications at El Alamein and with laying the engineering plans that made possible General Montgomery's swift advance through Libya. He was killed near Sousse, Tunisia, April 11.

Kiska: *see* ALASKA; WORLD WAR II.

Kiwanis International.

Kiwanis International is composed of all Kiwanis clubs in the United States and Canada. Membership in each club is limited to two men from each business, professional and agricultural classification. The first Kiwanis club was organized in Detroit, Mich., Jan. 1915. In Canada the first club was organized in Hamilton, Ont., Nov. 1916. In Dec. 1943, there were 121,670 members in the 2,197 Kiwanis clubs. The name "Kiwanis" suggests the unselfish and constructive service of Kiwanians; the motto of the organization is "We Build." In Dec. 1941 war work was added to the continuing programs of youth service, community welfare and rural-urban relations.

The general office in 1943 was at 520 N. Michigan ave., Chicago, Ill.

President (1943–44) was Donald B. Rice, Oakland, Calif. Secretary, O. E. Peterson, Chicago, Ill.

(W. A. D.)

Kleist, Paul Ludwig von

(1881–), German army officer, was born Aug. 8 in Braunfels, Prussia. Product of a German military school, he served as a lieutenant of hussars and regimental commander in World War I. After the armistice, he was a cavalry instructor in Hanover, but during Hitler's rule he was lifted from the obscurity of the classroom to command of an army corps. Kleist participated in successful operations in Poland, 1939, France, 1940, and led the mechanized column that took Belgrade in the Yugoslav campaign, 1941. Early in the Russian campaign, his tank army led the nazi attack on Kiev and the advance through the Ukraine. Kleist's armies also captured Dnepropetrovsk in Aug. 1941, but this proved a pyrrhic victory, since the Russians had destroyed the famous dam there before retiring. In Nov. 1941 Kleist's armies captured Rostov, only to lose it a week later when General Timoshenko launched a counteroffensive. When the nazis renewed their offensive in the summer of 1942, Kleist's 1st German tank army drove through to the foothills of the Caucasus. In 1943, when the Russians were pushing the Germans back, Kleist's name faded from the dispatches.

Knight, Eric

(1897–1943), British author, was born April 10 in Menston, Yorkshire. At the age of 12 he was working half-time in the Yorkshire mills as a bobbin-setter and went to school the remainder of the time. Sensitive about his cultured accent, he quickly picked up the colourful dialect and flavourful speech of his new environment—Skircoat Green—which was to figure as the "Powkithorpe Brig" setting in his Sam Small stories. Before he went to America, he had already worked in textile mills and steelworks. In the United States, he worked as copy boy on a Philadelphia newspaper, studied art at the Boston Museum of Fine Arts and the New York Academy of Design and knocked about the country as reporter on various newspapers. Chiefly noted for his best-selling novel, *This Above All* (1941), written after a visit to England during the nazi air blitz, he already had to his credit *Song on Your Bugles* (1937) and a whimsical Yorkshire story, *The Flying Yorkshireman* (1938). The latter work met with such success that he wrote a sequel, *Sam Small Flies Again* (1942). He was a member of the Canadian "Princess Pat" Light Infantry regiment in World War I and received a commission as major in the U.S. army special services section in July 1942. He was killed in the crash of a transport plane in the jungle near the coast of Surinam Jan. 15, while on a foreign mission.

Knights of Columbus.

Organized in 1882, this fraternal order of men is dedicated to the preservation and championship of Catholic and traditional American principles. There were tens of thousands of Knights of Columbus in the armies of their respective countries.

The total membership as of Aug. 1943 was 437,924, an increase of more than 9,000 over the previous year. The associate members numbered 221,943; insurance members 215,981. There were 2,495 local councils in 48 states, U.S. territories and possessions, Canada and Latin America. Total assets were reported as $53,492,032.24, total liabilities $48,122,214.35, leaving a surplus of $5,369,817.89. Total income was stated as $8,011,268.85, and benefits paid by insurance claims and old age benefits paid out were $4,270,142.44.

The 61st supreme convention was held Aug. 17–19 at Cleveland, Ohio; 279 delegates from 270 state and regional jurisdictions attended. The report showed a vast increase in membership of 9,101 over the previous year. Officers re-elected for another term were: supreme knight, Francis P. Matthews; deputy supreme knight, John E. Swift; supreme secretary, Joseph F. Lamb; supreme advocate, Luke E. Hart; supreme chaplain, Rt. Rev. Leo M. Finn.

The order in 1943 engaged deeply in war activities. War bonds were sold to the value of $89,266,307 or 360% of the assigned quota, and the order invested in excess of $20,000,000 in war bonds of U.S. and Canada. Knights of Columbus Catholic army huts were operated in U.S., Great Britain, Canada, Newfoundland, Iceland, North Africa, Sicily, Italy. A chapel with a resident chaplain was established in London. Four hotels were provided for Canadian servicemen on leave in London, and a new hostel was provided in place of that destroyed by fire at St. John's, Newfoundland, in Dec. 1942.

At the supreme convention a resolution was adopted pledging the homage of the order to the martyred Polish nation. A second resolution requested the president of the United States to entrust administration of Italian affairs to persons sympathetic to the culture and religion of Italy. A third resolution placed the order on record as opposed to anti-Catholic representation in the press and motion pictures.

Youth guidance was carried on for the 20th successive year by trained workers. The Columbian Squires, lads too young for membership, were active through their councils in the gathering of scrap and selling war stamps. Fifteen additional circles, including two in Mexico, were organized, bringing up the membership of the Columbian Squires to 15,380, and each circle developed its own civilian defense program. In 1943 the order provided 18 scholarships at the Catholic University of America. The correspondence school for members and their families completed its 20th year of service.

National headquarters in 1943 were at New Haven, Conn. *Columbia,* a monthly illustrated magazine, and *News,* a weekly, are the official publications. (J. LAF.)

Knox, (William) Franklin

(1874–), U.S. publisher, statesman and soldier, was born Jan. 1 at Boston and was educated at Alma (Mich.) college. He joined Theodore Roosevelt's Rough Riders, with whom he served from April to Sept. 1898. He was in France from May 1918 to Feb. 1919 and became colonel in the 365th field artillery. His newspaper career began on the Grand Rapids, Mich., *Herald* shortly after the Spanish-American war. He was successively publisher of the Sault Ste. Marie, Mich., *News,* 1901–12; controlling owner of the Manchester, N.H., *Union and Leader;* general manager of the Hearst newspapers; and, from 1931, publisher of the *Chicago Daily News.* Knox was Republican candidate for vice-president in 1936. Roosevelt named him secretary of the navy, June 20, 1940, when war was threatening. He flew to Pearl Harbor immediately after the Jap attack and reported to the nation on the damage done there. At the end of 1942 Knox stated that the U.S. navy was larger and more powerful than it was the day before Pearl Harbor. Eleven months later, when the 27,000-ton carrier "Wasp" was delivered on Nov. 24, 1943, Knox announced that the warship strength of 838 vessels was exactly double what it had been at the beginning of the year, the "Wasp" being the 419th ship delivered during 1943. On Dec. 14 he stated that "preliminaries" in the Pacific were over and that major blows against Japan were being prepared.

Knudsen, William Signius

(1879–), U.S. industrialist, was born in Copenhagen, Denmark, on March 25 and as a youth worked in a bicycle shop in his native town. At the age of 20 he emigrated to the United States, where he found work in a shipyard in New York. After working in a railroad shop, he went to Buffalo, where he ultimately became superintendent of a mill. He then worked for

Ford Motor company and became associated with Chevrolet Motor company, of which he was made vice-president in 1922 and later president. From 1933 to 1937 he was executive vice-president of General Motors corporation, and in the latter year he became president. On May 28, 1940 President Roosevelt appointed him commissioner of industrial production for the national defense advisory commission.

When President Roosevelt created the Office of Production Management Jan. 7, 1941, he named Knudsen director general. Knudsen continued to be the "top man" in the production phase of national defense until Jan. 1942, but gradually matters of general policy were delegated to other agencies such as the Office of Price Administration and the War Production board. On Jan. 16, 1942, he was appointed production director of the war department and made a lieutenant general. During the following two years he spent much of his time in the field, visiting and counselling industries, and otherwise expediting production. In Aug. and Sept. 1943, he visited Hawaii, Australia, New Zealand and other Pacific points.

Koga, Mineichi

(1885–   ), Japanese naval officer, was born in September in Saga-ken. He was graduated from the Naval Staff college, 1906, and rose to prominence in the Japanese navy. He was an attaché at the Japanese embassy in Paris, 1926–27, and on his return home was given the captaincy of a warship. After holding a post as commander of a training squadron, he was made vice chief of staff of the Naval Staff board, 1937, and just before the attack on Pearl Harbor, he was head of the Japanese fleet in China waters. At the outbreak of war in Dec. 1942, Adm. Koga's naval units supported the Hongkong and Malaya operations, and in 1943 he was commander of the important Yokusoka naval station. After the death of Adm. Isoroku Yamamoto in the spring of 1943, Adm. Koga was made commander in chief of the Japanese fleet.

Korea: see CHOSEN.

Krueger, Walter

(1881–   ), U.S. army officer, was born in Flatow, Germany, Jan. 26. Brought to the U.S. as a child, he attended the Cincinnati Technical school from 1896 to 1898 and left school to enlist as a private at the outbreak of the Spanish-American war. He later saw action during the Philippine insurrection, on the Mexican border, and during World War I. From 1921 to 1938 he filled various posts at army schools and on the general staff. Promoted through the grades, he became a brigadier general in 1936, major general in 1939, and lieutenant general in 1941. In May 1941, Gen. Krueger assumed command of the 3rd army, which later in the year defeated Gen. Ben Lear's 2nd army in practice manoeuvres in Louisiana. When the 6th army in the Southwest Pacific was organized early in 1943, he was sent to Australia to take command. In December the 6th army, under Gen. Krueger's command, invaded the island of New Britain.

Kruger-Gray, George: see GRAY, GEORGE KRUGER.
Kure (Ocean) Island: see PACIFIC ISLANDS, U.S.
Kuwait: see ARABIA.

Kyanite.

Shipments of kyanite from United States mines rose to 8,708 short tons in 1942, against 8,335 tons in 1941. No information was available in 1943 on imports.

(G. A. Ro.)

Labor, U.S. Department of: see GOVERNMENT DEPARTMENTS AND BUREAUS.

Labor Relations Board, National: see NATIONAL LABOR RELATIONS BOARD.
Labour: see AGRICULTURE; AMERICAN FEDERATION OF LABOR; CHILD WELFARE; CONGRESS OF INDUSTRIAL ORGANIZATIONS; EMPLOYMENT; INTERNATIONAL LABOUR ORGANIZATION; LABOUR UNIONS; LAW; MOTION PICTURES; NATIONAL LABOR RELATIONS BOARD; NEGROES (AMERICAN); RADIO; RELIEF; SHIPBUILDING; STRIKES AND LOCK-OUTS; SUPREME COURT OF THE UNITED STATES; UNITED STATES; WAGES AND HOURS; WAR LABOR BOARD, NATIONAL; WAR PRODUCTION, U.S. See also under various states.

Labour Party.

The British Labour party continued in 1943 to work under the conditions of political truce imposed by the war, and to be represented in the war cabinet and the government. Cabinet changes caused Clement Attlee to retire from the dominions office and replace Sir John Anderson as chairman of the cabinet committee on home affairs, while remaining deputy prime minister. Arthur Greenwood continued to lead the party in the house of commons, and George Ridley became chairman of the party executive.

The affiliated membership of the Labour party showed a small further fall in 1942, due mainly to the calling-up of members and the dislocation of some of the local labour parties by war conditions. The total was 2,453,000 as against 2,485,000 in 1941 and 2,663,000 in 1939. The decline was mainly in the individual membership of local parties, which had fallen from 409,000 in 1939 to 219,000 at the end of 1942. The rise in trade union membership was not reflected in the Labour party totals, as most of the new members had not yet become subscribers to the political funds of their trade unions. The development of the Labour party's membership was hampered by the party's failure to give a clear lead. A considerable floating section of left-wing opinion, especially among young people, was attracted away to Common Wealth, which, with a program very similar to the Labour party's, was unhampered by the truce and had been free to contest by-elections. The main body of the party was, however, fully determined to maintain the truce, in order not to put its members in the government into a difficulty, and not to lay itself open to any suspicion that it is not whole-hearted in its support of the war. The party conference in 1943 therefore decided to ban Common Wealth by making membership of that body inconsistent with membership of the Labour party; but this decision would be very difficult to enforce. The Labour party conference also rejected, by 1,951,000 votes to 712,000, a renewed proposal to accept the Communist party into affiliation. The conference approved a number of resolutions dealing with various aspects of reconstruction policy, elaborating the general conclusions of the reconstruction report approved in 1942. The most acrimonious discussion arose over a resolution and amendment dealing with the treatment of Germany after the war. The main object of the amendment was to draw a sharp distinction between the nazis and the German people and to demand that the whole people of Germany should not be treated as criminals on account of the nazis' misdeeds. But errors in tactics led to the defeat of the amendment. This attitude was reversed when the same issue came before the Trades Union congress in September, and it seems clear that this later decision more correctly expressed the real state of Labour opinion.

During the year, the Labour party in parliament showed increasing activity in criticizing the government, especially for its failure to formulate decisions on postwar policy. Both the parliamentary party and the conference gave strong support to the Beveridge social security proposals, and also pressed for a favourable government decision on the Uthwatt, Barlow and other reports dealing with basic problems of reconstruction. Colonial questions also occupied an increasing amount of Labour attention. (*See* also CABINET MEMBERS.) (G. D. H. C.)

Labour Unions.

United States.—The status and reputation of unions were deeply affected by a considerable increase in strikes during 1943. After a relatively quiet year, when less than 1,000,000 employees were involved in strikes, the number of strikes in 1943 rose to more than 3,500, the numbers on strike to nearly 3,500,000, and man-days lost through strikes to 14,000,000. The largest and most important of the strikes were called in vital war industries—coal, rubber and steel.

The primary cause of this outbreak of labour disturbances was a revolt against the principles of wage control devised and administered by the National War Labor board and other federal agencies. The kernel of the board's wage policy was the limitation of wage increases to 15% above the level of wages prevailing in Jan. 1941. The aim of this policy was to maintain the purchasing power of wages at their Jan. 1941 level and its underlying assumption was that the government's machinery of price control would keep the rise in the cost of living from exceeding 15%. Successful as price regulation, compared with the experience during World War I, was, the official index of living costs actually increased nearly 25% and unofficial figures collected by the unions showed a substantially greater advance. Throughout the year, therefore, organized labour became increasingly critical of the government's wage formula and from time to time strikes broke out to force a change in public policy.

It fell to the lot of John L. Lewis, however, to bring this whole question to a climax. In common with other labour leaders Lewis was being subjected to mounting pressure for higher wages by his union's members. Early in the year the anthracite miners struck against an increase in union dues and to get them back to work Lewis promised a substantial advance in wages. With the approaching termination on April 1 of the union's agreement with the coal industry, the United Mine Workers demanded a wage increase of $2 a day. Although this demand included pay for travel time (portal to portal), granting it would clearly have violated the official wage policy. Consequently, the miners' representatives refused to appear before the War Labor board and submit their case to it. When the coal operators turned down the union demands, strikes spread through the mines. Intervention by the president proved futile. Finally the government took over the mines and the men returned to work. But the wage dispute remained unsettled. On four occasions the mines were shut down. Prolonged negotiations were held between the union and the fuel administrator and the union and the operators. On Nov. 5, the War Labor board approved a wage increase amounting to $1.75 a day.

This settlement, regarded by the whole of organized labour as a surrender to John L. Lewis, brought on a nation-wide movement for the abandonment of the official ("Little Steel") wage formula. The steel, automobile and textile unions asked for increases running from 10 to 20 cents an hour. The conservative railroad unions brought a long-pending and complex wage dispute to a head by taking a strike vote and setting the date for a strike. Only intervention by the president and turning the roads over to the army averted a stoppage of rail transport. At the end of December the organized steel workers, launching their campaign for higher wages, struck important steel producers and threatened to tie up the whole industry.

Even before the strikes of 1943, the public had shown signs of fearing the growing power of organized labour and congress had on several occasions attempted to adopt regulatory legislation. But these efforts were blocked by the president. The new wave of

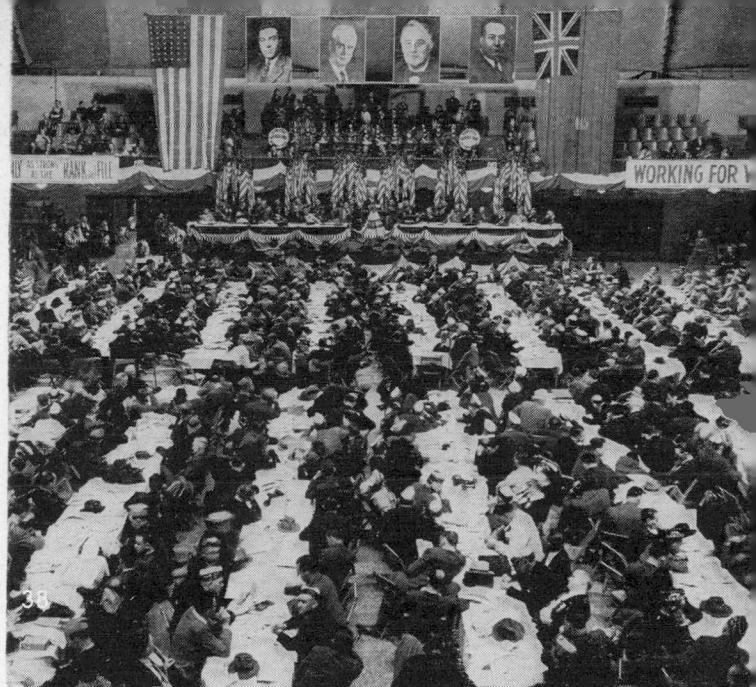

THE ANNUAL CONVENTION of the United Automobile Workers at Buffalo Oct. 4–10, 1943, voted support for Pres. Roosevelt in 1944 if he took an active stand against opponents of the New Deal. The two centre photographs above the rostrum are of C.I.O. President Philip Murray and President Roosevelt; at the left, Sec'y-Treasurer George Addes of the U.A.W.; at the right, the U.A.W.'s president, R. J. Thomas

strikes and their threat to war production impelled congress to action. On June 12 the Smith-Connally (Anti-Strike) bill was passed and several weeks later both houses of congress overrode the president's veto by large majorities. This act, aimed primarily to prevent strikes in war industries, set forth the conditions under which strikes might be called, the authority of the government to operate struck plants, and the powers of the War Labor board. In addition, the act forbade labour organizations, as well as corporations, to make political contributions in connection with elections to federal office.

How far public opinion had swung against organized labour was suggested by the results of the congressional and local elections held in November. Both the A.F. of L. and the C.I.O. had made careful preparations for the fall elections, had declared themselves against anyone who had supported the Smith-Connally bill, and had made strong efforts to get out the labour vote. The result was a considerable Republican victory in all parts of the country, the greatest upset being the election of a Republican governor in the normally Democratic state of Kentucky.

Inside the labour movement the two major factions, the A.F. of L. and the C.I.O., drifted farther apart. Peace negotiations, under way the year before, were abandoned. A dispute between the metal trades' unions of the A.F. of L. and the shipbuilders' union of the C.I.O. over the unionization of the employees of the Kaiser shipyards not only resulted in an overwhelming victory for the federation but also caused congressional action denying the right of the National Labor Relations board to nullify existing labour contracts. These defeats of the C.I.O. aggravated the already strained relations between it and the A.F. of L. Fuel was added to the fire when an application for membership in the federation by the United Mine Workers was warmly received. Although the resolution of difficult jurisdictional issues delayed action on the miners' application, it was generally believed that they would shortly be reaffiliated with the A.F. of L.

Owing again to the favourable economic conditions of war and the friendly policies of the administration, the membership of all branches of organized labour continued to increase, but at a slower rate than in the earlier war years. At the end of 1943, total membership probably exceeded 12,000,000 by a small amount and embraced approximately one-third of the country's wage-earners and lower salaried employees. (*See* also AMERICAN FEDERATION OF LABOR; BUSINESS REVIEW; CONGRESS OF INDUSTRIAL ORGANIZATIONS; LAW; NATIONAL LABOR RELATIONS BOARD; STRIKES AND LOCK-OUTS.) (L. Wo.)

Great Britain.—By the end of 1942 the trade unions affiliated to the British Trades Union congress had increased their membership to 6,024,411, as compared with 5,432,644 the previous year and 4,866,711 in 1939. The increase was specially marked among the unions in the metal and engineering trades and among those catering for general workers, which in practice enrol a high proportion of the less skilled workers in the engineering and other armament industries. There were four unions with a membership of over 500,000—Transport and General Workers (806,000), General and Municipal Workers (721,000), Amalgamated Engineering union (645,000), Mineworkers' federation (599,000). Two other unions—the National Union of Railwaymen and the Distributive Workers—exceeded 250,000, and four others 100,000. Of the total affiliated membership, 1,220,000 were women.

The Trades Union congress includes most of the important unions. The civil servants, including the post office workers, were still excluded from affiliation by the 1927 Trade Unions act. There was a renewed attempt in 1943 to get the ban on the affiliation of the civil service unions removed. The largest of these, the Union of Post Office Workers, applied for affiliation; and the T.U.C. general council agreed to recommend the congress to accept it in defiance of the law. The government thereupon threatened disciplinary action against all employees who remained in membership of the U.P.W.; and after negotiations with the Labour members of the government and with the Labour party it was decided to postpone acceptance of the U.P.W. affiliation and to make a further effort to secure an agreed modification of the law.

The T.U.C. and its affiliated bodies continued to give full support to the war effort, and to be represented on numerous committees set up by the government in connection with the various departments. In particular, there was a rapid growth during the year of factory joint production committees, and the trade unions established regional machinery and a special advisory service for the co-ordination of their efforts. There were at this time joint production committees in most of the large factories engaged on war work.

Interest at the Trades Union congress of Sept. 1943 was centred largely on discussions with the trade unions in the United States and the soviet union. There was great disappointment over the refusal of the American Federation of Labor either to enter into a joint committee with the T.U.C. and the Soviet All-Union Council of Trade Unions, or to widen the membership of the Anglo-American Trade Union committee so as to include the Congress of Industrial Organizations and the Railroad brotherhoods. The T.U.C. general council had made it clear to the American Federation of Labor that it was strongly in favour of both these things, but had been unable to influence the American Federation of Labor to modify its attitude. The T.U.C., in face of this report, reluctantly consented to the continuance of the Anglo-American committee on its existing basis. Discussions took place between the British and soviet trade union delegates in both London and Moscow. The soviet delegates brought forward a proposal to widen the Anglo-Soviet committee by the inclusion of delegates from other European countries as well as from the United States; but the T.U.C. regarded such a move as premature and as needing special consideration in the light of the position and prospects of the International Federation of Trade Unions, to which the T.U.C. belonged. The soviet delegates also strongly pressed the British trade unions to declare emphatically in favour of an immediate large-scale second front in Europe; but the

British delegates took the view, which was endorsed at the congress in September, that they could not take the responsibility of pronouncing on the correct timing of a military operation about which only the military authorities and the government could have the requisite knowledge. Accordingly, the T.U.C. would not go beyond declaring in favour of the second front at the earliest practicable date.

During the autumn months of 1943 there were a number of strikes, chiefly among miners and munition workers, which received a great deal of publicity in the press. Actually, these strikes were all small and local, and the time lost by strike action continued to be low—substantially lower than in World War I. Attempts were made to represent these strikes as due to the activities of political agitators; but there was no real evidence for this view, and the communists especially had been strongly against strike action and everywhere advised the strikers to return to work. The main cause was undoubtedly sheer weariness, aggravated by the unwise attempts of the government to discourage holiday-making during the summer. Discontent at the government's failure to make up its mind about the vital issues of reconstruction might have been a small contributory cause, but did not seem to have played a major part. In the coal mines there were special sources of unrest, arising out of the failure of the reorganization plans of the ministry of fuel and power to achieve any considerable results and out of wage-troubles, especially among the younger men.

A notable feature of the year's Trades Union congress was the rejection of a "Vansittartite" resolution and the acceptance of an amendment drawing a sharp distinction, in respect of "war guilt," between the nazis and the German people. This decision reversed that reached earlier in the year at the annual conference of the Labour party (*see* LABOUR PARTY) and undoubtedly represented better the majority view in British labour and trade union circles.

The Trades Union congress was making, through a number of committees, its own study of reconstruction problems. It had cordially endorsed most of the proposals made in the Beveridge report on the social services. It maintained its general ban on association with the Communist party; but the congress of 1943 agreed to modify it by lifting the ban on local trades councils which admitted Communist delegates. (G. D. H. C.)

Labrador: *see* NEWFOUNDLAND AND LABRADOR.

Lacrosse.
Despite the fact that the scope of its program during 1943 was cut down by the shortage of undergraduate manpower, the United States Intercollegiate Lacrosse association voted to carry on a full season in 1944, including the annual north-south game, provided the latter proved feasible when the 1944 season reached its climax. It was the north-south game which proved the highlight of the 1943 campaign with the Southern Collegiate All-Stars defeating the north 9–5. The north squad was made up of players from Army, Princeton, Yale, Rutgers, Pennsylvania, Stevens Tech, Lehigh, City College of New York, Drexel, Cornell, Syracuse and Springfield. The Southern All-Stars were a composite of navy, Maryland and Johns Hopkins.

The two best teams in the country were Navy and Maryland. On the distaff side, Philadelphia clinched its tenth National Women's Lacrosse association tournament title by defeating the Etceteras 12–2. The latter squad was made up of college girls.

A committee of the U.S. Intercollegiate Lacrosse association discussed with army and navy officials the use of Lacrosse as a part of training camp programs, believing that it was second only to football as a conditioner. Up to the end of 1943 this had not been adopted officially by the services. (T. J. D.)

La Fontaine, Henri

(1854-1943), Belgian lawyer and politician, was born April 22 in Brussels. A senator from 1894 to 1936, and vice-president of the senate, La Fontaine also was a professor of international law at the University of Brussels and the City College of New York. He was awarded the Nobel peace prize in 1913. La Fontaine presided over 20 world peace congresses and drew up a "magnissima charta" calling for a "United States of the World." He was named head of the International Bureau of Peace in Brussels, 1907, was president of the Juridical committee of the Inter-Parliamentary union, and represented his country at the League of Nations in 1920 and 1921. A Berne dispatch of May 26 carried a report of his death.

Land, Emory S.

(1879-   ) U.S. naval officer and government official, was born Jan. 9 in Canon City, Colo. He was graduated from the University of Wyoming, 1898; Annapolis, 1902; and the Massachusetts Institute of Technology, 1907. During World War I, he served on the staff of Adm. William Sims in London. Associated with problems of naval construction after 1904, he was assistant chief of the navy's bureau of aeronautics, 1926-28; chief of the bureau of construction and repair, 1932-37. Made a rear admiral when he retired from the navy in 1937, he was named commissioner of the U.S. maritime commission in 1937, and succeeded Joseph Kennedy as chairman in 1938. Under his administration during the next five years a tremendous program of shipbuilding developed. On Sept. 24, 1943, he stated that the program begun in 1938 would total 50,000,000 dead-weight tons by the end of 1944. There were then 100 yards, employing 750,000. On Jan. 3, 1944, he announced that 1,896 ships, with a dead-weight tonnage of 19,238,626, had been built in 1943. Soon after the U.S. entered World War II, Adm. Land was also made administrator of the War Shipping administration. On Aug. 11, 1943, his maritime commission named a committee to plan a postwar shipping program.

Landsteiner, Karl

(1868-1943), U.S. medical research scientist, was born June 14 in Vienna, Austria. He received his M.D. at the University of Vienna, 1891. At the invitation of the Rockefeller Institute for Medical Research in 1921, he went to the United States, where he became a naturalized citizen. In 1930, he received the Nobel prize for medicine for his discovery of the human blood groups, a work which made possible the successful use of blood transfusion. His discovery of the four blood groups and his subsequent research showed that by matching the patient's blood group with that of the donor, many of the dangers of blood transfusion could be eliminated. Dr. Landsteiner, who was a member of the Rockefeller institute from 1922 until his retirement in 1939, extended his research to immunology, bacteriology, virus diseases and drug allergy. He wrote extensively on these subjects and was honoured by many of the leading scientific organizations over the world. He continued his medical research at the institute after his retirement and died while working in his laboratory in New York city, June 26.

Laos: see FRENCH COLONIAL EMPIRE.

Laparra, Raoul

(1876-1943), French composer, was born May 13 in Bordeaux. He received his early musical training at the Paris conservatory, was awarded the Prix de Rome in 1903, and won international fame with one of his early compositions, *La Habañera*, 1908, an opera set in old Castile. His other operas included *Peau d'Ane* (1899), *La Jota* (1911), *Le Joueur de Viole* (1926) and *L'Illustre Fregona*

(1931). He wrote in addition several librettos, songs, piano and orchestra works and a number of publications including *La Musique Populaire en Espagne* (1914) and *Bizet et l'Espagne* (1935). He was killed during a bombing raid over France, April 4, according to a Paris radio broadcast.

La Puma, Vincenzo,

CARDINAL (1874-1943), Italian cardinal, was born Jan. 22 in Palermo. He attended Palermo seminary and studied at the University of Rome, receiving doctor's degrees in philosophy, theology and law. Titular archbishop of San Cosmos and Damian, he was created a cardinal on Dec. 16, 1935. He died in Rome Nov. 4.

Lard.

The production of lard in 1943 increased to an all-time high record of 2,874,000,000 lb., as estimated by the U.S. department of agriculture, compared with 2,455,000,000 lb. in 1942. The heavy marketing of hogs in the fall of 1943 was reflected in this increase. Only once had this high record been approached—in 1933, when 2,475,000,000 lb. were produced. The lard yield in 1943 was relatively low in relation to the weight of the hogs slaughtered, indicating that packers did not trim closely, being able to sell more of the fat as meat. The output of lard bears a close relation to the weight of hogs slaughtered, however, which enables estimates to be made on the number of hogs needed to meet lard demands. For 1944 a yield of 130 lb. of pork and 30 lb. of lard per hog on 104,000,000 head was expected to provide 3,120,000,000 lb. of lard. (*See* also HOGS; MEAT; VEGETABLE OILS AND ANIMAL FATS.)   (J. C. Ms.)

Latin America: see ARGENTINA; BOLIVIA; BRAZIL; BRITISH GUIANA; BRITISH HONDURAS; CHILE; COLOMBIA; COSTA RICA; ECUADOR; FRENCH COLONIAL EMPIRE; GUATEMALA; HISPANIC AMERICA AND WORLD WAR II; HONDURAS; INTERNATIONAL LAW; NICARAGUA; PANAMA; PARAGUAY; PERU; SALVADOR, EL; SURINAM; URUGUAY; VENEZUELA.

Latter Day Saints: see MORMONS.

Latvia.

One of the Baltic states of northeastern Europe, north of Lithuania, south of Estonia, formerly a republic; in 1941 it became part of the German "Ostland." Area, 25,016 sq.mi.; pop. (est. Jan. 1, 1939), 1,994,506. Capital, Riga (385,063 in 1935); the other principal city is Liepaja (57,098). Language, Latvian. Religion, Christian (Protestant, 56%; Roman Catholic, 24.5%; Greek Catholic, 9%; Greek Orthodox, 5.5%). The country was ruled, after the German occupation in 1941, by Commissioner-General Otto Heinrich Drechsler for Latvia, and Reichscommissar Hinrich Lohse, whose seat of government not only for Latvia but for the entire Ostland (*q.v.*) was established in Riga.

History.—Like her neighbours Estonia and Lithuania (*qq.v.*), Latvia was forced to bow first to one, then another, of the warring great powers: from June 1940 to June 1941 she was occupied and largely collectivized by the U.S.S.R.; in July 1941 she was occupied and "new ordered" by the nazi reich. Mass deportations were carried through by both the conquerors, and the economy was forced through violent changes.

The German masters of the country required the Latvians to produce for the German war effort, systematically regulating labour, banks, industry. Agriculture, partially collectivized during the Russian occupation, was not completely reorganized by the Germans, though some Danish and Belgian colonists were established on the land. Most of the Latvian ships at large were sunk before the end of 1943, but some Latvian sailors continued to operate in the Atlantic sea-lanes.

A communist government-in-exile was established in Moscow,

and the representatives of the prewar government continued to function in the western capitals in 1943. The latter pledged allegiance to the Atlantic Charter and the cause of the United Nations and hoped for the re-establishment of Latvian independence after the war. No clear-cut statements on this issue had been promulgated by the great states at the end of 1943. The silence of the Moscow and Tehran conferences on this point was in itself significant.

Statistics of education, finance and economic conditions ceased to be issued in Latvia after the soviet occupation in 1940; the latest available figures at the end of 1943 applied for the most part to 1938 and 1939.

Education.—In 1938–39 there were 1,987 elementary schools and 122 secondary schools. Enrolment at the University of Riga was 7,281. Total educational enrolment numbered 271,197— one-seventh of the population with 13,106 teachers. There were 912 public libraries.

Finance.—The monetary unit is the lat (=19.3 U.S. cents at par, established as equivalent to the Swiss franc in 1921). Effects of German control were still uncertain at the end of 1943. In 1939 the budget estimates envisaged revenue of 190,878,000 lats and expenditures of 190,481,000 lats.

Trade and Communication.—Imports in 1938 were 227,336,-000 lats; exports 227,204,000 lats. Chief articles of import were industrial machinery, agricultural machinery, automobiles and accessories, coal, cotton textiles, cotton (raw) and wheat. Chief articles of export were timber, flax, plywood and butter. Exports went chiefly to Great Britain, Germany, the U.S.S.R. and the Netherlands. Imports were primarily from Germany, Great Britain, the U.S.S.R., Sweden and the United States. In 1940 the Latvian state railways operated over 2,200 mi.; bus lines over 2,800 mi. The principal harbours are Riga, Liepaja and Ventspils.

Agriculture.—The principal crops with their yields (in short tons) were as follows in 1939: rye, 493,830; barley, 245,041; oats, 534,395; wheat, 233,247; potatoes, 1,807,882; flax, 54,123. Livestock included 414,470 horses, 1,271,730 cattle, 1,469,570 sheep, 891,470 pigs, 4,729,120 poultry, 222,460 beehives. About 66% of the employed were in agriculture.

Manufacturing.—After the decline in 1931 and 1932, Latvia's industrial production rose rapidly to a general index figure of 148 in 1937 (based on 100 in 1930). Strong efforts were made up to 1939 to increase the self-sufficiency of the country.

At the beginning of 1939 some 5,970 industrial establishments employed 98,500 persons, and in 1938 produced a value of 695,000,000 lats. About 15% of the employed were in industry and 5% in commerce. Chief industries were foodstuffs, wood and paper and textiles.

BIBLIOGRAPHY.—Alfred Bilmanis, *The Baltic States and the Baltic Sea* (Washington, 1943); *Latvia under German Occupation* (mimeographed, by Latvian Legation, Washington, 1943). (F. D. S.)

Laval, Pierre

(1883–   ), French statesman, was born June 28 at Châteldon, Puy-de-Dôme. For a brief biographical sketch, see *Encyclopædia Britannica*. Laval had remained in comparative obscurity after the start of war in 1939 until Marshal Pétain, after France's defeat, named him his successor as well as vice-premier. An opportunist, Laval consulted with Hitler on several occasions in 1940 and displayed obvious pro-nazi inclinations. A rift between Pétain and Laval occurred, and the latter was abruptly dropped from the Vichy cabinet Dec. 13, 1940. Laval was not reinstated until April 18, 1942, when he formed a new cabinet and assumed the title of chief of government. He followed a straight pro-nazi policy. He insisted that Frenchmen go to Germany to work in factories, thus helping to "crush bolshevism," and to release French prisoners. On Nov. 18, 1942, a week after the Germans had occupied all of France, Pétain gave Laval dictatorial powers to make laws and decrees on his own responsibility. Laval delivered a violent tirade against the British and proclaimed his confidence in an eventual axis victory. In the spring of 1943, Gen. Giraud, threatening eventual invasion of France, warned Laval: "You have lost the right to call yourself a Frenchman." On June 5, Laval called for 200,000 more workers to go to Germany. On June 25, the German radio announced that he had ordered the 100,000 Jews that had been naturalized since 1927 deprived of citizenship.

Law.

Aspects of war were reflected in every type of litigation. Conflicts arose between military and civil authorities over curfew and exclusion orders in defense areas, the suspension of the writ of *habeas corpus* under a declaration of martial law and the trial of soldiers for offenses against civilians. The courts faced new problems also in determining the status of aliens who came from countries taken over by the nazis and in applying emergency laws concerning selective service, inflation control and war labour disputes.

Some litigants put forward novel claims and defenses inspired by war conditions. Tenants not only sought the protection of OPA regulations in eviction cases in rent control areas, but also resorted to a new doctrine of "frustration" (similar to the old defense of impossibility of performance) in order to escape liability for rent on leases of business property where its use for the purpose intended was wholly or partly interrupted by war regulations. In a personal injury suit the defendant car owner unsuccessfully raised the defense that the plaintiff had assumed all risks by becoming a fellow passenger in a share-the-car plan brought about by gas rationing. A manufacturer who ran his plant in a manner disturbing to neighbours contended that his operations should not be restrained as a nuisance because he was engaged in war work, but the Massachusetts supreme court rejected this plea.

The trend of U.S. supreme court decisions was to support the vastly increased powers delegated by congress to the executive department and administrative agencies and not to interfere with state legislation and court decisions except when there were serious conflicts with federal authority or civil rights were endangered.

Only the more important and interesting legal developments of a less technical nature are noted in this article.

Administrative Law.—Both by necessity and inclination the supreme court continued its hands-off policy toward the administrative process. Agency regulations and rulings have added such a vast undergrowth to the law's "wilderness of single instances" that the courts cannot review administrative proceedings in detail.

The court declined to interfere with the discretion exercised by the Federal Power commission, the Federal Security administrator, the National Labor Relations board and the Interstate Commerce commission in orders issued by those agencies based on findings of fact arrived at after the consideration of carefully accumulated evidence, much of it highly technical in character. In an NLRB case the court ruled that there could be no judicial review of questions not presented in the original hearing before the administrative agency (*Marshall Field & Co.* v. *NLRB*, 318 U.S. 253). Nor should the courts interfere with the orders of administrative tribunals until all administrative remedies are exhausted, it was held in *Illinois Commerce Commission* v. *Thomson*, 318 U.S. 675. An injunction had been granted against proceeding with a rate hearing before the state commission on the ground that the Interstate Commerce commission had already approved an increase of rates. The supreme court held that the injunction should have been denied because the petitioner had not come to the end of his remedies before the state agency.

Chain broadcasting regulations formulated by the Federal Communications commission were upheld against attacks by the two major radio networks (*N.B.C.* v. *U.S.*, 319 U.S. 190 and *Columbia Broadcasting System* v. *U.S.*, 319 U.S. 190). The regulations provided that broadcasting licences should not be granted to stations having certain business relations with the networks and they were designed to prevent practices which the commission had found, after extensive investigation, to be "detrimental to the public interest." The court held that in giving the FCC power to license and regulate broadcasting "in the public interest, convenience and necessity," congress did not limit the commission's power merely to dealing with technical and engineering problems. Nor were the regulations a denial of free speech.

The doctrine of "exclusive primary jurisdiction" was applied by the court in sustaining the power of the secretary of labour to subpoena a contractor in a hearing under the Walsh-Healey Public Contracts act. The contractor asked the federal district court to decide whether the act applied to his business, but the supreme court held that it was primarily the duty of the secretary of labour to determine this question (*Endicott-Johnson* v. *Perkins,* 317 U.S. 501).

In a series of cases involving railroad reorganizations under the Bankruptcy act, approved by the Interstate Commerce commission, the supreme court held that the federal courts should consider only the general fairness and legal validity of such plans. They need not examine the details.

Administrative agencies, however, cannot justify their orders on "broad equitable principles," the court said in setting aside an order of the Securities and Exchange commission in connection with the reorganization of a public utility holding company. "An administrative order cannot be upheld unless the grounds upon which the agency acted in exercising its powers were those upon which its action can be sustained" (*S.E.C.* v. *Chenery Co.*, 318 U.S. 80).

In two 5-to-4 decisions, the court declined to permit the interference by federal courts with orders of state administrative agencies. It held that U.S. district court had no jurisdiction to set aside orders of the Texas Railroad commission, since the Texas statutes provided a well organized system for judicial review in the state courts.

Aliens and Citizenship.—The cancellation of a naturalization certificate granted in 1927 to an admitted communist was set aside by the supreme court. The government charged that he was not attached to the principles of the constitution because of his membership in a party which advocated the overthrow of the government by violence. Justice Murphy, speaking for the majority of the court, applied the "clear and present danger" test announced by Justice Holmes in the famous World War I sedition case of *Schenck* v. *U.S.*, 249 U.S. 47. The government had not proved with requisite certainty, he said, that the attitude of the Communist party at the time when the petitioner was naturalized created a "clear and present danger of public disorder." The facts and the law should be construed as far as reasonably possible in favour of citizenship. It should not be presumed in construing the denaturalization act "that congress meant to circumscribe liberty of political thought." Justices Stone, Roberts and Frankfurter dissented on the ground that "congress, which has the power to deny citizenship to aliens altogether, may safeguard the grant of this privilege." No question of freedom of speech was involved, they said. Wendell L. Willkie represented the petitioner (*Schneiderman* v. *U.S.*, 320 U.S. 118).

A U.S. district court in California ruled that the membership of Harry Bridges in the Communist party justified the attorney-general in ordering his deportation to Australia. The Alien Registration act of 1940 requires the deportation of aliens who at or after the time of their entry have been members of any organization which advocates, or has in its possession literature, advocating the overthrow of the U.S. government by force. The attorney-general had found that Bridges was a member of two subversive organizations. The court held that neither the statute nor the deportation order violated the free speech guarantees of the constitution.

The supreme court sustained the conviction of an American citizen of Japanese descent for wilful violation of a curfew order of the western defense command which required all persons of Japanese ancestry within a designated military area to remain at home between 8 P.M. and 6 A.M. It was within the constitutional authority of congress and the president, acting together, to prescribe a curfew as a war emergency measure. Ruling that such an order was not unjust discrimination, the court said, "Distinctions between citizens solely because of their ancestry are by their very nature odious to a free people whose institutions are founded on the doctrine of equality," but "the adoption by the government, in the crisis of war and threatened invasion, of measures for the public safety, based upon the recognition of the facts and circumstances which indicate that a group of one national extraction may menace that safety more than others, is not wholly beyond the limits of the constitution" (*Hirabayashi* v. *U.S.*, 320 U.S. 81). Briefs were filed by the American Civil Liberties Union and Japanese-American Citizens' League as friends of the court.

Two U.S. district courts in the eastern defense area, however, held that there was not sufficient danger of espionage and sabotage to justify military orders excluding naturalized citizens of German origin from that area. Such orders were held to violate the constitutional right of citizens to move from state to state.

Two circuit court of appeals decisions construed the effect of the *anschluss* of Austria with Germany in 1938 on the status of aliens.

An Austrian citizen, who arrived in the U.S. in 1936 as a Czechoslovakian quota immigrant and was residing in the U.S. at time of *anschluss* but never accepted German sovereignty, was not an enemy alien subject to internment (*U.S. ex rel. Schwarzkopf* v. *Uhl,* 137 F. [2d] 898). On the other hand, a person born in Austria, who resided in France from 1919 to 1939 and then went to the U.S., was a "native" of Germany subject to restraint as an enemy alien because of state department rulings that Austria became part of the reich by the *anschluss* (*U.S. ex rel. D'Esquiva* v. *Uhl,* 137 F. [2d] 903).

The problem of deporting a Greek seaman who had overstayed his permissible period in the U.S. was solved in a circuit court decision by ordering him sent to the "Greek government in exile" in England as the "country whence he came." Congress afterward by statute established this as the proper method of dealing with such aliens.

Civil Rights.—At the insistence of members of Jehovah's Witnesses, the supreme court overruled its previous "flag salute" and "handbill" decisions. A state law, prescribing "the commonly accepted salute to the flag" as a regular part of the program of public schools, was held to violate the 1st and 14th amendments in *West Virginia Board of Education* v. *Barnette,* 319 U.S. 624. Justice Jackson, speaking for a majority of six, said that the flag salute is a form of utterance, the affirmation of a political creed. To coerce the expression of any creed through such a ritual is a violation of freedom of speech. It is not a permissible means of achieving national unity. The court thus overruled its 1941 decision in the *Gobitis* case.

The court also reversed the conviction of a Witness for violating a state statute making it a crime to disseminate literature tending to create "an attitude of stubborn refusal to salute, honour and respect" the national and state flags and governments (*Taylor* v. *Mississippi*, 319 U.S. 583).

Laws interfering with the right of Jehovah's Witnesses to spread their beliefs "publicly and from house to house" were held invalid. A Dallas ordinance forbidding the scattering of handbills was not a reasonable exercise of police power when applied to a religious broadside entitled, "Peace, Can it Last?" (*Jamison* v. *Texas*, 318 U.S. 413). An ordinance of another Texas town, making it unlawful to sell books or materials in residential districts without the issuance of a permit by the mayor, if he deemed it advisable "after a thorough investigation," abridged freedom of religion, speech and press (*Largent* v. *Texas*, 318 U.S. 418). In these two cases the court was unanimous. But in *Martin* v. *Struthers*, 319 U.S. 141, the Witnesses, by the margin of a 5-to-4 decision, won the right to ring door-bells and otherwise arouse householders and their families for the purpose of proselytizing and distributing religious dodgers in spite of an ordinance forbidding the practice. Even if such activities were obnoxious to a majority of the citizens they could not legally be banned. In *Murdock* v. *Pennsylvania*, 319 U.S. 105, the court held, on the same day and by the same vote, that a 40-year-old ordinance requiring canvassers to procure a licence and pay a fee was invalid when applied to religious colporteurs. Cities may prohibit the use of their streets for purely commercial enterprises, but the fact that religious literature is sold rather than given away does not make the enterprise commercial. To charge a licence fee for such evangelism violates the 1st and 14th amendments. In several of the handbill cases briefs were filed by such organizations as the American Civil Liberties Union, the Bill of Rights committee of the American Bar association, the American Newspaper Publishers' association and the Society of Seventh Day Adventists, as friends of the court, urging the position finally taken by the majority of the court. In a brief filed in the flag salute case the American Legion supported the view taken by the dissenting members of the court.

The extent to which an employer may express his opinions about labour unions without being guilty of unfair practices in violation of the National Labor Relations act was considered in several circuit court decisions. These and cases involving freedom of speech under statutes and ordinances regulating union activities are reported under *Labour* in this article.

Constitutional Law. *Federal Power.*—In several cases the supreme court was called upon to determine the extent of the government's power to control wages and hours under the Fair Labor Standards act. The act, by its own terms, applies only to employees who are "engaged in commerce or in the production of goods in commerce." This language, the court held, is narrower than that of other statutes, like the National Labor Relations act, which extend federal control to business "affecting" interstate commerce. The court therefore declined to apply the wages and hours act to employees whose work was only indirectly connected with interstate commerce. (*See* cases reported under *Labour* in this article.)

In two cases the court sustained the power of federal agencies to regulate public utility companies whose facilities were hooked up with those of companies in other states. Federal authority over the transmission of electricity was held in *Jersey Central P.&L. Co.* v. *FPC*, 319 U.S. 61, not to be limited to companies which themselves own interstate power lines. The court sustained the jurisdiction of the Federal Power commission over a utility company which owned and operated facilities within one state, which connected with facilities of a second company also within

that state, whose facilities in turn connected with those of a third company outside the state. The same theory won out by a 5-to-3 decision in another case. An Ohio utility company bought gas from another company for delivery by pipeline from West Virginia for use in Ohio. In a hearing before the Ohio public utilities commission over the rates to be charged by the Ohio company an order was entered on the West Virginia company to present information as to the reasonableness of its charges for gas furnished the Ohio company. The West Virginia company contended that the Ohio commission had no jurisdiction over it and brought suit in a federal district court to enjoin the enforcement of the commission's order. While the suit was pending congress enacted the Natural Gas act which gave the Federal Power commission jurisdiction over interstate gas shipments. The court subsequently granted the injunction, which was sustained by the supreme court (*Pub. Ut. Comm. of Ohio* v. *United Fuel Gas Co.*).

The court seemed to recognize the existence of a national common law which has developed outside of statutory rules. It held in *Clearfield Trust Co.* v. *U.S.*, 318 U.S. 363, that "the rights and duties of the United States on commercial paper which it issues are governed by federal rather than by state law" and "in the absence of an applicable act of congress, it is for the federal courts to fashion the governing rule according to their own standards." The famous decision in *Erie* v. *Tompkins*, 304 U.S. 64, that there is no federal common law was held not to apply. On the other hand in *Palmer* v. *Hoffman*, 318 U.S. 109, the *Erie* v. *Tompkins* doctrine was applied in a grade crossing accident case tried in a federal court because of diversity of citizenship. The burden of establishing contributory negligence must be determined by state law, the court ruled.

Federal-State Relations.—In several cases of a technical nature the supreme court followed the established rule that federal and not state law controls in the application of federal statutes. The right of a farmer-debtor in Alabama to redeem after the foreclosure of a mortgage must be determined under the terms of the Bankruptcy act and not by state law. What rights are created by state law must be decided by the bankruptcy court "regardless of the characterization which may be applied to them by state statutes and decisions" (*Wragg* v. *Federal Land Bank*, 317 U.S. 325). The procedure specified by state laws was upheld by the court, however, in reversing convictions in two criminal cases on confessions obtained from the defendants while they were detained in violation of a Tennessee statute. Nor will the federal courts ordinarily restrain state officers from collecting state taxes where there is an adequate remedy under local law. The supreme court affirmed the refusal of the district court to entertain the petition to have the Louisiana Unemployment Compensation law declared unconstitutional as applied to a taxpayer and its maritime employees (*Great Lakes Dredge & Dock Co.* v. *Huffman*, 319 U.S. 293).

In accordance with this abstention doctrine the court ruled against the granting of an injunction to restrain a criminal prosecution in a state court for the violation of a city licensing ordinance by a member of Jehovah's Witnesses, even though the ordinance was held unconstitutional by the court in other cases on the same day (*Douglas* v. *Jeannette*, 319 U.S. 157).

The court worked out a reconciliation of conflicting national and state interests in holding that California's Agricultural Prorate act does not violate either the commerce clause of the constitution or the Sherman act and Agricultural Marketing Agreement act (*Parker* v. *Brown*, 317 U.S. 341). California produces almost half of the world's raisin crop, and between 90% and 95% of the raisins grown in California are shipped in interstate and foreign commerce. The California Agricultural Prorate act set up a program for marketing state agricultural products to restrict competition among growers and maintain prices. The Sherman act did not apply because it was directed against individual action in restraint of trade, and the action here was by a state. Nor did the California program conflict with the Agricultural Marketing act since "the two acts were co-ordinate parts of a single plan for raising farm prices to parity levels." The state program was, in fact, adopted in collaboration with officials of the federal department of agriculture and aided by loans from the Commodity Credit corporation. State regulations affecting interstate commerce are to be sustained, the court said, if upon consideration of all relevant facts, the matter seems to be one appropriate for local control without materially obstructing the free flow of commerce. The court thus applied the doctrine of "accommodation" which is accomplished by "comparing the relative weights of the national and local interests involved."

A slightly different form of accommodation between national and state authority was applied in *Terminal Association* v. *Trainmen,* 318 U.S. 1. A union which was under contract to furnish labour to a railroad, asked that cabooses be provided for the health and safety of switchmen. When the railroad failed to do so, the union applied to the Illinois Commerce commission, which directed that cabooses be supplied. The railroad contended that the National Railroad Adjustment board had jurisdiction over the dispute since it involved interstate commerce. The court conceded that the federal board might have had jurisdiction also, but neither the Interstate Commerce act, nor the federal Railway Labor, Boiler Inspection or Safety Appliance acts precluded the state commission from acting.

The court arrived at opposite results in two cases involving the right of state agencies to regulate the price of milk furnished to the army. In *Penn Dairies* v. *Milk Commission,* 318 U.S. 261, it was held that milk sold for use of the army on land leased from the commonwealth of Pennsylvania was subject to prices fixed by the state milk control commission. But in *Pacific Coast Dairies* v. *Dept. of Agriculture of California,* 318 U.S. 285, state authorities were held to have no right to revoke a dealer's license for selling and delivering milk at prices below the local minimum to the army at Moffitt field, which was owned exclusively by the United States. "The conclusions may seem contradictory," said Justice Roberts, "but in preserving the balance between national and state powers, seemingly inconsequential differences often require diverse results."

The court again held the government immune to state taxation in ruling that the Florida Commercial Fertilizer law does not apply to fertilizer owned by the United States and shipped into Florida for distribution by the department of agriculture as part of the soil conservation program. The government had a right to an injunction against the enforcement of the state tax and taging requirements (*Mayo* v. *U.S.,* 319 U.S. 441).

The federal courts must exercise great caution in dealing with disputes between states, said Justice Roberts in a case involving conflicting claims between Kansas and Colorado over the use of the Arkansas river which flows across both states. Overruling a master's findings in favour of Kansas, the supreme court stressed that both states have equal rights in such waters. The benefits of irrigation should be secured to one state without depriving the other of the use of the flowing stream (*Colorado* v. *Kansas,* 319 U.S. 729).

Criminal Law.—An advisory committee, appointed by the supreme court and headed by Arthur T. Vanderbilt, completed a draft of 56 rules of criminal procedure for the federal courts. The proposed rules include such simplifications as a short form of indictment to replace the involved forms which have been in use for a century and a single motion to dismiss instead of vari-ous technical motions. The surprise element in alibi defenses is removed by requiring the defendant, upon the government's demand, to disclose before trial the place where he claims to have been at the time of the crime. The cost of appeals is reduced by permitting counsel to print, as an appendix to his brief, only such part of the record as he desires the appellate court to read.

The conviction of the German propagandist, George Sylvester Viereck, under the Foreign Agents' Registration act was reversed by the supreme court on the ground that the statute only required the disclosure of activities of a registrant "as agent of a foreign principal" and the activities charged against the defendant were on his own behalf. Certain remarks to the jury by the prosecuting attorney were disapproved by the court as appeals to passion and prejudice (*Viereck* v. *U.S.,* 318 U.S. 236).

The supreme court also reversed two convictions based on confessions. Three members of a clan of Tennessee mountaineers were sentenced to 45 years' imprisonment for the murder of a federal revenue officer who was taking part in a night raid on a cache of "moonshine" whisky hidden near the family cemetery. The defendants were held two days for questioning before being brought before a U.S. commissioner for commitment as provided by statute. Confessions obtained during that period were improperly used against the defendants (*McNabb* v. *U.S.,* 318 U.S. 332). In the second case persons accused of conspiring to seek the destruction of federal property were held by a sheriff and FBI men for six days' questioning which was held to violate a state statute forbidding imprisonment prior to examination by a magistrate (*Anderson* v. *U.S.,* 318 U.S. 350).

Wilful failure to file an income tax return or pay the tax was held to be a misdemeanor, not a felony. A wilful and positive attempt to evade or defeat the tax is a felony (*Spies* v. *U.S.,* 317 U.S. 492). The conviction of the owner of a network of gambling houses in Chicago for large scale evasion of income taxes was approved by the supreme court.

Pretending to be an FBI agent in order to get information about a particular person violated the federal statute against impersonating an officer with "intent to defraud," even though the information thus obtained was valueless to the accused (*U.S.* v. *Lepowitch,* 318 U.S. 702).

The notorious Louis Buchalter, Emanuel Weiss and Louis Capone asked the supreme court to review their conviction of first degree murder for alleged errors during their nine-weeks' trial in a New York court, but their petition was denied. The court held that the states are free to enforce their criminal laws under such statutory provisions and common law doctrines as they deem appropriate. The supreme court will reverse the judgments of state courts in such cases only when they are inconsistent with the fundamental principles of liberty and justice.

The conviction of Boss Thomas J. Pendergast of Kansas City of a criminal contempt of court was reversed by the supreme court on the grounds that the alleged misbehaviour was barred by the three-year statute of limitations. Pendergast had been charged with taking part in a fraudulent scheme to distribute a fund deposited with a custodian by certain insurance companies in Missouri pending the outcome of rate litigation (*Pendergast* v. *U.S.,* 317 U.S. 412). This case should not be confused with the prosecution of Pendergast for income tax evasion. In another decision the court held that a federal court may punish for contempt by fine or imprisonment but not by both.

The supreme court held invalid the section of the Federal Firearms act which provides that a defendant's prior conviction of a crime of violence and his present possession of a firearm creates the presumption that such article was received by him in interstate or foreign commerce subsequent to the effective date of the statute. Such a statutory presumption violates the due process clause, because it leaves the jury free to act on the presumption alone once the specified facts are proved (*Tot* v. *U.S.*, 319 U.S. 463).

A defendant, charged with using the mails to defraud, waived his right to trial by jury and was found guilty by the court after conducting his own defense. On an appeal made on his behalf, the supreme court ruled that a defendant under indictment for felony may waive his right to a jury even though he has not had the advice of counsel. He may also waive his right to the help of counsel (*Admas* v. *U.S. ex rel. McCann*, 317 U.S. 269).

Domestic Relations.—Reverberations of the U.S. supreme court's 1942 decision in *Williams* v. *North Carolina*, 317 U.S. 287, were heard in divorce proceedings throughout the land. In the *Williams* case a man and woman had been convicted by a North Carolina court of "bigamous cohabitation." They had actually been married in Nevada after obtaining divorces in that state from their former spouses in proceedings where there was no personal service on the defendants who lived in North Carolina. The supreme court held that full faith and credit required North Carolina to recognize the Nevada divorce decrees, thus overruling the famous case of *Haddock* v. *Haddock*, 201 U.S. 562, in which a husband had left his wife in New York and got a divorce in Connecticut, serving her with notice of the suit by publication only. Upon his return to New York his wife sued him for divorce, and he set up the Connecticut decree as a defense, but the U.S. supreme court in 1906 held that full faith and credit did not require the New York court to recognize a decree obtained without personal service on the defendant. Under the *Williams* decision this is no longer the law.

Trial courts in several states held that the *Williams* decision merely eliminates the requirement of personal service on the defendant in out-of-state divorces, and that it does not preclude them from questioning the validity of such divorces where neither of the spouses was genuinely domiciled in the state granting the divorce. On this theory some courts revived the practice of enjoining the prosecution of "foreign" divorce actions against residents of their own states where it appeared that the domicile of the plaintiff was fictitious or falsely alleged.

A New York court denied custody of a child to the mother because of adultery and to the father because he was "contaminated with the germ of naziism."

Labour. *Anti-Strike Act.*—The War Labor Disputes act, also known as the Smith-Connally act, was passed by congress over the president's veto on June 25 and became effective July 1. It gave statutory recognition to the War Labor board, which had been created by the president's order. The board has jurisdiction to decide wages, hours and all other issues in any labour dispute which may lead to substantial interference with the war effort. The act also provides that when a strike is threatened in a war plant, the workers' representatives must notify the secretary of labour, the War Labor board and the National Labor Relations board, and submit a statement of the issues involved. For the next 30 days production must continue. If the dispute is not settled during this cooling-off period, then on the 30th day the NLRB shall take a secret vote to determine whether a majority of the workers wish to strike. The president is empowered to take possession of any war plant on behalf of the government whenever its operation is interrupted by a labour disturbance. The plant must be returned to its owners, however, within a period of 60 days after the restoration of its productive efficiency. Anyone who induces or instigates a strike, lock-out, slow-down or other interference with the operation of a government-controlled plant, may be punished by a fine of not more than $5,000, or imprisonment for not more than one year, or both.

An amendment to the Corrupt Practices act of 1925 was in-cluded in the War Labor Disputes act, making it unlawful for a labour organization to furnish campaign contributions in connection with any election at which presidential electors, senators or representatives are to be voted for.

Closed Shop.—A closed-shop agreement was held invalid by a federal district court in New York because the court found that it had led to a stoppage of work at an air base, thus interfering with vital war production. A Florida circuit court ruled the same way in a case that was almost identical. But the supreme court of Florida sustained a closed-shop agreement against attack by *quo warranto* proceedings in a case where a shipbuilding company was charged with an illegal conspiracy to grant a labour monopoly. The court pointed out that there had been no proof that compliance with the closed-shop agreement retarded any war work. The union had signed a no-strike pledge as part of the agreement. Moreover, such matters properly belong under federal jurisdiction through regulatory statutes (*Watson* v. *Tampa Shipbuilding Co.*).

Picketing.—Decrees of a New York court enjoining the picketing of two cafeterias were reversed by the supreme court. The lower court found that the pickets carried signs stating that the cafeterias were "unfair to organized labour" although they were actually operated by the members of a partnership without any employees. The pickets also told prospective customers that the cafeterias served bad food, and that by patronizing them "they were aiding the cause of fascism." The lower court injunctions were based on the theory that pickets should not be permitted to injure places of business by representations they knew to be false, and that the New York anti-injunction act did not apply because there was no "labour dispute." The supreme court, however, disagreed, ruling that the right to picket cannot be taken away "merely because there may have been isolated instances of abuse falling far short of violence" (*Mesevich* v. *Angelos*, Nov. 22, 1943).

An injunction against picketing was sustained by the New York court of appeals in another case because of false representations. The owner of a shoe store had a collective bargaining agreement with a union of his employees satisfactorily covering wages and working conditions. A rival union peacefully picketed the store in an attempt to force the owner to deal with it and to retaliate against the first union for picketing shoe stores employing members of the rival union. The court held that there was no labour dispute within the meaning of the state anti-injunction act. The store owner was entitled to an injunction since the signs carried by the pickets saying that he was unfair to the rival union were false (*Dinny and Robbins* v. *Davis*, 290 N.Y. 101).

The Massachusetts supreme court held that a strike for a closed shop is illegal, and that picketing by a union in order to force a closed-shop agreement upon an employer is not protected by the state picketing statute (*Fashioncraft* v. *Halpern*, 48 N.E. [2d] 1).

A contract coercively obtained from a theatre owner by a musicians' union on the threat of calling a strike of stage hands and picketing the theatre was set aside by the Michigan supreme court as invalid. The owner had a contract with the stage hands, but when he refused to employ an orchestra of six musicians, which he did not need or desire, agents of unions representing both groups of workers served a strike ultimatum on the theatre two hours before a performance was scheduled to begin. His signature to a contract obtained under such duress was not binding. There was no bona fide labour dispute (*Lafayette Dramatic Productions* v. *Ferentz*, 305 Mich. 193).

State Laws.—The Texas supreme court refused to relieve the president of a C.I.O. union from a fine and jail sentence for contempt of court in violating an injunction against his soliciting membership without first obtaining an organizer's card from the secretary of state as required by the Texas Labor act. This provision was not a restraint on freedom of speech. The supreme court of Florida, however, ruled that a municipal ordinance forbidding labour unions to solicit fees for membership, in public places, was an unconstitutional restraint on the right of employees to organize and the right of free speech (*Pittman* v. *Nix*).

A Colorado trial court held that provisions of the state Labor Peace act, requiring unions to incorporate, was unconstitutional as a prior restraint on freedom of speech, press and assembly in violation of the 1st and 14th amendments. The remainder of the act restricting boycotts, picketing and unauthorized strikes was constitutional as a reasonable exercise of police power.

Unfair Practices.—A sweeping order of the National Labor Relations board was upheld in *Virginia Electric and Power Co.* v. *NLRB,* 319 U.S. 533. The board had directed the disestablishment of a company-dominated union, the reimbursement of dues checked off to that union, and the reinstatement of employees. The court held that the board had full power to order such affirmative action as would effectuate the policies of the National Labor Relations act.

In another case before the NLRB, while a hearing was pending on charges of unfair labour practices against an electric company, the transmission poles and towers of the company were dynamited. The hearing ended in findings against the company and the company asked the board to reopen the case and hear evidence that union officers and members committed the dynamiting. The board refused, but on appeal to the circuit court the board was ordered to reopen the case, hear the offered evidence of sabotage and report its findings to the reviewing court. The supreme court affirmed this order (*NLRB* v. *I. and M. Electric Co.,* 318 U.S. 9).

An employer who persuaded employees to sign individual contracts in order to eliminate outside unions as collective bargaining agents was found by the NLRB to be engaged in unfair labour practices and was directed to cease giving effect to such contracts. This order was sustained on appeal to the circuit court (*Western Cartridge Co.* v. *NLRB*). In another opinion the same court held that an employer could not refuse to bargain with a union on the ground that his relations with his employees were controlled by contracts which were made before the time when the NLRA went into effect (*NLRB* v. *Case Co.*).

The extent to which employers may express their opinions about unions was considered in several circuit court opinions. In one case it was held that a newspaper publisher had the right to tell his employees that a particular union was "terrible" and not a reputable organization. This was not an unfair labour practice since it did not amount to threats tending to coerce his employees. It was also held proper for another employer to express his opinion about the selection by his employees of a certain union as a bargaining agent as long as he did not threaten reprisals against those who might disagree. But statements that a union was organized by racketeers, that workers would gain nothing by joining it, and that a former employee was discharged for strike activity, did constitute unfair practices in violation of the NLRA, according to another circuit court ruling.

Wages and Hours.—The status of employees under the Wages and Hours act depends upon the nature of the activity of the workers rather than upon the business of the employer. In determining whether a particular type of activity came within the act, the court applied the test of the "continuity of the flow of goods in interstate commerce." In *Walling* v. *Jacksonville Paper Co.,* 317 U.S. 564, employees who handled intrastate deliveries of paper were held subject to the Wages and Hours act since the paper was procured outside the state and remained only temporarily in the employer's warehouses within the state. The paper retained its character of goods in interstate commerce even though the actual sales and deliveries were wholly within the state. In *Higgins* v. *Carr Bros. Co.,* 317 U.S. 572, however, the court held that the FLSA did not apply to employees of a produce concern which obtained its goods both from local producers and dealers outside the state but unloaded them for redistribution in the local trade. Here the interstate movement had ended. The fact that the employer was in competition with wholesalers doing an interstate business was not relevant. The employees in the *Walling* case were covered by the act because they delivered goods brought into the state from outside under a specific prior agreement. In the *Higgins* case the employees handled goods originating both inside and outside the state which were ordered to meet the demands of general local trade.

The problem was simpler in *Overstreet* v. *North Shore Co.,* 318 U.S. 125, where the court held that the FLSA applies to employees of a company operating a toll road and a drawbridge used for the passage of goods in interstate commerce. But in *McLeod* v. *Threlkeld,* 319 U.S. 491, it was held that a cook who served maintenance-of-way employees of an interstate railroad was not covered by the Wages and Hours act. His work was further removed from the interstate flow of goods, since the men he served were merely servicing the means for interstate transportation. In another case, which the supreme court declined to review, it was held that porters employed by the owner of an office building are not brought under the FLSA merely because the tenants of the building are engaged in interstate commerce. Similarly the New York court of appeals ruled that a porter employed by a national bank to clean its building was not subject to the Wages and Hours act, even though part of the bank's business was interstate.

The FLSA was held to apply, however, to common labourers in a machinery repair shop which mainly serviced interstate commerce. The fact that the employees sometimes drove trucks to the employer's farm and did work not related to interstate business was not enough to change their classification since there was no actual separation of such services from their interstate duties.

In a case tried before the federal district court in New York, the child labour provisions of the FLSA were applied to an interstate telegraph company in spite of its contention that its messages were not "shipments in interstate commerce" and that the act applies only to producers of tangible goods which can actually be shipped.

An indictment under the Civil Rights act of 1870 against employers and union officials for conspiracy to violate the FLSA overtime provisions was held improper. The charge was that the employees had been intimidated into refraining from asserting their rights under the FLSA. The district court said this was not covered by the Civil Rights act which was designed to punish infringement of rights guaranteed by the 14th and 15th amendments. The prosecution should have been brought under the penal provisions of the FLSA.

Military Jurisdiction.—Conflicts between the military and civil authorities were resolved in several cases. A U.S. citizen in Hawaii was imprisoned by military authorities upon the suspicion that he was engaged in disloyal activities. The governor, with the president's approval, had declared martial law and suspended the writ of *habeas corpus.* The circuit court held that such measures were properly taken in the interest of public safety in wartime (*Zimmerman* v. *Walker,* 132 F. [2d] 442).

The supreme court held that the federal courts have no jurisdiction to try soldiers for criminal offenses committed on land acquired by the U.S. unless the government has accepted jurisdiction by filing notice with the governor of the state in which the land is situated or by similar appropriate action, since such procedure is specified by a federal statute. The court therefore ruled that the conviction of three soldiers by a federal district court for rape committed at an army camp in Louisiana was improper because the government had never formally accepted jurisdiction over the land (*Adams* v. *U.S.*, 319 U.S. 312). The court, however, did not indicate in its opinion that there had been any controversy between military and civil authorities in this case.

The warden of the city prison was ordered by a New York court to turn over to army authorities a soldier charged with assault on a civilian. In times of peace the civil authorities have precedence in the trial of such defendants, the court said, but in wartime they are subject to military law. Similarly a federal district court held that a civilian employee of an aircraft company working at a military depot in Eritrea was subject to court martial on a charge of stealing jewellery. He was a person "accompanying the army in the field" subject to military law under the articles of war even though all of his work was on British aircraft.

A civilian cook working for a steamship company operating a ship under contract with the U.S. government discovered that he was subject to army court martial for desertion when he left the ship without the consent of the captain just before it sailed from an army base as a troop transport. The fact that he intended to take service on a merchant vessel and was not informed that the ship was to be a transport before he joined it, was no defense, according to a district court decision. He was properly tried by an army rather than a navy court martial.

A different conclusion was reached in Alabama. A soldier, charged with rape, was arrested and held by state officers. The federal district court refused a writ of *habeas corpus* for delivery of the soldier to military authorities for trial. The articles of war, the court said, require military authorities to surrender to state officers persons in military service charged with certain offenses, "except in time of war." But this exception does not give the army exclusive jurisdiction in wartime or require the state to surrender jurisdiction on demand of the military.

Patents.—The National Patent Planning commission, established in 1941 by executive order to conduct a survey and study of the United States patent system, issued a report proposing changes in the law. Among them are provisions (1) that all patent agreements must be recorded with the patent office, so that secret, improper and illegal agreements may be exposed; (2) for the cancellation of patents which later information shows should not have been issued; (3) for a public register of patents under which the owners are willing to grant licences on reasonable terms; (4) that if the court finds in an infringement suit that the manufacture of the invention by the infringer is necessary to the national defense or required by public health or safety, the patent owner may be limited to the recovery of reasonable compensation without stopping the continued use of the invention; (5) that congress should establish an objective test for the patent ability of an invention on the basis of its value in advancing the arts and sciences; (6) that the present term of 17 years for a patent be retained, but that the protection of the patent laws shall not extend for more than 20 years beyond the time when a patent is first applied for, so that delays of more than three years in the prosecution of an application would shorten the 17 year term to a corresponding extent; and (7) that the court of customs and patent appeals be designated as the sole tribunal to review the denial of a patent by the patent office.

Public Contracts.—The supreme court sustained a judgment of $315,000 against electrical contractors for collusive bidding on PWA projects in the Pittsburgh area. The suit was brought by informers under the 1863 false claims statute which entitled

them to one-half of the amount recovered. The fact that the defendants had already been fined $54,000 in a criminal action for the same fraud was not a defense to the informers' suit which did not place them twice in jeopardy within the meaning of the 5th amendment (*Marcus* v. *Hess*, 317 U.S. 537). Informers in a subsequent suit against different defendants did not fare so well. Federal attorneys intervened by filing both civil and criminal proceedings against the defendants and asked for a stay of the prior suit brought by the informers. The circuit court of appeals, 8th circuit, held that the government was entitled to precedence in the trial of such cases, if it has proceeded with due diligence. It should not be placed in a position of having to rush into court without careful preparation in order to forestall action by informers.

All contracts for sales in excess of $100,000 to the war, navy and treasury departments and to the maritime commission were subject to renegotiation under the Renegotiation act. By amendments adopted in July, congress extended the act to four subsidiaries of the Reconstruction Finance corporation and redefined "sub-contracts." The government agencies involved in the renegotiation process adopted a policy of allowing a greater profit margin to contractors who succeeded in lowering the cost of war goods through greater production efficiency.

A corporation executive was convicted of violating the criminal provisions of the Renegotiation act in connection with contracts with the navy department. In response to a request for a statement of the actual cost of production, he had referred a government representative to the corporation's books, knowing that they contained improper items of expense.

Social Security.—The provision of the Federal Social Security act, which exempts maritime employers from the federal tax does not operate to exempt them from the New York unemployment insurance taxes, according to a supreme court decision (*Standard Dredging Co.* v. *Murphy*, 319 U.S. 306).

The supreme court of the state of Washington held that trainmen members of a minority union were not directly interested in a strike called by a majority union of logging loaders so as to preclude them from the benefits of the unemployment compensation act (*Wicklund* v. *Com'r. of Unemp. Comp.*, June 17).

The Utah supreme court ruled, however, that members of a minority union which objected to a strike called by a majority union were not entitled to unemployment compensation under the state act which denies benefits to workers of the "grade, class or group" of those fomenting a strike (*Iron Workers Union* v. *Industrial Comm. of Utah*, June 25).

The N.J. Unemployment Compensation law was upheld by the state supreme court against charges that it violated the 14th amendment (*Wiley Motors, Inc.* v. *Unemployment Compensation Comm. of N.J.*).

The Pennsylvania supreme court held invalid a law granting bonuses to the dependents of state employees, who went into war service, characterizing the statute as "fraternalism run riot" (*Kurtz* v. *Pittsburgh*).

The Vocational Rehabilitation act, which provides federal aid to states for the rehabilitation of persons disabled in industry and their return to employment, was amended. Congress set up specific standards for state plans for rehabilitation which must be approved by the federal security administrator before a state can qualify for such federal aid.

Taxation.—The pay-as-you-go system went into effect under the Current Tax Payment act of 1943 which provides for the payment of income and victory taxes for the current year in quarterly instalments. The law requires certain employers to withhold (on behalf of the government) 20% of wages and salaries in excess of exemptions to apply on the taxes of em-

"PICK ONE OUT, Ma, So I Can Go Back to Work." The indecision of Congress about passing a pay-as-you-go tax plan before adopting the final bill in June 1943, expressed in this cartoon by Lewis in the *Milwaukee Journal*

ployees. Some classes of employees are not subject to the withholding provisions. In order to lighten the burden of changing over to a current basis, taxpayers are forgiven 75% of their 1942 or 1943 tax, whichever is smaller. An anti-windfall provision cuts down the amount of forgiveness on large incomes resulting from war conditions. Special exemptions and allowances are given to members of the armed forces. The new law, however, does not change previous tax rates nor apply to the incomes of estates, trusts and corporations. Taxpayers must still file final returns on or before March 15 for income during the preceding year. The rate of the victory tax was lowered by amendments adopted Oct. 28.

The supreme court refused the government's request that *Eisner* v. *Macomber*, 252 U.S. 189, be overruled, re-affirming its position that a stock dividend is not income unless it changes the holder's proportionate interest in the corporation (*Helvering* v. *Sprouse*, 318 U.S. 604, and other cases). The courts also passed on various other technical phases of the income tax laws.

In an opinion of interest to real estate buyers and mortgagees, the supreme court held that a federal estate tax lien attaches to real estate at the date of a decedent's death without assessment demand or recording. Such liens are superior to the liens of subsequent mortgages even though the mortgagee lends money in good faith without knowledge of the lien (*Detroit Bank* v. *U.S.*, 317 U.S. 329). Similarly a federal estate tax lien on real estate takes precedence over later liens for state, county and city taxes (*Michigan* v. *U.S.*, 317 U.S. 338).

The attempt of the Tennessee legislature to repeal the state poll tax was held invalid by the state supreme court on a technical point of constitutional law (*Biggs* v. *Beeler*). The Ohio supreme court held that sales of trailers to out-of-state buyers are subject to the Ohio sales tax. Collection of the tax was not a violation of the interstate commerce clause of the federal constitution (*Trotwood Trailers* v. *Evatt*). Offices of a company in Texas where mail orders were accepted and forwarded to its main office are chain stores taxable as such, ruled the Texas supreme court (*Montgomery Ward* v. *Texas*). The ruling in *Grosjean* v. *American Press Co.*, 297 U.S. 233, was applied by the Florida supreme court in holding that a municipal ordinance imposing an annual licence tax on newspapers on a graduated scale based on volume of circulation was unconstitutional as a restraint on press freedom (*City of Tampa* v. *Tampa Times*). Inheritance taxes imposed by

Oklahoma on estates of deceased members of the Five Civilized Tribes was validly applied to cash and securities held for the Indians by the secretary of the interior (*Okla. Tax Comm.* v. *U.S.*, 319 U.S. 598).

Trade Regulation.—Two medical societies were convicted of conspiring to violate the Sherman act by obstructing the business of Group Health, a non-profit corporation organized by government employees in the District of Columbia to provide medical care and hospitalization on a risk-sharing prepayment basis. Group Health employed full-time physicians paid by salaries. The medical societies were charged with trying to prevent Group Health from carrying on its business by restraining their own members from working for Group Health or consulting with doctors employed by Group Health and by persuading hospitals in Washington, D.C., to refuse their facilities to patients of Group Health's doctors. In sustaining the conviction of the medical societies, the supreme court held that it was not necessary to decide whether the practice of medicine was a trade. Group Health was engaged in "trade" within the meaning of the Sherman act. Nor was the dispute between the medical societies and Group Health one "concerning terms and conditions of employment," within the meaning of the Clayton act as expanded by the Norris-LaGuardia act, so as to exempt the medical societies from the operation of the Sherman act (*American Medical Ass'n* v. *U.S.*, 317 U.S. 519).

The much-publicized prosecution of the Associated Press under the Sherman and Clayton acts before a three-judge district court resulted in a decree restraining the defendant press association from "continuing to enforce its by-laws in their present form." It was left open to the A.P. to adopt substitute by-laws restricting admission to membership, "provided that members in the same field with the applicant shall not have power to impose, or dispense with, any conditions upon his admission, and that the by-laws shall affirmatively declare that the effect of admission upon the ability of an applicant to compete with members in the same field shall not be taken into consideration in passing upon his application." The by-laws which were found objectionable provided that if an applicant is operating in the same field as an existing member, and his application is approved by a majority of members, he may be admitted upon paying 10% of the regular assessments paid to the association members in that field from Oct. 1, 1900, to the time of his election. This was held to be an unreasonable restraint of trade. Two other actions of the association, which the government complained of, were held not to violate the anti-trust laws, namely, the purchase of all the shares of Wide World Photos and an alleged "cartel" with the Canadian Press association under which each organization agreed to furnish its news to the other to the exclusion of nonmembers (*U.S.* v. *A.P.*, 52 F. Supp. 362).

In *Parker* v. *Brown*, 317 U.S. 341 (discussed under *Constitutional Law*), the court held that a state may create a combination in restraint of trade without violating the federal antitrust laws.

An exchange of information among members of a wholesalers association in order to blacklist manufacturers who were selling directly to retailers was held by a circuit court to violate the Sherman act. A district court ruled that an agreement between a union and employers restricting the use of spray equipment for painting was a reasonable health measure and not an antitrust law violation. A 100% monopoly of the business of furnishing sleeping car service to railroads was held by another district court to be a violation of the Sherman act even though "nonpredatory." A manufacturer who agreed with a retailer not to sell coats to the retailer's competitor, in consideration of a promise of indemnity against loss, violated the New York antitrust law, according to the state's court of appeals.

The Kansas Filled Milk act, banning the use of non-milk fats in milk products, was upheld by the state supreme court in a case involving the use of cottonseed oil. The law was a proper exercise of legislative judgment in the interest of public health.

The North Dakota supreme court held that a statute designed to regulate the practice of professional photography, through examination and licensing, was unconstitutional as an improper exercise of police power.

The Wisconsin act establishing a "State Bar of Wisconsin" to which all lawyers practicing in the state must belong was approved by the state supreme court but the effective date for its operation was postponed till the end of World War II.

The supreme court of Ohio held a Cincinnati ordinance limiting business hours of barber shops unconstitutional as an improper exercise of police power. It had no real relation to health, safety, morals or general welfare of public.

The federal trade commission properly ordered a manufacturer to cease and desist from using the letters "M.D." either alone or in conjunction with the picture of a doctor, nurse or a cross on medicated powder, since it conveyed the false impression that the product was indorsed by the medical profession or the Red Cross (*Stanley Lab*. v. *FTC*). So, too, an order of the commission was upheld which directed a manufacturer to cease using "Scout," "Boy Scout" and "Scouting" in connection with knives sold because it gave the false impression that they were sponsored by the Boy Scouts of America.

The federal security administrator has the power to promulgate regulations fixing reasonable "standards of identity" for foods under their common names to prevent the misleading of consumers, the supreme court held.

Treason.—The conviction of the Detroit traitor, Max Stephan, for harbouring a German war prisoner who had escaped from Canada and supplying him with food, clothing and money, was sustained by the circuit court of appeals, 6th circuit, in the first treason case to reach the courts. The supreme court refused to review the decision. The treason conviction of Anthony Cramer for aiding the nazi saboteurs, Thiel and Kerling, who landed from a U-boat, was also sustained. But the circuit court for the 7th circuit reversed the conviction for treason of the father, mother, uncle, aunt and two friends of another saboteur, Hans Max Haupt, because of the use in evidence of admissions made by the defendants during a period of several weeks in custody of the FBI. The defendants should have been brought before a committing officer immediately after their arrest as required by statute. This provision is mandatory on the arresting officers and cannot be waived by the defendants as the government contended it had been.

War Regulations.—The government continued to exercise wartime controls over communications, transportation, manpower, labour disputes, foreign commerce and credits, property of enemy aliens, food, fuel, rents and prices, wages and hours, materials and production. Business men faced an increasing volume of paper work resulting from the necessity for organizing and applying economic resources most effectively for the prosecution of the war. No person escaped the effects of this marshalling of industrial and human forces.

Price and Rent Control.—The Office of Price Administration broke all federal bureau records in the bulk of its output of legalistic literature. This was no doubt inevitable in view of the enormous task delegated to this agency of devising and enforcing price schedules and techniques for rent control and rationing. According to Justice Magruder, a member of the emergency court of appeals created by the Price Control act: "The administrator had to move promptly, on the broadest possible front; he had to get out regulations covering great numbers of commodities,

affecting a wide range of industries, the full comprehension of each of which is a lifetime study. He could not afford to be a perfectionist in getting the program started."

In a unanimous decision the supreme court ruled that the emergency court of appeals has exclusive jurisdiction to restrain the enforcement of regulations or price orders under that act subject, however, to review by the supreme court. The action of the district court in dismissing the application of wholesale meat dealers for an injunction against a maximum price regulation was affirmed. The petitioners should have pursued the administrative remedy provided by the statute, namely, to file a protest with the price administrator, and if the protest were denied, to appeal to the emergency court (*Lockerty* v. *U.S.*, 319 U.S. 182). From this and circuit court decisions it would appear that the emergency court has exclusive jurisdiction to determine the validity of price regulations. The emergency court held that rent control is not a violation of the due process clause nor an improper delegation of legislative power.

The California supreme court held that an action by a consumer to recover a $50 penalty for an overcharge of 25 cents in connection with a tire inspection was maintainable in a state court. The validity of the price regulations may not be challenged in such a case.

Defendant may, however, attack the constitutionality of the act, but the court held that it was not an illegal delegation of legislative power (*Miller* v. *Municipal Court*). On the same theory the Pennsylvania supreme court sustained a judgment for treble damages for a price violation. But such a suit must be brought in good faith. A defendant who was sued for treble damages in a New York court successfully raised the defense that the complainants conspired among themselves to induce him to violate the act. He claimed that he was ignorant of the price ceiling and that the complainants had persuaded him to violate the regulations for the sole purpose of suing him for damages for such violation. No man may take advantage of his own wrong, said the court in dismissing the suit. Another collusive suit, but this time between a landlord and tenant who agreed upon this method of testing the constitutionality of the Price Control act, was dismissed by a federal district court on motion of government counsel. The supreme court affirmed the dismissal (*U.S.* v. *Johnson*, 319 U.S. 302).

A district court held that a deputy of the price administrator's office has no right to conduct secret hearings for the examination of buyers of meat products. Witnesses, called for such examination, may be accompanied by counsel and a stenographer who may take notes as members of the public. But counsel has no right to interrupt or take part in the proceedings.

Utility rates are excluded from the matters over which the price administrator was given power except that he has the right to intervene and to be heard in rate cases, according to a decision of the court of appeals of the District of Columbia.

Selective Service.—The supreme court held that a registrant's contention that an appeal board had rejected his claim through a misconstruction of the Selective Service act was not a proper defense to a prosecution for failure to obey an induction order where it appeared that the director of selective service had ruled as a matter of fact that the registrant was not a bona fide conscientious objector (*Bowles* v. *U.S.*, 319 U.S. 33).

A registrant who was under arrest for failure to obey an induction order tried to get a review of his draft classification by *habeas corpus* proceedings on the ground that his local board had been arbitrary and unfair, but the circuit court of appeals held that compliance with an induction order is a prerequisite to contesting a registrant's classification in court. A registrant, however, who furnished his board with the address of his maritime union as his forwarding address was not guilty of knowing failure to keep his board advised of the address where mail could reach him since the union office was part of a chain of forwarding addresses (*Bartchy* v. *U.S.*, 319 U.S. 484).

Opposition to war "not on political considerations but on a general humanitarian concept . . . essentially religious in character" may entitle a registrant to classification as a conscientious objector, according to a circuit court of appeals decision. But objection to military service for philosophical and political reasons pertinent only to the present war was held by a district court not to exempt another registrant "by reason of religious training and belief."

Soldiers' and Sailors' Relief Act.—The supreme court held that the stay of court proceedings against persons serving in the armed forces provided by statute, is discretionary with the trial court. A defendant, who was a commissioned officer and had taken part in the trial of a case as an attorney and trustee, did not have the absolute right to a continuance under the relief act (*Boone* v. *Lightner*, 319 U.S. 561). (*See also* AGRICULTURE; BANKING; BUSINESS REVIEW; CONSUMER CREDIT; PATENTS; PUBLIC UTILITIES; RELIEF; TAXATION; WAR LABOR BOARD, NATIONAL; WAR PRODUCTION BOARD.) (M. DN.)

Lawn Tennis: *see* TENNIS.

Lead. There were no new data available for addition to the accompanying table of world production of lead, and many of the figures for 1940 and 1941 shown are estimates; only those carrying a decimal point are reported outputs.

World Production of Lead
(In thousands of metric tons)

	1929	1937	1938	1939	1940	1941
Australia	177.3	234.4	235.7	252.4	280	315
Belgium	62.2	88.0	90.5	96.0	55	20
Canada	148.0	186.4	185.7	177.9	215	220
Germany	97.9	162.4	171.7	181.4	200	225
Burma	81.5	78.9	81.4	78.6	83	84
Mexico	248.8	231.2	242.7	215.7	196.3	155.3
Spain	133.3	30.0	36.0	27.0	56	57
U.S.S.R.	6.2	55.0	69.0	75.0	80	90
United States	624.2	426.3	344.4	381.4	389.2	438.2
World Total	1,756.8	1,719.6	1,704.2	1,722.7	1,800	1,850
Ex. U.S.	1,132.6	1,293.3	1,359.8	1,341.3	1,511	1,412

There was an increase in mine production of lead in the United States, from 461,426 short tons of recoverable metal in 1941 to 492,435 tons in 1942, an improvement of 7%. Increases totaling 47,262 tons were reported from 12 states, while the same number had decreases totaling 16,253 tons, leaving a net increase of 31,009 tons. The only producing area to show an appreciable increase in output was southwestern Missouri; the combined increases in other areas were offset by the decreases. The output of refined lead decreased from 470,517 tons in 1941 to 467,367 tons in 1942, but antimonial lead more than compensated for this drop, with an increase from 40,237 tons to 51,762 tons. No data was received for 1943, but apparently the shortage of manpower resulted in some decrease, since it was reported that after the first quarter of the year some withdrawals from the stockpile were found necessary.

Lead still remained listed with the metals of which there was a surplus of supply, available for substitution for scarcer metals, but at the end of 1943 it was several points higher in the list, as a result of the reduction in supply. Apparently the reduction was not considered to be a threat of impending scarcity, since it was announced at the end of October that premium prices had been withdrawn for certain classes of mines.

Advance estimates indicated a decrease in consumption of lead in small arms ammunition in 1944, but this was expected to be offset by increases in other uses, giving a final figure not much if any different from that of 1943. The mine production was expected to furnish only about 40% of the total consumption, the remainder coming from imports and secondary lead.

It was unofficially reported that lead production in Canada in 1942 was 243,800 short tons. (*See also* BUSINESS REVIEW.) (G. A. Ro.)

League of Nations. It is doubtful if the nonpolitical organs of the League of Nations, functioning in four separate countries, had ever done more important work than during 1943. The economic department at Princeton furnished the Hot Springs conference with a report on the league's work on nutrition, which was the documentary background of the most successful international conference during World War II. The economic and financial departments produced a remarkable series of studies on postwar problems: *Wartime Rationing and Consumption, Money and Banking, Relief Deliveries and Relief Loans, Trade Relations Between Free Market and Controlled Economies.* But their two outstanding reports were *The Transition from War to Peace Economy,* admittedly the most authoritative outline of the domestic and international measures needed to avert postwar depressions and maintain high levels of production and employment; and *Europe's Overseas Needs, 1919-1920, and How They Were Met,* with its lessons drawn from the failure then to develop promptly an international plan for providing basic needs for the economic rehabilitation of devastated areas. These staff plans, as it were, for winning the peace attracted great attention among the United Nations, each serving a special purpose in connection with the United Nations' plans for giving effect to the Atlantic charter and other declarations of common policy.

Vital work on medical treatment was being done by the health section, in the standardization of sera, vitamins, and products like heparin, the recent preventive against blood clotting. Standard specimens were prepared at the National Institute of Medical Research, Hampstead, London, and sent from there to all Allied and neutral countries. The Permanent Opium board continued in collaboration with the Opium Supervisory body, Washington, to keep close check on the production, manufacture, and distribution of narcotics. In spite of the secrecy maintained by Germany and Japan about their narcotic production—the latter was still deliberately trying to poison China with drugs—the board received statistics from German-occupied countries and even Hungary and was able to keep the machinery for world-wide drug control working. Taking it all round, the value of the league's ability to provide scientific statistics, on which policies could then be based, had never been more in evidence.

The Supervisory commission, entrusted in wartime with control of the league's business, adopted a budget for 1944, amounting to some £580,000, of which 59% was to be paid by the British commonwealth on a prewar basis of contribution, as was also the case with the U.S.A., as far as concerns the International Labour Office. All the Allied countries were to contribute proportionately, with token or other payments, according to the exigencies of war. The league remained solvent, with funds sufficient for those sections of its organization which were still functioning. Geneva was still the headquarters, from which the secretary general, Sean Lester, directed the various activities, mostly by telegraphy. (*See also* DRUGS AND DRUG TRAFFIC; MANDATES; REFUGEES.) (M. FE.)

Leahy, William Daniel (1875–), U.S. naval officer, was born at Hampton, Ia., on May 6. He was graduated from the U.S. naval academy in 1897. In

1912 he was chief of staff of the Nicaraguan occupation armies and in 1916 chief of staff in the Haitian campaign. Commissioned rear admiral in 1930, he became commander of the destroyers' scouting force in 1931, chief of the bureau of navigation in 1933 and chief of naval operations in 1937. He was commissioned vice-admiral in 1935 and admiral in 1936.

Upon his retirement from the navy in 1939, he was appointed governor of Puerto Rico. In Nov. 1940, President Roosevelt named him ambassador to the French government at Vichy. In April 1942, Roosevelt summoned Leahy to Washington "for consultations." Though one purpose of this move was to express disapproval of Vichy's policies, his primary purpose was to appoint Leahy chief of staff to the commander-in-chief. Leahy was named to this newly created post on July 21, 1942. In this capacity he accompanied the president to the international conferences held during 1943 at Quebec, Cairo and Tehran. On March 6, 1943, the president appointed Adm. Leahy to a special committee which held hearings on manpower problems.

"Lease-Lend" Act (H.R. 1776): *see* FOREIGN ECONOMIC ADMINISTRATION.

Leather.

The United States leather industry was unable in 1943 to continue the record high rate of production which had been maintained through 1942. Demand for all types of leather continued as great as during the preceding year, but the inventory reserves of raw stock, tanning materials and finished leathers which had enabled the industry to meet practically all of the demands made upon it in 1942 had been used up before 1943 was well under way.

With inventory reserves eliminated, tanners were forced to depend upon reduced domestic production and declining imports of cattle hides, kipskins and calfskins, and production of these leathers in 1943 was well below that of 1942. In other types of leathers the production decline was not generally as serious as in cattle-hide leathers, but it was estimated that total production of all leathers during the year was around 25% below 1942. There was no information available for publication at the close of the year on leather production outside the United States.

Increased output of domestic chrome ore eased the chrome situation somewhat in 1943, and sufficient quantities of chromium chemicals were available through the year to meet the industry's needs. However, in September the War Production board issued new allocation orders covering chromium chemicals and there was some fear expressed in the tanning industry that another serious situation might develop in that quarter.

The WPB in February imposed controls on the distribution and use of vegetable tanning materials under Order M-277. The use of vegetable tanning materials was confined to the tanning of shoe, belting, harness, strap and other leather and to the manufacture of pharmaceutical products and water treatment materials. The use of vegetable tanning materials was prohibited for tanning furs and in the manufacture of crude petroleum oil or other products. In addition, the use of chestnut wood tanning materials was prohibited for the manufacture of water treatment materials. The order specifically listed both domestic and imported raw materials covered by the control.

The greatest problem in the production of domestic tanning materials in 1943 was the difficulty encountered in securing labour to provide the wood and tanning extracts. This was emphasized in the case of chestnut extract, with the situation in regard to this important tanning material becoming so serious that the WPB placed it under allocations control at the end of the year.

Many of the chemicals and other materials, as well as some

dyestuffs, that were formerly used in substantial quantities by the industry were restricted, subject to allocations or in unpredictable supply through the year.

The industry also experienced shortages of most oils and greases used in tanning, and the use of many of these was further controlled by government regulations from time to time during the year.

Maintenance of tanning machinery and equipment was a problem, since replacements were practically halted by WPB regulations on production and sale of new and used equipment, and the industry found it difficult to obtain repair parts promptly.

The sole leather problem continued unabated through 1943, and resulted in the introduction of numerous substitute materials which served the double purpose of alleviating the sole leather shortage and of enabling the shoe industry to make nonrationed types of footwear. Many of these substitutes were purely experimental, many were of highly questionable value, but a few were expected to continue in use after the war.

The National Bureau of Standards tested hot oil and wax treatments intended to increase the wear life of sole leather and reported that these extended the life of the leather 15% and 40% respectively over that of untreated leather. The WPB recommended these treatments for adoption by the shoe industry. The WPB also included specifications for minimum quality of shoe soles in a revision of Conservation Order M-217 (Footwear).

Producers of side and kip upper leathers were limited by the WPB to a monthly production quota of 70% of average 1942 monthly output for side leathers and 90% for kip leathers. In addition, numerous government restrictions were imposed on the use of side and kip leathers, with military and lend-lease requirements getting first call, followed by essential civilian requirements, with the diversion of as much leather as possible into the manufacture of footwear.

Calf-leather production was first restricted to a monthly quota of 90% of the 1942 rate, and this was reduced later in the year to 80% in an effort to secure equitable distribution of available raw-stock supplies. Tanners of calf leather were required to process into leather for navy footwear all raw stock suitable for that purpose, and deliveries of military weights and grades were reserved exclusively for manufacturers of navy shoes. This created a broad gap in the calf-leather supply which the spreading out of other weights and grades of calf leather, and the substitution of side and kip leathers, did not fill.

The most important factors affecting kid and goat leathers in 1943 were the reopening of some important raw-stock supply sections and government measures taken through the year to make more of these leathers available for footwear by curbing their use for other purposes. Requirements for goatskin leathers for military garments in 1943 eased off from the preceding year, but requirements for these leathers for work gloves and other essential civilian purposes increased.

Domestic production of sheep and lambskins was high in 1943, and large imports added to the supply of raw stock for sheepskin leather tanners. Restrictions on the use of shearlings were removed by the government, making available for civilian uses large quantities of shearlings that had previously been demanded for military clothing and other military equipment.

The most significant labour developments of 1943 were the inclusion of insurance benefits in contracts negotiated by the International Fur and Leather Workers union (C.I.O.) with two Chicago tanners and a schism in the ranks of the same union in the important tanning district around Salem and Peabody, Mass. The intra-union strife resulted in a general strike called by insurgent members and their refusal to obey orders from the

War Labor board and the president to return to work and resume production of critical military leathers. The president then ordered the army to seize 13 of the 32 affected tanneries. This action was followed by a return of the strikers, referral of the dispute to the WLB for action, and the subsequent return of the tanneries to their owners. (*See also* SHOE INDUSTRY.)

(R. B. B.)

Lebanon.
Independent republic, formerly French mandated territory, bordering the eastern Mediterranean. Area 3,475 sq.mi.; pop. (est.) 900,000; chief town: Beirut (cap.), 180,000. President: Sheikh Beshara el Khoury (1943). Language: Arabic; religion: mainly Mohammedan.

History.—The restoration of the constitution was proclaimed by Gen. Georges Catroux on March 18, 1943, and Dr. Ayoub Tabet was appointed head of the state with two "ministers of state," Emir Khaled Chehab and Jawad Boules, to assist him. The law empowering the government to nominate one-third of the chamber was abolished. On July 21 Tabet resigned and was succeeded by Petro Trad, a member of the Greek Orthodox community. Elections were held on Aug. 29, a dispute regarding representation in the chamber of deputies having been settled by giving 30 seats to the Christians and 25 seats to the Moslems. The new chamber met on Sept. 21 and elected Beshara el Khoury president of the republic and Sabri Hamadeh president of the chamber.

In the absence of Jean Helleu, the delegate general, at Algiers for consultation with the French Committee of National Liberation, the chamber on Nov. 8, 1943, unanimously passed a bill revising the clauses of the constitution which were incompatible with full sovereignty. On Nov. 11 Pres. Khoury, the prime minister and seven other ministers were arrested by French troops on the orders of Helleu, now returned, who dissolved the chamber and suspended the constitution, calling on Emil Eddé to carry on the administration. A general strike was called and demonstrations and rioting occurred, resulting in civilian casualties. Gen. Catroux arrived in Beirut on Nov. 16 with full powers to negotiate a settlement, R. G. Casey, British minister of state in the middle east, having already arrived on Nov. 13. On Nov. 22 President Khoury, the prime minister and other ministers were released and resumed work. The chamber met again on Nov. 24 and Riyadh as-Sulh, prime minister and minister of finance, indicated that the revision of the constitution voted on Nov. 8 was considered still to be in force. It was reported that Gen. Catroux had previously told the president that the French Committee of National Liberation, while recognizing the Riyadh as-Sulh government, did not accept the revision of the constitution. An ordinance issued by Yves Chataigneau, who replaced Helleu on Nov. 22, was announced Nov. 24, repealing the ordinance suspending the constitution. Gen. Catroux returned to Algiers Nov. 30. For financial, trade, agricultural data, *see* SYRIA.

Leeward Islands: *see* WEST INDIES, BRITISH.
Legislation: *see* LAW.

Lehman, Herbert H.
(1878–   ), U.S. politician, was born March 28. He was graduated from Williams college in 1899. He later entered the textile business and in 1908 became a partner in Lehman Brothers banking house, where he remained until World War I. At the beginning of the war, he acted as treasurer and vice chairman of the Jewish Joint Distribution committee and then assisted, in a civilian capacity, Franklin Delano Roosevelt, then assistant secretary of the navy. He joined the army in Aug. 1917, was commissioned a captain and assigned to the general staff. He eventually attained the rank of colonel in the quartermaster corps and was awarded the D.S.M. in 1919. After the war Lehman returned to the banking business. In the elections of 1928, he was voted into office as lieutenant governor of New York and won re-election in 1930. He was elected governor in 1932, and won re-election in 1934 and 1936. In 1938, he ran again, defeating Thomas Dewey, to win New York's first four-year term as governor. Lehman declined a renomination in 1942 and was appointed director of foreign relief and rehabilitation by President Roosevelt. On Nov. 11, 1943, he was elected and assumed office as director general of the United Nations Relief and Rehabilitation administration.

Leland Stanford Junior University: *see* STANFORD UNIVERSITY.

Lemons and Limes.
The United States 1943 lemon crop, almost all of which was grown in California, was estimated by the U.S. department of agriculture at 14,274,000 boxes compared with 14,940,000 in 1942. This was a relatively large crop, since the average for 1932–41 was only 10,146,000 boxes while the record year of production was 1940 with 17,236,000 boxes. Prices of lemons were high and prices received by growers were more than 50% above those of the previous year. Imports of lemons or lemon products from the Mediterranean countries were practically nothing.

The 1943 crop of limes, produced only in Florida, was estimated at 190,000 boxes compared to 175,000 in 1942. This was much above the average of 1932–41 of only 58,000 boxes.

(J. C. Ms.)

"Lend-Lease" Act: *see* FOREIGN ECONOMIC ADMINISTRATION.
Lend-Lease Administration, Office of: *see* AGRICULTURE; FOREIGN ECONOMIC ADMINISTRATION.

Leonard, Adna Wright
(1874–1943), U.S. clergyman, was born Nov. 2 in Cincinnati, O. He was ordained in the Methodist Episcopal Church in 1899, after graduating from New York university. He continued his studies at Drew Theological seminary and in Rome and received his D.D. at Ohio Northern in 1909. He was created bishop in 1916 and served in San Francisco, Buffalo and Pittsburgh. In 1939 he became bishop in the Washington area after the union of the Methodist Episcopal Church, South, and the Methodist Protestant Church. During World War II he served as chairman of the General Commission of U.S. Army and Navy Chaplains and in that capacity represented 31 U.S. Protestant denominations during an inspection tour of overseas U.S. camps. Bishop Leonard was killed in a plane crash in Iceland, May 3, after completing a tour of the British Isles—the first lap of a projected inspection trip which was to have included Iceland, North Africa, India and China.

Lepidolite: *see* LITHIUM MINERALS.

Leprosy.
In a hospital for leprous patients, 20 volunteers were given a therapeutic trial of sulfanilamide. Six received two courses and 14 one course. The courses lasted from 6 to 12 weeks. It was the opinion of the physicians that the drug effected no improvement in the leprous condition of the patients, but that ulcers infected with other bacteria improved. These workers tried sulfanilamide therapy in 12 patients suffering with pseudoerysipelas, a severe complication of leprosy. Prompt improvement resulted in all cases. One group of experimenters treated with sulfanilamide and sulfathiazole rats and mice which had been inoculated with "rat leprosy." They con-

cluded that the drugs inhibited the development of the disease in these animals, but as soon as the medication was discontinued the leprous nodules began to grow.

Though cases of leprosy have occurred from time to time in immigrants living in the United States, the disease has shown a tendency to perpetuate itself only in the Gulf states of Florida, Louisiana and Texas. Between 100 and 200 cases of leprosy developed among Scandinavian immigrants who settled in Minnesota and adjacent states. Although no special measures were taken to prevent the spread of leprosy in these states, only seven known cases developed in the first generation of American born persons and a single doubtful case in the second generation. A similar condition existed in California where 475 cases of leprosy were reported between 1906 and 1940. Only 14 of these were thought to have contracted the disease there; the others probably were infected in their native country. More than 100 cases of leprosy were discovered in New York city but only two of these could possibly have contracted the disease there.

It is the opinion of many members of the medical profession as well as of persons not medically trained that chaulmoogra oil and its derivative are specifically curative drugs for the treatment of leprosy. An author who for many years was interested in the leprosy problem discussed the evidence relative to the employment of chaulmoogra oil in the treatment of leprosy and found no acceptable scientific data to justify its use. He explained the alleged favourable results reported for this drug by the fact, well known to experienced leprologists, that many cases of leprosy improve spontaneously even though therapy has not been instituted.

BIBLIOGRAPHY.—G. H. Faget, F. A. Johansen and Sister Hilary Ross, "Sulfanilamide in the Treatment of Leprosy," *Public Health Reports* 57:1892–1899 (1942); C. Krakower, P. Morales-Otero and J. H. Axtmayer, "Effect of Sulfanilamide on Experimental Leprosy," *Journal of Infectious Diseases,* 72:1-10 (1943); G. W. McCoy, "Observations on the Epidemiology of Leprosy," *Pub. Health Rep.* 57:1935–1943 (1942); "Chaulmoogra Oil in the Treatment of Leprosy," *ibid.,* 57:1727 (1942).   (C. H. BD.)

Lettuce.

The production of lettuce in 1943 was estimated by the U.S. department of agriculture at 20,788,000 crates, or 14% below the total of 23,604,000 crates grown in 1942. The acreage was reduced from 156,490 in 1942 to 135,970 in 1943, which was in accord with the recommendations of the U.S. department of agriculture. This compared with an average acreage of 154,500 for the 10-year period of 1932–41. While

U. S. Seasonal Acreage and Production of Lettuce, 1943 and 1942

	Acreage		Production (Crates)	
	1943	1942	1943	1942
Early	34,700	38,300	5,335,000	5,690,000
Second early	38,280	60,750	5,184,000	6,904,000
Intermediate	4,200	3,950	838,000	836,000
Late (1)	26,260	23,490	4,579,000	5,209,000
Late (2)	32,530	30,000	4,857,000	4,965,000
Total	135,970	156,490	20,788,000	23,604,000

the demand continued high and prices were at ceiling levels, the shipments were restricted. The production of the early crop was above the average but the intermediate and late crops were reduced. Much of the demand was supplied by victory gardeners. The consumption of lettuce steadily increased after the sandwich lunch was adopted in cities and factories.

(J. C. Ms.)

Lewis, John Llewellyn

(1880–   ), U.S. labour leader, was born Feb. 12 in Lucas, Ia., the son of a Welsh coal miner. After seven years of schooling he was compelled, because of his family's financial need, to desert

U.S. CARTOONISTS almost without exception raged at John L. Lewis as he ordered coal miners to strike April 30, 1943. This cartoon by Bishop of the *St. Louis Star-Times* is captioned "All the Land Mines are Not in Europe"

his studies and enter the mines. His success as legislative agent for the United Mine Workers of Illinois (1908–11) led to his appointment as American Federation of Labor organizer (1911–17). He returned to the U.M.W.A. as vice-president in 1917, became acting president in 1919 and since 1920 has held the post of president. Lewis had long favoured industrial organization of open-shop mass production industries, contrary to traditional A.F. of L. craft unionism. In 1935 he formed the Committee for Industrial Organization. When he refused to heed the A.F. of L. executive council's order to dissolve the committee, the participating unions in the C.I.O. were suspended in 1936 and the following year were expelled from A.F. of L. membership.

Lewis supported Roosevelt in 1936, the C.I.O. donating $500,-000 to the Democratic campaign funds. However, there was a distinct cooling-off between the two men after Roosevelt in 1937 refused to give more than lukewarm support to his labour adherents. Embittered by Roosevelt's change of attitude, Lewis supported Willkie in 1940, and promised to resign if Willkie lost. He made good his promise although he retained the U.M.W.A. presidency.

Lewis made several attempts to regain lost prestige and power, and early in 1942 endeavoured to bring 3,000,000 dairy farmers into his catch-all union, District 50. His antagonism to C.I.O. President Philip Murray had become so great that at the convention in Oct. 1942, he led the U.M.W.A. out of the C.I.O. and in 1943 he negotiated for re-entry into the A.F. of L. The period from May to Nov. 1943, was marked by a series of mine workers' walkouts. Lewis demanded wage increases to offset rising prices and rejected the decisions of the WLB, which held to the "little steel formula." After the fourth walkout in a six-month period, the miners reached an agreement on Nov. 3, 1943.

Liberal Party.

The Liberal Parliamentary party expressed dissatisfaction with the government's attitude towards the Beveridge report and subsequently, through the organization in the country, the Liberal party made it clear that they accepted wholeheartedly the proposals for social security which Sir William Beveridge, himself a Liberal, had effectively established as a major political issue.

At the annual assembly of the party the restatement of postwar Liberal policy, begun the previous year, was completed by the presentation of the reports of many research committees. During the autumn the prospects of a speaker's conference aroused hopes amongst Liberals that by improved electoral machinery the house of commons in the postwar period of reconstruction might come to represent public opinion more closely than in the period between the wars.

At the beginning of 1943 E. H. Gilpin became chairman of the executive of the party. Most of the group of Liberal ministers were fully engaged in tasks connected with the prosecution of the war—Sir Archibald Sinclair at the air ministry, Major Gwilym Lloyd George transferred from the food ministry to that of fuel and power, Dingle Foot at the ministry of economic warfare, and Harcourt Johnstone in the department of overseas trade.

While the future of the Liberal party as an organized political force was still conjectural there could be little doubt that Liberal sentiment had widely increased and a fair comment by the hypothetical "man in the street" would be that the Liberal party had a great opportunity before it.   (W. Rs.)

Liberia. This Negro republic on the west coast of Africa, founded by philanthropic societies from the United States in 1820 as a homeland for free Negroes, is bounded on the northwest by the British colony of Sierra Leone, and on the north and east sides by French West Africa. Area, c. 43,000 sq.mi. Pop. (est.), 2,500,000—of which approximately 25,000 are Americo-Liberians (descendants of the original American Negro immigrants), and the remainder are the indigenous tribes, uncivilized, and little touched by the outside world. Capital city, Monrovia (est. pop., 10,000). President in 1943, Edwin J. Barclay. Language: official, English; various tribal tongues spoken by the natives of the hinterland. Religion: official, Christian; tribal, pagan and Mohammedan chiefly.

History.—During 1943 Liberia continued to serve as an important link in the Allied war effort. Though no declaration of war was made, this little republic opened its doors completely to the military of the United States which established important air bases in the country for use in ferrying planes to Africa, the near east and the far east. Large and complete repair and service shops were set up at these air fields, and roads were built by units of the U.S. army to connect these air bases. A substantial number of American troops was kept in Liberia during 1943, many of them being Negroes.

In Jan. 1943 President Franklin D. Roosevelt flew to Liberia from the Casablanca meeting with Churchill. He was received by President Barclay, and while there, reviewed the American troops. In June 1943, President Barclay of Liberia paid a state visit to the White House in Washington, and was entertained by President and Mrs. Roosevelt. While in the United States, Mr. Barclay received medical treatment and underwent an operation at one of the American hospitals.

The year 1943 saw another presidential election in Liberia, in which the Whig party, which elected every candidate in the past, continued in power, electing its candidate, Wm. V. S. Tubman, who took office the first week of Jan. 1944.

Firestone Plantations company had planted in Liberia more than 75,000 acres of rubber of which, at the end of 1943, there was in production more than 45,000 ac. Rubber produced from the plantations of Firestone Plantations company in 1943 was approximately 35,000,000 lb. and the production from the plantations owned and operated by Liberian citizens was approximately 500,000 lb. The number of Liberian employees on the daily payroll of Firestone Plantations company, at the end of 1943, exceeded 23,000 persons.

Education.—In 1943 there was little change in the educational program of the country which is designed to serve chiefly the Americo-Liberian children on the coast. A few government schools continued to operate in the hinterland, but with difficulty. There were in 1943 an estimated 100 schools of all types in the republic. The leading institutions are the College of West Africa, Liberia College, and the Booker Washington Agricultural and Industrial Institute at Kakata, all of which were founded by American philanthropic societies.

Banking and Finance.—The revenues in 1942 fell off sharply in the early months because of the difficulty of securing shipping facilities, but regained the usual figure later in the year. Liberian government revenues for the calendar year 1942 (1943 were not available) were as follows: Hut tax, Liberian $278,171; other internal revenue, Liberian $332,260; customs revenue, Liberian $595,895; total revenue for 1942, $1,206,326. There was an increase in the amount of gold exported. The presence of American troops and the personnel of the American air bases, all brought increased amounts of money into the country. The funded foreign debt as of Nov. 30, 1942, was U.S. $1,193,000. The internal floating debt (April 30, 1943) was Liberian $112,800. Currency: effective Jan. 1, 1944, British sterling was no longer legal tender in Liberia but was replaced by the United States currency. As of Jan. 1, 1944, U.S. $1.00 equalled Liberian $1.00. Formerly £1 sterling equalled Liberian $4.80, equalled approximately U.S. $4.00. Chief Bank: the Bank of Monrovia, controlled by the Firestone Plantations company.

Trade.—Overseas trade in 1943 was limited almost completely to the United States, and increased over the previous year because of improved shipping facilities which came with the curtailing of the U-boat menace in the South Atlantic. No figures were available for the imports and exports. The chief export products during 1943 were rubber, gold, piassava, palm nuts. Foreign trade for 1942 was as follows: exports of rubber and latex $7,353,050, all other exports $797,973, total exports $8,151,-023. Total imports 1942 $4,800,936. Financial adviser to the republic was John Dunaway in 1943.

Communications.—The Liberian government owns and operates a powerful radio station in Monrovia, and the Firestone Plantations company operates one on its plantations in the hinterland. There is a French cable station. The construction of motor roads was pushed by the American army engineers in 1943 in order to connect the air bases and the ports. There is an estimated 300 miles of motor roads in the republic. There are no railroads. There is air service from county to county. There are no harbours.   (J. H. Fy.)

Liberty Ships: *see* SHIPBUILDING; SHIPPING, MERCHANT MARINE.

Libraries. American libraries large and small, from the great research library to the small public library, were doing all in their power to further the successful prosecution of the war by supplying books and information required by the armed forces, by government, by industry, and, not least, by civilians. Much thought had been given to plans for postwar developments in library service, to building programs, and to the acquisition of books that would be needed for research when normal studies might be resumed. Wartime demands gave a new impetus to the use of microfilm in copying printed materials to be sent to all parts of the world. Following the pattern of the American Library in London, the British division of the Office of War Information established small reference libraries in Sydney and Melbourne, Australia; Wellington, New Zealand; Johannesburg, South Africa, and Bombay, India, to provide information about the history, institutions and culture of the United States.

Staff losses in all grades in the U.S. were so serious that many libraries were forced to curtail activities and shorten hours. Losses were greater at the clerical than at the professional level. Inadequate salaries were largely responsible in the case of those who left library positions for employment in government service or industry. In general, however, library incomes were not reduced, and many libraries were able to raise salaries. There was an encouraging extension of state aid to libraries, and some increase in appropriations to state library agencies. The total enrolment (March 1, 1943) in the 34 schools of various types accredited by the board of education for librarianship (A.L.A.) was 1,258, including 126 advanced, and 134 special or nonmatriculated students. This was a decrease of 419 as compared with 1942. The fall of 1943 saw a further drop in enrolment.

The 1943 Victory Book campaign collected 7,000,000 books of which 4,500,000 were distributed to military establishments and organizations serving the armed forces and the merchant marine at home and abroad. These books supplemented the collections provided by government funds. Books were needed for training and recreation, and there was ample testimony to the place the library fills in camps, training centres and on shipboard.

New library buildings were opened at Carroll college (Waukesha, Wis.), Davidson college (N.C.), MacAlester college (St. Paul, Minn.), and at the University of South Carolina. Three important gifts were received by the Library of Congress: a new collection of the papers of General William Tecumseh Sherman, the papers of Booker T. Washington, and the magnificent Lessing J. Rosenwald collection of manuscripts and early printed books. The Rockefeller foundation and the Carnegie corporation continued their generous support of library activities in many fields. Lists of these grants are to be found in their annual reports. A survey of the United States Army Medical library (Washington, D.C.) was made under the direction of Keyes D. Metcalf, director of the Harvard university library, with funds provided by the Rockefeller foundation. Mr. Metcalf and Dean T. C. Blegen of the University of Minnesota completed a survey of the relationship between the State Historical society of Wisconsin and the University of Wisconsin library.

Sixty of the 170 volumes of the Library of Congress *Catalog of Printed Cards* (printed by photo offset process) had been delivered to subscribers at the end of the year. Some 40 large libraries agreed to compare their own holdings with this printed catalog, and to report to the national union catalog titles not recorded therein. This project would probably add as many as 5,000,000 titles to the 6,000,000 listed. The second edition of the *Union List of Serials in Libraries of the United States and Canada* was published in June.

Size of Collections or Statistics of Libraries.—Nineteen libraries contained more than 1,000,000 volumes each: the Library of Congress, 6,349,157 volumes (June 30, 1941); the New York Public library, 4,449,192 volumes (comprising reference department, 2,899,790 volumes; circulation department, 1,451,249 volumes; Municipal Reference library, 98,153 volumes) (Dec. 31, 1942); Harvard university, 4,400,870 volumes (June 30, 1942); Yale university, 2,351,236 volumes (June 30, 1942); Cleveland (Ohio) Public library, 2,161,049 volumes (Dec. 31, 1942); Chicago (Ill.) Public library, 1,993,604 volumes (Dec. 31, 1942); Columbia university, 1,887,034 volumes (June 30, 1942); Boston (Mass.) Public library, 1,714,910 volumes (1942); Los Angeles (Calif.) Public library, 1,644,921 volumes (June 30, 1942); University of California, 1,568,743 volumes (comprising 1,170,738 volumes at Berkeley [June 30, 1942], and 398,000 volumes at Los Angeles [1942]); University of Chicago, 1,369,206 volumes (June 30, 1942); Cincinnati (Ohio) Public library, 1,365,348 volumes (Dec. 31, 1942); University of Illinois, 1,306,-561 volumes (June 30, 1942); Brooklyn (N.Y.) Public library, 1,229,894 volumes (June 30, 1942); University of Michigan, 1,168,612 volumes (June 30, 1942); University of Minnesota, 1,221,987 volumes (June 30, 1942); Cornell university (Ithaca, N.Y.), 1,094,117 volumes (June 30, 1941); Carnegie library of Pittsburgh (Pa.), 1,085,117 volumes (Dec. 31, 1942); Detroit (Mich.) Public library, 1,054,984 volumes (June 30, 1942). Four libraries possessed more than 900,000 volumes each: St. Louis

(Mo.) Public library, 997,951 volumes (April 30, 1943); Princeton university, 990,657 volumes (June 30, 1942); University of Pennsylvania, 979,919 volumes (June 30, 1942); Milwaukee (Wis.) Public library, 934,978 volumes (Dec. 31, 1942).

These figures were very uncertain standards of comparison because of differences in methods of counting, and because public libraries with many branches contained many copies of new and standard books.

Librarians.—Charles C. Williamson, director of libraries and dean of the school of library service of Columbia university since 1926, retired June 30. His great work at Columbia was the organization in 1926 of the school of library service, formed by the merger of the New York State library school at Albany and the library school of the New York Public library, the co-ordination of the Columbia libraries, and the planning of the new library building, South Hall, the gift of Edward S. Harkness, which was opened in 1934. The Columbia school of library service was a direct outgrowth of Williamson's significant report, *Training for Library Service*, 1923, prepared for the Carnegie corporation. Dr. Williamson was succeeded by Carl M. White, director of the library and the library school of the university of Illinois, who in turn was succeeded by Robert B. Downs, director of libraries of New York university since 1938.

Frank K. Walter, librarian of the university of Minnesota since 1921, retired June 30, and was succeeded by E. W. McDiarmid, associate professor in the university of Illinois library school. Homer Halvorson was appointed to the librarianship of Johns Hopkins university Sept. 1 upon the retirement of John C. French, librarian since 1927. John B. Kaiser, librarian of the Oakland (Calif.) Public library, became librarian of the Newark (N.J.) Free Public library on April 16 in place of Beatrice Winser, retired. H. M. Lydenberg took charge in August of the International Relations office of the American Library association in Washington. He was succeeded at the Biblioteca Benjamin Franklin in Mexico City by Prof. R. H. Gjelsness who would also direct the preparation of a union catalog of library resources in Mexico City, financed by a grant of $13,000 from the Rockefeller foundation. Eldon R. James, librarian of the Harvard law school from 1923 to 1942, was appointed law librarian of congress.

Henry O. Severance, librarian of the university of Missouri from 1907–37, died Oct. 10, 1942. In Feb., 1943, occurred the deaths of Franklin O. Poole, librarian of the association of the bar of the city of New York since 1905, and of W. N. C. Carlton, librarian of Williams college from 1922–39. John T. Vance, law librarian of congress since 1924, died on April 11. Frederick P. Keppel, president of the Carnegie corporation from 1923 to 1941, died on Sept. 8. During his administration the corporation gave generously to develop libraries and to promote education for librarianship. J. M. C. Hanson, great cataloger and organizer, long connected with the Library of Congress and the university of Chicago, died on Nov. 8 at the age of 79. Zaidee B. Vosper, editor of the A.L.A. *Booklist* since 1927, died on Nov. 16, and Lutie E. Stearns, pioneer library organizer in Wisconsin, on Dec. 27. (*See* also AMERICAN LIBRARY ASSOCIATION; CATHOLIC LIBRARY ASSOCIATION; SPECIAL LIBRARIES ASSOCIATION; etc.)

BIBLIOGRAPHY.—For further information about American libraries consult: *Bulletin* of the American Library association (Chicago); Library Journal (New York); *College and Research Libraries* (Chicago); *Library Quarterly* (Chicago). Important contributions to library literature were: A.L.A. Board on Salaries, Staff and Tenure, *Classification and Pay Plans for Libraries in Institutions of Higher Learning* (1943); Pierce Butler, ed., *The Reference Function of the Library: Papers Presented Before the Library Institute at the University of Chicago, June 29 to July 10, 1942* (1943); J. M. Flexner, *Making Books Work: a Guide to the Use of Libraries* (1943); Deoch Fulton, ed., *Bookmen's Holiday: Notes and Studies Written and Gathered in Tribute to Harry Miller Lydenberg* (1943); Chalmers Hadley, *John Cotton Dana* (1943); G. D. McDonald, *Educational Motion Pictures and Libraries* (1942); John VanMale, *Resources of Pacific Northwest Libraries* (1943); C. C. Williamson and A. L. Jewett, ed., *Who's Who in Library Service*, 2nd ed. (1943). (C. F. McC.)

Great Britain.—The great demands made upon all libraries—national, public, university, school and special—increased with the passing of another year of war. The libraries of the country served the needs of a country at war, not spectacularly perhaps, but nevertheless positively and objectively. Much increased use was made, not only of recreational literature, but also of books on almost every subject in the field of knowledge. As well as readers in search of entertainment and information, the users included government departments, factories, business houses and industrial undertakings, and the services. Interest in, and appreciation of, the library service were keen and were sharpened by the publication in the autumn of *The Public Library Service, its postwar reorganization and development: proposals by the Council of the Library Association.* The publication of these far-reaching proposals, which followed detailed consideration of the *McColvin Report* issued in 1942, might well lead, it was thought, to the elimination of existing variations in standards of efficiency and the development of a well-organized, sound and generous service, in which all elements would rise to a level not known before.

Building activity was restricted, but over the country additional service points were established to meet rising demands, mainly by the conversion of shops, dwelling-houses, and schools.

The indiscriminate destruction of books collected in response to salvage appeals was halted. The keynote of the national book recovery campaign, launched at the end of 1942, was an appeal for books *as books,* not as waste paper, and the organization ensured that all books were carefully scrutinized so that those suitable for the restoration of war-damaged libraries at home and abroad, for H.M. forces, and certain other purposes, might be saved from destruction and set aside for allocation to appropriate libraries and institutions. (D. C. H. J.)

Libya: *see* ITALIAN COLONIAL EMPIRE; WORLD WAR II.

Liechtenstein.
An independent, tiny European state, northeast of Switzerland, to which it is united by a customs union. Area, 65 sq.mi.; pop. (census Dec. 1941) 11,102. Chief town, Vaduz (capital, pop. 2,020). Ruler: Prince Franz Joseph II, b. 1906, was given ruling authority by his 84-year-old uncle, Prince Franz I, on March 30, 1938 and after the latter's death was crowned prince on May 29, 1939. Language, German; religion, mainly Roman Catholic; products: corn, wine, fruit, wood and marble. There is no army. Posts and telegraphs are administered by Switzerland. (S. B. F.)

Life Insurance: *see* INSURANCE.
Life Span: *see* BIRTH STATISTICS; DEATH STATISTICS; INFANT MORTALITY; SUICIDE STATISTICS.
Lighting: *see* ELECTRICAL INDUSTRIES; MOTION PICTURES.

Lime.
Production of lime in the United States in 1942 increased slightly over 1941, to 6,103,791 short tons, another new record high. Of the total, 79% was quicklime and 21% hydrated lime; agricultural uses took 7%, building 13%, metallurgical uses 26%, chemical uses 36% and refractory uses 20%. A drop of 35% in the use of building lime was offset by increased demand in industrial uses. Canadian production totalled 884,830 short tons in 1942, an increase of 3% over 1941; 93% of the output was used in the chemical industry. Production through Aug. 1943 was 7% ahead of the same period of 1942. (G. A. Ro.)

Limes: *see* LEMONS AND LIMES.
Limestone: *see* STONE.

Lindsey, Benjamin Barr
(1869–1943), U.S. judge and social reformer, was born Nov. 25 in Jackson, Tenn. (For his early career see *Encyclopædia Britannica.*) Judge Lindsey devoted most of his career on the bench to reform of juvenile court procedure. He became a storm centre of criticism when he advocated "companionate marriage" as a means of eliminating undesirable factors in family life and environment which contributed to juvenile delinquency. Judge Lindsey was a superior court judge in Los Angeles, Calif., from 1934 until his death on March 26, 1943, in Los Angeles.

Linen and Flax.
The demand for flax fibre and linen products in the prosecution of the war encouraged the growing of flax on almost every continent in 1943. When Russia's supply was stopped in the early days of 1940 and 1941, experimental flax growing started with renewed interest in Ireland, the United States of America, Canada, New Zealand and South Africa. In South America, Peru and Brazil made their plans. During 1943, the results of this new interest in flax growing were indicated in crop reports from widely scattered areas. In Peru, a total export of 2,238,600 short tons of fibre during the first eight months was larger than expected but farmer interest was lagging because of relatively low yield. In Chile, the cultivation of flax was slowly expanding, 125 ac. being planted in Cautin province in 1943, for the first time, although the industry itself had started there in 1903. Argentina was reported in Sept. 1943, as having found after four years of experimentation a desirable flax fibre called "Mapum M. A." which had proved resistant against epidemics or plagues and gave high yields. The two-year-old linen industry in Brazil, centred at Florianopolis, had developed extensive flax cultivation in the Itagui district and, by 1943, had more than 50 flax cleaning and processing plants in the state of Parana. Suitings, canvas and dress goods were being manufactured in increasing quantities, all of them consumed domestically, as Brazil had formerly imported approximately $5,000,000 worth of linen from Ireland and England annually before World War II. Brazilian authorities stated that close to $500,000 had been invested in the cultivation of flax alone.

The Canadian flax industry, started in Quebec, developed in 1943 in British Columbia. The first fibre flax crop was harvested in early August, and was of high quality as the flax was tank-retted rather than field-retted. The processing plant, constructed during the summer of 1943, at Vernon, B.C., at a cost of $100,000 was prepared to handle 1,400 to 1,500 ac. of flax and it was expected the production would be about 1,200 ac. in 1943. The anticipated value of the 1943 crop was $180,000 for the fibre and an additional $25,000 of flaxseed.

In the United Kingdom, 7,500 ac. of flax were raised in 1943 for scutching at Northampton where the flax processing mill was described as the largest in the British empire. The quantity was more than double that grown in all of Great Britain five years before. An innovation in the Northampton plant was the use of flax shive (waste) as a fuel. No other fuel was employed. In Denmark, incidentally, flax shive was reported in 1943 as being used in producing gas for automobiles and trucks. It was dried and pressed into briquettes for burning.

Scotland's golf courses were partially plowed up in 1943 for flax production. Half of the 18-hole courses and one-third of the 9-hole courses were utilized. In Lincolnshire, it was reported that a group of schoolboys from 7 to 16 years of age, raised two and a quarter tons of flax on their playing field.

In Eire (Ireland), the traditional home of flax and linen, three acres of flax were planted in 1943 to one in 1942. The total production in 1943 was 27,500 ac. Flax spinning also began again in 1943 after a lapse of several years for the purpose of producing linen thread and twine.

As an encouragement to farmers growing flax and workers in flax factories, the ministry of supply in Great Britain announced in Oct. 1943, that a mobile exhibition of flax plants and fibre would tour Britain's flax growing area. Because of the war, it was stated, the total acreage of 400 in 1939 had grown to 52,000 ac. in 1943, and new factories had been equipped and opened throughout the country to handle the abundant harvests and prepare flax for the manufacture of war weapons. One of the most essential uses was in the webbing for the paratroopers' chute harness.

The importance of adequate processing machinery in securing the maximum return on the flax acreage was emphasized in the 1943 report from New Zealand where large strides were made during the first war years. In 1941–42, 15,000 ac. were planted and in 1942–43, this had increased to 22,000 ac. In May 1943, however, the New Zealand war cabinet asked for volunteers from military forces to help in preparing the crop and final results for 1943 were expected to be greatly reduced over the previous year.

In the United States of America, the experiments conducted by the Georgia School of Technology, the Georgia State Engineering Experiment station and the Tennessee Valley authority were concentrated on production of low-grade fibres suitable for use in bagging and cordage to meet wartime demand. The flax fibres were used as a substitute for jute, hemp, henequen and sisal. Whether the production costs, at a wartime emergency level in 1943, could be reduced to meet civilian peacetime competition with other fibres was considered a problem for the future, according to a report given by the research director at Atlanta, Ga., in July 1943. The current production was done on cotton mill equipment although some experiments were made unsuccessfully on jute spinning equipment.

Among other countries reporting flax production during 1943 were Morocco, with 135,600 ac. planted compared with 45,840 ac. in 1934 to 1938; Tanganyika Territory, Africa, with 16,418 ac., and Turkey which sold 800 tons of flax to the United Kingdom. In Rumania, a company was formed in 1943 with a working capital of 20,000,000 lei to supervise flax growing and the ministry of agriculture announced plans to establish 15 factory centres for flax processing.

BIBLIOGRAPHY.—*Foreign Commerce Weekly*, U.S. Department of Commerce (Washington, D.C.); *Daily News Record* (New York); *Textile Recorder* (Manchester, England).   (I. L. BL.)

Link, Mrs. Adeline DeSale

(1892–1943), U.S. chemist, was born Jan. 4 at Omaha, Neb. She was graduated from Vassar, 1914, and received her doctorate in philosophy from the University of Chicago, 1917. She taught at Lawrence college, Appleton, Wis., 1917–21, was chemistry instructor at the University of Chicago, 1921–29, and assistant professor at the latter institution from 1929 to the time of her death. Regarded as one of the outstanding women chemists in the United States, Mrs. Link made important contributions to the study of chemical reactions. She died Nov. 20 in Chicago.

Lin Sen

(1864–1943), president of China, was born at Foochow, Fukien. As a youth, he studied with U.S. missionaries and later received a traditional Chinese education at a private college. He lived in San Francisco for several years and while in the United States became a member of the Kuomintang, then a secret society. Returning to China shortly after the revolution, he won a seat in the senate of the first parliament—a post he held until 1923. He became a member of the central executive committee of the Kuomintang in 1924, was named to the state council of the national government, 1928, and was vice-president of the legislative Yuan, 1928–31. He succeeded to the presidency of that body in March 1931. Lin Sen became president of the national government in 1932, when a candidate was sought whose position in Kuomintang circles would qualify him to unify dissenting factions of the Nanking government and the Canton group. Lin Sen successfully bridged the political gap and was revered by the Chinese people as an elder statesman. Despite his high office, he withdrew from the limelight and led a life completely devoid of ostentation. His position as president was a nominal one, for Chiang Kai-shek, who relinquished the presidency in late 1931, still controlled the real reins of government. Lin Sen died in Chungking, Aug. 1.

Lions Clubs, International Association of.

The International Association of Lions Clubs was founded by Melvin Jones on June 7, 1917. It is a nonpolitical, nonsectarian association of service clubs whose purpose is to recognize the needs of the community and by independent effort and through co-operation with other agencies meet those needs; also, to do everything possible to help achieve a United Nations victory. The activities of the clubs cover eight classifications: Boys and girls; citizenship and patriotism; civic improvements; community betterment; education; health and welfare; safety; sight conservation and blind. From May 1, 1942, to April 30, 1943, 66,507 separate activities were carried out.

The membership of the clubs is composed of business and professional men, and in 1943 numbered approximately 155,000. There were 4,350 clubs in 14 countries: Canada, China, Colombia, Costa Rica, Cuba, El Salvador, Guatemala, Honduras, British Honduras, Mexico, Nicaragua, Panama, the United States and Venezuela. Headquarters for the association in 1943 were at 332 S. Michigan ave., Chicago, Ill., and were directed by Secretary General Melvin Jones.

Dr. E. G. Gill of Roanoke, Va., was the 1943–44 international president. The association issues a monthly publication, the *Lion Magazine*, and the 1943 international annual meeting was held at Cleveland, Ohio.   (M. Jo.)

Liquors, Alcoholic.

The United States had been for many years the country of greatest production and consumption of potable spirits. Because of existing war conditions, production in practically all foreign countries was considerably curtailed, in most instances (as in Scotland) entirely suspended. Consumption in these countries also was materially reduced. Accurate records for the years after 1939—the war years—were not obtainable.

In the United States the general situation of the alcoholic liquor industry began to change toward the end of the year 1941. Production, distribution and consumption underwent in turn and in gradual acceleration quite radical and far-reaching adjustments. Most whisky distilleries began to use their available facilities for the production of industrial alcohol (grain spirits at 190 proof).

At first the opinion prevailed that this alcohol was needed solely, or at least principally, in the manufacturing process of smokeless powder. It developed, however, that the unexpectedly large requirements for high octane gasoline created a shortage of raw material for the rapidly growing synthetic rubber industry, which had to turn to alcohol as a substitute. At the same time, shipping conditions caused a practically complete interruption in the importation of molasses which had constituted the principal raw material for distillation of industrial alcohol. By government order all distillation of grain for beverage purposes was terminated as of Oct. 8, 1942, and as rapidly as possible all beverage distilleries were converted to production of alcohol for smokeless powder, synthetic rubber, medical supplies, chemicals and many other vital war materials.

Of the total government requirement of alcohol for 1943, estimated at 525,000,000 gal., the beverage industry would have supplied 225,000,000 gal. In 1944 war necessities would require 625,000,000 gal. of alcohol, of which the beverage distillers were expected to supply 240,000,000 gal.

Whisky is normally by far the predominant alcoholic beverage in the United States.

The normal yearly production was somewhat above 120,000,000 gal. The volume of production of other alcoholic beverages was much smaller, for brandy about 30,000,000 gal., gin 5,500,000 gal., rum 3,000,000 gal. and liqueurs and divers other spirits 20,000,000 gal.

Kentucky was the state of largest production, accounting for 53% of the production, with Illinois 17%, Indiana 12%, Pennsylvania 7%, Maryland 6% and other states 5%.

No whisky was produced in the United States during 1943. On the other hand, the demand for consumption increased. Normally the annual consumption of all alcoholic liquors amounted to about 170,000,000 gal. at various proofs ranging predominantly from 86 proof to 100 proof. Of this total nearly 135,000,000 gal. was domestic whisky. At the beginning of 1943 somewhat over 400,000,000 gal. of whisky remained in the bonded storage warehouses.

Importation of Scotch whiskies (from aged stock) continued at almost the same rate as in previous years, about 8,000,000 gal.

Total importations of distilled spirits rose from 9,760,000 proof gallons in the fiscal year ending June 1942 to 15,430,000 proof gallons in the year ending June 1943, due to increased production in and importation of rum, gin and beverage alcohol from Cuba and the West Indies. (A. J. Li.)

Liquor Control.—During the year 1943, the salient feature of liquor control was the shift toward federal and, to a lesser degree, industry control, in an effort to adjust the production, distribution and sale of liquor to war conditions.

In the 17 monopoly states official rationing systems were established, and in the licence states voluntary rationing systems were the rule. The distiller rationed the distributor; the distributor, the retailer; and, in turn, the retailer rationed the consumer. Pronounced effects of the rationing induced by the shortage were threefold: a turn to rum and gin imported in rapidly increasing quantities from Cuba, Jamaica, Puerto Rico and Mexico, a new impetus to the activities of bootleggers and a considerable mortality among retailers who were unable to get merchandise.

Federal control manifested itself in 1943 in the establishment of price ceilings by the Office of Price Administration; a substantial increase in federal taxes, the exact amount not determined by Dec. 1943; and increased activity of the Alcohol Tax Unit. The OPA price ceilings affected liquor in bulk and package goods. They did not at first affect the price of individual drinks to the consumer. The distributor was allowed a 15% mark-up above cost of sales on package goods to the retailer, and the retailer was, in turn, allowed a $33\frac{1}{2}$% mark-up on sales to the consumer. Mark-ups varied slightly in the case of wines and cordials.

Later in the year ceilings on cost of drinks to the consumer were established.

Insufficient personnel greatly hampered enforcement, although a number of suits were filed. Leading distillers, by advertising ceiling prices, endeavoured to co-operate with the OPA in seeing that the ceiling prices were observed. They also made a vigorous effort to ensure a fair distribution of merchandise by giving to all accounts a like proportion of the 1942 sales. Distillers and distributors established a voluntary quota system.

Government requirements made it extremely difficult for wine producers to get the necessary raw materials. There was also a serious shortage of tank cars.

The year 1943 saw the largest production of beer since repeal. This was in spite of the fact that the amount of malt available to breweries was restricted to 65% of the 1942 quota and a government order reserved 15% of production for the armed forces.

The shortage of liquor found the monopoly states in a less favourable situation than the licence states because of absence of reserves. This, at least temporarily, impeded the progress of the adoption of the monopoly system, which had gotten a very good start.

Two states, Washington and Oregon, in order to ensure adequate supplies of liquor, purchased distilleries in Kentucky. This action, however, was taken to secure the whisky in bulk on hand in the distilleries, and it was probable that ownership would not be permanently retained by the states.

Increase in the federal tax per gallon to whatever figure was to be decided upon ($9.00 probably) would mean a further widening in the difference of incidence between state and federal taxation.

Social problems connected with liquor, such as sales to minors, sales to drunks, closing hours, issuance, limitation and revocation of licences were under the jurisdiction of the cities and states and would probably remain so. Licence fees during 1943 underwent small change. There was a vigorous movement to increase the fees, both of retailer and distributor.

An unusual feature which developed during 1943 was the declaration of dividends, payable in liquor, by some fairly large distilleries. Such action involved a number of legal questions yet to be determined and might give rise to new methods of control.

Advertisements pointed out in 1943 that no whisky had been distilled since Oct. 8, 1942; that distillery plants were entirely devoted to the manufacture of alcohol essential to the war effort; that of an inventory of approximately 399,000,000 gal. as of Oct. 31, 1943, nearly 96,000,000 gal. disappeared through shrinkage and evaporation; that a reserve of not less than 100,000,000 gal. had to be set up for postwar requirements and that the amount available, about 203,000,000 gal., would be consumed, at the 1943 rate of demand, in less than a year if it were not that every distiller had followed a self-imposed rationing program. (*See* also BREWING AND BEER; INTOXICATION, ALCOHOLIC; WINES.)

(M. LB.)

Literary Prizes.
The literary prizes for the year 1943 were as follows:

International.—NOBEL PRIZE FOR LITERATURE not awarded since 1939.
United States.—AMERICAN ACADEMY OF ARTS AND LETTERS AND THE NATIONAL INSTITUTE OF ARTS AND LETTERS, AWARDS IN LITERATURE, $1,000 each to Carson McCullers, José Garcia Villa, Virgil Geddes and Joseph Wittlin.
JOHN ANISFIELD AWARDS (*Saturday Review of Literature*), $1,000 each to Zora Neale Hurston for *Dust Tracks on a Road* (Lippincott), the best book concerned with racial problems in the field of creative literature; to Donald Pierson for *Negroes in Brazil* (University of Chicago), the best scholarly book in the field of race relations.
ATLANTIC MONTHLY PRESS AND LITTLE, BROWN & COMPANY, $5,000 for the most interesting non-fiction having to do with the war. No prize awarded.
A. S. BARNES & Co.—Poetry prizes to service men. First prize of $250 to John Ackerson, of the merchant marine; second prize of $100 to Corporal Harold Applebaum, U.S.A. medical detachment. There were 123 additional prizes. The 125 poems were published in book form under the title *Reveille-War Poems*.
CAREY-THOMAS AWARD (*Publishers' Weekly*) for the best example of creative publishing. A scroll to Farrar & Rinehart for their "Rivers of America" series.

CATHOLIC LITERARY AWARD (Gallery of Living Catholic Authors) for the outstanding book of Catholic interest. A scroll to John Farrow for his *Pageant of the Popes* (Sheed & Ward).

COMMONWEALTH CLUB OF CALIFORNIA.—GOLD MEDAL FOR GENERAL LITERATURE to Oscar Lewis for *I Remember Christine* (Knopf); GOLD MEDAL FOR SCHOLARSHIP AND RESEARCH to James Westfall Thompson and Bernard J. Holm for *The History of Historical Writing* (Macmillan); SILVER MEDAL FOR POETRY to H. L. Davis for *Proud Riders* (Harper); SILVER MEDAL FOR A JUVENILE to Hildegarde Hawthorne for *Long Adventure* (Appleton). SILVER MEDALS were also awarded to Hector Chevigny for *Lord of Alaska* (Viking); to Frank Waters for *The Man Who Killed the Deer* (Farrar & Rinehart); to Lillian B. Ross for *The Stranger* (Morrow).

DOUBLEDAY, DORAN—CURTIS BROWN WRITERS' CONFERENCE PRIZE, $400 for the best novel by a student at one of the writers' conferences, to Joyce Horner of the University of New Hampshire Writers' Conference, for *The Wind and the Rain*.

DODD, MEAD PRIZES.—$1,000 RED BADGE DETECTIVE STORY PRIZE to Ruth Sawtell Wallis for *Too Many Bones;* $1,000 PRIZE FOR THE BEST WAR NOVEL to John Lodwick for *Running to Paradise;* THIRD INTERCOLLEGIATE LITERARY FELLOWSHIP PRIZE to Catherine Lawrence for *One of the Masses*.

E. P. DUTTON & COMPANY.—THOMAS JEFFERSON SOUTHERN AWARD, $2,500 to Jesse Stuart for his novel, *Taps For Private Tussie.* LEWIS AND CLARK NORTHWEST CONTEST, $1,500 for the best book by a northwest author to Clyde F. Murphy for his novel, *The Glittering Hill*.

FRIENDS OF AMERICAN WRITERS AWARD to promote high standard in American writing, $750 to Kenneth L. Davis for his novel, *In the Forests of the Night* (Houghton).

GUGGENHEIM FELLOWSHIPS, 64 awards amounting to about $2,500 each. Among the winners were Muriel Rukeyser, Edward Weismiller, Jeremy Ingalls, José Garcia Villa (Filipino poet), Vladimir Nabokov (Russian-born novelist), Vladimir Pozner (French-born), Dr. Hugh MacLennan (Canadian). An award went to Signe Kirstine for a biography of Emanuel Swedenborg; to Dr. David Willson for a life of James I, King of England; to Madeleine Stern for a book on Louisa May Alcott; and to Dr. Randall Stewart for a book on Nathaniel Hawthorne. Dr. William Charvat will do a study of the profession of authorship in 19th century America; Dr. John Flanagan, a history of the literature of the middle west; Dr. Harry Levin, an analysis of the symbolist technique in American fiction.

HARPER PRIZE NOVEL AWARD, $10,000 to Martin Flavin for *Journey in the Dark*.

HARPER'S MAGAZINE PRIZE for the best first-hand war experience article submitted to *Harper's Magazine* up to July 1942, $1,000 to Bob Fairhaul and his collaborator, Richard G. Hubler, for *The Bomb Hit the Cruiser*, appearing in the Dec. 1941 issue.

O. HENRY MEMORIAL AWARD PRIZE STORIES OF 1943 (Doubleday).— First prize, $300 to Eudora Welty for "Livvie Is Back" (*Atlantic Monthly*); second prize, $200 to Dorothy Canfield for "The Knot Hole" (*Yale Review*); third prize, $100 to William Fifield for "The Fishermen of Palzcuaro" (*Story Magazine*); a first story prize, $100 to Clara Laidlaw for "The Little Black Boys" (*Atlantic Monthly*).

AVERY HOPWOOD AWARD for the best novel by a student in the University of Michigan, to Jay McCormick for *November Storm* (Doubleday).

HOUGHTON, MIFFLIN LIFE-IN-AMERICA SERIES AWARD, $2,500 to Roi Ottley for his native son's picture of life in Harlem, *New World A-Coming; Inside Black America*.

ALFRED A. KNOPF LITERARY FELLOWSHIPS, $2,500 each to Mrs. Fawn Brodie for a projected life of Joseph Smith, the founder of the Mormon Church, and to Donald W. Mitchell for his proposed history of the "new" United States navy from 1883 to the present.

LATIN-AMERICAN LITERARY PRIZE (Farrar & Rinehart and the Division of Intellectual Co-operation of the Pan American Union), $2,000 to Pierre Marcelin and Philippe Thoby-Marcelin, two cousins from Haiti, for their novel *Canapé-Vert;* $2,000 non-fiction award to Argentina Diaz Lozano of Honduras for her *Peregrinaje;* $1,000 to Fernando Alegría of Chile for her juvenile, *Lautaro.* Farrar & Rinehart will publish the books in translation.

NATIONAL EDUCATION ASSOCIATION JOURNAL, selection of the book which if read generally by the people would bring a new outlook to our republic, *A Time of Greatness* by Herbert Agar (Little, Brown).

NEW YORK DRAMA CRITICS CIRCLE AWARD, a plaque presented to Sergeant Sidney Kingsley for *The Patriots*.

NEW YORK HISTORICAL SOCIETY, gold medal for achievement in history to Dr. George C. D. Odell in recognition of his *Annals of the New York Stage*, now in its thirteenth volume.

PARENTS MAGAZINE AWARDS, medals for outstanding books for parents, to Anna W. M. Wolf for *Our Children Face War* (Houghton); to Dorothy W. Baruch for *You, Your Children and War* (Appleton-Century).

MARY ROBERTS RINEHART MYSTERY NOVEL AWARD (Farrar & Rinehart and *Collier's Weekly*), $2,000 to C. W. Grafton for *The Rat Began to Gnaw the Rope*.

SHELLEY MEMORIAL AWARD for an American poet's work as a whole, to Percy MacKaye and Robert Penn Warren, jointly.

CONSTANCE LINDSAY SKINNER AWARD (Women's National Book Association), a bronze plaque, made by Alice E. Klutas, to Mary Graham Bonner for her many excellent books for children and more particularly for *Canada and Her Story* (Knopf).

SOUTHERN WOMEN'S NATIONAL DEMOCRATIC ORGANIZATION IN NEW YORK for the most distinguished book by a southern writer, to Douglas Southall Freeman for his *Lee's Lieutenants* (Scribner).

UNIVERSITY OF MINNESOTA FELLOWSHIPS, newly established through a grant from the Rockefeller foundation, for written interpretations of life in the central northwest. Among the winners of the first series of awards were Vera Kelsey, Meridel Le Sueue, Florence and Francis Lee Jacques.

Great Britain.—JAMES TAIT BLACK MEMORIAL PRIZES to Arthur Waley for his translation of the Chinese novel, *Monkey*, by Wu Ch'êng-ên (John Day); to Arthur Ponsonby for his biography, *Henry Ponsonby: Queen Victoria's Private Secretary* (Macmillan).

Children's Books.—CALDECOTT MEDAL FOR A PICTURE BOOK to Virginia Lee Burton for her illustrations in her own book, *The Little House* (Houghton).

CARNEGIE MEDAL (British) to D. J. Watkins-Pitchford for *The Little Grey Men*.

DOWNEY AWARD for the finest American children's book written in the Catholic tradition, to Covelle Newcomb for *The Red Hat* (Longmans), a biography of Cardinal Newman.

JULIA ELLSWORTH FORD FOUNDATION AWARD, $1,250 to Gladys Malvern for her *Valiant Minstrel: The Story of Harry Lauder* (Messner).

HERALD TRIBUNE CHILDREN'S SPRING BOOK FESTIVAL PRIZES, three awards of $200 each to Hugh Troy for *Five Golden Wrens* (Oxford), the best book for younger children; to Laura Ingalls Wilder for *These Happy Golden Years* (Harper), the best book for middle-aged children; to Elizabeth Yates for *Patterns On The Wall* (Knopf), the best book for older children.

JUNIOR SCHOLASTIC MAGAZINE GOLD SEAL for a juvenile book considered to be an enriching experience in the lives of young Americans, to Gregor Felsen for *Submarine Sailor* (Dutton).

JOHN NEWBERY MEDAL (American Library Association) to Elizabeth Janet Gray for *Adam of the Road* (Viking).

YOUNG READER'S CHOICE AWARD (Pacific Northwest Library Association) to Eric Knight for *Lassie Come-Home* (Winston), selected by vote of grade school children as the book which they enjoyed most in 1943.

(B. GM.)

Literature: *see* AMERICAN LITERATURE; CANADIAN LITERATURE; ENGLISH LITERATURE; FRENCH LITERATURE; GERMAN LITERATURE; ITALIAN LITERATURE; LITERARY PRIZES; PUBLISHING (BOOK); RUSSIAN LITERATURE; SPANISH-AMERICAN LITERATURE; SPANISH LITERATURE.

Lithium Minerals.

Lepidolite, spodumene and amblygonite are produced mainly in South Dakota, with some smaller output in North Carolina, and lithium-sodium phosphate is recovered from the brines of Searles lake, Calif. The combination of the output of minerals with a comparatively low lithium content with the much richer salt gives a figure which does not have a great deal of significance and the value is a better measure of relative output. The total shipments of minerals and salts in 1942 was 5,405 short tons ($243,516), as compared with 3,832 tons ($115,718) in 1941. The increase of 41% in weight as against 110% in value would indicate a larger proportion of salts in the 1942 total. (G. A. Ro.)

Lithuania.

A Baltic country of northeastern Europe, N. of Poland; in 1941 it became a part of Germany's "Ostland." Area, 22,959 sq.mi. (1940); pop. (Jan. 1, 1940) 2,879,070. Chief cities of Lithuania are: Vilnius (Vilna, capital, 207,750); Kaunas (actual seat of administration, 152,365). Religion, predominantly Roman Catholic (85%). Ruler in 1943 was Commissioner General Adrian von Renteln, who was responsible to Reichscommissar Hinrich Lohse of the Ostland.

History.—The kaleidoscopic changes of centuries of Lithuanian political history were epitomized in 1940–43: Under the control of the U.S.S.R. from June 15, 1940, to June 23, 1941, the Lithuanians then staged a revolution and declared independence; the German armies reached Kaunas on June 24, 1941; but allowed the independent Lithuanian government to function for only about seven weeks; on Aug. 5 this government resigned and the nazi control was complete.

Under the German occupation the promises made by the reichscommissar of "order . . . construction and civilization . . . a supervised economy" had scarcely been fulfilled at the end of 1943. Private property was only partly restored, and in a proclamation of March 17, 1943, Hinrich Lohse definitely declared that only those who participated in the "War against Bolshevism" would be allowed to regain property. The same order closed the universities, avowedly because of the anti-nazi activities of the Lithuanian intellectuals. The library "revision" carried out by the nazis in Lithuania as in Poland and the other Baltic states deprived two Kaunas libraries of 10,000 and 17,000 volumes respectively; the library of the University of Vytautas the Great

f 23,000 volumes, and the library of the Academy of Sciences
in Vilnius of over 40,000 volumes. Reports indicated a systematic
annihilation of the educated class by arrest or execution. At the
beginning of 1943 there were some 100,000 Lithuanian labourers
in Germany, and new demands for troops as well were made in
the spring of 1943. Large numbers of men and boys refused to
register and took to the woods where they organized as guerrilla
bands. Open revolt was reported in March, and Heinrich Himmler
himself went to Lithuania to try to quell the spreading violence.

Lithuanian representatives in the United Nations placed their
hopes for national rejuvenation in the Atlantic Charter and the
policies of the democratic countries. Another government-in-
exile functioned in Moscow. The political future of the country
remained uncertain, with no specific statement emanating from
the United Nations, with the soviet union seemingly assuming
that Russian occupation must be re-established, and with the
Lithuanians themselves rebellious but powerless to express their
will in any decisive fashion. There was the possibility that if the
Germans were forced to withdraw they might declare Lithuania
independent as a parting gesture. Lithuanian units with the Red
army were reported to have destroyed 13,000 Germans, and to be
fighting heroically. Toward the end of 1943 the battle lines came
close to the Lithuanian frontier with the Russian drive past
Vitebsk.

Statistics of education, finance and economic conditions were
not issued after the soviet occupation in 1940, and the latest available figures at the end of 1943 pertained mostly to 1938 and 1939.

Education.—In 1938–39 there were 2,335 private schools with
298,429 scholars, and 83 secondary schools and gymnasia with
19,539 scholars. Part of the university at Kaunas was moved
back to Vilna Jan. 15, 1940.

Finance.—The monetary unit is the lita (=16.1 U.S. cents at
par, established in 1922 as one-tenth the U.S. gold dollar). At the
end of 1939 the foreign debt was 68,915,300 litas, and the domestic debt of the government was 65,231,200 litas. In 1939 the
budget estimate of the government balanced at 341,785,274 litas.

Trade and Communication.—In 1938 imports amounted to
223,686,000 litas, and exports to 233,200,000 litas. Chief articles
of import were cotton yarn and thread, woollen yarn and thread,
cotton fabrics, woollen fabrics, coal and fertilizers. Chief articles
of export were meat, butter, flax fibre, pigs and eggs. Almost
40% of the exports went to Great Britain, 27% to Germany,
5.7% to the U.S.S.R. Imports came 31% from Britain, 24.5%
from Germany, 6.7% from the U.S.S.R. In 1938 telephones
numbered 26,591; radio sets 53,667; broadcasting stations 2.

Agriculture.—Almost 77% of the population is engaged in
agriculture, and 49% of the land is arable. Chief products in
1939 and their output in short tons were as follows: rye 726,636;
wheat 282,850; barley 282,740; oats 450,841; potatoes 2,290,469;
flax fibre 31,416; butter 21,890. The 1939 estimate of livestock
was: horses 521,000; cattle 1,004,000; sheep 1,224,000; pigs
1,224,000; poultry 5,130,920.

Manufacturing.—In 1938 some 1,441 industrial establishments
employed 40,818 people. Meat and fish products were valued at
44,919,000 litas; manufactured timber 12,532,000 litas; tissues
and yarns 28,131,000 litas; machines, etc. 13,215,000 litas;
leather goods 14,374,000 litas. Lithuania increased industrial production from an index of 100 in 1929 to 354 in 1939. Total industrial production of 1939 was 405,749,000 litas.

BIBLIOGRAPHY.—Gregory Meiksins, *The Baltic Riddle* (1943); Joachim
Joesten, "German Rule in Ostland," *Foreign Affairs,* XXII, No. 1, pp. 143–
147 (Oct. 1943).   (F. D. S.)

Litvinov, Maxim Maximovich

(1876–   ), Russian pol-
itician, was born July 17
in Bialystok, Russia. He joined the Social-Democratic party in
1898 and supported Lenin and the bolshevists in the factional
clash of 1904. After the revolution (1917) he was the party's
plenipotentiary in London, where he was imprisoned as a hostage.
He took part in conferences at Genoa and the Hague, led soviet
delegations at the 1927, 1928 and 1929 sessions of the preliminary
disarmament commissions of the League of Nations and in 1928
signed the Kellogg pact for the U.S.S.R. He was made commissar for foreign affairs in 1930 and championed collective security
at League of Nations sessions. He was suddenly dropped from
his foreign office post May 3, 1939, in the midst of negotiations
with Britain and France for a general mutual assistance pact;
the mystery of his ouster was solved in Aug. 1939 when Germany
concluded a nonaggression pact with the U.S.S.R. He was expelled from the communist party Feb. 21, 1941, but returned to
favour after the nazis attacked the U.S.S.R., June 22, 1941, and
was appointed soviet ambassador to the U.S. Nov. 6, 1941.

On Aug. 21, 1943, Litvinov was replaced as ambassador to the
United States by Andrei Gromyko. The suddenness of this move,
coupled with the removal of Ivan Maisky from his post as ambassador at London, led many observers to believe that Stalin
was dissatisfied with Anglo-U.S. failure to open a second front.
Credence was lent to this view because of the customary soviet
practice of removing envoys from countries whose policies did
not meet with Kremlin approval.

Livestock.

The total number of all livestock on United States
farms in 1943 as estimated by the U.S. depart-
ment of agriculture exceeded all previous records, the increase in
hogs and cattle more than offsetting the decreases in sheep, horses
and mules. When the large increases made during the year in
hogs and poultry were included, the total annual supply reached
an entirely new record high. In terms of animal units the total
on Jan. 1, 1943, was 5% larger than a year earlier and 11% above
the ten-year average. When these numbers are converted to grain-
consuming animal units, the increase during 1942 was about 11%

AUCTION OF CATTLE at Ellicott City, Md., Sept. 16, 1943, which realized
a total of $383,700 for 230 animals—a U.S. livestock record

Numbers of Livestock on U.S. Farms, 1943, 1942 and 10-Year Average

	1943 (Jan.)	1942 (Jan.)	1932–41 av.
Horses	9,678,000	9,907,000	11,409,000
Mules	3,712,000	3,813,000	4,542,000
Cattle	78,170,000	75,162,000	68,418,000
Milk cows	26,946,000	26,398,000	25,316,000
Sheep	55,089,000	56,735,000	52,386,000
Hogs	73,660,000	60,377,000	51,508,000
Chickens	540,107,000	474,910,000	420,201,000
Turkeys	6,549,000	7,623,000	6,510,000

and in terms of hay and pasture units, 2%. This record number was to a large extent the result of a large supply of grain and hay after five years of good crops. The production of feed grains and hay in 1942 was high and the carry-over stocks were large, with the result that on Jan. 1, 1943, farm feed grain supplies were the largest in 20 years and 3% above the five-year average, while hay was 6% above the same average. The increase in hogs was the largest, amounting to 22% in 1942. The total number of cattle was at a new high record, over 3,000,000 head more than the previous record. Numbers of sheep decreased about 3% after having advanced continuously for five years. The number of horses and mules continued the decline which began in 1915 with the beginning of the use of the power tractor. The numbers of poultry increased in 1942 and continued at a rapid rate through 1943. (*See also* AGRICULTURE; CATTLE; HOGS; HORSES; MEAT; POULTRY; SHEEP.)   (J. C. Ms.)

Livestock Shows: *see* SHOWS.

Loftus, Marie Cecilia ("CISSIE") (1876-1943), British actress, was born Oct. 22 in Glasgow, Scotland, the daughter of vaudeville actors. She grew up backstage, helped as her mother's off-stage maid, and at the age of 16 was a sensation on the London stage with her impersonations. Her dramatic talent won quick fame, and for 50 years she was an outstanding figure in New York and London theatrical circles. She joined Mme. Modjeska's company in 1900, played leading woman to E. H. Sothern and succeeded Ellen Terry in Sir Henry Irving's company. In the United States she appeared with Sothern in *Hamlet* and took the feminine lead in *If I Were King*, written by her first husband, Justin H. McCarthy. She scored hits in such diversified fields as James Barrie's *Peter Pan* and in the Ziegfeld Follies. Miss Loftus made her talking picture debut in *East Lynne*, 1931, and subsequently appeared in *The Old Maid*, *The Blue Bird*, *It's a Date* and *Lucky Partners*. She died in New York city, July 12.

London. London's wartime life appeared to change little during 1943 despite the welcome ubiquity of U.S. soldiers and airmen and such minor new discomforts as wooden slatted utility seats in new buses. The year's outstanding event was the publication of the County of London plan which concerned London's future.

Prepared for the London County council at the request of the government by J. H. Forshaw, the L.C.C. architect, in consultation with Prof. Patrick Abercrombie, the plan was the first comprehensive design for London since Wren's scheme after the great fire. It outlined developments for the succeeding 50 years. Working on a fundamental "neighbourhood" principle, the town planners proposed to enlarge the community life of the 28 London boroughs by dividing them into groups of units of from 6,000 to 10,000 people each. A unit would have its own schools, shops, public buildings, amusements, residential areas and industrial districts. Each unit would be as self-contained as possible for all ordinary purposes. Westminster would remain the pivot of national and religious life. Bloomsbury would form the University "precinct." The south bank of the Thames from Westminster bridge to London bridge would be "a river pleasaunce" with open

A VARIETY OF USES was made of London's bombed buildings in 1943. Here a band is giving a public concert in the foundation of a demolished structure

spaces for recreation and a cultural centre for art and music.

The plan adapted itself to existing London arterial roads by having two ring roads for the county area: an inner ring encircling the imperial, cultural and commercial core of London and linking the main line railway terminals; and an outer ring linking docks, marshalling (freight) yards and industrial centres. Nine new arterial roads radiating from Westminster were designed to cross the ring roads while avoiding the "neighbourhoods."

On the plan's basis of 4 ac. to every 1,000 people, London county's open spaces would grow from 7,888 ac. to 13,316 ac. To this end roughly two-thirds of the L.C.C.'s intended new housing would have to be flats and the rest chiefly terraced houses. It was calculated that in 20 years' time the existing county population of 4,000,000 would fall to 3,400,000, chiefly through removals. This estimate permitted the plan to fix population densities from a maximum of 200 per residential acre in the west central district to 100 in the outer districts.

The published scheme was conditioned by a larger London regional design for the 9,000,000 population of greater London under preparation by Professor Abercrombie. It did not include the "square mile" of the city of London, whose corporation was devising its own plan to recreate its heavily bombed areas. Much legislation would need to be passed by parliament before any of these plans could be carried out, but it was anticipated that reconstruction of some of the worst-bombed areas of east London could begin within the ambit of the county plan immediately after the war ended. The plan could make no estimate of cost. It was later calculated by the Finance committee of the L.C.C. that the 100,000 new residences needed would cost around £80,000,000.

Meanwhile Waterloo bridge, opened after five years' construction costing £1,250,000, stood as a symbol of a new London. Designed by Sir Giles Scott and five engineers, it has five spans of 240-ft. clear compared with nine spans of 120-ft. in Rennie's bridge of 1817 which it replaced.

London was practically immune from heavy air raids during 1943. In the autumn there were several series of brief raids by high-speed enemy aircraft which indiscriminately dropped bombs that nearly all fell in the suburbs, causing little damage to property and, with a few exceptions, little loss of life. The immunity and Londoners' cool attitude towards the raids allowed most tube shelters to be closed temporarily. In March, during a raid, 173 people were crushed and suffocated to death on a flight of stairs leading to a tube shelter. The tragedy was believed to have been caused when a woman with a bundle and a baby tripped, but the report of the official inquiry was not published.

London's evacuated population continued to return to the county throughout the year. The number of children in L.C.C. schools grew to over 240,000, leaving roughly 100,000 in the county. The latter included 62,000 children with whom the L.C.C. education department had lost touch, and special machinery was set up to trace the "lost" evacuees.

A report by the L.C.C. Chief Inspector of Education in May disclosed a serious decline in the educational standard of senior children. Of 2,000 children aged 13 years, 7 months, tested in English, arithmetic, history and geography, about half were found to be below standard. In cases of children moved from place to place since the war began, retardation was said to be between 6 months and 12 months. Following the report, special tuition was started for backward scholars.

There was no reported sign of physical deterioration among L.C.C. school children.

The health of London adults was considered satisfactory in the light of wartime circumstances. Deaths from all causes—to give the latest published figures available in 1943—dropped from 43,577 in 1941 to 36,057 and births increased from 33,944 to 40,654 in the same period. The customary population statistics were not available.

The L.C.C. began its 1943–44 year with a surplus of £6,000,000 and the county rate, which is distinct from borough rates, remained at 6/9½ in the £. A gross expenditure of roughly £42,450,000 was estimated. It included a reduction in the cost of civil defense from £18,000,000 to an estimated £12,000,000.

London's traffic became noticeably light during 1943 because of gasoline restrictions. Privately-run cars almost disappeared. Bus mileage increased to a quarter more than the prewar figure, largely through war workers' journeys. Women replacements of London's male bus conductors increased to 90%. When more buses were provided for London, it was difficult to find conductoresses for them because of other calls on women for war work.

During a "Wings for Victory" week, London set out to raise £150,000,000 for official war investment. The final figure of contributions of all sources, from commercial corporations to private citizens, was £162,015,869.   (P. Bn.)

London University.

During 1943 the emphasis shifted from wartime emergency planning to planning for the postwar period. Several more schools made arrangements to return to London at the end of the session. The number of internal students was 9,800, an increase of 650, and the number of external students was 13,061, the largest number ever registered. The educational work for prisoners of war was greatly extended, and the extra-mural department which was doing valuable work for the armed forces initiated special courses dealing with the life and culture of the Allied nations. Most of the vacant chairs and readerships remained unfilled because of war conditions. Harold Claughton was appointed principal of the university, Dr. D. R. Pye became provost of University college and Dr. R. V. Southwell rector of Imperial college. The honorary degree of LL.D. was conferred on President Roosevelt at Ottawa by the governor-general of Canada as chancellor of the university. The university contingent of the Senior Training corps was restarted in London.

Los Angeles.

Fifth largest U.S. city, with a population of 1,504,277 in 1940, Los Angeles, Calif., ended 1943 with an (Los Angeles Chamber of Commerce) estimated population of 1,775,000. Mayor (Dec. 31, 1943) Fletcher Bowron.

The Los Angeles metropolitan area was rated (by the U.S. bureau of the census) as the nation's third most populous in 1943 and its industrial area, with total government war contracts, according to the War Production board, aggregating more than those of any other industrial area of the U.S. in value, excepting only that of Detroit, Mich., approached peak production of aircraft, parts, ships, tanks, guns, ammunition and various other war equipment and supplies.

In spite of the fact that the number of factory workers in the industrial area increased from a prewar total of 136,000 to approximately 500,000—and the subsequent overcrowding of housing facilities by rapidly-expanding population—Los Angeles county in 1943 escaped being classified as a "boom area" by the National Industrial Conference board.

Production began during the fall of 1943 in Henry J. Kaiser's $83,000,000 Fontana steel plant, and synthetic rubber was added to the area's aluminum production, thus creating three basic industries to serve the entire western United States.

Four major tire factories, two synthetic rubber factories, four plants producing synthetic rubber ingredients and 41 other establishments turning out still other rubber products were located in Los Angeles county.

Not only were extra hours devoted by civic and industrial leaders to the problem of finding an increased labour supply to achieve and continue peak war production in 1943, but they also found time to give thought to postwar planning, with the result that many war plant operators announced blueprints ready for almost immediate conversion to peacetime production.

The end of 1943 found completion of regional organization of the Metropolitan Opera guild, with offices for southern California located in Los Angeles, and the Philharmonic orchestra had as permanent musical director a former member, Alfred Wallenstein.

Assessed valuation for the city in the fiscal year 1943–44 was $1,376,569,775. The city tax rate was $5.1931 per $100. The budget for 1943–44 was $46,447,872, exclusive of the water and power and harbour departments. Bonded indebtedness, as of Nov. 30, 1943, was $118,676,462.10.   (F. P. Dy.)

Louisiana.

One of the west south central states of the United States of America, admitted to the union in 1812 as the 18th state, Louisiana is popularly known as the "Pelican state," "Creole state" or "Bayou state." Area 48,523 sq.mi., of which 45,177 sq.mi. are land. Pop. (1940) 2,363,880, of which 1,383,441 or 58.5% were rural and 980,439 or 41.5% urban; 64% native whites, 34.3% Negroes and 1.7% foreign born. Capital, Baton Rouge (34,719). Other important cities: New Orleans (494,537), Shreveport (98,167), Monroe (28,309), Alexandria (27,066), Lake Charles (21,207).

History.—The legislature did not meet in 1943. The new state civil service system went into operation on Jan. 1, after the supreme court had upheld its constitutionality. A program of economy and efficiency in state affairs was continued, in spite of political opposition in the form of several court actions brought to test the constitutionality of certain reform statutes or the legality of some administrative policies.

The national war effort caused increased industrial activity in Louisiana in 1943. Established industries engaged in war production were expanded by the addition of new units, and several new defense plants were put into operation. Housing facilities were greatly expanded near the chief industrial centres and the numerous military training camps.

State officers in 1943 were Sam Houston Jones, governor; Mark M. Mouton, lieutenant governor; James A. Gremillion, secretary of state; A. P. Tugwell, treasurer; L. B. Baynard, auditor; Eugene Stanley, attorney general.

Education.—In 1943 the 895 public schools for whites enrolled 200,546 elementary and 79,475 high school pupils and employed 10,255 teachers; the 107 public schools for Negroes enrolled 26,860 elementary and 17,453 high school pupils and employed 1,220 teachers. The 172 private schools for whites enrolled 39,331 elementary and 9,676 high school pupils and employed 1,603 teachers; the 15 private schools for Negroes enrolled 4,556 elementary and 2,063 high school pupils and employed 180 teachers.

State expenditures exceeded $18,000,000 (exclusive of local funds) for public elementary and secondary schools and $8,000,000 for state-supported colleges and universities. Wartime conditions caused a decrease in enrolments in all Louisiana colleges.

Public Welfare, Charities, Correction.—Louisiana expended about $16,000,000 in 1943 in paying old-age benefits to 37,000 persons, aiding dependent children in 13,000 families, assisting 1,400 blind persons and extending general relief to 4,600 unemployables. The labour shortage and the high wages prevailing in industry and agriculture greatly reduced the expenditures for general relief and unemployment insurance as compared with 1942.

The state maintained the following institutions in 1943: charity hospitals at New Orleans, Shreveport, Lafayette, Monroe, Pine-

LOUISIANA STATE GUARDSMEN were called out Oct. 9, 1943, to seat a sheriff in Plaquemines parish when the sheriff's foes declared that his appointment was illegal. The guardsmen are shown here removing a barricade on the highway

ville, Independence and Bogalusa; insane hospitals at Jackson and Pineville; a tuberculosis sanitarium at Greenwell Springs; schools for the blind and deaf at Baton Rouge; training school for the feeble-minded at Alexandria; soldiers' home at New Orleans. There were also numerous private and endowed hospitals and orphanages in operation. The state maintained two prison farms for its 3,300 adult offenders and separate training institutes for about 300 juvenile delinquents. Maintenance expenditures for charitable and correctional institutions exceeded $9,500,000 in 1943, while an additional $1,300,000 was expended on permanent improvements at the charitable institutions.

Communication.—In 1943 Louisiana had 18,200 mi. of public highways, 14,410 of which were state-maintained, 10,140 being gravelled and 4,270 paved; the expenditure for highways was less than $12,000,000, because of shortage of materials for new construction. There were 4,400 mi. of railways and 4,800 mi. of navigable waterways. New Orleans, Baton Rouge and Lake Charles are ports for ocean-going commerce, with combined tonnage of 7,515,000 foreign and 11,556,000 coastwise in 1940. There were 26 airports for land planes and 11 seaplane bases and anchorages in 1943. There were nearly 265,000 telephones in service in Louisiana in 1943.

Banking and Finance.—Louisiana had 30 national banks in 1943, with deposits of $780,000,000 and resources of $825,000,000; and 116 state banks, with deposits of $330,000,000 and resources of $355,000,000. There were 67 savings and loan associations, with total resources of about $80,000,000. State budget for fiscal year 1942–43: receipts $106,431,399; expenditures $85,391,172. Gross state debt $170,000,000; net debt $165,000,000.

Agriculture.—Total value of agricultural production in 1943 was $244,000,000, compared with $190,000,000 in 1942; total acreage harvested was 4,200,000, compared with 4,124,000 in 1942. Cash income from crops and livestock was $275,000,000 in 1943, compared with $225,000,000 in 1942; from government

Table I.—*Leading Agricultural Products of Louisiana, 1943 and 1942*

Crop	1943	1942
Cotton, bales	735,000	593,000
Corn, bu.	22,786,000	24,412,000
Rice, bu.	23,978,000	25,758,000
Sugar cane, tons	5,700,000	4,935,000
Sweet potatoes, bu.	8,330,000	5,808,000
Irish potatoes, bu.	3,599,000	2,520,000
Oats, bu.	3,406,000	3,150,000
Hay, tons	375,000	393,000
Pecans, lbs.	8,640,000	6,400,000
Peanuts, lbs.	9,900,000	8,840,000
Peaches, bu.	176,000	335,000
Pears, bu.	78,000	239,000
Oranges, boxes	260,000	340,000

payments, $12,000,000, compared with $13,200,000 in 1942. War conditions stimulated agricultural production in Louisiana in 1943. Crop yields were not unusual, but the weather was generally favourable for agriculture, and the prices for agricultural commodities were somewhat higher than in 1942.

Manufacturing.—The production of chemicals, refined petroleum, synthetic rubber, lumber and cottonseed derivatives was greatly increased by the urgent demand for war supplies, and a few other types of manufactures showed a smaller increase in 1943. Nearly 2,000 industrial establishments, employing 150,000 workers and paying $200,000,000 in wages, produced finished products worth $1,155,000,000 in 1943, as compared with $990,-000,000 in 1942.

Mineral Production.—War demands stimulated mineral production in Louisiana in 1943, and the total value of the minerals produced was estimated at $260,000,000, as compared with $250,-000,000 in 1942. Some small new oil fields were opened during the year.

Table II.—*Principal Mineral Products of Louisiana, 1943 and 1942*

Mineral	1943	1942
Petroleum (bbl.)	127,135,000	122,432,000
Natural gas (M. cu.ft.)	455,000,000	475,000,000
Natural gasoline (bbl.)	2,418,500	2,300,000
Sulphur (long tons)	640,000	600,000
Salt (short tons)	830,000	700,000

(W.Pr.)

Love, Nancy Harkness (1914–), U.S. commander of the Women's Auxiliary Ferrying Squadron (WAFS), was born Feb. 14 in Houghton, Mich. She learned to fly when she was 16 years old and while a student at Vassar, 1931–34, qualified for a commercial pilot's licence. She was air marking pilot for the U.S. bureau of air commerce, 1935–37. Later she became a test pilot, and in 1941 she joined her husband's aviation company as sales director. On Sept. 11, 1942, Sec'y. of War Stimson announced plans to establish a unit of women fliers to ferry army planes from factories to airfields, thus relieving male pilots for other duties. The unit, known as the Women's Auxiliary Ferrying Squadron (WAFS), was put under command of Mrs. Love. During the summer of 1943 the WAFS were incorporated in the Women's Airforce Service Pilots (WASP), and Mrs. Love was appointed to the staff of the commanding officer of the ferrying division, air transport command.

Lowden, Frank Orren (1861–1943), U.S. politician, was born Jan. 26 at Sunrise City, Minn. (For his early career, see *Encyclopædia Britannica*.) Lowden, known as a "favourite son" in midwest Republican circles, was regarded as the outstanding G.O.P. candidate for president at the Chicago convention in 1920, but lost to Warren G. Harding, a "dark horse" after an 11th hour switch in votes. He declined the nomination as vice-president and running mate to Calvin Coolidge in 1924 and withdrew as Republican presidential candidate in 1928 when his farm plank for the party platform was rejected. He later retired to his Sinnissippi farm in Oregon, Ill. He died in Tucson, Ariz., March 20.

Lowell, Abbott Lawrence (1856–1943), U.S. educator, was born Dec. 13 in Boston. Brother of Amy Lowell, poetess, and Percival Lowell, astronomer, he was president of Harvard university from 1909 to 1933. He donated $1,000,000 for the establishment of a Harvard Society of Fellows to give financial assistance to post-graduate students. After retiring in 1933 he became head of the Motion Picture Research council. His later books include *Conflicts of Principle* (1932), *At War with Academic Traditions* (1934),

Biography of Percival Lowell (1935) and *What a College President Has Learned* (1938). He died at his home in Boston, Jan. 6. (See *Encyclopædia Britannica*.)

Luce, Clare Boothe (1903–), U.S. playwright and member of congress, was born in New York city April 10. Graduated in 1917 from St. Mary's school at Garden City, Long Island, N.Y., and in 1919 from Miss Mason's Castle school at Tarrytown-on-the-Hudson, she later received an honorary degree from Colby college. She was associate editor of *Vogue* in 1930, and associate editor and managing editor of *Vanity Fair* from 1930 to 1934. In 1935 she married Henry R. Luce, magazine publisher. As Republican nominee for congress from the 4th district of Connecticut (Greenwich) in 1942, she conducted a colourful campaign, and was elected Nov. 3. Mrs. Luce was appointed in Jan. 1943 to the house military affairs committee and on Feb. 10, she made nation-wide headlines in referring to Vice-President Wallace's views on global thinking as "globaloney." She lashed the administration's foreign policy, declaring that it was tied to the coattails of the British foreign office, expressed concern over the "political muddle" on the home front, assailed Churchill for regarding freedom as a "white man's monopoly" and called for liberation of India. She praised the Moscow accords but denied that her approval was inconsistent with her stated views on "globaloney." She is the author of *Stuffed Shirts* (1933) and *Europe in the Spring* (1940), and such plays as *The Women* (1937), *Kiss the Boys Goodbye* (1938) and *Margin for Error* (1939).

Lumber. Lumber continued as one of the most important and critical materials on the home front as well as for the conduct of the war. In fact it became so critical for particular uses such as shipbuilding, boxes and crating materials and aeroplane stock that special campaigns were conducted to increase production at the various mills. Labour continued to be the bottleneck of the problem. Large numbers of men were taken by the draft or attracted to other and higher paying war industries so that many logging and sawmill operations were seriously curtailed through the lack of available manpower, and in some of these sawmills women were used. Formerly, women had practically never been used in the sawmills or in the woods operations because of the hazardous and heavy work involved. Consumption for 1943 in the U.S. was about 36,000,000,000 bd.ft., of which approximately 29,500,000,000 bd.ft. was of softwoods and 6,500,000,000 bd.ft. of hardwoods.

In spite of priority ratings issued by the War Production board and increased ceiling prices for lumber as issued by the Office of Price Administration in Washington, the production of lumber did not meet all of the requirements of the army, navy, and other armed services as well as industrial requirements for war purposes.

Difficulties in securing sufficient machinery, tires, trucks, and other necessary equipment for the operation of logging work in the woods as well as in the operation of sawmills were considerably relieved. The production of Douglas fir on the north Pacific coast was curtailed due to the loss of employees to both the shipbuilding and aircraft factories. However, the industry there made an excellent record in meeting the requirements as far as possible. The increased demand for lumber for landing barges, patrol boats, mine sweepers, mine layers, submarine chasers, salvage tugs and containers increased vastly, particularly in the Douglas fir and southern pine regions. Southern pine continued as the most important species produced, followed in order of importance by Douglas fir, ponderosa pine, oak, white pine and hemlock.

A large number of small sawmills increased their production or started operations after being dormant throughout the recent economic depression.

The largest, most symmetrical, and the highest value logs produced in the Douglas fir forests continued to be in great demand for the manufacture of veneers used in making plywood. The production of plywood from hardwoods and southern pine was increased considerably. In some parts of the country the selection of the best logs for plywood curtailed the volume of logs available for lumber production. The increasing and critical demands for pulpwood, particularly in the northeast and in Canada, also affected somewhat the production of lumber. In some cases, prices for lumber, especially for some species like spruce, were so attractive that considerable volume of this species normally used for the manufacture of paper was used for the production of various kinds of lumber.

Dunnage was in especially great demand for the stowing and protection of various kinds of war cargoes shipped to foreign shores. In fact, the demand for boxes and other forms of containers used for the shipment of munitions increased so greatly that upper grades of lumber not normally used for these purposes were widely shipped and utilized under the extreme emergency situations created by the war. (N. C. B.)

British Empire.—Notwithstanding the unprecedented fellings in the forests and woodlands of Great Britain in the earlier war years, production of home-grown timber in 1943 showed no diminution. Actually production figures were expected to establish a new high record. Statistics were not made public. By the end of 1942 it was estimated that home-grown production was meeting about 75% of Great Britain's requirements. In the later months of 1943 Britain was producing about three-eighths of its sawn softwood requirements, three-fourths to four-fifths of its sawn hardwoods, and practically all its mining timbers.

The 1942 production targets set by the government home timber production department were exceeded by the trade mills, military forestry units, and the departmental operations. Results were: sawn hardwoods, 126% of target figures; sawn softwoods 107%; sawn mining timbers 114%; round mining timber 99%. For 1943 the same targets were set, except that in round mining timber an expansion of 10 to 15% was called for. Trend of production during 1943 is shown by the following midyear (1943) results: sawn hardwoods 132% of target; sawn softwoods 110%; sawn mining timber 113%; round mining timber 101%. Britain proved to have much more growing timber than was commonly supposed, especially hardwoods. In licensing timber for use many consumers were directed to use hardwoods for work that would normally use softwoods.

To Britain's home production were added in 1943 greatly valued imports from the United States, Canada, Brazil, British Guiana and other countries. During the year an official U.S. Timber mission visited Great Britain to discuss matters of common interest in connection with the control and production of timber and economy in use. Canada's production, estimated at 4,000,000,000 bd.ft. kept up well, despite great manpower difficulties. Shipments to Great Britain from the United States and Canada helped greatly the maintenance of national stocks in Great Britain to meet all vital war necessities. How great these were may be gathered from a statement by the British timber controller that civilian consumption had been brought down to between 10 and 15% of prewar volume.

Postwar housing needs in Britain were much discussed during 1943, and increasing attention was given to the possibility of providing unit-built or prefabricated dwellings for which timber is admirably suitable.

Europe.—From the European timber-producing countries—except from Sweden—little information was available, though it was known that in countries overrun by the Germans the invaders were pursuing ruthless felling in the forests. Sweden, neutral in the war, was still cut off from her main markets. Germany was her only large customer; quotas for Denmark, the Netherlands and Belgium were very small in 1943. Sweden's exports had fallen from about 750,000 standards of sawn and planed goods, including boxboards, before the war, to 365,000 standards in 1942—the lowest total for 75 years. In 1943 Sweden's exports up to the end of August were approximately 190,000 standards. A greatly increased consumption of timber in Sweden itself provided some compensating balance for the industry. (*See* also FORESTS.) (N. F.)

Lutherans. The year 1943 was another long year of suffering and endurance for the millions of Lutherans in the northern and central countries of Europe with almost no communication with Lutherans in other parts of the world.

In America the Lutheran churches recorded very substantial gains in membership and in material support. In addition to increases in support of the regular work of missions, education and charity, the Lutherans in America contributed more than $1,750,-000 for work among the men in the armed forces of the country.

The Board of Foreign Missions of the United Lutheran Church in America organized a school for its missionaries on furlough, especially those on forced furlough from Japan and China, at which there was a basic study, by the missionaries and members of the board, of the whole missionary enterprise, out of which a plan was developed to project similar schools into all congregations.

A notable event was the most inclusive mid-summer conference of Lutheran theological teachers ever held in America, which convened at Rock Island, Ill.

Another event of wide interest was the purchase of the residence of the late John Pierpont Morgan, on Madison avenue, New York city, for the future national headquarters of the United Lutheran Church in America. (W. H. G.)

Lutz, Frank Eugene (1879-1943), U.S. entomologist, was born Sept. 15 in Bloomsburg, Pa. He was graduated from Haverford college, 1900, and in 1902 was appointed a member of the staff of the Brooklyn institute's biological laboratory. The following year he was made an assistant in the zoological department of the University of Chicago. He was resident investigator for the experimental evolution station at Cold Harbor, L.I. (maintained by the Carnegie institution), 1904-09. In 1909 he became assistant curator of the department of invertebrate zoology of the American Museum of Natural History, and was associate curator, 1916-21. When the museum created an independent department of entomology in 1921, Dr. Lutz was appointed curator, a post he held until his death. Under his guidance, some 2,000,000 specimens of insects were collected and assembled. He wrote *A Lot of Insects* (1941) and *Field Book of Insects* (1917). Dr. Lutz died Nov. 27 in New York city.

Lutze, Viktor (1890-1943), German storm trooper chief, was born Dec. 28 in Bewergen, Germany. A veteran of World War I, he was forced to leave his job in the German post office, because of the loss of an eye, and turned to politics. An early believer in national socialism, he was one of the first to join the storm troopers. When Hitler became chancellor, Lutze was made police president and later provincial governor and state counsellor of Hanover. After Hitler purged the nazi party ranks in June 1934, Lutze succeeded Ernst Roehm as head of the S.A. (Sturm Abteilung) troops. It was rumoured that he was rewarded with the post because of his willingness to curb the rising power of the organization he had helped to build, for remunerative considerations—he was said to have been one of the richest nazi leaders. Lutze ruthlessly cleansed the S.A., ousted all non-party members and all followers of the ill-fated von Schleicher and Roehm. He then recast his paramilitary force into an anti-Christian, "philosophical" group. His death in Potsdam, May 2, followed an auto accident, the details of which were not disclosed. He was posthumously awarded the highest grade order of the German Eagle by Hitler.

Luxembourg.

A grand duchy situated between France, Germany and Belgium. Area, 999 sq.mi.; pop. (est. 1942) 301,000; chief city, Luxembourg (cap. 59,000); language, Luxembourgian (idiomatic) and (officially) French and German; religion, 98% Roman Catholic. Ruler in 1943 (since 1919): Grand Duchess Charlotte.

The grand duchess was forced to flee on May 10, 1940, as German troops swept into the country and placed it under martial law. In a plebiscite on Oct. 10, 1941, asking the people to vote to become German citizens, 98% refused. The loyal Luxembourgers still adhered to the sentiment of their patriotic national song, "We want to remain what we are."

On Aug. 30, 1942, Luxembourg was incorporated by decree into the German reich, and a mobilization order summoned its citizens to military service in the German army. This action was vigorously protested by the workers who called a general strike. As a result, orders were given that strikers were to be sentenced to death, and many were deported into Germany. In their place many Russian prisoners were brought in to work in the mines, but in 1943 the average iron ore output per day per worker fell from $13\frac{1}{2}$ to $8\frac{1}{2}$ tons.   (S. B. F.)

Lynchings.

The lynching record, which showed a slight increase in 1942, turned downward again toward the vanishing point in 1943, with only three victims reported. Three states were involved, Florida, Georgia and Illinois. All the victims were Negroes. The respective offenses alleged were: resisting arrest; killing a white man; and insulting white women by telephone. One of the victims was clubbed to death by a sheriff, his deputy and a county policeman; one was taken from jail and shot by four masked men; the third, a soldier, was shot to

death by a mob of farmers when he attempted to escape from a farmhouse. The outcome of the first case was unusual in that the three officers involved were tried and convicted by a jury of their fellow Georgians and sentenced to prison by a Georgia judge. Nine cases were reported in six southern states in which officers of the law prevented attempted lynchings, and one in New Jersey in which civilians restrained a threatening mob of sailors. Following are brief stories of the three lynchings of the year:

Newton, Ga., Jan. 29: Robert Hall, young Negro mechanic charged with stealing an automobile, was arrested and turned over to Sheriff Claude Screws, of Baker Co. Later that night, severely beaten and bearing 21 abrasions, contusions and cuts, Hall was taken from the jail to a hospital in Albany, where he died next morning. The officers claimed that he had been beaten while resisting arrest and trying to shoot the sheriff. On April 9 a federal grand jury indicted the sheriff, his deputy, Jim Kelly, and Frank Jones, a county policeman. In October the three were convicted in federal court of violating civil liberties statutes, and each was sentenced by Judge Bascomb Deaver to three years' imprisonment and a fine of $1,000.

Marianna, Fla., June 16: Cellos Harrison, 31-year-old Negro awaiting trial on the charge of killing a filling station operator, was taken from the county jail by four masked men. According to the jailer, the four gained admittance to the jail by telling him they wished to lock up a drunken man. Some hours later Harrison's dead body, severely beaten, was found in a ditch five miles from Marianna. The masked men were not identified, no arrests were made and no indictments returned.

Fulton Co., Ill., Nov. 7: Pvt. Holley Willis, Negro soldier from Camp Ellis, was shot to death at midnight by a posse of white farmers. He was attempting to escape from a farmhouse, where, it was claimed, he had made insulting telephone calls to several families in the community. Four members of the mob confessed participation, but were exonerated by the coroner's jury, which rendered a verdict of "justifiable homicide."

(R. B. E.)

Lyttelton, Oliver

(1893–   ), British government official, was born in England and educated at Eton and at Trinity college, Cambridge. He saw continuous active duty in World War I, 1915–18, serving as brigade major with the Grenadier Guards. Awarded the military cross and the D.S.O., he was demobilized with the rank of captain. After the war he entered business, became managing director of the giant British Metal Corp., Ltd. With the onset of World War II, in Sept. 1939, he entered the ministry of supply as the controller of nonferrous metals. In Oct. 1940, Prime Minister Churchill appointed him president of the board of trade. Since a parliamentary seat had to be found for him, he was elected M.P. for Aldershot. In 1941, he became a minister of state and a member of the war cabinet. Churchill established precedent by sending him as British representative to the middle east, the first time in history that a full-ranking cabinet officer had been established in overseas headquarters. He was recalled in 1942, to assume the post of minister of production. To pool the production resources of the U.S. and Great Britain, he and WPB Director Donald Nelson were named co-administrators of a combined production and resources board. In Aug. 1943 Lyttelton announced that British aircraft production for the second quarter of 1943 had exceeded the same period for 1942 by 44%.

McAdie, Alexander George

(1863–1943), U.S. meteorologist, was born Aug. 4 in New York city. He was graduated from the College of the City of New York, 1884, and received his M.A. degree from Harvard university, 1885. Prof. McAdie, who served overseas during World War I as an aerographic officer for the navy, was associated with weather bureaus in several large cities. He was lecturer in physics at Clark university, Worcester, Mass., 1889–90, and was later professor of meteorology at Harvard and director of the Blue Hill Meteorological observatory, Milton, Mass. Prof. McAdie, who retired in 1931, was credited with pioneer work in establishing the foundations for contemporary methods of weather forecasting employed by bomber and fighter pilots.

McAdie died Nov. 1 in his home near Hampton, Va.

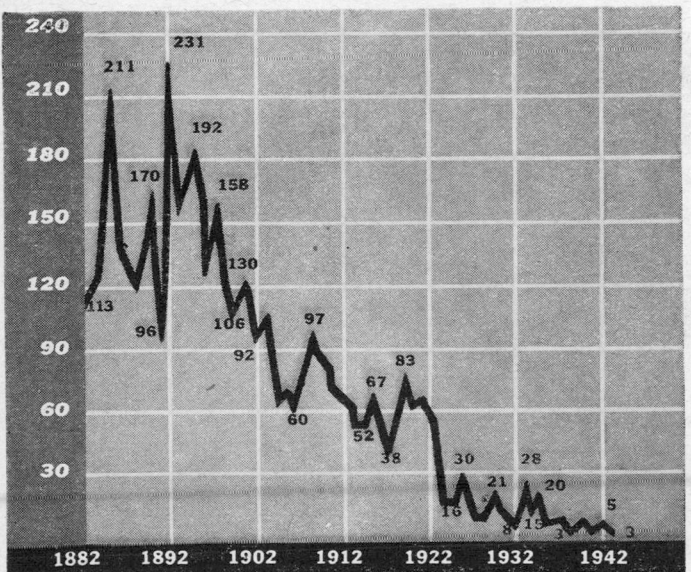

LYNCHINGS in the U.S. from 1882 to 1943, based on figures of the department of records and research, Tuskegee institute

McAfee, Mildred H.

(1900–   ), commander of the U.S. women's naval reserve unit (WAVES), was born on May 12 in Parkville, Mo., and was graduated from Vassar in 1920. She was acting professor of economics and sociology at Tusculum college, Greeneville, Tenn., 1923–26, and received her master's degree at the University of Chicago in 1928. She was dean of women at Centre college, Danville, Ky., 1927–32, and at Oberlin college, 1934–36, and was appointed president of Wellesley college in 1936. After the outbreak of World War II, she was named a member of the education advisory committee for the navy training program, working with naval personnel on plans for a women's reserve. When President Roosevelt signed the bill creating a women's naval reserve on July 30, 1942, Miss McAfee was chosen to head the WAVES (Women Appointed for Volunteer Emergency Service) (see WOMEN'S RESERVE OF THE NAVY) and she was sworn in Aug. 3, 1942, with the rank of lieutenant commander. On Jan. 15, 1943, the navy announced that 4,500 officers and 31,000 enlisted men would be replaced by WAVES. Six months later a goal of 91,000 by the end of 1944 was set.

On Aug. 2, during a three-day celebration of the first anniversary of the unit, Comdr. McAfee and Mrs. Roosevelt reviewed 2,500 WAVES at the naval training station, Hunter college, New York city.

Macao: *see* PORTUGUESE COLONIAL EMPIRE.

MacArthur, Douglas

(1880–   ), U.S. army officer, was born Jan. 26 in Little Rock barracks, Ark., the son of Lt. Gen. Arthur MacArthur. Graduated from West Point in 1903, he was commissioned in the engineer corps.

(See *Encyclopædia Britannica.*)

Following Japan's attack on the Philippines he was renamed a full general by President Roosevelt, Dec. 19, 1941, and led Filipino and American forces in the defense of the islands. Although heavily outnumbered in men and material, MacArthur slowed the Japanese advance and retired to the Bataan peninsula. He left the Philippines on Roosevelt's orders and reached Australia on March 17, 1942, to assume command of the United Nations' armies in the Southwest Pacific. In the fall of 1942, U.S. and Australian troops launched a counter-offensive to reconquer New Guinea.

By the end of 1943, the Japanese had been driven from the strategic Huon gulf and MacArthur's armies had landed on New Britain. MacArthur had urged "swift, massive strokes" rather than island-hopping to achieve victory and subsequently expressed disappointment over Allied tardiness to launch a counter-offensive in the Pacific After disclosure that Lord Louis Mountbatten had been given command of the Southeast Asia war theatre, MacArthur asserted that he would be content with a minor role in the interest of common victory. On Dec. 22, 1943, it was disclosed that MacArthur and Gen. George C. Marshall had met in New Guinea for a conference on Pacific strategy. Although MacArthur had declared in Oct. 1942 that he had no political ambitions, some Republican leaders regarded him as presidential timber and had started a minor MacArthur boom in late 1943. In Dec. 1943, the war department ruled that officers could accept a draft nomination for the presidency.

McGill, Frank Scholes

(1894–   ), Canadian airman, born in Montreal, June 20, was educated at McGill university (1911–13). In World War I he joined the royal naval air service, in which his distinguished and varied service at so early a period put him in the line of later leadership. He served especially with the seaplane carrier "Vindex," with the Dover patrol and in many fields. After the war McGill was associated with the Dominion Linoleum Co. of Montreal, becoming director and secretary. Even before war broke out in 1939 McGill organized No. 115 auxiliary (air) squadron. His active service began immediately with the war (Sept. 1939) and from that date he played a leading part in the organization and training of Canadian airmen and is generally regarded as among the most distinguished and efficient war leaders of Canada. He was commanding officer at Camp Borden, Uplands and Trenton. Entering as squadron leader, McGill passed through the various grades of promotion to become air vice marshal in 1942.

(S. LEA.)

Machinery, Farm: *see* AGRICULTURE.

Machinery and Machine Tools.

Shipments of tools from builders' plants in the United States during 1943 totalled about $1,183,000,000,

FROM A FLYING FORTRESS, Gen. Douglas MacArthur personally directed the mass landing of Allied paratroopers behind the Japanese lines northwest of Lae Sept. 5, 1943. This surprise attack led to the capture of Lae

which was a little less than the all-time record of $1,321,748,000 established by that industry during 1942. The tremendous expansion in production facilities and manufacturing efficiency which made possible these production records could, in a measure, be indicated by the fact that in the war-boom year of 1918 this industry shipped a total of about $220,600,000 worth of its products.

The year 1943 also saw a great expansion in the productive efficiency of other branches of the metalworking industry, almost all of which was diverted to the manufacture of combat and service equipment for the fighting forces of the United Nations. During the year the aeroplane manufacturing industry produced from 86,000 to 87,000 military aeroplanes. In this connection, it is of interest to note that in the three-year period ending with 1943, aircraft production increased 42 times while production per worker was practically doubled during 1943. Other industries showed accomplishments just as important to the war effort.

As during 1942, the demand for high war production during 1943 stimulated the development of new and improved methods. Included in this trend was the greatly increased use of induction heating equipment for forging, heat-treating, annealing and brazing operations. Another development which was given considerable impetus during the year was that of increasing milling production rates by using cutters having negative rake and helix angles. Cutters were operated at surface speeds up to about 900 ft. per min. and at feeds up to 60 in. per min. when milling steel. When milling aluminum alloys and other nonferrous metals, similar cutters were operated at speeds of more than 10,000 ft. per min. with feeds in excess of 200 in. per min. The milling cutters employed for these operations all had cutting edges tipped with tungsten-carbide. Usually, such milling cutters had fewer teeth than was common practice in more conventional milling operations.

Another development which received much attention during 1943 was the sub-zero cold-treatment of steels for austenitic decomposition after heat-treatment in order to produce greater hardness, and for the "stabilization" of gauges so they would maintain their size for a longer time. While there was considerable variation in the procedures employed by various users of this process, the successful application of sub-zero refrigeration equipment indicated the value of additional research work along this line. Increasing use also was made of mechanical refrigeration equipment capable of maintaining temperatures down to −120° F. for making precision shrink fits. With this equipment, it was possible to assemble ball and roller-bearing races and other parts in machine units by merely slipping them in position after chilling.

As was the case during 1942, manufacturers of machine tools and other production equipment for the metalworking industry concentrated on the production of standard models during 1943, in order to facilitate increased production. Development of new units and the improvement of older models again was delayed until engineering time could be devoted to such projects without hindering the war effort. Of course, it was necessary for the machine tool industry to develop and build special units to meet increased production demands for some war products which could not be made fast enough with standard equipment. Typical of these were a number of special machines designed and built for certain operations on parts for aircraft engines and similar units.

TUBES OF U.S. ANTI-AIRCRAFT GUNS, cast in one piece by a revolutionary method developed by the army ordnance department. Molten or liquid metal is poured into a chill mould which is rotated at a high speed so that centrifugal force causes the metal to take the shape of the mould before it solidifies, leaving a hollow in the centre. The casting is removed from the chill mould as soon as it is solid and rigid enough to keep its shape during handling. After cooling, it is heat treated to get the desired crystalline structure of the metal and then machine finished and further heat treated

415

416 McINTYRE, M. H.—McNAUGHTON, A. G. L.

In these cases, the special engineering required for the development of the units was justified by the fact that the necessary increased production was achieved, with an accompanying reduction in productive workers needed.

Among the new standard units made available during 1943 was a precision thread grinder in which either a single-ribbed wheel or a multi-ribbed wheel could be used for grinding single or multiple lead, right or left-hand threads with any pitch up to 60 threads per inch. This machine grinds either by traversing of the wheel along the work, or by plunge cutting. In the plunge cutting operation, a multi-ribbed wheel sufficiently wide to equal the thread length is fed into the full depth of the thread, and the threaded increment is formed in one pass, with the stock making $1\frac{1}{3}$ to $1\frac{1}{2}$ turns. This machine will grind in one pass two, three or four multiple-start threads in most cases.

Also made available during 1943 was a precision thread rolling machine of unusual type with which either tapered or straight threads can be rolled on bolts, studs, grooves and other parts made of high-tensile strength steels. The principal feature of this machine is the use of two steel rolls of large diameter, having on their faces negative multiple threads of the same profile, pitch and helix angle as the thread to be rolled. These rolls are pressed with gradually increasing hydraulic pressure into the workpiece or blank. All threads are rolled simultaneously. Rolling pressure and speed of the rolls can be adjusted to suit the metal and the pitch and diameter of the thread. The sustained rolling pressure made possible with the design of this machine condenses the metal forming the thread, and produces a strong thread that is burnished to a mirror-like polish.

Said to be the largest machine of its type ever built, a gear shaving machine developed during the last part of 1943 had capacity for gears from 24 to 96 in. in pitch diameter and up to 97 in. outside diameter. The maximum shaving range from the headstock spindle was $110\frac{1}{2}$ in. This machine was designed for finishing gears for large steam turbine reduction units, as well as timing gears for large diesel engines.

Two sizes of a turret lathe with a completely automatic machining cycle were placed on the market during 1943. Built into each of these machines was a flexible hydraulic system that provided an independent feed for each face of the turret. Multiple cutting and various combinations of machine movements could be performed readily with these machines. Speed changes are made automatically and can be changed at any time while the machine is in operation, during the cut, or at the end of the turret stroke. Constant headstock temperature for precision spindle alignment is maintained in these machines by a thermostatically-controlled heating system.

An electronic instrument for checking and sorting metals and alloys for metallurgical properties was announced during 1943. This instrument performs both qualitative and quantitative metallurgical tests on ferrous and nonferrous metals by nondestructive means. Machinability, toughness and internal stresses are among the physical properties which can be successfully evaluated. Such factors as structure, analysis and heat-treatment determine penetration hardness and affect readings of the instrument. For instance, the extent of age hardening in aluminum alloys or decarbonization of ferrous alloys may be evaluated. The instrument operates on the principal that metallurgical properties cause variations in the core loss of a tuned pick-up coil in which the part is placed. These variations affect the shape of a visible pattern shown on the instrument's indicator screens, or can be made to control an automatic solenoid-operated mechanism for sorting large quantities of parts. The instrument is not an all-purpose tool, since it must be correlated for the duties to be performed in order that dependable readings may be obtained.

In addition, a number of interesting developments were made in the fields of mechanical handling equipment in order to make it possible to employ women in metalworking plants on jobs formerly beyond their strength. Many jobs had been confined to men because of the weight-lifting factor. Therefore, much attention was paid in a number of plants to the development of work-handling devices that would permit the employment of women on jobs otherwise beyond their strength or unsuited to their physical characteristics. Among these were transfer units for moving relatively heavy parts from conveyor lines to machine tools, and then back onto the conveyor line after a machining operation was completed. (*See also* AUTOMOBILE INDUSTRY IN THE WAR.)

(B. C. B.)

McIntyre, Marvin Hunter (1878–1943), U.S. newspaperman and secretary to President Roosevelt, was born Nov. 27 in La Grange, Ky. He started newspaper work at the turn of the century and became editor of the *Washington Times*. In 1917, he entered the navy department as public relations officer and made the acquaintance of Franklin Delano Roosevelt, then assistant secretary of the navy. In 1932, McIntyre helped handle publicity for Mr. Roosevelt during the presidential campaign. After the election McIntyre was given the post of assistant secretary and in 1937, after the death of Louis Henry Howe, he was made secretary, a post he held until his death, Dec. 13, 1943, in Washington.

McKenna, Reginald (1863–1943), British banker and politician, was born July 6 in London. After finishing his studies at King's college, London, and at Cambridge, he practised law until 1895, when he was elected as Liberal candidate to the house of commons from North Monmouthshire. He held various cabinet posts from 1905 to 1916 and left the government when the Asquith cabinet fell in 1916. The following year he became director of the London and Midland bank and held the chairmanship of this institution from 1919 until his death. He died in London Sept. 6.

Mackenzie King, William Lyon: *see* KING, WILLIAM LYON MACKENZIE.

McNair, Lesley James (1883–   ), U.S. army officer, was born May 25 in Verndale, Minn. A graduate of West Point, 1904, he served with the Funston expedition to Veracruz, 1914, and the Pershing expedition to Mexico, 1916. During World War I, he saw duty with the First division in France, was attached to general headquarters of the A.E.F. and was awarded the D.S.M. Gen. McNair attended the Army War college, 1928, and became commandant of the Command and General Staff school, 1939. With war imminent, he was assigned to duty at the Army War college in Washington. After reorganization of the war department general staff in 1942, McNair became commanding general of the army ground forces. He saw active duty in the North African campaign. While at a forward observation post in Northern Tunisia, he was wounded by shell fragments and returned to the U.S. for treatment. He resumed command of the ground forces, May 26, 1943.

McNaughton, Andrew George Latta (1887 –   ), Canadian army officer and scientist, was born at Moosomin (Sask.) Feb. 25; he was educated at McGill university and served conspicuously in World War I. In May 1919, McNaughton was appointed member of the committee for the reorganization of the military forces of Canada, and in 1922 deputy chief of the Canadian general staff. In 1922 he was promoted to chief of the general staff, a position which he held until he became president of the Canadian National Research council (1935). He served in that capacity till Oct. 1939, when he was appointed commander of the Canadian active service forces. In Dec. 1939 Gen. McNaughton landed in Great Britain with the 1st Canadian division. He was responsible for the intensive training and scientific arming of the Canadian forces both at home and abroad; the Canadian troops which served at Dieppe (Aug. 19, 1942) were trained by him. On Dec. 26, 1943, it was announced that Gen. McNaughton had given up the command of the Canadian active service forces and was retiring, owing to ill-health. (J. I. C.; S. LEA.)

McNutt, Paul Vories
(1891–   ), U.S. politician and government official, was born July 19 in Franklin, Ind. Educated at Indiana university (A.B., 1913) and at Harvard (LL.B., 1916), he served on the faculty at Indiana university law school, 1917–25, and was dean of the law school, 1925–33. He became national commander of the American Legion in 1928, governor of Indiana in 1933, high commissioner of the Philippines in 1937, and first administrator of the Federal Security administration in 1939. On April 18, 1942, President Roosevelt made McNutt head of the War Manpower commission, a new agency to assure swift mobilization and distribution of the nation's manpower in war industries. In December, WMC powers were enlarged, and McNutt was given authority over the Selective Service system. On April 17, 1943, he ordered the "freezing" of 27,000,000 workers in essential jobs. Protests were widespread and vigorous. On May 3, the order was rescinded and arrangements put in effect for accomplishing the same ends on a regional basis. In Dec. 1943, a new draft bill, which deprived McNutt of his power over Selective Service, became law.

Madagascar: *see* FRENCH COLONIAL EMPIRE.
Magazines and Periodicals: *see* NEWSPAPERS AND MAGAZINES.

Magee, John Benjamin
(1887–1943), U.S. educator, was born July 19 in Albion, Ia. He received his Ph.D. from Upper Iowa University in 1909 and his S.T.B. from Boston university in 1912. Ordained in 1910, he served in the educational department of the Methodist Episcopal Board of Sunday Schools, 1912–13, and held various pastorates from 1913 to 1939. He was named president of Cornell college, Mount Vernon, Ia., in 1939 and held that post until his death. Dr. Magee died at Excelsior Springs, Mo., April 6.

Magnesite.
The mine production of crude magnesite in the United States in 1942 increased 12% over 1941, to 497,368 short tons; sales during the year included 35,485 tons of caustic calcined and 273,661 tons of refractory magnesia, obtained from sea water, bitterns and dolomite, brucite and magnesite. Sales of dead-burned dolomite increased from 1,069,887 short tons in 1941 to 1,229,357 tons in 1942. Production of other magnesium compounds, chloride, sulphate, hydroxide and precipitated carbonate, from the same sources as the magnesite output totalled 362,892 short tons in 1942, as compared with 103,906 tons in 1941. (G. A. Ro.)

Magnesium.
There was no official report on the annual magnesium output after 1940 in the United States, when it totalled 6,412 short tons, but an extensive program of ex-

HUGE CONTAINER OF MAGNESIUM being carried over retort furnaces at the plant of The Permanente Metals corporation near San Francisco. This plant, managed by Henry J. Kaiser, was in full production in 1943

417

pansion was inaugurated, mostly in government-owned plants, which was scheduled for completion in 1943. In 1941 enough new capacity was added to produce an estimated 20,000 to 25,000 tons during the year, and this was greatly increased in 1942, but no figures on output were reported. The only basis on which to estimate the 1943 status of the industry was an official announcement in Aug. 1943, that in the seven months, January to July, output had totalled 116,770 short tons. The July output was given as 17,450 tons in government-owned plants and 1,750 tons in privately-owned plants.

The January to June total averaged only 16,550 tons per month, against 17,450 tons in July, indicating that an appreciable amount of new capacity had been added in the first half of 1943, but whether the new plant capacity was all in full-scale operation by July was not known. In any case, the January-July output as reported, plus the remaining five months of the year at the July rate would give a total of 204,000 tons for the year, which might be increased for the year, if all plants had not been in full operation in July. The press reported that the scheduled output was at a rate of 265,000 tons a year.

This increased output resulted in several decreases in the price of the metal, which dropped from 27 cents per pound in Aug. 1939, to 20½ cents. (*See also* BUSINESS REVIEW; METALLURGY.)

(G. A. Ro.)

Mail-Order Business: *see* BUSINESS REVIEW.

Maine.

The extreme northeastern state of the United States, admitted as the 23rd state in 1820, and popularly known as the "Pine Tree state." Land area 31,040 sq.mi.; water area 2,175 sq.mi.; pop. (1940) 847,226. Rural dwellers numbered 504,169, while 343,057 were classed as urban. The capital is Augusta (19,360). The largest cities are Portland (73,643); Lewiston (38,598); Bangor (29,822).

History.—The state legislature met in Jan. 1943 for its regular session and adjourned in April. Most of the bills passed were concerned with routine matters or amendments to existing law. Fish and game laws were simplified and a postwar planning fund established. The state personnel board granted a general pay increase in all departments, after the legislature had appropriated larger amounts for personal services for the biennium beginning July 1, 1943. Numerous individual increases were also granted by the board, but rapid turnover and shortages continued to be serious, especially in state institutions. Republican governor Sumner Sewall of Bath began his second term (1943–44) and announced that he would not be a candidate for a third term.

Education.—The University of Maine, Bates, Bowdoin and Colby colleges operated with reduced civilian enrolments, but were aided by army and navy programs designed to train meteorologists, fliers, engineers, etc. Elementary and secondary schools suffered a teacher shortage, and a few schools closed at the opening of the fall term. The net enrolment of the state's 2,014 elementary schools in 1940–41 was 122,528; that of the 275 secondary schools, 46,121. There were 6,899 teachers employed in the state during that year.

Public Welfare, Charities, Correction.—The 13 state institutions (correctional, insane hospitals, sanatoria) were generally overcrowded and under-staffed in 1943. High employment levels resulted in a low unemployment compensation case load. Public assistance in large part took the form of aid to the aged, aid to the blind, aid to dependent children and World War I relief, with the first category containing by far the largest number of cases (15,742 in June 1943). The largest average monthly grant was to those receiving World War I relief ($40.28 in June 1943).

Communication.—The total mileage of the state's highways

at the end of the year 1941 was 21,862. During 1942 there were 221,371 registered motor vehicles in Maine.

Banking and Finance.—As of June 30, 1942, the Maine banking department supervised 168 fiscal institutions including 32 mutual savings banks (with 2 branches), 31 trust companies (with 54 branches), 34 building and loan associations, 8 loan companies, 5 credit unions and 1 industrial bank (with 1 branch). The assets of these institutions totalled $326,292,778 and those of the 35 national banks in the state $153,323,000.

State receipts, expenditures and bonded debt for the fiscal year beginning July 1, 1942, were as follows: total funds available, $47,107,166; total authorized, $33,456,142; bonded debt, $24,305,500. On Dec. 31, 1942, the state valuation totalled $704,000,491. The valuation per capita was $831 and the state tax rate $7.25 per $1,000.

Agriculture.—A moist 1943 season contributed to produce luxuriant farm crops and victory gardens, although harvesting of hay was difficult because of rainy and cloudy weather.

Leading Agricultural Products of Maine, 1943 and 1942

Crop	1943 (est.)	1942
Corn, bu.	640,000	672,000
Wheat, bu.	48,000	40,000
Oats, bu.	3,315,000	4,017,000
Barley, bu.	120,000	112,000
Buckwheat, bu.	140,000	119,000
Hay, tons	863,000	901,000
Potatoes, bu.	73,485,000	42,660,000
Apples, bu.	704,000	813,000
Beans, tons (dry)	3,250	4,150

Manufacturing.—The total value of manufactures (1939 census, last before World War II) was $345,368,595. Total employment was 81,995, and wages paid $82,026,503. No reliable figures were available to show the effect of war on industry in 1943. Maine shipyards continued at full production until Dec. 1943, when the seven day week was discontinued and barge production stopped, by order of the U.S. Maritime commission.

Mineral Production.—The total value of minerals produced in Maine in 1939 was $3,769,671, as compared with $3,548,638 in 1938. Stone, sand, and gravel production was low in 1943, while feldspar and peat production was up. (E. F. D.)

Maize: *see* CORN.

Malaria: *see* EPIDEMICS AND PUBLIC HEALTH CONTROL.

Malaya, British: *see* FEDERATED MALAY STATES; STRAITS SETTLEMENTS; UNFEDERATED MALAY STATES; WORLD WAR II.

Malta: *see* MEDITERRANEAN, BRITISH POSSESSIONS IN THE.

Manchuria

("MANCHOUKUO"). An empire, in practice a Japanese dependency, located in northeastern Asia, bounded N. and E. by soviet Siberia, W. by soviet Siberia, Outer Mongolia and China, S.E. by Chosen. Area, 548,000 sq.mi.; pop. (1939), 39,454,026, including 642,300 Japanese, 1,162,000 Koreans and 1,035,525 Mongols. Before the Japanese occupation in 1931–32, Manchuria contained the three northeastern provinces of China, Fengtien, Kirin and Heilungkiang, and was administered separately from China proper by Chang Hsueh-liang, who succeeded his father, Chang Tso-lin. Capital, Hsinking (the former Changchun). The largest cities (Dec. 1939) were Mukden (863,515), Harbin (517,127), Hsinking (415,264), Antung (220,587). Later estimates credited Mukden with a population of more than 1,000,000 and Harbin with about 650,000 inhabitants. The principal religions of Manchuria, in the order of numbers of adherents, were Buddhism, Taoism, Lamaism, Mohammedanism and Christianity. There were about 130,000 Roman Catholics and about 125,000 Christians of other denominations. The emperor in 1943 was Kang Teh.

History.—Manchuria remained outside the area of active warfare in the far east in 1943, and no events of outstanding importance were recorded during the year. The state of "Manchoukuo," never recognized by the United States, Great Britain, China and most of the United Nations, came into existence as a result of the military aggression of the Japanese army, which seized Mukden, the seat of the former Manchurian administration, on Sept. 18, 1931. This occupation was subsequently extended to the entire country. A committee of Manchurians who were ready to accept Japanese domination proclaimed an independent state Feb. 18, 1932. Henry Pu Yi, a scion of the Chinese Manchu dynasty, was inaugurated as chief executive of the new government on March 9, 1932. He was proclaimed emperor, under the name of Kang Teh, on March 1, 1934.

The Japanese army remained the actual power behind the administration of "Manchoukuo." The commander-in-chief of the Kwantung army, the Japanese force of occupation, became *ex officio* Japanese ambassador in Hsinking. The chief executive organ (no representative legislative body was set up) was the state council. A privy council was also established, with a mainly decorative function, as a consultative organ for the emperor. The Concordia association, which claimed a membership of 1,137,883 in 1939, became a pale copy of the single ruling party idea; one of its avowed purposes was to "establish inseparable relations between Japan and Manchoukuo." While most of the ministers named were Manchurians, actual power went to Japanese vice-ministers; and Japanese officials were in the majority in the powerful general affairs board. By a decision of the Cairo conference in Nov. 1943 Manchuria was to be returned to China after the end of the war.

Education.—Manchuria in 1939 possessed 15,877 primary schools, with 1,589,169 pupils. There were 238 middle schools, with 54,768 students; 40 normal schools, with about 8,000 students; and 13 institutions for higher education, with 3,820 students. Government expenditure on education in 1939 was 45,967,000 yuan.

Finance and Banking.—The yuan, unit of currency, is equivalent in value to the Japanese yen, pegged at 23.48 U.S. cents in Dec. 1941. The budget for 1940 was 573,550,000 yuan, as against 403,377,000 yuan in 1939. Japanese rule at first brought currency stability, but inflationary price symptoms were becoming evident by the end of the '30s.

Trade and Communication.—Exports during the first nine months of 1940 were 544,629,000 yuan; imports were 1,397,715,000 yuan. This unfavourable visible balance of trade reflected the heavy inflow of Japanese capital for industrial and military purposes. There were about 6,710 mi. of railways in 1940 and about 30,000 mi. of highways, of which 13,000 mi. were suitable for motor traffic. There was considerable construction of new railway lines, especially in the north and east of the country,

under the new regime.

Agriculture and Mineral Production.—Manchuria's staple crop is the soybean, production of which varies from 130,000,000 to 210,000,000 bu. annually. There were 1,683,000 cattle, 2,000,000 sheep, 1,250,000 goats, 5,500,000 hogs, and 2,000,000 horses in 1937. The country produced 685,000 tons of rice and 74,667 bales of cotton in 1940.

Coal and low-grade iron are the principal mineral deposits; the output of coal in 1939 was 19,000,000 tons.

(W. H. Ch.)

Mandated Pacific Islands: *see* PACIFIC ISLANDS, MANDATED.

Mandates. The mandates section of the secretariat of the League of Nations spared no pains to keep all available official and unofficial documentary material up to date throughout 1943. There was no break in continuity. Though unable to meet, owing to the war, the mandates commission received the mandatory powers' annual reports.

The moral and practical value of this international experiment remained undoubted; for the principles on which the mandatory system was based could not be ignored in the future study of colonial problems. These principles were, briefly, consideration of the social, moral and political welfare of natives as the primary object of administration; custodianship of peoples not yet able to stand by themselves, with the ultimate aim of self-government; collective supervision (with possibilities of wide extension) by an international body; application of economic equality to mandated territories.

The accompanying table lists the mandated territories with their mandatory powers and former administration. (*See* also NEW GUINEA.)

(M. Fe.)

Mandated Territories

Territory	Area Sq.mi.	Date of Mandate	Mandatory Power	Former Title	Former Administration
South West Africa, including Caprivi Zipfel, formerly part of Bechuanaland Protectorate . .	323,000	Dec. 17, 1920	Union of South Africa	German Southwest Africa	German Empire
Togo, comprising: (1) Togoland, *i.e.*, western section, excluding the seaboard .	13,041	July 20, 1922	Great Britain	Togo	German Empire
(2) Togo, *i.e.*, eastern section and seaboard .	21,809		France		
Cameroons, comprising: (1) Cameroons adjoining Nigeria	34,081	July 20, 1922	Great Britain	Kamerun	German Empire
(2) Cameroons adjoining French-Equatorial Africa	162,892		France		
Tanganyika . . . . *Ruanda-Urundi*	363,000 21,230	July 20, 1922	Great Britain Belgium	German East Africa	German Empire
Palestine . . . . *Trans-Jordan*	10,159 34,740	Sept. 29, 1923	Great Britain Great Britain	Palestine Part of the Wilayat of Syria	Ottoman Empire
*Syria and Lebanon	76,030		France	Syria	
New Guinea, Territory of, comprising: (1) Northeastern New Guinea (*i.e.*, the northern section of southeast New Guinea) (2) Bismarck Archipelago (New Britain, New Ireland, the Admiralty Isles, etc.) (3) Certain of the Solomon Islands (Bougainville, Buka, etc.)	93,000	Dec. 17, 1920	Commonwealth of Australia	Kaiser Wilhelm's Land Bismarck Archipelago German Solomon Islands	German Empire
Western Samoa, comprising Savaii, Upolu, etc..	1,133	Dec. 17, 1920	New Zealand	German Samoan Islands	German Empire
Nauru	8	Dec. 17, 1920	British Empire—Great Britain, New Zealand, and Australia, the present administrator	Nauru	German Empire
Pacific Islands North of the Equator, comprising: (1) Marianne or Ladrone Islands (except Guam) (2) Caroline Islands, comprising the Eastern Carolines and Western Carolines, together with Yap Island and Pelew (3) Marshall Islands	830	Dec. 17, 1920	Japan	No change	German Empire

**Syria and Lebanon were recognized by Great Britain and the Fighting French as independent republics in Sept. and Nov. 1941 (see LEBANON; SYRIA). In 1943 most of the subjects reserved for control under the mandate were relinquished by General Georges Catroux, for the French National committee, to the Syrians and Lebanese, whose full independence was, therefrom, only a question of time.

Mandel, Georges

(1885–1943), French politician, was born June 5 at Chatou, France. Like many able Frenchmen of political ambitions, Mandel climbed the stepladder of journalism into the chamber of deputies. He followed the rising star of Georges Clemenceau, became the latter's assistant chief of cabinet during the first Clemenceau ministry in 1906 and continued to be a devoted friend and aid to the old "Tiger" throughout his lifetime. He was Clemenceau's chief of cabinet during World War I and was credited with maintaining internal order at a crucial period when French workingmen and soldiers showed signs of wearying of the war. After the war, Mandel became a deputy for the department of the Gironde. In 1938 he was appointed to the colonial ministry in the Daladier cabinet and in June 1940, while the German invasion was in full force, minister of interior in the cabinet of Paul Reynaud. After the Vichy government came into power, Marshal Pétain ordered the arrest of Mandel. The latter, however, fled to Morocco, was there arrested by Gen. Noguès and returned to France, where he was imprisoned. Mandel, who was of Jewish faith, was soon transferred to Germany, and a Geneva newspaper of June 5 reported his death in a German concentration camp.

Manganese.

Items of information on manganese were few during 1943. That ferromanganese was kept throughout the year on the list of materials of which there was a surplus of supply might be taken as an indication that on the whole the United States supply was maintained in a satisfactory condition, but there were also indications that the strenuous attempts to build up any appreciable domestic output were not

World Production of Manganese Ore
(In thousands of metric tons)

	1937	1938	1939	1940	1941
Brazil	253	222	193	226	433
Cuba	131	124	102	120	251
Egypt	186	153	120	?	?
Gold Coast . . .	536	329	342	?	?
India	1,068	983	858	?	?
South Africa . .	631	552	420	412	460?
U.S.S.R.	2,752	2,273	?	?	?
Others	565	580	450?	?	?
Totals	6,120	5,200	4,600?	?	?

very successful.

The results with high-grade ores were apparently fairly good, but the work on low-grade ores did not make much progress, so far as could be learned, though no specific statements could be made about either, since no reports were available on outputs in either class.

Neither were reports made on imports, but it was learned from South Africa that shipments from there were greatly hampered by lack of shipping, and it seemed probable that Brazil and Cuba supplied the bulk of the imports.

In spite of shipping troubles, production kept up in South Africa; some of the surplus over exports was absorbed by increased local sales, and the remainder was stocked, ready for shipment at any time that shipping space could be secured.

Brazil was engaged in 1943 in the development of a local steel industry which would take some of the manganese output, but the amounts needed would not be large enough to make any very serious cut in exports to the United States, even though production could not be increased to cover the home demand. There would seem to be a goodly amount of wishful thinking in a German comment which implied that the new steel industry would require such large amounts of manganese that the Brazilian government would no longer be interested in fostering exports to the United States.

The German excursion into southern Russia did not bear much fruit in the shape of access to manganese supplies. The Germans failed to reach the major producing areas in the Caucasus, and the disastrous retreat had put back into Russian hands the smaller deposits of the southern Ukraine, which had been in German hands for some months, but probably not long enough for them to have done much with them, especially if the Russians in their original retreat from this section followed their usual scorched earth policy.

(G. A. Ro.)

Manitoba.

A central province of Canada; area 246,512 sq.mi. (26,789 sq.mi. water); pop. (1941 final census figures) 729,744; urban 44%; Canadian-born 73%. Capital, Winnipeg (221,960). Other cities are St. Boniface (18,157), Brandon (17,383) and Portage la Prairie (7,187).

History.—Stuart S. Garson took the oath of office as 12th premier on Jan. 14, 1943, succeeding John Bracken, who became leader of the Progressive-Conservative party of Canada, and who had created the present coalition government which continued. No changes in the cabinet took place. Five by-elections during the year resulted in the coalition government's winning three (one by acclamation) and the Co-operative Commonwealth Federation party, two.

Education.—Pupils in elementary grades in 1942 numbered 105,170 and in secondary grades 21,440. Government graded correspondence students numbered 1,836. Public school teachers numbered 4,484.

Agriculture.—The Winnipeg Grain exchange was closed on Sept. 28 under order of the federal government as a war measure. Total (gross) agricultural production reached a peak in provincial history of $230,000,000 due to increased production in coarse grains, hogs, butter and eggs, and increased prices generally.

Manufacturing, Minerals, Fisheries, Furs.—Manufactures (1941) were valued at $211,534,751; minerals (1942) $14,643,-269; fisheries (1942) $3,843,331 (increase in value of 17%, decrease in production of 8½%); furs (1942–43), wild catch $2,012,-746; farms $1,111,187; processed in Manitoba $997,733; processed in and exported from Manitoba, $7,990,961.

Communication.—In 1943 railways totalled 7,831 mi. Highways: surfaced, including trans-Canada, 8,745 mi. (gravelled, 8,208, bituminous, 500, concrete, 37). The government-owned telephone system had 88,257 subscriber stations, 131 exchanges and a total wire mileage of 325,237; it operated two radio stations, one of 15,000 watts at Winnipeg and one of 1,000 watts at Brandon.

(J. L. J.)

Manpower, War: *see* WAR MANPOWER COMMISSION.
Manufacturers, National Association of: *see* NATIONAL ASSOCIATION OF MANUFACTURERS.

Maple Products.

The production of syrup and sugar from the maple tree declined in 1943 com-

Maple Trees Tapped and Syrup and Sugar Production, by States

State	Trees Tapped		Sugar Made, lb.		Syrup Made, gal.	
	1943	1942	1943	1942	1943	1942
Vermont	3,800,000	4,000,000	354,000	320,000	1,072,000	1,310,000
New York . . .	2,893,000	3,111,000	124,000	177,000	839,000	933,000
Ohio	786,000	854,000	2,000	5,000	193,000	177,000
Michigan . . .	542,000	488,000	6,000	19,000	134,000	102,000
Pennsylvania . .	375,000	441,000	27,000	40,000	95,000	128,000
Wisconsin . . .	283,000	333,000	2,000	2,000	48,000	90,000
New Hampshire .	239,000	254,000	22,000	44,000	66,000	66,000
Massachusetts .	198,000	200,000	26,000	28,000	66,000	64,000
Maine	131,000	128,000	7,000	8,000	27,000	27,000
Maryland . . .	34,000	38,000	8,000	11,000	15,000	18,000

pared with 1942 chiefly because a smaller number of trees were tapped, due to the shortage of labour. Only 9,281,000 trees were tapped compared with 9,847,000 in 1942 and an average of 11,-279,000 trees in the period 1932–41. The production as estimated by the U.S. department of agriculture was 2,555,000 gal. of syrup in 1943 compared with 2,915,000 gal. in 1942 and a 10-year average of 2,534,000 gal.

The sugar crop was 578,000 lb. in 1943 compared with 654,000 lb. in 1942 and an average of 800,000 lb. for the period 1932–41.

(J. C. Ms.)

Marble: see STONE.
Margarine: see OLEOMARGARINE.
Marigny, Alfred de: see OAKES, SIR HARRY.

Marine Biology.

Biologists all over the world noted with profound regret the report[1] of the destruction of the Naples marine station and aquarium by the retreating German army as it evacuated the city early in October, 1943. The station, conceived by its founder and long-time director, Anton Dohn, was begun in 1872, at a cost of more than $100,000, and was built with the idea of establishing an institution, partly for the purposes of exhibiting in display tanks the beautiful and varied marine forms of the Mediterranean sea (the Aquarium), but mainly for the study of sea life under the best experimental conditions. The original station was a three-story stone structure with the aquarium of some 26 illuminated glass-fronted tanks occupying the first floor. The upper stories were given over to offices, library and laboratory rooms. Being one of the oldest and finest institutions devoted to Marine research on the European continent, it was the mecca for international biologists for more than 70 years. While the loss of the physical plant was considerable, the destruction of long-time type specimen collections and invaluable books, separates and manuscripts robbed marine biology of a rich heritage indeed, and one that can never be replaced.

Although seaweeds have been used for human and animal food for untold ages, exact scientific facts concerning their life histories and composition have been of very recent origin. A review of the status of many of the common seaweeds appeared in some detail in *Nature*.[2] In addition to fodder and fertilizer in rural provinces, quantities find their way into commercial uses. Out of potash and mineral extractions have come many diverse derivatives of a basic thick, shiny substance known as "algin," subsequent treatment of which with reagents results in the formation of a rubbery mass—a substitute for "hard rubber." Treated somewhat differently, a film similar to cellophane and suited for wrapping can be made. It can also be treated and drawn into thread which may be spun into a fabric known as artificial silk.

Treated yet again somewhat differently, it forms a white powder which serves well as a base for cosmetics, transparencies, plastics, auto polishes, creaming agents, as well as a suspension medium for powdered milk and cocoa. It is a source of glue, gel and mucilage. These and other facts prompt many issues of harvesting and transport as well as manufacturing and marketing of seaweeds.

In a word, the botanist, the ecologist, the biochemist, the technician and the financier will find new avenues over which to spread their talents.

Reports on the algae collected on the Swedish Antarctic and Magellanic expeditions[3] were available in 1943. Besides the well-known species of the "kelp belt," many unknown and hitherto undescribed species are listed.

The red algae dominate the deeper waters, while the shore forms are mostly brown.

Workers in South Africa[4] successfully made agar from three abundant seaweeds viz., *Gelidium cartilagineum* Gallion, *Gracilaria confervoides* Grer and *Sukria vittata* Ag.

Notes of alarm were sounded by the British government and two of its widely separated dominions, stressing the fact that overfishing of their adjacent waters must be rectified if serious consequences are to be averted. A paper before the Royal Society of London[5] called attention to the practice of overfishing (cod, haddock, hake, place, *et al.*) in the waters of the British Isles and the North sea. Technical improvements in ships and gear were seriously diminishing the supply. One suggestion to restore a biological balance was to enlarge the mesh so that immature specimens might not be caught. Another related to international agreements so drawn that each fishery area might be assured of a steady yield. A paper on fisheries research in Canada indicated that a similar series of problems confronted the Canadian government.[6]

The Australian Council for Scientific and Industrial Research[7] made public several bulletins, one of which reported that in spite of the war, which affected its people greatly, the sea-mullet was being overfished and suggested several steps to be taken to remedy the practice.

With the reconquest of the Mediterranean[8] it was hoped that the United Nations might immediately revive the fishing industry, institute modern methods of handling and thus relieve the transport system in feeding the undernourished and starving peoples of southern Europe.

It was thought that Sardinia's sardines and Sicily's tuna canneries might again be put into operation and expanded so that the output might be more adequate to the demands for sea food.

The director of the Marine Biological laboratory at Woods Hole, Mass., in his annual report stated among other things that only one-half of the normal number of students attended the current session.

Announcement was made by the Royal Canadian navy[9] of the development of "pink pills" for the prevention of or cure for seasickness. This remedy, while developed for use in the naval personnel, would no doubt in normal times be used extensively by the scientist as well as the layman where sea travel is imperative. Another discovery of a "sea-water de-salter" was announced by the U.S. Naval Medical Research institute. The new chemical briquet, about the size of a candy bar, quickly absorbs the salts and thus produces water that is fit to drink. Not only was such a de-salter to be used in case of shipwreck, but all overseas combat and commercial planes were to be provided with the new life-saving equipment since each briquet weighs only one-sixth as much as the drinking water it produces and occupies only one-tenth as much space. (*See also* ZOOLOGY.)

BIBLIOGRAPHY.—E. S. Russell, *The Overfishing Problem* (Cambridge, 1942); *Biological Results of the Last Cruise of the Carnegie*, Carnegie Institute of Washington, D.C.; H. U. Sverdrup, M. W. Johnson, and R. H. Fleming, "Oceanographic Observations on the E. W. Scripps Cruises of 1938," *The Oceans; Their Physics, Chemistry, and General Biology* (1942); Easter E. Cupp, *Marine Plankton Diatoms of the West Coast of North America* (1942); *Bulletin*, Scripps Institute of Oceanography, 5:1 (1943); J. Y. Gilbert and W. F. Allen, "Phytoplankton of the Gulf of California," *Journal of Marine Research*, 5:2 (1943). (F. M. B.)

[1] *Time* (Oct. 12, 1943).
[2] *Nature*, 152: 149 (1943).
[3] *Nature*, 151: 26 (1943).
[4] *Nature*, 151: 532 (1943).
[5] *Nature*, 151: 337 (1943).
[6] *Science*, 98: 117 (1943).
[7] *Nature*, 152: 110, for this and other bulletins.
[8] *Science*, 98: 12 (1943).
[9] *Science Supplement* (Nov. 26, 1943).

FUNERAL MASS for U.S. soldiers and marines killed on Guadalcanal

Marine Corps.

On Nov. 10, 1775, the first Continental congress established the marine corps as an integral part of the U.S. navy for duty afloat or ashore. The average strength is kept at about 20% of the naval personnel and on Dec. 15, 1943, it was about 325,000 total officers and enlisted men. Enlisted men are detailed from the selective service enrolment and from voluntary enlistment of men from 17 to 18 years of age. Officers are commissioned from graduates of the U.S. Naval academy and distinguished military colleges, from qualified enlisted men and from selected civilians for special duties. The ranks of officers and enlisted men correspond to those of the navy but the titles are those of the army from private to general.

Four distinct missions are assigned the marine corps: maintenance of marine detachments aboard battleships, cruisers and aircraft carriers as parts of the regular crews; maintenance of amphibious striking forces as parts of the fleets; garrison duties at naval stations at home and abroad; and provision of landing forces for the navy. The normal duty of the marines is with the navy but the statutes provide that any portion of it may be transferred to the army for temporary service.

The organization and training of the corps to meet these requirements includes infantry, artillery, aviation afloat and ashore, paratroops and tanks, and supply troops.

Fleet marine forces under the orders of the admirals of the fleets are made up of heavily armed and armoured triangular divisions specially outfitted and trained for overseas operations with a fleet or its task forces, provided with special transports, landing boats and amphibious tanks, with attached aviation squadrons.

During 1943, divisions were active in battle in the Southwest Pacific, especially the force under Lieut. Gen. A. A. Vandegrift at Guadalcanal and Bougainville islands with the naval forces of Admiral William F. Halsey, Jr., and the force under Maj. Gen. Holland M. Smith with the naval forces of Admiral Chester W. Nimitz in the Gilbert Islands and the capture of Tarawa.

To train the marines for their varied duties large recruit training stations are operated at Parris Island, S.C., and San Diego, Calif., and large divisional training centres are located at Camp Lejeune, New River, N.C., San Diego, Calif., and Quantico, Va.

Aviation units for training are maintained at these stations and also with the naval aviation training centres ashore and with naval aviation afloat.

On Dec. 31, 1943, Lieut. Gen. Thomas Holcomb was transferred to the retired list after seven years' service as commandant of the marine corps and he was succeeded in that office by Lieut. Gen. Alexander Archer Vandegrift. Upon retirement the outgoing commandant received promotion of one grade giving him the rank of general, the highest rank ever held by a marine officer.

Marine Corps Women's Reserve.—During 1943 a force of women was authorized for service in the marine corps reserve to be raised by voluntary enlistment and to be trained for service at shore stations of the corps in suitable positions, relieving men of the corps for active field service.

This women's reserve, consisting of 500 officers and 12,000 enlisted women (Dec. 15, 1943), was commanded by Lieut. Col. Ruth Cheney Streeter, the authorized strength for July 1, 1944, being 1,000 officers and 18,000 enlisted. The main training station for the force is at Camp Lejeune, New River, N.C.

They were being assigned to clerical and administrative work in offices at headquarters of the corps and other shore stations, to the ground crews of marine aviation servicing, overhauling and repairing planes and packing parachutes, and driving and repairing trucks and motor cars. They were also relieving men of the marine corps at supply depots and stations and as trumpeters and drummers, and were to be assigned to other duties when training made them available.

Marine Insurance: *see* INSURANCE.

Market Gardening.

The total production of vegetable crops for the fresh market in the United States, including potatoes and beans, was the largest on record in 1943. This increase was due to the large crops of potatoes and beans while the totals of other vegetable crops grown for market and processing was about 10% less than in 1942, but more than for any previous year except 1941.

The total commercial production of truck crops for shipment to the fresh market was estimated by the United States department of agriculture at 6,508,000 tons for 1943 which was about 7% less than was produced in 1942, but 4% more than the ten-year average. Much of the planted acreage was lost due to freezes and floods. The smaller commercial supplies of fresh vegetables compared with 1942 were offset to a large extent by greatly increased production in victory gardens. The smaller supplies and high consumer purchasing power resulted in a higher level of prices than in 1942 by about one-third. Temporary ceilings were placed on several fresh vegetables at certain markets and the highest prices were in those products not under the ceilings.

In view of the strong demand, the War Food administration called for an increase of about 6% for the crops of 1944, though it appeared doubtful if the production could be increased without

Commodity	Unit	1943	1942
Artichokes	boxes	826,000	864,000
Asparagus	crates	9,770,000	9,213,000
Beans, lima	bu.	1,206,000	1,574,000
Beans, snap	bu.	17,057,000	15,980,000
Beets	bu.	2,203,000	2,128,000
Cabbage	tons	1,031,000	1,276,000
Cantaloupes	crates	8,667,000	9,610,000
Carrots	bu.	26,911,000	20,216,000
Cauliflower	crates	7,569,000	9,481,000
Celery	crates	15,938,000	17,335,000
Corn, sweet	ears	264,000,000	273,900,000
Cucumbers	bu.	3,690,000	4,872,000
Eggplant	bu.	1,147,000	922,000
Garlic	sacks	131,000	217,000
Kale	bu.	734,000	440,000
Lettuce	crates	23,977,000	23,412,000
Onions	sacks	14,816,000	18,781,000
Peas, green	bu.	6,058,000	6,214,000
Peppermint	lb. oil	815,000	1,435,000
Peppers, green	bu.	4,699,000	4,896,000
Shallots	bu.	450,000	682,000
Spearmint	lb. oil	239,000	349,000
Spinach	bu.	14,531,000	14,815,000
Tomatoes	bu.	26,101,000	26,647,000
Watermelons	melons	47,948,000	56,526,000

a very good season and high yields. An increase in victory gardens was also suggested. The goal for 1944 was set at 22,000,000 gardens compared with 18,000,000 in 1943. With better supplies of fertilizer and the experience of gardeners, better returns were expected. (*See* also LETTUCE; POTATOES; TOMATOES; TRUCK FARMING.)   (J. C. Ms.)

Marmon, Howard C.

(1876–1943), U.S. automobile manufacturer, was born May 24 in Richmond, Ind. After graduating from the University of California in 1898, he entered his father's machinery factory, then established his own automobile factory. He designed the first Marmon automobile in 1902, and shortly afterwards became vice-president and chief engineer of the Marmon Motor company. In the early years of motor racing, Marmon's cars took many top honours. His Marmon Wasp won the first 500-mile international sweepstakes on the Indianapolis Speedway in May 1911, making an average of 74.61 miles an hour for the distance. During World War I, he served on several aeroplane missions to Europe and was adviser on the construction of the Liberty aeroplane motor. He died at Fort Lauderdale, Fla., April 4.

Marriage and Divorce.

There were two opposite social trends of greatest concern to the family. On the one hand there was evidence that the war stress affected the family even more in 1943 than in 1942 and that the strain was cumulative as it influenced family disorganization. As a result of this the year 1943 brought also wider public realization of the difficulties of families and more effort among U.S. social leaders to strengthen the home life of the nation that it might successfully meet its stress. The most spectacular indication of the first trend was the increase of juvenile delinquency, especially that of the teen-age girl. Although this problem had other causes than the breakdown of family functioning, it was chiefly an expression of the demoralization of many individual homes. J. Edgar Hoover's report on arrests for the first six months of 1943 showed an increase in the delinquency of girls under 21 years of age, of 64.7% over that of the first half of 1942. More impressive was the fact that there were more arrests during this six months' period than for the entire 1941 calendar year. For offenses against common decency the number of girls under 21 years of age arrested during the first half of 1943 increased 89.5%. From every section of the nation, especially from cities and communities near war camps, social workers reported a noticeable increase in the problem of maladjustment among youth and especially among girls. The most startling evidence of this was the increase in reported cases of syphilis among boys

and girls between 15 and 20 years of age. The New York Health department reported that primary and secondary syphilis increased 37% during 1942 in this group as compared with the period 1939–41. The child-labour situation also revealed effects of the war that were greatly influencing family life and the conduct of youth, especially when minors in war work earned as much or more than their fathers. During 1943, 44 legislatures met in regular sessions. Sixty-two acts were passed affecting the employment of minors in 27 states. Fifty-four of these enactments contained backward steps, although 40 of these were limited to the war period. In addition two of these states and one other issued 15 administrative rulings, all but one of which relaxed somewhat the previous child-labour regulations.

The constructive trend was especially evident along the lines of maternal and infant care. It was estimated that there would be approximately 3,000,000 births during 1943, the highest number of births, although not the highest rate of increase, in the history of the nation. Retailers reported their sale of maternity dresses during 1943 would be from 50 to 100% greater than for 1942. Congress recognized the nation's responsibility for the health of expectant mothers and their babies by an appropriation, later increased, which provided allotments for the care of the wives and infants of men serving in the lower grades of military service. The need of this appeared when a comparison was made between the states in their provision for the care of the pregnant woman and her child. For example the proportion of cases not having the care of a physician ranged from practically none in some states to approximately half in Mississippi. There were similar differences in the proportion of non-hospitalized cases extending from 6% in Connecticut to 83% in Mississippi. The Children's bureau program for community action for children in war time had the following six objectives:

1. A well-baby clinic in every community.
2. Care for children of employed mothers.
3. School lunches in every school.
4. Schooling for every child.
5. Play and recreation programs in every community.
6. Employment safeguards for every boy and girl.

According to the statistical bulletin of the Metropolitan Life Insurance company, the number of marriages during 1943 would probably total 1,725,000, 75,000 less than the peak number of 1942. This would be the first decrease since 1938.

It appeared that the decline in the war marriage boom apparent in New York city as 1943 came to an end would prove true for the nation as a whole. Licences were granted in 11 months to only 71,250 couples, the lowest in four years. A comparison of the marriage rates of World War I and II based on New York city populations of 5,400,000 and 7,377,300 follows:

Year	Number of Marriages	Rate (in 1,000)
1917	59,210	11.0
1918	56,733	10.3
1941	83,012	11.0
1942	81,454	10.8

The prevailing divorce confusion in the United States was further clouded by a chancery court decision in New Jersey which refused, in spite of the ruling of the United States supreme court the previous December that all states must recognize divorces granted in other states, to recognize a Nevada divorce decree on the basis that the six weeks' residence requirement was not a legal and honest domicile in Nevada. On Dec. 13, Justice Morris Eder of the New York supreme court made a similar ruling holding that when a husband or wife establishes a Nevada residence merely for the purpose of obtaining a divorce the intent of the domicile is fictitious and the decree therefore illegal. Regarding the United States supreme court decision of 1942 in the

Table I.—Families by Race and Nativity of Head, with Total Population by Race and Nativity, and Population per Family by Race, for the U.S.: 1940, 1930, 1920, 1900, and 1890.[1]

Subject	1940	1930	1920	1900	1890
FAMILIES					
All families . . .	35,088,840	29,904,663	24,351,676	15,963,965	12,690,152
White	31,794,000	26,982,994	21,825,654	14,063,791	11,255,169
Native	26,389,800	21,043,417	16,407,983	10,206,500	8,021,434
Foreign born . .	5,405,100	5,939,577	5,417,671	3,857,291	3,233,735
Negro	3,164,200	2,803,756	2,430,828	1,833,759	1,410,760
Other races	129,740	117,913	95,194	66,415	24,214
Percent	100.0	100.0	100.0	100.0	100.0
White	90.6	90.2	89.6	88.1	88.7
Native	75.2	70.4	67.4	63.9	63.2
Foreign born . .	15.4	19.9	22.2	24.2	25.5
Negro	9.0	9.4	10.0	11.5	11.1
Other races	0.4	0.4	0.4	0.4	0.2
POPULATION					
Total.	131,669,275	122 775,046	105,710,620	75,994,575	*62,622,250
White	118,214,870	110,286,740	94,820,915	66,809,196	54,983,890
Native	106,795,742	96,303,335	81,108,161	56,595,379	45,862,023
Foreign born . .	11,419,138	13,983,405	13,712,754	10,213,817	9,121,867
Negro	12,865,518	11,891,143	10,403,131	8,833,994	7,470,040
Other races	588,887	597,163	426,574	351,385	168,320
Percent	100.0	100.0	100.0	100.0	100.0
White	89.8	89.8	89.7	87.9	87.7
Native	81.1	78.4	76.7	74.5	73.2
Foreign born . .	8.7	11.4	13.0	13.4	14.6
Negro	9.8	9.7	9.9	11.6	11.9
Other races	0.4	0.5	0.4	0.5	0.3
POPULATION PER FAMILY					
Total	3.8	4.1	4.3	4.8	4.9
White	3.7	4.1	4.3	4.8	4.9
Negro	4.1	4.2	4.3	4.8	5.3
Other races	4.5	5.1	4.4	5.3	7.0

*Exclusive of 325,464 persons specially enumerated in Indian territory and on Indian reservations, for whom family data are not available.
[1]Sixteenth Census of the United States, 1940, p. 3.

Table II.—Median Size of Family by Tenure, for the United States, by Regions. Urban and Rural (with Colour for the South): 1940 and 1930.[2]

Region and Tenure	All Families		Urban		Rural-Nonfarm		Rural-Farm	
	1940	1930	1940	1930	1940	1930	1940	1930
United States. . . .	3.15	3.40	3.00	3.26	3.12	3.28	3.71	4.02
Owner	3.21	3.49	3.17	3.48	3.01	3.14	3.51	3.89
Tenant	3.10	3.35	2.90	3.12	3.23	3.47	3.92	4.21
Northeastern states . .	3.19	3.42	3.17	3.43	3.18	3.32	3.44	3.65
Owner	3.31	3.60	3.38	3.73	3.08	3.21	3.37	3.56
Tenant	3.12	3.31	3.08	3.27	3.30	3.52	3.66	4.03
North central states . .	3.08	3.33	2.99	3.24	2.93	3.07	3.49	3.83
Owner	3.11	3.38	3.15	3.44	2.79	2.89	3.32	3.71
Tenant	3.05	3.29	2.88	3.09	3.13	3.41	3.75	4.06
South—Total. . . .	3.36	3.68	2.98	3.25	3.82	3.54	3.97	4.28
Owner	3.39	3.75	3 14	3.46	3.24	3.46	3.82	4.26
Tenant	3.35	3.66	2.89	3.14	3.39	3.64	4.10	4.34
South—White . . .	3.41	3.79	3.06	3.40	3.38	3.69	3.98	4.35
Owner	3.41	—	3.18		3.26		3.80	—
Tenant	3.41	—	2.99		3.48		4.16	—
South—Nonwhite . . .	3.17	3.28	2.65	2.71	2 99	2.09	3.94	4.07
Owner	3.24	—	2.85	—	3.09	—	4.00	—
Tenant	3.14	—	2.58	—	2.94		3.93	—
West	2.72	2.96	2.55	2.82	2.86	3.01	3.29	3.55
Owner	2.92	3.15	2.84	3.07	2.90	3.07	3.23	3.48
Tenant	2.51	2.80	2.37	2.62	2.81	3.00	3.41	3.78

[2]Sixteenth Census of the United States, 1940, p. 5.

North Carolina versus *Williams* case, he stated, "I find nothing in the prevailing opinion of the court which overrides the existing rule, that the full faith and credit clause does not estop the court in which it is sought to assert the judgment of the foreign court, from inquiring into and investigating its validity to ascertain and determine if it is entitled to be given valid recognition under that provision." An authoritative symposium on the law of divorce by Roscoe Pound appeared in the *Iowa Law Review*, Jan. 1943.

Missouri, Nebraska, Idaho and Wyoming in 1943 increased to 30 the number of states requiring some sort of premarital examination for venereal disease, while Idaho, Nebraska, Georgia and Kansas by requiring prenatal examinations also increased the number of states having laws to protect the unborn against syphilis to 30. The state of New York strengthened its premarriage examination law by providing that the statement of the physician making such tests, "shall include the name and address of the applicant; a statement that a serological test for syphilis was performed; the date on which the specimen was taken and the name and location of the laboratory in which such test was made." The physician's statements must accompany the application for a marriage licence. The bill provides, however, that the result of the serological test shall not be included in such statement but that a detailed report of the laboratory test when positive shall be filed with the local health authorities and held in "absolute confidence" and not open to public inspection. The new California law allowing divorce for more than three years' duration of insanity, passed in 1942, went into effect on Aug. 4, 1943. The spouse seeking the divorce, however, must make satisfactory arrangements for the support of the insane partner for life.

American religious leadership throughout the year at various church conferences recognized the strain on family life during war time and emphasized the need of conserving both marriage and the family. At the 54th Triennial General convention of the Protestant Episcopal Church, a report was submitted proposing the revising of the divorce regulations to permit the diocesan bishop to grant permission for a divorced person to remarry after consulting a pastor or priest, a lawyer and a physician. This change, approved by the lay delegates, was defeated by a narrow margin in the clerical order of the Church's house of deputies, 38 voting "Yes," 32 "No," and 9 divided. A majority vote is required to authorize the change.

Although interest in problems of marriage and the family was never greater, war conditions during 1943 prevented some of the conferences which otherwise would have been held, such as the National Conference for Family Relations, which was to have been held at Cleveland, and the Annual April Conference on the Conservation of Marriage and the Family at Chapel Hill.

Representative of gatherings that were held are the Iowa Conference of Family Relations at Cornell College, the Pacific Northwest Conference of Family Relations at the University of Washington, the Family Relations Conference of Northern California at Berkeley, the Second Annual Conference of Negro Colleges on Conservation of Marriage and the Family at the State College for Negroes at Durham, N.C., the Institute for Family and Child Care Services at Vassar college, and the Annual Institute of the Child Study Association of America at New York, having as its subject, "The American Family Faces the Second War Year."

Tables I and II reveal the present family population of the United States in comparison with the four preceding decades, and the median size of family in comparison with the situation of ten years ago.

(*See* also CENSUS, 1940.)   (E. R. G.)

Marshall, George Catlett (1880–), U.S. army chief of staff, was born at Uniontown, Pa., on Dec. 31. Commissioned second lieutenant of infantry Feb. 2, 1901, after completing his studies at Virginia Military institute and the Army Staff college, he advanced through the grades to brigadier general in 1936. In 1902 and 1903 he served in the Philippines, also from 1913 to 1916. He was with the American expeditionary forces in France in 1917, on the general staff of the 1st division, as chief of operations of the 1st army and as chief of staff of the 8th army corps. After the war he was aide-de-camp to Gen. John J. Pershing for five years. From 1924 to 1927 he was stationed in China; in 1933 he was appointed commander of the 8th infantry and in 1936 commanding general of the 5th brigade. On July 1, 1939, Marshall took office as acting chief of staff. The appointment was made permanent on Sept. 1, the day that Hitler invaded Poland, and Marshall was made a full general. In the war years following he demonstrated remarkable ability to co-ordinate diverse elenents and points of view, while retaining the goodwill of practically everyone, including members of congress. He was an early supporter of the Burke-Wadsworth selective service bill, and after its enactment into law directed and co-ordinated the enormous load of activity that attended the first peacetime military conscription in U.S. history. In 1941 he endorsed aid to Britain. When war actually came on Dec. 7, 1941, Marshall had under his command an army of 1,500,000 green soldiers. In his biennial report, released Sept. 8, 1943, he revealed that there were 8,000,000 U.S. soldiers, many in actual fighting on fronts all over the world. Later in the month he stated that the army planned to have an estimated 2,250,000 men serving outside the U.S. by the end of 1943, and 5,000,000 by the end of 1944. Late in 1943 it was widely rumoured that Marshall would be replaced as chief of staff and given the position of supreme commander of Anglo-American armies in Europe, but the appointment was given to Gen. Dwight D. Eisenhower. Marshall attended the Casablanca, Quebec, Cairo and Tehran conferences during the year. After he left Tehran, he returned to the U.S. by way of Asia and the Pacific, where he conferred with high officers in New Guinea, the Solomons, Hawaii and elsewhere. He completed his round-the-world trip of more than 30,000 mi. on Dec. 23.

Marshall, Tully

(1864–1943), U.S. actor, was born William Phillips in Nevada City, Calif., on April 13. He left college to join a vaudeville troupe in San Francisco, later graduating to the legitimate stage. In 1887 he went to New York city, where he played minor roles with Modjeska and E. H. Sothern. He scored his greatest footlight success in *The City* (by Clyde Fitch), which enjoyed a two-year run in New York city, 1909–11. He also directed and starred in two plays written by his wife, Marion Fairfax, *The Builders*, 1907, and *The Talker*, 1912. He left Broadway for Hollywood in 1915, "stole the show" in the picturization of Emerson Hough's *The Covered Wagon* and thereafter was in wide demand as a feature player. Because of his extensive stage experience, Marshall easily bridged the changeover from silent to talking pictures. In his later years, he appeared in such motion picture hits as *Black Fury, A Tale of Two Cities, Stand In, Ball of Fire* and *This Gun for Hire*. He died at his home in Encino, Calif., March 10.

Martinique: *see* FRENCH COLONIAL EMPIRE.

Marvin, Charles Frederick

(1858–1943), U.S. meteorologist, was born Oct. 7 in Putnam, O. He graduated from Ohio State university in 1883 and the next year joined the weather forecasting service as civilian member of the army signal corps. He was chief of the U.S. weather bureau from 1913 until his retirement in 1934. During his long career he invented many meteorological instruments, including devices for measuring and automatically recording rainfall, snowfall, sunshine and atmospheric pressure. In addition he did notable work in the investigation and standardization of the anemometer for measuring wind velocities and pressure. He was among the first to start a special weather report service for pioneering transatlantic aviators and was the inventor of the clinometer, to determine the exact height of clouds, especially valuable to airports. He was the author of numerous papers on meteorology and simplification of the calendar. He died in Washington, June 5.

Maryland.

A south Atlantic state and one of the original 13 states, popularly called the "Old Line" state. Total area 10,577 sq.mi., land area 9,887 sq.mi., water 690 sq.mi.

Population (1940) 1,821,244; urban 1,080,351, rural 740,893; white 1,518,481; nonwhite 302,763. Capital, Annapolis (pop. 13,069); other cities: Baltimore (859,100), Cumberland (39,-483), Hagerstown (32,491), Frederick (15,802).

History.—The governor, Herbert R. O'Conor, was re-elected in 1942 for a second term. The Maryland legislature met for its biennial session, Jan. to April, 1943. Outstanding bills passed included a constitutional amendment reorganizing the court of appeals—as recommended by the Bond Committee report. The juvenile court of Baltimore city was reconstituted so that all juvenile delinquents would be dealt with in the department of welfare. Provision was made for the construction of two chronic disease hospitals after the war. The state conservation program was strengthened by passage of a bill providing for a co-operative crab-conservation program with Virginia and by the defeat of two bills, one to open the Potomac to oyster dredging and the other to break down the fin-fish conservation program.

The fiscal system was strengthened by a report by a special committee which led to legislative scrutiny of the budget and a revised budget estimate by the governor providing a carefully integrated fiscal program. A bill providing a bonus for school teachers and state employees was passed. An emergency measure reducing the income tax 33% was passed for 1942 and a reduction of 50% was made for the 1943 tax.

Education.—In 1943 there were 965 elementary and occupational (Baltimore only) schools in Maryland including 330 Negro schools. The total elementary enrolment was 205,016, of which 45,960 were Negro. Teaching staff 5,290, including 1,237 Negro. There were 214 secondary and vocational schools (including 39 Negro) with an enrolment of 75,550 (including 11,730 Negro) and a teaching staff of 3,925 of which 977 were Negro.

Public Welfare, Charities and Correction.—General public assistance including foster home care was given in Oct. 1943 to 3,916 persons (cost, $1,504,683 for Jan.–Oct. inclusive); old age assistance to 13,461 ($3,056,488); aid to needy blind, 477 ($127,-064); aid to dependent children 8,919 ($1,285,247). Unemployment compensation benefits amounted to $824,544.

Correctional institutions and the average number of inmates in 1943 were as follows: Maryland penitentiary (1,172); Maryland house of correction (1,145); Maryland state penal farm (396); women's prison of Maryland (118). There were also four juvenile institutions.

Communication.—The State Roads commission expended during the period from Oct. 1942, to June 30, 1943, a total of $11,314,837. The total mileage maintained by the state was 4,362; connecting links not state-maintained 99.95. An important highway construction project of 1943 was a full cloverleaf grade separation at intersection of state Route 20 and state Route 150, to expedite traffic movement to industrial areas of Sparrows Point and Middle River. On Dec. 31, 1941, there were 1,361 mi. of railroads in Maryland. There were 21 airports and 5 seaplane ports in the state in 1941. Telephones in service in Maryland numbered 387,732 as of Nov. 1, 1943.

Banking and Finance.—On June 30, 1943, there were 112 state banks and trust companies and branches with total deposits of $590,555,744 and total resources of $644,203,176; and there were 11 mutual savings institutions and total deposits of $248,-199,796 and total resources of $278,327,297. There were 63 national banks with total deposits of $581,861,000 and total resources of $618,027,000. State appropriations for the fiscal year ending June 30, 1943, were $55,371,982.84; expenditures $45,-366,830.78; bonded indebtedness $33,619,000; surplus in general funds $12,600,932. These figures are for nine months only, since Maryland changed the end of its fiscal year from Oct. 31 to June 30.

Table I.—Leading Agricultural Products of Maryland, 1943 and 1942

Crop	1943 (est.)	1942	Crop	1943 (est.)	1942
Corn, bu.	12,744,000	16,344,000	Tame hay, tons	529,000	553,000
Wheat, bu.	4,935,000	5,986,000	Potatoes, bu.	1,800,000	2,019,000
Oats, bu.	1,012,000	1,110,000	Tobacco, lb.	19,525,000	31,008,000
Barley, bu.	1,800,000	2,365,000			

Agriculture.—Maryland's cash income from farm products in the months from Jan.–Sept. 1943, totalled $127,529,000, of which $57,883,000 represented the income from crops and $69,646,000 that from livestock and livestock products. The 1943 figure was $32,585,000 higher than that for the same period in 1942, during which time the total cash income from crops reached only $43,-731,000, and that from livestock and livestock products $51,213,-000.

Manufacturing.—Manufacturing industries reporting to the state commissioner of labour and statistics showed a per cent change in employment of +4.6 and +20.3 in combined payrolls from Oct. 1942 to Oct. 1943. Average weekly earnings amounted to $50.33 and average hours worked per week amounted to 46.7 hours.

Mineral Production.—The total value of mineral production

Table II.—Leading Mineral Products of Maryland, 1941 and 1940

Product	1941, Value	1940, Value	Product	1941, Value	1940, Value
Clay	$2,042,000	$1,856,000	Sand and gravel	$4,446,850	$2,763,322
Coal	4,088,426	3,171,243	Stone	2,218,478	1,395,373

in 1941 was $17,291,523, as compared with $12,605,701 in 1940. Leading mineral products and their values are shown in Table II.

(C. B. S.)

Massachusetts.
A north Atlantic state of the U.S.A., admitted to the union Feb. 6, 1788. Area, 8,093 sq.mi., including 254 sq.mi. of inland water; pop. (1940) 4,316,721, of which 3,859,476 was urban, 457,245 rural; 4,257,596 white, 55,391 Negro. Capital, Boston (770,816). Other principal cities: Worcester (193,694); Springfield (149,554); Fall River (115,428); Cambridge (110,879); New Bedford (110,341); Somerville (102,177); Lowell (101,389) and Lynn (98,123).

History.—Officers of the state in 1943 included: Governor Leverett Saltonstall (Rep.), who was inaugurated for his third two-year term on Jan. 6; lieutenant governor, Horace T. Cahill (Rep.); secretary of state, Frederic W. Cook (Rep.); treasurer and receiver general, Francis X. Hurley (Dem.); auditor, Thomas J. Buckley (Dem.); attorney general, Robert T. Bushnell (Rep.).

During the 1943 session of the legislature, which meets biennially, the senate consisted of 26 Republicans and 13 Democrats, and the house of representatives of 139 Republicans and 97 Democrats. Legislation in 1943 was largely concerned with provisions to facilitate the eventual postwar readjustment. Five special commissions, requested by the governor, were directly employed in advance preparation for the problems of reconversion to a peacetime economy. The Post-War Readjustment committee devoted itself to working with private industries of the state in their postwar planning. The Commission on Emergency Public Works assembled and evaluated plans for public works by the state itself and stimulated cities and towns to plan projects. The Post-War Highway commission studied the order of priority in which projected new highways should be undertaken. A committee on transportation studied the revamping of the Boston metropolitan transportation system. The committee on veterans' rehabilitation and re-employment was charged with the specific task of assisting returning veterans. The legislature also set up its own legislative commission on postwar rehabilitation to act as a liaison agent between the executive and the legislative branches in dealing with the problems of returning veterans.

The financial position of both the state and municipal governments in Massachusetts at the end of 1943 was strong. The net direct debt of the state government by Nov. 30, 1943, had been reduced to $5,663,861 from a peak of about $40,700,000 in 1938. The combined debt of Massachusetts cities and towns at the close of 1943 stood at less than $215,000,000, a drop of more than $100,000,000 from the 1932 peak of $316,484,599.

Education.—In 1943 Massachusetts maintained 1,887 elementary school buildings, with 358,459 pupils and 13,713 teachers; 169 junior high school buildings, with 92,948 pupils and 4,010 teachers; 271 senior high school buildings, with 139,-638 pupils and 6,754 teachers; 9 teachers' colleges, with 1,917 students and 313 teachers; and the State college at Amherst, with 1,484 students, including 750 army air force cadets; and 249 members of the professional staff.

Massachusetts maintains the State college at Amherst, the Massachusetts Maritime academy and the Art school in Boston, three textile schools, and a teachers' college at Bridgewater, Fitchburg, Framingham, Hyannis, Lowell, North Adams, Salem, Westfield and Worcester.

Public Welfare, Charities, Correction.—State welfare aid (totals estimated on the basis of 11 months ending Nov. 30) reached an average of 119,410 cases with an approximate expenditure of $46,460,000, a drop of 106,950 cases, and of approximately $18,000,000 from the 1942 figures. Types of assistance were: old age, $29,157,000; aid to dependent children, $6,826,000; general relief, $5,700,000; aid to the blind, $341,000; child guardianship, $2,065,000; unemployment compensation, $2,370,-196.

The five state correctional institutions in 1943 included a state prison, a state prison colony, a reformatory for men, a reformatory for women, and a state farm including accommodations for the criminally insane.

Communications.—Total mileage of highways in 1942 was 23,516 of which 17,439 mi. were rural. State highway expenditures in 1942 were $10,903,000, of which $8,517,000 was for construction, maintenance and administration. Railroad mileage in operation in 1942 was 4,234, a figure which included sidetrack and privately owned industrial track. There were 1,072,197 telephones in use in Sept. 1943.

Banking and Finance.—Of the 902 state banking institutions in 1943, 191 were savings banks, 181 co-operative banks, 68 trust companies and 462 credit unions. In addition, there were 124 national banks operating in the state. Total banking deposits were $6,649,920,000 and total banking assets $8,503,508,000. The 26 federal savings and loan associations had resources of $144,718,-508, on Dec. 31, 1943.

State government receipts for the year ending Nov. 30, 1942, were $132,624,093; and expenditures for the same period were $125,411,797. The state debt on Nov. 30, 1943, was $6,959,300 (gross direct), $5,663,861 (net direct).

Agriculture.—Gross income of agricultural production in 1942 was $118,929,000, of which $42,940,000 was from crops, $75,-179,000 from livestock and $810,000 from government payments. Cash income from crops in 1942 was $38,772,000 and from livestock $71,107,000. Fish landed in Boston in 1943 totalled 143,-

Table I.—Principal Agricultural Products of Massachusetts, 1943 and 1942

Crop	1943 (est.)	1942
Tobacco, lb.	8,185,000	9,024,000
Cranberries, bbl.	485,000	560,000
Apples, commercial, bu.	2,228,000	3,400,000
Potatoes, bu.	3,375,000	2,945,000
Asparagus, crates	149,000	158,000
Onions, bags	258,000	338,000
Hay, all, tons	568,000	582,000
Corn, grain, bu.	336,000	308,000
Corn, silage, tons	308,000	308,000

450,493 lb. and were valued at $12,656,150.

Mineral Production.—The production of principal minerals in 1942, in short tons, was: coke and by-products, 1,176,400; lime, 37,537; stone, 1,800,600; sand and gravel used, 5,179,419.

(L. Sl.)

Massachusetts Institute of Technology.

During 1943, the institute carried on war research and development work under 162 contracts, of which approximately one-third were with industrial firms and two-thirds with government agencies.

The institute's financial operations during its fiscal year 1942–43 involved an expenditure of about $23,000,000, as compared with prewar annual expenditures of about $4,000,000. The war activities of the institute had required the addition to its educational and research plant of 450,000 sq.ft. of floor space by new construction and 260,000 sq.ft. by rental.

To meet conditions created by the war and to co-ordinate with the army and navy college training programs, the institute in June 1943 adopted a new academic program for all civilian students consisting annually of three consecutive terms of approximately 16 weeks each. In accordance with this program a new civilian freshman class was admitted in June. Without any relaxation of admission standards, this new freshman class totalled 580, only 20 less than the normal quota of 600 for entering classes. For statistics of enrolment, endowment, faculty members, etc., see UNIVERSITIES AND COLLEGES. (K. T. C.)

Material Coordinating Committee (U.S. and Canada): see CANADIAN-U.S. WAR COMMITTEES.

Mathematics.

There are normally two reliable criteria for the degree of mathematical activity in the United States: the number of papers presented at meetings of the American Mathematical society, and the quantity of research published in the various journals. A lack of papers presented in 1943 was not immediately reflected in the amount of publication due to a backlog of papers on hand, but a definite drop in publication appeared to be imminent.

In spite of this rather gloomy prediction it is gratifying to be able to observe that the American Mathematical society and the Mathematical Association of America were united in a policy which called for a continuation of their meetings. This policy was also that of the English societies.

Moreover, this prediction was no indication of a genuine lack of mathematical activity in these abnormal times, for there was a tremendous amount of war work being done by mathematicians. All such research was to remain unpublished for the duration.

Mathematical activities for 1943 will be summarized in two parts: addresses and publications.

The speaking event of the year was the Colloquium lectures sponsored by the society. This year the lectures were delivered by Professor E. J. McShane on "Existence Theorems in the Calculus of Variations." His book was awaited with interest. At the annual meeting of the society the retiring presidential address, "New Settings for Topology in Analysis," was delivered by Professor Marston Morse. It is almost impossible to speak of significant lectures abroad except to mention that Professor M. H. Stone, president of the American Mathematical society, lectured extensively throughout South America.

Publications are more difficult to enumerate, but along with other results which attracted attention are the following. It was shown that the theory of group extensions is a powerful tool in the study of homologies in infinite complexes and topological spaces (Samuel Eilenberg and Saunders MacLane). Results were announced and published along the lines of H. Hopf's classical discovery on relations between the fundamental group and the second Betti group (Samuel Eilenberg, Saunders MacLane and R. H. Fox). Progress was made on the Kline problem—a characterization of the sphere (D. W. Hall). Important work was done on the theory of surfaces of zero area (T. Radó). A new development in surface theory was the definition of an essential area (P. V. Reichelderfer). Kolmogoroff's celebrated law for the iterated logarithm was generalized (W. Feller). The fundamental theorem on the density of sums of sets of positive integers was proved after having remained an unsolved problem for the past decade (H. B. Mann, simplifications by E. Artin and P. Scherk). A detailed proof of results on the Artin-Riemann hypothesis was expected to appear soon (André Weil). It was shown that all sufficiently large integers can be represented as the sum of seven cubes (U. V. Linnik). Results on trigonometric sums were sharpened (I. M. Vinogradow).

Several prizes were awarded. Professor Jesse Douglas won the Bôcher prize for his research in analysis. The Sylvester medal was presented to Professor J. E. Littlewood for his discoveries in the analytic theory of numbers.

An important new journal, *Quarterly of Applied Mathematics*, appeared under the sponsorship of Brown university.

A partial list of new books follows. *The Problem of Moments*, J. A. Shohat and J. D. Tamarkin. *The Theory of Rings*, N. Jacobson. *Vectors and Matrices*, C. C. MacDuffee. *Introduction to Non-Linear Mechanics*, N. Kryloff and N. Bogoliuboff. *Meromorphic Functions and Analytic Curves*, Hermann Weyl. *Eratosthenian Averages*, A. Wintner. Several important volumes were reprinted in the public interest by authority of the Alien Property custodian.

BIBLIOGRAPHY.—*The American Mathematical Monthly*, vol. 50; *Bulletin of the American Mathematical Society*, vol. 49; *The Journal of the London Mathematical Society*, vol. 17; *Mathematical Reviews*, vol. 4; *Science*, vol. 98.
(J. W. T. Y.)

Maurice and Laura Falk Foundation, The: see FALK FOUNDATION, THE MAURICE AND LAURA.
Mauritania: see FRENCH COLONIAL EMPIRE.
Mauritius: see BRITISH EAST AFRIC

Meat.

The total output of all meats in the United States in 1943 (not including poultry) was estimated to be 24,000,000,000 lb., 13% above 1942 and 50% above the average of 1935–39, which was 16,182,000,000 lb. Of this total for 1943 about 15,815,000,000 lb. was consumed by civilians and 6,330,000,000 lb. by noncivilians, with the remainder going into reserve and carryover into 1944. Military and lend-lease requirements amounted to about 25% of the total production. The amount available for civilians was about 128 lb. per capita on the average, which was almost 6 lb. less than the average for 1942.

The large pig crop of 1943 with heavy fall marketing provided a total pork production of 13,082,000,000 lb., the largest on record, and after about one-third of the total went to noncivilian uses left about 64 lb. per capita, or 5 lb. more than in 1942.

Of beef the total production was estimated to be 8,780,000,000 lb. or 325,000,000 lb. more than in 1942, while the production of veal dropped to about 1,000,000,000 lb. This total, less the increased requirements for military and lend-lease uses, left only about 60 lb. per capita for civilians, compared with 68 lb. in 1942 and an average consumption of 63 lb. in the 5-yr. period 1935–39. The goal for 1944 was set at about 11,800,000,000 lb. of beef and veal to meet an expected increase of noncivilian uses.

The total production of lamb and mutton was estimated to be 987,000,000 lb. in 1943, compared with 1,036,000,000 lb. in 1942. Of the total of 987,000,000 lb., about one-third or 268,000,000

TWO THOUSAND BROOKLYN BUTCHERS, unable to obtain meat from wholesale houses, staged a near riot March 25, 1943, before mounted police dispersed them

lb. was required for noncivilian uses. The amount remaining for civilians would provide about 5.2 lb. per capita, compared with an average of 6.7 lb. consumed in 1935–39.

The large cold storage stocks of frozen and cured meats in Dec. 1943 reflected the heavy production of the year. Total stocks of meats on Dec. 1 amounted to 703,775,000 lb., compared with 603,243,000 lb. in 1942 and 499,758,000 lb. as the average of 1932–41. Of this total 183,096,000 lb. was beef, 376,072,000 lb. was pork and 31,074,000 lb. lamb and mutton. Heavy shipments were being made to the army and under lend-lease, so that the normal indications of the stored stocks were obscured. Under reversed lend-lease, Australia and New Zealand shipped the

Livestock Slaughter in Plants under Federal Inspection (January to October), 1943 and 1942

	1943 numbers	1942 numbers
Hogs	48,893,000	42,096,000
Sheep	18,735,000	17,324,000
Cattle	9,237,000	10,347,000
Calves	4,056,000	4,783,000

American forces in the Pacific area a large amount of meat, amounting to 61,484,000 lb. from Australia and 49,650,000 lb. from New Zealand. (*See* also BACON; CATTLE; HOGS; LIVESTOCK; POULTRY; RATIONING; SHEEP.)   (J. C. Ms.)

Mediation Board, National: *see* NATIONAL MEDIATION BOARD.

Medical Association, American: *see* AMERICAN MEDICAL ASSOCIATION.

Medicine.
Penicillin.—Medical attention in 1943 was focused particularly on penicillin. Twenty-two pharmaceutical companies were licensed by the Office of Scientific Research and Development, through its committee on research, and by the War Production board to manufacture and distribute this substance. The limitations on supply made it necessary to restrict the product to the armed forces and to certain experimental studies.

Announcement was made that a technique had been developed for growing penicillin on surgical gauze, so that it could be grown by any laboratory and applied in this way. However, subsequent studies indicated that the necessity for standardiza-

tion and sterilization of products applied to wounds made it impossible to recommend this procedure. For medical uses, penicillin, which is a form of mould, must be grown, dried, standardized, and then used, either as a powder directly on wounds or as a solution by injection into the muscles, the blood, or the spinal fluid.

Penicillin is especially effective in streptococcic, gonococcic and meningococcic infections. Its outstanding use was its application to persistent infections of the bones in osteomyelitis, particularly of the jaw and the head. Cases of gonorrhoea which were resistant to treatment with sulfonamides were successfully treated with penicillin. Announcement was made that penicillin can change a positive Wassermann test in syphilis to negative in a short time. The Wassermann test remained negative in many such cases for several months. The ultimate value would be determined only when postmortem examinations became possible on persons who had been cured of syphilis by this method. Announcement was made that subacute bacterial endocarditis, a condition heretofore considered almost invariably fatal, had been treated successfully with a combined injection of heparin, a drug which dissolves blood clots, and penicillin. (*See* PENICILLIN.)

Anaesthesia.—Especially significant in 1943 were advances in anaesthesia, including particularly spinal anaesthesia and the injection of anaesthetic substances directly into the blood. The navy adopted these techniques in place of inhalation anaesthesia.

Obstetrics.—Continued development of continuous caudal analgesia in childbirth made possible the report of 10,000 cases with a low incidence of failure and a small number of complications. Through the facilities of the United States Public Health service educational courses were established for training physicians and anaesthetists in this technique.

Malaria.—Medical enemy No. 1 in the war was malaria. Research indicated a technique for control, involving the use of quinine, atabrine and plasmochin. American production of atabrine rose from 50,000 tablets per year to more than 2,000,000,000 tablets annually. The United States assumed largely the burden of supplying all of this drug to the United Nations. Investigators continued to search for a new drug capable of preventing malaria, also for a new technique to control the mosquito.

An insect repelling bomb was produced and was in 1943 available to the forces of the United Nations. The insect-repellent agents include freon, used in household refrigeration, and pyrethrum. So great was the demand for this material that the use of the insect repelling bomb was limited to the armed forces until after the war.

Sulfonamides.—New investigations showed that the sulfonamides are efficient in controlling meningitis, bringing the total number of deaths from 17 for each 100 cases to 3 for each 100 cases in various epidemics. Physicians in one large army camp stopped the spread of an epidemic by giving regular doses of sulfathiazole to all of the soldiers who might be exposed to the infection.

Deaths from pneumonia in the army were less than 1%. In civilian life the number of deaths was reduced from 27 out of each 100 cases to 7 out of each 100 infected.

Doctors tested a mixture of sulfadiazine in chewing gum for infections in the throat, but objection was made because of the possibility of sensitizing people to the drug. Sprays containing mixtures of sulfadiazine and a constricting agent were recommended for the treatment of colds. Experts were convinced that the sulfonamide drugs are not especially efficient against the virus of colds. They would, however, prevent the growth of secondary germs, like the streptococcus.

New sulfonamides were developed, including sulfamerazine, which was said to be less toxic than previous forms, and which was recommended particularly for use where there might be complications related to the kidney. Research showed that baking soda or sodium bicarbonate taken previous to the giving of the sulfonamide drugs tends to prevent such kidney complications.

The sulfonamides were found to be especially effective in the treatment of dysenteries and diarrhoeas. The most frequently used sulfa drug for general purposes was sulfadiazine. Other forms undergoing experimentation included sulfasuxidine and sulfapyrazine.

Another derivative of the sulfonamides, called diasone, was advanced for use in tuberculosis, after it was shown that it could successfully control experimental infections with tuberculosis in guinea-pigs. Experiments also continued with another derivative, called promin, advanced for tuberculosis.

The rate for tuberculosis rose all over the rest of the world, and even slightly in some portions of the United States. Particularly important in the attack on tuberculosis was the uniform x-raying of all inductees in the army and navy, with the permanent filing of miniature X-ray photographs with the examination of every man in the armed forces. (*See* TUBERCULOSIS.)

Venereal Diseases.—The venereal disease rates in the army and navy were lower than ever before, but they rose considerably among the civilian population, in some areas in association with a rise in juvenile delinquency. By a combination of heat treatment and the sulfonamide drugs, cases of gonorrhoea were controlled in from two to three days. By the use of the heat cabinet and mapharsen, a derivative of arsenic, cases of syphilis were reported cured, in many instances, in periods varying from a few days to 21 days, according to the system of treatment adopted.

Experiments in the intensive treatment of syphilis by these techniques, by mapharsen alone, by penicillin alone, were being conducted in intensive treatment centres set up by the United States Public Health service. Special attention was given to selection of cases to be given such treatments, since they were known to carry a considerable hazard. (*See* VENEREAL DISEASES.)

Neuropsychiatry.—The most frequent cause of discharge and rejection from the armed forces was neuropsychiatric disturbance, representing as high as 45% of all cases of disability. Special divisions of the medical department of the army and navy and the air forces were established to study and control this situation.

The Selective Service system developed a special technique, involving educational, psychologic and occupational study of selectees by trained social workers with a view to eliminating admission to the army and navy of men not qualified from a mental point of view. Several tests were developed for psychologic study, including one called the Minnesota Multiphasic Personality Inventory, which was found useful in industry for determining persons likely to have nervous breakdowns or accidents.

Continued experiments with shock treatment for various forms of mental derangement or mental depression indicated the chief usefulness of such methods was in depression psychosis. Electric shock seemed to be preferable to either insulin or metrazol shock. The methods have not lived up to what seemed to be their early promise.

Experiments continued with the operation on the frontal lobe of the brain—lobotomy—as a means of treating mental disease, particularly cases of anxiety or emotional upsets. The electro-encephalograph or brain wave machine was applied to the study of epileptics, most of whom had abnormal electroencephalograms. More than 50% of the members of the immediate families of epileptics are likely to have abnormal tracings with this brain wave machine.

Among the pilots and air force personnel a condition called aeroneurosis was described, characterized by gastric disturbance, nervous irritability, insomnia and minor psychiatric disturbances. (*See* PSYCHIATRY.)

Vitamins.—Continued studies of the vitamins showed the one

PATIENT WITH A BROKEN LEG demonstrating his ability to walk shortly after the bone has been set and immobilized by a Stader splint. A pair of pins is drilled into the bone above and below the fracture, and the leg is set by means of mechanical adjustments. When the adjustments are complete (tightening all screws, turnbuckle, etc.) the reduction device automatically becomes a splint

most lacking in American diets was thiamine, called vitamin B_1 of the vitamin B complex. This vitamin is developed in the bowel of most persons by the action of intestinal bacteria. Some people are not able to develop enough thiamine to meet the body's needs. Drugs, like the sulfonamides, will destroy the intestinal germs which create this vitamin from food. Not all mothers provide the same amount of thiamine in their milk. The giving of thiamine to a mother by injection or increase of the vitamin in her diet will cause a rapid increase in the amount of thiamine in the mother's milk.

Experiments made in 1942 resulted in the claim that large doses of vitamin A would cause a lowering of blood pressure. In 1943, extended studies, including tests on human beings, proved that large doses of vitamin A cannot be depended on to lower blood pressure.

Many studies were made to show the vitamin content of most commonly used foods and the circumstances under which the vitamins are lost from food. (*See* VITAMINS.)

Surgery.—In surgery, attention was focused, because of the war, on the treatment of infected wounds and on shock. The exceedingly low mortality rate for the wounded was accredited to several factors—mechanization of the medical department, making medical corps service available practically in the front lines. When a man was wounded he received immediately the necessary blood plasma to overcome shock and loss of blood. He might inject himself with a narcotic drug, using a new device which permitted any wounded soldier to inject material, like a sterile solution of morphine, immediately. Rapid transportation by motorized vehicle or aeroplane took the wounded soldier promptly to a hospital far in the rear.

The sulfonamide drugs were given by mouth and in some instances applied directly to the wounds to lower the rate of serious infection. The mortality among the wounded in World War II was less than 3% and in many engagements less than 1%, contrasted with a death rate as high as 7% to 9% in previous wars.

The studies made on shock indicated that the administration of plasma was the important lifesaving measure. Scientists reversed their views on the treatment of shock by stopping the use of heat in shock and resorting to the use of a simple blanket to prevent chill. Research indicated that damaged tissues of the body are invaded by anaerobic germs and that the poisonous products of these germs may be the shock-producing substance.

Discoveries.—Vitallium, a new alloy, was used in medicine to bridge gaps in the bile ducts in operations on the gall bladder. Tantalum, a noncorrosive, malleable, nonabsorbable metal, was used to cover defects in the skull resulting from injury. Nerves were repaired by taking a section of nerve from a corpse and using it as a splint between broken ends of the nerves. Gum acacia or clotted blood was used to hold the splint in place. British and American war surgeons agreed that tourniquets do more harm than good in first-aid work.

Erysipelas was found quite controllable by the sulfonamide drugs and penicillin. A drug called thio-urea, which has the effect of lowering the basal metabolic rate and reducing the nervous irritability in excessive action of the thyroid gland, diminished the number of cases of hyperthyroidism and goiter in which surgery is necessary.

Sprains and strains were treated by anaesthesia and continuous use rather than by enforced rest. British surgeons applied electric stimulation which produces contractions and relaxation of muscles in the treatment of sprains and strains. Refrigeration as a means of producing anaesthesia developed considerable use in hospitals as a means of freedom from pain during amputation of limbs, but was not found practical in military surgery.

The army found that for ordinary burns boric acid treatment is best. More serious burns were treated with paraffin applications, plaster-of-Paris casts, and various pliofilm and other coverings.

Nutrition.—The attention of experts in nutrition turned away from vitamins and toward minerals and amino acids as essential substances. It was found that only 8 out of more than 22 amino acids are necessary to maintain the nitrogen required for the health and growth of the human body. The amino acids, in 1943, considered essential for the health of the human being were isoleucine, leucine, lysine, methionine, threonine, valine, phenylalanine and trytophane.

Public Health.—The outstanding epidemic conditions for 1943 were influenza, virus pneumonia, and infantile paralysis which reached a new high level in the United States, meningitis which regularly increases during war periods, and venereal diseases which also increase in wartime.

The birth rate for 1943 was the highest in the history of the United States, increasing to 24 births per 1,000 population. Nineteen forty-three was the fourth year in succession in which the birth rate increased The number of babies born is 200,000 greater than in 1942, and nearly 1,000,000 greater than the low point of 1933. (*See* also ALLERGY; ANAESTHESIA; BACTERIOLOGY; BIOCHEMISTRY; BIRTH CONTROL; CANCER; CHEMISTRY; CHEMOTHERAPY; DIETETICS; DRUGS AND DRUG TRAFFIC; ENDOCRINOLOGY; EPIDEMICS AND PUBLIC HEALTH CONTROL; HOSPITALS; INDUSTRIAL HEALTH; NERVOUS SYSTEM; PHYSIOLOGY; UROLOGY; VETERINARY MEDICINE; X-RAY. Also *see* articles on specific diseases.)

BIBLIOGRAPHY.—Champ Lyons, "Penicillin Therapy of Surgical Infections in the U.S. Army," *J.A.M.A.*, *123*:1007–1018 (1943); E. K. Gubin, "Penicillin, the Wonder Drug," *Hygeia*, 21:642 (1943); R. A. Hingson and Waldo B. Edwards, "Continuous Caudal Analgesia," *J.A.M.A.*, 123:538–546 (1943); Frank L. Gunderson and Ross A. Gortner, Jr., "Several Important Trends in Food and Nutrition," *Special Report by Cereal Inst.* (Nov. 24, 1943); *Fundamentals of Anesthesia*, American Medical Association, 1942; *Statistics—Birth*, Metropolitan Information Service (Dec. 27, 1943); *J.A.M.A.* vols. 121, 122 and 123; *Quarterly Cumulative Index Medicus*, vols. 33 and 34 (1943). (M. FI.)

Military Medicine, U.S.—Numerous military medical advances were realized while others were conceived and were in the developmental stage. An important advance was the creation and use in combat of the small portable hospital which was carried forward near the battle front, by hand if necessary, in order to provide emergency surgical aid soon after soldiers are wounded. This and similar methods which bring medical aid nearer the front lines were factors in bringing about a pronounced reduction in the mortality rates of American fighting men when contrasted to those of World War I.

Another medical achievement more extensively used near the front during 1943, sometimes even in foxholes, was blood plasma for cases of shock and the severely wounded. The blood which the people at the home front generously donated through the facilities of the Red Cross thus became a means of saving many fighting men who, if similarly wounded in World War I, would have died.

The evacuation by air of patients from the front to hospitals in the rear and to the homeland was more extensively used during 1943.

Wounded and sick soldiers greatly benefited also by more extensive use of the sulfa drugs which were taken with them to the front. The sulfonamides prevented many serious systemic infections. They were important in reducing the mortality rate in meningitis from 39% in World War I to a 1943 rate of about 4%, and in reducing the pneumonia mortality rate from 25% to 4%. They radically improved the management in the army of the gonorrhoea problem and greatly reduced the complications of streptococcal infections, scarlet fever and measles.

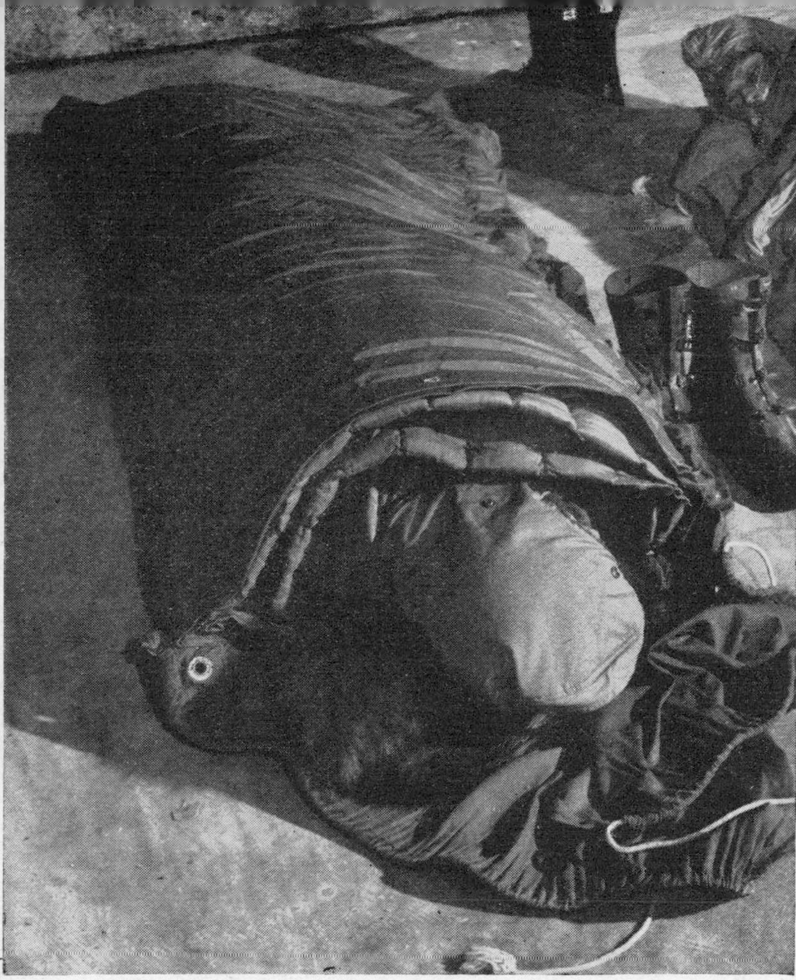

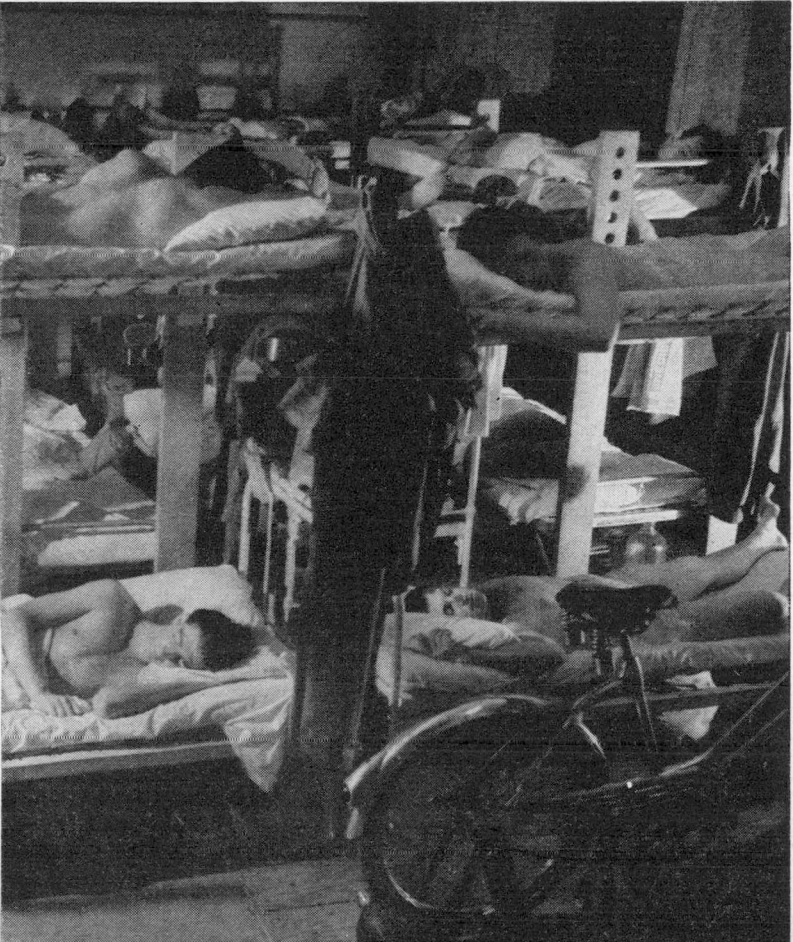

TO STUDY THE EFFECTS OF EXTREME COLD on U.S. soldiers, men at Armored Medical Research laboratory, Fort Knox, Ky. are placed in a cold room with temperature of —30° F. Here they are bundled in sleeping bags

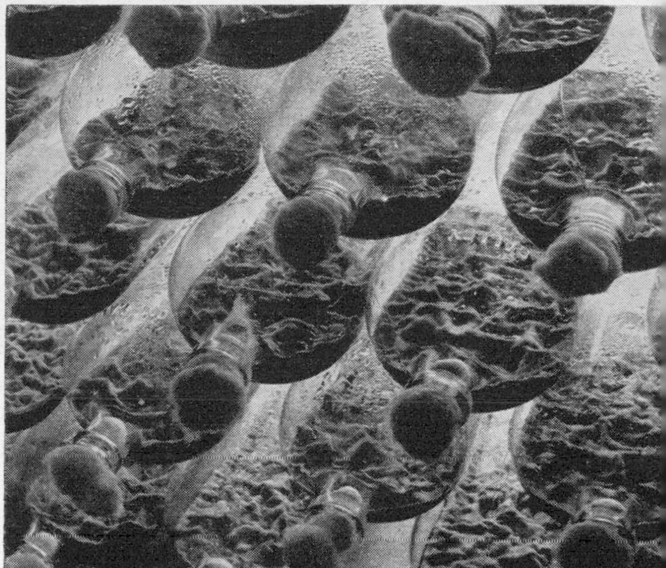

"HOT ROOM" in which the U.S. Armored Medical Research laboratory observes the effects of extreme heat on soldiers

PENICILLIN MOULD CULTURES growing in bottles placed in incubators. Penicillin, a powerful antibacterial compound, was produced and used in increasing quantities during 1943, mostly for the U.S. armed forces

A RECORD PARACHUTE JUMP of 40,200 ft. was made by Lieut. Col. William Randolph Lovelace II, U.S. army flight surgeon, June 24, 1943, near Ephrata, Wash. Col. Lovelace, here shown breathing oxygen as he dressed in warm clothing before taking off, made the jump to demonstrate the safety of bailing out with proper equipment at stratospheric levels

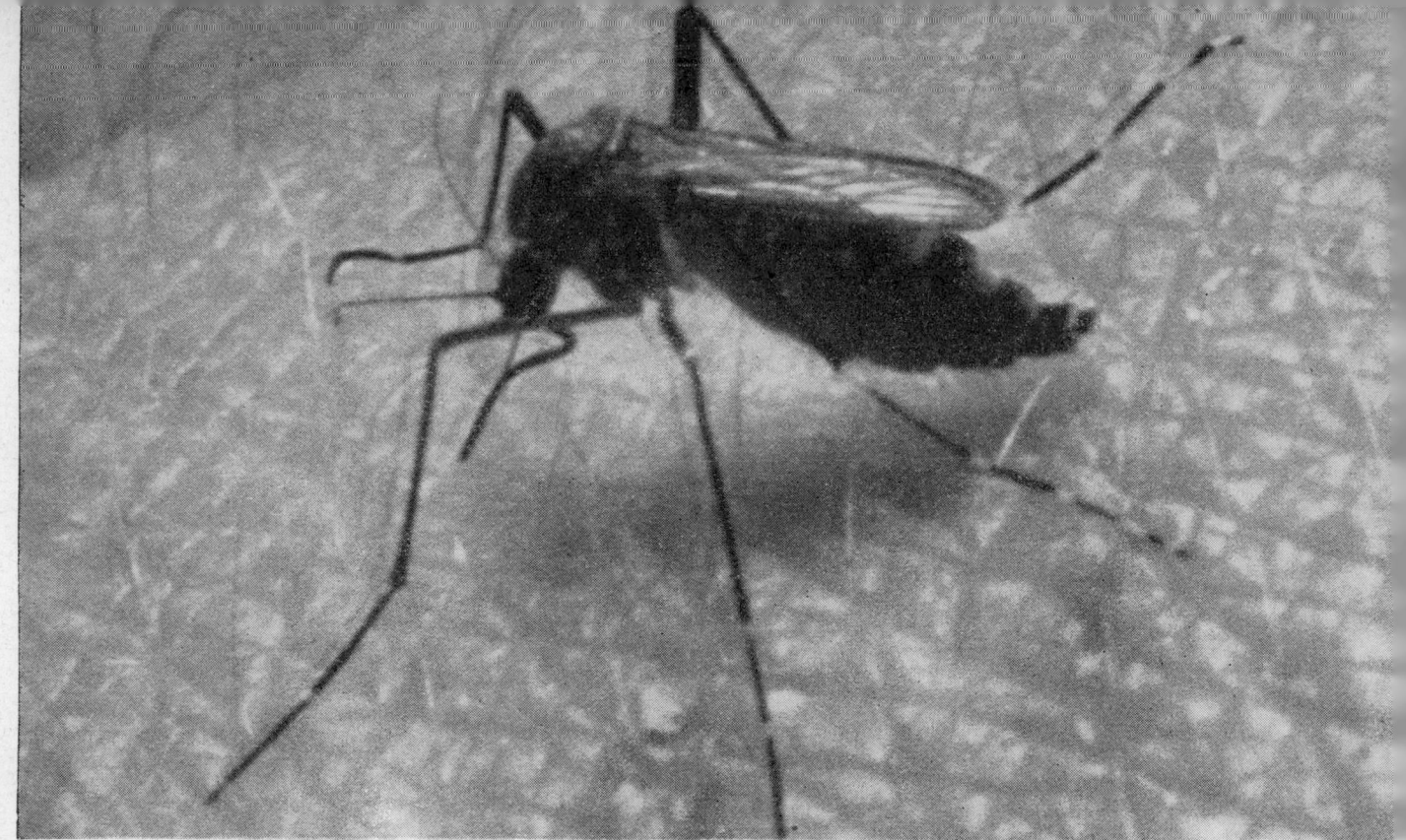

AËDES AEGYPTI, carrier of yellow fever and dengue, photographed on the arm of a medical researcher (linear magnification, 20 times). Increased and speedy traffic with countries where these diseases are endemic intensified control methods in the United States in 1943

Penicillin, an extract of cultures of a common mould (*Penicillium notatum*) was a new therapeutic agent which has potent bactericidal properties. Amazing results in the treatment by penicillin of certain infections were obtained. Further purification of the extract by the manufacturers together with additional extensive clinical studies of its effects offers great promise. The surgeon general of the army during 1943 sponsored clinical studies of penicillin therapy in surgical infections in a number of army hospitals, with the co-operation of the committee of medical research of the office of scientific research and development. The report of the treatment of septic gunshot fractures with penicillin indicated that dramatically successful results might be achieved by the meticulous surgeon who combined penicillin, effective blood transfusions and conservative surgical procedures into a program of thoughtful management of individual cases. Well-planned clinical and laboratory investigation also revealed that a major deficiency of red blood cells and haemoglobin occurred in such cases. The regeneration of red cells and haemoglobin depends on control of the infection. Penicillin was found to be "dramatically" effective in rapidly establishing this phase of convalescence. Penicillin permitted a direct surgical approach to the management of septic gunshot fractures. Its role in this regard, however, was analogous to the use of vitamin K in patients with obstructive jaundice. Such a concept, the report stated, emphasized the limitations of penicillin therapy and designated the supplemental position of penicillin in the over-all surgical program.

Typhus fever wrought havoc in armies and civilian populations in the past. It was prevalent in Russia and central Europe during World War I. While no proven cases appeared in the American Expeditionary Forces in World War I, many troops in World War II served in typhus-infected areas. Louse-borne typhus steadily increased among the native populations of North Africa, the near and middle east, and elsewhere. Had the American army not foreseen the possibility of outbreaks of typhus and taken precautionary measures, epidemics might have occurred among U.S. troops. The surgeon general's office constantly watched the typhus situation long before American troops invaded Africa, and as that event approached, the need for definite typhus control measures became clear. The president therefore, by executive order, on Dec. 24, 1942, established the United States of America Typhus commission, the forward echelon of which was in Cairo. During 1943 the Typhus commission collected many strains of typhus virus. U.S. troops serving in or preparing to go into typhus-infected areas were vaccinated against typhus. There was developed at the Army Medical school a means whereby the prevailing types of typhus in a region could be determined. By this means—the complement fixation test—epidemic typhus was discovered in a South American country and surveys were being made in other countries. Previously it had not been possible to differentiate by this method between epidemic and endemic typhus antisera. Serologic evidence was obtained to substantiate the theory advanced by Zinsser that Brill's disease represented a recrudescence of an old attack of typhus fever. The implications were that mild cases of epidemic typhus actually existed in the United States and that one attack of typhus did not confer lifelong immunity, as had been generally believed. The observations on Brill's disease, Plotz said, strongly suggested that man serves as the reservoir for epidemic typhus between outbreaks, as the rat does in endemic typhus. The surgeon general's office had developed an agent which would completely delouse clothes in 30 minutes using very simple equipment in comparison to the cumbersome and time-consuming method used in World War I. In addition, a powder was developed which when sprinkled once in the seams of clothing would keep insects away for at least two weeks. Thus the typhus prevention program was far advanced during 1943.

American troops in Africa up to the close of 1943 had been practically free of typhus fever.

The National Research council sponsored extensive studies in various clinics on the treatment of burns. Progress on this important subject was expected to develop; it was agreed that the prevention and treatment of shock in every severe burn was the first indication and should precede any definitive treatment. The most important early general complication was loss of plasma volume as a result of plasma leakage into the interstitial spaces. This, it was found, could be largely prevented by firm pressure bandaging and controlled by plasma transfusion. In all, about 80 methods of burn therapy were published up to 1944 and there was some disagreement regarding the best therapy; however, the pressure method was rapidly gaining in popularity. The studies under way by the several burn projects and the National Research council, no doubt when assembled and analyzed, would give valuable therapeutic, pathologic and bacteriologic data on this controversial subject.

Among important advances in surgical technique in the treatment of wounds of the colon, apart from the transverse colon, was the exteriorization at the time of the primary operation of the damaged loop of colon through a small lateral incision in the iliac fossa or the hypochondriac regions. The exploratory central incision was then closed quickly. The colonic loop having been pulled out through the small lateral incision was at that time not subjected to further surgery but allowed to serve as a colostomy. This made safer and simpler the primary operation on soldiers with wounds of the large bowel and reduced the danger of sepsis.

The surgeon general's office was very much interested in research, a fact further evidenced by the rapid expansion of the Virus laboratory at Walter Reed hospital, studies of the medical aspects of tank warfare at the Armored Forces Medical laboratory at Ft. Knox, studies at the Medical Equipment laboratory at the Field Service school at Carlisle barracks, and research at the Army Industrial Hygiene laboratory at Johns Hopkins university, which, among other things, investigated the equipment and materials used by the army with reference to toxicologic considerations and, at the same time, offered its services to all army installations for the chemical analysis of materials with reference to the presence of toxic substances; numerous improvements in medical equipment and supplies were made, including the first overseas type of hospital train to be built in the United States and specially designed for use in combat areas. Trains of this type were for the removal of sick and wounded from the evacuation hospitals, which were usually within 25–50 miles of the front lines, to the larger general hospitals perhaps hundreds of miles in the rear. (*See* also NURSING, WAR.)

BIBLIOGRAPHY.—George A. Marks, "Portable Surgical Hospital at Buna," *Bulletin of the U.S. Army Medical Department* no. 71, pp. 43–55 (Dec. 1943); Champ Lyons, "Penicillin Therapy of Surgical Infections," *J.A.M.A.* 123:1007–1018 (1943); James S. Simmons, "The Present State of the Army's Health," *J.A.M.A.*, 122:916–923 (1943); Stanhope Bayne-Jones, "United States of America Typhus Commission," *Army Medical Bulletin*, no. 66, p. 4 (July, 1943); Harry Plotz, "Complement Fixation in Rickettsial Diseases," *Science*, vol. 97, pp. 20–21 (1943); Alan O. Whipple, "Basic Principles in Treatment of Thermal Burns," *Annals of Surgery*, 118:187–192 (1943); "Colostomy," *Bulletin of the U.S. Army Medical Department* (in type); James S. Simmons, "The Preventive Medicine Program of the United States Army," *American Journal of Public Health*, vol. 33, pp. 731–940 (August 1943); "Expression of Gratitude," *Bulletin of the U.S. Army Medical Department*, no. 71, p. 15 (Dec. 1943).
(J. F. H.)

Mediterranean, British Possessions in the.

These comprise Gibraltar, the Maltese islands and Cyprus, of which the accompanying table gives certain statistics. (*See* also BRITISH EMPIRE.)

History.—*Gibraltar.*—Conditions in 1943 were naturally improved as a result of the Allied victories in the Mediterranean theatre. In Gibraltar it was announced on March 8 that men under 55 fit for sedentary work and men under 50 fit for other work essential to the colony's economy, who had been evacuated in 1940, might apply to return. A scheme was also begun in July for Gibraltar civilian workers to spend 6 weeks' leave with their families evacuated to England; about 1,300 out of a total of nearly 3,000 with evacuated families were affected, the other families being in Jamaica or Madeira.

There was some trouble from sabotage during the summer, and two Spanish dockyard workers were sentenced to death, the one for causing an oil fire in the dockyard, and the other for attempting to cause a dockyard explosion.

Malta.—The North African victories raised the siege of Malta and, in the words of the governor, turned the island from a "beleaguered and battered fortress" into a "vengeful citadel." Enemy air raids were few and caused little damage. From Sept. 1939 to June 1943 civilian air raid casualties totalled 1,436 killed and 3,415 injured, with 6,952 buildings destroyed or damaged.

On July 7 the colonial secretary announced in parliament the British government's intention immediately after the war to restore responsible government in internal affairs to the Maltese people, and Col. Strickland, the leader of the elected majority in the Maltese council of government, urged that the preliminary work should be begun at once. Other tributes to Malta's heroic defense included the granting of a Rhodes scholarship every year instead of once every three years and of a British council architectural scholarship. Educational development continued during the year; the British institute did good work, and an institute was also opened on the island of Gozo.

Supplies became much more plentiful on the island, and from Oct. 28 for the first time since the siege began restaurants and snack bars were allowed to serve light meals. Fruit, wines and esparto grass, badly needed by the fishermen, were also being sent. The rising cost of living caused some labour trouble, however, and during September some 20,000 dockyard and other workers struck work in a demand for an adjustment of war bonuses. At the beginning of October they agreed to return to work and not to strike for the duration of the war, provided adequate conciliation and arbitration machinery were set up and the living conditions of civil and defense employees were levelled up.

Cyprus.—Like Malta, Cyprus became a formidable base for attack, and large forces gathered there from all parts of the empire brought the island a temporary wartime prosperity. The rising cost of living caused some labour troubles, and there were strikes in January and August. Measures were undertaken to tax the

British Possessions in the Mediterranean

Territory and Area in sq. mi.	Population	Principal Products 1939 (in metric tons)	Imports and Exports (in thousand £)	Road, Rail and Shipping	Revenue and Expenditure (in thousand £)	Education, Elementary and Secondary 1938
GIBRALTAR, 1⅞ .	(1938) 20,139	..	free port; no statistics kept	(1938) shpg. cleared, 13,748,978 tons net	(1939) rev. 204 exp. 275	elem. schools 13; scholars 2,714; sec. schools 4; scholars 450
MALTA, 122 . . .	(1939) 270,000	potatoes, 31,500 wheat, 7,600 barley, 4,500	(1938) imp. 3,866 exp. 219 re-exp. 468	(1939) rds. Malta 267 mi. Gozo 68 mi.	(est. 1939–40) rev. 1,524 exp. 1,517	elem. schools 82; scholars 29,118; sec. schools 3; scholars 1,244
CYPRUS, 3,572 . .	(1940) 382,000	wines, 158,000 hectolitres; pyrites (1938), 776,000; barley, 49,200; wheat, 68,300; potatoes, 31,300	(1941) imp. 2,515 exp. 977 re-exp. 98	(1939) rds. 864 mi. rlys. 71 mi.	(1940) rev. 951 exp. 1,146	elem. schools: Christian 492; Muslim 212; scholars: Christian 37,-646; Muslim 7,493; sec. schools 34; scholars 4,463

higher incomes, to subsidize essential goods and to raise the lower wages, and afforestation and irrigation schemes were under way for agricultural improvement; the 1943 harvest promised to be the best for 10 years.

In March the first municipal elections in 13 years were held, with an adult poll of over 90%, and the colonial secretary announced in parliament on March 31 that everything was being done to encourage democratic institutions and self-government. This question raised difficulties, however, since the Greek population demanded union with Greece, while the Muslim minority reaffirmed its desire to remain under British rule.

The budget deficiency of £250,000 was covered by a grant from the British government, with further grants for subsidies to reduce living costs. Sir E. Jackson, lieut.-governor of Malta, was appointed chief justice of Cyprus on Feb. 21.　　(C. M. Cl.)

Mei Lan-fang (1893–1943), Chinese actor, noted for his performances in female roles, was one of China's biggest box office attractions. Both his grandfather, court idol of the middle 19th century and outstanding impersonator of female roles, and his father, were celebrated actors. Mei Lan-fang made his professional debut at the age of 13, soon won the title of "king of actors" among Chinese audiences and was acknowledged the peer of even the greatest Chinese actresses. In 1930, he took his company of 22 actors on a tour of the United States and was received at the White House by President Hoover. An unconfirmed report of his death from poisoning in Shanghai, Aug. 8, was picked up in Chungking from a Japanese radio broadcast.

Mello Franco, Afranio De (1870–1943), Brazilian statesman, was born Feb. 25 in Paracatu, in the state of Minas Gerais, Brazil. He studied law at the University of São Paulo and later taught philosophy and international law. He was Brazil's representative at the League of Nations, 1923–26, and was twice president of the league council. In 1926, he announced Brazil's withdrawal from the league because the nation had been refused a permanent seat on the council. He served as judge of the Permanent Court of International Justice, The Hague, 1923–29. He became foreign minister in the Vargas government when the latter seized power in 1930 but resigned three years later. A recognized authority on international law, he was named chairman of the American Neutrality commission meeting at Rio de Janeiro. Later, when the United States became involved in World War II, and this commission was transformed into the Inter-American Juridical committee, he continued as president. The committee was created for the purpose of co-ordinating American legislation and policy on international problems brought about by the war. He died in Rio de Janeiro, Jan. 1.

Meloney, Marie Mattingly (Mrs. William Brown Meloney) (1883?–1943), U.S. editor, was born in Bardstown, Ky., the daughter of the former Sarah Irwin, founder and editor of the *Kentucky Magazine*. After her career as a concert pianist was cut short by an accident, she turned to writing and journalism. Before her marriage to the late William Brown Meloney, an editor of the *New York Sun,* in 1904, she wrote a column for that newspaper called "Men About Town." She began her 16-year association with the *New York Herald Tribune* in 1926, became executive director of the *Herald Tribune* Home institute and organized the annual *New York Herald Tribune* Forum on Current Problems, of which she was chairman. She also became editor of the *Herald Tribune's* Sunday magazine in 1926, con-

tinued at that post when the publication became known as *This Week* and brought its weekly circulation up to 6,000,000. She resigned in June 1942 and was named its editorial director. Mrs. Meloney died at her home in Pawling, N.Y., June 23.

Merchant Marine: *see* Shipping, Merchant Marine.

Mercury. Although mercury was classed as a strategic metal when this group was organized, and was expected to make trouble through shortness of supply in emergency, the industry made a much better record than had been thought possible. Production in the United States was rapidly built up to a point where it met the demand, and instead of the country being dependent on imports for a large share of the consumption, probably more metal was exported than imported. At the same time stocks were accumulated to such a point that during 1944 both production and imports were expected to be reduced by 30%. The metal during the latter part of 1943 was listed as one with a surplus of supply over essential demands, and some of the controls on uses were to be relaxed.

A small output was developed in Canada as a war measure, from deposits in British Columbia, and was so successful that it supplied the domestic demand, with some for export. Some of this surplus was shipped to the United States under contract with the Metals Reserve company, but the contract was cancelled in October, when stocks had reached the desired level.

No definite figures were reported on Spanish output, but it was said to have exceeded the 85,500 flasks produced in 1941. After the shift of Italy from the axis to the United Nations, there was interest manifested in the effect that this would have on the production and disposal of the mercury output, when the producing areas were cleared of German occupation.　　(G. A. Ro.)

Metallurgy. In the 1943 developments along metallurgical lines the chief emphasis was on the saving of time, labour and metals, rather than on the usual commercial angles of costs and profits; the latter would follow automatically when the new methods and processes created under war demand would be applied to peacetime operations.

Corrosion Prevention.—An improved process electroplates silver on magnesium as a protection against atmospheric corrosion.

High-Temperature Alloys.—The temperature at which steam can be used was raised to 1800° F. by the development of new alloys.

Inspection Methods.—A mass production method was developed for the X-ray inspection of aeroplane castings which produces a photographic record of six castings every 30 seconds, or at the rate of 17,000 per day.

Metal Shaping.—Methods were devised for precision forging of automotive gears, saving the time formerly required for machining. Machining operations, in general, were speeded up, with special attention given to the construction of combination machines which could perform a whole series of operations, applying the principles of the automatic screw machine to a highly complicated succession of different operations, such as the conversion of a rough casting into a finished aeroplane engine cylinder. Precision casting methods were developed which will give an accuracy of 0.001 inch on small parts, resulting in savings of metal, time, tooling costs, machining time and man-hours.

New Applications.—The familiar bimetallic disc used for several years as a control in electrical heating devices was adapted for fire protection devices in war planes.

Welding.—New methods and applications for welding were being developed. One of these was the "stitching" of stainless steel sheets by special resistance welding machines.

Copper.—A copper-clad steel wire, developed for use in high-frequency communication lines, was found to be as efficient as solid copper.

Lead.—A novel method of making moulds for the shaping of thermo-setting plastic consisted of dipping the pattern in a bath of melted lead, forming a thin coating of lead on the surface of the pattern, which is then withdrawn, or by die casting if the pattern is complicated. After using for forming the plastic, the mould is stripped off and remelted for use again.

Lead powder mixed with a high viscosity grease was satisfactorily used as a lubricant for heavy gears.

Steel.—Large quantities of copper and zinc were saved by the development of a steel cartridge case for ammunition. After the original development in the United States, the steel case was adopted by Great Britain also.

Possibly the greatest single step in the saving of strategic steel-alloying metals was accomplished by the development of an extensive series of so-called "NE" (national emergency) steels. These are low-alloy steels designed to take the place of the standard types of alloy steels with higher alloy content. These steels were so successful that they would account for about one-third of the 1943 output of alloy steels in the United States.

Substitutes.—Plastic printing plates were developed to take the place of aluminum and zinc needed for other uses. Electrolytic iron can be used as a substitute for copper or nickel in electrotype plates and in the surface hardening of stereotype plates.

Substitution of steel for copper, brass and aluminum would, when fully adopted, effect savings in excess of 300,000 short tons of copper, 200,000 tons of zinc and 50,000 tons of aluminum.

Lead-base die castings were being extensively substituted for brass, aluminum and zinc-base castings. It appeared that lead-base bearing metals might also be used to replace similar alloys containing tin.

Tin.—Rapid and continuous methods of electroplating tin on sheet strips for can manufacture were saving from one-half to three-quarters of the tin required by the old hot-dip process.

(G. A. Ro.)

Metal Prices and Production: *see* MINERAL AND METAL PRODUCTION AND PRICES.

Meteorology.
With some modifications dictated by experience, the applications of organized meteorology to military needs progressed during 1943 on essentially the same basis as in 1942. Within the United States the civilian weather bureau continued to operate the basic service for synoptic observations and forecasts, while the military services, with their own personnel and facilities, applied these basic values to such military purposes as aviation training, manoeuvres, handling of supplies, the conduct of coastal air and maritime patrol, destruction of enemy submarines, transoceanic air transport, and convoying operations in the Atlantic and Pacific. For the staffing of military meteorological units abroad, the army and navy continued intensive training of meteorological cadets and officers; and active meteorological services were put in operation as rapidly as the U.S. military control of foreign areas progressed. The value and importance of these services as guides to tactical operations—aerial, maritime and land-surface alike—were abundantly demonstrated in active practice.

In a joint project of the army, navy and weather bureau, work was completed during December on a 40-year series of daily sea-

AIR FORCE CADETS sending up a radiosonde balloon at the meteorology department of New York university

435

Table I.—Monthly and Annual Mean Temperature and Extremes in °F., 1943, in Cities of the United States

Cities	Jan.	Feb.	Mar.	Apr.	May	June	July	Aug.	Sept.	Oct.	Nov.	Dec.	Year	An. Dept.*	Highest	Lowest
Albuquerque	38.6	43.6	48.2	60.9	65.8	74.0	79.0	78.4	70.2	56.8	44.3	32.0	57.6	+2.3	100	4
Bismarck	-2.0	15.3	18.6	47.0	51.4	62.2	72.6	69.4	57.4	49.0	29.0	22.7	41.0	+2.0	95	-38
Buffalo	21.2	25.8	30.3	36.9	51.8	65.7	71.6	68.8	60.8	48.4	37.5	26.6	45.4	-1.6	92	-16
Charleston	50.4	50.9	55.5	63.5	73.7	82.4	82.0	81.2	74.8	65.6	56.4	50.4	65.6	-0.4	99	17
Chicago	22.6	27.8	32.2	45.6	56.6	72.2	75.7	75.0	61.6	53.7	36.2	27.6	48.9	+0.5	97	-13
Del Rio	51.8	60.2	62.0	74.4	78.6	83.0	86.8	88.7	77.6	68.6	58.6	50.0	70.0	+0.4	105	20
Helena	6.4	21.6	21.0	47.3	49.0	56.2	67.6	66.4	57.6	47.4	32.8	23.2	41.4	-1.1	96	-33
Houston	52.5	59.8	59.2	70.8	77.2	82.6	83.2	84.0	76.3	70.0	59.2	53.7	69.0	-0.1	99	17
Knoxville	42.4	42.1	46.2	57.0	69.8	79.9	79.0	79.0	67.9	56.8	46.8	39.8	58.8	+1.4	101	9
Los Angeles	57.6	60.1	58.8	61.4	65.5	66.4	70.7	71.3	70.6	65.3	65.0	56.8	64.2	+1.8	103	39
Memphis	41.6	46.4	46.8	62.0	73.0	81.6	83.8	84.0	70.5	60.8	48.8	40.7	61.7	+1.1	105	10
Miami	70.0	64.4	70.1	71.6	76.7	79.6	80.4	81.2	80.3	75.2	70.7	67.1	73.9	-0.5	90	36
Mobile	52.1	54.6	57.8	67.6	77.0	82.5	83.4	83.3	75.7	65.8	56.2	52.4	67.4	+0.1	98	22
New York	30.8	34.1	39.6	45.4	61.3	74.4	75.8	74.5	66.2	55.0	44.8	32.6	52.9	+0.6	96	-8
Norfolk	43.3	44.6	49.0	55.1	70.3	80.0	79.1	78.6	70.8	60.2	51.5	42.8	60.4	+0.9	98	13
North Platte	25.9	36.8	32.8	53.4	55.7	68.8	77.7	77.8	63.0	51.8	38.9	31.2	51.2	+2.9	102	-19
Oklahoma City	37.3	46.6	45.2	64.8	65.8	80.4	85.0	87.2	74.2	61.4	50.2	36.8	61.2	+1.8	106	-2
Portland, Me.	17.6	22.9	29.6	38.4	52.8	64.7	68.6	65.4	57.6	49.1	37.4	27.0	43.7	-1.8	94	-39
Portland, Ore.	35.0	46.3	47.2	55.6	56.6	61.4	67.8	66.7	67.8	56.4	48.6	42.0	54.3	+1.2	92	11
San Francisco	51.9	54.8	55.6	55.6	58.6	57.4	59.0	59.8	63.4	61.2	59.2	53.6	57.5	+1.4	96	39
Sault Ste. Marie	11.3	16.4	16.8	33.5	48.2	58.4	64.8	62.6	53.6	44.2	31.2	18.8	38.3	+0.3	92	-25

* Annual departure.

Table II.—Monthly and Annual Rainfall, in Inches, 1943, in Cities of the United States

Cities	Jan.	Feb.	Mar.	Apr.	May	June	July	Aug.	Sept.	Oct.	Nov.	Dec.	Year	Annual Dept.
Albuquerque	0.25	0.26	0.23	0.06	1.41	1.20	1.19	1.33	0.39	0.22	0.14	0.94	7.62	- 0.44
Bismarck	0.75	0.53	1.31	0.87	2.05	6.44	2.15	2.72	0.23	1.54	0.58	0.33	19.50	+ 3.16
Buffalo	1.98	2.30	2.44	3.72	3.52	2.77	1.73	2.59	3.45	4.01	2.57	0.69	31.77	- 4.23
Charleston	3.49	0.64	5.49	2.69	2.79	2.93	8.61	1.35	2.41	0.05	1.25	4.47	36.17	- 9.05
Chicago	2.12	1.34	2.47	3.37	7.08	1.47	5.14	5.20	0.92	1.49	1.39	0.34	32.33	- 0.54
Del Rio	0.58	0.05	0.57	1.37	4.87	1.28	2.51	0.00	2.47	1.55	1.72	1.58	18.55	- 1.35
Helena	1.09	0.38	0.39	1.45	0.67	2.49	0.18	0.89	0.78	0.51	0.23	0.19	9.25	- 2.30
Houston	3.48	1.04	3.99	0.74	6.27	1.40	13.53	1.32	4.41	1.31	14.10	3.80	55.39	+ 8.34
Knoxville	2.09	4.83	5.17	3.48	2.88	3.55	9.29	1.48	3.51	3.70	2.02	2.33	44.33	- 3.05
Los Angeles	7.98	3.07	4.55	0.50	T	0.01	T	0.00	T	0.18	0.05	6.23	22.57	+ 7.34
Memphis	1.23	0.72	7.45	2.89	6.02	2.02	0.01	0.60	5.56	0.45	3.42	3.72	34.09	-13.63
Miami	4.04	0.94	3.29	2.26	3.32	5.68	5.86	5.31	5.98	3.91	2.38	1.85	44.82	-10.84
Mobile	6.45	2.63	10.34	3.09	4.39	5.26	7.37	4.21	7.17	0.83	4.69	5.04	61.47	- 0.14
New York	3.22	1.67	3.86	2.25	4.71	3.17	3.87	2.95	2.17	9.24	1.97	1.42	40.50	- 2.49
Norfolk	2.80	1.81	4.18	2.77	3.83	4.26	10.27	1.00	6.08	3.90	1.36	2.01	44.27	+ 0.18
North Platte	0.21	0.08	0.50	2.33	2.04	3.45	2.10	1.79	0.21	1.35	0.24	0.04	14.34	- 4.05
Oklahoma City	0.03	0.89	1.45	2.79	9.76	2.07	0.31	0.77	2.87	1.28	0.37	2.92	25.51	- 5.64
Portland, Me.	2.14	2.81	2.43	3.34	6.09	2.42	3.78	3.27	1.64	6.55	5.56	1.00	41.03	- 0.91
Portland, Ore.	6.30	4.04	7.26	2.56	1.65	3.04	0.59	1.19	0.09	6.21	2.20	3.03	38.16	- 3.46
San Francisco	6.15	1.95	3.18	1.88	0.13	0.13	T	0.00	0.02	0.74	0.80	2.69	17.67	- 4.35
Sault Ste. Marie	1.35	1.40	3.22	1.80	3.89	6.51	1.59	2.71	0.86	2.72	3.91	1.54	31.50	+ 1.56

T=Trace: less than 1/100 of an inch.

Table III.—Duration of Sunshine, in Hours, 1943, in the United States

Cities	Jan.	Feb.	Mar.	Apr.	May	June	July	Aug.	Sept.	Oct.	Nov.	Dec.	Year	Annual Dept.
Albuquerque, N.M.	208	264	277	342	342	354	347	336	273	302	264	143	3454	+ 32
Bismarck, N.D.	140	186	237	303	250	290	415	320	287	215	99	142	2884	-226
Buffalo, N.Y.	82	146	236	170	214	385	300	293	270	160	91	61	2408	+150
Charleston, S.C.	191	245	217	320	354	359	294	317	300	280	259	220	3356	+415
Chicago, Ill.	129	215	242	266	230	344	330	288	233	230	133	168	2808	+168
Del Rio, Tex.	194	210	203	249	242	279	343	386	188	226	176	166	2922	+215
Helena, Mont.	143	167	203	191	208	266	376	332	280	161	104	152	2583	- 92
Houston, Tex.	156	176	184	256	273	266	298	301	139	262	191	148	2650	- 58
Knoxville, Tenn.	115	189	194	200	281	273	251	320	264	224	216	116	2643	+ 30
Los Angeles, Calif.	206	231	225	260	298	316	348	344	314	264	258	180	3244	+ 43
Memphis, Tenn.	183	185	210	263	249	334	336	331	194	235	237	143	2900	+129
Miami, Fla.	244	257	294	269	306	270	251	245	217	215	176	173	2917	- 44
Mobile, Ala.	147	194	200	298	316	292	263	296	188	279	255	165	2893	+145
New York, N.Y.	136	199	224	290	260	343	320	330	237	182	209	187	2917	+241
Norfolk, Va.	152	191	216	263	300	334	305	347	238	248	247	182	3022	+299
North Platte, Neb.	186	209	247	262	231	302	384	337	304	272	170	189	3093	+ 18
Oklahoma City, Okla.	205	253	234	280	186	332	365	371	244	244	239	185	3138	+129
Portland, Me.	165	190	196	266	261	327	344	257	210	130	155	181	2682	+111
Portland, Ore.	124	169	131	238	247	233	334	272	285	105	124	131	2393	+139
San Francisco, Calif.	211	218	247	305	371	350	318	324	249	261	212	155	3221	+293
Sault Ste. Marie, Mich.	89	94	186	233	221	203	342	188	147	185	75	68	2031	+103

level weather maps of the northern hemisphere. Bearing representative weather observations from all areas north of the equator, the maps were analyzed by the most modern air-mass and frontal techniques, and show the development and movement of important weather conditions and their interrelations and seasonal variations. Printed in book form for the use of meteorologists in active forecasting assignments with the armed services, this convenient assembly of data should later prove of immense value in meteorological research and practice. Supplementary maps for the 3, 10, 13 and 16 kilometer levels were also prepared for a portion of the 40-year period of the sea-level series. Studies of the two sets in conjunction disclosed significant and hitherto unknown relationships between upper-level and surface-level weather—suggesting, for example, that the southward movement of stratosphere air from the polar regions and the northward movement of the relatively colder stratosphere air from the tropics are directly associated with the development of severe cold waves.

During Nov. 1943, the domestic censorship of weather information was discontinued for all types of current weather data and forecasts except for such elements as might still be useful in hostile submarine or aerial operations affecting United Nations interests. A legitimate safeguard during the uncertain stages of the war immediately following the attack on Pearl Harbor and during the height of German submarine activity off the Atlantic coast, the censorship caused widespread inconvenience from the domestic standpoint. It likewise brought into sharp relief a large number of specific uses and applications of weather information in the operations of industry, transportation, utilities management and agriculture. To meet the needs of such activities, the U.S. weather bureau instituted a system of operational advices, designed to omit meteorological information and at the same time to guide operations affected by weather. The effects of this development would undoubtedly be visible henceforth in an improved form of forecasting, applying more directly to actual operating procedures such as the management of gas and electric loads, the timing of fruit spraying and harvesting crops, and the protection of perishables in railroad transit.

An important service to aviation was accomplished during 1943 in the organization of the weather bureau's flight advisory weather service. This service was to be directly associated with the operations of the airway traffic control of the Civil Aeronautics administration, which is responsible for the safety of aircraft in flight. Meteorologists, skilled in the interpretation of weather data, would be assigned to all the airway traffic control units, to assure that the latter are at all times supplied with (a) the latest available information on existing meteorological conditions aloft, (b) trends of weather change of significance to current flights, and (c) specific information on anticipated developments upon which orders for the continuation or stoppage of flights may be based by the traffic controllers. These advisory weather units, under organization at the close of the year, were to be established at the 23 civilian airway traffic control centres which, in direct liaison with army air forces control units of similar purpose, actively supervised the aviation of the United States.

Another important contribution to the protection of aviation, particularly with respect to landings at the larger air fields, was the congressional approval of the installation of ceilometers at 112 additional airport stations of the weather bureau. This instrument, designed to measure the heights of cloud ceilings during daylight as well as at night, proved its worth as a much-needed safety device. Also, a pronounced advance in observational procedure was launched during the Texas coast hurricane in late July by Col. Joseph D. Duckworth and Lts. Ralph M. O'Hair and Wm. H. Jones-Burdick of the army air forces instructors' school at Bryan field, Texas, when they flew in an AT-6 aeroplane around and through the centre of the hurricane to observe its size, intensity, location and the mechanics of its temperatures, pressures, winds and clouds. Forecasting of these larger storms had depended largely upon observations from ships in the vicinity of the storm—an advantage often reduced or lost by the efforts of ships' masters to avoid the storms as widely as possible. The successful flight of these officers proved the practicability of aeroplane reconnaissance flights for the purpose of first-hand observation of hurricanes in action, and doubtless marked the first step in a systematized program for obtaining essential information by this method.

In research, weather bureau studies of the dynamics of large-scale air currents in middle latitudes produced a new technique for forecasting the trajectory of particles of air over three-day periods; and the method was applied to the forecasting of winds at three kilometres in the midlatitude band of westerlies. New empirical formulas were developed also for forecasting the movements of long waves in the westerlies, and these waves were found to be related to the surface-weather tendency to vary in trends lasting for periods of a week or more. Studies conducted by the weather bureau in collaboration with the war department's corps of engineers continued the development of techniques for analyzing storms and estimating the maximum amount of precipitation that can fall in a given river basin from the most severe and long-lasting storm.

A direct and effective impetus to meteorological progress in the western hemisphere was accomplished during 1943 by the institution of a training class for Latin American meteorological students at Medellin, Colombia. Conducted under the auspices of the state department and the weather bureau in co-operation with the Colombian government, the course ran for seven months beginning in February and concentrated directly upon the basic sub-professional subjects of instrumentation, observations, weather map plotting and analysis, mathematics, physics and English. Some 200 Latin American students attended and the teaching staff consisted of 10 Latin Americans and an equal number of North Americans. Of the graduation group, 40 were chosen for advanced meteorological training in the United States and six diverted to further training in agricultural meteorology. This professional training was to be followed by an internship of several months at active forecast offices in the weather bureau. The advanced training was financed by funds provided by congress and the granting of 22 scholarships by the universities to which the students were assigned. There was also established at San Juan, P.R., an Institute of Tropical Meteorology to give concentrated study to weather conditions in the Caribbean and adjacent areas, particularly as these apply to aviation and the inception, development and movement of hurricanes.

In intent and fact these extensions of meteorological study for application beyond continental borders represented the first active steps in the trend toward international meteorological co-operation that must inevitably follow the war. Results of that trend could not be anticipated, but speculation was already decidedly active among meteorologists on questions of communications, observational contents, timing and distribution that would be more necessary than ever for the protection of world-wide air commerce in the future. The scope of meteorological requirements for this commerce embraced the fundamental necessity to extend, integrate and standardize the basic network of synoptic weather stations throughout the world. Also required would be a large number of new stations in the so-called blind areas, on land as well as at sea. It would be necessary to organize, for uniform operation throughout the world, an in-flight radio reporting system to supply weather reports (from aircraft in flight) upon conditions of cloud, wind, icing, humidity, etc., prevailing in the higher atmospheric levels. The required rapidity of distribution of current weather reports to assure adequate synoptic mapping over large portions of the earth's area would need the aid of an unprecedented operating efficiency in international communications to cope with the abundance as well as the combined need for uniformity, speed and accuracy in observation transmissions. Agreement among governments and air-transport operators must be soundly established and actualized to the end that all types of

Table IV.—Monthly Rainfall in Inches Outside the United States, Oct. 1942—Sept. 1943

Cities	Oct.	Nov.	Dec.	Jan.	Feb.	March	April	May	June	July	Aug.	Sept.
London	3.4	2.0	2.2	4.7	1.4	0.3	0.7	1.9	1.3	1.4	1.4	2.3
Edinburgh	2.5	0.6	1.2	2.1	1.3	1.6	1.0	3.3	1.7	2.5	3.5	1.2
Stockholm												
Lisbon	3.7	2.2	5.2	6.7	1.4	4.3	2.0	0.2	0.02			
Calcutta	7.4	0.3	0.0	0.7	1.4	0.6						
Bombay	0.0	0.0	0.3	0.3	0.0	0.0						
Baghdad	—											
Singapore												
Cape Town	1.3	0.2	0.4	1.7	0.5	1.0	2.2	2.7	1.7	3.4	3.7	1.8
Johannesburg												
Salisbury (Rhodesia)	3.1	3.1	7.9	10.2	6.5	11.6	1.6	1.9	0.03	0.0		
Quebec	4.5	5.0	4.1	2.6	2.5	4.6	3.6	3.8	6.1			
Toronto	2.9	2.7	4.2	2.9	2.3	4.4	3.3	4.6	2.9	3.0	2.5	1.4
Winnipeg	0.3	0.7	1.3	1.4	0.7	1.5	0.3	3.2	3.8	3.5	2.9	1.6
Victoria, B.C.	1.3	4.8	5.4	2.7	2.0	2.5	1.4	1.1	0.7	0.3	0.7	0.2
Sydney	6.3	5.5	3.7		0.5	1.0	1.9	14.3	1.0	0.3	7.7	8.7
Melbourne	2.3	3.8	1.3	2.8	1.6	0.5	2.2	0.6	2.3	1.2		
Perth	1.7	0.3	1.5	0.8	0.5	2.2	2.5	2.3	6.1	6.3		
Wellington, N.Z.	2.6	3.1	2.7	3.0	4.3	0.5	1.5	3.2	10.0	5.5	6.8	9.7

Table V.—Monthly Mean Temperatures in °F. Outside the United States, Oct. 1942—Sept. 1943

Cities	Oct.	Nov.	Dec.	Jan.	Feb.	March	April	May	June	July	Aug.	Sept.
London	52.5	42.3	44.3	42.0	42.5	45.2	52.9	56.1	59.9	63.9	62.7	57.4
Edinburgh	49.2	42.1	43.5	38.9	43.3	43.5	48.7	50.1	56.0	57.7	56.0	53.3
Stockholm												
Lisbon	65.1	56.3	53.9	54.8	52.9	56.5	63.0	65.8	70.4			
Calcutta	82.3	76.5	69.0	70.4	70.0	81.3						
Bombay	83.6	79.7	77.3	74.1	77.1	81.3						
Baghdad												
Singapore												
Cape Town	62.7	68.1	68.6	68.5	67.8	70.2	63.5	57.8	55.3	52.8	55.1	57.5
Johannesburg												
Salisbury (Rhodesia)	67.4	69.0	69.2	68.3	67.1	66.7	66.0	60.9	56.2	58.2		
Quebec	48	32	12	8	17	21	32	51	62			
Toronto	51.3	39.9	24.9	19.5	25.7	30.0	39.1	55.1	69.3	71.1	68.7	59.7
Winnipeg	45.7	21.0	1.4	-8.3	5.5	9.9	39.7	48.6	58.6	70.7	65.4	53.5
Victoria, B.C.	53.5	44.0	42.9	34.7	43.7	43.8	50.9	51.9	56.7	59.0	59.9	60.8
Sydney	62.1	66.5	69.3		72.3	71.1	64.1	59.5	52.7	52.4	52.3	57.9
Melbourne	58.7	62.1	66.9	69.1	66.4	65.1	56.9	52.3	48.5	49.4		
Perth	59.6	68.3	72.9	72.0	73.3	72.4	65.9	59.9	57.5	53.1		
Wellington, N.Z.	55.6	56.3	57.5	59.9	62.1	59.1	56.7	49.4	48.5	45.3	45.3	49.5

meteorological information from all sources should be freely available to all users in the common support and protection of the commerce. Finally, international research, designed to fit the borderless nature and action of weather, would necessarily command a co-ordinated international interest in the general improvement of meteorological practice.

The Weather of 1943.—In general, the weather of 1943 was warmer, drier and sunnier than usual, and over large areas decidedly different in several respects from that of 1942. It was somewhat less favourable for agriculture, principally because of untimely spring frosts, excessive wetness during the planting and early haying season and, later, harmful dryness in some areas. There was much less rainfall than during the preceding year which curtailed crop production in some sections, but in most of the principal agricultural states favourable conditions prevailed, and the general farm output, while considerably below that for 1942, was larger than normal. The less favourable crop weather is emphasized by the fact that while the combined acreage for 52 crops harvested in 1943 was more than 9,000,000 ac. in excess of 1942, total production was 6% less.

Following the general temperature trend in evidence for a good many years, the winter of 1942–43 was warmer than normal in nearly all sections of the country. However, notwithstanding this general warmth, the winter brought some extremely cold weather, the lowest temperature reported being −60° at Island Park dam, Idaho, on Jan. 18.

Spring frosts and freezes did much damage, especially in the south-central and southern parts of the U.S. where fruit and early vegetables were killed over large areas. As a result, unusually small crops of apples, peaches, cherries, apricots and strawberries survived for harvest.

East of the Mississippi river the spring season, in addition to the untimely frost, brought frequent heavy rains to many sections which seriously hampered farmers in the planting of corn, haying and other seasonal work. Thus, the corn crop got off to a late start but the summer brought higher than normal temperatures and much sunshine to the principal producing states which hastened development. Corn matured with no material frost damage and the fall season was unusually favourable for harvest.

The summer had above normal temperatures in nearly all sections of the U.S., and most of the principal agricultural states had sufficient moisture to produce good crops. In considerable areas, especially the middle Atlantic states and a large south-central section, it was one of the warmest summers of record. However, while most central and northern states had timely summer rains, unfavourable dryness developed in central-eastern sections and much of the south. The highest temperature recorded for the summer was 124° in July, reported from two stations in California.

The outstanding feature of the fall and early winter was widespread dryness, in marked contrast to the two preceding falls. The New England states, New York, Mississippi and Louisiana were the only states with as much as normal rainfall for the three fall months. It was one of the driest falls of record over large areas. While this was decidedly favourable for the harvesting of crops and made possible maximum returns from a minimum of harvesters, the dryness was unfavourable for the seeding and germination of winter grains, especially in the western winter wheat belt and the south. In the central and southern plains the dry weather restricted the acreage that could be seeded to wheat, delayed seeding, and greatly reduced the usual fall grazing of livestock on wheat fields. This, together with reduced grazing on other pastures, accentuated the feed shortage and increased the liquidation of livestock, especially in the southwest.

About the middle of December another severe freeze overspread the south, resulting in more or less damage, heavy in localities, from Texas eastward to Florida and the Carolinas. Florida suffered most with a loss of truck crops, many ready for market, valued at more than $4,000,000. Temperatures were not low enough to seriously harm citrus fruit and they escaped with negligible damage.

The year, mainly the first half, brought extensive flood damage. The most noteworthy floods occurred in May, affecting seven states from Oklahoma to Michigan and causing extensive damage to rich agricultural and industrial areas. In parts of the Arkansas and Osage rivers the floods were the greatest in 100 years, with near-record stages reached in the middle Mississippi, the Illinois, Wabash and Maumee rivers. An outstanding storm of the year was a tropical hurricane in southeastern Texas on July 26–29, which did some $15,000,000 damage. (*See also* DISASTERS; FLOODS AND FLOOD CONTROL.)　　(F. W. RR.)

Other Countries.—The values for monthly rainfall and monthly mean temperatures given in the accompanying tables referring to countries outside the United States are provisional and may in some cases require a small correction. On account of war conditions it was not possible to give complete data for some of the stations. Gaps in the tables indicate that the data could not be obtained.　　(D. BRU.)

Methodist Church. Prior to Dec. 1, 1943, the Methodist Church sent 1,000 ministers into the army as chaplains and 300 into the navy, about two-thirds of its quota; had raised more than $2,000,000 for purposes related to the war; and had set up a plan for exerting pressure upon the peace-framing agencies of the government. The Crusade for a New World Order, popularly called the "Bishops' Crusade" because initiated by the council of bishops, started Jan. 1, 1944, and through an elaborate program of meetings, broadcasts, study classes and house to house visitation aimed to stir the minds of Methodists, so that they would express themselves by showers of post cards to congress, urging that certain Christian principles be embodied in the postwar reconstruction of the world. Subsidiary to this end was a Conference on Bases of a New World Order held at Delaware, O., in March 1943, when the subject was presented by distinguished speakers.

The die-hard group in the former Methodist Episcopal Church, South, experienced a setback on Aug. 26, when the supreme court of South Carolina ruled that the plan of union was valid, and that unification was soundly based in the law. The second part of the decision denied to the Methodist Church the exclusive right to the use of the title "Methodist Episcopal Church, South." The issues were to be taken to the federal courts.

The council of bishops in session in Princeton, N.J., in December, elected Bishop H. Lester Smith of Cincinnati, president and G. Bromley Oxnam, secretary.

The Statistical centre was removed from New York to 740 Rush st., Chicago; and Albert C. Hoover replaced Thomas P. Potter as director. There were 24,176 Methodist ministers serving 42,000 congregations, on 21,031 pastoral charges. Sunday school enrolment continued to decline, having reached 5,093,558. Adult baptisms 143,314; children 124,104. So-called active members in the United States 6,640,424, a gain of 80,829; "nonresident members" (1,173,467) gave a total on July 1, of 7,713,891. Receipts for ministerial support were $35,342,931. Local churches raised for current expenses $43,693,423 in the fiscal year ending May 31, 1943; the Commission on Overseas Relief took in $464,049. Total war emergency receipts were $1,400,000. Scattered reports from many localities showed that debt-paying was easy. One third of the Methodist Church debt in Missouri was liquidated.

Total sales for the Methodist Publishing House reached $6,326,-144. Its Abingdon-Cokesbury line of nondenominational books was exceptionally popular; the circulation of its 24 Sunday school periodicals ran above 6,000,000, and the weekly *Christian Advocate,* with 250,000 circulation, led all denominational weeklies. Out of the produce of the business $250,000 was appropriated for distribution to the retired ministers. Similar amounts were being used to reduce the debt incurred during the bad years, and to create a reserve for improved machinery.

The Division of Foreign Missions, which staggered under a debt of about $3,000,000, paid the last dollar of the remainder, $341,-728. The church supplied money enough to pay for the repatriation of scores of mission workers from the war-torn lands. In co-operation with Overseas Relief and the Woman's Division of Christian Service, it was possible to send $15,000 a month for the aid of Methodist workers of China.

For world service in 1943 the Methodist Church gave $4,659,-830, an increase of $492,063 over the previous year. This was apportioned among the 12 boards and commissions according to a fixed ratio. The Board of Missions and Church Extension received 69.30%, board of education 14.55% and the remaining one-sixth went to the ten minor causes, eight of them getting less than $50,000 each. The foreign division reckoned as one of the major decisions of the year the setting apart of the proceeds of the Collins bequest, approximating $3,000,000 in standing timber, as a reserve on which to base an adequate plan for pensioning retired missionaries.

Methodist philanthropies which began in the U.S. in 1883 attained considerable magnitude. Hospitals in U.S. 79, bed capacity 13,248, operating expenses $19,717,790, value of property $66,-134,163; child welfare 56 homes with 6,847 inmates, and property worth $12,721,143; 47 homes for aged with 3,777 inmates with $11,734,207; homes for business girls and young women, 24 accommodating 1,165, in property valued at $1,265,134. Of the Methodist hospitals 73% were rated Grade A by the American College of Surgeons.

Financially the educational event of the year was the bequest of Walter Murphy to Northwestern university, amounting to $20,000,000. Executive changes of importance were: the resignation of President McConaghy of Wesleyan university; he was succeeded by Dean Victor L. Butterfield; in place of John B. Magee, deceased, Dr. Russell D. Cole became president of Cornell college; Dr. Hugh C. Stuntz succeeded President J. L. Cunningim at Scarritt college; Rev. Robert O. McClure was elected president of Ohio Northern university.

From collections and endowments, local and national, $3,810,-167 was distributed in 1942 to 14,060 retired Methodist preachers and their dependents. The total of the vested funds was $28,822,361.   (J. R. J.)

Metropolitan Museum of Art: *see* ART EXHIBITIONS; ART GALLERIES AND ART MUSEUMS.

Mexico.
A federal republic of North America lying between the United States and Central America. Area, 767,168 sq.mi.; pop. est. 20,623,826 (19,473,741 census 1940). Approximately 55% of the population was mestizo, 29% Indian, 15% white, with foreigners and others making up less than 1%. The language is Spanish, but an estimated 14% speak only Indian tongues. There is no official state religion, but the people are overwhelmingly Roman Catholic. The capital is Mexico City (pop. 1,464,556). Other principal cities are: Guadalajara, 228,049; Monterrey, 180,942; Puebla, 137,324; Mérida, 98,334; León, 86,089; Tampico, 81,334; Aguascalientes, 81,124; San Luis Potosí, 78,042; Torreón, 76,613; Veracruz, 70,958; Chihuahua, 57,456;

Pachuca, 52,387. The president in 1943 was Gen. Manuel Avila Camacho (took office Dec. 1940).

History.—In its second year at war with the axis powers, Mexico was still rendering economic and spiritual assistance to the cause of the Allied Nations rather than engaging in active military participation. Nevertheless, considerable feeling was rising for forming an expeditionary force so that Mexico could take a more important place among the Allied Nations. Generally speaking, a lack of war materials deterred Mexico from entering more actively into the combat.

One of Mexico's early moves had been the arrest and segregation of dangerous enemy aliens. Under Miguel Alemán, youthful and energetic minister of the interior, the more dangerous of the aliens had been interned. However, it was estimated in Jan. 1943 that approximately 4,500 Japanese nationals remained scattered throughout the population. Evidence of subversive activities by these hidden elements was watched for constantly.

Growth of the army in Mexico continued steadily. The class of 1924 was called to the colours on Flag day, March 2, at which time throughout the country impressive ceremonies were held.

Besides the army itself, Mexico encouraged civilians to train and drill with a goal in view of 2,000,000 trained reserves. Under the decree of Aug. 11, 1942, all able-bodied men were required to have military instruction. However, by the summer of 1943 the president decided that military drill should be voluntary. Civilian military training fell off abruptly in the cities, although remaining almost unchanged in the rural areas.

In Mexico City one of the largest military displays of 1943 was held on Independence days (Sept. 15 and 16). Parades were reviewed by President Avila Camacho, Minister of National Defense Gen. Lázaro Cárdenas, United States Chief of Staff Gen. George C. Marshall, Coordinator of Inter-American Affairs Nelson Rockefeller, and the representative of the president of Cuba, Gen. Manuel Benítez. At that time the latest inductees were marched by the reviewing stand as symbols of the rapidly growing Mexican army.

Rearming and preparing its western coast for defense against possible Japanese attack also occupied much of Mexico's attention in 1943. Mazatlán became a war district. Manzanillo was converted into a naval base by the ministry of marine, under Gen. Heriberto Jara, secretary of navy. Furthermore, many naval installations and refuelling stations were established along the western coast line.

Plans for further strengthening the war effort were laid at a meeting of the president of the United States and President Avila Camacho in Monterrey, Mexico in April. One of the most important accomplishments of the conference was the formation of the Joint Commission for Economic Co-operation, consisting of two representatives from each country. Other projects were discussed, including the progress of Mexico's various war industries.

Railroads caused great concern in Mexico during 1943. With neglected roadbeds, insufficient rolling stock, and old and inadequate locomotives, railroad difficulties became constantly more acute. A United States commission, headed by Oliver M. Stevens, was appointed to assist in solving the problem. Safety measures, such as speeds compatible with the state of the roadbed, more efficient control over train movements, and a continuous inspection of the tracks were adopted as a result of suggestions by the commission. Some contracts for materials were negotiated, but clearance for deliveries was delayed.

Part of Mexico's difficulty in adjusting to a war economy lay in her foreign trade. Exports, mostly destined for the United States, so consistently outstripped imports that a very heavy reserve of dollar credits accumulated. Total imports and exports reached a new high of 1,744,400,000 pesos in 1942, and preliminary counts indicated that the 1943 figures would be even higher. The danger of inflation from the large dollar credits appeared very real to the heads of the National Bank of Mexico.

War plans in agriculture were especially successful in 1943. Although Mexico did not produce as much as it consumed, there was nevertheless a remarkable improvement in agricultural matters. Upon entrance into the war, a plan for mobilizing agriculture in the republic of Mexico was instituted. The results of the 1942 program were very satisfactory in that the plan was surpassed by 1,316,510 ac. under cultivation. The grand total stood at 16,595,930 ac. of which 148,200 were newly placed under irrigation. The total crop production exceeded the plan in a similar manner. During 1943 heavy yields were also obtained, even though the weather was very unfavourable.

To assist both industry and agriculture, Foreign Minister Ezéquiel Padilla had some success in negotiating for allocations of machinery to Mexico. United States machines and equipment made idle by war industries could be put to use in Mexico. Also, a more liberal quota of farm machinery for the agriculture program was obtained.

Industry was greatly stimulated by the war effort. In order to improve planning, two United States engineers were engaged to make a survey of the general business structure. The establishment of plywood plants, paper mills, a high-octane refinery, iron and steel plants all marked the move toward industrialization. Also, a special bid was made for United States capital by Mexico's consul general in New York city. As a result, a new investment trust was formed in May 1943 composed of United States and Mexican financiers.

Of significance surpassed by no other part of its economic life was Mexico's mining industry. Production of strategic metals including zinc, copper and silver increased or stayed firm. Petroleum, however, caused some concern. (See *Mineral Production,* below.)

Increased economic activity brought a rapid rise in prices in Mexico. Wholesale prices reached a high in 1943 of 162% of the 1929 average, and retail prices rose even more. Real estate values and stock market prices went up even faster, causing considerable concern to the officials attempting to curb inflation.

Price control measures were put into effect for many items. Farm produce, foodstuffs, cloth, toilet articles and automobile tires were included on the list. In order to control the grain market, an association of merchants with the Federal Office of Distribution under the ministry of agriculture and economy was established. The country was divided into economic zones, in which, in co-operation with state governments, the association bought and sold grain so as to maintain a stable market.

Another method of holding off inflation was attempted by the sale for peso bank notes of especially minted gold coins (without legal tender value). The purpose of the drive to sell gold was to reduce the amount of paper money in circulation and to absorb some of the new purchasing power of the country. Similarly, a 200,000,000 peso government loan was floated to take care of the increasing surplus of credits. Both financial attempts met with marked success.

Politics, despite the stresses of wartime living, continued in much the same vein as previously. On July 4, 1943, a new chamber of deputies was elected. Again the official party of the Mexican Revolution (P.R.M., *Partido de la Revolución Méxicana*) held the overwhelming majority. During July and August the electoral college considered the cases of the various candidates whose elections were disputed. When the chamber of deputies was installed, 144 of the 147 new representatives were of the official party. None of the independent candidates represented

either of the principal opposition parties, the rightist *Acción Nacional* and the communist *Liga de Acción Política.*

The slow shifting of the president, and with him Mexico's politics, to a centre-of-the-road policy was demonstrated in many ways. The supreme court especially supported the politics of the president in moderating some of the more drastic laws. However, small landowners who had received expropriated property were assured that their rights would be protected, and that the *ejidos* (communal lands) would be left untouched.

A more conservative note was sounded when Octavio Vejar Vásquez succeeded leftist Luis Sánchez Pontón as minister of education. Vejar Vásquez was held to be both conservative and a strong supporter of the church. He abolished co-education in Mexican schools and also ordered all school teachers to abandon their political activity.

Similar trends were shown in labour. Vincente Lombardo Toledano was replaced as secretary of Mexico's most powerful trade-union alliance (the C.T.M.) by Fidel Velázquez. Lombardo Toledano still maintained, however, his control over the Confederation of Latin American Workers.

One group in Mexico's population which was making a significant contribution economically and socially was the Spanish refugee. Almost every trade, profession and walk of life was represented by the Spanish elements, who were slowly fitting themselves into Mexican life. The refugees had proved to be an important counterbalance to the pro-axis and anti-United Nations Spanish Falange. Various parties and subdivisions of the Spanish refugees were welded together as the Democratic Spanish union. The union was headed by Antonio Velao, liberal Republican minister in the former Spanish government. A focal point for the Spanish refugees was thus provided. In order to give greater support to the war effort, the newly organized Spaniards offered a battalion of trained, disciplined, and well officered troops to President Avila Camacho.

Another step in the unifying of the Spanish refugees was undertaken when Spanish Republicans elected Diego Martínez Barrio as president of a government-in-exile. The new government, although challenged by other refugee groups, principally in London, asked for formal recognition. However, the Martínez Barrio group was destined for disappointment, for in Nov. 1943 it was decided that a Spanish government could not be allowed in Mexico under the constitution. Some support was given to the new movement when one week earlier a Committee of San Sebastián (named from the place in Spain where the Revolutionary committee was formed to begin the Spanish republic) was created for the purpose of overthrowing the Franco regime in Spain. This committee was supported by the chiefs of all Mexican parties, except the communist.

Relations with the United States were better during 1943 than at almost any other time in the history of Mexico. Much of the credit for this circumstance was given to Foreign Minister Ezéquiel Padilla. A reciprocal trade agreement with the United States was put into effect on Jan. 30. Arrangements were made whereby workers were furnished United States areas suffering labour shortages, and even the oil question was largely solved. The biggest United States claimant, Standard Oil of New Jersey, accepted on Oct. 1, 1943, $22,000,000 awarded under the agreement.

Of more local concern to Mexico was the extensive health program, begun in 1936, which received special impetus after the entrance of Mexico into World War II. Victor Fernández Manero directed the program as head of the department of public health. Educational programs were undertaken, and public and group medical care was provided. Regional sanitariums, hospitals and medical centres were developed. In addition to the civil-

SOMEWHAT REMINISCENT of Russia's May Day celebration were the huge festivities in commemoration of Mexican independence before the national palace at Mexico City Sept. 16, 1943

ian facilities, a network of military hospitals was built under the direction of Gen. Ignacio Sánchez Neira of the ministry of national defense.

Closely allied with the public health program were the plans advanced by the United States to spend $1,178,000 on health projects along the Pan-American highway. Water and sewage service for the towns along the highway accounted for most of the expenditure. Methods of combating blindness and tropical diseases occupied the remainder of the budget.

Construction on the Pan-American highway continued. Progress was mostly in the area south of Mexico City, pressing towards the Guatemala border. Steep mountainous country and volcanic rock caused most of the engineering difficulties.

A colourful addition to life in Mexico City came with the construction of the new *Hipódromo de las Américas* track for horse racing. The track occupied an important place in the social life of the Federal District, although some criticism from labour circles was levied at the display at the Hipódromo.

Perhaps the most dramatic incident of 1943 in Mexico was the sudden eruption of a new volcano in the fields near San Juan Parangaricutiro in the state of Michoacan. The volcano rose from the level fields in less than a week, beginning on Feb. 20, to a height of over 140 ft., and threatened the village of Parangaricutiro with a flow of lava almost 50 ft. high. However, after a week the volcano subsided in activity, and the flow of lava ceased.

Education.—Education is free, compulsory and divorced from religion. Private schools, however, are allowed to teach religion, and officially the government in 1943 was more lenient toward the church than formerly. Mexico had approximately 25,000 primary schools with over 2,000,000 enrolment. Secondary schools in 1942 had about 80,000 enrolment and the country's ten universities around 30,000. There were more than 100 technical schools, including 30 vocational agricultural schools for Indians and 91 for adult education. Illiteracy was estimated at a little less than 45%. Rural education was supported by the federal government, urban by the states and municipalities.

Finance.—The monetary unit is the peso (value in 1943 approximately 20.65 cents U.S.). In 1943 bank circulation rose to 2,585,600,000 pesos and reserve bank deposits to 650,000,000

pesos (250,000,000 pesos in Aug. 1942).

In line with Mexico's war activities the 1943 budget as presented by Finance Minister Eduardo Suárez was the largest in the financial history of the country. A total of 707,845,000 pesos was appropriated. To national defense went 177,300,000 pesos, education, 97,200,000 pesos, public debt, 95,500,000 pesos, agriculture and development, 94,900,000 pesos, presidency, 1,400,000 pesos. Bonds for 125,000,000 pesos were authorized of which 100,000,000 pesos were earmarked for highways and 25,000,000 pesos were designed for railroad rehabilitation. On the other side of the ledger, taxes on income, liquor, petroleum and gasoline were substantially increased.

Indicative of the boom times were the effects on the treasury. Receipts for 1942 were approximately 900,000,000 pesos, and investors in Mexico's foreign loans began receiving payments in July after a default of 15 years.

Trade and Communication.—Exports in 1943 exceeded imports until September, when imports and exports became approximately equal. Preliminary estimates were that the total volume of imports and exports in 1943 would be greater than the record year of 1942.

Exports in 1942 totalled 991,900,000 pesos (728,800,000 pesos in 1941). This was even higher than the 1940 peak of 960,000,000 pesos. Gold, silver, copper, lead, zinc and oil comprised the bulk of Mexico's export goods. Beef, henequen, tomatoes and *huaraches* (sandals) also stood high on the export list. Chicle, coffee, chick peas, cotton, vanilla, guayule, vegetable wax and fodder were also exported in appreciable quantities.

Imports in 1942 were 752,500,000 pesos (914,500,000 pesos in 1941 and 668,400,000 pesos in 1940). Manufactured articles, including machinery, composed the largest single category of imports. Some food was also imported during 1943. The above figures do not include munitions of war.

External communications are by sea, especially through Veracruz; by three main railways to the United States and one to Guatemala; by air to all parts of the hemisphere; and by a growing network of motor highways.

The national railway system (14,500 mi.) linked the more important population and industrial centres. There were more than 36,000 mi. of improved roads in 1942, of which 4,500 mi. were paved.

Agriculture.—Mexico has an estimated 37,050,000 ac. of tillable land, of which 13,410,556 ac. were under cultivation in

1940 and 16,595,930 ac. in 1942 (3.5% of the total area of the country). Forest land comprised 25,893,993 ac. and grazing land 69,713,715 ac. In 1940 (census) there were 26 irrigation districts comprising 6,774,988 ac. of which 2,057,115 ac. were irrigable, and 1,101,208 ac. were under actual irrigation. In 1942 an additional 148,200 ac. were brought under irrigation.

Agricultural production in 1942 was (in short tons): 2,590,405 tons of maize, 552,252 tons of wheat, 511,467 tons of refined sugar (1943), 123,458 tons of rice (154,322 tons estimated for 1943), 205,028 tons of beans, 303,133 tons of bananas, 170,061 tons of tomatoes, 186,289 tons of cotton seed, 91,491 tons of chick peas, 93,696 tons of sesame, 44,092 tons of pineapple (marketed), 19,841 tons of grapes, 59,524 tons of coffee, 122,355 tons of henequen, 6,614 tons of chicle, 66,138 tons of guayule (7,716 tons only had been forecast).

Timber produced in 1942 was: 35,315,000 cu.ft. of pine, 1,317,250 cu.ft. of mahogany, 1,045,320 cu.ft. of red cedar, 432,600 cu.ft. of white cedar, 91,820 cu.ft. of primavera. Charcoal, resins and other products equalled 45,600 tons.

Manufacturing.—During 1943 the expansion of Mexican industry continued. A high-octane refinery was established. Certain new industries such as plywood and pulpwood were begun, and a Mexican-United States group of financiers undertook the establishment of branches of certain United States manufacturing firms in Mexico. Employment was high and prices were rising.

Mineral Production.—Basic to Mexico's economy is mining. In 1942 Mexico ranked first in world silver production, second in lead and fourth in gold. Total production of precious metals was 2,937 tons valued at 291,322,422 pesos; of industrial metals was 621,187 tons at 446,522,197 pesos; and of metalloids was 47,734 tons, at 16,493,043 pesos. Of this amount, 519,000 tons were classed as strategic war metals. Silver production in 1942 was 74,000,000 oz., most of which was purchased by the United States.

Petroleum production continued to decline. Total production of crude in 1941 was 43,304,179 bbl. as against 34,813,659 bbl. in 1942. Even more drastic reduction was noted during 1943. Statistics for 1942 were: six new producing wells with a daily initial capacity of 15,051 bbl.; exports, 6,540,889 bbl.; consumption, 28,490,033 bbl.; petroleum derivatives, 40,513,155 bbl. (*See* also INTERNATIONAL LAW.)

BIBLIOGRAPHY.—Secretaría de la Economía Nacional, Dirección General de Estadística, *Anuario estadístico de los Estados Unidos Mexicanos, 1940* (1942); Banco Nacional de México, *Review of the Economic Situation of Mexico* (Mexico City, monthly); H. B. Parkes, *History of Mexico* (1939); Frances Toor, *Guide to Mexico* (rev. ed. 1940); Anita Brenner, text, and George R. Leighton, photographs, *The Wind That Swept Mexico: The History of the Mexican Revolution, 1910–1942* (1943); Ezéquiel Padilla, *Free Men of America* (1943).   (C. L. G.)

Mica. Consumption of high-grade mica sheets in the United States during the first eight months of 1943 was more than 50,000 lb. monthly in excess of receipts, and depletion of stocks was so heavy that in October further restrictions on use were announced, under which consumption from Dec. 1 was restricted to the rate during the first three quarters of 1943. However, the grades below "good stained" were more plentiful; stocks of "stained" mica increased during the same period from 370,000 lb. on Jan. 1 to 1,160,000 lb. on Aug. 1, 1943. A new buying schedule was put into effect in May, designed to encourage greater production of small sizes.   (G. A. Ro.)

Michigan. One of the north central group of states, Michigan was the 26th state admitted to the union; it is popularly known as the "Wolverine state." Area, 97,940 sq.mi. (including 39,960 sq.mi. of Great Lakes' water surface);

pop. (1940) 5,256,106; 3,454,867 were urban, 1,801,239 rural. Whites comprised 95.9% of the population, nonwhites 4.1% (215,934). Capital, Lansing (78,753). Larger cities were Detroit (1,623,452), Grand Rapids (164,292), Flint (151,543), Saginaw (82,794).

History.—War production continued to play the dominant role in Michigan history in 1943. Population congestion in the Detroit area continued, constituting an important factor in bringing on the most significant event in 1943 Michigan history: the race riot which broke out in Detroit on the evening of Sunday, June 20. (*See* DETROIT; RACE RIOTS.)

The legislature convening in regular session in Jan. 1943 and ending March 26 was composed of 25 Republicans and 7 Democrats in the senate, 73 Republicans and 27 Democrats in the house of representatives. Despite the fact that a considerable portion of the session—shortest since the Civil War—was devoted to argument over the question of return to standard time and to futile attempts to reorganize state highway administration, the legislature passed 265 measures, 9 of which were vetoed by Gov. Harry F. Kelly. Appropriations totalled $137,000,000; a six-member state commission of labour and industry was created; for the first time since 1925, seats in the house of representatives were reapportioned; a new compilation of Michigan statutes (first since 1929) was ordered; the Michigan council of defense, created early in 1941, was abolished, and the direction of its system was transferred to one man, a director of civilian defense (Gov. Kelly appointed Capt. Donald S. Leonard to this position); and for the first time in 30 years, the workmen's compensation law was revised. Gov. Kelly's program for the "streamlining" of the government by the merging of departments was deferred. However, considerable authority for the consolidation of state agencies was entrusted to the newly created department of business administration, to the headship of which Gov. Kelly named Robert S. Ford, director of the University of Michigan's bureau of government. An effort in the legislature to reverse Michigan's century-old anti-capital punishment position failed of success.

In the April 1943 election, Republican candidates for state offices were uniformly successful: R. Spencer Bishop and Ralph A. Hayward were chosen regents of the University of Michigan; Eugene B. Elliott, superintendent of public instruction (re-elected); Stephen S. Nesbit, member of the state board of education (re-elected); W. G. Armstrong and Sarah Van Hoosen Jones, members of the state board of agriculture; Charles M. Ziegler became the first Republican in 10 years to win the position of state highway commissioner. In the nominally nonpartisan election of justices of the state supreme court, Neil E. Reid and Emerson R. Boyles, endorsed by the Republicans, were successful, though the latter's plurality over Democrat-endorsed Burt D. Chandler was only 2 votes in a total of over 350,000, making this election the closest of any for state office in Michigan's entire history.

Recurring charges of corruption in state legislatures led, late in the summer, to the initiation of a one-man grand jury investigation under the direction of Judge Leland W. Carr. Two other events of importance during 1943 were court martial proceedings following the shooting of a Negro private by the commandant of Selfridge field, and the completion of the MacArthur lock in the St. Mary's ship canal at Sault Sainte Marie.

Education.—There were 5,260 elementary schools and nearly 800 secondary schools in the state public school system with a total enrolment of about 950,000 pupils; their teaching staffs numbered 32,492 members. The 1943 legislature appropriated $50,000,000 for the support of the public schools.

Public Welfare, Charities, Correction.—The State Social Welfare commission reported that the general relief load decreased 39.6% from Nov. 1942 to Nov. 1943, as compared with a decrease of 39.0% from Nov. 1941 to Nov. 1942; the active load of persons receiving relief was 21,153 during Nov. 1942; 12,785 during Nov. 1943. During Nov. 1942, 90,082 persons received old-age assistance; during Nov. 1943, 87,784; during this period the total number of families receiving aid to dependent children decreased from 18,198 to 13,719; recipients of aid to the blind declined in number from 1,369 to 1,290. For all programs, a total of $40,930,465.36 was expended in assistance from Dec. 1942 to Nov. 1943. Of this, 38.5% represented federal participation, 53.6% state participation and 7.9% local county participation.

The 10 state institutions supervised by the Hospital commission cared for nearly 21,000 patients in 1943, committed to custody because of mental illness or deficiency. Three prisons conducted by the Corrections commission had a population of more than 7,200 in 1943, including the State Prison of Southern Michigan.

Communication.—With state highway department revenue dropping from $31,704,320 in 1942 to approximately $22,000,000 in 1943 and heavy increases in maintenance costs, highway building was considerably restricted in 1943. Chief expenditures in a $15,500,000 construction program were devoted toward the completion of the Detroit-Willow Run expressway and access roads in war production areas, with the federal government providing from 50% to 75% of the funds. Michigan in 1943 had some 9,400 mi. of trunk line highways and more than 88,000 mi. of county roads. A wartime "production miracle" was the completion, early in the summer, of the great new MacArthur lock in the Soo canal. Despite the shortening of the shipping season by a month, because of weather conditions, 85,000,000 tons of iron ore passed through the canal; 28% more wheat, 76% more in other grains, 21% more soft coal passed through than in 1942.

Banking and Finance.—On Oct. 18, 1943, the total resources of the 345 state commercial banks and 4 industrial banks amounted to $1,586,265,957.74, showing an increase of 2.3% since the first of the year; the deposits of state banks had reached an all-time peak.

As of Dec. 21, 1943, 94% of the average deposit dollar impounded during the banking holiday period of 10 years before had been returned to the depositor-creditors.

Agriculture.—A 57-year record rainfall during the planting season brought widely varying effects to production records in the chief crops raised by Michigan's 168,000 farmers. Oats, corn, wheat and barley suffered heavily.

Table I.—*Leading Agricultural Products of Michigan, 1943 and 1942*

Crop	1943 (est.)	1942
Corn, bu.	52,604,000	69,703,000
Oats, bu.	35,053,200	67,410,000
Wheat, bu.	11,200,000	16,322,000
Barley, bu.	3,792,360	7,293,000
Navy beans, 100-lb. bags	5,310,000	4,832,000
Potatoes, bu.	22,365,000	16,562,000
Buckwheat, bu.	800,000	391,000
Eggs	1,412,000,000*	1,319,000,000*

*First eleven months.

Manufacturing.—An enormous increase in manufacturing took place in 1943; the previous year had seen new processes undertaken for war production; 1943 witnessed impressive accomplishment in the form of production completed. Because of war conditions, official statistics are not available beyond 1939. In that year the total value of manufactures was $4,348,223,244. Figures released by the War Production board in September revealed that of a total of $109,886,573,000 in major war supply contracts to that date, Michigan's share was $11,469,576,000, or 10.5%, placing it ahead of every other state in this respect.

Mineral Production.—As in 1942, war-production needs

Table II.—*Principal Mineral Products of Michigan, 1941 and 1940*

Mineral	Value, 1941	Value, 1940
Iron ore	$43,765,164	$40,474,951
Petroleum	21,900,000	20,150,000
Pig iron	21,384,383	18,472,588
Coke	18,213,048	15,445,452
Cement	13,333,850	11,389,191
Salt	10,975,872	7,479,905
Copper	10,959,840	10,214,748
Natural gas	8,722,000	8,339,000
Gypsum	1,090,309	1,017,126

stimulated increase in the development of Michigan's varied mineral resources in 1943. Fifteen oil and gas discoveries were made during the first 11 mo. of 1943, although no large pools or fields were found.

During the year the producing oil wells on state property numbered 192; gas wells, 15; they yielded $900,000 to the general fund of the state.

BIBLIOGRAPHY.—*Michigan, A Guide to the Wolverine State* (American Guide Series, 1941); *The Michigan History Magazine,* quarterly; press releases and printed reports of the various governmental offices; *Michigan Official Directory and Legislative Manual,* published by the secretary of state biennially.
(L. G. V. V.)

Michigan, University of. During 1943 the teaching facilities of the University of Michigan were increasingly utilized for instructing military and naval personnel while the enrolment of civilian students declined. A Division for Emergency Training was organized in Dec. 1942, to negotiate with government agencies, arrange and manage the courses, and a number of units were introduced in Jan., March, and April 1943. For the army the university taught engineering, pre-meteorological subjects, languages, civil administration and several specialized medical subjects, such as thoracic surgery, epidemiology and medical laboratory techniques; the Judge Advocate General's school was moved to Ann Arbor in Sept. 1942. The navy, marine and coast guard contingents were mostly in the basic, pre-medical and engineering curricula of the navy V-12 course, and practically all the medical and dental students were enlisted in either the army or the navy. The navy's postgraduate school of naval architecture was brought to Ann Arbor from Annapolis in July 1943. In addition there were offered throughout the year a great number of courses for civilians to meet war conditions, including basic science for student nurses, a course for tabulating machine supervisors, and those classed as Engineering, Science and Management War Training courses. Between July 1942, and Aug. 1943, 1,649 persons were enrolled in full-time courses of this character and 2,671 in part-time courses. Nearly 200 research projects were carried on for government agencies and war industry. The School of Public Health occupied its new building in May and June 1943. For statistics of enrolment, etc., see UNIVERSITIES AND COLLEGES.
(A. G. R.)

Microphotography: see PHOTOGRAPHY.
Microscope, Electron: see PHOTOGRAPHY.
Midway Islands: see PACIFIC ISLANDS, U.S.

Mikhailovitch, Draja (1893–   ), Yugoslav army officer, was born in Shumadija, a village near Belgrade. He fought in the Balkan War, 1912–13, and in World War I. He saw action on the Salonika front, was thrice wounded, decorated for bravery and was promoted to a captaincy. He then attended the higher military academy and the general staff school. After the swift nazi conquest of Yugoslavia in April 1941, Mikhailovitch fled to the mountains, where he rounded up scattered Yugoslav detachments and welded them into a guerrilla force of considerable strength. His initial operations were successful and he was rewarded with the post of minister of war in the Yugoslav government-in-exile, Jan. 1942. In early 1943, Mikhailovitch restricted his operations against the Germans, and his Chetniks clashed frequently with the Yugoslav partisans, a rival organization. Mikhailovitch was widely publicized abroad, but within Yugoslavia his intense Serb nationalism repelled rather than attracted popular support from the heterogeneous racial elements in the country; as a result his armies fell to less than 25,000 in numbers, while the partisans boasted more than 200,000 guerrillas in their ranks. The partisans, who consistently charged that Mikhailovitch had "sold out" to the axis, not only won the bulk of popular support in Yugoslavia but backing from the Allies as well. King Peter II admitted, Oct. 16, 1943, that Mikhailovitch was not doing "sufficient fighting" against the Germans, but declared that the Chetnik leader had promised to activate his military operations and had agreed not to fight the partisans.

Mikolajczyk, Stanislaw

(1901–   ), Polish politician, was born in Gelsenkirchen, Germany, the son of a farm labourer who emigrated from Poznan province in western Poland to find work in the Westphalian mines. The family returned to Poland, where Mikolajczyk as a youth found work in a sugar-beet factory, and became active in political organizations. He was wounded during the Russo-Polish war in 1920. After the war, he entered politics and at the age of 29 was elected to the sejm, serving from 1930 to 1935. He was vice-president of the Polish Peasant party and was made its president in 1937. When the nazis invaded Poland in Sept. 1939, he saw military action in the unsuccessful defense of Warsaw. He fled to Hungary, where he was interned, but later escaped to France. He became President Ignace Paderewski's deputy in the Polish parliament in exile and upon the latter's death succeeded to the presidency. In 1941, he was appointed minister of home affairs and deputy prime minister in Premier Sikorski's government-in-exile. He became prime minister when Sikorski was killed in a plane crash, July 5, 1943. In his first address before the Polish national council, he affirmed the "historic necessity" for collaboration with soviet Russia. He insisted, however, upon restoration of all territory within Polish borders before the war.

Milk.

Total milk production in the United States in 1943 was estimated at 118,000,000,000 lb. by the United States department of agriculture, compared with the record production of 119,240,000,000 lb. in 1942 and 107,903,000,000 lb. for the average of 1937–41. The need for milk could not be met by this amount of production because of the great increase in demand by civilians for fluid milk and for military and lend-lease uses. The War Food administration had set 122,000,000,000 lb. as the goal, but because of a lower return per cow this goal was not attained. This was due to less favourable prices for milk compared to the cost of feed and the limited supplies of feed in some dairy regions. The number of cows continued to increase.

The production of cheese and other manufactured products declined in 1943 because of the strong demand for fluid milk. Civilian per capita consumption of all major dairy products was reduced below the prewar averages in 1943. Consumption of fluid milk in cities in 1943 was estimated to be 15% above the 1942 level and 34% above the 1935–37 average. The government moved in early fall to develop a payment program to stop the downward trend in milk production and to raise it if possible. Payments amounting to 30 to 50 cents per 100 lb. were offered dairymen. The rates were higher in areas where the quantity of purchased feed was large and feed costs advanced the most, and also where milk prices were low just preceding the war. Limitations of milk sales were ordered by the War Food administration

in some markets. The feed shortage in New York's milkshed led the state government to protest vigorously to the national authorities to move feed supplies into the area. A severe shortage of milk in New York city was forecast for 1944. The drought in the summer of 1943 reduced the supply of dairy feeds in the middle Atlantic coast states and cut down milk production until late fall when feed wheat and other grains were shipped into the area. The price of milk was at such levels that the cash farm income from milk and dairy products was expected to be 20% higher for 1943 than 1942. Farm costs, wages in particular, were higher in 1943 than in 1942 and the supply of labour much more limited. The demand for milk for civilian uses was estimated to be sufficient to use 120,000,000,000 lb. in 1944. The added needs for military uses, and for relief in Europe, should World War II end in 1944, would greatly exceed the possible production and make strict economies necessary, if not a rationing plan. (*See* also BUTTER; CHEESE; DAIRYING.)   (J. C. Ms.)

Millerand, Alexandre

(1859–1943), French Socialist and politician, was born Feb. 10 in Paris. During his half-century in politics, Millerand was responsible for the introduction of important social legislation in France. After resigning from the presidency in 1924, he served as senator from 1925 to 1940. He died at Versailles, April 6, according to a Berne report. (See *Encyclopædia Britannica*.)

Millstones: *see* ABRASIVES.

Milyukov, Paul Nikolayevich

(1859–1943), Russian politician and historian, was born Jan. 27 in St. Petersburg (Leningrad). A former leader of the liberation movement in Russia and a member of Prince Lvov's provisional government, he fled to Kiev after the bolsheviks seized power and then went to Paris. There he edited a Russian daily newspaper, *Dernières Nouvelles,* and a monthly magazine and continued his writings on Russian history. He died at Aix-les-Bains, France, March 31, according to a Berne report of April 15. (See *Encyclopædia Britannica*.)

Mineral and Metal Production and Prices.

The comparatively few data on production in 1942 have been added to the accompanying tables, supplementing the figures of earlier years which must be used in most cases. A production table including figures scattered over the years 1938 to 1942 is admittedly not particularly desirable, but it is the best that can be done for the war years; while it lacks much of the value of a table made up entirely of figures for the latest year, it at least shows the latest data that have been received for the various countries.

A second table presents the opening and closing price quotations for 1943 on the London and New York markets for the leading minerals, ores and metals. With most of the prices under governmental control, and subject to little if any variation, the former practice of including the high and low prices for the year has been discontinued for the time being, as they would in most cases merely be repetition.

The *Mineral Industry* index of aggregate world mineral production, which has formerly been quoted as a measure of over-all mineral output from year to year, has become a war casualty through lack of sufficient data on which to base calculations, but similar data are available for a few individual countries in the *Monthly Bulletin* of the League of Nations. Even though not directly comparable because of different bases and coverage, the tabulation of the data from the two sources in Table III gives a

Table I.— World Mineral and Metal Production in 1942

(Metric tons unless otherwise specified; Th. indicates thousands and Mi., millions of units.)

Country	Aluminum (Th.)	Bauxite (Th.)	Antimony (Th.)	Asbestos (Th.)	Cadmium (Th. Lb.)	Chromite (Th.)	Coal (Mi.)	Coke (Mi.)	Copper in Ore (Th.)	Copper (Blister) (Th.)	Diamonds (Th. carats)	Gold (Mi. Oz.)	Iron Ore (Mi.)	Pig Iron (Mi.)	Steel (Mi.)	Lead in Ore (Th.)	Lead (Th.)
Algeria			[1.0]				p		p							[4.6]	
Angola											791						
Australia		{1.7}	[0.6]	(0.5)	[376]	[1.0]	17.5	1.4	[19.8]	(22.7)		1.18	[0.49]		(1.25)	[278.8]	{315}
Belgian Congo							p		(148.6)	168	6,018	[0.49]					
Belgium					[1,168]		29.8	5.2		[65.9]			[0.2]	[3.07]	(2.23)		{20}
Bolivia			{14.9}	{0.2}					{7.2}			(0.01)				15.7	
Brazil		{20}	[0.1]	{0.5}		(4.6)			p		300	(0.32)	[0.26]	[0.19]			
Burma			p				{1.4}		{3.4}			p				[78.6]	{84}
Canada	{200}		p	(313.5)	[940]		17.1	3.0	[270.1]	(281.2)		4.84		2.06	2.78	[176.3]	244
Chile							1.9		(352.0)	453.6		(0.34)	(1.75)			(0.8)	
China				(5.5)			{17.8}	P	p			p			p		
Colombia							{0.4}					(0.61)		[1.0]			
Czechoslovakia		[0.8]	[1.2]	[2.7]			[30.5]	2.4	p			(0.01)	[1.84]	[1.0]			
France	{60}	{500}	p		[256]		[51]	7.8	p			[0.09]	[33.14]	[7.9]	(5.45)	[5]	{10}
Germany	{270}	{135}	[0.1]		[952]		[433]	43.5	35.8	66.0		p	[10.94]	[20.3]	(25.13)	[96]	{225}
Gold Coast		(180)									1,000	(0.79)					
Greece			p			[55]	[0.1]						[0.31]			[4.1]	[4.9]
Guiana, Brit.		(900)									27	(0.04)					
Guiana, Neth.		(1,100)										(0.02)					
Hungary	{3}	{600}					(10.7)	p	p				[0.37]	[0.46]	(0.74)		
India		(15)	p	[0.3]		[49.9]	26.0	1.9	5.6	(6.9)	p	(0.26)	[3.12]	[2.02]	(1.37)		
Indo-China							0.8						[0.03]				
Italy	{40}	{380}	[0.9]	6.9	[182]	[52]	3.1	1.7		[3.0]		p	[0.99]	[1.0]	(2.5)	[39.5]	{45}
Japanese Emp.	{49}		p	(1)	[52]	[39]	?		(129)	(125)		(1.93)	[1.0]	[3.0]	(6.34)	[12]	17
Luxembourg													[5.14]	[1.8]	(1.30)		
Malaya		(63.8)					(0.8)					(0.04)	[1.87]				
Manchoukuo													[0.12]	(0.7)			
Mexico			{11.1}		{1,994}		{0.9}	[0.5]	{48.7}	40.9		0.80	[0.11]	(0.07)		{155.3}	{160}
Morocco, Fr.			[0.1]				0.1						[0.27]			[19]	
Neth. E. Indies		{100}					(2.5)		p			p	[0.08]				
New Caledonia						(55.8)			p								
Norway	{35}						p		(20.0)	(7.3)		p	[1.43]	[0.17]		p	p
Peru			{1.5}		[204]				{35.4}	35.1		(0.29)				{54.8}	{43.0}
Philippines						(194.4)			{0.4}	p		1.16					
Poland					[538]		[38.1]	[2.5]	{9.9}				[0.87]	[1.0]		[5.3]	[5.6]
Portugal			[0.1]				0.4					p					
Rhodesia, No.			[0.1]						[259.4]	[231.3]		0.76	p	p			
Rhodesia, So.				52.9		(300)	1.1					p					
Siam (Thailand)												[0.01]					
Sierra Leone											850	(0.03)	[0.88]				
South Africa			p	(20.1)		[163.6]	(17.3)	[0.2]	(13.4)	(17.0)	106	14.12	(0.64)	(0.30)	(0.4)	[14.7]	(0.7)
So.-West Africa						[71]			(1.5)		60	p	(0.02)				
Spain	{1}						10.3	0.8	P	(4.5)			(2.9)	0.53	(0.75)	[57.9]	{57}
Sweden	{2}						{0.6}	[0.1]	{9.6}	(12.5)		(0.20)	[13.79]	[0.69]	(0.88)	[8.7]	[23.4]
Tunisia													[0.76]			[17.2]	
Turkey			[0.6]			(110.0)	2.4		(8.7)	(8.7)		p	[0.24]			[7.6]	p
United Kingdom	{35}		{0.4}	22.1	[275.4]		207.3	[13.0]	p	(4.5)			[12.05]	[8.3]	(13.4)	[30.2]	{10}
United States	472.7	{900}	{0.4}		[275]	(2.7)	580.9	64.0	972.6	987.1		3.58	107.7	55.25	78.04	446.8	424.8
U.S.S.R.	{50}	(270)		[86]	[275]	[217]	247	(16.5)				4.4?	(26.53)	[15.2]	(19.47)	[69]	{90}
Venezuela									(157)	(157)		(0.15)					
Yugoslavia	{1}	{400}	[4.2]		[250]	[59.5]	[6.1]		[64.2]	(43.0)		[0.34]	0.67	[0.06]		(68.8)	(14.0)
World Total	{1,045}	{5,500}	{34}	?	[9,200]	(1,250)	1,600+	?	2,500?	2,720?	9,254?	40.4?	208?	(106.4?)	(143.4?)	?	{1,850?}

Country	Magnesite Ore (Th.)[1]	Manganese Ore (Th.)	Mercury (Th. Lb.)	Nickel (Th.)	Petroleum (Mi. Bbl.)	Phosphate Rock (Th.)	Platinum (Th. Oz.)	Potash (Th.)[2]	Pyrite (Th.)	Salt (Mi.)	Silver in Ore (Mi. Oz.)	Sulphur (Th.)[3]	Tin in Ore (Th.)	Tin (Th.)	Tungsten Conc.[4] (Th.)	Zinc in Ore (Th.)	Zinc (Th.)
Algeria			[7]			(362)		[44]		[0.1]	[0.08]					[3.3]	
Angola										p							
Australia	[19.8]	p	p			p	p	{55}		0.1	[14.68]		[3.5]	[3.3]	{0.4}	[224]	(85)
Belgian Congo		[7.7]				p	p			p	[2.09]		{14}	[2.1]		[3.0]	
Belgium						[34]								[3.1]			(65)
Bolivia			p		0.3						(5.63)	(4.0)	{41}		{5.1}	7.3	
Brazil		{433.3}	[0.3]		0.2	p				0.6	(0.02)						
Burma			[0.9]		2.1					p	(6.18)		[5.8]		{8.3}	[29.6]	
Canada		p	P	[102.6]	10.2	1.9	[149]	[207]		0.6	19.75						216
Chile		{23}			(32)						(1.52)	(29.5)					
China		(216)				(8)			[3]	[0.20]	(0.26)		[11]	10.9	{9.3}		
Colombia					10.9		[39]			[0.2]	(0.26)						
Czechoslovakia	[74.7]		[100]		0.1					[0.2]	[1.19]					[0.8]	[8.9]
France					0.6	(10)		[582]	[147]	1.6	[0.57]					[35]	
Germany	[439]	p	[65]	[0.6]	4.5	[3]		[1861]	[405]	3.3	[7.01]			[0.3]		[185]	[225]
Gold Coast		[341.7]									[0.02]						
Greece	[168.2]	[11.2]		[1.3]				[217]		[0.1]	[0.34]					[3]	
Guiana, Brit.																	
Guiana, Neth.																	
Hungary		22.2			4.7						[0.04]						
India	[26.0]	[858.2]			2.4	p		[4]		(1.5)	[0.02]				{0.5}		
Indo-China		[2.4]				(22)						p	[1.6]	[0.2]		(5.6)	[5.3]
Italy	[6.2]	[48.3]	[2315]	[0.1]	0.5	p		[930]	{2000}	1.5	[0.81]	[355]	{1.6}	[0.2]	{2.0}	[77.6]	(40)
Japanese Emp.		[70]	[21]	p	2.7	[365]	p	P		0.9	[10.3]	[172]	{1.7}	[1.7]			(60)
Luxembourg																	
Malaya		[32.0]								p			{83}	[81.5]	{0.5}		
Manchoukuo	[331]																
Mexico		p	{798}		35.1	(714)				[0.1]	[78.36]	[1]	[0.3]		{0.2}	{122.8}	(40)
Morocco, Fr.		[86.6]								p	[0.21]						
Neth. E. Indies		[12.1]		[0.8]	11.5	(34)				[0.1]	[0.62]	(17.2)	{54}	[14.8]			
New Caledonia				[17.5]		[5]											
Norway	[2.1]			[1.2]					[1025]		[0.30]					[4.5]	(20)
Peru		(58.0)			12.6					16.6	{1.24}	(0.6)		p	{0.2}	20.3	
Philippines						p				p							
Poland					3.3	[10]		[108]	[92]	[0.6]	[0.06]					(66.6)	(120)
Portugal		[3.0]							[372]	p	[0.02]		[1.5]	p	2.9		
Rhodesia, No.		[3.0]								[0.08]						(12.7)	(15)
Rhodesia, So.			p	p				[27]		(0.19)			[0.4]	p	p		
Siam (Thailand)										[0.1]			{16.5}	p	{0.5}		
Sierra Leone						p				p							
South Africa	[2.6]	(412.1)	[0.4]			p	[40]		(37)	[0.1]	[1.29]		[0.5]		p		
So.-West Africa						(1)				p	[0.46]		[0.1]			[29.0]	
Spain			[1842]	p		(125)			[957]	[0.60]	[0.6]				0.9	{29.0}	(12)
Sweden		[5.9]	[9]			[6]			[192]		[1.22]				{0.2}	[28.9]	
Tunisia						(936)				[0.1]						[0.4]	
Turkey	[0.8]	[3.3]	[12]							[0.3]	[0.58]	[2.6]				[10.1]	
United Kingdom					0.7			[4]		2.7	[0.07]			[1.8]	[0.1]	[9.6]	(60)
United States	451.2	{77}	3864	(0.5)	1385.5	4718.5	[38]	617.8	707.9	12.4	55.86	3,178.6		[1.8]	[37.4]	689.7	571.5
U.S.S.R.	P	{2272}	[300]	[2.5]	200	(1461)	[170]	[266]	[980]	(4.4)	[8.0]			?	{6.5}	?	(85)
Venezuela	[39.3]				222.9					p			p				
Yugoslavia									[146]	p	[2.29]					(18.8)	[4.2]
World Total	?	[4,600?]	[5,500?]	136?	2,024	10,000?	[460?]	?	?	265?	?	?	{250?}	[170.7]	{47?}	?	(1,732?)

NOTES: A figure in braces is for 1941, and one in parentheses is for 1940, 1942 or 1941 data not being available; one in brackets is for a preceding year, 1939, or the latest available. A figure without decimals is an estimate, except with cadmium, mercury, potash and pyrite. The letter "p" indicates a production unknown or smaller than the minimum base of the table, while "P" indicates an output of greater size.

[1] Crude magnesite. [2] K2O equivalent of salts produced. [3] Mainly crude sulphur, but includes some ore, where sulphur content is not reported; also includes some sulphur recovered from industrial gases, especially from the roasting of sulphide ores. [4] 60% WO3 basis.

Table II.—*Mineral and Metal Prices in 1943*

New York market as reported by *E&MJ Metal and Mineral Markets*					London market as reported by the *Metal Bulletin*							
Open	Close	Grade	Units		Grade	Units	Open £	Open s.	Open d.	Close £	Close s.	Close d.
15.00 ¢	15.00 ¢	99% ingot	Pound	Aluminum	98–99%	Long ton	110	.	.	110	.	.
$ 2.15		50–55% Sb.	S.T. unit	Antimony, Ore	50–55% Sb	Unit	.	nom.	.	.	nom.	.
16.049 ¢	15.839 ¢	Domestic, cased	Pound	Antimony	Domestic, 99%	Long ton	120	.	.	120	.	.
16.50 ¢	16.50 ¢	Chinese	,,		Chinese	,,	.	nom.	.	.	nom.	.
4.0 ¢	4.0 ¢	White oxide	,,	Arsenic	Foreign, 99%	,,	44	.	.	60	.	.
$ 15.00	$ 15.00	4% Be (a)	,,	Beryllium-copper alloy	Strip	Pound	.	9	6	.	9	6
$ 1.25	$ 1.25	Ton lots	,,	Bismuth		,,	.	6	3	.	6	3
90 ¢	90 ¢	Commercial sticks	,,	Cadmium		,,	.	5	5	.	5	5
$ 43.50	$ 43.50	48% Cr_2O_3, 3 Cr:1 Fe	Long ton	Chromium, Ore	Rhodesian, 1st grade	Long ton	11	19	.	11	19	.
89 ¢	89 ¢	97%, spot	Pound	Metal	98–99%	Pound	.	4	6½	.	4	6½
13 ¢	13 ¢	4–6% C, 66–70 Cr (a)	,,	Ferro-alloy	4–8% C.	Long ton	45	.	.	59	.	.
19.5 ¢	19.5 ¢	2% C, 67–72% Cr (a)	,,	Ferro-alloy	2% C. (a)	Pound	.	1	½	.	1	6
$ 1.50	$ 1.50	97–99% Co	,,	Cobalt		,,	.	8	6½	.	8	6½
11.775 ¢	11.775 ¢	Domestic	,,	Copper	Fire ref., high gr.	Long ton	61	10	.	61	10	.
11.700 ¢	11.700 ¢	Export	,,		Electrolytic	,,	62	.	.	62	.	.
$ 35.00	$ 35.00		Ounce	Gold	Official	Ounce	.	168	.	.	168	.
$165.00	$165.00	Sponge, powder	,,	Iridium		,,	32	10	.	36	5	.
$ 4.45	$ 4.45	Mesabi, non-bessemer	Long ton	Iron, Ore	50% No. African	Long ton	.	nom.	.	.	nom.	.
$ 23.50	$ 23.50	Basic	,,	Pig	Basic	,,	6	0	6	6	0	6
$ 68.64	$ 76.54	80%, Joplin, Mo.	Short ton	Lead, Ore	80% R/C	,,	.	nom.	.	.	nom.	.
6.50 ¢	6.50 ¢	New York	Pound	Metal	Foreign, soft	,,	25	.	.	25	.	.
22.5 ¢	20.5 ¢	99.8% car lots	,,	Magnesium, ingots		Pound	.	1	6	.	1	6
29.5 ¢	27.5 ¢		,,	Sticks		,,	.	1	10	.	1	10
76.8 ¢	76.8 ¢	46% Brazilian	L.T. unit	Manganese, Ore	50–52% Mn	Unit	.	1	2	.	1	3⅜
$135.00		78–82%	Long ton	Ferro-alloy		Long ton	18	10	.	18	10	.
$ 36.00	$ 36.00	19–21% Mn	,,	Spiegel	18–22% Mn	,,	11	1	.	11	1	.
$197.00	$181.00	(76 lb.)	Flask	Mercury	(76 lb.)	Flask	69	2	6	69	2	6
45 ¢	45 ¢	90% MoS_2 (b)	Pound	Molybdenum, Ore	85% MoS_2	Unit	.	43	9	.	43	9
95 ¢	95 ¢	55–65% Mo (a)	,,	Ferro-alloy	70–75% Mo, C free (a)	Pound	.	6	.	.	6	.
35 ¢	35 ¢	Cathodes	,,	Nickel	Refined	Long ton	192	10	.	192	10	.
$ 24.00	$ 24.00		Ounce	Palladium		Ounce	5	15	.	5	17	6
$ 75.00	$ 75.00	24% P	Long ton	Phosphorus, Ferro-	20–25% P.	Long ton	15	.	.	15	.	.
$ 36.00	$ 35.00		Ounce	Platinum		Ounce	8	15	.	8	16	3
$125.00	$125.00		,,	Rhodium		,,	34	.	.	33	10	.
$ 1.75	$ 1.75	99.5%	Pound	Selenium		Pound	.	8	6	.	8	6
14.75 ¢	14.75 ¢	97+% Si, spot	,,	Silicon	98–99% Si	Long ton	85	.	.	85	.	.
$ 74.50	$ 74.50	50% Si	Long ton	Ferro-alloy	45% Si	,,	23	10	.	27	10	.
$135.00	$135.00	75% Si	,,	,,	75% Si	,,	36	10	.	43	.	.
44.75 ¢	44.75 ¢	Foreign, New York	Ounce	Silver	Official, spot	Ounce	.	.	23½	.	.	23½
$ 1.75	$ 1.75		Pound	Tellurium		Pound	.	7	.	.	7	.
52.00 ¢	52.00 ¢	Straits	,,	Tin	Standard, cash	Long ton	275	10	.	275	.	.
$142.50	$142.50		Short ton	Titanium, Ferrocarbon-	15–18% Ti	Pound	.	.	8¾	.	.	8¾
$ 26.00	$ 26.00	Domestic	S.T. unit	Tungsten, Ore	}65%	Unit	.	77	6	.	77	6
$ 24.00	$ 24.00	Chinese	,,	,,								
$ 1.90	$ 1.90	75–80% W (a)	Pound	Ferro-alloy	80–85% W (a)	Pound	.	9	8	.	9	3
$ 2.625	$ 2.625	99% W	,,	Powder	98–99% W	,,	.	9	9½	.	9	9½
27.5 ¢	27.5 ¢	(c)	,,	Vanadium, Ore	10–12% V_2O_5	Unit	.	nom.	.	.	nom.	.
$ 2.825	$ 2.825	(a)	,,	Ferro-alloy	35–60% V. (a)	Pound	.	15	6	.	15	6
$ 55.28	$ 55.28	60%, Joplin, Mo.	Short ton	Zinc, Ore	52% R/C	Long ton	.	nom.	.	.	nom.	.
8.25 ¢	8.25 ¢	St. Louis	Pound	Metal	G.O.B., foreign	,,	25	15	.	25	15	.

(a) Per pound of base metal contained. (b) Per pound of MoS_2 contained. (c) Per pound of V_2O_5 contained.

rough guide to current progress, the 1943 figures being only for the month indicated.

The U.S. bureau of mines estimated the gross value of mineral output in the United States in 1943 at $8,030,000,000, a rise of 6% over $7,569,000,000 in 1942. Mineral fuels increased 12% in dollar value and metallic products 6%, while nonmetallics other than fuels dropped 14%, largely through the decline in demand for materials used in the building industry.

Table III.—*Index to Mineral Production, 1940–43 for a few countries*

		1940	1941	1942	1943
World	*Mineral Industry*	159	163	?	?
United States	Minerals	111	118	122	132–Sept.
Canada	Mining	117	182	186	287–Aug.
Chile	Mining	105	124	121	109–May
Mexico	Base metals	90	98	117	?
Sweden	Iron and steel	105	106	112	111–Aug.

(*See* also STRATEGIC MINERAL SUPPLIES, and the reviews of the various metals and minerals.) (G. A. Ro.)

Mineralogy.

The continued disrupted international conditions forced many mineralogists to suspend, temporarily, investigations which could be published and devote their energies to the war effort. This change in activities and the critical shortage of paper resulted in a reduction in the size or in the number of issues of some important mineralogical journals. Nevertheless, the number of significant publications in mineralogy during 1943 was impressive.

In his address as retiring president of the Mineralogical Society of America, A. F. Buddington discussed "Some Petrological Concepts and the Interior of the Earth," (*American Mineralogist*, March). The new mineral, gamagarite, a vanadium compound of barium containing iron and manganese, from Postmasburg district, Union of South Africa, was described by J. E. deVilliers (*ibid*, May). R. A. Hatch presented data on the phase equilibrium in the lithium aluminosilicate system (*ibid*, Sept.–Oct.), and M. A. Bredig on the phase relations in the calcium orthosilicate-orthophosphate system (*ibid*, Nov.–Dec.). Publications in book form included: (a) *World Minerals and World Peace*, by C. K. Leith, J. W. Furness and Cleona Lewis (Brookings institute, Washington), an important study of the greatly increased production and consumption of minerals and their role in international affairs; (b) *Optical Crystallography*, by E. E. Wahlstrom (New York), a timely and valuable contribution because of the many current applications of crystal optics and the polarizing microscope; (c) *Minerals and Rocks*, by R. D. George (New York) emphasizes mineral economics.

Gem Minerals.—Widely consulted articles on the uses of the diamond appeared in the second "Symposium on Diamonds" (*American Mineralogist*, March), as follows: "Diamond Production," by S. H. Ball; "Gem Diamonds and Their Present Trends," by Lazare Kaplan; "Diamond Dies," by Alexander Shayne; "Diamond-set Tools," by C. B. Slawson, and "Recent Development of Bonded Diamond Wheels," by A. A. Klein. The absorption bands and the luminescence phenomena of the diamond were discussed by B. W. Anderson (*The Gemmologist*, London, Jan., Feb., April). The war greatly increased the use of diamonds in industry and information concerning the variations in hardness in the diamond was of much importance. These variations were reviewed by Paul Grodzinski (*Industrial Diamond Review*, London, Feb.,

March). There was an unprecedented demand for quartz crystals for use as oscillating plates in radio, electronic and other apparatus which are essential in war matériel. During 1943 many specialized articles on various phases of the industrial use of quartz appeared in *Electronics, Communications,* and other technical journals. The production of quartz crystal plates with specified properties was on a large scale and of great strategic importance.

The discussion as to whether or not the diamond had ever been successfully produced in the laboratory was reopened by F. A. Bannister and K. Lonsdale in their article "An X-ray Study of Diamonds Artificially Prepared by J. B. Hannay in 1880" (*Mineralogical Magazine,* London, June). Bannister and Lonsdale studied by modern X-ray methods specimens purported to have been the results of experiments carried on by Hannay, and found that they possessed the properties of the diamond. While the results of this study were not to be questioned, there still remained considerable doubt as to the authenticity of the specimens. Whether or not Hannay actually succeeded in producing diamonds could not be proven conclusively until the methods used by him over 60 years before were repeated with success. (*See also* MINERAL AND METAL PRODUCTION AND PRICES.)

(E. H. KR.)

Miniature Photography: *see* PHOTOGRAPHY.

Minnesota.

A north central state of the United States, popularly known as the "Gopher state." Area, 84,068 sq.mi., of which 4,059 are water. Pop. (1940) 2,792,300. The rural population was 50·2% of the total. Capital, St. Paul (287,736). The only city in the state with a larger population was Minneapolis (492,370); Duluth had 101,065. The native-born white inhabitants in 1940 numbered 2,474,078, foreign-born, 294,904 and Negro, 9,928.

History.—Officers of the state in 1943 were: governor, Edward J. Thye; secretary of state, Mike Holm; treasurer, Julius A. Schmahl; auditor, Stafford King; attorney general, J. A. A. Burnquist; and chief justice, Henry M. Gallagher. Harold E. Stassen, who was serving his third term as governor, resigned to enter the United States navy. Edward J. Thye, lieutenant governor, was sworn in as governor in April 1943.

The 1943 session of the legislature passed more laws (666) than any Minnesota legislature since the adoption in 1891 of the constitutional amendment prohibiting special legislation. Much of this increase was due to the tremendous number of salary increase laws, made necessary by the rise in the cost of living.

A war-powers act was passed giving the governor special emergency powers. A state department of aeronautics was established and charged with the licensing of pilots and the administration of the airport laws. The Metropolitan Airport commission was created to develop airports for the Twin Cities. A number of laws were passed for the relief of servicemen, and a fund of $2,500,000 was to be set aside to aid returning war veterans and their families.

Other legislation included acts establishing the Iron Range and Rehabilitation commission, to recommend approval of expenditures and projects for rehabilitation purposes. Occupation and royalty tax on iron ore was increased from 9 to 10½% for the two-year period beginning July 1, 1943.

The income tax law was revised, and the act increased the credit of unmarried persons to $10 and of married persons to $30. The allowance for dependents was increased from $5 to $10. The money and credit tax was completely suspended for 1943–44 and no returns were required for those years. Old-age pensions were increased to $40 instead of $30, and aid to dependent children

was also raised. The unemployment compensation law was revised to raise the maximum benefits from $16 to $20 a week. An act to extend workmen's compensation to cover all occupational diseases instead of the restricted list on the statute books was passed. Real estate levy was cut from 9 mills per year to 6 mills the first year of the biennium and to 5½ the second year.

Education.—In 1942–43, Minnesota had 8,257 elementary, 660 secondary schools, and 13 junior colleges. Enrolment was 315,224, with 12,546 teachers in the elementary grades; 178,807, with 7,953 teachers in the secondary grades; 1,900, with 152 teachers in junior colleges; 8,063 in adult-education classes, with 257 teachers; and 478 in teacher training departments, with 36 teachers. The total public school expenditure for 1942–43 was $54,787,998.

EDWARD J. THYE, Republican, was sworn in as governor of Minnesota in April 1943 to succeed Harold E. Stassen, who had resigned to enter the U.S. navy

Public Welfare, Charities and Correction.—During the year ending June 30, 1943, $3,394,721 was spent on general relief, the average number of cases being 12,250; on old-age assistance, $17,193,116, the average number of recipients being 61,938. A total of $3,340,104 was spent on dependent children; this sum cared for an average of 7,803 families and 18,881 children. An average of 1,025 persons received $356,526 as aid to the blind. For the same period, the state prison, two state reformatories, and two training schools for delinquents had a total of 2,491 inmates and an aggregate expense of $1,377,081. Unemployment compensation paid out was $2,192,350 in 1943, compared with $6,531,939 in 1942.

Communication.—Highway mileage totalled 11,247 at the end of 1943. Railway mileage at the end of 1941 was 8,365. There were 29 airports and landing fields in the state and 7 seaplane bases and anchorages in 1941.

Banking and Finance.—On July 1, 1943, there were 484 state banks, one mutual savings bank, and four trust companies in Minnesota with deposits of $457,624,607 and resources of $497,328,152; 185 national banks with deposits of $1,310,906,000 and resources of $1,399,324,000; 44 building and loan associations with resources of $39,251,825. The state revenue and expenditure for the year ending June 30, 1943, were as follows: receipts, $33,991,346 plus transfers, warrants cancelled, and cash balances, making an available total of $57,391,493; payments, $44,170,492, plus transfers and adjustments, making a total of $49,301,125; balance, $8,749,986. The unpaid bonds and certificates of indebtedness on June 30, 1943, totalled $98,770,284. The state's four principal trust funds as of June 30, 1943 totalled $125,837,239.

Agriculture.—In Minnesota the cash income from farm marketings for the first seven months of 1943 totalled $451,674,000 compared with $349,103,000 in 1942.

Manufacturing.—Official figures later than 1939 were not available in 1943. According to the U.S. biennial census of manufactures in that year, there were 4,008 manufacturing establishments, employing 92,084 persons. Wages earned amounted to $125,442,031 and the output was valued at $845,771,514.

Leading Agricultural Products of Minnesota, 1943 and 1942

Crop	1943 (est.)	1942
Corn, all, bu.	195,619,000	207,190,000
Oats, bu.	160,099,000	177,567,000
Barley, bu.	35,490,000	50,327,000
Wheat, all, bu.	17,814,000	23,170,000
Potatoes, bu.	17,710,000	19,380,000
Flaxseed, bu.	17,700,000	15,950,000
Tame hay, tons	5,413,000	5,473,000
Rye, bu.	1,784,000	3,345,000

Mineral Production.—The 1943 output of iron ore in Minnesota was estimated at 83,655,340 tons. A late opening of inter-lake navigation resulted in delays in getting the iron ore movement at maximum of capacity.

BIBLIOGRAPHY.—Minnesota *Legislative Manual,* 1943.   (L. BE.)

Minnesota, University of.

An institution of higher education at Minneapolis, Minn. Enrolment of regular collegiate civilian students, which reached a peak of 15,807 in 1939, continued its decline in 1943. Because of army and navy trainees, however, the total number receiving instruction on the campus was slightly larger than in 1942. Women constituted 79% of the freshmen. The school of nursing, in the fall of 1943, enrolled the largest number of students in the cadet nurse corps of any institution in the U.S. During the years the Board of Regents extended the term of President Walter C. Coffey to June 30, 1945—one year beyond the normal retirement age and also created two vice-presidencies, academic and business. Dr. Errett W. McDiarmid from the University of Illinois assumed the post of librarian, replacing Frank K. Walter, who retired after 27 years of service. Gifts to the university during the year totalled $1,015,686.13. Staff members on leave for service in the armed forces or for other war-related work totalled 569 through Nov. 20, 1943; of this total, 288 were from the academic staff. (For statistics of enrolment, faculty, library volumes, etc., *see* UNIVERSITIES AND COLLEGES.)   (W. C. C.)

Minor League Baseball: *see* BASEBALL.
Mint, United States: *see* COINAGE.
Miquelon: *see* FRENCH COLONIAL EMPIRE.

Missions, Foreign.

In 1943 additional developments were brought to foreign missions, both Roman Catholic and Protestant, in consequence of the world-wide war. Yet these were not as sharp or as startling as had been those of the earlier years of the conflict. This was largely because the area of the conflict had already reached its widest dimensions and the tide of axis invasion and occupation had become stationary and here and there had been forced into recession. More missionaries were repatriated from Japan and from the portions of China occupied by the Japanese. There was little or no repatriation from some of the Japanese occupied lands, notably the East Indies. Japanese Christians, both Roman Catholic and Protestant, increased their efforts to effect close relationships with their fellow believers in the vast territories held by their country's armed forces. In spite of the difficulties of transportation, scores of new missionaries were being sent from the United States and the British Isles to South America, Africa, India and free China. A few missionaries who had been on furlough or who had been driven out by war managed to make their way back to their fields. If that field had been in China, it was, of course, to free and not to occupied China that they returned. In Great Britain and the United States giving to missions increased. From the Protestants of these lands, largely through the Orphaned Missions fund of the International Missionary council, remittances were maintained to Protestant missionaries from the continent of Europe who had been cut off from their supporting constituencies. Similarly, in the United States the provinces of various Roman Catholic orders continued to come to the assistance of the missions of the European provinces which had been cut off from their overseas missions. In Protestant circles in the United States there was much planning for the postwar years.

(K. S. L.)

Mississippi.

A southern state of the U.S.A., admitted to the union in 1817, popularly known as the "Magnolia state"; area, 47,716 sq.mi. (47,420 sq.mi. land and 296 sq.mi. water); pop. (1940), 2,183,796; capital, Jackson (62,107). Other cities: Biloxi (17,475); Greenville (20,892); Gulfport (15,195); Hattiesburg (21,026); Laurel (20,598); Meridian (35,481); Natchez (15,296); Vicksburg (24,460). Of the state's population in 1940, 432,882, or 19.8%, were urban. In 1940 there were 1,106,327 whites; 1,074,578 Negroes; 2,177,324 native born; 6,472 foreign.

History.—For 1940–1944 the elected officers of the state were: governor, Paul B. Johnson; lieutenant governor, Dennis Murphree; secretary of state, Walker Wood; attorney general, Greek L. Rice; state tax collector, Carl N. Craig; state treasurer, Lewis S. May; superintendent of education, J. S. Vandiver; state audi-

THOMAS L. BAILEY, Democrat, elected governor of Mississippi Nov. 2, 1943

tor, J. M. Causey. In the Aug. 24, 1943 primary, Thomas L. Bailey with 143,153 votes defeated Former Governor Martin S. Conner with 125,882, for the office of governor. For 1944–1948 the elected officers of the state, chosen in the Democratic primaries in Aug. 1943, were: governor, Thomas L. Bailey; lieutenant governor, Fielding L. Wright; secretary of state, Walker Wood; attorney general, Greek L. Rice; state tax collector, Carl N. Craig; state treasurer, Newton James; superintendent of education, J. S. Vandiver; state auditor, Bert J. Barnett. On Dec. 26, 1943, Governor Paul B. Johnson died at his home in Hattiesburg, and was immediately succeeded by Lieutenant Governor Dennis Murphree for the duration of his unexpired term.

Education.—In 1943 there were 1,319 white elementary schools in Mississippi and 3,637 Negro elementary schools, a total of 4,956. The enrolment in elementary schools in 1942–1943 was 512,959, of whom 235,508 were whites and 277,451 Negroes. The state had 575 white high schools and 100 Negro high schools, with a total enrolment of 74,344. There were 9,530 white elementary and high school teachers, and 6,879 Negro elementary and high school teachers, a total of 16,409 teachers. The total enrolment in white elementary and high schools was 295,896; in Negro elementary and high schools, 291,407.

Public Welfare.—In 1943 approximately 300,000 workers were covered by unemployment insurance. Benefits paid to persons covered by unemployment insurance amounted to $370,366. From July 1, 1942 through June 30, 1943, the state department of public welfare paid $2,818,649 to 29,040 recipients of old age assistance; $169,448 to 1,443 recipients of aid to the blind; $602,469 to 3,261 families for aid to 8,356 dependent children.

The Work Projects administration's total expenditures for the year were approximately $3,068,269, its average employment per month from Jan. 1943 through its liquidation in June 1943 was approximately 4,165.

Agriculture.—In 1943 there were 291,092 farms covering 30,348,800 ac., with a total acreage of 7,018,000 harvested. The total value of agricultural production in 1942 amounted to $334,429,000; in 1943, to $367,403,000.

Cash income from crops in 1942 amounted to $241,658,000; from livestock, to $52,252,000; from government payments, to $28,947,000.

Table I.—*Leading Agricultural Products of Mississippi, 1943 and 1942*

Crop	1943	1942
Cotton, bales	1,840,000	1,968,000
Cottonseed, tons	820,000	878,000
Corn, bu.	43,508,000	49,198,000
Oats, bu.	9,000,000	9,000,000
Hay, tons	1,007,000	1,127,000
Sweet potatoes, bu.	6,970,000	6,460,000
Sugar-cane syrup, gal.	2,992,000	3,300,000
Sorghum syrup, gal.	1,495,000	1,800,000
Peanuts, lb.	23,000,000	25,000,000
Lespedeza seed, lb.	1,900,000	3,300,000
Peaches, bu.	476,000	974,000
Pecans, lb.	5,300,000	5,400,000

Communications.—In 1943 the state maintained 6,443 mi. of highways and the counties approximately 64,000 mi. The total state expenditure for highways in 1943 amounted to $4,305,-836.07; in 1942, to $5,552,046.54. The county expenditure for maintenance costs only amounted to $7,380,744.55 in 1943; to $8,069,506.06 in 1942.

The total mileage of railroads in the state on Dec. 31, 1943, was 3,947.33 mi.

Banking and Finance.—On Dec. 31, 1943, there were 179 state banks in Mississippi, with 22 branch banks and 27 branch offices. There were 22 national banks in Mississippi. The resources of the state banks were $364,081,370.42 and deposits were $340,916,295.16; the resources of the national banks were $153,-756,194.32 and deposits were $145,031,512.32. The general fund account as of Jan. 1, 1943, amounted to a balance of $11,989,-739.17. On Dec. 31, 1943, the balance was $22,967,989.60. The special fund account showed a balance of $5,952,053.94 on Dec. 31, 1943. On Dec. 31, 1943, the general fund debt of the state was $22,606,000 (direct obligation bonds); outstanding highway bonds amounted to $51,097,000, making a total state debt of $73,703,000.

Manufacturing.—The value of manufactures in the state in 1937 was $190,670,510; in 1939 (the last federal biennial census as of 1943), $174,937,294. The number of persons employed in 1937 was 49,246; in 1939, 50,014.

The wages paid in 1937 amounted to $32,091,639; in 1939, $34,083,646.

Mineral Production.—The total value of mineral production in 1942, including natural gas, sand and gravel, crude oil and other mineral products, determined from tax paid, was $29,726,-143. In 1942 approximately 28,614,235 bbl. of petroleum were

Table II.—*Principal Mineral Products of Mississippi, 1942*

Mineral	Value 1942
Natural gas	$ 219,600
Sand and gravel	3,020,822
Crude oil	26,358,825
Other mineral products	126,896

produced; in 1943, 18,853,067 bbl. In 1942 2,084,061,000 cu.ft. natural gas were produced; in 1943, 1,300,000,000 cu.ft. On Dec. 31, 1943, there were approximately 375 producing oil wells in the state. (C. Cs.)

Missouri. A west north central state of the U.S.A., admitted to the union in 1821; popularly known as the "Show Me" state. Area, 69,674 sq.mi., of which 404 are water. Pop. (1940) 3,784,664 (51.8% urban, 48.2% rural); 3,425,062 (90.5%) native white, 114,125 (3%) foreign-born white, 224,386 (5.9%) Negro. Capital, Jefferson City (24,268). Largest cities: St. Louis (816,048), Kansas City (399,178), St. Joseph (75,711), Springfield (61,238).

History.—The 62nd Missouri general assembly (Jan. 6–Aug. 23, 1943) was in session longer than any previous assembly. The senate was evenly divided politically, with 17 Democrats and 17 Republicans, but its presiding officer, the lieutenant governor, was a Democrat; the house was overwhelmingly Republican (95 to 55). The legislature appropriated more than $255,000,000 for the 1943–44 biennium, the largest sum in Missouri's history. Of this amount, it allotted $52,750,000 for old-age assistance ($11,550,-000 above the 1941–42 fund), and $11,450,000 for general relief and dependent children (a $3,550,000 decrease). The legislature enacted laws providing for: a three-day waiting period for the issuance of marriage licences; serological tests for marriage licence applicants; a revision of the civil procedure and corporation codes; a permanent joint committee on legislative research; the establishment of teachers' pension and retirement funds by the three largest cities; a soil conservation commission; a revision of the Missouri food and drug laws; an absentee ballot for members of the armed forces. The legislature defeated the governor's proposals to establish a state merit system and to consolidate the state's tax collection agencies.

The legislature proposed two constitutional amendments: the first, which was subsequently approved by the voters at a special election on April 6, 1943, provided that all laws, except appropriation laws, should become effective 90 days after enactment; the second, to be passed upon by the voters in Nov. 1944, gives the legislature power to direct the investment or disbursal of county school funds for public school purposes.

At the special election on April 6, 1943, the voters chose 83 delegates to a convention to revise the state constitution. This constitutional convention, the sixth in Missouri's history, convened at Jefferson City on Sept. 21, 1943, and was still in session in Jan. 1944.

The major state officers (1943), all Democrats except the Republican governor, were: Forrest C. Donnell, governor; Frank G. Harris, lieutenant governor; Dwight H. Brown, secretary of state; Forrest Smith, auditor; Wilson Bell, treasurer; Roy S. McKittrick, attorney general.

Education.—For the school year ending June 30, 1943, the public school system consisted of 7,740 elementary schools, with 508,529 pupils and 17,358 teachers; 867 secondary schools, with 159,549 pupils and 7,867 teachers; 2 state universities (white and Negro); 5 state teachers' colleges; schools for the deaf and blind; and a Negro vocational school.

Public Welfare, Charities, Correction.—For the year ending June 30, 1943, unemployment compensation totalled $4,695,772, and the government employment services made 456,339 placements. For the same period WPA earnings amounted to $7,615,-993; old-age assistance $23,890,282; aid to dependent children $4,938,410; general relief $2,176,355; blind pensions $979,157. In June 1943, 108,708 persons received old-age assistance; 29,084 aid to dependent children; 15,488 general relief; 3,032 blind pensions. On Dec. 31, 1942, the state penitentiary had 3,067 inmates, and the four state correctional institutions a total of 1,044 inmates.

Communication.—On Dec. 31, 1942, Missouri had 16,116 mi. of state highways and 100,671 mi. of rural roads. During 1942 the state highway department spent $23,824,532 (state and federal funds), of which $8,371,345 was for construction, and $4,268,-166 for maintenance. In 1941 railroad mileage totalled 7,042 mi.

Banking and Finance.—On June 30, 1943, Missouri had 483 state banks, with deposits of $1,162,702,000 and resources (loans and investments) of $1,080,237,000; 83 national banks, with deposits of $799,852,000 and resources (loans and investments) of $863,260,000; 206 building and loan associations, with resources of $140,236,922.

Total receipts of the state treasury during 1943 amounted to $113,795,420; disbursements for 1943, $99,680,502; gross state debt, Jan. 1, 1943, $83,008,000; net state debt, Dec. 31, 1943, $76,255,000.

Agriculture.—The value of Missouri's 1943 crops, harvested from 12,994,200 ac., was estimated at $362,326,000, an increase of 17% over the value of 1942. Production of most crops in 1943 was below 1942, but was above any other recent year; the acreage harvested was 5% above 1942. Floods destroyed 700,000 ac. of Missouri's crops in May and June, when the Mississippi river at St. Louis reached its highest mark (38.94 ft.) since 1844.

Table I.—Leading Agricultural Products of Missouri, 1943 and 1942

Crop	1943 (est.)	1942
Corn, bu.	139,810,000	146,899,000
Tame hay, tons.	3,575,000	4,368,000
Cotton, bales.	295,000	417,000
Oats, bu.	51,750,000	59,427,000
Winter wheat, bu.	12,649,000	9,035,000
Soybeans (for beans), bu.	8,696,000	7,065,000

Manufacturing.—During 1939, Missouri's industries manufactured products valued at $1,388,056,267, employed 178,538 wage earners and 24,275 salaried persons, and paid $190,735,851 in wages and $58,937,137 in salaries.

Table II.—Principal Industries of Missouri, 1939 and 1937

Industry	Value, 1939	Value, 1937
Meat packing (wholesale)	$107,254,213	$116,576,053
Footwear (except rubber)	100,346,106	103,253,379
Iron and steel (excluding machinery)	89,059,177	77,681,234
Wearing apparel	85,297,177	76,998,667
Malt liquors	41,412,301	34,272,016
Drugs, medicines	23,006,499	24,335,460

Mineral Production.—The value of Missouri's mineral production in 1940 was estimated at $50,325,000, 10.3% more than in 1939. In 1941 Missouri produced 165,900 tons of lead (36% of the U.S. output), and 6,328,000 bbl. Portland cement, 27.3% more than in 1940.

Table III.—Principal Mineral Products of Missouri, 1940 and 1939

Mineral	Value, 1940	Value, 1939
Lead	$17,205,200	$14,690,414
Cement	Fig. not available	7,420,013
Bituminous coal	Fig. not available	6,124,000
Stone	6,176,867	4,589,986
Clay (raw and products)	Fig. not available	3,931,065
Lime	3,184,293	2,800,379
Barite	1,216,069	1,163,870

(R. P. Br.)

Mohammedanism: *see* ISLAM.

Molotov, Vyacheslav Mikhailovich

(1890 –), Russian statesman, was educated at Petersburg polytechnic and during his youth organized bolshevik student groups and worked for the newspaper *Pravda*. February of 1917 found him a member of the Petrograd soviet executive committee. In 1920 he was appointed secretary of the central committee of the communist party of the Ukraine, and in the following year he held this office for the whole of the U.S.S.R. He was appointed president of the soviet of people's commissars in 1930 and was named foreign commissar May 3, 1939, to succeed Maxim Litvinov. The latter appointment foreshadowed the temporary shift in soviet foreign policy which led to the nazi-soviet pact of nonaggression, signed by Molotov in Moscow, Aug. 24, 1939.

On May 6, 1941, Molotov resigned as premier of the U.S.S.R. and was succeeded in this office by Stalin; he remained as foreign commissar, however, and took over the vice-premiership. On July 1, ten days after the German invasion started, Stalin named him vice-chairman of the soviet defense committee, to which was delegated the full authority of state. On July 13, Molotov signed the British-U.S.S.R. mutual-aid pact in which each nation agreed not to make a separate peace. In the spring of 1942, Molotov went to England and on May 26 he and Anthony Eden signed a 20-year Russo-British mutual assistance pact. Molotov then flew to Washington, where, after conferences from May 29 to June 4, he and President Roosevelt signed a lend-lease agreement. In August, Molotov was named vice-chairman of the people's council of commissars.

On April 26, 1943, Molotov announced the suspension of relations with Poland. In reply to charges of mass murders of Polish officers, he accused the Poles of collaboration with Germany in an effort to force territorial concessions from the U.S.S.R. Later in the year, Oct. 19–30, he presided at a tripartite conference with Anthony Eden and Cordell Hull in Moscow. On Dec. 12, Molotov signed a mutual assistance pact with Czechoslovakia.

Moltke, Hans Adolf von

(1884–1943), German diplomat, was born Nov. 29 of a distinguished Junkers family. His father, Friedrich von Moltke, was a state minister of Prussia; his great uncle was Count Helmuth von Moltke, Prussian field marshal who led Bismarck's armies against France in 1870. Hans von Moltke was educated at the universities of Berlin, Heidelberg and Königsberg. He entered the diplomatic service in 1913, joined the German army at the outbreak of World War I and re-entered the diplomatic corps at the war's end, as embassy counsellor at Constantinople (now Istanbul). He was attached to the foreign office, 1928–31, and was appointed minister to Poland, 1931. After Poland signed its non-aggression pact with Germany in 1934, Hitler raised the status of his legation in Warsaw to an embassy and Von Moltke became Reich ambassador. Von Moltke was recalled after the German invasion of Poland in 1939; he was credited with having compiled German "documents" putting the war guilt on the Allies. He was sent to Madrid as ambassador in Jan. 1943. It was reported that Hitler had instructed him to use every power at his means to alienate Gen. Franco from the Allies and to try to lure the Spanish dictator into the axis camp. Von Moltke's efforts in this direction never bore fruit. He died in Madrid, March 22.

Molybdenum.

Although molybdenum started 1943 in the list of materials short in supply, this shortage was remedied. Consumption demands were not only met, but a stockpile was accumulated covering a six months' supply. During the first six months of 1943 the new supply included about 29,000,000 lb. of domestic output and 2,200,000 lb. of imports, a total of 31,200,000 lb., double the world output of as late as 1937. Consumption for 1943 was estimated at 52,400,000 lb., 10% less than the production rate for the year. Requirements for 1944 were estimated at 44,551,000 lb., including a continuation of 1943 fourth-quarter rate of exports. Lend-lease and Canadian requirements totaled 7,917,000 lb. in the first half of 1943.

An official announcement stated that Canada was in 1943 producing a substantial portion of her requirements, with three mines producing. (G. A. Ro.)

Monaco.

A principality on the Mediterranean coast, bounded on the land side by French (occupied) territory. Area 375 ac. (0.59 sq.mi.); pop. (census 1939), 23,973. Chief towns: Monaco, La Condamine, Monte Carlo; ruler: Prince Louis II; language: French. The chief occupation is catering for visitors, who, before war broke out in 1939, numbered more than 2,000,000 annually.

Monazite.

No information was available on production or imports of monazite in the United States, but at the end of 1943 cerium salts were listed as balanced as to supply and essential demand. The working of beach sands in Florida for titanium and zirconium give a small byproduct recovery of monazite. Normally India and Brazil are the chief sources of supply. (G. A. Ro.)

Monetary Units: *see* EXCHANGE CONTROL AND EXCHANGE RATES.

Mongolia

(INNER AND OUTER). A vast, arid, sparsely populated tableland in northeastern Asia, with several deserts, of which the Gobi is the largest. Estimated area 956,844 sq.mi. It is bounded N. by Siberia, E. by Manchuria ("Manchoukuo"), W. by Sin Kiang (Chinese Turkestan), S. by China. Mongolia was included in the boundaries of the Chinese Empire and the Chinese Republic never renounced its claim to sovereignty in this area. But in practice Outer Mongolia was controlled by the soviet union after 1921 and Japan dominated Inner Mongolia after 1937. Of these two divisions, Outer Mongolia is the larger in size (622,744 sq.mi.), but Inner Mongolia (334,100 sq.mi.) is more closely settled, with some industry, agriculture and mining along with the vast stretches of grazing land which are the basis of the typical pastoral economy of the nomadic Mongols.

Outer Mongolia.—Population (est. 1941) 850,000. Capital Ulan Bator, formerly Urga (pop. 100,000). This immense territory after World War I was almost completely isolated from the outside world, except for the soviet union. Soviet troops, pursuing the anti-Bolshevik forces of Baron Ungern-Sternberg, which had utilized Outer Mongolia as a base for raids into Siberia, entered Outer Mongolia in 1921 and co-operated with a few educated Mongol revolutionaries in setting up a people's revolutionary government. From that time Outer Mongolia was closely controlled from Moscow. When diplomatic relations were resumed between the soviet and Chinese governments in 1924 the soviet government recognized Outer Mongolia as an integral part of China and promised to withdraw its troops from that region. In practice, however, China was unable to exercise administrative sovereignty. A treaty of alliance was concluded between the soviet union and Outer Mongolia in 1936 and there was apparently close military co-operation between the two regimes in border clashes with Japanese and Manchurian troops during the '30s. The most serious of these was at Nomonhan in 1939. The Soviet-Japanese treaty of neutrality of April 1941 contained a clause under which Japan promised to respect the territorial inviolability of Outer Mongolia, the soviet union undertaking a similar obligation in relation to Manchuria; and there were no reports of border troubles during 1943.

Under a constitution which was promulgated in 1924 and which closely followed the general outline of the soviet constitution, although with some allowances for the primitive character of Mongolian economy and ways of life, Outer Mongolia constitutes a people's republic, with power vested in a representative assembly called the Great Huruldan, which selects from its members a smaller group, the Little Huruldan, for more frequent sessions. The Little Huruldan elects a committee of five, which is in charge of current affairs.

Economic Developments.—Outer Mongolia's trade connections continued to be exclusively with the soviet union in 1943. Russian financial advisers helped work out a new currency system, the basic unit being the *tugerik,* valued at 90 kopecks. Most of the wealth of Outer Mongolia consists of herds and flocks. It is estimated that there were 1,340,000 horses, 270,000 camels, 1,500,000 oxen and 10,600,000 sheep in the country in 1942. There were some disturbances and uprisings in the country between 1929 and 1932 because severe measures were employed to promote collectivist ownership of cattle. Some of the wealthier Mongols fled across the frontier into China. These measures were subsequently modified.

Wool, hides, bristles and casings are leading Outer Mongolian exports. The soviet union supplies the country with oil, chemicals, cement, textiles and manufactured goods. Trade is financed through the Mongol Bank, in which the soviet government owns half the capital. The chief commercial organization is the Mongolian Central Co-operative society. There is an air line between Ulan Bator and Verkhne-Udinsk in Siberia, and there is a highway between Ulan Bator and the Siberian border town of Kyakhta.

There are no railways in the country. Northwest of Outer Mongolia is the little soviet protectorate of Tannu-Tuva, area 64,000 sq.mi., pop. 65,000, capital Kysylchoto, with communication with Siberia by way of the Yenisei river, which rises in Outer Mongolia.

Inner Mongolia.—Inner Mongolia includes the three northern Chinese provinces of Chahar, Suiyuan and Ningsia (Sitao). The Japanese invasion of North China in 1937 led to the creation, under strong Japanese tutelage, of a new state called Mengchiang (Federated Council of the Mongol Borderland), claiming authority over the three provinces, with their mixed Chinese and Mongol population of five to seven million.

Because of the differing racial composition and economic character of the region, the new state was organized in the form of a federation of three regimes, with capitals at Hohohoto (formerly Suiyuan), Kalgan and Tatung. The regime at Hohohoto was composed of representatives of the Mongol "banners," or clans and represented the fruition of a long period of Japanese intrigue among the Mongol chiefs of North China, designed to take advantage of the political and economic friction between the agricultural Chinese and the nomadic Mongols, who sometimes resented the encroachment of Chinese settlers on their grazing lands.

Tatung is the principal town of North Shansi and the centre of a huge but very imperfectly developed coal region. Kalgan is an old trading town northwest of Peking.

The Japanese authorities hoped to insure a regular supply of wool from this region after it had been brought under their political control; but economic development was hampered by guerrilla warfare and by floods and drought. The Meng-chiang yuan is of the same nominal value as the Japanese yen (23.48 U.S. cents) and Meng-chiang trade is channelled entirely through Japanese sources. The Peking-Suiyuan railway affords the principal means of communication for Inner Mongolia and is carefully guarded by Japanese troops. Japanese peace offers to China always specified Inner Mongolia as a region where Japan should possess special political and economic rights. The principal products of Inner Mongolia are wool, furs, coal, iron, opium, cereal and linseed. (W. H. CH.)

Montana. A northwestern state of the United States, popularly known as the "Treasure state." Area, 147,138 sq.mi.; pop. (1940): 559,456. The urban population was 211,535 or 37.8%. Capital, Helena (15,056). Other cities of 10,000 or more were: Butte (37,081); Great Falls (29,928); Billings (23,261); Missoula (18,449); Anaconda (11,004). Of the total population there were 540,468 whites, of whom 484,826 were native-born and 55,642 were foreign-born. The Indian population numbered 16,841.

History.—In the general election of 1942 the Republicans had gained control of both houses of the state legislature. Sam G. Ford, elected for a four-year term in 1940, was the first Republican governor since 1920. Other state officials in 1943 were Ernest T. Eaton, lieutenant governor; Sam Mitchell, secretary of state; John J. Holmes, auditor; R. V. Bottomly, attorney general; Elizabeth Ireland, superintendent of public instruction.

A $70,000,000 postwar public works program to aid private industry in providing jobs for returning veterans and give the state needed improvements, was drafted by the Montana planning board in 1943. Highway construction, irrigation of semi-arid farm lands, extension of rural electrification, and new buildings and improvements at the state institutions were listed as the main projects to be undertaken. Strenuous opposition developed throughout the state against the army engineers' plan to raise the level of Flathead lake 17 ft. or more, the chief objection being the claim that the economic and social life of some 50,000 Montana people would be disrupted. State agencies, however, co-operated with the federal government in developing plans for two large water conservation projects—the Hungry Horse dam on the South Fork of the Flathead river, and the Canyon Ferry dam on the Missouri river near Helena.

Education.—There were 1,786 elementary schools in Montana in 1943, with an enrolment of 69,236 and a teaching staff of 3,514. There were 195 high schools with an enrolment of 27,329 and 1,425 teachers. The cost of operating these schools was $12,895,233.

Public Welfare, Charities, Correction.—Through federal and state aid, approximately 21,000 persons received public assistance in 1943. Grants totalling $4,965,538 were distributed as follows (figures in parentheses indicate the average number of recipients per month): Old age assistance (11,845), $3,590,702; aid to dependent children (6,322), $703,640; aid to needy blind (313), $101,196; general relief (1,436), $320,000; medical care (331), $40,000; hospitalization (285), $175,000; burials (45), $35,000. Unemployment compensation benefits of $109,239—less than one tenth the amount for 1942—were paid to 1,194 persons, an average of $11.68 per week for 7.83 weeks, or $91.49 per claimant. Correctional institutions with their average population and total expenditures in 1943 were: Montana State prison, 403 inmates, $181,383; State Industrial school, 95 inmates, $70,930; Vocational School for Girls, 79 inmates, $43,025.

Communication.—Approval during 1943 of the Federal Aid Secondary system added nearly 1,400 mi. to the state highway system, bringing the total mileage under the state highway commission up to 7,951. State highway expenditures in 1943 were $4,490,930. There were 13 designated airports and 63 emergency landing fields, including those used by the forest service. The number of telephones was estimated at 77,500.

Banking and Finance.—There were 110 banks in the state in 1943. The 41 national banks had total deposits of $165,670,000, and their total resources were $175,554,000. State banks had total assets of $126,254,254 and their total deposits were $117,836,620. There were 16 building and loan associations with assets of $12,981,350. For the fiscal year 1942–43, the net state income was $41,203,692 and the total expenditures were $33,856,801. The gross debt of the state was $8,421,725 and the net debt, $6,942,657.

Agriculture.—Crop production in Montana in 1943 was 4% higher than in 1942 and the greatest in the state's history. The value of all main crops was $184,292,000 as compared with $139,869,000 in 1942—a 32% valuation increase due mainly to price increases. The cash income from livestock and livestock products was $125,829,000. Government payments were $12,500,000.

Table I.—*Leading Agricultural Products of Montana, 1943 and 1942*

Crop	1943	1942
Wheat, bu.	74,335,000	73,783,000
Hay, tons	2,499,000	2,759,000
Barley, bu.	15,039,000	12,330,000
Flaxseed, bu.	4,544,000	2,475,000
Oats, bu.	18,760,000	20,319,000
Sugar beets, tons	581,000	915,000
Corn, bu.	3,230,000	3,800,000
Potatoes, bu.	2,645,000	1,725,000
Seed peas, 100-lb. bags	627,000	492,000
Dry beans, 100-lb. bags	549,000	338,000
Alfalfa seed, bu.	97,000	90,000
Mustard seed, lb.	31,300,000	34,000,000

Manufacturing.—The total value of products manufactured in Montana in 1939 was $151,885,026 as compared with $176,278,814 in 1937. Persons employed in manufacturing numbered 10,898 in 1939 and were paid salaries and wages amounting to $15,832,241. Information through the U.S. biennial census for manufactures was not available in 1943 for the years since 1939.

Mineral Production.—The 1943 production of gold, silver, copper, lead and zinc in Montana was valued at $53,671,500, a decrease of 11% under that of 1942. There was a decrease in the output of each metal, but the value of the copper output was greater, owing to the average higher price of the metal.

Table II.—*Principal Mineral Products of Montana, 1943 and 1942*

Mineral	Value, 1943	Value, 1942
Copper	$34,775,000	$34,168,948
Zinc	8,316,800	10,176,990
Silver	6,144,000	7,955,995
Lead	2,353,200	2,686,700
Gold	2,082,500	5,141,220
Total	$53,671,500	$60,129,853

Crude oil production amounted to approximately 8,000,000 bbl. in 1943 as compared with the all-time state record of 8,093,972 bbl. produced in Montana in 1942. (E. E. B.)

Montenegro. A former kingdom in the northwest Balkan peninsula, Montenegro had voted its union with Serbia Nov. 25, 1918, in the then newly formed kingdom of the Serbs, Croats and Slovenes, later Yugoslavia. As a province within Yugoslavia, Montenegro had an area of 3,733 sq.mi. With the redistribution of Yugoslav administration in 1930, Cetinje, which had a population of 6,367 on March 31, 1931, became the capital of the Zetska banovina or province.

When Yugoslavia disintegrated as the result of German aggression in April 1941, the country was occupied by Italians. This occupation came to an end with the collapse of Italian fascism in July 1943, and the subsequent Italian surrender to the Allies. Throughout the two years of Italian occupation the inhabitants of Montenegro and its mountain fastnesses, a proud and freedom-loving people who had resisted for centuries the pressure of Turkey and kept their independence, refused to submit to the "new order" imposed by the axis. Though very little authentic news came from Montenegro in 1943, there is no doubt that after the downfall of Italy the patriot forces, both those of General Draja Mikhailovitch and those of General Tito (Josip Brozovitch) continued to harass the German garrisons which replaced the Italians and to occupy very large parts of Montenegrin

territory. (*See* also CROATIA; DALMATIA; YUGOSLAVIA.)
(H. Ko.)

Montgomery, Bernard Law
(1887–   ), British army officer, was born Nov. 16. The son of an Ulster clergyman, he joined the Royal Warwickshire regiment as a second lieutenant in 1908. He fought in France during World War I, was wounded twice and received the distinguished service order. After the war, he was a battalion commander, served in Palestine as division commander and was instructor at the Staff college in Quetta, India, remaining until 1937. A month before the outbreak of World War II, in Aug. 1939, he was appointed to command the third division which went to France with the B.E.F., and helped evacuate his troops from Dunkirk in June 1940. In 1942, when Rommel had driven the British constantly eastward in North Africa until the whole middle east was threatened, Churchill announced on Aug. 18 the appointment of Lt. Gen. Montgomery as commander of the British 8th army. Under his leadership, the 8th army stopped and turned the Afrika Korps at El Alamein. Three months later, Jan. 23, 1943, Montgomery captured Tripoli, 1,200 mi. to the west. On Feb. 11, Montgomery and his then renowned 8th army were placed under Gen. Dwight Eisenhower's unified command. Montgomery broke the Mareth line on March 29, and took part in the capture of Tunis and Bizerte early in May. The 8th army continued its drive across the Mediterranean into Sicily and Italy, and when the year ended was driving up the eastern Italian coast toward Rome. On Dec. 24, coincident with Roosevelt's announcement of Eisenhower as invasion commander, London announced that Montgomery would return to London to serve under him as commander of British ground forces.

Montreal.
A city in the province of Quebec, Canada, first called Ville Marie, founded in 1642 on the site of the Indian village of Hochelaga, is situated on an island at the confluence of the Ottawa and St. Lawrence rivers, approximately 1,000 mi. from the Atlantic ocean and 2,760 mi. from Liverpool. Being at the head of ocean navigation, it is the terminus for lake vessels from the Great Lakes and is served by three canal systems—the St. Lawrence canals (1,230 mi. to the Great Lakes), the eastern United States canals, via the Richelieu river and Lake Champlain (127 mi.) and the Ottawa river canals (119 mi.).

The population of the city proper, according to the census of 1941, was 903,007, and of greater Montreal 1,105,359. At the beginning of 1944, as estimated by *Lovell's Directory*, it was, for the city proper, 1,326,305, and for greater Montreal 1,522,757.

Default in the payment of the principal of certain of the city's bonds caused the Quebec municipal commission, a provincial organization, to be placed in charge of certain parts of the city administration. Interest on all bonds has been paid regularly and a plan for refunding is under consideration.

In Dec. 1943, the police and firemen went on strike, in protest against the city's refusal to give effect to the majority award of a board of arbitration. The strike lasted only a few hours. The clerical staff later went on strike, this strike lasting about 23 days.

The port of Montreal is the largest in Canada. War conditions accelerated its activity in 1939–43, but statistics are unavailable because of war censorship.

In 1943 building permits were issued for 1,102 new projects, having a value of $6,186,804, and for 1,861 repair jobs, having a value of $3,109,544. Bank deposits (for 11 months ended Nov. 30, 1943) were $12,548,546,772 and bank clearings (for 9 months ended Sept. 30, 1943) were $5,848,975,421. The assessed value of real estate as of April 30, 1943, was $1,250,128,640, of which $337,204,619 was exempt from taxation.   (J. A. MA.)

Montserrat: *see* WEST INDIES, BRITISH.
Moravia: *see* BOHEMIA AND MORAVIA.

Mordacq, Jean-Jules-Henri
(1868–1943), French army officer and biographer of Georges Clemenceau, was born Jan. 12 in Clermont-Ferrand. Educated at St. Cyr Military academy, General Mordacq came to play an important role in World War I. He was chief of Premier Clemenceau's military aides and his principal assistant from 1916 to 1918. When an armistice was imminent, he consistently held, despite popular disapproval, that the Allies continue the war until Germany surrendered unconditionally. After the war, he commanded an army of occupation in the Ruhr. When Clemenceau retired, General Mordacq, who had incurred many political enemies, passed into oblivion. He committed suicide by drowning in the Seine river in Paris, April 12, according to a Paris broadcast.

Morgan, John Pierpont
(1867–1943), U.S. financier and banker, was born Sept. 7 at Irvington, N.Y. (For his early career see *Encyclopædia Britannica*.) Morgan shunned publicity, but his appearance before the Pecora banking committee in 1933 was turned into a public spectacle. The hectic sessions, likened to a circus sideshow, made photographic history when a press agent planted a midget on Morgan's lap while photographers snapped pictures. When the Banking Act of 1933 was passed, the Morgan firm dropped its security underwriting and continued with its private deposit banking. The investment business was turned over to a new firm headed by Mr. Morgan's son, Henry, and two partners. Further changes were made in 1940. The Morgan partnership was dissolved and the "House of Morgan" was recreated as an incorporated bank with Morgan as chairman of the board.

Morgan died of a heart ailment while vacationing in Boca Grande, Fla., March 13.

Mormons.
During the year the temple in Idaho Falls, Ida., was completed and was ready for dedication, planned for the spring or early summer of 1944.

Welfare.—The Church Welfare program steadily developed over the church. There were 14,578 ac. of land farmed during the year by voluntary, gratuitous labour to produce food for the needy. Some 65 canneries were operated, and 598 livestock "projects." People were urged to can and otherwise preserve as much food as possible. The people responded by working in groups; housewives worked at home. These groups processed 1,253,000 cans. Strictly welfare canning amounted to 849,000 cans, a total of 2,102,000 cans. Careful estimates indicated that families canned and stored an additional 42,625,000 cans, a total for the church of 44,727,000 cans in the wards and stakes. Adding to this the canning by families in the missions, the total would approximate 50,000,000 cans, which represented more than 1,000,000,000 points, a material assistance to the food problem in affected areas.

Buildings.—The church building program was seriously curtailed owing to the difficulty of getting building materials. Normally the church builds an average of 100 churches per year, at an approximate prewar cost of $2,000,000. New building almost ceased because of operation of priorities.

Priesthood Work.—Intensive efforts were carried forward for upbuilding priesthood organization work, particularly in developing an increased brotherhood among the members. The different priesthood organizations were urged to institute "projects" for the care of their own needy members, which resulted in 213 crop "projects," 157 livestock "projects," and 30 manufacturing and processing "projects" (total 400), for aiding needy members of the priesthood of the church, which includes all male members of the church over 12 years of age. (*See* also CHURCH MEMBER-SHIP.)   (J. R. CL.)

Morocco: *see* FRENCH COLONIAL EMPIRE; SPANISH COLONIAL EMPIRE.

Morrison, Herbert Stanley
(1888–   ), British states-man, was born at Brixton, London, Jan. 3, 1888. Having left elementary school at 14, he passed through a variety of jobs. From 1913 onwards he took up politics as a full-time occupation, first as a journalist, later as secretary to the London Labour party. After a year as mayor of Hackney (1919–20) he was elected, in 1922, to the London county council which remained the main sphere of his activities and in-fluence for the next 18 years. After a brief spell in parliament (1923–24) Morrison was re-elected in 1929 and joined the sec-ond Labour government as minister of transport. Out of parlia-ment from 1931 until 1935, he was again elected in 1935. As leader of the L.C.C. he was responsible for the smooth working of the evacuation of London school children upon the outbreak of war. In May 1940 he became, as minister of supply, one of the three Labour members of the Churchill coalition government. In October he was put in charge of the home office and ministry of home security, offices which he still held in 1943, since 1941 as a member of the war cabinet. At the Labour party conference of 1943 he was defeated in the election for treasurer, but by a series of vigorous and widely discussed speeches on postwar problems he staked a solid claim to the party leadership at the end of the war.   (H. W. AT.)

Mortgages, Farm: *see* FARM CREDIT ADMINISTRATION.
Mortgages, Home: *see* NATIONAL HOUSING AGENCY.

Moscow.
When the history of Moscow in wartime comes to be written, one outstanding feature will be re-corded, that of the close collaboration of the mass of the popula-tion with the authorities in overcoming the difficulties consequent on siege. The story of the 80,000 Muscovites, many of them women, who in the autumn of 1942 went to the forests with the aim of securing the city's fuel supply, is only one of the many examples of this spirit of collaboration. Hundreds of thousands of people became allotment-holders, mutually helping in the cultivation of allotments. The Trade Union committee frequently arranged with suburban vegetable farms for supplies of farm products to be sent to factories or office canteens. During the winter of 1942–43, with the help of the government, over 2,000 well-equipped rooms or flats in Moscow had been given to fam-ilies of front line fighters, over 200 new kindergartens and 100 crèches had been opened. In special dining halls for weaker chil-dren, over 20,000 children of men at the front were regularly fed.

With the help of the active participation of the population was "ensured smooth distribution of food supplies and queuing is very little in evidence."

For rationing purposes people fell into three categories. The first and by far the largest category consisted of the industrial workers. They received more bread, butter and meat than either office employees or adult dependents not engaged in industry. Scientists and artists were also placed in the category for work-ers. The bread ration for the man and woman working in an office was about 1¼ lb. per day, while that of the factory worker was 1½–1¾ lb. per day. The Moscow ration of cereals for men or women in industry was double that of the office employees, the same ap-plied to butter and other fats. Most of the factory and office employees dined at factory or office canteens or at hotel restau-rants or cafés allocated to them. No coupons were surrendered for potatoes and vegetables at dinner and often not even for meat, so that dinner for workers and employees could in the main be regarded as additional food to the ration.

The population of Moscow could also supplement their ration by purchasing food on collective farm markets, "but while pre-war prices prevail for rationed food, prices in the kolkhoz markets are comparatively high. On the whole, our meals are frugal but they do contain the necessary vitamins and calories that enable us to keep on working hard—hard enough to keep the Red Army well supplied" (Soviet *Monitor*).

This concentration of all efforts of the Moscow population to assure the smooth flow of supplies to the Red army and to "increase and educate well-trained reserves for the Red Army" was the main motive in the life of the Moscow population in 1943.   (A. M. BV.)

Moscow, Pact of: *see* UNION OF SOVIET SOCIALIST REPUBLICS.

Motion Pictures.
The motion picture industry in the U.S. turned in a record-breaking performance in 1943. Despite shortages of man power and essentials, the industry was in a more flourishing condition at the year's end than at any previous period.

Gross earnings of producing companies were at an all-time high. RKO, for example, which showed a deficit in 1942, changed this into a surprisingly high profit in 1943. Theatre receipts reached unprecedented levels, with a trend toward substantially increased admission prices. On the other side of the ledger were heavy taxes, increased pay rolls for rank-and-file workers and mounting costs for materials going into picture-making.

Production expenses soared above anything the industry had ever known. Increases naturally varied with the circumstances of the individual pictures, with estimates ranging from 25% to 100%. In December, William F. Rodgers, Metro-Goldwyn-Mayer's general sales manager, addressing a meeting of exhibi-tors, was quoted as saying that his company's production costs were twice those of a year ago; that pictures which under ordi-nary circumstances would have taken 7 or 8 weeks to produce now required 14 or 15 weeks.

Financial authorities, viewing the general motion picture scene, inclined to the view that receipts would continue to take up the slack of mounting taxes and costs and that, insofar as prophecy was possible, optimistic prospects extended into the postwar era.

The industry kept a wary eye on television, in which some studios already had interested themselves financially. Also, the view was widely held that if Hollywood, after the war, was to continue to dominate the cinemas of the world, Hollywood would have to fight to do it. It was felt that, aside from the economic aspect, motion pictures had shown themselves to be so important in the fields of propaganda and morale that all governments in a position to do so would encourage to the limit their countries' picture production and distribution.

The capital investment of the motion picture industry in 1943 was practically unchanged from that of 1942, war conditions hav-ing prevented any appreciable constructive progress.

Theatres	$1,900,000,000
Studios	125,000,000
Distribution	25,000,000
	$2,050,000,000

Reliable statistics were lacking at 1943's end. One financial authority estimated that amusement industry earnings in 1943 showed the greatest increase in the nation—60.9%. Estimates based on government admission taxes for October indicated a daily film box-office take of $5,000,000.

The industry was in an unusually fluid state in 1943. Changing conditions made rigid planning impossible. Studios generally made it plain that production forecasts were just that—that the number and kind of pictures would be subject to revision as circumstances warranted.

Backlogs of completed but unreleased product reached a new high. The trend was toward fewer releases, since pictures were held longer in theatres and fewer prints for distribution were made, because of the governmental raw film stock allocations. As a result, there was some complaint of product shortage by smaller and subsequent-run houses. Their problem was met in part by re-issues of old pictures. Illustrative of increased playing time: New York city's Radio City Music Hall, the world's largest theatre, screened only 12 pictures in 1943, including one which had started its run in 1942. In 1933, its first year of operation, 46 pictures were shown; 26 in 1941.

As was natural in a boom period, 1943 saw an unusual increase in the number of independent producing companies. The Production Code administration approved 403 feature pictures, of which 18 were foreign, through Dec. 18, 1943. Indicative of the decline in feature production, 322 were approved during the first ten months of 1943, as compared with 450 for the corresponding period in 1942.

In 1943 more and more world-famous names blinked out on the marquees, as additional male stars went into the service. Studios indulged in unusual co-operation to cope with the actor shortage, with loan-outs of stars and featured players increasing. More and more the play became the thing. Story prices went up as the stars departed. Best-sellers and stage hits were purchased at skyrocket heights.

Increase in production value was sought through the use of colour, which had its biggest year. It was expected that colour would be utilized even more after the war.

Indicative of the casting situation was the conclusion to be drawn from a study of *Motion Picture Herald's* ten top money-making stars of 1942. Eight places were won by men (Abbott and Costello were dualled in the poll) and of these war service drew two from before the cameras—Clark Gable, second, and Gene Autry, seventh; in other words, 25% of the top-draw male stars. In the ranks of the younger actors, departures naturally were more numerous. (Actors in service at the end of 1943 were estimated at 1,400.)

The *Motion Picture Herald's* poll for 1943 found a woman at the top—Betty Grable, whose vehicles were Twentieth Century-Fox Technicolor musical comedies. She was followed by Bob Hope, Abbott and Costello (the 1942 champions), Bing Crosby, Gary Cooper, Greer Garson, Humphrey Bogart, James Cagney, Mickey Rooney and Gable, who had a picture released before going into the army. As to types of pictures, there were no pronounced trends discernible during 1943. Musicals, as a leading form of "escapist" fare, were very popular, but a survey showed that public favour was not confined to any particular variety of film.

The industry was continually stirred by protests that it was turning out too many war pictures. But here again the old rule held good. Some war pictures were stand-out hits, others flopped ingloriously.

So, too, with the old problem of low-budgeted pictures. The trend away from "B" films continued. Yet—to confound the analysts—*Hitler's Children*, produced by RKO at a cost of $187,-000, and a war picture to boot, was one of 1943's sensational box-office successes.

The most discussed pictures of the year were Paramount's *For Whom the Bell Tolls*, Warner Bros'. *This Is the Army*, Twentieth Century-Fox's *The Song of Bernadette*, Metro-Goldwyn-Mayer's *Madame Curie* and Walt Disney's United Artists release, *Victory Through Air Power*.

The last-named, a picturization of the book of the same name by Alexander P. de Seversky, again revealed Disney as a trail-breaker in the realm of films. His production might best be described as a "motion picture lecture" on the controversial subject of the aeroplane's role in war.

The Movies and the War.—American motion pictures in 1943 performed great services for the government, receiving in return little save the greatest benefit of all—comparative freedom of action. The industry had feared attempts at propaganda control and had maintained vigilance. In 1943 it breathed more easily. It was felt that the government generally was confining its attempts at regulation to the necessities dictated by war.

It was estimated at the end of 1943 that of the 18,000 males normally employed in the actual production of motion pictures, nearly 7,000 were in the armed forces.

Always, beneath the glamour and glitter that the world associates with motion pictures, is solid, skilled, ingenious craftsmanship. It was this characteristic which, in 1943, enabled the industry to turn out a splendid assortment of product despite the disabilities imposed by war conditions. Much of the credit for this belongs to the technical workers. In fact, Hollywood was saying proudly that there was no task beyond the abilities of its technical corps. And therefore Hollywood's contribution to the war effort was especially important. The qualities which make film technicians invaluable to picture-making are among the qualities which are invaluable to war-making.

So the film capital could contribute in quantity specialists whose services were sorely needed—cameramen, still photographers, camouflage experts, sound department technicians specializing in radio work and aeroplane detection, laboratory technicians, precision machinists, electrical experts and many others.

It is possible to touch only briefly on industry war service such as documentary films and government trailers, inter-American relations films, training of technicians, support of war loan and relief drives, entertainment of servicemen by star appearances at camps and overseas.

War training films were turned out by the studios at cost. Prints of 16-mm. films were given for free exhibition to the armed forces abroad. It was estimated at the end of 1943 that such prints supplied to the war department would total 10,200 features and 11,890 short subjects. Reconditioned 16-mm. projectors also were supplied.

Entertainment for Service Men.—Entertainment abroad deserves more than passing notice, however. Stars of both sexes found themselves in regions more strange than any in which they had play-acted on motion picture sets. They faced dangers by land and sea and air. They visited England, Africa, the South Pacific, the Caribbean, Alaska, Newfoundland, India, China. Those who gave of their time and money and comfort and safety are too numerous to name. But in a record of outstanding service, Joe E. Brown's name is outstanding. Other especially noteworthy entertainment names were those of Bob Hope, Jack Benny, Al Jolson, Martha Raye, Carole Landis, Mitzi Mayfair, Kay Francis and Gary Cooper.

A graphic description of the part played by motion pictures in war was given by the special service division, Overseas Motion Picture service, United States army, in a release dated Nov. 16, 1943. This stated that "Hollywood's latest movies are now being seen by an average of 630,000 overseas men in uniform each night. . . . On one night selected as representative, that of Oct. 1, a total of 1,269 movie shows were presented in army camps around the globe. Attendances ranged from 15,000 in an open-air New Guinea amphitheatre to 11 men in a lonely Quonset hut in an Alaskan outpost."

Awards.—Academy of Motion Picture Arts and Sciences Awards for 1942 (for the principal 1943 awards see p. 457):

(for the principal 1943 awards see p. 457)

Irving G. Thalberg award, for most consistent high quality production achievement by an individual producer, Sidney Franklin; outstanding picture, *Mrs. Miniver*, Metro-Goldwyn-Mayer; performances—actor, James Cagney in *Yankee Doodle Dandy*, Warner Bros.; actress, Greer Garson in *Mrs. Miniver;* supporting actor, Van Heflin in *Johnny Eager*, Metro-Goldwyn-Mayer; supporting actress, Teresa Wright in *Mrs. Miniver;* best direction, William Wyler for *Mrs. Miniver;* best original motion picture story, Emeric Pressburger for *The Invaders* (British), Ortus, Columbia; best (adaptation) screen play, Arthur Wimperis, George Froeschel, James Hilton and Claudine West for *Mrs. Miniver;* best original screen play, Ring Lardner, Jr. and Michael Kanin for *Woman of the Year*, Metro-Goldwyn-Mayer; best art direction—black and white, Richard Day and Joseph Wright for *This Above All*, Twentieth Century-Fox; colour, Richard Day and Joseph Wright for *My Gal Sal*, Twentieth Century-Fox; best cinematography—black and white, Joseph Ruttenberg for *Mrs. Miniver;* colour, Leon Shamroy for *The Black Swan*, Twentieth Century-Fox; best sound recording, Nathan Levinson for *Yankee Doodle Dandy;* short subjects—cartoon, *Der Fuehrer's Face*, Walt Disney; one-reeler, *Speaking of Animals and Their Families*, Paramount (Fairbanks and Carlisle, producers); two-reeler, *Beyond the Line of Duty*, Warner Bros. (Gordon Hollingshead, producer); best film editing, Daniel Mandell for *The Pride of the Yankees*, Samuel Goldwyn, RKO-Radio; best scoring of a musical picture, Ray Heindorf and Heinz Roemheld for *Yankee Doodle Dandy;* best scoring of a dramatic picture, Max Steiner for *Now, Voyager*, Warner Bros.; best song, "White Christmas," from *Holiday Inn*, Paramount (music and lyrics by Irving Berlin); best special effects, *Reap the Wild Wind*, Paramount (Gordon Jennings, Farciot Edouart, William L. Pereira for photography, Louis Mesenkop for sound); best interior decoration (certificates of merit given to the decorators of the productions receiving the award for art direction)—black and white, Thomas Little for *This Above All;* colour, Thomas Little for *My Gal Sal;* certificates for distinctive achievement were presented to Charles Boyer, "for his progressive cultural achievement in establishing the French Research foundation in Los Angeles as a source of reference for the Hollywood motion picture industry"; Noel Coward, "for his outstanding production achievement, *In Which We Serve*"; Metro-Goldwyn-Mayer studio "for its achievement in representing the American way of life in the production of the 'Andy Hardy' series of films"; plaques for distinctive achievement in documentary production were presented to *Kokoda Front Line!*, *Battle of Midway*, *Prelude to War* and *Moscow Strikes Back.*

Outstanding pictures of 1943 included—

This Is The Army, Heaven Can Wait, For Whom the Bell Tolls, The Song of Bernadette, Madame Curie, So Proudly We Hail, Sweet Rosie O'Grady, Claudia, The Human Comedy, The More the Merrier, Watch on the Rhine, Behind the Rising Sun, Lassie Come Home, Shadow of a Doubt, Victory Through Air Power, The Ox-Bow Incident, Hitler's Children, Guadalcanal Diary, Princess O'Rourke, Johnny Come Lately, Casablanca and *Air Force.*

Among the outstanding films also should be included a number of documentary pictures. Productions of this type attained a new importance in 1943, in some cases occupying a position on theatre screens usually filled by a straight entertainment feature. Outstanding documentaries were *Desert Victory* (British), *Report from the Aleutians, Battle for Britain* and *Battle of Russia.*

Battle-action documentaries were not obtained without risk and in some instances casualties in the photographic units ran high.   (L. O. P.)

Technical Developments.—Restrictions on manpower and material increased, thus again preventing normal technical developments within the motion picture industry. A few developments previously well under way were continued to completion. The very nature of the restrictions placed on the industry forced changes in the technical processes and equipment which are worthy of note. Fewer pictures were made but the tendency was toward more elaborate and thus more expensive productions.

Set Construction.—The War Production board limitation of $5,000 in new material for set construction in any one production had two interesting results. Sets were definitely planned for use in several productions and second-hand material was employed wherever possible. Various studios purchased and demolished old buildings in order to secure the material for set construction. Paramount purchased a lumber mill in Oregon which was roofed with straight grain boards 6 in. thick by 12 in. to 16 in. wide. These timbers were remilled and provided considerable excellent

lumber. The use of plastics increased materially. A part of this increase was the result of the inability to secure materials, particularly metal, but was also a natural growth resulting from the increased knowledge of plastics and their ready adaptability to motion picture requirements. Primary uses of plastics in the industry are for set dressing, hardware and costumes.

Dim-out Restrictions.—When the entire Pacific coast was dimmed out as a wartime measure, night photography on outside sets was banned. Thus all night shots were either photographed on covered sets with artificial lights or with natural light and suitable filters. The use of filters for securing night effects in the daytime is not new and is not entirely satisfactory. The best results were secured on outdoor sets which could be completely covered with canvas, thus largely but not completely eliminating natural light. Night shots so made were considered by many to be better than night shots photographed at night with artificial light because natural light filtering through the canvas permitted some desired background detail. Thus the practice of photographing night shots under daylight conditions with artificial light in canvas-covered sets may continue even though the dim-out regulations have been lifted.

Location Sets.—Restriction on transportation forced a reduction in location work. Some location shooting was, of course, continued but wherever possible it was replaced by miniature and processing photography.

Optics.—The use of antireflection coating on camera and projector lenses continued to increase. Processes for lens coating were further improved, particularly with respect to durability.

Camera lenses having the same focal length and the same f./ rating vary considerably in their efficiency of light transmission. Thus two lenses presumed to be alike may actually produce considerably different exposures of the film when photographing the same subject simultaneously. Since film laboratories develop on a time-and-temperature basis, consistent photographic results can only be obtained by accurate control of film exposure in the camera. Cameramen must work with different lenses, hence a knowledge of light efficiency of the lenses is necessary. This problem was solved at various studios, notably at Twentieth Century-Fox, by setting up one camera lens at a given f./ stop as a standard and calibrating all other lenses from this reference. By this process, the f./ system ceases to be a simple mathematical calibration and becomes an actual calibration based on equivalent light efficiency. Thus for the first time all lenses so calibrated and set at the same f./ stop will produce the same exposure when photographing the same subject.

Film.—No new films were introduced but fine grain films were further improved and their use was considerably increased throughout the industry. All major studios now release fine grain prints.

Film Processing Laboratories.—At Twentieth Century-Fox one new developing machine was placed in operation. It is basically of the Eastman-Capstaff design with modifications developed by Twentieth Century-Fox laboratory technicians. This machine is noteworthy because for the first time there is no measurable evidence of developer drag or directional effect.

Process Photography.—The slide projector developed at Paramount in 1942 was further improved in 1943 by the addition of a shutter similar to that employed on projectors except that the blades were made of Alco glass. Thus the shutter provides a reduction in heat on the slide almost equivalent to that which could be obtained with a metal blade shutter, while at the same time producing considerably less visual flicker on the screen. Photographically, of course, this flicker is not objectionable since it is timed with the camera shutter, but it is trying on the actors. In order to use this projector with Kodachrome transparencies,

Above, left: KATINA PAXINOU (left) with Gary Cooper (second from right) in *For Whom the Bell Tolls*. Miss Paxinou was named 1943's best supporting actress by the Academy of Motion Picture Arts and Sciences

Above, right: PAUL LUKAS (right) was voted best actor of 1943 for his role in *Watch on the Rhine*. Bette Davis (centre) was also starred

Right: MICKEY ROONEY (left) and Frank Morgan in William Saroyan's *The Human Comedy*, which won the Academy award for the best original picture story of 1943

Below, left: INGRID BERGMAN in *Casablanca*, which received the Academy award as the best motion picture of 1943

Below, right: JENNIFER JONES was the winner of the 1943 Academy award as best actress of the year for her role in *The Song of Bernadette*

Paramount developed a system for rephotographing such transparencies to correct them for size and colour. They then developed a process for transferring the Kodachrome image from its film base to a glass base since the film base would obviously not stand the heat of this projector.

Colour.—The year 1943 found a general increase in the use of colour photography. Technicolor's Monopack process, while still in the experimental stage, was used in several productions. Monopack employed a three-colour process in which the picture is originally photographed on a single film containing three emulsions. This film is developed to a positive and is therefore similar to the well-known Kodachrome process. From this positive, the present technique provides for the making of three separation negatives from which prints are made by the Technicolor imbibition process. Ansco continued the development of a three-colour process where a single film carrying three emulsions is exposed in the camera and developed to a negative from which contact prints may be made in the usual manner. While this process was said to be in wide use for military purposes, it was not available to the motion picture industry in 1943. The process of photographing in 16-mm. Kodachrome and blowing this up for release in 35-mm. Technicolor continued to increase, notable examples being *At the Front in North Africa* and *Report from the Aleutians*.

Sound.—In spite of war restrictions, several studios modified their variable density recording equipment to permit original recording on 200-mil push-pull sound tracks, thus gaining the advantages of push-pull recording and an increase in signal to noise ratio. This material must, of course, be rerecorded to obtain a normal release negative. Many variable density users also added limiter amplifiers to their production channels. These amplifiers were variable gain devices designed to prevent excessive overload on high level signals. Variable area users employed a variable gain amplifier having a gradual characteristic of gain change vs. level and the limiter is an adaptation of this device. For many years it was the practice in some studios to record vocalists on a separate sound track from that on which the orchestra is recorded. Separation between the voice and the orchestra was obtained by use of uni-directional or bi-directional microphones and was never particularly satisfactory. In 1943 several studios constructed small rooms in conjunction with their scoring stages so that the vocalist might be acoustically isolated from the orchestra. The vocalist sees the picture and the orchestra through a suitable window and by means of headphones or controlled acoustical methods also hears the orchestra.

Increased use was made of a small dynamic type of receiver with a moulded plastic earpiece. These were similar to those employed in hard-of-hearing aids and provided better response, because of the close coupling with the ear.

Republic introduced a device for providing audible indication of the failure of synchronous camera motors to run at their correct speed.

Lighting.—No new lights or lighting methods were introduced but Paramount developed a light meter designed to measure accurately the actinic value of the light. Previous light meters had been sensitive primarily in the red or infrared range where the film had little sensitivity.

As a measure of conservation, Twentieth Century-Fox adopted the practice of protecting arc and incandescent lights with a shield of Tufflex glass. This is a tempered glass highly resistant to thermal shock. It prevents wind or rain from damaging the light itself.

Industry and Technical Contributions to the War.—A considerable percentage of the technical personnel of the motion picture industry entered the armed forces. Others affiliated with war research, development and manufacturing activities, thus reducing the available technical personnel in the studios to a minimum. Military personnel was trained by the studios in camera work. Training films continued to be produced in the industry although the army and navy were handling a large percentage of this work themselves. Sixteen-millimetre releases on selected pictures were provided for the military at the cost of the prints. Such releases were reported to be shown wherever U.S. military men were located.

The Research Council of the Academy of Motion Picture Arts and Sciences sponsored the development of a special portable sound-recording equipment for the signal corps. The design of this system was largely the work of the MGM sound engineers. Manufacturing companies who normally supplied sound recording, camera, lighting and similar equipment to the motion picture industry were engaged almost entirely in the manufacture of war equipment. New sound-recording, camera and lighting equipment would, no doubt, become available to the industry as the result of this wartime work.   (W. V. W.)

Educational Motion Pictures.—In 1943 the U.S. government became the world's largest producer, distributor and user of films. Government expenditures for army, navy, air force, industrial and scholastic training films were approximately $20,000,000, or an average of about a dollar per trainee for the year. Experts estimated that films increased the speed of training 25% to 35%. Of greatest significance to educators was the new emphasis on techniques of utilization. The U.S. Office of Education ended the year with 98 films completed, 100 in production and 300 in plan-

ALEXANDER DE SEVERSKY'S BOOK, *Victory Through Air Power*, was turned into a Technicolor animated cartoon by Walt Disney in 1943. These three scenes show the British evacuation at Dunkirk under a protecting canopy of planes, a cemetery of German bombers in Britain, and the concentrated Allied bombing of Hitler's "European fortress"

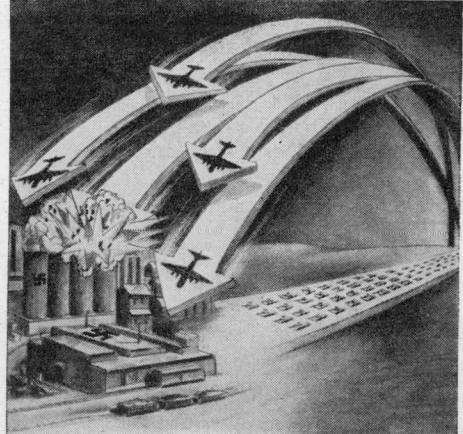

ning stages. Utilization of each subject was based on a definitive visual aid unit. By the end of the year 25 such units were being distributed, including a 16-mm. sound film, a silent filmslide strip of 20 to 50 key shots from the film and an illustrated instruction manual. Federal Security Administrator Paul V. McNutt, in a statement on Dec. 28, 1943, declared: "These war training films, designed as a new type of teaching tool, are making educational history by teaching workers essential skills *motion by motion.* For example, engine lathe training requires 17 films; aircraft manufacturing skills will require more than 30 films." The USOE films during 1943 were made by 23 producing units in 8 states. The business of distribution was handled by contract with one firm, which sold by the end of the year about 30,000 prints.

For the armed forces the most active film production centre was that of the army signal corps, whose studio at Astoria, N.Y., completed with the aid of Hollywood experts some 500 subjects within 12 months, establishing a record in the documentary-film field. The U.S. navy bureau of personnel, through its staff of 80 audio-visual officers at all domestic and foreign bases, did outstanding work in film utilization.

While most film expenditures for training inductees were charged off as war expense, the Office of Education film program was put on a self-liquidating basis, in line with a congressional act providing for the amortization of the cost of USOE films in about five years. (W. Ln.)

The notable wartime success of teaching army recruits and industrial workers by means of sound films was expected to result in the greatly expanded use of films in civilian schoolwork after the war. To meet this anticipated need *Encyclopædia Britannica,* on Dec. 11, 1943, formed a subsidiary company to be called Encyclopædia Britannica Films, Inc., which acquired the personnel and the approximately 200 teaching films of the Erpi Film Co., formerly the property of Western Electric Co. (*See also* PHOTOGRAPHY.)

Motor-Boat Racing.
Motor-boat racing in the United States was virtually at a standstill throughout 1943, due to wartime restrictions on the use of gasoline for pleasure purposes and for competitive events. There were no regattas of national importance and outboard racing was confined chiefly to some local races in the middle west.

Only racing event of general interest was the 11th annual running of the Hearst Perpetual Gold Trophy Speedboat regatta, held at Long Beach, California, in August, and attended chiefly by California drivers and speed boat owners.

The winners were:

Class	Driver	Boat
Class A hydroplanes	Orville Brisbin	"Chiz-Briz"
Class B hydroplanes	R. S. Hooper	
Class C hydroplanes	William Schuyler	"If"
Class M hydroplanes	Howard Newton	"Baby Fox"
Class C racing runabouts	Lester Missall	
Class F racing runabouts	L. A. Ratikin	"Torpedo"
Class C service runabouts	Jos. Leanardo	"My Shadow"
Class 225-Cubic Inch	Kenneth Ingram	"Guess Who"
Class 135-Cubic Inch	Thomas Ince	"Dynamite"
Pacific Coast One Design	Elmer Cravener	"Pudgy"

(H. L. St.)

Motor Buses: *see* AUTOMOBILE INDUSTRY IN THE WAR; MOTOR TRANSPORTATION.

Motor Cars: *see* AUTOMOBILE INDUSTRY IN THE WAR.

Motor Transportation.
Despite shortages of manpower, materials and vehicles and the limitation of speed under which they were permitted to operate, the U.S. motor carriers in 1943 showed notable records of performance. To cite one instance, intercity buses carried in 1943 an increase of 44.1% in the number of passengers over the number carried in 1942 with an increase of 33.5% in passenger miles and revenue. The 31,000,000 passenger miles rolled up in 1943 included transportation of inductees to induction centres, members of the military travelling under individual orders and on furlough, and civilian travellers.

As far as the bus was concerned, a survey covering all classes of operation for the first nine months of 1943 indicated that all classes of carriers were carrying greatly increased loads, with more people being handled per bus than ever before. Passenger revenue per mile of line for city companies in 1943 ran at the rate of about 26% over 1942 with the revenue for the intercity carriers at nearly double that of 1943. Total operating revenue of the industry for 1943 was placed at about $1,006,000,000 and the number of passengers at 8,600,000,000.

As 1943 drew to a close passenger travel by bus and by train approached double that of the year previous. It was about four times as great as before World War II. Trains and buses operated with about the same amount of equipment they had before the war. So far as the bus and the truck were concerned there was promise at the end of 1943 that relief would be afforded by additional vehicles and in the amount of replacement materials. In the bus field, at the end of 1943, prospects pointed to the industry being permitted to build 6,960 new integral buses during 1944 compared with only 1,500 delivered in 1943 and about 11,000 in 1942. Actually the industry could absorb a great many more buses considering the more favourable prospect for replacement parts and appurtenances during 1944. The new figure of authorization was taken to mean that a maximum of 1,740 buses would be assigned to the intercity lines with a possible minimum of 1,392. Another hopeful prospect was that this figure might be revised upward due to probable windfalls in material and in the likelihood of an increase in manpower and in manufacturing facilities. The pressure for more buses for use in cities, especially war industry cities, was terrific. In the local or city field there was some restoration of service by street car where tracks and overhead were still in place. In all such instances, the buses so released were assigned to help out on routes already overcrowded or were used to establish new routes as an aid to the war effort.

In the truck field the production of 123,000 new commercial vehicles was approved for 1944. Of this number, however, only about 90,000 were to be for civilian use. The rest were for the U.S. Maritime commission, the U.S. Foreign Economic administration, the dominion of Canada and other noncivilian purposes. This 90,000 might be compared to normal prewar replacement production of 450,000 vehicles annually. The new trucks were to go into the civilian truck pool, which at the end of 1943 was virtually exhausted. They were to be doled out only for needs directly related to the war effort or to uses necessary to the civilian economy. In addition, the construction of 12,250 commercial truck trailers was authorized.

The Office of Defense Transportation reiterated its advice that truck operators redouble their maintenance efforts and regard their present vehicles as probably the last which they would be able to obtain until the end of 1944. As in the case of the bus industry ODT emphasized the need on the part of management to direct its efforts to preventive maintenance and the drivers to careful habits in handling vehicles entrusted to them. In 741 war plants checked in the fall of 1943, 65% of all incoming freight was carried by truck.

Both the bus and the truck industries were plagued through the year by the manpower problem. This was true in respect to both drivers and mechanics. In World War II, a war of movement by motor vehicle, there was great need by the armed forces for all classes of mechanics. Faced with the drain on its personnel the bus industry made good use of women both in the shops and on the vehicles. In helping to ease this situation the Office of Defense Transportation set up well-organized training programs intended to develop personnel for use in both these categories. Thus on Dec. 6, 1943, the Office of Defense Transportation issued "Transportation Training," the first of a series intended primarily to acquaint transportation company officials with training programs and information of help to them in meeting their manpower problems. In addition the bulletin discussed the upgrading or supplementary training for employees already in the service and set forth new methods and techniques for meeting the problem of recruiting new employees. Help in meeting the critical manpower situation was also forthcoming in tangible form as a result of the 130 Office of Defense Transportation-War Manpower special training classes conducted throughout the country for motor mechanics. In Nov. 1943, it was announced that men and women students were soon to be available from the 72 cities in which the ODT and the WMP had been conducting classes. It was estimated that the intercity bus carriers needed 22,000 workers for replacements and local transit lines 55,000.

Shortages of tires, repair parts, new equipment and manpower, plus restrictions on road speed and other regulations, limited the carrying capacity of trucks, buses and automobiles to a point far below the demands of service they render. These findings from a source outside of the industry (the Truman committee investigating the national defense program) are cited because they emphasized the record which both the bus and the truck made under the most unfavourable operating conditions.

On Oct. 11, 1943, the War Production board amended its limitations order so as to assign a priority rating equal to military production to parts for medium and heavy trucks, trailers and buses. In the opinion of the Truman committee the War Production board delayed the parts production program by not having a survey as soon as the problem became apparent. To permit a vehicle lacking only one vital functional part to be laid up and rendered useless while a new one was being built seemed poor economy. The extent to which the parts shortage worked to the detriment of the industry is indicated by citing figures compiled by the Office of Defense Transportation which disclosed that 292% more vehicle-days were lost by buses in Aug. 1943, because of parts shortages than in Aug. 1942, 271% more lost by for-hire trucks and 175% more lost by private trucks.

In any discussion of motor buses sight must not be lost of the place which these vehicles play in the national economy as an aid essential to the educational program. There were in 1943 about 85,000 school buses and on them 4,000,000 children were transported daily. No accessions were made to this fleet. It is true that the school buses had priority on supplies of parts and of gasoline, but that alone was not enough. The problem was tackled early and vigorously. Of great help to the educators and the public officials who had to wrestle with it were the general suggestions set down in pamphlet form as a result of the work conferences held at Yale university and at Washington in the summer of 1942. (*See also* AUTOMOBILE INDUSTRY IN THE WAR; HORSES; MUNITIONS OF WAR.)   (C. W. S.)

Other Countries.—Since more up-to-date figures were not available and, even if available, would be useless as a guide to the motor transport on the roads, the numbers of motor vehicles in the principal countries of the world in 1939 are given.

The year 1943 showed no great change in the numbers of vehicles as compared with 1942. Such change as there was continued the decline in numbers. In Italy, for instance, in that part under German control, all private cars were commandeered, and

Motor Vehicle Registrations, Exclusive of U.S., in Early 1939

Country	Private Cars Taxis '000's	Trucks Buses '000's	Total '000's
United Kingdom	1,916	626	2,542
France	1,750	500	2,250
Germany	1,306	402	1,708
Canada	1,161	220	1,381
Australia	552	252	804
U.S.S.R.	85	593	678
Italy	303	86	389
Union of South Africa	294	45	339

the position in France was little better. In Great Britain all gasoline for private cars could be used only for purposes which were particularized, and the quantities allowed were cut to a point which made it a matter of difficulty to make the allowance adequate for the work to be done. The purposes which supported a claim for a supply of gasoline tended to be examined more closely and to be further curtailed. This applied to public services as well as private cars. Bus services in Great Britain for instance were reduced somewhat during the year. (*See also* ACCIDENTS; RAILROADS.)   (W. T. ST.)

Motor Vehicles: *see* AUTOMOBILE INDUSTRY IN THE WAR; FEDERAL BUREAU OF INVESTIGATION.

Mountbatten, Lord Louis

(1900–), British naval officer, was born June 25 in Windsor, England, as Louis Francis Albert Victor Nicholas of Battenberg. His mother, Princess Victoria, was a daughter of Louis IV, grand duke of Hesse, and a granddaughter of Queen Victoria. His father, Austrian-born Prince Louis of Battenberg, grandson of Louis II of Hesse, resigned as an admiral of the British navy in 1917 because of anti-German sentiment and changed his name to Mountbatten. Lord Louis entered the British navy as a midshipman at the age of 13 and served throughout World War I. He rose through the grades until, in March 1942, he was made acting vice admiral. Early in World War II his gallantry and daring attracted attention when he brought the destroyer "Kelly" to port twice after it was damaged, first by a mine and the second time, apparently hopelessly, by a torpedo. In the fall of 1941 he was ordered to the United States to take over the command of the "Illustrious," which was undergoing repair. Before he was able to take his new command out of port, however, he was ordered back to England for an undisclosed assignment. Not until April 1942, was it revealed that Lord Louis had succeeded Sir Roger Keyes as leader of the Commandos, whose daring raids over western Europe had become legendary. His title was Chief of Combined Operations, and in March he had been made acting vice admiral. During 1943 he attended the Casablanca and Quebec conferences. At the latter, in Aug. 1943, was announced the creation of the new Southeast Asia command and the appointment of Mountbatten as its commander in chief. On Sept. 10 he was made acting admiral for the duration of his post. In December he announced that he had merged the British and American units under the command of Air Chief Marshal Sir Richard Pierse.

Mount Holyoke College.

An institution for the higher education of women in liberal arts, founded in 1837 by Mary Lyon and situated at South Hadley, Mass. In 1943 the naval reserve midshipmen's school (WR), established on the campus in 1942, was changed to the Naval Training school (WR) for graduate WAVES, Marines and SPARS. Some of the college facilities were turned over to the United States navy without decreasing the college enrolment. For statistics of student enrolment, faculty, endowment, library volumes, etc., *see* UNIVERSITIES AND COLLEGES.   (R. G. HA.)

Mowinckel, Johan Ludwig (1870–1943), Norwegian politician, was educated at Oslo university and at schools in Germany, England and France. A shipowner, he entered politics in 1899 as town councillor of Bergen and held, concurrently, the post of president of the Bergen council. He later became a member of the Norwegian Storting and served as president of that body from 1913 to 1921. He was president of Norway's League of Nations delegation, 1928–30 and 1933–34, and president of the League council in 1933. He was prime minister and minister of foreign affairs, 1925–27, 1928–31, and 1933–35. He went to the United States after the nazi occupation of Norway in 1940 and died at New York city, Sept. 30, 1943.

Mozambique: *see* PORTUGUESE COLONIAL EMPIRE.
Mules: *see* HORSES.

Municipal Government.

The outstanding trend in local U.S. government in 1943 was the swing in emphasis from "war" to "postwar" in official municipal thinking. The year ended in a plethora of postwar plans, culminating in the much heralded $100,000 fee plan of New York Park Commissioner Robert Moses and staff for the Portland, Oreg., local government area. Financial conditions appeared bright on the surface without, however, encouraging much confidence that any permanent basis of improvement had been laid. The marked reaction which set in against federal or state domination was officially reflected in the resolutions adopted by the American Municipal association at its annual conference in October, which among other matters called for the return to local governments of all local functions assumed by the state and federal governments during the depression and war emergencies, and the maintenance and encouragement of independent local government under plans for the sharing of federal and state collected revenues with local governments.

Activities Related to the War Effort.—Civilian defense measures continued in effect, though with dwindling emphasis as dimout regulations were removed in coastal cities toward the close of the year. The larger cities carrying war damage insurance had for the most part expressed their intention to renew. Victory gardens were encouraged through availability of city-owned land. Intermunicipal co-operation was greatly accelerated, particularly in police and fire services; 20 or so states expressly authorized such co-operation in health, personnel, planning, police, fire and other services.

The major war problem centred on the excessive burdens placed on local government in the congested war industry areas. Additional funds ($200,000,000) were authorized by congress under the Lanham act to help finance the public works and other community facilities so urgently needed; also ($300,000,000) for the greatly increased construction during 1943 of war housing for in-migrant workers. A federal Committee for Congested Production Areas, consisting of representatives from the war and navy departments and other federal wartime agencies, headed by Harold Smith, director of the budget, was established in April in the executive office of the president, to co-ordinate federal activities affecting problems arising out of congestion and to supplement the efforts of state and local governments in meeting the economic and social problems involved. By the end of the year the committee had assisted in the procurement of ice manufacturing facilities, sewer construction authorization, child care program development, a Negro recreation centre, garbage removal, and construction of access roads to industries. It had established area representatives in the following six areas: Hampton Roads, Va.; San Francisco bay; Puget sound; San Diego; Portland, Oreg.-

Vancouver, Wash.; and Mobile, Ala. Reporting in December, a house naval subcommittee which investigated critical housing, health, food, transportation and other conditions in the congested Los Angeles-Long Beach sector, urged the addition to the federal committee of a representative for that area as soon as possible.

Personnel.—By October, representatives of federal, state and local civil service agencies reported that from approximately 3% to approximately 25% of civil service personnel were on military leave, or about 10% in the majority of jurisdictions. Most agencies were making war service appointments, that is, temporary appointments without civil service status. In municipal police and fire personnel, already 11% undermanned, a possible further loss of one-third following the drafting of fathers was anticipated. Some cities were successful in securing deferment for police and fire personnel, and some not: they were obliged in every case to take up the matter on an individual basis with local draft boards. In Miami and Norfolk military police and shore patrolmen were used to relieve the shortage of regular police officers.

Women were employed in a variety of capacities normally reserved for men: as street car and bus operators, traffic officers, fire inspectors, fire fighters, street cleaners, garbage collectors, park workers and personal property tax appraisers. A few communities experimented with employing high school boys in garbage and refuse collection, at city nurseries, even as regular firemen.

Wage and salary increases for municipal personnel continued apace. Local governments were expressly exempted from compulsory federal control of salaries and wages, though expected to conform to the national stabilization policy. Wartime pay adjustment plans were for the most part on a sliding scale, a flat percentage, or a cost-of-living basis. Detroit, facing intense industrial competition, achieved the distinction of having the highest paid municipal personnel in the country.

The turnover in municipal personnel increased the need for in-service training programs, particularly in such services as fire and police, confronted as they were with new social, economic and defense problems calling for training in the use of new types of equipment and of new techniques. A noteworthy manual, *Techniques of Law Enforcement Against Prostitution,* was compiled by the National Advisory Police committee, set up by the Federal Security administrator, and distributed to mayors, city managers and police chiefs, describing the best procedures developed throughout the United States in the control of venereal disease. In the civilian defense field, information reported early in 1943 indicated that more than 1,000 cities had trained a total of 201,617 auxiliary policemen—an average of 27 for each 10 regular employees—and 194,854 auxiliary firemen—or 29 for each 10 employees.

The American Municipal association and American Society of Planning Officials, in co-operation with state leagues of municipalities, inaugurated "postwar planning institutes" designed to aid municipal officials in the making of really comprehensive postwar plans. The University of Pennsylvania sponsored in-service training courses for state and local public officials under the direction of the Institute of Local and State Government. An in-service training course in fuel conservation was given by New York city to employees responsible for operating heating installations for the city. Many former municipal administrators, after receiving military commissions, attended the U.S. Army School of Military Government at Charlottesville, Va., and were in 1943 functioning in occupied areas abroad.

Finances.—Municipal finances presented the most favourable picture in many years. Revenues on the whole were satisfactory, with slight gains reported here and there from non-property tax sources, also some losses in the returns from gasoline taxes, automobile use taxes, parking meters, and business and occupation taxes. Several states allocated new or increased shares of state collected taxes to municipalities and other local units. California and Washington made direct appropriations to local governments for the relief of emergency war conditions. Any undercurrent of anxiety pertaining to revenues related more to the uncertainties of the postwar period than to current conditions.

Expenditures were not generally increased, with the exception of the heavy war industry cities where marked increases in such essential services as street maintenance and repair, garbage and refuse collection and disposal, and street cleaning costs were reported.

The question of tax losses due to federal acquisition of real property for war purposes loomed to the fore. Proposals for a solution were offered by the Federal Real Estate board in its *Federal Contributions to States and Local Governmental Units with Respect to Federally Owned Real Estate,* which the president duly transmitted to congress (House Document no. 216). The situation regarding payments in lieu of taxes on government-financed war housing projects also brightened considerably, with an estimated $13,000,000 to be paid in lieu of 1943 taxes, all cities being put on a common basis in this respect.

Current tax collections continued high. Tax rates decreased an average of $.35 per $1,000 of assessed value for the year 1942–43 for all cities of over 30,000 population, while assessed values enjoyed a slight average increase. This trend did not hold, however, for the group of cities over 1,000,000 in population, where tax rates increased an average of $.56 and assessed values continued their decline.

Municipal borrowing continued at a low ebb. The total of state and municipal sales for the year approximated only $505,000,000, the bulk of which were refunding and not new issues. Municipal bond yields reached an all-time low of 1.69% on Nov. 1, according to the *Bond Buyer's* index based on bonds of larger cities. On Dec. 1, the index stood at 1.82%. The net long-term debt of all cities of over 25,000 population, approximating $8,000,000,000, declined 4.2% during 1942–43, and was less than in any year since 1932. Short-term debt declined even more precipitately, totalling about $261,000,000, a decline of 6%. New York city reduced its net long-term debt by about $100,000,000.

In March of 1943 the special Committee on Intergovernmental Fiscal Relations appointed by the secretary of the treasury issued its monumental study, available from the superintendent of documents as Senate Document no. 69, 78th congress, 1st session under the title: *Federal, State, and Local Government Fiscal Relations.* The recommendations of the committee received wide publicity in local government fields. The Municipal Finance Officers association went on record at its annual conference as commending this report, which was subsequently termed comparable to the famous Rowell-Sirois report in 1940 on Canadian Dominion-Provincial Relations. Of the committee's recommendations, the proposal to create a permanent three-man federal-state tax commission to work out methods of central-local tax co-operation and the proposal for supplementing the municipal property tax with a rental tax on occupiers aroused the most widespread interest.

Postwar Planning.—Under the auspices of a special advisory committee on wartime and postwar planning set up by the International City Managers' association, an illuminating survey of postwar planning activities in 92 city manager cities was undertaken in May 1943. The great majority were found to be assembling data on postwar conditions regarding population, employment, conversion of war industries and public works. Most of the larger cities had official planning agencies. Nearly all had established reserves for the postwar period, by setting aside cash

from surplus funds, investing surplus funds in war bonds, setting up depreciation accounts for replacements and repairs, or by paying off debt.

In a symposium conducted by the *American City* magazine in nine issues from Nov. 1942, to Sept. 1943, 249 municipalities in all parts of the United States reported on planning improvements to be undertaken after the war; 140 of these were setting up financial reserves for this purpose.

Twelve additional states enacted legislation authorizing municipalities to set up postwar reserves, bringing the total of such states to 21. Such reserves were established also in other states by cities under home rule charter provisions and other state laws regulating investment of local funds.

On the federal level, the National Resources Planning board in its *National Resources Development; A Report for 1943* encouraged the making of plans by municipalities, in co-operation with the state and federal government (Part I: Postwar Plan and Program). After the liquidation of that board by congress, the enactment of federal measures on postwar planning, including financial aid to cities, was dropped, presumably pending issuance of a report by the Senate Committee on Postwar Economic Policy and Planning. However, two measures contemplating aid to cities for urban rebuilding, the Thomas bill and the Wagner bill, were introduced.

Proportional Representation Elections.—The 1943 proportional representation election in New York city resulted in a reduction in size of the city council from 26 to 17, because of the fixed quota provisions of the charter, and in the election of two Communists and a left-wing labour leader to the council. The other eight American cities holding P.R. elections in 1943 were: Cincinnati, Toledo and Hamilton, Ohio; Cambridge and Lowell, Mass.; Yonkers, N.Y.; Wheeling, W.Va.; and Boulder, Colo. P.R. was adopted for the first time in the little resort of Long Beach, Long Island, N.Y.

Council-Manager Cities.—Nine American cities adopted manager government during the year; three others which had previously done so were counted for the first time, making a total of 555 cities and seven counties under manager government in the United States.

Miscellaneous.—In tacit acknowledgment of municipal home rule, the wage stabilization policy, unemployment stabilization regulations, and 48-hour work week requirements of the federal government, were not made binding on cities, though a number voluntarily co-operated. On the other hand, a pending measure to provide federal aid to education was vigorously opposed on the ground of endangering home rule. Opposition to federal proposals for urban rehabilitation developed for similar reasons. Much of the local initiative in postwar planning was inspired by fear that the state or federal governments might otherwise take the lead after the war. (*See* also HOUSING.)   (A. M. Ds.; L. Gu.)

Munitions Assignment Board (U.S. and Great Britain): *see* BRITISH-U.S. WAR BOARDS.

Munitions of War. The finest body of men that could be assembled is powerless to wage and win wars if the tools of war are not furnished.

The record of the United States for 1943 in the procurement and production of munitions of war was one to be proud of. Applied to fighting on world-wide fronts, the term "munitions" covers some 700,000 different items, ranging from tanks and cannon to shoelaces and spoons. To review the status of the entire scale is obviously impossible. However, data concerning a representative cross section of the munitions field will throw some light on the production effort in America in 1943. In the first five months of 1943, the volume of tonnage moving in and out of installations in the United States averaged slightly over three and one-third million tons per month. This is significant, since prior to 1939 there was no armament industry.

Fortunately, the necessary plans and specifications had been prepared and were in readiness in the files of the United States army ordnance department. These plans were keyed to the extremes of the industrial world—the plant with less than 100 employees had its place in the scheme of things alongside the industrial giant with thousands on its payrolls. The need of factory conversion to war production had been recognized and blue-printed in advance; the mechanics of contracting and subcontracting had also been carefully integrated. How well ordnance department planning met the challenge of war can be realized in some degree from figures released late in 1943 in "Army Ordnance Report No. 3," wherein it was shown that, based upon dollar for dollar production, the United States ordnance department in just two years had grown over 35 times greater than the General Electric Co. had in 43 years.

During the year 1943, the war department announced that awards of army-navy "E" for excellence in production of war materials for exactly one year amounted to 1,910, of which 1,188 were nominated by the army and 722 by the navy. A total of 1,598 companies were represented, 1,042 manufacturing primarily for the army and 556 for the navy. The awards covered plants composed of a single employee to one hiring more than 126,000 workers.

To the Munitions Assignments board fall all problems concerned with the entire science of logistics. These problems ranged from the assignment of equipment to guerrilla bands to shipment of railroad locomotives. When the British 8th army went into action it had, in addition to British-produced munitions, the latest American tanks and self-propelled, high calibre American anti-tank guns.

Comparative figures at like calendar points in 1942 and 1943 showed the tremendous increase in munitions procurement and production. Taking April 1942 and April 1943 as marker points, it can be shown that the ordnance department accepted delivery in 1943 of ordnance material valued at $1,112,206,000 as compared with $444,324,000 the preceding year; more than three times the number of tank and combat vehicles were accepted; deliveries of self-propelled artillery were in some instances 16 times greater; deliveries of all types of artillery were up 258%; more than 10 times as many light antiaircraft guns were accepted, while acceptances of 75-mm. and 105-mm. howitzers jumped almost 50%; there was a threefold increase in deliveries of 60-mm. and 81-mm. mortars; deliveries of bombs, shells and bullets kept pace with a triple increase.

The character of munitions delivered displayed the ability of American factories to meet the needs of war. General Sherman 32-ton tanks were emphasized rather than the preceding year's General Stuart 13-ton tank. In the realm of self-propelled artillery there were produced the M-12 tank destroyer, a 155-mm. gun mounted on a medium tank chassis, and a 105-mm. howitzer mounted on M-7 tank chassis. The infantry mortars delivered won renown in Tunis, where they were reputed to have dropped their shells "into the hip pockets" of the axis infantry. Types of bombs and shells produced ranged from 20-mm. shells and small incendiary bullets to 16-in. coast artillery shells and 2- and 4-ton block busters. Antitank and antipersonnel mines were produced in huge quantities. Antiaircraft artillery with a lethal 60,000-foot vertical range was produced. Included in the year's deliveries were some items not produced at all the preceding year—fragmentation bomb clusters, medium and heavy howitzers, new types of tank destroyers and self-propelled guns, armoured reconnaissance cars and heavy tank-recovery vehicles designed to bring in

disabled tanks from the battlefields. For 1943, provision was made for the United States ordnance department to buy $17,-300,000,000 worth of artillery, tanks, motor vehicles, bombs, rifles, ammunition, machine guns and aircraft cannon. One piece of artillery was being provided for every 46 soldiers in World War II, as compared with one piece for every 1,100 soldiers in World War I.

Munitions developments for the year included:

Ammunition.—In 1918, the United States produced small arms ammunition at the rate of 278,000,000 rounds a month; in 1943, that amount was produced every week. For World War I, the United States produced 2,700,000 artillery shells a month; for World War II, 18,000,000 a month. In January, more than 70,-000 aircraft bombs of 1,000-lb. size or larger were produced by American industry. In February, the United States produced 1,932,000 high explosive shells of all calibres, 419,000 bombs, and 1,244,000,000 cartridges of calibre .30, .45 and .50 ammunition. Thus, the United States in 1943 produced enough rifle and machine-gun ammunition each month to fire 83 rounds at every individual soldier in the axis. Production of ammunition for 1943 increased 550% over the preceding year. In one arsenal alone, each employee produced for the 12-mo. period an average of more than 47,000 rounds of small arms ammunition of calibres .30 and .50. A deadly bullet christened the "Blue Goose" was developed. It is fired from a .50-calibre machine gun, pierces gasoline tanks, to explode inside, where it starts a chemical fire of intense heat.

Armour.—As protection against bursting ack-ack shells, many airmen wore in 1943 infantry helmets along with flexible armour from neck to hips, with a sporran protecting the thighs.

Artillery.—Artillery may be classified as horse-drawn, pack, truck-drawn, self-propelled, railway, coast defense, aircraft and antiaircraft. Bombing planes are, in effect, long-range artillery and artillerymen are no longer the sole persons to man artillery. The smallest cannon, the 20-mm., was an aircraft weapon. Rated as infantry and cavalry weapons were the 37-mm. gun M-3 (antitank), the 60-mm. mortar M-2 and the 81-mm. mortar M-1. Field artillery is classified as: light—pieces up to and including the 105-mm. howitzer; medium—such as the 155-mm. howitzer and the 4.5" gun; and heavy—the 155-mm. gun, the 8" and 240-mm. howitzers and seacoast artillery ranging from 8" to 16". The development of true "flying artillery" really takes field weapons "upstairs."

One of the surprising weapons of 1943 was the 4.2" chemical mortar. It is a rifled weapon with a 2-mi. range and was designed originally to throw smoke shells, particularly white phosphorus, whose particles burn in air after bursting and cling flaming to any surface. However, it was found that the mortar handled a 25-lb. shell, packed with an 8-lb. high explosive charge, exceptionally well, and invasion forces in Sicily and Italy used the mortar with excellent results; in fact, it was referred to by the enemy as a "miracle gun." In the heavy artillery class, the army put the M-10 into mass production. This weapon was designed as a tank destroyer and was, in effect, a land cruiser capable of coping with anything in battle. In its manufacture, sections were fabricated from armour plate wherever possible and machine welding was extensively used to save time. Another heavy antitank weapon was the M-12, a 155-mm. gun mounted on a medium tank chassis and capable of attaining the speed of a medium tank. This weapon, exceedingly mobile, could hurl a 95-lb. projectile more than 10 mi. with sufficient force at that range to knock out any tank or sink a battle cruiser. In North African fighting, self-propelled weapons brought down enemy planes and violently disrupted German communications lines. The ordnance department standardized gun motor carriages for 37-mm., 75-mm. and 105-mm. howitzers. In the smaller armament realm, there was noted a production record in one month of 7,000 aircraft cannon of 2-mm. calibre. Armament of aircraft demonstrated how far the United States had come along since 1918, when the ordnance department announced the installation of 75-mm. cannon in army air force planes. First tested from B-18 aircraft, it was finally proved practicable, so that in 1943 it was a fact that a gun of the same size but of greater power than the field artillery most in use in World War I could be fired from aeroplanes with speeds of more than 300 mi. per hour. This weapon knocked out any tank in use, could sink any lightly armoured warship and destroy enemy gun emplacements. Two other important aircraft weapons were the 37-mm. automatic cannon and the .50-calibre aircraft machine gun with its incendiary and armour-piercing ammunition.

Battery.—Most chemicals which activate a "dry" cell become virtually inert at subzero temperatures. Experimentation during 1943 sought to develop a battery that would not become less active at low temperatures. The meteorological section, signal corps, hit upon the plan of keeping batteries at normal temperatures by containing them in a thermos bottle.

Bazooka.—This Yank-christened instrument enabled the individual soldier to stand his ground against any tank. In African operations, one shot from a bazooka forced the surrender of a small but strong fort. This weapon was a metal tube slightly over 50 in. long and a little less than 3 in. in diameter, open at both ends. Attached to the tube were a shoulder stock and front and rear grips for the firer, together with sights and an electric battery which set off the rocket propelling charge when the launcher trigger was squeezed. The bazooka was operated by a two-man team—one the firer, the other the loader. When the bazooka was in firing position, the loader was at the right and rear of the firer. After loader placed rocket in tube he turned a contact lever to the "fire" position, signalled "ready" to the firer, then dropped down and away from rear end of the tube. When firer squeezed the trigger, the rocket propelling charge was ignited and flashed from rear of tube. The rocket itself was heavier than a hand

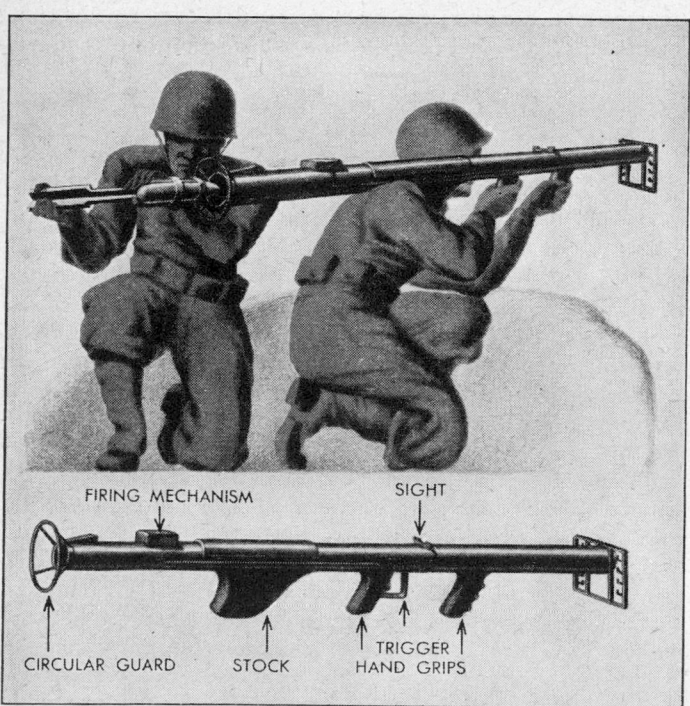

FIRING MECHANISM   SIGHT

CIRCULAR GUARD   STOCK   TRIGGER HAND GRIPS

THE BAZOOKA or rocket gun enables a foot soldier to operate effectively against armoured vehicles. The drawings show the weapon itself and a two-man bazooka team, consisting of a firer and a loader, in action. Although it is only about 50 in. long and weighs about the same as a Springfield rifle, the bazooka fires a projectile which can penetrate 3 in. of armour

grenade and was nearly 2 ft. long. It was highly effective against tanks and pillboxes.

Binoculars.—Optical glass manufacturers co-operated to standardize the types of binoculars fabricated for issue. Thousands of splendid instruments were turned in gratuitously by civilians for military use.

Brass.—By reason of a process perfected at the Evansville ordnance plant and Frankford arsenal it was possible to substitute steel for brass in the manufacture of .45-calibre ammunition. This made possible the saving of 1,774 lb. of brass for each 100,000 rounds of this type ammunition.

A further savings, estimated at 365,000 lb. of brass annually, was made possible by substituting plastic for brass in enlisted men's uniform buttons and collar insignia. In addition to the metal savings effected, the plastic material had the added advantages of not reflecting light and of being nontarnishable.

Canisters.—Gas mask canisters, formerly filled with activated charcoal produced from hard-to-get cocoanut shells, were to be filled with charcoal produced from sawdust, wood, coke and even coal. The new product was superior to the old in its ability to absorb toxic gases.

Drinking Water.—In New Rochelle, N.Y., manufacture was begun of a device called "Sunstill" to convert sea water into drinking water. A new water testing kit devised by the army determined the calcium hypochlorite content of water by use of the chemical agent known as orthotolidine.

Duffel Bag.—Patterned after the marine corps bag, this new type duffel bag was designed for troops going overseas. It was made of single-ply No. 10 duck, was 37 in. high on a 12-in. square base; it had a snap-fastening device at the top, was equipped with a carrying strap and was dark olive-drab in colour.

Engine.—A new tank engine was satisfactorily tested. It was 500-h.p., 8-cyl., liquid cooled and relatively light-weight because of secondary aluminum used in its construction.

The Packard Motor Car Co. built a new engine for P-51 planes. It had greater than 1,500 h.p. and its perfection had the effect of raising aerial warfare nearly two mi.

Gas Mask.—A new light-weight gas mask was developed as suitable for desert and jungle warfare. It had a 20-in. hose connecting face piece to a canister which gave protection against all known gaseous agents. There was also developed a new, waterproof gas mask kit.

A new type gas mask was developed for horses and mules. There were two types, M-4 designed for pack and draft animals, and M-5 for cavalry horses. Both were very light and had close-fitting muzzle pieces connected by flexible hose to canisters. They resembled human gas masks and animals were afforded enough air to walk, trot or gallop in comfort while adequately protected against field concentrations of known chemical agents.

Gasoline.—The fuel and lubricants division, office of the quartermaster general, working in co-operation with the ordnance department, perfected an all-purpose, all-weather gasoline designed to meet year-round combat requirements of all army ground force vehicles. It was standardized at 80-octane and its development was the result of three years' experimentation.

Gasoline Tank.—To be used in starting equipment in very cold weather, a two-compartment gasoline tank was devised; one tank contained 1 qt. of high vapour pressure priming gasoline, the other tank held a gallon of ordinary gasoline. The starting mechanism was needled with the high test gas and then switched to the ordinary type.

Glass.—Chemists of the American Optical Co. invented a coating which made glass nonreflecting and practically invisible. Glare was eliminated. For the duration of the war, use of this coating process was restricted to military purposes.

RUSSIAN ROCKET GUNS ranged in batteries, being fired at the Germans before Stalingrad. They are called "Katiushas"

U.S. SOLDIERS examining the famous German "Tiger" tank

CONCRETE BARRICADES at Picatinny arsenal, Dover, N.J., separate buildings to lessen the effects of explosions

U.S. MOBILE 155-MM. GUN, mounted on a medium-tank chassis, was the latest version of self-propelled artillery in 1943. Throwing a 95-lb. shell ten miles, it could knock out any tank in existence

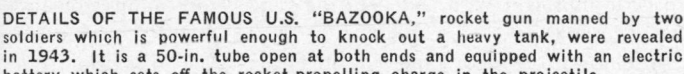

DETAILS OF THE FAMOUS U.S. "BAZOOKA," rocket gun manned by two soldiers which is powerful enough to knock out a heavy tank, were revealed in 1943. It is a 50-in. tube open at both ends and equipped with an electric battery which sets off the rocket-propelling charge in the projectile

Grenades.—Rifle grenades, previously fired only from Springfield rifles, were fired by a special type of blank cartridge from Garands and from carbines. These grenades were practically one-man tank busters.

The Chemical Warfare service developed coloured smoke grenades which throw off a dense smoke for 2 or 3 min. They came in brilliant colours and in black. They could be set off on the ground or dropped from a plane to flame in air. Different signal requirements could be met by combining colours and, by prearranged code, friendly tanks or other units could make appropriate answers to signals from friendly aeroplanes.

Gyro.—A tank gyro stabilizer was developed to improve gunner's aiming chances. This device functioned satisfactorily while tank was driven at full speed across the battlefield.

Hangar.—A portable hangar was fabricated of cold, formed steel, with coverings and doors of specially treated dark canvas. In cold climates, wood sheathing was to be substituted for canvas. A portable, oil-fired, circulating air heating unit was also developed for heating this hangar.

Helmet.—The Chicago quartermaster depot was named as sole source of war department procurement for the new U.S. army M-1 steel helmet liner. This had three parts, (1) the steel shell fabricated and procured from special bullet and shrapnel resisting alloy steel, (2) a lightweight, rigid moulded plastic liner which is worn minus the steel shell in out-of-combat areas and (3) a head and neck band.

Hospital Train.—There was exhibited in Washington, D.C., during November, an all-steel, overseas type hospital train. It consisted of 10 cars, including 6 ward cars, a kitchen car, utilities car and two personnel cars for officers and enlisted men. Each car was slightly more than half the length of an ordinary railway car and was designed to negotiate the sharp curves, narrow bridges and tunnels of foreign railways. The train had a pressure ventilating system, complete sterilization units and operating areas in each ward car. It was used principally to remove patients from evacuation hospitals and the train was a complete unit in itself. The utilities car furnished electric current from two diesel generators, while two oil-fired steam boilers provided heat and hot water.

Each ward car could accommodate 16 bed patients.

Hydrosizing.—Shells for the 4.2″ chemical mortar were body-sized by a new method. Instead of turning the shells on a lathe the sizing was done by hydraulic pressure. The time was reduced from 6 min. per shell by the old method to 30 sec. per shell by the new.

Material saved by hydrosizing amounts to 205 tons of metal on each 100,000 shells.

Inner Tubes.—Glenn L. Martin Co., aircraft manufacturer, announced the development of a new plastic which made better inner tubes than natural rubber. It had no resemblance to rubber but was, instead, a vinyl chloride plastic. It could be processed on standard rubber-working machinery and did not need to be vulcanized.

This substitute material was called Marvinol and its basic ingredients were coal, air, salt and water.

Jungle Kit.—In a 10-oz. waterproof kit, jungle aids were assembled for the soldier. The kit contained: a printed waterproof sheet of "Ten Rules for Jungle Safety," a pocket knife, a fish hook and line, a length of strong twine, a length of strong wire, a compass, a glass for starting a fire, iodine crystals in a waterproof container, matches in a waterproof container, and mosquito net for head covering.

Kitchen.—A kitchen railway car was designed to provide food for more than 250 persons at one sitting. It had two coal burning stoves, a huge sink, two water tanks, closets, large ice box and

storage batteries for operating the lighting system.

Knife.—A new trench knife resembling an oversized hunting knife was designed. It had a corrugated raw-hide handle. The blade was 6¾ in. long, one cutting edge running the full length of the blade, the other extending only 2¾ in., after which the steel widens for strength. A new leather sheath, provided with metal plates, protected the wearer from the cutting edge of the knife in case of a fall.

Leather.—Savings in this item were effected by long-range planning. By switching to an unlined horsehide riding glove and by altering the cuff design, a total of 1,028,000 sq. ft. of leather was saved. Through substitution of 3,399,377 sq. ft. of cattle hide splits, a total of 11,484,300 sq. ft. of horsehide splits and 153,125 sq. ft. of grain leather horsehides was saved in making heavy leather gloves. Height of uppers on soldiers' shoes was decreased to effect a saving of 9,871,088 sq. ft. of grain cattle hides. Incidentally, this change saved great lengths of shoelaces and, by the elimination of four eyelets on each shoe, made possible a saving of 282,032 lb. of steel. Shoulder strap hand bags carried by nurses and Wacs were made of arctic sealskin, a noncritical item and a means of saving 3,262,410 sq. ft. of cowhide. Another 1,100,295 lb. of strap leather was saved by replacing the all-leather machete sheath by one of water-repellent cotton duck. Canvas carbine covers saved 1,060,285 lb. of leather.

Lights.—A submarine searchlight was developed capable of withstanding immersion in cold water one minute after burning and likewise able to resist the shock of firing a heavy calibre gun only a few feet away from its mounting.

Since bodies of water absorb rather than reflect light, it was necessary to fashion floating lights to define water runway areas for safe landings on dark nights. Westinghouse technicians devised an intense, battery-operated fluorescent lamp mounted on a floating rubber doughnut.

Bicycle tail lights were attached during the year as a part of equipment for parachutes.

Lubricants and Fuel Oil.—By sharp rationing of crude oil and refined gasoline, particularly on the eastern seaboard of the United States, an estimated 500,000 bbl. of gasoline a day were saved. However, army demands made this still a very critical matter. Crude oil requirements were estimated at 4,150,000 bbl. a day, or about 130,000 bbl. more than could efficiently be produced.

The government's Automotive and Power branch tested a new synthetic lubricant with an operating range from minus 100° to plus 300° F.

Machine Guns.—In January and February of 1943, American shops produced 150,000 machine guns and 134,000 submachine guns as against 132,000 machine guns of all calibres in all of World War I.

A new submachine gun was put into mass production. It weighed less than 9 lb. and might be taken down in three principal pieces, none of which was over 1 ft. long. This gun, M-3, was so small it could be carried in an ordinary brief case. It was a .45-calibre weapon, all-metal construction with collapsible metal stock. Working parts were fully enclosed against dirt, water and mud. This gun was found exceptionally reliable in operation, even after immersion in sea water. It was capable of firing 450 rounds per minute, cost less than $20 to manufacture, and after firing 49,600 rounds in test showed no decrease in accuracy.

Mats.—Aladdin's magic carpet came to light in the widespread use of interlocking steel mats by means of which landing fields and take-off runways were built almost as if by magic. In the month of January, alone, more than 37,000,000 sq. ft. of metal landing mats were produced, and later in the year it was estimated that production of this item had increased 353% over the

GERMAN ANTIPERSONNEL MINE

Push or pull detonator mechanism screws on here

Inner mine explodes, sending bullet-like steel balls in all directions

Inner shell

Outer shell

350 polished steel balls

Detonator ignites jumping charge which in turn ignites powder train to TNT

BLAST FROM INNER MINE

INNER SHELL MINE

Jumping charge in outer shell throws inner shell mine into the air

BLAST FROM JUMPING CHARGE

Pushing down detonator mechanism ignites mine

MINE

OUTER SHELL

OUTER SHELL

THE ANTIPERSONNEL BOUNDING MINE (Silent Soldier) explodes when the detonator mechanism is pushed or pulled. This German model explodes twice, the second time in the air, at which time the inner shell scatters its contents of 350 steel balls as far as 200 yards

output for the year 1942.

Microphone.—A tiny lip microphone was devised to be worn on the upper lip for use in tanks and other places where users of communications must have their hands free. This instrument fitted easily under gas masks and dust respirators.

Packaging.—Formerly, U.S. tanks shipped to British ports had to be de-slushed of heavy coats of grease which had been smeared on to prevent rust during the ocean voyage. While lying helpless at dockside throughout this process, they were easy targets for nazi bombers who took advantage of the targets afforded. In 1943, tanks were shipped wrapped in plastic film with a drying agent inside the wrapper. Arrived at port of debarkation, the wrapping was ripped off and the tank driven quickly away from the dock.

Pipelines.—Portable pipelines for military service were developed by the corps of engineers in co-operation with private industry. These lines solved the problems of bringing liquid fuels and water to front line troops, the latter especially valuable in arid regions. This new pipeline was nearly as portable as a tank truck. It could be laid at the rate of 20 mi. per day and it was movable to allow coverage of rapidly shifting battle fronts. One mile of the line, including pumping stations, weighed only 13 tons. The pipe sections could be laid on top of any terrain accessible to trucks.

Plastics.—The army tested plastics for temperature variations ranging from −55° to +85° C.

Powder.—A new process was evolved whereby wood pulp was used in the manufacture of smokeless powder. The development was undertaken by the Hercules Powder Co. because it was recognized that the U.S. cotton supply was inadequate. The new process was estimated to have saved $20,000,000 manufacturing costs in its first year of operation.

In addition to sulfanilamide tablets, U.S. soldiers carried a tin of powder a small amount of which would de-flea them. Along with this was a small vial of fumigator with which they could quickly delouse their clothing in sealed paper sacks.

Rifles.—Production of the Garand rifle was stepped up to the point of producing 80,000 of them a month.

Rubber.—The normal natural rubber consumption was estimated on an annual basis at 600,000 tons. The army's rubber conservation program reduced the use of crude rubber in war material by 45% on the basis of the amount of rubber in the same material as of Dec. 7, 1941. Eleven principles of conservation were established: designs; constructions and compounds; factory inspection of finished products; packaging; procurement; storage; issue; application; preventive maintenance; reconditioning and reclaiming and co-ordination. Polyvinyl resins replaced rubber for cable and electric wire insulation. Butyl was used to replace natural rubber for floats, boats, rafts and other inflatable items. Buna S replaced natural rubber in tires. In November the war department announced that, henceforth, all army rubber footwear would be manufactured from Buna S, saving about 180,000 lb. of natural rubber per month.

Searchlights.—This engineer item showed a 525% production increase for the year.

Shoes.—In January and February, 5,000,000 pairs of marching shoes were built for the military service. Early in the year, army shops were rebuilding 250,000 pairs of shoes per month and repairing another 525,000 pairs. For the year it was estimated that approximately 6,500,000 pairs were rebuilt, effecting a savings of $7,000,000 plus 20,000,000 sq.ft. of leather.

Shoe-pac.—A new type was designed with rubber feet and leather tops intended for use in snow or on wet terrain. It had a nonskid rubber heel, ridged for easy attachment of snow shoes.

Soap.—A new all-purpose soap was perfected by the army. It was mild, nonirritant and efficient under all conditions.

Spectacles.—A new type was devised for use with gas masks.

Statistics.—Certain statistics are of interest in connection with the production of munitions. Emergency construction, real estate and maintenance programs for the army of the United States represented an outlay of approximately $11,000,000,000 since beginning of these activities in June 1940. Nearly 15,000 separate projects were undertaken, including air bases, tactical air fields, schools and depots. Posts, camps and stations occupied a total area of approximately 14,500 sq.mi., or the combined area of Massachusetts, Rhode Island and Connecticut. The army built more than 480,000,000 sq.yd. of roads, airfield runways and parking spaces—the equivalent of 13 New York-to-Seattle highways each 21 ft. wide. The army also operated 3,340 mi. of railroad.

In September, percentage-of-increase figures were published showing the rise in production since Sept. 1939, viz.: petroleum 66%; soft coal 40%; chemicals 300%; iron ore 125%; hydro-electric power 79%; and steel 106%. The month of July 1943 was a turning point, since it showed for the first time in months an over-all increase in production of munitions—the gain stood at 3%.

Figures released in September showed actual output since May 1940 of: aeroplanes 123,000; tanks 53,000; trucks 1,233,000; and small arms 9,500,000.

For the manufacture of munitions, the small manufacturers of the country received 48.8 cents out of every procurement dollar spent by the army service forces, and an additional 25.2 cents of each dollar was received by small plants through "first-tier" subcontracts.

Steel.—One of the toughest problems in the history of military production was solved by the General Motors Corp. (Buick division) working with army ordnance experts. Demand for conservation of copper made mandatory the evolving of a process for the manufacture of steel shell cases. The four different processes which solved the problem involved extension and cold working of bar stock steel, drawing it into size and shape of an artillery shell case, giving it at the same time the high physical properties required in firing. It was hot-extruded and cold-drawn from a billet of steel $3\frac{1}{8}$ in. in diameter by $1\frac{3}{4}$ in. deep, and perfect surface was secured by grinding. Inspection by magnaflux method checked all internal imperfections.

At the Fontana plant of Henry Kaiser in San Bernardino valley, Calif., was produced California's first "home-grown" steel, from ore to finished plate. In August the first sheared plate was made and fitted into the deck of a Kaiser Liberty ship.

Stereofluoroscope.—This was a newly developed instrument whereby a surgeon got a three-dimensional picture when he probed for bullets or shell splinters in a soldier's body. He was able to look at the embedded foreign matter and, by using a slim sterilized needle, reach to the fragment for removal purposes.

Stethoscope.—A new acoustic stethoscope introduced sounds to the doctor's ears never before heard in the human body. The device registered sounds of the human body ranging from 40 to 4,000 sound cycles.

Tanks.—During World War I, the United States produced a total of just 80 tanks; in a two-month period in 1943, production of tanks stood at 5,000.

Telephone.—A sound-powered telephone, operated without cumbersome batteries, proved to be one of the most useful pieces of equipment on Guadalcanal. Power in the telephone was generated by the human voice and was capable of a 5-mi. radius of transmission under almost any circumstances—10-mi. radius under favourable conditions. It was more compact and durable than battery-powered phones and combatted tropical humidity. Signalling was accomplished by whistling into the transmitter.

Trucks.—In January and February, more than 28,000 army trucks and, in February, 7,800 weapon-bearing combat vehicles were produced. A new product of the year was the "truck amphibian, $2\frac{1}{2}$-ton, 6x6, DUKW-353." Promptly christened "the duck," it could carry both troops and cargo on sea as well as on land.

Turret.—A power turret was designed for aircraft. It was technically a gun mount, power-operated. This turret overcame the slipstream (air driven back by the propellers), thus enabling the gunner to hold a steady sight on his target. The steady aiming thereby afforded was called "tracking," and, coupled with American advanced sighting devices, made it almost impossible for the aircraft gunner to miss.

Uniforms.—Developments in this field were based on a "layering" principle by which successive layers of clothing might be donned to suit the climate. Basic fabric was a 9-oz. rip-proof material known as "5-harness" sateen. It was extremely tough and had excellent wind- and water-resisting characteristics. An army field jacket was made of this material, reversed side out, with a 5-oz. poplin lining. All buttons were covered with flaps to prevent catching on objects. For cold climates, warm pile-cloth was used, and for extremely cold areas, two suits were provided, worn, one with pile side of cloth in, the other with pile side out.

Tailored two-piece slack suits were prescribed for Army nurses on duty on hospital ships, hospital trains and in warmer climates overseas. This uniform provided greater freedom of movement than was possible with skirts and dresses and also afforded better protection from insects.

Walkie-talkie.—There was perfected a new series of radio communications set, light enough to hold in one hand and almost as easy to operate as a telephone handset. It was used with outstanding success in North African operations. Fitted with an improved superheterodyne, its range was triple that of old models. The set used miniature radio tubes and was known to function after being completely rain-soaked.

X-ray Machine.—Westinghouse engineers developed a new X-ray machine capable of inspecting as many as 17,000 aeroplane castings in a 24-hr. day. This unit produced an exposed film of six castings every 30 sec.

Certain definite army unfilled needs were brought out in the munitions field. Some of them were: a device to locate nonmetallic land mines; a harmless method of darkening aluminum so as not to reflect light; a method of waterproofing vehicles so that engines would not stall while fording streams; an inexpensive durable metal for soldiers' dishes; and a method of absorbing or eliminating poisonous carbon monoxide.

Navy.—Vessels of the U.S. navy completed in the three years between July 1940 and July 1943, when added to existing tonnage, made it the mightiest surface fleet in the world's history. Building for the three-year period included 333 combat vehicles, 1,274 mine craft and patrol craft, 151 auxiliaries, 654 yard and district craft and 12,964 landing craft. The degree of step-up in 1943 is shown in the figures for June, which showed that the number of vessels completed in that month approximated the total number finished in the entire first 18 mo. of the defense building program. During the first half of 1943, navy yards and private shipbuilders, including the record-making and breaking Henry Kaiser, built more than 6,000 naval craft of all classes. This was an increase of 250% over the number of vessels completed in the same period in 1942. Ships built cost approximately $2,500,000,000 and represented 1,000,000 standard displacement tons. Included in this construction group were the first vessels of a new combatant type, the destroyer escort. Production of PT boats was seven times that of the preceding year. Noted in construction work for the year was virtual completion of the reconstruction job on the vessels crippled at Pearl Harbor in 1941, along with the righting of the giant liner, the "Lafayette" (ex-"Normandie"). It was estimated that in 1943 the United States had afloat more than 5,000,000 tons and ships of all kinds were coming off the ways for the navy at the rate of five per day. Figures estimated for the fiscal year 1944 (ending June 30, 1944) showed a total vessel strength of 41,179 divided by types as 4,153 combatant, patrol, mine and auxiliary ships; 2,994 district and yard craft; and 34,032 small landing craft and special boats.

Big ship balance was restored by commissioning of the aeroplane carrier U.S.S. "Saratoga" and the launching on Dec. 7 of the 52,000-ton battleship "Wisconsin." A new class of carriers (CVB) 45,000-ton, inaugurated in 1942, saw two keels laid down in 1943 and a third planned for 1944. The "Saratoga," the biggest aeroplane carrier afloat was originally intended to be built as a battle cruiser. An interesting bit of historic construction during the year was the refitting, regunning and remanning of the former presidential yacht "Mayflower," which was put into service as a coast guard cutter on Oct. 19, 1943. For the British navy, the Bethlehem-Hingham shipyard at Hingham, Mass., completed a destroyer escort ship 25 days after its keel was laid.

Antiaircraft fire power on modern battleships was 100 times greater than it was three years ago. Of this type of ship armament, four gun-and-mount assemblies constituted 97% of the dollar value of all ship installations for antiaircraft fire:

    20-mm. antiaircraft guns
    40-mm. antiaircraft guns
    3"/50 calibre double-purpose guns
    5"/38 calibre double-purpose guns

Of the above, only one, the 5", was American designed.

Amphibious attacks on Sicily, Italy, Attu, Kiska, Rendova and Tarawa showed how well the navy was equipped with landing craft to meet army requirements. The several types of these craft were: LST—landing ship tank, really a medium-sized ocean freighter (372 ft. long; 5,500 tons), whose bows open up like huge jaws when discharging cargo; LCI-L—landing craft infantry-large, able to navigate by itself on high seas (155 ft. long) and can carry 200 infantrymen; LCV—landing craft vehicle and LCP —landing craft personnel, with space sufficient to carry 50 men or equivalent cargo to shore (36 ft. long); LCM—landing craft mechanized (50 ft. long), carries a medium tank and crew of four; LCT—landing craft tank (100 ft. long), designed to carry large tanks with their crews.

Navy chemists developed plastic shipbottom paint which materially reduced fouling, so much so that very appreciable savings in fuel oil were effected.

General utility, semicircular steel buildings were fabricated for navy use. They weighed complete 25,000 lb. each and could be packed for shipping in crates occupying only 369 cu. ft.

Waters off Cape Fear, N.C., witnessed the testing of many diverse types of life-saving equipment, all of which showed revolutionary advance in items provided to sustain life during long periods of time if cast adrift at sea.

In the realm of merchant ships, William Francis Gibbs, co-operating in a program of standardization to speed up mass production, reduced merchant ship types from 6 to 3; types of geared turbines from 27 to 8; and turbogenerators from 77 to 17. It was believed that future merchant ships would be powered with geared turbines giving them speeds of over 15 knots per hr. These Victory ships would supplant the Liberty ships and, with the same cargo-carrying capacity, would be able to outrun submerged submarines.

Salvage.—The importance of systematic salvage in relation to the munitions program was stressed by war department circular 399, Dec. 9, 1942, which stated in part that ". . . used ammunition components be recovered and turned in for salvage in best possible condition. . . ." Early in January, it was announced that the army had collected at overseas bases and returned to the United States approximately 1,348,000 lb. of brass cartridge cases. At overseas bases there were collected tires, tubes, scrap rubber, scrap metals, clothing and textiles. When received in the United States, repairable property was channeled into repair facilities while metal scrap was sent into channels of industry. There was a steady flow to the United States of 300 tons of battle scrap a month. This scrap was in addition to ferrous scrap which the navy was salvaging in shore installations at the rate of 25,000 tons a month. In the navy, items of salvage extended from pliofilm for aeroplane engine covers to antifreeze radiator liquids. Waste lumber was given for fuel to needy families; electric light bulbs were salvaged for brass; tin cans returned to tin and steel components; garbage was fed to piggeries; metal was salvaged from photo film rolls and typewriter ribbon spools; and scrap cordage was used in manufacturing tough fibre paper serving as a substitute for silk in small parachutes used for dropping aeroplane flares.

To encourage household savings of kitchen fats, the war department reprinted and distributed the DuPont Co. conversion scale showing that: 100 lb. of scrap fats and oils could be converted into more than 6 lb. of glycerine and, then, nearly 15 lb. of nitroglycerine. In turn, this would make enough dynamite to bring down 1,500 tons of soft coal or enough iron ore to provide steel to make 2,000 100-lb. bombs. (See also AIR FORCES OF THE WORLD; NAVIES OF THE WORLD; SUBMARINE WARFARE.)

BIBLIOGRAPHY.—United States: *Army and Navy Journal; Army Ordnance; Bulletin of the Army Ordnance Association; Command and General Staff School Military Review; Army and Navy Register; Time; Newsweek; War Department Press Digests, Bulletins, Releases,* and *Radio Digest; Life.* Great Britain: *The Times.* Germany: *Deutsche-Wehr; Militar Wochenblatt.* U. S. S. R.: *Krasnaya Zvesda.* (R. S. T.)

Murphy, Robert Daniel

(1894–), U.S. foreign service official, was born Oct. 28 in Milwaukee. He entered the foreign service in 1917 as a clerk in the Berne legation and held consular posts in Zurich, Munich and Seville until 1930, when he was transferred to the Paris embassy as consul and later first secretary. After the collapse of French armies in June 1940, he followed the Pétain government to Vichy, there becoming a counsellor in the U.S. embassy and chief U.S. representative in French North Africa. Murphy was credited with having played an important role in preparing the groundwork for the U.S. invasion of French North Africa in Nov. 1942. For this work he was given the D.S.M. and was raised to the rank of minister. During the early part of 1943, under a storm of criticism from the U.S., Murphy worked toward a settlement of Giraud-de Gaulle differences, his goal being French unity and the establishment of a governing body that the U.S. would be willing to recognize. Finally, the French Committee of National Liberation was set up, and conditional recognition by the U.S. was achieved Aug. 26. When the advisory council to the Allied Control Commission for Italy was formed in November to replace the Allied Mediterranean commission, Murphy was appointed as the U.S. member with the personal rank of ambassador. His duties as American representative to the French Committee for National Liberation were taken over by Edwin C. Wilson, former ambassador to Panamá.

Murray, Philip

(1886–), U.S. labour leader. A native of Scotland, he was born in Blantyre May 25 and emigrated to the United States in 1902. Naturalized in 1911, he became a member of the international board of the United Mine Workers of America the next year, president of the union's fifth district in 1916, and international vice-president in 1920. During World War I he was a member of Pennsylvania's regional war labour board and served also on the National Bituminous Coal Production committee. In 1935 he was named to the National Industrial Recovery board and to the advisory council of the National Recovery administration. Murray, choice of John L. Lewis, succeeded him as C.I.O. president, Nov. 22, 1940, when Lewis fulfilled his pledge to quit if Roosevelt were re-elected. But Murray did not follow Lewis in his bitter opposition to Roosevelt's foreign policy. A split developed, which became an open break in May 1942, when Lewis ousted Murray as U.M.W.A. vice-president. Murray fought back, and the C.I.O. went along with him; Lewis and the Mine Workers walked out. In 1942, Murray proposed industry councils in which labour, management and government would be equally represented. While this plan was not adopted, WPB did sponsor labour-management committees throughout the nation's war plants. In 1943 Murray fought actively for various things: to maintain the no-strike policy, to use manpower more efficiently, to streamline the War Labor board, to stabilize prices, etc. When congress refused to go along, and instead enacted the Smith-Connally anti-strike bill and was hesitant about taxes and subsidies, the C.I.O. set up a political action committee, with $750,000 funds, to aid the candidate it supports in the 1944 presidential election. In his Labor day address, Murray asked that labour be given greater voice in determining national policies. Late in 1943, he was emphatic in his demands that, since taxes and subsidies adequate to stabilize prices had not been provided, the "little steel formula" should be scrapped and wages permitted to rise. Murray was re-elected president of C.I.O. on Nov. 5.

Museums of Art: *see* ART GALLERIES AND ART MUSEUMS.

Music. In 1943 most musicians came to realize that the aesthetics of 10 and 20 years before would not suffice for the new world ahead.

Certainly, the tenets of "pure art" were already under attack. The effects of this attack were to be seen in the music from Russia. Sergei Prokofiev, the composer of the *Classical Symphony* and of much performed violin and piano concerti was composing an opera on Tolstoy's *War and Peace*. He produced a cantata— *Ballad of the Unknown Boy* and a *Symphonic Suite, 1941.* Vissarion Shebalin wrote a *Slavonic Quartet* and a *Russian Overture.* Reinhold Glière completed not only a *Concerto* for coloratura soprano with orchestral accompaniment, but also a popular vocal number, *End of Hitler.* Nyoskovsky's *Kirov Is With Us* is a cantata based on the Leningrad siege. Dmitri Shostakovich sold to an orchestra in the United States for $10,000 the first performance rights to his new *Eighth Symphony,* which, like the seventh, is based directly on the great Russian offensive in the war. The fact that the "International," the song of world-wide revolution, was abandoned by the U.S.S.R. in 1943 for a nationally contained anthem, might in some way serve to mark the change that was taking place.

Aaron Copland wrote his *Lincoln Portrait,* though perhaps his *Piano Sonata,* given its first performances during 1943, remained his most provocative new work. A new *Sonata for Violin and Piano* was heard in January of 1944. Daniel Gregory Mason produced *A Lincoln Symphony.* Robert Palmer set Vachel Lindsay's *Abraham Lincoln Walks at Midnight.* Lincoln and Jefferson served Earl Robinson with material for radio cantatas. "Songs can be bullets," said Robinson. Four choruses for men's voices by Randall Thompson setting writings of Thomas Jefferson were

FRANK SINATRA, popular radio singer of 1943, singing with the New York Philharmonic at Lewisohn stadium, New York city, Aug. 3

performed at the 200th anniversary of his birth. William Schuman, winner of the newly formed Pulitzer prize (no longer a scholarship for study but a prize for the best work of the year), produced *Prayer—1943* and *A Free Song,* a cantata on words by Walt Whitman. William Grant Still, whose *In Memoriam of Colored Soldiers Who Died for Democracy* the New York Philharmonic Symphony Orchestra was to perform, made a setting of an anti-fascist poem by Katherine Garrison Chapin, *Plain Song for America.* Ross Lee Finney wrote a *Symphony Communiqué* and *Pole Star for This Year,* a setting of a poem by Archibald Mac Leish. Paul Creston, whose *First Symphony* won the New York Music Critics' award for the finest orchestral work by an American composer having its New York *première* during the season, composed *Chant of 1942.* Roy Harris in his program notes for his *Fifth Symphony,* given first performance by Sergei Koussevitzky and the Boston Symphony Orchestra and dedicated to the Russian army, showed the composer's desire "to express qualities of our people . . heroic strength, determination, will to struggle, faith in our destiny."

It must not be supposed, however, that such works give the complete picture for 1943. Many composers, just as moved by the events of the times, completed works which revealed no outward indication of these events. A *Duo for Violin and Piano* by Roger Sessions had its first performance. Frederick Jacobi completed a three-act opera *The Prodigal Son* based on four early American prints. His *Ode* for orchestra was presented in 1943 by the San Francisco and the Boston Symphony Orchestras. David Diamond completed a *Second Symphony.* Howard Hanson's *Fourth Symphony* was given a New Year's broadcast. A *Second Symphony* was completed by John Verral. One can enumerate concerti, symphonies, quartets and various other forms that show the continuing interest of the composer in objective musical organization.

The music of South and Central America perhaps inevitably was less influenced by changing times. That the work of 1943 seemed less different from the work of ten years before might be due to several causes. For one thing, national feeling marked South American music very strongly; the music of Mexico in particular was deeply concerned with the mass audience. Then also, perhaps, the effects of the conflict were less strong and less immediate there than elsewhere. In Mexico new symphonies by Edward Hernandez Mancada and Condelario Huizar and new piano concerti by Blas Galindo and Jesé Rolon were presented. Creative activity was vigorous also in Chile, Brazil and Argentina.

European composers living in the Americas were active. A *Second Symphony,* a *Piano Quartet* and a *Suite Concertante* attracted attention to the works of Bohuslav Martinu. A new symphony by Darius Milhaud was presented by the NBC Symphony Orchestra. This composer was working on a new opera *Bolivar.* Ernst Krenek wrote a series of choral works to Latin texts. Karol Rathaus was working on a *Third Symphony.* Igor Stravinsky's *Dances Concertantes* was given its *première* at the Museum of Modern Art in New York city.

There was little to review in the musical life of continental Europe in 1943.   (R. L. Fy.)

Popular Music.—The year 1943 was on the whole more encouraging than discouraging in the field of popular music. Its chief discouragement was the ban on recordings and transcriptions issued by James Caesar Petrillo, who said that this action had thus far cost the members of his union over $7,000,000 in fees.

A fair amount of popular music managed to get on records nevertheless, the popular Frank Sinatra making some with choral accompaniment, with Decca finally capitulating to the Petrillo demands and thus getting the jump on the other record manufacturers. The immediate effect of the record shortage was seen in the revival of old hits and a new emphasis on the music of motion pictures and stage productions.

Richard Rodgers and Oscar Hammerstein II were the heroes of the year on the creative side of popular music. The enormous success of the Theatre guild's musical play, *Oklahoma!*, for which these two men were chiefly responsible, brought a new dignity and prestige to a business that sadly needed both, and almost eliminated the old dividing line between "popular" and "classical" music. Hammerstein provided an additional sensation with his up-to-date adaptation of Bizet's *Carmen* under the title of *Carmen Jones,* produced by Billy Rose with an all-Negro cast.

The best popular song of the year was unquestionably the Rodgers-Hammerstein "People Will Say We're in Love," from *Oklahoma!* That the public appreciated its merits was proved by a record of 25 appearances in the Hit Parade, three times at the top, seven times in second place and three times in third, with every evidence of continued popularity for 1944. Toward the close of the year, this outstanding hit was actually passed by the earthy waltz song, "Oh, What a Beautiful Morning," from *Oklahoma!* while other numbers from the same opera had a more than average success.

A motion picture tune, "You'll Never Know," was in the Hit Parade 24 times, with nine appearances at the top of the list. "As Time Goes By," achieving new life through the film *Casablanca,* made 21 appearances in radio's Hall of Fame, four times at the top. Other frequent visitors to this established sanctum of popular music were the Disney good neighbour ditty, "Brazil," the air-minded "Comin' in on a Wing and a Prayer," "It Can't Be Wrong," "Sunday, Monday or Always," "There are Such Things," "Taking a Chance on Love" (featured in both the play and the motion picture, *Cabin in the Sky,* by Vernon Duke), Cole Porter's "You'd Be So Nice to Come Home To," and the frankly nonsensical "Pistol-Packin' Mama," which might be called the novelty song of 1943.

It is highly probable that the biggest seller of sheet music and records was Bob Miller's hillbilly patriotic number, "There's a Star Spangled Banner Waving Somewhere," which had already made an amazing record in 1942 and still commanded a circulation of which the connoisseurs seemed utterly unaware. Its complete absence from the Hit Parade was a mystery.

The films succeeded in reviving such good old-timers as "For Me and My Gal" (with the help of Judy Garland) and "Put Your Arms Around Me, Honey," while the 25-year-old "Paper Doll" surprised even its publishers with a new and active life.

Other hit songs of 1943 were "Moonlight Becomes You," "I Had the Craziest Dream," "I've Heard That Song Before," "That Old Black Magic," "Don't Get Around Much Any More," "Let's Get Lost," "All or Nothing at All" and "In the Blue of Evening." Irving Berlin's "White Christmas" maintained its popularity into the new year and came back strongly for the holiday season of 1943–44. Arthur Schwartz added his bit toward a definitely higher standard with the witty "They're Either Too Young or Too Old," introduced, strangely enough, by Bette Davis on the screen, and showing a real popularity by the end of the year.   (S. Sp.)

A poll conducted by the musicians' publication *Down Beat* among swing-band musicians to determine their favourite male singer of 1943 had the following results: Frank Sinatra, 4,992; Bing Crosby, 3,942; Bob Eberly, 1,197. Benny Goodman was voted "king of swing" as the outstanding swing-band leader of the year. (*See* also PERFORMING RIGHT SOCIETIES; RADIO.)

Music Library Association.
The Music Library association was organized in 1931, with promotion of the establishment, growth and use of

YEHUDI MENUHIN and the London Philharmonic orchestra gave a special concert for 5,000 U.S. soldiers and guests at Albert Hall, London, in March 1943

music libraries and collections of music as its primary objective. Membership in 1943 included some 200 individuals and 100 institutions throughout the U.S. and Canada. Edward N. Waters, Library of Congress, was president for 1943. The work of the organization is carried on by its executive board, consisting of the president, vice-president, secretary-treasurer and two members-at-large; by regional chapter chairmen and by various committees, among which are publications, inter-library relations, inter-American library relations, photoduplication, personnel and employment, and periodical indexing. In normal times an annual mid-winter meeting is held, devoted to reports, elections and discussions. A summer meeting is held in conjunction with the annual conference of the American Library association.

Publications include the association's quarterly periodical, *Notes; Music and Libraries,* a volume of selected papers presented at the 1942 meetings; a *Code for Cataloging Music,* comprising five chapters and a supplement on cataloguing phonograph records.

Important bibliographical work for the U.S. army included lists of both music and books for camp libraries, the latter list mimeographed and distributed by the war department.

The M.L.A. is affiliated with the American Library association, and a member of the National Music council and the Council of National Library associations.   (C. V. N.)

Mussolini, Benito
(1883–   ), Italian statesman and dictator. For his earlier career, see *Encyclopædia Britannica.* Il Duce chose June 10, 1940, as the pro-

"A BUST." This cartoon by Costello of the *Knickerbocker News* (Albany, N.Y.) appeared after the fall of Tripoli, Jan. 23, 1943

pitious date for entering World War II, doing so with the declaration that "our conscience is entirely clear." After a few desultory thrusts at defeated France he consulted with Hitler at Munich June 18 on the terms of peace. Italian military activities then remained in relative abeyance until the beginning of the campaigns in North Africa (Sept. 12, 1940) and in Greece (Oct. 28). Both these operations were soon thrown into reverse, and on Dec. 6, 1940, Mussolini reorganized his military command.

The later events of Mussolini's career fell into a general pattern: conferences with Hitler; shake-ups of the army; explanations of defeats; and threats against the common enemies of the axis. In June 1941, he joined Hitler in declaring war on Russia and in the same month boasted that U.S. intervention would not alter the outcome of the war.

During 1943, Mussolini's prestige and popularity among the Italian people dwindled to the vanishing point. Flagging Italian morale alarmed even Hitler, and on July 19, 1943, the fuehrer conferred with the duce at Verona. It was the 14th and perhaps the most crucial meeting between the two dictators. Mussolini presumably intimated that he was losing his grip on his countrymen. Six days later, on July 25, Mussolini was ousted from the office he had held for 20 years, after a stormy meeting with his cabinet and King Victor Emmanuel III. Marshal Pietro Badoglio, who had succeeded to the post of premier, had the ex-duce incarcerated, but a few days after the Allied invasion of Italy, German paratroopers staged a bold raid on the prison, liberated Mussolini and took him back safely to axis territory. On Sept. 23, 1943, he formed a new "Republican fascist" government under German protection and exhorted Italian people to rally to his cause. (*See* also FASCISM; ITALY.)

Mustard Seed: *see* SPICES.

Muti, Ettore (1902–1943), Italian air officer and politician, was born May 22. He volunteered in the Italian army during World War I, fought with D'Annunzio's troops at Fiume and returned home a bemedalled hero. Muti joined the fascist ranks before the march on Rome and was known as the "strong-arm" leader of Mussolini's palace guard, although nominally he was ranked as a minor fascist official. He served as lieutenant colonel in the Ethiopian campaign, participated in the Spanish civil war and the Italian campaigns in Albania and Greece, becoming one of Italy's most decorated air heroes. Muti's "devotion" to the fascist party and his ruthless personality were recognized in 1937 when Mussolini named him secretary general of the fascist party. When Il Duce resigned in July 1943, it was reported that Muti fled to escape the wrath of his anti-fascist victims. His death was announced by an Italian news agency, Aug. 24.

Nagano, Osami (1880–   ), Japanese naval officer, was born in June at Kochi, Japan. After graduating from the naval academy in 1900, he attended the naval staff college. In 1913, he was a language officer in the U.S., where he studied law at Harvard university and took courses at the War college. As naval attaché in Washington, 1920–23, he participated in the Washington naval conference of 1921–22. In 1928, he commanded a Japanese naval training squadron which visited Annapolis and was received by President Hoover. Known for his shrewd diplomacy, he represented his government at a number of international conferences. He attended the Geneva conference in 1932 and proposed elimination of aircraft carriers and long-range submarines, as well as restriction of the number of capital ships. At the London naval conference, 1935–36, Nagano sealed the doom of the 5-5-3 ratio. He rejected President Roosevelt's proposal of a 20% reduction, and when his demands for Japanese parity were refused, he led the Japanese delegation from the conference. Nagano was appointed minister of the navy in the Hirota cabinet, 1936. He apologized for the sinking of the U.S. gunboat "Panay" in 1937, insisting it had been an "accident." He became chief of the Japanese naval general staff, April 19, 1941.

Narcotics: *see* DRUGS AND DRUG TRAFFIC.

Nash, Patrick A. (1863–1943), U.S. politician, was born in Chicago, and made his fortune as contractor in the sewer building business established by his father. He was Democratic ward committeeman of the 14th (later the 28th) ward and its "boss" for over 40 years. He was appointed to the Board of Assessors in 1915 and elected to the Board of Review in 1918, but was defeated for reelection to the latter post in 1924. When the assassination of Anton Cermak left Chicago mayorless in 1933, Nash was instrumental in winning the vacant post for his close friend and hand-picked candidate, Edward J. Kelly. The two formed a political partnership, the nationally known "Kelly-Nash machine," which flourished for the next 10 years. Nash died in Chicago, Oct. 6.

National Academy of Sciences. A body of scientists incorporated by act of congress approved by President Lincoln in 1863 for the purpose of investigating and reporting upon scientific subjects whenever called upon to do so by any department of the United States government, with the proviso that the academy shall receive no compensation for services to the government but may be reimbursed for the actual expenses incurred in making such investigations and reports. Membership in the academy is limited to 450 active members, who must be citizens of the United States, and 50 foreign associates. Names voted upon in the election of new members are nominated by the section covering the branch of research in which the individual is working, upon a two-thirds vote of that section. There are no applications for membership, as the proposed names originate upon suggestion by the existing membership. In 1943 the academy was engaged to a large extent on government problems concerned with scientific matters related to the war. These reports were confidential and were not published by the academy.

The academy meets twice a year. The annual meeting is held in Washington on the fourth Monday of April, and the autumn meeting is generally held in the east and west in alternate years. For the duration of the war, both meetings are held in Washington and are confined to business sessions for members only. Upon cessation of the war, scientific sessions to which the public is invited were expected to be resumed.

From the income of a number of trust funds given to the academy for that specific purpose, the academy awards medals in recognition of outstanding scientific research, or grants small sums of money to worthy investigators to enable completion of scientific research projects in special fields, according to the terms stipulated by the donors of these funds. At the 1943 annual meeting the following medals were presented: Henry Draper medal for 1943 to Ira Sprague Bowen; Agassiz medal for 1942, with accompanying honorarium of $300, to Columbus O'Donnell Iselin, II; Daniel Giraud Elliot medals, with accompanying honoraria of $200, for 1935 to Edwin H. Colbert, for 1936 to Robert Cushman Murphy; John J. Carty medal and accompanying award, $4,000, to Edwin Grant Conklin.

Twenty-six new members were elected at the 1943 annual meeting: Leason Herberling Adams, Abraham Adrian Albert, Jesse Wakefield Beams, Arthur Francis Buddington, Leonard Carmichael, William Henry Chandler, Edwin Joseph Cohn, John Nathaniel Couch, Theodosius Dobzhansky, Lee Alvin DuBridge, Leslie Clarence Dunn, Wallace Osgood Fenn, Paul Darwin Foote, Louis Plack Hammett, William Vermillon Houston, Walter Pearson Kelley, Warfield Theobald Longcope, Eli Kennerly Marshall, Jr., Leonor Michaelis, William Albert Noyes, Jr., Oswald Hope Robertson, Carl-Gustaf Arvid Rossby, Calvin Perry Stone, Charles Vincent Taylor, Hubert Bradford Vickery and Vladimir Kosma Zworykin. Six new foreign associates were elected at the same time: Alfonso Caso, Mexico; Sir Harold Spencer Jones, England; Richard Vynne Southwell, England; Charles Edward Spearman, England; Sir D'Arcy Wentworth Thompson, Scotland; Hendrik Johannes van der Bijl, South Africa.

The academy publishes an annual report, scientific memoirs, biographical memoirs of deceased members and monthly proceedings devoted to condensed reports of recent scientific discoveries. The academy building, 2101 Constitution ave., Washington, is closed to the public for the duration of the war.

(P. Bt.)

National Archives: *see* ARCHIVES, NATIONAL.

National Association of Manufacturers.

The National Association of Manufacturers, an organization of individuals, firms and corporations engaged in manufacturing, was founded in 1895 with the following general objectives: (1) the promotion of the industrial interests of the United States; (2) the fostering of the domestic and foreign commerce of the United States; (3) the betterment of relations between employers and their employees; (4) the protection of the individual liberty and rights of employer and employee; (5) the dissemination of

information among the public with respect to the principles of individual liberty and ownership of property; (6) the support of legislation in furtherance of those principles and opposition to legislation in derogation thereof. Membership, 10,000. President: Robert M. Gaylord, president of Ingersoll Milling Machine company; chairman of the board, F. C. Crawford; chairman of the executive committee: William P. Witherow; executive vice-president: Walter B. Weisenburger; secretary: Noel Sargent; treasurer: Theodore G. Montague.

Headquarters: 14 West 49th street, New York city. Branch offices: Investment building, Washington, D.C.; 111 Sutter street, San Francisco, California.

The N.A.M. also established the Economic Principles commission which was making intensive studies and analyses of the nature, operations, achievements and problems of the free enterprise system, and was in 1943 under the chairmanship of Robert R. Wason. Another important activity was headed up by the Better America program which was organized in 1943 to reduce the association's basic thinking and its constructive recommendations on long-range governmental policies to a series of visual presentations which could be used to crystallize industrial opinion, and which industrialists in turn could use to give congressmen and other government officials an impressive picture of industrial thinking. It was in 1943 under the chairmanship of H. W. Prentis, Jr.

Operating as an affiliated part of the National Association of Manufacturers, the National Industrial council included some 300 industrial associations of three categories: State associations, Manufacturing Trade associations, and Industrial Relations associations. The council provided an effective industrial contact with collective manufacturing membership in each section of the country.

(N. S.)

National Association of State Libraries.

The National Association of State Libraries is one of the oldest library associations in America. It was organized at a meeting in St. Louis in 1899 and elected as its first president, Melville Dewey, the author and inventor of the Dewey Decimal System of Library Classification. In the intervening years annual meetings have been held in various parts of the country, and almost every state in the union has had representation in the list of officers.

Forty-two state libraries throughout the country comprise the institutional members. There are in addition a limited number of associate and individual members whose interests are allied with state library work. Although state libraries are not all alike they do have many similar activities which makes an interchange of service and an exchange of publications particularly desirable. This is particularly true in the fields of legislative research and public documents. As the result of working together, it is now possible for each state library to secure from every other state whatever state publications are required.

In order to help in the cataloguing of these publications the association has in recent years published a series of check lists of session laws, statutes and legislative journals. These are kept up to date by the issuance of supplements as they are required. In 1943 a supplement was issued to the Check List of Legislative Journals and in the previous year a supplement was issued to the Check List of Session Laws.

In conjunction with the American Library association the state libraries were co-operating with the national libraries of Central and South American countries in order that they might be provided with such state publications as were needed.

The National Association of State Libraries is a member of the Council of National Library associations and participates in the work of collecting large numbers of scientific and research publications, which after the war will be distributed to devastated libraries in Europe, Asia and Africa.

The annual meetings of the association were cancelled for the duration. In 1943 the officers were: president, Dennis A. Dooley, state librarian of Massachusetts; first vice president, Alfred Decker Keator, director, State Library of Pennsylvania; second vice president, Mrs. Virginia G. Moody, state librarian of South Carolina; secretary-treasurer, Mrs. Gladys F. Riley, former state librarian of Wyoming; executive committee, the officers named above and the most recent past president, Miss Helene H. Rogers, assistant state librarian of Illinois.   (D. A. DY.)

National Catholic Community Service: see CATHOLIC COMMUNITY SERVICE, NATIONAL.

National Catholic Rural Life Conference: see CATHOLIC RURAL LIFE CONFERENCE, NATIONAL.

National Catholic Welfare Conference: see CATHOLIC WELFARE CONFERENCE, NATIONAL.

National Debt. The national debt of a country generally refers to the total financial obligations of the state arising out of the issuance of public securities. It does not include the debt of all governmental units and agencies but only the obligations of the central government. The national debt usually indicates the extent to which the central government has resorted to borrowing over the years to make up the deficit between its outlays for government services and investment and its revenues from taxation and various minor sources. As the manner of keeping official accounts varies from country to country, however, there are many exceptions to this definition. On the one hand, agencies or corporations of the central government are sometimes set up outside the budget so that their debt does not appear in the national debt. On the other hand, obligations are sometimes assumed by the government and included in the official national debt statistics which did not originate in a borrowing operation. The adjusted service bonds issued to veterans are an example of this type of obligation included in the national debt total of the United States.

The course of the national debt in the United States from 1913 to 1944 is shown in Table I. The debt first reached substantial proportions during World War I, with a peak of over $25,000,000,000 at the end of the fiscal year 1919. During the following decade, about one-third of the debt was liquidated. With the onset of the world-wide depression in 1929 and the subsequent use of government expenditures as a method of fighting economic depression, the debt expanded rapidly throughout the 1930s to reach almost $43,000,000,000 at the end of the fiscal year 1940.

With the sharp rise in government expenditures which attended the rearmament program begun in the middle of 1940, the history

Table I.—National Debt of the United States, 1913-44

June 30	(Millions of dollars)	June 30	(Millions of dollars)
1913	$ 1,193	1929	$ 16,931
1914	1,188	1930	16,185
1915	1,191	1931	16,801
1916	1,225	1932	19,487
1917	2,976	1933	22,539
1918	12,244	1934	27,053
1919	25,482	1935	28,701
1920	24,298	1936	33,545
1921	23,976	1937	36,427
1922	22,964	1938	37,167
1923	22,350	1939	40,445
1924	21,251	1940	42,971
1925	20,516	1941	48,961
1926	19,643	1942	72,422
1927	18,510	1943	136,696
1928	17,604	1944	197,000

Source: Data from 1913 to 1943 are from U.S. treasury department, daily treasury statement (revised); 1944 estimated.

Table II.—Public Debt of the United States, Direct and Guaranteed
(Millions of dollars)

	December 31		
	1941	1942	1943
Direct public debt, total*	$57,938	$108,170	$165,877
Interest-bearing debt, total	57,451	107,308	163,508
Public issues:			
Bonds, total	40,000	64,868	96,128
U.S. savings bonds†	6,140	15,050	27,363
All other	33,860	49,818	68,766
Notes, total	8,468	16,247	19,761
Regular and national defense series	5,997	9,863	11,175
Tax and savings series	2,471	6,384	‡8,586
Certificates of indebtedness	..	10,534	22,843
Bills	2,002	6,627	13,072
Special issues	6,982	9,032	12,703
Non-interest-bearing debt	487	862	1,370
Guaranteed obligations not owned by the treasury	6,327	4,301	4,230
Total direct and guaranteed debt	64,265	112,471	170,108

*Includes $11,278,000,000 as of Dec. 31, 1941, $5,201,000,000 as of Dec. 31, 1942, and $7,853,000,000 as of Dec. 31, 1943, advanced to government agencies for which their obligations are owned by the treasury.
†At current redemption values except Series G which is stated at par.
‡Of this total, $8,302,000,000 represents savings notes.
Source: Daily statement of the U.S. treasury.

of the United States debt entered a new period. New tax measures increased government revenues substantially, but the scale of armament expenditures was so large that the national debt rose approximately $15,000,000,000 by the end of the calendar year 1941.

This was just a foretaste of what came after the nation's actual entry into the armed conflict. Vigorous steps were immediately taken to mobilize the entire economic structure of the country for the greatest war production program in all history. While tax revenues increased substantially in both 1942 and 1943, they could not keep pace with the flood of expenditures which the war effort required. As a consequence the national debt rose approximately $50,000,000,000 in 1942 and almost $58,000,000,000 in 1943. At the end of 1943 the debt was $165,877,278,992 and it was expected to reach $197,000,000,000 by June 1944.

Late in 1942 the treasury began the policy of raising the bulk of its required financing in short war loan drives, during the first of which total securities of almost $13,000,000,000 were sold. In 1943 two war loan drives were conducted, the first in April and the second in September, which yielded a total of $37,500,000,000. The September drive differed in one important respect from the two previous drives in that it was confined to non-banking investors. Despite this fact, the treasury sold almost $19,000,000,000 of securities, about the same total as in the April drive during which more than $5,000,000,000 of the sales were accounted for by commercial banks. Since the policy of the government was to secure as much of its financing as possible from individuals in order to minimize the inflationary effect of the huge government deficit, the sales of securities to individuals were stepped up considerably with each succeeding war loan drive. (See also WAR BONDS.)

One of the main features of the treasury's policy of securing non-inflationary sources of funds was the emphasis placed upon the sale of war bonds and stamps to individuals. In 1943 the amount of savings bonds outstanding rose from $15,050,000,000 at the beginning of the year to $27,363,000,000 at the end of the year. This constituted a sizeable increase in net sales to approximately $1,000,000,000 savings bonds per month in 1943 from $750,000,000 in 1942. In the course of the year there was, however, a disturbing increase in the rate of redemptions on these bonds. It was to be expected, of course, that redemptions would increase as the amount outstanding increased. However, they rose more than proportionately to outstandings. As compared with redemptions in the closing months of 1942 of about $4.50 out of every $1,000 outstanding, the monthly rate of redemptions in the latter part of 1943 was about $9.50 for every $1,000 outstanding.

An important factor behind the increase in savings bonds sales was the fairly widespread adoption of the payroll deduction plan which was sponsored by the treasury. The savings bonds purchased in 1943 by means of regular deduction from payrolls accounted for a large proportion of total sales in that year. Toward the end of the year about 27,000,000 employees were participating in the program and having $450,000,000 or 9% of their pay deducted each month for the purchase of war bonds. At the end of the preceding year there were only 20,000,000 employees participating in the program and the average deduction amounted to only 7%.

The maintenance of a low interest rate policy by the treasury was one of the outstanding developments in the financing of the public debt during the war. Up through the end of 1943 the war was being financed at an average rate of interest of slightly less than 1.75% on the securities issued compared with an average rate of about 4.25% on the securities issued to finance World War I. Interest rates during the war period rose only moderately above the level prevailing during the depression of the '30s, the highest rate for long-term market issues being 2.5%. As a special inducement to individuals to increase their savings and thus assist in the government's anti-inflation program, the interest rate on savings bonds if held to maturity was fixed at 2.9%.

For securities outstanding in the fiscal year 1943 the computed annual rate of interest amounted to 1.98% compared with 2.29% in the fiscal year 1942. As may be seen in Table II, the major factor in this decline was the proportionate rise in certificates of indebtedness and notes outstanding. Although these securities carried a low interest rate, they were a popular outlet, because of their high degree of liquidity, for business funds being built up during the war. This development meant, of course, that a substantial amount of refinancing would have to be done after the war.

Despite the decline in the rate of interest on outstanding securities, actual interest on the public debt rose substantially in 1943 because of the large rise in the total debt. From a figure of $1,452,000,000 in 1942, interest on the public debt rose to $2,191,000,000 in 1943.

State and Local Government Debt.

The figures on the debt of state and local governments, 1929–43, are shown in Table III. Because of the many government subdivisions in the United States and the many functions of government remaining in the hands of local government units, the state and local government debt has always been an important component of total government debt. It arose largely from the financing of the various types of public works, although during the period of declining economic activity from 1929–33 the falling-off of revenues and increasing expenditures for relief added to the debt total. From 1933 on state and local debt varied little, as the federal government took over the major burden of relief and also financed much

Table IV.—*National Debt of Various Countries*

Country	Date of Latest Comparable Debt Figures	Total Debt in Local Currency* (000,000)
Africa		
Egypt	1/31/43	78,341.3 pounds†
Union of South Africa	3/31/43	416.0 pounds
America, North		
Canada	3/31/43	7,893.4 dollars
Mexico	3/31/41	3,460.2 pesos
United States	12/31/43	165,877.3 dollars
America, South		
Argentina	12/31/40	5,316.5 pesos
Brazil	12/31/40	20,150.8 milreis
Chile	12/31/40	4,409.1 pesos
Colombia	12/31/39	204.7 pesos
Ecuador	12/31/40	434.4 sucres
Peru	6/30/41	625.8 soles
Asia		
India	3/31/43	12,658.6 rupees
Japan	3/31/42	40,470.0 yen
Europe		
Belgium	3/31/43	188,600.0 francs
Bulgaria	10/31/41	28,894.3 leva
Czechoslovakia	12/31/38	52,950.0 koruny
Denmark	3/31/41	1,211.6 kroner
Finland	8/31/41	22,000.0 markkas
France	8/31/43	1,231,522.0 francs
Germany	12/31/43	260,000.0 marks
Greece	1/31/40	52,874.7 drachmas
Hungary	6/30/39	1,937.4 pengos
Italy	9/30/35	108,636.6 lire
Netherlands	12/31/40	5,329.6 guilders
Norway	6/30/39	1,528.4 kroner
Poland	3/31/39	5,317.8 zlotys
Portugal	12/31/40	6,489.7 escudos
Rumania	3/31/41	100,148.0 lei
Spain	12/31/41	28,901.5 pesetas
Sweden	11/30/43	9,739.0 kroner
Switzerland	12/31/40	4,956.9 francs
Turkey	5/31/39	619.4 pounds
United Kingdom	12/11/43	19,103.0 pounds
Yugoslavia	3/31/39	24,620.0 dinars
Oceania		
Australia	6/30/43	2,164.9 pounds
New Zealand	3/31/43	503.3 pounds

Sources: Statistical yearbook and monthly statistical bulletins of the League of Nations; Federal Reserve bulletin; official government reports.
*For approximate value of various currencies see EXCHANGE CONTROL AND EXCHANGE RATES.
†Egyptian pounds.

of the public works of state and local governments. After 1940 state and local debt declined as revenues increased with the rising tide of national income and as scarcity of materials placed severe restrictions on public works expenditures. This trend was continued in 1943.

While the reduction of state and local debt during the war years was not as large as the potentialities of the situation could have made possible, the financial situation of these government units was somewhat improved toward meeting postwar problems.

Other Countries.

Latest figures available for the national debt of leading countries are given in Table IV. That throughout history war has been the primary cause of the growth of national debts was borne out by the advance in debts during World War II. The debt of all belligerent countries, of course, rose precipitously and even some of the neutral countries had to increase government expenditures to an extent that made borrowing necessary. By and large, the one area of the world not subject to rising national debt totals during the war period was Latin America.

For the belligerent countries the national debt rose, because of the large scale of military operations, higher than in any previous war. The debt of the United Kingdom, for example, rose from £8,301,100,000 in 1939 to £19,103,000,000 at the end of 1943. Over this same period the national debt of Canada increased from $3,638,300,000 to $7,893,400,000, while in Australia the national debt of £A1,295,000,000 increased to £A2,164,969,307 by the end of June 1943.

Some conception of the financial drain of the war upon the occupied countries may be gained from the case of France, where the national debt advanced from 352,210,000,000 francs in 1939 to 1,231,522,000,000 francs in 1943. For most of the occupied countries, however, no reliable statistics on the public debt have been available in recent years.

Table III.—*Debt of State and Local Governments, United States*
(Millions of dollars)

End of fiscal year	Total	State	County	Municipal	School district and Special district
1929	17,234	2,300	2,270	9,259	3,405
1930	18,459	2,444	2,434	9,929	3,652
1931	19,534	2,666	2,564	10,458	3,846
1932	19,804	2,896	2,565	10,483	3,860
1933	19,985	3,018	2,521	10,577	3,869
1934	19,286	3,201	2,477	9,730	3,878
1935	19,429	3,331	2,433	9,778	3,887
1936	19,662	3,318	2,389	10,058	3,897
1937	19,594	3,276	2,345	10,067	3,906
1938	19,576	3,309	2,282	9,923	4,062
1939	19,996	3,343	2,219	10,215	4,219
1940	20,246	3,526	2,156	10,189	4,375
1941	20,183	3,370	2,046	10,210	4,557
1942	19,643	3,163	1,846	10,079	4,554
1943	18,645	2,862	1,634	9,784	4,365

Source: U.S. department of commerce.

The national debts of the axis powers were not, in 1943, known as accurately as those of the Allied nations, since the reported debt figures were not complete. In the case of Germany the official national debt rose from r.m. 30,737,000,000 in 1939 to r.m. 260,000,000,000 at the end of 1943. It was unofficially estimated, however, that the total German public debt had reached about r.m. 400,000,000,000 by that time. In Italy no official figures had been issued since 1935, but it was unofficially estimated that the debt in 1943 was 415,000,000,000 lire compared with 108,636,600,000 lire at the time of the official release. (*See* also BUDGET, NATIONAL; GREAT BRITAIN; NATIONAL INCOME AND NATIONAL PRODUCT; TAXATION.)   (M. GT.)

National Education Association
of the United States moved forward during 1943 into an enlarged program to meet the educational problems resulting from wartime conditions. It conducted a campaign to raise a $600,000,000 emergency war and peace fund—one-third for the various state education associations, two-thirds for the N.E.A. to strengthen its work on behalf of the war and the peace. The Educational Policies commission distributed widely a number of important publications, including *Education and the People's Peace*. The campaign for federal aid to keep the schools open and to equalize educational opportunity as embodied in Senate Bill 637 was intensified as it became apparent that more than 100,000 teachers left the schools after Pearl Harbor. "Victory through Education" was the theme of American Education week, Nov. 7–13, 1943.

Because of the wartime need for conserving travel facilities the association's winter convention scheduled to be held in St. Louis was canceled and the summer convention gave way to a business meeting of the Representative assembly at Indianapolis, June 27–29.

The association was organized in Philadelphia in 1857. It had, in 1943, a membership of 219,334 and its affiliated state associations had a membership of 753,082. The official organ is *The Journal of The N.E.A.*, edited by Joy Elmer Morgan, and issued to all members monthly except June, July and August. The president for 1943–44 was Mrs. Edith B. Joynes, principal of the Robert Gatewood Elementary school, Norfolk, Virginia; executive secretary, Willard E. Givens. (*See* also EDUCATION.)

(J. E. Mo.)

National Foundation for Infantile Paralysis: *see* INFANTILE PARALYSIS.
National Gallery of Art: *see* SMITHSONIAN INSTITUTION.

National Geographic Society.
Organized in 1888 by a small group of professional geographers resident in Washington, D. C., this society's purpose was set forth in its charter as that of "increasing and diffusing geographical knowledge." Gilbert Grosvenor, the president in 1943, assumed the direction of the organization's activities in 1899 and broadened the scope of its researches to appeal to the layman interested in scientific accomplishments. The membership of the society, which was less than 1,000 in 1899, was 1,200,000 in 1943.

As one method for carrying out the purpose for which it was established, the society issues monthly its official publication, the illustrated *National Geographic Magazine*. During the 55 years of its existence, the society has sent numerous expeditions to various parts of the earth to gather data in the fields of geography, geology, volcanology, glaciology, archeology, astronomy, meteorology and other sciences associated with geography. The scientific results of these expeditions have been recorded in a series of published monographs.

In 1943 the society continued archeological investigations in southern Mexico in co-operation with the Smithsonian institution. The field party, under the direction of Dr. Matthew W. Stirling, excavated beneath mounds on the site of a former centre of religious pilgrimages at La Venta, state of Tabasco. Near the point at which artifacts of ordinary jade were found in 1942, the excavators made the surprising discovery of art objects fashioned from emerald-green gem jade, the equal of the famous Burmese gem jade, standard of world excellence. This jade uncovered at La Venta is the only gem jade yet found in the western hemisphere.

Other discoveries at La Venta in 1943 included room-size mosaic floors made of polished green serpentine tiles, massive flat-topped altars decorated with carvings and a four-foot monkey-god carved from green serpentine.

One of the most spectacular discoveries made at La Venta in the three years of work there—a colossal sculptured human head—was represented in Washington in 1943 by a plaster cast added to the museum items in the Society's Administration building. The original head of basalt, more than 20 ft. in circumference and weighing some 20 tons, could not be moved from the discovery site.

Foreign field studies during 1943 included W. Robert Moore's investigations of war-essential minerals in Brazil, B. Anthony Stewart's records of cryptostegia rubber production in Haiti and the Dominican Republic and Luis Marden's observations of industrial and military establishments in Costa Rica and Nicaragua.

Continuing to place special emphasis on co-operation in the war effort, the society made available to the armed forces and other government agencies the facilities, records and data assembled at its Washington headquarters. These included its library, its unpublished manuscripts and photographs relating to all parts of the world and its maps and cartographic notes. Assistance was given in the preparation of manuals and guides for the use of invasion troops. As a special project the society published in the *National Geographic Magazine* 1,700 illustrations in colour showing identification insignia, service ribbons, badges, medals and decorations of the United States armed forces and other services, including women's insignia.

As supplements to the *National Geographic Magazine,* five large-scale, ten-colour maps were published: Africa; Northern and Southern Hemispheres; Europe and the Near East; Pacific Ocean and the Bay of Bengal; and the World, the latter on a special projection showing the land masses and seas in a unified picture.

News bulletins, giving background information—geographic, economic and historic—of places brought into the news by war developments, were supplied to more than 500 daily newspapers in the United States. *Geographic School Bulletins* were furnished to 31,000 schoolrooms during the educational year to aid in keeping the teaching of geography up to date.   (G. GR.)

+National Guard.
In the spring of 1943, the chief of staff of the army announced that the American army had assumed globular offensive in all theatres. Offensive operations began in 1942, and it was in 1942 that war department press releases showed that in every offensive national guard units participated, notably, the 164th infantry regiment from North Dakota participated with the marines on Guadalcanal, and when the marines were relieved from that area, other national guard units from the American division, under General Alexander Patch, replaced them. The 34th infantry division from Minnesota, Iowa and South Dakota participated in the landing in North Africa and in the heavy fighting that followed there. They were joined later by the 45th infantry division, the 36th infantry divi-

sion, and many anti-aircraft regiments and separate battalions, with some national guard regiments attached to other task forces operating in Sicily and on into Italy where all of these troops distinguished themselves.

From the southwest area, General MacArthur announced the participation of the troops of the 32nd infantry division (Wisconsin and Michigan), and the 41st infantry division (Oregon, Washington, Idaho, Montana and Wyoming), operating with the Australian units in subduing New Guinea, particularly, Buna and the Milne bay areas. At various times in 1943, the brilliant work of the 37th infantry division was reported and the 43rd infantry division (New England), participated in activities in the capture of Rendova and others of the Solomon Islands.

In Dec. 1943, announcement was made that the 27th infantry division (New York), particularly the 165th regiment known as "The Fighting 69th" of World War I and Civil War fame, had retaken Makin Islands.

From Alaska came the news that national guard combat teams helped retake the islands of Amchitka, Attu and Kiska. In all areas, divisions were not the only national guard troops involved. All were accompanied by anti-aircraft battalions and special artillery and engineer units which were originally national guard organizations carrying the standards of those organizations.

In the middle of December the war department news release again mentioned "National Guard units from Texas" participating in the occupation in Arawe in New Britain. These units were part of what was known as the "Texas Cavalry Brigade." The 36th infantry division, at that time, was operating brilliantly in Italy and that division was known as "Texas' Own." Other divisions were gradually being moved to the front in the combat zones and as the year 1943 drew to a close, the bulk of the national guard with three years intensive training, reorganization, re-equipment, had actively participated. The 29 air squadrons of the national guard all had met the enemy and many of their officers had been highly decorated. Under state control there were no national guard troops either in 1942 or 1943.

State Guards.—As the national guard of the states and territories entered the federal service, it was found necessary to provide for internal security and protection and the organization of other troops which bore the name "State Guards" The formation of these troops was authorized by congress in Oct. 1940, and it was not until 1941 that they came into existence in full measure. Many states had no provision in state law for such emergency units. The governors of many states had to appear for the first time to obtain sanction of their state assemblies for the emergency measures which they had taken and to justify expenditures which the states had made toward the formation, training and equipment of state guards. In many states the legislatures modified the actions of the governors and there was much reorganization and stabilizing throughout 1943. However, the states provided for increased training and particularly for special schools for officers and non-commissioned officers, and some degree of field training.

The turn-over of personnel in the state guards was, in some cases, 100% annually, due largely to the induction of its personnel into federal service. The increased tempo of selective service virtually compelled the state guards to find its manpower in boys who were under 18 and men who were over 45, and among men who had been rejected for even limited field service in the forces of the United States.

The state guards were active in the suppression of riots in Detroit, Mich., Mobile, Ala., Beaumont, Texas, and many other places. All through the middle west, thousands of them combatted the flood waters of the Ohio, Mississippi and Missouri, and saved millions of dollars worth of property. In West Virginia they went into the mines to bring out the dead and living in mine disasters. In California, and along the Atlantic seaboard, they patrolled beaches and other vital points releasing combat troops of this responsibility. At the end of the year there were more than 150,000 standing ready for emergency, subject to the orders of their state executives. They were better armed, better equipped and better trained than at any previous time.

(J. F. Ws.)

National Housing Agency.

During 1943 the major concern of the National Housing agency continued to be the provision of housing for war workers. As a result of its efforts it was possible to say, as the year drew to a close, that the war housing program had reached an advanced stage and in many localities had caught up with the immediate need. Since the start of the emergency in mid-1940, some 1,350,000 units of war housing had been completed, another 210,000 were in various stages of construction, and over 1,500,000 in-migrant war workers had been housed in existing private structures. During the first ten months of 1943, a total of 392,423 units of war housing had been started and total completions in the same period amounted to 489,329.

These substantial accomplishments were made possible by the conversion of the house building industry to a complete war basis and by the closer integration of the war housing program with the total war effort.

Complete war status for the house building industry was achieved through a variety of steps. One of the most important was the very substantial savings in the use of critical materials. The National Housing agency worked closely with the industry and with other governmental agencies to eliminate every unessential use of metal, particularly, in housing construction, and to develop wherever possible substitutes for the most critical items. A corollary of this conservation program was the redoubling of efforts by the National Housing agency to accommodate an ever-increasing number of war workers in structures already in existence. This was done through share-your-home campaigns and also through efforts to get property owners to convert their structures into additional housing accommodations either with their own or with government funds. Also the National Housing agency co-operated closely with private industry and private finance to develop their maximum participation in the war housing program.

The year 1943 was the first full year of operation under the consolidated National Housing agency, which had been formed early in 1942 to focus and direct the urban housing activities of the federal government. Into the agency had been consolidated the housing activities formerly carried on by some 16 agencies and administrative units. The new set-up resulted in a streamlining of the organization on a functional basis. The office of the administrator (John B. Blandford, Jr., in 1943) performed the over-all, fact-finding and planning functions which consisted primarily of formulating war housing policy and programming war housing, including its postwar disposition. (J. B. Bl.)

Federal Housing Administration.—The Federal Housing administration (one of the three major units of the National Housing agency) continued to gear its activities to the national war effort in 1943. Under its program, private investment funds totalling around $7,341,171,462 were mobilized to finance war housing projects, to place existing home mortgages on a sound amortized basis, and to make possible essential repairs, fuel conservation installations, and conversion projects to provide additional dwelling units to house war workers.

FHA field offices processed private war housing priority requests on behalf of the War Production board and made compliance inspections of privately financed war housing built under War Production board priorities to determine conformity of the construction with regulations regarding the use of critical materials. FHA technical facilities were used to the utmost to further sound housing construction under war restrictions and shortages of critical war materials. Commissioner in 1943 was Abner H. Ferguson.

Congress twice amended title VI (War Housing insurance) of the National Housing act under which FHA principally operated in 1943 by increasing from $800,000,000 to $1,600,000,000 the aggregate amount of mortgages insurable under this title, and by extending the expiration date of title VI insurance authority from July 1, 1944, to July 1, 1945.

Congress also amended title I of the act by extending the expiration date of the insurance authority from July 1, 1944, to July 1, 1947, and by increasing the maximum permissible premium under title I from three-quarters of one percent to one percent.

Title II was amended by extending the authorization to insure mortgages on existing construction from July 1, 1944, to July 1, 1946.

Insurance of all types written during 1943 amounted to $942,-493,149 compared with the high record of $1,136,473,238 written in 1942. This brought the total insurance written from June 1934, through Dec. 1943, to $7,341,171,462. These funds were advanced by private financial institutions, for the FHA lends no money. Income for 1943 was $26,574,355, of which $11,101,970 went to FHA operating expenses and $15,472,385 to the various insurance funds.

New dwelling units started in 1943 under FHA inspection totalled 137,841, compared with the previous high record of 220,344 started in 1941. Practically all of the units started in 1943 were in the officially designated critical war housing areas.

Under section 203 of title II the FHA during 1943 insured 52,408 small-home mortgages for $244,514,138, compared with 149,635 for $691,445,427 in 1942. This amount brought the net total as of Dec. 31, 1943, to 1,034,865 mortgages insured for $4,-519,019,688. These mortgages are protected by the Mutual Mortgage Insurance fund, which as of Dec. 31, 1943, had net resources of $68,514,553.

Under section 207 of title II, one large-scale housing mortgage for $139,000 was insured in 1943, compared with 11 for $5,701,-000 in 1942. As of Dec. 31, 1943, mortgages insured numbered 356 and amounted to $145,878,206. A total of 38,272 dwelling units was provided by the 356 projects insured from the beginning of operations. The Housing Insurance fund protecting these mortgages, as of Dec. 31, 1943, had net resources of $2,773,416.

Under section 603 of title VI, 113,659 war housing mortgages on one-to-four family dwellings for $517,656,180 were insured in 1943, compared with 68,706 for $267,015,578 in 1942. As of Dec. 31, 1943, mortgages insured under this section totalled 186,143 in number and amounted to $798,103,008.

Under section 608, mortgages on 273 large-scale war housing projects totalling $100,570,200 had been insured as of Dec. 31, 1943, with firm commitments outstanding to insure 51 more for $15,221,500. A total of 27,659 dwelling units will be provided by the 324 projects. These figures compare with mortgages covering 31 projects and totalling $16,760,200, insured from May 26, 1942, the effective date of the amendment creating section 608, through Dec. 31, 1942.

The War Housing Insurance fund protecting mortgages insured under sections 603 and 608, as of Dec. 31, 1943, had net resources of $2,014,774.

In addition to the protection of the funds, debentures issued under titles II and VI of the National Housing act are guaranteed unconditionally as to principal and interest by the United States.

Under title I, a total of 308,161 property improvement loans for $96,373,831 was reported for insurance in 1943, compared with 432,755 for $155,551,033 reported in 1942, bringing the grand total to 4,437,977 for $1,777,600,360.   (A. H. F.)

Federal Home Loan Bank Administration.—The FHLB administration directs the home-financing and related activities of agencies which were under the supervision of the Federal Home Loan Bank board prior to an executive order of the president of Feb. 24, 1942. These agencies are the Federal Home Loan Bank system, the Federal Savings and Loan Insurance corporation and the Home Owners' Loan corporation.

The executive order was issued under authority of the First War Powers act, 1941, approved Dec. 18, 1941. It consolidated the urban housing activities of the government under the newly established National Housing agency and designated John H. Fahey, former chairman of the Federal Home Loan Bank board, to direct the Federal Home Loan Bank administration with the title of commissioner. By the same order, the United States Housing corporation was placed under the Federal Home Loan Bank administration for liquidation. Commissioner of the FHLB administration in 1943 was John H. Fahey.

Federal Home Loan Bank System.—The Federal Home Loan Bank system was created by act of congress approved July 22, 1932, to provide reserve credit facilities for thrift and home-financing institutions—namely, savings and loan associations and institutions of similar type, mutual savings banks and life insurance companies engaged in home mortgage finance. The system in 1943 functioned through 12 regional Federal Home Loan banks, located in Boston, New York, Pittsburgh, Winston-Salem, Cincinnati, Indianapolis, Chicago, Des Moines, Little Rock, Topeka, Portland and Los Angeles.

Institutions approved for membership were required to invest in the capital stock of their respective regional banks. Of the aggregate stock of the banks, as of June 30, 1943, approximately 69% was held by the government. In addition to their capital stock, the regional banks obtained their funds from the public sale of debentures and by accepting deposits from member institutions.

The funds of each regional bank were used mainly in 1943 to make short- and long-term advances to member institutions for the purpose of providing additional accommodations for first mortgage loans on homes.

The growth and present resources of the bank system are evidence of its value in the field of home mortgage finance.

On Jan. 1, 1933, it had but 101 member institutions, with estimated assets of $217,000,000. By June 30, 1943, membership had increased to 3,774, of which 2,261 were state-chartered savings and loan associations, 1,468 federal savings and loan associations, 23 life insurance companies, and 22 mutual savings banks; their combined assets were approximately $6,045,000,000. On the same date, the paid-in capital stock of the regional banks amounted to $179,461,850 and their consolidated assets totalled $260,628,000.

Under the leadership of the 12 regional Home Loan banks, the member institutions of the system in 1943 took an active part in the financing of homes for workers in the areas of war industries and in promoting the sale of war bonds and other government securities.

Federal Savings and Loan Insurance Corporation.—The Federal Savings and Loan Insurance corporation, a permanent instrumentality of the United States, was created by congress in 1934.

DWELLINGS FOR WAR WORKERS in San Francisco, Calif., under the supervision of the National Housing agency. Variation was achieved through different types of balconies and gables

It was established to insure the safety of investments, up to $5,000 per investor, in each federal savings and loan association and in each state-chartered institution of the savings and loan type which applied and qualified for this protection. As of June 30, 1943, associations to the number of 2,428 and with total assets of $3,880,000,000 had become insured, of which 1,468 were federal savings and loan associations and 960 were state-chartered institutions. On June 30, 1943, the corporation had accumulated reserves amounting to nearly $42,000,000, in addition to its capital of $100,000,000, originally provided by congress.

Home Owners' Loan Corporation.—The Home Owners' Loan corporation was created by congress in 1933 to make loans, during a three-year period, directly to distressed urban home owners by taking over their delinquent mortgages. Since its lending operations ceased in 1936, the corporation has been engaged principally in collections on its loans and in the sale and rental of the properties it was forced to acquire.

Loans were made at an interest rate of 5%, later accepted at 4½%, and were to run for a period not over 15 years and be retired through monthly payments. In 1939 the law was amended to permit the corporation to extend its loans to a maximum of 25 years in justified cases.

Provided with $200,000,000 initial capital, HOLC was authorized to issue U.S. guaranteed bonds in an amount not to exceed $4,750,000,000, of which $3,489,453,550 were issued. A total of $1,735,509,700 in bonds was outstanding as of June 30, 1943.

HOLC made more than 1,000,000 loans, which, with later advances to borrowers for taxes, and other costs, increased its cumulative investment from the beginning of operations through June 1943, to $3,484,000,000. By monthly collections and continuous sale of the corporation's acquired properties, this amount had been reduced to $1,632,000,000, as of June 30, 1943. In other words, on that date the corporation was liquidated by 53.1%. More than 243,000 loans had been paid off in full. Over the same time, the corporation acquired 195,643 properties, of which 170,652 had been sold by June 30, 1943. During 1943, HOLC was liquidating its assets at a faster rate than in any year since it began its liquidation program in 1936.

United States Housing Corporation.—The United States Housing corporation was created in May 1918, to provide housing for war workers during World War I. On June 30, 1943, the corporation held an interest in real estate with an approximate value of $543,743. The major portion of these assets represents properties in Philadelphia, the final liquidation of which had been delayed by tax litigation. Originally under supervision of the secretary of labour, the corporation was transferred to the secretary of the treasury in 1937, to the Federal Works agency in 1939, and then to the Federal Home Loan Bank administration in 1942 to complete its liquidation.   (J. H. FA.)

Federal Public Housing Authority.—Created by presidential executive order Feb. 24, 1942, the Federal Public Housing authority is the constituent unit of the National Housing agency responsible for fiscal and construction activities in connection with public housing. Under the executive order, the authority assumed the housing functions of the United States Housing authority, Defense Homes corporation, Farm Security administration (except farm housing), divisions of defense housing and mutual ownership of the Federal Works agency, Public Buildings administration, and war and navy departments (except on army and navy reservations or posts). On Sept. 30, 1943, the Federal Public Housing authority had under its jurisdiction or control a total of over 700,000 units. The great majority, 80%, were war housing units while the remaining 20% were low-rent units formerly administered by the United States Housing authority and the Farm Security administration.

Commissioner of the FPHA in 1943 was Herbert Emmerich.

On Sept. 30, 1943, approximately $2,000,000,000 had been provided by congress or made available under legislation for public war housing. From these funds a total of 716,000 public war housing units had been programmed. Of these totals, approximately $1,800,000,000 (90%) had been allotted to the FPHA and 575,000 units (80%) were under its jurisdiction or control. The remainder of the war housing program was primarily carried out under the direction of the army and navy on military posts and reservations. Essentially all of the war housing produced in 1943 was of temporary construction in order to hold the use of materials and labour to a minimum. A temporary family dwelling for war workers contained 1,917 lb. of critical materials, only 20% of the 9,712 lb. of such materials which went into a prewar house. Of the 575,000 war housing units under the jurisdiction of the FPHA on Sept. 30, 1943, 72% had been completed; 19% were under construction and scheduled for completion within a few months, leaving only 9% in the planning or land acquisition stage. Family dwellings comprised 453,000 units or 79% of the war housing program; 79,000, or 14% were dormitory units; 43,000 or 7% were trailers.

The Federal Public Housing authority also performs the functions previously carried out by the United States Housing authority which operated under the United States Housing act of 1937. This act authorized the United States Housing authority to make loans in an amount not to exceed $800,000,000 to local housing authorities to enable them to build low-rent housing projects for families in the lowest income group and for whom there was a lack of decent, safe and sanitary housing within their means. These loans may be made for as much as 90% of the capital cost of projects and may be repaid with interest over a period of up to 60 years. Actually, however, on June 30, 1943, the end of the fiscal year, the FPHA, on loans finally closed, had loaned but 70% of the cost of projects. In addition to an authorization for loans the United States Housing act of 1937, as amended, authorized the United States Housing authority to make annual contributions to local housing authorities to reduce rents in an aggregate amount not exceeding $28,000,000 a year. Although on June 30, 1943, the FPHA had outstanding commitments for the maximum amount, it was actually liable for only $13,000,000 during the year because a number of projects were suspended for the duration of World War II, and others were diverted to war housing use during the emergency. On June 30, 1943, the total units in the FPHA program under the United States Housing act amounted to 187,000 units. Of these, 163,000 units were in an active status and 24,000 had been suspended for the duration of the war. Of the units in active status, 106,000 units were in the low-rent program and 57,000 units had been diverted to war purposes. In addition to the low-rent units under the United States Housing act, the FPHA in 1943 had under its jurisdiction 22,000 family dwellings which were built by the Public Works administration, and 5,000 units which were transferred to the FPHA from the Farm Security administration.

Despite the fact that a large proportion of the FPHA war housing program was in exceedingly small communities where there were no local housing authorities, 137,000 or 41% of the war housing units completed on June 30, 1943, had been developed by local housing authorities and 197,000, or 59% were under local housing authority management. Of all housing, both war and low-rent, which had been completed and which was under FPHA jurisdiction as of June 30, 1943, a total of 321,000 units, or 69% of the entire program, was being managed by local housing authorities. (*See* also HOUSING.) (H. EH.)

National Income and National Product.

As the U.S. economy moved forward to the virtual peak of mobilization for war in 1943, the national income continued the phenomenal rise initiated in 1940. The new high record of national income reached in 1943 was $147,200,000,000, compared with the 1942 total of $119,800,000,000. The preliminary estimate of the gross national product for 1943 was $187,500,000,000 as compared with the total of $151,700,000,000 for 1942. In 1939 the national income was $70,800,000,000 while the gross national product was $88,600,000,000.

Meaning of National Income and Gross National Product. —National income as understood in this survey represents a summation of the net earnings of the various factors of production derived from their association in current economic production. Both money income and income in kind are included, so long as they are derived from participation in current production. Such income receipts as relief, unemployment benefits, pensions, gifts, capital gains or losses, and gains from illegal activities are excluded since they do not represent earnings derived from current productive activity. The incomes included in the compilation are net incomes; that is, in the case of business enterprises, the incomes are counted after deduction of costs of doing business and after allowance for depreciation and

business taxes. In the case of corporations the income is taken after allowance for income and excess profits taxes. The estimates are limited to those incomes which are ordinarily derived from the market economy. Thus, the value of the services of housewives is not included, whereas the income derived from government employment or government obligations is included. It is well to emphasize that the national income is not simply the sum of money incomes of all persons in the nation, such as might be reported for income tax purposes.

The gross national product, as measured by the U.S. department of commerce, represents a summation of three major components: (1) the market value of goods and services flowing to consumers, (2) the value of the gross output of capital goods retained by private business, and (3) the cost value of the goods and services produced or purchased by government. The gross national product differs from the national income in that no allowance is made for depreciation and other reserves (which constitute business expenses in the computation of income) or for taxes paid by business.

Changes in U.S. National Income, 1919–43.—Estimates of national income from 1919 to 1943 are shown in Table I. It will be noted that the economic boom associated with World War I reached its high point in 1920. There followed a sharp and short liquidation in 1921 and then an almost continuous upsurge of economic activity during the prosperous '20s, with a new high for national income in 1929 not surpassed until 1941. The magnitude of the disastrous depression of the early '30s may be seen in the fact that the national income was more than halved between 1929 and 1932.

Table I.—National Income in Current and Average 1935–39 Dollars

Year	Current dollars	1935–39 dollars*	
	Total (In 000,000,000s of dollars)	Total (In 000,000,000s of dollars)	Per capita ($)
1919	67.6	47.8	455
1920	69.7	44.1	414
1921	52.6	40.8	377
1922	60.4	49.5	451
1923	70.0	56.7	508
1924	70.0	56.4	499
1925	74.6	59.5	518
1926	76.8	60.7	521
1927	76.2	61.9	524
1928	80.1	64.8	541
1929	83.3	68.1	566
1930	68.9	58.0	471
1931	54.5	51.0	411
1932	40.0	41.6	334
1933	42.3	45.7	364
1934	49.5	50.6	400
1935	55.7	56.1	440
1936	64.9	65.2	509
1937	71.5	69.0	536
1938	64.2	64.2	494
1939	70.8	71.9	549
1940	77.8	78.5	591
1941	95.6	90.1	677
1942	119.8	105.1	780
1943†	147.2	123.7	906

Source: U.S. department of commerce.
*Adjusted for price changes by use of a combination of cost of living indexes of urban workers and farmers and price index of capital goods.
†Preliminary.

The estimates in the accompanying tables are in terms of dollars and consequently are affected by the general level of prices as well as by the physical quantity of goods and services produced. Since for many purposes the physical quantity of national production, or real national income, is required, a series depicting this volume is also shown in Table I, average prices of 1935–39 being used as a base. Entirely adequate price information for adjusting the national income in current dollar terms was not available in 1943, but the estimates in Table I are sufficiently accurate for most purposes.

There are two interesting points to be observed in connection with these estimates of real national income. The first is that the year-to-year changes in the total are considerably less violent than in the estimates of national income in current dollars. The depression of 1921, for example, was largely accounted for by a drop in prices rather than by a decline in physical output. The depression of the early '30s was also partly a result of price movements, although in this instance the decline in real income was very substantial. On the other hand, the recession of 1938 was to a smaller degree accounted for by a decline in prices. It may be noted, however, that the volume of net output after adjustment for price changes was higher in 1939 than in 1937, whereas the reverse was true of national income in current dollars.

The second point is that the comparison between the general level of national income in the '30s as against the '20s is more favourable to the latter decade if real output is used than if the money value is used. In other words, the lower level of the national income in the '30s is partly accounted for by the lower prices prevailing in that period. It is striking, for example, that the real national income in both 1937 and 1939 exceeded that of 1929. Furthermore, the real national income in 1939 was 50% above that of 1919, whereas the current dollar value showed less than a 5% increase. This large rise in real income is a reflection of the increase in the capital and labour resources being utilized in the productive process and also of the tremendous advances in productive efficiency occasioned by technological development. So far as the importance of the latter factor is concerned, it is significant that the larger quantity in 1939 over 1919 was achieved with a smaller percentage utilization of the available productive capacity of both men and machines.

In assessing the importance of the rise in national income over time, it is also essential to take account of the increase in population. As population rises there are, of course, more persons to share in the goods being produced for present and future consumption and also more hands available for contributing to total output. The changes in income produced per capita, after adjustment for fluctuating prices, are shown in Table I.

The outbreak of World War II marked 1939 as the end of a definite phase in the economic life of the nation. The stimulus provided by the great U.S. defense effort was already evident in 1940, when the national income rose more than $6,000,000,000, even though the program was not inaugurated until the middle of that year. It was not until 1941, however, that the full impact of the rearmament program became apparent. In that year the national income rose by $17,000,000,000.

With the actual outbreak of war at the end of 1941 the efforts to obtain the maximum output of armaments in the United States were intensified, leading to an ever greater use of available economic resources. As a consequence, the national income continued to expand in 1942, with a gain for the year of almost $22,000,000,000.

The sharp upward movement was continued during the first half of 1943, but during the latter months of the year there was a decided levelling off in the rate of income gain. Nonetheless, for the year as a whole, the national income showed a substantial rise of over $27,000,000,000. As may be seen from the statistical data in Table I, the rise in the national income after 1940 was in part due to the rising trend of prices, but the larger part of the expansion represented an increase in real income.

Distributive Shares of the U.S. National Income.—An analysis of the national income in terms of shares of income paid or accruing in the various factors of production is presented in Table II. Because of certain conditions and controls of wartime, the changes recorded for the various distributive shares in later years departed from the pattern which was customary under peacetime prosperous conditions.

Total salaries and wages continued to rise precipitously in 1943. This component of the national income exceeded $100,-000,000,000 in 1943 for the first time in the nation's history,

Table II.—*National Income by Distributive Shares*
(In 000,000,000s of dollars)

Item	1929	1932	1939	1940	1941	1942	1943*
Total National Income	$83.3	$40.0	$70.8	$77.8	$95.6	$119.8	$147.2
Total Compensation of Employees	53.1	31.7	48.1	52.4	64.6	83.7	105.0
Salaries and Wages	52.6	31.0	44.2	48.7	60.9	80.3	101.7
Supplements to Salaries and Wages	.5	.6	3.8	3.7	3.7	3.4	3.3
Net Income of Corporations	7.2	−3.6	4.2	5.8	7.7	7.6	8.7
Net Dividends	5.9	2.7	3.8	4.0	4.4	4.0	4.0
Corporate Savings	1.3	−6.4	.4	1.8	3.3	3.6	4.7
Net Income of Noncorporate Business	13.6	4.8	11.2	12.2	15.5	20.1	23.9
Agriculture	5.2	1.5	4.3	4.4	6.2	9.7	12.7
Other	8.5	3.4	6.9	7.8	9.3	10.4	11.2
Net Interest	5.9	5.6	5.1	5.1	5.3	5.4	5.9
Net Rents and Royalties	3.6	1.5	2.3	2.3	2.6	3.1	3.6

Source: U.S. department of commerce, bureau of foreign and domestic commerce, national income unit.
*Preliminary.

more than double the figure of 1940. Although the salary and wage total was affected by rising wage rates over this period, the record-breaking expansion represents mostly the fact that new millions of persons were put to work and that the employed population as a whole was working considerably longer hours than was the case two years earlier. Also, the poorer paid industries tended to shrink relative to the higher paid heavy goods industries, the latter having expanded tremendously to meet the requirements of total war. Of course, the absolute increase in wages and salaries was the largest of any component of national income, but this result was merely due to the fact that wages and salaries bulked so large in the total.

All through the war period the net income of agricultural proprietors recorded the largest percentage gain among the distributive shares of national income. In 1943 agricultural net income reached a record total of $12,700,000,000. This compared with $9,700,000,000 in 1942 and constituted an almost three-fold increase over agricultural net income in 1939. The precipitous increase in agricultural income over these years was partly accounted for by record-breaking output of food and other farm products, though by far the more important influence there was a substantially higher level of agricultural prices.

The net income of other noncorporate business continued to advance in 1943 though in less spectacular fashion than in the case of wages and salaries or farm income. The total of $11,200,-000,000 for this component of the national income in 1943 represented a rise of 8% over the previous year and 65% over 1939. Both the interest and rent components of the national income were relatively stable in 1943 though over the entire war period there occurred a quite substantial increase in aggregate net rents.

In the absence of new legislation with respect to corporate taxes in 1943, net income of corporations advanced with the increase of the total volume of business. This contrasted with the situation in 1942 when the heavy increase in both corporate income and excess profits tax rates held profits to their 1941 level. Over the entire war period, though corporate profits had doubled by 1943, the increase was much less than customary for this volatile component of the national income. This again was a reflection of the considerably higher taxes levied on corporation income and excess profits.

Industrial Origin of National Income.—Statistics on the industrial origin of national income are presented in Table III. In this breakdown of the national income the effect of wartime conditions is clearly evident. Most noticeable are the huge gains that were made in income originating in manufacturing, government activities and agriculture. Because wartime requirements

Table III.—U.S. National Income by Industrial Origin

(In 000,000,000s of dollars)

Industry	1929	1932	1939	1940	1941	1942	1943*
Total National Income	$83.3	$40.0	$70.8	$77.8	$95.6	$119.8	$147.2
Agriculture	6.8	2.4	5.2	5.3	7.3	11.0	14.3
Mining	1.9	.5	1.4	1.8	2.1	2.4	2.8
Manufacturing	20.9	6.2	17.0	20.3	27.6	36.7	47.5
Contract Construction	3.5	.9	1.9	2.1	3.5	4.9	4.2
Transportation	7.0	3.6	5.0	5.4	6.5	8.0	9.5
Power and Gas	1.4	1.1	1.5	1.6	1.8	1.7	1.7
Communication	1.0	.7	.9	.9	1.0	1.1	1.2
Trade	11.9	5.6	11.0	12.2	14.4	15.7	17.1
Finance	10.1	5.3	6.8	7.0	7.7	8.3	9.0
Government	6.4	6.6	10.0	10.3	11.5	16.4	25.1
Service	8.3	4.7	7.0	7.4	8.0	9.2	10.0
Miscellaneous	4.0	2.4	3.2	3.5	4.2	4.5	4.8

Source: U.S. department of commerce, bureau of foreign and domestic commerce, national income unit.
*Preliminary.

centred so largely in manufacturing output, this component of national income became an increasingly large percent of total national income in the course of the war. By 1943 it accounted for about one-third of total income, whereas in 1939 it was less than one-quarter. The huge rise in income originating in government activities, likewise a wartime development, reflected not only the expansion of the armed forces of the nation but also the increased activities in government arsenals and navy yards. Income originating in only one industrial component in national income, namely contract construction, declined from 1941 to 1943, the reason being the passing of the peak in the construction phase of the war production program.

Gross National Product.—The statistical components of the gross national product are shown in Table IV. The outstanding development revealed by the table is the spectacular increase in total gross national product after 1940. By 1943 the gross national product reached the amazing total of $187,500,000,000, in comparison with $97,000,000,000 in 1940. Of course, it is well known that part of this increase was caused by a rise in prices rather than by expansion in a physical volume of goods and services produced. These two factors cannot be separated in an entirely satisfactory manner for a period which covers the transition from a peacetime to a war economy. However, approximate measures indicate that more than two-thirds of the expansion in the value of the gross national product represents additional goods and services produced, and that less than one-third represents the effects of inflation. There is little doubt that the productive potential of the U.S. economy was realized in the course of the war to an extent that would not have seemed possible a few years earlier.

The driving force behind the expansion was federal government expenditures for goods and services required in the rearmament and war efforts. (The figures shown in the table for

Table IV.—Gross National Product or Expenditure, 1939-43

(In 000,000,000s of dollars)

Item	1939	1940	1941	1942	1943*
Gross national product or expenditure	$88.6	$97.0	$119.2	$151.7	$187.5
Government expenditures for goods and services	16.0	16.7	25.7	61.7	96.1
Federal Government	7.9	8.8	17.8	54.3	89.3
War	1.4	2.7	12.5	49.3	84.5
Nonwar	6.5	6.1	5.3	5.0	4.8
State and local government	8.1	7.9	7.8	7.4	6.8
Output available for private use	72.6	80.4	93.5	89.9	91.4
Private gross capital formation	10.9	14.7	19.0	8.0	1.0
Construction	3.6	4.3	5.4	2.9	1.5
Producers' durable equipment	5.5	6.9	8.9	5.1	2.1
Net change in business inventories	.9	1.8	3.5	−.6	−1.3
Net exports of goods and services	.8	1.4	.9	.4	−1.2
Net exports and monetary use of gold and silver	.2	.3	.2	.1	−.1
Consumers' goods and services	61.7	65.7	74.6	82.0	90.5
Durable goods	6.4	7.4	9.1	6.4	6.6
Nondurable goods	32.6	34.4	40.1	48.0	54.6
Services	22.7	23.9	25.4	27.6	29.4
MEMO: Consumers' expenditures in average 1939 dollars	61.7	65.1	70.0	69.8	72.6

*Preliminary.

war expenditures are not the same as total government outlays for war purposes since some of these outlays might not have been for currently produced goods and services.) While there was a significant increase in war output during 1940, owing to the inauguration of the defense program in the middle of that year, the real results of the defense program became fully evident in 1941, when war expenditures exceeded $11,000,000,000. Pearl Harbor brought an intensification of the war effort and the setting of new goals for war production, which in 1942 carried war expenditures to the spectacular total of approximately $50,000,000,000, a figure constituting about one-third of the gross national product.

In 1943, when the virtual peak of the war production program was reached, war expenditures totalled almost $85,000,000,000, and accounted for 45% of the gross national product. The success of the nation's economic mobilization for war is amply demonstrated by these figures.

It may be observed that both in 1940 and 1941 the expansion of war production did not require any curtailment of goods and services available for private use. As a matter of fact, in both those years nonwar production was steadily increased. This was the case with both capital formation and consumers' goods and services, and was possible because at the beginning of the rearmament program the nation had available a huge pool of unemployed economic resources, both men and machines. In 1942 and 1943, however, this situation came to an end, and the value of war output increased more than the total gross national product. Both federal nonwar and state and local government utilization of current production were decreased. The major cut, however, came in the field of private capital formation, where the record-breaking 1941 total of over $19,000,000,000 was reduced to $1,000,000,000 by 1943. Both private construction and private purchases of machinery and equipment were drastically curtailed. Furthermore, business inventories were curtailed in both 1942 and 1943 in contrast to the substantial accumulation in 1941 and a change in the same direction occurred with respect to the nation's export balance (excluding lend-lease).

In terms of actual dollars spent, consumers' purchases of goods and services actually increased in 1942 and 1943. This rise, however, merely reflected the influence of rising prices; in terms of dollars of constant purchasing power, the goods and services received by consumers was relatively stable after 1941. That it was possible to maintain consumers' goods and services at so high a level in the face of the tremendous requirements of the war program was due to two important factors. In the first place, the total of consumers' purchases was larger than current production by virtue of the drawing down of business inventories of consumers' goods. In the second place, the fact that the United States did not reach an overall manpower shortage until 1943 meant that the restrictions on consumers' goods output were due entirely to shortages of raw materials and imported commodities. Because the war program consisted mostly of munitions and munitions' manufacturing facilities, the material shortages were largely confined to durable goods. It may be seen that consumers' durable goods declined fairly sharply, and this decline would have been very much greater had it not been for previously accumulated inventories. While there were isolated shortages among the nondurable goods, on the other hand, many of these commodities as well as virtually all consumers' services were increased. The decline in consumers' durable goods, therefore, was entirely offset by increases in nondurable goods and services.

Consumer Income and Savings.—Table V contains a breakdown of the national income by use of funds. The primary purpose of a breakdown of this sort is to show the impact of taxes

Table V.—*Disposition of National Income, 1939-43*
(In 000,000,000s of dollars)

Item	1939	1940	1941	1942	1943*
National income	$70.8	$77.8	$95.6	$119.8	$147.2
Add: Transfer payments	2.4	2.6	2.5	2.6	3.1
Less: Corporate savings	.4	1.8	3.3	3.6	4.7
Contributions to social insurance funds	2.0	2.1	2.6	3.3	3.9
Equals: Income payments to individuals	70.8	76.5	92.2	115.5	141.8
Less: Personal taxes and non-tax payments	3.1	3.3	4.0	6.6	16.8
Federal	1.3	1.4	2.0	4.7	14.9
State and local	1.9	1.9	1.9	1.9	1.9
Equals: Disposable income of individuals	67.7	73.2	88.2	108.8	125.0
Less: Consumer expenditures	61.7	65.7	74.6	82.0	90.5
Equals: Net savings of individuals	6.0	7.5	13.7	26.9	34.6

*Preliminary.

upon the flow of personal income and the proportionate allocation of income after taxes between expenditures for consumption and savings. These data are of particular importance in time of war since they indicate the magnitude of the inflationary pressure generated by the huge volume of government war expenditures.

In 1943 the flow of income to individuals continued to rise sharply as it had during the earlier years of the war. The total of $141,800,000,000 was more than double the income flow in 1939. Partly offsetting the rise in income was a large advance in tax payments. However, the increase in taxes was far from large enough to offset completely the advance in individual income, so that income after taxes rose from $108,800,000,000 in 1942 to $125,000,000,000 in 1943.

As previously mentioned, the quantity of goods and services available for consumers' purchase remained relatively stable in 1943. The consequence of this fact together with the continued rise in disposable income was to continue the heavy pressure on consumers' goods prices. As a result, consumer expenditures rose from $82,000,000,000 in 1942 to over $90,000,000,000 in 1943, with the increase representing higher prices paid rather than more goods and services received. Nonetheless, the administrative mechanisms of price control and rationing were fairly effective in limiting price advances so that net savings of individuals again rose substantially. It is interesting to note that consumer expenditures rose by about the same amount in both 1942 and 1943 (with about the same quantity of goods being available in both years) although the rise in income after taxes was somewhat larger in the earlier year. Savings, therefore, rose by $13,000,000,000 in 1942 but only by $8,000,000,000 in 1943. (*See* also BUDGET, NATIONAL; BUSINESS REVIEW; NATIONAL DEBT; WEALTH AND INCOME, U.S. DISTRIBUTION OF.)

(M. GT.)

National Labor Relations Board.
More than 9,500 cases were filed with the board in 1943, the third largest number in the board's history. This number was exceeded only in 1941, when industry was expanding to meet defense needs and in 1938, when a pent-up flood of cases was released by the supreme court's upholding of the constitutionality of the Labor Relations act. In 1943, the board's close relation to war production was seen in the fact that 50% of the new cases were concentrated in seven industries, all essential to the war effort: iron and steel, machinery, aircraft, food, shipbuilding, chemicals, and electrical machinery.

Of the 9,543 new cases filed, election cases numbered over 6,000, the largest number received in any of the eight years of the board's activity. Charges of employer unfair labour practices decreased to 3,400, the lowest number filed in any of the five preceding years. The shift to election cases was accentuated by frequent agreement of all parties that the board's election facilities be utilized. Thus, more than half of the representation cases were characterized by agreements of employers and labour organizations that a question of representation existed and should be resolved without the necessity of formal hearings and directives of the board. As a consequence, they agreed on all the details of the referendum, indicated that they would abide by the results, and availed themselves of the board's election machinery.

As in preceding years, an overwhelming number of unfair labour practice cases were closed by the board without the necessity for formal proceedings. In 1943, the board closed 86% of such cases in the informal stages by means of withdrawal, dismissal and settlement of charges made against employers.

A total of 4,153 elections were conducted by the board during the year. Valid votes were cast by 1,126,501 workers. Of the 4,153 elections, 1,766 were won by affiliates of the Congress of Industrial Organizations, 1,398 by American Federation of Labor unions, 416 by unaffiliated labour organizations, and in 573 elections a majority of votes was not received by any of the organizations appearing on the ballot.

Remedies in unfair labour practice cases closed in 1943 were varied. Company-dominated unions were disestablished in 205 cases. A total of 8,361 workers was reinstated after discriminatory discharges and after strikes caused by unfair labour practices. Back pay amounting to $2,284,593 was paid to 5,115 workers who had been the victims of discriminatory practices. Notices of compliance with the act were posted in 1,110 cases.

The liaison procedures with other federal agencies, established in the defense and early war periods, were extended in 1943. Among the agencies with which the board exchanged information were the war and navy departments, the War Production board, the War Shipping administration, the National War Labor board, and the Conciliation service of the department of labour. Essentially, the board's function in relation to war plants in which other agencies were interested was to act with speed and to assign these cases a priority in handling.

Distinction must be drawn between the basic functions of the National Labor Relations board and of the National War Labor board (*q.v.*). The former was entrusted by congress with the duty of preventing and remedying unfair labour practices and to determine representatives for collective bargaining. The War Labor board was established to settle wartime disputes involving wages, union security, and other substantive provisions of labour agreements. The NLRB co-operated closely with the WLB by exchange of information and a close integration of efforts. Typically, determination by the NLRB of bargaining representation in many plants was a first step to the settlement by WLB of disputes concerning wages and conditions of employment.

In 1943, as in 1942, litigation in the courts was concerned chiefly with enforcement of board orders. The United States supreme court and the various circuit courts of appeals reviewed 100 board orders. In the supreme court, three of the four board orders were upheld and enforced in full. In the circuit courts of appeals, 87 of the 96 cases reviewed resulted in enforcement of board orders. In several cases the problem was whether anti-union statements made by an employer were protected by the constitutional guarantee of freedom of speech or whether such statements were violations of the National Labor Relations act. The supreme court refused to grant certiorari in three such cases, leaving in effect these lower court rulings: Where an employer's action consisted solely of an expression not containing any expressed threat and the record of his activities did not reveal any other anti-union activities, such utterance was protected by the Fifth amendment. Where the written or oral conduct of an employer constituted a threat, such utterance was not protected by the Fifth amendment. Where an employer made statements, written or oral, as well as committing other anti-union acts, the total activities of the employer (including the letter or statement) amounted to unlawful coercion under the act.

During 1943 the board figured in three legislative enactments.

In the first, congress imposed, through an amendment to the Appropriation Act of 1944 and for the duration of the fiscal year, a limitation upon board use of funds so as to prevent it from acting in any unfair labour practice case arising over a labour agreement which had been in existence for three months or longer before a charge was filed. In the second, the board was entrusted with the new task of protecting the rights and benefits of employees affected by the merger of domestic telegraph carriers, under an amendment to the Communications Act of 1934. In the third, the board was assigned the duty of conducting strike votes in accordance with section 8 of the War Labor Disputes act. In the first six months of this new law, often referred to as the Smith-Connally act, 654 strike notices were filed, 444 were withdrawn and 117 strike votes were conducted. (*See* also LABOUR UNIONS; LAW; STRIKES AND LOCK-OUTS.)   (H. A. Ms.)

National Lawyers Guild.

The National Lawyers guild held its national convention in Chicago on Feb. 20, 21 and 22, 1943. A major project decided upon by the national executive board was to take steps toward the convening of a meeting of representatives of the bars of the United States, Great Britain and the soviet union for discussions on subjects of assistance to the United Nations in the prosecution of the war and looking toward permanent collaboration in the postwar period. The guild announced this program at dinners in honour of Sir Donald Somervell, attorney general of Britain and Wales, held in Washington, D.C., and New York in September. Simultaneously, a memorandum on this subject was submitted to the commissar of justice of the soviet union through the soviet embassy in Washington, D.C. The matter was under discussion in London and Moscow.

Among its other war activities the guild succeeded in securing a change in the policy of the war department which henceforth would make possible the granting of commissions in the judge advocate general's department to qualified Negro lawyers.

National officers re-elected for 1943 were president, Attorney General Robert W. Kenny of California; executive secretary, Martin Popper of New York; vice-presidents, Osmond K. Fraenkel of New York, Mitchell Franklin of Louisiana, Edward Lamb of Ohio, Louis F. McCabe of Pennsylvania; treasurer, Benedict Wolf of New York. Newly elected vice-presidents were Bartley C. Crum of California, Judge William H. Hastie of Washington, D.C., Judge William H. Holly of Illinois, and Judge Ira W. Jayne of Michigan.   (M. PR.)

National Mediation Board.

The National Mediation board, an independent federal agency in the United States created June 21, 1934 by an amendment to the Railway Labor act of May 20, 1926, was charged with investigation of representation disputes and mediation of disputes over rates of pay, rules and working conditions on carriers by rail and air, thus to avoid interruptions to interstate commerce by rail or air transport.

During 1943, the Mediation board received 390 cases. It disposed of 360 cases, 167 representation disputes and 193 disputes involving changes in rates of pay, rules or working conditions.

On Nov. 22, 1943, the United States supreme court decided three cases involving interpretation of the Railway Labor act. In one of these decisions it was held that the Mediation board's determinations and certifications in representation proceedings were final and not subject to review by the courts. In the other two cases it was held that jurisdictional disputes between unions did not present questions justiciable in the courts, and that the Railway Labor act intended that such disputes are to be settled by negotiation, mediation or voluntary arbitration.

National Railway Labor Panel.—The Railway Labor act provided for the appointment of an Emergency board by the president upon recommendation of the National Mediation board to investigate and report to the president on any dispute unsettled through mediation or arbitration which threatened substantially to interrupt interstate commerce. To supplement the act during the war emergency, the president by Executive Order 9172 of May 22, 1942 established the National Railway Labor Panel, consisting of 20 members, from which Emergency boards were to be selected by the chairman of the Panel in cases where the employees refrained from taking strike votes and setting strike dates. Ten Panel Emergency boards were appointed during the year 1943 and nine of these boards filed their reports before the end of the year. (*See* also RAILROADS; STRIKES AND LOCK-OUTS.)   (W. M. L.)

National Monuments: *see* NATIONAL PARKS AND MONUMENTS.

National Parks and Monuments.

During 1943 the national park service continued to make definite contributions to the war program in addition to fulfilling its primary function of protecting the 22,000,000-ac. national park system entrusted to its care.

That the national parks, national monuments, and allied areas

SOLDIERS lunching among the sequoias in the Mariposa grove of big trees, Yosemite national park, Calif., in 1943

constituting the national park system are important to U.S. citizens was attested to by the fact that, notwithstanding travel handicaps, visitors to these areas during the travel year ended Sept. 30, 1943, totalled approximately 7,000,000. Nearly 2,000,000 were members of the armed forces.

More than 300 authorizations for wartime use of park facilities and resources were granted by the service during 1943. As heretofore, inconvenience to park administration and to visitors, or remediable damage to park property were not considered sufficient reasons for denying such use. Only where the proposed uses would destroy or impair distinctive park features or qualities did the service feel justified in asking whether all reasonable alternatives had been exhausted and if the demand was based upon critical necessity.

With the intensified demands for lumber to meet war requirements, particularly Sitka spruce for aeroplane construction, the magnificent virgin forests of Olympic national park were in grave jeopardy. The service, with the strong support of the secretary of the interior, held steadfast to the principle that no trees should be cut in the park until proof was furnished that no other practicable source was available. While discussions were under way with the War Production board the situation eased as a result of cancellation of plans for a number of types of wooden planes, increased spruce aircraft lumber production in British Columbia and Alaska, and increased supplies of aluminum for aeroplane construction. As a consequence, the secretary received word from the War Production board that Sitka spruce in the park was not needed for warplane construction and that unless unforeseen circumstances arose none probably would be needed through March 1944.

In 1943 two units were added to the national park system— Jackson Hole national monument, Wyoming, established by presidential proclamation of March 15, and the Thomas Jefferson national memorial, Washington, D.C., established April 13, the 200th anniversary of Jefferson's birth and the date of the memorial's dedication by President Roosevelt. In addition, two structures in non-federal ownership—Independence hall in Philadelphia, Pa., and St. Paul's church in Eastchester, N.Y.—were designated as national historic sites.   (N. B. D.)

National Railway Labor Panel: see NATIONAL MEDIATION BOARD.
National War Fund: see WAR RELIEF, U.S.
National War Labor Board: see WAR LABOR BOARD, NATIONAL.

National Youth Administration.
The National Youth administration provided training to youth between the ages of 16 and 24 who were out of school, to qualify them for jobs in war industries in which there was a present or potential shortage of labour.

Students in secondary schools and colleges were given part-time employment for small wages to enable them to continue their education.

The National Youth administration operated war production training projects through which out-of-school youths were employed in workshops to learn mechanical unit skills under conditions similar to those which are found in industry. NYA shops were operated on a multiple-shift basis and provided training in metal and machine shop work, forge and foundry work, aviation mechanics, radio and electrical work, welding and similar occupations vital to the war effort. During the twelve-month period ending June 30, 1943, the National Youth administration provided training in these skills to more than 400,000 youths.

The War Manpower commission, under whose jurisdiction the NYA operated in 1943, determined the types of training to be provided; the U.S. Employment service registered all NYA youths as an aid to their placement in industry.

The NYA program for needy students attending non-profit making, tax-exempt schools, colleges and universities provided monthly wages ranging from $3 to $6 in secondary schools and $10 to $25 in colleges and universities in return for useful work performed under the direction of the school officials. Employment was given on the basis of scholastic merit and proved need. Both programs were administered by the NYA through 11 regional offices co-ordinated through the national office in Washington, D. C. The National Youth administration was established by executive order of the president on June 25, 1935. Originally set up within the Works Progress administration, the NYA was transferred to the Federal Security agency in 1939 and came under the jurisdiction of the War Manpower commission Sept. 17, 1942. After its inception through June 30, 1942, the NYA provided jobs for almost 2,700,000 youths on the out-of-school program and more than 2,100,000 youths on the student work program.

In June 1943 the congress directed the NYA to terminate all its training activities and to complete liquidation not later than Jan. 1, 1944. The National Youth administrator was Aubrey Williams.   (A. Ws.)

Natural Gas: see GAS, NATURAL.
Nauru: see MANDATES; PACIFIC ISLANDS, MANDATED.

Navies of the World.
An inevitable result of the widespread war at sea was to stimulate the development of new tactics, new types of ships, new weapons and new methods of using weapons.

In order to get over the losses sustained in the early part of the war through the efficiency of the British "asdic" method of detection, U-boats followed fresh tactics. After 1939 most of their attacks were made on the surface at night, when their low silhouettes were difficult to spot. Star-shells, originally devised to counter destroyer attacks in darkness, were employed by escort vessels guarding convoys to reveal the submarines; and later a special type of searchlight for use by aircraft was similarly employed, the aircraft acting in concert with the escort vessels.

New types of warships included the corvette, the original design of which was based on that of the well-known whale catchers used in the antarctic. After a large number of these corvettes had been built, an improved and enlarged design superseded them; this type was known in the United States as a destroyer-escort and in the United Kingdom as a frigate. Large numbers were built for both the royal navy and the United States navy. Another new type was the escort aircraft carrier, smaller and slower than the big fleet aircraft carriers, but of great value in dealing with the submarine menace. Use of these vessels bridged the mid-Atlantic gap between the extreme ranges of shore-based aircraft, enabling every mile of the convoy route between the U.S.A. and Europe to be patrolled by aircraft. Motor torpedo boats and motor gunboats, referred to by the British admiralty under the comprehensive term "light coastal craft" also developed considerably. Not only the Allies, but also Germany and Italy made extensive use of them, though the latter country's vessels, classed as M.A.S. (*motoscafi anti-summergibili*) accomplished but little in the Mediterranean. Nor was another Italian device, a torpedo in a light framework attached to a skiff with an outboard motor, very effective. Japan contributed the midget submarine, manned by two or three men, which was used without success at Pearl Harbor, Sydney and Diego Suarez in 1941 and 1942. A British type of midget submarine, of which little is known, proved a better invention, the biggest German battleship, the "Tirpitz," being crippled by this means. Yet another type which underwent development was the anti-aircraft ship, outstanding examples of which were the British cruisers of the "Dido" class and the U.S. cruisers of the "San Diego" type.

The magnetic and acoustic mine, and various combinations of these devices, caused many losses at sea. Originally an enemy weapon, these were laid extensively in the Baltic by the R.A.F. in 1942–43, and soon became a serious source of trouble to the Germans. The latter also produced torpedoes of novel types, one being an electric weapon which leaves no perceptible track, and the other one of acoustic pattern, which is attracted by the vibrations of a propeller.

Torpedo attack from the air underwent great development, though it was in the experimental stage during World War I. In Nov. 1940, the Italian fleet at Taranto was disabled by this means; and the destruction of the German battleship "Bismarck" in the Atlantic in 1941 was the fruit of damage caused by torpedoes from royal naval aircraft. Japan also made extensive use of this weapon, which she first employed at Pearl Harbor, in the sinking of H.M.S. "Prince of Wales" and "Repulse," and in the destruction of the U.S.S. "Hornet," "Lexington" and "Chicago."

In the tactics of night fighting, the technique developed by the royal navy in prewar days was employed with conspicuous success by Sir Andrew Cunningham's fleet at the battle of Matapan. It was imitated by the Japanese in the battle of Savo Island, when the U.S.S. "Astoria," "Quincy" and "Vincennes," and H.M.A.S. "Canberra" were sunk. In the following November the tables were turned by Admiral Halsey, who inflicted a severe defeat on the enemy in the battle of Guadalcanal. Three cruisers were believed to have been destroyed by the gunfire of the U.S.S. "South Dakota" on this occasion during a night action.

During 1943 two U.S. battleships of 45,000 tons, the "Iowa" and "New Jersey," passed into service, bringing the total of capital ships in the U.S. navy up to 22. This included the "Oklahoma," under reconstruction after capsizing at Pearl Harbor.

Aircraft carriers continued to prove their value in various directions. It is estimated that by the end of 1943 the U.S. navy would include 15 fleet carriers, some of the heavy type and others of the lighter design evolved from 10,000-ton cruiser hulls. Japan was without the shipbuilding resources to equal this, though it was suspected that four large armoured ships might have been converted into aircraft carriers in an effort to replace losses more rapidly. Many escort aircraft carriers, converted from mercantile hulls, were added to both the royal and U.S. navies, and proved useful in the Mediterranean as well as in the protection of convoys from attack by submarines in mid-Atlantic. Neither Germany nor Italy had any aircraft carriers in service.

Both Allied and enemy navies incurred numerous cruiser casualties, but only the former effectually replaced them. In 1943 the royal navy lost but a single cruiser, H.M.S. "Charybdis," and the U.S. navy two, the "Chicago" and "Helena," a contrast to the preceding years. The first of the six battle cruisers laid down for the U.S.N. in 1941 had been launched and named "Alaska." There was no confirmation of the report that she might be completed as an aircraft carrier.

There was no evidence to show how far Japan had progressed in replacing her heavy losses. It was believed that at least two big new battleships of over 40,000 tons had been delivered, and new aircraft carriers and cruisers were also suspected to be ready. Destroyers and submarines were being turned out steadily at the estimated rate of 20 of each per annum.

Naval operations in the Baltic, Black sea and Arctic ocean by the soviet navy were on a small scale in 1943, being confined to submarine attacks on transports and supply ships, and occasional minor encounters between light warships.

Though losses in 1943 were on an unprecedented scale, and the rate of replacement was believed to have declined, it would not be safe to assume that the number of German submarines in service at the end of 1943 was less than 300. Not more than about one-quarter of these would normally be operating at sea at the same time. Italian losses in this category up to the time of the armistice were stated to have reached a total of 84. Japanese submarines had not shown themselves very active, though they were believed to have been used for the evacuation of Kiska, in the Aleutians.

Despite losses, British submarine strength was believed to have increased during the year. Undoubtedly the activity of H.M. submarines in the Mediterranean contributed materially to axis defeats in North Africa and Sicily. U.S. submarines increased their numbers to a much greater extent, and their unceasing campaign against Japanese shipping in the Pacific was believed to be causing the enemy serious concern, as tonnage was being destroyed faster than it could be replaced.

British Naval Strength.—It was stated in 1943 by the first lord of the admiralty that all losses incurred during the war had been replaced by new ships. These losses included 5 capital ships; 5 aircraft carriers; 26 cruisers; 3 fast minelayers; 107 destroyers; 58 submarines; 13 sloops; 1 frigate; 12 fleet minesweepers; 23 corvettes; 1 monitor; 9 river gunboats; 21 light coastal craft; 2 escort aircraft carriers; 2 depot ships; 14 armed merchant cruisers; 12 auxiliary minesweepers; 14 armed yachts; 168 trawlers and whalers; 18 drifters; 4 fleet tugs; and 23 miscellaneous auxiliaries.

After allowing for these losses, and for such ships as were believed to have been due for completion by the end of 1943, the strength of the royal navy at that date might be reckoned at 15 battleships (including one battle cruiser); 8 fleet and 25 escort aircraft carriers; 64 cruisers (including one cruiser-minelayer); 320 destroyers; 80 submarines; 66 sloops; 80 frigates; over 200 corvettes; about 200 fleet minesweepers; 4 monitors; 2 aircraft tenders; 2 netlayers; 9 river gunboats; 6 coastal motor gunboats, motor torpedo boats and motor launches. Trawlers, drifters, armed yachts, depot ships and mercantile auxiliaries of every description were too numerous for an estimate to be possible.

There had been no news of the completion of the four battleships of about 40,000 tons which were on order at the outbreak of war, though this did not necessarily imply that none of them had been completed.

Naval forces of the dominions, including the royal Indian, royal Australian, royal Canadian and royal New Zealand navies, as well as those of Newfoundland, South Africa, Burma, Ceylon and Kenya, are incorporated as far as possible in the above figures. Their personnel was known to have been increased greatly since war began; in the case of the R.C.N., it was expected to reach 90,000 by the end of 1943. Canada built small warships such as frigates, corvettes, minesweepers and patrol vessels in very large numbers, not only for her own service but also in some measure for the royal navy and United States navy; while Australia, besides providing for her own needs in the way of destroyers and minesweepers, had also constructed sloops for the royal Indian navy.

United States Naval Strength.—The largest program of naval construction in the history of the United States, designed to produce a "two-ocean" navy, was nearing its peak. Ships in service at the end of 1943 were estimated to be at least 22 battleships; 15 fleet and 20 escort aircraft carriers; 49 cruisers; 360 destroyers and destroyer escorts; 175 submarines; 12 gun-

U.S. BATTLESHIP "CALIFORNIA," sunk at Pearl Harbor, putting to sea in 1943, refitted and stripped of outdated equipment

GERMAN BOMB scoring a near hit immediately astern of a U.S. transport during the initial invasion of Sicily July 10, 1943

LEAVING A HEAVY WAKE of oil, a Japanese destroyer fruitlessly shifts its course to avoid Allied bombs in the battle of the Bismarck sea March 2–4, 1943. An entire convoy of 10 warships and 12 transports was wiped out by the Allies in the three-day battle

THE "GEEHEEBEE," also nicknamed "jahemy," "le Tourneau" and "jeramy," was an ingenious U.S. naval contraption introduced in 1943. Its varied uses included lifting boats and barges, clearing earth, and pulling heavy objects. Here it is shown in action on Attu Island, pulling a damaged landing craft ashore

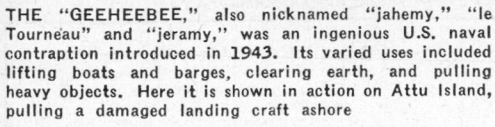

THE U.S. LANDING CRAFT "LST" (landing ship—tank) made its fighting debut in 1943. Huge doors swing open as the ship is "beached," permitting men, tanks and supplies to move rapidly ashore

boats; 50 escort vessels (frigates); 40 patrol vessels (ex-yachts); 800 submarine chasers; 15 minelayers; 650 minesweepers; 200 motor torpedo boats; 22 seaplane tenders, and immense numbers of other fleet auxiliaries. There were also the vessels of the U.S. coast guard, including some 40 ocean-going ships besides numerous coastal craft.

Under construction or on order were 9 battleships (though 5 of these were not being proceeded with for the present); 6 battle cruisers; and an unknown number of aircraft carriers, cruisers, destroyers, escort vessels and auxiliaries of every category. Some idea of the immense strides made may be gathered from the fact that between July 1, 1940, and the corresponding date in 1943 there were completed for the U.S. navy 333 combatant vessels aggregating 1,117,054 tons and costing over $3,000,000,000; 1,274 mine and patrol craft of 199,765 tons, costing $20,000,000; 151 auxiliaries, 654 yard and district craft, and 12,964 landing craft. No naval construction program of comparable size and speed had ever been accomplished. Altogether the fleet thus created amounted to 15,376 new ships of more than 2,200,000 tons.

Total personnel on duty at July 31, 1943, was 1,782,000 officers and men of the navy, plus 315,200 marine corps and 151,200 coast guard. By the end of the year it was expected these figures would have been raised to 2,294,000 navy, 399,700 marine corps and 171,500 coast guard.

Japan.—For years past great secrecy characterized Japan's naval preparations, and this had been intensified after Dec. 1941. Allowing for the uncertainty thus produced, it was probable that at the end of 1943 there were in service 10 or 12 battleships; 6 to 8 aircraft carriers; 20 cruisers; over 100 destroyers; about 100 submarines; 15 to 20 seaplane carriers; 5 coast defense ships; and a large but uncertain number of ancillary vessels, such as minelayers, minesweepers, submarine chasers and gunboats. An unknown number of battleships, aircraft carriers, cruisers, destroyers, submarines, etc., might be assumed to be under construction.

France.—The majority of the seaworthy ships of the French navy were under the control of the Committee of National Liberation, which had its headquarters at Algiers. These included 5 battleships, 1 aircraft carrier, 10 cruisers, between 20 and 30 destroyers and about 20 submarines, besides minor war vessels such as sloops, corvettes, etc. Nearly every vessel of importance in the hands of the German-occupied administration at Vichy was scuttled or otherwise disabled at Toulon in Nov. 1942, and it was not likely that many of these could be put into service under present conditions. A cruiser and a few small craft might have passed under Japanese control at Saigon, in Indo-China. Little or no progress appeared to have been made with the few warships that were under construction in French yards before the enemy occupation.

Italy.—Excluding a few damaged or incomplete ships in German hands, the Italian navy was at the end of 1943 entirely at the disposal of the United Nations. Ships intact were believed to comprise 5 battleships, 8 or 9 cruisers, nearly 50 destroyers and between 20 and 30 submarines, with sundry auxiliaries.

Germany.—German naval strength at the end of 1943 amounted to 3 battleships, one of which was damaged and another under reconstruction; 2 armoured ships, known popularly as "pocket battleships," one of which had also been damaged; 1 aircraft carrier, apparently unfit for service; 6 cruisers; not more than 40 destroyers and seagoing torpedo boats; 2 coast defense ships; and an uncertain number of submarines (estimated at about 300), motor torpedo boats and minesweepers. Of late the enemy relied on its submarines and small craft to carry on the war afloat.

U.S.S.R.—Little more was recorded of Russian naval strength than before the war. It included 3 obsolete battleships, 2 of them in the Baltic and the other in the Black sea; 6 or 7 cruisers, of which 2 were in the Baltic and 4 or 5 in the Black sea; about 90 destroyers and seagoing torpedo boats; 200 or more submarines; a small seaplane carrier; and over 100 motor torpedo boats and motor launches. Vessels in the latter categories were divided between the Baltic, the Arctic, the Black sea and the far east.

Other European Countries.—The government of the Netherlands had at its disposal at the end of 1943 a total strength of 3 cruisers, 4 destroyers, 12 submarines, 3 sloops, 1 frigate, 1 corvette, 4 minelayers, 2 minesweepers, 10 torpedo boats (mostly of the modern motor type), a gunboat and a submarine chaser.

Norway retained under control of her government in London 4 destroyers, 2 large torpedo boats, 2 submarines, 4 corvettes, 8 patrol vessels, 8 motor torpedo boats, 4 motor launches, 1 submarine chaser and a number of small minesweepers.

The Danish fleet, with the exception of some small craft which had taken refuge in Swedish waters, was either under German control or lay scuttled in its home ports. Prior to Aug. 29, 1943, it had included 2 coast defense ships, 17 torpedo boats and 12 submarines. Two destroyers were nearing completion at Copenhagen.

Sweden for some years past had been carrying out a program of naval expansion. At the end of 1943 it possessed 2 cruisers, 7 coast defense ships, 24 destroyers and large torpedo boats, 26 submarines, 2 minelayers, 42 minesweepers, 17 motor torpedo boats, and a number of patrol vessels and fleet auxiliaries. Under construction were 2 cruisers, 2 destroyers and some smaller craft.

In the Finnish navy there remained a coast defense ship, 5 submarines, 10 coastal minelayers, 7 motor torpedo boats and some craft of less importance.

Poland had 1 cruiser, 6 destroyers, 5 submarines (3 of them interned), and 3 motor gunboats.

Spain could dispose of 6 cruisers, 16 destroyers, 8 submarines, 6 old torpedo boats, 6 minelayers and 2 sloops.

Portugal possessed 5 destroyers, 3 submarines, 1 large torpedo boat and 6 sloops.

Navies of the World as of December 1943

Country	Battleships and battle cruisers	Fleet aircraft carriers	Escort aircraft carriers	Cruisers	Coast defense ships	Destroyers and seagoing torpedo boats	Submarines
British Empire	15	8	25	64	4	320	80
U.S.A.	22	15	20	49	..	360	175
Japan	11	8	?	20(?)	5	100(?)	100(?)
Italy	5	..	..	9	..	50	30(?)
France	5	1	..	10	..	22	20(?)
Germany	3	1	..	6	2	40(?)	300(?)
Russia	3	..	..	7	..	90	200
Turkey	1	..	..	2	..	8	12
Spain	..	..	..	6	..	16	8
Sweden	..	..	..	2	7	24	26
Netherlands	..	..	..	3	..	4	12
Greece	..	..	..	1	..	11	2
Poland	..	..	..	1	..	6	5
Norway	..	..	..	..	..	4	2
Denmark	..	..	..	..	1	1	..
Finland	..	..	..	..	1	..	5
Portugal	..	..	..	..	..	5	3
Rumania	..	..	..	..	..	2	3
Yugoslavia	..	..	..	..	..	3	4
Argentina	2	..	..	3	4	15	3
Brazil	2	..	..	2	..	10	4
Chile	1	..	..	3	..	8	9
Peru	..	..	..	2	..	2	4
Colombia	..	..	..	..	..	2	..
Thailand	..	..	..	..	4	11	4

Owing to the war, figures relating to the first seven countries named above could not all be taken as exact. The navies of Denmark, Finland, Rumania, Yugoslavia and Thailand were under enemy control. Old torpedo boats no longer in seagoing condition, and motor torpedo boats (coastal craft) are not included in the above table. The two German "pocket battleships" are counted under the head of cruisers. French ships scuttled at Toulon have been omitted, for though they were lying in shallow water, they could not be made serviceable for a long time to come. This also applied to Danish ships scuttled in 1943. French, Italian, Norwegian, Danish and Yugoslav ships in enemy hands are not included in the figures for those countries. Russian figures have been estimated approximately in the absence of official information.

Turkey had an old battle cruiser, 8 destroyers, 12 submarines, old cruisers used for training, 5 minelayers and 3 motor torpedo boats.

In the royal Hellenic navy were 1 old cruiser, 11 destroyers, submarines, 4 corvettes, 1 submarine chaser and 3 old torpedo boats.

Rumania had 2 or 3 destroyers, 3 submarines, 1 minelayer, 1 motor torpedo boat and some old vessels of minor importance, all under German control. Bulgaria, also subservient to Germany, had 2 motor torpedo boats and some other small craft. In the Yugoslav fleet there were 3 destroyers, 4 submarines, 9 motor torpedo boats and sundry other ships of less importance. With the exception of one submarine operating with the Allies, all these were under Italian control up to Sept. 1943; some might since have fallen into Allied hands, while others might have been appropriated by the Germans.

South America.—In the Argentine navy at the end of 1943 were 2 old battleships, 3 cruisers, 15 destroyers, 3 submarines, 4 old coast defense ships, 14 minesweepers and some fleet auxiliaries. Two sloops under construction remained incomplete owing to non-delivery of their engines, ordered from Germany. In the Brazilian fleet there were 2 old battleships, 2 cruisers, 10 destroyers and seagoing torpedo boats, 4 submarines, 6 corvettes, 3 minelayers, 2 minesweepers and 11 submarine chasers. Six destroyers were under construction at Rio. Chile had 1 battleship, 3 cruisers, 8 destroyers, 9 submarines and 1 sloop.

Other South American navies possessed fleets of relatively small importance. Peru had 2 cruisers, 2 destroyers and 4 submarines. Colombia had 2 destroyers and 3 gunboats. Mexico's fleet comprised 5 sloops and some small patrol craft; Cuba had 2 sloops and some patrol vessels; Uruguay, 1 sloop and 3 patrol vessels; Venezuela, 4 gunboats; Ecuador, 3 or 4 patrol vessels; and Paraguay, 3 river gunboats. The Dominican Republic, Haiti and Nicaragua disposed respectively of 3, 2 and 1 patrol vessels.

Asia.—China lost the bulk of her navy in resisting Japanese aggression, but retained 12 small vessels, mostly river gunboats, of which 3 were presented by the British government and 1 by that of the United States. At Nanking was a quisling administration set up by the Japanese, which nominally disposed of 2 small cruisers, 1 sloop and 7 gunboats.

The Siamese navy—the term Thai, meaning free, can scarcely be applied to that country since it passed under Japanese domination—included 4 coast defense ships, 1 destroyer, 10 torpedo boats, 3 submarines, 2 sloops and 8 motor torpedo boats. Two cruisers ordered in Italy were never delivered, and were believed to remain incomplete. Manchuria, another Japanese vassal state, had an old destroyer and about 30 river patrol vessels. Persia, which under Riza was known as Iran, possessed 2 sloops and 4 gunboats, and Iraq 4 river patrol craft.   (F. E. McM.)

Navy, U.S. Department of: *see* GOVERNMENT DEPARTMENTS AND BUREAUS.

Nazis: *see* ANTI-SEMITISM; FASCISM; GERMANY.

N.E.A.: *see* NATIONAL EDUCATION ASSOCIATION.

Nebraska.
One of the states formed from the territory of the Louisiana Purchase, Nebraska lies in the lower Missouri valley in the west north central part of the United States; admitted to the union in 1867; land area, 76,653 sq.mi.; water area, 584 sq.mi.; pop. (1940) 1,315,834, a decrease of 62,129 from 1930; capital, Lincoln (81,984). In 1940, 39.1% of the population was urban. About 1% of the total population is Negro and about 8% foreign-born.

History.—Dwight Griswold, Republican, was re-elected governor of Nebraska Nov. 3, 1942, for the term 1943–45. Other state officers elected for 1943–45 were: lieutenant governor, Roy W. Johnson; auditor, Ray C. Johnson; secretary of state, Frank Marsh; treasurer, Carl G. Swanson; chief justice, Robert G. Simmons. Alone among the 48 states, Nebraska has a one-house legislature, the 43 members of which are chosen biennially on a non-partisan ballot.

Education.—Elementary and secondary education is largely under the control of local school districts, of which there were more than 7,000 in 1942, with but slight supervision by a state superintendent of public instruction. The total enrolment in elementary and secondary schools in 1942 was 257,664 and the teaching staff numbered 13,319. Expenditures amounted to $20,991,682.

Public Welfare, Charities, Correction.—The state appropriation for public assistance for 1943–45 was $23,765,490. In July 1943 the number of persons receiving general relief was 2,104 and the amount spent for the year ending June 30, 1943 was $837,557. At the same time, recipients of aid to dependent children numbered 8,204 and received during 1942–43, $1,660,228; 636 blind persons received $183,602. The state maintained 7 correctional institutions with a total of 1,097 inmates in June 1943 and 10 others for dependents with a population of 6,644; 3,278 inmates were on parole at the same date. The total appropriation for the 17 institutions for the period 1943–45 was $5,847,949.

Communication.—The total highway mileage of the state in 1943 was 100,987. Of this, 11,320 mi. had been designated as part of the state system of highways and 9,157 mi. had been marked and were maintained by the state. Of this latter figure, 3,984 mi. were hard surfaced, 4,915 gravelled and 258 of earth. State expenditures for highway purposes during 1941–43 amounted to $18,434,000 while the budget carried $10,447,250 for the biennium 1943–45. As of Nov. 1, 1942, there were 22 civil airports in the state, 20 of which were managed by municipalities, in addition to an undisclosed number of federally-maintained auxiliary landing fields. Total railway mileage in the state in 1943 was 8,457. Thirteen radio stations operated from points within the state in Nov. 1943, six of which were located in Omaha and Lincoln.

Banking and Finance.—State banks numbered 273, a decrease of six from 1942. Total assets in 1943 were $177,060,177. There were also 47 building and loan associations with assets of $57,914,372; and 175 co-operative credit associations with assets of $5,983,310. National banks at the same date numbered 132 with resources of $613,000,000.

The total assessed value of the state in 1943 was $2,123,882,890. The tax rate for state purposes was set at 2.48 mills, calculated to produce $5,059,841. Receipts for the biennium 1941–43 amounted to $82,538,264 including $18,179,140 of federal funds. Expenditures were $59,026,333. Total appropriations for 1943–45 were $54,257,727 including estimated federal funds of $15,191,571. There was no state tax on personal or corporate incomes or on sales. The state had no bonded debt, though that of the local subdivisions in 1943 amounted to $73,954,411. This figure did not include the indebtedness of the public power districts, which in 1943 amounted to more than $89,000,000.

Agriculture.—The total acreage harvested for the crops listed in Table I in 1943 was 15,624,000. In addition, an undetermined number of acres of wild hay was exploited. The total farm income in 1942 was $495,703,000, divided as follows: crops, $123,616,000; livestock, $335,648,000; government payments, $36,439,000. Agricultural income for the first half of 1943 was $307,825,000. A large annual deficiency in rainfall during the period 1931–41 was reflected in a sharp decline in the cash incomes of producers. Better growing conditions in 1942 and 1943 resulted in much larger yields.

Table I.—*Leading Agricultural Products of Nebraska, 1943 and 1942*

Crop	1943	1942
Corn, bu.	216,632,000	242,708,000
Wheat, bu.	61,285,000	69,908,000
Oats, bu.	71,676,000	58,278,000
Barley, bu.	27,918,000	38,258,000
Potatoes, bu.	12,090,000	12,876,000
Sugar beets, tons	568,000	930,000
Alfalfa hay, tons	1,343,000	1,593,000

Manufacturing.—The value of all manufactured products in 1939—the last year for which complete figures were available in 1943—was $273,524,500. In that year, 1,161 establishments employed 3,642 salaried persons and 18,810 wage earners and paid salaries and wages amounting to $28,135,500. World War II greatly increased manufacturing activity in the state, but no figures were available in 1943 as to the value of products or wages paid.

Table II.—*Principal Industries of Nebraska, 1939 and 1937*

Industry	Value of products	
	1939	1937
Meat packing.	$117,743,576	$112,708,382
Creamery butter	21,133,891	23,291,846
Flour and mill products	17,485,317	25,524,100
Poultry dressing and packing	8,807,209	5,949,969

Mineral Production.—The state has no mineral wealth of consequence. Petroleum was discovered late in 1939 and by Nov. 1943, 87 wells had produced about 4,000,000 bbl. This, however, is not a significant part of the national output.   (L. W. L.)

Necrology: *see* OBITUARIES.

Negroes (American).
Accelerated induction of Negroes into the armed forces during 1943 brought the Negro quota near to its population ratio; approximately 700,000 Negroes were in the army, of whom 5,000 were officers, including some 300 chaplains; 74,000 in the navy, 4 pursuit squadrons and 1 bomber fighter group in the air corps, and the 51st defense battalion in the marine corps. Integrated training was extended from officer-training centres to several army student training centres successfully, but in spite of continued public protests, the traditional policy of racial segregation was maintained elsewhere in the armed forces, resulting in sporadic disturbances in several of the camps in the U.S. and in England. The 99th pursuit squadron participated creditably in June in the North African campaign, in July in Sicily, and brigaded with the British 8th army took part in the Italian campaign. Its commanding officer, Col. B. O. Davis, Jr., relinquished command to Capt. Geo. Roberts, to return to the U.S. to take charge of the 332nd fighter group in training. Other combat units, like the 450th anti-aircraft artillery, saw action; others were ready for action—the 92nd and 93rd infantry divisions, the 795th tank destroyer battalion, the 931st field artillery battalion and the 349th coast artillery (AA); but public protests urged the increased employment of Negro soldiers in combat duty, although a number of quartermaster and transportation units served creditably in combat areas, with group and individual citations. In the merchant marine, integrated full quota employment continued successfully, with six Liberty ships, including the "Booker T. Washington," the "George Washington Carver," the "Frederick Douglass," and the "Paul Laurance Dunbar," named for outstanding Negroes, also the U.S. destroyer, "Leonard Harmon," named for a Negro cited for heroism in Pacific naval action.

Civil and Economic.—In war industry, increased pressure o[f] the Fair Employment Practices commission, twice reorganized an[d] implemented by another presidential order, No. 9346, raised th[e] Negro quota of employment in war industries from 5.8% to 7.3%[.] But upgrading and merited entry to skilled classifications were n[o]t proportional. There was considerable employer and union opposi[-] tion, notably, the citation of 21 railroads by the FEPC for discrim[-] inatory employment practices. Labour and residential friction als[o] resulted in a number of race riots, the most serious of which oc[-] curred in Mobile; Detroit; Beaumont, Texas; and a Negro protes[t] riot in New York city. Following these, there was marked effort t[o] reduce friction through the appointment in many states an[d] cities of bi-racial committees and inter-racial commissions. Th[e] war labour migration of Negroes was estimated at 800,000 an[d] the rough gain in new job employment at 500,000. Increased ten[-] sions, coupled with considerable constructive effort to adjus[t] them, carried race relations to a new prominence in public affair[s] and discussion. The anti-poll-tax fight, the Federal Education Ai[d] bill and the soldier vote legislation all pivoted critically on th[e] race issue. In politics, an increased number of Negro candidate[s] were successful in municipal and state elections, including th[e] re-election of a Negro to the New York city council, of Justic[e] Francis Rivers to the city court of New York. The America[n] Bar association revoked its colour bar by the election of Judg[e] James Watson to membership, and James W. Johnson was ap[-] pointed collector of internal revenue for the 3rd New York dis[-] trict. Truman Gibson Jr., succeeded William H. Hastie a[s] civilian aide to the secretary of war, upon the latter's protest res[-] ignation from that position over the continued segregation o[f] Negroes in the armed services. Hastie's protest was recognized b[y] the National Association for the Advancement of Coloured Peo[-]

RIOTERS dragging a Negro from a streetcar during the Detroit race riot of June 20–22, 1943

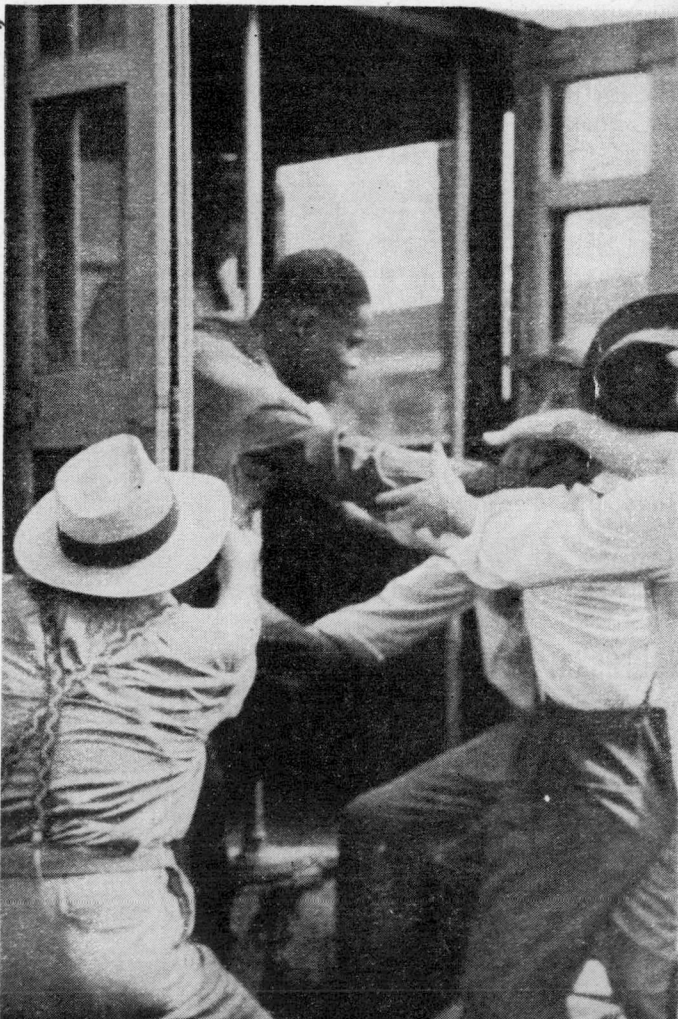

le's award of the Spingarn medal for 1943. State visits were made to the U.S. by the president and president elect of Liberia, nd by President Lescot of Haiti, both of which set favourable precedents.

Educational and Cultural.—The *Crisis* annual survey reorted 3,756 Negro college graduates, among them 3,185 from Negro schools with an enrolment of 27,273 students. Of these 58 received professional and higher degrees. Dr. W. E. B. DuBois, noted publicist and sociologist, was elected a member of he National Institute of Arts and Letters, the first Negro to be so chosen; and Marian Anderson, the singer, was awarded the Order of African Redemption by the Liberian government. Paul Robeson starred with sensational success in the role of Othello, produced on Broadway by Margaret Webster and the Theatre Guild. Roi Ottley's *New World A-Coming; Inside Black America*, won the $2,500 Houghton Mifflin Life in America series ward, and had an unusual best-seller circulation. (*See also* LYNCHINGS.)

BIBLIOGRAPHY.—Roi Ottley, *New World A-Coming;* Edwin Embree, *Brown Americans;* Chas. S. Johnson, *Patterns of Segregation;* Guy W. Johnon, *Race and Rumors of Race;* Bucklin Moon, *The Darker Brother;* Gunar Myrdal, *An American Dilemma: The Negro Problem and Modern Democracy;* John Lafarge, *Racial Justice;* Rackham Holt, *Geo. Washington Carver.* (A. LeR. L.)

Nehru, Jawaharlal

(1889–   ), Indian statesman, was born of wealthy parents and was educated in England at Harrow and Old Trinity college, Cambridge. Nehru learned to speak several Indian tongues fluently, and on his return to India he immediately took up the cause of Indian independence. He became a member of the All-India Congress committee in 1918, was arrested repeatedly for political offenses and was associated with the various civil disobedience movements in India after 1921. He was twice president of the Indian Congress party, 1929 and 1936, and was generally regarded as, next to Gandhi, the most important Indian leader. His autobiography, written in prison, was widely circulated in Great Britain and in the United States, where it was published under the title *Toward Freedom*. Nehru demanded for India, not dominion status, but complete independence. After the Japanese attack on Pearl Harbor, he came out for the Allied cause. He was nevertheless arrested and imprisoned, Aug. 9, 1942, along with Gandhi and a large group of Congress party leaders. William Phillips, special presidential envoy from the United States, tried to see him early in 1943, but was denied access. On April 22 a New Delhi federal court declared these political imprisonments without trial contrary to law. The British viceroy, however, overruled this court action. Nehru continued in prison, closely guarded, practically incommunicado.

Nelson, Donald Marr

(1888–   ), U.S. business executive, was born Nov. 17 at Hannibal, Mo., and was graduated from the University of Missouri in 1911. The next year he was employed by Sears Roebuck and company as a chemical engineer. In 1927 he was appointed general merchandise manager of the company, in 1930 vice president in charge of merchandising, and in 1939 executive vice president and chairman of the executive committee. He served with the National Defense Advisory commission in 1940, and as director of purchases for the Office of Production Management in 1941. On August 28 of that year, President Roosevelt named Nelson executive director of the Supply Priorities and Allocations board. This agency was supplanted on Jan. 13, 1942, by the War Production board, with Nelson as chairman, and with authority over the whole war procurement and production program. Nelson's position, therefore, became the counterpart of Bernard M. Baruch's in World War I. During the next two

years WPB had some difficulties, both with industry and with army and navy procurement agencies, but it maintained its dominant position. During 1942, as war production expanded and civilian production was curtailed, the problem of allocating materials became increasingly acute. A "controlled materials plan" was put into effect late in the year. On Nov. 11, Nelson named Ferdinand Eberstadt vice chairman of materials and Charles E. Wilson, former General Electric president, vice chairman of production. Friction developed. On Feb. 16, 1943, Nelson removed Eberstadt and concentrated the whole organization under Wilson as executive vice chairman. From then on affairs ran fairly smoothly. War production mounted steadily. By the end of 1943 the production battle was largely won. In late autumn Nelson visited Europe, where he conferred with Stalin and inspected Russian war plants. On Nov. 12, shortly after his return, Wilson resigned. Nelson accepted the resignation, but Pres. Roosevelt overruled him, and Wilson stayed on.

Nepal.

An independent kingdom (area *c.* 54,000 sq.mi., est. pop. 5,600,000) lying between India and Tibet—and including Mt. Everest—ruled in fact by the prime minister, Maharaja Joodha Shamsher Jung Bahadur Rana.

Substantial help to the British war fronts continued to be given by the Gurkha regiments of the Indian army, their experience being especially valuable in the dense jungles of the Assam-Burma border. General officer commanding the Nepalese contingents in India was General Krishna Shamshere Jung Bahadur Rana.

Nepal continued a brisk trade with India in 1943, exporting chiefly hides, jute, tobacco and timber, and importing cotton goods, salt and metals.

The British envoy, Lt.-Col. G. L. Betham, resided at the capital Khatmandu (pop. *c.* 80,000).

Nervous System.

Generally speaking the advances made in 1943, regarding the nervous system, were chiefly concerned with those problems found and met with in the prosecution of the war. These were:

Military Neuropsychiatry.—In the circular letter No. 176 released by the war department, psychiatric casualties in the combat zone fell into the following main groups: (1) Psychoneurosis under which are included anxiety, hysteria and psychasthenia; (2) psychoses; (3) psychopathic personality; (4) mental deficiency; (5) organic disease of the brain and spinal cord. In this letter the attention of all medical officers was invited to their responsibility for the mental as well as the physical health of the military personnel. Early recognition and treatment were stressed so that the individual could recover quickly whenever possible. Many involved persons recovered.

War Wounds of the Peripheral Nerves.—Most cut or injured nerves were treated surgically by uniting both cut ends by sutures. The injured limb was then immobilized so that the repaired nerve was not stretched. This method seemed to have produced the best results for nerve regeneration.

Treatment of Head Wounds Due to Missiles.—In a surgical division in the middle east an experience of two years in the treatment of missile wounds of the head revealed the following data: of 516 patients seen only 9% died while 71% returned to duty. A certain technique of surgical procedure resulted in a minimum amount of complications, infections and reduced time disability. The results were very gratifying.

BIBLIOGRAPHY.—The War Department, Washington, D.C., "Early Recognition and Treatment of Neuropsychiatric Conditions in the Combat Zone," Circular Letter No. 176; E. H. Parsons, "Military Neuropsychiatry in the Present War," *Ann. Int. Med.*, 18:935 (June 1943); Winchell M. Craig, "War Wounds of the Peripheral Nerves," *U.S. Naval M. Bull.*, 41:613 (May 1943); P. B. Ascroft, "Treatment of Head Wounds Due to Missiles,"

The Lancet, 245:211 (Aug. 21, 1943). (T. T. S.)

Netherlands.

A kingdom of northwest Europe. Bounded N. by the North sea, E. by Germany, S. by Belgium, and W. by the North sea. Occupied by German armed forces in May 1940. National flag, red, white and blue, in equal horizontal stripes. Area 13,440 sq.mi.; pop. (est. Dec. 7, 1941) 9,000,000. Chief towns (pop. Dec. 31, 1938): Amsterdam (cap. 793,526); Rotterdam (612,372); The Hague (pre-war seat of the government 495,518). Language: Dutch; religion: Christian (1930 census, Dutch Reformed Church 2,732,333; Roman Catholic, 2,890,022). Ruler: Queen Wilhelmina; president of the council of ministers, Prof. P. S. Gerbrandy.

History.—During the winter of 1942–43 the construction of defense works in the western part of the country, with the destruction of buildings and the evacuation of defense zones caused much hardship. The advertising of the East company continued; and subsidiary companies, for instance one for dredging and draining, were announced; but no more support was forthcoming than before. The main effort of the Germans was the forced deporting of labour. Shortly before the New Year it was announced that Mussert was to be leader of the Dutch people. A comprehensive decree on public order laid down the principles of a quasi-martial law which might be applied in an emergency. At the end of January Mussert announced the creation of a secretariat of state in which eight of his principal followers had functions in spheres of activity resembling those of government departments. This was not a puppet government, but an auxiliary machine to force the subjugation of the civil service, especially with a view to the deporting of labour. Professor Gerbrandy, the prime minister with the government in London, consequently broadcast an appeal to civil servants to resist the German measures. Popular indignation was expressed in attacks on the delegates. Within a few months of their appointment several of them were shot dead or died of wounds.

In the spring the Germans called up for labour all students except the small minority who signed a document of submission. On April 29 General Christiansen ordered all soldiers of the Netherlands army to report for re-internment as prisoners. The prime minister called upon them to disobey the order, which was furiously resented. A wave of strikes and sabotage spread through the whole country. Martial law was proclaimed and for a few days there was severe repression. After quiet had been restored, the Germans (as they had done earlier in Norway) forbade the use of wireless sets to any except their own supporters. In order to cut off listening to London they thus had to throw away the principal instrument of their own propaganda. In the summer a dispute with the medical profession marked the failure of the attempt to organize it on National Socialist principles. In September Roskam, the head of the agricultural organization, resigned, thus admitting his failure with the farmers. In October it was announced that the members of the N.S.B., the Dutch National Socialist party, who had hitherto been allowed to carry arms, were now to have arms issued to them. Terrorism thus worked towards a climax. On the other hand underground organizations flourished and there were many attacks on the N.S.B. besides acts of sabotage such as the destruction of registers needed for the labour call-up. Between July 1 and Oct. 6 the Germans announced 94 executions. (G. N. C.)

Education.—In 1938: elementary schools, 7,812; scholars, 1,242,778; secondary schools, 288; scholars, 62,301; high schools (1937–38), 4; scholars, 3,037; universities (1937–38), 6; scholars, 9,471.

Finance.—Revenue, ordinary (est. 1940) 741,096,000 florins; expenditure, ordinary (est. 1940), 740,548,189 florins; public debt (May 31, 1942) 7,449,000,000 florins; notes in circulation (Oct. 10, 1942), 2,724,143,000; gold reserve (Oct. 10, 1942) 917,809,474 florins; exchange rate (average 1940), 1 florin = 53.19 U.S. cents.

Trade and Communication.—Trade (merchandise) imports 1938: 1,414,768,000 florins; 1939: 1,516,651,000 florins; exports 1938: 4,039,156,000 florins; 1939: 966,215,000 florins. Communications and transport, 1938: roads, suitable for motor traffic 8,534 mi.; railways, open to traffic, 2,278 mi.; rivers and canals navigable, 4,817 mi.; airways, distance flown, 6,629,000 mi.; shipping (June 30), 2,855,400 gross tons; launched (July 1938–June 1939), 246,400 gross tons; entered with cargoes, 27,606,524 net tons; cleared with cargoes, 23,151,428 net tons. Motor vehicles licensed (Aug. 1, 1938): cars, 94,000; buses, 4,088; trucks, 50,988; cycles, 55,140; wireless (June 30, 1939): registered receiving sets, 839,542; connections with radio-distributing systems, 368,710.

Agriculture, Manufactures, Mineral Production.—In metric tons (1939 actual figures): wheat, 416,523; rye, 603,532; barley, 146,041; oats, 449,241; pulse, 185,891; sugar beet, 1,716,052; flax, 152,487; cotton goods (1938), 136,565,000 guilders; machinery (1938), 99,821,000 guilders; coal, 12,861,000; salt, 199,800; pig iron and ferro-alloys (1938), 276,600; zinc, 20,500. (*See* also CURAÇAO; NETHERLANDS COLONIAL EMPIRE; NETHERLANDS INDIES; SURINAM.)

Netherlands Colonial Empire.

Total area excluding mother country (approx.) 789,700 sq.mi.; total pop. excluding Netherlands (est. Dec. 31, 1940) 70,760,000.

The table on p. 493 lists the colonial possessions of the Netherlands, together with statistics appropriate to each of them.

History.—During 1943 considerable progress was made in economic reconstruction and organizing the war effort in the part of Dutch New Guinea still in Dutch control. Civilian conscription and training schemes were introduced; and the various races of the island, including the Papuans, showed a gratifying spirit of co-operation. Authentic news from the great areas of the Netherlands Indies occupied by the Japanese was scanty. Economic conditions were certainly bad. There were shortages of food and clothing and much unemployment. Rice was rationed; but, by pressing for the growing of war materials such as cotton instead of food crops, the Japanese made the situation still worse. Their attempts to win over the peoples to voluntary collaboration were unsuccessful. It appears, for instance, that only 39 British Indians enlisted in Chandra Bose's "Independence army." Soekarno, whom the Japanese appointed "Leader" of the occupied territories, set up a number of bodies such as a defense corps and a women's defense corps in which his followers were enrolled.

A pretense was made of granting self-government to the Indonesians. An advisory council for Java was set up, of which all the members were Indonesians, together with 7 provincial councils and one for Batavia; but 23 of the 43 members of the council for Java were nominated, while the 18 elected members were elected only by the provincial councils of which, in turn, half the members were nominated. In October an industrial council was established with the object of co-ordinating industry for the purposes of the Japanese in the war. About the same time another measure was taken which indicated greater pressure on manpower: all Indo-Europeans were ordered to register. Javanese labour was deported for mine work in Borneo.

The Japanese appear to have been disappointed with the results of their efforts. They seem to have obtained no appreciable quantity of oil. Early in the year they strengthened their control by adding civilian administrators to their naval and military

Overseas Territories of the Netherlands and Essential Statistics

Country and Area, sq. miles (approx.)		Population est. Dec. 31, 1940 (000's omitted)	Capital	Status	Governors, Premiers, etc.
ASIA					
NETHERLANDS INDIES, including Java and Madura, Sumatra, Celebes, Borneo (D.), New Guinea (D.), Timor (D.), etc.	735,300	70,476	Batavia	colony	Under Japanese occupation, 1943
AMERICA					
CURAÇAO	403	106	Willemstad	colony	*Governor:* Dr. P. A. Kasteel
SURINAM (Dutch Guiana), etc. . . .	54,000	178	Paramaribo	colony	*Governor:* Dr. J. C. Kielstra

headquarters, and there were some executions. In July Premier Hideki Tojo paid a two-day visit to Java. The administration continued to be under the Great Asian Affairs department of Aoki. Throughout the year the Netherlands West Indies co-operated smoothly in the United Nations war effort.

(*See also* CURAÇAO; NETHERLANDS INDIES; SURINAM; WORLD WAR II.)   (G. N. C.)

Netherlands Indies.

This, the largest Netherlands colonial possession, was in 1943, and had been since March 1942, under Japanese military occupation (except for part of New Guinea). The Netherlands Indies is a huge archipelago, with several very large islands, Java, Sumatra, Celebes, Borneo and New Guinea (part of Borneo is British and the eastern half of New Guinea is under Australian administration), and many smaller ones. The archipelago is located between 6° N. and 10° S. latitude and the climate is tropical. Area, 733,681 sq.mi.; pop. (census of 1930) 60,727,233; (est. 1940) 70,476,000, of whom 48,416,000 lived in densely settled Java and the adjacent small island of Madura, while 22,060,000 lived in the so-called Outer Islands, the less settled and developed regions of the archipelago. Capital, Batavia (437,000). Other large cities: Surabaya (313,000); Bandung (167,000). The great majority of the natives are Moslems, although an admixture of Hindu and pagan practices is found in some regions. There are about 2,500,000 Christians, about 1,000,000 Buddhists and a number of Animists. Governor general (appointed in 1936) until the Japanese occupation: Jonkheer A. W. L. Tjarda van Starkenborgh-Stachouwer.

History.—Except for occasional air raids on outlying stations, the Japanese occupation was not disturbed during 1943. The objectives of the occupation authorities were apparently to create a semblance of political support among the natives, to Japanize the administration and the educational system, to bring in Japanese banks to assist in financing operations, to make the economy more self-sufficient and to make preparations for possible United Nations attacks, especially in Sumatra, exposed to air and naval offensives launched from India.

Telephone conversations in Java were permitted only in Japanese or Malay, Dutch and English being barred. Japanese language schools with six-year courses were started for Indonesian children in April 1943. Radio telephone service between Macassar, on the island of Celebes, and Tokyo was opened on Feb. 1. The streets of Macassar were given Japanese instead of Dutch names.

Japan announced a program of "autonomy" for the Netherlands Indies in August 1943. Its main feature was the establishment of "a central council which will have the right to advise and submit proposals connected with administrative affairs to the Japanese military authorities." Elections for regional and municipal councils of the same type were held in September.

Japanese broadcasts in Oct. 1943 indicated that Indonesians were being urged to join a "defense corps" that would relieve the

Japanese army of police duties. There were attempts to recruit Indonesian labour on a large scale for shipbuilding in Batavia and for the repairing of roads and other transportation facilities in Sumatra. The Japanese slogan of "co-prosperity" was at least temporarily shelved in favour of self-sufficiency, because shipping difficulties prevented a normal exchange of goods among the far-flung territories of Japan's newly conquered empire. In normal times the Netherlands Indies had exchanged large surpluses of such raw materials as rubber, tin, tobacco, coffee, quinine, etc. for manufactured goods from abroad. In 1943 the Japanese apparently found the surplus stocks of rubber and tobacco an embarrassment and tried to put the archipelago on a more self-sufficient basis by substituting rice for rubber and some other export crops in some cases. There was also a shortage of new clothing, because of the lack of cotton and the inability of the Japanese to bring in textile goods from Japan in any large quantity.

The Netherlands Indies authorities established a school for civil servants in Melbourne, Australia, under the direction of Prof. Frederik David Holleman, in July 1943. The minimum training course was six months; the subjects taught included Malay language and dialects, Islamic institutions and Malay social institutions and traditions. The purpose of the school was to train civilian administrators qualified to take over after Allied reoccupation of the Indies. A commission, appointed by the governor general before the Japanese invasion, and headed by F. H. Visman, was working on constitutional projects which would make the Netherlands Indies in the future more independent of direct control from the Netherlands and would broaden the previous suffrage qualifications, although the Netherlands Indies still was considered an inseparable part of the Netherlands empire.

Education.—In Aug. 1943 there were 12,000 elementary schools in the Netherlands Indies, with 1,900,000 pupils, besides 32 secondary schools, five high schools, 20 vocational schools, one agricultural college, 7 fine-art schools for girls, one normal college, one medical college and one technical college, according to a statement of the Japanese Domei News agency. Dutch sources asserted that under the Netherlands administration there were more than 20,000 native schools with over 2,500,000 pupils, besides 628 western schools, with 150,000 pupils; 7.2% of the population was literate in 1930.

Finance.—The Japanese yen was introduced as the currency of the Indies during 1943 and was given an arbitrary value of parity with the Dutch guilder, the former unit of currency. (Formerly the yen had been worth .44 guilders.) The Java bank, which had formerly controlled the note issue, and all other Dutch financial institutions were liquidated. The Bank of Japan, the Yokohama Specie bank, the Bank of Taiwan and the Mitsubishi bank began to operate in the Netherlands Indies. The last Dutch budget, of 1942, called for revenue of 750,918,773 guilders and expenditures of 813,802,815 guilders.

Trade and Communication.—Imports in 1940 were 444,300,000 guilders (value of the guilder 53 U.S. cents); exports were 873,500,000 guilders. The principal exports in 1940 were rubber (328,254,000 guilders), oil and petroleum products (169,577,000 guilders), tin and tin ore (72,218,000 guilders), sugar (52,041,000 guilders), tea (50,925,000 guilders).

There were, in 1940, 43,450 mi. of highways and 4,620 mi. of railways, 3,387 in Java, 1,233 in Sumatra. There were 94,000 motor vehicles of all types in 1941; 10,870 steamers, with a total tonnage of 12,456,664, cleared irom tne ports of the colony in 1939. The Royal Netherlands Airways was formerly one of the main lines of air communication between Europe and the orient.

Agriculture.—Figures of production for some of the principal crops, in 1940, were as follows: sugar, 1,587,364 tons; rubber, 546,021 tons; palm oil, 241,702 tons; tea, 81,986 tons; coffee, 77,647 tons; tobacco, 27,414 tons; quinine, 16,371 tons; cocoa, 1,553 tons.

Manufacturing and Mineral Production.—Although the Netherlands Indies had always been primarily a source of raw materials, local industries were encouraged during the '30s and gained stimulus when the outbreak of World War II in 1939 cut off or curtailed the supply of imported manufactures. Among these local industries were batik, spinning and weaving, tobacco, ceramics, paint, soap, chemicals, cement, wood, glass and paper. Figures of output for the principal mineral products in 1939 were as follows: oil, 7,949,000 tons; tin, 31,000 tons; coal, 1,781,000 tons; gold, 2,500 tons; silver, 19,200 tons. The Japanese made special efforts to restore oil production, in view of the deficiency of this vital fuel in Japan. (*See* also JAPAN; NETHERLANDS COLONIAL EMPIRE.) (W. H. CH.)

Neutrality: *see* INTERNATIONAL LAW.

Nevada.
A far western state of the U.S., admitted to the union Oct. 31, 1864. Popular name is the "Sagebrush" state. Area 110,540 sq.mi., including 738 sq.mi. of water. Pop. (1940) 110,247. The population in 1943 was estimated at 141,813, the increase being due to the establishment of wartime industries in Mineral and Clark counties. Of the population 39.3% were urban; 93,431 were native white; only 10,599 were foreign-born white. Capital, Carson City (2,478); other cities: Reno (21,317); Las Vegas (8,422); Sparks (5,318).

History.—The forty-first session of the legislature in 1943 was featured by legislation retiring all outstanding bonds and the creation of a million dollar postwar fund. Other acts passed by the legislature in 1943 included the following: the Flight Strip act, authorizing the department of highways to co-operate with the Public Roads administration of the U.S. in the construction and maintenance of flight strips and of certain classes of highways; the Nevada State Police act, which provided for the creation and organization of a Nevada state police force consisting of one inspector, 3 sergeants, 5 subordinate police officers and 250 reserves.

In 1943 the elected officers of the state were: governor, E. P. Carville; lieutenant governor, Vail Pittman; secretary of state, Malcolm McEachin; attorney general, Alan H. Bible; state treasurer, Dan W. Franks; state controller, Henry C. Schmidt; superintendent of public instruction, Mildred Bray. Chief Justice of the state was William E. Orr.

Education.—In 1943 there were 210 elementary schools with a total enrolment of 19,367 pupils, staffed by 696 teachers. On Jan. 1, 1944 there were 46 high schools with a total enrolment of 6,237 pupils, staffed by 299 teachers. On Jan. 1, 1944 the total school enrolment was 26,866, including 1,262 kindergarten pupils.

Public Welfare, Charities, Correction.—The amount spent for social security and old-age assistance was $843,151.17. For the year ending Dec. 31, 1943, the state spent $39,520.00 for unemployment compensation. On Jan. 1, 1944 the state prison had 241 inmates, 4 of whom were women; total expenditures of the fiscal year ending June 30, 1943, were $97,002.27. The state industrial home had 50 inmates; expenditures $20,761.26; the state hospital for mental diseases had 344; expenditures were $99,968.92; the orphans' home had 45 inmates on Jan. 1, 1944, and expended $37,239.86 during the fiscal year.

Communication.—There were 5,518 mi. of roads in the state-designated highway system in 1943, 3,064 of which were hard-surfaced and approximately 2,500 improved but not paved. On Jan. 1, 1944, there were 11 standard airports reservations.

Banking and Finance.—On. Jan. 1, 1944, there were four state banks. The Nevada Bank of Commerce at Elko had in addition two branches; total deposits as of Oct. 1943 were $11,825,089.63, total resources $12,619,700.21. The First National Bank of Nevada had nine branches, with total deposits as of Jan. 12, 1944, of $74,812,126.54 and total resources of $78,083,814.85; the Ely National bank with one branch had total deposits as of Oct. 1943 of $73,119,157.82 and total resources of $77,707,-771.72. State receipts for the year ending June 30, 1943, were $8,082,529.74, and expenditures $6,934.915.92. On Jan. 10, 1944, the cash balance was $2,685,898.05. The postwar fund totalled $1,092,000.00, and Nevada's assessed valuation for 1943 was $241,094,990, an increase of $19,862,458 over 1942. Nevada had no state debt in 1943.

Agriculture.—Nevada's wartime agricultural production for 1943 exceeded the five-year average annual production for 1937–1941. On this comparative basis the wheat acreage showed an increase of 11%; corn acreage an increase of 33%; acreage in oats an increase of 50%; acreage in barley an increase of 67%; acreage in potatoes an increase of 100%. Crops harvested in 1943 were valued at approximately $12,990,000 as compared with $9,500,000 in 1942.

Table I.—*Leading Agricultural Products of Nevada, 1943 and 1942*

Crop	1943 (est.)	1942
Barley, bu.	984,000	828,000
Potatoes, bu.	585,000	403,000
Hay, tons	603,000	636,000
Oats, bu.	320,000	320,000
Wheat, bu.	548,000	484,000

The state's barley production was by far the heaviest crop ever produced in the state; the production of potatoes was the largest since 1930. Marketing of surplus cattle greatly increased in 1943, and the condition of the state's herds of cattle was reported by the U.S. department of agriculture as well above the average for the preceding 10-year period. Above-normal precipitation was enjoyed during the year 1943 on most of the Nevada range.

Manufacturing.—The total value of manufactures in 1941 was $20,582,000. The number of employees was 1,093 and the total wages paid was $1,000,642. The number of manufacturing establishments was 105 and the principal manufactures were printing products; brick, clay and iron and steel products; and automobile parts.

Mineral Production.—The total value of gold, silver, copper, lead and zinc production in 1943, as reported by the U.S. bureau of mines, was $27,770,047. Gold, silver, lead and copper decreased, zinc alone showing a large increase.

Table II.—*Principal Mineral Products of Nevada, 1943 and 1942*

Mineral	Value, 1943	Value, 1942
Gold	$4,830,000	$10,328,920
Silver	1,105,777	2,647,776
Copper	18,083,000	20,246,446
Lead	708,180	720,384
Zinc	3,043,090	1,896,642
Totals	$27,770,047	$35,840,168

Nevada produced magnesium in substantial amount. An increase in the production of tungsten, mercury and vanadium was noted. Tin was produced in small quantities. Gypsum, fluorspar and coal developments created interest. Gem-stone production increased, with turquoise in active demand. (E. C. D. M.)

New Brunswick.
One of the three maritime provinces of the dominion of Canada (*q.v.*), admitted to the union in 1867; area 27,985 sq.mi.; pop. (1941) 457,401, of whom 97% were native born. Capital, Fredericton (10,062). Other cities are Saint John (51,741) and Moncton (22,763). The lieutenant governor in 1943 was W. G. Clark and the premier was J. B. McNair.

Education.—The number of students in provincially controlled public schools in 1942 was 96,470; in private schools, 3,015; in institutions of university standard, 1,297.

Communication.—The mileage of surfaced highways in 1942 was 8,455; earth highways 3,840; provincial expenditure on highways, $1,193,404. The railroad mileage was 1,848 in 1942; the number of telephones, 35,798.

Finance.—The ordinary receipts in 1942 were $12,459,611; expenditure, $11,921,467. The direct debt (less sinking funds) was $97,043,223; indirect liabilities (less sinking funds) $2,741,509.

Agriculture.—The acreage of field crops in 1943 was 922,700; gross values of field products, $28,497,000.

Leading Agricultural Products of New Brunswick, 1942 and 1941

Crop	1942	1941
Oats, bu.	6,895,000	5,983,000
Potatoes, cwt.	6,818,000	5,736,000
Turnips, cwt.	3,157,000	3,634,000
Hay and clover, tons	970,000	880,000

Manufacturing.—The gross value of manufactured products in 1940 was $89,281,008; net value, $38,253,475; number of employees, 16,859; salaries and wages, $17,639,789. (J. C. HE.)

New Caledonia: see FRENCH COLONIAL EMPIRE.
New Deal: see UNITED STATES.

Newfoundland and Labrador.
A British colony of North America, with suspended constitution. Area: Newfoundland 42,000 sq.mi.; Labrador 110,000 sq.mi.; total 152,000 sq.mi.; pop. (est. Dec. 31, 1938): Newfoundland, 290,660; Labrador, 4,780. Chief town and capital: St. John's (pop. 1941: 39,886). Governor (1943): Sir Humphrey Walwyn; language: English; religion (1935 census): Roman Catholic, 93,925; Church of England, 92,732; United Church, 76,100; Salvation Army, 18,054.

History.—Work on defense projects undertaken by the U.S. and Canadian armed forces continued to bring unprecedented prosperity to Newfoundland in 1943 and almost doubled the national income. A wartime boom in the fishing industry also helped to solve the unemployment problem, and, apart from a temporary stoppage in one of the mining operations, due to a shortage of shipping, there was no able-bodied relief throughout the year. Moreover there were more than 10,000 men serving abroad, and one Newfoundland regiment was in action in Tunisia.

Higher wages and the danger of a considerable shortage of essential supplies set the cost of living rising, and steps to deal with this were announced by the public welfare commissioner on Feb. 15, including the removal of the import duty on potatoes, remission of the $7\frac{1}{2}$% war import duty on about 80 essential foodstuffs and other commodities such as medical supplies and fishing equipment, and fixing the price of tea and molasses (both rationed). Coal rationing was also imposed on Feb. 10.

A revenue surplus of $3,681,650 was announced in the budget speech of April 27; owing to the alteration of the financial year to end on March 31, the period under review was one of nine months only. From the previous three years' surpluses interest-free loans of some $6,500,000 had been made to Britain for the duration of the war, in addition to $1,200,000 from the sale of savings certificates.

Considerable dissatisfaction was felt during the year with the commission government, and on March 8 the board of trade passed resolutions protesting against the new income and profits tax proposals and demanding a return to some form of representative government. A petition, backed by many sections of the community, was later sent to the king, requesting the appointment of a royal commission to inquire into the island's constitutional and financial position. The dominions secretary stated in parliament on June 10, however, that, during his visit to Newfoundland in 1942, he had found that the main body of opinion there considered it inexpedient to carry out constitutional changes in wartime. (C. M. CL.)

Education.—In 1940: schools 1,898; scholars on rolls 66,508; average attendance 70.2%.

Banking and Finance.—Revenue, est. (1942–43) $18,744,100; expenditure, est. (1942–43) $17,722,300; public debt (June 30, 1941) $2,412,773 and £19,980,012; notes in circulation (June 30, 1941) $13,535; exchange rate as Canadian dollar.

Trade and Communication.—Overseas trade 1940–41 (merchandise) imports $35,484,323; exports $36,723,352; re-exports $606,463. Communications (Dec. 31, 1938): roads, main 1,150 mi.; secondary and local 6,000 mi.; railways, open to traffic 747 mi.; motor vehicles licensed (1940) 10,588.

Mineral Production and Fisheries.—Fisheries 1940: cod (inshore, deep sea and Labrador) 87,549 metric tons; seal $205,030; salmon (export) 3,750,336 lb.; lobster (export) 2,477,289 lb.; fish oils (export) 1,826,377 lb. In metric tons (1940): wood pulp (1938) 242,000; iron ore (metal content) 797,000; lead ore (metal content) 25,500; silver 46.5; gold 678 kg.

New Guinea.
One of the largest islands in the world, with an estimated area of 312,329 sq.mi., stretching from the equator in the N.W. to 12° 5′ S. in the S.E. and from 130° 50′ E. to 151° 30′ E., separated from Australia by the shallow Torres strait and Arafura sea. On its eastern side lies the Bismarck archipelago.

New Guinea is divided between three administrations: (1) Dutch New Guinea, area 151,789 sq.mi.; pop. (est.) 195,460, of whom 237 were Europeans (1940) (*see* NETHERLANDS INDIES). (2) British New Guinea (Territory of Papua), area 90,540 sq.mi., pop. 338,822 (1940) is under the governor-general of Australia, with a lieutenant governor of its own and a centre of administration at Port Moresby. It comprises roughly the southeastern corner of the island and is an exporter of rubber and copra, while copper is mined in the vicinity of Port Moresby. (3) Northeastern New Guinea and the adjacent islands of the Bismarck archipelago, including Bougainville and Buka in the northern Solomons, were German colonial possessions before World War I. After Dec. 17, 1920, this area was administered by Australia under a mandate from the League of Nations. Area 93,000 sq.mi.; pop. (1940) 668,871 natives, besides an unknown number in the unexplored interior; 6,498 non-natives, including 3,345 British, 2,061 Chinese, 430 Germans, 159 Dutch, 145 Americans, 38 Japanese. Administrator of the mandated territory in 1943 was Brig. Gen. Sir Walter Ramsay McNicoll (appointed Sept. 13, 1934). The headquarters of the administration are normally at Rabaul.

History.—In the course of their invasion of the South Pacific the Japanese occupied all the foreign settlements in the mandated territory and established their main advanced base in the South Pacific at Rabaul, where the Germans had formerly de-

Above: U.S. PARACHUTE ATTACK in Japanese-held Markham valley of New Guinea Sept. 5, 1943, shielded by a smoke screen (background). In this official air force photograph, scores of paratroopers are shown jumping at low altitude from C-53 transport planes, at the height of the attack

Right: CAT NAPPING U.S. SOLDIERS near the front line at Buna mission before their capture of the Buna area early in 1943

Below, left: AUSTRALIANS entering a U.S. "LST" (landing ship—tank) for transport to Lae, New Guinea, where they landed Sept. 4, 1943

Below, right: U.S. SOLDIERS BATHING in water-filled shell holes at Buna mission a few hours after capturing this Japanese stronghold in New Guinea in the first week of Jan. 1943

veloped a good harbour, on New Britain Island. At the high tide of the Japanese advance in this area, in the autumn of 1942, their troops crossed the high Owen Stanley range, which cuts across New Guinea in a northwestern-southeastern direction, and threatened Port Moresby, the last important United Nations base north of Australia. However, U.S. and Australian troops under the command of Gen. Douglas MacArthur checked this advance and, making skilful use of airborne troops, took the offensive in turn, driving the Japanese in 1943 from such bases as Lae, Salamaua and Fischhafen and, toward the end of the year, effecting a double landing on New Britain with the apparent purpose of pressing on toward Rabaul, which was threatened from another direction by landings of U.S. forces under the command of Adm. William F. Halsey on Bougainville, in the northern Solomons.

Agriculture, Mineral Production, Trade.—As might be inferred from the small number of foreign residents, economic development has been slight. The total area under cultivation in 1940 was 276,000 ac., although it is estimated that the mandated territory contains about 34,200,000 ac. of land suitable for cultivation. Much the greatest part of the cultivated area was under coco-nut plantations and copra was the main product and export. The territory produced 73,716 tons of copra, of a value of £A.847,734 in 1938. Secondary crops, the output of which is of minor importance, are cocoa, coffee, rubber, kapok and tobacco. Gold, silver and platinum are mined, the first being the most important mineral product. The foreign trade of the mandated territory was £A.1,610,967 in imports, £A.2,980,360 in exports in 1938.

Social and Economic Changes.—Although New Guinea may still be considered one of the most remote parts of the world, the total isolation from foreign contacts in which most of the natives lived in the past began to break down under such varied pressures as the activity of the missions, the increasing area patrolled by government officials and the growing demand for native labour on the plantations. There were ten missions (three Roman Catholic, three Lutheran, two Methodist, one Anglican, one Seventh Day Adventist), with a combined staff of more than 600, in New Guinea in 1938. There were 41,849 natives in indentured service in 1938, 20,855 on plantations, 7,189 on mines, 7,511 in shipping, commerce and industry, 4,477 in domestic service, 1,747 in administration service and 70 in miscellaneous occupations. There were also 883 native members of the police force. World War II brought further changes and upheavals to this remote region; and the primitive Melanesian natives were used as bearers and for labour service by both sides. (*See* also WORLD WAR II.)   (W. H. CH.)

New Hampshire.
One of the New England group of states and one of the original states of the union, popularly known as the "Granite state"; area, 9,304 sq.mi., including 9,024 sq.mi. of land and 280 sq.mi. of water; population (1940) 491,524. Of the total population, 283,225 or 57.6% were urban and 208,299 rural. Total estimated civilian population Mar. 1, 1943, was 454,490. In 1940 there were 490,989 whites, including 422,693 native and 68,296 foreign-born. Capital, Concord (27,171). Other cities: Manchester (77,685), Nashua (32,927), Berlin (19,084), Dover (14,990), and Portsmouth (14,821).

History.—The general court was in session from Jan. 6 to May 20, 1943. Measures passed included an act granting broad emergency war powers to the governor and council; an act creating a state veterans council, to aid returning soldiers and to ensure them preference in public employment; and an act providing for a soldiers' bonus, to be paid any resident of the state serving more than 90 days in the armed forces, such bonus

to amount to $10 a month for each month of service, the total not to exceed $100. To finance bonus payments, the existing poll tax was increased by $3.

State officers in 1943 were governor, Robert O. Blood; secretary of state, Enoch D. Fuller; state treasurer, F. Gordon Kimball; commissary general, Charles F. Bowen; and acting attorney general, Stephen M. Wheeler, all Republican.

Education.—In 1942-43, there were 1,812 public schools, classified as follows: kindergartens 46; mixed schools 273; classified schools 1,311; junior high schools 44; senior high schools 95; opportunity schools 15; evening schools 28. The total number of elementary pupils was 50,241, with 2,114 teachers; the number of high school pupils 19,537, with 1,006 teachers. Total payments for public education during the year ending June 30, 1943, were $7,650,635. Owing to the loss of several hundred teachers because of war conditions, a critical shortage developed during the course of the year 1942-43.

Public Welfare, Charities, Correction.—The burden of general relief showed a continued downward trend during 1943 because of increased opportunities for employment. In Sept., 1942, there were 4,259 cases on general relief, with an expenditure of $107,112, as compared with only 3,059 cases in Sept. 1943, with an expenditure of $84,449. Expenditures for public assistance under the Social Security act continued to increase, the total for Sept. 1943 being $241,322, as compared with $224,087 for Sept. 1942. By far the greatest part of this increase was in the category of old-age assistance, aid to dependent children and needy blind showing little change.

On Jan. 1, 1940, there were 259 persons in prison and reformatory in New Hampshire. The appropriation for the state prison at Concord for the fiscal year 1943-44 was $182,791; and for the Industrial School for Committed Minors at Manchester, $93,555.

Communication.—Rural highways and urban extensions amounted to 3,635 mi. at the close of 1940. State highway funds disbursed in 1941 totalled $8,743,000. In 1940 there were 1,002 mi. of steam railroads in the state.

Banking and Finance.—As of June 30, 1943, there were in New Hampshire 52 national banks with deposits of $118,217,000 and resources of $133,888,000, as compared with deposits and resources, respectively, on June 30, 1942, of $93,734,000 and $108,971,000. Fifty-five state-chartered banks reported deposits of $229,263,187.48 and resources of $257,217,137.66. There were 25 building and loan associations with total resources of $13,980,-803.90. Forty-three savings banks and savings departments of eight trust companies reported deposits of $220,086,300.91 as of June 30, 1943.

Cash receipts of the state treasury department for the fiscal year ending June 30, 1943, $25,862,337.04; cash disbursements, $26,114,254.01; cash balance, June 30, 1943, $5,151,940.36. Gross fixed bond and note debt, June 30, 1943, $14,135,000; net fixed bond and note indebtedness, $11,543,408.25. Average property tax rate for 1943 was $30.30 per $1,000 of assessed valuation.

Agriculture.—The principal crops showed declines in yields in 1943, with the exception of potatoes and corn, as shown in the table.

Manufacturing.—Total estimated value of manufactures in

Leading Agricultural Products of New Hampshire, 1943 and 1942

Crop	1943 (est.)	1942
Corn, bu.	630,000	630,000
Oats, bu.	266,000	273,000
Tame hay, tons	413,000	425,000
Potatoes, bu.	1,402,000	1,088,000
Apples, bu.	778,000	961,000
Maple sugar, lb.	...	44,000 (est.)
Maple syrup, gal.	...	66,000 (est.)

1939, last federal biennial census before World War II, was $237,396,015. Salaried personnel, including officers and employees, 4,593; salaries, $10,483,983; wage earners 55,781; wages paid $52,735,240. War industries led to rapid population increases in some communities, Portsmouth, Somersworth, Laconia and Claremont having been particularly affected.

Mineral Production.—Total value of minerals produced in 1940 was $1,065,000 (estimated). Mica mining on a substantial scale was resumed in New Hampshire in 1942, to help in meeting war requirements.   (W. E. Ss.)

New Hebrides: *see* PACIFIC ISLANDS, BRITISH; FRENCH COLONIAL EMPIRE.

New Jersey. Sometimes called the "Garden state," New Jersey is one of the three middle Atlantic states. Area, 7,836 sq.mi., including 314 sq.mi. of water; pop. (1940) 4,160,165. Capital, Trenton (124,697). The largest city is Newark (429,760); second is Jersey City (301,173).

History.—The elections of 1943 completed the Republican conquest of major elective offices in New Jersey. Walter E. Edge was elected to the governorship by a majority of 127,000 over Mayor Vincent J. Murphy of Newark, the Democratic nominee. The Republicans retained control of the legislature by overwhelming majorities in both branches, the assembly standing 44 Republicans to 16 Democrats and the senate 18 Republicans to three Democrats. In December the death of United States Senator W. Warren Barbour left the Democrats in possession of this office by virtue of the appointment by Governor Edison of Arthur Walsh of South Orange to the vacancy. The 1943 elections also marked the first concrete step toward the adoption of a new constitution for which an intermittent fight had been waged since the governorship of Woodrow Wilson. A referendum was adopted by a majority of 154,000, directing the 1944 legislature to write a new constitution, retaining the state bill of rights, for ratification or rejection at the 1944 general election. The referendum was opposed by Mayor Frank Hague of Jersey City, Democratic state leader, and by rural politicians on the ground that no change in the constitution should be ordained until the war was over. The gubernatorial and legislative campaigns found the Democratic party weakened by the Edison-Hague feud. Mayor Hague had tried without success to persuade A. Harry Moore, three-time governor, to run again as the Democratic nominee. Three weeks before the deadline for filing nominating petitions, Mayor Hague turned to Mayor Murphy and agreed to support him. Governor Edison did likewise. Mayor Murphy was supported also by the C.I.O. and the leaders of the railway unions. Edge, backed by a united party which averted a primary contest for the nomination, carried 18 of 21 counties. Mayor Murphy won only in Camden, Middlesex and Hudson, the home of the Hague organization, and by reduced majorities.

During 1943 the validity of the railroad tax legislation, which had brought the Edison-Hague break into the open, was attacked in the court of chancery, and Vice Chancellor Wilfred H. Jayne ruled that it was unconstitutional because it remitted interest amounting to more than $20,000,000. The case against the railroad legislation was prosecuted by Attorney General Wilentz and was defended by special counsel authorized by the legislature to act for the state treasurer. An appeal from the chancery decision was taken immediately to the court of errors and appeals.

Education.—For the fiscal year 1941–42, total enrolment of day students in public schools was 719,623, a decrease of 13,326. Teachers numbered 29,513. Total salaries were $61,673,907, averaging $2,123 a year. Total school buildings numbered 2,090.

WALTER E. EDGE, Republican, was elected governor of New Jersey Nov. 2, 1943

There were 19,345 adult given instruction in various war training programs by 451 teachers Total cost of the public school system was $108,607,744.

Public Welfare, Charities, Correction —Direct relief commitments by the state to municipal governments for the first ten months of 1943 totalled $2,110,341 as against $4,556,177 in 1942.

In 1943 the number of relief cases fell below 12,000 for the first time since public assistance reports for the state at large have been available.

Communication.—Although highway construction was curtailed because of the war, the state had at the end of 1942 more than 1,680 mi. of paved roads, many of six lanes. In 1939 there were 2,123 mi. of steam railways in New Jersey.

Banking and Finance.—The 158 financial institutions under jurisdiction of the state department of banking and insurance reported total deposits, at the close of the state's fiscal year June 30, 1943, of $1,766,751,500, an all time high. The report was made by 133 trust companies and state banks, 22 savings banks and 2 savings associations.

Agriculture.—Harvests in 1942 broke all previous records, when crop value reached $179,800,000, and the state department of agriculture estimated in November 1943 that the 1943 harvest and prices would surpass that total.

Leading Agricultural Products of New Jersey, 1943 and 1942

Crop	1943 (est.)	1942
Wheat, bu.	984,000	1,175,000
Corn, bu.	6,808,000	8,370,000
Oats, bu.	1,118,000	1,290,000
Barley, bu.	182,000	270,000
Rye, bu.	224,000	278,000
Potatoes, bu.	11,502,000	10,136,000
Apples, bu.	2,262,000	3,239,000
Tame hay, tons	399,000	379,000

Manufacturing.—Employment in New Jersey industries reached a record high in 1942. More than 800,000 were gainfully employed, according to preliminary reports to the state department of labour from 1,785 plants. The figures indicated an increase of 19% over 1941. Average weekly earnings ran to a record high of $43.79, and more than 5,000 plants were engaged in war production.

Mineral Production.—The total value of New Jersey's mineral production in 1939—the latest year for which federal figures were available in 1943—was $30,271,293. The leading products, in order of value, were zinc, clay, sand and gravel, stone and iron ore.   (W. R. Ck.)

New Mexico. Fourth largest state in the southwestern United States, popularly known as the "Sunshine state"; admitted to the union in 1912. Total area, 121,666 sq.mi. (121,511 sq.mi. land, 155 sq.mi. water); pop. (1940) 531,818 (25.6% increase since 1930), divided among rural, 355,417; urban, 176,401 (33.2%); native white, 477,065; Negro, 4,672; foreign born, 15,247.

History.—The administration, legislature and congressional representation were Democratic in 1943. The chief officers of the state elected on Nov. 3, 1942, were: governor John J. Dempsey; lieutenant governor, James B. (Jawbone) Jones; secretary of state, Cecilia Tafoya Cleveland; auditor, J. D. Hannah; treasurer, Guy Shepard; attorney-general, Edward P. Chase; superintendent of public instruction, Georgia L. Lusk; commissioner of public lands, H. R. (Ray) Rodgers.

Legislation passed in 1943 to equalize state employees' salaries; to forbid legislators to hold additional state jobs; to provide child vaccination against diphtheria; to permit limited child labour under age 16 during the war; to create a state purchasing agent; and to levy a tobacco tax for needy aged people's support.

Education.—For the school year 1941–42, 710 rural schools, with 58,253 pupils and 1,754 teachers, cost $4,118,476.33; 247 municipal schools, with 73,089 pupils and 1,989 teachers, cost $5,737,214.28.

Public Welfare, Charities, Correction.—For the fiscal year ending June 30, 1943, the WPA spent $2,629,311 for labour and material. During the calendar year 1943, $29,102 was paid out for unemployment benefits. On June 30, 1943, $223,000 had been spent for old-age and survivors insurance, and $2,564,743 for public assistance.

The penitentiary appropriation was $130,480 for 519 inmates (Sept. 1, 1943); insane asylum, $325,000, 889 inmates; School for Mental Defectives, $47,480, 76 inmates; Industrial school, $49,-000, 110 inmates; Girls' Welfare home, $60,000, 116 inmates (Dec. 1943).

Communication.—New Mexico had an estimated 62,896.3 mi. of roads in 1943; 9,351.5 constituted the state highway system. For the fiscal year ending June 30, 1943, the state highway department expended $3,004,386.76.

Steam railway companies operated 2,598 mi. of main track (1942).

There were 57 airports, and approximately 850 mi. of airways operated by two scheduled air carriers. There were about 50,550 telephones.

Banking and Finance.—On June 30, 1943, there were 22 national banks with deposits of $98,026,000; loans, $16,307,000; investments, $49,678,000; and 19 state banks with deposits of $32,775,000; loans, $5,550,000; investments, $14,560,000. Total resources of 12 building and loan associations in 1942 were $4,436,805.86 and of 7 federal savings and loan associations, $3,084,684.

The total of all state receipts for the fiscal year ending June 30, 1943, was $31,587,668.27; expenditures, $28,208,252.04. The gross and net debt were respectively $23,634,000 and $23,-342,585.

Table I.—*Leading Agricultural Products of New Mexico, 1943 and 1942*

Crop	1943 (est.)	1942
Tame hay, ton	420,000	432,000
Grain sorghums, bu.	1,422,000	4,060,000
Wheat, bu.	2,405,000	4,813,000
Corn, bu.	2,930,000	3,792,000
Beans, bags	792,000	1,070,000
Cotton, bales	111,000	122,000

Table II.—*Principal Mineral Products of New Mexico, 1943 and 1942*
(Year ending Oct. 31)

Mineral	Value, 1943	Value, 1942
Copper	$18,504,489	$19,245,964
Potash	12,271,470	10,393,317
Zinc	10,055,836	6,767,425
Coal	6,136,364	4,929,458
Silver	239,625	408,963
Lead	733,956	535,952
Gold	75,603	338,924

Agriculture.—The total value of agricultural production in 1943 was estimated at $46,928,000; acreage harvested, 1,542,000. Livestock was valued at $116,873,000, Jan. 1, 1943.

Manufacturing.—Manufactured products were valued at $25,-123,641 in 1939; an average of 3,250 employees received $2,912,-993 in wages.

Mineral Production.—As in preceding years, copper was New Mexico's chief mineral in 1943. The total value of minerals produced was $50,057,314. (F. D. R.)

New South Wales.
A state of the Australian commonwealth, lying in the southeast and occupying 309,432 sq.mi.; pop. (est. Dec. 31, 1941) 2,812,321. Chief cities (pop. est. Dec. 31, 1940): Sydney, capital (1,310,530); Newcastle (119,590). Governor (1943): Captain the Rt. Hon. Lord Wakehurst.

History.—The most contentious bill introduced by William J. McKell, the Labour premier, during 1943 embodied his proposals to reconstitute the legislative council (upper chamber). As then constituted, it was elected by members of both chambers, who voted as a single electoral body at simultaneous sittings of both chambers, members being elected for a period of 12 years, of whom one quarter retired each three years. Other measures of note included: alterations in the machinery for industrial arbitration; the grant of £A.100,000 for a cancer research institute in Sydney; a £A.100,000 grant for stepping-up milk production; a £A.100,000 grant for the provision of tractors and machinery to be hired out to small dairy farmers; and the reservation of an area 100 mi. long and 22 mi. wide in the southern Alps as a national park. Special committees on postwar public works were set up and plans submitted covering the expenditure of £A.50,-000,000 over 20 years. Water conservation was to cost £A.1,000,000 a year over this period. There was a budget surplus for the fiscal year ended June 30 of £A.1,113,000, largely due to increased earnings by the government-owned railway system and the success of other government business undertakings.

Education.—In 1940: public schools 3,209; teachers, 12,877; scholars on roll, 359,777; average attendance, 296,924; expenditure by state, £A.4,882,000.

Finance.—In 1941–42: revenue, £A.65,865,000; expenditure £A.64,824,000; debt outstanding (June 30, 1942), £A.365,095,-000.

Communication.—Roads (1940), 126,058 mi.; railways, government (Dec. 1942) 6,127 mi.; tramways (June 1941) 172 mi. Motor vehicles licensed (March 31, 1943): cars 174,154; commercial vehicles 72,334; cycles 14,395. Wireless receiving set licences (March 1943), 536,795.

Telephones (June 1941): exchanges, 2,018; instruments connected, 280,161.

Agriculture, Manufacturing, Mineral Production.—Production in 1942–43: wheat, 52,000,000 bu.; butter, 89,000,000 lb.; wool, greasy, 547,000,000 lb.; maize, 3,142,000 bu.; coal (1942) 12,223,000 tons; gold (1939), 87,189 fine oz. Industry and labour, 1941–42: factories, 10,166; employees (average) 298,245; gross value of output £A.339,488,312; unemployment (trade union returns) (March 1943) 1.4%. (W. D. MA.)

Newspapers and Magazines.
Paper shortage was the outstanding problem of American newspapers during 1943. Circulations increased at least 2.6%, attaining an all-time record of nearly 44,000,000 daily. National and classified advertising increased materially, offsetting a slight decline in local retail advertising. Manpower shortage was a serious problem which was somewhat eased by reduction in business, and by a great increase in the employment of women. Most newspaper meetings were concerned with government re-

NEWS DESK of the *Stars and Stripes*, the U.S. army's European daily, in the offices of the *Times* of London

strictions and threats to freedom of the press. In spite of these problems, the number of casualties among newspapers was smaller than normal and, because of adequate handling of war news, newspaper prestige with the public increased remarkably.

That war was the absorbing news topic of the year was shown by the selection of "Big Stories of 1943" announced on Dec. 31, 1943, by the news agencies. The Associated Press list was: (1) Overall blueprint for winning the war and keeping the peace; (2) Russia turns the tide; (3) Germany invaded through the roof; (4) Italy surrenders, wars on Germany; (5) America strikes back in Pacific; (6) Mussolini topples; (7) Pay-as-you-go taxes voted; (8) De Marigny murder case; (9) Coal strikes imperil war production; (10) U-boats lose battle of Atlantic. Other big stories included in the United Press and International News Service lists were: Four Allied conferences at Casablanca, Quebec, Cairo and Tehran; conquest of North Africa and Sicily; capture of Attu and Kiska; New Deal reverses and Republican gains; Jap execution of U.S. fliers; U.S. builds world's biggest air fleet and navy; preparation for opening of European second front; domestic manpower crisis including draft of fathers; anti-inflation battle and rise of black markets; Errol Flynn trial.

The year brought a succession of cuts in paper supply and rises in paper cost, made more difficult by rising circulations. The 25-man Newspaper Industry Advisory committee, and a similar magazine committee, conferred constantly with the War Production board on systems of rationing to reconcile the needs of the small newspapers and the huge demands of the metropolitan

Sunday newspapers. During the first quarter of the year, the cut limited all newspapers except very small ones to the amount used during the same period in 1941. During the second quarter, all papers were cut 2½% below 1941. For the third quarter a sliding scale spread the saving from 2½ to 5% for various papers, and for the fourth quarter a new sliding scale brought the total reduction of 1943 to 10% below 1941. In November a new sliding scale for 1944 set up an annual reduction ranging from 4% for weeklies to 24% for metropolitan dailies. Meanwhile, on March 1, the Office of Price Administration authorized a price rise of $4 a ton; a similar rise in September brought the price to $58 a ton.

To meet the paper shortage, various expedients were announced: for instance, the tabloid New York *Daily News* raised its sales and advertising prices and urged readers to borrow copies; the Chicago *Tribune* eliminated classified advertising pages in editions going 50 mi. out of the city; many newspapers "froze" circulation and refused new subscribers; many newspapers rationed advertising; the Milwaukee *Journal* reduced its Saturday paper to an 8-page Victory edition; and finally the Chicago *Daily News* omitted all commercial advertising from Dec. 23 to Jan. 3. Scripps-Howard and other newspapers experimented with 30-lb. paper (instead of 32) with such success that the largest American paper-maker in December put the lighter paper on the market and congress was changing the tariff to admit lighter paper from Canada, which provides 75% of the American supply. Also, "ersatz," or de-inked, newsprint was tried by various newspapers.

Because of alarm among newspaper men concerning increasing wartime controls by government, almost every newspaper meeting of the year had the central theme of defense of freedom of the press; for example: the American Society of Newspaper Editors in Washington, Feb. 12–13; the Associated Press in New York, April 19, to which Kent Cooper, general manager, urged a world-wide crusade for freedom of news; the American Newspaper Publishers association in New York, in April, which appointed a 5-man Press Freedom committee; the 10th annual convention of the American Newspaper guild, in Boston, June 14–18, representing 20,000 members; the 58th annual convention of the National Editorial association, in Cincinnati, June 20, representing weekly newspapers in 42 states; 275 Associated Press editors meeting in Chicago, Sept. 9; the 4th annual Newspaper Week, Oct. 1–8, with the slogan, "Free Press—Free People—An Unbeatable Team"; the memorial to John Peter Zenger at St. Paul's Free Press shrine, East Chester, N.Y., during Bill of Rights week, Dec. 12–18. The American Society of Newspaper Editors, on Oct. 4, saluted the underground publishers of nazi-dominated Europe.

Voluntary censorship under Byron Price continued to work smoothly throughout the year, but there was increasing complaint against army and navy censorship and constant difficulty with Elmer Davis and the Office of War Information. In July, Mr. Price omitted his 6-month revision of the censorship code, because it was working so well, and in December he liberalized the code and warned against "unauthorized censorship." In October, the ban on radio and press weather forecasts was removed. In June, congress reduced the OWI domestic activities budget so sharply that Davis closed 62 regional offices and dismissed 794 of his writers; in July, Davis created an OWI advisory group of nine leading newspaper editors, urged President Roosevelt to release more war news, and in September startled the country with a series of "horror pictures" of army casualties. The press took great pride in "keeping the secret" of various important events which had been "released in advance": for example, the news of the Casablanca meeting of Roosevelt and Churchill in January was kept secret for 32 hours; in April, the press was silent about the president's southern trip; the secret of the landing in Sicily in July was kept for more than a month; and in December, America "held the release" on the meetings of Allied leaders in Cairo and Tehran, although Reuters in Lisbon and Tass in Russia broke the release and German radio spread the "rumour" story. Mr. Roosevelt on his return forbade further "release in advance" on such events. The greatest flurry over censorship resulted from a White House order limiting press coverage of the United Nations Food conference in Hot Springs, Va., in March; considering this a precedent for future international conferences, the press fought so vigorously that the meeting was finally opened to them almost completely.

The anti-trust suit against the Associated Press, which was filed on Aug. 28, 1942, by the federal department of justice at the instance of Marshall Field of the Chicago *Sun,* continued through the year without conclusion. Three judges of the U.S. circuit court of appeals of New York—Judges Learned Hand, Augustus N. Hand and Thomas W. Swan—were on Jan. 7, 1943, named as an "expediting court" to handle the case. At a special meeting on Feb. 9, the A.P. further eased its by-law concerning election of members. Between January and June the government presented 545 questions of fact to A.P. for answer, and A.P. presented the government with 40 similar requests—piling up a record of over 2,000,000 words. Both sides agreed on May 29 to a "summary judgement" based on written evidence, filed their lengthy briefs, and on July 8 argued the case in court. The majority opinion in the court's 2-1 decision, handed down on Oct. 6, stipulated necessary revisions in A.P. admission rules to avoid the charge of "monopoly"—Judge Swan dissented. The department of justice filed its "proposed judgement for the court" on Nov. 12, and the A.P. was given 30 days—later extended to Jan. 3—to answer. Meanwhile, during December, various newspaper spokesmen urged A.P. to appeal the case, rather than file an answer, arguing that the decision tended to treat news-gathering as a "public utility" in violation of the constitutional free press guarantee, and of the sanctity of property right in "copy." On Dec. 15, the Chicago *Sun* again applied for membership.

Few other important legal battles affecting the press developed in 1943. One unprecedented case was the action on April 13 of a U.S. district court in fining 15 New York department stores $80,-000 under the Sherman anti-trust act, because of their combined action in withholding advertising from the New York *Times* in protest against a raise in rates; the action was brought by the attorney general on the grounds that "readers feared the lack of advertising meant shortage of merchandise due to the war." Newspapers applauded as a victory for press freedom the 5-4 decision of the U.S. supreme court on May 4 annulling a city ordinance of Jeannette, Pa., which restrained Jehovah's Witnesses from distributing their pamphlets. The Federal Communications commission continued its investigation of newspaper ownership of radio stations, which it began in March, 1941, and in November the Newspaper-Radio committee protested to congress, arguing that newspapers controlled only 169 out of the 801 radio stations. In November, Press Wireless, a co-operative company formed by American newspapers in 1929, filed with FCC a protest against any proposed merger of international communications under government control, and charged government interference with transmission of war news. Much discussion centred about the Bankhead bill introduced in U.S. senate in May to authorize the U.S. treasury to spend annually $30,000,000 on newspaper advertisements of war bonds, allocating at least 50% to weekly newspapers. Some 93% of the weeklies supported the bill, but the daily newspapers opposed it as a "dangerous subsidy." After amending the bill on Nov. 16 to provide only $15,000,000 for non-dailies in small cities, the senate passed it by a small majority,

but in December it was finally shelved.

Tabulations of newspaper achievements to aid the war effort ran into huge figures. The carrier boys of 900 newspapers, after selling 566,159,323 war stamps in 1942, sold 900,000,000 more by the end of Sept. 1943, and were credited with selling one-sixth of all Third Loan stamps. Tabulations announced by the U.S. treasury indicated that the daily and weekly newspapers printed 73,-938 advertisements, totalling 114,682,123 lines and valued at $4,564,270 in the Second War Loan, in May, and almost double that amount in the Third Loan in September; newspapers donated over 40% of the space and merchants the rest. Some 1,600 newspapers in 27 states in August joined in a campaign to urge farmers to cut 2,500,000 cords of pulpwood to relieve the paper situation. Later, 1,100 dailies co-operated in November to collect 8,000,000 tons of waste paper. The annual threat of higher newspaper postal rates, appearing in March, again failed. Although the draft administration in January classified all newspaper employees as 3B "necessary men," by August only four newspaper jobs remained on the "essential list"; in April all newspaper workers were "frozen" to their jobs.

The casualty list of war correspondents was 15 dead and 69 wounded by December 1943 (28 held as prisoners up to April). This represented a casualty rate of 22% as against the army's 5%. Three correspondents had received military decorations, and by November 11 Liberty ships had been named after dead correspondents. As so many of the casualties were on bombing missions, newspapers in April ordered their men to avoid such risks. During the year, American newspapers had 370 reporters and 65 photographers with the armed forces overseas, and had 250 ready to cover the proposed second front. By April, correspondents had published more than 100 "I Seen It" books, and more appeared later. Most striking was the popularity of Ernie Pyle, of Scripps-Howard Newspaper alliance, whose war column in 162 newspapers (circulation, 9,000,000) and whose book made his name a household word. In the home offices, 822 daily newspapers in October reported an honour roll of 156 former employees killed in military service; 766 dailies reported 40,000 former employees in the army or navy and staff losses of as much as 30%.

Among other outstanding newspaper events of the year were: 25 American editors visited England during the summer as guests of the British ministry of information; the University of Missouri cancelled Journalism Week and instead published a book, "Journalism at War"; Linwood I. Noyes, of the Ironwood, Mich., *Globe* (circ. 7,500) was the first small daily publisher to be elected president of the American Newspaper Publishers association; the Milwaukee *Journal* in May increased its employee-ownership to 40% (600 employees own $3,000,000 of stock); a $20,000,000 Gannett foundation was set up in June to perpetuate the Gannett newspaper group; on Oct. 7 the 92-year-old Western Union Telegraph company absorbed the 62-year-old Postal Telegraph and became the largest wire and cable company in the world; at the request of the National Council on Education for Journalism, 12 schools of journalism set up emergency short courses for women and others adopted accelerated programs.

Magazines.—American magazines showed the effects of war more than newspapers, not only in the large weight of war in their content, but in shortages of paper and advertising. All except the smallest reduced their paper consumption at least 10% below 1942 and for 1944 faced a reduction of 25% below 1942; all popular magazines were much smaller in size or format and many adopted paper of lighter weight or inferior quality. Magazines were forced to refuse millions of dollars worth of advertising; *Life,* limited to 104 pages, rejected $4,500,000; *Fortune* reduced its page format. Circulations continued high; one over 4,000,000; four others over 3,000,000; six others over 2,000,000;

FIRST PRIZE WINNER: The most widely circulated and the most commented upon news photograph of the year, was that of Mrs. Roosevelt being given the traditional Maori "hongi" or nose kiss by her native guide, Rangi, when the first lady visited Whakarewarewa in New Zealand in September. Photograph by J. Thompson of Rotorua, N.Z., for *Look* magazine

SECOND PRIZE WINNER: "Slingin' Sammy" Baugh, great halfback of the Washington Redskins weeps after being removed in the first half of the annual professional football championship game at Chicago, Dec. 26. Baugh returned to the game in the second half and threw two passes for touchdowns, but the final score was: Bears 41, Redskins 21. Photograph by Mickey Rito of the *Chicago Times*

THIRD PRIZE WINNER: A year before Pearl Harbor, Bob Moore left his drugstore in Villisca, Iowa (pop. 2,011), and joined the army. Three years later he had become a captain. In Feb. 1943 he also became a hero. For bravery at Faid pass he was made a lieutenant colonel and in July was sent home on furlough to his wife and daughter. "Hero's Return" was chosen by *Britannica* as one of the most poignant 1943 news photographs. Photo by Earle L. Bunker of the *Omaha World-Herald*

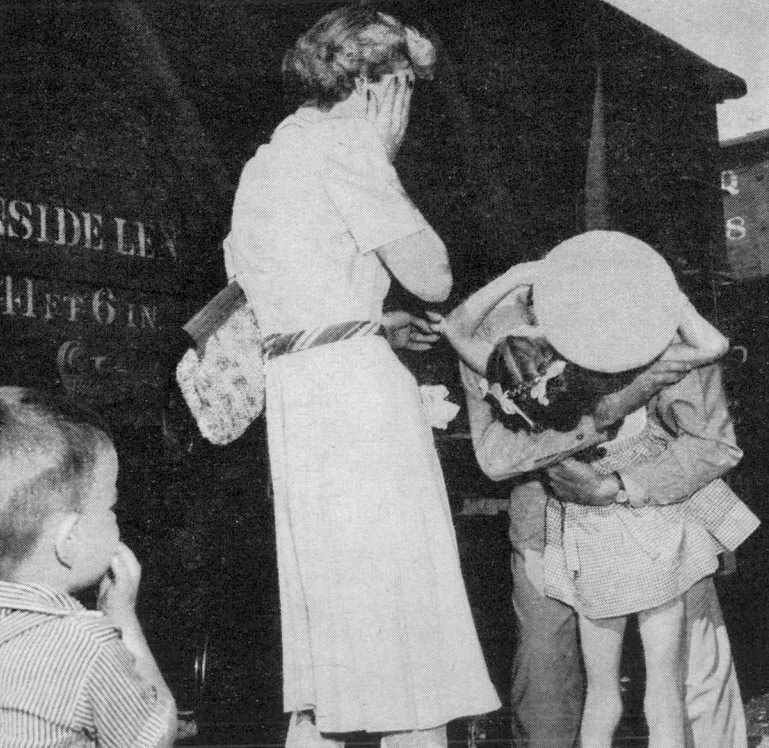

and five others over 1,000,000. The pace set by 30 large magazines, in carrying free advertising of the 1st War Loan in 1942 was continued during the two loans of 1943. Co-operating, 100 national magazines appeared on the stands on Labor day with covers boosting women's civilian war work. In one July issue, *Life* devoted an entire section to printing the current war casualty list of 15,000 men, with home towns. *PM* of New York dropped colour from its format in November. The post office in September threatened to bar *Esquire* from the mails on charge of obscenity (the Varga nudes) but after hearings the postal board voted 2–1 to drop the charge; however, on Dec. 30, Postmaster General Frank C. Walker annulled *Esquire*'s second class postal privilege, effective Feb. 28, 1944, on the grounds that the magazine was "not devoted to useful information" worthy of mail subsidy. (G. M. Hy.)

Great Britain.—By the middle of 1943 more than 160 American journalists were operating in London in connection with the war.

J. H. Brebner, director, news division, ministry of information, went to Cairo early in the year to reorganize the ministry of information in the middle east, following upon many complaints of inefficiency and inadequacy.

In August, the country's stock of newsprint had reached its lowest level. Two new ships were built and launched by the Newsprint Supply company with special government permission. Two additional ships were under charter, making a fleet of five, including one original vessel. By October the stock of newsprint was increased to more than 20 weeks' supply. The government agreed that newspapers should slightly increase their permitted consumption of newsprint from October onwards for increasing circulation, and not for the printing of more pages. Including this increase, the weekly consumption of newsprint was still under 5,000 tons, as against 24,000 tons prewar. The controlled price of newsprint in October was £32 5s. per ton, and the equalized price obtained through the Newsprint Supply company £31 12s. per ton. This compares with the controlled price of £24 per ton on June 30, 1940.

Notwithstanding the newsprint difficulty, 181 foreign language newspapers were published in Britain. Of the grand total there were 41 Polish, 28 Czechoslovakian, 17 French, 14 Spanish, 13 German and 12 Dutch. There were also papers for the Chinese, Belgians, Austrians, Greeks, Hungarians, Italians, Norwegians, Rumanians, Swiss, Latvians and Danes in Britain.

A new monthly magazine, *Transatlantic,* was first published in October—"to assist the British and American peoples to 'walk side by side in majesty, in justice and in peace.'" Its editor, Geoffrey Crowther, was also the editor of the *Economist.* Arrangements were well in hand for the reappearance of the famous *Cornhill* in Jan. 1944 under the editorship of Peter Quennell.

It was announced that the *Manchester Guardian* had been vested in seven trustees to ensure that the general principles guiding the conduct of the paper would be maintained in the future. The *Economist* celebrated its centenary on Sept. 2 and the *News of the World* on Oct. 1.

Among important appointments during 1943 were that of J. W. Haley, joint managing director of the Manchester Guardian and Evening News, Ltd., as editor-in-chief of BBC and of Wilson Midgley, formerly New York correspondent of the London *Daily News* and *Star,* to the editorship of *John O'London's Weekly.*

Increasing use was made by the government of the advertising columns of the press to recruit for coal-mining and nursing, and for calling on the public to save still more for the war effort; for economy in the use of the railways, fuel, telephones and telegraphs; to guard against careless talk. A special campaign was undertaken to fight the venereal disease menace.

Newspaper profits were well maintained. The previous year's figures are in brackets: London Express Newspapers, Ltd., showed a trading profit of £247,956 (£247,789); Odhams Press, Ltd., £698,428 after the clearing of debenture and other interest; Benn Bros., net profit of £58,552; Manchester Guardian, £30,283 (£12,338); George Newnes, Ltd., £138,123 (£120,387); Associated Newspapers, Ltd., £567,124 (£535,124); Daily Mirror, £208,758 (final figure £202,804); and Sunday Pictorial, £222,573 (£192,497). (*See also* ADVERTISING; PRINTING.) (S. R. C.)

New York. One of the original 13 states of the union, popularly known as the "Empire state," New York covers an area of 49,576 sq.mi., of which 1,647 sq.mi. are water. With a population of 13,479,142 (federal census, 1940) it retained its place as the most populous of the states. It had in that year a foreign-born population of 2,853,530, which included 584,075 born in Italy and 316,800 born in Germany. The capital is Albany, with a population of 130,577. Among the other cities are New York, with a population of 7,454,995, or about twice as many as any other city in the U.S.; Buffalo, 575,901; Rochester, 324,975; Syracuse, 205,967; Yonkers, 142,598; Utica, 100,518; Binghamton, 78,309; Troy, 70,304. Because of the influx of workers in war industries, the population of New York city increased greatly after 1940. The urban population of the state was 11,165,893 and the rural population, 2,313,249.

History.—The legislature, which continued in session until March 26, 1943, changed the date of the opening of the fiscal year from July 1 to April 1, raised the pay of state employees 7½% and 10%, appropriated $25,000 for child care centres under the state council for children whose mothers were engaged in war work, continued the Commission on Postwar Planning, put disabled veterans of World War II on the same basis as veterans of World War I, permitted the continuance of free lunches in the schools, removed the stigma of conviction of crime in the case of deserving youth between the ages of 16 and 19, created an Emergency Food commission and reapportioned the legislative districts.

Although the only state official to be elected was the lieutenant governor to fill the vacancy caused by the death of the incumbent in the summer, the election attracted national attention as it was believed that the result would foreshadow to a certain extent the outcome of the presidential election in 1944. The Republicans nominated State Senator Joseph R. Hanley and the Democratic candidate was Lt. Gen. William N. Haskell, who was also supported by the American Labor party. Hanley was elected by a majority of about 350,000 over Haskell. The principal officers in 1943 were Thomas E. Dewey, governor; Joseph R. Hanley, lieutenant governor; John J. Bennett, Jr., attorney general, and George D. Stoddard, commissioner of education.

Education.—During the fiscal year ending June 30, 1942, the last year for which complete figures had been assembled in 1943, there were 972 high schools with 741,596 pupils, and 8,537 elementary schools, with 1,427,151 pupils. The total cost of maintaining the schools, exclusive of money raised by the issue of bonds, was $357,923,285. In addition to the public schools there were 88 colleges and universities, including 11 teachers' colleges, with 151,000 students and a teaching staff of 16,197.

Public Welfare, Charities, Correction.—The number of persons receiving public assistance in August, 1943, was 202,117,

LITTERED STREETS OF HARLEM, New York city, after Negro looters had stripped stores during the riot of Aug. 1–2, 1943

for whose relief $7,484,225 was contributed as compared with $9,784,000 in Oct. 1942. The amount spent for home relief during the month was $2,585,574 or 51% less than in the same period of 1942. The amount spent for old age assistance was $3,610,557; $1,199,005 were spent to aid dependent children and $89,089 to assist the blind. There were eight state prisons, three reformatories, three institutions for defective delinquents and three hospitals for the criminal insane.

Communication.—There were in the state on Jan. 1, 1942, exclusive of streets in cities and incorporated villages, 84,591 mi. of highways, of which 71,836 were town and country roads. Of the total 58,620 were classified as improved. The state spent in 1942 $3,331,991 for construction and reconstruction, $9,303,779 for maintenance and repairs, $2,248,175 for engineering, administration and materials and $204,501 for engineering studies and planning, making a total of $15,088,446. Of this amount, $2,294,978 were contributed by the federal government. The state maintained a system of 525 mi. of canals including the Erie, 339 mi.; the Oswego, 24 mi.; the Cayuga-Seneca, 92 mi. and the Champlain, 60 mi. Although no tolls are charged, the canals yield a revenue of more than $500,000,000 a year for the use of terminals, the sale of water power and the operation of grain elevators.

Banking and Finance.—On Jan. 1, 1943, there were 132 savings banks with deposits of $5,574,423,000 and resources of $6,263,588,000; 126 state banks with resources of $245,970,000 and $220,896,000 in deposits; 155 trust companies with resources of $16,858,153,000 and deposits of $15,416,687,000; 5 private banks with resources of $174,239,000 and deposits of $149,103,000 and 14 industrial banks with resources of $73,310,000 and deposits of $66,233,000.

Agriculture.—According to the census of 1940 there were 153,238 farms in the state with a total acreage of 17,170,337. The value of the products sold was $274,175,053 of which $167,052,240 was received from the sale of livestock and livestock products.

Table I.—*Leading Agricultural Products of New York, 1943 and 1942*

Crop	1943 (est.)	1942
Corn, bu.	23,177,000	27,600,000
Tobacco, lb.	660,000	1,450,000
Potatoes, bu.	29,127,000	27,405,000
Apples, bu.	12,250,000	18,997,000
Grapes, tons	44,000,000	69,600,000

Manufacturing.—In 1939, according to the biennial manufacturing census (none was taken during World War II) there were 34,506 manufacturing establishments employing 957,844 persons, paying $1,163,785,198 in wages and producing goods valued at $7,134,400,147.

Table II.—*Principal Industries of New York, 1939 and 1937*

Industry	Value of products	
	1939	1937
Boots and shoes	$104,144,500	$125,819,448
Bread and bakery products	204,500,887	243,386,287
Clothing	917,562,506	847,556,856
Steel products	197,884,816	157,809,733
Printing, including periodicals	416,760,806	576,731,299

Mineral Production.—The value of minerals produced in 1940 was $159,794,483 and in 1941 it was $190,319,185.

Table III.—*Principal Mineral Products of New York, 1941 and 1940*

	Value, 1941	Value, 1940
Cement	$16,673,726	$11,687,089
Coke	32,808,937	29,549,871
Pig iron	66,718,244	54,150,107
Petroleum	13,300,000	11,000,000
Salt	7,416,734	6,423,775
Stone	10,806,450	10,308,401
Zinc	5,766,900	4,496,436

(G. W. Do.)

New York City. The largest city in the U.S.A., New York had a population of 7,454,995, according to the census of 1940. Mayor: Fiorello H. LaGuardia. Results disconcerting to the politicians arose from the peculiarities of New York city's election laws in 1943. Both Republican and Democratic conventions nominated Thomas A. Aurelio to the supreme court. But after the conventions adjourned it was reported that Aurelio had thanked an alleged racketeer for his support. The conventions then met a second time and repudiated Aurelio; the Republicans nominated George Frankenthaler and the Democrats indorsed the American Labor party candidate, Matthew M. Levy.

The courts were asked to decide if a convention could repudiate a nomination made in accordance with law and they held that a nomination once made could not be withdrawn; therefore Aurelio was the regular Republican and Democratic candidate for the bench and his name had to appear as such on the party tickets. This decision forced Frankenthaler to run as an independent. Levy, as the Labor party candidate with indorsement of the Democrats, also ran as an independent. In view of the court decision that the name of Aurelio had to appear on the ballots of the two leading parties the result was foreseen, for the electors are in the habit of voting the straight party ticket. Aurelio won by a handsome majority over the combined opposition, and this, too, in spite of the unsuccessful attempt before the election to have him disbarred for alleged connection with racketeers.

The peculiarities of the law also resulted in the election of three Communist members of the city council. The voter is supposed to indicate on the ballot his first, second and third choices. The candidate who is first choice on 75,000 ballots wins. He wins also if he has a majority of the votes for first choice among the first three. The Communists confined their voting to first choice candidates with the result indicated. As there are only about 100,000 Communist voters in the city out of a total registration of about 2,200,000, they won a disproportionate share of seats in the council. It was planned during the year to ask the legislature to change the law so as to make a repetition of this thing impossible.

The prevalence of youthful crime in the Bedford-Stuyvesant section of the borough of Brooklyn led a meeting of representatives of 21 organizations of young people to adopt a resolution calling on the mayor to clean up the section and provide recreational facilities. It was charged that the arrest of girls under 21 for offenses against decency had increased 69.9% over 1942 and that the arrest of girls for crimes against property had increased 33.6%. It was also charged that more than half of the

urglaries were the result of the activities of youth under 21 and
hat 29% of the arson cases, 27% of the forgeries and 13% of
he murders were due to the same youthful group. (*See also*
MUNICIPAL GOVERNMENT.) (G. W. DO.)

New York University. A nontax-supported, privately governed institution of higher education occupying six principal centres of instruction in New York city. While student enrolment in 1943 had declined more than a third since 1940, the enrolment of women showed stability and some recovery was noted in the recession of enrolment in graduate divisions. There were more than 3,000 military students in training under government contract in various departments. Pearl Harbor day, Dec. 7, 1943, was observed with a student mass-meeting tribute to the more than 30,000 alumni and former students and 400 faculty members serving with the armed forces, and the estimated 200 who had lost their lives in such service. An Institute on Post War Reconstruction, embracing public forums, research and publication was established, and conferences supported by various exile governments were held on postwar educational problems of Europe. Special short-course conventions dealing with wartime problems of various related areas of government, law and business were held. The training of army post exchange personnel was launched under government auspices. The former Savage School of Physical Education of New York city was absorbed and consolidated with the university's teacher-training department of health and physical education. Gifts during the year exceeded $600,000, the principal item being $100,000 from the George F. Baker charity trust for the college of medicine. Degrees and certificates were conferred upon 3,615 candidates. Joseph H. Park succeeded John Musser as dean of the graduate school of arts and science, and with Frank H. Sommer's retirement Arthur T. Vanderbilt was appointed dean of the school of law. For statistics of enrolment, faculty, library volumes, etc., see UNIVERSITIES AND COLLEGES. (H. W. CH.)

New Zealand, Dominion of. A British dominion, consisting of a group of islands lying in the south Pacific between 34° 25′ and 47° 17′ S. and between 166° 26′ and 178° 36′ E. Area: Dominion proper 103,415 sq.mi.; other islands, 519 sq.mi.; pop.: Dominion proper (est. March 31, 1943), 1,640,191, including Maoris (93,116); Cook and other Pacific islands (census 1936), 16,350. Chief cities (pop. est. April 1, 1941): Auckland (223,700); Wellington (cap. 160,500); Christchurch (135,500); Dunedin (82,200). Language: English. Religion: Christian (1936 figures, excluding Maoris: Church of England 600,786; Presbyterian 367,855; Roman Catholic 195,261; Methodist 121,012). Governor general in 1943: Air Marshal Sir Cyril Newall; ruler: King George VI.

History.—The best indication of the progressive improvement in the war situation was provided by the fact that it was found possible to hold a general election in September. The Labour government headed by Peter Fraser was returned to power, though its majority was substantially reduced. A number of parties took the field but their candidates were roundly defeated, losing their deposits in practically every case. The "Democratic Labour" party of left wing dissidents from the Labour party was headed by J. A. Lee, who had the biggest majority in the 1938 elections when he stood as an orthodox Labour candidate. On this occasion he was heavily defeated. All his other followers forfeited their deposits, but their votes in five cases turned the scale against the government and let Nationalist candidates in. The National party went to the poll with a pledge, if elected, to form a non-party government and prosecute the war effort to the full. It promised to maintain the social security system introduced by the Labour government, removing "anomalies and injustices," but urged New Zealanders to entrust their economic destiny to the system of free private enterprise rather than government bureaucracy. The government took its stand on its war record and made a special appeal to soldiers serving overseas, whose votes were recorded, based on what had already been done to conserve their interests. This appeal apparently had considerable effect, for in several cases the servicemen's vote swayed contests in Labour's favour. Labour retained its hold on the cities, but lost ground in the semi-rural constituencies. The state of parties at the close of 1943 was: Labour 45, National 34, Independent 1.

Walter Nash, finance minister, returned from Washington to present the budget in June. War expenditure, it revealed, amounted to £144,000,000 for 1942–43, the main items being navy £8,500,000; army £88,000,000; air £24,000,000. Reverse lend-lease cost £7,000,000. Revenue receipts totalled £42,800,000. Net increase of debt in 1942–43 totalled £78,427,000, of which £73,908,000 was internal. The war overdraft from the United Kingdom government was £15,400,000, of which £8,000,000 was repaid during the year. Since March 1936, the ordinary debt domiciled in London had been reduced by more than £10,500,000. War expenditure for 1943–44 was estimated at £148,000,000 including reverse lend-lease £20,000,000. Estimated receipts were £46,000,000, payments by United Kingdom £12,000,000, local borrowings £50,000,000, and lend-lease £40,000,000. Provision was made for pensions increases. Disablement pensions were raised from £2 to £3 per week and other adjustments were made so that a totally disabled man with a wife and two children would receive £6 16s. a week. Pensions for widows of servicemen were also raised, so that a widow with two children would receive £4 16s. weekly free of tax. Mr. Nash, speaking of the economic position, said adequate measures had been taken to control manpower. Factory out-put for 1941–42 reached the record total value of £155,000,000—35% above prewar production. Primary production still exceeded prewar records.

To check the danger of inflation due to a rise of £50,000,000 in the national income while available goods had decreased by 40% an Economic Stabilization commission was appointed with A. T. Donnelly as chairman. It was given powers to control prices of 110 items from groceries to furniture and also wages and salaries.

Major C. F. Skinner returned from North Africa to become minister of rehabilitation. J. G. Coates, a former prime minister, and a member of the war cabinet, died suddenly in his office. He was succeeded by William Perry, president of the Returned Services association.

The New Zealand division took a prominent part in the expulsion of Axis forces from Africa, earning an eloquent tribute from Mr. Churchill when he addressed them at Tripoli. The Victoria cross was awarded to Second Lieut. Moana-Nui-a-Kiwa Ngarimu for great gallantry during the action at Tebaga gap, March 26, 1943. He was the first Maori to receive the award.

Education.—(Dec. 1941) state elementary schools, 2,230; scholars, 245,655; secondary, 197; scholars, 50,029. University of New Zealand has six constituent colleges, including two agricultural colleges at Lincoln and Palmerston North, grouped together as the New Zealand School of Agriculture; university students, 5,266. Total cost (year to March 31, 1942) £5,218,618.

Finance.—Revenue, consolidated fund, year to March 31, 1943, £42,361,009, expenditure, £38,206,431. Public debt (March 31, 1943) £463,825,371 (due in London £158,274,297, Australia £862,300, balance internal). Note circulation March 1943, £25,577,349; reserve (in Reserve bank) gold £2,801,878, exchange £25,002,266. Net overseas funds, May 31, 1943, £38,710,294.

Total expenditure on World War II to March 31, 1943, £239,-000,000. Exchange rate: £N.Z. 125 equal £100 sterling. Deposits ir. post office and trustee savings banks (March 31, 1943) £102,-790,182; depositors 1,383,136.

Trade and Communication.—Overseas trade: total merchandise exports, year ended March 1943, £75,702,878 (compared with £69,163,121 in 1942); total merchandise imports, year ended March, 1943, £60,781,375 (compared with £50,589,652 in 1942). Communication and transport: roads paved or surfaced (including main highways 12,381 mi.) 44,271 mi.; not paved or surfaced 9,108 mi.; railways 3,400 mi., passenger journeys, year to March 31, 1942, 28,610,945 (compared with 26,276,923); goods traffic 8,473,765 tons (compared with 8,426,182). Shipping (1941) entered 2,323,264 tons net, cleared 2,309,469 tons net. Motor vehicles licensed (March 1943) 298,635 (including 194,715 cars). Wireless licences, March 31, 1943, 368,942. Telephone subscribers 231,640.

Agriculture.—1941–42 acreages: wheat for threshing 258,002; oats for threshing 70,796; chaff and hay 143,218, not harvested, fed off, etc., 68,394; barley for threshing 36,026, total 41,088; maize for threshing 8,779, not harvested 5,229; linseed 859; peas for threshing 30,976; potatoes 15,201; onions 825; perennial rye grass 53,903; linen flax 20,200; western wolths and Italian rye-grass 11,789; cocksfoot 10,624; tobacco 2,435. Yields, total and per acre, wheat 8,671,244 bu. (33.61); oats 3,444,812 bu. (48.66); barley 1,296,630 bu. (35.99); maize 444,249 bu. (50.60); peas 852,077 bu. (27.51); potatoes 89,604 tons (5.89); onions 8,418 tons (10.20); perennial rye-grass 16,289,670 lb. (302). Dairy produce (1939–40): butter 3,103,797 cwt. (173,-811 short tons); cheese 2,033,506 cwt. (113,876 short tons). Livestock in dominion, 1942: horses 261,611; cattle 4,641,714 (including 1,777,239 dairy cows in milk); pigs 688,677 (including 91,338 breeding-sows); sheep 31,751,660 (including 20,030,933 breeding-ewes).

Manufacturing.—Factory production, 1941–42: number of establishments, 6,367; employees 117,214; salaries and wages paid, £29,504,299; value of products, £155,566,193; value of land, buildings, machinery and plant, £87,127,932. (A. J. Hp.)

NHA: *see* NATIONAL HOUSING AGENCY.

Nicaragua.
A republic of Central America, bounded on the north by Honduras and on the south by Costa Rica. Area 57,143 sq.mi., including a water area of 3,475 sq.mi.; pop. (1940 census) 983,160. The capital is Managua (83,546); other leading cities (with pop.) are: León (30,573); Granada (24,843); Masaya (19,827); Chinandega (14,967); Matagalpa (8,506). Language: Spanish. President in 1943: General Anastasio Somoza.

History.—The political scene remained quiet in Nicaragua during 1943. War policies had been established early in the war and required no modification beyond a decision, announced on April 17, to inaugurate compulsory military service. In the summer legislation was introduced into congress which would amend the constitution to permit the re-election of President Somoza, strictly forbidden under existing provisions. In addition it was proposed that the provisions of the Atlantic charter be incorporated into the national constitution.

A planned health project was started in 1943, with the United States to spend $500,000 in aiding in malaria control, establishment of a nursing school in Managua and health centres in other cities, and for other assistance in improvement of health conditions. There was again talk of construction of a Nicaragua canal to relieve pressure on the Panama canal.

Economically, the year proved to be a boom period for Nica-

NICARAGUAN CADETS of the republic's military academy being reviewed b President Anastasio Somoza in 1943

ragua, in spite of priorities and scarcities of goods. Governmen income was such that it was possible to retire in June bond issue: not due for redemption until several years later. In spite of cessa tion in October of work on the Inter-American highway, employ ment circumstances remained satisfactory. Inflation was a threat and living costs steadily mounted in spite of price controls.

Education.—In 1941 Nicaragua had approximately 650 ele mentary schools (about 550 state and 100 private) with a tota enrolment of 61,000 (average attendance was much lower, how ever). Secondary schools numbered 12 (3 national, 9 private): enrolment, 1,250.

Finance.—The monetary unit is the córdoba, fixed in value a 20 cents U.S. A surplus of 300,000 córdobas was announced fo the fiscal year ending June 30, 1943. In 1941 the total publi debt was 8,672,419 córdobas.

Trade and Resources.—The year was an exceptionally goo export year; the increase in trade compared with 1942 was esti mated at as much as 226%. Exports in 1942 were valued at 71,-632,985 córdobas; imports at 33,861,365 córdobas. The favour able trade balance with the United States for nine months end ing Sept. 30, 1943, amounted to $4,801,000.

The latest crop estimates for the 1942–43 year showed: coffe 189,393 bags (a bit low because of early heavy rains); rice 6,-000,000 lb.; sesame 8,000,000 lb.; corn 33,000,000 lb.; beans 10,000,000 lb.; cotton 19,000,000 lb.; cacao 700,000 lb.

Gold is normally the most important item of export (61% in 1941); production was beginning to suffer in 1943 from worn-out equipment. For the first 10 months of 1943 gold exports were $6,-646,923 (4% under the same period of 1942). From May 2, 1942, to May 31, 1943, it was estimated that nearly $1,000,000 worth of crude rubber had been exported.

Communication.—In 1942, Nicaragua had 270 mi. of railway, and some 2,000 mi. of highway (most of it unimproved). Inter-American road-building projects improved highways, but to an extent as yet unspecified. Construction on the Inter-American highway ceased in October. Air service is supplied by Pan American Airways and T.A.C.A. Steamer service improved during the year.

BIBLIOGRAPHY.—Dana G. Munro, *The Five Republics of Central America* (1918); Chester Lloyd Jones, *The Caribbean since 1900* (1936); Isaac Joslin Cox, *Nicaragua and the United States* (1927).   (D. RD.)

Nickel.
Production figures on nickel were lacking from 1938 on, but rough estimates placed the world total at 149,913 short tons in 1941, 136,685 tons in 1940, and 130,071 tons in 1939, as compared with 121,804 tons in 1938. Production in Canada was officially announced as increasing to a new record high in each of the war years, but there was no basis for an estimate of the amount of the increase in 1942 over 1941. The Canadian production capacity was increased by 25,000 short tons, but because of labour shortage the full capacity was not utilized. In spite of this, war demands of the United Nations were met, though during the latter part of 1943 output dropped 10% below the peak. Various exploration projects discovered considerable tonnages of low grade nickel ore at several localities in the United States, but the nickel content was so low in all instances that there was small chance for commercial exploitation, even under war conditions.

The new development at Levisa bay on the north coast of Cuba was scheduled to start operations before the end of 1943, using a new process for the treatment of silicate ores, producing nickel oxide which would be shipped to the United States for further treatment.   (G. A. RO.)

Nielsen, Alice
(1876–1943), U.S. singer, was born June 7 in Nashville, Tenn. "Discovered" in a church choir where her bell-like soprano stood out clear and strong, Miss Nielsen decided on a singing career and went to study voice in San Francisco. In 1893, she sang with a Gilbert and Sullivan troupe, later joining an opera company in San Francisco. She then went east, had indifferent success in Boston and New York until she was discovered by Victor Herbert, who engaged her as the leading lady for his operetta, *The Serenaders*. Miss Nielsen was an instantaneous success. Mr. Herbert then composed two light operas, *The Fortune Teller* and *The Singing Girl,* especially for his new star. But her ambitions to become a prima donna in grand opera led her to forsake operettas and she studied in Italy making her operatic debut in Naples, 1903, as Marguerite. Returning to the United States, she made her debut in 1905 at the Casino theatre, New York city, as Norina in *Don Pasquale.* She was soon accepted as one of the elite among the operatic giants of that "golden age"—Caruso, Tetrazzini, Melba, et al. From 1910 to 1915, she played with the Boston Opera company and also appeared with the Metropolitan and Civic opera in Chicago. She made her last public appearances in light opera in 1917. Miss Nielsen died in New York city, March 8.

Niger: *see* FRENCH COLONIAL EMPIRE.
Nigeria: *see* BRITISH WEST AFRICA.

Nimitz, Chester William
(1885–   ), U.S. naval officer, was born Feb. 24 in Fredericksburg, Tex., and was graduated from Annapolis in 1905. An experienced submarine officer, during World War I he was chief of staff to the commander of the Atlantic fleet's submarine force. He was promoted to rear admiral, June 23, 1938. On Dec. 17, 1941, the navy high command was overhauled after the surprise attack on Hawaii, and Admiral Nimitz was made commander-in-chief of the Pacific fleet, with the rank of admiral. He assumed his post at Pearl Harbor on Dec. 31, 1941.

On Dec. 7, 1942—the first anniversary of Pearl Harbor—he predicted that the Pacific fleet would soon carry the war to Japan's home waters.

On Oct. 5 it was announced that Adms. King, Nimitz and Halsey had completed a series of conferences at Pearl Harbor. At a press conference in November, Adm. Nimitz told newspapermen that Japan's final defeat would probably be launched from China.

Nitrogen, Chemical.
Although nitrate deposits were known to exist in at least 23 states of the United States, all of them were too small and too low in grade for any commercial recovery. Chile still remained the sole source of natural nitrates, but the bulk of the consumption of chemical nitrogen was from coal via by-product coke ovens, and from plants for the fixation of atmospheric nitrogen. Normal prewar consumption of chemical nitrogen in the United States was about 500,000 short tons, 80% in agriculture and the remainder in industrial uses; how much this amount was increased by war demands it was impossible to say, but the available supply was reported to be inadequate, and all commercial nitrogen compounds were under allocation by the War Production board. Synthetic plant capacity was heavily increased and among others the plant at Muscle Shoals, Ala., built during World War I, but not completed in time for use, was modernized in 1942 and was making ammonium nitrate for explosives and fertilizers. Other new plants produced ammonia, ammonium nitrate and sodium nitrate.   (G. A. RO.)

NLRB: *see* NATIONAL LABOR RELATIONS BOARD.
NMB: *see* NATIONAL MEDIATION BOARD.

Noguès, Auguste
(1876–   ), French army officer, was born in the Haute-Pyrenees department, France. He entered the École Polytechnique at the age of 21 and was commissioned as a lieutenant. He was stationed in Africa, 1908–14, saw field service in World War I and participated in the Rif campaign, 1924–26. He was named resident general of Morocco in 1936 by Léon Blum, popular front chieftain. At the outbreak of World War II, Noguès was made commander in chief of all French forces in North Africa. After the establishment of the Vichy regime, he pledged fealty to Marshal Pétain, but in Oct. 1940, he warned both Spain and the axis countries that he would not surrender North Africa to any invading force, even if Pétain ordered him to do so. At the time of the U.S. landings in North Africa in Nov. 1942, Noguès ordered French troops to fire on U.S. soldiers debarking at Casablanca. However, after Allied occupation of North Africa became a fait accompli, he returned to Algiers and assertedly persuaded other recalcitrant French colonial officers to effect a compromise with De Gaulle's Fighting French armies. After the assassination of Darlan, Noguès was appointed to Gen. Henri Giraud's imperial war council, Dec. 27, 1942, and was retained as governor general of Morocco. In Feb. 1943, Noguès expressed amazement that he was "unpopular" with the Americans and insisted that he did the "honourable" thing in opposing the Allied landings. On June 4, Noguès, who was on Gen. De Gaulle's blacklist as a pro-fascist and pro-Vichyite, submitted his resignation as governor general.

North Borneo: *see* BRITISH EMPIRE.

North Carolina.
A south Atlantic coast state, popularly known as the "Old North state" or the "Tar Heel state," North Carolina is one of the original 13 states of the union; area 52,712 sq.mi. (49,142 sq.mi. land, 3,570 sq.mi. water); pop. (1940), 3,571,623, of which 974,175 (27.3%) were

urban, 2,597,448 (72.7%) rural and 1,005,501 (28.2%) nonwhite. Capital, Raleigh (46,897); other cities: Charlotte (100,899); Winston-Salem (79,815); Durham (60,195); Greensboro (59,-319); Asheville (51,310).

History.—The first wartime legislature of North Carolina since 1865 adjourned on March 10, 1943 after 55 days of labour. Notable legislative actions were the nine months' public school law, the granting of emergency war powers to the governor and council of state, the creation of a state school for delinquent Negro girls, the first authorization of state financial support for art and music, the establishment of unified administrative control of public schools, of state correctional institutions and of state institutions for mental defectives, the creation of a state postwar reserve fund of $20,000,000, and the enactment of record maintenance appropriations with no increase in taxes.

During 1943, an average of more than 300,000 young men were constantly in training in nearly fifty military and naval installations in the state.

At Kitty Hawk on Dec. 17, 1943, was celebrated the 40th anniversary of the first successful flight by the Wright brothers.

State officers in 1943 were: J. Melville Broughton, governor; R. L. Harris, lieutenant governor; Thad Eure, secretary of state; George Ross Pou, auditor; C. M. Johnson, treasurer; Clyde A. Erwin, superintendent of public instruction; Harry McMullan, attorney general; W. P. Stacy, chief justice.

Education.—In 1941–42 there were 3,602 public elementary schools with 18,448 teachers and principals and 671,614 enrolled pupils and 1,004 public high schools with 7,854 teachers and principals and 206,299 enrolled pupils, operated at a cost of $36,-684,670, more than three-fourths of which was contributed by the state government. The state provided bus transportation for 341,135 school children at an average cost of $7.71 per pupil.

Public Welfare, Charities, Correction.—In Oct. 1943, public grants amounting to $382,207 were made to 35,672 persons for old-age assistance; $132,487 to 7,104 families for aid to dependent children; $34,914 to 2,219 blind persons; and $23,164 to 2,693 cases for general relief (by the county governments). During the year ending June 30, 1943, the total amount of public relief funds distributed was $7,785,725; and in 1942 unemployment benefits amounted to $2,984,220. In 1943 the state maintained nine charitable institutions with 9,575 inmates on Nov. 1; five correctional institutions with 831 inmates; and state highway prison camps with 6,467 prisoners.

Communication.—In 1943 the state highway and public works commission maintained 11,385 mi. of state highways, of which 9,905 mi. were hard-surfaced, and 49,046 mi. of county roads, of which 2,446 mi. were hard-surfaced. There were 4,581 mi. of railroads, 324 mi. of city bus routes, 10,277 mi. of passenger bus routes and 11,525 mi. of freight vehicle routes in 1943.

Banking and Finance.—On Oct. 18, 1943, there were 44 national banks with deposits of $278,636,000 and resources of $295,788,000, and 182 state banks with deposits of $873,002,522 and resources of $932,002,903. In 1942 there were 152 building and loan associations operating under state charters with total assets of $90,952,087. In 1941–42 state receipts were $210,081,-593; disbursements, $154,388,246. On June 30, 1942, the state gross bonded and net debts were $133,736,500 and $113,942,103, respectively. The assessed value of property was $2,496,247,967 in 1941. In the state general fund there was a cash surplus of $39,370,000 on June 30, 1943.

Agriculture.—Stationary acreage, reduced production, and increased value due to higher prices characterized 1943 wartime agriculture in North Carolina. The total value of production harvested from 6,534,000 ac. was approximately $500,000,000, of which tobacco alone accounted for $222,300,000. The cash in-

Table I.—*Leading Agricultural Products of North Carolina, 1943 and 1942*

Crop	1943 (est.)	1942
Tobacco, lb.	553,680,000	574,400,000
Cotton, bales	595,000	727,000
Corn, bu.	51,018,000	47,068,000
Tame hay, tons	1,263,000	1,163,000
Peanuts, lb.	317,100,000	332,100,000
Wheat, bu.	5,812,000	8,014,000
Sweet potatoes, bu.	7,760,000	8,855,000
Irish potatoes, bu.	12,099,000	9,434,000
Oats, bu.	5,977,000	6,625,000
Soybeans, bu.	2,313,000	3,484,000
Lespedeza seed, lb.	31,000,000	34,500,000
Peaches, bu.	252,000	2,463,000
Apples, bu.	499,000	1,086,000
Pecans, lb.	2,700,000	2,500,000

come of North Carolina farmers in 1942 was $373,848,000 from crops, $67,346,000 from livestock and livestock products, and $22,443,000 from government payments. The value of the lands and buildings on the 278,276 farms in 1940, 44% of which were operated by tenants, was $736,708,125.

Manufacturing.—In 1939 manufacturing establishments numbering 3,225 employed 270,210 wage earners at wages of $199,-289,501 and made products valued at $1,421,329,578. War needs and higher prices boomed North Carolina industrial production to about $2,000,000,000 in 1943.

Mineral Production.—The mineral production for North Carolina in 1941 was valued at approximately $19,000,000. In quantity production of mica, feldspar and bromine, North Carolina ranked first among the states; but in value of all minerals produced, it ranked thirty-fifth. The war brought increased mining activity in 1943, especially in mica and manganese.

Table II.—*Principal Mineral Products of North Carolina, 1941, 1940 and 1939*

Mineral	Value, 1941	Value, 1940	Value, 1939
Stone	$4,806,623	$4,850,277	$6,979,426
Clay products	5,356,000	4,629,000	4,761,867
Sand and gravel	2,345,165	1,439,457	1,101,369
Feldspar	552,386	426,784	397,031
Mica		391,481	253,721
Talc and pyrophyllite	567,921	298,382	283,789

BIBLIOGRAPHY.—U.S. Census; reports of state agencies; 1943 Session Laws.
(A. R. N.)

North Dakota.

A west north central state of the United States, popularly known as the "Flickertail state." Land area, 70,054 sq.mi.; water area, 611 sq.mi.; pop. (1940) 641,935. The rural population was 510,012; urban, 131,923. Capital, Bismarck (15,496). The chief cities are Fargo (32,580); Grand Forks (20,228); and Minot (16,577).

History.—The chief officers of the state in 1943 were as follows: governor, John Moses; lieutenant governor, Henry Holt; secretary of state, Thomas Hall; state auditor, Berta E. Baker; state treasurer, Carl Anderson; attorney general, Alvin C. Strutz; commissioner of insurance, Oscar E. Erickson; commissioner of agriculture and labour, Math Dahl.

Education.—Elementary schools in 1943 had an enrolment of 95,226; secondary schools, 30,128. The total number of schools was 3,928. The institutions of higher learning were the state university and school of mines, the agricultural college, three state teachers' colleges, two normal schools, a school of forestry and a school of science. The total enrolment in these institutions in 1943 was 5,589 and their teaching staffs numbered 365.

Public Welfare, Correction.—The WPA during the fiscal year ending June 30, 1942, expended $4,171,742 of federal funds and employed an average of 6,382 per month. The number of correctional institutions in 1942 was seven and the average number of inmates was 565. The cost of maintenance was $1,500,000.

Communication.—Mileage on state highways on Jan. 1, 1943 was 7,073.1; of rural highways on Jan. 1, 1942, 98,509.6. State expenditures of the highway department for the year ending June 30, 1943 were $3,932,210.93. The total railway mileage in the state in 1942 was 6,211.92.

Banking and Finance.—On Dec. 31, 1942, there were 115 state banks and one trust company, with resources of $90,392,-564.72 and deposits of $84,702,824.44. Twelve savings and loan associations had resources of $10,564,042.18 for 1942. For the year ending June 30, 1943 state receipts were $37,419,319.66, and expenditures were $29,164,181.99. The bonded indebtedness of the state on Dec. 31, 1943 was $20,397,350.62.

Agriculture.—The total farm acreage harvested in 1943 was 17,534,000 (excluding wild hay). The cash income from crops and livestock was (1942) $306,654,000, including benefit payments of $23,010,000. Cash income from livestock (1942) was $121,219,000.

Table I.—*Leading Agricultural Products of North Dakota, 1943 and 1942*

Crop	1943	1942
Spring wheat (other than durum), bu.	121,486,000	112,180,000
Durum, bu.	32,670,000	37,664,000
Corn, bu.	25,335,000	29,000,000
Oats, bu.	70,924,000	74,925,000
Barley, bu.	63,648,000	67,454,000
Rye, bu.	4,014,000	16,082,000
Flax, bu.	15,052,000	9,184,000
Potatoes, bu.	22,100,000	17,955,000

Manufacturing.—The total value of manufactures in 1939 was $43,767,082, and the total employment was 3,435. The estimated value of creamery butter for 1942 was $24,921,000. The value of flour and grain mill products in 1939 was $5,303,788; of publishing and printing, $2,255,874.

Table II.—*Principal Mineral Products of North Dakota, 1939 and 1938*

Mineral	Value, 1939	Value, 1938
Coal	$2,425,000	$2,380,000
Sand and gravel	128,279	151,824
Natural gas	29,000	27,000

Mineral Production.—For the year ending July 1, 1942, the production of lignite coal was 2,469,364 tons, valued at $3,099,-633.68. The total value of mineral production in 1939 was $2,689,627; in 1938 it was $2,653,473.   (O. G. L.)

Northern Ireland: *see* IRELAND, NORTHERN.
Northern Rhodesia: *see* RHODESIA.

Northern Territory

OF AUSTRALIA. Area 523,620 sq.mi.; pop. (June 30, 1940): aboriginals, full-blooded, 13,901; half-caste, 902; white (est. Dec. 31, 1941), 9,615. Capital, Darwin (pop. Dec. 31, 1940, 3,900).

History.—The Northern Territory remained a "proclaimed defense area" throughout 1943. Troops stationed there proved that areas which were formerly regarded as useless country could be made highly productive.

Finance.—Revenue (1942–43), estimated, £A.47,000; from Central Australia railway (1942–43) £A.1,900,000; from North Australia railway (1942–43) £A.495,000. Expenditure, ordinary appropriation (1942–43) £A.329,650; new works, etc. £A.174,000.

Production and Communication.—Production, 1939–40: pastoral industry, £A.587,821; gold, £A.233,789; wolfram, £A.47,-836; pearl shell, £A.15,998. Railways, government (Dec. 31, 1941), 508 mi.   (W. D. MA.)

Northwestern University.

An institution of higher learning at Evanston and Chicago, Ill. The university comprises the following divisions: the college of liberal arts, the graduate school, the technological institute and the schools of music, education, speech, commerce and journalism, all located in Evanston (suburb of Chicago) on a campus bordering Lake Michigan; the medical, law and dental schools and the evening departments of the university, all on Chicago's near north side, on a campus six blocks from the loop business

district. A total of 1,829 degrees were awarded during 1943.

For the fiscal year ending Aug. 31, 1943, gifts to the university totalled $876,858, exclusive of the $20,000,000 bequest of Walter P. Murphy for the development of the new technological institute.

During the year the university strengthened its programs in medicine and home economics by taking over the Illinois Social Hygiene League and the School of Domestic Arts and Science in Chicago.

With approximately 80% of their students in uniform, the medical and dental schools concentrated most of their efforts in training men for the armed forces. An increasing amount of confidential research was carried on for the government in the technological institute and other divisions of the university. Training for war industries was given to hundreds of men and women. Two naval schools were maintained: the naval reserve midshipmen's school on the Chicago campus, and the radio operators' school on the Evanston campus. The navy V-12 college training program was established on July 1, 1943.

A total of 266 members of the faculty were in military or governmental service. Over 8,000 alumni of the university were in the armed forces, and 68 of them had died in service. The university made plans for the erection after the war of a memorial chapel in honour of its war dead. For statistics of enrolment, faculty, library volumes, etc., *see* UNIVERSITIES AND COLLEGES.

Northwest Territories.

The Northwest Territories comprise the territories formerly known as Rupert's land and the Northwestern territory, except such portions thereof as form the provinces of Manitoba, Saskatchewan and Alberta and the Yukon territory, together with all British territories and possessions in North America and all islands adjacent thereto, not included within any province, except

FORT NORMAN REFINERY on the Mackenzie river, Northwest Territories, Canada. A 550-mi. pipe line—the Canol project—was under construction in 1943 by the U.S. army to carry the huge petroleum reserves of the Mackenzie basin to the Alaska highway and beyond. The cost of the project was under investigation by a U.S. senate committee at the end of the year

the colony of Newfoundland and its dependencies. Area, 1,309,-682 sq.mi.; pop. (1941 census) 12,028; seat of government, Ottawa. For administrative purposes, the Territories in 1918 were subdivided into the provisional districts of Mackenzie, Keewatin and Franklin. The Northwest Territories act (1927) provides for a territorial government composed of the commissioner of the Northwest Territories, the deputy commissioner and five councillors appointed by the governor general in council. The Northwest Territories council in 1943 was composed as follows: commissioner, Charles Camsell; deputy commissioner, R. A. Gibson; members of council, A. L. Cumming, K. R. Daly, H. L. Keenleyside, H. W. McGill, S. T. Wood; secretary, D. L. McKeand.

Transportation and Communication.—Inland water transportation on the Mackenzie river system from railhead at Waterways, Alberta, to points in the Mackenzie district was provided by three companies, two of which maintained passenger services. These companies carried a large volume of freight on boats and barges, in addition to that handled by Marine Operators, Ltd., for the Canol project. Regular commercial air services, which also carry mail, were maintained from Edmonton, Alberta, to numerous settlements. Construction of new landing fields at key points permitted operation of wheel-equipped aircraft the year round. Medical centres, trading posts and other places in the eastern Arctic were served by the annual supply ship from Montreal, Quebec, which also carried mail. Auxiliary boat services from Churchill, Manitoba, were also provided. Radio communication was maintained between important settlements and trading posts in the Territories and outside points through government and private commercial radio stations.

Fur Trade.—The fur trade and mining are the principal industries of the Territories. The value of pelts harvested for the year ended June 30, 1942, was $2,840,701. Fur trading is controlled by regulation and is open only to those who have been issued permits and who have established permanent posts. Natives and half-breeds living the life of natives enjoy free hunting and trapping privileges. Of the white residents, only those who, under the regulations, are included in an established eligible list are permitted to hunt and trap and such individuals require an annual license. Reindeer herding in the northern Mackenzie district was continued in the interests of the native population.

Mineral Production.—The search for strategic minerals to meet wartime demands was a feature of mining activity in the Northwest Territories in 1943. Geological parties of the department of mines and resources successfully carried on exploratory and detailed field work in the Yellowknife district, and a number of mining companies also engaged in exploration and prospecting. As a result, a large number of claims were staked. The mill at the pitchblende-silver property of Eldorado Mining and Refining Company, Ltd., at Great Bear lake was operated at full capacity to meet the demand for concentrates from which radium and uranium salts are produced. Labour shortages brought about by war conditions and the transfer of men to base metal workings in other parts of Canada resulted in a curtailment of gold production in the Yellowknife area. Milling operations at the Con and Rycon mines of Consolidated Mining and Smelting Company of Canada, Ltd., were discontinued in August, and Thompson-Lundmark Gold Mines, Ltd., property was closed down temporarily in Sept. 1943. Production, however, was maintained at Negus Mines, Ltd. The approximate average monthly value of gold production from these mines for the first eight months in 1943 was: Con, $107,610; Rycon, $12,610; Negus, $67,000; Thompson-Lundmark, $68,000. The total value of gold production in the Northwest Territories for the five-year period ended August 31, 1943, was approximately $13,685,000.

Canol Project.—A development in 1943 was the extensive drilling program carried out at Norman Wells in the lower Mackenzie region as part of the Canol project. This project, authorized by an exchange of notes between the governments of Canada and the United States, was a joint defense undertaking involving (1) a program of development to increase the production of oil in the Northwest Territories to supply the requirements of the armed forces in Canada and Alaska and for use along the Alaska highway; (2) the construction of a pipeline to convey crude oil from Norman Wells to Whitehorse, Y.T., and (3) erection of an oil refinery at Whitehorse. Drilling was being carried out to determine the extent of the oil field. Until completion of the pipeline, production was restricted to meet local needs, and as a result no sustained test of the capacities of the wells brought in was, up to the close of 1943, possible.

(R. A. G.)

Norway. A country of northern Europe, bounded N. by the Arctic ocean, E. by Finland and Sweden, S. and W. by the North sea. Area 124,556 sq.mi.; pop. (est. 1939) 2,921,-000. Capital, Oslo (253,124). Other principal cities, with 1930 populations, are Bergen (98,303); Trondhjem (54,458); and Stavanger (46,780). Religion, Lutheran Christian. Ruler in 1943: King Haakon VII (q.v.). Prime Minister: Johan Nygaardsvold (in exile in London). Norway was occupied by Germany in 1940, and was administered in 1943 through Reichscommissar Josef Terboven and Premier Vidkun Quisling, with General Nikolaus von Falkenhorst of the army and William Rediess of the gestapo.

History.—During 1943 Norway was the scene of varied military activity. Raids such as the ones at Larvik and Florö sank nazi ships and destroyed factories. At Rjukan the nitrate works was blown up, reportedly by paratroopers. Later the area was bombed and the great electrolysis plant demolished. The large aluminum plant at Heröya was likewise bombed as was the molybdenum mine at Knaben near Stavanger, and the U-boat base at Trondhjem. A combined British and United States naval force struck Bodö in the far north on Oct. 4, 1943 and in surrounding waters sank nine nazi merchant vessels. One of the most daring feats of the war was the attack by British midget submarines on the "von Tirpitz" in Alten fjord (Sept. 22); it left the German battleship incapacitated for at least several months. Later, off North cape (Nordkapp), a British convoy escort sank the "Scharnhorst." Fighting also took place at Spitsbergen, where a German force raided the Norwegian garrison on Sept. 8, evidently attempting unsuccessfully to put the meteorological station out of commission.

The peoples' war within Norway gathered strength during the year despite repression and a steady stream of executions (189 acknowledged). Hostages were taken, but this seemed not to deter sabotage. Concentration camps in Norway were crowded with about 12,000 inmates, and about 1,500 had been taken to Germany by November, prior to the arrest of the Oslo students. Some 2,300 Jews arrested late in 1942 had their property confiscated and about 1,500 of them were sent to Poland. Many young men continued to escape to England or to Sweden. Some 17,000 Norwegians were in Sweden by the summer of 1943, but the border was becoming increasingly difficult to cross. The teachers arrested in 1942 were released except for about 40.

The Germans had great difficulty with the students and faculty at the University of Oslo. In March 1943, when the students refused to recognize the nazi student organization, the university was closed and the students sent to do forest work. In the fall the government attempted to enforce new politically determined admission requirements. When a number of the faculty protested they were sent to a concentration camp. But the students also

HAAKON VII, Norway's exiled king (centre), laughing at a remark by the lord mayor of Cardiff, Wales, at a luncheon for Norwegian merchant sailors in July 1943

objected, and too clearly showed their lack of appreciation of the "new order"; hence the mass arrest of 1,200 students on Nov. 30. This act aroused resentment and vigorous protests from Sweden and Switzerland (among the few free peoples who were still on any kind of speaking terms with the nazis), but a large number (at least 300) were nevertheless transported to Germany, where they were promised a special camp.

On Aug. 16, 1943 Quisling issued a decree recognizing a *de facto* state of war in Norway; under it an Oslo police official, Gunnar Eilifsen, was immediately executed, and the entire force of 500–550 men was required to swear loyalty to the regime on pain of death for refusal. The cause of the difficulty was supposedly the refusal of the police to arrest girls to be taken to Germany for labour service. On Oct. 1 a new decree stipulated the death sentence for any disobedience of orders. Still there could be, and was, effective opposition; when an additional 35,000 labourers were demanded, people gave false names and addresses and by various means cut the available number to 3,500; then they fired with gasoline the building containing 90,000 of the record cards.

However, fortification and road building were pushed forward. 100,000 Norwegians were doing forced labour, and probably an additional 100,000 foreigners. In addition Norway had to support an occupying army of about 200,000 men. Total costs for three years of "protection" ran to 9,000,000,000 kroner, and the national debt rose from 1,500,000,000 kr. to 4,000,000,000 kr. Funds taken from the Bank of Norway amounted to 6,600,000,-000 kr.

One of the encouraging events of 1943 to Norwegians was the Swedish order of August forbidding the transit and leave traffic for German materials and soldiers on Swedish railroads. This meant inconvenience for the Germans, and it meant above all the removal of the chief sore point in the relations between Norway and Sweden.

The food situation in the country was bad. The farmer's capital was exhausted, his help was gone, horses were scarce, there was little machinery and no fuel, and commercial fertilizers were not to be had. The forests were being denuded rapidly. The resultant food shortage caused in turn a sharp increase in disease (especially tuberculosis, rickets and "hunger-dropsy") and a general lowering of vitality.

Abroad the Norwegian government-in-exile in London decreed decisive action against all traitors as soon as the war permitted action. Nygaardsvold's government also, however, pledged that it would present itself to the people as soon as an election could be held, and stand or fall by the democratic verdict. The Norwegian merchant marine, though sadly depleted, continued to do magnificent service, as did the Norwegian air force, which claimed to have returned in full to Germany the tonnage of bombs which the Germans gave Norway in 1940. The Norwegian navy, especially the corvettes, was making itself effective against submarines, and an army was organized and ready for action.

Education.—In 1937–38 there were 357,793 students and 10,-521 teachers in the elementary schools; 31,127 students and 1,809 teachers in the middle schools and gymnasia, and 16,033 students in continuation schools. The 11 universities had a combined enrolment of 4,998. The total state budget for educational purposes in 1939–40 was 65,364,000 kr.

Finance.—The monetary unit is the krone (23.4 U.S. cents in 1939). Budgetary income and expenses for 1937–38 balanced at

572,135,000 kr.; the proposed budget of 1939–40 was 595,627,000 kr. The government in London planned expenditures of 142,827,-636 kr. in the first six months of 1941 and of about 92,000,000 kr. in the second six months of 1942. Nearly one-sixth of this was for payments on the state debt. Income was largely from the merchant fleet, requisitioned early in the war.

Trade.—In 1939 exports were valued at 808,172,000 kr.; imports, 1,361,835,000 kr. The imports rose rapidly in the last three months, while Norway built up stocks for the war period.

Communication.—In 1939 there were 2,335 mi. of state railways and 25,677 mi. of highways (11,857 mi. improved, 13,820 unimproved). In 1938 there were 107,657 motor vehicles. Norwegian air lines flew a total of 85,000 mi. in 1938. Telephones numbered 122,664; telegraph lines extended 21,875 mi.; radio receivers (licensed) numbered 400,623.

Agriculture.—The total value of agricultural products in 1938 was 384,207,000 kr.; of animal products (eggs, milk, wool, etc.), 428,000,000 kr.; furs, 30,000,000 kr. Landholdings numbered 562,407 (298,360 operating units) with a value of 2,410,101,000 kr. Leading crops were wheat 15,791,000 kr., rye 2,197,000 kr., barley 22,382,000 kr. and oats 31,479,000 kr. In 1938 total productive forest area was one-quarter of the total land area, or 18,700,000 ac.

Fisheries.—The total catch of fish in 1937 was 903,646 tons, the value of which was 92,272,000 kr.; 523,000 tons of the total was herring of various kinds.

Manufacturing.—In 1937 there were 4,306 establishments which turned out products valued at 2,023,551,000 kr. According to value of the product, the most important industries were food and tobacco 411,109,000 kr., paper, cellulose 309,733,000 kr., iron and metal 308,169,000 kr., mining 216,511,000 kr., textile 144,488,000 kr., and wood, furniture, etc. 140,756,000 kr.

Mineral Production.—In 1938 the principal mineral product was iron ore, valued at 26,665,000 kr. Pyrites, valued at 18,168,-000 kr., and copper, valued at 5,013,000 kr., were respectively the second and third minerals.

BIBLIOGRAPHY.—Tor Myklebost, *They Came As Friends* (New York, 1943).   (F. D. S.)

Nose: *see* EAR, NOSE AND THROAT, DISEASES OF.

Notre Dame, University of.
An institution of higher education at Notre Dame (South Bend), Indiana.

Principal gifts of the year were the $100,000 I. A. O'Shaughnessy Foundation in Fine Arts, the gift of $107,404 as the first annual alumni fund and a substantial bequest from the estate of Martin Gillen, Wisconsin lawyer.

The most significant academic changes were the great reduction in the number of civilian students and the introduction (July 1) of the navy V-12 program with 1,851 trainees, composed of apprentice seamen, Naval R.O.T.C. and marines. The United States navy reserve midshipmen school continued as a separate program housed and fed on the campus. The university's program of night courses in the ESMWT curricula also continued.

Thomas F. Woodlock of the *Wall Street Journal* was named Laetare medalist for 1943.

A nationwide commemoration of Notre Dame's 72 dead in World War II and 11 missing, was held in December by alumni. Five thousand Notre Dame men were in service.

Outstanding guest lecturer of the year was Roscoe Pound who delivered a series of lectures on "Fifty Years' Growth of American Law." New courses in air law and tax law were introduced. The university year, beginning with July, marked the new 48-week operation under the navy program. For statistics of enrolment, faculty, library volumes, etc., *see* UNIVERSITI AND COLLEGES.

Nova Scotia.
One of the three maritime provinces of tl Dominion of Canada, admitted to the union 1867; area 21,428 sq.mi.; pop. (1941), 577,962. Capital, Ha fax (70,488); estimated wartime population 1943, 106,480. Oth cities are Sydney (28,305) and Glace Bay (25,147) both centr of coal, iron and steel industries. The lieutenant governor 1943 was H. E. Kendall; the premier A. S. MacMillan.

Education.—The number of students in provincially controll schools in 1942 was 122,378; in private schools, 3,459; in ins tutions of university standard, 2,389.

Communication.—The mileage of surfaced highways in 19 was 6,234; earth highways, 8,853; provincial expenditure highways, $1,746,369. The railroad mileage in 1942 was 1,39 the number of telephones, 52,251.

Finance.—The ordinary receipts in 1942 were $16,443,94 ordinary expenditure, $15,497,608. The direct debt (less sinki funds) was $98,478,264; indirect liabilities (less sinking funds $3,181,812.

Agriculture.—The acreage of field crops in 1943 was 519,60 gross value of field products, $16,316,000.

Table I.—*Leading Agricultural Products of Nova Scotia, 1942 and 1941*

Crop	1942	1941
Oats, bu..	2,622,000	2,356,000
Turnips, cwt..	3,920,000	4,020,000
Potatoes, cwt.	2,496,000	1,887,000
Hay and clover, tons	663,000	632,000

Manufacturing.—The gross value of manufactured produc in 1940 was $113,814,650; net value, $40,548,446; number c employees, 21,062; salaries and wages, $21,519,617.

Table II.—*Principal Industries of Nova Scotia, 1939 and 1938*

Industry	Value of products	
	1939	1938
Steel works.	$15,223,484	$11,183,267
Fish packing	6,531,571	6,471,510
Pulp and paper	5,523,373	5,933,523
Railway rolling stock	2,507,399	3,246,033
Sawmills	2,954,498	3,013,284

Mineral Production.—The value of the mineral production i 1942 was $31,652,244. The Inverness field had been closed.

Table III.—*Principal Mineral Products of Nova Scotia, 1940 and 1939*

Mineral	Value	
	1940	1939
Coal.	$28,766,195	$25,611,271
Gypsum	1,302,347	1,340,830
Gold	855,432	1,082,170

BIBLIOGRAPHY.—*The Royal Gazette; Journal of Education; Public A counts; Report of Department of Industry and Publicity; Canada Yea Book, 1942.*   (J. C. HE.)

Nursery Schools: *see* EDUCATION.

Nursing, War.
To meet the nation's critical wartime nursin shortage, the president of the United States on June 15, 1943, approved the Bolton act, public law 74, whicl had been passed unanimously by the 78th congress.

Graduate nurses, responding to the call of the armed forces had left the staffs of hospitals, health and welfare agencies schools and institutions. War industries and public health agencie needed larger nursing staffs. The civilian shortage of nurses ha reached dangerous proportions in war-boom areas. Hospitals, car rying peak loads of patients, were pressed for additional service at the very time their staffs were being depleted. In short, the civilian hospital system of the country, early in 1943, was faced with a threatened collapse, due to the shortage of nurses.

The nurse training program, initiated in 1941 as part of the national defense health activities had been successful within the limitations imposed by law, but the need for more substantial government aid in the recruitment of nurses became acute when the army and navy issued a call for an additional 37,899 nurses in 1943.

Leaders in nursing, nurse education and hospital fields studied the problem and appealed for aid from government agencies concerned—army, navy, U.S. public health service, Federal Security agency, and Veterans' administration. Representing the consensus of all interested groups, the Bolton act was drafted with the full co-operation of the profession, after a series of conferences attended by representatives of the National Nursing Council for War Service, the American Hospital association and governmental agencies concerned.

Congresswoman Frances P. Bolton, Ohio, sponsored the act, "to provide the training of nurses for the armed forces, governmental and civilian hospitals, health agencies and war industries, through grants to institutions providing such training and for other purposes." Under this act, the U.S. cadet nurse corps was established. Federal funds were appropriated for carrying out a national nurse recruitment and nurse education program. In addition to undergraduate training, aid for graduate and refresher courses was authorized. Administration was placed under the U.S. public health service. Recruitment is carried on through the National Nursing Council for War Service.

The Federal Security administrator appointed an advisory committee to advise the surgeon general, U.S. public health service, concerning the rules and regulations authorized by law. The division of nurse education was established in the office of the surgeon general, to direct the program. Miss Lucile Petry, granted leave of absence from her position as dean of the Cornell university-New York hospital school of nursing, was appointed director.

A minimum of 65,000 new student nurses was set up as a national recruitment quota for the fiscal year, July 1, 1943, to June 30, 1944. The 1,255 schools of nursing accredited by the American College of Surgeons were invited to accelerate their curricula, expand their facilities and participate in the U.S. cadet nurse corps program. As of Dec. 31, 1943, 974 schools had applied and been approved for participation. The schools already accepted expected to admit 44,439 new cadets and to have a total cadet enrolment of 91,013 during the fiscal year 1943–44.

Under the provisions of the Bolton act, cadet nurses received complete nursing education through accelerated programs ranging from 24 to 30 months. The pre-cadet period was the first 9 months, the junior cadet period the next 15 to 21 months, depending on the school's curriculum. In those states and/or schools where regulations required 36 months for graduation, a senior cadet period was provided, during which the student practised nursing, under supervision, in the home school of nursing, or other civilian, military or governmental institution or agency. The choice was hers. In general, the standards of the National League of Nursing Education were used as a guide. Upon graduation, a cadet was eligible to become a registered nurse and to enter any field of nursing.

In addition to national recognition for rendering a war service, cadet nurses received full scholarships covering the cost of tuition, fees, books, maintenance, uniforms and monthly cash allowances: $15 during the pre-cadet period; $20 during the junior period; and at least $30 as a senior cadet.

Young women between the ages of 17 or 18, depending on state and school regulations, and 35, who are graduates of an accredited high school with satisfactory grades, and in good health, may qualify to become members of the U.S. cadet nurse corps. An increasing number of nursing schools are enrolling married students. Any member of the corps enrolled 90 days prior to the cessation of hostilities will be permitted to complete her training under the U.S. cadet nurse plan.

In return for advantages received through the corps, cadet nurses promise that, health permitting, they will remain in nursing, either essential civilian or military, for the duration. They are not required to pledge themselves to military service alone.

Corps members were not placed on the payroll of the federal government. Schools of nursing approved under the requirements of the Bolton act received allotments from the U.S. public health service to help meet the cost of equipping and instructing cadet nurse corps members. This was a grant-in-aid program.

The official outdoor uniform for 1943–44 of the corps included a gray wool suit, two gray and white striped cotton suits, a wool topcoat, a raincoat and berets to match the suits. Markings were regimental red epaulets and sleeve insignia. Silver buttons, lapel and epaulet insignia and cap device were also furnished. Indoor uniforms were those of the school attended. The woven insignia of the U.S. cadet nurse corps might be worn on the left sleeve.

The Bolton act provided postgraduate and refresher training to approximately 4,000 graduate nurses in the first six months of the program. Postgraduate programs in universities and colleges qualified graduate nurses for nursing service positions, faculty positions and specialized work in the various clinical fields. Refresher courses, designed to round out or make up deficiencies in basic nursing training, prepared inactive graduate nurses to return to practice.

A nursing section was established during 1943 in the procurement and assignment service of the War Manpower commission. This section had as its objectives (1) to procure nurses to meet the needs of the armed forces, having due consideration for civilian nursing needs; (2) to bring about the equitable distribution of the remaining nurses in order to maintain the best possible nursing service for the civilian population and non-military governmental agencies. (T. Pn.)

Nutmegs: *see* Spices.

Nutrition: *see* Dietetics; Food Research; Medicine; Vitamins.

Nutrition and Home Economics, Bureau of: *see* Agricultural Research Administration.

Nuts. The acreage of planted nut trees was estimated to be 565,000 ac. in 1942, having increased steadily from about 407,000 ac. in 1932. The principal nuts produced in the United States are pecans, walnuts, almonds and filberts. Pecans are much the most important and are produced chiefly in the southeastern states and Texas, while walnuts are grown in California and Oregon, almonds in California, and filberts in Oregon and Washington.

The pecan crop in 1943 in the 12 principal states was 114,747,000 lb. compared to 77,200,000 lb. in 1942 and a 10-year average 1932–41 of 91,113,000 lb. The 1943 crop was 15% above the average. Improved varieties yielded 49,223,000 lb. while the seedlings produced a crop of 65,526,000 lb. compared to 31,670,000 in 1942. The Texas and Oklahoma crops, consisting mostly of seedlings, were three times the light crop of last year; the Georgia crop, the largest in the southeast, was 17% smaller than last year's record crop of 26,500,000 lb.

The California walnut crop in 1943 was 57,000 tons, the same as in 1942, while the Oregon crop was 5,700 tons compared to

U.S. Production of Pecans by States, 1943 and 1942

State	Improved Varieties		Wild Varieties	
	1943 lb.	1942 lb.	1943 lb.	1942 lb.
Georgia	18,480,000	22,300,000	3,520,000	4,200,000
Alabama	8,300,000	7,900,000	2,200,000	2,000,000
Mississippi	5,300,000	3,100,000	3,700,000	2,300,000
Texas	4,200,000	1,500,000	23,800,000	8,800,000
South Carolina	3,000,000	2,700,000	450,000	400,000
Louisiana	2,620,000	1,900,000	6,880,000	4,500,000
Florida	2,579,000	2,700,000	1,945,000	1,900,000
North Carolina	2,380,000	2,200,000	320,000	300,000
Arkansas	1,200,000	900,000	3,400,000	2,500,000
Oklahoma	1,100,000	300,000	17,400,000	3,440,000
Missouri	52,000	20,000	1,348,000	580,000
Illinois	12,000	10,000	563,000	490,000

U.S. Production of Oats, 1943 and 1942

State	1943 bu.	1942 bu.	State	1943 bu.	1942 bu.
Iowa	184,012,000	196,270,000	North Carolina	5,977,000	6,625,000
Minnesota	142,791,000	177,567,000	California	5,408,000	5,696,000
Illinois	113,091,000	137,787,000	Colorado	5,355,000	5,647,000
Wisconsin	100,347,000	100,577,000	Wyoming	3,999,000	3,906,000
Nebraska	71,676,000	58,278,000	Alabama	3,936,000	4,800,000
North Dakota	70,924,000	74,925,000	Louisiana	3,712,000	3,150,000
South Dakota	70,500,000	90,400,000	Tennessee	3,339,000	3,105,000
Missouri	51,750,000	59,427,000	Maine	3,315,000	4,017,000
Kansas	47,424,000	46,232,000	Virginia	2,860,000	3,510,000
Indiana	33,212,000	52,392,000	Utah	1,890,000	1,638,000
Ohio	29,424,000	51,824,000	Kentucky	1,760,000	1,760,000
Michigan	23,898,000	67,410,000	West Virginia	1,599,000	1,848,000
Oklahoma	22,914,000	23,940,000	Vermont	1,188,000	1,061,000
Texas	21,980,000	11,210,000	New Jersey	1,100,000	1,290,000
Montana	18,760,000	20,319,000	Maryland	1,032,000	1,110,000
Pennsylvania	14,878,000	26,010,000	New Mexico	816,000	924,000
South Carolina	14,102,000	13,461,000	Nevada	369,000	320,000
Oregon	11,363,000	10,064,000	Arizona	243,000	252,000
Georgia	10,120,000	10,152,000	New Hampshire	210,000	273,000
New York	9,724,000	33,440,000	Massachusetts	155,000	198,000
Washington	9,264,000	10,560,000	Florida	150,000	168,000
Mississippi	9,000,000	9,000,000	Connecticut	120,000	136,000
Idaho	7,400,000	7,898,000	Delaware	100,000	132,000
Arkansas	6,850,000	7,904,000	Rhode Island	31,000	34,000

(J. C. Ms.)

3,600 tons in 1942. The total crop of the two states was about 3% larger than in 1942 and 17% above the 10-year average of 53,440 tons. The California harvest was slower than usual and the quality of the nuts was reduced by an unusually large percentage of shriveled kernels.

The almond crop of California was 16,000 tons, which was 6,000 tons smaller than the 1942 record crop of 22,000 tons, but larger than the 10-year average 1930–39 of 12,590 tons.

The filbert crop of Oregon and Washington was 7,260 tons or 70% larger than the 1942 crop of 4,570 tons. The 10-year average was 2,397 tons. (*See also* Coco-Nuts; Peanuts.)   (J. C. Ms.)

NWLB (National War Labor Board): *see* War Labor Board, National.

NYA: *see* National Youth Administration.

Nyasaland: *see* British East Africa.

Nylon: *see* Rayon and Other Synthetic Fibres.

Oakes, Sir Harry

(1874–1943), British millionaire, was born Dec. 23 in Sangerville, Me. A gold prospector in his youth, he travelled throughout the world in search of ore for 15 years before striking a lode at Kirkland Lake, Ontario. He became a British subject in 1915, while he was a resident of Canada and when he moved to Nassau, Bahamas, in 1937, he became a citizen of that colony. Sir Harry, who was made a British baronet in 1939, was believed to have been one of the world's richest men. He was found dead, July 8, 1943, in his palatial Nassau home. Police investigators were called in, and it was disclosed that apparently the wealthy baronet had been beaten and clubbed to death. On July 10 the Nassau police arrested his son-in-law, Alfred de Marigny, who had married Nancy Oakes, daughter of Sir Harry. De Marigny was booked on charges of murder. His trial opened Oct. 18; the prosecution attempted to prove that the defendant clubbed his father-in-law to death because he feared he would lose his chance to share in the huge Oakes fortune. During the 22 sessions many lurid details regarding activities of the "fast set" in the Bahamas were revealed.

On Nov. 11, 1943, the jury hearing the murder charge voted nine to three for acquittal of de Marigny but also recommended his immediate deportation.

Oats.

The oat crop of 1943 was estimated by the United States department of agriculture at 1,143,867,000 bu. compared with 1,349,547,000 bu. in 1942 and a 10-year average of 1,018,783,000 bu., 1932–41. This 15% decline from the previous year was due to lower yields, the average being about 30 bu. per acre in 1943 compared with almost 40 bu. in 1942, though above the 10-year average of 28 bu. Good harvesting weather in the western states favoured the yield and offset lower yields in central and eastern states. Stocks of oats carried over were less than a year earlier due to the great demand for feed resulting from the large increase in livestock numbers.

Obituaries.

The following is a list of men and women who died during 1943. An asterisk (*) marks those for whom biographical notices are to be found in regular alphabetical position.

Name	Birth date	Death date
*Abd-el-Aziz IV, sultan of Morocco	Feb. 24, 1878	June 9
*Aberhart, William, Canadian politician	Dec. 30, 1878	May 23
Ailsa, Archibald Kennedy, 4th Marquess of, British lawyer, soldier	May 22, 1872	Feb. 27
Alger, John Lincoln, U.S. educator	Nov. 20, 1864	Jan. 11
Allen, Edgar, U.S. anatomist, educator	May 2, 1892	Feb. 3
*Ames, Joseph Sweetman, U.S. physicist, educator	July 3, 1864	June 24
Anderson, Alexander Pierce, U.S. botanist, chemist	Nov. 22, 1862	May 7
Anderson, John, U.S. dramatic critic	Oct. 18, 1896	July 16
*Andrews, Charles McLean, U.S. historian, educator	Feb. 22, 1863	Sept. 9
*Andrews, Frank Maxwell, U.S. army officer	Feb. 3, 1884	May 3
Andrews, John Bertram, U.S. economist	Aug. 2, 1880	Jan. 4
Angus, Samuel, Irish educator and theologian	Aug. 27, 1881	Nov.17(?)
*Antoine, André, French actor-manager	Jan. 31, 1851	Oct. 21 (?)
Apanasenko, Joseph R., Russian army officer	(?)	Aug. (?)
*Appleyard, Rollo, British consulting engineer	Jan. 1, 1867	Mar. 1
*Armitage, Albert Borlase, British explorer	July 2, 1864	Nov. 2
Arniches, Carlos, Spanish dramatist	1866	Apr. 15
Arny, Henry Vinecome, U.S. chemist and university dean	Feb. 28, 1868	Nov. 3
*Aronson, Naoum, Russian sculptor	1872(?)	Sept. 30
Babb, Max Wellington, U.S. industrialist	July 28, 1874	Mar. 13
Babcock, Edward Silas, U.S. educator	Apr. 17, 1867	May 21
Ball, Elmer Darwin, U.S. entomologist	Sept. 21, 1870	Oct. 5
Ball, Frank Clayton, U.S. manufacturer	Nov. 24, 1857	Mar. 19
Barber, Charles Williams, U.S. army officer	Sept. 21, 1872	Jan. 7
Barbour, Henry Gray, U.S. pharmacologist, educator	Mar. 28, 1886	Sept. 23
*Barbour, W. Warren, U.S. politician	July 31, 1888	Nov. 22
*Barclay, McClelland, U.S. illustrator	May 9, 1893	July (?)
*Barker, Lewellys Franklin, U.S. physician, educator	Sept. 16, 1867	July 13
Barlow, Reginald, U.S. actor	1867(?)	July 6
*Barr, Norman Burton, U.S. welfare worker	Jan. 27, 1868	Apr. 1
Barton, Pamela, British women's golf champion	1917(?)	Nov. 13
*Baur, Harry, French actor	1880(?)	Apr. 8(?)
*Beatty, Sir Edward Wentworth, Canadian railroad executive	Oct. 16, 1877	Mar. 23
Becker, William Dee, U.S. politician	1874(?)	Aug. 1
*Beers, Clifford Whittingham, U.S. pioneer in mental hygiene	Mar. 30, 1876	July 9
Bell, Edward Price, U.S. newspaperman	Mar. 1, 1869	Sept. 23
Ben Avi, Ittamar, Palestine editor	1883(?)	Apr. 18
*Benét, Stephen Vincent, U.S. poet	July 22, 1898	Mar. 13
Bergalli, Marcelino, Uruguayan army officer	1882(?)	Apr. 18
*Bernie, Ben, U.S. orchestra leader, actor	1891(?)	Oct. 20
*Bevan, Arthur Dean, U.S. surgeon	Aug. 9, 1861	June 10
*Binyon, Laurence, British poet, critic	Aug. 10, 1869	Mar. 10
*Birch, Reginald Bathurst, U.S. artist, illustrator	May 2, 1856	June 17
Blackie, Ernest Morell, British bishop	Aug. 19, 1867	Mar. 1
Blake, Edgar, U.S. clergyman	Dec. 8, 1869	May 26
Blanco-Galindo, Carlos, Bolivian army officer, politician	Mar. 12, 1882	Oct. 2
Blatchford, Robert, British author and socialist	Mar. 17, 1851	Dec. 17
*Bledsoe, Julius (Jules) C., U.S. Negro singer	Dec. 29, 1898	July 14
Bolton, Mother Margaret, U.S. educator	Feb. 12, 1873	Feb. 28
Bordes, Pierre, French politician	Dec. 28, 1870	July 24(?)
*Boris III, king of the Bulgarians	Jan. 30, 1894	Aug. 28
Boris, Grand Duke Boris Vladimirovich, Russian aristocrat and cousin of Czar Nicholas II	Nov. 18, 1877	Nov. 8
*Bosworth, Hobart Van Zandt, U.S. actor	Aug. 11, 1867	Dec. 30
*Boutens, Peter Cornelis, Netherlands poet	Feb. 20, 1870	Mar. 14
Bowie, Edward Hall, U.S. meteorologist	Mar. 29, 1874	July 29
*Bracco, Roberto, Italian dramatist	Nov. 10, 1861	Apr. 21
Bragg, Caleb S., U.S. flier, auto racer	Nov. 26, 1886	Oct. 24
*Bridgman, George B., U.S. artist and art teacher	Nov. 5, 1864	Dec. 16
Brigham, Carl Campbell, U.S. educator	May 4, 1890	Jan. 24
Brockman, Ann (Mrs. William C. McNulty), U.S. artist	Nov. 6, 1899	Oct. 18
Broderick, Bonaventure Finnbarr, U.S. clergyman	Dec. 25, 1868	Nov. 18
Brown, William Adams, U.S. clergyman	Dec. 29, 1865	Dec. 15
Bull, Ernest M., U.S. steamship executive	Oct. 2, 1875	Oct. 6
*Bumpus, Hermon Carey, U.S. educator	May 5, 1862	June 21

Name	Birth date	Death date
BUNGE, ALEJANDRO E., Argentine economist and financier	Jan. 8, 1880	May 24
BUNGE, AUGUSTO, Argentine physician, politician	Apr. 25, 1877	Aug. 2
BURNHAM, WILLIAM ARNOLD WEBSTER LAWSON, 3RD BARON, British army officer	Mar. 19, 1864	June 15
*BURNS, JOHN, British politician	Oct. 20, 1858	Jan. 24
BURRARD, SIR SIDNEY GERALD, British geologist, geographer	Aug. 12, 1860	Mar. 16
BUSCH, CARL, U.S. musician, composer	1862(?)	Dec. 19
*BYRON, ARTHUR WILLIAM, U.S. actor	Apr. 3, 1872	July 16
*CADY, HAMILTON PERKINS, U.S. chemist, educator	May 2, 1874	May 26
CALDER, FRANK, Canadian sports official	Nov. 17, 1877	Feb. 4
CALDERON, LUIS FELIPE, Colombian diplomat	Sept. 25, 1864	Aug. 19
CALDWELL, WILLIAM EDGAR, U.S. gynaecologist	Feb. 23, 1880	Apr. 1
CALKINS, GARY NATHAN, U.S. scientist, educator	Jan. 18, 1869	Jan. 4
CAMDEN, HARRY POOLE, JR., U.S. sculptor	Mar. 10, 1900	July 29
CAMPBELL, CHARLES MACFIE, U.S. psychiatrist, educator	Sept. 8, 1876	Aug. 7
CAMPBELL, GEORGE ALEXANDER, U.S. clergyman	Jan. 27, 1869	Aug. 17
CANABAL, TOMAS GARRIDO, Mexican politician	1890(?)	Apr. 8
CANNON, SYLVESTER QUAYLE, U.S. church official, construction engineer	June 10, 1877	May 29
CARLISLE, ARTHUR, Canadian clergyman	Nov. 29, 1887	Jan. 5
CARLTON, WILLIAM NEWNHAM CHATTIN, U.S. librarian, author	June 29, 1873	Feb. 3
CARLYLE, ALEXANDER JAMES, British clergyman and educator	July 24, 1861	May 28
CARRUTH, WILLIAM MASSEY, U.S. educator	Apr. 22, 1879	Jan. 23
*CARVER, GEORGE WASHINGTON, U.S. chemurgist	1864(?)	Jan. 5
*CATTANI, FEDERICO, CARDINAL, Italian prelate	Apr. 17, 1856	Apr. 12
CATTERALL, ARTHUR, British musician	1884	Nov. 28
CAYZER, SIR AUGUST BERNARD TELLEFSEN, British shipping executive	Jan. 21, 1876	Mar. 1
*CAZALET, VICTOR ALEXANDER, British M.P.	Dec. 27, 1896	July 4
CHAMBERLAIN, CHARLES JOSEPH, U.S. botanist, educator	Feb. 23, 1863	Jan. 5
CHESTER, FREDERICK DIXON, U.S. bacteriologist, chemist	Oct. 8, 1861	Jan. 1
*CHITTENDEN, RUSSELL HENRY, U.S. physiological chemist	Feb. 18, 1856	Dec. 26
*CHURCH, SAMUEL HARDEN, U.S. industrialist	Jan. 24, 1858	Oct. 11
CHU SHEN, Chinese politician	1879	July 4(?)
*CLAIR, MATTHEW WESLEY, U.S. Negro clergyman	Oct. 21, 1865	June 28
CLARK, BARZILLA WORTH, U.S. politician	Dec. 22, 1881	Sept. 21
*CLAWSON, RUDGER, U.S. Mormon church leader	Mar. 12, 1857	June 21
CLIFFE, ALICE BELMORE, British actress	1870(?)	July 31
*COATES, JOSEPH GORDON, New Zealand statesman	1878	May 27
COFFROTH, JAMES WOOD, U.S. boxing promoter	Sept. 12, 1872	Feb. 6
*COLLES, HENRY COPE, British music critic, author	Apr. 20, 1879	Mar. 4
COLLINGWOOD, ROBIN GEORGE, British educator	1889	Jan. 11(?)
COLLINS, JAMES J. (JIMMY), U.S. baseball star	1870(?)	Mar. 6
CONNAUGHT AND STRATHEARN, ALASTAIR ARTHUR, DUKE OF, British army officer	Aug. 9, 1914	Apr. 26
COOK, WALTER WHEELER, U.S. educator and law professor	June 4, 1873	Nov. 7
CORDEAUX, SIR HARRY EDWARD SPILLER, British government official	Nov. 15, 1870	July 2
COTSWORTH, MOSES B., British advocate of calendar reform	Dec. 3, 1859	June 4
COTTENHAM, MARK EVERARD PEPYS, 6TH EARL OF, British peer	May 29, 1903	July 20(?)
COULTER, STANLEY, U.S. educator	June 2, 1853	June 26
CRABITÈS, PIERRE, U.S. judge, author	Feb. 17, 1877	Oct. 9
CREAL, EDWARD WESTER, U.S. congressman	Nov. 20, 1883	Oct. 13
*CREMONESI, CARLO, CARDINAL, Italian ecclesiast	Nov. 4, 1866	Nov. 25
*CRILE, GEORGE WASHINGTON, U.S. surgeon, scientist	Nov. 11, 1864	Jan. 7
*CRUMIT, FRANK, U.S. stage and radio star	1889	Sept. 7
*CUDAHY, JOHN, U.S. diplomat	Dec. 10, 1887	Sept. 6
*DAFOE, ALLAN ROY, Canadian physician	May 29, 1883	June 2
*DANCHENKO, VLADIMIR NEMIROVICH, Russian theatrical producer	1858(?)	Apr. 25
DARDEL, NILS DE, Swedish artist	1888(?)	May 25
*DARWIN, LEONARD, British economist, eugenist	Jan. 15, 1850	Mar. 21
DAVIS, CHARLES B., U.S. jurist	Mar. 9, 1877	Mar. 3
DAVIS, JONATHAN MCMILLAN, U.S. politician	Apr. 26, 1871	June 27
*DE GEER, GERARD (JAKOB), BARON, Swedish geologist	Oct. 2, 1858	July 23
*DELAFIELD, E. M. (MRS. ELIZABETH M. DASHWOOD), British novelist	1891	Dec. 2
*DENNIS, CHARLES HENRY, U.S. newspaper editor	Feb. 8, 1860	Sept. 25
DENNY, COLLINS, U.S. clergyman	May 28, 1854	May 12
DETT, ROBERT NATHANIEL, U.S. composer	Oct. 11, 1882	Oct. 2
*DICKINSON, LUREN DUDLEY, U.S. politician	Apr. 15, 1859	Apr. 22
*DICKINSON, WILLOUGHBY HYETT DICKINSON, 1ST BARON, British statesman	Apr. 9, 1859	June 1
DINAND, JOSEPH NICHOLAS, U.S. clergyman	Dec. 3, 1869	July 29
DINWIDDIE, COURTENAY, U.S. sociologist	Oct. 9, 1882	Sept. 13
*DITTER, J. WILLIAM, U.S. congressman	Sept. 5, 1888	Nov. 21
DIXEY, HENRY E., U.S. actor	Jan. 6, 1859	Feb. 25
DOBSON, WILLIAM ALEXANDER, U.S. naval architect	Aug. 31, 1853	June 3
DOCKWEILER, JOHN FRANCIS, U.S. lawyer, politician	Sept. 19, 1895	Jan. 31
DOHAN, EDITH HALL, U.S. curator, author	Dec. 31, 1877	July 14
DORET, GUSTAVE, Swiss composer	Sept. 20, 1866	Apr. 19
DRAIN, JAMES ANDREW, American Legion commander	Sept. 30, 1870	May 30
*DUNCAN, SIR PATRICK, British politician	Dec. 21, 1870	July 17
*DU PONT, RICHARD CHICHESTER, U.S. glider champion	Jan. 2, 1911	Sept. 11
DYKE, CORNELIUS G., U.S. radiologist	1900(?)	Apr. 23
*ELY, RICHARD THEODORE, U.S. economist	Apr. 13, 1854	Oct. 4
EMSLIE, ROBERT D. (BOB), Canadian baseball umpire	Jan. 27, 1859	Apr. 26
ENGLEBRIGHT, HARRY LANE, U.S. congressman	Jan. 2, 1884	May 13
ENGLISH, ROBERT HENRY, U.S. naval officer	Jan. 16, 1888	Jan. (?)
ERB, DONALD MILTON, U.S. educator	Aug. 3, 1900	Dec. 23
EWERS, HANNS HEINZ, German author	Nov. 3, 1871	June 17(?)
*EWING, JAMES, U.S. pathologist	Dec. 25, 1866	May 16
FAIRCHILD, HERMAN LE ROY, U.S. geologist and educator	Apr. 29, 1850	Nov. 29
FALCONER, SIR ROBERT ALEXANDER, Canadian educator and university president	Feb. 10, 1867	Nov. 4
FARNHAM, SALLY JAMES, U.S. sculptor	(?)	Apr. 28
FARRELL, JAMES AUGUSTINE, U.S. steel executive	Feb. 15, 1863	Mar. 28
FEDELE, PIETRO, Italian historian, educator	1873	Jan. 11
FELT, EPHRAIM PORTER, U.S. entomologist	Jan. 7, 1868	Dec. 14
*FISH, BERT, U.S. foreign service official	Oct. 8, 1875	July 21
*FITZROY, EDWARD ALGERNON, British politician	July 24, 1869	Mar. 3(?)
FLEMING, ALBERT GRANT, Canadian educator, public health leader	Apr. 23, 1887	Apr. 9
*FORD, EDSEL BRYANT, U.S. automobile manufacturer	Nov. 6, 1893	May 26
*FREEMAN, JAMES EDWARD, U.S. clergyman	July 24, 1866	June 6
*FREEMAN, RICHARD AUSTIN, British writer	1862	Sept. 30

Name	Birth date	Death date
FREMANTLE, SIR FRANCIS EDWARD, British M.P.	May 29, 1872	Aug. 26
FREUD, ALEXANDER, Austrian educator	Apr. 18, 1866	Apr. 22
*FUQUA, STEPHEN OGDEN, U.S. army officer	Dec. 25, 1874	May 11
*GAGER, CHARLES STUART, U.S. botanist	Dec. 23, 1872	Aug. 9
*GALWAY, GEORGE VERE ARUNDELL MONCKTON-ARUNDELL, 8TH VISCOUNT, Irish peer	Mar. 24, 1882	Mar. 27
GARRELS, ARTHUR, U.S. consul	Jan. 3, 1873	June 29
*GEORGE OF BAVARIA, PRINCE, Bavarian churchman	Apr. 2, 1880	June 1(?)
GILCHRIST, HARRY LORENZO, U.S. army officer	Jan. 16, 1870	Dec. 26
GIL FORTOUL, JOSÉ, Venezuelan diplomat	1862	June 15
GILLET, LOUIS, French art critic, writer	Dec. 11, 1876	July 1(?)
GILLMORE, FRANK, U.S. actor, union executive	May 14, 1867	Mar. 29
*GLYN, ELINOR (MRS. CLAYTON GLYN), British author	Oct. 17, 1864	Sept. 23
GOODERHAM, ALBERT EDWARD, Canadian industrialist	Oct. 16, 1885	Jan. 23
GOODSPEED, ARTHUR WILLIS, U.S. educator	Aug. 8, 1860	June 6
GRACE, WILLIAM RUSSELL, U.S. corporation official	Apr. 11, 1878	Mar. 31
GRAHAM, GEORGE PERRY, Canadian politician	Mar. 31, 1859	Jan. 2
GRAND, SARAH (MRS. FRANCES ELIZABETH CLARKE MACFALL), British novelist, suffragist	1855(?)	May 12
GRANET, SIR (WILLIAM) GUY, British railroad executive	Oct. 13, 1867	Oct. 12(?)
GRANTLEY, JOHN RICHARD BRINSLEY NORTON, 5TH BARON, British M.P.	Oct. 1, 1855	Aug. 5
*GRAY, GEORGE KRUGER, British artist	Dec. 25, 1880	May 4(?)
*GREGORY, JACKSON, U.S. author	Mar. 12, 1882	June 12
GUERNUT, HENRI ALFRED, French politician	1876	May 30
GUITERMAN, ARTHUR, U.S. writer	Nov. 20, 1871	Jan. 11
GUYER, ULYSSES SAMUEL, U.S. congressman	1869(?)	June 5
HAGGARD, STEPHEN, British actor, novelist	Mar. 21, 1911	Mar. 3(?)
*HALL, RADCLYFFE, British novelist, poet	1886(?)	Oct. 7
*HALL, SIR (WILLIAM) REGINALD, British naval intelligence officer	June 28, 1870	Oct. 22
*HAMMERSTEIN-EQUORD, KURT VON, BARON, German army officer	Sept. 16, 1878	Apr. 24
*HARPER, SAMUEL NORTHRUP, U.S. educator	Apr. 9, 1882	Jan. 18
HARRINGTON, GORDON SIDNEY, Nova Scotian politician	Aug. 7, 1883	July 4
*HART, ALBERT BUSHNELL, U.S. educator	July 1, 1854	June 16
HART, GEORGE HENRY CHARLES, Netherlands economist	Aug. 9, 1893	Sept. 3
*HART, LORENZ (LARRY), U.S. musician and songwriter	May 2, 1895	Nov. 22
*HARTLEY, MARSDEN, U.S. painter	Jan. 4, 1877	Sept. 2
HARTLIEB, J. FREDERICK, U.S. business executive	1877(?)	Jan. 26
*HASSANI, MOHAMED TAGEDDINE EL, SHEIK, Syrian politician	1886	Jan. 17
HATFIELD, WILLIAM HERBERT, British steel scientist	Apr. 10, 1882	Oct. 17
HAUCK, MRS. LOUISE PLATT, U.S. author	Aug. 15, 1883	Dec. 10
HAWES, CHARLES HENRY, U.S. anthropologist	Sept. 30, 1867	Dec. 13
*HAWKES, HERBERT EDWIN, U.S. educator	Dec. 6, 1872	May 4
*HAYASHI, SENJURO, Japanese army officer, statesman	Feb. 23, 1876	Feb. 4(?)
HEADFORT, GEOFFREY THOMAS TAYLOUR, 4TH MARQUESS OF, British politician	June 12, 1878	Jan. 29
HEDRICK, EARLE RAYMOND, U.S. mathematician	Sept. 27, 1876	Feb. 3
HERBERT, SIR JOHN ARTHUR, British civil servant and governor of Bengal	1895	Dec. 11
HERLIN, EMIL, U.S. cartographer	Jan. 28, 1904	Jan. 6
*HEWARD, LESLIE HAYS, British musician, composer	Dec. 8, 1897	May 3
HEWART, GORDON, 1ST VISCOUNT HEWART OF BURY, British lord chief justice	Jan. 7, 1870	May 5
HEYMANN, LIDA GUSTAVA, German educator	Mar. 15, 1868	Aug. (?)
HEYWARD, DUNCAN CLINCH, U.S. politician	June 24, 1864	Jan. 23
*HILBERT, DAVID, German mathematician	Jan. 23, 1862	Feb. (?)
*HINSLEY, ARTHUR, CARDINAL, British prelate	Aug. 25, 1865	Mar. 17
HIRAGA, YUZURU, Japanese ship designer, educator	Mar. 8, 1878	Feb. 17
HIRST, HUGO, 1ST BARON OF WITTON, British utility executive	1863	Jan. 22
HOGAN, ALOYSIUS GONZAGA JOSEPHUS, U.S. ecclesiast and educator	Aug. 5, 1891	Dec. 17
HOOD, SOLOMON PORTER, U.S. clergyman, diplomat	July 30, 1853	Oct. 12
HORWOOD, SIR WILLIAM THOMAS FRANCIS, British army officer and police commissioner	Nov. 1868	Nov. 16
HOUGH, HENRY HUGHES, U.S. naval officer	Jan. 8, 1871	Sept. 9
HOVEY, GEORGE RICE, U.S. educator	Jan. 17, 1860	Jan. 28
*HOWARD, LESLIE, British actor	Apr. 3, 1893	June 1
*HRDLICKA, ALES, U.S. anthropologist	Mar. 29, 1869	Sept. 5
*INGRAM, WILLIAM, U.S. marine officer, football coach	1897(?)	June 2
IRVINE, SIR WILLIAM HILL, Australian politician	July 6, 1858	Aug. 20
ISHAM, NORMAN MORRISON, U.S. architect	Nov. 12, 1864	Jan. 1
*JACOBS, WILLIAM WYMARK, British author	Sept. 8, 1863	Sept. 1
JAQUITH, HAROLD CLARENCE, U.S. educator	May 25, 1888	Apr. 20
JEFFREYS, ELLIS (MINNIE GERTRUDE), British actress	May 17, 1872	Jan. 21
*JESPERSEN, JENS OTTO HARRY, Danish philologist, educator	July 16, 1860	Apr. 30
*JESSCHONNEK, HANS, German army officer	Dec. 10, 1898	Aug. 20(?)
JEWETT, JAMES RICHARD, U.S. educator	Mar. 14, 1862	Mar. 31
JOHNSON, PAUL BURNEY, U.S. state governor	Mar. 23, 1880	Dec. 26
JONES, SIR ROBERT ARMSTRONG-, British surgeon	Dec. 2, 1857	Jan. 30
JULES-BOIS, H. A., French writer	1869(?)	July 2
*JUSTO, AGUSTÍN P., Argentine statesman	Feb. 26, 1876	Jan. 10
KEEN, EDWARD LEGGETT, U.S. newspaperman	Jan. 19, 1870	Oct. 7
KELLAS, ELIZA, U.S. educator	(?)	Apr. 10
*KELLY, HOWARD ATWOOD, U.S. surgeon, radiologist	Feb. 20, 1858	Jan. 12
KENMARE, VALENTINE EDWARD CHARLES BROWNE, 6TH EARL OF, British newspaperman	May 29, 1891	Sept. 20
*KENT, RAYMOND ASA, U.S. college president	July 21, 1883	Feb. 26
KEOGAN, GEORGE, U.S. athletic coach	(?)	Feb. 17
*KEPPEL, FREDERICK PAUL, U.S. educator	July 2, 1875	Sept. 8
KHARITONOFF, FEDOR MIKHAILOVICH, Russian army officer	1899(?)	May 27
KILBY, THOMAS ERBY, U.S. politician	July 9, 1865	Oct. 22
KIMBALL, ARTHUR LIVINGSTONE, U.S. physicist	Feb. 22, 1886	Mar. 20
*KINNICK, NILE CLARKE, JR., U.S. football star	1919(?)	June 2(?)
*KISCH, FREDERICK HERMANN, British army officer	Aug. 1888	Apr. 11
KLENZE, CAMILLO VON, U.S. educator	Mar. 22, 1865	Mar. 17
*KNIGHT, ERIC, British author	Apr. 10, 1897	Jan. 15
KONIJNENBURG, WILLEM ADRIAAN VAN, Netherlands painter	Feb. 11, 1868	Mar. 5(?)
KUMMER, FREDERIC ARNOLD, U.S. author and playwright	Aug. 5, 1873	Nov. 22
LACIAR, SAMUEL LINE, U.S. music critic	July 26, 1874	Jan. 14
LADD, CARL EDWIN, U.S. educator	Feb. 25, 1888	July 23
*LA FONTAINE, HENRI, Belgian politician	Apr. 22, 1854	May 26(?)
LANDES, MRS. BERTHA KNIGHT, U.S. politician, mayor of Seattle, Wash.	Oct. 19, 1868	Nov. 29
*LANDSTEINER, KARL, U.S. medical research scientist	June 14, 1868	June 26
LANE, SIR WILLIAM ARBUTHNOT, British surgeon	July 4, 1856	Jan. 16

Name	Birth date	Death date
*Laparra, Raoul, French composer	May 13, 1876	Apr. 4
*La Puma, Vincenzo, Cardinal, Italian ecclesiast	Jan. 22, 1874	Nov. 4
Laughlin, Frank C., U.S. jurist	July 20, 1859	Jan. 18
Leath, Vaughn de, U.S. singer, composer	Sept. 26, 1900	May 28
Lenihan, Mathias Clement, U.S. clergyman	Oct. 6, 1854	Aug. 19
Lenygon, Francis Henry, British interior decorator	May 11, 1877	June 12
*Leonard, Adna Wright, U.S. clergyman	Nov. 2, 1874	May 3
Levin, Meyer, U.S. bombardier	June 6, 1916	Jan. 7
Lilina, Maria Petrovna, Russian actress	1866(?)	Aug. 24
Limerick, May, Countess of, British welfare worker	(?)	Mar. 11
*Lindsey, Benjamin Barr, U.S. judge	Nov. 25, 1869	Mar. 26
*Link, Mrs. Adeline De Sale, U.S. chemist	Jan. 4, 1892	Nov. 20
*Lin Sen, Chinese president	1864	Aug. 1
Linton, Frank Benton Ashley, U.S. artist	Feb. 26, 1871	Nov. 13
Littell, Philip, U.S. writer and journalist	Aug. 6, 1868	Oct.31(?)
Lockhart, Henry, Jr., U.S. financier	Sept. 30, 1877	Apr. 14
*Loftus, Marie Cecilia (Cissie), British actress	Oct. 22, 1876	July 12
*Lowden, Frank Orren, U.S. politician	Jan. 26, 1861	Mar. 20
*Lowell, Abbott Lawrence, U.S. educator	Dec. 13, 1856	Jan. 6
*Lutz, Frank Eugene, U.S. entomologist	Sept. 15, 1879	Nov. 27
*Lutze, Viktor, German Storm Troop chief	Dec. 28, 1890	May 2
*McAdie, Alexander George, U.S. meteorologist	Aug. 4, 1863	Nov. 1
McArthur, Duncan, Canadian government official	Mar. 17, 1885	July 20
McClaughry, Wilfred Ashton, British air vice marshal	Nov. 26, 1894	Jan. 4
MacDougall, William Dugald, U.S. naval officer	June 20, 1868	Mar. 5
MacEwen, Walter, U.S. artist	Feb. 13, 1860	Mar. 20
Macfarlane, John Muirhead, U.S. botanist, educator	Sept. 28, 1855	Sept. 16
McFarlane, Lewis Brown, Canadian telephone executive	1852(?)	June 9
Machado de Castro e Silva, José, Brazilian navy chief of staff	1866(?)	June 10
*McIntyre, Marvin Hunter, U.S. journalist and secretary to Pres. F. D. Roosevelt	Nov. 27, 1878	Dec. 13
Mack, Julian William, U.S. judge	July 19, 1866	Sept. 5
*McKenna, Reginald, British financier, politician	July 6, 1863	Sept. 6
*Magee, John Benjamin, U.S. educator	July 19, 1887	Apr. 6
Magidoff, Jacob, U.S. editor, journalist	June 22, 1869	Aug. 26
Magie, William Francis, U.S. educator	Dec. 14, 1858	June 6
Main, Charles Thomas, U.S. engineer	Feb. 16, 1856	Mar. 6
Mallory, Hervey Foster, U.S. educator	Oct. 18, 1866	July 22
*Mandel, Georges, French politician	June 5, 1885	June (?)
Manion, Robert James, Canadian government official	Nov. 18, 1881	July 2
Mapes, Victor, U.S. writer	Mar. 10, 1870	Dec.11(?)
Marett, Robert Ranulph, British anthropologist	June 13, 1866	Feb. 18
*Marmon, Howard C., U.S. motor car manufacturer	May 24, 1876	Apr. 4
Marquis, Albert Nelson, U.S. editor and publisher	Jan. 10, 1854	Dec. 21
*Marshall, Tully (William Phillips), U.S. actor	Apr. 13, 1864	Mar. 10
Martin, Lillien Jane, U.S. psychologist	July 7, 1851	Mar. 26
*Marvin, Charles Frederick, U.S. meteorologist	Oct. 7, 1858	June 5
Masliansky, Zvei Hirsh, U.S. Zionist leader	May 16, 1856	Jan. 11
May, Charles Henry, U.S. ophthalmologist and eye surgeon	Aug. 7, 1861	Dec. 7
Mee, Arthur, British editor	July 21, 1875	May 28
*Mei Lan-fang, Chinese actor	1893	Aug. 8(?)
*Mello Franco, Afranio de, Brazilian statesman	Feb. 25, 1870	Jan. 1
*Meloney, Marie Mattingly (Mrs. William Brown Meloney), U.S. editor	1883(?)	June 23
Merritt, Abraham, U.S. editor, author	Jan. 20, 1884	Aug. 21
Merry del Val, Marquis, Spanish diplomat	1864	May 26
Meston, Lord James Scargie, British M.P.	June 12, 1865	Oct. 7
Metzler, William Henry, U.S. educator	Sept. 18, 1863	Apr. 18
Millay, Kathleen, U.S. author	1897(?)	Sept. 21
Miller, Richard E., U.S. painter	Mar. 22, 1875	Jan. 23
*Millerand, Alexandre, French politician	Feb. 10, 1859	Apr. 6
*Milyukov, Paul Nikolayevich, Russian politician, historian	Jan. 27, 1859	Mar. 31
Mitchell, Howard Hawkes, U.S. mathematician	Jan. 14, 1885	Mar. 13
Moffat, Jay Pierrepont, U.S. diplomat	July 18, 1896	Jan. 24
Moisseiff, Leon Solomon, U.S. consulting engineer	Nov. 10, 1872	Sept. 3
*Moltke, Hans Adolf von, German diplomat	Nov. 29, 1884	Mar. 22
Moore, Edward Caldwell, U.S. theologian	Sept. 1, 1857	Mar. 26
Moore, Fred R., U.S. Negro editor	1858(?)	Mar. 1
*Mordacq, Jean-Jules-Henri, French army officer	Jan. 12, 1868	Apr. 12
*Morgan, John Pierpont, U.S. financier	Sept. 7, 1867	Mar. 13
Morton, Sir James, British dye manufacturer	Mar. 24, 1867	Aug. 22
Motherwell, W. R., Canadian government official	Jan. 6, 1860	May 24
*Mowinckel, Johan Ludwig, Norwegian politician	1870	Sept. 30
Murphy, J. Edwin, U.S. journalist	Apr. 16, 1876	Mar. 29
*Muti, Ettore, Italian air officer, politician	May 22, 1902	Aug.24(?)
Nakano, Seigo, Japanese journalist, politician	Feb. 1885	Oct.27(?)
*Nash, Patrick A., U.S. politician	1863	Oct. 6
Nevin, Arthur Finley, U.S. composer	Apr. 27, 1871	July 10
Nichols, Neil Ernest, U.S. naval officer	Sept. 16, 1879	June 23
*Nielsen, Alice, U.S. singer	June 7, 1876	Mar. 8
Nogues, Pablo, Argentine engineer, politician	Sept. 16, 1878	Jan. 14
*Oakes, Sir Harry, British baronet	Dec. 23, 1874	July 8
*O'Brien, Frank Michael, U.S. newspaper editor	Mar. 31, 1875	Sept. 22
O'Brien, Michael Joseph, Canadian clergyman	July 29, 1874	Aug. 30
*O'Day, Caroline Goodwin, U.S. congresswoman	June 22, 1875	Jan. 4
O'Donnell, Pat, U.S. author	1896	Apr. 19
Ogilby, Remsen Brinckerhoff, U.S. educator	Apr. 8, 1881	Aug. 7
O'Gorman, James A., U.S. congressman	May 5, 1860	May 17
*O'Hare, Edward Henry, U.S. naval air officer	Mar. 13, 1914	Nov.(?)
*Olds, Robert, U.S. army air officer	June 15, 1896	Apr. 28
*Olivier, Sydney Olivier, 1st Baron of Ramsden, British statesman	Apr. 16, 1859	Feb. 15
*Onegin, Sigrid, German-Swedish opera singer	June 1, 1891	June18(?)
*Oppenheimer, Franz, German sociologist and politician	Mar. 30, 1864	Sept. 30
*Orlebar, Augustus H., British air officer	1897(?)	Aug. 4
Overman, Lynne, U.S. actor	Sept. 19, 1887	Feb. 19
Pabst, Gustave, U.S. brewer	Nov. 26, 1866	May 29
Packard, Winthrop, U.S. naturalist	Mar. 7, 1862	Apr. 1
*Paddock, Charles William, U.S. editor, track star, marine corps officer	Aug. 11, 1900	July 21
Palmer, Edgar, U.S. business executive	Nov. 12, 1880	Jan. 8
Palmer, Potter, U.S. capitalist	Oct. 8, 1875	Sept. 3
Parsons, Edward Smith, U.S. educator	Aug. 9, 1863	Apr. 22
Parton, Lemuel Frederick, U.S. writer	Oct. 1, 1879	Jan. 30
Partridge, Frank Charles, U.S. politician	May 7, 1861	Mar. 2
Paton, William, British church official	Nov. 13, 1886	Aug. 21
Pearce, Haywood Jefferson, U.S. educator	Aug. 26, 1871	May 1
Pearson, Thomas Gilbert, U.S. ornithologist	Nov. 10, 1873	Sept. 3
Pease, Joseph Albert, Lord Gainford, British politician	Jan. 17, 1860	Feb. 15

Name	Birth date	Death date
*Peek, George Nelson, U.S. manufacturer and agricultural expert	Nov. 19, 1873	Dec. 17
*Pellegrinetti, Ermenegildo, Cardinal, Italian prelate	Mar. 27, 1876	Mar. 29
Perret, Frank Alvord, U.S. volcanologist	Aug. 2, 1867	Jan. 12
*Phelps, William Lyon, U.S. educator, author	Jan. 2, 1865	Aug. 21
Phillips, Sir Frederick, British financial expert	1884	Aug. 16
Phillips, John C., U.S. politician, lawyer	Nov. 13, 1870	June 25
Picknell, George W., U.S. artist	June 26, 1864	Apr. 1
Pier, Garrett Chatfield, U.S. archaeologist	Oct. 30, 1875	Dec. 30
Pierce, Ulysses Grant Baker, U.S. clergyman	July 17, 1865	Oct. 10
Plaisted, Frederick William, U.S. politician	July 26, 1865	Mar. 4
Plymouth, Ivor Miles Windsor-Clive, 2nd Earl of, British M.P.	Feb. 4, 1889	Oct. 1
Polk, Frank Lyon, U.S. lawyer, politician	Sept. 13, 1871	Feb. 7
Pollock, Courtenay Edward Maxwell, British sculptor, inventor, author	(?)	June 7
Portland, William John Arthur Charles James Cavendish-Bentinck, 6th Duke of, British sportsman	Dec. 28, 1857	Apr. 26
Poulton, Sir Edward Bagnall, British zoologist and entomologist	Jan. 27, 1856	Nov. 21
*Pound, Sir (Alfred) Dudley (Pickman Rogers), British naval officer	Aug. 29, 1877	Oct. 21
Powell, William D., U.S. army officer	Nov. 11, 1893	Oct. 6
Powers, James T., U.S. comedian	Apr. 26, 1862	Feb. 10
Price, James H., U.S. attorney and former governor of Virginia	1882(?)	Nov. 22
*Rachmaninoff, Sergei Vassilievitch, U.S. pianist, composer	Apr. 2, 1873	Mar. 28
Rambonnet, Jean Jacques, Netherlands statesman	1864(?)	Aug. 4
*Ramey, Howard Knox, U.S. army air officer	Oct. 14, 1896	Apr. (?)
Rathbone, Albert, U.S. lawyer	July 27, 1868	Aug. 20
Ratshesky, Abraham C., U.S. banker, diplomat	Nov. 6, 1864	Mar. 15
*Ray, Charles, U.S. motion picture actor	Mar. 15, 1891	Nov. 23
*Ray, Edward (Ted), British golf champion	1877	Aug. 27
Reich, Nathaniel Julius, U.S. Egyptologist	Apr. 29, 1882	Oct. 5
*Reinhardt, Max, U.S. theatrical producer	Sept. 9, 1873	Oct. 31
Reuter, Ludwig von, German naval officer	1868(?)	Dec. 21
Rhoades, John Harsen, U.S. banker	Feb. 6, 1869	Jan. 15
*Rice, Cale Young, U.S. poet, dramatist	Dec. 7, 1872	Jan. 24
Rice, Merton Stacher, U.S. clergyman	Sept. 5, 1872	Mar. 17
*Richards, Laura Elizabeth, U.S. author	Feb. 27, 1850	Jan. 14
Richardson, Friend William, U.S. politician	1865(?)	Sept. 5
Ridgway, Erman Jesse, U.S. publisher	Aug. 6, 1867	June 16
Ripley, Alfred Lawrence, U.S. banker	Nov. 6, 1858	Oct. 13
*Roberts, Sir Charles George Douglas, Canadian author and poet	Jan. 10, 1860	Nov. 26
Roberts, Percival, U.S. steel executive	July 15, 1857	Mar. 6
Robins, Edward, U.S. author, historian	Mar. 2, 1862	May 21
*Roosevelt, Kermit, U.S. explorer, author, soldier	Oct. 10, 1889	June 4
*Roper, Daniel Calhoun, U.S. politician	Apr. 1, 1867	Apr. 11
*Rosenfeld, Kurt, German lawyer, politician	Feb. 1, 1877	Sept. 26
Ross, David E., U.S. inventor, manufacturer	Aug. 25, 1871	June 28
*Rowan, Andrew Summers, U.S. army officer	Apr. 23, 1857	Jan. 11
Rowntree, Cecil, British surgeon	1880(?)	Oct. 14
Roy, Camille, Canadian clergyman	Oct. 22, 1870	June 24
Russell, Clinton W., U.S. army officer	May 6, 1891	Mar. 23
Sadler, Sir Michael Ernest, British educator	July 3, 1861	Oct. 14
Safford, Harry Robinson, U.S. railway executive	Feb. 7, 1875	Apr. 10
Sarraut, Maurice-Guillaume, French editor and politician	Sept. 22, 1869	Dec. 3(?)
Schillinger, Joseph, Russian composer	Aug. 31, 1895	Mar. 23
*Schlesinger, Frank, U.S. astronomer	May 11, 1871	July 10
Scott, James Brown, U.S. lawyer, educator	June 3, 1866	June 25
Sears, Charles Hatch, U.S. church official	Nov. 21, 1870	May 3
Sears, Richard D., U.S. tennis champion	1862(?)	Apr. 8
*Selincourt, Ernest de, British educator, writer	Sept. 24, 1870	May 22
Sergent, Emile, French physician	July 11, 1867	May 24(?)
Sexton, Walton Roswell, U.S. naval officer	Sept. 13, 1876	Sept. 9
Shannon, Joseph B., U.S. politician	Mar. 17, 1867	Mar. 28
Sharton, Alexander R., U.S. newspaper publisher	1880(?)	Jan. 30
*Shaw, Mrs. George Bernard, wife of British playwright	(?)	Sept. 12
Sherard, Robert Harborough, British author	Dec. 3, 1861	Jan. 30
Shimazaki, Haruki (Toson), Japanese writer	Feb. 17, 1872	Aug. 22(?)
Shiozawa, Koichi, Japanese naval officer	Mar. 1888	Nov.17(?)
Shute, Henry A., U.S. judge, author	1856(?)	Jan. 25
*Sikorski, Wladyslaw, Polish politician, army officer	May 20, 1881	July 4
*Slemp, Campbell Bascom, U.S. politician	Sept. 4, 1870	Aug. 7
Smith, Harry de Forest, U.S. educator	Jan. 22, 1869	Feb. 2
Smith, Reed, U.S. educator	Jan. 16, 1881	July 24
Snell, Henry Bayley, U.S. artist	Sept. 29, 1858	Jan. 17
*Spykman, Nicholas John, U.S. educator	Oct. 13, 1893	June 26
*Steagall, Henry Bascom, U.S. politician	May 19, 1873	Nov. 22
Stearns, Harold Edmund, U.S. writer	May 7, 1891	Aug. 13
*Stein, Sir Aurel, British archaeologist	Nov. 26, 1862	Oct. 28
*Stimson, Frederic Jesup, U.S. legal scholar and statesman	July 20, 1855	Nov. 19
Stockley, William F. P., Irish educator, politician	1859	Aug. (?)
*Stoessel, Albert Frederic, U.S. musician	Oct. 11, 1894	May 12
Stolz, Karl Ruf, U.S. educator	Jan. 9, 1884	Mar. 29
Stone, John S., U.S. electrical engineer	Sept. 24, 1869	May 20
Strakosch, Sir Henry, British banker	May 9, 1871	Oct. 30
*Sueyro, Saba H., Argentine politician, naval officer	1890(?)	July 17
Swan, Russell Henry Jocelyn, British surgeon	July 20, 1876	Mar. 6
Swartwout, Egerton, U.S. architect	Mar. 3, 1870	Feb. 18
Swift, Gustavus Franklin, U.S. meatpacker	Mar. 1, 1881	Oct. 28
*Taft, Helen Herron (Mrs. William Howard Taft), widow of U.S. president	June 2, 1861	May 22
Taft, Horace Dutton, U.S. educator	Dec. 28, 1861	Jan. 28
Taitt, Francis Marion, U.S. clergyman	Jan. 3, 1862	July 17
Tanner, Richard J. (Diamond Dick), U.S. wild west hero	Nov. 29, 1869	July 2
Tawresey, John Godwin, U.S. naval officer	Jan. 23, 1862	Feb. 17
Taylor, Ivon Roy, U.S. physiologist, educator	Nov. 14, 1897	Sept. 20
*Tesla, Nikola, U.S. inventor	July 10, 1856	Jan. 7
Thomen, August A., U.S. physician, author	Jan. 16, 1892	Sept. 11
Thomson, Sir St. Clair, British laryngologist	July 28, 1859	Jan. 29
Tillett, Benjamin, British politician, labour leader	Sept. 11, 1860	Jan. 27
*Trebitsch-Lincoln, Ignatius, Hungarian-born Buddhist monk	1879	Oct. 7
Trees, Joe Clifton, U.S. oil and gas operator	Nov. 10, 1869	May 19
*Trygger, Ernst, Swedish politician	1857(?)	Sept. 23
Turrell, Walter John, British electrotherapist	Apr. 9, 1865	Jan. 27

Name	Birth date	Death date
*Tussaud, John Theodore, British sculptor	May 2, 1858	Oct. 13
Twitmyer, Edwin Burket, U.S. psychologist	Sept. 14, 1873	Mar. 3
*Ulyanov, Dmitri, Russian politician, medical research scientist	1874	July 16
Underwood, Bert Elias, U.S. photographer	Apr. 29, 1862	Dec. 27
*Upshur, William Peterkin, U.S. marine corps officer	Oct. 28, 1881	July 21
Valencia, Guillermo, Colombian politician, writer	Oct. 29, 1873	July 8
Vance, John Thomas, U.S. librarian	Aug. 24, 1884	Apr. 11
Van Dyke, Woodbridge Strong, U.S. motion picture director	1890(?)	Feb. 5
*Veidt, Conrad, British actor	Jan. 22, 1893	Apr. 3
*Veiller, Bayard, U.S. playwright	1869	June 16
*Vidal y Barraquer, Francis of Assisi, Cardinal, Spanish prelate	Oct. 3, 1868	Sept.14(?)
Vogt, Alfred, Swiss ophthalmologist	Oct. 31, 1879	Dec. 10
Waite, Alice Vinton, U.S. educator	Jan. 16, 1864	Apr. 6
Wakasugi, Kaname, Japanese diplomat	July 1883	Dec. 10
Walden, Percy Talbot, U.S. educator	June 29, 1869	Apr. 15
Waldo, Richard H., U.S. editor	Sept. 28, 1878	June 11
Waldorf, Ernest Lynn, U.S. bishop	May 14, 1876	July 27
Walker, Kenneth N., U.S. army air force officer	July 17, 1898	Jan. 5(?)
Waller, Arthur Craig, British naval officer	June 18, 1872	Feb. 21
*Waller, Thomas W. ("Fats"), U.S. musician and composer	1904(?)	Dec. 15
Ward, Charles Howell, U.S. osteologist	Oct. 28, 1862	Jan. 18
Ward, Freeman, U.S. geologist, educator	Aug. 9, 1879	Sept. 14
Ward, Henry Levi, U.S. naturalist and palaeontologist	Oct. 8, 1863	Dec. 17
*Warren, Whitney, U.S. architect	Jan. 29, 1864	Jan. 24
Waterman, Julian Seesel, U.S. educator	Sept. 9, 1891	Sept. 18
*Webb, Beatrice Potter, British socialist, author	Jan. 22, 1858	Apr. 30
*Webster, Leslie Tillotson, U.S. medical research scientist	July 23, 1894	July 12
*Wedgwood, Josiah Clement Wedgwood, 1st Baron, of Barlaston, British M.P.	Mar. 16, 1872	July 26
*Wells, Harry Gideon, U.S. pathologist	July 21, 1875	Apr. 26
*Wertheimer, Max, German psychologist, philosopher	Apr. 15, 1880	Oct. 12
West, Andrew Fleming, U.S. educator	May 17, 1853	Dec. 27
Wheat, Alfred Adams, U.S. judge	June 13, 1867	Mar. 11
White, Henry Seely, U.S. educator	May 20, 1861	May 20
White, Horace, U.S. lawyer and New York governor	Oct. 7, 1865	Nov. 27
Whitehouse, Sir Harold Beckwith, British surgeon	Oct. 26, 1882	July 28
*Widener, Joseph Early, U.S. turfman, financier	Aug. 19, 1872	Oct. 26
*Wigmore, John Henry, U.S. educator	Mar. 4, 1863	Apr. 20
*Wiley, Henry Ariosto, U.S. naval officer	Jan. 31, 1867	May 20
Willet, Anne Lee, U.S. artist	1866(?)	Jan. 18
Willoughby, Charles Clark, U.S. anthropologist	July 5, 1857	Apr. 21
*Wood, Sir Kingsley, British statesman	1881	Sept. 21
*Woollcott, Alexander, U.S. author	Jan. 19, 1887	Jan. 23
Worsley, Frank Arthur, British explorer	1872	Feb. 1
Wright, William Mason, U.S. army officer	Sept. 24, 1863	Aug. 16
Wynne, Sir Henry Arthur, Irish solicitor	June 14, 1867	Aug. 21
*Yamamoto, Isoroku, Japanese naval officer	Apr. 4, 1884	Apr. (?)
*Yaroslavsky, Emelyan, Russian historian and politician	1878(?)	Dec. 5(?)
*Yersin, Alexandre Émile John, Swiss bacteriologist	Sept. 22, 1863	Mar.2(?)
Yon, Pietro Alessandro, U.S. musician and organist	Aug. 8, 1886	Nov. 22
*Young, Arthur Henry (Art), U.S. artist, cartoonist	Jan. 14, 1866	Dec. 29
Young, Gilbert Amos, U.S. educator	June 24, 1872	June 27
Young, Karl, U.S. educator and author	Nov. 2, 1879	Nov. 17
Zamperini, Louis, U.S. track champion	1918(?)	May 27(?)
*Zeeman, Pieter, Netherlands physicist	May 25, 1865	Oct. 9
Zernatto, Guido, Austrian politician	1904(?)	Feb. 8
Zimmer, Henry Robert, German educator	Dec. 6, 1890	Mar. 20

O'Brien, Frank Michael

(1875-1943), U.S. newspaper editor, was born March 31 in Dunkirk, N.Y. He made his journalistic start in Buffalo, worked up to reporter and later city editor of the Buffalo *Express*. He came to the attention of New York newspapers with his coverage of the assassination of President McKinley at the Buffalo exposition in 1901, and eventually was employed by the New York *Sun* in 1904. He gave up that job to become secretary to the mayor of New York city (1906-10). Returning to newspaper work, he was editor of the New York *Sun*, 1926-43. O'Brien wrote many short stories and won the Pulitzer prize for an editorial "The Unknown Soldier," which appeared in the old New York *Herald* in 1921. He also wrote *The Story of the Sun* (1918) and *New York Murder Mysteries* (1932), a compilation of celebrated New York crimes. He died in New York city, Sept. 22.

Obstetrics: *see* Gynaecology and Obstetrics.
OCD (Office of Civilian Defense): *see* Civilian Defense.
Oceanography: *see* Marine Biology.

O'Day, Caroline Goodwin

(1875-1943), U.S. congresswoman, was born June 22 in Perry, Ga. After graduating from Lucy Cobb institute, Athens, Ga., she studied art in Paris, Munich and Holland, and later won fame as a magazine illustrator and fashion designer. After her marriage, she took an active role in social work and was on the board of the Henry Street settlement. Mrs. O'Day worked dili-

gently for women's suffrage and was regarded as the champion of labour and welfare organizations. After women won the right to vote, she joined the Democratic party organization in Westchester county and was leader of the Democratic women in New York from 1923 until her death. She was elected delegate-at-large to four Democratic national conventions, at several of which she headed the New York state delegation. An ardent supporter of President Roosevelt, Mrs. O'Day supported his New Deal policies during her tenure in congress as New York's representative-at-large, 1935-42. She refused, however, to vote for repeal of the arms embargo in the Neutrality measure, 1939, and voted against the Selective Service bill in 1940. She did, however, vote for a declaration of war after Pearl Harbor. Mrs. O'Day retired from politics in the summer of 1942, because of ill health, and died in Rye, N.Y., Jan. 4.

OEM: *see* Emergency Management, Office for.
OEW: *see* Foreign Economic Administration.
Office for Emergency Management: *see* Emergency Management, Office for.
Office of Civilian Defense: *see* Civilian Defense.
Office of Defense Transportation: *see* Defense Transportation, Office of.
Office of Economic Stabilization: *see* Economic Stabilization, Office of.
Office of Education, U.S.: *see* Education.
Office of Price Administration: *see* Price Administration, Office of.
Office of Scientific Research and Development: *see* Scientific Research and Development, Office of.
Office of War Information: *see* War Information, Office of.

O'Hare, Edward Henry

(1914-1943), U.S. naval air officer, was born March 13 at St. Louis, Mo. Known as "Butch," he attended Western Military academy, Alton, Ill., and was graduated from the U.S. Naval academy at Annapolis, 1937. In 1942, as a fighter pilot with the U.S. Pacific fleet, he was decorated with the congressional medal of honour by President Roosevelt for shooting down, Feb. 20, 1942, five Japanese bombers and for saving his carrier, the "Lexington," from destruction. He was later promoted to lieutenant commander. On Nov. 20, 1943, O'Hare was officially listed as missing. His group of carrier planes attacked a Japanese formation somewhere in the Pacific and his comrades reported that they believed his plane had been shot down.

Ohio.

A north central state of the United States, popularly known as the "Buckeye state." Area, 41,222 sq.mi., including 100 sq.mi. of water; pop. (1940) 6,907,612, of whom 2,294,626 were rural and 4,612,986 urban; native white 6,047,265, foreign-born white 519,266, Negro 339,461, other races 1,620. Capital, Columbus (306,087). Other cities of more than 100,000 were Cleveland (878,336), Cincinnati (455,610), Toledo (282,349), Akron (244,791), Dayton (210,718), Youngstown (167,720) and Canton (108,401).

History.—The 95th general assembly convened Jan. 4, 1943 for what most of its members thought would be a short session, but which stretched out to 25 weeks with adjournment *sine die* coming on June 24. It was one of the longest biennial sessions in the state's history. About 200 bills of the 722 considered were enacted. Among the most important of those enacted were measures which: approved the highest appropriation bill in the history of the state to date; returned the state to Eastern Standard time; authorized liquor rationing; relaxed employment regulations for females and minors; levied an unemployment surtax on pay rolls of manufacturers expanded by war production; provided prison terms for operators of the "numbers" gambling racket; permitted the state highway director to keep secret his engineers' estimates of highway costs and to award contracts in excess of bids; increased state subsidies for schools more than $5,000,000; required the state to relieve counties of the expense of caring for indigent patients in institutions for the feeble-minded; established a postwar planning commission and set aside about $23,000,000 for a postwar welfare building program; increased 1943–44 old-age pension funds by $10,000,000; and extended for two years the liquid fuel, cigarette and utility excise taxes.

Gov. John W. Bricker started his third term Jan. 11, 1943, the only Republican to be elected governor of Ohio three times in succession. In his inaugural address he advocated immediate repeal of the sales tax on food served in restaurants, a suggestion which the general assembly refused to adopt, and announced that the state's net surplus was about $42,000,000. On Nov. 10, 1943 Bricker formally announced that he would be a Republican candidate for president in the Ohio primaries, foregoing a bid for a fourth term as governor.

Other chief officers of the state in 1943 were: Lieut. Gov. Paul M. Herbert, Treasurer Don Ebright, Attorney General Thomas J. Herbert, Secretary of State Edward J. Hummel, Auditor of State Joseph T. Ferguson.

Education.—Ohio in 1943 had 3,828 elementary schools with a total enrolment of 704,477 and a total teaching staff of 21,385; 1,250 secondary schools (including 127 junior high schools) with a total enrolment of 448,988 (including 82,369 pupils in junior high schools) and a total teaching staff of 18,033 (including 2,768 junior high school teachers). Ohio had five state universities with a total enrolment of 25,478 and a total teaching staff of 1,561.

Public Welfare, Charities, Correction.—The average number of general relief cases in Ohio in 1943 was 16,142 and the total spent was $6,720,000; average number of cases of aid for the aged, 134,009 at a total cost of $47,000,000; average number of cases of aid to dependent children, 25,171 at a total cost of $5,727,950; average number of cases of aid to the blind, 3,560 at a total cost of $1,144,000; number of weeks of unemployment compensated (11 months) 117,991, the net amount of benefit payments being $1,430,324. In 1943 the four penal institutions had an average population of 7,077. The two industrial schools had an average population of 1,342. The 22 institutions, including hospitals for the insane and epileptics and homes for the feeble-minded, under the supervision of the department of public welfare, were operated during 1943 at a total cost of $12,000,000.

Communication.—Ohio had 88,895 mi. of highways in 1943 outside municipalities. Of this total, 18,490 mi. were classified as state, 28,409 mi. as county and 41,996 mi. as township. Estimated expenditures on the state highway system in 1943 were $32,000,000. The state had 8,870.26 mi. of railroads, 117 airports and landing fields and 1,580,239 telephones.

Banking and Finance.—There were 443 state banks in Ohio with deposits (Oct. 18, 1943) of $2,882,115,530 and resources of $3,089,632,463. There were 241 active national banks in Ohio with deposits (Oct. 18, 1943) aggregating $2,313,212,000 and resources $2,475,720,000. State-chartered savings and loan associations numbered 540 with total resources (June 30, 1943) of $697,151,689. There were 122 federal savings and loan associations with total assets (Jan. 1, 1943) of $267,634,451.

The state budget for the 1943–44 biennium was $369,034,569. At the close of 1943 Ohio had a surplus in excess of $68,000,000.

Agriculture.—The total acreage harvested in Ohio in 1943 was 10,505,000; in 1942, 10,359,500. Total value of crops in the state

Table I.—*Leading Agricultural Products of Ohio, 1943 and 1942*

Crop	1943	1942
Corn, bu.	174,042,000	185,752,000
Wheat, bu.	26,449,000	36,205,000
Oats, bu.	29,424,000	51,824,000
Barley, bu.	800,000	1,785,000
Rye, bu.	1,140,000	1,870,000
Soybeans, bu.	27,993,000	24,398,000
Potatoes, bu.	8,550,000	9,180,000
Apples, bu.	2,422,000	6,384,000
Tame hay, tons	3,505,000	3,659,000
Tobacco, lb.	21,067,000	24,056,000

in 1943 was $417,391,000; in 1942, $369,756,000. Total value of livestock and livestock products in 1942 was $458,890,000. Total farm cash income in Ohio in 1942 was $599,831,000. Of this, $162,189,000 came from crops; $408,724,000 from livestock and livestock products; $28,918,000 from government payments. In spite of the handicaps of insufficient manpower, lack of mechanical equipment and unfavourable weather in the planting season, Ohio broke some of its production records in 1943 and maintained fifth place among the states in agricultural output.

Manufacturing.—The total value of manufactures in Ohio in 1939 was $4,584,665,659; total employment, 686,089; total wages and salaries paid, $1,033,426,673.

Mineral Production.—The total estimated value of mineral

Table II.—*Principal Mineral Products of Ohio, 1942 and 1941*

Mineral	Value, 1942	Value, 1941
Bituminous coal	$69,200,000*	$58,344,497
Cement	12,517,870	11,988,884
Sand and Gravel	10,570,888	9,230,358
Stone	13,546,490	12,469,498

*Estimated.

production in Ohio in 1942 was $167,207,457.　(P. By.)

Ohio State University.
An institution of higher education at Columbus, Ohio. Formally established as a land-grant institution in 1870, it opened its doors on Sept. 17, 1873, to a student body of 17. The university admits both women and men. It has ten colleges: agriculture, arts and sciences, commerce and administration, dentistry, education, engineering, law, medicine, pharmacy and veterinary medicine; a graduate school; and five special schools: home economics, journalism, nursing, optometry and social administration. Graduate work is offered through the doctor of philosophy degree. Special curricula in 1943 prepared women for secretarial service and for homemaking. A new school of aeronautics was created. Latest additions to the physical plant were a 400-acre airport and a war research laboratory. The university for 20 years had operated on a four-quarter plan, enabling most students to complete their studies in three calendar years. For statistics of enrolment, faculty, etc., see UNIVERSITIES AND COLLEGES. Dr. Howard L. Bevis, president, took office Feb. 1, 1940.　(H. L. B.)

Oil: see PETROLEUM.

Oils and Fats, Vegetable and Animal: see VEGETABLE OILS AND ANIMAL FATS.

Oklahoma.
A west south-central state and the 46th of the United States. The people of the state are popularly known as "Sooners," from the name applied to those who crossed the starting line sooner than the time fixed by the government for the first land run into Oklahoma, April 22, 1889. Area, 69,919 sq.mi., including 636 sq.mi. of water; pop. (1940) 2,336,434. The rural population numbered 1,456,771; urban, 879,663. Approximately 87% was native white, 7% Negro, 4% Indian and 2% foreign born, Mexican and miscellaneous. The state's two largest cities are Oklahoma City (204,424), the capital, and Tulsa (142,157).

History.—The administration of Governor Leon C. Phillips ended with the beginning of 1943. At the Nov. 1942 election, Robert S. Kerr had been chosen to succeed Phillips as governor. Others elected were: lieutenant governor, James E. Berry; secretary of state, Frank C. Carter; state auditor, C. C. Childers; attorney general, Mac Q. Williamson; state treasurer, A. S. J. Shaw; state superintendent of public instruction, A. L. Crable.

Education.—In the public schools in 1941–42 (latest figures available in 1943) 528,293 pupils were enrolled, with 19,390 teachers. Of these pupils, 128,603 were enrolled in the 854 high schools. The expenditure for the maintenance of public schools, elementary and secondary, during the fiscal year amounted to $32,015,747. The state maintained a university at Norman, a state agricultural and mechanical college at Stillwater, the Panhandle Agricultural and Technical college at Goodwell, two junior agricultural and mechanical colleges, four agricultural and mechanical colleges, a college for women, five state colleges primarily for teachers, an agricultural, mechanical and normal university for Negroes at Langston, an institute of technology at Weatherford, a military academy and one college preparatory school and junior college. There were 19 junior colleges with municipal support. In addition, there were six accredited senior colleges and three junior colleges with church affiliations.

Public Welfare, Charities, Correction.—As of Jan. 1944, 77,160 persons were the recipients of old-age assistance, 1,944 blind persons received aid, and 13,890 families were given aid for 33,209 children. The hospitals and eleemosynary institutions in 1943 included three tuberculosis sanitariums, five mental hospitals, two orphans' homes, one school for the deaf and one for the blind. There was also one penitentiary, one reformatory and four schools of detention and correction.

Communication.—Oklahoma contained approximately 101,000 mi. of state and rural highways in 1942, not including streets in towns and cities. Annual expenditures for roads were approximately $23,000,000. Within the state at the end of 1943 there were 6,150 mi. of railroad.

Agriculture.—The year 1943 was marked by severe floods in the eastern part of the state in the spring and an extended drought in the late summer.

Leading Agricultural Products of Oklahoma, 1943 and 1942

Crop	1943	1942
Wheat, bu.	31,711,000	57,370,000
Corn, bu.	23,350,000	35,631,000
Broomcorn, tons.	8,800,000	11,900,000
Grain sorghums, bu.	5,355,000	10,614,000
Barley, bu.	3,750,000	10,625,000
All hay, tons	1,657,000	1,990,000
Cotton, bales	385,000	708,000

Manufacturing.—Total value of manufactures in 1939, the year of the last federal biennial census of manufactures before World War II, was $312,168,499. State industries employed 33,528 persons; salaries of $11,090,299 and wages of $30,465,185 were paid.

Mineral Production.—The total value of mineral production in 1941 was estimated at $260,000,000, as compared with $236,000,000 in 1940. Petroleum production declined in 1941 and 1942 in some of the older pools, but the number of new pools and extensions was developed.   (J. W. Mt.)

Old-Age Insurance: *see* SOCIAL SECURITY.
Old-Age Pension: *see* RELIEF; SOCIAL SECURITY. *See also* under various states.

Olds, Robert (1896–1943), U.S. army air officer, was born June 15 in Woodside, Md. During World War I, he was flying instructor in the United States and at the Cler-mont-Ferrand instruction centre, France, where he was made officer in charge of training. After the war, he served in the Hawaiian department and with the War Plans Division office of the chief of air corps. One of the army's early exponents of heavy bombardment, he was later given command of the 2nd bombardment group at Langley Field, Va. While at that post, he was assigned to lead two good-will missions of Flying Fortresses on nonstop flights to South America, 1938, 1939—for which he received the D.F.C. In June 1941, he was given the task of organizing the ferry command and supervising delivery of bombers to England. In recognition of his success, he was promoted to brigadier general and received the D.S.M. In 1942, he was advanced to major general and put in command of the 2nd air force, with headquarters at Fort George Wright in Washington. Ill health forced him into inactivity in Feb. 1943, and he died at Tucson, Ariz., April 28.

Oleomargarine (MARGARINE). The production of oleomargarine in the United States reached a record high point in early 1943 but declined sharply almost to the level of 1942 following fat rationing in March. The use of fats and oils in oleomargarine for civilian use had been subject to government restriction since Sept. 1942. The total production of oleomargarine had been fairly constant since 1934, fluctuating between 260,000,000 and 320,000,000 lb.

The increase in 1942 brought the total to the record high point of 426,000,000 lb. and the total for 1943 was expected to reach 650,000,000 lb.

Scarcity of butter caused an increase in oleomargarine manufacture to the maximum permitted, which would be 167% of average production in 1940 and 1941. The coloured oleomargarine was produced almost entirely for export while the uncoloured production was for domestic civilian consumption. The coloured production had been only a small part of the total in recent years, less than 1% on the average, because of the heavy tax on its manufacture. This federal tax was 10 cents per lb. on coloured oleomargarine and $\frac{1}{4}$ cent per lb. on the uncoloured product with exports tax-free. The federal tax was controlled by the bureau of internal revenue, which issued all permits for withdrawal for export or domestic consumption. The growing demand for a butter-substitute in 1942 led to an increase in the proportion of coloured oleomargarine produced and by July 1943, the coloured proportion rose to about 50% of the total. This relationship was not expected to continue, however, and showed a decline in the later months of 1943. The materials used in the manufacture of oleomargarine were principally cottonseed oil, soybean oil, milk and oleo oil. The use of such tropical vegetable oils as coco-nut oil, palm oil, etc. ceased when the supplies of these were cut off by the war in the Pacific. Proposals to repeal the tax on oleomargarine were made in congress and aroused vigorous opposition by dairy farmers and others interested in preventing the use of butter substitutes.

Legislation taxing and otherwise controlling the manufacture of oleomargarine had been in effect since 1900.

(J. C. Ms.)

Olivier, Sydney Olivier, 1ST BARON, OF RAMSDEN (1859–1943), British statesman, was born April 16. The former secretary of state for India (1924), was known as the "foster parent of the Labour party," and was an active member and officer of the Fabian society in the late '80s. He died at his home, Wychwood, Bognor Regis, Feb. 15. (See *Encyclopædia Britannica*.)

Oman and Muscat: *see* ARABIA.

Onegin, Sigrid

(1891–1943), German-Swedish opera singer, was born June 1 in Stockholm of German parents. She studied voice in Germany and Italy and later with her husband, Baron Onegin, Russian composer. The statuesque young singer made her operatic debut in Stuttgart in 1912 as Carmen singing opposite Enrico Caruso, and during her first season there appeared in 12 different operatic roles. She gained her reputation, however, in such Wagnerian roles as Erda, Brangaene, Fricka and Waltraute. In her later years she developed her rich, velvety contralto voice so that she was able to add bright coloratura soprano roles to her repertoire. She was discovered by Giulio Gatti-Casazza while singing with the Munich Opera company and taken to America to make her operatic debut at the Metropolitan in *Aida,* 1922. From 1926 to 1933, she was a member of the Berlin Opera and afterwards went to live in Zurich. She made her final New York appearance in a recital in 1938. She died in Magliaso, Switzerland, according to a Berne report of June 18.

Ontario.

One of the two central provinces of the Dominion of Canada (*q.v.*), admitted to the union in 1867; area, 412,582 sq.mi.; pop. (1941) 3,787,655. Capital, Toronto (667,-457). The population in 1941 was 80% native born and 62% urban. The lieutenant governor in 1943 was Albert Matthews; the premier G. A. Drew.

Education.—The number of students in provincially controlled public schools in 1942 was 708,180; in private schools 21,264; in institutions of university standing 19,185.

Communication.—The mileage of surfaced highways in 1942 was 56,309; of earth highways 16,137; provincial expenditure on highways $16,081,059. The railroad mileage in 1942 was 10,562, number of telephones 660,002.

Finance.—The ordinary receipts in 1942 were $106,384,870; ordinary expenditure $109,618,967. The direct debt (less sinking funds) was $729,815,356; indirect liabilities (less sinking funds) $129,603,233.

Agriculture.—The acreage of field crops in 1943 was 10,089,-000; gross value of field products $208,357,000.

Manufacturing.—The gross value of manufactured products

Table I.—Leading Agricultural Products of Ontario, 1942 and 1941

Crop	1942	1941
Wheat, bu..	24,252,000	15,884,000
Oats, bu..	84,538,000	64,845,000
Barley, bu..	12,179,000	10,447,000
Corn, bu.	13,622,000	11,337,000
Potatoes, cwt.	7,161,000	7,579,000
Turnips, cwt.	12,696,000	12,056,000
Hay and clover, tons	5,962,000	4,296,000

Table II.—Principal Industries of Ontario, 1939 and 1938

Industry	Value of products	
	1939	1938
Smelting and refining	$134,726,912	$166,012,623
Automobiles	102,102,931	133,315,645
Meat packing	79,480,472	75,917,387
Electrical supplies	67,733,158	74,510,006
Flour and feed	58,336,183	70,815,603
Pulp and paper	65,486,349	72,948,378
Butter and cheese	52,663,274	54,744,598

Table III.—Principal Mineral Products of Ontario, 1940 and 1939

Mineral	Value	
	1940	1939
Gold	$125,574,988	$111,533,873
Copper		32,637,305
Nickel	94,576,434	50,920,305
Lead		1,240
Zinc		
Silver	5,563,101	472,675

in 1940 was $2,302,014,654; net value $1,004,529,583; number of employees 372,643; salaries and wages $479,399,188.

Mineral Production.—The value of the mineral production in 1942 was $258,423,267.   (J. C. He.)

OPA: *see* PRICE ADMINISTRATION, OFFICE OF.
Opera: *see* MUSIC.
Opium: *see* DRUGS AND DRUG TRAFFIC.

Oppenheimer, Franz

(1864–1943), German sociologist and political economist, was born March 30 in Berlin. He took his medical degree from the University of Freiburg. Convinced that he could do more for the general well-being of his patients by improving their social and economic conditions, he quit his medical practice, returned to school and graduated with a Ph.D. in economics and sociology at the University of Berlin. He wrote widely and was best known for a short book, *The State* (1908), which was translated into many languages, and for his *System of Sociology,* a four-volume work (1922–29). Oppenheimer, who advocated the partitioning of the large Junker estates in Prussia, launched several co-operative communities in rural areas in an effort to demonstrate that poverty and mass unemployment could be solved if proper social remedies were applied. After the advent of Hitlerism, he fled Germany and lectured at the University of Kobe, Japan. He was admitted to the United States and became research associate of the University of California in 1938. He died in Los Angeles, Sept. 30.

Oranges.

Total United States production of oranges, including tangerines, for the 1943–44 season was estimated at 96,290,000 boxes by the United States department of agriculture, which was 8% more than the large production of last year and 13% above the production of 1941–42. The Florida crop of oranges and tangerines was 22,000,000 boxes, of which 3,200,000 were tangerines. Shipments were nearly double the movements of the previous year to the same date. A strong de-

U.S. Production of Oranges by States, 1943 and 1942

State	1943 boxes*	1942 boxes*
California		
Valencias.	30,800,000	30,055,000
Navels and miscellaneous	18,530,000	14,241,000
Florida		
Early and midseason	22,000,000	19,100,000
Valencias.	17,500,000	18,100,000
Tangerines	3,200,000	4,200,000
Texas	3,100,000	2,550,000
Arizona	900,000	730,000
Louisiana	260,000	340,000

*Net content per box of oranges in California and Arizona approximates an average of 77 lb.; in Florida, Texas and other states, 90 lb.

mand, partly due to the smaller crop of apples, resulted in relatively high prices. Army and lend-lease requirements were strong particularly for juices and other processed forms.   (J. C. Ms.)

Oregon.

A Pacific state of the U.S.A., admitted to the union Feb. 14, 1859. Area, 96,350 sq.mi.; pop. (1940) 1,089,684. Capital, Salem (30,908); chief city, Portland (305,-394).

History.—Oregon made a substantial contribution to the war effort in 1943 in ship construction. Six major yards in the Portland area, including Vancouver, Wash., launched 356 steel ocean-going vessels. The total of 3,222,375 tons was estimated as being nearly one-sixth of the nation's production outside of yards building wholly for the navy. These new ships when ready for service would have an estimated value of $837,000,000. About 115,000 men and women were employed in their construction.

The three Maritime commission yards operated by the Kaiser

organization launched 272 steel vessels, totalling, 3,126,000 tons. Of these 25 were for the navy and the others were cargo and tank ships. Three smaller yards in Portland operating under navy direction launched 84 vessels, mostly of smaller sizes but some of complicated design. In addition to the ships launched, there were many repair and conversion projects in the Portland area, including seven aircraft escort carriers. A variety of marine construction was carried on at Astoria, Coos Bay and other places not included in the above figures. In 1942, the Portland area yards launched 193 vessels, totalling 1,360,000 tons.

In the fall of 1943 the Oregon Shipbuilding corporation began construction of the first of the new Victory ships. The first ship in this series, the "United Victory," was launched in Portland on Jan. 12, 1944.

Another important contribution to the war effort in Oregon was the production of lumber. While much of this went into direct military construction, there was a greatly increased demand for crating and box material. Packing requirements for overseas shipments increased tremendously.

Three large army camps were operated in 1943, as well as a number of smaller army and navy establishments. In the summer and fall of 1943 central Oregon was the scene of extensive army manoeuvres with about 75,000 troops, drawn from the Pacific coast area.

The Oregon legislature met in Jan. 1943. Total appropriations for the biennium of 1943–45 amounted to $23,723,365, an increase of about $2,800,000 over the previous biennium. An act was passed providing for a reduction in the state personal income tax rates as the taxable income increased in volume. Late in 1943, the state tax commission announced that the rate applicable for the 1943 tax would be reduced by 75%.

The legislature also referred a sales tax proposal to a popular vote to be held at the general election in Nov. 1944.

Housing problems in the Portland metropolitan area and in other Oregon communities were not entirely satisfactory, but many new housing units were made available and the tension was greatly relieved.

The year 1943 was Oregon's centennial year for the first large immigration over the Oregon Trail in 1843. Extensive celebrations were impracticable on account of war conditions, but many local meetings were held.

A number of Portland public and civic organizations subscribed a fund of $100,000 in 1943 and employed Robert Moses of New York city to investigate Portland's postwar problems. Moses and his staff spent much time in Portland and late in the year presented a detailed plan calling for the expenditure of $75,000,000 for postwar projects. Most of these projects were designed to improve local traffic conditions.

Education.—During the school year 1941–42 there were 214,640 pupils in public schools, including 60,503 in high schools. There were 7,997 teachers. For the school year 1941–42 the value of school properties was $62,160,201.

Communication.—On December 31, 1943, there were 4,806 mi. of primary state highways, of which 4,612 were surfaced. Highway expenditures for 1943 were $13,504,005, of which $2,470,246 was for interest and debt retirement. As of Dec. 31, 1942, there were 3,662 mi. of steam railways, not including second main track, sidings, etc.

Finance.—As of Nov. 1, 1943, Oregon's state gross bonded debt was $24,089,425, against which there were sinking funds and other applicable assets amounting to $17,382,149, leaving a balance of debt of $6,707,276.

Agriculture.—The total cash income of Oregon farmers in 1942 was $213,642,000, of which $6,585,000 represented government payments.

Principal Agricultural Products of Oregon, 1943 and 1942

Crop	1943 (est.)	1942	Crop	1943 (est.)	1942
Corn, bu.	1,862,000	1,742,000	Barley, bu.	9,125,000	10,075,000
Oats, bu.	11,020,000	10,064,000	Wheat, all, bu.	19,500,000	19,953,000

Manufacturing.—The census of 1939 showed 2,248 manufacturing establishments in Oregon; 69,880 persons employed; salaries and wages, $91,326,581; value of products, $365,374,436. Major items: logging camps, $23,363,038; sawmills, $108,663,140; planing mills, $8,122,845; meat packing, $15,178,448; paper mills, $15,698,747. (L. A. McA.)

Orlebar, Augustus H. (1897?–1943), British air officer, was born at Higham Ferrers, Northamptonshire. He became a test pilot during World War I, later studied at the R.A.F. staff college from which he was graduated in 1926. He was leader of British aviators who competed for the Schneider cup in 1929 and 1931 and set a speed record of 357.7 miles per hour in the 1929 meet. In World War II, he commanded an R.A.F fighter group on cross-channel sweeps and directed flight training. An acting air vice marshal, he was made deputy chief of combined operations in March 1943 and was third in command of the service headed at that time by Lord Louis Mountbatten. He died in London, August 4.

OSRD: *see* SCIENTIFIC RESEARCH AND DEVELOPMENT, OFFICE OF.

Osteopathy. Research work continued to be a feature of osteopathic progress, the most important publications during 1943 relating to physiological problems. Steps were taken for closer correlation of activities and exchange of information among those engaged in research.

The osteopathic profession in 1943 set an all-time record in the number in the profession, 10,820, and likewise in membership in the American Osteopathic association and in the divisional (state and provincial) societies. The annual meeting at Detroit was a war service conference, and the 1944 meeting to be held in Chicago was to be of the same nature.

Additional boards were set up for the certification of those who practice specialties, the complete list of boards now including examiners in pathology, internists, neurology and psychiatry, obstetrics and gynaecology, ophthalmology and otolaryngology, pediatrics, proctology, radiology, surgery (with a sub-board on anaesthesiology).

Funds appropriated for the army and the navy included provision of osteopathic care for personnel in those branches. In reacting to this situation, and undertaking to maintain and increase the quality of osteopathic physicians and surgeons available, the osteopathic colleges went beyond the provisions already made for expansion. All of them were adding to laboratories and libraries, and increasing their faculties in 1943, and some building programs were getting under way. (R. G. Hu.)

Ottawa. The capital of the Dominion of Canada (*q.v.*) and the seat of the supreme court, is situated on the right bank of the Ottawa river near the mouth of the Rideau, both rivers having very beautiful falls. The city itself is divided into an upper and a lower town by the Rideau canal. The parliament buildings are situated on a series of high bluffs which overlook the river, in one direction toward the Chaudière falls and in the opposite direction toward the Rideau falls. The population of the city was 154,951 in 1941. The gross value of manufactured products in 1941 was $28,582,935. The city's most important educational institution is the Université d'Ottawa.

BIBLIOGRAPHY.—*The Canada Year Book, 1941.* (J. C. He.)

Outer Mongolia: *see* MONGOLIA.

OWM: *see* WAR MOBILIZATION, OFFICE OF.

Oxford University.

The academic year 1942–43, which began with 2,615 undergraduates in residence, ended with 2,728. The numbers of men matriculating in Hilary (218) and Trinity terms (399) were much above even the high figures of the previous year. Sixty-nine per cent of the men matriculating were below the age of 18½. This was a substantial increase over the previous year's figure, but there were indications that the proportion would in the future be constant at about 70%.

For the first time the regulations calling up for national service caused many women (302) to enter for the special wartime examinations in Trinity term 1943. Unlike men, most women would not be liable to be called up at the end of a bye-term but would normally stay up for two full academic years. Most of the occupations upon which they would then enter, having been approved by the Minister of Labour, would probably be reckoned as national service for the purpose of qualifying for war degrees.

Scholarship examinations in classics and history were held by one group of seven colleges in September, 1943; another group of seven examined in Dec. 1943; and the third group (six colleges) were to examine in March 1944. The dates of examinations in other subjects were not affected by the war.

A standing committee of scientists with some lay members was appointed to advise on biological problems affecting estate management. This committee was modelled on the committee on building problems of which the establishment was recorded in 1942. The university and colleges are among the biggest owners of agricultural land in the country.

Benefactions, apart from those which renewed existing grants, included £10,000 from Mr. and Mrs. P. Vaughan Morgan in memory of their daughter Violet to endow scholarships in English literature, and a bequest of £12,000 from Dr. H. E. D. Blakiston for the purchase of works of graphic art. The university also acquired partly by gift from R. W. Ffennell and partly by purchase from him 2,840 ac. (out of 3,108) of the Wytham abbey estate. In Oct. 1943 the numbers of matriculations were 991 men and 335 women. (D. V.)

Japanese occupation, to Col. Marchant, the British resident commissioner, and the other Europeans who remained on the islands. Japanese attempts to ingratiate themselves with the natives failed completely; and when the Allied offensive began, the islanders proved invaluable scouts and played a conspicuous part in the fighting.

Measures were being undertaken in the liberated areas to repair the damage done by the Japanese. On July 20 O. C. Noel, former administrative officer, Uganda, was appointed to succeed Col. Marchant as resident commissioner of the Solomons. The Japanese had exterminated whole villages in an attempt to coerce the natives into working for them, and an anthropologist was dispatched to the islands to help the native communities to reorganize themselves. There was urgent need for the re-establishment of adequate medical services as there had been serious outbreaks of disease during the Japanese occupation.

It was also important to get the vegetable gardens and plantations back into production and an agricultural officer toured the most seriously devastated areas to supervise the work of replanting.

On April 23 the U.S. Navy department announced that U.S. forces were in occupation of the Ellice Islands on the supply line to the S. Pacific and Australia, and subsequently the islands were frequently bombed by the Japanese. Japanese positions in the N. Gilbert islands, particularly the island of Tarawa, were attacked several times by Allied aircraft before U.S. forces recaptured the islands Nov. 23 in an assault which cost the U.S. Marines more than 1,000 dead and more than 2,500 wounded in a total force of 4,000–5,000. The Japanese garrisons were virtually annihilated.

In Fiji the labour welfare board continued its work of endeavouring to raise the standard of living, while improving the health services. Defense preparations continued, and early in the year the first battalion of the Fijian Infantry regiment left for the battle areas.

On June 1 Major Ratu J. L. V. Sukuna was appointed adviser on native affairs in Fiji, a post carrying with it membership on the Executive council. He was the first Fijian civil servant to attain so high a post.

On Oct. 11 Queen Salote of Tonga celebrated the Silver Jubilee of her coronation. (*See* also SOLOMON ISLANDS.) (C. M. CL.)

Pacific Islands, British.

Territories of the British empire in the Pacific ocean, of which certain statistics are given in the accompanying table. *See* BRITISH EMPIRE for population, capital towns, status and governors.

History.—Fighting continued throughout the year with the Allied offensive in New Guinea and the Solomons, and most of the central Solomons were regained; in November the U.S. Marines retook the Gilbert islands after a fierce 76-hour battle. (*See* WORLD WAR II.) In May the Colonial office published a report from the high commissioner, Sir Philip Mitchell, giving an account of the loyalty of the Solomon Islanders, during the

Pacific Islands, British

Territory and Area Square Miles	Principal Products	Imports and Exports (in thousand £)	Revenue and Expenditure (in thousand £)	Education: Elementary and Secondary
FIJI, 7,055	gold (1940) 3,600 kg. (exports 1940) sugar £F. 1,285,191 copra £F. 125,063 bananas £F. 41,747	(1940) imp. £ Fiji 1,826 exp. £ Fiji 2,679	(1940) rev. £ Fiji 938 exp. £ Fiji 948	(1940) schls., 417; scholars, 31,530
PAPUA (administered by the Commonwealth of Australia; *see* also PACIFIC ISLANDS, MANDATED) 87,786 (mainland); 2,754 (islands)	rubber (1939–40 exports) £152,487 gold (1940) 1089 kg. copra (1939) metric tons 9,500	(1940–41) imp. £A. 539 exp. £A. 493	(1940–41) rev. £A. 189.5 exp. £A. 189.3	Mission schools with compulsory attendance for native children (1939–40) Europ. schls., 3; schls., 63
GILBERT AND ELLICE ISLANDS COLONY (including the Gilbert group; the Ellice group; Ocean island [seat of administration]; Fanning, Washington and Christmas islands; and the Phoenix group*). *c.* 200 .	(metric tons) natural phosphates (1939) 325,000 copra (1938) 4,900	(1938–39) imp. 138 exp. 282	(est. 1939–40) rev. 73.1 exp. 82.7	(1939) schls., 236; schls., 6,828
NEW HEBRIDES (a condominium administered jointly by the British and French Governments†) 5,700	(1939) tons copra 14,569 cocoa 1,935	(1939) imp. 118.6 exp. 123.9	(1939–40) rev. 24.3 exp. 22.7	Numerous Presbyterian and Catholic mission native schls., 1 Fr. Govt. schl., and 1 Catholic mission schl. for whites
BRITISH SOLOMON ISLANDS PROTECTORATE, 11,458	(1940–41) copra 12,991 tons	(1940–41) imp. 134.4 exp. 121.9	(1940–41) rev. 51.3 exp. 65.8	(1937–38) elem. schls., 6; schls., 4,697
TONGAN ISLANDS PROTECTORATE. *c.* 250 .	(export 1941) copra 4,258 tons bananas, 54,210 cases	(1941) imp. 71.9 exp. 56.5	(1939–40) rev. 45.3 exp. 51.9	(1940) schls., 125; schlrs., 9,324

*Canton and Enderbury Islands, in the Phoenix group, are shared with the U.S.A. under the Anglo-American pact, Aug. 10, 1938.
†New Hebrides adhered to the Fighting French cause of General de Gaulle in 1940.

Pacific Islands, French.

The latest statistics available in 1943 for this French colony are given herewith: area (Society, Tuamotu, Tubuai and Marquesas isls.), 1,540 sq.mi.; pop. (est. Dec. 31, 1939) 45,000 (whites, *c.* 3,700). Chief town: Papeete (in Tahiti), cap. 8,460. Governor (1943): Col. Orselli.

Finance.—Local budget (est. 1939) 27,560,000 francs.

Trade.—(1939): imports 80,-482,000 francs; exports 63,536,-000 francs. Roads 1937: Tahiti 48 mi.; Raiaeta 19 mi.; shipping (1938) cleared, 162,927 net tons.

Production.—Export: copra (1939) 25,353 short tons; natural phosphates (1940) 190,698 short tons. (*See* also SOLOMON ISLANDS.)

Mandated Pacific Islands

Territory and Area Square Miles	Population and Status	Principal Products	Imports and Exports (000's omitted)	Revenue and Expenditure (000's omitted)
NEW GUINEA, mandated territory (69,700) including Bismarck Archipelago (19,200) and Solomon Is. (4,100)	(1940) native 668,871; European 4,399; Asiatic 2,099. Under mandate of the Commonwealth of Australia	Exports: gold (1940) 7,800 kg. Copra (1938) 74,400 metric tons	(1939–40) imp. £A.1,268 exp. £A.3,674	(1939–40) rev. £A.497 exp. £A.501
WESTERN SAMOA (1,133)	(1940) 61,249 (white 410) Under mandate of New Zealand	(Export 1940) copra 5,644 tons; bananas £N.Z. 84,706	(1940) imp. £N.Z.165 exp. £N.Z.222	(1940–41) rev. £N.Z.108 exp. £N.Z.110
MARIANNE IS., CAROLINE IS., PALAU, and MARSHALL IS. (811)	(1936) 107,137 (Japanese, 56,496) Under Japanese mandate	cane sugar (1938–39) 70,300 metric tons; phosphates (export 1938) 104,000 metric tons	(1936) imp. 13,866 yen exp. 25,108 yen	(1939) rev. 9,904 yen exp. 9,675 yen
NAURU (8)	(1940) 3,460 (European 171, Chinese 1,512). Under British mandate, held jointly by Great Britain, New Zealand and Australia, the present administrator	natural phosphates (export 1940) 808,-400 tons	(1940) imp. £A.192.7 exp. £A.541.2	(1940) rev. £A.27.1 exp. £A.26.2

Pacific Islands, Mandated.

The former German possessions in the western Pacific comprise part of New Guinea with adjacent archipelagos, Western Samoa, the Marshall, Caroline, Palau and Ladrone, or Marianne islands, and the islet of Nauru. Statistics for these territories are given in the accompanying table. For capital towns and governors of New Guinea, Western Samoa and Nauru, *see*

BRITISH EMPIRE. After the Japanese entry into the war in 1941, these islands became the scene of hostilities, for which *see* WORLD WAR II. (*See* also NEW GUINEA.)

Pacific Islands, U.S.

In addition to such large island possessions in the Pacific as Hawaii, the Aleutians, American Samoa and Guam (the latter occupied by the Japanese in 1943) the United States possesses a dozen tiny islands in the Pacific, negligible in size and economic value, but important, both in peace and in war, from the standpoint of aviation and naval security. Increasing interest was shown in these formerly neglected islets in the later '30s, as air flights across the Pacific were organized on a regular commercial basis and as the threat of war with Japan became more evident.

U.S. LIBERATOR BOMBER over the Japanese-held island of Nauru. Clouds of smoke are rising from three phosphate plants bombed during a raid April 21, 1943

Midway and Kure (Ocean) Islands.—The Midway Islands are a group in the North Pacific, 1,200 mi. northwest of the Hawaiian Islands. Area of the group: 28 sq.mi. Pop. (1936) 118. Midway consists of two low-lying islands, Sand (area 850 acres) and Eastern (328 acres). These are surrounded by a coral reef five miles in diameter and by numerous islets. Sand and Eastern islands are little more than sand-spits, but they acquired importance, first as the site of a trans-Pacific cable station (installed 1903), second as a stopping point on the Pan American Airways route from San Francisco to the Philippines via Hawaii, Midway, Wake and Guam (inaugurated 1935), third, as an important U.S. air and naval station in the war against Japan. One of the first big Japanese defeats was sustained in a three day battle in the neighbourhood of Midway, fought June 4–6, 1942.

Midway was discovered by a Captain N. C. Brooks in 1859 and was first known as Brooks Island. The name was later changed to Midway, because of the group's position in the mid-Pacific, 2,800 mi. from California and 2,200 mi. from Japan. It was formally declared a U.S. possession in 1867. Kure (Ocean) Island is a coral reef 14.7 mi. in circumference, lying 56 mi. northwest of Midway. It was placed under the control of the navy department by an executive order of Feb., 1936.

Wake Island.—Wake Island, famous as the scene of a gallant last-stand defense by a garrison of a few hundred U.S. marines against a greatly superior Japanese attacking force in Dec. 1941, consists of three islets, Wake, Peale and Wilkes, and is located in the North Pacific, 2,130 mi. due west of Honolulu. The total land area of the islets is about 2,600 acres (4 sq.mi.), Wake, the largest, being about 2 sq.mi. It was formally annexed to the United States on Jan. 17, 1899. For many years it was neglected and uninhabited, except for occasional visits of Japanese birdhunters; but it was placed under U.S. navy department jurisdiction in 1934 and later contained an air station, a hotel for air travelers and quarters for a small garrison of marines. It was discovered by the British ship, "Prince William Henry," in 1796.

Johnston Island.—Johnston Island consists of two islets on an eight-mile reef, located 600 mi. southwest of Hawaii. It was discovered by the British naval vessel "Cornwallis" in 1807 and named after the vessel's captain, Charles James Johnston. Competing U.S. guano interests lent some activity to this barren sand bar in the '50s and '60s of the 19th century. The final U.S. assertion of claim to the island was an Executive Order of June 29, 1929, placing the island under the control and jurisdiction of the department of agriculture as a refuge for native birds. An appropriation of $1,150,000 was provided by congress for the construction of seaplane facilities.

Kingman Island.—Kingman reef, 150 ft. long by 120 ft. wide at high tide, is the smallest land area in the world over which the United States claims sovereignty. The reef is about 8 mi. long and 5 mi. wide, counting in submerged shoals. Two other tiny islets in the reef appear at low tide. The strategic importance of this desolate reef lies in the fact that it is the only possible seaplane base between Honolulu (1,067 mi. to the N.) and Pago Pago, in American Samoa (q.v.), 1,797 mi. to the S.W.

Palmyra Island.—A U-shaped atoll, with its 53 islets containing an area of about 500 acres, located 960 mi. S.W. of Hawaii. Its possession was disputed for a time between the United States and the kingdom of Hawaii; it was specifically mentioned when the U.S. annexed Hawaii in 1898; but sporadic British claims to the possession of the island were put forward later. It is a possible air base on the route from Hawaii to New Zealand.

Swains Island.—A coral atoll, one sq.mi. in area, pop. 150, of Polynesian race, formally brought under the jurisdiction of American Samoa in 1925 after remaining for a time under the patriarchal rule of a U.S. whaling captain named Eli Jennings, who had himself accepted as a local chief, and his descendants.

Howland, Jarvis and Baker Islands.—Baker and Howland Islands are small coral atolls, located where the international date line crosses the equator. Jarvis Island is 1,150 mi. further E. and slightly below the equator. Rectangular Baker Island is 1 mi. long and 1,500 yd. wide, elongated Howland Island is 2 mi. long and 750 yd. wide. Both were discovered by U.S. whaling captains early in the 19th century. Jarvis Island, a bare coral plateau, 1.8 mi. long and 1.3 mi. wide, was discovered in 1821. These islands were "colonized" by students of a Hawaiian boys' school in 1935 and placed under the jurisdiction of the depart-

WAKE ISLAND was the target of one of the most concentrated and devastating air raids of World War II Oct. 5–6, 1943, when U.S. naval planes and ships rained more than 700 tons of bombs and shells on the Jap-held base

ment of the interior in 1936. Radio and aerological stations were established there.

Canton and Enderbury Islands.—Geographically part of the Phoenix group and located 1,850 mi. S.S.W. of Hawaii, Canton (area 8.5 sq.mi.) and Enderbury (2.5 sq.mi.) figured in a prolonged dispute as to ownership between the U.S. and the British empire. Aviation experts consider Canton an excellent base for seaplanes and Enderbury suitable for land planes. The dispute was settled on Aug. 11, 1938, when the United States and British governments jointly announced an arrangement for "the use in common" of the islands, "for purposes connected with international aviation and communication." (*See* also GUAM; HAWAII; PHILIPPINES; SAMOA, AMERICAN.) (W. H. CH.)

Pacifism. The arrangement between the United States Selective Service administration and the National Service Board for Religious Objectors, representing the Friends, Mennonite and Brethren churches, the Federal Council of Churches of Christ in America, the Association of Catholic Conscientious Objectors, the interdenominational Fellowship of Reconciliation and other religious groups, under which alternative civilian service is performed by draftees recognized as sincere conscientious objectors was continued during 1943. At the end of the year about 7,000 such men were in Civilian Public Service. Sixty per cent of this number were in camps engaged mainly in forestry, soil conservation, prevention and fighting of forest fires. These men not only received no pay but had to provide their own maintenance or had to have it provided for them by the religious agencies administering Civilian Public Service. To meet the objection of a considerable number of conscientious objectors to serving under a "religious" or denominational agency, the Selective Service administration opened a camp under its own management at Mancos, Colo. Conscientious objectors could elect whether to serve under religious agency or direct government management.

The remainder of Civilian Public Service men were on "detached service," more than 1,000 in mental hospitals from which considerable success in the application of pacifist techniques was reported. Several other groups served as "guinea pigs" in experiments in typhus control, treatment of pneumonia, control of salt water intake by shipwrecked persons, and other problems, under the direction of universities or research agencies. These men received their maintenance but no pay.

Much dissatisfaction over failure of the government to provide pay and at least maintenance for all conscientious objectors (C.O.s) who did not deliberately choose to donate their services and maintenance developed. As the draft of fathers went into effect, an acute situation arose for a considerable number of dependents of conscientious objectors. Criticism increased when the comptroller general ruled that wages paid by private farmers to conscientious objectors in Civilian Public Service who volunteered to relieve labour shortages had to be paid over to the treasury of the United States. The only concession granted was that such money should be held in a separate account, the disposition of which was to be determined after the war.

The religious agencies under which most C.O.s served complained that the Selective Service administration was intervening to such an extent in the discipline in Civilian Public Service camps as to place the agencies in the position of becoming instruments of coercion. Great disappointment was also felt when, after President Roosevelt himself had authorized organization of a C.O. unit for difficult and dangerous relief and rehabilitation work in China, a "rider" to a congressional appropriation bill forbade the use of any federal funds either for work of C.O.s abroad or for any training for such work.

During the year the department of justice reported that of the 6,116 persons convicted up to June 30, 1943, of violations of the Selective Service act, it listed 2,071 as conscientious objectors. Of that number 1,630 were still in prison on that date. This included 964 Jehovah's Witnesses, however, who seek status as ministers of religion rather than as conscientious objectors. The latter included a considerable number of men generally admitted to be sincere but regarded as not qualifying as conscientious objectors by virtue of "religious training and belief," who refused induction into the army but were eager to render alternative service under civilian auspices. Two types of parole are theoretically open to conscientious objectors in prison, a special parole under the Selective Service act and the general parole available to federal prisoners on the expiration of one-third of their term. In practice, however, very few were granted. Furthermore, a considerable number of C.O.s who had already completed a term, on refusal to abandon their "absolutist" position, were convicted a second time and returned to prison. Such developments, as well as the censorship of mails in federal prisons and the practice of segregation of Negro and white inmates, led to work-strikes on the part of a minority among imprisoned C.O.s and also to hunger-strikes, lasting in at least two instances for many weeks with the authorities resorting to forcible feeding.

Public concern over many of these developments led to the formation during 1943 of a National Committee on Conscientious Objectors by the American Civil Liberties Union. It took steps to test a number of issues in the federal courts. In general, however, there was no governmental interference with the work of pacifist churches or other agencies.

BIBLIOGRAPHY.—Reports of the National Service Board for Religious Objectors; publications of the Commission to Study the Bases of a Just and Durable Peace, Federal Council of Churches of Christ in America; Official Statements of Religious Bodies Regarding the Conscientious Objector, compiled and published by the Department of International Justice and Goodwill, Federal Council of Churches; General Lewis B. Hershey, *Selective Service in Wartime: Second Report of the Director of Selective Service, 1941–42;* Julien Cornell, *The Conscientious Objector and the Law* (1943); *Conscience and the War: A Report on the Treatment of Conscientious Objectors in World War II,* American Civil Liberties Union (Sept. 1943). (A. J. M.)

Paddock, Charles William (1900–1943), U.S. editor, track star and marine corps officer, was born Aug. 11 in Gainesville, Tex. Known as the "world's fastest human" in the '20s, Charlie Paddock held the National A.A.U. record for the 100-yard outdoor sprint, 0:09.6, in 1921 and 1924. He also set a national record for the 220-yard run on an outdoor track in 1924. He represented the U.S. at the Olympic games at three different times, but only at Antwerp in 1920 did he succeed in beating his competitors in the 100-metre race. In private life Paddock was manager of two California newspapers. Commissioned a captain in the marine corps in July 1942, he served on the staff of General Upshur as aide and public relations officer. He was killed in the crash of a naval aeroplane at Sitka, Alaska, which took Gen. Upshur and four others to their death, July 21.

Painting. In spite of the limitations imposed by war conditions, painting in the United States during 1943 showed a notably increased vitality. Several factors played their part in this. Thanks to war needs, there was a definite narrowing of the nation's art production with a healthy trimming away of the less convinced aspirants. It is true that the war exerted a severe drain on the art schools of the country. It took several of the most promising younger painters temporarily away from their easels. But it also provided other work for many, young and old, who painted more by avocation than from inner necessity. And the essentially propagandist illustrators of "the American scene" and "social" or "party-line" schools that had flour-

"GREGOR PIATIGORSKY" by Wayman Adams of New York city won first prize at the U.S. exhibition of the Carnegie institute at Pittsburgh, Pa. in Oct. 1943

ished in the '30s found more remunerative and honorific fields for their abilities outside the fine arts. Pictorial imagination once more began to show itself more freely. With Pearl Harbor, domestic interest in the "social" school of art had faded. Emphasis on "the American scene" had long since lost its shibboleth value. Pictorial "realism" at its starkest could not rival the grim realities reproduced photographically in the newspapers. Painting was thrown back on a fuller exploitation of its own means of expression and for subject matter on the romantic imagination. The refugee artists whom naziism had driven to these shores had begun to take a place in their new world. Their first unfamiliarity with the new scene had worn off; they had begun to respond to their new environment, or at any rate to work less self-consciously in it. The younger Americans had now had time to become acquainted with the work of these Europeans produced in their midst and many were beginning to take profitable lessons from it. An increased public buying power, untapped by foreign markets, afforded a substantial encouragement to the artists through increased private and institutional purchases, an intensified interest in new painters, larger and more frequent exhibitions of contemporary American art. While the federal government was naturally forced to withdraw from the mural field, part of its work of patronage was taken over by private enterprise. The Springfield Art museum arranged a $4,500 competition for a mural which was won by a soldier, Private Sante Graziani of Camp Robinson, Arkansas. *Life* magazine and the Abbott Laboratories both fostered ambitious essays at reporting the war on canvas. And a new plan, proposed as a model for the establishment of collections of contemporary art in universities throughout the country, was initiated at the University of Arizona, where a donor spent $20,000 for 100 contemporary American paintings.

Besides this increased liveliness in the general scene, the most striking feature of American painting during 1943 was a renewed vitality in the work of many of the established artists. Max Weber, for example, in his 1943 work turned to new fields of colour interest—light warm washes emphasizing the atmospheric glow of his forms and replacing the colder, clearer architecture of his earlier forms. The expressionistic treatment that marked

his work during the last few years had pointed in this direction. But the tortured forms of those canvases have taken a calm, restful character in his latest paintings. He has brought them by subtle distortions and this quieter palette into the plane of the picture-surface. Yet no vitality has been sacrificed, in this reduction of three-dimensional emphasis, thanks to increased variety of his tonal modulations. And the sullen mineral colours of his preceding work have now given way to mellower, if still melancholy, gamuts. Another of the older generation, John Marin, in his 1943 oils continued to develop his vigorous technique in marine and Maine coast studies. In this medium he proceeds with always a bolder hand to slash out brush-stroke patterns that add a suggestion of muscular rhythms to the formal and chromatic features of his compositions. At the same time his water-colours have lost none of the idyllic calm of his earlier days though his latest are somewhat less patternistically assertive. Georgia O'Keeffe, a fellow-exhibitor with Marin at Alfred Stieglitz' An American Place in New York, opened 1943 with a large retrospective exhibition at the Art institute in Chicago. And in the canvases she brought back from a summer in New Mexico she evinced a new strength of colour and confidence in an expression based on nature but closely approaching the abstract. "Cliffs Beyond Abiqui, My Backyard" and "Head with Broken Pot—1943" point to an interest in sharply delineated, tightly built compositions in warm earth-colours, deep greens, blacks and ultramarines, that promise a great advance over the softer, seductive, feminine qualities which have so often characterized her work in the past.

Another essential picture-maker, of a very delicate but subtle sensibility, who came emphatically to the fore in 1943 is Milton Avery. Although Avery has never studied abroad, he is perhaps more closely related to the French artist Bonnard in his colour sense and pictorial organization than any other American painter. He had been quietly developing an extremely personal idiom over the last 15 years without any general recognition. But an exhibition of his recent work in the late spring brought him considerable notice, and the oils he produced during the summer offer an even greater freedom of drawing and brushwork than previously and a fresher use of arbitrary colours richly harmonized in an extremely personal way.

Two other younger men with a sensibility to delicate effects, Julian Levi and Yasuo Kuniyoshi, both continued to develop their personal manners. Kuniyoshi's main interest remains the refinements of textural expression, but Levi continued to widen his enterprise in the field of portraiture without abandoning any of his grasp of painterly quality. At the same time the Philadelphian, Franklin Watkins, turned in 1943 almost wholly from his interest in baroque composition to portraiture. In this field Watkins is steadily taking a pre-eminence as the artist who combines perhaps best a psychological sense of the sitter's character with a feeling for the fundamental pictorial effect. But perhaps the most surprising portrait of the year was Charles Sheeler's self-portrait, "Charles Sheeler Looks at Painting," in which he combined certain reminiscences of the forms abstracted from nature of his early work with his more familiar meticulous puritanic, realism in a witty, carefully painted canvas affording a warmth of humanity rare in Sheeler's work of recent years.

Shortly before his sudden death during the summer, Marsden Hartley showed a group of his most recent oils in New York. In these canvases Hartley's personalization of the German expressionistic manner was given an even broader treatment. His rather heavy-handed love of paint was still to the fore—a structural concept above all with little interest in the subtleties of handling. During the year another younger expressionist, Abraham Rattner, showed a marked advance toward a tighter composition without slighting in any way the boldness of his colour oppositions. Walter Quirt, whose gifts have always been visible through an extremely uneven production, began to show signs of controlling his effects through a more convinced expression. But Karl Zerbe may be said to offer the richest variety of the "expressionists," to which is added a fine colour sense and an enlivening vigour.

In the field of fantasy, Raymond Breinin of Chicago was most successful with his misty dream landscapes, with wraithlike, haunting figures. Julio de Diego found a world idiom somewhat reminiscent of Paul Klee which he managed to personalize through his personal palette. And Morris Kantor's series of war fantasies displayed his characteristic expression on a small scale with considerable quiet poetry.

Of the older abstractionists Stuart Davis was easily the most impressive. The nature reductions of his earlier landscapes and city views have now been further condensed. The resultant abstract compositions have all the decorative charm of his earlier work without the distraction of a representational content which always made itself felt without adding anything to the pictorial effect.

Among the younger painters who were brought forward for the first time in one-man exhibitions, Jackson Pollock of Wyoming is the most individual. He has a rich colour sense and the ability as well as the courage to undertake large compositions. There are still reminiscences of admiration for Picasso in his work. But in approaching a subject, he employs a startling freedom of rhythmic brush-work and through it composes extremely individual abstract compositions. Another younger abstractionist, Irene Rice Pereira, after a long abstention from painting due to illness, showed a group of new work in which her form researches have been given a new direction. In place of her former concentration on textural contrasts of mosaic-like squares parallel to the surface plane, we now see a use of larger elements and an exploration of means for suggesting space within the picture and its architectural composition. Matta Echaurren, the young Chilean surrealist, continued his researches in Redonesque light effects contrasted with tenuous structural elements. While he has not yet found the ability to handle a large canvas satisfactorily, certain passages show an extreme sensibility, and his smaller canvases and water-colours continue to keep him one of the most promising younger men. The Mexican Ruffino Tamayo continued strong, savage fresco-like work without any notable loss or gain in expression. But at the same time Arshile Gorky, whose work has always held a certain promise, buried though it has been in reminiscences of Picasso, Miro and others, seems to have definitely found himself in a series of water-colours painted during the past summer. Here Gorky has finally managed to put his predecessors' work completely out of mind in going direct to nature and has succeeded in transforming his vision of flowers and grass into striking abstract space compositions within a freedom of transcription and meticulous detail that give them a rich individuality.

Among the refugee artists, the most striking production was "Broadway Boogie-Woogie" by Piet Mondrian. In this canvas Mondrian left the static effects of his work of the last 20 years for an organization of restless, contrasting colour squares held together on a stable base of rectangular lines. Marc Chagall likewise seems to have eventually found himself at home in the United States. His work exhibited in 1943 shows him clearly out of the uncertainty which has marked his canvases of the last decade. In an oil such as "The Juggler," although the iconography seems little changed, he has recovered a freshness of outlook and a lively vigour which perhaps represents his response to his new environment better than any representational motives could. Fernand Léger in New York and L. Moholy Nagy in Chicago

both continued to find new, if characteristic formal organizations in their individual veins. And of the younger men, Masson and Tanguy produced work in 1943 which began to show signs of recovering the quality of their finest European periods, while George Kepes, in certain camouflage studies produced some of the most interesting researches in pictorial texture-contrasts shown during the year. (*See* also SCULPTURE.)   (J. J. Sw.)

Paints and Varnishes.
United States sales of paint in 1943 were expected to approximate those of 1941. These sales would be 5–10% better than 1942.

Because of the over-all vegetable oil shortage, the oil content of civilian paints was limited by government regulations. Drying oils continued scarce because of the large production of military and civilian coatings and the large domestic and foreign requirements for edible oils and hydrogenated fats, in spite of a 6% increase over 1942 in total 1943 domestic fat and oil production and an all-time record production of 900,000,000 lb. of domestic linseed oil. Linseed oil was burned as fuel in Argentina because of the lack of shipping space.

Castor oil again became of major importance to coating compositions, because of increased shipping from Brazil and increased acreages in Mexico and the United States. Tung oil stocks and their replacement prospects decreased further and forced replacement in many military uses, thereby restricting tung oil to such items as food can coatings, electrical insulating and naval paints.

The gap between the rubber and paint industries was narrowed by large commercial production of elastomers, from drying oils and their acids, to replace rubber in gaskets and other moulded products not requiring high tensile strength.

In general, the use of high grade synthetic resins and solvents was carefully controlled by government regulations. A report of naval stores showed that considerable turpentine was used in 1943 for manufacture of synthetic resin. New and improved resins from petroleum by-products appeared in good commercial quantities. Rosin supplies toward the end of the year were not readily available because of widespread use throughout the war program.

In the field of pigments, ammonium ferrous phosphate was introduced and advocated as a corrosion inhibiting flake pigment because of its impermeability, oxygen and acid acceptance, and competed with red lead and zinc chromate as a component of paints for metal protection. Refined and treated tall oils appeared on the market as a partial replacement for the vegetable oil shortage since tall oil was not classified as a vegetable oil in government regulations.

Containers continued to be a problem in the industry, with the limited use of glass bottles and part fibre containers. Light gauge metal containers, however, were somewhat more available.

Military finishes continued to be a big factor in the industry. The boat-building program in particular affected the supplies of synthetic resins and pigments. This had a pronounced effect on the availability of titanium oxide and zinc chromate pigment for other types of finishes. The lustreless paints used for the majority of military equipment underwent minor refinements and continued in good volume. Considerable reformulation of paints for military needs was necessary to take advantage of available raw material.   (A. B. Ho.)

Pakistan: *see* INDIA.

Palaeontology.
In the United States, Samuel Paul Welles in a monographic study of the long necked

plesiosaurs gave a detailed description of the skeletal anatomy of four new genera, all from the Upper Cretaceous of California. The paper concluded with a revision of the elasmosaurian plesiosaurs that resulted in the naming of five new genera. C. Lewis Gazin published a paper in which the important mammalian faunas of the San Pedro valley, Arizona, were fully discussed. A brief sketch of previous investigations and a discussion of their age and environment was followed by a systematic description of the Benson and Curtis ranch faunas. Two genera and four species were described as new. Lore Rose David in an extended paper described the Miocene fish faunas from many California localities. Part VI dealt with the fish of the famous Lompoc diatomaceous earth deposits. It was found to consist of 31 families, 39 genera and 42 species, a harmonious assemblage of a warm temperate coastal sea. This study revealed there was greater similarity between the fish faunas of the Pacific and Atlantic coasts of America during Miocene time than exists today. A paper by Charles W. Gilmore described all of the known lizard specimens assembled by the Central Asiatic expeditions in their explorations of Inner Mongolia. Seven genera and eight species were named as new. Two of the specimens pertained to North American genera, and a burrowing lizard marks the first occurrence of an Amphisbaenidae in a fossil state outside of the United States.

Charles L. Camp, D. W. Taylor and S. P. Welles issued their *Bibliography of Fossil Vertebrates* covering the years 1934 to 1938 inclusive. This volume of 663 pages of vital importance to all vertebrate palaeontologists, continues a coverage of world literature on vertebrate palaeontology covered previously by a volume published in 1940.

A most interesting discussion relating to the first discovery of fossil vertebrates in North America was published by George G. Simpson. He reached the conclusion that the first discovery of scientific standing was made by Charles Le Moyne, whose party found mastodon remains along the Ohio river in 1739. He points out, however, that the Indians should be credited with the first authentic discovery of "great bones" as early as 1519 in Mexico.

In invertebrate palaeontology in the United States, E. O. Ulrich, Aug. F. Foerste and A. K. Miller published Part II Brevicones of their joint report on the Ozarkian and Canadian cephalopods. This systematic study of all available materials resulted in the discovery of no less than seven genera and 145 new species. The paper is full and well illustrated.

Vladimir J. Okulitch issued a paper on the Pleospongia of North America, in which all of the Cambrian fossil sponges were described and illustrated. Their geographic and stratigraphic distribution, ecology and faunal associations were fully considered. A paper by Philip W. Reinhart dealt with the description, stratigraphic and geographic occurrences and relationships of the molluscan family Acidae as represented on the Pacific slope. Nine genera and 85 species were recognized, more than half of which occur in the recent fauna. A few species were described as new.

In a paper describing stemless crinoids from the Lower Cretaceous of Texas, Raymond E. Peck discovered they developed from a stemmed ancestor and became highly modified for a passive floating existence. Four genera and many species were described as new.

In palaeobotany in the United States, Roland W. Brown published a short paper describing a climbing fern from the Upper Cretaceous of Wyoming, the earliest authentic record from North America. Carroll Lane Fenton in a study of Palaeozoic algae discussed the problems involved in the recognition, preservation and nomenclature of early algae. J. H. Hoskins and A. T. Cross published a monographic study of the cone genus *Bowmanites*. This is a review of the genus and a description of several new species.

In South America, Joaquin Frenguelle published a paper on the Triassic flora of Argentina, in which 10 new plant forms were described.

BIBLIOGRAPHY.—Samuel Paul Welles, "Elasmosaurid Plesiosaurs with Description of New Material from California and Colorado," *Mem. Univ. Calif.*, vol. 13, no. 3 (1943); C. Lewis Gazin, "The Late Cenozoic Vertebrate Faunas from the San Pedro Valley, Arizona," *Proc. U.S. Nat. Mus.*, vol. 92 (1942); Lore Rose David, "Miocene Fishes of Southern California," *Geol. Soc. Amer. Special Paper No. 43* (Jan. 1943); Charles W. Gilmore, "Fossil Lizards of Mongolia," *Bull. Amer. Mus. Nat. Hist.*, vol. 81, art. iii (1943); C. L. Camp, D. N. Taylor and S. P. Welles, "Bibliography of Fossil Vertebrates 1934–1938," *Geol. Soc. Amer. Special Paper No. 42* (Nov. 1942).
George G. Simpson, "The Discovery of Fossil Vertebrates in North America," *Jour. Paleont.*, vol. 17 (Jan. 1943); E. O. Ulrich, Aug. F. Foerste and A. K. Miller, "Ozarkian and Canadian Cephalopods, pt. ii, Brevicones," *Geol. Soc. Amer. Special Paper No. 49* (Aug. 1943); Vladimir J. Okulitch, "North American Pleospongia," *Geol. Soc. Amer. Special Paper No. 48* (July 1943); Philip W. Reinhart, "Mesozoic and Cenozoic Archidae from the Pacific Slope of North America," *Geol. Soc. Amer. Special Paper No. 47* (June 1943); Raymond E. Peck, "Lower Cretaceous Crinoids from Texas," *Jour. of Paleont.*, vol. 17 (Sept. 1943); Roland W. Brown, "A Climbing Fern from the Upper Cretaceous of Wyoming," *Washington Acad. Sci. Jour.*, vol. 33 (1943); Carroll L. Fenton, "Pre-Cambrian and Early Paleozoic Algae," *Amer. Midland Naturalist*, vol. 30 (1943); J. H. Hoskins and A. T. Cross, "Monograph of the Paleozoic Cone Genus Bowmanites (Sphenophyllates)" (1943); Joaquin Frenguelle, "Contribuciones al conocimiento de la flora del Gondwana superior en la Argentina," Notas del Museo de La Plata, *Paleontologia*, vol. 7 (1942).   (C. W. Gi.)

Palestine. Palestine lies on the western edge of Asia and is bounded on the west by the Mediterranean, on the southwest by Egypt, on the south by the gulf of 'Aqaba, on the east by Trans-Jordan, on the northeast by Syria and on the north by the Lebanon. Area 10,100 sq.mi.; pop. (est. Dec. 31, 1940) 1,545,000. Chief towns: (pop. est. 1939): Jerusalem (cap. 129,800); Haifa (104,800); Jaffa (77,400); Tel-Aviv (130,300). High Commissioner (1943); Sir H. A. MacMichael; languages: English, Arabic, Hebrew; religions: (1939) Mohammedan 848,933; Jewish 424,373; Christian 114,624.

History.—The fear that war might sweep over Palestine was fading by the beginning of 1943, and the thoughts of both Arabs and Jews were returning to the problem of the country's political future.

The internal security of the country was not seriously troubled in 1943, though four British constables were fatally shot during the first nine months. But the underlying tension between the Arab and Jewish populations was vividly illuminated in August and September, when a military court convicted two British soldiers and two Jewish civilians on charges connected with the theft of military equipment from Allied stores. Some 125,000 rounds of ammunition and 300 rifles had been stolen from camps or depots in Palestine and Egypt, and from the docks at Suez. The defending counsel for the two soldiers, each of whom was sentenced to 15 years' imprisonment, pleaded that they had fallen into the power of a wealthy gun-running organization which was connected with the Jewish agency. These allegations were indignantly denied by the agency, which challenged the defending counsel to substantiate them before an independent court of inquiry. Meanwhile the trial of the two civilians, one of whom was a trade union official, was running its six-weeks' course. On Sept. 27 the court sentenced them to imprisonment for ten and seven years respectively, finding at the same time that the existence of a secret organization dangerous to the peace of the country and detrimental to the war effort had been established. The Zionist leaders continued to protest, and attributed sinister motives to the prosecution. In November there were widespread demonstrations of protest against the action of the police and military in searching a Jewish settlement where arms were believed to have been hidden.

THE BEACH at Tel Aviv, Palestine, in 1943

Zionists came into conflict with the British authorities on another occasion during 1943, on the issue of postwar reconstruction. Sir Douglas Harris was transferred in March to the post of reconstruction commissioner, and the high commissioner subsequently defined his task in terms which emphasized the predominantly agricultural character of the Palestinian economy and envisaged a decline from the wartime level of industrial production. This was interpreted by the Zionist general council as a reaffirmation of the policy laid down in the White Paper of 1939, and it declared that the Jewish community would not co-operate in planning on that foundation.

The support of the majority in organized U.S. Jewry for Zionism was expressed in a resolution carried at the beginning of Sept. 1943 by a representative U.S. Jewish conference. This demanded that the Jewish agency should be given authority to regulate immigration into Palestine and to develop the country's resources, these measures being "the essential prerequisites for the attainment of a Jewish majority and for the re-creation of the Jewish Commonwealth."

Meanwhile the leading statesmen of neighbouring Arab countries were reminding the world of their interest in the future of Palestine. The prime ministers of Egypt and Iraq each visited Palestine shortly before their conversations in Cairo to discuss the possibility of Arab union, and each assured the Arab population that they were watching over its interests.

The more immediate preoccupations of both government and people were much the same as in 1942. First place was still taken by the cost of living, which was shown by the official index to have risen from a figure of 100 on the eve of the war to 215 in January and 248 in June 1943. This resulted in higher costs of industrial production, and a fear that military orders, which had amounted to £P.10,000,000 in 1942, would begin to fall off even before the cessation of hostilities. The government was urged to subsidize the prices of necessities more generously. The 1943 estimates already provided £P.1,000,000 for this purpose, in addition to such other emergency expenses as the loans to citrus farmers, cost-of-living allowances and civil defense measures. There were increases of taxation, including the imposition of surtax on incomes of over £P.2,600.

The White Paper had provided for the admission of 75,000 Jewish immigrants before the end of March 1944, after which date further immigration would depend on Arab acquiescence. At the end of Sept. 1943, owing to the difficulty of escaping from Europe and to shortage of transport, only 44,000 of these immigrants had arrived in Palestine. His majesty's government therefore decided to suspend the time limit for the remaining 31,000.

Education.—(1939–40): Arab public system maintained by government, 402 schools (12 with secondary sections), 54,367 scholars; Muslim schools, private 178 (2 with secondary sections) with 14,204 scholars; Jewish public schools (1940) 419 (including 6 training colleges and 18 secondary, 5 trade and vocational schools) with 56,900 scholars; Jewish private schools 320 (including 22 secondary schools and 2 training colleges) with 25,700 scholars; Christian schools 195 with 25,274 scholars; Hebrew university, Jerusalem 130 teachers, 1,106 students.

Banking and Finance.—Revenue and expenditure (1941–42) revenue £P.8,325,553; expenditure (1941–42) £P.7,463,602; public debt (March 31, 1942) £P.4,475,000; notes in circulation (Jan. 31, 1943) £P.24,700,000; exchange rate £P.1 = £1 sterling = $4.03 U.S. in 1943.

Trade and Communication.—Overseas trade (merchandise): (1941) imports £P.12,038,000; exports £P.1,362,000; (1940) imports £P.11,035,454; exports, domestic £P.2,114,584; re-exports £P.176,195. Communications and transport: roads (1939) all weather 1,451 mi.; seasonable 985 mi.; railways (1940) broad gauge 333 mi.; narrow (Hedjaz rly.) 271 mi.; airways (1938): passengers 600, mail 86.9 tons; shipping (1939) entered 1,857 vessels; 4,370,085 net tons. (Dec. 31, 1940) motor vehicles licensed: 5,062 private cars, 1,198 public cars, 936 buses; 3,180 trucks and vans, 1,331 cycles; tractors 20; wireless receiving set licences (1938) 35,708; telephone subscribers (1940), 10,716.

Agriculture and Mineral Production.—Production 1939 (in short tons): potash (exports) £P.381,162; citrus fruits (exports) £P.3,807,570; barley (1940) 113,500; wheat (1940) 149,900; olive oil (1940) 3,970; wine (1938) 792,500 gal.; maize 6,830; tobacco (1940) 1,100; potatoes 11,460; sesamum 4,190.

Palmyra Island: *see* PACIFIC ISLANDS, U.S.

Panamá. A republic of Central America, nearest to South America. It is bisected by the Canal Zone, leased to the United States. Area: 32,933 sq.mi.; pop. (1940 census): 631,637, exclusive of the Canal Zone (pop. 1940 census: 51,827). The capital is Panamá city (111,893); other cities are: Colón (44,393); David (9,222); Chitré (4,790); Santiago (4,253). President in 1943: Dr. Ricardo Adolfo de la Guardia.

History.—The most noteworthy political news from Panamá in 1943 was the decision to suspend the coming presidential election. Under war conditions it was felt that the hazards of changing administrations would be too great for the safety of the republic, and on Jan. 4 the Panamá national assembly voted to continue President Ricardo Adolfo de la Guardia in office for two more years, without an election being held. A possible threat of revolution was removed late in August when Dr. José Pezet, former minister of education in the administration of President Arnulfo Arias, was arrested, together with others suspected of conspiracy against the government (Pezet claimed that under the Panamá constitution he should have succeeded to the office vacated by Arias but assumed by de la Guardia).

In April the senate of the United States approved a 1942 agreement by which certain water and sewage systems and real estate in the cities of Colón and Panamá were to be turned over to the republic, and a $2,700,000 debt for Panamá's share of a strategic highway project liquidated.

A department of public works was established Aug. 25, to care for the national construction program.

Economic conditions in Panamá were good during the major part of the year. While the export trade continued low, only a small part of the normal volume of bananas and coco-nuts being shipped, import trade was high. The large number of service men at the Canal Zone, and the extensive defense construction there, meant large pay roll expenditure in Panamá, effectively offsetting the loss of peacetime tourist trade. Late in the year employment in the Zone slackened, with purchasing power in the republic declining accordingly.

The agricultural program inaugurated in 1941–42 continued to develop although slowed down by lack of labour, farm and irrigation machinery, and particularly shortage of fuel and tires for essential transportation. Price control remained in effect, and gasoline use was severely restricted. Shortage of meat made necessary the advocation of "meatless Mondays."

Education.—In 1940, Panamá had 550 primary schools (enrolment 55,000); 7 post-primary schools (enrolment 4,500) and a National university with 500 students. Panamá is also the site of a new Inter-American university. Expenditures for education in 1941 were $2,513,000.

Finance.—The monetary unit is the balboa, equal in value to the U.S. dollar. The budget for the biennium ending Dec. 31, 1944, was set at $39,378,714 (revenue for 1942: $22,310,000; expenditure: $21,347,000). Income for the first half of 1943 was $13,037,757. There was no internal debt by 1943; the external debt (July) was $18,337,100.

Trade and Resources.—Exports for 1942 were valued at $2,-229,028, a decline of 48% from the previous year. Imports for 1942 were $37,579,517, up 14%.

Panamá has embarked upon a diversified agriculture program which it is hoped will make her independent for basic foodstuffs. In 1942, production of major crops was: rice 1,356,892 quintals; corn 228,654 quin.; beans 63,033 quin.; bananas 685,218 stems; plantains 4,048,000 stems; coco-nuts 455,754 (smallest output since 1910); cacao 2,161 short tons; abacá 254 tons; sugar 8,864 tons. There were 6,691,956 lb. of honey produced.

Communication.—Highway mileage in 1942 was 750 mi.; railway mileage, 257 mi. Communication with the outside world is by sea and air. (*See also* CENTRAL AMERICA; HISPANIC AMERICA AND WORLD WAR II.)   (D. RD.)

Pan-American Highway: *see* ROADS AND HIGHWAYS.

+ **Pan American Union.** The Pan American union is an international organization created in 1890 at the First International Conference of American States and maintained by the 21 American republics to promote peace, commerce and friendship among the republics. The union is supported by annual contributions from member countries in amounts proportional to population. It is controlled by a governing board composed of the secretary of state of the United States, who is chairman, and the diplomatic representatives in Washington of the other republics. Headquarters: Washington D.C.; director general in 1943, Dr. L. S. Rowe; assistant director, Dr. Pedro de Alba.

The Pan American union serves as the permanent secretariat of the International Conferences of American States and organizes many of the technical inter-American conferences convened to consider specific subjects. The union is also a centre of information on the American republics and on inter-American relations.

At the meeting of ministers of foreign affairs of the American republics held at Rio de Janeiro in 1942, the Pan American union was requested to organize several special agencies to deal with problems arising out of the participation of American republics in the war. Among these was the Inter-American Defense board, which continued to function at Washington during 1943, with the participation of military, naval and aviation experts of the 21 republics.

The Emergency Advisory Committee for Political Defense composed of seven representatives designated by the governments of Argentina, Brazil, Chile, Mexico, the United States, Uruguay and Venezuela, was established in Montevideo to control subversive activities in the American republics. During 1943 the committee made consultative visits to many of the countries of the continent, and worked out with officials of each country a program for the effective application of the committee's recommendations. National committees for political defense were established in all the countries visited.

The Inter-American Financial and Economic Advisory committee, organized in 1939 immediately following the outbreak of the war, continued its activities at the Pan American union during 1943, giving major attention to the resolutions of a financial and economic character adopted at the Rio de Janeiro meeting of foreign ministers. A special subcommittee was set up to map plans for the Inter-American Technical Economic conference, provided for in one of the Rio resolutions, to consider present and postwar economic problems. Through the Inter-American Coffee board, established by the committee in 1941, the plan for the division of the coffee market of the United States among the 14 coffee-producing countries of Latin America on the basis of their proportionate share of total production, was extended for another year to Oct. 1944.

The Executive Committee on Postwar Problems of the governing board of the Pan American union prepared a study of basic principles of the inter-American system, and undertook the preparation of a report on recent trends in inter-American economic co-operation. The preliminary recommendation on postwar organization formulated by the Inter-American Juridical committee of Rio de Janeiro in 1942, was sent to all the governments of the American republics, several of which during 1943 set up national committees to undertake studies and formulate projects on problems of postwar organization.

At the meeting of the governing board of the Pan American union held on Nov. 3, the Hon. Cordell Hull, secretary of state of the United States, was re-elected chairman of the board for the year 1944. The ambassador of Honduras, Dr. Julian R. Cáceres, was elected vice-chairman, succeeding the Bolivian ambassador, Dr. Luis F. Guachalla. (*See also* HISPANIC AMERICA AND WORLD WAR II.)   (L. S. RO.)

Paper and Pulp Industry. In 1943 the paper and pulp industry found itself in the

Table I.—United States Paper Production Capacity for 1942

Kind of paper	Capacity*
Newsprint	1,080,000
Groundwood	700,000
Book**	2,105,300
Writing	758,000
Cover	30,000
Text	16,200
Sulphite and other wrapping . . .	1,250,000
Kraft wrapping	1,700,000
Tissue	893,000
Paperboard	8,650,000
Building	938,000
All other	260,000
Total	18,380,500

*Including idle mills and equipment (short tons).
**Including coating raw stock and machine-coated papers.

Table II.—United States Paper Production, 1939-42

In Short Tons (1938-40 U.S. Census) (1942 A.P.P.A.)

Kind	1939	1940	1941	1942
Newsprint	954,259	1,056,304	1,045,269	981,000
Book papers	1,534,591	1,655,423	2,026,291	1,830,000
Paperboard	6,104,968	6,449,548	8,246,576	7,600,000
Wrapping	2,238,993	2,500,818	2,745,815	2,742,000
Writing	594,594	599,452	737,827	827,000
Cover	19,401	26,944	61,570	52,000
Tissue	665,723	761,712	960,309	1,050,000
Groundwood	121,717	129,410	641,409	596,000
Building	659,000	682,460	721,312	750,000
All other	625,306	621,638	117,765	94,000
Total—all grades	13,509,642	14,483,709	17,304,143	16,522,000

Table III.—U.S. Production and Consumption of Paperboard and Paper

Year	U.S. population	Production—short tons		Per capita consumption—pounds	
		Paperboard	Paper	Paperboard	Paper
1904	82,601,384	559,700	2,546,900	13.6	61.7
1909	90,691,354	883,100	3,238,500	19.5	71.3
1914	97,927,516	1,291,800	3,860,900	26.4	78.8
1919	105,003,065	1,867,100	4,099,000	35.5	78.1
1925	114,867,141	3,286,600	5,895,600	55.5	102.7
1930	123,090,000	4,060,700	6,108,400	65.9	99.4
1935	127,521,000	4,695,900	5,783,200	73.6	90.7
1940	131,669,275	6,550,000	7,822,000	99.6	118.9

middle of a war economy. With steel, tin, aluminum and other materials diverted almost entirely to armaments many products heretofore made of these materials found paper and paperboard as substitutes. In the packaging of foods alone the requirements of paper products had to meet tremendous demands. On the other hand the industry had to meet large losses through paper curtailment of other industries such as the automobile, refrigerator, radio, etc. whose reduced requirements were reflected in paper and paperboard production In all branches of business great accomplishments were made in reducing paper requirements.

Throughout 1943 the shortage of wood pulp, caused largely by reduced manpower in the woods, made it necessary to allocate pulp to mills on the basis of essential paper production. Many mills increased their re-use of waste paper. Rayon pulp requirements increased from 72,000 tons in 1930 to 316,308 tons in 1942. Nitrocellulose as an outlet was a new and large user of wood pulp, it having previously been made from cotton. Because

Table IV.—United States Production and Consumption of Paper, Wood Pulp, and Pulpwood

Year	Paper (Short tons)		Wood pulp (Short tons)		Consumption of Pulpwood (Cords)		
	Production	Consumption	Production	Consumption	Domestic	Imported	Total
1899	2,167,593	2,158,000	1,179,525	1,216,254	1,617,093	369,217	1,986,310
1909	4,216,708	4,224,000	2,495,523	2,856,503	3,207,653	793,954	4,001,607
1920	7,334,614	7,846,827	3,821,704	4,696,035	5,014,513	1,099,559	6,114,072
1925	9,182,204	10,590,000	3,962,217	5,590,304	5,005,445	1,088,376	6,093,821
1930	10,169,140	12,314,819	4,630,308	6,463,185	6,089,852	1,105,672	7,195,524
1935	10,506,195	12,490,886	4,944,226	6,877,860	6,590,942	1,037,332	7,628,274
1940	14,483,709	16,620,632	8,851,740	9,724,643	12,564,180	1,435,820	13,742,958
1941	17,280,000	19,768,325	9,978,400	10,801,223	15,400,000	1,292,640	16,692,640
1942	16,522,000	. . .	10,227,720	11,047,906	. . .	. . .	16,800,000

Table V.—U.S. Wood Pulp Production

(Short tons)

Year	Unbleached sulphite	Bleached sulphite	Total sulphate	Ground-wood	Soda	All others	Total
1925	790,510	612,576	409,768	1,612,019	472,647	64,697	3,962,217
1930	815,897	751,166	949,513	1,560,221	474,230	79,281	4,630,308
1935	634,947	944,620	1,467,749	1,355,819	485,162	144,002	5,032,299
1938	601,855	1,004,621	2,443,057	1,333,308	394,307	155,418	5,933,560
1940	990,668	1,601,016	3,725,135	1,762,821	548,047	164,940	8,851,740
1941	1,193,700	1,703,300	4,387,837	1,867,000	609,300	217,263	9,978,400
1942	1,212,354	1,718,192	4,725,133	1,889,607	453,459	228,975	10,227,720

Table VI.—Cellulose Consumption by the U.S. Rayon Industry

(Short tons)

Year	Total pulp	Wood pulp		Linters pulp		Raw cotton linters Bales
		Tons	%	Tons	%	
1930	72,000	45,000	62	27,000	38	115,000
1935	137,000	86,000	63	51,000	37	218,000
1939	194,500	145,000	75	53,000	25	211,000
1940	238,000	178,000	75	60,000	25	256,000
1941	287,500	214,500	75	73,000	25	312,000
1942	330,000	280,500	85	49,500	15	211,000

Table VII.—Canadian Paper Production

(Short tons)

Kind	1940	1941	1942
Newsprint	3,503,801	3,519,733	3,257,000
Book and writing paper . .	102,696	117,444	121,000
Wrapping paper	139,716	162,581	166,000
Paperboard	500,094	652,314	619,000
Tissue	34,054	35,725	38,000
Other paper	39,053	42,344	41,000
Total .	4,319,414	4,530,141	4,242,000

Table VIII.—Canadian Wood Pulp Production

(Short tons)

Kind	Production		
	1940	1941	1942
Groundwood	3,305,484	3,494,922	3,236,983
Sulphite bleached	543,987	590,812	603,300
Sulphite unbleached . . .	936,558	1,073,704	1,157,138
Sulphate	371,569	426,743	460,986
Screenings, chemical . . .	42,741	48,270	51,294
Screenings, mechanical . .	62,725	55,363	51,277
All other pulp	27,698	31,033	33,728
Total	5,290,762	5,720,847	5,594,796

Table IX.—World Production of Chemical Pulp

1938 (thousands of short tons)

United States	4,596	Estonia	87
Sweden	2,620	Lithuania	60
Finland	1,621	Rumania	52
Germany	1,469	Switzerland	50
Canada	1,147	Netherlands	46
Japan	643	Italy	45
U.S.S.R.	600	Newfoundland	41
Norway	502	Latvia	32
Austria	300	Yugoslavia	23
Czechoslovakia . . .	280	Great Britain	16
France	139	Mexico	3
Poland	120	Total	14,492

of steel and other priorities no new mills were built in 1943.

Canada.—In 1941 pulp and paper ranked first with respect to wage and salary distribution, capital investment and net value of production; it was second to the non-ferrous metal smelting and refinery group with respect to gross production and second to sawmills with respect to employment. There were 105 mills in operation in 1942.

United Kingdom.—No statistics were available to show paper production in Great Britain after the war began. Having depended largely on Scandinavian mills for raw materials, considerable adjustment was necessary in operations since only a limited amount of pulp was available from America. Straw and old papers became the major raw materials. There was a critical shortage of rosin and esparto. The government controls eliminated most unessential uses for papers and Great Britain learned how to get along with the quality and quantity of papers produced.

(R. G. M.)

Papua: *see* BRITISH EMPIRE; NEW GUINEA; PACIFIC ISLANDS, BRITISH.

Paraguay.
An inland republic in southern South America. Area, 154,165 sq.mi.; pop. (1938 official estimate: 954,848) was unofficially computed at nearly 1,100,000 in 1943. The official language is Spanish, but Guaraní, the indigenous tongue, is more widely spoken outside the capital. The capital is Asunción (pop., 1943 unofficial est., 123,000). Other important cities, with approximate populations, are Villarrica (35,000), Concepción (13,000), and Encarnación (15,000). Religion: overwhelmingly Roman Catholic. President in 1943: Gen. Higínio Morínigo.

History.—In May, Pres. Morínigo visited Brazil, returning an earlier official visit by Pres. Vargas; the following month he made a journey to the United States, visiting most of the other American republics on the same occasion. Commercial treaties with Brazil and Bolivia were made; a similar agreement with the United States was under formal discussion. A trade treaty with Argentina in November was followed the next month by an official visit to that country. Internal development continued to be fostered through United States financial and technical aid to a sanitation and health program, agricultural research, highway improvement and other projects.

Education.—Paraguay has some 2,000 primary schools and a national university (at Asunción). The educational system, however, is not well developed. Illiteracy is officially estimated at about 50%; however, reliable foreign observers put it at 60% or higher.

Finance.—Until 1943, the monetary unit was the peso (value: 302 to the U.S. dollar), divided theoretically into 100 centavos. The lowest coin was the 50-centavo ($\frac{1}{2}$ peso) piece, the highest bill 1,000 pesos. Effective Nov. 7, 1943, a new unit was established, the *guaraní* (value 33 cents U.S.), equal to 100 of the former pesos. The gold peso (value: 68.66 cents U.S.) was used for foreign transactions.

Trade.—In 1942, exports were 16,539,588 gold pesos, 9.3% over 1941 and 45.3% over 1940 totals; going to Argentina in transit, 44.9% (1941: 42.7%; 1940: 36.4%), Great Britain 18.8% (19.1%; 12.7%), United States 14.7% (19.0%; 20.9%), Argentina 13.6% (13.4%; 22.5%), Uruguay 6.4% (5.3%; 3.2%). Imports were 17,161,673 gold pesos, 41.6% over 1941 and 15.2% over 1940, Argentina supplying 44.8% (1941: 50.5%; 1940: 45.1%), Brazil 24.6% (4.4%; 3.1%), United States 19.4% (19.6%; 21.4%), Great Britain 6.1% (8.5%; 8.6%). Preserved meats made up 22.4% of all 1941 exports (1940: 15.1%), quebracho extract 19.2% (22.2%), hides 12.6% (12.5%), cotton 10.5% (11.0%), woods 6.2% (6.1%), petitgrain oil 4.9% (4.4%), yerba maté 4.7% (12.9%), sugar 3.5% (0.6%), tobacco 2.4% (3.2%). Imports are approximately 20% foodstuffs, practically all the balance manufactures.

Communication.—Both external and internal communications are inadequate. Only air service approaches adequacy. Air transport is maintained by Pan American Airways system to Buenos Aires, Rio de Janeiro, and Corumbá (Brazil), and by an Argentine air line. Weekly Brazilian military-postal planes provide airmail service from Brazil. During 1943, application was mad in the United States by Eastern Air Lines for a New York Buenos Aires service to pass through Asunción. There is n internal air service. The country's main dependence is upon wate transport. The chief access to world markets is by an Argentin shipping line by way of the Paraguay and Paraná rivers to Bueno Aires. A Brazilian line maintains services to Montevideo and t Corumbá (Brazil). Small river steamers serve Paraguayan port on the Alto Paraná and Paraguay rivers.

The principal land communication is by rail from Asunción t Encarnación, where it connects by train-ferry across the Paran and Posadas, and thence to Buenos Aires. Some short lines exis in the Chaco. Total railway mileage approximates 713 mi.

Highway communication is generally poor except for th Estigarribia Highway from Asunción to Villarrica, which is bein extended toward Encarnación through United States financial aid

Resources.—Cotton, sugar, tobacco, rice, peanuts and cor are extensively cultivated, both for domestic consumption an (except corn) for export. Competition in world markets i hampered, however, by high shipping costs. The same facto: adversely affects development of citrus fruits. Petitgrain oi (from bitter orange leaves) is, however, well developed as a export. Some tung oil is produced. Yerba maté is cultivate especially for domestic consumption. Among forestal product: quebracho, source of tannin, is extensively exploited for export as are some miscellaneous valuable cabinet-woods.

Cattle raising is important, with canned meats, meat extracts and hides important export items. In 1943, Great Britain purchased all canned meat exports for United Nations war needs Mineral resources are negligible. In 1943, however, extensive surveys were made for petroleum in the Chaco.

Manufacturing.—Manufacturing is but slightly developed except for tannin extraction and meat processing. Some *ñandutí* (Paraguayan lace) is manufactured for export.

Parents and Teachers, National Congress of.
The National Congress of Parents and Teachers, an organization of more than 2,500,000 members in about 28,000 local parent-teacher associations, was organized and functioning in 1943 in each of the 48 states, the District of Columbia, Hawaii and Puerto Rico. Founded in 1897 in Washington, D.C., as the National Congress of Mothers, the Congress is dedicated to the care and protection of children and youth. Membership is available to anyone interested. The organization's program includes activities dealing with education in all its phases, health, home and family life, citizenship, juvenile protection, etc. An extensive program of war activities was carried on, based on the regular, long-range program of the Congress.

The organization maintains an extensive publications program. The *National Parent-Teacher*, official magazine, is published ten times a year. *The National Congress Bulletin*, published monthly, goes to every local association and to individual subscribers. *Community Life in a Democracy, Schools for Democracy* and *The Parent-Teacher Organization: Its Origins and Purposes* were important book publications.

Special projects of the Congress included the summer round-up of the children, the community school lunch, the national radio project, and the traffic safety education project. The Congress carried on a constant program of study of legislation affecting children and youth, co-operating with both government and citizen organizations in many phases of the work. The office of the National Congress is at 600 S. Michigan blvd., Chicago 5, Ill. President (1943–46), Mrs. William A. Hastings of Madison, Wis.

(M. A. Hs.)

3ort

3rt

Paris. Capital and largest city of France, pop. (1936) 2,829,746; of greater Paris, including the belt of suburban factory towns, 4,933,855 There was a mass exodus from Paris at the time of the German occupation on June 14, 1940, but most of the refugees later returned to their homes. During 1943 there was no return of the French government to Paris, perhaps because the Germans regarded that city as likely to be in the advanced zone of hostilities when the Allied invasion of the continent took place.

Paris had suffered no major damage during the war and occasional Allied bombings of the Renault automobile works and other factories working on German war orders had not touched the city's famous architectural monuments and artistic treasures by the end of 1943.

Paris during 1943 continued to be cut off from direct contact with the non-axis world. The German military governor was General Otto von Stulpnaegel, and he repeatedly resorted to shooting of hostages in an effort to curb terrorist attacks on German soldiers and acts of sabotage inspired by the French underground resistance movement. One of the better known victims of these shootings was Gabriel Peri, a writer on foreign affairs for the communist newspaper, *L'Humanité*.

But the underground movement, far from being crushed, gained strength as the tide of war turned against Germany in 1943. With its revolutionary traditions and its large population of students and workers, Paris contributed its full share of volunteers and martyrs to the underground resistance. The German attack on Russia in 1941 had brought a considerable number of workers in the industrial suburbs of Paris into the camp of national resistance.

French industry in Paris and elsewhere was more and more compulsorily integrated into the nazi economy. Germany was obtaining tanks from the Renault plant and shells, grenades, bombs and army cars from the big Citroën automobile works, along with planes from the Potez factory in Amiens. There was also a good deal of pressure to obtain skilled French workers for munitions factories in Germany.

Life for the great majority of Parisians was bleak, cold and hungry under the enemy occupation, although the rationing system prevented downright starvation. French food rations, as of 1942, were as follows:

Bread, 68 oz. a week; meat, 6½–9 oz.; fats and oils, 3½ oz.; potatoes, irregular. Clothing was very scarce and a new pair of shoes could be bought legally only if convincing evidence was presented that the owner had completely worn out any old pairs. A black market where extremely high prices prevailed was patronized by wealthy people. There was a lively speculation in objects of permanent value, paintings, furniture, rare editions of books, stamp collections, antiques of all kind, fine porcelain. This reflected the growing distrust of the paper franc which, at last accounts as of 1943, was quoted at 210 to the dollar on the free market, as against an official value of 43.50 to the dollar.

Motor transportation continued very much diminished in Paris, and the motor vehicles on the curiously quiet streets were mostly German staff cars and army trucks and trucks engaged in municipal services. The Metro (subway) continued to function and was jammed to capacity. A few horse-cabs appeared on the streets.

Places of amusement, the Opera and the Opera Comique, concert-halls, theatres, motion-picture theatres and dance-halls remained open and German officers, "collaborationists" and the French who had retained some of their former wealth furnished a clientele for the famous restaurants, most of which, including Maxim's, the Lido and the Boeuf sur le Toit, continued to function in 1943. (W. H. Ch.)

Parks and Monuments: *see* NATIONAL PARKS AND MONUMENTS.

Parliament, Houses of. The eighth session of the 37th parliament of the United Kingdom of Great Britain and Northern Ireland was opened, with the usual wartime simple ceremony and without previous announcement, by the king accompanied by the queen, on Nov. 11, 1942.

Changes in the highest offices of the commons were caused by the resignation in January of Sir Dennis Herbert, chairman of committees, followed on March 4 by the death while still in office of Edward A. Fitzroy, the speaker. Col. Douglas Clifton-Brown, Conservative M.P. for Hexham, for five years deputy chairman of committees, had become chairman on Jan. 20. On March 9, when the house reassembled after five days' interruption of business, he was unanimously elected speaker. By simultaneous steps, Major James Milner, Labour M.P. for S.E. Leeds, became deputy and then chairman of committees. Charles Williams, Conservative M.P. for Torquay, was chosen deputy chairman and the vacancy on the chairmen's panel was filled by Charles G. Ammon, Labour M.P. for Camberwell North.

An important reshuffling of war cabinet offices, but without change in personnel, came about in September through the sudden death of Sir Kingsley Wood As chancellor of the exchequer Sir Kingsley was not in the war cabinet, but Sir John Anderson, who passed from lord presidency of the council to succeed him, was and remained so. Clement Attlee, the deputy premier, took over the lord presidency, with its chairmanship of the cabinet committee on home affairs, but gave up his dominions portfolio to Viscount Cranborne, who as leader in the lords already had special access to the cabinet. The new lord privy seal was Lord Beaverbrook, but his return to the government did not restore his cabinet place. (*See* CABINET MEMBERS.) By other changes Richard Law, promoted in the foreign office to the rank of minister of state, was succeeded as parliamentary secretary by George Hall, transferred from the admiralty and replaced by J. P. L. Thomas. N. A. Beechman became junior lord of the treasury.

Further changes on Nov. 12 enlarged the war cabinet by the inclusion of Lord Woolton, on his appointment as minister of reconstruction. As food minister he was succeeded by Col. J. J. Llewellin, whose post as minister resident for supply in Washington, D.C., was filled by Ben Smith. H. U. Willink, brought from the Conservative back bench to be minister of health followed Ernest Brown who remained in the government as chancellor of the duchy of Lancaster. A. T. Lennox-Boyd became the new under secretary for aircraft production.

On the passing of the bill setting up the new ministry of town and country planning, W. S. Morrison, minister-elect, became a full member of the government. (*See* GOVERNMENT DEPARTMENTS AND BUREAUS.)

In spite of the political truce two seats were lost to the government at by-elections. West Belfast passed from the Ulster Unionists to J. Beattie of the Irish Labour party, and Eddisbury (Cheshire) won from the National Liberals by J. E. Loverseed, gave the Common Wealth party its second M.P.

Lady Apsley's election for Bristol Central to follow her husband, who was killed on active service, brought the number of women M.P.'s to 14. Two other members, Col. Cazalet and Major Whiteley, were killed with Gen. Sikorski, the Polish premier, in a plane crash at Gibraltar.

No censure motion had to be resisted by the government during the year but strenuous opposition from the Conservatives to the bill which set up wages boards in a reorganized catering trade delayed that measure in committee till some concessions were made. Women members won a notable victory by securing for women compensation equal to that which men receive as a result of civilian war-injuries. The strongly-expressed will of the house obtained important improvements in widows' and old age pensions.

House of Lords.—On becoming viceroy of India, Sir Archibald Wavell was created a viscount and similar rank which would normally have been bestowed on a retiring speaker was granted to Mrs. Fitzroy on her husband's death. Of the five new barons, Sir Roger Keyes became the fourth admiral of the fleet in the upper house and Sir Hugh Dowding's honour commemorated the air victory won under his command in the battle of Britain. (L. Du.)

Patch, Alexander McCarrell, Jr. (1889–), U.S. army officer, was born Nov. 23, at Ft. Huachuca, Ariz., the son of an army officer. He was graduated from West Point in 1913 and was commissioned a second lieutenant. During World War I, he saw active duty in France and on his return to the U.S. he became a member of the faculty at Staunton Military academy, Virginia, 1920–24. He attended the Command and General Staff school, 1924–25, and returned to Staunton, where he continued until 1928. In 1930 he received further training at the Army War college. Promoted to the rank of major general in March 1942, Patch commanded the U.S. troops which co-operated with the Free French forces to forestall Japanese seizure of New Caledonia. He was placed in command of operations on Guadalcanal in Jan. 1943, when the army relieved Gen. Alexander A. Vandegrift and his marine units. By Feb. 10 the Japanese had been driven from Guadalcanal, and on March 7 Patch was awarded the navy's D.S.M. with a citation by Secretary of the Navy Frank Knox for his participation in the Guadalcanal action.

Patents. Larger and more significant co-operation with the war and navy departments marked the activities of the patent office in 1943. Of special importance and value were first, its scrutiny of pending applications to determine the military usefulness and the commercial worth of the mechanisms and compositions these covered and secondly, its fulfilment of the provisions of statutes requiring that all such inventions and discoveries be subjected to secrecy to preclude their revelation to the enemy. In 1943 there were issued 4,155 secrecy orders, and from July 1, 1940, to Dec. 31, 1943, a total of 7,875 such restrictions. In this function the commissioner had the collaboration of the war and navy departments, the War Production board, the Office of Scientific Research and Development and other agencies.

In the fiscal year ended June 30, 1943, net receipts of the office were $3,563,616.97, and expenditures $4,610,780.45. There was a decrease in earnings largely attributable to a decline in the number of applications for patents and for trademark registrations. Applications for patents, including those for designs and reissues, totalled 48,724, and for trademark registrations 8,552. Patents granted numbered 33,502. Trademarks registered were 5,596. (*See* also INTERNATIONAL LAW; LAW.) (C. P. Co.)

Patterson, Robert Porter (1891–), U.S. government official, was born Feb. 12 in Glens Falls, N.Y. He was graduated from Union college, 1912, took his law degree from Harvard, 1915, and practised law in New York city. He saw military action in the Mexican campaign, 1916, and in World War I, during which he rose to the rank of major and was awarded the D.S.C. Patterson was ap-

pointed judge of the U.S. district court for the southern New York district, 1930, and became judge of the U.S. circuit court of appeals, 1939. He resigned his seat on the bench in July 1940 to accept an appointment as assistant secretary of war and five months later became undersecretary of war. In Feb. 1943, Patterson clashed with Rubber Director William M. Jeffers when he charged that Jeffers was furthering the rubber program at the expense of more vital military projects. In November, Patterson defended the construction by the war department of the Canol oil pipeline in northern Canada. While the Truman senate investigating committee revealed that the $134,000,000 project was producing 479 bbl. daily, Patterson insisted that the extremely critical need for oil justified the cost.

Patton, George Smith, Jr. (1885–), U.S. army officer, was born Nov. 11 in San Gabriel, Calif. He was graduated from West Point, 1909, began his army career as cavalry lieutenant, 1913, and was aide-decamp to General Pershing in Mexico, 1916–17, and in England, 1917. An expert on mechanized warfare, he was made a tank brigade commander in July 1940. On April 4, 1941, he was promoted to major general and two weeks later he was made commander of the 2nd armoured division. Soon after Pearl Harbor, he was made corps commander in charge of both the 1st and 2nd armoured divisions and organized the desert training centre at Indio, Calif. Patton was commanding general of the western task force during the U.S. operations in Africa in Nov. 1942, and handled the landing of U.S. forces on the western coast of Africa.

Named for promotion to lieutenant general on March 11, 1943, Patton fought through the major portion of the Tunisian campaign. On May 8, it was announced that he had been superseded by Gen. Omar N. Bradley. Patton meanwhile organized new forces for the impending invasion of Sicily, during which he commanded the U.S. Seventh army, but did not participate in the Italian campaign in 1943. Patton was widely criticized in Nov. 1943 when it was revealed that he had twice struck an enlisted man suffering from shell shock in an evacuation hospital in Sicily in August. Severely upbraided for this action by Gen. Dwight Eisenhower, Patton apologized not only to the victim of his outburst but to his seventh army troops as well. Eisenhower subsequently defended his retention of Patton in a post of responsibility on grounds that he was a loyal and valuable leader.

"Pay-as-you-earn" System: *see* TAXATION.

Peaches. The 1943 peach crop of the United States was estimated by the U.S. department of agriculture to be only 42,060,000 bu. compared to 65,365,000 bu. in 1942, a decline of 37% from 1942 and 24% below the ten-year (1932–41) average. Only seven states, all of them in the western groups, had above-average crops in 1943. Colorado had a record crop and Utah the largest in recent years. The New Jersey crop was below average and the crops of Pennsylvania and Michigan only fair. Most other states had very small crops. Production in the ten southern peach states was 5,378,000 bu. compared to 19,591,000 bu. in 1942 and the ten-year (1932–41) average of 15,108,000 bu.

U.S. Peach Production in Leading States, 1943 and 1942

State	1943 bu.	1942 bu.	State	1943 bu.	1942 bu.
California . .	25,127,000	28,752,000	Texas	900,000	1,610,000
Washington .	2,052,000	2,108,000	Arkansas . .	738,000	2,337,000
Colorado . .	1,978,000	1,490,000	Alabama . .	649,000	1,595,000
Georgia . . .	1,593,000	6,177,000	South Carolina	392,000	3,500,000
Michigan . .	1,452,000	2,150,000	North Carolina	252,000	2,463,000
Pennsylvania .	1,176,000	1,771,000	Virginia . . .	172,000	1,936,000
New Jersey .	918,000	1,228,000	New York .	95,000	1,615,000

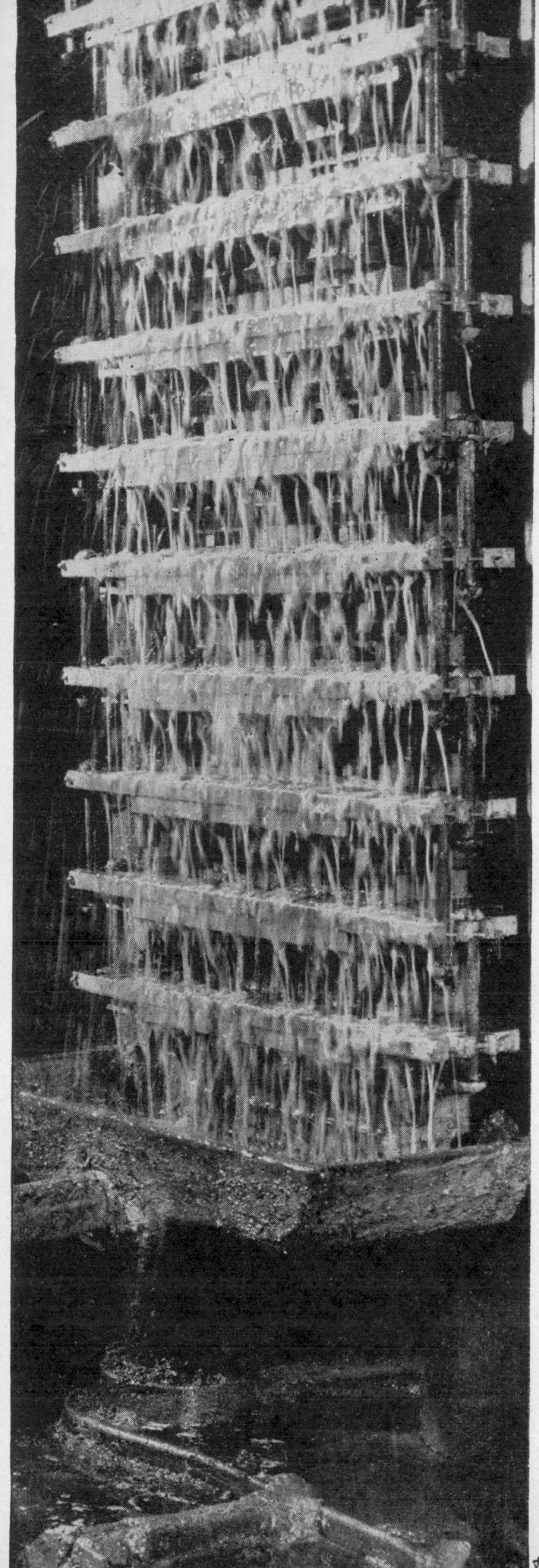

In California production of all varieties was less than in 1942 though above the ten-year average. Clingstone production was 16% less than 1942 while freestone production was 7% smaller. Production in all other states was less than 1,000,000 bu. apiece.

(J. C. Ms.)

Peanuts. The increase in peanut production needed in the war emergency was met in 1943 by a total crop of 2,561,610,000 lb. as estimated by the U.S. department of agriculture which was about 16% more than the 2,211,535,000 lb. crop of 1942 and about double the ten-year average (1932–41) of 1,214,777,000 lb. In the old commercial areas of the southeastern states yields were near a record. Lower yields were reported from

U.S. Production of Peanuts by States, 1943 and 1942

State	1943 lb.	1942 lb.	State	1943 lb.	1942 lb.
Georgia	910,080,000	627,690,000	Oklahoma	92,750,000	151,050,000
Alabama	499,875,000	335,400,000	South Carolina	46,800,000	28,875,000
Texas	344,705,000	430,080,000	Mississippi	23,750,000	30,000,000
North Carolina	317,100,000	332,100,000	Tennessee	15,750,000	6,750,000
Virginia	193,875,000	175,950,000	Arkansas	12,300,000	15,200,000
Florida	94,500,000	69,600,000	Louisiana	10,125,000	8,840,000

the southwest indicating that the crop had been expanded onto poorer lands less suitable to the crop. In Oklahoma unfavourable weather delayed harvest particularly of late planted peanuts which were damaged by unusually early frosts. While the acreage more than doubled after 1941, a further increase of about 30% was suggested by the War Food administration for 1944 to get the much needed oil. The principal retarding factors were labour and machinery.

(J. C. Ms.)

Pears. Production of pears increased to a record crop of 32,000,000 bu. in 1938, but declined to 31,000,000 in 1942 and was estimated by the U.S. department of agriculture at 23,761,000 bu. in 1943. This amount compares with an average crop of 27,938,000 bu. for the period 1932–41. The production of Bartlett pears in California, Washington and Oregon was about the same as in 1942 but 13% larger than the average. In these

U.S. Pear Production in Leading States, 1943, 1942 and 10-Yr. Average
(In thousands of bushels)

State	1943	1942	10-yr. average	State	1943	1942	10-yr. average
California				New York	528	1,241	1,192
Bartlett	11,209	8,834	8,413	Michigan	481	1,000	1,156
Other varieties	1,250	917	1,250	Texas	211	508	361
Washington				Georgia	138	507	323
Bartlett	3,906	5,063	4,158	Mississippi	136	519	322
Other varieties	1,360	1,612	1,848	Virginia	26	528	336
Oregon							
Bartlett	1,449	1,824	1,431				
Other varieties	1,462	2,504	2,157				

same leading pear producing states other varieties than Bartlett yielded about 21% below the average. The crop in the rest of the states was much below average. Prices were about 50% higher in 1943 than in 1942.

All other states produced less than 500,000 bu. each in 1942 and less in 1943.

(J. C. Ms.)

Peat. Lack of imported supplies stimulated peat production in the United States to an increase from 70,097 short tons in 1940 to 86,503 tons in 1941, but in 1942 output dropped back to 71,500 tons. About 75% of the supply is used as a soil conditioner, 20% in mixed fertilizers, and 5% in other uses, including litter in barns and poultry yards, and packing material for fruits, vegetables and shrubs, so that practically the entire supply

PEANUT OIL pouring from a hydraulic press in Terrell county, Ga. A source of glycerine for munitions, production of the oil was speeded up in 1943

is used in agriculture, and none as fuel, which is the main use in the important European producing countries.　　(G. A. Ro.)

Pecans: *see* NUTS.

Peek, George Nelson

(1873–1943), U.S. industrialist and government official, was born Nov. 19 in Polo, Ill. After graduating from the Oregon (Ill.) high school in 1891 he attended Northwestern university. He entered private industry in 1893, soon became an executive and served in that capacity with several agricultural implement companies until 1923. In 1918 he was with the War Industries board as commissioner of finished products. The following year he acted as chairman of the industrial board in the U.S. department of commerce. As president of the American council of Agriculture, 1925–28, Peek gained a knowledge of farm problems which proved valuable when he was appointed administrator for the newly formed Agricultural Adjustment administration in May 1933. In 1934–35 he acted as special adviser on foreign trade to President Roosevelt while serving as head of the Export-Import Bank of Washington. He was the author of several articles and pamphlets dealing with national agricultural policy and foreign trade. He died at Rancho Santa Fe, near San Diego, Calif., on Dec. 17.

Pellegrinetti, Ermenegildo

(1876–1943), Italian cardinal, was born March 27 at Camaiore, Italy. He entered a seminary at Lucca and had served in an inconspicuous capacity until 1919 when he accompanied the late Msgr. Achille Ratti, Papal Nuncio, to Warsaw as secretary. When the latter became pope in 1922, he selected Pellegrinetti to represent the Vatican as Nuncio to Yugoslavia. In his new post, Pellegrinetti found himself surrounded with anti-Italian and anti-Vatican sentiment. Although ratification of a concordat which he negotiated in 1936 was deferred by the Yugoslav senate, his work, nevertheless, was said to have improved the status of the Roman Catholic Church in that country. He was made titular archbishop of Adana in 1922, a cardinal in 1937, and was mentioned as possible successor to Pope Pius XI. Cardinal Pellegrinetti died in Rome, March 29, according to a Rome broadcast recorded in London.

Pemba: *see* BRITISH EAST AFRICA.

Penicillin.

Penicillin is an extremely powerful germ-killing substance. It is obtained by growing a mould known as *Penicillium notatum* in a suitable liquid medium and then extracting the active substance from the liquid. It is such a potent agent that in dilutions of 1 part in 100,000,000, the growth of such death-dealing organisms as the staphylococcus is prevented.

Penicillin was first described by Dr. Alexander Fleming in 1929. For ten years it received little attention. It was difficult to produce and it was extremely unstable. From 1940 on, however, there was great interest in this agent, since it is an effective weapon against a wide variety of infections common among wounded soldiers. Its production and investigation in the United States and in England were a part of the war effort. In the United States, the production of penicillin and its clinical application was stimulated by the Committee on Medical Research of the Office of Scientific Research and Development.

Penicillin is relatively nontoxic. It can be injected into the veins, the muscles, or the subcutaneous tissues without causing any undesirable reactions. It cannot be given by mouth since it is destroyed by the gastric juice. It is excreted rapidly in the urine and in the bile. In view of its rapid excretion it is necessary to give it either continuously or at frequent intervals.

PENICILLIN-PRODUCING MOULD (*Penicillium notatum*) growing on the surface of a sugar nutrient in a bottle.

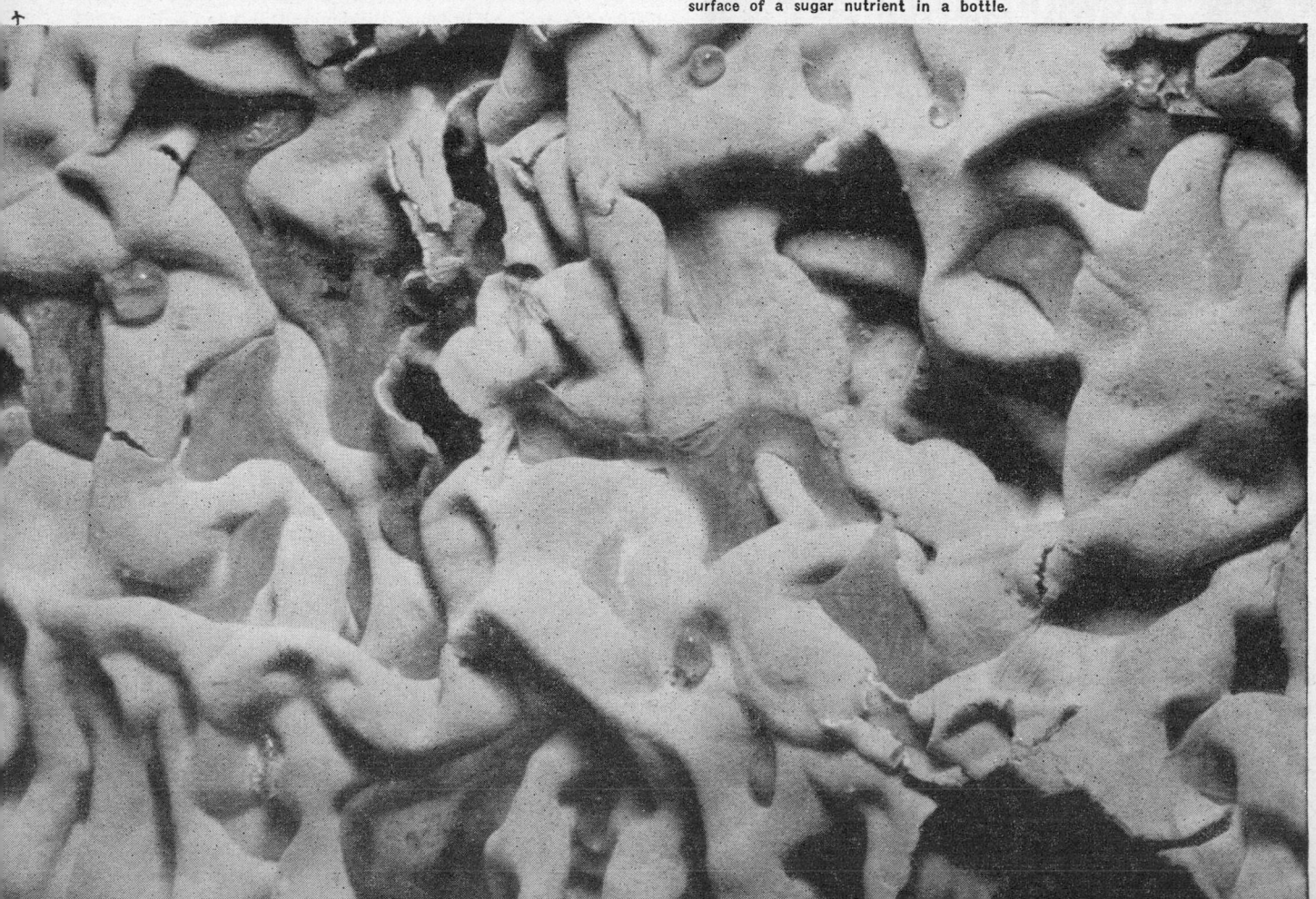

The beneficial effects of penicillin in the treatment of many infections can no longer be doubted. A large number of patients were treated and the results were recorded.

In the treatment of blood stream infections, bone infections, lung infections, eye infections, gonorrhoea and syphilis the results were dramatic in many cases. In the case of staphylococcic blood stream infections the fatality rate before the sulfonamides was between 80% and 85% With the sulfonamides it dropped to between 65% and 70%. With penicillin there were good reasons for believing that the death rate would be in the neighbourhood of 20% or 25%.

Infections due to the organism causing gonorrhoea were overcome in 24 to 48 hours even after they had resisted the sulfonamides.

Unfortunately, penicillin alone was ineffective in the treatment of bacterial endocarditis, an infection of the valves of the heart.

The limiting factor in the use of penicillin was its production on a large scale. Prodigious efforts were made to increase production, and progress was made and continued in 1943. Large quantities of the mould must be grown either in bottles or vats for a number of days. Then the active material must be extracted from the medium and purified so that it can be injected in man without causing reactions. Relatively small amounts of penicillin were obtained from large amounts of liquid, so that it frequently required the processing of 250 gal. of liquid to obtain enough material to treat a single patient. Another disadvantage was the instability of the product once it was obtained. All of the processes of manufacture were improved and the facilities for producing larger amounts were being enlarged (*See* also CHEMOTHERAPY.)

BIBLIOGRAPHY.—A. Fleming, "On the Antibacterial Action of Cultures of a penicillium, with Special Reference to Their Use in the Isolation of B. Influenzae," *Brit. Jour. Exper. Path.*, 10:226 (1929); E. Chain, H. W. Florey, A. D. Gardner, M. A. Jennings, J. Orr-Ewing and A. G. Sanders, "Penicillin as a Chemotherapeutic Agent," *Lancet*, 2:226 (1940); A. N. Richards, Chairman, "Penicillin. Statement released by the Committee on Medical Research," *J.A.M.A.*, 122:235 (1943); W. E. Herrell, "Further Observations on the Clinical Use of Penicillin," *Proc. Staff Meet. Mayo Clin.*, 18:65 (1943); C. S. Keefer, Chairman, F. G. Blake, E. K. Marshall, J. S. Lockwood, W. B. Wood, "Penicillin in the Treatment of Infections. A report of 500 cases," *J.A.M.A.*, 122:1217 (1943); F. G. Blake and B. Craige, "Penicillin in Suppurative Disease of the Lungs," *Yale Jour. Biol. & Med.*, 15:507 (1943); J. F. Mahoney, C. Ferguson, M. Buchholtz and C. J. Van Slyke, "The use of Penicillium Sodium in the Treatment of Sulfonamide-Resistant Gonorrhea in Men," *Am. J. Syph., Gon., and Ven. Dis.*, 27:525 (1943); Champ Lyons, "Penicillin Therapy of Surgical Infections in the U.S. Army," *J.A.M.A.*, 123:1007 (1943). (C. S. KR.)

Pennsylvania. A Middle Atlantic state and one of the original 13 states of the union, popularly known as the "Keystone state." Area, 45,333 sq.mi. including 288 sq.mi. of water; pop. (1940) 9,900,180, of whom 8,453,729 were native born white, 973,260 foreign born white and 470,172 Negroes. The Negro population increased after World War II began because of the influx of workers from the south attracted by the high wages in the war industries. The white population in 1940 included 80,111 of German birth and 197,281 of Italian. The urban population numbered 6,586,877 and the rural 3,313,303. Capital, Harrisburg (83,893). Cities with a larger population: Philadelphia (1,931,334); Pittsburgh (671,659); Scranton (140,404); Erie (116,955); Reading (110,568); Allentown (96,904); Wilkes-Barre (86,236).

History.—The legislature, which began its biennial session Jan. 5, 1943, continued in session until May 9, passing many important bills. It reduced taxation by $45,000,000 in spite of increased appropriations for welfare and education and appropriations to the police pension fund in Philadelphia and other cities. It suspended the operation of the civil service regulations in state departments for the duration of the war, transferred 400 jobs from the Democratic-controlled attorney general's office to the Republican secretary of revenue, permitted the employment of school children 14 years old on farms in case of a shortage of adult labour, authorized the state council of defense to aid in the elimination of black markets, made an estimated reduction of $3,000,000 in automobile license fees, empowered the governor, with the approval of a legislative committee, to suspend state laws when the legislature is not in session on the request of the federal government, created a postwar planning commission to plan a public works program to provide work for returning soldiers, and increased from 44 to 48 hours a week the permissible time for the employment of women and children in war industries.

The principal officers in 1943 were: Edward Martin, governor; James H. Duff, attorney general; G. Harold Wagner, treasurer, and George W Maxey, chief justice.

Education.—According to the latest figures available in 1943 there was an enrolment of 1,879,736 pupils in the public schools, including 96,824 in the kindergartens, 1,106,275 in the elementary and 676,637 in the secondary schools, with 87,045 teachers in the elementary schools and 22,562 in the secondary. Approximately $200,000,000 was spent for the support of the system.

Public Welfare, Charities, Correction.—An appropriation of $121,024,400 was made for public assistance for 1941-2. This was used to provide relief for 309,000 WPA workers and 102,178 aged and for pensions for 10,686 blind persons. The state maintains seven penal and correctional institutions, for the support of which a biennial appropriation of $247,347.59 was made in 1940-41.

Communications.—Of the approximately 100,000 mi. of highways in 1943, 40,510 mi. were under the control of the state. Of the latter mileage, 32,947 were improved, including 675 mi. in cities, 2,100 in boroughs and 37,782 in townships. Included in the total were 5,700 mi of city streets. The department of highways spent $121,355,846 during the biennium 1941–43. There were 11,950.4 mi. of steam and 1,866.7 mi. of electric railroads in 1943.

Banking and Finance.—There were 399 state banking institutions including 8 savings banks in 1943, with total resources of $3,391,186,556 and deposits of $2,686,191,018. In addition there were 1,313 building and loan associations with assets of $77,670,929. There were 688 national banks with assets of $3,758,013,000, demand deposits of $1,369,985,000 and time deposits of $1,068,266,000. Appropriations for the biennium ending June 30, 1943, were $331,147,595, including $198,000,000 for public relief. The estimated receipts from taxation were $414,141,822. The gross debt was $108,426,000, which securities in the sinking fund reduced to a net of $76,740,932.29.

Agriculture.—The total farm income for 1942 was $362,504,000, in which is included $6,240,000 received from the federal government. The leading agricultural products for 1942 and the estimated crops for 1943 were as shown in Table I.

Table I.—*Leading Agricultural Products of Pennsylvania, 1943 and 1942*

Crop	1943	1942
Wheat, bu.	13,843,000	15,301,000
Corn, bu.	52,026,000	55,685,000
Oats, bu.	16,820,000	36,010,000
Barley, bu.	2,928,000	4,000,000
Buckwheat, bu.	2,443,000	2,145,000
Hay, tons	2,765,000	3,300,000

Manufacturing.—There were 17,366 manufacturing establishments in the state, according to the census of 1940, employing 1,419,041 persons to whom $1,940,045,800 was paid in wages. The capital invested was $4,223,471,300 and the value of the goods produced was $6,991,966,000. The value of the product of the principal industries for 1940 and 1937 is shown in Table II.

Table II.—*Principal Industries of Pennsylvania, 1940 and 1937*

Industry	Value of Products	
	1940	1937
Metals	$1,944,848,400	$1,958,279,000
Textiles	795,457,200	819,402,500
Food	740,901,600	770,319,300
Chemicals	518,062,300	409,395,500
Paper and printing	372,074,400	350,436,600
Leather	174,963,900	175,288,000
Tobacco products	92,272,300	85,513,300

Mineral Production.—The latest available figures put the total value of the mineral production at $1,822,389,500. The value of the principal products in 1938 and 1939 was:

Table III.—*Principal Mineral Products of Pennsylvania, 1939 and 1938*

Mineral Products	Value	
	1939	1938
Bituminous coal	$188,900,000	$160,965,000
Anthracite	187,175,000	180,600,167
Pig iron	186,392,533	191,266,844
Petroleum	36,200,000	32,762,000
Natural gas	35,268,000	29,544,000
Cement	34,332,649	28,242,913

The department of the interior reported that the value of anthracite mined in 1940 was $192,539,600 and of bituminous coal was $218,504,200. There are more than 80,000 oil wells from the yield of which 2,095,350,858 gal. of gas were distilled.

(G. W. Do.)

Pennsylvania, University of.

An institution of higher learning at Philadelphia, Pa. Carrying on the policy begun in 1941, when the entire faculties and facilities of the university were placed at the government's disposal, the university continued research projects, and additional ones were initiated in chemistry, engineering, physics, medicine, psychology and surgery. Most of these projects dealt with war problems. Some 15,000 war workers in nearby factories had taken advantage of the training programs supervised by the engineering departments and the Wharton school.

More than 300 members of the faculty had entered the government service, the majority having been called to fill positions of administration or research in Washington or elsewhere. Established on the campus were units of the Army Specialized Training program, the Women's Army corps, the Navy College Training program and the Naval Flight Preparatory school. Area-language groups were in training at the University museum, army medical officers at the Graduate School of Medicine and Cadet corps nurses at the University hospital. For statistics of enrolment, faculty, endowment, library volumes, etc., see UNIVERSITIES AND COLLEGES.

(T. S. G.)

Pensions, Army and Navy: *see* VETERANS' ADMINISTRATION.
Pepper: *see* SPICES.

Performing Right Societies.

Performing right societies exist in the principal countries of the world. They are founded on the principle of copyright law that the right to control public performance is vested in the owner of music copyright. The chief performing right society in the United States and sole affiliate in the United States of the principal foreign societies is the AMERICAN SOCIETY OF COMPOSERS, AUTHORS AND PUBLISHERS, familiarly known under its alphabetical designation of ASCAP. In its 30th year in 1943, ASCAP had become the world's most important performing right society, with 1,600 writer members (including 135 women) and 200 publisher members.

ASCAP's entry into the serious music field, its preparation for postwar licensing of music in industry, and its initiation of litigation to bring the great juke-box field within scope of its licensing activities were important developments of 1943. It announced that during the year it had achieved complete coverage of the commercial musical performance field in the United States, and had put into operation an equalized rate policy that had greatly improved its customer relations. Infringement suits had dropped from a former total of several hundreds to less than 40 at the end of the year.

Heretofore ASCAP had exercised only the popular music rights of its members, covering chiefly songs and dance music. Inclusion of serious music in its repertoire carried a similar enlargement of repertoires of its foreign affiliates, including many familiar old world copyrights widely used in symphonic and concert programs.

Rapid development of the use of music in industrial plants had been world-wide for several years. During 1943 the Performing Right society of England litigated this matter, winning favourable decisions in the highest court in two test cases, with the result that the government itself was to pay a lump sum (£25,000 annually) to PRS for unrestricted use of its repertoire in war plants. In the United States, ASCAP adopted a hands-off policy as a contribution to the war effort, merely asserting its rights and waiving collection of fees for the duration of the war.

Two test suits brought by ASCAP against juke-box operators had not progressed beyond the pleading stage. ASCAP's claim was that the specific exemption of coin-operated machines in the 1909 copyright law was not applicable to juke-box operations.

Because of the war, much of ASCAP's international business was done through the U.S. alien property custodian. England's society (PRS) was the only European organization to continue direct exchange of collections. Other international operations were chiefly of a bookkeeping nature.

Wartime restrictions and accompanying transportation difficulties closed many establishments formerly using ASCAP licenses, but expanding musical policies in those that continued to operate and better coverage combined to keep the total number of licenses up to more than 30,000 and to maintain better than 1942 income.

ASCAP's main office is at 30 Rockefeller Plaza, New York city. There were 22 branches in 1943. Deems Taylor was president in 1943 and John G. Paine general manager.

Perkins, Milo Randolph

(1900–), U.S. government official, was born Jan. 28 in Milwaukee, Wis. A salesman and part owner of a burlap bag business, Perkins became assistant secretary in the department of agriculture in the early days of the New Deal, and by 1935 was Secretary Henry Wallace's right-hand man. Named assistant director of the Farm Security administration in 1937, he handled the rehabilitation loan program and cut the cost of government housing for farmers. In Jan. 1939 he was transferred to the Agricultural Adjustment administration as associate administrator and was also named president of the Federal Surplus Commodities corporation. In 1941 he was appointed executive head of the Economic Defense board, retaining that post when this agency was reorganized as the Board of Economic Warfare on Dec. 17, 1941. In April 1942 he was given control of the government program to acquire critical war materials.

In July 1943, a bitter open dispute developed between Perkins' chief, Wallace, and Secretary of Commerce Jesse H. Jones. In Wallace's absence from Washington, Perkins joined in the fray, denouncing Jones.

President Roosevelt ended the quarrel by wiping out the Board of Economic Warfare.

Permanent Joint Board on Defense (U.S. and Canada): *see* CANADIAN-U.S. WAR COMMITTEES.

Persia: *see* IRAN.

Peru.

A republic on the west coast of South America between Ecuador and Chile, and contiguous also with Colombia, Brazil and Bolivia. Area: 482,133 sq.mi. Pop. (1940 census): 7,023,111; whites and mestizos form 52.89% of the population, Indians 45.86%. Capital city: Lima (533,645); other cities are: Callao (84,438); Arequipa (79,185); Cuzco (45,158); Trujillo (38,961); Iquitos (34,231); Chiclayo (32,646); Huancayo (28,-679); Cerro de Pasco (19,187). President in 1943: Manuel Prado y Ugarteche.

History.—During 1943 Peruvian problems continued to be largely internal. Lack of shipping and priorities limited imports, and in April and June food shortages, partly caused by a poor rice crop the previous year, caused some unrest. It was necessary for the government to take over all supplies of rice and beans, and to fix prices on these staples. On Aug. 27 a central price control board was established in an attempt to hold down rapidly rising prices as much as possible.

The government likewise attempted to direct agricultural effort away from production of cotton and sugar and toward diversified food crops. On May 19 a co-operative agreement was signed with the United States designed to increase this latter type of production, with the United States to furnish technical aid. A herd of zebu, which had been purchased in Brazil to be crossed with native cattle, arrived in Peru in July.

An important industrial project got under way during 1943 in the formation of the government-directed Santa corporation, with a $15,500,000 capitalization. It was hoped that the concern could develop Peru's untouched iron ore deposits and accessory transportation facilities to such an extent that the republic would be independent in iron and steel needs.

With axis property taken over by the government, many enterprises were being purchased by Peruvian capital. The Japanese population (estimated at 25,000–30,000) caused some concern because of their key position in some fields of production, and their actions were rigidly limited.

On May 10 a fire, possibly intentional, caused the destruction of the National Library of Peru, with the loss of many priceless manuscripts. A drive was subsequently started to try to restore the collection by gift insofar as this was possible.

Education.—While by law primary education is free and compulsory, in some sections schools are not available. In 1939 there were 4,727 elementary schools with an enrollment of 492,989; about 216 secondary schools and 5 universities.

Finance.—The monetary unit is the sol, valued at 15.38 cents U.S. in 1943. Total reserves in the Central bank amounted to 138,000,000 sols on June 30, 1943. The foreign debt (June 30, 1941) 546,078,000 sols; the total internal debt: 379,739,000 sols.

Trade and Communication.—No 1943 figures on total trade were available; 1940 imports were valued at $51,668,000; exports at $65,782,000. At this time the United States supplied 53% of imports, and took 43% of exports; Great Britain supplied 9%, and took 12%. In 1943 trade with neighbouring American states increased.

Communication by sea and air in normal times is excellent, and there is a rail connection to Bolivia. There are some 1,900 mi. of railways. The highway system amounts to 15,700 mi. of good roads. In 1943 the 522 mi. highway connecting the Pacific coast with Iquitos on the Amazon side of the Andes was opened Sept. 7; other trans-Andean links are planned. Possibly 22,000 mi. of Peruvian rivers in the Amazon valley are navigable.

Agriculture.—Cotton, sugar and rice are the leading agricultural crops, with coffee, maize, wheat, cocoa, tea, quinine, flax and tagua nuts also of significance. The cotton crop for 1943 was estimated as less than in 1942 because of insect damage (1943: 56,000 short tons; 1942: 77,000 short tons). Other crop estimates were: sugar, 474,000 short tons; rice, 83,000–94,000 short tons (in 1942, a bad year, 71,650 short tons were produced); flax, 3,968 short tons; dry tea, 250,000 lb. The coffee quota for the year starting Oct., 1943, was set at 30 short tons.

Estimates on wool production for 1943 were: sheep wool, 7,900 tons; alpaca hair, 3,500 tons; llama, huarizo and vicuña hair, 350 tons. For 6 months of 1943, hide and skin output was: cattle, 90,000; sheepskins, 530,000; goatskins, 235,000.

Minerals.—Petroleum production for three quarters of 1943 was 11,505,557 bbl. (total output for 1942: 14,632,530 bbl.). Coal output (1942) amounted to 132,276 short tons. Other minerals (1941) were: copper, 40,589 short tons; silver, 15,100 troy oz.; gold, 260,980 troy oz.; lead (all forms) 69,079 short tons; zinc 29,-597 short tons; vanadium, 1,949 short tons; bismuth, 362 short tons. Guano production (1943) was 67,243 short tons, 10% under 1942 output. (*See* also HISPANIC AMERICA AND WORLD WAR II.)

(D. RD.)

Pétain, Henri Philippe

(1856–   ), French soldier and statesman. See *Encyclopædia Britannica* for his biography. He was called from virtual retirement in 1939 to become French ambassador to Spain after Franco's triumph in the civil war and remained in this post after the beginning of war in 1939 until May 18, 1940, when, with France's army falling back in a retreat approaching a rout, he was summoned to Paris to act as vice-president of the government council and adviser to the minister of war. On June 16, 1940, he succeeded Paul Reynaud as premier, and the next day he was forced to sue for peace. He then began the painful task of reconstruction under the watchful eye of France's conquerors. Moving his government to Vichy July 2, he secured from the national assembly authorization to prepare a new constitution. On July 10, 1940, Pétain assumed dictatorial powers.

In 1941, Pétain apparently followed a two-way policy in which he alternately submitted to Germany, then resisted German demands for the French fleet and for French bases in North Africa. But on critical issues, where the Germans raised the iron fist and made peremptory demands, Pétain offered little or no opposition. His failure in 1942 to prevent the Germans from seizing masses of Frenchmen for deportation to German factories did not add to his waning popularity. The aging marshal bitterly protested the Allied occupation of French North Africa on Nov. 8, 1942, and severed diplomatic ties with Washington. By the same token, he protested the total occupation of France by German troops three days later as a breach of the armistice terms. On Nov. 18, 1942, Pétain granted dictatorial powers to Pierre Laval to make all laws and decrees. During 1943, Pétain was no longer in the foreground of Vichy politics. While he denounced the United States for "unjustifiable" bombings of French soil in April 1943, the majority of his countrymen welcomed the attacks as harbingers of the invasion to come. In May 1943, he admitted that "open opposition" to his policies had slowed the "reconstruction" of France and in Nov. 1943, Swiss dispatches said the marshal had been on the verge of resigning as chief of state because the German authorities had prevented him from promulgating a new "democratic" constitution. It was also reported that Pétain had wanted to renounce Laval as his successor.

Petroleum.

The year 1943 saw Russia successfully defend the Caucasian oil fields against the invading nazis and wrest Maikop, an important but minor Russian oil

DITCH for the "Big Inch" petroleum pipe line, linking Longview, Tex., and the eastern states. It was completed in 1943

field, from German hands. By the end of the year soviet armies were pressing axis forces toward the Polish and Rumanian borders, thus putting the oil fields of those countries, which were the only large sources of natural petroleum within the home and conquered territories of Germany, within striking distance of air forces—and even of ground forces should the Russian offensive continue to roll on.

Of no less strategic importance was the successful Allied campaign in North Africa and Sicily, which cleared the Mediterranean and shortened the supply lines of the Allied armies. Coupled with the successes attained against German submarines in the Atlantic, these campaign results meant virtually uninterrupted flow, with very little loss, of oil to the armies and navies of the United Nations and for the war industries of Britain. The Russian and African successes also took off threat of invasion and removed the partial blockade existing against the Iraq and Iranian oil fields, giving the United Nations a chance to draw more heavily upon these sources.

The accompanying table shows the world production of petroleum and of petroleum substitutes, 1941 and 1942, divided as to production sources available to Allied nations and to axis nations.

The United States was producing oil at an all-time high of 4,600,000 bbl. a day, but even with that huge rate of production the demand was so great that stocks of both crude oil and petroleum products above ground gradually went down until they reached the minimum for safe working stocks. Actual oil shortage was feared.

It was estimated that in the United States proved oil reserves total 20,000,000,000 bbl. Normally new sources of proved reserves must be found continuously in order to take the place of fields that were being depleted and whose rates of daily production were declining. The major burden of supplying the great current market demand fell on new fields, and—this was what concerned the government's Petroleum Administration for War and the oil industry—the rate of new discovery and the bringing in of new fields was not equal to the drain on existing fields since 1940. It was estimated that 1,500,000,000 bbl. would be produced from reserves in 1943.

Foreign Operations.—One result of this situation was the

projected expansion of American activities in oil fields outside the United States. The U.S. army made commitments of $130,-000,000 on what was known as the Canol project in northern Canada where the drilling of a number of wells in the Fort Norman district and the building of a pipe line over the mountains to Whitehorse were undertaken as a means of supplying oil for motor vehicles moving over the Alaska highway and for possible use in military operations based on Alaska.

The most significant move, however, was that based upon the operations of the Petroleum Reserves corporation. As pointed out by Petroleum Administrator for War Harold L. Ickes, in the past American oil companies established themselves in the foreign oil business, obtained rights to oil reserves, constructed refining and pipe line facilities, and engaged in world-wide distribution of oil and its products—all entirely as a result of private initiative with the government simply extending its good offices. On the other hand, the other principal nations, or most of them, conducted their foreign oil business through corporations or agencies entirely or partly owned or in effect controlled by the government itself.

Believing that government assistance and participation might be necessary for American companies, the Petroleum Reserves corporation was available for these purposes. The directors of the corporation were the secretaries of state, war, navy and interior, and the administrator of the Foreign Economic administration. That the greater utilization of oil from the near and middle east, including the expansion of production and the provision of additional refining facilities in that area, would be among the first results of this government-sponsored activity was forecast. E. L. De Golyer, former assistant deputy petroleum administrator, and W. E. Wrather, director of the U.S. Geological Survey, both noted petroleum geologists, were sent on a mission to the near and middle east in the fall of 1943.

World Production of Crude Petroleum and Its Substitutes
(Thousands of Barrels)

Countries	1941			1942*		
	Crude	Petroleum Substitutes	Total	Crude	Petroleum Substitutes	Total
Allied Nations:						
U.S.A.	1,404,180	67,680	1,471,860	1,385,000	79,000	1,464,000
U.S.S.R.	240,000	1,500	241,500	212,000	2,000	214,000
Venezuela	223,000	1,200	224,200	145,000	1,500	146,500
Iran	78,000	1,000	79,000	76,000	1,000	77,000
Mexico	41,200	1,000	42,200	35,000	800	35,800
Colombia	24,400	900	25,300	10,600	900	11,500
Argentina	21,800	500	22,300	22,000	600	22,600
Trinidad	21,200	200	21,400	24,500	200	24,700
Peru	12,900	1,000	13,900	13,500	1,000	14,500
Canada	6,300	3,700	10,000	6,400	3,900	10,300
Iraq	12,500	.....	12,500	14,800	.....	14,800
Egypt	7,700	200	7,900	8,000	300	8,300
Burma	7,800	100	7,900	2,400	100	2,500
Bahrein Island	6,900	200	7,100	7,800	200	8,000
United Kingdom	.....	7,000	7,000	.....	7,500	7,500
Sarawak	1,340	.....	1,340	500	.....	500
Brunei	5,460	.....	5,460	1,000	.....	1,000
Saudi Arabia	5,870	.....	5,870	6,000	.....	6,000
British India	2,270	.....	2,270	2,500	.....	2,500
Ecuador	1,500	50	1,550	1,800	100	1,900
Miscellaneous	500	2,200	2,700	600	2,200	2,800
Total Allied	2,124,820	88,430	2,263,250	1,975,400	101,300	2,076,700
Axis Nations:						
Rumania	40,500	2,000	42,500	41,000	2,000	43,000
Germany	5,240	32,000	37,240	5,400	46,000	51,400
France	500	4,100	4,600	500	4,800	5,300
Poland	3,310	200	3,510	3,400	300	3,700
Hungary	2,600	100	2,700	3,800	200	4,000
Italy and Albania	1,200	300	1,500	1,500	400	1,900
Japan*	3,300	5,500	8,800	3,400	6,900	10,300
Netherlands Indies	62,120	1,000	63,120	9,000	200	9,200
Miscellaneous	200	2,000	2,200	200	2,100	2,300
Total Axis	118,970	47,200	166,170	68,200	62,900	131,100
World Total	2,243,790	135,630	2,379,420	2,043,600	164,200	2,207,800

*Estimated.
Data taken from *AIME Transactions*, vol. 151, entitled "Petroleum Development and Technology, 1943," page 262.

World-Wide Programming.

World-Wide Programming.—Deputy Petroleum Administrator Ralph K. Davies at the Nov. 1943 meeting of the American Petroleum institute, referred to the "necessity for world-wide programming in the effort to make ends meet in the matter of oil supply." Oil demand estimates were made for at least two years ahead from various sources, with the Army and Navy Petroleum board estimating military requirements. The PAW program division had the assistance of the British through the British counterpart of PAW. The war demands were met from sources nearest the area of consumption. Obviously, with limited shipping facilities, the short haul principle was desirable. But shipping could not always be the determining factor as frequently there were other equally real physical limitations such as the quality and quantity of particular products which could be refined at a given point.

War Demand for Petroleum Products.—In 1942 only 12.5% of the total gasoline made in American refineries east of the Rocky mountains went to the military. In the first quarter of 1943, the military took 21.4%; in the second quarter, 23.1%, and the percentage for the last half of 1943 was estimated by PAW at 30.6.

These figures held no promise for civilian consumers in the United States of more liberal gasoline rationing. As more war products were needed out of a barrel of crude oil, less gasoline for motor cars was being made. Each U.S. barrel of crude oil contains 42 gal. The proportions of different products made from it were changed to meet new wartime needs.

Automobile gasoline production was reduced from 18 gal. out of each barrel to 12 gal. Of the 6 gal. making up the difference that went into motor car fuel in peacetime, 3½ gal. in 1943 went into aeroplane fuel, synthetic rubber, explosives and special army gasoline.

Two of the 6 gal. went into additional fuel oils needed by the navy, Liberty ships, war factories and the like. Even a part of the production of 12 gal. per barrel of ordinary gasoline was used by the army's vast fleet of trucks, jeeps and other mechanized equipment.

The remainder had to be divided largely among farm tractors, school buses, industrial trucks and essential passenger car use by war workers.

Refineries Converted for War.—Wartime conditions caused great change in petroleum refining. Quantities and quality of super-aviation fuel by American refineries reached high records which must remain a military secret.

In Jan. 1942, there were 22 refineries in the United States making 100-octane or some major ingredient thereof, such as base stock or blending agent. In June 1943, there were 47 such refineries, of which 28 were being supplemented by still more new refineries.

When all of the construction work was completed on these 47 refineries, they would be able as a group to produce 85% more aviation gasoline than they did June 1942. There were 26 other refineries under construction which were scheduled to make 100-octane. In addition to all of these, there were 53 refineries in June 1943, making some raw material of 100-octane, and some of these produced the completed product as well. Thus, there was a net figure of 126 domestic refineries which were or would by the spring of 1944 contribute to the vast aviation gasoline program. In Oct. 1943, it was stated that production of 100-octane aviation gasoline was more than four times greater than in the early months of 1943 and that within a few months it would be about eight times greater.

Altogether approximately $900,000,000 was being invested in production facilities for 100-octane gasoline; more than 75% of this investment being by the oil companies and remainder by the government.

Petroleum for Synthetic Rubber.—Butadiene, a petroleum derivative, forms the principal ingredient of Buna-S, the synthetic rubber made under the U.S. government's synthetic rubber program. Before Pearl Harbor there were no more than 30,000 tons of synthetic rubber being made in the United States. Through the Defense Plants corporation, the government undertook to erect new plants and finally laid out a program for over 800,000 tons yearly of Buna-S synthetic rubber. The annual rate of 800,000 tons was achieved late in 1943.

Of the total butadiene required for this huge program, petroleum was supplying 75%; alcohol the balance. As of Nov. 1943, some 30 butadiene and styrene plants had been constructed or were nearing completion. Most of these plants producing materials for synthetic rubber were financed by the government but were company-operated.

Pipe Line Construction.—The oil transportation system in the United States for transporting over 1,500,000 bbl. a day from the mid-continent and Gulf coast to the eastern seaboard was transformed after Pearl Harbor. The tanker service which had moved 95% of this oil was badly disrupted because of submarine warfare and the necessity of using tankers in other areas. In June 1942, the War Production board approved construction of a pipe line two feet in diameter—the "Big-Inch Line"—from Texas to Illinois and later authorized its extension to the Atlantic coast.

The building of this line, the world's biggest, with a capacity of 300,000 bbl. daily, was carried out by an organization drawn from the oil industry and was an epic achievement in construction. The main line, 1,381 mi. in length, laid through swamps, over mountains and across rivers, despite floods and storms and the worst winter conditions, was completed in 350 days in June 1943.

A second 20-in. line was being built over practically the same route. The two lines were expected to move more than 500,000 bbl. of oil daily and, with other measures adopted for increasing deliveries by tank car and barge, this would mean a greater volume of oil possible to be shipped into the Atlantic seaboard than ever received by the tanker route. Many other government-sponsored pipe line projects were underway or completed. The total cost of this pipe line program was estimated at approximately $250,000,000, and includes both government and private financing.

Petroleum Substitute Measures in U.S.—There was wide interest and support in proposed measures for the government to authorize the bureau of mines to build large pilot demonstration plants for making oil from coal.

According to Dr. A. C. Fieldner, chief of the technological branch of the bureau, the plants contemplated would have a capacity of about 100 bbl. of gasoline a day each and would cost about $3,000,000.

(*See also* Business Review.) (L. M. F.)

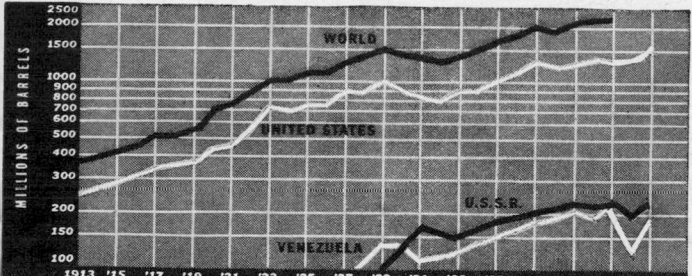

TOTAL WORLD PRODUCTION OF PETROLEUM and output of the three principal producing countries, as compiled by *The Mineral Industry*

Peyrouton, Marcel B.

(1888–), French government official, was an ambitious civil servant who rose quickly in the French colonial service. He became secretary general of the government of Algeria, 1930, resident general of Tunisia, 1933, and resident general of Morocco, 1936. While visiting Italo Balbo in Libya in 1936, Peyrouton paid tribute to the "creative spirit of fascism." The popular front government found this a singular sentiment in a republican official; Peyrouton was removed from his Moroccan post and sent to Argentina as ambassador. In June 1940, he was again appointed resident general of Tunisia, but hastened home to join the Vichy government after the fall of France. By Sept. 1940, he was Vichy interior minister and he embarked on a series of moves that earned for him the hatred of French underground and anti-nazi groups. He ordered the arrest of Paul Reynaud and Georges Mandel, signed Vichy's anti-Jewish laws and employed strong punitive measures to crush the underground movement. After a bitter quarrel with Pierre Laval, Peyrouton resigned in Feb. 1941; Adm. Jean Darlan then returned him to Argentina as Vichy's ambassador, but when Laval returned to Pétain's favour, Peyrouton quit his post. On Jan. 19, 1943, Gen. Henri Giraud named Peyrouton to the post of governor general of Algeria. De Gaullists attacked the appointment, charging that Peyrouton was a Vichyite and fascist. As a result of De Gaulle's increasing influence, Peyrouton was compelled to resign, June 1, 1943. In November, he appeared before a French commission probing treason charges and on Dec. 21, Peyrouton was arrested and imprisoned on charges that he suppressed French underground groups during his tenure as Vichy interior minister.

Phelps, William Lyon

(1865–1943), U.S. educator and author, was born Jan. 2 in New Haven, Conn. He was graduated from Yale in 1887, took his Ph.D. from the same school in 1891. In the latter year, he also took his A.M. degree from Harvard and remained there for a year lecturing on English. Later, he returned to Yale where he was a member of the English department for 41 years, and served as Lampson professor from 1901 until his retirement in 1933. For many years he was voted Harvard's most inspiring professor and young collegians jammed his classes in contemporary drama and Tennyson and Browning. In 1895, he started the first modern novel class at Harvard and was credited with introducing Russian novelists to English readers. His genial humour and sense of the dramatic made him popular as lecturer and critic. His contributions to magazines and his syndicated newspaper column, "A Daily Thought," brought him a reader audience calculated in the millions, and his annual list of the best of current literature appeared regularly in the nation's newspapers. His books, chiefly on English literature, old and new, include: *The Beginnings of the English Romantic Movement* (1893), *Essays on Modern Novelists* (1910), *Browning* (1915), *The Advance of the English Novel* (1916), *The Advance of English Poetry, The Twentieth Century Theatre* (1918), *Reading the Bible* (1919), *Essays on Modern Dramatists* (1920), *Some Makers of American Literature, As I Like It* (1923), *What I Like in Prose, What I Like in Poetry* (1934) and *Autobiography with Letters* (1939). Dr. Phelps died in New Haven, Aug. 21.

Philadelphia.

Third largest city in the U.S.A. and the largest city in Pennsylvania, Philadelphia had a population of 1,931,334 by the federal census of 1940. It was estimated that this had grown to 2,200,000 in 1943 largely because of the influx of white and Negro workers from the south attracted by the high wages paid in war industries. On the death of Mayor Robert E. Lamberton in the summer of 1941, Bernard Samuel, Republican, president of the city council, became acting mayor under a provision of the city charter, to serve for the remainder of the term for which Mr. Lamberton had been elected. Mr. Samuel was nominated by his party for the full term in 1943 to run against the Democratic candidate, William C. Bullitt, former ambassador to Russia and to France. Mr. Samuel was elected by a majority of about 65,000 and the Republicans retained control of the council by a large majority. In accordance with the policy to keep the courts out of partisan politics ten sitting judges were re-elected with the support of both parties. The assessed valuation of taxable property was $2,369,916,667 in 1943 and the city debt was $476,000,000. The appropriation for current expenses of all kinds was $92,678,761. A wage tax of 1½% yielded $18,666,667 in 1943. This tax was reduced to 1% for 1944. Three members of the election board and a watcher from a division in the 47th ward were tried on charges of making false election returns and found guilty. Two of them were also convicted of fraudulently writing names on the certificates of voters. Efforts of the federal government to check the activities of German sympathizers resulted in a court order directing a leader of the German-American Bund in the city to leave the eastern defense area and in the cancellation of the citizenship of another leader of the bund. (G. W. Do.)

Philately.

Philatelists will probably remember 1943 as the year inflation hit stamp prices! For stamps are luxury items, with no ceilings or other let or hindrance, and prices soared. Supplies were definitely limited, since none of the usual accumulations that formerly followed the best markets could move from country to country; and since the United States was avid for stamps and without imports, there was no reason during 1943 for prices to do aught but soar.

War wages and lack of other luxury goods placed philatelists in a position to bid against each other for available items, and the lack of other amusements turned many former collectors back to their albums.

With the centenary of the first United States stamps, those of 1847, but four short years away, fine items of that emission were particularly in demand.

The auction of the holdings of the late Col. E.H.R. Green, which began in 1942, continued throughout 1943 and was not expected to be concluded until 1944. The trend of prices was clearly shown by this, for the estimates made of values in 1942, which were rather accurately reached in the first sales of that year, proved too low by an estimated 20% in 1943, and stamp dealers predicted further increases over the early estimates before 1944 closed.

Stamp issues of the axis and its satellites being forbidden, both by common sense and the decrees of many of the United Nations (including the United States), the trend previously marked in 1942 continued in 1943—fewer stamps were issued. The Standard catalogue recorded fewer than 1,000 new varieties added in 1943, and it was notable that many of these fell definitely into what might be termed "propaganda" stamps. Though it was long evident that many commemoratives served as advertising, stamps were increasingly being used frankly to carry messages of policy and expression of governmental issues.

The "Four Freedoms" Stamps.—For one example, in 1943 the United States issued a one-cent stamp designed by a sculptor, Paul Manship. It shows a warrior carrying the torch of freedom with a tablet commemorating the Four Freedoms enunciated by President Roosevelt and Winston Churchill in the Atlantic charter in these short words: "Freedom of Speech and Religion, from Want and Fear."

Less happy was the choice of design for the series of five-cent values honouring the "Overrun Nations"—those unhappy victims of the war's ferocity. One frame, of undistinguished merit, was used for the entire series, all in the same queer shade resembling gray, and the flag of the nation honoured was placed in full colour therein.

Breaking the custom of 50 years, the stamp was partially printed by contract. The frame was prepared by the treasury's bureau of printing and engraving, but the coloured flag was added by the American Bank Note company, the same firm which last held a contract for the production of U.S. stamps in 1893.

The Mysterious A.M.G. Stamps.—Shortly after the occupation of Sicily by Allied troops, there were rumours of "Allied Military Government" stamps in use in that area. Later, these rumours were confirmed. A set of stamps in Italian currency was issued in 1943, bearing the caption "Allied Military Postage" and the value in figures, with the words "Italy" and the currency above and below, respectively. The values were 15, 25, 30, 50 and 60 centesimi, 1, 2, 5 and 10 lire.

Apparently, these stamps were issued for the use of the civilian population of the occupied areas of Italy, for military mail needs no stamps and is handled through army post offices. Though these stamps were the product of the U.S. bureau of printing and engraving, they were not U.S. emissions, being for the Allied Nations. They were for sale only in the occupied regions. Presumably they would be considered as "occupation of Italy stamps."

The War.—The war-inspired issues of the United States have already been mentioned. Russia found time, despite valiant efforts in the field of battle, to produce some more colourful emissions depicting the actions and the care of soldiers. The Tehran conference of the leaders of Russia, Britain and the United States was also marked by Russia with stamps. Curaçao issued some semi-postal stamps to raise funds for prisoners of war.

Italy, besides being the guinea pig for the A.M.G. stamps, also had the anomalous condition of using stamps in German-occupied states bearing the portrait of King Victor Emmanuel III, who surrendered to the Allied Nations! During the last week of 1943, rumours leaked out of German-held Italy that the remaining stamps would be "blacked out," the king's portrait being obliterated and the stamps given some sort of Fascist surcharge.

Commemoratives.—Brazil, the first country of the Americas to issue postage stamps, commemorated that fact in 1943 with an issue reproducing the original stamps of 1843 as part of the design. Brazil also commemorated numerous other events, mostly of purely local interest. A disquieting note was the appearance of many minor varieties of these issues. Before the revolution late in 1943, Bolivia issued a series commemorating the centenary of the department of El Beni. The various French colonies, not content with "France Libre" and "France Combattante" issues, commemorated many events.

Literature.—The Barry Bowl, a cup given annually for the outstanding stamp department in a daily newspaper (named in honour of the late Ralph A. Barry, who conducted such a column) was awarded to the New York *Sun* and its stamp editor, Franklin J. Bruns, Jr.

The Standard catalogue continued in 1943 its experiment of publishing three editions; one for the stamps of America and the British commonwealth, one for the rest of the world, and a combined edition. Protests over the new arrangement continued. Because of the long lag between rapidly changing prices and the catalogue values, the publishers were releasing lists of recognized changes to the philatelic press each few weeks.

The interest in essays and proofs that had long been evidenced by serious philatelists blossomed in a new Essay-Proof society, organized in the latter months of 1943. Nearly 100 members were

enrolled for the first meeting, and the society planned to publish a quarterly journal, beginning in the first quarter of 1944. Clarence Brazer, of New York, whose articles on proofs and essays appeared in the *Collectors' Club Philatelist* in 1942 and 1943 was both president of the new society and editor of its journal.

(M. HA.)

Philippines, Commonwealth of the.

The commonwealth of the Philippine Islands comprises the archipelago of the same name ceded by Spain to the United States in the treaty of Paris, 1898. The chain of approximately 7,100 islands with a total area of 115,600 sq.mi. falls between north latitudes 4° 21' and 21° 10' and between east longitudes 116° and 127°. Lying about 800 mi. off the east coast of Asia, the Philippines stretch from Formosa on the north to Borneo on the south. By regular steamship routes, Manila is 631 nautical miles southeast of Hongkong, 1,757 mi. southwest of Yokohama, 1,370 mi. northeast of Singapore, 4,838 mi. west of Honolulu and 6,929 mi. southwest of San Francisco.

The Philippines are acknowledged to have a strategic geographic position. They command the principal trade routes connecting the north Pacific coasts of America and Asia with Southeast Asia, the East Indies and India, and they offer a suitable western anchorage for a system of modern air and naval bases extending from Pearl Harbor through the Marshall, Caroline and Marianas islands.

The total area is 115,600 sq.mi. The last official census, 1939, gave the population as 16,000,313, including the following non-Filipino nationalities: Chinese 117,487; Japanese 29,057; Americans (U.S., exclusive of armed forces) 8,709; Spanish 4,627; Germans 1,149; British 1,053. Calculated on recent rates of increase without allowance for the effects of war and invasion, the population at end of 1943 should have been somewhat in excess of 17,900,000. Principal religions according to census of 1939: Roman Catholic, 12,603,365; Aglipayan (Independent Philippine Catholic), 1,573,608; Mohammedan, 677,903; Protestant, 378,-361. In addition about 680,000 were pagans following various animistic cults. The principal cities and their populations were: Manila, the political and commercial capital on the northern large island of Luzon, 623,492 (not including several large suburbs); Cebu, 146,817; Iloilo, 90,480; Legaspi, 41,468.

History.—The political organization of the Philippines is determined by the Philippine Independence act of 1934 (48 Stat. 456) as amended. Under this act an autonomous commonwealth was established on Nov. 15, 1935, and independence was set for July 4, 1946. During the commonwealth period the United States remains sovereign with final control over the public debt, currency, trade relations, immigration, foreign affairs, armed forces and military and naval reservations and bases, and with the right to intervene for the preservation of government, the protection of life, property and individual liberty, and the discharge of government obligations. All Filipinos owed allegiance to the United States, and every officer of the commonwealth was required to declare under oath "that he recognizes and accepts the supreme authority of and will maintain true faith and allegiance to the United States." The chief officer was the United States high commissioner to the Philippine Islands, a representative of the president of the United States, required to be recognized as such by the commonwealth government, by the commanding officer of the military forces, and by all other officers of the United States in the islands.

The commonwealth government had a constitution adopted under the terms of the Independence act. In form and style it was that of a highly centralized, representative, tri-power republic,

MANILANS staged a parade during the visit of Premier Hideki Tojo to the Philippines in 1943. The pictures of Tojo's visit, received through neutral sources, were the first photographs from the Philippines to reach the United States after the islands' fall in 1942

with reservations covering U.S. sovereignty. The executive consists of a president and vice-president elected at large. The legislature is a senate elected at large and a house of representatives elected by districts. The judiciary consists of municipal courts, courts of first instance (provincial), a court of appeals and a supreme court (with provision for appeal to the United States supreme court). All judges are appointed by the executive. There are no juries and decisions are directly given by the judges themselves. For purposes of local government and central government administration the country is divided (census of 1939) into 49 provinces and 9 chartered cities; the provinces into 1,170 municipalities; the cities and municipalities into 16,939 barrios or villages.

In 1943 the authority of the high commissioner was vested in Harold L. Ickes, secretary of the interior. The commonwealth president was Manuel L. Quezon, and the vice-president was Sergio Osmeña. Other officers were the resident commissioner to the United States, J. M. Elizalde, who was a delegate to the United States congress; and the auditor general, Jaime Hernandez. These officers, together with an appointed wartime cabinet, resided in Washington, D.C.

President Quezon and Vice-President Osmeña were inaugurated for their second terms on Dec. 30, 1941, at Corregidor, and on their arrival in Washington in May 1942, they set up the official executive establishment of the commonwealth. Due to a constitutional eight-year limitation on the presidential term of office, President Quezon would have surrendered his office on Nov. 15, 1943, and Vice-President Osmeña would have succeeded automatically. However, at the request of the commonwealth government in exile the U.S. congress in Public 186, approved Nov. 12, 1943, amended the Philippine constitution in such manner as to continue Quezon in office as president of the commonwealth "until the president of the United States shall proclaim that constitutional processes and normal functions of government shall have been restored in the Philippine Islands." The act provides that upon such proclamation the vice-president shall become president and serve until his successor is elected.

In addition, the U.S. congress passed through the senate and had pending in the house two resolutions. The first of these resolutions provides for: (a) U.S. land, sea and air bases in the Philippines, and (b) for advancing the date of independence when the enemy shall have been expelled and democratic processes of government restored. The second provides for a joint U.S.-Philippine economic commission to consider questions of postwar rehabilitation, finance, economy and trade relations.

The commonwealth government was in 1943 considered to be one of the United Nations and participated in various of the conferences held under its auspices.

By the end of 1942 presumably all important coastal points in the principal inhabited islands were under enemy control, but reliable reports indicated that attacks from guerrilla bands operating in isolated or mountainous up-country districts continued actively throughout 1942 and 1943. Several prisoner of war camps were established on Luzon, Palawan and Mindanao islands. More than 3,500 civilians (approximately 2,500 Americans and 1,000 British and other Allied citizens) were held in Manila at Camp Santo Tomas. Other civilian concentration camps were at Baguio and Davao.

Filipinos, allowed limited freedom of residence, occupation and religion, were subjected to a carefully designed policy of attraction. The Japanese reopened a few elementary schools, but all textbooks were censored and the curricula were distorted to include the Japanese language and to suppress U.S. and native history, civics and culture.

Jorgé Vargas, formerly executive secretary to President Quezon, with cabinet rank, was appointed late in Jan. 1942 by the Japanese commander in chief in the Philippines to be chairman of the executive commission. This commission assisted the Japanese military authorities in the establishment of "Central Administrative Organs and Judicial Courts" which apparently consisted of 7 departments and 40 or more bureaus and courts. The departments were reportedly headed by Filipinos formerly holding high positions in the commonwealth government.

The Japanese prime minister, Tojo, announced in May 1943 that "independence" would be granted the Philippines before the end of the year. In June the military administration with the collaboration of the Vargas executive commission formed a committee to prepare for independence. A totalitarian constitution was drawn up and "independence" was proclaimed on Oct. 15, 1943. The "president" was José P. Laurel, a member of the former legitimate supreme court. He was assisted by a group of "ministers of state" comprising practically the same officers as those in the Vargas executive commission. Vargas became "ambassador" to Japan. The new puppet government avowed its position to be that of a "full-fledged member of the Greater East Asia Co-prosperity Sphere"; it advocated drastic elimination of all elements of western culture and active defense against the return of the United States to the islands. To facilitate the latter aim the constabulary was being increased to an army of 50,000 or more, and an alliance had been entered into with Japan. A single national fascist party, the "Kalibapi," was organized. Its members controlled the legislative, administrative and judicial branches of the puppet government.

Underground reports indicated that the mass of the common people of the Philippines, as well as a majority of the wealthier, educated classes, held the puppetry in great contempt. It appeared to be tolerated only so far as it forced itself on the people through control of the distribution of rice and other necessities. Attempts on the part of the Japanese and the puppet government to capture guerrillas, or to attract their surrender through repeated extensions of amnesty laws, met with little success.

The following digest of education, finance, trade, etc. is based upon the last available data prior to the Japanese invasion. Reports as to current conditions under the enemy, while too fragmentary and unreliable for publication, indicated that nearly all schools were closed, that the islands were suffering an enormous inflation due to the circulation of Japanese military currency, that trade even with Japan was negligible and that agriculture, manufacturing and mineral production were well below normal.

Education.—Public schools, March 1940: number 12,057; enrolment, primary 1,572,639; intermediate 277,574; secondary 90,579; collegiate (normal and technical) 3,777; total 1,944,569. Private schools, June 30, 1940: number 439; enrolment, kindergarten 2,844; primary 41,861; intermediate 22,578; secondary 51,055; collegiate 31,153; total 149,491; in addition, recognized schools (136) offering special vocational courses had 9,188 enrolment.

Finance.—The monetary unit is the peso, fixed at a mint par of U.S. $0.50; exchange rates showed only negligible fluctuations from the par rate in 1941. Estimated general fund balance, June 30, 1942, on deposit in the U.S., 100,000,000 pesos. Total bonded indebtedness, June 30, 1941, 149,507,000 pesos; total sinking fund reserve 77,484,863 pesos. Currency dollar reserves on deposit in the U.S. as of June 30, 1942: cash surplus exchange standard fund plus cash balance treasury certificate fund U.S., $134,169,734. Currency in circulation and available per circulation as of Sept. 30, 1941, 222,407,808 pesos, including notes of the Bank of the Philippine Islands (1,358,385 pesos) and of the Philippine National bank (2,299,816 pesos).

Trade.—During 1941, Philippine overseas markets, except in the U.S., were virtually closed on account of limited tonnage and restrictive control of foreign exports and funds. Overseas trade values Jan. 1 to Sept. 30, 1941, were: Shipments to U.S. 227,000,000 pesos (of which 77,000,000 pesos were gold and silver bullion and concentrates); exports to foreign countries 41,000,000 pesos; total outward 268,000,000 pesos; shipments from U.S. 180,000,000 pesos; imports from foreign countries 43,000,000 pesos; total inward 223,000,000 pesos. The total overseas trade value, 491,000,000 pesos, was 11% in excess of that for the same period in 1940 and only 16% under the total for the entire year of 1940. Outward values of principal commodities, Jan. through Sept. 1941: coco-nut oil 22,000,000 pesos; copra 17,000,000 pesos; desiccated coco-nut 9,000,000 pesos; abacá 29,000,000 pesos; cordage 3,000,000 pesos; embroideries 6,000,000 pesos; logs, lumber 7,000,000 pesos; gold and silver bullion and concentrates 77,000,000 pesos; other minerals 12,000,000 pesos; centrifugal sugar 48,000,000 pesos; refined sugar 7,000,000 pesos; cigars 4,000,000 pesos; pineapples 3,000,000 pesos. Similarly for inward commodities: wheat flour 10,000,000 pesos; rice 1,000,000 pesos; other foodstuffs 25,000,000 pesos; iron and steel 15,000,000 pesos; automotives 8,000,000 pesos; machinery 17,000,000 pesos; nonmetallic minerals and chemicals and manufactures thereof 43,000,000 pesos; textiles 50,000,000 pesos.

Communication.—In 1940: railroads, 840 mi.; highways (kilometres) first-class 11,771.9; second-class 7,393; third-class 3,795.1; trails 4,912.1. Motor vehicles registered: automobiles 33,898; trucks 20,236, motorcycles 630. Airways: 1,171,453 passenger miles; 20,407 passengers; 3,083,415 lb. air express; 15,855 lb. air mail. Telephones, 31,419. Telegraph lines 14,716,930 kms. Broadcasting stations 6. International cable and radio services 5.

Agriculture.—The total estimated value of crops in 1938 was 417,144,000 pesos. Area planted and value, leading crops; palay (rough rice) 4,722,640 ac., 136,423,000 pesos; sugar cane 563,160 ac., 113,559,000 pesos; coco-nut 1,588,210 ac., 92,126,000 pesos; abacá 1,254,760 ac., 22,672,000 pesos; corn 1,736,410 ac., 19,424,000 pesos; bananas 227,240 ac., 10,312,000 pesos; tobacco 185,250 ac., 4,125,000 pesos. Livestock and poultry (1939) were valued at 141,514,451 pesos. Number and value: carabaos 2,918,730, 78,826,516 pesos; hogs 4,348,515, 26,100,326 pesos; cattle

1,349,264, 20,077,610 pesos; chickens 25,365,102, 8,994,591 pesos; horses 340,433, 6,222,661 pesos; goats 402,173, 874,155 pesos; ducks 690,868, 418,592 pesos.

Manufacturing.—Chief manufactures are centrifugal sugar, copra, coco-nut oil, desiccated coco-nut, cordage, cigars and cigarettes and embroideries. Production of sawmills in 1940 was 332,908,721 bd.ft.; number of mills 148.

Mineral Production.—Total estimated value of minerals produced in 1940 was 91,626,384 pesos. Chief products: gold 1,096,745 fine oz., 76,563,888 pesos; iron 1,221,126 long tons, 5,633,728 pesos; copper 20,014,918 lb., 3,487,701 pesos; chromite 189,919 long tons, 2,661,764 pesos; silver 1,394,736 fine oz., 1,874,094 pesos; manganese 48,036 long tons, 1,287,011 pesos; lead 2,080,381 lb., 117,927 pesos; platinum 6.03 troy oz., 271 pesos. (*See* also JAPAN; WORLD WAR II.) (E. D. H.)

Philosophy. In 1943 many philosophers turned to the great simplicities. The destiny of man, the ways of life, the hope for human culture: what can be said of them in time of crisis? Though little that is revolutionary appeared in formal works of philosophy, there was a good deal of overhauling, new evaluation, and reversal of emphasis.

The Nature and Destiny of Man by Reinhold Niebuhr presents a doctrine of sin and salvation, final judgment and transcendent ends that surprised many who knew the author as a social liberal and religious modernist. In the same way *Education Between Two Worlds* by Alexander Meiklejohn surprised those who knew the author as an educational progressive. He attacks John Dewey on the grounds: (1) that he tends to reduce intelligence to scientific method, (2) that the state for him has a negative function, (3) that he gives no meaning to "fair" or "objective" and thus has no criterion of criticism. Meiklejohn repudiates Locke and returns to the unity of knowledge and civilization of Comenius. He rejects relativism, pragmatism, James, and what he terms the disintegrations of Protestant-Capitalist culture. In *Education at the Crossroads*, by Jacques Maritain, the Catholic philosopher, there is on the other hand a definite, if unrecognized, sympathy with the pragmatic, experimental point of view from which Meiklejohn moves away. In *The Destiny of Western Man*, Walter Terence Stace emphasizes the primacy of reason and of sympathy in democracy and its accord with the true nature of man, while in *Paths of Life, A Preface to a World Religion*, Charles Morris courageously proposes Maitreyism, a post-Buddhist faith, to orient men in and beyond the contemporary ideal.

In the arts, too, valuations were revised. *Art and Freedom* by Horace Kallen is a generous effort to orient art in respect to the great human values. In *The Aesthetic Process*, Bertram Morris conceptually analyses art as process. In *The Language of Poetry*, edited by Allen Tate, an important effort is made by four distinguished men of letters to interpret poetry, not as emotion and response, but as a kind of language. *Music and the Line of Most Resistance*, by Artur Schnabel, is an enlightening study by a pianist who knows his field operationally as well as symbolically. *Romanticism and the Modern Ego*, by Jacques Barzun, is a brilliant support and generalization of the romantic thesis.

Schelling's Letze Philosophie, by Horst Fuhrmans, is an important addition to the literature of German idealism. *America's Progressive Philosophy*, by Wilmon Henry Sheldon, is a significant and original study of modern philosophies of process. *The Philosophy of G. E. Moore*, edited by Paul Arthur Schilpp, was the year's addition to the well-known *Library of Living Philosophers*. *Metaphysics and the New Logic* by Warner Arms Wick and *The Moral Ideals of Our Civilization* by Radoslav Andrea Tsanoff are efforts to co-ordinate some philosophical thinking with new ideologies.   (B. B.)

Phoenix Islands: *see* PACIFIC ISLANDS, BRITISH.

Phosphates.
Mine production of phosphate rock in the United States in 1942 was 4,818,938 long tons, and deliveries 4,644,240 tons, small decreases from 1941. Mine production was greater than sales, and producers' stocks were at the highest level in a decade, 1,867,000 tons.

Production in northern Africa (Algeria, Tunisia, Morocco and Egypt) is normally greater than in the United States, but was in 1943 presumably disorganized by the extension of the war to this area.   (G. A. Ro.)

Photography.
Photography was put to its greatest test during 1943. With the entire world at war, practically every phase of photography was called upon to help bring the whole conflict to an early conclusion. Photographers were trained by the thousands and were actively working with the armies in every fighting country. Britain and America led the field in the production of new techniques as well as new cameras, films and paper. The electron microscope revealed previously unseen structures in war metals or served in detecting minute organisms in fighting disease. New lenses, a new lens cement and even a new optical glass with a high index were only a few of the important improvements.

The photographic manufacturers were producing all their products in greater quantities than ever before. The amateur photographer was sharply curtailed in his use of photographic goods. However, there was enough film and photographic paper available so that the average amateur could still carry on his interests on a limited scale. Toward the end of 1943 some products, such as photoflood bulbs, were more easily obtained than at the beginning of the year.

The output of the camera and lens plants of the Eastman Kodak company was almost entirely confined to the armed services, and enormous quantities of sensitized materials of all kinds were made for the forces. The camera and optical-goods factories were expanding and adapted to the large-scale manufacture of nonphotographic articles requiring a high degree of precision. Kodak also developed a new Spectrum Analysis No. 2 plate, which had greater speed than the previous ones. The Kodagraph Magenta contact screen was placed on the market for making screen negatives for use in photolithography by the albumin process. The year 1943 marked the 20th birthday of the Ciné-Kodak and the first practical system of making home movies.

Previously a large number of lenses cemented with natural Canada balsam were broken, discoloured and rendered useless because of extremes in temperature met with in desert fighting and stratosphere flying. After two years of research, Kodak produced a new cement which met every condition of extreme heat and cold and high humidity more satisfactorily than any previously known cement.

Ansco colour film, previously available only to the armed forces, was offered to essential war industries to meet the demand for a colour film that could be processed by the consumer immediately following exposure. Ansco colour paper was also introduced to both the armed forces and essential industries. This material has a multilayer emulsion, with incorporated colour components which couple with the developer by-products to produce direct colour prints. Colour prints can be made from either colour-separation negatives (successively exposed through three colour-separation filters) or from complementary colour negatives (single exposure). An interesting and practical application of Ansco colour paper was the making of machine drawings, wiring diagrams, etc. in quantity, the lines being differentiated by colour for facilitating line production of intricate devices. The armed forces adopted Ansco colour paper as an adjunct in the preparation of military maps in colour.

War Photography.—Many important photographic developments were applied directly to war work. The largest and most complete naval photographic laboratory in the world designed for the navy by the Eastman Kodak company and incorporating apparatus in research instruments was in operation at Anacostia, D.C. More than a hundred of the navy personnel of the laboratory were given special training at the Kodak Park works in Rochester, N.Y. A smaller naval photographic laboratory was also completed at Norfolk, Va. Portable units, for the signal corps photo outfits, were built around the Kodak 35-mm. camera, the Kodak portable miniature enlarger and the Kodak day-load tank. All extra space was used to store securely all necessary equipment, such as trays, timers, film, paper, etc. This portable outfit could be used for enlarging or copying. The outfit was enclosed in a good-sized suitcase and could be set up or closed in less than one minute.

Sixteen-millimeter ciné cameras were used extensively in making combat pictures and training films. In many instances photographic reticles were used instead of engraved reticles on war and peacetime instruments. The Eastman Kodak company was producing large numbers of these for the armed forces. Because it is unaffected by heat, cold or moisture, Kodapak, a relative of safety film base was being used for insulating plane wires (instead of rubber) and field communication wires and for wrapping field rations.

Kodak developed a tropical prehardener which enables the processing of photographic negative materials at prevailing temperatures in the tropics without producing any deleterious effects, physically or sensitometrically. An extensive investigation of the washing of photographic film and paper products was also completed; recommendations for the complete removal of the last traces of silver and hypo retained from the fixing process were made. Probably the most useful fact obtained, from the viewpoint of the armed services, was the remarkable decrease in washing time effected by the use of sea water.

A new so-called spray emulsion was introduced by the Ansco company to coat metal sheets or other material with a sensitive layer for photographic template production, used extensively in many war factories. This technique had the advantage over transfer methods, in that sheets of any size and shape could be sensitized.

The Ansco research laboratory proposed an improved procedure for measuring contact printing density.[1] In connection with this study an investigation of the spectral transmission characteristics of optical wedges was carried out, and it was shown that wedges made of photographic silver are superior to those made of colloidal carbon.

The previously described Ansco-Sweet photoelectric densitometer was made commercially available. In practice the instrument proved to be more precise than visual densitometers, faster operating and capable of giving more reproducible data.

Aerial Photography.—One of the most important uses of photography in World War II was in the field of aerial work. Tens of thousands of photographs were made to reveal before and after conditions in enemy territory. Along with this accelerated use of photography in the air came new equipment, some of which was not ready for public release.

One of the sensational developments was the new shutterless

---

[1] M. H. Sweet, "The Spectral Characteristics of Optical Wedges." *Jour. Optical Soc. of Amer.*, 33: 194–208 (April 1943).

continuous-strip aerial camera. This camera makes a continuous picture as the film passes across a narrow slit at a speed which is synchronized with the image which passes below the lens. The camera will take about 200 ft. of film at one loading. One continuous negative could be made or short lengths of the film strip could be made. Colour film or black and white could be used as required. This continuous-strip aerial camera had various important applications for aerial reconnaissance work.

During peacetime, it was anticipated, this camera would find many commercial uses for aerial surveys. The geologist, for example, when using colour film might be able to trace the outcroppings of a fault that might give evidence of a new oil field.

During the year the Eastman Kodak company announced the production of Kodacolor aerial reversible film for military aerial photography. This colour film could be processed by military personnel in the field. The film is fast enough to permit exposures at $\frac{1}{50}$ sec. at f/8, or approximately a Weston 32-exposure factor. For the first time it was possible to make colour photographs from high altitudes using this new Kodacolor film and special filters that counteract the effective haze.

Mobile photographic trailers for the army air forces to permit quick developing and printing operations in the field were designed by Eastman processing engineers. Several dozen air force personnel were trained at Kodak Park for service as instructors in the operation of the darkroom-trailer equipment.

Lenses made of Kodak's rare-element optical glass, giving greater speed without loss of definition and covering power, stepped up considerably the effectiveness of aerial photography. This was the first basic discovery in the optical-glass field for more than half a century and made it possible for aerial cameramen to do their jobs from a safer height and at the same time obtain better pictures. The new aerial lenses made by Eastman included 40-in. telephoto lenses, and lenses of aperture f/2.5 in 12-in. and 7½-in. focal lengths.

New fast aerofilms were introduced by Kodak for the armed services during the year. The infrared film for aerial photography was nearly as fast as the fast panchromatic films.

During 1943 the Polaroid corporation, together with the marine corps and the U.S. navy respectively, worked out an extremely rapid technique for the preparation of large areas of stereoscopic mosaics. The procedure was suitable for field use in preparing large-area vectographs for staff study. One of the novel features of the technique was the use of water in place of an adhesive to hold the prints down. The large-area vectograph film introduced by the Polaroid corporation was 11 x 14 in. in size. This was the film used in reproducing the stereoscopic aerial mosaics.

New equipment, especially designed for the army air forces in collaboration with their photographic laboratories, included a contact printer with cold Argon lamps so constructed that the illumination is adjustable for printing trimetragon aerial negatives of nonuniform density; a compact optical printer for rectifying aerial negatives; a portable universal developing tank for 16-mm. and 35-mm. film; and a continuous 35-mm. strip printer.

Vast improvements were made in Ansco Direct Copy film—speed increased four times, gradation scale extended and made linear over a useful density range—providing more practical means for direct duplication of negatives by single exposure and development.

High-speed Photography.—Because of the accelerated war demands, high-speed cameras were developed and improved upon.

An important development was perfected by Dr. Robert W. Cairns, director of the Hercules Experiment station, Wilmington, Del. Dr. Cairns made the rotating-drum camera which is used to photograph the detonation waves of explosions, which travel 5 to 25 times as fast as sound. This camera records ex-

plosions of 1-kg. charges that are about 6 in. long. A slow explosion is one that lasts about 100-millionths of a second. This high-speed camera was used to record all the details of the activity of many war explosions.

The photo lamp department of the General Electric company reported that the rated peak lumens were increased on five of their photoflash bulbs. The Midget flashbulbs, such as Nos. 5, 6 and the S.M., were finding greater use in war photography as well as among the amateurs and news photographers. Quality of the flashlamps was maintained despite the use of substitute materials, which had been very difficult to work with. Substitution of brass-plated steel for brass lamp bases, substitution of a lower tin content solder for the conventional prewar solder in order to conserve tin, and substitution of iron leads for nickel and copper as a conservation measure had to be considered.

X-ray photography was applied more extensively for medical and industrial uses than in any previous time. One of the important developments was the use of 35-mm. film in an appropriate camera for copying the fluorescent screen on an X-ray machine. With this equipment it was possible to obtain X-ray records of thousands of workers as well as to give periodic checkups for members in the military forces. Also, a special film base was treated for the making of stereoscopic X-rays. Two images are photographed on the same area of film, the only difference being that they are not superimposed on each other but slightly separated in relation to the stereoscopic viewer.

The Ansco company developed special film for industrial radiography, having a higher speed to X-radiation and finer grain.

The Museum of Modern Art in New York city opened its new photography centre and announced the appointment of Willard D. Morgan, editor of the department of photography and of the centre. To photographers, students, critics, collectors, teachers and historians, the photography centre offers its resources of information. Its growing archives include biographical and technical material gathered from photographers themselves; wide contemporary and historical information in the manuals, albums, periodicals, exhibition catalogues and special publications in the library; the illustrated card catalogue of the museum's collection of photographs and similar catalogues of other important collections; and lantern slides, either for individual selection or lecture sets accompanied by text. Large and small exhibitions presenting important trends in creative photography are major functions of the department.

The Radio Corporation of America developed a new small model of the electron microscope which would undoubtedly make this revolutionary instrument available to a wider field of users.[2]

The Polaroid corporation produced polarizing coloured photographic filters. They combine in a single filter the functions of a standard coloured filter and a polarizing filter. A typical filter of this type is a polarizing yellow filter for use in obtaining dark sky effects. To the effect of the yellow filter is added the effect of the polarizer which, by rotation, can be used to control the apparent brightness of polarized sky light. Up to the close of 1943, the use of these filters was confined to military applications on visual and photographic instruments. Three dimensional instruction diagrams and photographs in vectograph form were developed for special military training purposes.

Microphotography.—Microphotography during the year continued to extend its usefulness in wartime in the fields of government, business and scholarship. Great progress was made in the V-mail or soldiers' mail plan and equally spectacular advances in the parallel and less publicized official mail on microfilm. Relatively little new equipment was presented for public inspection.

[2]V. K. Zworykin and James Hillier, "A Compact High-Resolving-Power Electron Microscope." *Jour. of Applied Physics* (Dec. 1943).

INDIVIDUAL TIES in the railroad tracks are discernible under a magnifying glass in this U.S. army photograph taken from an altitude of 10,000 ft.

OPERATORS indexing a strip of Army Air Force tri-metrogon photography onto an aeronautical chart

U.S. ARMY AIR FORCES high altitude photograph taken at approximately 38,000 ft. with a 40-in. telephoto lens. Detail in this photograph is not visible to the human eye at this altitude

TAKEN FROM A SINGLE-SEATER U.S. ARMY RECONNAISSANCE PLANE flying 310 m.p.h. at an altitude of 150 ft., this photograph has amazingly clear details. The film unrolls past a slit in the shutterless camera at a rate which varies with the speed and altitude of the plane

Several new and improved devices, however, were placed in operation and would presumably be made generally available at the close of World War II. Postwar planning activities were in full swing and a number of companies manifested a desire to introduce new equipment. Experimental and pilot models in some cases were already in existence.

Colour microfilm, although expensive, was becoming less so and was used for a number of projects. Outside this field, there were few developments in sensitive materials. One factor, however, of supreme importance was the enunciation by the National Bureau of Standards of a "Standard for Permanent Record Photographic Microcopying Film" and its corollary, "Standard for Temporary Record Photographic Microcopying Film."

The legal aspects of federal microfilming were changed somewhat by the repeal of the act of Sept. 24, 1940, entitled "Public Law No. 788, 76th Congress, Chapter 727, 3d Session, H.R. 10026," and the enactment into law of "Public Law No. 115, 78th Congress, Chapter 192, 1st Session, H.R. 2943." The latter incorporates all of the provisions of the former legislation and in addition specifies certain procedural changes and requirements intended to streamline the uses of the technique. State legislation for the record use of microphotography was extended by passage of similar acts by several states. The state of Illinois, for example, passed two separate acts legalizing the use of microphotography.

V-mail, which was developed by Kodak, reached its greatest usefulness during 1943. The Kodak company continued to give instruction courses in the processing of V-mail film and paper to the appropriate branches of the services. During the latter part of the year the war department released special information to promote a wider use of V-mail. It informed the public that the V-process insured the letter against loss, V-mail saved 98% of the space that ordinary mail would use on planes and ships for vital medical, food and munitions cargo, and that it saved time because it had priority over most types of mail.

Kodak made a number of new developments in recording materials, particularly a new paper for reflex copying.

The Ansco company (formerly known as Agfa Ansco) increased the speed of Ansco Direct Copy film four times. The gradation scale was extended and made linear over a useful density range, thus providing more practical means for direct duplication of negatives by single exposure and development. (*See also* MOTION PICTURES; NEWSPAPERS and PERIODICALS; X-RAY.)

BIBLIOGRAPHY.—*The Complete Photographer*, National Educational Alliance (1943), Willard D. Morgan, ed.; Morgan and Lester, *Graphic Graflex Photography* (1943 ed.) and *The Leica Manual* (9th ed., 1943).
(W. D. MN.)

Physics.

Research on all phases of military and naval science continued in 1943. More of it was based on the classical phenomena of physics than on the latest discoveries in the field of atomic structure. Such war work did not, of course, find its way into current literature, but it brought many new recruits to physics. Looking ahead, the American Institute of Physics, acting for the several societies of physicists in the United States, purchased a national headquarters for physicists at 57 E. 55th St., New York city. Early in 1944, this building was to house the editorial offices of the professional journals. The institute's important tasks were to encourage friendly co-operation among the numerous specialized groups of physicists and to play the role of co-ordinator in matters affecting professional standards, professional welfare and the support of scientific research.

Cosmic Rays.—Cosmic rays, as they are found in the earth's atmosphere, consist in the main of two portions. One of these, the soft component, is made up of electrons which can be stopped by a few centimetres of lead. Since the earth's atmosphere is equivalent in absorbing power to nearly 100 cm. of lead, these electrons must be of local origin. They are, in fact, produced in bunches here and there in the atmosphere and in other absorbing material by a very penetrating component of the rays. This penetrating component itself is created in the high atmosphere by primary rays which appear to come from interstellar space, whose exact nature was in 1943 still uncertain. Part at least of the penetrating component was known to consist of fast-moving mesotrons, particles of mass about 180 times that of the electron, which create "showers" of electrons as they pass downward. These mesotrons are, however, unstable, having a lifetime of about two-millionths of a second. This fact alone certifies that they must be of atmospheric origin. If their source were far away they would disintegrate before they reached the earth, changing, it was believed, into an electron and a neutrino, both moving with high kinetic energy derived from the mass-energy of the mesotron. New experiments to determine the mesotron's half life were reported by B. Rossi and N. Nereson. Their estimate was $2.15 \pm 0.07 \times 10^{-6}$ sec. Therefore, even if mesotrons moved with practically the speed of light, the chance is very small that one of them would survive a 20-mile journey. Nevertheless, enough survive for accurate measurement at sea level and in deep mines.

It is important to know if these ionizing mesotrons are the only source of the soft component of cosmic rays. As a result of experiments carried out underground, V. C. Wilson and D. J. Hughes deduced that mesotrons alone are responsible for the soft component below sea level, to depths as great as 600 m. in the earth. In the atmosphere, however, V. H. Regener's experiments lead to a different conclusion. With an ingenious arrangement of electrical counting tubes, he was able to record on photographic film the approximate paths of penetrating cosmic rays and of other rays created by them. In many cases showers of soft secondary rays were produced in the absence of any ionizing penetrating ray. At an altitude of 10,000 ft. he found that showers were produced nine times as frequently by nonionizing parent rays as by ionizing mesotrons. At lower altitudes, the ratio grew progressively smaller. Thus the penetrating component of cosmic rays must consist of two parts, one being composed of mesotrons, the other of some nonionizing radiation. However, the nonionizing radiation must be absorbed much faster than mesotrons in order that Regener's experiments may be consistent with those of Wilson and Hughes.

In 1943, R. A. Millikan, H. V. Neher and W. H. Pickering published a second report on their world-wide cosmic ray survey, which was designed to provide new information about the source of the rays. By measuring the intensities of the rays at different geomagnetic latitudes and at various elevations they were, in effect, using the magnetic field of the earth as a giant spectrograph to separate rays of different energies. Since many of the rays are charged particles, they tend to be deflected away from the earth at the equator but come to the earth's surface readily at the north and south magnetic poles. The three authors measured the energy-distribution of the rays. Then they compared their findings with the results which would be anticipated if the rays were created in interstellar space by the annihilation of the very sparsely distributed atoms there. The observations and predictions agreed very well. Hence it is reasonable to consider Millikan, Neher and Pickering's assumption as a good working hypothesis concerning the origin of cosmic rays, which are therefore the only observable relics of the annihilation process. What initiates this transformation of energy, and in what form it travels to the earth, were in 1943 unsolved problems.

Thermal Diffusion.—The law of force between two molecules cannot be written down in exact mathematical form. Certain facts concerning intermolecular forces are, however, obvious. The magnitude of the force decreases with increasing separation of the particles, provided they are more than a certain distance apart. Molecules also resist very strongly any attempt to bring them closer than a certain distance, as may be deduced from the difficulty of compressing to smaller bulk such a substance as water. In treating the behaviour of molecules by mathematical arguments it is therefore necessary to use plausible approximations, which are usually in the form of inverse power laws. Certain molecules, which behave somewhat like hard elastic spheres, are classed as "hard" molecules; others, in which a repulsive force builds up gradually as the molecules approach, are termed "soft" molecules. The theory was in 1943 still far from rigorous, but was reliable enough to be used as a guide in interpreting the results of thermal diffusion experiments. W. W. Watson and D. Woernley enclosed a mixture of ordinary and heavy ammonia in two glass bulbs connected by a long narrow tube. After keeping one hotter than the other for some hours, a greater concentration of the heavy component was found in one bulb, in agreement with the general predictions of the theory. After repeating the experiment in various temperature ranges it was possible to find out how the separation of the components of the gaseous mixture was affected by temperature. Here a new observation was made. A reversal in the direction of separation occurred at about 20° C., which means that if one bulb were held at 100° C. and the other at −60° C., no separation would occur by thermal diffusion. A similar result was recorded in 1942 for neon-ammonia mixtures. The cause of this puzzling behaviour can be found in the lack of spherical symmetry of the ammonia molecule. Indeed, the method is a promising one for investigating long-range molecular forces.

Cerenkov Radiation.—A new radiation accompanying the passage of very fast electrons through transparent materials was found by the Russian physicist Cerenkov in 1934. After the first announcement several papers were published dealing with the dependence of its properties on electron velocity and on the refractive index of the medium. Cerenkov radiation cannot be produced unless electrons move with a velocity greater than that of light in the transparent medium. In the words of J. E. Henderson, the radiation may be regarded as the electromagnetic bow wave of an electron, analogous to the bow wave of a boat which moves faster than the waves which it sets up on the surface of the water. Like the bow wave of a boat, Cerenkov radiation travels and can be observed only in certain directions with respect to the moving electron; in all other directions it is destroyed by interference. The direction of emission is connected with speed of the electron and the refractive index of the medium by a simple relation which was verified by the experiments of H. O. Wyckoff and J. E. Henderson in 1943 and of G. B. Collins and V. C. Reiling in 1938.

Electron Microscopy.—In the standard type of electron microscope, only objects suitable for forming into or being mounted upon extremely thin films can be investigated directly. The surface of a solid cannot, therefore, be examined unless a replica of the surface is first made on a thin film. A film of the metal itself cannot be used because it has properties quite different from those of the same metal in bulk. A new technique developed by R. D. Heidenreich and V. G. Peck promised to be very useful. The process is a two-stage one. First, plastic polystyrene is moulded on to the metal surface and squeezed in a press. Then the excess metal is cut and dissolved away, leaving a negative imprint of the metal's surface on the plastic. Next, the plastic is mounted in a vacuum above a small heating coil from which silica is quickly evaporated on to the cold polystyrene. Silica mole-

cules are extremely mobile on polystyrene, so they penetrate into little crevices and cover the surface completely. The silica film is removed from the plastic by dissolving the latter away. It is then ready for mounting on a frame for insertion in the microscope.

In this series of processes, some detail is inevitably lost, but the final resolution obtainable with such replicas is between 150A and 200A, surpassing that of an optical microscope some twenty-fold. So many problems of surface structure await solution in this range that a new electron microscope was designed expressly for the task. The first model was built by C. H. Bachman and S. Ramo. In this instrument extremely high resolving power was consciously sacrificed for simplicity, compactness and mobility. It operated entirely on electrostatic principles and needed none of the precise current and voltage regulation required for an electron microscope with magnetic lenses. An image is first formed by an electron beam on a fluorescent screen, which is then photographed through a good optical microscope. The magnification due directly to the electron beam is therefore comparatively small, but the intermediate image possesses the high resolution necessary for further enlargement by the optical system.

New High-pressure Cloud Chamber.—One of the most direct ways of investigating the behaviour of charged particles is to photograph the tracks of ions which they leave in their wake as they traverse a cloud chamber. In the case of cosmic rays, in which interesting events occur only rarely, the accumulation of useful data by a cloud chamber operated at atmospheric pressure is a wearisome undertaking. A few high-pressure chambers have, indeed, been built, and their good performance has suggested that it would be advantageous to have chambers which could operate at several hundred atmospheres. The chief problem of design was solved by T. H. Johnson, S. DeBenedetti and R. P. Shutt of the Bartol Research foundation, who enclosed their new chamber completely in a bath of transparent oil, contained in a 5-ton steel casting strong enough to withstand the large forces involved. In this way the pressures inside and outside the chamber itself are nearly equal. Photographs are made through a small window in the casting and expansion is effected by releasing a little of the surrounding oil. Already photographs had been made between 100 and 200 atmospheres in argon. One such picture showed at once all that happens in the atmosphere over a vertical area of some 20,000 sq. ft. Furthermore, a chamber operated at such high pressure has a sensitive period much longer than that of a low-pressure chamber. The harvest of information per picture is, of course, proportional to the pressure and to the time of sensitivity. With this important new instrument, data concerning rare events such as mesotron disintegration might be expected rapidly. (*See also* X-RAYS.)

BIBLIOGRAPHY.—The reader who desires fuller information on physics in 1943 will do well to look up the topics mentioned here in the index to vol. 63 and 64 of the *Physical Review*, whence he will be led to original papers in that and in other journals.   (T. H. O.)

Physiology. **Thyroid Gland.**—Interest was aroused in a possible new treatment for hyperthyroidism by the observation that certain sulfonamides as well as thiourea and its derivatives lowered the basal metabolic rate when fed to rats for several weeks. A large number of compounds were tested and it was found that a substance called "thiouracil" was most effective in decreasing metabolism. This substance was subsequently tried clinically on a number of patients with hyperthyroidism. The preliminary results were encouraging but more extensive studies are necessary before a final evaluation of the drug can be given. In regard to the mechanism of action of thiouracil, the evidence indicated that it prevented the thyroid gland from utilizing iodine in the synthesis of the thyroid hormone; thiouracil did not interfere with the action of the thyroid hormone when the latter was given in a preformed state.

Vitamins.—One of the toxic manifestations of the sulfonamide drugs is the occurrence of anaemia and leucopenia (a reduction in the number of white blood cells). Recent work has indicated that one of the members of the vitamin B complex may be useful in preventing these effects. This substance, folic acid, was discovered in 1941. It was shown that the administration of this compound cures the anaemia and leucopenia produced in rats by the administration of sulfonamide drugs.

Evidence was obtained indicating that vitamin B₁ (thiamine) is synthesized by bacterial action in the human intestinal tract. This was known to occur in certain other animal species but it had not yet been demonstrated in man. An interesting and perhaps clinically important observation was the fact that certain sulfonamide drugs employed in the treatment of intestinal disorders (succinylsulfathiazol) prevented this intestinal synthesis from occurring. (*See* also VITAMINS.)

Gastrointestinal Tract.—It was known for some time that extracts of the upper intestinal mucosa contained a substance called enterogastrone which inhibits gastric secretion and motility. The possibility that patients might be "immunized" against the recurrence of peptic ulcer by injections of enterogastrone received some encouraging support during 1943. The development of gastrojejunal ulcer in Mann-Williamson dogs was prevented for one year by enterogastrone injections. In the Mann-Williamson operation, a gastrojejunostomy is performed and the alkaline bile and pancreatic juice is diverted into the terminal ileum; this allows unbuffered and gastric juice to come in contact with the jejunal mucosa. Ninety-eight per cent of these animals die with ulcer within one to nine months if untreated. After preventing ulcer in these animals for a period of a year, the enterogastrone injections were discontinued. In spite of this, however, ulcer failed to develop in these dogs even after a period of a year without treatment. This was a surprising result because in previous work with aluminum phosphate and gastric mucin, ulcer developed within one to four months after treatment was stopped. The mechanism of this enterogastrone "immunization" is not clear. It is not due to a markedly reduced secretion of acid or pepsin by the gastric glands. It may be due to an increased resistance of the jejunal mucosa to irritation.

The effect of coffee and caffeine on gastric secretion was studied. It was found that these substances stimulate gastric secretion in the cat and in man but not in the dog. In the cat, acute and chronic ulcers of the stomach and duodenum could be produced by the daily administration of five grains of caffeine. On a body weight basis, this would correspond to 30 to 60 grains for man (a cup of coffee contains about one and one-half grains of caffeine). Thus if the human stomach behaves like the cat's stomach, abuse of coffee or other caffeine containing beverages may be a direct cause of ulcer in susceptible subjects. In man, caffeine and alcohol manifest a synergistic stimulation to gastric secretion.

Thus the practice of drinking coffee in relation to alcoholic beverages places the stomach and duodenum of the person susceptible to peptic ulcer under considerable strain.

Environmental Stress.—In World War II men were frequently exposed to extremes of heat and cold and were often forced to exist for prolonged periods without adequate sources of food or water. During 1943 intensive studies were carried out in the Mojave desert in California with regard to the water requirements of men under conditions of extreme heat. The water requirements were found to depend upon the amount of body activity and the daily temperature. At 95° F., a man required at least three quarts of fluid a day, and one who worked hard in the sun needed as much as seven quarts. At 110° F., six quarts were required at rest and as much as 10 to 12 quarts in 24 hours were needed by men doing strenuous work in the sun. When the water supply was limited, it was found that more than twice as much work could be accomplished by men working only during the coolest part of the 24 hours (*i.e.*, at night) than by those who worked during the day when the heat was most intense.

Other studies were made upon men adrift at sea in rubber life rafts. Some of the conclusions reached from this study were: (1) When water is scarce, dehydrated or heavy foods should not be eaten. (2) It was found to be advantageous to drink large quantities of water prior to being cast adrift. (3) When water became available after a period of prolonged dehydration, it was found to be better to drink as much as one could comfortably hold at once instead of drinking smaller amounts at wider intervals. (4) Keeping the clothing saturated with sea water was found to help prevent dehydration.

BIBLIOGRAPHY.—E. B. Astwood, "Chemical Nature of Compounds Which Inhibit the Function of the Thyroid Gland," *J. Pharmacol. & Exper. Therap.*, 78:79 (1943); E. B. Astwood, J. Sullivan, A. Bissell and R. Tyslowitz, "Action of Certain Sulfonamides and of Thiourea upon the Function of the Thyroid Gland of the Rat," *Endocrinology*, 32:210 (1943); E. B. Astwood, "Treatment of Hyperthyroidism with Thiourea and Thiouracil," *J.A.M.A.*, 122:78 (1943); C. G. Mackenzie and J. B. Mackenzie, "Effect of Sulfonamides and Thioureas on the Thyroid Gland and Basal Metabolism," *Endocrinology*, 32:185 (1943); R. H. Williams and G. W. Bissell, "Thiouracil in the Treatment of Thyrotoxicosis," *Science*, 98:156 (1943); V. A. Najjar and E. J. Holt, Jr., "The Biosynthesis of Thiamine in Man," *J.A.M.A.*, 123:683 (1943); A. C. Ivy, "Some Recent Developments in the Physiology of the Stomach and Intestine which Pertain to the Management of Peptic Ulcer," The Ludwig Kast Lecture, 16th Graduate Fortnight of the New York Academy of Medicine, Oct. 1943; E. S. Judd, Jr., "Experimental Production of Peptic Ulcer with Caffeine," *Bull. Am. College of Surgeons*, 28:46 (1943); D. J. Sandweiss, "The Immunizing Effect of the Anti-Ulcer Factor in Normal Human Urine (Anthelone) Against Experimental Gastrojejunal (Peptic) Ulcer in Dogs," *Gastroenterology*, 1:965 (1943); "When Thirsty—Drink," *Science News Letter*, 44:198 (1943); "Adrift for Science," *Science News Letter*, 44:314 (1943). (A. C. I.)

Pig Iron: *see* IRON AND STEEL.

Pigs: *see* HOGS; LIVESTOCK.

Pittsburgh. Tenth in population (671,659) among cities of the United States in 1940, Pittsburgh, Pa., had an area of approximately 54.3 sq.mi. at the end of 1943. It is in the southwestern part of Pennsylvania at the junction of the Monongahela and Allegheny rivers. Mayor (Jan. 1, 1944), Cornelius D. Scully.

In 1943, production at factories in the region centred in Pittsburgh, already representing near-capacity levels in 1941 and 1942, was further increased. There were completed in the region during 1943 a significant enlargement of iron and steel capacity, expansion of plants producing small war craft, and an important new unit producing materials for synthetic rubber. Accompanying the larger industrial output was a record dollar volume of retail trade.

With brisk industry and trade, utility loads in the district were heavy in 1943, but with limited interruption and delay, the loads were carried, local transportation in rush periods being relieved somewhat by more staggering of office and school hours. A new electric generating plant in the Pittsburgh area, with a capacity of 60,000 kw., was dedicated early in 1943.

Although deeply involved in war, the community took important steps in 1943 toward planning for peace. The city of Pittsburgh and the county of Allegheny, through their planning commissions and their works departments, increased their efforts in the planning of public works.

The assessed valuation of taxable real estate in Pittsburgh, for city and school taxes of 1943, was $1,044,010,664, land valuation being $471,359,772 and building valuation $572,650,892. City tax rates were 22.5 mills on land and 11.25 mills on buildings; school rate, 11.75 mills on combined valuation. The county rate of 7.625 mills within the city related to a somewhat lower assessed value.

Expenditures and debt to the nearest dollar for the city of Pittsburgh, the Pittsburgh school district and the county of Allegheny were as follows: expenditures, except debt retirement, calendar year 1943, $18,080,774 for the city, $12,122,105 for the school district, $16,281,814 for the county; bonded debt less cash and bonds in sinking funds, end of 1943, $53,264,661 for the city, $18,010,369 for the school district, $82,485,613 for the county. It is necessary to note that only 54.8% of the county's assessed valuation of taxable real estate was in Pittsburgh.   (J. G. Bo.)

Pius XII

(1876–   ), the 262nd successor of St. Peter in the See of Rome, was elected by the cardinals in conclave on his 63rd birthday, March 2, 1939, and was crowned as pope on March 12. (For details of his early life, see *Encyclopædia Britannica*.) In his office as pope he is held to be the Vicar of Christ on earth, and he is the spiritual pastor over an estimated 400,000,000 Catholics in all parts of the world. These were to be found in 1943 in all the warring nations, though countless thousands were either slaughtered or died in concentration camps.

The course of the war in 1943 was brought very close to the person of the pope himself, though it was reported that His Holiness had refused to take refuge outside the war zone (*see* VATICAN CITY STATE). Among the outstanding events connected with the pope was a quotation from his peace appeal made in April in the British house of lords, and the association with papal ideals for world peace voiced by high prelates of the Church of England.

Among the many benefactions made by the pope during 1943 in the direction of war relief were: $50,000 given for the restoration of Catholic churches destroyed in air raids in Great Britain; $20,000 given for church restoration in Malta; $2,000 given for internees in the Isle of Man. Papal delegates in Finland and Rumania were ordered to distribute food and clothing to Russian prisoners of war. A version of the Gospels was published in Serbian for war prisoners.

The pope addressed a letter to Cardinal Marchetti-Selvaggiani on the bombing of Rome, July 20, 1943. On Aug. 15 he appealed to world Catholics to pray for peace, and addressed a peace appeal on the fourth anniversary of the war, Sept. 1. Dec. 8 was designated by the pope as a day of public prayers for peace throughout the Catholic world.

On March 12 the pope celebrated the fourth anniversary of his coronation. Two encyclicals were published in 1943: *Mystici Corporis,* on the Mystical Body of Christ, June 29, and *Divino Afflante Spiritu,* on the study of Holy Scripture, Sept. 30.

The Vatican *Gold Book* was published by the Vatican Polyglot Press, covering the activities of the Holy See for the years 1941–42 in the fields of diplomacy, the ministry and works of charity.

The pope presided at the opening of the academic year of the Pontifical Academy of Sciences. On Oct. 30 he broadcast in Spanish to the Peruvian National Eucharistic congress. In his pre-Lenten discourse to the clergy of Rome the pope urged them to preach Sunday observance. On his name-day, June 2, he received the respects of the cardinals in Rome, when he deplored persecutions, paid tribute by name to the Poles, and recalled his own efforts to secure peace. On June 13 the pope addressed 20,000 Italian workers on social security as the basis of harmony in society. The broadcast of the pope's midnight mass on Christmas eve was cancelled, because of the 6 P.M. curfew enforced by the German occupation forces in Rome.

In his Christmas message, broadcast to the whole world on Christmas eve, Pius XII prayed that a just peace may be celebrated in 1944. The pope called for a normal measure of power sanctions, but warned that true peace can never be a harsh imposition supported by arms alone. (*See* also ROMAN CATHOLIC CHURCH; VATICAN CITY STATE.)

BIBLIOGRAPHY.—J. W. Naughton, *Pius XII on World Problems* (America Press); H. C. Koenig, editor, *Principles for Peace* (Washington, D.C.).
(J. LAF.)

Plague, Bubonic and Pneumonic.

The published reports of the first nine months of 1943 indicate that bubonic and pneumonic plague recurred in the people or rodents of Africa, Asia, South America, Oceania and the United States. Its occurrence among troops of the nations at war was not recorded but it was present in Casablanca, Dakar, Port Said, Madagascar and Hawaii, which were sites of military operations. Serious outbreaks of epidemic proportions did not occur in 1943, although there were several instances of the development of the pneumonic form of the disease among a few individuals of each of several widely separated areas.

One author attributed the decreasing frequency with which pneumonic plague assumes epidemic intensity to the infrequency of the occurrence of cough and expectoration among patients in whom the lungs become involved.

Observations continued from year to year on rats of rural areas in Hawaii made it apparent that infection occurs and recurs in a rather circumscribed area, while similar observations among

POPE PIUS XII exhorting a multitude of Romans after the second U.S. air raid on Rome Aug. 13, 1943

field rodents in continental United States suggested that there is a gradual easterly extension of the disease toward the Great Plains section. These deductions seemed to be strengthened by experiences of 1943 during which an active epizootic recurred within an area of approximately 30 sq.mi. on the island of Hawaii, and the disease was found for the first time in areas of the eastern third of the states of Montana, Wyoming, Colorado and New Mexico which had been surveyed during previous years by the same procedures.

The continued studies on the role of fleas in the spread of the disease among rodents confirm the wide dissemination of the Indian rat flea (*Xenopsylla cheopis*) in the world; the identification of eight flea species in Canada which are probable vectors; and the experimental determination that two species which are prevalent in rural areas of central United States have a capacity as vectors equal to that of the Indian rat flea.

Tests were made on the Indian rat flea and on *Diamanus montanus*, which is common to the California ground squirrel (*Citellus beecheyi beecheyi*), to determine the probable number of plague bacteria (*Pasteurella pestis*) which would be ingested by a flea under favourable circumstances. An average of 3×10^5 organisms were obtained from specimens of such species shortly after feeding on an infected mouse; and it was also observed that an average of 200 organisms were expelled in their faeces during subsequent periods of 24 hr.

Technical investigations of the biochemical requirements of the plague bacterium suggested that its sources of nitrogen may be supplied by inorganic salts. The confirmation of this conclusion might result in simplification of the procedures used in detecting the organism.

A re-examination of the use of carbon bisulphide in the control of rodents when introduced into their burrows as a spray confirmed its lethal effect on the animal but indicated that its fleas were not killed.

BIBLIOGRAPHY.—"World Distribution of Cholera, Plague, etc.," *Public Health Reports* (U.S. Public Health Service), 58:1638 (1943); R. Pollitzer and C. C. Li, "Some Observations on the Decline of Pneumonic Plague Epidemics," *Journal of Infectious Diseases*, 72:160-172 (1943); L. Jackowski, "The Oriental Rat Flea, *X. cheopis*, in Michigan," *Journal of Parasitology*, 29:300 (1943); O. Hecht, "The Fleas of Rats in Venezuela," *Rev. Sanidad y Asistencia Social* (Caracas), 7:811-820 (1942); G. A. Mail and G. P. Holland, "Siphonaptera of Western Canada in Relation to Sylvatic Plague," *Proceedings of the 6th Pacific Sci. Cong.*, 5:122-125 (1942); F. M. Prince, "Report on the Fleas *Opisocrostis bruneri* (Baker) and *Thrassis bacchi* (Roth) as Vectors of Plague," *Public Health Reports* (U.S. Public Health Service), 58:1013-1016 (1943); J. R. Douglas and C. M. Wheeler, "The Fate of *Pasteurella pestis* in the Flea," *Jour. Infec. Dis.* 72 (1):18-30 (1943); M. Doudoroff, "Studies on the Nutrition and Metabolism of *Pasteurella pestis*," *Proceedings of the Society of Experimental Biology and Medicine*, 53:73-75 (1943); M. A. Stewart, "Carbon Disulphide in Control of Sylvatic Plague Vectors," *American Journal of Hygiene*, 36:243-246 (1942).   (N. E. W.)

Plant Industry, Soils and Agricultural Engineering, Bureau of: see AGRICULTURAL RESEARCH ADMINISTRATION.

Plastics Industry.

The second year of war shifted the plastics industry around in such an amazing manner as to actually portend the ushering in of the "Plastic Age." In 1942, plastics played an emergency role in substituting for and replacing the strategic metals and rubber. The war job performed was so excellent, the conversions so numerous, that many plastics also became critical materials, available only for war usage. This affected such synthetic resins and plastics as phenolics, vinyls, styrenes, acrylics and ethyl cellulose.

Total U.S. production of synthetic resins and plastics during 1942 was about 426,731,106 lb., or more than 213,000 tons. Figures for 1943 production were not available, but it could be presumed that plastics production more than held its own despite curtailment of consumer goods. Considering the new capacity brought in for the production of phenol and styrene, just to men-

PLASTIC ROPE, braided with strong filaments of Saran, was applied to many marine and wartime uses in 1943

tion two resins, it was estimated that 1943 production was close to 600,000,000 lb.

Phenol formaldehyde plastics were perhaps the most widely used in war production. They were lightweight, stable under rapid temperature changes, good insulators, impervious to weathering and had high impact resistance. In planes, phenolic materials were fabricated into pulleys, fairleads, for control cables which pass to every part of the structure, cabin air controls, propeller parts and propellers themselves, aileron control quadrants, illuminated dials and name plates for night flying. These same materials saw active service on the sea as well. A warship in 1943 was a veritable electric power plant with everything operated electrically—elevators, gun turrets, gun light switches, radios, pumps, junction boxes, etc. In all such assemblies, the plastic played an important part, and had to function precisely and without failure.

The need for moulding materials of exceptional mechanical strength to replace strategic metals greatly stimulated the use and further development of compounds known as high or medium impact phenolics. Plastic of this type successfully passed the test for 37 mm. dummy fuses, and for the 75 mm. mortar shell fuse. In the Browning machine gun it replaced the black walnut used for grip handles. Booster tubes for demolition bombs were made of phenolics. And even the traditional duck from which army tents had been made was treated with phenolic formaldehyde resins, which not only increased the life of the duck material, but improved its water permeability and protected the fire-resistant finish against weathering or deterioration in storage. Melamine resins, which were but recently perfected, were used for buttons which withstood the gruelling tests prescribed by the quartermaster corps. Previously all buttons were made from imported vegetable ivory. Melamine resin was also the basis of a new treatment for paper pulp, and imparted extraordinary strength to sheets made from it, and at the same time increased the resistance of the sheet to folding. This new paper lent itself to such unusual uses as clothing, army tents, sandbags, etc. It also was experimented with in the food field, where it was used for crate liners, for locker bags, for frozen foods, etc.

The two years of war witnessed a vast increase in the manufacturing of acrylic plastics, as well as the expansion of the facilities for fabricating aircraft parts. The aircraft industry continued to use a large percentage of the sheet production, turning out more planes per month and using a larger area of acrylics per plane. New developments included an acrylic power turret which could be revolved mechanically to aim multiple machine guns. The new bombers also carried another acrylic innovation, a gunner enclosure practically in the tail of the plane.

Acrylics saw active service in all phases of the war. Even blackout lights on army trucks and jeeps were made from acrylics. Tank sight windows were cut from sheet acrylics. Navy PT boats had acrylic machine-gun housings, as well as acrylic windows. Sea-going dials and gauges were protected from the effects of salt water by moulded or fabricated acrylic covers.

In the report issued by the Baruch committee on the rubber situation, it was stated that vinyl resins, as a substitute, saved the equivalent of 22,000 tons of crude rubber per year. Despite great increases in vinyl production capacity, there was not enough in 1943 to satisfy military needs.

Wartime applications for polyvinyl compounds increased faster than they could be made. Polyvinyl butyral, long used only as the plastic sandwich for laminated safety glass in automobiles, coated the fabric from which lightweight raincoats were made for soldiers. Polyvinyl alcohol was moulded into heat-resisting tubing and gaskets for trucks. Polyvinyl acetate was used instead of rubber latex in mid-soles for shoes. Polyvinyl chloride was used in making degaussing cables to protect ships against magnetic mines and for general use for insulation for primary and secondary cables for army as well as navy aircraft.

In replacing natural rubber in army raincoats, polyvinyl butyral saved 1¾ lb. of crude rubber in each raincoat. It was also used in bags for transporting drinking water to thirsty soldiers, hospital sheeting for military and civilian use, life belts for the navy and merchant marine, food bags and waterproof, oil-resistant suits for seamen. In extruded form, polyvinyl butyral replaced rubber in tubing, in clamps to prevent vibration of fuel lines on aeroplanes, and in a host of other military applications.

Cellulosic materials were extensively employed in gas mask parts including lenses, knobs, starter buttons, blackout lenses and protective surfaces for maps and documents. Cellulose acetate sheeting found a large war use in windows for trainer aeroplanes, for gliders, and for windshields for motorcycles. Fluorescent cellulose acetate sheeting was used for lighting fixtures in war equipment, where visible lighting could not be used. Cellulose acetate and cellulose acetate butyrate moulding powders were becoming more and more important in the manufacture of war and essential civilian materials. The butyrate and the high acetic acid content cellulosic plastics were being used for applications requiring improved water resistance and dimensional stability. Among such uses were gas mask lenses, hose nozzles, pistol grips, flashlight cases, first aid kits, stirrup pump parts, shaving brush handles. The mechanical strength and ease of moulding these products made them extremely valuable as substitutes for metal, rubber and glass, and as materials for construction of articles for which metal and rubber are not satisfactory.

One of the best known of all plastic materials was polystyrene, even though it was relatively new in the United States. During 1943 productive capacity for the manufacturing of monomeric styrene for polymerization into the plastic was a fortuitous circumstance, since this product was available for the manufacturing of the Buna-S type of rubber. This further demonstrated one of the many contributions the plastics industry made to the war effort. Petroleum and coal are the raw materials from which styrene is made, which is further polymerized to make polystyrene. Its most remarkable characteristic is extreme resistance to chemical attack. For example, hydrochloric acid which will dissolve glass has no effect on polystyrene. It absorbs practically no moisture and is an excellent insulator, a sheet of one-thousandth of an inch thick resisting up to 3,000 volts. In war it was applied to battery boxes, radio insulations, coaxial cable insulation, resin modifiers for wire coating, etc.

Ethyl cellulose was designed originally for peacetime applications. Its outstanding properties are water resistance, toughness, high impact, dimensional stability, low density and general resistance to weathering. It was in 1943 under strict allocation by WPB because of its adaptation to military use, the chief of which was as a fabric coating for braided ignition cable, fire- and water-proofing dyes, artificial leather, etc. In sheeting form it made transparent face shields for gas masks, goggles, envelopes for shop prints, and recording surfaces for airport and general communication monitors. One development was ethyl rubber made of ethyl cellulose combined with an oil plasticizer. It is flexible, has elastic properties, and shows better resistance to abrasion, ozones and to gasoline than natural rubber, but less resilience, elongation or resistance to permanent deformation. It could be used instead of natural rubber for gun covers, electrical or junction tape, water tubing to replace brass, raincoats, hospital sheeting, gloves, footwear, etc.

The chief reason for the early failure of wood parts in aircraft construction was due to the inferiority of animal and vegetable glues which had very poor resistance to water, as well as being subjected to fungus growth. These factors weakened the structure to such a degree as to destroy its value entirely. The development of synthetic resin adhesives which offered excellent bonding characteristics and complete resistance to moisture and fungus growth opened a new and entirely successful field to use in aeroplane parts.

Plastic plywood in 1943 was becoming increasingly important as a major structural material for war use, and low pressure moulding methods were being used for speedy, efficient low cost production of lightweight training planes, assault boats, floating ramps, pontoons, and for the PT motor torpedo boats. All of these were fabricated of lightweight resin bonded plywood which filled the gap of a serious aluminum shortage. Pilot seats of plastic plywood were an important recent development. These seats were made of a phenolic impregnated fabric composition, as were the helmet liners used by the armed forces.

Since their introduction in 1940, the vinylidene chloride resins (Saran) aroused considerable interest, because of their unusual properties—water, chemical and solvent resistance combined with toughness, durability and

appearance. It was in 1943 finding its way into such varied end product as piping for use in plumbing fixtures, to replace brass and copper in defens housing, for electric fixtures and installations. And such was the versatilit of plastic material, that it could be extruded into fibres or monofilament to be woven into a wide variety of upholstery fabrics, these fabrics magi cally endowed with endless resistance to weather, dirt and abrasives, ane even to fire, wonderfully strong, resilient and brightly hued. It replace rattan in subway seats, and was expected to be used in restaurants, theatre and hotels, and the interiors of tomorrow.

The safeguards of censorship prevent extensive descriptions of many o the wartime arrivals in the materials field. But a brief survey of some o these newcomers may be offered:

Synthetic replacements for natural mica—one of the most critical wa materials because it is a vital component of radio and electrical apparatu —were being developed by several companies. One of these produced a series of commercial products called Polectron. Polectron was said to hav an unusual combination of low dielectric loss, high temperature stabilit and superior water resistance, although the mechanical strength of the resir made in 1943 was still relatively poor. Immediate uses for the material such as dielectric sheets in condensers, did not call for a high degree o mechanical strength.

An inorganic mineral element, silica, was combined with organic radical composed of carbon and hydrogen to produce a new group of plastics calle Silicones. Silicones are said to be resistant to temperatures as high a 500° F., which suggests their suitability for use in electrical insulatio where such conditions may be encountered.

Another new material, as yet a little-known name on the plastics roster was Penacolite. This was said to be a phenolic-type thermosetting resir which cures rapidly at temperatures from 60° to 150° F. under nearly neutral conditions. This type of resin might eliminate many of the difficulties in assembly gluing of wood or plastic-plywood parts for use continuously exposed to the weather.

Polystyrene fulfilled many difficult assignments in wartime electronic and aircraft equipment. Styraloy, a recently developed elastomeric styrene derivative, was reported to have properties which made it eminently suitable for electrical applications at both high and low temperatures.

A long-awaited entry in the plastics field was an adhesive which would permit the bonding together of metal, wood, plastics, ceramics, fibres and rubber in any desired combination. A possible solution to this problem was found in Cycleweld and Reanite cements, thermosetting plastics which were applied to the surfaces of the units to be bonded and then cured under heat and pressure.

This process was said to form structures which were stronger, lighter and cheaper than those joined by conventional methods.

Reinforced plastics which permitted large-volume production of low-cost, lightweight, high-strength structures offered many advantages beyond the replacement of critical aluminum and magnesium. Several new resins which would form satisfactory bonds at low or contact pressures and thus eliminate the need for costly dies were created, and special papers, cotton and rayon fabrics, and glass fibre cloths were developed as reinforcing materials. These low-pressure laminated plastics attracted interest because they made possible the fabrication of huge structures heretofore considered impractical

RADIO INSULATORS and coil forms of Lucite, for military high-frequency equipment

and even impossible for plastics.

Resin-impregnated wood became an important factor in maintaining an adequate supply of propellers for the expanding air forces. A plant with facilities for producing 50 times the volume of Pregwood available prior to the war, was in operation. The resin-impregnated and compressed maple boards were bonded by means of electrostatic high-frequency heating of thermosetting phenolic glues into blocks from which the propeller is carved. Other applications of this wood-plastic material included electrical insulation, bearing plates, skis and ventilating fans.

A new rubber-like product, Paracon, made by the condensation of dibasic acids with glycols or by the condensation of hydroxy acids was announced. The elongation at break of these polyesters was said to average 400% with an average tensile strength of about 1,700 lb. per square inch. Important progress was also made in the production and application of polyethylene and its derivatives, but the publications on the subject were limited to the patent literature.

(*See also* CHEMISTRY; MUNITIONS OF WAR; PAINTS AND VARNISHES; RAYON AND OTHER SYNTHETIC FIBRES; RUBBER.)　　(C. A. BN.)

Platinum.

No information was received on platinum production, except that the chief producer in Colombia reported the recovery of 17,603 oz. of crude in the first three-quarters of 1943. The Canadian nickel output was maintained, and unless there was some difficulty to hold up recovery and refining of the platinum slimes from the nickel refinery, platinum output should keep up as well. However, some decrease in supply, accompanied by increased demand in electronics and the manufacture of fibre glass during the last half of 1943 disturbed the former balance between supply and demand, and platinum was moved to the head of the list of metals short in supply. Steps were taken to improve scrap and inventory control provisions, and unless the situation showed prompt improvement, allocation would be required. In December it was reported that the supply had improved somewhat, but that the position was still uncertain.　　(G. A. RO.)

Plums and Prunes.

The total fresh basis production of plums and prunes in 1943 was estimated by the U.S. department of agriculture to be 682,000 tons in the commercial producing states which was 10% above that of 1942 but 3% below the 10-year (1932–41) average. California produced 68,000 tons of plums compared to 72,000 tons in 1942 and Michigan 3,400 tons against 5,300. The dried prune crop of California, Oregon and Michigan, where most of the crop is growing, was 206,100 tons in 1943 (dry basis) compared with 177,100 tons in 1942 and a 10-year average of 215,320 tons. There was an increase of drying in each state. The tonnage of Oregon and Michigan prunes canned and cold packed increased greatly and was estimated at 47,800 tons or 95% more than in 1942. Of this total about 10,000 tons were cold packed. Smaller quantities were marketed fresh, particularly in Idaho where production for

Table I.—U.S. Production of Prunes in Tons, by States, 1943 and 1942

State	1943 (fresh basis)	1942 (fresh basis)
Western Oregon	94,800	55,000
Eastern Oregon	10,200	15,500
Eastern Washington	12,600	17,200
Western Washington	11,600	7,400
Idaho	3,900	18,200

Table II.—Quantities of Prunes Used Fresh, Canned and Dried,* in Tons

State	1943	1942
Used fresh (fresh basis)		
Oregon	18,400	19,600
Washington	10,800	16,400
Idaho	3,900	18,900
Canned (fresh basis)		
Oregon	38,500	18,700
Washington	9,300	5,800
Dried (dry basis†)		
California	191,000	171,000
Oregon	14,000	6,000
Washington	1,600	100

*Includes quantities sold and used on the farm for household consumption.
†The drying rate in Oregon and Washington ranges from 3 to 4 lb. of fresh fruit to 1 lb. of dried; in California, 2½ lb. fresh fruit to 1 lb. dried.

fresh use was only 3,900 tons in 1943 compared with 18,900 tons in 1942.　　(J. C. MS.)

Pneumonia.

During the early months of 1943 there was a much sharper rise in the death rate from pneumonia than in previous years. This was observed among civilians as well as in army camps. Most of the increase was probably accounted for by the greater number of cases of so-called "primary atypical pneumonias" of unknown aetiology, which were presumably caused by viruses. The case fatality rate in this group remained low, but those who died of this disease were young and middle-aged adults as compared with the older age groups of the fatal cases of the usual bacterial pneumonias.

While complications of these atypical pneumonias continued to be infrequent as compared with those observed in cases of bacterial pneumonia, certain severe complications were encountered. These involved, predominantly, the nervous system and the heart and its linings. Bacterial superinfections, formerly thought not to be a feature of this disease, were also observed quite frequently.

Measles epidemics occurred in the army camps just as they did during World War I. In World War II, however, fatalities were rare, whereas in World War I the mortality from measles was next only to that from influenza. In both of these diseases deaths were due chiefly to the complicating pneumonias. The low fatality rate might well be ascribed to the widespread use of the sulfonamide drugs. They not only cured most of the complicating bacterial pneumonias but probably also cut down the chances of a spread of the virulent bacteria to other susceptibles. Thus the possibility of secondary pneumonias in the cases of measles was markedly reduced.

No specific treatment was found for the primary atypical pneumonias. In the bacterial pneumonias sulfadiazine continued to be the drug of choice. Some new derivatives and closely related compounds of sulfadiazine having similar activity and efficacy were released during the year. The most important of these were sulfamerazine which is a monomethyl derivative of sulfadiazine, and sulfapyrazine which has the closely related pyrazine substitute for the pyrimidine of sulfadiazine. Penicillin proved more effective than the sulfonamides chiefly in infection with the staphylococcus. This organism played an increasingly important role in the aetiology of pneumonias, particularly those secondary to virus diseases and to other serious conditions. Penicillin also proved effective against pneumococci which are resistant to sulfonamide action. The use of this drug remained in the experimental stage.

Laboratory investigators came forth with a number of new viruses which they considered as possible aetiological agents of the primary atypical pneumonias. In every instance, however, the evidence for the causal relationship was not complete. Furthermore, the viruses described by the various observers differed fundamentally from one another. The viruses of pigeons (ornithosis) and of parrots and other exotic birds (psittacosis) proved to be related to the prevalent "virus" pneumonias in only a small minority of the cases (10% to 25% in the experience of different observers).

Of interest was the discovery that most of the cases of primary atypical pneumonia developed a peculiar property in the blood known as "cold agglutinins." Their blood serum causes their own red blood cells, as well as those of other blood groups and of other animals, to clump in the cold and the clumps break up at body temperature. This property is a rare one and was described in a number of other conditions but the only disease with which it was described as occurring with great regularity is trypanosomiasis. In the latter disease a specific parasite is found in the blood and the central nervous system. (*See also* CHEMOTHERAPY.)

(M. FD.)

BIBLIOGRAPHY.—Mary Gover, "Influenza and Pneumonia Mortality in a Group of 90 Cities in the United States, August 1935—March 1943," *Pub. Health Rep.*, 58:1033–1061 (1943); "Recent Increase in Pneumonia Mortality," *Statistical Bull.*, Metropolitan Life Ins. Co., vol. 24, no. 4 (1943); "Health in American Army Camps," *ibid.*, vol. 24, no. 6 (1943); Osler L. Peterson *et al.*, "Cold Agglutinins (Autohemagglutinins) in Primary Atypical Pneumonias," *Science*, 97:167 (1943); John H. Dingle *et al.*, "Primary Atypical Pneumonia, Etiology Unknown," *War Med.*, 3:223–248 (1943); Francis G. Blake *et al.*, "Feline Virus Pneumonia and Its Possible Relation to Some Cases of Primary Atypical Pneumonia in Man," *Yale J. Biol. and Med.* 15:139–166 (1942); Harry M. Rose and Eleanora Malloy, "Observations Concerning the Etiology of Primary Atypical Pneumonia," *Science*, 98:112–114 (1943).

Poetry: *see* AMERICAN LITERATURE; CANADIAN LITERATURE; ENGLISH LITERATURE; FRENCH LITERATURE; LITERARY PRIZES; PUBLISHING (BOOK); RUSSIAN LITERATURE; SPANISH-AMERICAN LITERATURE; SPANISH LITERATURE.

Poland.

A republic in northeastern Europe, invaded by the Germans and partitioned by Germany and the U.S.S.R. in 1939; the whole of Poland was conquered by Germany in 1941 after the outbreak of the German-Russian war. Area (Sept. 1, 1939) *c.* 150,820 sq.mi.; pop. (official est. Jan. 1, 1939, including Teschen) 35,100,000. Capital: Cracow (259,000). Other chief cities: Warsaw (1,289,000); Lodz (672,000), Lwow (318,000); Poznan (272,000); Vilna (209,000). Prime minister: Stanislaw Mikolajczyk (from July 1943).

History.—The year 1943 was marked for Poland by two dramatic events: the rupture of Polish-soviet diplomatic relations and the death of General Wladislaw Sikorski, Polish prime minister and commander-in-chief, in an air crash at Gibraltar on July 4.

On April 25, in Moscow, Vyacheslav Molotov, Russian commissar for foreign affairs, handed to Tadeusz Romer, the Polish ambassador, a note stating that "the soviet government has decided to sever relations with the Polish government." Although the immediate cause for the severing of diplomatic relations was described in Molotov's note as the "entirely abnormal" behaviour of the Polish government in connection with the German "discovery" of a mass grave of Polish officers in the Katyn forest near Smolensk, the crisis had been steadily growing for more than a year, owing to the difficulties encountered in the implementation of the provisions of the 1941 treaty. The prisoners and deportees release of whom had been agreed upon under the treaty were freed, but the Polish authorities claimed to be unable to trace 8,300 officers taken prisoner after Sept. 17, 1939. At the same

time the soviet authorities began to raise the question of the citizenship of the deportees. The final stage in prolonged discussions and correspondence was a soviet note of Jan. 16, 1943, stating that henceforth all the deportees would be considered as soviet citizens.

The crisis created by the dispute over citizenship did not facilitate the organization of the Polish army in Russia, which also had been agreed upon under the 1941 treaty. Seventy-five thousand of the men already recruited had been sent to Iran in two groups, in March and Aug. 1942. In March 1943 a "Union of Polish Patriots" was formed in Moscow under the chairmanship of Mme. Wanda Wasilewska, a Polish communist, who started to publish a weekly called *Wolna Polska* (*Free Poland*) to express "the genuine opinion of the Polish people."

When, on April 12, 1943 the Germans announced their Katyn forest "discovery," the Polish government thought that an investigation by the International Red Cross would deprive them of any political advantages they had hoped to gain by playing up their "discovery"; for on April 15 the Russians had announced that the Polish officers, who had been in a labour camp near Smolensk, had fallen into the hands of the Germans and been put to death. Following the Polish government's request to the International Red Cross at Geneva the U.S.S.R. broke off relations with Poland. A few days later, on May 9, Moscow radio announced that the council of people's commissars had acceded to the request made by the union of Polish patriots to form a Polish division.

Following General Sikorski's death a new Polish government was formed on July 14, 1943, with 12 ministers. The new government was representative of the Polish nation, for the four parties represented in it commanded the vast majority of votes and controlled the underground movement in Poland. The new commander-in-chief of the Polish forces (in Britain, the middle east and the Polish underground army) was General Kazimierz Sosnkowski.

(K. SM.)

In Dec. 1943 the U.S.S.R. and Czechoslovakia formed a defensive alliance, pledging mutual assistance in the event of any further German drive to the east and leaving the way open for the admission to the pact of any third power bordering on either country and representing an object of German aggression. This clause presumably referred to Poland. The Polish government-in-exile, however, professed disinterest unless Russia would agree to guarantee Poland's pre-1939 eastern boundary, which included in Poland the western portions of White Russia and the Ukraine. On Jan. 11, 1944, Russia announced it would annex the whole of these two territories, declaring that the disputed territory would thenceforth be apportioned to the country by whose nationals it was predominantly populated. This, Russia alleged, would set Poland's eastern border approximately at the so-called Curzon line, established after World War I. The soviet government at the same time offered to help Poland make up the loss of territory on the east by assisting her to regain territory on the west, including a corridor to the Baltic sea, and invited Poland to become a party to the Czech-soviet treaty.

(X.)

The Underground Front.—The resistance of the Polish nation to the invader continued to be a total one. The Polish government in London had its own delegate in Poland, working in conjunction with the political representatives of the four main political parties, whose leaders were members of Mikolajczyk's government. A declaration dated Aug. 15, 1943, addressed to the Polish prime minister, which was published in the principal Warsaw underground paper, *Rzeczpospolita Polska* (*Polish Republic*), recommended to the members of the London government "full national solidarity" and collaboration with the Allies.

In a statement issued in London on Nov. 22, 1943, Ignacy

THE TREK OF POLISH REFUGEES from the U.S.S.R. into Iran continued in 1943—the fourth year of their exile

chwarzbart, Jewish member of the Polish national council, re-ealed that the population of the Warsaw ghetto—already re-uced in 1942 from 350,000 to 120,000 by deportations and mass .aughter—was completely liquidated in the spring of 1943. A milar fate befell the Jews in ghettoes in other towns in Poland.

The Struggle Outside Poland.—The Polish minister of defense announced in a report of Aug. 1943 that the Poles had nearly 0,000 fully equipped and trained troops in the middle east, un-er the command of Lt.-General Wladyslaw Anders. They were art of the second army organized by Poles in exile, the rest eing in the British Isles. Polish losses in killed, wounded and risoners since Sept. 1, 1941, had amounted to 903,000. From the ummer of 1940 until the end of Sept. 1943 the Polish fighter quadrons operating from bases in Britain and the middle east not down 605 enemy planes. (K. SM.)

Banking and Finance.—(In thousands of zlotys): revenue est. 1939–40) 2,428,700; expenditure (est. 1939–40) 2,486,500; ublic debt (March 31, 1939) 5,317,800; gold reserve (Aug. 31, 939) 443,000. Bank notes in circulation (Aug. 31, 1939) 1,928,-oo. Exchange rate (Aug. 1939) 1 zloty=18.75 U.S. cents.

Trade and Communication.—Foreign trade (in thousands of lotys): imports, merchandise (1938) 1,299,600; (Jan.-July 1939) 62,300. Exports, merchandise (1938) 1,184,400; (Jan.-July 939) 781,500. Communications: roads (1937) 36,689 mi.; rail-ays, main lines (1937) 11,223 mi.; shipping (July 1, 1939) 63 essels, totalling 121,630 tons gross.

Agriculture, Mineral Production, Manufacturing. — (In hort tons) (1939): wheat, 2,502,200; barley, 1,631,400; rye, ,411,000; oats, 3,174,600; (1938) maize, 139,100; potatoes, 38,-93,500; beet sugar, 426,600; coal, 42,002,000; petroleum, 558,-oo; pig-iron and ferro-alloys, 1,067,000; steel, 1,720,400.

ole Vaulting: *see* TRACK AND FIELD SPORTS.

Police. During 1943 the conditions of police service through-out the world were controlled in large measure by he war. In the occupied countries under axis domination, civil olice were held within the firm administrative grasp of the quasi-ilitary police authorities in Berlin. But as the Allied powers ex-ended their dominion to all of North Africa, to the Italian islands f the Mediterranean, and to the southern half of Italy, the Allied Iilitary Government forces took over Italian police units and laced them under direct military control.

Compulsory military service in many lands was a major factor n diverting trained police into military channels, and many were he official efforts to put an end to this gradual attrition of pro-essional police resources. Nevertheless, as the year ended there vas as yet no slackening in the transfer of men from police to nilitary service, with strong indications that the same tendencies vould continue into 1944 in so far as Germany, Great Britain nd the United States were concerned.

In those Allied and axis-controlled areas which were subject to requent aerial bombardment, police were confronted by par-icularly heavy burdens in clearing debris, assisting in the care of he injured, identification of large numbers of dead, and main-aining free circulation of traffic under extremely adverse condi-ions. Even outside of the bombardment zone, and in belligerent nd neutral countries alike, there was an increasing burden im-osed on police in maintaining surveillance over aliens, and ccelerating the transport of motor convoys of men, equipment nd supplies.

Wherever reductions in the number of trained police, or in-reases in the multiform tasks of law enforcement and military raffic threatened to overwhelm the regular police establishments, ecourse was had to the use of untrained and part-time auxiliaries.

Comprehensive data on these developments are available only for the United States. There an inquiry in cities over 25,000 popula-tion indicated a personnel turnover during the 18 months preced-ing June 30, 1943, that ranged in specific forces from 5.7% to 60.0%. The median was 22.9%. Despite such major shifts in personnel, these cities averaged 1.77 police employees per 1,000 inhabitants, a reduction of only 3.1% in police strength from the preceding year. The conclusion seems inescapable that there had been much police recruiting during 1943, which had undoubtedly been accompanied by a decline in the quality of police personnel.

In addition, auxiliary police had been increased 10% by April 30, 1943, when they outnumbered regular police in a ratio of 2.03 to 1. Most of these were enrolled as air-raid defense workers, though generally available for any type of war emergency situ-ation.

Comparative data on police department employees in more than 400 cities having a combined population in excess of 50,000,-ooo appear in Tables I and II.

Table I.—Numerical Strength of U.S. Municipal Police Forces, 1941-43
(Number per 1,000 inhabitants)

Population Groups of Cities	1941	1942	1943
Group I—Over 250,000	2.12	2.13	2.07
Group II—100,000 to 250,000	1.45	1.50	1.47
Group III—50,000 to 100,000	1.37	1.46	1.40
Group IV—25,000 to 50,000	1.23	1.29	1.24

Table II.—Geographic Distribution of the Numerical Strength of U.S. Municipal Police Forces Arranged by Population Groups
(Number per 1,000 inhabitants)

Geographic Divisions	Group I Over 250,000	Group II 100,000 to 250,000	Group III 50,000 to 100,000	Group IV 25,000 to 50,000	General Ratio
New England	2.80	1.91	1.63	1.47	1.92
Middle Atlantic	2.37	1.69	1.63	1.38	2.15
East North Central	1.90	1.15	1.31	1.08	1.61
West North Central	1.79	1.11	1.00	0.97	1.45
South Atlantic	2.34	1.54	1.38	1.35	1.79
East South Central	1.18	1.21	1.41	1.20	1.43
West South Central	1.28	1.14	1.15	1.09	1.20
Mountain	1.31	1.16	1.58	1.03	1.24
Pacific	1.80	1.55	1.31	1.28	1.65
Totals	2.07	1.47	1.40	1.24	1.77

Among crimes against the person, 81.7% were cleared by arrest of the offender in 1942, while 26.5% of crimes against property were successfully handled in this fashion. Table III shows the recent record in crime clearances.

Table III.—Per Cent of Crimes Cleared by Arrest in U.S. Cities, 1940-42

Offenses	1940	1941	1942
Murder and non-negligent manslaughter	88.7	88.1	90.6
Negligent manslaughter	83.4	86.6	86.1
Rape	79.4	76.2	81.2
Robbery	41.8	40.4	43.3
Aggravated assault	73.7	75.0	80.5
Burglary; breaking or entering	33.1	32.0	31.5
Larceny (theft)	23.4	22.7	25.0
Auto theft	23.8	24.4	24.6

Attention is particularly directed to the generally improved record of clearances in 1942 as compared with the two preceding years. In that year, the ratio of police to population reached an all-time high in the United States.

The annual congress of the International Association of Chiefs of Police was held in Detroit in Aug. 1943. While attendance from the United States and Canada heavily predominated, there were numerous delegates from Central and South America and from the British Isles. The congress set a new high attendance record.

Chief preoccupation of the delegates was with war-connected police activities, particularly in maintaining effective liaison with such national agencies as the Federal Bureau of Investigation (U.S.) and the provost-marshals of the several allied armies. Occupational draft deferments for police and ways and means for giving effect to police priorities in securing essential equipment also attracted much attention as did the detailed discussions of race riots in Detroit and New York city earlier in the year. (*See* also CRIME; FEDERAL BUREAU OF INVESTIGATION; KIDNAPPING; SECRET SERVICE, U.S.)

BIBLIOGRAPHY.—*Uniform Crime Reports* (quarterly) for 1941, (semi-annually) for 1942, and the first half of 1943 (Federal Bureau of Investigation, Washington). *Municipal Year Book, 1943* (International City Managers' Association, Chicago). (BR. S.)

Poliomyelitis: *see* INFANTILE PARALYSIS.
Political Parties, Great Britain: *see* COMMUNISM; CONSERVATIVE PARTY; LABOUR PARTY; LIBERAL PARTY.
Political Parties, U.S.: *see* COMMUNISM; DEMOCRATIC PARTY; REPUBLICAN PARTY; SOCIALISM.

Polo. The United States Polo association, governing body of the game, suspended, following the declaration of war by the United States against Germany, Japan and Italy, all championships and nationally sponsored tournaments; these not to be resumed until the conclusion of hostilities. Polo played in the United States during 1943 was of an informal character and much of it at army posts by men in the armed forces.

Approximately 80% of the handicapped players were in the armed forces and several were reported killed, wounded in action or held as prisoners of war. During 1943 the association lost one of its officers when Lt. Commander Gouverneur Morris Carnochan, secretary and treasurer, was killed while on active duty in an aeroplane somewhere in the South Pacific.

The affairs of the association continued to be administered by F. S. von Stade as acting chairman and by W. Thorn Kissel as acting secretary-treasurer. (R. F. K.)

Population, Movements of: *see* REFUGEES.
Populations of the Countries of the World: *see* AREAS AND POPULATIONS OF THE COUNTRIES OF THE WORLD.
Porto Rico: *see* PUERTO RICO.

Portugal. A republic of western Europe, forming part of the Iberian peninsula and bounded on the N. and E. by Spain and on the S. and W. by the Atlantic ocean. Area (including Azores and Madeira), 35,670 sq.mi.; pop. (census Dec. 12, 1940) 7,702,000. Chief towns: Lisbon (cap. 594,300), Oporto (232,280). President: Gen. Antonio Carmona; premier in 1943: Dr. Oliveira Salazar; language: Portuguese; religion: Christian (mainly Roman Catholic).

History.—While maintaining the best of relations with the two belligerents to whom, in the words of Dr. Salazar (April 27, 1943), she was "bound by close ties of political comradeship or deep affection"—Brazil and Britain—Portugal continued to observe strict neutrality in World War II and strengthened her bonds with Spain. On Feb. 22, 1943, a new trade agreement was signed with Spain under which each country was to send the other nearly double the previous year's amount of supplies and five times the annual average amount before the Spanish Civil War. Among other international events were the inauguration of a direct telegraphic service with Argentina in March and the sending of a military, naval and air mission to the United States in April.

On Oct. 12 it was announced, in Lisbon and in London, that at the request of the British government the Portuguese government had agreed to grant Britain temporary facilities in the Azores which would provide increased protection for merchant shipping in the Atlantic, the arrangements made to include British assistance in furnishing essential material and supplies to the Portuguese armed forces and the maintenance of the Portuguese national economy. All British forces would be withdrawn from the Azores at the end of hostilities.

On April 13 was passed an important law concerning the nationalization of capital. All new public utility companies were required to be Portuguese-controlled, with a Portuguese board of directors, and 60% of the capital had to be Portuguese.

Daily life in Portugal was still difficult in 1943. Cotton shortage threatened to throw 60,000 persons out of work. Port wine exports in two years had fallen from 32,000,000 litres to 6,500,000. Meat was scarce; bread, milk and tobacco supplies were further limited; olive oil, soap and charcoal were rationed; wheat, maize, millet and potato crops were the smallest in 10 years. Smuggling and profiteering reached grave proportions. Food prices had risen by as much as 100% since 1940 and wages had increased but little. In July these conditions led to industrial disturbances which had to be severely dealt with, while the government frankly warned the country that the drought of the early summer, the worst for over a century (which also destroyed thousands of acres of forest), would mean more and more restriction as the year went on. To help provide for the future, Portugal purchased 54,000 tons of German shipping lying in ports in Angola and Mozambique and 6,000 tons from Costa Rica.

Though the country's credit balance was rather lower than in the previous year, owing largely to heavy expenditure on armaments, the financial position as a whole was considered better. The war profits tax gave twice its expected yield and a new government loan of £10,000,000 at 2¾%, announced in May, was well taken up.

Social measures included (Feb. 20, 1943) the extension of family allowances (Aug. 13, 1942) to civil servants; the establishment of a plan for the building of new primary schools, the cost to be equally divided between state and local authorities; and an extension of the scheme established 10 years previously for the construction of state-subsidized dwellings.

A new ambassador in London, the duke of Palmella, succeeded Dr. Armindo Monteiro in 1943. (E. A. P.)

Education.—Elementary (1938–39) schools 7,962; scholars 462,854; secondary schools 42; scholars 18,242; universities 3; students 5,182.

Banking and Finance.—Revenue, ordinary (est. 1942) 2,132,900,000 escudos; expenditure, ordinary (est. 1942) 2,126,600,000 escudos; public debt (Dec. 31, 1940) 6,489,700,000 escudos; notes in circulation (April 30, 1943) 5,434,000,000 escudos; gold reserve (April 30, 1943) 1,394,000,000 escudos; exchange rate (average 1941) 1 escudo = 4.002 cents U.S.

Trade and Communication.—External trade 1942 (merchandise): imports 2,413,200,000 escudos; exports 3,859,200,000 escudos. Communications and transport (Dec. 31, 1937): roads first and second class 8,858 mi.; railways, open to traffic, 2,187 mi.; motor vehicles licensed (Dec. 31, 1937): cars 34,442; commercial 11,410; cycles 4,536; shipping (June 30, 1939) 269,000 gross tons.

Agriculture and Other Production.—Production 1940 (in metric tons): wheat 285,100; maize 367,900; wine 5,187,000 hectolitres; coal 310,000; rye 76,100; oats 25,000; rice (1939) 71,600; barley 26,200; potatoes 616,700; olive oil 34,500; sea fisheries (excluding cod-fishing) 195,000. (*See* also PORTUGUESE COLONIAL EMPIRE.)

Portuguese Colonial Empire. Total area (approx.) 839,506 sq.mi.; total population (est. Dec. 31, 1939) 9,930,000, excluding Portugal.

Country & Area sq.mi. (approx.)	Population est. Dec. 31, 1939 (000's omitted)	Capital, Status, Governors, Premiers, etc.	Principal Products (in metric tons)	Imports & Exports 1940 (in thousand escudos)	Road, Rail & Shipping 1939	Revenue and Expenditure est. 1942 (in thousand escudos)
AFRICA Angola (Portuguese West Africa) 481,351	3,500	Luanda, colony, *governor-general:* Vasco Lopes Alves.	maize (1938–39) 316,800 cane sugar (1940–41) 40,600	(1941) imp. 223,205 exp. 434,011	rds. 22,708 mi. rly. 2,080 mi. shpg. (1936) entered, 5,330,087 tons	rev. and exp. 262,525
Cape Verde Is. 1,546	170	Praia, colony, *governor:* Joao Figueiredo.	(export 1937) salt 29,843 preserved fish 325 coffee (E. 1939) 137,-000 kg.	imp. 110,981 exp. 156,279	rds. 493 mi. shpg. (1939) cleared, 3,127,315 tons	rev. and exp. 19,021
Portuguese Guinea 13,946	420	Bissau, colony, *governor:* Luiz António de Carvalho Viegas.	(export 1940) ground-nuts 29,300; palm kernel oil, 2,800	imp. 27,864 exp. 49,407	rds. 1,863 mi. shpg. (1940) cleared, 70,482 tons	rev. and exp. 35,545
São Tomé and Principe Isl. 386	60	S. Tomé, colony, *governor:* Amadeu Gomes de Figueiredo.	cacao, coffee, coco-nut	imp. 21,327 exp. 43,030	rds. 179 mi. rly. 10 mi. shpg. cleared, 339,638 tons	rev. and exp. 11,580
Mozambique (Portuguese East Africa) 297,729	4,500	Lourenço-Marques, colony, *governor-general:* General Tristão de Bettencourt	cane sugar (1936–37) 115,100; ground-nuts (export 1940) 18,600	imp. 431,891 exp. 171,126	rds. 17,504 mi. rly. 1,128 mi. shpg. (Beira) cleared, 2,377,713 tons	rev. and exp. 488,214
ASIA Portuguese India 1,538	600	Nova Gôa, colony, *governor-general:* José Cabral.	fish, spices, salt	imp. 104,933 exp. 1,646	rds. 730 mi.; rly. 51 mi.; shpg. (1938) cleared 1,729,866 tons	rev. and exp. 46,488
Macao 8	200	Macao, colony, *governor:* Gabriel Mauricio Teixeira.	fish, cement, preserves	(1936) imp. 108,158 exp. 62,818	shpg. (1938) cleared, 3,117,571 tons	rev. and exp. 46,799
Timor 7,332	480	Dilly, colony, *governor:* Manuel de Abreu Teixeira de Carvalho.	coffee, sandalwood, wax	imp. 3,880 exp. 4,154	rds. 677 mi. shpg. cleared, 91,215 tons	rev. and exp. 9,230

he Azores and Madeira. Certain essential statistics of the colonial possessions of Portugal are given in the accompanying table.

History.—At the beginning of 1943 Dr. Vieira Machado, minster for the colonies, returned to Lisbon from a seven months' our in Angola, Mozambique and the Belgian Congo. On his return he took part in an empire week, observed throughout Portugal, to inculcate a realization of the country's imperial responsibilities, which had a special significance as being the first such observance since the unification of the empire in July 1942. On the anniversary of the Portuguese revolution (May 28) occasion was taken to pay homage to the 160 heroes of the campaigns of occupation who were still living. At the Praça do Império, the group was publicly received, and, after an address by the cardinal-patriarch of Lisbon, decorations were conferred on representative members.

As a first step towards the economic valorization of the entire colonial empire there was created in Angola a council of technical and economic co-ordination.

For the agreement of Oct. 12 by which Portugal granted Britain facilities in the Azores, *see* PORTUGAL. (E. A. P.)

Portuguese East Africa: *see* PORTUGUESE COLONIAL EMPIRE.
Portuguese Guinea: *see* PORTUGUESE COLONIAL EMPIRE.
Portuguese West Africa: *see* PORTUGUESE COLONIAL EMPIRE.

Post Office.
The audited revenues of the post office department for the fiscal year 1943, as stated in the records of the comptroller general of the United States, amounted to $966,227,288.51. This was the highest in postal history and $106,409,797.63 higher than in 1942, which was the next highest.

There were also reported to the treasury department the items stated in the act of June 9, 1930, indicating the estimated postage that would have been collected if the services had been on a regular pay basis, in the case of penalty and franked mail, free-in-county mail, differentials in second-class mail matter and free matter for the blind. These amounted to $122,343,916.00.

The expenses of the department for the fiscal year as audited amounted to $952,535,379.06, of which amount $20,347,154.72 was on account of prior years. There was $32,704,513.28 to be paid on account of the 1943 fiscal year. This left a total expense for the fiscal year 1943 of $964,892,737.62, resulting in a gross operating surplus on an accrual basis of $1,334,550.89.

Effective March 27, 1942, free mail privileges were granted to members of the armed forces. It was estimated that 2,121,-974,400 pieces of first-class mail were being mailed annually by U.S. soldiers and sailors. The revenue which would have been derived from this mail at the rate of 3 cents apiece would have amounted to $63,659,232.

The tremendous increase in the volume of mail handled by the post office department for other branches of the government had been a matter of concern to congress and the department for a number of years. Thousands of tons of forms, pamphlets, circulars and supplies were being sent by government departments and establishments free of postage under the "penalty privilege." Congress enacted laws prohibiting, with certain exceptions, the sending free of postage of books, reports and bulletins without a request therefor. The records disclosed that during the fiscal year 1943 there were mailed free 1,956,073,568 pieces, weighing 295,711,589 lb., an increase of 440,058,124 pieces and 59,182,574 lb. over the previous year.

The intensive bond and stamp sales program, inaugurated May 1, 1941 in co-operation with the treasury department, was greatly expanded after U.S. entry into the war. On June 30, 1943, war savings stamps were on sale at 43,680 post offices. Sales from July 1, 1942, to June 30, 1943, amounted to $537,861,246.80.

From March 1, 1935, when the United States savings bonds were placed on sale at post offices, to June 30, 1942, there were sold through the postal service 35,128,618 bonds, having a sale value of $4,309,937,575. During the fiscal year ended June 30, 1943, 41,042,540 bonds, having a sale value of $1,495,509,025 were sold. At the close of the year bonds were on sale at 21,340 post offices, including 1,200 branches and stations, a net increase of 1,384 over the preceding year.

Through its 42,680 post offices and 4,087 stations being conducted under contract agreement, as well as 1,878 classified

AS PART OF THE 25TH ANNIVERSARY CELEBRATION of regular U.S. air-mail service, this army helicopter hovered in front of the capitol at Washington, D.C., May 15, 1943

stations and branches, there were received, transported and delivered more than 33,000,000,000 pieces of mail matter during the fiscal year, having a weight of more than 3,500,000 tons, representing an increase over the previous fiscal year of more than 3,000,000,000 pieces of mail and more than 300,000 tons.

On June 30, 1943, there were 4,087 stations being conducted under contract agreement. The average cost per contract unit was $478, and the total cost of operation during the fiscal year amounted to $1,928,902, whereas the receipts from the sale of stamps at these contract stations amounted to $40,675,779 during the calendar year 1942.

During the fiscal year, city delivery service was established in 61 additional cities, thereby increasing to 3,408 the number of cities in which this service was in operation. It was extended to 14,645 blocks of territory serving 412,307 families and 7,254 new places of business.

Postmasters.—During the fiscal year there were 3,322 postmasters confirmed by the senate and appointed without term by the president. There were 2,178 presidential postmasters reappointed upon the expiration of their commissions and 400 reappointed due to advancement of their offices from the fourth class to the presidential grade, which necessitated new appointments. Of the postmasters appointed, 2,322 were due to the expiration of four-year terms, 496 to advancement of offices from the fourth class to the presidential grade, 164 to resignations, 118 to deaths, 73 to removals, 74 to retirement, 73 to transfers to other classified positions, 2 to failure of postmaster to qualify after appointment. Fourth-class postmasters were commissioned to 2,310 offices during the year as vacancies occurred through various causes.

Dead Letters.—During 1943 15,437,258 letters were impossible of delivery, an increase of more than 2.9% over the previous year. This increase reflected to some extent the increased volume of mail handled but was due more to the large number of incorrectly addressed letters for the military and naval forces and for civilians who moved incident to changes in location due to war work. A total of 2,968,510 letters was returned to the senders, of which 279,176 were found to contain valuable enclosures and 49,007 of them contained money, amounting to $115,322. A total of 12,371,296 letters was destroyed as undeliverable. Money found loose in the mails amounted to $36,943. There were also 531,484 unclaimed parcels and articles found loose in the mails. These parcels were sold at public auction and $110,292 realized.

Air Mail.—On June 30, 1943, there were 45,304 mi. of domestic air mail routes, an increase of 681 mi. over June 30, 1942. During the year two new domestic air mail routes were established.

The air mail service, established as one of the most vital postal services, owing to the need it fills in connection with the wartime demand for speed, handled a volume of mail approximating an 80% increase in pound-miles over the preceding year with about one-half the number of aircraft, a large number of the commercial transport planes having been withdrawn for transfer to the military service.

There was a large increase in the volume of mail carried by foreign air mail routes during 1943 which operated with a high percentage of performance. This was particularly true of the important air mail service to South America which was maintained to both the east and west coasts on daily schedules. At the close of the fiscal year the length of certified foreign air mail routes was 54,530 mi.

Rural Delivery.—The rural delivery routes in operation on June 30, 1943, required a total daily travel of 1,425,860 mi. by rural carriers in providing service to approximately 29,319,347 patrons. The policy of consolidation of rural routes to absorb vacancies was continued. Operation of the rural delivery service resulted in an expenditure of $91,812,942 for the fiscal year as compared with $91,634,811 for the previous year, an increase of but $178,131 over 1942. The amounts saved through consolidation of routes were utilized to establish new routes and provide extension of existing routes. Thereby 4,889 more miles were covered by rural carriers at the close of the fiscal year 1943 than in 1942. Rural delivery service was transferred from the jurisdiction of the second assistant postmaster general to the first assistant postmaster general on July 1, 1942, to co-ordinate it better with other delivery services.

Postal Savings.—The postal savings system continued to merit a widespread public demand for its services; the depositors numbered 3,064,054 for 1943, an increase of 8.93% from the preceding year. The balance due depositors represented by outstanding certificates of deposit was $1,577,409,942, an increase of $261,999,540, or about 19.96%. In addition, there was held in trust for depositors accrued interest of $45,004,355.96, and unclaimed deposits of $115,668, making a total of $1,622,529,965.96.

t the end of the year, postal savings certificates were on sale 8,060 depositories, including 861 branches and stations; but vings stamps were on sale at all post offices and practically l branches and stations.

Buildings.—During the fiscal year ended June 30, 1943, the st office department operated 3,258 government-owned build-gs. Owing to the war and the cessation of the public-building rogram, no new buildings were completed during the fiscal year. hrough reassignments of space within these buildings, agencies the government which were or had intended occupying com-ercial quarters were accommodated, with a saving of $94,743.64. ecause of the war, the public building program was suspended. xpiring leases numbering 869 were renewed in 1943. Where ecessary to meet increased service needs, larger quarters and perior facilities were obtained, and in other cases necessary im-rovements were secured in the occupied quarters. The square ot cost of renewing leases was increased from 73.8 cents in 942 to 74.6 cents in 1943. Fifty-five new leases were made, in-uding 35 for offices previously occupying space on a monthly ental basis, the new contracts providing improved quarters and many instances complete new equipment.   (I. Gg.)

Great Britain.—The 1943–44 budget estimate of expenditure, 110,632,000, was £8,100,000 above the 1942–43 figure; but as dditional war expenditure was being met from vote of credit omparisons were difficult. The revenue estimate, £111,032,000, xcluded the value of telegraph and telephone services for gov-rnment departments, estimated at £17,000,000, for which cash ayments ceased on March 31, 1943: this change was to save an-power. Allowing for this, the estimate showed an increase of 5,500,000 over that for 1942–43 (£13,000,000 above actual re-eipts). These sums excluded wireless licence revenue, which was ccounted for separately, but included war surcharges which were ncreased in the 1943–44 budget. Commercial accounts were sus-ended to save work.

There was remarkable progress in every branch of savings. By ec. 31, 1942, balances in the post office savings bank had eached a total of £1,005,431,000; investments standing at the redit of holders on the post office register £656,332,000 and Na-ional Savings certificates £966,857,000 (excluding interest).

In order to release labour for vital war work, postal deliveries nd collections were further curtailed and the business reply ervice was suspended. Overseas surface mails were steadily main-ained in spite of attacks on shipping.

The excessive use of the airgraph and air-letter services indi-ated that these speedy means of communicating with the armed orces and merchant navy personnel overseas were greatly ap-reciated.

Notwithstanding further dilution of operative and engineering taff the telephone and telegraph organizations successfully met he expanding needs of the fighting and defense services and war ndustry. Some restriction was unavoidable. The community was rged to be sparing in the use of both services and the popular reetings telegram facility had to be withdrawn.

The volume of postal traffic remained below the prewar level, nainly by the reduction in circular advertising, but wartime work t public counters combined with pressure in the telegraph and elephone services required additional staff, and in July 1943 the otal had reached 294,000. Of the prewar total (283,000) about 1,000 (including 2,500 women) had joined the forces and 5,000 vere on loan to other government departments. Temporary sub-titutes being mostly women, the number of women rose to 129,-00. (*See also* PHILATELY.)   (S. R. C.)

Postwar Planning.

Immediately after Pearl Harbor, and during the year 1942, planning for the peace in the United States had been distinctly unpopular. But as the flood of nazi advances in the U.S.S.R. and Africa was first stopped, and then turned back, and as the hope of an Allied vic-tory developed into a certainty, the popularity and practice of postwar planning rapidly increased. By the summer of 1943 the Office of Public Opinion Research reported that 60% of the American people favoured planning for the peace, even before victory was won; and the Twentieth Century fund listed 28 gov-ernmental and 109 private planning agencies operating on a national basis—not counting a multitude of regional and local bodies and individual commercial concerns. Their fields of inter-est included international and regional problems, business and finance, economic and social questions, education, agriculture, labour and law.

The amount of planning for the postwar period under way in 1943 far exceeded that which was carried on during World War I. In the previous war the planning that was done lacked any single objective. In 1943 a "full-employment" economy when the war was over was accepted by widely diverse interests as their basic aim.

The two outstanding 1943 events in the field of international governmental postwar planning were the food conference held in Hot Springs, Va., from May 18 through June 3 and the formation in November of the United Nations Relief and Rehabilitation administration (*q.v.*). The first conference of the UNRRA dele-gates, representing 44 nations, was held at Atlantic City toward the end of 1943, and a program of joint operations on a global scale was worked out.

In sharp contrast to the nation-wide interest of Americans in postwar planning during 1943 was the action of congress which wrecked the National Resources Planning board by cutting off its funds beginning July 1, 1943.

The senate, however, recognized the importance of postwar problems by setting up in March 1943 a special committee on postwar economic policy and planning, under the chairmanship of Senator Walter F. George of Georgia. Before the end of the year the committee had published two brief reports summarizing the activities of public and private agencies in the field and the prob-lems with which they were dealing.

U.S. postwar planning agencies active in 1943 could be classi-fied in three main groups: (1) government, including federal, state and city bodies; (2) private nonprofit organizations; and (3) business concerns and trade associations.

In the field of government planning the most important event in 1943 was the appointment of Bernard M. Baruch early in No-vember as adviser on postwar adjustment to the war mobilization director. Baruch was instrumental in the formation of a Joint Contract Termination board which at the end of the year had worked out a uniform and consistent policy to be followed by government agencies in the termination of contracts. The dis-posal of surplus stocks and government-owned plants were among other postwar problems being studied by Baruch. The postwar planning activities of other government agencies in 1943 were, briefly, as follows:

The bureau of labour statistics studied postwar employment opportunities, the problems met after World War I in returning to a peacetime economy, the machinery and consequences of the coming demobilization and the probable postwar output of leading industries in relation to employment. The department of com-merce carried forward an analysis of the possible expansion in the postwar period of markets for goods and services if the coun-try achieves maximum employment, studied the problems of transforming war production into high-level peacetime output, and through its 13 regional branches, made special regional stud-ies of postwar employment and profit opportunities.

The department of agriculture was engaged in building complete "atlases" of agricultural information covering nine regions; estimating food requirements and possible output after the war and the general economic conditions under which agriculture would operate; formulating long-run goals for agriculture and postwar plans for the conservation and development of U.S. natural resources; planning adequate health and medical service for farm families, and studying the postwar interrelation of agriculture and industry.

The Public Roads administration developed plans with state highway departments for reconditioning and expansion of the nation's roads; the Maritime commission studied the problems and resources of American shipping after the war; the Rural Electrification administration worked on plans for postwar expansion of electric service and equipment; the National Housing agency made estimates of housing demands and resources after the war; the division of special research of the state department studied problems of postwar international economic and political reconstruction; the divisions of research and statistics of the treasury and of the Federal Reserve board worked intensively on problems of postwar finance; and the Social Security board submitted a report to congress recommending a social security program providing a bulwark against all major risks to those who work for a living.

State and municipal governments were also active in postwar planning during 1943. All the states set up planning commissions and most of the larger cities developed programs for action after the war. In the case of cities this work was largely the formulation of plans and specifications for public works. (*See* Town and Regional Planning.)

Among the private postwar planning activities of 1943 the following were especially significant:

The Committee for Economic Development (*q.v.*), a nonprofit educational institution run by and for business under the chairmanship of Paul G. Hoffman, president of the Studebaker corporation, was organized "to maximize the productive employment to be provided by business in this country" through the stimulation of postwar planning by individual companies, and through research on some of the central economic problems of the postwar period. The chamber of commerce of the United States and the National Association of Manufacturers were also active in postwar planning in 1943—the chamber through its economic policy committee and the association through its postwar problems committee—studying problems and publishing reports of their findings. On the side of labour both the American Federation of Labor and the Congress of Industrial Organizations recognized the need for postwar planning by appointing special committees to study problems of the peace.

In the commercial field most of the large companies set up special planning committees among their executives to study postwar reconversion plans, market possibilities, the development of new products and materials, etc. Many trade associations also began systematic planning activities covering their own industries.

The National Planning association and the Brookings institution were devoted to research on a wide range of postwar problems, while the Commission to Study the Organization of Peace and the Twentieth Century fund were active in the field of public education. The latter two co-operated with the National Broadcasting company in a series of coast-to-coast radio programs on postwar problems entitled "For This We Fight." Most of the leading national membership organizations—the Y.'s, the General Federation of Women's Clubs, Rotary, etc.—carried on extensive educational work on postwar issues with their members.

In addition to the work of planning itself, several agencies—including the committee on postwar economic policy and planning of the senate, the National Planning association, the Twentieth

Century fund, and the United Nations Information office—studied, catalogued and classified the organizations which were doing the planning. Also libraries, including the Library of Congress and the Woodrow Wilson library, made extensive collection of postwar planning materials and functioned as central information centres. (*See* also United States.)   (E. Ck.)

Potash. During World War I, consumers of potash in the United States were forced on short rations, because at that time the bulk of the supply came from Germany. Thereafter, the United States developed a domestic potash industry that put the country on a basis of self-sufficiency. After 1939, exports exceeded imports. A report prepared by the industry in 1942 estimated the probable domestic demand for the year at 577,000 short tons of contained K_2O, as against a plant capacity of 620,000 tons; as a matter of fact, production for 1942 turned out to be 679,206 tons of contained K_2O; this figure was 10% greater than the estimated plant capacity, 29% greater than the 1941 output, and 118% greater than the 1939 output.

No information was received from any of the European centres of production which normally account for almost all the world output outside of the United States. Germany nominally controlled not only the German sources, but also those of France and Poland, but it was likely that shortages of labour, materials and shipping facilities seriously handicapped operations. Nothing was known of conditions in Russia and Spain after the beginning of the war in 1939, except that the Spanish industry, which was closed by the civil war, was reopened on a small scale in 1940. (*See* also Fertilizers.)   (G. A. Ro.)

Potatoes. A record production of potatoes was harvested in 1943 because of increased acreage and yields. The acreage was increased 24%, to a total of 3,363,000 ac., as estimated by the U.S. department of agriculture, compared with 2,711,000 in 1942 and an average of 3,131,000 in the period 1932–41. The crop was estimated to be 469,092,000 bu., compared with 371,150,000 bu. in 1942 and the 10-yr. average of 363,332,000 in 1932–41. The yield was 139.5 bu. per acre in 1943, compared with 136.9 in 1942 and an average of 116.9 in 1932–41. Harvesting was completed in most areas before frost damage, except in Idaho where the late planted crop was damaged by an October freeze and about 5% of the crop was damaged so as to be a loss. As a whole the losses from frost were not serious except in a few localities.

Table I.—U.S. Production of Potatoes by States, 1943 and 1942

State	1943 bu.	1942 bu.	State	1943 bu.	1942 bu.
18 surplus late potato states			Vermont	1,825,000	1,473,000
			New Hampshire	1,472,000	1,088,000
Maine	73,485,000	42,660,000	Arizona	1,170,000	562,000
Idaho	43,470,000	30,590,000	Rhode Island	1,085,000	975,000
New York	29,678,000	27,676,000	New Mexico	480,000	340,000
Minnesota	23,571,000	18,050,000	*7 intermediate potato states*		
Michigan	22,305,000	16,562,000			
North Dakota	22,100,000	17,955,000	New Jersey	11,431,000	10,136,000
Colorado	18,705,000	17,020,000	Virginia	9,594,000	7,242,000
Pennsylvania	18,656,000	17,584,000	Kentucky	4,664,000	4,173,000
Wisconsin	16,368,000	10,050,000	Missouri	3,827,000	4,560,000
Washington	13,200,000	7,800,000	Kansas	2,970,000	2,700,000
Nebraska	12,090,000	12,876,000	Maryland	1,980,000	2,019,000
California	11,480,000	10,880,000	Delaware	308,000	335,000
Oregon	10,335,000	6,825,000	*12 early potato states*		
South Dakota	3,680,000	2,816,000			
Utah	3,430,000	2,312,000	California	16,450,000	12,250,000
Montana	2,645,000	1,725,000	North Carolina	12,099,000	9,434,000
Wyoming	2,175,000	2,240,000	Texas	6,450,000	4,675,000
Nevada	680,000	483,000	Alabama	5,264,000	3,996,000
12 other late potato states			Arkansas	4,661,000	3,619,000
			Tennessee	4,380,000	3,564,000
Ohio	8,550,000	9,180,000	Florida	3,703,000	4,116,000
Iowa	5,238,000	6,600,000	Louisiana	3,599,000	2,520,000
Indiana	4,100,000	6,480,000	South Carolina	3,193,000	3,108,000
Massachusetts	3,375,000	2,945,000	Oklahoma	2,501,000	2,244,000
Connecticut	3,190,000	3,016,000	Georgia	2,135,000	1,782,000
West Virginia	2,775,000	3,808,000	Mississippi	1,904,000	1,917,000
Illinois	2,170,000	3,528,000			

Table II.—*U.S. Sweet Potato Production by Leading States, 1943 and 1942*

State	1943 bu.	1942 bu.	State	1943 bu.	1942 bu.
Georgia	9,375,000	8,000,000	Virginia	2,976,000	3,875,000
Louisiana	8,856,000	5,808,000	Kentucky	1,826,000	1,656,000
North Carolina	7,760,000	8,855,000	Arkansas	1,620,000	1,700,000
Alabama	7,680,000	6,006,000	Florida	1,608,000	1,190,000
Mississippi	6,970,000	6,460,000	California	1,500,000	1,250,000
South Carolina	6,960,000	5,890,000	New Jersey	1,440,000	2,720,000
Texas	5,616,000	3,825,000	Maryland	960,000	1,440,000
Tennessee	4,752,000	3,600,000			

The demand for potatoes for civilian consumption increased. The government's requirements for military and lend-lease purposes were larger than in the previous year. More seed potatoes were set aside for an increased acreage in 1944. All these demands absorbed the supply except in some localities where storage facilities were inadequate to handle the larger crop. Special efforts were made to induce consumers to buy in quantity and store in private cellars. The government's price-support program resulted in heavy purchases which were mostly diverted to canners, starch manufacturers and dehydrators and for relief purposes. Because of storage and transportation difficulties prices were somewhat below ceilings in some localities. Demand for potatoes was expected to continue to increase and a larger crop was recommended by the War Food administration for 1944.

Sweet Potatoes.—A crop of sweet potatoes of 75,801,000 bu. was estimated by the U.S. department of agriculture for 1943, compared with 65,380,000 bu. in 1942, an increase of 16%, and a 10-yr. average of 69,291,000 bu., an increase of 9%. Only once, in 1935, has production exceeded this amount, when 81,249,000 bu. were grown. The yield per acre in 1943 was below the average because of hot, dry weather in August throughout the principal growing areas. Civilian consumption was about as usual—near the average of 23 lb. per capita. Growers were assured minimum prices for the 1943 crop by the government, with loans on potatoes stored in approved warehouses. (J. C. Ms.)

Poultry. At the beginning of 1943 the principal poultry numbers on farms—chickens and turkeys—were estimated by the U.S. department of agriculture to be: chickens, 440,107,000 head; turkeys, 6,549,000 head.

The number of chickens represented a new high record total, 5% above a year earlier and 28% above the 10-yr. average 1932-41. High egg prices compared with feed prices had encouraged growers to increase their flocks in 1942, particularly for eggs for drying. Egg production was far ahead of any previous year—a total of about 5,000,000,000 dozen, about 12% more than in 1942 and 45% above the average. The number of laying hens were at record levels in all parts of the country. During the last half of the year a heavy culling of flocks was begun which not only improved the average of the flocks and saved feed but also added to the supplies of poultry meat on the markets.

Because of the heavy consumption of poultry near the sources of supply the increase in marketing did not show in the larger city markets. Because of this culling and good feeding the rate of production per laying hen was near the record of 1942 in spite of a decline in quantity and quality of feed. The average was 110 eggs per hen compared with 111 in 1942 and a 10-yr. average of 100 eggs.

An important factor in the improvement of poultry was the National Poultry Improvement plan under the U.S. department of agriculture, which operated to improve greatly the average quality of the chicks raised. Hatcheries and flock owners had to attain certain minimum standards of breeding, disease control and management, to participate in the plan. In 1942-43 there were 69,569 flocks in this plan, covering an egg capacity for hatching 147,048,000, which is equivalent to about 30% of the total capacity of hatcheries in the U.S. Another improvement program, called the Victory Cockerel program, was started in 1943 to improve the male birds in hatchery flocks. It was reported to have reached over 18% of the hatcheries participating in the national plan.

Turkey production was restricted by a shortage of eggs for hatching in the spring and the number raised was about the same as in 1942 and short of the goal of 560,000,000 lb. dressed weight. The crop of 1943 was estimated to be only 480,000,000 lb., or 85% of the goal. While turkey production was above the pre-war average, it was much below the demand because of the requirements for the military.

Prices of poultry and eggs were higher than in 1942 and both products sold at or near ceiling prices throughout the year. The production of dried eggs increased about 20% in 1943 over 1942 and was six times as large as in 1941. This use absorbed about 16% of the U.S. production of shell eggs. About 800,000,000 dozen eggs were dried in 1943. (*See* also Eggs.) (J. C. Ms.)

Pound, Sir (Alfred) Dudley (Pickman Rogers)

(1877-1943), British first sea lord, was born Aug. 29 and was educated at Fonthill, East Grinstead, and at The Limes, Greenwich. He was in command of H.M.S. "Colossus" at the Battle of Jutland May 31, 1916, and was mentioned in dispatches for his part in the engagement. From 1922 to 1925 he was director of the admiralty's plans division, and from 1925 to 1927 chief of staff to Admiral Sir Roger Keyes, then commander-in-chief of the Mediterranean fleet. After two years as assistant chief of the naval staff (1927-29) and two years as rear admiral in command of a battle cruiser squadron (1929-31), he was appointed in 1932 as second sea lord and chief of naval personnel at the admiralty. He was advanced to admiral in 1935 and the next year he was named commander-in-chief of the Mediterranean fleet. On May 17, 1939, he was appointed first sea lord and chief of the British naval staff to succeed Admiral Sir Roger Backhouse.

During World War II, he attended all the principal conferences between Prime Minister Churchill and President Roosevelt and participated in the United Nations staff talks. Shortly after his return from the Quebec conference in the summer of 1943, he took ill and on Oct. 4 resigned his naval post. He died in London, Oct. 21.

Presbyterian Church.

The Reformed churches holding the Presbyterian system, within the United States of America, were 12 in number in 1943, and included 18,034 ministers, 18,183 churches, and 3,748,350 communicant members, with approximately 7,500,000 adherents. Outside of continental United States they had, in 1942, 2,148 American foreign missionaries and 13,958 national workers in 21 countries, with a communicant membership of 240,528.

During the year the churches of the Presbyterian family intensified their individual and co-operative work demanded by war conditions. By Dec. 31, 1943, 996 of their ordained ministers were in service as chaplains with the armed forces after approval by the General Commission on Army and Navy Chaplains, of which the churches were members. Unitedly and individually the churches provided material and spiritual help to the chaplains. Through the general commission and other interdenominational agencies, they sent high churchmen on visits to the army chaplains in the various service commands in the United States, and on the invitation of President Roosevelt sent the chairman of the general commission, Dr. William Barrow Pugh, a Presbyterian clergyman, to visit the chaplains on a three months' tour of the theatres of war operations in Europe, Africa, Asia and South

America. Several million dollars in special funds were contributed for spiritual work among soldiers and sailors and in war industry communities, for relief in China, for support of foreign missions cut off from their normal European church income, and for the aid of churches in occupied lands of Europe.

In the oecumenical field, a proposal was being considered for organic union between the Evangelical and Reformed Church and the Congregational-Christian Churches. Further progress was made in negotiations for union between the Presbyterian Church in the United States of America and the Presbyterian Church in the United States (Southern), and between the former church and the Protestant Episcopal Church. Through all of 1943 the churches celebrated, in numerous meetings, the tercentenary of the convening in July 1643, of the Westminster assembly of divines, which formulated the doctrinal standards still being used by Presbyterian churches throughout the world.

Europe.—The national synod of the Reformed Church of France was able to hold its first meeting as a single body since 1939. In session at Paris May 18–20, 1943, the synod sent a formal appeal to the church members for faithful endurance, in a land of "measureless suffering." General enthusiasm greeted the publication earlier in the year of a proposed plan of church reconstruction which included a suggestion for the ordination of a lay clergy. A shortage of ministers was hindering the work in France as in other occupied countries because of forced labour, of internment and of imprisonment, affecting the clergy and theological students. The church continued its aid to refugees in France.

In Hungary, 25 Reformed Church and Lutheran Church leaders, meeting at Budapest June 25, formed the Hungarian Oecumenical council. Its purpose was to intensify the co-operation between the two churches and to establish closer relations with churches of other lands through the World Council of Churches. In Rumanian Transylvania, the situation of the Hungarian Reformed Church was extremely difficult. Handicapped by the prevalent shortage of pastors, the churches were permitted to carry on none of their work except in church buildings, and then only with police present. Despite the losses to the ministry, aggravated by deportation of many theological students to Germany, the Reformed churches of the Netherlands were alert and active. A strengthening of the parishes in preparation for the difficult post-war task of the church was proceeding vigorously. In Belgium also the Reformed Church continued its work, though under the handicap of German occupation. (W. B. Pu.)

Presidents, Sovereigns and Rulers.

The following list includes the names of those holding chief positions in their countries at the beginning of 1944.

Country	Name and Office	Accession
Afghanistan	Muhammad Zahir, Shah	1933
Albania	Zog I, King (German Regency)	1928
Arabia, Saudi	Abd-ul-Aziz ibn Sa'ud, King	1926
Argentina	Gen. Pedro Pablo Ramírez, President	1943
Australia	Alexander Gore Arkwright, Baron Gowrie, Governor General[1]	1936
	John Curtin, Prime Minister	
Belgium	Leopold III, King (German occupation)	1934
Bolivia	Maj. Gualberto Villarroel, President of the Junta	1943
Brazil	Dr. Getulio Vargas, President	1931
Bulgaria	Simeon II, King (Regency)	1943
	Dobri Boshiloff, Prime Minister	
Burma	Sir Reginald Hugh Dorman-Smith, Governor (Japanese occupation)	1941
Canada	Earl of Athlone, Governor General	1940
	W. L. Mackenzie King, Prime Minister	
Chile	Juan Antonio Ríos, President	1942
China	Gen. Chiang Kai-shek, President of National Gov't	1943
	President of Executive Yuan	1939
Colombia	Dr. Alfonso López, President	1942
Costa Rica	Rafael A. Calderón Guardia, President	1940
Cuba	Gen. Fulgencio Batista y Zaldivar, President	1940

Country	Name and Office	Accession
Czechoslovakia	Dr. Eduard Beneš, President (German occupation)	1940
Denmark	Christian X, King (German occupation)	1912
Dominican Rep.	Gen. Rafael Leónidas Trujillo Molina, President	1942
Ecuador	Carlos Arroyo del Río, President	1940
Egypt	Farouk I, King	1936
Eire	Dr. Douglas Hyde, President	1938
	Eamon de Valera, Premier	1932
Ethiopia	Haile Selassie I, Emperor	1930
Finland	Risto Ryti, President	1940
France	Henri Philippe Pétain, Chief of State, Marshal of France (German occupation)	1940
Germany	Adolf Hitler, Fuehrer and Reich Chancellor	1933
Great Britain	George VI, King and Emperor	1936
	Winston Churchill, Prime Minister	
Greece	George II, King (German occupation)	1935
Guatemala	Gen. Jorge Ubico, President	1931
Haiti	Elie Lescot, President	1941
Honduras	Gen. Tiburcio Carías Andino, President	1933
Hungary	Admiral Nicholas Horthy de Nagybánya, Regent	1920
	Nicholas von Kallay, Premier	
Iceland	Sweinn Björnsson, Regent (U.S. Protection)	1941
India	Sir Archibald P. Wavell, Viceroy, Governor General	1943
Iran	Mohammed Reza Pahlevi, Shahinshah	1941
Iraq	Feisal II, King (Regency)	1939
Italy	Victor Emmanuel III, King	1900
	Pietro Badoglio, Premier, Chief of Gov't, Sec'y of State	
Japan	Hirohito, Emperor	1926
	Gen. Hideki Tojo, Premier	
Lebanon	Cheil Bechara El Khoury, President	1943
Liberia	W. V. S. Tubman, President	1944
Liechtenstein	Franz Joseph II, Sovereign Prince	1938
Luxembourg	Charlotte, Grand Duchess (German occupation)	1919
"Manchoukuo"	Henry Pu Yi ("Emperor Kangte")	1934
Mexico	Manuel Avila Camacho, President	1940
Monaco	Louis II, Prince	1922
Morocco	Sidi Mohammed ben Youssef, Sultan	1927
Netherlands	Wilhelmina, Queen (German occupation)	1890
Newfoundland	Sir Humphrey T. Walwyn, Governor	1936
New Zealand	Sir Cyril Newall, Governor General	1941
	Peter Fraser, Prime Minister	
Nicaragua	Gen. Anastasio Somoza, President	1937
Norway	Haakon VII, King (German occupation)	1905
Oman	Sir Sayyid Sa'id bin Taimur, Sultan	1932
Palestine	Sir Harold Alfred MacMichael, High Commissioner	1938
Panamá	Ricardo Adolfo de la Guardia, President	1941
Paraguay	Gen. Higinio Morínigo, President	1943
Peru	Manuel Prado y Ugarteche, President	1939
Philippines	Manuel Luis Quezon, President (Japanese occupation)	1935
Poland	Wladislaw Raczkiewicz, President (German occupation)	1939
Portugal	Gen. António Oscar de Fragoso Carmona, President	1926
	Dr. António de Oliveira Salazar, Premier	
Rumania	Michael I, King	1940
	Ion Antonescu, Premier-Dictator	
Salvador, El	Gen. Maximiliano Hernández Martínez, President	1931
South Africa	N. J. de Wet, Officer Administering the Government	1943
	Gen. Jan C. Smuts, Premier	
Spain	Gen. Francisco Franco Bahamonde, Chief of State, Prime Minister	1936
Sudan	Lt. Gen. H. J. Huddleston, Governor General	1940
Sweden	Gustaf V, King	1907
Switzerland	Walter Stampfli, President	1944
Syria	Shukri Kuwatli, President	1943
Thailand	Ananda Mahidol, King (Regency) (Japanese occupation)	1935
Trans-Jordan	Abdullah ibn Hussein, Emir	1928
Tunisia	Sidi Mohammed Lamine Pasha, Bey	1943
Turkey	Ismet Inönü, President	1938
U.S.S.R.	Mikhail Ivanovich Kalinin, President	1936
	Joseph V. Stalin, Premier	
United States	Franklin D. Roosevelt, President	1933
Uruguay	Juan José Amezaga, President	1943
Vatican City	Pius XII, Pope	1939
Venezuela	Gen. Isaias Medina Angarita, President	1941
Yemen	Zaidi Imam Yahya ben Muhammed ben Hamid ed Din, Imam, King of the Yemen	1934
Yugoslavia	Peter II, King (German occupation)	1934
Zanzibar	Seyyid Sir Khalifa bin Harub, Sultan	1911
	Sir Henry Guy Pilling, British Resident	1940

[1]The Duke of Gloucester was appointed governor general of Australia Nov. 15, 1943, to take office in July 1944.

Price Administration, Office of.

By the end of 1943 nearly the whole price structure of the United States had been brought under control through the General Maximum Price Regulation and more than 500 individual maximum price regulations. Ceilings on animal feeds, fresh fruits and vegetables, used commodities, and on various primary products, most important of which was live hogs, had closed most previous gaps in the price control structure. Maximum prices had been established for most of the materials going into armament production as well as for essential semi-fabricated and fabricated industrial products. Ceilings had been established on residential rents in defense rental areas in which 80,000,000 people lived.

The Office of Price Administration was created April 11, 1941, by executive order of the president to prevent "price spiraling, rising costs of living, profiteering, and inflation." The agency, known until Aug. 1941 as the Office of Price Administration and Civilian Supply, took over the price stabilization and consumer protection work started by the Advisory commission to the Council of National Defense. On Jan. 30, 1942, the president signed the Emergency Price Control act of 1942 giving the OPA clear statutory powers and providing it with specific authority to enforce its orders. The close to 100 "price schedules" became regulations under the act. On April 28 OPA issued the General Maximum Price Regulation, which set the highest prices charged in March 1942 as ceiling prices on most commodities sold to the American consumer. Price control still remained seriously incomplete, however, chiefly because statutory limitations permitted ceilings on only 60% of the foods in the consumer budget. The Stabilization act, amending the earlier statute, which received the president's signature Oct. 2, 1942, enabled the extension of price control to about 90% of all foods.

In April 1943 the president issued an order directing the price administrator to place ceilings on all cost-of-living commodities, to prevent any further increases so far as possible and to reduce excessively high prices. Following this order a four-point program was entered upon by the OPA:

1. to extend price control across the board, to include a number of formerly exempt commodities such as fish and fresh fruits and vegetables;
2. to reduce prices which had got out of hand, including prices of meats, butter, and fresh fruits and vegetables;
3. to extend the use of specific dollars-and-cents ceilings to include retail foods; and
4. to provide more vigorous enforcement of the program.

Under the third of these points, the community price program was launched during the late spring and summer. This was designed to remedy a serious defect of the General Maximum Price Regulation and the "formula type" regulations under which many commodities had been taken out of the general regulation. This defect, which made compliance at retail difficult, was the lack of a clear and stated price which seller and buyer alike could know to be the legal price. Under the GMPR, ceiling prices were those of a base date and varied from retailer to retailer. Under the formula type regulations, standard calculations were applied to individual cost data, and the resulting calculated price varied from one retailer to another. Under the community price program, the established formulas were applied to costs typical of each class of retail food outlet to arrive at specific prices. These prices, calculated separately for each community, were required to be posted in the retail stores where all parties could readily consult them. At the close of 1943 prices had been set under this program on about 700 food and grocery items in 600,000 retail food stores, 94% of the nation-wide total. Communities covered by the orders included 96% of the population.

Under the new program, ceiling prices for the most important items in the consumer food budget were set on a community basis. Specific dollars-and-cents prices were set for four classes of retail outlets, classified according to volume of business and type of service.

The extension of the dollars-and-cents ceilings was paralleled during the first part of 1943 by the increasing use of quality standards in price regulations. The passage of the Taft amendment to the Commodity Credit Corporation act on July 16, however, prohibited the OPA from requiring grade labelling in any case and from requiring standards except where "absolutely essential to an effective system of fixing prices." Grade labelling

requirements were thereupon removed from 20 regulations, and other regulations were revised to assure complete conformity with the congressional mandate. The director of the Office of Economic Stabilization, however, ordered continued the federal grading and marking of carcasses and wholesale cuts of beef, veal, lamb and mutton, which had been recommended and approved by the meat industry.

By the time the "hold-the-line" program had been put into effect, prices on a number of commodities had risen so steeply that emergency measures had to be taken. Rollbacks of some prices were accomplished by reducing inflated margins of distributors and producers. In other cases, however, prices could not be reduced without also reducing margins or farm returns below reasonable levels. In such cases subsidies were authorized by the director of the Office of Economic Stabilization in order that the reduction of retail prices would still permit a fair return to producers and distributors. The reductions were financed by the Commodity Credit corporation and other agencies having funds available for the purpose. Subsidies introduced during 1943 kept down the retail prices of a very significant group of cost-of-living staples, including meats, butter, cheese and milk, apples, bread and flour, peanut butter and certain canned vegetables. The net result of the program as a whole was apparent in the fact that, despite rising inflationary pressures, the cost of living, as reported by the bureau of labour statistics, rose only 3½% during 1943, as compared with 9% in 1942 and 10% in 1941. Whether or not subsidies would be continued in the control of food prices was still to be decided by congress at the end of 1943.

Rationing during 1943 assumed an increasingly significant place in American life with the inclusion under the program of shoes, processed foods and meats, fats, oils and cheese. In general, commodities like fuel oil, automobiles, supplementary gasoline, etc., were rationed differentially according to individual need and essentiality to the war program. The basic gasoline ration, shoes and all foods, however, were rationed according to the principle of equal division of available supply among all consumers. During the summer of 1943, local boards were given authority to grant additional quantities of food ration points to people living or working in isolated areas who could not otherwise get a nutritionally adequate diet.

An important development in the rationing program during 1943 was the growth of the ration banking plan worked out in co-operation with the American Bankers' association. The plan enabled retailers, wholesalers, primary suppliers, bulk consumers, and institutional and industrial users to deposit their ration currency in co-operating banks and to make and receive ration payments in the form of checks. About 84% of the U.S. commercial banks participated in the program. Most of the banks that did not participate were small ones in rural areas where there was no need for the program.

Administrative policy during 1943 stressed the elimination of complex administrative procedures, the simplification of regulations, and the reduction of paper work. Marked emphasis was laid on the need for decentralizing the program. During the last months of the year there was considerable restaffing of the Price department in order to comply with the legislative provision incorporated in the appropriation act for 1944 that all key policy positions in the agency be held by men who "in the judgment of the administrator . . . shall be qualified by experience in business industry or commerce."

Active co-operation and participation of the general public in the OPA program was more fully enlisted during the year. Price panels, made up of local volunteers, were established in the War Price and Rationing boards throughout the United States to promote compliance with the regulations among retailers and consumers in the community and to provide a channel for the consideration and settlement of consumer complaints. Closer relations with industry were brought about through a substantial increase in the number of industry advisory committees set up to iron out special problems and to further the exchange of viewpoints between the agency and the business world. A labour office and an Industry council had been established prior to 1943. An agricultural relations advisor was appointed during the year to promote better understanding between the OPA and U.S. farmers.

A Consumer Advisory committee was also appointed to study the effects of OPA policies on the consumer and to advise with operating people on how policies and regulations might be made more effective.

Leon Henderson, who had been OPA administrator for nearly two years, resigned on Jan. 20, 1943, and was succeeded by Prentiss M. Brown. On Nov. 8, Mr. Brown resigned and Chester Bowles, who had been general manager since July, became the third OPA administrator. (*See also* CANADA, DOMINION OF; PRICES; RATIONING; WAR PRODUCTION, U.S.) (C. Bs.)

Prices.

The general level of U.S. commodity prices moved higher in 1943, but the trend of prices for particular commodities varied widely from this general level. Inflationary forces appeared in the expansion of governmental purchases for war needs, the rapid rise in the quantity of money in circulation in purse and pocket, the abnormal increase in the amounts held by individuals and corporations as demand bank deposits against which checks could be drawn, and in the rapid rise in the amount of paper money in common use. These factors were re-enforced by influences tending to increase the prices of particular goods, in the form of black markets, increasing scarcities of civilian supplies, and the abrupt increases in items over which price control measures were not taken by the government, such as furs, whisky, used cars, jewellery, corporate stock and land values.

During 1943 certain inflationary offsets developed, such as a decline in the velocity of circulation of money, the withholding of consumers' purchasing power under the tax collection process of the individual income tax, improvement in administration of price control, rationing of consumers' goods, adjustments under the controlled materials plan, and increased individual and corporate savings and investments in war bonds. Taking into consideration only items entering into the cost of living index, the effectiveness of price control over particular prices was found in the declining rate of increase from 3% per quarter in 1942 to 2% per quarter in 1943.

The demand factors underlying 1943 price changes could be observed in the expansion of consumers' purchasing power, as seen in Table I. The danger of inflation was a common topic of study in 1943. The amount of money that the consumer had in his pockets and at the bank was an important factor determining what he could but not what he would pay in his demand for goods supplied. The billions of dollars in circulation shown in Table I indicates that the amount of money in consumers' pockets tended to rise throughout 1942 and continued unbroken through 1943. Considering only the dollars per capita in circulation, the inflationary trend was still more striking, rising from $116 in January to $141 in October. The rate of increase, however, tended to decline in 1943. The velocity of the bank deposits, showing the number of times during the month that a dollar had been exchanged for goods and services, showed a definite downward trend. The turnover of dollars was based on the relation of debits of individual accounts to net demand deposits in member banks reporting weekly for the 100 leading cities.

The 1943 dollar passed through fewer hands than did the dollar of 1942 or 1941. The monthly average for 1941 showed a turnover of 22.5, for 1942 of 21.5 and for 1943 of 21.1. The purchasing power of the dollar declined slightly during the first quarter of 1943, but perhaps no data indicated more clearly the extent of the success of price control, taxation and rationing, than the stability of purchasing power of the dollar for the remainder of the war year.

Despite the increase in pocket money and in bank deposits, constituting what many financial experts called the "inflationary potential," the value of the dollar remained sufficiently stable to allay fears of inflation for 1943.

The greatest single U.S. buyer in 1943 was the federal government. The expenditures of the United States constituted a powerful demand influence, and as these monthly expenditures increased, the strain upon price control became correspondingly greater. On the other hand, the receipts from taxes indicated the extent to which the government was mopping up the consumers' purchasing power shown in Table I. Federal taxes were deflationary; federal expenditures were inflationary. Since the federal government commanded four-fifths of physical production in 1943, the fiscal policy was inevitably related to the price control policy. Table II affords a clear-cut understanding of the relative importance of the deflationary effect of taxes, and the inflationary effect of expenditures for the war years.

Although federal expenditures exceeded revenues every month during 1943, the increased funds pouring into the treasury after July became a substantially larger proportion of outlays. The

Table I.—*Composition and Comparative Trends of Purchasing Power, 1943 and 1942*

Month	Money in Circulation				Deposits (except inter-bank accounts) (in billions)		Velocity of bank deposits		Purchasing power of dollar as measured in wholesale prices	
	Billions at end of month		Dollars per capita							
	1943	1942	1943	1942	1943	1942	1943	1942	1943	1942
Jan. . .	$15.6	$11.1	$116	$83	$57	$48	19.6	22.4	78.9	83.8
Feb. . .	16.1	11.4	119	86	54	41	18.7	22.6	78.5	83.2
Mar. . .	16.2	11.5	120	86	65	49	19.6	22.6	77.8	82.4
Apr. . .	16.6	11.7	123	88	73	46	21.8	20.9	77.5	81.5
May . .	17.1	12.0	126	90	64	48	19.6	21.6	77.3	81.4
June . .	17.4	12.4	128	92	66	50	18.8	21.3	77.9	81.6
July . .	17.9	12.7	131	95	65	51	18.6	21.1	77.9	81.5
Aug. . .	18.5	13.2	135	98	60	55	17.2	19.5	78.1	81.1
Sept. . .	18.8	13.8	138	102	75	58	23.1	20.8	78.1	80.8
Oct. . .	19.2*	14.2	141	106	..	..	..	20.8	..	80.2
Nov. . .	..	14.8	..	110	..	53	..	21.6	..	80.2
Dec. . .	..	15.4	..	115	..	61	..	23.1	..	79.6

Federal Reserve *Bulletin.* Purchasing power of dollar computed by bureau of foreign and domestic commerce, on basis of 1935-39 wholesale prices. *Estimated.

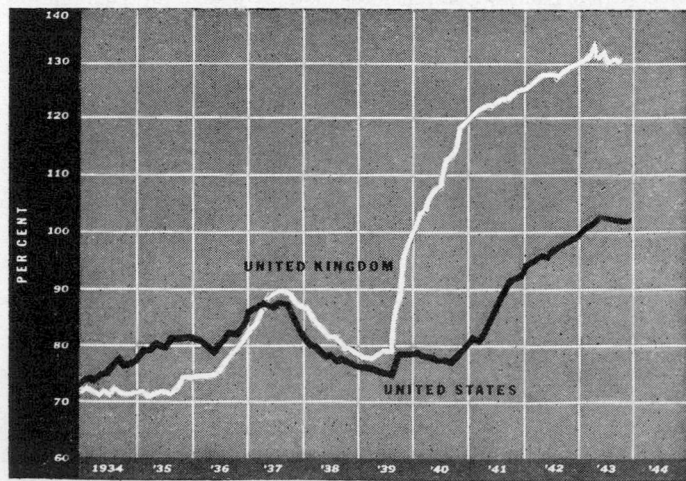

Fig. 1.—WHOLESALE PRICES IN THE UNITED KINGDOM AND THE UNITED STATES, 1934–43 (Sources: United Kingdom—Board of Trade, converted to 1926 base; United States—Bureau of Labor Statistics). War conditions in the United Kingdom made many price quotations nominal; undoubtedly the index for that country understates the price rise after August 1939

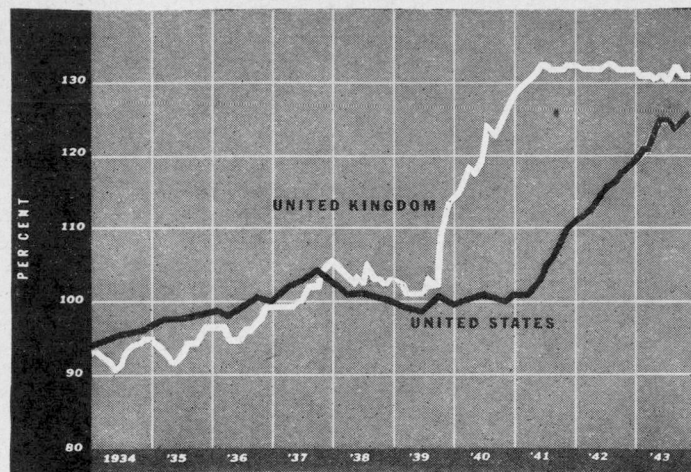

Fig. 2.—RETAIL PRICES IN THE UNITED KINGDOM AND THE UNITED STATES, 1934–43. (Sources: Cost of living indexes. Ministry of Labour, converted to 1935–39 base, first-of-month data; Bureau of Labor Statistics, mid-month data, selected dates before Sept. 1940.) Because of the war, the price rise shown for the United Kingdom after 1939 and, to a lesser extent, for the United States after 1941, is probably understated

withholding method of income tax collection strengthened the anti-inflationary power of taxation to the extent shown in Table II. As this difference between the inflationary effects of expenditures and the deflationary effects of taxation became less and less, federal fiscal policy became an important price control factor.

The Office of Economic Stabilization (*q.v.*) confronted two difficult price problems, in the form of demands for increased wages, based upon alleged increases in living costs, and requests of producers of particular commodities for price increases to cover rising costs of production. The president's order to "hold the line" was rigidly followed by both the War Labor board and the Office of Price Administration. The Little Steel formula, basing wages on living costs, came under severe strain in the fourth quarter of 1943, with demands from coal miners, steel workers, and railroad brotherhoods, where increased costs of fuel and transportation would have been widely reflected in costs of other goods. The shortage of crude petroleum led to a demand for an increase of 35 cents per barrel by producers, but the request was refused because profit margins were favourable, the industry showed good earnings for 1943, the cost of oil entered too extensively into other costs, and it was doubtful if such an increase would have added substantially to successful explorations of new reserves. During the fourth quarter of 1943, however, more requests for price increases were granted in particular industries than at any other time during the year.

Subsidies for price control purposes were used more extensively during 1943 than in previous years. The U.S. government purchased abroad such important metals as antimony ore, copper,

Table II.—*Comparison of Federal Inflationary Expenditures and Deflationary Taxes, 1941-43*

	Expenditures by months (in billions)			Revenues by months (in billions)		
	1943	1942	1941	1943	1942	1941
January	$6.37	$2.63	$1.12	$ .82	$ .61	$.34
February	6.12	2.63	1.08	1.19	.94	.67
March	7.35	3.44	1.40	5.21	3.55	1.57
April	7.47	3.76	1.32	1.51	.73	.57
May	7.44	3.96	1.14	1.48	.56	.54
June	8.33	4.53	1.55	4.57	2.49	1.28
July	7.11	5.16	1.60	2.05	.79	.46
August	7.62	5.22	1.56	3.01	.80	.55
September	7.54	5.93	1.88	5.45	2.53	1.14
October	7.41	5.94	2.09	..	.65	.49
November	7.79 *	6.36	1.80	..	.83	.73
December	..	6.50	2.50	..	2.70	1.21
Total	..	56.06	19.15	..	17.38	9.55

U.S. Department of Commerce, *Survey of Current Business.*   *Estimated.

tin, bauxite, chrome, manganese and mercury, which were then sold in domestic markets at ceiling prices, but below landed costs. Since these metals were resold largely on government account, the losses were largely fictitious whenever the government sold below cost for public use. Public opposition to direct governmental purchases and resale led to direct payments to sellers and producers. The "roll-back program" of May and June, 1943, was designed to roll back the prices of meat, coffee and butter by 10% to check rising living costs. Payments were made to processors, *e.g.*, creameries and slaughterers, who in turn agreed to sell to retailers at lower prices. Farmers protested that these subsidies did not benefit them but only the processors who obtained windfall gains therefrom.

Other Countries.—Compared with the prewar average (Jan. to June, 1939) the prices of goods entering into the cost of living index of the League of Nations had risen in the second quarter of 1943 as follows: 274% in Turkey; Palestine, 237%; Iran, 203%; Bolivia, 206%; India, 95%; Finland, 86%; Chile, 84%; Spain, 66%; Norway and Sweden, 50%; Mexico, 49%; Peru, 43%; Japan, 33%; United Kingdom, 28%; the United States, 24%; Argentina, 21%; Canada, 18%; Germany, 11%. In Chungking, China, the cost of living in 1942 was 2,149% above 1939 levels. Between Aug. 1942 and 1943, the wholesale price index of the London board of trade rose from 128.2 to 130.9, indicating that firm price control had been in effect in England. (*See* also AGRICULTURE; BUSINESS REVIEW; CONSUMER CREDIT; PRICE ADMINISTRATION, OFFICE OF; STOCKS AND BONDS; and articles on individual commodities.)   (E. H. HE.)

Primary Education: *see* EDUCATION.

Prince Edward Island.
The smallest of the Canadian provinces lies in the Gulf of St. Lawrence. The island is about 130 mi. long, and has an average width of 21 mi. Pop. (1941) 95,047, predominantly rural. The largest city is Charlottetown (14,460), the provincial capital.

History.—On Sept. 15, 1943, the provincial general elections were held. These resulted in the continuance in power of the Liberal party, which gained practically a two to one majority over its chief opponent, the Progressive Conservative. The prime minister in 1943 was T. Walter Jones, who succeeded Thane Campbell on the latter's elevation to the chief justiceship of the province in May.

Education.—The two chief educational institutions of Prince Edward Island are Prince of Wales college and St. Dunstan's university, both situated at Charlottetown.

Communication.—Communication with the mainland across Northumberland strait is maintained by powerful railway ferryboats. The Trans-Canada airway also provides communication by plane twice daily between Charlottetown and Moncton.

Agriculture, Fisheries, Fur Production.—About 85% of the entire surface of the island is arable. During 1943, farming conditions were good, with the hay and grain crops excellent. The potato crop, because of excessively wet weather, was below average. The fishing industry represented a considerable advance. In 1942, the total value of the catch was $1,148,367 as compared to $758,464 in 1940. The fur haul of the island in 1941–1942 represented a value of $735,189.   (J. I. C.)

Princeton University.
An institution of higher learning at Princeton, N.J. During 1943— its 197th year—Princeton became practically a military installation. It was a "pilot" institution for the basic and area and language courses of the army specialized training program and later received engineering and reserve details. Units of the navy and

marine corps college training programs (V-12 and pre-medical) were also assigned to it. In addition, it continued to provide accommodations for a navy school for the indoctrination of officers and an army post exchange school. While the campus population was 1,000 larger than it had ever been, the civilian enrolment was reduced to one-quarter of normal.

In addition to carrying the increased burden of instructing the uniformed students, the faculty members continued to pursue war research projects and to lend their assistance to government agencies. Under wartime pressure the new department of aeronautical engineering was rapidly developed and new buildings were erected for it. Programs of study in the near east and Latin America were expanded. First steps were taken in the framing of a postwar plan of study and curriculum. For statistics of enrolment, faculty, library volumes, etc., *see* UNIVERSITIES AND COLLEGES. (H. W. Do.)

Principe: *see* PORTUGUESE COLONIAL EMPIRE.

Printing. With U.S. manufacturers concentrating on warmaking equipment and materials, no big printing machine development was announced during 1943.

Interesting developments—some with reasonably high potentialities—centred around substitutes for zinc and copper, widely used in war and printing alike.

As substitutes for electrotypes (copper face on lead base) and for offset press plates (ordinarily of zinc or aluminum) plastics were noted in 1942. Use was extended in 1943; the material was found practical for moulding electrotypes, accepting the copper shell (face) by electro deposition with silver the conductor rather than black lead used with customary wax mould. The silver, incidentally, eliminates dirt accompanying black lead.

A method of depositing iron as well as copper or nickel was evolved. The Sept. 1943 *Better Homes and Gardens* was produced from plates the shells of which were formed by alternating layers (deposits) of nickel, iron and copper respectively, saving considerable copper. Iron being three to four times harder than nickel, an iron shell of one to one and one-half thousandths of an inch is sufficiently tough to give extremely long press mileage.

Soon, it was predicted, neither zinc nor copper (or any combination of the two) would be used for original photo-engraved plates. Experiments with soft iron, Dow metal, magnesium and other metals were made. It was predicted that such originals would be engraved faster and more economically by electric etching, eliminating use of nitric acid. Three newspapers set up to make plates in this fashion but the supply of zinc was reduced by half and the nitric acid situation was relieved. The etching of plastic materials was not found practical up to the close of 1943, but development was going on.

During 1943 duPont announced "Dacolyte" for copper electro forming applications. The addition of but one-third to two-thirds ounce per gallon of solution contributed toward improved deposits; surface irregularities of the copper were practically eliminated and the deposit was tougher and harder.

A similar material, B.C.F. addition agent, developed particularly for electrotypes, effected a considerable saving in copper. Because of the increased hardness, a thinner copper plate shell could stand the same, or increased, press wear. Use of this product enabled electrotypers to produce one-third more square inches per pound of copper than the average 1942 production on which allotment of material was based.

A quite notable advance in colour photography came with development of Ansco colour paper print. It was said to be the first paper from which finished colour prints could be made by exposure to three colour separation negatives in turn and devel-

opment in an ordinary dark room. Essentially the base paper carried three emulsion layers, each having a colour-forming compound which coupled with the reaction products of development. The result was a transparent die image.

Inability of operators of fast multicolour presses ("wet" printing) to match engraver's colour proofs (different colours being proofed slower than on production presses) had long been troublesome. To permit the printer to match engraver's colours with proof presses which were not too high-priced, a new 2-colour proof press using a single impression cylinder with inking units arranged to ink the plates immediately before impression, was built by Vandercook. A 4-colour proofer was in development.

(J. L. F.)

Printing Office, U. S. Government. The office was established by authority of congress in 1860 to execute printing and binding for congress, the executive and judicial departments. The total area occupied by the government printing office proper in 1943 was 1,396,973 sq.ft., or 32.1 ac. In addition, the government printing office occupied 7 warehouses in various sections of the U.S. covering 125,237 sq.ft. of floor space or 2.9 ac. During the fiscal year 1943 it was necessary to place orders with outside contractors for printing in the amount of $25,944,709.57, as the government printing office was unable to handle the volume of printing necessary in connection with the war. The value of the government printing office buildings in 1943 was $9,634,825; machinery and equipment $6,236,731, making the total value of the plant $15,871,556. At the close of the fiscal year 1943, there were 7,973 employees on the rolls with a pay roll of approximately $21,900,000. During the fiscal year 1943, this office made charges for 821,787,445 copies of publications of all classes. This total included 9,087,829 copies of the *Congressional Record*, 5,191,000 copies of the *Federal Register*, 4,394,822 copies of specifications of patents, trademarks, designs, etc., and 251,726 copies of the patent office *Official Gazette* and annual indexes. The number of postal cards printed amounted to 2,268,321,000 and money orders 297,083,308. The stores division and warehouses handled 7,668 carloads of paper weighing 345,204,321 lb. The division of public documents mailed out 802,384,327 publications and forms; its receipts from the sale of government publications during the year amounted to $2,366,897.04. The total charges made to congress and all other government agencies during the fiscal year were $77,837,186.54. (A. E. Gɪ.)

Priorities and Allocations. Wartime industrial production in the U.S. brought adoption of various systems by the War Production board, each of which was designed to bring about orderly flows of materials to manufacture of military and essential civilian products. As a background to 1943 developments, the Office of Production Management had instituted the simple priorities system of a first-things-come-first variety. This method of distributing materials was successful during the early prewar period, when real materials scarcities had not appeared in the U.S.

Manufacturers of most urgently needed war and civilian items needed assurance that their orders would be filled in preference to orders from manufacturers whose output was not as important. As a consequence, the system of preference ratings was adopted. Orders for materials bearing the highest preference ratings were required, under rules and regulations of OPM to be filled prior to orders bearing lower ratings.

The system originally included preference ratings of A-1, A-2, A-3, A-4, A-5, etc. These ratings were assigned to important war and essential civilian items on the basis of relative urgency patterns laid down by the War Production board and military agencies. However, the pressure from various groups of producers soon brought about a classification of more items among the top preference ratings than was actually warranted. Since many producers received ratings of A-1 or A-2, it was impracticable to lower the ratings applicable to their operations from the relatively high classes to lower ones. Therefore, it was decided to establish intermediate ratings between the A-1 and A-2 groups, including A-1-a, A-1-j, and A-1-k, etc.

Ultimately, the priorities system was still further "inflated" through inclusion of large segments of war and civilian production programs in these higher ratings groups so that eventually, it became necessary to modify the entire system by establishing a new group of ratings, to top all other ratings. This new group included AA-1, AA-2, AA-3, AA-4, AA-5, etc. In addition an AAA preference rating was established for use in cases of emergency only.

At the same time that the AA preference rating scheme was established, the A group was retained as a lower series of ratings. Eventually, an intermediate rating between AA-2 and AA-3 was established as AA-2X, in order to permit adjustments between the highest classification of relative urgency.

As materials became increasingly short in the U.S. productive system, the demands of producers holding relatively high preference ratings became so great that all of their demands for basic materials could not be met from available supplies. As a consequence, it became necessary to take steps to assure that the amounts of basic materials which might be purchased through the use of preference ratings was no greater than the available supply. There had to be a balancing of demands for materials with supplies of them, in order that the most essential war and civilian programs might be met, according to a prearranged time schedule.

The Production Requirements plan was developed during 1942 to make materials for production of war and civilian items available under quantity controls on a plant basis. The quantities of materials which plants might purchase for production of the items they were manufacturing, however, were unrelated insofar as the end products themselves were concerned. For example, under PRP, the X company might be eligible to purchase 500 tons of steel for the manufacture of 1,000 parts for an aeroplane. At the same time, the Y company might be eligible to purchase only 200 tons of aluminum for the manufacture of 300 parts for the same aeroplane. There was no co-ordination between the numbers of parts which might be made for a given war program—the aircraft program for example. As a result, a situation eventually developed wherein a production period would end and there would be aeroplanes without propellers on hand, tanks without tracks, and ships without fittings. In order to correct this situation, it became necessary to make materials available to war and essential civilian industries on a program basis. Thus, materials in 1943 were made available for the production of aeroplanes, rather than to individual plants for the production of unrelated numbers of parts for aeroplanes.

This method of program distribution was implemented by the Controlled Materials plan, announced in Nov. 1942, and placed in operation during the second quarter of 1943. It became popularly known as CMP. In its essentials, CMP was a method of vertical allocation of basic critical materials—specifically, copper, steel and aluminum in specified forms and shapes. The plan also included the preference rating structure, under which other materials required for production programs were made available within quantity controls. CMP worked as follows in 1943:

Statements of supply of and demand for controlled materials, on the basis of production programs, were made to the WPB requirements committee. Estimates of supply were made available to the committee from products of controlled materials—and producers of other critical materials playing an important role in production of war and essential civilian goods.

Statements of demand were presented to the requirements committee by the claimant agencies (war department, army ordnance, navy department, Maritime commission, Aircraft Resources Control office (agent for army air forces and bureau of aeronautics of United States navy), Office of Lend-Lease administration, Office of Economic Warfare, Office of Civilian Requirements, department of agriculture, Office of Defense Transportation, Office of Rubber Director, Petroleum Administration for War, National Housing agency, Office of War Utilities Director). In 1943 these were U.S. government agencies responsible for planning war and civilian production.

The statements of supply and demand were then compared and adjusted in order that more materials would not be allotted for production than were actually estimated to be available for a coming quarterly production period. As a result of this adjustment, programs of the various claimant agencies were adjusted in order that they would fall within the available supplies of materials allotted to them by the requirements committee. The claimant agencies then, on the basis of applications for allotments filed with them, made allotments of controlled materials to class A product manufacturers, consumers of controlled materials.

In addition, the requirements committee made allotments of controlled materials to WPB industry divisions, which in turn made allotments to manufacturers of class B products.

A distinction between products was drawn, because of the fact that it was feasible to make allotments of materials on a vertical basis in only some instances—chiefly where large end items were involved, with relatively large component parts. Class B products were usually products of a relatively standardized nature, having the general character of shelf goods. While this distinction was not specific, the classification of products was of necessity somewhat arbitrary. Practically, to determine the distinction, it was necessary to refer to the official CMP class B product list. This list indicated what items were class B products. Any item which did not appear on the list was a class A product.

The distinction was important, because it indicated the method to be used in making allotments—class A products being subject to the vertical allotment procedure down a chain of manufacturers, and class B products being allotted for directly by WPB industry divisions. In essence, an allotment of controlled materials was authority to purchase the items covered by it. In the case of class A products, the manufacturer of the end item (for example, tanks, or aeroplanes, or ships) obtained his authority to purchase controlled materials from a claimant agency. He then was in a position to place an authorized controlled materials order with a producer or distributor of controlled materials. He was also in a position to grant allotments (authority to purchase controlled materials) to other producers supplying him with class A products.

When a manufacturer received an allotment of controlled materials, he also received an authorized production schedule and a preference rating. With the preference rating he could purchase class B products and other items (other than class A products or controlled materials) in amounts necessary to fill his authorized production schedule under the allotment which he had received.

Class B product manufacturers received allotments of controlled materials, authorized production schedules, and preference ratings direct from the industry divisions of WPB. They, in turn, could make allotments of controlled materials to manufacturers who supplied them with class A products, use the allotments, or parts of them to place authorized controlled materials orders with controlled materials producers or distributors, and use their preference ratings for the purchase of class B products and other items (except class A products and controlled materials) in amounts necessary to meet their authorized production schedules. Manufacturers of class A products had to receive an allotment of controlled materials, a preference rating, and an authorized production schedule in order to be in a position to produce and deliver class A products. However, manufacturers of class B products need only to have had a preference rated order in order to make deliveries of their class B products.

The over-all basic idea of CMP in 1943 was control of the entire basic raw materials distribution system through rigid control in the form of allotments of specified forms and shapes of three basic materials and through related controls governing the remaining materials.

While CMP was the outstanding example of the allotment procedure in 1943, other materials were subjected to specific types of allotment. For example, chemicals, textiles and woodpulp were subject to allotment procedures not forming an integral part of CMP, but operating along with it.

These forms of allotments followed the general scheme laid down under CMP, but did not always include the vertical aspects. In most instances, allotments were direct from WPB industry divisions to users of the products covered. (*See also* BUSINESS REVIEW; PRICE ADMINISTRATION, OFFICE OF; RATIONING; WAR PRODUCTION, U.S.; WAR PRODUCTION BOARD.)

+Prisoners of War.
Although there were no official figures available for the total number of prisoners of war during 1943, it was estimated that more than 4,000,000 were held captive during the year. The largest part consisted of Russians held by Germany and axis forces held by the U.S.S.R., but estimates of actual numbers were erratic. Some 200,000 former French prisoners of war in Germany were transferred to other categories during the year, reducing the number of French prisoners of war to 872,000. Proportionately, the largest increase in prisoners during the year was in the number of Americans held in Europe. Whereas in 1942 it was estimated that there were 500 such prisoners, the 1943 figures total some 11,000, consisting of survivors of planes shot down over Europe and captives taken during the North African and Italian campaigns. Figures for prisoners of other Allied nationalities held in Europe remained fairly constant, including 142,000 British, 140,000 Yugoslavs, 66,000 Belgians, 55,000 Poles, 9,500 Dutch, 1,500 Greeks and 1,100 Norwegians. Among axis prisoners held by the United Nations, it was estimated that 193,000 were held by the United States, 74,000 in Great Britain and 27,000 in Canada. In the Far East, estimates showed that Japan was holding approximately 20,000 American prisoners, 148,000 British and 45,000 Dutch, as well as some 50,000 civilian internees.

In accordance with the terms of the Geneva Prisoners of War convention of 1929, ratified by most of the belligerents of World War II, representatives of the protecting powers and of the International Red Cross committee continued to visit prison camps and to report on the application of the convention. In general, these reports indicated that the convention was being observed.

The convention, which had not been ratified by Russia or Japan but which Japan agreed to observe without formal ratification, established certain standards for the treatment of war prisoners. Food was to be the equivalent of that of troops of the detaining power at base camps. Sanitary and medical facilities were to be provided. Prisoners might be held in compounds but not individually confined except under unusual circumstances. Officers were to receive pay, generally on the same scale as officers of corresponding rank in the army of the detaining power. Prisoners other than officers might be required to work at an agreed-upon rate of pay, but the work should have no direct relation to war operations. Neutral representatives might visit the camps.

Facilities for the exchange of correspondence with relatives at home were to be provided and prisoners might receive packages. Exemption from postal charges was granted. The convention further provided for the exchange of information about prisoners through bureaus in each belligerent country and a central information bureau in a neutral country.

Supplies of food, uniforms, medicines, to supplement those of the detaining power, and educational, recreational and religious articles continued to be supplied to war prisoners by governments, Red Cross societies and other agencies through the intermediary of the International Red Cross committee. Regular shipments were made on vessels operated by the committee to and from Europe, but the Japanese government continued to interpose objections to the establishment of regular shipments of such supplies to the Far East. Substantial quantities were sent to Japanese-controlled territory during 1943, via the exchange ships which met at Goa in India in Sept. 1943. Reports received late in 1943 showed that these supplies were reaching Allied prisoners and civilian internees in Japan and Japanese-occupied territory, including the Philippines.

Various proposals were made to Japan by Allied governments and Red Cross societies to establish facilities for the regular dispatch of relief supplies for prisoners in the Far East. Stores were built up in Vladivostok in the hope that Japan would agree to their onward passage and distribution. By the end of 1943, however, the Japanese had not yet agreed to any of these proposals. Efforts by the Allied governments and Red Cross societies were being continued.

Delegates of the International Red Cross committee observed the distribution of supplies in prison camps, and receipts signed by the prisoners and their representatives were returned to the senders. It was estimated that less than 1% of the relief supplies sent to prisoners of war failed to reach the proper destination. Neutral representatives of the Young Men's Christian association continued to be allowed permission by most of the belligerents to visit prison camps and assist in educational, recreational and religious activities.

Some improvements were made during 1943 in the facilities for the exchange of correspondence between prisoners and their families, although the only provision for sending parcels to prisoners in the Far East was on the one sailing of the exchange ship "Gripsholm." Instructions for communicating with and sending parcels to prisoners were changed occasionally, but in the United States the latest information was obtainable from post offices, Red Cross chapters and the office of the provost marshal general, Washington, D.C. (*See also* RED CROSS.)

(P. E. R.)

Prisons.
Reports revealed that U.S. state prisons in 1943 manufactured products for armed forces amounting to $14,000,000 (in addition to $21,000,000 worth for state use) from Aug. 1942, to Nov. 1943. They included: bomb noses; bomb racks; shirts and other clothing; tool boxes; submarine nets; blankets, etc. The federal institutions produced war matériel valued at over $18,000,000 for the year ending July 30, 1943.

In addition, various penal farms raised about $25,000,000 worth of produce (meats, vegetables and fruits), and in many instances, inmates volunteered to work on private farms because of manpower shortages. No escapes were reported. Institutions also did laundry, salvage and repair work for nearby army camps.

It should be emphasized that patriotism on the part of the inmates, not compulsion, was responsible for this record. As of Nov. 1943, the prison industries branch of the War Production board awarded National Service certificates (comparable to the army and navy "E") to 44 institutions.

GIRL CLOTHING WORKER in Montreal, Canada, measuring a jacket for an axis prisoner. A large red circle on the back identifies the wearer as a war prisoner

ITALIAN PRISONERS wading out to a U.S. landing craft off the shore of Sicily. They were captured during the first battles near Gela in July 1943

U.S. MILITARY POLICEMAN standing guard at the German prison camp, Camp Chaffee, Ark., in 1943

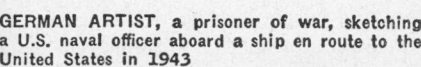

GERMAN ARTIST, a prisoner of war, sketching a U.S. naval officer aboard a ship en route to the United States in 1943

Additional reports revealed that thousands of inmates gave blood to Red Cross banks; some acted as "guinea pigs" to the cause of science (one died as a result). Prisoners also purchased more than $1,000,000 worth of war bonds from their paltry earnings in prison industries.

To facilitate the induction of inmates into the army when their sentences expired, selective service boards were set up in all federal and state prisons during 1943. Not all released felons, though, were inducted. Those convicted of the more serious crimes, as well as alcoholics, sex perverts, drug addicts and habitual offenders, were barred Some states (Kentucky, Oklahoma, Texas, New Jersey, Michigan) which enacted legislation soon after Pearl Harbor permitting the parole of worthy inmates *prior* to the expiration of their sentences (if the army would accept them) continued that practice, with excellent results. Only a handful of men so paroled relapsed into crime.

Because of the war—and the consequent restricted use of vital materials, no new buildings were erected in the prisons. In many, though, educational facilities were extended—particularly in vocational fields—to prepare inmates for war work within the prison, or upon their release.

With the exception of England, no information was available about prisons and crime in Europe. In that country, juvenile delinquency, rampant after the outbreak of the war, decreased considerably due to co-ordinated efforts on the part of social agencies and groups of interested citizens. And in the prisons, the inmates continued to aid in the war effort They produced considerable matériel and worked on either institutional or private farms. (*See also* CHILD WELFARE; CRIME.)   (L. E. L.)

Private Schools: *see* EDUCATION.
Prizes: *see* LITERARY PRIZES.
Production, Industrial: *see* BUSINESS REVIEW; WAR PRODUCTION, U.S.
Profits, Company: *see* BUSINESS REVIEW; TAXATION.
Progressive Education: *see* EDUCATION.
Proportional Representation: *see* MUNICIPAL GOVERNMENT.

Protestant Episcopal Church.
During the year 1943 the continuance of the world-wide war deeply affected the life of the Episcopal Church. So many of the clergy volunteered for service as chaplains in the armed forces that the proportional quota of chaplains assigned by the war department to the Episcopal Church was more than filled.

The statistics for the year showed increases in some items, decreases in other items. The total number of baptized persons, 2,188,573, and the total number of communicants, 1,520,394, were the largest ever reported in the history of the church but the number of confirmations showed a slight decrease and the number of church school pupils showed a decrease of more than 35,000. The total of contributions for all purposes, $38,288,766, was an increase of $2,977,456 over that of 1942.

Because of war conditions, the triennial general convention, held this time in Cleveland, Ohio, was shortened to a period of only eight working days, but the necessary business was accomplished. A budget of $2,615,382 was adopted for the general missionary work of the church in 1944 with provision for increases in 1945 and 1946. In the adoption of this missionary budget special emphasis was placed on the need for more effective work among the Negro population of the United States and upon the great missionary opportunity open in China.   (W. T. M.)

Prunes: *see* PLUMS AND PRUNES.

Psychiatry.
Shock Therapy.—The three forms of "shock" therapy used in the treatment of mental diseases were evaluated. A series of 15 or 20 insulin "shocks" are usually given to each patient over a period of a few weeks. When used to treat schizophrenia or dementia praecox, the recovery rate exceeds that found following any other type of treatment.

Little more than 1% of the 48,772 patients with dementia praecox in New York civil state hospitals in 1941 recovered under all other forms of treatment. More than 350 patients, however, treated by the insulin shock method, recovered; 28% more showed major improvement and another 28% were somewhat improved. This drastic form of treatment, therefore, increased the recovery rate by ten times. It was five times more efficient than electric shock or the convulsive treatment initiated by metrazol injections. The drug was ineffective in restoring to usefulness mental defectives, the aged, or patients deteriorated by structural brain disease. Electric shock, a convulsive agent which largely replaced metrazol, appeared to have particular value in affection disorders and in the involutional states. Both metrazol and electric convulsive therapy, most observers agreed, are of small value in the treatment of schizophrenia. Although shock treatments in general did not live up to the claims of their early sponsors, an important therapeutic method was added to the small stock of agents formerly known to change the course of mental disease.

Psychosurgery.—Operation on the frontal lobe of the brain as a means of treating mental disease was first introduced by Moniz in 1935. The technique of prefrontal lobotomy or leucotomy, as the operation is called, was modified. M. C. Petersen, who treated 41 patients, without any fatalities, found that many showed a relief from anxiety and were able to be cared for in their homes. Walter Freeman and J. W. Watts noted that their patients exhibited certain characteristics different from their prepsychotic self. The patients were more likely to be indolent, often were outspoken, saying the first thing that came into their heads, and were often hasty, undiplomatic and tactless. They were sorry for their attitude and often apologized. Emotional reactions were brisk, shallow and short-lived. The brooding, melancholy, hurt feelings and grim silences, characteristic of their preoperative state, entirely disappeared. They harboured no grudges. The intellect was intact. With the passage of time, there was often further improvement in social adaptation, even through the third to the fifth year. In general, the operation gave better results than formerly anticipated, and in selected cases of chronic depression of long-standing where the prognosis was particularly poor, prefrontal lobotomy was the treatment of choice.

Epilepsy.—Most epileptics have abnormal electroencephalograms, a condition known as cerebral dysrhythmia. Brain waves, moreover, have individuality and the pattern is an hereditary trait. W. G. Lennox showed that similar twins have indistinguishable electroencephalographic records. In members of the immediate family of epileptics abnormal tracings were found in over 50%, a much higher incidence than in the general population. These studies led to the conclusion that epilepsy is not inherited, but that a predisposition or susceptibility is inherited Behind the abnormal pulsations of the brain lies the unknown chemistry of discharging nerve cells. Studies of arterial and venous blood from the brain area indicated that in epilepsy there is a lower concentration of carbon dioxide in the blood and the brain burns less glucose per unit of oxygen than in normal people.

Group Psychotherapy.—Group treatment of the neuroses was developed in many clinics and hospitals. Alfred Hauptmann reported that 90% of the neurotics ordinarily encountered by physicians and seen in the out-patient department of hospitals can be treated successfully by this method. Each patient should be guaranteed, however, individual approach before he enters the class and in some cases this is necessary. Subordination to the class leader is one of the main curative principles, and it can be achieved more easily by group than by individual treatment. Teaching is primarily by lectures. Donald Blair tried the same method in the treatment of the neuroses in the war cases. He used general typewritten statements for distribution, individual interviews, autobiographies and a series of ten lectures. The results were satisfactory and group psychotherapy appeared to be well worthy of trial in the medical departments of the fighting forces.

Alcoholism.—A growing interest in the medical aspects of alcoholism is reflected in the current literature on the subject. The *Quarterly Journal of Studies on Alcohol*, established in 1939, became a focal point for the publishing of scientific contributions. William Fleeson and E. F. Gildea analysed such a group. The largest number were "exogenous drinkers," with heterogeneous origins of their drinking habits and without any single personality type predominating. Many in this classification were able to make personality adjustments to their drinking habits. A smaller group were the true addicts, who suffered from addiction at the beginning of their use of alcohol. Although they might have good insight into the problem, their personality make-up would not allow them to give up drinking. The smallest group were the "symptomatic drinkers," also endogenously determined. The underlying cause was usually a psychosis, their inebriety being only a secondary manifestation of a more profound psychological state. After many years of exogenous or symptomatic drinking, moreover, patients may become secondarily addicted.

Joseph Thimann reported on his use of the conditioned reflex in the treatment of the abnormal drinker. The unconditioned stimulus was an emetic, consisting of a solution of emetine, pilocarpine and ephedrine. The conditioning treatment required many other controlled factors, including a special room excluding all extraneous auditory, olfactory and visual stimuli. The positive auditory stimuli were at the same time reinforced, such as the clinking of bottles and glasses, the sound of poured liquor and the effects of retching and vomiting. Treatment was given in session on four to seven successive days, and repeated after one to 12 months. The results depended largely on the selection of patients, not being good in psychopathic cases. Under expert hands, with a careful evaluation of the patients and with fully controlled environmental conditions, the method, as reported by Thimann and others, was effective.

The clinical aspects of alcoholism were summarized by E. M. Jellinek in a book devoted to studies on the aetiology and treatment of abnormal drinking and to the mental and physical disorders associated with it. The volume is the first of a projected series on the "Effects of Alcohol upon the Individual," undertaken by the Research Council on Problems of Alcohol, organized in 1937 and affiliated with the American Association for the Advancement of Science.

War Psychiatry: Selection of Recruits.—The great number of neuropsychiatric casualties in World War I, the prolonged and costly care of the veteran with nervous and mental disease in all countries and the growing awareness of the problem in field units as well as hospital organizations, in line officers and doctors in World War II led to a more careful selection of men before induction into the service than at any time in the history of medicine. The "screening" in the United States and elsewhere was not entirely successful. The reason in the U.S. lay largely in the fact that psychiatric resources were not evenly spread throughout the country. Competent psychiatrists were not avail-

able in many parts of the country. There was an attempt, however, to eliminate the unfit during the training period, but in places where there was official apathy many men remained in the service, only to break down under the great strain of modern, active combat. Some neuropsychiatrists tended to over-exaggerate the importance of neuropsychiatry as a part of military medicine, but in general line officers were expressing a willingness to recognize functional and mental disorders, in contrast to the attitude prevalent in World War I. Psychiatrists with actual battle experience, as pointed out by G A. Blakeslee, tended to eliminate a larger percentage of recruits than those who had never seen men break down under fire.

L. R Gowan showed that from one-half to two-thirds of the men who developed neuroses in the army were predisposed to such a disability before induction. There was no place in the army for the so-called "problem" boy. Military service did not eliminate these problems, but only tended to aggravate them, resulting in more serious or often permanent disabilities. War brings about many situations that require the individual to make extensive emotional adjustments. War neurosis, as stated by Gowan, is not a new disease, but merely the appearance of previously existing neurotic tendencies brought to the surface and organized into form by exposure to war's demands. To discover these tendencies in a recruit should be the primary function of an examining psychiatrist.

The Nature of the War Neurosis.—W. R. D. Fairbairn found in his examination of British cases, that in nearly every man treated there was a history of previous psychopathologic experiences. The war only served to activate a pre-existing, if latent, abnormal reaction. The chief symptom was a separation-anxiety, which he found always present in war neurotics. The capacity to endure danger usually varied with the extent to which the individual had outgrown the stage of infantile dependence. The compulsion to return home was often displayed, sometimes in the form of a fugue or in a consciously executed flight. The author found that the group spirit was the essence of morale, the phenomenon of panic in a military unit being basically one of separation-anxiety affecting all or usually all members of the group simultaneously. High morale, moreover, within a group exercised a profound influence in counteracting the ill effects of infantile dependence among its members.

Alexander Simon and Margaret Hagan also reported, after a study of 400 psychiatric casualties in United States navy and marine corps men, that previous mental illness, broken homes, psychosis in the family, faulty education, occupational maladjustment, antisocial behaviour and alcoholism were found in a study of complete social histories. Broken homes occurred in nearly one-half of the cases.

Sodium amytal narcosis, according to L. L. Altman, became of increasing importance in the treatment of war neuroses. Its use was first emphasized by Sargant. The use of the drug must be preceded, accompanied and followed by psychotherapy in the form of investigation, explanation, positive suggestion and reassurance.

E. R. Smith stressed the great strain under which modern warfare is carried out. During the occupation of Guadalcanal by the United States marine corps, sleep and eating were almost impossible Weight losses ran as high as 45 lb. Rain, heat, insects and malaria contributed to the disorder of thinking and living. This strain persisted and increased for months. The complaints and symptoms were identical for each individual—headaches, lowered thresholds to sharp noises, periods of amnesia and of panic, sensory somatic complaints, marked muscular hypertonicity, tremors and palsies. Intellectually normal, the men were emotionally unstable and showed unbelievable neuromuscular tension. Fear of cowardliness was almost universal. Few cases could be returned to full or combat duty, but most of the men leaving service, in the author's opinion, should be able to return successfully to civilian life.

Aubrey Lewis examined some of the more severe neurotics after they had returned to civil life and found that a large number were able to take their usual place in society.

Aviation Medicine.—E. G. Reinartz, commanding officer of a United States school of aviation medicine, reported that, while the exigencies of the air service beget no novel or unique psychological phenomena, they increase the incidence of certain syndromes. Aeroneurosis is a chronic functional nervous and psychic disorder characterized by gastric distress, nervous irritability, insomnia and minor psychic disturbances. It is, moreover, likely to occur in the professional or experienced pilot and is commonly known as "staleness." Emotional stress is the principal exciting factor, since in order to fly it is necessary for a pilot to repress many thoughts which provoke emotional reactions. If such repression is not successful, conflicts will arise, for the instinct of self-preservation which is frequently stimulated in aviation arouses many profound emotional disturbances. Even if fear is repressed subconsciously, pilots are affected by it every time they go into the air. The flight surgeon detects signs of aeroneurosis quickly, often before the pilot himself is aware that anything is the matter. A second syndrome, according to Reinartz, is "flying fatigue." This is the result of highly abnormal flying strain such as occurs in battle conditions and is not characterized by emotional factors such as appear in aeroneurosis. The onset is slow, but once started development is often rapid, leading to deterioration and disintegration of mental and physical faculties. In order to diagnose the condition in its earliest state, the flight surgeon must be closely associated with the pilot's case. These two conditions are separated from aeroembolism produced by rapid decrease of pressure below one atmosphere. The symptoms depend on bubbles of nitrogen escaping from the blood and lodging in various parts of the body. It appears in high-altitude flying and, as was pointed out by M. N. Walsh, there is considerable individual variation with regard to the ability of pilots to withstand high altitudes. Ordinarily, mental symptoms do not occur when flying below 9,000 ft. Above 12,000 ft. symptoms occur with rapidity, such as a decrease in acuteness of hearing and vision, blunting of judgment, impaired critical perception, indolence of thought, forgetfulness and absentmindedness. There may be changes in mood and diminution or loss of the will to perform certain duties, although the ability to perform them may be essentially unimpaired. The pilot himself is often unaware of these effects. When flying above 18,000 ft. all symptoms are exacerbated. These reactions are reversible by the administration of oxygen if given in time, but at a level of 40,000 ft. the time is only 30 to 60 seconds and only 15 seconds if activity is being carried out. In high-altitude flying an uninterrupted supply of oxygen was, therefore, indispensable for pilots operating above 12,000 ft. In addition, there were the grave accidents which occurred because of nitrogen emboli and the execution of turns and dives might produce anaemia with structural damage to the brain.

BIBLIOGRAPHY.—Benjamin Malzberg, "The Outcome of Electric Shock Therapy in the New York Civil State Hospitals," *Psychiatric Quarterly,* 17:154–163 (1943); Nolan D. C. Lewis, "The Present Status of Shock Therapy of Mental Disorders," *Bull. of the New York Academy of Medicine,* 19:227–244 (1943); M. C. Petersen, "Prefrontal Lobotomy in the Treatment of Mental Disease," *Proc. of the Staff Meetings of the Mayo Clinic,* 18:368–371 (1943); Walter Freeman and James W. Watts, "Prefrontal Lobotomy," *Bull. of the New York Academy of Medicine* 18:794–812 (1942); E. L. Hutton, "Results of Prefrontal Leucotomy," *The Lancet,* 1:362–366 (1943); William G. Lennox, "Newer Knowledge of Epilepsy," *Annals of Internal Medicine,* 18:145–153 (1943); Alfred Hauptmann, "Group Therapy for Psychoneuroses," *Diseases of the Nervous System,* 4:22–25 (1943); George L. Wadsworth and Robert A. Clark, "Individual and Group Treatment in Institutional Psychiatry," *Diseases of Nervous System,* 4:53–59 (1943); Donald Blair, "Group Psychotherapy for War Neuroses," *The Lancet,* 1:204–205 (1943); William Fleeson and Edwin F. Gildea, "A Study of the Personalities of 289 Abnormal Drinkers," *Quarterly Journ. of Studies on Alcohol,* 3:409–432 (1942); Jose Thimann, "The Conditioned Reflex as a Treatment for Abnormal Drinking; Its Principle, Technic and Success," *New England Jour. of Medicine* 228:333–335 (1943); E. M. Jellinek, ed., *Alcohol Addiction and Chronic Alcoholism* (1942); George A. Blakeslee, "Neuropsychiatry in War Time," *Bull. of the New York Academy of Medicine,* 18:775–793 (1942); L. Gowan, "Psychiatric Aspects of Military Disabilities," *United States Navy Medical Bull.,* 41:129–137 (1943); W. Ronald D. Fairbairn, "The War Neuroses: Their Nature and Significance," *British Medical Jour.,* 1:183–186 (1943); Leon L. Altman, "Neuroses in Soldiers: Use of Sodium Amytal as an Aid to Psychotherapy," *War Medicine,* 3:267–273 (1943); Alexander Simon and Margaret Hagan, "Social Data in Psychiatric Casualties in the Armed Services," *American Journ. of Psychiatry,* 99:348–3 (1942); E. Rogers Smith, "Neuroses Resulting from Combat," *American Jour. of Psychiatry,* 100:94–97 (1943); Aubrey Lewis, "Social Effects Neurosis," *The Lancet* 1:167–170 (1943); Eugene G. Reinartz, "Some Mental Aspects of Aviation Medicine," *Jour. of Aviation Medicine* 14:7 83 (1943); M. N. Walsh, "Neuropsychiatric Aspects of Aviation Medicine," *Archives of Neurology and Psychiatry,* 49:147–149 (1943).

(H. R. V.)

Psychology. American psychology during 1943 had a three dimensional orientation: (1) its continued application in the prosecution of the war; (2) its attention to peace and postwar problems; (3) the continued development of pure psychological research.

As in World War I American psychologists were called upon for solutions of the problems involved in the classification of military personnel in the armed forces of the United States. The committee on classification of military personnel, a group of prominent psychometricians under the chairmanship of Walter V. Bingham, acts as an advisory body to the adjutant general

SELF-ANALYSIS was advanced as one of the methods of experimental depth psychology by Dr. Werner Wolff, expatriate German psychologist in the United States, in his book *The Expression of Personality* (Harpers, 1943). In one test, the subject is asked to comment upon two composite photographs of himself, taken without his knowledge. The portrait is split down the middle, reversing one half, and fitting it against the remaining half. The subject's reactions to his "left" and "right" faces, usually strongly negative or positive, provide definite clues to his personality, according to Dr. Wolff

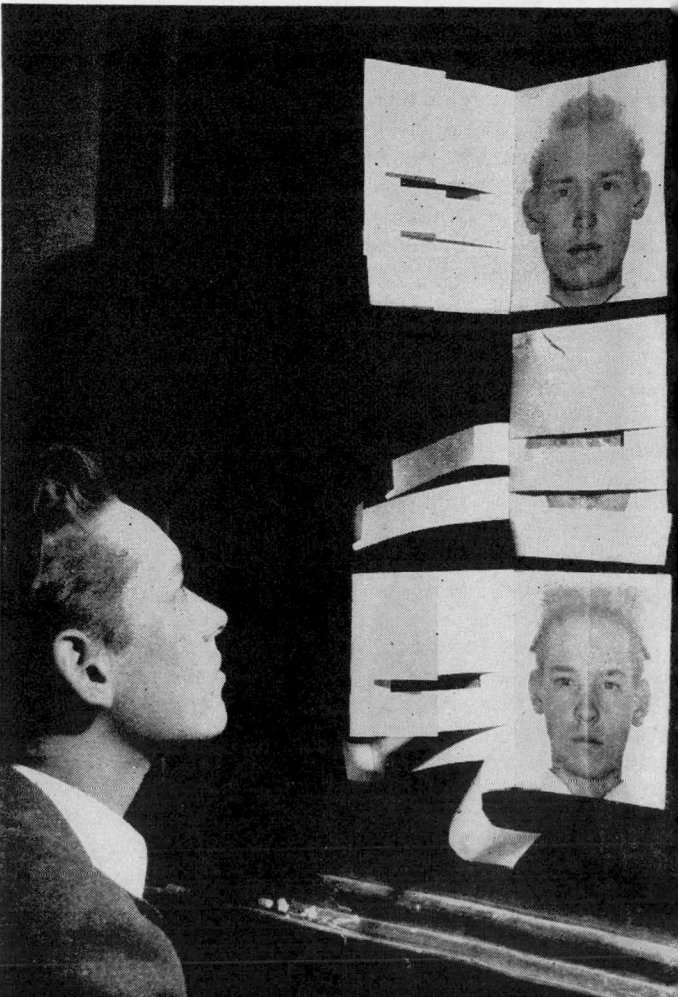

who was directed by the secretary of war, in June 1940, to assume central authority for the classification of all men in the army.

The actual administration of personnel procedures in the army was handled by the classification and enlisted replacement branch under the adjutant general's office. The officers who administered the program in the field were psychologists and personnel technicians who had special training at the adjutant general's school established in 1941 at Fort Washington, Md. The more significant psychological contribution, however, was made by the personnel research section of the classification branch under the direction of M. W. Richardson. This section constructed and revised the many tests demanded by the army's general and specialized needs. These demands could not be met by the rigid application of old psychological instruments. They required a program of constant research and experimentation which had, however, to be concerned solely with actual and urgent army situations. In addition to tests, the section prepared standardized aids for the field work of the army's classification officers: manuals of test administration, interview schedules and rating forms.

The first important step in the classification of the army recruit was the administration of a minimum literacy test to detect the men who would not be able to absorb army training—a large part of which was based on manuals and other written material. Men failing the literacy test were given a visual classification test to select the illiterates with sufficient native ability to learn military duties. The next step for literate men was the army general classification test on the basis of which soldiers were grouped into five categories according to their learning capacity. In addition, men took the mechanical aptitude test and the radio telegraph operator aptitude test and their scores helped determine their assignment to specialist training in mechanics or radio-telegraphy. Experiment showed the best single test for radio-telegraphy to be a work sample test of code learning. Auditory discrimination proved to be not quite as significant.

Initial assignments of men were based both upon test scores and upon the results of a standardized interview yielding data on such items as education, languages, occupational history, hobbies, leadership experience and previous military training.

Slow learners were placed in special training units under experts who had developed a good deal of original instructional material designed to increase motivation by its freedom from rigid and static content. In this way psychological training salvaged many recruits who would otherwise have been dismissed as mentally unqualified.

The need for highly trained technicians and officers was so great that the army utilized the resources of the country's universities in establishing the army specialized training program. Under the terms of this program soldiers were assigned to those colleges where the army had set up a curriculum. The ASTP included a basic phase and an advanced phase, the latter of which was divided into various specialized curricula. Criteria for admission to the ASTP included high scores on the army general classification test and on an educational achievement test also prepared by the personnel section.

The advanced phase of ASTP offered a curriculum in personnel psychology during 1943 at 11 leading U.S. universities for the purpose of increasing the number of trained personnel psychologists in the army. The total number of men assigned to these schools in 1943 was 1,350.

The National Research council's emergency committee in psychology established a sub-committee on a textbook of military psychology in 1942 to prepare a textbook for men in the armed forces. This volume appeared during 1943 as the co-operative effort of 59 psychologists with E. G. Boring, editor-in-chief. The book is a nontechnical presentation for the soldier of psychological facts and principles which bear upon military problems. Major attention is given to perception and the sense organs; but individual differences, training, efficiency, motivation, adjustment, mobs and rumours are also included.

The selection and classification of pilots was under the direction of the office of the air surgeon, army air forces. Aviation applicants had to pass, first, the aviation cadet qualifying examination which was primarily a test of pilot aptitude. Later the cadet took the aviation cadet classification tests, a series of 20 tests taking two days to administer. These tests were developed and were in the process of experimental modification by a large staff of psychologists. They measured the following types of function: (1) intelligence, judgment and proficiency, (2) alertness, observation and speed of perception, (3) personality, temperament and interest, (4) visual-motor co-ordination.

During 1943 the belief grew among psychologists that the winning of the war and the winning of the peace were different aspects of the same process. The general hypothesis that the nature of victory was related to a durable peace not only received acceptance but the emergence of specific postwar reconstruction problems before the end of the war became apparent. For example, the returning soldiers discharged because of physical injury or mental illness were challenging psychological resources for rehabilitation. In March 1942 the first rehabilitation clinic was held at Yale university for purposes of vocational and psychological counselling and in the course of the following 15 months over 60% of the clients tested were placed in jobs. In 1943 Stanford university established a course in psychology for rehabilitation workers emphasizing the physiological psychology of motor functions, optimal procedures for making and breaking motor habits, psychological adjustment and the mental hygiene of the hospitalized person.

One expression of this interest in postwar problems was manifest in the creation of a committee on the psychological aspects of postwar planning by the Society for Psychological Study of Social Issues under the chairmanship of Gardner Murphy. This committee co-ordinated research and information on major psychological obstacles to permanent peace; on the school systems of the various world powers as they bore on the development of war and peace attitudes; on American attitudes toward the postwar world. The implementation of research into psychological areas of understanding and attitude was furnished in part by the Office of Public Opinion Research of Princeton university which had been systematically sampling the opinions of the American public on a nationwide basis on postwar problems. This research institute reported that the majority of the American public in all major income groups wants co-operative national planning after the war in which government, business, labour and agriculture will participate. Other nation-wide attitudinal research was in agreement that the American people favoured international organization to preserve the peace but that their thinking was unstructured concerning the instrumentalities for achieving this end. Thus many clung to specific beliefs in high tariff barriers and immigration restrictions while accepting the general desirability of international co-operation. This was consistent with previous psychological research which indicated that the acceptance or rejection of general symbols could be accompanied by contradictory beliefs concerning specific, related proposals.

Another indication of the growing interest in psychological peace problems appeared in the April number of the *Journal of Abnormal and Social Psychology* which was given over to articles on "Psychological Considerations in Making the Peace," with contributions from E. C. Tolman, K. Lewin, C. Buhler, F. Schreier, K. Bode, O. H. Mowrer and R. Stagner. The discussion covered such problems as: how can psychological identification with a world state be achieved?; how can German forfeiting of freedom through overemphasis upon general abstract concepts be remedied educationally?; how should an unrealistic pacifist reaction after the war, which turns away from the basic problems, be met?; to what extent could church groups within Germany assist in re-education after the war?

Finally, the fundamental question concerning the basis of war in human nature received renewed study. In 1943 Mark May summarized the work of the Yale Institute of Human Relations on this problem in *A Social Psychology of War and Peace*. This volume denies that war is the inevitable outcome of human nature. It holds that though aggressive tendencies are unavoidable due to the frustrations in the socialization process and in social interaction, nevertheless it has been possible to control overt conflict within the in-group. Hence aggression is possible to control between groups. The only assured way to prevent armed conflict, however, would be to extend the boundaries of the peace group to include all nations, that is, to build an international order.

In addition to war-oriented research, steady psychological advances continued during 1943 in the study of the physiological basis of behaviour, of learning and motivation, and of social functions. Extirpation experiments established the independence of the optic cortex and the superior colliculi in the mediation of visual functions. The cerebral mechanisms of vision furnish the basis for focal pattern vision; the lower centers are the basis for pattern vision of moving contours as well as brightness discrimination and flicker vision. In the field of learning the hypothesis that anticipatory goal reactions are symbolic processes of a higher level than the goal gradient was strengthened by the removal of the prefrontal cortical areas in rats with a resulting persistence of the goal gradient and the disappearance of the anticipatory reaction. Unusual results were reported in experiments on incidental memory with an *intent* group showing no better scores after a 19-day interval than a *non-intent* group. A genuine contribution to the dynamics of attitude formation appeared in T. Newcomb's *Personality and Social Change*, a study of the personal basis of attitude change in a college community. The role and status of the individual in the group proved a central factor in attitude change. The extension of controlled psychological techniques in field situations was demonstrated by a study of Italian acculturation by I. Child. (*See also* NERVOUS SYSTEM).

BIBLIOGRAPHY.—Staff, Personnel Research Section, AGO, *Psychological Bulletin*, 40:129–135, 205–211, 271–279, 357–371, 429–435, 499–508 (1943); M. A. Seidenfeld, *Psychological Bulletin* 40:279–281 (1943); D. Wolfle, *Psychological Bulletin*, 40:780–786 (1943); E. G. Boring, *Psychology for the Fighting Man* (1943); Staff of the Psychological Branch, Office of the Air Surgeon, *Psychological Bulletin*, 40:759–769 (1943); G. W. Allport and H. R. Veltfort, *Journal of Social Psychology*, 18:165–233 (1943); D. C. Marquis, *Psychological Bulletin*, 40:687–700 (1943); J. S. Bruner, *Public Thinking on Post-War Problems* (1943); M. May, *A Social Psychology of War and Peace* (1943); K. U. Smith and M. Bridgman, *Journal of Experimental Psychology*, 33:165–187 (1943); M. A. Epstein and C. T. Morgan, *Journal of Experimental Psychology*, 32:453–463 (1943); W. C. Biel and R. C. Force, *Journal of Experimental Psychology*, 32:52–63 (1943); T. Newcomb, *Personality and Social Change* (1943); I. Child, *Italian or American* (1943).   (D. KA.)

Public Assistance: *see* CHILD WELFARE; RELIEF; SOCIAL SECURITY.

Public Buildings Administration: *see* FEDERAL WORKS AGENCY.

Public Health Engineering.
Air Sanitation.—In 1943, the reality of air-borne infection appeared to have become rather generally accepted among sanitarians. Accumulating evidence had shown that, beyond the range of "droplet infection"—direct contact with droplets result-

ing from coughing and sneezing—there is air carriage of bacteria resulting from the evaporation of the smaller droplets to dr nuclei. These may float for hours or days and be carried ove considerable distances.

Once in this suspended form, the fate of the bacteria is deter mined by their own ability to withstand the adverse conditions o desiccation and of sunlight, direct or diffused. It is known o good experimental evidence that many of the pathogens of th nose and throat will survive under these conditions, either as fre floating particles or as deposited dust for a sufficient length c time. The subject was well summarized up to 1942 by Leo Buchbinder.

Recognition of these facts led to extensive investigation upo both sides of the Atlantic into methods of air disinfection. Mos of these studies, during the war years, were conducted under gov ernmental auspices, British and American, and the results wei utilized in connection with military and civilian activities on th war front and little publicity was given to the newer develop ments.

Improvements were made in the use of aerosols, vapours o mists of disinfectant sprayed into the room. Ultraviolet ligh was also applied in large-scale experimental work. These studie were expected undoubtedly to have an important bearing upo public health practice in the postwar years.

Water Supply.—For some years previous to 1943, there ha been a gradual accumulation of evidence that contaminate drinking water might be a means of communicating poliomyelitis Briefly, this evidence was as follows:

1. The gastrointestinal tract is a possible portal of entry to the huma body. The older views had held that the sole portal entry is the naso pharynx and the olfactory nerves.
2. Active virus is recoverable from stools of patients and from cit sewage.
3. The virus lives in sewage for a considerable time and in pure wate for at least 100 days.
4. Ordinary processes of water purification do not destroy the viru completely.
5. In many cases of epidemics, the chronological distribution amon cities in a river valley has followed the river downstream.

Up to 1943, it had not been generally believed that publi water supplies were implicated in any of the major epidemics o this disease, but the possible responsibility of contaminated wate —as well as milk and other foods—for occasional sporadic case could not be eliminated. A considerable anxiety was felt among those responsible for water and sewage treatment as was evi denced by several scientific studies dealing with the effects of the various standard processes employed upon the virus. These studies were summarized up to 1943 by H. J. Carlson, *et al.*

City Planning.—Among the several lines of postwar planning undertaken up to 1943, none had greater public health implica tions than the planning for new housing construction and for city and town development.

Harland Bartholomew, engineer of the City Planning commis sion of St. Louis, Mo., summarized the opportunities and the needs that might be expected to develop as the result of housing shortage and need for speedy re-employment of men released from war activities, military and civil.

There are three levels of planning: the city as a whole, the neighbourhood, and the individual home. Zoning, with reference to more orderly development, open spaces and recreational cen tres deals with the community as a whole. It segregates industry, provides purer air in residential areas and reduces congestion. Neighbourhood planning results in decreasing traffic hazards, con venient access to shops, schools and playgrounds and elimination of slums. Housing deals with the internal arrangements of the household, especially such details as living space, sanitary facili ties, light and air.

BIBLIOGRAPHY.—Leon Buchbinder, "The Transmission of Certain Infections of Respiratory Origin. A Critical Review," *J.A.M.A.*, 118:718–730 (1942); H. J. Carlson, G. M. Ridenour, and C. F. McKhann, Jr., "Effects of the Activated Sludge Process of Sewage Treatment on Poliomyelitis Virus," *Am. Jour. Pub. Health*, 33:1083–1087 (1943); Harland Bartholomew, "Public Health Implications in City and Regional Planning," *Am. Jour. Pub. Health*, 33:481–489 (1943). (E. B. PH.)

Public Health Service: *see* FEDERAL SECURITY AGENCY; VENEREAL DISEASES.

Public Housing Authority, Federal: *see* NATIONAL HOUSING AGENCY.

Public Libraries: *see* AMERICAN LIBRARY ASSOCIATION; LIBRARIES.

Public Roads Administration: *see* FEDERAL WORKS AGENCY; ROADS AND HIGHWAYS.

Public Utilities.

In 1943 performance by the public utility industry of the United States was dominated as in 1942 by war influences. Early in the year the War Production board reorganized its organization for wartime public utility control when J. A. Krug assumed his new duties as wartime administrator of utility services. With the placing of local electric railway and motor bus services under the control of the Office of Defense Transportation by executive order, the merging of the control of all nontransport utilities under the new WPB set-up simplified the dual system of regulation under the war powers and of regulation under the police powers. The courts were also upholding the power of the OPA under federal anti-inflation legislation to prevent increases in the rates of common carrier and other public utilities after Sept. 15, 1942, by federal, state or municipal authority without 30 days' notice to OPA and opportunity to intervene.

The most significant influence of OPA on public utility regulation was shown by the reduction in freight rates ordered by the Interstate Commerce commission in April. This reduction removed increases of 6% which the commission had granted early in 1942. In carrying out the purposes of the stabilization act of Oct. 1942, the commission found that the passenger rate advances of 10% did not need to be disturbed and that despite the freight rate decreases the resulting service revenues would be sufficient to meet all costs. Similarly, the OPA was attempting to prevent increases in other public utility prices, especially those which flowed automatically from contractual or technical requirements like the various types of fuel clauses. In spite of this influence, rate increases were granted when it became necessary to provide increased revenues in order to keep up good service.

Coming to a head in 1943, though announced on Jan. 3, 1944, the decision of the U.S. supreme court in the case of the Hope Natural Gas company against the Federal Power commission reaffirmed the position it had already taken in the Natural Pipeline cases. The conflict between the reproduction cost theory and the prudent investment theory of rate-base determination was, if anything, even more pronounced in this case because the circuit court of appeals had set aside the rate reduction order of the FPC because it was not based on reproduction cost. It was now generally agreed that the decision would further serve to support the FPC and any other federal and state commissions which proposed to regulate rates on a prudent investment basis. It should also support the FPC in its work continued throughout 1943, relating to reclassification of fixed capital accounts and in its original-cost studies, with the view of eliminating "write-ups" in these plant accounts.

Expansion in the jurisdiction of the FPC was likewise upheld by a U.S. supreme court ruling in the Jersey Central Power and Light company case. Here the court expanded its definition of interstate commerce by using the potential sale of breakdown power across state lines as the basis for extending the com-

mission's jurisdiction to intrastate utilities connected with companies having interstate tie-lines.

The year was also memorable because for the first time the electric energy output of the United States, under the influence of war production, reached and passed the 200,000,000,000 kw.hr. mark. With 221,000,000,000 kw.hr. generated by means of an installed capacity of slightly less than 50,000,000 kw., the nation's producing power reached a peak from which it is more than likely that the future must show a recession. It was also important to note that the upsurge in the supply of publicly owned generating facilities reached about 20% of the national total, with hydro power more than holding its own with the expanding steam power. It was the federal portion of the public supply which had been expanding, particularly in hydro facilities. The tenth and last unit was installed at Bonneville in December, bringing that project's capacity to its ultimate of 516,400 kw. at a cost of $81,000,000. Private enterprise also set a new mark with the installation in the Fisk generating station at Chicago of a record breaking steam turbine of 147,000 kw.

A major problem of postwar adjustment was expected to come when administrative arrangements were worked out to co-ordinate public supply with private supply of power. The bureau of reclamation was decentralized into six area components. Contracts providing for the sale of power from Reclamation's Shasta dam to Pacific Gas & Electric company were signed. A Southwestern Power administration was established to sell power from Norfork, Pensacola and Denison dams. And in the background the Securities and Exchange commission was continuing its work of supervising the corporate simplification of holding company systems and their dissolution into newly integrated operating units.

In March the Federal Communications commission granted final authorizations for the Bell Telephone Company of Pennsylvania to acquire the Keystone Telephone system of Philadelphia and for the New Jersey Bell Telephone company to acquire the Eastern Telephone and Telegraph company and the Camden and Atlantic Telephone company. Of similar import is congressional legislation, now signed by the president, which authorized the merging of the Western Union and Postal Telegraph systems, plans for which were worked out and approved by the FCC during the year. (*See also* DAMS; ELECTRICAL INDUSTRIES; LAW; RURAL ELECTRIFICATION; TENNESSEE VALLEY AUTHORITY.) (M. G. G.)

Public Works Administration: *see* FEDERAL WORKS AGENCY.

Publishing (Book).

In a year in which fewer titles were issued in all but five of the classifications into which U.S. books are divided, books on philosophy and ethics showed the only substantial numerical increase, with 131 more books published in this classification in 1943 than in 1942. The number of books on technical and military subjects, the category which in 1942 registered the only sizable numerical gain over the preceding year, declined nearly 14% in 1943, although total sales remained large. Books of poetry and drama suffered the greatest numerical decrease, but marked decreases also occurred in the classifications of fiction, children's books and, unexpectedly in a war year, history, geography and travel. The year's total of new books and new editions was only 8,325—1,200 fewer than in 1942 and 2,787 fewer than in 1941. Table I, compiled by *Publishers' Weekly*, summarizes U.S. book publication for 1942 and 1943.

Best Sellers.—The year 1943's two fiction best sellers, Lloyd C. Douglas' *The Robe* and Marcia Davenport's *The Valley of Decision*, were both published in Oct. 1942, and remained on the best seller list throughout 1943. In third place was *So Little Time*, by John P. Marquand, followed by *A Tree Grows in Brooklyn*, by Betty Smith. *The Human Comedy*, by-

Table I.—U.S. Publication of Books, 1942 and 1943

International Classification	1942 New Books	1942 New Editions	1942 Total	1943 New Books	1943 New Editions	1943 Total	Net Change
Philosophy, Ethics . . .	72	12	84	188	27	215	+131
Religion, Theology . . .	610	46	656	541	60	601	− 55
Sociology, Economics .	557	63	620	541	44	585	− 35
Law	82	30	112	59	19	78	− 34
Education	200	17	217	234	22	256	+ 39
Philology	222	58	280	170	44	214	− 66
Science	305	92	397	324	125	449	+ 52
Technical and Military Books	606	185	791	549	136	685	−106
Medicine, Hygiene . . .	309	134	443	224	107	331	−112
Agriculture, Gardening .	79	21	100	71	27	98	− 2
Domestic Economy . . .	83	29	112	91	26	117	+ 5
Business	205	56	261	109	37	146	−115
Fine Arts	170	17	187	153	22	175	− 12
Music	54	13	67	58	18	76	+ 9
Games, Sports	121	28	149	78	11	89	− 60
General Literature . . .	338	62	400	265	36	301	− 99
Poetry, Drama	533	61	594	371	22	393	−201
Fiction	1,108	555	1,663	933	545	1,478	−185
Juvenile	793	71	864	646	44	690	−174
History	571	75	646	465	74	539	−107
Geography, Travel . . .	222	37	259	178	37	215	− 44
Biography	482	60	542	424	49	473	− 69
Miscellaneous	64	17	81	92	29	121	+ 40
Total	7,786	1,739	9,525	6,764	1,561	8,325	−1,200

William Saroyan, and *Mrs Parkington*, by Louis Bromfield. *The Song of Bernadette*, by Franz Werfel, 1942's fiction best seller, was in tenth place in 1943. *One World*, by Wendell L. Willkie was the nonfiction leader in 1943, with John Roy Carlson's exposé of fascist activities in the U.S., *Under Cover*, in second place. *Journey Among Warriors*, by Eve Curie, *On Being a Real Person*, by Harry Emerson Fosdick, *Guadalcanal Diary*, by Richard Tregaskis, and *Burma Surgeon*, by Lt. Col. Gordon Seagrave, followed. Marion Hargrove's 1942 nonfiction best seller, *See Here, Private Hargrove*, remained, like Werfel's book, on the 1943 list in tenth place. Although no figures were released on sales of individual books, *Publishers' Weekly* stated that a substantially larger number of copies of the 20 best sellers of 1943 had been sold than of the 20 best sellers of 1942.

Great Britain.—1943 was the sixth consecutive year in which the number of books published in Great Britain fell below that of the preceding year. The 6,705 titles issued in 1943 represented a decrease of 536 from the 1942 figure as well as a total smaller by several hundred than the expected publication figure of 7,000 books. However, three classifications showed numerical increases over 1942, and works on aeronautics, on naval and military subjects and on veterinary science, farming and stockkeeping appeared in greater numbers during 1943 than in prewar years. Of

Table II.—British Publication of Books, 1941, 1942 and 1943

Classification	1941	1942	1943
Aeronautics	118	159	148
Biography and Memoirs	356	295	281
Children's Books	520*	595*	671
Educational	340	384	312
Fiction	2,342	1,559	1,408
History	199	213	192
Medical and Surgical	238	303	212
Naval and Military	158	246	229
Poetry and Drama	286	249	329
Political	556	678	596
Religion	446	495	425
Travel	112	108	102
Veterinary Science, Farming and Stock-keeping	37	46	73
Other	1,873	1,911	1,727
Total	7,581	7,241	6,705

*Includes minor fiction.

1943's production, 1,201 titles were reprints and new editions and 5,504 were new books. Table II, compiled by the publishers of *The Bookseller*, gives detailed statistics of British book production for 1941–43. (*See* also NEWSPAPERS AND MAGAZINES; AMERICAN LITERATURE; ENGLISH LITERATURE; etc.)

⊦Puerto Rico.
A United States insular dependency in the West Indies; area, 3,400.6 sq.mi.; pop. (1940): 1,869,255, a 21.1% increase over 1930. Whites comprised 76.2%, Negroes, 23.8%. The chief cities are San Juan, the capital (169,247); Ponce (65,182); Mayagüez (50,376); Caguas (24,377); Arecibo (22,134); Río Piedras (19,935). Languages: Spanish and English; religion: predominantly Roman Catholic. Governor in 1943: Rexford Guy Tugwell.

History.—The year 1943 was one of considerable strain, economically and politically, for Puerto Rico. Depredations by axis submarines and dislocations of normal sources of supplies and food through wartime restrictions and operations brought about great shortages; agricultural crops were lighter than in the two previous years; military installations were largely completed, thus throwing unemployed labour onto the market; and the colonial government itself was called into question. Both in the United States and in the island pressure was increased for autonomy or independence.

An investigating committee headed by Senator Dennis Chavez (Dem., N.M.) arrived in Puerto Rico from the United States in Feb. 1943, to hold an enquiry into social, economic and political conditions. Governor Rexford Guy Tugwell was called upon to make a general report on affairs in the island. In his comprehensive report, Tugwell strongly endorsed the policy of granting autonomy to Puerto Rico, especially in regard to the election of governor. This point became one of the principal recommendations of the Chavez committee.

In March, President Roosevelt requested congress to amend the organic act to permit the people of Puerto Rico to elect their own governor, and appointed a special advisory committee composed of Puerto Ricans and continental residents to study the matter. The committee was headed by Secretary of the Interior Harold L. Ickes. Senator Millard Tydings (Dem., Md.), however, pressed for complete independence for the island, except that military bases would be retained by the United States.

A matter of great concern to the Puerto Ricans came with a threat of suspension of the FWA work relief program. Although some reduction in the total rolls was effected, a means was found to prepare an insular work program to assume full responsibility for emergency work relief. Rapidly rising prices, aggravated scarcities, and the completion of military construction made a reduction in work relief a serious problem for the large low income groups, such as the landless "agregados."

Shortages of food and consumers goods, fortunately, were gradually alleviated after March 1943, through the successful campaign against the axis submarines and through an increased allocation of shipping to the island. Also, an extensive "victory garden" program helped somewhat to improve the food situation. However, the efforts of a Food Distribution administration were needed to avoid famine and suffering.

Lack of sufficient chemical fertilizer for the sugar cane and tobacco plantings, and a severe storm on Oct. 14, 1943, which damaged food crops, created many agricultural problems. However, these factors were compensated to a large degree by the extraordinary rise in the production and exportation of rum. By September, rum production had reached a peak of 944,164 gal. per month. Income from the tax on rum and general improvement in shipping caused the insular treasurer to estimate revenue for the 1943–44 fiscal year at $53,775,000—a possible surplus of more than $28,000,000.

Education.—In 1943, there were 1,939 public schools with an enrolment of 321,932. It was estimated that of the children ages 6–14, more than 400,000 were not attending school. There were 1,622 elementary, 92 rural vocational ("second unit"), 17 trade, 158 junior high, and 42 high schools. The University of Puerto Rico had almost 5,000 students in 1943.

Finance.—The monetary unit is the United States dollar. Private deposits in banks had more than doubled since 1940, reaching a total in Oct. 1943, of $99,800,000.

Trade and Communication.—During 1943, shipping restrictions were gradually relaxed until by September, imports had reached two-thirds of the 1940 average (imports in 1940 were valued at $107,030,482—93% from the United States). Export shipping was only slightly below normal by the end of the fiscal year. Imports were principally of foodstuffs—rice, fish, meat, beans, corn, flour, and vegetable oils and fats; also imported were textiles and various manufactures. Export shipments were of sugar, rum (five times normal), tobacco, needlework and fruits.

Daily air service with the United States and Panamá continued. Internal communication was by railway (387 mi.) and by 1,487 mi. of main highway supplemented by local and military roads. Radio-telephone and cable service connected Puerto Rico with the United States and other countries. Also, there were six radio broadcasting stations and six newspapers.

Agriculture.—Agriculture is the principal economic pursuit. Most important products in 1943 were: sugar, 1,039,237 short tons; tobacco 8,200,000 lb.; coffee 17,541,500 lb.; cotton 3,200,-000 lb.; pineapples 500,000 crates; coco-nuts 10,057,000 nuts; grapefruit and oranges (for local consumption). In 1940, there were 51,494 work and 112,585 other cattle, and 22,709 horses, mules and donkeys. There were approximately 1,200,000 ac. of tillable land.

Manufacturing.—Manufacturing is for domestic consumption except for rum production, needlework, sugar processing and cigar and cigarette making. (C. L. G.)

Pugilism: *see* BOXING.

Pulitzer Prizes.

The Pulitzer prizes in journalism and letters were established by the late Joseph Pulitzer, founder of the school of journalism of Columbia university, and are awarded annually in the spring by the trustees of the university on the recommendations of an advisory board of the school. In 1943 all monetary awards were for $500 each; three travelling scholarships were granted to students and one

scholarship worth $1,500 was granted an art student. The prize awards were: for a distinguished American novel, to Upton Sinclair for *Dragon's Teeth*; for a distinguished book on the history of the United States, to Esther Forbes for *Paul Revere and the World He Lived In*; for the best American biography, to Samuel Eliot Morison for *Christopher Columbus; Admiral of the Ocean Sea*; for a distinguished volume of verse, to Robert Frost for *A Witness Tree*; for an original American play, produced in New York, to Thornton Wilder for "The Skin of Our Teeth"; for a distinguished musical composition, to William Schuman for *Secular Cantata No. 2, A Free Song*. The awards in journalism were: for a meritorious public service by an American newspaper ($500 gold medal), to the Omaha *World Herald* for its original plan for the collection of scrap metal; for a distinguished example of reporting, to George Weller of the foreign staff of the Chicago *Daily News*; for distinguished articles of national or foreign correspondence, to Ira Wolfert, North American Newspaper Alliance, for three articles on the fifth battle of the Solomons and to Hanson W. Baldwin, New York *Times*, for articles on the South Pacific battle areas; for distinguished editorial writing, to Forrest W. Seymour of the Des Moines *Register and Tribune*; for a distinguished cartoon, to Jay N. Darling, of the New York *Herald Tribune*; and for a distinguished news photograph, to Frank Noel, of the Associated Press. (*See also* LITERARY PRIZES; THEATRE.) (H. HA.)

Pulp Industry: *see* PAPER AND PULP INDUSTRY.
Pulpstones: *see* ABRASIVES.
Pumice: *see* ABRASIVES.

Purdue University.

An institution of higher education at Lafayette, Ind., founded May 6, 1869, as the Indiana link in the chain of land-grant colleges and universities. Degrees in 1943 were offered in agriculture, home economics, pharmacy, science, physical education, education, and the following branches of engineering: civil, electrical, chemical and metallurgical, mechanical and aeronautical, public service and engineering law; trade and industrial education.

Like many other institutions of learning, Purdue in 1943 was geared to the U.S. war effort, with the school calendar changed from two semesters of 18 weeks and a summer term to three full terms of 16 weeks each, so that a student might graduate in two and two-thirds calendar years.

While the type of training offered in Purdue fitted definitely into the war program, there were in addition to the regularly enrolled student body in 1943 hundreds from the navy or army taking special courses. The normal civilian enrolment of about 7,000 continued to drop, but there were 1,250 in the navy V-12 training program; 800 in the naval electricians' school; 1,500 in the army's specialized training programs; 150 in training at the Purdue airport as navy flight instructors or in preliminary flight training; 42 South American fliers in training under the inter-American program, etc.

Research in agriculture and industry as well as the teaching and extension programs were also directed into the nation's war effort. For statistics on enrolment, faculty, library volumes, etc., *see* UNIVERSITIES AND COLLEGES.

THE 1942 PULITZER PRIZE CARTOON: "What a Place for a Waste Paper Salvage Campaign" by J. Norwood Darling of the *New York Herald Tribune*. Columbia university announced the prize May 3, 1943

Pyrite.

The production of pyrite in the United States rose from 722,688 short tons in 1941 to 806,807 in 1942; production increased by 12% and value of output by 23%. Output was reported to have increased again in 1943, but no details were available. Before the war, imports, chiefly from Spain, were almost as large as the domestic output, but Spanish shipments were cut by shortage of shipping, and imports from

Canada took their place. Canadian production, largely by-product from the concentration of copper ores, increased heavily. Australia could produce large tonnages of by-product pyrite from copper, lead and zinc ores, but the domestic demand is small and distance from other points of consumption plus shortage of shipping blocks the recovery of more than is required to meet the domestic consumption. Portugal for a time was a heavier producer than the United States, but here, too, lack of shipping curtailed operations. The Spanish output was irregular, between 33,000 and 66,000 short tons monthly; a total of 151,200 tons in the last quarter of 1942 declined to 116,600 tons in the first quarter of 1943.   (G. A. Ro.)

Quakers: see FRIENDS, RELIGIOUS SOCIETY OF.

Quebec. One of the two central provinces of the dominion of Canada (q.v.), admitted to the union in 1867; area 594,534 sq.mi.; pop. (1941) 3,331,882, of whom 65% were urban. Capital, Quebec (147,908); largest city, Montreal (890,234). The lieutenant governor in 1943 was Eugene Fiset; the premier, Adelard Godbout.

Education.—The number of students in provincially controlled schools in 1942 was 610,792; in private schools 57,593.

Communication.—The mileage of surfaced highways in 1942 was 19,250; of earth highways 18,918; provincial expenditure on highways $21,389,804. The railroad mileage in 1942 was 4,804.

Finance.—The ordinary receipts in 1942 were $59,153,857; ordinary expenditure $66,441,201. The direct debt (less sinking funds) was $387,747,347, indirect liabilities (less sinking funds) $38,554,517.

Agriculture.—The acreage of field crops in 1943 was 6,599,900; gross value of all field crops $153,152,000.

Table I.—Leading Agricultural Products of Quebec, 1942 and 1941

Crop	1942	1941
Wheat, bu.	603,000	533,000
Oats, bu.	50,580,000	47,291,000
Barley, bu.	3,881,000	3,715,000
Corn, bu.	994,000	695,000

Manufacturing.—The gross value of manufactured products in 1940 was $1,357,375,776; net value $595,552,909; number of employees 252,492; salaries and wages $277,639,876.

Table II.—Principal Industries of Quebec, 1939 and 1938

| Industry | Value of products | |
	1939	1938
Pulp and paper	$103,564,981	$88,990,115
Smelting and refining	86,005,322	78,954,445
Cotton, yarn and cloth	49,176,421	39,568,088
Tobacco, cigars and cigarettes	39,986,847	39,156,515

Mineral Production.—The value of the mineral production of Quebec in 1942 was $104,749,101.

Table III.—Principal Mineral Products of Quebec, 1940 and 1939

| Mineral | Value | |
	1940	1939
Gold	$42,409,020*	$41,939,552†
Copper	...	11,831,749
Nickel	14,476,814	...
Lead	...	...
Zinc	...	882,606
Silver	1,340,540	472,675
Asbestos, etc.	16,931,476	15,858,492

*1942.   †1941.   (J. C. HE.)

Queensland. A state of the Australian commonwealth lying in the northeast and occupying 670,500 sq.mi.; pop. (est. Dec. 31, 1941) 1,036,830. Chief cities (pop. Dec. 31, 1940): Brisbane, cap., 335,000; Rockhampton 35,500; Townsville 31,450. Governor (1943): Sir Leslie Orme Wilson.

History.—The Labour government under the premiership of F. A. Cooper remained in office throughout 1943. The state smeltery at Chillagoe—the last of the state enterprises established during World War I—was closed in July. Legal history was made in March when a jury of seven was empanelled in criminal proceedings in Brisbane. This followed special legislation passed to permit smaller juries consequent on the manpower shortage. Sugar production during 1943 was estimated at 607,000 tons, the lowest for several years. The year's cotton crop was also expected to be lower owing to unfavourable weather conditions.

The postwar reconstruction committee submitted plans to the state government for extending the state's irrigation and water conservation resources involving a capital outlay of £A14,000,000 to £A15,000,000.

Education.—In 1940: schools, 1,914; scholars, 171,391.

Finance.—Revenue (1941–42) £A23,662,947; expenditure (1941–42) £A23,599,175. Debt outstanding (June 30, 1942) £A131,171,752.

Communication.—Roads (1940) 125,095 mi.; railways (Dec. 31, 1942) 6,497 mi. Motor vehicles licensed (March 31, 1943), 63,948 cars; 44,756 commercial; 5,378 cycles. Wireless receiving set licences 176,947. Telephones, 85,847.

Agriculture, Manufacturing, Mineral Production.—Production in 1941–42: sugar cane 800,000 tons; wheat 3,000,000 bu.; maize 3,733,424 bu.; wool 194,200,000 lb.; gold (1939) 145,667 fine oz.; silver (1939) 3,600,000 oz.; coal (1942) 1,708,000 tons. Industry, manufacturing, 1940–41: factories 2,972; employees (average) 57,269; production, gross value of output £A70,236,464; unemployment (trade union returns) (March 1943), 1.5%.   (W. D. MA.)

Quicksilver: see MERCURY.

Race Riots. When the Alabama Dry Dock and Shipbuilding company of Mobile promoted 12 Negro workers May 25, 1943, the white workers objected. As the Negro workers left the plant they were attacked, and 11 of them were so badly injured that they had to be treated at a hospital. Order was not restored until a detachment of troops arrived.

Rioting began in Los Angeles, Calif., on June 4 when soldiers and sailors attacked Mexicans and Negroes who were wearing "zoot" suits; the rioting continued for six days, and the city council passed an ordinance forbidding the wearing of zoot suits, but on June 7, before the ordinance was passed, a mob of about a thousand service men and civilians raided a theatre and drove the Mexicans and Negroes into the street, where they were assaulted.

Rioting began in Beaumont, Tex., on June 19 when it was rumoured that a white woman had been assaulted by a Negro. Negroes were attacked whenever they appeared on the streets, and many hundred workers in the Pennsylvania company's shipyard went out and refused to return to their jobs until order was restored. Ten persons had to receive hospital treatment for the injuries received.

Rioting began in Detroit, Mich., on Sunday, June 20, with an attack on Negroes employed by the Packard company. Attracted by the high wages in the war industries, more than 300,000 whites and Negroes from the south had migrated to the city, taking with them the southern feeling about race relations. Early in June some Negroes employed by the Packard company had been promoted. Agitators charged with being members of the Ku Klux Klan incited the white southern workers to protest against the promotion of the Negroes. Many Negro workers were unable to get to the plant on Monday because they were attacked by roving mobs composed chiefly of boys and young men. The mobs not only attacked the Negroes but also broke the show windows of stores and carried off the goods from the shelves. On Monday night eight Negroes were riding on a Woodward avenue car. A police inspector with eight patrolmen boarded the car and told the Negroes that a mob was coming toward it and that he would protect any Negro who wished to be guarded against mob violence. Four of the men left the car with the police, but when they reached the street they were beaten and generally abused. Mobs of from 800 to 1,000 roamed the streets attacking Negroes in their automobiles, overturning the cars and burning them. Thirty-five persons were killed during the trouble, 29 of whom were Negroes. More than 600 were injured, most of them Negroes and 85% of the 1,832 persons arrested were also Negroes.

On Sunday, Aug. 1, according to New York city police, a Negro army M.P. interfered with a policeman who attempted to arrest a woman in the lobby of a hotel in the Harlem district. The policeman shot and slightly wounded the Negro. It was at once rumoured that a policeman had killed a Negro soldier, and rioting began with attacks upon Negroes. During the trouble five Negroes were killed and 561 persons, many of them Negroes, were injured. (G. W. Do.)

Rachmaninoff, Sergei Vassilievitch
(1873 – 1943), U.S. pianist, composer and conductor, was born April 2, on his father's estate, Oneg, in the Novgorod district, Russia. He made his home in the United States after World War I, and though he appeared as conductor on several occasions, his popularity rested on his mastery of the piano and on his compositions. His works, ranked among the most important 20th century compositions, were described as purely "Russian" and as typical of the Slav folk spirit. Most popular of his compositions, a prelude in C sharp minor, was written when he was only 20 years old. He became a naturalized U.S. citizen, Feb. 1, 1943. An attack of pneumonia and pleurisy cut short his last concert tour and he died at his home in Beverly Hills, Calif., March 28. (See *Encyclopædia Britannica*.)

Racing and Races: *see* DOG RACING; HORSE RACING; TRACK AND FIELD SPORTS.
Radar: *see* RADIO DETECTION.

Radio.
Industrial Developments.—Civilian radio manufacture in the U.S. was at a virtual standstill during 1943, with no new radio receiving sets or transmitters of any character produced for other than wartime use. But a tremendous new radio-electronics industry was established, with military production reaching the total of $250,000,000 a month during 1943 as against $30,000,000 a month a year before.

The total number of radio receiving sets at the end of 1943 was 57,000,000, a decline of some 2,300,000 as compared with the preceding year. But the number of radio homes increased from an estimated 30,800,000 in 1942 to 32,500,000 in 1943, reaching an all-time high. The decline in sets in use was attributed to multiple sets in the same home out of working order because of shortages in replacement tubes and batteries (primarily on farm or non-electrified areas).

With 32,500,000 of the nation's 35,000,000 homes radio-equipped, according to a survey made by the Office of Civilian Requirements in Dec. 1943, roughly nine out of each ten families had radio service. OCR also estimated in Dec. 1943 that 8.5% of receiving sets were out-of-order. Scheduling of production for tubes and parts, ordered by WPB in December

for the first two quarters of 1944, was expected to restore large numbers of out-of-order sets to operation.

The total investment in the radio manufacturing industry as of Jan. 1, 1944 (devoted 100% to military, lend-lease and other wartime production) was placed at $350,000,000. Annual gross revenue was estimated to be $3,500,000,000. The total number of employees was 400,000, with an estimated annual payroll of $900,000,000.

Radio distributors, dealers and other establishments had a total investment at the end of 1943 of $280,000,000, with annual gross revenues of $200,000,000. They employed approximately 100,000 people, with an annual payroll of $150,000,000.

Because of wartime restrictions, no data was available at the year-end on exports of receivers to Latin American countries for civilian use. In 1942, consistent with the government's hemispheric solidarity program, about 2,500,000 sets were delivered to countries in Latin America, increasing the total number of receivers in those countries to an estimated 6,000,000. Another 3,000,000–5,000,000 sets, standardized export models capable of short-wave reception, probably were delivered to these nations during 1943.

On Jan. 1, 1944, in the United States there were 912 standard broadcast stations licensed and in operation. This compared with 917 a year before. Several stations, unable to operate because of wartime restrictions and lack of manpower, turned in their licences.

The "freeze" on construction of new stations, which became effective on April 27, 1942, continued in force during 1943. While several new stations were licensed, these were in areas considered underserved from the military standpoint. Similarly, improved facilities were authorized where a minimum of critical material was needed, to provide necessary coverage in underserved areas.

Wartime restrictions also prevented further development of television and frequency modulation (FM) broadcasting during the year. Operations on a quasi-experimental basis, however, continued, with these new services poised to expand as soon as restrictions were lifted. Large scale plans for postwar allocations in all radio fields envisaged some 3,000 FM stations and 1,000 television stations a decade following cessation of hostilities.

There were 42 commercial FM stations licensed as of Jan. 1, 1944, while seven other companies held construction permits to build such stations as soon as equipment becomes available. There were five commercial television stations authorized, while three construction permits were outstanding. In addition, 21 companies held experimental television licences while six others had construction permits. International shortwave stations in operation, with the government underwriting the programming for propaganda purposes, totalled 18 at the end of 1943. Seven other stations, however, were under construction.

As in years past, radio's chief sources of advertising revenue were foods, drugs (including soaps and similar housekeepers' supplies) and tobacco. These commodities represented about three-fourths of the total income of the national networks. The broadcasting industry continued its steady growth during 1943, with the "sold out" sign for desirable daytime and evening hours displayed by practically all metropolitan area stations and the networks.

National and regional advertisers, still limited as to production in most cases, continued their campaigns largely along institutional or "brand name" lines. They sought to maintain public prestige and to preserve continuity of their choice program time on the national networks, looking to the war's end. Many large manufacturing concerns, engaged in wartime production, began use of radio for institutional purposes. Moreover, rationing of paper for newspapers and magazines resulted in some "windfall" business for radio.

Throughout 1943, broadcasters found themselves at grips with the Federal Communications commission and with labour unions. Primary activity, however, was in congress, where the senate interstate commerce committee, in Dec. 1942, completed hearings on proposed new radio legislation, to spell out the powers of the FCC. The house select committee to investigate the FCC, created in Jan. 1943, held hearings during the year, and charged the commission with exceeding its powers.

War effort programs were the rule during 1943. Estimates of the Office of War Information made in November were that time valued at $103,000,000 had been donated by the industry for government programs.

For the first time in history, a major network changed hands. In October, Radio Corporation of America sold the Blue Network to Edward J. Noble, chairman of the Life Savers Corp., for $8,000,000 cash. In December, *Time Magazine* purchased a $12\frac{1}{2}\%$ interest in the Blue Network Co. Chester J. LaRoche, advertising agency executive, also purchased a $12\frac{1}{2}\%$ interest in the network.

Revenue and Finance.—During 1942 (1943 figures were not available) the broadcasting industry maintained its consistent pace of increasing business from year to year, with an increase of approximately 6.1% over the 1941 figure. This was slightly less than half the rate of increase during 1941 over the preceding year. Rough industry estimates for 1943 indicated net time sales of $215,000,000 as against $191,000,000 in 1942. There were no accurate figures on talent sales but they run between $40,000,000 and $45,000,000 annually.

BOB HOPE (right) and Frances Langford at a U.S. bomber base in England. The popular radio stars made numerous appearances at U.S. military bases and in war zones during 1943. In this photograph, censors deleted part of the placard (in black) behind which they are standing

Table I.—Radio Advertising Revenue, 1942 and 1941

	1942	1941
Major and regional network advertising revenue...	$89,500,000	$82,373,607
National "spot" advertising*	49,500,000	45,681,959
Local advertising†	52,000,000	51,697,651
Total	$191,000,000	$179,753,217

*Advertising by nationwide distributors placed over individual stations (as opposed to chain, or network, advertising).
†Advertising placed by local advertisers over the individual stations in their market areas.

Before all discounts, the advertising revenue of the industry was divided, as shown in Table I.

The Federal Communications commission, which from 1938 on produced annual compilations of radio business and expenses, did not develop complete data for 1942 by the close of 1943, because of restrictions on government statistical production and of the manpower shortages. The detailed data was expected to be available sometime in 1944, covering the 1942 calendar year.

The industry's 1942 balance sheet, as produced in preliminary form by the FCC, varied slightly from the industry estimates, though the overall totals are approximately the same. The balance sheet is shown in Table II.

Table II.—Revenue and Expenses of Radio Industry in 1942

	1942	Pct. change over 1941
Station revenue:		
Sale of time to major and regional chains	$34,419,071	+ 7.2
Sale of time to national spot advertisers	51,059,159	+13.2
Sale of time to local advertisers	53,898,916	+ 4.2
Total sale of station time	$139,377,146	+ 7.6
Network revenue:		
Revenue retained after paying affiliated stations . . .	$50,769,906	+ 4.4
Total industry time sales	$190,147,052	+ 6.7
Deduct commission to advertising agencies	26,504,107	+ 8.2
Total industry net time sales	$163,642,945	+ 6.5
Incidental revenue	15,196,554	—
Total net industry revenues	$178,839,499	+ 5.9
Expenses:		
Total deductions	$134,207,261	+ 8.3
Broadcast Service Income (Total Revenue in Excess of Expenses before Taxes)	$44,632,238	— .4

The figures in Table II are based on returns received by the FCC from 819 stations, the national and regional networks, including nine key stations of the major networks, and 23 managed and operated stations. They are not projected to cover the entire roster of 912 stations, leaving 61 stations which failed to file reports out of the compilation.

The FCC analysis shows the trend in increased radio overhead. While total broadcast revenues increased from approximately $168,779,000 in 1941 to nearly $179,000,000 in 1942, expenses jumped from $124,000,000 to $134,000,000. Thus, the total broadcast service income, before federal taxes, remained relatively the same—$44,839,000 in 1941 as against $44,632,000 in 1942. But the higher tax rates were expected to diminish appreciably net profits after taxes.

Trade estimates of gross billings, which are projected from one-time rates of stations and networks, showed gross billings for 1942 of $254,800,000 as against $237,600,000 in 1941. Gross billings for 1943 were estimated at $280,000,000. Of the 1942 estimated gross billings, $121,500,000 was assigned to major and regional networks; $69,500,000 to national spot and $63,800,000 to local advertising.

Radio was the only medium to come through the first year of the war comparatively unscathed with regard to its economic position. All other media had experienced losses. But during 1943, all media showed significant increases, with many newspapers and national magazines forced to "ration" space. Because of the "sold out" status of leading station and desirable network time, radio also was in the position of picking and choosing accounts during 1943.

Profit.—No profit figures were available for 1943, because of the delay entailed in FCC production of this data. In 1942 an excess of revenues over expenses of $44,632,238 was reported. In 1941, the excess of revenue over expenses totalled $33,438,118. This was an average of $42,650 per station.

The economic structure of radio generally was regarded as improved during 1943 as compared with the preceding year. A number of small stations, regarded as "chronic losers" still were in that category during the year. But aggregate losses were not expected to exceed $500,000 for the some 150 stations usually in this category, or about $3,000 per station.

Industry Assets.—The tangible property of the entire broadcasting industry in 1942 and 1943 remained relatively unchanged, in view of the WPB-FCC freeze order on new construction.

The tangible property of the broadcasting industry as shown in 1941 had a composition as shown in Table III.

Table III.—Composition of Tangible Property of Radio Industry in 1941

	817 stations	Major networks	Regional networks	Total
Original cost	$67,917,706	$9,934,697	$121,960	$77,974,363
Depreciated cost	39,416,993	5,596,815	97,189	45,110,997

Programming.—*Network Commercial Programs.*—The ten most popular network programs as of Dec. 1 were[1]:

1943	1942
1. Fibber McGee & Molly	1. Chase & Sanborn Program (Edgar Bergen)
2. Bob Hope	2. Fibber McGee & Molly
3. Lux Radio Theatre	3. Jack Benny
4. Chase & Sanborn Program (Edgar Bergen)	4. Bob Hope
5. Kraft Music Hall	5. Kraft Music Hall
6. Red Skelton	6. Lux Radio Theatre
7. Sealtest Village Store	7. Red Skelton
8. Maxwell House Coffee Time	8. Maxwell House Coffee Time
9. Aldrich Family	9. Aldrich Family
10. Kay Kyser Hit Parade	10. Kay Kyser

There was further emphasis on war programming during 1943. In addition to the contributed sustaining time valued at more than $100,000,000 for government programs, many commercial programs took on a war-public service connotation. All programs in the war effort category were cleared through the Office of War Information, radio branch. A regular weekly schedule of campaigns to be emphasized on the air, broken down as to networks and various groups of affiliated stations, was inaugurated during the year.

An increase in international pickups, with broadcasts direct from the headquarters of war theatres, also was evident during the year in news and special events coverage. All networks increased war news staffs.

One innovation was the wire recorder, a compact instrument using a magnetized wire for recording and reproduction, which was dispatched to the fighting fronts through the war department's radio branch. Several programs, employing actual pickups from the fighting lines, were broadcast during the year in this new phase of "documentary" radio reporting.

The perennial controversy over so-called "soap operas," serial strips continued during 1943. There developed, also, a heated discussion over "editorializing" on the air by commentators and analysts who express personal opinions. The controversy resounded from congress to the FCC and throughout the networks. While no hard and fast rules developed, it was generally agreed that freedom of expression on the air should be retained as synonymous with press freedom, but that commentaries should be labelled for what they are—editorial, analysis or straight news reporting.

Network Programs by Types.—The general composition of network evening programming, based on latest available information, appears in Table IV.

Table IV.—General Composition of Network Evening Programs

Type of program	1943 % of time on the air	1942 % of time on the air
Drama, serial drama.	27.9	31.4
Audience participation.	14.3	14.5
Variety	18.1	22.6
Commentators, news and talks	18.6	10.9
Popular music	12.6	12.6
Familiar music	5.8	5.2
Classical, semiclassical music	2.0	2.8
Children's programs.	.7	(No record)

Data supplied by the Co-operative Analysis of Broadcasting.

Note: Each program type has been allotted the number of hours which all programs in that type represent. The chart is based on the table of program types. 15-minute programs broadcast 5 times a week have been considered as 1¼ hours per week for the number of weeks investigated, 15-minute programs 3 times a week ¾ hour, etc.

Talent Costs.—Accurate data was not computed covering aggregate talent costs of network commercial programs. Trade estimates, however, covering the 1942–43 period were in the neighbourhood of $40,000,000 for nighttime programs and $8,000,000 for daytime programs. Costs generally increased by virtue of widespread introduction of union scales for performers and announcers, not only in key operating cities but in virtually all metropolitan areas.

Individual Station Programming.—The most decided trend in individual station programming during the year revolved around the war. Many stations adopted variations of "home front" features, based on reports of local fighting men overseas or in training camps. These supplemented network pickups of the same broad character. With rationing of food products, gasoline and other items, stations also built regular features covering point rationing. Sponsors were found readily available for such features in local areas.

Looking toward the war's end, stations generally put on drives for local retail advertising. Department stores spend the bulk of their budgets in newspapers. Under the auspices of the National Association of Broadcasters, a nationwide tour was made in the fall and winter of 1943, covering 120 cities, to exhibit the motion picture production "Air Force and the Retailer."

News programming settled down during 1943. In 1942 Associated Press, through its subsidiary PA, entered the field and there was lively competition for station clients. United Press, International News Service and Transradio Press, pioneers in radio news distribution, broadened their operations also, with a general speeding up of news service to individual stations and networks. Many stations supplemented their national news coverage through creation of local reportorial staffs. Several larger stations and all of the networks maintained full-time correspondents or bureaus in Washington.

Programs During the War.—When war came in Dec. 1941, broadcasters were fearful of the effect of government censorship, particularly since radio had never gone through a war. The reverse was true. Only scattered incidents involving censorship developed. "Man In the Street" broadcasts and certain types of audience participation shows had to be discontinued or modified. But voluntary censorship worked so well that a revised code of wartime practices for broadcasters was issued Dec. 10, 1943, lifting many of the former restrictions. Weather broadcasts, banned from the war's outbreak, were restored in the fall.

Despite out-of-order sets, as a result of wartime conditions, official estimates indicated that the radio audience continued to

---

[1] These ratings are supplied through the courtesy of A. W. Lehman, manager of the Co-operative Analysis of Broadcasting, and are copyrighted by the latter. The CAB is the industry's major fact-finding body in the field of programming.

increase during 1943. Approximately 32,500,000 American families, or 89% of the total, had one or more radio sets in use, according to a survey made by the Office of Civilian Requirements in Dec. 1943. President Roosevelt continued as the nation's leading radio personality, with his addresses reaching from some 45% to 75% of the radio audience. On several occasions in 1942, his audience reached 83%, a figure he did not eclipse in 1943, as far as the records go.

The average daytime audience for network programs, whether of the serial (soap opera) or non-serial type, reached an all-time high during 1943, according to a year-end review released in December by C. E. Hooper Inc., radio research organization. The average daytime audience was more than 6% larger, in the last quarter of 1943 than for the corresponding period of 1942.

Although the volume of daytime serial dramas had held constant at about 50 hours per week for 16 months, there developed a rapid rise in the volume of non-serial programs from 6½ hours during week days in January to the Dec. 1943 figure of 22¾ hours weekly.

Radio v. Government.—*The Network "Monopoly" Case.*— On May 10, 1943, the U.S. supreme court upheld the right of the FCC to regulate practically everything that is radio, by sustaining the jurisdiction of the commission to regulate contractual relations of the major networks with their affiliates. The effect of the supreme court's split decision was to sustain the commission's right to issue regulations preventing the networks from optioning more than a fixed percentage of the time of affiliated stations; to bar them from entering into exclusive contracts with affiliates and to prevent operation of more than one network by a single company.

The issue had been in litigation for a half dozen years. The supreme court opinion, however, went beyond the mere network regulations and appeared to give the commission authority to control general business practices of networks and stations and also inferred some degree of program control. The latter contention, however, was vigorously disputed by the FCC, and more particularly its chairman, James Lawrence Fly, who contended that broadcasters had plucked a phrase from the opinion out of context. This mooted phrase was "composition of that traffic" which broadcasters interpreted as giving the commission implied control over programs.

At hearings before the senate interstate commerce committee, which ran from Nov. 3 until Dec. 16, 1943, the broadcasting industry, through spokesmen for the National Association of Broadcasters, two of the networks and independent station groups, appealed to congress in effect to "repeal" the supreme court opinion and limit the FCC to control of physical aspects of radio.

Immediately upon completion of the hearings, the committee began executive sessions to draft new legislation to spell out the FCC's functions. Impressed by predictions made for the development of remarkable new services, such as FM, television and facsimile transmission by radio, the committee pondered the question of writing a series of simple amendments to the Communications Act of 1934, in lieu of an entirely new bill. An integrated act, covering radio's ultimate service, which would see voice transmission, motion pictures and an electronics printing process (facsimile) in the same cabinet, probably would await the peace.

As a direct result of the FCC's network regulations, RCA, which had operated both the NBC Red and Blue networks from 1926 and 1927 on, respectively, separated the two projects on Jan. 9, 1942 and divorced Blue operations from those of NBC. Subsequently, on Oct. 14, Edward J. Noble formally took over the Blue network and became its board chairman. He paid a cash figure of $8,000,000 for it. On Dec. 28, Mr. Noble announced sale of a 12½% interest each to Time Inc. and advertising executive LaRoche for $500,000 each, cash. Mark Woods, president, and Edgar Kobak, executive vice-president of the Blue Network Co., each acquired small stockholdings at the same time.

Following the supreme court action in the network cases, the department of justice dismissed anti-trust proceedings on practically the same issues filed against RCA, NBC and Columbia Broadcasting system on Dec. 31, 1941. Also dismissed by the federal district court in Chicago was a $19,000,000 triple damage suit against RCA-NBC filed by Mutual Broadcasting system, which claimed its growth had been impeded by RCA's operation of two networks.

Other FCC Investigations.—Faced with two separate investigations in congress during 1943—one before the senate interstate commerce committee and the other by the house select committee—the FCC dusted off a pair of old orders toward the end of the year which brought protests both from members of congress and from the industry. On Nov. 23, 1943 it resurrected a 2½-year-old order, banning multiple ownership of broadcast stations in the same area, affecting some 40 existing combination ownerships, or situations where there was overlapping service (*i.e.* the signals of one station overlap those of another owned by the same interests). The new order was made effective June 1, 1944. While no outright transactions had been completed at the year's end, negotiations were in progress for station sales or exchanges, to conform with the order.

There were projects for organized resistance, however, on the ground that the commission over the years had licensed these stations and renewed their licenses, finding that public interest thereby would be served. Owners contended that dual operation did not tend toward monopoly because competition existed with other stations in the same service areas in practically every case as well as with newspapers.

The second proposed regulation was that designed to ban newspaper ownership of broadcasting stations as tending toward monopoly in public opinion. Pressed by members of congress about its lethargy in deciding this issue, pending since March 1941, the commission, in the waning days of 1943 tentatively approved a policy allowing newspapers to own stations. Final action, however, did not crystallize as the year closed.

House Investigation.—When 1943 ended, the house select committee to investigate the FCC, created the preceding January, was still functioning. Originally given a $60,000 appropriation, the house authorized another $50,000 fund in November, to complete the inquiry. Originally headed by Rep. Eugene E. Cox (Dem., Ga.) the committee precipitated one of the most sanguinary fights in Washington political history in its attack upon the commission and more particularly its chairman, James Lawrence Fly. Rep. Cox resigned chairmanship of the committee in September and Rep. Clarence F. Lea (Dem., Calif.) was named his successor. The investigation was launched by the house, after Rep. Cox had levelled charges of incompetence, inefficiency and alleged wrong-doing against the FCC and more particularly its chairman.

Board of War Communications.—All wartime communications policy determinations, other than those directly affecting the military, were cleared through the Board of War Communications during 1943.

Practically all of the activities of the Board of War Communications were secret. During the year it issued a number of orders dealing with civil activities in all branches of communications. Restrictions placed upon the operations of broadcast stations to conserve materials were promulgated through this board and remained in force throughout the year. The ban on operations of amateur radio stations in the short waves was retained as a national security measure.

Musical Property.—Broadcasters experienced no serious musical copyright troubles during 1943, perhaps for the first time since radio became a national service. Music troubles revolved around the dispute with the American Federation of Musicians (34,000 members) and at the year's end, more trouble appeared to be brewing. James C. Petrillo, president of the federation, on Aug. 1, 1942 similarly banned the making of transcriptions and phonograph records by union members, alleging unfair competition with live musicians. Despite a congressional inquiry and National War Labor board arbitration, this impasse, which broadcasters prefer to call a "strike," was not broken until Sept. 24 when Decca Records Inc. and World Broadcasting system agreed to the Petrillo demands for payment of royalties direct to the union for "unemployment relief." Subsequently, independently operated transcription and record companies agreed to somewhat similar terms and were authorized to resume recording. RCA, in behalf of its Victor Co. and the recording division of NBC, another subsidiary, and Columbia Recording Corp., subsidiary of Columbia Broadcasting system, refused to accept the Petrillo terms on the ground that a "private WPA" would be established.

Portents of a national strike of musicians performing for the radio networks was seen as the year ended. Contracts of the major networks with the federation were to expire Feb. 1, 1944. Petrillo had advised locals not to negotiate new contracts with network key stations, pending action by the transcription and record subsidiaries of RCA and Columbia Broadcasting system on the royalty demands. It was generally thought that if the recording ban was not reconciled by the date of expiration of union contracts, the federation might be disposed to withdraw all staff orchestras from network key stations.

Employment.—With average weekly compensation to its 25,515 full-time employees of $55.75, the broadcasting industry in 1943 maintained its standard of high compensation—a gain of 6.6% over the preceding year. While no comparable industry figures were available, it was stated semi-officially in Washington that this represented the highest average wages and salaries of any United States industry. The average weekly payroll (for the week of Oct. 17, 1943) totalled $1,366,687 for full-time employees. Excluding executives, the average per full-time employee was $49.50, or an increase of 7.3%. Station employees in executive capacities received the following average weekly salaries: general managers, $132.73; technical, $67.15; program, $67.29; commercial, $102.49;

THE BRITISH EQUIVALENT of "Information Please" in 1943 was a quiz program called "Any Questions?" Four of the program's stars, here shown left to right, were C. E. M. Joad, Julian Huxley, Sir William Beveridge and the master of ceremonies, Donald McCullough

publicity, $65.32. In non-executive positions, station technical operating personnel averaged $48.53 per week; announcers, $45.-76; staff musicians, $53.83; outside salesmen, $76.85; script writers, $37.60. Part-time employees totalled 4,862 average weekly and were primarily in the talent group. Network and network-owned stations paid this talent group of part-time employees $80.44 per week, while stations paid $30.25.

Television and Frequency Modulation.—The technical progress of these two arts is discussed below in *Scientific Developments* and in TELEVISION.

In Dec. 1941, it was estimated there were 500,000 FM receivers in use, and about 10,000 television receivers. During the year, nine U.S. television stations were broadcasting on regular schedule—three in New York, one in Schenectady, one in Philadelphia, two in Chicago and two in Hollywood. New television sets, it was generally predicted, would be available within six months after peace in Europe. The first models of sight and sound receivers probably would range from $200 to $700. One manufacturer said he would offer a $150 table model television set.

FM, providing a "staticless" type of transmission and reception which insures higher fidelity of reproduction, was expected to open up virtually unlimited competition in broadcasting after the war, according to its proponents. Under existing standards of allocation, 3,000 new FM sound broadcasting stations could be established. These would represent a capital investment of roughly $150,000. To launch FM with greatest possible expedition, two separate organizations were formed. One, FM Broadcasters Inc., was a trade association designed to encourage development of FM and to co-ordinate operations; the second, American Network Inc., proposed to create a nationwide network of FM stations to compete with the established AM (amplitude modulation) networks. FM receivers, it was predicted, would sell in about the same price range as regular receivers.

Radio in the Western Hemisphere.—Little or no change in the status of radio on the North American continent was effected during 1943, because of the frozen state of allocations. Most Latin American countries procured their radio equipment from manufacturers in the United States. This was so particularly after the beginning of World War II. Before then, Telefunken, German radio manufacturing and operating cartel, had important outlets in South and Central America.

The benefits of the North American Regional Broadcasting agreement, which became effective in March 1941, were fully realized in 1943. Because medium wave channels used for standard broadcasting (540 kc.-1600 kc.) have an interference range over the continent, scientific allocations to the various countries

in the hemisphere was necessary, along with uniform methods of operation.

World Conferences.—Need for an international radio conference and possibly a worldwide telecommunications conference immediately after the war was generally foreseen. In the post-war era, radio networks, both sound and television, might be extended internationally. Although it appeared fairly certain that such networks would not extend beyond the western hemisphere or even to South America for some time to come, the technical considerations should not be overlooked in planning domestic services, according to government engineers.

Much would be gained by allocating the same frequency bands to television on an international basis and also in adopting international standards for both program broadcasting and network relay systems (by short-wave radio). If such plans were not made, it might be impossible to set aside common bands of frequencies for maritime and air navigational aids, looking toward globe-girdling aviation service, wherein radio would serve both as its eyes and ears. Moreover, if different bands and technical standards were used in different regions of the world, problems respecting sale of apparatus and exchange of international programs might become well-nigh unsolvable.

Military Radio.—Smashing of barriers of distance, psychological as well as geographical, the army developed in 1943 the largest improvised network in the world to bring radio to American troops in all theatres of war. Every medium of radio, from 100,000-watt short-wave transmitters to the old acoustic spring-wound playback phonographs, was used by the armed forces service to bring soldiers, sailors and marines entertainment either direct or by recording. Thousands of hand-operated playback machines were sent to areas where no electricity was available and transcriptions of programs were supplied by transport plane for reproduction of these recorded programs.

In addition to broadcasting stations set up under military jurisdiction wherever feasible, short-wave transmitters operated by the overseas branch of the Office of War Information carried American radio service features. Special performances of radio stars, usually transcribed, regularly were featured. In places where radio could not be received, turntables and public address systems carried the programs. Army hospital ships and troop transports were supplied at the year's end with two hours of running time of transcriptions daily. Similar arrangements were made for submarines. (*See* also RADIO DETECTION.)

U.S.-Latin-American Broadcasts.—Use of radio in psychological warfare continued apace in 1943. The greatest activity, however, was in short-wave transmission to Latin America under the joint direction of the Office of War Information and the co-ordinator of Inter-American Affairs. OWI was charged with broadcasts to all nations other than South America, with the latter area in the hands of CIAA. In Nov. 1942, programming of all short-wave stations was taken over by the government, though the transmitters were owned independently and operated by the private licensees. An average of some 40 hours daily of program material was broadcast over a dozen transmitters in Spanish, Portuguese and English.

The press division of CIAA prepared and teletyped to various station alignments some 40,000 words daily of news and news commentary in three languages. In addition, program interchanges with Latin America gained impetus and began regular features on the national networks.

Another trend during the year was the development of Spanish language programs on many domestic stations under the general title "How to Speak Spanish." Instruction was largely an adaptation of the phonetic method. These programs were in keeping with the overall effort toward the good neighbour policy. (S. TF.)

Scientific Developments (U.S.).—Air, military and naval applications and developments of radio techniques during 1943 necessarily overshadowed all other possibilities. The security requirements of the war prevented release and discussion of the scientific advances, in specific and quantitative terms, but there seemed little doubt that when the results of the new work could at last be applied to peacetime services there would be found to be available many new tools that would add to radio's value to humanity. Most people think of radio only in connection with the mass-communication or "broadcasting" aspect of its ability to transmit intelligence. Even in that field 1943 saw confirmation of earlier suggestions that the newer proposals of frequency modulation and television would become still more important shortly after hostilities cease. Testimony before a senate committee, which was studying the problems of revising existing legislation as to radio, brought out that in the broadcasting of speech and music it appeared that frequency modulation would be likely to supersede ordinary broadcasting for all local or regional operations, but that present methods would probably be retained for maximum uses including service to rural areas. It was also indicated that the visual broadcasting services of television and facsimile (the so-called "magic printing press") might well be expected to provide new and important industrial activity in the postwar period, particularly in view of the technical improvements in both systems that had been attained in order to meet military requirements.

In point-to-point communication also, 1943 saw a realization that it would be reasonable to expect faster and more accurate service over even greater distances, together with the possibilities of much expanded short-distance services. The announced use of satisfactory portable short-wave radio telephone in battle areas immediately suggested that similar instruments would be valuable to state and municipal fire-fighting and police organizations and, with the extension of the useful spectrum of radio waves, might perhaps even lead to the possibility of vastly extended person-to-person radio communication.

In non-communication radio applications, there was a flurry of announcements with respect to "radar"; generally known to be a radio direction-finder capable of determining not only the bearing of an objective, but also its distance, without requiring the co-operation of two stations for triangulation studies. Such reports gave rise to expectations that in postwar marine navigation the fog obstacle would be largely overcome, and that in flying there would be fewer hazards due to uncertainty as to safely available space. (*See* also ADVERTISING; FEDERAL COMMUNICATIONS COMMISSION; RADIO DETECTION.) (J. V. L. H.)

Great Britain.—On Nov. 14, 1943, the British Broadcasting corporation celebrated its 21st birthday. In 21 years it had grown from a staff of 31 of the first British Broadcasting company to one of over 12,000.

During the year the chief events of internal organization were the retirement of Sir Cecil Graves owing to ill health and the consequent changes in the higher officers of the corporation. Robert W. Foot, hitherto joint director-general with Sir Cecil, was appointed sole director-general, and a new post was created under him, that of editor-in-chief. The first holder of this post was W. J. Haley, till then joint managing director of the *Manchester Guardian* and *Evening News* and also a director of Reuters and the Press association. Sir Noel Ashbridge, previously controller of the engineering division, became deputy director-general.

Among the chief developments during the year were the growth of rebroadcasting of BBC programs by American stations, which by November were taking 175 hours per week; the increase of exchange programs between the BBC and stations in the U.S.A. and Canada, such as "Trans-Atlantic Call," and the creation of permanent BBC offices in Cairo, San Francisco and Canada. Seymour Joly de Lotbinière was appointed to take charge of the last.

All these are instances of the BBC's avowed policy of making radio a means of international communication in the fullest and most reciprocal sense. With these developments can be linked the virtual doubling of the broadcasting time given to the Latin-American service. This service hitherto had consisted of five hours which had to be divided between the Portuguese and Spanish tongues, one service, owing to the lack, in wartime, of transmitters and their associated apparatus and labour, having to go off the air in order to make way for the other. These difficulties finally having been overcome, in November the Latin-American Spanish and the Latin-American Portuguese services were enabled to run independently of each other with broadcasting hours of five and a half Spanish and four Portuguese.

A further development occurred in the empire service with the introduction in June of the general overseas service, a scheme of programs specially designed not for residents in various parts of the empire but for the many thousands of exiles and servicemen from Britain then scattered all round the globe, especially in the middle east and adjacent territories. This was further expanded in November.

In a quite different way, too, the BBC made its programs known all over the globe through the development of a special department—the London transcription service—which sent out records of selected programs to some 30 or 40 broadcasting companies in the English-speaking world. Most important of these was the complete series of "The Man Born To Be King," the radio dramatic version of the life of Jesus, written by Dorothy Sayers. This had created much controversy before it came on the air in the home service children's hour in 1941. The early objections tailed into insignificance, however, when the series was actually heard, and the BBC was commended by leading churchmen of all denominations for its contribution to Christian knowledge.

During the year there were several notable expansions of the services in foreign languages, one being that for the Japanese. This service, starting on July 4, gave news in the Japanese language four days every week. On the other three days the program consisted of news and commentary in English. On the same date the service in English for Europe was extended to include five-minute daily lessons in colloquial English; and eight days later the European news services were expanded by the addition in English, French and Dutch of special bulletins for the information of the editors of the "underground" newspapers of the continent. Similar bulletins in German, largely for Polish editors, followed in October. In that month, also, two fresh bulletins in French were broadcast daily for all Europe, with especial attention to listeners in eastern and southeastern Europe and in parts of the middle east. At the same time 15 minutes each were added to the Portuguese and Spanish transmissions, these being rebroadcasts of "America Calling Europe" from New York. This rebroadcast service was thus raised from 16 to 18 languages, including English. The total European service broadcast in 24 languages, and for 44 hours in the 24.

Other high lights of the year included the BBC's announcement of the fall of Mussolini only five minutes after the first statement from Rome radio; a service as rapid giving the news of the surrender of Italy; and the remarkable broadcast by Wynford Vaughan Thomas from records which he made in a Lancaster bombing Berlin. Various editions of these records were put out in the home and all the empire services.

On Nov. 29, 1942, the BBC publication, *The Radio Times*, had achieved its 1,000th number; and on Dec. 14, 1942, the BBC published T. O. Beachcroft's *Calling All Nations*, telling the story of the growth of the overseas services from the first tentative empire service of ten years before to the present broadcasting of 48 languages. On Jan. 2, 1943, another pioneering effort celebrated its 2,000th performance—the daily program, "Music While You Work," specially devised to help factory workers.

Radio Detection. The curtain which hid one of the most secret of technical war developments was slightly lifted for a brief period when a joint army-navy release on April 25, 1943, revealed the existence of "radar" and described its early development. On July 13 the chief of the review branch of the war department bureau of publication issued instructions prohibiting further publicity on the subject.

According to the release of April 25, "The term 'radar' means radio-detecting-and-ranging. Radars, then, are devices which the Allies used to detect the approach of enemy aircraft and ships, and to determine the distance (range) to the enemy's forces."

Such devices, used by the British and called "radio-locators," were instrumental in saving England during the aerial blitz in 1940–41 by indicating the approach of German raiders long before they reached target areas. Thus the R.A.F. and the ground forces were given time to prepare their defenses. At Pearl Harbor on the morning of Dec. 7, 1941, radar detected the Japanese planes 45 minutes before they struck, while they were 135 mi. away, but its indications were ignored.

The system operates with ultra-high-frequency radio waves (of wave-length below 10 metres) which, like light, can be focused in a beam and swept around, covering air and sea. Striking a ship or aeroplane, they are reflected back like an echo, and the returning signal is detected with appropriate equipment. Since the waves travel with the speed of light (186,000 mi. per sec.) the round trip takes a very brief period of time, yet it can be measured accurately, and the range determined.

A navy statement issued May 23 said that the birth of radar was the discovery in mid-Sept. 1922, by Dr. A. Hoyt Taylor and

TESTING RADAR TRANSMITTERS at a U.S. war plant before shipment to the U.S. navy in 1943

Leo C. Young of the Naval Aircraft Radio laboratory, that radio signals were reflected from steel buildings and metal objects. They then suggested that this effect might be employed to detect from one warship the presence of enemy vessels, irrespective of fog, darkness or smoke screen. Later it was found that aircraft crossing a line between a radio transmitter and a receiver operating directionally gave a characteristic effect which showed the presence of the aircraft.

Experimentation continued, and in Jan. 1931, the radio division of the bureau of engineering of the navy ordered the Naval Research laboratory to "investigate the use of radio to detect the presence of enemy vessels and aircraft." The war department was informed of the possibilities of these methods in 1932, the comment being made that "a system of transmitters and associated receivers might be set up in a defense area to test its effectiveness in detecting the passage of hostile aircraft into the area. Such a development might be carried forward more appropriately by the army than by the navy."

By 1932, aeroplanes in motion nearly 50 mi. away from the transmitter had been detected. A report on the work up to the middle of that year stated that the object of the investigation was to develop instruments for the collection, automatic recording and correlating of data to show position, angle and speed of approach of objects in the air. The types of apparatus and systems for detecting enemy aircraft and vessels had developed to such a degree by March 1933, that the Naval Research laboratory was able to outline in detail the theoretical military applications.

With the aid of an appropriation of $100,000 made in 1935 upon the initiative of the naval appropriations committee of the house of representatives, and with the co-operation of the national bureau of standards and representatives of the army, the work continued. In June 1936, Admiral Harold G. Bowen, then chief of the navy bureau of engineering, directed that plans be made for the installation of a complete set of radar equipment aboard ship.

It was on Feb. 17, 1937, that the assistant secretary of the navy, Charles Edison, and the chief of naval operations, Admiral Leahy, witnessed a demonstration of aircraft detection by the first radar set developed in the United States. Two years more were required for the design and construction of a practical shipboard model. Such a set was installed on the U.S.S. "New York" late in 1938. It was tested at sea during the winter cruise and battle manoeuvres carried on during the first three months of 1939.

The apparatus was so successful that in Oct. 1939, additional sets were ordered, on a bid basis, from commercial sources, and the following year other manufacturers were called in to aid in supplying the armed forces with needed equipment. After that, practically every important unit in the electronics industry was working on one phase or another of this important project. Some of these companies had previously worked on allied researches, such as the use of a reflected radio wave to determine the altitude of an aeroplane above the ground.

While the later phases of the work in the United States were taking place, the British "radio-location" system was developed, mainly under the direction of Sir Robert A. Watson-Watt. Members of the British technical mission, in Sept. 1940, held a series of conferences with representatives of the navy department and the Naval Research laboratory and much information was exchanged.

"During the conference with the British technical mission," the navy's statement of May 23 revealed, "it was found that the British equipment was similar in many respects to the equipment developed by the Naval Research laboratory, and members of the British mission stated that the British development had resulted from articles reporting the preliminary work between 1926 and 1930 of Dr. Taylor and Mr. Young, of the Naval Research laboratory, and Dr. Breit and Dr. Tuve, of the Carnegie Institution of Washington, studying the height of the Kennelly-Heaviside layer. With this preliminary study as a base, the British independently had developed their radar system and independently had arrived at frequencies and circuits very similar to those developed in this country."

Though the most spectacular use of radar was in the detection of aeroplanes, it also had value against ships, as was shown by the accuracy with which, in May 1941, the German battleship "Bismarck" successfully aimed its first salvo against H.M.S. "Hood," quickly sinking the British ship, although it was 13 mi. away. This was attributed to the use of some radio detection system. In night action in the Solomons, a United States battleship was able to locate and sink a Japanese ship 8 mi. away, although the enemy was not seen until actually on fire.

Undoubtedly such methods would find wide application after the war, particularly in allowing aeroplanes and ships to navigate safely in all kinds of weather, in darkness and in fog.

(J. Sto.)

Radiology. In the field of diagnostic radiology the roentgenologic characteristics of atypical (virus) pneumonia were worked out, and the value of roentgenography in the differential diagnosis was established. Serial roentgenograms made during the course of the disease were found to be of aid in clarifying its course and pathology.

Further studies of the heart and great vessels by the roentgen ray, with the aid of an opaque medium, or angiocardiography, revealed the value of this procedure in the diagnosis of congenital heart lesions.

The technique of venography was improved. As this method of examination has been more widely used, its value has been shown to be greater and considerable knowledge has been added as to the pathology of venous thrombosis.

Other technical advances include the development of a stereoscopic method for the localization of opaque foreign bodies in the orbit; a new method for the making of stereoscopic films, and a technique for better soft-tissue visualization.

In treatment, more adequate reports on the effects of supervoltage therapy appeared. Treatment with roentgen rays generated in the region of 1,000,000 volts was shown to give a larger depth dose and a decreased dose to the skin, so that the treatment was in general better tolerated. Statistical studies, however, which covered a period of over five years, showed that the results are only a trifle better than at 200,000 volts.

The most conspicuous development in the therapeutic field was the report of the physical studies of the radiations from the betatron. This instrument produces either cathode rays or X-rays. The cathode rays produced at 20,000,000 volts have the power of penetrating 10 cm. of tissue. Studies of the X-rays produced at various voltages from 5,000,000 to 20,000,000 showed that the point of maximum dose becomes deeper as the voltage is raised, so that at 20,000,000 volts it lies between 3 and 4 cm. below the surface and is considerably higher than the surface dose. While these radiations were not yet applied to the treatment of disease, the physical observations raised hopes that the betatron might develop into a more efficient instrument for the treatment of deep-seated cancer than any so far evolved.

BIBLIOGRAPHY.—A. E. Seeds and M. L. Mazer, "Virus Pneumonia," *Am. J. Roentgenol.*, 49:30–38 (1943); F. C. Curtzwiler and B. E. Moore, "Primary Atypical Pneumonia of Unknown Etiology," *Radiology*, 40:347–360 (1943); H. M. Weber, "Angiocardiography," *Am. J. M. Sc.*, 205:747–753 (1943); M. F. Steinberg, A. Grishman and M. L. Sussman, "Angiocardiography in Congenital Heart Disease. II Intracardiac Shunts," *Am. J. Roentgenol.*, 49:766–776 (1943), III "Patent Ductus Arteriosus," *Am. J. Roentgenol.*, 50:306–315 (1943); H. A. Yenikomshian and W. H. Shehadi, "Duodenal Ulcer Syndrome Caused by Ankylostomiasis," *Am. J. Roentgenol.*, 49:39–48 (1943); G. R. Krause and J. A. Crilly, "Roentgenologic Changes in the Small Intestine in the Presence of Hookworm," *Am. J. Roentgenol.*, 49:719–729 (1943); M. L. Sussman and E. Wachtel, "Factors Concerned in Abnormal Distribution of Barium in the Small Bowel," *Radiology*, 40:128–138 (1943); H. Mahorner, "A Method for Obtaining Venograms of the Veins of the Extremities," *Surg., Gynec. & Obst.*, 76:41–42 (1943); A. Lesser and L. Raider, "Venography with Fluoroscopy in Venous Lesions of the Lower Limb," *Radiology*, 41:157–163 (1943); J. R. Watson, J. M. Lichty, J. M. Hill and R. B. Miller, "Use of Venograms for the Localization and Study of Arteriovenous Fistula," *Surg., Gynec. & Obst.*, 76:659–664 (1943); M. E. DeBakey, G. F. Schroeder and A. Ochsner, "Significance of Phlebography in Phlebothrombosis," *J.A.M.A.*, 123:738–744 (1943); E. P. Griffin, C. Gianturco and S. Goldberg, "A Stereoscopic Method for the Localization of Intraorbital Foreign Bodies," *Radiology*, 40:371–374 (1943); E. Klein, M. Klein, H. Klein and A. T. Newman, "An Investigation into Some Practical Aspects of Stereoptics," *Am. J. Roentgenol.*, 49:682–690 (1943); J. de Carvajal-Forero and M. R. Thompson, "Roentgenography of Soft Tissues by Monochromatic Roentgen Radiation and Color-Forming Developers," *Am. J. Roentgenol.*, 50:248–257 (1943); W. L. Watson and J. Urban, "Million Volt Roentgen Therapy for Intrathoracic Cancer: Palliative Effects in a Series of 63 Cases," *Am. J. Roentgenol.*, 49:299–306 (1943); H. E. Schmitz, "Further Study of Supervoltage X-Ray Therapy in Carcinoma of the Cervix," *Radiology*, 40:458–462 (1943); F. H. Colby and M. D. Schulz, "A Review of Carcinoma of the Bladder Treated by Supervoltage X-Rays over a Five-Year Period," *Radiology*, 41:371–376 (1943); H. W. Koch, D. W. Kerst and P. Morrison, "Experimental Depth Dose for 5, 10, 15 and 20-Million Volt X-Rays," *Radiology*, 40:120–126 (1943).

(S. J. Hy.)

Radium. A small amount of radium is recovered in the United States as a by-product in the treatment of ores mined primarily for vanadium and uranium, but the bulk of the world output is derived from the ores of the Belgian Congo and Canada. Ore from the Eldorado mine at Great Bear lake in Canada is treated at the company's refinery at Port Hope, Ont. In 1940 some 1,200 short tons of Congo ore were sent to the United States after the refinery in Belgium fell into German hands, but it was not known whether this was continued. It was demonstrated by field use that the Geiger-Mueller counter of gamma-ray emissions could be used as a prospecting instrument, not only for pitchblende veins but also for mildly radioactive host rocks in large scale reconnaissance surveys. (*See* also URANIUM.) (G. A. Ro.)

Railroad Retirement Act: *see* SOCIAL SECURITY.

Railroads. The outstanding facts in the railroad record of 1943 in the U.S:

(1) The volume of traffic, both freight and passenger, and the gross revenues, were higher than in any previous year.

(2) The transportation demands of the army, the navy, the war production plants, and the lend-lease administration were met in a manner which brought ready praise from their high officers.

(3) Notwithstanding the heavy demands of the war agencies the civilian freight traffic was satisfactorily handled and, while many passenger trains were badly crowded and frequently late, the painful expedient of rationing of passenger travel was avoided.

(4) New high records in rail operating efficiency were recorded. The more effective utilization of locomotives, cars, trackage and terminals made possible the production in 1943 of nearly 80% more ton miles and 25% more passenger miles than in 1918 (World War I) notwithstanding the fact that in 1943 the locomotives and passenger train cars were about one-third less, and the freight cars were about one-quarter less than in 1918.

(5) In protest against wage increase awards of boards appointed by the president under the Railway Labor act and modifications ordered by the director of economic stabilization, the unions of the non-operating and operating railroad employees issued strike orders to take effect on Dec. 30. On Dec. 24 the non-operating unions and two of the operating unions agreed to the arbitration of their pending disputes by the president and

rescinded their strike orders. Three of the non-operating unions rejected presidential arbitration. On Dec. 27 President Roosevelt, acting under authority of the same 1916 law utilized by President Wilson in Dec. 1917, ordered the secretary of war to take over and operate all railroads in the United States. The executive order commandeering the railroads stated as reason for the unexpected action that "the continuous operation of transportation service in the nation is necessary for the movement of troops, materials of war, necessary passenger traffic, and supplies and food for the armed forces and the civilian population, and is otherwise essential to the successful prosecution of the war," and that "the continuous operation of some transportation systems is threatened by strikes called to commence Dec. 30, 1943."

As of midnight, Jan. 18, 1944, the roads were restored to private operation after the recalcitrant unions had accepted a settlement worked out by the president and approved by the director of economic stabilization.

Taking these subjects in the order given we may first note certain specific detail in traffic volume. The 1943 results, in Table I, may be compared with the immediately preceding year, the year 1939, the last year unaffected by national defense, and lend-lease activities, and 1918, the last year of World War I.

Table I.—Volume of Traffic
(in thousands of millions)

Item	1943*	1942	1939	1918
Revenue ton miles	725	638	333	405
Passenger miles	85	54	23	43

*Figures for 1943 partially estimated.

The large volume of traffic in 1943 naturally resulted in a new high in gross revenues although large parts of the tonnage and passengers were government freight and members of the armed forces which, in substantial part, moved under reduced rates. The cancellation by the Interstate Commerce commission of the freight rate increases of approximately 6%, authorized by the commission in 1942, also held down gross revenues.

The condensed income account given in Table II shows that the increase in revenues in 1943 over 1942 was less in amount than the sum of the increases in operating expenses and taxes, and that the net income available for dividends and other appropriations from income was less than in 1942.

Table II.—Condensed Income Account—Class I Railroads
(in millions)

Item	1929	1939	1942	1943*
Operating revenues	$6,279	3,995	7,466	9,075
Operating expenses	4,506	2,918	4,601	5,650
Taxes	397	356	1,199	1,850
Net railway operating income	1,252	589	1,485	1,380
Per cent return on investment	4.81	2.25	5.50	5.60
Net income after fixed & contingent charges	897	93	902	880
Dividends paid	490	126	202	215

*1943 partially estimated. From *Railway Age*, Jan. 1, 1944.

In support of the assertion herein made that the adequacy and quality of rail service in 1943 met the military needs, the opinions of high-ranking officers may be quoted. Lt. General Brehon Somervell, the head of the Army Service Forces, wrote for the *Railway Age* of July 24, 1943:

American railroads and American railroad men are accomplishing one of the most brilliant achievements in this global war. With limited equipment, with constantly diminishing manpower, with forceful leadership through the Association of American Railroads, with elimination of peacetime competition, the carriers have pooled their brains and their equipment to move the army as demanded. It has been by far the largest moving job in the history of America. It has been done with outstanding efficiency.

The views of the navy were published in the same issue of *Railway Age* in an article by Vice-Admiral S. M. Robinson, chief, Office of Procurement and Material, who wrote:

The navy has been obliged to call on the railroads to perform seemingly impossible feats in the transportation of personnel and munitions. In every case the railroads have risen to the occasion.

In operating efficiency the commendable record of 1942 was continued and in most items improved upon. The freedom from congestion in freight service and the more effective utilization of freight cars were attributable in large part to the co-operation of shippers and the helpful co-ordinating influence of the ODT and the ICC. The significant items indicative of freight performance were:

Table III.—*Freight Car and Freight Train Performance*

Item	9 Months ended Sept. 30		
	1939	1942	1943
Tons per loaded car	26.5	31.4	33.5
Car miles per serviceable car day	34.5	47.5	49.8
Per cent loaded of total car miles	62.3	62.7	63.7
Ton miles per car day	501	906	1,036
Per cent cars unserviceable	9.4	5.2	2.4
Tons per freight train	792	1,021	1,111
Speed of trains (m.p.h.)	16.8	16.0	15.5
Ton miles per train-hour	13,300	16,300	17,200
Locomotive miles per locomotive day	103	122	125
Per cent locomotives unserviceable	30.7	13.6	11.8

Other important developments during the year include the reports of the board of investigation and research, set up under the Transportation Act of 1940, and the improvement in the financial condition of the railroads. On Sept. 24 the board issued a report favouring uniform freight rate scales throughout the country, and thus brought to public attention the time-honoured controversy over discrepancies between eastern, southern, and western rates.

During 1943 four railroads were discharged from receivership or bankruptcy, while two small companies entered trusteeship, so that as of the end of the year 85 companies were in the hands of receivers or trustees, of which 30 were "Class I" roads operating 27% of total "Class I" mileage. A series of supreme court decisions during the year upheld the methods of valuation used by the Interstate Commerce commission in reorganization cases, in a number of which the stockholders' equity was eliminated. Reduction of debt made possible by increased earnings left the industry in an improved financial condition. (*See* also BUSINESS REVIEW; INTERSTATE COMMERCE COMMISSION; NATIONAL MEDIATION BOARD.) (W. J. C.; H. E. DL.)

Other Countries.—During 1943 the outstanding feature of railway developments throughout the world was the proof that railways are an integral part of the war machine of the various belligerents, as might be witnessed by their high priority as a target for air attack. Further the theory, steadily gaining ground during the two inter-war decades, that alternative means of land transport were gradually replacing railways as the prime means of moving masses of people and commodities by land, was falsified, owing to the restrictions effective in so many countries on the consumption of oil products and rubber. This background, almost universal in five continents, explains why the main problem facing railways in the vast majority of countries was that of attempting to deal with overloads of traffic, and, indeed, restricting as much non-essential traffic as possible.

Great Britain.—The British railways proved no exception to this general rule, but in a country where, though population is dense on the average, hauls are comparatively short and no large centres are far from a coast possessing good harbour facilities, the question did not become quite so acute as in other countries. Britain was well provided with urban and country bus routes, and some of these had been converted to gas producer working, consequently, the load on the railways was to that extent eased, though interurban and long distance services, being duplicate with railway routes, were discontinued. Additionally, the close correlation through railway financial integration of the railroad passenger services enabled widespread economies to be effected in vehicle mileage.

In general, the most serious problem arose through the withdrawal of skilled staff, chiefly to the armed forces, thereby limiting the train mileage possible, though extensive recruitment of temporary women employees eased the gravity of the position. Since 1939 no official operating figures had been published, but, in general, a study of timetables reveals that passenger train services had been reduced by approximately 30%, and, doubtless, freight train mileage had risen by an important percentage as compared with the prewar figure. Overall percentages do not give a correct picture because areas differ widely, and the changed flows of traffic since 1939, owing to civil evacuation and military activities, overloaded certain railway facilities little used in prewar years; other facilities were not being called upon to carry their due quota. Shortage of staff creates difficulty in every branch of railway working, making for slower station working with delays to trains and their connections, a reduced output in repair shops with more motive units awaiting attention, a reduced standard of track maintenance and inability to effect much needed refurnishing, cleaning and painting of rolling stock, stations and buildings.

Britain was still a front line war area with rigid black-out restrictions and liable to air attack at any point at any hour; yet withal, the accident record of the British railways was not far short of the peacetime standard, and smooth running of the faster trains revealed that, in spite of difficulties, the reduction in standard of equipment, track and signalling was not openly noticeable. Every effort was made to reduce unnecessary travel, but the summer week-end holiday peaks were heavy, and the attraction of a holiday at home to people who had worked overtime for four years had, somewhat naturally, lost its appeal. Zoning orders in regard to food distribution helped to ease freight traffic loads as did heavier loading of wagons, of which there had been no general shortage, probably assisted by the completion of small but useful track and yard facilities at the bottlenecks created by new traffic routes.

Normal programs of construction and improvements, such as electrification, had long been held up; on the other hand, few instances occurred where even branch lines had been dispensed with and tracks removed. Locomotive construction was limited to standard types and, naturally, the bulk of output was in the heavy freight category. The U.S. built "Austerity" type 2-8-0 class locomotives and their British counterparts were much in evidence throughout Britain. Long non-stop runs, such as Carlisle–London, 199 mi., still remained a feature of British working, as did financial profit-earning capacity, and, though the rental figure paid by the British government remained at about £43,000,000, it was likely that the surplus of net revenue over this figure accruing to the government would not be lower in 1943 than the £45,000,000 retained in 1942. As a typical example of substitute materials concrete blocks were being used for timber sleepers or ties in sidings.

Continental Europe.—With the exception of Switzerland, Sweden, Spain and Portugal, and a small mileage of the Turkish state railways in Europe, the railway systems of continental Europe formed an integral part of the German war machine and provided the transport arteries of the German armies. Under such conditions physical improvements were limited to those required for strategic purposes and little data were available as to changes in 1943. The Italian state railways became a battleground with the southern sections in Allied hands and the northern rail gateways, such as Genoa, Turin, Milan, Bologna, Bolzano and Trieste as objectives of air attack. In France much branch line and other mileage was known to have been removed and despatched to the U.S.S.R. for military lines, and the same applied in Belgium.

Progress was made with electrification of the Brive–Montauban section of the line from Paris to the Spanish frontier at Cerbère/Portbou, otherwise electrified throughout from Paris to Sète. Preparatory work continued on the conversion of the Paris–Lyon main line to electric traction. French and Belgian locomotive builders were fully occupied in turning out German standard locomotives suited to working in eastern Europe and the Balkans, and some progress was made in extending the "Metro" underground lines in Paris and eliminating level crossings. Many sections of French and Belgian railways were exposed to frequent air attack to prevent the movement of troops and military stores: civil traffic was cut to the minimum and lack of motive power and equipment was said to be acute.

In Germany heavy air attacks extensively damaged railway facilities, especially in the industrial Ruhr and the Rhineland, while the railway load was eased where possible by diversion to the inland waterways. Evacuation of industrial production to Austria and Czechoslovakia necessitated improvements in the freight handling facilities in those countries and to a lesser extent in Hungary, while the strategic importance of the main line to Salonika and Athens, frequently damaged by patriot activities, was understood to have necessitated additional accommodation at several junctions. In general, bridges damaged in the fighting of 1940–41 had been almost completely repaired, and in Bulgaria progress had been made in the construction of new lines of strategic importance, such as Gueschevo–Kumanovo, Simeti–Demir Hisar and Montchilgrad–Gümüljina. Rumanian state railway trains were reported to be running into Odessa, the schedule from Bucharest requiring about 21 hours.

In Switzerland further sections of the Swiss Federal system were electrified, notably Winterthur–Schaffhausen and Neuchâtel–Les Verrières, but the most difficult problem was that of handling the heavy coal traffic from Germany to Italy via the Gotthard and Simplon–Loetschberg routes; this traffic presumably had nearly ceased by September. The Swedish state railways faced equally with a serious fuel shortage made further progress with electrification—45% of state railway mileage carrying 85% of the total traffic was reported as electrified. Conversion of the Hälsingborg-Hässleholm and Eslöv routes was due for completion in 1943. Further company-owned railways in the Malmö area were to be taken over by the state. In Spain the Santiago section of the new Zamora–Corunna railway was opened, embodying many heavy engineering works, and satisfactory progress was made with the output of new locomotives and equipment; heavy arrears of repairs had still to be undertaken before the pre-civil war situation would be fully restored. Electrification of the Madrid–Avila main line progressed but slowly, though the Villalba–El Escorial section was nearing completion in spite of materials difficulties.

Africa.—No data were published covering new railway mileages opened by the Allied forces controlling North Africa, and the need for the Mediterranean–Niger route southwards from Kenadza had grown less with the victories of the United Nations in Tunisia. In Portuguese East Africa construction was understood to be proceeding with the new lines in the Tete area north of the Zambezi. The line from Hercules to Koedoespoort in the Pretoria area was opened by the South African railways in June 1943. A line from Kena (Nile valley) to Safaga (Red sea) was reported as completed by Egypt, where many locomotives had been converted to burn oil fuel. A standard Beyer-Garrett type of locomotive was in production in Britain, suitable for working on many African lines laid with light 60-lb. rails.

Asia.—Definite information was not available regarding the progress made by Japan in linking more closely the Siamese railway system with those of Malaya and Indo-China. The head-

quarters of the South Manchurian railway had been moved from Dairen to Hsinking. Equally U.S.S.R. railway construction in Asia was not publicized. The Turkish state railways opened in July 1943 their new line from Diarbekir through Bismil and Cizre towards the Iraq frontier, and progress was made with the Mamuret el Aziz route via Palu to Karpahur, now open to traffic. Thence onwards via Mush and Van to Iran the line was under construction.

South America.—The link between the Argentine and Chilean railways via Salta made further progress and reports stated that trains were running to a point 190 miles from Salta; there were 158 miles further to the Chilean frontier at Paso de Socompa, whence Antofagasta is 211 miles distant; the route throughout was unlikely to be completed until 1945, and on the Chilean side the railhead was still 52 miles from the Argentine frontier. Argentina in Aug. 1943 agreed to reconstruct the Transandine railway. Fuel shortage continued very serious for locomotive purposes in Argentina. Many improvements were being effected on the Brazilian railways, thanks to American help, especially in the case of the Victoria–Minas line.

Australia.—The New South Wales government railways conducted trials with a new semi-streamlined 4-6-2 "Pacific" type locomotive, known as class C 38, and working at the high pressure of 248 lb. per sq.in. With Australia and New Zealand both virtually theatres of a war area it was not possible to give data on railway improvements or additions, but, as in so many other countries, the main problem to be faced was that of attempting to carry the heavy traffics offering with limited facilities for the construction of new equipment and repairs to older units. The transfer of coastal traffic to the railways and the restriction of highway movement to conserve gasoline and tires were partial causes of the increased railway load, while the various breaks of gauge limited the possible transfer of motive power units between the various state systems.

Canada.—Still increasing traffics and revenue were the outstanding features of the working of the two large Canadian railways in 1943, but with the rise in expenditure for salaries, wages, stores and fuel the increase in net revenue, predominant during the earlier war years, commenced to slacken. The latest Canadian National figures revealed an increased net revenue over 1942, but the Canadian Pacific figures indicated that the net revenue for 1943 would approximately equal that of the preceding year. Events of importance were the opening in July of the great new passenger terminal of the C.N.R. to replace the old Bonaventure station at Montreal, thus bringing to fruition a scheme planned and commenced over 15 years before, and the close correlation between the C.N.R. and its famous air subsidiary the Trans-Canada Airlines. The C.P.R. was also developing its airlines which are more of the shorthaul feeder character. Both systems received important additions to their heavier motive power classes and electric locomotives operated trains in the new station area at Montreal. Further Canadian mileage was being equipped with automatic signals. (*See also* DISASTERS; UNITED STATES.)

(C. E. R. S.)

Rainfall: *see* METEOROLOGY.

Ramey, Howard Knox

(1896–1943), U.S. army air officer, was born Oct. 14 in Mississippi. He served in the signal corps, aviation branch, in World War I, and later attended the air service photography school, the air corps tactical school and the command and general staff school. Regarded as one of the outstanding heavy bombardment officers of the U.S. army air force, Brig. Gen. Ramey was commander of the 5th bomber command of the 5th U.S. air force, a post to which he succeeded the late Brig. Gen. Kenneth M. Walker in Jan. 1943.

General MacArthur announced from Allied headquarters in Australia on April 3 that Gen. Ramey and his crew had been reported missing in action after failing to return from a recent mission.

Ramírez, Pedro Pablo

(1884–   ), Argentine army officer, was born Jan. 10 at La Paz, Entre Ríos province, Argentina. He was graduated from the Argentine Military college in 1904, and was commissioned a first lieutenant in 1910. He studied in Germany, 1911–13, serving with Kaiser Wilhelm's famous Fifth Hussars. He resumed his military career on returning to Argentina and rose to the rank of general. In 1930, he mobilized the army to help Gen. José F. Uriburu overthrow the liberal Irigoyen regime. But in 1932, Uriburu and his cohorts were overthrown in turn, and Ramírez suffered a temporary eclipse. The Argentine general, who expressed admiration for Italian fascism, helped organize the Milicia Nacionalista, modelled after the Italian blackshirts. In 1942, he was appointed war minister by Pres. Ramón S. Castillo but was subsequently ousted from this position. On June 4, 1943, Gen. Arturo Rawson with the aid of Ramírez, overthrew the Castillo regime; Rawson, president for three days, stepped down in favour of Ramírez on June 7. In his first public statement, Ramírez pledged to retain the republican form of government, co-operate with American nations and continue neutrality "for the moment." Throughout 1943, however, he jettisoned freedom of speech and the press, established a dictatorship, instituted anti-Jewish measures, suppressed newspapers that criticized his rule and in Jan. 1944 decreed the dissolution of all political parties.

Rapid Transit: *see* ELECTRIC TRANSPORTATION.
Rates of Exchange: *see* EXCHANGE CONTROL AND EXCHANGE RATES.

+Rationing.

Consumer rationing began in the United States in 1942, to meet shortages in supplies of certain civilian goods needed for, or curtailed by, the war program. The legal basis for rationing had been laid in 1941 in the Priorities and Allocations act of May 31, 1941, and was clarified and elaborated in the Second War Powers act of March 27, 1942. The president delegated his rationing authority, with respect to food, to the War Food administration, and with respect to all other matters, to the War Production board. In making its decisions, the WPB is guided by the recommendation of certain so-called supply agencies, notably the Petroleum Administration for War in the case of gasoline and fuel oil, and the Rubber director in the case of tires. In the case of some commodities, however, such as petroleum, where PAW rather than WPB has power to decide, the determination is made by a so-called supply agency. The Office of Price Administration rations pursuant to delegations of authority issued by the WFA and WPB.

Tires, automobiles and typewriters were among the first commodities upon which the impact of war was felt. They were rationed by certificate, as were bicycles, because eligibility to purchase the commodity must be determined separately in each individual case. Coupon books, on the other hand, were used when the commodity was distributed equally to all citizens or to all those in a given class, such as owners of automobiles or of oil-burning heating or cooking equipment.

War Ration Book I, put in use in May 1942, first provided coupons for sugar, then also for coffee and shoes. A separate coupon book was issued for rationed gasoline and coupon sheets for rationed fuel oil.

The rationing program was greatly extended in 1943, so that by the end of the year it covered a large proportion of U.S. food, including virtually all meats, processed foods, canned

"WAITER TROUBLE." Cartoonist Parrish's explanation of U.S. food scarcity in 1943 and the reasons therefor, published in the *Chicago Tribune*

goods and many dairy products. A most important development during the year was that of point rationing. Numerous modifications made the program simpler to carry out, and often more equitable to the consumer. Growth of the ration banking system was a significant contribution to the simplification and workability of the program.

The scarcity of leather, especially of imported hides, and the large demands of the armed forces made shoe rationing a necessity early in 1943. On Feb. 7 the War Production board directed the Office of Price Administration to ration shoes and the order was put into effect the same day. The mechanics of the program were simple. Certain stamps in the War Ration Books were designated as shoe stamps and every individual in the U.S. was entitled to one. At first each succeeding shoe stamp had a four-month period of validity. Later, with the validation of a new stamp, the period was abolished and the stamp was made usable at any time. Consumers were thus relieved of end-of-period pressure to use their current stamps. At the same time it was announced that no further stamp would be validated for six months. Special provision was made to take care of individual hardship cases.

The extension of rationing in March to processed foods, meats and fats was necessitated mainly by the rapidly increasing needs of our armed forces and our fighting Allies. Because canned foods are compact and easily stored, government purchases, especially for overseas shipment, are extremely high. Government requirements were approximately 35% of the total pack for 1943, while the proportion of total dried fruits, dehydrated vegetables and soups ran even higher. At the same time, civilian demand increased while the total output of canned goods was restricted because of the shortages of tin, steel, rubber and manpower. In addition to the decline in allocable civilian supplies of processed foods, the need for rationing was further accentuated by panic buying and consumer hoarding during the nine months prior to rationing.

Meat production, unlike that of canned goods, increased steadily from 1941, with a record production in 1943. Enormous government requirements, however, coupled with the rise in consumer income which led to a greatly increased consumer demand made rationing a necessity. Fats and oils and later canned milk and almost all cheeses were included under the meat program.

War Ration Book II was issued simultaneously with the start of the processed foods program. Blue stamps were reserved for processed foods; red stamps for meats and fats. War Ration Books III and IV consisted of point coupons for meats, processed foods and other commodities, and unit stamps for sugar, shoes and possible future programs. Book III was distributed by mail June 15–July 15, and Book IV through individual registration in October.

Point rationing was introduced with the processed foods program, which went into effect on March 1, 1943. A separate rationing program for each commodity would have been extremely cumbersome and would have made no allowance for regional or individual food preferences. Under the point system, coupons designated for groups of food were valid for a certain number of "points," and the amount of goods that could be purchased was determined by the point value assigned to each item. These point values were changed from time to time according to the supply situation and as the character of demand became clear from experience under the program. Point values tended to perform the same function that dollar prices normally perform in bringing supply and demand into equilibrium.

An outstanding feature of rationing was the "flow-back" of ration currency. Local War Price and Rationing boards issued books of ration stamps to consumers and granted certificates to institutional, industrial and other bulk users. Stamps and cer-

tificates flowed to retailers, wholesalers, processors and primary distributors, the surrender of ration currency being required with each exchange of goods at each level in the trade. The last two groups were required to turn over all ration currency to OPA and the currency they turned over had to match the value of the rationed goods they transferred.

The mechanism of the "flow-back" of ration points was simplified during 1943 by the use of a ration banking plan worked out in co-operation with the American Bankers' association. About 84% of U.S. commercial banks participated in the program, which enabled retailers, wholesalers, primary suppliers, bulk consumers and institutional and industrial users to deposit their ration currency in co-operating banks and to make and receive payments in the form of checks. It was estimated that approximately 50,000,000 deposits would be made annually and about 637,000,000 items would be handled by the banks each year. The ration banking program relieved local boards throughout the U.S. of a tremendous burden of counting, auditing and exchanging stamps and coupons for certificates of larger denomination. The producers and distributors of rationed goods benefited likewise from the time and cost-saving features instituted by ration banking.

The second half of 1943 was characterized not so much by the extension of rationing as by its modification. Forms and procedures were simplified considerably. Operating techniques were improved through co-operation with both industry and consumers. One of the improved techniques worked out was that of enumerating stamps by weight rather than by counting. Formerly the retailer had to count an enormously large volume of stamps. After intensive research it was found that large quantities of stamps could be enumerated more accurately by weighing than by counting and the change relieved the retailer of a real hardship. All the programs were amended in various ways which made it simpler to attend to individual needs. For example, local boards were given authority to grant additional quantities of food ration points to people living or working in isolated areas who could not otherwise get a nutritionally adequate diet. A plan for supplementing ration stamps with plastic tokens was scheduled to go into effect early in 1944. Under the proposed plan each stamp, regardless of original face value, was to have a value of 10 points in each program, which would eliminate the time-consuming job of sorting stamps. Change would be given consumers in the form of tokens which would remain valid indefinitely. The expiration date of ration stamps would be extended for much longer periods. Under the token plan it was expected that War Ration Books III and IV would last two years.

By the end of 1943, OPA was rationing new automobiles, bicycles, tires, gasoline, fuel oil, coal and oil heating stoves, some solid fuels, typewriters, rubber footwear, shoes, sugar, canned and processed foods, meats, fats and some dairy products. Coffee, after having been rationed for seven months, was released from rationing during the year. Plans had been completed for rationing coal, should it become necessary. Dates upon which rationing began: 1941—new tires and tubes, Dec. 30. 1942—recapped and recapping tires, Feb. 19; new automobiles, March 2; typewriters, March 13; sugar, April 28; gasoline in 17 eastern states, May 12; nation-wide mileage rationing, Dec. 1; bicycles, July 9; rubber footwear, Sept. 29; fuel oil, Oct. 22; coffee, Nov. 29 (released July 29, 1943); coal and oil heating stoves for private dwellings in 30 states, Dec. 19 (nation-wide Aug. 24, 1943). 1943—shoes, Feb. 7; processed foods, March 1; meats, fish, fats, oils, cheese, March 29; canned milk, June 2; soft cheese, June 6; firewood in Pacific northwest, March 1; coal in Pacific northwest, Sept. 20; jellies and preserves, Oct. 31. (*See also* BUSINESS REVIEW; PRICE ADMINISTRATION, OFFICE OF.) (C. Bs.)

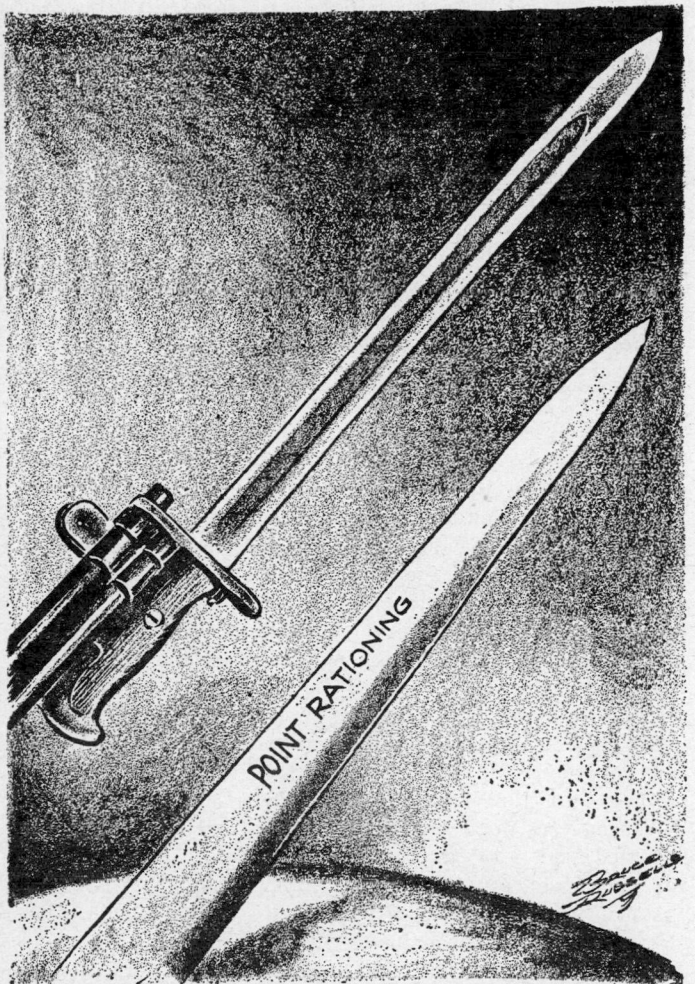

"HOME FRONT BAYONET," by Russell of the *Los Angeles Times*

Ray, Charles

(1891–1943), U.S. actor, was born in Jacksonville, Ill., on March 15. He received his early schooling in theatricals in stock shows and vaudeville and worked in motion pictures as an extra. Ray rose to motion-picture fame as a homespun hero and was at the height of his career in the early 1920s. His name later gradually disappeared and with the advent of sound pictures Ray could find only subordinate roles. He toured vaudeville houses in an effort to boost his waning popularity, but returned to Hollywood in 1934 and thereafter was cast in minor parts. Among his better-known films were: *String Beans, The Sheriff's Son, The Coward, The Busher, The Girl Dodger, The Egg-Crate Wallop, Greased Lightning, Bill Henry, Crooked Straight, Forty-Five Minutes from Broadway, The Old Swimmin' Hole, Scrap Iron, A Midnight Bell, The Girl I Loved,* and *The Courtship of Myles Standish.* Ray died Nov. 23 in Hollywood, Calif.

Ray, Edward (Ted)

(1877–1943), British golf champion, was born in Jersey, one of the Channel Islands. Ted Ray and the late Harry Vardon, also a Jersey native, made up one of the greatest professional golf combinations in Britain. Ray's skillful technique won him many golf competitions including the British Open championship, 1912, and the American Open championship, 1920. Both he and Vardon were beaten by a young amateur, Boston's 20-year-old Francis Ouimet, in a highly publicized three-way play-off at an open championship at Brookline, Mass., in 1913. Ouimet's victory over the veteran English golfers was a startling upset that caught the imagination of the American people and started the game of golf on the road to popularity in the United States. Ray, however, continued to be a formidable opponent and participated in many American and continental matches. He died in London, Aug. 27.

Rayon and Other Synthetic Fibres.

By Dec. 1943, rayon fabrics and yarn had become so important to the world at large that in the United States of America, the War Production board issued an allocation quota order setting aside for export to friendly countries 4% of the yarn and fabric produced. From South America and from the various countries in the United Nations group came demands for American-made rayon fabrics or the yarns from which to make fabrics or hosiery. In return for food, shelter and labour provided American forces stationed in such outlying points as New Zealand and Iceland, civilians in those countries were supplied rayon fabrics under the lend-lease agreements. South American hosiery and fabric mills, established during 1940–42, needed yarn to supply their domestic needs.

The production of rayon in the United States in 1943 exceeded the 1942 record year. Preliminary estimates indicated that the total consumption of rayon yarn in 1943 would exceed the previous high year of 1942 by 5.5%. Of this, the filament yarn consumption would exceed the 1942 record by 5% and the staple fibre by about 6%. Aside from the increased production of regular yarn, five of the rayon producers, who in 1942 had been ordered by the United States government to convert part of their facilities to production of special yarn for tire cord, had completed the necessary expansion by Nov. 1943 and expected an annual production rate of 240,000,000 lb. of high tenacity yarn for this purpose by the middle of 1944.

Military use of rayon yarns continued in 1943. It was estimated that approximately 50% of the viscose process yarn and from 10 to 15% of the acetate yarn went into such channels during 1943. Staple fibre rayon was used only in a limited way to augment the wool supply in the early part of the year. This was not important in the later months as the wool supply had

Table I.—Estimated World Rayon Production
(In millions of pounds)

	1939			1942		
	Filament	Staple	Total	Filament	Staple	Total
Europe						
Germany*	171.0	449.0	620.0	220.0	880.0†	1,100.0
Italy	119.0	191.0	310.0	132.0	330.0†	462.0
France	56.2	15.5	71.7	69.5	128.0†	197.5
Belgium	13.0	2.5	15.5	17.6	17.6†	35.2
Netherlands	24.2	—	24.2	26.5	11.0	37.5
Norway	0.4	—	0.4	1.0	None	1.0
Hungary	0.1	—	0.1	1.5	None	1.5
Rumania	2.7	0.1	2.8	4.4	7.7	12.1
Finland	0.5	0.6	1.1	1.1	2.2	3.3
Sweden	2.1	2.3	4.4	3.3	6.6	9.9
Switzerland	11.7	0.1	11.8	13.2	22.0	35.2
Spain	3.0	—	3.0	8.8	19.8	28.6
Great Britain	120.0	60.0	180.0	90.0	45.0	135.0
Greece	0.7	—	0.7	1.0	—	1.0
Portugal	0.4	—	0.4	0.5	—	0.5
U.S.S.R.	17.0	—	17.0	30.0	—	30.0
Total Europe	542.0	721.1	1,263.1	620.4	1,469.9	2,090.3
North America						
Canada	14.2	—	14.2	18.5	—	18.5
Mexico	—	—	—	0.5	—	0.5
United States	328.6	51.3	379.9	479.3	153.3	632.6
Total North America	342.8	51.3	394.1	498.3	153.3	651.6
South America						
Argentina	5.8	—	5.8	8.3	—	8.3
Brazil	15.1	0.2	15.3	17.0	2.5	19.5
Chile	—	—	—	1.0	—	1.0
Colombia	0.2	—	0.2	1.2	—	1.2
Total South America	21.1	0.2	21.3	27.5	2.5	30.0
Asia						
Japan	239.3	309.5	548.8	300.0	400.0	700.0
Turkey	0.2	—	0.2	1.0	—	1.0
Total Asia	239.5	309.5	549.0	301.0	400.0	701.0
World Total	1,145.4	1,082.1	2,227.5	1,447.2	2,025.7	3,472.9

Source: 1939 data is from the June 1941 *Organon*, pages 90–91.
1942 data: For the European countries, Germany to Spain inclusive, the data are from the Textile Unit, Bureau of Foreign and Domestic Commerce, United States Department of Commerce; the unit emphasizes that the data are estimated based on the most reliable information obtainable, but that the figures cannot be guaranteed. Other countries' data are estimated by the Textile Economics Bureau. Data for Great Britain estimated at 75% of the 1939 rate. Figure for the U.S.S.R. is a pure guess. Data for United States and Canada is actual. Data for South American countries reasonably accurate, based on trade information. Japanese data a pure guess based on capacity operation of the industry previously reported in the 1937–38 period.
*Data for Germany includes Austria, Poland and Czechoslovakia.
†Lanital (casein wool) included for Germany, France, Italy and Belgium.

improved to such an extent that restrictions on the use of raw wool were lifted by the War Production board in Nov. 1943. However, staple fibre and acetate filament yarn were the main supplies for civilian fabrics, an important part of essential textile requirements for clothing and household articles.

One of the most colourful uses of rayon for military purposes was the successful employment of fragmentation bomb parachutes during the campaigns of 1943 in the South Pacific and in North Africa. Especially in the South Pacific, the low-level flying made possible by the use of the parachute bombs, proved most effective in the capture of important enemy positions in New Guinea and other Pacific island strongholds. The use of rayon fabric provided an inexpensive, lightweight parachute that enabled the bombing crew to escape from their low altitude before the bomb exploded. The slowly drifting bomb was of the type that scattered explosive instead of penetrating the earth. American rayon fabric mills supplied not only their own but Allied forces as well with these effective implements of war.

Not only in the United States was rayon production attaining new importance. In Dec. 1943, statistics of world production, the first since June 1941, were issued by the Textile Economics bureau in New York showing that world total rayon production increased from 2,227,500,000 lb. in 1939 to 3,472,900,000 lb. in 1942, a gain of 56%. Of the 1942 production, 1,447,200,000 lb. was filament yarn and 2,025,700,000 lb. was staple fibre. The filament yarn showed an increase of 26% and the staple fibre an increase of 87% over 1939. The latter increase was due primarily to the use of staple fibre as a substitute for wool and

Table II.—*United States Rayon Production in Millions of Pounds*

	1943	1942	1941	1940	1939	1938
Rayon filament yarn . .	501.1	479.3	451.2	390.1	328.6	257.6
Rayon staple fibre . . .	162.0	153.3	122.0	81.1	51.3	29.9

Table III.—*United States Consumption in Millions of Pounds*

	1943	1942	1941	1940	1939	1938
Cotton	5,236.4	5,618.6	5,208.5	3,961.7	3,629.7	2,918.7
Silk	not available	not available	25.3*	35.8	47.3	51.7
Wool	527.7†	597.4*	652.2	411.1	396.5	284.5
Rayon	656.2	468.8	452.4	388.7	359.7	274.1

*11 months actual, one month estimated.
†10 months actual, two months estimated.

cotton in the axis countries. In Germany, Italy and France, the total staple fibre production was 1,338,000,000 lb. compared with the United States production of 153,300,000 lb. in 1942. Japan also exceeded American production of staple fibre with a total poundage of 400,000,000. In the production of filament yarn, however, the United States produced more than any other single country, manufacturing 29% of the world's total in 1939 and 33% in 1942. In total production of filament and staple fibre, Germany in 1942 led with 1,100,000,000 lb. (32% of the total), Japan second with 700,000,000 lb. (20% of the total) and the United States making a close third with 632,600,000 lb. (18% of the world total).

This total would probably be less for Germany in 1943 because of the bombings of rayon plants which, according to military reports, were hard hit in the heavy attacks during the latter months of 1943.

The general world picture of rayon production is given in Table I.

The introduction of other types of synthetic fibres continued during 1943. Nylon was not available for civilian use except for approximately 2,000,000 yd. of nylon parachute cloth rejected by the army air forces for parachutes and ordered sold by the War Production board for essential civilian use. Most of this was treated with a special finish to make underwear or infants' wear. Fibreglass, a spun glass cloth, was being used in a coated fabric in place of cotton. It had the advantage of being non-flammable and extremely flexible. Fibreglass was found to be extremely strong within a relatively small area, a two-ply standard yarn being the equivalent in diameter of a 100-denier rayon. In the fibrous form, it was roughly twice the strength of steel piano wire. In a flare chute used in 1943 bombings over Germany, the fibreglass was used as reflector or screen between the blinding white light of the flare and the lightweight rayon parachute used to carry it down. The use of the screen prevented pilots and bombardiers in following planes from being blinded.

Velon was featured in 1943 by a former silk manufacturer who was developing its use in upholstery fabrics both for the home and for automobiles. Velon fabrics showed no stains and were non-flammable. It was impervious to the effects of salt water, heat, cold or tropical conditions. Aralac, the synthetic yarn that was most like wool, previously used only in blends, was offered in 1943 by its producers for use alone or in combination with other yarns. The longer staple of aralac offered special advantages over wool.

Production of all types of synthetic yarns, including rayon, was uncertain by the end of 1943 because of the shortages of wood pulp and chemicals. Manpower was the cause of pulp shortage, the same conditions causing the shortage in paper supplies. The chemical shortages were particularly important in acetate yarn but also were expected to affect pigmented yarn, largely used in civilian fabrics. Plastic yarns, such as cellulose acetate, nylon,

vinyon, etc., contained essential chemicals needed for the war effort. The prospects at the end of the year were for a drastically decreased civilian supply. (*See also* SILK; TEXTILE INDUSTRY.) (I. L. BL.)

Receipts, Government: *see* BUDGET, NATIONAL.
Reciprocal Trade Agreements: *see* INTERNATIONAL TRADE.
Reclamation: *see* CANALS AND INLAND WATERWAYS; FLOODS AND FLOOD CONTROL; FORESTS; IRRIGATION; SOIL EROSION AND SOIL CONSERVATION.

Reconstruction Finance Corporation.

The Reconstruction Finance corporation was created by congress on Jan. 22, 1932, and started operations on Feb. 2, 1932.

Its original purpose was to aid in financing agriculture, commerce and industry, which were then under great economic stress. Its main activities included the strengthening of the banking structure of the nation through, first, the making of loans and, later, the purchase of and loans on preferred stock and capital notes and debentures in banks, trust companies, insurance companies and mortgage loan companies; loans to railroads; for self-liquidating public works; to business; to mining and fishing industries; for refinancing drainage, levee and irrigation districts and public school districts; for the carrying and orderly marketing of agricultural commodities and livestock and exportation of agricultural and other products; also the purchase of securities from the Public Works administration. The RFC Mortgage company was formed by RFC on March 14, 1935, to aid in the re-establishment of a normal market for sound mortgages on income-producing urban property. The Disaster Loan corporation was created by an act of congress Feb. 11, 1937, and was organized by RFC on Feb. 15, 1937, for the purpose of making loans to those who had suffered by reason of floods or other disasters.

The Federal National Mortgage association was established by RFC on Feb. 10, 1938, to maintain a market for first mortgages insured by the Federal Housing administration under Title II of the National Housing act.

With the necessity for national defense, the following subsidiaries were formed:

Defense Plant corporation	Aug. 22, 1940
Defense Supplies corporation	Aug. 29, 1940
Metals Reserve company	June 28, 1940
Rubber Reserve company	June 28, 1940

The Defense Plant corporation was organized to assist in financing the construction and equipping of defense plants and projects throughout the country and to operate them if necessary, while the Defense Supplies corporation and Metals Reserve company were formed to acquire stockpiles of strategic and critical war materials from all over the world. The Rubber Reserve company was created to build up our stockpile of raw rubber and to develop and supervise the operation of facilities for the production of synthetic rubber.

The Defense Homes corporation (not a subsidiary of RFC but managed by it) was incorporated pursuant to a letter of the president to the secretary of the treasury on Oct. 18, 1940, allocating funds to the federal loan administrator to provide homes of a permanent type for war workers and their families.

The War Damage corporation was created by RFC on Dec. 13, 1941, for the purpose of offering reasonable insurance protection against loss of or damage to property resulting from enemy attack in the United States and its possessions.

The United States Commercial company was created by RFC March 27, 1942, its original purpose being to compete with enemy countries for the purchase of materials which might be of use to the enemy. It was transferred to the Foreign Economic

Reconstruction Finance Corporation—Summary of Activities Feb. 2, 1932, through Dec. 31, 1943

	Authorizations	Disbursements	Repayments and Other Reductions
For benefit of agriculture	$ 2,603,733,430.83	$ 1,452,180,464.11	$ 1,450,690,620.58
To open banks to meet demands of depositors	1,334,880,161.08	1,138,251,619.27	1,092,957,177.95
For distribution to depositors in closed banks	1,419,531,473.07	1,056,883,720.04	1,040,525,167.93
For bank capital (including Export-Import banks $176,500,000, and Federal Home Loan banks $124,741,000)	1,647,160,539.00	1,471,521,311.56	815,049,462.11
For self-liquidating projects (including PWA municipal securities) .	1,297,532,405.62	1,072,390,065.85	957,046,102.78
To business enterprises	684,026,741.40	348,002,811.70	255,904,855.34
For loans to national defense	14,343,603,048.33	11,486,731,869.18	4,886,072,979.54
For loan to Great Britain and Northern Ireland	425,000,000.00	390,000,000.00	61,334,740.74
For purchases of stock—national defense	125,000,001.00	26,000,001.00	
To drainage, levee and irrigation districts	148,999,798.64	100,370,198.25	44,400,000.84
To railroads (including PWA railroad securities)	1,626,986,435.54	1,049,298,714.70	651,782,075.76
For loans to and capital of mortgage loan companies (including $25,000,000 capital the RFC Mortgage company and $11,000,000 capital Federal National Mortgage association)	887,342,930.95	735,582,073.01	560,517,059.54
For loans to and capital of insurance companies	151,589,750.19	137,843,209.81	105,605,282.73
To building and loan associations (including receivers)	179,874,559.59	139,898,067.90	136,698,246.85
To public school authorities	25,689,050.00	23,242,175.00	22,784,900.00
For catastrophe rehabilitation loans	16,184,520.95	12,003,055.32	11,347,543.65
To state funds for insurance of deposits of public moneys . . .	13,087,715.88	13,064,631.18	13,064,631.18
For mining, milling and smelting businesses	19,019,100.00	8,989,409.40	3,748,883.38
For loan to Export-Import bank	25,000,000.00	25,000,000.00	25,000,000.00
For other purposes	669,057.07	614,813.85	614,813.85
Total—By directors of the corporation	$26,974,910,779.14	$20,687,868,211.13	$12,135,153,634.75
Allocations and loans to other governmental agencies and for relief by direction of congress	3,819,327,821.87	3,545,583,239.51	3,104,027,771.60*
GRAND TOTAL	$30,794,238,601.01	$24,233,451,450.64	$15,239,181,406.35†

*Includes $2,783,040,007.21 of corporation's notes cancelled pursuant to act of congress approved Feb. 24, 1938.
†Includes $46,724,308.14 credited on indebtedness for property taken over for debt.

administration July 15, 1943

The Rubber Development corporation was created by RFC on Feb. 20, 1943, for the purpose of developing sources of rubber outside of the United States. This organization was transferred to the Foreign Economic administration on July 15, 1943.

The Petroleum Reserve corporation was created by RFC June 30, 1943, to acquire petroleum, petroleum products and petroleum reserves outside the United States. It was transferred to Foreign Economic administration July 15, 1943.

The Federal Loan agency came into being through the president's reorganization plan No. 1, of April 25, 1939. Grouped under Federal Loan agency were the Reconstruction Finance corporation and its subsidiaries above mentioned and in addition the Federal Home Loan Bank board, Home Owners' Loan corporation, Federal Savings and Loan Insurance corporation, Federal Housing administration, Electric Home and Farm authority (now in liquidation) and Export-Import Bank of Washington (now a part of the Foreign Economic administration). In Feb. 1942 the activities of the Federal Loan agency were placed by executive order under the direction and supervision of the secretary of commerce for the duration of the war, with transfers of the Defense Homes corporation, Home Owners' Loan corporation, Federal Home Loan Bank board, Federal Savings and Loan Insurance corporation and the Federal Housing administration being effected to the National Housing agency. (C. B. H.)

Red Cross.

United States.—Red Cross services and supplies, in 1943, were carried to every part of the globe occupied by United States troops. In Europe, North Africa, the middle east, India, Australia and the islands of the Pacific, thousands of specially trained Red Cross men and women—field directors, hospital, club and recreation workers—were by the side of the fighting men. They accompanied invasion forces into new combat areas or followed close behind—always within earshot of cannon fire. In continental United States and insular possessions there were other thousands of Red Cross workers on duty in camps and naval stations and military hospitals. Their number was being constantly augmented to keep pace with expansion by the army and navy.

The number of overseas Red Cross service clubs, rest homes and recreation centres grew to 350 during 1943. An innovation was the clubmobile, a bus equipped as a clubroom which solved the problem of bringing Red Cross services and supplies to remote camps and outposts in Great Britain, North Africa, Sicily, Italy, Australia and other places. The demand of army and air force officers for more frequent visits by Red Cross clubmobiles to their camps and airfields led to the inauguration of a new service—aeroclubs and camp clubs. Still another development during the year was the establishment of rest homes for aviators in need of relaxation after they had been on many bombing missions.

Important as were these activities for the able-bodied, far more vital was the service to the sick and wounded servicemen in the military hospitals at home and overseas. In the war zones Red Cross hospital workers shared the hardships and risks with the nurses, doctors and patients. Hospital service and the work performed by field directors constitute the basic services of the Red Cross in this war. Field directors were available to servicemen and women everywhere.

Millions of Americans served their country on the home front as volunteer Red Cross workers. There were 4,000,000 workers in volunteer special services alone. They made 12,000,000 garments and 2,500,000 kit bags for uniformed men and women and rolled more than 900,000,000 surgical dressings. They drove cars, ambulances and trucks in city, country and army camp. They served many thousand mass emergency meals to troops and civilians, and worked as typists, clerks and utility helpers in Red Cross and other war aid centres.

During 1943 the U.S. Red Cross enrolled about 27,000 nurses for service in the army and navy nurse corps. A hundred thousand trained volunteer nurse's aides served in veterans' and civilian hospitals. About 400,000 women and girls were taught Red Cross home nursing, while an expanding nutrition program helped strengthen the home front.

More than 17,000,000 members of the American Junior Red Cross produced millions of comfort and recreation articles ranging from hospital tray favours to furniture for army recreation rooms.

Of the more than 1,500,000 Red Cross first aid certificates issued in 1943 to persons who completed a prescribed training course, a large percentage went to war plant workers in every part of the country.

During the year, the Red Cross blood donor service grew to a nation-wide project with 35 blood donor centres and 63 mobile units, collecting approximately 100,000 pints each week. More than 4,000,000 donations were made through the Red Cross during the year, bringing the total donations to more than 5,000,000 from the time the service was inaugurated at the request of the surgeons general of the army and navy in 1941. The quota for 1944 was 5,000,000 pints.

The year 1943 saw the opening of four large packing centres in Philadelphia, New York, Chicago and St. Louis for the packing of Red Cross food parcels for American and Allied prisoners of war. In these plants 4,000 women volunteers packed nearly 7,000 Red Cross standard food packages. They were consigned to the International Red Cross committee at Geneva, Switzerland, for distribution principally in Europe. In Sept. 1943, the diplomatic exchange ship "Gripsholm" sailed from New York carrying a cargo of food packages, medicines and other supplies valued at $1,500,000 for the United States and Allied prisoners of war in the far east. An *American Red Cross Prisoner of War Bulletin* of which 100,000 copies were issued each month was launched during 1943. So was another publication, the *Red Cross News*, printed in small type on onion skin paper and sent by air through the International Red Cross committee to Americans in prison camps in Europe.

In March 1943, the Red Cross filed over 6,000 claims for veterans' pensions. Six months later the number had jumped to 25,000 a month. Requests for Red Cross assistance in filing claims for government benefits continued to increase in proportion to the number of men discharged from military service. The bulk of cases handled by Red Cross were filed for servicemen by Red Cross field directors attached to army and navy hospitals in the United States. When men were discharged from hospitals and returned to their homes, Red Cross chapters took over the responsibility of aiding veterans and their families who were in need during the period pending settlement of claims for government benefits.

All chapters maintained their service units in readiness to meet natural disasters of all types—windstorms, floods, fires and famine—and to assist local emergency defense councils with civilian aid in case of enemy action. Rehabilitation was offered to those victims who, through their own resources, were unable to recover from the effects of disasters. (G. S. Br.)

The World.—The 63 national Red Cross societies and their two international organizations, the International Red Cross committee and the League of Red Cross societies, found increased opportunities for service in a world at war.

Information was exchanged between national societies through the Geneva headquarters of the League of Red Cross societies—the federation of the national Red Cross and Red Crescent societies. The League's secretariat sent missions to societies both in Europe and in the western hemisphere, and through its publications encouraged the development and expansion of national activities. The League's Pan-American bureau, with headquarters in Santiago, Chile, supplied materials and advice to the societies of Latin America, and arranged field visits to extend disaster relief and nursing programs.

The International Red Cross committee continued to discharge its basic wartime responsibility as a benevolent neutral intermediary between belligerents. Through its headquarters in Geneva, Switzerland, continued to flow personal messages exchanged between civilians across enemy lines, bringing the wartime total of such messages by Sept. 1943, to over 3,000,000. The committee's delegates in warring nations visited prison camps, observed the application of the Geneva Prisoners of War Convention, and distributed relief supplies to prisoners and civilian internees. Ships operated by the international committee, sailing under safe conduct, carried relief supplies for prisoners of war on a regular schedule across the Atlantic, and the flow of such supplies through the committee's warehouses in Switzerland was larger than in any preceding year. (*See* also PRISONERS OF WAR.) (P. E. R.)

Re-employment of War Veterans: *see* SELECTIVE SERVICE, U.S.

Reforestation: *see* FORESTS.

Reformed Church: *see* PRESBYTERIAN CHURCH.

Refugees. The year 1943 brought no surcease to the refugees trapped on the continent of Europe. When Germany occupied southern France in Dec. 1942, virtually all avenues of escape from Europe were closed. Inside Europe the deportations of Jewish refugees from the western countries to the east, which had been initiated by the Germans in Aug. 1942, in Paris, continued without abatement. At the end of the year 1943 it was generally accepted that practically all central European Jews, who had earlier sought haven in France and the Low Countries, had been shipped eastward along with many nationals of these countries.

Deportations were carried out with determination and ruthlessness. Families were separated, wives from husbands and children from parents. The old and infirm were collected along with others, first in concentration centres and then into deportation trains with minimum supplies of food and personal belongings. The deportations developed some resistance in the civilian population, particularly in France. Church groups, charitable institutions and individual families aided in hiding and protecting children especially, even at the risk of their own lives and security.

Concurrently with the deportations of Jews the recruiting of labourers for the war industries in Germany was intensified. The number of foreign involuntary workers drawn from other countries in Europe to Germany increased during the year to approximately 5,000,000. The ranks of the workers were increased substantially by the discharge of many Allied prisoners of war, who were immediately re-enlisted as civilian workers.

Even before the final closing of the borders of southern France at the end of 1942, the physically able among the refugees had established routes of illegal egress over the Pyrenees into Spain. At the beginning of the year some 15,000 refugees, predominantly French but including most of the nationalities of Europe, were in Spain endeavouring to make their way to north Africa or overseas to the western hemisphere. Their number was aug-

YOUNG FRENCH REFUGEE, son of a French war prisoner, enjoying a hearty meal at a home for refugee children in Geneva, Switzerland

mented daily by accretions of 50 to 100 who managed to cross the mountains even during the winter months at the beginning of 1943.

In North Africa the Allied occupation brought release and re-employment to some thousands of refugees who had escaped to that area earlier. Included were approximately 5,600 Spanish refugees, a small fraction of the estimated 120,000 caught in southern France by the German occupation. An Inter-Allied commission co-operating with the French authorities in North Africa arranged for their release from internment camps and immediate employment, chiefly in the labour corps of the Allied armies.

The persistent reports of mass executions of refugees in eastern Europe and of mounting death rates from starvation coupled with the complete stoppage of emigration from Europe resulted in public demands in the spring of 1943 in England and the United States for more effective governmental action on behalf of refugees.

In April 1943 the Anglo-American conference met in Bermuda to consider the problem. Recommendations were made to the American and British governments that the membership of the Intergovernmental Committee on Refugees, organized as a result of the Evian conference called by President Roosevelt in 1938, be enlarged and that its scope be extended to include authority to act on behalf of all refugees wherever they might be found, who had been obliged to leave their homes during the war for reasons of race, religion or political belief. This reorganization of the Intergovernmental committee and the extension of its mandate was accomplished at a meeting of the committee in London in Aug. 1943.

Hopes aroused by the Bermuda conference that intergovernmental action might result in the removal to neutral countries—Sweden, Switzerland, Spain and Turkey—of larger numbers of refugees from the occupied areas were doomed to disappointment. In spite of repeated efforts directed particularly to the rescue of children from Bulgaria and Rumania the exits of axis Europe remained closed to the refugees. The single exception was in the escape to Sweden of some 6,000 refugees from Denmark upon the German occupation of that country in the fall of 1943. Over 1,000 Danish Jews had previously been deported to the east.

The neutral countries had generally received refugees who crossed their borders clandestinely. Switzerland had accepted over 20,000 refugees from France and Germany, and Sweden some 20,000 Finnish children, more than 15,000 refugees from Norway and 4,000 from Germany. These were in addition to numbers of military refugees from France and Norway.

The movement of Polish refugees through Iran and India to temporary camps in east Africa and Mexico probably constituted the largest movement of refugees outside Europe during 1943. Some 33,000 Polish refugees had trekked in 1942 from eastern Poland through Soviet Russia to Tehran. From there they were transferred to Karachi and Bombay, India. More than 1,200 were removed by boat to Palestine. During 1943, 21,000 were placed in camps in Uganda, Kenya and Tanganyika; 1,500 were transported across the Pacific to Mexico to await repatriation to Poland after the war.

Smaller numbers of Greek refugees found asylum in the near east, 5,000 on the island of Cyprus, 2,000 in Syria, 2,000 in Egypt, 1,000 or more in Ethiopia and others in temporary camps in east Africa and the Belgian Congo.

The withdrawal of Italian troops from southern France following the collapse of Italy in the fall of 1943 precipitated a new movement of refugees into Switzerland. Central European refugees, previously comparatively safe in the Italian occupied zone of southern France, joined others from northern Italy and Italian

military personnel to increase the refugee group in Switzerland to approximately 63,000. There were repercussions to the changed status of Italy in the war also in the near east. Greek refugees, some of Italian nationality, numbering over 10,000 fled from Samos and other islands relinquished by Italian troops to Palestine and Syria.

The refugee situation in the far east did not change substantially during 1943. The westward movement from central and eastern China continued at a slower pace. Estimates of the numbers of persons involved indicated displacements comparable to those in Europe. The war in the southern Pacific uprooted many overseas Chinese who fled from Burma, Malaya, Thailand, the Netherlands Indies and French Indo-China to Australia, India and China.

On Nov. 9, 1943 the representatives of 44 nations signed an agreement at Washington establishing the United Nations Relief and Rehabilitation administration. At the first session of the council of the new international relief organization which followed immediately at Atlantic City, New Jersey, the discussion of the problems of displaced persons in Europe and the far east clearly demonstrated the concern of governments to find early solutions for their uprooted populations. (*See* also CHILD WELFARE; JEWISH RELIGIOUS LIFE.)

BIBLIOGRAPHY.—Sir John Hope Simpson, *The Refugee Problem* (London 1939) and *Refugees, A Review of the Situation since September 1938* (London 1939), issued under the auspices of the Royal Institute of International Affairs; "Refugees," *The Annals of The American Academy of Political and Social Science* (May 1939); Louise W. Holborn, "The Legal Status of Political Refugees, 1920–1938," *American Journal of International Law*, 32:680–703 (1938); *Survey Graphic* supplement Nov. 1940, March 1941, Sept. 1941, and other articles; Eugene M. Kulischer, *The Displacement of Population in Europe, 1943,* (International Labour Office, Montreal). (G. L. W.)

Rehabilitation and Occupational Therapy for Wounded Soldiers.

The medical rehabilitation of disabled ex-members of the armed forces in the 94 hospitals of the Veterans' administration in operation in 1943, supplemented the efforts of the internist and surgeon by an integrated program of physical therapy, occupational therapy, physical exercises, recreation and library activities. Group therapy was conducted for mentally ill patients whose condition unfitted them for individual assignment to an occupational therapy project.

Physical Therapy.—Physical therapy was extensively employed in the treatment of subacute and chronic conditions and in the restoration of impaired function. There were 95 physical therapy units in field stations of the Veterans' administration: 51 in hospitals for medical and surgical disorders, 29 in hospitals for neuropsychiatric patients, 13 in hospitals for tuberculous beneficiaries, and 2 in regional offices. Each unit was centrally located, completely equipped with modern appliances, and well lighted and ventilated. A physician was in charge of each, and the technicians under his direction were specially trained for this work.

The physical therapy measures used in the three different types of hospitals varied considerably. In all of them thermotherapy, massage, active and passive exercises, ultra-violet rays, galvanic, faradic and sinusoidal treatments were available. Hydrotherapy rooms were installed in the hospitals for medical and surgical and for neuropsychiatric patients, and were equipped with electric light cabinets, control table, shower, arm and leg whirlpool baths and sitz baths. Continuous flow tubs and pack rooms and swimming pools were provided for disturbed psychotic patients. In the hospitals for neuropsychiatric beneficiaries a well developed program of physical exercise and recreation was carried on by physical directors. The hospitals for tuberculous patients were equipped for heliotherapy—by solariums, indoor and out, and mobile ultra-violet ray lamps. Mineral baths were available at

Above, left: RED CROSS WORKER helping a convalescent U.S. soldier construct a model plane in the army's Halloran General hospital, Staten Island, N.Y.

Above, right: U.S. SOLDIER, wounded in North Africa, being taught correct weaving technique at an army hospital in the United States

Below, left: PAINTING CLASS for U.S. soldiers recovering from wounds in an army hospital in 1943

Below, right: WOUNDED U.S. CORPORAL flexing the muscles of his hand, burned during the crash of a bomber. The finger ladder is part of the equipment in the physical therapy department of Lovell General hospital, Ft. Devens, Mass.

the hospital in Saratoga Springs, N.Y.; and at a Florida facility (Bay Pines), the beach and warm water were used for helio-therapy and exercise.

Because the great preponderance of the beneficiaries were men who served in World War I, the physical measures employed were gradually modified to accord with their average age and its attendant disorders. The incidence of arthritis and peripheral vascular diseases naturally increased, and special facilities for their treatment were amplified. Fever therapy was employed as required.

The admission of patients from the armed forces in World War II, which was expected to accelerate greatly, would give renewed impetus to physical therapy.

Occupational Therapy.

Occupational therapy had an exceptional development under the Veterans' administration. As the name signifies, it was primarily a treatment measure, organized and administered for that purpose. It was prescribed and supervised by physicians. Any vocational training that might accrue, although considerable, was regarded as incidental and secondary. Occupational therapy projects were assigned only after careful consideration was given to the interest and aptitudes of the patients concerned, and to their physical, mental and emotional condition. Although many of the activities in occupational therapy had direct relation to the maintenance requirements of the hospitals where they were carried on, the assignments were never thought of as "work." There was consistent adherence to the administration's concept and definition of occupational therapy as "any mental or physical activity that is prescribed for, directed, and supervised to promote recovery from disease or injury, and to aid in the hospital or extramural adjustment of patients."

Besides the projects in arts and crafts conducted in hospitals for general medical and surgical, tuberculous and neuropsychiatric patients, occupational therapy projects of the industrial type also were carried on in connection with the fabrication and repair of pajamas, mattress covers, cooks' aprons, neckerchiefs, bedshoes, brushes, brooms, toothbrush cabinets, cement blocks, dustpans, tub-hammocks and covers for continuous flow tubs, repairs to library books, mops, rubber mats, printing and mimeographing, shoe repairs, head bands, shoeshining boxes, typewriter desks, venetian blinds, dishwashing racks, window drapes, raffia hats, linen trucks, library trucks, laundry trucks, convalescent gowns, wristlets, restraint belts, rubber pillowcases, furniture repairs and other repairs. Projects in landscaping, vegetable gardening, general agriculture and other outdoor activities were used and emphasized whenever this type of treatment could be utilized to advantage.

Habit-training and kindergarten types of occupational therapy for mentally deteriorated patients were further developed and extended in the neuropsychiatric facilities, under occupational therapy personnel with special training and experience in this type of treatment. Co-ordinated with this were the activities resulting from programs of recreational therapy, group therapy and physical exercise.

BIBLIOGRAPHY.—Bonnie E. Balott, "Occupational Therapy," *School Arts*, 43:17–18 (1943).   (C. M. G.)

Reinhardt, Max

(1873–1943), U.S. theatrical producer, was born Sept. 9 in Baden, near Vienna. Reinhardt, whose staging of *The Miracle* made him internationally famous as a producer, left Berlin in 1933 after nazi officialdom ousted him from the German State theatre because of his Jewish birth. Almost penniless, he went to the United States, where he staged the Hollywood production of *A Midsummer Night's Dream*, 1935. At the time of his death he was supervis-ing the production of *La Belle Hélène* for the New Opera company and a successful revival of his production of the operetta, *Rosalinda*, had entered its second year on Broadway. Reinhardt, who became a naturalized U.S. citizen in 1940, died in New York city, Oct. 31. (See *Encyclopædia Britannica*.)

Relay Racing: *see* TRACK AND FIELD SPORTS.

Relief.

The outstanding fact in the field of relief in 1943 was the great demand for workers in all belligerent countries, so insistent that every able-bodied person could get a job, if free to take it, and the need was so urgent that persons on the old-age assistance rolls left to take jobs, mothers or guardians of small children made special arrangements for the care of their children so they might accept positions and even some of the blind were drawn into wage earning.

The number of the unemployed in the United States dropped to an altogether unanticipated low of less than 1,000,000, as against a theoretical minimum of 2,000,000 which had been assumed as the ultimate reduction possible in that category. Those who had been freely stigmatized as shirkers and paupers on work relief projects, such as the Works Progress administration, were in 1943 working in defense industries, absorbed in the military services or otherwise risen to the ranks of independence, leaving only the physically and mentally handicapped, the aged and children with their guardians on the relief rolls.

Up to the middle of 1942, assistance to the aged in the United States had increased from about 500,000 recipients in 1936 to about 2,250,000 in July 1942, aid to dependent children from about 110,000 families to 386,000 and aid to the blind from about 57,000 to 78,000. After July 1942, all these trends not only had ceased to continue in their upward direction, but had actually been reversed, the least pronounced being among the blind and the most among families with dependent children.

In the class of general relief, the unemployables and the unemployed not cared for by the above provisions, the decrease in total number receiving assistance began earlier, as industrial conditions began to absorb the unemployed. In Jan. 1940, it stood at about 1,600,000 families and dropped to only slightly more than 300,000 cases in the fall of 1943.

As the number of cases decreased, certain changes in character of cases and in methods of administration emerged. Obviously, everyone capable of securing a job was off the rolls, and therefore those left presented more difficult problems. Services looking toward rehabilitation occupied a larger share of the attention of public and private assistance workers than ever before. A substantial number of states in the United States placed their general relief grants on a cash basis to families, as it had been in the special categories such as aid to the blind, the aged and dependent children.

Contributions to community funds, or to war chests continued to rise in Canada and the United States as they had in 1942. In Canada 15 chests collected $4,895,385 in 1943 as compared with $3,777,058 in 1942. In the United States 247 war chests raised in 1943 $118,438,178, compared with $101,633,241 in 1942. There was no solicitation for funds for the Red Cross in the United States in 1942; but in 1943 a special appeal, largely for relief due to World War II, was made for $125,000,000, and more than $141,000,000 was raised. These substantial increases in contributions to private agencies in the two English-speaking countries of North America were in the face of drastically increased taxation, draining off excess profits of corporations and extra earnings of individuals. They cannot be offered as conclusive evidence of the confidence which these private agencies enjoyed, but they are valid evidence that high taxes did not reduce the willingness, or perhaps the ability, of corporations and persons to give in a period of high industrial activity and its sequential widely spread improvement in the income of workers.

The publication of *Social Insurance and Allied Services in England* by Sir William Beveridge in England, and of the *Report of the National Resources Planning Board* in the United States in the latter part of 1942 broke new ground in the theory and administration of public assistance. While both documents were interested primarily in insurance provisions whereby wage earners might be adequately protected in old age, illness, invalidity, unemployment and the other predictable contingencies which reduce them to dependence, each recognized that all plans for the anticipation of need by insurance or other means must envisage a general assistance program capable by its flexibility and adequacy of caring for those whose needs do not fall within the anticipated categories. The Beveridge report said, "The State cannot be excluded altogether from giving direct assistance. However comprehensive an insurance scheme, some . . . will fall through the meshes of any insurance." For this residual group he proposed a national assistance program, based on the means test, with aid somewhat less adequate than insurance benefits, but with no requirements as to residence as a criterion of eligibility.

The National Resources Planning board (U.S.) made practically the same recommendations, modified only by the governmental structure of the United States, which places ultimate responsibility for public assistance upon the different states. The device used by the federal government to bring about uniformity in benefits and public assistance within the more than 50 jurisdictions was to offer grants-in-aid for assistance, among other purposes, conditioned upon the states' meeting certain conditions. It recommended that the system of categorical assistance be enlarged to include all assistance, granted without reference to the residence of the applicant within the jurisdiction in which he becomes dependent. This report, however, followed the precedent of the United States in recommending provision for a flexible work relief resource for the unemployed, which English policy discarded over a half century ago.

The reception of these reports in the two countries was almost diametrically opposite. In England all parties, Tory and Labour alike, urged the adoption of the various provisions of the Beveridge report; the conservative group offered minor restrictive amendments which the liberal group opposed; but the divergence of opinion as to the wisdom of adopting it substantially as submitted was all but universally held. Contrariwise, the congress of the United States, on receipt of the report, immediately cut out the appropriation for the board's work and refused to consider its recommendations. The Wagner-Murray senate bill No. 1161 incorporated some of its recommendations into a proposed law; but only the most optimistic expected the bill to reach passage in the 78th congress. (*See also* CHILD WELFARE; MUNICIPAL GOVERNMENT; SOCIAL SECURITY.)

BIBLIOGRAPHY.—Social Security Bulletin, Oct. 1943; *Canadian Welfare* (Oct. 1943); *Community* (Dec. 1943); Sir William Beveridge, *Social Insurance and Allied Services* (1942); National Resources Planning Board, *Security, Work and Relief Policies*, U.S. Government Printing Office (1942).
(F. J. B.)

Relief, War: *see* WAR RELIEF, U.S.
Relief and Rehabilitation Administration, United Nations: *see* UNITED NATIONS RELIEF AND REHABILITATION ADMINISTRATION.

Religion. The emergence of religion of a diffused, popular sort, as a reflection of the vicissitudes of multitudes of people under the war stress, was unquestionably the outstanding development in the religious field in 1943. It appeared in the widespread resort to prayer by soldiers facing danger and by their families at home, in the appointing of special days for formal public prayer and in the vast outpouring of religious sentiment by the radio in response to sensitiveness to what the public wants. Much of this manifestation of religion was outside of churchly forms and matched the unconventional and "scrambled" religious ministries of war chaplains to soldiers of varying faiths.

The year was also marked by highly significant inter-faith action. A statement of fundamental principles for a postwar world order, issued in the United States by 38 Roman Catholics, including archbishops and bishops, 48 Jews and 48 Protestant leaders, marked a form of collaboration unprecedented for America. The declaration found basic common ground in the conviction that "a moral law must govern the world order," and theologians were putting new stress on the doctrine of a natural revelation of God expressed in all faiths and appealing to the consciences of Christians, Jews and pagans alike. This was the 1943 theme of the meeting of the American Theological society. The latest sessions of the Conference on Science, Philosophy and Religion continued to give respectful recognition to religion on the part of the intellectual world.

Even more significant was the realization by nations that religion is essential to their solidarity and peace. The White Paper setting forth the British government's plans for educational reconstruction indicated

a very general wish that religious education should be given a more defined place in the schools, springing from the desire to revive the spiritual and personal values in our society and in our national practices. . . .

"We are concerned," the White Paper continued, "to see preserved, or born, a genuinely Christian civilization . . . one in which the Christian belief in God and all that is derived from it . . . shall set the tone of society."

Easily the most spectacular event of the year in the religious world was the reversal of Russian policy which permitted and regularized the election of the Metropolitan Sergei as patriarch of the Russian Orthodox Church, after a hiatus in that office for nearly 20 years, due to the government's opposition to religion. This move apparently assured freedom of religious worship, especially for the recognized church, and probably also some provision for theological education and a limited amount of publication; it did not mean general freedom of religious education or propaganda. Even so the government's action was a clear recognition of the integral place of the church in the social and cultural life of the Russian people.

The failure of this more liberal policy to include the Russian minority religions—some of which are akin to certain strong American denominations—together with the continued suppression of minority churches in many totalitarian countries and the renewed tension between Roman Catholic and Protestant churches with respect to missions in Latin America, combined to bring the matter of religious freedom to the fore in church circles. A tentative demand was voiced for the inclusion of a "charter of religious liberties" in the formal treaty agreements under which the postwar world was expected to be reconstituted.

The chief preoccupation of the churches' thinking during 1943 was with a group of Christian ethical principles on which they sought to mobilize world sentiment for the ordering of the postwar world, together with practical measures of reconstruction for religious institutions throughout the world which had been damaged or destroyed by war. The effort to develop a common Christian world view, through correspondence and exchange of papers by international commissions working under a co-ordinated plan through the World Council of Churches, only partly succeeded. It did not prevent the development of somewhat divergent trends of thought between the churches of the English-speaking world on the one hand, and those, especially, of the European continent on the other.

Unhappily the heightened sense of religion's responsibility for its world task, together with a certain rivalry with respect to the control of funds, occasioned a fresh flare-up in several denominations in the United States of the controversy between "fundamentalist" groups and the more moderate majority party in control of the churches. This threatened disruption of the agencies of certain denominations, caused numerous local congregations to cease to co-operate with their denominations and led to the organization of a nonecclesiastical national fundamentalist organization seeking to duplicate the Federal Council of Churches.

A compilation of nation-wide religious statistics for the 1943 *Yearbook of American Churches* showed that church membership increased faster than population and that the churches included in their membership a larger portion of the population of the U.S. than ever before. A challenging revelation of these statistics was the fact of the extraordinary growth, relative to the longer-established churches, of the emotional sects. Generally speaking, these expected the speedy return of Christ to earth, sought holiness through a radical break with the world and claimed supernatural gifts of speech, healing, etc. Thirty-four denominations of this type increased their memberships after 1926 four times as fast as the old-line churches. In spite, however, of their very great rate of gain, the irregular denominations all told constituted not more than 5% of the total church membership of the nation. (*See* also CHRISTIAN UNITY; CHURCH MEMBERSHIP; also under separate churches.) (H. P. D.)

Religious Denominations: *see* CHURCH MEMBERSHIP.
Relocation, Japanese: *see* ALIENS; WAR RELOCATION AUTHORITY.
Representatives, House of: *see* CONGRESS, UNITED STATES; ELECTIONS.

Republican Party.
The Republican party subscribed to a program of full United States co-operation with other democratic and peace-minded nations in the postwar era.

The minority members of congress supported all measures for effective prosecution of the war against the axis, but they frequently combined with conservative Democrats to reject administration proposals dealing with domestic questions. With 208 members in the house and 38 in the senate for the first 10 months of the year, the G.O.P. exerted more influence in national affairs than it had in a decade.

The Republicans formally charted their course in both foreign and domestic fields when their Postwar Advisory council staged what amounted to an off-year, party convention at Mackinac Island, Michigan, on Sept. 7, 1943. That body adopted these main principles with respect to the war and eventual world reorganization:

1. Prosecution of the war by a united nation to conclusive victory over all our enemies, including
  (a) Disarmament and disorganization of the armed forces of the axis;
  (b) Disqualification of the axis to construct facilities for the manufacture of the implements of war;
  (c) Permanent maintenance of trained and well equipped armed forces at home.
2. Responsible participation by the United States in postwar co-operative organization among sovereign nations to prevent military aggression and to attain permanent peace with organized justice in a free world.

The G.O.P. formally underwrote these pledges when the minority representation voted overwhelmingly for the Fulbright resolution in the house and for the Connally resolution in the senate. The Fulbright resolution was adopted by a vote of 360 to 29, with

OPENING SESSION, Sept. 6, 1943, of the Republican Postwar Advisory council at Mackinac Island. At the conference, 43 delegates, including 18 state governors, approved a compromise declaration favouring U.S. participation "in postwar co-operative organization . . . through regular constitutional channels"

three Democrats and 26 Republicans in opposition.

Five senators opposed the Connally pronouncement. They were Hiram W. Johnson of California, William Langer of North Dakota, Henrik Shipstead of Minnesota, Burton K. Wheeler of Montana and Robert R. Reynolds of North Carolina. Although the first three are listed as Republicans, they have never been classified as regular party men.

The Fulbright resolution declared that "the congress hereby expresses itself as favouring the creation of appropriate international machinery with power adequate to establish and maintain a just and lasting peace among the nations of the world, and as favouring participation by the United States therein through its constitutional process."

The Connally declaration paraphrased the house edict, but it also included the following paragraph from the agreement negotiated at Moscow on Nov. 1, 1943, by the foreign ministers of the United States, Great Britain and Russia:

Resolved that the senate recognizes the necessity of there being established at the earliest practicable date a general international organization, based on the principle of sovereign equality of all peace-loving states, and open to membership by all such states, large and small, for the maintenance of international peace and security.

The Mackinac convention, however, condemned the administration's domestic program. After advocating greater encouragement of "private enterprise" and postwar "termination of rationing, price-fixing and all other emergency powers," the advisory council said:

The present program of the New Deal administration, with the enlargement thereof set forth in the reports of the National Resources Planning board, would wreck the country because the only remedy it proposes is unlimited government spending of borrowed money. It would socialize business, agriculture and the professions. It would extend the power of government until ultimately no man or woman could act, write or speak without approval. It would substitute for American liberty the regimented existence of a subject people.

The Mackinac meeting named the following study committees and chairmen: Foreign Policy and International Relations—Senator Arthur H. Vandenberg of Michigan; Postwar Enterprise, Industry and Employment—Governor John W. Bricker of Ohio; Social Welfare and Security—Governor Earl Warren of California; Finance, Taxation and Money—Senator Robert A. Taft of Ohio; Reform of Government Administration—Governor Thomas E. Dewey of New York; Labour—Representative Charles A. Halleck of Indiana; Agriculture—Senator Charles L. McNary of Oregon; International Economic Relations—Representative Daniel A. Reed of New York.

Senator McNary continued as Republican senate leader, and Representative Joseph W. Martin Jr. of Massachusetts remained as house minority leader.

Harrison E. Spangler of Iowa headed the Republican National committee, devoting full time to the job—the first occupant of the post to do so in many years. He placed the headquarters on an all-year-around basis, whereas in the past it had been inactive except for a few months before congressional or presidential elections.

Representative J. William Ditter of Pennsylvania, who was killed in an aeroplane accident on Nov. 21, 1943, was succeeded as chairman of the Republican Congressional committee by Representative Halleck. Former Senator John G. Townsend Jr. of Delaware was reappointed chairman of the Republican Senatorial committee. (*See* also UNITED STATES.)　(R. Tu.)

Retail Sales: *see* BUSINESS REVIEW.
Réunion: *see* FRENCH COLONIAL EMPIRE.

Rhode Island.
A north Atlantic state of the United States, in New England; one of the 13 original states; popularly known as "Little Rhody." Area, 1,214 sq.mi. (smallest of the United States); pop. (1940) 713,346. The urban population was 653,383 (91.6%). Capital, Providence (253,504). Other cities include Pawtucket (75,797); Woonsocket (49,303); Cranston (47,085); Newport (30,532); Warwick (28,757); Central Falls (25,248).

History.—At the regular 1943 session of the legislature, leading measures passed included the following:

An act authorizing the governor to shorten the business week because of the fuel shortage; an act extending the governor's emergency war powers for a year; an act providing for military leaves and separation pay for certain persons employed in the service of the state; an act exempting residents of the state from the payment of interest on delinquent property taxes while such residents are in the military or naval service of the United States; an act providing penalties for an employer who refuses to restore a job to a member of the armed services if the member applies within 40 days of discharge and the employer is in a position to rehire him; an act appropriating $20,000 to establish canning centres in various parts of the state to tie in with the food conservation program; an act creating a commission to study the matter of bonuses for men and women now in the armed services; an act authorizing inmates of the state prison to participate in war production; an act freezing unemployment compensation credits of Rhode Islanders in the armed services until two years after the war; an act relating to hours and conditions of employment of women and minors—chiefly restricting employment of minors under 16 years of age; an act allowing employees to draw cash sickness insurance benefits even though they are paid for absences by their employers; an act empowering the governor to lower cash sickness benefits and reduce the number of payments in the event of an epidemic or other emergency; an act creating a second injury indemnity fund; an act setting up a curative cen-

tre for injured workmen; an act making appropriations of $17,759,970.06 for the support of the state for the fiscal year ending June 30, 1944; an act increasing from 3% to 4% the excise tax on financial institutions; an act placing a tax ceiling of 27.5 cents on each $100 of deposits in savings banks and a tax ceiling of 10 cents on each $100 of deposits in credit unions, but granting credit unions a $100,000 exemption, plus exemptions on loans to members; an act revising the unincorporated business tax so that businesses will pay $1 per $1,000 on gross receipts over $5,000, excepting wholesalers who will pay 50 cents on $1,000; an act authorizing cities and towns to set up reserve funds to be spent on capital expenditures after the war; an act authorizing the city of Providence to create the office of budget director; an act relative to the assignment of accounts receivable; an act allowing theatres in several communities to open an hour earlier on Sunday; an act regulating the practice of electrolysis and providing for licences therefor; an act regulating the sale, distribution and use of biological products; an act opening a specific area of the Sakonnet river to power dredging and providing for the opening of a comparable substitute area in Narragansett bay when the Sakonnet river is over-fished; an act to provide for the conservation of soil and soil and forest resources and the prevention and control of erosion; an act creating a state board of inspection of horse riding schools and defining its powers and duties.

The chief executive officers of the state, all re-elected in Nov. 1942 for 1943–44 were: J. Howard McGrath, governor; Louis W. Cappelli, lieutenant governor; Armand H. Cote, secretary of state; John H. Nolan, attorney general; Russell H. Handy, general treasurer. In the 1942 gubernatorial election, McGrath (Dem.) received 139,407 votes; McManus (Rep.), 98,741. Edmund W. Flynn was chief justice of the supreme court.

Education.—During 1942–43 there were in the public elementary schools 60,216 pupils and 2,115 teachers; in junior high schools 20,954 pupils and 933 teachers; in senior high schools (three years) 15,581 pupils and 754 teachers; in senior high schools (four years and vocational) 4,809 pupils, of whom 551 were vocational, and 204 teachers.

Public Welfare, Charities, Correction.—The total number of persons receiving relief in all categories (excluding incapacitated fathers) in Nov. 1943 was 15,266, or about 2.1% of the state's 1940 population. The total amounts paid out during the year Dec. 1, 1942–Nov. 30, 1943, were as follows: general public assistance $929,142; soldiers' relief $68,478; old-age assistance $2,357,732; aid to dependent children $828,335; aid to the blind $28,717. In unemployment compensation, the gross amount of benefits paid during 1943 was $1,350,400.09 to 11,577 different individuals. The amount paid into the fund during 1943 was $15,081,868.92. There were 785 inmates in correctional institutions in Oct.-Nov. 1943, and 4,724 patients in charitable institutions and institutions for defectives.

Communication.—The total mileage of highways on Dec. 31, 1943 (excluding city streets), was 2,680.86, of which the state highway system comprised 806 mi. At the close of the year 1942 railroads were operating 185.9 mi. of road, and electric railways 78.504 mi. Water-borne commerce of the state for 1941 was 7,220,697 tons of which 530,970 tons were foreign commerce (imports, 370,156 tons; exports, 160,814 tons) and 6,689,727 tons were coastwise (receipts, 5,982,731 tons; shipments, 706,996 tons). Airways totalled 120 mi.; there were one airport and two landing fields. In Jan. 1942, there were 138,762 telephones in service.

Banking and Finance.—There were 35 banking institutions in 1943. Resources of 23 banks under state supervision totalled $563,172,899.46 and of 12 banks under federal supervision, $223,642,649.75. Savings deposits (exclusive of club accounts) in savings banks and trust companies (the 23 state banks) amounted to $343,644,438.31 on June 30, 1943. In addition, six loan and investment companies had resources of $8,103,032.50; eight building and loan associations, $47,007,889.87; 23 credit unions, $6,090,953.59.

At the close of the fiscal year, June 30, 1943, total state receipts were $22,979,600.22; expenditures and encumbrances $20,-168,056.75; surplus from operation $2,811,543.47. The state gross debt was $28,363,000; net debt $22,633,254.66.

Agriculture.—The total estimated value of agricultural production was $15,984,000 in 1943 and actual value was $15,704,000 in 1942. Total acreage harvested was 50,000 in 1943. Cash income from crops in 1943 was $4,064,000; from livestock $10,-820,000; from government payments $100,000, a total of $14,-984,000.

Leading Agricultural Products of Rhode Island, 1943 and 1942

Crop	1943	1942
Corn for grain, bu.	39,000	42,000
for silage, tons	57,000	57,000
Hay (tame), tons	45,000	49,000
Alfalfa, tons	2,000	2,000
Potatoes, bu.	1,085,000	975,000
Oats, bu.	31,000	34,000
Apples (commercial), bu.	281,000	332,000
Peaches, bu.	1,000	16,000
Pears, bu.	4,000	6,000
Grapes, tons	150	200
Livestock and Livestock Products		
Cows and heifers, 2 years and over	23,000	23,000
All cattle and calves	29,000	29,000
Hens, 3 months and over	548,000	504,000
Sheep and lambs	2,000	2,000
Hogs	8,000	7,000
Milk produced, lb.	135,000,000	140,000,000
Eggs produced, doz.	5,900,000	5,800,000
Chickens raised, no.	1,100,000	908,000
Turkeys raised, no.	26,000	25,000

Manufacturing.—The total estimated value of manufactures was $516,390,541 for 1939 and $517,196,193 for 1937. Employment in 1939 totalled 106,269 wage earners and 12,005 salaried personnel. The number of establishments was 1,460. Wage earners received $105,406,950 and salaried personnel $27,940,576. (Figures for 1943 were not obtainable from bureau of the census). Report of state department of labour for Dec. 1943, showed 84,463 wage earners and weekly payroll of $3,217,584 with a statement that survey covered over 75% of total number of wage earners employed in all manufacturing industries in Rhode Island.

Mineral Production.—The value of mineral production in Rhode Island is small, exceeding only that of Delaware and the District of Columbia. Value in 1939 was $980,916; in 1940, $994,-997. Stone ($558,944 in 1939 and $511,620 in 1940) and sand and gravel ($265,631 in 1939 and $333,612 in 1940) are the principal products. Production of stone reached 320,780 tons in 1939 and 201,380 tons in 1940; sand and gravel 383,557 tons in 1939 and 515,129 tons in 1940.   (M. C. Ml.)

Rhodesia. The territory extending from
the Transvaal border northward to the boundaries of the Belgian Congo and of Tanganyika Territory. It is bounded on the east by Portuguese East Africa, Nyasaland and the Tanganyika Territory, and on the west by Belgian Congo, Portuguese West Africa and Bechuanaland. Area 440,-656 sq.mi.; comprises two territories of the British empire; viz., Southern Rhodesia and Northern

Rhodesia. Southern Rhodesia is a self-governing member of the British commonwealth, but supervision over native rights is reserved to the imperial government. Northern Rhodesia remains a dependency of the crown. Certain essential statistics are given in the accompanying table. (*See also* BRITISH EMPIRE.)

History.—Intensive production in both Rhodesias of crops and basic metals in 1943 accentuated the shortage of African labour. Both territories enjoyed considerable prosperity, but costs of living rose owing to the limitation of imports. The financial position improved considerably; Southern Rhodesia was able to offer Great Britain a loan of £3,000,000 free of interest, and the revenue of Northern Rhodesia showed a large surplus at the beginning of the year.

Southern Rhodesia.—In June the Southern Rhodesian parliament passed a bill to prolong its life for 12 months to avoid a general election. On the appointment of R. C. Tredgold as high court judge, Captain Bertin was appointed minister of justice in his place, and Sir G. Huggins took over the defense ministry. Captain Bertin was responsible for internal security and internment and refugee camps. Professor Wallis, who was appointed editor of archives, was to publish a series of volumes of historical documents of Rhodesian history under a scheme financed by Sir Ernest Oppenheimer to be known as the "Oppenheimer Series." The 50th anniversary of the occupation of Matabeleland was celebrated by the issue of a special postage stamp. Many more Rhodesians were joining the forces; numbers were serving in the Black Watch, the Cheshires and in other well-known British regiments. A battalion of Rhodesian African rifles was added to the East African command, comprised chiefly of Matabele and Mashona. Much attention was being paid to the encouragement of sound farming; a subsidy was paid for maize grown according to approved methods.

Northern Rhodesia.—The rationing of food and other commodities was avoided, but supplies of articles for native consumption were scarce and efforts were made to increase imports. A river route opened through Lake Bangweulu facilitated transport of supplies to the northeastern districts. A state maize-growing project to increase production was rejected owing to difficulties of equipment and labour. A meat cold-storage plant was opened in Livingstone to assist the cattle industry. Copper production during the first nine months of 1943 exceeded that for the same period in the previous years and vanadium production increased by 15%.   (J. L. K.)

Ribbentrop, Joachim von
(1893–   ), German statesman, was born April 30 at Wesel on the Rhine and was educated at the gymnasium at Metz. In 1910 he went to Canada as an independent merchant. At the outbreak of war in 1914 he returned to Germany, enlisted in a Hussar regiment, advanced to lieutenant colonel and by the end of the war was attached to the war ministry. After the war he

Rhodesia

Territory and Area in sq. mi.	Principal Products	Imports and Exports (in thousand £)	Road and Rail	Revenue and Expenditure (in thousand £)	Education: Elementary and Secondary 1938
NORTHERN RHODESIA 290,323	copper (smelter production 1939) 215,100 metric tons (export 1940) copper, blister, £7,452,644 copper, electrolytic, £1,270,638	(1941) imp. 5,639 exp. 10,937	(1940) All rds. 8,775 mi. rly. 629 mi.	(est. 1942) rev. 2,657 exp. 1,919	Eurpn. schls., 18, schlrs., 1,320; African schls., 431, schlrs., 35,570
SOUTHERN RHODESIA 150,333	(1941) maize 118,475 metric tons coal 1,874,975 tons gold 790,442 oz.	(1941) imp. 9,829 exp. 15,395	(1941) Main rds. 1,621 mi. rly. 1,361 mi.	(est. 1942-43) rev. 7,050 exp.: ord. 4,335 war 4,106	(1941) Eurpn. schls., 78, schlrs., 11,106; Asiatic and coloured schls., 12, schlrs., 1,734; native (1940) schls., 1,392, schlrs., 111,686.

returned to private business as a wine merchant. He first became identified with the nazi party as a worker in 1930. At his home in Berlin-Dahlem were held the important meetings that preceded Hitler's appointment as chancellor of the reich, Jan. 30, 1933. In 1935 Ribbentrop was appointed ambassador-at-large, and from 1936 to 1938 he was ambassador to Great Britain. He became foreign minister, Feb. 4, 1938, and from then on played a prominent role in the diplomatic manoeuvring that co-ordinated with German military operations. In 1939 he made the deal with Russia that kept peace until Germany was ready to invade. In 1940 he negotiated the three-power pact with Italy and Japan. From 1941 to 1943 he participated, with Hitler and others, in numerous conferences with leaders of satellite and conquered states

On Aug. 6, 1943, Ribbentrop went to Italy to confer with Premier Pietro Badoglio and Foreign Minister Raffaele Guariglia, but was unsuccessful in his effort to keep them lined up with the axis.

Rice, Cale Young

(1872–1943), U.S. poet and dramatist, was born Dec. 7 in Dixon, Ky. He received degrees from Cumberland and Harvard universities and soon afterwards turned to writing as a career. He wrote two novels, *Youth's Way* (1923) and *Early Reaping* (1929), and numerous poetic and prose dramas. Among his 21 volumes of poetry are *From Dusk to Dusk* (1898), *With Omar and Song Surf* (1900), *Nirvana Days* (1908), *Many Gods* (1910) and *Far Quests* (1912). His poetic dramas include *Charles di Tocca* (1903), *David* (1904), *Yolanda of Cyprus* (1906), upon which an opera score was based, and *A Night in Avignon* (1907). He also wrote his autobiography, *Bridging the Years* (1939). He was the husband of the late Alice Hegan Rice, author of *Mrs. Wiggs of the Cabbage Patch*. Mr. Rice was found dead in bed in Louisville, Ky., Jan. 24, from a gunshot wound below the heart. A revolver was found beside him.

Rice.

A crop of 70,025,000 bu. of rice in the United States in 1943 exceeded the crop of 1942, 64,549,000 bu., by 8% and the ten-year (1932–41) average of 47,334,000 bu. by 48%. The acreage was 1,500,000, much the largest on record and 10% above the goal set by the government for 1943. The yield per acre, 46.7 bu., was above 1942 and near the average of 48.4. The southern rice area produced nearly 56,000,000 bu. compared with 52,000,000 bu. in 1942. California produced about 14,200,000 bu., its largest crop on record owing to expanded acreage as well as favourable conditions. More machinery was used for harvesting and drying, offsetting the shortage of labour. The Arkansas and Louisiana growers suffered from water shortage early in the season followed by floods late in the season. Texas had a good crop except in the hurricane belt.

U.S. Production of Rice by States, 1943 and 1942

State	1943 bu.	1942 bu.	State	1943 bu.	1942 bu.
Louisiana . . .	23,908,000	23,370,000	California . . .	14,030,000	12,627,000
Texas	20,196,000	15,910,000	Arkansas . . .	11,891,000	12,642,000

Rice production in South America continued to increase under the stimulus of war demand. Brazil early in 1943 reported a large surplus for export though the total crop was not expected to exceed that of 1942 amounting to 14,700,000 bu. In 1942 a total of about 196,000,000 lb. was exported. Peru was reported in the fall of 1943 to have a crop of about 6,000,000 bu. for harvest compared with the small crop of 3,889,000 bu. of 1942. Efforts were made to expand the acreage of rice in Peru by improving the water resources. Ecuador was reported to have a crop of 7,300,000 bu. in 1943 compared with an average of 3,400,000 bu. for the five-year period 1936–40. Ecuador was the third largest exporter of rice in the western hemisphere, exceeded only by the United States and Brazil. Cuba's needs for rice amounting to about 460,000,000 lb. are supplied by imports from the United States and Ecuador.

Efforts to increase the crop in Cuba were not successful because of the scarcity of water for irrigation. Yields are low on dry lands.

The rice crop of China was reported as larger in the Free China areas, but some localities had poor crops and in late 1943 faced famine conditions. In India the failure of the crop because of storm damage, harvesting difficulties and other troubles resulted in a shortage in the Bengal area so acute as to have resulted in the starvation of several hundred thousand people.

(J. C. Ms.)

Richards, Laura Elizabeth

(1850–1943), U.S. author, was born Feb. 27 in Boston, the daughter of Julia Ward Howe, author of the "Battle Hymn of the Republic," and of Dr. Samuel G. Howe, head of Boston's Perkins institution. Mrs. Richards embarked on a literary career by writing nursery rhymes for her children, which were published in 1873. She later wrote children's stories, the most famous of which is *Captain January* (1890). Collaborating with her sisters, she wrote a biography of her mother, *Julia Ward Howe, 1819–1910*, which was published in 1915 and won the Pulitzer prize for biography, 1917. Mrs. Richards also wrote a biography of her father in 1935. Her own autobiography, *Stepping Westward*, was published in 1931. She died at her home in Gardiner, Me., Jan. 14.

Rivers and Harbours.

Federal improvement and maintenance of rivers and harbours and other waterway channels in the continental United States and its territories and island possessions are carried out by the corps of engineers, U.S. army, under the direction of the secretary of war and the supervision of the chief of engineers in accordance with the plans authorized by congress. Reports requested by congressional directives to ascertain the advisability of further improvements of this nature are also made by the corps of engineers. The water transportation facilities provided by these works are vital to the commercial and economic development of the United States in normal times and are of the utmost importance to the nation in time of war.

In conformity with national policy governing wartime construction in the interest of conservation of manpower, equipment and materials, the work program on river and harbour projects for navigation and allied purposes was restricted to improvements having direct importance to the war effort. Improvements and maintenance operations were carried out on 323 separate projects of which six projects were fully completed. During the fiscal year ending June 30, 1943, the principal items of new work operations included the continuation of dredging and rock removal in the Kennebec river from the mouth to Bath, Me.; removal of ledge rock and dredging in the main channel of Portland harbour, Me.; dredging of anchorage areas in New York harbour; dredging and rock removal in the Kill van Kull section of the New York and New Jersey channels; rock removal in the Delaware river channel leading from Philadelphia to the sea; bank protection work in the deep cut section of the Chesapeake and Delaware canal; enlarging channel dimensions in sections of the Sabine-Neches waterway; deepening of the final middle section completing the through waterway extending from Lake Michigan to Sturgeon bay, Mich.; construction of the Mac-

Arthur lock in the St. Mary's river at Sault Ste. Marie, Mich., which was completed during Aug. 1943; completion of the power-house extension at the Bonneville dam on the Columbia river, the tenth and final power generating unit having been placed in operation in Dec. 1943, adding 74,000 additional horsepower, and increasing the power capacity of the Bonneville multipurpose project to 518,400 kw.; completion of the initial power generating unit of 35,000 kw. capacity at Fort Peck dam, Mont., on the Missouri river, the production of power having commenced on July 1, 1943; widening of a section of the Cuyahoga river, Ohio, and enlargement of the turning basin; closing of the gap in the west breakwater at Oswego harbour, N.Y.; continuation of construction of the breakwater extension at Los Angeles and Long Beach harbours; and construction of a breakwater extending from Waadah island to the westerly shore of Neah bay, Wash.

In addition to the maintenance of channels previously completed, and the above-mentioned new work projects, important channel and harbour improvements were also effected on waterways and at ports on the Atlantic, Gulf, and Pacific coasts, on inland rivers, and on the Great Lakes. These included improvements at Weymouth Back river, Mass.; Providence river and harbour, R.I.; Connecticut river below Hartford, Conn.; Hudson river, N.Y.; Great Lakes to Hudson River waterway, N.Y.; Fishing creek, Md.; Norfolk harbour, Va.; Caloosahatchee river and Lake Okeechobee drainage areas, Fla.; Southwest pass and South pass, Mississippi river, La.; Mississippi river between the Missouri river and Minneapolis, Minn.; Missouri river from the mouth to Sioux City, Ia.; Ohio river; Allegheny river, Pa.; Manitowoc harbour, Wis.; Calumet harbour and river, Ill. and Ind.; Indiana Harbor, Ind.; Illinois waterway, Ill.; Buffalo harbour, N.Y.; San Pablo bay and Mare Island strait, Calif.; and Bodega bay, Calif. (*See also* AQUEDUCTS; CANALS AND INLAND WATERWAYS; DAMS; FLOODS AND FLOOD CONTROL.) (E. RD.)

Other Countries.—Ports play so important a role in war transport operations that secrecy in regard to their equipment and methods of exploitation was essential in World War II, and no information could be divulged in this regard.

That there was widespread activity during 1943 in the expansion of facilities at certain ports of strategical importance could not be doubted and it was well known that in the middle east, for instance, new ports and harbours were created and brought into commission, mainly for war purposes. "Camp X," for example, was the wartime designation of a modern seaport which arose during the year on a bay of the Egyptian coast, where the year before there was little more than desert sand, and it was typical of a number of new ports in various stages of development scattered along the coastline of the middle east.

To this active expansion of port facilities there was a counterbalance in the practical destruction (due to R.A.F. raids) of well known European ports, formerly of the highest trading importance. The fate of Hamburg, Naples, Genoa, and, in some lesser degree, a score of others was known.

Although port developments in actual progress in Great Britain cannot be discussed, allusion to postwar projects to be put in hand when circumstances were favourable is permissible. Quite a number of British ports had schemes under consideration, some of them of considerable magnitude. Notable among them were plans for the expansion and development of the harbours and docks at the ports of Dundee and Greenock. Both of these were set out fully in reports published in the press, particularly in *The Dock and Harbour Authority,* the scheme for Dundee in the June 1943 issue and the scheme for Greenock in the Sept. 1943 issue.

There was considerable activity at Marseilles, where a scheme of some magnitude was in progress, and also at Cape Town,

where the new Duncan dock was completed. The new basin added 290 acres to the sheltered accommodation for shipping at the port. The naming ceremony of the dock took place on April 19, 1943. Just prior to this event, on March 13, the first pile was driven for the enclosure cofferdam within which was to be constructed a large new graving dock, with an effective length of 1,212 ft., an internal width of 150 ft. and a depth over all of 40 ft. at low water. Work on the site was actually commenced in May of 1942, when dredging operations were begun.

Another new graving dock was projected for the port of East London, with a length of 750 ft., a width of 80 ft. and a depth over sill of 29 ft. Port improvement works to cost £900,000 were in hand at the port of Durban, Natal.

Kindred developments took place in East Africa, where at the port of Mombasa two new deep-water berths were provided and at Beira the depth of water at Pungwe wharf was increased.

(B. CU.)

+ Roads and Highways. Notable highway construction throughout the world in 1943 was limited to routes urgently needed for movement of men and materials in the prosecution of the war. Men, materials and equipment were not available for general highway construction. Highway networks in all of the countries at war played an important part in transport for war production and feeding of armed forces and civilian populations. The highways were maintained as a necessary war measure but not to the high standards of peacetime maintenance. Normal replacements of old roads nearing the end of useful life were not made. The war brought a gradual decline in the condition of roads throughout most of the world.

Alaska Highway.—This highway, extending 1,483 mi. from Dawson Creek, B.C., to Fairbanks, Alaska, was the greatest single highway construction job undertaken up to Jan. 1, 1944. Work was begun in the spring of 1942 by 7 regiments of U.S. army engineers and the civilian forces of 52 contractors working under the Public Roads administration. By the beginning of winter the combined forces had pushed through a pioneer road for the entire length of the route.

During the winter of 1942–43 work was carried on in the cold and darkness of the subarctic region, building barracks, shops and major bridges across the Peace, Kiskatinaw and Sikanni Chief rivers on the south end of the project. This work was rushed in anticipation of the large volume of hauling from Dawson Creek to begin with the first mild weather.

A highway adequate for all military purposes was completed during the construction season of 1943. In general the route followed along the pioneer road built in 1942 but a number of relocations materially shortened the distance. Work was done by 14,000 men employed by 81 contractors from the United States and Canada and by one regiment of U.S. engineers. Nearly 6,000 units of heavy road building equipment were kept going by two shifts of men working 10 or 11 hours each.

Floods in the early spring and summer took out most of the temporary bridges constructed in 1942. These were replaced by permanent structures. In all there were 86 permanent bridges to build. A few of the larger steel structures were not to be completed until 1944 because of delays in obtaining and delivering steel.

A large volume of traffic flowed over the highway in 1943 to supply and expand the airports and emergency fields on the air route to Alaska.

United States.—Highway work in 1943 consisted almost entirely of road construction and services having a direct connection with the conduct of the war. Governmental restrictions on the use of manpower and materials practically terminated

Above, left: TRAFFIC CONTROL HEADQUARTERS of the Alaska highway at Dawson Creek, B.C., Canada. The position of every army truck on the road is indicated on the board

Above, right: CLEARING SNOWDRIFTS in front of a line of trucks used on the Alaska highway in 1943

Right: FILLING STATION on the Alaska highway

Below, left: WEATHER STATION on the Alaska highway

Below, right: SNOW CLEARED on the Alaska highway, near Squanga lake

the normal highway construction program but considerable work was done in building roads to war plants and training centres. In Sept. 1943, traffic on main rural highways in most states had declined 40% to 50% from the 1941 level. Estimates of motor vehicle registration indicated a decline in automobile registrations from the 1941 figure of 10.7% while trucks declined only 2.7%. With a more intensive use of trucks and somewhat larger loads there was no material reduction in the amount of freight hauled by highway.

In the federal road building program 8,445 mi. of road of all classes were completed during the fiscal year ending June 30, 1943, as compared with 12,936 mi. in the fiscal year 1941. The highways completed in the fiscal year 1943 included 2,836 mi. of access roads to war industries and military establishments, 4,148 mi. on the federal-aid system, 1,056 mi. of secondary federal-aid roads, 106 mi. in connection with the elimination of railroad grade crossings, 168 mi. of national forest highways, and 131 mi. of miscellaneous construction. These classifications were indicative of the source of the funds used in making the improvements. Practically all of the projects completed were urgently needed in the war effort. The total cost of all completed work was $274,801,799 of which the federal government paid $196,600,272.

Federal aid in the amount of $60,000,000 was made available for planning postwar highway projects and nearly 500 planning projects were initiated. The total mileage involved amounted to about 5,000 mi. and $5,800,000 in federal planning funds were involved. Major city arteries, alternate routes around cities, and limited access highways had an important place in this program. A master plan for highway improvement was outlined by the president's National Interregional Highway committee.

Inter-American Highway.—Great progress was made during 1943 in closing the gaps in this 3,300-mi. highway from Laredo, Texas, to the Panama Canal Zone. Mexico continued work on closing the two gaps totalling 500 mi. between Oaxaca and the Guatemala border. Because of the strategic importance of this highway, particularly in defending the Panama canal against air attack, agencies of the United States government gave considerable aid in closing the gaps south of Mexico. The Defense Highway act of 1941 authorized $20,000,000 for work between the Mexico-Guatemala border and Panama. Co-operation was conditioned upon the payment of at least one-third of construction costs by governments desiring assistance. It was originally planned to spread the work over a 5-year period but the war significance of the project made it necessary to accelerate the work. Agreements were entered into with the various governments and during the year construction was begun on about 275 mi. of road and a number of bridges. This work was under the direction of the Public Roads administration of the Federal Works agency. The most spectacular construction was in Costa Rica where the continental divide is crossed at an elevation of 10,930 ft. At the end of 1943 the only large gaps in the Inter-American highway were in southern Mexico and in Costa Rica.

Pan-American Highway.—That portion of the Pan-American highway north of Panama was also called the Inter-American highway and progress on this section is described above. Work was done on one of the three remaining gaps in Ecuador. There were no other major construction projects along the route. The general progress being made on the system as a whole was indicated by the fact that it was possible in 1943 to drive from Lima, Peru, to Buenos Aires in the dry season, and in any season to drive from Caracas, Venezuela, to a point south of Quito in Ecuador. The 8,097 mi. of highway in the South American section between the Colombia-Panama border and Buenos Aires, Argentina, (alternate routes included) had improvements as follows

in 1943: Paved, 2,015 mi. or 25%; all weather surfaces, 4,14 mi. or 51%; dry weather surfaces, 1,646 mi. or 20%; and un suitable for motor vehicles, 289 mi. or 4%.

Other Work in the Americas.—Peru was completing the las link in a 572-mi. highway from the Pacific port of Callao acros the Andes mountains to the headwaters of one branch of th Amazon. This route crosses the Andes at an elevation of 15,90 ft. It passes through a region suitable for growing rubber, te and other products that have been imported from the orient Colonization was taking place rapidly in the vicinity of Tinge Maria.

In Bolivia, engineers from the United States assisted th Bolivian Development corporation in surveying and preparin plans for a road from Cochabamba in the high plateau country to Santa Cruz on an Amazon tributary. This road, when built was expected to make available to the more populated section o the country many agricultural products that have been imported

Brazil continued the gradual development of main highway from Rio de Janeiro to Porto Alegre to the south, to Belo Hori zonte to the west, and to Baia to the north. The population o Brazil is spread mainly along the Atlantic coast and depends upon ocean transport to a considerable extent. Submarine attacks on this commerce made the nation conscious of the need for more rapid improvement of its coastal highways. For some time Brazi imported a considerable quantity of bulldozers, graders and other modern road-building equipment. These machines were scattered throughout the settled portion of the country and were extending the road network.

Argentina ranked high among South American countries in road improvement. That country in 1943 was covered by a network of highways that were improved in some degree. General improvement of these highways continued.

Europe.—In Great Britain the existing highways were subjected to a heavy war traffic. An excellent organization was created for immediate repair of war damage to highways. In one instance a 270-ft. bridge was wrecked and replaced in 120 hours. Many miles of service roads for military installations were built but construction of general use highways was deferred until after the war. Highways had a prominent place in postwar planning activity. A plan to remodel London was presented for consideration by the London county council in July 1943. The authors of the plan, J. H. Forshaw and Prof. Patrick A. Abercrombie, stated that the road plan is based on the Bressey-Luytens plans of 1937 but that they introduced modifications "to bring the road system into conformity with a plan which embraces all aspects of redevelopment-housing, industry and open spaces as well as transport." The plan included main arterial radial roads with three ring roads. Tunnels would be used at the centre of the city.

The French road system was reported to be deteriorating because of lack of maintenance. The French press reported some 50,000 mi. of highway in bad condition and likely to disintegrate because it was not possible to obtain tar for maintenance work

A road from Narvik in northern Norway to the port of Petsamo, Finland, under construction for nearly two years, was reported as completed early in 1943. The work was done by prisoners of war and conscripted Norwegians.

Press reports from German-occupied countries described plans for the construction of great road systems in France, Hungary, Czechoslovakia and Yugoslavia to be undertaken in the near future. There was no evidence that this was anything more than propaganda to build up the hopes of people under German domination.

Other Countries.—In Turkey highways from Mersin to Ankara and from Erzurum to Ankara were scheduled for completion in 1943. The 312-mi. highway from Ankara to Istanbul was also scheduled for completion.

One of the spectacular road jobs of 1943 was the improvement of the highway in Iran from the Persian gulf to the Caspian sea. This highway, a railroad and terminal facilities, known as the Persian supply corridor were operated by U.S. army engineers to supply the soviet armies with great quantities of war supplies. The corridor was about 700 mi. long. A primitive road across 180 mi. of desert where the temperature rises to 150° and through mountains at an elevation of 8,000 ft. was converted into a road suitable for heavy truck hauling. In Aug. 1943, trucks were hauling five times the amount hauled eight months previously and 11 times the tonnage moved over the Burma road in its peak month of operation. Supplies moved to the soviet army as fast as it could take them away from the port on the Caspian sea.

Early in 1943 a force of 5,000 men was at work on a new motor road that will shorten the distance from Peshawar, India, to Kabul, Afghanistan, from 195 mi. to 165 mi.

The 621-mi. road across central Australia from the railhead at Alice Springs to a connection with the railroad extending south from Darwin was put to intensive use. This road was opened to traffic in Sept. 1940, and it was reported that truck travel amounted to 3,000,000 mi. a month. Hauling costs dropped from 9.15 cents per ton-mile in the first month of operation to 4.48 cents per ton-mile. Because of the great importance of this war-supply highway it was being extended to Darwin, a distance of 1,000 mi. from Alice Springs.

Many miles of military road were built behind the fighting fronts in North Africa, the Solomon Islands, the Aleutian Islands, Sicily, the soviet republics and in northeast India. Roads over which military vehicles may move are essential in modern warfare. Most of these roads, of necessity, were hurriedly constructed, and they were kept in use in wet weather only by extreme efforts. While they might later have some peacetime uses they did not constitute an important addition to the world's highways. (*See* also MOTOR TRANSPORTATION.) (T. H. MACD.)

Robert, Georges Achille Marie-Joseph

(1875–   ), French naval officer, was born Jan. 31. He entered the navy, 1893, rose to the position of vice admiral, 1930, and had been commander of the Mediterranean squadron. When war broke out in Sept. 1939, he was sent to the Antilles as high commissioner of Martinique and Guadeloupe. In June 1940, after the fall of France, Pétain vested Robert with dictatorial powers for the rule of all French possessions in the western hemisphere. Robert immediately ousted de Gaullists from posts of power, instituted strict controls over the press and radio, established a secret police and created concentration camps for political prisoners. Facing the possibility of famine in the islands under his rule, Robert reached an agreement with the U.S. in Nov. 1940. The U.S. shipped food to the starving islands, and Robert immobilized some of the French warships in the harbours. The U.S. attitude toward his regime stiffened following reports that German U-boats were given refuge and refuelling rights in Martinique ports, and on April 26, 1943, Washington formally severed all relations with Robert's regime. Lack of food and growing unrest among the people of the islands compelled the French admiral to end his regime in July 1943. A Vichy dispatch, Dec. 30, said that Robert had arrived in Vichy for conferences with Marshal Pétain.

Roberts, Sir Charles George Douglas

(1860–1943), Canadian poet and author, was born Jan. 10 in Douglas, York county, near Fredericton, N.B., and graduated ↑

from the University of New Brunswick, 1879. He was headmaster of the Chatham grammar school, 1879, and a faculty member of King's college, Windsor, Nova Scotia, 1885–95. In the early 1900s he was recognized as an outstanding Canadian author and had several volumes of poetry and fiction to his credit. During World War I he served in France and was mustered out after the armistice with the rank of a major. He was knighted in 1935. His better-known works of poetry are *Orion and Other Poems* (1880) and *Songs of the Common Day* (1892). Among his novels are: *The Forge in the Forest* (1897), *The Heart of the Ancient World* (1900), *The Kindred of the Wild* (1902), *Red Fox* (1905), *The Heart That Knows* (1906), *Kings In Exile* (1909), *Hoof and Claw* (1913), *The Wisdom of the Wilderness* (1923) and *Lovers in Acadie* (1924). Sir Charles died Nov. 26 in Toronto.

Rockefeller Foundation.

The foundation was chartered in 1913 for the permanent purpose of "promoting the well-being of mankind throughout the world." Its program is concerned with certain definite problems in the medical, natural and social sciences, the humanities and public health. During 1943 the foundation appropriated approximately $7,685,000 for work in its various fields of interest. The chairman of the board of trustees in 1943 was Walter W. Stewart; the president, Raymond B. Fosdick; and the secretary, Norma S. Thompson.

The General Education Board was incorporated by act of congress in 1903, with the stated object of "promoting education within the United States of America without distinction of race, sex, or creed." Its program is restricted largely to the support of education in the southern states. During 1943 appropriations approximating $2,573,000 were made by the board. The chairman of the board of trustees in 1943 was Walter W. Stewart; the president, Raymond B. Fosdick; and the secretary, William W. Brierley. (H. B. V. W.)

Roentgen Ray: *see* RADIOLOGY.

Rokossovsky, Konstantin

(1905?–   ), Russian army officer, first saw action against the Germans during World War I. After the Russian revolution, he joined the communists, fought in the civil wars, 1918–20, and in the Russo-Polish campaign of 1920. After peace was restored, Rokossovsky, who had displayed talent for tactics and leadership, was sent to the Frunze Military academy, where he studied tank and air warfare. During the battle for Moscow, 1941, Rokossovsky commanded one of the seven Russian armies defending the capital and acquitted himself with merit. He waited until the Germans had exhausted their reserves in their final attempt to reach Moscow and then launched a savage counteroffensive, hurling back the invaders on a wide front. One of the "younger generals" and a capable leader, Rokossovsky won his greatest renown at the battle of Stalingrad, 1942–43. He was in command of the six soviet armies on the Don front that first trapped and then annihilated the 22 divisions of the German 6th army commanded by Field Marshal Friedrich von Paulus in Feb. 1943. When Stalin took over the post as commander in chief of all Russian armies in 1942, he broke up the large and unwieldy fronts into smaller sectors and assigned a command to Gen. Rokossovsky on the Don front. In Sept. 1943, when the Russian armies were driving the Germans westward, Rokossovsky was head of an army on the central part of the front.

Roman Catholic Church.

The pope, Pius XII (*q.v.*), is recognized as the supreme

ruler of the Roman Catholic Church. Appointed by the pope are the cardinals, archbishops, bishops, vicars and prefects apostolic who govern the ecclesiastical jurisdictions throughout the world. The college of cardinals consists of 70 members with its full complement. Through 1943 no new cardinals had been created by Pius XII since he became pope in 1939. The Sacred college consists of 6 cardinal bishops, 50 cardinal priests, 14 cardinal deacons. At the beginning of 1943 the College of Cardinals consisted of 49 members. The complement was reduced to 43 by six deaths, and at the close of the year the cardinals numbered 25 Italians and 18 non-Italians.

The Catholic population of the world in 1943 was estimated at between 399,000,000 and 400,000,000. The number of patriarchates was 14; 7 of the Latin rite, that of the West Indies being vacant, and 7 of the Oriental rites. The number of residential sees in the Catholic Church in 1943 was 1,226, including archbishoprics and bishoprics. Vicariates and other jurisdictions numbered 517. Ecclesiastical jurisdictions in the Americas were: United States 118; Brazil 101; Canada 50.

The number of Catholics on the American continents was estimated to be about 112,000,000 in 1943. Catholics in the United States and territories numbered some 22,945,247. There were 2 cardinals, 21 archbishops, 131 bishops and apostolic vicars. The clergy numbered 24,031 secular priests and 12,939 regular. Public churches and chapels numbered 18,976; high schools 1,522, parochial schools 7,647. Seminaries were reduced by ten to 193, and universities and colleges for men to 139—a reduction of nine. During 1943, 40 bishops died and 4 new dioceses were created.

Chaplains in the United States forces numbered about 3,000 at the end of 1943. During the year 17 Catholic chaplains died in action or in line of duty.

Catholics in England and Wales were estimated at 2,406,419; in Scotland 614,469. Clergy of Great Britain were 3,903 secular and 1,981 regular. Chaplains in the services were 679. Catholic members of the house of lords were 48; of the house of commons 22. Catholics in Eire and Northern Ireland were estimated at 3,285,659. Canada, with 50 episcopal jurisdictions, had 7,137,069 Catholics in 1943. Catholics in Australasia, including Australia and New Zealand numbered 1,696,954. Total Catholics in the British commonwealth were estimated at 20,438,856. Total number of Catholics in the English-speaking countries were 56,301,820 in 1943.

Bishop Bernard W. Griffin, auxiliary of Birmingham, was named Dec. 22 as archbishop of Westminster and Catholic primate of England, in succession to the late Cardinal Hinsley.

The Church and World War II.—Stubborn resistance to the totalitarian order by the church prevailed throughout 1943. In Belgium Canon Cardijn, labour union leader, was imprisoned by the nazis. Seizure of church bells by the nazis was denounced by the bishops, who again assailed the invaders in a joint pastoral March 21. Abbé Cordonnier was executed for aiding British airmen. Mgr. Van Wayenbergh, rector of Louvain university, was sentenced to imprisonment. The blind Franciscan priest, Father Agnelli, was sent to internment in Germany. The bishop of Namur excommunicated the Rexist leader Léon Degrelle, and the bishop of Tournai denounced nazi seizure of his cathedral.

The Rt. Rev. Thomas Megan, U.S. missionary, was appointed head of the Chinese social service by Generalissimo Chiang Kai-shek. An outspoken pronouncement of the French bishops on March 7 condemned the deportation of French workers to Germany.

It was stated in 1943 that 2,943 friars of the Franciscan order had been conscripted into the German army as combatants; and during the year 1,200 German priests and members of religious orders were known to have been interned in concentration camps.

In a strongly worded protest Bishop Dietz of Fulda accused the nazis of pantheism; and on Aug. 19 the Catholic bishops in conference at Fulda accused the nazis of religious persecution. A further denunciation of the nazi attack on human rights was made by Bishop Von Preysing of Berlin; and the German bishops sent a joint message to the pope regretting the bombing of Vatican City on Nov. 5.

Stubborn resistance to the invaders was continued by Catholics of the Netherlands. The Dutch bishops issued a joint pastoral forbidding co-operation with the nazis Feb. 17. On Feb. 21 the bishops published a denunciation of the activities of the German occupation authorities. The plans of the nazis for sterilization of certain members of the population was sternly rejected by the Christian doctors of the Netherlands. On May 12 the bishops again accused the nazis of propagating anti-Christian concepts. The famous Jesuit college at Valkenburg was taken over by the nazis and the church was closed to worshippers.

Cardinal Seredi, prince-primate of Hungary and archbishop of Esztergom, in a forthright statement condemned the master race propagandists as tools of Satan.

Italian prelates and clergy were placed in a precarious position by the nazi occupation and the invasion by the United Nations. After the bombing of Rome Italian cardinals gave guidance and reassurance to their various flocks. In the centre and north of Italy priests who condemned terror and pillage were seized by the gestapo. The monks of the famous Benedictine abbey of Monte Cassino, founded by St. Benedict himself, were ordered by the nazis to leave their abbey and seek refuge in Rome. Famous treasures, both of the abbey and others sent for safe keeping from many parts of Italy, were seized by the nazis and sent to Germany. Cardinal Schuster, archbishop of Milan, whose city was occupied by the Germans, denounced the nazis as godless hordes of bandits on Nov. 27.

Catholic bishops of Lithuania, who were promised respect for their religion by the occupiers, accused the nazis of violating their promises. In Mexico the archbishop of Mexico City begged the pope to intervene in behalf of Bulgarian Jews.

In Poland the persecution of the church continued. Some 3,000 Catholic priests were reported to have been executed by the Germans. A nazi decree ordered that baptism could be administered only by German priests, and nazi governors in Poland issued orders that hymns and prayers referring to Poland were prohibited. The well known Catholic Lublin university, whose faculty and students were dispersed, was adopted by Fordham university in New York city.

Slovakia also made its voice heard against its nazi ally when the Slovak bishops on March 21 denounced the nazi law forbidding the baptism of Jews.

Vatican City on April 19 began a weekly broadcast in Russian to war prisoners and persons in occupied territory. Radio Vatican stated categorically that the Holy See did not recognize any wartime creation of new states. The same radio broadcast a statement condemning Japanese atrocities.

Papal Official Acts.—Preparations were made by the Sacred Congregation of Rites, and approved by the pope, for the beatification or canonization of Vincenta Maria Lopez; Innocenzo da Berzo; Peter Donders; John Nepomuc Tschiderer; Imedla Lambertini; Placido Baccher; Michel Garicoits; Placido Riccardi; Caterina Volpicelli; Jeanne de Valois; Nicolas von der Flue; Maria Eustochio Verzeri; Popes Innocent XI, Benedict XIII, Pius IX, Pius X. The Sacred Congregation of the Sacraments broadcast to all countries new instructions for caring for the Blessed Sacrament during war emergencies. Designated laymen were authorized to seek out the Sacred Hosts that were scattered by bombing. The Holy Office permitted the use of water divining s a scientific experiment.

United States.—According to Brig. Gen. W. R. Arnold, U.S. Catholic chaplains in 1943 exceeded 25% of the quota and were estimated to number about 3,000 at the end of the year. Archbishop Francis J. Spellman of New York, during his visits to the fronts, addressed the U.S. forces in North Africa March 14. V. Rev. Patrick A. O'Boyle was appointed by the bishops as executive director of war relief agencies.

The following events occurred in the U.S. hierarchy during 1943: Bishop Edward F. Hoban was installed as coadjutor of Cleveland, O., Jan. 21; Most Rev. William T. McCarty, C.SS.R., was consecrated assistant military bishop Jan. 25; Most Rev. Martin J. O'Connor was consecrated auxiliary of Scranton, Pa. Jan. 27; Most Rev. Edwin V. Byrne was appointed archbishop of Santa Fe, N.M. June 15; Most Rev. Joseph A. Burke was consecrated auxiliary of Buffalo, N.Y. June 29; Most Rev. Matthew A. Niedhammer was consecrated bishop for Nicaragua June 29; Most Rev. James A. McFadden was installed as first bishop of Youngstown, O.; Most Rev. Johannes Gunnarsson, S.M.M. was consecrated bishop for Iceland July 7; Archbishop Walsh of Newark, N.J. celebrated his episcopal silver jubilee July 29; Most Rev. Bryan J. McEntegart was consecrated bishop of Ogdensburg, N.Y. Aug. 23; Most Rev. Francis J. Haas was consecrated bishop of Grand Rapids, Mich. Nov. 18; Most Rev. James P. Davis was consecrated bishop for San Juan, P.R.

Twenty-three Catholic archbishops and bishops joined with Protestant and Jewish leaders in signing a seven-point declaration on world peace. The Catholic hierarchy supported food relief for nazi-occupied lands in senate resolution 100 Nov. 27.

The Mendel medal for scientific achievement was awarded to Dr. Speri Sperti. The James J. Hoey medal for interracial justice was presented to Philip Murray, president of the C.I.O., and Ralph H. Metcalfe of the National Catholic Community service. Francis P. Matthews, supreme knight of the Knights of Columbus, received the Catholic Action medal, and the Laetare medal was presented to Thomas F. Woodlock, editor and financier of New York.

Catholic periodicals showed a circulation of 10,008,874, an increase of 883,219 over 1942.

Missions.—One Catholic missionary priest was executed by the Japanese in Shansi province in China, and several churches were burned. Six Dutch and Belgian missionary bishops and other missionaries were interned by the Japanese in China. Japanese troops occupied the house of the Paris foreign missions at Hongkong, and the missionaries were transferred to Chungking. Supervision of all prayer books was ordered by the Tokyo government, as well as all official documents of the church. Vatican radio stated that all Oblate mission priests in the Philippines had been interned and their houses confiscated or destroyed. Eighty-one U.S. Jesuit missionaries, among them Bishop Hayes, were interned by the Japanese at the Ateneo de Manila, P.I. Japanese authorities in the Philippines removed all foreign missionaries from their local religious work. Foreign missionaries in China also were re-interned. (*See also* CATHOLIC COMMUNITY SERVICE, NATIONAL; CATHOLIC LIBRARY ASSOCIATION; CATHOLIC ORGANIZATIONS FOR YOUTH; CATHOLIC RURAL LIFE CONFERENCE, NATIONAL; CATHOLIC WELFARE CONFERENCE, NATIONAL; PIUS XII; VATICAN CITY STATE.) (J. LaF.)

Rome. Until July 19, 1943, the capital of Italy had been immune to all air raids in World War II. Rome was an important rail centre as well as the seat of Mussolini's government, but St. Peter's cathedral and Vatican City were located there, and any strategic advantage which might be gained by bombing the city would be more than counter-balanced by grief

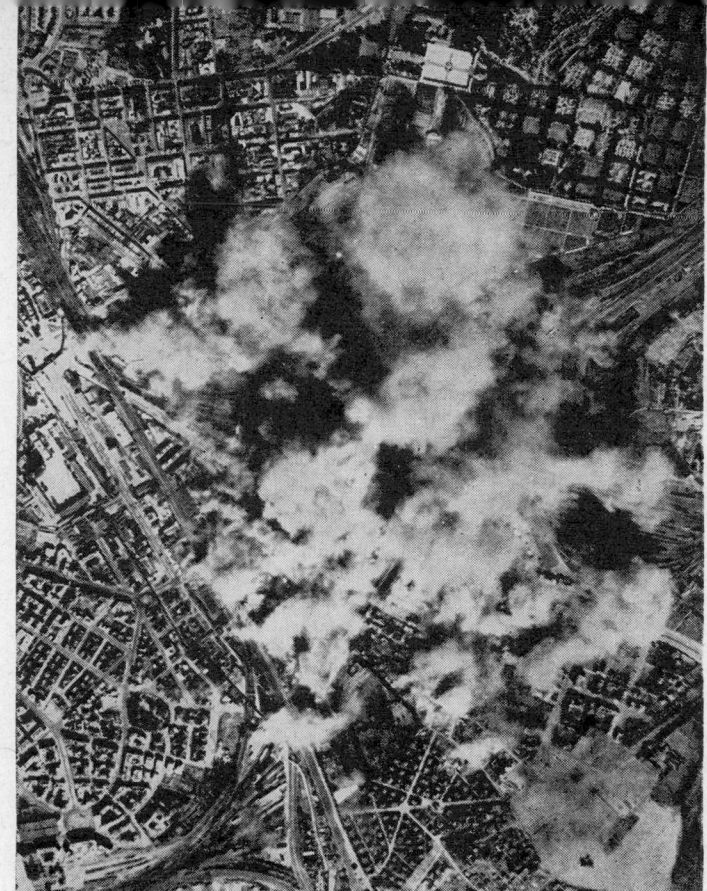

THE FIRST BOMBING OF ROME, July 19, 1943. Billows of smoke are rising from the San Lorenzo freight marshalling yards, four miles east of Vatican city, during the attack by 500 U.S. bombers

and possible anger throughout the Catholic world if sacred Christian shrines should be destroyed.

But three new factors intervened: the invasion of Sicily and the necessity of interrupting the constant reinforcement of axis troops, the desirability of driving out Mussolini as quickly as possible; and precision bombing as practised by Americans in broad daylight, thus guaranteeing the security of the more important religious monuments. And so the U.S. bombers flew to the attack, their object the rail yards, four miles distant from Vatican City.

The raid was pre-eminently successful as a military venture. Liberators wrought ruin at the Littorio yards north of Rome, and Flying Fortresses did likewise at the Lorenzo yards on the eastern edge of the city, pulverizing rail connections, demolishing rolling stock and buildings. But one basilica close to the Lorenzo yards unfortunately was hit, and when the pope as bishop of Rome visited his church the axis press raised the cry of sacrilege This was not ineffective, for aside from a second raid which speedily followed, the Allied air fleet left Rome severely alone during the subsequent months of 1943. Stray bombs afterwards fell upon Vatican City, doing minor damage, but whether they were Allied or axis bombs it was impossible to say.

The Germans did not occupy Rome directly upon Mussolini's downfall, since Victor Emmanuel still professed loyalty to the axis. But the Germans were highly suspicious, and both the king and Marshal Badoglio escaped just in time to avoid capture by the incoming nazis. The latter immediately proclaimed that they would protect the pope; they also threatened to treat Rome as they had Naples. Meanwhile all Jews were rounded up and hauled away to unknown destinations. Hitler's gestapo was impowered to hunt down anti-fascists. (W. P. HL.)

Rommel, Erwin (1891–   ), German army officer, fought on the western front and the Italian front in World War I. He joined the postwar reichswehr and fought as a storm-troop leader in the nazi party. He advanced rapidly in the German army and his brilliant strategy and tactics in mechanized warfare won him early recognition. In the battle of France, Rommel's tank units smashed through the Maginot line at Sedan in May 1940 and swept to the coast at Abbeville, closing a ring around 1,000,000 Allied soldiers in northern France and Belgium.

Rommel, who was made commander of the German desert armies in 1940, added to his reputation as a strategist in his battles against the British in Africa during 1941-42. But in Oct. 1942 the British launched an offensive that compelled Rommel to retreat more than 1,000 miles and yield all of Libya for a last-ditch stand in Tunisia. In March 1943, it became apparent that the Afrika Korps was hopelessly trapped in Tunisia; at this juncture Rommel was called back to Germany for "reasons of health." Gen. Juergen von Arnim superseded him as commander of the axis forces in Tunisia. In Sept. 1943, after the Allied invasion of Italy, it was revealed that Marshal Rommel had been given command of German forces in North Italy. A month later, German press dispatches said that Rommel had been given full charge of the army in Italy and of axis operations in Yugoslavia. Subsequent German reports hinted that Rommel was to be given the task of meeting Allied invasion armies on the "invasion coast."

✛ Roosevelt, Franklin Delano (1882–), 32nd president of the United States (see *Encyclopædia Britannica* for extended biography).

President Roosevelt devoted himself almost wholly to war and postwar problems in the critical year of 1943. He delegated supervision of domestic questions to a group of officials who came to be known as his "War Cabinet."

The president gave a preview of his year's program in his opening message to congress on Jan. 7, 1943. He reported that the Allies were on "the road to victory," and he outlined a postwar world in which, he said, Americans would have assurance of freedom from want "from the cradle to the grave." He also promised freedom from fear through the defeat and disarmament of Germany, Japan and Italy, or any other nation which coveted a neighbour's territory.

In January Mr. Roosevelt made the first of several foreign visits designed to knit more closely the military and political plans of the United Nations. On the 26th of that month the world was startled by the announcement that the president and Prime Minister Churchill had conferred for ten days at Casablanca, North Africa, with their full military and naval staffs.

The meeting followed logically, they explained, on the expulsion of the German and Italian forces from Africa. They said that they had mapped the 1943 campaign against Germany, and in a press interview Mr. Roosevelt added that the offensive would end only in the "unconditional surrender" of the axis.

In April the chief executive made another eventful trip. On the 20th of that month he met President Avila Camacho of Mexico at Monterrey, Mexico. It was the first meeting between the heads of these two countries since William Howard Taft conferred with Porfirio Diaz at Juarez in 1909.

Mr. Roosevelt, at a formal dinner in his honour, assured Mexico of American good will, and repudiated for both nations any selfish or imperialistic designs. Camacho, in response, called for a peace that would eliminate "the old faults of ambition, of imperialism, of inequity and sordid privilege."

In August Mr. Roosevelt met Mr. Churchill again at Quebec, and the military and naval experts were present in full force. Allied successes in Sicily and Italy, it was explained, necessitated the making of more detailed and integrated arrangements for the invasion of Europe, and major discussions centred on that topic. While in Ottawa, President Roosevelt addressed the Canadian parliament.

In late November Mr. Roosevelt attended another of these historic assemblages, this time at Cairo. There he conferred with Churchill and Generalissimo Chiang Kai-shek on the far eastern phase of the conflict. The three announced on Dec. 1 their determination to strip Japan of all the islands she had "seized or occupied" since World War I, the territory she had stolen from China, the Korean peninsula and all the areas she had conquered in World War II.

Stalin did not attend the Cairo meeting because his nation was not at war with Japan, so President Roosevelt and Prime Minister Churchill flew directly to Tehran, the capital of Iran, for a conference with the soviet dictator. It was the first meeting between the American chief executive and the occupant of the Kremlin. The official announcement's most significant passage was:

"We express our determination that our nations shall work together in war and in the peace that shall follow. . . . We have reached complete agreement as to the scope and timing of the operations (against Germany) to be undertaken from the east, west and south. . . . We came here with hope and determination. We leave here friends in fact, in spirit and in purpose. Signed: Roosevelt, Churchill and Stalin."

In a radio report to the nation on Christmas Eve, President Roosevelt elaborated on the arrangements made at this series of conferences for permanent preservation of world peace. He declared that the United States, Great Britain, Russia and China would act in concert, not to enslave the German people, but to get rid "once and for all of nazism and Prussian militarism." He said "if force is necessary to keep international peace, international force will be applied—for as long as may be necessary."

Preoccupied with foreign affairs, President Roosevelt created on May 28 an agency designed to free him of concern with domestic problems. He established a central organization known as the Office of War Mobilization with a mandate to "keep both our military and civilian economy running at top speed and to eliminate friction from rival agencies."

As head of the new agency he named James F. Byrnes, who resigned from the supreme court late in 1942 to become economic stabilizer. Other members were Secretary of War Henry L. Stimson, Secretary of Navy Frank B. Knox, War Production Board Chairman Donald M. Nelson, Munitions Assignment Board Chairman Harry L. Hopkins and Fred M. Vinson, who succeeded Mr. Byrnes as economic stabilizer. So much authority was transferred to this board that Mr. Byrnes was given the unofficial title of "Assistant President."

Marvin F. Jones of Texas, who resigned from the U.S. court of claims in January to become Mr. Byrnes' aide, was named food administrator in June, succeeding Chester C. Davis. The latter, who was on leave from his post as president of the Federal Reserve bank at St. Louis, quit because, as he wrote the White House, there was too great a division of authority in this field. As evidence of difficulties in a related realm, Mr. Roosevelt had three price administrators in 12 months—Leon Henderson, ex-Senator Prentiss M. Brown of Michigan and Chester A. Bowles of Massachusetts.

In midsummer Vice-President Henry A. Wallace precipitated another reorganization of various agencies associated directly or indirectly with prosecution of the conflict. As head of the Board of Economic Warfare, he charged in an open and tart letter that Jesse H. Jones, secretary of commerce and chairman of the Reconstruction Finance corporation, had handicapped his foreign operations. Mr. Jones denied the allegation in an equally sharp letter.

In a communication interpreted as a rebuke to both officials, the president abolished the Board of Economic Warfare, and established the Office of Economic Warfare, which later became the Foreign Economic administration. Leo T. Crowley, alien property custodian and head of the Federal Deposit Insurance corporation, was placed in command of the new unit.

The Foreign Economic administration was eventually expanded to embrace the Lend-Lease administration, several RFC subsidiaries engaged in developing or purchasing raw materials abroad, the Board of Economic Warfare's old functions and the Office of Foreign Relief and Rehabilitation. As further evidence of the increasing importance of economic problems, Mr. Roosevelt named Edward R. Stettinius Jr., under secretary of state, in place of Sumner Welles, resigned. Former board chairman of U.S. Steel, Mr. Stettinius had served as Lend-Lease administrator.

As allied might pointed toward 1944 as a year of decision at least in the European theater, President Roosevelt showed growing concern over a postwar program. He placed Bernard M. Baruch in charge of the problem of reconverting plants from wartime to civilian production. He asked Herbert H. Lehman, former governor of New York, to head the Office of Foreign Relief and Rehabilitation. In that capacity Mr. Lehman arranged for an international conference that was held at Atlantic City in November.

The conferees organized a United Nations Relief and Rehabilitation administration, with Mr. Lehman as director.

Mr. Roosevelt found it necessary to cope with domestic troubles as the year drew to a close. When railroad unions dissatisfied with his aides' handling of their wage increase petition called a nationwide strike for Dec. 30, he ordered Secretary Stimson to take over and operate the lines. Two days later, on December 27, the strike order was withdrawn by the unions.

Mr. Roosevelt's apparent indifference toward his domestic program of social and economic reform disquieted his liberal aides and followers during 1943. On Dec. 28 he seemed to confirm their fears. He announced at his press conference that he intended to scrap the "New Deal" as a slogan, and to substitute a "Win the War" declaration as a White House motto.

"Dr. New Deal," he explained, was needed to cure the patient that was the United States in 1933. But, he continued, the convalescent required a new kind of physician after Dec. 7, 1941—Pearl Harbor—and, therefore, he had called in "Dr. Win the War." He indicated, however, that a "Super New Deal" might appear after the war to rebuild the social and economic structure of this country and the world. He warned that the United States could never again isolate itself—politically, militarily or economically. (*See also* UNITED STATES.)   (R. Tu.)

⊢Roosevelt, Kermit

(1889–1943), U.S. explorer, author and soldier, was born Oct. 10 at Oyster Bay, N.Y., the son of the late Theodore Roosevelt, 26th president of the U.S. He was educated at Groton and Harvard and as a youth accompanied his father on a big game expedition to Africa and on an exploration trip of the "River of Doubt," subsequently named the Roosevelt river by the Brazilian government. He later returned to South America where he spent several years in engineering work and banking. In 1917, he joined the British army, was commissioned captain and served in Mesopotamia and Palestine. When the U.S. entered the war, he transferred to the A.E.F. and was in command of an artillery battery. After the war, he went into the shipping business and eventually formed the Roosevelt Steamship company which was merged with the International Mercantile Marine company in 1931 with Mr. Roosevelt becoming vice president. He resigned in 1938 and the next year sailed to England to enlist again in the British

army. He was commissioned a major with the Middlesex regiment. Except for a brief period in 1940 when he helped recruit volunteers for the Finnish army, he remained with the British army serving in Norway and Egypt until invalided to England in Dec. 1940. He returned to the U.S. for treatment and following his recovery received an assignment to intelligence with the U.S. army, with rank of major. He was sent to Alaska in July 1942. Mr. Roosevelt was the author of *War in the Garden of Eden* (1919), *The Happy Hunting Grounds* (1920), edited *Quentin Roosevelt: A Sketch With Letters* (1921) and with his brother, Theodore, wrote *East of the Sun and West of the Moon* (1926) and *Trailing the Giant Panda* (1929). He died in Alaska of unrevealed causes, June 4.

Roper, Daniel Calhoun

(1867–1943), U.S. politician, was born April 1 in Marlboro county, S.C. He was graduated from Duke university, 1888, had a brief try at teaching school and then entered politics. He gained a seat in the South Carolina house of representatives, 1892–94. Mr. Roper joined the Wilson bandwagon in 1916, became chairman of the organizing bureau during the Wilson campaign and was rewarded with the office of vice chairman of the tariff commission, March-Sept. 1917. Subsequently, Roper, known as a "dry," was named commissioner of internal revenue and made the first unsuccessful attempt to enforce the prohibition law. He resigned in 1920 to practise law in Washington but returned to the national scene four years later to stump for William Gibbs McAdoo, presidential aspirant. In 1933, President Roosevelt appointed him secretary of commerce. Roper's office came under a barrage of criticism when its two important branches, the bureau of air commerce and the bureau of navigation and steamboat inspection, were accused of negligence because of an unprecedented number of airliner crashes and the Morro Castle disaster. A conservative among New Dealers, Mr. Roper managed to retain the confidence of the administration brain-trusters as well as big business. He resigned his post in 1938 and the next year served briefly as minister to Canada. He wrote his autobiography, *Fifty Years of Public Life* (1941), with Frank H. Lovette. Mr. Roper died in Washington, D.C., April 11.

Rosenfeld, Kurt

(1877–1943), German lawyer and politician, was born Feb. 1 in Marienwerder, Germany. He studied law and economics at Freiburg and Berlin universities and was admitted to the Berlin bar in 1906. During his legal career he defended such German revolutionists as Rosa Luxemburg, Kurt Eisner, Georg Lebedour and Karl von Ossietzky and at one time, during a libel trial in Munich where he was cross-examining Adolf Hitler, he compelled the court to fine the future fuehrer 1,000 marks for contempt when he declined to answer a question coming from Rosenfeld because the latter was a Jew. Rosenfeld was municipal councillor in Berlin, 1910–20, a member of the Reichstag, 1919–33, served on its foreign relations committee and was Prussian minister of justice, 1918–19. A staunch Social-Democrat, he served in World War I, but propagandized against the kaiser's government and after the armistice sought a democratic peace for Germany. He was chairman of the Socialist Labour party in Germany, 1931–33, and in the latter year was disbarred and deprived of his property and citizenship by the nazi government. He fled to the United States in 1934 and died in Sunnyside, Queens, New York, Sept. 26, 1943.

Rosenwald Fund, The Julius.

The Rosenwald fund differs from other large U.S. foundations in that the trustees not only are permitted to spend capital as well as income at any time but are compelled to expend all its funds within 25 years of the death of its founder, that is, before Jan. 6, 1957. During the 25 years following its establishment in 1917 by Julius Rosenwald, this fund expended approximately $18,000,000, which amounted to all of its income from year to year and about seven-eighths of its principal fund. At the close of the fiscal year June 30, 1943, the assets of the fund (held chiefly in capital stock of Sears, Roebuck and Co. of Chicago) had a value of approximately $3,000,000. The chief program of the fund during its early years was aid in the building of rural public schools for Negroes. The main programs in 1943 were: (1) improving the content and quality of rural education in both white and Negro schools in the south; (2) fellowships for Negroes and for white southerners and (3) efforts to improve race relations, especially the relations between white and Negro citizens throughout the United States. During the year 1942-43 the fund expended $475,000 upon these and related programs.

Rotary International.

Rotary International is the world-wide organization of all Rotary clubs. In spite of war conditions throughout the world, Rotary had a gain of 10,221 members in 1943, and in this same period, 139 new Rotary clubs were organized in 13 countries of the Americas, and in Australia, China, England, India, New Zealand, Northern Ireland, South Africa and Sweden. On Dec. 14, 1943, there were 5,235 Rotary clubs in more than 50 countries of the world, with a membership in excess of 220,000.

Officers for the fiscal year 1943-44 were: president, Charles L. Wheeler, San Francisco, Cal., U.S.A.; vice-presidents, Carlos M. Collignon, Guadalajara, Mexico, and Harry C. Bulkeley, Abingdon, Ill., U.S.A.; secretary, Philip Lovejoy, Chicago, Ill., U.S.A.; treasurer, Rufus F. Chapin, Chicago, Ill. Headquarters in Chicago, Ill.; additional offices in London, England; Zurich, Switzerland; and Bombay, India.

During 1943, Rotary activities included general community betterment undertakings, work for crippled children and under-privileged children, the establishment and supervision of camps and clubs for boys and girls, assistance to students through scholarships and student loan funds, the promotion of high ethical standards in businesses and professions, and the development of international good will and understanding. In addition, Rotary clubs actively co-operated with their governments in rationing, salvaging and fund-raising campaigns, and in all phases of civilian defense, and engaged in activities for the alleviation of war suffering. In May 1943, the U.S. War Production board presented a citation to Rotary International in recognition of the meritorious salvage activities of the 3,400 Rotary clubs in the United States.

In the U.S.A. and Canada, 207 "Institutes of International Understanding" were sponsored by Rotary clubs, presenting to community forums and to high school audiences outstanding speakers on vital world problems. The 34th annual convention of Rotary International was held in St. Louis, Mo., U.S.A., May 17-20, 1943.

The official magazine of Rotary International is *The Rotarian*, which has a Spanish edition, *Revista Rotaria*. In addition, there are numerous regional Rotary magazines published throughout the world in several different languages.   (P. Ly.)

Rowan, Andrew Summers

(1857-1943), U.S. army officer, and bearer of the historic "message to Garcia," was born Apr. 23 at Gap Mills, W.Va. A graduate of West Point, 1881, he was commissioned as 2d lieutenant and later was appointed military attaché to Chile. He was ordered to Jamaica in April 1898, at the outbreak of the Spanish-American war, and there received instructions from the Military Intelligence bureau to deliver a message to Gen. Calixto Garcia, rebel Cuban leader. Rowan's task was to find Garcia in his mountain hideout, to get vital information on the strength of the insurgent armies and to arrange for their co-operation with American troops. Skirting the coast in an open sailboat, he crossed to Santiago, Cuba, hid in jungles and swamps and scaled difficult mountain terrain until he reached Bayamo where he found Garcia. Following his successful parleys with the rebel leader, Rowan returned to the U.S. and delivered to the war department the information which helped speed the American victory in Cuba. Rowan was promoted to lieutenant colonel, was publicly congratulated by Pres. McKinley and became a national hero. His feat was popularized in the celebrated work of Elbert Hubbard, *A Message to Garcia* (1899), which sold over 30,000,-000 copies and was widely translated. Lt. Col. Rowan retired from the army in 1909 and in 1922 received the D.S.C. for his heroic exploit. He died in San Francisco, Jan. 11.

Rowing.

Because of the war, the Poughkeepsie regatta was cancelled for the fifth time since its inception in 1895. Of the annual cup races, only the Adams Cup and Childs Cup were held, both with added starters to insure competition for all college boating crews. The Dad Vail regatta was cancelled, Rutgers university being the only member of the Dad Vail association to carry on the sport. Of the major rowing colleges, all boated crews with the exception of Syracuse and Yale.

The 1943 intercollegiate rowing season opened on the Pacific coast where, on March 26, the University of Washington varsity and junior varsity 150-lb. crews defeated the University of British Columbia heavy varsity and freshman crews by three and two lengths respectively over the one-and-one-half-mile Fraser river course in British Columbia.

On April 17 the eastern season opened at New Brunswick, N.J. with Princeton, Rutgers and Columbia over the one-and-five-sixteenths-mile Raritan river course. Conditions were excellent. Princeton won the varsity race in 7:2 by three-quarters of a length over Rutgers, with Columbia third. In the only other race the Columbia freshmen defeated the Rutgers junior varsity by two lengths in 7:35. Princeton and Columbia crews rowed in shells borrowed from Rutgers, but used their own oars.

Harvard and Massachusetts Institute of Technology opened the following Saturday, April 24, with a dual regatta over the one-and-five-sixteenths-mile Charles river course at Boston, Mass. Wind and choppy water made conditions slow. Harvard swept the regatta, winning the varsity race by one-half length in 6:58, the junior varsity by one and one-half lengths in 7:8, the 150-lb. varsity and junior varsity in 7:11 and 7:8 respectively, and the Harvard third varsity defeated the M.I.T. freshmen by one-half length. On the same day Columbia's varsity crew defeated Navy over the one-and-three-quarters-mile Harlem river course at New York city by the narrow margin of four-tenths of a second in the fast time of eight minutes flat. In the only other event the Navy plebes nosed out the Columbia freshmen by about the same margin in 8:22.2. In the third regatta of the day, Princeton won its second victory of the year, this time over Pennsylvania and Rutgers, over the one-and-five-sixteenths-mile Schuylkill river course at Philadelphia, Pa. The Princeton varsity's winning time was 7:16, one-fifth second ahead of Pennsylvania. Rutgers finished third, one length back. Pennsylvania won the junior varsity race by one length over Princeton, with Rutgers third, and the 150-lb. race over Princeton by the same margin.

On May 1, Harvard, Navy and Pennsylvania met in the Adams Cup regatta, with Cornell opening its season as an added starter. All races were over the one-and-five-sixteenths-mile Schuylkill river course, Philadelphia, Pa. After trailing Navy up to the last 100 yards the Harvard varsity sprinted well to win by inches, thus retaining the Adams Cup for the sixth consecutive year. Cornell finished third, three and one-quarter lengths behind Navy and only a foot or two ahead of Pennsylvania. Time—6:42. This ended Harvard's brief but undefeated season and left them once again the mathematical champion in the east. Navy won the junior varsity race in 6:39 with Harvard, Cornell and Pennsylvania finishing in that order. The Navy plebes defeated the Pennsylvania freshmen in a dual race and Cornell won the 150-lb. event with Pennsylvania and Princeton tied for second and M.I.T. fourth. On the same day, at New York, Columbia and Rutgers reversed the results of their first meeting, Columbia winning the varsity race by three-quarters of a length in 7:56.4 and the Rutgers junior varsity winning from the Columbia freshmen by one-half length. Distance—one and three-quarters miles. In the west, California opened its season against Stanford at two miles on the Oakland estuary, Oakland, Calif. California won all three races, varsity, junior varsity and freshman over green Stanford crews.

On May 8 Princeton, Pennsylvania and Columbia met on the Severn river, Annapolis, Md. at one and three-quarters miles, for the Childs Cup. Navy and M.I.T. were added starters. Princeton won the cup but finished third behind Navy, the winner in 9:41.3, and M.I.T. Pennsylvania was fourth and Columbia fifth. The Harvard, M.I.T. and Cornell 150-lb. crews met on the same day at one and five-sixteenths miles on the Charles river. Harvard won handily with M.I.T. second and Cornell third.

The annual Pacific coast regatta between Washington and California was held on May 15 over the three-mile Oakland estuary course. The Washington varsity, hard hit by losses to the armed forces, trailed by seven and one-half lengths at the finish. The winning time of the good California crew was 15:02.5. There was no junior varsity race. Washington won the two-mile freshman race by two-tenths of a second in 10:14. Cornell and Navy rowed their annual dual race over the one-and-three-quarters-mile Severn river course, Cornell winning the varsity event by a deck length in 9:48 and the freshman race by one-tenth of a second in slow time. Navy won the junior varsity race easily by two lengths.

On May 22 the California varsity defeated the University of California at Los Angeles varsity over a 2,000 metre course at Los Angeles in a dual regatta by six lengths in six minutes flat, and the California junior varsity won from the U.C.L.A. junior varsity by two lengths in 6:18.

During the summer several of the rowing schools took advantage of the Navy V-12 program to hold crew practice through the summer and early fall. As a result Navy and Columbia held an informal race on Sept. 4, varsity crews only, over the one-and-five-sixteenths-mile Severn river course at Annapolis. Navy won by one-half length in the first intercollegiate crew race in which Navy V-12 students participated.

On Oct. 9 the Harvard and M.I.T. crews rowed a dual regatta at one and five-sixteenths miles on the Charles river, M.I.T. winning the varsity and junior varsity races for their first victory on record over like Harvard crews. The M.I.T. varsity was but one second off the course record of 6:40. Harvard won the 150-lb. and freshman races, bringing the 1943 season to a close.

(R. H. SD.)

Ruanda and Urundi: *see* BELGIAN COLONIAL EMPIRE; MANDATES.

Rubber. The main task facing the U.S. rubber industry at the beginning of 1943 was that of speeding the conversion of products from natural to synthetic rubber in order to re-

RAW RUBBER being unloaded from a river boat at Manáos, Brazil, in 1943. Brazilian wild rubber contributed increasingly to the stock pile of the United States and its Allies during the year

duce the consumption of the former sufficiently to conform to the amount currently obtainable. From cultivated areas in the United States, about 1,120 tons of guayule rubber were produced in 1943. This, together with increased production of rubber from trees growing wild in tropical America and Africa, increased the annual U.S. receipts of natural rubber to approximately 67,200 short tons. Additional quantities from Africa and rubber obtained by abnormally intensive tapping in Ceylon supplied England's requirements of the natural product. Development of cryptostegia plantations in Haiti was vigorously pushed, but little rubber was expected from this project until late 1944. Although industry and the rubber director's staff co-operated fully in making these conversions, the stock pile on Dec. 31, 1943, had dwindled to only half of that a year prior to that date.

The scrap and spare tires collected by the government in 1942 and 1943 supplied adequate material for all reclaimed rubber needed during the year and furnished about 12,000,000 usable tires, one-third of which were utilized in conserving the stock of new tires. On Sept. 30, 1943, sufficient scrap was available for 18 months' requirements of reclaimed rubber at the then current rate of consumption.

The most serious task of the rubber director's office was bringing into production the government factories for the manufacture of butadiene and styrene, and plants for converting these into GR-S rubber, as well as plants to produce neoprene and butyl rubber. The total capacity contemplated from government plants was 952,000 short tons. On Oct. 31, 1943, the rated capacity of plants then completed was 723,520 tons, divided as follows: 655,-200 of GR-S, 44,800 of neoprene and 23,520 of butyl. The output of neoprene plants had equalled expectations, and some of the GR-S plants had exceeded the anticipated rates of production. Unfortunately, the expected output of butyl rubber was not attained. Only 2,576 tons of this variety were made in 1943. As frequently occurs with new processes, difficulty was encountered in turning out raw materials and synthetic rubber of uniform quality. Considerable progress was made during the year, however, in narrowing the range of variability.

The development of required quality in goods made with GR-S calls for increased supplies of certain other materials less essential for products made with natural rubber. One of these, carbon black made from natural gas, is needed to produce in GR-S compositions a degree of strength obtainable from natural rubber without this pigment. Moreover, since GR-S compositions generate more heat than natural rubber when repeatedly flexed, truck and bus tires made with GR-S and cotton cords fail at abnormally low mileages. Cords of special high-tenacity rayon proved to be far superior to cotton in resisting the effects of heat, and the production of serviceable tires of these large sizes from synthetic rubber depended on the use of rayon cords. Plants producing carbon black, high-tenacity rayon and certain essential auxiliary chemicals were enlarged or converted during 1943 in order to supply the increased amounts which would be required in 1944 for the synthetic rubber program.

The use of extenders, materials possessing a degree of rubberiness, which when mixed with synthetic rubber in considerable proportions ostensibly improve its processing characteristics without detracting from the excellence of the vulcanized material, rose rapidly and then waned equally suddenly in 1943 when it was found that the service of compositions containing extenders was in many cases not satisfactory. Some extenders, however, possess value with synthetic rubber.

In order to reduce the amount of new rubber used, more stringent restrictions were imposed in the issuance of permits for the purchase of tires for replacement purposes, and retreading was encouraged by making available increased quantities of camelback (re-capping material). The wear on passenger cars of retreads containing no new rubber, early specified as a conservation measure, proved so unsatisfactory that about 40% synthetic was added to retreading materials. The resulting improvement in quality not only reduced the amount of retreading material required, but by prolonging the life of recapped tires postponed the replacement with new tires of rubber in other parts of the structure. Distribution of camelback in 1943 totalled 226,000,000 lb., compared to 105,000,000 lb. in 1942. Other conservation measures were the banning of new rubber, both natural and synthetic, completely from articles for which other materials could be satisfactorily substituted, and in many others restricting the amounts of new rubber permissible. The successful accomplishment of this program was secured by exchange of information among the technical staffs of the rubber manufacturers through a co-ordinator in the rubber director's office. Unfortunately tires, the product using the greatest tonnage of rubber, were among the most difficult to convert. Passenger car tires containing GR-S

rubber, when driven at conservative speeds, will render long service; but bus and truck tires of similar compositions, because of their thicker walls and heavier loadings, heat excessively and up to the end of 1943 had required from 10% to 30% of natural rubber to produce serviceable quality. As additional means of conserving tires in use, driving pools for workmen and car speeds not exceeding 35 m.p.h. were strongly urged. Lack of butyl rubber for use in auto tubes made necessary the use of some natural rubber for this purpose also.

Estimates of total supplies and consumption of rubber were modified during 1943. In January it appeared that the stock pile at year's end would be but 116,480 tons; in May the estimate was 159,040 tons. A report from the rubber director's office on Nov. 10, 1943, based on nine months' operation, predicted an inventory of 229,600 tons; which, though less than half of the inventory a year previous, was about double the January estimate.

The need of submitting to practical trial many promising suggestions for the improvement of synthetic rubber by modifying either the manufacturing procedure or the composition of polymerizable mixtures, and the desirability of thorough evaluation of these and other rubber-like materials led the rubber director to provide a plant where new ideas and new rubbers might be subjected to careful examination to determine their real value. Buildings to house a government-owned pilot plant and evaluating laboratory were erected in Akron, Ohio during 1943. (*See* also Business Review; Chemurgy; Petroleum; Rationing.)

(J. W. Sc.)

Rugby: *see* Football.
Rulers: *see* Presidents, Sovereigns and Rulers.

Rumania.

A kingdom in southeastern Europe. Area on Jan. 1, 1941 *c.* 74,000 sq. mi.; pop. *c.* 16,000,000. Capital, Bucharest. Principal cities: Bucharest (648,162); Yassy (104,-471); Galatz (102,232); Timisoara (89,872). Religion, mostly Greek Orthodox. King (1943): Michael (Mihai); prime minister: Gen. Ion Antonescu (*q.v.*).

History.—Little news penetrated from Rumania to the outside world in 1943—less concerning internal conditions than from any other axis satellite. The dictatorship of Gen. Ion Antonescu continued, yet the opposition in the country seemed to gain in strength, especially in connection with the German retreat in the U.S.S.R. and the allied successes in the Mediterranean. By the end of 1943 the Russian armies were approaching the territory which Rumania had annexed in 1941 when, as an ally of Germany, she had helped invade soviet Russia. This territory, 16,-000 sq.mi. between the rivers Dniester and Bug, had been organized as a Rumanian province, Transnistria. The Russian advance not only threatened the Rumanian control of Transnistria, but also raised the claim of soviet control over Bessarabia, the land between the rivers Dniester and Pruth, and northern Bukovina which Rumania had been forced to cede in 1940 to the U.S.S.R.

Of the major German satellite countries Rumania was probably the most unhappy in 1943. She was not only more directly threatened by the Russian advance than any other, but was also involved in a bitter dispute with another satellite, Hungary, over Transylvania, a province of Rumania which in 1940 had been divided, on Germany's order, between Hungary and Rumania, both of which claimed control over the whole province. Of all the satellites, perhaps with the exception of Finland, Rumania took the most active part in the war against the U.S.S.R., and her army suffered exceedingly heavy losses before Stalingrad and in southern Russia at the time of the retreat of the invading forces. The whole political and economic life of Rumania was under German control and was made entirely subservient to the German war effort.

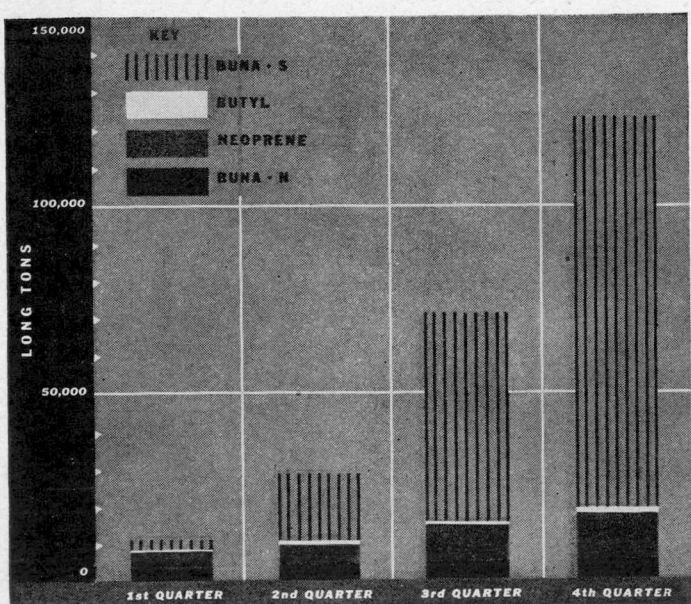

ESTIMATED U.S. PRODUCTION of synthetic rubber by types in 1943

FLYING AT CHIMNEY HEIGHT, a fleet of 175 U.S. Liberator bombers raided Rumania's Ploesti oil refineries Aug. 1, 1943, causing huge damage to Germany's chief source of fuel

In the beginning of 1943 a plot of the Iron Guard against Antonescu's regime was discovered, numerous arrests were made and a number of leaders of the projected uprising were executed. On Jan. 10, Ion Antonescu conferred with Adolf Hitler at the latter's field-headquarters. Antonescu was accompanied by his nephew and deputy premier Mihai Antonescu. The official communiqué maintained that a full agreement of opinion with regard to the conduct of the war had been reached. Yet war weariness continued to spread in 1943. Leaders of the opposition, like Dr. Julius Maniu, head of the Transylvanian peasant party, tried to organize the opposition in the country. In mid-April Prime Minister Antonescu again visited Chancellor Hitler in Berlin. Though the official communiqué did not mention it, the meeting probably dealt with the growing bitterness in Hungarian-Rumanian relations and with the need for increased production in Rumania, especially in the field of oil.

U.S. bombers had bombed the oil fields and oil refineries in Rumania from their bases in the middle east. About 175 big bombers took part in a low-level raid on Ploesti Aug. 1 which cost about 20% of the planes, but caused great damage to the oil fields there.

Agriculture, Minerals and Trade.—Rumania is predominantly an agricultural country. The few industries which exist, like flour milling, brewing and distilling, are directly connected with agriculture. The chief crops of the country are maize, wheat, barley, rye and oats. The principal minerals are petroleum and natural gas, iron and copper ores, salt and lignite. The output of natural gas in 1937 amounted to 62,175,022,462 cu.ft.; the output of crude oil amounted in 1938 to 7,286,000 short tons, while it decreased, in spite of all German efforts, to 5,511,000 tons in 1942. In 1940 only 1,532,000 tons of petroleum were exported, as against 3,075,000 tons in 1939.

The monetary unit is the leu, nominally 10 milligrams gold (.900 fine). In 1938 the total imports amounted to 18,767,000 lei, the exports to 21,532,000 lei. The chief importing countries were Germany, Czechoslovakia, Great Britain, France and Italy, while the chief exports went to Germany, Great Britain, Czechoslovakia, Italy and France.

The estimated ordinary revenue for 1942–43 amounted to 71,-200,000,000 lei, the expenditure to 72,500,000,000 lei. The public debt on April 1, 1939, was 104,127,428,054 lei. (*See* also WORLD WAR II.)   (H. Ko.)

Ruml Plan: *see* TAXATION.

Rundstedt, Karl Rudolf Gerd von (1875–   ), German army officer,

was born Dec. 12 at Aschersleben, descendant of a noble family of Brandenburg. He served in Alsace and Poland during World War I and acquired military fame in 1939 during the Polish campaign. He was in command at the fall of Cracow, Lodz and Przemysl. The battles of the river San and the bend of the Vistula, and the entry into Warsaw were further milestones in Gen. Rundstedt's career. For these accomplishments and for his successes during the invasion of the Low Countries and France in 1940 he was created marshal of the reich July 19, 1940. Rundstedt commanded the southern group of German armies in the Russian campaign of 1941, suffering the first major German defeat of World War II at Rostov. He was shifted to France in 1942 and put in command of the Atlantic coast defenses and the forces occupying France. On Nov. 27, after the French fleet was scuttled at Toulon, Hitler made Rundstedt military ruler of France. He continued during 1943 to strengthen defenses against the expected second front attack. Late in 1943 he conferred with Field Marshal Erwin Rommel.

Rural Electrification. The electrification of rural areas

in the United States, which progressed at an accelerated rate after the establishment of the Rural Electrification administration in 1935, continued during 1943 at a reduced rate because of the war and the resulting shortage of critical materials for new line construction. War regulations were liberalized during the year so that electric service could be extended to qualified farms, as certified by local war boards, for use in war food production activities and in alleviating rural labour shortages. As a consequence, many farmers who had been wanting electric power in order to step up their food production and to replace labour that had gone into military service and war factories applied for service. During the year there was a significant increase in the use of electricity in the production of foods, particularly milk, poultry and livestock, and in the processing and preservation of foodstuffs. In June 1943 the average farm connected to an REA-financed power line used 14 kw. hr. more electricity than in June 1942. It was estimated that approximately 2,500,000 farms were receiving central station service on Dec. 31, about 41% of the total, in comparison with approximately 2,420,000, or 39.7%, at the end of 1942.

The growth of rural electrification is shown by the approximate number and percentage of electrified farms, as follows: Dec. 1934, 744,000, 10.9%; June 1936, 840,000, 12.3%; June 1937, 1,070,000, 15.8%; June 1938, 1,300,000, 19.1%; June 1939, 1,513,000, 22.1%; June 1940, 1,870,000, 27.1%; June 1941, 2,126,000, 34.9%; June 1942, 2,337,000, 38.3%. A considerable part of the accelerated progress after 1935 was accounted for by rural electric, non-profit co-operatives. Nearly 95% of the loans of the Rural Electrification administration were made to these quasi-public co-operative enterprises which were essentially community-owned and -operated enterprises, governed by boards of directors selected by the consumer members.

By the end of 1943 Rural Electrification administration had allotted approximately $474,000,000 to finance on a self-liquidating basis the construction of nearly 420,000 miles of distribution lines and other electric facilities to serve nearly 1,375,000 rural consumers. At the close of the year, 810 systems had in operation 388,000 miles of line serving over 1,080,000 consumers in comparison with 378,000 miles serving 1,012,000 consumers at the end of 1942. To a considerable extent, this increase reflected the recognition given electric power as a farm production tool by the war agencies charged with allocation of critical materials. Approximately 80% of the consumers were farms; the balance consisted of non-farm residences, industrial and commercial enterprises, and community institutions. During 1943 the rural electric co-operatives increased their financial stability, as was indicated by payments in advance of due date of about $14,000,000 on their debts to the government in contrast to about $175,000 overdue more than 30 days at the year end.

On REA-financed systems in the heavy food-producing states, for instance, the average monthly use of power per consumer increased up to 26 kw.hr. over the previous year. Many essential war activities such as military establishments, air beacons, mines and industrial plants located in rural areas were dependent on electric service for their operation.

Wider application of electric power to farm operations continued to receive considerable attention of research agencies and others although many new developments in electrical farm equipment were not manufactured because materials were not made available. To meet their need for equipment for food production there was an active interest in homemade equipment and many farmers were making items of electrical equipment that were no longer available in the markets, such as stock tank heaters and brooders for chickens and pigs. (R. T. B.)

Russell Sage Foundation.
This foundation was established in 1907 by Mrs. Russell Sage for the improvement of social and living conditions in the United States. It has an endowment of $15,000,000. It conducts studies aimed through the spreading of information to help

in correcting adverse living conditions on the one hand and in promoting healthful and helpful conditions on the other. About 65% of its income in 1943 was devoted to work carried on by its own staff; the remainder was granted to work by other agencies.

The foundation had published well over 100 books and over 200 pamphlets by 1943. Among its publications were: *The WPA and Federal Relief Policy*, by Donald S. Howard; *Social Work Year Book*, edited by Russell H. Kurtz; *A Study in Public Relations*, by Harold P. Levy, and *Salaries and Qualifications of Child Welfare Workers*, by Ralph G. Hurlin.

The offices of the foundation are at 130 E. 22nd st., New York city. (S. M. HA.)

Russia: *see* UNION OF SOVIET SOCIALIST REPUBLICS.

Russian Literature.
Throughout 1943 literature in the soviet union continued to be dominated by the war. Themes connected with World War II or with Russia's past ousted practically everything else. Soviet writers looked upon their work as part of the total war effort. The bulk of this war literature took the form of short stories, front sketches or publicistic articles. Among the collections of stories one of the most memorable is Nikolay Tikhonov's volume of stories about Leningrad during the siege. A novel by Arkady Perventsev, *Ispytanie* (*The Ordeal*), deals with the evacuation of an aircraft factory from the war zone to the Urals. No soviet author had so far attempted to give a picture of the war as a whole in a large-scale novel, but Sholokhov was said to be engaged on a vast war epic.

There were also many war plays. Korneychuk's *Front* is interesting rather for its subject-matter than for its literary or dramatic qualities. It portrays the conflict between two different mentalities among Red army generals: the old, smacking of revolutionary "romanticism" of the civil war, and the new, realistic and scientific. Leonov's two plays—*Nashestvie* (*Invasion*) and *Lenushka* (described as "a popular tragedy")—are memorable and intense creations. In both, the action is set in the front zone: in the former, in a German-occupied town; in the latter, among soviet guerrillas. Both verge rather dangerously on melodrama. There is a curious synthesis, in Leonov, of Dostoievski and Gorky, and the war seen through this double prism assumes a strange "Goya-esque" aspect.

Among historical novels one must mention *Ivan Grozny* (*Ivan the Terrible*) by V. Kostylev and *Brusilovsky proryv* (*Brusilov's Breakthrough*) by Sergeyev-Tsensky. Less monumental than the author's earlier epic of the Crimean war (*The Ordeal of Sevastopol*), the latter deals with the Russian summer offensive of 1916 and its background in epic and objective tones.

Patriotic motives prevailed also in soviet poetry. Many poets were writing patriotic songs which enjoyed great popularity, but one agrees with N. Aseyev, one of the older soviet poets, who thought the general level of this war poetry not very high. A long semi-narrative, semi-lyrical poem by Vera Inber about wartime Leningrad (*Pulkovsky meridian*—*The Meridian of Pulkovo*) belongs to that author's best. Boris Pasternak, the greatest of the living soviet poets, made a new translation of *Romeo and Juliet*.

It is necessary to note the revival of émigré literature with its centre in New York. A new quarterly review (*Novy Zhurnal*) succeeded in rallying many former collaborators of the Parisian *Sovremenniya Zapiski*. Its first five issues contained unpublished stories by Bunin (who in 1943 was in France), the beginning of a new historical novel by M. Aldanov (*Istoki*—*The Fountainhead*) with Bakunin as one of the characters, and some new work by V. Nabokov-Sirin, which includes a daring but felicitous attempt to write the concluding scene of Pushkin's unfinished verse drama *Rusalka*.   (G. St.)

Russian S.F.S.R.: *see* UNION OF SOVIET SOCIALIST REPUBLICS.

Rutledge, Wiley Blount, Jr.

(1894–), U.S. jurist, was born July 20 in Cloverport, Ky. He attended Maryville college, Tenn., received his B.A. degree from the University of Wisconsin, 1914, and his law degree from the University of Colorado, 1922. He was admitted to the Colorado bar in 1922 and practised in Boulder. He was professor of law at the University of Washington, 1926–35, and professor of law and dean of the law college at the University of Iowa, 1935–39. Regarded as an outstanding legal scholar and widely known for his liberal views, he was nominated associate justice of the U.S. court of appeals for the District of Columbia in April 1939, and entered his new duties the following month. On Jan. 11, 1943 President Roosevelt named him to fill the U.S. supreme court vacancy left by the resignation of Justice James F. Byrnes. Justice Rutledge, who was only 48 years old at the time, was the second youngest member of the court. (Justice William O. Douglas, the youngest member, was then 44.)

Ryder, Charles W.

(1892–), U.S. army officer, was born Jan. 16 in Kansas. After graduating from West Point, 1915, he was commissioned a 2nd lieutenant. During World War I he fought on the western front, was cited for extraordinary heroism and was awarded a number of decorations. After the war he was stationed in China and served for awhile in military intelligence. Commanding the force that landed at Algiers on Nov. 8, 1942, Major General Ryder negotiated surrender terms with the French garrison commander 16 hours after the initial landings. For his "exceptionally meritorious service" in Algeria he was awarded the distinguished service medal, Dec. 31, 1942. After the Tunisian victory it was announced that Gen. Ryder had commanded the 34th national guard division in the drive on Bizerte.

Rye.

The 1943 rye crop was estimated by the U.S. department of agriculture at 33,314,000 bu. compared with 57,341,000 bu. in 1942 and a 10-year average (1932–41) of 38,589,000 bu. This decrease was due to a much lower yield per acre, 11.6 bu., than in 1942 when it was 14.9 bu., as well as a drastic reduction in acreage of almost 1,000,000 ac., or about 75%. This change resulted from a shift of acreage by farmers to other

U.S. Production of Rye in Leading States, 1943 and 1942

State	1943 bu.	1942 bu.	State	1943 bu.	1942 bu.
South Dakota .	5,220,000	13,872,000	Ohio	1,140,000	1,870,000
Nebraska . . .	5,052,000	5,026,000	Oklahoma . .	897,000	1,188,000
North Dakota .	4,014,000	16,082,000	Michigan . . .	748,000	1,160,000
Minnesota . .	1,538,000	3,345,000	Illinois . . .	682,000	539,000
Indiana	1,416,000	1,944,000	Pennsylvania .	624,000	841,000
Kansas	1,354,000	1,287,000	Missouri . . .	605,000	495,000
Colorado . . .	1,323,000	1,375,000	Montana . . .	435,000	720,000
Wisconsin . . .	1,144,000	1,620,000	Virginia	429,000	585,000

crops believed to be more essential in the war period. The 1943 goal set by the War Food administration was only 90% of 1942. Stocks of old rye were in strong demand at the end of 1943 because of the general feed shortage.   (J. C. Ms.)

Sabotage: *see* FEDERAL BUREAU OF INVESTIGATION.
St. Christopher: *see* WEST INDIES, BRITISH.
St. Croix: *see* VIRGIN ISLANDS.
St. Helena and Ascension Islands: *see* BRITISH WEST AFRICA.

St. John: *see* VIRGIN ISLANDS.
St. Kitts-Nevis: *see* WEST INDIES, BRITISH.

St. Louis.

Eighth largest city of the United States, St. Louis, Mo., had a population of 816,048 by the federal census of 1940, with an additional 541,567 persons living within the greater metropolitan district. Mayor (Jan. 1, 1944): Aloys P. Kaufmann (Rep.).

While 5,000 spectators watched at Lambert-St. Louis field Aug. 1, 1943, a glider towed in an army air force anniversary demonstration lost a wing and crashed. Among the 10 occupants killed were Mayor William Dee Becker (elected in 1941), the city's deputy comptroller, the director of public utilities and Thomas N. Dysart, president of the St. Louis Chamber of Commerce. Aloys P. Kaufmann, 40, who three months earlier had been elected president of the board of aldermen, succeeded Becker as mayor.

St. Louisans voted (April 6, 1943) for aldermen by wards, instead of at large, for the first time since 1914. Republicans gained a 21-to-7 majority in the board of aldermen by winning 8 seats, plus the presidency, while the Democrats won 7.

During 1943 the city adopted a redistricting plan to equalize the 28 wards in size and population, levied a 2-cent tax on each package of cigarettes (expecting $750,000 yearly revenue), and tentatively planned a $60,125,000 postwar improvement program.

The beginning of the 1943–44 fiscal year (April 12, 1943) found St. Louis not only with a balanced budget for the first time since 1928, but with a surplus of $513,174. Bonded indebtedness was $62,720,500; legal borrowing power, $115,696,-701; assessed valuation of real and personal property, $1,074,-810,000; tax rate (city, state and schools), $2.75 on $100, and the city budget (for all purposes), $34,205,760.   (E. L. R.)

St. Lucia: *see* WEST INDIES, BRITISH.
St. Pierre and Miquelon: *see* FRENCH COLONIAL EMPIRE.
St. Thomas: *see* VIRGIN ISLANDS.
St. Vincent: *see* WEST INDIES, BRITISH.

Salazar, António de Oliveira

(1889–), Portuguese statesman, was born at Santa Comba Dão (Coimbra) on April 28, 1889. In 1916 he became professor of economics at Coimbra university. Shortly after the revolution of May 1926, the Portuguese president, General Carmona, invited him to join the government as finance minister; he accepted the post, but, finding himself unduly restricted, resigned within a week. Less than two years later, after stipulating that complete freedom within his department should be given him, he reassumed office on April 27, 1928. In 1930 Dr. Salazar founded the civil organization known as the National Union. On July 5, 1932, he became president of the council of ministers; in the following year the new corporative constitution of the Portuguese republic was submitted to the country in a plebiscite and a national assembly elected. In 1936 Dr. Salazar assumed the portfolios of war and foreign affairs.

Several weighty speeches were made by Dr. Salazar during 1943, but his outstanding pronouncement was the comprehensive broadcast made on the 15th anniversary of his appointment as finance minister (April 27, 1943). Of the British alliance he said: "We did not fail to reaffirm it at a dark and difficult moment." Of Spain: "In the policy of friendship with her we have found precious support which bore fruit in what has been termed the Peninsular Bloc." Of neutrality: "It is not maintained without care, effort and expense. . . . Except . . . in the still outstanding incident of Timor, our neutrality has been respected by all; and I believe that we too have honoured it." (*See* PORTUGAL.)

Sales, Retail and Wholesale: *see* BUSINESS REVIEW.

Salt. The production of salt in the United States in 1942 increased 8% over 1941, to 13,693,284 short tons. Of the total, 7,373,165 tons were in the form of brine, 3,517,832 tons in evaporated salt, and 2,802,287 tons in rock salt. Purely industrial uses took 9,839,191 of the total, while the food industry and table use accounted for 1,963,457 tons.

In Canada the 1942 output was 653,672 short tons, 17% more than in 1941, while that of the first 8 months of 1943 was 7% greater than for the same period of 1941.   (G. A. RO.)

Salvador, El. A republic on the west coast of Central America, without a Caribbean littoral. It is the smallest Central American republic (area 13,176 sq.mi.) but the most densely populated per square mile (pop., off. est. 1939, 1,-744,535). Capital: San Salvador (pop., 1939 census, 105,494). Other cities are: Santa Ana (86,667); San Miguel (46,569); Santa Tecla (34,313); Ahuachapán (32,220); Sonsonate (21,-484); San Vicente (30,000); Zacatecoluca (28,081). The prevailing religion is Roman Catholic. President in 1943: Gen. Maximiliano Hernández Martínez.

History.—El Salvador continued war policies as developed in 1942. The state of siege, started at the beginning of the war and continued every 90 days, remained in effect in 1943.

Economic conditions in the first part of the year were less favourable than later. In August the exportation of basic foodstuffs was prohibited, and the ban was not lifted until November. A price control plan was established Sept. 2, covering some 50 items. Some profiteering had been in evidence before this time. Wages in all industries had been raised by October, except for government employees. The gasoline shortage was serious in El Salvador, with at least 35% of all private cars with no allowance at all, and with bus traffic down 50%.

Education.—Primary schools in 1941 numbered about 1,300, with an average attendance of approximately 75,000. Secondary schools numbered 26; enrolment 1,650. The 1943 budget estimated educational expenses at 2,246,000 colones (1942: 2,211,000).

Finance.—The monetary unit is the colón (value in 1943, 40 cents U.S.). The 1943 budget estimated revenue at 23,901,000 colones; expenditures at 23,896,000 colones. The public debt (July 1, 1942) was 44,947,000 colones (39,132,000 colones external; 5,815,000 colones internal). The gold reserve was estimated at near 35,000,000 colones. Because of a shortage of small coins, United States dimes were made legal tender in September (at 25 centavos, one-fourth of a colón).

Trade and Resources.—No figures for 1943 on total trade were available; imports and exports for 11 months of 1943 had increased over 1942, however. Coffee, normally 90% of exports, was estimated at 917,690 bags for 1942–43; the quota was increased during the year from 753,578 bags to 1,064,264 bags and would be filled from stocks on hand. Total national production in 1942 was estimated to value $55,362,000 (agriculture 82.5%, industry 15.5%, mining 2%). Principal crop estimates were as follows: cotton 68,140 quintals; cottonseed 6,500 tons; sugar 412,600 quin.; castor beans 2,000 tons; sesame 1,000 tons, rice 23,000 tons. The favourable trade balance with the United States for nine months of 1943 was $9,947,000.

Communication.—Communication by sea improved in 1943. Air service was supplied by TACA and Pan American Airways. Railway mileage was estimated at 375 mi., highways at 3,700 mi. (1,600 mi. unimproved).

BIBLIOGRAPHY.—Dana D. Munro, *The Five Republics of Central America* (1918); Chester Lloyd Jones, *The Caribbean since 1900* (1936).
(D. RD.)

Salvage Drives, U.S. The War Production board, through its Salvage division, actively engaged over 16,000 volunteer salvage committees operating through homes, farms and industry throughout cities, counties and states. In addition to these volunteer workers, national and local organizations such as the Boy Scouts, American Legion, Salvation Army, Kiwanis clubs, etc. were mobilized for the purpose of generating and collecting salvage materials needed for essential purposes during the war. Normal trade channels were used to the utmost at all times, and all types of waste material dealers contributed to the collection, segregation and preparation of these materials.

U.S. Salvage Collected in 1943
(in net tons)

Item	Amount
Tin cans	255,513
Collapsible tubes	2,380
Household fats	43,919
Waste paper*	6,066,554
Iron and steel scrap†	26,207,000

*Consuming mill receipts.
†Consumers' receipts.

The principal scrap materials sought in 1943 were: *Iron and steel scrap,* the flow of which had to be maintained to meet the greatest all-time total in steel production the United States has ever known.

Wastepaper.—The paperboard industry encountered difficulties because of shortage of manpower necessary to produce wood pulp and pulpwood. A wastepaper collection effort was intensified and an impending disaster averted by putting innumerable publicity forces to work and by arranging for the collection and disposition of wastepaper in counties and communities throughout the U.S.

Used household fats and greases were a subject of considerable salvage effort. Late in 1943 the OPA arranged to give two meat points for each pound of fat returned to the butcher. By virtue of this and other efforts, the collection of waste fats increased.

Tin was made available in quantity because of the collection of tin cans, automobile radiators, and collapsible tubes used for toothpaste, shaving cream, etc. The tin cans served a double purpose, furnishing both steel and tin once they were returned to detinning plants. The collapsible tubes, while not providing steel, did make available a substantial amount of tin.

Collection of silk and nylon hosiery was discontinued during 1943, but only after 2,964,656 lb. had been obtained for use in making powder bags, parachute lines and other similar articles.

Copper scrap was moved at a greatly accelerated rate because of salvage efforts in automobile graveyards, industrial plants, public utilities and other sources. (*See also* IRON AND STEEL; RUBBER; WAR PRODUCTION, U.S.)   (H. M. FT.)

Salvation Army. An army of 5,000,000 workers attacked the problem of human needs in 98 countries in 1943: 20,667 hospitals, lodging places and other centres throughout the globe served humanity in 1943: many of the Salvation Army's 27,417 officers—each an ordained minister—marched with Allied forces on 23 fighting fronts. When faced, during the great depression in Britain, with thousands of hungry persons the Salvation Army put cooking facilities in a few trucks and motored to meet the need. From this simple, direct action grew the mobile canteen. In 1943 the Salvation Army had 500 mobile canteens on 24-hour call throughout Britain alone.

Meeting emergency needs led to the establishment of rehabilitation homes for inebriates, hospitals for unmarried mothers, prison parole activities, free or low-cost lodging places, boys' clubs and fresh air camps and all the rest of the social services.

In 1943 all these were continued in the United States without let-up, in spite of added war services.

The year was marked by increased efforts to meet the rising child delinquency needs, overcrowding of the 178 lodging places, increased strain on the 42 maternity homes and hospitals.

Workers in 1,867 organized centres in the U.S. continued all religious services, also the knitting and sewing for persons in-or-out of uniform. The personal visitation to the sick and bereaved and the giving of cheer baskets increased. Considerable attention was given to migrant wives of service men.

The year witnessed an increase in emergency war services, not only in the U.S. but, through the global network of Salvation Army centres and canteens (called Red Shield units), to Americans and Allies on 23 fronts. The Salvation Army, through its international organization, provided $1,000,000 for war service in the Australian area alone. Advancing with MacArthur's men, Red Shield workers established 13 recreational centres in New Guinea.

The Red Shield work, originating in 1899, included in 1943 more than 2,000 clubs in the war zones and an untotalled number of mobile canteens and foot marchers. Red Shield workers in 1943 carried the Salvation Army flag back onto Italian territory with the invasion forces; it had been banned during the fascist regime.

In the United States, in 1943, the number of Red Shield units rose to 160. The number of service centres assigned by the United Service Organizations, Inc., for operation by the Salvation Army (one of its six constituent agencies) rose to 167.

(E. J. PA.)

Samoa, American.
A group of six islands and one uninhabited coral atoll in the South Pacific, a U.S. possession by virtue of a tripartite treaty with Germany and Great Britain regulating the disposition of the Samoan archipelago, concluded in Nov. 1899. Area, 76 sq.mi. Pop. (1940) 12,908. The capital is Pago Pago, on the island of Tutuila. The six inhabited islands are Tutuila, Aunuu, Ofu, Olosega, Tau and Swains. The uninhabited coral atoll, Rose Island, is located 70 mi. east of its nearest neighbour.

American Samoa is governed by a naval officer, commissioned as governor by the president. There is a native governor in each of the three administrative divisions of American Samoa; and these native governors appoint the county chiefs, who select the village chiefs. The natives are of the Polynesian race and more than doubled in numbers during the period of American rule. In 1943 there were 36 public schools with an enrolment of about 3,000, and 6 private mission schools.

The chief product of American Samoa is copra, of which about 1,100 tons are exported annually. The islands are fertile and well watered and produce taro, breadfruit, yams, coco-nuts, pineapples, oranges and bananas. About 70% of the land consists of forests.

Construction of a naval air base at Pago Pago was started in 1940. While news of further air and naval development was restricted in the interest of military secrecy, American Samoa became an important and valuable link in the chain of naval and air bases between the west coast and Hawaii and Australia, New Zealand and the combat theatres of the South Pacific.

(W. H. CH.)

Samoa, Western: see MANDATES; PACIFIC ISLANDS, MANDATED.

Sand and Gravel.
The United States production of sand in 1942 was 107,371,000 short tons, and of gravel 196,975,000 tons, a total of 304,346,000 tons; these are respectively increases of 3%, 6% and 5% over 1941. Building construction took 46% of the sand, road paving 36%, foundries

8%, and railroads used 4%, partly as ballast, and partly as engine sand. Of the gravel output building took 24%, paving 59% and railroad ballast 12%. (G. A. Ro.)

Sandstone: see STONE.

San Francisco.
Twelfth United States city, San Francisco, Calif., had a population in 1940 of 634,536, federal census. Estimates by the San Francisco department of public health placed the population at 775,000 in July 1943. Mayor (Dec. 31, 1943): Angelo J. Rossi (Roger D. Lapham, mayor-elect, took office Jan. 8, 1944).

In the manufacturing industries of the San Francisco industrial area, employment rose 46% and payrolls 68% during 1943, and were 231% and 500%, respectively, above the 1940 prewar level. The 11 months' cumulatives for 1943 for San Francisco revealed new records established, with financial transactions up 27%, postal receipts 47%, retail trade 20%, wholesale trade 9%, carloadings 16%, cost of living 7%, and general business activity up 21%. Retail sales in 1943 were estimated at over $1,000,000,-000, wholesale trade at $2,500,000,000, and manufacturing at nearly $2,000,000,000.

Proclaimed the nation's foremost shipbuilding centre for the war program and one of the principal ports of military embarkation, the San Francisco area shipbuilding industries in 1943 employed more than 150,000 workers and had since 1940 been awarded contracts for 790 ships and other shipbuilding facilities totalling $2,250,000,000.

San Francisco's funded debt on Sept. 30, 1943, was $125,054,-100, leaving an actual margin for future bond issues of $102,-804,510. The complete budget for the 1943–44 fiscal year amounted to $95,601,035 with total tax charges of $36,760,949. Total assessed valuation for the 1943–44 period was $1,176,221,-757. Tax rate for the same period was $4.36 per $100 assessed valuation. Tax delinquency for the fiscal year ended June 30, 1943 was at an all-time low of 0.76%, and the lowest in the U.S. among large cities. (R. B. KR.)

Santo Domingo: see DOMINICAN REPUBLIC.
São Tomé: see PORTUGUESE COLONIAL EMPIRE.

→Saracoglu, Shukru
(1890?–   ), Turkish statesman, was born in Odemis, Turkey. He was educated in Turkish civil service schools and studied law at Lausanne university, Switzerland. He enlisted in the Turkish army during World War I, joined with Mustafa Kemal Pasha (Kemal Ataturk) after the armistice and fought against the Greek forces in 1921. After the destruction of the Greek armies and the abolition of the sultanate, Saracoglu became a member of the national assembly as deputy from Izmir, and rose swiftly in the ranks of Mustafa Kemal's party. An advocate of westernization for Turkey, he instituted many legal reforms during his tenure as justice minister, 1932–38. After Ataturk's death in Nov. 1938, Saracoglu was named foreign minister. He followed a consistent policy of neutrality during the first years of World War II. In July 1942, he was named prime minister. After the re-election of President Inönü in March 1943, Saracoglu headed a reorganized cabinet.

Sarawak: see BRITISH EMPIRE.

Saskatchewan.
The central of the three Canadian prairie provinces, Saskatchewan was created a province in 1905 by the Canadian parliament. Area, 251,700 sq.mi, comprising open country in the south, and broken wooded land in the north. Pop. (1941 census) 895,992. Local administra-

tion is in the hands of a provincial parliament. The chief cities of Saskatchewan (population based on the 1941 census) are as follows: Regina, provincial capital (58,245); Saskatoon (43,027); Moose Jaw (20,753); Prince Albert (12,508); Weyburn (6,179). Saskatoon is the seat of the University of Saskatchewan, a provincial institution.

History.—In the general elections of 1938, William Patterson, the Liberal premier, had been returned to office; there was no change of political importance in 1943. Saskatchewan returns to Ottawa 21 members to the house of commons and six senators.

Agriculture, Forests, Fisheries.—In 1943 the wheat crop was expected to reach about 155,000,000 bu., or about one-half of the 1942 crop. Other crops (computed as of Nov. 1943) were as follows: oats 23,747,991 bu.; barley 14,771,214 bu.; flaxseed 8,460,299 bu.; sunflower seed 8,700,000 bu. Sunflower seed was distinctly a wartime production, the commodity having great industrial and food value. As in previous years, there was difficulty in finding labour for harvesting in 1943. The problem was met by moving in some 2,000 farmers and farm labourers from central Canada. The forests of Saskatchewan in 1941 produced lumber to the value of $3,322,733; the fur haul for 1941–42 represented the sum of $2,245,275.   (J. I. C.)

Saudi Arabia: *see* ARABIA.
Savings and Loan Insurance Corporation, Federal: *see* NATIONAL HOUSING AGENCY.
Savings Banks: *see* BANKING.
Schizophrenia: *see* PSYCHIATRY.

Schlesinger, Frank

(1871–1943), U.S. astronomer, was born May 11 in New York city. He was educated in New York, receiving his B.S. from City college, 1890, and his M.A., 1897, and Ph. D., 1898, from Columbia. An authority on determining stellar distances by photography, Dr. Schlesinger, while astronomer at Yerkes observatory, 1903–05, developed a method of measuring distances between stars on photographic plates taken with long-focus telescopes. He also designed a measuring engine to make his computations on distance more precise; this device is now regarded as standard equipment in observatories. While director and professor of astronomy at the Allegheny observatory, University of Pittsburgh, 1905–20, he designed a photographic telescope with 30-inch lens. He was director of Yale university's observatory from 1920 until his retirement in 1941. He died at Lyme, Conn., July 10.

Scientific Research and Development, Office of.

The Office of Scientific Research and Development (OSRD) was created in the Office for Emergency Management (*q.v.*) by executive order 8807 of June 28, 1941. Dr. Vannevar Bush of the Carnegie institution of Washington was appointed director. Within the OSRD were set up the National Defense Research committee (NDRC) and the Committee on Medical Research (CMR), the former to assist the director of the OSRD in the mobilization of the scientific personnel and resources of the U.S., and the latter to advise and assist with special reference to the medical personnel and resources of the U.S. The NDRC operated as a committee of the Council of National Defense from June 27, 1940, until June 28, 1941, during which time it entered into a number of contracts which were assumed by the OSRD.

As in preceding years the OSRD in 1943 operated largely through contracts with scientific laboratories in academic and industrial establishments. Of the 364 separate contractors, 119 were academic institutions and 245 industrial establishments.

Most of the work of the OSRD was started at the direct request of the armed services. Practically all of it was of a confidential nature, which made it impossible to reveal details. In May 1943 it was stated that more than 200 devices or formulas developed through OSRD had been turned over to the armed services and that many of them were being used against the enemy. Army and navy orders for OSRD-developed equipment placed through May 1943 aggregated more than $2,000,000,000. The congressional appropriation to support OSRD activities for the fiscal year ending June 30, 1944, was $135,982,500.   (I. ST.)

Scotland: *see* GREAT BRITAIN AND NORTHERN IRELAND, UNITED KINGDOM OF.
Scrap: *see* SALVAGE DRIVES, U.S.; SECONDARY METALS.

Sculpture.

The art of sculpture faced a difficult period in 1943 as a result of the increased demands of the war upon manpower and materials. Many sculptors turned to war work; and others, especially those of the younger generation, were drawn into the armed services. Individual sculpture production and exhibition activity were consequently much curtailed; and what continuation of work there was was carried on largely by the older artists. On the whole there appeared few opportunities or incentives to important or large-scale activity.

A main restrictive factor was the drastic limitation of the use of metal for sculpture work. With bronze, nickel, aluminum and other sculpture materials imperatively needed for armament production, the casting of sculpture in metal was reduced to an almost negligible quantity, leading bronze founders in some instances to estimate depreciation of normal production by as much as 90% to 100%. Sculptors however turned to work in stone, wood and terra cotta, or simulated bronze for temporary purposes by colouring fragile plaster; but small figures and portraits were the rule and little monumental work was completed during the year.

Exhibition activity thus was limited somewhat, largely to the showing of previously completed work and to new productions in the less enduring earth mediums. Most noteworthy among the exhibitions were several shows of the work of individual sculptors. A comprehensive display of architectural and decorative sculpture by Carl Milles, noted Swedish-born sculptor, was presented in May by the American Academy of Arts and Letters which further signalized the artist's achievement by awarding him the academy's medal of merit and $1,000 prize for 1943. Several original pieces were shown but the exhibition was limited by wartime transportation problems mainly to large photographs of Milles's principal plastic achievements.

In January there was another notable showing made by the Whitney Museum of American Art (since amalgamated with the Metropolitan museum) of the work of the museum's late founder, the sculptor Gertrude Vanderbilt Whitney. Arranged as a memorial, it consisted of small bronzes and more monumental work in stone, bronze and other material and illustrated much of the artist's entire production from 1905 to 1940. The sculpture, largely traditional in style, was beautifully shown and very sympathetically received by the public. Maria Martins, wife of the Brazilian ambassador, had a stimulating show of modern sculpture early in the year at the Valentine gallery in New York, demonstrating sources of inspiration in the primitive folklore of her native land, and a robust style in its interpretation. Another show of similar character, exhibiting technical authority and power, presented a well known French refugee sculptor, Jacques Lipchitz, at the Buchholz gallery in February. Both events introduced recent work with fresh trends in ideas.

One of the most popular and entertaining groups was that of

Alexander Calder, American modern sculptor, who had a large retrospective display of his work at the Museum of Modern Art in September. Consisting of "mobiles" and "stabiles" it contained fascinating and light-hearted creations in abstract forms, some of them motivated by electrical power and others susceptible of movement by a breeze of air. Hundreds went to see these brightly painted, animate objects in metal and wood which the artist had created during a period of about 15 years.

The National Sculpture society made its major moves in two group exhibitions representing traditional art forms. One was the annual bas-relief exhibition, in which Miss Janet de Coux of Philadelphia received the Lindsey Morris memorial prize for medallic sculpture, her subject being a design for a "China service medal." Tenth in a series devoted to small relief sculpture, the exhibition was made by 42 members of the society from New York and other cities. The other presentation during this period was a display of enlarged photographs of important American sculpture at the New York Historical society. It was entitled "American Patriots" and designed to show the quality of the best public sculptural monuments to national heroes such as Washington, Lee, Theodore Roosevelt, John Paul Jones and Admiral Farragut. Many of the society's famous members, past and present, were represented by these statues in many cities throughout the country.

A few public monuments, commemorative busts and memorials, were completed during 1943 and dedicated in different cities. In Washington two busts of statesmen were unveiled under official auspices, one being a bust of the late Thomas B. Reed, onetime speaker of the house, by the late Gutzon Borglum, which was dedicated in the house of representatives last January; and a bust of John N. Garner, former vice-president, unveiled in a ceremony at the capitol in April. A five-ton granite statue of Mary Todd and Abraham Lincoln by Frederick C. Hibbard, was provided as a gift to the city of Racine, Wis., and was erected in that city. Other sculpture projects included a bronze portrait of Prof. Albert Einstein, noted scientist, completed by the New York sculptor Eleanor Platt, which was to be presented to the Hebrew university in Palestine after World War II by a group of American friends of the university and of the scientist.

Museum acquisitions included notable sculpture. The National Gallery of Art in Washington received the gift of an 18th century French terra cotta statue entitled "La Surprise," by Claude Michel (called "Clodion"), from Mrs. Jesse Isidor Straus in memory of her late husband who was American ambassador to France from 1933 to 1936. The Metropolitan Museum of Art also acquired a distinguished 12th century stone lintel, depicting in deeply carved relief the Holy Women of the Sepulchre and the Entombment of Christ. The sculpture was a gift to the museum's branch, The Cloisters, from John D. Rockefeller, Jr., and is one of the largest single pieces of mediaeval carving in the United States. (*See* also ART EXHIBITIONS.) (C. Bu.)

SEC: *see* SECURITIES AND EXCHANGE COMMISSION.
Secondary Education: *see* EDUCATION.

Secondary Metals.

Information available on the recovery of secondary metals in the United States is presented in the accompanying table. All metals in the list show clearly the effect of increased demand, to supplement primary production in the war program. Some of these metals are recovered from junked materials, but with increased industrial activity an increasing percentage comes from scrap made in the fabricating plants, and so has never been in use.

Nonferrous metal scrap shipped to consumers by dealers in 1942 totalled 951,057 short tons, including 488,436 tons of cop-

Secondary Nonferrous Metals Recovered in the United States

	1937	1938	1939	1940	1941
Copper—Thousands of short tons					
As metal	285.6	192.4	151.4	170.8	135.9
In alloys	246.5	167.4	345.1	351.8	580.7
In chemical compounds	?	?	3.2	9.4	9.8
Total	532.1	359.8	499.7	532.0	726.4
Percentage*	62–78	60–74	62–57	53–63	?–57
Lead—Thousands of short tons					
As metal	154.5	119.4	86.9	59.6	75.3
In alloys	120.6	105.5	148.8	200.8	322.1.
In chemical compounds	?	?	5.8		
Total	275.1	224.9	241.5	260.3	397.4
Percentage*	41	41	36–87	33–87	?–96
Zinc—Thousands of short tons					
As metal	64.5	42.3	36.0	69.0	89.7
In alloys	62.8	44.8	98.9	112.3	143.2
In chemical compounds	?	?	54.8	40.8	48.5
Total	127.3	87.1	189.6	222.0	284.0
Percentage*	21	21	33–24	31–29	?–39
Tin—Thousands of short tons					
As metal	8.3	4.9	4.4	5.1	5.9
In alloys	20.3	17.3	23.0	26.5	36.1
In chemical compounds	1.7	1.4	0.7	0.7	1.1
Total	30.3	23.6	29.2	32.2	42.0
Percentage*	35	47	42–58	44–62	?–70
Aluminum—Thousands of short tons					
As metal	29.4	16.7	2.9	5.6	8.3
In alloys	33.2	22.1	51.0	74.7	97.6
Total	62.6	38.8	53.9	80.4	106.9
Percentage	38	26.5	38–70	41–57	?–41
Nickel—Thousands of short tons					
As metal	0.9	0.8	} 2.9	5.2	5.3
In alloys†	1.5	1.5			
Total	2.4	2.3	2.9	5.2	5.3
Percentage*	5	10	5–35	6–46	?–40
Antimony—Thousands of short tons					
As metal	11.5	7.8	} 9.8	11.4	21.6
In alloys	0.8	0.7			
Total	12.3	8.5	9.8	11.4	21.6
Percentage*	69	77	83–98	60–98	?–99+
Platinum—Thousands of troy ounces	55.9	44.7	45.4	47.7	?
O.P.M.‡—Thousands of troy ounces	16.4	19.7	18.0	18.8	?
Gold—Thousands of troy ounces	?	870.9	895.1	?	?
Silver—Thousands of troy ounces	?	18,438.8	24,972.3	?	?

*Ratio of secondary recovery to consumption of new metal; where a second figure appears, this is the percentage of the total secondary metal recovered from *old* materials, the remainder having come from the reworking of new plant scrap.
†Includes some in chemical compounds. ‡Other platinum group metals.

per, 306,192 tons of lead and tin, 100,796 tons of aluminum, 50,435 tons of zinc, 3,297 tons of nickel and 1,871 tons of magnesium. At the end of the year dealers' stocks were 112,142 tons, against 90,928 tons at the beginning of the year and a low of 77,776 tons in February. Through Aug. 1943, similar shipments increased by 5% over the corresponding period of 1942, to 646,225 tons.

The consumption of ferrous scrap in the United States in 1942 showed an increase of 2% over 1941, with a total that reached 60,251,151 short tons—a new record high; in this total was 33,129,322 tons of plant scrap and 27,135,779 tons of purchased scrap. During the first eight months of 1943 plant scrap amounted to 20,715,000 tons and purchased scrap to 15,856,000 tons, both small increases over the same period of 1942. There was a shortage of scrap throughout the year, as is indicated by these figures; in normal operation plant scrap and purchased scrap are used in about equal quantities. At the end of Aug. 1943, only about two months' supply was on hand. During the fourth quarter an intensive drive for the collection of all kinds of metal scrap was under way. (G. A. Ro.)

Second World War: *see* WORLD WAR II.

Secret Service, U. S.

Because its "Know Your Money" campaign cut counterfeit money losses 97% in six years, the treasury department's secret service in 1943 applied the same principles to a "Know Your Endorsers" campaign, designed to prevent thefts and forgeries of government checks by exposing the methods of check thieves and forgers to their potential victims. Seeking to protect recipients of nearly 200,000,000 government checks issued during the fiscal year, representing army and navy allowances and allotments, social security benefits and other federal payments, secret service agents arranged for publication of news stories and warnings against check forgers in newspapers and magazines with a combined circulation of 204,922,409 and for the production and distribution of 596,774,346 copies of pamphlets, placards and other material printed by banks and private business establishments. The inscription: "Know Your Endorser—Require Identification," now being printed on government checks, was widely adopted by banks, corporations and state and local governments for use on private checks, at the suggestion of the secret service.

The 32-page secret service booklet, "Know Your Money," was adopted as a unit of study by 11,922 high schools throughout the United States, for study by 3,396,687 students under the guidance of 72,784 teachers. The "Know Your Money" study course was formally endorsed by the Americanism Commission of the American Legion, and a group of its educators compiled a comprehensive course of study which they sent to 6,000 high school teachers and post commanders with the request that "Know Your Money" be made a part of the curricula of high schools in their communities. The "Know Your Money" film was shown to 2,103,918 persons, including 1,265,925 high school students.

In protecting the president of the United States, secret service agents were faced with new problems during his unprecedented journey to Casablanca in January. Movements were executed according to careful advance arrangements and were kept a closely guarded secret until the news was officially released. Great care was also taken to insure the president's security during his trip to Mexico and his unpublicized inspection tours of the war plants of the nation, one of which took him through more than 20 states.

During the year plants for the production of counterfeit $1, $10 and $50 notes were captured by agents, who also seized 8 metal counterfeit plates, 30½ metal molds and 137½ plaster molds for all denominations of bogus coins, 36 film negatives, 1 glass negative for counterfeit Canadian gasoline ration stamps, 2 power presses and one hand press, 16 zinc plates for counterfeit "B" gasoline ration stamps, 20,859 counterfeit sugar ration stamps, 27,102 counterfeit "T" gasoline ration stamps, 14,180 counterfeit U.S. internal revenue stamps and 1,110 counterfeit Canadian excise stamps.

Agents seized counterfeit and altered notes with a total representative value of $44,909. Of this amount, $13,572 was captured before it reached circulation. Of the balance, only $22,079 represented losses suffered by victims of counterfeit note-passers.

Counterfeit coins seized had a representative value of $20,783, of which $1,340 was seized before they reached circulation. Of the balance, $16,309 represented losses to the public.

During the year there were 26,892 investigations disposed of. A total of 1,789 offenders were arrested, and convictions were obtained in 98% of the 1,515 criminal cases brought to trial.

(F. J. W.)

Securities: *see* BUSINESS REVIEW; STOCKS AND BONDS.

Securities and Exchange Commission.
As of June 30, 1943, the commission was composed of the following members: Chairman Ganson Purcell and Commissioners Robert E. Healy, Sumner T. Pike, Edmund Burke, Jr., and Robert H. O'Brien. The commission's headquarters were located at Philadelphia, Pa., and regional offices were located at Atlanta, Ga.; Baltimore, Md.; Boston, Mass.; Chicago, Ill.; Cleveland, O.; Denver, Colo.; Fort Worth, Tex.; New York, N.Y.; San Francisco, Calif.; and Seattle, Wash. A liaison office was maintained in Washington, D.C. The several acts administered by the commission are discussed below.

During the fiscal year ended June 30, 1943, 150 registration statements were filed with the commission under the Securities

act of 1933, which provided for the filing of financial and other information concerning securities proposed to be offered to the public, bringing to 5,176 the total number of registration statements filed under the act to that date. One hundred fifteen registration statements became effective during the year, registering securities in the aggregate amount of $659,480,015.

Under the Securities Exchange act of 1934, providing for the regulation of securities trading practices both on securities exchanges and in the over-the-counter markets, 19 national securities exchanges were registered with the commission at the close of the year, and 6 exchanges were exempted from registration. There were 2,244 issuers who had 3,866 separate security issues listed and registered upon national exchanges. There were 4,913 brokers and dealers who engaged in the over-the-counter securities business registered with the commission; the registrations of 24 brokers and dealers were revoked by the commission, and 4 applications for registration were denied. The National Association of Securities Dealers, Inc., with a membership of 2,221 at June 30, 1943, and having powers of self-discipline over its membership, remained the only such association registered with the commission.

On June 30, 1943, 129 holding companies with consolidated assets aggregating $16,079,000,000 were registered with the commission under the Public Utility Holding act of 1935. There were 1,217 holding, sub-holding, and operating companies included in the system companies registered with the commission. Between Dec. 1, 1935 (when the registration requirements of the act became effective), and Nov. 15, 1943, public utility holding companies disposed of their interests in 223 electric, gas, and non-utility companies with assets of approximately $3,233,000,000. Necessary corporate reorganization and simplification, as well as a more equitable distribution of voting power, was approved or ordered by the commission during the year in cases involving 29 companies and action by 12 major holding company systems to effect compliance with the integration requirements of the act was also ordered.

During the year the commission participated, under Chapter X of the Bankruptcy act, in the reorganization proceedings for 130 companies having total assets of approximately $93,770,000 and aggregate indebtedness of approximately $70,693,000.

Under the Trust Indenture act of 1939, 45 indentures covering securities of an aggregate principal amount of $399,800,429 were filed with and examined by the commission.

Three hundred ninety investment companies were registered with the commission as provided in the Investment Company act of 1940, on June 30, 1943, with estimated assets aggregating approximately $3,000,000,000. The act provided for the protection of investors through disclosure of finances and investment policies of these companies. Three important court actions were instituted under the act during the year. Two of these actions alleged gross misconduct and gross abuse of trust by the companies' managements; one case resulted in an adjudication in bankruptcy, and the other, involving three companies, was awaiting trial on the merits. The third action was based upon an abandonment of the company by its management, leaving an "orphan" trust, and in that case a liquidating receivership was obtained.

The registrations of 698 investment advisers were in effect at the end of the year under the Investment Advisers act of 1940.

During the year 1942–43, 947 cases of alleged fraudulent securities transactions were under investigation by the SEC; 48 companies and individuals were permanently enjoined from continuing practices violative of provisions of the acts administered by the commission; and 189 persons were indicted and 127 convicted for fraudulent activities violative of said acts. (*See* also

STOCKS AND BONDS.) (G. PL.)

Sedition: *see* FEDERAL BUREAU OF INVESTIGATION.

Seeing Eye, The

This organization, which teaches dogs to guide blind persons, began in 1928 when Morris Frank brought his German shepherd, Buddy I—bred and trained by Mrs. Harrison Eustis and Elliott S. Humphrey in Switzerland—to New York and proved that American street traffic could not baffle the expert animal. In 1943, some 800 blind men and women, from every state in the union, were using dogs educated by the Seeing Eye at Morristown, N.J., and were thus made capable not only of earning their livings but of helping their country, 100 of them directly in war industries. Many dog-reliant blind persons were using their second or third dogs; for a dog's life is short, and Seeing Eye guarantees not to let slip back into dependency anyone whom a guide dog has once set free.

After Pearl Harbor, Seeing Eye resolved to "at no expense to the federal government, endeavour to provide Seeing Eye dog guides for eligible persons who . . . have lost their sight in line of duty." Only a few of 1943's graduates were blinded soldiers; but Morris S. Frank, guided by "Buddy," visited 39 army, navy and veterans' hospitals, telling how the newly blinded can learn to live again. (B. TA.)

Seismology.

Seismology adapted itself to war conditions, especially to the fact that so much of the major earthquake belts are in active war zones. An unknown number of observing stations were destroyed or forced to suspend. However, the principal earthquakes were located and information was supplemented by study of the instrumental record at distant stations. While there was no major earthquake there were about 10 in which loss of life or property occurred, Turkey suffered most with three earthquakes of which the most severe was on Nov. 27, 1943. One new seismograph station was established in the United States and one in Mexico. Several suspended operation. Two stations were maintained in Greenland. There was co-operation in the location of earthquakes from Greenland, Canada, the United States, Mexico, Colombia, Peru, Samoa, New Zealand and Australia. Records were obtained in the central regions of several slightly destructive earthquakes, especially that of San Jose, Calif., on Oct. 25.

Results of earlier investigations were published which confirmed the accuracy of strong motion measurements and provided means for their utilization in the design of structures to resist earthquake damage. Some vibration measurements were made to aid in solution of problems of structural design.

No geodetic resurveys were made to determine crustal movements possibly associated with earthquakes but new surveys provided many additional points for use in future determinations. Tilt measurements continued but no earthquake occurred to test their value. No seismic sea wave was recorded on the tide gauges of North and South America. No purely investigation work was undertaken, but this was offset by the probable development of new devices which might prove useful. The activities of international seismological organizations was reported as continuing on a curtailed basis. (*See* also DISASTERS.) (N. H. H.)

Selective Service, U.S.

On Dec. 1, 1943, the Selective Service system reported that the combined strength of the U.S. armed forces was estimated at 10,100,000 men and women. At the same time, Selective Service said it estimated it would be required to call between 1,900,000 and 2,100,000 more men by July 1, 1944, to bring the military establishment up to its planned strength of 11,300,000 and to supply the replacements for those who would die and those who would be discharged.

The year 1943 imposed a severe burden on the Selective Service system and the 190,000 people, mostly volunteer workers, who carried out its work. These people, working on appeal boards, as advisory board members, government appeal agents, medical and dental examiners, re-employment committeemen, and on the 6,437 local boards were the real administrators of the program.

From its inception in Sept. 1940, until Feb. 1943, the Selective Service system called men for the army only. On Feb. 1, 1943, however, to carry out the provisions of an executive order of Dec. 5, 1942, the system began to furnish all men inducted into the navy, marine corps and coast guard as well as the army. Assignments for general service men were made on ratios determined by the needs of the respective services.

The requirement that all men between 18 and 38 needed by all of the armed forces should be inducted through Selective Service channels imposed an additional task on Selective Service local boards. It had one definitely beneficial effect, however. Prior to Feb. 1, 1943, when Selective Service was furnishing men for the army only, it was not unusual for men to be enlisted by the navy even after they had been classified as available for army service. Therefore, local boards might believe that they had a certain number of men available for forwarding to an army induction station on a given date. When the roll was called, however, they were likely to find that some of the men had enlisted in the navy and that the army requirements would not be met that day. That procedure adopted in Feb. 1943, prevented this situation from occurring.

While the reduction in the age limit from 45 to 38 curtailed the manpower pool in 1943 to a considerable degree, there was another factor that substantially reduced the supply of available men. On Dec. 31, 1943, Selective Service announced that 1,750,000 men had been deferred in Classes II-C and III-C, the former for men regularly engaged in an agricultural occupation or endeavour but without dependents, the latter for men so engaged but also having dependents. Of the 1,750,000 some 397,000 were between 18 and 22 years of age and were non-fathers. At the same time, only 122,500 men between 18 and 22 who were non-fathers were deferred because of occupations in war production or war supporting activities.

Under the executive order of Dec. 5, 1942, the Selective Service became a part of the War Manpower commission and operated as a bureau of the commission until Dec. 1943, when congress, in legislating amendments to the Selective Training and Service act of 1940, included a provision which stated that the president could delegate his authority under the act to the director of Selective Service only. On Dec. 23, 1943, the president issued an executive order setting up the Selective Service system as a separate agency again, and once more delegated his authority to the director of Selective Service.

On May 1, 1943, there were approximately 8,000,000 18 to 38 year-old registrants deferred because of their dependency. Two months later, on July 1, 1943, the total number of registrants deferred because of dependency had been reduced to 6,600,000 as the increasing demands of the armed forces necessitated the calling of men who had collateral dependents or wives only.

Then on Aug. 3, the chairman of the War Manpower commission announced that local boards should begin the reclassification of fathers who had been deferred because of the dependency of their children and that the induction of such fathers would begin Oct. 1, 1943. By Jan. 1, 1944, Selective Service announced that 99,000 registrants having children conceived prior to Dec. 8, 1941, or

Table I.—*Classification of Registrants, 18 Through 37 Years of Age, Sept. 15 and Dec. 1, 1943*
(Continental United States)
(Preliminary)

Selective Service Classification	Sept. 15, 1943						Dec. 1, 1943					
	Number of registrants			% of total reg.			Number of registrants			% of total reg.		
	Total	White	Negro	Total	White	Negro	Total	White	Negro	Total	White	Negro
Total living registrants	22,076,133	19,723,568	2,352,565	100.0	100.0	100.0	22,137,864	19,775,436	2,362,428	100.0	100.0	100.0
Class I-C	8,526,580	7,841,638	684,942	38.6	39.8	29.2	8,970,302	8,224,722	745,580	40.7	41.6	31.5
Class IV-F	3,083,046	2,477,584	605,462	14.0	12.6	25.7	3,353,052	2,685,367	667,685	15.1	13.6	28.3
Classes I-A, I-A-O, I-A(L) and I-A-O(L)	1,037,148	797,261	239,887	4.7	4.0	10.2	1,089,702	857,229	232,473	4.9	4.3	9.8
Classes III-A, III-B and Unclassified	6,247,042	5,686,811	560,231	28.3	28.8	23.8	4,636,624	4,228,480	408,144	20.9	21.4	17.3
Classes II-A and II-B	1,355,483	1,305,548	49,935	6.1	6.6	2.1	2,194,424	2,105,120	89,304	9.9	10.6	3.8
Classes II-C and III-C	1,585,018	1,389,117	195,901	7.2	7.0	8.3	1,639,228	1,436,367	202,861	7.4	7.3	8.6
Class III-D	76,197	73,008	3,189	0.3	0.4	0.1	89,463	85,254	4,209	0.4	0.4	0.2
Other classes	165,619	152,601	13,018	0.8	0.8	0.6	165,069	152,897	12,172	0.7	0.8	0.5

so-called pre-Pearl Harbor fathers had been inducted into the armed forces between Oct. 1 and Jan. 1. Furthermore, the pool of men deferred because of their dependents on Dec. 1, 1943, had been reduced to 4,500,000 and local boards were continuing the reclassification of such registrants at a rate between 750,000 and 1,000,000 per month.

Many of the registrants who had been deferred because of their children, however, were not placed in a class available for service but were reclassified into deferred classes by reason of their occupations in war production or in support of the war effort. In Oct. and Nov. 1943, 1,400,000 fathers were classified out of their dependency classification. Of that number, 900,000 were immediately placed in other classifications and deferred by reason of their occupations, indicating that local boards were continuing to follow the Selective Service policy of deferring men with children as long as possible.

Congress, in 1943, made two major legislative moves for the benefit of men with dependents.

The first was adopted on Oct. 26, 1943, when the Serviceman's Dependents Allowance act of 1942 was amended to increase the amounts payable to dependents of men in the armed forces.

As amended, the Serviceman's Dependents Allowance act provided:

SEC. 101. The dependent or dependents of any enlisted man in the army of the United States, the United States navy, the marine corps, or the coast guard, including any and all retired and reserve components of such services, shall be entitled to receive a monthly family allowance for any period during which such enlisted man is in the active military or naval service of the United States on or after June 1, 1942, during the existence of any war declared by congress and the six months immediately following the termi-

Table II.—*Classification of All Registrants, 18 Through 37 Years of Age, By States, Dec. 1, 1943**
(Preliminary)

State	Total living registrants		Class I-C		Class IV-F		Classes I-A, I-A-O, I-A(L) and I-A-O(L)		Classes III-A, III-B and Unclassified		Classes II-A and II-B		Classes II-C and III-C		Class III-D		Other classes	
	Number	Per cent	Number	Per cent	Number	Per cent	Number	Per cent	Number	Per cent	Number	Per cent	Number	Per cent	Number	Per cent	Number	Per cent
United States (Continental)	22,137,864	100.0	8,970,302	40.7	3,353,052	15.1	1,089,702	4.9	4,636,624	20.9	2,194,424	9.9	1,639,228	7.4	89,463	0.4	165,069	0.7
Alabama	486,598	100.0	162,418	33.2	97,764	20.1	34,393	7.1	88,360	18.2	48,032	9.9	52,101	10.7	743	0.2	2,787	0.6
Arizona	86,047	100.0	32,401	37.9	12,946	15.0	3,908	4.5	22,132	25.7	8,991	10.4	4,504	5.2	638	0.7	527	0.6
Arkansas	325,625	100.0	112,050	34.4	69,416	21.3	20,787	6.4	64,980	20.0	13,372	4.1	42,664	13.1	420	0.1	1,936	0.6
California	1,239,857	100.0	524,327	42.4	151,164	12.2	45,157	3.6	315,157	25.4	120,189	9.7	53,761	4.3	3,571	0.3	26,531	2.1
Colorado	178,497	100.0	71,569	40.2	24,158	13.5	8,445	4.7	30,916	17.3	22,744	12.7	18,514	10.4	227	0.1	1,924	1.1
Connecticut	306,792	100.0	138,086	44.9	40,395	13.2	9,450	3.1	67,189	21.9	42,116	13.7	5,698	1.9	2,117	0.7	1,741	0.6
Delaware	146,545	100.0	19,477	41.8	7,023	15.1	2,250	4.8	10,137	21.8	4,958	10.7	2,391	5.1	122	0.3	187	0.4
District of Columbia	146,181	100.0	63,051	43.1	31,809	21.8	11,012	7.5	26,742	18.3	10,517	7.2	280	0.2	768	0.5	2,002	1.4
Florida	323,228	100.0	122,822	37.9	68,137	21.1	30,723	9.5	60,745	18.8	24,590	7.6	13,738	4.3	623	0.2	1,850	0.6
Georgia	543,483	100.0	174,216	32.0	102,495	18.9	41,121	7.6	122,603	22.6	29,484	5.4	69,277	12.7	1,078	0.2	3,209	0.6
Idaho	91,177	100.0	31,273	34.4	7,936	8.7	5,280	5.8	14,956	16.4	12,985	14.2	17,594	19.3	127	0.1	1,026	1.1
Illinois	1,322,013	100.0	570,713	43.1	171,785	13.0	78,150	5.9	268,366	20.3	145,597	11.0	72,458	5.5	6,289	0.5	8,655	0.7
Indiana	565,659	100.0	227,906	40.4	82,916	14.7	22,693	4.0	136,602	24.1	53,356	9.4	35,916	6.3	2,031	0.4	4,239	0.7
Iowa	384,387	100.0	146,915	38.3	42,822	11.1	11,965	3.1	67,865	17.7	25,290	6.6	86,637	22.5	562	0.1	2,331	0.6
Kansas	269,722	100.0	111,152	41.2	27,577	10.2	12,329	4.6	38,744	14.4	30,041	11.1	47,069	17.5	285	0.1	2,525	0.9
Kentucky	462,419	100.0	172,315	37.2	88,155	19.1	21,674	4.7	116,691	25.2	20,372	4.4	39,353	8.5	1,281	0.3	2,578	0.6
Louisiana	416,060	100.0	157,684	37.9	79,422	19.1	23,023	5.5	82,653	19.9	31,607	7.6	39,095	9.4	475	0.1	2,101	0.5
Maine	128,531	100.0	52,990	41.3	17,775	13.8	6,792	5.3	22,170	17.2	20,112	15.6	7,414	5.8	499	0.4	779	0.6
Maryland	334,148	100.0	129,258	38.6	53,674	16.1	18,748	5.6	70,705	21.2	42,375	12.7	15,401	4.6	939	0.3	3,048	0.9
Massachusetts	674,013	100.0	315,781	46.8	98,221	14.6	25,787	3.8	131,168	19.5	84,205	12.5	7,516	1.1	6,731	1.0	4,604	0.7
Michigan	914,803	100.0	367,171	40.1	127,172	13.9	34,576	3.8	206,187	22.5	130,743	14.3	41,113	4.5	3,239	0.4	4,602	0.5
Minnesota	440,788	100.0	175,718	39.8	55,179	12.5	16,280	3.7	75,057	17.0	28,492	6.5	86,203	19.6	731	0.2	3,128	0.7
Mississippi	362,773	100.0	130,916	36.0	56,041	15.4	26,929	7.4	54,031	14.9	24,516	6.8	67,658	18.7	675	0.2	2,007	0.6
Missouri	594,348	100.0	241,995	40.6	95,977	16.1	29,596	5.0	109,844	18.5	47,860	8.1	62,974	10.6	1,547	0.3	4,555	0 8
Montana	93,338	100.0	36,518	39.0	10,893	11.7	3,646	3.9	13,229	14.2	14,366	15.4	13,872	14.9	192	0.2	622	0.7
Nebraska	195,089	100.0	74,974	38.4	22,829	11.7	7,479	3.8	23,344	12.0	18,052	9.3	46,616	23.9	346	0.2	1,449	0.7
Nevada	21,606	100.0	9,836	45.5	2,593	12.0	1,340	6.2	3,213	14.9	3,075	14.2	1,355	6.3	49	0.2	145	0.7
New Hampshire	73,995	100.0	32,355	43.8	10,959	14.8	4,108	5.6	13,151	17.8	9,873	13.3	2,836	3.8	163	0.2	550	0.7
New Jersey	725,763	100.0	343,719	47.3	94,226	13.0	29,510	4.1	162,180	22.3	77,990	10.7	10,608	1.5	3,443	0.5	4,087	0.6
New Mexico	89,517	100.0	34,106	38.0	12,886	14.4	6,760	7.6	13,087	14.6	12,494	14.0	9,187	10.3	253	0.3	744	0.8
New York city	1,274,962	100.0	611,397	48.0	210,319	16.5	75,442	5.9	258,582	20.3	91,837	7.2	1,118	0.1	15,571	1.2	10,696	0.8
New York state (excl. N.Y.C.)	941,134	100.0	420,714	44.7	118,872	12.6	35,347	3.8	177,277	18.8	125,737	13.4	51,946	5.5	4,418	0.5	6,823	0.7
North Carolina	635,029	100.0	197,326	31.1	133,450	21.0	39,644	6.2	144,933	22.8	40,873	6.4	74,127	11.7	1,606	0.3	3,070	0.5
North Dakota	103,500	100.0	35,040	33.9	11,975	11.6	3,784	3.7	7,563	7.3	8,122	7.8	36,378	35.1	88	0.1	550	0.5
Ohio	1,154,779	100.0	508,756	44.0	165,527	14.3	43,485	3.8	295,407	25.6	82,905	7.2	45,779	4.0	5,698	0.5	7,222	0.6
Oklahoma	364,135	100.0	135,945	37.3	57,587	15.8	15,380	4.2	78,415	21.5	29,487	8.1	43,974	12.1	935	0.3	2,412	0.7
Oregon	175,587	100.0	75,089	42.8	18,335	10.4	6,748	3.8	39,132	22.3	23,339	13.3	10,636	6.1	300	0.2	2,008	1.1
Pennsylvania	1,686,919	100.0	729,162	43.2	232,719	13.8	67,252	4.0	429,060	25.4	164,662	9.8	45,117	2.7	8,910	0.5	10,037	0.6
Rhode Island	116,631	100.0	56,844	48.8	17,770	15.2	6,460	5.5	13,593	11.7	19,744	16.9	1,148	1.0	442	0.4	630	0.5
South Carolina	341,088	100.0	101,560	29.8	75,759	22.2	23,987	7.0	82,572	24.2	23,139	6.8	31,488	9.2	957	0.3	1,626	0.5
South Dakota	98,182	100.0	33,288	33.9	10,592	10.8	2,991	3.0	11,593	11.8	6,382	6.5	32,561	33.2	103	0.1	672	0.7
Tennessee	507,063	100.0	187,136	36.9	93,270	18.4	29,586	5.8	127,642	25.2	29,069	5.7	35,816	7.1	1,854	0.4	2,690	0.5
Texas	1,101,690	100.0	419,665	38.1	167,176	15.2	69,027	6.3	256,761	23.3	82,312	7.5	97,150	8.8	2,507	0.2	7,092	0.6
Utah	92,063	100.0	35,157	38.4	8,778	9.5	6,007	6.5	21,025	22.8	13,104	14.2	6,288	6.8	410	0.4	1,294	1.4
Vermont	53,422	100.0	19,405	36.4	8,509	15.9	3,019	5.7	7,239	13.5	7,121	13.3	7,737	14.5	121	0.2	271	0.5
Virginia	491,996	100.0	171,517	34.9	107,706	21.9	24,640	5.0	111,366	22.6	43,924	8.9	28,327	5.8	1,967	0.4	2,549	0.5
Washington	289,509	100.0	113,853	39.2	30,163	10.4	9,305	3.2	22,173	7.7	92,213	31.9	17,005	5.9	588	0.2	4,209	1.5
West Virginia	329,576	100.0	134,167	40.6	54,786	16.6	17,378	5.3	89,307	27.1	24,490	7.4	7,436	2.3	827	0.3	1,185	0.4
Wisconsin	495,654	100.0	184,238	37.1	61,559	12.4	14,716	3.0	22,903	4.6	122,366	24.7	84,665	17.1	1,936	0.4	3,271	0.7
Wyoming	41,943	100.0	16,331	39.0	3,855	9.2	1,593	3.8	7,877	18.8	5,204	12.4	6,729	16.0	61	0.1	293	0.7

*Excludes registrants born prior to Dec. 1, 1905.

nation of any such war.

SEC. 102. The monthly family allowance payable under this title to the dependent or dependents of any such enlisted man shall consist of the government's contribution to such allowance and the reduction in or charge to the pay of such enlisted man except as to the initial family allowance provided by section 107 (a) thereof.

SEC. 103. The dependents of any such enlisted man to whom a family allowance is payable under the provisions of this title shall be divided into three classes to be known as "Class A," "Class B," and "Class B-1" dependents. The Class A dependents of any such enlisted man shall include any person who is the wife, the child, or the former wife divorced of any such enlisted man. The Class B dependents of any such enlisted man shall include any person who is the parent, brother, or sister of such enlisted man and who is found by the secretary of the department concerned to be dependent upon such enlisted man for a substantial portion of his support. The Class B-1 dependents of any such enlisted man shall include any person who is the parent, brother, or sister of such enlisted man and who is found by the secretary of the department concerned to be dependent upon such enlisted man for the chief portion of his support.

SEC. 104. A monthly family allowance shall be granted and paid by the United States to the Class A dependent or dependents of any such enlisted man upon written application to the department concerned made by such enlisted man or made by or on behalf of such dependent or dependents. A monthly family allowance shall be granted and paid by the United States to the Class B or Class B-1 dependent or dependents of any such enlisted man upon written application to the department concerned made by such enlisted man, or upon written application to the department concerned made by or on behalf of such dependent or dependents in any case in which the secretary of the department concerned finds that it is impracticable for such enlisted man to request the payment of such allowance. The payment of a monthly family allowance to any Class B or Class B-1 dependent or dependents of any such enlisted man shall be terminated upon the receipt by the department concerned of a written request by such enlisted man that such allowance be terminated.

SEC. 105. The amount of the monthly family allowance payable to the dependent or dependents of any such enlisted man shall be—

To Class A dependent or dependents: A wife but no child, $50; a wife and one child, $80, with an additional $20 for each additional child; a child but no wife, $42, with an additional $20 for each additional child; a former wife divorced but no child, $42; a former wife divorced and one child, $72, with an additional $20 for each additional child.

To Class B dependent or dependents, payable only while there is no allowance payable to any Class B-1 dependent, $37.

To Class B-1 dependent or dependents: One parent but no brother or sister, $50; two parents but no brother or sister, $68; one parent and one brother or sister, $68, with an additional $11 for each additional brother or sister; two parents and one brother or sister, $79, with an additional $11 for each additional brother or sister; a brother or sister but no parent, $42, with an additional $11 for each additional brother or sister.

SEC. 106. (a) For any month for which a monthly family allowance is paid under this title to the dependent or dependents of any such enlisted man the monthly pay of such enlisted man shall be reduced by, or charged with, the amount of $22, and shall be reduced by, or charged with, an additional amount of $5 if the dependents to whom such allowance is payable include more than one class of dependents. The amount by which the pay of any such enlisted man is so reduced or with which it is so charged shall constitute part of the monthly family allowance payable to his dependent or dependents.

(b) Whenever a division is made of payments of monthly family allowance among dependents of a class, the total amount payable under the provisions of section 105 of this title to or for the benefit, respectively, of two or more children, of two parents, of a former wife divorced and one or more children, or of two or more brothers and sisters, shall be equally divided among the respective children, parents, former divorced wife, or brothers and sisters, or shall be otherwise apportioned and paid within the respective groups as the secretary of the department concerned may direct. The monthly family allowance to Class B dependents shall be payable to only one designated dependent unless the secretary of the department concerned shall direct that the prescribed amount be apportioned among and paid to two or more of such dependents.

(c) Notwithstanding any other provisions of this title, in any case in which a family allowance is granted under this title—

(1) to a wife living separate and apart from the enlisted man under a permanent or temporary court order or decree or written agreement, the amount of the family allowance payable to such wife shall not exceed the amount provided in such order, decree, or written agreement to be paid to such wife, and if such order, decree, or written agreement provides no amount to be paid to such wife, no family allowance shall be payable to her; or

(2) to a former wife divorced, the amount of the family allowance payable to such former wife divorced shall not exceed the amount fixed in the court order or decree as the amount to be paid to such former wife divorced.

In any case in which the application of the provisions of this subsection results in payment to a dependent or dependents of an enlisted man in an amount less than $22, the amount by which the pay of such enlisted man is reduced or with which it is charged shall be the amount of such payment. In every other case in which application of this subsection alone or in conjunction with other provisions of this title results in a payment or payments of $22 or more the amount of such reduction or charge shall be as provided in subsection 106 (a).

Another major move made by the congress for the benefit of registrants with children was the adoption on Dec. 5, 1943, of amendments to the Selective Training and Service act, of 1940, as amended, which provided that in so far as possible fathers should not be called until available non-fathers were called.

SENATOR BURTON K. WHEELER (centre) testifying against the drafting of U.S. fathers in 1943, at a joint session of the senate and house military affairs committee

This provision, however, stipulated that the induction of fathers should not be delayed if such action would interfere with the calling of men required by the armed forces.

The amendments also eliminated the listing of so-called non-deferrable occupations and the induction of men with dependents by reason of the fact that they engaged in nondeferrable activities and occupations. Under this practice, certain registrants, such as bartenders, night club employees, etc., had been inducted, without regard to their dependency status, unless they changed from their nondeferrable occupation to one not listed as nondeferrable.

The legislation also provided for the appointment by the president of a five-man medical commission which was charged with responsibility of investigating the physical, mental and moral standards for admission to the armed forces. It also was requested to investigate the situation with respect to use of limited service personnel in the armed forces and to make recommendations to the president as to whether or not additional numbers of limited servicemen could be utilized by the armed forces without impairing their effectiveness.

One section of the amending legislation provided for pre-induction physical examination at the request of registrants whose induction was shortly to occur. In order to give effect to that section, Selective Service in conjunction with the war and navy departments, put into effect a revised procedure for physical examination. The new procedure provided that instead of a registrant's being inducted immediately after passing his physical examination at the induction station and thereafter being sent home as an enlisted reservist on inactive duty, for 21 days in the case of the army and 7 days in the case of the navy, the registrant would be given a pre-induction examination. If he passed it, he was not to be inducted immediately but was to be returned home in a civilian status and would not have to report for induction until at least 21 days after his examination, regardless of whether he was to be inducted into the army or the navy. Although this procedure was to go into effect on Feb. 1, 1944, in order to commence building up the pools, registrants were to be ordered to report for pre-induction examinations during January in addition to registrants being ordered to report for induction under the old procedure until Feb. 1, 1944. It was hoped that sufficient numbers of persons would be given pre-induction examinations long enough before their actual induction so that by building up large enough pools a period in excess of the initial 21 days could be granted.

The amending legislation also contained a provision that in all cases where a registrant was employed in a Selective Service appeal board area which did not encompass the area of his local board and he was deferred by reason of his occupation, his case should be referred to the appeal board of his principal place of employment for review. This action was taken by the congress with the expressed intent of curtailing the deferment by local boards of men employed in areas far distant from their place of registration.

One of the most far-reaching moves made by Selective Service was the announcement that after Feb. 1, 1944, no registrants between 18 and 22 years old would be granted occupational deferments except in certain cases approved by the director of Selective Service or state directors or in the case of certain students, the merchant marine, and the army transportation corps.

Re-employment.—As the total size of the military establishment increased in 1943, so too did the number of discharges from the armed forces, either through normal attrition or through the casualties of war.

In the Selective Training and Service act of 1940, as amended, is the provision that men who have satisfactorily completed their training and service and who are physically able to return to their former employment shall be returned if it is possible for their former employer to rehire them. The act also provides for the creation within the Selective Service system of a division to carry out the re-employment provisions.

The re-employment division of the Selective Service system decentralized its operation down to the local level and to each local board there was assigned at least one re-employment committeeman responsible for obtaining re-employment benefits of the act for the veterans in his local board. The committeemen also was to work with the representatives of other agencies, government and private, interested in the employment and rehabilitation of men discharged from the armed forces.

In 1942 some 80,000 men were discharged from the military establishment as unfit for further service. By Dec. 31, 1943, the number had been increased to 750,000, of whom 200,000 had been discharged from army and navy hospitals as complete disability cases. Of the latter, 62% were reported on Dec. 31 to have been employed, rehabilitated, or as not requiring assistance. The remainder were reported to be in process of being employed, or rehabilitated, or for other reasons their cases were unclosed. Of those who sought to return to their old jobs, only one sought redress in the courts, as provided in the Selective Training and Service act of 1940, as amended, because his former employer refused to rehire him. But that case did not go to the trial stage because when the former employer was advised of that possibility, he rehired the man and paid him back wages.

The re-employment provisions of the Selective Training and Service act apply not only to men discharged from the armed forces but to the women as well and to men of the merchant marine.

In the accompanying tables the classification of registrants 18 to 37 years of age is shown. The selective service classifications listed and their meaning are, Class I-C, member of land or naval forces of the United States; Class IV-F, physically, mentally or morally unfit for service; Class I-A, available for military service; Class I-A-O, available for noncombatant military service (conscientious objector); Class I-A(L), available for limited military service; Class I-A-O(L) available for limited noncom-

batant service; Class III-A, formerly deferred by reason of maintaining bona fide family relationship (dependency); Class III-B, formerly deferred by reason of dependency and activity (this class was abolished but a few registrants therein had not been reclassified in Dec. 1943); Classes II-A and II-B, man necessary in support of war effort, and man necessary in war production; Class II-C, man deferred by reason of his agricultural occupation or endeavour; Class III-C, man deferred both by reason of dependency and agricultural occupation or endeavour; Class III-D, man deferred by reason of extreme hardship and privation to wife, child or parent.

Pay.—The Pay Readjustment act of 1942 which in 1943 applied to the WACS, WAVES, SPARS and Marines, established uniform rates of base pay for enlisted men of the army, navy, marine corps and coast guard.

The act provided:

The monthly base pay of enlisted men of the army, navy, marine corps and coast guard shall be as follows: Enlisted men of the first grade, $138; enlisted men of the second grade, $114; enlisted men of the third grade, $96; enlisted men of the fourth grade, $78; enlisted men of the fifth grade, $66; enlisted men of the sixth grade, $54; and enlisted men of the seventh grade, $50. Chief petty officers under acting appointment shall be included in the first grade at a monthly base pay of $126.

(*See* also FEDERAL BUREAU OF INVESTIGATION; HEART AND HEART DISEASES; INDIANS, AMERICAN; MEDICINE; NERVOUS SYSTEM; REHABILITATION AND OCCUPATIONAL THERAPY FOR WOUNDED SOLDIERS; WAR MANPOWER COMMISSION.)

(J. SN.)

Selenium. The production of selenium in the United States in 1941 increased 85% over 1940, to 681,650 lb., but dropped back to 316,613 lb. in 1942, 14% less than in 1940. The United States and Canada are the main contributors to a world output estimated at 600 short tons, smaller producers being Russia, Japan, Rhodesia, Mexico and possibly Sweden.

(G. A. RO.)

Selincourt, Ernest de (1870–1943), British educator and writer, was born Sept. 24 in Streatham, England. He was educated at University college, Oxford, and was a lecturer on English language, literature and poetry at Oxford, Cambridge, Belfast and Birmingham universities. At the latter school he served also as dean of the faculty of arts, 1919–30, and as vice-principal, 1931–35. Dr. de Selincourt collected, arranged and edited the voluminous correspondence between William Wordsworth and his sister, Dorothy. Six volumes were devoted to these letters, one was published in 1935, two in 1936 and three in 1938. He wrote a biography, *Dorothy Wordsworth* (1933), *Oxford Lectures on Poetry* (1934) and edited *Wordsworth's Poetical Works* from the manuscripts (1940), *Journals of Dorothy Wordsworth*, 2 vols. (1941), and collected and edited the works of Keats and Spenser. Dr. de Selincourt died at Kendal, Westmorland, May 22.

Senate: *see* CONGRESS, UNITED STATES; ELECTIONS.
Senegal: *see* FRENCH COLONIAL EMPIRE.
Serbia: *see* YUGOSLAVIA.

Serum Therapy. For the serums now used in medicine in the United States, official potency standards and tests have been established by the National Institute of Health for the following products: botulinus antitoxin, diphtheria antitoxin, Clostridium histolyticum antitoxin, Clostridium oedematiens antitoxin, staphylococcus antitoxin, tetanus antitoxin, scarlet fever streptococcus antitoxin, perfringens antitoxin, vibrion septique antitoxin, diphtheria toxin-antitoxin mixture, antidysenteric, antimeningococcic and type specific antipneumococcic serums. These are the products that are known to be useful in the treatment of various diseases. Most of them are made by inoculating an animal with the germs or with the toxin or poison developed by the germs and thereafter collecting the blood from the animal and separating the serum which contains the antisubstances.

Thus the serums included cover snake-bite poisoning, botulism, diphtheria, erysipelas, gas gangrene, tetanus, scarlet fever and staphylococcic infections, also anthrax, dysentery and pneumonia.

In addition to these serums which are made by utilizing the blood of animals, serums are prepared from human blood taken from patients who have recently recovered from various diseases. These serums include the serums used against measles, scarlet fever and infantile paralysis. These are commonly called convalescent serums.

The use of serums and serum preparations is sometimes followed by reactions which are due to sensitivity of the person concerned to animal products, especially the serum of the horse. In certain cases these reactions may be avoided by the use of serums which have been altered by the reaction of enzymes or by using serums from bovine species or sheep and goats. Serums and antitoxins, unless made by the inoculation of the horse, must show on the label the species of animal used.

As a part of the war effort, serums were also being developed for use against some of the special conditions concerned in the war. These were, however, still in an experimental stage.

For pneumonia, serum is obtained from the blood of an animal which has been immunized with cultures of a pneumococcus. It was known in 1943 that there are many different varieties of the pneumococcus so that it is necessary to have a serum that is specific against the type concerned. Antipneumococcic serum obtained from rabbits has been shown to have less of certain disadvantages than does the serum obtained from horses. In 1943, by special techniques rabbit serums were made against many different types of pneumonia.   (M. F.)

Service Organizations, United: *see* UNITED SERVICE ORGANIZATIONS.

Seychelles: *see* BRITISH EAST AFRICA.

Sforza, Carlo, COUNT (1872–), Italian statesman, was born at Lucca. He entered the diplomatic service, was minister at Peking, 1911, and at Belgrade, 1916. He served as Italian high commissioner in Turkey, 1918 and under-secretary for foreign affairs, 1919. In 1919 he was created senator. He became minister of foreign affairs in the Giolitti cabinet June 1920, and negotiated the treaty of Rapallo between Italy and Yugoslavia, Nov. 1920. He remained foreign minister until July 4, 1921 and in Feb. 1922 was appointed ambassador in Paris. After Mussolini's accession to power, he resigned and became one of the chief leaders of the anti-fascist opposition in the senate. Following the murder of Matteoti in 1924, Count Sforza left Italy and went into self-imposed exile. He lived on the continent and travelled to the United States where he lectured frequently at American universities. In Aug. 1942, at the Italian anti-fascist congress in Montevideo, he was proclaimed leader of the newly formed Free Italian National council. After the downfall of Mussolini, Sforza, who had been in the U.S., returned to Italy, Oct. 1943. He subsequently repudiated the Badoglio government, declaring that he could not support a government which was not chosen by the Italian people. On Nov. 3, Sforza declared in a press interview that he would take a post in the Badoglio government only if King Victor Emmanuel and Crown Prince Umberto abdicated, asserting that the house of Savoy, through its close association with Mussolini, had become "obnoxious"

symbols of fascism. On Nov. 20, he suggested that a regency under the six-year-old Prince of Naples would be the most appropriate reconstruction government for Italy.

Shaposhnikov, Boris Mikhailovich (1882–), Russian army officer, was born Oct. 4 in Zlatoust, Russia. He won a scholarship to the imperial academy of the general staff, was graduated in 1910 at the top of his class and was commissioned an officer in the Czarist army. In May 1918 he offered his services to the red army and was appointed an assistant commissar by Lenin and Trotsky. In 1921 he was awarded the order of the red banner. He served in the red army for 13 years before joining the communist party. In 1937 he became chief of the general staff and a member of the powerful central executive committee of the U.S.S.R. He became generally recognized as the chief strategist of the red army when he succeeded in breaking Finnish resistance in the winter of 1940. In recognition of his achievements in the Finnish campaign, Stalin conferred on him the rank of marshal in May 1940. He was said to have been the author of the three-front plan of defense against Hitler's armies in the German-Russian war, and on Oct. 31, 1941, he was recalled as soviet chief of staff. Shaposhnikov was also said to have contrived the strategy that enabled the Russians to hurl back the nazis at the Volga river and Stalingrad in 1942. National recognition of his achievements was evidenced by the nation-wide observance of his birthday on Oct. 4, 1942. In April 1943 it was announced that owing to protracted illness Shaposhnikov had been replaced as chief of staff by Marshal A. M. Vasilevsky.

Sharpening Stones: *see* ABRASIVES.

Shaw, Mrs. George Bernard (?–1943), wife of the British playwright, was born Charlotte Frances Payne-Townshend, daughter of a millionaire Irishman. She and Shaw, who first met at the home of the Sidney Webbs, were married in 1898. Mrs. Shaw thereafter devoted all her time to caring for her celebrated husband, a job which, she once confided in a friend, took up one-third of her time. She was one of his valued critics and acted as his official interpreter on their visits abroad. A philanthropist and lover of music and the arts, she also translated several French plays and collected a book of selected passages from her husband's works. She died in London, Sept. 12.

Sheep. The number of sheep in the United States declined in 1942 as shown by the U.S. department of agriculture estimates of Jan. 1, 1943. This followed an increase through several years to a high record total in Jan. 1942. The total number of sheep and lambs on farms at the beginning of 1943 was 55,089,000 head compared with 56,735,000 head in 1942 and an average of 52,386,000 head for the period 1932–41. This total appeared to be about a maximum of numbers of sheep for the United States since almost equal numbers were reported in the past in 1884, 1900 and 1930. After reaching a low point of 32,-597,000 in 1923, however, there was a fairly steady increase in numbers.

The 1943 lamb crop was estimated at 31,100,000 head which was about 1,500,000 head less than in 1942 and the lowest since 1939. The total sheep and lamb production of 1943 was therefore 86,189,000 compared with 87,200,000 in 1942. This decrease reflected the labour shortage in the important sheep states since weather and feed conditions were not much different in the two years.

Requirements for lamb and mutton were estimated to be 965,-

000,000 lb., or about 5.2 lb. per capita. This amount was produced in 1943 and the goal for 1944 was about 70,000,000 lb. below that amount. The War Food administration suggested goals which would maintain the total number of sheep at the level expected on Jan. 1, 1944, which was near the average of 1938–43, 52,000,000 head. (*See* also LIVESTOCK; MEAT; WOOL.)

(J. C. Ms.)

Shigemitsu, Mamoru

(1887–), Japanese statesman, was born July 29 in Oita-ken. He received his law degree from Tokyo Imperial university. He entered the foreign service in 1911 and held minor diplomatic posts in Germany, England and the United States, 1911–18. He was a member of the Japanese delegation at the Paris peace conference, 1919, and was associated with the Japanese foreign office, 1920–24. Shigemitsu was sent abroad again, serving in China, 1925, and Germany, 1927, and was minister plenipotentiary to China 1929–30. In 1932 he was hit by fragments of a bomb hurled by a Korean patriot at Shanghai and lost a leg. He was made vice minister of the foreign office, 1933, and was appointed ambassador to the U.S.S.R. in 1936. Two years later, he was named ambassador to England. In 1941, Tokyo ordered him to leave his British post and return home; he paid a "courtesy" visit to Washington on his way back to Japan. Two days after the Japanese attack on Pearl Harbor, Shigemitsu was appointed ambassador to the puppet regime at Nanking. In April 1943, Tojo reshuffled his cabinet and selected Shigemitsu as his foreign minister. Prior to Pearl Harbor, Shigemitsu was reported in favour of Japanese co-operation with Britain and the United States and was said to be highly critical of the ruling Japanese military clique.

＋ Shipbuilding.

United States statistics on shipbuilding for the merchant marine were available to the public, but for other nations they were discontinued for the duration. Some general information on naval building in the U.S. was released, but the publishing of detailed information as to numbers and types of ships was forbidden.

Up to Dec. 1, 1943, 1,691 sea-going commercial vessels of 17,217,525 deadweight tons were delivered by the shipyards of the United States, or at an average rate, for the 11 months, of five vessels a day. The total output of seagoing commercial vessels for 1943 would approximate 19,000,000 deadweight tons, or more than twice the record production of 1942 which was 8,088,732 deadweight tons. It was known that other nations were producing commercial vessels, but their total output for the year 1943, at best, was but a small percentage of the output of the United States.

The president's message to congress on Sept. 17, 1943, in speaking of the magnitude of naval building by the industry, made the following statement:

The number of fighting ships and auxiliaries of all kinds completed since May 1940, is 2,380, and 13,000 landing vessels.

In the 2½ years between Jan. 1, 1941, and July 1, 1943, the power plants built for installation in navy vessels had a horsepower equal to all the horsepower of all hydroelectric plants in the United States in Jan. 1941.

The completions of navy ships during the last six months were equal to completions in the entire year of 1942.

We have cut down the time required to build submarines by almost 50%.

Losses of world merchant tonnage, due to torpedoing by submarines, aircraft bombing, mines and other casualties were greatly reduced in 1943 as compared with 1942. Statistics were not available for publication as to losses by types, sizes or tonnage.

Substantially all of the shipyard and ship repair plant facilities in the United States for the construction of new vessels and for the repair of vessels which had been projected through 1942

were completed and in production. Several building yards, which were under construction in 1942 came into operation in the early part of 1943, and were building vessels of several classes.

Shipbuilding output in the United States of both merchant and naval vessels was in 1943 at about the maximum possible with the personnel, materials, machinery and equipment allocated to shipbuilding.

A new type of ship, the Victory ship of approximately the same deadweight tonnage, but of superior design and of higher speed than the Liberty ship, was developed during 1943, and the production of a large number of them before the end of 1944 was contemplated. The ships would be 4 to 6 knots faster than the Libertys and equipped with steam turbines instead of steam reciprocating engines installed in the Liberty type.

From Dec. 30, 1941, to Dec. 1, 1943, 1,662 EC-2 type Liberty ships were delivered. These vessels were of a standard design, and sizable contracts were awarded to each yard building them. By reason of the multiple production of ships of this type, the time from keel-laying to delivery was continually reduced from month to month. The first few vessels took over 200 days to build. The records for Sept. 1943 indicated that for 106 Liberty ships built in all yards, an average time from keel-laying to delivery was only 41½ days.

More than one-third of the merchant ships produced were vessels other than Liberties. These categories were divided between oil tankers, C-type ships for the long range program and other types such as special auxiliaries, coastal cargo ships, tankers and barges.

Synthetic and substitute materials were extensively developed during the war to take the place of standard materials used in peacetime. Among the substitutions were steel for copper, plywood in place of steel for the construction of small floating craft, plastics in place of aluminum, synthetic rubber and many other materials. Some of these substitutes, of course, might be discarded after World War II. Self-propelled and non-propelled vessels of re-enforced concrete were being built.

The advantages of multiple production were only to be obtained where large numbers of vessels of the same type were built. Most of the time-saving developments were expected to disappear in normal times when only a very limited number of vessels of the same type in every respect would be under construction at one time.

Employment in the industry in the United States continued to increase, and, for the construction and repair of vessels of all types and all sizes in 1943 approximated 1,500,000, with a probable equal number employed in allied industries engaged in the making of materials and in the building of equipment for incorporation in vessels.

The employment of women in the industry was accelerated during the year and in September approximated 9½%. In general the wage rate was the same for women as for men.

In Sept. 1943 (latest statistics available) the average hourly earning rate in the industry was $1.336, the highest wage rate prevailing in any of the durable goods industries, and the average weekly earnings in the industry during that month were $63.48, on a 47.8-hour week; the next closest rate being that for "aircraft engines" which was $61.14 on a 47.2-hour work week.

Shipbuilding became an inland as well as a seacoast industry. Many of the smaller shipyards of the U.S., not only on the seacoasts, but on the great rivers and on the Great Lakes, were participating extensively in the production of smaller vessels of many types for the war effort. (*See* also SHIPPING, MERCHANT MARINE.)

(H. G. S.)

Great Britain.—The most conspicuous feature of the shipbuilding year was the greatly increased number of fast ships built by the Allied countries. The increased success of the anti-submarine measures greatly reduced the losses, so that immediate delivery was not of such paramount importance and there was a reasonable reserve of slow ships for bulk cargoes. The construction of fast and specially designed ships had never been entirely abandoned, although for security reasons little publicity was given to it, and at the beginning of 1943 the British yards were building as many as they could without upsetting the balance of production. It was officially pointed out that it took 50% more time, material and labour to build a 15-knot ship than an 11-knotter of similar capacity.

In Britain some of the faster ships were built by individual shipowners under licence, the authorities maintaining very strict control over the design and all its features, but a considerable number were built by the government itself. Ships of extreme design, with speculative features or demanding priority material, were strongly discouraged.

The fast ships built to government order included meat ships, troop transports, etc., and these did excellent work, their design being usually a simplification of prewar practice. The latest type of which some details were officially released was a 3-deck fast cargo liner of 12,000 tons deadweight capacity and accommodation for 12 passengers, with excellent hull form for speed and seakindliness. She was fitted with excellent deck gear for handling cargo. The speed was unofficially estimated at comfortably over 15 knots. Some were propelled by double reduction geared turbines with watertube boilers burning oil fuel, while some were Diesel driven, the hull and general features being identical.

Builders in the British dominions were also turning to a faster type as their programs of standard ships were delivered. In Canada the new ships were akin to the American "Victory" type while the Australians were building a smaller and faster cargo vessel suitable for the coasting and Pacific island trade.

British shipbuilding was hampered by a most unfortunate increase in the number of labour disputes during 1943, resulting in a very large number of man-hours being lost both directly and through sectional disputes holding up the work of others. These strikes were practically all sectional and unofficial, against the advice of the workers' own unions and deliberately ignored the official measures which proved adequate for the settlement of practically every legitimate dispute. Many of the strikes were for the purpose of annulling disciplinary measures.

At the beginning of 1943 the average British shipyard worker's earnings were over 81% higher than they had been before the war, but in the late summer fresh demands for increased wages were lodged with the employers and discussed.

The proportion of women in the British yards increased and they proved capable of undertaking, with conspicuous success, a wide range of work. A great number of lads eagerly applied for apprenticeship. There was more dilution, and steady progress by agreement with the unions was made on the understanding that it was to be a war measure only in breaking down the rigid lines of demarcation.

Prefabrication and welding were employed more and more. The amount of welding was largely influenced by weather conditions but its use was increased sufficiently to alarm the riveters about the permanence of their position. Prefabrication was largely governed by the labour available. Several shipyards closed during the slump, and their machinery dispersed, were re-opened for prefabricated building.

It was officially announced that it had been agreed with the United States that, to a considerable extent, British yards should specialize in naval vessels and American in merchantmen.

Great attention was paid to the salvage of ships and their fittings and excellent work was done, keeping the repair side of the

TEEN-AGE BOYS were employed by some U.S. shipyards in 1943 not as trainees, but as full-time employees at standard wages

industry very busy. Improved organization of labour greatly reduced the waste while men are standing by for repair jobs, although it cannot be eliminated altogether.

Neutral Countries.—Although practically all the neutrals were endeavouring to build ships, the only ones of importance were Spain and Sweden. In the former country they were continuing the government program laid down in 1942, covering a wide range of types, but they had to face great difficulties with both material and labour, and ships urgently required meant the suspension of work on other ships. Swedish shipbuilding, although by far the most active, was handicapped by further German arrears in the delivery of steel plates and, after German threats to the country, by the mobilization of skilled men into the forces. Swedish shipbuilders and engineers were carrying out a great deal of experimental work for postwar types. Propellers with reversing blades were fitted in ships of unprecedented size and in view of the shortage of oil great progress was made with producer gas engines, although the most striking instance came from Denmark, where producer gas engines were put into a 3,000-ton ship.

Axis Countries.—In the axis and enemy-occupied countries, although definite information was difficult to obtain, progress appeared to have been slow in all cases in spite of the urgent need. Italy complained that her shipbuilding had been handicapped by Germany not delivering the coal and materials promised; after the armistice with Italy it was found that ships which had been described as being at sea were still far from completion. German shipbuilding appeared to have been almost entirely limited to submarines, destroyers and small naval types despite the shortage on their sea communications with Sweden and occupied territories. Danish shipbuilding had been forced almost exclusively into German work which finally so exasperated the workers that the sabotage campaign was directed largely against the shipyards. Similarly, the French had been able to obtain little material except for German work and the big Messageries Maritimes liner "Marechal Pétain," laid down in 1939, was still uncompleted in 1943. Japan had been making every effort to use the building resources of occupied territories and published huge programs of wooden auxiliaries and other small craft to relieve the full-powered steel ships with better ships built in the seized yards in Hongkong and the Netherlands Indies. (*See also* BUSINESS REVIEW.)
(F. C. Bo.)

Shipping, Merchant Marine.
United States.—The end of 1943 found United States shipping and shipbuilding industries in step with other phases of war production to meet the constantly increasing output necessary after the United States was plunged into war. Movement of men and war materials from the United States and importation of strategic raw materials made ocean transportation the most vital factor in victory for the United Nations.

Revision of the United States' shipping industry and creation of the United States Maritime commission followed the Merchant Marine act of 1936, stating that the United States should have a merchant marine adequate for both the national defense and development of its foreign and domestic commerce. Vessels were to be American owned, constructed and manned and were to be the best-equipped, safest and most suitable types.

Obsolescence in the merchant marine was the chief weakness found in an economic survey in 1937. To form a steadily expanding, modern and superior fleet, the maritime commission inaugurated a long-range construction program which called for the completion of 500 vessels during the next 10 years. Without this program as a basis, the commission shipyards could not have met the demands for increased construction at the outbreak of war in Europe in 1939.

Since facilities for manufacturing geared-turbine propulsion machinery for the C-types of the construction program were overloaded, the maritime commission adapted and adopted a design called the EC-2 emergency cargo vessel, known as the Liberty ship, as the basis of its wartime merchant fleet. These vessels were powered by triple-expansion reciprocating steam engines which could be built at many plants throughout the country. The standardized design of the ship and its parts was readily adapted to fast production because of prefabrication of large sections of the ship and extensive use of welding instead of riveting. It also permitted rapid training of workers.

Important accomplishment was reduction of the national average time to build a Liberty ship from 241.3 days in Jan. 1942 to 41.2 days in Sept. 1943.

When the commission made its survey in 1937 only 10 shipyards with 46 ways capable of producing ocean-going vessels over 400 ft. long were in operation. These facilities were enlarged and new shipyards built under the direction and financing of the commission. In late 1943 approximately 70 shipyards with more than 300 ways on the east, west and Gulf coasts and on the Great Lakes were building and repairing ships. Also, during 1943 approximately 1,500 factories in about 32 states employed almost a million persons to produce equipment and accessories.

Shortages of materials, machinery and trained manpower had to be met. A centralized purchasing plan helped to eliminate competitive buying on the part of shipyards and established control over distribution of parts to shipyards. In Oct. 1943 there were around 700,000 workers, 14% of whom were women, helping to build the U.S. merchant fleet. Approximately 90% of these inexperienced employees had to be trained for their jobs.

Early in the year the president directed that 8,000,000 dead-weight tons of shipping be built during 1942. This goal was exceeded with 8,089,732 dead-weight tons, consisting of 746 vessels delivered.

The output for 1943 was set at approximately 19,000,000 dead-weight tons. In mid-November the 24,000,000 dead-weight ton goal for the two years ending Dec. 31, 1943, had been met. By Dec. 1, 1943, 17,194,387 dead-weight tons, comprising 1,688 vessels, had been delivered to the maritime commission. This included 1,118 Liberty ships, 146 C-types, 215 tankers, 1 passenger-cargo vessel, 31 coastal-cargo vessels, 41 ocean-going tugs, 16 ore carriers, 97 special types and 23 barges.

Early in 1944 a part of the Liberty ship program was to be superseded by deliveries of another type of standardized cargo vessel, the Victory ship. It was faster and more efficient than the Liberty, making it much better for war service and a far better ship for peacetime trade competition.

Maintenance and repair of the vast merchant fleet was also an important phase of the over-all program. During the first six months of 1943 there were approximately 8,300 vessels of 1,000 gross tons or more repaired in the United States. This included keeping vessels in service, installing defense equipment and even returning to service ships that had been blown in half and sunk. As of June 30, 1943, more than 125,000 persons were employed in major ship repair yards around the coasts of the United States.

For every ship sliding down the ways an average complement of 42 merchant seamen was needed to carry on its operations. A systematic training program was organized following the Merchant Marine act of 1936. Its purpose was to formalize the training of marine officers and to maintain high standards of personnel and education.

Since 1891 American vessels had carried youthful American citizens as cadets in training to become merchant marine officers. Other officers were supplied, at the rate of about 200 a year, from state nautical schools.

In March 1938 the commission set up the United States Merchant Marine Cadet corps for training officers. Four months later the United States Maritime service was established and administration was placed with the coast guard, under rules and regulations made by the maritime commission.

In forming a course of study in 1939 the commission abstracted the best features of systems which other governments had found useful. Ship operators desired an extension of the cadet training system with higher standards for enrollees and more adequate training. Also needed was a plan to permit li-

APPRENTICE SEAMEN at a maritime training station in 1943, aboard a "training ship" on concrete. After the U.S.A. entered World War II, the U.S. maritime service introduced a 13-week course that was soon turning out thousands of trained sailors each year

DRILL in the use of life suits is required for apprentice seamen of the U.S. maritime service until they can slip into the suits within 30 seconds

DECK HANDS at a U.S. maritime training station undergoing basic training

LIFEBOAT PRACTICE at a U.S. maritime training station

censed officers to equip themselves for advancement.

Training facilities were enlarged and the program accelerated along with ship construction. The training system in 1943 included the merchant marine cadet corps, maritime service and state academies. For the duration, operation of the merchant fleet was delegated to the War Shipping administration. This included recruitment and training of personnel to sail the ships.

Merchant Marine Cadet Corps.—Training in the cadet corps covered a period of 18 months for duration of the war, lowered from the peacetime term of three years plus a year as cadet officer. The course was divided into (a) three months' preliminary training at Cadet Basic schools at Pass Christian, Miss., San Mateo, Calif. or the United States Merchant Marine academy at Kings Point, N.Y.; (b) at least six months aboard merchant ships; and (c) nine months' advanced training in academic courses at the Merchant Marine academy.

Maritime Service.—Eight training stations for unlicensed maritime personnel and for licensed officer candidates were operated by the maritime service. Four of these gave a three to six months' course for apprentice seamen in the deck, engine and steward departments. They were at Hoffman Island, N.Y., Sheepshead Bay, N.Y., St. Petersburg, Fla. and Avalon, Calif. Officer candidate schools were maintained at Fort Trumbull, New London, Conn. and Alameda, Calif. They were open to seamen with a minimum of 14 months' sea experience who wished to qualify for a third-assistant rating. Also, a number of upgrading schools for licensed and unlicensed personnel were maintained by maritime service.

State Academies.—Five state academies, in Bronx, N.Y., Philadelphia, Pa., San Francisco, Calif., Hyannis, Mass. and Castine, Me., had some 1,200 cadets enrolled during 1943. Practically all of these men would become maritime officers before the end of 1944.

Combined training in these schools made available to the merchant marine from 1938 to Sept. 1, 1943, 9,169 officers, of which 1,157 were from the cadet corps, 6,767 from maritime service and 1,245 from state academies. Also, 1,261 radio operators and 36,568 unlicensed seamen in all ratings were trained for the merchant marine. This made a total of 46,998 men.

Besides delivering men and war materials to battle shores, the United States merchant marine helped to maintain the flow of lend-lease goods to the Allies. From the time of passage of the Lend-Lease act in March 1941 until July 31, 1943, lend-lease goods and services to other Allied countries totalled $13,973,339,-000. As of June 1943 about 30% of the dry cargo space was given to these shipments. (*See also* SHIPBUILDING; WAR SHIPPING ADMINISTRATION.) (E. S. L.)

Great Britain.—Although there was no reason for complacency, the shipping situation during 1943 was considerably easier and the improvement was progressive. This was partly due to reduced sinkings by the enemy, partly to increased deliveries by the shipyards and partly to improved organization. On the financial side the reduced sinkings and the large number of submarines destroyed meant great relief in the expense of war risk insurance. All rates were greatly reduced, on some routes by as much as 75% and on a great many by between 50% and 60%.

The improved use and routing of ships by the Allied authorities was also striking. Far less time was lost through official orders and although there was still an uneconomical number of ballast voyages on the North Atlantic westward, greater use was made of returning army and navy supply ships for commercial cargo. Reciprocal arrangements to feed and supply Allied forces, for instance, the American forces, in the Pacific from Australia also led to a great saving in merchant tonnage.

The amount of tonnage used for feeding the British Isles was

reduced by intensive farming, but the sinking of specially designed refrigerated ships, and their diversion to other purpose was only partially overcome by dehydration and the transport of bacon and certain meats in slow tramp-type ships with small refrigerating plant and insulation confined to the blanket system on the sides and bulkheads of the lower holds only. I the temperature of these holds is lowered as much as possibl during loading, a small refrigerating machine is sufficient to keep 50,000 cu.ft. of bacon good for 20 days.

During the year the supply services to the forces in Nortl Africa, Sicily, Italy and Russia made conspicuously big demand on commercial tonnage, but the slow, tramp-type ships prove most useful and the losses in convoy were far less than migh have been expected. The re-opening of the Mediterranean route which immediately followed the axis defeat in North Africa and was made more secure by the collapse of Italy, was admitted by German official sources to be worth 2,000,000 tons of shipping to the Allies. The supply of munitions to Russia went on without intermission, although every White sea convoy expected to be attacked and in some cases the losses were considerable. As the year progressed a growing proportion of these munitions went through the Persian gulf for use on the southern and central fronts, while Russian ships carried large quantities from the United States to Vladivostok without molestation by the Japanese, although it was perfectly well known that they were for use against Japan's ally, Germany.

Co-operation between the Allies made most of the manning and other resources available. In the summer it was announced that between 150 and 200 American ships, their type varying with the needs of the moment, were being "bare-boat" chartered to Britain during 1943, and British crews were sent out for them. Both Britain and the United States continued to reinforce the smaller Allied fleets in order that their seamen might sail under their own flags. Norway received 20 American ships, for the duration of the war only, as well as some from Britain, while France, Belgium, Holland and Greece were similarly supplied, the type of ship varying with her war purposes and the crew which was to handle her. China also received tonnage and immediately put it to good use.

All the British dominions increased their merchant fleets by new construction or other means. The Canadian was the most conspicuous and the government announced its hope that the service would be permanent. They experienced considerable difficulty in manning the numerous ships built. As far as the ratings were concerned, the supply was excellent through well-managed training establishments, but the question of the officers was more difficult. A number were borrowed from the British reserve pool and in the meantime a number of ships were "bare-boated" to the United States and Britain. Australia used many of her ships for the coastal sea transport of raw materials, while South Africa maintained a number of ships, including prizes from the enemy, transporting supplies for her war factories.

Considering all things, the Allies' manning difficulties were remarkably few, mainly on account of excellent planning and the magnificent spirit of the great majority of the men. The supply of recruits was almost unlimited except from the occupied countries, where they had no chance of getting away. Very few volunteers were accepted without some form of pretraining, for which there was ample opportunity both in Britain and in the dominions. The efficiency of men already at sea was also improved by various training establishments; the firemen's schools had excellent results in reduction of the smoke which had given away the position of so many convoys and in the saving of fuel.

The most troublesome feature of the manning side was the shortage of marine engineers, especially those with the higher

THE "NORMANDIE," former French liner which had burned at her pier in the Hudson river and keeled over in Feb. 1942, was refloated 18 months later. The ship was divided into watertight compartments, from which water was removed by controlled pumping. Pumping began early in Aug. 1943, and by Aug. 9 the bow had been raised 41 ft. out of the water (above). It was turned over to the navy on even keel Oct. 27

certificates of competency. This shortage undoubtedly increased in spite of the numerous certificated men who returned to the sea from positions ashore. One reason for this was the difficulty of studying for technical certificates under the strain of war service, the same strain which accelerated the natural wastage of the older men, while the casualties among engineers were higher than among deck officers. Secondary matters of concern were the increase in tuberculosis among seamen, the normal difficulties of efficient ventilation at sea having been greatly increased by the necessity of blackout precautions, and a tendency for Asiatic seamen—Indian, Malay and Chinese—to cause trouble. That is recognized as being very largely due to the long periods away from home on war service.

There was a very gratifying increase in the proportion of torpedoed seamen who were saved: well over 80%. This was partly due to improvements in the build and equipment of lifeboats and life rafts, although it was realized that there was a danger of introducing so many useful fittings that there would be little room for the men. The officers' and seamen's organizations acted in close co-operation with the shipowners in putting life-saving suggestions before the government, and many were approved after test. Remarkable progress was made in the evolution of really practical distilling apparatus suitable for fitting into lifeboats, where thirst caused more terrible deaths than anything else. The authorities carefully tested numerous types; most of them proved unsuitable, either because they were too complicated or because they and their fuel weighed too much, but some gave remarkable results.

The number of lifeboats burned through oil or petrol from torpedoed tankers catching fire on the surface of the water led to the order that tankers should be fitted with steel lifeboats, in spite of certain disadvantages and the difficulties of supply. To overcome these, experiments were made with considerable success to evolve a fire-resisting wooden lifeboat. The design of life rafts was also greatly improved.

The merchant services of the Allies continued to work independently but in close co-operation with Britain and the United States. Generally speaking, their material decreased, for the allocations made did not completely cover the losses; but the morale of their crews kept up wonderfully and the successes in North Africa, with the strengthening of French feeling after the complete occupation of the country, greatly increased the number of French ships at the Allies' disposal. The men generally strongly preferred to serve in the Fighting French navy rather than in merchant ships.

Neutral Shipping.—As in World War I, Germany divided the neutrals into those who mattered and those who did not, but none was immune from attack and many ships were sunk on purely neutral voyages. During the year 1943 this applied even to Spain, whose sympathies were reckoned as being with the axis and whose ships had frequently been accused of unneutral service. These casualties greatly increased the supply problems of the country. The Swiss government acquired as many ships as possible, mostly at an exorbitant price, but had great difficulty with their polyglot crews. In South America the shortage of tonnage was felt most keenly in the Argentine, where great quantities of grain were used as fuel in lieu of imported coal. The Turkish fleet, which had been depleted by a number of small vessels sunk by the axis in the Black sea, was strengthened by several cargo ships transferred from Britain and by the acquisition of the crack Rumanian government liners "Bessarabia" and "Transylvania" which had been sheltering in Istanbul for a long period in spite of German efforts to get them transferred to the trooping service.

The Swedish merchant marine started the year with about 40% of its prewar tonnage lost by war risk and the great majority of its new ships laid up. Even before relations between Sweden and Germany became strained, and while the Germans were obtaining great benefit from Swedish concessions, the German press was complaining bitterly that Sweden was utterly selfish in building motorships for postwar work, which had to be laid up for lack of oil, instead of coal-burning steamers, which could be used on the German supply services. All through the year Swedish seamen of all grades, in spite of the generous bonus which they drew, showed a growing dislike for these services, which culminated in the summer in many of them refusing to sail to the North sea ports. They maintained that the Germans always gave them the most dangerous jobs and put them in the worst positions in the convoys, in order to preserve their own ships.

Early in the year Sweden was greatly handicapped by the sudden German withdrawal of her safe conduct to "permit ships," which had been allowed to pass through both belligerent blockades for the revictualling of Sweden from South America. The Germans maintained that any of these ships which were lost —their number was considerable—should be replaced from those in Allied hands and not from the ships in Swedish waters, but the Allies naturally did not agree. Considerable hardship was caused to Sweden until Berlin abandoned the attitude and the safe conducts were renewed.

Axis Shipping.—All the enemy powers suffered acutely from a shortage of shipping through attacks of Allied submarines, speedboats and aircraft, and the difficulty of maintaining the remaining ships in an efficient and seaworthy condition. In Germany there also appeared to be considerable disaffection among the crews, although such reports had to be accepted with reserve. There was no doubt that the Italian merchant seamen were strongly objecting to the Mediterranean supply services before the fall of Tunisia, and Germany had to send crews for the great majority of the French steamers which were seized when the south of France was occupied. Most of the remainder were manned by the Italian navy. The Japanese government was also forced to admit the acute shortage of shipping in the Pacific, in spite of every effort, and used this as an excuse to the disappointed public for the small quantity of loot from the occupied territories which had reached Japan.

British shipping finance was very worrying to the owners and of little interest to investors. With general requisitioning, each ship lost automatically reduced the receipts of the company and it was fully realized that with shipbuilding costs steadily rising, the money received from war risk insurance was less than ever adequate to replace casualties. In Germany, Italy and Spain government control made published accounts meaningless and in Sweden most profits were put aside for postwar development.

(F. C. Bo.)

Shipping Administration, War: *see* WAR SHIPPING ADMINISTRATION.

Shock Treatment: *see* PSYCHIATRY.

Shoe Industry.
The world-wide shortage of shoes in 1943 was estimated at 1,000,000,000 pairs due to war wear, waste, plant destruction and global economic pressures. Leather, the seventh essential material for warfare, was in acute shortage the world over for it was used in more than 400 items directly and indirectly associated with the war effort. Civilian restraint, by rationing, by regulation and by enforced denial reduced production in all lands below the point of physical needs.

The most serious shortage was in children's shoes, complicated by growth as well as wear, to the point of real menace to health. Priorities for production were expected to correct, in part, this serious situation in 1944—in England and the United States and

Comparative Statistics of U.S. Shoemaking, 1941, 1942 and 1943

Production of Shoes by Major Types (000's omitted)							
Year	Women's	Men's	Misses' and Children's	Youths' and Boys'	Infants'	All Other	Total
1941	184,915	120,519	47,912	19,159	28,175	82,417	483,097‡
1942	181,685	102,100	41,285	17,107	25,657	75,161	442,995‡
1943*† . . .	161,500	84,500	32,400	19,200	25,000	87,400	410,000‡

Estimated Consumption of Shoes by Major Types (000's omitted)							
1941	181,387	107,343	45,566	17,525	24,097	62,216	438,134‡
1942	192,798	103,155	43,732	18,339	27,274	79,941	465,239‡
1943*† . . .	179,500	91,300	41,000	20,800	27,000	102,400	462,000‡

Per Capita Production of Shoes by Major Types (Pairs per capita)							
1941	3.89	2.42	3.71	1.46	3.14	0.62	3.64‡
1942	3.60	2.02	3.40	1.36	2.81	0.56	3.31‡
1943*† . . .	3.17	1.65	2.98	1.49	2.74	0.65	3.03‡

Estimated per Capita Consumption of Shoes by Major Types (Pairs per capita)							
1941	3.66	2.15	3.63	1.35	2.87	0.47	3.30‡
1942	3.82	2.04	3.38	1.41	2.97	0.60	3.47‡
1943*† . . .	3.52	1.79	3.16	1.58	2.86	0.76	3.46‡

1941 Military	15,285,000 pairs
1942 Military	40,875,000 pairs
1943 Military	45,600,000 pairs

*Includes rationed and non-rationed types.
†Estimated.
‡Excludes shoes for military purposes.

countries not directly under fire.

In 1943 a Joint Leather commission, consisting of British, Canadian and U.S. experts, surveyed hide and skin resources in the Argentine, Uruguay and Brazil and collected world statistics on availability of raw stock supply. The Combined Raw Materials board, after receiving the report of the Footwear, Leather and Hides mission sent to England, established a flexible formula for the allocation of world leather on agreed ratio of civilian and military needs.

The percentage of foreign hides necessary to allocate to the countries on such a formula was dependent upon the estimated supply position, for the period in question, of the respective domestic markets and the exportable surplus from all other markets. For example, assuming that the following would be the number of hides available in any one year: United States domestic hides—20,000,000; United Kingdom domestic hides—2,000,000; foreign hides—10,000,000; total—32,000,000. Under a 3.5 to 1 ratio the United States would be entitled to about 25,000,000 hides, of which 5,000,000 would be imported, *i.e.*, 50% of the foreign hides.

International co-operation was expected to survive the cessation of hostilities for some indeterminate period of time because the leather shortage would continue until store and consumer stocks were replenished.

United States production of leather shoes decreased at an alarming rate in the closing months of 1943 due to reduction of manpower from 200,000 prewar to 177,000 workers in October. In the ten-month period of January to October, men's work shoes showed a percentage decline of 15% and men's dress shoes 20%; youths' and boys' increased 13.5%, misses' and children's shoes dropped 22% and infants' decreased 2%. Output of women's shoes was 12% less; part-leather and part-fabric shoes decreased 27% and all-fabric, non-rationed shoes showed an increase of 437% during this period.

Rationing of shoes in the United States, at the rate of one pair per person per period, started Feb. 9, 1943; second coupon June 15 and third coupon Nov. 1, 1943 to be valid indefinitely, was calculated to restrain consumer shoe buying. But the non-rationed field of shoemaking became an avenue of escape for manufacturers, merchants and public and showed an increase of 437% production, which would indicate that shoes made of materials other than leather could be marketed and worn as extra foot coverings despite their short wear-hour utility.

Rubber footwear was limited to stern necessity—requisitions being demanded for rubber boots and heavy work types. Civilian rain gear was in minimum supply and no tennis or gymnasium type shoes were manufactured for civilian sale. Some relief in children's rubber type footwear was expected in 1944. (*See* also LEATHER.) (A. D. AN.)

Shows. **Dogs.**—There was an increased demand in the United States in 1943 for pet and companion dogs. Breeding specimens were in demand, the top sale being that of a boxer for $7,500.

The highlight of the year was the extensive training of dogs as part of the armed forces, at five training camps. Approximately 1,500 dogs were sent out monthly from these camps for service on various battlefields throughout the world.

Dog shows suffered a decline of about 20% in number. The leading show was the New York city event in February—the Westminster Kennel club, with 2,351 dogs entered.

In field trials, the pointer Ariel captured the chief "bird dog" honour, placing first at the Grand Junction, Tenn., field trial. In retrievers, the same black labrador that won the championship in 1942, repeated—Shed of Arden. Registrations saw the merry little cocker still in top place on American Kennel club records with beagle, boston, scottie and wire following in order. The *American Field*, registering mostly "bird dogs," listed approximately 12,000 for the year, pointers leading. (W. JU.)

Horses.—All kinds of horse shows continued to be sharply restricted in 1943 due to several causes: limitations on public meetings; the use of buildings and grounds by the military for defense purposes; the absence of horse owners on war duties; and restrictions on shipment of horses by rail or truck. Race meets were an exception, most races being held as usual with large attendance. Most of the great state fairs were omitted or held on a very small scale because their grounds and buildings were being used by the government. New York and Ohio held no fairs, Wisconsin, Illinois, Indiana and Iowa held only small exhibitions without animals.

The International Livestock Exposition and Horse show at Chicago and the American Royal Livestock and Horse show at Kansas City were cancelled. The National Horse show at New York was reduced to a small exhibition of juniors conducted for war-activities benefit purposes. Some of the hunt clubs and riding societies held small meets for local benefits. Those in the vicinity of New York, Philadelphia and in Kentucky attracted considerable crowds. The absence of many leading horsemen in the services and on special war work left the exhibitions largely in the hands of the juniors. The declining place of the horse in modern warfare was mentioned as a factor in some circles. Notwithstanding the limitations on motoring, the light horse did not gain greatly in popularity. (J. C. MS.)

Livestock.—War exerted even more restrictions on the normal schedule of fairs and expositions, and their attendant livestock shows, in 1943 than in the preceding year. One of the few exceptions was Denver's National Western Stock show which annually opens the calendar year of American livestock shows in January. This exposition took place Jan. 16 to 23. It was one of the largest and most successful Denver shows ever held.

This show is famous for its large competitions featuring range-bred feeder cattle and purebred bulls of the beef breeds. It is an important source of supply for bulls required for range service as well as for quality beef calves that move, under normal conditions, from this event into corn belt feed lots each year.

The oldest livestock show in the United States is the South-

western Exposition and Fat Stock show, held annually in Ft. Worth, Texas, in March. In 1943 this showing was reduced to an exhibition of market animals only, stock that was moved to slaughter direct from the show.

With the exception of Denver, all of the national and sectional livestock expositions were confined to market animal shows only in 1943, in most instances because of a loss of show facilities.

These, in addition to Ft. Worth, were the Pacific International Livestock exposition in Portland; the American Royal Livestock show in Kansas City; and the Aksarben Livestock and Horse show in Omaha, all of which were confined to exhibitions of market stock.

Since it was founded in 1900, the largest livestock exposition in the United States, and the world, has been the International Livestock exposition, held annually, up to the war, during the first week of December at the Chicago stockyards. The international show was cancelled both in 1942 and 1943. The International amphitheatre, one of the country's most modern exhibition buildings, built as a permanent home for the exposition, was taken over by the army shortly after the outbreak of war.

In place of the International Livestock exposition, an exhibition of fat stock only was held during the same week the full exposition would have taken place. Known as the Chicago Market Fat Stock and Carlot competition, this show was held in sheds and pens of the Chicago market. Even thus restricted, a total entry of 4,558 head of steers, lambs and hogs was shown here in 1943 by stockmen from 14 states and Canada, comprising the largest livestock showing of the year. This show was held from Nov. 29 to Dec. 2.

Canada's two largest annual livestock shows, the Royal Winter fair and the Canadian National exhibition, both held in Toronto, were cancelled in 1943, as in 1942, because of the war. The largest Canadian show held in 1943 was the Calgary Exhibition and Stampede at Calgary, Alberta, July 5 to 10.

The purebred dairy cattle industry was even more restricted than was the beef cattle industry through the cancellation in 1943 of both the National Dairy show and the National Dairy Cattle congress, the two national shows that normally reflect progress in the dairy industry on a nation-wide basis. The National Dairy show is an itinerant exhibition and the National Dairy Cattle congress had been held each year in Waterloo, Iowa.

In 1943 all but five state fairs were cancelled. Two fairs, the Indiana and South Dakota state fairs were reduced to 4-H club exhibits. Of the series of midwest fairs, normally the country's largest, only one, the Wisconsin state fair, was held. This show took place in Milwaukee, Aug. 21 to 27. The other states holding fairs in 1943 were Kansas, Missouri, Nebraska and Oklahoma.

The only show of importance in Great Britain that survived the war was the annual Perth Show and Sale in Scotland, featuring Shorthorn and Aberdeen-Angus cattle, the two major breeds in Scotland. The 1943 show and sale was held in February. A six-day show, three days each were apportioned to the judging and sale of these two breeds.

The oldest livestock show in the world is the Highland Agricultural show of Scotland. After 108 years of continuous progress, it had not taken place since 1939; and the Royal Agricultural show of England was discontinued the same year, after 98 continuous years, because of the war.

South America's leading agricultural show, the Palermo, was again held in Buenos Aires in Aug. 1943. In 1943 the Palermo show was termed an international exhibition, as it is every fifth year. It occasionally draws entries from Great Britain and other South American countries on these fifth year renewals but owing to war conditions, exhibits in 1943 were confined to those from

Argentina and Uruguay. The Palermo is the world's largest showing of Shorthorn cattle and is also noted as an exhibition of Aberdeen-Angus and Hereford cattle, as well as sheep. Lesser emphasis is placed on the exhibits of Holstein-Friesians and Guernseys, the principal dairy breeds of the Argentine.   (W. E. O.)

Siam: *see* THAILAND.
Sierra Leone: *see* BRITISH WEST AFRICA.

Sikorski, Wladyslaw

(1881–1943), Polish politician and army officer, was born May 20 in Tyszowce, Narodovy, Austrian Galicia, and studied engineering at the Lwów University Technical college, graduating in 1908. One of the leaders of the prewar nationalist movement in Poland, he was trained in the Austrian army, 1905–06, commanded a regiment of the Polish legions in World War I and fought in the Polish-Russian conflict, 1920. After the assassination of Polish President Narutowicz, Gen. Sikorski, then chief of the general staff, was made premier and interior minister, 1922–23. He served as war minister, 1924–25, then returned to army service as commander of the Lwów military area. His dismissal from the army in 1928 was only one of the many personal changes effected by Marshal Pilsudski in the civil and army administrations after he took power. Sikorski subsequently went to France where he wrote extensively on political and military matters.

At the outbreak of the war with Germany in Sept. 1939, his request for an assignment to active service was refused. After the collapse of Poland, however, he became premier of the Polish government-in-exile; in addition, he was made commander in chief of the Polish legions that fought on battlegrounds in France, Britain and the middle east. Politically, he mended his fences with the Czechoslovak government-in-exile, but ran into a snag on the thorny issue of relations with Russia. On June 23, 1941, Gen. Sikorski secured an agreement with Moscow which invalidated the Soviet-German pact partitioning Poland in 1939. But dissatisfied with the conduct of anti-Russian elements within the Sikorski cabinet, the Russians ruptured diplomatic relations in April 1943. Sikorski's continued efforts to mend relations with the soviet union were interrupted by his death in a plane crash, July 4, while en route from Gibraltar to London.

Silk.

China, in 1943, began to lay plans for postwar development of its silk market, which the Chinese anticipated would replace the Japanese market as the chief source of supply for United States and European manufacturers. After the convention of United Nations representatives on food distribution, held in the United States in May and June, Chinese delegates conferred in Washington with government officials and former silk industry executives as to what the silk market might be after the war and how China could capture it. Also present were representatives of producers of synthetic fibres, for China did not ignore the fact that the return of silk to textile products was made questionable by the inroads of synthetic fibres during the war period. This was especially true of nylon in the manufacture of women's hosiery. It was the opinion of American silk people present that the silk demand after the war would be limited to a few special fabrics, such as neckwear for men, better dress fabrics, etc., but that the hosiery market would be almost completely taken over by the synthetic fibres. To what degree the Chinese could supply even the small potential demand depended upon the condition of their mulberry groves and filatures (reeling factories) after the defeat of the Japanese (since the major silk sections were in enemy hands) and upon the ability of the Chinese to adapt their reeling methods so as to reel silk of the size and standards of quality needed for American-type machin-

ery. The Chinese had customarily reeled very fine silk that could be used on the slower weaving and knitting machinery of European mills but was not efficient for high-speed American machinery operated by high-wage workers.

Statistical data about silk in 1943 was nil except for scattered reports from less important centres of production. In China, determined efforts were being made in Sinkiang to preserve silk raising by importation of mulberry saplings from the soviet union and 551 lb. of eggs from interior China. The 1943 yearly production was estimated at 347 short tons. In Yunnan province, 8,144,000 new mulberry trees were planted in the first six months of 1942 but results of that planting were not of use in 1943. However, approximately 59 piculs (1 picul equals 133⅓ lb.) of low-grade and 150 piculs of high-grade silk were produced by one of the larger operators in that area. The total investment of the sericultural industry of Yunnan province was estimated, in 1943, at $25,000,000 (national currency). In India, where the raising of silk for weaving into parachute cloth for the United Nations was started in 1941 and 1942, a new three-year program was started in 1943 for enlarging of mulberry groves at an expense of 1,250,000 rupees annually. A conditioning house was established at Kashmir, the centre of the silk industry in India, and it was said that 4,000 families in the Kashmir area derived their entire livelihood from the raising of silk. In addition, it provided a part-time industry for 50,000 more families. Indian industrialists also made inquiries in the United States for the names of the best engineering firms in the textile industry with the idea of modernizing weaving equipment in order to enter the postwar fabric markets in a substantial way.

In the near east, a silk-reeling plant was installed at Cyprus during 1943 to take over the reeling of a part of the cocoon crop of that island although it was said that the greater part of the expanding production would continue to go to Syria and Lebanon, where the weaving of silk fabrics was well established, for local consumption. Bulgaria was reported to have started a special two-year sericultural course during 1943 to encourage more modern methods of silkworm raising and cocoon reeling.

Even in the Belgian Congo, a silkworm gut industry, begun just prior to the war, reported in 1943 a production of 2,200,000 strands compared with 80,000 strands in 1940. Silkworm gut is a valuable commodity for use in surgical sutures.

In the western hemisphere, the several projects started in 1941 and 1942 to raise silk met with varying degrees of success in 1943. No further reports came from Venezuela although prospective American buyers of that country's cocoons for manufacture into spun silk stated that the price was entirely out of line with market prices on manufactured yarn. Brazilian efforts were moving slowly but in Dec. 1943, a New York department store had enough manufactured Brazilian silk fabrics to put them on display at a price of about $6.75 a yard. The same fabrics, according to reports from Rio de Janeiro in October, sold at $2.00 a yard there. Five weaving plants were making the all-silk fabric and the government was encouraging the production of silk by furnishing free mulberry plants to farmers in São Paulo and Minas Gerais.

In the United States, the War Production board conducted a country-wide campaign in 1943 to collect used silk stockings for manufacture into yarn for cartridge-bag cloth, utilized in holding the powder charges for big guns. This yarn was formerly made of pierced cocoons, but spinners discovered a process of using silk stockings for the same purpose. As a result, by Sept. 30, the salvage division of the War Production board announced a total of 49,000,000 pairs or 2,965,000 lb. of silk and nylon stockings had been received. The supply of silk hosiery was ample, it was understood, to cover powder-bag cloth requirements over the next three years. (*See* also RAYON AND OTHER SYNTHETIC FIBRES; TEXTILE INDUSTRY.) (I. L. BL.)

Silver.

Returns on world silver production were so few that it is impossible to make any estimate of the 1942 world total; such figures as were received will be included in the text discussion, without making any addition to the following table.

World Production of Silver
(In millions of fine ounces)

	1937	1938	1939	1940	1941
Canada	23.0	22.2	23 2	23.8	21.8
United States . . .	71.3	61.7	63 9	68.3	65.8
Mexico	84.7	81.0	75.9	82.6	78.4
Other N. America .	4 8	5.0	6.0	6.0	6.1
Peru	17.5	20.6	18.8	19.9	17.5
Bolivia	9.5	6.4	7.2	5.6	7.4
Other S. America .	4.2	4.3	4.7	5.3	5.6
Germany	6.8	7.0	7.0		
U.S.S.R.	7 2	8.0	7.0	22.0	?
Other Europe . . .	7.2	8.5	9.2		
Japan	12.6	13.0	14?	13?	?
Burma	6.2	5.9	6.2	7.0	?
Other Asia	1.9	2.4	1.7	3.4	?
Africa	5.2	5.7	4.7	4 6	?
Oceania	14.8	15.1	15.5	15.6	?
Total	277.7	267.7	265.1	277.0	265?

Following the ruling of the War Production board in Oct 1942, closing all gold and silver mines not having material outputs of essential base metals, the output for the year showed a decline from 72,336,029 oz. in 1941 to 56,090,855 oz. in 1942. Figures for 1943 were correspondingly low, with a total of 36,262,000 oz. through October, against 47,521,000 oz. in the same period of 1942. At this rate the total for the full year should be about 43,514,000.

The passage of the Greene act during 1943 made about 1,000,-000,000 oz. of U.S. treasury stocks of silver available for certain specified essential war uses. The so-called "free silver" in the treasury, that is, metal not held as backing for silver certificates issued, was available for war uses shortly after Dec. 1941, and was extensively used, but efforts to include monetized silver as well were blocked by the silver interests. The act finally passed seemed to be a move in the right direction, but apparently permitted uses were so restricted that the measure would have little real effectiveness; or at least one would judge this to be the case from the fact that to the end of the year purchase permits had been issued for only about 25,000,000 oz., of which about 3,000,-000 oz. went to Great Britain under lend-lease. The need for greater freedom of use for treasury silver was also confirmed by the fact that since both domestic output and imports declined, there was no surplus of supply of either, beyond the current demand for permitted uses.

Silver production in Canada in 1942 suffered much less decline

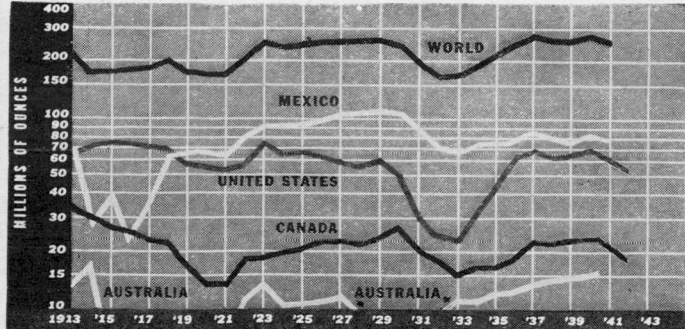

SILVER PRODUCTION of the major producing countries and of the world, as compiled by *The Mineral Industry*

than in the United States, dropping to 12,138,000 oz. in the first eight months of 1943, as compared with 13,482,000 oz. in the same period of 1942 The total for 1942 was 19,752,000 oz.

Through Aug. 1943, silver output in Peru totalled 10,850,000 oz., or at an average rate of 16,325,000 oz. for the year, as compared with 16,600,000 oz. in 1942 (*See* also MINERAL AND METAL PRODUCTION AND PRICES.) (G. A. Ro.)

Simeon II

(1937–   ), king of Bulgaria, was born June 16. On Aug 28, 1943, his father, Boris III, died under mysterious circumstances—his death being reported variously as due to a heart attack, to poisoning and to shooting—and the six-year-old crown prince ascended the throne. In September a regency was named, consisting of King Boris' brother Cyril, former war minister Lieut Gen. Nikola Michov and former premier Bogdan Filov, who had resigned with his cabinet shortly before

Sinclair, Sir Archibald

(1890–   ), British politician, was born Oct. 22 in London. Educated at Eton and Sandhurst, he joined the army in 1910, but later resigned to enter politics In 1922 he was elected to commons as a Liberal party member for Caithness and Sutherland. He was chief Liberal whip, 1930–31, and served as secretary of state for Scotland, 1931–32. After the party split over the issue of joining the Baldwin government, Sir Archibald became head of the Independent Liberals. Blunt and forthright, he thundered against Britain's hesitant stand on the Ethiopian issue and lashed Chamberlain's appeasement policy. When Churchill became premier in May 1940 he made Sir Archibald secretary of state for air. Early in 1942 he promised 1,000-plane raids over Germany, and he more than kept that promise. He told the commons in March 1943 that British air power had wrecked or damaged 2,000 nazi factories. In June Sir Archibald accompanied King George VI to the North African front.

Sinkiang

(CHINESE TURKESTAN) Largest and most remote of the provinces of China, bounded N. and W. by the soviet union, N. by Mongolia, S. by India and Tibet, E. by China. The name means New Dominion. Area, 705,769 sq.mi.; pop. (estimate of Chinese ministry of interior, 1936) 4,360,020. Capital Urumchi (Tihwa) (50,000) in the northern part of the region The two other largest towns, Kashgar (80,000) and Yarkand (75,000) are in the south. Religions: Confucianism, Taoism, Mohammedanism Governor in 1943 (since 1933) General Sheng Shih-tsai. Chinese constitute about 10% of the population, and there are 14 other ethnic groups, mostly Turki tribes. Sinkiang is in large part an arid country and the small proportion of land under cultivation is mostly located in oases and river valleys. Among the principal export products are wool, cotton, furs, skins, sheep, cattle and horses. Machinery and manufactured goods are purchased in the soviet union. Some 2,440 mi. of motor roads were built in Sinkiang during the decade 1932–42, but there were no railways in 1943. The air route from Chungking to Moscow lies across Sinkiang, with stops at Hami, on the eastern frontier of the province, and at Urumchi.

Sinkiang experienced an interesting shift of power and influence during 1943. After 1934 Russian political and economic influence had been very strong, although at no time was Chinese sovereignty abrogated And in 1943 this sovereignty became more genuine than it had been for many years. As a result of secret negotiations, the details of which were not fully known, there was a large-scale Russian political, economic and military evacuation from Sinkiang. Russian soldiers withdrew from their station at Hami, Russian economic equipment was dismantled and removed. Signs of the changing atmosphere were the widespread display of portraits of Chiang Kai-shek and Kuomintang slogans, the return of traffic to the left side of the road, as in China (it had been routed, Russian fashion, on the right side) and the opening of U.S. and British consulates in Urumchi, which had hitherto been regarded as an exclusive Russian sphere of influence. (W. H. Ch.)

Sister Kenny Treatment: *see* Infantile Paralysis.
Skating: *see* Ice Skating.

Skiing. All national ski championships of 1943 were called off because of the war, leaving the 1942 collection of champions in possession of the various titles and restricting the sport almost exclusively to the Atlantic coast.

If any unofficial title recognition was in order for 1943, the honours belonged to Arthur Devlin. The 20-year-old Syracuse university freshman dominated the eastern, jumping until the time he became an army air cadet midway in the season. Devlin's performances, which included second place in the 1942 national championship, brought him recognition as the United States' outstanding native-born ski-jumper. He started the 1943 season by winning the downhill and 40-metre jumping events of Lake Placid's 22nd annual collegiate meet. He set a meet record of 136 ft. on the 40-metre hill—called the Olympic jump. He also defeated Sergeant-Pilot Ola Aangesen, the 1942 national champion, with a jump of 206 ft. in an exhibition at Lake Placid's long hill. Just before going into the armed service, Devlin won the President Roosevelt trophy at Bear Mountain, N.Y., with a jump of 153 ft. The Roosevelt trophy meet revealed poignantly the influence of the war and gas rationing upon ski-meet attendance.

In 1942 a crowd of 19,500 attended the Bear Mountain classic; in 1943 the crowd numbered 1,500.

The University of New Hampshire won the 34th Dartmouth Outing club carnival, combined with the Senior Intercollegiate Ski union championships. New Hampshire scored 567.5 points to 562.5 for the host school. The defeat for Dartmouth in the Intercollegiate union championships was its first since 1935. Individually, Bill Distin of Dartmouth was the meet's standout with victories in the downhill and cross-country and seconds in the slalom and jump.

Skiing's main tragedy of 1943 came late in the season when John Neal, 17-year-old Lake Placid skier, died of injuries received in a fall. Neal won the Washington birthday jump at Lake Placid.

Weather and transportation problems forced cancellation of almost all competitive skiing in other sectors of the country. Late in 1943 the Norge Ski club of Chicago made plans for a mild revival of midwest ski jumping by scheduling an exhibition tournament at Wrigley field, home of the Chicago Cubs of the National Baseball league. (M. P. W.)

Skin Diseases: *see* Dermatology.

Slate. The production of dimension slate in the United States showed a marked decrease in 1942, dropping 41% to 107,030 short tons, while ground material increased 11% to 483,740 tons, a total of 590,770 tons, valued at $6,360,223. The heaviest drops were in roofing slate (49%) and billiard table tops (31%), while electrical slate and ground slate each increased 10%. (G. A. Ro.)

Slemp, Campbell Bascom (1870–1943), U.S. politician, was born Sept. 4 in Turkey

Cove, Va. He was graduated from the Virginia Military institute, 1891, and studied law at the University of Virginia. After a period of teaching mathematics and practising law, he entered the business world and was president of the Slemp Coal company and other large corporations. He made his debut in politics in 1905, when he was named chairman of the Virginia Republican State Committee of Virginia, and rapidly became a G.O.P. power in the south. In 1907 he was elected to the United States house of representatives to fill the unexpired term of his father, who had died, and was re-elected during a 14-year period running from 1909 to 1923. During the 1920 presidential campaign, Slemp was leader of the Harding drive to crack the Democrats of the solid south. From 1923 to 1925, he was secretary to President Coolidge, acting as the president's conciliator before congress, and helped him win the Republican nomination in 1924. In 1928 Slemp supported Hoover, but the setting of the Republican sun during the depression years led Slemp to resign as chairman of the party's committee in Virginia and he never regained the limelight as a political figure. He died of a heart ailment in Knoxville, Tenn., Aug. 7.

Slovakia. A nominally independent republic in Central Europe, a part of Czechoslovakia until its secession, with German help, in March 1939, after which it placed itself under German protection. Area 14,848 sq.mi.; pop. 2,800,000, of whom the great majority are Slovaks, a Slav people closely akin racially and linguistically to the Czechs. The majority are Roman Catholics, but there is a considerable Protestant minority. Capital, Bratislava (132,852); chief cities: Trnava (24,000); Nitra (21,250). President (1943): Msgr. Joseph Tiso; premier, Dr. Bela Tuka.

History.—In 1943 the clerical fascist regime in Slovakia continued in closest collaboration with Germany, shaping its policy entirely after the nazi model. But many Slovaks protested against the anti-democratic and anti-Czech policy of the Slovak government and worked actively for the re-establishment of the Czechoslovak republic.

Leading Slovaks participated in the Czechoslovak government established in England under Dr. Eduard Beneš.

The clerical fascist regime in Slovakia perfected during 1943 its anti-Semitic legislation according to the nazi model. Minister of the interior Sano Mach declared in a speech on Feb. 8 that all Jews would be deported to eastern Poland. At that time it was estimated that only 20,000 of the original 90,000 Jews were still left in Slovakia.

The Slovak Protestants under Dr. Samuel Osusky, bishop of the Slovak Evangelical church, petitioned the government on April 17 to recall the Slovak division from the Russian front. It was later reported that large parts of the Slovak troops had been recalled or had joined the Russians. (*See* also Bohemia and Moravia; Czechoslovakia.) (H. Ko.)

Smith College. An institution of higher education for women at Northampton, Mass. In 1943–44 the college continued emphasis on the humanities, history, art and languages, with interest in science and mathematics increasing. Beginning in 1943, students were offered a choice of graduation in four years or in three years if they chose to attend two summer sessions. During the summer vacation of 1943 the majority not thus accelerating their studies assisted the war by work on farms or in industry. Extracurricular activity in first aid, home nursing, nutrition, etc., continued. WAVES continued their training program on the campus. For statistics of enrolment, faculty, library volumes, etc., *see* Universities and Colleges. (H. F. D.)

Smithsonian Institution.

The institution was founded in 1846 through the bequest of James Smithson, an English scientist, "for the increase and diffusion of knowledge among men." The governing body is the board of regents, comprising the chief justice, the vice-president, three senators, three representatives, and six eminent private citizens; the executive officer, the secretary, Dr. Charles Greeley Abbot. The institution administers six government bureaus that grew directly out of its early activities, and also the Freer Gallery of Art; the National Gallery of Art is a bureau of the institution but is administered by a separate board of trustees.

With the United States at war, the institution devoted itself mainly to aiding with its specialized knowledge the army, navy and other war agencies. Technical information in the fields of geography, anthropology, biology, geology and engineering, and laboratory investigations of special problems were involved. Exceedingly effective, and greatly in demand by the army, the navy, the universities and the public, was the new series of pamphlets entitled "War Background Studies." Most of these authoritative papers deal with the geography, peoples and resources of the regions penetrated by the war. Others treat of the evolution of nations, the natural-history background of camouflage, and the poisonous reptiles of the world. Sixteen of these publications were printed, and the total distribution covering the year 1943 exceeded 150,000.

In co-operation with three other scientific agencies, and with moderate financial support from foundations, the institution took part in establishing the Ethnogeographic board, a nongovernmental agency set up to act as a clearinghouse for technical information within its scope requested by the army, navy and war agencies. The institution gave office space and compensation of the director, and also assigned to it the service of three members of the institution's permanent staff. This board was in position to obtain spot information in widely divergent fields to meet the constant and urgent calls of the armed services. Thousands of such inquiries were quickly and satisfactorily answered by immediate reference to the host of well-informed experts with whom the board had contacts. It also furnished at the request of the army and navy extended reports by experts on strategic areas.

As the repository of nearly 18,000,000 specimens of national value, present and for the future, the institution, of course, continued their care and the care of the buildings. To guard against loss by air raids, a selection of the most valuable irreplaceable specimens was removed to a distant repository where they are under guard.

The Astrophysical observatory maintains its three solar observing stations on distant desert mountains, to keep unbroken its unique record of the variation of the radiation emitted by the sun, on which all life and weather depends. Much progress has been made in the study of the relations of solar variation and weather. At Washington the laboratories of the observatory were mainly occupied with special war problems.

The art treasures of the National Gallery of Art were greatly augmented by gifts during 1943, including the Widener, Dale, and Rosenwald collections. The gallery gave Sunday evening musical concerts, lectures and accompanied tours for service men and women and their friends. The Zoological park, National museum and National Gallery of Art were visited in the fiscal year ending June 30, 1943, by 1,974,500; 1,355,269; and 1,508,081 persons, respectively. Of these visitors approximately one-fourth represented the armed services. (C. G. A.)

Soap, Perfumery and Cosmetics.

Progress of the war had a direct effect on all three of these industries in 1943, primarily on the distributive side. Early in 1943 the U.S. public was permitted to believe that short supply of fats for munitions might necessitate the rationing of soaps. There followed inevitably a consumer "run" on the retail market particularly for kitchen and laundry soaps.

But soap rationing did not materialize and as householders stocked themselves ahead, the run was dissipated so that by the end of 1943 the situation was about normal.

The main distributive outlet for this class of soaps was, of course, the grocery trade. Equally with all other retail business the grocery trade felt the increasing scarcity of consumer goods. And, again like all other tradesmen, grocers looked around outside their accepted field, for lines of goods with which to augment their dwindling stocks.

Toilet soaps, cosmetics and perfumes found much favour in the grocers' eyes and appeared on grocery shelves to a hitherto unequalled extent.

However, in general those cosmetics and perfumes which appeared in the grocery stores were not established lines save only as these might find their way into the grocery stores through obscure channels.

Established cosmetics and perfume manufacturers on the one hand would not willingly jeopardize the good will of their normal distributors (usually the drug, department and chain stores) by seeking this unconventional outlet; and, on the other hand, because of the restrictions on sales volume imposed by continued government limitations of raw materials and supplies, were in no position to open new accounts.

A further factor in this situation was the greatly expanded demand for all kinds of luxury goods resulting from the expansion of consumer buying power and the contraction of civilian goods markets.

Although alcohol continued in short supply, manufacturers of cosmetics and perfumes continued as in 1942 to promote perfumes rather than cosmetics, since in the overall perfumes presented fewer production problems than cosmetics. The solid perfumes which appeared in 1942 made little market headway in 1943 since they shared to a large extent the production difficulties of cosmetics.

The end of the campaign in North Africa and the invasion of Italy, notably the Sicilian campaign, while having had an immediate effect on prices of African and Italian essential oils and other perfume materials, had not by the end of 1943 produced any substantial increase in supplies from these sources although it was, of course, to be expected that such increases must ultimately appear. (H. T.)

Soapstone: see TALC.

Soccer.

The Brooklyn Hispano soccer club scored a "double" in major soccer play during 1943, winning the American league championship and the national open cup title. The Brooklyn team won the open crown, 4 to 3, over the Morgan-Strasser club of Morgan, Pa., after its first game with the western champions had ended in a 2–2 tie. The Morgan-Strassers won the national amateur championship, defeating Santa Maria of the Baltimore Knights of Columbus in the final.

The Vikings of Chicago won the International league, while the Milwaukee Falks captured the Midwest cup. Maccabi A.C. won both the Eastern league title and the Junior cup of the New York State Football association. The Senior cup of the N.Y. Football association went to Eintracht A.C. The Philadelphia Americans won the Lewis cup, while the Celtic Circles gained the Dr. G. R. Manning cup and the Jewish All-Stars won the Meyer Levine cup. (M. P. W.)

Socialism.
The year 1943 saw no international reorganization of socialist forces and while socialist parties in various countries made encouraging gains there was no emergence of organized socialism as the moulder of the coming peace.

United States.—The Socialist party reiterated its desire to further the building of some such mass party as the Canadian Co-operative Commonwealth federation. It declared its intention, despite the increasing difficulties of getting on the ballot in many states, to run a presidential ticket in 1944, with or without allies. In off-year elections Jasper McLevy was re-elected mayor of Bridgeport, Conn., as the candidate of the Connecticut Socialist party which is not affiliated with the national organization. Reading, Pa., Socialists elected J. Henry Stump, a former mayor, to that office, and voted to reaffiliate with the national party with which they had previously co-operated in elections. A member of the Socialist Democratic federation—to be distinguished from the Socialist party—Gertrude Weil Klein, actively connected with the Amalgamated Clothing Workers, was re-elected to the council from the Bronx with the endorsement of the American Labor party.

The most important socialist developments during the year occurred in nations included in the British Commonwealth of Nations.

Australia.—The socialistic Australian Labour party in Aug. 1943 scored an impressive victory by electing 49 representatives to parliament, an increase of 13 over its previous representation and almost double the number of the three opposition parties combined. It also was to have 22 of 36 seats in the senate by July 1944. John Curtin remained as prime minister and interpreted the vote as a mandate against a coalition cabinet. The ministry of postwar reconstruction in his government, established at the end of 1942, set up several commissions during 1943 to plan for industrial and rural reconstruction. Brief dispatches of Dec. 18, 1943, reported that the triennial conference of the party had approved a new policy by the government which was described as a sharp break "with the long-standing tendency of labour towards isolationism and exclusionism."

New Zealand.—In Sept. 1943 the Labour party government under Prime Minister Peter Fraser and Vice-Premier Walter Nash (well known in the U.S. as minister to Washington) was returned to power with a clear, though reduced majority in parliament. The Communists supported it despite opposition to a number of its policies. As in Australia, the Labour party refused to form a coalition government on the ground that it had won endorsement from the people. In November the party representatives urged a program of vacations with pay for all workers, equal pay for equal work, the establishment of a minimum family income and greater socialization of industry. In the previous month the war cabinet had approved a ten-year plan for increasing the national hydroelectric organization.

Canada.—The swing toward the Co-operative Commonwealth federation, first noted in 1942, was emphasized by the success of the party in the Ontario provincial elections of 1943, when it increased its representation in the legislature from 0 to 34 as against 38 members for the Progressive-Conservative party and 15 for the Liberals. The C.C.F. was strongly backed by labour and the farmers, but was not dominated to the degree of the British Labour party by the bloc voting of big unions. It was a socialist party in philosophy and campaigned on the basis of need of "social and economic planning on a bold and comprehensive scale." The party also won two by-elections for the federal parliament, and was endorsed at the September convention of the Canadian Congress of Labour as "the political arm of labour."

Great Britain.—There was no marked change in the position,

policy or standing of the British Labour party. It continued to be represented in the Churchill cabinet. The party conference in June 1943 voted by a bigger margin than the previous year to continue the electoral truce and to support the Beveridge plan. Once more it voted (by a card vote of 1,951,000 to 721,000) against the affiliation of the British Communist party. George Ridley, editor of the *Railway Service Journal*, was elected chairman of the party and Arthur Greenwood, acting leader of the Parliamentary Labour party, treasurer over the home secretary Herbert Morrison. Morrison was also rebuffed when, in the late fall, the party executives dissociated the party from his action in releasing Sir Oswald Mosley on the score of ill-health from the prison in which he had been confined without charges and without trial under an emergency war act. The leftist Independent Labour party continued to have an influence beyond its parliamentary strength. The new Common Wealth party Socialist but not Marxist, not bound by an electoral truce, made some progress.

The Trade Union congress at Southport, in the fall of the year, pledged itself to fight for a minimum of "four decencies" —in jobs, homes, social security, and educational opportunity for all British children.

Switzerland.—In the only parliamentary elections held on the European continent, the Social Democratic party, advocating more social legislation, increased its representation in the national council (parliament) from 45 to 56 seats out of a total of 194, thus becoming the largest single party. It renewed its campaign in the federal council of 7.

Sweden.—The coalition government, predominantly Social Democratic, while continuing its policy of neutrality, felt able to give active help to refugees, to oppose many nazi demands, and to refuse longer to permit transit of war materials and furloughed soldiers between Germany and Norway via Sweden. It proposed closer co-operation after the war with other northern countries and Russia, and in late September restored full privileges to the communist paper, barred from the mails since the Russo-Finnish War of 1939–40.

Finland.—In February, President Risto Ryti, following his re-election, asked the Social Democratic leader and speaker of parliament, V. Hakkila, to form a coalition cabinet. He failed because of the non-co-operation of the Agrarians, but Socialists accepted representation in the cabinet that was formed. In late September, V. A. Tanner, Social Democratic finance minister, urged an "honourable permanent peace" with Russia, but in December Stockholm dispatches indicated a break in negotiations because of Stalin's insistence on unconditional surrender.

Denmark.—In occupied Denmark Social Democrats were active in the stiffened opposition to nazi rule both before and after the nazi declaration of martial law and the great anti-German demonstrations of Aug. 1943. Social Democrats had previously terminated all connection with the Danish government, and in Denmark as in other parts of occupied Europe were driven into underground activity.

Italy.—Following the fall of Mussolini there was a surprising public manifestation of socialist strength. Socialists were co-operating with other democratic forces in demanding a more complete purge of fascism and the abdication of the house of Savoy.

France.—French Socialists were represented in the provisional consultative assembly meeting in November in Algiers. In occupied France they succeeded in underground publication and distribution of anti-nazi literature. Leon Blum and other prominent French Socialists were presumably held prisoners in Germany to which they were removed in the spring of 1943.

Latin America.—In the Latin-American countries there were no important changes in the socialist position and policies. In Argentina Socialists continued their agitation for the restoration of civil liberties and parliamentary democracy, both before and after the army coup d'état of June 1943. In Chile, Socialists remained in the Democratic Alliance and held cabinet posts although in the fall they precipitated a parliamentary fight with some of their allies by urging an emergency bill establishing drastic controls over private capital. (*See* also COMMUNISM; LABOUR PARTY.)   (H. W. L.; N. T.)

Socialist Soviet Republics: *see* UNION OF SOVIET SOCIALIST REPUBLICS.

Social Security.
As in other fields of economic activity, the effects of a country at war were felt in the U.S. in every phase of the social security program during 1943. Applications for the various social insurance and public assistance programs decreased drastically, while the reserves of the two social insurance plans—unemployment and old age insurance— were greatly augmented. Under both systems, however, the insured population and the future benefit liabilities increased as more people were drawn into industry at higher wages.

The year 1943 witnessed increasing public interest in social security, mainly due to the introduction of companion congressional bills for a co-ordinated federal social insurance program providing benefits for unemployment, old age, survivors', permanent disability, temporary illness, maternity and death. Sponsored by Senators Robert F. Wagner of New York and James E. Murray of Montana and Representative John P. Dingell of Michigan, the measures would greatly extend the covered population and provide protection for the families of the insured. Despite the increasing discussion, no major social security changes were enacted in congress during 1943. Certain seamen were brought under the Social Security act and an attempt was made to postpone again the scheduled increase in the old age insurance contributions from 1% to 2% each by employers and workers. By the end of 1943, the final action on again freezing

the rates for 1944 had not been taken. In the state unemployment insurance laws, however, there were a number of amendments, many of them providing increases in the upper levels of benefits and in their duration.

At the end of 1943, the status of the various social security programs was as follows:

National System of Old Age and Survivors' Insurance.—At the end of June 1943, estimates placed the number of persons with account numbers under this system at 66,400,000, or 63.2% of the population 14 years and over, as compared with 48.7% in 1940. In the fiscal year ending June 30, 1943, $149,304,000 were expended in benefits under this system. On that date, the total assets reached $4,268,296,000, an increase of about $1,000,000,-000 over the previous fiscal year.

At the end of Aug. 1943, the system had in force 826,591 benefits valued at $15,058,517. Approximately 15% of these benefits were being held up for a month or more because the beneficiaries were earning $15 or more a month from employment covered by the system. While the August benefits in force grew from 626,170 in Aug. 1942, it was estimated that approximately 600,000 aged persons were eligible for old age insurance benefits but were not applying for them because they were working.

Of the 706,270 beneficiaries who were paid $13,174,563 during Aug. 1943, 296,643, or 42.0%, were persons 65 years of age and over granted annuities in their own right. Supplementary benefits to the wives and children of retired workers numbered 97,249, or 13.8% of the total. In addition, the August roll of beneficiaries included 40,554 widows who had attained age 65; 68,067 younger widows with minor children; 200,091 children age 16, or 18 if attending school, and 3,666 parents. The average payment to a retired worker during Aug. 1943 amounted to $23.19; that of their wives, to $12.34; children, $12.26; aged widows, $20.14; widows with children, $19.66, and parents, $13.09. Lump-sum payments of six times the primary benefits were also made during August on behalf of 10,201 deceased insured workers at a total cost of $1,416,280. These grants are made only when no eligible dependents survive.

Railroad Retirement System.—Under the special national retirement program instituted for the railroad workers, 161,169

THE BEVERIDGE PLAN was a principal issue in a parliamentary by-election of Bristol, England, Feb. 18, 1943. Spectators are shown pausing to look at a candidate's banner in the centre of the bombed city

benefits for $10,356,298 monthly were in force at the end of Aug. 1943. The largest number of grants, 83%, were paid to annuitants who became eligible under the Railroad Retirement act. These beneficiaries received an average of $66.16 in that month. A constantly decreasing number of persons formerly pensioned by the railroads were also protected by this program. In August, there were 23,770 such pensioners receiving an average of $59.08, as well as 3,467 survivor annuities averaging $31.86. Death-benefit annuities numbered 625 and averaged $35.55 while lump-sum death benefits averaging $362.27 were paid on behalf of 1,285 deceased insured persons. In the fiscal year 1942–43, benefits under this system totalled $130,465,000 and receipts amounted to $220,578,000. Assets on June 30, 1943, amounted to $194,896,000.

Unemployment Insurance.—Unlike the two systems described above, unemployment insurance is a federal-state function, with the states and territories administering the programs. The 51 state and territorial plans expended $345,514,909 in benefits during 1942, approximately the same amount as in 1941. While the number of persons who received first payments in 49 jurisdictions decreased from 3,311,386 in 1941 to 2,680,153 in 1942, the average weekly total unemployment benefit rose from $11.06 to $12.66 and the average annual payment from $101.74 to $128.92 between 1941 and 1942. The 1942 average annual payment was $27.18 above that of 1941, $28.77 above 1940, and $44.68 above 1939. The higher payments of 1942 reflected both the higher wages prevailing during 1941 and the liberalization of benefits and their duration. Improvement was also revealed by the decreasing number of states with low weekly benefits. Thus in 1941, 24 jurisdictions paid average total-unemployment benefits below $10 and 10 jurisdictions below $8 while the totals for 1942 were 17 and 2 jurisdictions, respectively. The rate of those who exhausted benefits before re-employment, reported by 47 jurisdictions, also fell somewhat, from 46.7% in 1941 to 40.2% in 1942. The 1942 exhaustions ranged from 16.3% in Alaska to 66.0% in Louisiana. For the country as a whole, benefits were paid for an average of 9.6 weeks of unemployment.

During the first eight months of 1943, unemployed workers received $64,247,329 or 77.3% less than in the corresponding period of 1942. In Aug. 1943, the average weekly number of beneficiaries, 88,848, represented 83.6% less than in the same month of 1942. At the end of Aug. 1943, the funds available for benefits rose to $4,337,308,137 for all the states and territories.

Railroad Unemployment Insurance.—In Aug. 1943, the special program for railroad workers provided 1,565 payments covering 2-week compensable periods. These payments amounted to $40,342 for the month, less than one-fifth the amount spent in Aug. 1942. On Aug. 31, 1943, there was a balance of $382,737,000 in the program's reserve.

National Employment Service.—The employment service, nationalized in Dec. 1941, and transferred to the War Manpower commission in 1942 placed 6,071,329 persons in nonagricultural jobs during the first 8 months of 1943, an increase of 38.9% over the same period in 1942.

Public Assistance.—Though not as drastic as in unemployment insurance, reductions in beneficiaries were recorded in all types of public assistance—old age pensions, aid to the blind, aid to dependent children and general relief. The first three plans operated on a federal-state basis; for the fourth, the states received no federal aid. The greatest decrease was, naturally, in general relief, where the 312,000 cases in Aug. 1943, represented a decrease of 43.3% from Aug. 1942. For the same month, there was a drop of about 23.5% in the number of children aided as compared with 1942. The decreases in the number of blind and of aged persons aided—2.5% and 3.9% respectively—reversed

the steady accretion in these rolls for many years. In the month of Aug. 1943, 2,163,954 aged persons received assistance amounting to $55,717,491, or an average of $25.75 per person. Average pensions of $27.55 were paid to 76,980 blind persons, who received $2,120,775 during that month. Aid to dependent children averaged $39.32 per family for the 711,776 children in 290,822 families aided while the general assistance average was $25.88 per case during August. The monthly average grant for the blind and for those on relief rose by less than $2 between Aug. 1942, and Aug. 1943, but the averages for the aged and the dependent children increased by $3.50 and $4.80, respectively. (*See* also LAW; RELIEF.)   (A. BM.)

Great Britain.—The report on social insurance and allied services submitted to the government by Sir William Beveridge in Nov. 1942, aroused exceptional public interest. In Feb. 1943, a debate was initiated in the house of commons when the then lord president of the council (Sir John Anderson) on behalf of the government accepted the general lines of development of the social services laid down in the report, which he described as a monumental work of great ingenuity, and paid tribute to its author and the high idealism which had inspired his work. Considerable pressure was put on the government by members of all parties to take immediate steps to appoint a minister of social security, but while accepting in principle the recommendations of the report, including the eventual establishment of a ministry of social security, the government at this stage preferred to proceed by using the machinery of the various departments concerned, so that the government might work out a scheme which could be presented as draft legislation for the consideration of parliament. The amalgamation of the various government insurance and assistance schemes into a single unified system, also embracing other aspects of insurance, such as workmen's compensation and burial payments, so far confined to private enterprise, was obviously a task of great magnitude and complexity. Government spokesmen already reported satisfactory progress, and far-reaching developments were anticipated. The term "social security," prior to the Beveridge report almost unknown to the British vocabulary, became a household word.

Parallel with consideration of the Beveridge proposals the general tendency to enlarge the benefits and scope of the existing state insurance and assistance schemes continued.

Following the extension of the income limit from £250 to £420, and increases in rates of benefit which became payable in 1942 under the National Health Insurance, Contributory Pensions and Workmen's Compensation act of 1941, a further important step forward was the Pensions and Determination of Needs act, 1943, which became operative on Aug. 30.

The main provisions of this act were: the extension of the supplementary old age pension scheme administered by the assistance board, to include widows receiving a widows' contributory pension in which is included an allowance for dependent children; a modification in the treatment of capital assets in the assessment of need, and the permissive extension of this to the calculation of outdoor relief by the poor law authorities; also the statutory application of the principles of a "personal" as against a "household" means test to the assessment of need under the poor law. The effect of the first provision relating to widows with dependent children was twofold. Previous to the act such widows who had not reached the age of qualification for an old age pension, and who found the widows' pension insufficient for their needs, had to look for assistance to the local poor law authorities. Such assistance was now available in the form of a supplementary pension from the assistance board, a department of the central government. With this change another stage had been reached in the disintegration of the poor law. War conditions doubtless contributed to making a considerable number of widows self-supporting, and the number transferred from the local poor law authorities to the central authority of the assistance board had not been large, approximately 10,000, but the shift of administration from local to central government was significant In addition, approximately 12,000 pensions were in payment to widows who had not previously applied to the poor law. The second provision greatly modified the manner in which money and investments treated as capital assets were to be computed by the assistance board for the purposes of assessing supplementary pensions and also other allowances granted by the board. The effect of this was further to widen the scope of the supplementary pensions and other schemes administered by the assistance board, by bringing in persons who were previously excluded by the possession of capital, and also increasing the amount of allowances and supplementary pensions paid to those possessing capital sums which did not exclude them.

The act permitted the poor law authorities to adopt the same rules relating to capital in the assessment of need for their purposes. There were indications that most, if not all, of the authorities would accept these provisions wholly or in part.

The third provision applied solely to the poor law authorities and was statutory. This required such authorities to adopt the principles laid down in the Determination of Needs act, 1941, as they applied to applicants for supplementary pensions administered by the assistance board. Consequently all applicants for assistance whether to local funds through the medium of the poor law authorities or to central government funds through the medium of the assistance board were now subjected only to a "personal" test of need (this included wife or husband and dependents) and not to a "household" test which in the past had usually included all members of the household. This was a far-reaching change which for the first time applied uniform principles to the calculation of need to be met from public funds.

A further important advance was the Workmen's Compensation (Temporary Increases) bill which received its third reading in the house of commons on Nov. 5. This was the fourth measure of workmen's compensation introduced since the start of World War II, the cumulative effect of which had been to increase the scales of compensation by broadly 75%, and to spread payments more evenly according to individual needs. Introducing this bill the secretary of state for the home department (Herbert Morrison) stated that it was merely a temporary measure and an anticipation of long-term legislation which the government had under consideration as part of the Beveridge scheme.

The general trend toward a comprehensive system of social security was further exemplified by the increasing tendency of the public assistance committees which directly administered the poor law to effect changes of name. These changes were evidence of new conceptions in the administration of the old poor law, with which were still associated in the minds of possibly the majority of people the rigorous and unsympathetic methods of 100 years before. The changes were much more than the adoption of a fashionable nomenclature; active measures were being taken by many authorities to make their public assistance services effective social services in every sense of the term. Attention was being given to such matters as the special training of staff, the provision of bright and comfortable premises free from "institutional" atmosphere, and to increasing the range and efficiency of their health services.

The development of a comprehensive national health service such as envisaged in the Beveridge proposals was the subject of discussion by the British Medical association which had accepted the principles outlined by Beveridge. Beyond this nothing definite emerged, but there were indications that the organization of a national health service for all citizens covering all requirements might be the most difficult to implement of all the Beveridge proposals. (J. McAt.)

Social Service: *see* CHILD WELFARE; RELIEF; SOCIAL SECURITY.

Societies and Associations: *see* under specific name.

Sociology.

Although the impact of World War II had earlier been plainly apparent in the social sciences, 1943 bore witness to the struggle in unprecedented degree, and sociology was one of those most affected.

Chief among the changes brought by the war was the introduction of "area" courses in over 200 American colleges and universities. These were part of the army specialized training program, forming a major share of the subdivision called the foreign area and language study curriculum. The area portion of the FA and LSC accounted for about one-half of the time of the student-soldier, and after several changes in prescribed content arrived at the point where sociology and social anthropology, together with their social-psychological correlates and other social sciences, had much to do with the instruction offered. The FA and LSC men were to be equipped for service as aides to civilian affairs administrators (military government), liaison and intelligence personnel, examiners of war prisoners, and so on. Not only was working knowledge of at least one foreign language necessary, but in addition extensive acquaintance with the physical and human geography, recent political, economic and social development, and the basic features of the social processes, groups and institutions of the culture area or civilization concerned was demanded.

Teams of specialists—geographers, economists, political scientists, sociologists, social psychologists, etc.—were called together, in the larger schools, to provide the instructional staffs. In almost all instances knowledge of the languages concerned was asked of the area specialists, but in some instances—Japanese, for example—the requirement could not always be met. Nevertheless, it is fair to say that those offering area courses ordinarily had high linguistic competence as background of their knowledge of the peoples and countries studied.

This was particularly true of the sociologists, for, with the coming of World War II, social scientists of every variety were expelled from the totalitarian countries and many of them found final refuge in the United States. Among these social scientists the sociologists were perhaps the most prominent, for the traits which led them to break with academic orthodoxy were largely the same as those which kept them from identification with the rising totalitarianisms. Henssler, Gerth, Honigsheim and a host of other emigrés did yeoman service for the FA and LSC. True, there were many persons reared in the United States among the area staffs; only a part of the knowledge of Europe and other world regions came from former inhabitants of those regions—but that part was exceedingly helpful.

The products of the program would unquestionably have much to do with the various undergrounds, revolutionary movements in the axis and satellite countries, the checking of sabotage and espionage, the relief and re-education of civilians, the control of defeated and demobilized armed forces, and the general task of "winning the peace." Whereas the FA and LSC was designed for privates and non-commissioned officers, with a sprinkling of possible later entrants in officers' candidate schools, the civilian affairs training program (CATP), exemplified in the Charlottesville School of Military Government and the ten universities offering courses along parallel lines, was designed for commissioned officers only. Many of them were commissioned directly from civilian life as having skills and aptitudes fitting them for the administration of civilian affairs under military law: former legislators, executives, business men and technicians. Sociologists and other social scientists had a large part in the training of these men as well, although some of the officers' time was absorbed by topics, such as military law, which did not enter the work of the FA and LSC.

During the summer of 1943 the Social Science Research council began studies of the possibilities of "world regions" as instructional and research foci when peacetime higher learning was resumed. The American Council of Learned Societies turned its attention in a similar direction. Deans and presidents began to assess the worth of area studies as possible means of vitalizing language and social science instruction and of eliminating needless overlapping of courses. The regionalism long associated with the department of sociology of the University of North Carolina seemed to offer some methodological guidance, but its close linkage with problems peculiar to the south apparently made transference to other regions difficult. Human geography also provided a possible organizing strand, as did likewise social history and cultural anthropology. It was clear that when and if area studies were adapted to the purposes of peacetime instruction, sociology would be only one among the many social and humanistic sciences to be drawn upon.

Where the more strictly disciplinary aspects of sociology were concerned, the year was significant in only a few fields. Race relations received much attention, primarily because of the mounting antagonisms manifested in the "zoot suit" and Negro-white riots in Los Angeles and Detroit. Charles T. Johnson's *Patterns of Negro Segregation*, Howard W. Odum's *Race and Rumors of Race*, Alfred M. Lee and Norman D. Humphrey's *Race Riot*, Roi Ottley's *New World A-Coming*, and S. M. Strong's "Social Types in a Minority Group," *American Journal of Sociology* (March) were among the most significant publications. Studies of ideologies from the sociology of knowledge standpoint continued to appear; important were Hans Kelsen's *Society and Nature*, DeGré's *Society and Ideology*, and C. Wright Mill's "The Professional Ideology of Social Pathologists," *American Journal of Sociology* (Sept.). Social-psychological researches such as those conducted by Mass Observation in Britain and the American and British Institutes of Public Opinion continued; an informative account of Mass Observation activities appeared in the *American Journal of Sociology* (Jan.).

An important *Dictionary of Sociology*, edited by Henry Pratt Fairchild, was published; it served a useful purpose in recording contemporary sociological terminology and in pointing out the patterns future standardization must take.

The annual meeting of the American Sociological society, cancelled in 1942 because of transportation difficulties, was held in 1943. Rupert B. Vance of the University of North Carolina had been elected president by mail ballot in June, but under the new constitution took office only after the December meeting of the society. The president for 1943, George A. Lundberg of Bennington college, planned the December program, which was significant primarily for the attention paid to war and postwar topics. The regional sociological societies staged several meetings during the year. At one of them Adolph S. Tomars of City College of New York presented a highly significant paper on "Some Problems in the Sociologist's Use of Anthropology," published in the *American Sociological Review* (Dec.). It bears witness to the fact that the ever-closer drawing together of the two disciplines will be characterized by mutual adjustment which may eventually bring about a consolidation of social and cultural anthropology, sociology, and that variety of social psychology springing from the Cooley-Mead tradition.   (H. Bec.)

Sodium Carbonate. Production of natural sodium carbonates in the United States in 1942 increased by 3% over 1941, to 150,619 short tons, all from California. This was only about 4% of the amount of sodium carbonate produced by chemical methods from other products.   (G. A. Ro.)

Sodium Sulphate. The output of natural sodium sulphate in the United States in 1941 was 157,524 short tons, a reduction of 16%. During 1942 production capacity was increased to offset heavy reductions in imports from Europe. Production increased to 175,033 tons in 1942, an amount still 7% under the 1940 figure. Canadian production was 128,912 tons in 1942.   (G. A. Ro.)

Softball. U.S. army, Camp Bakersfield, Calif., won the national men's championship, while the national women's title went to the New Orleans Jax. Aside from the title tournament at Detroit, little championship softball was contested during 1943. The game, however, was immensely popular in army camps, and softball adherents point with pride to the fact that an army league was formed six days after United States troops had landed in Africa.   (M. P. W.)

Soil Erosion and Soil Conservation.

The year 1943 marked a definite trend among enlightened peoples of the world toward agricultural development based on conservation of land and water resources and higher standards of nutrition for human beings. Evidences of such an agricultural revolution were brought into the open for the first time by the United Nations Conference on Food and Agriculture which was held May 18–June 3 in the United States. Representatives of 44 participating nations recognized that soil erosion had in the past destroyed or severely damaged vast areas of the world's land. The conference agreed that if the food needs of all peoples were to be met in future times, the present and potential agricultural land of the planet must be adequately protected from erosion and from other serious damage by effective measures for conserving and rebuilding the fertility of the soil.

United States.—The national soil and water conservation program, started in 1933, advanced more rapidly in 1943 than in any previous year. Technicians of the soil conservation service, U.S. department of agriculture, helped farmers to install conservation-production measures on an additional 27,000,000 ac., with the double objective of increased production of war crops and minimum damage to the land. Of this area, 11,000,000 ac. were within soil conservation districts, and the remaining 16,000,000 ac., representing 365,000 farms, were outside the districts. This brought to 67,000,000 ac. the total area under soil and water conservation programs of varying intensity.

Conservative estimates showed the increased production of strategic crops in 1943 as a result of conservation practices on the 67,000,000 ac. of farm and range land to be three times greater than in 1942.

By the end of the 1943 plowing season, it seemed unlikely that there would be any flagrant widespread plow-up of unarable land. Some thousands of acres of dry land in the southwest were plowed for beans, and pastures in some regions were broken and planted to feed crops; but in most instances rotation systems were established or the land was protected by contouring with properly protected waterways.

Public approval of the principle of wise land use was evidenced by the spread of soil conservation districts during the year. As of Nov. 15, 1943, 970 soil conservation districts, covering

552,830,000 ac. in 2,480,807 farms, had been organized in 43 of the 45 states which had enacted a soil conservation districts law. This represented an increase for the year of 73,701,000 ac. in districts. Over 99½% of the total farm and range land in the United States was in the 45 states which had passed districts legislation.

The soil conservation service held a series of orientation schools and apprenticeship classes in all parts of the U.S. to train personnel in carrying out important conservation jobs requiring minimum equipment, labour and fuel, and having an immediate effect on war crop production. More than 6,000 of these classes were held.

Soil and water conservation work accomplished during the year is described in the following summaries:

The surveying and mapping work of the soil conservation service was continued, and approximately 32,000,000 ac. were covered throughout the year by farm plan surveys.

An intensive program was carried out to encourage farmers in all regions to grow and harvest seed of grasses and legumes for use in setting up crop rotations and to help meet scarcities of chemical nitrogen for fertilizer. As a result, millions of pounds of seed of some 20 grasses and legumes were available for treating 2,548,745 ac. with adequate rotations.

Threefold and fourfold increases in corn yields following kudzu and sericea lespedeza were reported, while increases of 500 lb. of peanuts and 15 bu. of oats per acre were obtained from growing crotalaria in the rotation.

Contour planting, a basic soil conservation practice in the United States, spread more rapidly during 1943 than in any previous year. The stubble mulch or subsurface type of tillage was used on several hundred thousand acres in the plains states and in wheat areas of the Pacific northwest to conserve moisture, prevent wind and water erosion, and increase yields.

During 1943, 29 soil conservation nurseries in operation in different parts of the country provided 65,000,000 plants for erosion control plantings. Reforestation work was reduced, chiefly due to labour shortages, but maintenance plantings of shelterbelts in wind erosion areas was continued, and assistance was given farmers in meeting increased needs for wood for farm and industrial requirements. Farm production of fish for food, also a phase of the soil conservation program, increased 44% over the preceding 3-year record: 1,375 farm ponds were stocked and put under management plans.

About 130 small drainage projects were planned or undertaken by soil conservation service engineers during the year, and conservation work in the field of irrigation farming reached a new peak: 750,000 ac. of irrigated lands were benefited by new structures, or other improvements allowing more efficient use of water.

In 1943 the total area of grazing land on which improvement in production had been accomplished through soil conservation methods was brought to 30,000,000 ac., mostly in the 17 western states.

Research and experimental work, essential to an extensive soil conservation program, were continued. Research workers of federal, state and other experiment stations and laboratories, carried on investigations on soil and water losses under various cropping practices and equipment uses; sedimentation as affecting water supply and agricultural use of bottomlands; causes of soil-creep and earth-flow; permissible velocities for field waterways and terrace outlets under different vegetative covers; erosion processes under irrigation; the domestic production of economic erosion control plants.

The Conservation Needs survey of the total agricultural land of the United States, started in 1942 by the U.S. soil conservation service, was completed in Aug. 1943. The survey, based on classification of land according to physical characteristics and best productive use, provides the most complete analysis of agricultural land resources ever undertaken by any country.

Great Britain.—The most intensive development of use of agricultural land ever recorded was carried on consistently in the United Kingdom throughout the first four years of World War II. By the close of 1943, nearly every available acre of ground was under cultivation and incorporated in crop rotation systems designed to maintain soil fertility through the period of war production. Per acre yields of many of the poorer soils of England and Wales were astonishing agriculturists throughout the United Nations: 55 to 60 bu. of wheat to the acre from soils but a few inches over chalk were not uncommon.

By mid-year it was announced that production of food and feed crops in Britain had been more than doubled by planned and controlled expansion of arable acreage coupled with soil fertility improvement methods. At the end of the plowing season the amount of arable land in the United Kingdom had increased to approximately 19,000,000 ac., bringing the increase during the war period to 34% Tillage had increased by 53%. The potato acreage had been doubled, and annual imports of feedstuffs had been reduced from 8,500,000 tons prewar to less than 1,000,000 tons. The grain crop grown in 1943 was more than two-thirds greater than at the beginning of the war, and the total cattle

GAUGE for measuring amount of soil erosion from a cultivated slope

population had increased although it was at an all-time high at the beginning of the war. The year's harvest produced 100,000,000 tons of food, an increase of 70% since 1939.

The unprecedented success of Britain's wartime farm program was attributed in large part to the grassland farming practised in England and Wales for centuries, the highly developed system of rotations, and the watershed control program that had been consistently maintained since passage of the Land Drainage act in 1930. Likewise, by the beginning of 1943 it had become apparent that the war had brought home to leaders and farmers of Britain the inestimable value of the factual data collected by the Land Utilization Survey in the 1930s and published in simplified form in 1941 for use during the emergency period. By employing these data on all phases of land conditions, covering the total land of the United Kingdom, it should be possible to determine the land-use conversions which can be maintained after the war-production crisis.

Having reached the peak of land conversion in 1943, Britain was able to isolate the most serious hazards of her emergency agricultural program. The mountain or rough hill land which covers two-thirds of Scotland, one-third of Wales, and large areas of England, was considered the country's number-one soil erosion problem. Some serious erosion was caused by clearing, plowing and planting these ancient "rough grazing lands" to potatoes or other row crops in 1941 and 1942 without adequate soil conservation measures. By 1943 simple procedures involving pioneer crops and special fertilization had been worked out in some counties so that normal yields of food crops were obtained, but on the whole the erosion hazard remained to be reckoned with in the postwar period. British experts, well aware of the dangers to the hill lands, were making plans to use modern soil conservation practices in reconverting or revitalizing the hill lands after the war. Several counties of the United Kingdom had already organized such programs by the harvest season.

Severe gullying, caused by up and down hill plowing on steep slopes, was reported from north England, indicating that contour strip cropping would be necessary if the steep drumlins and other lands were to continue in cultivation. Blowing fenland resulting from too much drainage, plus intensive cultivation without windbreaks or proper cover, caused serious loss of high-value soils, and often dust storms.

Canada.—With some 58,000,000 ac. in war crops, and more than twice that amount classed as potentially agricultural, the people of Canada were becoming increasingly aware of the necessity for protecting their lands during the period of rapid expansion. The work of the Prairie Farm Rehabilitation administration which benefited millions of acres in Manitoba, Saskatchewan and Alberta, included conversion of submarginal areas from cropland use to community pastures; water supply development for farm uses and irrigation; and soil and water conservation research through 7 experimental farms, 47 district substations, 17 land reclamation projects, more than 800 regrassing projects, 4 large tree-planting experiments, and 228 farmers' groups known as agricultural improvement associations.

The land utilization phase of the administration's work was proving tremendously successful. In 1943, community pastures covering almost 1,000,000 ac. were in operation, other pastures totalling approximately 300,000 ac. were ready for use or under construction, and work to establish pastures on 2,100,000 ac. had begun. Irrigation had been provided for 221,891 ac., and during the year a program to extend irrigation to approximately 3,000,000 ac. was begun.

In Ontario, action was taken during the year to set up a conservation and rehabilitation program as recommended by the Guelph conference in 1942. Preliminary studies for starting runoff and erosion experiments were under way in the latter half of 1943. Surveys of several areas in Ontario showed drying up of streams and springs, seasonal damaging floods, sheet and gully erosion, and silting and pollution of waters resulting from cutting and grazing of forests, ill-advised drainage schemes, and unwise use of farm land for crops.

Mexico.—The department of soil conservation, established in 1942 to function as a part of the Comision Nacional de Irrigacion, issued reports of preliminary erosion surveys of the entire country and more detailed surveys of two regions. Physical, climatic, social and economic factors were considered in setting up land-capability classes for adapting soil and water conservation methods to the various land types. Erosion was found to be extremely serious in many sections of Mexico. More than 200,000 ac. of formerly cultivated land in the state of Tlaxcala was reported to be completely ruined for further cropping, while erosion had become a major problem on many lands still in cultivation. Extensive reforestation was planned to cover the ruined areas. Terracing, contour cultivation, rotations and soil-improvement measures, particularly by use of leguminous crops as green manure, were recommended for all lands remaining in cultivation.

Surveys similar to the Tlaxcala studies, were in progress in other states during the latter half of 1943.

Australasia.—In Australia 94,000,000 ac. were in agricultural use, with 30,000,000 ac. in crops. Only 8,000,000 ac. of this land, largely in the coastal regions, was considered first-class agricultural land. More than 200,000,000 additional acres were classed as potential agricultural land.

Serious erosion in the form of soil drift resulted from cultiva-

tion, without soil conservation methods, in the Mallee districts of Victoria and South Australia. This drew the attention of the State Rivers and Water Supply commission and as an emergency safeguard a soil drift control competition was conducted, offering prizes to farmers using control methods. Many farmers participated in the competition, with the result that drifting was greatly diminished. The practices of leaving stubble on the ground and sowing rye-corn for grazing and drift control spread rapidly during the year.

The Soil Conservation and Rivers Control Council of New Zealand reported that during the year a limited amount of stop-banking was carried out, sand-dune reclamation was continued on a reduced scale, and river-control and protection were undertaken at three or four points.

The problem of erosion in New Zealand was regarded as serious. One-third of the land was subject to accelerated erosion in varying stages, and of 15,000,000 ac. of forest land cleared, largely by burning, in the past 94 years, only 852,196 ac. had been reforested. Studies showed that much of the hill land never should have been cleared. Little, if any, effort had been made to apply erosion control, and overgrazing, burning off, and exploitation of the high country still continued.

China.—Extensive studies on the soils and soil erosion, land utilization, and soil and water conservation needs of the northwestern provinces of Shensi, Kansu and Tsinghai were made during 1943 by Dr. W. C. Lowdermilk, assistant chief of the U.S. soil conservation service, and a staff of eight Chinese soil experts. Demonstration projects and experimental plots were set up, and the first Soil Conservation Association of Farmers ever to be formed in China held its first formal meeting in October. Work of demonstration projects was closely co-ordinated with that of the National Conservancy bureau, including the Yellow River commission, and the ministry of agriculture and forestry.

The National Conservancy bureau of China had completed seven projects to supply water to 282,450 ac. of land suited for irrigation in Shensi. Projects to irrigate an additional 155,100 ac. were under construction. However, the water-supply program, started in 1930 to eliminate the hazards of famine in the region, by watering 2,100,000 ac. of loessial soils rich in fertility, was found to be handicapped for lack of a soil conservation program. The steep slopes were eroding, and it was generally believed that three rivers of the region, the Wei, King and Lo, were supplying most of the silt flowing into the Yellow river.

Heavy cultivation of steep slopes was found throughout the northwestern provinces by Dr. Lowdermilk and his staff members, and return of the land to appropriate uses was recommended. It was proposed that gullied slopes and badlands of great extent be planted to grasses, legumes, willowherbs and trees, and that many thousands of soil-saving dams be built along streams. Much of the gently sloping land could be cultivated with such erosion safeguards as contouring, strip cropping, bench terracing and diversion trenches to carry off unabsorbed rainfall. Many of the bottomlands, where rice and other crops are grown, should be farmed by level terracing.

Field data collected by the survey party headed by Dr. Lowdermilk were submitted to the Executive Yuan in Dec. 1943, together with recommendations for a soil and water conservation program for northwestern China.

U.S.S.R.—Research in soil science, natural meadow compositions and plant migrations, forest soils as affected by various methods of cutting, winter crops, and other phases of conservation farming were continued on many of the government-owned-and-operated state farms of the soviet union. Upwards of 4,000 state farms, comprising approximately 10% of the tilled lands, were in operation during the first two years of invasion. Their major function, experimental work, proved of inestimable value in evacuating old crops to new regions, in extending cultivation to new areas, and in co-ordinating soil science and land utilization for collective farmers engaged in reclaiming war-torn lands. Under guidance of the state farms, all 1943 spring plowing and sowing in the central and eastern regions was done strictly according to the most approved scientific methods, including soil conservation and fertility-improvement practices. Productivity of the soil rose 30% between 1913–43, and the sown area increased by the same percentage.

Land restoration in recaptured areas proceeded rapidly throughout the year. Seed produced by regional seed production farms and collective farmers far in the rear of the fighting was available to farmers returning to liberated areas; fruit tree seedlings and other plants were supplied by soviet botanical gardens; and farm cattle which had been evacuated to safe areas in 1941 and 1942 were being returned to liberated collective farms with pastures and feed sufficient to maintain them.

Africa.—Only about 20% of the continent is considered potentially arable, and not more than 2% of the arable land is first-class agricultural land. Serious erosion in many parts of the continent was recognized and had led to aggressive action in several African countries to stop soil erosion and water waste even before World War II.

In the Union of South Africa, the soil and veld conservation division of the department of agriculture gave technical advice and aid to farmers in application of soil conservation methods; in reducing cattle grazing on over-stocked areas; in planting grass on eroded areas; and in conducting educational campaigns to induce farmers to protect arable land from erosion by means of contour banks, contour hedges and other measures.

By the close of 1943 studies of the erosion problems of ten areas of varying sizes had been reported, including recommendations for water conservation, diversion of flood waters and protection of watersheds by revegetation. Thirteen thousand dams had been built as a part of the erosion control program, and a vigorous program to improve soil fertility by use of legumes in irrigated areas was well under way. Erosion was known to be serious and damaging in Natal, the Karroo districts, and the mountains of western Cape province where destructive fires had been common for many years.

In the Transvaal, Orange Free State and Rhodesia, badly eroded land was taken out of cultivation and erosion control projects were started. In 1943, the legislative assembly of Rhodesia enacted a law to set up a program for checking erosion damage, particularly with reference to the Mazoe valley. Likewise in Rhodesia, a government decision to pay less for maize grown on eroded land than that from conserved land awakened interest in a more progressive conservation policy. The Central Food Production committee of Rhodesia was co-operating with the Natural Resources board in aiding farmers to follow a long-term policy of production combined with maintenance of soil fertility.

Considerable acreages of sheet erosion and gullying were reported in Central province, Tanganyika, during the 1930s, and by 1943 contour banks were being used to retard the flow of water, and hedges were being planted to protect soils and crops from wind erosion. In Teso district, Uganda, where cultivation of cotton had impaired the soil, strip-cropping, construction of dams, reforestation of steep hills and other anti-erosion measures continued to be applied to the land.

South America.—During the year 1943 the legislative bodies of Colombia, Venezuela and Argentina passed national soil conservation legislation. A soil conservation service was set up in Colombia, to function in the ministry of national economy. In Bolivia and Peru there was evidence that educational programs would be necessary before legislation could be introduced. The ministry of agriculture of Chile was engaged in an extensive program of surveys and experimentation preliminary to launching demonstrations in different phases of soil conservation. A project was under way in Uruguay for creation of a conservation service to be advisory to several ministries of the government. In Brazil, in the state of São Paulo, the experimental station at Campinas already had initiated contour farming and other conservation measures over large areas. Argentina, the only South American country that suffers from extensive wind erosion as well as water erosion, was expected to set up a nation-wide soil conservation program during 1944.

The erosion problems of Latin America were clarified during 1943 through reports from and discussions with representatives of several of the republics who visited the United States to study soil and water conservation methods or to seek technical aid in initiating surveys or demonstrations. The most serious erosion in the northern half of the continent was known to be in the highlands of Colombia and Venezuela, the Andes region of Ecuador, the heavily populated departments of Huanuco and Junin in Peru, and the northeastern states of Brazil where droughts are common.

In the southern half, wind erosion in La Pampa, parts of San Luis and Cordoba, and southern Santa Fe and western Buenos Aires provinces had reached the stage of disastrous dust storms, abandonment of homes, and formation of sand dunes on over-grazed lands and over-cultivated wheat lands, which were left bare during seasons of high winds. Erosion by water was pronounced severe in the territory of Misiones, Argentina, where the annual rainfall is about 100 in. Uruguay, faced with a serious problem of advancing beach sands, had made extensive pine tree plantings in the effort to combat it.

Yields of wheat in many parts of southern Chile were reported reduced by one-half to three-fourths as a result of erosion caused by past farming practices. This led the Chilean ministry of agriculture during the year to project a plan to convert large areas of eroded wheat lands to pasture, and to plant other wide areas in eucalyptus to establish forests and control erosion on badly damaged slopes. (*See also* AGRICULTURE; AQUEDUCTS; DAMS; DROUGHT; IRRIGATION.)

BIBLIOGRAPHY.—*Final Act and Section Reports*, United Nations Conference on Food and Agriculture (1943, Washington, D.C.); *Production and Distribution of Food in Great Britain*, British Information Service (Oct. 1943); *Fertility, Productivity and Classification of Land in Britain*, Land Utilization Survey of Britain, 1941 and 1943; *Journal of the Ministry of Agriculture* (Sept. 1943, London); *Journal of the Royal Society of Arts* (1943, London); *Nature* (1943, London); *Herbage Abstracts*, Welsh Plant Breeding Station, Aberystwyth; *The Geographical Journal* (London); *Country Life* (1943, London); *Farming in South Africa*, Department of Agriculture and Forestry (1943, Johannesburg); *Forestry Abstracts*, Imperial Forestry Bureau (1943, Oxford); Reports of United States embassies in China, Canada, New Zealand, 1943, Office of Foreign Agricultural Relations, U.S. Department of Agriculture (Washington, D.C.); *New Zealand Science Review* (June 1943); Report by Guelph Conference on Conservation of Natural Resources of Ontario; *Publicity Series*, 1943, Department of Agriculture and Forestry (Pretoria, South Africa); *War Bulletin No. 4*, Welsh Plant Breeding Station; *Agriculture*, Journal of Ministry of Agriculture (Sept. 1943, Rhodesia); *The East African Agricultural Journal* of Kenya, Tanganyika, Uganda and Zanzibar (1943); *The Geographical Magazine* (May 1943, New York); *Journal of the Royal African Society* (Oct. 1942); *Journal Department of Agriculture* (Victoria); *Scientific Monthly* (May 1943); *Scientific Agriculture* (Dec. 1942, Canada); *Agriculture in the Americas*, U.S. Department of Agriculture (July 1943); Comision Nacional de Irrigacion, Mexico; U.S.S.R. Information Service; *Boletin Tecnico N.4*, Ministerio de Agricultura (Jan. 1943, Chile); Soil Conservation Service, U.S. Department of Agriculture. (H. H. BE.)

Solar System: *see* ASTRONOMY.
Soldiers' Bonus: *see* VETERANS' ADMINISTRATION.

Solomon Islands.
An archipelago in the western Pacific, included in Melanesia and forming a chain (in continuation of that of the Admiralty Islands and New Mecklenburg in the Bismarck archipelago) from N.W. to S.E.

U.S. INVASION BARGES landing on the beaches of Rendova Island in the New Georgia group, Solomon islands, early in the morning of June 30, 1943. The Americans ousted the Japanese garrison after a short but bitter fight

between 154° 40′ and 162° 30′ E., 5° and 11° S., with a total land area of 17,000 sq.mi. Administratively the islands are divided between the British Solomons (a colonial possession of Great Britain, with a land area of 11,700 sq.mi. and a pop. [1931] of 94,105, of whom 497 were Europeans) and the northern islands of the group, of which Bougainville is the largest. These belonged to Germany before World War I and were assigned to Australia under a League of Nations mandate after that conflict. Powers of government in the British Solomons are vested in a British resident, whose seat of administration is located on Tulagi Island, off the south coast of Florida Island.

The Solomons constitute a double row of large mountainous volcanic islands, flanked by some small atolls to the north, east and south. They extend for a distance of 900 mi. from Bougainville strait in the northwest to Fakata, or Mitre Island, in the neighbourhood of the Santa Cruz Islands to the southeast. Their northern extremity is marked by the atoll Ontong Java or Lord Howe, their southern by Rennell Island; the intervening distance is 430 mi. The great majority of the natives belong to the Melanesian race, but some 4,000 inhabitants of the outlying atolls are Polynesians.

History.—The strategic importance of the Solomons had been realized in some quarters in Australia after World War I, but the terms of the league mandate forbade fortification of the northern islands, and the British government took no steps to create air and naval bases in the British Solomons. The base at Singapore was supposed to provide adequate protection for what seemed, before the Japanese onslaught in 1941, a safe and remote part of the world.

The central Solomons area marked the farthest southward penetration of Japanese ground, air and naval forces. A turn of the tide in this combat theatre was marked when U.S. marines seized Tulagi and the important Henderson airfield on Guadalcanal in Aug. 1942. For some time the marines were hard pressed by superior Japanese forces and confined to a relatively narrow beachhead; but decisive naval victories in October and November of that year eased the American position and made it increasingly difficult for reinforcements and supplies to reach the Japanese forces on Guadalcanal.

A steady but slow process of clearing the Japanese from the part of the archipelago which they had occupied went on during 1943, and by the end of the year the Japanese were on the defensive in the last of their major strongholds in the Solomons area, the large northern island of Bougainville. Deadly modern weapons were brought into action on islands where naked savages had formerly fought out their tribal feuds with spears and bows and arrows, and air duels were fought over volcanic islands and small coral atolls. Difficult health and climatic conditions were encountered, and malaria ranked with the Japanese as an enemy. The forward movement in the Solomons was co-ordinated with the clearing of the Huon peninsula in northeastern New Guinea, and with landings, at the end of 1943, in New Britain, an important objective of both drives being the major Japanese base of Rabaul, in New Britain. (*See* also WORLD WAR II.)

Finances, Trade, Education.—Revenue in 1940–41 was £51,320 sterling, expenditure was £65,848. Exports during 1940–41 were £131,938. Among the principal products of the Solomons are bêche-de-mer, copra, ivory nuts, trochas shell, used for pearl buttons, cocoa, rubber, sweet potatoes, pineapples, bananas, yams. Education is in the hands of five missions.

(W. H. CH.)

Somaliland, British: *see* BRITISH EAST AFRICA.
Somaliland, French: *see* FRENCH COLONIAL EMPIRE.
Somaliland, Italian: *see* ITALIAN COLONIAL EMPIRE.

Somervell, Brehon Burke (1892–), U.S. army officer, was born May 9 in Little Rock, Ark., and was graduated from West Point in 1914. During World War I, he was a divisional chief of staff of personnel and operations on the western front, 1918–19, and was assistant chief of staff of supplies of the American occupation force in Germany, 1919–20. During the postwar years, he supervised a number of civilian engineering and construction projects in the United States and in Europe and was WPA administrator for New York city, 1936–40. He was made assistant chief of staff in charge of the army supply division on Nov. 25, 1941, and supervised the shipment of supplies to U.S. armed forces all over the world. On March 2, 1942, Lt. Gen. Somervell was made commander of the army supply services. During 1942 and 1943 he supervised a rapid expansion of quartermaster and ordnance activities. On Oct. 1, 1943, he was nominated by President Roosevelt for the permanent rank of major general. He attended a war conference in Chungking, Oct. 16–20, and later accompanied President Roosevelt to Cairo and Tehran.

Soong, T. V. (1894–), Chinese statesman, was born in Shanghai, the eldest son of Charles Jones Soong, wealthy Bible publisher, and the brother of Mme. Chiang Kai-shek. He attended Vanderbilt university, Harvard and Columbia, where he specialized in economics, and later he worked in New York banking houses. On returning to China in 1917, he worked as adviser to a large coal company in Shanghai; six years later, he became director of the department of commerce with the nationalist government established in Canton. As finance minister, 1928–33, Soong established many reforms, including a budget system, central banking and unified currency. In 1936 he founded the Bank of China. Chiang Kai-shek named him foreign minister, Dec. 23, 1941, while he was in Washington, D.C., as a special envoy. He did not return to China until the following October, having signed a lend-lease agreement with Secretary Hull in the meantime. Soong also spent much of 1943 in the United States. He conferred with Roosevelt and Churchill in Washington in May and participated in the Quebec conference in August.

Soong Mei-ling: *see* CHIANG KAI-SHEK, MADAME.
Sorghum: *see* SYRUP, SORGO AND CANE.
South Africa, British: *see* BRITISH SOUTH AFRICAN PROTECTORATES.

South Africa, The Union of. A self-governing dominion of the British commonwealth of nations. The four provinces of which it consists, the Cape of Good Hope, Natal, the Transvaal and the Orange Free State, extend from the southernmost point of the African continent to the Limpopo in the north. The former German colony of South-West Africa (pop.: European 33,600; Bantu and Coloured 287,731) is administered under mandate as an integral part of the union, but this territory has not been incorporated as a province. Area 472,550 sq.mi. (incl. Walvis bay, 430 sq.mi.); pop. (est. June 30, 1941), 10,521,700 (Europeans, 2,188,200; Bantu, 7,250,700; Coloured, 844,400; Asiatic 238,400). Chief towns (pop. census 1936): Cape Town (seat of legislature) (344,223); Johannesburg (519,384); Durban (259,606); Pretoria (seat of government) (128,621); Port Elizabeth (109,841). Governor-general in 1943: Rt. Hon. M. J. de Wet; premier: Field Marshal Jan C. Smuts. Languages: English, Afrikaans. Religion: European population: Christian (Dutch Reformed Churches 55%; Anglican, 19%; Methodists, 6%; Presbyterians, 5%).

History.—During 1943 South African affairs again fell under the three interlocked categories of war, industrial development and party strife. Prime Minister Smuts warned his people that the hardest fighting was still to come but that they must be "in at the finish" in Berlin. Thereafter he looked forward to sharing in the task of restoration as the union's "reparation policy." Having recognized the French committee of National Liberation and drawn a sharp distinction between the nazis and "another and better Germany," he went to London (Oct.) to take his seat in the British war cabinet.

The union had begun to feel the pinch of the war toward the close of 1942, when the cost of living had risen 20% above that of 1939. Smuts's United party ministry was strained by grumbling at its new "austerity" policy, and friction between its Labour left wing and its Dominion party right. Dr. Daniel F. Malan, the Nationalist leader, still confident of a German victory, played up to the British section of the electorate by harping on soldiers' grievances and tried in vain to re-unite all the opposition factions on a stop-the-war Afrikander basis. His position had been strengthened by the death of his rival, General J. B. M. Hertzog, in Nov. 1942. The ministry was further shaken by the momentary resignation of J. H. Hofmeyr, its second in command, who ac-

SOUTH AFRICA'S FIRST DIVISION was welcomed home in Cape Town in 1943. These troops cracked the nazi defenses at El Alamein in Oct. 1942

cepted the renewal of a "pegging" bill, which forbade Indian traders in Transvaal towns to penetrate European areas during a term of years but objected to its extension to residential areas in Durban (Natal). Smuts refused to accept his resignation, and thereafter the ministry was helped by the course of the war and a hopeful budget. Increases were made in excise, postage, income tax surcharge, special contributions from the diamond and gold mines (the latter now standing at $22\frac{1}{2}\%$), personal and savings fund levies, state railway fares and a 50% increase of the tax on foreign shareholders.

Smuts won a resounding victory on the war issue at a general election in which the soldiers took part (July). His United party did unexpectedly well in the Afrikander rural areas and gained a majority of 89 to 64 over all other parties. Labour gained markedly. The Communists failed completely in spite of their appeals to the harassed Negroes. Nicolaas Havenga's Afrikaner (Neutrality) party was wiped out. Oswald Pirow's New Order party, perhaps prudently, boycotted this democratic election. Malan's Nationalists at least formed a solid block, which might grow if times are bad after the war. The state of the parties was: United party, 89 (72); Labour, 9 (4); Dominion, 7 (8); Independents, 2 (0); Europeans representing the natives, 3 (3); a total of 110 in support of the war policy against the Nationalists, 43 (41). A few days after the election Sir Patrick Duncan, the governor-general, died.

An Industrial and Agricultural Requirements commission foreshadowed a fairly speedy decline in gold production, saw small hope of agriculture's coming to the rescue and noted that the remarkable wartime scale of secondary industries can hardly be maintained when prices again become an object.

The budget devoted the entire proceeds of native taxation to native education and made a beginning of giving all school children of whatever colour one square meal a day. Meanwhile the union's industries maintained an army of 150,000, out of an "occupied" European population of 750,000, and sent much to the Allies. A joint Union-United Kingdom-United States supply council was formed to carry this work farther (Sept. 1943).

Finally the legislative council of Mandated South-West Africa asked unanimously for incorporation as the fifth province of the union (Sept.). Smuts replied that this would be considered but that the League of Nations must be approached first.

(E. A. Wr.)

Education.—In 1939: state and state-aided primary and secondary: European schools, 4,014; scholars, 391,056; non-European schools, 5,131; scholars, 620,384; universities, average number of students 10,505.

Banking and Finance.—Revenue (est. 1942–43) £91,400,000; expenditure (est. 1942–43): ordinary £63,700,000, war £80,000,-000; revenue (est. 1943–44) £108,500,000; expenditure (est. 1943–44): ordinary £67,500,000, war £96,000,000; public debt (Dec. 31, 1942) £425,000,000; notes in circulation (Feb. 28, 1943) £40,300,000; gold reserve (Feb. 28, 1943) £63,500,000; exchange rate (average 1943) £1 SA=$3.98.

Trade and Communication.—External trade (1940) (exclusive of goods in transit and of gold bullion and specie): imports (total) £105,099,234; exports (domestic) £28,562,207; re-exports £5,528,430. Communication and transport: roads fit for motor traffic (1938–39) 87,495 mi.; railways, including South-West Africa (March 31, 1940), 13,645; airways, including South-West Africa (1939): passengers carried, 35,578; freight and mails carried, 2,640,984 lb.; mileage flown 1,751,453; shipping (1940) entered, 6,598; net tonnage 25,504,068; cleared, 6,554; net tonnage 25,315,168. Motor vehicles licensed (Dec. 31, 1940): cars and taxis, 317,958; vans and lorries, 51,215; tractors 1,044; cycles 21,725; wireless receiving set licences (1940) 283,119; telephones, instruments in use (1940) 202,753.

Agriculture, Manufacturing, Mineral Production.—Production (1940–41) (in metric tons): gold (1942) 14,120,617 fine oz., declared value £118,613,108; (1941) 14,386,361 fine oz.; declared value £120,845,424; diamonds (1939) 1,269,828 metric carats; maize 2,159,100; coal (1940) 17,493,000; sheep, number (Aug. 31, 1939) 38,289,430; cattle, number (Aug. 31, 1939) 11,-852,736; wool (1940) 125,000; wheat, European cultivation, 466,-800; cane sugar, refined, 467,800; iron ore (metal content) (1940) 396,000; pig iron and ferro-alloys (1940) 304,000; steel

(1939) 314,000; silver (1940) 40.2; manganese ore (metal content) (1940) 174,500; chrome ore (chromic oxide content) (1940) 73,300; asbestos (1938) 21,900; wine (1938–39) 1,555,-000 hectolitres; tobacco, European cultivation, 13,800; potatoes (1938–39), European cultivation, 196,800; oats, European cultivation (1939–40), 80,700; barley, European cultivation (1938–39), 20,500; mohair (1940), export, 1,900; copper (smelter production) (1940) 13,600; ground-nuts (1938–39), European cultivation, 13,500; benzol (1939) 1,700; superphosphates of lime (1937) 164,000. Industry and labour: (census 1939) establishments 9,837; employees, European, 117,056; others 189,087; value of gross output, £172,764,000; value added to materials used, £85,108,000. Employment index (average 1929=100) average 1941, 164; Feb. 1942, 172.

South America: *see* Argentina; Bolivia; Peru; etc.

South Australia.

A state of the Australian commonwealth 380,070 sq.mi. in area, bounded by longitudes 129° E. and 141° E., and by latitude 26° S. and the southern coast of the continent. Population (est. Dec. 31, 1941) 605,689. Chief city and capital (pop. Dec. 31, 1940), Adelaide, 330,000. Governor in 1943: Sir Charles Malcolm Barclay-Harvey.

History.—The industrialization of the state consequent upon the demands of war and in spite of acute manpower problems continued during 1943. Figures released for factory output during 1942 showed more than 35% increase over the previous year. Among new industries established in 1943 was a £600,000 plant for reforging scrap steel and a £500,000 chemical plant which, after the war, was to be converted for the production of fertilizers. Seasonal conditions were excellent and rural production consequently high. The wheat crop returned a record yield of 18.18 bu. per ac. The government announced a five-year postwar road plan for the construction of 3,000 mi. of roads at a cost of £A3,500,-000. The plan covers more than 100 roads in all parts of the state.

Education.—In 1939: state primary schools 1,004; teachers 2,556; average daily attendance 55,672.

Finance.—In 1941–42: revenue £A15,002,000; expenditure £A13,715,000; debt outstanding (June 30, 1942) £A109,190,000.

Communication.—Roads (March 31, 1940): 52,330 mi. Railways (1942): government, 2,547 mi. Motor vehicles licensed (March 31, 1943): cars 54,401; trucks 22,794; cycles 6,131. Wireless set licences (March 1943) 147,145.

Agriculture and Manufacturing.—Wheat (1942–43) 37,000,-000 bu.; barley (1941–42) 11,700,000 bu.; wine (1941–42) 11,-140,000 gal.; currants (1941–42) 9,872.6 short tons; wool (1941–42) 105,000,000 lb.; butter (1941–42) 20,370,000 lb. Industry (1941–42): factories 2,233; employees 67,000; gross value of output £A61,000,000; unemployment (March 31, 1943) 1.0%.

(W. D. Ma.)

South Carolina.

A south-Atlantic state of the United States, and eighth of the original 13 to ratify the constitution, 1788; popularly known as the "Palmetto state." Area, 31,055 sq.mi., including 461 of inland waters; pop. (1940) 1,899,804; white 1,084,308; Negro 814,164; others 1,332; 75.5% rural; 0.3% foreign-born. Capital, Columbia (62,396). Other cities include Charleston (71,275); Greenville (34,734); Spartanburg (32,249).

History.—Olin D. Johnston, elected governor in Nov. 1942, was inaugurated Jan. 19, 1943. Having served from 1935–39, he was the first to serve a second term after the term was raised from two years to four with immediate re-eligibility forbidden.

The legislature extended state support for schools from eight months to nine; raised teachers' salaries (which any district might supplement) 15%, and assumed practically the entire expense for bus transportation of pupils; appropriated $186,000 for school lunches; raised state employees' pay 10%; voted $50,000 for postwar planning; appropriated $6,800,000 to reduce state debt; eliminated primary election laws for fear of federal action on the rule excluding Negroes from the Democratic party, thus leaving primary regulations to private party action; passed a law requiring physically fit males 16–60 to work or fight; discontinued the low state tax on general property, leaving this to local governments, which were also given state aid. In addition, the governor vetoed a marriage protection act on the ground that it was too feeble to be effective, and the legislature defeated an effort to permit the $57,000,000 Santee-Cooper hydro-electric authority to buy two large companies for $40,000,000, fearing politico-economic monopoly power. A suit to compel equal pay for white and Negro teachers brought no results.

The total state appropriations of $18,161,555 were the largest in the state's history. Highway gasoline revenues, however, fell to about half. Farm wages were the highest in 20 years.

Mrs. Sue Logue, executed together with several men for murder, was the first woman to be electrocuted in the state, but not the first to be executed. The only one of the penal officials charged with corruption so far tried was acquitted, though bad conditions were undoubted. A sheriff was sent to jail for 60 days for depriving a prisoner of federal constitutional rights. The 250 Catawba Indians (largely mixed with white and Negro blood) were by agreement with the U.S. provided at joint expense with more land, schools, and direct support, admitted to citizenship, and transferred to federal supervision.

The state supreme court ruled that Methodists refusing membership in the reunited church might use the name Methodist Church South, but not any of its property. Dissenters number a few hundred.

Education.—Enrolment in white elementary schools for the year ending June 30, 1943, was 186,230 (a decrease of 2,070); Negro 186,236 (a decrease of 5,317); high schools, white 71,294 (a decrease of 2,986); Negro 21,692 (an increase of 615). White elementary teachers 6,310, high school 3,011; Negro teachers 5,188 and 667 respectively; expenditures $16,753,801 for whites, $3,618,591 for Negroes. All men's colleges were taken over during the year for the training of soldiers.

Public Welfare, Charities, Correction.—In the year ending June 30, 1943, federal allocation for needy persons totalled $1,752,000, to which the state added $100,000. The amount of $1,319,500 went to the aged, $390,000 to dependent children; 27,777 persons were assisted. Total allocation for the year ending June 30, 1944 was $2,349,500. State unemployment trust fund rose to $27,264,933 by Dec. 31, 1943, supplied entirely by employers, while payments to unemployed during 1943 dropped to $566,770, a decline of 70%. Payments for the 12 months ending June 30, 1943, totalled $940,219. Patients in the state hospital (for mentally diseased) on June 30, 1943, numbered 4,688; on parole, 775; in feeble-minded school, 853. Prisoners in penitentiary and state farms June 30, 1943, 1,084; legal executions during year ending same date, 9.

Communications.—Paved highways on June 30, 1943, comprised 7,230 mi.; earthen state highways, 4,747 mi.; railroads, 3,563 mi.

Banking and Finance.—On June 30, 1943, there were 22 national banks (plus 19 branches), 84 state banks (plus 4 branches), 39 cash depositories with deposits and resources as follows: national banks and branches, $220,375,000 and $233,671,000; state banks, branches and depositories, $107,272,986 and increased resources. Resources of federal building and loan associations totalled $25,890,773; state associations, $11,848,331. State debt

June 30, 1943 was $68,246,511, of which $61,958,913 was for highways. Federal internal revenues collected year ending June 30, 1943, $105,673,000.

Agriculture.—Value of crops in 1943 was $231,315,000, 17% above the 1942 figure and the highest since 1919, when crops were valued at $360,000,000. Labour and equipment shortages were considerable. Of total crop values, vegetables supplied $12,432,000; 90% of the peach crop was frozen in April.

Table I.—Leading Agricultural Products of South Carolina, 1943 and 1942

Crop	1943 (est.)	1942
Corn, bu.	24,720,000	21,330,000
Wheat, bu.	3,002,000	3,377,000
Oats, bu.	14,102,000	13,461,000
Hay, tons	479,000	550,000
Irish potatoes, bu.	3,193,000	3,108,000
Sweet potatoes, bu.	6,960,000	5,890,000
Tobacco, lb.	87,400,000	96,750,000
Cotton, bales	695,000	699,000
Cotton seed, tons	309,000	311,000
Peaches, bu.	392,000	3,500,000

Manufacturing.—The total value of manufactures for the year ending June 30, 1943, was $1,062,402,844; employees numbered 167,718; wages, $208,195,102.

Table II.—Principal Industries of South Carolina, 1943 and 1942

Industry	Value, 1943	Value, 1942
Textiles	$771,575,622	$623,870,751
Lumber and products (boxes, paper pulp, etc.)	71,113,724	61,116,950
Electricity	25,602,965	23,080,314
Clothing (including knitted)	20,620,709	15,341,032

Mineral Production.—Production for 1943, chiefly stone and clay, aggregated $4,493,522. (D. D. W.)

South Dakota.
A north-central state, admitted to the union Nov. 2, 1889; popularly called the "Coyote state." Area, 77,615 sq.mi. (land area, 76,536 sq.mi.); pop. (1940), 642,961; urban population, 158,087; rural population, 484,874; average number of inhabitants per sq.mi., 8.4. Capital, Pierre (pronounced "Peer" by South Dakotans) (4,322). Largest city, Sioux Falls (40,832). Ten cities had a population above 5,000 in 1940. In 1943 the state's population was substantially reduced by migration to defense centres. An estimate by the director of the state census placed the total population as of Dec. 31, 1943, at 550,000.

History.—M. Q. Sharpe, governor (Rep.), took office Jan. 5, 1943. All partisan state elective offices were held by Republicans. The legislature, made up of 100 Republicans and 10 Democrats, was in session from Jan. 5 to March 5. In addition to routine legislation, administration-backed laws were passed providing for tithes from specified departments; establishing a department of audits and accounts under a comptroller; reducing the unemployment commission to one member; and authorizing a study of compulsory education through high school. The tithing law met vigorous opposition from sportsmen and from gasoline taxpayers. An action in the state supreme court nullified the law as it applied to the highway department and permitted it to be referred. Although opponents of the law circulated petitions to refer it, the referendum was denied on the grounds of insufficient legal signers. A hearing on the question of the law's constitutionality was set for the Jan. 1944 term of the supreme court.

Education.—The school census, ages 5–21, was 164,976 in 1943 compared with 186,258 in 1940.

Finance.—Total receipts for the fiscal year 1942–43 were $38,000,000; disbursements were $33,700,000; balance, $16,400,000. The net bonded state debt was $28,367,191.85.

Agriculture.—In 1943 the crop value was $244,170,000, an in-

Principal Agricultural Products of South Dakota, 1943 and 1942

Crop	1943 (est.)	1942	Crop	1943 (est.)	1942
Corn, bu	87,800,000	103,214,000	Wheat, bu.	32,545,000	45,274,000
Oats, bu.	73,300,000	90,400,000	Hay (tame and wild), tons	2,242,000	3,009,000
Barley, bu	36,414,000	59,364,000			

crease of $10,000,000 over 1942. In the nation, South Dakota was first in rye; second in durum wheat; third in barley, flax and wild hay; fourth in all spring wheat; fifth in sorghum forage; seventh in all wheat and oats; eleventh in corn. The total production was sharply reduced over 1942 but was well above the ten-year average for the state. (L. K. F.; X.)

Southern California, University of.
An institution of higher education at Los Angeles, Calif., comprising 25 schools and colleges.

During 1943 it endeavoured to preserve and advance the traditional academic program; nevertheless a rather strictly wartime campus prevailed, and the educational work was adjusted to train men and women for war service. The calendar year was divided into three major terms of 16 weeks each, the accelerated program preparing more men in less time.

The 1,200 men in the navy V-12 curriculum, including 300 marines, and 200 N.R.O.T.C. trainees, were supplemented by 400 army premedical and predental students. More than 4,000 adults enrolled in night classes in engineering, science and war training, sponsored by the U.S. department of education.

Special work was offered in occupational therapy, nursing and nursery school education, aviation medicine, and psychological clinic. Certain major divisions (engineering, mathematics, medicine, dentistry, chemistry, physics) overflowed with students, while other departments suffered decimation.

Alumni numbering 5,000 were in the service of the armed forces in 1943; 150 staff members were on special leave for war effort. For statistics of faculty, student enrolment, library volumes, etc., *see* UNIVERSITIES AND COLLEGES. (R. D. Hu.)

Southern Rhodesia: *see* RHODESIA.
South-West Africa: *see* MANDATES; SOUTH AFRICA, THE UNION OF.
Sovereigns, Presidents and Rulers: *see* PRESIDENTS, SOVEREIGNS AND RULERS.
Soviet Republics: *see* UNION OF SOVIET SOCIALIST REPUBLICS.
Soviet Union: *see* UNION OF SOVIET SOCIALIST REPUBLICS.

Soybeans.
The soybean by 1943 had risen to a prominent place as a wartime crop in the United States, as it had in Europe. As a food for animals and man, and particularly as a source of oil, its culture in the United States increased almost 400% over the prewar average. The War Food administration set a goal of 12,000,000 ac. for 1943 and the crop was estimated to be 95% of the production goal. Total 1943 production was estimated by the U.S. department of agriculture to be 206,117,000 bu. compared with 209,559,000 bu. in 1942 and 51,571,000 bu. as the 10-year average, 1932–41. While the acreage was increased in 1943 to 11,480,000 from 10,762,000 in 1942, the yield was only 17.9 bu. per ac. in 1943 as compared to 19.5 bu. per ac. in 1942. In areas outside the central states large areas were cut for hay because heat and drought damaged the prospects for beans and also because of a shortage of other hay crops.

Prices for soybeans were supported by the government through arrangements with the oil-seed crushers which required them to pay the minimum price of $1.00 per bu. for No. 1 beans. All beans purchased by crushers were required to be sold to the Commodity Credit corporation and then repurchased at certain

U.S. Soybean Production by Leading States, 1943 and 1942

	1943 bu.	1942 bu.		1943 bu.	1942 bu.
Illinois	70,602,000	66,400,000	Kansas	2,318,000	2,544,000
Iowa	39,332,000	35,451,000	North Carolina	2,313,000	3,484,000
Ohio	27,993,000	24,398,000	Mississippi . .	1,704,000	2,842,000
Indiana . . .	27,084,000	26,380,000	Michigan . . .	1,596,000	2,114,000
Missouri . . .	8,696,000	7,065,000	Virginia . . .	1,056,000	1,782,000
Minnesota . .	3,321,000	3,549,000	Wisconsin . .	1,054,000	780,000
Arkansas . . .	2,536,000	3,255,000	Kentucky . . .	858,000	1,066,000

All other states produced less than 1,000,000 bu. of beans. Soybeans grown for hay not included.

fixed prices designed to enable the old type plants to operate and to secure the maximum oil output. Even with the full use of all available plants in the soybean growing area, a part of the crop had to be shipped to the south and west for crushing, the extra cost of transport being paid by the government. The growing need for oil was shown by the increase in goals set up for 1944 by the War Food administration which called for 14,000,000 ac. compared to the 12,000,000 ac. goal for 1943. It was expected that by 1944 farm machines for soybean culture and handling would be available in quantity sufficient to care for the increase in the crop. In Iowa and Illinois, where most of the crop is grown, it was expected to take the place of oats and pasture. (*See* also CHEMURGY.)   (J. C. Ms.)

Spaatz, Carl A. (1891–   ), U.S. army air officer, was born June 28 in Boyertown, Pa. He was graduated from West Point in 1914, studied at the aviation school in San Diego in 1915 and participated in the Mexican campaign a year later. During World War I, he commanded a pursuit squadron in the St. Mihiel offensive in 1918 and was decorated for shooting down two enemy planes. After the war he was stationed at various U.S. flying fields, and in 1929 he piloted the army plane that established a record of 150 hr. and 40 min. in an endurance flight over Los Angeles. Advancing rapidly in the air corps, he was chief of staff to Gen. Henry H. Arnold in 1941, and soon after Pearl Harbor he took over the air force combat command. In July 1942, he was named U.S. air commander in Europe. Early in 1943 he was shifted to the Mediterranean theatre as commander of the 12th U.S. air force and of the United Nations' Northwest Africa air forces. In November, Algiers announced creation of a new U.S. 15th air force, also under command of Lt. Gen. Spaatz, to concentrate on bombing, from Mediterranean bases, targets in Germany and occupied Europe. A raid on a Messerschmitt assembly plant in Austria was the first mission. On Dec. 24, 1943, President Roosevelt announced the appointment of Gen. Spaatz as commander of "the entire American strategic bombing force operating against Germany" from all directions. The command of the 15th air force was taken over by Maj. Gen. Nathan F. Twining.

Spain. A southwestern European state, occupying about 84% of the Iberian peninsula. Area (including the Balearic and Canary Islands): 194,804 sq.mi. Pop. (1940 census): 25,877,971; in 1930 it was 23,563,867. The capital is Madrid (1,088,647). Other leading cities are: Barcelona (1,081,175); Valencia (450,756); Seville (312,123); Málaga (238,085); Zaragoza (238,601); Córdoba (143,296); Granada (155,405); Murcia (193,731); Valladolid (116,024). The language is Spanish, the state religion, Roman Catholic. Chief of state, or caudillo, in 1943: Gen. Francisco Franco.

History.—When 1943 ended Spain had still managed to retain her status as one of the few officially neutral (or rather non-belligerent) nations in a world at war. As in 1942, a heavy political and financial debt to the axis powers, a position in uncomfortable proximity to German military might, and a definite affinity to

totalitarian philosophy inclined her leaders toward support of the axis. At the same time her exposed position in regard to Allied attack, in case of belligerency (in 1943 even more apparent as the attack on Italy developed), her desperate poverty after her own civil war, and her need for certain essential items from the Allies, made it impossible for her to risk an Allied attack.

Insofar as the nations at war were concerned, both sides were content with Spanish neutrality for the time being. Germany could obtain some supplies from Spain, and if she tried to secure a Spanish entry into the war on the axis side, might open another sector demanding defense. The United Nations had enough to concentrate upon in other areas, and gains would not be commensurate with risks and expenses involved in an attempt to force Spanish support of their side. For these reasons it was logical that United States Ambassador Carleton Hayes could announce in January that the United States was not trying in any way to oust the Franco regime, and that Great Britain and the United States could agree to deliver to Spain 50,000 tons of cotton in the first part of the year. By August somewhat more pressure was in evidence, with a demand by the British ambassador, Sir Samuel Hoare, that Spain assume an actual rather than a nominal neutrality. Likewise the United States in the same month refused to sell arms and ammunition to Franco when such a purchase was proposed. In the last few weeks of the year news stories seemed to foreshadow a possible economic boycott of Spain in 1944.

The United Nations particularly objected to the participation of the Spanish "Blue Division" in the German operations in Russia. This force, officially only a private group of volunteers, had been large enough so that its losses in Russia were reported as high as 7,000 men. A general of the division, Agustín Muñoz Grande, a Falangist and strongly pro-axis, was at the head of the Spanish military cabinet in the early months of the year, and there was little doubt of Spanish governmental backing of the unit. Due to Allied representations, by September members of the division were returning to Spain in some numbers, and in October it was unofficially reported that Franco had decided to withdraw the force completely.

On April 16 Spain officially offered her "good services" as mediator to the two parties at war in World War II, but for obvious reasons the offer was ignored by the United Nations.

Rumours that the monarchy was to be restored by Franco were heard fairly frequently, as in 1942, since many of his strongest supporters were monarchists. In August, however, news reports indicated that Don Juan, prince of the Asturias and claimant to the throne, had broken off all contacts with Franco and was to try to work for restoration independently.

Political prisoners were released in 1943 in somewhat greater numbers. In June it was announced that over 3,000 would gain freedom, with double that number to follow, and in July the government stated that some 10,000 more would be released. That real opposition to the Franco regime was still in existence, however, was evidenced by a successful effort of saboteurs at El Ferrol, the northern Spanish naval base, where fires were set on May 20 that did much damage to docks and installations, and possibly to two cruisers and several destroyers.

On Dec. 20 the Falange (the only recognized party in Spain) announced that the party militia would be dissolved and that the army would take over its work. It was also stated that liberty of the press would be established and that some modification of the party organization would take place.

In spite of poverty at home, Spain managed to maintain service on her external debt. An announcement was made in July that the Spanish Foreign Exchange institute planned to arrange for payments on American commercial accounts for obligations incurred prior to July 18, 1936, which were still in arrears. The government also proposed to reconstruct University City at Madrid, wrecked during the civil war of 1936–39, at a cost of 225,000,000 pesetas, with another 75,000,000 pesetas assigned to improvements in other universities.

Barter agreements were discussed with Switzerland and Sweden during the year, particular effort being made by Spain to dispose of the Malaga raisin crop. The German-controlled airline in Spain officially was turned over to Spanish operation, but there was doubt as to whether the transfer was genuine. An agreement over blocked credits with Cuba foreshadowed improved commercial relations with that country.

Internal shortages continued, although news reports contained mention of official projects involving much industrial construction of all types, but particularly of chemical plants, shipyards, and electrical installations, all designed to make Spain more nearly self-sufficient.

Education.—Education is nominally compulsory and free; the church has a part in religious instruction. Extensive reconstruction of Spanish universities was projected during the year.

Finance.—The official monetary unit is the peseta (value in 1943: approx. 9 cents U.S.). The currency is artificially controlled. Currency in circulation June 30, 1943, was 15,192,937,654 pesetas. Expenditures for 1943 were set in the budget at 9,456,-475,296 pesetas (1942: 7,969,778,147 pesetas). During the year the income tax system was revised, with the federal "renta" or special income tax increased on higher incomes, and the state special income tax (the "cedula") repealed, with the federal government compensating the provinces for the loss.

Trade and Communication.—General trade figures for recent years were not released (1940 exports: $128,839,000; imports: $202,754,000). Estimates on the export of bitter oranges were 263,750 cases in amount (1942: 285,000 cases). Nut exports were comparatively small. Cotton imports for the first 9 months of 1943 amounted to 6,962,442 short tons (total for 1942: 7,694,-693 short tons). Dried bean imports (87% of which came from Argentina, the United States, and Mexico) totalled 51,023 short tons.

Some improvement in communication was claimed; in Nov. 1942, locomotives in service numbered 2,550 as against 1,837 in 1939. A link of the new Coruña-Madrid railway line was opened in April 1943. Electrification of many lines was being continued. Much activity in ship construction was reported, with 187 vessels on order and a number of these under actual construction. Shipyards were authorized at Bilbao and Alicante during the year, and 43 harbour improvement projects were carried out. A merchant fleet of 1,056,875 tons was claimed to be in operation.

Agriculture.—Production in 1943 was still under normal years. Cereal crops in 1942 were estimated as follows (in short tons): wheat, 3,269,466; oats, 722,717; rye, 591,593; barley, 2,004,224; corn, 774,469; rice, 160,533. Potato production amounted to 3,728,320 short tons. The bean crop (1942) amounted to 165,345 short tons; chickpeas or garbanzas amounted to 107,474 short tons; lentils to 16,535 short tons; peas to 33,069 short tons. Edible oil production amounted to 220,460 short tons of olive oil (1942–43); 1,764 short tons of filbert oil; 441 short tons of almond oil; also 528 gal. of fish liver oil were extracted. The queen olive crop for the 1942–43 season was estimated at 50,000–60,000 hogsheads; manzanilla olives at 25,000–30,000 hogsheads. In the case of almonds (1943 crop: 33,029 short tons) and raisins, there were heavy stocks on hand carried over from the previous year. Wool production for 1942 was 2,776 short tons; domestic cotton, 6,790 short tons. Total rosin and derivative oil output was 29,762 short tons.

Mineral Production.—Few figures on mineral production

were available. Steel production (1942) totalled 702,392 short tons; nickel, 617 short tons. Mercury output (unoff. est. 1941) was 85,500 flasks. In addition to domestic necessities, the production of lead allowed an export of 13,228 short tons in 1942. Hard coal production, for 5 months of 1943, was 3,747,820 short tons (1942 corresponding period: 3,527,360 short tons). (*See also* WORLD WAR II.)

BIBLIOGRAPHY.—Charles E. Chapman, *A History of Spain* (1918); E. Allison Peers, *Spain, the Church and the Orders* (London, 1939); *Foreign Commerce Weekly; Foreign Policy Reports.* (D. RD.)

Spangler, Harrison E.

(1879–), U.S. lawyer and politician, was born June 10 in Guthrie county, Iowa. He was graduated from Iowa university law college and was admitted to the bar in 1905. Active in Republican party activities since his youth, Spangler worked his way up to state leadership and in 1931 became a member of the Republican national committee. He directed Alfred Landon's presidential campaign for the midwest area in 1936. After the retirement of Joseph W. Martin as chairman of the Republican national committee in 1942, Spangler was selected for the post. He was active throughout 1943 in preparation for the 1944 presidential election. On Sept. 6 Spangler opened the meeting of the Republican Post-war Advisory council at Mackinac Island, Mich.

Spanish-American Literature.

It is in the field of the novel that the literary production of Spanish America was most fortunate in the year 1943 and the name of Joaquín Edwards Bello must be placed at the head of the year's list. His book *En el viejo Almendral*, in which one renews acquaintance with the characters of *Valparaíso, la ciudad del viento*, combined the well-known Edwards realism and a melancholy and reminiscent atmosphere that fits very well with the novel's period, 1900, and its background, the speculating commercial middle classes of a port destined, due to the opening of the Panama canal, never again to be what it once had been. Edwards Bello received in 1943 the Chilean national prize for literature for the ensemble of his already long work, a fitting recognition of a successful career. As if this writer, who always seems in his works somewhat autobiographical, had set the mood for the year's production, there were several other more or less autobiographical novels: in Chile, Benedicto Chuaqui's *Memorias de un emigrante*, given the 1943 Santiago municipal prize, is the romanced autobiography of a Syrian immigrant; the Venezuelan Mariano Picón Salas also looked to the past in *Viaje al amanecer*, a remembrance of his childhood in the Andes; and the Mexican writer Agustín Yáñez, who in 1942 in *Flor de juegos antiguos* pictured a provincial Mexican infancy, in his 1943 book *Archipiélago de mujeres*, subtitled "Adolescence's ports of call," successfully presented a young man's discovery of woman. Another Mexican, José Revueltas, representing a different conception of the novel, published in 1943 a distinguished work under the title of *El luto humano*. The historical novel had not been too popular in Latin America in late years, but in 1943 Gerardo Gallegos in *Beau Dondon conquista un mundo* made an excellent attempt at it. The Chilean Reinaldo Lomboy's *Ránquil* would fit in both the historical and the social revolt types of writing. Using as basis of his plot a real life incident, Lomboy develops the tragedy of a group of farmers expelled from their land, driven to misery and rebellion and bloodily crushed by the forces of the state; occasionally Lomboy loses the thread of his story in his delight in description of landscape, and the effectiveness of his effort becomes thus somewhat diluted. One might also mention some other novels published in 1943: the Ecuadorian Demetrio Aguilera Malta's *La isla virgen*, the Mexican Diego Cañedo's *El referí cuenta nueve*, the Argentinean Abelardo

Arias' *Álamos talados,* the Colombian Eduardo Caballero Calderón's *El arte de vivir sin soñar.*

In the short story, Argentina led the field in 1943 with two books, *Como naufragó el Capitán Olssen* and *La señora Enriqueta y su ramito,* by the devoted director of the "Teatro del Pueblo" and grand writer, Leonidas Barletta. His stories are subtle and entertaining, carrying their message deep in their apparently commonplace occurrences. The Peruvian Serafín Delmar in *Los campesinos y otros condenados* described the men and the landscape of his native land as he painfully remembered them during his long term behind prison walls. The great descriptive narrator Mariano Latorre published a new book of Chilean short stories and poems entitled *Mapu.* The Cuban Lino Novás Calvo collected in a volume *La luna nona y otros cuentos* some of his fine short stories, and his compatriot Ramón Guirao gathered some Afro-Cuban folklore materials in *Cuentos y leyendas negros de Cuba.* From Central America came Juan Ulloa's *Vidas humildes, Cuentos salvadoreños.*

Poetry was in 1943 as assiduously cultivated as ever in Spanish America. In Mexico, the Honduran Don Rafael Heliodoro Valle published a book of poems, *Contigo,* which, in the words of González Martínez, is "a book of plenitude," written by a fully developed man and scholar, sensitive, sincere and profound; Efrén Hernández's *Entre apagados muros* was the appreciable first poetic work of a well-established short-story writer, and Octavio Paz in *A la orilla del mundo* gathered his poems of different years, permitting the reader to follow the evolution of one of the most promising men of the younger generation of Mexican poets. From Central America came some verse *plaquettes* of interest: for instance, the Guatemalans Raúl Leiva's *En el pecado* and Otto Raúl González's *Voz y voto del geranio.* The Colombian poet Germán Pardo García collected his poems in a book, *Sacrificio,* in which the musical quality so characteristic of his country's poetry does not fail him. In Venezuela, Otto D'Sola published *El viajero mortal,* pervaded with the author's sense of anguish before the world's agony. In Chile, the venerable Don Samuel A. Lillo published *El río del tiempo,* verses full of the mildness of heart of a man who can look back on a very long life; in the same sentimental trend was Felix Armando Núñez's *Canciones de todos los tiempos;* in contrast, Pablo de Rokha's *Multitud* and *Morfología del espanto* expressed often violently his social and political preoccupations. Although formally written in prose, though it is a poetical prose, mention should be made of Augusto d'Halmar's *Mar, Historia de un marino y de un pino*

marítimo. Argentina's Francisco Luis Bernárdez reached a new point in his poetic orbit with the publication of *Poemas de carne y hueso,* an attempt at the humanization of a poetry formerly dehumanized. To the rather hard and cold pole of purely intellectual poetry belonged some other Argentinean books: *La columna y el viento* by Vicente Barbieri, *Ángel trocado* by Elena Duncan, *Persuasión de los días* by Oliverio Girondo. Closer to the tones of emotion was *Orilla nocturna* by González Carbalho, a new maker of delicate and essential poetry, as was also Silvina Ocampo's *Enumeración de la patria,* adorned with a gift for original and rapid imagery, and Juan Burghi's *Pájaros nuestros.* Verging on archaism was Antonio Pérez Valiente de Moctezuma's *Sol en la niebla* and on symbolism, Macedonio Fernández's *Muerte es beldad.*

World War II had not found a more vigorous singer in the Spanish language than the great Chilean Pablo Neruda nor a better poem than his *Nuevo canto de amor a Stalingrado.*

For those who love the past, one should not fail to mention the appearance of a hitherto unpublished little book of poems written in his last days by Amado Nervo and which, under the title *La última luna,* was included in the Mexican review *Ábside.*

In the field of essay-writing or in that of more erudite endeavours, it was stimulating to observe all over Spanish America men deeply interested in the continued search for the real meaning and significance of their countries in a world in transformation. Some approached this study from the philosophical point of view and thus are found Mexicans searching the history of Mexican thought: Samuel Ramos in *Historia de la filosofía en México,* Leopoldo Zea in *El positivismo en México.* The Chileans approached the problem historically: Norberto Pinilla in *La generación chilena de 1842;* or looked more physically to their land: Luis Durand in *Presencia de Chile;* or examined the popular manifestations of their national spirit: Pablo Garrido, in *Biografía de la cueca.*

In Cuba, the learned Don Fernando Ortíz looked into an economic event of the island's history in *La hija cubana del iluminismo.* (L. Mo.)

Spanish Colonial Empire.
Total area (approx.) 128,100 sq.mi.; total population excluding Spain (est. Dec. 31, 1939) 1,005,000.

The accompanying table lists the colonies, protectorates, etc., of Spain (*q.v.*) with certain essential statistics appropriate to each of them.

Spanish Colonial Empire

Colony and Area sq.mi. (approx.)	Population Estimated Dec. 31, 1939 (000's omitted)	Capital, Status, etc.	Principal Products (in short tons)	Imports and Exports (in thousand pesetas)	Road, Rail and Shipping	Revenue and Expenditure (in thousand pesetas)
Ceuta and Melilla, 77	115	Madrid, administered as part of Spain	exports (1934) raw materials 991,577; manufactures 14,211	(1934) imp. 47,546 exp. 14,500		
Morocco, Spanish, 8,080	750	Tetuan, protectorate *High Commissioner:* General Carlos Asensio	(1938) iron ore (metal content) 887,352; (1938) antimony ore (metal content) 89	(1938) imp. 123,146 exp. 71,143	rds. *c.* 500 mi. rly. 80 mi.	(1938) rev. and exp. 111,785
Spanish Guinea, including Fernando Po, Rio Muni and four small islands, 10,380	120	Santa Isabel, colony	cocoa (1937–38) 14,771	(1930) imp. 17,625 exp. 21,970		(1932) rev. and exp. 11,020
Western Sahara, including Ifni, Rio de Oro and Spanish Sahara, 109,600 . .	20	Villa Cisneros, colonies	fish and dates			(1929) rev. and exp. 6,947

Spanish Guinea: *see* SPANISH COLONIAL EMPIRE.

Spanish Literature.
Spanish literary production in 1943 suffered from material shortages arising from war conditions. American publishing houses, particularly those of Argentina, assumed a large share of the burden of publishing the Spanish works mentioned below.

The output of novels was unusually low. Juan Antonio Zunzunegui won wide acclaim for his second novel, *El hombre que iba para estatua.* Pérez de Ayala's *Bajo el signo de Artemisa* was published in Buenos Aires; numerous reprints of the novels of Pérez Galdós anticipated the centenary of this writer's birth; and there were reprints of most of the novels of Pérez y Pérez. *Los héroes universales de la literatura española* was the work of Juan Cabal; and in *La novela picaresca en España* Valbuena Prat continued his noteworthy work as critic.

In poetry, anthologies and criticism were more abundant than original poems. Notable in the former group was Dámaso Alonso's *Poesía de la edad media.* Sustained interest in Menéndez Pelayo resulted in the reprinting of the *Antología de poetas líricos castellanos.* Rafael Alberti contributed *El poeta en la España de 1931* and Angel Battistessa studied *Poetas y prosistas españoles.* Some 300 poems of Pedro Salinas were collected in *Poesía junta,* published in 1942.

Jacinto Grau's *Unamuno y la España de su tiempo* evidenced the lasting interest in the versatile sage of Salamanca. Palacio Valdés' *Album de un viejo* was reprinted, as were essays of Pío Baroja (*Pequeños ensayos*); and F. Madrid produced a biography of Valle Inclán. Ramón de la Serna's *Mi tía Carolina Coronado* is a study of a modern poet.

The Consejo Superior de Investigaciones Científicas continued to sponsor literary and historical research. Noteworthy among the monographs appearing under its auspices were Sánchez Alonso, *Historia de la historiografía española* and Ramon Cenal, *Teoría del lenguaje de Carlos Bühler.* The Real Academia de Ciencias Morales y Políticas issued *La época del mercantilismo en Castilla,* the *discurso de recepción* of José Larraz López, onetime finance minister.

Spanish letters included the writings of a goodly company of expatriates, whose work gradually merged with the stream of Hispanic literature. Madariaga returned to fiction with *El corazón de piedra verde* and wrote a *Guía del lector del Quijote.* Jiménez de Asua contributed a volume on *Cüestiones penales de eugenesía, filosofía y política,* while Sánchez Albornoz and Ots Capdequi wrote in the field of historical-legal criticism. There were political treatises by or concerning three former presidents: Doin, *El pensamiento político de Azaña;* Aguirre, *De Guernica a New York;* and Ossorio, *Vida y sacrificio de Companys. Orígenes del frente popular* was the work of Martínez Barrio.

Proscribed in Spain, the Catalan language and literature found another refuge in the Casal Català, established in London. At Oxford, Joan Gili published an *Introductory Catalan Grammar.*

(R. S. S.)

Spanish Morocco: *see* SPANISH COLONIAL EMPIRE.
Spanish West Africa: *see* SPANISH COLONIAL EMPIRE.
Spars: *see* COAST GUARD, U.S.

Special Libraries Association.
Founded in 1909 to further the purpose of special libraries in business and industrial organizations, and to promote the collection, organization and dissemination of information in specialized fields; to develop usefulness and efficiency of special libraries and other research organizations; and to encourage the professional welfare of its members. As of Sept. 30, 1943, the association had 3,023 members in the United States, Canada and overseas. These members represent banking, advertising, insurance, finance, social welfare, publishers, newspapers, manufacturers, museums, specialized departments of colleges and universities, business branches of public libraries and technical libraries. The official journal, *Special Libraries,* is published monthly September to April, with bimonthly issues May to August. The association has 19 chapters in the U.S. and two in Canada. An annual convention is held yearly in June. The association carries on a publications program which is professional in character and is taking part in the war effort. *Special Library Resources,* vol. 1, was published in 1941 with three additional volumes planned for 1944 publication.

(K. B. S.)

Spellman, Francis Joseph
(1889–), archbishop of the diocese of New York, was born May 4 in Whitman, Mass. After receiving an A.B. degree from Fordham university in 1911, he studied for five years at the University of the Propaganda at Rome. On his ordination in 1916 he returned to serve in Boston. In 1925 he again went to Rome, this time to serve as an attaché in the office of the secretary of state and translator of papal broadcasts and encyclicals. He remained in this post until 1932, when he was made auxiliary bishop of Boston. In April 1939, he was appointed archbishop of New York, the wealthiest Catholic see in the world. On Dec. 11 he was named military vicar of American Catholics in the armed forces. In this capacity Archbishop Spellman started, in Feb. 1943, on a six-month, 45,000-mi. aeroplane trip covering four continents. He visited the Pope, Prime Minister Churchill, and officials of a number of countries, as well as many military hospitals. The letters written to his father during this trip, relating his experiences and impressions, were published in *Collier's* magazine under the title "Action This Day."

Spelman Fund of New York
was chartered in 1928. The fund, during 1943, continued its program directed at the improvement of the methods and techniques in the field of public administration. The Chairman of the Board of Trustees in 1943 was Charles E. Merriam.

(C. MH.)

Spices.
Supplies decreased sharply during 1943. French Indo-China, Netherlands Indies and China, the principal producing areas, continued under enemy control, and no statistics as to imports, countries of origin, etc., were released by the U.S. government. The U.S. War Production board's Regulation M-63 as amended Aug. 7, 1943, controlled imports of black and white peppers, cinnamon, ginger, nutmegs, allspice, mace, paprika, vanilla beans, celery and sesame seeds by a permit system. To retard the disappearance of scarce items, the U.S. Food Distribution administration on July 1, 1943, ordered that deliveries

should not exceed the following percentages of 1941 totals:

Black pepper	Not more than 40%	Mace	Not more than 40%
Cinnamon (cassia)	Not more than 35%	Nutmegs	Not more than 60%
Cloves	Not more than 90%	Pimento (allspice)	Not more than 115%
Ginger	Not more than 100%	White pepper	Not more than 40%

Black pepper ordinarily constitutes about 50% of the spice business. Stocks in U.S. warehouses were large in 1943, probably enough to meet consumer demand through 1945. In Feb. 1942 the Office of Price Administration imposed a ceiling price on whole black pepper of six and one-half cents per pound. Ceilings usually had been determined after officials had met representatives of different branches of an industry, but in the case of pepper, such a hearing was not held. Holders owned their pepper at a cost of eight cents or more, so the loss of one and one-half cents per lb. would exceed $510,000 on the approximate 15,360 tons (2,240 lb. each) stored in public warehouses in 1943. Trading ceased, bringing a new limitation order (see *above*) lowering the deliverable percentage from 60% to 40%.

Much pepper was imported in 1939, 1940 and 1941 as a hedge against inflation. Pepper was ideal for this purpose, as there was no import duty. Added advantages were long-keeping quality and constant domestic/export demand.

The growing of spices in the U.S. did not proceed well in 1943. There were two exceptions, mustard and hot red peppers. In the states of Washington, Montana and California there were good mustard seed harvests, estimated by the department of agriculture above 44,000,000 lb. Until a few years previously, almost all mustard seed originated in the European and Asiatic war areas. As shortages of butter, meats and oils were emphasized by the requirement of more ration points, new uses for prepared mustard appeared. Added to butter or oleomargarine, these may be stretched about 40%. Red pepper growing became profitable in the south and quality excellent. Aromatic seeds, herbs and paprika fared badly because of fantastically high production costs.

Imports of useful spice seeds and turmeric from India in 1943 were almost impossible as native prices, due to inflation, were much above U.S. ceilings.

Negotiations whereby coriander, cummin and fenugreek seeds and marjoram might again be obtained from North Africa proceeded during 1943. Evaluation of the franc in terms of the dollar was one of the problems. Little information was available to indicate when trading would be resumed with Morocco, Algeria and Tunisia. (C. A. T.)

Spirits: see LIQUORS, ALCOHOLIC.

Spodumene: see LITHIUM MINERALS.

Sports and Games: see ANGLING; ARCHERY; BADMINTON; BASEBALL; BASKETBALL; BILLIARDS; BOWLING; BOXING; CHESS; CRICKET; CURLING; CYCLING; FENCING; FOOTBALL; GLIDING; GOLF; GYMNASTICS; HAND-BALL; HORSE RACING; ICE HOCKEY; ICE SKATING; LACROSSE; MOTOR-BOAT RACING; POLO; ROWING; SHOWS; SKIING; SOCCER; SOFTBALL; SQUASH RACQUETS; SWIMMING; TABLE TENNIS; TENNIS; TRACK AND FIELD SPORTS; TRAPSHOOTING; WRESTLING; YACHTING.

Spruance, Raymond Amos

(1886–), U.S. naval officer, was born July 3. He entered the navy in 1903 and was promoted through the ranks to rear admiral in Oct. 1940. He was assistant chief of staff to the commander of the naval forces in Europe, 1924–25, and was chief of staff and aide to the commander of a destroyer scouting force, 1933–35. After acting as commandant of the 10th naval district, San Juan, Puerto Rico, 1940–41, he returned to the office of the chief of naval operations at Washington and was sent to the Pacific theatre of operations at the outbreak of war

with Japan in Dec. 1941. Adm. Spruance was in complete charge of operations during the landings of the U.S. marines on the Gilbert Islands of Makin and Tarawa, Nov. 20–23, 1943. At that time, it was also disclosed that he had been made chief of a newly created Central Pacific command.

Spykman, Nicholas John

(1893–1943), U.S. educator, was born Oct. 13 in Amsterdam, the Netherlands. He attended the Universities of Delft and Cairo and received his Ph.D. degree from the University of California in 1923. In his youth, Dr. Spykman had been a journalist in the far east, and was at one time managing editor of a Netherlands Indies journal. He taught at the University of California in 1923, went to Yale in 1925 as assistant professor of international relations and became a naturalized U.S. citizen in 1928. He became chairman of the Yale department of international relations in 1935 and first director of the Yale Institute of International Studies, holding both posts until 1940. After the entrance of the United States into World War II, Dr. Spykman gave courses at the University of Virginia's special school for military administration of occupied areas. An authority on geopolitics, Dr. Spykman created controversy with his work, *America's Strategy in World Politics* (1942). He emphasized that the preservation of some balance of power was a prerequisite to the security of the western hemisphere. Dr. Spykman died in New Haven, Conn., June 26.

Squash Racquets.

Although no official national championship was held in squash racquets during 1943, H. Sherman Howes of Boston was generally recognized as U.S. champion as a result of his victory in the National Red Cross championships held in New York city. Howes defeated Germain Glidden of Englewood, N.J., 7–15, 15–11, 15–12, 15–14, in the final. Glidden, a national champion in 1936, 1937 and 1938, upset Charles Brinton of Philadelphia, the 1942 titlist, in the semifinals. The veterans' championship, held as a part of the Red Cross tournament, was won by A. M. Sonnabend of Boston, who held the national veterans' title in 1938. Sonnabend defeated Bradford C. Durfee of New York city, 16–15, 15–12, 15–10, in the final of the 1943 Red Cross Veterans' meet.

The only other squash racquets event of major importance was the international test with Canada for the Lapham trophy. The Canadians regained the trophy, 8 matches to 4. John C. Holt II, of Yale, won the national intercollegiate championship, replacing Brinton who in 1942 competed for Princeton. The New York state championship was won by H. W. Pell of the Princeton club.

Squash tennis, equally hard hit with squash racquets and racquets because of the rubber shortage, also held a National Red Cross tournament to replace its official national championship. Joe Lordi of the New York Athletic club, national champion in 1941, won the Red Cross event. (M. P. W.)

Stainless Steels: see METALLURGY.

Stalin, Joseph Vissarionovich

(1879–), Russian statesman, was born in Georgia and succeeded Lenin as virtual dictator of the soviet union in 1924 (see *Encyclopædia Britannica*). On May 6, 1941, shortly before the German invasion, Stalin assumed the premiership of the U.S.S.R. after the resignation of Vyacheslav Molotov from that office.

Throughout 1942 and 1943, Marshal Stalin repeatedly appealed to the Allies to open a second front and asserted on several occasions that Allied aid was not commensurate with Russia's con-

"THE PEACE PLANNERS." The best-laid schemes of U.S. postwar planners would go awry without the assent of Joseph Stalin, pointed out Darling of the *New York Herald Tribune* in 1943 prior to the pacts of Moscow and Tehran

tribution in engaging the greater bulk of the nazi army. It was believed, however, that most of Stalin's suspicions regarding Anglo-U.S. motives were dissolved after the Tehran conference in the last days of Nov. 1943. At this historic parley, Stalin and Roosevelt met for the first time, Stalin and Churchill for the second. The three United Nations chiefs agreed on a master plan to destroy the German military power. The subsequent appointment of Gen. Dwight D. Eisenhower as invasion commander allayed Russian apprehension over the second front. (*See* also UNION OF SOVIET SOCIALIST REPUBLICS.)

Stamp Collecting: *see* PHILATELY.

Standards, National Bureau of.

The national bureau of standards, established by act of congress March 3, 1901, was made up in 1943 of nine scientific and technical divisions, three divisions dealing with commercial standardization, and a special division set up as a war measure, and concerned wholly with military problems. The regular divisions are the following: electricity, weights and measures, heat and power, optics, chemistry, mechanics and sound, organic and fibrous materials, metallurgy, clay and silicate products, simplified practice, trade standards and codes and specifications. On June 30, 1943, the bureau staff consisted of 2,263 employees and 51 research associates. The regular appropriation for the fiscal year was $2,440,200. In addition, $304,100 was made available in deficiency items.

The war affected all the bureau's activities. An increasing proportion of the personnel and of laboratory facilities were transferred to war projects until it was estimated that 90% were so employed. However, certain normal activities proved fully as useful in war time as in peace. This was true, for instance, of the standard frequency radio broadcasts which were extended and improved, largely for the benefit of the military services. The testing of weighing and measuring equipment increased greatly; 30,000 master length gauges, and 32,000 pieces of glass volumetric apparatus were measured and certified. The scarcity of many engineering and construction materials was reflected in the problems submitted to the bureau. Substitutes for metals were being sought in wood, concrete and plastics. Buildings erected at the bureau were fabricated from concrete and wood, using very little steel.

The bureau demonstrated that often a scarce metal can be replaced by one not so high on the priorities list, possibly treated in some way to give it special properties for the work in hand. An example was the development of exhaust pipes for aeroplane engines, made of steel coated with vitreous enamel to replace the scarce stainless steels. The necessity of conserving fuel oil was the cause of many tests of "conversion grates" intended to make possible the use of coal in oil-burning heating boilers. A few of these were found to have real possibilities.

The complete elimination of the usual sources of jewel bearings for electrical and other instruments resulted in a synthetic sapphire industry in the United States. The bureau aided manufacturers in overcoming many problems, and one company alone was producing more than 2,000,000 carats of spinel and sapphires a month. Crystalline quartz for the manufacture of oscillators was tested in large quantities; 500,000 pounds were inspected during June 1943. Supplementing this work, a research project was started to insure maximum utilization of all grades of crystals. The number of standard samples of pure substances (used as controls in industrial laboratories) ordered during 1943 was 24,000; more than 150 standards were available.

A new publication on the physical properties of metals and alloys was prepared to replace a circular issued in 1924 and still in demand. It was of great value to engineers forced to use unfamiliar construction materials during the emergency.

Many determinations of the properties of synthetic rubbers were made, and samples of articles manufactured from these materials were tested. The bureau developed standard test procedures by which to evaluate the products of the newly built synthetic rubber plants, so that full utilization of every grade of material would be insured. In the course of the bureau's work on plastic windows and enclosures for aircraft, it was shown that a common constituent of sun-tan lotions, when incorporated in the plastic, would greatly reduce deterioration from the ultraviolet rays in sunlight and protect the plane's crew from sunburn. Certain alkaline methods were found feasible for treating low-grade bauxites and common clays in order to recover alumina of sufficient purity to meet the rigid requirements of the aluminum industry. At the bureau's branch laboratories more than 18,000,000 barrels of cement were tested for use on government construction projects.

The War Production board and the Office of Price Administration requested the bureau's assistance in developing simplification programs intended to conserve materials and manpower. The bureau was associated with WPB in the development of 130 limitation and 25 conservation orders. Twenty-one Commercial Standards were translated into Spanish and Portuguese. An important standard affecting domestic business covered the retreading of automobile tires.

Four circulars on elevator maintenance during the war period were prepared by a special committee and published by the bureau. Other results of the year's work appeared in 222 papers by members of the staff—152 in the bureau's own series and 70 in scientific and technical journals. (L. J. BR.)

Standley, William Harrison

(1872–), U.S. naval officer and diplomat, was born Dec. 18 at Ulciah, Calif. He was graduated from the U.S. Naval academy, 1895, was commissioned an ensign, saw service in the Spanish-American war, and was a naval captain during World War I. He was raised to the rank of rear admiral in 1927, was assistant chief of naval operations, 1928–30, commander of destroyer squadrons, 1930–31 and commander of a cruiser division with the rank of vice-admiral, 1931–33. He was commander of a battle force in 1933, ranking as an admiral, and was chief of naval operations, 1937–38. Although he retired with the rank of rear admiral, 1937, he was recalled to active duty in March 1941. In the fall of 1941, he served as a member of a mission to the U.S.S.R. to confer with British and Russian officials on means of speeding aid to the U.S.S.R. He was appointed ambassador to Moscow, Feb. 9, 1942. While Adm. Standley was favourably impressed with the Russians, he nevertheless criticized their failure to publicize the amount of aid they were receiving from the U.S. As a result, soviet newspapers devoted more space to the quantity of U.S. war materials sent to the U.S.S.R. Adm. Standley returned to Washington in late September and his resignation as ambassador was announced Oct. 1.

Stanford University

(THE LELAND STANFORD JUNIOR UNIVERSITY), an institution of higher education near Palo Alto, Calif.

On Sept. 1, 1943, Dr. Donald Bertrand Tresidder took office as president of the university, succeeding Dr. Ray Lyman Wilbur, who no longer was an administrative officer but remained as chancellor. Gifts amounting to $1,000,000 were received during the fiscal year ending Aug. 31, 1943. On May 7–8, the first annual conference was held under the auspices of the school of humanities on "The Humanities Look Ahead." By autumn the university's facilities were taxed to the utmost to handle, in addition to the civilian students, 3,000 soldier students under the army specialized training program and the civil affairs training school —with units in medicine (including premedical), basic and advanced engineering, personnel psychology, quartermaster corps, foreign area and language studies (European and Asiatic), and Women's Army corps (for physiotherapy aides). Appointments of professors in geography and anthropology were made to work on these war programs. Aside from improvements in buildings for housing and boarding students no structural changes were made. For the duration of the war all fraternity houses were taken over as part of the dormitory system and named after the presidents of the United States. Intercollegiate athletics were eliminated in accordance with the army program. With the pressures of war there came the continuous session, newer methods of teaching languages, and other changes in courses that seemed likely to have a permanent effect on higher education at Stanford. For statistics of enrolment, faculty, library volumes, etc., *see* UNIVERSITIES AND COLLEGES.   (R. L. W.)

Stanley, Oliver Frederick George

(1896–), British politician, and the son of the 17th earl of Derby, was educated at Eton and Oxford. As an artillery major, he served with distinction in World War I and was awarded the military cross and the croix de guerre. After the armistice, he was admitted to the bar, 1919. Stanley, who held cabinet posts in the MacDonald, Baldwin, Chamberlain and Churchill governments, was parliamentary undersecretary to the home office, 1931–33, minister of transport, 1933–34, minister of labour, 1934–35, president of the board of education, 1935–37, and president of the board of trade, 1937–40. In 1940, Chamberlain named him secretary of state for war, but

he was dropped by Churchill when the latter became prime minister in May 1940. In Nov. 1942, Churchill reshuffled his government and Stanley returned to the cabinet as colonial secretary. In March 1943, he was the object of some criticism from liberal elements in England and the U.S. for his statement rejecting any kind of scheme of international administration of British colonies after the war. His views on this subject were identical with those of Churchill.

Stark, Harold Raynsforo

(1880–), U.S. naval officer, was born at Wilkes-Barre, Pa., on Nov. 12. Graduated from the U.S. Naval academy in 1903, he was commissioned ensign two years later and served on various ships and at various naval stations from 1903 to 1917. During World War I he was on the staff of Admiral William S. Sims, commander of the U.S. naval forces in European waters. On March 15, 1939, he was appointed chief of naval operations with the rank of admiral. He was persistent and successful in his pleas to congress for a larger fleet, making possible a two-ocean navy. On March 9, 1942, Admiral Ernest J. King, commander in chief of the U.S. fleet, became chief of naval operations and Stark was made commander of U.S. naval forces in European waters, the same position that Admiral Sims had held in World War I. As such, he was liaison officer between the British admiralty and Washington. In the summer of 1943 he rendered outstanding diplomatic service in his negotiations with Gen. Charles de Gaulle and the French Committee of National Liberation. With de Gaulle's assistance, Stark was able to obtain the co-operation of French officials, both civil and military, with U.S. armed forces in New Caledonia and New Hebrides. He also negotiated mutual lend-lease arrangements between the Free French and the U.S. which gave to the U.S. essential supplies from New Caledonia, Madagascar, Africa and other French colonies in return for assistance to French forces in the Pacific theatre. Stark had much to do with the agreement achieved in 1943 by Generals de Gaulle and Giraud.

Stars: *see* ASTRONOMY.
State, U.S. Department of: *see* GOVERNMENT DEPARTMENTS AND BUREAUS.
State Guard: *see* NATIONAL GUARD.

Steagall, Henry Bascom

(1873–1943), U.S. politician, was born May 19 in Clopton, Dale county, Alabama. He graduated from the University of Alabama in 1893, and held a number of political offices in the state. He was elected to the U.S. congress in 1915 as representative from the 3rd Alabama district and was re-elected 13 consecutive times. Steagall was influential in the house during the closing days of the Hoover administration and throughout the first 10 years of the Roosevelt presidency. As chairman of the house banking and currency committee, many important financial measures passed through his hands. He was co-author of the Glass-Steagall emergency banking bill for expanding credit and the Glass-Steagall banking reform act, and was leader of the house's powerful farm bloc. He died in Washington, Nov. 22.

Steamships: *see* SHIPBUILDING.
Steel: *see* IRON AND STEEL.

Stein, Sir Aurel

(1862–1943), British archaeologist, was born Nov. 26 in Budapest. During his more than 30 years of research in remote parts of Asia, he uncovered a wealth of material on ancient civilizations which he recorded in books and a score of technical papers. His last publication, *On Old Routes of Western Iran,* appeared in 1940. Sir Aurel died in Kabul, Afghanistan, Oct. 28. (See *Encyclopædia Britannica.*)

Stellar System: *see* ASTRONOMY.

Stettinius, Edward R., Jr.

(1900–   ), U.S. business-man and statesman, was born in Chicago Oct. 22, son of Edward R. Stettinius, partner in the firm of J. P. Morgan and company. He studied at the University of Virginia, but left to enter the employ of General Motors in 1924. In 1931 he became a vice-president of that corporation. In 1934 he resigned from General Motors to become vice-chairman of the finance committee of the U.S. Steel corporation; two years later he became chairman of the committee and a director of the corporation, and in 1938 he was made chairman of the board. In May 1940, he was appointed a member of the advisory commission to the Council of National Defense, and a few days later he resigned all his offices with the U.S. Steel corporation. This was not his first connection with the federal government, for in the latter half of 1933 he had been liaison officer between the NRA and the industrial advisory board of the NRA, and in 1939 he had been made chairman of the War Resources board. From Jan. to Aug. 1941, he served as chairman of the priorities board and director of the priorities division of the OPM. On Aug. 28, following the resignation of Harry L. Hopkins, Stettinius was appointed lend-lease administrator.

He remained in this post until Sept. 25, 1943, when Pres. Roosevelt named him to succeed Sumner Welles as under-secretary of state.

Stilwell, Joseph W.

(1883–   ), U.S. army officer, was born March 19 at Palatka, Fla. He was graduated from West Point, 1904, and served with the A.E.F. in France during World War I. After the armistice, he studied Chinese at the University of California, spent three years at Peiping mastering several Chinese dialects and served as military attaché in China, 1932–39. After Pearl Harbor, he was promoted to lieutenant general, Feb. 1942. He served a month as General Chiang Kai-shek's chief of staff and in March 1942 Chiang gave him command of the 5th and 6th Chinese armies fighting the Japanese invading Burma. Beaten by stronger and better-equipped Japanese, Stilwell retreated toward India. After the fall of Burma in May 1942, Stilwell led a group of 400 refugees through 140 mi. of jungles and mountains to safety in India; the trip took them 20 days. After turning up at Allied headquarters in New Delhi, Stilwell said: "I claim we got a hell of a beating. We got run out of Burma and it was humiliating as hell. I think we ought to find out what caused it, go back and retake it." During 1943, as U.S. commander in southeastern Asia under Lord Louis Mount-batten, he was busy preparing to do so.

Stimson, Frederic Jesup

(1855–1943), U.S. diplomat and legal scholar, was born July 20 at Dedham, Mass. He studied law at Harvard university, graduating in 1878, and held a number of political posts in Massachusetts. He was professor of comparative legislation at Harvard, 1903–14. In 1914, Stimson was named U.S. ambassador to Argentina, a post he held until 1921, and he was also special ambassador to Brazil, 1919. Among his works are: *The Law of the Constitutions, State and Federal* (1907), *Popular Law-Making* (1910), *The American Constitution, As It Protects Private Rights* (1923), *The New Deal under the Constitution* (1936), and *Critique of Pure Science* (1938). He died at Dedham, Nov. 19.

Stimson, Henry Lewis

(1867–   ), U.S. statesman, of whom a biographical sketch appears in *Encyclopædia Britannica.* A Republican, he became an ardent admirer of Cordell Hull's policies as secretary of state (the office Stimson had held in Pres. Hoover's cabinet) and was always quick to defend Hull's actions against criticism. He favoured in particular a strong stand for the United States against Japan, Germany and Italy. Pres. Roosevelt appointed him secretary of war on June 20, 1940. Like his fellow cabinet-member, Frank Knox, Stimson favoured a militant foreign policy in 1940 and 1941. Stimson continued to direct an ever-expanding program in 1942 and 1943. One of his last official acts of the latter year was to take control of the railroads on Dec. 27, when strikes threatened.

Stock Exchanges: *see* STOCKS AND BONDS.

Stocks and Bonds.

Stocks.—Although U.S. stock market price movements for 1943 were somewhat more extensive than during 1942, the extent of the fluctuations was comparatively small considering the extraordinary economic events of a domestic and international character. Except momentarily, the market as a whole seemed unaffected by war events, the imposition of increased taxes or the effects of rationing and control systems. Probably most of the war events of 1943 and their accompanying economic effects were anticipated and largely discounted by the market. Throughout 1943 the average price level of stocks remained extremely low, in view of large corporate earnings and dividend distributions, a situation strongly incompatible with the large amount of talk concerning the prospects of inflation, as well as the huge postwar activity to meet depleted backlogs of needed goods, repairs and new construction. In fact, the most noticeable feature concerning stock market movements during the last half of the year was the drooping tendency of the market periodically whenever talk of peace or exceptionally favourable military events figured heavily in the press. Moreover, throughout the year the market was unusually sluggish as regards the volume of transactions. For all of the leading groups of stocks, the average price level rose gradually from January to July and thereafter showed a slight decline to the end of the year.

Using the Standard & Poor's barometric figures (average for each month based on daily closing prices) the average monthly price of 20 representative railroad stocks stood at 30.2 for Jan.

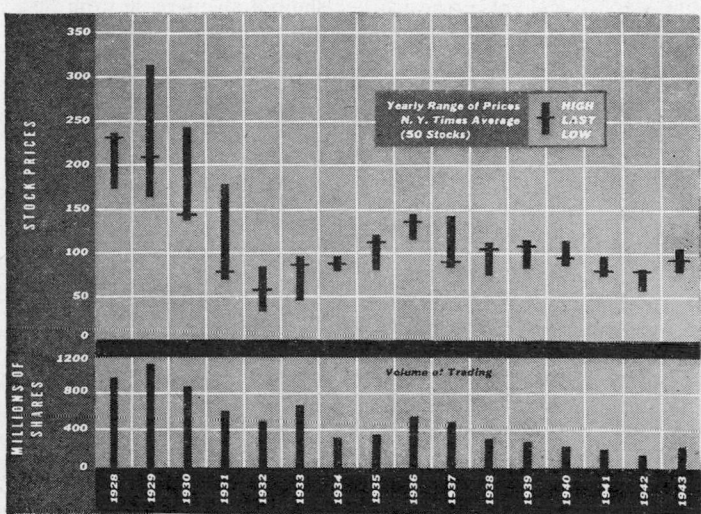

TRADING IN STOCKS on the New York Stock exchange: yearly range of prices and number of shares sold, exclusive of odd-lot and stopped sales

Table I.—*U.S. Security Market Prices*

	Railroads 20 stocks		Industrials 50 stocks		Public Utilities 20 stocks		Copper and Brass 7 stocks		Stocks 90 stocks	
	1943	1942	1943	1942	1943	1942	1943	1942	1943	1942
Jan.	30.2	28.1	101.8	89.2	38.2	35.4	*75.2	*88.3	80.2	70.9
Feb.	31.6	28.0	107.7	86.4	41.3	33.9	*80.0	*85.1	84.9	68.7
March	35.1	26.2	110.9	82.1	42.9	30.8	*84.1	*81.4	87.9	64.9
April	37.7	24.8	114.0	79.0	45.4	28.8	*85.8	*76.9	90.9	62.2
May	39.4	24.6	118.3	79.8	47.1	29.8	*84.8	*70.8	94.4	62.9
June	38.3	24.0	121.0	84.4	47.8	31.1	*80.2	*71.4	96.1	66.1
July	39.4	25.8	122.5	87.9	51.4	30.6	*82.3	*76.1	98.1	68.6
August	36.7	26.7	116.2	87.3	49.9	30.0	*77.4	*75.6	93.2	68.2
Sept.	37.3	27.2	118.6	88.1	51.3	30.4	*76.2	*75.3	95.2	68.9
Oct.	37.6	29.7	117.3	94.1	51.0	33 7	*77.4	*80.9	94.3	74.0
Nov.	34.9	29.6	112.1	95 2	48.8	35.7	*74.3	*76.4	90.0	75.2
Dec.	35.0	28.2	113.8	96.5	48.9	34.9	*72 7	*71.6	91.2	75.6

*Copper and Brass figures use 1935–1939 as a base period. All other figures use 1926 as a base period.
The above figures are an average for the month based on daily closing prices, except for Copper and Brass, which are weekly prices.
(Source of data—Standard & Poor's *Trade and Securities, Current Statistics.*)

1943, as compared with 28.2 and 28.1 for December and January of 1942. Thereafter a gradual rise occurred until May and July, when for each of those months the monthly average stood at 39.4. The gradual nature of the rise for railroad shares is indicated by the monthly averages of 31.6 for February, 35.1 for March, 37.7 for April, 39.4 for May, 38.3 for June and 39.4 for July. Following July, the monthly average declined slightly to 36.7 for August, 37.3 for September and 37.6 for October. The monthly average increased by 30.5% from January to July, and subsequently declined by 4.8% during the next three months.

In the field of industrial stocks, using Standard & Poor's average for 50 leading issues, the average monthly price stood at 101.8 for Jan. 1943, as compared with 96.5 and 89.2 for December and January of 1942. From January to July of 1943, this monthly average rose from 101.8 to 122.5, or an increase of 20.2%. Following July, the average monthly price level declined slightly to 117.3 in October, or by 4.2%.

Similar price movements by months occurred in the public utility and copper and brass groups of stocks. For 20 public utility stocks, the Jan. 1943 average stood at 38.2, as compared with 34.9 and 35.4 for December and January of 1942. Following Jan. 1943, the average monthly price increased from 38.2 to 51.4 for July, an increase of 34.5%. Thereafter the price declined inappreciably to 49.9 for August and was 51.3 for September and 51.0 for October. The copper and brass stocks monthly average price stood at 75.2 for Jan. 1943 as compared with 71.6 and 88.3 for December and January of 1942. By April 1943 this average stood at 85.8, the highest monthly average for the year. Following April, a moderate decline occurred, namely, to 77.4 for October.

Combining all of the aforementioned groups of stocks (90 representative shares), the market showed an increase from 80.2 for January to 98.1 for July, or more than 22%. Subsequently, the price level declined from 98.1 to 94.3 for October, or by 3.8%.

On Jan. 1, 1943, the market value of all listed shares on the New York Stock exchange stood at $38,016,706,000, with an average market price per share of $26.39. On Dec. 1, 1943, this market value stood at $45,101,778,943, with an average market price of $32.44. An appreciation in value of approximately 18.7% was thus shown for the year.

Number, Volume and Amount of Stocks.—According to the New York Stock exchange's compilation, the total of stocks listed on that exchange on Dec. 1, 1943, stood at 1,486,877,195 shares, with a total market value of $45,101,778,943. This value compares with $37,374,000,000 and $37,882,000,000 at the corresponding dates of 1942 and 1941. Of 1943's total (on Nov. 1), U.S. stocks aggregated 1,445,000,000 shares, valued at $47,279,000,000, and stocks of other countries 40,473,000 shares valued at $899,249,000. The total of shares was distributed over 1,218 separate United States issues and 17 issues of other countries, representing a total of 868 issuing corporations.

Total shares traded on the New York Stock exchange during 1943 amounted to 274,039,185 (up to Dec. 27), as compared with 125,677,963 during 1942; 170,534,363 during 1941; 207,605,359 during 1940; 262,015,799 during 1939; and 1,124,991,000 during 1929, the largest total on record. The 1943 market, as was also the case in 1942, was relatively stagnant, although total sales were more than double those of 1942. March was the largest month on the New York Stock exchange in 1943, with 36,997,000 shares, while October was the smallest, with only 13,923,000 shares. The New York Curb market had sales during 1943 of 70,228,763 shares (up to Dec. 27), as compared with 22,327,822 shares during 1942 and 34,690,900 shares during 1941.

Bonds.—Using the Standard & Poor's barometer figure for composite bonds (average for each month based on daily closing prices), the average high price stood at 106.4 for Jan. 1943 and 107.4 for February. Thereafter, for the rest of the year, the monthly high average price varied between 111.3 for July and October and 106.4 for January. Moreover, the monthly fluctuation between high and low was very meagre. Only during January was there a range between high and low as great as 1.90 points.

The yearly price movement thus showed a remarkably stable bond market during 1943, and an exceedingly high price level. According to the New York Stock exchange's record, bond and note flotations of United States corporations during the first 10 months of 1943 totalled only $792,618,000; but exclusive of refunding issues, investment trusts and holding companies, the total flotation amounted to only $242,605,000. Both of these figures were substantially similar to the small totals of 1942.

Number, Volume and Amount of Bonds.—According to the New York Stock exchange's compilation, the total par value of bonds listed on that exchange at the beginning of Nov. 1943 stood at $91,003,712,000, with a market value of $90,501,769,000. These figures compared with $67,155,675,000 and $64,543,971,000, respectively, for Dec. 1942. The increase in the par value of bonds during 1943 was largely attributable to the issue of large amounts of new United States government securities. Of 1943's total, United States corporation bonds amounted to (at the beginning of November) $16,603,934,000 par value, with a market value of $14,366,125,000; company bonds of other countries with

Table II.—*1943 Price Range of 25 Representative U.S. Common Stocks*

Stock	High	Low	Last (Dec. 27)
Allied Chemical & Dye	165	140½	148
American Car & Foundry	45½	24¼	34¼
American Smelting & Refining	47⅞	36½	36¾
American Telegraph & Telephone	158¼	127¼	155½
American Tobacco	63¾	42½	56⅝
Anaconda Copper	31⅞	24⅛	24¾
Bethlehem Steel	69⅛	54	55¾
Chrysler corporation	85⅜	67⅝	81½
Douglas Aircraft	73½	44	48⅜
E. I. du Pont de Nemours	159¼	134	140
General Baking	9¼	5¾	7¾
General Electric	39⅞	30¾	36⅞
General Motors	56	44⅛	51½
Goodyear Tire & Rubber	41⅞	25⅛	38⅜
Great Northern railway	32⅞	21⅞	25⅜
Illinois Central railroad	16¾	8	10⅛
International Harvester	74¾	56⅝	71¾
Montgomery Ward	50	33¼	44¾
National Dairy Products	21⅞	14⅝	19⅜
New York Central railroad	20	10⅜	15⅝
Pennsylvania railroad	32⅛	23½	25⅝
Standard Oil of Indiana	38¾	28⅛	33⅛
Standard Oil of New Jersey	60	46½	54
Union Pacific railroad	102½	80¼	93
United States Steel	59⅜	47⅜	51

a par value of $828,604,000 and a market value of $744,491,000; United States government bonds (inclusive of corporations and subdivisions) with a par value of $71,518,751,000 and a market value of $74,060,154,000; and other governments (inclusive of subdivisions) with a par value of $2,052,423,000 and a market value of $1,330,999,000. The total listed bonds of United States corporations were distributed over 824 issues with 442 issuers; of United States government bonds with 83 issues and 5 issuers; and other governments with 157 issues and 52 issuers. Total bonds traded on the New York Stock exchange during 1943 amounted to $3,207,300,425 (up to Dec. 27), as compared with $2,182,625,800 during 1942, $2,114,098,550 during 1941, and $1,671,598,875 during 1940.

Stock Exchanges.—Important changes made by the New York Stock exchange in its rules and practices during 1943 were comparatively few. The most important changes may be grouped under the following five headings:

Merchandising of Securities.—On April 1, 1943, the special committee on merchandising of blocks of securities recommended to the board of governors of the exchange, which approved the report, a "continuation of the Exchange's policy to supplement the auction market, when necessary, by authorizing special offerings and secondary distributions of securities and to discuss with the SEC certain changes that would bring special offerings more closely into conformity with secondary distributions." Again, on June 18, the board of governors adopted amendments to the rules to permit dealings in securities on a "when distributed" basis, under certain prescribed conditions. The first instance was reported to have attended the distribution of nearly 2,000,000 shares of Public Service of New Jersey common stock by the United Gas Improvement company under the Public Utility Holding Company act.

A "special offering method of trading" was first approved on a temporary basis on Feb. 16, 1942. On July 2, 1943, the board of governors amended the rules governing special offerings and made this method of distribution a permanent adjunct of the auction market by the SEC. The amendment included "permission to over-allot up to 10% and to include in offering stock acquired in stabilization during offering; prohibiting members from receiving any part of the special commission for any purchase; elimination of requirement to reconfirm on account statements essential details of offering; to make more specific disclosure to customers; to simplify information requirements in application for special offering permission; to provide 15-minute effective period and require Exchange approval for termination of uncompleted offering and removal of three-hour time limit."

Table III.—*U.S. Bond Prices for 1943*
Composite Bonds
Dollars per $100
(Standard Statistics Company)

Month	High	Low	Month	High	Low
Jan.	106.4	104.5	July	111.3	110.4
Feb.	107.4	105.8	Aug.	110.6	110.2
March	109.0	107.4	Sept.	110.6	110.2
April	109.5	109.0	Oct.	111.3	110.1
May	110.5	109.5	Nov.	111.8	110.7
June	110.6	109.1	Dec.	112.6	111.4

Table IV.—*1943 Price Range of 25 Leading U.S. Domestic Bond Issues*

Name	High	Low	Last (Dec.27)
American Telegraph & Telephone 3¼s 66	110½	107⅛	108
American Tobacco 3s 62	105	100⅞	103¾
Atchison, Topeka & Santa Fe 4s 95	120¼	111¼	119⅛
Bethlehem Steel 3¼s 65	105¾	102½	105
Chesapeake & Ohio railroad 4½s 92	137½	130½	132⅛
Commonwealth Edison 3½s 68	111¾	108⅞	110
Erie 4s 95	102	92⅞	101¾
Firestone Tire & Rubber 3s 61	105	99	102
Goodrich 4¼s 56	109	103¾	106½
Great Northern railway 5½s 52	112½	102⅝	112¼
Louisville & Nashville 4½s 2003	105⅛	94½	104½
National Dairy 3¼s 60	108⅛	105½	105⅞
National Distillers 3½s 49	108½	102⅝	106¼
New York Edison 3¼s 65	110⅛	107¾	108⅛
Norfolk & Western railroad 4s 96	132½	124⅝	128
Pennsylvania railroad gen 5s 68	117	108	114¾
Republic Steel 4½s 56	106	101½	106
Southern Pacific 3¾s 46	101 3/16	93½	100 15/16
Standard Oil of New Jersey 3s 61	107½	104	105
Tex. Corp. 3s 65	107	105⅜	105½
Union Pacific 1st 4s 47	109⅜	107⅝	107⅞
United States Steel 2.40s 52	102½	101½	101½
Western Union 5s 51	102¾	87⅛	102½
Westinghouse El. & Mfg. 2⅛s 51	102½	101¼	101¾
Young S. & T. 3¼s 60	101¾	95½	101½

Transfer Taxes and Commissions.—The state of New York, on April 20, 1943, adopted legislation eliminating the requirement that brokers affix tax stamps to transferred securities. Instead, registered stock exchanges or affiliated clearing corporations were authorized to collect the tax, thus relieving brokers of the necessity of maintaining large stocks of stamps, paid for in advance. Similarly, on Oct. 15, the federal department of internal revenue amended its regulation respecting documentary stamp taxes, effective Nov. 1, so that the payment of federal transfer taxes would be made by the Stock Clearing corporation, instead of by the use of stamps by each member firm. On Nov. 23, the New York exchange appeared before the Senate Committee on Banking and Currency and the House Committee on Interstate and Foreign Commerce, in support of an amendment to eliminate the payment of the registration fee on dealings in government securities on national securities exchanges. Both committees approved the legislation.

For a number of years the annual financial report of the New York Stock exchange and affiliated companies had shown a considerable loss. To strengthen its financial position, the constitution of the exchange was amended to read: "when receipts from the stock exchange charge of 1% on members' net commissions, received and retained by members and member firms on transactions effected on the exchange, exceed $500,000 in any year, the rate will be reduced to ½ of 1%, and the charge will be discontinued for the remainder of the year when $750,000 has been received." On June 3, 1943 the board of governors approved an amendment to the constitution removing the aforementioned restrictions on total receipts from the 1% assessment charge.

Renegotiation Contracts of Listed Corporations.—On May 5, 1943, and again on July 28, the presidents of listed corporations were advised by the New York exchange that upon completion of any renegotiation proceedings, they should report to stockholders any effect that the settlements might have on the operating figures.

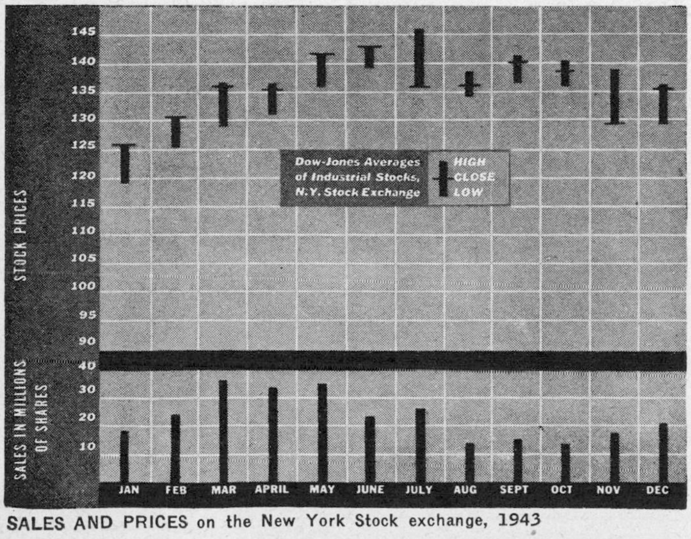

SALES AND PRICES on the New York Stock exchange, 1943

Regulations with Respect to War Loans.—Announcement was made by the New York exchange, on Sept. 15, 1943, that "for a period of fifteen days after Third War Loan Bonds are delivered to subscribers, no member firm may carry them on margin unless the customer (1) agrees to pay off the debit balance against such bonds within six months or less and (2) does not contemplate selling the security prior to full payment." Mention should also be made of the exchange's special advertising campaign of the Third War loan.

Other Actions.—Five such actions of 1943 deserve special mention, namely: (1) The amendment of the general margin rule of the exchange to the effect that "on and after April 1 purchases of securities selling below 5 may only be made on a cash basis." (2) The amendment by the SEC of the short sales rule so that "in determining the price at which a short sale may be effected in a security that has gone ex-dividend, ex-right or ex-any other distribution, all sale prices for the security prior to the 'ex' date may be reduced by the value of the distribution." (3) Disapproval, on June 18, in answer to a special poll, of the plan to admit corporations as members of the exchange. The canvass disclosed that 67% of members of the exchange and 76% of member firms registered such disapproval. (4) The suggestion by the New York exchange, on Oct. 14, to presidents of listed corporations "that stock dividends received not be recorded as income and that stockholders be notified of the amount of earnings or earned surplus capitalized by stock dividends when issued by a corporation." (5) Announcement of the exchange, on Dec. 2, that "to enlarge the usefulness of the Exchange, studies and preliminary research had been initiated looking toward the development of plans for mobilization of private capital to aid in world reconstruction after the war is won." (*See also* BUSINESS REVIEW.)   (S. S. H.)

Stoessel, Albert Frederic

(1894–1943), U.S. conductor, composer and violinist, was born Oct. 11 in St. Louis, Mo. Widely known as a teacher, Mr. Stoessel headed the New York university music department, 1923–30, and was a faculty member of the Juilliard Graduate school, 1930–43. He was also music director of the Chautauqua Symphony orchestra, 1920–43, and conductor of the Oratorio Society of New York, 1921–43. He directed the Worcester festival, 1925, and the Westchester County Musical festival, 1927–33. His compositions include *Suite Antique, Cyrano de Bergerac, A Festival Fanfare, Hispania Suite, Concerto Grosso* and an opera, *Garrick* (1936). He collapsed on the stage of the American Academy of Arts and Letters in New York city, May 12, while conducting an orchestra at the annual ceremony of the academy and the National Institute of Arts and Letters, and died shortly afterwards. (See *Encyclopædia Britannica*.)

Stomach Disorders: *see* ALIMENTARY SYSTEM, DISORDERS OF.

Stone.

The following table lists the production of the various types of stone in the United States, so far as data were available at the close of 1943.

Production of Stone in the United States
(In thousands of short tons or thousands of dollars)

Name of Stone	1942			1941		
	Dimension	Crushed	Total	Dimension	Crushed	Total
Basalt	13	17,613	17,626	10	17,927	17,937
Granite	522	13,543	14,064	782	13,517	14,299
Limestone	463	142,025	142,488	814	132,350	133,164
Marble	49	121	170	69	107	176
Sandstone	233	6,468	6,701	183	7,409	9,592
Others	68	14,766	14,835	89	9,851	9,940
Total	1,347	194,537	195,884	1,947	181,161	183,108
Value	$16,702	$188,300	$205,002	$21,396	$173,942	$195,338

Dimension Stone.—Sales of dimension stone in 1942 were 31% less in quantity than in 1941, but only 22% less in value. Building construction used 76% of the total, with small percentages going to monumental work (marble and granite only), paving, curbing and flagging. In addition to the stone listed above, 107,030 tons of slate were sold as dimension stone in 1942.

Crushed Stone.—Sales of crushed stone in 1942 increased 7% over 1941, while value increased 8%; this does not include 47,657,000 tons of crushed limestone used in the production of cement, 12,208,000 tons used in making lime, or 483,740 tons of crushed slate. Concrete and road metal took 55% of the total, metallurgical and refractory uses 17%, agricultural uses 7% (all limestone), and railroad ballast 9%.   (G. A. Ro.)

Straits Settlements.

A British crown colony, under Japanese occupation Feb. 1942, one of the three principal administrative divisions of British Malaya, the others being the Federated and Unfederated Malay States

SCHOOL FOR SINGAPORE RESIDENTS in which they are required to learn the Japanese language. This photograph was released by the Japanese to neutral sources in 1943

(*qq.v.*). Area of Straits Settlements, 1,356 sq.mi.; pop. (1941) 1,435,895, divided racially as follows: Europeans 18,101, Malays 315,629, Eurasians 13,540, Chinese 927,003, Indians 148,851, others 12,771. The capital is Singapore and the large population, in relation to area, of the Straits Settlements is explained by the fact that it includes the two largest cities and trading centres of British Malaya, Singapore and Penang, the latter located on an island off the west coast of the Malay peninsula. The Japanese changed the name of Singapore to Shonan (Light of the South) and carried out propaganda among Indian prisoners of war and among the local Indian population with a view to organizing a "fifth column" Indian army under the direction of the pro-axis Indian nationalist leader, Subhas Chandra Bose.

Education, Finance, Communication.—There were 420 schools, with 83,078 students and pupils, in 1940. The unit of currency before the Japanese occupation was the Straits dollar, equivalent to 47.51 U.S. cents in 1941. The pound sterling was often used in financial estimates. Revenue in 1941 was £5,501,790 and expenditure £7,056,729. At the end of 1940 there were 1,073 mi. of metalled roads and 133 mi. of gravelled roads in the colony.

There were radio broadcasting stations at Singapore and for Penang in Province Wellesley.   (W. H. CH.)

Strategic Mineral Supplies.

As 1943 ended there were in the U.S. some metals, formerly short in supply, that shifted to a position of adequacy for essential demands, or to a moderate surplus. Furthermore, this position was made all the more secure by the fact that none of these shifts was announced merely on the basis of a current balance between supply and essential demands, but only after there was accumulated a surplus stock sufficient to cover the demands for six months or more.

The periodical "Material Substitution and Supply List" of the War Production board classified the essential material under these three groups:

I. Those insufficient in supply to meet war and essential industrial demands.
II. Those with approximate balance between supply and demand.
III. Those with an excess of supply over demand.

During the latter half of 1943, the following shifts were made in the classification of metal and mineral products, the list being confined to raw materials only, and not including any semi-manufactured materials in which a shortage was created by lack of processing plants or equipment, rather than by shortage of the primary raw material.

From Group I to Group II: Aluminum, chromium, magnesium, molybdenum, tungsten, vanadium, zinc, cryolite, graphite, mica and spodumene.

From Group I to Group III: Cobalt and talc.

From Group II to Group III: Calcium, mercury, palladium, titanium, zirconium and vermiculite.

On the other hand, it was found necessary to shift columbium, platinum and natural gas from Group II to Group I, and coal and petroleum from Group III to Group II.

Metals remaining classified in Group I through the year were arsenic, beryllium, bismuth, cadmium, copper, nickel, tantalum, tin, high-grade asbestos, high-grade bauxite, low-grade chromite, corundum, fluorspar, fuel oil, gasoline, nitrates and quartz crystals.

The improvements in supply outlined above were in many cases sufficient to permit the relaxation of control methods, and in others complete removal of control. Prospects promised continued improvement in the supply situation of other metals in 1944, and material increases in the amounts available for civilian supplies.

(G. A. Ro.)

Stratton, Dorothy Constance

(1899–   ), U.S. coast guard officer, was born in Brookfield, Mo., March 24. Beginning as a teacher of history in Brookfield, she became (1924) vice-principal and dean of girls at the San Bernardino, Calif., senior high school. In 1933 she joined the faculty of Purdue university as associate professor of psychology and dean of women; in 1940 she was made a full professor. During her incumbency she was instrumental in securing improvements for women students, including the establishment of residence halls and an employment service. In the summer of 1942, after helping to select one of the first groups of recruits for the Women's Army Auxiliary corps, she joined the Women's Naval reserve (WAVES) as a lieutenant. In September she became assistant to the commanding officer at the training centre for radio operators at Madison, Wis. When the Women's Reserve of the coast guard was created, Lieut. Stratton was selected to head the new unit and was promoted to the rank of lieutenant commander. She was sworn in on Nov. 24, 1942. The nickname SPARS, officially accepted as a designation for this unit, was coined by Lieut. Com. Stratton.

Lieut. Com. Stratton wrote *Problems of Students in a Graduate School of Education* (1933) and was co-author of *Your Best Foot Forward* (1940).

Streeter, Ruth Cheney

(1895–   ), officer of U.S. Marine Corps Women's reserve, was born Oct. 2 in Brookline, Mass. Educated in Boston and Paris schools and Bryn Mawr college, she married Thomas Winthrop Streeter, lawyer, in 1917 and settled in Morristown, N.J. Mrs. Streeter became increasingly active in state and local affairs, serving on a number of welfare boards. As World War II approached, her interests turned toward national defense. In 1941–42 she was a member of the aviation committee of the New Jersey Defense council, and in 1942–43 she was an adjutant in the Civil Air patrol, having obtained her private pilot's license in 1940 and her commercial pilot's license in 1942. In 1942–43 she was also chairman of the Citizens' Committee for Army and Navy, Inc., for Fort Dix. When the women's reserve of the marine corps was organized early in 1943, Mrs. Streeter was chosen as director, and in February she was inducted with the rank of major. Together with her mother, Mrs. W. H. Schofield, Major Streeter was the donor of the Cheney award given to army aviators for "unusual valour and self-sacrifice" in memory of a brother killed in World War I.

Strikes and Lock-outs.

The United States, Canada and Great Britain published, for many years, current statistics of strikes and lock-outs, their causes and results, together with detailed reports upon the more important strikes of each year. In 1943, the strike information gathered by these countries was much less complete, because of war conditions. Most of the other nations' reports are less complete and less accurate.

The Canadian department of labour published a report on strikes throughout the world in the *Labour Gazette,* March 1937.

The political situation in Germany, Italy, Russia and Japan made it "inadvisable" for wage earners to undertake strikes during recent years. World War II added Czechoslovakia, Poland, France, Norway, Denmark, the Low Countries, Bulgaria, Ru-

ANTHRACITE MINERS loitering near a Pennsylvania colliery entrance in Jan. 1943 after striking against John L. Lewis' demand for increased dues to the United Mine Workers union. President Roosevelt intervened Jan. 19 and ordered the miners back to work

JURISDICTIONAL STRIKE RING

"LADIES AND GENTLEMEN—THE WINNAH." This cartoon by Lewis in the *Milwaukee Journal* appeared shortly after John L. Lewis called a national coal strike April 30, 1943

mania, Greece, Finland, to the area in which strikes would be ruthlessly suppressed.

Table I.—United States: Number of Strikes, Workers Involved and Man-days Lost, 1935-1942*

Monthly Labor Review, United States Bureau of Labor Statistics (May 1943)

Year	Number of Strikes Beginning in Year Indicated	Workers Involved in Strikes Beginning in Year	Man-days Idle During Year
1935	2,014	1,117,213	15,456,337
1936	2,172	788,648	13,901,956
1937	4,740	1,860,621	28,424,857
1938	2,772	688,376	9,148,273
1939	2,613	1,170,962	17,812,219
1940	2,508	576,988	6,700,872
1941	4,228	2,362,620	23,047,556
1942	2,968	839,961	4,182,557

*Strikes involving fewer than 6 workers or lasting less than 1 day are not included in this table nor in the following tables. Notices or leads regarding strikes are obtained by the Bureau from more than 650 daily papers, labour papers, and trade journals, as well as from all government labour boards. Letters were written to representatives of parties in the disputes asking for detailed and authentic information. Since answers to some of these letters had not been received, the figures given for the late months are not final.

Table II.—United States: War Industries' Strikes, 1942 Compared by Months; Also All Strikes, Jan.-June 1943*

Month	Number Strikes		Workers Involved		Man-days Lost	
	All Industries	War Work	All Industries	War Work	All Industries	War Work
1942						
January	156	27	26,929	11,605	330,567	46,197
February	181	50	58,122	24,587	357,333	118,700
March	234	66	67,292	34,957	401,739	166,680
April	277	91	56,038	26,255	367,400	173,513
May	285	125	68,820	44,891	322,085	137,330
June	345	171	109,611	78,627	586,408	254,653
July	388	198	99,676	74,812	416,741	233,614
August	330	195	92,122	70,352	448,712	266,353
September	274	156	87,904	71,912	387,150	318,892
October.	207	93	61,593	38,321	243,756	167,865
November	144	91	52,481	43,422	128,164	91,925
December	147	96	59,269	48,571	192,502	119,572
1943						
January	195	†	90,000	†	450,000	†
February	210	†	42,000	†	170,000	†
March	260	†	72,000	†	230,000	†
April	395	†	200,000	†	675,000	†
May	395	†	620,000	†	1,275,000	†
June	400	†	950,000	†	4,750,000	†

Compiled from *The Monthly Labor Review*, U.S. Bureau of Labor Statistics.

*Strikes affecting war work not separately compiled after Dec. 1942. Monthly strike statistics suspended, because of budgetary necessity, after June 1943. Only Oct. 1943 figures available, but incomplete. †Publication of data for second, fourth and sixth columns discontinued after Dec. 1942.

The year 1937 was still the record year in number of strikes since 1917. The number of strikes began to increase in 1933 and rose steadily through 1937.

Table III.—Relative Frequency and Size of Labour Disputes in Great Britain in 1943 and 1942

Month	Number of Disputes Started in Month		Number of Work People Involved in All Disputes during Month		Working Days Lost in Labour Disputes during Month	
	1943	1942	1943	1942	1943	1942
January	73	57	18,700	17,100	37,100	59,000
February	75	63	16,100	13,700	34,000	29,000
March	152	66	47,400	14,300	122,000	44,000
April	121	91	31,900	36,400	68,000	66,000
May	139	187	63,500	97,500	178,000	312,000
June	123	144	39,800	130,500	112,000	360,000
July	103	75	34,300	18,800	97,000	42,000
August	137	123	56,100	22,100	139,000	38,000
September	190	128	88,700	26,000	337,000	55,000
October	..	110	..	58,500	..	337,000
November	..	130	..	40,300	..	93,000
December	..	87	..	25,300	..	90,000

Compiled from British *Labour Gazette*.

Table IV.—Causes of Labour Disputes in Great Britain, 1943, by Months, and Monthly Average for 1942*

Cause	Average, 1942	J	F	M	A	M	J	J	A	S
Demands for wage increases.	31	18	13	40	35	24	27	19	29	57
Resistance to wage reductions	4	.	3	6	7	13	9	6	7	10
Other wage questions . .	28	19	18	33	32	41	28	35	42	43
Hours	3	2	4	6	4	10	3	2	6	.
Employment of particular classes of people or individuals	13	7	10	26	17	19	17	12	18	24
Other working arrangements	16	20	22	35	21	31	28	26	27	31
Questions involving trade union principles	1	6	5	2	1	1	4	1	.	4
Sympathetic strikes	.6	1	.	4	4	.	7	2	8	11

Compiled from British *Labour Gazette*, Oct., 1943.

*Figures for September are provisional and subject to revision. Those for previous months have been revised (from previous *Year Book* figures) in accordance with more recent information.

Table V.—Results of Labour Disputes in Great Britain Settled in 1943

Results of Strikes	Average 1942	J	F	M	A	M	J	J	A	S
Settled in favour of labour	15	12	15	20	16	27	17	13	27	26
Settled in favour of employers	48	33	35	67	63	71	65	36	77	98
Settled by compromises .	20	15	19	31	24	17	22	21	19	37
Negotiations pending, but work resumed	18	12	10	30	17	25	18	18	16	20

Compiled from British *Labour Gazette*, Feb.-Oct., 1943.

Table VI.—Number and Time Loss in Canadian Labour Disputes, 1943 and 1942

Month	1943			1942		
	No. of Strikes	No. of employees involved	Time loss in working days	No. of Strikes	No. of employees involved	Time loss in working days
January . .	34	19,857	166,707	13	2,715	46,606
February .	32	5,243	24,306	16	2,901	23,997
March . .	28	17,008	31,183	18	3,770	23,191
April . . .	37	30,526	102,685	17	6,838	20,403
May . . .	39	15,351	46,792	32	6,904	18,047
June . . .	55	22,331	140,885	55	16,275	41,593
July . . .	42	15,984	66,971	68	21,736	53,498
August . .	50	35,201	236,948	59	21,434	49,951
September .	42	11,076	36,896	43	13,357	37,808
October . .	36	5,923	25,496	26	6,107	20,926
November .	..	..	..	27	20,490	103,770
December .	..	..	..	13	1,434	6,016
Total . .	395	178,500	878,869	387	123,961	451,806

Compiled from *Canadian Labour Gazette*. All 1943 figures are preliminary.

Table VII.—Trend of Labour Disputes in Canada, 1931–42

Year	Number of disputes	Number of workers involved	Time loss in man-working days
1931	88	10,738	204,238
1932	116	23,390	255,000
1933	125	26,558	317,547
1934	191	45,800	574,519
1935	120	33,269	284,028
1936	156	34,812	276,997
1937	278	71,905	886,393
1938	147	20,395	148,678
1939	122	41,038	224,588
1940	168	60,619	266,318
1941	231	87,091	433,914
1942	354	113,916	450,202

Compiled from *Canadian Labour Gazette*.

The monthly reports on strikes issued by the U.S. bureau of labour statistics indicated that close to one-half of the strikes of 1941 involved some question of union recognition, with wages the other major issue. In 1943, the principal cause was wage disputes. In Great Britain a very large percentage of the strikes end definitely in favour of the employers, and disputes over union recognition are far less common than in the United States.

Canada had only 192 strikes in 1940 involving 63,469 workers and but 268 involving 97,580 employees in 1941. (*See also* LABOUR UNIONS; NATIONAL LABOR RELATIONS BOARD; UNITED STATES; WAR LABOR BOARD, NATIONAL.) (D. D. L.)

Strontium.
Shortage in the supply of strontium in the United States was relieved during 1943, and the year ended with the supply in balance with essential demands. The latest available figures on production in the United States were: 4,724 short tons of strontium minerals in 1941, and imports of about the same size, both heavy increases over 1940. The demand was due to the use of strontium salts in tracer bullets and signal flares. (G. A. Ro.)

Submarines: *see* NAVIES OF THE WORLD.

Submarine Warfare.*
Axis Submarine Campaign.—As the year 1942 ended the U-boat campaign in the Atlantic loomed large as the major threat to a United Nations' victory. On the land fronts things were going well; the epic of Stalingrad had turned the tide in Russia, General Eisenhower's combined forces were well established in North Africa, and even in the South Pacific the all-conquering Japanese were being driven back from their farthest outposts. But the wolf-packs of U-boats still, as shown in the record of shipping losses for 1942, were having their innings in the Atlantic.

*All assertions or opinions contained in this article are the private ones of the writer and are not to be construed as official or reflecting the views of the U.S. navy department or of the naval service at large.

EXPLODING DEPTH CHARGE from the U.S. coast guard cutter "Spencer," on convoy duty in the north Atlantic in 1943. As the convoy (background) proceeded on its course, the "Spencer" tracked down and sank a German submarine

They remained the chief obstacle to successful conclusion of the European war, and that the menace was fully appreciated by the heads of governments of the United Nations was borne out not only by their statements but by the urgent actions taken to counter it. Even to the layman it was clear that, unless the U-boat's supremacy could be checked, the Allied forces in North Africa and Britain would not be properly supplied or augmented, and that the flow of lend-lease supplies to Russia would be insufficient to keep that valiant ally girt with the sinews of war.

Official quarters still remained silent on losses of merchant tonnage but, at the end of 1942, unofficial sources in close touch with the situation estimated that a minimum of 4,000,000 gross tons was lost to the Allies during the year. Some estimates (by the Truman committee of the U.S. senate) ran as high as 12,000,000 tons, an average of 1,000,000 a month, but this probably referred to deadweight tons—equivalent to about 8,000,000 gross tons. Secretary of the Navy Frank Knox admitted that Allied merchant losses were 1,000,000 gross tons greater than the combined gross tonnage of all cargo vessels built by the United Nations during 1942. As the United States alone built approximately 5,400,000 gross tons in 1942, and as the other Allies probably accounted for more than 1,000,000 more, it may safely be assumed that the total loss of United Nations' merchant shipping approximated 7,000,000 gross tons. This figure, however, was not as staggering as the admission that valuable bottoms and crews were still being destroyed at a rate considerably in excess of their replacement.

That Hitler was fully aware of the value of his underseas arm as his most likely hope of victory was evidenced in Jan. 1943 by his appointment of Admiral Karl Doenitz, his submarine specialist, to be grand admiral, succeeding to supreme command of the entire German navy. This appointment highlighted the role the U-boat was expected to play in the forthcoming campaign, for Doenitz was known as an able, crafty strategian who would get the utmost from the powerful weapon he had forged. The new grand admiral promptly announced his intention to "put the entire concentrated strength of the navy into the submarine war, which will be waged with still greater

vigour and determination."

Thus the curtain rose on the campaign of 1943. The might of the U-boat fleet was feared by all the United Nations and those months of early spring, when the full weight of the wolf-packs might be expected, assumed a nightmarish aspect. It was presumed that Hitler had available at least 400 U-boats, and some estimates ran as high as 700. To pit against these the Allies had a rapidly increasing number of antisubmarine weapons, but as yet these were new and untried. The outlook was dismal.

January, with high and wintry seas, was a bad month for the U-boats. Nine merchantmen were sunk during the first week, but these were mostly in the comparatively placid waters off South America. Eight more cargo bottoms were later reported sunk in the western Atlantic, then, at month's end, four more in the South Atlantic. Counting other scattered sinkings, the loss during January probably totalled close to 250,000 gross tons. Germany claimed a gross of 408,000 tons.

Early in February Secretary of the Navy Knox stated that there were then more U-boats at sea than during the critical month of June 1942; he added that the navy was "straining every effort to produce sufficient antisubmarine vessels." The United States was shocked by the torpedoing of two American passenger-cargo ships in the North Atlantic with a loss of 850 lives, mostly service personnel. But few other losses were reported, and in one week it was officially stated that there were no sinkings whatever in the western Atlantic—the first such week since Pearl Harbor. It is probable that total shipping losses in February were about 200,000 tons, and it was generally felt that Doenitz was saving his knockout blow for more propitious spring weather.

March, living up to expectations, started off with heavy U-boat blows in the western Atlantic, the nazis claiming 23 ships in the first five days. The wolves were out in force and were exacting a toll—at what price could only be guessed, but the results were serious. Official reports from both sides of the Atlantic indicated that antisubmarine craft were in attendance on the vital convoys in increasing numbers, but still the losses were so great that the outcome was in grave doubt. There were indications that March sinkings totalled close to 500,000 gross tons.

But April, usually the best month for U-boats, proved a surprise. Early in the month Berlin claimed the sinking of 14 Allied merchantmen in the Atlantic and Mediterranean, and 16 more in later wolf-pack attacks on northern convoy routes. U-boats were again active sporadically off the coast of the United States and in the Caribbean, but it was evident that the antisubmarine drive of the United Nations was at last taking effect. Whereas many experts expected disaster to the tune of at least 1,000,000 tons in April, the total sinkings are known to have been less than those of March and were probably in the vicinity of 350,000 gross tons. Even Germany claimed only 423,000.

Such a turn in the tide of battle was almost unbelievable and victory over the U-boat could not be claimed until borne out by a steadily decreasing rate of shipping losses in succeeding months. In May, Germany admitted its recent lack of success, blaming it on "extraordinarily bad weather, too many convoy lanes, and strong escorts"—an unusually honest estimate. Official Allied sources stated that now all transatlantic convoys were covered by an "air umbrella" throughout their entire passage, and the conduct of all convoys in the northwest Atlantic was concentrated in the hands of Rear Admiral L. W. Murray, an antisubmarine expert of the Canadian navy. Concurrently the 10th fleet, U.S. navy, was formed, composed of various types of antisubmarine craft in the Atlantic and under the direct command of Admiral E. J. King, commander in chief, U.S. navy, with Rear Admiral F. S. Low, U.S.N., acting as chief of staff with immediate supervision over its activities; the relationship

between the 10th fleet and Admiral Murray's command remains unexplained, but is undoubtedly very close. The U-boat bag for May was probably about 300,000 gross tons, and a German radio broadcast alibied that there were "simply not enough ships which could be sunk."

June remained quiet and it became apparent that the nazis, suffering severe reverses, were recalling their U-boats from previously happy hunting grounds and were probing for more lucrative areas for attack. Two full weeks passed without a single sinking in the western Atlantic. Reports of killings of U-boats began to trickle in, adding up to so impressive a total that it appeared the submarines were finally on the defensive. It was reliably stated that escort craft (surface and air) were now present in such numbers that they could engage in active searching for U-boats at a distance from the convoys, keeping them almost immobilized beneath the surface and unable to close with their prey. Losses in June dropped to the lowest in 19 months, about 120,000 tons. Days passed without the sinking of an Allied cargo vessel in any ocean and there was no discounting the remarkable victory over the U-boat. Prime Minister Winston Churchill, after announcing heavy losses of U-boats during May and June, added: "Staggered by these deadly losses, the U-boats have recoiled to lick their wounds and mourn their dead." It was generally believed that they were withdrawn from the now lethal North Atlantic to be refitted with more effective defensive gear and new tactics. They would return again to the fight.

In July, Rear Admiral W. P. Blandy, U.S.N., chief of ordnance, let fall hints of a new antisubmarine weapon. He stated that something very secret, but much more effective than depth charges, was now being employed against U-boats. In spite of this, however, there was an abrupt increase in shipping losses in isolated areas. Wolf-packs were reported off Brazil, torpedoings flowered in the Mozambique-Madagascar area, and there was considerable activity in the Caribbean and off the African coast. It is probable that about 300,000 tons were sent to the bottom—a considerable rise over June. North Atlantic convoys were unmolested.

August was notable for the first official announcement of U-boat losses. President Roosevelt and Prime Minister Churchill issued a joint statement that, during May, June and July, the Allied forces had definitely destroyed more than 90 U-boats. This news brought home to the public the decided turn for the better, and English-speaking peoples everywhere breathed more easily. It was emphasized, however, that the battle was not yet completely won, that there were still tremendous U-boat reserves which could be expected to return to battle refreshed and refurbished with a better defense. During August steps were taken to improve convoy escorts in the South Atlantic, with the result that total losses for the month were reduced to approximately 200,000 gross tons. The Office of War Information (U.S.) stated that now more U-boats were being sunk than merchantmen.

September was still better. Mr. Churchill said that during four months no ship had fallen prey to U-boats in the North Atlantic, and added that during the first two weeks of September "no Allied ships were sunk by U-boat action in any part of the world." Submarines were still active in scattered areas, however, and at month's end there were again reports of wolf-packs prowling the North Atlantic. In spite of this, and of German claims exceeding 300,000 tons, the total loss of cargo bottoms was probably not more than 150,000 gross tons.

Despite the decisive turn in the tide, the underseas weapon still offered the greatest promise of strategical success for Germany, and this was recognized by Hitler and Doenitz. Portugal's permission for the Allies to use the Azores for antisubmarine bases was, however, a heavy blow to nazi hopes, for this made possible continuous air coverage over the convoy routes to the

THE LEON TORPEDO, a version of which was possibly used by the Germans during 1943 in submarine attacks on allied shipping, was designed to correct miscalculations made by a submarine gunnery officer in aiming torpedoes at enemy ships. The diagram shows a submarine (2) at a distance of several miles from the target vessel (4). The line 5 represents the line of sight from the submarine's periscope (3) to the enemy ship. The submarine's gunnery officer, basing his calculations on the speed and direction of the target vessel, assumes that it will reach the position 4' by the time the gyroscopically-steered torpedo (7) has reached it. The torpedo is therefore aimed along the line 6. However, such unforeseeable circumstances as a change in the speed or direction of the target vessel may enable it to reach, for example, the position 4" by the time the torpedo arrives at the position 4'. The Leon torpedo corrects any error in the torpedo's direction after the missile has been fired. It contains, in addition to its gyroscopic steering device, a mechanism which is sensitive to the vibrations set up in the water by the propeller of the target ship. When it picks up these vibrations, it takes over the functions of the gyro (at the point 8) and steers the torpedo along the course 9 directly into the propeller of the target ship

Mediterranean. Again in October the U-boats launched mass attacks to feel out the situation in the North Atlantic, but with little success. Such few sinkings as were accomplished, added to scattered losses, totalled probably not more than those in September—150,000 gross tons.

The curve of merchant sinkings seemed now to have flattened out at about 150,000 tons a month, and this was probably close to the nazi toll again in November. December started with a big spurt, but this was largely the result of the sneak air raid on the crowded harbour of Bari, Italy; U-boats had but little connection with the losses. After a long hiatus, however, they were again active in the Gulf of Mexico and off Cape Hatteras, accounting for one ship in each area, and in the Caribbean, where they destroyed five merchantmen during the month. Berlin claimed a toll of 225,000 tons, but it is probable that again it stayed close to the monthly average of 150,000 gross tons sunk by all methods.

At the end of 1943, German broadcasts asserted that 3,784,500 gross tons of Allied merchant shipping were sunk during the year by all methods, the U-boat being the principal weapon of destruction. In previous years nazi claims were about twice the amount of actual losses. But now, possibly due to despondency over the failure of the U-boat, their claims were not so extravagant. It is probable that actual losses for the year were approximately 2,700,000 gross tons—a discrepancy of about 1,000,000 tons favouring the United Nations. This was little more than half that of the best previous full year of the war, and probably only about one-third of the loss during 1942. Fully to realize the implications of these figures one must remember that 1943 was conceded to be the critical year of U-boat warfare, the year in which Germany reached the peak of her submarine might, the

year when Doenitz expected to hurl back decisively the threat from America. The U-boat was convincingly defeated on its own battleground, and this Allied victory assumes equal stature with the crushing of nazi hordes in Russia during the same period. In fact, the latter was to a large extent dependent on the former.

It seems worthwhile to examine the causes of this crucial victory. To achieve it required the mustering of many weapons, the perfecting of old ones and the invention of new ones. By the combination and co-ordination of all these weapons in a magnificent spirit of aggression the battle was won.

First, the intensified production of cargo vessels on both sides of the Atlantic, but especially in the United States. This is a negative form of action—it increases merchant bottoms in the attempt to keep pace with sinkings, but does nothing to decrease U-boat activity. In 1942 the production of new ships was less than those sunk, but in 1943, when almost 12,500,000 gross tons of new merchantmen were produced in America alone, production so outstripped destruction that it attained a commanding lead. The opening of the Mediterranean in June acted, in effect, to increase considerably the tonnage available to the United Nations by materially shortening the long lines of supply to the middle east and India. The danger of lack of shipping seemed in 1943 to be forever past.

Second, mass production of escort and other antisubmarine craft. This had been greatly accelerated after the entry of the United States into the war. In Britain the frigate superseded the smaller corvette, while in America a new type, called a destroyer escort, was designed for the sole purpose of hunting U-boats on the high seas; this latter type is almost as large as a destroyer but lends itself to production-line manufacture while lacking the speed and armament of its big sister. By March these hunters had taken their stations about convoys in such numbers that they were able to forsake traditional defense measures and form offensive groups to search out the underseas enemy. Patrol craft and submarine chasers were also being commissioned in large numbers. By October's end the situation was so well under control that Secretary of the Navy Knox announced that contracts for 427 antisubmarine craft had been cancelled, 305 of these being destroyer escorts. No more pertinent commentary on the state of the U-boat campaign could have been promulgated.

Third, shore-based air patrols. After the outbreak of war in 1939 the coastal command of the royal air force played a vital role in the battle against the U-boat. Handicapped at first by lack of range, it managed by dint of hard flying to keep the waters about Britain clear of underseas bandits. As successively longer-ranged planes became available the U-boat was driven ever farther into the Atlantic. The United States and Canada soon augmented these patrols, flying from frigid bases in Newfoundland, Greenland, Iceland, until in 1943 only short stretches of ocean were not covered by the huge observation and bombing planes of the Allies. When bases in the Azores were obtained in October the middle Atlantic routes also came under their protection. Another unheralded group of planes kept constant watch over the Bay of Biscay, and these avenging angels were responsible for holding down the U-boats enroute to or from their bases in occupied France.

Fourth, auxiliary carriers. Not until 1943 did these merchantmen, converted into aircraft carriers, really get into the fight. They ranged mid-ocean, where land-based planes could not reach, covering with their brood of planes areas far ahead and on the flanks of the convoy, and operating to keep the U-boats down just when they most needed their surface speed to reach attack positions. The first real news of the "baby flat-tops" came in March when Secretary Knox announced that dozens of them were already in operation. From then on they were much in the public eye. They haunted those sea stretches where the U-boat was most active and, in addition to keeping it immobilized, were credited with more than their share of sinkings. In this writer's opinion the auxiliary carriers were more responsible for the U-boat's defeat than any other one factor.

Fifth, bombing at the source. The battering by United Nations' bombers of U-boat construction yards and repair bases in Germany, France and Norway was pursued vindictively during the winter and spring months, and the precision daylight bombing by the 8th U.S. air force was particularly effective. It is doubtful if many U-boats, protected by bombproof pens, were themselves severely damaged, but the devastation inflicted on building and repair facilities had the unquestioned effect of greatly extending the stay of the U-boats in port. To escape these deadly bombings Germany transplanted some building yards to the eastern Baltic; evacuation of civilians from the operating bases at Lorient, Brest and St. Nazaire was also necessary. After May such raids were less frequent—a silent commentary on the state of the U-boat campaign. Toward the end of the year the 15th U.S. air force, from bases in the Mediterranean, heavily raided the U-boat lairs at Marseilles and Toulon, indicating that axis submarines were becoming obnoxious in the middle sea.

Sixth, blimps. While these are short-ranged and used only for coastal convoys, they, because of their ability to hover over a danger spot, have proved invaluable. They were produced in increasing numbers and the U.S. navy boasts that no merchant ship has been lost from a blimp-protected convoy. The same, however cannot be said of the blimps; in July, off the Florida coast, one was shot down by a U-boat.

Seventh, technological advances. Scientists of the United Nations pitted their wits against those of the axis to keep anti-submarine measures a jump ahead of the U-boat. While most of this work was of a secret nature it seemed that they had been successful. Electronic devices were developed for both surface and submerged work, and these were probably of vital importance to the escort and aircraft in locating the U-boat. Depth charges were stepped-up to cope with strengthened hulls, and new methods of laying them were devised. The chief new nazi weapon was the acoustic torpedo, which is directed to its target and exploded under its stern by the target's propeller noises, crippling both motive and steering power and leaving the mer-

chantman a helpless victim to a later orthodox torpedo. As yet there was no hint of the nature of the amazing new weapons stated by Admiral Blandy to be in service. The British, however, stated that aircraft in 1943 were carrying searchlights of such intensity that U-boats were forced to remain submerged even at night.

British Submarines Against Supply Lines.—The splendid work carried on in the Mediterranean in 1942 against Field Marshal Erwin Rommel's lines of supply to North Africa was maintained valiantly during 1943. Aided by a few Greek, Polish, Dutch and Yugoslav submarines operating under the British high command, the British undersea force achieved phenomenal results. Working in narrow waters under constant surveillance by enemy aircraft, they rendered the short passage of axis supply ships and transports so dangerous that possibly less than half of them got through unscathed. Realizing that the fate of the empire rested on them, the submarine captains exerted every effort to stem the flow of munitions to Africa. Their success was epitomized by the understatement of Admiral of the Fleet Sir Andrew B. Cunningham, R.N., Mediterranean commander in chief: "Our submarines had a very good time—and some made surprising bags." At the time of the September invasion of the Italian mainland British submarines had reportedly sunk a total of 1,335,000 gross tons since the beginning of the campaign. They continued to take a steady though lighter toll, pursuing axis cargo carriers into the Tyrrhenian, Adriatic and Aegean seas. During the height of the Mediterranean campaign most of Britain's submarine fleet was probably operating there. But results warranted such a concentration, and it is unquestionable that they played a decisive role in the defeat and expulsion of Rommel's Afrika Korps, and in clearing the vital Mediterranean lifeline.

U.S. Submarines in the Pacific.—In the far western reaches of the Pacific was waged throughout 1943 a war of attrition against the Japanese which was a miniature of the U-boat campaign in the Atlantic but which greatly outstripped its nazi counterpart in comparative success. Operating from Hawaii against Japan's home waters, from Australia against Japanese supply lines in the conquered Indies, and from Aleutian bases against the Kuriles and northern routes, fine American submarines, acting mostly as lone wolves, struck heavy blows at the lifelines essential to the maintenance of Japanese control. To appreciate fully the strategical necessity of this campaign one must understand Japan's shipping predicament. It was reliably estimated in 1941 that Japan had slightly in excess of 7,000,000 tons of cargo bottoms, counting those United Nations' ships that were confiscated in oriental ports. This was more than sufficient to serve the nations' normal needs but, with the rapid expansion of empire southward, it was entirely incapable of coping with the complex burden of supplying advanced bases, moving armies, and carrying loot, in the form of raw materials, back to the homeland. Quickly recognizing that here was the Achilles' heel of Japan, Admiral C. W. Nimitz, U.S.N., commander in chief Pacific, a submarine pioneer, directed that this weakness be fully exploited. Although some submarines were diverted to patrol and reconnoitre off enemy bases, the main force was concentrated on this attenuated line of supply.

Results were excellent. On Jan. 2, 1943, the navy department reported the sinking of the 112th Japanese ship, and on Dec. 28 the total sunk was announced as 386—a net increase for the year of 274 ships. In addition to these almost sure losses (the navy analyzes each reported sinking and accepts only those that are foolproof) there were 36 more probably sunk and 114 damaged. These losses included the few combatant ships that succumbed to pig-boat torpedoes, but the great majority were cargo carriers, either merchant or naval. Between these dates United

States submarines haunted the coastal routes along the main Japanese islands and occupied China, the waters about the Philippines and Malaysia and, in one case, were reported in the sacrosanct and narrow Straits of Tsushima, separating Japan from Korea. Daring feats and large bags featured the press releases from the navy department; presidential unit citations were awarded a number of underseas raiders, as in the case of the renowned "Wahoo" which, in a 14-hour battle with a heavily armed convoy, sank all four of the valuable ships in it—a total of 31,890 gross tons.

In estimating the amount of Japanese tonnage lost during the war it must be remembered that the great majority of Japanese cargo carriers are in the coastal trade and are accordingly of relatively low tonnage. It is known that the Jap resorted to the use of junks and barges, and started building these in large numbers in the shipyards of occupied China. In September, Secretary Knox estimated that more than 2,500,000 tons of Japanese shipping had gone down, this total amounting to one-third of that available, counting what had been seized, salvaged and repaired; 77% of the sinkings were accomplished by submarines, including a few Hollanders. This tonnage loss is probably a bit high, and based on over-optimistic reports from submarine skippers. Assuming the average Japanese cargo bottom to be somewhat under 5,000 gross tons, it would appear that not more than 1,250,000 tons were sunk in 1943, making a grand total of about 1,750,000 gross tons since Pearl Harbor. Even these reduced figures, considering the parlous state of Japanese shipping, were reassuring, for estimates of new construction in the mikado's empire varied from 400,000 to 700,000 tons a year. The United Nations were surely making serious inroads into this irreplaceable merchant fleet, and that this was appreciated by the high command was indicated in November by the promotion of Rear Admiral C. A. Lockwood, U.S.N., commander submarines Pacific, to the rank of vice admiral.

Japan's Submarine Effort.—The sizable submarine fleet of Japan is circumscribed in its efforts by geography. Early in the war it made desultory jabs at shipping along the American Pacific coast and on the route to Hawaii. But these proved unworthy of the expenditure of fuel and time and were largely discontinued. The important U.S. supply lines to Australia proved a luscious target and the initial steps were taken to attack this route in force. But the United States' acquisition of bases in the Fijis and New Hebrides, and the 1942 campaign against the southern

Solomons, deprived the Japs of any really effective bases for such operations. There remained only the coastal route along eastern Australia, and here the underseas craft of Japan were reported active in May and again in October. General Douglas MacArthur, U.S.A., stated that wolf-pack tactics were employed, and his spokesman (unidentified) admitted a loss of 2% of shipping in the southwest Pacific, but this percentage was probably effective only during a relatively brief period. In May the Australian hospital ship "Centaur," properly marked and lighted, fell prey to a Japanese pirate, the loss of life being fairly light —299 doctors, nurses and crew. Some of the sinkings in the western Indian ocean, generally credited to U-boats, were possibly the work of Japanese submarines, but even so, their success against shipping lanes was inconsequential and their chief efforts were directed against naval objectives.

Russian Submarines in Commerce Warfare.—There is always a paucity of news regarding all submarine operations, but from Russia, known to have sizable underwater flotillas, there came complete silence. About 50 submarines were working in the Black sea and, although any knowledge of results was lacking, it was probable that these continuously harassed the Rumania-Crimea supply line. Other Russian boats were known to be operating in the Barents sea against German lines to northern Norway and Finland, and the fact that the luftwaffe heavily

DECK OF GERMAN SUBMARINE, raked by shellfire and about to sink, after the U.S. coast guard cutter "Spencer" had encountered it in the north Atlantic in 1943. A single crewman is left on the deck; the others have jumped in the sea or been killed

bombed Russian submarine bases indicated that this campaign had more than nuisance value. At least 50 submarines were known to have been stationed at Vladivostok in the Pacific; while these were inactive as long as Japan and Russia remained at peace, they constituted a real threat in case of an eventual break.

Blockade.—Blockade is, of course, another form of warfare against shipping. In the past it was a nonviolent method, sanctioned by international law, of preventing a neutral nation from supplying one's enemy with the sinews of war. It was enforced by proclamation, coercion and, as a last resort, force. To be binding it must be effective; that is, naval craft must be off the blockaded coast in sufficient force to ensure compliance. In World War I the U-boat soon rendered a close blockade too dangerous to be practical. Further, in its all-out attack on both enemy and neutral shipping, it discarded the accepted rules of visit and search because they were not in concord with the nature of a submarine. Consequently such blockades as remained were conducted along the shipping routes far from the enemy's coasts and merchantmen were coerced into proceeding to belligerent control ports for examination and possible condemnation. The coming of the aeroplane further sounded the death knell of the old-style blockade.

In World War II, Britain imposed much the same sort of distant blockade; it was never, however, legally declared. But, as most neutral nations themselves became involved in hostilities, there remained but few merchantmen against whom a blockade could be imposed—for enemy cargo carriers are always legitimate game. The warfare carried on by U-boats against transatlantic shipping and by the U.S. submarines against the Japanese lifelines might be termed, in an unorthodox sense, blockade. But there was in 1943 no legal use of blockade as an economic weapon. Blockade still existed, however, in a real sense, as evidenced by the continuing use of United Nations seapower to prevent overseas trade with Germany or any of its satellites. Germany struggled to escape full pressure of this throttling grip by dispatching blockade runners. In 1943, these went, as far as was known, only to Japan, and some were said to be specially constructed submarines of low cargo capacity. While it is doubtful if these achieved any measure of success, such expeditions were sure indications of the extremity of nazi economy.

Submarines in Naval Actions.—In addition to their unending war on shipping, submarines play an important role in naval warfare. Even when destruction of cargo carriers is their primary mission, they never fail to grasp an opportunity to attack an enemy man-of-war. They are also employed in a calculated war of attrition; if submarines are sprinkled liberally enough throughout naval operating areas they are bound eventually to sink a few combatant ships. They see wide employment as scouts, searching in advance of fleets or task forces, or reconnoitring off enemy bases. They have definite value in a fleet action (though not yet so used) to deny certain areas to the enemy, and, following in the wake of battle, to pick off stragglers. Many odd chores fall to the lot of this versatile type—anything that requires stealth and secrecy. By and large, submarines were singularly unsuccessful against men-of-war during 1943, but such uses of this nature as occurred are recorded, as far as secrecy will permit, below.

Germany and Italy.—In February, Germany claimed the U-boat sinking of a "Dido"-class British cruiser in the eastern Mediterranean; this remains unverified. In April, the British destroyer "Harvester" was sunk by U-boat action, and later in the same month the German high command claimed the sinking of the U.S. aircraft carrier "Ranger" in the Atlantic; the navy department vigorously denied that this or any other combatant ship had been sunk, so the episode remained a mystery in 1943. In October, the United States reported the loss of three de-stroyers and a minelayer from "underwater explosion"; possibly these craft were also U-boat victims. In November, the old U.S. destroyer "Borie" sank after a long death struggle with a U-boat, in which her adversary was also lost.

Great Britain.—In April, a British submarine in the Mediterranean blew the bow off an Italian cruiser; its fate was not divulged. In May, an Italian destroyer was sunk in the Mediterranean. In September, midget submarines launched an attack on the pride of the nazi navy, the battleship "Tirpitz," in Alten fjord in northern Norway. Reconnaissance photographs indicated that the "Tirpitz" was badly injured and would be immobilized for months. This was the first public intimation that the British indulged in midget submarines, and nothing is known of their characteristics. The operation was carried out over 1,000 mi. from the nearest base and involved the passage of intricate minefields, nets and obstructions. Three of the midgets were lost. British submarines were also used, chiefly in the Mediterranean, for varied bombardment missions.

Japan.—As previously mentioned, Japan found it difficult to operate against Allied supply lines, so the majority of her submarines were concentrated in combatant areas. The Coral sea and adjacent waters were infested with them in hopes of attacking the omnipresent naval forces or, if attack proved impossible, to wear them down by keeping them constantly on the alert. Few actual sinkings of combatant U.S. vessels were reported and, in view of the navy department's record of candour, it is probable that all that occurred were admitted. It is also likely that some warships were torpedoed but not sunk and that, for reasons of security, these casualties were kept secret. Early in July, the new destroyer "Strong" was sunk in Kula gulf under circumstances that point to a submarine as the offender. Shortly thereafter the transport "McCawley" was sunk, after having been damaged by a bombing which made her an easy prey to a submarine lurking off Rendova island. A few nights later the U.S.S. "Helena," a 10,000-ton 6-inch cruiser, laden with battle honours, was lost in the American victory off Kula gulf; she went down under the impact of three torpedoes in rapid succession, indicating that they came not in the wide spread from a distant destroyer but were fired from a fortunately placed submarine close aboard. In November, at the invasion of Tarawa, the auxiliary carrier "Lipscombe Bay" exploded as the result of a submarine torpedo hit and sank with a large loss of life. The Japanese made masterly use of the submarine in ferrying supplies and reinforcements to Guadalcanal and other beleaguered islands. They were probably used in the evacuation of Kiska. That they were being regularly employed in reconnaissance and as scouts was common knowledge, and that some carry aircraft was verified by the sighting, over Sydney and near Hawaii, of single small Japanese float planes. Japanese submarines were also used for isolated nuisance bombardments. In spite of the lack of merchant targets they were put to a very effective use.

United States.—The main effort being directed against shipping, Japanese men-of-war were, for U.S. submarines, largely targets of opportunity. Such targets, however, loomed up fairly regularly on the crosswires of American periscopes. In October, the navy department reported that a total of 3 cruisers, 22 destroyers, 2 tenders and 12 other combatant ships (all Japanese) had gone to the bottom as the result of submarine torpedoes. How many of these were sunk in 1943 was not stated. Among the "others" was the unnamed gunboat, rammed by the submarine of Commander Howard Gilmore who, lying wounded on his bridge, ordered his mate to "Take her down!" at the expense of his own life but saving his ship and crew. No Japanese submarines were officially listed as lost in those weird "submarine versus submarine" encounters although there were unauthenticated reports that two had been so sunk. American submarines were probably also used on scouting and reconnaissance missions, and there were rumours of their landing shock troops at the beginning of various offensive operations.

Submarine Losses.—*Germany and Italy.*—During 1943, antisubmarine measures (*see* above) became really effective. Even during the bad winter months sure sinkings of U-boats were reported in increasing numbers. With the advent of spring, reports of still heavier submarine losses made the headlines, and these were verified by the joint statement of President Roosevelt and Prime Minister Churchill in August that during the three preceding months there were "over 90" sure sinkings of U-boats. Thereafter, due to the recall of the U-boats from the convoy lanes to new areas and for refitting, the rate dropped. Sinkings continued to be reported in the press, but no more official figures were vouchsafed until October, when another joint statement announced the loss of 60 U-boats during July, August and September. The rate of sinkings, then, was 25 axis submarines a month during the six most propitious months of 1943—undoubtedly greater than the rate at which they were being built. It may be assumed that the rate for the remaining six months was at least half as great, and that not less than 135 axis submarines were destroyed during the year. To this must be added those Italian submarines that fell into United Nations' hands with the capitulation of Italy—probably about 50. The blow to Doenitz' campaign was stupendous and it is remarkable that U-boat morale stood the shock so well. No figures on axis losses were forthcoming from Germany.

Great Britain.—The loss of eight submarines ("Utmost," "Sahib," "Traveller," "P222," "Splendid," "Saracen," "Parthian," "Trooper") was noted during the year—also one Greek and one Fighting French submarine, both operating with British forces in the Mediterranean. In September, the admiralty announced (their figures have always been trustworthy) that a total of 56 British submarines had been sunk during the war; it is doubtful if the figure had reached 60 at year's end.

Japan.—An estimate of Japanese submarine losses is difficult. Individual claims during the year had been noted to a total of 17, and in February the Associated Press tabulation estimated the number sunk since Pearl Harbor at 29. Yet, in October, the navy department reported only 6 sure sinkings since the beginning of the war. On the other hand official Japanese sources have admitted a total loss of 11 submarines through November. As Japanese admissions regarding other categories of ships had been found to be quite accurate there was reason to believe that their figures were the best available. The low number of Japanese sinkings, however, indicated either (1) skilful submarine captains, (2) excellent defensive qualities, (3) inadequate antisubmarine measures by the United States, or (4) lack of full employment of Japanese submarines.

United States.—Eleven U.S. submarines were announced as overdue and probably lost during the year ("Argonaut," "Amberjack," "Grampus," "R-12," "Triton," "Pickerel," "Grenadier," "Dorado," "Runner," "Wahoo," "Grayling"). The giant "Argonaut," after being damaged by depth charges, went down in a blazing gun duel with Japanese surface craft. The "R-12" was lost while on a routine training cruise. The others, including the famous "Wahoo," disappeared without trace in the western Pacific. These losses are approximately double those of 1942 but it was probable that the ratio of losses to submarines operating had changed but little. It was expected, however, that this rate would increase in the future because of the tremendous expansion of the submarine force and the consequent dilution of experienced personnel, and of improved Japanese antisubmarine measures. It is interesting to note that Japan's navy war minister, Admiral

Shimada, announced the sinking during the war of 128 U.S. submarines.

New Construction.—*Germany.*—Estimates of the monthly rate of U-boat construction vary widely. The maximum rate was probably achieved in 1942, about 25 a month. New construction in 1943 was on the wane for two reasons: (1) the heavy bombardments of building yards and parts factories, (2) the necessity for building larger U-boats to reach unprotected areas. While no definite figures were available, it seemed likely that not more than 15 new boats were being produced each month, and that the size of the U-boat fleet in 1943 was approximately 350. The rate of destruction definitely passed the rate of construction. Reliable sources stated that construction of the 517-ton class was suspended and that the majority of new boats were of the more versatile 740-ton type. These have an endurance of 16,000 mi. and achieve a surface speed of nearly 20 knots. It was reported that they were fitted with additional topside armour to permit them to remain on the surface during strafing attacks. They were also being fitted, in addition to their 4.1-in. guns, with an increased number of anti-aircraft weapons, ranging in calibre up to 40-mm. During the year the use of supply submarines (known as "milk cows") was confirmed. These were broadbeamed, unwieldy submersibles, designed to carry quantities of diesel oil, torpedoes, ammunition, water and provisions, and to deliver these to operating U-boats at secret rendezvous at sea. A few large U-boats of more than 1,000 tons, for extreme range and minelaying purposes, probably continued to be built, and rumours were also heard of experimentation with midget types, but these had not been reported in action.

Great Britain.—No reliable information was available. New submarine construction in 1943 had probably not greatly exceeded losses.

Japan.—No data.

United States.—Because of the remarkable success of U.S. submarines against Japanese lines, American shipyards were probably turning out new boats at record speed. They were near the top of the priority list. Secretary Knox stated that "new submarines completed this year would be equal to 30% of the submarine fleet in existence on Jan. 1, 1943." It was estimated that approximately 150 U.S. submarines were in commission in 1943, and this number was steadily increasing.

U.S.S.R.—No data. Probably little new construction.

Submarine Personnel.—*Germany.*—In May, unofficial Allied sources estimated that 12,000 U-boat officers and men were either lost or prisoners. Since that time probably 6,500 more suffered like fates. Such casualties would surely affect the efficiency of remaining U-boat crews; already their increasing lack of daring and proficiency was noted in 1943. From Sweden came reports of U-boat mutinies at Norwegian bases and disturbances at Kiel. Rear Admiral Low stated that Germany found it necessary to draft submarine crews. Experienced U-boat personnel was apparently being spread very thin, accomplished skippers were few, and veteran crewmen formed but a nucleus for a complement of green hands. But there were in 1943 no indications of a general cracking of morale, and it was expected that the U-boat menace would continue in decreasing intensity as long as Germany remained a belligerent.

Great Britain.—Not having experienced rapid expansion, British submarine personnel remained, as far as is known, capable and daring.

Japan.—Results against combatant ships indicated that Japanese submarine crews were well-trained and had a high morale.

United States.—The American submarine force underwent a rapid expansion, and a dilution of veteran personnel was inevitable. Because, however, of the highly selective nature of this duty in peacetime, and of the thorough and strenuous training, new submarines could be expected to be provided with adequate crews.

Submarine Tactics.—Except in Germany, nothing new developed, as far as was known, in submarine tactics. Early in 1942 it appeared that Grand Admiral Doenitz was reverting to the tactics of the wolf-pack, this time throwing as many as 20 to 30 submarines, in echelons, into a single continuing attack on a convoy. Reports were meagre, but it is probable that these echelons were staggered, about 100 mi. apart, across possible convoy tracks. The first U-boat to sight the convoy fell in astern of it, making no attack but "homing" her consorts on the target by radio direction finders. When the horde was assembled about the convoy the signal to attack was given, usually at evening twilight. Two or more U-boats would feint from ahead, attracting the attention of the convoy's escorts and drawing them off in pursuit. When these were in full chase the remaining U-boats would launch their attacks from the flanks and astern, approaching in the awash condition and slamming torpedoes at any targets that crossed their paths. In order to prosecute successfully this plan the U-boats must use their high surface speed during daylight to make and retain contact with the convoy. The obvious counter to this attack was to keep them submerged during the critical hours of concentration, and the answer was found in a heavy screen of aircraft circling at some distance about the convoy. This protection was afforded by long-range planes from shore bases, and by planes from small auxiliary carriers when in mid-Atlantic. As soon as this "air umbrella" was perfected, sinkings of merchant ships dropped off precipitously while U-boat losses soared.

If the U-boat were to continue to be a dangerous weapon new tactics must be designed. In desperation Admiral Doenitz withdrew his flotillas from the North Atlantic and sent some of these in search of less well-protected areas. Others he recalled to their bases for refitting. Here they were provided with heavy anti-aircraft batteries, and their crews were trained to use them; radio echoing devices for the earlier location of Allied aeroplanes were installed; topside armour was added. They were then, in September, sent back into the fray to battle their way on the surface through opposing aircraft to the vital convoys. They again launched heavy and concerted attacks, using these new weapons and tactics; again they were largely unsuccessful, although they did manage to bring down a number of Allied planes. There were no further innovations, but the U-boats could be expected to sally forth again and again, with new methods of attack, as long as Germany remained in the war, and it was likely that some of these would bring a temporary measure of success. Only by eternal vigilance could the U-boat be held in check. (*See also* NAVIES OF THE WORLD; SHIPBUILDING; WORLD WAR II.)   (E. E. HA.)

Subsidies: *see* AGRICULTURE.
Substitute Materials: *see* WAR PRODUCTION, U.S.
Sudan: *see* ANGLO-EGYPTIAN SUDAN.

Sueyro, Saba H. (1890?–1943), Argentine naval officer and politician, completed his studies at the Argentine Naval college in 1910 and later went to the United States for further naval training. A torpedo and mine expert, he held several naval commands, eventually reached the rank of rear admiral and commanded the Rio Santiago Naval base. He had served as naval attaché to Washington and in 1942 headed the Argentine military purchasing commission to the U.S. to negotiate for the purchase of arms. He was named vice president of Argentina following the *coup d'état* of Gen. Arturo Rawson in June 1943, and continued at that post when Gen. Pedro Pablo Ramírez took over the government several days later. He died in Buenos Aires, July 17.

Sugar. The total production of sugar from sugar cane and sugar beets combined in 1943 was estimated by the U.S. department of agriculture to be more than 200,000 tons below 1942 because of the decreased beet sugar crop The acreage of sugar cane was larger in 1943 and the yield higher—21.5 tons per ac. compared with 18.5 tons per ac. in 1942 and 18.6 for the ten-year average. The acreage and crop grown for seed was above the average. In addition to the sugar, 42,423,000 gal. of molasses, including blackstrap, were produced from the cane. Most of the crop was harvested before Dec. 1, although crushing usually extends into January. Factories were unable to operate steadily because of the shortage of labour to cut the cane.

The production of beet sugar as reported by the factories was 938,000 short tons in 1943 compared with 1,613,000 tons in 1942 and a ten-year average of 1,452,000 tons in 1932–41. The acreage of sugar beets was only 552,000 compared with 945,000 in 1942 and 833,000 as the ten-year average. The yield per acre was also less than in 1942 but equal to the average. The crop as a whole was about 44% less than the near record crop of 1942 and the smallest since 1922. The causes of this bad year were the unfavourable weather at planting time, the scarcity of labour, difficulties in harvesting the 1942 crop which discouraged growers, and the competition for the use of the land for other crops requiring less labour. In Michigan and Ohio there was much abandonment because of late planting and poor stands. The reduced acreage was harvested without serious loss due to labour shortage.

Sugar rationing continued through 1943 with little change, although imports of Cuban sugar improved early in the year. In July the allotment for commercial canning was raised to 100% of 1941 usage. Other measures for relief of home canners pro-

SUGAR BEET REFINERY at Picture Butte, Alberta, Canada

Table I.—U. S. Production of Beet Sugar by States, 1943 and 1942

State	1943 short tons	1942 short tons	State	1943 short tons	1942 short tons
Colorado . . .	244,000	321,000	Utah	64,000	82,000
California . .	168,000	347,000	Michigan . . .	49,000	172,000
Montana . . .	102,000	141,000	Wyoming . . .	27,000	62,000
Idaho	78,000	145,000	Ohio	7,000	54,000
Nebraska . . .	76,000	104,000	Other states . .	123,000	185,000

Table II.—U. S. Production of Cane Sugar, 1942, 1943 and 10-Year Avg.

State	1942 Short tons	1943 Short tons	Average 1932–41 Short tons
Louisiana	400,000	454,000	329,000
Florida	60,000	100,000	61,000

vided a maximum of 25 lb. per capita for persons with large fruit supplies. Supplies of sugar were large enough at the end of the year 1943 to provide adequate stocks and provide for consumption and export considerably larger than in 1942.

The world sugar markets were divided into three major areas by the war,—Japanese-controlled Asia, German-controlled Europe and the United Nations areas. There was no trade between these areas, which left the United Nations primarily dependent on the production of the western hemisphere. Prior to the war this was a surplus area to the extent of about 1,300,000 tons which was mostly shipped to Europe. The estimated supply of sugar available at the end of 1943 in the principal western hemisphere countries was about 10,000,000 tons, which was 5.1% above 1942 and 14.4% above the average of the three prewar years. This increase in supply was mainly in the increased Cuban stocks, held back by shortage of shipping. Sugar production in the western hemisphere in 1943 as a whole was estimated at 6,900,000 tons or 14% less than 1942 but about 5% less than the three prewar years. The principal decline was in United States beet-sugar production and about an equal decline in the Cuban cane-sugar crop. (*See also* BEE-KEEPING; MAPLE PRODUCTS, RATIONING; SYRUP, SORGO AND CANE.) (J. C. Ms.)

Suicide Statistics.
Mortality from suicide in the United States during 1943 was probably the lowest in two decades, according to current indications provided by the experience of the millions of industrial policyholders of the Metropolitan Life Insurance company. The final rate for 1943 was expected to be more than 10% under that of 1941 (the latest year of record by the bureau of the census), when there were 17,102 deaths and the death rate was 12.8 per 100,000 population. In 1942 Canada had 834 deaths from suicide, with a rate of 7.2 per 100,000, and England and Wales recorded 3,802 deaths, the rate being 9.2 per 100,000. Large towns in Germany had 7,647 deaths from suicide in 1942, almost 20% more than in 1939.

Considered geographically, mortality from suicide in 1941 in the United States was highest in the Pacific coast states, where the rate was 21.7 per 100,000. Following that, in descending order, were the mountain states, 16.4; east north central, 14.2; middle Atlantic, 13.6; west north central, 13.4; New England, 12.9; south Atlantic, 10.5; west south central, 8.9; and lowest, east south central, 7.9.

Death rates per 100,000 according to race and sex during 1941 were as follows (in each case, the first figure relates to males and the second to females): white, 20.7, 6.8; Negro, 5.7, 1.6; Indian, 9.3, 3.7; Chinese, 54.0, 9.9; Japanese, 41.7, 14.6; all other races, 25.4, 13.8.

The death rates per 100,000 from suicide among white males in 1941 ranged from 0.5 at ages 10 to 14, to a high of 66.5 at ages 75 and over. The rate for white females ranged from 0.3 at ages 10 to 14 to a maximum of almost 13 at ages from 45 to 59, the later ages showing lower rates.

A study of the United States death records for 1940 showed that contributory causes of death were mentioned in only one-fifth of the cases, or 3,631 out of a total of 18,957. In this group of 3,631 cases, mental diseases and deficiency were mentioned in two-fifths of the total, diseases of the circulatory system in one-fifth, intracranial lesions of vascular origin in one-tenth, with influenza and pneumonia, and diseases of the heart ranking next in importance.

In the July 1943 issue of the *Psychiatric Quarterly*, A. B. Siewers and E. Davidoff presented the results of a study of the characteristics of patients referred to a general hospital and to a psychopathic hospital because of attempted suicide. In the general hospital group, only one-fifth were suffering from psychoses, while nine-tenths of those in the psychopathic hospital group were so afflicted. Almost one-third of the persons in each group had some organic disease. The distribution of the two groups according to sex and marital status were very similar; about three-fifths were women and a like proportion were married. The average age of the females admitted to the general hospital was 30 years, and of those to the psychopathic hospital, 40 years. The authors state that the higher age of the latter group "corresponds closely to the age of onset of climacteric manifestations or involutional psychoses in females." Persons unemployed or unskilled were much more frequent in the general hospital group than in the psychopathic hospital group; skilled or professional persons were most frequent among the latter. The apparent motives for the attempt at suicide as stated by the patients were about the same for both groups.

BIBLIOGRAPHY.—L. I. Dublin and B. Bunzel, *To Be or Not To Be* (1933); U.S. Bureau of the Census, *Vital Statistics—Special Reports and State Summaries* (issued irregularly), *Annual Reports of Vital Statistics*, and *Vital Statistics Rates, 1900–1940*; Metropolitan Life Insurance Company, *Statistical Bulletin* (issued monthly). (A. J. Lo.)

Sulfonamide Drugs: *see* MEDICINE.

Sulphur.
The production of sulphur in the United States in 1942 increased by 10% over 1941, to 3,460,362 long tons, while shipments decreased 8% to 3,132,408 tons. With the production rate maintained in the face of declining demand from Aug. 1942 to Feb. 1943, stocks at the mines rose to 5,114,486 tons at the year-end. During the second and third quarters of 1943, demand increased to figures greater than the production rate. Production during the first eight months of 1943 was 1,726,548 tons, shipments 1,970,050 tons, and stocks 4,815,220 tons.

Canada has no output of native sulphur, but the sulphur-bearing gases from roasting pyrite are utilized in the production of sulphuric acid, liquid sulphur dioxide and elemental sulphur. (G. A. Ro.)

Sumatra: *see* NETHERLANDS COLONIAL EMPIRE; NETHERLANDS INDIES.

Sunday Schools.
No world's Sunday school convention was held after that at Oslo in 1936, which reported 369,510 Sunday schools in 129 countries, with 3,145,895 teachers and 34,139,624 pupils. This enrolment decreased because of the dislocations of war, and because Sunday schools were banned in countries under German control. Yet the Sunday schools have continued. "The Christian front in Norway is the hardest to conquer," the Quisling newspaper stated; and in that front were the teachers of the Norwegian Sunday schools. More young people were enrolled in classes for the training of Sunday school teachers in Sweden in 1943 than before the war. The Swedish Sunday School association aided Sunday school

work in Finland by sending literature for use in those schools. Literature for the French Sunday School union was being published in Switzerland and found its way monthly to the pastors and Sunday school workers in France. Sunday schools were maintained in Czechoslovakia, especially among Bohemians and Moravians.

The India Sunday School union appointed for the first time a native of India as its general secretary, in succession to a European missionary. In west China, the National Committee for Christian Religious Education found increased opportunities from its new headquarters at Chengtu. The National Sunday School union of England initiated a four-year advance program embracing the reorganization of local unions, an effort to enrol children who were not attending Sunday schools, and placing greater emphasis on teacher-training and educational evangelism.

The organization of the Latin American Union of Evangelical Youth was consummated through action taken by interdenominational youth organizations in 8 countries—Argentina, Bolivia, Chile, Colombia, Cuba, Mexico, Puerto Rico and Uruguay —which thus became its charter members.

The World's Sunday School association held a conference on Christian education for world order in May 1943, at Schwenksville, Pa., with delegates representing 20 countries. It launched a World Fellowship in Christian Education, to promote the systematic interchange of correspondence and information in this period when travel was sharply curtailed. While the president of the International Council of Religious Education, Lieutenant Commander Harold E. Stassen, former governor of Minnesota, was on duty in the United States navy, James L. Kraft of Chicago served as acting president. At its annual meeting this organization, which represented the Protestant churches of the United States and Canada, reported a total of 177,066 Sunday schools with 21,366,083 teachers and pupils. (*See* also CHURCH MEMBERSHIP.) (L. A. WE.)

Superphosphates.

The production of superphosphates in the United States in 1942 was 5,144,484 short tons of all grades, an increase of 19% over 1941. The sales of phosphate rock to producers of superphosphates totalled 3,631,-812 short tons, an increase of 15% over 1941. (G. A. Ro.)

Supreme Court of the United States.

Personnel.—With the appointment of Wiley Blount Rutledge, the supreme court in 1943 was a court entirely nominated by President Roosevelt except for Justices Roberts and Stone, and the latter was nominated as Chief Justice by the president.

The latest incumbent of the high court, Wiley Blount Rutledge,

associate justice of the U.S. court of appeals, Washington, D.C., was nominated, and confirmed by the senate on Feb. 8, 1943, to fill the vacancy left by James Francis Byrnes when the latter was made director of economic stabilization.

Issues.—The 1942–43 term of the U.S. supreme court was characterized by a great number of concurring opinions and more dissenting votes than at prior terms. The court overruled a number of precedents:

In the field of domestic relations law, its 36-year-old decision in *Haddock* v. *Haddock,* long a landmark in divorce law was rejected when the court held that a Nevada divorce is entitled to full faith and credit in all other states.

The court reversed itself in flag salute cases holding that states may not penalize conscientious refusal to salute the flag. The court distinguished between due process of law as applied to restraints upon property interests and due process applied to freedom of speech, press, assembly and ownership. In the case of property the test is whether the legislature had a rational ground for the restraint. In the case of persons freedom may not be restrained on such slender grounds.

It upheld claims of individual constitutional rights against a state's restriction through handbill ordinances prohibiting distribution of literature. The court restored "to their high constitutional position the liberties of itinerant evangelists who disseminate their religious beliefs and the tenets of their faith through the distribution of literature."

In considering the problem of interned citizens of Japanese ancestry, the court concluded that while as American citizens they were entitled to all the privileges, immunities and guarantees which are enjoyed under the constitution and statutes by other citizens of the United States, as a precaution against invasion and in view of the strategic importance of our west coast area their internment was deemed to be justifiable. Such use of preventive martial law was not deemed to be an unconstitutional taking of property.

The court refused to divest of citizenship one who was a member of the Communist party 12 years prior to the time when proceedings were initiated to cancel his citizenship.

The court greatly strengthened the hands of labour when it decided that picketing was permissible even though the representations made were untrue and disparaging. It was said that statements to the effect that the cafeterias' food was bad and that their patronage aided the cause of fascism was not sufficient to justify the granting of the injunction; that the "loose language or undefined slogans" were "part of the conventional give and take in our economic and political controversies" and did not constitute falsification of facts.

Further indicating the trend of labour law the court stressed the facts: that misconduct of a union did not disqualify it from filing charges with the Labor board that an employer engaged in

THE U.S. SUPREME COURT in 1943. Seated, left to right: Stanley F. Reed, Owen J. Roberts, Chief Justice Harlan F. Stone, Hugo L. Black, Felix Frankfurter. Standing: Robert H. Jackson, William O. Douglas, Frank Murphy, Wiley B. Rutledge, Jr.

unfair labour practices; that such misconduct did not deprive the board of jurisdiction to hear the case, although the board could consider such misconduct as material to its own decision to entertain and proceed upon the charge; that a backpay order of the board does not permit the employer to deduct from the wages due discharged employees the amount of benefits received by them under state unemployment compensation; that the board having found that an employer dominated an unaffiliated union could order the employer to reimburse employees for dues checked off their wages.

The profession of medicine found itself afoul of the law when the supreme court sustained the circuit court of appeals in finding that a concerted activity of the American Medical association and a local medical society against certain practitioners because of their group health association violated the Sherman Anti-Trust act. Even the sanctity of the press and the inviolate right of freedom of speech were not beyond attack, as was illustrated by the decision against the Associated Press.

Federal regulatory bodies were on the whole upheld: the Power commission in seeking enforcement of its orders against a public utility, the Communications commission in regulations pertaining to chain broadcasting as required in the "public interest, convenience or necessity," the National Labor Relations board in ordering reimbursement of dues paid to a company-dominated union, and the ICC in upholding an order authorizing railroads to discontinue loading charges.

In the 31 opinions handed down in the field of criminal law it sustained the constitutionality of the Federal Fire Arms act, upheld the conviction under the Harrison Narcotic act of manufacturing wholesalers for selling substantial amounts of morphine-sulphate tablets, and sustained an indictment charging one with impersonating an FBI officer. It held that tax evasion constituted a misdemeanour not a felony, and that one found guilty of contempt could not be sentenced to fine *and* imprisonment since the statute provides alternative punishment *i.e.*, fine *or* imprisonment only. The court also held that extra-judicial confessions of a defendant were not admissible against the accused and justified reversal of the conviction.

The court ruled that the Copyright act does not prevent an author from assigning his interest in a copyright renewal before he has secured it at the end of the original 28-year copyright grant. In determining that the Copyright act did not nullify an agreement by an author made during the original copyright terms to assign his renewal, Mr. Justice Frankfurter observed that it was not for the court to deny to authors the same freedom to dispose of their property as is enjoyed by others.

Statistics.—In the 1942–43 term there were 169 majority opinions disposing of 221 cases.

Number of Opinions, U.S. Supreme Court, 1942-43 Term

	Favourable to Government	Against Government
Federal tax cases	14	4
Federal labour cases	4*	2*
Federal regulation cases (other than labour)	11	4
Federal criminal cases (not including those arising out of war)	7	10
Federal war cases	3	2
Federal public contracts cases	4	
Federal miscellaneous cases	11*	6*
Total	54	28
State tax cases	3*	3*
State regulation cases	6	8
State criminal cases	2	3
Total	11	14
Total federal and state government cases (107)	65	42

*Rulings both for and against the federal or state government or in favour of one and against the other were entered in one opinion.

Affirmances and Reversals.—Decisions of courts below were affirmed in 44% of the cases decided by opinion. Affirmances were entered in 76 instances; reversals in 78 instances; and modification of the decision below in one case, the judgment below being affirmed as modified. In eight instances the court by opinion dismissed appeals or denied certiorari, and in seven cases no decision was entered on the merits of the case.

There were 165 dissents from a total of 70 majority opinions. The number of dissents were Stone 13, Roberts 28, Black 23, Reed 16, Frankfurter 18, Douglas 22, Murphy 26, Jackson 17, Rutledge 2.

There were fewer 5-to-4 decisions than in the previous term.

The court evolved a new type of dissent which became more accentuated in recent terms. Acts of congress were generally not overridden. The thought was that the supreme court justices must be statesmen as well as jurists and determine the direction of legislative growth rather than arrest it. The day of the major dissent appeared to have vanished.

A statistical summary of the court's work indicated: *Original Docket:* Total cases 15; cases disposed of 5; cases remaining 10. *Appellate Docket:* Total cases 1,103; cases disposed of 992; cases remaining 111. *Totals:* Total cases 1,118; cases disposed of 997; cases remaining 121. (*See also* LAW.) (B. WE.)

Surgery. The maintenance of blood supply to a tissue is as important as the maintenance of a supply line to an army and whenever either is stopped, disaster results. Many arms and legs are lost because the main artery supplying the part has been injured. Arthur H. Blakemore, Jere W. Lord and Paul L. Stefko showed that by using a vitallium tube lined by a vein, satisfactory repair of vessels can be made. Vitallium is a metal which produces no reaction in tissues. The tube is lined with a piece of vein, the ends of the vein being brought out over the end of the tube. The vein-lined tube is then tied into the defect in the artery. In this way the blood supply of the extremity is maintained. In order to improve the blood supply to the heart in patients who have had coronary thrombosis, Claude S. Beck, several years before, suggested methods which would increase the number of vessels supplying the heart muscle. He originally advocated a rather extensive procedure of placing a chest muscle on the heart muscle, but he showed also that many less extensive procedures resulting in the development of adhesions between the chest wall and the heart increased the blood supply to the heart muscle. Whereas, as shown in a report by Harold Feil, the immediate mortality is relatively high, those who survived the operation received definite benefit. In an attempt to increase the blood supply to the brain when this had been cut off by a haemorrhage or plugging, due to a clot, of the artery supplying that portion of the vein, Frederick E. Kredel suggested a procedure similar to that which was used by Beck, namely, the use of a flap of muscle placed against the brain which had been deprived of its blood supply, and in this way the paralysis and other symptoms resulting from a stroke were lessened or even obviated.

During 1943, considerable advances were made in the treatment of burns. It was shown quite definitely that tannic acid in the treatment of burns is undesirable, not only because it causes a crust under which infection can progress, but also because from an extensive burn surface there occurs sufficient absorption of tannic acid to produce severe liver damage, and in a number of fatal cases death was the result of the liver damage rather than of the burn. The administration of plasma in burns and the treatment of the burn as a wound, that is, by cleanliness, the prevention of infection, and the compression, remained the best methods of treatment. Sanford M. Rosenthal showed that there is apparently a disturbance in the sodium balance in burns, because he showed that animals with severe burns could be kept alive by the administration of sodium chloride introduced intraperitoneally. Fox used this treatment in humans and found that by the administration of large amounts of sodium lactate by mouth to severely burned patients excellent results were obtained with a marked diminution in mortality.

Vitallium was used for a number of years as a metal which might be implanted in tissue; it was valuable because it produced little or no reaction. A new metal, tantalum, was suggested, which apparently has all of the advantages of vitallium, but does not have some of its disadvantages. Vitallium has to be cast to fit the part, but it has been possible with tantalum to cut, bend and hammer it, making it easier to use. O. H. Fulcher reported on the use of tantalum in the repair of skull defects and found it very valuable. Tantalum was also made into fine thread which was used for the repair of nerves, the advantage being that it produced no reaction and was, therefore, well tolerated by the tissues.

In the grafting of skin it is essential that the graft be maintained in close approximation to the defect until healing has occurred. Machteld E. Sano suggested using constituents of human blood as a cement substance to aid in this process. She took the extract from the white cells of the blood and painted this on the undersurface of the skin graft. The area to be grafted was painted with plasma and as soon as the graft was applied, it became firmly adhered. She reported excellent results with this treatment because the tissue extract and plasma form a medium for the growth of cells and actually stimulate healing. Lawrence W. Smith and Alfred E. Livingston showed that chlorophyll, which is the green colouring matter in plants, exerted a definite stimulating influence on the healing of wounds and that when compared with other substances used to stimulate wound healing, the other substances were practically without value.

Osteomyelitis, which is a severe systemic infection involving the blood stream but producing abscesses in the bone, claimed a high mortality rate. Robertson reported that excellent results were being obtained by treating the condition not only locally, when an abscess forms, but also by the administration of large doses of sulfonamides early in the condition. In this way the invasive properties of the infection could be controlled and much better results were obtained.

The control of haemorrhage from surfaces which ooze and which cannot be sutured is a real problem to many surgeons, particularly neurosurgeons. Although thrombin which is necessary for the clotting of blood is available and can be applied to the surface, it is difficult many times to maintain the thrombin in place for clotting to occur. If one used ordinary gauze, the clot became detached when the gauze was removed. Virginia K. Frantz prepared an oxidized cellulose which is absorbable and this was used by Tracy J. Putnam together with thrombin to control haemorrhage from bleeding brain surfaces. Since the oxidized cellulose is absorbable, it is not necessary to remove it after clotting has occurred and excellent results have been reported.

William Andrus, Lord and Stefko showed both experimentally and clinically that the acidity of the stomach was decreased when a pedicle graft of the jejunum, which is the upper part of the small intestine, is placed in the stomach. This is particularly important in patients with stomach ulcer in whom the recurrence of ulcers is due to the persistence of a high acid content. (See also ANAESTHESIA; INDUSTRIAL HEALTH; MEDICINE.)

BIBLIOGRAPHY.— William DeWitt Andrus, Jere W. Lord and Paul L. Stefko, "Effects of Pedicle Grafts of Jejunum in the Wall of the Stomach on Gastric Secretion," *Ann. Surg.*, 118:499–522 (Oct. 1943); W. Wayne Babcock, "The Sano Method of Accelerated Wound Healing" (editorial), *S.G. and O.*, 77:556–557 (Nov. 1943); Claude S. Beck, "Principles Underlying the Operative Approach to the Treatment of Myocardial Ischemia," *Ann. Surg.*, 118:788–806 (Nov. 1943); Arthur H. Blakemore, Jere W. Lord and Paul L. Stefko, "Restoration of Blood Flow in Damaged Arteries: Further Studies on a Nonsuture Method of Blood Vessel Anastomosis," *Ann. Surg.*, 117:481–497 (April 1943); David Bodian, "Repair of Traumatic Gaps in Nerves," *J.A.M.A.*, 121:662–664 (Feb. 27, 1943); Loyal Davis, John Scarff, Neil Rogers and Meredith Dickinson, "High Altitude Frostbite; Preliminary Report," *S.G. and O.*, 77:561–575 (Dec. 1943); Harold Feil, "Clinical Appraisal of the Beck Operation," *Ann. Surg.*, 117:807–815 (Nov. 1943); Virginia K. Frantz, "Absorbable Cotton, Paper, and Gauze (Oxidized Cellulose)," *Ann. Surg.*, 118:116–126 (July 1943); O. H. Fulcher, "Tantalum as a Restoration of Blood Flow to Repair Cranial Defects," *J.A.M.A.*, 121:931–933 (March 1943); Henry N. Harkins, "Treatment of Shock from War Wounds," *Ill. Med. J.*, 83:325–331 (May 1943); Frederick E. Kredel, "Collateral Cerebral Circulation by Muscle Graft," *South. Surg.*, 11:235–244 (April 1942); Tracy J. Putnam, "The Use of Thrombin on Soluble Cellulose in Neurosurgery," *Ann. Surg.*, 118:127–129 (July 1943); D. E. Robertson, "The Medical Treatment of Hematogenous Osteomyelitis," *Ann. Surg.*, 118:318–328 (Aug. 1943); Sanford M. Rosenthal, "Experimental Chemotherapy of Burns and Shock," *Public Health Reports*, 58:1429–1436 (Sept. 24, 1943); Machteld E. Sano, "A Coagulum Contact Method of Skin Grafting as Applied to Human Grafts," *S. G. and O.*, 77:510–513 (Nov. 1943); Lawrence W. Smith and Alfred E. Livingston, "Chlorophyll: An Experimental Study of its Water Soluble Derivatives in Wound Healing," *Am. J. Surg.*, 62:358–369 (Dec. 1943). (A. O.)

+Surinam

(DUTCH GUIANA). A Netherlands colony in northeastern South America. The area is 54,291 sq.mi.; the population, according to official estimates, was 177,980 in 1939. Around 45% of the population is East Indian in origin (26.8% British East Indians and 18.8% Javanese), the largest such proportion in the western hemisphere. The chief cities are Paramaribo, the capital (pop. 54,853), and Nieuw Nickerie (3,800). Government is under an appointed governor and a partially-elected council. The governor in 1943 was Dr. J. C. Kielstra (succeeded on Jan. 3, 1944, by J. C. Brons, acting governor).

History.—With the decline of the axis submarine menace in western Atlantic and Caribbean waters, trade conditions eased and shortages became less acute. Meanwhile, bauxite mining activity and presence of United States troops in Surinam provided economic stimuli. The former, however, was expected to decline somewhat as a result of huge United Nations stock piles, with consequent effects on the colony.

Surinam was visited in November by Crown Princess Juliana of the Netherlands, first of the royal house of Orange ever to

NATIVE WOMEN of Surinam, members of the Dutch colonial army auxiliary, parading in 1943

come to the colony. Earlier in the year a Surinam economic mission visited Brazil; the first Brazilian consul ever accredited to the colony arrived at Paramaribo on May 13.

On Oct. 25, Gov. Kielstra celebrated his tenth anniversary as governor. Shortly thereafter it was announced that he would retire on Jan. 3 to become Netherlands minister to Mexico. His incumbency had been marked by sharp change in the colony's fiscal condition, from a budget of 7,000,000 guilders, 3,000,000 of which was met by a home government subsidy, to one of 13,500,000 guilders, raised entirely from the colony's own resources. Local government had been reorganized, a strong military force built up, and many social reforms introduced.

On Aug. 3, Surinam's first daily newspaper, *Het Nieuws,* began publication.

Education.—Surinam had, in 1943, 114 elementary schools (44 of them public), with nearly 22,000 enrolment, over half in Paramaribo, and four secondary schools. In addition there were 33 schools for bush Negroes and Indians in the interior.

Finance.—The monetary unit is the guilder (value approx. 53¢ U.S.). During 1943 the colony was faced by an acute shortage of subsidiary coins, which was relieved by assistance from the United States mint.

Trade.—The basic exports are mineral. Bauxite, first developed in 1922, dominated in 1943. In 1941, 1,093,764 tons of bauxite were exported, practically all to the United States, nearly double prewar totals. Exports in 1942 and 1943 were unofficially reported to be greater. Gold, whose production is no longer reported, was the second export. Agricultural exports included sugar, coffee and rice. Some balata was exported. Exports in 1941, the latest available, were 11,398,377 guilders value, of which 93.4% went to the United States, 4.2% to Great Britain. Imports were 9,429,922 guilders value, the United States supplying 71.9%, Trinidad 5.4%, Argentina 4.6%, and Great Britain 4.2%. The Netherlands supplied about 50% of prewar imports. The principal imports are manufactures and foodstuffs.

Communication.—External communication is by steamship and air. Pan American Airways and "KLM" (Royal Netherlands Airways) maintain regular air transport service. There were 8 mi. of railway in 1943 and fairly good roads along the coast. Interior communication is entirely by trails and navigable rivers.

Resources.—Sugar was once the main economic basis, but has steadily declined in importance. Normal production is around 9,000 to 10,000 tons. Annual production of first quality coffee approximates 9,000 bags (of 132 lb.). Considerable low grade is also produced. Bananas, cacao, rice, coco-nuts and citrus fruits are also cultivated. Export of orange juice and pulp is on the increase.

Bauxite, the main mineral resource, is increasing in importance. In 1940 it provided 87% of all export values against 35% in 1935 (*see* above). Gold production averages around 400,000 grams a year.

The interior forests contain many valuable unexploited hardwoods. Balata is gathered in appreciable quantities. During 1943 surveys were made of the colony's rubber resources.

BIBLIOGRAPHY.—Netherlands Information News, *Netherlands News* (New York, fortnightly); J. K. Wright and William van Royen, *The Netherlands West Indies: Curacao and Surinam* (1941); J. W. Nystrom, *Surinam: a Geographic Study* (c. 1942).

Swains Island: *see* PACIFIC ISLANDS, U.S.; SAMOA, AMERICAN.
Swaziland: *see* BRITISH SOUTH AFRICAN PROTECTORATES.

Sweden.
A democratic monarchy of northern Europe. Area, 173,341 sq.mi.; pop. (est. 1940) 6,370,538. Capital, Stockholm (est. [1943] 615,975). Other principal cities,

with populations (1943), are Göteborg (Gothenburg) (285,732), Malmö (159,708), Norrköping (72,039), Hälsingborg (63,250). Religion, Lutheran Christian. Ruler in 1943: King Gustavus V (*q.v.*); prime minister: Per Albin Hansson.

History.—On Jan. 18, 1943, Premier Per Albin Hansson not only announced again that Sweden would resist any invasion but declared that if invasion came Swedes should pay no attention to any orders to cease firing. This stiffening tone was the keynote of Swedish policy and action through the year.

The reasons for this change from earlier policy were many. Partly, no doubt, the stronger tone was due to events like the Russian advance and the Allied landing in North Africa. Partly, it was due to the strengthening of Sweden herself. In 1943 Sweden had 26 destroyers actually in service; 70 naval vessels had been added since 1939, plus 140 merchant vessels, and the Göta-Verken and other shipbuilding establishments were still busy. In December Gen. Helge Jung painted a very encouraging picture of Swedish powers of self-defense. Industry had to a very large extent adapted itself to the production of nonimportable essentials. The food situation was somewhat improved. Despite the long-standing lack of fodder and a poor hay crop in 1943, the livestock census showed 200,000 more cattle and 130,000 more pigs. Eighty-four thousand acres were used to produce oleaginous plants, greatly aiding the edible fat situation.

Toward Germany people, press and government became increasingly hostile. In the trade negotiations with Germany even the temporary credits formerly granted were refused. The nazis sent Hans Thomsen, former chargé d'affaires in Washington, as minister to Sweden in Feb. 1943 to try to develop better relations. But the Swedish government ruled that two armed Norwegian merchant vessels laid up at Gothenburg might leave if they wished, and Germany at once retaliated by cutting off her permission for the Swedish safe-conduct ships to and from the Americas. The loss of a Swedish submarine, "Ulven," probably by hitting a mine, and the firing on another submarine, "Draken," by a German ship, inflamed Swedish opinion and brought a stiff protest by the government. The German reply was not very satisfactory, but in May the safe-conduct traffic was again allowed (but was cut off again on Oct. 28). The Swedes totalled their sea losses since 1939 to 167 merchant ships with a gross tonnage of 482,576, and lives numbering 1,133. New incidents continued to occur, such as the attack on two fishing boats off the Danish coast on Aug. 25, and the shooting down of a passenger plane from Britain on Oct. 22 ("Gripen"). Beginning in August the government took action which the people had been demanding for months: On Aug. 15 the transportation of war materials for the Germans to Norway and Finland on Swedish railways was stopped; on Aug. 20 the leave transit of German troops and the use of Swedish lines for transit between Trondhjem and Narvik was forbidden; and on Oct. 1 the transportation of German oil through Sweden was ended.

Sentiment in Sweden was affected not only by incidents involving her own people, but by the increasing severity of German activities in Denmark and Norway. When on Aug. 29 the Germans took over direct control in Denmark and a month later started to round up the Jews there, the Swedish government protested vigorously and offered asylum to all the hunted people. The Germans did not appreciate this neighbourly intervention, but more than 8,000 Danes escaped to Sweden, largely children and old people. An organization was quickly established in Sweden providing homes for all and jobs for as many as possible.

The arrest and threatened deportation to Germany of 1,200 students of the University of Oslo further inflamed Swedish opinion. German Foreign Minister Joachim von Ribbentrop returned a curt reply to the Swedish protest, refusing to discuss it and telling Sweden to cease interference with German affairs. The Swedish reply to this was a warning that continuance of German policy would result in increasing deterioration in Swedish-German relations.

Neutrality showed some of its advantages when Gothenburg became the exchange port for some 842 totally disabled German war prisoners and 5,175 British. Sweden was host to about 50,000 foreigners, including some 20,000 Finnish children and 8,000 Danish refugees.

Sweden did much thinking and planning for the postwar world. Her shipyards built ships which could not run till the war was over, and plants were expanded in the wood pulp, iron ore and steel industries. New air routes were planned. But repeatedly press and leaders expressed the responsibility of neutral Sweden to give aid after the war for the reconstruction of her neighbours' industry and commerce. On Oct. 18 the minister of finance, Ernst Wigforss, asked the riksdag for an initial appropriation of 100,000,000 kr. for direct aid in food and other necessities to the needy after the war—precedence to be given to Sweden's own northern people.

Education.—In 1937–38 there were 567,579 pupils and 27,858 teachers in the elementary schools and 90,087 students in secondary schools. In the five universities, 7,606 students were enrolled in 1940. Sweden's budget for educational expenses in 1941–42 was 256,387,000 kr.

Finance and Banking.—The monetary unit is the krona (26 U.S. cents at par, 23.94 cents on Nov. 8, 1941). The fiscal year ending in June 1942 left a government deficit of 2,205,000,000 kr. National income was about 12,000,000,000 kr., of which about 5,000,000,000 kr. went into state and municipal taxes. The national debt Aug. 31, 1943, was 9,125,000,000 kr., more than double that of three years earlier. In 1940 there were 28 private banks with deposits of 4,793,477,000 kr. Gold reserves in Dec. 1942 reached an all-time record of 1,404,000,000 kr. ($351,000,-000).

Trade.—The two notable things about Swedish trade, both natural wartime phenomena for a country so situated, were the decline in total commerce and the increased share of Germany in that trade: from 25% of Sweden's imports in 1939 to 46% in 1942, and from 19.5% of Sweden's exports in 1939 to 40% in 1942.

Because of the difficulties of obtaining coal (for Germany could not maintain promised deliveries), the Swedes like the Danes began cutting peat on a large scale; 1942 production was 700,000 tons. Industrial use of coal was cut from 250,000 tons per month to 50,000 tons per month, and crude oil consumption went to almost zero. Automobiles burned "producer-gas," supplied from 10,463,600 cu.yd. of wood annually. Water supply for power production was increased from 1,800,000,000 kw.h. in 1939 to 2,800,000,000 kw.h. in 1943.

Communication.—On Dec. 31, 1940, there were 10,231 mi. of railroads. By 1943 railway electrification served half the trackage and 85% of freight volume. In 1939 there were 53,787 mi. of highways, practically all listed as "improved." Motor vehicles

Table I.—Sweden's Imports 1939-1942 By Commodity Groups

Commodity Groups	1939		1940		1941		1942	
	*Kr.	%	*Kr.	%	*Kr.	%	*Kr.	%
Foodstuffs, etc.	387.6	15.5	306.4	15.3	236.2	14.1	381.5	21.6
Minerals and metals	884.1	35.4	675.6	33.7	519.6	31.0	509.3	28.8
Chemical products	232.6	9.3	176.3	8.8	162.4	9.7	185.2	10.4
Textiles, leather, rubber	472.3	18.9	374.6	18.7	381.9	22.8	368.2	20.8
Forest products	51.7	2.1	30.1	1.5	27.8	1.7	32.5	1.8
Machines, vehicles, etc.	470.4	18.8	441.5	22.0	346.2	20.7	293.3	16.6
Total	2,498.7	100.0	2,004.5	100.0	1,674.1	100.0	1,770.0	100.0

*Value in millions of kronor. (*Sweden, A Wartime Survey*, p. 89.)

Table II.—Sweden's Exports 1939-1942 By Commodity Groups

Commodity Groups	1939		1940		1941		1942	
	*Kr.	%	*Kr.	%	*Kr.	%	*Kr.	%
Foodstuffs, etc.	132.6	7.0	72.5	5.5	67.8	5.0	21.9	1.7
Minerals and metals	584.5	30.9	495.5	37.3	544.3	40.5	488.8	37.2
Chemical products	58.1	3.1	42.6	3.2	34.2	2.5	26.4	2.0
Textiles, leather, rubber	59.8	3.2	33.1	2.5	12.7	0.9	14.7	1.1
Forest products	715.8	37.9	474.7	35.8	490.2	36.5	539.4	41.1
Machines, vehicles, etc.	337.8	17.9	209.1	15.7	196.0	14.6	221.6	16.9
Total	1,888.6	100.0	1,327.5	100.0	1,345.2	100.0	1,312.8	100.0

*Value in millions of kronor. (*Sweden, A Wartime Survey*, p. 90.)

licensed (Dec. 1940) numbered 81,334. Airways (1939) flew 1,536,000 mi. and carried 60,000 passengers. Telephones (Dec. 31, 1941) numbered 980,000 (about 150 per 1,000 persons), putting Sweden second only to the U.S. in the per capita ratio of telephones. Telegraph mileage was 11,040. There were 1,470,375 licensed radio sets and 35 broadcasting stations. The Swedish merchant marine consisted of 1,605,000 gross tons in 1938.

Agriculture.—In 1942 the bread-grain harvest, still 10% below normal, was almost double the 1941 crop. Fodder was 13% below normal, but provided for a 4,000,000-ton milk production, for cheese production at the existing rate and for a butter increase of 16% to about 95,000 tons. Egg production was about 60% of the 10-year average, and meat also about 60%. The potato harvest of 1942 was above normal, as were the sugar-beet and pea crops.

Manufacturing.—The total value of production in 1939 was 8,151,768,000 kr. There were 644,360 workers in 19,092 establishments. The chief manufactures were machinery and metal, 2,518,576,000 kr.; wood and paper, 1,489,655,000 kr.; foods, 1,395,787,000 kr.; clothing and textiles, 801,799,000 kr.; chemicals, 392,569,000 kr.; electrical equipment, 302,984,000 kr.; beverages, 230,845,000 kr.; stone, etc., 229,054,000 kr.; and leather, 228,717,000 kr.

Mineral Production.—Production of the leading minerals in 1939 was as follows: iron ore, 15,197,633 tons; iron and steel, 1,300,900 tons; cast iron, 709,923 tons; coal, 489,085 tons; arsenic ore, 267,065 tons; sulphur pyrites, 211,352 tons; fireclay, 153,168 tons. Silver production amounted to 7,226,855 oz.; gold, 2,149,220 oz.

BIBLIOGRAPHY.—Joachim Joesten, *Stalwart Sweden* (1943); Kurt Singer, *Duel for the Northland* (1943); *Sweden, A Wartime Survey* (1943); Naboth Hedin, "Sweden, The Dilemma of a Neutral," *Foreign Policy Reports*, XIX, No. 5 (May 15, 1943).   (F. D. S.)

Sweet Potatoes: *see* POTATOES.

Swimming.

Increased effort on the part of belligerent nations to provide schooling in watermanship for service men and women made of 1943 a year of notable progress in swimming. Competitive swimming and water polo were curtailed in the open field because of the war, but they gained greater favour than ever as features of the athletic and recreational activities at service training stations and, whenever possible, behind the many fronts.

World's records continued to fall and it deserves mention that the feats achieved bettered not only the listed marks but also those claimed since the *Federation Internationale de Natation Amateur*, in charge of the supervision of world's standards, ceased to function at the start of hostilities.

Swimmers of the United States turned in six of the new records and of chief interest was the exploit of Alan Ford, a college freshman, in covering 100 yd. free style in 50.7 sec., a performance which clipped the oldest record on the international table, John Weissmuller's of 51 sec., set in 1927. Ford also helped Richard Baribault, Brewster Macfadden and Richard Lyon, his Yale uni-

A 16-YEAR SWIMMING RECORD fell Jan. 30, 1943, when Alan Ford of Yale university swam the 100-yd. free style in 50.7 sec., breaking the mark of 51 sec. set in 1927 by Johnny Weissmuller. Ford is shown in a practice swim, using a mirror to detect flaws in his stroke

versity fellow students, to lower the time for the 400 yd. relay to 3 min. 26.2 sec.

Harry Holiday shaded the back stroke figures for 100 yd. to 57 sec. and 200 m. to 2 min. 22.9 sec., while Emmett Cashin cut the breast stroke marks for 200 yd. to 2 min. 19 sec. and 200 m. to 2 min. 33.7 sec., but the national committee withheld recognition of the latter feats pending further investigation.

The European Swimming league announced its acceptance of a string of European records, four of which rate as world's best also. Denmark's famous ace, Ragnhilde Hveger, who held all but 2 of the 15 free-style standards registered for women, surprised by slashing the time for 400 m. back stroke to 5 min. 38.2 sec. Anna Kappel, of Germany, brought down the breast stroke records for 400 m. to 6 min. 8.2 sec. and 500 m. to 7 min. 43.4 sec. Artem Nakache, of France, lowered the men's breast stroke mark for 200 m. to 2 min. 36.7 sec., but the fate of his achievement obviously would depend on whether or not Cashin's quoted performance in 2 min. 33.7 sec. was recognized.

Leonid Meskov, of the Russian army, equalled the record of 5 min. 43.8 sec. for 400 m. breast stroke. The soviet union, however, was not affiliated with the F.I.N.A., so Meskov's effort did not qualify.   (L. DE B. H.)

Switzerland.
A republican confederation of 22 cantons of west-central Europe, bounded N. and E. by Germany, S. by Italy and W. by France. Flag, white cross on red background. Area 15,944 sq.mi.; pop. (1941 census) 4,260,-179. Chief towns: Berne (cap. 129,331), Zürich (333,829), Basle (161,380), Geneva (124,442), Lausanne (92,000). Languages (census 1930): German 2,924,314; French 831,100; Italian 242,-034; Romansch 44,204 and others 24,797. President (Jan. 1, 1944) Dr. Walter Stampfli.

History.—Switzerland was still able in 1943 to maintain her position as a haven of comparative peace and security in the midst of a war-torn Europe. But her political and economic position was very difficult. Constantly threatened by Germany, surrounded on all sides by axis territory, and dependent on Germany for coal and other raw materials, Switzerland was compelled to pay high prices for her imports and to sell her food and machinery to Germany at low prices. This caused a constantly unfavourable balance of trade for the Swiss.

After the United States and many other American states went to war with the axis powers in the winter of 1941–42, the Swiss government consented to assume the burden of looking after their diplomatic interests, in addition to representing numerous other countries already at war. Switzerland also became the great centre for the work of the Red Cross in arranging the exchange of prisoners.

Education.—Managed locally by the cantons and communities, education is obligatory and free. In 1939–40 the pupils in primary schools numbered 455,561, and those in secondary and middle schools 73,422, in addition to various cantonal and technical schools. The seven universities (Basle, Zürich, Berne, Geneva, Lausanne, Fribourg and Neuchâtel) had a total of 9,649 matriculated students in the winter of 1940–41.

Finance.—The franc, the Swiss monetary unit, was devalued about 30% in 1936, so that it contained about 200 mg. of fine gold and had in 1942 an exchange value of 23.40 U.S. cents. The budget estimates for 1941 were 517,700,000 francs of revenue, and 592,300,000 francs of expenditure, and the total debt, including railway debt, was 6,130,656,000 francs.

Trade and Communications.—Imports and exports in 1942 were 2,071,000,000 francs and 1,595,000,000 francs respectively. Swiss railways, 3,218 mi. in length, carried 23,300,000 metric tons of freight and 144,000,000 passengers. There were, in 1943, three main and three local broadcasting stations.   (S. B. F.)

Symphony Orchestras: *see* MUSIC.
Synthetic Products: *see* CHEMISTRY; PETROLEUM; PLASTICS INDUSTRY; RAYON AND OTHER SYNTHETIC FIBRES; RUBBER; STANDARDS, NATIONAL BUREAU OF.
Syphilis: *see* MEDICINE; VENEREAL DISEASES.

Syria.
An independent republic, formerly French mandated territory, bordering the eastern Mediterranean. Area, 73,587 sq.mi.; pop. (est.) 2,800,000; chief town: Damascus (cap. 225,000). President (1943): Shukri al Quwatli. Language: Arabic; religion: mainly Mohammedan.

History.—The president, Sheikh Mohamed Tageddine el Hassani, died Jan. 17, 1943. A new government was reported on March 26 with Atta Ayubi as prime minister. Powers were granted in January to General Georges Catroux, Fighting French delegate-general, to re-establish a constitutional regime and to hold parliamentary elections. Jean Helleu was appointed as his successor in June. The primary elections were held on July 10 and the secondary on July 26. The chamber of deputies, which numbered 124, elected Shukri al Quwatli president. The new ministry was composed of seven Sunni Moslems and one Greek Orthodox Christian. Faris Alkhuri was elected president of the chamber. On Nov. 28, the foreign affairs committee urged that Article 16 of the constitution, giving special powers to the French, should be abolished and control secured over public security, customs and the army. Yves Chataigneau's appointment as delegate-general was announced on Nov. 22. Currency in circulation at the end of March 1943 was £ Syrian 101,000,000 and by May the gold pound had risen from 45 to 70 Syrian pounds.

The following statistics refer to Syria and Lebanon jointly:

Finance.—Monetary unit, the Syrian pound (divided into 100 piastres). Revenue 1938 (at the rate of 20 francs = one Syrian pound) 588,787,596 francs. Expenditures 509,085,433 francs. Notes in circulation (June 30, 1939) £ Syrian 35,600,000; reserves (June 30, 1939), gold £ Syrian 3,500,000, foreign assets £ Syrian 31,800,000.

Trade and Communication.—Imports (1940) £ Syrian 57,-000,000; (1941) £ Syrian 38,000,000; exports (1940) £ Syrian 19,000,000; (1941) £ Syrian 11,000,000. Roads (1939) c. 1,900 mi.; railways (1939) 890 mi.

Agriculture.—(1940) short tons; wheat 737,990; barley 424,-385; maize (1938) 30,312; oats (1939) 5,950; potatoes (1938) 45,855; tobacco (1938) 3,748; wine (1938) 1,136,000 gal.; cotton 7,165; cotton seed 16,645; sesamum (1938) 5,842; olive oil 14,-330; wool (1938) 10,913; raw silk 220.

Syrup, Sorgo and Cane.

The United States production of sugar cane syrup in 1943 was estimated by the U.S. department of agriculture at 19,240,000 gal., somewhat more than either 1941 or 1942, though less than

Table I.—U.S. Production of Cane Syrup by States, 1943 and 1942

State	1943 gal.	1942 gal.	State	1943 gal.	1942 gal.
Louisiana . . .	5,640,000	5,760,000	Florida	2,040,000	1,760,000
Georgia . . .	4,250,000	3,900,000	Texas.	700,000	665,000
Mississippi . .	2,992,000	3,300,000	South Carolina .	648,000	485,000
Alabama . . .	2,875,000	2,645,000	Arkansas . . .	95,000	95,000

Table II.—U.S. Production of Sorgo Syrup in Leading States, 1943 and 1942

State	1943 gal.	1942 gal.	State	1943 gal.	1942 gal.
Alabama . . .	2,048,000	1,767,000	Tennessee . . .	1,239,000	1,134,000
Mississippi. . .	1,495,000	1,800,000	North Carolina .	732,000	1,065,000
Georgia	1,320,000	1,220,000	Arkansas . . .	722,000	1,155,000

the average of 20,818,000 gal. for the period 1932–41. The production of sorgo syrup in 1943 at 11,760,000 gal. was about 2,000,000 gal. below 1942 and only 81% of the 10-year average. (*See* also BEE-KEEPING; MAPLE PRODUCTS.)   (J. C. Ms.)

Table Tennis.

Paradoxically the war, which continued to handicap organized table tennis in 1943, promised to give it a postwar fillip through the world-wide distribution of star players among the armed forces and introduction of the game in virgin territory. Two examples, somewhat fantastic, were a U.S. army private playing singles with the shah of Iran in the latter's palace, and Australian troops teaching the game to "fuzzy-wuzzies" on a South sea isle. With cancellation of the world championships for the fourth consecutive year, the U.S. championships were of prime importance. Petty Officer William Holzrichter, U.S. navy, won the men's singles; Sergeant Laszlo Bellak and Private Tibor Hoffmann (Hazi), two former Hungarians who joined the U.S. army, the men's doubles; and Sally Green, the women's singles for the fourth straight year. The U.S. Table Tennis association recognized the game's growing appeal among youth by establishing a junior boys' singles event.   (C. Z.)

Taft, Helen Herron

(MRS. WILLIAM HOWARD TAFT) (1861–1943), widow of the former U.S. president and chief justice, was born June 2 in Cincinnati, O. She was educated in public schools in Cincinnati and taught school there for several years. She was married to Mr. Taft in 1886 and four years later accompanied him to the Philippines where he served as governor. Mrs. Taft, who has been credited with planning her husband's public career, advised him against accepting a seat on the supreme court bench offered to him by President Theodore Roosevelt in 1903 on grounds that it would mar his chances as presidential candidate. During the time she was First Lady, Mrs. Taft instituted many changes in White House management and had planted the famous cherry trees in the vicinity of the Washington monument. A talented musician, she founded the Cincinnati Symphony orchestra in 1896 and was at one time president of the organization. She died at her home in Washington, May 22.

Tahiti: *see* PACIFIC ISLANDS, FRENCH.
Taiwan: *see* FORMOSA.

Talc.

The record sales of 416,369 short tons of talc and related minerals produced in the United States in 1941 declined by 7% in 1942, when a total of 387,963 tons was reached. The bulk of this total was ground talc. Increases in use were made in paint, roofing and insecticides, all other uses showed declines. Canadian production included 15,499 tons of talc and 14,369 tons of soapstone.   (G. A. Ro.)

Tanganyika: *see* BRITISH EAST AFRICA; MANDATES.
Tanks, Military: *see* MUNITIONS OF WAR; WORLD WAR II.

Tariffs.

In 1943, as in 1941 and 1942, war dominated the field of tariffs as it did all other fields of activity. There were many tariff reductions in 1943, particularly in Canada, in Central and South America, and in the colonies. Sharp reductions and transfers to the free list prevailed. But most of them were limited—either the duty was suspended, not repealed, or the imports had to be made by a state agency or they were limited seasonally or by quotas, or they were restricted to specific uses—for example, making containers for exporting the produce of the country. Some related explicitly to war shortages and were limited to the duration of the war or to the duration of the shortage. Costa Rica published an extensive list of duty decreases (and also increases) on Nov. 21, but the decreases were not to become effective until Jan. 1, 1944. Paraguay reduced its ad valorem rates in October in order to prevent an increase in duty expressed in a new currency unit.

Decrees or laws increasing tariff rates were somewhat less numerous than those giving decreases or exemptions, but they seemed likely to endure longer. Most of them were intended to raise revenue rather than to shelter domestic industries, although the latter type was not absent. Liquors, tobacco and "luxuries" were prominent in the particularized increases, but several countries imposed or increased the rates of surtaxes, sales taxes, or other charges affecting most of their imports. Uruguay raised official values by 30%. Paraguay more than trebled the additional charges on imports by raising the ad valorem charge from 7% to 15% and changing the conversion ratio. Costa Rica raised duties on a long list of luxuries and also doubled the surtax (from 5% to 10% of duty) and made it applicable to all products not bound by trade agreements. Chile raised her additional tax on "dispensable" products from 10% to 15% of duty-paid value. Turkey increased her sales tax on most domestic and imported products from 12½% to 15% ad valorem. Egypt doubled her specific duties of 1941.

Mexico on Dec. 18 decreed many increases in duties and a few decreases, the changes to become effective Jan. 17, 1944. Some rates were only slightly increased but others were raised by a third or a half or even doubled. The United States department of commerce summarized the changes in three pages.

Changes in export duties were relatively few. Several decreases were reported and a larger number of increases, as always occurs with rising prices. Madagascar's war tax illustrated the progressive type of export duty, the rate being 3% of the amount by which the value of a commodity exceeds the official value fixed for the third quarter of 1939. El Salvador increased the export duty on coffee from 43 cents to $1.25 per 100 lb. and provided for an annual adjustment according to prices during the last 15 days of October. The higher export duty took the place of other taxes, including certain income taxes. Tunisia developed a novelty—retroactive export taxes. That on wool carpets and rugs (100 or 160 francs per net kilogram) was published Jan. 7, 1943, but retroactive from Dec. 6, 1941. Most of the export duties were imposed or raised in order to collect more revenue, but numerous embargoes were imposed to reserve supplies for domestic use so that the burden of shortage rested on foreign countries. Cuba, however, restricted domestic consumption of beef so as to make a greater contribution to the war.

European countries continued to make and remake (sometimes every six months) barter and compensation agreements indicating the classes of goods and the quantities or values to be exchanged—the total trade usually to be carefully balanced.

The American countries continued to exchange most-favoured-nation pledges and to make agreements for tariff reductions. The United States on Jan. 1 and Jan. 30, 1943, put into effect its trade agreements with Uruguay and with Mexico, and on Nov. 19 with Iceland. The trade agreement of April 8, 1943, with Iran, however, had not been ratified by Iran at the end of the year. Negotiations with Bolivia and with Paraguay had been announced, but since then there was a change of government in Bolivia.

Colombia and Ecuador expanded the list of concessions made by their agreement of July 1942. Paraguay exchanged a few concessions with Brazil, and on Nov. 17, 1943, signed trade and financial treaties with Argentina covering all aspects of commercial and financial relations and stipulating many tariff concessions on both sides. Argentina agreed with Chile for ten years to buy only natural sodium nitrate and not to construct a synthetic nitric acid plant.

Of potentially much greater significance than the new concessions exchanged among American countries was the disposition to consider closer future relations including customs unions. Argentina and Chile agreed on Aug. 24 to appoint a mixed commission to report within a year on possible bases of a customs union. "This customs union will be open to the adherence of any neighbouring country and will constitute a first step toward a continental economic organization including the reduction or the abolition of customs barriers" according to a declaration of the two governments. Likewise, Chile and Peru proposed to establish commissions to study possible free trade between them, and Chile and Brazil agreed on a permanent mixed commission to stimulate production and trade.

Chile, on Feb. 10, 1943, ratified the treaty of Oct. 17, 1941, by which Chile and Peru exchanged tariff concessions, and the two governments declared in a protocol their intention to maintain the exclusive character of these concessions. On March 1, Chile signed a most-favoured-nation treaty with Brazil, as had been done the year previously with Mexico (proclaimed by the Mexican government April 30, 1943). Both of these treaties excepted from the pledge of equal treatment the special treatment that might be accorded to a neighbouring state or which might be accorded to a partner in a customs union. But both Mexico and Brazil accepted this exception only with a list of exceptions to the exception, that is, lists of products in which they were respectively especially interested, which should always receive in Chile the treatment of the most-favoured-nation, whether or not that nation was in customs union with Chile.

A contrary tendency may be noted. Haiti denounced the preferential customs treaty of 1941 with the Dominican Republic so that it was to expire on March 8, 1944, and Guatemala announced that the free trade agreement of 1941 with El Salvador would not be extended beyond its initial term ending Nov. 6, 1943. (*See* also INTERNATIONAL TRADE.) (B. B. W.)

Tasmania. A state of the Australian commonwealth, forming an island 26,215 sq.mi. in area to the southeast of the mainland, from which it is separated by 140 mi. of Bass strait. Pop. (est. Dec. 1941) 241,171. Chief cities: Hobart (cap.,

66,620); Launceston (33,250). Governor (1943): Sir Ernest Clark.

History.—The premier, R. Cosgrove, twice introduced a bill to grant wider powers to the federal government for a limited period after the war, but on each occasion the bill was rejected by the legislative council after having been passed by the lower house.

Tasmania's large prewar fresh apple export trade was largely replaced by the manufacture of apple juice for the services. More than 1,000,000 gallons were supplied during 1943. The federal government decided to establish an aluminum ingot industry based on Tasmanian and Victorian bauxite deposits.

The postwar reconstruction committee's plans for housing, water and sewerage, hydroelectric extensions and reafforestation to cost £A.9,000,000 were approved by the cabinet.

Education.—In 1939: state primary schools 420; average daily attendance 25,538; state high schools 5; average attendance 1,783.

Finance.—Revenue (1940–41), £A.2,920,000; expenditure £A.3,110,000; public debt (June 30, 1942), £A.28,737,000.

Communication.—Roads (1940) 9,386 mi.; railways: government (Dec. 1942), 642 mi.; private, 132 mi. Motor vehicles licensed (March 31, 1943): cars 15,703; trucks 5,505; cycles 2,442. Wireless receiving set licences (March 31, 1943) 49,030. Telephones (June 30, 1941) 19,565.

Manufacturing.—Production 1939–40: primary £A.8,185,110; secondary £A.6,253,029. Labour 1941–42 average: factory employment, 17,556 employees; unemployment (March 1943) 1.3%.
(W. D. Ma.)

Taxation. **United States.**—Employers in the United States became tax collectors on a grand scale in July 1943, when the pay-as-you-earn scheme of harvesting the bumper crop of tax dollars was put into effect by the government.

Under the revolutionary provisions of the Current Tax Payment act of 1943, signed by President Roosevelt on June 9, a 20% withholding of taxable income at source became effective July 1 for all wage and salary earners. Employers, who had been given a few years of experience in tax collection technique through the small percentage withheld from wages and salaries under the Social Security act, were now charged with collecting and remitting to the treasury's designated depositaries the bulk of revenue due from individual taxpayers.

The transition to pay-as-you-earn was accomplished with comparatively little disturbance to the economic equilibrium of the nation. Yet, 1943 as a whole was a year of tax turmoil. Generally speaking, the public was confused by the complexities of the tax situation. Millions more citizens had become "tax conscious" through the withholding from wages of the 5% Victory tax during the first half of the year but they found it difficult to comprehend the workings of the tax abatement clause and other features of the Current Tax Payment act.

Congress found practically no surcease from the gruelling task of revising the revenue code. Consideration of the withholding tax legislation extended over the first five months of the year, and scarcely had the ink of the president's signature dried on that historic document than treasury plans were being discussed for a second major tax law—this one designed to raise additional revenue (effective on income received in the calendar year 1944) of between $10,000,000,000 and $12,000,000,000 a year. Furthermore, bills were introduced in congress to boost social security tax rates to 6% each on employee and employer, thus raising an annual sum estimated at more than $12,000,000,000, most of which would be immediately available for general purposes. However, on Dec. 16, 1943, congress froze existing social security rates at 1% each on employer and employee until March 1, 1944.

On Oct. 3, the treasury recommended to congress additional taxes of $10,500,000,000, of which $6,500,000,000 would come out of the pockets of individuals. The plan contemplated repeal of the 5% Victory tax, which would free about 9,000,000 persons from income tax payments; repeal of the 10% earned income credit; reduction in exemptions of individuals; sharp increase in surtax rates applicable to both individuals and corporations; graduation of rates of withholding tax so as to collect substantially the full liability in the higher salary and wage brackets; increase in estate and gift tax rates and reduction of exemptions; and increase in excise tax rates all along the line. Congress received these proposals coldly, and 1943 ended with new tax legislation still the subject of debate.

The house of representatives on Nov. 23, 1943, passed a bill to add approximately $2,142,000,000 to federal taxes, making only minor changes in rates, except those applying to excise taxes on toilet preparations, liquors, transportation tickets, communication services and luxury items generally. On Dec. 23, the senate finance committee reported a measure designed to raise $2,300,000,000 in new taxes, which the committee estimated would bring total revenue over a full year's time up to $43,600,000,000. With congress in holiday recess, action on the bill had not been taken by the end of 1943.

"Pay-as-you-earn" System.—The Current Tax Payment act of 1943, as its title implies, provided new machinery for the collection of U.S. federal income taxes. It was not a new *tax* law in the sense of revising existing rates, but it instituted the most radical changes in the income tax situation made in more than a quarter of a century. Moreover, it was regarded as a *permanent* change —not to be classed in the category of a war emergency measure as so many revisions in the tax structure of the United States had been since 1939.

The outstanding feature of the new law was the provision compelling employers to withhold 20% of wages and salaries, after specified exemptions reflecting the family status, from pay roll checks, and to deposit such withheld sums to the credit of the government in local banks designated as depositaries. The 20% deduction from pay rolls represented the normal income tax of 17% and 3% of the Victory tax. The 5% Victory tax imposed under the Revenue act of 1942 was not repealed, but only 3% was collected currently after July 1, 1943, on the theory that the remaining 2%, due March 15, 1944, probably would be cancelled out by refunds to be granted for purchases of war bonds, payment of life insurance premiums, or reduction of personal indebtedness, as provided in the 1942 act.

A provision requiring employers to pay all withheld taxes into the depositaries within ten days after the close of each calendar month enabled the treasury to come into quick possession of these taxes. Employers were compelled also to file quarterly reports of such payments with the collector of internal revenue, accompanied by depositary receipts for the full amount of taxes

withheld. A prodigious amount of additional bookkeeping was thus imposed on employers.

Withholding Exemptions.—Employees were charged with the responsibility of filing exemption certificates with employers. For withholding purposes, exemption allowances were fixed in tables included in the Current Tax Payment act, as in Table I.

In no event shall the tax to be withheld be less than 3% of the excess of each wage payment over an exemption determined in accordance with the following schedule:

VICTORY TAX WITHHOLDING EXEMPTION SCHEDULE

Pay roll period	Withholding exemption
Weekly	$12.00
Biweekly	24.00
Semimonthly	26.00
Monthly	52.00
Quarterly	156.00
Semiannual	312.00
Annual	624.00
Daily or miscellaneous (per day of such period)	1.70

Relief for Armed Forces.—Excluded from the withholding provisions were members of the armed forces, farm workers, casual labourers, domestic help, ministers of the gospel and services by nonresident aliens. Members of the armed forces also received a special exemption of $1,500 on base pay, in addition to regular exemptions allowed civilians under the 1942 revenue act.

Employers were given the option of computing the exact amount of tax to be withheld from the pay of each employee as provided by the intricate terms of the law, or of using the figures set out in tables shown in the statute for various wage or salary levels and dependency situations. (*See* TABLE II.) Employers were required to furnish each employee within 30 days after the close of each calendar year a statement of the total amount of taxes withheld.

Although the new law accomplished a considerable degree of current tax collection in 1943, it was estimated by the treasury that only 17,000,000 of the 44,000,000 taxpayers affected would become fully current during the year, with the remaining 27,000,000 not becoming fully current until 1945, when they paid off the 25% portion of their "abatement year" tax liability that had not been "forgiven."

Tax Abatement.—The much-discussed "tax-forgiveness" clause of the so-called Ruml plan was incorporated in modified form in

ORDINARY CITIZEN'S view of the pay-as-you-go tax bill passed by Congress in June 1943. Cartoon by Bishop in the *St. Louis Star-Times*, entitled "Whistling as He Works"

Table I.—*Family Status Withholding Exemption Schedule*

Pay roll period	Single person	Married person claiming whole of personal exemption for withholding or head of family	Married person claiming half of personal exemption for withholding	Married person claiming none of personal exemption for withholding	Each dependent, other than the first dependent in the case of the head of a family
Weekly	$12.	$24.	$12.	0	$6.
Biweekly	24.	48.	24.	0	12.
Semimonthly	26.	52.	26.	0	13.
Monthly	52.	104.	52.	0	26.
Quarterly	156.	312.	156.	0	78.
Semiannual	312.	624.	312.	0	156.
Annual	624.	1,248.	624.	0	312.
Daily or miscellaneous (per day of such period)	1.70	3.40	1.70	0	.85

Table II.—*Wage Bracket Withholding Table, for Use by Employers in Complying With Provisions of U.S. Current Tax Payment Act of 1943*

(Weekly pay roll period)*

When the wages are		And, (1) such person is a married person claiming none of personal exemption for withholding and has—									
		No dependents	One dependent	Two dependents	Three dependents	Four dependents	Five dependents	Six dependents	Seven dependents	Eight dependents	Nine dependents
		Or, (2) such person is a married person claiming half of personal exemption for withholding and has—									
				No dependents	One dependent	Two dependents	Three dependents	Four dependents	Five dependents	Six dependents	Seven dependents
		Or, (3) such person is a single person and has—									
				No dependents	One dependent	Two dependents	Three dependents	Four dependents	Five dependents	Six dependents	Seven dependents
At least	But less than	Or, (4) such person is a married person claiming all of personal exemption for withholding and has—									
						No dependents	One dependent	Two dependents	Three dependents	Four dependents	Five dependents
		Or, (5) such person is head of a family and has—									
						No dependents or one dependent	Two dependents	Three dependents	Four dependents	Five dependents	Six dependents
		The amount of tax to be withheld shall be—									
$ 0.00	$10.00	$1.00	—	—	—	—	—	—	—	—	—
10.00	15.00	2.50	$1.30	$0.10	—	—	—	—	—	—	—
15.00	20.00	3.50	2.30	1.10	$0.20	$0.20	$0.20	$0.20	$0.20	$0.20	$0.20
20.00	25.00	4.50	3.30	2.10	.90	.30	.30	.30	.30	.30	.30
25.00	30.00	5.50	4.30	3.10	1.90	.70	.50	.50	.50	.50	.50
30.00	40.00	7.00	5.80	4.60	3.40	2.20	1.00	.70	.70	.70	.70
40.00	50.00	9.00	7.80	6.60	5.40	4.20	3.00	1.80	1.00	1.00	1.00
50.00	60.00	11.00	9.80	8.60	7.40	6.20	5.00	3.80	2.60	1.40	1.30
60.00	70.00	13.00	11.80	10.60	9.40	8.20	7.00	5.80	4.60	3.40	2.20
70.00	80.00	15.00	13.80	12.60	11.40	10.20	9.00	7.80	6.60	5.40	4.20
80.00	90.00	17.00	15.80	14.60	13.40	12.20	11.00	9.80	8.60	7.40	6.20
90.00	100.00	19.00	17.80	16.60	15.40	14.20	13.00	11.80	10.60	9.40	8.20
100.00	110.00	21.00	19.80	18.60	17.40	16.20	15.00	13.80	12.60	11.40	10.20
110.00	120.00	23.00	21.80	20.60	19.40	18.20	17.00	15.80	14.60	13.40	12.20
120.00	130.00	25.00	23.80	22.60	21.40	20.20	19.00	17.80	16.60	15.40	14.20
130.00	140.00	27.00	25.80	24.60	23.40	22.20	21.00	19.80	18.60	17.40	16.20
140.00	150.00	29.00	27.80	26.60	25.40	24.20	23.00	21.80	20.60	19.40	18.20
150.00	160.00	31.00	29.80	28.60	27.40	26.20	25.00	23.80	22.60	21.40	20.20
160.00	170.00	33.00	31.80	30.60	29.40	28.20	27.00	25.80	24.60	23.40	22.20
170.00	180.00	35.00	33.80	32.60	31.40	30.20	29.00	27.80	26.60	25.40	24.20
180.00	190.00	37.00	35.80	34.60	33.40	32.20	31.00	29.80	28.60	27.40	26.20
190.00	200.00	39.00	37.80	36.60	35.40	34.20	33.00	31.80	30.60	29.40	28.20
$200 or over		20% of the excess over $200 plus									
		$40.00	$38.80	$37.60	$36.40	$35.20	$34.00	$32.80	$31.60	$30.40	$29.20

If the number of dependents is in excess of the largest number of dependents shown, the amount of tax to be withheld shall be that applicable in the case of the largest number of dependents shown reduced by $1.20 for each dependent over the largest number shown, except that in no event shall the amount to be withheld be less than 3 per centum of the excess of the median wage in the bracket in which the wages fall (or if the wages paid are $200 or over, of the excess of the wages) over $12, computed, in case such amount is not a multiple of $0.10, to the nearest multiple of $0.10.

*Similar tables are provided in the act for biweekly, semimonthly, monthly and daily pay rolls.

the Current Tax Payment act. To ease the burden of transition to current tax collection, the act provided for at least 75% abatement of 1942 or 1943 tax liability (whichever was smaller) for everybody and 100% tax abatement in the lower brackets. A taxpayer owing less than $50 in taxes for either 1942 or 1943 was relieved of any tax liability. Each taxpayer whose tax bill under the abatement plan was between $50 and $66.67 was freed of paying $50 of the amount, the remainder to be paid in two installments—on March 15, 1944, and March 15, 1945. Abatement of 75% was made applicable to all persons whose tax liability exceeded $66.67, the remaining 25% of the tax to be paid one-half on March 15, 1944, and the other half on March 15, 1945, in addition to current taxes. The withholding levy did not apply to income derived from sources other than wages or salary, such as dividends, interest, etc.

The abatement provisions did not have the effect of reducing taxes due in 1943 or 1944, as many had anticipated. It was pointed out by the treasury department that the taxpayer generally would not benefit immediately unless his income fell off, but that he would have the satisfaction of knowing that at death he would owe no income tax. As a matter of fact, treasury officials estimated the new collection system would add about $3,000,000,-000 to tax collections for the fiscal year ending June 30, 1944, due in large measure to current collection of taxes on the higher levels of individual incomes in 1943 and 1944.

Quarterly Estimates of Income.—The law provided for filing of quarterly estimates and partial payments by taxpayers in certain categories, with a final complete return and adjustment on March 15 of each year. As applied to 1943, an estimate of income for the full year and remittance of taxes due was required on or before Sept. 15 from single persons whose wages or salary exceeded $2,700 a year, married persons with pay in excess of $3,500 annually, or those receiving more than $100 income a year from sources other than wages or salary, regardless of the amount of such wages. A penalty of 6% interest was provided for failure to estimate within 80% of the correct tax liability for the year, but leave was granted the taxpayer to revise his estimate on or before Dec. 15 and thus escape the penalty if his revised estimate was not more than 20% below the correct amount to be determined in the complete return to be filed March 15, 1944. Special provision was made for farmers, who were not required to file an estimate in September but did have to file on or before Dec. 15, 1943. The penalty in the case of the farmer applied only if his estimate was less than 66⅔% of his tax liability as determined by the final return March 15, 1944.

State and Local Taxes.—The general trend of revenue legislation on the part of state governments during 1943 was toward a recognition of the unprecedented burden imposed upon the average taxpayer by heavy wartime federal income taxes and the purchase of war bonds. Various types of relief were instituted. Thirty states enacted laws affecting the payment of state income taxes. Pay for service in the armed forces was exempted from taxation in Arkansas, California, Indiana, New York, North Carolina, North Dakota and Wisconsin. Similar exemption of amounts under $2,000 was made by Minnesota, and under $3,000 by Oregon. South Dakota and West Virginia repealed their income tax laws altogether. Pension annuities and allowances for disability resulting from military service were exempted from gross income tax by Maryland. Collection was deferred in Montana and Vermont in cases where ability to pay was impaired by war service. Eight other states extended for various periods the deadline for filing returns on income other than service pay. Indiana exempted such income from all taxes in event of death while in service.

Postwar planning and financial preparation for the transition to peace times received attention in practically all of the 44 states where legislative sessions were held during 1943. New official boards were set up to deal with the fiscal problems involved. Long-term development projects were authorized and funds provided to carry out the work. Wisconsin, for example, extended the privilege dividend tax and the tax on tobacco products to 1945 to create revenue for postwar rehabilitation of discharged soldiers. Cities in various states were given authority to build up cash reserve funds. New Hampshire levied an additional $3 poll tax to pay bonuses to veterans.

A 1% war emergency gross income tax for 1943 and 1944 was enacted by Delaware, in addition to the net income tax already in effect. A credit of $624 a year was allowed. Temporary increase to 6% in the corporation franchise tax rate in New York was extended until Nov. 1, 1944. The temporary additional taxes on individual incomes in Massachusetts were extended through 1946. Several states followed the example of the federal government in abolishing the requirement for sworn returns. Pennsylvania eliminated credit to corporations for federal income or excess profits taxes. Among deductions provided for by state statutes were: Limited medical and hospital expenses by Iowa, Maryland, New York, North Dakota, Oklahoma and Wisconsin; contributions for charitable or educational purposes, in varying degrees, in Alabama, North Carolina and South Carolina.

The situation resulting from renegotiation of war contracts received attention in several states. Connecticut provided for the filing of amended returns by the taxpayer following notice by the U.S. government of an adjustment affecting profits. Credits and refunds were allowed in Alabama, California, Kentucky, Massachusetts, Virginia, Wisconsin, and to a limited degree in Minnesota and New York. The maximum income tax rate was reduced in California to 6% on income in excess of $25,000 and personal exemptions were raised. Iowa indulged in a little "forgiveness" by providing for a settlement in full for 1942 and 1943 taxes on the basis of 50% of the amount due. Maryland allowed a credit of 33⅓% against taxes due for 1942, 1943 and 1944. Oregon's corporation income tax rate was cut from 8% to 5%, contingent upon enactment of a sales tax. Normal income taxes were reduced and the surtax repealed, also subject to approval by the electorate of an act providing for a 3% tax on gross income of retailers from sales of tangible personal property. South Dakota rendered its income tax ineffective by repealing the rate-fixing section. The personal income tax was repealed by West Virginia.

New taxes or revision upward of rates on alcoholic beverages was the order of legislation in 28 states that made changes in their liquor laws during 1943. Legislation affecting gasoline and petroleum products was confined principally to administrative regulation changes. Life insurance premiums were subjected to a 2% tax in Massachusetts, and Arizona imposed a 5% net income tax on all banks doing business within the state. The bank tax in Rhode Island was increased from 3% to 4%. Various unimportant changes were made in property taxes and motor vehicle taxes by several states. Sales taxes were continued in most states where a time-limit applied. (*See also* BUDGET, NATIONAL.)

Great Britain.—As in the United States, the taxation policy of the British government in 1943 veered further toward the prevention of inflation through soaking up as much of the excess income of the people as possible. The Budget White Paper in April showed that there had been a remarkable increase in income of wage earners between 1939 and 1943. More than 85% of net income (after payment of income taxes) went to weekly wage earners in 1943. Government taxes (central and local) in Great Britain rose from £1,100,000,000 in the 1938–39 fiscal year to an estimated total of more than £3,000,000,000 ($12,000,000,000) in 1943–44. The standard rate of individual income tax in effect in 1943 was 10s. in the £—50%. The surtax rate was graduated. Individuals were subject to income tax and surtax. The income tax began on earnings of £110 ($440) a year for the single person, and on income of £156 ($624) a year for a married person; married, with one child, £211; with two children, £267; three children, £322. After certain allowances, such as for incapacitated relatives, housekeepers, and life insurance premiums, the first £600 of "taxable income" was taxed at the rate of 32½% and the remainder at 50%. A system of tax withholding by employers was in effect with respect to weekly wage earners, with special provisions to relieve "hardship" cases. Postwar credits were made applicable to a portion of taxes paid.

The individual surtax was assessed against all income over £2,000. A rate of 10% applied to the first £500 of surtax income, with a gradual rise until all persons with income in excess of £20,000 paid surtaxes at the rate of 47½%. The combined tax rate on all incomes above £20,000 a year was 97½%. Estate taxes ranged from 1% on estates of £100 to 36% on estates of £25,000, 52% on £1,000,000, and 65% on £2,000,000.

The British system of taxing business profits in 1943 was severe. An excess profits tax of 100% was imposed on all profits in excess of those made in specified "standard years," subject to a 20% refund after the war. This refund would be taxable at the rate current at that time. As an alternative, a tax of 5% on incorporated business and 4% on unincorporated business was collected if the yield would be greater. The 50% standard rate of income tax applied to all remaining profits. Dividends were subjected to a double tax in that the recipient was required to include in his income, not the sum he received but the amount that would have been paid to him by the corporation had it not been required to pay the income tax of 50%.

The excise taxes remained heavy and the "purchase" tax, based on the wholesale cost of commodities, rose as high as 100% on luxuries such as jewellery, furs and silk dresses.

As outlined by the financial secretary of the treasury on Sept. 22, 1943, the British government decided to introduce a "pay-as-you-earn" system of income tax collection for the fiscal year beginning April 6, 1944, to apply to all persons paid weekly. As described in a special White Paper, "the tax deducted from earnings *in* any financial year will represent the liability *for* that year, measured by the actual earnings *of* that year, and the deductions of tax week by week will keep pace with the accruing liability." Under the plan accepted, the "code number" of each wage earner was to be sent to his employer who, in addition, would be issued "tax tables" showing for each "code" the "cumulative" tax payable on any given aggregate amount of wages up to the end of each week of the fiscal year. The "cumulative" tax shown in the tax tables for aggregate earnings up to a given week of the financial year would take account of the tax-free allowances up to that date, as well as the tax-free allowance of one-tenth on earned income (maximum allowance £150) and of the lower rate of tax (6s.6d. in the £ instead of the standard rate of 10s. in the £) on the first £165 of taxable income. On the basis of the code the employer would be able to record the earnings and tax payable by each wage earner.

Canada.—Under the new pay-as-you-earn system put into effect in Canada in 1943, the individual taxpayer was required to pay somewhat larger amounts than in an ordinary year, despite a 50% "forgiveness" of 1942 income tax. Corporation taxes were practically unchanged. Excise taxes, already high, were increased in some instances. The impost on spirits and tobacco was boosted —spirits from $9 to $11 per proof gallon, raw leaf tobacco from 20 cents to 28 cents a pound, manufactured tobacco from 51 cents to 67 cents, cigarettes from $8 to $10 per 1,000, cigars from $4.25 to $9.25 per 1,000.

Direct and indirect taxes were greatly increased as a result of the war. Direct taxes raised eight times as much revenue in the fiscal year ending March 31, 1943, as in the last full peacetime year. During that period the number of persons paying taxes increased from 300,000 to more than 2,000,000 The minimum rate on corporations was 40% of profits and the rate on excess profits was 100%, with 20% refundable after the war.

The pay-as-you-earn method of collection began April 1, 1943. In making adjustments in payments, 50% of the tax liability for 1942 was wiped out. Part of the income tax payments represented a saving portion to be refunded to the taxpayer after the war, with interest at 2%. Luxury taxes were increased. (*See* also BUSINESS REVIEW; LAW; NATIONAL DEBT.)　　(C. A. SR.)

Tea. The general supply of tea continued to be ample through 1943 and the new crop plus the carryover assured an ample supply for 1943–44. The principal sources, India and Ceylon, had good crops although smaller crops were reported in East Africa. Under agreement, the British food ministry bought these crops and allotments were made by the Combined Food board. The U.S. allotment was about 65,000,000 lb. for 1943, most of it for civilian use, since relatively small amounts were used by the U.S. military forces, except those stationed in Great Britain and Africa. While tea consumption declined in 1941–42 it appeared to be approaching normal in 1943. The shift from tea to coffee by many consumers appeared to be permanent however as the coffee restrictions were lifted.　　(J. C. Ms.)

Tedder, Sir Arthur William (1890–　　), British air officer, was graduated from Magdalene college, Cambridge in 1912, and served with the royal flying corps in France during World War I. He attended the Royal Naval Staff college, 1923–24, headed the air armament school at Eastchurch and directed training at the air ministry. In 1936, he became air officer commanding the R.A.F. in the far east and in 1940, he was promoted to deputy commander in chief of the R.A.F. in the middle east. As commander in chief in 1941, he was credited with having smoothed over the friction between air, land and naval forces on the desert front. In 1942, Tedder made great progress in co-ordinating air with ground forces, first in the campaign in April against Marshal Erwin Rommel, which ended in defeat, and later in the great British offensive which started in Oct. 1942, and ended in victory. He was knighted "for distinguished services" and became vice-chief of the air staff. On Feb. 11, 1943, he was named air chief in the Mediterranean theatre, and on the following Dec. 28 he was named deputy supreme commander of the invasion forces under Gen. Dwight Eisenhower.

Tehran, Declaration of: *see* UNITED STATES.

Telegraphy. During the year 1943 the task of handling the large volume of telegrams and cablegrams required for the conduct of the war continued to be the first consideration of the telegraph industry. The telegram and the cablegram were used primarily for war purposes. The war, of course, put a heavy burden on the U.S. telegraph system. In the output of every instrument for war, the telegraph played a part. The telegraph company handled more than 200,000,000 telegrams and 10,000,000 telegraph money orders in 1943, despite the fact that some 7,000 of its employees entered the military services and there was a lack of essential materials for expanding its equipment.

By the end of 1943, the company had provided telegraph facilities for more than 4,000 projects for the army, the navy, the civil aeronautics administration and other government agencies and war plants. Many of these involved the construction of lines to isolated spots where new war plants, camps and bases were located.

The telegraph company's laboratories also were devoted largely to the development of special equipment for war purposes, but most of this equipment is secret.

The most important development of the year in the communications field was the merger of the Western Union Telegraph company and Postal Telegraph, Inc., which became effective at midnight, Oct. 7, 1943. The merger fulfilled the principle upon which Western Union was founded: namely, that a proper telegraph service calls for a system reaching all important points, under a single management, with a fixed tariff and uniform standards of efficiency. Until 1943, the law had prohibited telegraph mergers, but permissive legislation was enacted by Congress in March following hearings in which a telegraph merger was advocated by the Federal Communications commission and all public agencies concerned, including the army and navy.

Following the consummation of the merger, co-ordination of management and administrative personnel of the two companies was promptly effected. All Postal main and branch offices were made Western Union branches. During the integration period, which was expected to require about two years, it was planned to maintain the trunk lines as well as most of the main offices of both companies. The Postal employees were transferred to the Western Union service rolls.

Western Union's plan for expanding and modernizing its plant was retarded by the war, but there were certain scheduled improvements, costing about $4,000,000, which were important to the war and which were being carried out.

A number of technical improvements were placed in wider use in 1943 and further increased the capacity of the telegraph trunk lines. These improvements included the extended use of direct circuits, carrier systems, the Varioplex, reperforator switching, improved repeaters, sub-center switching and facsimile telegraphy. All these facilitated the handling of the swollen volume of wartime traffic. In particular, the extended use of leased wire switching systems was found to be an essential war requirement.

Statistics.—Reliable statistics covering the telegraph systems of the world in 1943 were not available but the latest comprehensive data for the land line wire telegraph systems of the United States (aside from that of telephone companies) follows:

Mi. of pole line	240,998
Mi. of underground conduit (single duct)	6,161
Mi. of aerial wire	1,823,323
Mi. of aerial cable wire	122,617
Mi. of underground cable wire	335,846
Mi. of land line submarine cable wire	6,562
Total mi. of land line wire (approximately 77% copper)	2,288,348

Number of telegraph offices	22,586
Approximate number of telegraph agencies	15,500
Approximate number of revenue messages transmitted	214,000,000
Approximate investment in operated land lines plant	$375,642,000

The submarine cable telegraph systems of the world, so far as indicated by the latest available data, consist of about 360,000 mi. of ocean cable, containing about 432,000 mi. of copper conductors and representing a capital outlay of about $400,000,-000. Approximately 80% of the total mileage of ocean cables was provided by private enterprise and the remainder by government administrations.　　　　　　　　　　(A. N. Ws.)

Telephone. During the year, the number of telephones in the United States increased from about 24,900,-000 to about 26,400,000. Telephone plant investment showed an increase of about $100,000,000. These gains, and other increases in the physical facilities employed in providing telephone service which might be cited, assume full significance only in the light of the fact that they were made at a time when many of the materials required in telephone manufacturing and construction were being diverted in large quantities to uses more directly involved in the war effort. Increases in these physical facilities were made by the telephone companies only on the basis of their necessity as contributions toward victory—toward the efficient handling of a rising tide of war telephone calls.

During 1943, toll and long distance telephone traffic continued to increase, from about 3,600,000 a day to around 4,100,000 a day, on an average. The total for the year of long distance messages involving the lines of the American Telephone and Telegraph company was about 150,000,000 as against about 59,000,000 in 1939, a typical prewar year, and about 114,000,-000 in 1942.

Handling this increasing wartime traffic, without being able to provide additional facilities in sufficient amounts, continued to be a major problem of the business. Typical of many steps taken during the year toward its solution was the more extensive use of carrier currents.

A new method, employing the crossbar principle, by which toll operators can dial calls, in much the same manner as numbers are dialled by subscribers, was introduced in a large area centring around Philadelphia.

Continued emphasis was placed by the telephone companies on the conservation of critical metals and other materials. Important savings were effected, for example, through the introduction of a device by which weathered drop wires can be repainted and protected from further deterioration, without removing them from the plant.

Contrasted with this simple tool is an extremely complex product of telephone research, experimentation and engineering, first demonstrated to the public late in the year. This is an electrical gun director which computes automatically the intricate mathematical problems involved in accurately directing anti-aircraft fire. Making allowances for such factors as temperature, barometric pressure, wind velocity and direction, latitude and height and speed of the plane, it tracks its target and aims a number of guns simultaneously.

These two devices, occupying opposite extremes of simplicity and complexity, were typical of many other developments by telephone organizations during 1943 which proved valuable contributions to the winning of the war.

The provision of telephone facilities for army camps, naval bases and other military establishments, as well as for war plants, was a problem of increasing scope and difficulty. In many cases, factories producing war materials were provided with special telephone equipment or routines which materially increased their speed of production.

During the year, the total number of service men instructed in plant schools maintained by the telephone operating companies grew to more than 8,000. Of nearly 55,000 Bell system employees in the armed forces at the end of the year, about 15,000 were in the signal corps, and many others in corresponding branches of the navy, the marine corps or the coast guard. Large numbers of employees of the independent telephone companies were also serving in the armed forces.

Appeals to the public, through an extensive advertising and publicity campaign, to avoid making unnecessary long distance calls to busy war centres, to limit the length of their conversations when circuits were busy and to refrain from making calls that might interfere with "service for service men" met with cordial co-operation.　　　　　　　　　　(W. S. G.)

Television. During 1943 television activities in the United States and abroad were wholly directed toward advancing the progress of the war. Although television broadcasting to home-installed televisors was maintained on a token basis, the programs were principally directed to meeting military requirements. Instruction of air-raid wardens, first aid workers and other civilian war workers was continued, in view of the fact that television provided effective means for bringing a single lecture before thousands rather than tens of interested observers. No additional television receivers were manufactured and sold during the year, because of war need for the materials that would have been involved, but supplemental service was provided by the donation of personally owned and home-installed sets to hospitals and other group centres, so that television transmission of sport events and telecasts of comparable entertainment programs were made available to audiences, including returned service men, much more widely than would otherwise have been possible.

Although the application of television's scientific principles revolved almost entirely around wartime uses, it was generally recognized that the future would see television broadcasting on a basis technically superior to anything available prior to Pearl Harbor. Among the anticipated improvements were increased service distances, based partly upon better synchronizing systems capable of operating in the face of more severe interference conditions, together with the availability of larger pictures projected upon flat screens of either home or theatre size. The expected advent of such satisfactory television service gave rise to speculation and, indeed, to planning as to the character of television programs that might be expected to fill the postwar requirements of a national audience. One result of activity along these lines was an experiment at Schenectady, N.Y., where a complete edition of a daily newspaper was presented to a television audience. First the pages of the newspaper were shown on the screen, and then each feature was "acted out" for the benefit of the observers. Seeing news commentators, cartoonists and advertising models come to life visually, and hearing their aural presentations simultaneously with their appearance, was judged as suggesting an additional program possibility that would probably be of widespread interest. Analysts of the future of home television seemed to feel that there would be available many types of useful and interesting programs, and that their production would not involve the high costs, probably prohibitive for television, that were usually associated with the making of feature films by the motion picture industry.

Thus, although the scientific aspects of television were so closely tied into direct wartime applications that they may not even be outlined, during 1943 there was moderately extensive study and discussion of how television might best be developed as a postwar public service. The need for co-ordinating current scientific developments into a sound industrial plan for the whole

radio, including television and facsimile, resulted in the organi-
:ion of the Radio Technical Planning board. This large group,
awn from the entire radio field, was not only set up to plan the
:ure of television as did the National Television Systems com-
ttee in 1940 and 1941, but to analyze in similar manner the
er branches of radio. Colour television, the transmission of
ger and more detailed pictures, co-ordination with recording
thods and the use of television principles for determining range
d direction were among the topics to be studied. Just as the
lustry-wide agreement as to television practices, reached
rough the work of the National Television Systems committee,
ulted in the initiation of commercial television on July 1,
41, the conclusions of the Radio Technical Planning board were
pected to provide a sound basis for new and expanded indus-
al activities in radio and television as production facilities are
dually released from direct war manufacturing. (J. V. L. H.)

Great Britain.—In the colour television systems successfully
monstrated in Britain (Baird) and America (Goldmark) the
ojection of successive colour frames was accomplished by the
e of a rotating filter disk interposed between the screen and
e observer. The presence of this filter disk introduced certain
advantages, particularly as the merit of the cathode-ray tube
a television reproducer lies in the absence of mechanical mov-
 parts.

Accordingly John L. Baird was experimenting with a colour
evision system in which successive images are projected
rough separate lenses and combined on the viewing screen.
ch lens is fitted with an appropriate colour filter, and the images
 reproduced one above the other on the screen of a projection
be. These images are then converged by the individual filters
d lenses on to the screen.

Proper registration of the pictures on the viewing screen pre-
ts the major difficulty of this system, which by 1943 had only
en demonstrated in two colours. The size of picture shown was
in. by 5 in. with 600-line definition.

Although general research on television was still restricted, the
rm in which an improved service would be resumed after the
r was the subject of much discussion. Although it was gen-
ally agreed that the British standard in operation at the out-
eak of war (425 lines, 50 fields, interlaced) did not approach
rfection, the view was expressed that it would be economically
sirable to re-establish it as early as possible and aim at mak-
g the fullest use of the available definition within the existing
nd of frequencies.

BIBLIOGRAPHY.—*Electronic Engineering* (Jan. 1943, July 1943, Sept.
43); *Wireless Engineer* (June 1943).　　(G. P.)

ellurium. There was an enormous expansion in the production and use of tellurium in the United States in
41, with output increasing 170% to 239,983 lb., but the 1942
tput dropped back to 98,798 lb., only 11% ahead of 1940.
　　(G. A. Ro.)

ennessee. A south central state, 16th to enter the union,
called the "Volunteer State." Land area 41,961
.mi., water area 285 sq.mi. Population (1940) 2,915,841; rural,
888,635; urban, 1,027,206; rural farm, 1,271,944; native white,
395,586; Negro, 508,736; foreign-born, 11,320; other races,
9. Capital Nashville (167,402). Other cities include Memphis
92,942); Chattanooga (128,163); Knoxville (111,580).

History.—Governor of Tennessee in 1943 was Prentice
ooper; secretary of state, Joe C. Carr; state treasurer, John W.
arton; comptroller of the treasury, Robert W. Lowe; adjutant
neral, Thomas A. Frazier; attorney general, Roy H. Beeler.
ommissioners were as follows: agriculture, C. C. Flanery; con-

servation, Paul S. Mathes; education, B. O. Duggan; finance and
taxation, George McCanless; highways and public works, C. W.
Phillips; institutions, W. O. Baird; welfare, William A. Shoaf;
insurance and banking, J. M. McCormack; labour, S. E. Bryant;
public health, Dr. R. H. Hutcheson; railroad and public utilities,
Porter Dunlap, Leon Jourolman and John C. Hammer.

Education.—In 1942, of 5,373 elementary schools, 1,495 had
three or more teachers; the number of one-teacher schools declined from 3,555 in 1927 to 2,425 in 1942. Enrolment in elementary schools in 1942 was 511,312. In 1942 there were 581
high schools with a total enrolment of 124,514; the number of
teachers, 5,428.

Public Welfare, Charities, Correction.—In June 1943, 69
WPA recipients received $15,362; 39,050 old-age recipients,
$556,167; aid to dependent children, 32,510 (12,832 families),
amount $264,999; aid to blind, 1,593, amount $20,650. In 1942–
43 there were eight correctional institutions with approximately
4,057 inmates; expenditures, $1,443,506. Separate schools were
maintained for the blind, the deaf, and the underprivileged;
three state hospitals for the insane; a home and training school
for feeble minded.

Communication.—In 1942, of about 82,000 mi. of public
road, 7,510 mi. comprised state highways; state expenditures
were $14,192,978 for the 1942 fiscal year. There were 3,503 mi.
of railroad in 1942. In Nov. 1943 there were 30 airports, of
which 18 were civil fields, 8 CAA intermediate fields and 4 army
fields; there were 720 mi. of designated airways. Of the 333,600
telephones in the state, 232,500 were residential and 101,100 business. Water-borne commerce on the Tennessee river in 1940
amounted to 2,206,913 short tons; Cumberland river, 852,138;
Mississippi river, 7,055,675 short tons from Ohio river to Baton
Rouge and 1,841,068 at Memphis.

Banking and Finance.—In June 1943, there were 69 national
banks with 17 branches and 226 (June 30, 1943) state banks with
31 branches; assets, $904,009,000 for national and $349,860,195
for state banks; deposits, $850,476,000 for national and $322,-
645,959 for state banks. Savings and loan associations in Dec.
1942 numbered 42, with assets of $38,881,300.

Total state revenue for the fiscal year 1942–43 was $53,105,680;
revenue shared with counties and cities, $7,759,289; revenue for
state purposes, $45,346,391. Direct bonded debt for the state
on June 30, 1943, was $94,923,000; highway reimbursement
debt, $12,002,156; gross debt, $106,925,156; unencumbered surplus in sinking fund, $21,930,969; net debt, $84,994,187.

Agriculture.—There were 247,617 farms in 1940 with a total
of 18,492,898 ac.; 6,158,662 ac. of cropland were harvested.
Gross value of agricultural production in 1942 was $327,614,000;
cash farm income, $254,761,000 (including government pay-
ments); cash farm income from crops was $127,147,000; from
livestock and livestock products, $114,189,000; government pay-
ments to farmers, $13,425,000. Gross farm income from crops
was $127,147,000 in 1942. The forest area is approximately
14,000,000 ac.

Table I.—*Leading Agricultural Products of Tennessee, 1943 and 1942*

Crop	1943*	1942
Corn, bu.	61,662,000	75,924,000
Tame hay, tons	2,076,000	2,339,000
Cotton, bales	510,000	625,000
Wheat, bu.	4,116,000	5,234,000
Tobacco, lb.	96,408,000	87,808,000
Potatoes, bu.	4,736,000	3,564,000
Sweet potatoes, bu.	4,590,000	3,600,000

*Estimated.

Manufacturing.—In 1939 (the latest data available in 1943)
2,289 manufacturing plants yielded products valued at $728,-
087,825, of which $320,341,902 was added by manufacture. The

number of wage earners increased from 107,645 in 1925 to 131,874 in 1939; wages paid in 1939, $109,661,769.

Table II.—*Principal Industries of Tennessee, 1939 and 1937*

Industry	Value of products	
	1939	1937
Rayon and allied products	$49,724,728	$49,132,660
Hosiery	33,798,963	29,219,241
Meat packing, wholesale	28,266,104	29,491,149
Chemicals	25,639,499	38,048,635
Cooking and other edible fats	19,787,646	36,457,022
Footwear (except rubber)	17,740,737	20,897,976
Flour and other grain mill products	16,147,788	22,673,578
Cottonseed oil, cake, meal linters	15,390,972	20,150,709

Mineral Production.—The total value of minerals produced in Tennessee in 1941 was $56,301,592, compared with $42,683,407 in 1940.

Table III.—*Principal Mineral Products of Tennessee, 1941 and 1940*

Mineral	Value 1941	Value 1940
Aluminum	*	$30,023,000
Coal	$16,454,539	12,024,742
Stone	9,157,673	6,674,710
Cement	8,520,284	5,655,635
Zinc	5,425,500	4,384,296
Sand and gravel	2,829,836	2,255,287
Lime	1,354,642	1,050,199
Coke	1,118,725	618,746
Clay products (other than pottery and refractories)	2,401,000	1,869,000

*Not included in total value of minerals in 1941.

(C. E. A.)

Tennessee Valley Authority. The TVA in 1943 continued its contributions to prosecution of the war in every field of its widespread activities. These included production of electric power, construction of new dams to provide new supplies of power, manufacture of munitions, research and education in wartime food processing and preservation, production and testing of phosphatic and nitrogenous fertilizers to increase farm output, assistance to industry and agencies of government by providing information and technical assistance, and construction of facilities to improve the wartime usefulness of the navigation channel.

Four new dams were placed in operation during the year, bringing the total constructed by TVA to 14 and the total in operation to 20. Douglas dam was placed in operation after a record-breaking construction period of 12 months and 19 days, and others completed were Fort Loudoun, Apalachia, and Ocoee No. 3. Filling of Fort Loudoun dam reservoir in Sept. 1943 extended the navigation channel in the Tennessee to its full commercial length of 650 mi., although accomplishment of the all-year full project depth to accommodate boats and barges of 9-ft. draft awaited closure of Kentucky dam in 1944 and completion of a small amount of dredging. Governing depths in low water periods pending completion of these jobs was 6 to 8 ft.

In 1943 the TVA constructed and operated four public use river terminals at Knoxville and Chattanooga, Tenn., and Decatur and Guntersville, Ala., and a coal terminal at Harriman, Tenn., in order to increase the wartime usefulness of the Tennessee channel which connects at Paducah, Ky., with the 8,000-mi. inland waterway system stretching from New Orleans and the Gulf coast to Minneapolis and St. Paul, Minn.; Pittsburgh, Pa.; Chicago, Ill.; and Kansas City, Mo. Traffic on the Tennessee increased from 138,400,000 ton-miles in 1941 to 161,500,000 ton-miles in 1942, as compared with 32,700,000 ton-miles in 1933, and cargoes included large amounts of petroleum products, grain from the midwest, coal, pig iron and military vehicles. The TVA multipurpose system of dams provided 8,000,000 ac.-ft. of storage for flood control at the close of 1943; the total will be increased to almost 14,000,000 ac.-ft. with completion of Kentucky

and Fontana dams in 1944 and 1945. Kentucky dam, which w have more than 4,500,000 ac.-ft. of useful storage for flood co trol on the lower Ohio and Mississippi rivers, was under constru tion near the mouth of the Tennessee. Fontana dam, being bu on the Little Tennessee in North Carolina in 1943, was plann to be the highest dam in the eastern United States, rising 460 from bedrock.

The power system, consisting at the close of 1943 of the multi-purpose dams built by the TVA, Wilson dam transferr from the war department in 1933, and five acquired dams, pl five supporting steam plants, one of which was built by TV was producing power at the rate of more than 9,000,000,0 kw.-hr. a year. About three-quarters of the total output w being used by war industry, served either directly from the TV transmission system or through 83 municipal and 45 co-operati distribution systems. Aluminum, copper, plastics, shells, arn clothing, aeroplanes and heavy chemicals were some of the pro ucts being manufactured by TVA power. Dams placed in oper tion plus additional installations at existing projects brought t total installed capacity of the system to more than 1,800,000 k by the close of 1943 as compared with 1,375,000 kw. on June 3 1942, and 1,639,000 kw. on June 30, 1943. Construction goi forward under War Production board allocations was expect to bring the installed capacity to about 2,100,000 kw. in 1945.

Total power operating revenues for the fiscal year 1943 exceede $31,500,000, and net income amounted to nearly $13,150,00 Net income plus interest paid on bonds represented a return average power investment of about 5%.

In its plants at Muscle Shoals, the TVA produced ammoniu nitrate and elemental phosphorus for munitions, calcium carbi for synthetic rubber, and concentrated phosphatic fertilizers strengthen wartime food programs both in the United Stat and abroad, where large quantities were shipped under lend-leas Ammonium nitrate, not needed for munitions, was released f use as fertilizer. A sample study in one state showed that tes demonstration farms using TVA phosphates had increased pr duction by 30% without additional manpower or machiner On June 30, 1943, 44,389 test-demonstration farmers in 28 stat were using TVA phosphate fertilizers.

In co-operative research, the TVA and the University of Te nessee developed equipment and techniques for both communit and home dehydration of fruits and vegetables and carried c educational campaigns to further their construction and prope use. The War Production board authorized use of materials t construct 40,000 units of a home dehydrator developed by th

INTERIOR OF THE AMMONIA PLANT at Nitrate Plant No. 2, Muscle Shoa Alabama, where ammonia was produced for explosives in 1943. Women worke were trained to do many of the jobs formerly held by men

TVA and the university, but production was limited. TVA provided technical advice to many food processors. Information was provided to both government and industry on availability of raw materials, plant sites, transportation and processing methods. The TVA was mapping strategic areas for the U.S. army and designing 13 dams for the Russian government under lend-lease.

A peacetime forest inventory yielded valuable information on location and availability of woods for ships' timbers, aeroplane veneer, tanning extracts and many other uses, and landowners were assisted in making their timber available for war uses in a manner to maintain the long-term usefulness of their forests.

As of June 30, 1943, TVA power was being distributed to more than 500,000 residential, farm, commercial and industrial consumers through the municipal and co-operative distribution systems. Cost of residential service under TVA rates fell to an average of 1.96 cents per kw.-hr., as compared with the United States average of 3.67 cents per kw.-hr. Average use per residential consumer for the fiscal year was nearly 1,600 kw.-hr., or over 50% higher than the national average.

The TVA made no request for additional appropriations for the fiscal year which commenced July 1, 1943, but is carrying on its operations with revenues and previously appropriated funds. The total funds made available to TVA from 1933 through the fiscal year 1943 were $733,041,770, consisting of $667,969,270 in congressional appropriations and $65,072,500 from sale of bonds.

Members of the TVA board of directors in 1943 were David E. Lilienthal, chairman, Harcourt A. Morgan, and James P. Pope. (*See also* DAMS; ELECTRICAL INDUSTRIES; PUBLIC UTILITIES.)

(W. L. S.)

Tennis. As in 1942, many tennis tournaments in the United States were cancelled either for lack of competitors or insufficient galleries or both. Some, however, were held much as usual, including several events on grass in the east. The national championships were played at the West Side Tennis club, Forest Hills, Long Island, in the first week of September. Entries were limited to 32 players in the men's and women's singles. John A. Kramer, former national doubles champion, defeated the only foreign threat in the semi-finals by beating Francisco Segura of Ecuador in five sets but lost in the finals to Lt. Joseph R. Hunt, USN, in five sets. Miss Pauline Betz repeated her 1942 triumph by winning the women's singles title over the same adversary, Miss Louise Brough. The men's doubles was won by Kramer and Frank A. Parker, and the women's by Miss Brough and Miss Margaret Osborne. (J. R. Tu.)

Termites: *see* ENTOMOLOGY.

Tesla, Nikola (1856–1943), U.S. electrical inventor, was born July 10 at Smiljan, Croatia (Yugoslavia). Of his claimed 700 inventions, his most important were developed before the turn of the century and included the induction motor, transformer and the principle of the rotary magnetic field. Handicapped by lack of funds and a poor business sense, he was compelled, for years, to conduct his experiments in hotel rooms. In an interview on his 78th birthday, he said that he had invented a "death beam" capable of destroying 10,000 aeroplanes at 250 miles' distance and of killing an army of 1,000,000 instantly. In ill health, he lived the last years of his life almost as a recluse and was found dead in his hotel room in New York city, Jan. 7. (See *Encyclopædia Britannica*.)

Texas. A south-central state of the United States, admitted to the union in Dec. 1845; popularly known as the "Lone Star state." Area, 263,644 sq.mi. (plus 3,695 sq.mi. of inland water surface); pop. (1940), 6,414,824. Rural population was 3,503,435 or 54.6% of the total. Negroes and other non-whites constituted 14.5% of the population. Since 1940, census bureau estimates indicate that growth of urban population ranges from 6.4% at Amarillo to 30.7% at San Antonio. Capital, Austin (87,930 in 1940). Three largest cities in 1943, as estimated by census bureau, based on registrations for war ration books were Houston, 588,175 (384,514 in 1940); Dallas, 440,888 (294,734 in 1940); San Antonio, 412,905 (253,854 in 1940).

History.—No general election was held in Texas during 1943, and there was little political activity or interest. The war disrupted normal life and, moving the people from one place and from one occupation to another, commanded most of their interest and energy. Cities and towns with army camps or defense plants continued to bulge with newcomers.

While the people remained apathetic, a strenuous campaign against the national administration and its major policies was carried on by the junior U.S. senator, W. Lee O'Daniel, the governor of the state, Coke R. Stevenson, and the lieutenant governor, John Lee Smith. The only state official of any importance who defended the administration was the attorney general, Gerald Mann. He resigned in December and was succeeded by his assistant, Grover Sellers. Other state officers were Jesse James, treasurer; James P. Alexander, chief justice of the supreme court; Bascom Giles, commissioner of general land office; J. A. McDonald, commissioner of agriculture; L. A. Woods, superintendent of public instruction; George H. Sheppard, comptroller.

Education.—For 1942–43 elementary schools had an enrolment of 796,336 white pupils and 174,171 Negroes. Secondary schools had an enrolment of 279,751 whites and 33,893 Negroes; total, 1,284,151. The total teaching staff was 47,334, of which 40,649 were whites and 6,685 were Negroes.

Public Welfare, Charities, Correction.—During 1943 the average number of old-age assistance recipients was 182,765. Case loads ranged from a peak of 183,367 cases to 180,511 cases. Payments to old-age assistance recipients amounted to $44,337,874.82. Average number of cases receiving aid to the blind was 4,427 in 1943, ranging from 4,106 to 4,681 cases with payments to recipients totalling $1,276,596 for the year.

An average of 11,604 families received aid to dependent children during 1943. The case load ranged from 12,168 families to 10,389 families. Payments to recipients totalled $2,967,554.

Eleemosynary institutions in the state numbered 22, of which 13 were hospitals for mental and nervous cases. During 1943 hospitalization for the insane was greatly facilitated by the completion of a 120-bed ward at Terrell State hospital and by renovation of the Confederate Veteran home at Austin to accommodate 375 mentally ill. The 47th state legislature appropriated $3,000,000 for building additional institutions for the insane, but wartime priorities prevented use of most of that sum.

The remaining eleemosynary institutions consisted of sanatoriums for tuberculars, schools for the blind and for the deaf (both white and Negro); two homes for delinquent children; two for white orphans and one for Negro orphans; one for crippled children.

Communications.—The state in 1943 had 26,883.37 mi. of highways, including 24,565.17 mi. maintained by the state, 607.20 mi. in urban areas, and 1,711 mi. not wholly maintained by the state. The amount spent by the state for regular maintenance was $4,892,983.11; for maintenance betterment, $750,233.36; and for traffic service, $1,778,356.10, making an over-all total of $7,421,572.57. Cash disbursed for highway construction, in the fiscal year Sept. 1, 1942–Aug. 31, 1943 was $18,707,473.84. There were more than 22,000 mi. of railway track in 1943.

Banking and Finance.—On Dec. 31, 1943 there were 391 state banks in Texas with total deposits of $536,326,600.69, and total resources of $595,009,572.89. On Dec. 31, 1943 there were 439 national banks in Texas. On Oct. 18, 1943 there were 438 national banks with total deposits of $3,113,803,000 and total resources of $3,296,422,000.

As of Aug. 31, 1943 the total cash balance in state funds (Aug. 31, 1942), plus deposit from revolving fund previously invested in Confederate pension warrants, plus total gross cash receipts for fiscal year 1943 totalled $354,821,921.88. Total gross cash disbursements, end of fiscal year 1943, totalled $290,371,429.09. Cash balance on hand, Aug. 31, 1943 amounted to $64,450,492.79. On Dec. 31, 1943 the state's gross bonded debt was $4,117,200, its cash sinking fund reserve, $15,000, its net bonded debt, $4,102,200. On the same date, its total warrants outstanding and unpaid in general revenue fund amounted to $25,574,326.21; its cash on hand for paying general revenue fund warrants was $7,126,454.42. Net warrant debt was $18,447,871.79.

Agriculture.—Total harvested acreage in Texas in 1943 was 28,921,000 as compared with 26,414,000 in 1942. The ten year average from 1932–41 was 27,417,000. Total cash income, 1943, was $1,087,217,000, almost $2,000,000 greater than in 1942.

Table I.—*Leading Agricultural Products of Texas, 1943 and 1942*

Crop	1943 (est.)	1942
Wheat, bu	35,697,000	47,438,000
Barley, bu.	3,682,000	4,818,000
Oats, bu.	15,694,000	11,210,000
Peanuts, lb.	423,200,000	430,080,000
Grain sorghums, all, bu.	59,475,000	59,675,000
Rice, bu.	20,196,000	15,498,000
Hay, all, tons.	1,419,000	1,661,000
Cotton (ginnings), 500 lb. bales.	2,850,000	3,038,000
Peaches, bu.	900,000	1,610,000
Pecans, lb.	23,250,000	10,300,000
Grapes, tons	2,200,000	2,200,000

Table II.—*Cash Income, Leading Livestock and Livestock Products of Texas, 1943 and 1942*

Product	1943	1942
Cattle	$180,784,000	$160,191,000
Milk products	99,271,000	76,715,000
Hogs	48,107,000	28,317,000
Calves	41,058,000	38,192,000
Wool	33,824,000	33,640,000

Manufacturing.—In 1943 value added by manufacturing exclusive of wages paid workers was, approximately, $500,000,000, as compared with $451,000,000 for 1942. Non-agricultural payrolls for 1943 were estimated at $2,800,000,000 as compared with $1,956,000,000 in 1942.

Mineral Production.—Texas led all other states in completion of wildcat oil wells in 1943. Average daily production of petroleum, the state's greatest source of mineral wealth, averaged over 1,000,000 barrels per day. Value of minerals in Texas in 1941 (latest available figures) was about $836,260,000. Since then, the development of the state's mineral resources for war production has greatly increased the value of its minerals.   (C. W. RA.)

Texas, University of.
An institution of higher education at Austin, Tex. The 61st annual session opened Sept. 1, 1943, under a new trimester calendar to meet navy requirements. More than 1,100 navy V-12 trainees were assigned to the university for college training July 1, bringing the naval contingent on the campus to more than 2,000, including a naval flight preparatory school stationed here in Jan. 1943, and a CAA-War Training service unit for naval aviation cadets, opened in 1940. The university school of dentistry at Houston was opened Sept. 1, 1943, as the Texas Dental college came under university operation, with Dean F. C. Elliott continuing as its executive officer. The school of dentistry graduated its first class of 31 students Dec. 13, all save five going directly into either army or navy service as commissioned officers. In October the college of nursing at Galveston inaugurated a U.S. cadet nurse corps program, to train student nurses for urgent military and civilian duty. Under its engineering, science and management war training program, the university trained more than 12,000 men and women for war industry in special short courses between Feb. 1941, and July 1943. Activities in the Latin-American field were intensified with the creation of a University Executive Committee on Inter-American Relations in Texas, headed by Dr. G. I. Sanchez as director; operation of a special six-weeks' co-operative field school in Mexico City by the University of Texas Institute of Latin-American Studies and the National University of Mexico; and establishment of a Latin-American workshop for teaching English as a second language. For statistics of enrolment, faculty, library volumes, etc., *see* UNIVERSITIES AND COLLEGES.   (H. P. R.)

Textile Industry.
Although the U.S. textile industry did not set a new record for mill activity in 1943, and in fact was slightly under 1942 in that respect, it was still a remarkably active year—the fifth in a series of five successive years of high production.

There was of course some reduction in government purchases of textiles towards the end of the year and there was expected to be even sharper reductions in 1944, but the prospect was that this would be offset by demands for lend-lease and rehabilitation.

One of the most important developments growing out of World War II was postwar implication of research on military textiles. Much of the work that was done would result in better fabrics for civilians. Efforts to make cloths proof against the many demands imposed by use in the arctic and in the jungle, and in the air and under the sea, was expected to result in the postwar production of fabrics which would be more effective in keeping the body warm, comfortable and dry.

One problem which faced the textile industry, and the consuming public, throughout 1943 was the ever-present threat of clothes rationing. That possibility was not completely removed but practically every responsible official connected with any phase of the war effort involving textiles appeared to be sincerely anxious to avoid rationing of clothes. (*See* also COTTON; RAYON AND OTHER SYNTHETIC FIBRES; WOOL.)   (D. G. Wo.)

Thailand (Siam).
A kingdom of southern Asia between Burma and French Indo-China, extending southwards into the Malay peninsula; area 198,247 sq.mi.; pop. (census 1937) 14,464,489 (est. March 1940) 15,717,000. Chief towns: (pop. 1937) Bangkok (former cap. 681,214); Chiengmai (544,001); Khonkaen (473,475); Chiengrai (443,476). Ruler (1942): King Ananda Mahidol; language: Siamese; religion: Buddhism.

History.—Thailand's status as Japan's satellite was reaffirmed by announcements early in 1943 that her troops were actively co-operating with the Japanese army on the Yunnan front, and in April the prime minister announced that Thai casualties had totalled 1,172 since the beginning of the war. This military collaboration received its reward during the visit of the Japanese premier to Bangkok in July, with Japan's recognition of "the long-cherished aspirations of Siam for new territory" and her agreement to Thailand's annexation of two Shan provinces, Kengtung and Mong-pan, just inside Burma's S.E. frontier, and of the four Malay states of Perlis, Kedah, Kelantan and Trengganu, an area of about 14,770 sq.mi., rich in tin, rubber and rice resources.

Dissatisfaction and hatred of Japan were reported to be growing in Thailand, however, and in April two well-known Liberal cabinet ministers, Major Kuang Aphai and Nai Tavi, resigned. Unrest was fomented by a severe rice shortage at the end of 1942, caused by disastrous floods in the Menam river valley, and the price of rice rose to about three times the normal level. Shortage of almost all goods made rationing essential, and a first experiment was made with matches.

"Co-prosperity" meant for Thailand increasing Japanese economic and political control. Early in 1943 it was announced that the Japanese southern affairs bureau was considering the disposition of enemy assets in Thailand and the mobilization of her raw materials, that 150 Thai students were to visit Japan, that a Japanese official would head a cultural institute in Bangkok, and so forth. Labour shortage remained acute, the price of gold rose, there was fear of inflation, and in March 1943 there were tirades from Bangkok radio against the "Jews of Siam" (probably Chinese), who were accused of profiteering and spreading rumours that the tical was to be devalued. A sweeping change came early in 1943 under Japanese inspiration with the banning of the national habit of betel-chewing.   (C. M. Cl.)

Education.—In 1938–39: government schools 429; scholars 61,297; local public and municipal schools 11,072; scholars 1,484,483; universities 2; students (1937) 11,525.

Banking and Finance.—(1942) revenue, 210,000,000 baht; expenditure 259,000,000 baht, expenditure, capital (est. 1941) 56,056,000 baht; public debt (March 31, 1940) 69,000,000 baht; notes in circulation (July 31, 1941) 226,000,000 baht; reserves (July 31, 1941): gold 97,000,000 baht; foreign assets (July 31, 1941) 152,000,000 baht; exchange rate (average 1940): 1 baht = 35.15 cents U.S.; (Sept. 1941) 1 baht = 36.97 cents U.S.

Trade and Communication.—Foreign trade 1940–41 (merchandise): imports 163,400,000 baht; exports 257,600,000 baht. Communication: roads, state highways completed (1938) 1,815 mi.; railways, open to traffic (1938), 1,925 mi.; airways, length of route opened (1938) 444 mi.; motor vehicles licensed (1937–38): total 11,439 (cars 5,910; trucks 4,233; buses 146; cycles 559); wireless receiving set licences (1938) 29,834.

Agriculture and Mineral Production.—Production (in metric tons): rice (1939–40) 5,082,700; rubber (1940 exports) 45,000; tin ore, metal content (export 1940) 17,700; tobacco (1938–39) 8,400; cotton ginned (1940–41) 2,400; maize (1938–39) 5,600.

Theatre.
The shortage in playhouses, in the U.S. in 1943, because of the theatre's unparalleled prosperity, became so acute both in New York and on the road that various theatres which had long been in disuse or had been given over to other enterprises were hastily reclaimed. Bookings during the second half of the year were at such a premium that desperate producers in several cases went to the extreme of housing their attractions out of town in buildings that previously had been devoted to lectures, concerts and the like. The box-office in the metropolis and outlying cities did such a land-office business even during the summer that surprised managers viewed the situation as a not entirely unmixed blessing, fearing that the war's end might suddenly bring with it a partial collapse of the boom and find them oversold on many an investment.

The boom was brought about by three things. First, the greatly increased earnings of workers in the war industries created a public that hitherto had not been able to afford the luxury of the theatre and that had been forced for its amusement subsistence to patronize the far less expensive motion pictures. Second, the curtailment of travel, both in the matter of trains and automobiles, not only kept many people at home and with the theatre as a substitute diversion but added to the amount of savings they had free for the purpose. And, third, it became more and more evident that a sizeable proportion of men and women

MARY MARTIN and Kenny Baker in *One Touch of Venus*, a successful musical of 1943 on Broadway

who once were satisfied with the films have been educated away from them or perhaps have simply become tired of their endless repetitions and have increasingly sought the theatre for relief. The general quality of drama, however, hardly kept pace with the theatre's income.

As the best new play of the 1942–43 season the New York Drama Critics' Circle awarded the palm to Sidney Kingsley's *The Patriots*, an eloquent handling of the theme of the young American democracy's fight for self-preservation. The principal characters were Jefferson, Washington and Hamilton. For its award, the Pulitzer committee selected Thornton Wilder's *The Skin of Our Teeth*, which the critics by a majority vote had dismissed from consideration on the ground that its originality had been widely questioned and that Wilder had allegedly borrowed his inspiration from James Joyce's little read novel, *Finnegans Wake*.

But if the more serious drama was lacking, there was no lack in amusing lighter fare. *The Doughgirls*, by Joseph Fields, a wartime farce laid in Washington, D.C.; *Dark Eyes*, by Elena Miramova in collaboration with Eugenie Leontovich, dealing with three eccentric Russian women week-ending on Long Island; and *Kiss and Tell*, by F. Hugh Herbert, a comedy of adolescence, offered amends in the laughter department. And in the way of musical shows *Oklahoma!*, with a lively score by Richard Rodgers; a satisfactory revival of Lehar's *The Merry Widow; Something For the Boys*, with tunes by Cole Porter; a modern paraphrase of Bizet's opera under the title *Carmen Jones* with a Negro cast; *One Touch of Venus* and several others assisted in making the public forget to a degree the torpor in the more sober dramatic department.

There continued to be no end to the war plays, most of which were worthless. *Cry Havoc,* by Allan R. Kenward, and *The Russian People,* by Konstantin Simonov, both of which appeared just as the curtain was about to descend on the previous year, were cheap melodramas, and these were followed by equally commonplace exhibits—all, like them, failures—called *A Barber Had Two Sons,* by Thomas Duggan and James Hogan; *Counterattack,* derived from the Russian by Janet and Philip Stevenson; *This Rock,* by Walter Livingston Faust; *Men In Shadow,* by Mary H. Bell; *The Family,* derived from Nina Fedorova's novel of the same name by Victor Wolfson; *Sons and Soldiers,* by Irwin Shaw; *Land of Fame,* by Albert and Mary Bein; *et al.* Only *Tomorrow the World,* by James Gow and Arnaud d'Usseau, treating of a small boy indoctrinated with the nazi philosophy and his moral rehabilitation, caught the public's fancy, which was in some measure deserved since the play was the only even relatively satisfactory one in the lot.

Many of the established American playwrights remained absent from the scene. There was no representation by Eugene O'Neill, although he had completed a number of new plays, nor by Robert Sherwood, Lillian Hellman, George Kaufman, Paul Green, Marc Connelly, and S. N. Behrman, among others. Elmer Rice came a critical cropper with a machine-made study of maternity, interlarded with his customary doses of social significance, called *A New Life.* Maxwell Anderson was represented at the end of the year by still another war play, *Storm Operation,* written at the suggestion of General Eisenhower, which was below his best mark. Rose Franken, author of *Another Language* and *Claudia,* distinguished herself, however, when all seemed lost, with a serious play titled *Outrageous Fortune.* John Van Druten supplied an additional pleasant comedy in *The Voice of the Turtle* and William Saroyan disappointed his admirers with an indifferent comedy called *Get Away, Old Man.*

Among the better known players, Helen Hayes wasted a first-rate performance on a poor biographical play about Harriet Beecher Stowe called *Harriet,* the work of Florence Ryerson and Colin Clements; Katharine Cornell and Raymond Massey devoted themselves to a trivial little comedy, *Lovers and Friends,* by the English Dodie Smith; George Coulouris offered a stock-company performance as the villainous Richard III in the Shakespeare drama of that name; Ethel Barrymore continued to display herself in Emlyn Williams' *The Corn Is Green,* originally produced in November, 1940; Maurice Evans abandoned the stage for the period and gave his services to the entertainment of the armed forces in Hawaii; Elisabeth Bergner, the German actress banished by Hitler, proved as artificial as heretofore in a cheap melodrama, *The Two Mrs. Carrolls;* and Elsie Ferguson, returning to the stage after a long absence, came off with honours in the Franken play above noted.

There were two exhibits by men in the armed services. *The Army Play-By-Play* consisted of five short plays written, acted and produced by soldiers from the various military camps. Several of the playlets were entertaining. Moss Hart, who had written no play for the Broadway stage, gave his efforts instead to fashioning a show called *Winged Victory* for the U.S. Army Air Forces, which was of small merit but which was enthusiastically received upon its presentation to Boston and New York audiences.

Among the many revivals there were, in the musical field, aside from the before-mentioned, *The Merry Widow, The Student Prince, Blossom Time, The Vagabond King, Porgy and Bess, A Connecticut Yankee,* and the continuing highly successful *Rosalinda (Die Fledermaus).* In the dramatic field there were reproductions of *The Milky Way, Boy Meets Girl, Run Little Chillun, The Petrified Forest,* and *Goodbye Again,* none of them successful. Only the Theatre Guild's revival of *Othello* with Paul Robeson as the Moor met the public's fancy.

Vaudeville, still essaying its renewed day in court, found favour in a show headed by Frank Fay, Bert Wheeler and Ethel Waters titled *Laugh Time.* An attempt called *Bright Lights,* however, ended in abrupt failure, despite the presence on the bill of Smith and Dale in their celebrated *Dr. Kronkhite* buffoonery and James Barton in his old favourite, *The Pest.*

The little summer theatres, because of the gasoline situation, were few and far between, and those that operated were considerably less successful than in previous seasons. And the New York amateur and semi-amateur organizations negotiated nothing in the way of real dramatic quality.

Among the better acting performances on the Broadway stage, aside from those of certain of the more established players, were those of Betty Field in *A New Life,* Eugenie Leontovich, in *Dark Eyes,* Cecil Humphreys in *The Patriots,* Virginia Gilmore in *Those Endearing Young Charms,* Rhys Williams in *Harriet,* young Skippy Homeier in *Tomorrow the World,* William Wadsworth in *Three Is a Family,* Morris Carnovsky in *Counterattack,* Terry Holmes in *Manhattan Nocturne,* Jose Ferrer in *Othello,* and Oscar Homolka in *The Innocent Voyage,* to name just a few.

In conclusion, the phenomenal *Tobacco Road* returned to Broadway, marking the eighth year of its showing, and *Life With Father* entered upon its fifth enormously successful year.

(G. J. N.)

Statistics of the Theatre in New York City, 1943 and 1942

	1943	1942
Productions	109	110
Musical comedies	30	26
Plays	79	84
Premières	71	73
Successful productions	20	17
Performers employed	1,856	1,679
Tickets sold	7,920,000	7,210,000
Approximate cost of productions	$2,500,000	$2,250,000
Number of shows booked for other cities	87	94

(X.)

Great Britain.—The British dramatists managed in 1943 to break through the idea that in times of total war managers should rely only upon light matters or old successes. J. B. Priestley in *They Came to a City* dramatized the hopes and fears of young and old when standing at the gateway of the future. Inevitably a play of this kind tends to be described as propaganda and doctrinaire; but, in this instance, there was a great deal of character, and not a little comedy as well as pathos, in the portrayal of various acutely drawn types, entranced or bewildered or even terrified by the prospect of a bright, adventurous new world.

James Bridie (Dr. Mavor of Glasgow) had so often disappointed his admirers by allowing his brilliant beginnings to wander on to lame or vague or elusive conclusions that his success with *Mr. Bolfry* gave general delight. For here was a comedy of ideas which remained an orderly, well-devised piece of playmaking and did not become, as so often with Mr. Bridie, a mad gambol of fantastic notions. The scene is a manse in the West Highlands of Scotland in wartime where some young people, oppressed by a Calvinist minister's godliness, manage to call up the devil in the form of Mr. Bolfry and there is much ado in getting rid of him. Another new play of consequence was *Lottie Dundass* by Enid Bagnold, the well-known novelist and creator of *National Velvet.* This was a gripping study of an overwrought girl with madness in her blood and a fiery ambition in her heart. One lovely feature of the piece was the performance of Sybil Thorndike as the girl's much-enduring mother. War-plays yielded Terence Rattigan's *Flare Path* which effectively communicated the comedy as well as the ardours and endurances of life at a bomber station.

Distinguished revivals in London included a very "starry" presentation of Congreve's *Love for Love,* in which John Gielgud led gaily a team of all the talents. Turgeniev's *A Month in the Country* also found great favour. Russian themes were naturally popular during the year, but there was more appetite for the pacific and amorous Russian scene of 1860, as Turgeniev so charmingly painted it, than for the prodigious battle-scape of Tolstoy's *War and Peace,* which was attempted in dramatic form with a multiple stage and huge cast. The story got lost in the stagecraft and signally failed to draw the public. Shaw was represented by *Heartbreak House,* in which popular revival Robert Donat, Edith Evans and other stars appeared. American importations continued to find large support: they included *Junior Miss, Arsenic and Old Lace* and *My Sister Eileen.*

In the country one of the year's most interesting developments was the provision of drama in the great hostels attached to the new ordnance and munition factories. These hostels housed many thousands of workers, mostly women, drawn from all over the country. They were of all classes and many of them had never seen an acted play before, being accustomed only to the cinema and mechanized entertainment. They began to respond most eagerly to the plays sent out on special hostel-circuit by C.E.M.A. (the Council for the Encouragement of Music and Arts). Several actors and actresses of high position became so interested in this pioneer work that they gave up many months to it. It was noteworthy that plays of a classical nature were among the most popular with hostel audiences, Ibsen's *Hedda Gabler* being one of them and Shakespeare's *Twelfth Night* (with Wendy Hiller and Walter Hudd) another.

In the provincial cities there were some hopeful experiences. The "Old Vic" company successfully reopened the Liverpool playhouse—one of England's most famous repertory theatres. Sir Barry Jackson did the same for the Birmingham playhouse, whose company had given so many stars of stage and screen to England and America. At Glasgow a new Citizens' theatre was inaugurated in the autumn—a brave innovation for wartime—and at Bristol the oldest English playhouse, the famous Theatre Royal known to Garrick, Kean, and most of the great figures of histrionic history, was saved from demolition by C.E.M.A., redecorated, and reopened successfully as a home for touring companies of special quality. (I. Br.)

Theatre Library Association.

Theatre Library association is an organization of persons in libraries and museums, as well as private collectors and members of the theatrical profession, who are concerned with preserving and making accessible to the public the records of the drama and kindred fields of entertainment. The association, an affiliate of the American Library association, had its inception at a meeting in New York in 1937, called by the then-director of the New York Public library, H. M. Lydenberg.

The publications of T.L.A. are the *Broadside* and the *Theatre Annual.* The *Broadside,* usually issued twice yearly, to present news of work-in-progress, exhibitions, books by members, and topical notes, is edited by Mrs. Sarah Chokla Gross, 11 Newkirk ave., East Rockaway, Long Island, N.Y. *Theatre Annual,* whose second issue appeared in Dec. 1943, publishes articles, translations and illustrative plates, of permanent interest but difficult to find elsewhere. Editor: Richard Ceough, 42 West 35th st., New York 1, N.Y.

Membership in 1943 was 109. Officers of the executive board, 1943-44: President, George Freedley, Theatre Collection, New York Public Library, 476 Fifth ave., New York 18, N.Y.; secretary, Mrs. Sarah Chokla Gross, McCord Theatre Museum of Dallas; treasurer, Mrs. Elizabeth P. Barrett, Theatre Collection, New York Public library.

A traveling exhibition of photographs of historic stage models made by Dr. Elemer Nagy of Yale; and a soviet drama exhibit in New York arranged by Dr. Franz Rapp, with an opening lecture on contemporary Russian drama by Prof. H. W. L. Dana, were highlights of T. L. A.'s 1943 program. (S. C. G.)

Therapy: *see* CHEMOTHERAPY; SERUM THERAPY.
Thyroid: *see* ENDOCRINOLOGY.

+ Tibet.

A country of central Asia, lying N. and N.E. of the Himalayas, mainly a high tableland. Nominally a Chinese dependency, it is in practice independent. Area, about 450,000 sq.mi.; estimates of the population vary, but 2,000,000 is a probable figure. The religion is Lamaism, a late form of Buddhism modified by animism and primitive magic, and education is in the control of the many monasteries. The ruler is the 14th dalai lama (born 1933) enthroned in 1940 as Lingerh Lamutanchu.

The most important event during 1943 in Tibet was the discovery in April of a "divine child" at Lihwa, Sikang, who was chosen as the true reincarnation of the late panchan lama, who died in 1937. The panchan lama is the religious head of the Lama Buddhist Church, spread across Tibet and a great part of Mongolia.

Tibet's neutrality in the war was maintained, but there was no mistaking the country's pro-Allied sympathies. On Nov. 20, 1942, the government had sent, on behalf of the dalai lama and regent, members of the cabinet and the whole people, congratulations to the government of India on the Allied victory in Egypt. Messages of friendship and congratulation on the Allied North African victories were also sent to President Roosevelt during the early summer of 1943. (C. M. CL.)

Timber: *see* LUMBER.
Timor: *see* PORTUGUESE COLONIAL EMPIRE.

Timoshenko, Semyon Konstantinovich

(1895–), Russian army officer, was born in Furmanka, Bessarabia, of peasant parents. He joined the Red army during the revolution of 1917, winning renown as a guerrilla leader. After the revolution he studied strategy in soviet military academies, and from 1935 to 1938 he commanded a number of Russian military districts. During the Russo-Finnish conflict, 1939–40, Timoshenko built a replica of the Mannerheim line just behind Russian positions and had his troops rehearse every operation before attacking the Finnish chain of fortresses. On May 8, 1940, he was appointed people's defense commissar and was given the rank of marshal, but he was transferred from this post July 20, 1941, and took active command of Russian armies on the western zone of the German-Russian front. On Oct. 23, 1941, he was shifted to the southern front, where he recaptured Rostov and Taganrog and routed the German armies. In Aug. 1942, after the recapture of this region by the Germans, Timoshenko was transferred to the northwestern front. A few months later, however, he returned to the southern front, where he commanded the drive that resulted in the second recapture of the Taman peninsula in Oct. 1943. For this achievement he was awarded the Order of Suvorov, first class.

Tin.

Surplus supplies were developed for a number of nonferrous metals during 1943; although tin was not one of this list, it was reported late in the year that the stocks of tin in the United States were of the order of 100,000 tons, which, considering the conditions that prevailed in 1942 and 1943, was a good showing, but not good enough to justify any relaxation of control or of limitations in uses.

World Production of Tin
(Long tons)

	1937	1938	1939	1940	1941
Belgian Congo ..	8,900	7,300	9,700	12,500	13,000
Bolivia	25,100	25,400	27,200	37,900	42,740
China	10,500	11,200	10,900	?	?
Dutch E. Indies..	39,800	21,000	31,400	44,400	53,000
Malaya	77,500	43,200	56,000	85,400	81,000
Nigeria	10,500	7,300	10,900	10,300	14,800
Siam	16,500	13,500	17,000	17,400	16,200
World total . . .	209,100	149,700	184,300	237,800	250,000

Bolivia was the only producing country from which production figures were received. Output declined from 42,887 long tons in 1941 to 38,901 tons in 1942. Although there was a decline in 1942 because of disturbed conditions in the industry, the 1941 figure was somewhat better than the estimate for that year included in the world table.

There were many conflicting reports as to the capacity of the Texas smelter, but it was usually considered to be 50,000 tons a year of metal. Bolivia was understood to be the main source of ore, of which a considerable stock pile was accumulated before the smelter went into operation. Since the reported capacity was well over the Bolivian output, it was evident that ore must have been received from some other source, or else the surplus was drawn from the stockpile. It was announced late in Dec. 1943, that $350,000 had been made available for additional equipment in the plant, which would hardly have been required if the plant was not being utilized to capacity; this brought the total investment in the plant to $6,650,000.

The contract for the purchase of Bolivian ores by Metal Reserve company expired at the end of June 1943. No renewal of the contract was completed in 1943, but deliveries were continued as usual, under a temporary agreement, with settlements made at the old contract rate of 60 cents per pound of metal. The delay was partly due to failure to agree on the price to be paid under a new contract, the sellers holding out for an increase to 60½ cents. After the change in the Bolivian government, which took place late in the year, a new contract could not be legally completed until the new government had been recognized by the government of the United States. (*See also* METALLURGY; MINERAL AND METAL PRODUCTION AND PRICES.)

(G. A. Ro.)

Titanium. Imports of titanium ores into the United States are no longer reported. Shortage of shipping space and the uncertain conditions prevailing in India, the main source of supply, led to the installation of a plant for the treatment of the titanium-iron ores of Essex county, New York, which was planned to have a capacity of 800 tons daily of ilmenite concentrates.

(G. A. Ro.)

Tito: *see* BROZOVICH, JOSIP (TITO).

Tobacco. The 1943 total tobacco crop of all types was estimated in December by the U.S. department of agriculture to be 1,403,275,000 lb. compared with 1,408,717,000 lb. harvested in 1942 and a ten-year average of 1,349,896,000 lb. Acreage was 6% more than in 1942 and the yield per acre was 960 lb. compared with 1,023 lb. in 1942 and the ten-year average of 878 lb.

Flue-cured tobacco production was slightly below the total of 1942 but above the average. The Virginia and North Carolina old belt crops were both larger than in 1942; Virginia, 81,900,000 lb. in 1943 compared with 77,900,000 lb. in 1942 and North Carolina 204,955,000 lb. in 1943 and 201,400,000 lb. in 1942. The

eastern North Carolina belt produced only 275,025,000 lb. in 1943 compared with 295,260,000 in 1942. There was also a decline in the South Carolina belt, 152,740,000 lb. in 1943 compared with 166,900,000 lb. in 1942. Georgia, Florida and Alabama each had larger crops together totalling 76,258,000 lb. in 1943 compared with 70,230,000 lb. in 1942.

The total of fire-cured types in Virginia, Kentucky and Tennessee was smaller; 68,523,000 lb. in 1943 compared with 71,510,-000 lb. in 1942 and an average of 108,045,000 lb. The principal decline was in Virginia, because of the drought.

The burley tobacco crop, grown in ten states, was 12% above 1942; 385,386,000 lb. compared with 343,509,000 lb. in 1942 and an average of 322,486,000 lb. The planting of burley tobacco was extended over a long period in the spring of 1943 because of the wet weather and shortage of labour. The leaf was heavy, however, and the yield 976 lb. per acre compared with an average of 855 lb. The acreage was large, 394,700 ac., compared with an average of 377,410 ac.

The Maryland tobacco crop was the smallest on record as the result of the drought. Production in 1943 was only 17,604,000 lb. compared with 28,120,000 lb. in 1942 and an average of 28,518,-000 lb. The acreage was reduced somewhat but the yield was only 540 lb. per acre compared with an average of 756 lb. in 1932–41. The dark air-cured crops of Indiana, Kentucky, Tennessee and Virginia were smaller than in 1942 and the average.

All cigar types of tobacco yielded a crop of 108,312,000 lb. in 1943 compared with 118,573,000 lb. in 1942 and a ten-year average of 114,928,000 lb. This was because of a reduction in acreage which was 80,600 ac. in 1943 compared with 89,700 ac. in 1942 and an average of 89,000 ac. The yield was better than average. Of these cigar types the decrease was 11% in the filler class and 9% in the binder class. Wrapper tobacco showed an increase of 6% over that of 1942. There was some hail damage in the Connecticut valley and from drought and frost in Pennsylvania. The total production of cigar filler types was 47,645,000 lb. compared with 53,620,000 lb. in 1942. All cigar binder types produced 50,840,000 lb. compared with 55,711,000 lb. in 1942 and slightly below the average. Cigar wrapper types totalled 9,827,000 lb. compared with 9,242,000 lb. in 1942 and an average of 8,608,000 lb. The crop of Louisiana perique was estimated at 150,000 lb. compared with 70,000 lb. in 1942 and an average of 149,000 lb.

Consumption of tobacco continued at high and increasing levels during 1943. Flue-cured tobacco was used in record quantities due to the high domestic consumption of cigarettes. Lend-lease shipments were smaller because of the policy not to supply civilians. The latter were supplied by sales through regular trade channels. Prices for this tobacco averaged near the 1942 level. The burley tobacco supply was somewhat lower than the average of 1940–42 and its use was increasing since about 50% of it was used in cigarettes. The production of the lower priced cigars and smoking tobacco declined in 1943 while the use of snuff and chewing tobacco increased because of the prohibition of smoking in munition plants. The general rising purchasing

U.S. Production of Tobacco by States, 1943 and 1942

State	1943 lb.	1942 lb.	State	1943 lb.	1942 lb.
No. Carolina .	553,680,000	574,400,000	Florida . . .	14,810,000	14,778,000
Kentucky . . .	328,811,000	289,495,000	Indiana . . .	9,505,000	8,880,000
Virginia . . .	106,878,000	104,105,000	Massachusetts	8,185,000	9,024,000
Tennessee . .	93,545,000	89,340,000	Missouri . .	5,740,000	5,100,000
So. Carolina .	87,400,000	96,750,000	West Virginia	2,450,000	2,244,000
Georgia . . .	65,004,000	59,710,000	New York . .	795,000	1,475,000
Pennsylvania .	39,715,000	42,120,000	Minnesota . .	600,000	720,000
Wisconsin . .	27,368,000	29,200,000	Alabama . .	265,000	215,000
Ohio	21,067,000	24,056,000	Kansas . . .	185,000	190,000
Connecticut .	19,518,000	19,680,000	Louisiana . .	150,000	70,000
Maryland . .	17,604,000	28,120,000			

power was reflected in the demand for higher priced cigarettes and cigars. Some of the cheap brands of cigars and cigarettes disappeared from the markets. (J. C. Ms.)

Tobago: *see* WEST INDIES, BRITISH.
Togoland: *see* MANDATES.

Tojo, Hideki

(1884–   ), Japanese army officer and statesman, was born in Tokyo, the son of Gen. Eikyo Tojo, master strategist of the Russo-Japanese war of 1904–05. A graduate of the Military Staff college, in 1915, he went to Germany in 1919 as military attaché and studied military strategy. On Oct. 18, 1941, Tojo, then a lieutenant general, became premier after Prince Konoye resigned under a bombardment of criticism for his failure to better relations with the United States without sacrificing Japan's ambitions to create a "new order" in the far east. Tojo also took over the war and home ministry portfolios. On Dec. 13, 1941, six days after Japan attacked Hawaii, Tojo said Japan was "fighting in self-defense and the cause of righteousness."

In Feb. 1943 Tojo was given dictatorial economic and political powers; a month later these powers were increased. In successive reorganizations of his cabinet he further added to them by assuming the portfolios of the minister of education and the minister of commerce and industry. Throughout the year his messages to the Japanese emphasized the gravity of the situation and the growing power of the Allies. On Dec. 8 he predicted a Japanese victory in 1944, but warned that the victory would not be an easy one.

Tokyo.

The capital and largest city of Japan. Pop. (1940) 6,778,804; area, 257 sq.mi.; situated at 35° 41′ N. and 139° 45′ E. at the head of the bay of the same name on the southeastern coast of Honshu, largest of the Japanese islands. There were 1,029,695 buildings and dwelling houses in the city (1937).

Except for the surprise raid of General James Doolittle's air force on April 18, 1942, there had been no direct attack on Tokyo up to the end of 1943. But toward the end of 1943 Premier Hideki Tojo and other high officials began to sound insistent warnings about possible future air attacks, and plans were announced for emergency civilian occupation, for widening of streets and for emergency fire-fighting measures.

Tokyo is a self-governing municipality, with an elected city council and board of aldermen and a mayor, selected by the city council, at the head of the administration. The municipal budget for 1939–40 was 256,394,000 yen. Elementary and middle schools, utilities and public services of various kinds are under the direction of the municipal administration. But police and fire protection measures are reserved for the prefectural authorities. There were 1,906 elementary and middle schools of all types in Tokyo in 1937, with 1,118,399 pupils. There were 104 higher schools, including 22 universities, with 107,302 students. At the end of 1936 Tokyo contained 14,329 factories, employing more than five workers each, with 403,095 workers. There were 29,633

YOKOSUKA NAVAL BASE photographed from one of the U.S. bombers that raided Tokyo April 18, 1942. The photograph was released shortly after the first anniversary of the raid in 1943

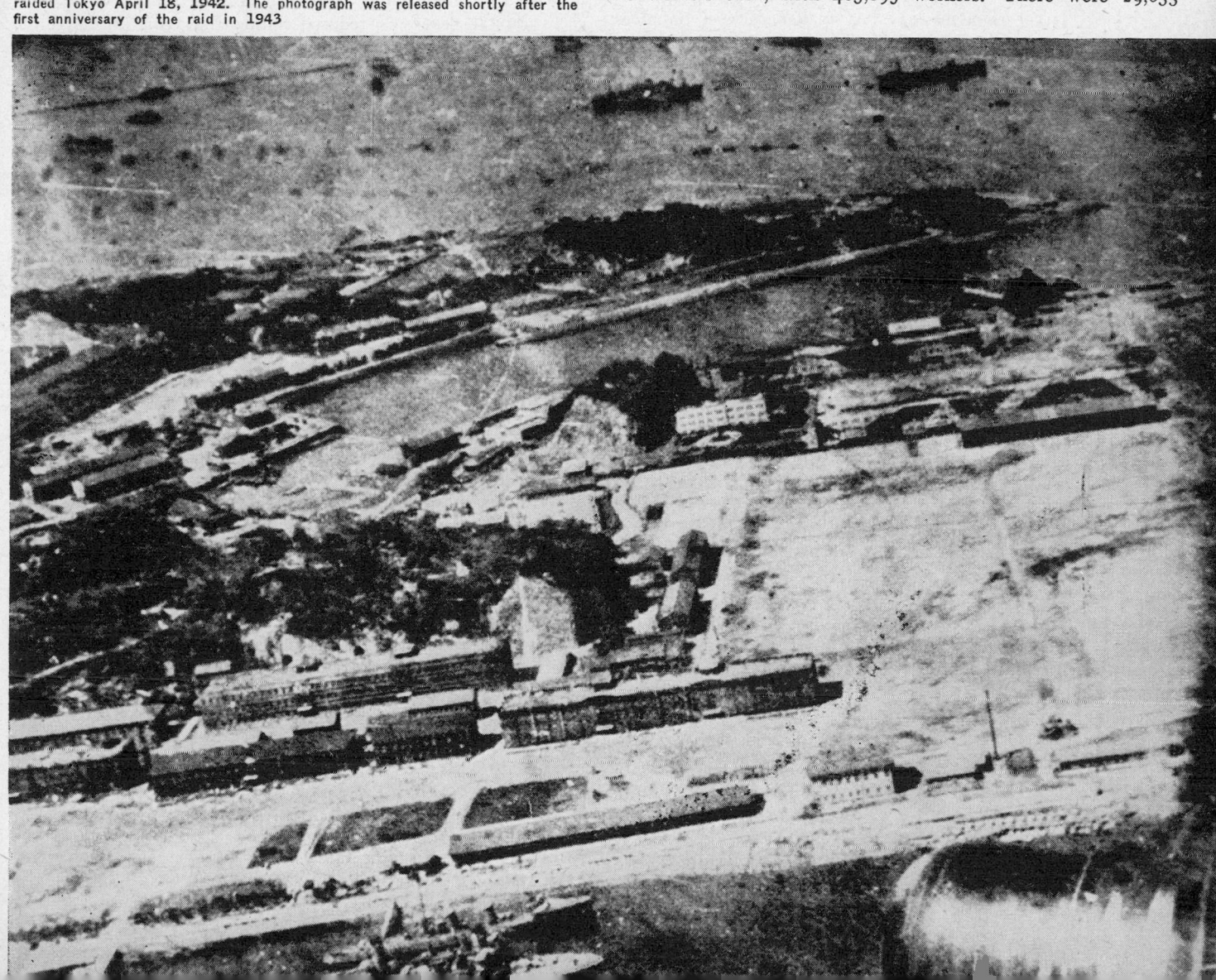

small workshops, with 47,251 operatives. These figures doubtless increased considerably in later years, because of the expansion of the munitions industries. (W. H. Ch.)

Tolbukhin, Fedor (? –), Russian army officer, was commander of one of the Russian armies that destroyed Marshal Friedrich von Paulus's Sixth German army at Stalingrad. An excellent tactician, Tolbukhin was highly regarded as one of the more able of the younger Russian commanders. His achievements were recognized by the Russian high command, and he was twice promoted in 1943, reaching the rank of colonel general. An expert in the use of cavalry and tanks, he crushed German defenses at Taganrog in 1943 in a daring manoeuvre. As a result, the Germans lost an estimated 35,000 dead on the Taganrog battlefield. His force laid siege to the city of Melitopol for 11 days and captured it on Oct. 23. The hand-to-hand fighting in Melitopol's streets was savage. His troops dashed across the Ukraine flatlands, plugged the German land outlet for its forces in the Crimea and seized Perekop Nov. 1.

Tomatoes. The total U.S. tomato crop of 1943 was somewhat less than in 1942 as estimated by the U.S. department of agriculture, primarily because of a smaller crop for canning, which offset the increase in production for the fresh vegetable market. The tomato crop for processing was put at 2,873,000 tons for 1943, compared with 3,166,700 tons in 1942 and an average of 1,813,800 tons for the period 1932–41. This was because of reduced yields, since the acreage in 1943 was considerably larger than in 1942. A smaller pack of tomatoes and tomato products resulted. Ceilings were fixed by the government and support prices provided to be maintained into 1944. Prices to growers ranged from 20% to 50% higher than in 1942. Between 25% and 30% of the pack was set aside for government purchases, including most of the new dehydrated lines, which were about three times as large as in 1942.

The tomato crop for market was estimated to be 37,102,000 bu. compared with 26,572,000 in 1942 and 22,634,000 for the 10-year period 1932–41. The increases were in the late crop since the early crop was much smaller in 1943 than in 1942. Prices

U.S. Seasonal Acreage and Production of Tomatoes for Fresh Market, 1943 and 1942

Crop	Acreage		Production	
	1943	1942	1943 bu.	1942 bu.
Fall	10,500	15,100	1,055,000	789,000
Early (1)	5,900	14,200	885,000	1,647,000
Early (2)	43,750	42,200	3,644,000	4,067,000
Second early	59,300	44,500	3,973,000	3,598,000
Intermediate	48,850	47,850	7,457,000	7,215,000
Late (1)	57,630	48,850	9,346,000	8,434,000
Late (2)	4,500	4,700	742,000	822,000

were on a generally higher level than in 1942 and temporary ceilings were applied in some cases. Demand continued high and some increase in acreage was suggested by the War Food administration for 1944. (*See* also MARKET GARDENING; TRUCK FARMING.) (J. C. Ms.)

Tongan Island Protectorate: *see* PACIFIC ISLANDS, BRITISH.
Tongking: *see* FRENCH COLONIAL EMPIRE.

Toronto. Second largest city of Canada and capital of the province of Ontario, Toronto had a population of 667,457 in 1941 and an estimated population of 669,130 in 1943. Area 35 sq.mi. In 1943, though the greater part of its facilities continued to be devoted to war purposes, Toronto maintained its importance as a manufacturing and distributing centre. Transcontinental and local railway services and the city-owned street

SOLDIERS ON FURLOUGH from Ft. Dix, N.J., helped unload trucks of tomatoes at a nearby canning factory in Aug. 1943

railway and bus lines functioned well in spite of greatly increased traffic, as did the hydroelectric distribution system, also city-owned. The municipal tax rate was lowered for 1943, and the city's capital debt was reduced during the year. The hydroelectric system rebated to its customers one-half of one monthly account. During 1943 a contract was made for the construction of a new sewage disposal works. Construction by the dominion government of a large hospital for war casualties was commenced on Armistice day, Nov. 11, 1943. The city donated the extensive grounds required. The world-famous Canadian National exhibition, after 63 years of continuous operation, was discontinued temporarily in 1943, the site of 350 ac. and numerous buildings being required for war purposes. (G. R. G.)

Torpedoes: *see* NAVIES OF THE WORLD; SUBMARINE WARFARE.
Totalitarian State: *see* GERMANY; SPAIN; UNION OF SOVIET SOCIALIST REPUBLICS.

Towers, John H. (1885–), U.S. naval officer, was born in Rome, Ga., January 30, and was graduated from Annapolis in 1906. One of the first men to qualify for naval aviation in 1911, he established a world's record endurance flight in a seaplane in 1912, and was assistant director of naval aviation during World War I. His competence in aviation was quickly recognized and in May 1919 he organized and led a unit of flying boats that made the first transatlantic flight in history. He was assistant chief of the navy department's bureau of aeronautics, 1929–31, was commanding officer of the United States aircraft carrier "Saratoga," 1937–38, and was made chief of the bureau of aeronautics in June 1939. In the same month, he was made a rear-admiral. Adm. Towers was long an advocate of naval air expansion and was in the vanguard of the air-minded officers who fought for a vast naval air expansion program. In Sept. 1942, he was promoted to rank of vice admiral and given command of the Pacific fleet air force.

Town and Regional Planning. In the United States, many cities prepared surveys and planned projects for the postwar period. These were facilitated by state legislation in more than 20 states to give local governments authority to build up postwar reserve funds, draw up master plans for redevelopment projects, and operate development authorities for special projects. Many cities, at the suggestion of the late National Resources Planning board, operating under the powers of the Federal Employment Stabilization act of 1931, prepared six-year programs for public works which could be undertaken after World War II.

Assisted by the magazine *Fortune,* the city of Syracuse, N.Y., undertook to prepare a modern plan with the active participation and support of its citizens. The National Resources Planning board, before its demise, co-operated with three cities—Tacoma, Wash.; Corpus Christi, Tex.; and Salt Lake City, Utah—to apply a new master plan procedure. There was much public discussion concerning methods of redeveloping the blighted districts which have grown up in most cities. Federal-aid legislation was introduced into congress to facilitate municipal action.

The Omaha *World-Herald,* following the Citizens Conference on Planning at Omaha in June 1943, published a series of postwar planning articles entitled "What Will We Do with Omaha?" The Dallas *News,* which had long supported planning, ran a series of 12 articles on the future of Dallas, in connection with the revised plan being prepared by Harland Bartholomew and S. Herbert Hare.

A number of cities and regions issued reports during 1943, including St. Louis county, San Francisco, Cleveland, Chicago and Portland, Oreg. In Eugene, Oreg., the *Register-Guard* and a group of citizens inaugurated a self-help program for postwar projects and the city voted to raise cash reserves ready for postwar use. The Chamber of Commerce of the United States issued an account of how Albert Lea, Minn., devised a procedure for community postwar planning, jobs and production. Almost all of the larger cities considered new plans for airports and practically every city was making plans for through highways which, under a federal law, might for the first time participate in the regular federal aid on the plan applied from 1916 on to state highway systems. (*See* POSTWAR PLANNING.)

In Great Britain there was great planning activity in 1943. The Barlow, Scott and Uthwatt reports published in 1942, if adopted, would exercise a profound influence on planning and land-use patterns of local communities. The county of London plan, prepared for the London County council is built around the neighbourhood as the unit and includes better road and rail connections, extended parks and parkways, and a new distribution of facilities. Many reports, booklets and articles on town and regional planning were published during 1943 in England. (*See also* HOUSING.)

BIBLIOGRAPHY.—*United States:* American Planning and Civic Association, *American Planning and Civic Annual* (1943); American Society of Planning Officials, *Proceedings* (1943); Boston City Planning Board, *Rehabilitation in Boston;* Chicago Plan Commission, *Building New Neighborhoods;* Cleveland City Planning Commission, *Things We Need;* Chamber of Commerce of the U.S., *Bibliography of Postwar Planning* and *A Procedure for Community Postwar Planning, Jobs and Production at the War's End, Albert Lea, Minnesota;* Robert Moses and Associates, *Portland* (Oregon) *Improved;* National Resources Planning Board, *National Resources Development Report* (Jan. 1943), *Puget Sound Region, War and Postwar Development* (May 1943), *Estimate of Future Population of the United States 1940–2000* (Aug. 1943); Eliel Saarinen, *The City, Its Growth, Its Decay, Its Future;* Saint Louis County Planning Commission, *It's Up to You, It's Your County, It's Your County Plan;* Saint Paul (Minn.) Central Business District Authority, *Downtown Saint Paul;* Twentieth Century Fund, *Postwar Planning in the United States, an Organization Directory. Great Britain:* Cadbury Bros. Ltd., *Our Birmingham;* L. B. Escritt, *Regional Planning;* J. H. Forshaw and Patrick Abercrombie, *County of London Plan,* prepared for the London County Council; Sir Gwelyn Gibbon, *Reconstruction and Town and Country Planning;* William Kerr, Corporation of Glasgow, *Memorandum on Postwar Planning of Glasgow;* Lewis Mumford, *Social Foundations of Physical Planning* (Replanning Britain Series no. 9); Royal Institute of Architects, *Replanning Britain.* Journals. *United States: American City* (monthly); *News Letter* (American Society of Planning Officials, monthly); *Planning and Civic Comment* (American Planning and Civic Association, quarterly); *Architectural Forum* (monthly) in Nov. 1943, inaugurated a new department called "Planning With You"; *Fortune* magazine (monthly) in May 1943, presented "Syracuse Tackles Its Future" and in November inaugurated a new series, "So You're Going to Plan a City." *Great Britain: The Housing and Planning News-Bulletin* (National Housing and Town Planning Council); *Journal of the Town Planning Institute* (London, bi-monthly); *Town and Country Planning* (London, quarterly).

(H. Js.)

Track and Field Sports.

Once again the distance running of Sweden's Gunder Haegg (or Hagg) and Arne Andersson and the pole-vaulting of California's Cornelius Warmerdam highlighted an otherwise curtailed track and field program on American and other tracks.

Haegg made an eight-race tour of the United States during June, July and August. Although out of condition from a long sea voyage on a tanker, the Swedish star did not lose a race during his U.S. campaign and wound up with American records in the mile, two mile and 1,500-metre runs. He started with the two mile in the National A.A.U. by winning over Greg Rice, stellar American distance runner, and 20 days later set an American record of 8 min., 53.8 sec. at Los Angeles. Later in the trip he lowered the mark to 8:51.3. The last half of Haegg's tour was devoted principally to the mile run, and late in July he set an American record of 4 min., 5.3 sec. Aside from establishing three U.S. records, the Haegg tour netted approximately $150,000 for the Army Air Forces Aid society.

While Haegg was barnstorming the United States, Andersson remained on native Swedish tracks to lower two of the world records Haegg set the previous year. Andersson's 4:02.6 in the mile was two full seconds below that of his compatriot, while his 3:45 in the 1,500 metre bettered Haegg's record time by 3.8 sec. A movement to bring Andersson to America during the summer failed, but a campaign was later started to have both Swedish stars perform in the United States during 1944.

After crashing the 15-ft. ceiling consistently for three years,

GUNDER HAEGG, Swedish track star who toured the United States in 1943, on a practice run near Välädalen, a Swedish sports centre

Warmerdam reached a new high of 15 ft., $8\frac{1}{2}$ in. in his last meet of the 1943 indoor season at Chicago.

Greg Rice, the former Notre Dame runner, was once again omnipresent in the distance events of the 1943 winter meetings. Rice ended the winter season with his 65th consecutive victory over the longer routes and registered a world indoor record of 8:51.

Harold Davis, former University of California sprinter (in 1943, with the Olympic club of San Francisco), again scored a "double" in the National A.A.U. championships. As in the 1941 Intercollegiate championships, when questionable starting blocks deprived him of a record-equalling 9.4 sec. in the 100-yd. dash, Davis had a possible record nullified because of a strong following wind. His near-record came in the 200 metre final which he won in 20.2 sec., one-tenth under Jesse Owen's recognized world mark. Bill Cummins of Rice joined Davis as the double winners of the A.A.U. championships, winning both hurdle events. Aside from Davis' repeats in the 100 and 200 metres and Cummins' in the 110-metre high hurdles, others to retain their championships were: Cliff Bourland of Southern California in the 400 metre; Gil Dodds of the Boston A.A. in the 1,500, Ensign Warmerdam of Del Monte Pre-Flight in the pole vault, Frank Berst of the New York A.C. in the 56-pound weight and Ensign Bill Brown of Bainbridge, Md., in the hop, step and jump.

Lieut. Joe McCluskey of the U.S. navy reserve, a 31-year-old veteran of the American track, won his 24th National A.A.U. championship in running away with the 3,000-metre steeplechase title. He started winning A.A.U. titles in 1930 and his total is an all-time record.

Although its squad included only four men, the University of Southern California won its ninth straight National Intercollegiate track and field championship with a clean-cut victory over a group of eastern, mid-western and Pacific coast favourites. U.S.C. scored 46 points to 39 for California and 36 for Rice. New York university, the eastern favourite as a result of its I.C.4-A. championship, finished fourth with 32. Cliff Bourland led the Trojans with a first in the 440 and a third in the 220, while Jack Trout also contributed 16 points to U.S.C. with seconds in the 100 and 220-yd. dashes behind Davis of California. Edsel Curry's second in the broad jump and Doug Miller's third in the javelin completed the team work of the Southern California athletes. U.S.C. and California stood out on the Pacific coast; Michigan won both the outdoor and indoor championships of the Big Ten, and New York university topped the east with team victories in the A.A.U. indoor and I.C.4-A. outdoor championships.

Indoor Track.—The consistent winning of Rice, Warmerdam and Hugh Short of Georgetown, plus the ever-changing supremacy in the classic mile, featured the 1943 indoor season. Short tied the world record of 1:10.2 in the 600-metre run and was unbeaten in the middle-distance event before he went into the army in mid-February.

Winter-long competition in the mile run found honours almost evenly divided among Frank Dixon of New York university, Gilbert Dodds of Boston A.A., Earl Mitchell of the University of Indiana, and Don Burnham of Dartmouth. Dixon won the National A.A.U. indoor title, but Dodds turned in the season's fastest time of 4:08.5.

Herbert Thompson of Jersey City led the indoor sprinting with a world record-equalling 6.1 in the 60-yd. dash of the National A.A.U. meet. He later lowered the 45-yd. mark to 4.8 sec., but the distance was not recognized as a legitimate test by the A.A.U.

New York university became the first college team to win the Indoor A.A.U. team crown by edging out New York Athletic club, the defending champion, 27 to 26. N.Y.U. easily won the Intercollegiate Indoor championships with 48 points to $20\frac{1}{2}$ for second-place Fordham.

Women.—Stella Walsh entered her 11th year of U.S. women's track and field dominance to carry the Polish Olympic Women's A.C. of Cleveland to the team championship in the annual A.A.U. tournament. Miss Walsh won three events—100-metre, 200-metre and broad jump—to score 30 points, the same total she contributed in 1942. Led by the former Olympic champion's contribution, the Cleveland Polish group dethroned Tuskegee institute as team champion with $87\frac{1}{6}$ points to $77\frac{1}{2}$ for the Negro school. Alice Coachman of Tuskegee was second in individual scoring with 28 points, including firsts in the 50-metre and high jump and a second in the 100-metre. Frances Gorn of Cleveland was the other double winner of the tournament with victories in the shot-put and discus throw.

(M. P. W.)

Best U.S. Track and Field Performances (Outdoor), 1943

100 Yards

9.5 sec.—Davis, California; Metcalf, Oklahoma Aggies; Parker, Jefferson, Tex., H.S.
9.6—Shy, Missouri; Pettit, Navy.

220 Yards

20.6 sec.—Parker, Jefferson, Tex., H.S.
20.9—Davis, California.
21.1—Morris, Army; O'Reilly, Corpus Christi air base.
21.2—Shy, Missouri; Patton, Los Angeles H.S.

440 Yards

48.1 sec.—Fulton, Stanford.
48.3—Morris, Army.
48.5—Bourland, So. California.
48.7—Barcena, Howard Payne college.
48.9—Kelley, Illinois.

880 Yards

1 min., 53.6 sec.—Nowicki, Fordham.
1:53.9—Klemmer, California.
1:55.3—Swanzey, Washington.
1:54 —Fulton, Stanford.
1:54.2—Hulse, New York A.C.

One Mile

4 min., 5.3 sec.—Haegg, Sweden.
4:08.7—Hulse, New York A.C.
4:16.4—Dodds, Boston A.A.
4:17.2—Porter, Rice.
4:17.6—Dunn, Illinois.

Two Miles

8 min., 51.3 sec.—Haegg, Sweden.
9:12.2—Rice, New York A.C.
9:15.7—Dodds, Boston A.A.
9:17.1—Thompson, Texas.
9:22.6—Wilt, Columbia Navy.

High Hurdles

14 sec.—Tate, Oklahoma Aggies.
14.1—Cummins, Rice.
14.4—Fiewger, Lawrence; Nichols, Oklahoma Aggies.
14.6—Biewenner, unattached, California

Low Hurdles

22.8 sec.—Dillard, Baldwin-Wallace.
23.0—Buschman, Michigan State.
23.5—Alexander, Missouri.
23.8—Cummins, Rice.
23.9—Haliburton, N.Y.U.

16-lb. Shot Put

54 ft., $9\frac{5}{8}$ in.—Audet, So. California.
$52.3\frac{3}{4}$—Aussieker, Missouri.
$51.7\frac{1}{4}$—Mayer, N.Y.U.
$51.3\frac{7}{8}$—Delaney, Olympic Club.
$50.2\frac{1}{2}$—Brown, U.S. Naval Acad.

Discus Throw

174 ft., $10\frac{1}{8}$ in.—Cannon, Staten Is. navy base.
162.9—Hiler, Army Medical corps.
$156.10\frac{3}{4}$—Gordien, Minnesota.
155.2—Debus, Nebraska.
$153.7\frac{3}{8}$—Fox, Olympic Club.

Pole Vault

15 ft. 4 in.—Warmerdam, Del Monte Pre-Flight.
14.1—Defield, Minnesota.
$14.0\frac{1}{2}$—Ganslen, Camp Crowder.
14.0—Morcom, New Hampshire; Moore, Olympic Club.

High Jump

6 ft., 8 in.—Watkins, Texas Aggies; Sheffied, Utah.
$6.7\frac{3}{8}$—Smith, Stanford.
$6.7\frac{1}{4}$—Donovan, Drake.
$6.6\frac{3}{8}$—Williamson, Camp Pickett.

Broad Jump

24 ft., 11 in.—Tate, Oklahoma Aggies.
24.10—Lewis, Rankin, C.C.
$24.8\frac{1}{4}$—Christopher, Rice.
24.3—Curry, So. California.
$24.2\frac{1}{2}$—Jurkovich, California.

Javelin Throw

203 ft., $8\frac{3}{4}$ in.—Marshall, Kirkland Field.
202.10—Henderson, Texas Aggies.
202.9—Smith, Tulane R.O.T.C.
202.5—Biler, Olympic Club.
$202.1\frac{1}{2}$—Gast, Iowa State.

Hammer Throw

169 ft., $11\frac{3}{4}$ in.—Cruikshank, Camp Pickett.
$165.0\frac{1}{2}$—Dreyer, New York A.C.
163.10—Williams, Olympic Club.
$163.2\frac{3}{8}$—Folwartshny, New York A.C.
$159.1\frac{1}{2}$—Huber, New York A.C.

Trade Agreements: *see* INTERNATIONAL TRADE.
Trade Commission, Federal: *see* FEDERAL TRADE COMMISSION.
Trade Unions: *see* LABOUR UNIONS.
Traffic Accidents: *see* ACCIDENTS.

Trailer Coaches.

From Oct. 1942 and during 1943, approximately 36,000 trailer coaches were manufactured for the purpose of temporarily housing war-workers and construction workers. These were purchased by the Federal Housing administration as a stop-gap housing expedient until more permanent accommodations could be provided.

Standard equipment of a trailer coach consisted of a mobile unit on either single or dual axles and wheels, 18 ft. to 24 ft.

long, 7 ft. 6 in. wide, 6 ft. 6 in. interior height. The interior could be divided into one, two or three rooms by means of movable partitions. Studio couches with sleeping accommodations for four persons, 6-volt and 110-volt wiring systems, oil heater, cooking stove, refrigerator, lighting fixtures, sink with attachments to be hooked up to city water supply, insulated floor, roof and walls, and adequate ventilation, were part of the regular equipment. Exterior coverings were of Homasote, Masonite, leatherette, steel or a number of other materials. Interiors were usually panelled in gumwood, birch, maple or mahogany.

Because of the lack of tires and axles in 1943, trailer coaches were moved to government locations where the running gear was removed and returned to a pool. This running gear could then be used to relocate trailers or move them from the factory to their destination. The trailer coach thus became a semi-permanent home, available for instant removal to other locations when necessity demanded. (P. E.)

Trans-Jordan.
Trans-Jordan lies to the east of Palestine, bounded on the north by Syria, on the northeast by Iraq, on the southeast and south by Saudi Arabia.

It is an Arab principality which, under a local Arab administration, forms part of the British-mandated territory of Palestine (q.v.). Like the land west of the Jordan, it continued in 1943 under the supervision of the British high commissioner for Palestine and Trans-Jordan, Sir Harold Alfred MacMichael, represented in Trans-Jordan by a British resident, Alec S. Kirkbride. The prince of Trans-Jordan is Emir Abdullah ibn Hussein; the prime minister (1943), Tawfiq Abdul Huda. Area: 34,740 sq.mi.; pop. c. 350,000. Religion: Mohammedan, with about 30,000 native Christians. Capital, Amman, the ancient Rabbat Ammon. Chief cities: Amman (25,000), Es-Salt, Maan.

History.—During 1943 the country continued to be an important bulwark of the British efforts to consolidate the middle eastern front against any expansion of axis influences. Emir Abdullah adhered faithfully to all his treaty obligations, and under his leadership the Arabic tribes of the country remained loyal to the alliance with Great Britain. The prime minister of Trans-Jordan visited Egypt and discussed there with the prime minister problems connected with the future unity of all Arab lands. These negotiations were part of those carried on during the whole year among Egypt, Saudi Arabia, Iraq and all the other Arab countries to lay the foundations for a common Arab policy after the war.

Finance, Education, Communication.—In 1940–41 revenue amounted to £388,455 and grants in aid from the British government to £95,110, the expenditure to £465,807 on the ordinary and £44,766 on the extraordinary budget. The value of the local currency is identical with that of British currency. The public debt is insignificant; it amounted in 1943 to £155,107. The economic life of the country is still primitive, many of the inhabitants leading a nomadic or semi-nomadic life. Important are the phosphate deposits and the potash found in the Dead sea. Illiteracy is still wide spread, but the government spent £27,874 on education, and in addition there were numerous private schools. The Hejaz railroad runs through the country from north to south, but it is of less importance than the newly built 1,400 mi. of good motor road connecting the country with Palestine, Syria and Iraq. (H. Ko.)

Transylvania: see HUNGARY; RUMANIA.

Trap-shooting.
The state of Ohio took possession of its 13th Grand American handicap in the 44-year history of the event when Jasper Rogers, 35-year-old Dayton war-plant toolmaker, won the 1943 title in a six-way shoot-off. Tied with five other marksmen with 97 targets out of a possible 100, Rogers knocked over 47 out of 50 to lead the shoot-off.

Paul Wagner of Lima, O., virtually had the Grand American handicap clinched in the extra shoot, but missed the last two targets to finish one behind Rogers.

The all-around championship of the annual shoot at Vandalia, O., went to Herschel Cheek, a police officer at Clinton, Ind., with 478 out of a possible 500. His father, Ben F. Cheek, won the Grand American in 1936. The younger Cheek also aided Indiana in winning the 1943 state team championship with 976 out of 1,000. Indiana also captured the champion of champions title on the performance of L. E. Smith of Peru. Smith was tied with Walter Tulbert of Detroit and Gene Wenz of Louisville, each with 99 out of 100, and won in the shoot-off with 49 in a possible 50. Further honours to Indiana came by the victory of Orla C. Booher of Farmland, Ind., in the North American Amateur championship. Booher broke 200 straight targets to win.

Rudy Etchen, shooting instructor at Navy Pier, Chicago, broke the last 65 targets in a row to repeat as National doubles champion. He scored 96 out of 100 as compared with his winning 94 last year. J. R. Hinkle of Corsicana, Tex., won the North American Professional title with 195 targets out of 200.

Skipper Winski, 17-year-old high school student from Wellsburg, W.Va., featured the women's firing in the annual tests with victories in the Grand American and the Preliminary handicap. She won both shoots with 90 targets out of 100. Miss Winski was the first woman to take two titles in the same year. James A. Sabata of David City, Neb., won the men's phase of the Preliminary handicap with 98 out of 100. Florence Mos of Cincinnati gave Ohio a place in the women's championships by winning the North American 16-yd. event. Tied with Mrs. George Cameron of Houston, Tex., the defending champion, in the regular shoot at 192, Miss Mos won the shoot-off with 23 targets to Mrs. Cameron's 22.

The 1943 Grand American was modified considerably because of war conditions. It was cut from four to three days and included 500 targets instead of the usual 950. (M. P. W.)

Treasury, U.S. Department of: see GOVERNMENT DEPARTMENTS AND BUREAUS.

Trebitsch-Lincoln, Ignatius
(1879–1943), Hungarian-born Buddhist, came from Paks, Hungary, of orthodox Jewish parentage. He left home at the age of 18, became a converted Protestant in Berlin, studied at the Anglican seminary in Montreal where he became qualified as a curate and found a position as vicar of a church in Kent, England. He later renounced his vows, became secretary to a rich manufacturer, and was elected to the house of commons in 1910. After a three-year term on charges of forgery (1916–19), he was stripped of his British citizenship and expelled. He went to the United States, was expelled in 1922, and then migrated to the far east, where he became financial adviser to the Chinese Marshal Wu Pei Fu and later counsellor to Pu-Yi, Japanese puppet ruler of Manchuria. He next turned up in the robes of a Buddhist monk in Peiping in 1926. He returned to Europe in 1932 to seek converts to Buddhism, but was politely and firmly escorted to the border of each country he visited. He closed the last years of his adventurous career in relative quiet in Shanghai, where he lived as a Buddhist monk.

Trebitsch-Lincoln died in Shanghai, Oct. 7, according to a Japanese news dispatch.

Trinidad: *see* West Indies, British.
Tripoli: *see* Abrasives.
Trolley Buses: *see* Electric Transportation.

Truck Farming.

Total production of 11 major vegetables grown for canning and drying in 1943 was about 14% smaller than in 1942 but 50% larger than the 10-year average 1932–41, reflecting the very rapid growth in the processing industry. The total canned pack of vegetables was expected to be three-fourths that of the 1942–43 season but slightly larger than the 5-year average. The 1943 harvested acreage of truck crops for processing was 1,902,150, a reduction of 3% from the 1942 harvest of 1,968,050 ac. but 49% above the 10-year average for 1932–41 of 1,275,960 ac. Lighter yields were due to droughts in the area extending from the Ozarks eastward into Tennessee and in the Atlantic coast states of Maryland and Delaware. Yields of all truck crops except asparagus and beets were below 1942 but on the average above the 10-year average.

Table I.—U.S. Production, Acreage and Price per Ton of 11 Truck Crops for Commercial Processing, 1943 and 1942

	Acres		Production		Price per Ton	
	1943	1942	1943 tons	1942 tons	1943	1942
Asparagus	40,400	48,460	44,040	51,820	$151.30	$118.15
Beans, lima (shelled)	63,750	66,080	28,340	37,830	103.21	84.59
Beans, snap	154,720	135,260	255,400	233,500	93.90	74.88
Beets	17,630	16,730	138,700	131,000	20.99	15.17
Cabbage (sauerkraut)	12,840	15,000	95,500	161,300	21.83	7.96
Corn, sweet (corn in the husk)	495,910	485,610	1,134,700	1,282,500	18.36	13.44
Cucumbers (pickles)	82,530	107,910	145,320	199,370	40.00	33.34
Peas, green (shelled)	433,780	434,120	403,080	423,910	80.03	63.71
Pimentos	8,910	11,440	8,570	14,650	50.53	41.84
Spinach	39,030	46,240	82,000	114,400	53.00	38.72
Tomatoes	551,650	601,200	2,645,600	3,166,800	26.14	19.70

Table II.—U.S. Cold-Storage Holdings of Frozen Vegetables, Dec. 1, 1943 and Dec. 1, 1942

Commodity	Dec. 1, 1943 lb.	Dec. 1, 1942 lb.
Asparagus	5,804,000	5,937,000
Beans, lima	11,731,000	15,220,000
Beans, snap	15,145,000	5,906,000
Broccoli, green	1,810,000	860,000
Corn, sweet	17,346,000	6,838,000
Peas, green	47,506,000	35,077,000
Spinach	11,491,000	5,470,000
Other vegetables	28,120,000	8,107,000
Classification not reported	55,417,000	32,430,000

Since one-fourth to one-third of the vegetable pack was set aside for government purchase from the 1943 crop, the amount for civilian consumption was sharply reduced. A larger quantity was dehydrated than in 1942, but most of that was reserved for military and lend-lease uses.

A price-support program was in effect on eight important truck crops in 1943—tomatoes, sweet corn, snap beans, lima beans, green peas, beets, carrots and cabbage. Prices ranged from 20% to 50% above those of 1942. To encourage canning, the War Food administration announced in July a program to purchase, until July 1944, all quantities of 10 products offered at 95% of the canners' net ceiling price.   (J. C. Ms.)

Trucks: *see* Automobile Industry in the War; Motor Transportation.

✛Truman, Harry Shippe

(1884–), U.S. politician, was born May 8 in Lamar, Mo. After finishing high school he worked at sundry jobs, enlisted in the army during World War I and served overseas as a captain. With the aid of the Pendergast machine, he became judge of the Jackson county court, 1922–24, and was presiding judge, 1926–34. Truman was elected to the national senate in 1934 and was returned in 1940. Although he was sponsored originally by Boss Pendergast, Truman's sincerity and record were unquestioned. During his first senate term, Truman emerged as an investigator of talent while serving with the committee investigating railroads. Early in his second term, he was made head of a special senate committee created in Feb. 1941 to investigate the U.S. national defense program. Empowered only to investigate and recommend, the committee soon became a powerful instrument against waste and corruption in the fulfilling of war contracts. It saved $250,000,000 on army construction, shed light on I. G. Farbenindustrie's alleged cartel agreement with Standard Oil Company of New Jersey, disclosed hoarding of contracts by large firms at the expense of small, bared fake inspections of inferior steel, revealed manufacture of defective warplanes by a large plant and criticized dollar-a-year men as lobbyists for industry. In Dec. 1943, Truman blasted the war department for construction of the Canol pipe line, disclosing that $134,000,000 had been expended on a project that produced only 479 bbl. of oil daily.

Trygger, Ernst

(1857?–1943), Swedish politician, was a jurist of long standing before going into politics in 1897 as member of the first chamber of the Swedish parliament. He held this seat for 40 years, was a leader in the Conservative party and succeeded to the premiership in 1923. This cabinet fell, however, in the following year. In 1928 he was named to the foreign affairs ministry, a post from which he resigned in 1930. He was a delegate to the League of Nations in 1929, but did not regard the League as a guarantee for peaceful peoples against aggressor nations. In the years following World War I he called for greater co-operation among Scandinavian countries, suggesting that they pool together as an organized force in European politics. He died in Stockholm, Sept. 23, according to an American-Swedish news exchange.

Tuberculosis.

Diagnosis and Case Finding.—Every reactor to tuberculin has tuberculosis in some stage of its evolution; therefore, Collins, Lotz, Lyght and others emphasized the necessity of the tuberculin test in all examinations for tuberculosis.

The following examinations and findings for pulmonary tuberculosis were reported: in Uruguay of 134,209 persons examined, 13.4%; in Rio Grande do Sul, Brazil of 8,893 state officers and employees examined, 1.45%; in Santiago, Chile of 25,556 employees examined, 899; in Buenos Aires, Argentina of 62,349 persons examined, 3.08%.

Among 75,000 royal air force personnel gross tuberculosis was present in 38 women and 196 men, while among 30,000 recruits for the women's auxiliary air force 102 had tuberculosis. In 53,400 examinations of men in the army of the United States, active tuberculosis of the lungs was found in approximately 10 of every 10,000 examined. It was stated that among inductees for all services 1% had been rejected. The New York City Health department examination of 114,130 national guardsmen and selective service registrants revealed 435 with active and 721 with arrested pulmonary tuberculosis. In U.S. war industries of 194,986 persons examined, 1.3% had tuberculosis, of whom 53.6% were in the minimal, 43.3% in moderately advanced, and 3.1% in the far advanced stage.

Special Organizations and Projects.—Many Kentucky counties made mandatory X-ray inspections of the chest of each tuberculin reactor before graduation from high school. In Peoria, Ill., this was extended to every member of the school personnel. Of 73,000 college students tested with tuberculin, 21.8% reacted. In 311 colleges with tuberculosis control programs, 744 new cases of tuberculosis were diagnosed among 558,075 students. The American School Health association devised a plan for certifying individual schools or whole school systems which met certain qualifications in the control of tuberculosis.

In New York state examination of 7,187 patients admitted to general hospitals (in whom tuberculosis was not suspected) disclosed 201 with reinfection type of disease. The Minnesota State Medical association recommended that all patients admitted to hospitals be examined for tuberculosis, as well as the personnel. Several states took cognizance of the seriousness of tuberculosis in institutions for the mentally ill and appointed full-time directors of these activities.

Examination of 1,000 pregnant Negro women at the Provident hospital in Chicago revealed 1.8% with active and 1.1% with inactive tuberculosis. This was approximately the same incidence as among non-pregnant women examined at the same hospital and in other parts of the country.

The Minnesota State Medical association continued to develop a state-wide tuberculosis control program, with Meeker county as its demonstration area. The Texas association developed a similar program. Eight Minnesota counties have been accredited, on the basis of low mortality and low infection rates.

Gross sale of tuberculosis Christmas seals in the United States amounted to $9,390,000 in 1942 and $11,000,000 was the 1943 goal. Most associations supported by seals worked on case-finding among industrial workers and following up rejectees.

Treatment.—In the United States there were 468 tuberculosis hospitals to which more than 100,000 patients were admitted. The problem of personnel was serious. This, with the discovery of large numbers of cases, made proper isolation facilities difficult in some places.

It was anticipated that many patients must be treated in their homes; hence, the National Tuberculosis association issued four manuals on *Home Care of Tuberculosis.*

In Chile 536 cases of pulmonary tuberculosis treated by ambulatory artificial pneumothorax did as well as 146 cases treated by pneumothorax in sanatoriums. This finding coincides with that of a number of tuberculosis workers in various parts of the world. Total surgical removal of a diseased lobe or an entire lung continued to attract considerable interest.

Investigations continued on the effects of the sulfonamides on tuberculosis in animals and man. Excellent results were obtained in animals. Encouraging reports were made on the effect on tuberculosis in man.

Mortality.—Throughout the world tuberculosis and malaria ran parallel as the first cause of death. In the South American nations tuberculosis was second.

In Rio de Janeiro it continued in first place, causing 17.76% of the deaths from all causes.

In Great Britain from 1939 to 1941 the increase in tuberculosis mortality was 11% for males and 13% for females. Tuberculous patients were evacuated from many institutions in Sept. 1939 and large numbers with contagious tuberculosis returned to society. The demand for labour brought into activity many persons evacuated from sanatoriums who still had contagious tuberculosis and spread it. The evacuation of town populations to the country resulted in children being supplied with raw milk containing tubercle bacilli. Among evacuated children up to the age of 10 there was a relative increase of 50% in mortality. The Medical Research council recommended: 1. All milk must be heated so that tubercle bacilli are killed. 2. Finding all unsuspected tuberculous persons. 3. Isolation of contagious cases. This was so effective that no more persons died in 1942 than in the prewar year 1938.

Among the French population tuberculosis increased 30% and

in Paris there was an alarming number of consumptives between the ages of 50 and 60 years.

Of the United Nations the United States was unique in its tuberculosis death rate. Among Metropolitan industrial policyholders for the first nine months of 1943, it was 3.5% below that of 1942.

Tuberculosis Among Animals.—In Great Britain about 40% of the cattle had tuberculosis and over 6% of all farms distributed milk containing tubercle bacilli.

The incidence of tuberculosis among cattle in Argentina was 5%, while among milk cows it ranged from 25% to 70%. In 1941 over 22,000,000 lb. of meat were condemned. In Buenos Aires 25% to 40% of samples of raw milk were found to contain tubercle bacilli; in La Plata 15% to 25%; in Cordoba 12.2%.

Wight reported that in the United States between 1917 and 1943 the tuberculin test was administered to 262,235,544 cattle; 3,854,078 reactors were slaughtered. Of the 9,308,936 tested in 1943, only 0.18% reacted. Smith showed decrease of tuberculosis in man in close association with the control of the disease among cattle.

Inspection of carcasses of 56,867,080 swine slaughtered in 1943 resulted in sterilization or condemnation of 26,711 for tuberculosis. From 1925 to 1943 the tuberculin test was administered to 296,475,771 fowls, of which 4.4% reacted.

Prevention.—With no dependable immunizing agent available, emphasis was placed on protection against exposure to contagious cases by finding, isolating and retaining them in institutions, and keeping the disease in animals under control.

In England the ministry of health intensified the offensive against pulmonary tuberculosis by examining large numbers of apparently healthy persons. The government provided for special maintenance allowances so that those found to have the disease could undergo treatment.

It had long been advocated that all immigrants be examined on or before admission to any nation. This was first accomplished when Mexican workers taken to the United States to harvest in California were examined in Mexico City.

The Michigan department of health supervised examinations in Dallas and San Antonio of migrant field workers who sought employment in Michigan and neighbouring states, in an effort to prevent the entry of tuberculous workers. These procedures were borrowed from the veterinarians, who have used them for decades to prevent tuberculosis among cattle.

BIBLIOGRAPHY.—A. G. Evans, "Incidence of Pulmonary Tuberculosis of Adult Type in the R.A.F.—Results of Mass Radiography of 75,000 Cases," *Brit. Med. J.* 1:565 (1943); Foreign Letters, London, "The Detection of Pulmonary Tuberculosis in Women," *J.A.M.A.*, vol. 123 (Sept. 4, 1943); Esmond R. Long and Wm. H. Stearns, "Physical Examination Induction," *Radiology*, 41:144 (1943); D. E. Ehrlich, I. A. Schiller and H. R. Edwards, "Army X-Ray Examination for Tuberculosis: Army Physical Examination Teams in Southern New York District, Second Corps Area," *Am. Rev. Tuberc.*, 47:113–120 (1943); H. D. Lees, "Tuberculosis Among College Students," *Journal Lancet*, 63:98 (1943); "Report of Committee on Childhood Tuberculosis, American School Health Association," *Jour. School Health* (Feb. 1943); W. B. Tucker and J. E. Bryant, "The Problem of Unsuspected Tuberculosis During Pregnancy in the Negro," *Am. J. Obst. & Gynec.*, 45:678 (1943); Medical Staff of Hospital-Sanatorio "El Peral," "Nuestra experiencia sobre neumotorax terapeutico ambulatorio," *Bol. d. Hosp.-San. "El Peral,"* 2:131 (1942); Moses Behrend, "Total Pneumonectomy for Pulmonary Tuberculosis," *J. Thoracic Surg.* 12:484 (1943); J. A. Pérez, R. Finochietto and G. Sayago, "Lobectomia por tuberculosis," *Rev. Asoc. méd. argent.*, 57:48 (1943); Heinz J. Lorge and Paul Dufault, "Pneumonectomy in Pulmonary Tuberculosis," *Am. Rev. Tuberc.*, vol. 48 (Oct. 1943); H. C. Hinshaw, "Treatment of Tuberculosis with Promin; Progress Report," *Am. Rev. Tuberc.*, 47:26–34 (1943); Chas. K. Petter and Werner S. Prenzlau, "Treatment of Tuberculosis with Diasone," *Am. Rev. Tuberc.* in press; Medical Research Council, His Majesty's Stationery Office (London, 1942) "Report of the Committee on Tuberculosis in War-Time"; "Public Health Under Hitler, Medicine and the War," *J.A.M.A.* vol. 122 (June 19, 1943); "Wartime Trends in Tuberculosis," *Statistical Bulletin,* Metropolitan Life Insurance Co., New York, 24:1–3 (May 5, 1943). (J. A. My.)

Tung Oil: *see* VEGETABLE OILS AND ANIMAL FATS.

Tungsten. The tungsten supply improved materially during 1943, after having been more or less short after the start of World War II. At the end of the year 1943 the supply was approximately in balance with the demand for war and essential industrial uses. While nothing was reported on output in the United States after 1941, it was known that new deposits were discovered and developed, to produce amounts of tungsten far greater than had been anticipated, and, in view of the conditions in China and Burma, it might well be that the United States was in 1943 one of the world's leading tungsten producers.

Portugal and Spain were the only sources of supply open to Germany. Both of these were at least nominally neutral countries, and there was sharp competition between British and German buyers, to secure the output, and prices ran up to fantastic figures. While the British supply was not all that it might be, it was far superior to the German, and British buying was as much a measure to keep the metal out of the hands of the Germans as to secure it for their own use. It was understood that the export regulations in Portugal permitted unlimited export of tungsten to either Great Britain or Germany, if it was produced in a mine owned by nationals of that country, but the output of other mines was allocated for export by the government. As a result of this ownership basis of export permits, it developed that in order to secure greater amounts for export to Germany, Germans were using devious legal manipulations in order to secure control of British-owned mines.

Spain was a less important producer than Portugal, the respective outputs of concentrates in 1942 being 1,045 and 3,175 short tons. During the first half of 1943 the output rate in Portugal dropped slightly, but in Spain it almost doubled.

Canada had only a relatively small output of tungsten, but developed some output as a war measure. The supply situation was improved to such an extent that no more government contracts would be placed, and the development work that was being done on some new properties was discontinued. (*See* also BUSINESS REVIEW; MINERAL AND METAL PRODUCTION AND PRICES.)

(G. A. Ro.)

Tunisia: *see* FRENCH COLONIAL EMPIRE.

Tunnels. There was no tunnel construction during 1943 except that which had some bearing on the worldwide conflict. World War I proved that tunnels as works of defense at fighting fronts were of doubtful value. However, in home defense the system of passenger transport tube tunnels at comparatively great depths below ground surface in London proved to be safe shelter from bombing raids; these tunnels lie within the non-water bearing earth stratum called London clay. On the other hand a tragic case of unsafe shelter in the highway tunnels under the river Elbe at Hamburg was reported in a Reuters dispatch of Aug. 24, which stated that 18,000 persons were drowned within these tunnels as a result of Allied air bombing. These iron-lined tunnels were in super-saturated sands of the riverbed.

New York city during the month of March 1943, placed 42 of its 85 mi. of Delaware Aqueduct tunnel into limited operation. This link of the project was in its final stages, lining of the rock bores with concrete at a rate of over 80 ft. per day.

The New York City Tunnel authority under an appropriation made by the state legislature made studies for the construction of a highway tunnel under the Narrows from Brooklyn to Staten Island; the tunnelling would be about 10,000 ft. long at great depth below the ship channel.

The first link of Chicago's passenger transportation tunnels was put in public operation during the month of October. This part

of the system was the so-called State street line about five miles long.

The U.S.A. pioneer and highly successful highway in the twin Liberty tunnels at Pittsburgh, built over 20 years before, was greatly rehabilitated in 1943 with an improved drainage system, renewed surfacing of roadways, glazed tile lining, new lighting and improved carbon monoxide recording apparatus. These twin tunnels, about 6,000 ft. long, in the elimination of severe grades and long detours were built through solid rock ridge.

The building of a tunnel for the Chesapeake & Ohio railway through the Blue Ridge mountains was continued and excavation advanced to near completion towards the end of the year. This tunnel superseded one built in the '50s to the plans of engineer Col. Claudius Grozet. The old tunnel became inadequate to accommodate large modern cars, therefore the government permitted this new work to continue because of its freight-carrying capacity in prosecution of the war.

In northern California the Pacific Gas & Electric company completed the 23,200 ft. of its Pit River No. 5 aqueduct tunnel. This is a 19-ft. diameter tunnel for hydroelectric power, adding in these times 160,000 k.v.a. to the war production effort.

The city of Denver, Colo., conducted preliminary work on behalf of a very extensive projected addition to its water supply and incidentally electric power service, in the form of a diversion project on the Blue river. The plan included a tunnel, 22 mi. long, from near Dillon to the north fork of the South Platte river.

Of the two enormous 50-ft. diameter spillway tunnels at Boulder dam, the one on the Arizona side of the river suffered extensive erosion by scour at the foot of its steep inclination from the great hydraulic descent of over 500 ft. Its counterpart on the Nevada side remained intact. This damage was discovered in Dec. 1941, after the tunnel had been about four months in operation. The matter of restoration involving exploration, study and the work itself presented an intricate problem with the result the work, under considerable difficulties, was not completed until April 1943.

In London the war shortage of metals such as cast iron so generally used as a structural lining in shield-driven tunnels led to the use of a substitute, ferro-concrete, in the construction of the London Transport board tubes within the London clay. This new type of lining was in every respect similar to the standard troughed cast iron lining with segments bolted together through flanges longitudinally and transversely. The thickness of flanges and skin were necessarily greater than for cast iron and to the extent of increasing the displacement diameter by only 3 in. and at a reputed saving in cost of about 20%. This substitution permitted the building of stretches of tunnel, for air-raid shelter, which later could be absorbed in future tunnel extension.

Mexico City, or more strictly the Federal District of Mexico, added to its existing means of drainage and in so doing was driving a tunnel of a capacity of 1,920 cu.ft. per second, 7 mi. long entirely in rock. This city was also constructing a great addition to its supply of drinking water by a large project requiring the construction of a tunnel in rock about 9 mi. long and of 191 cu.ft. per second capacity. In the state of Puebla, Mexico, adjoining the city of Puebla, a tunnel in rock of a capacity of 1,765 cu.ft. per second and about 7 mi. long was being constructed for the purpose of irrigation.

(J. FE.)

Turkestan, Chinese: *see* SINKIANG.

Turkey. A republic in southeastern Europe and western Asia. Area 296,500 sq.mi.; pop. (Oct. 20, 1940) 17,-869,901. Capital, Ankara. Chief cities: Istanbul (789,346); Izmir (184,362); Ankara (155,544); Seyhan (89,990); Bursa

(77,348); Eskişehir (60,614); Gaziantep (57,314). Religion, Mohammedan. President (1943), General Ismet Inönü; Premier, Şükrü Saracoğlu.

History.—On March 8, 1943, General Ismet Inönü was unanimously re-elected by the Turkish parliament for a second four-year term as president of the Turkish republic. Shortly afterwards elections were held. The new chamber, like the preceding ones, was composed of members of the Republican People's party, the official party. The cabinet remained on the whole the same except for four minor changes.

During the year Turkey reaffirmed in a more and more determined way her alliance with Great Britain and drew closer to the United States and to the soviet union. This shift in Turkish policy from neutrality to non-belligerency on the side of the United Nations coincided with the growing strength of the latter. After his conference with President Roosevelt at Casablanca, Prime Minister Churchill went to Turkey as a guest of the Turkish government and met President Inönü at the end of January at Adana near the Syrian border. As a result of this meeting "the bonds of friendship and mutual good will and understanding between Turkey and the United Kingdom (were) confirmed and still further strengthened. . . ." In continuing these talks, the British commander-in-chief in the middle east, General Sir Henry Maitland Wilson, visited Ankara from April 15 to April 19, to arrange for a flow of Allied war material to Turkey.

This new confirmation of the alliance with Britain was followed as a result of British and American diplomatic efforts by a rapprochement between Turkey and the soviet union, which was officially confirmed by the Turkish premier in a speech delivered on June 15 before the final session of the sixth congress of the Turkish Republican People's party.

The climax in the improved relations between Turkey and the United Nations was reached when the Turkish president met with President Roosevelt and Prime Minister Churchill in Cairo on Dec. 4–6, 1943. The official communiqué stated that the Cairo meeting bore "striking testimony to the strength of the alliance which unites Great Britain and Turkey, and to the firm friendship existing between the Turkish people and the United States of America and the soviet union. The study of all problems in a spirit of understanding and loyalty showed that the closest unity existed between the participating countries in their attitude to the world situation. The conversations have consequently been most useful and most fruitful for the future relations between the four countries concerned." The closer alliance between Turkey and the United Nations did not fail to produce a deep impression on the peoples of the Balkans, especially on the axis satellites, and by the end of the year feverish German military preparations in Bulgaria, and Turkish counter-measures were reported.

A tax law adopted in Dec. 1942 had provided that tax payers who did not settle their debts within one month would be compelled to labour on public works until they had completely settled their debt. Unfortunately the tax was assessed in 1943 in secret commissions without the right of appeal and was handled in such a way that while it was applied most leniently towards Mohammedans, it was so severely handled in the case of Greek and Yugoslav nationals and the Christian (mostly Greek and Armenian) and Jewish minorities of Turkish nationality, that many of them were forced out of business and were transported to labour camps in the distant parts of eastern Anatolia. This procedure aroused protests, not only by the Turkish minorities but also by the Greek and other governments whose nationals were involved, and Turkey decided on Dec. 2, 1943, to release the tax defaulters, whose number was estimated at 30,000.

Education.—In 1940 there were 9,739 schools with 26,282 teachers and 1,049,816 students. The total expenditure on edu-

TURKISH TROOPS unloading crates of U.S.-made bombs shipped to Turkey under lend-lease agreement in 1943

cation by the government in 1940 was £T.32,507,374. There were two universities, one in Istanbul and one in Ankara.

Finance.—Revenue for 1942–43 was estimated at £T.394,-328,340, expenditure at £T.394,326,938. The public debt amounted on May 31, 1939 to £T.619,385,681. The monetary unit is the Turkish pound (£T.) valued at approximately 76 cents U.S. in 1942.

Trade and Communication.—Trade naturally showed the fluctuation of wartime conditions. In 1940 imports amounted to £T.68,900,000 and exports to £T.11,400,000. The chief importers to Turkey in 1940 were Italy, Great Britain, Germany and the United States, while the Turkish exports went to Italy, United States, Great Britain and Germany. Turkey imported mineral oils and coal, machinery, iron and steel manufactures, cotton piece goods, paper and paper manufactures, chemicals, tea, coffee and cocoa, and rubber manufactures. The principal exports were tobacco, cotton, hazelnuts, mohair, olive oil, raisins, wool, opium, chrome, barley.

Turkey had on July 1, 1940 a merchant marine of 290 ships of 217,381 gross tons. The length of the railway lines on Dec. 31, 1940 was 4,609 mi., of which 4,339 mi. were owned by the state.

Agriculture and Industry.—The Turkish government in the early 1920s undertook a program of industrialization, and a number of modern textile, paper, glass and other factories were constructed. Yet the main industry of the country remained agriculture, which also was being modernized with the help of the government. Besides cereals, tobacco, opium, figs, raisins, nuts and almonds are grown. Silk, mohair, skins and hides and olive oil are important products, and the breeding of sheep and goats is of great importance.   (H. Ko.)

Tussaud, John Theodore

(1858–1943), British sculptor and director of Mme. Tussaud's famous Waxworks museum in London, was born May 2 in Kensington. He was the great-grandson of Mme. Tussaud, founder of the original museum which included models of the victims of the French revolution, a collection originally carved in wood to withstand the rigours of travel. Tussaud contributed over 1,000 models of famous celebrities of his period and wrote *The Romance of Madame Tussaud's* (1920). Tussaud died in London, Oct. 13.

TVA: *see* TENNESSEE VALLEY AUTHORITY.

Twentieth Century Fund.

A nonprofit organization in the U.S. for research and public education on economic questions, it was founded in 1919 and endowed by the late Edward A. Filene, Boston merchant and philanthropist. The entire income of the fund is devoted to its own research and educational work.

The fund is governed by a board of trustees—composed of leaders in education, business, government and the professions—who serve without compensation and are zealous in maintaining the nonpartisan character of all fund activities.

The fund's basic aim is to help the American people solve some of their chief economic problems by objective fact finding and the formulation of programs for action. For each survey a research staff is set up to find the facts. The research findings are reviewed by a special committee of qualified citizens of diverse views who then formulate policies in the public interest. The fund itself expresses no views in its publications and the research staffs and committees are given complete freedom in their work. Both the factual findings and the program for action are published in book form and are further given the widest possible circulation through the press, pamphlets, radio programs, etc. Surveys deal with such subjects as taxation, the costs of distributing goods, housing, collective bargaining, the electric power industry, and postwar economic problems and activities.

After 1942, a major part of the fund's resources was devoted to the economic problems to be faced in the postwar era. The officers of the fund in 1943 were: John H. Fahey, president; Henry S. Dennison, chairman, executive committee; Percy S. Brown, treasurer; Evans Clark, executive director; J. Frederic Dewhurst, economist. Address: 330 West 42nd street, New York 18, New York. (E. CK.)

U-Boats: *see* SUBMARINE WARFARE.
Uganda: *see* BRITISH EAST AFRICA.
Ulster: *see* IRELAND, NORTHERN.

Ulyanov, Dmitri

(1874–1943), Russian politician and medical research scientist, younger brother of Nikolai Lenin, was born in Simbirsk (now Ulyanovsk). He studied at the Simbirsk gymnasium, at Kazan and Samara universities and was graduated from the latter school in 1893. The following year he entered the medical faculty of the University of Moscow. He became a revolutionary after the death of his eldest brother, Alexander, who was executed in 1891 for having belonged to the terrorist group that attempted, unsuccessfully, to assassinate Tsar Alexander III. Dmitri Ulyanov joined the Marxist student circle at the University of Moscow and became actively connected with the workers' revolutionary committee. He was jailed in 1897, paroled the next year, and completed his medical studies at Yurevski university, 1901. He then joined the state service as physician. He held his revolutionary activity in check during his brother's exile and in 1903 joined the staff

of the *Iskra* (*The Spark*), a newspaper founded by Lenin. Dmitri Ulyanov joined the bolshevists and was a member of the bolshevist centre in Kiev. He was again arrested in 1904 and again imprisoned for his revolutionary activity. During the bolshevist revolution, he was staff member of a bolshevist newspaper in Sevastopol; in 1919 he became a member of the revolutionary committee of the Communist party and later replaced Bela Kun as vice-chairman of the Crimean Soviet republic. After the revolution, he resumed his medical work and served successively with the Commission of Health, the Communist Institute for Health and the scientific department of the Polyclinic at the Kremlin. He died at Gorki, July 16.

Unemployment: *see* EMPLOYMENT.
Unemployment Insurance: *see* SOCIAL SECURITY.

✛Unfederated Malay States.

One of the three principal subdivisions of British Malaya (*see* also STRAITS SETTLEMENTS and FEDERATED MALAY STATES). Area, 22,276 sq.mi.; pop. (excluding Brunei), est. 1939, 1,918,831. These principalities were occupied by Japan in the first months of 1942. Four of them, Kedah, Perlis, Trengganu and Kelantan, were transferred to the possession of Thailand by a decision of the Japanese government in 1943. In normal times the states are under indirect British rule, with native Sultans accepting advice on matters of policy and administration from British residents. The largest, richest and most populous of these states is Johore, at the southern tip of the Malay peninsula. Its revenue in 1940 was 24,737,590 Straits dollars, its expenditure 23,548,568 dollars. Its exports were 138,214,062 Straits dollars, re-exports 1,933,979 dollars, imports 57,275,959 dollars. The area, population and capitals of the land states in 1940 (no later figures were available at the end of 1943) were as follows: Johore, 7,330 sq.mi., pop. 737,590, capital Johore City; Kedah, 3,660 sq.mi., pop. 515,758, capital Alor Star; Kelantan, 5,750 sq.mi., pop. 390,332, capital Kota Bharu; Trengganu, 5,050 sq.mi., pop. 211,041, capital Kuala Trengganu; Perlis, 310 sq.mi., pop. 57,776, capital Kangan. The inhabitants of these states are mostly Malays, except in Johore, where the Chinese outnumber the Malays. After rubber the most important products are rice and coco-nuts. (*See* also JAPAN.) (W. H. CH.)

Union of South Africa: *see* SOUTH AFRICA, THE UNION OF.

Union of Soviet Socialist Republics.

A state of eastern Europe and northern and central Asia. Area (Aug. 1939) 8,175,500 sq.mi., over one-fifth of which lies within the polar circle; pop. (Jan. 17, 1939 census), 170,467,186. The general increase in the population of the U.S.S.R. for the period of 12 years to Jan. 1939 amounted to 23,439,271, or 15.9%, the rate of increase varying throughout the period. Sixty-four per cent of the population of the soviet union lived in the Russian Soviet Federated Socialist Republic (78% of the U.S.S.R. territory), the remaining 36% of the population being distributed almost in equal halves between the Ukrainian S.S.R. (2% of the territory) and the nine other union republics (total territory 20%). In Jan. 1939, Great Russians constituted 58.4% of the population (as against 53% at the end of 1926); Ukrainians 16.6% (21.2%); White Russians, 3.1% (3.2%); Uzbeks, 2.9% (2.7%); Kazaks, 1.8% (2.7%); Tatars, 2.5% (2%); Jews, 1.8% (1.8%); Azerbaijanis, 1.3% (1.2%); Georgians, 1.3% (1.2%); Armenians, 1.3% (1.1%). Altogether some 60 different ethnic groups are comprised in the union. The 140-odd languages and dialects spoken in the U.S.S.R. belong to the following groups: Indo-European, Caucasian, Semitic, Ural-

FOREIGN COMMISSAR VYACHESLAV MOLOTOV of the U.S.S.R. signing the Four-Power Pact of Moscow, terms of which were announced Nov. 1, 1943. Others seated at the table, left to right, are Fu Ping Sheung, Chinese Ambassador to the U.S.S.R., U.S. Secretary of State Cordell Hull and British Foreign Minister Anthony Eden

Altaic (Finno-Ugrian, Samoyede, Turkic, Mongolic, Tungusic), Palaeo-Asiatic and Far Eastern. Capital: Moscow (4,137,018). Ten other cities had a population of more than 500,000 in 1939: Leningrad (3,191,304), Kiev (846,293), Kharkov (833,432), Baku (809,347), Gorki (644,116), Odessa (604,223), Tashkent (585,005), Tiflis (519,175), Rostov-on-Don (510,253), Dnepropetrovsk (500,253). Premier: Joseph Stalin (q.v.).

History.—In the military field, 1943 opened with the raising of the siege of Leningrad on Jan. 18. The summer of the year was to see the defeat of the German offensive against the Kursk salient, followed in the autumn by the recapture by the Red army of Kharkov, the Don basin, Briansk, Smolensk, Kiev and Gomel, and the clearing of the Taman peninsula and a German retreat beyond the line of the Dnieper.

Economic Situation.—On the economic side, 1943 was chiefly notable as the year in which soviet war industries were able to achieve a superiority, as regards the output of tanks, planes and artillery, over the war industry of Germany; as the year in which attention could once again be directed to improving the output of consumer goods industries, thereby relieving somewhat the burden of stringency that war and invasion had imposed on the civilian population; and as a year when the tasks of reconstruction, in the liberated areas, were begun. The year 1942 had seen soviet war industry, much of it (including one-third of all munition factories) evacuated during the previous winter from the war zone, firmly established in its new centres in the Trans-Volga region, in the Urals and in Siberia. Already in the summer of that year official statements had claimed that the production of arms and munitions in the new centres exceeded the prewar figure.

In October, *Pravda* claimed that in the course of the previous 12 months the output of pig-iron had grown 20%, of steel 12% and of coke 17%. It was officially stated that the output of ammunition during the first half of 1943 was 50% above that of the first half of 1942, while the output of certain types, such as new shells of unusually great armour-piercing capacity, increased by five, six or seven times. It appears that this increased output actually took place on the basis of a diminished labour force, since it was also stated that labour productivity increased between 70 and 80% over the same period. The arms workers of the Sverdlovsk district actually quadrupled their output in the first half of 1943, and proceeded to set themselves the target of improving on that achievement by 50 to 100% in the second half

of the year. Statistics of tank and aircraft production were not made public; but there was reason to believe that increases in their case had also reached impressive dimensions. When the serious losses in economic potential that the U.S.S.R. had suffered from the German invasion are borne in mind, this resilience of soviet war production stands out as one of the most amazing features of the war.

Rehabilitation Problems.—With the German retreat from the Kuban and the Don regions in the winter, the problem arose of restoring, not only communications, but also civilian life in the ravaged and depopulated areas. With the soviet offensive of the late summer, liberating half the Ukraine, the problem acquired high priority on the agenda of immediate tasks. As one example, it was announced in April by the people's commissar of education of the Russian republic that some 5,000 schools, caring for nearly 500,000 children, had already been reopened in the liberated areas; and in the Rostov region alone 128 out of some 230 schools destroyed by the enemy were reported well on their way to restoration. Rebuilding was undertaken largely in the form of temporary wood structures, rapidly assembled from prefabricated parts, transported from regions where these could be mass-produced. A good deal of attention was paid to the question of improvised and novel building methods. At a conference of architects held at Moscow in the summer it was stated that already some 10,000 new buildings of all kinds had been erected since the start of war, and, as regards industrial building, a special research institute in Moscow had introduced numerous innovations in wood, concrete and stone construction as well as in the use of substitutes for cement and brick and in the extended utilization of three-ply boarding. A parallel institute concerned with house building was experimenting with "Orgalite" building blocks made from waste paper, with building blocks made from slag, and with aluminum-foil coatings for walls in postwar building. On Aug. 22 a special decree of the council of people's commissars outlined in considerable detail "immediate measures" to be taken "for the restoration of national economy in the districts liberated from German occupation." Chief among these was the return of evacuated livestock: some 600,000 horses, cattle, sheep and goats were scheduled as due to be re-evacuated by the middle of October, transfer in some cases to be from as far away as eastern Kazakstan. Between 5 and 10% of the tractors previously available in these regions was to be allocated to them to help in restarting mechanized agriculture on the collective farms, and the supply departments of the army were instructed to allocate captured booty wherever practicable to equip machine tractor stations in these areas.

RUSSIAN CARTOONIST'S DISPARAGEMENT of the famed German "Tiger" tank. The title is "Even a Tiger Does Not Save the Situation." The upper poster reads, "The German general offensive." Goebbels's poster reads, "It is not Germans who launch offensive, but the Soviet troops." The cartoon, by Boris Efimov, appeared in the *Krasnaya Zvezda*

Among financial measures, on June 10 the finance commissar was able to announce that the second 20-year state war loan, amounting to 12 milliard roubles, had been over-subscribed by 50% within one week of issue. This loan was divided into two parts: the one consisting of noninterest-bearing lottery certificates was issued to private individuals, the other consisting of interest-bearing paper was issued only for collective subscription by bodies such as collective farms and industrial institutions. From abroad, assistance in the shape of lend-lease supplies of war materials continued at least on the scale of the year 1942; and on Jan. 20 Edward R. Stettinius, Jr., announced that up to Jan. 1, 1943, lend-lease shipments to the U.S.S.R. from the U.S.A. had totalled over 3,000 tanks, nearly 2,600 planes and 81,000 vehicles, in addition to which Great Britain had supplied more than 2,600 tanks and over 2,000 planes.

The liberation of occupied territory also brought to light new evidence of the ruthless cruelty of the German authorities in relation both to war prisoners and the civilian population—cruelty which far surpassed ordinary wartime atrocities and revealed itself as a systematic policy, designed in high places, to enslave and exterminate on a scale unparalleled since the middle ages. These discoveries became the subject of a number of notes by the soviet government to foreign powers in the course of the year. Already on Nov. 4, 1942, a special commission of investigation had been set up, which included the metropolitan of Kiev, Nikolai Shvernik, of the trade unions, Andrei A. Zhdanov, Professors Burdenko, Tarlé and Trainin and the writer Alexei Tolstoy; and on Dec. 19, 1942, Foreign Commissar Vyacheslav Molotov had issued a note on "The Persecution of the Jews and Other Atrocities in the U.S.S.R." It stated that his government had "authentic information proving a fresh intensification of the Hitlerite regime of bloody massacre of the peaceful population throughout the territories of Europe occupied by the German-fascist invaders. . . ." Soon after the invasion of Riga, it was stated, the Germans shot more than 60,000 Jews, many of whom had been deported thither from Germany, so that there were "now no more than 400 Jews in Riga, living in a ghetto surrounded by barbed wire, access to which is prohibited," and

"doomed to death by starvation." Similar massacres had occurred in Lithuania; at Lutsk in the Ukraine 20,000 Jews were herded together under pretext of re-registration and were shot; at Kiev and Dnepropetrovsk 60,000 people, including old women and children, of Jewish nationality "were exterminated in the first month of the occupation." In April 1943 the report of the commission of investigation at Vyazma, Gzhatsk and Rzhev named a series of German officers and gestapo chiefs, together with two N.C.O.s in charge of war prisoner camps, as responsible for atrocities occurring in these places, adding that "history knows no such wholesale extermination of a people." On May 11 Molotov submitted a further note to the ambassadors of foreign powers "regarding the mass deportation of soviet civilians into German-fascist slavery and on the responsibility of German authorities and private individuals for these crimes." It revealed details from German documents of the forcible seizure and transfer of some 2,000,000 persons into forced labour in Germany.

Foreign Relations.—In soviet Russia's relations with other powers the outstanding events in the course of 1943 were the rupture of relations between the soviet government and the Polish government in London; the holding in October of a three-power conference of the foreign ministers of the U.S.S.R., Britain and the U.S.A. in Moscow and, ending Dec. 1, the four-day conference of President Roosevelt, Prime Minister Churchill and Marshal Stalin at Tehran, Iran.

On Feb. 25 the foreign affairs committee of the Polish National council had issued a declaration that "from the moment of the conclusion of the Polish-Soviet treaty of July 30, 1941," they had "maintained the unchangeable attitude that so far as the question of frontiers between Poland and soviet Russia is concerned the *status quo* previous to Sept. 1, 1939, is in force." At the same time the declaration repudiated any hostile intentions towards the U.S.S.R. and denied that the Polish government harboured

ROLES REVERSED. Cartoon of 1943 by Shoemaker of the *Chicago Daily News* entitled "Russian Peace Plan"

any designs to extend Poland's eastern frontiers to the Dnieper and the Black sea. This evoked the reply through the soviet news agency that the declaration bore witness to "the fact that the Polish government refuses to recognize the historic rights of the Ukrainian and White Russian peoples to be united within their national states." On April 12 the German news agency announced the discovery near Smolensk (in the Katyn district) of mass graves of 10,000 Polish officers whom they alleged had been killed by the Russians in 1939, an announcement characterized by the soviet information bureau as a "vile fabrication." The day following the soviet denial, the Polish minister of national defense, General Marjan Kukiel, issued a statement calling for an investigation into the Katyn graves by the International Red Cross, in view of the "detailed information given by the Germans concerning the finding of the bodies"; while the Polish cabinet announced that on the previous day they had already applied to the International Red Cross for an investigation. The International Red Cross intimated that it had received applications in the same sense from both the Polish government and the German Red Cross, but declined to act in the matter. The soviet press proceeded to charge General Wladyslaw Sikorski's cabinet with "swallowing a carefully baited hook thrown out by the German propaganda agencies"; and on April 25 Foreign Commissar Molotov handed a note to the Polish ambassador, Tadeusz Romer, severing diplomatic relations with the Polish government, on the ground that "the recent behaviour of the Polish government with regard to the U.S.S.R." was "entirely abnormal and violated all regulations and standards of relations between two allied states." This was followed by a statement by Andrei Vishinsky to the representatives of the British and U.S. press, attacking the Polish government for "provoking the soviet suspension of diplomatic relations under the influence of the pro-Hitler elements within it and within the Polish press"; denying that the soviet authorities were hindering Polish subjects from leaving the U.S.S.R., or had any intention of forming another Polish government on soviet soil; and accusing representatives of the Polish embassy of having conducted espionage activities in the U.S.S.R. under the guise of charitable activities. Six days later, on May 13, the formation was announced in Moscow of a body known as the Union of Polish Patriots in the Soviet Union, which published a declaration of aims in the paper called *Wolna Polska,* including the following: "to help the Polish people under German occupation to achieve their liberation; to wage war side-by-side with the Red army against the enemy; to strive for the independence and sovereign rights of the Polish state and its parliamentary and democratic structure, and for the material and cultural well-being of Poles in the U.S.S.R.; and to strengthen the bonds between the soviet and Polish peoples." On the same day the formation was announced of a Polish division, the Kosciusko division, on soviet soil, under the command of Colonel S. Berling, formerly chief of staff of the 5th Polish division at Cracow. This was to be under the operational command of the Red army, though not part of it, and was to be recruited from among Poles from the Ukraine and from volunteers among Poles living in the U.S.S.R. prior to Sept. 1939.

On Nov. 1 the terms were announced in Moscow of the agreement reached at the Three-Power conference. These consisted of five main declarations; and as concrete immediate proposals it was agreed to set up a European advisory commission in London, with representatives of all three powers, with the object of consulting on all matters arising from the military occupation of Europe by the forces of the United Nations. (For the text of the pact of Moscow and related documents, *see* UNITED STATES.)

The meeting of the foreign ministers was followed in less than a month by a conference of Stalin, Churchill and Roosevelt at

HAULING PEAT for the supply of Leningrad. The German ring around the beleaguered city was broken Jan. 18, 1943

Tehran, Iran, Nov. 28–Dec. 1, 1943. For the first time since the Revolution, Stalin left the U.S.S.R., accompanied only by Foreign Commissar Molotov and a single military adviser—Marshal Klementiy Voroshilov. This long-expected meeting of the "Big Three" resulted in a declaration, dated Dec. 1, in which the three powers pledged mutual assistance "in the war and in the peace that will follow . . ." and concerted action to bring about the final destruction of all German armed forces. No mention was made of Japan; a separate statement guaranteed independence and postwar economic assistance to Iran (*q.v.*). (*See* UNITED STATES for the text of the Declaration of Tehran.)

A further political event of considerable importance affecting the relations between the soviet government and other nations was the adoption on May 15 of a resolution dissolving the Comintern by the executive committee of that body in Moscow.

Diplomatic events in the course of the year included the recall of Ivan Maisky as ambassador in London, following his appointment as a deputy commissar for foreign affairs, and his replacement by Fyodor Gusev, who had previously been appointed as first soviet minister to Canada in Oct. 1942, and also the recall of Maxim Litvinov as ambassador extraordinary to the government of the U.S.A. and in his place the promotion to ambassador of Andrei Gromyko, who had already acted as chargé d'affaires at the soviet embassy in Washington. Early in February an agreement was signed in Washington between Litvinov and the foreign minister of Colombia for an exchange of ambassadors between their two countries; and in April it was announced that both the Greek and Belgian governments had decided to raise their diplomatic missions in the U.S.S.R. to the status of embassies with reciprocal action on the part of the soviet government. On June 21 Constantine Oumansky, formerly soviet ambassador in Washington, presented his credentials to the President of Mexico as first soviet ambassador to the Mexican government; while Alexander Bogomolov, soviet ambassador to the Allied governments in London, presented his credentials to King Peter of Yugoslavia on June 8 (following a similar presentation of credentials to

WOMEN REMOVING DEBRIS from ruined Stalingrad in the summer of 1943 as the tide of German invasion receded farther and farther west. At the right is the shell of the department store where Marshal von Paulus surrendered the German 6th army to the Russians Jan. 31, 1943

President Eduard Beneš of Czechoslovakia in January). In the autumn it became known that the Czechoslovak government in London wished to enter into negotiations with the soviet government for a mutual assistance pact between the two countries; but at the request of the British government the visit of President Beneš to Moscow for this purpose was postponed until December.

The year 1943 also witnessed an increased attention in the U.S.S.R. to postwar problems in the international sphere; although stress continued to be laid repeatedly on the primacy of the military task of united struggle against fascism and the urgent necessity for creating a second front on the continent of Europe. The discussion journal, newly published in Moscow, entitled *War and the Working Class,* devoted considerable space to such questions; and the reference of Marshal Stalin, in his above-quoted reply to Reuters' correspondent, to "the future organization of a companionship of nations based upon their equality" was regarded by English commentators as possessing considerable significance. In May a soviet delegation participated in the United Nations conference on postwar food problems at Hot Springs, Va. Alexei Krutikov, chairman of the soviet delegation, in his address to the conference emphasized that "food supply problems are of great importance to the U.S.S.R. at the present moment, firstly because we require food now to supply the large army we maintain to defeat Germany, and secondly because food is needed to maintain the life and health of the plundered and impoverished people of the regions which the Red army is liberating. . . ."

Orthodox Church.—During September an event occurred which significantly affected the status of the Orthodox church in the U.S.S.R. With the prior agreement of the soviet government, a church council was held with the object of electing a patriarch, Metropolitan Sergii being duly elected as patriarch of Moscow and all Russia, and formally installed in his office in a ceremony at the Bogoyavlensky cathedral in Moscow on Sept. 12. At the end of the same month a visit was paid by the archbishop of

York to Moscow as a gesture of friendship between the Church of England and the Russian church, and to lay the basis of regular communication. (M. Do.)

Education.—Elementary and secondary school children in the educational year 1941–42 were estimated to reach a total of approximately 36,200,000 (an increase of 3.4% over the 1940–41 total); the number of university students was estimated at 657,-000 for 1941–42 (an increase of 13%); libraries (1940), 75,000 with 160,000,000 books; newspapers, 9,000 (in 70 languages), with a circulation of 38,000,000; printed books, 700,000,000 copies. Theatres, 790; cinemas, 30,461 in towns and 18,991 in villages.

Finance, Banking, Trade.—Estimates for 1940: Capital investments in industry, agriculture and transport from the all-union budget and other sources, 36.1 milliard roubles (15% increase over 1939). State revenue, 182,600,000,000 roubles (17.1% increase over 1939); state expenditure, 179,700,000,000 roubles (including defense services, 57,066,200,000; national economy 57,117,500,000; cultural services, 42,875,400,000, of which education, 23,195,000,000). Banks: 37,120 branch banks and agencies; deposits in savings banks, c. 7,000,000,000 roubles. Subscription to third five-year plan loan, 9,310,800,000 roubles. Gross retail trade turnover in 1939, 163,456,000,000 roubles. Foreign trade figures were not available for 1939, 1940, 1941 and 1942. Merchant marine (vessels of 100 tons and over) (1939) 1,316,000 gross tons.

Agriculture, Manufacturing, Mineral Production.—(Metric tons) Grain crops (1938): wheat 40,880,000; rye 20,930,000; oats 16,990,000; barley 8,200,000; maize 2,690,000; rice 317,000; potatoes (1938) 41,960,000; beet sugar (1940) 2,145,800; tea (1940) 12,900; cotton (1940) 800,000; cotton seed (1940) 1,720,-000; wool (1938) 137,400; flax (1939) 633,000; hemp (1939) 110,000; raw silk (1940) 1,700; rayon (1940) 7,700; wood pulp (1938) 10,800,000; crude petroleum (1940) 29,700,000; natural gas (1938) 2,600,000,000 cu.ft.; coal (1940) 146,800,000; iron ore (metal content) (1940) 14,000,000; pig iron and ferro-alloys (1940) 14,950,000; steel ingots and castings (1940) 19,100,000; manganese ore (metal content) (1940) 1,300,000; bauxite (1938)

250,000; aluminum (1940) 55,000; chrome ore (1940) 96,000; silver (1938) 218,000; gold (1937) c. 150,000 kilograms.

Industry and Labour.—While the total population of the U.S.S.R. increased by 16% between 1926 and 1939, skilled workers and intellectuals increased by the following number of times: mechanics 3.7, turners 6.8, millwrights 13.0, locomotive drivers 4.4, plasterers 7.0, tractor drivers 215.0, engineers 7.7, agronomists 5.0, scientists 7.1, teachers 3.5, physicians 2.3.

The social composition according to the 1939 census returns was: workers and employees 49.7%; peasants on collective farms and handicraftsmen in producers' co-operatives, 46.9%; independent peasants and handicraftsmen, 2.6%; nonworkers, 0.04%; groups not shown, 0.7%.

Unitarian Church.

The general conference in Nov. 1943, nominated Senator Harold H. Burton of Ohio, one of the authors of the Ball-Burton-Hatch-Hill resolution, for moderator of the denomination, to take office in May 1944.

Decentralization in the administration of denominational affairs progressed, with the result that seven regional organizations, which included 97% of all Unitarian churches, were set up. A New England Unitarian council was established in 1943.

The organized young people of the churches adopted the name, "American Unitarian Youth." The first national meeting, outside of Massachusetts, was held in the summer of 1943 at Lake Geneva, Wis. Five of the younger clergymen visited the college campuses throughout the country during the winter (1943–44), where "Unity Groups" were in process of formation. During the summer four farm camps for high-school boys and girls, and two industrial camps for college women, were carried on "to train young people in leadership, aid them in solving problems in group living, and offer opportunity for constructive community service."

The Unitarian Service committee had stations in 12 countries, on 5 continents. It opened a temporary office in the Dominican Republic, to assist the Spanish refugees there to establish themselves elsewhere. In Ecuador, an office was to receive, settle and care for refugees from Europe and Africa with the co-operation of the government of Ecuador. The staff in Geneva, Switzerland, was increased because of the thousands of refugees who came over the border during the year. In co-operation with the British Unitarians, six centres for rest and recreation for Allied soldiers, called Hibbert Houses, functioned in 1943: two in Cairo, two in Alexandria, one in Palestine and one in Syria.

Through the War Service council, more than 2,000,000 copies of the pamphlet for service men, "Think on These Things," were distributed, and the Salvation Army voted to make this pamphlet its contribution to the U.S.O. reading kit for soldiers. The first pamphlet for women in the services was circulated, under the title, "Your Chaplain Welcomes You."

On the home front, a Japanese Relocation committee was set up to help solve the many problems confronting loyal Americans of Japanese descent.

The attitude of the Unitarian Church toward its members who were conscientious objectors is worthy of note. Dr. Frederick M. Eliot, president of the American Unitarian association, said, "The majority among us have special obligation to respect the minority, who with equal fortitude and courage, follow the line of duty which their consciences dictate." (*See* also CHURCH MEMBERSHIP.)   (J. H. L.)

United Church of Canada.

The United Church of Canada, which in 1925 united the Presbyterian Church in Canada, the Methodist Church (Canada) and the Congregational Churches of Canada, reported for 1942 a membership of 721,184 with 1,713,186 persons under pastoral oversight, a Sunday School enrolment of 484,712 and 7,042 preaching places. The church owned property worth more than $85,567,035 and raised a total of $12,250,863 for all purposes.

The missionaries in West China were in a dangerous financial position owing to the inflation which prevailed and promised to grow worse. The missionary and maintenance givings of the church showed an increase of $57,879 over those of the year 1941.

The effort to liquidate a deficit of $1,700,000, which accumulated during the depression years, was meeting with success.

Among the important features in the life of the United Church during the year were the carrying on of a campaign of education to secure support for the pension fund by a system of assessments upon pastoral charges; the steady work of "The Commission on the Church, Nation and World Order" which will report to the next general council; the decision to join the Canadian Council of Churches in process of formation; the setting up of a commission to confer with the commission on re-union appointed by the Church of England in Canada; and the creation of a commission to study the possibility of a more extensive use of the radio as a part of the church's ministry.

About 200 ministers were in 1943 serving as chaplains in the Canadian armed forces. About 25 ministers were serving in the auxiliary services of the Canadian Legion and the Y.M.C.A.; 30 were listed as combatants, making a total of 255. This created a serious shortage of ministers for the normal work of the church.
   (G. A. Sı.)

United Kingdom: *see* GREAT BRITAIN AND NORTHERN IRELAND, UNITED KINGDOM OF.

United Nations (Dec. 31, 1943): *see* AUSTRALIA, COMMONWEALTH OF*; BELGIUM*; BOLIVIA; BRAZIL; CANADA, DOMINION OF*; CHINA*; COLOMBIA; COSTA RICA*; CUBA*; CZECHOSLOVAKIA*; DOMINICAN REPUBLIC*; ETHIOPIA; GREAT BRITAIN AND NORTHERN IRELAND, UNITED KINGDOM OF*; GREECE*; GUATEMALA*; HAITI*; HONDURAS*; INDIA*; IRAN; IRAQ; LUXEMBOURG*; MEXICO; NETHERLANDS*; NEW ZEALAND, DOMINION OF*; NICARAGUA*; NORWAY*; PANAMA*; PHILIPPINES, COMMONWEALTH OF THE; POLAND*; SALVADOR, EL*; SOUTH AFRICA, THE UNION OF*; UNION OF SOVIET SOCIALIST REPUBLICS*; UNITED STATES*; YUGOSLAVIA*. Those marked * were signatories to the original declaration of the United Nations Jan. 1, 1942. Ethiopia, Mexico and the Philippines adhered subsequently in 1942; Bolivia, Brazil, Iran, Iraq and Colombia signified their adherence in 1943.

United Nations Information Board.

This board, with headquarters in New York city, was one of the first United Nations organizations, established in Nov. 1942. It grew out of an organization called the Inter-Allied Information committee, created in Sept. 1940. The original purpose of this committee was to gather together in the United States representatives of the information services of the various Allies and co-ordinate their work.

The committee was financed and controlled during 1941 by Great Britain, her sister dominions, and the European allies. After the entry of the United States into the conflict and the merging of the Pacific and European wars, first China and then the United States took their places in the organization.

Following the development of the concept of the United Nations, in Nov. 1942, the title United Nations Information board was adopted, and all United Nations not yet members were invited to join; by Dec. 1943, 19 such nations were associated with the agency.

Parallel with these developments in the U.S., a similar international agency grew up in Britain—first as the Inter-Allied Information committee and later as the United Nations Information organization.   (W. B. M.)

United Nations Relief and Rehabilitation Administration.

The United Nations Relief and Rehabilitation administration came into being on Nov. 9, 1943, when representatives of 44 nations united and associated in World War II signed an agreement at the White House in Washington, D.C. In the preamble of that agreement they stated their determination that "immediately upon the liberation of any area by the armed forces of the United Nations or as a consequence of retreat of the enemy the population thereof shall receive aid and relief from their sufferings, food, clothing and shelter, aid in the prevention of pestilence and in the recovery of the health of the people, and that preparation and arrangements shall be made for the return of prisoners and exiles to their homes and for assistance in the resumption of urgently needed agricultural and industrial production and the restoration of essential services." UNRRA was created with a view to giving effect to this determination.

Having signed the agreement, the delegates gathered in Atlantic City, N.J., for the first council session of the administration, and throughout the remainder of the month laboured to turn their general purpose into a definite plan. As one of its first acts the council appointed Herbert H. Lehman, former governor of New York and head of the Office of Foreign Relief and Rehabilitation Operations since its inception, director general of UNRRA.

The conference further reached agreement upon a practicable program of defined scope, formulated a plan for financing the program, and devised a procedure for ascertaining and meeting needs. Principal among the policies established was that of nondiscrimination. Relief and rehabilitation was to be distributed fairly on the basis of the relative needs of the population in an area, and without discrimination because of race, creed or political belief.

The resolutions and reports adopted by the council constituted a guide for the director general. The work of the administration was to be further facilitated by appointment of its permanent committees: the committees on supplies and on financial control, the committees of the council for Europe and for the far east, and the committees on agriculture, displaced persons, industrial rehabilitation, and welfare. Administration headquarters were established in Washington, where an administrative staff of international experts was being brought together at the end of 1943. (*See* also POSTWAR PLANNING.)   (H. H. L.)

United Service Organizations.

The United Service Organizations, Inc., (U.S.O.) was formed Feb. 4, 1941, by the following member agencies: Young Men's Christian associations, National Catholic Community service, Salvation Army, Young Women's Christian associations, Jewish Welfare board and National Travelers Aid association. Its purpose was to provide off-duty recreational, spiritual and welfare services to the armed forces, and to workers in overburdened war production centres, as requested by the government.

In 1941 and 1942 U.S.O., supported entirely by public subscription, obtained $14,353,666 and $32,586,501 respectively through its own campaigns. In 1943, with 16 other major war-related agencies, it was a member of the National War fund, which set a goal of $125,000,000. U.S.O.'s quota of that amount was $61,227,000.

On Dec. 20, 1943, there were 2,779 U.S.O. clubs and other services including both agency and community conducted operations. Of these, 1,790 were operated by the U.S.O. member agencies and 989 by local communities in affiliation with U.S.O. These services fell into the following principal classifications:

Clubs in continental United States, including those conducted by member agencies and local communities in affiliation with U.S.O., numbering 1,716 and located in 48 states and the District of Columbia. Standard equipment included lounges, writing rooms, showers, snack bars, game rooms, libraries, musical instruments and auditoriums. Giving limited U.S.O. services were 514 smaller centres.

Troops-in-Transit Service operated 125 lounges in rail and bus terminals, supplemented by 152 U.S.O.-Travelers Aid services.

Mobile Service units numbered 130. They served men on outpost duty along Atlantic and Pacific coasts, as well as troops on manoeuvres.

Overseas Division maintained 126 clubs, 16 smaller centres, and 24 mobile units in western hemisphere bases from Alaska and Newfoundland to Brazil and also in Hawaii.

U.S.O.-Camp Shows, an affiliate, had 85 units touring army camps and navy posts in continental United States and 35 in western hemisphere bases and combat zones.

Attendance at clubs and lounges was approximately 28,000,000 a month. U.S.O.-Camp Shows performed before an average monthly audience of 2,000,000.

Information and counsel on personal problems constituted an important part of U.S.O. services in 1943. Opportunities were provided for service men and women to continue customary church attendance and association with churchmen and church members. Religious counsel, as requested, was also available. Special programs were held for the wives of service men, such as social gatherings and classes in pre-natal and child care, sewing, nutrition and cooking.

The work of 800,000 volunteers in 1943 was indispensable at clubs and lounges, not only in assisting professional staffs but also in providing companionship to men and women in service at programs and social events.

In addition to serving men and women in the armed forces, U.S.O. extended services to war workers and their families in certain overcrowded war production centres. Programs were patterned after those for the armed forces, with emphasis on classes for women similar to those for the wives of service men.

U.S.O. officers in 1943 were: Chester I. Barnard, president; John D. Rockefeller, Jr., honorary chairman; Walter Hoving, chairman of the board; W. Spencer Robertson, chairman of the executive committee; Francis P. Matthews, Frank L. Weil and Mrs. Henry A. Ingraham, vice-presidents; Randall J. LeBoeuf, Jr., secretary; and John F. Hickey, treasurer. National headquarters were in the Empire State building, 350 Fifth ave., New York 1, N.Y.   (C. I. B.)

United States.

The population of the United States in 1940, by the federal census, was 131,669,275. This figure represented an increase of 8,894,229 over the census of 1930. With possessions included, the population was 150,621,231 in 1940. On Jan. 1, 1943, the census bureau estimated the population of the U.S. proper at 135,645,969. The area of continental U.S.A. is 3,022,387 sq.mi. For population figures of the states, *see* the articles on the separate states. See also BIRTH STATISTICS; CENSUS, 1940; CHURCH MEMBERSHIP; DEATH STATISTICS; INDIANS, AMERICAN; NEGROES (AMERICAN).

Politics and Parties.—The most significant trend in U.S. domestic politics during 1943 was the ebb of the power of the

New Deal. This was evidenced not only by the substantial Republican gains made in the November elections of 1943, but also in the attitude of many prominent Democrats who became increasingly critical of "government by directive" and advocated a larger measure of congressional independence, initiative and control over the various administrative agencies of the New Deal. In September a conference of prominent Republican leaders met at Mackinac Island, Michigan, to plan the party's strategy for the presidential contest of 1944. In full confidence in a coming Republican victory, the conference pledged the party to a vigorous prosecution of the war and to the participation of the United States in postwar co-operation with the other members of the United Nations to prevent military aggression. The next month Wendell Willkie, the Republican standard bearer of 1940, in an address at the Kiel auditorium in St. Louis, declared that the freeing of enterprise for expanding productivity could be accomplished only by a change of government at Washington. The election of a Republican governor in Kentucky in 1943, for the first time in 16 years, increased the confidence of the party that it would carry the presidential election of 1944.

Congress.—The first session of the 78th congress convened on Jan. 6, 1943, and, except for a vacation from June 8 to Sept. 14, sat until Dec. 21. It contained 222 Democrats to 209 Republicans in the house and 57 Democrats to 38 Republicans in the senate, as against 267 to 162 and 66 to 28 respectively in the 77th congress. The close of the year saw the Democratic majority reduced by deaths and by-elections to the barest margin. At the same time, the November elections showed that after Jan. 1, 1944, there would be Republican governors in 26 of the 48 states —states which include 60% of the population and 342 of the 531 electoral votes, and had cast 37,700,000 of the 49,500,000 popular votes in the presidential election of 1940. The president's message to congress in Jan. 1943, dealt chiefly with the war effort, citing the astonishing figures of production in the war industries, and commenting: "I suspect that Hitler and Tojo will find it dif-

ficult to explain to the German and Japanese people just why it is that decadent, inefficient democracies can produce such phenomenal quantities of weapons and munitions and fighting men." The major measures which occupied the attention of congress during 1943 were, on the domestic front, the renewal of lend-lease which was due to expire on June 30; legislation to end the menace of strikes, especially in the coal fields; the control of the threatening spectre of inflation; and the elaboration of a tax bill to include the pay-as-you-go principle, drain off considerable amounts of excess money ("dangerous dollars," as Secretary Morgenthau called it) in the hands of the spending public, and provide, both by raising the rates and lowering the exemptions, for the addition of thousands of millions of dollars to the treasury. Congress also wrestled with the question of the continued government subsidies to farmers under the program of the Commodity Credit corporation; the drafting of pre-Pearl Harbor fathers (those men who became fathers before Sept. 1, 1942); and the liquidation (July 1) of the WPA, which since 1935 had spent over $10,000,000,000. On the war front congress showed every disposition to support the president, regardless of party affiliation. The vote on the renewal of lend-lease (March 11) until June 30, 1944, was 82 to 0 in the senate and 407 to 6 in the house, as against 60 to 31 and 260 to 165 on the original bill of 1941. It was revealed that a total of $9,632,000,000 had been allotted under the lend-lease program up to March 1, 1943, including $4,430,-000,000 to the United Kingdom, $1,825,000,000 to the U.S.S.R., but only $157,000,000 to hard-pressed China. The administrator, Edward R. Stettinius (in August to succeed Sumner Welles as undersecretary of state) estimated that about one-third of U.S. production in planes and tanks was going to lend-lease. Some excitement was caused when William H. Standley, U.S. ambassador to the U.S.S.R., publicly charged the soviet government with minimizing the aid which the United States was giving to Russia; but Stalin's handsome acknowledgment at the Tehran conference of Roosevelt, Churchill and Stalin at the end of November that without the aid of the United States the war could not be won fully atoned for any misgivings as to the appreciation of the help given to the soviet government.

In response to the stiffening public opinion in condemnation of the series of strikes staged by John L. Lewis' United Mine Workers (see *Labour,* below), congress on June 25 passed the Connally-Smith bill, which aimed at putting an end to strikes in industries vital to the prosecution of the war. The bill did not completely outlaw strikes, but provided that no strike ballot should be taken until 30 days after certifying the dispute to the secretary of labor, the War Labor board and the National Labor Relations board. Though the president agreed to seven of the sections of this War Labor Disputes act and was ready to have the Selective Service act so amended as to compel strikers in war plants to resume work under military compulsion, he vetoed the bill both on the ground that it prohibited campaign contributions from labour unions and made provision for a strike ballot, whereas labour had given a pledge after Pearl Harbor not to strike during the war. The president maintained that the pledge had been kept by all the unions except the United Mine Workers and that only one-twentieth of 1% of man hours had been lost by strikes since Pearl Harbor—a record which "had never before been equalled in our country and was as good or better than the record of any of our Allies in war time." Nevertheless, congress, by votes of 244 to 108 in the house and 56 to 25 in the senate immediately passed the bill over his veto. It was the first time since June 1940, that congress had overridden the presidential veto, and was regarded as a significant proof of congressional independence.

The task of preventing runaway inflation by a rapid rise in prices and a corresponding demand for higher wages in industry

"WE ALWAYS SUSPECTED," by Manning in the (Phoenix) *Arizona Republic.* Uno Who is the cartoonist's ordinary U.S. citizen

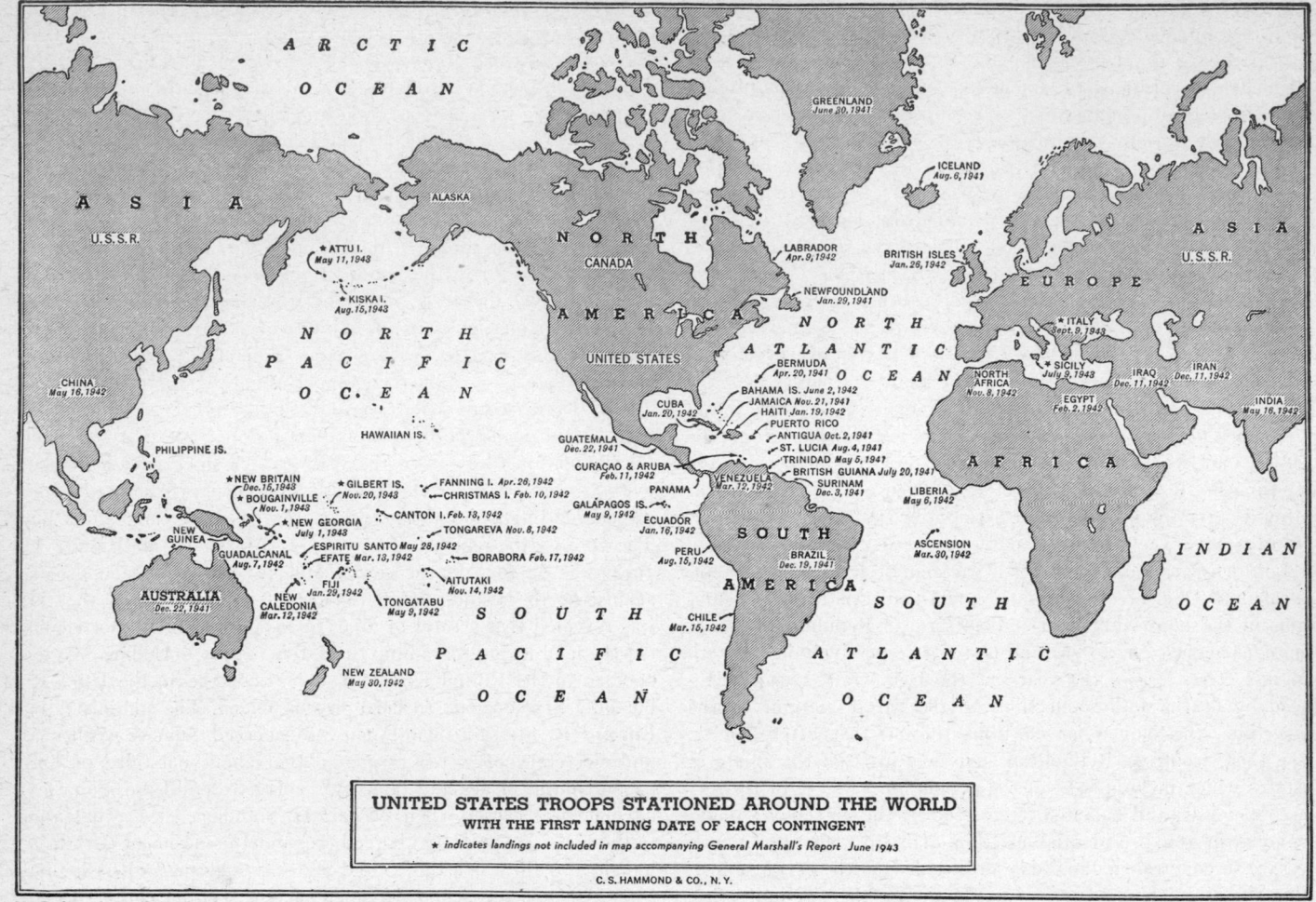

UNITED STATES TROOPS STATIONED AROUND THE WORLD
WITH THE FIRST LANDING DATE OF EACH CONTINGENT
★ indicates landings not included in map accompanying General Marshall's Report June 1943

C. S. HAMMOND & CO., N. Y.

MAP based on Gen. George C. Marshall's report of the progress of the United States' participation in World War II through June 1943. Subsequent landings through Dec. 1943 are starred

fell largely to the administrative agencies of the Office of Price Administration (headed by ex-Senator Prentiss Brown and later by Chester Bowles) and the War Labor board (chairman, William H. Davis). But that part of the task of "holding the line" against inflation which depended on the tax program of course fell to the province of congress, which alone has the power of raising revenue. Congress debated the tax program during all of 1943, with eyes fixed partly on the needs of the treasury, partly on the fight against inflation, and partly on the elections of 1944. We shall note later some details of the program (see *Taxes,* below); but here it is enough to state that, while congress had reached agreement on the method of taxation, it had not fully determined the rates by the end of 1943. The method sought to combine the pay-as-you-go plan (a modification of the project proposed originally by Beardsley Ruml) with the arrears of the taxes on incomes of 1942.

The question of the continuance of farm subsidies, some 40 of which were administered by the Commodity Credit corporation, was still unsettled as 1943 came to an end, the senate postponing action on it in order to get on with the tax bill. In spite of an impassioned radio plea for subsidies by the "economic czar," James F. Byrnes, and the support of the director of economic stabilization, Fred M. Vinson, the house of representatives, in the first week in December defeated subsidies by the large majority of 278 votes to 117. They had already approved the extension of the CCC to July 1, 1945, but cut out food subsidies after Dec. 31, 1943. The opposition to subsidies came largely from the farm bloc, which one might expect to approve the government's pay-

ment for the added costs of farm production. But the farmers objected to the stabilization of price ceilings on their crops, fearing that when the war was over the subsidies would cease, leaving the public conditioned to the lower farm prices. They preferred to let prices rise, despite Byrnes' declaration that the cost to the taxpayers of something over $1,000,000,000 a year would be far less than the cost in inflationary prices of food products. But the farm bloc, remembering the slump of 1920 in farm prices, was deaf to his plea. Senator Taft of Ohio proposed a compromise measure of $600,000,000 for farm subsidies, but it was ignored by congress. (*See also* ELECTIONS.)

The Budget and Finance.—In his budget message of Jan. 1943, President Roosevelt asked for something over $100,000,-000,000, of which $97,000,000,000 was to be for war expenditures for the fiscal year 1943–44. He also asked for an increase of $16,-000,000,000 in taxes. The war cost, he said, had increased four-fold since Pearl Harbor, from about $2,000,000,000 to $8,000,-000,000 a month. The debt limit was raised from $125,000,000,000 to $210,000,000,000, and a rider by Representative Wesley Disney (Dem., Okla.) was attached revoking the executive order of the president limiting incomes to $25,000 after taxes were paid. On Nov. 27 the budget director, Harold D. Smith, announced a cut of $11,000,000,000 in the 1944 budget, bringing it down to $92,000,000,000, and estimated the deficit at the end of 1943 at $57,000,000,000 and the public debt at $194,000,000,000. Purchases of war bonds and stamps for 1942 amounted to but $9,000,-000,000, or less than 8% of the national income of $116,000,000,-000. The war loan drives of Dec. 1942 ($12,000,000,000), April 1943 ($13,000,000,000) and Sept.-Oct. 1943 ($15,000,000,000), each of them double or more the great third Liberty Loan drive of

1918, were readily subscribed; and a fourth drive was announced for Jan. 1944. (*See* WAR BONDS.) It was evident that the enormous expense of the war, which by the end of 1943 was taking some two-thirds of the national income, would have to be met largely by borrowing, though it was hoped that the higher tax rates and the addition of more than 20,000,000 new taxpayers in 1943 would bring into the treasury close to $50,000,000,000, or approximately one-third of the national income, as against less than one-fourth in 1942. It was pointed out that in Britain 43% and in Canada 52% of the national income was paid in taxes. U.S. war expenses at a rate of almost $100,000,000,000 a year at the end of 1943 exceeded those of Germany, Great Britain, the U.S.S.R., Italy and Japan combined. (*See* also NATIONAL DEBT.)

Taxes.—In his budget message of 1943, as noted above, the president asked for $16,000,000,000 in new taxes. This figure was later pared down to $12,000,000,000, and again to $10,500,000,-000, which was Secretary Morgenthau's irreducible minimum demand. After debating the subject for months, the house in the late autumn passed a bill calling for only a $2,139,000,000 increase over the tax assessment of 1942 (which, incidentally, had raised taxes by $9,000,000,000). The senate had not reached its final decision before the end of 1943. The reasons for this meagre response to the requests of the president and the secretary of the treasury were various. Some congressmen believed that the wealthier taxpayers could not bear the proposed increases in the higher brackets without serious detriment to business enterprise. Others held that since four-fifths of the national income went to persons with $5,000 a year or less, a 3% tax on low incomes should be levied. Still others advocated a federal sales tax, which added to the sales tax levied in several of the states, would increase the burden on the poor. All of the congressmen doubtless had an eye fixed on the approaching elections of 1944, and were

affected by the perennial reluctance of congress to increase taxes on the eve of a presidential year. Randolph Paul, the expert adviser of the treasury department, was chiefly concerned with the threat of inflation in an inadequate tax assessment. He pointed out that while incomes had mounted by some $80,000,000,000 since Pearl Harbor, personal taxes had increased by only $19,-000,000,000. Though the American people had paid off $4,000,-000,000 of debts since Dec. 1941, had accumulated $10,000,000,-000 in social security and insurance funds, had bought $20,000,-000,000 more of government bonds, they still had over $18,000,-000,000 more in bank deposits and currency than they had at the time of Pearl Harbor. This vast amount of spendable money was serving to widen the "inflationary gap," that is, the discrepancy between the dwindling amount of civilian goods purchasable and the cash in hand for buying. The administration still held to the increased tax program as the best check on inflation, but the refusal of congress to levy more than about one-fifth of the added taxes asked by the treasury department left to administrative agencies (the OPA and the OES) the task of keeping down prices as best they could through ceilings. (*See* also PRICES; TAXATION.)

Industry.—When President Roosevelt in his Jan. 1943, message to congress declared that "the arsenal of democracy is making good," he spoke no idle words. By the close of the year the goals set for 184,000 manufacturing plants were more than reached. The national production figures had risen from $54,-000,000,000 in 1940 to $119,000,000,000 in 1942, and $151,000,-000,000 in 1943. U.S. war production equalled that of all the enemy countries combined. Since the beginning of the war the United States had increased petroleum output by 66%, coal by 40%, chemicals by 300%, iron ore by 125%, hydroelectric power by 79%, and steel by 106%. In order to develop still further a unified program for the maximum use of the nation's industrial resources for both military and civilian needs, the president in May

MARSHAL STALIN, PRESIDENT ROOSEVELT AND PRIME MINISTER CHURCHILL at the Tehran conference, Nov. 28–Dec. 1, 1943

created the Office of War Mobilization with James F. Byrnes as head and secretaries Stimson and Knox, Donald M. Nelson, Fred M. Vinson and Harry Hopkins as members. This was essentially an economic war cabinet, vested with a control over the nation's industries not unlike that of Bernard Baruch's War Industries board of 1917. Byrnes was made a sort of czar over all the special directors of industrial production: Jeffers (rubber), Ickes (fuel), Eastman (transportation), Bowles (OPA), McNutt (manpower), Nelson (WPB), Wickard (agriculture), William H. Davis (WLB), and Elmer Davis (OWI). Monthly production of planes rose from 2,500 at the beginning of 1942 to nearly 9,000 at the end of 1943; tonnage of merchant ships from 7,000,000 to 27,-000,000, and of naval vessels from 213,854 to 1,091,368. (*See also* BUSINESS REVIEW; WAR PRODUCTION, U.S.)

Labour.—During almost the entire year 1943 the administration, congress and the public were kept in a state of indignant unrest by the defiant attitude of John L. Lewis, president of the United Mine Workers of America. Three times Lewis called out the miners on strike, causing the eventual loss of 40,000,000 tons of coal, with serious consequences for the war industries and transportation. The miners' contract with the operators expired on April 1, and the union demanded an increase of $2 a day in wages to meet the increased cost of living. Lewis flouted the "little steel formula" of July 1942, which had limited wage increases to 15% above the level of Jan. 1941, and refused to recognize the authority of the War Labor board, which he called "a jealous and vindictive body." The "surrender" to Lewis was widely condemned in the country. By his successful defiance he had put the WLB in an embarrassing position and given encouragement to other unions to break the non-strike pledge following Pearl Harbor. The president, who had constantly been charged with too great leniency toward organized labour, did not refrain from expressing his disapproval of the tactics of the miners' union, nor did James F. Byrnes, in a nation-wide radio address on the anniversary of Pearl Harbor (Dec. 7).

Near the end of 1943 another major conflict loomed in the labour field. The 350,000 operating and 1,100,000 non-operating railroad employees had been for some months seeking a raise of 30% in wages to compensate for the higher cost of living. Utterly dissatisfied with the increase of 4 cents an hour offered them by the emergency board of the Railway Labor act, the five railway brotherhoods (engineers, firemen, conductors, trainmen and switchmen) took a strike ballot in the second week of December, in which 97.7% of their members voted to quit work on all the lines of the country. The seriousness of such a threat at the time when the roads were at the peak of their job could not be exaggerated. President Roosevelt moved immediately to meet the situation by summoning to a conference at the White House on Dec. 19 the heads of the five railroad brotherhoods and the wage committees of the carriers who had the power to make wage agreements with the unions. The seriousness of the situation was enhanced by the fact that no help could be expected from congress, since the legislators voted to adjourn from Dec. 21 to Jan. 10. The upshot of several conferences among the representatives of the brotherhoods and the carriers, the president and Economic Stabilization Director Vinson was that on Christmas Eve the strike was called off. At the same time a threatened strike of 350,000 workers in the steel industry was averted when Philip Murray, president of the C.I.O., announced that the men would continue work. (*See also* LABOUR UNIONS; STRIKES AND LOCKOUTS.)

The Food Problem.—The U.S. farm still remained the "biggest war plant" in 1943. The whole world had come to depend on it for food supplies for the various fighting forces. The president in his budget message of Jan. 1943, asked for $991,996,154 for agri-

"FIVE MINUTES IN A FOXHOLE Would Be Enough!" Cartoon by Temple of the *Times-Picayune* of New Orleans in 1943

culture in the fiscal year 1943, partly for soil conservation and partly for parity payments. Though U.S. farm production for 1943 exceeded that for 1942 by about 5%, he warned that the military forces and lend-lease would require close to 50% more, and predicted a stricter rationing of food supplies for civilians, which "might hurt our taste but not our health." For there would still be an ample supply of dairy products (except butter), meat, poultry, and fresh fruits and vegetables. Food Administrator Wickard announced in Feb. 1943 the extension of rationing to canned soups, fruits and vegetables, dried fruit, margarine, butter, meat and oils. The farmer's income was steadily rising (an increase of 90% since 1941), but there were three serious difficulties with which he had to cope. First, there were the perennial uncertainties of weather. In the spring, continuous excessive rains threatened to make serious inroads on the corn and grain crops; but warm sunny weather following dispelled the fear, and the actual returns exceeded those of 1942. However, the shortage in manpower to work the farms and in agricultural machinery created unprecedented difficulties. The importation of workers from Mexico, the utilization of prisoners of war and of some trainees released by the selective service, and the employment of school children in vacation time helped the situation; but these sources furnished only a small addition to the agricultural forces. Furthermore, the government was steadily cutting down the allotment of material for the building of new agricultural machines and the repair of those in use. Farmers were obliged to operate often with worn-out seeders, tractors, binders and reapers, patched up with scrap and tied with twine. It was not inadequate prices from which they were suffering, as in the years following World War I. Their income was higher than ever before. But money could not buy the help or the material they needed. (*See also* AGRICULTURE.)

Manpower.—The agricultural situation was but one aspect of the general problem of manpower with which McNutt, Hershey and Byrnes were wrestling. The goal set for 1943 was the augmentation of the 6,000,000 in the armed forces at the beginning of the year by some 4,500,000, and the increase of about 7,000,000 workers in munitions and essential war industries. The 8,000,000 unemployed employables at the time of Pearl Harbor had practically all been absorbed by the war demands, and the problem became one of better budgeting of the available man- and womanpower. Some critics of the selective service insisted that the educational and physical requirements for induction into the army and navy could be lowered somewhat without prejudice to the morale of the troops. After congress reassembled in Sept. 1943, the main debate on the subject of manpower was on the necessity of calling up the pre-Pearl Harbor fathers. Late in November the congress voted for conscription of the pre-Pearl Harbor fathers, but put them at the bottom of the list; and the president agreed to the bill. A distinctive feature of 1943 was the great increase in the number of women workers, both in the ranks of the uniformed women (the WACS, WAVES, SPARS, and the marine and ferry corps) and in the war industries. By the end of 1943, about one-third of the women between the ages of 18 and 64 were engaged in some kind of war work, and it was estimated that 18,000,000 more were available. Colonel Oveta Culp Hobby of the WACS, for example, declared that she could use ten times the 50,000 women already serving in her organization. Reports from some 8,000 manufacturing plants showed that the women workers had risen 184% in the aircraft industry, 161% in steel and 36% in iron. In World War I women had served as nurses and ambulance drivers and had replaced men as ticket collectors, trolley conductors, elevator operators and a number of other light occupations; but now they were doing men's jobs at almost all the factories, mills and shipyards in the United States.

Transportation.—*The Railroads.*—In spite of heavy handicaps, the railroads in 1943 surpassed even the "magnificent record" of the previous year. With 38% fewer locomotives and 25% fewer cars, they carried 80,000,000 passenger miles and 735,000,000 freight miles of traffic, as compared with the corresponding figures of 54,000,000 and 638,000,000 in 1942. They moved an average of 2,000,000 soldiers and sailors a month. The burden on the railroads was increased over that in World War I by the fact that they had now to devote more than 30% of their service to the ports of the Pacific coast, as against only 7% in the former war. However, two of the handicaps under which the roads were operating in 1942 were reduced during 1943. In the first place, the submarine menace waned; the significance of the victory over the submarines can be realized by the fact that before their raids began about 95% of the oil used in U.S. industries was brought from the wells of Texas, Oklahoma and California by water. The railroads rose to the occasion when the oil famine threatened, and increased their haulage from some 180,000 bbl. to 800,000 bbl. a day. Along with the relief in the U-boat menace came the completion in July 1943 of the "big inch," the 1,341-mi. oil pipeline from Texas to New Jersey, across eight states and under 20 rivers, with a capacity of delivering 350,000 bbl. a day. Considerable excitement was caused by a speech of Vice-President Wallace at Dallas, Tex., on Oct. 20, in which he warned against an attempted monopoly of transportation by the railroads at the expense of trucks and buses, and was answered with some heat by President John J. Pelley of Association of American Railroads. But the serious event in the railroad situation came in the last days of 1943, when the operating and non-operating railroad employees threatened to strike (*see above*). The upshot of the dispute was a presidential order to Secretary Stimson on Dec. 27 for the army to take over the railroads. Ere the year closed, as we have seen, the railroads called off the strike, agreeing to arbitra-

tion by the government which they were confident would satisfy their wage demands. (*See also* RAILROADS.)

Shipping.—To the 8,000,000 tons of merchant vessels built in 1942, the U.S. added 16,000,000 in 1943. By the end of Sept. 1943, more than 2,000 ships had been launched, and the goal for 1944 was 5,000 ships with a tonnage of 50,000,000—or more than half the total tonnage of the world in 1939. In Dec. 1943, the rate of building was 130% higher than in 1942, and was proceeding at an enormously increased figure over the sinkings, which at the beginning of the year had averaged six ships a day. (*See also* SHIPBUILDING; SHIPPING, MERCHANT MARINE.)

Aviation.—Production in the aircraft industry rose from $6,400,000,000 in 1942 to more than $20,000,000,000 in 1943, a figure equal to one-seventh of the U.S. national income. Though most of the planes were for the armed forces, about one-fourth were transport planes capable of conversion for civilian use. Work was under way in 1943 on the largest airfield in the world, on Long Island, N.Y.: a field five times as large as La Guardia field, with 13 mi. of runways and a capacity of 1,000 flights a day. The 21 domestic and international commercial airlines for the most part kept in operation during 1943; and although TWA, for example, saw its commercial fleet reduced by 57%, it lost only 23% of plane mileage. Workers in the aircraft plants increased from 390,000 men in 1941 to 1,200,000 men and women in 1943, when the entire plane output of the axis powers was exceeded. On the second anniversary of Pearl Harbor the 150,000th plane was completed. (*See also* AIR FORCES; WAR PRODUCTION, U.S.)

The Army and Navy.—During 1943 the demands of the chief of staff, General George C. Marshall, rose from an army of 7,500,000 to one of 10,700,000. Ten out of every 14 able-bodied men between the ages of 18 and 38, it was estimated by manpower commissioner McNutt, were in the armed forces at the close of 1943. The contest between the army, the navy, industry and agriculture for men was bound to be keen. Germany had put 13.5% of her population into the field, a proportion which would mean forces of 17,500,000 for the United States. The military appropriations for the year totalled $99,147,000,000 ($71,510,000,000 for the army and $27,637,000,000 for the navy). The army air forces at the end of the year contained 2,500,000 men, or more than all the U.S. armed forces in World War I; and the naval air force had grown from 1,744 planes to 18,269. Fighting ships

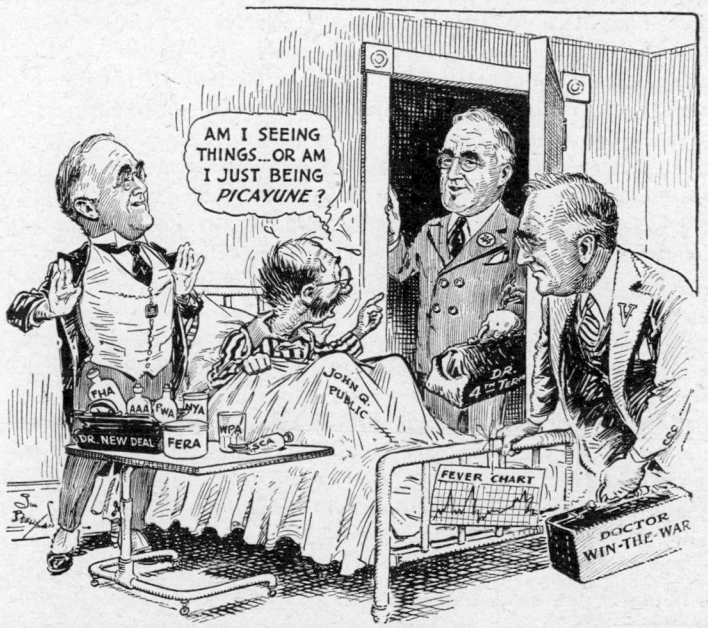

"THERE'S AN ODD FAMILY RESEMBLANCE AMONG THE DOCTORS" said Jim Berryman of the *Washington Evening Star*

numbered 2,674 at the close of 1943, as against 953 a year earlier and 674 in 1941. In those three years the United States built 2,200,000 tons of naval ships, added 23,000 planes, and completed $500,000,000 worth of shore facilities. (*See* also AIR FORCES; NAVIES OF THE WORLD; SELECTIVE SERVICE.)

International Affairs.—The text of U.S. policy in foreign relations might be found in President Roosevelt's Lincoln day (Feb. 12, 1943) speech at Washington: "Unless the peace that follows the war recognizes that the whole world is one neighbourhood and does justice to the whole human race, the germs of another world war will remain as a constant threat to mankind." To co-ordinate the efforts of the United Nations, especially the four great ones, the United States, Britain, U.S.S.R. and China, which contained three-fourths of the population of the world, was the constant concern of the president. In May 1943, he held his fifth conference with Prime Minister Winston Churchill since they had together written the Atlantic Charter of Aug. 1941. And in August they met again at Quebec, with Secretary Hull and Foreign Minister Eden attending. On Feb. 21 Madame Chiang Kai-shek addressed congress (the first private citizen ever to do so) and pleaded for the defeat of Japan without waiting until the Germans gave in. But in spite of the admiration of everyone for the courage with which China had withstood the assault of the far better equipped forces of Japan for more than six years, the strategy of the United Nations favoured concentrating the main attack on Hitler's far-flung forces. From Sept. 1 on hardly a week passed without some important conference bearing on the problems of winning the war and providing for the postwar world. Congress, which reconvened in the middle of September (soon after the conference of the Republican leaders at Mackinac Island) showed a far different attitude toward co-operation in a program to insure lasting peace than it had displayed after the armistice of World War I. A group of senators led by Burton, Ball, Hatch and Hill (the so-called B2H2 group) was urging the participation of the United States in a concert of the United Nations for a durable peace; and the house, by a vote of 360 to 29 on Sept. 26, adopted a resolution of Congressman James W. Fulbright of Arkansas, favouring U.S. participation in the creation of appropriate international machinery "with power adequate to establish and maintain a just and lasting peace among the nations of the world." A resolution of similar intent by Chairman Tom Connally (Dem., Tex.) of the foreign relations committee was before the senate. On Nov. 27 there met at Atlantic City the council of the United Nations' Relief and Rehabilitation Administration (ex-governor Herbert H. Lehman of New York, chairman) which laid plans for the expenditure of some $2,000,000,000 for the relief of destitution in the war-torn countries, each to contribute 1% of its national income for the preceding year. It was estimated that the United States would bear $1,350,000,000 of this expense, and that the needs of the 35 countries with 500,000,000 inhabitants would take some 46,000,000 tons of food and other supplies. (*See* also POSTWAR PLANNING.)

Meanwhile a series of historic conferences among the world leaders was taking place. At the end of October Secretary Hull flew to Moscow to meet foreign secretaries Eden of Great Britain and Molotov of the soviet union for discussions preliminary to the conference of the principals, Roosevelt, Churchill and Stalin, a few weeks later. (D. S. MU.)

The text of the joint four-nation* declaration signed Nov. 1, 1943, at Moscow was as follows:

The governments of the United States of America, the United Kingdom, the soviet union and China:

United in their determination, in accordance with the declaration by the

United Nations of Jan. 1, 1942, and subsequent declarations, to continue hostilities against those axis powers with which they respectively are at war until such powers have laid down their arms on the basis of unconditional surrender;

Conscious of their responsibility to secure the liberation of themselves and the peoples allied with them from the menace of aggression;

Recognizing the necessity of ensuring a rapid and orderly transition from war to peace and of establishing and maintaining international peace and security with the least diversion of the world's human and economic resources for armaments;

Jointly declare:

1.—That their united action, pledged for the prosecution of the war against their respective enemies, will be continued for the organization and maintenance of peace and security.

2.—That those of them at war with a common enemy will act together in all matters relating to the surrender and disarmament of that enemy.

3.—That they will take all measures deemed by them to be necessary to provide against any violation of the terms imposed upon the enemy.

4.—That they recognize the necessity of establishing at the earliest practicable date a general international organization, based on the principle of the sovereign equality of all peace-loving states, and open to membership by all such states, large and small, for the maintenance of international peace and security.

5.—That for the purpose of maintaining international peace and security pending the re-establishment of law and order and the inauguration of a system of general security, they will consult with one another and as occasion requires with other members of the United Nations with a view to joint action on behalf of the community of nations.

6.—That after the termination of hostilities they will not employ their military forces within the territories of other states except for the purposes envisaged in this declaration and after joint consultation.

7.—That they will confer and co-operate with one another and with other members of the United Nations to bring about a practicable general agreement with respect to the regulation of armaments in the postwar period.

The declaration of the Moscow conference regarding Italy was as follows:

The foreign secretaries of the United States, the United Kingdom and the soviet union have established that their three governments are in complete agreement that Allied policy toward Italy must be based upon the fundamental principle that fascism and all its evil influence and configuration shall be completely destroyed and that the Italian people shall be given every opportunity to establish governmental and other institutions based upon democratic principles.

The foreign secretaries of the United States and United Kingdom declare that the action of their governments from the inception of the invasion of Italian territory, in so far as paramount military requirements have permitted, has been based upon this policy.

In furtherance of this policy in the future the foreign secretaries of the three governments are agreed that the following measures are important and should be put into effect:

1.—It is essential that the Italian government should be made more democratic by inclusion of representatives of those sections of the Italian people who have always opposed fascism.

2.—Freedom of speech, of religious worship, of political belief, of press and of public meeting shall be restored in full measure to the Italian people, who shall also be entitled to form anti-fascist political groups.

3.—All institutions and organizations created by the fascist regime shall be suppressed.

4.—All fascist or pro-fascist elements shall be removed from the administration and from institutions and organizations of a public character.

5.—All political prisoners of the fascist regime shall be released and accorded full amnesty.

6.—Democratic organs of local government shall be created.

7.—Fascist chiefs and army generals known or suspected to be war criminals shall be arrested and handed over to justice.

In making this declaration the three foreign secretaries recognize that so long as active military operations continue in Italy the time at which it is possible to give full effect to the principles stated above will be determined by the commander in chief on the basis of instructions received through the combined chiefs of staff.

The three governments, parties to this declaration, will, at the request of any one of them, consult on this matter. It is further understood that nothing in this resolution is to operate against the right of the Italian people ultimately to choose their own form of government.

Following is the text of the declaration on Austria signed at Moscow:

The governments of the United Kingdom, the soviet union and the United States of America are agreed that Austria, the first free country to fall a victim to Hitlerite aggression, shall be liberated from German domination.

They regard the annexation imposed on Austria by Germany on March 15, 1938, as null and void. They consider themselves as in no way bound by any changes effected in Austria since that date. They declare that they wish to see re-established a free and independent Austria and thereby to open the way for the Austrian people themselves, as well as those neighbouring states which will be faced with similar problems, to find that political and economic security which is the only basis for lasting peace.

Austria is reminded, however, that she has a responsibility, which she cannot evade, for participation in the war at the side of Hitlerite Germany, and that in the final settlement account will inevitably be taken of her own contribution to her liberation.

*This was the only declaration of the Moscow Conference to which China was a signatory.

The following statement on atrocities, released concurrently with the other Moscow declarations, was signed by President Roosevelt, Prime Minister Churchill and Premier Stalin:

The United Kingdom, the United States and the soviet union have received from many quarters evidence of atrocities, massacres and cold-blooded mass executions which are being perpetrated by Hitlerite forces in many of the countries they have overrun and from which they are now being steadily expelled. The brutalities of nazi domination are no new thing, and all peoples or territories in their grip have suffered from the worst form of government by terror. What is new is that many of these territories are now being redeemed by the advancing armies of the liberating powers and that in their desperation the recoiling Hitlerites and Huns are redoubling their ruthless cruelties. This is now evidenced with particular clearness by monstrous crimes on the territory of the soviet union which is being liberated from Hitlerites and on French and Italian territory.

Accordingly, the aforesaid three Allied powers, speaking in the interests of the 32 United Nations, hereby solemnly declare and give full warning of their declaration as follows:

At the time of granting of any armistice to any government which may be set up in Germany, those German officers and men and members of the nazi party who have been responsible for or have taken a consenting part in the above atrocities, massacres and executions will be sent back to the countries in which their abominable deeds were done in order that they may be judged and punished according to the laws of these liberated countries and of the free governments which will be erected therein. Lists will be compiled in all possible detail from all these countries, having regard especially to invaded parts of the soviet union, to Poland and Czechoslovakia, to Yugoslavia and Greece, including Crete and other islands; to Norway, Denmark, the Netherlands, Belgium, Luxembourg, France and Italy.

Thus, Germans who take part in wholesale shooting of Polish officers or in the execution of French, Dutch, Belgian or Norwegian hostages or of Cretan peasants, or who have shared in slaughters inflicted on the people of Poland or in territories of the soviet union which are now being swept clear of the enemy, will know they will be brought back to the scene of their crimes and judged on the spot by the peoples whom they have outraged. Let those who have hitherto not imbued their hands with innocent blood beware lest they join the ranks of the guilty, for most assuredly the three Allied powers will pursue them to the uttermost ends of the earth and will deliver them to their accusers in order that justice may be done.

The above declaration is without prejudice to the case of German criminals whose offenses have no particular geographical localization and who will be punished by joint decision of the governments of the Allies.

The Moscow meeting was important for its demonstration of the complete accord between the three nations to wage the war to the end against the nazis; and on Nov. 5 the United States senate, by the overwhelming vote of 85 to 5 adopted almost word for word article 4 of the Moscow declaration.

In November, President Roosevelt and Prime Minister Churchill met Generalissimo Chiang Kai-shek at Cairo (Nov. 22–26) and agreed to divest Japan of all the territory she had stolen since she began her career of aggression in the far east.

The text of the Cairo statement, dated Dec. 1, 1943, was as follows:

The several military missions have agreed upon future military operations against Japan.

The three great Allies expressed their resolve to bring unrelenting pressure against their brutal enemies by sea, land and air. This pressure is already rising.

The three great Allies are fighting this war to restrain and punish the aggression of Japan.

They covet no gain for themselves and have no thought of territorial expansion.

It is their purpose that Japan shall be stripped of all the islands in the Pacific which she has seized or occupied since the beginning of the first World War in 1914, and that all the territories Japan has stolen from the Chinese, such as Manchuria, Formosa and the Pescadores, shall be restored to the Republic of China.

Japan will also be expelled from all other territories which she has taken by violence and greed.

The aforesaid three great powers, mindful of the enslavement of the people of Korea, are determined that in due course Korea shall become free and independent.

With these objects in view, the three Allies, in harmony with those of the United Nations at war with Japan, will continue to persevere in the serious and prolonged operations necessary to procure the unconditional surrender of Japan.

From Cairo Roosevelt and Churchill flew to Tehran, Iran, where they met Marshal Stalin and in a four-day conference mapped the plan of an all out attack on Hitler's "European Fortress."

The text of the declaration signed by President Roosevelt, Prime Minister Churchill and Premier Stalin at Tehran is as follows:

We, the President of the United States of America, the Prime Minister of Great Britain, and the Premier of the soviet union, have met in these four days past in this the capital of our ally, Tehran, and have shaped and confirmed our common policy.

We express our determination that our nations shall work together in the war and in the peace that will follow.

As to the war, our military staffs have joined in our round-table discussions and we have concerted our plans for the destruction of the German forces. We have reached complete agreement as to the scope and timing of operations which will be undertaken from the east, west and south. The common understanding which we have here reached guarantees that victory will be ours.

And as to the peace, we are sure that our concord will make it an enduring peace. We recognize fully the supreme responsibility resting upon us and all the United Nations to make a peace which will command good will from the overwhelming masses of the peoples of the world and banish the scourge and terror of war for many generations.

With our diplomatic advisers we have surveyed the problems of the future. We shall seek the co-operation and active participation of all nations, large and small, whose peoples in heart and in mind are dedicated, as are our own peoples, to the elimination of tyranny and slavery, oppression and intolerance. We will welcome them as they may choose to come into the world family of democratic nations.

No power on earth can prevent our destroying the German armies by land, their U-boats by sea, and their war plants from the air. Our attacks will be relentless and increasing.

Emerging from these friendly conferences we look with confidence to the day when all the peoples of the world may live free lives untouched by tyranny and according to their varying desires and their own consciences.

We came here with hope and determination. We leave here friends in fact, in spirit, and in purpose.

Signed at Tehran, Dec. 1, 1943.

ROOSEVELT, STALIN, CHURCHILL.

The text of the statement on Iran, signed at Tehran, is as follows:

The President of the United States of America, the Premier of the U.S.S.R., and the Prime Minister of the United Kingdom, having consulted with each other and with the Prime Minister of Iran, desire to declare the mutual agreement of their three governments regarding relations with Iran.

The governments of the United States of America, the U.S.S.R. and the United Kingdom recognize the assistance which Iran has given in the prosecution of the war against the common enemy, particularly by facilitating the transportation of supplies from overseas to the soviet union. The three governments realize that the war has caused special economic difficulties for Iran and they agreed that they will continue to make available to the Iran government such economic assistance as may be possible, having regard to the heavy demands made upon them by their world-wide military operations and to the world-wide shortage of transport, raw materials and supplies for civilian consumption.

With respect to the postwar period, the governments of the United States of America, the U.S.S.R. and the United Kingdom are in accord with the government of Iran that any economic problem confronting Iran at the close of hostilities should receive full consideration along with those of other members of the United Nations by conferences or international agencies, held or created, to deal with international economic matters.

The governments of the United States of America, the U.S.S.R. and the United Kingdom are at one with the government of Iran in their desire for the maintenance of the independence, sovereignty and territorial integrity of Iran. They count upon the participation of Iran, together with all other peace-loving nations in the establishment of international peace, security and prosperity after the war, in accordance with the principles of the Atlantic Charter, to which all four governments have continued to subscribe.

Both President Roosevelt and Vice-President Wallace visited Latin American countries in 1943, the president stopping off at Brazil on his way back from Africa in February, and the next month conferring with President Camacho at Monterrey, Mexico. Both visits resulted in valuable negotiations on the aid which those countries could furnish to the cause of the United Nations in their contribution of indispensable metals, airfield facilities, and general co-operation. In March and April, Wallace, an enthusiastic student of Spanish, made a good-will tour of South America (bypassing only Argentina, whose disposition toward the United States and the United Nations was far from friendly). On Sept. 15 the 21 republics of the continent were represented in an educational conference at Panama. The United States continued, in spite of some severe criticism, to spend large sums of money to secure the good will of the Latin American countries. (*See* also HISPANIC AMERICA AND WORLD WAR II.)

For the progress of the war *see* WORLD WAR II.

In a radio address on Christmas eve President Roosevelt reported to the nation on his meetings with the statesmen at Cairo and Tehran, and announced that General Dwight D. Eisenhower would be transferred from Cairo to London to direct the "second-front" assault on the continent. He warned that a bitter battle was before the American people; but he was confident of the outcome. (D. S. Mu.; X.)

Education.—*See* the articles EDUCATION; UNIVERSITIES AND COLLEGES.

Defense.—For information about the armed forces of the United States in 1943, *see* AIR FORCES OF THE WORLD; MARINE CORPS; NATIONAL GUARD; NAVIES OF THE WORLD; WORLD WAR II. *See also* CIVILIAN DEFENSE.

Finance and Banking.—Statistics pertaining to the United States will be found in such articles as BANKING; BUDGET, NATIONAL; BUSINESS REVIEW; NATIONAL DEBT; NATIONAL INCOME AND NATIONAL PRODUCT; STOCKS AND BONDS; TAXATION; WEALTH AND INCOME, U.S. DISTRIBUTION OF.

Foreign Trade.—The U.S. department of commerce announced in Jan. 1942 that it would cease publication of its monthly summaries of U.S. foreign commerce, as of Oct. 31, 1941, in order to prevent giving vital information to the enemy. For such information as was available in 1943, *see* BUSINESS REVIEW; FOREIGN ECONOMIC ADMINISTRATION; INTERNATIONAL TRADE.

Communication.—For statistics, *see* the articles AVIATION, CIVIL; CANALS AND INLAND WATERWAYS; ELECTRIC TRANSPORTATION; MOTOR TRANSPORTATION; POST OFFICE; RADIO; RAILROADS; SHIPBUILDING; SHIPPING, MERCHANT MARINE; TELEPHONE.

Agriculture.—Statistical material pertaining to this subject may be found under AGRICULTURE; also in the articles on separate crops and agricultural products.

Manufacturing.—The report of the department of commerce biennial census of manufactures for 1939, issued Jan. 15, 1941, estimated the number of establishments at 184,244; salaries and wages at $11,631,967,995 and value of products at $56,828,807,223. The 1941 census was not taken because of World War II, and after the U.S. entrance into the war, no complete overall figures for U.S. industrial production were issued. *See* BUSINESS REVIEW and WAR PRODUCTION, U.S. for industrial trends in 1943.

Labour.—For data on labour in 1943, *see* the articles AMERICAN FEDERATION OF LABOR; CONGRESS OF INDUSTRIAL ORGANIZATIONS; LABOUR UNIONS; RELIEF; SOCIAL SECURITY; STRIKES AND LOCK-OUTS; UNEMPLOYMENT; WAGES AND HOURS.

Mineral Production.—The U.S. department of the interior, for reasons of military security, issued no statistics on U.S. mineral production in 1942–43. (For such information as was passed by the censor in 1943, *see* the articles on individual minerals; also MINERAL AND METAL PRODUCTION AND PRICES; STRATEGIC MINERAL SUPPLIES.) (X.)

BIBLIOGRAPHY.—Books published in 1943 of significance in American history:

History. The United States and Its Place in World Affairs, 1918–1943; ed. Allan Nevins and L. M. Hacker; S. V. Benet, *Western Star;* H. A. Wallace, *The Century of the Common Man;* J. T. Adams, *The American;* W. E. Binkley, *American Politics and Parties;* J. P. Nichols, *Twentieth Century United States;* E. B. Greene, *The Revolutionary Generation;* J. C. Miller, *The Origins of the American Revolution;* C. A. Beard, *The Republic;* B. De Voto, *The Year of Decision;* D. S. Freeman, *Lee's Lieutenants* (vol. 11); I. Stone, *They Also Ran;* H. Basso, *Mainstream;* G. W. Johnson, *American Heroes and Hero Worship;* M. Curti, *The Growth of American Thought.*

Biography. F. Biddle, *Mr. Justice Holmes;* R. Holt, *George Washington Carver;* S. K. Padover, *The Complete Jefferson;* H. S. Canby, *Walt Whitman, an American;* W. L. Cross, *Connecticut Yankee;* H. Ickes, *The Autobiography of a Curmudgeon;* R. S. West, *Gideon Welles;* G. S. Seagrave, *Burma Surgeon;* J. Daugherty, *Abraham Lincoln;* H. Fast, *Citizen Tom Paine;* DeL. Ferguson, *Mark Twain, Man and Legend;* R. B. Nixon, *Henry W. Grady;* F. Greenslet, *Under the Bridge;* R. D. Meade, *Judah P. Benjamin;* H. Hull, *Mayling Soong Chiang;* T. Maynard, *Orestes Brownson;* M. Lerner, *The Mind and Faith of Justice Holmes;* H. W. Van Loon, *Simon Bolivar;* A. U. Pope, *Maxim Litvinoff.*

Economics and Sociology. J. R. Bellerby, *Economic Reconstruction;* C. E. Noyes, *Economic Freedom;* D. Hinshaw, *The Home Front;* S. Chase, *Where's the Money Coming From;* C. A. Ward, *Those Raw Materials;* H. M. Wriston, *The Challenge to Freedom;* C. Crow, *The Great American Customer;* R. T. Flewelling, *The Survival of Western Civilization;* J. Seidman, *Union Rights and Union Duties;* E. M. Queeny, *The Spirit of Business Enterprise;* E. R. Embree, *Brown Americans;* R. Ottley, *New World*

A-Coming; C. McWilliams, *Brothers Under the Skin;* G. A. Kennedy, *Who Are the Americans;* G. Lawton, ed., *New Goals for Old Age;* R. Davis-Dubois, *Get Together America.*

The War. F. Monaghan, *World War II* (vol. 2); S. Johnston, *Grim Reapers;* B. Mathews, *United We Stand;* H. Handleman, *Bridge to Victory;* Eve Curie, *Journey Among Warriors;* R. Ingersoll, *The Battle Is the Pay-Off;* F. V. Drake, *Vertical Warfare;* H. Matthews, *The Fruits of Fascism;* R. M. Coudenhover-Kalergi, *Crusade for Pan-Europa;* O. D. Tolischus, *Tokyo Record;* W. L. White, *Queens Die Proudly;* P. van Paassen, *The Forgotten Ally;* E. Pyle, *Here Is Your War;* E. Shiber, *Paris Underground;* K. Baring, *Our Army Today;* J. K. Taussig and H. F. Cope, *Our Navy;* A. Crane, ed., *Marines At War;* J. R. Carlson, *Under Cover;* H. St. G. Saunders, *Combined Operations;* E. Hungerford, *Transport for War;* A. G. Clifford, *The Conquest of North Africa;* R. Tregaskis, *Guadalcanal Diary;* M. Werner, *Attack Can Win In '43;* D. F. Zanuck, *Tunis Expedition;* J. Driscoll, *War Discovers Alaska;* R. L. Scott, *God Is My Co-Pilot;* T. Lawson, *Thirty Seconds Over Tokio;* N. W. Ross, *The Waves;* J. M. Redding and H. I. Leyshon, *Skyways to Berlin;* E. J. Kahn, *G. I. Jungle;* W. B. Clausen, *Blood for the Emperor;* H. Pol, *The Hidden Enemy.*

Latin America. E. P. Hanson, ed., *New World Guides, South America;* L. D. Baldwin, *The Story of the Americas;* S. F. Bemis, *The Latin-American Policy of the United States;* A. P. Whitaker, *Inter-American Affairs;* T. H. Reynolds, *The Progress of Pan-Americanism;* J. W. White, *Our Good Neighbor Hurdle;* C. Beals, *Dawn Over the Amazon;* W. Frank, *South American Journey;* A. Brenner, *The Wind that Swept Mexico;* J. Jobim, *Brazil in the Making;* J. P. Normano and A. Gerbi, *Japanese in South America;* J. H. Kemble, *Panama Route.*

Foreign Affairs. W. Lippmann, *U.S. Foreign Policy;* W. Willkie, *One World;* A. Shaw, *International Bearings of American Policy;* K. Colegrove, *The American Senate and World Peace;* R. N. Amahen, ed., *Beyond Victory;* L. Balogh, *Chaos or Peace;* J. T. Whitaker, *We Cannot Escape History;* B. Newman, *The New Europe;* H. C. Cassidy, *Moscow Dateline;* H. P. Howard, *America's Role in Asia;* E. Ben-Horin, *The Middle East;* S. Greenbie, *Asia Unbound;* I. Brant, *The Road to Peace and Freedom;* G. A. Borgese, *Common Cause;* V. Sheehan, *Between the Thunder and the Sun;* C. P. Romulo, *Mother America;* W. D. Herridge, *Which Kind of Revolution?;* C. Gill, *World Republic.* (D. S. Mu.)

United States-British War Boards: *see* BRITISH-U.S. WAR BOARDS.

United States-Canadian War Committees: *see* CANADIAN-U.S. WAR COMMITTEES.

United States Government Departments and Bureaus: *see* GOVERNMENT DEPARTMENTS AND BUREAUS. Also *see* under specific name, *i.e.* COAST GUARD, U.S., etc.

United States Housing Authority (USHA): *see* NATIONAL HOUSING AGENCY.

U.S. Investments Abroad.

There was no complete survey of American investments abroad after 1940, when holdings were valued at approximately $11,000,000,000, as indicated in the table on page 721. However, the United States treasury department conducted during 1943 the most comprehensive census of American property in foreign countries ever undertaken. All persons owning property in foreign countries were required to report their holdings on or before Dec. 1, 1943, with certain relatively minor exceptions—chiefly holdings in specified categories valued at less than $10,000. The results of this census, when tabulated, were expected to provide almost complete data on foreign assets, information which would be extremely valuable to business men, government officials, and all others interested in international economic relations.

The United States government emerged as the major supplier of American capital to foreign countries, as huge sums were placed abroad to facilitate the production of many and varied commodities vital to the successful prosecution of the war. Most of these enterprises were financed by the various subsidiaries of the Reconstruction Finance corporation, although the $130,000,000 Canol project, providing petroleum facilities in northwestern Canada, was an army undertaking. Another major enterprise in Canada was the Shipshaw plant of the Aluminum Company of Canada, Ltd., constructed with funds supplied in part by the Metals Reserve company in the form of advance payments for future production. Rubber developments were promoted by the United States government in various Latin American countries, and the cultivation of abaca and other fibre plants was encouraged to replace lost far eastern supplies. In addition, of course, large sums were "invested" in military and semi-military installations around the world. Investments and other expenditures by United States government agencies in Latin America became a subject of political controversy during the closing months of the year, the debate serving to focus public attention on these matters and to bring to light correct data regarding the financial extent of the operations.

United States Investments Abroad, December 31, 1940
(In millions of dollars)

| Area | Long-Term Investments | | | | | Short-Term Investments |
| | Direct Investments | Portfolio Investments | | | Total Long-Term | |
		Foreign Dollar Bonds	Miscellaneous Foreign Securities	Total		
Canada and Newfoundland	2,103	1,390	285	1,675	3,778	46
West Indies	674	74	5	79	753	
Central America and Mexico	546	26	—	26	572	129
South America	1,551	893	5	898	2,449	
Europe	1,420	506	130	636	2,056	109
Asia	422	155	5	160	582	120
Oceania	120	95	3	98	218	
Africa	131	2	17	19	150	6
International*	33	—	—		33	
Total	7,000	3,141	450	3,591	10,591	410

*Investments not geographically allocable.

Sources: *American Direct Investments in Foreign Countries*, U.S. Department of Commerce, 1942; *The Balance of International Payments of the United States in 1940*, U.S. Department of Commerce, 1941; "Status of United States Investments in Foreign Dollar Bonds, End of 1940," in *Foreign Commerce Weekly*, July 19, 1941, p. 3; "U.S. Investments in Foreign Dollar Bonds," in *Foreign Commerce Weekly*, Sept. 26, 1942, p. 8; *Bulletin* of the Treasury Department, March 1941.

In spite of the war, the years 1942 and 1943 produced considerable activity on the part of private American capital seeking new investment outlets abroad. Stimulated by rising prices for Canadian bonds in the U.S. and perhaps by anticipation of a return to par of the Canadian dollar, purchases by American investors of outstanding Canadian securities amounted to some $97,000,000 in 1942 and $119,000,000 in the first nine months of 1943, according to the dominion bureau of statistics. The participation of American capital in the exploitation of the Steep Rock iron deposits in Canada was accomplished through a public offering of securities of the Canadian corporation developing the properties, and during the year it was also announced that work was proceeding on U.S.-owned iron ore properties in Venezuela, with scheduled development and construction costs of about $25,000,000 envisaged. Other acquisitions or expansions included a pharmaceutical concern and a pulp mill in Canada, an air line, a plant for manufacturing flavouring syrups for soft drinks, and several finance-investment firms in Mexico, tire plants in the last-named country and in Cuba, and a substantial interest in the TACA air routes in the Caribbean. While the amount of capital involved in these enterprises was small in comparison to the great exodus of American capital in the '20s, it was evident that private funds were still available for foreign investment if the attendant circumstances appeared favourable.

On Sept. 29, 1943, the state department announced that an agreement had been reached with Mexico, by which the government of the latter country would pay some $29,000,000 for most of the American-owned petroleum properties expropriated in 1938. Acceptance of the settlement by the principal claimant, the Standard Oil Company of New Jersey, was announced on Oct. 1, thus apparently bringing to a close one of the bitterest disputes in the history of American industry abroad. One of the other major companies involved, the Sinclair Oil corporation, had settled its claims directly with the government of Mexico in 1940, and received the final installment of an $8,500,000 award

in 1943.

By decree law no. 6019, dated Nov. 23, 1943, the government of Brazil established a new plan for the servicing of the external debt of that country which was considerably more liberal in its terms than the one prevailing in recent years. The decree was the outcome of extended negotiations between the government and representatives of the bondholders and presumably represented a definitive and final settlement, providing, as it did, for regular annual amortizations of the principal amounts outstanding.

The government of El Salvador, in a decree dated Nov. 12, 1943, imposed an increased export duty on coffee, the proceeds of which were to be devoted to servicing the external debt, in default since 1937.

Details of the application of these funds remained to be determined by negotiation.

Perhaps the most significant development during 1943 affecting U.S. foreign investments was the rather widespread attention being devoted to the postwar role of American capital abroad. The department of commerce, in its publication *The United States in the World Economy*, stated: "In view of our high standard of living and enormous capacity for saving, it is both natural and logical that American capital should resume investment activity abroad on a scale large enough to sustain this country's export trade and concurrently support reconstruction and development programs in foreign countries." This point of view seemed to have been widely accepted on the ground that it would be to the mutual advantage of debtor and creditor alike if future investments take the form of direct participation in the ownership and management of industrial and commercial enterprises, rather than the public flotation of bond issues of foreign governmental entities—national, provincial or municipal.

Another phase of the problem that received attention was the question of joint participation with local capital in the countries where investments are to be made. A trend in this direction was especially noticeable during the decade of the '30s in Great Britain, where many leading American-owned companies offered securities to the British public. Several of the financial firms organized in Mexico in 1943 represented joint ventures of United States and Mexican capital. In an article in the *Harvard Business Review*, Kuang Tai Hu, a Chinese graduate student at the university, expressed the opinion that foreign capital would be welcomed in China after the war only on terms which would leave a considerable share of the investment and voice in the management in the hands of the Chinese.

Official importance attached to postwar international capital movements and the related problem of exchange stability was evidenced by the drafting of elaborate, though tentative, plans for international stabilization funds and a world bank. These plans, prepared by both British and American government experts, were widely discussed in the press, and in financial and economic journals. At the close of the year, however, the extent and character of the international movement of capital in the postwar period still remained to a large degree unforeseeable, although there was little, if any, lack of agreement as to the importance of the problem and the necessity for discovering a workable solution. (R. L. Ss.)

Universities and Colleges.
The following seven pages carry a selected list of universities, colleges and junior colleges in the U.S. and Canada, with location, year founded, chief executive, enrolment, size of faculty, endowment and number of library volumes, for the academic year 1943–44. An asterisk denotes 1942–43 data; two asterisks denote data previous to 1942–43. (*See also* EDUCATION.)

Institution and Location	Year Founded	Chief Executive	Full Time Students	Number Army & Navy Students	Faculty	Endowment	Library Volumes
A							
Abilene Christian College, Abilene, Tex.	1906	Don H. Morris	450	—	37	—	16,334
Acadia University, Wolfville, Nova Scotia, Canada	1838	Frederic W. Patterson	510	70	45	$ 1,459,258	86,000
Adams St. Tch. Col., Alamosa, Colo.	1921	Ira Richardson	—	—	25	—	18,600
Adelphi College, Garden City, Long Island, N.Y.	1896	Paul Dawson Eddy	633	—	58	46,000	39,000
Adrian College, Adrian, Mich.	1845	Samuel J. Harrison	112	—	24	150,000	10,000
Agnes Scott College, Decatur, Ga.	1889	James R. McCain	555	—	67	2,227,959	41,000
Akron, University of, Akron, Ohio	1870	H. E. Simmons	900	375	118	145,000	64,851
Alabama Polytechnic Inst., Auburn, Ala.	1872	Luther N. Duncan	1,710	1,500	207	325,471	93,555
Alabama State College for Women, Montevallo, Ala.	1896	A. F. Harman	650	—	100	585,122	46,000
Ala. State Teachers College, Florence, Ala.	1872	J. A. Keller	726	—	40	—	50,000
Ala. State Teachers Col., Jacksonville, Ala.	1883	Houston Cole	250	—	45	—	30,000
Ala. State Teachers Col., Livingston, Ala.	1883	T. K. Sisk	50	—	16	—	22,729
**Ala. State Teachers Col., Montgomery, Ala.	1874	H. C. Trenholm	1,336	?	79	—	11,026
Alabama, University of, University, Ala.	1831	Raymond R. Paty	2,300	2,800	300	5,100,000	275,000
Alaska, University of, College, Alaska	1922	Charles E. Bunnell	225	—	16	—	20,000
Alberta, Univ. of, Edmonton, Alta., Can.	1908	Robert Newton	1,980	292	221	1,205,167	80,000
Albertus Magnus Col., New Haven, Conn.	1925	Sister M. Uriel	160	—	30	—	17,500
Albion College, Albion, Mich.	1835	John L. Seaton	456	250	55	1,987,995	60,265
Albion State Normal School, Albion, Ida.	1897	Raymond H. Snyder	192	—	23	1,500,000	14,000
Albright College, Reading, Pa.	1856	Harry V. Masters	232	—	37	641,448	22,870
Alcorn Agri. & Mech. Col., Alcorn, Miss.	1871	William H. Bell	346	—	57	209,872	15,000
Alderson-Broaddus Col., Philippi, W.Va.	1871	John W. Elliott	61	—	17	45,000	6,800
Alfred University, Alfred, N.Y.	1836	J. Nelson Norwood	278	400	76	1,043,708	62,782
Allegheny College, Meadville, Pa.	1815	J. R. Schultz	533	400	58	1,568,417	94,000
**Allen University, Columbia, S.C.	1870	Samuel R. Higgins	365	?	23	48,000	4,365
Alliance Jr. Col., Cambridge Springs, Pa.	1912	John J. Kolasa	30	—	9	3,000,000	8,002
Alma College, Alma, Mich.	1886	Roy W. Hamilton	372	186	28	—	51,000
Amarillo College (Jr.), Amarillo, Tex.	1929	Ernest C. Shearer	200	—	19	—	9,000
American Inter. Col., Springfield, Mass.	1885	Chester S. McGown	302	—	32	—	11,000
**American University, Los Angeles, Calif.	1921	Frederick H. Clapp	180	?	9	—	3,800
American University, Washington, D.C.	1893	Paul F. Douglass	296	—	66	901,125	110,080
Amherst College, Amherst, Mass.	1821	Stanley King	180	960	100	18,737,474	230,000
Andrew College (Jr.), Cuthbert, Ga.	1854	S. C. Olliff	110	—	14	50,000	4,500
Antioch College, Yellow Springs, Ohio	1853	A. D. Henderson	816	400	65	1,800,000	65,000
Appalachian St. Teachers Col., Boone, N.C.	1903	B. B. Dougherty	360	—	40	—	40,000
Arizona, University of, Tucson, Ariz.	1885	Alfred Atkinson	1,617	304	196	63,489	164,530
Ark. Agri., Mech. & Norm. Col., Pine Bluff, Ark.	1873	Lawrence A. Davis	243	—	54	—	6,393
Arkansas College, Batesville, Ark.	1872	John D. Spragins, Jr.	75	—	19	60,000	12,000
Arkansas Polytechnic Col. (Jr.), Russellville, Ark.	1909	J. W. Hull	752	105	35	—	25,000
Arkansas State College, Jonesboro, Ark.	1909	H. E. Thompson	373	—	56	—	19,000
Arkansas, University of, Fayetteville, Ark.	1871	A. M. Harding	1,200	1,382	176	—	199,662
Armstrong Junior College, Savannah, Ga.	1935	Foreman M. Hawes	111	—	10	—	5,000
*Asheville College, Asheville, N.C.	1887	Frank C. Foster	180	?	18	—	15,000
Ashland College, Ashland, Ohio	1878	Edward G. Mason	140	—	30	377,116	19,000
Assumption, College de l', L'Assomption, P. Q., Canada	1832	La Corporation du Collège de l'Assomption	311	70	34	11,960	18,100
Athens College, Athens, Ala.	1842	E. R. Naylor	164	—	12	250,000	12,408
Atlanta Center—Univ. System of Georgia (Jr.), Atlanta, Ga.	1932	George M. Sparks	2,004	—	61	—	15,000
Atlanta University, Atlanta, Ga.	1867	Rufus E. Clement	82	—	24	3,868,341	71,800
Atlantic Christian College, Wilson, N.C.	1902	Howard S. Hilley	365	—	20	335,427	14,717
Atlantic Union Col., So. Lancaster, Mass.	1862	G Eric Jones	450	—	38	100,000	20,000
Augsburg College & Theological Seminary, Minneapolis, Minn.	1869	Bernhard Christensen	200	—	22	72,000	20,000
Augusta, Junior College of, Augusta, Ga.	1925	Eric W. Hardy	195	—	24	—	11,000
Augustana College & Theological Seminary, Rock Island, Ill.	1860	Conrad Bergendoff	357	250	118	69,112	84,899
Aurora College, Aurora, Ill.	1893	Theodore P. Stephens	75	—	18	67,282	27,000
Austin Peay Norm. Sch., Clarksville, Tenn.	1927	P. P. Claxton	225	90	26	—	13,000
Averett College (Jr.), Danville, Va.	1859	Curtis V. Bishop	338	—	32	40,726	7,541
B							
Baker University, Baldwin City, Kan.	1856	Nelson P. Horn	193	—	27	1,221,732	67,254
Baldwin-Wallace College, Berea, Ohio	1845	Louis C. Wright	760	420	58	2,000,000	60,000
Ball State Teachers College, Muncie, Ind.	1918	W. E. Wagoner	786	551	112	—	92,069
Barber-Scotia College (Jr.), Concord, N.C.	1867	L. S. Cozart	159	—	17	375,000	7,190
Bates College, Lewiston, Me.	1863	Clifton D. Gray	395	283	57	2,149,104	79,209
Baylor University, Waco, Dallas, and Houston, Tex.	1845	Pat M. Neff	1,314	500	105	1,757,607	102,658
Beaver College, Jenkintown, Pa.	1853	Raymon Kistler	441	—	55	30,000	21,000
Belhaven College, Jackson, Miss	1894	G. T. Gillespie	275	—	32	400,000	18,000

Institution and Location	Year Founded	Chief Executive	Full Time Students	Number Army & Navy Students	Faculty	Endowment	Library Volumes
Belmont Abbey Col. (Jr.), Belmont, N.C.	1878	Vincent G. Taylor	278	80	31	—	40,000
Beloit College, Beloit, Wis.	1846	W. Bradley Tyrrell	321	—	52	$ 2,274,506	131,129
**Benedict College, Columbia, S.C.	1870	J. J. Starks	525	?	25	140,000	19,000
Bennett College, Greensboro, N.C.	1873	David D. Jones	363	—	31	555,710	17,039
Bennett Junior College, Millbrook, N.Y.	1891	Courtney Carroll	150	—	35	20,000	9,764
Bennington College, Bennington, Vt.	1932	Lewis Webster Jones	295	—	42	100,093	23,300
Berea College, Berea, Ky.	1855	Francis S. Hutchins	700	300	78	10,380,794	100,000
Berry Schools, The, Mt. Berry, Ga.	1902	Gardner L. Green	800	200	150	—	30,000
Bessie Tift College, Forsyth, Ga.	1847	C. L. McGinty	200	—	25	325,000	13,500
Bethany College, Bethany, W.Va.	1840	W. H. Cramblet	192	331	36	2,287,814	37,000
Bethany College, Lindsborg, Kan.	1881	Emory Lindquist	167	—	29	396,711	21,693
Bethany-Peniel College, Bethany, Okla.	1909	S. T. Ludwig	?	—	27	?	15,000
Bethel College, McKenzie, Tenn.	1842	Ewell K. Reagin	100	—	12	415,000	11,000
Bethel College, North Newton, Kan.	1887	Edmund G. Kaufman	162	—	28	450,000	22,500
Bethune-Cookman College (Jr.), Daytona Beach, Fla.	1904	James A. Colston	323	—	22	160,912	13,500
**Billings Polytechnic Institute, Billings, Mont.	1908	Ernest T. Eaton	500	?	35	400,000	25,000
Birmingham-South. Col., Birmingham, Ala.	1856	George R. Stuart	298	320	54	800,000	56,000
Bishop College, Marshall, Texas	1881	Joseph J. Rhoads	233	—	27	13,957	17,000
Bishop's College, University of, Lennoxville, Que., Can.	1853	A. H. McGreer	126	—	18	1,230,820	25,000
Blackburn College (Jr.), Carlinville, Ill.	1857	William M. Hudson	285	—	20	1,126,350	15,000
Black Hills Teachers College, Spearfish, S.D	1883	Russell E. Jonas	100	300	40	—	22,331
Bluefield St. Tch. Col., Bluefield, W.Va.	1895	Henry L. Dickason	306	—	23	—	10,000
Blue Mountain Col., Blue Mountain, Miss.	1873	Lawrence T. Lowrey	337	—	26	400,000	16,200
**Blue Ridge College, New Windsor, Md.	1843	Homer E. Cooper	150	?	19	—	5,000
Bluffton College, Bluffton, Ohio	1900	L. L. Ramseyer	97	—	25	201,000	16,000
Bob Jones College, Cleveland, Tenn.	1927	R. R. (Bob) Jones	800	—	70	—	14,000
Boise Jr. Col., Boise, Idaho	1932	Conan E. Mathews	165	—	17	—	6,200
Boston College, Chestnut Hill, Mass.	1863	Wm. J. Murphy	474	386	88	607,000	219,000
Boston University, Boston, Mass.	1839	Daniel L. Marsh	10,870	1,084	664	5,288,508	225,000
Bourget College, Rigaud, Que., Can.	1850	Father Louis-Joseph Lefebvre	509	86	65	24,000	38,000
Bowdoin College, Brunswick, Me.	1794	K. C. M. Sills	159	660	53	8,123,370	193,000
Bowling Green St. Univ., Bowling Green, O.	1910	Frank J. Prout	842	464	87	—	69,226
Bradford Junior College, Bradford, Mass.	1803	Dorothy M. Bell	263	—	32	150,750	15,240
Bradley Polytechnic Inst., Peoria, Ill.	1897	Frederic R. Hamilton	562	400	65	2,383,880	56,095
Brenau College, Gainesville, Ga.	1878	A. C. Wheeler	405	—	41	545,380	20,000
Brewton-Parker Jr. Col., Mt. Vernon, Ga.	1904	R. L. Robinson	166	—	10	25,000	4,000
Bridgewater College, Bridgewater, Va.	1880	Paul H. Bowman	143	—	23	503,990	15,000
Brigham Young University, Provo, Utah.	1876	Franklin S. Harris	950	250	120	200,000	130,000
British Columbia, Univ. of, Vancouver, B.C.	1915	Leonard S. Klinck	2,449	85	260	502,687	130,000
Brooklyn Polytechnic Inst., Brooklyn, N.Y.	1854	Harry S Rogers	441	488	92	1,587,970	24,025
Brownsville Jr. Col., Brownsville, Texas	1926	Ben L. Brite	76	—	12	—	10,000
Brown University, Providence, R.I.	1764	Henry M. Wriston	872	810	211	11,807,000	625,000
Bryn Mawr College, Bryn Mawr, Pa.	1880	Katharine E. McBride	594	—	87	7,196,030	185,000
Bucknell University, Lewisburg, Pa.	1846	Arnaud C. Marts	785	556	111	1,300,000	95,000
Bucknell Univ. Jr. Col., Wilkes-Barre, Pa.	1933	Eugene S. Farley	105	250	20	20,000	8,892
Buena Vista College, Storm Lake, Iowa	1891	Henry Olson	675	—	30	250,000	20,000
Buffalo, University of, Buffalo, N.Y.	1846	Samuel P. Capen	850	899	432	6,156,283	195,784
Butler University, Indianapolis, Ind.	1850	M. O. Ross	968	1,100	86	2,994,360	76,017
C							
California Inst. of Tech., Pasadena, Calif	1891	R. A. Millikan	394	727	150	13,500,000	58,516
California, University of, Berkeley, Calif.	1868	Robert G. Sproul	11,800	3,000	2,400	33,378,000	1,800,000
Calvin College & Seminary, Grand Rapids, Mich.	1876	Henry Schultze and Louis Berkhof	382	—	25	191,567	27,500
**Campbell College, J. P., Jackson, Miss.	1890	S. L. Greene	169	?	13	—	680
Campbell College (Jr.), Buies Creek, N.C.	1887	L. H. Campbell	430	—	33	180,000	8,000
Camrose Lutheran College, Camrose, Alberta, Canada	1911	Georg Moi	141	16	5	—	1,200
Canal Zone Jr. Col., Balboa Heights, C.Z.	1933	Roger C. Hackett	116	1	6	—	8,000
Canisius College, Buffalo, N.Y.	1870	Timothy J. Coughlin	259	350	67	—	37,277
Capital University, Columbus, Ohio	1850	Otto Mees	555	250	74	625,000	37,000
Carbon College (Jr.), Price, Utah	1938	E. B. Sessions	175	—	16	—	3,250
Carleton College, Northfield, Minn.	1866	Donald J. Cowling	589	700	90	3,459,276	135,795
*Carnegie Inst. of Tech., Pittsburgh, Pa.	1900	Robert E. Doherty	2,261	?	400	17,031,983	34,000
Carroll College, Helena, Mont.	1910	E. J. Riley	25	270	21	500,000	18,000
Carroll College, Waukesha, Wis.	1846	G. T. Vander Lugt	251	—	28	880,518	25,000
*Carson-Newman Col., Jefferson City, Tenn.	1851	James T. Warren	225	200	28	575,000	26,000
Case School of Apld. Sc., Cleveland, Ohio	1880	Wm. E. Wickenden	689	249	103	4,475,830	35,000
**Catawba College, Salisbury, N.C.	1851	Howard R. Omwake	427	?	37	386,520	18,000
Catholic Univ. of Amer., Washington, D.C.	1887	Patrick J. McCormick	1,191	500	250	3,172,407	305,505
Cedar Crest College, Allentown, Pa.	1867	Dale H. Moore	335	—	37	115,000	25,000
Centenary College of La., Shreveport, La.	1825	Paul M. Brown	388	500	45	475,000	25,000
Centenary Jr. Col., Hackettstown, N.J.	1929	Hurst R. Anderson	174	—	21	—	8,850

Institution and Location	Year Founded	Chief Executive	Full Time Students	Number Army & Navy Students	Faculty	Endowment	Library Volumes
Central College (Jr.), Conway, Ark.	1892	Edwin S. Preston	100	—	15	—	5,004
Central College, Fayette, Mo.	1855	Harry S. DeVore	253	311	32	$ 1,128,538	60,000
Central College, Pella, Iowa	1853	Irwin J. Lubbers	354	133	28	319,340	20,000
Central Mich. Col. of Ed., Mt. Pleasant, Mich.	1892	C. L. Anspach	1,164	600	105	—	50,000
Central Mo. St. Tch. Col., Warrensburg, Mo.	1871	George W. Diemer	659	374	66	—	63,564
Central Normal College, Danville, Ind.	1878	P. R. Hightower	63	—	12	—	10,922
*Central State College, Edmond, Okla.	1890	R. R. Robinson	787	?	66	—	16,821
Cent. Wash. Col. of Edu., Ellensburg, Wash.	1891	Robert E. McConnell	660	400	68	—	38,000
Central YMCA College, Chicago, Ill.	1919	Edward J. Sparling	2,022	—	44	24,000	27,045
Centre College, Danville, Ky.	1819	James H. Hewlett	138	450	22	1,833,347	39,000
Chaffey Jr. Col., Ontario, Calif.	1916	Gardiner W. Spring	271	600	31	—	35,000
*Chapman College, Whittier, Calif.	1920	George N. Reeves	56	?	64	119,000	14,000
Charleston, College of, Charleston, S.C.	1770	George D. Grice	209	—	20	500,000	30,964
Chattanooga, Univ. of, Chattanooga, Tenn.	1886	David A. Lockmiller	600	350	50	800,000	100,000
Chestnut Hill, Col. of, Philadelphia, Pa.	1871	Sister Maria Kostka	335	—	47	—	30,000
Cheyney Training School for Teachers, Cheyney, Pa.	1837	Leslie Pinckney Hill	134	—	15	—	17,000
Chicago, University of, Chicago, Ill.	1891	Robert M. Hutchins	5,615	—	832	69,423,973	1,436,244
Chico State College, Chico, Calif.	1889	Aymer Jay Hamilton	268	—	37	—	31,258
Christian College (Jr.), Columbia, Mo.	1851	James C. Miller	330	—	35	100,000	12,000
Cincinnati, University of, Cincinnati, Ohio	1819	Raymond Walters	2,068	2,450	589	10,111,055	551,991
Citadel, The, Charleston, S. C.	1842	C. P. Summerall	600	1,450	128	—	30,000
Claflin College, Orangeburg, S. C.	1869	Joseph B. Randolph	148	—	15	165,000	15,000
Clark University, Worcester, Mass.	1887	Wallace W. Atwood	219	300	51	—	170,000
Clarke College, Dubuque, Iowa	1843	Sister Mary Ambrose	342	—	40	—	25,000
Clarkson College of Tech., Potsdam, N. Y.	1896	John A. Ross, Jr.	210	—	32	1,298,152	11,718
Cleary College, Ypsilanti, Mich.	1883	P. R. Cleary	266	—	10	—	7,000
Clemson Agri. Col., The, Clemson, S. C.	1889	Robert Franklin Poole	731	1,523	131	286,756	64,290
Coe College, Cedar Rapids, Iowa	1881	Charles A. Anderson	309	800	50	1,823,648	52,158
*Coker College, Hartsville, S. C.	1894	C. Sylvester Green	261	?	34	756,000	18,000
Colby College, Waterville, Me.	1813	J. S. Bixler	328	500	71	3,000,000	100,000
Colby Junior College, New London, N. H.	1837	H. Leslie Sawyer	367	—	38	300,000	16,000
Colgate University, Hamilton, N.Y.	1819	Everett N. Case	140	1,100	90	5,900,000	130,000
College Catholique, Le, Gravelbourg, Sask., Can.	1917	Aimé Lizée	114	46	21	—	3,000
Collège Ste-Anne, Church Point, N.S., Can.	1890	W. Haché	165	35	16	—	10,000
Colorado College, Colorado Springs, Colo.	1874	Charlie Brown Hershey	365	443	45	2,517,000	128,000
Colorado School of Mines, Golden, Colo.	1870	M. F. Coolbaugh	214	529	61	—	60,000
Colorado State College of Agriculture and Mechanic Arts, Fort Collins, Colo.	1870	Roy M. Green	586	1,510	134	—	108,304
Colorado St. Col. of Edu., Greeley, Colo.	1889	George W. Frasier	629	623	83	—	111,600
Colorado, University of, Boulder, Colo.	1876	Reuben Gilbert Gustavson	2,449	1,104	319	469,762	511,490
Colorado Woman's College (Jr.), Denver, Colo.	1888	J. E. Huchingson	386	—	40	103,029	8,000
**Columbia College, Columbia, S.C.	1854	J. Caldwell Guilds	347	?	30	485,000	15,000
Columbia University, New York, N.Y.	1754	Nicholas M. Butler	10,672	1,436	2,396	89,135,729	1,934,512
Compton Jr. Col., Compton, Calif.	1927	Scott Thompson	3,100	500	88	—	25,000
Concord State Tch. Col., Athens, W.Va.	1875	Joseph Franklin Marsh	276	200	38	—	19,798
Concordia College, Moorhead, Minn.	1891	J. N. Brown	434	—	43	560,616	29,000
Concordia Theol. Seminary, St. Louis, Mo.	1839	Louis J. Sieck	342	—	20	75,000	35,000
Concordia Teachers Col., River Forest, Ill.	1864	Arthur W. Klinck	186	—	27	—	15,000
Concordia Teachers Col., Seward, Neb.	1894	A. O. Fuerbringer	63	—	15	—	9,461
Connecticut, University of, Storrs, Conn.	1881	Albert N. Jorgensen	3,922	850	243	308,182	114,000
Connecticut College, New London, Conn.	1911	Dorothy Schaffter	759	—	95	2,218,000	100,583
Connecticut, Junior College of, Bridgeport, Conn.	1927	E. Everett Cortright	110	—	14	—	7,000
*Conn. Teachers Col., New Britain, Conn.	1849	Herbert D. Welte	375	?	74	—	23,000
Converse College, Spartanburg, S.C.	1889	Edw. M. Gwathmey	388	—	45	602,834	32,000
Cooper Union, New York, N.Y.	1859	Edwin S. Burdell	1,917	—	152	9,381,151	106,698
Copiah-Lincoln Junior College, Wesson, Miss.	1915	J. M. Ewing	200	—	30	—	7,000
Cornell College, Mount Vernon, Iowa	1853	—	420	600	72	2,386,177	60,000
Cornell University, Ithaca, N.Y.	1865	Edmund Ezra Day	3,409	3,796	1,245	33,110,464	1,142,563
**Cortland State Normal Sch., Cortland, N.Y.	1866	H. DeW. DeGroat	470	?	44	—	28,000
Cottey Jr. Col. for Women, Nevada, Mo.	1884	Marjorie Mitchell	157	—	20	50,000	8,000
Creighton University, Omaha, Neb.	1878	Jos. P. Zuercher	780	500	195	—	138,775
Culver-Stockton Col., Canton, Mo.	1853	W. H. McDonald	121	—	23	858,365	28,000
D							
Dakota Wesleyan Univ., Mitchell, S.D.	1885	Joseph H. Edge	250	—	30	633,708	28,872
Dalhousie Univ., Halifax, N.S., Canada	1818	Carleton Stanley	627	291	139	2,782,337	65,811
Dana Col. and Trinity Theol. Sem., Blair, Neb.	1884	Lawrence Siersbeck	76	—	14	172,000	11,000
Danbury State Tch. Col., Danbury, Conn.	1904	Ralph C. Jenkins	177	—	42	—	22,000
**Daniel Baker College, Brownwood, Texas	1889	Thomas H. Hart	304	?	22	181,000	11,000
Dartmouth College, Hanover, N.H.	1769	Ernest M. Hopkins	363	2,010	231	19,715,276	557,613
Davidson College, Davidson, N.C.	1837	John R. Cunningham	246	500	45	3,089,000	42,000
Davis & Elkins College, Elkins, W.Va.	1903	R. B. Purdum	62	200	18	$ 184,193	14,500
Dayton, University of, Dayton, Ohio	1850	John A. Elbert	383	250	90	—	40,000
Defiance College, Defiance, Ohio	1884	H. D. Hopkins	43	—	20	210,345	16,000
*Delaware, University of, Newark, Del.	1833	Walter Hullihen	786	?	164	721,797	93,420
Delta State Tch. Col., Cleveland, Miss.	1924	William M. Kethley	135	—	32	—	20,000
Denison University, Granville, Ohio	1831	Kenneth I. Brown	602	600	80	3,225,882	160,000
Denver, Univ. of, Denver, Colo.	1864	Ben Mark Cherrington	3,500	—	350	2,643,250	175,000
DePaul University, Chicago, Ill.	1898	M. J. O'Connell	1,466	1,351	224	2,000,000	74,086
DePauw University, Greencastle, Ind.	1837	Clyde E. Wildman	899	1,004	93	6,207,853	101,900
Detroit Inst. of Tech., Detroit, Mich.	1891	Paul Hickey	1,700	—	41	100,000	9,800
Detroit, University of, Detroit, Mich.	1877	Charles H. Cloud	909	469	165	1,640,000	120,630
Dickinson College, Carlisle, Pa.	1773	Fred P. Corson	225	700	48	1,600,000	72,000
Dillard University, New Orleans, La.	1930	A. W. Dent	218	—	31	—	30,000
Dixie Junior College, St. George, Utah	1917	Glenn E. Snow	225	—	26	—	9,050
Doane College, Crete, Neb.	1872	Bryant Drake	113	596	35	1,074,730	27,605
Drake University, Des Moines, Iowa	1881	Henry Gadd Harmon	1,589	950	125	1,790,495	107,389
Drew University, Madison, N.J.	1867	Arlo Ayres Brown	376	200	57	6,066,871	191,045
Drexel Inst. of Tech., Philadelphia, Pa.	1891	George Peters Rea	1,076	729	121	2,863,160	79,796
Dropsie College, Philadelphia, Pa.	1905	Abraham A. Neuman	52	—	7	1,298,264	49,828
Drury College, Springfield, Mo.	1873	J. F. Findlay	313	200	36	978,327	60,282
Dubuque, University of, Dubuque, Iowa	1852	Dale D. Welch	206	252	36	717,236	13,951
Duchesne College, Omaha, Neb.	1881	Mother Helen Casey	126	—	16	44,640	16,768
*Duke University, Durham, N.C.	1838	Robert Lee Flowers	3,647	?	511	38,963,698	659,044
Duluth Junior College, Duluth, Minn.	1927	Raymond D. Chadwick	103	—	20	—	8,000
Duluth State Tch. Col., Duluth, Minn.	1895	Herbert Sorenson	251	—	46	23,400	24,940
Duquesne University, Pittsburgh, Pa.	1878	Raymond V. Kirk	548	350	151	2,000,000	45,671
D'Youville College, Buffalo, N.Y.	1908	Sister Grace	300	—	27	—	24,102
E							
Earlham College, Richmond, Ind.	1847	Wm. C. Dennis	258	—	35	1,387,533	65,417
East Carolina Tch. Col., Greenville, N.C.	1907	Leon R. Meadows	939	—	66	—	44,639
East Central Jr. Col., Decatur, Miss.	1914	L. O. Todd	363	—	21	—	6,500
East Central State College, Ada, Okla.	1909	A. Linscheid	739	440	63	—	44,899
Eastern Ill. St. Tch. Col., Charleston, Ill.	1895	Robert G. Buzzard	281	—	70	—	54,000
Eastern Ky. St. Tch. Col., Richmond, Ky.	1906	W. F. O'Donnell	269	911	73	—	66,721
Eastern Mont. St. Norm. Sch., Billings, Mont.	1927	L. B. McMullen	50	—	16	—	15,000
Eastern Nazarene Col., Wollaston, Mass.	1918	G. B. Williamson	256	—	24	—	12,166
Eastern Oregon College of Education, La Grande, Ore.	1929	Roben J. Maaske	110	483	47	—	18,701
Eastern Wash. Col. of Ed., Cheney, Wash.	1890	Ralph E. Tieje	184	—	46	—	50,000
Edinburg Junior College, Edinburg, Texas	1927	H. A. Hodges	102	—	20	—	9,975
Elizabethtown Col., Elizabethtown, Pa.	1899	A. C. Baugher	152	—	17	175,000	13,000
Elmhurst College, Elmhurst, Ill.	1871	Timothy Lehmann	216	—	19	235,999	38,649
Elmira College, Elmira, N.Y.	1855	William S. A. Pott	300	—	46	876,240	53,834
Elon College, Elon College, N.C.	1889	Leon E. Smith	380	250	32	500,000	31,000
Emerson College, Boston, Mass.	1880	Harry Seymour Ross	185	—	22	—	12,766
Emmanuel College, Boston, Mass.	1919	Sister Teresa Patricia	561	—	61	—	26,000
Emmanuel Miss. Col., Berrien Spgs., Mich.	1874	A. W. Johnson	429	—	35	300,000	29,000
Emory and Henry College, Emory, Va.	1836	Foye G. Gibson	81	300	22	549,741	14,500
Emory Junior College, Oxford, Ga.	1929	George S. Roach	214	—	18	—	5,000
Emory University, Emory University, Ga.	1836	Goodrich C. White	932	884	104	7,000,000	216,968
Emporia, College of, Emporia, Kan.	1882	D. A. Hirschler	110	—	25	—	24,272
Erskine College, Due West, S.C.	1839	Robert C. Grier	148	400	35	362,393	26,000
Evangelical Theological Seminary, Naperville, Ill.	1873	H. R. Heininger	76	—	7	582,489	10,500
Evansville College, Evansville, Ind.	1854	Lincoln B. Hale	224	70	31	450,000	20,315
Eveleth Junior College, Eveleth, Minn.	1919	C. H. Gibson	54	—	8	—	12,000
F							
Fairmont St. Tch. Col., Fairmont, W.Va.	1867	Joseph Rosier	530	65	42	—	26,000
*Fayetteville State Tch. Col., Fayetteville, N. C.	1877	J. W. Seabrook	576	—	27	—	16,770
Fenn College, Cleveland, Ohio	1881	Cecil V. Thomas	228	680	71	809,060	20,509
Finch Junior College, New York, N.Y.	1900	Jessica G. Cosgrave	223	—	32	—	7,500
Findlay College, Findlay, Ohio	1882	C. A. Morey	59	—	12	473,094	20,000
*Fisk University, Nashville, Tenn.	1866	Thomas E. Jones	461	?	49	3,194,948	76,000
Flat River, Junior Col. of, Flat River, Mo.	1922	Irvin F. Coyle	65	—	17	—	9,000
Flint Junior College, Flint, Mich.	1922	W. S. Shattuck	160	—	10	—	11,000
Fla. Agri. & Mech. Col. for Negroes, Tallahassee, Fla.	1887	J. R. E. Lee	1,208	—	119	—	16,022
Florida Normal & Industrial Institute (Jr.), St. Augustine, Fla.	1892	William H. Gray, Jr.	470	—	47	—	12,308
*Florida Southern College, Lakeland, Fla.	1885	Ludd M. Spivey	780	?	64	528,000	24,000
Fla. State Col. for Women, Tallahassee, Fla.	1905	Doak S. Campbell	1,992	—	198	—	99,089
Florida, University of, Gainesville, Fla.	1853	John J. Tigert	805	1,468	206	300,000	180,000
Fordham University, New York, N.Y.	1841	Robert I. Gannon	1,193	778	213	717,000	222,245
Fort Hays Kansas State College, Hays, Kansas	1900	Lyman Dwight Wooster	300	400	75	—	50,000

Institution and Location	Year Founded	Chief Executive	Full Time Students	Number Army & Navy Students	Faculty	Endowment	Library Volumes
Frances Shimer College (Jr.), Mount Carroll, Ill.	1853	Albin C. Bro	174	—	20	$ 180,000	12,000
Franklin & Marshall Col., Lancaster, Pa.	1787	Theodore August Distler	744	581	52	1,395,867	91,500
Franklin College, Franklin, Ind.	1834	William G. Spencer	164	—	31	925,000	33,000
Fresno State College, Fresno, Calif.	1911	Frank W. Thomas	981	—	89	—	51,437
Friends University, Wichita, Kan.	1898	W. A. Young	200	—	26	565,000	23,000
Furman University, Greenville, S.C.	1826	John Laney Plyler	638	400	54	2,802,555	55,000
G							
Gallaudet College, Washington, D.C.	1864	Percival Hall	141	—	17	—	10,000
Geneva College, Beaver Falls, Pa.	1848	M. M. Pearce	219	300	37	646,986	35,000
Geo. Peabody Col. for Tch., Nashville, Tenn.	1785	Sidney C. Garrison	671	600	76	5,100,000	157,000
*Georgetown College, Georgetown, Ky.	1829	Samuel S. Hill	165	?	22	500,000	16,000
Georgetown Univ., Washington, D.C.	1789	Lawrence C. Gorman	669	1,784	627	258,887	200,000
Georgetown Visitation Convent (Jr.), Washington, D.C.	1799	Sister Jane Frances Leibell	70	—	18	—	10,000
Geo. Washington Univ., The, Washington, D.C.	1821	Cloyd H. Marvin	11,145	219	412	2,510,000	145,000
George Williams College (Jr.), Chicago, Ill.	1890	Harold Coe Coffman	112	300	49	200,000	18,000
George Williams Col., Sir, Montreal, Can.	1873	K. E. Norris	487	—	100	—	13,190
Georgia Military College (Jr.), Milledgeville, Ga.	1879	J. H. Jenkins	488	—	33	—	2,750
Georgia Sch. of Technology, Atlanta, Ga.	1886	Marion L. Brittain	2,871	2,100	165	550,000	62,000
*Georgia State Col., Industrial College, Ga.	1892	Benjamin F. Hubert	473	?	35	—	12,000
Ga. State Col. for Women, Milledgeville, Ga.	1889	Guy H. Wells	814	800	101	—	32,000
Ga. State Womans Col., Valdosta, Ga.	1906	Frank R. Reade	309	—	24	—	19,097
Georgia, University of, Athens, Ga.	1785	Harmon W. Caldwell	1,581	2,600	169	945,000	172,834
Gettysburg College, Gettysburg, Pa.	1832	Henry W. A. Hanson	300	550	42	825,000	54,035
Glenville State College, Glenville, W.Va.	1872	D. L. Haught	275	—	20	—	20,000
Gonzaga University, Spokane, Wash.	1887	Francis J. Altman	230	291	30	—	42,673
Gordon Military College (Jr.), Barnesville, Georgia	1852	J. E. Guillebeau	350	90	21	50,000	3,650
Gorham Normal School, Gorham, Me.	1878	Francis L. Bailey	170	—	28	—	12,000
Goshen College, Goshen, Ind.	1893	Ernest Edgar Miller	227	—	27	119,458	25,300
Goucher College, Baltimore, Md.	1885	David A. Robertson	524	—	73	2,132,660	78,201
Graceland College (Jr.), Lamoni, Iowa	1895	G. N. Briggs	195	—	22	250,000	18,300
Grand Rapids Junior College, Grand Rapids, Michigan	1914	Arthur Andrews	283	—	23	—	12,956
Grand Rapids, University of, Grand Rapids, Mich.	1936	Paul F. Voelker	440	—	18	—	5,000
Grand Séminaire Mazenod, Gravelbourg, Saskatchewan, Canada	1931	Rev. Wilfrid Piédalue	9	—	5	—	1,200
*Great Falls, Col. of, Great Falls, Mont.	1932	J. J. Donovan	400	?	34	—	30,000
Green Mountain Junior Col., Poultney, Vt.	1834	Jesse Parker Bogue	200	—	25	81,000	12,000
Greensboro College, Greensboro, N. C.	1838	Luther L. Gobbel	407	—	36	512,060	24,000
**Greenville College, Greenville, Ill.	1892	H. J. Long	220	?	20	125,000	13,000
Grinnell College, Grinnell, Iowa	1846	Samuel N. Stevens	325	1,000	70	3,114,845	111,000
Grove City College, Grove City, Pa.	1876	Weir C. Ketler	483	530	96	837,812	43,000
Guilford College, Guilford College, N.C.	1837	Clyde A. Milner	186	—	21	592,973	25,150
Gulf Park College (Jr.), Gulfport, Miss.	1921	Richard G. Cox	250	—	30	—	6,699
Gustavus Adolphus Col., St. Peter, Minn.	1862	Walter A. Lunden	129	401	37	561,480	30,621
H							
Hamilton College, Clinton, N.Y.	1812	W. H. Cowley	51	550	88	6,996,361	201,192
Hamline University, St. Paul, Minn.	1854	Charles Nelson Pace	479	—	52	2,005,300	44,400
Hampden-Sydney Col., Hamp.-Sydney, Va.	1776	E. G. Gammon	63	250	19	373,000	33,000
Hampton Institute, Hampton, Va.	1868	Ralph P. Bridgman	785	702	107	—	68,000
**Hannibal-LaGrange Col., Hannibal, Mo.	1857	A. E. Prince	143	?	20	50,000	6,985
Hanover College, Hanover, Ind.	1827	Albert G. Parker, Jr.	150	—	15	1,600,000	43,000
Hardin College (Jr.), Wichita Falls, Texas	1922	James B. Boren	319	120	28	350,000	7,000
**Harding College, Searcy, Ark	1924	George S. Benson	523	?	36	25,500	18,000
Hardin-Simmons Univ., Abilene, Tex.	1891	Rupert N. Richardson	618	—	45	1,250,000	30,000
Harris Teachers College, St. Louis, Mo.	1904	Charles H. Philpott	350	—	34	—	23,146
Hartwick College, Oneonta, N.Y.	1928	H. J. Arnold	110	—	23	120,000	15,000
Harvard University, Cambridge, Mass.	1636	James B. Conant	1,706	8,000	1,814	150,000,000	5,000,000
Hastings College, Hastings, Neb.	1882	Wm. M. French	182	200	32	698,549	32,000
Haverford College, Haverford, Pa.	1833	Felix Morley	129	373	58	4,380,188	157,000
Hawaii, University of, Honolulu, Hawaii	1907	Gregg M. Sinclair	1,500	299	123	35,468	151,614
Hebrew Union College, Cincinnati, Ohio	1875	Julian Morgenstern	58	—	11	2,150,000	100,000
Heidelberg College, Tiffin, Ohio	1850	Clarence E. Josephson	496	250	35	970,400	33,000
Henderson St. Tch. Col., Arkadelphia, Ark.	1929	Matt L. Ellis	223	250	44	—	24,891
Hendrix College, Conway, Ark.	1884	John Hugh Reynolds	239	250	40	1,000,000	45,250
**Hesston Col. & Bible Sch., Hesston, Kan.	1908	Milo F. Kauffman	185	?	12	35,000	5,500
Hibbing Junior College, Hibbing, Minn.	1916	H. A. Drescher	176	150	22	—	5,384
Highland Park Jr. Col., Highland Park, Mich.	1917	H. Herbert Harbison	127	90	11	—	6,500
High Point College, High Point, N.C.	1924	Gideon I. Humphreys	257	200	28	137,218	14,841
Hillsdale College, Hillsdale, Mich.	1844	Harvey L. Turner	175	—	22	752,489	28,500

Institution and Location	Year Founded	Chief Executive	Full Time Students	Number Army & Navy Students	Faculty	Endowment	Library Volumes
*Hillyer Jr. Col., Hartford, Conn.	1883	Alan S. Wilson	160	?	69	$ 100,000	5,000
Hinds Jr. Col., Raymond, Miss.	1917	George M. McLendon	287	—	21	—	5,400
Hiram College, Hiram, Ohio	1850	Paul H. Fall	180	250	28	1,004,294	40,000
Hobart and William Smith Colleges, Geneva, New York	1822	John Milton Potter	217	377	59	1,436,361	114,986
Hollins College, Hollins College, Va.	1842	Bessie C. Randolph	331	—	39	441,552	37,400
Holy Cross, Col. of the, Worcester, Mass.	1843	Joseph R. N. Maxwell	254	621	90	—	130,000
*Holy Heart Seminary, Halifax, N.S., Can.	1895	Julien Deville	68	?	8	68,000	8,600
Holy Names, Col. of the, Oakland, Calif.	1868	Sister Mary Loyola	299	—	42	—	—
Holy Names College, Spokane, Wash.	1907	M. Elizabeth Clare	131	—	24	—	14,500
Hood College, Frederick, Md.	1893	Henry I. Stahr	436	—	47	413,167	25,000
Hope College, Holland, Mich.	1866	Wynand Wichers	276	250	36	825,000	36,000
Houghton College, Houghton, N.Y.	1883	Stephen W. Paine	293	—	32	274,929	19,000
Houston College for Negroes, Houston, Tex.	1927	E. E. Oberholtzer	399	—	22	—	7,789
Houston, University of, Houston, Texas	1927	Edison E. Oberholtzer	1,073	549	41	—	20,821
**Howard College, Birmingham, Ala.	1842	Harwell G. Davis	648	?	54	750,000	32,000
Howard Payne College, Brownwood, Tex.	1889	Thomas H. Taylor	473	—	28	610,000	23,000
Howard University, Washington, D.C.	1867	M. W. Johnson	2,567	534	265	1,025,119	202,784
Hunter College, New York, N.Y.	1870	George N. Shuster	5,638	—	380	129,276	148,700
Huntingdon College, Montgomery, Ala.	1854	Hubert Searcy	500	—	30	400,000	20,000
Huntington College, Huntington, Ind.	1896	Elmer Becker	67	—	16	95,000	13,522
Huron College, Huron, S.D.	1883	George F. McDougall	80	82	22	732,111	23,760
I							
**Idaho, The College of, Caldwell, Ida.	1891	William W. Hall, Jr.	300	?	29	525,000	18,000
Idaho, So. Branch of the Univ. (Jr.), Pocatello, Ida.	1927	John R. Nichols	705	400	78	—	23,000
Idaho, University of, Moscow, Ida.	1889	Harrison C. Dale	870	1,300	193	2,300,000	103,000
Illinois College, Jacksonville, Ill.	1829	H. Gary Hudson	96	250	34	1,133,710	32,486
Illinois Institute of Technology, Chicago, Ill. (formerly Armour Institute [1892] and Lewis Institute [1877]	1940	H. T. Heald	1,103	1,173	242	2,034,093	90,306
Illinois State Normal Univ., Normal, Ill.	1857	R. W. Fairchild	1,078	299	170	—	102,000
Illinois, University of, Urbana, Ill.	1868	Arthur C. Willard	13,472	5,166	2,364	1,454,645	1,759,851
Ill. Wesleyan Univ., Bloomington, Ill.	1850	William E. Shaw	318	110	43	1,400,000	45,000
Immaculate Conc. Sem. Huntington, L.I., N.Y.	1926	Patrick J. Barry	209	—	17	—	50,000
Immaculata Jr. College and Seminary, Washington, D.C.	1905	Sister Eugenia Clare	360	—	20	—	8,000
Incarnate Word Col., San Antonio, Tex.	1900	Sister M. Columkille	508	—	67	—	33,147
Indiana Central Col., Indianapolis, Ind.	1902	I. J. Good	140	—	23	98,161	15,451
Ind. State Tch. Col., Terre Haute, Ind.	1865	Ralph Noble Tirey	666	380	80	—	—
Indiana University, Bloomington, Ind.	1820	Herman B. Wells	3,557	3,153	450	2,638,426	500,000
Iowa State College, Ames, Iowa	1858	Charles E. Friley	4,500	3,500	600	1,200,000	350,000
Iowa State Tch. Col., Cedar Falls, Iowa	1876	Malcolm Price	818	—	120	—	123,492
Iowa, State University of, Iowa City, Ia.	1847	Virgil Hancher	2,884	3,641	746	1,002,075	604,746
*Iowa Wesleyan Col., Mt. Pleasant, Ia.	1842	Stanley B. Niles	302	?	26	574,738	27,500
Ithaca College, Ithaca, N.Y.	1892	Leonard B. Job	225	—	41	—	5,000
J							
Jackson Jr. College, Jackson, Mich.	1928	G. L. Greenawalt	54	—	14	—	4,960
James Millikin University, Decatur, Ill.	1901	John C. Hessler	276	300	50	1,039,703	36,000
James Ormond Wilson Tch.Col., Wash.D.C.	1873	Walter E. Hager	253	—	44	—	22,020
Jamestown College, Jamestown, N.D.	1884	B. H. Kroeze	163	600	42	1,058,399	16,700
Jean-de-Brébeuf, Collège, Montreal, Que., Can.	1928	Jean Laramée	635	—	50	—	14,500
John B. Stetson University, De Land, Fla.	1883	William S. Allen	305	440	52	900,000	45,000
John Brown Univ., Siloam Springs, Ark.	1919	John E. Brown	300	—	40	2,000,000	12,000
John Carroll University, Cleveland, Ohio.	1886	Thomas J. Donnelly	79	400	40	2,500,000	35,707
John McNeese Jr. Col., L.S.U., Lake Charles, La.	1939	Rodney Cline	200	200	28	—	4,000
John Tarleton Agri. Col. (Jr.), Stephenville, Texas.	1917	J. Thomas Davis	335	500	70	133,000	29,389
Johns Hopkins Univ., Baltimore, Md.	1876	Isaiah Bowman	698	650	650	30,667,644	689,024
Johnson C. Smith Univ., Charlotte, N.C.	1867	Henry L. McCrorey	352	—	24	465,162	24,808
Joliet Junior College, Joliet, Ill.	1901	Roosevelt Basler	176	—	26 p't time	—	11,420
Jones County Jr. Col., Ellisville, Miss.	1927	J. B. Young	717	—	35	—	13,631
Judson College, Marion, Ala.	1838	John Ingle Riddle	215	—	32	520,000	18,000
Juniata College, Huntingdon, Pa.	1876	Charles C. Ellis	239	—	29	717,376	50,000
K							
Kalamazoo College, Kalamazoo, Mich.	1833	Paul L. Thompson	214	225	37	1,265,602	34,434
Kansas City, Jr. Col. of, Kansas City, Mo.	1915	A. M. Swanson	700	—	43	—	21,000
Kansas City, Univ. of, Kansas City, Mo.	1929	Clarence R. Decker	689	60	117	1,000	100,000
Kan. State Col., Manhattan, Kan.	1863	Milton S. Eisenhower	1,350	1,625	330	505,000	145,300
Kan. St. Tch. Col., Emporia, Kan.	1863	James F. Price	381	500	108	—	84,000
Kan. State Teachers Col., Pittsburg, Kan.	1903	Rees H. Hughes	424	250	93	—	70,684
Kansas, University of, Lawrence, Kan.	1865	Deane W. Malott	4,107	2,131	300	256,000	350,000

Institution and Location	Year Founded	Chief Executive	Full Time Students	Number Army & Navy Students	Faculty	Endow-ment	Library Volumes
*Kansas Wesleyan University, Salina, Kan.	1886	Edgar K. Morrow	441	—	35	$ 521,322	20,000
Keene Teachers College, Keene, N.H.	1909	L. P. Young	202	93	41	—	25,000
Kemper Military School (Jr.), Boonville, Mo.	1844	A. M. Hitch	522	—	50	—	8,250
Kemptville Agricultural School, Kemptville, Ont., Can.	1917	M. C. McPhail	44	—	5	—	300
Kent State University, Kent, Ohio	1910	Raymond M. Clark	—	570	130	—	77,724
Kentucky St. Col., Frankfort, Ky.	1886	Rufus B. Atwood	283	—	38	—	18,000
Kentucky, Univ. of, Lexington, Ky.	1865	Herman Lee Donovan	1,352	1,208	234	184,075	337,000
Kentucky Wesleyan Col., Winchester, Ky.	1866	Paul Shell Powell	94	—	18	93,466	17,421
Kenyon College, Gambier, Ohio	1824	Gordon K. Chalmers	91	400	61	1,657,222	72,000
Keuka College, Keuka Park, N.Y.	1890	Henry E. Allen	286	—	34	346,848	23,301
Kilgore College (Jr.), Kilgore, Tex.	1935	B. E. Masters	548	100	25	—	7,460
King College, Bristol, Tenn.	1867	R. T. L. Liston	55	160	15	100,000	5,000
King's College, Univ. of Halifax, N.S., Can.	1789	A. Stanley Walker	46	—	10	900,000	30,000
Kletzing College, University Park, Iowa	1906	C. W. Butler	90	—	14	30,000	15,000
Knox College, Galesburg, Ill.	1837	Carter Davidson	346	600	61	2,639,357	67,280
Knoxville College, Knoxville, Tenn.	1875	Wm. Lloyd Imes	200	—	30	600,000	12,500
L							
Lafayette College, Easton, Pa.	1826	William M. Lewis	240	1,161	103	4,065,000	120,000
LaGrange College, LaGrange, Ga.	1831	Hubert T. Quillian	210	—	18	—	12,850
Lake Erie College, Painesville, Ohio	1856	Helen D. Bragdon	148	—	25	793,115	31,822
Lake Forest College, Lake Forest, Ill.	1857	Ernest A. Johnson	200	400	30	1,354,074	53,116
Lamar College (Jr.), Beaumont, Tex.	1923	John E. Gray	820	—	21	—	4,787
Lambuth College, Jackson, Tenn.	1924	R. E. Womack	118	—	16	10,000	8,000
Lander College, Greenwood, S.C.	1872	John Marvin Rast	240	—	28	214,880	16,000
Lane College, Jackson, Tenn.	1882	James F. Lane	386	—	25	30,000	12,500
**Langston University, Langston, Okla.	1897	G. L. Harrison	562	?	75	—	8,892
LaSalle-Peru-Oglesby Jr. Col., LaSalle, Ill.	1924	Frank A. Jensen	62	—	21	—	10,000
La Sierra College (Jr.), Arlington, Calif.	1922	L. R. Rasmussen	367	—	45	—	10,350
Laval University, Quebec, Canada	1852	Cyrille Gagnon	3,711	1,766	651	2,500,000	544,000
LaVerne College, LaVerne, Calif.	1891	C. Ernest Davis	81	—	22	52,902	8,752
Lawrence College, Appleton, Wis.	1847	Ralph J. Watts	427	300	50	1,518,500	69,000
Lebanon Valley College, Annville, Pa.	1866	Clyde A. Lynch	203	—	25	806,504	27,419
**Lehigh University, Bethlehem, Pa.	1865	Clement C. Williams	1,748	?	155	6,901,207	248,165
Leland College, Baker, La.	1870	James M. Frazier	370	—	20	110,000	6,500
LeMoyne College, Memphis, Tenn.	1871	Hollis F. Price	262	—	30	—	20,000
Lenoir-Rhyne College, Hickory, N.C.	1891	P. E. Monroe	361	100	34	671,331	26,530
Lesley School, Cambridge, Mass.	1909	Marguerite Franklin	69	—	27	—	—
Lévis, Collège de, Lévis, Province de Quebec, Canada	1853	Léopold Roberge	775	190	74	—	33,000
Lewiston State Norm. Sch., Lewiston, Ida.	1893	Glenn W. Todd	101	100	30	—	17,000
Limestone College, Gaffney, S.C.	1845	R. C. Granberry	350	—	35	515,000	1,900
Lincoln College (Jr.), Lincoln, Ill.	1865	William D. Copeland	50	—	12	275,000	11,000
Lincoln Institute, Lincoln Ridge, Ky.	1911	Walter K. Belknap	270	—	16	225,000	5,144
Lincoln Memorial Univ., Harrogate, Tenn.	1897	S. W. McClelland	201	—	28	859,206	19,989
Lincoln University, Jefferson City, Mo.	1866	Sherman D. Scruggs	396	—	61	—	23,047
Lincoln University, Lincoln Univ., Pa.	1854	Walter L. Wright	140	—	20	1,027,198	38,000
Lindenwood College, St. Charles, Mo.	1827	Harry Morehouse Gage	489	—	51	2,277,291	26,345
Little Rock Junior Col., Little Rock, Ark.	1927	J. A. Larson	200	76	18	1,000,000	16,000
*Linfield College, McMinnville, Ore.	1858	Wm. G. Everson	368	?	34	929,282	28,742
Livingstone College, Salisbury, N.C.	1879	William J. Trent	269	—	19	46,500	19,043
Long Beach Jr. Col., Long Beach, Calif.	1927	George E. Dotson	534	—	23	—	30,000
Long Island University, Brooklyn, N.Y.	1886	Tristram W. Metcalfe	549	—	75	500,000	26,600
Lon Morris Col. (Jr.), Jacksonville, Texas	1873	C. E. Peeples	94	90	14	110,000	7,550
Loras College, Dubuque, Iowa	1839	M. J. Martin	348	90	38	1,400,000	92,000
*Loretto Heights College, Loretto, Colo.	1891	Paul J. Ketrick	141	?	34	—	15,465
Los Angeles City College (Jr.), Los Angeles, Calif.	1929	Rosco C. Ingalls	3,087	1,025	150	—	53,729
**Louisburg College, Louisburg, N.C.	1779	Walter Patten	296	?	23	61,000	6,578
Louisiana College, Pineville, La.	1906	Edgar Godbold	275	—	25	313,015	13,208
Louisiana Polytechnic Inst., Ruston, La.	1894	Claybrook Cottingham	1,623	600	110	—	29,997
La. State Norm. Col., Natchitoches, La.	1884	Joe Farrar	575	700	125	—	43,662
Louisiana State Univ. and A. & M. College, Baton Rouge, La.	1860	C. B. Hodges	3,976	1,726	492	14,556	327,732
Louisville, Univ. of, Louisville, Kentucky	1837	Einar William Jacobsen	1,945	967	289	1,040,535	119,233
**Lowell Textile Institute, Lowell, Mass.	1895	Charles H. Eames	290	?	40	—	2,915
Loyola College, Baltimore, Md.	1852	Edward B. Bunn	306	—	27	1,350,000	34,000
Loyola College, Montreal, Que. Can	1895	Edward M. Brown	585	—	27	—	20,642
Loyola University, Chicago, Ill.	1870	Joseph M. Egan	3,540	520	750	1,252,450	104,855
Loyola University, Los Angeles, Calif.	1865	Edward J. Whelan	320	250	48	—	34,000
Loyola University, New Orleans, La.	1912	Percy A. Roy	505	140	154	5,000,000	102,346
Lutheran College and Seminary, The, Saskatoon, Saskatchewan, Canada	1913	N. Willison	9	—	5	2,200	4,300
Luther College, Decorah, Iowa	1861	O. J. H. Preus	220	—	22	531,609	72,000
Lynchburg College, Lynchburg, Va.	1903	R. B. Montgomery	145	260	25	296,949	22,000
Lyons Township Jr. Col., La Grange, Ill.	1929	Ross Holt	120	—	4	—	17,000

Institution and Location	Year Founded	Chief Executive	Full Time Students	Number Army & Navy Students	Faculty	Endow-ment	Library Volumes
M							
Macalester College, St. Paul, Minn.	1885	C. E. Ficken	420	—	63	$ 2,350,000	40,000
McGill University, Montreal, Canada	1821	F. Cyril James	2,813	250	564	23,470,474	421,984
**McKendree College, Lebanon, Ill.	1828	Clark R. Yost	179	?	22	300,000	16,000
McMaster Univ., Hamilton, Ont., Can.	1887	George P. Gilmour	651	50	51	1,750,000	56,000
MacMurray College for Women, Jacksonville, Ill.	1846	C. P. McClelland	715	—	61	3,820,535	35,924
**McMurry College, Abilene, Texas	1921	Frank L. Turner	410	?	34	60,000	13,500
McPherson College, McPherson, Kan.	1887	W. W. Peters	131	—	21	334,701	15,000
Madison College, Harrisburg, Va.	1908	Samuel P. Duke	1,016	—	81	45,000	36,446
Madison College, Madison College, Tenn.	1904	E. A. Sutherland	164	—	22	—	23,000
Maine St. Normal School, Farmington, Me.	1864	Lorey C. Day	455	—	32	—	10,000
Maine, University of, Orono, Me.	1865	Arthur A. Hauck	884	916	136	1,091,104	197,346
Manchester College, No. Manchester, Ind.	1889	Vernon F. Schwalm	360	—	35	593,100	30,000
Manhattan College, New York, N.Y.	1863	Brother A. Victor	572	574	88	—	90,000
*Manhattanville Col. of Sac. Hrt., N.Y.	1847	Grace C. Dammann	387	?	68	346,720	46,750
Manitoba, The University of, Winnipeg, Manitoba, Canada	1877	Sidney Earle Smith	2,335	—	225	967,982	110,500
Marian College, Indianapolis, Indiana	1937	Mother M. Clarissa	140	—	24	—	17,500
**Marietta College, Marietta, Ohio	1797	Harry Kelso Eversull	318	?	38	1,274,861	119,056
Marin Junior College, Kentfield, Calif.	1926	Ward H. Austin	124	—	20	—	12,500
Marion College, Marion, Ind.	1920	Wm. F. McConn	260	—	20	75,000	16,000
Marquette University, Milwaukee, Wis.	1881	R. C. McCarthy	1,389	1,031	438	2,062,674	136,000
Mars Hill Jr. Col., Mars Hill, N.C.	1856	Hoyt Blackwell	657	—	46	124,593	18,500
**Martin Luther Col., New Ulm, Minn.	1884	Carl L. Schweppe	212	?	13	—	10,000
Mary Baldwin College, Staunton, Va.	1842	L. Wilson Jarman	323	—	31	539,373	29,066
Marygrove College, Detroit, Mich.	1910	Sister M. Honora	705	—	72	—	39,540
Mary Hardin-Baylor College, Belton, Tex.	1845	Gordon G. Singleton	298	—	36	825,000	33,500
Maryland Col. for Women, Lutherville, Md.	1853	Wm. H. Moore, III	180	—	16	—	11,000
Maryland St. Tch. Col., Bowie, Md.	1867	William E. Henry	107	—	12	—	10,930
Maryland, Univ. of, College Park, Md.	1807	H. C. Byrd	1,726	1,051	851	2,200,000	170,000
Marymount College, Salina, Kan.	1922	Mother Chrysostom	193	—	28	—	18,000
Marymount College, Tarrytown, N.Y.	1907	M. Therese Dalton	260	—	39	1,000,000	26,750
Maryville College, Maryville, Tenn.	1819	Ralph W. Lloyd	421	300	42	1,857,248	51,423
Maryville Col. of the Sac. Heart, St. Louis, Mo.	1872	Mother Marie Odeide Mouton	189	—	28	300,000	20,805
Mary Washington Col., Fredericksburg, Va.	1908	Morgan L. Combs	1,995	—	156	—	60,000
Marywood College, Scranton, Pa.	1915	Sister M. Sylvia	374	—	44	60,000	34,327
Mason City Junior Col., Mason City, Iowa	1918	James Rae	—	—	13	—	6,000
Mass. Inst. of Tech., Cambridge, Mass.	1861	Karl T. Compton	1,579	2,016	683	26,655,637	365,000
Mass. State College, Amherst, Mass.	1863	Hugh P. Baker	734	—	135	—	130,181
Mass. State Tch. Col., Bridgewater, Mass.	1840	John J. Kelly	305	—	39	15,000	20,185
Mass. State Tch. Col., Fitchburg, Mass.	1894	Charles M. Herlihy	200	100	42	—	29,000
Mass. State Tch. Col., Framingham, Mass.	1839	Martin F. O'Connor	417	—	35	—	18,000
Mass. State Tch. Col., Hyannis, Mass.	1897	Anson B. Handy	60	200	18	—	14,000
Mass. State Tch. Col., Salem, Mass.	1854	Edward A. Sullivan	312	—	40	—	15,000
Mass. State Tch. Col., Westfield, Mass.	1839	Edward J. Scanlon	70	—	24	—	16,500
Mass. State Tch. Col., Worcester, Mass.	1871	Clinton E. Carpenter	121	—	19	—	16,000
Memphis State College, Memphis, Tenn.	1909	Jennings B. Sanders	188	—	57	—	35,000
Mercer University, Macon, Ga.	1833	Spright Dowell	386	325	46	1,500,000	69,000
Mercyhurst College, Erie, Pa.	1926	Mother M. Borgia	250	—	32	1,600,000	16,000
Meredith College, Raleigh, N.C.	1891	Carlyle Campbell	468	—	38	553,396	26,875
Miami, Univ. of, Coral Gables, Fla.	1925	Bowman Foster Ashe	616	897	63	—	65,350
Miami University, Oxford, Ohio	1809	A. H. Upham	1,649	650	223	—	179,500
Michigan, University of, Ann Arbor, Mich.	1817	Alexander G. Ruthven	6,225	3,650	821	16,122,339	1,193,486
Mich. Col. of Mng. & Tech., Houghton, Mich.	1885	Grover C. Dillman	146	490	80	—	45,000
Michigan State Col. of Agriculture and Applied Science, E. Lansing, Mich.	1855	John A. Hannah	3,100	3,500	506	1,871,015	173,304
Mich. State Normal Col., Ypsilanti, Mich.	1849	John M. Munson	641	300	171	70,000	112,225
Middlebury College, Middlebury, Vt.	1800	Samuel S. Stratton	561	457	64	4,205,000	152,497
Middlesex University, Boston, Mass.	1849	Samuel H. Wragg	550	—	80	—	6,000
Midland College and Western Theological Seminary, Fremont, Neb.	1887	F. C. Wiegman	162	—	30	161,142	22,583
Middle Tennessee State College, Murfreesboro, Tenn.	1909	Q. M. Smith	350	300	52	—	28,000
Miles College, Birmingham, Ala.	1907	W. A. Bell	348	—	22	—	10,000
Milligan College, Milligan College, Tenn.	1875	C. E. Burns	—	300	24	130,000	16,449
Mills College, Oakland, Calif.	1852	Lynn T. White, Jr.	614	—	89	2,084,960	90,000
Millsaps College, Jackson, Miss.	1892	Marion L. Smith	283	380	40	760,000	35,000
Milton College, Milton, Wis.	1867	J. G. Meyer	160	—	15	225,000	16,000
Milwaukee-Downer Col., Milwaukee, Wis.	1851	Lucia R. Briggs	349	—	49	2,180,740	44,146
Milwaukee School of Eng., Mlwke., Wis.	1903	Oscar Werwath	500	—	29	—	—
Minn., University of, Minneapolis, Minn.	1851	Walter C. Coffey	8,122	—	1,632	23,266,507	1,309,176
Minn. State Tch. Col., Bemidji, Minn.	1913	A. C. Clark	141	—	36	—	21,000
Minn. State Tch. Col., Mankato, Minn.	1868	Frank D. McElroy	330	—	57	—	27,000
Minn. State Tch. Col., St. Cloud, Minn.	1869	Dudley S. Brainard	330	404	75	—	49,000
Minn. State Tch. Col., Winona, Minn.	1858	A. T. French	209	—	38	—	22,000
Misericordia College, Dallas, Pa.	1925	Sister Mary Borromeo	200	—	40	1,100,000	19,800
*Mission House College, Plymouth, Wis.	1862	Paul Grosshuesch	125	?	20	68,000	25,440

Institution and Location	Year Founded	Chief Executive	Full Time Students	Number Army & Navy Students	Faculty	Endow-ment	Library Volumes
Mississippi College, Clinton, Miss.	1826	D. M. Nelson	545	350	30	$ 651,000	28,000
Miss. So. Col., Hattiesburg, Miss.	1910	J. B. George	300	700	85	—	30,000
Miss. State Col., State College, Miss.	1878	G. D. Humphrey	400	—	100	239,787	88,523
Miss. St. Col. for Women, Columbus, Miss.	1884	B. L. Parkinson	900	—	80	—	58,000
Mississippi, University of, Oxford, Miss.	1844	Alfred B. Butts	625	1,100	100	—	110,000
Missouri, University of, Columbia, Mo.	1839	F. A. Middlebush	1,789	2,760	350	1,992,327	475,000
Missouri Valley College, Marshall, Mo.	1889	William Roy Mitchell	329	264	25	561,390	27,191
**Mitchell College, Statesville, N.C.	1853	Grace K. Ramsay	200	?	15	10,000	5,204
Modesto Junior College, Modesto, Calif.	1921	Chas. D. Yates	337	—	34	—	22,717
Monmouth College, Monmouth, Ill.	1853	James Harper Grier	250	600	67	1,837,316	40,000
Montana School of Mines, Butte, Mont.	1893	Francis A. Thomson	350	328	25	800,000	20,000
Montana State College, Bozeman, Mont.	1893	Roland R. Renne	935	1,000	175	1,894,838	63,167
Montana State Normal Col., Dillon, Mont.	1893	Sheldon E. Davis	40	—	9	—	26,000
Montana State Univ., Missoula, Mont.	1893	Charles W. Leaphart	660	1,000	81	863,339	252,818
Monticello College (Jr.), Godfrey, Ill.	1838	George I. Rohrbaugh	317	—	35	—	17,000
Montréal, Collège de, Montreal, Que., Can.	1767	Emile Lépine	400	32	34	—	25,000
Montréal, Université de, Mont., Que., Can.	1876	Olivier Maurault	8,729	2,252	950	—	75,000
Moorhead St. Tch. Col., Moorhead, Minn.	1887	O. W. Snarr	214	500	61	—	27,778
Moravian Sem. & Col. for Wom., Beth., Pa.	1742	Edwin J. Heath	285	—	35	285,000	11,000
Morehead St. Tch. Col., Morehead, Ky.	1922	W. H. Vaughan	125	600	46	—	24,353
Morgan Park Junior College, Chicago, Ill.	1933	Albert G. Dodd	130	—	15	—	4,500
Morgan St. College, Baltimore, Md.	1867	D. O. W. Holmes	435	—	28	—	3,821
Morningside College, Sioux City, Iowa	1889	Earl A. Roadman	371	—	63	313,486	48,454
Morris Brown College, Atlanta, Ga.	1881	W. A. Fountain, Jr.	432	—	31	107,476	5,706
Morris Harvey College, Charleston, W.Va.	1888	Leonard Riggleman	200	—	30	300,000	11,000
Morton Junior College, Cicero, Illinois	1924	William P. MacLean	130	—	225	—	14,602
Mount Allison Univ., Sackville, N.B., Can.	1840	George J. Trueman	521	50	60	1,217,649	51,054
Mt. Angel Col. & Sem., St. Benedict, Ore.	1887	Thomas Meier	85	—	20	48,000	36,000
Mount Holyoke Col., So. Hadley, Mass.	1837	Roswell G. Ham	1,056	250	140	5,482,339	186,034
**Mount Royal College, Calgary, Alta., Can.	1910	George W. Kerby	165	?	20	—	2,000
**Mt. St. Jos.-on-the-Ohio, Col. of, Cincin., O.	1920	Mother Mary Regina	276	?	41	635,000	18,000
Mt. St. Mary Sem., Norwood, Ohio	1825	James W. O'Brien	195	—	16	—	—
Mt. St. Mary's Col., Emmitsburg, Md.	1808	John L. Sheridan	420	320	41	350,000	52,000
Mt. St. Mary's Col., Los Angeles, Calif.	1925	Mother Marie de Lourdes	200	—	35	—	16,000
Mt. St. Scholastica Col., Atchison, Kan.	1863	Mother Lucy Dooley	313	—	37	—	24,000
*Mt. St. Vincent, College of, New York, N.Y.	1910	Sister Catharine Marie	376	?	48	—	27,211
Mount Union College, Alliance, Ohio	1846	Charles B. Ketcham	281	300	39	1,517,358	70,000
Muhlenberg College, Allentown, Pa.	1848	Levering Tyson	140	562	51	1,000,600	65,000
Multnomah College (Jr.), Portland, Ore.	1897	Edward L. Clark	111	—	15	25,500	6,384
Mundelein College for Women, Chicago, Ill.	1930	Sister Mary Justitia Coffey	602	—	58	—	23,684
Murray State Teachers Col., Murray, Ky.	1923	James H. Richmond	321	600	87	—	40,000
Muskegon Junior Col., Muskegon, Mich.	1926	A. G. Umbreit	103	—	12	—	140,000
Muskingum College, New Concord, Ohio.	1837	Robt. N. Montgomery	400	300	70	900,000	35,000
N							
Nasson College, Springvale, Me.	1912	Dawn N. Wallace	150	—	20	—	5,000
National College of Edu., Evanston, Ill.	1886	Edna Dean Baker	341	—	48	117,717	28,980
**National University, Washington, D.C.	1869	Leslie C. Garnett	—	?	52	—	14,000
*Nazareth College, Nazareth, Mich.	1924	Sister M. Kevin	196	?	39	—	22,000
Nazareth College and Academy (Jr.), Nazareth, Ky.	1814	Sister Margaret Gertrude	171	—	31	—	16,000
Nebraska Central Col., Central City, Neb.	1899	O. W. Carrell	43	—	7	50,000	5,000
Neb. State Teachers Col., Chadron, Neb.	1911	Wiley G. Brooks	486	86	42	—	28,000
Nebraska, University of, Lincoln, Neb.	1869	C. S. Boucher	2,654	2,105	467	42,340	389,141
Neb. Wesleyan Univ., Lincoln, Neb.	1887	Benj. F. Schwartz	235	—	38	967,953	33,208
Nevada, University of, Reno, Nev.	1874	C. H. Gorman	412	—	75	459,986	67,577
*Newark Col. of Engin., Newark, N.J.	1881	Allan R. Cullimore	795	?	76	97,505	18,343
Newark, University of, Newark, N.J.	1934	George H. Black	491	—	18	162,557	25,000
Newberry College, Newberry, S.C.	1856	James C. Kinard	140	330	32	330,000	21,000
New Bruns., Univ. of, Fredericton, N.B., Can.	1800	Norman MacKenzie	365	75	26	—	30,000
Newcomb Mem. Col., New Orleans, La.	1886	Frederick Hard	755	—	72	2,748,541	300,000
New Hampshire, Univ. of, Durham, N.H.	1866	Fred Engelhardt	1,061	891	172	1,275,108	123,493
New Haven St. Tch. Col., N. H., Conn.	1893	E. W. Ireland	302	—	24	—	20,000
**N. J. State Tch. Col., Newark, N.J.	1913	Roy L. Shaffer	468	?	42	—	35,655
N. J. State Tch. Col., Trenton, N.J.	1855	Roscoe L. West	751	—	70	—	42,000
N. J. St. Tch. Col., Montclair, N.J.	1908	Harry A. Sprague	561	—	49	—	46,000
N.M. Col. Agri. & Mech. Arts, St. Col., N.M.	1889	J. W. Branson	177	412	85	416,419	48,000
New Mex. Mil. Inst. (Jr.), Roswell, N.M.	1893	Daniel C. Pearson	565	—	33	—	20,000
New Mex. School of Mines, Socorro, N.M.	1889	R. H. Reece	14	300	21	—	6,000
N. Mex. St. Tch. Col., Silver City, N.M.	1893	Haddon W. James	101	—	41	—	27,625
New Mex., Univ. of, Albuquerque, N.M.	1889	James F. Zimmerman	1,025	753	125	—	96,749
New Rochelle, Col. of, New Rochelle, N.Y.	1904	Francis W. Walsh	805	—	68	41,794	50,878
N. Y., Col. of the City of, N. Y., N.Y.	1848	Harry N. Wright	5,164	2,200	550	531,847	281,515
N. Y. St. Col. of Forestry, Syracuse, N.Y.	1911	Samuel N. Spring	112	1,000 p't time	33	—	14,768
N. Y. St. Col. for Tch., Albany, N.Y.	1844	John M. Sayles	917	—	96	—	34,300
New York State Teachers College, Brockport, N.Y.	1867	E. C. Hartwell	275	—	37	—	18,000

Institution and Location	Year Founded	Chief Executive	Full Time Students	Number Army & Navy Students	Faculty	Endow-ment	Library Volumes
N. Y. State Tch. Col., Buffalo, N.Y.	1872	Harry W. Rockwell	842	—	79	—	27,923
N. Y. St. Tch. Col., Fredonia, N.Y.	1866	Leslie R. Gregory	313	—	44	—	16,000
New York State Teachers College, Geneseo, N.Y.	1867	James B. Welles	317	—	49	—	30,100
New York State Teachers College, New Paltz, N.Y.	1886	Benjamin H. Matteson	414	—	48	—	13,600
New York State Teachers College, Oneonta, N.Y.	1889	Charles W. Hunt	313	—	41	—	23,030
N. Y. St. Tch. Col., Oswego, N.Y.	1861	Ralph W. Swetman	226	300	45	—	23,932
New York State Teachers College, Potsdam, N.Y.	1866	Clarence O. Lehman	427	—	46	—	21,000
New York University, New York, N.Y.	1831	Harry W. Chase	12,308	2,862	2,041	$ 8,778,342	649,152
Niagara Univ., Niagara Univ., N.Y.	1856	Joseph M. Noonan	390	550	94	—	59,781
Nicolet, Séminaire de, Nicolet, Que., Can.	1803	Robert Charland	345	—	30	15,000	34,000
N. C., Agri. Col. of, Greensboro, N.C.	1891	Ferdinand D. Bluford	913	400	88	—	29,022
N. C. College for Negroes, Durham, N.C.	1910	James E. Shepard	583	—	35	—	27,663
North Carolina, University of, Chapel Hill, N.C.	1789	Frank Porter Graham	1,788	1,550	385	3,045,178	434,020
North Central College, Naperville, Ill.	1861	Edward E. Rall	303	208	39	1,202,990	30,000
N D. Agri. Col., Fargo, N.D.	1890	Frank L. Eversull	486	650	100	1,567,603	67,850
*N.D. Sch. of Forestry, Bottineau, N.D.	1907	Albert F. Arnason	84	?	9	—	5,000
*N. D. St. Nor. & Ind. Sch., Ellendale, N.D.	1889	John C. McMillan	211	?	22	—	18,000
*N. D. St. Sch. of Sc., Wahpeton, N.D.	1903	E. F. Riley	300	?	46	—	8,000
N. D. St. Tch. Col., Dickinson, N.D.	1918	Chas. E. Scott	346	189	30	—	15,000
N. D. St. Tch. Col., Mayville, N.D.	1889	Cyril W. Grace	117	—	23	—	20,000
N. D. St Tch. Col., Minot, N.D.	1913	C. C. Swain	293	300	52	—	32,699
N. D., University of, Grand Forks, N.D.	1883	John C. West	652	1,150	108	—	97,000
N. E. Jr. Col., La. St. Univ., Monroe, La.	1931	Clyde C. Colvert	657	300	48	—	7,500
N. E. Mo. St. Tch. Col., Kirksville, Mo.	1867	Walter H. Ryle	856	126	60	—	75,105
Northeastern St. Col., Tahlequah, Okla.	1909	John Vaughan	250	—	40	—	35,120
Northeastern Univ., Boston, Mass.	1898	Carl Stephens Ell	1,701	—	139	440,020	17,476
Nor. Ill. State Tch. Col., DeKalb, Ill.	1895	Karl Langdon Adams	441	—	65	—	53,827
Nor. Mich. Col. of Edu., Marquette, Mich.	1899	Henry A. Tape	208	—	61	—	39,338
Northern Montana Col. (Jr.), Havre, Mont.	1929	G. H. Vande Bogart	116	—	14	—	15,852
Nor. State Tch. Col., Aberdeen, S.D.	1901	N. E. Steele	169	300	40	—	27,034
North Georgia Col. (Jr.), Dahlonega, Ga.	1873	J. C. Rogers	370	300	35	—	10,746
Northland College, Ashland, Wis.	1892	John A. Reuling	125	80	14	100,000	25,000
North Park College (Jr.), Chicago, Ill.	1891	Algoth Ohlson	488	—	40	321,000	17,200
*North Tex. Agri. Col. (Jr.), Arlington, Tex.	1917	E. E. Davis	1,173	?	68	—	20,616
Nor. Tex. State Tch. Col., Denton, Tex.	1890	W. Joseph McConnell	1,800	250	150	—	140,000
Northwestern College, Watertown, Wis.	1864	Erwin E. Kowalke	88	—	17	83,300	21,800
Northwestern State College, Alva, Okla.	1897	Sabin C. Percefull	285	400	43	—	17,897
Northwestern University, Evanston, Ill.	1851	Franklyn B. Snyder	5,900	4,500	900	57,750,000	735,000
N. W. Mo. State Tch. Col., Maryville, Mo.	1906	Uel W. Lamkin	250	400	60	—	35,000
Northwest Nazarene Col., Nampa, Ida.	1913	Lewis T. Corlett	375	—	21	—	12,000
**Norwich University, Northfield, Vt.	1819	John M. Thomas	519	?	44	739,981	36,000
Notre Dame College, South Euclid, Ohio	1922	Mother Mary Vera	225	—	31	—	21,594
Notre Dame of Md., Col. of, Balti., Md.	1895	Sister Mary Frances	280	—	41	27,217	23,000
Notre Dame, Univ. of, Notre Dame, Ind.	1842	Hugh O'Donnell	2,500	1,850	210	1,010,000	238,370
O							
Oakland City Col., Oakland City, Ind.	1890	W. P. Dearing	48	—	10	50,000	18,000
Oberlin College, Oberlin, Ohio	1833	Ernest H. Wilkins	1,229	674	175	20,158,582	434,129
Occidental College, Los Angeles, Calif.	1887	Remsen D. Bird	365	393	58	1,150,000	69,362
**Oglethorpe University, Atlanta, Ga.	1913	Thornwell Jacobs	300	?	35	—	60,000
Ohio Northern Univ., Ada, Ohio	1871	Robert O. McClure	156	—	27	356,112	34,250
Ohio State University, Columbus, Ohio	1870	H. L. Bevis	6,445	3,450	800	1,782,976	650,076
Ohio University, Athens, Ohio	1804	W. S. Gamertsfelder	1,273	—	253	69,719	145,235
Ohio Wesleyan Univ., Delaware, Ohio	1842	H. J. Burgstahler	1,857	1,000	112	3,698,910	167,480
**Okla. Agri. & Mech. Col., Stillwater, Okla.	1891	Henry G. Bennett	6,500	?	347	—	138,000
Okla. Baptist Univ., Shawnee, Okla.	1910	John W. Raley	400	500	36	—	21,000
Okla. Col. for Women, Chickasha, Okla.	1908	C. Dan Procter	750	—	60	—	33,000
Oklahoma, University of, Norman, Okla.	1890	Joseph A. Brandt	1,856	1,770	284	3,757,700	237,793
Olivet College, Olivet, Mich.	1844	Joseph Brewer	135	—	19	209,415	37,511
Olivet Nazarene College, Kankakee, Ill.	1908	A. L. Parrott	600	—	36	—	9,000
Omaha, Municipal Univ. of, Omaha, Neb.	1909	Rowland Haynes	387	—	43	86,158	75,000
Ontario Agri. Col., Guelph, Ont., Can.	1874	George I. Christie	238	202	80	—	45,792
Oregon Col. of Ed., Monmouth, Ore.	1856	C. A. Howard	147	—	40	—	29,668
Oregon State College, Corvallis, Ore.	1868	A. L. Strand	1,949	1,279	300	261,430	195,044
Oregon, University of, Eugene, Ore.	1872	Donald M. Erb	1,733	1,044	201	821,630	340,000
Ottawa, University of, Ottawa, Ont., Can.	1848	Philippe Cornellier	1,928	—	220	134,332	132,500
Ottawa University, Ottawa, Kan.	1865	Andrew B. Martin	165	—	25	443,932	19,000
Otterbein College, Westerville, Ohio	1847	J. Ruskin Howe	289	—	37	1,194,081	31,662
Ottumwa Heights College (Jr.), Ottumwa, Iowa	1925	Mother Mary Geraldine Upham	94	—	20	—	10,000
Ouachita College, Arkadelphia, Ark.	1886	James Richard Grant	550	250	45	550,000	25,000
Our Lady of Elms, Col. of, Chicopee, Mass.	1928	Thomas M. O'Leary	164	—	—	—	—
Our Lady of the Lake Col., San Ant., Tex.	1912	John L. McMahon	99	—	52	254,080	46,310
Ozarks, The Col. of the, Clarksville, Ark.	1891	Wiley Lin Hurie	225	750	25	398,928	22,000

Institution and Location	Year Founded	Chief Executive	Full Time Students	Number Army & Navy Students	Faculty	Endowment	Library Volumes
P							
Pacific College, Newberg, Ore.	1891	Emmett W. Gulley	75	—	14	$ 280,000	11,000
*Pacific, College of the, Stockton, Calif.	1851	Tully C. Knoles	297	?	64	570,000	40,000
Pacific Union College, Angwin, Calif.	1909	Henry J. Klooster	434	—	38	—	24,399
Pacific University, Forest Grove, Ore.	1849	Walter C. Giersbach	129	—	20	286,506	35,000
Packer Collegiate Institute (Jr.), Brooklyn, N.Y.	1845	Paul D. Shafer	430	—	60	697,000	14,634
Paine College, Augusta, Ga.	1882	Edmund C. Peters	271	—	20	35,000	19,000
Palm Beach Junior College, West Palm Beach, Fla.	1933	John I. Leonard	114	—	6	—	4,773
Paris Junior College, Paris, Texas	1924	J. R. McLemore	227	—	19	—	7,000
Park College, Parkville, Mo.	1875	William L. Young	275	400	45	1,369,391	34,836
Parsons College, Fairfield, Iowa	1875	Herbert C. Mayer	73	—	28	636,116	23,424
Pasadena College, Pasadena, Calif.	1902	H. Orton Wiley	300	—	25	—	14,000
Pasadena Jr. College, Pasadena, Calif.	1924	John Wesley Harbeson	3,407	1,000	193	—	40,000
Pearl River Jr. Col., Poplarville, Miss.	1912	R. D. McLendon	90	—	20	—	5,000
Pembroke State College for Indians, Pembroke, N.C.	1887	R. D. Wellons	75	—	16	—	5,000
Pa. Col. for Women, Pittsburgh, Pa.	1869	Herbert L. Spencer	326	—	40	601,000	26,158
Pa. Military College, Chester, Pa.	1821	Frank K. Hyatt	450	125	34	—	9,000
Pa. State College, The, State College, Pa.	1855	Ralph D. Hetzel	3,111	2,205	639	517,000	250,000
Pa. State Teachers College, California, Pa.	1855	Robert M. Steele	186	—	32	—	23,300
Pa. State Tch. Col., Clarion, Pa.	1867	Paul G. Chandler	201	300	34	—	20,000
Pa. State Tch. Col., E. Stroudsburg, Pa.	1893	Joseph F. Noonan	203	—	32	—	18,263
Pa. State Teachers Col., Edinboro, Pa.	1861	L. H. Van Houten	108	76	25	—	22,000
Pa. State Tch. Col., Indiana, Pa.	1871	Joseph M. Uhler	832	—	100	—	24,205
Pa. State Tch. Col., Kutztown, Pa.	1867	Q. A. W. Rohrbach	243	375	43	—	25,000
Pa. State Tch. Col., Lock Haven, Pa.	1878	Richard T. Parsons	269	100	34	—	32,000
Pa. State Tch. Col., Mansfield, Pa.	1862	James G. Morgan	310	—	45	—	25,000
Pa. State Tch. Col., Millersville, Pa.	1855	D. L. Biemesderfer	196	—	36	—	29,291
Pa. State Tch. Col., Shippensburg, Pa.	1871	Albert L. Rowland	167	—	27	—	24,000
Pa. State Tch. Col., Slippery Rock, Pa.	1889	John A. Entz	189	500	59	—	20,800
Pennsylvania, Univ. of, Philadelphia, Pa.	1740	Thomas S. Gates	5,650	3,500	1,441	22,913,366	991,366
Pestalozzi Froebel Tch. Col., Chicago, Ill.	1896	Herman H. Hegner	134	—	29	—	5,800
Pfeiffer Junior College, Misenheimer, N.C.	1928	G. G. Starr	170	—	18	500,000	7,000
Philander Smith Col., Little Rock, Ark.	1869	M. LaF. Harris	230	—	26	149,500	16,000
Phillips University, Enid, Okla.	1906	Eugene S. Briggs	489	—	40	750,683	37,000
*Phoenix Junior College, Phoenix, Ariz.	1920	Harry B. Wyman	318	?	23	—	14,529
Piedmont College, Demorest, Ga.	1897	M. B. Dana	200	—	13	225,000	16,000
Pikeville College (Jr.), Pikeville, Ky.	1889	A. A. Page	133	—	13	300,000	8,000
Pine Manor Jr. Col., Wellesley, Mass.	1911	Marie Warren Potter	222	—	60	—	6,000
Pittsburgh, Univ. of, Pittsburgh, Pa.	1787	John G. Bowman	3,716	2,775	893	3,169,556	350,659
Plymouth Teachers Col., Plymouth, N.H.	1870	Ernest L. Silver	119	—	17	—	18,000
Pomona College, Claremont, Calif.	1887	Elijah Wilson Lyon	504	550	91	3,863,251	110,944
*Pomona Jr. College, Pomona, Calif.	1892	Johnston E. Walker	771	?	43	—	11,000
Port Huron Jr. Col., Port Huron, Mich.	1923	Howard D. Crull	74	—	8	—	7,000
Portland, Univ. of, Portland, Ore.	1901	Chas. C. Miltner	394	64	47	—	25,000
Potomac State School (Jr.), Keyser, W.Va.	1901	E. E. Church	148	—	18	—	8,150
Prairie View State Col., Prairie View, Tex.	1876	W. R. Banks	1,153	185	93	—	21,640
Pratt Institute, Brooklyn, N.Y.	1887	Charles Pratt	1,000	675	150	12,000,000	146,378
Presbyterian College, Clinton, S.C.	1880	William P. Jacobs	148	400	25	190,000	24,455
Prince of Wales College and Normal School, Charlottetown, P.E.I., Can.	1860	George-Douglas Steel	432	—	25	88,450	4,300
Princeton University, Princeton, N.J.	1746	Harold W. Dodds	550	—	350	37,000,000	1,100,000
Principia Col. of Lib. Arts, The, Elsah, Ill.	1898	Frederic E. Morgan	334	—	26	798,608	42,500
Providence College, Providence, R.I.	1919	John J. Dillon	165	466	70	90,000	31,729
Prov. Inst. Tech. & Art, Calg., Alta., Can.	1916	J. Fowler	1,053	496	45	—	2,693
Puerto Rico, Univ. of, Rio Piedras, P. R.	1903	Jaime Benítez	3,336	50	320	1,247,438	83,000
Puget Sound, College of, Tacoma, Wash.	1888	R. Franklin Thompson	322	250	46	1,200,000	43,483
Purdue University, Lafayette, Ind.	1869	Edward C. Elliott	6,385	3,800	650	—	175,339
Q							
Queens College, Charlotte, N.C.	1857	Hunter B. Blakely	345	—	39	324,866	20,065
Queen's University, Kingston, Ont., Can.	1841	Robert C. Wallace	1,564	369	147	3,570,287	205,319
R							
Rabbi Isaac Elchanan Theological Seminary and Yeshiva Col., New York, N.Y.	1897	Samuel Belkin	825	—	80	550,000	71,000
Radcliffe College, Cambridge, Mass.	1879	Wilbur K. Jordan	890	150	400 part time	5,525,099	95,000
Randolph-Macon College, Ashland, Va.	1830	J. Earl Moreland	59	315	23	981,366	39,405
Rdlph.-Macon Wom. Col., Lynchburg, Va.	1893	Theodore H. Jack	680	—	72	1,254,431	58,000
Redlands, University of, Redlands, Calif.	1907	Elam J. Anderson	867	393	72	2,645,119	65,082
Reed College, Portland, Ore.	1904	Arthur F. Scott	280	200	46	1,627,350	79,000
Regina College, Regina, Sask., Can.	1911	Stewart Basterfield	87	—	10	—	8,900
Regis College, Denver, Colo.	1888	John J. Flanagan	54	300	22	46,950	45,204
**Regis College, Weston, Mass.	1927	Sister Honora	508	?	50	—	20,000
Rensselaer Poly. Inst., Troy, N.Y.	1824	Livingston W. Houston	1,723	1,191	143	9,947,100	36,500
R. I. Col. of Edu., Providence, R.I.	1920	Lucius A. Whipple	278	—	55	—	21,053
Rhode Island State Col., Kingston, R.I.	1892	Carl R. Woodward	450	600	135	—	70,824

Institution and Location	Year Founded	Chief Executive	Full Time Students	Number Army & Navy Students	Faculty	Endowment	Library Volumes
Rice Institute, The, Houston, Texas	1912	Edgar O. Lovett	631	514	90	$ 16,300,000	168,000
Richmond, University of, Richmond, Va.	1832	F. W. Boatwright	594	400	65	3,200,101	110,000
Ricker Junior College, Houlton, Maine	1848	Roy M. Hayes	210	—	11	—	5,000
Ricks College (Jr.), Rexburg, Idaho	1888	Hyrum W. Manwaring	145	—	15	—	8,039
Rio Grande College, Rio Grande, Ohio	1876	R. Lloyd Pobst	62	—	11	73,000	9,500
Ripon College, Ripon, Wis.	1851	Clark G. Kuebler	177	475	55	875,215	41,044
River Falls St. Tch. Col., River Falls, Wis.	1874	J. H. Ames	251	—	37	—	23,200
Riverside Jr. Col., Riverside, Calif.	1916	A. G. Paul	137	—	26 p't time	—	17,021
Roanoke College, Salem, Va.	1842	Charles J. Smith	167	105	25	675,000	22,000
Rochester, University of, Rochester, N.Y.	1850	Alan Valentine	1,636	1,003	313	52,780,467	406,198
Rockford College, Rockford, Ill.	1847	Mary Ashby Cheek	330	—	32	985,500	31,180
Rockhurst College, Kansas City, Mo.	1910	William Hugh McCabe	100	—	30	—	20,000
Rosary College, River Forest, Ill.	1922	Sister Mary Peter	608	—	67	101,244	48,300
Rosemont College, Rosemont, Pa.	1922	Mother M. Cleophas	275	—	42	—	42,631
Rose Polytechnic Inst., Terre Haute, Ind.	1874	Donald B. Prentice	157	248	34	2,000,000	23,500
Russell Sage College, Troy, N.Y.	1916	Helen M. McKinstry	626	—	70	1,027,117	39,461
Rutgers University, New Brunswick, N.J.	1766	Robt. C. Clothier	2,871	1,528	421	5,100,000	347,314
S							
Sacramento Jr. Col., Sacramento, Calif.	1916	Nicholas Ricciardi	865	275	60	—	27,000
Sacré-Coeur, Collège du, Sudbury, Ont., Can.	1913	Guy Courteau	303	78	30	50,000	10,000
Sacré-Coeur, L'Université du, Bathurst, N.B., Can.	1899	Jules Comeau	350	100	32	—	15,000
St. Ambrose College, Davenport, Iowa.	1882	Ambrose J. Burke	70	400	30	—	30,000
Ste-Anne-de-la-Pocatière, Collège of, Sainte-Anne-de-la-Pocatière, Que., Can.	1827	W. Lebon	750	150	105	—	80,000
St. Anselm's College, Manchester, N.H.	1893	Bertrand C. Dolan	40	200	30	—	15,000
**St. Benedict, College of, St. Joseph, Minn.	1913	Mother R. Pratschner	229	?	37	—	30,000
St. Benedict's College, Atchison, Kan.	1859	Cuthbert McDonald	103	—	37	—	100,000
St. Bonaventure Col., St. Bonvtre., N.Y.	1859	Thomas Plassmann	103	321	41	—	59,000
St. Catherine, College of, St. Paul, Minn.	1911	Sister Antonius	738	—	70	607,574	65,000
St. Charles' Seminary, Sherbrooke, Que., Can.	1875	Michel Couture	593	110	65	—	24,343
St. Dunstan's Univ., Charlottetown, P.E.I., Can.	1855	R. V. MacKenzie	205	—	14	—	8,000
St. Edward's University, Austin, Texas	1885	William Robinson	115	—	20	—	21,000
St. Elizabeth, Col. of, Convent Sta., N.J.	1899	Sister Marie J. Byrne	440	—	45	—	29,000
St. Francis College, Brooklyn, N.Y.	1884	Brother Columba	47	—	12	750,000	11,000
St. Francis, College of, Joliet, Ill.	1925	Sister M. Aniceta	234	—	42	16,000	21,273
**St. Francis College, Loretto, Pa.	1847	John P. J. Sullivan	214	?	28	1,100,000	17,000
St. Francis Xavier University, Antigonish, N.S., Can.	1853	D. J. Macdonald	468	260	26	480,792	33,000
St. Helen's Hall Junior Col., Portland, Ore.	1932	Sister Mildred Eleanor	75	—	11	—	5,840
St. Hyacinthe, Séminaire de, St. Hyacinthe, P.Q., Can.	1811	J. Arthur Vézina	567	106	55	—	60,000
St. John's College, Annapolis, Md.	1696	Stringfellow Barr	136	—	23	300,000	40,191
St. John's College, Winnipeg, Man., Can.	1866	R. J. Pierce	40	—	13	230,474	7,000
**St. John's Lutheran Col., Winfield, Kan.	1893	Carl S. Mundinger	160	?	16	20,000	12,000
St. John's University, Brooklyn, N.Y.	1870	William J. Mahoney	806	250	192	500,000	65,686
St. John's University, Collegeville, Minn.	1857	Alcuin Deutsch	216	300	40	—	68,714
Saint Joseph College, West Hartford, Conn.	1932	Sister M. Rosa	290	—	36	—	15,700
St. Joseph Jr. Col., St. Joseph, Mo.	1915	Nelle Blum	210	—	20	—	7,000
St. Joseph's College, Emmitsburg, Md.	1809	Sister Paula Dunn	150	—	26	—	16,300
St. Joseph's College, Philadelphia, Pa.	1851	Thomas J. Love	147	—	35	—	15,000
St. Joseph's Col. for Women, Brooklyn, N.Y.	1916	William T. Dillon	321	—	39	—	18,226
St. Joseph, Séminaire, Mont-Laurier, P.Q., Can.	1915	Aime Joyal	248	—	26	4,500	18,000
St. Joseph, Séminaire, Trois Rivières, Que., Can.	1860	Joseph Desilets	650	140	52	—	2,000
St. Joseph's Univ., St. Joseph, N.B., Can.	1864	J. Hervé Morin	452	—	56	—	20,000
St. Lawrence University, Canton, N.Y.	1856	Millard H. Jencks	336	350	57	2,236,839	80,000
St. Louis University, St. Louis, Mo.	1818	Patrick J. Holloran	2,903	1,124	650	2,162,165	444,717
Ste. Marie, Collège, Mon., Que., Can.	1848	Roméo Bergeron	571	—	42	—	80,000
St. Mary College, Xavier, Kan.	1923	Arthur M. Murphy	317	—	45	—	26,000
St. Mary of the Lake Sem., Mundelein, Ill.	1921	Reynold Hillenbrand	285	—	37	—	70,000
St. Mary-of-the-Woods Col., St. Mary-of-the-Woods, Indiana	1840	Mother Mary Bernard	237	—	40	600,000	63,879
St. Mary's Col., NotreDame, HolyCross, Ind.	1844	Sister Mary Madeleva	380	—	57	100,000	30,216
**St. Mary's College, St. Mary's Col., Calif.	1863	Brother Albert	503	?	55	—	70,000
St. Mary's College, St. Mary's, Kan.	1848	Daniel H. Conway	189	—	21	—	34,567
**St. Mary's College, Winona, Minn.	1912	Brother Leopold	333	?	32	—	20,000
St. Mary's Junior College, O'Fallon, Mo.	1919	Mother M. Ancilla	19	—	6	—	11,760
St. Mary's Junior College, Raleigh, N.C.	1842	Mrs. Ernest Cruikshank	290	—	30	163,900	9,000
St. Mary's Seminary, Baltimore, Md.	1791	John J. Lardner	475	—	29	800,000	60,000
St. Mary's University, San Antonio, Tex.	1852	Walter F. Golatka	100	—	30	—	24,888
St. Michael's College, Winooski Park, Vt.	1904	James H. Petty	67	—	16	32,414	30,000
St. Olaf College, Northfield, Minn.	1874	Clemens M. Granskou	676	600	90	828,193	54,636
St. Paul's Poly. Inst., Lawrenceville, Va.	1888	J. Alvin Russell	1,012	—	65	150,000	8,250
St. Petersburg Jr. Col., St. Petersburg, Fla.	1927	Robert B. Reed	95	100	20	—	10,500

Institution and Location	Year Founded	Chief Executive	Full Time Students	Number Army & Navy Students	Faculty	Endowment	Library Volumes
St. Peter's College, Jersey City, N.J.	1878	Vincent J. Hart	172	—	20	—	30,000
St. Rose, College of, Albany, N.Y.	1920	Edmund Gibbons	318	—	40	—	11,335
St. Teresa, College of, Winona, Minn.	1910	Sister M. A. Molloy	364	—	40	—	30,000
Ste. Thérèse, Séminaire de, Ste. Thérèse de Blainville, Que., Can	1825	Philippe Chartrand	300	90	32	—	30,000
St. Thomas, College of, St. Paul, Minn.	1885	James H. Moynihan	97	259	36	$ 1,150,000	35,410
St. Vincent College, Latrobe, Pa.	1846	Alfred Koch	140	350	40	2,500,000	64,147
Salem College, Salem, W.Va.	1888	S. Orestes Bond	88	250	16	127,457	14,000
Salem College, Winston-Salem, N C	1772	H. E. Rondthaler	327	—	40	467,971	25,946
San Angelo Junior Col., San Angelo, Tex.	1928	Wilson H. Elkins	146	—	14	—	6,000
**San Antonio, Univ. of, San Antonio, Tex	1894	W. W. Jackson	230	?	20	—	9,100
San Bernardino Valley Junior College, San Bernardino, Calif.	1927	John L. Lounsbury	300	—	35	—	25,000
San Diego State College, San Diego, Calif.	1897	Walter R. Hepner	855	—	65	—	82,000
San Francisco Col. for Wom., SanFran ,Cal.	1930	Mother Leonor Mejia	259	—	36	—	107,000
**San Francisco, Univ of, San Fran , Calif.	1855	William J. Dunne	900	?	77	—	55,000
San Jose State and Jr. College, San Jose, Cal.	1862	T. W. MacQuarrie	1,620	—	140	—	90,000
San Mateo Jr. Col., San Mateo, Calif.	1922	C. S. Morris	305	—	30	—	10,750
Santa Ana Jr. Col., Santa Ana, Calif.	1915	John H. McCoy	200	—	25	—	15,778
Santa Barbara St. Col , Santa Barbara, Cal	1909	Clarence L Phelps	700	—	60	—	50,000
Santa Clara, Univ. of, Santa Clara, Calif.	1851	Charles J. Walsh	107	375	51	—	52,300
Sarah Lawrence College, Bronxville, N.Y.	1926	Constance Warren	296	—	68	510,120	41,575
Saskatchewan, Univ. of, Saskatoon, Sask., Can.	1907	James S. Thomson	1,654	240	167	50,000	75,000
Schreiner Institute (Jr.), Kerrville, Tex.	1923	J. J. Delaney	345	100	25	175,000	8,000
Scranton-Keystone Jr. Col., La Plume, Pa.	1868	Byron S. Hollinshead	145	—	15	—	13,000
Scripps College, Claremont, Calif.	1926	Frederick Hard	230	—	25	900,567	26,955
Seattle College, Seattle, Wash	1892	Francis E. Corkery	2,800	—	72	—	28,000
Seattle Pacific College, Seattle, Wash	1891	Chas. Hoyt Watson	290	—	27	80,000	17,000
*Seton Hall College, South Orange, N.J.	1856	James F. Kelley	563	?	91	—	23,500
Seton Hill College, Greensburg, Pa.	1918	James A. Reeves	447	—	56	500,000	27,682
Shaw University, Raleigh, N.C.	1865	Robert P. Daniel	475	—	42	357,000	18,000
**Shenandoah College, Dayton, Va.	1875	Wade S. Miller	150	?	20	45,945	5,391
Shorter College, Rome, Ga.	1873	Paul M. Cousins	211	—	25	487,000	19,264
Shurtleff College, Alton, Ill.	1827	Guy Wimmer	138	—	23	170,251	30,000
Simmons College, Boston, Mass.	1899	Bancroft Beatley	1,500	—	139	3,138,148	92,988
Simpson College, Indianola, Iowa	1860	Edwin E. Voigt	189	—	24	1,388,570	30,000
Sioux Falls College (Jr.), Sioux Falls, S.D.	1883	Othniel A.Pendleton,Jr	55	—	14	136,578	16,000
Sisters College of Cleveland, Cleveland, O.	1928	Jos. Schrembs	171	—	30	—	21,290
Skidmore Col., Saratoga Springs, N.Y.	1911	Henry T. Moore	816	—	79	840,346	52,436
Smith College, Northampton, Mass.	1871	Herbert Davis	2,055	—	247	6,681,870	305,133
Snead Junior College, Boaz, Ala.	1935	Festus M. Cook	151	—	22	310,000	8,750
**Snow College (Jr.), Ephraim, Utah	1888	James A. Nuttall	165	?	23	—	8,000
South Dakota State Col., Brookings, S.D.	1881	Lyman E. Jackson	404	1,600	131	561,088	—
So. Dak. Sch. of Mines and Tech., Rapid City, S.D.	1885	Joseph P. Connolly	142	325	42	250,000	16,600
South Dakota, Univ. of, Vermillion, S.D.	1882	I.D. Weeks	423	—	101	—	110,612
Southeastern State College, Durant, Okla.	1909	T. T. Montgomery	283	—	40	—	31,118
S E.Mo.St.Tch.Col., Cape Girardeau, Mo.	1873	Walter W. Parker	1,200	335	65	—	80,000
Southeastern Univ., Washington, D C.	1917	James A. Bell	1,492	—	39	—	14,000
So. Calif., Univ. of, Los Angeles, Calif.	1879	R. B. von KleinSmid	2,497	1,700	900	1,600,000	314,228
So. Ill. Normal Univ., Carbondale, Ill.	1874	Roscoe Pulliam	722	—	124	—	54,432
Southern Jr. Col., Collegedale, Tenn.	1916	Kenneth A. Wright	275	—	15	—	9,100
Southern Methodist Univ., Dallas, Texas	1911	Umphrey Lee	1,000	350	116	2,452,671	155,810
Southern Oreg. Col. of Educ., Ashland, Ore.	1926	Walter Redford	60	—	20	—	12,831
Southern St. Norm. Sch., Springfield, S.D.	1881	Wm. A. Thompson	63	—	22	119,517	16,000
So.Uni.& Agri.& Mech.Col., Scotlndvl , La.	1880	F. G. Clark	678	—	62	—	24,475
So. Georgia College (Jr.), College, Ga.	1907	J. M. Thrash	176	—	18	—	6,224
**South, University of the, Sewanee, Tenn.	1858	Alexander Guerry	355	?	31	1,750,000	53,003
S.W.Tex.St.Tch.Col., San Marcos, Tex.	1901	John Garland Flowers	572	500	92	—	70,000
Southwestern College, Memphis, Tenn.	1848	Charles E. Diehl	365	250	36	471,356	50,355
Southwestern College, Winfield, Kan.	1885	Chas. E. Schofield	150	—	40	596,000	26,000
Southwestern In. of Tech., Weatherford, Okla.	1903	G. S. Sanders	235	—	47	—	32,130
Southwestern La. Inst., Lafayette, La.	1898	Joel L. Fletcher	1,770	736	148	—	44,325
Southwestern Univ., Georgetown, Texas	1840	J. N. R. Score	288	400	51	642,524	58,000
Spelman College, Atlanta, Ga.	1881	Florence M. Read	458	—	33	3,119,794	70,000
Springfield College (International YMCA College), Springfield, Mass.	1885	Ernest M. Best	63	500	55	1,107,000	29,226
Springfield Jr. Col., Springfield, Ill.	1929	Mother Mary Barbara	106	—	15	—	9,858
Spring Hill College, Spring Hill, Ala.	1830	Wm. D. O'Leary	185	200	38	207,000	43,000
Stanford Univ., Stanford University, Calif.	1885	Donald B. Tresidder	2,500	2,700	750	30,435,000	870,000
Stanstead Col., Stanstead, Que., Can.	1872	Errol C. Amaron	300	75	25	100,000	4,000
State Agri.& Mech. Col.(Jr.), Magnolia, Ark.	1910	Chas. A. Overstreet	180	—	20	—	12,169
*Stephens College (Jr.), Columbia, Mo.	1833	James M. Wood	1,700	?	190	150,000	45,000
Sterling College, Sterling, Kan.	1887	Hugh A. Kelsey	108	—	24	444,429	20,200
Stevens Inst.of Tech., Hoboken, N.J.	1870	Harvey N. Davis	290	513	76	—	35,000
Stout Institute, The, Menomonie, Wis.	1893	Burton E. Nelson	272	—	41	—	27,195
**Sue Bennett College (Jr), London, Ky.	1896	Kenneth C. East	126	?	12	—	9,500

Institution and Location	Year Founded	Chief Executive	Full Time Students	Number Army & Navy Students	Faculty	Endowment	Library Volumes
Sullins College (Jr.), Bristol, Va.	1870	Wm. E. Martin	410	23	42	$ 225,000	12,400
Sul Ross State Tch. Col., Alpine, Tex.	1920	Horace W. Morelock	159	290	23	—	21,200
Susquehanna Univ., Selinsgrove, Pa.	1858	G. Morris Smith	127	—	33	439,170	21,372
Swarthmore College, Swarthmore, Pa.	1864	John Nason	801	335	93	8,016,000	132,448
Sweet Briar College, Sweet Briar, Va.	1901	Meta Glass	454	—	52	670,803	59,441
*Syracuse University, Syracuse, N.Y.	1870	William P. Tolley	5,465	?	678	4,645,930	287,020
T							
Talladega College, Talladega, Ala.	1867	Buell G. Gallagher	246	—	27	1,300,000	26,000
Tarkio College, Tarkio, Mo.	1883	M. Earle Collins	62	—	18	657,493	17,945
Tch. Col., Athenaeum of O., Cincinnati, O.	1928	Carl J. Ryan	30	—	18	—	24,375
Temple University, Philadelphia, Pa.	1884	Robert L. Johnson	3,215	800	637	187,719	235,000
Tenn. Agri. & Indus. St. Tch. Col., Nashvle, Tenn.	1911	W. S. Davis	700	—	60	—	30,000
Tenn. Jr. Col., Univ. of, Martin, Tenn.	1927	Paul Meek	207	90	30	—	12,306
Tennessee Poly. Inst., Cookeville, Tenn.	1915	Everett Derryberry	306	400	53	—	28,000
Tenn. State Tch. Col., East, Johnson City, Tenn.	1911	Charles C. Sherrod	280	200	55	—	40,000
Tennessee, Univ. of, Knoxville, Tenn	1794	James D. Hoskins	1,651	1,269	221	490,000	192,298
Tenn. Wesleyan Col. (Jr.), Athens, Tenn.	1866	James L. Robb	135	—	14	140,000	12,000
Texarkana College (Jr.), Texarkana, Texas	1927	H. W. Stilwell	111	—	12	—	5,638
Tex., Agri.& Mech.Col. of, Col. Station, Tex.	1871	F. C. Bolton	2,000	5,000	311	215,664	105,000
Texas Christian Univ., Fort Worth, Tex.	1873	M. E. Sadler	1,400	465	120	4,000,000	75,000
**Texas College, Tyler, Texas	1894	D. R. Glass	475	?	45	—	9,500
Tex. Col. of Arts and Indus., Kingsville, Tex.	1925	E. N. Jones	415	250	62	—	29,665
Tex. Col. of Mines and Metal., El Paso, Tex.	1913	Dossie M. Wiggins	561	250	53	508,730	31,214
Tex. Lutheran College (Jr.), Seguin, Tex.	1892	William F. Kraushaar	120	—	12	20,000	16,500
Texas St Col. for Women, Denton, Tex.	1901	Louis H. Hubbard	2,270	—	150	—	87,000
Texas Technological Col., Lubbock, Tex.	1923	Clifford B. Jones	1,590	—	217	—	86,529
Texas, University of, Austin, Tex.	1881	Homer Price Rainey	6,700	1,100	406	48,816,170	729,319
Texas Wesleyan College, Fort Worth, Tex.	1892	Law Sone	389	—	27	147,000	18,000
Thornton Junior College, Harvey, Ill.	1927	William E. McVey	85	—	15	—	10,000
Tillotson College, Austin, Texas	1877	Mary E. Branch	488	—	28	—	19,175
Toledo, University of, Toledo, Ohio	1872	Philip C. Nash	1,042	500	101	25,000	115,306
Toronto, University of, Toronto, Ont., Can.	1827	Henry J. Cody	6,877	568	1,081	15,000,000	413,300
Tougaloo College, Tougaloo, Miss.	1869	Judson L. Cross	505	—	40	40,000	13,000
Transylvania College, Lexington, Ky.	1780	L. A. Brown	132	200	29	796,000	45,000
Trinity College, Hartford, Conn.	1823	Arthur H. Hughes	127	406	47	3,639,190	136,000
Trinity College, Sioux City, Ia.	1913	Francis J. Friedel	31	—	7	—	15,000
Trinity College School, Port Hope, Ont., Can.	1865	P. A. C. Ketchum	263	190	20	—	5,000
*Trinity Univ., San Antonio, Texas	1869	Monroe G. Everett	288	?	36	450,000	30,171
**Trinity University, Waxahachie, Tex.	1869	F. L. Wear	316	?	30	713,677	21,588
**Tri-State College, Angola, Ind.	1884	Burton Handy	950	?	35	—	7,000
Tufts College, Medford, Mass.	1852	Leonard Carmichael	2,585	1,669	625	7,499,156	200,000
Tulane University, New Orleans, La.	1834	Rufus C. Harris	3,672	1,837	428	10,130,202	350,000
Tulsa, University of, Tulsa, Okla.	1894	C. I. Pontius	509	—	69	1,240,031	121,700
Tusculum College, Greeneville, Tenn.	1794	John McSween	189	—	26	1,000,000	17,000
Tuskegee Inst., Tuskegee Institute, Ala.	1881	F. D. Patterson	1,280	—	107	6,968,622	54,409
Tyler Jr. College, Tyler, Tex.	1926	J. M. Hodges	110	—	10	—	10,000
U							
Union College, Barbourville, Ky.	1879	Conway Boatman	125	—	21	474,039	16,295
Union College, Lincoln, Neb.	1891	E. E. Cossentine	444	—	37	—	32,000
Union College, Schenectady, N.Y.	1795	Dixon Ryan Fox	250	600	85	3,858,000	118,000
Union University, Jackson, Tenn.	1834	John J. Hurt	156	300	34	396,000	16,000
U.S. Coast Guard Acad., New London, Conn.	1876	James Pine	1,495	—	155	—	20,000
U. S. Military Academy, West Point, N.Y.	1802	Francis B. Wilby	2,426	—	711	—	121,000
U. S. Naval Academy, Annapolis, Md.	1845	John R. Beardall	3,266	—	405	—	100,000
Upper Iowa University, Fayette, Iowa	1857	V. T. Smith	113	—	17	516,493	15,902
**Upsala College, East Orange, N.J.	1893	E. B. Lawson	444	?	32	200,000	22,000
Ursinus College, Collegeville, Pa.	1869	Norman E. McClure	340	200	42	700,000	31,000
Ursuline College, Louisville, Ky.	1938	Mother M. Roberta Zehe	368	—	38	—	17,067
Ursuline Col. for Women, Cleveland, Ohio	1871	Mother Marie Sands	203	—	31	—	18,000
Utah State Agri. Col., Logan, Utah	1888	Elmer G. Peterson	3,290	1,530	157	—	80,000
Utah, University of, Salt Lake City, Utah	1850	LeRoy E. Cowles	2,758	1,000	298	750,909	166,000
V							
Valleyfield, Séminaire de, Valleyfield, Que., Can.	1893	Lionel Deguire	350	34	31	—	12,573
Valparaiso University, Valparaiso, Ind.	1859	O. P. Kretzmann	328	—	40	544,434	49,000
Vanderbilt University, Nashville, Tenn.	1872	Oliver C. Carmichael	936	739	380	27,049,719	423,953
Vassar College, Poughkeepsie, N.Y.	1861	Henry N. MacCracken	1,400	—	175	—	—
Vermont State Norm. Sch., Castleton, Vt.	1867	Ermo Houston Scott	66	—	10	—	10,060
Vermont St. Norm. Sch., Johnson, Vt.	1867	D. W. McClelland	65	—	11	—	7,200
Vermont St. Norm. Sch., Lyndon Center, Vt.	1921	Rita L. Bole	42	—	10	—	9,000
Vermont, Univ. of, and State Agric. Col., Burlington, Vt.	1791	John S. Millis	650	1,280	249	3,389,838	161,397
Villanova College, Villanova, Pa.	1842	E. V. Stanford	303	612	90	3,031,410	73,000
**Vincennes University, Vincennes, Ind.	1806	W. A. Davis	124	?	12	150,000	25,000
Virginia Intermont Col. (Jr.), Bristol, Va.	1884	Hugh G. Noffsinger	391	—	43	328,000	10,500
Virginia Junior College, Virginia, Minn.	1921	Floyd B. Moe	106	—	25	—	16,500

Institution and Location	Year Founded	Chief Executive	Full Time Students	Number Army & Navy Students	Faculty	Endow-ment	Library Volumes
Virginia Military Inst., Lexington, Va.	1839	C. E. Kilbourne	279	543	63	$ 289,512	66,348
Va. Polytechnic Inst., Blacksburg, Va.	1872	Julian A. Burruss	950	2,000	243	349,312	117,127
Va. St. Col. for Negroes, Ettrick, Va.	1883	L. H. Foster	896	—	136	173,000	26,555
Virginia State Tch. Col., Farmville, Va.	1884	Joseph L. Jarman	795	—	52	—	37,200
Va. State Tchr. Col., Radford, Va.	1910	David Wilbur Peters	358	—	42	—	27,819
**Va. Theol. Sem. & Col., Lynchburg, Va.	1888	Wm. H. R. Powell	70	?	20	—	4,000
Virginia Union University, Richmond, Va.	1899	John Malcus Ellison	445	—	27	788,089	31,000
Virginia, Univ. of, Charlottesville, Va.	1819	John L. Newcomb	660	1,000	39	11,697,066	405,036
*Visalia Jr. Col., Visalia, Calif.	1926	L. J. Williams	464	?	34	—	5,700
Viterbo College, La Crosse, Wis.	1931	Mother M. Engelberta	43	—	14	—	12,989
W							
Wabash College, Crawfordsville, Ind.	1832	Frank Hugh Sparks	48	289	31	2,281,555	88,000
Wagner Mem. Luth. Col. Staten Island, N.Y.	1883	C. C. Stoughton	214	—	22	333,855	34,610
Wake Forest College, Wake Forest, N.C.	1834	Thurman D. Kitchin	618	—	142	3,010,770	65,080
Walla Walla College, College Place, Wash.	1892	George W. Bowers	538	—	42	—	21,000
Ward-Belmont Sch. (Jr.), Nashville, Tenn.	1865	Joseph E. Burk	682	—	51	—	14,700
Wartburg College, Waverly, Iowa	1868	E. J. Braulick	170	—	22	34,159	25,625
Washburn Municipal University of Topeka, Topeka, Kan.	1865	Bryan S. Stoffer	696	430	81	1,149,869	55,492
Washington & Jefferson Col., Wash., Pa.	1780	Ralph C. Hutchison	86	400	38	1,615,211	62,350
Washington and Lee Univ., Lexington, Va.	1749	Francis P. Gaines	118	885	35	3,128,765	128,016
Washington College, Chestertown, Md.	1782	Gilbert W. Mead	180	—	30	—	2,500
Washington Miss. Col., Takoma Pk., Md.	1904	Benj. G. Wilkinson	400	—	40	40,000	29,000
Washington, State Col. of, Pullman, Wash.	1890	Ernest O. Holland	1,512	2,200	263	5,810,204	450,000
Washington St. Norm. Sch., Machias, Me.	1909	C. O. T. Wieden	60	—	13	—	2,535
Washington University, St. Louis, Mo.	1853	George R. Throop	2,647	1,575	609	20,429,494	501,623
Washington, University of, Seattle, Wash.	1861	Lee Paul Sieg	4,556	1,625	561	—	528,705
*Wayland College, Plainview, Texas	1909	George W. McDonald	140	?	11	15,000	6,000
Wayne University, Detroit, Mich.	1868	Warren E. Bow	4,584	426	791	—	214,000
*Weatherford College, Weatherford, Texas	1873	Clarence A. Sutton	101	?	14	46,363	6,455
*Weber College (Jr.), Ogden, Utah	1889	H. A. Dixon	750	?	46	—	17,650
Webster College, Webster Groves, Mo.	1915	George F. Donovan	216	—	53	15,478	25,056
Wellesley College, Wellesley, Mass.	1870	Mildred H. McAfee	1,536	400	187	10,876,729	219,200
Wells College, Aurora, N.Y.	1868	William E. Weld	262	—	43	1,441,619	96,081
Wentworth Mil. Acad. (Jr.), Lexington, Mo.	1923	J. M. Sellers	90	—	12	—	6,100
Wesleyan College, Macon, Ga.	1836	N. C. McPherson, Jr.	551	—	53	458,334	27,300
Wesleyan University, Middletown, Conn.	1831	Victor L. Butterfield	150	750	81	8,054,190	297,407
*West Chester St. Tch. Col., West Chester, Pa.	1871	Chas. S. Swope	1,157	?	83	—	35,000
Westbrook Junior College, Portland, Maine	1925	Milton D. Proctor	305	—	27	65,700	6,430
*Western Carolina Tch. Col., Cullowhee, N.C.	1889	Hiram T. Hunter	340	?	20	—	17,000
Western College for Women, Oxford, Ohio	1853	Mary M. D. Thomson	271	—	42	768,894	43,216
Western Ill. St. Tch. Col., Macomb, Ill.	1899	F. A. Beu	611	—	80	—	55,617
West. Ky. St. Tch. Col., Bowling Green, Ky.	1906	Paul L. Garrett	513	431	93	—	67,588
Western Maryland Col., Westminster, Md.	1867	Fred G. Holloway	425	321	60	891,245	41,569
West. Mich. Col. of Ed., Kalamazoo, Mich.	1904	Paul V. Sangren	2,000	900	220	—	59,026
West. Ontario, Univ. of, London, Ont., Can.	1878	W. Sherwood Fox	1,348 all p't time	95	267	462,435	164,682
Western Reserve Univ., Cleveland, Ohio	1826	Winfred G. Leutner	4,419	1,000	652	13,372,239	560,000
West. St. Col. of Colo., Gunnison, Colo.	1911	Chas. C. Casey	167	—	24	—	32,864
Western Union College, LeMars, Iowa	1900	David O. Kime	135	109	21	227,147	14,000
West Liberty St. Tch. Col., W. Liberty, W.Va.	1937	Paul N. Elbin	155	—	24	—	20,183
Westminster College, Fulton, Mo.	1851	Franc L. McCluer	360	275	23	900,000	42,000
Westminster Col., New Wilmington, Pa.	1852	R. F. Galbreath	410	400	63	750,000	30,000
Westminster Col. (Jr.), Salt Lake City, Utah	1875	Robert D. Steele	65	—	10	120,000	14,600
West Texas St. Tch. Col., Canyon, Tex.	1910	J. A. Hill	1,061	400	70	—	41,843
*West Virginia State Col., Institute, W.Va.	1891	John W. Davis	835	?	53	—	25,909
West Virginia Univ., Morgantown, W.Va.	1867	Charles E. Lawall	1,396	1,258	270	$105,300	185,547
West. Wash. Col. of Edu., Bellingham, Wash.	1899	W. W. Haggard	250	—	52	—	63,286
Wheaton College, Norton, Mass.	1834	J. Edgar Park	468	—	70	1,202,016	52,200
Wheaton College, Wheaton, Ill.	1860	V. R. Edman	1,131	250	85	607,612	80,000
Whitman College, Walla Walla, Wash.	1859	Winslow S. Anderson	617	263	56	1,185,975	74,700
Whittier College, Whittier, Calif.	1901	H. F. Spencer	283	—	39	600,000	45,000
Whitworth College, Spokane, Wash.	1890	Frank F. Warren	265	90	24	35,000	14,000
Wichita, Municipal Univ. of, Wichita, Kan.	1926	William M. Jardine	710	—	65	95,855	69,719
Wiley College, Marshall, Texas	1873	E. C. McLeod	316	—	40	600,000	17,863
Willamette University, Salem, Ore.	1842	G. Herbert Smith	674	258	44	1,740,846	40,000
William and Mary, Col. of, Williamsburg, Va.	1693	John Edwin Pomfret	898	800	100	1,500,000	175,000
William and Mary, Col. of, Vir. Polytechnic In., Norfolk Div. (Jr.), Norfolk, Va.	1930	C. J. Duke, Jr.	220	—	18	—	9,000
Wm. Jennings Bryan Univ., Dayton, Tenn.	1930	Judson A. Rudd	61	—	10	—	30,000
William Jewell Col., Liberty, Mo.	1849	Walter Pope Binns	285	600	56	1,228,355	53,963
William Penn Col., Oskaloosa, Iowa	1874	Errol T. Elliott	105	—	16	110,000	26,000
Williams College, Williamstown, Mass.	1793	James P. Baxter	108	1,003	92	11,234,153	192,875
*William Smith Col., Geneva, N.Y.	1908	John M. Potter	187	?	54	1,402,882	110,375
Williamsport Dickinson Junior College, Williamsport, Pa.	1812	John W. Long	300	350	35	350,000	12,000
William Woods College (Jr.), Fulton, Mo.	1890	Harlie L. Smith	315	—	31	800,000	10,000
Willimantic State Teachers College, Willimantic, Conn.	1889	George H. Shafer	140	—	44	—	—
Wilmington College, Wilmington, Ohio	1870	S. Arthur Watson	120	5	17	300,000	18,000
Wilson College, Chambersburg, Pa.	1870	Paul Swain Havens	400	—	50	827,127	50,000
Winthrop College, Rock Hill, S.C.	1886	Mowat G. Fraser	1,542	320	97	—	75,453
Wisconsin State Tch. Col., Eau Claire, Wis.	1916	W. R. Davies	340	300	52	—	25,671
Wisconsin St. Tch. Col., LaCrosse, Wis.	1909	Rexford S. Mitchell	360	—	45	—	35,000
Wisconsin St. Tch. Col., Milwaukee, Wis.	1880	Frank E. Baker	830	200	86	—	60,000
*Wisconsin State Tch. Col., Oshkosh, Wis.	1871	Forrest R. Polk	485	?	48	—	30,000
Wisconsin State Tch. Col., Platteville, Wis.	1866	Chester O. Newlun	218	—	35	—	28,867
Wisconsin St. Tch. Col., Central, Stevens Point, Wis.	1894	William C. Hansen	270	350	49	—	38,000
Wisconsin State Tch. Col., Superior, Wis.	1893	Robert C. Williams	222	250	55	—	35,302
Wisconsin St. Tch. Col., Whitewater, Wis.	1868	Claude M. Yoder	328	—	45	—	40,000
Wisconsin, University of, Madison, Wis.	1848	Clarence A. Dykstra	5,264	3,500	1,163	1,912,923	1,100,000
Wittenberg College, Springfield, Ohio	1845	Rees E. Tulloss	304	700	55	2,173,600	71,102
Wofford College, Spartanburg, S.C.	1854	Walter K. Greene	100	500	25	826,772	39,105
Woodrow Wilson Jr. Col., Chicago, Ill.	1934	John A. Bartky	945	—	46	—	60,000
Woodstock College, Woodstock, Md.	1869	David Nugent	246	—	47	—	225,000
Wooster, College of, Wooster, Ohio	1866	Charles F. Wishart	538	600	81	3,480,000	96,855
Worcester Poly. Inst., Worcester, Mass.	1865	Wat T. Cluverius	316	328	64	4,644,809	27,000
Wyoming, University of, Laramie, Wyo.	1887	J. L. Morrill	652	1,063	153	4,046,213	113,900
X							
Xavier University, Cincinnati, Ohio	1831	Celestin J. Steiner	204	500	63	—	80,080
Y							
Yale University, New Haven, Conn.	1701	Charles Seymour	1,860	3,000	825	106,124,503	2,401,000
Yankton College, Yankton, S.D.	1881	William C. Lang	127	90	30	701,518	36,000
York College, York, Neb.	1890	D. E. Weidler	89	—	16	91,835	17,000
Young L. G. Harris College (Jr.), Young Harris, Ga.	1886	J. W. Sharp	275	—	12	100,000	12,000
Youngstown College, Youngstown, Ohio	1908	Howard W. Jones	289	78	25	—	27,125
Yuba Junior Col., Marysville, Calif.	1927	Pedro Osuna	150	—	25	—	10,000

UNRRA: *see* UNITED NATIONS RELIEF AND REHABILITATION ADMINISTRATION.

Upshur, William Peterkin

(1881–1943), U.S. marine corps officer, was born Oct. 28 in Richmond, Va. After graduating from the Virginia Military institute, 1902, he was commissioned a 2nd lieutenant in the marine corps. He won several awards including the congressional medal of honour for his service in Haiti in 1915. During World War I, he went to France to take charge of the military prison at Bordeaux; later he was shifted to command of the guard camp at Bassens. A graduate of the U.S. Army Command and General Staff school, the Naval War college and the Army War college, he was made a brigadier general in 1938, and given command of the fleet marine force. He had been on duty in the Philippines and China, at Washington headquarters of the marine corps and saw service at sea. In Oct. 1939 he was promoted to major general, was later put in charge of the marine corps base at San Diego and in Nov. 1941 was named commanding general of the marine corps department of the Pacific with headquarters at San Francisco. He was killed July 21 in the crash of a naval aeroplane near Sitka, Alaska.

Uranium. Comments made under the subject of radium, vanadium (*q.v.*) also apply to uranium, and little additional information was available in 1943. It was rumoured that German scientists were working intensively on the isolation of U235 from uranium, and the development of energy by atomic disintegration in the hope that something practical could be accomplished in time to be of help in winning the war. (*See* also RADIUM.)

(G. A. Ro.)

Urology. According to data published regarding the treatment of gonorrhoeal urethritis in the armed forces, the sulfonamides proved to be effective agents in combating a disease which had defied treatment over the centuries. It was estimated that infection in the urethra with *Neisseria gonorrhoeae* can be eliminated by medication with sulfonamide compounds, if they are adequately employed, in from 80% to 90% of cases. It was recognized, however, that in approximately 10% of the cases of gonorrhoeal urethritis sulfonamide therapy fails. It was found that this failure is due largely to inherent qualities of the *Neisseria gonorrhoeae* which render them sulfonamide resistant in varying degrees. The degree of resistance to sulfonamide compounds could in 1943 be determined by means of comparatively simple laboratory tests.

During 1943 it was shown that penicillin also will eliminate gonorrhoeal urethritis and apparently even more efficiently than the sulfonamides. In fact, it was found that penicillin will overcome gonorrhoeal infection in at least 98% of cases and, of even greater importance, the infection will be eliminated within about 48 hours. Owing to the scarcity of penicillin, its use was confined largely to those cases of gonorrhoeal urethritis in which the infections were resistant to sulfonamide medication. In all of these resistant cases reported thus far the gonorrhoeal infection was eliminated by penicillin. The absence of any toxic reaction following the administration of penicillin is an important advantage of penicillin over sulfonamide medication. Penicillin, besides being used in treatment of gonorrhoeal urethritis of the male, also was used in the treatment of gonorrhoeal infection in the female pelvis and of gonorrhoeal proctitis, with equally good results.

Pyrogen free penicillin, dissolved in a physiologic solution of sodium chloride, may be administered either intravenously by the drip method, or intramuscularly at intervals of three hours. The administration of penicillin must be continuous or nearly continuous in the treatment of severe gonorrhoeal infections. Because of the difficulty of production, penicillin compounds, unfortunately, were not universally available in 1943.

Early clinical results following bilateral orchiectomy (excision of both testicles) in cases of carcinoma of the prostate gland were often so favourable that it was thought the operation might control the malignant lesion permanently. Further observations on late results of orchiectomy in the treatment of prostatic carcinoma, however, raised some doubt as to the efficacy of the procedure. In fact, postoperative results were disappointing in so many cases that many urologists questioned the advisability of routine orchiectomy in these cases. Some observers went so far as to claim that orchiectomy seems to stimulate the malignant process after an early stage of improvement.

Many urologists claimed that the clinical results of the administration of female hormones in cases of prostatic carcinoma are as good as, or better than, those after orchiectomy. They were of the opinion that androgenic stimulation can be controlled in this manner more completely than by orchiectomy. One of the advantages claimed for administration of estrogenic compounds is the fact that the estrogenic hormone will neutralize androgenic secretion in tissues other than the testicle. Orchiectomy alone will eliminate only such androgenic stimulation as has its origin in testicular tissue. The amount of estrogenic drug needed to neutralize androgenic stimulation was not in 1943 standardized. Some clinicians advised a dosage of only 1 or 2 mg. daily, while others employed much larger amounts. Some urologists employed orchiectomy and followed it up by the administration of estrogenic drugs. Some clinicians believed that the potency of estrogenic therapy is not as great when a preparation containing estrogenic hormone is administered following orchiectomy. The administration of estrogenic drugs may be difficult in some cases because of systemic reaction, characterized by hot flushes, nausea, weakness, or pain with swelling in the mammary gland.

Opinions differed as to when these measures should be employed in the treatment of prostatic carcinoma. Most clinicians favoured immediate employment of these measures in order to prevent progress of the malignant lesion. Others favoured postponement of both orchiectomy and administration of estrogenic hormones until there is clinical evidence of metastasis.

The results of the treatment of interstitial cystitis and other forms of painful cystitis with instillations of silver nitrate indicated that this method offered permanent relief in approximately 60% of cases. In some cases in which symptoms recurred, a repetition of treatment with silver nitrate at intervals controlled the symptoms. The combination of wide overdistention of the bladder, while the patient was under general anaesthesia, with subsequent instillations of silver nitrate, gave permanent relief in other cases. In some cases continuous lavage of the bladder with a solution of silver nitrate (1:1,000) for several days brought relief. (W. F. BR.)

Uruguay. A republic on the southeastern coast of South America, between Argentina and Brazil. It is the smallest republic on the continent (area: 72,153 sq.mi.), but the most densely populated (pop., official est. Dec. 31, 1940: 2,164,000). Capital city: Montevideo (pop. est. 1941: 770,000); other cities, with estimated populations: Paysandú (50,000); Salto (48,000); Mercedes (33,000); Lavalleja (30,000); Tucuarembo (30,000); Artigas (28,500); Rivera (22,000); Treinta y Tres (21,500). President in 1943 (inaugurated March 1): Juan José de Amézaga.

History.—Uruguay's new Liberal president, Juan José de Amézaga, assumed the executive office on March 1, and continued the active collaboration in inter-American defense laid down by his party in 1941 and 1942. In January the vice-president-elect, Alberto Guani, visited the United States, and while there signed agreements with the Export-Import bank covering a loan of $20,000,000, to be used in a public improvements program in Uruguay. The Uruguayan government announced early in 1943 that diplomatic relations would be resumed with Russia, with whom such contacts had been broken in 1936. Relations with Vichy France, however, were severed on May 12.

The new administration started its internal program with severe handicaps to overcome. In addition to the usual problems of wartime, Uruguay was faced with the most severe drought in a number of years. In an effort to decrease unemployment the government inaugurated a public works construction program, and on May 3 the president proposed legislation which would control monopolies and would serve as a basis for price and wage control. During the first half of the year the labour situation remained unsatisfactory in view of low wages, a steady increase in living costs, and only slight improvement in regard to employment. Toward the latter part of the year, however, conditions improved. The drought was broken and agricultural prospects became brighter; wool production proved to be excellent in both quality and quantity. In July the Board of Economic Warfare in the United States released the ban on South American wools which had been in effect, and Uruguay was allowed to ship to the United States 60% of the amount of the 1941–42 export. The United States also started to import once more Uruguayan sheepskins. In October Great Britain signed a contract for the United Nations to take meats available for export in Uruguay for the year.

The steadily increasing favourable foreign trade balance caused some concern over inflation, with some leaders favouring nationalization of foreign-owned utilities as a desirable measure to prevent it, and others desiring the surplus to go into repatriation of the sterling debt of £18,000,000.

Rationing continued in force during 1943, notably on gasoline and kerosene, and price control was applied on many items.

Education.—Education is compulsory and free; the system is considered one of the more progressive of South America. Primary schools numbered approximately 1,700 (in 1941); enrolment was more than 200,000.

Finance.—The monetary unit is the peso (value in 1943: approximately 52⅔ cents U.S.). The 1943 budget estimated revenue at 112,912,000 pesos; expenditures at 112,649,000 pesos. It was expected that 1943 would end with a deficit of 20,000,000 pesos; 1944, with a deficit of 30,000,000 pesos. The funded public debt (Dec. 31, 1941) was 449,531,175 pesos, with an additional 94,500 peso international debt.

Trade and Communication.—For the first half of 1942 exports were valued at $33,147,779; imports at $32,517,549. In 1943 imports from the United States (about 26% in 1941) and the United Kingdom (15% in 1941) declined, and imports from Latin American countries increased. Uruguay had a favourable trade balance with the United States, for nine months of 1943, of $27,370,000. Wool exports from Oct. 1, 1942–Sept. 30, 1943, amounted to 103,605 bales (1941–42: 57,009 bales). Coal imports for the year ending June 30, 1943, were 265,654 short tons. Because of the drought Uruguay had to import potatoes.

External communication is by sea and air, with rail connection to Brazil and Argentina. Highway mileage is 22,500 mi., of which 1,500 mi. is paved. Bus and truck traffic was seriously curtailed in 1943 by lack of gasoline. There are 1,527 mi. of railways; speeds were reduced on these in order to conserve irreplaceable steel rails.

Agriculture and Manufacturing.—Uruguay is primarily pastoral (sheep and cattle). An unofficial estimate indicated that 20,000,000 to 22,000,000 sheep were being raised; the wool clip (Oct. 1, 1942–Sept. 30, 1943) was 67,168 short tons (1941–42: 55,945 short tons). Stock slaughterings (nine months ending Sept. 30, 1943) were: cattle, 1,030,146 head; sheep, 972,454 head. Agricultural production for the first half of 1943 (in short tons) was: wheat 364,034; rice 15,225; corn 40,091; barley 9,666; oats 33,983; potatoes 45,984; flax 51,223. Linseed production for the 1942–43 year was officially estimated at 54,013 short tons.

The more important manufacturing industries include meat-packing products, textiles, leather goods (for domestic consumption), hats, and wines in their output. During 1943 the textile mills exported many shipments to South Africa. (*See* also ARGENTINA; HISPANIC AMERICA AND WORLD WAR II.)

(D. RD.)

U.S.O.: *see* UNITED SERVICE ORGANIZATIONS.
U.S.S.R.: *see* UNION OF SOVIET SOCIALIST REPUBLICS.

Utah. A Rocky mountain state, admitted to the union in 1896, popularly known as the "Mormon state." Area 84,916 sq.mi. (82,346 sq.mi., land; 2,570 sq.mi., water); pop. (1940) 550,310. The rural (nonfarm) population was 150,465, (farm) 94,352; urban 305,493, with the following origins: white (native) 510,662, (foreign born) 32,298; Negro (native) 1,225, (foreign born) 10. Capital, Salt Lake City (149,934). Other principal cities are Ogden (43,688), Provo (18,071) and Logan (11,868).

History.—In 1943 the administration of the Democratic governor, Herbert B. Maw, co-operated with federal authorities in essential war measures, while business and industrial interests aided in the expansion of mining and metallurgical industries which were stimulated by war exigencies.

In 1943 E. E. Monson continued as secretary of state; Reese M. Reese, auditor; Oliver G. Ellis, treasurer; Grover A. Giles, attorney general; and Charles H. Skidmore, superintendent of public instruction.

Education.—There were 143,448 children in the public schools in 1943, a drop of 5,184 from the 1942 figure. The total cost of education was $13,197,010.38, with $11,377,231.18 devoted to operating expenses. There were 4,102 teachers and 434 principals.

Public Welfare, Charities, Correction.—Total obligations of $8,449,718.20 incurred in 1943 for public assistance were distributed as follows: old-age assistance, $5,564,421.14; aid to dependent children, $1,383,415.44; aid to blind, $53,537.54; general $672,191.53. A total of 15,780 households were receiving assistance in June 1943 as compared with 21,508 in Dec. 1941.

Services to children of working mothers, started in Feb. 1943, totalled $10,746.58.

Communication.—Highway mileage in 1943 was as follows: state, 5,450; county, 15,633; city, 2,412. There were 2,005 mi. of steam railway in 1942. State expenditures for roads in 1942 were approximately $6,051,071.14. Utah had 33 airports and fields in 1943.

Banking and Finance.—Fifty-seven banks, 45 state and 12 national, had total assets of $407,163,177.78 in 1943, and total bank deposits reached $384,020,790.45. In 1942 the state's 15 building and loan associations had aggregate assets of $20,926,166.17. State receipts for the year ending June 30, 1942 were $40,400,517.83; expenditures were $37,383,310.21. The total of outstanding bonds in 1942 was $1,695,000, with this amount available from the state liquor control fund for retirement of all outstanding bonds.

Agriculture.—Cash income from farm marketings was $71,506,000 during Jan.–Sept. 1943 as compared with $53,083,000 for the same period in 1942. Producers increased the farm yield as part of the war program. Value of 1943 truck and canning crops was $5,882,000; for 1942, $4,036,000. Value of canning tomatoes in 1943 was $1,621,000, and shipping tomatoes, $286,000.

Table I.—*Principal Agricultural Products of Utah, 1943 and 1942*

Crop	1943	1942
Hay (tame and wild), tons	1,158,000	1,174,000
Potatoes, bu.	3,430,000	2,312,000
Sugar beets, short tons	478,000	572,000
Celery, crates	183,000	132,000
Tomatoes, fresh, bu.	130,000	35,000
" processing, tons	73,000	82,700
Onions, 100-lb. sacks	300,000	264,000
Peas, tons	25,520	20,080

Manufacturing.—The upward trend in manufacturing continued in 1943, with new industries enabling Utah not only to hold its population but to attract newcomers to defense industries. Workers numbered 30,700 in 1942 as compared with 20,300 in 1941, and only 15,982 in the first quarter of the latter year. Total pay rolls in manufacturing were estimated at $67,569,943 in 1943 as compared with $50,939,000 in 1942.

Mineral Production.—The United States war program gave sharp impetus to the state's greatest industry, with important production of copper, lead, and zinc and activity in vanadium, tungsten and potash. In gold production, Utah jumped from fourth to first place among the states of the union because of its copper mines, which produce both metals. In 1943 the state had an estimated production of 381,763 fine ounces of gold and 9,308,520 fine ounces of silver, as compared with 391,544 fine ounces of gold in 1942 and 10,574,955 fine ounces of silver in the same year.

Table II.—*Mineral Production of Utah, 1943 and 1942*

Mineral	1943 (est.)	1942
Copper, lb.	646,100,000	613,382,000
Lead, lb.	132,500,000	143,860,000
Zinc, lb.	93,534,000	91,086,000
Value of all ores	$124,348,439	$113,552,848

Activity continued in connection with expansion of the pig iron plant and coking coal mine near Cedar City. (F. W. GA.)

Utilities, Public: *see* PUBLIC UTILITIES.

Vanadium.
Explorations developed new deposits of vanadium in Idaho and Wyoming, and other areas might provide some supply if methods could be devised to recover the metal from low-grade ores. These sources would supplement the domestic supply formerly obtained from Colorado and Utah. Peruvian production capacity was enlarged in order to assure an adequate supply. During 1943, vanadium was shifted from the list of metals short in supply to those with adequate supply for essential requirements.   (G. A. Ro.)

Vandegrift, Alexander A.
(1887–   ), commandant of the U.S. marine corps, was born March 13 in Charlottesville, Va. He entered the corps as a second lieutenant in 1909, took part in the landing in Nicaragua in 1912 and at Veracruz in 1914. In World War I, however, it was his fate not to fight against Germany but to stay in Haiti, helping keep peace there. Vandegrift first came to public attention in 1927 on the China coast when he sent marine planes into the air to threaten Japanese observation planes which, despite his warnings, persisted in photographing U.S. fleet manoeuvres. Fifteen years later, a major general and assistant commandant of the marine corps, he engaged the Japs in earnest as leader of the Solomon Islands campaign and "hero of Guadalcanal." His victories won for him the congressional medal of honour and promotion to lieutenant general. On Nov. 1, 1943, he led the marines again in their first landing at Bougainville. Shortly afterward he was recalled to Washington to succeed Lt. Gen. Thomas Holcomb, retired, as commandant of the marine corps on Jan. 1, 1944.

Varnishes: *see* PAINTS AND VARNISHES.

Vasilevsky, Alexander Mikhailovich
(1897?–   ), Russian army officer, was a Czarist soldier during World War I and joined the proletariat during the revolution of 1917. A product of the Russian general staff schools, he helped reorganize the soviet armies after the Russo-Finnish war, 1939–40. Attached to the Russian high command since 1941, Vasilevsky served under Marshal Georgi Zhukov, who later became subordinate to his former aide as chief of the operational staff. Vasilevsky, who held the rank of major general in 1941, rose to the rank of marshal in 18 months, and in Nov. 1942 he succeeded Marshal Boris Shaposhnikov, who was reported in ill health, as Russian chief of staff. The appointment of Vasilevsky was part of Stalin's plan to revitalize and reorganize his general staff. The soviet premier dropped the old triumvirate of Budenny, Timoshenko and Voroshilov from their former positions of prominence and replaced them with seven of his "younger generals"; Vasilevsky was regarded as the best fitted for the position of chief of staff. Under his guidance, the younger generals scored brilliant successes at Stalingrad, in the Russian summer offensive of 1943 and the winter campaign of 1943–44.

Vassar College.
A college for women at Poughkeepsie, N.Y., founded by Matthew Vassar in 1861. As an emergency measure in order to train students more quickly for war work and reconstruction activities, the college put into operation in Sept. 1943 a three-year course for the bachelor's degree. The academic year was lengthened to 40 weeks.

The curriculum was revised to adapt it to both the three-year and the four-year schedule and to realize more fully the basic Vassar aim of education for social use, but there was no change in the quantity or quality of work required for the degree. The curriculum still lay wholly within the field of the liberal arts. New courses introduced during 1941–43 as specific preparation for war service, such as meteorology, radio and vacuum tube applications, and intensive work in translation of foreign languages were continued. To foster individual and group competence and responsibility, as well as to meet the labour shortage and to reduce cost of education to the student, every student gave an hour a day to household work. This co-operative system was organized under student supervision in close relation to the student government. For statistics of the faculty, student enrolment, endowment, etc., *see* UNIVERSITIES AND COLLEGES.   (H. N. MacC.)

↑Vatican City State.
A sovereign independent state, established by the Lateran treaty between the Holy See and the royal Italian government, Feb. 11, 1929. The treaty is recognized in international law, and the reigning pope is the sovereign. The area of Vatican City is 108.7 ac. It has its own railroad station, radio station, postal and aerial system and currency. Total issue of bronze, nickel, silver and gold coins is not to exceed 1,000,000 lire. Executive powers are exercised by the governor, responsible only to the pope; administrative power is exercised by a commission of cardinals, which in 1943 rearranged the civil service in 11 distinct groups.

The population of Vatican City in 1943 numbered in excess of 800, to which was added the Vatican diplomatic colony representing the nations who broke off relations with the axis powers.

Ambassadors and ministers accredited to the Vatican in 1943 were 37. Ambassadors and ministers of China, Italy, Finland and Rumania presented their credentials to the pope. Archbishop Godfrey, apostolic delegate to Britain, was appointed Vatican chargé d'affaires to the Polish government in London.

Allied planes bombed Rome July 19, and the patriarchal basilica of San Lorenzo fuori le Mura, Vatican property, was severely damaged. Immediately following the bombing the pope visited the bombed district. Blood spots were observed on the pope's white cassock. Radio Vatican denied German and Italian reports that the pope had protested to President Roosevelt on July 24. German troops assumed protection of the Vatican Sept. 10, and on Sept. 15 restricted the use of Radio Vatican. The pope protested Sept. 16 to Gen. Albert Kesselring against the closing of St. Peter's to Italians, and on Sept. 21 church dignitaries entering Vatican City were held by the Germans. On the same day ten cardinals were reported to be under house arrest by order of the German commander, and on Sept. 24 German troops were placed at the entrance to Vatican City.

Papal guards were increased Oct. 7, and later Hitler's reported offer of asylum in Lichtenstein or Germany was rejected by the pope. Notices of inviolability were posted at the entrance to Vatican City Oct. 13, but on Oct. 29 Germany pledged to respect the person of the pope and the neutrality of Vatican City.

Vatican City was bombed by an unidentified plane Nov. 6, damaging buildings, but there were no casualties. Gen. Dwight Eisenhower, U.S.A., declared no Allied planes were over Rome that day.

In the city of Rome there were 446 churches in 1943, of which 106 were parish churches. (*See also* PIUS XII; ROMAN CATHOLIC CHURCH.)   (J. LaF.)

Vatutin, Nikolai Fedorovich
(1900?–   ), a Russian army officer, was a private in World War I. During the revolution of 1917, he joined the bolsheviks and rose to the rank of a cavalry division commander. He was commander of one of the Russian armies that recaptured

Kharkov in 1943. After the Russians launched their big drive in the summer of 1943, Vatutin was in command of soviet armies that cracked German defenses in the Ukraine, crossed the Dnieper river, captured Kiev and later swept through Korosten and Zhitomir. His advance was too rapid for his slower-moving supply lines and he was compelled to evacuate both Korosten and Zhitomir in Nov. 1943 under the impact of a strong German counterblow. Vatutin quickly shifted his strategy, whittled down the strength of the German drive and had halted the nazi offensive by December. His army then resumed the offensive, recaptured Korosten and Zhitomir and by Jan. 1944 had crossed over the boundaries of prewar Poland.

Vegetable Oils and Animal Fats.

The production of fats and oils in the United States increased in 1943 to an estimated total of 11,200,-000,000 lb. compared with an output of 10,600,000,000 lb. in 1942, according to revised estimates by the U.S. department of agriculture. Stocks at the beginning of the season, Oct. 1, were 80,000,000 lb. larger in 1943 than in 1942 and there was also an increase in imports. The principal forms of fats and oils included in the supply were: lard and pork fats 3,200,000,000 lb.; butter 1,960,000,000 lb.; inedible tallow and greases 1,650,000,000 lb.; cottonseed oil 1,240,000,000 lb.; soybean oil 1,300,000,000 lb.; linseed oil 900,000,000 lb.; corn oil 240,000,000 lb. and peanut oil 185,000,000 lb. There were also smaller amounts of olive, wool oil, tung, fish, etc. The greatest increase was in soybean oil, which nearly tripled in three years. Pork fats accounted for a large part of the increase in 1943, a product of the great increase in hog numbers. Lard production reached a new high point since 1919, cottonseed was below the level of 1926–36 and butter production declined. Peanut-oil production did not increase like the crop, since most of this increase was used for peanut butter, candy and salted nuts.

Requirements for fats were increasing in 1943. Lend-lease shipments were heavy, military needs expanded and preliminary steps were being taken to build up some stocks for relief. Domestic consumption of food fats and oils were about 46 lb. per capita in 1943 compared with a prewar average of about 48 lb. in 1935–39. The principal decline was in butter, which was down about 4 lb. from the 1935–39 average. This was partially offset by an increase of 1 lb. in margarine. The use of lard and rendered pork fat was up to 14.3 lb. per capita, compared with the average of 11 lb. Shortening was down to 9.1 lb. compared with 11.9 in 1935–39. Exports were about 50% greater in 1943 than in 1942 and a larger quantity was taken for the manufacture of munitions. Even with price ceilings in effect the continued high level of employment resulted in a strong demand.

The production of oil-bearing crops, soybeans, peanuts and cottonseed must be increased in 1944 to meet the growing needs and provide any surplus for relief purposes, should large areas be liberated in Europe in 1944. Both soybeans and peanuts increased in 1943 but the crop of cottonseed was down about 11%

U.S. Production of Principal Fats and Oils
(Millions of Pounds; Department of Agriculture Estimates)

	Year Beginning	1940–41	1941–42	1942–43	1943–44*
Butter	Oct.	2,287	2,142	2,112	1,960
Lard	Oct.	2,285	2,440	2,739	3,200
Inedible tallow and greases	Oct.	1,492	1,733	1,600	1,650
Corn oil	Oct.	186	242	240	240
Cottonseed oil	Aug.	1,425	1,250	1,400	1,240
Linseed oil	July	494	546	729	900
Olive oil	Nov.	11	8	10	10
Peanut oil	Oct.	174	78	133	185
Soybean oil	Oct.	564	707	1,198	1,300
Tung oil	Dec.	4	2	5	3

*Estimated.

from the previous year. The plans for 1944 called for further expansion in oil seeds of all kinds, soybeans 20% and peanuts 30%. This increase in the oil-bearing crops was considered of vital importance because of the expected decline in butter and pork-fat production. (*See* also BUTTER; COCO-NUTS; COTTON; PEANUTS; SOYBEANS.) (J. C. Ms.)

Vegetables: *see* AGRICULTURE; CORN; HORTICULTURE; LETTUCE; MARKET GARDENING; POTATOES; TOMATOES; ETC.

Veidt, Conrad

(1893–1943), British actor, was born Jan. 22 in Berlin. He received his early theatrical training under Max Reinhardt and had a successful stage career before appearing in motion pictures. Tall, slim, of aristocratic bearing and a skilled linguist, Veidt portrayed "villains" with such consummate skill that he frequently "stole the show" from the stars. He went to the United States in 1926 to appear in a movie version of François Villon and though he had hoped some day to return to Germany to continue his career, the rise of naziism changed his plans. He became a British citizen in 1938. His first important motion picture role was in *The Cabinet of Dr. Caligari*. He was later seen in *Power, Dark Journey, I Was a Spy, The Passing of the Third Floor Back, All Through the Night, U-Boat 29, A Woman's Face, Whistling in the Dark, The Men in Her Life, Escape, Blackout, Rome Express, The Devil is an Empress, Nazi Agent* and *Casablanca*. He died in Hollywood, Calif., April 3.

Veiller, Bayard

(1869–1943), U.S. playwright, was born in Brooklyn, N.Y. His early interest in the theatre was dampened by an unfavourable criticism of his first script and he gave up his college career and turned to reporting. He moved westward, became in turn a logger and stock company manager. Returning to the theatre, he produced a great number of his own plays, the most successful of which were *Within the Law* (1912), *The Thirteenth Chair* (1916) and *The Trial of Mary Dugan* (1927). For the movies, he wrote *Guilty Hands* and *Unashamed* and supervised the motion picture versions of *The Trial of Mary Dugan* and *The Thirteenth Chair*. He wrote an autobiography, *The Fun I've Had* (1941). Veiller died in New York city, June 16.

Venereal Diseases.

Congress appropriated $12,500,000 for venereal disease control during the fiscal year 1943. State, local and other funds budgeted for this purpose totalled $8,772,578. There was a total of $19,368,458 available to the states and territories.

The aim of control activities was considered as not only the prevention of the usual wartime increases in the incidence of venereal disease but also the development of a foundation for strong and adequate resources for postwar control. This was in order to avoid repetition of the disastrous experience following World War I, when there was a virtual abandonment of many control measures.

In spite of war-induced shortages of personnel and supplies, the state health departments continued the steady expansion of their activities (Table 1). Increases were reported in the amount of drugs distributed; the number of clinics was increased; the number of clinic admissions for syphilis and for gonorrhoea totalled considerably more than in 1942.

Outstanding in the field of research was a report from the Venereal Disease Research laboratory, Staten Island, N.Y., upon investigations of the use of penicillin in the treatment of human syphilis. Syphilis prophylaxis in rabbits was being studied, using penicillin, arsenicals and other preparations. This led to the treatment of four human cases of primary syphilis with penicillin. The four cases showed satisfactory clinical responses with no indications of any relapses, and the penicillin investigations were continued. Another report of interest from the same laboratory dealt with the use of penicillin sodium in sulfonamide-resistant gonorrhoea in men. The chemical was found to give evidence of being of great value (74 of 75 patients studied responded in a satisfactory manner with practically no reaction to the drug).

Perhaps the chief development of the year 1943, however, was the establishment by the public health service in co-operation with state departments of health and other public and private agencies of a network of rapid treatment centres, where infected persons—chiefly women—received intensive venereal disease therapy. Conceived as a wartime measure to check the spread of syphilis and gonorrhoea among the armed forces, war workers and selective service registrants, these institutions were primarily hospitals where the newer techniques in the treatment of syphilis and gonorrhoea were applied. The en masse demonstration of the effectiveness of the various intensive therapies afforded by the centres was considered as of paramount importance in that the medical profession might profit by the accumulated experience and the proving of techniques that might result. By the end of 1943 there were over 30 of these centres established over the United States, the Canal Zone, Puerto Rico and the Virgin Islands.

The public health service provided consultation services and supplied specially trained physicians, nurses and technical personnel to operate the centres. Former Civilian Conservation corps camps and National Youth administration resident centres and other types of existing buildings, renovated and adapted, were utilized. Syphilis treatment schedules under investigation during 1943 in these hospitals consisted of: One-day fever plus chemotherapy, 5-day drip, 10–20 Schoch method, 10–12 week Eagle, and variations of these. Sulfathiazole and sulfadiazine continued to be the drugs of choice in the treatment of gonorrhoea and were used in the rapid treatment centres. However, evidence accumulated in the centres in 1943 indicated that the proportion of so-called sulfa-resistant cases had increased; investigations were initiated to determine the causes in order to overcome this phenomenon.

In another phase of the national control program, a "national round-up" of Selective Service registrants with positive blood tests for syphilis was inaugurated toward mid-1943. The plan was designed to aid state health officers in achieving co-ordinated action between local health agencies and local Selective Service boards with the objective of making available for service a large number of men previously unavailable. Essential features of the plan were as follows: (1) Rapid medical reclassification by local health officers of each registrant with a positive blood test, and (2) notification to local boards of the medical availability of the registrant insofar as syphilis was concerned.

In 1943 considerable progress was made in the field of venereal disease control in industry. The recommendations of an advisory committee to the public health service, containing current authoritative information and formulating sound, basic principles applicable to any program of venereal disease control in industry, were presented to management, labour, the medical profession and public health authorities. For the first time a framework of adequate, uniform principles upon which to base desirable control programs in industry was therefore available. These principles proved generally acceptable and positive action upon them throughout the U.S. ensued. With continuing growth throughout 1944 in this field, a nationwide venereal disease control program in industry, integrated with the general health programs through the active co-operation of local health departments, was en-

Table I.—*Venereal Disease Control Activities of State Health Departments*

Fiscal Year	No. of Clinics	Clinic Admissions		Serologic Tests[†]	Drugs Distributed	
		Syphilis Cases	Gonorrhoea Cases		Doses of Arsenicals[†]	Sulfonamide Tablets[†]
1939 ..	2,405*	249,464	62,835	5.6	4.7	3.5‡
1940 ..	2,887*	288,778	66,811	10.2	6.9	5.3
1941 ..	3,245	340,615	84,418	16.5	8.2	7.2
1942 ..	3,569	343,312	104,421	20.6	8.7	13.8
1943 ..	3,852	430,302‡	133,784‡	18.0	11.4	22.2

*End of calendar year.   †In millions.   ‡Estimate.

visioned as one of the major advances in venereal disease control. (*See* also EPIDEMICS AND PUBLIC HEALTH CONTROL.)

(J. R. HR.)

Venezuela. A republic of northern South America, with a coast line extending from Colombia on the west to British Guiana on the east. Area: 352,170 sq.mi.; pop. (1941 census): 3,847,051, not including approx. 100,000 Indians. Capital city: Caracas (268,808). Other cities (1936 census figures): Maracaibo (110,010); Valencia (49,214); Barquisimeto (36,429); Ciudad Bolívar (25,134); Puerto Cabello (20,622). President in 1943: General Isaías Medina Angarita.

History.—The year proved to be a fairly satisfactory one for Venezuela, with no change in general political policy taking place. The administration of President Medina Angarita retained most of the seats in congress in elections held Jan. 19, 1943.

The most significant development of the year was the enactment on March 13 of a new oil law settling the somewhat strained relations which had existed between the oil companies and the government, and to the general satisfaction of both sides. Under the new plan all companies and concessions were placed in an equal position under the law. Taxes were increased on surface lands, and some immunities from customs charges enjoyed by the companies were eliminated; the income of the government would be increased by 80% by these changes (the corporations likewise paid some 25,000,000 bolívars in disputed back taxes). At the same time the oil companies had their concessions lengthened to a period of 40 years, and their position was far more secure than before. The agreement also provided for an increase in production to about 200,000 bbl. per day, after the war.

On April 15 President Medina Angarita authorized the formation of a new political party, to be named the Partidarios de la Política del Gobierno, and designed to support the administration program. The move was partly in anticipation of the presidential election campaign of 1945 (President Medina Angarita in May stated that he would not be a candidate). Venezuela's other party is the Acción Democratica, some nine years old; it was believed the conservatives might form another organization for the coming campaign. In cabinet appointments made in May the administration showed a trend toward the left by inclusion of three men from liberal groups.

Economic conditions continued satisfactory in 1943, in spite of shortages. Ship arrivals increased, aiding retail trade.

Education.—The school system numbered (1942) some 5,600 elementary schools, with 295,400 students; 90 secondary and technical schools, enrolment over 7,000. There were two universities; modernization of the Central university at Caracas was being planned in 1943. The 1942–43 budget allotted 22,892,000 bolívars to education; in 1943–44 the amount was increased to 23,830,000 bolívars.

Finance.—The monetary unit is the bolívar, value approximately 30 cents U.S. in 1943. In the budget for 1942–43, revenues were estimated at 301,673,000 bolívars; expenditures at 319,553,000 bolívars; for 1943–44, revenue was estimated at 316,693,000 bolívars; expenditures 347,958,000 bolívars. In both budgets loans were planned to cover deficits. The national debt amounted to 15,494,577 bolívars (Dec. 31, 1942), all internal. Note circulation amounted to 256,076,000 bolívars on June 30, 1943.

Trade.—In 1941 exports totalled 1,061,565,000 bolívars in value, of which petroleum formed 94.2% of the total. Other products exported were coffee, cacao, gold, hides and skins, pearls, balatá. Imports were valued at 287,736,000 bolívars, and were mainly foodstuffs, textiles and manufactures. Both imports and exports were down in volume in 1942, largely because of lack of shipping.

Resources.—Petroleum is the most important item produced in Venezuela; the output in 1942 was 155,800,000 bbl.; in 1941 it was 228,100,000 bbl. The drop in 1942 was due to the shortage of tankers. In normal times Venezuela is the third largest producer in the world.

Coffee forms the largest agricultural export. The 1942–43 crop was damaged by heavy rains; while the original estimate of production was for around 900,000 bags, in the period Oct. 1, 1942–Aug. 31, 1943, only 459,543 bags were harvested. The 1942–43 cotton crop was 3,779 short tons, about half of the expected crop, with much damage due to insects. Cacao output (1941) was 13,547 short tons. Normal production of salt is 24,802 tons; of coal, 5,512 tons.

Communication.—External communication is by steamer, Pan American Airways, and Royal Dutch Airways. Highways total 5,883 mi., with 3,600 mi. surfaced and improved. Due to lack of tires, it was estimated in 1943 that 6,000 cars were laid up. Railway mileage is 589 mi. The line called the "German railway" was blacklisted in Nov. 1943, and unable to operate because of lack of fuel was taken over by the government Nov. 16. There is likewise internal communication by domestic airlines, and on the Orinoco river and its tributaries by boat. (D. RD.)

Vermiculite.
Sales of vermiculite in the United States in 1942 more than doubled over 1941, to 57,848 short tons. Prices increased slightly from the decline in 1941, the reported increase in total value being 155%, against one of 147% in tonnage. (G. A. RO.)

Vermont.
A north Atlantic state of the U.S.A., the only one of the six New England states with no sea coast; popularly known as the "Green Mountain state." Area 9,718 sq.mi., of which 440 sq.mi. are water. Pop. (1940) 359,231, later greatly depleted by the exodus of thousands to the armed services and to war industries in other states. In 1940 there were 327,079 native whites, 31,727 foreign-born, 384 Negro, 41 of other races. The two largest cities are Burlington, on Lake Champlain (27,686), and Rutland (17,082). The capital is Montpelier (8,006).

History.—The state legislature convened in 1943 and granted emergency powers to the governor, who in turn created the office of civilian defense and the Council of Safety. There were no changes in the constitution. State officers in 1943: governor, William H. Wills; lieutenant governor, Mortimer R. Proctor; secretary of state, Rawson C. Myrick; state treasurer, Levi R. Kelley.

Education.—Approximately 1,000 elementary schools were in operation during 1943, or 100 less than in the preceding year. The enrolment dropped 4,991, reached 39,104 pupils; number of teachers, 1,814. In the 91 secondary schools of the state there were 14,964 pupils enrolled, a decrease of 1,101 from the preceding year. Teachers in the secondary school numbered 708.

Public Welfare, Charities, Correction.—The Public Welfare department has jurisdiction over all penal institutions in the state, the state hospital for the insane, the tuberculosis sanitariums, the state industrial school. Old-age assistance is set up under a director and a board of three members. The expenditure of this division for the fiscal year ending June 30, 1943, was $1,269,576. Expenditures for the year ending June 30, 1943, were as follows: aid to dependent children $265,458.08, 645 cases, 1,669 children; committed children $143,740.42, 1,022 cases; blind assistance $42,132.50, 150 cases; general relief, not including hospital, burial or overnight transients, $1,074, 2,439 persons; penal institutions $189,980. As of July 1, 1943, there were in the house of correction 64 men; in the state prison 141; in the women's reformatory 25. For the Weeks school for juvenile delinquents, expenditures were $12,256 (pop. 186).

Communication.—Railroad mileage in the state totalled 968.4 in 1943. There were 64,276 telephones in the state. Total number of miles in public highways was 14,204.5, of which 1,780.3 mi. were listed as state highways, 2,744.0 mi. as state-aid highways and 9,680.2 mi. as town highways. Total state expenditure for state highway work for the fiscal year ending June 30, 1943, was $4,300,000.

Banking and Finance.—At the close of the fiscal year, June 30, 1943, there were 57 state and national banks in Vermont, 8 mutual savings banks, 33 savings banks and trust companies, 10 co-operative savings and loan associations and 3 credit unions. There was an increase in bank deposits in 1943 of $10,514,725.63. Total bank deposits $126,157,910. Total number of banks 41.

Receipts of the state as of June 30, 1943 totalled $16,702,157.35; disbursements $15,020,191.67; obligations $5,493,431.90; unappropriated surplus $1,176,664.29.

Agriculture.—The total number of cattle in 1943 was 398,763, of which 264,361 were milk-producing. Wartime restrictions in dairy products impelled the governor to appoint the commissioner of agriculture, E. H. Jones, "milk co-ordinator for the existing emergency" in 1943.

Leading Agricultural Products of Vermont, 1943 and 1942

Crop	1943 (est.)	1942	Crop	1943 (est.)	1942
Corn, bu.	2,508,000	2,800,000	Maple syrup, gal.	1,072,000	1,310,000
Potatoes, bu.	1,846,000	1,473,000	Apples, bu.	705,000	731,000
Oats, bu.	1,440,000	1,961,000	Maple sugar, lb.	354,000	320,000
Tame hay, tons	1,147,000	1,161,000			

Manufacturing.—The number of manufacturing plants in Vermont in 1943 was 850; the number of workers about 110,000, of whom about 50,000 were industrial workers. Total wages paid industrial employees were about $55,000,000. Total value of products produced was estimated at well over $175,000,000. The principal products manufactured are machine tools, woodworking, lumber and furniture, marble, granite, textiles, paper, talc, asbestos, slate, scales and clothing. War manufacturing expanded pay rolls to a considerable extent in 1943.

Mineral Production.—The outstanding event of geological interest in Vermont in 1943 was the development of copper mines, abandoned 40 years previously, in the copper-bearing belt extending north and south over a known distance of approximately 20 mi. The six basic mineral industries of the state, asbestos, granite, limestone, marble, slate and talc, were variously affected by the war. The mining of asbestos was extremely active in 1942–43, as was marble. Slate was at low ebb and most of the quarries were closed. Lime was mined at about 80% of normal, owing to conditions in the paper industry. Talc companies were also operating at about 80% of normal. The critical condition of the rubber industry greatly restricted the use of Vermont talc.

(L. M. A.)

Veterans' Administration.
Medical Treatment and Domiciliary Care.—On June 30, 1943, the Veterans' administration was operating hospital

Table I.—*U.S. Veterans on Roll, June 30, 1943*

War	On roll, June 30, 1943	Disbursements, Fiscal Year 1943
Yellow fever experiments		
Participants	9	$ 13,500.00
War of 1812		
Deceased veterans	1	240.00
Mexican War		
Deceased veterans	82	49,324.00
Indian Wars—total	4,794	2,408,854.11
Living veterans	1,475	1,156,235.90
Deceased veterans	3,319	1,252,618.21
Civil War—total	33,177	16,553,415.09
Living veterans	625	870,564.63
Deceased veterans	32,552	15,682,850.46
Spanish-American War—total . .	204,484	122,988,548.48
Living veterans	140,093	99,457,260.43
Deceased veterans.	64,391	23,531,288.05
Regular establishment—total . .	56,858	22,812,363.79
Living veterans	43,197	17,162,826.52
Deceased veterans	13,661	5,649,537.27
World War I—total	545,330	270,956,692.75
Living veterans	428,964	208,107,227.65
Service connected	341,505	165,865,297.31
Nonservice connected . . .	84,878	37,879,290.87
Emergency officers, etc. . .	2,581	4,362,639.47
Deceased veterans.	116,366	62,849,405.10
Service connected	89,925	51,660,113.69
Nonservice connected . . .	26,441	11,189,351.41
World War II—total	15,173	6,359,405.68
Living veterans	7,037	2,589,141.75
Deceased veterans	8,136	3,770,263.93
Reserve Officers—living veterans .	181	231,475.97
Grand total—pensions and compensation. . .	860,089	442,373,819.87
Living veterans	621,572	329,574,732.85
Deceased veterans	238,508	112,785,587.02
Participants, yellow fever experiments . .	9	13,500.00

facilities at 93 locations in 45 states and the District of Columbia. There were 61,764 beds for hospital treatment and 18,455 for domiciliary care. In addition, 1,693 hospital beds in other government facilities were being utilized. The hospital load of the Veterans' administration at that time was 56,897 patients, of whom 56,641 were United States veterans, 24 were allied veterans of World War I and 232 were miscellaneous beneficiaries. Of the United States veterans, 54,013 were in Veterans' administration facilities, 1,680 in other government hospitals and 948 in state or civil institutions. Approximately 74.98% of these United States veterans were receiving treatment for disabilities not of service origin. During the fiscal year 1943, 9,835 United States veterans were admitted for observation and treatment of tuberculosis, 9,952 for psychotic or mental diseases, 12,642 for other neurological disorders and 127,805 for general medical and surgical conditions. The veteran population in domiciliary status June 30, 1943, totalled 8,997. Of this number, 5,582 veterans were disabled by general medical conditions, 3,273 by neuropsychiatric diseases and 142 by tubercular ailments. During the fiscal year 1943, an average of 4,898 veterans eligible for care in Veterans' administration facilities were cared for in state or territorial homes. These homes are reimbursed by the federal government at the rate of $240 a year for each of such veterans domiciled therein. During the year, dental care was provided for 31,460 hospital patients, 6,831 domiciliary members and 2,976 outpatients in clinics maintained by the Veterans' administration.

Pensions and Compensation.—Table I shows the number of cases on the rolls as of June 30, 1943, and the net disbursements during the fiscal year 1943 from the appropriations "ARMY AND NAVY PENSIONS."

Vocational Rehabilitation.—Public No. 16, 78th congress, approved March 24, 1941, provided vocational rehabilitation to any person who served in the active military or naval service at any time after Dec. 6, 1941, and prior to the termination of World War II, who (1) was honourably discharged from such service; (2) has a disability incurred in or aggravated by such service for which pension is payable or would be but for the receipt of retirement pay and (3) is in need of vocational rehabilitation to overcome the handicap of such disability. As of June 30, 1943, only a few applications for training had been received.

Guardianship.—The guardianship load of the Veterans' administration, June 30, 1943, was 78,064 wards, of whom 43,172 were incompetents and 34,892 minors. The value of estates of these wards approximated $155,709,290.63.

Insurance.—As of June 30, 1943, there were 586,590 United States government life insurance policies in force representing $2,499,603,842 of insurance. Monthly payments were being made to 10,808 policyholders for permanent and total disabilities. Disbursements for this type of insurance during the fiscal year 1943 totalled $39,814,670.28. On June 30, 1943, monthly payments of yearly renewable term insurance policies were being made to 9,717 permanently and totally disabled veterans and to the beneficiaries of 4,683 deceased veterans. Monthly payments on automatic insurance policies were being made to 224 veterans and the beneficiaries of 19 deceased veterans. Disbursements for term and automatic insurance during the fiscal year totalled $14,489,489.50, including $5,345,996.16 transferred to the U.S. Government Life Insurance Trust fund for cases traceable to hazards of war. As of June 30, 1943, there had been approved 9,565,088 applications for national service life insurance aggregating $66,506,754,500. An act approved Oct. 17, 1940, provided for suspension of enforcement of certain civil liabilities of persons serving in the armed forces of the United States. Article IV of the act provided that the government would, on application by the insured, guarantee to commercial insurance companies premiums on insurance carried with such companies by policyholders while in active service. Through June 30, 1943, 67,054 applications for this benefit had been received, of which 53,080 representing $127,575,186.53 of insurance had been approved.

Finance.—The actual net disbursements from appropriations and trust funds of the Veterans' administration (including adjustments on lapsed appropriations) during the fiscal year 1943 were as shown in Table II. (*See also* REHABILITATION AND OCCUPATIONAL THERAPY FOR WOUNDED SOLDIERS.)

Table II.—*Net Disbursements of Veterans' Administration in Fiscal Year 1943*

Appropriations	Disbursements
Salaries and expenses	$111,401,127.42*
Emergency fund for the president, national defense (allotment to Veterans' administration)	2,968,212.36
Printing and binding	292,792.13
Hospital and domiciliary facilities and services (Veterans' administration)	2,694,330.81
Public Works Administration act of 1938 (allotment to Veterans' administration, 1938–43)	26,158.49
Emergency relief (transfers from WPA), 1941–43	139,811.86
Army and navy pensions	442,373,819.87
Military and naval insurance (World War I)	14,489,489.50§
National service life insurance (World War II)	18,295,029.69†
Adjusted service and dependent pay (World War I)	167,728.42
Vocational rehabilitation (World War I)	–3,452.55
Military and naval family allowance	–2,680.23‡
Miscellaneous	260.35
Trust funds	
U. S. government life insurance fund	39,814,670.28
National service life insurance (World War II)	6,549,351.07
Adjusted service certificates (World War I)	996,953.80
Army allotments	39.00
General post fund	34,156.86
Funds due incompetent beneficiaries	89,187.24
Personal funds of patients, Veterans' administration	3,078,508.21
Total	$643,406,394.64

*Includes adjustments on lapsed appropriations—medical and hospital services, credit of $215.78.

†Represents net amount transferred by vouchers to national service life insurance trust fund for payment of claims traceable to the extra hazards of military or naval service. Does not include $12,849,767.15 transferred by transfer appropriation warrants from July 1 through Aug. 31, 1942.

‡Credits to appropriations.

§Includes $5,345,996.16 transferred to U. S. government life insurance trust fund for hazardous cases.

Note: "Salaries and expenses," "Public Works administration" and "emergency relief" include net disbursements of $633,879.08 from allotments made to other government agencies. Allotments were made to the war department and Federal Works agency.

(F. T. HI.)

→Veterans of Foreign Wars.

Adoption of a nationwide program of war service and the formulation of a 10-point postwar veteran welfare program comprised a major share of the activities of the Veterans of Foreign Wars of the United States during the year 1942–43.

Based on resolutions adopted by the various V.F.W. state conventions early in the summer of 1943—resolutions which later were endorsed by the 44th V.F.W. national encampment at New York city—the V.F.W. outlined the following comprehensive program:

(1) Continuation of pay, within certain limits, for a period of six months after honourable discharge at the close of World War II, for all persons serving in the armed forces of the United States, based on a minimum of $100 a month.

(2) Educational aid by the federal government to honourably discharged veterans of the war whose educations were interrupted or prevented by military or naval service.

(3) Adequate Veterans' administration hospital facilities for medical treatment and hospitalization of honourably discharged veterans of any recognized war, campaign or expedition, with at least 90 days' service.

(4) Pension and compensation payments to be established and maintained on a fair and reasonable cost of living index.

(5) Effective, workable veteran preference in employment on federal, state, county and municipal jobs.

(6) All supply and construction contracts between the federal government and private firms or contractors to contain a clause that 3 employees of every 10 or major portion thereof, of said private firms or contractors, shall be honourably discharged veterans.

(7) Pension entitlement to widows and orphans of honourably discharged, deceased veterans of any recognized war, campaign or expedition, where said veteran had at least 90 days' service, regardless of service-connected disabilities.

(8) Pension entitlement to honourably discharged veterans of any war, campaign or expedition who had at least 90 days' service and who are (a) unemployable, (b) unable to secure gainful and sustaining employment and (c) disabled to a degree of 10% or more, regardless of service connection of said disability.

(9) Special recognition for honourably discharged veterans of any recognized war, campaign or expedition, who served on foreign soil or had sea duty in hostile waters, by a special allowance of 20% above standard rates for compensation, pension and retirement pay and a five-point addition above standard additions in veteran preference on classified civil service examination grades.

(10) Continuation and expansion of the Veterans' administration as an independent federal agency with full jurisdiction over vocational rehabilitation for service-connected disabled veterans; medical treatment, hospitalization, pensions and compensation for all eligible veterans and continuation and expansion of the Veterans' Employment service to render special assistance to all honourably discharged veterans in need of or seeking employment.

More than 150,000 veterans or men still in the armed forces of World War II joined the V.F.W. during the fiscal year ended Aug. 31, 1943, marking the greatest year of expansion the organization had experienced since its founding in 1899.

The constitution and by-laws provide that V.F.W. eligibility to membership is earned by armed service, in time of war "on foreign soil or in hostile waters." Thus, immediately upon the United States' declaration of war upon Japan and Germany, thousands of members of the U.S. army, navy and marine corps became eligible to V.F.W. membership as soon as they had left the continental limits of the United States. Many of these World War II members became affiliated, for the duration of the war, with V.F.W. "field units" established on 65 battle fronts throughout the world in 1943.

CREW OF THE "MEMPHIS BELLE," famous U.S. bomber which completed its 25th mission over Europe in 1943, being inducted into the Veterans of Foreign Wars at Detroit, Mich.

Others, including many who had received medical discharges, became active members of the 3,600 local V.F.W. posts throughout the country.

The V.F.W.'s 44th year also was distinguished by record-breaking achievements in other activities. The 22nd annual Buddy poppy distribution, in behalf of disabled veterans and their dependents, reached an all-time high in the sale of 9,253,275 poppies throughout the country. The V.F.W. aviation cadet recruiting program, undertaken at the request of the war department, resulted in a total of 45,000 young men being qualified for training in the army air forces, and an additional 37,000 for other branches of the armed forces.

Attainment of several long-standing legislative objectives also marked the 1942–43 year, notably in the enactment of H.R. 1749, the broadest bill on veterans' hospitalization ever passed by congress. H.R. 1749, which became Public Law No. 10, granted to veterans of World War II the same hospitalization, domiciliary care and burial benefits already available to veterans of previous wars. Another accomplished objective was enactment of Public Law No. 16, which completely separated disabled war veterans from disabled civilians as to vocational rehabilitation. There were in 1943 more than 2,500 ladies' auxiliary chapters.

"Unity for Peace" was the keynote of the 1943 national encampment, Sept. 28–30, 1943, at New York, at which Carl J. Schoeninger, electrical engineer of Detroit, Mich., was elected commander-in-chief.

(B. Y.)

Veterinary Medicine.
A noteworthy trend in the application of veterinary science was its upward turn in the face of decreasing animal transportation in the military service. In the civilian circles of Great Britain and the United States, the expansion was due to increasing the number of food-producing animals and to more alert attention to mastering the diseases which reduce food poundage. In the military forces, there was extension of meat and milk inspection in home and far-flung theatres where trained veterinary officers, under the direction of medical corps, not only supervised the safety of army rations but also superintended the health of the domestic animals surrounding military stations. The American pattern of food inspection, enforced by the surgeon general of the United States army, attracted wide attention among the forces of the United Nations operating in Iceland, the near east, and Australia where the civilian veterinary services and agricultural interests willingly co-operated with veterinary officers in eradicating transmissible diseases from the farm animals concerned.

Veterinary War Conference.—The American Veterinary Medical association convened a session at St. Louis in August to study the more important animal-disease problems of war in the western hemisphere. Officially appointed delegates from Canada and Mexico participated. The object was to fortify disease-control measures among farm animals and to recommend practical means of nourishing them regardless of declining sources of adequate proteins. The government's plan of merely stepping up the number of animals without corresponding plans of providing the essentials of normal nutrition and housing was frowned upon.

The War-Dog Service.—The war-dog service organized in the army of the United States in 1942 was enlarged to many thousands of dogs. Elaborate training stations and numerous dog trainers and veterinary officers were provided to develop the project. The dogs were donated by the citizenry under the sponsorship of Dogs for Defense, Inc., a private nonprofit corporation of New York. Trained dogs of selected breeds were assigned in large numbers to armed forces in field and factory. They served as sentries, patrols, and transport animals, in the latter role as sledge dogs in northern army posts. The yeoman service rendered by trained dogs since ancient times was thereby redemonstrated in the global war of 1943.

Veterinary Education.—World War II exposed the shortcomings of the veterinary educational system of Great Britain and the United States. Left to private enterprise, unmanaged through lack of public interest and support until recent years, the adequacy, cleanliness and wholesomeness of food derived from animals received little consideration as populations increased and civilization developed. Sufficient manpower had not been furnished to supervise the safety of the food man eats, granted that this is one of the purposes of veterinary science. The legislature of New York published a book drawing attention to the filthy, insanitary abattoirs of that state; the Chicago *Herald-American* published a series of illustrated articles depicting a similar situation in Illinois. The United States public health service established its "standard milk ordinance" where there is no supervision of the cows whence the milk comes. The Illinois legislature passed a law to curb the incidence of bovine brucellosis and undulant fever (human) but the state veterinarian did not have sufficient veterinary personnel to enforce it. Meanwhile the American veterinary schools turned away hundreds of applicants for veterinary degrees without taking steps to broaden the fields in which trained veterinarians should be working.

The Sulfonamides in Veterinary Medicine.—Although sulfanilamide and the allied compounds proved useful in acute streptococcal infections of animals, the response of chronic infections to their action was practically nil. Chronic mastitis, chronic endometritis, brucellosis, actinomycosis, and the pasterelloses were not perceptibly improved by the use of these drugs. On the other hand, the salmonelloses affecting the digestive tract were recognizably improved by the slow absorbing group, of which sulfaguanidine is an example. The use of sulfapyridine in acute pulmonary infections of animals was disappointing.

Trichomoniasis of Cattle.—Increasing importance was placed in the role played by *Trichomonas foetus* in interrupting reproduction in cattle. Improved methods of diagnosing this widespread venereal disease of cattle were developed by scientists of the University of Wisconsin. Attempts by the zoological division of the United States bureau of animal industry to immunize cows against the disease failed.

Hog-Cholera Vaccination.—The swine population of the United States was increased from the ten-year average of 55,000,-000 head to 125,000,000 in 1943. The increment was made possible by the extensive use of anti-hog-cholera serum and virus, the production of which was the largest of record. The use of crystal-violet vaccine (attenuated virus) in lieu of serum-virus vaccination gained ground during the year but represented but a small percentage of total hogs vaccinated against cholera.

Rabbit Production.—The raising of rabbits in the United States and Great Britain, for food and fur, was increased in 1942 and 1943, together with scientific research into the nature of their ailments. The potentiality of the "backyard rabbitry" as a source of delectable food was never before realized in these two countries. The fish and wildlife service of the United States and the ministry of agriculture and fisheries of Britain furnished useful information on the husbandry of domestic rabbits and the handling of their common maladies. Light was shed on coccidiosis, spirochetosis, ecto- and endoparasites, mucoid enteritis, and the inevitable accidents of reproduction. That the domestic rabbit is not the victim of tularemia (although not exempt to experimental inoculations) was emphasized.

Meat-Inspection Service Removed from the Bureau of Animal Industry.—Federal meat inspection established in 1890 and improved by congress in 1906 which was always directed by the chief of the bureau of animal industry, United States department of agriculture, and manned by veterinarians of civil service classification was transferred to the Food Distribution administration, that is, from scientific to commercial command. The transfer aroused nation-wide protests mainly on the ground of excellent record and the sense of security the American people had always felt under the former direction. The protests came from stockmen, expert hygienists and veterinarians. Unaware of the object of such changes the public showed meagre interest in the transfer.

Relocation of Veterinarians.—The Procurement and Assignment Service recommended voluntary relocation of veterinarians not engaged in essential practice or positions. That is, doctors of veterinary medicine engaged exclusively in pet-animal practice or nonessential commercial pursuits should relocate in rural districts densely populated with food-producing animals in order to be deferred from military service. Veterinarians in the civilian service, federal or state, or engaged in practice among farm animals were given preferential rating by local draft boards. Students taking the pre-veterinary course or the curriculum leading to the degree of doctor of veterinary medicine in a recognized college were given preferential rating provided their individual effort so justified.

BIBLIOGRAPHY.—W. A. Hagan, "Veterinary Education in the Postwar World," *J.A.V.M.A.*, 53:269–274 (1943); Editorial, "Postwar Veterinary Education," *ibid.*, 53:298–299 (1943); "Veterinary War Conference, Current Reports, *ibid.*, 53:234–261 (1943); *The Meat You Eat*, New York State Trichinosis Commission (1942); R. F. Bourne, "Sulfonamides in Veterinary Medicine," *Proceedings*, Eastern Iowa Veterinary Association (In press); G. G. Garlick, D. E. Bartlett and D. M. Hammond, "Trichomoniasis of Cattle," *Amer. J. Vet. Research*, no. 14 (1944); Personal communication, Corn States Serum Company, Omaha, Neb. (1943); Edward L. Vail and E. F. Kenny, "Rabbit Production," Fish and Wildlife Service, U.S. Department of the Interior, *Bull.* 31; Meat Inspection Service Removed from the Bureau of Animal Industry, Proceedings War Conference, *J.A.V.M.A.*, 53:246 (1943); Relocation of Veterinarians: Veterinary Medicine and the War, News Item, *ibid.*, 53:233 (1943). (L. A. M.)

Vichy. A town of central France, department of Allier, located on the right bank of the Allier river, 33 mi. southeast of Moulins; pop. (1939) 20,000. The town first came into political prominence when it was selected in 1940 as the seat of the French government, formed after the loss of the war to Germany and headed by Marshal Henri Philippe Pétain (*q.v.*) as chief of state. The town was convenient as a temporary seat of administration because of the number of hotels and sanitariums which could be converted to use as government offices. What was originally conceived as a makeshift arrangement of short duration still continued at the end of 1943, because no definitive peace treaty had been signed between Germany and France.

Victoria. A state of the Australian commonwealth, area 87,-844 sq.mi.; pop. (est. Dec. 31, 1941), 1,952,152. Chief cities (pop. Dec. 31, 1940): Melbourne (cap. 1,076,700); Geelong (40,100); Ballarat (38,590); Bendigo (30,150). Governor: Maj. Gen. Sir W. J. Dugan.

History.—The Country party government under the leadership of Albert Dunstan completed eight years of office in April and was returned to power at the general elections in June. The net result of the elections was that the United Australia party—supporting the government—lost 3 seats, 1 each to the Country party and Labour party and 1 to the Independents. In September, however, the government was defeated on a vote of no confidence in connection with the redistribution of parliamentary seats. A Labour government was sworn in on Sept. 14, but resigned less than 48 hours later, on the refusal of the governor to grant a dissolution. The governor thereupon commissioned Albert Dunstan to form a coalition government with T. T. Holloway, the leader of the United Australia party.

The state budget which was introduced in August revealed a surplus of £A.755,000 for 1942–43 and provided for an estimated surplus of £A.56,000 during the current fiscal year. Features of the budget were increases in expenditure on education (£A.211,000), hospitals (£A.216,000) and a £A.100,000 fund for the encouragement of secondary industries in rural areas.

Education.—In 1939: state primary schools 2,585; scholars on roll 221,219; average attendance 155,441. State secondary schools 154; scholars on roll 42,104; average attendance 34,176.

Finance.—In 1942–43 (estimated) revenue £A.32,541,000; expenditure £A.32,456,000; debt outstanding (June 30, 1942) £A. 177,716,484.

Communications.—Roads and streets (1940) 103,929 mi. Railways (1941–42) 4,764 mi. Motor vehicles licensed (March 31, 1943); cars, trucks, etc., 214,888; cycles 15,996. Wireless receiving set licences (March 31, 1943) 387,667. Telephones (June 30, 1941) 228,936.

Agriculture, Manufactures, Mineral Production.—Production in 1942–43: wheat 42,000,000 bu.; wool (1940–41) 185,000,000 lb.; coal, brown (1940) 3,994,515 tons; gold (1939) 156,522 fine ounces. Industry and labour, 1941–42: factories 8,916; employees 257,369; gross value of output £A.256,112,647; unemployment (trade union returns) (March 1943), 0.8%.

(W. D. MA.)

Victory Gardens: see HORTICULTURE.
Victory Tax: see TAXATION.

Vidal y Barraquer, Francis of Assisi
(1868–1943), Spanish cardinal, was born Oct. 3 in Cambrils. He entered the priesthood in 1899, was appointed successively bishop of Pentacomia, 1913, apostolic administrator of Solsona, 1914, archbishop of Tarragona, 1919 and cardinal, 1921. Politically an anti-falangist, he refused to endorse the pastoral letter which gave its blessing to the Franco cause during the early days of the Spanish Civil War and was obliged to leave the country for his own safety. Italian consular officials helped him escape and he found haven in Italy. Cardinal Vidal died while on a visit to Fribourg, Switzerland, according to a news report from that city, Sept. 14.

Vinson, Frederick Moore
(1890–   ), U.S. politician, was born Jan. 22 at Louisa, Ky. He was graduated from Kentucky Normal college, 1908, received his B.A., 1909, and his law degree, 1911, from Centre college and practised law in Louisa in 1911. He was commonwealth attorney of the 32nd judicial district of Kentucky, 1921–24, and served seven terms in the national house of representatives. A key man in congress during the early days of the Roosevelt administration, Vinson helped formulate revenue legislation as a member of the house ways and means committee. His record was strongly prolabour, he voted for legislation approving establishment of the NLRB and was instrumental in putting through congress the bill on the undistributed profits tax. In 1937, he accepted President Roosevelt's offer of the post of associate justice in the U.S. court of appeals for the District of Columbia and assumed his new duties in May 1938. Vinson was named director of the Office of Economic Stabilization in May 1943. The following month, he vetoed the 8-cent per hour increase asked for by 1,100,000 nonoperating employees of the railroad brotherhoods. On Nov. 16, 1943, Vinson warned that the "little steel" wage formula would be destroyed if the 8-cent increase was approved by congress.

Virginia.
Southernmost of the middle Atlantic states, the "Old Dominion" was one of the 13 original United States. Area 40,815 sq.mi., including 916 sq.mi. of water. Pop. (1940) 2,677,773, 35.3% urban and 64.7% rural. The civilian population was estimated in April, 1943 at 2,883,945. An estimate by the population study of the state planning board showed a civilian white population of 2,250,345, nonwhite of 633,600. Capital, Richmond (193,042 in 1940 and 231,000 in April 1943). Other cities include Norfolk (144,332 and 205,946), Roanoke (69,287 and 64,866), and Portsmouth (50,745 and 64,996).

History.—The state's shipyard industry soared in 1943, and the population of Newport News increased from 35,000 to more than 55,000. Shipyard workers numbered close to 30,000, of whom 1,600 were women. War brought a marked redistribution of the state's population, as the rapid expansion of industrial localities sucked labour from farm areas. There was no session in 1943 of the general assembly, which meets biennially in even-numbered years, although interim commissions were active in such fields as small-loan legislation, co-operatives, medical licensing requirements and public health. The state department of corrections, which was established in 1942, ended its first year of operation with 501 prisoners on parole and 600 on probation. A general election in Nov. 1943 resulted in 15 new members in the state senate and 35 new members in the house of delegates. The governor (elected in Nov. 1941) was Colgate W. Darden, Jr.; William M. Tuck was lieutenant governor.

Education.—In 1942–43, elementary school enrolment was 428,466, teaching staff 12,165; secondary school enrolment 128,244, teaching staff 5,924.

Public Welfare, Charities, Correction.—For the year ended June 30, 1943, 12,480 persons received $858,296.70 in general relief; 21,892 persons received $2,403,285.85 in old-age assistance; 6,153 families with 17,693 dependent children, $1,168,404.25; 1,208 blind, $167,930.68; and in 1943 (January through November) 70,421 unemployment compensation checks were written for $829,538.59. This represented only 25% of the number and amount of unemployment checks in the same period of 1942. An average daily population of 4,000 were in five penal institutions for adults, and 717 were in four industrial schools for juveniles at the end of the fiscal year in June 1943.

Communication.—On Jan. 1, 1942, there were 9,607.6 mi. of highway in the state's primary system; on July 1, 1943, there were 37,675 mi. in the secondary system. During the year ended June 30, 1943, the state spent $23,528,097.17 on the highways. Railroad mileage in Virginia was 4,203.2 on Jan. 1, 1943. There were 327,842 telephones in Virginia on Nov. 30, 1943.

Banking and Finance.—On Oct. 18, 1943, Virginia had 184 state banks with 63 branches and five "facilities," and 130 national banks and branches. On Oct. 18, 1943, deposits in state banks totalled $506,034,477 and assets $551,892,354. On June 30, 1943, deposits of national banks were $725,971,000, and assets $784,935,000. Resources on Dec. 31, 1942, of 19 industrial loan associations were $6,793,864; of 58 building and loan associations, $34,937,414; of 32 credit unions, $1,524,093. The state budget for the fiscal year ended June 30, 1943, showed receipts of $147,572,307, some 12% above the previous year, and expenditures of $126,820,685, 11% above the previous year. The gross debt on June 30 was $18,599,351; there was no net debt, since a sinking fund of $19,252,294 left an excess of $692,942. The fiscal year ended with a surplus of $21,699,419.

Agriculture.—The value of Virginia's principal crops in 1943 was estimated at $205,000,000, an increase of 16% over 1942. Acreage harvested advanced 1% above the 1942 figure to 3,905,000 ac. A shortage of farm labour and a prolonged drought combined to reduce the volume of 11 of the 13 principal crops. The farm income in 1943 was estimated at more than 37% higher than in 1942, when the income was $222,106,000.

Manufacturing.—The total value of manufactured products for the year ending Sept. 30, 1942, was $1,755,767,694. Wage

Table I.—*Leading Agricultural Products of Virginia, 1943 and 1942*

Crop	1943 (est.)	1942
Tobacco, lb.	106,878,000	104,150,000
Cotton, lint, bales	25,000	34,000
Corn, bu.	33,275,000	35,586,000
Oats, bu.	2,860,000	3,510,000
Barley, bu.	1,575,000	2,120,000
Apples, commercial, bu.	5,220,000	14,094,000
Peaches, bu.	172,000	1,936,000
Wheat, winter, bu.	5,863,000	7,520,000
Hay, all tame, tons	1,420,000	1,498,000
Lespedeza seed, lb.	5,000,000	9,200,000
Potatoes, bu.	9,594,000	7,242,000
Sweet potatoes, bu.	2,976,000	3,875,000
Peanuts for nuts, lb.	193,875,000	175,950,000
Soybeans for beans, bu.	1,056,000	1,782,000

Table II.—*Principal Industries of Virginia, 1942 and 1941 (Oct. 1-Sept. 30)*

Industry	Value of Products	
	Oct. 1, 1940-Sept. 30, 1941	Oct. 1, 1941-Sept. 30, 1942
Tobacco products	$528,130,587	$424,198,041
Food and kindred products	187,787,984	135,308,438
Textiles and their products	254,302,193	179,711,490
Wood products	112,912,574	79,869,851
Paper and printing	124,993,180	96,924,436
Chemical products	144,828,853	73,131,229
Metals and machinery	61,391,282	38,787,922
Transportation equipment	276,730,874	183,784,622

earners were paid $272,512,356 in this period, while total salaries amounted to $54,535,281; an estimated 234,130 persons were engaged in manufacturing at the end of this period. The principal industries were tobacco products, food and kindred products, transportation equipment, textiles, paper and printing and chemical products.

Mineral Production.—Production of coal in the year ended Sept. 30, 1942, was valued at $38,494,104, up 30% from the previous year; coke was valued at $1,884,051, up 50%; stone and slate, $6,391,841; and sand and gravel, $1,551,441. Progress was made in the development of magnesium and mica mines in several localities. (J. S. Br.)

Virginia, University of.
A state institution for higher education at Charlottesville, Va. The original university was designed and built by Thomas Jefferson. There are six departments: two academic—the college and department of graduate studies; and four professional—law, medicine, engineering and education. The total budget for 1943-44 was $3,052,850. The corporate name of the university is "The Rector and Visitors of the University of Virginia." For statistics of student enrolment, faculty members, endowment, library volumes, etc., see UNIVERSITIES AND COLLEGES. (J. L. N.)

Virgin Islands.
A United States dependency in the West Indies, east of Puerto Rico, comprising St. Croix (pop. 12,902), St. Thomas (11,265) and St. John (722) islands. Area, 133 sq.mi.; pop. (1940) 24,889, 13.1% more than in 1930, with whites 9%, Negroes 69% (1930: 78.3%), "mixed and other races" 22% (1930: 12½%). The chief cities are: Charlotte Amalie, the capital, on St. Thomas, 9,801 (1930: 7,036); Christiansted, 4,495 (1930: 3,767) and Frederiksted, 2,498 (1930: 2,698) on St. Croix. The governor in 1943 was Charles Harwood.

History.—The Virgin Islands during 1943 generally felt the pressure of wartime dislocations and shipping restrictions. Supplies of food to the islands were largely effected through the Food Distribution administration. Food shortages, however, had been overcome by the end of 1943. In order to avoid unemployment after the completion of defense construction, Governor Harwood proposed an extensive public works plan involving a water storage project in St. Croix, water supply facilities in St. Thomas, and highway construction generally in the islands.

Education.—Public and private elementary and secondary schools had an enrolment in June 1943 of 2,813. Charlotte Amalie high school had 498 students.

Finance.—The monetary unit is the United States dollar. A United States government subsidy of $159,800 was required to defray the expenses of St. Croix. However, the islands of St. Thomas and St. John operated without a federal deficit appropriation for the second successive year.

Trade.—Under wartime conditions in 1943 official policy was to withhold full trade statistics. A general retrogression from the 1942 high was felt in the Virgin Islands as a result of shipping restrictions and the completion of defense installations. Production and sale of both rum and sugar, however, rose considerably during 1943.

Communication.—External communication is by steamer and Pan American Airways, through Charlotte Amalie. Inter-island traffic is by boat. Radio-telephone service was established with the United States during 1943.

Agriculture.—Agriculture supplements shipping to support St. Thomas. St. Croix and St. John are largely agricultural. In 1940 (census) there were 828 "farms" of 3 ac. or more, totalling 55,228 ac. St. Croix produced practically the entire sugar crop of the islands, which amounted to 2,250 tons in 1943—a 150% increase over 1942. Grazing was encouraged by a government-built abattoir on St. Croix and a cold storage market on St. Thomas. Vegetables, orchard products (guava, cacao, coco-nuts, limes, lemons and oranges), and livestock comprised the principal agricultural products other than sugar. (C. L. G.)

Virgin Islands, British: see WEST INDIES, BRITISH.
Viruses: see INFANTILE PARALYSIS; MEDICINE; PNEUMONIA.
Vital Statistics: see BIRTH STATISTICS; CENSUS, 1940; DEATH STATISTICS; INFANT MORTALITY; MARRIAGE AND DIVORCE; SUICIDE STATISTICS.

Vitamins.
Food shortages and rationing along with educational work by numerous agencies made people more food conscious. Unfortunately exaggerated claims and implications concerning the widespread prevalence of malnutrition, especially of various vitamin deficiencies, were enthusiastically used to bombard the public with misleading advertising concerning the need and value of vitamin preparations. Good nutrition is a prerequisite for good health, but vitamins are only part of nutrition. Good nutrition comes from consuming a variety of wholesome food, not from a poor diet supplemented with costly vitamin preparations.

Many reports showed that the seeds of cereal grains, which are low in ascorbic acid, can develop significant amounts of this vitamin by sprouting. The use of bean sprouts by the Chinese is well known, and studies have shown that the field soybean not only acquires improved dietary qualities by sprouting, but it is more readily cooked and useful as food for man. Burkholder summarized a study of the vitamins of the B complex before and after germination of oats, wheat, barley and corn. This shows that germination results in a marked increase in riboflavin and niacin; the thiamin content was not changed appreciably. The possibilities of making the best use of the available cereal foods still remained to be explored.

Dehydrated foods have obvious advantages when it comes to transporting large quantities of food a considerable distance. It is not a simple problem to dehydrate food products so that upon rehydration they will possess a reasonable degree of original appearance, taste and nutritive value. As ascorbic acid is readily destroyed by oxidation, and vitamin A is also susceptible to this process, it is likely that these nutrients are diminished in most dehydrated products. Numerous investigations have shown that the ascorbic acid content of dehydrated products is practically zero and that vitamin A is appreciably decreased. As we depend heavily on vegetables as a source of vitamin A, in the form of carotene, means of stabilizing this nutrient in the dehydration process were under intensive investigation.

Several studies on the relation of vitamin intake to physical fatigue due to hard muscular work were made. Such studies were of direct importance to the war, both with regard to the armed forces and civilian workers. It was shown that excessive amounts of the various vitamins are of no advantage in combating fatigue, but insufficient amounts of the vitamin B complex will cause earlier fatigue and a falling off in physical efficiency. Barborka, Foltz and Ivy reported the results of study on four well trained young men which confirmed the latter observation. They concluded that vitamin B complex added to a vitamin B complex inadequate diet restores work output to efficient levels. It was generally believed that thiamin is probably the principal "B vitamin" concerned with fatigue, yet Keys and co-workers in studies on normal young men reported that at a low level of thiamin, 0.23 mg. per 1,000 calories, muscular and metabolic functions were in no way limited. Hard physical work, particularly in warm climates, is accompanied by considerable perspiration, and since sweat is an aqueous medium, it is important to know whether significant amounts of the water soluble vitamins are lost by this means.

The best evidence available suggested that only small amounts of vitamins are lost in sweat, and that water and salt are the only practical losses which require attention.

Certain vitamins are synthesized by the intestinal bacteria. These microorganisms are thus of considerable importance to the nutrition of animals and of human beings because the vitamins synthesized are available to the host. Vitamin K is produced by bacteria in the intestinal tract in sufficient quantities to meet the normal needs of man and most animals. Biotin, one of the vitamins of the B complex, is provided to man in larger quantities by intestinal bacteria than by the diet. Man may not develop deficiencies of biotin, pantothenic acid, pyridoxine, folic acid, and most likely certain other essential nutrients because these substances are made for him by microorganisms in the intestinal tract. But should the intestinal flora be altered, as by the administration of drugs, radical changes in the diet, or by diseases of the gastrointestinal tract, diseases primarily nutritional in aetiology may result.

One of the vitamins mentioned in the preceding paragraph, folic acid, which is required by the rat only when the bacterial flora is interfered with, as by the feeding of sulfaguanidine, was shown to be required in the diet of the chick and the monkey. A deficiency in the chick leads to lack of growth, poor feathering and anaemia, while monkeys show an anaemia and a severe leukopenia (decrease in the number of white blood cells below the normal range). Hogan and collaborators summarized the work on this vitamin in the chick, and also reported the preparation of this compound in pure form. Its chemical formula was not reported in 1943.

The investigations on folic acid in the nutrition of monkeys was done principally by Waisman and Elvehjem.

The role that various vitamins, and other nutrients, might have in resistance to infection has long given rise to much speculation. There was no evidence in 1943 that amounts of any nutrient above such levels as are necessary for good nutrition will give increased resistance to disease, though there was abundant evidence that good nutrition is a requisite for a maximum degree of resistance. Trager made the interesting observation that one of the vitamins, biotin, may play a specific role in resistance to malaria. The observations on this finding were limited to experiments on ducks and chicks and whether they would be of practi-

cal significance to man was not known in 1943. Biotin deficiency in man under natural conditions was unknown; however, in countries where malaria is endemic, it is more severe in times of famine.

For some years enzyme chemists have developed a concept that substances possessing a chemical structure similar to the active or "prosthetic" group of the enzyme may compete with the active group for adsorption on the surface of the same protein, thereby interfering with the formation of the enzyme and hence decreasing enzyme activity. This interesting concept was applied in various vitamin researches. Thus thiopanic acid which is similar in structure to the vitamin pantothenic acid prevents growth of certain microorganisms. In animals, the administration of dicoumarin or salicylic acid, presumably because of their chemical relationship to vitamin K, produces hypoprothrombinemia. In each case a competitive action between the vitamin and the inhibitory substance was demonstrated. Woolley and White demonstrated the production of thiamin deficiency in mice by the administration of a pyridine analogue of thiamin, pyrithiamin, and Woolley and Krampitz described a condition in mice and rats similar to scurvy which was produced by feeding a compound structurally related to ascorbic acid. The use of these "anti-vitamins" or vitamin-inhibitors opened up a new field of vitamin research, and a field which ultimately might yield much of practical importance to the study of disease.

While the essential amino acids are not classed as vitamins, they are for all practical purposes similar to vitamins in that they are substances required by the body and which must be obtained ready-made, either from food or perhaps from synthesis by intestinal bacteria. Rose was investigating the amino acid requirements of man and found that nitrogen equilibrium might be maintained in young adults for periods of two weeks on a diet in which the only source of protein was eight pure amino acids.

These investigations are fundamental to a better understanding of human nutrition.

For those interested in comprehensively following progress in vitamin research and other phases of the science of nutrition, attention should be called to a series of excellent review articles which appeared in the *Journal of the American Medical Association* and were to be published in book form under the title of *Handbook of Nutrition*, and also to the publication by the Nutrition foundation of a new type of journal called *Nutrition Reviews*. This is a monthly publication which undertakes to provide an authoritative, unbiased review of the world's current research progress in nutrition.

(*See* also ALIMENTARY SYSTEM, DISORDERS OF; BIOCHEMISTRY; CHEMISTRY; DIETETICS; FISHERIES; FLOUR AND FLOUR MILLING; MEDICINE; PHYSIOLOGY.)

BIBLIOGRAPHY.—P. R. Burkholder, "Vitamins in Dehydrated Seeds and Sprouts," *Science*, 97:562–564 (1943); C. J. Barborka, E. E. Foltz and A. C. Ivy, "Relationship between Vitamin B Complex Intake and Work Output in Trained Subjects," *J.A.M.A.*, 122:717–720 (1943); A. Keys *et al.*, "The Performance of Normal Young Men on Controlled Thiamine Intakes," *J. Nut.*, 26:399–415 (1943); A. G. Hogan *et al.*, "Isolation of the Antianemia Factor (Vitamin Bc) in Crystalline Form from Liver," *Science*, 97:404–405 (1943); H. A. Waisman and C. A. Elvehjem, "The Role of Biotin and 'Folic Acid' in the Nutrition of the Rhesus Monkey," *J. Nut.*, 26:361–375 (1943); W. Trager, "The Influence of Biotin upon Susceptibility to Malaria," *J. Exper. Med.*, 77:557–581 (1943); D. W. Woolley and A. G. C. White, "Production of Thiamine Deficiency Disease by the Feeding of a Pyridine Analogue of Thiamine," *J. Biol. Chem.*, 149:285–289 (1943); D. W. Woolley and L. O. Krampitz, "Production of a Scurvy-Like Condition by Feeding of a Compound Structurally Related to Ascorbic Acid," *J. Exper. Med.*, 78:333–339 (1943); W. C. Rose *et al.*, "Further Experiments on the Role of the Amino Acids in Human Nutrition," *J. Biol. Chem.*, 148:457–458 (1943). (F. J. SE.)

V-Mail: *see* PHOTOGRAPHY.

Vocational Education: *see* EDUCATION.

Von (in personal names): *see* under proper names.

Voroshilov, Klementiy E.

(1881–), Russian army officer, was born Feb. 4 in Verkhnyi, Ukraine. In 1903 he joined the Social-Democratic party. He was exiled to Archangel in 1907 for revolutionary activities but escaped to Baku. During World War I he was a revolutionary organizer, but after the bolsheviks seized power he entered active military life. He led guerrilla detachments against German armies in the Ukraine in 1918. He was people's commissar of the army and navy in 1925 and was a member of the Communist party central committee after 1921. On May 8, 1940, Voroshilov was named vice-premier and Marshal Timoshenko succeeded him as defense commissar. In Aug. 1941 Marshal Voroshilov was in command of the northwestern front which included Leningrad, and in Oct. 1941 he was charged with formation of new Russian armies. He was then returned to the Leningrad area and was one of the commanders there when the siege was broken in Jan. 1943. He attended the Churchill-Stalin conference in Moscow in Aug. 1942 and the Molotov-Eden-Hull conference in the same city in Oct. 1943.

WAC: *see* WOMEN'S ARMY CORPS.

WAFS: *see* WOMEN'S AIRFORCE SERVICE PILOTS.

Wages and Hours.

During 1943, as well as 1942, employment and pay rolls in manufacturing and non-manufacturing industries improved substantially as a result of World War II orders and the U.S. war program as well as foreign orders. Both hourly wages and weekly earnings increased markedly. The acceleration of work within plants, caused by the adoption of three shifts and large overtime bonuses increased total pay rolls and gave workers throughout many industries much higher weekly earnings. Practically all industries engaged in war production or affected by war orders reported a high percentage of overtime.

Table I shows the employment indexes for 1942 and the first nine months of 1943 in all manufactures, and for durable goods and nondurable goods groups, by months. These indexes were arrived at by the use of 1939 as the base.

Table II shows the average hours and earnings in the two sample months of Jan. and July, 1943, in the principal manufacturing and nonmanufacturing industries. Table II shows clearly the high level of wage-earners' weekly "take-home" in 1943, through the combination of high rates and long hours.

Table III shows a steady rise in average hourly earnings from 1939 to 1943. The increase is greater than the rise in hourly rates since a steadily increasing amount of time-and-one-half and double-time overtime rates appreciably increased hourly average earnings. There was no way of separating the increment

Table I.—Employment and Weekly Wages Indexes for All Manufacturing Industries of the U.S. in 1943 (9 months) and 1942

(Indexes are based on 1939 average and adjusted to census of manufacturers. They are not comparable to indexes published prior to Dec. 1942 by the Bureau of Labor Statistics)

Months	All Manufacturers				Durable Goods				Nondurable Goods			
	Employment		Pay Roll		Employment		Pay Roll		Employment		Pay Roll	
	1943	1942	1943	1942	1943	1942	1943	1942	1943	1942	1943	1942
Jan.	165.0	139.8	290.9	200.7	218.1	169.1	399.9	255.9	123.1	116.8	184.4	146.8
Feb.	166.4	142.3	297.5	208.2	221.5	172.3	410.0	265.8	123.0	118.6	186.9	151.9
Mar.	167.6	144.3	304.5	215.1	224.3	175.8	421.0	276.2	123.3	119.4	190.7	155.4
Apr.	167.6	146.3	309.6	221.4	225.6	180.0	430.4	287.2	122.0	119.8	191.5	157.0
May.	167.2	148.0	313.5	228.7	225.9	184.1	437.1	300.0	121.0	119.8	192.6	159.0
June.	168.8	149.9	317.1	234.5	228.5	188.9	441.6	312.1	121.7	119.2	195.4	158.7
July.	169.8	153.4	315.6	242.7	227.9	193.9	443.7	323.9	122.6	121.4	194.2	163.3
Aug.	170.9	157.1	322.4	254.8	230.4	199.2	448.5	342.0	124.0	123.9	199.1	169.5
Sept.	170.2	159.6	328.3	261.8	230.7	202.5	461.3	352.4	122.6	125.9	198.3	173.3
Oct.	—	160.7	—	270.9	—	206.7	—	366.2	—	124.5	—	177.7
Nov.	—	161.9	—	280.4	—	210.4	—	382.8	—	123.8	—	180.3
Dec.	—	142.3	—	287.7	—	215.5	—	391.2	—	124.4	—	186.5

This table compiled from statistics released by the *Monthly Labor Review*, United States Bureau of Labor Statistics, Washington, D.C.

Table II.—Average Weekly Earnings, Average Weekly Hours, and Average Earnings per Hour in Major Industrial Classifications, January and July, 1943 in the U.S.

Industry	Average Weekly Earnings (1943)		Average Weekly Hours (1943)		Average Hourly Earnings (1943)	
	Jan.	July	Jan.	July	Jan. Cents	July Cents
ALL MANUFACTURING	$40.62	$42.76	44.2	44.4	91.9	96.3
Durable goods	46.68	48.76	45.9	46.0	101.7	106.0
Nondurable goods	32.03	33.89	41.7	42.1	76.8	80.5
Iron and steel	44.91	47.14	45.0	45.5	99.8	103.6
Electrical machinery	44.70	44.86	47.0	40.2	95.1	97.1
Machinery, not electrical	50.69	51.08	49.6	48.1	102.2	106.2
Transportation equip, except automobiles	53.65	55.93	46.9	46.8	114.4	119.5
Automobiles	55.85	57.18	45.7	46.0	122.2	124.3
Nonferrous metals	45.30	46.84	45.9	46.1	98.7	101.6
Lumber basic	27.10	31.59	39.8	42.8	68.1	73.8
Furniture	29.68	32.48	42.7	43.6	69.5	74.5
Stone, clay and glass	34.15	35.49	41.7	41.8	81.9	84.9
Textile-mill products	26.85	27.09	41.3	40.8	65.0	66.4
Apparel products	24.49	26.05	37.1	36.9	66.0	70.6
Leather	28.90	29.13	40.3	39.2	71.7	74.3
Food	33.18	35.52	43.2	44.4	76.8	80.0
Tobacco	24.07	27.41	39.4	42.1	61.1	65.1
Paper & allied products	34.21	35.55	44.2	44.6	77.4	79.7
Printing & publishing	38.65	40.08	39.8	40.2	97.1	99.7
Chemical products	39.38	42.04	44.5	45.3	88.5	92.8
Products of petroleum	45.42	51.14	41.1	44.9	110.5	113.9
Rubber products	43.25	44.94	44.5	44.1	97.2	101.9
NONMANUFACTURING						
Coal Mining:						
Anthracite	31.25	39.69	31.0	37.7	100.7	106.3
Bituminous	37.55	42.76	34.7	37.1	108.5	115.0
Metalliferous mining	41.16	43.43	43.3	43.7	94.1	98.6
Quarrying	33.34	36.72	44.3	46.5	75.9	79.1
Crude petroleum	42.82	49.41	39.9	43.3	105.9	111.7
Telephone & telegraph	34.51	35.94	41.2	42.2	84.0	85.5
Electric light & power	42.05	44.86	40.5	42.0	102.6	106.0
Street railways & buses	42.49	44.30	49.3	49.4	85.2	88.1
Wholesale trade	37.40	39.44	41.4	42.4	90.8	93.3
Retail trade	24.37	25.48	41.3	41.7	64.5	67.5
Hotels	19.60	20.18	44.6	44.8	42.4	44.9
Building construction	46.03	47.97	37.1	39.0	124.0	123.1

Compiled from *Monthly Labor Review*, United States Bureau of Labor Statistics, Washington, D.C.

added to hourly earnings by overtime work from the prevailing rates paid for standard hours of employment.

The bureau of labour statistics figures showed a downward trend of hours in most industries from 1937 to 1939 because of reduction in hours-standards effected by union agreements. But in 1941 to 1943 average hours increased, particularly in the heavy industries, because so much overtime was worked as a result of the war.

The much higher hourly earnings in some industries are due to one or more of the following factors: (1) character of the labour supply employed, as to sex, age and skill, (2) productivity of the industry, principally determined by its degree of modernization, technical equipment and proportion of skilled workers, (3) degree to which union working conditions prevail, (4) necessity of paying high wages to attract labour supply.

Weekly earnings are really of greater significance than hourly rates, from the point of view of living standards. There were 23 industries of the 31 studied in which average weekly earnings exceeded $30 per week in July 1943, and the maximum was $57.18 in the automobile industries. The lowest weekly earnings were in hotels: $20.18. In July 1943, there were 16 industries in which average weekly earnings exceeded $30 and six where they exceeded $40 per week. Four of these were: $57.18 in the automobile industry; $55.93 in transportation equipment; $51.08 in machinery; and $47.97 in construction. The lowest, hotels, were but $20.18. The average weekly earnings of durable goods manufacturers were $48.76 in July 1943 compared with $44.62 a year earlier and $31.24 in 1941.

Four industries fell between $20 and $25 per week and four between $25 and $30; none below $20 in July 1942.

The wages of farm labour were higher in 1943 than in 1942, judging by the reports of the U.S. bureau of agricultural economics; both monthly and daily wages. (*See also* AGRICULTURE; BUSINESS REVIEW; CANADA; CENSUS, 1940; LAW.)

Table III.—*Rise in Hourly Earnings Rates in U.S.A., 1939-43*

Industry	Hourly earnings in August				
	1939	1940	1941	1942	1943
Manufactures in general	$.634	$.668	$ .745	$ .864	$ 96.5
Durable goods manufactures	.699	.731	.830	.966	106.0
Nondurable goods	.585	.613	.658	.738	81.1
Iron and steel	.757	.777	.871	.967	103.7
Machinery	.721	.745	.844	.976	106.3
Lumber and products	.502	.526	.588	.677	74.4
Food and kindred products	.596	.615	.658	.732	80.5
Tobacco products	.472	.492	.520	.587	65.8
Rubber products	.770	.779	.861	.936	101.5
Anthracite mining	.928	.926	.989	.992	107.3
Bituminous mining	.890	.887	1.033	1.061	114.7
Wholesale trade	.711	.736	.798	.861	94.4
Building	.924	.956	1.001	1.174	124.6

(D. D. L.)

Great Britain.—The most recent official statistics of wages in Great Britain referred to Jan. 1943. At that date, weekly *rates* of wages, as distinct from earnings, had risen on the average by 26% to 27% above the level prevailing in Oct. 1938, the date used by the government as a basis for prewar conditions.

Earnings had naturally increased a good deal faster than rates of wages, owing both to the spread of systems of payment by results and the intensification of output and to the working of longer hours, including large amounts of overtime and week-end work. As against this, the proportion of women employed was higher than before the war; and the lower earnings of the women had a tendency to depress the general average. Over all the industries covered by the return gross earnings (before deduction of income tax or insurance contributions) were higher by about 65% in Jan. 1943 than in Oct. 1938. For adult men only, the increase was a little under 65%. For women, it was 80%, the figure being considerably affected by the payment of the men's rates to women directly replacing male workers on jobs normally done by men. For boys and youths under 21 the average increase was nearly 73%; and it has to be borne in mind that the average age in this group was lower than it was before the war, owing to the extensive calling up of youths of 18 and upwards. For girls under 18 the average rise was 73.4%. Average earnings in 1938 and 1943 respectively were, for men 69/- and 113/9d., for women 32/6d. and 58/6d., for boys and youths 26/1d. and 45/1d., and for girls 18/6d. and 32/1d. The increases within these averages varied considerably for different trades, being naturally highest in the metal and engineering trades. The lowest increases were in the public utility services and in the printing and paper trades. In the building trades there was a tendency for earnings to fall, after sharp increases up to 1942. This reversal of the previous tendency was due mainly to restrictions on uneconomic overtime and week-end work since the completion of the main war-time program of factory and aerodrome construction. In particular, the very high earnings which were accruing to boys and youths in the building and constructional trades had for the most part ceased.

The returns summarized in the preceding paragraph cover rather over 6,000,000 workers, mainly in factory and other constructional trades. They do not include miners or transport workers or workers in the clerical and distributive trades. Probably the inclusion of the excluded groups would not greatly affect the general averages. For coal miners, earnings per shift are known to have increased by about 65% between the first quarter of 1939 and the first quarter of 1943. Agricultural workers (adult males) in 1943 had a national minimum rate of 60/- a week, and women of 45/-. Earnings in the public services rose substantially less than the average, and earnings on the railways probably at about the average rate.

These changes in money wages have to be compared with an official figure of 28% for the rise in the cost of living between 1938 and 1943. This official figure, however, understated the actual increase, owing to the very sharp rise in the cost of semi-luxuries not included in the index (tobacco, beer, all kinds of personal goods not subject to rationing, furniture, and so on). The official figure was kept down by the fact that all the main elements in the cost of living that were being held down by government subsidies were included in it. The effect of this system, and of the methods of rationing applied, was to keep nutrition at a satisfactory standard for most of the population; but there were serious declines of quality in clothing, especially boots, and in standards of housing, partly owing to blitz damage, but still more because of the cessation of building and the concentration of population in certain areas in which great industrial developments occurred.

Wages were still settled in the main by collective bargaining between trade unions and employers' associations, with reference to arbitration, either by the wartime National Arbitration Tribunal or by *ad hoc* bodies, where agreement was not reached. Wages in 1943 were fairly stable, with only a small upward tendency. Strikes, though much noticed in the press, were few and small, and turned mainly on local grievances or on questions arising out of the interpretation of national arbitration awards. The time lost by stoppages of work was very small, despite a good many protests against the refusal to grant increases, especially to skilled timeworkers whose earnings lagged behind those of pieceworkers doing less skilled work.

Hours of labour in general remained unaltered, with some tendency to reduce the excessive amounts of overtime and Sunday work previously enforced. The working of very long hours by juveniles between 16 and 18 was largely checked, especially in the constructional trades. Average hours of work were still considerably in excess of prewar hours; but the strain was partly relieved by some improvement in conditions of travel to and from work. The movement for holidays with pay was further extended, the most important recent agreement covering the workers in the building and civil engineering industries.

In connection with all figures of wages and earnings it should of course be borne in mind that direct taxation had by this time been extended to cover the main body of adult wage-earners. The system of collection on the basis of the year's earnings, having given rise to many difficulties, was being superseded for most manual workers by a "pay-as-you-earn" method. It was estimated (Oxford University Institute of Statistics *Bulletin*, June 1943) that in 1942 wages took 42% of the national income, as against 39% in 1938 (or 46% as against 40% if military pay is included with wages). (*See* also LABOUR UNIONS; PRICES.)

(G. D. H. C.)

Wake Island: *see* PACIFIC ISLANDS, U.S.
Wales: *see* GREAT BRITAIN AND NORTHERN IRELAND, UNITED KINGDOM OF.

Wallace, Henry Agard

(1888–   ), vice-president of the United States. (*See Encyclopædia Britannica.*) Wallace was secretary of agriculture in the cabinet of Franklin D. Roosevelt from March 4, 1933, until Sept. 5, 1940, when he resigned to campaign for the vice-presidency, to which he was elected the following Nov. 5.

In the summer of 1941 he became an important figure in the U.S. defense program. President Roosevelt appointed him head of the Economic Defense board (later the Board of Economic Warfare) on July 31 and chairman of the Supply Priorities and Allocations board on Aug. 28. In Dec. 1942 a dispute between Wallace and Jesse Jones, chairman of the Reconstruction Finance corporation, from which the BEW obtained funds to purchase war materials abroad, was first made public in testimony before a senate committee. The quarrel came to a head on June 29, 1943, when Wallace accused Jones of obstructing the war effort by hampering the BEW in its efforts to secure vital materials from foreign sources. On July 15 President Roosevelt abolished the BEW and transferred all subsidiaries of the RFC engaged in financing foreign purchases to a new Office of Economic Warfare (later the Foreign Economic administration). Early in 1943 Wallace made a good will tour to seven South American countries, where he addressed several national congresses. His book *The Century of the Common Man,* containing many of his principal speeches and writings, appeared in July 1943.

Waller, Thomas W.

("FATS"), (1904?–1943), U.S. musician and composer, was the son of a Negro pastor and grandson of a noted Negro violinist. As a child, he studied the bass viol, violin and piano. In 1924, he published his first song, "Squeeze Me." In 1925 he launched his own band, which became popular with the start of the swing music era. From night clubs and cabarets he went to the radio, produced records and appeared in the movies. He composed part of the score for the musical comedy *Keep Shufflin',* 1927, the music for *Ain't Misbehavin',* 1928 and *Honeysuckle Rose,* 1928. He also wrote the score for *Early to Bed,* a Broadway hit in 1943, and was the composer of some 400 songs. He was taken ill on a train bound for Kansas City and was found dead in his berth, Dec. 15.

War Boards, British-U.S.: *see* BRITISH-U.S. WAR BOARDS.

War Bonds.

Unprecedented sums were sought from the American people by their government for support of the U.S. war effort in the Second and Third War Loans of 1943. But neither sum—$13,000,000,000 in the Second loan, $15,000,000,000 in the Third—was an adequate measure of the public's loan-subscribing willingness and capacity. Against the goal of $13,000,000,000, the Second loan produced $18,600,000,-000. For the Third loan, the goal was raised to $15,000,000,000,

and the country's voluntary response was $18,900,000,000. As a collateral result of the combined total of $9,500,000,000 in oversubscriptions, Secretary of the Treasury Henry Morgenthau Jr., was enabled to postpone the Fourth War Loan until 1944.

The Second War Loan was launched April 12 and completed May 1. The Third loan began Sept. 9 and continued through Oct. 2. The $37,500,000,000 thus raised by the government in six weeks compared with $21,000,000,000 raised by five drives in a total of 18 weeks for World War I, 1917–19.

Commercial banks provided not a penny of the Third loan's $18,900,000,000 yield, and only $5,000,000,000 of the Second loan. The importance, as an anti-inflation safeguard, of the sale of securities to nonbanking investors and particularly to individuals was stressed by the treasury in both loans.

Sales of Series E, F and G war bonds to the extent of $5,400,-000,000 were included in the Second and Third loan totals. In the first 11 months of 1943 there were additional Series E, F and G sales of $7,500,000,000, through operation of the pay roll savings plan and other month-to-month treasury war bond promotions.

Second War Loan, Third War Loan and regular war bond sales therefore amounted in 1943 to a grand total of $45,000,-000,000, not counting war bond sales for the month of December. Participation by commercial banks in the Second loan was limited by the treasury to approximately $5,000,000,000; the banks actually oversubscribed this share several times. In a financing operation supplementary to the Third War Loan, but conducted separately, the treasury made a limited offering of marketable securities to commercial banks, and announced cash sale allotments totalling $3,200,000,000 upon subscriptions totalling $10,900,000,000. For the entire calendar year net absorption of government securities by commercial banks and federal reserve banks amounted to approximately $24,000,000,000, and net absorption by all others, excluding special issues to trust funds, etc., amounted to approximately $30,000,000,000.

The extent to which various categories of nonbanking subscribers participated in the Second and Third loans is shown in the table:

Nonbanking Subscriptions to Second and Third U.S. War Loans, 1943
(millions of dollars)

Class of Investor	Second War Loan	Third War Loan
Individuals, partnerships and personal trust accounts	$3,290	$5,377
Insurance companies	2,408	2,620
Mutual savings banks	1,195	1,508
State and local governments	503	795
Dealers and brokers	544	894
Other corporations and associations	5,145	7,120
U.S. government agencies and trust funds	391	630

The types of securities offered were essentially the same for the two loans. Combined sales to nonbanking investors for both loans were, in rounded figures: Series E savings bonds, $3,900,-000,000; Series F and G savings bonds together, $1,500,000,000; Series C savings notes (formerly tax notes), $4,100,000,000; $2\frac{1}{2}\%$ long term bonds (1964–69 maturities), $7,500,000,000; 2% medium term bonds (1950–52 and 1951–53 maturities), $8,100,-000,000; $\frac{7}{8}\%$ treasury certificates of indebtedness (one year), $7,200,000,000.

Second War Loan sales to commercial banks were: 2% bonds, $2,100,000,000; $\frac{7}{8}\%$ certificates, $2,100,000,000; treasury 90-day bills, $810,000,000.

Of the three savings bonds, commonly referred to as war bonds, the Series E "people's bond" continued to lead heavily in sales, with a total of $9,600,000,000 for the first 11 months

A MILITARY PARADE on Fifth avenue, New York city, signalized the opening of the third U.S. war loan drive Sept. 9, 1943

of 1943. Nearly 53,000,000 units of these bonds were sold in the Third loan. Bonds of the $25 denomination accounted for approximately a third of all Series E sales.

Redemptions of savings bonds during the first 11 months of 1943 were: Series E, $1,194,000,000; Series F, $30,000,000; Series G, $79,000,000. Amounts of each series outstanding as of November 30 were: Series E, $15,404,673,000; Series F, $1,548,705,000; Series G, $6,128,924,000.

In each bond-selling campaign the treasury had the aid of millions of volunteer salesmen and saleswomen. Sales organizations functioned by federal reserve districts for the Second War Loan, as they had for the First or Victory Fund drive in Dec. 1942. In preparation for the Third War Loan, Secretary Morgenthau announced the "streamlining" of the sales forces on a state basis, with the chairmen of state war finance committees reporting to the secretary through the national director of the treasury's war finance division. Within the states, the former volunteer Victory Fund committees and the treasury's war savings staffs were combined, and state chairmen and their associates took charge of local war finance committees formed along city and county lines. It was estimated that by the end of the year, war bonds had been sold to more than 50,000,000 persons.

Under Secretary of the Treasury D. W. Bell announced in Dec. 1943 that the war had been financed at an average rate of slightly less than $1\frac{3}{4}\%$, compared with an average rate of about $4\frac{1}{4}\%$ on the securities issued to finance World War I. (*See* also BANKING; NATIONAL DEBT.)   (F. SM.)

War Chest: *see* COMMUNITY CHEST; RELIEF.
War Committees, Joint (U.S. and Canada): *see* CANADIAN-U.S. WAR COMMITTEES.

War Communications, Board of.

During 1943 the Board of War Communications (created by executive order Sept. 1940 as the Defense Communications board) issued 18 orders designed to co-ordinate, strengthen and speed essential wartime communications in the U.S. Priority systems were inaugurated for telephone, teletypewriter and telegraph messages important to the war effort. The need for flexible, efficient systems of radiotelegraph communications to theatres of Allied military operations in North Africa and elsewhere occupied considerable attention of the board. Effective May 1943, American international wire or radio carriers had to obtain board approval before opening negotiations with any foreign administration regarding new communications circuits from the United States.

James Lawrence Fly, chairman of the Federal Communications commission, continued as chairman of the board in 1943. Other members were Major General Harry C. Ingles, chief signal officer of the army; Rear Admiral Joseph R. Redman, director of naval communications; Hon. Breckinridge Long, assistant secretary of state; and Hon. Herbert E. Gaston, assistant secretary of the treasury and BWC secretary. The board had no paid personnel or appropriations. It operated through a co-ordinating committee and a law committee staffed by personnel from the five agencies represented on the BWC. A number of committees, made up of industry, government and labour representatives, experts in all fields of wire and radio communications, served the board as advisers. (*See* also FEDERAL COMMUNICATIONS COMMISSION; RADIO.)   (J. L. FY.)

War Crimes.

United Nations Commission for the Investigation of War Crimes. This commission held its first meeting on Oct. 20, 1943. Its creation was a result of the Inter-Allied declaration signed at St. James's palace, London, on

"WRITTEN IN BLOOD." The indelibility of German war crimes as seen by Angelo of the *Philadelphia Inquirer*

Jan. 13, 1942, by representatives of the governments of Belgium, Czechoslovakia, Greece, Luxembourg, the Netherlands, Norway, Poland and Yugoslavia and of the Free French National committee, after a conference in which representatives of Australia, Canada, China, Great Britain, India, New Zealand, South Africa, the United States, and the U.S.S.R. participated as guests. Previously, on Oct. 25, 1941, President Roosevelt and Prime Minister Churchill had issued simultaneous statements calling for retribution against the perpetrators of war crimes. The declaration was followed by a series of collective notes and memoranda of evidence presented to the governments of Great Britain, the United States and the U.S.S.R. by the signatories.

On Aug. 21 and Oct. 7, 1942, President Roosevelt again publicly declared the intention of the United States "that just and sure punishment shall be meted out" to those responsible for organized atrocities, and stated that the American government was prepared to co-operate in establishing the commission. On Oct. 7 also, the lord chancellor (Viscount Simon) reiterated in the house of lords the same intention on the part of the British government, and emphasized that technical aspects such as gathering evidence, reviewing applicable rules of law, etc., were not being neglected. Associated with the commission, which had offices in London, in 1943, were representatives appointed by the United Nations, to assist in its work of investigation, research and the collection of the information on which action against individual war criminals can be based. Herbert C. Pell, former Ambassador to Portugal and Hungary, was the United States representative. Sir Cecil Hurst represented Great Britain. Due to technical questions which had not yet been settled, the U.S.S.R. was not represented on the commission, but had already given notice of her intention to prosecute war criminals by calling for the trial of Hess and actually trying and executing several persons found guilty of war crimes in portions of Russia liberated from the Germans. At the Moscow conference, a statement was issued on Nov. 1, 1943 signed by President Roosevelt, Prime Minister Churchill and Premier Stalin, "speaking in the interests of the 33 United Nations," solemnly declaring that at the time of the granting of any armistice, German officers and men and members of the nazi party responsible for or having taken a consenting part in atrocities, would be sent back to the countries where the crimes were committed, to be judged and punished by the laws of these countries, and that lists would be compiled "in all possible detail." In addition, German criminals "whose offenses have no particular geographical localization" would be punished by joint decision of the governments of the Allies, a point designed to prevent the escape of political offenders through legal loop-holes.

(W. B. M.)

War Damage Corporation: *see* INSURANCE.
War Damage Insurance: *see* INSURANCE.

War Debts.

A statement follows showing the World War I indebtedness of foreign governments to the United States as of July 1, 1943.

Country	Principal	Accrued Interest	Total Indebtedness
Funded debts:			
Belgium . . .	$ 400,680,000.00	$ 86,267,077.60	$ 486,947,077.60
Czechoslovakia .	165,241,108.90	656,255.60	165,897,364.50
Estonia	16,466,012.87	6,880,627.93	23,346,640.80
Finland	8,032,756.97	800,254.36	8,833,011.33
France	3,863,650,000.00	588,894,204.40	4,452,544,204.40
Germany (Austrian indebtedness)[1]	25,980,480.66	44,058.93	26,024,539.59
Great Britain . .	4,368,000,000.00	1,743,864,782.58	6,111,864,782.58
Greece	31,516,000.00	4,485,855.00	36,001,855.00
Hungary	1,908,560.00	699,637.73	2,608,197.73
Italy	2,004,900,000.00	37,349,009.34	2,042,249,009.34
Latvia	6,879,464.20	2,757,079.90	9,636,544.10
Lithuania . . .	6,197,682.00	2,435,323.92	8,633,005.92
Poland	206,057,000.00	86,109,584.20	292,166,584.20
Rumania	63,860,560.43	7,435,480.08	71,296,040.51
Yugoslavia . . .	61,625,000.00	1,155,468.78	62,780,468.78
Total	$11,230,994,626.03	$ 2,569,835,600.35	$ 13,800,830,226.38
Unfunded debts:			
Armenia	11,959,917.49	14,235,170.10	26,195,087.59
Russia	192,601,297.37	236,217,810.82	428,819,108.19
Total	$ 204,561,214.86	$ 250,452,980.92	$ 455,014,195.78
Total of above . .	$11,435,555,840.89	$ 2,820,288,581.27	$ 14,255,844,422.16
Germany[2] Army costs (reichsmarks)	997,500,000.00	45,458,676.50	1,042,958,676.50
Awards of Mixed Claims Commission (reichsmarks)	2,040,000,000.00	135,150,000.00	2,175,150,000.00
Total (reichsmarks)	3,037,500,000.00	180,608,676.50	3,218,108,676.50
Total (in dollars at 40.33 cents to the reichsmark) . .	$ 1,225,023,750.00	$ 72,839,479.23	$ 1,297,863,229.23

[1] The German government had been notified that the government of the United States would look to the German government for the discharge of this indebtedness of the government of Austria to the government of the United States.
[2] Indebtedness to the United States under agreements of June 23, 1930 and May 26, 1932.

(D. W. B.)

War Department, U.S.: *see* GOVERNMENT DEPARTMENTS AND BUREAUS.

Warfare, Incendiary.

For the intensive bombing of Berlin in Nov. and Dec. 1943, a greater weight of incendiary bombs than of explosive bombs was dropped. The effects produced by incendiaries also were greater. Some neutral observers reported that as high as 90% of the devastation of Berlin, caused by RAF and AAF bombing late in 1943, resulted from incendiary damage.

Incendiary damage from air attack was caused almost entirely by specially designed incendiary bombs; the fires caused by explosive bombs were insignificant when compared to the staggering values in real property in all theatres of operation that were destroyed by incendiaries.

A liquid and three solids were the principal incendiaries used: oil; and white phosphorus, magnesium and thermit.

With any one of these four incendiary agents employed in an aerial bomb, the technical objective was simply to place fire, burning at sufficiently high temperature, against a burnable target; and to maintain this intense heat sufficiently long to induce combustion. For a point target of high inflammability, a single fire thus induced was usually sufficient to destroy the structure. Where area bombing was undertaken, the tactical objective was to generate an appropriate number of separate fires, sufficiently close together so that they would coalesce into a general conflagration before they could be extinguished.

The ultimate objective of incendiary attack—that is, the generation of a conflagration—was attained with greater frequency in 1943 than in any previous year. On numerous occasions bombers returning to renew attack of an area target reported fires still burning several days after previous attacks.

Increasing altitudes from which aerial attacks were launched, necessitated use of bombs of larger size, because even in area bombing operations the small magnesium incendiary bomb weighing approximately 2 lb. gave excessive dispersion in falling 20,000 or more feet. Another objection to scattering large quantities of small bombs was the increasing number of bombers simultaneously present over a target area.

Thus tactical considerations were more important than technical factors; the placing of incendiary bombs successfully at the target in step with the increasing tempo of aerial attack was of primary concern.

In planning incendiary attacks, thought was still given to the quality and extent of fire-fighting organization within the target area, although passive defense against incendiary warfare became less and less effective as intensity of bombing operations increased. Three factors were seen to hamper fire fighting, or the efforts of the defender to nullify the destructive effectiveness of incendiary bombs:

a. The sheer weight of explosive bombs dropped toppled buildings and impeded access to fires, disrupted water supplies and demoralized fire fighters.
b. Extensive use of delay action (explosive) bombs had the result of prolonging attacks long after bombers had returned to their bases, and thus further interfering with fire control measures.
c. Follow-up aerial attacks were timed to cause fire fighters' to take cover while fires were still blazing.

The antipersonnel incendiary bomb which was first used extensively in 1942, assumed less importance in 1943, partially because of developments in strategy of air attack. Increased intensity of attacks and the frequency with which metropolitan targets, particularly in the European theatre, were bombed combined to render the explosive feature of incendiary bombs less significant.

Renewed interest was noted in white phosphorus as an incendiary agent. Military advances made by the United Nations during 1943 placed under Allied control the principal global resources for producing this incendiary. Although not as effective a fire kindler as magnesium, white phosphorus is a powerful antipersonnel agent, since it usually scatters in showers of burning particles which imbed in flesh and cause painful burns. During 1943 white phosphorus was widely used, both in aerial bombs and in shell, for its combined casualty and incendiary effect.

The flame thrower also was brought from military obscurity to considerable prominence during 1943. The flame thrower proved valuable in attacking bunkers and pillboxes having narrow and usually camouflaged firing apertures.

Improvements in the flame thrower noted in 1943 were: *a.* extended range of the fire jet (to over 50 yd.), and *b.* use of solid fuels which cling to and burn on the target. The latter tended to enhance the incendiary value of the flame thrower, although the primary tactical use of this weapon was still antipersonnel rather than antimatériel.

Although the possibility of incendiary attack of communities of the United States mainland diminished during 1943 because of curtailment of axis air power, at the same time the vulnerability of American cities to fire from the air was noted and some long range planning was proposed, particularly by the National Fire

Protection association, to diminish this risk.   (G. J. B. F.)

War Food Administration.

The work of the War Food administration in 1943 was designed to help farmers produce the largest possible supply of food; to allocate the food in a way that would be most effective in prosecuting the war; and to help processors, handlers and consumers distribute the civilian supply of food as evenly and fairly as possible. Farmers wrote an astounding record of production in 1943. (*See* AGRICULTURE.)

In making the plans for the production of 1943, farmers were assisted by goals placed before them by the Agricultural Adjustment agency's farmer committeemen. They also were assisted in making plans of needed war crops by support prices which gave assurance as to the return that could be counted on for each pound or bushel or bale of output. Support prices are the equivalent for farmers of the contract prices to producers of other war materials such as guns, ships, tanks, clothing, etc.

After the farm plans were made early, attention was turned to one of the great problems of the year—shortage of experienced labour. The number of people working on farms at the beginning of 1943 was the lowest on record. Yet with more food and fibre produced than ever before, there were no significant losses of farm production that could be attributed to labour shortage. The farm people were chiefly responsible for this accomplishment. Reports show that during the summer of 1943 farmers increased their working hours even above the long hours they worked in 1942. Also, an estimated 400,000 year-round farm workers who otherwise would have entered the armed services were kept on the farms during 1943 by deferments granted by selective service boards under the so-called Tydings amendment.

However, the farm families and their regular help could not do the whole job. It was necessary to provide a great deal of volunteer help from towns and cities. This work was administered by agencies of the War Food administration. Starting in May 1943, about 4,000,000 placements of workers were made under this program. This involved 1,500,000 different workers. In addition, more than 65,000 Mexicans, Jamaicans and Bahamians were imported by the War Food administration for work on American farms. Twenty thousand United States farm workers were transported from their home states to other states at the expense of the government, and 27,000 farm workers were transported from one place to another within their home states. Even so, the United States achieved its record 1943 production with nearly 4,000,000 fewer people on farms than in World War I.

Some pinches in supply of machinery were inevitable during 1943, when the unparalleled munitions program was using up metals and other critical materials and necessarily had first call on them. Realizing that more machinery had to be made available in 1944, the War Food administration by July 1, 1943, had successfully presented to the War Production board the next year's requirements, and the WPB had authorized the manufacture of 80% of as much new machinery as was manufactured in 1940.

Fertilizers (except nitrogen, which was needed for explosives) were supplied above prewar levels, while adequate insecticides and fungicides were available to protect commercial crops and victory gardens. They were distributed equitably to meet the crop needs in various areas.

The record food output created a serious problem of transportation in 1943. However, the railroads, the water-borne carriers, the War Shipping administration, and other agencies co-operated with WFA, and this problem was solved. In 1943, one-fifth more cars of grain and grain products were moved than in 1942; one-eighth more carloads of livestock were moved; grain imports from Canada were many times greater.

To get the huge crop and livestock output processed required co-operation of WFA with the food-processing industries in presenting their case for machinery. Consultations were held with food industries and machine manufacturers. Schedules of production and minimum needs for new equipment were drawn up, and WPB released the necessary materials. As a result, the food-processing industries handled 49% more meat in 1943 than in the average prewar year; 63% more chickens; 50% more egg products; 14% more dairy products; 29% more fats and oils; and 63% more canned vegetables.

This great output of raw and processed foods was allocated by WFA in 1943 as follows: 75% for civilians, 13% for United States military services, 12% for U.S. allies and other friendly nations.

Food distribution orders were the means of implementing this allocation, and 919 orders were issued during 1943, covering nearly every important phase of food distribution. Some of the orders enforced economies in processing and distribution to keep down the cost, save manpower, materials and transportation. Some held back supplies for the military services. Some allocated scarce foods for better distribution. Each order was for a specific need and was withdrawn when its purpose had been served.

The War Food administration worked closely with the armed services in co-ordinating all government buying of food in 1943. Through the establishment of an Inter-Agency Food Procurement committee, supplies were provided at the right time at the right place in the right amounts. The food buying program was operated in substantial part by the War Food administration. More than 80 food industry advisory committees helped with the procurement and processing machinery and various other problems involved.

Local civilian shortages of some foods developed during 1943, particularly in congested areas. In several congested areas WFA helped establish or expand feeding facilities in industrial plants and to improve the meals served to industrial workers. In other areas, where temporary local surpluses developed, foods were purchased to support producer prices; new markets or processing outlets were found; warehouse accommodations were obtained, or programs were developed to stimulate the sales of these foods at the times when heaviest supplies arrived on the market. Spoilage of food was kept at a minimum.   (M. Js.)

War Frauds: *see* FEDERAL BUREAU OF INVESTIGATION.

War Information, Office of.

The Office of War Information, under the terms of executive orders of June 13, 1942, and March 9, 1943, was authorized "to formulate and carry out . . . information activities designed to facilitate the development of an informed and intelligent understanding, at home and abroad, of the status and progress of the war effort and of the war policies, activities and aims of the government."

The overseas branch was organized to disseminate information to allied, neutral and occupied nations throughout the world and, in conjunction with the military establishment, direct propaganda warfare against enemy countries. Operations of the overseas branch in 1943 included radio broadcasting on a 24-hour schedule in virtually every language to every nation in the world, the distribution of news, pamphlets and leaflets, motion pictures, magazines, photographs and other information materials both from the continental United States and from outposts at strategic points throughout the world. The domestic branch directed and co-ordinated the release of all government information about home front

Dit is 'n soldaat in
die Amerikaanse Leër . . .

Este es uno de los infantes
de marina norteamericanos . . .

Voici l'étoile qui
symbolise la Liberté.

PROPAGANDA BOOKLET for small children issued by the Office of War Information in several languages in 1943. Specimen pages, left to right, show pictures of a U.S. tank crew member (Africaans or Boer language: "This is a soldier in the American army . . ."); a marine (Spanish: "This is one of the [North] American marines . . .") and a U.S. star (French: "This is the star symbolizing liberty.")

activities to the press, radio and other media of public information.

Elmer Davis, former news analyst of the Columbia Broadcasting system, was named director of OWI in June, 1942. Robert Sherwood, newspaperman and playwright, was named director of the overseas branch. Palmer Hoyt, publisher of the *Portland-Oregonian,* became director of the domestic branch in June, 1943.

(G. A. Bs.)

War Labor Board, National.

During 1943 government stabilization controls, though threatened by powerful groups seeking increased prices and wages, held in check the forces of inflation.

The wage regulations of the economic stabilization program were administered by the National War Labor board. In addition, the board was responsible for settlement of wartime labour disputes.

The wage stabilization powers of the board were defined by the Anti-Inflation act of Oct. 1942, and by subsequent orders from the president and the director of economic stabilization. The WLB wage program provided first, a limitation upon changes in the general level of wages, by application of the "little steel" formula, and second, a basis for allowing increases in rates to correct inter-plant and intra-plant wage relationships, substandard wages and obsolete wage structures which hindered the flow of manpower to critical war industries.

Gross average weekly and hourly earnings of factory workers continued to rise significantly in 1943. However, a considerable proportion of the rise was attributable to lengthening of the work week in meeting production schedules, with resulting overtime pay; to the effect of higher wages in war industries, and to upgrading from lower-paid to higher-paid jobs.

These factors, which increased the earnings of manufacturing workers, were an inevitable consequence of stepped-up war production. They were not subject to the control of the War Labor board, which sought to regulate only basic wage rates and to permit shift differentials, incentive plans, promotions and reclassifications, and certain other wage components which did not affect basic rates. A measure of the effect of board action on wages was provided by a comparison of the increase in gross earnings and in basic rates. Of the 10.2-cent gain in gross average hourly factory earnings in the first year of wage stabilization, 1.1 cents was attributable to increases ordered or approved by the board for basic wage rates.

A dramatic illustration of increased earnings without an increase of wage rates was provided by the agreement between the secretary of the interior and the United Mine Workers in the bituminous coal case. The original demand of the United Mine Workers was for an increase of $2 a day for no more work. The contract that was finally approved allowed $1.50 a day for one hour more work under the old wage scales, plus a small weekly adjustment for travel time after 40 hours. Wage rates were not increased but hours were added to the week, thus increasing the miners' earnings and also stepping up vitally needed coal production.

The second major function of the War Labor board was the peaceful settlement of labour disputes. Right after Pearl Harbor labour and industry pledged no strikes or lock-outs for the duration and agreed that a National War Labor board should be set up to settle all disputes. Executive order 9017 officially established the board and defined its powers. The War Labor Disputes act of June 1943, gave the board additional authority to order the terms and conditions governing the relations between the parties and subpoena witnesses or documents. Executive order 9370 provided penalties for noncompliance with directive orders of the board.

On the whole, the no-strike pledge was observed. The bulk of the strikes in 1943 were wildcat stoppages unauthorized by national union officials. Of the 13,500,000 man-days lost in 1943, 8,500,000, or 63%, were due to the four major coal strikes. While the number of strikes in wartime was higher than in years before the war, they were shorter and the number of people involved was smaller than in peacetime disputes.

One of the most frequent issues in dispute was the open shop-closed shop controversy.

The board largely resolved this issue with the maintenance of membership formula.

On the basis of its experience during 1943 in administering the voluntary maintenance of membership provision, the board, in Nov. 1943, adopted a standardized procedure. This included a simple explanation of maintenance of membership to be posted in plants, a revised form of union security order, and a procedure for administering the maintenance of membership provision.

The work load of the War Labor board in both stabilization cases and disputes increased sharply during 1943. From Jan. through Dec. 1943, the board and its agencies turned out final rulings in 122,000 voluntary applications for pay adjustments, involving over 6,000,000 employees.

During the same period the board decided more than 3,900 labour dispute cases involving more than 3,500,000 workers. (*See* also LAW; NATIONAL LABOR RELATIONS BOARD; STRIKES AND LOCK-OUTS.)

(W. H. Ds.)

War Manpower Commission.

Despite the vast authority vested in the War Manpower commission and the broad scope of its control, the shortage of labour in the United States reached an acute stage in 1943 and at the year's end continued to be one of the nation's most serious unsolved problems. Heavy demands for workers to meet the increasingly heavy schedules of war production and the severe drain on the labour force by the monthly Selective Service calls aggravated an already critical situation in the labour market. Existing manpower was being depleted by inductions into the armed forces at a rate that would soon exhaust the available supply. With nearly every draftable single man or "post-Pearl Harbor" father scheduled for military service, the drafting of "pre-Pearl Harbor" fathers was ordered in October.

This precipitated a climax in the long public controversy over the drafting of fathers, and congress in Dec. 1943, by legislative action, withdrew the Selective Service system from the authority of the WMC. However, the immediate effect of this legislation was negligible, inasmuch as the Selective Service director, on instructions from the president, continued to operate closely with the WMC on matters of policy.

Coincidental with the extension of the draft, a renewed campaign was instituted to recruit a million more women, chiefly housewives, for war-useful jobs and to transfer more workers from less essential activities. In July 1943, out of a total of 63,600,000 persons either at work or in the armed forces, 17,200,000 were women. This was the largest number of United States workers ever employed at one time and also by far the largest number of women engaged either in the armed forces or in gainful occupations.

In an effort to overcome the manpower crisis, stringent regulations were enforced on an ever-widening scale. Critical shortages of labour developed in many parts of the United States—much more severe in some areas than in others. To meet this situation, a policy of employment stabilization had been adopted whereby areas were classified under various headings. The aim was to reduce turnover and the unnecessary migration of workers and to direct the flow of scarce labour where it was most needed. All hiring was channelled through the United States Employment service and certain other recognized placement agencies. Special emphasis was placed on the need of organizing community action to improve housing and transportation conditions.

In Group I were placed areas of acute labour shortage. Group II embraced areas wherein a labour shortage could be anticipated within six months. By WPB directive, procurement agencies were restricted in awarding contracts in these areas. Group III included areas in which a general labour shortage was foreseeable after six months, and Group IV consisted of areas of adequate labour supply. By Dec. 1943, more than 70 areas were classified in Group I. In this category a minimum 48-hour week became mandatory in November.

To aid employers in achieving the most productive use of labour, a bureau of manpower utilization was established in February, with technically-equipped consultants to make plant surveys, but only at request of employers. These surveys were credited with accomplishing concrete savings in manpower. Nevertheless, labour turnover remained excessively high in 1943, separations averaging 8.2% a month throughout the nation and in some areas as high as 29% and 39%. On the Pacific coast, where a large proportion of vital aircraft manufacture and shipbuilding was concentrated, the labour situation was such as to require special attention of the WMC. Wage differentials and labour-hoarding were among the conditions causing trouble. On Sept. 15, the Office of War Mobilization announced the so-called West Coast plan, which provided for area production committees

and labour practice committees to determine which establishments had first claim on available manpower. Indications were that the basic pattern thus established would be adopted by other labour shortage areas.

Employment stabilization standards were revised, effective Oct. 15, by the so-called "job freezing" regulation. Under this order no worker engaged in an essential or locally-needed activity could be hired by another employer unless such hiring aided the prosecution of the war and no worker could be hired for work in a critical occupation except through referral by the USES. Along with this program was issued a list of critical occupations and activities and also an expanded non-deferrable list.

The WMC in 1943 continued under the chairmanship of Paul V. McNutt, federal security administrator. It included representatives of the war, navy, agriculture and labour departments and various government agencies. (*See also* BUSINESS REVIEW; SELECTIVE SERVICE, U.S.; WAR PRODUCTION, U.S.).

(C. A. SR.)

War Medicine: *see* MEDICINE; PSYCHIATRY; SURGERY.

War Mobilization, Office of.

To develop wartime policies and programs and unify activities on the home front, President Roosevelt, in an order dated May 27, 1943, created the Office of War Mobilization, with James F. Byrnes, former associate justice of the United States supreme court, as director. The executive order set up a committee of war mobilization with the director as chairman. Other members in 1943 were: Secretary of War Henry L. Stimson, Secretary of Navy Frank Knox, Fred M. Vinson, Director of Economic Stabilization, WPB Chairman Donald M. Nelson, and Harry L. Hopkins, chairman of the Munitions Assignments board. Marvin Jones, who became War Food administrator June 30, was later added to the committee.

Director Byrnes was vested with tremendous authority (a) to develop unified programs for the maximum use of the nation's natural and industrial resources, manpower not in the armed forces, and the stabilization of civilian economy; (b) to unify the activities of federal agencies concerned with the production and distribution of military and civilian supplies, and (c) to issue necessary directives to federal agencies.

As a climax to the disagreement between Vice-President Henry A. Wallace and Secretary of Commerce Jesse H. Jones, the president on July 15 assigned to OWM the task of co-ordinating the policies and programs of the agencies engaged in foreign economic affairs. The controversy between Wallace and Jones was but one of several public airings of differences between government officials. In settling this dispute, the president directed heads of agencies to submit controversies to him or Director Byrnes. If disputes were aired in public, the president called on the agency heads involved to submit their resignations at the same time they issued a statement to the press.

At the suggestion of Director Byrnes, the war department, the navy department and the War Shipping administration set up committees to screen their respective programs. The Office of War Mobilization is represented on these committees. As a result of re-examination of war programs and realigning them with changing war needs, there have been cutbacks totalling $16,000,000,000.

On June 9, 1943, Director Byrnes announced the appointment to the OWM of Bernard M. Baruch "without title or salary." On Nov. 6, 1943, Director Byrnes set up within OWM a new unit headed by Baruch and John Hancock to deal with war and postwar adjustment problems and to develop unified demobilization policies and programs.

REASONS FOR ABSENTEEISM being checked by special telephone operators at a U.S. aircraft plant in 1943

War Prisoners: *see* PRISONERS OF WAR.

War Production, U.S.

In 1943, U.S. war production reached a peak, and many of the raw-materials bottlenecks which had developed in 1942 were broken.

By the end of 1943 plane production reached the goal set by President Roosevelt shortly after Pearl Harbor—more than 8,800 a month. The 86,000 planes delivered in 1943 represent a phenomenal increase over the 6,000 delivered in 1940, the 20,000 in 1941 and the 48,000 in 1942.

In the first six months of 1943 more merchant vessels were delivered than in all of 1942. Month after month thereafter the total climbed, until in December the rate of merchant ship construction was many times higher than the rate of sinkings. In the second half of 1940, only 33 merchant ships slid down American ways. In 1941 the total was 103; in 1942 it reached 727; and the estimated total for 1943 was about 1,750.

Between Jan. and July 1943 100 warships came off the ways, and shortly after the middle of the year Secretary of the Navy Frank Knox estimated that by the end of 1943 the U.S. naval fleet would be double its size at the beginning of the year.

Production of ground ordnance and signal equipment continued to exceed all previous records. Average monthly production in 1943 was about 14 times that of 1941.

Increases in war production were paralleled by increases in war expenditures. The average daily rate of war expenditures, which had jumped from $81,200,000 to $235,600,000 in 1942, progressed from $240,500,000 in Jan. 1943 to $299,800,000 in November.

The immediate task of the War Production board (*q.v.*) after its establishment Jan. 16, 1942, was threefold: (1) to convert the huge U.S. industrial plant from the production of pleasure cars, metal kitchen items and other peacetime goods to the production of goods needed for war; (2) to expand industrial facilities; (3) to increase the supply of raw materials.

By the autumn of 1942, the rapid, straight-line production techniques of the automobile, refrigerator, vacuum cleaner, radio and other consumer durable-goods industries were being applied to the manufacture of guns and tanks, ships and planes. The production of hundreds of other everyday articles had practically been stopped by orders prohibiting the use of copper, steel and other scarce materials, and the manufacturers of these articles had gone into war work. In 1943 conversion was no longer a major problem.

By Jan. 1943, America's government-financed war plant was 61% completed. The industrial facilities program—including construction, machinery and equipment—which had been put in place by the end of 1942 reached a total of approximately $12,294,000,000 and was expected to reach $17,564,000,000 by the end of 1943. Throughout 1943 the rate of facilities construction moved along a planned decline, with the result that more and more of the nation's resources could be thrown into direct production of munitions.

By July 1943 the facilities program was more than 80% completed. At the year's end, except for certain special programs and some special machinery, the United States had all the machine tools and the capital equipment it needed to produce everything necessary to defeat the enemy.

Materials.—A continuing problem after U.S. entry into World War II was that of providing sufficient raw materials. Domestic production of materials had to be increased, available foreign sources had to be developed and strict economy had to be practised in the use of all materials, so that the goals for the production of finished war goods could be met. Though many difficulties remained to be surmounted at the end of 1943, great strides had been made in increasing the materials supply, and many obstacles that had seemed insurmountable in 1942 were hurdled in 1943. For a discussion of critical materials, *see* STRATEGIC MINERAL SUPPLIES; METALLURGY; BUSINESS REVIEW; also the individual articles on metals and minerals important to U.S. war production in 1943, especially ALUMINUM; CHROMITE; COPPER; IRON AND STEEL; MAGNESIUM; MOLYBDENUM; NICKEL; TIN; TUNGSTEN; VANADIUM; and ZINC. *See* also PAPER AND PULP INDUSTRY; PETROLEUM; RUBBER.

Scheduling and Adjusting Production.—To insure a measured, steady flow of raw materials to war plants, WPB devised the controlled materials plan, announced in Nov. 1942 and placed in operation in April 1943. Under this plan, WPB in 1943 divided the available controlled materials—copper, steel and aluminum, in specified forms and shapes—among the "claimant agencies," such as the army, navy, maritime commission and others, charged with procuring the essential military and civilian needs of the United States and the other United Nations. Each claimant agency, in turn, adjusted its program to fit its share of materials and divided it among the manufacturers, who fabricated it into finished products according to prearranged time schedules.

But the plan, though it solved the biggest, if not the toughest, problem of scheduled production—that of material shortages—did not ensure that all the necessary parts, particularly the critical ones, with wide uses in war production, would be available for fabrication into a plane or tank or essential civilian item at the time and place required. For lack of enough bearings, a fan or a compressor, a vital war machine might not be assembled according to schedule.

Scheduling production of hard-to-get parts, or "critical components," as they were commonly called, was WPB's biggest production job in 1943. It was accomplished by means of scheduling procedures established in a general scheduling order issued in February. The order required manufacturers to indicate realistic delivery dates for parts in insufficient supply and assured that the plants best able to produce particular types of critical parts would produce those parts and leave production of other types to other plants.

These procedures were similar to the scheduling devices of the controlled materials plan, except that specified critical components, instead of raw materials, were channelled to the war plants. The measure of their success was clearly indicated by the steadily rising curve of war output.

Over-all scheduling of production, of major importance from the first, in 1943 became more necessary than ever. Scheduling became the keynote of efficiency, and the only way the United States could produce what was demanded, and in the proper proportions, was to make increasingly better use of plants, materials and manpower already employed in war production.

The slack experienced in 1942 had been pretty well taken up by the end of 1943. Manpower was particularly short. Millions of additional workers were needed to produce aircraft, ships, munitions and other war equipment in accordance with the goals set for 1944.

It was a fairly simple matter, in the beginning, to transfer resources from nonessential to essential uses. By the end of 1943 a more difficult choice—between essential and more essential uses—had to be made. Increasing the production of one weapon of war may mean reducing the output of another.

Adjustments in the production machine had to be more exact than ever before. Because the raw materials used in one type of product were more urgently needed for another type of product, plants in many cases had to be shifted from one type of production to another. When the immediate requirements for one kind of war goods were met, production of those goods was often discontinued or reduced temporarily.

A considerable amount of reconversion had already been effected in 1943. One plant, built to make recoil mechanisms for cannon, was changed over to make struts for aircraft landing gear. Another plant, constructed to make tank armour, shifted to production of engine cylinders. Certain ammunition plants began producing aircraft engine parts and accessories. Other plants, built for the production of aircraft engine accessories, were producing small arms for the army.

Besides adjustments such as these, other adjustments were needed in 1943 to mesh the U.S. war production program into the production programs of the other United Nations, in accordance with over-all military requirements. Co-ordination and integration on an international basis were effected through the Combined Production and Resources board and the Combined Raw Materials board, made up of representatives from the United Kingdom, Canada and the United States, working in close collaboration with the combined chiefs of staff.

The combined boards in 1943 surveyed the over-all demands of the United Nations in relation to the available supply of critical materials and products, such as rubber, coal, steel, copper, hides and leather, wheeled vehicles, internal combustion engines and others. Their recommendations for combined action, designed to achieve maximum utilization of available resources as well as the most economical use of shipping facilities, were then passed on to the production agencies of the nations involved.

For example, a recommendation of the combined boards with respect to effecting increased output of coal in British mines was to be carried out through the offices of WPB in 1944. About one-fourth of the requirements of the British coal-mining mechanization program for 1944 were to be met by U.S. production. (*See* Britısh-U.S. War Boards; Canadıan-U.S. War Committees.)

Conservation of Materials.—Simultaneously with the step-up in demand for raw materials, the importance of enlarging and replenishing the U.S. stockpiles through conservation increased during 1943.

For example, in 1942 a nation-wide fuel conservation campaign had been initiated. In Sept. 1943 WPB in conjunction with other government agencies and private industry found it necessary to launch another nation-wide program, to induce every industrial and commercial plant as well as every private citizen in the United States to conserve not only coal, oil and gas but also electricity, water and communication and transportation facilities.

Even a reasonably economical use of coal for domestic and commercial heating was expected to save more than 20,000,000 tons annually. A 10% reduction in use of electricity would save over 4,000,000 tons of coal or its equivalent and more than 75,000,000 lamp bulbs. A 10% reduction in the use of manufactured gas would save more than 1,500,000 bbl. of fuel oil.

As the materials, facilities and manpower needed for production of shipping containers became increasingly scarce during 1943, re-use of existing containers developed into a "must." Metal was so urgently needed for war purposes that none could be used for containers unless no other material would serve. The consumption of wooden containers was 25% ahead of all available supplies. The production of fibreboard for corrugated containers was running thousands of tons a week behind actual consumption. Narrowmouthed glass jars were 18% oversold, and widemouthed jars 26% oversold. Importation of textiles for bags was difficult, and domestic production facilities were inadequate to meet the increased demand.

To give immediate impetus to the conservation of shipping containers through their re-use by manufacturers, wholesalers and retailers everywhere in the United States, the containers division, WPB, launched its container re-use program in October.

Another new campaign aimed to alleviate the serious shortage of good quality rope and cordage. The Cordage institute developed the campaign in co-operation with WPB, launching it on Oct. 1, 1943, only two months after the idea was originally broached by the war advertising council. The campaign was directed primarily to manufacturers of rope and cordage and through them reached users with the message that their existing supplies of rope had to be carefully handled so that the hard fibre content would "last and last and last." The campaign material was paid for by the industry.

A program to conserve cutting tools was in operation during 1943 and received new impetus from the growing shortage of labour for making replacement tools.

Since the beginning of the war, thousands of tons of critical materials as well as countless man hours had been made available for war production by simplifying and standardizing the designs, models and sizes of industrial products, by substituting less scarce materials for the more scarce, by salvaging materials that prewar U.S.A. threw onto the junk pile and by revising specifications.

Simplification and Standardization.—As in 1942, simplification—the elimination of unessentials from an item or a line of items—and standardization—the restriction of production to certain specified types of items in a given line—were effected in various lines of goods in 1943.

After March 15, 1943, new wood furniture patterns were prohibited, and after July 1 each manufacturer was limited to production of 35% of the patterns he offered in Sept. 1941, or 24 patterns in all, whichever was greater. Simplification enabled the furniture manufacturer to make the most efficient use of still available materials and labour.

Luggage production was limited to 7 standard types, but each manufacturer was permitted to produce these types in as many as 14 different styles.

Similar simplification and standardization orders were issued to cover silver-plated flatware, greeting cards, various types of tools and hardware, blankets, knitwear and other items.

Equipment for the armed forces likewise was simplified and standardized wherever possible, not only to save materials, labour and facilities but also to facilitate replacement of parts. For example, early in 1943 the number of basic air-cooled gasoline-engine models was reduced by 50%, and each basic model produced by a given manufacturer was made to take a single type of carburettor, muffler, air cleaner, spark plug and other parts. A uniform parts-and-maintenance manual was also accepted.

Substitution.—Synthetic rubber, brought into higher production in 1943, was employed for an increasing number of uses as a substitute for natural rubber, notably in tires, in 1943. The camelback for recapping tires was made of a combination of reclaimed rubber and 40% Buna-S and was available in greater quantity and better quality. Buna-S was also standard for tires for motorcycles, bicycles, tractors, wheelbarrows and other implements and truck and bus tires in the smaller sizes.

Ceramics and glass continued to replace metals for such items as cooking utensils and dress accessories. In the early part of 1943, research was begun in connection with ceramic stoves, and by the end of the year a satisfactory ceramic cooking-stove model, weighing less than one-third as much as the 1,085-lb. prewar metal type which it supplanted, had been developed.

Wood and paper continued to be used as substitutes, but the increased demand for these materials, in the face of a declining supply of manpower, caused a scarcity of these in turn, and their use as substitutes was limited. Plastics, formerly regarded as substitutes, became so critical that they could be used only where they could serve a particular purpose better than the material they replaced. Certain other materials, though critical, also came into use as substitutes because they were relatively less scarce than the materials they replaced. Steel, for instance, replaced copper in the new-style penny, carbon steel took the place of stainless steel in kitchen cutlery, and shoe eyelets, formerly of brass, were made of zinc-coated steel.

An important saving was accomplished in packing boxes for calibre .45 ammunition. Formerly lined with terneplate (steel covered with an alloy consisting of approximately 25% tin and 75% lead), they now had a wax-dipped liner. By the elimination of solder, along with terneplate, an additional 7 lb. of tin for each 100,000 rounds was saved.

Facilitation of production through the use of castings, pressings, assemblies and stampings instead of large forgings was a type of substitution which enabled the navy to specify alloys and products that were more easily manufactured, to replace those involving longer and more expensive methods.

Another example of substitution by the navy was that of the use of reclaimed and synthetic instead of crude rubber in the manufacture of self-sealing tanks for planes.

Salvage.—Salvage of waste paper and collection of iron and steel scrap were the most urgent problems of 1943 fostered by the salvage division of WPB. At the same time that military and industrial uses of paper skyrocketed, manpower shortages in the forests kept the production of wood pulp for containers and other products almost 25% below that of 1942. Waste paper salvage was of crucial importance in alleviating the wood-pulp shortage.

New impetus was given to the continuing program for the collection of iron and steel scrap by the inauguration on Oct. 1, 1943, of the "victory scrap bank," a special drive to bring lagging collections to a total of 15,000,000 tons for the last six months of the year.

Collection of household fats, initiated in Aug. 1942, reached a peak of almost 8,500,000 lb. in June 1943 and then declined slightly.

Though by the end of the year the impressive total of 200,000,-000 tin cans, or 20,000 tons, was being collected for detinning and other war purposes each month—20 times as many as at the beginning of the program—two out of three tin cans that went into homes were still being lost to the war effort. The salvage of silk and nylon stockings for use in the manufacture of powder bags, parachutes and other military items was discontinued Sept. 30, 1943, after a grand total of more than 50,000,000 pairs had been donated by the women of America in the 11 months during which the campaign was in operation. (*See also* SALVAGE DRIVES, U.S.)

Revision of Specifications.—Government specifications had to be continually revised and new requirements established in order to keep pace with rapidly shifting stockpiles of vital war materials in 1943. Working closely with the army, navy and other interested government departments, WPB's conservation division, by means of its specification projects, tackled the problem of conserving materials in limited supply, finding substitutes for the most critical materials and bringing specifications into line with the changing supply.

The number of government department specifications already revised or under development was well past the 800 mark in Dec. 1943. The materials and products for which federal specifications were completed or being prepared included: brass and bronze castings and ingots, aluminum alloy castings, salt spray corrosion tests, paint colours, rubber, plastics, paper, 55-gal. steel drums for gasoline, brushes and certain types of containers.

Civilian Requirements.—In 1943, for the first time since U.S. entry into the war, the problem of providing civilians with the goods they needed to maintain health and working efficiency began to reach an acute stage with respect to certain categories of items.

Until the middle of 1942, inventories were sufficiently large and the war program left enough resources free to supply aggregate civilian demands at an expanding volume. At the same time, the increased individual incomes obtained from war production and related activities insured that these expanding demands would result in actual purchases.

Later, inventories began falling, while manpower and facilities for civilian production and distribution were seriously reduced. Peak war schedules were placing additional claims on U.S. national resources.

Office of Civilian Requirements.—This office, successor to the Office of Civilian Supply, WPB, in fulfilling its function of maintaining production and distribution of all essential civilian goods in so far as was consistent with demands upon materials, facilities and manpower for war production, was taking various steps to correct this situation.

By directing manufacturers or distributors of such urgently needed items of farm equipment as shovels, forks and the like to set specified quantities of these products aside for farmers, OCR was making it easier for farmers to get the equipment they needed to meet the high food-production goals.

Priority assistance was also given to manufacturers of needed types of baby goods, to replenish the falling supply.

A continuing project of OCR in 1943 was a nation-wide survey, culminating in the questioning of 5,739 households and conducted according to the best modern survey techniques, to determine what shortages in civilian goods were causing actual hardship, what products in short supply were in most acute demand and whether available supplies were being fairly distributed. (*See* also AUTOMOBILE INDUSTRY IN THE WAR; BUDGET, NATIONAL; BUSINESS REVIEW; NATIONAL INCOME AND NATIONAL PRODUCT;

WAR PRODUCTION BOARD—WAR RELOCATION AUTHORITY 753

PRIORITIES AND ALLOCATIONS; RATIONING; SALVAGE DRIVES, U.S.; UNITED STATES; WAR LABOR BOARD, NATIONAL; WAR MANPOWER COMMISSION; WAR PRODUCTION BOARD; WORLD WAR II.)

War Production Board.
War production in 1943 was approximately double that of the previous twelve months. During the period of this accomplishment the War Production board, headed for the second successive year by Chairman Donald M. Nelson, underwent a number of organizational changes. First and principal was creation of the office of executive vice-chairman. To this vitally important post Nelson appointed Charles E. Wilson, president of General Electric company, who had joined the board in 1942 as production vice-chairman. Wilson, charged with responsibility for conduct of war production programs and operations, appointed a program vice-chairman and an operations vice-chairman. At the end of 1943, these positions were filled, respectively, by J. A. Krug, a top executive in WPB and its predecessor, the Office of Production Management, and Lemuel W. Boulware. Boulware, who joined the board early in 1942, was serving as deputy controller of shipbuilding at the time of this appointment. Krug also became chairman of the requirements committee.

Other new offices established under the executive vice-chairman during the year included those of vice-chairmen for manpower requirements, labour production, metals and minerals, and that of a vice-chairman in charge of field operations, facilities bureau, bureau of planning and statistics, procurement policy division, Office of Production Research and Development and the resources protection committee. Filling the latter position was Donald D. Davis, formerly operations vice-chairman. Davis was also chairman of the facilities committee.

The two new vice-chairmen for labour problems were Clinton S. Golden, Pittsburgh, Pa., working on labour scarcities and surpluses, and Joseph D. Keenan, Chicago, Ill., responsible for labour productivity. Golden went to the board from the position of assistant to President Philip Murray of the United Steelworkers of America (C.I.O.). Keenan was secretary of the Chicago Federation of Labor (A.F. of L.).

In Dec. 1943, Arthur H. Bunker, former chief of the aluminum and magnesium division, became vice-chairman for metals and minerals and as such became directing head of the steel, copper and aluminum divisions, the minerals bureau and the minerals resources co-ordinating division and its related committees. Also reporting directly to Wilson was a new war production drive division, established to stimulate plant productivity through the setting up and operation of labour-management committees.

During the year William L. Batt became vice-chairman for international supply. Batt also was Chairman Nelson's representative on the Combined Production and Resources board and, by appointment by President Roosevelt, American member of the Combined Raw Materials board, of which he served as chairman.

New agencies set up during 1943 and directly responsible to Chairman Nelson were the Office of War Utilities, Smaller War Plants corporation and the Office of Civilian Requirements. The first was headed by J. A. Krug, the second by Albert M. Carter as acting chairman, while Arthur D. Whiteside, president of Dun and Bradstreet, was the vice-chairman heading the office which, as a claimant agency, represented the needs of the civilian population in a war economy.

An important development of the year was the increasing responsibility given the 13 WPB regional offices. Starting with a grant of authority to approve or reject applications for priority assistance in certain limited categories, the decentralization program was extended until, by the end of 1943, within policies laid down in Washington, the regional directors were exercising a considerable degree of discretionary judgment. (See also BUSINESS REVIEW; HOUSING; PRIORITIES AND ALLOCATIONS.)

War Relief, U.S.
The President's War Relief Control board was established by executive order No. 9205 July 25, 1942 to further, for the duration of World War II and six months thereafter, the productive use of voluntary contributions for the relief of war sufferers in foreign countries, or for the welfare of the personnel of the armed forces and the merchant marine of the United States.

The solicitation and collection of public contributions were controlled by the registration or licensing of agencies authorized to administer foreign war relief and national military welfare programs approved by the board. Approval was based upon these major considerations: the necessity for the specific relief or welfare; whether the purpose to be served was adequately fulfilled or might be adequately fulfilled by existing programs and organizations; whether it could be carried out under existing political, economic and military limitations; the estimated costs and the relationship to accepted budgets; the appropriateness of the suggested means of financing; considerations of foreign policy, including export of commodities and transfer of funds; character and scope of the relief and welfare programs financed by the United States government and the American Red Cross abroad and at home; availability of supplies and shipping; and the protection of normal home charities.

Violation of conditions and regulations, or undue costs of administration, were made grounds for the suspension or revocation of the licence to operate.

The major voluntary agencies registered with the board came together in 1943 as a federation of war philanthropies financed through community war chests. The federation, known as the National War fund, was organized with the co-operation of the President's War Relief Control board. The programs of the member agencies were co-ordinated, after budget hearings, to permit one annual country-wide appeal for funds to support war charities other than those of the American Red Cross.

Registered organizations numbered 126 at the end of 1943, of which 101 were for foreign war relief activities. During the year there was contributed to registered agencies for foreign war relief a total of $47,852,035 in cash, and $12,708,145 as the value of goods in kind. Of the cash received, $42,088,225 was transmitted abroad and goods in kind valued at $9,928,947 were shipped. The chief beneficiaries of these private relief resources were Great Britain, China, the soviet union and Greece. It should be understood that the totals do not include the value of shipments of food, medicines and clothing provided through the operations of lend-lease and the American Red Cross.

In addition to the 101 agencies registered with the board for foreign war relief, there were 25 registered agencies engaged in domestic welfare on behalf of the armed forces and the merchant marine. Their total contributions were not available, but $65,352,000 was included in the National War Fund campaign for 1943 for these services. (See also PRISONERS OF WAR; RED CROSS; RELIEF.)
(J. E. Ds.)

War Relocation Authority.
Established by executive order of the president March 18, 1942, the War Relocation authority was set up primarily to provide for the 110,000 people of Japanese ancestry who were evacuated by military order from the Pacific coast region in the spring and summer of 1942. The agency's prime objective was to relocate as many of these evacuated persons as possible on farms and in cities outside the restricted west coast zone. While

resettlement went forward, WRA maintained the evacuated people in barracks cities known as relocation centres, and provided them with food, shelter, medical care, work opportunities and standard education for the children.

Relocation of the evacuated people out of these centres into normal communities began on a significant scale in the early months of 1943 and continued at an average rate of about 400 departures a week throughout the summer. By the end of 1943, more than 16,000 former residents of the centres had resettled across the country, and during the year 8,500 went out of the centres on seasonal agricultural jobs. A considerable portion of the latter group were expected to locate year-round jobs and apply for indefinite leave from the centres.

Focal areas for relocation were in the Great Lakes states and the intermountain west, with largest numbers in Chicago, Denver, Salt Lake City and Cleveland. Lesser numbers were residing in scores of other communities throughout the intermountain region, the middle west and the east.

Under WRA regulations leave permits were granted, upon application, to any residents of the centres not considered in any way dangerous to the security of the country. Information from federal intelligence agencies and from records developed by WRA were used in determining eligibility for leave. Those evacuees who applied for repatriation or who refused to pledge unqualified loyalty to the United States, or whose past records cast doubt on their loyalty were separated from the others and located at a single centre at Tulelake in northern California, where a series of disorders broke out early in Nov. 1943, and caused officials to call out regular army troops and declare temporary martial law Nov. 13–14. (*See also* ALIENS.)　　　　(D. S. MR.)

Warren, Whitney

(1864–1943), U.S. architect, was born Jan. 29 in New York city. Designer of railway, business and residential buildings and hotels, Mr. Warren in 1920 was commissioned to restore the Louvain library in Belgium destroyed by the Germans in 1914. His plan to complete the balustrade with a Latin inscription: "Furore Teutonico Diruta: Dono Americano Restituta" (Destroyed by German Fury: Restored by American Generosity) met with a great deal of controversy from pacifist groups. The library was again demolished in the Nazi blitzkrieg in May 1940 and its 700,000 volumes went up in flames. Mr. Warren retired from the architectural firm of Warren and Wetmore in 1933. He died in New York city, Jan. 24. (*See Encyclopædia Britannica.*)

War Risk Insurance: *see* INSURANCE.
War Savings Stamps: *see* POST OFFICE.

War Shipping Administration.

The War Shipping administration was established Feb. 7, 1942, by executive order of President Roosevelt. Broad powers in acquisition, use and operation of ships were given the agency to supervise, for the duration of the war, the operations of all United States merchant vessels.

Organization of the War Shipping administration began with the appointment of Rear Admiral E. S. Land, U.S.N. (retired), chairman of the Maritime commission, as administrator. Many executive positions were filled by officials from the Maritime commission, thus forming an interlocking directorate for the two agencies in dealing with wartime maritime policy.

In conjunction with the British ministry of transport, War Shipping administration assumed control of movements of vessels in the United Nations shipping pool and made allocations of tonnage where needed.

The War Shipping administration also acquired the responsi-

bility of properly and adequately manning ships, making surveys of crew requirements at all ports and forecasting the nation's maritime manpower needs. Besides training merchant marine crews and officers, it recruited many men from private life with marine experience to return to sea duty.　　　　(E. S. L.)

Washington.

A state in the extreme northwest United States, popularly known as the "Evergreen state," admitted to the union Nov. 11, 1889. Total area, 68,192 sq.mi. of which 66,977 sq.mi. are land; pop. (1940) 1,736,191 (1943 est. —1,848,255); native, 1,525,812; foreign born, 210,379. Capital, Olympia (13,254). According to 1943 estimates the three largest cities had grown perceptibly since 1940; Seattle from 368,302 to 485,000 (est.); Spokane from 122,001 to 154,365 (est.); Tacoma from 109,408 to 142,000 (est.). The urban population in 1940 was 921,969 or 53.1%.

History.—The state legislature in its 28th session responded in 1943 to a popular initiative petition and passed a measure authorizing public utility districts to combine and acquire electric power projects through eminent domain procedures. Opponents of the bill filed a referendum petition. The state supreme court sustained their contention that the emergency clause in the act was not valid and therefore did not militate against a referendum on the bill. The court also declared that children suspended from a school because they did not give the flag salute were not delinquent, providing they were not disrespectful to the national emblem.

State officials in 1943 were: governor, Arthur B. Langlie; lieutenant governor, Victor A. Meyers; secretary of state, Belle Reeves; treasurer, Otto A. Case; attorney-general, Fred E. Lewis, acting, Smith Troy on leave; chief justice of state supreme court, George B. Simpson.

Education.—During the school year 1942–43, average daily attendance in elementary and secondary schools was 265,880; the number of teachers was 11,661. Total current expenditures were $35,183,543.12 (est.) and the cost per pupil in attendance was $132.33 (est.). Salaries of teachers, including superintendents, averaged $1,908.19.

Public Welfare, Charities, Correction.—The total amount spent upon public assistance in the state, including federal direct expenditures and state aid was $40,234,436.45 during the period of Oct. 1942 to Sept. 1943 inclusive. An average number of 96,147 persons received a total of $38,107,122.71 in all forms of assistance. An average number of 62,422 old persons received a total of $19,476,942.51. An average number of 14,551 children received a total of $2,952,401.19. An average number of 921 blind persons received aid totalling $375,778.46. On Sept. 30, 1942 there were nine state charitable institutions, with a total population of 9,508, and four correctional institutions with a total population of 2,080 inmates.

Communication.—In 1940 there were 6,297 mi. of highways in the state and 5,268 mi. of railroad.

Banking and Finance.—The total assessed valuation of all real and personal property subject to tax for 1943 was $1,212,960,-741. On April 1, 1943 the state cash balance was $51,997,742.78. The bonded indebtedness on Dec. 1, 1943 was $9,454,000, easily covered by various bond retirement funds. Total tax receipts for the fiscal year ending March 31, 1943 were $147,582,736.07, and disbursements were $127,697,402.34. One hundred and thirty-two banks in the state reported a total capital of $31,228,500; capital surpluses and undivided profits of $62,175,500; deposits of $1,578,638,000; and assets of $1,654,016,700.

Agriculture.—Income from crops in 1942 was $195,812,000; from livestock $129,992,000; from government payments $7,951,-000.

Manufacturing.—In 1939, latest year for which complete fig-

Leading Agricultural Products of Washington, 1943 and 1942

Crop	1943 (est.)	1942
Wheat, bu	52,193,000	55,148,000
Apples, bu	23,184,000	27,552,000
Hay (wild and tame), tons	1,899,000	1,966,000
Peas (100 lb. bags)	5,110,000	4,199,000
Pears, bu	5,266,000	6,723,000
Potatoes, bu	10,865,000	7,800,000
Hops, lb	13,376,000	11,788,000
Barley, bu	9,287,000	12,560,000
Oats, bu	9,261,000	10,080,000

ures were available in 1943, the total value of manufactured products was $636,649,809; 101,136 salaried persons and wage earners received a total of $143,412,064. Shipbuilding and plane construction probably equalled or exceeded lumber and sawmill products as the state's leading industries in 1943.

Mineral Production.—Mining statistics were a military secret in 1943 but probably exceeded the 1941 figure of $31,590,023, a post-depression high. Copper and zinc, of which metal a new rich vein was discovered, were exploited to the very limit.

(H. J. DE.)

+**Washington,** DISTRICT OF COLUMBIA, national capital of the U.S.A., and 11th largest of U.S. cities, with a population of 663,091 by federal census of 1940. In 1943 the estimated population was 900,000. In the metropolitan area the population increased from 900,000 in 1940 to an estimated 1,300,000 in 1943. The federal government in 1943 owned outright about one-fourth of the 44,320 ac. in the District of Columbia. Private taxable property in the district amounted for the fiscal year 1943–44, to $1,354,348,720—$495,378,491 for land and $858,970,229 for improvements. The federal government's land was valued at $359,803,472 with $336,723,350 for improvements. The district owned lands and improvements to the value of $90,466,248, and property exempt from taxation, such as churches and schools, amounted to $114,110,505. No taxes are paid on federal or district property, but the federal government in 1943–44 made, according to custom, a $6,000,000 lump sum appropriation to supplement revenues from private property, highway and water funds to meet a budget of $56,517,465. The property tax rate of $1.75 per $100 on a full-valuation assessment gave a levy of $23,701,336. The District of Columbia had no bonded indebtedness in 1943, and arrangements had been made to retire a debt of less than $5,000,000 by 1945.

The constitution of the U.S. gave congress the exclusive legislative authority over the district, which is administered by a commission of two citizens appointed by the president and an engineer nominated from the corps of engineers, U.S. army.

Many residents of the District of Columbia vote in the states from which they came, but no franchise is exercised in the district, which belongs to all the people of the U.S. During 1943, proposals were revived to provide for residents of the district who do not vote elsewhere a vote for president of the United States and possibly for some form of representation in congress. Legal opinion was announced to the effect that so-called home-rule would run counter to the provisions of the constitution.

From 1934, when the Alley Dwelling act was passed by congress, to 1943, $865,000 was expended on slum clearance and $15,000,000 for low-cost housing. On the defense program, $3,200,000 was expended before Pearl Harbor and in the following two years $11,000,000 was spent on demountable homes and $3,500,000 on demolishable and temporary structures. The National Capital Housing authority estimated in 1943 that there would be a postwar need for $100,000,000 worth of public housing over a period of 15 or 20 years to supply housing to low-income families.

The National Capital Park and Planning commission during 1943 drafted postwar plans to secure a co-ordinated program of public works, to secure legislative authority for the redevelopment of the blighted and decadent areas, and to formulate a program of planning projects for the Washington region as a whole. The District Recreational department proposed in 1943 a $15,000,000 recreational improvement program on a postwar six-year basis.

(H. Js.)

WASP: *see* WOMEN'S AIRFORCE SERVICE PILOTS.

Wavell, Archibald Percival, VISCOUNT (1883–), British soldier, born in May, was the son of Maj. Gen. A. G. Wavell. Following his father's career, he enlisted in the Black Watch in 1901 after studying at the royal military college and the staff college and saw action in the Boer War, in India and in World War I. He then served with the Egyptian expeditionary force until 1920. In 1938 he was promoted to lieutenant general. From 1937 to 1938 he commanded the British troops in Palestine and Trans-Jordan, and in 1940 he became commander in chief of the British forces in the middle east. His small force of empire soldiers swept the Italians out of Cyrenaica in Libya, and he supervised the operations in East Africa which recaptured British Somaliland and took Italian Somaliland, Eritrea and Ethiopia from the Italians. He suffered serious reverses at the hands of the Germans, however, in Libya, Greece and Crete, and on July 1, 1941, he was succeeded as middle east commander by Gen. Sir Claude Auchinleck, whose post as commander of the British forces in India Wavell thereupon took over. In August, Wavell directed the British campaign which resulted in the joint British-Russian occupation of Iran. On Jan. 3, 1942, a month after the Japanese attack on Pearl Harbor, Sir Archibald was named supreme commander of allied armies in the far east, but in March of the same year, he was returned to command of his former post, the India-Burma area. On June 19, 1943, he was appointed viceroy of India and on July 1, was elevated to the peerage as Viscount Wavell. A few months after his new appointment, he defended Britain's record in India, declaring on Sept. 23 that while Britain had made mistakes in administration, it had made few blunders of greed and fear. Wavell took office in inauspicious times. He was faced with one of the worst famines in India's history and with general apathy of the population toward the United Nations war effort. (*See* also INDIA.)

WAVES: *see* WOMEN'S RESERVE OF THE NAVY.

Wealth and Income, U. S. Distribution of.

Despite wide interest in this subject and its recognized importance, no completely satisfactory study of the size distribution of income in the United States had been made up to the close of 1943. The most comprehensive study was that issued by the National Resources committee on the distribution and disposition

Table I.—Percentage Distribution of Aggregate Money Income and Expenditure of Consumers, 1935-36, 1941, and 1942*
(Preliminary national estimates including both urban and rural consumers)

Net Money-Income Class	All Families†			Aggregate Consumer Money Income			Aggregate Consumer Expenditure		
	1935-36	1941	1942	1935-36	1941	1942	1935-36	1941	1942
0 to $500	25	16	16	5	2	2	8	4	4
$500 to $1,000	28	19	16	15	7	5	18	8	7
$1,000 to $1,500	20	16	15	18	9	7	20	11	10
$1,500 to $2,000	11	14	14	15	12	9	15	13	12
$2,000 to $3,000	10	20	20	17	24	20	17	26	24
$3,000 to $5,000	4	10	13	11	18	19	10	18	21
$5,000 and over	2	5	6	19	28	38	12	20	22
Total	100	100	100	100	100	100	100	100	100

Source: Bureau of Labor Statistics and Bureau of Home Economics.
*Annual rate for 1942 based on first quarter.
†Includes families of two or more persons and single consumers.

Table II.—Average Money Expenditures of City Families and Single Persons for Current Consumption, by Money Income Class, 1941

	Under $500	$500–1,000	$1,000–1,500	$1,500–2,000	$2,000–2,500	$2,500–3,000	$3,000–5,000	$5,000–10,000
Total	$420	$750	$1,215	$1,671	$2,103	$2,516	$3,246	$4,704
Food. . . .	167	295	433	558	674	784	973	1,311
Housing . . .	103	177	271	344	405	456	534	682
Household operation . .	20	33	50	71	92	112	152	275
Furnishings . .	8	22	50	89	123	153	193	228
Clothing . . .	29	71	128	184	242	303	421	673
Automobile . .	16	33	81	148	210	265	353	496
Other transportation . . .	8	16	26	34	42	50	70	152
Personal care .	8	17	26	36	45	55	72	108
Medical care .	26	32	58	77	96	115	153	236
Recreation . .	20	20	35	54	77	103	158	293
Tobacco . . .	7	19	31	38	46	55	72	105
Reading . . .	4	8	13	17	21	25	33	49
Formal education . .	3	4	4	7	12	18	36	85
Other items. .	1	3	9	14	18	22	26	31
Per cent of money income								
Total	136.5	100.9	97.5	95.5	93.9	91.8	87.0	75.8
Food. . . .	54.3	39.7	34.8	31.9	30.1	28.6	26.1	21.1
Housing . . .	33.3	23.9	21.7	19.7	18.1	16.6	14.3	11.0
Household operation . .	6.5	4.5	4.0	4.1	4.1	4.1	4.1	4.4
Furnishings . .	2.7	3.0	4.0	5.1	5.5	5.6	5.2	3.7
Clothing . . .	9.5	9.5	10.2	10.5	10.8	11.0	11.3	10.9
Automobile . .	5.1	4.4	6.5	8.4	9.4	9.7	9.4	8.0
Other transportation . . .	2.5	2.2	2.1	1.9	1.8	1.8	1.9	2.1
Personal care .	2.7	2.2	2.1	2.0	2.0	2.0	1.9	1.7
Medical care .	8.3	4.3	4.7	4.4	4.3	4.2	4.1	3.8
Recreation . .	6.6	2.6	2.8	3.1	3.4	3.8	4.2	4.7
Tobacco . . .	2.3	2.6	2.5	2.2	2.1	2.0	1.9	1.7
Reading . . .	1.4	1.1	1.0	1.0	1.0	.9	.9	.8
Formal education. .	0.8	.5	.4	.4	.5	.7	1.0	1.4
Other items. .	0.5	.4	.7	.8	.8	.8	.7	.5

of income for the year 1935–36.

In 1942, however, the bureaus of labor statistics and home economics conducted small studies of the distribution of income and expenditures for 1941 and the earlier part of 1942 in order to provide more current data. Some of the basic information from these studies is presented in Tables I and II. It will be noted that even for the latest period there was a high degree of inequality in the distribution of income. Families with incomes of $1,500 and less, for example, constituted 47% of all families in 1942, whereas they received only 14% of total income. On the other hand the 6% of all families having incomes of $5,000 and over received 38% of total income.

It is apparent from Table I, however, that the sharp increase in total income that occurred during World War II brought a striking change in the distribution of income that was moving families out of the smallest income classes into the larger income classes. In 1935–36 the largest single group of income recipients was that which received between $500 and $1,000, while in both 1941 and 1942 the largest group was that receiving between $2,000 and $3,000.

Inasmuch as the rise in incomes tended to take families out of the smallest income groups, the families receiving $1,500 or less obtained a much smaller proportion of the aggregate consumer income in 1941 and 1942 than they did in 1935–36. As can be seen in the table, families with $1,500 or less received 38% of

aggregate income in 1935–36 but only 14% in the early part of 1942. This does not mean, as is sometimes thought, that the low income families failed to participate in the increase in income but rather that, by participating in the increase in income, they were taken out of the smallest income groups.

The distribution of expenditures by income-size class is shown in Table II for 1941. The outstanding fact in this table is the very high percentage of total income accounted for by food and housing expenditures for the lowest income classes. On the other hand, many other types of expenditure formed a remarkably constant percentage of income from one income class to another with the exception of the group with incomes under $500.

The data on this size-distribution of income were on a family basis; that is, all the income of the various members of a given family was lumped together as one income. For some problems, however, distribution of income arranged on the basis of individual income recipients is most appropriate, notably in connection with tax questions. Such a distribution of income, submitted by the treasury department to congress in connection with the 1943 Revenue act, is shown in Table III. Of course, in this table a much smaller percentage of income recipients are in the group above $5,000 than was the case in Table I, since a family with several income recipients might easily be in the class above $5,000, even though no one of the income recipients was in that class. The table shows the sharp cut made in the high income group by the heavy taxes being imposed during the war. It also brings out how large a proportion of income recipients (almost 90%) had incomes of less than $3,000—even under conditions of wartime prosperity.

State Distribution of Income Payments.—Statistics on the geographic distribution of income in the United States are provided by the department of commerce's annual estimates of income payments to individuals in the various states, as shown in Table IV. Both total and per capita incomes vary substantially from one region of the country to another. By and large, lower levels of income are characteristic of the predominantly agricultural states. It must be kept in mind, however, that these statistics relate to dollar incomes and consequently do not take account of the geographic differences in the cost of living.

The per capita income of $852 for the United States in 1942 was by far the largest ever reached, comparing with $680 in 1929 and $693 in 1941. In 1939 average per capita income was

Table III.—Estimated Distribution, by Net Income Classes, of Income Recipients, Income Payments and Personal Taxes Paid in the Calendar Years 1943 and 1944
(Number of Income Recipients in Millions; Dollar Figures in Billions)

	Total	Distribution by net income classes[1]						
		0–$1,000	$1,000–2,000	$2,000–3,000	$3,000–5,000	$5,000–10,000	$10,000–25,000	$25,000 and over
		Calendar year 1943						
Number of income recipients[2] . .	65.3	24.6	22.9	10.2	5.6	1.4	.4	.1
Total income payments[3]	142.0	21.2	40.3	29.4	25.8	11.5	7.0	6.9
Less personal taxes[4]	17.9	.6	3.5	2.7	3.4	2.2	2.0	3.5
Total income payments after personal taxes	124.1	20.6	36.8	26.7	22.3	9.3	5.0	3.4
		Calendar year 1944						
Number of income recipients[2] . .	67.3	21.6	24.4	12.2	6.7	1.8	.5	.1
Total income payments[3]	157.0	19.2	42.4	34.6	30.7	14.5	8.1	7.4
Less personal taxes[4]	22.0	.5	4.1	3.4	4.3	2.8	2.4	4.4
Total income payments after personal taxes	135.1	18.7	38.3	31.2	26.4	11.7	5.7	3.0

Source: U.S. Treasury Department.
Note. Figures are rounded and will not necessarily add to totals.
[1]The classification by net income brackets is in accordance with net income as determined by the Current Tax Payment act of 1943.
[2]Includes only the income recipients who would be potential income-tax paying units if there were no exemptions and if the present advantage to filing separate returns were retained. The income of income recipients who are dependents for purposes of the federal individual income tax is included, although the number of such income recipients is excluded.
[3]Income payments are as defined by the department of commerce.
[4]Refers to the personal taxes paid under present law in the calendar year rather than liability for personal taxes incurred in the calendar year. Personal taxes consist of federal, state and local individual income taxes, estate, inheritance and gift taxes, property taxes (excluding taxes on business property and rented houses), taxes and licences on motor vehicles not used in business, miscellaneous personal taxes and nontax payments to government.

only $539.

The precipitous rise in per capita income during the war years tended to bring the poorest states closer to the level of income prevailing in the richer states. For example, in 1939 per capita in the southeast region of $303 was only 43% of the per capita income in the middle east region. By 1942, however, the per capita in the southeast region had risen to 50% of that prevailing in the middle east region.

Table IV.—Distribution of Income Payments by States

Region and State	Aggregates ($000,000)			Percentage increase in total income payments		Per capita income payments ($)	
	1939	1941	1942	1939–1942	1941–1942	1939	1942
United States....	70,601	91,910	114,039	62	24	539	852
New England.....	5,728	7,422	8,780	53	18	680	1,026
Connecticut	1,300	1,812	2,308	78	27	764	1,296
Maine.........	400	521	664	66	28	474	786
Massachusetts ...	3,107	3,928	4,482	44	14	719	1,024
New Hampshire ..	268	316	343	28	9	548	719
Rhode Island....	480	636	743	55	17	678	1,016
Vermont.......	173	209	241	39	15	483	698
Middle East	22,783	28,640	33,403	47	17	709	1,039
Delaware......	203	286	332	63	16	771	1,186
District of Columbia	813	1,023	1,310	62	28	1,031	1,164
Maryland	1,075	1,509	1,953	82	29	634	1,077
New Jersey.....	2,859	3,720	4,531	58	22	816	1,304
New York......	11,301	13,717	15,468	37	13	804	1,106
Pennsylvania ...	5,819	7,455	8,694	49	17	589	894
West Virginia...	713	928	1,115	56	20	378	598
Southeast	8,413	11,388	15,187	80	33	303	522
Alabama.......	682	1,010	1,429	110	42	242	480
Arkansas.......	478	655	1,034	116	58	246	514
Florida.......	819	1,047	1,363	66	30	442	655
Georgia.......	902	1,224	1,613	79	32	290	498
Kentucky......	839	1,051	1,343	60	28	297	477
Louisiana......	829	1,052	1,372	66	30	354	534
Mississippi.....	436	626	915	110	46	201	407
North Carolina ...	1,088	1,424	1,877	72	32	308	523
South Carolina ...	492	669	918	87	37	261	459
Tennessee	852	1,194	1,455	71	22	295	492
Virginia......	996	1,436	1,869	88	30	402	697
Southwest	3,756	4,777	6,583	75	38	386	661
Arizona.......	228	284	417	83	47	461	832
New Mexico	178	218	279	57	28	341	558
Oklahoma.....	796	977	1,332	67	36	340	598
Texas........	2,554	3,298	4,554	78	38	401	677
Central States ...	20,089	26,482	32,237	60	22	565	891
Illinois........	5,284	6,770	7,908	50	17	671	979
Indiana.......	1,689	2,373	2,903	72	22	495	827
Iowa	1,185	1,556	2,022	71	30	468	823
Michigan......	3,054	4,238	5,361	76	26	591	960
Minnesota.....	1,378	1,655	2,034	48	23	497	761
Missouri......	1,832	2,379	2,920	59	23	486	762
Ohio.........	4,153	5,532	6,676	61	21	603	957
Wisconsin.....	1,514	1,979	2,413	59	22	485	786
Northwest	3,102	4,110	5,646	82	37	419	792
Colorado......	564	684	877	56	28	505	785
Idaho........	214	277	365	71	32	411	758
Kansas.......	693	974	1,429	106	47	383	814
Montana.......	288	386	450	57	17	515	860
Nebraska......	524	658	965	84	47	397	774
North Dakota ...	209	331	425	103	28	325	721
South Dakota ...	228	300	429	89	43	351	725
Utah	242	324	484	100	50	443	850
Wyoming......	141	176	223	58	26	567	883
Far West	6,729	9,091	12,203	81	34	692	1,157
California	5,047	6,716	8,735	73	30	741	1,167
Nevada	84	108	180	115	67	767	1,352
Oregon	587	796	1,128	92	42	544	1,046
Washington	1,012	1,472	2,160	114	47	588	1,166

Source: United States Department of Commerce.

Although all states participated in the wartime income increase, the gains varied from a low of 28% for New Hampshire to 116% for Arkansas. In general, states in the southeast, southwest, northwest and far west regions showed increases in income greater than the national average. The reasons for the better-than-average gains in income were not the same in all regions. In the south, for example, an important factor was the increase in income due to the influx of population arising from the location of army camps in that region. In the far west, on the other hand, there was an unusually sharp increase in income contributed by manufacturing industries, whereas in the northwest the increase in farming income played a dominant role. Through-

out the country agricultural income rose more substantially than did income of other types. Furthermore, the increase in agricultural income was not accompanied by an increase in number of persons engaged in that industry, in contrast to the increase in wage and salary income, so that the rise in real prosperity of the agricultural regions was very material.

The changes in the geographic distribution of income during the war period followed to a considerable degree the trends established during the prewar years. Industrialization of the south and the far west was notable. While the trends during the war were accelerated, they had been basically in evidence for many years. The only significant exceptions to the continuance of prewar trends in geographic shifts of income were Colorado, Montana and Wyoming. (*See* also BUDGET, NATIONAL; CENSUS, 1940; NATIONAL INCOME AND NATIONAL PRODUCT.)

(M. GT.)

Weather: *see* METEOROLOGY.

Webb, Beatrice Potter

(1858–1943), British Socialist and author, was born Jan. 22 in Cotswold Hills, Gloucester, England. The daughter of a wealthy railway executive, she tired of her aimless social life and early in her youth found new interest in social work. Her investigations into the living conditions of the working classes took her to London, where she made studies of the dock area, of cotton operatives and the sweat shops in the east end. She herself took a job in a tailoring establishment to learn first-hand the conditions of the workers. When the Fabian society came into being in the 1880s, she became identified with the Socialist group and in 1892 married Sidney Webb, one of its leaders. Together they continued their work toward social reform and collaborated extensively on social and economic publications. (*See* SIDNEY WEBB, *Encyclopædia Britannica.*) The two were constantly surrounded by a swarm of secretaries, who gathered facts and statistics and compiled data which the Webbs used in their exhaustive studies. When Mr. Webb received the title of the 1st Baron Passfield in 1929, she refused to use the title, preferring to be known as Mrs. Webb. Her autobiography, *My Apprenticeship*, was published in 1926. She died at her home, Passfield Corner, in Liphook, Hampshire, April 30.

Webster, Leslie Tillotson

(1894–1943), U.S. medical research scientist, was born July 23 in New York city. He received his M.D. from Johns Hopkins medical school in 1919, spent the next year there as assistant in the pathology department and later in 1920 served in a similar capacity with the Rockefeller Institute for Medical Research. He was made a member of the institute in 1934. Dr. Webster, using laboratory mice to determine the mechanism of the spread of diseases, was credited with creating a branch of epidemiology known as "experimental epidemiology." He also carried out extensive research on rabies, devised tests for early diagnosis and for determination of the quantitative potency of anti-rabic vaccines. His book, *Rabies*, was published in 1942. He died in Scarsdale, N.Y., July 12.

Wedgwood, Josiah Clement Wedgwood,

1ST BARON, OF BARLASTON (1872–1943), British M.P., descendant and namesake of the famous potter, was born March 16. He served in the Boer War and World War I and was sent on a mission to Siberia in 1918 with temporary rank of colonel. He first joined the British Labour party ranks after the war, was vice chairman, 1921–24, and was chancellor of the Duchy of Lancaster in the Ramsay MacDonald government. In parliament he represented Newcastle-under-Lyme, 1906–42, and in the latter year was raised to the peerage as first Baron Wedgwood of Barlaston. An active crusader for many years, he urged the establishment of Palestine as a Jewish homeland with dominion status, and during an unofficial visit to the United States in June 1941 advocated a union of Great Britain and the U.S. as a democratic barrier against the totalitarianism then engulfing Europe. He was the author of *Local Taxation in the Empire* (1928), *History of Parliament, 1439–1509,* and books on Staffordshire history and pottery. He died in London, July 26.

Welles, Sumner
(1892–   ), U.S. undersecretary of state, was born Oct. 14 at New York city and was educated at Groton (Mass.) school and at Harvard. In 1922 he was U.S. commissioner to the Dominican Republic, and in 1924 he was President Coolidge's personal representative in Honduras, then in the throes of revolution. Welles was appointed assistant secretary of state April 6, 1933, and except for a short period as ambassador to Cuba in 1933 held this office until his appointment May 21, 1937, as undersecretary of state. In the spring of 1940 he undertook a "fact-finding mission" to Germany, Italy, France and Great Britain. During 1941 he held innumerable interviews with various European and Asiatic diplomats, with particular attention to the status of unoccupied France in its relationship to Germany.

Welles headed the U.S. delegation to the Pan-American conference held at Rio de Janeiro early in 1942. During the spring of 1943 he was chairman of a state department committee that drafted a document which, with few changes, was adopted as the official agreement of the Moscow conference in October.

Increasing friction between Welles and Secretary of State Cordell Hull and public differences on policy were said to have led to Welles' resignation, announced Sept. 25, 1943, and the appointment of Edward R. Stettinius, Jr., as his successor.

Wellesley College.
A women's college in Wellesley, Mass., founded in 1870 by Henry Fowle Durant, Wellesley occupies 400 ac. A four-year liberal arts college, Wellesley is pre-eminently for candidates for the B.A. degree but offers also the degrees of M.A., M.A. in Education, M.S. and a certificate in Hygiene and Physical Education. By the addition of courses and new combinations of courses in the curriculum, students are enabled to prepare for positions immediately concerned with the war and postwar effort. The president of the college, Mildred H. McAfee, continued on leave of absence in 1943 (since Aug. 1942) to serve as director of the Women's Reserve of the U.S. Naval Reserve. In Oct. 1943, the Navy Supply Corps school at Harvard university opened a branch school at Wellesley college, with 400 officers in training.

For statistics of enrolment, endowment, library volumes, etc., *see* UNIVERSITIES AND COLLEGES.   (M. H. McA.)

Wells, Harry Gideon
(1875–1943), U.S. pathologist, was born July 21 at New Haven, Conn. A graduate of the Sheffield Scientific school (Yale) in 1895, he held degrees from Lake Forest university and Rush Medical college and received his Ph.D. from the University of Chicago in 1903. An authority on cancer and tuberculosis, Dr. Wells began his life-long association with the department of pathology at the University of Chicago in 1901, was made professor of pathology in 1913 and became professor emeritus in 1940. He was dean in medical work, 1904–14, director of medical research at the Otho S. A. Sprague Memorial institute, Chicago, twice president of the American Association for Cancer Research and at one time

headed the Association of Pathology and Bacteriology. Dr. Wells was the author of *Chemical Pathology* (1907), *Chemistry of Tuberculosis* (1923) and *Chemical Aspects of Immunity* (1925, 1929). He died in Chicago, April 26.

Wertheimer, Max
(1880–1943), German psychologist and philosopher, was born April 15 in Prague. He held professorships in philosophy and psychology at Berlin university, 1920–29, and at Frankfurt-on-Main university, 1929–33. Shortly after Hitler came to power, he left Germany and went to New York city, where he served as professor of psychology on the graduate faculty of the School of Political and Social Science (The University in Exile). One of the founders of the Gestalt school of psychology and co-originator of a psychological deception test based on an association of words, Dr. Wertheimer was an authority in experimental perception, the psychology of thinking and social psychology. He was the author of *Productive Thinking* and edited and published *Psychologische Forschung* in Berlin from 1921 to 1936. He died at his home in New Rochelle, N.Y., Oct. 12.

West Africa, British: *see* BRITISH WEST AFRICA.

Western Australia.
A state of the Australian commonwealth; area 975,920 sq.mi.; pop. (est. Dec. 31, 1941) 467,082. Chief city: Perth (pop. Dec. 31, 1940—including Fremantle) 228,000. Governor: (vacant in 1943); lieutenant governor in 1943: Sir James Mitchell.

History.—The Labour government, under the premiership of J. C. Willcock, remained in office during 1943. Under the federal government's regulations for the planning of production to conform to war requirements and the best utilization of manpower, there was a compulsory reduction by $33\frac{1}{3}\%$ of the area under wheat cultivation. A new factory and chemical works was set up by the state government for the production of potash in sufficient quantity to supply the entire needs of Australia. Before the war imports of potash were 13,000 tons p.a. The state government also undertook the building of a number of 350-ton wooden ships. The gold-mining industry was adversely affected by labour diversions to the armed forces and to war industries; production had fallen by more than 25% since the outbreak of war.

Education.—In 1940: state primary schools 804; average attendance 50,198. State secondary schools 6; average attendance 1,796.

Finance.—Revenue (1941–42), £A11,940,000; expenditure, £A11,938,000; debt outstanding (June 30, 1942), £A97,359,000.

Communication.—Roads (June 30, 1940) 29,722 mi.; railways (Dec. 1942): government, 4,381 mi.; motor vehicles licensed (March 31, 1943): cars 29,229; trucks 20,688; cycles 3,710. Wireless receiving set licences (March 31, 1943) 96,288.

Agriculture and Manufacturing.—Production: wheat (1942–43) 20,700,000 bu.; wool (1941) 74,985,000 lb.; gold (1942) 848,180 fine oz. Industry and labour (1940–41): factories 2,056; employees 22,734; gross value of output £A21,824,974; unemployment (trade union returns) (March 1943) 1.6%.

(W. D. Ma.)

West Indies.
An archipelago between South America and Florida, embracing the Greater Antilles (Cuba, Hispaniola, Puerto Rico, Jamaica, and adjacent small islands), the Lesser Antilles chain of small islands between Puerto Rico and the South American mainland, and some other, more distant islands, including Curaçao and Aruba. The archipelago has a total land area of around 99,000 sq.mi. The population (estimated roughly as nearly 13,000,000 at the end of 1943) is 75%

white and 25% Negroid in Cuba and Puerto Rico, 80% to 99% Negro and mulatto elsewhere, except in Trinidad, where 40% is East Indian. Languages: Spanish, English, French and Netherlandish. Religion: generally Roman Catholic. Politically, the area is divided into three republics, six British, one Netherlands, and two French colonies, and two United States dependencies. The United States has naval and military bases under lease in a number of the islands.

History.—Politically, the main event was the shift in political status of the French colonies from Vichy allegiance to a quasi-adherence to the French Committee of Liberation (*see* FRENCH COLONIAL EMPIRE: *French Possessions in America*). With this shift the entire archipelago was, for the first time in its history, at war against a common enemy. It was still a combat area, but the intensity of the submarine warfare which had marked 1942 was notably relaxed. Commerce and trade were less hampered and on a sounder basis. Nevertheless, war strain was still felt, with some of the islands, as Trinidad, a centre of war production and other activity, flourishing, and Jamaica still stunned from her inability freely to ship her produce.

Trade and Production.—Normally trade is mainly with the United States and Canada and, in the European colonies, with their respective metropolises. During 1943, however, this trade was distorted by war factors. War goods were being produced at capacity, nonwar production was in the doldrums. Sugar is the dominant export crop in most of the islands. Cacao, bananas (in Jamaica), cotton, citrus fruits and spices are likewise important. Except in Trinidad and Curaçao, and to a degree in Cuba, agriculture is the sole economic basis. Petroleum and asphalt are important in Trinidad, and some metals are found in Cuba and Hispaniola. Curaçao is a leading world oil-refining centre.

Communication.—External communication is by sea and air. The leading islands are directly connected with the Pan American Airways world network. The British West Indian Airways and K.L.M. (Royal Netherlands Airways) both extended their insular services during 1943, and the latter announced plans for inclusion of St. Martin as a regular port of call in 1944. (*See* also CUBA; CURAÇAO; DOMINICAN REPUBLIC; FRENCH COLONIAL EMPIRE; HAITI; HISPANIC AMERICA AND WORLD WAR II; PUERTO RICO; VIRGIN ISLANDS; WEST INDIES, BRITISH.)

BIBLIOGRAPHY.—*Canada-West Indies Magazine* (Montreal, monthly); *Crown Colonist* (London, monthly); *West Indies Year Book for 1943* (London, New York, 1943).

West Indies, British.
The several British islands in the West Indies have an area aggregating 8,240 sq.mi. Their total population was estimated at more than 2,300,000 at the end of 1943. Except for Jamaica, where a census was taken during 1943 (with results only partially available), there had been no census after 1931, and in some colonies none after 1921. Racially the population ranges from 75% to 99% Negro and mulatto except in Trinidad. There it is 40% East Indian and 1% Chinese. The chief cities are the colonial capitals (*see* table on page 760), but only Kingston, Port-of-Spain, and to an extent Bridgetown are important beyond the limits of their respective colonies.

Politically, the islands are administered separately or in groups as British crown colonies (*see* table). After 1940 the island colonies, with British Guiana and British Honduras, had a common comptroller for development and welfare, with whom were associated some other officials with special duties. Each colony has a governor or other chief executive (in the Leeward Islands a "president" subordinated to the governor of the group) and lesser officials appointed by the crown. (For names of governors, *see* BRITISH EMPIRE.) Barbados has the third oldest representa-

tive assembly in the British empire. Trinidad and Jamaica are in process of reorganizing their political structure on a broader, more representative basis, with elected majorities in the legislative assemblies. The smaller colonies usually have appointed majorities. The trend throughout, however, is toward an eventual federation, possibly including British Guiana and British Honduras, with greater local self-government.

The United States, under an agreement effected March 27, 1941 (supplanting a previous provisional one of Sept. 3, 1940), maintains several military, naval and air bases under 99-year lease. These are in Jamaica, Trinidad, Antigua and St. Lucia.

History.—With the lessening menace of axis submarines in West Indian waters, shipping shortage was not so acutely felt as in 1942. Trinidad, centre of petroleum, defense activity and air transport, suffered from a manpower shortage which adversely affected harvesting. Heavy pay rolls from United States defense building continued to swell savings-banks deposits. Living costs were 89% over 1935, and rationing and price control were necessary on many commodities.

Jamaica, on the other hand, was faced with an unemployment problem. An imperial subsidy of £500,000 a year was continued for the banana industry, whose export trade was around 6% of 1938 levels. Jamaican foreign trade was reportedly generally improved during the first half of 1943. Relief projects employed 12,000 persons. In mid-year 9,435 Jamaican agricultural labourers went to the United States under contract. Before the end of the year their remittances home had exceeded £100,000. Meanwhile, living costs were 60% greater than in 1939 despite £218,-000 in subsidies, with a further £500,000 allocated for the year ending Sept. 30, 1944.

The West Indian colonies continued to be the principal recipients of colonial development and welfare loans and grants during 1943, being allotted over £2,500,000 of a £4,500,000 total. These included projects for road construction in the Leewards, rural health, a food storage plant in Grenada and numerous others.

Politically, interest centred in the long-drawn-out question of a new constitution for Jamaica. Adult suffrage, local government reform and popular control of the assembly were agreed upon but the exact form of the constitution was undetermined at the close of 1943.

Education.—In 1943 there were approximately 1,378 elementary schools, with an estimated 329,355 enrolment, as well as secondary schools. Jamaica, with 667 elementary schools, had 164,000 enrolment. Higher education is provided at Codrington college, near Bridgetown, Barbados, and at the Imperial College of Tropical Agriculture, St. Augustine, Trinidad. The latter, supported by imperial subsidy and grants from tropical British West African and West Indian colonies, is outstanding.

Finance.—The pound sterling is legally standard except in Trinidad, where the Trinidad dollar is exchangeable at 4s. 2d. (normally equivalent to the U.S. dollar; 1943 value: 83.4 cents U.S.). The Trinidad or "West Indian" dollar is the most widely used currency in the British West Indies. Trinidad government and bank notes circulate freely through the islands and are legal tender in Grenada, St. Lucia and the Leeward colonies. The Jamaica government and Leewards and Barbados banks issue dollar notes. The normal subsidiary currency is British; only in Jamaica is there a local coinage.

Trade and Communication.—In general 1941 statistics were the latest available with any degree of completeness. During 1943 British West Indian external trade was generally recovering from the sharp disruptions experienced in earlier years, particularly in 1942, but had by no means returned to normal. Trinidad and Tobago, with heavy demands for its oil and other war goods, continued to have a heavily swollen trade. Even there agricultural

Area and Population Estimates, British West Indies

Colony	Area (sq. mi.)	Pop. (latest est.)	Capital (with est. pop.)
Barbados	166	197,956	Bridgetown (70,500)
Jamaica and dependencies			
Jamaica	4,450	1,250,000	Kingston (80,000)
Cayman Islands	104	6,850	Georgetown (1,400)
Turks and Caicos	169	6,500	Grand Turk (1,600)
Leeward Islands			
Antigua (including Barbuda, 62 sq.mi. and Redonda)	171	39,036	St. John's (10,000)
Montserrat	32	13,332	Plymouth (2,000)
St. Kitts-Nevis (St. Christopher, 68 sq.mi.; Nevis, 50 sq. mi.; Anguilla, 34 sq.mi.) . .	152	38,848	Basseterre (8,000)
Virgin Islands (British) . .	67	6,720	Road Town (400)
Trinidad and Tobago (Tobago, 116 sq.mi., pop. 31,100)	1,980	506,316	Port of Spain (97,531)
Windward Islands			
Dominica	304	53,202	Roseau (8,000)
Grenada (including Carriacou, 13 sq.mi., pop. 9,358)	133	90,586	St. George's (6,500)
St. Lucia	233	71,232	Castries (9,000)
St. Vincent (including the Lesser Grenadines)	150	61,447	Kingstown (3,900)

export suffered from shortage of shipping space, a factor common to all the islands. Jamaica, normally depending heavily on its space-consuming banana and other bulky agricultural exportation, continued to be hardest hit.

In the five-year prewar period 1934–38, exports for all the British West Indies averaged $64,154,000 value, imports $76,-015,000 value, with Trinidad and Tobago accounting for $33,891,-000 and $42,924,000 respectively, or well over half, although their population is less than a quarter of the whole. In 1941 external trade, based on incomplete figures, with estimates for the balance, totalled (in Trin. dollars): exports, $47,295,284 and $57,-485,563 value respectively. The sharp rise in value represented heavy increase in unit values rather than in volume, which generally declined.

Prewar external trade was dominated by Great Britain, Canada, and the United States, with Great Britain usually leading as a supplier and the United States as a purchaser. Under war conditions both the United States and Canadian proportions tended to increase notably, at British expense. Until 1939 foodstuffs approximated 22% of all import values, textiles, other manufactures and petroleum most of the balance. The principal exports were: sugar and derivatives 32%, petroleum (entirely from Trinidad) 31%, bananas (almost entirely from Jamaica) 17%, with cacao 4½%, spices 2½% and citrous products 2⅓%. Sugar products made up 90% of Barbadian exports and more than half those of St. Lucia and the Leeward Islands. Wartime emphasis on production for domestic consumption has strongly influenced export production.

External and internal communication is by water and by air. Railways are of consequence only on the largest islands. Trinidad, Antigua and Jamaica are regular calls on the Pan American Airways service. Trinidad itself is one of the leading air transport junctions in the American tropics. During 1943 the K.L.M. (Royal Netherlands Airways) expanded its West Indian service to connect Trinidad and Jamaica directly with Miami, Curaçao and Venezuelan points.

The most important system from the islands' standpoint, however, is the British West Indian Airways, whose service to Tobago, Barbados and Jamaica was extended in 1943 to include most of the more important British Leeward and Windward islands and Miami. During the year, 50% of the B.W.I.A. shares was acquired by the Trinidad government for sale by popular subscription or to such British West Indian colonial governments as might be interested.

Water transportation is inadequate in normal times and has been very seriously affected by war conditions. Interisland maritime communication is by small steamer, motorboat and sail.

Only Jamaica (214½ mi.) and Trinidad (123 mi.) have any railway lines of consequence. Antigua has two small sugar lines (48

mi.), used mainly for freight, and St. Kitts a similar 36-mi. railway.

Except in the two largest islands, highways are scantily developed. Jamaica has the best road network, with 2,458 mi. of parochial roads, suitable for light motor traffic, and 2,301 mi. of cart and bridle roads.

Agriculture.—Nearly all the islands are heavy sugar producers. Barbados, Antigua, St. Kitts and Nevis depend primarily on sugar. In 1942 a total of 432,497 tons of sugar was produced in six colonies (Jamaica 155,262 tons, Barbados 109,042 tons, Trinidad 104,359 tons), of which 50,887 tons was consumed locally. Production in St. Vincent averages around 1,200 tons. A widely varying proportion of sugar cane is converted into molasses and rum. Jamaica is especially important for rum and annually exported about 900,000 gal. in prewar years. Exports declined to 442,003 gal. in 1941 and 415,469 gal. in 1942, but production was understood to have remained normal, with large quantities stored for postwar shipment. In Trinidad sugar-growing suffered a sharp decline, largely because of labour shortage and wartime shipping difficulties. Against 154,218 tons in 1937 and a "normal" of 140,-000 tons, it was estimated at 70,000 tons or less in 1943 in the face of ideal weather conditions.

More than 97% of banana acreage, or 72,909 ac. in 1942, is in Jamaica, normally the world's largest banana exporter. In 1938, 23,811,337 stems were exported, but war difficulties reduced the total to 5,588,555 in 1941 and 1,347,324 in 1942. To sustain the industry, an imperial subsidy is given. St. Vincent, St. Lucia, Grenada and Dominica also produce bananas. Cacao is grown especially in Trinidad and Tobago (210,000 ac.) and in Grenada (20,500 ac.) and St. Lucia (4,250 ac.). Coco-nut acreage aggregates in excess of 105,000 ac., half of it in Trinidad and Tobago. Jamaica, however, is the heaviest exporter (1938: 33,415,379 nuts; 1941: 17,134,950 nuts), followed by St. Vincent, St. Lucia and Trinidad. Cotton is important, with some 22,000 ac. planted in 1941, 18,066 ac. in sea-island cotton. St. Vincent, St. Kitts-Nevis, Grenada, Montserrat and Antigua are the leading cotton islands.

Citrus fruits, especially oranges, limes and grapefruit, are grown in most of the colonies. More than half of Dominica's export values are made up by citrus fruit. Jamaica formerly exported oranges and grapefruit extensively, largely to Great Britain, but war conditions compelled a shift to orange pulp. The most important West Indian citrus product is the lime. Dominica, St. Lucia, Trinidad and Montserrat together account for most of the world's lime-juice production.

Arrowroot accounts for half to two-thirds of St. Vincent's export values. This land dominates world production (1941 exports: 11,224,002 lb., valued at £142,992). Spice production is especially important in Grenada, where nutmeg (1940 value: £79,596) and mace (£39,602 value) make up half of export values. Jamaica is the sole source of pimento ("allspice"), with a 1941 export of 3,246,994 lb. (value £151,662), and is an important producer of ginger.

Jamaica's "Blue mountain" coffee is regarded as one of the world's finest. Other varieties, however, are of low quality. In 1941, 18,000 bags (of 132 lb.) were exported. Trinidad (1941: 10,780 bags) produces some coffee.

Mineral Production.—Except in Trinidad, where petroleum and asphalt all but dominate economic life, and in Barbados, where some small petroleum deposits are known to exist, the British West Indies lack mineral resources. No official release is given petroleum-production data in Trinidad. During 1943, however, the industry was reported to be working at full capacity.

Fishing.—Commercial fishing is carried on in all the islands, although frequently on a part-time basis only. The Barbados overnment, however, allocated £2,250 in 1943 to aid the industry rough loans. Previous loans on a smaller scale had raised the umber of commercial fishing boats from 358 to 404.

Manufacturing.—Except for petroleum refining in Trinidad nd sugar processing there is little manufacturing. Under war ress, however, government policies have been to encourage local anufacturing, such as cassava milling, wherever possible.

BIBLIOGRAPHY.—*West Indies Year Book, 1943; Canada–West Indies agazine* (Montreal, monthly); *Crown Colonist* (London, monthly); *olonial Review* (London, quarterly); *West India Committee Circular* London, fortnightly).

West Virginia.
A state in the Appalachian mountain region in the eastern part of the United States. West Virginia was formed from Virginia during the Civil War nd admitted to the union June 20, 1863. Area, 24,282 sq.mi. including 150 sq.mi. of water); population (1940) 1,901,974, of hich 1,742,320 were white (41,782 foreign born). Its total rban population was 534,292. Its capital is Charleston (pop. 7,914). Its other chief cities are Huntington (78,836) and Vheeling (61,099).

History.—The chief state officers in 1941–42 were: governor, Mansfield M. Neely; secretary of state, William S. O'Brien; reasurer, R. E. Talbott; auditor, Edgar B. Sims; attorney-general, Clarence W. Meadows. All except the governor were re-lected in Nov. 1940.

Education.—The pupil enrolment (net) in the 4,589 state ele-nentary schools for 1942–43 was 292,608. In the 383 state high chools it was (net) 134,509. The number of teachers was 10,519 n the elementary schools and 5,312 in the high schools. The otal state appropriation for elementary and secondary education n 1942–43 was $15,225,000.

The state supports seven teacher-training colleges which in 1942–43 had a total student enrolment of 3,251 and a total in-tructional membership of 273. It also supports West Virginia university.

Public Welfare, Charities, Correction.—For the year end-ng July 1, 1943 the total expenditure for old-age assistance was $4,553,337; for the blind, $258,431; for dependent children, $3,-042,600. Including the cost of administration, the total cost of public assistance was $9,619,376. The total general relief fund was $3,264,488.

Communication.—In 1942–43 the state had about 4,171 mi. of steam railway (about 6,654 mi. including all sidings), 116.8 mi. of electric railway and an extensive system of improved highways (approximately 16,890 mi., of which more than 10,396 mi. were hard-surfaced). The total mileage of air lines in the state was 750 (450 miles passenger-carrying). The total number of telephones was 199,543 (excluding 3,185 of local unconnected lines).

Banking and Finance.—On June 30, 1943, the total deposits of the 103 state banks and trust companies were $234,274,849. The total deposits of the 77 national banks in the state were $288,633,589. Resources of 22 federal savings and loan associa-tions were $20,547,507. Resources of 37 state building and loan associations were $10,992,139.

State receipts for 1942–43 were $134,203,048; disbursements, $130,399,804; balance, June 30, 1943, $28,193,961. On July 1, 1943, the total state funded indebtedness was $73,963,000. Total state debt, gross, $71,053,000 (net, $65,788,050).

Agriculture.—Total cash income from farm crops and live-stock in 1942 was $64,698,000; income from government pay-ments was $2,595,000. The number of farms by the census of 1940 was 99,282 (acreage 8,908,803), valued at $269,827,285.

Manufacturing.—In 1940, the state had 3,188 reporting in-dustrial establishments, which employed 230,726 persons and paid $396,884,878.99 in wages. These plants had a total production of about $898,722,285.80. The chief industries were steel, glass, chemicals, petroleum refining, stone, potteries and porcelain, ce-ment, lumbering, woodworking and flour.

Mineral Production.—In 1942 oil production was 3,430,000 bbl.; natural gas production was 240,000,000,000 cu.ft.; coal pro-duction was 156,742,598 short tons. Total coke production (both bee hive and by-product) was estimated at 3,017,881 in 1943.

BIBLIOGRAPHY.—*West Virginia Bluebook* and various official depart-mental reports.
(J. M. CA.)

Whaling: *see* FISHERIES.

Wheat.
The 1943 wheat crop of the United States was esti-mated by the U.S. department of agriculture at 836,-298,000 bu., which is 14% less than the 1942 crop of 974,176,000 bu. and 13% greater than the ten-year average, 1932–41. The yield per acre averaged 16.5 bu. which had been exceeded only twice since 1918. The total acreage harvested in 1943 was 50,554,000 ac., slightly more than in 1942 but 4,000,000 ac. less than the ten-year average. Winter wheat production was 529,-606,000 bu. with an average yield of 15.6 bu. per acre from 33,-952,000 ac. Durum wheat was estimated at 36,204,000 bu. from an acreage about the same as in 1942. All other spring wheat amounted to 270,488,000 bu., a new high record. The acreage 14,472,000 was 24% greater than in 1942 due to the change in government policy in early 1943 when acreage restrictions on wheat were removed.

The great surplus of wheat in the United States which reached a record total stocks of 632,000,000 bu. in 1942 began to dis-appear rapidly in 1943. Although stocks were still second only to the high record of 1942, in 1943 at 618,000,000 bu. the increased use for feed and alcohol was expected to bring them down to a normal level of about 250,000,000 bu. by July 1944. The unex-pected uses which developed in 1942 and 1943 were the demand for wheat for stock feed and for the manufacture of alcohol for rubber and powder. Early in 1943 the policy of the government to limit acreage was suddenly removed and by the middle of the year a 26% increase in acreage for the 1943 crop was proposed. Thus within a little more than a year a burdensome surplus be-came a very useful reserve supply. The total supply at the begin-ning of the crop year July 1, 1943 amounted to about 1,453,000,-000 bu. compared with 1,613,000,000 bu. in 1942 and 1,328,-000,000 bu. in 1941. The total disappearance for all uses, food, feed, industrial uses, etc., was 1,203,000,000 bu. compared with 995,000,000 bu. in 1942 and 696,000,000 bu. in 1941. The esti-mated amount used for food was above average amounting to 537,000,000 bu. compared with an average of about 480,000,000 bu. for 1933–43. The amount used for feed in 1943 was estimated to be 427,000,000 bu. compared with only 109,000,000 bu. in 1940, and industrial uses took 239,000,000 bu. in 1943 compared with about 100,000,000 bu. average in the prewar periods.

Wheat prices advanced late in 1943 to the highest levels in 15 years. They did not reach the levels of the World War I period however since there was a scarcity of wheat at that time. Loan rates to farmers for 1943 wheat were based on $1.23 per bu., wheat represented 85% of parity at the beginning of the year. Previous years' loan rates were: 1942, $1.14; 1941, 98 cents; 1940, 65.5 cents; and 1939, 64 cents. In November the stabiliza-

Principal Agricultural Products of West Virginia, 1943 and 1942

	1943 (est.)	1942
Corn, bu.	13,761,000	14,042,000
Wheat, bu.	1,053,000	1,457,000
Oats, bu.	1,722,000	1,848,000
Buckwheat, bu.	216,000	209,000
Hay (Tame), tons	964,000	946,000
Apples, bu.	2,178,000	4,686,000
Potatoes (Irish), bu.	2,850,000	3,808,000
Barley, bu.	209,000	312,000

Table I.—*U.S. Production of Wheat by States, 1943 and 1942*

State	1943 bu.	1942 bu.	State	1943 bu.	1942 bu.
North Dakota	154,156,000	149,844,000	Virginia	5,863,000	7,520,000
Kansas . . .	144,241,000	200,101,000	North Carolina	5,812,000	8,014,000
Montana . .	74,335,000	73,783,000	Utah	5,417,000	5,010,000
Nebraska . .	61,285,000	69,908,000	Maryland . .	4,913,000	5,986,000
Washington .	51,667,000	55,148,000	New York .	4,528,000	7,559,000
Texas . . .	36,366,000	47,438,000	Tennessee . .	4,116,000	5,234,000
South Dakota	32,057,000	45,274,000	Kentucky . .	3,902,000	5,194,000
Oklahoma . .	31,711,000	57,370,000	South Carolina	3,002,000	3,377,000
Colorado . .	31,540,000	27,406,000	Iowa	2,994,000	4,192,000
Ohio	26,449,000	36,205,000	New Mexico. .	2,405,000	4,813,000
Idaho . . .	22,720,000	21,261,000	Georgia . . .	2,123,000	2,530,000
Oregon . . .	19,500,000	19,764,000	Wisconsin . .	1,345,000	1,717,000
Minnesota . .	18,008,000	23,170,000	West Virginia .	1,053,000	1,457,000
Illinois . . .	16,821,000	12,837,000	New Jersey . .	920,000	1,128,000
Indiana . . .	15,274,000	14,052,000	Nevada . . .	542,000	484,000
Pennsylvania .	13,436,000	15,301,000	Arizona . . .	462,000	575,000
Missouri . .	12,649,000	9,035,000	Mississippi . .	224,000	161,000
Michigan . .	11,196,000	15,322,000	Arkansas . . .	198,000	242,000
California . .	8,436,000	9,916,000	Maine	48,000	40,000

Table II.— *World Wheat Production, 1939–43*

	1943	1942	1941	1940	1939
	(In Million bushels)				
United States. . .	836	981	943	813	741
Canada	294	557	315	540	521
Mexico	14	16	12	13	15
Europe (30 countries) .	1,540	1,380	1,425	1,300	1,694
North Africa . . .	116	111	117	118	151
Asia	576	504	523	581	552
Argentina	312	235	224	299	131
Australia.	100	156	167	83	210
Union South Africa	17	19	15	16	15
Total	3,805	3,959	3,741	3,763	4,030

tion director authorized a flour subsidy to enable millers to pay parity prices for wheat and at the same time sell flour at ceiling prices. The price of wheat in the principal exporting countries was greatly out of line due to transportation restrictions ranging in November as follows: United States, $1.68 per bu.; Canadian, $1.28; Argentine 81.3 cents; and Australian, 78.2 cents.

World Wheat Production.—The world wheat crop in 1943 was estimated by the U.S. department of agriculture at about 5% smaller than in 1942, not including U.S.S.R. and China. The reductions in Canada and the U.S. were offset by increases in Europe, Argentina, India and Turkey. The Canadian wheat crop was about 294,000,000 bu., much below the 557,000,000 bu. crop of 1942 though near the prewar average of 309,000,000 bu. per year. Mexico produced only 14,000,000 bu. compared with 16,-000,000 bu. in 1942. Europe as a whole, 30 countries, produced about 1,540,000,000 bu. which was near to the ten-year average, 1932–41. The axis countries increased acreage and were favoured with good growing conditions. Droughts somewhat reduced yields in Portugal, Spain and southern France. Prospects in Argentina indicated a record crop while Australia had reduced prospects at the end of 1943. In all countries the governments proposed increases in acreage in 1944 to meet an anticipated increased demand as hostilities cease. World exports of wheat and flour were reduced to less than 400,000,000 bu. in 1943 compared with 638,-000,000 bu. in 1938–39, the last prewar year. The total stocks in the four large exporting countries, United States, Canada, Argentina and Australia, were expected to exceed 1,200,000,000 bu. in 1944 which would be ample to meet all expected demand. (*See* also FLOUR AND FLOUR MILLING.) (J. C. Ms.)

Whisky: *see* LIQUORS, ALCOHOLIC.
Wholesale Trade: *see* BUSINESS REVIEW.

Wickard, Claude Raymond

(1893–   ), U.S. secretary of agriculture, was born near Delphi, Ind., on Feb. 28. After his graduation from Purdue university in 1915 he took over management of a farm near his birthplace. In 1933 he was appointed to the staff of the Agricultural Adjustment administration as assistant chief of the corn-

hog division. On Feb. 1, 1940, he was appointed under-secretary of agriculture, and on Aug. 19, after the resignation of Henry A. Wallace, President Roosevelt nominated him secretary of agriculture. In March 1941, Wickard took charge of the production and distribution of food to Britain and her allies under provision of the lend-lease act. He pressed the "food for freedom" program with vigour, stressing the need of increased production for lend-lease aid to Britain. On Dec. 6, 1942, President Roosevelt made Wickard war food administrator. On March 25, 1943, however, the president named Chester C. Davis to the position, stipulating that he report to Wickard. The arrangement did not work. Davis resigned three months later; Marvin Jones succeeded him. An advisory committee, named by Wickard to study the tangled situation, pointed to the "maze of committees, agencies, directives, cross-purposes, jealousies, etc." No basic organizational changes were made. On Oct. 29, the president named Wickard "neutral chairman" of the United Nations' war food board.

Widener, Joseph Early

(1872–1943), U.S. turfman and art collector, was born Aug. 19 in Philadelphia, and attended the University of Pennsylvania and Harvard. From his father, P. A. B. Widener, he inherited an immense fortune and a priceless art collection. The younger Widener, who also acquired his father's interest in art, added to the collection many paintings of the old masters, tapestry, sculpture, rare porcelains, jewels and crystals. In 1942, he presented the entire collection, variously estimated as worth between $15,000,-000 and $50,000,000, to the National Gallery of Art in Washington. Widener was also possessor of three famed racing stables. He was principal owner of the Belmont Park race track and the Hialeah Park race track. Widener died in Elkins Park, Pa., Oct. 26.

Wigmore, John Henry

(1863–1943), U.S. educator, was born March 4 in San Francisco. He took his law degree from Harvard in 1887, practised law for two years and then accepted an invitation to join the law faculty at Keio university, Tokyo. Dr. Wigmore later returned to the United States and from 1893 until his retirement in 1929, was associated with Northwestern University's Law school. He began as professor of law and was dean from 1901 to 1929. Dr. Wigmore won international honours for his contribution to international jurisprudence. He founded and was a former president of the American Institute of Criminal Law and Criminology, served on numerous committees and commissions, was a member of the Illinois Commission on Uniform State Laws and published the Modern Criminal Science series, 1910–15. He was also the author of *Treatise on Evidence* (10 vols.), 1904–05, 1923 and 1940. During World War I, he helped frame the National Draft law and later served on the staff of the judge advocate general. In 1930, his name was mentioned for a seat on the Permanent Court of International Justice. Dr. Wigmore died in Chicago, April 20.

Wild Life Conservation.

Wild life conservation in the United States in 1943 was characterized by a wartime curtailment of many normal activities, an interruption of long-time programs, and the direction or redirection toward war objectives of nearly all the operations and programs that were continued or undertaken. There was, however, some attention paid to the development of postwar programs that would help meet anticipated economic and social objectives of the nation and at the same time provide for a better preservation and wiser utilization of wild life resources. There

ere also evidences of a continuing public interest in wild life and its conservation, and conservationists—including administrators of public programs—continued to advocate, with encouraging responses, the principles that guided their peacetime programs. Some tendencies toward exploitation were combated, but conservationists were in general disposed to consider the year in retrospect as one of encouraging accomplishments. The conservation "movement" had remained mobilized, and its agencies for action had continued to function. The effects of war had not been so severe as had been feared. And, with hopes for the future, this result was attributed in part to the fact that the fears had been faced with vigilance and with determination to overcome their causes.

The Eighth North American Wild Life Conference—the 1943 meeting in a series that had established itself as the outstanding forum for wild life conservationists—was held in Denver, Colo., Feb. 15 to 17, with 424 registered in attendance—85 more than had met in Toronto in 1942. Sponsored by the American Wildlife Institute, the conference, according to J. Paul Miller, secretary of the institute, "helped to maintain an active interest in the conservation of our natural resources at a time when there was a very decided tendency to consider wild life and related problems of minor significance." Demands for ammunition to be used by hunters were co-ordinated at the conference, contributing to the later government action making limited supplies so available. As at earlier annual conferences many and various aspects of wild life conservation were discussed both in technical and general sessions, yet the demands for ammunition and the pointed emphasis in connection with them on increases in wild life populations and on the food values of game received greatest attention by the public.

These questions became the issues in one of the year's characteristic discussions among conservationists. Regarding the reports of wild life abundance and even in local areas overabundance, *Nature Magazine,* published by the American Nature association, declared, for example: "Recent years have seen a generally successful program of building up stocks of some wild life species while continuing the shooting of most species. In the case of only a few species, and then only locally, have we had too much wild life. Less hunting and wise hunting for the duration will unquestionably speed the recovery of many reduced species. In any cases of overabundance, the surplus can be removed in a properly supervised fashion."

Emphasizing the food values of wild life was criticized as weakening "the lock on the door that has been closed on the commercialization of game by conservationists and all good sportsmen," and such emphasis was opposed by some conservationists by minimizing the importance of this food supply. Referring to the federal estimate that "during the 1942–43 season, hunters took 255,404,000 lb. of usable meat for home consumption," the director of the National Audubon society, for example, pointed out in *Audubon Magazine* that "any such poundage of meat as 255,000,000 is but an inconsequential drop in the bucket by comparison with the poundage of meats available from domestic livestock."

The issues relating to the large numbers of wild life in local areas—particularly big game on federal public lands—were debated with special reference to a bill introduced in congress by Senator Pat McCarran of Nevada to extend federal control over wild life. The bill would have made it possible for administrators of federal lands to advise state officials to reduce game numbers in specific areas, or to effect the reductions themselves and dispose of the meat. Fearing possibilities for commercializing game, many conservation groups opposed the bill, a number of public hearings were held, and early in December Senator McCarran announced a withdrawal of his own support of the bill, declaring that its major purposes had been accomplished in focusing attention on the problems involved and bringing about co-operative federal-state action to meet the needs for reducing excessive populations.

The general wartime food situation did, however, give added importance to the table value of game, and the hunting limitations imposed by difficulties in transportation and relaxation made wild life increases seem more conspicuous. These increases were considerable. Waterfowl numbers, which in 1934 had been below 30,000,000, were estimated in the spring of 1943 to have increased to between 115,000,000 and 120,000,000, and there followed a favourable breeding season. Big-game animals, numbering about 6,748,000 at the close of 1941, according to the latest estimates compiled by the fish and wildlife service, were also increasing. The numbers of upland game birds were likewise believed to have been augmented, partly as a result of the federal aid in wild life restoration program, which though reduced in scope by war conditions continued to function.

Legal regulations of hunting were little changed. The migratory-bird hunting regulations—the only federal rules applied throughout the country—did lengthen the shooting day by allowing hunting to begin a half-hour before sunrise, but the 70-day seasons on waterfowl were continued and only slight adjustments were made in other provisions. No general conspicuous trends were noted in the state regulations of other game hunting. Widespread efforts were made to salvage for war use the fat, tallow, feathers and hides of game.

The extent of hunting in the United States was indicated by the fish and wildlife service's estimate that in 1942 the take of game birds and mammals was more than 141,000,000. This estimate included 614,000 deer, 34,000 elk, 9,000 antelope, and smaller numbers of other big game species. The bag of upland game, including rabbits, squirrels, raccoons, opossums and woodchucks was estimated at more than 71,000,000 and that of upland game birds—quail, pheasants, grouse, and the like—at more than 41,000,000. The take of waterfowl—mostly ducks—was 16,700,000, and of other migratory game birds, 11,518,000, according to these estimates.

No estimates were available at the close of the year regarding the number of hunters in 1943, the latest compilations being those for the seasons of 1941–42, when 8,532,354 hunting licenses were issued—607,532 more than in the preceding year. In the comparable period 8,423,218 fishing licenses were reported, many of these being issued to sportsmen who also purchased hunting licenses.

Fishing not only for sport but for food was promoted during the year, with attention to the needs for conservation, by the continued encouragement of "farm fish ponds," 3,000 of these having been built and stocked during the year ended June 30, 1943, by the fish and wildlife service in co-operation with the soil conservation service and at least an equal number already in existence having been stocked with sunfish, crappies, catfish and other pondfish, despite the closing of 12 federal fish hatcheries since Pearl Harbor.

In 1942, requisitioning of fishing boats by the navy and the army, shortage of materials for new boats, enlistment of fishermen in the navy and merchant marine, and shortages of rope, twine and fish-net materials resulted in a decline of more than 1,000,000,000 lb. in the yield from United States commercial fisheries—from a 5,000,000,000-lb. catch in 1941. The Office of the Co-ordinator of Fisheries was established to cope with these problems, and in Dec. 1943, the fish and wildlife service reported: "The commercial fisheries have shown a steady comeback in production from the low point which resulted from the first impact of war on the industry."

BIBLIOGRAPHY.—Among the most encouraging indications of continued public interest in wild life conservation was the year's output by book publishers. *Wildlife Refuges*, by Dr. Ira N. Gabrileson, director of the fish and wildlife service, the first book-length discussion on this subject, provided not only a history and an authoritative explanation of policies but also described the refuge systems of North America and assembled statistical information. *The Ducks, Geese and Swans of North America*, by Francis H. Kortright, with illustrations by T. M. Shortt (300 in color), published by the American Wildlife institute, was received as the best single volume on its subject. *The Mammals of Eastern United States* by William J. Hamilton, Jr., published by the Comstock Publishing company, provided a reading and reference work comparable with regional bird books, and *Meeting the Mammals*, by Victor H. Cahalane (Macmillan), with excellent illustrations by Walter A. Weber, dealt with national park areas west of the Mississippi. *The American Land: Its History and Its Uses*, by William R. Van Dersal (Oxford University press), synthesized a wealth of information about agricultural and other rural and wild land uses into a volume useful, interesting, inspiring and provocative. *Extinct and Vanishing Mammals of the Western Hemisphere with the Marine Species of All the Oceans*, an authoritative 620-page treatise by Glover M. Allen, dealing not only with extermination but also with possibilities for saving species now threatened, was published by the American Committee for International Wild Life Protection.

The principal source for current and other information on wild life in the United States was the fish and wildlife service (both a research and an administrative agency), United States department of the interior, Merchandise Mart, Chicago, Ill., which had available lists of federal publications and compilations, including a newly revised list of national, international and state officials and organizations. Among private organizations were the American Nature association, 1214 16th st., Washington, D.C.; the American Wildlife institute, Investment building, Washington, D.C., sponsor of co-operative research projects, special investigations, the annual continental wild life conferences, and monographs; the Izaak Walton League of America, Inc., 2801 South Halsted st., Chicago, Ill., concerned with conservation in general but particularly active in promoting improved streams and waters; and the National Audubon society, 1006 Fifth ave., New York, N.Y., sponsor of nature education programs, publications, an annual Christmas bird census, and sanctuaries. Scientific periodicals published during the year included the *Journal of Wildlife Management*, the *Journal of Mammalogy*, and *The Auk: A Quarterly Journal of Ornithology*. (H. Z.)

Wiley, Henry Ariosto

(1867–1943), U.S. naval officer, was born Jan. 31 in Troy, Ala. A graduate of Annapolis Naval academy, 1888, he saw service in the Spanish-American War and prior to World War I had command of various battleships. He was attached to the Sixth Battle squadron of the British Grand fleet with temporary rank of rear admiral, 1918, and after the war, was commander of destroyers with the U.S. Pacific fleet, 1919–20. He was made a vice admiral, 1923–25, and was later commander of the United States fleet with rank of admiral, 1927–29. Although he retired in Sept. 1929, he was called back to serve on the Maritime commission, 1936–40, and later headed the Navy Board for Production Awards. He was the author of an autobiography, *An Admiral from Texas* (1934). He died in Palm Beach, Fla., May 20.

†Wilhelmina

(WILHELMINA HELENA PAULINE MARIA OF ORANGE-NASSAU) (1880–), queen of the Netherlands, daughter of William III, king of the Netherlands, and Queen Emma, was born Aug. 31, 1880. She succeeded to the throne in 1890, under the regency of her mother, and was enthroned in 1898. She married Henry, duke of Mecklenburg-Schwerin (d. 1934), in 1901, and in 1909 Princess Juliana, heiress to the throne, was born.

When Germany invaded the Netherlands May 10, 1940, the royal family with members of the government sought refuge in London. Princess Juliana, who in 1937 had married Prince Bernhard Leopold of Lippe-Biesterfeld, left subsequently for Canada with her two daughters, while Prince Bernhard remained in England with the queen. On May 13, 1940, Queen Wilhelmina proclaimed that the seat of government of the Netherlands had been transferred to London.

During 1943 Queen Wilhelmina continued to maintain contact with the occupied Netherlands by broadcasting and by receiving personally all those who escaped. In August she appointed a recent arrival from the Netherlands, J. A. W. Burger, as minister without portfolio, to direct plans for the return of the government. In May, Queen Wilhelmina visited Canada and inspected Dutch troops stationed there. She also visited the United States and spent a week-end at the residence of President Roosevelt. In August she opened Netherlands house in London as a meeting place for British and Dutch people, run under the joint auspices of the British council and the Dutch government. She was presented on Oct. 15 with the degree of doctor of law, *honoris causa*, at the university of Oxford.   (G. J. R.)

Willkie, Wendell Lewis

(1892–), U.S. attorney, business executive and politician, was born Feb. 18 in Elwood, Ind. After being graduated from the University of Indiana with an A.B. degree in 1913, he taught history in the high school at Coffeyville, Kan. In 1916 he received his law degree from the University of Indiana and joined his father's law firm in Elwood. During World War I he was a captain in the 325th field artillery in France. In 1929 he joined the legal staff of Commonwealth and Southern, a large utilities holding company. Four years later he was president of the company.

His nomination for the presidency by the Republican convention June 28, 1940, was described as a political "miracle." He was defeated by a substantial margin in the election of Nov. 5, 1940, although he received 22,333,801 votes.

In the late summer of 1942, Willkie made a world tour as special representative of President Roosevelt, visiting Churchill, Stalin and Chiang Kai-shek. His book, "One World," based on this trip, was published in April 1943, and immediately climbed to the top of the best-seller lists. His attitude on foreign policy, expressed shortly after his tour, was objectionable to many Republicans and threatened to turn the party against him. He was late in 1943 one of the leading candidates for the 1944 Republican nomination for the presidency.

Wilson, Charles Edward

(1886–), U.S. industrialist, was born Nov. 18 in New York city. After a meagre grade school education, he went to work when he was only 12 years old as a shipping clerk with the General Electric company. He worked his way up through the ranks until he became president of the organization on Jan. 1, 1940. Wilson was selected by Chairman Donald Nelson for the post of vice-chairman of the War Production board in full charge of production, Sept. 17, 1942. Soon a policy dispute developed between Wilson and Ferdinand Eberstadt, vice-chairman in charge of materials. On Feb. 16, 1943, Chairman Donald M. Nelson removed Eberstadt, transferring his duties to Wilson, who thereupon became executive vice-chairman. On Nov. 12, 1943, shortly after Nelson's return from a European tour, Wilson, believing the production battle to be substantially won, resigned to return to the General Electric company. Nelson accepted his resignation, but Byrnes and Roosevelt declined to do so. Wilson stayed on with WPB. Bernard Baruch commented: "The agencies that wound up the U.S. economy for war should unwind it."

Wilson, Sir Henry Maitland

(1881–), British army officer, was educated at Eton and received a commission in the Rifle brigade in 1900. Before he was 20 he was on active service in South Africa. During World War I he fought in France and Belgium, serving both with his regiment and on the staff. After the war, he held appointments at the Royal Military college, Sandhurst, and the Staff college, Camberley. In 1938 he was promoted lieutenant-general and was sent to command Britain's army of the Nile in 1939. There, under General Wavell, he directed the advance which, covering 450 mi. in 57 days, swept the Italian forces from Cyrenaica. After this campaign General Wilson was made G.O.C.-in-C. and military governor of Cyrenaica. A few weeks later he was leading the United Kingdom and Empire troops under the orders of General Papagos in Greece. On a front of 60-70 mi. in eastern Greece he was faced by overwhelming German forces which, having broken through the Greek troops on his flank, seriously threatened to surround his little army. By skilful leadership he was able to extricate much of the greater part of his force in accordance with the expressed wishes of the Greek government. After this, in June–July 1941, in a campaign lasting only five weeks, he led the Allied forces which thwarted Vichy's support for a projected Nazi *coup d'etat* in Syria. In Aug. 1942 he was appointed the first commander-in-chief, Persia-Iraq. In Feb. 1943 he returned to Egypt to become commander-in-chief, middle east, in succession to General Alexander.

Winant, John Gilbert

(1889–   ), U.S. diplomat, was born Feb. 23 in New York city. He attended Princeton university and in 1912 became a teacher of English and assistant rector at St. Paul's school. In 1917 he entered the United States air service, becoming captain of the 8th observation squadron in France. After the war he was elected to the New Hampshire legislature, serving in both the house and the senate between 1917 and 1923. In 1925 he was elected for the first of his three terms as governor of New Hampshire. From 1935 to 1941 he was assistant director, then director, of the International Labour office. He resigned from this post to accept Pres. Roosevelt's appointment as ambassador to Great Britain, Feb. 6, 1941. In Dec. 1942 Winant arrived in Washington for a series of conferences, remaining through March, when he took part in the meetings between Pres. Roosevelt and Anthony Eden. In October he signed, in London, a mutual lend-lease agreement between the U.S., Britain, Canada and the U.S.S.R.

Windward Islands: *see* WEST INDIES, BRITISH.

Wines.

In spite of the world war which raged in most of the wine growing countries of Europe, the gathering of grapes and making of wine continued in 1943. Official figures were impossible to obtain from any of the European countries except Spain and Portugal, but from unofficial but reliable sources it was learned that the 1943 vintage was most satisfactory in so far as quantity is concerned and, in general, very satisfactory in quality in Austria, Hungary and France. No information of the German vintage was available, but from Italy it was learned that the vintage took place in the liberated territory, in many instances even while the towns adjacent to vineyards were under bombardment. It was not known whether or not it was possible to make wines in the central and northern parts of Italy (still under German domination in 1943) which normally produce the major portion of the Italian crop.

Because of unusually fine weather, the vineyards in the Bordeaux district of France were free from disease in spite of the lack of sulphate of copper with which the vines are usually sprayed. Unofficial reports indicated that the vintage was 50% greater in 1943 than in 1942, and that the quality was outstandingly fine. No reports were received from the burgundy or champagne districts, but it was known that the vineyards in the burgundy district were not short of labour and that the vintage took place at the usual time.

In Spain the weather during the vintage was favourable, but excessive heat in July and August caused considerable damage to the vineyards and greatly reduced the crops in the Jerez, Puerto and Sanlucar districts. Just as in the U.S., there was also a greater consumption of grapes for eating purposes in Spain in 1943 than in previous years, and in the southern part of Spain,

therefore, the total output of wines was about 60% of normal. The wine was of exceedingly good quality, the grapes having had a high sugar content and the alcoholic strength in consequence was higher than usual. In the central and northern parts of Spain the vintage was, like the Bordeaux vintage, above the average in quantity and in good quality. In Malaga on the south coast, and in Tarragona on the east coast, there was extremely good weather during the vintage, and there was better than a normal crop both in quantity and quality.

In Portugal the weather was, up to the end of July, most favourable resulting in a prolific budding of the vines. However, extreme heat in August and early September made an early vintage necessary and while the grapes had an excessive amount of sugar, the quantity produced was not as great as had been expected. The final result was a normal vintage in quantity, and extremely good quality. The government office in control of vintage authorized the production in 1943 of 50,000 pipes of port wine, the balance of the wine being fermented out for use as table wine.

In Algeria and Tunisia the yield was less than 50% of the average, the quality on the whole was inferior, and there was a great scarcity of white wines. The whole vintage in Algeria was blocked at the wineries by government order on the ground that the wines would be required for export to France. The lack of sufficient sulphur over a period of years seriously endangered the future of the Algerian vineyards.

In Australia the production was approximately 20% above normal with the quality good. The demand for Australian wines, particularly in Great Britain, was large but lack of shipping facilities prevented the growers from taking full advantage of the improved markets for their wines. Statistics from South Africa were not available.

In the western hemisphere there was an increase in production both in Chile and in Argentina. In Argentina the grape crush was the largest that it had ever been, with a resulting production of 10,661,756 hectolitres, or approximately 50% more than in 1942. Of this production (285,635,000 gal.) approximately 90% were table wines, quality being generally better than in 1942. In Chile, the vintage was considerably larger than in 1942, the production amounting to 2,710,200 hectolitres, equivalent to 72,633,360 gal. The quality was somewhat better than in 1942.

In the United States, the official figures were not released by the close of 1943, but estimates were, that the production was 25% to 30% heavier than in 1942. In California alone, which furnishes approximately 90% of the production of the United States, approximately 775,000 tons were crushed in 1943 as against 600,000 tons in 1942, producing from 75,000,000 to 80,000,000 gal. against 54,000,000 gal. in 1942. The grape crop was the largest in history, approximately 2,600,000 tons of all varieties of grapes, making the 1943 grape crop in California worth approximately $159,557,000. The figure for the first time made grapes the most valuable of all fruit crops in California. Quality was excellent.

In other states, qualities were also excellent, but production considerably below the average, and considerably below that of 1942. The 1943 consumption was estimated at between 80,000,000 and 90,000,000 gal. as against 112,000,000 gal. in 1942. (*See* also LIQUORS, ALCOHOLIC.)   (O. J. W.)

Wisconsin.

One of the north-central states, Wisconsin, popularly called the "Badger state," entered the union in 1848. Area, 56,154 sq.mi., of which 54,715 sq.mi. are land. The federal census of 1940 gave its population as 3,137,587, an increase of 6.8% over 1930, but the estimated civilian population on March 1, 1943 was 2,956,860, a decrease from 1940 of

5.7%. The urban population in 1940 was 1,679,144 and the rural, 1,458,443. Only 24,835 were non-white. Foreign-born whites numbered 288,774. Capital, Madison (pop. 1940, 67,447). The largest city, Milwaukee, had a population of 587,472, and other large cities are Racine (67,195), Kenosha (48,765), Green Bay (46,235), La Crosse (42,707) and Sheboygan (40,638).

History.—The legislature, urged by the acting governor to put Wisconsin on a war footing and to set aside the money pouring in from the income tax for postwar construction and rehabilitation of war veterans, passed 566 acts in a session of 8 months during 1943. Though legislature and acting governor were both Republican, 21 of his 36 vetoes were overridden, one more than the total number overridden in the entire previous history of the state, and the legislature insisted upon reconvening on Jan. 12, 1944.

Yet much of the acting governor's program was obtained. The 60% emergency surtax on incomes was not reenacted, but its yield for 1942 ($6,300,000) was set up as a postwar rehabilitation trust fund to provide medical, educational and economic rehabilitation for returning war veterans. A state trunk highway fund, estimated to contain $17,450,000 by the end of the 1943–45 biennium, was created for the purposes of postwar construction. The Wisconsin state council of defense was reorganized, and R. S. Kingsley was replaced as its chief by John Cudahy, who, on his death, was succeeded by G. R. Howitt. The state Civil War debt of $1,183,700 was retired. Unemployment insurance contribution rates as well as payments were increased, as were workmen's compensation payments. State aid to high schools was raised from $1,385,000 to $3,500,000 yearly. State civil service employees were voted a cost-of-living bonus, a pension-retirement plan, and a regulated system of annual increases. A controversial bill requiring all attorneys to be members of the state bar of Wisconsin was passed over a veto and upheld by the supreme court.

The state officers in 1943 were all Republican: W. S. Goodland, acting governor; F. R. Zimmerman, secretary of state; J. M. Smith, treasurer; J. E. Martin, attorney general; and John Callahan, superintendent of public instruction. The chief justice of the supreme court was M. B. Rosenberry.

Education.—There were 6,879 elementary schools, 462 secondary schools and 9 teachers' colleges in 1941–42. The enrolment was 361,599 in elementary schools and 158,248 in secondary schools. There were 15,312 elementary school teachers and 5,924 secondary school teachers.

Public Welfare, Charities, Correction.—The number of cases receiving public assistance as of June 1943 was as follows: general relief 8,669; old age assistance 50,495; aid to dependent children 8,034; aid to blind 1,728—a total of 59,478 households. Expenditures for public assistance in the year ending June 30, 1943, were as follows: general relief $4,791,307; WPA $5,537,673; old-age assistance $15,544,138; aid to dependent children $5,049,708; aid to the blind $539,470; and administration of the last three items, $938,630—a total of $32,400,926. Unemployment benefit payments in 1942 were $4,119,562 as against $2,927,466 in 1941. The contributions for 1942 were $18,857,125; for 1941, $13,509,273. Wisconsin's 17 charitable, penal and allied institutions were operated in the year ending June 30, 1942 at a cost of $3,998,357 (less fees, repairs, etc.). The average daily population for June 1943 was 20,254.

Communication.—The number of miles of highways as of Jan. 1, 1943, was 84,937 (towns), 2,392 (villages) and 5,899 (cities). The total was 93,228 mi. The expenditure on highways during July 1942–June 1943 was $28,689,086. The total railway mileage on Jan. 1, 1942, was 6,617. The number of airports was 58. On Jan. 1, 1943, there were 612,048 telephones.

Banking and Finance.—At the end of 1942 there were 46? state and 98 national banks. The number of credit unions wa 595. The deposits in state banks totalled $671,643,860; the asset were $737,528,685. National banks had deposits of $779,289,00? and assets of $839,466,000. The credit unions listed assets o $13,875,599. There were 120 building and loan associations wit? assets of $113,861,795.

The state receipts during the fiscal year ending June 30, 1943 were $141,028,304. The disbursements were $129,122,687. The state had no outstanding indebtedness in 1943. The state budge for state departments (excluding state aid to local units) for the biennium 1943–45 was $72,701,405, but appropriations of $9,108,595 were made in addition to the Executive Budget act.

Agriculture.—The total acreage harvested in 1942 was 9,009,000. The gross farm income was estimated at $615,171,000, consisting of $67,426,000 from crops and $547,745,000 from livestock and its products, including $289,376,000 from milk. The total was an increase of 31% over 1941 and was 17% above the previous high year (1919). This increase was partially caused by prices, which were 166% of the 1910–14 average, but production of farm products was the highest ever achieved in Wisconsin. The land used in producing cash crops was small compared with the land used for feed crops, a result of the state's great dairy industry.

Table I.—Leading Agricultural Products of Wisconsin, 1943 and 1942

Crop	1943 (est.)	1942
Corn (bu.)	109,968,000	103,544,000
Oats (bu.)	102,180,000	100,577,000
Canning peas (lb.)	257,080,000	260,480,000
Tobacco (lb.)	28,230,000	29,200,000
All tame hay (tons)	7,025,000	7,513,000
All clover and timothy (tons)	4,585,000	4,291,000
Alfalfa (tons)	2,132,000	2,859,000

Manufacturing.—The total value of Wisconsin manufactured products in 1939 was $1,604,507,356. The wages paid were $251,946,993. The number of wage earners was 200,897 (average for the year). Wisconsin, with an extremely diversified industry, ranked first in the manufacture of cheese, milk products, malt and canned peas in 1939.

Between June 1940 and Sept. 1943, Wisconsin manufacturers received $3,507,019,000 in major war supply and facility contracts. In 1942 the estimated average number of wage earners in Wisconsin manufacturing establishments was 312,700 and the estimated weekly payrolls, $11,928,000.

Table II.—Value of Mineral Products of Wisconsin, 1941 and 1940

Mineral	1941	1940
Stone	$5,666,120	$5,030,263
Iron ore	3,998,287	3,290,389
Sand and gravel	3,398,039	2,304,197

Mineral Production.—In 1940, the last year for complete figures as of 1943, the total value of mineral production was $13,554,000 compared with $12,704,942 in 1939.   (E. P. A.)

Wisconsin, University of.
An institution of higher education at Madison, Wis. More than 1,600 students received degrees at Wisconsin's June 1943 commencement, the 90th in the university's 93-year history.

Up to Nov. 1943, the university had trained 7,520 young men and women for the U.S. armed forces. Still in training at the university were 1,000 sailors and 250 WAVES in radio code and communications; 140 naval aviation cadets; 450 naval engineering students; 1,000 soldiers under the army specialized training program; 175 army and navy medical students; 100 officers in

...e Civil Affairs Training school; and 16 WACS being trained in ...ysiotherapy. The university also continued as the centre of ...e Institute of Correspondence study for both the army and ...avy, with more than 70,000 registrations received from soldiers ...d sailors in all parts of the world by Nov. 1943.

Under the federal engineering, science, management war train-...g program, the university continued its operation of 500 classes, ...rolling more than 10,000 students in 966 Wisconsin businesses ...d industries in 37 cities of the state for special training in war ...dustries to speed production.

For statistics of enrolment, faculty, library volumes, etc., *see* ...NIVERSITIES AND COLLEGES. (R. Fs.)

Withholding Tax: *see* TAXATION.

WLB: *see* WAR LABOR BOARD, NATIONAL.

Woman's Christian Temperance Union, National.

...uring 1943 the Department of Work for Soldiers and Sailors, ...hich had been carried on in peace as well as wartime, continued ... be augmented. The W.C.T.U. had by 1943 sent to the Red ...ross as one of its contributions more than $32,000 to purchase ...mbulances, mobile blood bank units, mobile canteens, station ...agons and clubmobiles. A "Safety School on Wheels," aptly re-...amed a "Physical Fitness Clinic," toured the camps for its third ...eason during the year, bringing entertainment and helpful drills ...nd information to the service men.

The two specific aims of the W.C.T.U., protection of the home ...nd abolition of the liquor traffic were actively carried on. ...uvenile delinquency, women drinking, support of and extension ...f education continued to receive special attention.

In 1943, 48,324 new members enrolled, and there was a total ...f 728 new organizations. The national officers for 1943–44 were: ...resident, Mrs. Ida B. Wise Smith, Evanston, Ill.; vice-president, ...rs. D. Leigh Colvin, New York city; corresponding secretary, ...liss Lily Grace Matheson, Evanston, Ill.; treasurer, Mrs. Mar-...aret C. Munns, Evanston, Ill.; recording secretary, Mrs. Nelle ... Burger, Springfield, Mo. (I. B. W. S.)

Women's Airforce Service Pilots.

Women's Air-force Service Pi-...ots (WASP), civilian pilots with the United States army air ...orces, began operations and training under the army air forces ...n the fall of 1942 with a nucleus of about 50 pilots. There were ...pproximately 1,000 in 1943.

WASP operations were at first limited to the ferrying of light ...iaison and training craft from factory to airfields within the ...United States. The first ferrying squadron was known as the ...VAFS (Women's Auxiliary Ferrying Service). Although the ...reater number in 1943 still flew the lighter craft, the WASP ...lso ferried all types of U.S. military planes in domestic use, ...vithin the United States and Canada. They were also engaged ...n other noncombat operations, such as target-towing, courier ...uty, tracking and testing.

WASP training in 1943 was concentrated at Avenger field, ...Sweetwater, Texas. Approximately 100 were enrolled each month ...s the same number were graduated and assigned to operations ...nder various commands of the air forces.

Recruits in 1943 had 35 hours' flying time and were between ...he ages of 18½ and 34.

Miss Jacqueline Cochran was director of women pilots on the ...rmy air forces in 1943.

The WASP in 1943 were on civil service status; trainees re-...ceived $150 per month base pay; the graduates, assigned to op-...erations, $250. In Nov. 1943, the official uniform of the WASP

was designated as a jacket and skirt of blue gabardine, a beret of the same material and a white cotton shirt with black tie.

(H. TA.)

Women's Army Corps.

The Women's Army corps (origi-nally known as the Women's Army Auxiliary corps) was created by act of congress in public law No. 554, dated May 14, 1942.

Members of the corps in 1943 performed noncombatant duties of an administrative nature in zones of operation as well as in the United States. Nomenclature for grades originally differed from that of the army, but equivalent pay was provided after the corps had been in existence six months by a pay equalization bill enacted by congress and signed by the president on Oct. 26, 1942. Mrs. Oveta Culp Hobby continued as the corps director in 1943.

Public law No. 110 was passed by congress and signed by the president on July 1, 1943, making the WAAC the Women's Army corps (WAC), and on July 5, 1943, Director Hobby was sworn in to the army of the United States with the rank of colonel. With this new legislation members of the WAC became eligible for government insurance rates, free mailing privileges, overseas pay, dependency allotments, and other army privileges. Though still a noncombatant organization, the new status made it pos-sible for WAC officers to take over operational and staff jobs in the army.

At the end of 1943 Wacs were doing 155 specific army jobs with general classifications including medical, personnel, science, photography, languages, drafting, communications, mechanics, radio, clerical, textiles, food, supply and many others.

Grades and pay scale for members of the WAC, like those of the men in the army, are as follows:

WAC Officers

Grade	Monthly base pay	Grade	Monthly base pay
Colonel (Director)	$333.33	Captain	$200.00
Lt. Colonel	291.67	1st Lieutenant	166.67
Major	250.00	2nd Lieutenant	150.00

WAC Enlisted Women

Grade	Monthly base pay	Grade	Monthly base pay
Master Sergeant	$138.00	Corporal	$66.00
Tech. Sergeant	114.00	Private 1st Class	54.00
Staff Sergeant	96.00	Private	50.00
Sergeant	78.00		

In 1943, as was true from the beginning of the WAC training program, all members took basic training corresponding to that given male army trainees, with the exception of those courses dealing with weapons and military tactics. Enlisted members received specialist training in army administration, motor trans-port, bakers and cooks schools, communications, medical, surgi-cal and dental technicians schools, army finance, and other courses of study. Officers came up from the ranks of enlisted women and were given an intensive officer candidate course before they were commissioned. Courses in various army officer specialist schools such as the Adjutant General's school, the Ordnance school, Special Services school and many others were opened to WAC officers also.

Limited at first to 25,000, the corps was increased by execu-tive order to 150,000 on Nov. 20, 1942, to meet the demands by various branches of the service for WAC personnel.

On Aug. 4, 1943, another executive order authorized the strength of the Women's Army corps not to exceed 200,000 members.

Women's Auxiliary Ferrying Service: *see* WOMEN'S AIR-FORCE SERVICE PILOTS.

Women's Clubs, General Federation of.

The General Federation of Women's Clubs in 1943 sponsored a campaign to place 20,000 student nurses in training. Individual clubs provided many students recruited with gift scholarships of approximately $250. In the year the scholarship fund totalled over $200,000. Selling war bonds to provide a fleet of bombers—composed of one from every state federation and others from district federations and clubs, each bearing the name of the group making it possible—was another 1943 objective. The bomber campaign fund totalled over $60,000,000.

Following a visit to state conventions throughout the U.S., Mrs. John L. Whitehurst, federation president, inaugurated a nation-wide campaign to reduce juvenile delinquency through co-operation of law-enforcement and welfare agencies, and the provision of worth-while spare-time activities for youth. Other important programs of the year included salvage drives; conservation and rationing programs; nutrition classes; nurses' aide, first-aid and home nursing courses; gardening and canning; recruitment of labour for farms and industry; recruitment of WACS, WAVES, SPARS, WAFS and marines; extension of Pan-American scholarships; and a study of peace and postwar planning.

In July and August, the federation president spent five and a half weeks in England, as the guest of the British government, studying war conditions, social problems and women's activities.

The legislative program included a concerted effort for renewal of the Reciprocal Trade Agreements act, for which the federation had been on record since 1938. One hundred leaders of the organization met in Swampscott, Mass., in June, to report war service activities, plan further projects and discuss peace and postwar planning. In 1943 the federation comprised 16,500 clubs in the United States and 30 foreign countries, with a total membership of more than 2,500,000 women. Headquarters are maintained at 1734 N street, Northwest, Washington, D.C.

(S. A. W.)

Women's Reserve of the Navy.

Members of the women's reserve of the United States naval reserve, popularly known as WAVES, were serving during 1943 in every bureau of the navy department and at shore stations in every naval district within the continental limits of the United States. Established by act of congress in July 1942, the women's reserve had grown to a membership of 47,600 by the end of 1943, and the goal for the end of Dec. 1944 was set at 92,400 women. Training facilities were increased during 1943 to meet the enlarged demands of the naval service.

Since Feb. 1943, recruit training had been concentrated at the Naval Training school, The Bronx, New York. After six weeks there, the enlisted women were assigned directly to duty stations or to one of 17 other navy schools for specialized preparation for jobs including those of storekeepers, yeomen, radiomen, mail clerks, key punch operators, and cooks and bakers, etc. A large number of women were also prepared to serve in billets in naval aviation as parachute riggers, aerographer's mates, control tower operators, aviation machinist's mates and aviation free gunnery instructors. WAVES of the hospital corps were on duty or in training in the offices, laboratories and wards of naval hospitals throughout the U.S.

All officers received their introduction to navy life at the Naval Reserve Midshipmen's school at Northampton, Mass. After two months of indoctrination, they were commissioned and were either ordered immediately to duty stations or to other schools. Specialized officer training was given in such fields as aerological engineering, radio, ordnance, communications, supply, air navigation instruction and the Japanese language.

768

CLASS OF WAVES AND MARINES receiving instruction in control tower operation at Gordon field, Ga., in 1943

Each class of officer candidates after June 1943 included a number of qualified enlisted women who were recommended for officer training upon completion of six months of service in an enlisted status. Already women who were seamen upon first assuming their duties had qualified for third class petty officer ratings and petty officers had advanced within the classes of their own specialties.

By virtue of an act of congress approved Nov. 9, 1943, officers and enlisted personnel of the women's reserve became entitled to all allowances or benefits available to navy men, with the exception of those allowed to or for a spouse. The same legislation removed the limitations which had been previously placed on rank and provided for one captain in the women's reserve. In accordance with the latter provision of the bill, the director of the women's reserve, Mildred H. McAfee, was promoted to the rank of captain.

Applicants for the women's reserve in 1943 had to be citizens of the United States with a minimum of two years of high school education and able to meet physical requirements and make a satisfactory score in an aptitude test. Wives of commissioned officers in the rank of ensign or above in the navy and women with children under 18 years of age were not acceptable in 1943. At the time of enlistment, officer candidates had to be between the ages of 20 to 49 inclusive, and enlisted women between the ages of 20 to 35 inclusive. In addition, officer candidates had to hold a college degree or have had two years of college with at least two years of acceptable business or professional experience; also two years of mathematics in high school or college.

(M. H. McA.)

Women's Reserve of the United States Coast Guard Reserve: *see* COAST GUARD, U.S.

Wood, Sir Kingsley

(1881–1943), British statesman, son of a Wesleyan minister, was admitted as a solicitor in 1903, entered public life as a London county councillor for Woolwich in 1911 and sat in parliament as Conservative member for Woolwich West after 1918. Between 1919 and 1929 he was parliamentary private secretary to various ministers of health; from Sept. to Nov. 1931 he was parliamentary secretary to the Board of Education in the national government. In Nov. 1931, he became postmaster-general and during his tenure effected many reforms which put the post office on a profit-making basis for the first time in many years. When Stanley Baldwin became prime minister in June 1935, Sir Kingsley was transferred to the ministry of health. He retained that office until 1938, when he succeeded Lord Swinton as minister for air. His policies and leadership in the air ministry were harshly attacked by both government and opposition leaders, and he was shifted to the post of chancellor of the exchequer in May 1940, where he was given the difficult task of financing Britain's war expenditures. A few hours before his death he was at work finishing details for an announcement to be made to parliament the following afternoon on a pay-as-you-go tax plan. Sir Kingsley, who had been knighted in 1918, died in London, Sept. 21.

Wool.

The quantity of wool shorn in the United States in 1943 was estimated at 376,822,000 lb. This quantity was 15,500,000 lb. or about 4% smaller than the record production in 1942, but about 11,000,000 lb. or 3% above the ten-year (1932–41) average. The decrease in production from 1942 was a result of the smaller number of sheep shorn, as the average weight of wool per sheep shorn was practically the same in 1943 as in 1942. The estimated number of sheep shorn was 47,674,000 compared with 49,784,000 in 1942 and the ten-year average of 45,691,000. The average weight of wool per sheep was 7.90 lb.

The consumption of greasy shorn wool for the first nine months of 1943 amounted to 863,938,000 lb. Of the 445,000,000 lb. of scoured wool consumed during this period, the National Association of Wool Manufacturers reported that 37% was of domestic origin and 63% imported. Production of wool cloth for the first three-quarters of 1943 was 10% less than that manufactured during the corresponding period in 1942; the consumption of apparel wool during those months rose 7% above last year's totals for the same period.

The Australian 1942–43 wool clip represented the fourth seasonal output handled under the arrangement whereby the United Kingdom government acquired the whole of the Australian product, other than the requirements of local manufacturers, for the duration of the war and one full wool year thereafter. The greasy wool appraised by members of the National Council of Wool Selling Brokers of Australia amounted to 3,294,323 bales, totalling 1,047,060,000 lb. The Argentine 1942–43 wool production amounted to 517,000,000 lb., the largest on record.

To assure the effective distribution of wool for the fulfillment of war and civilian requirements in the United States, the War Food administration, on April 17, 1943, issued an order requiring that domestic grown wool which had not been sold prior to April 25 must, with certain exceptions, be sold to and purchased only by the Commodity Credit corporation. The order applied to both shorn and pulled domestic wool, the wool being purchased through handlers on the basis of ceiling prices, less handling costs. It then would be sold directly to manufacturers at ceiling prices. The wool was appraised by committees composed of three members appointed by and working under the director of food distribution. Appraisals were made on the basis of grade, shrinkage, length of staple and other factors affecting the value. Up to Dec. 11, 234,000,000 lb. of wool had been appraised.

In addition to the purchase of approximately 250,000,000 lb. of domestic grown wool, an additional amount of foreign grown wool was purchased by the government. This stockpile consisted of 290,000,000 lb. of Australian; 6,000,000 lb. of Argentinean; 32,000,000 lb. of Uruguayan, 20,000,000 lb. still remaining in Uruguay at the end of 1943. This total of 328,000,000 lb. of for-

eign wool did not include an estimated amount of 525,000,000 lb. of Australian, New Zealand and South African wools owned by Great Britain and stored in the United States which, if necessary, could have been used for domestic consumption. Sizable quantities of the British stockpile of wool were transshipped to England.

On Dec. 15, 1943, an announcement was made by the War Production board for proposals for orderly withdrawals from the government-owned stockpile of wool acquired through the Defense Supplies corporation. Reasons for considering such withdrawals were to the effect that the shipping situation had improved to such an extent that potential obstacles to continued importation of wool from the primary sources of supply had been largely overcome and that it was essential that storage space in the U.S. utilized for the wool stockpile be freed for use in storing urgently needed commodities of strategic importance. Also, it was pointed out that by making this stockpiled wool on a "spot" basis it was anticipated that part of the shipping space used for the importation of wool could be shifted to other products, as well as ease the strain on port and railway facilities. (See also Sheep; Textile Industry.) (C. M. An.)

Woollcott, Alexander

(1887–1943), U.S. author, critic and actor, was born Jan. 19 in Phalanx, N.J. After graduating from Hamilton college, New York, 1909, he joined the staff of the New York *Times* as a cub reporter. Five years later, he succeeded to the post of dramatic critic and subsequently he worked on nearly every newspaper in New York. In 1929, he branched out into the radio field as "Town Crier" of the air and established a nationwide reputation as raconteur, gossip, conversationalist, wit and man-about-town. As a literary critic, he wielded tremendous influence on the nation's book-buying public. Mr. Woollcott also played in the title role of *The Man Who Came to Dinner*, 1940, a play in which he himself was lampooned. He was the author of *Mrs. Fiske—Her Views on Acting* (1917), *Two Gentlemen and a Lady* (1928), *While Rome Burns* (1934) and publisher of two anthologies, *The Woollcott Reader* (1935) and *Woollcott's Second Reader* (1937). He was stricken with a heart attack while participating in a radio forum in New York city, Jan. 23, and died a few hours later.

Words and Meanings, New.

English is the language of which it may least be said that it ever stands still. In wartime, with nearly all the English-speaking peoples engaged in the conflict, its growth is vastly accelerated. Most of the added terms, or new meanings of old terms, quickly fade as their usefulness dies out; others remain, but have little more than historic value; a few become active members of the community of words. The following were selected out of the many that were born, or gained popularity, from 1940 to 1943, because they seemed to offer the greatest promise of survival, or because they were most typical of the period.

The names of coiners, as far as they were ascertained, appear in italics. Dates, unless otherwise specified, are those of the initial appearance of the term or new meaning; a preceding hyphen (-1939) means that the term or meaning is at least as old as the date given.

activate. To bring into active existence, as "to activate an air corps squadron"; to put into practise, get busy on, as "to activate a reconversion program." (Orig. military, -1941.)

aeropolitics. Political and economic development as influencing, and as influenced by, the development and application of aviation. (*Burnet Hershey*, Feb. 28, 1943.)

bazooka. A firearm, consisting of a metal tube slightly over 50 inches long and under 3 inches in diameter, with a shoulder stock, front and rear grips, sights, electric battery to set off the charge, and trigger, designed to launch rocket projectiles. It is operated by two men, one holding and firing the gun, the other loading. (*Major Zeb Hastings*, 1942, after the musical instrument invented by Bob Burns, 1905.)

block-buster. The 4,000-lb. bomb dropped by British Lancaster planes beginning in March 1942; a similar heavy bomb. (1942.)

brief. To give formal instructions, regarding a scheduled military operation, to those about to engage in it. (-1940.)

brownout. A voluntary, partial dimout. (Australia, 1942; U.S., 1943.)

cargoliner. A transport plane carrying freight exclusively. (1943.)

chin turret. A gun turret mounted beneath the nose of bombers. (1943.)

co-belligerent, *adj.* Fighting together (with another power) without a formal alliance, as "co-belligerent Italy." *n.* A country so fighting. (-1813.)

commando. A unit of British soldiers trained in close-range fighting for raids on enemy territory; loosely, a member of such a unit, or of a similar unit of another nationality. (*Winston Churchill*, Oct. 10, 1941, from Portuguese or Spanish *comando* adopted as name for defense units of Boer Republic.) Compare **ranger.**

enrich. To supply with added food value, esp. with vitamins and minerals. A government standard (promulgated May 1941; July 3, 1943) exists for enriched flour. (*Frank L. Gunderson*, summer 1940, from *Quaker Oats Co.*, 1932.) **enrichment.**

expediter, expeditor. An official charged with keeping uninterrupted the flow of materials or of routine work in industry and government. Some expediters are agents of the U.S. army and navy; others are in direct employ within industries and government bureaus such as the War Production Board. (*General Electric Co.*, c. 1925)

extend. To make a scarce or expensive food go farther by preparing in combination with a cheaper or more plentiful food, as "to extend meat with cereal." (-1934 as "to adulterate.") **extender.**

featherbedding. The limiting of work or output in order to spread jobs and thus prevent unemployment. **featherbed rules.** Union regulations to accomplish featherbedding.

feather merchant. A slacker. (After comic-strip characters of *Billy De Beck*, 1937, from earlier senses.)

GI, GI Joe, *n.* An American soldier. *GI* is to the army as a whole what *doughboy* is to the infantry. (Short for GI soldier, -1941.) *adj.* Pertaining to the army services, or ministering to its needs, as "GI food," "a GI dance." (General issue.)

glide-bomb. To bomb, from an aeroplane, by descending at an angle of less than 65° from the horizontal when releasing bombs. Steeper dives are called *dive-bombing.* (-1940.)

globaloney. Nonsense about matters affecting the world as a whole. (**Global** baloney. *Rep. Clare Luce*, Feb. 9, 1943.)

handie-talkie, *military.* A portable two-way radio telephone weighing about five lb. (-1942.) Compare **walkie-talkie.**

homeostasis. The tendency of living organisms to maintain a relatively stable condition by means of mechanisms which compensate for disturbing factors. (*Walter B. Cannon*, 1926.) A similar function elsewhere, as in the social organism. (-1941.)

incentive pay. Wages paid in accordance with various "incentive plans" or "systems" which reward increased production; in particular, a piece-work or modified piece-work system. (-1907.)

longram, *telegraphy.* A deferred day message with a minimum charge for 100 words. (**Long telegram.** Dec. 1942; service effective Feb. 1, 1943.)

mission. The objective of an operational flight, esp. where bombing is involved; the flight itself. (-1942.)

mock-up. A model of an aircraft, constructed of inexpensive material and usually full-size, for the purpose of prearranging or studying details of construction and use. (-1938.) A similar model of other items of military equipment. (-1942.) A model in general. (1943.)

newsmap. A map issued periodically with current events depicted on it, and with accompanying text and illustrations. (**News Map** *of the Week*, a copyrighted periodical. 1938.)

pathfinder. A flare capable of illuminating the ground for bombing purposes, even through fog, when dropped by attacking planes. Called also *TI* (target-indicator). (Nov. 1943.)

pattern-bomb. To bomb, from a number of aircraft, in such a way that the relative position of the craft determines the "pattern" of the bombs when they strike, so as to cover the target in a desired manner.

pesticide. An agent for controlling farm or garden pests of whatever sort. The Canadian Fertilizers and Pesticides administrator was commissioned Jan. 20, 1942. (*Grant S. Peart*, Sept. 18, 1940.)

pin-up girl. A girl with whose picture men, esp. soldiers, like to decorate their quarters. (-1941.)

probable. A supposed casualty, esp. referring to military craft, as "there were ten destroyed and five probables."

ranger. A member of a battalion of American soldiers, formed Dec. 1941, trained in close-range fighting for raids on enemy territory. (1942.) Compare **commando.**

restore. To bring back a food to the original nutritive value of its ingredients. (1939.)

scuttlebutt, *naval slang.* Gossip; a rumour. (-1938. **Scuttle-butt** story, -1901; scuttle butt, drinking fountain on board ship, -1843.)

Seabees (*gen. plural*). The U.S. navy construction battalions, comprising welders, carpenters, mechanics, and other personnel skilled in building and supplementary trades, trained to fight as well as work in the field. (1942.)

shuttle, *combining form.* Involving vehicles, esp. aircraft, making repeated trips between fixed points, as "shuttle bombing," "shuttle raid," "shuttle plane." *v.* To move a vehicle or by a vehicle in such trips. (-1941, from **shuttle train,** -1891.)

snafu, *military slang.* In a mess, haywire. (**S**ituation **n**ormal: **a**ll **f**ouled **up.**)

sortie. An operational flight by one military aircraft. Each return to base for replenishment is counted as the end of one sortie.

stretch, stretcher. See **extend.**

suntans. Summer uniform worn by American soldiers.

TI. See **pathfinder.**

trainasium. A conglomerate structure of metal bars, resembling a large bird-cage, used to develop muscular co-ordination in military students. (**Train**ing gymn**asium.** -1942.)

triphibian. Adapted to or using the three elements, land, water and air, as "a triphibian assault." (**Tri**+am**phibian.** *Winston Churchill*, Aug. 31, 1943.)

triphibious. See **triphibian.** (**Tri**+am**phibious.** *Leslie Hore-Belisha*, 1941.)

underground, *n.* An outlawed political or military movement or organization operating in secret; such organizations collectively, as "the European underground will strike against naziism"; underground fortifications, materials or equipment protected under ground against attack. *adv.* Into hiding, into the underground, as "the patriots had to go underground." **undergrounder.** A member of the underground.

upgrade. To raise (the name or number of a quality) without improving the quality itself, as "cheaper meats were illegally upgraded." (-1941.)

walkie-talkie, walkee-talkee, walky-talky, *military.* A two-way radio telephone small enough to be transported on horseback; a smaller set carried on the back of one man. (-1940.) Compare **handie-talkie.**

wolf. A determined would-be seducer, a man "on the make." (-1937, esp. 1942, from an older underworld sense.) (D. L. BR)

Work Projects Administration: *see* FEDERAL WORK AGENCY.

Works Agency, Federal: *see* FEDERAL WORKS AGENCY.

World War II.

This article is divided into the following sections:

I.—INTRODUCTION

In 1943, the industrial and military might of the United States, the amazing power of the Red army and the destructive force of the R.A.F. began to pay dividends which surpassed all expectations and started the turning of the tide of World War II. American men and materials flowed to all theatres of war in great convoys and were instrumental in enabling Allied forces to take the offensive. The Red army not only engaged the bulk of the wehrmacht on the eastern front, but destroyed its offensive power as well. In turn, the R.A.F., taking vengeance for the battle of Britain, crippled the reich's war industry and played havoc with German civilian morale. In the Pacific, the burden of the war against the Japanese was carried by American naval, air and land forces and the attack on Truk in Feb. 1944 indicated that an assault on Japan proper was in the making. As the year 1943 ended, the axis powers, failing in their physical attempts to halt the growing military power of the Allies, turned on their propaganda machine in full force in a supreme effort to sow dissension among the United States, Great Britain and the soviet union.

Theirs was the desperate hope that the "Big Three" would become divided over political issues and slacken in their joint war effort. The Allies, however, were determined to push political controversy into a back seat until the axis was defeated. At conferences in Washington, Cairo and Tehran, they agreed on concerted action to destroy the military power of Germany and Japan.

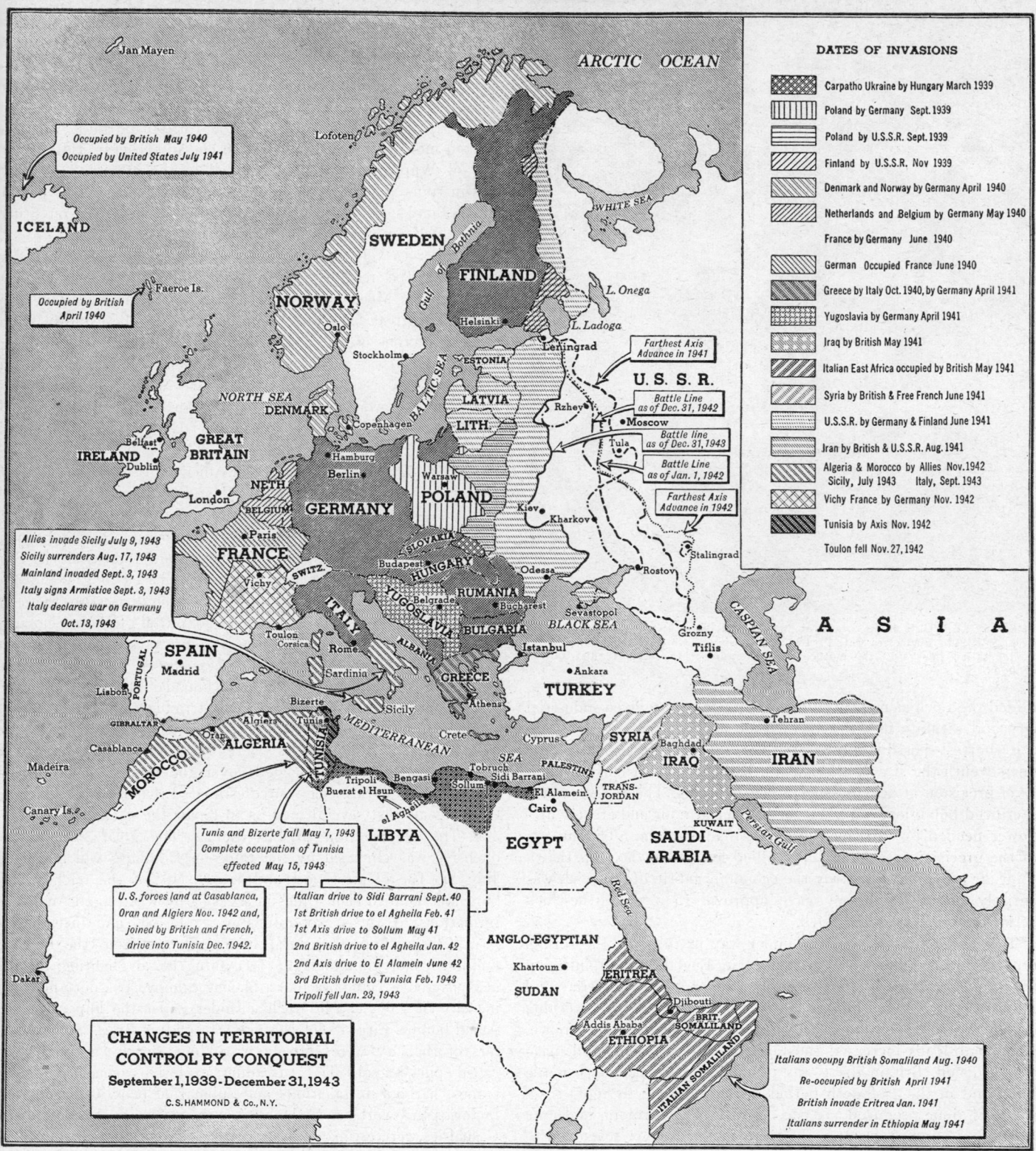

DATES OF INVASIONS

Carpatho Ukraine by Hungary March 1939

Poland by Germany Sept. 1939

Poland by U.S.S.R. Sept. 1939

Finland by U.S.S.R. Nov 1939

Denmark and Norway by Germany April 1940

Netherlands and Belgium by Germany May 1940

France by Germany June 1940

German Occupied France June 1940

Greece by Italy Oct. 1940, by Germany April 1941

Yugoslavia by Germany April 1941

Iraq by British May 1941

Italian East Africa occupied by British May 1941

Syria by British & Free French June 1941

U.S.S.R. by Germany & Finland June 1941

Iran by British & U.S.S.R. Aug. 1941

Algeria & Morocco by Allies Nov. 1942
Sicily, July 1943   Italy, Sept. 1943

Vichy France by Germany Nov. 1942

Tunisia by Axis Nov. 1942

Toulon fell Nov. 27, 1942

Occupied by British May 1940
Occupied by United States July 1941

Occupied by British April 1940

Farthest Axis Advance in 1941

Battle Line as of Dec. 31, 1942

Battle line as of Dec. 31, 1943

Battle Line as of Jan. 1, 1942

Farthest Axis Advance in 1942

Allies invade Sicily July 9, 1943
Sicily surrenders Aug. 17, 1943
Mainland invaded Sept. 3, 1943
Italy signs Armistice Sept. 3, 1943
Italy declares war on Germany
Oct. 13, 1943

Tunis and Bizerte fall May 7, 1943
Complete occupation of Tunisia
effected May 15, 1943

U.S. forces land at Casablanca,
Oran and Algiers Nov. 1942 and,
joined by British and French,
drive into Tunisia Dec. 1942.

Italian drive to Sidi Barrani Sept. 40
1st British drive to el Agheila Feb. 41
1st Axis drive to Sollum May 41
2nd British drive to el Agheila Jan. 42
2nd Axis drive to El Alamein June 42
3rd British drive to Tunisia Feb. 1943
Tripoli fell Jan. 23, 1943

**CHANGES IN TERRITORIAL
CONTROL BY CONQUEST**
September 1, 1939–December 31, 1943

C. S. HAMMOND & Co., N.Y.

Italians occupy British Somaliland Aug. 1940
Re-occupied by British April 1941
British invade Eritrea Jan. 1941
Italians surrender in Ethiopia May 1941

II.—AIR WAR OVER EUROPE

I. Introduction.—In 1943 the Allied air offensive was producing terror and devastation in Germany. Blockbusters fell in
mounting numbers on Hitler's Festung Europa, demolishing entire cities, razing war plants, destroying rail centres and breaching
dams. Thousands of homeless civilians were evacuated from the
stricken industrial areas. Civilian morale was seriously undermined and popular resentment against the nazi regime became so
widespread that the gestapo was compelled to employ its customary brutal measures to silence the growing undercurrent of
defeatism. Air power, first applied by the nazis to batter civilian
populations into submission became, in 1943, a Frankenstein that
turned against its inventors and threatened to destroy them.

From the strategical point of view the Allied air offensive was
eminently successful. The destruction of war plants robbed the
nazi armies in Russia and Italy of vital supplies. The luftwaffe,
compelled to maintain larger forces at home to counter the Allied
air blows, weakened its formations in Russia and Italy.

In early 1943 the royal air force was still the principal offensive
weapon of the Allied air command and was used primarily as an
area-bombing force. The huge formations of British bombers that

THE FOCKE-WULF plane plant at Marienburg, East Prussia, after bombing by U.S. Flying Fortresses Oct. 9, 1943. British Air Chief Marshal Sir Charles Portal called this raid "the most perfect example of the accurate distribution of bombs"

raided the reich at night would concentrate over a given industrial city and saturate it with several thousands of tons of bombs in the shortest possible time. The U.S. 8th air force, then only one-seventh the size of the R.A.F., had the task of making high-level precision attacks on specific nazi targets. The U.S. bombers sacrificed bomb-load capacity for heavier armour and greater fire-power needed to ward off the enemy fighter planes. The success of the precision attacks inclined Allied leaders to the view that a joint air offensive to destroy the economic fabric of the reich was entirely feasible and they gave approval to a round-the-clock aerial offensive over the reich.

This new offensive was well under way in 1943. By the spring, the combined Allied air force based in England was raining an ever-increasing tonnage of explosives over reich industrial and military objectives. Flights of 700 or more planes sweeping across the channel were nearly a daily—or nightly—occurrence. The bomb-loads increased substantially and the area of damage was widened. Britain itself was producing more planes than the reich and in the 20-month period from Jan. 1942 to Sept. 1943, the U.S. alone produced 110,000 aircraft. Furthermore, under its building program for 1944, American factories were scheduled to turn out more than 150,000 planes, the greater part of which were destined for the European theatre of operations. By the end of the year, it appeared that the once-mighty luftwaffe was hopelessly outnumbered and was facing extinction, since one of the major objectives of the Allied strategy was destruction of the German air force.

2. The Ruhr Valley Raids.—One of the chief targets of the Allied bomber squadrons was the Ruhr valley, industrial arsenal of the reich, which was hit with terrific force. In the month of June alone, the R.A.F. dropped 15,000 tons of bombs on Germany, mostly over the Ruhr. Of the Ruhr cities having populations of 100,000 or more, all but one had been bombed at least

once, some scores of times, by the summer of 1943. More than 1,000 acres of Duesseldorf were devastated in a single raid on June 11, 1943. The giant Krupp munitions works in Essen were paralyzed by repeated Allied aerial blows and in the city proper more than 4,000 acres had been laid waste. Cologne, the first city to feel the destructive weight of the 1,000-plane raid, had been blasted more than 120 times by the end of the year. Half of the city of Wuppertal had been levelled to the ground, Dortmund was in ruins and the commercial centre of Duisburg was demolished. Bombs also rained with monotonous regularity on Stuttgart, Muelheim, Krefeld, Bochum and Oberhausen.

In order to kill "20 birds with one stone," R.A.F. planes flew deep into the reich, May 16, and dropped dynamite-charged mines on the Moehne and Eder dams, two of the biggest in Germany. The great river walls were breached by the explosives and millions of tons of water spilled into the upper Ruhr and Weser valleys. The cities of Dortmund, Wuppertal, Soest, Kassel and Gelsenkirchen were inundated. Swedish travellers reported that nearly all war work in the Ruhr had been brought to a standstill by the floods and that the raid on the dams was 20 times more destructive than an ordinary air attack.

3. Long-Distance Raids.—The Allied raids were not confined exclusively to the Ruhr. Industrial and military establishments throughout axis Europe were battered by Allied planes. Long-distance bombers struck at objectives as far distant as Trondhjem in Norway and Crete in the Mediterranean. Industrial cities in Italy were heavily bombed by formations based in England and North Africa while Russian air fleets from bases to the east struck furiously at East Prussian targets. One of the spectacular raids of the European air war was a bold attack staged by a formation of 177 U.S. Liberator bombers, based in North Africa, against the oil refineries at Ploesti, Rumania. The Ploesti raid on Aug. 1, 1943, one of the longest round-trip flights of the year, was costly. Fifty-three of the bombers were lost and 400 men were casualties. But the results were satisfactory. Although the bombers spent only 60 seconds over the target, they crippled five of the refineries. One source estimated that it would take the Germans at least several months to repair the damage.

4. The Destruction of Hamburg.—The great summer air offensive was climaxed by the raids on Hamburg which started July 24. The greatest port and second city of the reich, Hamburg was bombed eight times in six days by R.A.F. and American formations. At least 8,000 tons of explosives and incendiaries struck the city in those 144 hours. Flames from the burning buildings shot thousands of feet into the air lighting up the heavens above Hamburg like a blazing canopy. The once-flourishing city of 1,692,000 lit up like tinder under the impact of the Allied bombs. Fires swept through street after street. Some quarters of the city were entirely wiped out; hardly a district escaped punishment. The cascading explosives smashed docks, cranes, harbour installations and submarine pens. Oil refineries, factories, gas works and telephone exchanges were also destroyed. Casualties were estimated at 14,000 killed and more than 400,000 people were reported left homeless. The nazi raids on Coventry —England's most heavily-bombed city—were trivial compared with the Allied blows on Hamburg. In their heaviest raid on Coventry 400 German planes dropped 450 tons in nine hours—a rate of almost a ton a minute. In the eighth and biggest raid on Hamburg, the R.A.F. dropped 2,250 long tons in 45 minutes—a rate of more than 50 tons a minute. A close examination of reconnaissance photographs subsequently revealed that about 77% of the city was destroyed. About 5,000 to 6,000 acres were totally devastated. The raids on Hamburg were a convincing demonstration of faultless co-operation between the day and night arms of the combined Allied air force. While the R.A.F. sledge-hammered the city by night, saturating wide areas, the U.S.A.A.F. followed up with pinpoint attacks on vital targets left unscathed by the British bombers. Speedy plywood Mosquito bombers filled the intervals with "psychological" attacks intended to wear down civilian morale and to keep the defenders off balance.

5. The Battle of Berlin.—The methodical destruction of Hamburg was a portent of things to come. It signified that the combined Allied air forces intended to obliterate Berlin by overwhelming mass aerial bombings. An Allied announcement to this effect led the nazi authorities to evacuate all residents, except workers in essential war industries and civilian activities, from Berlin. The capital of the reich and the greatest manufacturing centre on the continent, Berlin had been raided over 60 times up to the late summer of 1943. In August the R.A.F. struck Berlin twice, Aug. 23 and Aug. 31. In each raid 1,500 tons of bombs were dropped on the city. Although this figure was about twice the tonnage loosed over Berlin in any previous raid, these blows were merely skirmishes in which the R.A.F. was testing its own sinews and the strength of enemy defenses. In the first raid the British lost 58 bombers, the heaviest R.A.F. loss in a single raid in 1943. In the second, the nazis gave evidence that they were fully determined to protect the capital. The luftwaffe had sent up 500 night fighters to meet the onrushing R.A.F. raiders. The German interceptor craft, many of which were fitted with searchlights in their noses, dropped white flares in geometrical patterns so that the British had to cross the lighted lanes, revealing themselves for attack. Although the British planes broke through the luftwaffe air defense, their losses were again high, and 47 bombers were missing. On Sept. 3, the British air command shifted its tactics to meet the strong nazi air defense. Instead of using the slower Halifaxes and Stirlings, they employed the speedier Lancaster bombers, which flashed across Berlin in 20 minutes, dropping their entire bomb load of 1,120 tons in that interval, and then streaked back to their home bases. Casualties in this raid were halved and only 22 bombers were lost over Berlin as well as in operations over the Rhineland and France and channel patrols.

The capital was then spared heavy raids until Nov. 18, when the battle of Berlin began in earnest. On that day, a great R.A.F. armada bombed both Berlin and Ludwigshafen-Mannheim with over 2,500 tons of bombs. Four days later the R.A.F. formations opened a new bombing cycle. Starting Nov. 22 the R.A.F. pounded the capital on five consecutive nights, loosing some 5,000 tons of explosives in all over the city. Two of the attacks were staged by R.A.F. Mosquitoes; the other three were full-dress raids. The R.A.F. mixed incendiary with explosive bombs to cause the greatest damage possible. Blockbusters were used to collapse walls, pierce water mains, snap electric power cables and break windows thus creating a draft to fan the flames. Then thousands of incendiaries were poured over the city. Once fires were started, more explosives were tumbled over Berlin to create enough blast and vacuum to spread the fire over unburned areas. A large section of the city lay in ruins. The centre of town was the worst hit. Three rail stations were reported destroyed. The foreign office on Wilhelmstrasse was burned to the ground and the German air ministry, as well as the British, French and U.S. embassies were demolished. The industrial areas suffered heavily, many Berliners were bombed out and thousands of homeless left the city.

In the 77-day period, starting Dec. 1, 1943, and ending Feb. 15, 1944, the R.A.F. cascaded more than 13,000 tons of bombs over the capital in 11 raids. This brought the total weight of explosives dropped from the beginning of the battle of Berlin, Nov. 18, 1943, to more than 28,000 tons. The R.A.F. bombing of Feb. 15, 1944, was one of the heaviest aerial attacks in history. On that date, an estimated 1,000 British bombers smothered Ber-

lin with more than 2,800 tons of bombs in a fiery 30-minute attack. Returning fliers said the capital was a solid wall of flames and that smoke columns plumed four miles into the air. By March 1, 1944, it was reported that Berlin was a dying city. Almost every utility from the Templehof aerodrome to the transit service was destroyed or severely damaged. Reich government offices were moved out and reports from neutral countries said that more than 50% of the city's dwellings had been demolished.

6. The Luftwaffe on the Defensive.—By the winter of 1943–44, the luftwaffe was waging a desperate but losing battle for survival. Hitler, compelled to withdraw many planes from Russia to protect the home front, frantically switched his bomber plants to production of fighter planes. But these last-minute measures were unavailing. The German fighter command suffered heavy losses and was unable to check the Allied air fleets, which in the month of July alone, dropped 26,000 tons of explosives on targets in Germany. As the luftwaffe was both quantitatively and qualitatively inferior to Allied air forces, it had no choice but to fight a defensive delaying action. Nevertheless, it was still an efficient and dangerous instrument for destruction and carried a deadly sting. German fighter squadrons generally took a substantial toll of attacking bombers and allied losses of 20 to 40 bombers on daylight raids were not uncommon. Accurate anti-aircraft fire was also responsible for bringing down many Allied warplanes.

Called on to develop defensive measures to counterbalance the topheavy Allied air superiority, the Germans speeded up fighter craft production in late 1943. At the same time, however, the number of German aircraft shot down by Allied formations also increased. In Oct. 1943 U.S. bombers alone destroyed a total of 784 planes during seven operational days that month, while all German planes shot down by the combined Allied air forces based in England during October numbered 1,079. Nazi aircraft losses in the Mediterranean and Russian theatres of war are not included in this figure. Although German aircraft plants substantially augmented the output of combat planes, it was doubtful whether they could produce enough planes to balance these losses.

Among the other defensive measures introduced by the Germans to overcome their deficiency in numbers was a radio-controlled rocket-propelled glider bomb. First reported in action in the Italian campaign by Allied officers, the new rocket bomb was towed by mother craft at high altitudes and then released toward the target. Steered by remote control radio, this spectacular missile was reported very deadly in effect.

7. The Growth of U.S. Air Forces.—The phenomenal growth of the U.S. bomber squadrons based in England was one of the amazing and brilliant accomplishments of the U.S. war effort in 1943. When the Allied military command decided to try out the efficacy of the yet untested precision daylight raid over French targets in the summer of 1942, the U.S. 8th air force had 12 Flying Fortresses available for the experiment. On Aug. 17 of that year these dozen bombers flew 50 mi. into France, dropped 18 tons of bombs on Rouen's freight yards, and returned without the loss of a single plane. The crucial experiment was a success and a good section of the American aircraft industry was geared to the production of thousands of bombers to increase the size of the U.S. 8th air force and make it a mighty offensive weapon. Exactly a year later, on Aug. 17, 1943, a U.S. aerial task force, this time totalling more than 350 Fortresses, penetrated deep into Germany, and divided into three sections. Two of the flying columns dropped 424 tons of bombs on Schweinfurt, damaging an important roller-bearing works, and battled their way back to Britain through dense flak and clouds of nazi interceptor planes. The third column continued on to Regensburg, paralyzed the big Messerschmitt factory with a bomb load of 298 tons, and shuttled straight across to North Africa. More than 800 American heavy bombers were in the aerial armada that struck Frankfurt-on-Main on Jan. 29, 1944, with 1,800 tons of explosives —the heaviest raid to that date carried out by the U.S. 8th air force. With the Frankfurt raid, the U.S. air forces in England had come of age and had reached parity with the royal air force.

During its first full year of operation, the U.S. 8th air force had carried out 124 attacks. Its targets were U-boat operating bases, building and repair yards. It also attacked luftwaffe airfields, installations and nazi plane factories as well as industrial plants and transport and shipping facilities. The weight and variety of the U.S. heavy bomber attacks grew steadily and the luftwaffe was compelled to double, in western Europe, the number of fighter craft whose specific job was to ward off the big daylight raiders.

The luftwaffe, nevertheless, did succeed in inflicting heavy losses on some formations. In the Regensburg-Schweinfurt raid, 60 Fortresses were lost with 581 crew members, of whom 346 were alive although prisoners in Germany. During the triple raid on Brunswick, Oschersleben and Halberstadt on Jan. 11, 1944, 60 bombers of the U.S. 8th air force, manned by an estimated 595 men, were shot down. The U.S. air command contended that the loss of the bombers in both raids was more than compensated by the destruction of vital German industrial plants.

By the winter of 1943–44, the U.S. 8th air force, employed solely on strategical missions, was joined by the U.S. 9th air force. A tactical air weapon, the 9th consisted mostly of medium bombers and fighters designed to soften coastal defenses for the scheduled invasion of western Europe.

8. Statistics.—The following figures graphically illustrate the scope and intensity of the Allied air bombardment of the reich during the last three months of 1943:

	Short tons
Tonnage of bombs dropped:	
By the R.A.F.	44,240
By the U.S.A.A.F.	28,227
Total	72,467
Number of Operations:	
Night Bombing (R.A.F.)	56
Day Bombing (R.A.F.)	41
Day Bombing (U.S.A.A.F.)	36
Total	133
Plane Losses:	
R.A.F.	672
U.S.A.A.F.	489
Total	1,161

The following table shows the tonnage of bombs dropped annually on Germany by the R.A.F. since July 1940. The first figure is for the last six months of 1940 only:

	Short tons		Short tons
1940	5,880	1942	41,440
1941	25,760	1943	152,448

III.—THE RUSSIAN FRONT

1. Introduction.—In 1943 the myth of invincibility that once cloaked the German wehrmacht had been ground into the dust of the Russian steppes, and with it was laid to rest Adolf Hitler's grandiose schemes for converting vast sections of the soviet union into nazi lebensraum. Like the armies of Napoleon 130 years before, the nazi forces were retreating from Russia. Allowed no rest by the constantly attacking Russians, they were battered and bled white and were falling back toward the Baltic states, Poland and Rumania. But unlike the ragged French troops that broke and ran in headlong flight during Napoleon's retreat from Moscow in 1812, the Germans retreated in order and literally had to be uprooted by the advancing Russians. Discipline was still strong among the nazi troops and their morale was firm. Yet, barring a miracle, it was evident at the beginning of 1944 that the defeat of the wehrmacht in Russia was inevitable and only a matter of time.

Many military observers contended that Hitler's gross underestimation of the strength of the Red army was the greatest single factor contributing to the downfall of nazi armies in Russia. Others argued that Hitler and the German general staff were well aware of Russia's growing military power and that the nazi invasion of June 1941 represented a desperate gamble to destroy it. Time will be required to settle this academic controversy, but the successes of the Red army, the military talents of its leaders and its apparently inexhaustible reservoirs of manpower and matériel were established contemporary facts in 1943. While no little credit for the Russian successes in 1943 was due the Allies who shipped substantial quantities of planes, tanks, guns and motorized equipment to the soviet union, the Russian victories were, for the greatest part, self-earned. They accepted hardships and sacrifices cheerfully and showed astonishing fighting spirit. In 1944 the Red army was the most powerful fighting force in Europe and it was amply stocked with matériel turned out by the transplanted factories in the Urals.

2. The Winter Campaign, 1942–43.—The turn of the tide in the Russian campaign occurred at Stalingrad. There the Germans lost the strategical initiative, never to regain it throughout 1943. They had bludgeoned their way into the city in the autumn of 1942, and after terrific fighting they captured most of it. But they failed to dislodge the Russians from the bunker-fortified Mamai Kurgan hill, a high bluff that rises up from the Volga. This strategic hill controlled the west bank of the Volga and the Russians clung to it tenaciously, compelling the nazis to consume manpower and matériel in their futile efforts to capture the bluff. While the Germans were absorbed in their gigantic effort to oust the Russians from Mamai Kurgan, six soviet armies held in reserve launched a lightning manoeuvre to encircle the attacking force. Overnight, the positions of the opposing forces had changed; the trappers became the trapped. The nazis, apparently, did not realize the peril of their situation and made no effort to withdraw. By Dec. 1, the German 6th army, commanded by Marshal von Paulus, was encircled and completely cut off from other nazi units to the west. In order to prevent the wehrmacht from massing enough strength to break through the ring forged around Stalingrad and rescue the 6th army, the Russians launched another offensive 400 mi. to the northwest against the strong nazi belt of fortifications in the Kursk-Kharkov area. While this drive was proceeding, the Russian forces surrounding Stalingrad slowly twisted the garrote about the German 6th army, whose full strength was estimated at 22 divisions, or about 330,000 men. By Jan. 1, 1943, the 6th army's position was hopeless. Wishing

RUSSIAN TROOPS IN KHARKOV after its first capture by Red army troops Feb. 16, 1943. The city was retaken by the Germans a month later, but occupied again by the Russians Aug. 23

to avoid needless slaughter, the Russians urged von Paulus to surrender. But he refused and the soviet armies continued the grim task of systematic annihilation. On Jan. 26 a Russian breakthrough split the German defending army into two groups. One group, with the 6th army's commander, von Paulus, surrendered on Feb. 1. The second gave up the following morning. Thus ended the battle of Stalingrad, one of the bloodiest in history. Some sources believed that von Paulus could have broken out of the Stalingrad trap during the first week of the Russian offensive. High German officers captured in the ruined city declared that they never received the order to do so from von Paulus. The German commander himself was silent on this question. There were reports, however, that Hitler for some "intuitive" reason ordered von Paulus to stay and battle on.

The final victory at Stalingrad proved the wisdom of the Russian course, followed in the early stages of the Don battle, to avoid direct contact with the superior nazi plane-tank combat team. The Russians adroitly manoeuvred away from frontal assaults and carefully husbanded men and material for future battles. Other salient features of the Stalingrad battle were the courage and doggedness of Russian troops, the proper timing of the Russian counteroffensive that caught the Germans off guard and the superiority of Russian artillery which blunted the sharp point of the German panzers. One Russian general said that the Germans at Stalingrad committed no tactical mistakes, but added that they made a "strategical mistake" in putting Hitler at the command of the wehrmacht.

Important though Stalingrad was, it represented merely one phase of the Russian winter offensive of 1942-43. The major Russian objectives were to reconquer lost territory, to break the main German line by destroying its anchor positions and to destroy the wehrmacht. In order to accomplish its aims, the Russians launched five offensives: (1) the drive on Stalingrad, Nov. 19, 1942; (2) the attack on the German pocket in the Rzhev-Vyazma sector, opened Nov. 28-29, 1942; (3) the smash against the Kharkov-Kursk line, started on Dec. 15, 1942; (4) the Caucasus offensive opened Jan. 4, 1943, and (5) the drive to lift the siege of Leningrad, launched Jan. 11, 1943.

All five offensives were successful. The Germans, their tank forces chopped to pieces by Russian "blitz-grinding" tactics, fell back on all fronts to shorten their lines and tighten their defenses. On the northern front, three Russian columns struck hard at German fortifications controlling Leningrad, forced a breakthrough and carved out a broad corridor 9 mi. wide and 6 mi. deep. This corridor enabled the Russians to establish a land route by which to supply Leningrad with food and substantially eased the German siege.

Below Leningrad three Russian spearheads cut the Rzhev-Smolensk railway, annihilated an estimated 75,000 Germans in Velikie Luki, and captured the town by Jan. 2, 1943. The fall of Velikie Luki weakened the German hold on the Rzhev-Vyazma pocket and the Russians, maintaining systematic pressure on this key area, captured Rzhev, March 3, and Vyazma, a strong nazi "hedgehog" fortification, March 12.

Below Moscow, on the broad sector running from Orel through Kursk and Belgorod and south to Kharkov, initial Russian operations were successful. The defenses of the great German base at Kursk collapsed under a savage artillery bombardment and Kursk was captured, Feb. 8. The following day Belgorod was taken by the Russians, and on Feb. 16, Kharkov was reoccupied.

To the south, soviet units recaptured Rostov, the fourth time this city had changed hands since the start of the war.

In the Kharkov-Belgorod area, however, the Russians had outraced their lines of supply and the Germans struck back with surprising speed in March. The soviet armies in this sector re-treated 80 mi. to protect their overextended communications and evacuated Kharkov by March 14, and Belgorod a week later.

Far south in the Caucasus another Red army offensive was meeting with success. Russian divisions were attacking with vigour the flanks of the thin nazi spearheads wedged into the Caucasus. The Germans fell far short of their original objective —the capture of the Baku oilfields—and were stalled 400 mi. short of their goal when the soviets opened their counteroffensive Jan. 4, 1943. The Russian plan was to isolate enemy forces in the Caucasus by cutting off their land escapes at Rostov and their waterway link with the Kerch peninsula. But rather than risk another Stalingrad entrapment, the Germans quickly folded back their lines and withdrew to the north. Five weeks after the start of their drive the Russians had retaken Mozdok, Georgievsk, Mineralne Vodi and other key cities in the Caucasus and had rewon most of the German footholds on the eastern shores of the sea of Azov. The nazis, however, still retained a bridgehead on the Kuban delta. Presumably they hoped to resume the Caucasus drive in the summer.

By April 1943 the five Russian drives had halted. The armies of both sides were obviously fatigued and required rest and replacements by fresh divisions. Spring thaws made the Russian roads impassable and both the Red army and the wehrmacht used this period of enforced inactivity to prepare for the summer campaigns.

During their second winter offensive, which lasted from mid-Nov. 1942 until the end of March 1943, the Russians had dealt a paralyzing blow to the nazi military machine. German casualties were huge. A Moscow statement said 850,000 nazis were killed and 350,000 more were taken prisoner during the four-month campaign. In addition to leaving thousands of dead on the battlefields of Russia, the nazis also abandoned an enormous quantity of war material and relinquished their grip on 185,000 sq.mi. of soviet territory. Of equal importance to the losses in men and material inflicted on the wehrmacht were the strategical gains of the Red army. The powerful German hedgehog line had been pierced at several points and the Russians were in a favourable position to launch flanking operations against the remaining German anchors.

3. The Summer Campaign, 1943.—Between April and July 5, 1943, land operations were restricted to local forays and exploratory sorties. Seasonal rains had softened the broad battle areas stretching from Leningrad to Novorossiisk into fields of oozing mud. In May, when the spring sun hardened airfields, the luftwaffe went out on strategical missions to disrupt and dislocate Russian communications deep in the rear. But the German bomber formations were met in mid-air by swarms of Russian fighter planes and scores of the nazi craft were destroyed before they ever reached their targets. At the same time Russian bombers proceeded on similar missions back of the German lines and had more success in carrying out their missions. This surprising reversal in the balance of air power on the eastern front was a bad omen for nazi plans for a new summer offensive. The luftwaffe had undergone a serious decline in power while inversely, the Russian air force had grown in strength until it was more than a match for its opposite number. The gradual weakening of German air power in Russia was due to: (1) the steady bombing of reich aircraft factories by Allied planes based in England, and (2) the diversion of German air-power to the Mediterranean and the European war theatres. At the same time the Red air force was strengthened by Allied aid—the U.S. alone had shipped 6,500 planes to the soviet union by the fall of 1943 —and the enormously increased output of Russian factories.

By the end of June both armies were preparing for a new test of strength. The Germans had an estimated 240 to 260 divisions

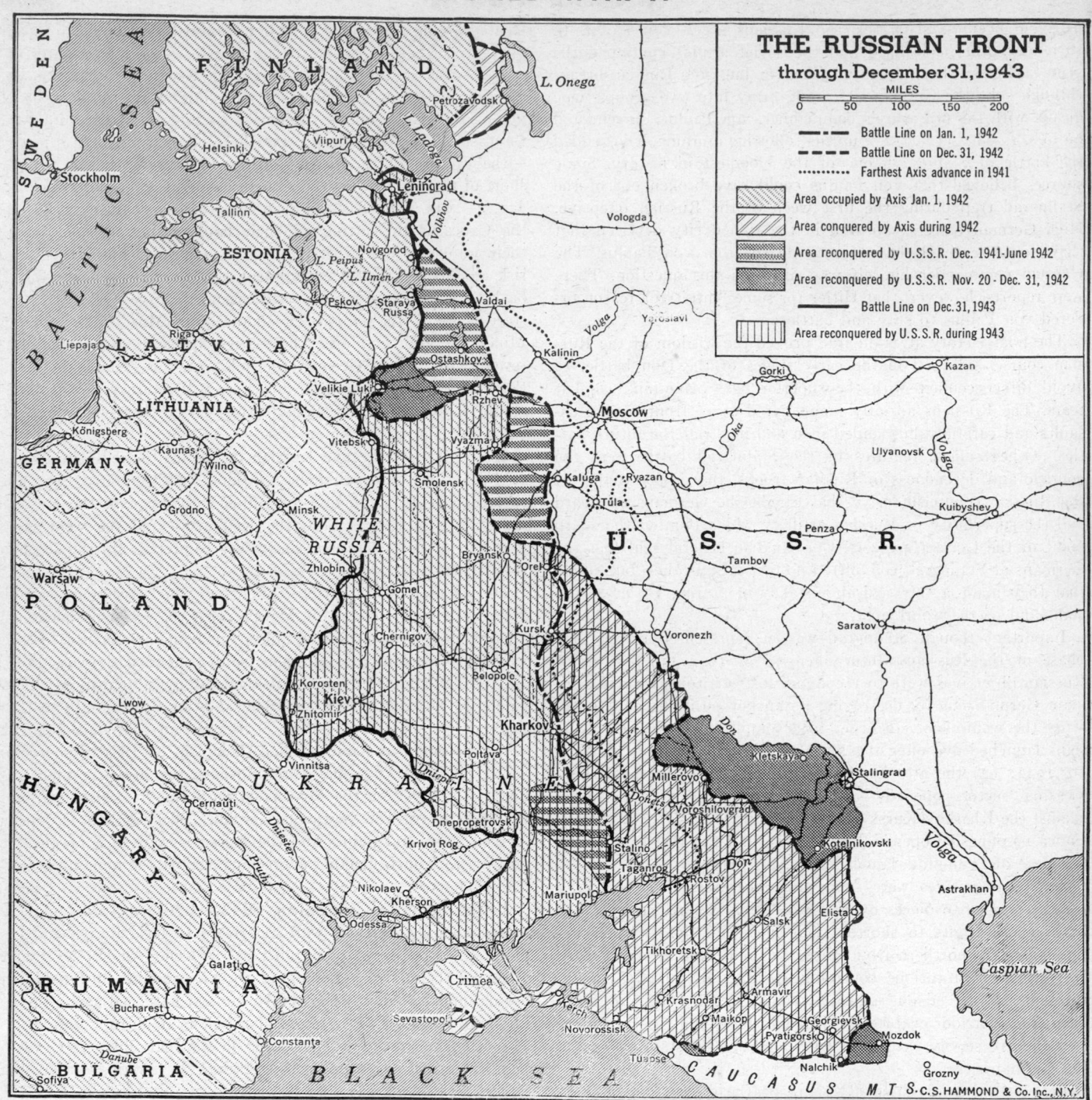

THE RUSSIAN FRONT
through December 31, 1943

MILES
0   50   100   150   200

— · — Battle Line on Jan. 1, 1942
— — — Battle Line on Dec. 31, 1942
········· Farthest Axis advance in 1941

Area occupied by Axis Jan. 1, 1942
Area conquered by Axis during 1942
Area reconquered by U.S.S.R. Dec. 1941-June 1942
Area reconquered by U.S.S.R. Nov. 20 - Dec. 31, 1942
——— Battle Line on Dec. 31, 1943
Area reconquered by U.S.S.R. during 1943

C.S. HAMMOND & Co. Inc., N.Y.

in Russia but the failure of the luftwaffe to gain ascendency over the Red air force crippled the efficacy of the strongest German offensive weapon—the plane-tank team. Although the wehrmacht was still a force to be reckoned with, it had suffered serious reverses over the winter and the morale of the individual soldier had been damaged. On the other hand, the Russian army was strong and ready, numbered between 250 and 275 divisions. Red army reserves were apparently limitless.

The third German bid to knock out the Red army was launched July 5, 1943. The wehrmacht attacked on the Orel-Belgorod front in areas where both armies had been concentrating troops for weeks. Hitler's commanders, hurling large forces of armour at the Russians, succeeded in denting soviet lines in the first week of battle. The wehrmacht command again used tanks to spearhead its drive with infantry following up. But the Russians, instead of leaving their positions, let the panzers pass through. Soviet in-

fantry then emerged from its trenches, repulsed the German foot-soldiers with heavy losses while batteries of rapid-fire guns chopped up the tanks in the rear. The German drive was stopped after a week of fighting. Employing their enormously superior fire-power, the Russians then mounted a powerful offensive of their own which was preceded by one of the heaviest artillery barrages in history. The bombardment opened before dawn on July 12 and was concentrated on a sector near Orel about 20 mi. long and 4 mi. deep. The Russians massed great numbers of guns—more than 10 times as many gun barrels per mile of front as had been used at Verdun during World War I—and literally burned out the stricken German sector. Then big Russian tanks protected by planes plunged over the charred ground. Lacking the firepower to halt the Russian tank assault, the nazis fell back. They could not stem the irresistible soviet surge over the flat country toward Orel and on Aug. 5 both Orel and Belgorod were captured by the Red army.

The fall of Orel endangered the entire German line below Smolensk. The soviet force then split into three columns. One sped toward Bryansk, another moved on Smolensk and a third oward Kharkov. All three columns pressed forward rapidly. The Germans retreated, albeit slowly and stubbornly. On Aug. 23, 1943, the Russians recaptured Kharkov, loosening another bolt in the collapsing nazi "hedgehogs" and hammered new spearheads into nazi defenses west of the city. This manoeuvre was designed to wrest the entire Donets basin from German control.

Having won three decisive battles—at the Kursk salient and at Orel and Kharkov—the Red army moved quickly westward in the hope of cracking the German defenses along the Dnieper river before the winter frosts set in. The key points of the German "Dnieper line" were, running north to south, Smolensk, Kiev and Dnepropetrovsk. But two nazi strongpoints stood in the path of the Russian push toward the Dnieper. To the north was Bryansk, a rail centre guarding the approaches to Smolensk and Kiev. To the south was Taganrog, a defense outpost wedged deep into Russian lines below Rostov. The Red army launched savage attacks on both of these key bastions. Taganrog was the first to fall. The Russians broke into the city Aug. 30 and wiped out the German garrison of 40,000 men in the Taganrog area in subsequent operations. A fortnight later, Sept. 17, the Russians took Bryansk. The soviet troops then stepped up their drive to the Dnieper. At the same time they launched a blistering attack on the German bridgehead on the Kuban delta, recapturing the naval base of Novorossiysk on Sept. 16. By this time the Red army offensive along the 700-mi. front from Smolensk to the axis bridgehead in the Caucasus gathered momentum. Shaken by the terrific force of the Russian blows, the Germans retreated steadily, giving up one vantage point after another. By Sept. 25 the nazis were compelled to evacuate Smolensk and retired to the west bank of the Dnieper. At the same time Russian forces were storming their way into the suburbs of Kiev and to the south were advancing on the Dnieper bend.

By Oct. 5 the Russians had made impressive gains due to their successful exploitation of German weak spots. Russian attacks would ripple up and down the German line until a lesion was found; then the attackers would hit that spot with a terrific hammer-blow. Lacking adequate reserves the wehrmacht could not cope with these tactics. The main nazi problem was to conserve manpower and to keep their armies intact. Although they had been badly mauled during the retreat to the Dnieper, the Germans had nevertheless conducted an orderly and skilful retirement. One factor was of negative help to the Germans. In retreating westward, they relinquished territory and shortened their lines. This shrinkage enabled them to release some forces used for policing occupied areas to fill gaps in the depleted ranks of the combat troops. During the first three months of their summer offensive, the Russians had reoccupied another 90,000 sq.mi. of territory. They recovered the Donets basin and its coal reserves, large sections of the fertile Ukraine and had put the oil of the Caucasus far beyond the German grasp.

4. The Winter Campaign, 1943–44.—The Russian winter offensive of 1943–44 was a continuation of the summer drive. The wehrmacht, weakened by heavy casualties, did not have sufficient strength to halt the soviet advances and to dig in behind a winter line. By contrast, the Red army was stronger than ever, had an abundance of arms and reserves and was able to continue its drive without stopping. On Oct. 5, the Russian line extended from Leningrad to Velikie Luki, then south to Gomel, whence it followed the configuration of the Dnieper to Zaporozhe. From Zaporozhe the line swung straight south to the German-held base at Melitopol and thence to the sea of Azov. At this time, the

Red army had five major offensives operating: (1) in the Nevel area above Smolensk, the Russians were striking toward the Baltic states, (2) in the Smolensk area, soviet troops were edging their way along the route toward Minsk in White Russia, (3) in the Kiev area, the Russians were preparing to cross the Dnieper, capture the key base of Kiev and traverse the gateway to Poland, (4) in the Ukraine, Red army units were battering at the German defenses on the west bank of the Dnieper, aiming at Dnepropetrovsk and (5) on the northern banks of the sea of Azov, soviet armies were pounding at German lines defending Zaporozhe and Melitopol.

In Oct. 1943 the Russians crossed the Dnieper at several places, thus hurdling a major obstacle in their campaign to drive the nazis out of soviet lands. In the southern Ukraine, they sealed off the last land escape for German forces in the Crimea by taking Perekop, and to the north they crowned their offensive triumphs with the capture of Kiev, Nov. 6. The reconquest of Kiev collapsed the German middle Dnieper defenses and put the Russians at the gate of an invasion route into central Europe via a land corridor between the Pripet marshes on the north and the Carpathian mountains on the south. Exploiting the advantage gained at Kiev, the Russian armies fanned out to the west and captured Zhitomir, Nov. 13. At this juncture, the Germans lashed back with a strong counterattack, chopping away at the overextended Russian communications and compelled Gen. Vatutin's 1st Ukrainian army to relinquish Zhitomir and fall back toward Kiev. The nazis pressed their attack and on Nov. 30, they recaptured nearby Korosten. In order to ease their direct frontal pressure at the western gates of Kiev, the Russians countered with fierce blows around the periphery of the Kiev bulge, capturing several strongholds in this area. This manoeuvre compelled the nazis to halt their drive at Kiev and shift troops to the threatened areas to stave off potential Russian break-throughs. Gen. Vatutin's forces in the Kiev sector, reinforced with great masses of artillery, then loosed a terrific bombardment of the German positions. Nazi tank phalanxes that attempted to force Russian lines in the Kiev area were tossed in the air by the scorching barrage and by Dec. 27 Vatutin's forces had resumed the offensive. They recaptured Zhitomir, Dec. 31, and by Feb. 10, 1944, they had penetrated prewar Poland. Meanwhile, to the north, a similar concentrated artillery barrage had crushed the German fortifications around Leningrad. Three Russian armies then opened a concerted offensive in Jan. 1944. The northern column completely cleared the Leningrad area and had crossed into Estonia. The central column swept around Lake Ilmen, capturing Staraya Russa and the southern column was driving toward the borders of Latvia. On the southern Ukraine front, the Russians had more difficulty in their attacks on the strong German defenses within the Dnieper bend. A German counteroffensive, started in mid-January, was launched against Russian positions north of Vinnitsa in an effort to relieve pressure on this outpost guarding the vital Odessa-Lwow railway. Instead of fighting this offensive, the Russians decided to attack elsewhere and in a surprise manoeuvre encircled 10 German divisions in the Korsun area. The Germans could not break this trap and lost more than 80,000 men in this miniature Stalingrad, which was liquidated by Feb. 17, 1944.

It was difficult to estimate the casualties of the Russian campaign; each side tended to exaggerate the other's losses and to minimize their own. In June 1943 a Russian communiqué stated that German casualties from the start of the war totalled 6,400,-000 killed and captured as against 4,200,000 Russians killed or wounded. A subsequent German statement that the Russians had lost 20,000,000 in dead, wounded and missing was dismissed as propaganda. The Russian figures corresponded roughly to an estimate made by the British ministry of economic warfare, Oct. 15, 1943, which put German losses at 4,000,000 in dead alone. Nine-tenths of the nazi casualties, according to this estimate, were sustained on Russian battlefields. This was twice the number of Germans killed in World War I. In the summer and fall offensives, the nazis claimed that Russian casualties were 1,300,000 dead, 1,570,000 wounded and 130,000 prisoners. The Russians said German losses in this same period were 900,000 dead, 1,702,000 wounded and 98,000 captured.

IV.—THE MEDITERRANEAN CAMPAIGN

1. The Tunisian Campaign.—In Jan. 1943 the Allied offensive in North Africa, which had gotten off to a running start two months before when Anglo-American forces landed in Morocco and Algeria, appeared none too promising. In Tunisia, axis armies, capitalizing on the slowness of the Allied units in taking the field, had established excellent defense positions. In Libya, the British 8th army was engaged in a vain chase of Marshal Rommel's Afrika Korps. The shrewd "desert fox" kept one step ahead of his pursuers and managed to keep his armies intact while falling back to the fortified Mareth line.

At first glance, the advantages appeared to lie with the axis. While the Allies were still floundering about in the early stages of the campaign, Hitler had rushed all the men and material he could spare to his African beachhead. By mid-January, the Germans had posted in their Tunisian garrisons a well trained army of seasoned troops. Combined with Rommel's Afrika Korps the German-Italian armies numbered about 200,000 men, most of whom were veteran nazi combat troops. The striking power of the axis force was built about three crack German armoured divisions supported by a luftwaffe fleet of about 1,000 planes based in airfields in Tunisia, Sicily and Italy. The Allied armies that originally landed in French North Africa numbered about 150,000 men, and were subsequently expanded by fresh reinforcements. Another force of between 100,000 and 150,000 troops, drawn from the French armies in Africa, was also available for Allied operations, but lacked equipment. Although figures on the size

of the Allied air arm were not disclosed, it was believed that the Anglo-American air forces far outnumbered the luftwaffe squadrons in this Mediterranean war theatre. In mechanized equipment too, the Allies had the edge, but with the exception of Gen. Bernard L. Montgomery's 8th army in Libya, the American and British tank crews in western Tunisia did not measure up to the Germans in experience and skill.

While the Germans possessed better defense positions and shorter supply routes, these tactical advantages were offset by the superior strategical position of the Allied armies. The Anglo-American-French troops under Gen. Dwight D. Eisenhower, then Allied commander of the Mediterranean war zone, had ample room for manoeuvre; whereas, the axis forces were crowded into a narrow corridor in Tunisia. The Germans dared not risk a major offensive to the west while the British 8th army threatened to bolt through their backdoor in the east.

As the year 1943 opened, the Allied and axis armies in Tunisia were sparring for position. Gen. Eisenhower's troops were deployed along a line running in a north-south direction from a coastal point 25 mi. west of Bizerte to the Djerid salt marsh on the south. The British 1st army, composed of American and British troops, held the northern flank, extending from the Tunisian coast to Mateur. The southern flank, held by the newly organized U.S. 5th army and French forces, ran from Mateur to the Djerid salt marshes.

During the first 15 days of January, operations in western Tunisia were hampered by the seasonal rains, which turned battlefields into knee-deep quagmires. In the Libyan theatre of war, the British 8th army pursued Rommel's armies in Tripolitania. By the middle of January, the 8th army was within 100 mi. of Tripoli, but its advance, though swift, was not all smooth sailing as Rommel had studded the path of his retreat with skilfully concealed minetraps which had to be cleared. On Jan. 23, 1943, Rommel evacuated the port of Tripoli, retreated into Tunisia and took up positions behind the Mareth line. A miniature Maginot defense system built by the French before the outbreak of World War II, the Mareth line was originally intended to prevent an Italian attack against Tunisia. Rommel's abandonment of Tripoli and retreat from Libya was a deliberate strategic manoeuvre. Rather than remain in the Libyan-Tripolitania sands where he risked certain defeat at the hands of a superior British force, he decided to fall back and join forces with the armies of Gen. Jurgen von Arnim in western Tunisia. He was thus able to concentrate his forces effectively to prevent the Allies from driving a wedge between the two axis armies in Tunisia.

As Rommel's troops were retreating toward the safety of sheltered positions behind the Mareth line, the axis forces took the offensive on the western Tunisian front. On Jan. 18, a strong German armoured force, spear-headed by Mark IV and Mark VI tanks attacked the French units west of Pont du Fahs. The French holding this strategic area buckled under the heavy tank assault. Allied armoured units rushed to their rescue, and the German panzers fell back. South of Ousseltia, the nazis launched another attack against the poorly equipped French detachments holding Faid, an important road pass. Again, Allied armour extricated the French from possible extermination.

Meanwhile, a third Allied armoured command, an American combat unit, smashed at Sened station, about 110 mi. south of Faid pass. Despite a furious dive-bomber attack and accurate enemy shell-fire, the Americans succeeded in taking Sened, Feb. 1, and drove within 6 mi. of the German stronghold at Maknassy. Although the American forces had made tactical gains, they had spread themselves perilously thin over a 200-mi. battlefront extending from Medjez-el-Bab on the north to Gafsa on the south. The U.S. troops halted abruptly to remedy this situation

THE TUNISIAN CAMPAIGN 1943
SCALE OF MILES
0   50   100   150
Railroads +++++   Roads

C.S. HAMMOND & CO., N.Y.

Map labels:
Tunis & Bizerte fall May 7
Marsala
Sicily
Agrigento
Bône occupied Nov. 12, 1942
C. Blanc
C. Serrat
Bizerte
Ferryville
C. Bon
Organized resistance ceases May 12
Tabarca
Mateur
Tebourba
La Calle
Béja
Tunis
Kelibia
Pantelleria
Bône
Souk-el-Arba
Medjez-el-Bab
Hammamet
Pont du Fahs
Zaghouan
Souk Ahras
Le Kef
Les Salines
Enfidaville
Gulf of Hammamet
Sousse
Line stabilized Jan. 12
Line restored by Mar. 22
Pichon
Kairouan
MEDITERRANEAN
Tébessa
Thala
Sbeitla
El-Djem
Mahdia
Lampedusa
Kasserine
Faid
SEA
Feriana
Area taken by Axis Feb. 14-16
Sfax
U.S. Patrols contact 8th Army Apr. 7
Maknassy
Kerkennah Is.
Gafsa
El-Guettar
Gulf of Gabès
Battle Line Mar. 30-Apr. 6
Tozeur
El Hamma
Gabès
Houmt-Souk
Chott el Djerid
Kebili
Djerba I.
Matmata
Mareth
New Zealand forces attack Mar. 22
MARETH LINE
Medenine
Tripoli falls Jan. 23
Foum-Tatahouine
Zuara
Tripoli
British attack Mareth Line Mar. 22
LIBYA
Garian
Battle Line Apr. 23-May 3

but before they could consolidate their positions, the Germans launched an all-out lightning drive against them, Feb. 14. Spearheaded by the big Mark VI tanks, which were fitted with 88-mm. guns, the German panzer divisions crashed through the lowlands between Faid pass and Sidi Bou Zid, virtually destroyed two U.S. armoured units and overran Allied artillery positions. Badly crippled by this surprise blow, the American forces withdrew rapidly, and evacuated Gafsa. The axis armour, following up its initial advantage, smashed boldly against the centre of the line and on Feb. 20, swept through Kasserine pass, one of the four vital mountain roads leading to the Algerian border. German mechanized columns then split in two and raced toward Algeria. This time, however, Allied armour lay in wait until the overconfident panzer crews sped to exposed ground near Thala, 25 mi. above Kasserine. Then Allied tanks, protected by air and land bombardments, launched a vicious counterattack which brought the panzers up short. This combined assault proved too much for the bewildered panzer divisions which turned tail and scooted back toward Sbeitla and Kasserine. Allied tanks gave chase and on Feb. 25, the Americans reoccupied Kasserine Gap without firing a shot. The Afrika Korps, badly mauled by these unexpected counterblows, retreated to the Sbeitla-Feriana line and the fighting subsided.

The Germans had failed in their objective—capture of Tébessa (in Algeria)—but they had inflicted a severe defeat on the Americans. The Allies lost more than 100 tanks in the Kasserine battle and their casualties were four times as large as those of the enemy. The Allies also learned several valuable lessons at Kasserine: (1) that the German dive-bomber was a formidable weapon against unseasoned forces, but was ineffective against veteran troops; (2) that armoured divisions were more effective when concentrated into sizable striking forces than when used in small and dispersed groups; and (3) that liberal sprinklings of avenues of retreat with mines and booby-traps can slow an attacking force. The application of overwhelming air power at precisely the right moment was an important factor in helping the Allies turn back the Germans at Kasserine pass. The success of the synchronized plane-tank-infantry attack in this battle set the pattern for subsequent Allied operations in Tunisia. By March of 1943 the Allied air force in the Mediterranean was united under a single command and then redivided, according to functional tasks, into tactical and strategic air forces.

By mid-March the Allies had recovered from the near-disaster of Kasserine pass and were gathering for an all-out offensive push to drive the axis out of Tunisia. The British 1st army and the U.S. 5th army (later reorganized as the 2nd American corps), which had gained in experience, and the British 8th, backbone of Allied power in Africa, were now functioning smoothly, jabbing and thrusting in alternation at the axis lines. On the northern front, the British 1st army troops were engaged in see-saw battles with the German regulars for control of the strategic hills commanding the approaches to Bizerte. On the central Tunisian front, American forces, employing the now familiar tactic of a relentless advance by infantry and tanks supported by destructive blows from the air, recaptured Gafsa on March 17 after a swift 30-mi. drive. Nearby El-Guettar and Sened fell in rapid succession and unable to weather the terrific land-and-air pounding, the axis armies fell back. While the British and Americans hammered the Germans in central Tunisia, Gen. Montgomery's 8th army breached the first of the three German defense positions in the Mareth line.

Meanwhile, the Allies poured relays of bombers over the axis lines. German airfields were plowed up and the luftwaffe's planes were destroyed, either in the air or on the ground, in such numbers that their replacement became virtually impossible. Further-

LONG STOP HILL (Djebel el Ahmera), a key to the approaches of Tunis, was captured by the Allies after a bitter three-day battle, April 23-26, 1943

more, the luftwaffe was drained by the enormous losses entailed in the Russian campaign and the Allied bombing of plane plants in Germany. The British 8th army then launched an all-out offensive against the Mareth line, March 20. After nine days and nights of furious fighting, the 8th army troops pierced the Mareth defenses and marched into the port of Gabes, March 30. Meanwhile, Gen. von Arnim, who succeeded Rommel as commander of the axis armies in Tunisia, beat a hasty retreat via the coast road to avoid being pinned back against the Gulf of Gabes.

After the Mareth battle the Allies launched a general offensive all along the mountainous Tunisian front. By April 5 they were hammering six wedges into the axis lines. On the north, Moroccan goumiers, who had captured Sedjenane and Cap Serrat, were pressing back axis units toward Mateur, an important road junction. Some 50 mi. to the south of Sedjenane a French force was slashing through German positions at Bou Arada in a drive for Pont-du-Fahs. In the Fondouk area, 100 mi. below Mateur, an American force was waging a savage battle to win heights commanding Kairouan. South of Fondouk another U.S. force cut through enemy columns near the Shott el Fedjedi. On April 7 this force effected a junction with the British 8th army which in turn was aided by a Fighting French unit that had made a 1,500-mi. trek from the Lake Chad area to join the Allied forces. The Allies then tightened their noose about the enemy forces who were being slowly strangled in the Tunisian "coffin corner." The Allies took Pichon, Fondouk and Sfax in rapid succession. By April 11 American troops stormed through Faid pass. The following day the 8th army captured Sousse. The axis line was shriveled to a mere 120 mi. in length and the Germans were fighting with their backs to the sea.

Von Arnim had hoped to make a stand at the port of Enfidaville on the coast, but the British 8th army units overran his

U.S. AMPHIBIOUS TRUCK plowing through a path cleared in a mine field on a beach near Gela, Sicily, July 10, 1943, shortly after the initial American landing forces had established a beachhead there to launch the invasion of the island. At the left is a jeep which has been destroyed by a Teller mine

positions and occupied the city by April 21. His troops were also driven from Long Stop hill, a vital defense on the road to Tunis, by the British and were fighting a losing battle against French units driving toward Pont-du-Fahs.

By the end of April the Tunisian battle was nearing its close. Thirteen miles west of Mateur, American troops cleared Djebel Tahent—Hill 609—by May 2, after an epic battle. Mateur itself fell to the Americans, May 3, and Bizerte was within range of Allied guns.

As the Allied armies were poised for the final kill Allied bombers and fighters made 2,500 sorties on May 6 over Tunisia and Sicily, pounding the reeling axis forces and supply lines. Stunned by the impact of the bombs and exploding shells fired at them by massed Allied artillery, the Germans staggered in retreat toward the sea. The following day, May 7, British, American and French forces smashed through the German lines. American troops captured Bizerte and grimy bare-waisted British Tommies marched into Tunis. The remnants of the axis forces fled toward Cap Bon with British armoured divisions in hot pursuit. Further axis resistance was both futile and impossible. On May 12 Gen. von Arnim surrendered and the battle for Africa had ended. Besides von Arnim, 16 other generals were taken prisoner and more than 200,000 axis troops, the majority of them Germans, were captured by the Allies.

2. Pantelleria and Sicily.—After driving the axis out of Tunisia, the Allied high command prepared to invade southern Europe via Italy, the weak link in Hitler's chain of fortifications girdling the continent. Three considerations governed the Allied decision to attack by way of Italy rather than western Europe. One was the flaccid morale of the Italian people. A second was the necessity of clearing the Mediterranean, which would shorten the distance of convoy shipments to the Allied bases in Africa. A third was the fact that German supply lines to the Italian boot were long and extenuated; in contrast nazi communications to possible invasion points in western France, Holland and Belgium were short and easily negotiated.

In order to invade Italy, the Allies first had to eject axis forces from the Mediterranean islands of Pantelleria, Lampedusa, Linosa and Sicily. As long as these outposts remained in axis control, Allied shipping in the Mediterranean was unsafe.

The reduction of Pantelleria was the first step in the Allied strategy of clearing the Mediterranean. This rockbound isle, 45 mi. square, was studded with heavy coastal guns, underground barracks and hangars, and was garrisoned by a force of more than 11,000 Italian troops. Strategically, Pantelleria was a stopper in the Mediterranean narrows and its role was to prevent passage of Allied shipping.

On May 20, 1943, the Allies started an aerial attack on Pantelleria. For 20 days and nights streams of bombers shuttled over Pantelleria dropping a tremendous weight of explosives on the island. In the last 13 days of the attack some 8,000 tons of bombs hit Pantelleria. On June 10, the heaviest day of the bombardment, Pantelleria was rocked by 1,500 tons of bombs. The Italian garrison found the air blitz unendurable and it surrendered on June 11. The following day Lampedusa gave up and the tiny force holding Linosa capitulated on June 13.

While some military theorists regarded the knockout of Pantelleria as proof that air power by itself could win a decision in war, others pointed out that special conditions enabled air power to win a victory in this battle. They maintained that the island fell because it was possible to isolate it completely from supporting mainland bases. These sources emphasized that Malta in three years of war had taken many times the weight of bombs dropped on the Italian outpost; but it survived because its supply lines were never severed.

The conquest of Pantelleria advanced the Allies toward their next objective—invasion of Sicily. Nearly 200 times the size of Pantelleria, Sicily had excellent ferry connections with the mainland and was dotted by 18 or 20 airfields. In addition, three or four more airfields on the toe of Italy were within easy fighter range of Sicily.

After Sicilian airfields, ports and railways had been thoroughly saturated by Allied bombings, an armada of 2,500 vessels, including warships, set out for the southern shores of Sicily. Covered by an intense sea-and-air barrage laid over axis defenses on the island, thousands of American, British and Canadian troops swarmed onto the southern shores of Sicily before dawn, July 10, 1943.

Gen. Eisenhower, who was in command of the Sicilian operations, divided his invasion forces into two armies, each numbering about 100,000 men. One, the 8th army, which included Canadian as well as British forces, led by Gen. Montgomery, landed on the southeast tip of Sicily; the other, the American 7th army, led by Gen. George S. Patton, Jr., landed at the southern shore. While the landings were successful, they were not unopposed and the Americans wading ashore at Gela, a small Sicilian port, had to battle hard against fierce German tank attacks which nearly drove them from several of their beachheads.

By July 12 the Allied forces had solidly established several bridgeheads on the island. The American 7th army controlled 70 mi. of the south coast. The British had won a 30-mi. stretch of the east shore and Canadian marines had won a foothold in between. The Allied forces then drove forward. The U.S. armies split up; two columns sped inland to the north, a third raced along the southern coast. The Italians offered little resistance to the spirited drive of the American troops, who by July 22 had captured Palermo, capital of Sicily, and had cut off the Italian forces on the western half of the island from German armies on the eastern half.

Although the British had captured Syracuse and Augusta by July 15, their drive in eastern Sicily was slowed by stubborn nazi resistance. The coast road to Catania, a port at the base of Mt. Etna, was narrow and it became clear that the Germans could hold it against a frontal assault. In order to dislodge them from these strong, natural positions, other British forces, as well as Canadian and U.S. troops released by the quick mop-up in western Sicily, started a drive to flank the German lines west of Mt. Etna. Allied progress was slow, as the Germans bitterly contested every foot of ground and littered the path of their retreat with countless minefields. They repelled several British attempts to break through the Catania bottleneck, but withdrew when Canadian troops, driving around the western slopes of Mt. Etna, threatened to snap off their communications with the Messina ferry to the north. The nazis retired from Catania on Aug. 5, and quickened their withdrawal toward Messina, the port closest to the Italian mainland and their most convenient escape exit.

Meanwhile, American, British, Canadian and French troops, as well as Moroccan Goums, launched a combined offensive toward Messina. Axis rearguard troops fought resolutely, but by Aug. 12, they were crowded into a narrow and untenable strip in the northeast corner of the island. Unable to halt the fierce Allied drive, the Germans evacuated what troops they could from Messina to the Italian mainland and on Aug. 17, U.S. forces captured Messina, thus ending the campaign of Sicily.

Although the Allies had conquered Sicily in the comparatively short space of 39 days, they suffered heavy casualties. The British lost 11,835 dead, wounded and missing, while American casualties were 7,400 and Canadian losses 2,388. Axis casualties were estimated at 30,000 killed and wounded and 130,000 captured.

The entire axis force at the start of the campaign consisted of 10 Italian and 4 German divisions totalling between 150,000 and 200,000 men. But from the very beginning of the invasion the Italians showed little heart for fighting and the entire burden of the defense of the island fell on the German forces, who were eventually outnumbered four or five to one.

3. Invasion of Italy.—While the Sicilian operation was merely an outpost battle in the Mediterranean, it enabled the Allies to establish an advanced base of operations for the attack on Italy. The basic objective in Allied plans was to knock Italy out of the war, thereby reducing the nazi foothold in the Mediterranean. Their secondary aims were to secure land bases for eventual operations against southern France and the Balkans and to establish advanced airfields from which to extend the Allied air offensive against the industrial vitals of Germany.

Heavy and increasingly destructive air raids over strategic and tactical targets in Italy preceded the actual land operations. Even before the Sicilian campaign had ended Allied bombers were hammering harbours and communications, destroying luftwaffe airfields and smashing Italian railways, upon which the Germans relied to speed men and material to any threatened point.

By mid-July 1943 the air blows on Italy rose in true Wagnerian crescendo. Bombers of the Allied strategic air force were reported to have reduced the cities of Genoa, Venice, Trieste, Leghorn, Naples, Taranto, Bari, Brindisi, Milan, Turin, Bologna and Florence to rubble. Meanwhile the tactical air force swarmed over the boot of Italy, wrecking ammunition dumps, setting fire to oil depots, smashing railway rolling stock and freight yards and bombing and strafing axis troop concentrations. This gigantic softening-up process came to a head on July 19, when 500 American planes attacked Rome—the first raid on the Italian capital since the war began. The attacking craft, carefully avoiding cultural and religious monuments, blasted a specific target—the city's railway marshalling yards. Rome, as the seat of fascism and a rail centre, was a legitimate target for air attack.

The Italian people, who had not expected that air warfare would be brought to their soil when Mussolini had cast his lot with Hitler in June 1940, were now appalled by the widespread destruction caused by Allied bombings. They clamoured so insistently for peace that the fascist regime was no longer master of the situation and Mussolini was ousted from power, July 25, 1943. Meanwhile Gen. Eisenhower offered peace terms to Mar-

MOPPING UP the streets of Messina was the last task of Allied troops in their conquest of Sicily in 1943

U.S. 5TH ARMY TROOPS halting momentarily in Naples while a labour corps clears away debris of bomb wreckage

shal Pietro Badoglio, the duce's successor, and the Allies temporarily suspended their air offensive while the new Italian government pondered the offer. Badoglio, however, was not able to persuade his German allies to leave Italy—a basic condition of Eisenhower's terms—and on July 31 the Allies warned that they would resume their bombings.

As a result, an estimated 3,000,000 Italian people fled from the urban centres to havens in the countryside. On Aug. 13 Rome was raided again and 500 tons of bombs were dropped on the city's two railroad yards. After this aerial attack, Badoglio declared Rome an open city, but Allied authorities rejected this unilateral declaration, demanding investigation by neutral authorities to determine whether Rome had been demilitarized. The Italians failed to heed the Allied demand.

Thenceforth, the Allied bombers concentrated on destruction of railways and aerodromes in the Italian boot. By Aug. 24 the railway system in southern Italy was virtually paralyzed and the enemy airfields were so thoroughly plowed up by bomb craters that the luftwaffe was compelled to fall back to bases in central Italy. Although the main blows against rail communications were in southern and central Italy, rail targets in the north were not immune from attack. On Sept. 3 a formation of U.S. bombers crippled rail traffic from the Brenner pass into Italy by bombing the line at Bolzano, Trento and Bologna. This attack was the finishing touch to Allied pre-invasion air blows against Italy's railway communications. On this same day the invasion began. Units of the British 8th army, containing Canadian as well as British troops, crossed the 2-mi.-wide water-gap separating the Sicilian port of Messina from the Italian mainland, established a beachhead in Calabria and occupied the towns of Reggio di Calabria and San Giovanni a few hours after landing.

The British 8th army met no resistance from the Italians—who surrendered in droves—as on the same day Marshal Badoglio had agreed to Allied terms to cease fighting. Five days later, on Sept. 8, Badoglio accepted Gen. Eisenhower's terms for unconditional surrender, under which the Italians agreed to give up their fleet, and Italy dropped out of the war as an axis partner. Reacting energetically to halt the deterioration of its military position in Italy, the German command poured thousands of reinforcements into the peninsula and on Sept. 10 German forces under Field Marshal Albert Kesselring occupied Rome after a battle of a few hours. In northern Italy, Field Marshal Rommel re-emerged on the scene of Mediterranean warfare. He seized the principal cities, rapidly subdued what little resistance the Italians offered and soon brought all strategic points under nazi control. At the same time the Germans announced that Kesselring had been put in command of their forces in central Italy and that Rommel, the "desert fox" of African fame, had been placed in charge of nazi armies in northern Italy.

While the alert German reaction to the armistice announcement saved the day for Hitler in central and northern Italy, the greater part of the Italian fleet escaped and surrendered to the British at Malta and Gibraltar. By Sept. 15 some 100 Italian warships, including five battleships, were in Allied hands. Although the Allies could not hope to use the Italian fleet against the Germans for some time, its surrender freed a large portion of Allied naval forces in the Mediterranean for duty elsewhere.

On Sept. 9, 24 hours after Italy's capitulation, units of the Allied 5th army landed on a beachhead below Salerno. The Allied strategy was to lure the Germans into rushing troops to meet the British 8th army in the south of Italy. Once this was accomplished, the Allies planned a landing to the north and a consequent quick dash across the waist of Italy to the Adriatic to cut off the German divisions in the south. In order not to alarm the Germans, announcement of the armistice was withheld until Sept. 8. The Germans, however, suspected a trap and refused to be drawn into it.

The landing on the Salerno beachhead was preceded by a naval barrage of considerable intensity. Both American and British troops, of the Allied 5th army, led by Lt. Gen. Mark Wayne Clark, quickly clambered up the

beach at 3:30 A.M. on Sept 9, only to find that the Germans were thoroughly prepared for their arrival. The first Allied troops to go ashore were cut to pieces by deadly patterned fire from concealed batteries of 88-mm. cannon and machine guns. Those that reached dry land were driven back by big German Tiger tanks and the beach became littered with Allied dead and dying and wrecked equipment. The Allied forces returned that night and established a bridgehead under a protective barrage from warships off shore while additional troops and supplies were landed the next morning. By Sept. 14 the British and American troops were established on a 25-mi.-wide strip of beach extending from Salerno to Agropoli on the south. Their position was by no means secure and they battled with their backs to the sea. While American and British warships kept up an incessant bombardment of the German lines above the beaches, all types of Allied aircraft were summoned to help the battered Allied troops on the beachhead below. They raked the German lines from end to end, rooting out the 88's camouflaged in the forests, spraying death on concealed machine-gun emplacements and accurately bombing enemy trucks and railway rolling stock.

This scorching assault from the air combined with a vicious shelling of German lines above the beaches by Allied warships and the stubborn refusal of the 5th army troops to yield their positions, turned the tide of the Salerno battle. By Sept. 15, after 150 hours of continuous fighting, the Germans started to withdraw from the Salerno salient. The following day the 5th army took the offensive, driving the Germans from the wide pocket between the Sele and Calore rivers. By Sept. 18 the British 8th army, which had been sweeping up the Adriatic coast turned part of its columns inland, effected a junction with the bruised 5th army and all Allied holdings in Italy were welded into a single front.

The Salerno battle was a Pyrrhic victory for the Allies at best. The casualties entailed—the U.S. forces alone lost 3,497 in dead, wounded and missing—in the first week of fighting were high and the nazis succeeded in fighting a delaying action that enabled Rommel and Kesselring to secure a firm grip on central and northern Italy.

At this stage of the campaign in Italy the Allies controlled the lower portion of the Italian boot. The Germans held Naples and virtually all Italian territory north of the city. Marshal Kesselring had about eight divisions massed for the defense of Naples and the road to Rome; by the end of the year this force was augmented by several armoured divisions. Rommel had another 15 to 20 divisions in northern Italy. Meanwhile, German forces in Sardinia, attacked by two Italian divisions, had evacuated the island and a French army under Gen. Giraud invaded Corsica on Sept. 14 and cleared all German troops from the island by Oct. 5.

After Salerno the Allied 5th army, aided by strong air support, swung around the Sorrento peninsula and occupied Naples on Oct. 1. On the Adriatic front, the British 8th army keeping pace with the Allied 5th army's advance, captured the great Italian air base of Foggia, Sept. 27, after a swift 25-mi. lunge over flat terrain. From Foggia, with its network of 13 airfields, Allied bombers were brought within striking distance of cities in southern Germany, Austria and the Balkans.

The Italian front hardened rapidly after the fall of Naples. The battle line, about 125 mi. long, stretched across the breadth of Italy from the Tyrrhenian to the Adriatic. The German "delaying action" strategy was aided by the rugged mountain terrain and the continuous autumn rains which bogged down Allied mechanized equipment and mired airfields. The Allied 5th army, holding the western section of the front, had succeeded by mid-October in crossing the Volturno river. The British 8th, holding the eastern sector, also made small gains. Expert in the strategic use of terrain for defensive operations, the Germans slowed the Allied advance to a walk by the winter of 1943–44. Their defense system was so arranged that it could be maintained by a relatively small number of troops. German artillery fire was expertly sighted while machine guns and mortars were artfully camouflaged in the heavily forested Apennines. By the end of the year the Italian campaign had settled down to a dreary repetition of the trench warfare of 1914–18, with neither side strong enough to effect a decisive breakthrough.

In an effort to break this deadlock, the Allies made a new landing below Rome on Jan. 22, 1944. British and American troops, supported by warships and planes, established beachheads on the Tyrrhenian coast about 30 mi. south of Rome, captured the port of Nettuno and then drove inland. They met little resistance during the first 48 hours, but the Germans rapidly reinforced their troops in this area and by March 1, the Allies were having difficulty in maintaining their new bridgehead.

Of some assistance to the Allied cause were the Italian guerrilla units operating behind German lines in central and northern Italy. Their activity was restricted, however, by the smallness of the territory in which they operated. The Badoglio government's declaration of war against Germany on Oct. 13, 1943, brought some recruits to the guerrilla detachments, but most of the Italian soldiers, dispirited by three years of futile service under the fascist regime, simply threw away their arms and returned to civilian life.

4. Balkan Operations.—A resurgence of activity among the guerrilla armies in the Balkans, notably Yugoslavia, attended the Allied invasion of Italy. Upon the surrender of the Badoglio government, the Yugoslav guerrillas attacked axis forces throughout the coastal areas. Their vigorous burst of activity forced Hitler to maintain troops in the Balkans badly needed elsewhere. The strength of the Yugoslav effort, however, was sapped by bitter factionalism that frequently flared into open civil war between the rival guerrilla forces. The Chetniks, led by Gen. Draja Mikhailovitch, numbered about 25,000 men and supported King Peter. They were sworn enemies of the partisan armies of Gen. Josip Brozovich, or Broz, known as Drug (Comrade) Tito, who rejected Peter. The partisans numbered upwards of 150,000 troops, were reported to be far more effective as a military force and carried the brunt of the fighting against the axis armies.

After the Allied invasion of Italy was underway, an Allied military mission went to Yugoslavia and served at the headquarters of both Tito and Mikhailovitch. Their purpose was to co-ordinate Yugoslav guerrilla activities with Allied strategy. At that time, the partisan armies were swarming through the Dalmatian coast. By the end of September they had occupied the key ports of Split, Susak and Senj and were launching fierce attacks on Trieste, Fiume and Dubrovnik. The German-Croat-

Ustachi garrisons sent out frantic appeals for help; the nazi high command responded by rushing four divisions to the threatened areas to stave off the partisan blows. By Oct. 1 the Yugoslav partisans were battling the German troops over a wide front. Tito's forces slashed into the outskirts of Trieste, encircled Zagreb, disarmed the Italian garrison at Fiume and engaged German armies at Split and Susak. The partisans, however, ran short of ammunition and subsequently evacuated Split, Fiume and Susak. As a result of the widespread guerrilla raids, the Germans were required to exert nearly as great an effort against the Yugoslavs as against the Allies in Italy. Twenty-one divisions, 12 German and 9 Bulgarian, were engaged against the Tito forces who threatened to overrun Yugoslavia's main east-west communication line.

Toward the end of October, a German offensive against Marshal Tito's armies was underway. By Dec. 1943 Marshal Tito's units had lost most of their Adriatic coastline to Marshal Rommel, who had been given command of the Yugoslav as well as the north Italy front. The partisan front in Dalmatia dissolved under the superior firepower of the nazi panzers and most of the guerrillas fell back to the interior. Deep inland there was no front line, and the war was made up largely of swift guerrilla actions by partisan bands.

Marshal Tito's greatest handicap was lack of sufficient ammunition to fight a long, pitched battle. Frequently his armies were compelled to withdraw from engagements nearly won because their bullets had run out. The partisans had few tanks, little artillery and no anti-tank or anti-aircraft guns. On many occasions they refrained from occupying cities because they lacked means to defend them from German bombers.

Guerrilla forces were also active in Greece, but again deep-seated political quarrels between democratic elements and royalists caused internecine strife and sapped the strength of the Greek guerrilla bands. As in Yugoslavia, periodic outbursts of civil war flared between the two factions and prevented establishment of a cohesive anti-axis front. The E.D.E.S. (Greek National Democratic army) fought spirited battles against a rival guerrilla army, the E.L.A.S., directed by the Greek Front of National Liberation. The E.L.A.S. faction charged that the E.D.E.S. group, which leaned toward King George, had attempted to negotiate an armistice with the German occupation authorities. The E.L.A.S., representing elements

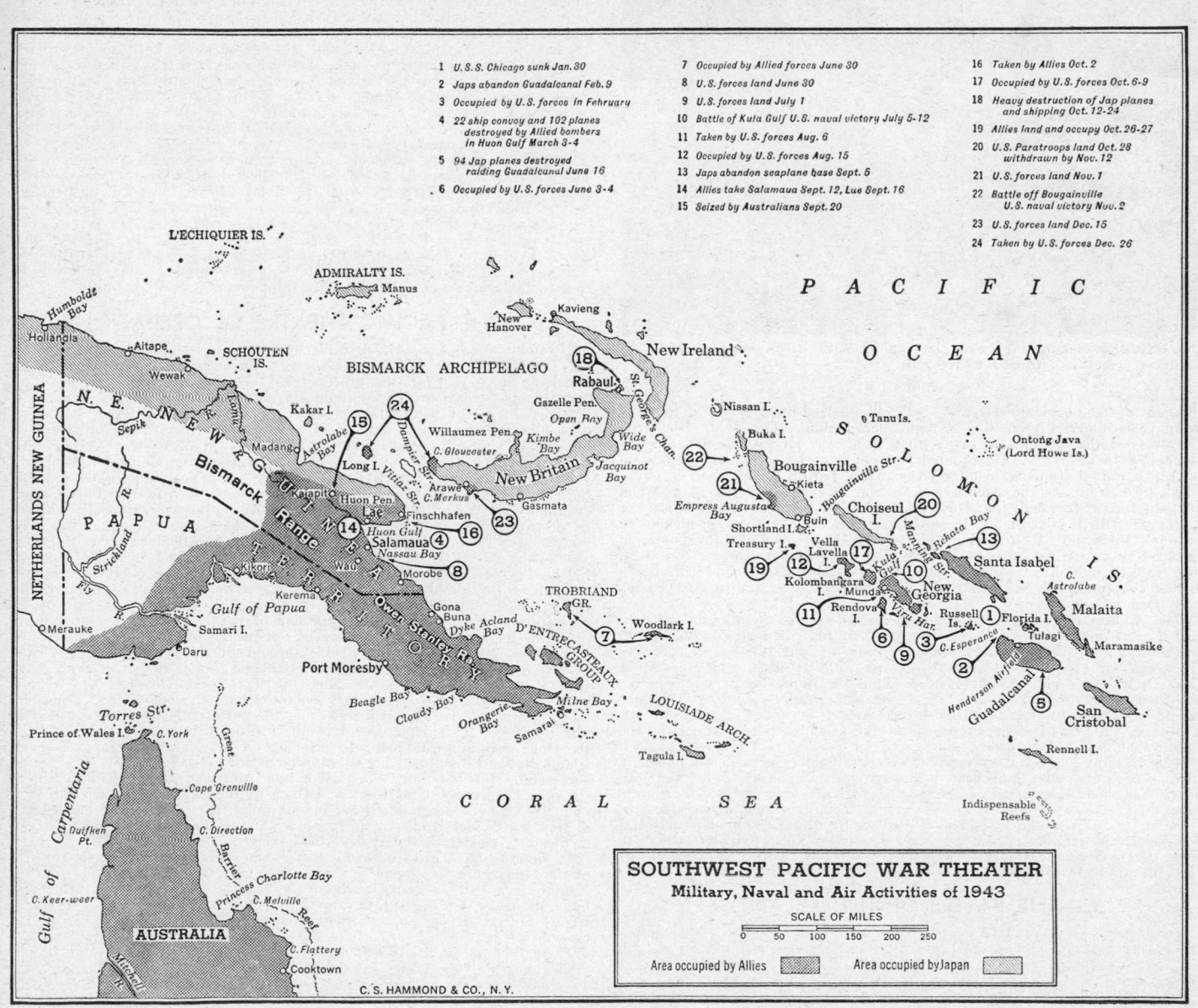

1 U.S.S. Chicago sunk Jan. 30
2 Japs abandon Guadalcanal Feb. 9
3 Occupied by U.S. forces in February
4 22 ship convoy and 102 planes destroyed by Allied bombers in Huon Gulf March 3-4
5 94 Jap planes destroyed raiding Guadalcanal June 16
6 Occupied by U.S. forces June 3-4
7 Occupied by Allied forces June 30
8 U.S. forces land June 30
9 U.S. forces land July 1
10 Battle of Kula Gulf U.S. naval victory July 5-12
11 Taken by U.S. forces Aug. 6
12 Occupied by U.S. forces Aug. 15
13 Japs abandon seaplane base Sept. 5
14 Allies take Salamaua Sept. 12, Lae Sept. 16
15 Seized by Australians Sept. 20
16 Taken by Allies Oct. 2
17 Occupied by U.S. forces Oct. 6-9
18 Heavy destruction of Jap planes and shipping Oct. 12-24
19 Allies land and occupy Oct. 26-27
20 U.S. Paratroops land Oct. 28 withdrawn by Nov. 12
21 U.S. forces land Nov. 1
22 Battle off Bougainville U.S. naval victory Nov. 2
23 U.S. forces land Dec. 15
24 Taken by U.S. forces Dec. 26

SOUTHWEST PACIFIC WAR THEATER
Military, Naval and Air Activities of 1943

SCALE OF MILES
0   50   100   150   200   250

Area occupied by Allies   Area occupied by Japan

C. S. HAMMOND & CO., N.Y.

U.S. TROOPS making the initial landing on Attu island May 11, 1943, as Japanese defenders retreated to the hills

The U-boats were torpedoing and sinking bottoms at such a rapid rate that combined U.S.-British construction in 1942 hardly offset the losses. The situation had become so grave that the U.S. and British governments had clamped an air-tight censorship on news of U-boat sinkings. This "silent" policy was evidently initiated in all good faith to conceal losses from the enemy; at the same time, however, it also prevented public opinion in the United Nations from realizing the gravity of the battle of the Atlantic. Obviously, the entire Allied war effort was in jeopardy. As long as the U-boat could disrupt sea communications at will, the Allies could not launch a full-scale offensive against Hitler's European fortress.

New measures to combat the German undersea raiders were imperative and in March 1943 U.S., British and Canadian officers met in Washington. They overhauled and renovated their anti-submarine campaign, scrapped older and traditional techniques for more modern methods in which air power played a more prominent part. On April 30, 1943, it was disclosed that Canada and Great Britain had been given full responsibility for convoying merchant shipping through the North Atlantic to British ports. Under this plan, U.S. and Canadian long-range bombers provided an air umbrella to an unspecified point somewhere in the mid-Atlantic; at this point British bombers took over and herded the convoys into United Kingdom ports.

This airguard over the full route proved extremely effective. U-boat sinkings, which, according to German high command reports, were 851,000 tons in March, fell to 415,000 tons in April and to 372,000 tons in May. In the month of June the German admiralty admitted that only 107,000 tons of Allied shipping were sunk. At the same time, the destruction of U-boats rose in inverse ratio to the decline in sinkings. The British admiralty announced in May that the number of submarines sunk exceeded output in that month, and in August President Roosevelt and Prime Minister Churchill revealed in a joint statement that axis submarines were sunk at the rate of one a day between May 1 and July 31, 1943.

By the fall and winter of 1943 the U-boat warfare waged by the Germans in the Atlantic was no longer a major problem. The German submarine command, striving to compete with the successful Allied strategy, developed new methods of attack. Anti-aircraft guns were installed on the undersea craft and the Germans used long-range aircraft to spot convoys and aid in concentrating U-boats against them. The new tactics were notable for their failure. On Dec. 9, 1943, Roosevelt and Churchill, in another joint statement, said that the number of U-boats destroyed exceeded the number of ships sunk. They also asserted that Allied merchant ship losses in November were the lowest of any month since May 1940.

One of the newer techniques used in protecting convoys and hunting down the U-boats was the pocket aircraft carrier. Planes based on these "baby flat-tops," officially known as escort carriers, would cruise the area in which a convoy was moving. Radio-telephonic communications enabled the planes to speed to positions where submarines were sighted. The submarine generally would be compelled to go into a crash dive to escape depth charges dropped from the planes. Other factors implementing convoy protection were the employment of destroyer-escorts, long-range patrol aircraft, new detection devices and improved depth charges. Additional factors were Portugal's agreement to let Great Britain use the Azores as a naval and air base, the increase in Russian air strength in the Murmansk area and the steady bombing of German submarine bases, construction yards and factories. (See also SUBMARINE WARFARE.)

VI.—THE PACIFIC THEATRE OF OPERATIONS

1. Introduction.—The Allied drive to reconquer the vast territory in the Pacific lost to Japan in the first six months of the war was well underway in 1943. But the process was slow and arduous. The road to Tokyo was strewn with geographical and logistical obstacles and was defended by a tough and clever army. While the Allied forces had succeeded in reconquering a number of Southwest Pacific islands of strategic importance, the Japanese still held Burma, Malaya, the Netherlands Indies, the East China coast and some sections of the Chinese hinterland. Japan's strategy to fight a gruelling delaying action was based on the hope that the Allies would tire of a protracted war in the Pacific and eventually sue for a negotiated peace. The Allies, however, were determined to destroy Japan, but not until Germany, the stronger of the two axis powers, was beaten first. As a result, the bulk of Allied war material was sent to the European theatre of war and the launching of an all-out assault in the Pacific necessarily had to wait upon completion of the European campaign. But despite the limitations placed on their offensive power in the far east, the Allies appeared to have achieved both air and naval superiority over the Japanese by the end of 1943. These two factors were of major importance and were largely responsible for the success of Allied amphibious operations in the Pacific throughout the year.

2. New Guinea.—A huge mountainous and jungle-ridden island, New Guinea was an important war zone in 1943. Gen. Douglas MacArthur, who was in command of military operations on the island, had launched an offensive to drive the Japanese from the northern coast of New Guinea. His purpose was to win control of the strategically situated coastline on the Huon gulf, and establish a base for operations against the Japanese-held island of New Britain. This drive, which had started in Sept. 1942, was successful. Jungle-trained Australian and American troops had captured the beachhead outposts of Buna and Gona by the end of 1942. On Jan. 22, 1943, the Allied forces seized Sanananda point, thus closing the first phase of the New Guinea campaign in which a Japanese army estimated at 15,000 men was virtually annihilated. Allied casualties were approximately half that figure. As the capture of Sanananda point perilled their control of the Huon gulf, the Japanese strove to redress their weakened position in New Guinea. In February a dozen Japanese troop transports, protected by a destroyer flotilla, sailed into the Bismarck sea, presumably to land troops on the Huon gulf. Allied scouting planes, however, sighted the convoy as it sneaked along the New Britain coast and a huge force of Allied bombers intercepted it. After a spectacular battle, the Allied planes destroyed the entire Japanese convoy, consisting of 10 warships and 12 transports. Some 15,000 Japanese aboard the vessels met their death by drowning or by the murderous strafing from the Allied planes. The

further to the political left, were believed pledged to a policy of ousting King George and establishing a republican regime. The fighting between the two bands became so bitter that Gen. Sir Henry M. Wilson was compelled to intervene. He ordered both sides to cease quarrelling and to present a united front against the German occupation forces.

A third front in the Mediterranean was opened in Sept. 1943, when British forces invaded the Dodecanese islands strung off the coast of Turkey. Allied control of these islands in the Aegean threatened to outflank the vaunted "iron ring" of German defenses in the Balkans from the east as the Allied invasion in Italy had outflanked them from the west. The initial British invasion efforts were successful and on Sept. 21 a British communiqué said that the key isles of Cos, Leros and Samos had been won.

The wehrmacht, however, was determined to reconquer the islands, which were far closer to German bases than to Allied supply sources in the middle east. The Dodecanese were only 50 and 100 mi. respectively from German-held Rhodes and Crete, but were at least 350 mi. distant from Cyprus, the closest British base. Thus the islands were within radius of German fighter planes but far beyond the radius of British fighter strength. Furthermore, the British occupation depended largely on the willingness of the Italian garrisons on the islands to participate in the fighting against their former allies.

The Italians, however, refused to co-operate and surrendered passively to the Germans who launched their counterattack on Oct. 3, 1943. In operations bearing a striking similarity to the successful nazi airborne invasion of Crete in May 1941, German parachutists and airborne troops, covered by aircraft and warships, landed on the three disputed islands and completely reconquered them by Nov. 22, 1943. The British attempt to seize the Dodecanese was criticized as a foolhardy venture in view of the fact that the air force was not able to give close support to the landing troops.

V.—THE BATTLE OF THE ATLANTIC

In early 1943 the U-boat campaign against Allied merchantmen plying the North Atlantic had reached a crisis. The German "wolf packs" were inflicting enormous losses on United Nations shipping and the Allies apparently were powerless to prevent it. Hitler's undersea raiders had sunk an average of 1,000,000 gross tons of shipping a month in 1942.

battle of the Bismarck sea, March 2-5, was a decisive victory of land-based aeroplanes over warships and crushed the Japanese hopes of re-conquering the Huon gulf area.

These successes in New Guinea and similar victories in the Solomons gave the Allies new springboards from which to launch new attacks on the Japanese bases in the Southwest Pacific. On June 30, 1943, the Allies opened a major offensive in both New Guinea and the Solomons to extend their grip on the arc-shaped island chain circling Australia's north coast. In New Guinea an Allied amphibious force landed at Nassau bay in an offensive aimed at Salamaua and Lae. Two months later another amphibious unit landed in the rear of both of these bases, completely isolating the Japanese garrison in this area. The Allied troops then systematically chopped up the trapped enemy forces and captured Salamaua, Sept. 12 and Lae, Sept. 16.

Occupation of these key bases enabled MacArthur to widen the target area of his fighter-planes and to give better air cover to his troops advancing up New Guinea's northern shoreline. Meanwhile, medium and long-range bombers intensified their attacks on the New Guinea bases of Finschhafen and Sattelberg. Land troops, moving steadily forward against bases shattered by Allied air blows, occupied Finschhafen, Oct. 2, and captured Sattelberg village, Nov. 26. The elimination of the scattered Japanese outposts in this New Guinea area enabled the Allied air forces to focus all their attention on the Japanese base of Rabaul, second in importance to Truk. MacArthur's next move was to neutralize Rabaul and air power was the weapon selected to accomplish this task. The air offensive against Rabaul and the neighbouring airfields and bases at Arawe, Gasmata and Cape Gloucester was launched in the autumn of 1943. Rabaul was pounded remorselessly; when it was adequately "softened," U.S. army troops invaded the southwest coast of New Britain Island on Dec. 15, 1943, and occupied the village of Arawe and its adjacent airfields after a few days of hard battle. Ten days later a detachment of U.S. marines landed in the Cape Gloucester area of New Britain on the island's northwestern tip. By the end of the year, the U.S. forces were pressing a hard drive to exterminate Japanese resistance on the island and to capture Rabaul.

3. The Solomon Islands.—The nip-and-tuck battle for control of the Solomons, a typical South Sea cluster of coral reefs and dank malaria-ridden islands, resolved itself in the favour of the American forces in 1943. After the decisive defeat of the Japanese naval forces in the battle of the Solomons in Nov. 1942, the U.S. regular army troops and marines drove the Japanese from Henderson field on Guadalcanal. By Feb. 10, 1943, the Americans had completely cleared the island of Japanese and the arduous six-month campaign had ended in a victory for U.S. arms.

After the Guadalcanal campaign, the Allied commanders, Gen. MacArthur and Admiral William F. Halsey, commander of Allied armed forces in the South Pacific, decided on a co-ordinated drive from both New Guinea and the Solomons. Their goal was to reduce the fortified enemy zones that protected the Japanese base at Rabaul. These zones consisted mostly of airfields located at strategic sites on both fronts and their destruction was imperative for the safety of an Allied offensive. This new double-barrelled offensive was opened June 30, 1943, four months after the conquest of Guadalcanal. While Gen. MacArthur's men pressed forward on the New Guinea coast, the troops under Adm. Halsey's command invaded new island groups in the Solomons north of Guadalcanal. The Americans quickly seized Trobriand and Woodlark Islands, wiped out the Japanese garrison on Rendova and then crossed the narrow water

gap to land on nearby New Georgia Island where they established secure bridgeheads under protection of a barrage from shore and naval guns.

The battle for New Georgia followed closely the pattern of the fighting for Guadalcanal. The Japanese fleet attempted to block the American landing forces but was soundly thrashed in the two battles of Kula gulf, July 6 and 12. Japanese resistance was stubborn in the initial phases of the New Georgia campaign, but weakened under the constant pressure brought to bear by the attacking forces. By Aug. 5 the Americans had won the coveted Munda air strip and by Aug. 26 all organized resistance on New Georgia had ended. Meanwhile, U.S. forces clamped a tight air and sea blockade around another island cluster—Arundel, Kolombangara, Vella Lavella and Santa Isabel—and cleared out all enemy troops by Oct. 15.

After the conquest of the central Solomons, Adm. Halsey lost no time invading the northern Solomons, where the remainder of Japanese strength was concentrated, and on Oct. 27, U.S. marines landed on tiny Mono and Stirling islands in the Treasury group. The following day, a larger force invaded Choiseul, but the Japanese withdrew rapidly without giving battle. The Choiseul landing set the stage for a larger operation, the invasion of Bougainville, where the Japanese at one time reportedly had a garrison of 40,000 men. On Oct. 31, a force of U.S. marines landed at Empress Augusta bay on Bougainville and were solidly entrenched on the island, and moved inland. By Feb. 15, 1944, the Allies had taken the Green Islands at the northern tip of Bougainville and started mopping-up operations against the 22,000 Japanese isolated in the central Solomons.

4. The Pacific Islands.—The success of the combined operations in New Guinea and the Solomons facilitated the next step in the Allied offensive in the Pacific—the flanking of Truk Island, Japan's major naval base in the South Pacific. The hub and heart of a concentric system of island bases, Truk was the Japanese equivalent of Pearl Harbor. A powerfully defended bastion, it guarded the Pacific lanes to the Japanese mainland. Its destruction was imperative as long as the Allies clung to the strategy of island-by-island conquest.

The drive to wrest the mid-Pacific islands from the Japanese had small beginnings. It started with the landing of U.S. troops on Funafuti, an Ellice island, in early 1943. This move brought U.S. bombers closer to the Japanese-held outposts in the Gilbert, Marshall and Caroline Islands. After a long softening process by bombers and warships had battered the Japanese defenses, U.S. marines and army troops invaded the Makin, Tarawa and Abemama atolls in the Gilberts, Nov. 20, 1943. Makin and Abemama fell easily to the attacking forces but Tarawa proved to be the costliest victory in the history of the U.S. marines. Of the several battalions that had to cross the exposed reefs in the initial assault on Tarawa, few survived the deadly Japanese fire. The attackers eventually gained the beach and annihilated the Japanese garrison estimated at between 4,000 and 5,000 men. The three islands were won by Nov. 23, the conquest of Tarawa cost the marines 1,026 dead and 2,557 wounded. U.S. losses on Makin were 65 dead and 121 wounded; on Abemama, 1 dead and 2 wounded.

Striking a little more than two months after the capture of the Gilberts, a powerful army and marine force of 30,000 men invaded the Marshall Islands on Jan. 31. A far larger operation than the Gilberts, the invasion of the Marshalls was also more expertly handled. The U.S. troops had won the Kwajalein atoll in less than a week and had inflicted losses of 8,122 dead and 264 captured on the Japanese; U.S. losses in Kwajalein were only 286 killed, 82 missing and 1,148 wounded.

5. Burma.—The reconquest of Burma ranked high in Allied war plans in early 1943. Its recapture was vital if the United Nations were to accomplish their task of shipping war materials to Chinese armies in

U.S. MARINES preparing to attack Japanese positions from their bitterly-won beachhead at Tarawa. The 76-hour battle for this coral atoll in the Gilberts in Nov. 1943 was the bloodiest in the history of the marine corps

UNLOADING SUPPLIES from a U.S. naval LCI (foreground) and LST (background) at Lae, New Guinea, in Sept. 1943

quantities large enough to permit them to mount a large-scale offensive against the Japanese. But several factors militated against early realization of the Allied plans. First and foremost was the lack of sufficient offensive power of British troops stationed on the western Burma frontiers and of Chinese forces strung along the Salween river sector in northern Burma. Second, was Allied unwillingness to risk opening a new front which would consume more war supplies than could be spared while preparations were underway to launch a second front in Europe. Nevertheless, the thin trickle of supplies that was hitherto allotted this "orphaned" war zone grew into a substantial stream in late 1943 and measures were taken to further speed up the flow of military material to the Burma area. In Sept. 1943 it was revealed that U.S. army engineers had been long at work on a new supply road to China. Officially known as the Ledo road, work on the highway was protected by seasoned Chinese troops and U.S. air forces. Meanwhile, the fighting in the Burma frontier regions was limited to local engagements. Four British attempts to break through Japanese defenses on the tip of the Mayu peninsula ended in failure, and in north Burma, the Japanese neutralized the Chinese troops in the Salween river sector from mounting an offensive for a southward drive.

6. China.—There was little change in the Chinese battlefronts in 1943. The Japanese attacked frequently, the Chinese counterattacked just as often and each side claimed to have inflicted heavy casualties on the other. But under the ebb and flow of battle, two facts emerged clearly: (1) the Chinese armies were still woefully weak in arms and war supplies and lacked the power for a sustained offensive against the Japanese; and (2) the Japanese, heavily committed in holding their conquests in the Southwest Pacific, were primarily interested in holding their gains and in exploiting the economic wealth of the Chinese territory they had conquered. As the Japanese armies in China were large and well-armed, they were enabled largely to realize this goal. Acting on the military maxim that the best defense is an offense, the Japanese launched several drives in China in 1943. Their principal objective was to prevent the Chinese from massing for large-scale action and to devastate the principal rice-growing areas. In the case of the Japanese push toward Yunnan, the Japanese hoped to prevent effective Chinese concentration for an attack on Burma. In the major drives south of the Yangtze river, the Japanese aim was to keep China on the edge of starvation by devastating the "rice bowl." This fertile rice-producing area, around Lake Tung-ting, produces an annual surplus of 650,000 tons of rice. Without the crops harvested from the rice bowl, Free China would cease to exist. The Japanese opened a drive toward Lake Tung-ting in Feb. 1943. By March they had occupied important trading centres, burned granaries and interfered with planting. After a temporary setback in June, the Japanese resumed their destructive raids and again devastated large rice-growing regions.

In early November the Japanese launched another drive into the rice bowl. This offensive reached its climax in the struggle for Changteh, which the Japanese occupied Dec. 3, and then relinquished after several days of bloody fighting. In their retreat from Changteh, the Japanese systematically looted warehouses where the new rice crop had been stored and burned what grain they could not carry away with them. By the end of the year the Japanese had been cleared out of the rice bowl but not before they had accomplished their aim of destroying large quantities of rice needed to feed Free China.

7. The Aleutians.—As the U.S. was too heavily involved in war theatres scattered throughout the globe in the summer of 1942, no serious effort was made to dislodge the Japanese from their positions in the Aleutian chain of islands straddling the Bering sea. In 1943, however, the U.S. industrial machine was turning out war weapons in great quantities and the American high command decided to oust the Japanese from their Aleutian foothold. Strong forces were organized in the inner chain

of the Aleutian Islands and on Jan. 12, 1943, the U.S. opened its Aleutian offensive with the occupation of Amchitka Island, only 70 flying miles from Japanese-occupied Kiska. Step no. 2 in the American offensive was the invasion by American ground forces of rocky Attu Island, May 11. After 19 days of battling fierce blizzards and determined Japanese resistance, the Americans won the island, annihilating the entire Japanese garrison, save for a few prisoners, by May 30. American planes and warships then softened Kiska, the largest and most important island held by the Japanese, with furious air and naval bombardments and on Aug. 15, a strong force of American and Canadian troops landed on Kiska. They met no opposition as all the Japanese had evacuated the island some time before rather than run the risk of annihilation.

(*See also* ADVERTISING; AGRICULTURE; AIR FORCES OF THE WORLD; ARCHITECTURE; BANKING; BUSINESS REVIEW; CHILD WELFARE; CRIME; DEATH STATISTICS; EDUCATION; EXCHANGE CONTROL AND EXCHANGE RATES; HISPANIC AMERICA AND WORLD WAR II; HOSPITALS; INTERNATIONAL LAW; INTERNATIONAL TRADE; IRON AND STEEL; MEDICINE; MINERAL AND METAL PRODUCTION AND PRICES; MUNITIONS OF WAR; NAVIES OF THE WORLD; NEWSPAPERS AND MAGAZINES; PACIFISM; POLICE; RAILROADS; REHABILITATION AND OCCUPATIONAL THERAPY FOR WOUNDED SOLDIERS; STRATEGIC MINERAL SUPPLIES; SUBMARINE WARFARE; WAR PRODUCTION, U.S. *See also* various countries.)

BIBLIOGRAPHY.—Antonin Basch, *The Danube Basin and the German Economic Sphere* (1943); William Henry Chamberlin, *The Russian Enigma* (1943); Hawthorne Daniel, *Islands of the Pacific* (1943); Edward Mead Earle, ed., *Makers of Modern Strategy* (1943); L. de Jong and Joseph F. W. Stoppelman, *The Lion Rampant* (1943); G. E. Hubbard, *British Far Eastern Policy* (1943); Walter Kerr, *The Russian Army* (1943); Herbert Matthews, *The Fruits of Fascism* (1943); Michael Padev, *Escape from the Balkans* (1943); Gaetano Salvemini and George La Piana, *What to Do with Italy* (1943); Jan Christiaan Smuts, *Toward a Better World* (1943); *Target: Germany*—the Army Air Forces' Official Story of the 8th Bomber Command's First Year Over Europe (1943); Lord Vansittart, *Lessons of My Life* (1943); Camille Cianfarra, *The Vatican and the War* (1944); Robert Goffin, *The White Brigade* (1944); Boris Skomorovsky and E. G. Morris, *The Siege of Leningrad* (1944); Jacques Stern, *The French Colonies* (1944).   (D. Ko.)

WPA: *see* FEDERAL WORKS AGENCY.

WPB: *see* WAR PRODUCTION BOARD.

WRA: *see* WAR RELOCATION AUTHORITY.

Wrestling. With the national intercollegiate wrestling championship called off because of the war, interest in amateur wrestling in 1943 centred in the annual A.A.U. championships at New York. The host, West Side Y.M.C.A., won the team title for the third time in four years, followed closely by Cornell (Ia.) college and Michigan State college. Cornell's three-man team scored 13 points to tie Michigan State for runner-up honours. New champions were crowned in all weight divisions, although several 1942 titlists, including Douglas Lee of the Baltimore Y. and Merle Jennings of Michigan State, were successful in heavier weight divisions. After being dethroned from the 191-lb. title in 1942, Henry Wittenberg regained his third championship in this division during 1943.   (M. P. W.)

WSA: *see* War Shipping Administration.
"W. W.": *see* Jacobs, William Wymark.

Wyoming. A Rocky mountain state, admitted to the union July 10, 1890, as the 44th state. Leadership in the extension of rights to women gave it the name "Equality state." Land area, 97,506 sq.mi.; water area, 408 sq.mi.; pop. (1940) 250,742. The rural population was 157,165; urban, 93,577; 229,-818 native white; 950 Negro; 17,107 foreign born. Capital, Cheyenne (22,474). Other cities of 10,000 or more: Casper (17,-964); Laramie (10,627); Sheridan (10,529).

History.—State officials in 1943 were: governor, Lester C. Hunt (D.); secretary of state, Mart T. Christensen (R.); auditor, William Jack (D.); treasurer, Earl Wright (R.); superintendent of public instruction, Esther Anderson (R.). In the general election of 1942, 30,771 Republican and 23,684 Democratic votes were cast. Wyoming supreme court justices in 1943 were: Ralph Kimball (R.), chief justice; Fred H. Blume (R.) and William A. Riner (R), associate justices.

Education.—In the 1942–43 school year there were 675 elementary schools, with an enrolment of 37,780 and with 1,725 teachers. The total salary for elementary teachers was $1,925,-912.02. There were 86 high schools and 28 permit high schools (2 years only) with an enrolment of 12,670 students and with 813 high school teachers. The high school teachers' salaries totalled $1,131,373.53.

Public Welfare, Charities, Correction.—The state department of public welfare reported the following estimate of expenditures for 1943: aid to dependent children, $222,810 (5,042 cases); old-age assistance, $1,230,236 (34,335 cases); aid to the blind, $103,976 (122 cases); general relief, $191,737 (568 cases). In 1943 Wyoming had three correctional institutions, one State Training school, one industrial institute for boys and one industrial girls' school. The state board of charities reported the following estimated expenditures for 1943: penitentiary, $333,756 (average of 211 inmates) (this amount also included expenditure for Saratoga Hot Springs and penitentiary farms); industrial boys' school, $65,331 (45 inmates); industrial girls' school, $41,-172 (94 inmates); State Training school, $110,620 (388 inmates); hospital for the insane, $164,112 (673 inmates). Other state institutions and their estimated expenditures for 1943 were: state children's home, $41,236.20; Wyoming general hospital, $177,174; Hot Springs State park, $13,261; tuberculosis sanatorium, $36,-760; soldier's and sailor's home, $29,840.

Communication.—In Nov. 1943, state highways totalled 4,082 mi.; rural highways, 20,012 mi.; railroads, 1,996.20 mi. (main tracks, taxable).

Banking and Finance.—In Nov. 1943 there were 30 state banks with deposits of $37,307,918.90; and resources of $40,589,-589.56. National banks numbered 26, with deposits of $94,975,-753.52, and resources of $101,871,481.04. There were eight insured savings and loan associations in June 1943. Total state receipts for the fiscal year were $15,074,848.30; disbursements, $11,939,162.76; gross bonded debt $2,520.00.

Ranching and Agriculture.—Wyoming livestock products

Table I.—*Leading Ranch and Farm Products of Wyoming, 1943 and 1942*

Product	1943 (est.)	1942
Cattle	947,000	885,000
Sheep	3,781,000	3,934,000
Wool, lb.	33,340,000	33,320,000
Hogs	125,000	84,000
Tame hay, tons	775,000	801,000
Wheat, bu.	3,439,000	4,259,000
Sugar beets, tons	270,000	451,000
Dry beans, cwt.	1,378,000	1,024,000
Corn, bu.	1,243,000	2,013,000
Potatoes, bu.	2,175,000	2,240,000

sold for approximately between $55,000,000 and $60,000,000, in 1943, and farm products were valued at between $10,000,000 and $15,000,000 for the same period.

Manufacturing.—The value of all manufactures, excluding oil refining and dairying, was estimated at $10,000,000 in 1942. No figures for 1943 were available at the end of the year.

Mineral Production.—The total value of Wyoming's principal mineral production in 1943 was estimated at $46,247,392. Petroleum was the principal mineral product. The largest producer among numerous fields was Lance Creek.

Table II.—*Principal Mineral Products of Wyoming, 1943 and 1942*

Mineral	Taxable valuation	
	1943	1942
Petroleum	$26,961,955	$24,642,310
Bituminous coal	16,362,739	13,159,992
Iron	2,722,550	2,804,551
Bentonite	201,149	112,893

(M. H. E.)

X-Ray. The use of the X-ray for diagnosis of protrusion of an intervertebral disk made further advance during 1943. Dandy advocated abolition of the use of contrast solutions in diagnosis of protruded intervertebral disk but this advice is applicable only to cases with typical symptoms. Confirmation of the diagnosis by X-rays made after injection of contrast solutions is considered advisable by most of the experienced surgeons in this field. Air as a contrast is unsatisfactory because of its low diagnostic accuracy.

A new contrast medium called "pantopaque" (ethyl iodophenylundecylate) was described. This is an iodized oil much lighter and less viscid than lipiodol. Because of its fluidity it can be manipulated into any locality within the membranes covering the spine and brain by tilting the patient on the movable horizontal table. Examination of the dorsal and cervical regions is thus facilitated.

The greatest advantage of "pantopaque" is the ease with which it can be withdrawn through the same needle with which it is injected when the diagnostic procedure is finished. There is a further advantage that even if a small amount remains in the spinal canal it disappears after a few weeks, either disseminated in the spinal fluid or possibly absorbed.

Angiocardiography.—Since Robb and Steinberg in 1938 described a method for rendering opaque the heart chambers and large intrathoracic blood-vessels considerable practical advance was made in the clinical use of the method. The conditions in which it was found of value are listed in a review by Weber. They included congenital heart disease, coarctation of the aorta, aneurysm, and various intrathoracic conditions with associated changes in the size and contour of the heart and great vessels. Taylor and Shulman and Steinberg, Grishman and Sussman reported on the use of this method in diagnosis of various heart diseases and Liberson and Liberson published an interesting experimental article on the use of the method to diagnose pulmonary embolism.

The method consists in the intravenous injection, usually into a vein of the arm, of diodrast (3.5 - diiodo -4- pyridone -N-acetic acid and diethanolamine). They used in the average case 35 cc. of a 70% solution of the drug (24.5 gm. of diodrast).

The method appeared to be harmless and doubtless would be increasingly used to aid in the diagnosis of the unusually difficult heart and vascular conditions which older methods failed to make clear.

Cholecystography.—A new contrast medium has recently been devised to replace tetraiodophenolphthalein for gall-bladder study. The name of the substance is priodax (beta-(4-hydroxg-3, 5- diiodophengl)-alpha-phenyl propionic acid). The advantages of priodax over tetraiodophenolphthalein were: 1. It does not contain phenolphthalein and does not act as a cathartic. This assures better absorption since it remains in the intestinal tract for a longer time. 2. It is less toxic. 3. It is almost completely absorbed from the intestinal tract and therefore does not produce opacities which conflict with the gall-bladder shadow. 4. It is easily and simply administered in tablet form. 5. The filling of the gall bladder is better than with other methods because of the complete absorption of the drug from the intestinal tract. (*See* also PHOTOGRAPHY; TUBERCULOSIS.)

BIBLIOGRAPHY.—Harry M. Weber, "The Present Status of Contrast Myelography," *Am. J. Med. Sc.* 206, 687–694 (Nov. 1943); idem "Angiocardiography," *Am. J. Med. Sc.* 205, 747–753 (May 1943); M. F. Steinberg, A. Grishman and M. L. Sussman, "Angiocardiography in Congenital Heart Disease. III. Patent Ductus Arteriosus," *Am. J. Roentgenol.* 50, 306–315 (Sept. 1943); Wm. A. Marshall, "Some Observations on Priodax. A New Contrast Medium for Visualization of the Gall-Bladder," *Am. J. Roentgenol.*, 50, 680–682 (Nov. 1943).   (A. C. CH.)

Yachting.

Fewer yachts were racing in 1943 than in 1942, due chiefly to the absence of many owners in the services or war work, but most of the recognized classes of smaller yachts were out and races were scheduled at most yachting localities. As in 1942, few of the larger yachts were out, being either in government service or laid up for the duration, except on the Great Lakes, where restrictions were fewer.

The two chief yachting events on the east coast, Larchmont race week, and the midsummer series at Marblehead, were held as usual, with a good showing in the smaller classes. At Larchmont, which held its 45th annual "week," 546 starts were recorded on the five days of racing, and at Marblehead, cradle of the sport on the New England coast, as many as 130 yachts started on several of the seven days of racing.

While the Star class sailed its chief event, the International championships, only two countries outside the United States were represented, Cuba and Venezuela, and all contestants sailed in boats furnished by the home fleet where the races were sailed, on Great South bay, Long Island. With 19 starters, sailing five races, the championship went to A. M. Deacon, representing Western Long Island sound, with 79 points. W. H. Picken, Jr., Great South Bay fleet, was second with 76 points, and C. de Cardenas, Cuba, third with 74. The Atlantic coast championship in the same class, was won by Horace Havemeyer, in "Gull II." Another important intersectional event was sailed as usual, the Barthel trophy race, representing the crew championship of the Great Lakes. Sailed on Lake St. Clair in 8-metre yachts, between crews representing Lakes Ontario, Erie and Michigan, it was won by the Lake Ontario crew headed by Elmer J. Doyle of Youngstown, N.Y., with Lake Erie second.

The Intercollegiate National Dinghy championship was sailed on Charles River basin, Boston, and was won by the Massachusetts Institute of Technology crew, 152 points, with Harvard second, 145 points. The McMillan trophy race, representing the Intercollegiate championship, sailed in June off Marblehead, was also won by M.I.T. with Harvard second. Other important intersectional championships were those in the Lightning class, sailed off Bay Head, N.J., which was won by Karl Smithers of Buffalo, and the Gulf Yachting association Lipton trophy, sailed in Fish class sloops, which was won by the Southern Yacht club crew with 35 points, Biloxi Yacht club crew second with 31 points.

Long-distance racing, always a popular part of a yachting season, was confined to the Great Lakes in 1943. Here, the two chief events of former years were sailed, the Chicago-Mackinac race of 333 mi. and the Port Huron-Mackinac, on Lake Huron. The former was sailed in two classes, racing and cruising. The Class Q sloop "Gloriant," owned by Vita Thomas, won the Mackinac cup in the racing class, while the sloop "Lassie," W. J. Lawrie, owner, took the Chicago-Mackinac trophy in the cruising division with "Tahuna," J. T. Snite, second.

In the somewhat shorter Port Huron-Mackinac race, "Apache," a N.Y.Y.C. 32-ft. class sloop, owned by Wilfred Gmeiner, was first in the racing-cruising class; the 8-metre "Shamrock," sailed by Ernest Grates took the racing class first prize, and in the cruising division, Andrew Langhammer's "Rambler VI" was the winner. All such events on the coasts had to be cancelled on account of war time restrictions.   (H. L. ST.)

Yale University.

An institution of higher education at New Haven, Conn. During 1943 the transfer to a war basis was completed. The army air force technical training command took over a large portion of the university's facilities and established a cadet school with an enrolment averaging 3,000. A navy V-12 program began July 1, with 1,500 undergraduates enrolled. At the same time, the army specialized training program was instituted with about 850 men, later increased to 1,500. After July 1943, except for certain students deferred as civilians for special essential training, or in 4-F, there were no undergraduates at Yale over 18 who were not in uniform. Yale was selected by the army for engineering, medical, and area and language training, the latter covering Japanese, Burmese, Chinese, Malay, Russian and Italian; advanced work was given for medical students, the military intelligence section and the civil affairs specialists training school. For the navy, courses were given in engineering and medicine, as well as in various basic studies.

Several committees in postwar planning were set up, and the research activities of the Institute of International Studies were expanded. Eight graduate fellowships of $2,500 a year each were established for advanced studies in the liberal arts.

Laboratory research was devoted to the war effort in many fields, including vitamin production, food dehydration, aeronautics, military clothing, high-altitude physiology and marine food resources. Among important acquisitions by the Yale library was the William Robertson Coe collection of Western Americana. The Yale Art gallery received the Maitland Griggs collection of early Italian paintings. For statistics of faculty, enrolment, endowment, etc., *see* UNIVERSITIES AND COLLEGES.

Yamamoto, Isoroku

(1884–1943), Japanese naval officer, was born April 4 at Nagaoka, Japan. He was graduated from the naval academy in 1904 and fought as an ensign in the Russo-Japanese war. He was naval attaché in the Japanese embassy in Washington, 1925. As Japanese delegate at the London naval conference in 1934–35, he successfully fought the Anglo-American proposal to extend the naval "holiday." Yamamoto thereafter won rapid promotion. Foremost Japanese advocate of combining air and sea power in naval attacks, he was promoted to commander-in-chief of the fleet in 1939. Referring to the Japanese surprise attack on Pearl Harbor, Domei (Japanese) news agency revealed in a dispatch on Dec. 17, 1941, that the strategy of surprise carried out by Adm. Yamamoto was planned by him earlier.

A Tokyo radio report announced that he had been mortally injured in action while directing naval operations from a plane on a "far southern front," in April 1943, and that he had died shortly afterwards. The fact that no major engagements had taken place in that theatre of operations during the month cast doubt on the Japanese reports as to the circumstances surrounding his death. While Yamamoto was on his deathbed, the emperor promoted him to fleet admiral on April 20. He was succeeded by Adm. Mineichi Koga.

Yamashita, Tomoyuki

(? -), Japanese army officer, was a close student of German military tactics. An able strategist, he trained Japanese soldiers in the technique of jungle warfare and conceived the military plan for the Japanese invasion of Malaya, 1941–42. His troops infiltrated the Malayan wilderness as independent units and, aided by native fifth-columnists, successfully marched through narrow jungle roads and paths that the British general staff thought were impenetrable. After a 10-week campaign, Singapore surrendered to Gen. Yamashita on Feb. 15, 1942. On March 9, after the failure of Gen. Masaharu Homma's drive to dislodge the U.S.-Filipino forces from the Bataan peninsula, Gen. Yamashita assumed command of the Philippines campaign. With a numerically superior army and air force, he won the battle of Bataan, April 9 and conquered the Corregidor island fortress, May 6, 1942. On Feb. 10, 1943, the Berlin radio broadcast a Tokyo dispatch that Yamashita, "supreme commander of forces in Malaya," had been promoted from lieutenant general to full general.

Yaroslavsky, Emelyan

(1878?–1943), Russian historian and politician, was one of the original members of the "Old Bolsheviks." He was president of the League of Militant Atheists from its inception in 1927 and waged a ceaseless "educational" war against religion in the U.S.S.R. He was also a member of the Russian Communist party's central executive committee and a deputy of the supreme soviet. After the German invasion of the U.S.S.R. in June 1941, Premier Stalin apparently ordered Yaroslavsky to soft-pedal his campaign so as not to offend Russia's allies, who were deeply concerned over the "Godless" aspect of Russian culture. Yaroslavsky's death was reported in a Moscow broadcast according to newspaper dispatches of Dec. 5.

Yemen: *see* ARABIA.

Yeremenko, Andrei Ivanovitch

(1892–), Russian army officer, was born Oct. 14 in Markova, the Ukraine. Drafted into the imperial Russian army in 1913, he became a corporal in 1914 and saw service in World War I on the eastern front. He became a guerrilla leader after the Brest-Litovsk peace signed by Germany and Russia, joined the red army during the revolution, and rose to the rank of officer in a cavalry unit. After the establishment of the soviet regime, Yeremenko, a student of strategy, attended the high cavalry school, the military-political academy and the Frunze military academy. During World War II, Yeremenko was given command of a field army on the northwest front, 1941–42 and in 1942–43 he was assigned to the Stalingrad front. During the bitter struggle for the Volga city, Yeremenko was wounded seven times and acquitted himself with valour.

He was decorated with the Order of the Red Banner, promoted to the rank of colonel general and in Aug. 1943, was raised to the rank of a full general.

Yersin, Alexandre Émile John

(1863–1943), Swiss bacteriologist, w a s born Sept. 22 at Rougemont, Switzerland. He did notable work on the diphtheria bacillus and diphtheria serum. He also discovered the bubonic plague bacillus and succeeded in making a serum to combat the disease. Since the 1890s, Dr. Yersin lived in the far east where he directed the Pasteur institute at Nhatrang, French Indo-China. He died in French Indo-China according to a Berne dispatch of March 2. (See *Encyclopædia Britannica*.)

Young, Arthur Henry

(1866–1943), U.S. artist and cartoonist, was born Jan. 14 near Orangeville, Stephenson county, Ill. He studied art in Chicago at the Academy of Design, 1884–86, and worked as illustrator and cartoonist for Chicago newspapers, 1884–94. He went to Denver in 1895, was co-editor of the *Masses*, 1911–19, was Washington correspondent for the *Metropolitan* magazine, 1912–17, and editor and publisher of *Good Morning*, 1919–21. He contributed illustrations and cartoons to many of the nation's best-known magazines and was contributing editor to the *New Masses*, Communist weekly. A talented and brilliant political cartoonist, he took an active part in campaigns for woman suffrage, labour organization, racial equality and abolition of child labour. Among his books are *Trees at Night* (1927), *On My Way* (1928), *Art Young's Inferno* (1933), *The Best of Art Young* (1936) and *Art Young, His Life and Times* (1939). He died in New York city, Dec. 29.

Young Men's Christian Association.

In 1943, Howard A. Coffin became president; Eugene E. Barnett was general secretary. At the end of 1943 there were 1,300 local associations and 1,200,000 members, of whom 60% were under 25, in cities, colleges, high schools, rural areas, railway and industrial centres. War emergency services dominated the program. As a principal agency of the United Service Organizations, the Y.M.C.A. was designated to operate work in 445 communities near military establishments and in 60 overburdened war production centres. Y.M.C.A. personnel were provided for U.S.O. operations in various off-shore bases. American service men in many parts of the world were served by Y.M.C.A. movements of those countries. Work among prisoners of war was continued and enlarged at a cost of about $2,000,000. Some 76 neutral representatives of the World's Committee of Y.M.C.A.'s visited prison camps for conference with camp leaders about prisoners' recreational, educational and religious needs. American co-operation through staff and emergency aid was given to indigenous association movements of Free China, India, Egypt, Palestine, Turkey and Latin America. Local associations in the United States stressed wartime youth needs despite absence of large numbers of members and group leaders in military service. Extensive co-operation was given to local defense efforts and other community organizations. Special physical fitness programs were conducted. Citizenship education for American responsibility for postwar world order was stressed

(O. E. P.)

Young Womens Christian Association.

The regular ongoing program of the Y.W.C.A. in the United States was adapted and expanded in 1943 to meet wartime conditions. As an international Christian women's organization, it was concerned not only with providing war service to women and girls in the United States but also to the many thousands who turn to the Y.W.C.A. in other countries for help. Through the World Emergency and War Victims fund, financial support and personnel was given to those associations to assist in meeting the needs of the women and girls in uniform as well as farm and factory workers; in providing youth centres for children of working mothers; and in the relief and restoration of war victims. Support for the World Emergency and War Victims fund comes in the main from the National War fund and in part from the Church Committee on Overseas Relief and Reconstruction. In the United States, the Y.W.C.A. as a member agency of the United Service Organizations, Inc., was responsible for 239 U.S.O. operations serving men and women in the armed forces and in war production industries. The year 1943 saw also the beginning of another special project, Y.W.C.A. War-Community

Service, organized for the purpose of providing necessary recreational and other facilities for women and girls in over-crowded war industry communities where such facilities do not exist or are inadequate to meet the need. This service was one of six national agency projects comprising American War-Community Services, Inc., and was financed by local war chests.

(M. S. Ss.)

Youth Administration, National: *see* NATIONAL YOUTH ADMINISTRATION.

Youth Movements.
Youth movements, organized efforts at political self-expression of young people, were dominated in 1943 by the universal war effort. In the totalitarian countries, whether communist or fascist, the youth movements continued strictly controlled by the respective governments as instruments of governmental policy. The efforts undertaken in 1942 to organize the youth in the democratic countries and in the axis countries for international action on a large scale were not renewed. The youth movements of the different religious organizations were carried on in the democratic countries, devoting much of their attention to the problems caused by the war and to the organization of the future peace. In fascist countries national youth organizations were formed to which all students must belong, while the world-wide Christian youth organizations like the Y.M.C.A, the Y.W.C.A and the Student Christian movement had been forbidden because of their international connections.

In the United States the newly organized United States Student assembly held its first meeting in May 1943. By its constitution it called itself "a confederation of autonomous democratic student groups, organized democratically and bound together by the common belief that democracy is the only just society." Communist organizations were barred from membership, when the Young Communist league tried to gain admission, because they were "not democratic by their very nature" and on account of their "mercurial foreign policy which changed according to the Moscow weather at any moment." The U.S. Student assembly called for "a dynamic revision of our society to banish political, economic and social insecurity" and for "a new America—not made new by changing our ideals, but by more complete acceptance of them." The assembly regarded itself as the American branch of the International Student assembly. The question of communist participation in democratic youth organizations came up again when the Young Communist league dissolved itself in Oct. 1943 and formed a new organization called "American Youth for Democracy" to unite communist and non-communist youth. The new organization called for an American-Soviet-British coalition, for the opening of a second front and for universal, obligatory military training for youth after the war. The democratic youth, however, did not join and regarded the formation of the new organization as an attempt of the communists to confuse the issues. (*See* also CATHOLIC ORGANIZATIONS FOR YOUTH.)   (H. Ko.)

Yugoslavia.
A kingdom in southeastern Europe, partitioned as a result of German aggression in 1941. Area 95,576 sq.mi.; pop. (est. Jan. 1, 1940) 15,703,000. Capital: Belgrade (266,849). Other chief cities: Zagreb (185,581); Subotica (100,058); Ljubljana (79,056); Sarajevo (78,173). Religion: 6,785,501 Greek Orthodox; 5,217,910 Roman Catholic; 1,561,166 Mohammedans; 231,169 Protestants; 68,405 Jews. King: Peter II; prime minister (1943): Bozhidar Puritch.

History.—The situation in Yugoslavia continued throughout 1943 in a troubled state, further complicated by the collapse of Italy. The unrest and bitterness produced by the occupation of

Yugoslavia was also much increased by the internal struggle among the Yugoslavs themselves. This disunity had two aspects, often so interconnected that it was difficult to gain a clear picture of the forces and trends at work. There was first the resistance movement against the armies of occupation, especially the German and (until Sept.) the Italian armies. This movement was, however, divided into two camps violently hostile to each other and often in bitter armed conflict. One of these patriot armies, the Chetniks, was led by General Draja Mikhailovitch, minister of war in the Yugoslav cabinet. The other, generally called the Partisans, was led by General Tito, a Croat communist, whose real name was Josip Brozovich. The forces of Mikhailovitch represented mainly the Serb army and guerrillas, while those of Tito included Serbs, Croats and Slovenes and were of a more leftist political conviction, often representing an agrarian communism, yet accepting in their ranks men of all parties and classes, peasants, workers, intellectuals, officers and priests. For some time it seemed as if Tito's forces were supported by soviet Russia while the United States and Britain supported the forces of Mikhailovitch.

The Yugoslav government in London, recognized as one of the United Nations, reflected during 1943 the internal tensions of the homeland and was frequently reorganized. On Jan. 2 a new cabinet was formed in which Professor Slobodan Yovanovitch was not only prime minister but also minister of the interior and of foreign affairs. The cabinet resigned on June 17 because it was unable to define a satisfactory postwar policy. On June 26 a new cabinet was formed with Milosh Trifunovitch, deputy leader of the Serb radical party, as prime minister and Milan Grol, leader of the Serbian democratic party, as minister of foreign affairs. In a broadcast on June 28, a national holiday of the Serbs, King Peter promised his people that after their liberation they would be free "to decide on their own fate in conformity with the principles of democracy."

As a result of Serb-Croat tension the cabinet of Trifunovitch resigned on Aug. 10 and was followed by a cabinet with Dr. Bozhidar Puritch, a Serb diplomat, as prime minister. The Yugoslav government transferred its seat at the beginning of October from London to Cairo. From there on Oct. 7 King Peter called on his people to "obey Mikhailovitch and other national leaders of your resistance to the enemy and refrain from internal struggle." Thereby the king recognized officially the existence of other liberation movements especially that of Tito. On Oct. 16 the Yugoslav government was broadened by the inclusion of three new members, two Croats and one Slovene.

Meanwhile the struggle in Yugoslavia went on. The patriotic armies were able to wrest important territory from German control and at times many important cities in Dalmatia and Bosnia were entirely under patriot control. But the attempts of creating a united front of the patriots failed.

At the beginning of the summer of 1943 the British government established military liaison with the Yugoslav partisans under Tito, according to an official statement of the British general headquarters for the middle east on July 21. The British were already in liaison with the forces of Mikhailovitch. In mid-September the Partisans controlled Fiume and Spalato on the Adriatic coast but soon they were forced out by superior German forces. They had seized some of the equipment of the Italians, but it was in no way sufficient to allow them major operations against the German army.

On Dec. 4 the Partisan movement announced that it had set up a provisional regime in opposition to the existing Yugoslav government in exile. It was reported that 140 delegates had created a parliament and government for the territory already won back from the Germans. Dr. Ivan Ribar, first president of the constitutional assembly of Yugoslavia after World War I, was elected head of the government, and General Tito was named fieldmarshal and chairman of the committee for national defense. A regular cabinet was formed, the three vice-presidents being respectively a Serb, a Croat and a Slovene. In the British parliament it was disclosed officially on Dec. 8 that the larger part of British supplies and arms sent to Yugoslavia had been going for some time to Tito's forces. On Dec. 14 Foreign Secretary Anthony Eden announced that the British military mission was headed by Fitzroy Maclean, a former member of the British foreign office. The soviet government followed the British example and announced on Dec. 14 that it would also send a military mission to Yugoslavia.

By the end of Dec. 1943, the hostility between Tito's Partisans and the government in exile which had supported Gen. Mikhailovitch took on more and more violent form. Tito's council issued a manifesto depriving the government in exile of all rights and accusing Mikhailovitch openly of a hostile attitude and of organizing civil strife. The government in exile denied these charges and maintained the legitimacy of its position. (H. Ko.)

Yukon Territory. Yukon Territory lies in the extreme northwest of continental Canada, bounded by Alaska, British Columbia, the Northwest Territories and the Arctic ocean. Area, 207,076 sq.mi.; pop. (1941) 4,914. Seat of government, Dawson. Local administration is in the hands of a territorial legislative council composed of three members elected triennially, and a controller. The Yukon is represented at Ottawa by one member in the house of commons. From June to October, steamships ply regularly from White Horse to Dawson.

The chief industry is mining, followed by fur trading and fishing. For the first nine months of 1943, gold production shrank to 30,111 oz., as compared with 53,137 oz. produced in the same period of 1942. The fur haul in 1941–42 represented a value of $398,132 as compared with a value of $373,399 for 1940–41. The fishing catch for 1942 was valued at $3,056. With the completion of the Alaska highway, the Yukon was brought into direct communication with the rest of the dominion. Communications within the territory are maintained chiefly by plane, and, during the season of navigation, by steamship. A railway from White Horse to Skagway (Alaska) gives access to the Pacific. (J. I. C.)

Zanzibar and Pemba: see BRITISH EAST AFRICA.

Zeeman, Pieter (1865–1943), Netherlands physicist, was born May 25 at Zonnemaire, Zeeland. The discoverer of the Zeeman effect, a phenomena produced in spectroscopy, and winner of the Nobel prize in 1902 he died in Amsterdam, Oct. 9, according to a broadcast from a German-controlled Netherlands station. (See *Encyclopædia Britannica*.)

Zeitzler, Kurt (1895–), German army officer, was born in Luckau, Brandenburg, Germany. He volunteered in World War I and served as infantry lieutenant, resigning his commission after the armistice. He rejoined the reichswehr in 1926 as a captain, became a major in 1934, a colonel in 1935, a major general early in 1942 and then a full general. He commanded an infantry unit during the Polish campaign in Sept. 1939, and was chief of staff to Gen. Von Kleist during the Battle of France, May–June 1940. He was also chief of staff to Gen. Von Rundstedt on the French invasion coast in 1942. In the winter of 1942 Zeitzler was made chief of the German general staff, replacing Gen. Franz Halder. During 1943 he was at some of Hitler's conferences, including one in January with the Rumanian premier, Antonescu, and a meeting with Mussolini in April.

Zhukov, Georgi Konstantinovich (? –), Russian army officer, joined the Russian imperial army as a private in 1915. After the revolution, he attended the Frunze military academy, where he received his military training under Gen. Boris Shaposhnikov, crack soviet strategist. He was named chief of the red army general staff and vice-commissar for defense, Feb. 1941. During the nazi drive on Moscow in the fall of 1941, Zhukov was given command of the capital's defense forces on Oct. 23, replacing Gen. Timoshenko, who was sent to the southern front. The German offensive at one time reached a point some 20 miles from Moscow, but there Russian armies held fast. Zhukov's armies launched a series of counterattacks; in December, German defenses cracked under the hammering Russian blows, and Hitler's armies fell back on nearly all sectors of the immense Moscow front. There he directed the counteroffensive at Stalingrad, for which he later received Stalin's personal congratulations. He did not remain to direct the last steps, however, for early in Jan. 1943 he was sent to Moscow to co-ordinate the forces for raising the siege of Leningrad. The siege was lifted Jan. 18, and on Jan. 29 Zhukov was awarded the Order of Suvorov, first degree, for his part in the campaign.

Zinc. Production figures for zinc after 1940 were received only from the United States, so that no data for 1941 and 1942 can be added to the world table.

World Production of Zinc
(In thousands of metric tons)

	1929	1937	1938	1939	1940
Australia	50.8	70.9	70.9	70.8	85.0
Belgium	197.9	225.6	210.4	185.7	65.0
Canada	78.1	143.9	155.7	161.8	180.0
France	91.6	60.4	62.2	60.3	35.0
Germany	102.0	163.3	192.5	212.3	225.0
Norway	6.4	41.3	46.5	45.0	20.0
Poland	169.0	109.3	110.8	117.9	160.0
U.S.S.R.	3.4	70.0	80.0	90.0	95.0
United Kingdom. .	59.2	63.1	56.2	50.4	60.0
United States . .	573.0	534.9	414.6	488.3	657.0
World Total . .	1,472.8	1,667.9	1,589.7	1,678.1	1,732.0
Ex. U.S.	899.8	1,133.0	1,175.1	1,189.8	1,148.0

The recoverable metal content of zinc ores mined in the United States increased from 749,125 short tons in 1941 to 760,210 tons in 1942, an increase of only slightly over 1%. Increases of output in Colorado, Missouri, New Mexico, New York, Idaho, Tennessee, Utah and five other states with minor changes totalled 68,946 tons; this was largely offset by decreases totalling 57,851 tons in Oklahoma, Kansas, Montana, Virginia, Nevada and three other states. In each list, the states are arranged in decreasing order of the magnitude of the tonnage change. In the tri-state district of Oklahoma, Kansas and southwest Missouri, the largest producing area, 8,513,000 tons of ore and 9,921,000 tons of tailings represented an increase of 6% in the tonnage treated during the year, but a decline in yield resulted in a drop of zinc produced from 258,837 tons in 1941 to 236,965 tons in 1942.

During 1942 and 1943 censorship prevented the publication of smelter output, but this restriction was removed in Dec. 1943. The smelter output in the United States from both domestic and foreign ores was 929,770 short tons in 1942, and 889,656 tons through Nov. 1943. The latter figure is at a rate of 970,512 tons for the year, an improvement of 4% over 1942. The returns for domestic ore in 1943 were not available at the close of the year, but in 1942 there was a drop to 629,957 tons, as compared with 652,599 tons in 1941. Domestic sales increased from 733,918 tons in 1942 to 742,916 tons through Nov. 1943, equivalent to a rate of 810,454 tons for the full year, and a rise of 10% over 1942.

In contrast, export sales dropped heavily, from 151,650 tons in 1942 to only 55,136 tons through Nov. 1943. Total sales in 1943 were at a rate of 870,601 tons, as compared with 885,568 tons in 1941. Stocks had been critically low throughout 1940 and 1941, and up to May 1942. Increased production and decreased sales built the stocks up from a low of 18,477 tons at the end of May 1942, to 65,268 tons at the end of the year, with even better results in 1943, reaching 159,853 tons at the end of November. Although this would be an abnormally high figure for stocks under normal conditions, it represented only about two months' average output under current conditions.

An unofficial report stated that the zinc output of Canada in 1942 was 216,000 short tons, equivalent to 20% of the combined output of the United Nations. (G. A. Ro.)

Zirconium.

No information was made public in the U.S. on zirconium in 1943, beyond the fact that the supply was improved; formerly listed as supply in balance with essential demand, the year closed with a surplus supply. How much of this improvement came from domestic output, and how much from imports, was not known. There were small-scale recoveries of zircon from beach sands in Florida for several years, and more extensive operations were planned. (G. A. Ro.)

Zoology.

The year 1943 saw curtailment of zoological science in some areas of the U.S. and expansion in others. The expansion dealt largely with the teaching of premedical zoology; particularly in those colleges and universities engaged in training army or navy cadets under government contract. Broadly, most of these programs required the teaching of general zoology (botany was included in naval programs but not in army), comparative vertebrate anatomy and vertebrate embryology. The details, of course, differed both between army and navy requirements as well as between institutions. These training programs served the double function of rapidly preparing pre-professional students in basic biological science and of making it possible for many zoologists to remain actively engaged in their profession on home grounds. Zoology also expanded in certain applied areas; especially as related to agriculture through economic entomology and to medicine through parasitology. The curtailment of zoology occurred along four lines: (1) In teaching not associated with medicine or veterinary medicine; (2) in loss of students and investigators to the war effort; (3) in basic research (although a commendable amount of this was done), and (4) in national and regional meetings and activities at summer biological stations. To document the last point, total attendance at the Marine Biological station (Woods Hole, Mass.) dropped from 461 in 1941 to 273 in 1942 to 228 in 1943. For another year the American Association for the Advancement of Science did not meet. Thus, members of such societies as the American Society of Zoologists and the Ecological Society of America could not get together for the exchange of ideas. However, certain organizations (the American Society of Zoologists, for example) published detailed abstracts of the current researches of its membership. These were widely circulated.

Research.—A problem that has long interested zoologists concerns the adjustments necessary for ocean animals to evolve into fresh water forms. The palaeontologist and morphologist advance evidence to show that the ancestors of the major phyla arose in the sea. In 1943, confirmatory evidence based on physiological considerations, appeared in a paper by L. C. Beadle. To invade fresh waters, marine animals must maintain a total body-fluid concentration greater than that of the external environment. Some animals, such as the marine worm *Nereis diversicolor,* show the beginnings of osmotic regulation. When in fresh or slightly salty water this species maintains for a time an internal salt concentration which is greater than that of the surrounding water. This permits the worms to enter brackish water. On the other hand, other forms such as certain crustacea withstand dilute sea water by virtue of another type of mechanism; one which prevents essential diminution in the concentration of body fluids. In such organisms this is accomplished by active absorption of salt from the medium through gills or other parts of the body surface. Thus, one type of physiological mechanism retains salt that is present (*Nereis*) while another brings in extra salt which then is stored in fluids and tissues (crustacea). It seems likely that devices such as these have been used by animals in their emancipation from the sea.

W. H. Johnson and E. G. Stanley Baker showed that the size of populations of a ciliate protozoan, *Tetrahymena,* was increased when vitamin B_1, thiamin hydrochloride, was added to the medium in certain concentrations. This greater population size was due, not to an acceleration of individual reproductive rate, but rather to an extension of the period of maximum cell division beyond that characteristic of controls in which thiamin was low or absent. Certain cultures, to which two other B-complex vitamins (riboflavin and pyridoxin) were added in addition to the thiamin, maintained the largest living populations. This research, dealing as it does with relatively simple one-celled creatures, demonstrated anew that the need for vitamins is not limited to "higher" forms but is something quite general among animals.

In 1943 W. F. Lamoreux studied the effect of light on the weight of white leghorn cockerels. In his experiments other factors such as food, temperature and genetic stock were controlled. He found that, when the birds were exposed to light for nine hours daily, they weighed significantly more after six weeks of such treatment than did birds exposed for 12 hours daily. Further, roosters that got only four hours of light in each 24 weighed more than did those that got 14 hours. Lamoreux reached the interesting conclusion that gains in the body weight of domestic fowl are greatest when the daily period of light is inadequate for the maximum stimulation of reproduction. Thus, midwinter light conditions, while excellent for inducing growth, are not favourable for the development of the gonads with consequent reproduction. (*See* also MARINE BIOLOGY.)

BIBLIOGRAPHY.—Joseph Needham, *Biochemistry and Morphogenesis* (1942); H. U. Sverdrup, Martin W. Johnson and Richard H. Fleming, *The Oceans. Their Physics, Chemistry and General Biology* (1942); Sherman C. Bishop, *Handbook of Salamanders* (1943); William J. Hamilton, Jr., *The Mammals of Eastern United States* (1943); Robert M. Yerkes, *Chimpanzees. A Laboratory Colony* (1943); L. V. Heilbrunn, *An Outline of General Physiology* (2nd edition) (1943); L. C. Beadle, *Biological Reviews,* 18 (1943); W. H. Johnson and E. G. Stanley Baker, *Physiological Zoology,* 16 (1943); W. F. Lamoreux, *Ecology,* 24 (1943). (T. PK.)

Zoological Gardens.—Postwar plans for zoos were being made, particularly in the United States. The New York Zoological society was planning a research centre for the study of animal diseases in relation to human diseases. It was to receive for this purpose $3,000,000 under a postwar program, and was to contribute $20,000 towards a $1,500,000 postwar aquarium or oceanarium at Coney Island, containing fresh- and salt-water animals from all over the globe. Dr. David L. Coffin was appointed to the Herbert Fox memorial fellowship in comparative pathology by the Zoological Society of Philadelphia. The fellowship provides for half-time work at the zoo by faculty members of the school of veterinary medicine interested in the diseases of wild animals.

In Great Britain, Winston Churchill was elected honorary fellow of the London Zoological society. The lion presented to him to commemorate his African visit was the father of cubs born in the zoo. H. Vinall collected fresh-water fish for the first wartime opening of the aquarium. Many tropical fish were to remain in the congenial temperature of the reptile house. (V. R.)

INDEX

The black type entries are article headings and cross references. These black type article entries do not show page notations because they are to be found in their alphabetical position in the body of the book, but they show the dates of the issues of the *Book of the Year* in which the articles appear. For example, "American Iron and Steel Institute 44, 43, 42, 41" indicates that the entry "American Iron and Steel Institute" is to be found in the *1944 Book of the Year*, the *1943 Book of the Year*, the *1942 Book of the Year* and the *1941 Book of the Year*. The reference "**Adult Education: see Education 44, 43, 42.** See **Education, Adult 41, 40**" indicates that the entry "Adult Education" is to be found in the article "Education" in the *1944 Book of the Year*, the *1943 Book of the Year*, and the *1942 Book of the Year*, and under the heading "Education, Adult" in the *1941 Book of the Year* and the *1940 Book of the Year*. All black type entries without dates indicate that the same entries appear in all previous issues. Examples, not **Advertising 44, 43, 42, 41, 40,** but **Advertising;** not **Academy of Arts and Letters, American:** see **American Academy of Arts and Letters 44, 43, 42, 41, 40,** but **Academy of Arts and Letters, American:** see **American Academy of Arts and Letters.**

The light type headings which are indented under black type article headings and cross references refer to articles elsewhere in the text (of this issue only) related to the entry listed in black type. The light type headings which are not indented refer to information in the text (of this issue only) not given a special article. All the light type headings show page references.

All headings whether consisting of a single word or more are treated for the purpose of alphabetization as single complete headings. Names beginning with "Mc" and "Mac" are alphabetized as "Mac"; "St." is treated as "Saint." All references below show the exact quarter of the page by means of the letters *a*, *b*, *c*, and *d*, signifying respectively the upper and lower halves of the first column and the upper and lower halves of the second column.

vancement of Science 52d; Anaemia 62a; Dietetics 236a; Veterinary Medicine 737d
Protestant Episcopal Church
Christian Unity 187b; Marriage and Divorce 424c; Presbyterian Church 564a
Prunes: *see* **Plums and Prunes**
Pryor, Arthur 43
Psychiatry
Commonwealth Fund, The 202c
Psychical Research 41, 40
Psychoanalysis: *see* **Psychiatry 42, 40**
Psychology
Psychology, Applied 41, 40
Public Assistance: *see* **Child Welfare 44, 43.** *See* **Relief; Social Security 44, 43, 42, 41, 40**
Public Buildings Administration: *see* **Federal Works Agency 44, 43, 42**
Public Health Engineering
Public Health Service: *see* **Federal Security Agency 44.** *See* **Medicine; Venereal Diseases 44, 43, 42.** *See* **Dietetics; Entomology; Hospitals 43, 42.** *See* **Public Health Services 41, 40**
Public Housing Authority, Federal: *see* **National Housing Agency 44, 43**
Public Libraries: *see* **American Library Association; Libraries**
Public Roads Administration: *see* **Federal Works Agency; Roads and Highways 44, 43, 42**
Public Utilities
Public welfare: *see* under various cities and states
Public Works Administration (PWA): *see* **Federal Works Agency 44, 43, 42.** *See* **Housing 40**
Publishing (Book)
Puerto Rico
Fisheries 284d; Four-H Clubs 295d
Pugilism: *see* **Boxing**
Pulitzer, Ralph 40
Pulitzer Prizes 44, 43. *See* **Literary Prizes; Theatre 42, 41, 40**
Pulp Industry: *see* **Paper and Pulp Industry**
Pulpstones: *see* **Abrasives 44, 43, 42**
Pumice: *see* **Abrasives 44, 43, 42.** *See* **Pumice 40**
Purdue University
Pusey, William Allen 41
PWA: *see* **Federal Works Agency 44, 43, 42.** *See* **Housing 40**
Pyrite
Quakers: *see* **Friends, Religious Society of 44, 43, 42, 41**
Quebec
Canada, Dominion of 150a; Jewish Religious Life 376d
Quebec conference: Arnold, Henry H. 79c; Canada, Dominion of 150c; China 183d; Churchill, Winston Leonard Spencer 188b; Geography 307b; Hopkins, Harry L. 339d; Hull, Cordell 334b; King, William Lyon Mackenzie 382c; Leahy, William Daniel 398a; Marshall, George Catlett 425a; Mountbatten, Lord Louis 460d; Newspapers and Magazines 500b; Pound, Sir (Alfred) Dudley (Pickman Rogers) 563d; Roosevelt, Franklin Delano 612b; Soong, T. V. 650c; United States 718a
Queensland
Quicksilver: *see* **Mercury**
Quidde, Ludwig 42
Quinine: Ecuador 244b; Japan 374c
Quisling, Vidkun Abraham 41
Rabaul, New Guinea 785a
Rabies: *see* **Veterinary Medicine 41, 40**
Race Riots 44
California 147b; Detroit 233d; Michigan 442c; Negroes (American) 490c; New York City 504a; Police 558a; Sociology 646a
Rachmaninoff, Sergei Vassilievitch 44
Racing and Races: *see* **Dog Racing 44, 43, 42.** *See* **Horse Racing; Track and Field Sports 44, 43, 42, 41, 40.** *See* **Air Races; Automobile Racing 43, 42, 41, 40**
Rackham, Arthur 40
Radar: *see* **Radio Detection 44**
Radio 44, 43, 42. *See* **Radio, Industrial Aspects of; Radio, Scientific Developments of, 41, 40**
Benton, William 107c; Burma 139b; Catholic Welfare Conference, National 162b; Censorship 163b; Christian Science 187a; Civilian Defense 191b; Federal Communications Commission 277c; Inter-American Affairs, Office of the Coordinator of, 357d; Law 389a; Netherlands 492b; Newspapers and Magazines 501b; Postwar Planning 562b; Religion 601c; Standards, National Bureau of, 659c; Supreme Court of the United States 677a; Television 688c; War Information, Office of, 747d; World War II 773d. *See* also under various states and countries
Radio Corporation of America 582a
Radio Detection 44
Radio Facsimile: *see* **Radio, Scientific Developments of 41, 40**
Radiology 44, 43, 42, 40
Radium
Industrial Health 353b; Northwest Territories 510b
Radziwill, Princess Catherine 42
Railroad Accidents: *see* **Disasters**
Railroad Retirement Act: *see* **Social Security 44, 43, 42, 41**
Railroads
Business Review 141d; Chicago 175a; Defense Transportation, Office of, 228b; Disasters 238a; Interstate Commerce Commission 363a; Labour Unions 385b; Mexico 439d; Roosevelt, Franklin Delano 613a; Sand and Gravel 621c; Stone 664c. *See* also under various states and countries
Rainfall: *see* **Floods and Flood Control; Meteorology**
Raisins: *see* **Grapes**
Ralston, James Layton 41
Ramey, Howard Knox 44
Ramírez, Pedro 44
Rapid Transit: *see* **Electric Transportation**
Rates of Exchange: *see* **Exchange Control and Exchange Rates**
Rationing 44, 43
Agriculture 24c; Allied Military Government 48d; American Bankers Association 53b; Automobile Industry in the War 87b; Bahamas 93c; Banking 95b; Bermuda 108b; Black Markets 112b; Boy Scouts 119b; Brazil 121a; British East Africa 127b; British Honduras 130a; Butter 146a; Candy 159a; Canning Industry 159d; Cheese 169a; Civilian Defense 190c; Clothing Industry 194b; Coffee 198b; Curaçao 218c; Egypt 251d; Elections 254c; Famines 273a; French Colonial Empire 299b; Great Britain 322c; Guatemala 327c; Hispanic America and World War II 336c; Insurance 355d; International Trade 362d; Jeffers, William M. 376a; Law 388c; Liquors, Alcoholic 405b; Moscow 454b; Munitions of War 466d; National Income and National Product 483b; Netherlands Colonial Empire 492d; Newfoundland and Labrador 495b; Newspapers and Magazines 500b; Oleomargarine 519c; Paris 533b; Portugal 558c; Price Administration, Office of, 565c; Prices 566b; Radio 581d; Rhodesia 604d; Rotary International 614b; Secret Service, U.S. 624b; Shoe Industry 636b; Soap, Perfumery and Cosmetics 641c; Sugar 674d; Textile Industry 692d; Thailand 693a; United States 716d; Uruguay 730d; Vitamins 740d. *See* also under various countries
Rautenburg, Robert 41
"Rawalpindi": *see* **European War; Great Britain 40**
Ray, Charles 44
Ray, Edward (Ted) 44
Rayburn, Sam 41
Rayon and other Synthetic Fibres 44, 43. *See* **Rayon 42, 41, 40**
Silk 638b
Read, Opie 40
Receipts, Government: *see* **Budget, National**
Reciprocal Trade Agreements: *see* **International Trade 44, 43.** *See* **Trade Agreements 42, 41, 40**
Democratic Party 230c; Women's Clubs, General Federation of, 768a
Reclamation: *see* **Canals and Inland Waterways; Floods and Flood Control; Forests; Irrigation; Soil Erosion and Soil Conservation 44, 43, 42, 41, 40.** *See* **Dry Farming 41, 40**
Reconstruction Finance Corporation
Reconversion of industry: Business Review 142b; Electrical Industries 255b; Postwar Planning 562b
Red Cross
Advertising 20b; Bank for International Settlements 94c; Baseball 98d; Bohemia and Moravia 113c; Boy Scouts 119c; Civilian Defense 191d; Cricket 214c; Daughters of the American Revolution 224d; Donations and Bequests 239d; Falk Foundation, The Maurice and Laura 272b; Poland 556c; Prisoners of War 570b; Prisons 572a; Relief 600d; Switzerland 681c; U.S.S.R. 709a; War Relief, U.S. 753c; Woman's Christian Temperance Union 767a
Re-Employment of War Veterans: *see* **Selective Service, U.S. 44**
Reeves, Jesse Siddall 43
Referendum: *see* **Initiative and Referendum 43, 42, 41, 40**
Reforestation: *see* **Forests**
Reformed Church: *see* **Presbyterian Church**
Christian Unity 187c
Refrigeration Treatment (Cancer): *see* **Cancer 40**
Refugees
Foreign Economic Administration 292d
Regnault, Jeanne Julia: *see* **Bartet, Jeanne Julia 42**
Rehabilitation and Occupational Therapy for Wounded Soldiers 44
Reichenau, Walter von 43, 41
Reinhardt, Max 44
Reisner, George Andrew 43
Relander, Lauri Kristian 43
Relay Racing: *see* **Track and Field Sports**
Relief
Community Chest 203d; Social Security 644b. *See* also under various cities and states
Relief, War: *see* **War Relief, U.S. 44, 43, 42**
Relief and Rehabilitation Administration, United Nations: *see* **United Nations Relief and Rehabilitation Administration 44**
Religion
Religious Denominations: *see* **Church Membership**
Relocation, Japanese: *see* **Aliens; War Relocation Authority 44**
Rennell, James Rennell Rodd 42
Reorganization, Governmental: for regrouping of U.S. offices and bureaus under Federal Security Agency, Federal Works Agency, Federal Loan Agency, etc., *see* listings under **Government Departments and Bureaus 44, 43, 42, 41, 40.** *See* **Legislation, Federal 40**
Representatives, House of: *see* **Elections 44, 43, 42, 41.** *See* **Congress, United States 44, 43, 42, 41, 40**
Republican Party
Elections 253d; United States 713a
Resins, Synthetic: *see* **Paints and Varnishes 44, 43, 42.** *See* **Plastics Industry 44, 43, 42, 41, 40.** *See* **Industrial Research 42, 40.** *See* **Chemistry, Applied 40**
Paints and Varnishes 527d; Plastics Industry 553b
Respirators: *see* **Infantile Paralysis 42**
Retail Sales: *see* **Business Review 44, 43, 42.** *See* **Retail Sales 41, 40**
Réunion: *see* **French Colonial Empire**
Revenue Act of 1939: *see* **Legislation, Federal 40**
Revenue Act of 1940: *see* **Legislation; Taxation 41**
Reynaud, Paul 41
Reynolds, George McClelland 41
Rheumatic Fever: *see* **Epidemics and Public Health Control 42**
Rheumatism: *see* **Arthritis 43, 42, 41, 40**
Rhode Island
Taxation 686c
Rhodes, Edgar Nelson 43
Rhodesia
Archaeology 70a; Cobalt 198a; Copper 210c; Dams 222a; Gold 317c; Selenium 628c; Soil Erosion and Soil Conservation 649a
Rhodes Scholarships 40
Ribbentrop, Joachim von
Ribeiro, Manoel 42
Rice, Alice Caldwell Hegan 43
Rice, Cale Young 44
Rice
Famines 272c; Formosa 295c; India 350b; Japan 375c; Netherlands Colonial Empire 492d; Thailand 692d
Richards, Laura Elizabeth 44
Richardson, James Otto 41
Richtmyer, Floyd Karker 40
Rickert, Thomas A. 42
Rickets: *see* **Medicine 42**
Riddle, John Wallace 42
Ridge, Lola 42
Riesman, David 41
Rio De La Plata Conference: *see* **Uruguay 42**
Rio de Oro: *see* **Spanish Colonial Empire**
Rio Muni: *see* **Spanish Colonial Empire**
Ríos Morales, Juan Antonio 43
Ripley, William Zebina 42
Ritchie, Neil Methuen 43, 42
Rivers and Harbours
Rivets, Explosive: *see* **Industrial Research; Metallurgy 42**
Roads and Highways
Federal Works Agency 281a; Sand and Gravel 621b; Stone 664c; Town and Regional Planning 699b. *See* also under various states and countries
Robert, Georges Achille Marie Joseph 44
Roberts, Sir Charles George Douglas 44
Roberts, Elizabeth Madox 42
Robinson, Frederick Bertrand 42
Robinson-Patman Act: *see* **Chain Stores 41, 40.** *See* **Law (Case) 41**
Roca, Julio Argentino 43
Rockefeller Foundation
Rodman, Hugh 41
Roebling Medal: *see* **Mineralogy 42, 41, 40**
Roentgen Ray: *see* **Radiology 44**
Rogers, James Harvey 40
Rogers, Norman McLeod 41
Rokossovsky, Konstantin 44
Roleo: *see* **Birling 43**
Roman Catholic Church
Rome 44
Italy 371d; World War II 781c
Rome-Berlin-Tokyo Axis: *see* **Chinese-Japanese War; Fascism; Hungary; Japan; Rumania; U.S.S.R.; United States 41.** *See* **Germany; Italy 41, 40.** *See* **European War; Strategy of the European War 40**
Rommel, Erwin 44, 43, 42
World War II 778a
Roosevelt, Franklin Delano
Arabia 68d; Archives, National 74d; Athlone, 1st Earl of, 83c; Bolivia 114a; Budget, National 134b; Camp Fire Girls 150a; Canada, Dominion of, 150c; China 183d; Chosen 186a; Clark, Mark Wayne 193b; Crowley, Leo Thomas 216b; Davies, Joseph Edward 225a; Davis, Chester Charles 225b; Davis, Elmer 225c; Education 247d; Egypt 252a; Elections 253d; Foreign Economic Administration 291b; Formosa 295b; France 297c; Hopkins, Harry L. 339c; Iran 365a; Italy 372b; Jones, Jesse Holman 378a; Liberia 401b; London University 409d; McIntyre, Marvin Hunter 416c; National Parks and Monuments 485b; Newspapers and Magazines 501a; Perkins, Milo Randolph 538d; Puerto Rico 578c; Radio 584a; Railroads 589c; Secret Service, U.S. 624a; Submarine Warfare 668d; Supreme Court of the United States 676b; Tibet 695c; Turkey 705a; United States 713b; War Crimes 745c; War Mobilization, Office of, 749c; War Production, U.S. 750b
Roosevelt, Gracie Hall 42
Roosevelt, Kermit 44
Roosevelt, Sara Delano 42
Roper, Daniel Calhoun 44
Roquer, Emma de: *see* **Calvé, Emma 43**
Rosenfeld, Kurt 44
Rosin: Forests 294b; Paints and Varnishes 527d; Paper and Pulp Industry 532a
Rosenwald Fund, The Julius
Rosny, Joseph Henry 41
Ross, James Delmage 40
Ross, John Dawson 40
Rostron, Sir Arthur Henry 41
Rotary International 44, 43, 42, 41
Rothermere, Harold Sidney Harmsworth 41
Rottenstone: *see* **Abrasives 43, 42**
Rourke, Constance Mayfield 42
Rowan, Andrew Summers 44
Rowell, Newton Wesley 42
Rowing
Royal air force 771d
Royal Canadian air force 151c
"Royal Oak": *see* **European War; Great Britain; Submarine Warfare 40**
Ruanda and Urundi: *see* **Belgian Colonial Empire; Mandates**
Rubber
Agricultural Research Administration 23a; Alcohol, Industrial 43c; Bolivia 114b; Botany 117b; Brazil 123a; British East Africa 127c; British West Africa 132a; Business Review 141c; Canada, Dominion of, 153b; Central America 168a; Chemistry 169d; Chemurgy 173d; Ecuador 244b; Federated Malay States 281c; Forests 294d; Haiti 329c; Honduras 339b; Japan 374c; Jeffers, William M. 376a; Jones, Jesse Holman 378b; Liberia 401b; Liquors, Alcoholic 404d; Los Angeles 409d; Marine Biology 421b; Munitions of War 467c; National Geographic Society 476c; Paints and Varnishes 527c; Petroleum 541c; Plastics Industry 553b; Shipbuilding 630d; Standards, National Bureau of, 659d; Thailand 692d; U.S. Investments Abroad 720d; War Production, U.S. 752a
Rubber, Synthetic: *see* **Rubber 44, 43, 42.** *See* **Chemistry; Standards, National Bureau of, 41**
Rubber Footwear: *see* **Shoe Industry 43, 42, 41, 40**
Rubens, Horatio Seymour 42
Ruckstull, Frederick Wellington 43
Ruff, Robert Hamric 43
Rugby: *see* **Football**
Rugh, James Torrance 43
Rulers: *see* **Presidents, Sovereigns and Rulers 44, 43, 42.** *See* **Sovereigns, Presidents and Rulers 41, 40**